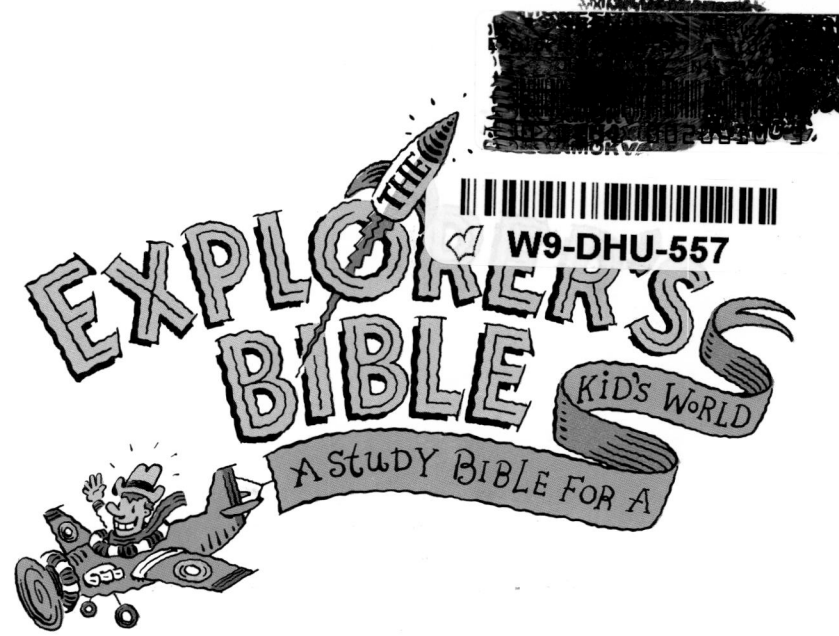

THE EXPLORER'S BIBLE
A STUDY BIBLE FOR A KID'S WORLD

This Is
My Bible

_____
(name)

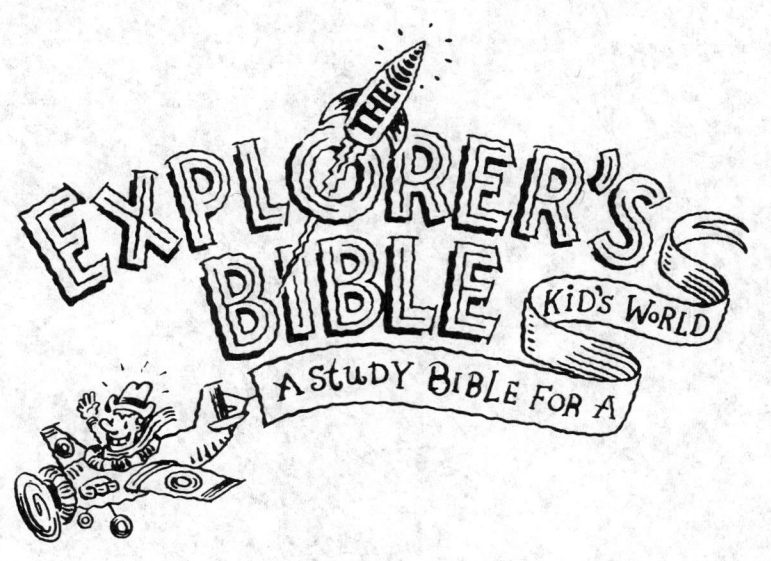

The Explorer's Bible

A Study Bible for a Kid's World

NEW KING JAMES VERSION

Thomas Nelson Publishers
Nashville

6/95

Photographs on pages 55, 639, 1156, 1221, 1379, 1471, 1532, 1556,
1651, and 1652, courtesy of Gustav Jeeninga; photograph on page 298,
courtesy of Willem A. VanGemeren; all others, courtesy of Howard Vos.

Title page logo: The triquetra (from a Latin word meaning "three-cornered") is an ancient symbol for the
Trinity. It comprises three interwoven arcs, distinct yet equal and inseparable, symbolizing that the
Father, Son, and Holy Spirit are three distinct yet equal Persons and indivisibly One God.

Bookstore

FOREWORD

The most significant and exciting book in the world is the Bible. But parts of it may be a little hard for children to understand and apply to their world. With five children, nineteen grandchildren, and three great-grandchildren of my own, I'm always looking for a fresh new approach to the old, old story of God's love. With this new study Bible designed especially for the needs of contemporary kids, I won't have any trouble helping them relate to the timeless stories of Bible people and places.

You see, Bible characters actually speak for themselves in language children can read and understand. In a unique format, front-page news articles leap off the pages, while kids learn definitions of hard words as they go and find out what Bible characters often learned the hard way.

Throughout, dynamic illustrations literally bring Bible history into a kid's world. It's a delightful touch!

Many a young person interested in exploring God's Word will become a stronger, more effective Christian for having used the tools provided here. Believe me, we are going to need all the strength and effectiveness God can give us if we are to survive the coming difficulties and bring glory to Him.

Read and enjoy! An adventure lies ahead for you!

Sincerely yours,

Ruth Bell Graham

October, 1991

TABLE OF CONTENTS

Dictionary—Concordance (with pronunciation guide)

Preface
FOR MOMS, DADS, AND OTHER TEACHERS

Good story Bibles for the very young are legion. But our conversations with parents and young leaders have impressed us with the need for a true study Bible that is also an exciting learning experience for early adolescents.

We come to know the people we meet by what they say and do. We also come to know God by what He says and does. Thus, the primary concern of Christian parents and teachers is to bring their children and students to know God by what He has said and done in His Word.

Because we share this concern, the authors have prepared the teaching materials for *The Explorer's Bible*. The materials are unique in their method of drawing the young reader into a feeling of first-hand knowledge of leading Bible personalities and events. The early learner is guided through lively first-person speeches by principal Bible characters, realistic "news breaks" of major biblical events, brief facts of special interest, definitions of Bible terms, and useful notes on Bible background and doctrine especially tailored for the pre-teen student.

The verbal teaching materials are functionally combined with maps and other visual aids and carefully located with their related Bible contexts. This mix of study elements accelerates the learning process in which young students quickly grasp the firm spiritual foundation upon which to build their lives when they enter young adulthood.

With such goals in view, it is our fond hope that *The Explorer's Bible* will become the best-loved Book on the family bookshelf, a Book to which parents can turn with confidence in guiding the reading of their children at home. The various features are designed for the learner's personal reading as well as for the family devotional time.

Here also is a Bible curriculum for the classroom teacher as well as for the parent-teacher in the home-school setting. The teacher will quickly see that the varieties of approach are not intended merely to entertain. Rather, the study materials present, in a unique form, the great truths of creation, redemption, and everyday living that Christians have always cherished.

Along with our labors have gone up the earnest prayers, not only of the authors, but also of dedicated parent-teachers like Forest Bahruth and Nina Sievert, that the study materials will be the work of God's own heart in reaching young people of our time. Now, more than ever, our children face a future of severe upheaval in spiritual values. But the Word of our faithful God will be their strong defense.

We wish to express our sincere thanks to our beloved editor, Merrie Noland, whose generous self-giving made possible many of the appealing qualities of *The Explorer's Bible*.

Bill and Jean McDowell
Orlando, 1991

vi

LET'S GO EXPLORING!

Explorers are daring and brave and adventurous. They like to climb, hike, search, investigate, go prospecting, and scout out the world around them. But explorers often need special tools to help them make their discoveries. For example, a backpack, a compass, some binoculars, a pick axe, and a magnifying glass make it easier to reach one's destination or to dig for treasure.

Now you are about to set out on the most exciting adventure of all—a journey through the Bible, God's Holy Word. You, too, will need some tools to help you reach your destination.

In sixty-six books, God has preserved everything He wants you to know about Himself, His world, and how you can be the boy or girl He created you to be. Sometimes He wrote the words in His own handwriting, such as The Ten Commandments, but most of the time He used people to record His thoughts. You will learn that God's Holy Spirit "inspired" them to write these sacred books and that He will be your Helper in understanding what you read. But, however He chose to do it, this Book is God's Word, not man's word!

Skim through these pages and find other special tools we have provided for you as you begin your journey:

1. DIGGING IN

These notes will help you "dig" for the rich treasure to be found in God's Word. They explain the background of familiar Bible stories and happenings. You will learn the meaning behind certain verses and passages. You will find out how Bible people lived and learn about the most recent archaeological discoveries in Bible lands.

Just look for the symbol of a shovel and pick axe and the words "Digging In" at the bottom of the page. The Scripture reference will tell you which verse or passage is being discussed.

Symbol for Note

Scripture
Reference
Callout

Learn how to
pronounce
hard words

⚒ DIGGING IN

3:1–14 Moses Meets God Moses had what it took to be a great hero of his people. He wasn't afraid to stand up for what was right.

But God could not use a man of anger. Moses murdered an Egyptian who was beating a Hebrew slave. This showed Moses that he had to learn patience and self-control. So God sent him into the desert of Sinai (pronounced *SIGH-nigh*) for 40 years. There he served as a shepherd for a wealthy sheep owner named Jethro.

This was a hard thin been a prince in Eg

Then one day Go in a burning bush th: sent Moses back t people from slavery that His true name met the true God nature like Egypt's g who is above every you know the I AM?

2. WORDFINDERS

Your "compass" to the meaning of hard-to-understand Bible names and terms. You will see that the word to be defined (in bold type) stands out from the rest of the Bible text. Then look for the definition at the bottom of the page.

Word to be
defined

Symbol for
definition

but have eternal life. ¹⁶For God so loved the world that He gave His only begotten Son, that whoever **believes** in Him should not perish but have everlasting life. ¹⁷For God did not send His Son into the world to condemn the world, but that the world through Him might be saved.

came to John and He who was with dan, to whom you hold, He is baptizi ing to Him!"

²⁷John answere can receive nothir given to him fro

🌀 WORDFINDER

3:16 Believes To accept what God has said in the

3. CAMEOS

Bible friends speak for themselves! Meet some men and women who will tell you about their lives, their families, and how God used them to work out His plan.

These personality profiles appear in boxes throughout the Bible, and are located near the title of a book or verse that contains the name. Sometimes you will see an artist's idea of what that Bible character looked like.

The Book of
RUTH

Mine is one of the most amazing stories of the Bible. Like Rahab, whom you read about in Joshua 2, I was not even a Hebrew. I was from Moab, which was an enemy nation of Israel. Another wonderful fact is that my husband Boaz was from the family of Rahab!

4. NEWS STORIES

If Bible-time people could have bought a daily newspaper in their town or area, headline news stories might have looked like this:

Giants Seen Across River?

Old Testament News Service

KADESH BARNEA—A huge number of Jews are camped south of Kadesh Barnea, poised and ready to cross over and take possession of the land God promised Abraham (see Genesis 1:7, 8).

As evidence, Joshua and Caleb brought back one cluster of grapes so large that it took two men to carry it!

Most of the spies disagree, however, and urge Moses not to proceed. "There

---

Read all about the dramatic events that took place in Bible times, as if they were this morning's news! And "listen" to eyewitness reports from "television" news teams as they give on-the-scene coverage of major happenings.

While our news may often seem like bad news, the Good News is still that God loves and cares for His people and provides a way for them to know Him.

5. QUESTIONS

Haven't you been curious about such things as "Why Was Methuselah the Oldest Man in the World?" and "What Was The Longest Day in History?"

One way to find answers is simply to ask. So we have placed in small boxes 100 questions about the Bible you have always wanted to ask.

As you read this Bible for yourself, other questions will be answered for you. Be sure to mark these passages in some way to remind yourself that God's Word contains all the answers to our deepest problems and needs.

Is this a question you have wanted to ask?

6. LESSONS

One tool that many people overlook is the study of what

Can Small Be Great?

We often think *bigness* is what matters. But God proves over and over that He likes to use very *small* things to do His great works. Remember David and Goliath? (See 1 Samuel 17.) God also used Gideon's army of three hundred men to show us we win only because God helps us.

someone else learned from an experience. Look for boxed items entitled "What _____ Learned" throughout the Bible text.

You will be very wise if you profit from the painful lessons learned by these Bible characters, so you won't have to repeat the experience!

You might want to make a list of all the lessons learned by these Bible friends, then ask God to show you how to use the lessons in your own life.

What Adam and Eve Learned

At first we were too heartbroken to understand all that happened. We had been so happy in the garden where God visited us every day. Now it was all over. The sky was filled with dark clouds, and the sunshine of our Father's love was hidden.

If only we had listened to our Friend, the Lord, how different everything would be now. Instead, we had obeyed Satan, our Enemy. Now we could not go back to those good times with God as before.

Afterward, we were really sorry for what happened, and our Father

BIBLE FRIEND	THE STORY	WHAT I CAN LEARN
Adam and Eve	Gen. 3:1-24	I will not listen to the Enemy when he tries to make me believe that disobeying God won't hurt anyone.

BE A TRAIL BLAZER

(16 Colorful Pages Packed with Riddles, Rhymes, and The Most Important Information You'll Ever Learn!)

Watch for these exciting activity pages with the picture of the young explorers looking for treasure:

• **BIBLE BOOKSHELF**—Find all the books of the Bible, grouped by category. For example, did you know that the Book of Ecclesiastes is a book of Poetry, or that the Book of Jonah is a book of Prophecy?

Learn the names of all 66 books and how to pronounce them. (See the Dictionary-Concordance at the back of the Bible.)

• **THE TEN COMMANDMENTS FOR YOUNG EXPLORERS**—Like stop signs and blinking lights in dangerous traffic areas, God's Ten Rules for Living were given to protect us and to help us live long and happy lives. (Look up the Ten Commandments in Exodus 20:1-17.)

• **HAPPY THOUGHTS FOR CHILDREN**— Jesus preached His best-loved Sermon (Matthew 5, 6, and 7) out of doors, on a beautiful grassy hillside near the Sea of Galilee a long, long, time ago. But His words are just as wonderful and important for us today.

• **LOVE LINES**—This familiar passage (1 Corinthians 13) has been adapted for you, using ideas and objects from your world. But the truth of its message on love is exactly the same today as when it was written nearly two thousand years ago.

• **BIBLE HEROES** (Old and New Testament)—Read the riddles about famous people from Bible times, then fill in the name of the hero or heroine. To learn more about this friend, turn in your Bible to the book and verse or verses mentioned.

- **SUPERHERO**—Kids love to read about the adventures of great people who have become known for their bravery, strength, or outstanding deeds. You may wish you could be just like them when you grow up. But there is only one Superhero who is worthy of being studied, imitated, and worshiped—Jesus!

In these pages you will read the highlights of Jesus' life on earth—from the time He was born as a baby in Bethlehem until the day He went back to heaven to live with His Father.

You will walk in His footsteps as He travels about the dusty countryside teaching, healing, and loving the crowds of people who followed Him. You will trace His path through the streets of Jerusalem during His last week, then get excited with the disciples who see Him with their own eyes after His resurrection from the dead!

- **THE ROAD TO HEAVEN** (How to Be Saved)—If you read only one of the "extra" pages in this study Bible, please read this one! Here, in five simple steps, is the secret to Everlasting Life. Look at the pictures and memorize the verse that goes with each one. Then follow the instructions!

- **EXERCISE YOUR SPIRITUAL MUSCLES**—You are growing taller and stronger each day, developing muscles that help you run and climb and play. But this page gives you a plan for developing your spiritual muscles, too. Find the Scripture verses that tell you how to be spiritually fit.

TAKE A TRIP THROUGH BIBLE LANDS

Throughout this study Bible, you will find nine illustrated maps. With each map is a story of a Bible traveler and a very important trip he made. Climb the mountains, sail the seas, and visit the towns and regions where these Bible friends met God and learned an important lesson.

HIDING GOD'S WORD

God has given you an incredible computer—your brain! You can store literally thousands and thousands of pieces of information there. Then, when you need that information, your memory is able to call it up.

While you are young and your mind is strong and fresh is the best time to store away parts of God's Word. Then, whenever you need comfort or protection or help, it is instantly available.

Look for the shaded verses and passages throughout this study Bible. There are over a thousand of them! Plan to memorize at least one verse a day (or week). You will be surprised how quickly God's Word will begin to make your life better and happier!

Son of Man be lifted up, 15 that whoever believes in Him should not perish but have eternal life. 16 For God so loved the world that He gave His only begotten Son, that whoever **believes** in Him should not perish but have everlasting life. 17 For God did not send His Son into the world to condemn

tween *some* of John's disciples and th Jews about purification. 26 And the came to John and said to him, "Rabb He who was with you beyond the Jor dan, to whom you have testified—be hold, He is baptizing, and all are com ing to Him!"

27 John answered and said, "A ma

THE LAST WORD(S)

In the back of this study Bible is a picture Dictionary-Concordance to help you find the meanings of words used in the Bible and to locate passages in which those words occur.

Some words will be pronounced for you, using a simple pronunciation guide: Big words are broken down into smaller words that are already familiar to you. And accented syllables are spelled in all capital letters. Ready, Set, Explore!

advocate One who speaks in defense of another. Christ is so called (1 Jn 2:1).

affliction Distress; pain; adversity. God has seen my a. Gen 31:42

agape (ah-GAH-pe) A Greek word meaning "love." It is also used to denote the "love feasts" of the early Christians (Jude 12).

Agrippa (ah-GRIP-uh) King of Judea before whom Paul appeared to plead his defense (Acts 25:13—26:32).

Ahab (AY-hab) An evil king of the northern kingdom of Israel in the time of Elijah; married Jezebel, a Sidonian princess, which caused religious turmoil; robbed Naboth of

The
Old Testament

What Is the Old Testament About?
The Bible is really one great story of salvation. The Old Testament of 39 separate books is the first part of that story. "Salvation" is God's long work of saving us from our sins. "Sin" is what happened when man decided to live his own way instead of God's way in the world that God created. That was when God began His great work of saving us from our sins.

To prepare the way, God had to destroy the whole world by a great flood, except for the family of Noah. Then God raised up a new people for Himself. They were the ancient Hebrews. God promised the Hebrews they would bring His salvation to the whole world.

The first five books of the Old Testament are mostly the story of how God chose the ancient Hebrews and taught them His laws. Following these are the twelve books that tell the history of the Hebrews. The next five are books of poetry and wisdom. One of these five books, the Psalms, is really a book of songs showing mainly how God wants to be worshiped.

The last seventeen books of the Old Testament were written by Hebrew prophets. These books tell about God's disappointment with the ancient Hebrews and His promise to bring them back to friendship with Him. The prophets also foretell a great surprise God was planning for the world—He was going to send His very own Son, the Messiah, to save us from our sins.

You can read all about this Messiah in the New Testament, which is the second part of the story of salvation.

The Book of
GENESIS

I am the One who gives you your life. I have lived forever, without beginning and without end. All things were made by Me. I set the sun, the moon, and the stars in their places, and I started the planets in motion.

Everything belongs to Me, because I am the Creator of all that lives in heaven and on earth. As you read this Book you will discover the truth about Me, about My world, and about yourself.

For example, you will learn that sin was the most unhappy event in the history of man. People turned away from the love and friendship of Me, their Creator.

But most of all I would like you to learn that I still love the universe I created. Yes, I even sent My very own Son to die so that you and I can be friends forever.

God creates the world

IN the beginning God **created** the heavens and the earth. ² The earth was without form, and void; and darkness *was* on the face of the deep. And the Spirit of God was hovering over the face of the waters.

³ Then God said, "Let there be light"; and there was light. ⁴ And God saw the light, that *it was* good; and God divided the light from the darkness. ⁵ God called the light Day, and the darkness He called Night. So the evening and the morning were the first day.

WORDFINDER

1:1 Created As used here, it means that God made the heavens and the earth from nothing. Compare with Genesis 2:7 where God only "formed" Adam from the dust of the ground.

God made the world out of nothing.

6 Then God said, "Let there be a firmament in the midst of the waters, and let it divide the waters from the waters." 7 Thus God made the firmament, and divided the waters which *were* under the firmament from the waters which *were* above the firmament; and it was so. 8 And God called the firmament Heaven. So the evening and the morning were the second day.

9 Then God said, "Let the waters under the heavens be gathered together into one place, and let the dry *land* appear"; and it was so. 10 And God called the dry *land* Earth, and the gathering together of the waters He called Seas. And God saw that *it was* good.

11 Then God said, "Let the earth bring forth grass, the herb *that* yields seed, *and* the fruit tree *that* yields fruit according to its kind, whose seed *is* in itself, on the earth"; and it was so. 12 And the earth brought forth grass, the herb *that* yields seed according to its kind, and the tree *that* yields fruit, whose seed *is* in itself according to its kind. And God saw that *it was* good. 13 So the evening and the morning were the third day.

14 Then God said, "Let there be lights in the firmament of the heavens to divide the day from the night; and let them be for signs and seasons, and for days and years; 15 and let them be for lights in the firmament of the heavens to give light on the earth"; and it was so. 16 Then God made two great lights: the greater light to rule the day, and the lesser light to rule the night. *He made* the stars also. 17 God set them in the firmament of the heavens to give light on the earth, 18 and to rule over the day and over the night, and to divide the light from the darkness. And God saw that *it was* good. 19 So the evening and the morning were the fourth day.

20 Then God said, "Let the waters abound with an abundance of living creatures, and let birds fly above the earth across the face of the firmament of the heavens." 21 So God created great sea creatures and every living thing that moves, with which the waters abounded, according to their kind, and every winged bird according to its kind. And God saw that *it was* good. 22 And God blessed them, saying, "Be fruitful and multiply, and fill the waters

⛏ DIGGING IN

1:26–28 God Created Man God did something different when He created people.

God made people to be like He is. No other earthly being has the ability to think and make new things as man can. God created everything in the vegetable and animal kingdom beautiful in its own way. And all animals are very gifted: The eagle carries his infant eaglet on his back high up into the air. Then he drops the little eagle and swoops down to catch it. He does this for as many times as it takes the eaglet to learn to fly.

But only man can make machines that fly, build great cities, and unlock the secrets of technology that instantly send pictures around the world.

God also created man with the ability to love Him and take care of all other created things. Do you love God and His world?

Adam and Eve, the first couple

in the seas, and let birds multiply on the earth." 23 So the evening and the morning were the fifth day.

24 Then God said, "Let the earth bring forth the living creature according to its kind: cattle and creeping thing and beast of the earth, *each* according to its kind"; and it was so. 25 And God made the beast of the earth according to its kind, cattle according to its kind, and everything that creeps on the earth according to its kind. And God saw that *it was* good.

26 Then God said, "Let Us make man in Our image, according to Our likeness; let them have dominion over the fish of the sea, over the birds of the air, and over the cattle, over all the earth and over every creeping thing that creeps on the earth." 27 So God created man in His *own* image; in the image of God He created him; male and female He created them. 28 Then God blessed them, and God said to them, "Be fruitful and multiply; fill the earth and subdue it; have dominion over the fish of the sea, over the birds of the air, and over every living thing that moves on the earth."

29 And God said, "See, I have given you every herb *that* yields seed which *is* on the face of all the earth, and every tree whose fruit yields seed; to you it shall be for food. 30 Also, to every beast of the earth, to every bird of the air, and to everything that creeps on the earth, in which *there is* life, *I have given* every green herb for food"; and it was so. 31 Then God saw everything that He had made, and indeed *it was* very good. So the evening and the morning were the sixth day.

God forms Adam and Eve

2 Thus the heavens and the earth, and all the host of them, were finished.

2 And on the seventh day God ended His work which He had done, and He rested on the seventh day from all His work which He had done. 3 Then God blessed the seventh day and sanctified it, because in it He rested from all His work which God had created and made.

4 This *is* the history of the heavens and the earth when they were created, in the day that the LORD God made the earth and the heavens, 5 before any plant of the field was in the earth and before any herb of the field had grown. For the LORD God had not caused it to rain on the earth, and *there was* no man to till the ground; 6 but a mist went up from the earth and watered the whole face of the ground.

7 And the LORD God **formed** man *of* the dust of the ground, and breathed into his nostrils the breath of life; and man became a living being.

8 The LORD God planted a garden eastward in Eden, and there He put the man whom He had formed. 9 And out of the ground the LORD God made every tree grow that is pleasant to the sight and good for food. The **tree of life** *was* also in the midst of the garden, and the tree of the knowledge of good and evil.

10 Now a river went out of Eden to water the garden, and from there it parted and became four riverheads. 11 The name of the first *is* Pishon; it *is* the one which skirts the whole land of Havilah, where *there is* gold. 12 And the gold of that land *is* good. Bdellium and the onyx stone *are* there. 13 The name of the second river *is* Gihon; it *is* the one which goes around the whole land of Cush. 14 The name of the third river *is* Hiddekel; it *is* the one which goes toward the east of Assyria. The fourth river *is* the Euphrates. 15 Then the LORD God took the man

⟨WORDFINDER⟩

2:7 Formed As used here, it means that God formed Adam from the dust of the ground. Compare with Genesis 1:1 where God made the heavens and the earth *from nothing.*

2:9 Tree of Life The tree God planted whose fruit Adam and Eve could have eaten and lived forever. We read about this tree again in Revelation 22:2.

God planted the tree of life in the middle of the Garden of Eden.

and put him in the garden of Eden to tend and keep it. ¹⁶ And the LORD God commanded the man, saying, "Of every tree of the garden you may freely eat; ¹⁷ but of the **tree of the knowledge of good and evil** you shall not eat, for in the day that you eat of it you shall surely die."

¹⁸ And the LORD God said, "*It is* not good that man should be alone; I will make him a helper comparable to him." ¹⁹ Out of the ground the LORD God formed *every* beast of the field and *every* bird of the air, and brought *them* to Adam to see what he would call them. And whatever Adam called each living creature, that *was* its name. ²⁰ So Adam gave names to all cattle, to the birds of the air, and to *every* beast of the field. But for Adam there

WORDFINDER

2:17 Tree of the Knowledge of Good and Evil   The tree God planted, but whose fruit Adam and Eve were forbidden to eat. By eating the fruit, they first experienced sin.

DIGGING IN

2:8–17 The Garden of Eden The garden God planted in Eden was a model of what God wanted the whole world to be like. It was the most beautiful nature park you could ever imagine. Adam and Eve lived happily there with God as their personal Friend.

In the world that God planned, there would be no disease and no death. We often think sickness and dying are just natural. But those things were not part of God's plan for us at the beginning.

Hatred and wars would not exist in the world as God made it. Instead of trying to be better than others, we would always be helping one another. Work would always be fun, not hard labor.

In God's plan, the wild animals would be as gentle as our favorite pets because they would never need to fear us. Weeds would not grow in our fields, and there would be no hunger. Yes, living in the world God planned would be like days of heaven on earth.

My name is Adam, which means "Ground," because God formed me out of the very elements of the earth. My wife is called Eve, meaning "Life-Giver," because she is the mother of all people.

Eve and I were very happy in the garden God made for us. Our world was like an immense park in which only the most elegant things lived and grew. The perfume of lilies and roses filled the air continually. Even the mighty lions played gently with us, and their cubs ate from Eve's hand.

Best of all, God Himself often came in the evening to walk and talk with us in the garden, and He taught us how to live in His world.

But one day everything went wrong. You can read about it in "What Adam and Eve Learned."

was not found a helper comparable to him.

21 And the LORD God caused a deep sleep to fall on Adam, and he slept; and He took one of his ribs, and closed up the flesh in its place. 22 Then the rib which the LORD God had taken from man He made into a woman, and He brought her to the man.

23 And Adam said:

"This *is* now bone of my bones
And flesh of my flesh;
She shall be called Woman,
Because she was taken out of Man."

24 Therefore a man shall leave his father and mother and be joined to his wife, and they shall become one flesh.

25 And they were both naked, the man and his wife, and were not ashamed.

Adam and Eve disobey God

3 Now the serpent was more cunning than any beast of the field which the LORD God had made. And he said to the woman, "Has God indeed said, 'You shall not eat of every tree of the garden'?"

2 And the woman said to the serpent, "We may eat the fruit of the trees of the garden; 3 but of the fruit of the

Who Was the Serpent?

How could a serpent speak? Why would anybody listen to a serpent? We usually stay away from snakes, but in the Garden of Eden no one had ever been bitten by one. So Satan used what seemed to be a beautiful serpent to deceive poor Eve. Satan took advantage of Eve's innocence.

⚒ DIGGING IN

3:2–13 How Sin Began *Who is your God?* This was the question Adam and Eve had to decide in the Garden of Eden. Satan, a disobedient angel, tricked our first parents into believing God should not rule over their lives.

Satan told Eve that she and her husband could be their own gods. Then they wouldn't need their Creator-Friend anymore. They could live forever without Him.

The Lord had told them to obey Him.

If they didn't obey Him, they would die, because all life comes from our Creator. Sickness, death, and all unhappiness in the world came because Adam and Eve decided to be their own gods. That's how sin began.

You must decide if the One who created you is going to be the God you give your life to. That is the most important decision you will ever make.

tree which is in the midst of the garden, God has said, 'You shall not eat it, nor shall you touch it, lest you die.' "

4 Then the serpent said to the woman, "You will not surely die. 5 For God knows that in the day you eat of it your eyes will be opened, and you will be like God, knowing good and evil."

6 So when the woman saw that the tree was good for food, that it was pleasant to the eyes, and a tree desirable to make one wise, she took of its fruit and ate. She also gave to her husband with her, and he ate. 7 Then the eyes of both of them were opened, and they knew that they were naked; and they sewed fig leaves together and made themselves coverings.

8 And they heard the sound of the Lord God walking in the garden in the cool of the day, and Adam and his wife hid themselves from the presence of the Lord God among the trees of the garden. 9 Then the Lord God called to Adam and said to him, "Where are you?"

10 So he said, "I heard Your voice in the garden, and I was afraid because I was naked; and I hid myself."

11 And He said, "Who told you that you were naked? Have you eaten from the tree of which I commanded you that you should not eat?"

12 Then the man said, "The woman whom You gave to be with me, she gave me of the tree, and I ate."

13 And the Lord God said to the woman, "What is this you have done?"

The woman said, "The serpent deceived me, and I ate."

14 So the Lord God said to the serpent:

"Because you have done this,
 You are cursed more than all cattle,
 And more than every beast of the field;
 On your belly you shall go,
 And you shall eat dust
 All the days of your life.
15 And I will put enmity
 Between you and the woman,
 And between your seed and her Seed;
 He shall bruise your head,
 And you shall bruise His heel."

16 To the woman He said:

"I will greatly multiply your sorrow and your conception;
 In pain you shall bring forth children;
 Your desire shall be for your husband,
 And he shall rule over you."

17 Then to Adam He said, "Because you have heeded the voice of your wife, and have eaten from the tree of which I commanded you, saying, 'You shall not eat of it':

"Cursed is the ground for your sake;
 In toil you shall eat of it
 All the days of your life.

🪓 DIGGING IN

3:15 A Cure for Sin God didn't just leave Adam and Eve to die when they sinned. He still loved them and He wanted them to love and enjoy Him.

The Lord gave Adam and Eve a promise when the sadness of their sin broke their hearts. Someday a Son would be born who would destroy Satan and take away all their sin. God called this Son the "Seed" of Adam and Eve, the One who would be their Savior.

Of course, you know this great Son was Jesus. He is the One who broke Satan's power. Jesus fought a mighty battle with Satan at the Cross. Satan tried to destroy the great Son of Adam who was also the Son of God. But the Son rose from the grave. Adam's sin brought death, but Jesus died to give you life forevermore. Adam and Eve believed God's promise. If you will trust in Jesus, you can have eternal life right now.

What Adam and Eve Learned

At first we were too heartbroken to understand all that happened. We had been so happy in the garden where God visited us every day. Now it was all over. The sky was filled with dark clouds, and the sunshine of our Father's love was hidden.

If only we had listened to our Friend, the Lord, how different everything would be now. Instead, we had obeyed Satan, our Enemy. Now we could not go back to those good times with God as before.

Afterward, we were really sorry for what happened, and our Father forgave us. Now we believe His promise to give us a new beginning, and that's what we learned!

From now on we will talk to God about everything we plan to do with our lives.

18 Both thorns and thistles it shall bring forth for you,
And you shall eat the herb of the field.
19 In the sweat of your face you shall eat bread
Till you return to the ground,
For out of it you were taken;
For dust you *are,*
And to dust you shall return."

20 And Adam called his wife's name Eve, because she was the mother of all living.

21 Also for Adam and his wife the LORD God made tunics of skin, and clothed them.

22 Then the LORD God said, "Behold, the man has become like one of Us, to know good and evil. And now, lest he put out his hand and take also of the tree of life, and eat, and live forever"— 23 therefore the LORD God sent him out of the garden of Eden to till the ground from which he was taken. 24 So He drove out the man; and He placed **cherubim** at the east of the garden of Eden, and a flaming sword which turned every way, to guard the way to the tree of life.

Cain kills Abel

4 Now Adam knew Eve his wife, and she conceived and bore Cain, and said, "I have acquired a man from the LORD." 2 Then she bore again, this time his brother Abel. Now Abel was a keeper of sheep, but Cain was a tiller of the ground. 3 And in the process of time it came to pass that Cain brought an offering of the fruit of the ground to the LORD. 4 Abel also brought of the firstborn of his flock and of their fat. And the LORD respected Abel and his offering, 5 but He did not respect Cain and his offering. And Cain was very angry, and his countenance fell.

6 So the LORD said to Cain, "Why are you angry? And why has your countenance fallen? 7 If you do well, will you not be accepted? And if you do not do well, sin lies at the door. And its desire *is* for you, but you should rule over it."

8 Now Cain talked with Abel his brother; and it came to pass, when they were in the field, that Cain rose up against Abel his brother and killed him.

9 Then the LORD said to Cain, "Where *is* Abel your brother?"

WORDFINDER

3:24 Cherubim Pronounced *CHER-uh-bim.* Plural of cherub. These are special angels who are always in the presence of God and continually praise Him.

What Cain Learned

I envied my younger brother Abel. He always seemed to do everything right. But no matter what I did, it seemed to go wrong. When God accepted my brother's offering instead of mine, that was the end! What was so special about his offering anyway?

So one day I just picked up a rock and knocked him down. I had never seen anybody die before, and when Abel didn't move, I was scared. He never did move again.

That was when God spoke to me. I was shattered with grief and guilt. Then I realized that all his life Abel had given God the best he had. But I had given the Lord only my leftovers.

God sent me away. But in my new home, I have decided God will always have my very best.

He said, "I do not know. Am I my brother's keeper?"

10 And He said, "What have you done? The voice of your brother's blood cries out to Me from the ground. 11 So now you are cursed from the earth, which has opened its mouth to receive your brother's blood from your hand. 12 When you till the ground, it shall no longer yield its strength to you. A fugitive and a vagabond you shall be on the earth."

13 And Cain said to the LORD, "My punishment is greater than I can bear! 14 Surely You have driven me out this day from the face of the ground; I shall be hidden from Your face; I shall be a fugitive and a vagabond on the earth, and it will happen that anyone who finds me will kill me."

15 And the LORD said to him, "Therefore, whoever kills Cain, vengeance shall be taken on him sevenfold." And the LORD set a mark on Cain, lest anyone finding him should kill him.

16 Then Cain went out from the presence of the LORD and dwelt in the land of Nod on the east of Eden. 17 And Cain knew his wife, and she conceived and bore Enoch. And he built a city, and called the name of the city after the name of his son—Enoch. 18 To Enoch was born Irad; and Irad begot Mehujael, and Mehujael begot Methushael, and Methushael begot Lamech. 19 Then Lamech took for himself two wives: the name of one was Adah, and the name of the second was Zillah. 20 And Adah bore Jabal. He was the father of those who dwell in tents and have livestock. 21 His brother's name was Jubal. He was the father of all those who play the harp and flute. 22 And as for Zillah, she also bore Tubal-Cain, an instructor of every craftsman in bronze and iron. And the sister of Tubal-Cain was Naamah.

23 Then Lamech said to his wives:

"Adah and Zillah, hear my voice;
Wives of Lamech, listen to my speech!
For I have killed a man for wounding me,
Even a young man for hurting me.
24 If Cain shall be avenged sevenfold,
Then Lamech seventy-sevenfold."

25 And Adam knew his wife again, and she bore a son and named him Seth, "For God has appointed another seed for me instead of Abel, whom Cain killed." 26 And as for Seth, to him also a son was born; and he named him Enosh. Then men began to call on the name of the LORD.

Adam's family

5 This is the book of the genealogy of Adam. In the day that God created

man, He made him in the likeness of God. 2 He created them male and female, and blessed them and called them Mankind in the day they were created. 3 And Adam lived one hundred and thirty years, and begot *a son* in his own likeness, after his image, and named him Seth. 4 After he begot Seth, the days of Adam were eight hundred years; and he had sons and daughters. 5 So all the days that Adam lived were nine hundred and thirty years; and he died.

6 Seth lived one hundred and five years, and begot Enosh. 7 After he begot Enosh, Seth lived eight hundred and seven years, and had sons and daughters. 8 So all the days of Seth were nine hundred and twelve years; and he died.

9 Enosh lived ninety years, and begot Cainan. 10 After he begot Cainan, Enosh lived eight hundred and fifteen years, and had sons and daughters. 11 So all the days of Enosh were nine hundred and five years; and he died.

12 Cainan lived seventy years, and begot Mahalalel. 13 After he begot Mahalalel, Cainan lived eight hundred and forty years, and had sons and daughters. 14 So all the days of Cainan were nine hundred and ten years; and he died.

15 Mahalalel lived sixty-five years, and begot Jared. 16 After he begot Jared, Mahalalel lived eight hundred and thirty years, and had sons and daughters. 17 So all the days of Mahalalel were eight hundred and ninety-five years; and he died.

18 Jared lived one hundred and sixty-two years, and begot Enoch. 19 After he begot Enoch, Jared lived eight hundred years, and had sons and daughters. 20 So all the days of Jared were nine hundred and sixty-two years; and he died.

21 Enoch lived sixty-five years, and begot Methuselah. 22 After he begot Methuselah, Enoch walked with God three hundred years, and had sons and daughters. 23 So all the days of Enoch were three hundred and sixty-five

---

Why Was Methuselah So Old?

Methuselah (pronounced *meh-THOO-suh-luh*) is the oldest person you will meet in the Bible. How could anybody live so long? Most of us don't even live a hundred years. You have already seen that sin is the real cause of death (see Genesis 2:19). As time went by, sin brought disease, weakness, and earlier death.

---

years. 24 And Enoch walked with God; and he *was* not, for God took him.

25 Methuselah lived one hundred and eighty-seven years, and begot Lamech. 26 After he begot Lamech, Methuselah lived seven hundred and eighty-two years, and had sons and daughters. 27 So all the days of Methuselah were nine hundred and sixty-nine years; and he died.

28 Lamech lived one hundred and eighty-two years, and had a son. 29 And he called his name Noah, saying, "This *one* will comfort us concerning our work and the toil of our hands, because of the ground which the LORD has cursed." 30 After he begot Noah, Lamech lived five hundred and ninety-five years, and had sons and daughters. 31 So all the days of Lamech were seven hundred and seventy-seven years; and he died.

32 And Noah was five hundred years old, and Noah begot Shem, Ham, and Japheth.

Noah builds the ark

6 Now it came to pass, when men began to multiply on the face of the earth, and daughters were born to them, 2 that the sons of God saw the daughters of men, that they *were* beautiful; and they took wives for themselves of all whom they chose.

3 And the LORD said, "My Spirit shall not strive with man forever, for he *is* indeed flesh; yet his days shall be one hundred and twenty years." 4 There

Maybe you've seen those funny pictures of Noah and the ark. Well, let me tell you, it wasn't very funny at all! I tried to tell everybody that God was going to send a big flood, but they only laughed and said I was out of my mind.

So I built my ark, just as God told me, and one day every kind of animal came pouring into it. After my family and I went in, it all started to happen—the frightening rain that fell and the underground springs that burst upward. You should have heard the pounding of the wind, the swirling waters—and I'll never forget the horrible cries of the drowning people!

But my family was saved, and the ark settled on Mount Ararat in Turkey. Then we began again to enjoy the life we had in the world before the Flood.

were giants on the earth in those days, and also afterward, when the sons of God came in to the daughters of men and they bore *children* to them. Those *were* the mighty men who *were* of old, men of renown.

5 Then the LORD saw that the wickedness of man *was* great in the earth, and *that* every intent of the thoughts of his heart *was* only evil continually. 6 And the LORD was sorry that He had made man on the earth, and He was grieved in His heart. 7 So the LORD said, "I will destroy man whom I have created from the face of the earth, both man and beast, creeping thing and birds of the air, for I am sorry that I have made them." 8 But Noah found grace in the eyes of the LORD.

9 This is the genealogy of Noah. Noah was a just man, perfect in his generations. Noah walked with God. 10 And Noah begot three sons: Shem, Ham, and Japheth.

11 The earth also was corrupt before God, and the earth was filled with violence. 12 So God looked upon the earth, and indeed it was corrupt; for all flesh had corrupted their way on the earth.

13 And God said to Noah, "The end of all flesh has come before Me, for the earth is filled with violence through them; and behold, I will destroy them with the earth. 14 Make yourself an ark of gopherwood; make rooms in the ark, and cover it inside and outside with pitch. 15 And this is how you shall make it: The length of the ark *shall be* three hundred cubits, its width fifty cubits, and its height thirty cubits. 16 You shall make a window for the ark, and you shall finish it to a cubit from above; and set the door of the ark in its side. You shall make it *with* lower, second, and third *decks.* 17 And behold, I Myself am bringing floodwaters on the earth, to destroy from

One cubit equals the length of a man's forearm.

Man Builds Strange Boat on Dry Land

Old Testament News Service

MESOPOTAMIA—A man named Noah is reported to be building a very strange boat. According to our reporters, the boat has no sail, no rudder, and no outside deck! Inside are hundreds of cages and pens for animals, plus a family living area.

There is no nearby body of water deep enough to float such a ship. But Noah insists that it is going to start raining any day now, and that there will be a great flood, though weather experts do not predict rain in this region for some time.

Noah claims that two of every kind of animal will begin to board the ship in the next few days. Though the source of all these animals is uncertain, the doors will remain open until they are all safely aboard, says Captain Noah. If he is right, this will be the largest collection of domestic and wildlife ever gathered under one roof!

under heaven all flesh in which *is* the breath of life; everything that *is* on the earth shall die. 18 But I will establish My covenant with you; and you shall go into the ark—you, your sons, your wife, and your sons' wives with you. 19 And of every living thing of all flesh you shall bring two of every *sort* into the ark, to keep *them* alive with you; they shall be male and female. 20 Of

God told Noah to build a big boat to hold his family and a floating zoo!

It rained for 40 days and 40 nights.

the birds after their kind, of animals after their kind, and of *every* creeping thing of the earth after its kind, two of *every kind* will come to you to keep *them* alive. 21 And you shall take for yourself of all food that is eaten, and you shall gather *it* to yourself; and it shall be food for you and for them."

22 Thus Noah did; according to all that God commanded him, so he did.

God sends the Flood

7 Then the LORD said to Noah, "Come into the ark, you and all your household, because I have seen *that* you *are* righteous before Me in this generation. 2 You shall take with you seven each of *every* clean animal, a male and his female; two each of animals that *are* unclean, a male and his female; 3 also seven each of birds of the air, male and female, to keep the species alive on the face of all the earth. 4 For after seven more days I will cause it to rain on the earth forty days and forty nights, and I will destroy from the face of the earth all living things that I have made." 5 And Noah did according to all that the LORD commanded him. 6 Noah *was* six hundred years old when the floodwaters were on the earth.

7 So Noah, with his sons, his wife,

⛏DIGGING IN

7:1–24 The Great Flood You have read how Noah might have described the great Flood in Genesis 6.

Some people wonder if the Flood really happened, but we have lots of proof that it did. The Flood is described in Genesis 7. Many other peoples of the world, even the Eskimos, also tell us about the ancient Flood.

Some people wonder if the Flood covered the whole world. The Bible says all the high mountains in Noah's area were covered. If the water was that high, it would have covered everything everywhere.

God told Noah to build a boat called an ark to float on top of the water. It was designed to carry Noah, his family, and two of every kind of animal God wanted to save. The ark was 450 feet long, almost as long as a city block, and 45 feet high, as tall as a five-story building.

The Flood lasted for a total of 371 days. The water came from great underground springs as well as from rain.

and his sons' wives, went into the ark because of the waters of the flood. 8 Of clean animals, of animals that *are* unclean, of birds, and of everything that creeps on the earth, 9 two by two they went into the ark to Noah, male and female, as God had commanded Noah. 10 And it came to pass after seven days that the waters of the flood were on the earth. 11 In the six hundredth year of Noah's life, in the second month, the seventeenth day of the month, on that day all the fountains of the great deep were broken up, and the windows of heaven were opened. 12 And the rain was on the earth forty days and forty nights.

13 On the very same day Noah and Noah's sons, Shem, Ham, and Japheth, and Noah's wife and the three wives of his sons with them, entered the ark— 14 they and every beast after its kind, all cattle after their kind, every creeping thing that creeps on the earth after its kind, and every bird after its kind, every bird of every sort. 15 And they went into the ark to Noah, two by two, of all flesh in which *is* the breath of life. 16 So those that entered, male and female of all flesh, went in as God had commanded him; and the LORD shut him in.

17 Now the flood was on the earth forty days. The waters increased and lifted up the ark, and it rose high above the earth. 18 The waters prevailed and greatly increased on the earth, and the ark moved about on the surface of the waters. 19 And the waters prevailed exceedingly on the earth, and all the high hills under the whole heaven were covered. 20 The waters prevailed fifteen cubits upward, and the mountains were covered. 21 And all flesh died that moved on the earth: birds and cattle and beasts and every creeping thing that creeps on the earth, and every man. 22 All in whose nostrils *was* the breath of the spirit of life, all that *was* on the dry *land,* died. 23 So He destroyed all living things which were on the face of the ground: both man and cattle, creeping thing and bird of the air. They were destroyed from

the earth. Only Noah and those who *were* with him in the ark remained *alive.* 24 And the waters prevailed on the earth one hundred and fifty days.

God dries the land

8 Then God remembered Noah, and every living thing, and all the animals that *were* with him in the ark. And God made a wind to pass over the earth, and the waters subsided. 2 The fountains of the deep and the windows of heaven were also stopped, and the rain from heaven was restrained. 3 And the waters receded continually from the earth. At the end of the hundred and fifty days the waters decreased. 4 Then the ark rested in the seventh month, the seventeenth day of the month, on the mountains of Ararat. 5 And the waters decreased continually until the tenth month. In the tenth *month,* on the first *day* of the month, the tops of the mountains were seen.

6 So it came to pass, at the end of forty days, that Noah opened the window of the ark which he had made. 7 Then he sent out a raven, which kept going to and fro until the waters had dried up from the earth. 8 He also sent out from himself a dove, to see if the waters had receded from the face of the ground. 9 But the dove found no resting place for the sole of her foot, and she returned into the ark to him, for the waters *were* on the face of the whole earth. So he put out his hand and took her, and drew her into the ark to himself. 10 And he waited yet another seven days, and again he sent the dove out from the ark. 11 Then the dove came to him in the evening, and behold, a freshly plucked olive leaf *was* in her mouth; and Noah knew that the waters had receded from the earth. 12 So he waited yet another seven days and sent out the dove, which did not return again to him anymore.

13 And it came to pass in the six hundred and first year, in the first *month,* the first *day* of the month, that the waters were dried up from the earth; and

Noah removed the covering of the ark and looked, and indeed the surface of the ground was dry. 14 And in the second month, on the twenty-seventh day of the month, the earth was dried.

15 Then God spoke to Noah, saying, 16 "Go out of the ark, you and your wife, and your sons and your sons' wives with you. 17 Bring out with you every living thing of all flesh that is with you: birds and cattle and every creeping thing that creeps on the earth, so that they may abound on the earth, and be fruitful and multiply on the earth." 18 So Noah went out, and his sons and his wife and his sons' wives with him. 19 Every animal, every creeping thing, every bird, and whatever creeps on the earth, according to their families, went out of the ark.

20 Then Noah built an altar to the LORD, and took of every clean animal and of every clean bird, and offered burnt offerings on the altar. 21 And the LORD smelled a soothing aroma. Then the LORD said in His heart, "I will never again curse the ground for man's sake, although the imagination of man's heart is evil from his youth; nor will I again destroy every living thing as I have done.

22 "While the earth remains,
Seedtime and harvest,
Cold and heat,
Winter and summer,
And day and night
Shall not cease."

God makes a promise to Noah

9 So God blessed Noah and his sons, and said to them: "Be fruitful and multiply, and fill the earth. 2 And the fear of you and the dread of you shall be on every beast of the earth, on every bird of the air, on all that move on the earth, and on all the fish of the sea. They are given into your hand. 3 Every moving thing that lives shall be food for you. I have given you all things, even as the green herbs. 4 But you shall not eat flesh with its life, that is, its blood. 5 Surely for your

lifeblood I will demand a reckoning; from the hand of every beast I will require it, and from the hand of man. From the hand of every man's brother I will require the life of man.

6 "Whoever sheds man's blood,
By man his blood shall be shed;
For in the image of God
He made man.
7 And as for you, be fruitful and multiply;
Bring forth abundantly in the earth
And multiply in it."

8 Then God spoke to Noah and to his sons with him, saying: 9 "And as for Me, behold, I establish My covenant with you and with your descendants after you, 10 and with every living creature that is with you: the birds, the cattle, and every beast of the earth with you, of all that go out of the ark, every beast of the earth. 11 Thus I establish My covenant with you: Never again shall all flesh be cut off by the waters of the flood; never again shall there be a flood to destroy the earth."

12 And God said: "This is the sign of the covenant which I make between Me and you, and every living creature that is with you, for perpetual generations: 13 I set My rainbow in the cloud, and it shall be for the sign of the covenant between Me and the earth. 14 It shall be, when I bring a cloud over the earth, that the rainbow shall be seen in the cloud; 15 and I will remember My covenant which is between Me and you and every living creature of all flesh; the waters shall never again become a flood to destroy all flesh. 16 The rainbow shall be in the cloud, and I will look on it to remember the everlasting covenant between God and every living creature of all flesh that is on the earth." 17 And God said to Noah, "This is the sign of the covenant which I have established between Me and all flesh that is on the earth."

18 Now the sons of Noah who went out of the ark were Shem, Ham, and Japheth. And Ham was the father of

Canaan. 19 These three *were* the sons of Noah, and from these the whole earth was populated.

20 And Noah began *to be* a farmer, and he planted a vineyard. 21 Then he drank of the wine and was drunk, and became uncovered in his tent. 22 And Ham, the father of Canaan, saw the nakedness of his father, and told his two brothers outside. 23 But Shem and Japheth took a garment, laid *it* on both their shoulders, and went backward and covered the nakedness of their father. Their faces *were* turned away, and they did not see their father's nakedness.

24 So Noah awoke from his wine, and knew what his younger son had done to him. 25 Then he said:

"Cursed *be* Canaan;
A servant of servants
He shall be to his brethren."

26 And he said:

"Blessed *be* the LORD,
The God of Shem,
And may Canaan be his servant.
27 May God enlarge Japheth,
And may he dwell in the tents
of Shem;
And may Canaan be his
servant."

28 And Noah lived after the flood three hundred and fifty years. 29 So all the days of Noah were nine hundred and fifty years; and he died.

Noah's family

10 Now this *is* the genealogy of the sons of Noah: Shem, Ham, and Japheth. And sons were born to them after the flood.

2 The sons of Japheth *were* Gomer, Magog, Madai, Javan, Tubal, Me-shech, and Tiras. 3 The sons of Gomer *were* Ashkenaz, Riphath, and Togar-mah. 4 The sons of Javan *were* Elishah, Tarshish, Kittim, and Dodanim. 5 From these the coastland *peoples* of the Gentiles were separated into their lands, everyone according to his lan-guage, according to their families, into their nations.

6 The sons of Ham *were* Cush, Mizraim, Put, and Canaan. 7 The sons of Cush *were* Seba, Havilah, Sabtah, Raamah, and Sabtechah; and the sons of Raamah *were* Sheba and Dedan.

8 Cush begot Nimrod; he began to be a mighty one on the earth. 9 He was a mighty hunter before the LORD; therefore it is said, "Like Nimrod the mighty hunter before the LORD." 10 And the beginning of his kingdom was Babel, Erech, Accad, and Calneh, in the land of Shinar. 11 From that land he went to Assyria and built Nineveh, Rehoboth Ir, Calah, 12 and Resen be-tween Nineveh and Calah (that *is* the principal city).

13 Mizraim begot Ludim, Anamim, Lehabim, Naphtuhim, 14 Pathrusim, and Casluhim (from whom came the Philistines and Caphtorim).

15 Canaan begot Sidon his firstborn, and Heth; 16 the Jebusite, the Amorite, and the Girgashite; 17 the Hivite, the Arkite, and the Sinite; 18 the Arvadite, the Zemarite, and the Hamathite. Af-terward the families of the **Canaanites** were dispersed. 19 And the border of the Canaanites was from Sidon as you go toward Gerar, as far as Gaza; then as you go toward Sodom, Gomorrah, Admah, and Zeboiim, as far as Lasha. 20 These *were* the sons of Ham, ac-cording to their families, according to their languages, in their lands *and* in their nations.

21 And *children* were born also to Shem, the father of all the children of Eber, the brother of Japheth the elder.

⊙WORDFINDER —————————————

10:18 Canaanites Pronounced *KAY-nuh-nights*. Descendants of Noah's grandson, Canaan. When Jacob and his family moved to Egypt, the dwellers in Palestine became known as Canaanites. Then Palestine was called Canaan.

Is This the Highest Tower in the World?

Old Testament News Service

PLAIN OF SHINAR—Work is underway on a new city. Building plans call for a tall tower to be erected nearby.

Eyewitnesses say the people of Babel are working day and night to raise their tower. Some are carrying bricks to the building site while others continue to build upward. Already the tower is more than a hundred feet high. Builders claim that, when it is finished, it will reach all the way up to heaven!

Our news office is watching events closely. At last report, thick clouds were beginning to form around the top of the tower. Frightening flashes of lightning and heavy thunder were increasing in the area, and the whole earth around the tower was shaking badly.

The view of this newspaper is that the city and the people working on the tower are in great danger.

22 The sons of Shem *were* Elam, Asshur, Arphaxad, Lud, and Aram. 23 The sons of Aram *were* Uz, Hul, Gether, and Mash. 24 Arphaxad begot Salah, and Salah begot Eber. 25 To Eber were born two sons: the name of one *was* Peleg, for in his days the earth was divided; and his brother's name *was* Joktan. 26 Joktan begot Almodad, Sheleph, Hazarmaveth, Jerah, 27 Hadoram, Uzal, Diklah, 28 Obal, Abimael, Sheba, 29 Ophir, Havilah, and Jobab. All these *were* the sons of Joktan. 30 And their dwelling place was from Mesha as you go toward Sephar, the mountain of the east. 31 These *were* the sons of Shem, according to their families, according to their languages, in their lands, according to their nations.

32 These *were* the families of the sons of Noah, according to their generations, in their nations; and from these the nations were divided on the earth after the flood.

The people build a tower

11 Now the whole earth had one language and one speech. 2 And it came to pass, as they journeyed from the east, that they found a plain in the land of Shinar, and they dwelt there. 3 Then they said to one another, "Come, let us make bricks and bake *them* thoroughly." They had brick for stone, and they had asphalt for mortar. 4 And they said, "Come, let us build ourselves a city, and a tower whose top *is* in the heavens; let us make a name for ourselves, lest we be scattered abroad over the face of the whole earth."

5 But the LORD came down to see the city and the tower which the sons of men had built. 6 And the LORD said, "Indeed the people *are* one and they all have one language, and this is what they begin to do; now nothing that they propose to do will be withheld from them. 7 Come, let Us go down and there confuse their language, that they may not understand one another's speech." 8 So the LORD scattered them abroad from there over the face of all the earth, and they ceased building the city. 9 Therefore its name is called Babel, because there the LORD confused the language of all the earth; and from there the LORD scattered them abroad over the face of all the earth.

10 This *is* the genealogy of Shem: Shem *was* one hundred years old, and begot Arphaxad two years after the flood. 11 After he begot Arphaxad, Shem lived five hundred years, and begot sons and daughters.

12 Arphaxad lived thirty-five years, and begot Salah. 13 After he begot Salah, Arphaxad lived four hundred and three years, and begot sons and daughters.

The people, trying to reach heaven, built a tall tower.

¹⁴ Salah lived thirty years, and begot Eber. ¹⁵ After he begot Eber, Salah lived four hundred and three years, and begot sons and daughters.

¹⁶ Eber lived thirty-four years, and begot Peleg. ¹⁷ After he begot Peleg, Eber lived four hundred and thirty years, and begot sons and daughters.

¹⁸ Peleg lived thirty years, and begot Reu. ¹⁹ After he begot Reu, Peleg lived two hundred and nine years, and begot sons and daughters.

²⁰ Reu lived thirty-two years, and begot Serug. ²¹ After he begot Serug, Reu lived two hundred and seven years, and begot sons and daughters.

🔨 DIGGING IN

11:1–9 The Tower of Babel There are remains of many ancient towers like the one Genesis calls the Tower of Babel (pronounced *BAY-bull*). Such a tower is called a ziggurat, (pronounced *ZIG-uh-rat*). One of those buildings that remains today could be the very tower in Genesis 11.

At the time of the Tower of Babel, after the great Flood, there was one race of people on the earth. Remember that these people still did not know much about astronomy. This is why they fool-

ishly imagined they could build a tower all the way up to the heavens.

Also, the people of Babel were sinners just like people today, and they wanted to test God's right to rule over their lives. The Tower of Babel was their way of telling God they could be just as high as He is! Sounds silly, doesn't it?

But people today still try to test God's right to rule their lives. When they break God's laws, they are telling Him, "I can do as I please!" Don't you think that's a foolish thing to say to God?

22 Serug lived thirty years, and begot Nahor. 23 After he begot Nahor, Serug lived two hundred years, and begot sons and daughters.

24 Nahor lived twenty-nine years, and begot Terah. 25 After he begot Terah, Nahor lived one hundred and nineteen years, and begot sons and daughters.

26 Now Terah lived seventy years, and begot Abram, Nahor, and Haran.

27 This *is* the genealogy of Terah: Terah begot Abram, Nahor, and Haran. Haran begot Lot. 28 And Haran died before his father Terah in his native land, in Ur of the **Chaldeans**. 29 Then Abram and Nahor took wives: the name of Abram's wife *was* Sarai, and the name of Nahor's wife, Milcah, the daughter of Haran the father of Milcah and the father of Iscah. 30 But Sarai was barren; she had no child.

31 And Terah took his son Abram and his grandson Lot, the son of Haran, and his daughter-in-law Sarai, his son Abram's wife, and they went out with them from Ur of the Chaldeans to go to the land of Canaan; and they came to Haran and dwelt there. 32 So the days of Terah were two hundred and five years, and Terah died in Haran.

God speaks to Abram

12 Now the LORD had said to Abram:

"Get out of your country,
From your family
And from your father's house,
To a land that I will show you.
2   I will make you a great nation;
I will bless you
And make your name great;
And you shall be a blessing.
3   I will bless those who bless you,
And I will curse him who curses you;
And in you all the families of the earth shall be blessed."

Where Was Ur of the Chaldees?

Ur was a city in the country of Babylonia (pronounced *bab-ih-LOW-nih-uh*). Usually Babylonia is called Chaldea (pronounced *kal-DEE-uh*) in the Bible. This was Abraham's early home. An ancient library and many beautiful treasures have been found in the city's ruins. The people of Ur worshiped the moon god.

WORDFINDER

11:28 Chaldeans The people who lived in Chaldea (pronounced *kal-DEE-uh*), a land found in the region of modern Iran and Iraq. Chaldea later included nearly all of Babylonia (pronounced *bab-ih-LOW-nih-uh*).

DIGGING IN

12:1–3 God's Great Promise Sometimes you may make promises you don't keep. But God can never break any of His promises.

People who have lived a long time in the world learn that God keeps every promise He ever made. He promises us, "I will never leave you nor forsake you." Friends fail us. Our bodies get sick. And someday we will die. But we can still say, "Surely goodness and mercy shall follow me all the days of my life, and I will dwell in the house of the Lord forever" (Psalm 23:6).

God made a very big promise to Abraham. First, God said He would give Abraham's people all the land of Palestine. Abraham's people still live there four thousand years later! That's the longest time any nation has lived anywhere.

Then God made a great promise that all people who trusted in Abraham's "Seed" would be blessed. The "Seed" of Abraham is Jesus who was born two thousand years after Abraham lived. So God will bless you forever if you trust in Jesus.

The ziggurat at Ur, Abraham's early home.

LACK OF FAITH

⁴ So Abram departed as the LORD had spoken to him, and Lot went with him. And Abram *was* seventy-five years old when he departed from Haran. ⁵ Then Abram took Sarai his wife and Lot his brother's son, and all their possessions that they had gathered, and the people whom they had acquired in Haran, and they departed to go to the land of Canaan. So they came to the land of Canaan. ⁶ Abram passed through the land to the place of Shechem, as far as the terebinth tree of Moreh. And the Canaanites *were* then in the land.

⁷ Then the LORD appeared to Abram and said, "To your descendants I will give this land." And there he built an altar to the LORD, who had appeared to him. ⁸ And he moved from there to the mountain east of Bethel, and he pitched his tent *with* Bethel on the west and Ai on the east; there he built an altar to the LORD and called on the name of the LORD. ⁹ So Abram journeyed, going on still toward the South.

¹⁰ Now there was a famine in the land, and Abram went down to Egypt to dwell there, for the famine *was* severe in the land. ¹¹ And it came to pass, when he was close to entering Egypt, that he said to Sarai his wife, "Indeed I know that you *are* a woman of beautiful countenance. ¹² Therefore it will happen, when the Egyptians see you, that they will say, 'This *is* his wife'; and they will kill me, but they will let you live. ¹³ Please say you *are* my sister, that it may be well with me for your sake, and that I may live because of you."

¹⁴ So it was, when Abram came into Egypt, that the Egyptians saw the woman, that she *was* very beautiful. ¹⁵ The princes of Pharaoh also saw her and commended her to Pharaoh. And the woman was taken to Pharaoh's house. ¹⁶ He treated Abram well for her sake. He had sheep, oxen, male donkeys, male and female servants, female donkeys, and camels.

¹⁷ But the LORD plagued Pharaoh and his house with great plagues because of Sarai, Abram's wife. ¹⁸ And Pharaoh called Abram and said,

An Egyptian plows his field.

Old Testament World

Abram (pronounced AY-brum) is about to make a very long trip. Where is Abram when God tells him to move? (11:31) Where does God tell him to go? (11:31) Why? (12:2–3)

Abram is not alone on this trip. Who goes with him? (12:5) Bible travelers either walked or rode camels or donkeys. Can you see the great cloud of dust stirred up by the footsteps and hoofprints as the wanderers journey northward?

The people stop first at Abram's family home. (11:31) You will see that they do not take a shortcut across the desert. Instead, they follow the Euphrates (pronounced you-FRAY-tees) River, which provides water for their families and flocks.

When they reach Canaan (pronounced KAY-nun), the land God has promised them, they stop at Shechem (pronounced SHE-kum 12:6), Bethel (BETH-ul), and Ai (AY-eye). (12:8) Find these cities on the map. What does Abram do here that pleases God?

"What *is* this you have done to me? Why did you not tell me that she *was* your wife? ¹⁹ Why did you say, 'She *is* my sister'? I might have taken her as my wife. Now therefore, here is your wife; take *her* and go your way." ²⁰ So Pharaoh commanded *his* men concerning him; and they sent him away, with his wife and all that he had.

Abram lives in Canaan

13 Then Abram went up from Egypt, he and his wife and all that he had, and Lot with him, to the South. ² Abram *was* very rich in livestock, in silver, and in gold. ³ And he went on his journey from the South as far as Bethel, to the place where his tent had been at the beginning, between Bethel and Ai, ⁴ to the place of the altar which he had made there at first. And there Abram called on the name of the LORD.

⁵ Lot also, who went with Abram, had flocks and herds and tents. ⁶ Now the land was not able to support them, that they might dwell together, for their possessions were so great that they could not dwell together. ⁷ And there was strife between the herdsmen of Abram's livestock and the herdsmen of Lot's livestock. The Canaanites and the Perizzites then dwelt in the land.

⁸ So Abram said to Lot, "Please let there be no strife between you and me, and between my herdsmen and your herdsmen; for we *are* brethren. ⁹ *Is* not the whole land before you? Please separate from me. If *you take* the left, then I will go to the right; or, if *you* go to the right, then I will go to the left."

¹⁰ And Lot lifted his eyes and saw all the plain of Jordan, that it *was* well watered everywhere (before the LORD destroyed Sodom and Gomorrah) like the garden of the LORD, like the land of Egypt as you go toward Zoar. ¹¹ Then Lot chose for himself all the plain of Jordan, and Lot journeyed east. And they separated from each other. ¹² Abram dwelt in the land of Canaan, and Lot dwelt in the cities of the plain and pitched *his* tent even as far as Sodom. ¹³ But the men of Sodom *were* exceedingly wicked and sinful against the LORD.

¹⁴ And the LORD said to Abram, after Lot had separated from him: "Lift your eyes now and look from the place where you are—northward, southward, eastward, and westward; ¹⁵ for all the land which you see I give to you and your descendants forever. ¹⁶ And I will make your descendants as the dust of the earth; so that if a man could number the dust of the earth, *then* your descendants also could be numbered. ¹⁷ Arise, walk in the land through its length and its width, for I give it to you."

¹⁸ Then Abram moved *his* tent, and went and dwelt by the terebinth trees of Mamre, which *are* in Hebron, and built an altar there to the LORD.

The burial place of Abraham and Isaac in Hebron.

Abram saves Lot

14 And it came to pass in the days of Amraphel king of Shinar, Arioch king of Ellasar, Chedorlaomer king of Elam, and Tidal king of nations, 2 *that* they made war with Bera king of Sodom, Birsha king of Gomorrah, Shinab king of Admah, Shemeber king of Zeboiim, and the king of Bela (that is, Zoar). 3 All these joined together in the Valley of Siddim (that is, the Salt Sea). 4 Twelve years they served Chedorlaomer, and in the thirteenth year they rebelled.

5 In the fourteenth year Chedorlaomer and the kings that *were* with him came and attacked the Rephaim in Ashteroth Karnaim, the Zuzim in Ham, the Emim in Shaveh Kiriathaim, 6 and the Horites in their mountain of Seir, as far as El Paran, which *is* by the wilderness. 7 Then they turned back and came to En Mishpat (that *is,* Kadesh), and attacked all the country of the Amalekites, and also the Amorites who dwelt in Hazezon Tamar.

8 And the king of Sodom, the king of Gomorrah, the king of Admah, the king of Zeboiim, and the king of Bela (that *is,* Zoar) went out and joined together in battle in the Valley of Siddim 9 against Chedorlaomer king of Elam, Tidal king of nations, Amraphel king of Shinar, and Arioch king of Ellasar— four kings against five. 10 Now the Valley of Siddim *was full of* asphalt pits; and the kings of Sodom and Gomorrah fled; *some* fell there, and the remainder fled to the mountains. 11 Then they took all the goods of Sodom and Gomorrah, and all their provisions, and went their way. 12 They also took Lot, Abram's brother's son who dwelt in Sodom, and his goods, and departed.

13 Then one who had escaped came and told Abram the Hebrew, for he dwelt by the terebinth trees of Mamre the Amorite, brother of Eshcol and brother of Aner; and they *were* allies with Abram. 14 Now when Abram heard that his brother was taken captive, he armed his three hundred and eighteen trained *servants* who were born in his own house, and went in pursuit as far as Dan. 15 He divided his forces against them by night, and he and his servants attacked them and pursued them as far as Hobah, which *is* north of Damascus. 16 So he brought back all the goods, and also brought back his brother Lot and his goods, as well as the women and the people.

17 And the king of Sodom went out to meet him at the Valley of Shaveh (that *is,* the King's Valley), after his return from the defeat of Chedorlaomer and the kings who *were* with him. 18 Then Melchizedek king of Salem brought out bread and wine; he *was* the priest of God Most High. 19 And he blessed him and said:

> "Blessed be Abram of God Most High,
> Possessor of heaven and earth;
> 20 And blessed be God Most High,
> Who has delivered your enemies into your hand."

And he gave him a tithe of all.

21 Now the king of Sodom said to Abram, "Give me the persons, and take the goods for yourself."

22 But Abram said to the king of Sodom, "I have raised my hand to the LORD, God Most High, the Possessor of heaven and earth, 23 that I *will take* nothing, from a thread to a sandal strap, and that I will not take anything that *is* yours, lest you should say, 'I have made Abram rich'— 24 except only what the young men have eaten, and the portion of the men who went with me: Aner, Eshcol, and Mamre; let them take their portion."

God makes a promise to Abram

15 After these things the word of the LORD came to Abram in a vision, saying, "Do not be afraid, Abram. I *am* your shield, your exceedingly great reward."

2 But Abram said, "Lord GOD, what

You are going to hear a lot more about me in the Bible. God changed my name from Abram (pronounced *AY-brum*), meaning "Great Father," to Abraham (pronounced *AY-bruh-ham*), meaning "Father of Many People." I lived two thousand years before Jesus was born.

The most important thing to remember is that God made some of His greatest promises to me. These promises are just as good today as they were in my own time.

God promised to lead me to a new country that would belong to my people forever—and God did just that! My people, the Hebrews, still live in Palestine today.

Not only that, but God also promised me a very great Grandson who someday would save you and me from our sins. You have probably heard of Him. His name is Jesus.

will You give me, seeing I go childless, and the heir of my house *is* Eliezer of Damascus?" ³ Then Abram said, "Look, You have given me no offspring; indeed one born in my house is my heir!"

⁴ And behold, the word of the LORD *came* to him, saying, "This one shall not be your heir, but one who will come from your own body shall be your heir." ⁵ Then He brought him outside and said, "Look now toward heaven, and count the stars if you are able to number them." And He said to him, "So shall your descendants be."

⁶ And he believed in the LORD, and He accounted it to him for righteousness.

⁷ Then He said to him, "I *am* the LORD, who brought you out of Ur of the Chaldeans, to give you this land to inherit it."

⁸ And he said, "Lord GOD, how shall I know that I will inherit it?"

⁹ So He said to him, "Bring Me a three-year-old heifer, a three-year-old female goat, a three-year-old ram, a turtledove, and a young pigeon." ¹⁰ Then he brought all these to Him and cut them in two, down the middle, and placed each piece opposite the other; but he did not cut the birds in

two. ¹¹ And when the vultures came down on the carcasses, Abram drove them away.

¹² Now when the sun was going down, a deep sleep fell upon Abram; and behold, horror *and* great darkness fell upon him. ¹³ Then He said to Abram: "Know certainly that your descendants will be strangers in a land *that is* not theirs, and will serve them, and they will afflict them four hundred years. ¹⁴ And also the nation whom they serve I will judge; afterward they shall come out with great possessions. ¹⁵ Now as for you, you shall go to your fathers in peace; you shall be buried at a good old age. ¹⁶ But in the fourth generation they shall return here, for the iniquity of the Amorites *is* not yet complete."

¹⁷ And it came to pass, when the sun went down and it was dark, that behold, there appeared a smoking oven and a burning torch that passed between those pieces. ¹⁸ On the same day the LORD made a covenant with Abram, saying:

"To your descendants I have given this land, from the river of Egypt to the great river, the River Euphrates— ¹⁹ the Kenites, the Kenezzites, the Kadmonites, ²⁰ the Hittites, the Perizzites, the Rephaim, ²¹ the Amorites, the Ca-

naanites, the Girgashites, and the Jebusites."

LACK OF FAITH

Abram's son Ishmael

16 Now Sarai, Abram's wife, had
borne him no *children.* And she had
an Egyptian maidservant whose name
was Hagar. ² So Sarai said to Abram,
"See now, the LORD has restrained me
from bearing *children.* Please, go in to
my maid; perhaps I shall obtain children by her." And Abram heeded the
voice of Sarai. ³ Then Sarai, Abram's
wife, took Hagar her maid, the Egyptian, and gave her to her husband
Abram to be his wife, after Abram had
dwelt ten years in the land of Canaan.
⁴ So he went in to Hagar, and she conceived. And when she saw that she had
conceived, her mistress became despised in her eyes.

⁵ Then Sarai said to Abram, "My
wrong *be* upon you! I gave my maid
into your embrace; and when she saw
that she had conceived, I became despised in her eyes. The LORD judge between you and me."

⁶ So Abram said to Sarai, "Indeed
your maid *is* in your hand; do to her
as you please." And when Sarai dealt
harshly with her, she fled from her
presence.

⁷ Now the **Angel of the LORD** found
her by a spring of water in the wilderness, by the spring on the way to Shur.
⁸ And He said, "Hagar, Sarai's maid,
where have you come from, and
where are you going?"

She said, "I am fleeing from the
presence of my mistress Sarai."

⁹ The Angel of the LORD said to her,
"Return to your mistress, and submit
yourself under her hand." ¹⁰ Then the
Angel of the LORD said to her, "I will
multiply your descendants exceed-

ingly, so that they shall not be counted
for multitude." ¹¹ And the Angel of the
LORD said to her:

"Behold, you *are* with child,
And you shall bear a son.
You shall call his name Ishmael,
Because the LORD has heard
   your affliction.
¹² He shall be a wild man;
His hand *shall be* against every
   man,
And every man's hand against
   him.
And he shall dwell in the
   presence of all his brethren."

¹³ Then she called the name of the
LORD who spoke to her, You-Are-the-
God-Who-Sees; for she said, "Have I
also here seen Him who sees me?"
¹⁴ Therefore the well was called Beer
Lahai Roi; observe, *it is* between Kadesh and Bered.

¹⁵ So Hagar bore Abram a son; and
Abram named his son, whom Hagar
bore, Ishmael. ¹⁶ Abram *was* eighty-six
years old when Hagar bore Ishmael to
Abram.

God gives Abram a sign of His promise

17 When Abram was ninety-nine
years old, the LORD appeared to
Abram and said to him, "I *am* Almighty
God; walk before Me and be blameless. ² And I will make My **covenant**
between Me and you, and will multiply
you exceedingly." ³ Then Abram fell
on his face, and God talked with him,
saying: ⁴ "As for Me, behold, My covenant is with you, and you shall be a
father of many nations. ⁵ No longer
shall your name be called Abram, but
your name shall be Abraham; for I

🔍 WORDFINDER

16:7 Angel of the Lord   Sometimes called the Angel of the Presence. This Angel
was really a way in which the Lord Himself was revealed to people.

17:2 Covenant   A legal agreement. God made a covenant with Abraham to give
the land of Canaan to his descendants and to make Abraham a blessing to the whole
world.

have made you a father of many nations. 6 I will make you exceedingly fruitful; and I will make nations of you, and kings shall come from you. 7 And I will establish My covenant between Me and you and your descendants after you in their generations, for an everlasting covenant, to be God to you and your descendants after you. 8 Also I give to you and your descendants after you the land in which you are a stranger, all the land of Canaan, as an everlasting possession; and I will be their God."

9 And God said to Abraham: "As for you, you shall keep My covenant, you and your descendants after you throughout their generations. 10 This is My covenant which you shall keep, between Me and you and your descendants after you: Every male child among you shall be circumcised; 11 and you shall be circumcised in the flesh of your foreskins, and it shall be a sign of the covenant between Me and you. 12 He who is eight days old among you shall be circumcised, every male child in your generations, he who is born in your house or bought with money from any foreigner who is not your descendant. 13 He who is born in your house and he who is bought with your money must be circumcised, and My covenant shall be in your flesh for an everlasting covenant. 14 And the uncircumcised male child, who is not circumcised in the flesh of his foreskin, that person shall be cut off from his people; he has broken My covenant."

15 Then God said to Abraham, "As for Sarai your wife, you shall not call her name Sarai, but Sarah shall be her name. 16 And I will bless her and also give you a son by her; then I will bless her, and she shall be a mother of nations; kings of peoples shall be from her."

17 Then Abraham fell on his face and laughed, and said in his heart, "Shall a child be born to a man who is one hundred years old? And shall Sarah, who is ninety years old, bear a child?" 18 And Abraham said to God, "Oh, that Ishmael might live before You!"

19 Then God said: "No, Sarah your wife shall bear you a son, and you shall call his name Isaac; I will establish My covenant with him for an everlasting covenant, and with his descendants after him. 20 And as for Ishmael, I have heard you. Behold, I have blessed him, and will make him fruitful, and will multiply him exceedingly. He shall beget twelve princes, and I will make him a great nation. 21 But My covenant I will establish with Isaac, whom Sarah shall bear to you at this set time next year." 22 Then He finished talking with him, and God went up from Abraham.

23 So Abraham took Ishmael his son, all who were born in his house and all who were bought with his money, every male among the men of Abraham's house, and circumcised the flesh of their foreskins that very same day, as God had said to him. 24 Abraham was ninety-nine years old when he was circumcised in the flesh of his foreskin. 25 And Ishmael his son was thirteen years old when he was circumcised in the flesh of his foreskin. 26 That very same day Abraham was circumcised, and his son Ishmael; 27 and all the men of his house, born in the house or bought with money from a foreigner, were circumcised with him.

The Lord promises Abraham a son

18 Then the LORD appeared to him by the terebinth trees of Mamre, as he was sitting in the tent door in the heat of the day. 2 So he lifted his eyes and looked, and behold, three men were standing by him; and when he saw them, he ran from the tent door to meet them, and bowed himself to the ground, 3 and said, "My Lord, if I have now found favor in Your sight, do not pass on by Your servant. 4 Please let a little water be brought, and wash your feet, and rest yourselves under the tree. 5 And I will bring a morsel of bread, that you may refresh your hearts. After that you may pass by, inasmuch as you have come to your servant."

They said, "Do as you have said."

6 So Abraham hurried into the tent to Sarah and said, "Quickly, make ready three measures of fine meal; knead it and make cakes." 7 And Abraham ran to the herd, took a tender and good calf, gave it to a young man, and he hastened to prepare it. 8 So he took butter and milk and the calf which he had prepared, and set it before them; and he stood by them under the tree as they ate.

9 Then they said to him, "Where is Sarah your wife?"

So he said, "Here, in the tent."

10 And He said, "I will certainly return to you according to the time of life, and behold, Sarah your wife shall have a son."

(Sarah was listening in the tent door which was behind him.) 11 Now Abraham and Sarah were old, well advanced in age; and Sarah had passed the age of childbearing. 12 Therefore Sarah laughed within herself, saying, "After I have grown old, shall I have pleasure, my lord being old also?"

13 And the LORD said to Abraham, "Why did Sarah laugh, saying, 'Shall I surely bear a child, since I am old?' 14 Is anything too hard for the LORD? At the appointed time I will return to you, according to the time of life, and Sarah shall have a son."

15 But Sarah denied it, saying, "I did not laugh," for she was afraid.

And He said, "No, but you did laugh!"

16 Then the men rose from there and looked toward Sodom, and Abraham went with them to send them on the way. 17 And the LORD said, "Shall I hide from Abraham what I am doing, 18 since Abraham shall surely become a great and mighty nation, and all the nations of the earth shall be blessed in him? 19 For I have known him, in order that he may command his children and his household after him, that they keep the way of the LORD, to do righteousness and justice, that the LORD may bring to Abraham what He has spoken to him." 20 And the LORD said, "Because the outcry against Sodom and Gomorrah is great, and because their sin is very grave, 21 I will go down now and see whether they have done altogether according to the outcry against it that has come to Me; and if not, I will know."

22 Then the men turned away from there and went toward Sodom, but Abraham still stood before the LORD. 23 And Abraham came near and said, "Would You also destroy the righteous with the wicked? 24 Suppose there were fifty righteous within the city; would You also destroy the place and not spare it for the fifty righteous that were in it? 25 Far be it from You to do such a thing as this, to slay the righteous with the wicked, so that the righteous should be as the wicked; far be it from You! Shall not the Judge of all the earth do right?"

26 So the LORD said, "If I find in Sodom fifty righteous within the city, then I will spare all the place for their sakes."

27 Then Abraham answered and said, "Indeed now, I who am but dust and ashes have taken it upon myself to speak to the Lord: 28 Suppose there were five less than the fifty righteous; would You destroy all of the city for lack of five?"

So He said, "If I find there forty-five, I will not destroy it."

29 And he spoke to Him yet again and said, "Suppose there should be forty found there?"

So He said, "I will not do it for the sake of forty."

30 Then he said, "Let not the Lord be angry, and I will speak: Suppose thirty should be found there?"

So He said, "I will not do it if I find thirty there."

31 And he said, "Indeed now, I have taken it upon myself to speak to the Lord: Suppose twenty should be found there?"

So He said, "I will not destroy it for the sake of twenty."

32 Then he said, "Let not the Lord be angry, and I will speak but once more: Suppose ten should be found there?"

And He said, "I will not destroy *it* for the sake of ten." ³³ So the LORD went His way as soon as He had finished speaking with Abraham; and Abraham returned to his place.

God destroys Sodom and Gomorrah

19 Now the two angels came to Sodom in the evening, and Lot was sitting in the gate of Sodom. When Lot saw *them,* he rose to meet them, and he bowed himself with his face toward the ground. ² And he said, "Here now, my lords, please turn in to your servant's house and spend the night, and wash your feet; then you may rise early and go on your way."

And they said, "No, but we will spend the night in the open square."

³ But he insisted strongly; so they turned in to him and entered his house. Then he made them a feast, and baked unleavened bread, and they ate.

⁴ Now before they lay down, the men of the city, the men of Sodom, both old and young, all the people from every quarter, surrounded the house. ⁵ And they called to Lot and said to him, "Where are the men who came to you tonight? Bring them out to us that we may know them *carnally.*"

⁶ So Lot went out to them through the doorway, shut the door behind him, ⁷ and said, "Please, my brethren, do not do so wickedly! ⁸ See now, I have two daughters who have not known a man; please, let me bring them out to you, and you may do to them as you wish; only do nothing to these men, since this is the reason they have come under the shadow of my roof."

⁹ And they said, "Stand back!" Then they said, "This one came in to stay *here,* and he keeps acting as a judge; now we will deal worse with you than with them." So they pressed hard against the man Lot, and came near to break down the door. ¹⁰ But the men reached out their hands and pulled Lot into the house with them, and shut the door. ¹¹ And they struck the men who *were* at the doorway of the house with blindness, both small and great, so that they became weary *trying* to find the door.

¹² Then the men said to Lot, "Have you anyone else here? Son-in-law, your sons, your daughters, and whomever you have in the city—take *them* out of this place! ¹³ For we will destroy this place, because the outcry against them has grown great before the face of the LORD, and the LORD has sent us to destroy it."

¹⁴ So Lot went out and spoke to his sons-in-law, who had married his daughters, and said, "Get up, get out of this place; for the LORD will destroy this city!" But to his sons-in-law he seemed to be joking.

¹⁵ When the morning dawned, the angels urged Lot to hurry, saying, "Arise, take your wife and your two daughters who are here, lest you be consumed in the punishment of the city." ¹⁶ And while he lingered, the men took hold of his hand, his wife's hand, and the hands of his two daughters, the LORD being merciful to him, and they brought him out and set him outside the city. ¹⁷ So it came to pass, when they had brought them outside, that he said, "Escape for your life! Do not look behind you nor stay anywhere in the plain. Escape to the mountains, lest you be destroyed."

¹⁸ Then Lot said to them, "Please, no, my lords! ¹⁹ Indeed now, your servant has found favor in your sight, and you have increased your mercy which you have shown me by saving my life; but I cannot escape to the mountains, lest some evil overtake me and I die. ²⁰ See now, this city *is* near *enough* to flee to, and it *is* a little one; please let me escape there (*is it* not a little one?) and my soul shall live."

²¹ And he said to him, "See, I have favored you concerning this thing also, in that I will not overthrow this city for which you have spoken. ²² Hurry, escape there. For I cannot do anything until you arrive there."

Lot's Wife—My story is one of the saddest in the Bible. My husband and I lived in Sodom (pronounced *SOD-um*), one of the most evil cities of our time. God tried to save Sodom and the nearby city of Gomorrah (rhymes with *to-MOR-row*), but nothing could persuade the people to change their ways. So God decided He would have to destroy the two cities.

God ordered our family to leave at once. He even sent two angels who warned us to hurry and not spend time looking back. But it was too hard for me to leave Sodom. All my nice things were in the city.

Suddenly brimstone and fire fell from the skies, and I was caught in that terrible storm. I instantly became a tall column of rock salt. That pillar of salt stands in its place to this day.

Boys and girls, listen to Jesus' warning: "Remember Lot's wife!" Sometimes we have to choose between God and *things*.

Therefore the name of the city was called Zoar.

23 The sun had risen upon the earth when Lot entered Zoar. 24 Then the LORD rained brimstone and fire on Sodom and Gomorrah, from the LORD out of the heavens. 25 So He overthrew those cities, all the plain, all the inhabitants of the cities, and what grew on the ground.

26 But his wife looked back behind him, and she became a pillar of salt.

27 And Abraham went early in the morning to the place where he had stood before the LORD. 28 Then he looked toward Sodom and Gomorrah, and toward all the land of the plain; and he saw, and behold, the smoke of the land which went up like the smoke of a furnace. 29 And it came to pass, when God destroyed the cities of the plain, that God remembered Abraham, and sent Lot out of the midst of the overthrow, when He overthrew the cities in which Lot had dwelt.

30 Then Lot went up out of Zoar and dwelt in the mountains, and his two daughters were with him; for he was

Lot's family escapes from Sodom, while his wife looks back and becomes a pillar of salt.

> **Sarah**—My name means "Princess." I was Abraham's first wife and the mother of Isaac.
>
> I am a lesson to all boys that they should promise to be fair to their wives when they marry. Abraham wasn't always fair to me. Twice he pretended I was only his sister, and both the Pharaoh (pronounced *FAY-row*) of Egypt and the king of Gerar (pronounced *GHEE-rar*) nearly got into a lot of trouble because of Abraham's lie.
>
> Sometimes I did what was wrong, too, like when I sent poor Hagar and her son Ishmael (pronounced *HAY-gar* and *ISH-may-el*) away. Although God forgave me, I have always been sorry. I'm glad to know that the Lord cared for Hagar and Ishmael in spite of my lack of love (see Genesis 17:20).

afraid to dwell in Zoar. And he and his two daughters dwelt in a cave. 31 Now the firstborn said to the younger, "Our father *is* old, and *there is* no man on the earth to come in to us as is the custom of all the earth. 32 Come, let us make our father drink wine, and we will lie with him, that we may preserve the lineage of our father." 33 So they made their father drink wine that night. And the firstborn went in and lay with her father, and he did not know when she lay down or when she arose.

34 It happened on the next day that the firstborn said to the younger, "Indeed I lay with my father last night; let us make him drink wine tonight also, and you go in *and* lie with him, that we may preserve the lineage of our father." 35 Then they made their father drink wine that night also. And the younger arose and lay with him, and he did not know when she lay down or when she arose.

36 Thus both the daughters of Lot were with child by their father. 37 The firstborn bore a son and called his name Moab; he *is* the father of the **Moabites** to this day. 38 And the younger, she also bore a son and called his name Ben-Ammi; he *is* the father of the people of **Ammon** to this day.

Abraham and King Abimelech

20 And Abraham journeyed from there to the South, and dwelt between Kadesh and Shur, and stayed in Gerar. 2 Now Abraham said of Sarah his wife, "She *is* my sister." And Abimelech king of Gerar sent and took Sarah.

3 But God came to Abimelech in a dream by night, and said to him, "Indeed you *are* a dead man because of the woman whom you have taken, for she *is* a man's wife."

4 But Abimelech had not come near her; and he said, "Lord, will You slay a righteous nation also? 5 Did he not say to me, 'She *is* my sister'? And she, even she herself said, 'He *is* my brother.' In the integrity of my heart and innocence of my hands I have done this."

6 And God said to him in a dream, "Yes, I know that you did this in the integrity of your heart. For I also withheld you from sinning against Me; therefore I did not let you touch her. 7 Now therefore, restore the man's wife; for he *is* a prophet, and he will pray for you and you shall live. But if you do not restore *her,* know that you shall surely die, you and all who *are* yours."

WORDFINDER

19:30–38 Ammonites and Moabites The nations that descended from Ammon and Moab, two sons of Lot.

What Lot Learned

Uncle Abraham's generosity made it easy for me to be greedy. You can read in Genesis 13 how he let me take the best of the land for myself. So I thought I did a smart thing that day.

Then I found out that things aren't always as good as they seem. The people in the cities where I lived were so wicked God had to destroy them. Even my poor wife became a pillar of salt.

Now I've had time to think it over, and I've decided to look before I leap next time. Uncle Abraham is an unselfish man. I'm asking the Lord to change me to be like Uncle Abraham. Now I just want to trust God with my whole life.

8 So Abimelech rose early in the morning, called all his servants, and told all these things in their hearing; and the men were very much afraid. 9 And Abimelech called Abraham and said to him, "What have you done to us? How have I offended you, that you have brought on me and on my kingdom a great sin? You have done deeds to me that ought not to be done." 10 Then Abimelech said to Abraham, "What did you have in view, that you have done this thing?"

11 And Abraham said, "Because I thought, surely the fear of God *is* not in this place; and they will kill me on account of my wife. 12 But indeed *she is* truly my sister. She *is* the daughter of my father, but not the daughter of my mother; and she became my wife. 13 And it came to pass, when God caused me to wander from my father's house, that I said to her, 'This *is* your kindness that you should do for me: in every place, wherever we go, say of me, "He *is* my brother." ' "

14 Then Abimelech took sheep, oxen, and male and female servants, and gave *them* to Abraham; and he restored Sarah his wife to him. 15 And Abimelech said, "See, my land *is* before you; dwell where it pleases you." 16 Then to Sarah he said, "Behold, I have given your brother a thousand *pieces* of silver; indeed this vindicates you before all who *are* with you and before everybody." Thus she was rebuked.

17 So Abraham prayed to God; and God healed Abimelech, his wife, and his female servants. Then they bore *children;* 18 for the LORD had closed up all the wombs of the house of Abimelech because of Sarah, Abraham's wife.

Isaac is born

21 And the LORD visited Sarah as He had said, and the LORD did for Sarah as He had spoken. 2 For Sarah conceived and bore Abraham a son in his old age, at the set time of which God had spoken to him. 3 And Abraham called the name of his son who was born to him—whom Sarah bore to him—Isaac. 4 Then Abraham circumcised his son Isaac when he was eight days old, as God had commanded him. 5 Now Abraham was one hundred years old when his son Isaac was born to him. 6 And Sarah said, "God has made me laugh, *and* all who hear will laugh with me." 7 She also said, "Who would have said to Abraham that Sarah would nurse children? For I have borne *him* a son in his old age."

8 So the child grew and was weaned. And Abraham made a great feast on the same day that Isaac was weaned.

9 And Sarah saw the son of Hagar the Egyptian, whom she had borne to Abraham, scoffing. 10 Therefore she said to Abraham, "Cast out this bond-

What Sarah Learned

When God promised Abraham and me a son, I laughed at the idea. We were too old to have children. But the Lord made me ashamed when He asked me, "Is anything too hard for the Lord?"

Of course, I believed God could do *almost* anything. After all, He was God. The most important thing was I didn't believe He could do anything for *me*!

What counts is believing God can do great things for *you*.

The Lord made me laugh again when He gave us Isaac (pronounced *EYE-zik*). But this time I laughed for joy. Never again would I doubt God's promises to Abraham and me.

woman and her son; for the son of this bondwoman shall not be heir with my son, *namely* with Isaac." 11 And the matter was very displeasing in Abraham's sight because of his son.

12 But God said to Abraham, "Do not let it be displeasing in your sight because of the lad or because of your bondwoman. Whatever Sarah has said to you, listen to her voice; for in Isaac your seed shall be called. 13 Yet I will also make a nation of the son of the bondwoman, because he *is* your seed."

14 So Abraham rose early in the morning, and took bread and a skin of water; and putting *it* on her shoulder, he gave *it* and the boy to Hagar, and sent her away. Then she departed and wandered in the Wilderness of Beersheba. 15 And the water in the skin was used up, and she placed the boy under one of the shrubs. 16 Then she went and sat down across from *him* at a distance of about a bowshot; for she said to herself, "Let me not *see* the death of the boy." So she sat opposite *him*, and lifted her voice and wept.

17 And God heard the voice of the lad. Then the angel of God called to Hagar out of heaven, and said to her, "What ails you, Hagar? Fear not, for God has heard the voice of the lad where he *is*. 18 Arise, lift up the lad and hold him with your hand, for I will make him a great nation."

19 Then God opened her eyes, and she saw a well of water. And she went and filled the skin with water, and gave the lad a drink. 20 So God was with the lad; and he grew and dwelt in the wilderness, and became an archer. 21 He dwelt in the Wilderness of Paran; and his mother took a wife for him from the land of Egypt.

22 And it came to pass at that time that Abimelech and Phichol, the commander of his army, spoke to Abraham, saying, "God *is* with you in all that you do. 23 Now therefore, swear to me by God that you will not deal falsely with me, with my offspring, or with my posterity; but that according to the kindness that I have done to you, you will do to me and to the land in which you have dwelt."

24 And Abraham said, "I will swear."

25 Then Abraham rebuked Abimelech because of a well of water which Abimelech's servants had seized. 26 And Abimelech said, "I do not know who has done this thing; you did not tell me, nor had I heard *of it* until today." 27 So Abraham took sheep and oxen and gave them to Abimelech, and the two of them made a covenant. 28 And Abraham set seven ewe lambs of the flock by themselves.

29 Then Abimelech asked Abraham, "What *is the meaning of* these seven ewe lambs which you have set by themselves?"

30 And he said, "You will take *these* seven ewe lambs from my hand, that they may be my witness that I have dug this well." 31 Therefore he called

Ishmael—My name is pronounced *ISH-may-el.* At first I didn't think any-body in the world wanted me. Isaac, my half-brother, was Abraham's legal son, and my mother and I weren't welcome in Abraham's house. So we had to leave home.

Then I found out about God's love. He supplied all our needs and promised that I would become the father of a great nation. God heard my cry that day, and that's why my name means "God Hears."

Perhaps you, too, feel alone in the world sometimes. Many children, like me, don't have two parents to care for them. Please let me tell you that God really cares for all children, and He cares about you. If you ask Him, God will be your Father always. Earthly fathers will die someday, but God will live forever.

that place Beersheba, because the two of them swore an oath there.

32 Thus they made a covenant at Beersheba. So Abimelech rose with Phichol, the commander of his army, and they returned to the land of the Philistines. 33 Then *Abraham* planted a tamarisk tree in Beersheba, and there called on the name of the Lord, the Everlasting God. 34 And Abraham stayed in the land of the Philistines many days.

Abraham proves his faith in God

22 Now it came to pass after these things that God tested Abraham, and said to him, "Abraham!"

And he said, "Here I am."

2 Then He said, "Take now your son, your only *son* Isaac, whom you love, and go to the land of Moriah, and offer him there as a burnt offering on one of the mountains of which I shall tell you."

3 So Abraham rose early in the morning and saddled his donkey, and took two of his young men with him, and Isaac his son; and he split the wood for the burnt offering, and arose and went to the place of which God had told him. 4 Then on the third day Abraham lifted his eyes and saw the place afar off. 5 And Abraham said to his young men, "Stay here with the donkey; the lad and I will go yonder and worship, and we will come back to you."

6 So Abraham took the wood of the burnt offering and laid *it* on Isaac his son; and he took the fire in his hand, and a knife, and the two of them went together. 7 But Isaac spoke to Abraham his father and said, "My father!"

And he said, "Here I am, my son."

Then he said, "Look, the fire and the wood, but where *is* the lamb for a burnt offering?"

8 And Abraham said, "My son, God will provide for Himself the lamb for a burnt offering." So the two of them went together.

9 Then they came to the place of which God had told him. And Abraham built an altar there and placed the wood in order; and he bound Isaac his son and laid him on the altar, upon the wood. 10 And Abraham stretched out his hand and took the knife to slay his son.

11 But the Angel of the Lord called to him from heaven and said, "Abraham, Abraham!"

So he said, "Here I am."

12 And He said, "Do not lay your hand on the lad, or do anything to him; for now I know that you fear God, since you have not withheld your son, your only *son,* from Me."

13 Then Abraham lifted his eyes and looked, and there behind *him was* a ram caught in a thicket by its horns. So Abraham went and took the ram, and offered it up for a burnt offering instead of his son. 14 And Abra-ham called the name of the place,

Isaac—My name is pronounced *EYE-zik* and means "Laughter." As Dad and I climbed the mountain together, he told me we were going to make a sacrifice to God. Making sacrifices was the custom in those days. But I was puzzled because we had no animal to sacrifice. When I asked him about it, my father only looked sad and said that God would provide His own sacrifice.

Suddenly my father picked me up and tied me to the altar. While I was still trying to understand what was happening, I heard the voice of God shouting, "Don't harm the boy, Abraham!"

Years later I found out that what happened that day was to show that God Himself would sacrifice His very own Son for our sins two thousand years later.

The- LORD-Will-Provide; as it is said *to* this day, "In the Mount of the LORD it shall be provided."

15 Then the Angel of the LORD called to Abraham a second time out of heaven, 16 and said: "By Myself I have sworn, says the LORD, because you have done this thing, and have not withheld your son, your only *son*— 17 blessing I will bless you, and multiplying I will multiply your descendants as the stars of the heaven and as the sand which *is* on the seashore; and your descendants shall possess the

God sends a ram for Abraham's sacrifice.

gate of their enemies. 18 In your seed all the nations of the earth shall be blessed, because you have obeyed My voice." 19 So Abraham returned to his young men, and they rose and went together to Beersheba; and Abraham dwelt at Beersheba.

20 Now it came to pass after these things that it was told Abraham, saying, "Indeed Milcah also has borne children to your brother Nahor, 21 Huz his first-born, Buz his brother, Kemuel the father of Aram, 22 Chesed, Hazo, Pildash, Jidlaph, and Bethuel." 23 And Bethuel begot Rebekah. These eight Milcah bore to Nahor, Abraham's brother. 24 His concubine, whose name was Reumah, also bore Tebah, Gaham, Thahash, and Maachah.

Sarah dies and is buried

23 Sarah lived one hundred and twenty-seven years; *these were* the years of the life of Sarah. 2 So Sarah died in Kirjath Arba (that *is,* Hebron) in the land of Canaan, and Abraham came to mourn for Sarah and to weep for her.

3 Then Abraham stood up from before his dead, and spoke to the sons of Heth, saying, 4 "I *am* a foreigner and a visitor among you. Give me property for a burial place among you, that I may bury my dead out of my sight."

5 And the sons of Heth answered Abraham, saying to him, 6 "Hear us, my lord: You *are* a mighty prince among us; bury your dead in the choic-

est of our burial places. None of us will withhold from you his burial place, that you may bury your dead."

7 Then Abraham stood up and bowed himself to the people of the land, the sons of Heth. 8 And he spoke with them, saying, "If it is your wish that I bury my dead out of my sight, hear me, and meet with Ephron the son of Zohar for me, 9 that he may give me the cave of Machpelah which he has, which *is* at the end of his field. Let him give it to me at the full price, as property for a burial place among you."

10 Now Ephron dwelt among the sons of Heth; and Ephron the Hittite answered Abraham in the presence of the sons of Heth, all who entered at the gate of his city, saying, 11 "No, my lord, hear me: I give you the field and the cave that *is* in it; I give it to you in the presence of the sons of my people. I give it to you. Bury your dead!"

12 Then Abraham bowed himself down before the people of the land; 13 and he spoke to Ephron in the hearing of the people of the land, saying, "If you *will give it,* please hear me. I will give you money for the field; take *it* from me and I will bury my dead there."

14 And Ephron answered Abraham, saying to him, 15 "My lord, listen to me; the land *is worth* four hundred shekels of silver. What *is* that between you and me? So bury your dead." 16 And Abraham listened to Ephron; and Abraham weighed out the silver for Ephron

---

⛏ DIGGING IN

22:15–18 God Keeps His Promise Some time ago we saw that God made a great promise to Abraham: Everybody who trusts in Abraham's "Seed" is blessed. That "Seed" was Jesus, who was born two thousand years after Abraham. God also promised Abraham that his son Isaac would be the great ancestor of Jesus.

Then one day God asked Abraham to sacrifice Isaac. How could God keep His promise if Abraham killed Isaac? Abraham didn't know for sure how the Lord was going to solve that riddle. But Abraham believed God just the same. So he went ahead with plans to sacrifice his son.

You know the end of the story. God really didn't let Abraham kill Isaac. It was just a test to see if Abraham believed God's promise about his son. And Abraham *did* believe God.

which he had named in the hearing of the sons of Heth, four hundred shekels of silver, currency of the merchants.

17 So the field of Ephron which *was* in Machpelah, which *was* before Mamre, the field and the cave which *was* in it, and all the trees that *were* in the field, which *were* within all the surrounding borders, were deeded 18 to Abraham as a possession in the presence of the sons of Heth, before all who went in at the gate of his city.

19 And after this, Abraham buried Sarah his wife in the cave of the field of Machpelah, before Mamre (that *is,* Hebron) in the land of Canaan. 20 So the field and the cave that *is* in it were deeded to Abraham by the sons of Heth as property for a burial place.

Rebekah is chosen to marry Isaac

24 Now Abraham was old, well advanced in age; and the LORD had blessed Abraham in all things. 2 So Abraham said to the oldest servant of his house, who ruled over all that he had, "Please, put your hand under my thigh, 3 and I will make you swear by the LORD, the God of heaven and the God of the earth, that you will not take a wife for my son from the daughters of the Canaanites, among whom I dwell; 4 but you shall go to my country and to my family, and take a wife for my son Isaac."

5 And the servant said to him, "Perhaps the woman will not be willing to follow me to this land. Must I take your son back to the land from which you came?"

6 But Abraham said to him, "Beware that you do not take my son back there. 7 The LORD God of heaven, who took me from my father's house and from the land of my family, and who spoke to me and swore to me, saying, 'To your descendants I give this land,' He will send His angel before you, and you shall take a wife for my son from there. 8 And if the woman is not willing to follow you, then you will be released from this oath; only do not take my son back there." 9 So the servant put his hand under the thigh of Abraham his master, and swore to him concerning this matter.

10 Then the servant took ten of his master's camels and departed, for all his master's goods *were in* his hand. And he arose and went to Mesopotamia, to the city of Nahor. 11 And he made his camels kneel down outside the city by a well of water at evening time, the time when women go out to draw *water.* 12 Then he said, "O LORD God of my master Abraham, please give me success this day, and show kindness to my master Abraham. 13 Behold, *here* I stand by the well of water, and the daughters of the men of the city are coming out to draw water. 14 Now let it be that the young woman to whom I say, 'Please let down your pitcher that I may drink,' and she says, 'Drink, and I will also give your camels a drink'—*let* her *be the one* You have appointed for Your servant Isaac. And by this I will know that You have shown kindness to my master."

15 And it happened, before he had finished speaking, that behold, Rebekah, who was born to Bethuel, son of Milcah, the wife of Nahor, Abraham's brother, came out with her pitcher on her shoulder. 16 Now the young woman *was* very beautiful to behold, a virgin; no man had known her. And she went down to the well, filled her pitcher, and came up. 17 And the servant ran to meet her and said, "Please let me drink a little water from your pitcher."

18 So she said, "Drink, my lord." Then she quickly let her pitcher down to her hand, and gave him a drink. 19 And when she had finished giving him a drink, she said, "I will draw *water* for your camels also, until they have finished drinking." 20 Then she quickly emptied her pitcher into the trough, ran back to the well to draw *water,* and drew for all his camels. 21 And the man, wondering at her, remained silent so as to know whether the LORD had made his journey prosperous or not.

Rebekah—My name is pronounced *ree-BECK-uh*. My father Bethuel and my brother Laban had told us about my Uncle Abraham who went to live in Palestine. Abraham and his wife Sarah had a son named Isaac.

One day Abraham's hired man came to visit us in Mesopotamia (pronounced *mess-uh-puh-TAY-mee-uh*) where Uncle Abraham also had grown up. I was coming to our well, and the hired man was standing there with his camels. When he asked me for a drink from our well, I offered to water his camels, too. Then he did a strange thing—he gave me jewelry and thanked God that he had found a wife for Isaac. I was speechless!

Later my father and brother both agreed that the hired man's actions were directed by the Lord, so I became Isaac's bride.

22 So it was, when the camels had finished drinking, that the man took a golden nose ring weighing half a shekel, and two bracelets for her wrists weighing ten *shekels* of gold, 23 and said, "Whose daughter *are* you? Tell me, please, is there room *in* your father's house for us to lodge?"

24 So she said to him, "I *am* the daughter of Bethuel, Milcah's son, whom she bore to Nahor." 25 Moreover she said to him, "We have both straw and feed enough, and room to lodge."

26 Then the man bowed down his head and worshiped the LORD. 27 And he said, "Blessed *be* the LORD God of my master Abraham, who has not forsaken His mercy and His truth toward my master. As for me, being on the way, the LORD led me to the house of my master's brethren." 28 So the young woman ran and told her mother's household these things.

29 Now Rebekah had a brother whose name *was* Laban, and Laban ran out to the man by the well. 30 So it came to pass, when he saw the nose ring, and the bracelets on his sister's wrists, and when he heard the words of his sister Rebekah, saying, "Thus the man spoke to me," that he went to the man. And there he stood by the camels at the well. 31 And he said, "Come in, O blessed of the LORD! Why do you stand outside? For I have prepared the house, and a place for the camels."

32 Then the man came to the house. And he unloaded the camels, and provided straw and feed for the camels, and water to wash his feet and the feet of the men who *were* with him. 33 *Food* was set before him to eat, but he said, "I will not eat until I have told about my errand."

And he said, "Speak on."

34 So he said, "I *am* Abraham's servant. 35 The LORD has blessed my master greatly, and he has become great; and He has given him flocks and herds, silver and gold, male and female servants, and camels and donkeys. 36 And Sarah my master's wife bore a son to my master when she was old; and to him he has given all that he has. 37 Now my master made me swear, saying, 'You shall not take a wife for my son from the daughters of the Canaanites, in whose land I dwell; 38 but you shall go to my father's house and to my family, and take a wife for my son.' 39 And I said to my master, 'Perhaps the woman will not follow me.' 40 But he said to me, 'The LORD, before whom I walk, will send His angel with you and prosper your way; and you shall take a wife for my son from my family and from my father's house. 41 You will be clear from this oath when you arrive among my family; for if they will not give *her* to you, then you will be released from my oath.'

42 "And this day I came to the well and said, 'O LORD God of my master

Abraham, if You will now prosper the way in which I go, ⁴³ behold, I stand by the well of water; and it shall come to pass that when the virgin comes out to draw *water*, and I say to her, "Please give me a little water from your pitcher to drink," ⁴⁴ and she says to me, "Drink, and I will draw for your camels also,"—*let* her *be* the woman whom the Lord has appointed for my master's son.'

⁴⁵ "But before I had finished speaking in my heart, there was Rebekah, coming out with her pitcher on her shoulder; and she went down to the well and drew *water*. And I said to her, 'Please let me drink.' ⁴⁶ And she made haste and let her pitcher down from her *shoulder,* and said, 'Drink, and I will give your camels a drink also.' So I drank, and she gave the camels a drink also. ⁴⁷ Then I asked her, and said, 'Whose daughter *are* you?' And she said, 'The daughter of Bethuel, Nahor's son, whom Milcah bore to him.' So I put the nose ring on her nose and the bracelets on her wrists. ⁴⁸ And I bowed my head and worshiped the Lord, and blessed the Lord God of my master Abraham, who had led me in the way of truth to take the daughter of my master's brother for his son. ⁴⁹ Now if you will deal kindly and truly with my master, tell me. And if not, tell me, that I may turn to the right hand or to the left."

⁵⁰ Then Laban and Bethuel answered and said, "The thing comes from the Lord; we cannot speak to you either bad or good. ⁵¹ Here *is* Rebekah before you; take *her* and go, and let her be your master's son's *wife,* as the Lord has spoken."

⁵² And it came to pass, when Abraham's servant heard their words, that he worshiped the Lord, *bowing himself* to the earth. ⁵³ Then the servant brought out jewelry of silver, jewelry of gold, and clothing, and gave *them* to Rebekah. He also gave precious things to her brother and to her mother.

⁵⁴ And he and the men who *were* with him ate and drank and stayed all night. Then they arose in the morning, and he said, "Send me away to my master."

⁵⁵ But her brother and her mother said, "Let the young woman stay with us *a few* days, at least ten; after that she may go."

⁵⁶ And he said to them, "Do not hinder me, since the Lord has prospered my way; send me away so that I may go to my master."

⁵⁷ So they said, "We will call the young woman and ask her personally." ⁵⁸ Then they called Rebekah and said to her, "Will you go with this man?"

And she said, "I will go."

⁵⁹ So they sent away Rebekah their sister and her nurse, and Abraham's servant and his men. ⁶⁰ And they blessed Rebekah and said to her:

"Our sister, *may* you *become*
  The mother of thousands of ten
    thousands;
  And may your descendants
    possess
  The gates of those who hate
    them."

⁶¹ Then Rebekah and her maids arose, and they rode on the camels and followed the man. So the servant took Rebekah and departed.

⁶² Now Isaac came from the way of Beer Lahai Roi, for he dwelt in the South. ⁶³ And Isaac went out to meditate in the field in the evening; and he lifted his eyes and looked, and there, the camels *were* coming. ⁶⁴ Then Rebekah lifted her eyes, and when she saw Isaac she dismounted from her camel; ⁶⁵ for she had said to the servant, "Who *is* this man walking in the field to meet us?"

The servant said, "It *is* my master." So she took a veil and covered herself.

⁶⁶ And the servant told Isaac all the things that he had done. ⁶⁷ Then Isaac brought her into his mother Sarah's tent; and he took Rebekah and she became his wife, and he loved her. So Isaac was comforted after his mother's *death.*

Esau and Jacob are born

25 Abraham again took a wife, and her name *was* Keturah. ² And she bore him Zimran, Jokshan, Medan, Midian, Ishbak, and Shuah. ³ Jokshan begot Sheba and Dedan. And the sons of Dedan *were* Asshurim, Letushim, and Leummim. ⁴ And the sons of Midian *were* Ephah, Epher, Hanoch, Abidah, and Eldaah. All these *were* the children of Keturah.

⁵ And Abraham gave all that he had to Isaac. ⁶ But Abraham gave gifts to the sons of the concubines which Abraham had; and while he was still living he sent them eastward, away from Isaac his son, to the country of the east.

⁷ This *is* the sum of the years of Abraham's life which he lived: one hundred and seventy-five years. ⁸ Then Abraham breathed his last and died in a good old age, an old man and full *of years,* and was gathered to his people. ⁹ And his sons Isaac and Ishmael buried him in the cave of Machpelah, which *is* before Mamre, in the field of Ephron the son of Zohar the Hittite, ¹⁰ the field which Abraham purchased from the sons of Heth. There Abraham was buried, and Sarah his wife. ¹¹ And it came to pass, after the death of Abraham, that God **blessed** his son Isaac. And Isaac dwelt at Beer Lahai Roi.

¹² Now this *is* the genealogy of Ishmael, Abraham's son, whom Hagar the Egyptian, Sarah's maidservant, bore to Abraham. ¹³ And these *were* the names of the sons of Ishmael, by their names, according to their generations: The firstborn of Ishmael, Nebajoth; then Kedar, Adbeel, Mibsam, ¹⁴ Mishma, Dumah, Massa, ¹⁵ Hadar, Tema, Jetur, Naphish, and Kedemah. ¹⁶ These *were* the sons of Ishmael and these *were* their names, by their towns and their settlements, twelve princes according to their nations. ¹⁷ These *were* the years of the life of Ishmael:

one hundred and thirty-seven years; and he breathed his last and died, and was gathered to his people. ¹⁸ (They dwelt from Havilah as far as Shur, which *is* east of Egypt as you go toward Assyria.) He died in the presence of all his brethren.

¹⁹ This *is* the genealogy of Isaac, Abraham's son. Abraham begot Isaac. ²⁰ Isaac was forty years old when he took Rebekah as wife, the daughter of Bethuel the Syrian of Padan Aram, the sister of Laban the Syrian. ²¹ Now Isaac pleaded with the LORD for his wife, because she *was* barren; and the LORD granted his plea, and Rebekah his wife conceived. ²² But the children struggled together within her; and she said, "If *all is* well, why *am I* like this?" So she went to inquire of the LORD.

²³ And the LORD said to her:

"Two nations *are* in your womb,
Two peoples shall be separated
    from your body;
One people shall be stronger
    than the other,
And the older shall serve the
    younger."

²⁴ So when her days were fulfilled *for her* to give birth, indeed *there were* twins in her womb. ²⁵ And the first came out red. *He was* like a hairy garment all over; so they called his name Esau. ²⁶ Afterward his brother came out, and his hand took hold of Esau's heel; so his name was called Jacob. Isaac *was* sixty years old when she bore them.

²⁷ So the boys grew. And Esau was a skillful hunter, a man of the field; but Jacob was a mild man, dwelling in tents. ²⁸ And Isaac loved Esau because he ate *of his* game, but Rebekah loved Jacob.

²⁹ Now Jacob cooked a stew; and Esau came in from the field, and he *was* weary. ³⁰ And Esau said to Jacob,

WORDFINDER

25:11 Blessed An adjective that means a person is favored by God and His kindness. Sometimes the word means the "happiness that God gives."

Jacob—My name is pronounced *JAY-kob* and means "Usurper." A usurper is someone who steals another person's position in the world.

Because my brother Esau was the oldest son, he was the legal heir to my father's property. But when my father Isaac was old and blind, I tricked him into believing I was Esau. So Isaac gave me what belonged to my brother.

Later I wrestled with an Angel all night long. That Angel was really the Lord who came to me in the form of a man. The Angel gave me a new name and a new heart. My new name, Israel, pronounced *IZ-ray-el,* means "Prince with God." Unworthy as I was, God kindly gave me the honor of being the father of the great nation of Israel.

The Lord is ready to give you a new heart, too, so that you can begin right now to learn more about Him. As you do this, you will become a prince or princess of God.

"Please feed me with that same red *stew,* for I *am* weary." Therefore his name was called Edom.

31 But Jacob said, "Sell me your birthright as of this day."

32 And Esau said, "Look, I *am* about to die; so what *is* this birthright to me?"

33 Then Jacob said, "Swear to me as of this day."

So he swore to him, and sold his birthright to Jacob. 34 And Jacob gave Esau bread and stew of lentils; then he ate and drank, arose, and went his way. Thus Esau despised *his* birthright.

Isaac and King Abimelech

26 There was a famine in the land, besides the first famine that was in the days of Abraham. And Isaac went to Abimelech king of the Philistines, in Gerar.

2 Then the LORD appeared to him and said: "Do not go down to Egypt; live in the land of which I shall tell you. 3 Dwell in this land, and I will be with you and bless you; for to you and your descendants I give all these lands, and I will perform the oath which I swore to Abraham your father. 4 And I will make your descendants multiply as the stars of heaven; I will give to your descendants all these lands; and in your seed all the nations of the earth shall be blessed; 5 because Abraham obeyed My voice and kept My charge, My commandments, My statutes, and My laws."

DIGGING IN

25:29–34 Esau Sells His Rights The laws of some countries state that God has given people certain rights that should not be taken from them. But Esau did a strange thing.

As the older son in the family, Esau had rights to the largest share of his father's things. But he sold his rights to his brother Jacob for just a pot of stew!

In one way, you are like Esau. God has made some great promises to you! If you aren't careful, you can lose these promises!

Sometimes things that are bad for you look very exciting. Friends may want you to take drugs, and drugs can make you feel great—for a while! Next thing you know, you can't do without the drugs, and your life is ruined. God wants better things for you. Don't sell those better things for a thrill that kills.

⁶ So Isaac dwelt in Gerar. ⁷ And the men of the place asked about his wife. And he said, "She *is* my sister"; for he was afraid to say, "*She is* my wife," *because he thought,* "lest the men of the place kill me for Rebekah, because she *is* beautiful to behold." ⁸ Now it came to pass, when he had been there a long time, that Abimelech king of the Philistines looked through a window, and saw, and there was Isaac, showing endearment to Rebekah his wife. ⁹ Then Abimelech called Isaac and said, "Quite obviously she *is* your wife; so how could you say, 'She *is* my sister'?"

Isaac said to him, "Because I said, 'Lest I die on account of her.' "

¹⁰ And Abimelech said, "What *is* this you have done to us? One of the people might soon have lain with your wife, and you would have brought guilt on us." ¹¹ So Abimelech charged all *his* people, saying, "He who touches this man or his wife shall surely be put to death."

¹² Then Isaac sowed in that land, and reaped in the same year a hundredfold; and the LORD blessed him. ¹³ The man began to prosper, and continued prospering until he became very prosperous; ¹⁴ for he had possessions of flocks and possessions of herds and a great number of servants. So the Philistines envied him. ¹⁵ Now the Philistines had stopped up all the wells which his father's servants had dug in the days of Abraham his father, and they had filled them with earth. ¹⁶ And Abimelech said to Isaac, "Go away from us, for you are much mightier than we."

¹⁷ Then Isaac departed from there and pitched his tent in the Valley of Gerar, and dwelt there. ¹⁸ And Isaac dug again the wells of water which they had dug in the days of Abraham his father, for the Philistines had stopped them up after the death of Abraham. He called them by the names which his father had called them.

¹⁹ Also Isaac's servants dug in the valley, and found a well of running water there. ²⁰ But the herdsmen of Gerar quarreled with Isaac's herdsmen, saying, "The water *is* ours." So he called the name of the well Esek, because they quarreled with him. ²¹ Then they dug another well, and they quarreled over that *one* also. So he called its name Sitnah. ²² And he moved from there and dug another well, and they did not quarrel over it. So he called its name Rehoboth, because he said, "For now the LORD has made room for us, and we shall be fruitful in the land."

²³ Then he went up from there to Beersheba. ²⁴ And the LORD appeared to him the same night and said, "I *am* the God of your father Abraham; do not fear, for I *am* with you. I will bless you and multiply your descendants for My servant Abraham's sake." ²⁵ So he built an altar there and called on the name of the LORD, and he pitched his tent there; and there Isaac's servants dug a well.

²⁶ Then Abimelech came to him from Gerar with Ahuzzath, one of his friends, and Phichol the commander of his army. ²⁷ And Isaac said to them, "Why have you come to me, since you hate me and have sent me away from you?"

²⁸ But they said, "We have certainly seen that the LORD is with you. So we said, 'Let there now be an oath between us, between you and us; and let us make a covenant with you, ²⁹ that you will do us no harm, since we have not touched you, and since we have done nothing to you but good and have sent you away in peace. You *are* now the blessed of the LORD.' "

³⁰ So he made them a feast, and they ate and drank. ³¹ Then they arose early in the morning and swore an oath with one another; and Isaac sent them away, and they departed from him in peace.

³² It came to pass the same day that Isaac's servants came and told him about the well which they had dug, and said to him, "We have found water." ³³ So he called it Shebah. Therefore the name of the city *is* Beersheba to this day.

34 When Esau was forty years old, he took as wives Judith the daughter of Beeri the Hittite, and Basemath the daughter of Elon the Hittite. 35 And they were a grief of mind to Isaac and Rebekah.

Isaac blesses Jacob

27 Now it came to pass, when Isaac was old and his eyes were so dim that he could not see, that he called Esau his older son and said to him, "My son."

And he answered him, "Here I am."

2 Then he said, "Behold now, I am old. I do not know the day of my death. 3 Now therefore, please take your weapons, your quiver and your bow, and go out to the field and hunt game for me. 4 And make me savory food, such as I love, and bring it to me that I may eat, that my soul may bless you before I die."

5 Now Rebekah was listening when Isaac spoke to Esau his son. And Esau went to the field to hunt game and to bring it. 6 So Rebekah spoke to Jacob her son, saying, "Indeed I heard your father speak to Esau your brother, saying, 7 'Bring me game and make savory food for me, that I may eat it and bless you in the presence of the LORD before my death.' 8 Now therefore, my son, obey my voice according to what I command you. 9 Go now to the flock and bring me from there two choice kids of the goats, and I will make savory food from them for your father, such as he loves. 10 Then you shall take it to your father, that he may eat it, and that he may bless you before his death."

11 And Jacob said to Rebekah his mother, "Look, Esau my brother is a hairy man, and I am a smooth-skinned man. 12 Perhaps my father will feel me, and I shall seem to be a deceiver to him; and I shall bring a curse on myself and not a blessing."

13 But his mother said to him, "Let your curse be on me, my son; only obey my voice, and go, get them for me." 14 And he went and got them and brought them to his mother, and his mother made savory food, such as his father loved. 15 Then Rebekah took the choice clothes of her elder son Esau, which were with her in the house, and put them on Jacob her younger son. 16 And she put the skins of the kids of the goats on his hands and on the smooth part of his neck. 17 Then she gave the savory food and the bread, which she had prepared, into the hand of her son Jacob.

18 So he went to his father and said, "My father."

And he said, "Here I am. Who are you, my son?"

19 Jacob said to his father, "I am Esau your firstborn; I have done just as you told me; please arise, sit and eat of my game, that your soul may bless me."

20 But Isaac said to his son, "How is it that you have found it so quickly, my son?"

And he said, "Because the LORD your God brought it to me."

21 Isaac said to Jacob, "Please come near, that I may feel you, my son, whether you are really my son Esau or not." 22 So Jacob went near to Isaac his father, and he felt him and said, "The voice is Jacob's voice, but the hands are the hands of Esau." 23 And he did not recognize him, because his hands were hairy like his brother Esau's hands; so he blessed him.

24 Then he said, "Are you really my son Esau?"

He said, "I am."

25 He said, "Bring it near to me, and I will eat of my son's game, so that my soul may bless you." So he brought it near to him, and he ate; and he brought him wine, and he drank. 26 Then his father Isaac said to him, "Come near now and kiss me, my son." 27 And he came near and kissed him; and he smelled the smell of his clothing, and blessed him and said:

"Surely, the smell of my son
Is like the smell of a field
Which the LORD has blessed.
28 Therefore may God give you

Of the dew of heaven,
Of the fatness of the earth,
And plenty of grain and wine.
29 Let peoples serve you,
And nations bow down to you.
Be master over your brethren,
And let your mother's sons bow
     down to you.
Cursed *be* everyone who curses
     you,
And blessed *be* those who bless
     you!"

30 Now it happened, as soon as Isaac had finished blessing Jacob, and Jacob had scarcely gone out from the presence of Isaac his father, that Esau his brother came in from his hunting. 31 He also had made savory food, and brought it to his father, and said to his father, "Let my father arise and eat of his son's game, that your soul may bless me."

32 And his father Isaac said to him, "Who *are* you?"

So he said, "I *am* your son, your firstborn, Esau."

33 Then Isaac trembled exceedingly, and said, "Who? Where *is* the one who hunted game and brought *it* to me? I ate all *of it* before you came, and I have blessed him—*and* indeed he shall be blessed."

34 When Esau heard the words of his father, he cried with an exceedingly great and bitter cry, and said to his father, "Bless me—me also, O my father!"

35 But he said, "Your brother came with deceit and has taken away your blessing."

36 And *Esau* said, "Is he not rightly named Jacob? For he has supplanted me these two times. He took away my birthright, and now look, he has taken away my blessing!" And he said, "Have you not reserved a blessing for me?"

37 Then Isaac answered and said to Esau, "Indeed I have made him your master, and all his brethren I have given to him as servants; with grain and wine I have sustained him. What shall I do now for you, my son?"

38 And Esau said to his father, "Have you only one blessing, my father? Bless me—me also, O my father!" And Esau lifted up his voice and wept.

39 Then Isaac his father answered and said to him:

"Behold, your dwelling shall be
     of the fatness of the earth,
And of the dew of heaven from
     above.
40 By your sword you shall live,
And you shall serve your
     brother;
And it shall come to pass, when
     you become restless,
That you shall break his yoke
     from your neck."

41 So Esau hated Jacob because of the blessing with which his father blessed him, and Esau said in his heart, "The days of mourning for my father are at hand; then I will kill my brother Jacob."

42 And the words of Esau her older son were told to Rebekah. So she sent and called Jacob her younger son, and said to him, "Surely your brother Esau comforts himself concerning you *by intending* to kill you. 43 Now therefore, my son, obey my voice: arise, flee to my brother Laban in Haran. 44 And stay with him a few days, until your brother's fury turns away, 45 until your brother's anger turns away from you, and he forgets what you have done to him; then I will send and bring you from there. Why should I be bereaved also of you both in one day?"

46 And Rebekah said to Isaac, "I am weary of my life because of the daughters of Heth; if Jacob takes a wife of the daughters of Heth, like these *who are* the daughters of the land, what good will my life be to me?"

Isaac sends Jacob to his Uncle Laban

28 Then Isaac called Jacob and blessed him, and charged him, and said to him: "You shall not take a wife from the daughters of Canaan. 2 Arise, go to Padan Aram, to the house of Bethuel your mother's father; and take yourself a wife from there of the daughters of Laban your mother's brother.

3 "May God Almighty bless you,
    And make you fruitful and
        multiply you,
    That you may be an assembly
        of peoples;
4   And give you the blessing of
        Abraham,
    To you and your descendants
        with you,
    That you may inherit the land
    In which you are a stranger,
    Which God gave to Abraham."

5 So Isaac sent Jacob away, and he went to Padan Aram, to Laban the son of Bethuel the Syrian, the brother of Rebekah, the mother of Jacob and Esau.

6 Esau saw that Isaac had blessed Jacob and sent him away to Padan Aram to take himself a wife from there, *and that* as he blessed him he gave him a charge, saying, "You shall not take a wife from the daughters of Canaan," 7 and that Jacob had obeyed his father and his mother and had gone to Padan Aram. 8 Also Esau saw that the daughters of Canaan did not please his father Isaac. 9 So Esau went to Ishmael and took Mahalath the daughter of Ishmael, Abraham's son, the sister of Nebajoth, to be his wife in addition to the wives he had.

10 Now Jacob went out from Beersheba and went toward Haran. 11 So he came to a certain place and stayed there all night, because the sun had set. And he took one of the stones of that place and put it at his head, and he lay down in that place to sleep. 12 Then he dreamed, and behold, a ladder *was* set up on the earth, and its top reached to heaven; and there the angels of God were ascending and descending on it.

13 And behold, the LORD stood above it and said: "I *am* the LORD God of Abraham your father and the God of Isaac; the land on which you lie I will give to you and your descendants. 14 Also your descendants shall be as the dust of the earth; you shall spread abroad to the west and the east, to the north and the south; and in you and in your seed all the families of the earth shall be blessed. 15 Behold, I *am* with you and will keep you wherever you go, and will bring you back to this land; for I will not leave you until I have done what I have spoken to you."

16 Then Jacob awoke from his sleep and said, "Surely the LORD is in this place, and I did not know *it*." 17 And he was afraid and said, "How awesome *is* this place! This *is* none other than the house of God, and this *is* the gate of heaven!"

18 Then Jacob rose early in the morning, and took the stone that he had put at his head, set it up as a pillar, and poured oil on top of it. 19 And he called the name of that place Bethel; but the name of that city had been Luz previously. 20 Then Jacob made a vow, saying, "If God will be with me, and keep me in this way that I am going, and give me bread to eat and clothing to put on, 21 so that I come back to my father's house in peace, then the LORD shall be my God. 22 And this stone which I have set as a pillar shall be God's house, and of all that You give me I will surely give a tenth to You."

Jacob marries Leah and Rachel

29 So Jacob went on his journey and came to the land of the people of the East. 2 And he looked, and saw a well in the field; and behold, there *were* three flocks of sheep lying by it; for out of that well they watered the flocks. A large stone *was* on the well's mouth. 3 Now all the flocks would be gathered there; and they would roll the stone from the well's mouth, water the sheep, and put the stone back in its place on the well's mouth.

4 And Jacob said to them, "My brethren, where *are* you from?"

And they said, "We *are* from Haran."

5 Then he said to them, "Do you know Laban the son of Nahor?"

And they said, "We know him."

6 So he said to them, "Is he well?"

And they said, "*He is* well. And look, his daughter Rachel is coming with the sheep."

7 Then he said, "Look, *it is* still high day; *it is* not time for the cattle to be gathered together. Water the sheep, and go and feed *them.*"

8 But they said, "We cannot until all the flocks are gathered together, and they have rolled the stone from the well's mouth; then we water the sheep."

9 Now while he was still speaking with them, Rachel came with her father's sheep, for she was a shepherdess. 10 And it came to pass, when Jacob saw Rachel the daughter of Laban his mother's brother, and the sheep of Laban his mother's brother, that Jacob went near and rolled the stone from the well's mouth, and watered the flock of Laban his mother's brother. 11 Then Jacob kissed Rachel, and lifted up his voice and wept. 12 And Jacob told Rachel that he *was* her father's relative and that he *was* Rebekah's son. So she ran and told her father.

13 Then it came to pass, when Laban heard the report about Jacob his sister's son, that he ran to meet him, and embraced him and kissed him, and brought him to his house. So he told Laban all these things. 14 And Laban said to him, "Surely you *are* my bone and my flesh." And he stayed with him for a month.

15 Then Laban said to Jacob, "Because you *are* my relative, should you therefore serve me for nothing? Tell me, what *should* your wages *be?*"

16 Now Laban had two daughters: the name of the elder *was* Leah, and the name of the younger *was* Rachel. 17 Leah's eyes *were* delicate, but Rachel was beautiful of form and appearance.

18 Now Jacob loved Rachel; so he said, "I will serve you seven years for Rachel your younger daughter."

19 And Laban said, "*It is* better that I give her to you than that I should give her to another man. Stay with me." 20 So Jacob served seven years for Rachel, and they seemed *only* a few days to him because of the love he had for her.

21 Then Jacob said to Laban, "Give me my wife, for my days are fulfilled, that I may go in to her." 22 And Laban gathered together all the men of the place and made a feast. 23 Now it came to pass in the evening, that he took Leah his daughter and brought her to Jacob; and he went in to her. 24 And Laban gave his maid Zilpah to his daughter Leah *as* a maid. 25 So it came to pass in the morning, that behold, it *was* Leah. And he said to Laban, "What is this you have done to me? Was it not for Rachel that I served you? Why then have you deceived me?"

26 And Laban said, "It must not be done so in our country, to give the younger before the firstborn. 27 Fulfill her week, and we will give you this one also for the service which you will serve with me still another seven years."

28 Then Jacob did so and fulfilled her week. So he gave him his daughter Rachel as wife also. 29 And Laban gave his maid Bilhah to his daughter Rachel as a maid. 30 Then *Jacob* also went in to Rachel, and he also loved Rachel more than Leah. And he served with Laban still another seven years.

31 When the LORD saw that Leah *was* unloved, He opened her womb; but Rachel *was* barren. 32 So Leah conceived and bore a son, and she called his name Reuben; for she said, "The LORD has surely looked on my affliction. Now therefore, my husband will love me." 33 Then she conceived again and bore a son, and said, "Because the LORD has heard that I *am* unloved, He has therefore given me this *son* also." And she called his name Simeon. 34 She conceived again and bore a son, and said, "Now this time my husband will become attached to

me, because I have borne him three sons." Therefore his name was called Levi. 35 And she conceived again and bore a son, and said, "Now I will praise the LORD." Therefore she called his name Judah. Then she stopped bearing.

Jacob has many children

30 Now when Rachel saw that she bore Jacob no children, Rachel envied her sister, and said to Jacob, "Give me children, or else I die!"

2 And Jacob's anger was aroused against Rachel, and he said, "*Am* I in the place of God, who has withheld from you the fruit of the womb?"

3 So she said, "Here is my maid Bilhah; go in to her, and she will bear *a child* on my knees, that I also may have children by her." 4 Then she gave him Bilhah her maid as wife, and Jacob went in to her. 5 And Bilhah conceived and bore Jacob a son. 6 Then Rachel said, "God has judged my case; and He has also heard my voice and given me a son." Therefore she called his name Dan. 7 And Rachel's maid Bilhah conceived again and bore Jacob a second son. 8 Then Rachel said, "With great wrestlings I have wrestled with my sister, *and* indeed I have prevailed." So she called his name Naphtali.

9 When Leah saw that she had stopped bearing, she took Zilpah her maid and gave her to Jacob as wife. 10 And Leah's maid Zilpah bore Jacob a son. 11 Then Leah said, "A troop comes!" So she called his name Gad. 12 And Leah's maid Zilpah bore Jacob a second son. 13 Then Leah said, "I am happy, for the daughters will call me blessed." So she called his name Asher.

14 Now Reuben went in the days of wheat harvest and found mandrakes in the field, and brought them to his mother Leah. Then Rachel said to Leah, "Please give me *some* of your son's mandrakes."

15 But she said to her, "*Is it* a small matter that you have taken away my husband? Would you take away my son's mandrakes also?"

And Rachel said, "Therefore he will lie with you tonight for your son's mandrakes."

16 When Jacob came out of the field in the evening, Leah went out to meet him and said, "You must come in to me, for I have surely hired you with my son's mandrakes." And he lay with her that night.

17 And God listened to Leah, and she conceived and bore Jacob a fifth son. 18 Leah said, "God has given me my wages, because I have given my maid to my husband." So she called his name Issachar. 19 Then Leah conceived again and bore Jacob a sixth son. 20 And Leah said, "God has endowed me *with* a good endowment; now my husband will dwell with me, because I have borne him six sons." So she called his name Zebulun. 21 Afterward she bore a daughter, and called her name Dinah.

22 Then God remembered Rachel, and God listened to her and opened her womb. 23 And she conceived and bore a son, and said, "God has taken away my reproach." 24 So she called his name Joseph, and said, "The LORD shall add to me another son."

25 And it came to pass, when Rachel had borne Joseph, that Jacob said to Laban, "Send me away, that I may go to my own place and to my country. 26 Give *me* my wives and my children for whom I have served you, and let me go; for you know my service which I have done for you."

27 And Laban said to him, "Please *stay,* if I have found favor in your eyes, *for* I have learned by experience that the LORD has blessed me for your sake." 28 Then he said, "Name me your wages, and I will give *it.*"

29 So *Jacob* said to him, "You know how I have served you and how your livestock has been with me. 30 For what you had before I *came was* little, and it has increased to a great amount; the LORD has blessed you since my coming. And now, when shall I also provide for my own house?"

Local Citizen Claims He Was Cheated

Old Testament News Service

HARAN—A wealthy rancher in the area has made a complaint against a member of his own family.

Rancher Laban (pronounced *LAY-bun*) claims that his nephew, Jacob (pronounced *JAY-kob*), who worked for him as a hired hand, has disappeared with Laban's two daughters, Leah and Rachel, and much of the livestock. It appears that Jacob has also taken the family gods.

A police report shows that Jacob worked for his uncle for twenty years— seven years for Leah, seven years for Rachel, and six years for the sheep and goats. It is believed that Laban agreed to this arrangement. Officials say that Laban received full value for the missing persons and livestock.

Although the gods have not been found, Laban and his nephew are settling their argument out of court. Jacob has returned to his own home in Canaan.

31 So he said, "What shall I give you?"

And Jacob said, "You shall not give me anything. If you will do this thing for me, I will again feed and keep your flocks: 32 Let me pass through all your flock today, removing from there all the speckled and spotted sheep, and all the brown ones among the lambs, and the spotted and speckled among the goats; and *these* shall be my wages. 33 So my righteousness will answer for me in time to come, when the subject of my wages comes before you: every one that *is* not speckled and spotted among the goats, and brown among the lambs, will be considered stolen, if *it is* with me."

34 And Laban said, "Oh, that it were according to your word!" 35 So he removed that day the male goats that were speckled and spotted, all the female goats that *were* speckled and spotted, every one that had *some* white in it, and all the brown ones among the lambs, and gave *them* into the hand of his sons. 36 Then he put three days' journey between himself and Jacob, and Jacob fed the rest of Laban's flocks.

37 Now Jacob took for himself rods of green poplar and of the almond and chestnut trees, peeled white strips in them, and exposed the white which *was* in the rods. 38 And the rods which he had peeled, he set before the flocks in the gutters, in the watering troughs where the flocks came to drink, so that they should conceive when they came to drink. 39 So the flocks conceived before the rods, and the flocks brought forth streaked, speckled, and spotted. 40 Then Jacob separated the lambs, and made the flocks face toward the streaked and all the brown in the flock of Laban; but he put his own flocks by themselves and did not put them with Laban's flock.

41 And it came to pass, whenever the stronger livestock conceived, that Jacob placed the rods before the eyes of the livestock in the gutters, that they might conceive among the rods. 42 But when the flocks were feeble, he did not put *them* in; so the feebler were Laban's and the stronger Jacob's. 43 Thus the man became exceedingly prosperous, and had large flocks, female and male servants, and camels and donkeys.

Jacob runs away from Laban

31 Now *Jacob* heard the words of Laban's sons, saying, "Jacob has taken away all that was our father's, and from what was our father's he has acquired all this wealth." 2 And Jacob saw the countenance of Laban, and indeed it *was* not *favorable* toward him

as before. 3 Then the LORD said to Jacob, "Return to the land of your fathers and to your family, and I will be with you."

4 So Jacob sent and called Rachel and Leah to the field, to his flock, 5 and said to them, "I see your father's countenance, that it is not *favorable* toward me as before; but the God of my father has been with me. 6 And you know that with all my might I have served your father. 7 Yet your father has deceived me and changed my wages ten times, but God did not allow him to hurt me. 8 If he said thus: 'The speckled shall be your wages,' then all the flocks bore speckled. And if he said thus: 'The streaked shall be your wages,' then all the flocks bore streaked. 9 So God has taken away the livestock of your father and given *them* to me.

10 "And it happened, at the time when the flocks conceived, that I lifted my eyes and saw in a dream, and behold, the rams which leaped upon the flocks *were* streaked, speckled, and gray-spotted. 11 Then the Angel of God spoke to me in a dream, saying, 'Jacob.' And I said, 'Here I am.' 12 And He said, 'Lift your eyes now and see, all the rams which leap on the flocks *are* streaked, speckled, and gray-spotted; for I have seen all that Laban is doing to you. 13 I *am* the God of Bethel, where you anointed the pillar *and* where you made a vow to Me. Now arise, get out of this land, and return to the land of your family.' "

14 Then Rachel and Leah answered and said to him, "Is there still any portion or inheritance for us in our father's house? 15 Are we not considered strangers by him? For he has sold us, and also completely consumed our money. 16 For all these riches which God has taken from our father are *really* ours and our children's; now then, whatever God has said to you, do it."

17 Then Jacob rose and set his sons and his wives on camels. 18 And he carried away all his livestock and all his possessions which he had gained, his acquired livestock which he had gained in Padan Aram, to go to his father Isaac in the land of Canaan. 19 Now Laban had gone to shear his sheep, and Rachel had stolen the household idols that were her father's. 20 And Jacob stole away, unknown to Laban the Syrian, in that he did not tell him that he intended to flee. 21 So he fled with all that he had. He arose and crossed the river, and headed toward the mountains of Gilead.

22 And Laban was told on the third day that Jacob had fled. 23 Then he took his brethren with him and pursued him for seven days' journey, and he overtook him in the mountains of Gilead. 24 But God had come to Laban the Syrian in a dream by night, and said to him, "Be careful that you speak to Jacob neither good nor bad."

25 So Laban overtook Jacob. Now Jacob had pitched his tent in the mountains, and Laban with his brethren pitched in the mountains of Gilead.

26 And Laban said to Jacob: "What have you done, that you have stolen away unknown to me, and carried away my daughters like captives *taken* with the sword? 27 Why did you flee away secretly, and steal away from me, and not tell me; for I might have sent you away with joy and songs, with timbrel and harp? 28 And you did not allow me to kiss my sons and my daughters. Now you have done foolishly in *so* doing. 29 It is in my power to do you harm, but the God of your father spoke to me last night, saying, 'Be careful that you speak to Jacob neither good nor bad.' 30 And now you have surely gone because you greatly long for your father's house, *but* why did you steal my gods?"

31 Then Jacob answered and said to Laban, "Because I was afraid, for I said, 'Perhaps you would take your daughters from me by force.' 32 With whomever you find your gods, do not let him live. In the presence of our brethren, identify what I have of yours and take *it* with you." For Jacob did not know that Rachel had stolen them.

33 And Laban went into Jacob's tent,

into Leah's tent, and into the two maids' tents, but he did not find *them*. Then he went out of Leah's tent and entered Rachel's tent. 34 Now Rachel had taken the household idols, put them in the camel's saddle, and sat on them. And Laban searched all about the tent but did not find *them*. 35 And she said to her father, "Let it not displease my lord that I cannot rise before you, for the manner of women *is* with me." And he searched but did not find the household idols.

36 Then Jacob was angry and rebuked Laban, and Jacob answered and said to Laban: "What *is* my trespass? What *is* my sin, that you have so hotly pursued me? 37 Although you have searched all my things, what part of your household things have you found? Set *it* here before my brethren and your brethren, that they may judge between us both! 38 These twenty years I *have* been with you; your ewes and your female goats have not miscarried their young, and I have not eaten the rams of your flock. 39 That which was torn *by beasts* I did not bring to you; I bore the loss of it. You required it from my hand, *whether* stolen by day or stolen by night. 40 *There* I was! In the day the drought consumed me, and the frost by night, and my sleep departed from my eyes. 41 Thus I have been in your house twenty years; I served you fourteen years for your two daughters, and six years for your flock, and you have changed my wages ten times. 42 Unless the God of my father, the God of Abraham and the Fear of Isaac, had been with me, surely now you would have sent me away empty-handed. God has seen my affliction and the labor of my hands, and rebuked *you* last night."

43 And Laban answered and said to Jacob, "*These* daughters *are* my daughters, and *these* children *are* my children, and *this* flock *is* my flock; all that you see *is* mine. But what can I do this day to these my daughters or to their children whom they have borne? 44 Now therefore, come, let us make a covenant, you and I, and let it be a witness between you and me."

45 So Jacob took a stone and set it up *as* a pillar. 46 Then Jacob said to his brethren, "Gather stones." And they took stones and made a heap, and they ate there on the heap. 47 Laban called it Jegar Sahadutha, but Jacob called it Galeed. 48 And Laban said, "This heap *is* a witness between you and me this day." Therefore its name was called Galeed, 49 also Mizpah, because he said, "May the LORD watch between you and me when we are absent one from another. 50 If you afflict my daughters, or if you take *other* wives besides my daughters, *although* no man *is* with us—see, God *is* witness between you and me!"

51 Then Laban said to Jacob, "Here is this heap and here is *this* pillar, which I have placed between you and me. 52 This heap *is* a witness, and *this* pillar *is* a witness, that I will not pass beyond this heap to you, and you will not pass beyond this heap and this pillar to me, for harm. 53 The God of Abraham, the God of Nahor, and the God of their father judge between us." And Jacob swore by the Fear of his father Isaac. 54 Then Jacob offered a **sacrifice** on the mountain, and called his brethren to eat bread. And they ate bread and stayed all night on the mountain. 55 And early in the morning Laban arose, and kissed his sons and daughters and blessed them. Then Laban departed and returned to his place.

Esau comes to meet Jacob

32 So Jacob went on his way, and the angels of God met him. 2 When

---

⬦ **WORDFINDER** _____

31:54 Sacrifice Pronounced *SACK-rih-fyce*. An offering to God. In the Old Testament, the people sacrificed the blood of animals for sin. In the New Testament, Christ is our only sacrifice for sin.

Jacob saw them, he said, "This *is* God's camp." And he called the name of that place Mahanaim.

3 Then Jacob sent messengers before him to Esau his brother in the land of Seir, the country of Edom. 4 And he commanded them, saying, "Speak thus to my lord Esau, 'Thus your servant Jacob says: "I have dwelt with Laban and stayed there until now. 5 I have oxen, donkeys, flocks, and male and female servants; and I have sent to tell my lord, that I may find favor in your sight." ' "

6 Then the messengers returned to Jacob, saying, "We came to your brother Esau, and he also is coming to meet you, and four hundred men *are* with him." 7 So Jacob was greatly afraid and distressed; and he divided the people that *were* with him, and the flocks and herds and camels, into two companies. 8 And he said, "If Esau comes to the one company and attacks it, then the other company which is left will escape."

9 Then Jacob said, "O God of my father Abraham and God of my father Isaac, the LORD who said to me, 'Return to your country and to your family, and I will deal well with you': 10 I am not worthy of the least of all the mercies and of all the truth which You have shown Your servant; for I crossed over this Jordan with my staff, and now I have become two companies. 11 Deliver me, I pray, from the hand of my brother, from the hand of Esau; for I fear him, lest he come and attack me *and* the mother with the children. 12 For You said, 'I will surely treat you well, and make your descendants as the sand of the sea, which cannot be numbered for multitude.' "

13 So he lodged there that same night, and took what came to his hand as a present for Esau his brother: 14 two hundred female goats and twenty male goats, two hundred ewes and twenty rams, 15 thirty milk camels with their colts, forty cows and ten bulls, twenty female donkeys and ten foals. 16 Then he delivered *them* to the hand of his servants, every drove by itself, and said to his servants, "Pass over before me, and put some distance between successive droves." 17 And he commanded the first one, saying, "When Esau my brother meets you and asks you, saying, 'To whom do you belong, and where are you going? Whose *are* these in front of you?' 18 then you shall say, 'They *are* your servant Jacob's. It *is* a present sent to my lord Esau; and behold, he also *is* behind us.' " 19 So he commanded the second, the third, and all who followed the droves, saying, "In this manner you shall speak to Esau when you find him; 20 and also say, 'Behold, your servant Jacob *is* behind us.' " For he said, "I will appease him with the present that goes before me, and afterward I will see his face; perhaps he will accept me." 21 So the present went on over before him, but he himself lodged that night in the camp.

22 And he arose that night and took

⚒ DIGGING IN

32:22–30 God Changes Jacob's Name A time comes in a young person's life when he or she must make a decision. God made you for Himself. Will you surrender your life to serve the Lord, whatever He calls you to be?

In his early life, Jacob ran away to serve his Uncle Laban in a far country. Then he promised his life to the Lord if He would bring him home again.

Now Jacob is almost home from serving his uncle. So God is asking Jacob to keep his promise.

Jacob struggles with God all night. In the morning Jacob is worn out, and has to give up. Then God gives Jacob a new name because now Jacob will be God's man. Jacob's new name is Israel (pronounced *IZ-ray-el*) and means "Prince with God."

God wants to give you a new nature, too. When you give in to His claims on your life, then you also will be a prince or princess of God. That will be the beginning of an exciting life for you.

Jacob wrestles with the Angel of the Lord.

his two wives, his two female servants, and his eleven sons, and crossed over the ford of Jabbok. 23 He took them, sent them over the brook, and sent over what he had. 24 Then Jacob was left alone; and a Man wrestled with him until the breaking of day. 25 Now when He saw that He did not prevail against him, He touched the socket of his hip; and the socket of Jacob's hip was out of joint as He wrestled with him. 26 And He said, "Let Me go, for the day breaks."

But he said, "I will not let You go unless You bless me!"

27 So He said to him, "What is your name?"

He said, "Jacob."

28 And He said, "Your name shall no longer be called Jacob, but Israel; for you have struggled with God and with men, and have prevailed."

29 Then Jacob asked, saying, "Tell me Your name, I pray."

And He said, "Why is it that you ask about My name?" And He blessed him there.

30 So Jacob called the name of the place Peniel: "For I have seen God face to face, and my life is preserved."

31 Just as he crossed over Penuel the sun rose on him, and he limped on his hip. 32 Therefore to this day the children of Israel do not eat the muscle that shrank, which is on the hip socket, because He touched the socket of Jacob's hip in the muscle that shrank.

Jacob and Esau make peace

33 Now Jacob lifted his eyes and looked, and there, Esau was coming, and with him were four hundred men. So he divided the children among Leah, Rachel, and the two maidservants. 2 And he put the maidservants and their children in front, Leah and her children behind, and Rachel and Joseph last. 3 Then he crossed over before them and bowed himself to the ground seven times, until he came near to his brother.

4 But Esau ran to meet him, and embraced him, and fell on his neck and kissed him, and they wept. 5 And he lifted his eyes and saw the women and children, and said, "Who are these with you?"

So he said, "The children whom God has graciously given your servant." 6 Then the maidservants came near, they and their children, and bowed down. 7 And Leah also came near with her children, and they bowed

Local Brothers Make Peace

CBN (Canaan Broadcasting Network)—For weeks, CBN has been keeping listeners informed about the quarrel between two of the most important men in the country—Jacob (pronounced *JAY-kob*) and Esau (*EE-saw*).

Twenty years ago Jacob fled the country when he was accused of stealing Esau's land rights. It was then reported that Esau planned to kill his brother on sight!

In the meantime, both men have gained power and popularity. Officials have been concerned that fighting might break out between the two brothers, drawing the whole country into a civil war.

Channel 7 is happy to report that Jacob and Esau have met and have made peace, and war has been avoided.

It is now reported that Esau has agreed to make his home in the mountains of the southland, while Jacob will live in the land of Canaan (pronounced *KAY-nun*) at Shechem (pronounced *SHE-kum*).

down. Afterward Joseph and Rachel came near, and they bowed down.

8 Then Esau said, "What *do you mean by* all this company which I met?"

And he said, "*These are* to find favor in the sight of my lord."

9 But Esau said, "I have enough, my brother; keep what you have for yourself."

10 And Jacob said, "No, please, if I have now found favor in your sight, then receive my present from my hand, inasmuch as I have seen your face as though I had seen the face of God, and you were pleased with me. 11 Please, take my blessing that is brought to you, because God has dealt graciously with me, and because I have enough." So he urged him, and he took *it*.

12 Then Esau said, "Let us take our journey; let us go, and I will go before you."

13 But Jacob said to him, "My lord knows that the children *are* weak, and the flocks and herds which are nursing *are* with me. And if the men should drive them hard one day, all the flock will die. 14 Please let my lord go on ahead before his servant. I will lead on slowly at a pace which the livestock that go before me, and the children, are able to endure, until I come to my lord in Seir."

15 And Esau said, "Now let me leave with you *some* of the people who *are* with me."

But he said, "What need is there? Let me find favor in the sight of my lord." 16 So Esau returned that day on his way to Seir. 17 And Jacob journeyed to Succoth, built himself a house, and made booths for his livestock. Therefore the name of the place is called Succoth.

18 Then Jacob came safely to the city of Shechem, which *is* in the land of Canaan, when he came from Padan Aram; and he pitched his tent before the city. 19 And he bought the parcel of land, where he had pitched his tent, from the children of Hamor, Shechem's father, for one hundred pieces of money. 20 Then he erected an altar there and called it El Elohe Israel.

Dinah's brothers take revenge

34 Now Dinah the daughter of Leah, whom she had borne to Jacob, went out to see the daughters of the land. 2 And when Shechem the son of Hamor the Hivite, prince of the country, saw her, he took her and lay with her, and violated her. 3 His soul was strongly attracted to Dinah the daughter of Jacob, and he loved the young woman and spoke kindly to the young woman. 4 So Shechem spoke to his father Hamor, saying, "Get me this young woman as a wife."

5 And Jacob heard that he had defiled Dinah his daughter. Now his sons were with his livestock in the field; so Jacob held his peace until they came. 6 Then Hamor the father of Shechem went out to Jacob to speak with him. 7 And the sons of Jacob came in from the field when they heard it; and the men were grieved and very angry, because he had done a disgraceful thing in Israel by lying with Jacob's daughter, a thing which ought not to be done. 8 But Hamor spoke with them, saying, "The soul of my son Shechem longs for your daughter. Please give her to him as a wife. 9 And make marriages with us; give your daughters to us, and take our daughters to yourselves. 10 So you shall dwell with us, and the land shall be before you. Dwell and trade in it, and acquire possessions for yourselves."

11 Then Shechem said to her father and her brothers, "Let me find favor in your eyes, and whatever you say to me I will give. 12 Ask me ever so much dowry and gift, and I will give according to what you say to me; but give me the young woman as a wife."

13 But the sons of Jacob answered Shechem and Hamor his father, and spoke deceitfully, because he had defiled Dinah their sister. 14 And they said to them, "We cannot do this thing, to give our sister to one who is uncircumcised, for that would be a reproach to us. 15 But on this condition we will consent to you: If you will become as we are, if every male of you is circumcised, 16 then we will give our daughters to you, and we will take your daughters to us; and we will dwell with you, and we will become one people. 17 But if you will not heed us and be circumcised, then we will take our daughter and be gone."

18 And their words pleased Hamor and Shechem, Hamor's son. 19 So the young man did not delay to do the thing, because he delighted in Jacob's daughter. He was more honorable than all the household of his father. 20 And Hamor and Shechem his son came to the gate of their city, and spoke with the men of their city, saying: 21 "These men are at peace with us. Therefore let them dwell in the land and trade in it. For indeed the land is large enough for them. Let us take their daughters to us as wives, and let us give them our daughters. 22 Only on this condition will the men consent to dwell with us, to be one people: if every male among us is circumcised as they are circumcised. 23 Will not their livestock, their property, and every animal of theirs be ours? Only let us consent to them, and they will dwell with us." 24 And all who went out of the gate of his city heeded Hamor and Shechem his son; every male was circumcised, all who went out of the gate of his city.

25 Now it came to pass on the third day, when they were in pain, that two of the sons of Jacob, Simeon and Levi, Dinah's brothers, each took his sword and came boldly upon the city and killed all the males. 26 And they killed Hamor and Shechem his son with the edge of the sword, and took Dinah from Shechem's house, and went out. 27 The sons of Jacob came upon the slain, and plundered the city, because their sister had been defiled. 28 They took their sheep, their oxen, and their donkeys, what was in the city and what was in the field, 29 and all their wealth. All their little ones and their wives they took captive; and they plundered even all that was in the houses.

30 Then Jacob said to Simeon and Levi, "You have troubled me by making me obnoxious among the inhabitants of the land, among the Canaanites and the Perizzites; and since I am few in number, they will gather themselves together against me and kill me. I shall be destroyed, my household and I."

31 But they said, "Should he treat our sister like a harlot?"

God blesses Jacob at Bethel

35 Then God said to Jacob, "Arise, go up to Bethel and dwell there; and make an altar there to God, who ap-

peared to you when you fled from the face of Esau your brother."

2 And Jacob said to his household and to all who *were* with him, "Put away the foreign gods that *are* among you, purify yourselves, and change your garments. 3 Then let us arise and go up to Bethel; and I will make an altar there to God, who answered me in the day of my distress and has been with me in the way which I have gone." 4 So they gave Jacob all the foreign gods which *were* in their hands, and the earrings which *were* in their ears; and Jacob hid them under the terebinth tree which *was* by Shechem.

5 And they journeyed, and the terror of God was upon the cities that *were* all around them, and they did not pursue the sons of Jacob. 6 So Jacob came to Luz (that *is,* Bethel), which *is* in the land of Canaan, he and all the people who *were* with him. 7 And he built an altar there and called the place El Bethel, because there God appeared to him when he fled from the face of his brother.

8 Now Deborah, Rebekah's nurse, died, and she was buried below Bethel under the terebinth tree. So the name of it was called Allon Bachuth.

9 Then God appeared to Jacob again, when he came from Padan Aram, and blessed him. 10 And God said to him, "Your name *is* Jacob; your name shall not be called Jacob anymore, but Israel shall be your name." So He called his name Israel. 11 Also God said to him: "I *am* God Almighty. Be fruitful and multiply; a nation and a company of nations shall proceed from you, and kings shall come from your body. 12 The land which I gave Abraham and Isaac I give to you; and to your descendants after you I give this land." 13 Then God went up from him in the place where He talked with him. 14 So Jacob set up a pillar in the place where He talked with him, a pillar of stone; and he poured a drink offering on it, and he poured oil on it. 15 And Jacob called the name of the place where God spoke with him, Bethel.

16 Then they journeyed from Bethel. And when there was but a little distance to go to Ephrath, Rachel labored *in childbirth,* and she had hard labor. 17 Now it came to pass, when she was in hard labor, that the midwife said to her, "Do not fear; you will have this son also." 18 And so it was, as her soul was departing (for she died), that she called his name Ben-Oni; but his father called him Benjamin. 19 So Rachel died and was buried on the way to Ephrath (that *is,* Bethlehem). 20 And Jacob set a pillar on her grave, which *is* the pillar of Rachel's grave to this day.

21 Then Israel journeyed and pitched his tent beyond the tower of Eder. 22 And it happened, when Israel dwelt in that land, that Reuben went and lay with Bilhah his father's concubine; and Israel heard *about it.*

Now the sons of Jacob were twelve: 23 the sons of Leah *were* Reuben, Jacob's firstborn, and Simeon, Levi, Judah, Issachar, and Zebulun; 24 the sons of Rachel *were* Joseph and Benjamin; 25 the sons of Bilhah, Rachel's maidservant, *were* Dan and Naphtali; 26 and the sons of Zilpah, Leah's maidservant, *were* Gad and Asher. These *were* the sons of Jacob who were born to him in Padan Aram.

27 Then Jacob came to his father Isaac at Mamre, or Kirjath Arba (that *is,* Hebron), where Abraham and Isaac had dwelt. 28 Now the days of Isaac were one hundred and eighty years. 29 So Isaac breathed his last and died, and was gathered to his people, *being* old and full of days. And his sons Esau and Jacob buried him.

Esau's family

36 Now this *is* the genealogy of Esau, who is Edom. 2 Esau took his wives from the daughters of Canaan: Adah the daughter of Elon the Hittite; Aholibamah the daughter of Anah, the daughter of Zibeon the Hivite; 3 and Basemath, Ishmael's daughter, sister of Nebajoth. 4 Now Adah bore Eliphaz to Esau, and Basemath bore Reuel. 5 And Aholibamah bore Jeush, Jaalam,

Building in Petra, the city carved out of rock by descendants of Esau.

and Korah. These *were* the sons of Esau who were born to him in the land of Canaan.

6 Then Esau took his wives, his sons, his daughters, and all the persons of his household, his cattle and all his animals, and all his goods which he had gained in the land of Canaan, and went to a country away from the presence of his brother Jacob. 7 For their possessions were too great for them to dwell together, and the land where they were strangers could not support them because of their livestock. 8 So Esau dwelt in Mount Seir. Esau *is* Edom.

9 And this *is* the genealogy of Esau the father of the Edomites in Mount Seir. 10 These *were* the names of Esau's sons: Eliphaz the son of Adah the wife of Esau, and Reuel the son of Basemath the wife of Esau. 11 And the sons of Eliphaz were Teman, Omar, Zepho, Gatam, and Kenaz.

12 Now Timna was the concubine of Eliphaz, Esau's son, and she bore Amalek to Eliphaz. These *were* the sons of Adah, Esau's wife.

13 These *were* the sons of Reuel: Nahath, Zerah, Shammah, and Mizzah. These were the sons of Basemath, Esau's wife.

14 These *were* the sons of Aholibamah, Esau's wife, the daughter of Anah, the daughter of Zibeon. And she bore to Esau: Jeush, Jaalam, and Korah.

15 These *were* the chiefs of the sons of Esau. The sons of Eliphaz, the firstborn *son* of Esau, were Chief Teman, Chief Omar, Chief Zepho, Chief Kenaz, 16 Chief Korah, Chief Gatam, *and* Chief Amalek. These *were* the chiefs of Eliphaz in the land of Edom. They *were* the sons of Adah.

17 These *were* the sons of Reuel, Esau's son: Chief Nahath, Chief Zerah, Chief Shammah, and Chief Mizzah. These *were* the chiefs of Reuel in the land of Edom. These *were* the sons of Basemath, Esau's wife.

18 And these *were* the sons of Aholibamah, Esau's wife: Chief Jeush, Chief Jaalam, and Chief Korah. These *were* the chiefs *who descended* from Aholibamah, Esau's wife, the daughter of Anah. 19 These *were* the sons of Esau, who is Edom, and these *were* their chiefs.

20 These *were* the sons of Seir the Horite who inhabited the land: Lotan, Shobal, Zibeon, Anah, 21 Dishon, Ezer, and Dishan. These *were* the chiefs of the Horites, the sons of Seir, in the land of Edom.

22 And the sons of Lotan were Hori and Hemam. Lotan's sister *was* Timna.

23 These *were* the sons of Shobal: Alvan, Manahath, Ebal, Shepho, and Onam.

24 These *were* the sons of Zibeon: both Ajah and Anah. This *was the* Anah who found the water in the wilderness as he pastured the donkeys of his father Zibeon. 25 These *were* the children of Anah: Dishon and Aholibamah the daughter of Anah.

26 These *were* the sons of Dishon: Hemdan, Eshban, Ithran, and Cheran. 27 These *were* the sons of Ezer: Bilhan, Zaavan, and Akan. 28 These *were* the sons of Dishan: Uz and Aran.

29 These *were* the chiefs of the Horites: Chief Lotan, Chief Shobal, Chief Zibeon, Chief Anah, 30 Chief Dishon, Chief Ezer, and Chief Dishan. These *were* the chiefs of the Horites, according to their chiefs in the land of Seir.

31 Now these *were* the kings who reigned in the land of Edom before any king reigned over the children of Israel: 32 Bela the son of Beor reigned in Edom, and the name of his city *was* Dinhabah. 33 And when Bela died, Jobab the son of Zerah of Bozrah reigned in his place. 34 When Jobab died, Husham of the land of the Temanites reigned in his place. 35 And when Husham died, Hadad the son of Bedad, who attacked Midian in the field of Moab, reigned in his place. And the name of his city *was* Avith. 36 When Hadad died, Samlah of Masrekah reigned in his place. 37 And when Samlah died, Saul of Rehoboth-*by*-the-River reigned in his place. 38 When Saul died, Baal-Hanan the son of Achbor reigned in his place. 39 And when Baal-Hanan the son of Achbor died, Hadar reigned in his place; and the name of his city *was* Pau. His wife's name *was* Mehetabel, the daughter of Matred, the daughter of Mezahab.

40 And these *were* the names of the chiefs of Esau, according to their families and their places, by their names: Chief Timnah, Chief Alvah, Chief Jetheth, 41 Chief Aholibamah, Chief Elah, Chief Pinon, 42 Chief Kenaz, Chief Teman, Chief Mibzar, 43 Chief Magdiel, and Chief Iram. These *were* the chiefs of Edom, according to their dwelling places in the land of their possession. Esau *was* the father of the Edomites.

Joseph dreams of greatness

37 Now Jacob dwelt in the land where his father was a stranger, in the land of Canaan. 2 This *is* the history of Jacob.

Joseph, *being* seventeen years old, was feeding the flock with his brothers. And the lad *was* with the sons of Bilhah and the sons of Zilpah, his father's

Joseph was Jacob's favorite son and often wore a special robe his father had given him.

wives; and Joseph brought a bad report of them to his father.

3 Now Israel loved Joseph more than all his children, because he *was* the son of his old age. Also he made him a tunic of *many* colors. 4 But when his brothers saw that their father loved him more than all his brothers, they hated him and could not speak peaceably to him.

5 Now Joseph had a dream, and he told *it* to his brothers; and they hated him even more. 6 So he said to them, "Please hear this dream which I have dreamed: 7 There we were, binding sheaves in the field. Then behold, my sheaf arose and also stood upright; and indeed your sheaves stood all around and bowed down to my sheaf."

8 And his brothers said to him, "Shall you indeed reign over us? Or shall you indeed have dominion over us?" So they hated him even more for his dreams and for his words.

9 Then he dreamed still another dream and told it to his brothers, and said, "Look, I have dreamed another dream. And this time, the sun, the moon, and the eleven stars bowed down to me."

10 So he told *it* to his father and his brothers; and his father rebuked him

Where Is Joseph?

World Press Wire Service

BETHEL—The eleventh son of a respected citizen of our city has been reported missing, supposedly the victim of foul play. The discovery of a many-colored coat, identified by Jacob (pronounced JAY-kob) as belonging to his son Joseph, has led to the belief that the boy may have been killed.

Further reports now indicate that Joseph may not be dead. Jacob's eldest son, Reuben, has told friends that he believes his brother may still be alive. The brothers all hated Joseph for his pride and arrogance, but not enough to kill him, Reuben insists. Reuben believes his other brothers may have done something else to Joseph. Possibly they have sold him as a slave to some trader passing through the country.

Area residents are asked to be on the lookout for clues leading to the whereabouts of Jacob's son.

and said to him, "What *is* this dream that you have dreamed? Shall your mother and I and your brothers indeed come to bow down to the earth before you?" ¹¹ And his brothers envied him, but his father kept the matter *in mind.*

¹² Then his brothers went to feed their father's flock in Shechem. ¹³ And Israel said to Joseph, "Are not your brothers feeding *the flock* in Shechem? Come, I will send you to them."

So he said to him, "Here I am."

¹⁴ Then he said to him, "Please go and see if it is well with your brothers and well with the flocks, and bring back word to me." So he sent him out of the Valley of Hebron, and he went to Shechem.

¹⁵ Now a certain man found him, and there he was, wandering in the field. And the man asked him, saying, "What are you seeking?"

¹⁶ So he said, "I am seeking my brothers. Please tell me where they are feeding *their flocks.*"

¹⁷ And the man said, "They have departed from here, for I heard them say, 'Let us go to Dothan.' " So Joseph went after his brothers and found them in Dothan.

¹⁸ Now when they saw him afar off, even before he came near them, they conspired against him to kill him. ¹⁹ Then they said to one another, "Look, this dreamer is coming! ²⁰ Come therefore, let us now kill him and cast him into some pit; and we shall say, 'Some wild beast has devoured him.' We shall see what will become of his dreams!"

Joseph's jealous brothers threw him in a pit, then sold him to some traders.

21 But Reuben heard *it*, and he delivered him out of their hands, and said, "Let us not kill him." 22 And Reuben said to them, "Shed no blood, *but* cast him into this pit which *is* in the wilderness, and do not lay a hand on him"— that he might deliver him out of their hands, and bring him back to his father.

23 So it came to pass, when Joseph had come to his brothers, that they stripped Joseph *of* his tunic, the tunic of *many* colors that *was* on him. 24 Then they took him and cast him into a pit. And the pit *was* empty; *there was* no water in it.

25 And they sat down to eat a meal. Then they lifted their eyes and looked, and there was a company of Ishmaelites, coming from Gilead with their camels, bearing spices, balm, and myrrh, on their way to carry *them* down to Egypt. 26 So Judah said to his brothers, "What profit *is there* if we kill our brother and conceal his blood?

27 Come and let us sell him to the Ishmaelites, and let not our hand be upon him, for he *is* our brother *and* our flesh." And his brothers listened. 28 Then Midianite traders passed by; so *the brothers* pulled Joseph up and lifted him out of the pit, and sold him to the Ishmaelites for twenty *shekels* of silver. And they took Joseph to Egypt.

29 Then Reuben returned to the pit, and indeed Joseph *was* not in the pit; and he tore his clothes. 30 And he returned to his brothers and said, "The lad *is* no *more*; and I, where shall I go?"

31 So they took Joseph's tunic, killed a kid of the goats, and dipped the tunic in the blood. 32 Then they sent the tunic of *many* colors, and they brought *it* to their father and said, "We have found this. Do you know whether it *is* your son's tunic or not?"

33 And he recognized it and said, "*It is* my son's tunic. A wild beast has de-

The pharoah and his queen sit on the throne of Egypt.

voured him. Without doubt Joseph is torn to pieces." 34 Then Jacob tore his clothes, put sackcloth on his waist, and mourned for his son many days. 35 And all his sons and all his daughters arose to comfort him; but he refused to be comforted, and he said, "For I shall go down into the grave to my son in mourning." Thus his father wept for him.

36 Now the Midianites had sold him in Egypt to Potiphar, an officer of Pharaoh *and* captain of the guard.

Judah and Tamar

38 It came to pass at that time that Judah departed from his brothers, and visited a certain Adullamite whose name *was* Hirah. 2 And Judah saw there a daughter of a certain Canaanite whose name *was* Shua, and he married her and went in to her. 3 So she conceived and bore a son, and he called his name Er. 4 She conceived again and bore a son, and she called his name Onan. 5 And she conceived yet again and bore a son, and called his name Shelah. He was at Chezib when she bore him.

6 Then Judah took a wife for Er his firstborn, and her name *was* Tamar. 7 But Er, Judah's firstborn, was wicked in the sight of the LORD, and the LORD killed him. 8 And Judah said to Onan, "Go in to your brother's wife and marry her, and raise up an heir to your brother." 9 But Onan knew that the heir would not be his; and it came to pass, when he went in to his brother's wife, that he emitted on the ground, lest he should give an heir to his brother. 10 And the thing which he did displeased the LORD; therefore He killed him also.

11 Then Judah said to Tamar his daughter-in-law, "Remain a widow in your father's house till my son Shelah is grown." For he said, "Lest he also die like his brothers." And Tamar went and dwelt in her father's house.

12 Now in the process of time the daughter of Shua, Judah's wife, died; and Judah was comforted, and went up to his sheepshearers at Timnah, he and his friend Hirah the Adullamite. 13 And it was told Tamar, saying, "Look, your father-in-law is going up to Timnah to shear his sheep." 14 So she took off her widow's garments, covered *herself* with a veil and wrapped herself, and sat in an open place which *was* on the way to Timnah; for she saw that Shelah was grown, and she was not given to him as a wife. 15 When Judah saw her, he thought she *was* a harlot, because she had covered her face. 16 Then he turned to her by the way, and said, "Please let me come in to you"; for he did not know that she *was* his daughter-in-law.

So she said, "What will you give me, that you may come in to me?"

17 And he said, "I will send a young goat from the flock."

So she said, "Will you give *me* a pledge till you send *it?*"

18 Then he said, "What pledge shall I give you?"

So she said, "Your signet and cord, and your staff that *is* in your hand." Then he gave *them* to her, and went in to her, and she conceived by him. 19 So she arose and went away, and laid aside her veil and put on the garments of her widowhood.

20 And Judah sent the young goat by the hand of his friend the Adullamite, to receive *his* pledge from the woman's hand, but he did not find her. 21 Then he asked the men of that place, saying, "Where is the harlot who *was* openly by the roadside?"

And they said, "There was no harlot in this *place*."

22 So he returned to Judah and said, "I cannot find her. Also, the men of the place said there was no harlot in this *place*."

23 Then Judah said, "Let her take *them* for herself, lest we be shamed; for I sent this young goat and you have not found her."

24 And it came to pass, about three months after, that Judah was told, saying, "Tamar your daughter-in-law has played the harlot; furthermore she *is* with child by harlotry."

So Judah said, "Bring her out and let her be burned!"

25 When she *was* brought out, she sent to her father-in-law, saying, "By the man to whom these belong, I *am* with child." And she said, "Please determine whose these *are*—the signet and cord, and staff."

26 So Judah acknowledged *them* and said, "She has been more righteous than I, because I did not give her to Shelah my son." And he never knew her again.

27 Now it came to pass, at the time for giving birth, that behold, twins *were* in her womb. 28 And so it was, when she was giving birth, that *the one* put out *his* hand; and the midwife took a scarlet *thread* and bound it on his hand, saying, "This one came out first." 29 Then it happened, as he drew back his hand, that his brother came out unexpectedly; and she said, "How did you break through? *This* breach *be* upon you!" Therefore his name was called Perez. 30 Afterward his brother came out who had the scarlet *thread* on his hand. And his name was called Zerah.

Joseph shows he is a leader

39 Now Joseph had been taken down to Egypt. And Potiphar, an officer of Pharaoh, captain of the guard, an Egyptian, bought him from the Ishmaelites who had taken him down there. 2 The LORD was with Joseph, and he was a successful man; and he was in the house of his master the Egyptian. 3 And his master saw that the LORD *was* with him and that the LORD made all he did to prosper in his hand. 4 So Joseph found favor in his sight, and served him. Then he made him overseer of his house, and all *that* he had he put under his authority. 5 So it was, from the time *that* he had made him overseer of his house and all that he had, that the LORD blessed the Egyptian's house for Joseph's sake; and the blessing of the LORD was on all that he had in the house and in the field. 6 Thus he left all that he had

in Joseph's hand, and he did not know what he had except for the bread which he ate.

Now Joseph was handsome in form and appearance.

7 And it came to pass after these things that his master's wife cast longing eyes on Joseph, and she said, "Lie with me."

8 But he refused and said to his master's wife, "Look, my master does not know what *is* with me in the house, and he has committed all that he has to my hand. 9 *There is* no one greater in this house than I, nor has he kept back anything from me but you, because you *are* his wife. How then can I do this great wickedness, and sin against God?"

10 So it was, as she spoke to Joseph day by day, that he did not heed her, to lie with her *or* to be with her.

11 But it happened about this time, when Joseph went into the house to do his work, and none of the men of the house *was* inside, 12 that she caught him by his garment, saying, "Lie with me." But he left his garment in her hand, and fled and ran outside. 13 And so it was, when she saw that he had left his garment in her hand and fled outside, 14 that she called to the men of her house and spoke to them, saying, "See, he has brought in to us a Hebrew to mock us. He came in to me to lie with me, and I cried out with a loud voice. 15 And it happened, when he heard that I lifted my voice and cried out, that he left his garment with me, and fled and went outside."

16 So she kept his garment with her until his master came home. 17 Then she spoke to him with words like these, saying, "The Hebrew servant whom you brought to us came in to me to mock me; 18 so it happened, as I lifted my voice and cried out, that he left his garment with me and fled outside."

19 So it was, when his master heard the words which his wife spoke to him, saying, "Your servant did to me after this manner," that his anger was aroused. 20 Then Joseph's master took

him and put him into the prison, a place where the king's prisoners *were* confined. And he was there in the prison. 21 But the LORD was with Joseph and showed him mercy, and He gave him favor in the sight of the keeper of the prison. 22 And the keeper of the prison committed to Joseph's hand all the prisoners who *were* in the prison; whatever they did there, it was his doing. 23 The keeper of the prison did not look into anything *that was* under *Joseph's* authority, because the LORD was with him; and whatever he did, the LORD made *it* prosper.

Joseph tells what dreams mean

40 It came to pass after these things *that* the butler and the baker of the king of Egypt offended their lord, the king of Egypt. 2 And Pharaoh was angry with his two officers, the chief butler and the chief baker. 3 So he put them in custody in the house of the captain of the guard, in the prison, the place where Joseph *was* confined. 4 And the captain of the guard charged Joseph with them, and he served them; so they *were* in custody for a while.

5 Then the butler and the baker of the king of Egypt, who *were* confined in the prison, had a dream, both of them, each man's dream in one night *and* each man's dream with its *own* interpretation. 6 And Joseph came in to them in the morning and looked at them, and saw that they *were* sad. 7 So he asked Pharaoh's officers who *were* with him in the custody of his lord's house, saying, "Why do you look *so* sad today?"

8 And they said to him, "We each have had a dream, and *there is* no interpreter of it."

So Joseph said to them, "Do not interpretations belong to God? Tell *them* to me, please."

9 Then the chief butler told his dream to Joseph, and said to him, "Behold, in my dream a vine *was* before me, 10 and in the vine *were* three branches; it *was* as though it budded, its blossoms shot forth, and its clusters brought forth ripe grapes. 11 Then Pharaoh's cup *was* in my hand; and I took the grapes and pressed them into Pharaoh's cup, and placed the cup in Pharaoh's hand."

12 And Joseph said to him, "This *is* the interpretation of it: The three branches *are* three days. 13 Now within three days Pharaoh will lift up your head and restore you to your place, and you will put Pharaoh's cup in his hand according to the former manner, when you were his butler. 14 But remember me when it is well with you, and please show kindness to me; make mention of me to Pharaoh, and get me out of this house. 15 For indeed I was stolen away from the land of the Hebrews; and also I have done nothing here that they should put me into the dungeon."

16 When the chief baker saw that the interpretation was good, he said to Joseph, "I also *was* in my dream, and there *were* three white baskets on my head. 17 In the uppermost basket *were* all kinds of baked goods for Pharaoh, and the birds ate them out of the basket on my head."

18 So Joseph answered and said, "This *is* the interpretation of it: The three baskets *are* three days. 19 Within three days Pharaoh will lift off your head from you and hang you on a tree; and the birds will eat your flesh from you."

20 Now it came to pass on the third day, *which was* Pharaoh's birthday, that he made a feast for all his servants; and he lifted up the head of the chief butler and of the chief baker among his servants. 21 Then he restored the chief butler to his butlership again, and he placed the cup in Pharaoh's hand. 22 But he hanged the chief baker, as Joseph had interpreted to them. 23 Yet the chief butler did not remember Joseph, but forgot him.

Pharaoh puts Joseph in charge of Egypt

41 Then it came to pass, at the end of two full years, that Pharaoh had a

dream; and behold, he stood by the river. 2 Suddenly there came up out of the river seven cows, fine looking and fat; and they fed in the meadow. 3 Then behold, seven other cows came up after them out of the river, ugly and gaunt, and stood by the *other* cows on the bank of the river. 4 And the ugly and gaunt cows ate up the seven fine looking and fat cows. So Pharaoh awoke. 5 He slept and dreamed a second time; and suddenly seven heads of grain came up on one stalk, plump and good. 6 Then behold, seven thin heads, blighted by the east wind, sprang up after them. 7 And the seven thin heads devoured the seven plump and full heads. So Pharaoh awoke, and indeed, *it was* a dream. 8 Now it came to pass in the morning that his spirit was troubled, and he sent and called for all the magicians of Egypt and all its wise men. And Pharaoh told them his dreams, but *there was* no one who could interpret them for Pharaoh.

9 Then the chief butler spoke to Pharaoh, saying: "I remember my faults this day. 10 When Pharaoh was angry with his servants, and put me in custody in the house of the captain of the guard, *both* me and the chief baker, 11 we each had a dream in one night, he and I. Each of us dreamed according to the interpretation of his *own* dream. 12 Now there *was* a young Hebrew man with us there, a servant of the captain of the guard. And we told him, and he interpreted our dreams for us; to each man he interpreted according to his *own* dream. 13 And it came to pass, just as he interpreted for us, so it happened. He restored me to my office, and he hanged him."

14 Then Pharaoh sent and called Joseph, and they brought him quickly out of the dungeon; and he shaved, changed his clothing, and came to Pharaoh. 15 And Pharaoh said to Joseph, "I have had a dream, and *there* is no one who can interpret it. But I have heard it said of you *that* you can understand a dream, to interpret it."

16 So Joseph answered Pharaoh, saying, "*It is* not in me; God will give Pharaoh an answer of peace."

17 Then Pharaoh said to Joseph: "Behold, in my dream I stood on the bank of the river. 18 Suddenly seven cows came up out of the river, fine looking and fat; and they fed in the meadow. 19 Then behold, seven other cows came up after them, poor and very ugly and gaunt, such ugliness as I have never seen in all the land of Egypt. 20 And the gaunt and ugly cows ate up the first seven, the fat cows. 21 When they had eaten them up, no one would have known that they had eaten them, for they *were* just as ugly as at the beginning. So I awoke. 22 Also I saw in my dream, and suddenly seven heads came up on one stalk, full and good. 23 Then behold, seven heads, withered, thin, *and* blighted by the east wind, sprang up after them. 24 And the thin heads devoured the seven good heads. So I told *this* to the magicians, but *there was* no one who could explain *it* to me."

25 Then Joseph said to Pharaoh, "The dreams of Pharaoh *are* one; God has shown Pharaoh what He *is* about to do: 26 The seven good cows *are* seven years, and the seven good heads *are* seven years; the dreams *are* one. 27 And the seven thin and ugly cows which came up after them *are* seven years, and the seven empty heads blighted by the east wind are seven years of famine. 28 This *is* the thing which I have spoken to Pharaoh. God has shown Pharaoh what He *is* about to do. 29 Indeed seven years of great plenty will come throughout all the land of Egypt; 30 but after them seven years of famine will arise, and all the plenty will be forgotten in the land of Egypt; and the famine will deplete the land. 31 So the plenty will not be known in the land because of the famine following, for it *will be* very severe. 32 And the dream was repeated to Pharaoh twice because the thing *is* established by God, and God will shortly bring it to pass.

33 "Now therefore, let Pharaoh select a discerning and wise man, and

set him over the land of Egypt. 34 Let Pharaoh do *this,* and let him appoint officers over the land, to collect one-fifth *of the produce* of the land of Egypt in the seven plentiful years. 35 And let them gather all the food of those good years that are coming, and store up grain under the authority of Pharaoh, and let them keep food in the cities. 36 Then that food shall be as a reserve for the land for the seven years of famine which shall be in the land of Egypt, that the land may not perish during the famine."

37 So the advice was good in the eyes of Pharaoh and in the eyes of all his servants. 38 And Pharaoh said to his servants, "Can we find *such a one* as this, a man in whom *is* the Spirit of God?"

39 Then Pharaoh said to Joseph, "Inasmuch as God has shown you all this, *there is* no one as discerning and wise as you. 40 You shall be over my house, and all my people shall be ruled according to your word; only in regard to the throne will I be greater than you." 41 And Pharaoh said to Joseph, "See, I have set you over all the land of Egypt."

42 Then Pharaoh took his signet ring off his hand and put it on Joseph's hand; and he clothed him in garments of fine linen and put a gold chain around his neck. 43 And he had him ride in the second chariot which he had; and they cried out before him, "Bow the knee!" So he set him over all the land of Egypt. 44 Pharaoh also said to Joseph, "I *am* Pharaoh, and without your consent no man may lift his hand or foot in all the land of Egypt." 45 And Pharaoh called Joseph's name Zaphnath-Paaneah. And he gave him as a wife Asenath, the daughter of Poti-Pherah priest of On. So Joseph went out over *all* the land of Egypt.

46 Joseph was thirty years old when he stood before Pharaoh king of Egypt. And Joseph went out from the presence of Pharaoh, and went throughout all the land of Egypt. 47 Now in the seven plentiful years the ground brought forth abundantly. 48 So he gathered up all the food of the seven years which were in the land of Egypt, and laid up the food in the cities; he laid up in every city the food of the fields which surrounded them. 49 Joseph gathered very much grain, as the sand of the sea, until he stopped counting, for *it was* immeasurable.

50 And to Joseph were born two

Wealthy Egyptians lived in homes like this one, with lovely courtyards and large columns.

Hebrew Man Is President of Egypt

World Press Wire Service

MEMPHIS, EGYPT—In a surprise move, the king of Egypt has named Joseph, a foreigner of Hebrew descent, president of this country, second only to himself. The Hebrew now wears the king's ring of power on his hand.

Joseph was in prison when Pharaoh learned of his ability to explain dreams. When Joseph was asked to explain a disturbing dream of the king, Joseph told him to expect seven years of good crops followed by seven years of famine. Joseph also said the king should appoint a wise person to manage the future food supply of the land.

In addition to his other duties, Joseph will be overseeing the storage of Egypt's surplus food supply to be used during the years of famine.

sons before the years of famine came, whom Asenath, the daughter of Poti-Pherah priest of On, bore to him. 51 Joseph called the name of the first-born Manasseh: "For God has made me forget all my toil and all my father's

Because God was with him, Joseph became an important official in Egypt.

house." 52 And the name of the second he called Ephraim: "For God has caused me to be fruitful in the land of my affliction."

53 Then the seven years of plenty which were in the land of Egypt ended, 54 and the seven years of famine began to come, as Joseph had said. The famine was in all lands, but in all the land of Egypt there was bread. 55 So when all the land of Egypt was famished, the people cried to Pharaoh for bread. Then Pharaoh said to all the Egyptians, "Go to Joseph; whatever he says to you, do." 56 The famine was over all the face of the earth, and Joseph opened all the storehouses and sold to the Egyptians. And the famine became severe in the land of Egypt. 57 So all countries came to Joseph in Egypt to buy *grain,* because the famine was severe in all lands.

Joseph's brothers travel to Egypt

42 When Jacob saw that there was grain in Egypt, Jacob said to his sons, "Why do you look at one another?" 2 And he said, "Indeed I have heard that there is grain in Egypt; go down to that place and buy for us there, that we may live and not die."

3 So Joseph's ten brothers went down to buy grain in Egypt. 4 But Jacob did not send Joseph's brother Benjamin with his brothers, for he said, "Lest some calamity befall him."

⁵ And the sons of Israel went to buy *grain* among those who journeyed, for the famine was in the land of Canaan.

⁶ Now Joseph *was* governor over the land; and it was he who sold to all the people of the land. And Joseph's brothers came and bowed down before him with *their* faces to the earth. ⁷ Joseph saw his brothers and recognized them, but he acted as a stranger to them and spoke roughly to them. Then he said to them, "Where do you come from?"

And they said, "From the land of Canaan to buy food."

⁸ So Joseph recognized his brothers, but they did not recognize him. ⁹ Then Joseph remembered the dreams which he had dreamed about them, and said to them, "You *are* spies! You have come to see the nakedness of the land!"

¹⁰ And they said to him, "No, my lord, but your servants have come to buy food. ¹¹ We *are* all one man's sons; we *are* honest *men;* your servants are not spies."

¹² But he said to them, "No, but you have come to see the nakedness of the land."

¹³ And they said, "Your servants *are* twelve brothers, the sons of one man in the land of Canaan; and in fact, the youngest *is* with our father today, and one *is* no more."

¹⁴ But Joseph said to them, "It *is* as I spoke to you, saying, 'You *are* spies!' ¹⁵ In this *manner* you shall be tested: By the life of Pharaoh, you shall not leave this place unless your youngest brother comes here. ¹⁶ Send one of you, and let him bring your brother; and you shall be kept in prison, that your words may be tested to see whether *there is* any truth in you; or else, by the life of Pharaoh, surely you *are* spies!" ¹⁷ So he put them all together in prison three days.

¹⁸ Then Joseph said to them the third day, "Do this and live, *for* I fear God: ¹⁹ If you *are* honest *men,* let one of your brothers be confined to your prison house; but you, go and carry grain for the famine of your houses.

²⁰ And bring your youngest brother to me; so your words will be verified, and you shall not die."

And they did so. ²¹ Then they said to one another, "We *are* truly guilty concerning our brother, for we saw the anguish of his soul when he pleaded with us, and we would not hear; therefore this distress has come upon us."

²² And Reuben answered them, saying, "Did I not speak to you, saying, 'Do not sin against the boy'; and you would not listen? Therefore behold, his blood is now required of us." ²³ But they did not know that Joseph understood *them,* for he spoke to them through an interpreter. ²⁴ And he turned himself away from them and wept. Then he returned to them again, and talked with them. And he took Simeon from them and bound him before their eyes.

²⁵ Then Joseph gave a command to fill their sacks with grain, to restore every man's money to his sack, and to give them provisions for the journey. Thus he did for them. ²⁶ So they loaded their donkeys with the grain and departed from there. ²⁷ But as one *of them* opened his sack to give his donkey feed at the encampment, he saw his money; and there it was, in the mouth of his sack. ²⁸ So he said to his brothers, "My money has been restored, and there it is, in my sack!" Then their hearts failed *them* and they were afraid, saying to one another, "What *is* this *that* God has done to us?"

²⁹ Then they went to Jacob their father in the land of Canaan and told him all that had happened to them, saying: ³⁰ "The man *who is* lord of the land spoke roughly to us, and took us for spies of the country. ³¹ But we said to him, 'We *are* honest *men;* we are not spies. ³² We *are* twelve brothers, sons of our father; one *is* no *more,* and the youngest *is* with our father this day in the land of Canaan.' ³³ Then the man, the lord of the country, said to us, 'By this I will know that you *are* honest *men:* Leave one of your brothers *here* with me, take *food for*

the famine of your households, and be gone. 34 And bring your youngest brother to me; so I shall know that you *are* not spies, but *that* you *are* honest *men.* I will grant your brother to you, and you may trade in the land.' "

35 Then it happened as they emptied their sacks, that surprisingly each man's bundle of money *was* in his sack; and when they and their father saw the bundles of money, they *were* afraid. 36 And Jacob their father said to them, "You have bereaved me: Joseph is no *more,* Simeon is no *more,* and you want to take Benjamin. All these things are against me."

37 Then Reuben spoke to his father, saying, "Kill my two sons if I do not bring him *back* to you; put him in my hands, and I will bring him back to you."

38 But he said, "My son shall not go down with you, for his brother is dead, and he is left alone. If any calamity should befall him along the way in which you go, then you would bring down my gray hair with sorrow to the grave."

Joseph's brothers return with Benjamin

43 Now the famine *was* severe in the land. 2 And it came to pass, when they had eaten up the grain which they had brought from Egypt, that their father said to them, "Go back, buy us a little food."

3 But Judah spoke to him, saying, "The man solemnly warned us, saying, 'You shall not see my face unless your brother *is* with you.' 4 If you send our brother with us, we will go down and buy you food. 5 But if you will not send *him,* we will not go down; for the man said to us, 'You shall not see my face unless your brother *is* with you.'"

6 And Israel said, "Why did you deal *so* wrongfully with me *as* to tell the man whether you had still *another* brother?"

7 But they said, "The man asked us

pointedly about ourselves and our family, saying, '*Is* your father still alive? Have you *another* brother?' And we told him according to these words. Could we possibly have known that he would say, 'Bring your brother down'?"

8 Then Judah said to Israel his father, "Send the lad with me, and we will arise and go, that we may live and not die, both we and you *and* also our little ones. 9 I myself will be surety for him; from my hand you shall require him. If I do not bring him *back* to you and set him before you, then let me bear the blame forever. 10 For if we had not lingered, surely by now we would have returned this second time."

11 And their father Israel said to them, "If *it must be* so, then do this: Take some of the best fruits of the land in your vessels and carry down a present for the man—a little balm and a little honey, spices and myrrh, pistachio nuts and almonds. 12 Take double money in your hand, and take back in your hand the money that was returned in the mouth of your sacks; perhaps it was an oversight. 13 Take your brother also, and arise, go back to the man. 14 And may God Almighty give you mercy before the man, that he may release your other brother and Benjamin. If I am bereaved, I am bereaved!"

15 So the men took that present and Benjamin, and they took double money in their hand, and arose and went down to Egypt; and they stood before Joseph. 16 When Joseph saw Benjamin with them, he said to the steward of his house, "Take *these* men to my home, and slaughter an animal and make ready; for *these* men will dine with me at noon." 17 Then the man did as Joseph ordered, and the man brought the men into Joseph's house.

18 Now the men were afraid because they were brought into Joseph's house; and they said, "*It is* because of the money, which was returned in our sacks the first time, that we are brought in, so that he may make a case

against us and seize us, to take us as slaves with our donkeys."

19 When they drew near to the steward of Joseph's house, they talked with him at the door of the house, 20 and said, "O sir, we indeed came down the first time to buy food; 21 but it happened, when we came to the encampment, that we opened our sacks, and there, *each* man's money *was* in the mouth of his sack, our money in full weight; so we have brought it back in our hand. 22 And we have brought down other money in our hands to buy food. We do not know who put our money in our sacks."

23 But he said, "Peace *be* with you, do not be afraid. Your God and the God of your father has given you treasure in your sacks; I had your money." Then he brought Simeon out to them.

24 So the man brought the men into Joseph's house and gave *them* water, and they washed their feet; and he gave their donkeys feed. 25 Then they made the present ready for Joseph's coming at noon, for they heard that they would eat bread there.

26 And when Joseph came home, they brought him the present which *was* in their hand into the house, and bowed down before him to the earth. 27 Then he asked them about *their* well-being, and said, "*Is* your father well, the old man of whom you spoke? *Is* he still alive?"

28 And they answered, "Your servant our father *is* in good health; he *is* still alive." And they bowed their heads down and prostrated themselves.

29 Then he lifted his eyes and saw his brother Benjamin, his mother's son, and said, "*Is* this your younger brother of whom you spoke to me?" And he said, "God be gracious to you, my son." 30 Now his heart yearned for his brother; so Joseph made haste and sought *somewhere* to weep. And he went into *his* chamber and wept there. 31 Then he washed his face and came out; and he restrained himself, and said, "Serve the bread."

32 So they set him a place by himself, and them by themselves, and the Egyptians who ate with him by themselves; because the Egyptians could not eat food with the Hebrews, for that *is* an abomination to the Egyptians. 33 And they sat before him, the firstborn according to his birthright and the youngest according to his youth; and the men looked in astonishment at one another. 34 Then he took servings to them from before him, but Benjamin's serving was five times as much as any of theirs. So they drank and were merry with him.

Joseph tests his brothers one last time

44 And he commanded the steward of his house, saying, "Fill the men's sacks with food, as much as they can carry, and put each man's money in the mouth of his sack. 2 Also put my cup, the silver cup, in the mouth of the sack of the youngest, and his grain money." So he did according to the word that Joseph had spoken. 3 As soon as the morning dawned, the men were sent away, they and their donkeys. 4 When they had gone out of the city, *and* were not *yet* far off, Joseph said to his steward, "Get up, follow the men; and when you overtake them, say to them, 'Why have you repaid evil for good? 5 *Is* not this *the one* from which my lord drinks, and with which he indeed practices divination? You have done evil in so doing.'"

6 So he overtook them, and he spoke to them these same words. 7 And they said to him, "Why does my lord say these words? Far be it from us that your servants should do such a thing. 8 Look, we brought back to you from the land of Canaan the money which we found in the mouth of our sacks. How then could we steal silver or gold from your lord's house? 9 With whomever of your servants it is found, let him die, and we also will be my lord's slaves."

10 And he said, "Now also *let* it *be* according to your words; he with

whom it is found shall be my slave, and you shall be blameless." 11 Then each man speedily let down his sack to the ground, and each opened his sack. 12 So he searched. He began with the oldest and left off with the youngest; and the cup was found in Benjamin's sack. 13 Then they tore their clothes, and each man loaded his donkey and returned to the city.

14 So Judah and his brothers came to Joseph's house, and he *was* still there; and they fell before him on the ground. 15 And Joseph said to them, "What deed *is* this you have done? Did you not know that such a man as I can certainly practice divination?"

16 Then Judah said, "What shall we say to my lord? What shall we speak? Or how shall we clear ourselves? God has found out the iniquity of your servants; here we are, my lord's slaves, both we and *he* also with whom the cup was found."

17 But he said, "Far be it from me that I should do so; the man in whose hand the cup was found, he shall be my slave. And as for you, go up in peace to your father."

18 Then Judah came near to him and said: "O my lord, please let your servant speak a word in my lord's hearing, and do not let your anger burn against your servant; for you *are* even like Pharaoh. 19 My lord asked his servants, saying, 'Have you a father or a brother?' 20 And we said to my lord, 'We have a father, an old man, and a child of *his* old age, *who is* young; his brother is dead, and he alone is left of his mother's children, and his father loves him.' 21 Then you said to your servants, 'Bring him down to me, that I may set my eyes on him.' 22 And we said to my lord, 'The lad cannot leave his father, for *if* he should leave his father, *his father* would die.' 23 But you said to your servants, 'Unless your youngest brother comes down with you, you shall see my face no more.' 24 "So it was, when we went up to your servant my father, that we told him the words of my lord. 25 And our father said, 'Go back *and* buy us a little

food.' 26 But we said, 'We cannot go down; if our youngest brother is with us, then we will go down; for we may not see the man's face unless our youngest brother *is* with us.' 27 Then your servant my father said to us, 'You know that my wife bore me two sons; 28 and the one went out from me, and I said, "Surely he is torn to pieces"; and I have not seen him since. 29 But if you take this one also from me, and calamity befalls him, you shall bring down my gray hair with sorrow to the grave.'

30 "Now therefore, when I come to your servant my father, and the lad *is* not with us, since his life is bound up in the lad's life, 31 it will happen, when he sees that the lad *is* not *with us,* that he will die. So your servants will bring down the gray hair of your servant our father with sorrow to the grave. 32 For your servant became surety for the lad to my father, saying, 'If I do not bring him *back* to you, then I shall bear the blame before my father forever.' 33 Now therefore, please let your servant remain instead of the lad as a slave to my lord, and let the lad go up with his brothers. 34 For how shall I go up to my father if the lad *is* not with me, lest perhaps I see the evil that would come upon my father?"

Joseph sends for Jacob

45 Then Joseph could not restrain himself before all those who stood by him, and he cried out, "Make everyone go out from me!" So no one stood with him while Joseph made himself known to his brothers. 2 And he wept aloud, and the Egyptians and the house of Pharaoh heard *it.*

3 Then Joseph said to his brothers, "I *am* Joseph; does my father still live?" But his brothers could not answer him, for they were dismayed in his presence. 4 And Joseph said to his brothers, "Please come near to me." So they came near. Then he said: "I *am* Joseph your brother, whom you sold into Egypt. 5 But now, do not therefore be grieved or angry with

Who Are the Strangers from Canaan?

ENBC (Egyptian National Broadcasting Corporation)—A caravan of strangers entering Egypt is now known to be from Canaan, the birthplace of Joseph, our Hebrew president. Following a private meeting of the eleven men and their families, sources close to the president say that he recognized them immediately as his brothers, whom he had not seen for many years.

Pharaoh, the king, has not only welcomed these foreigners to our land, but plans to invite them to live here. The king is expected to explain his views on this matter later today.

It is thought that this decision will not receive full national approval. The Egyptian people are craftsmen and farmers, while the Hebrews are shepherds and keepers of cattle. Flocks and herds of animals have never been welcome here.

Stay tuned to this channel for a royal announcement during the six o'clock news.

yourselves because you sold me here; for God sent me before you to preserve life. 6 For these two years the famine *has been* in the land, and *there are* still five years in which *there will be* neither plowing nor harvesting. 7 And God sent me before you to preserve a posterity for you in the earth, and to save your lives by a great deliverance. 8 So now *it was* not you *who* sent me here, but God; and He has made me a father to Pharaoh, and lord of all his house, and a ruler throughout all the land of Egypt.

9 "Hurry and go up to my father, and say to him, 'Thus says your son Joseph: "God has made me lord of all Egypt; come down to me, do not tarry. 10 You shall dwell in the land of Goshen, and you shall be near to me, you and your children, your children's children, your flocks and your herds, and all that you have. 11 There I will provide for you, lest you and your household, and all that you have, come to poverty; for *there are* still five years of famine."'

12 "And behold, your eyes and the eyes of my brother Benjamin see that *it is* my mouth that speaks to you. 13 So you shall tell my father of all my glory in Egypt, and of all that you have seen; and you shall hurry and bring my father down here."

14 Then he fell on his brother Benjamin's neck and wept, and Benjamin wept on his neck. 15 Moreover he kissed all his brothers and wept over them, and after that his brothers talked with him.

16 Now the report of it was heard in Pharaoh's house, saying, "Joseph's brothers have come." So it pleased Pharaoh and his servants well. 17 And Pharaoh said to Joseph, "Say to your brothers, 'Do this: Load your animals and depart; go to the land of Canaan. 18 Bring your father and your households and come to me; I will give you the best of the land of Egypt, and you will eat the fat of the land. 19 Now you are commanded—do this: Take carts out of the land of Egypt for your little ones and your wives; bring your father and come. 20 Also do not be concerned about your goods, for the best of all the land of Egypt *is* yours.'"

21 Then the sons of Israel did so; and Joseph gave them carts, according to the command of Pharaoh, and he gave them provisions for the journey. 22 He gave to all of them, to each man, changes of garments; but to Benjamin he gave three hundred *pieces* of silver and five changes of garments. 23 And he sent to his father these *things:* ten donkeys loaded with the good things of Egypt, and ten female donkeys loaded with grain, bread, and food for his father for the journey. 24 So he sent his brothers away, and they departed; and he said to them, "See that you

do not become troubled along the way."

25 Then they went up out of Egypt, and came to the land of Canaan to Jacob their father. 26 And they told him, saying, "Joseph is still alive, and he is governor over all the land of Egypt." And Jacob's heart stood still, because he did not believe them. 27 But when they told him all the words which Joseph had said to them, and when he saw the carts which Joseph had sent to carry him, the spirit of Jacob their father revived. 28 Then Israel said, "It is enough. Joseph my son is still alive. I will go and see him before I die."

Jacob moves to Egypt

46 So Israel took his journey with all that he had, and came to Beersheba, and offered sacrifices to the God of his father Isaac. 2 Then God spoke to Israel in the visions of the night, and said, "Jacob, Jacob!"

And he said, "Here I am."

3 So He said, "I am God, the God of your father; do not fear to go down to Egypt, for I will make of you a great nation there. 4 I will go down with you to Egypt, and I will also surely bring you up again; and Joseph will put his hand on your eyes."

5 Then Jacob arose from Beersheba; and the sons of Israel carried their father Jacob, their little ones, and their wives, in the carts which Pharaoh had sent to carry him. 6 So they took their livestock and their goods, which they had acquired in the land of Canaan, and went to Egypt, Jacob and all his descendants with him. 7 His sons and his sons' sons, his daughters and his sons' daughters, and all his descendants he brought with him to Egypt.

8 Now these were the names of the children of Israel, Jacob and his sons, who went to Egypt: Reuben was Jacob's firstborn. 9 The sons of Reuben were Hanoch, Pallu, Hezron, and Carmi. 10 The sons of Simeon were Jemuel, Jamin, Ohad, Jachin, Zohar, and Shaul, the son of a Canaanite woman.

11 The sons of Levi were Gershon, Kohath, and Merari. 12 The sons of Judah were Er, Onan, Shelah, Perez, and Zerah (but Er and Onan died in the land of Canaan). The sons of Perez were Hezron and Hamul. 13 The sons of Issachar were Tola, Puvah, Job, and Shimron. 14 The sons of Zebulun were Sered, Elon, and Jahleel. 15 These were the sons of Leah, whom she bore to Jacob in Padan Aram, with his daughter Dinah. All the persons, his sons and his daughters, were thirty-three.

16 The sons of Gad were Ziphion, Haggi, Shuni, Ezbon, Eri, Arodi, and Areli. 17 The sons of Asher were Jimnah, Ishuah, Isui, Beriah, and Serah, their sister. And the sons of Beriah were Heber and Malchiel. 18 These were the sons of Zilpah, whom Laban gave to Leah his daughter; and these she bore to Jacob: sixteen persons.

19 The sons of Rachel, Jacob's wife, were Joseph and Benjamin. 20 And to Joseph in the land of Egypt were born Manasseh and Ephraim, whom Asenath, the daughter of Poti-Pherah priest of On, bore to him. 21 The sons of Benjamin were Belah, Becher, Ashbel, Gera, Naaman, Ehi, Rosh, Muppim, Huppim, and Ard. 22 These were the sons of Rachel, who were born to Jacob: fourteen persons in all.

23 The son of Dan was Hushim. 24 The sons of Naphtali were Jahzeel, Guni, Jezer, and Shillem. 25 These were the sons of Bilhah, whom Laban gave to Rachel his daughter, and she bore these to Jacob: seven persons in all.

26 All the persons who went with Jacob to Egypt, who came from his body, besides Jacob's sons' wives, were sixty-six persons in all. 27 And the sons of Joseph who were born to him in Egypt were two persons. All the persons of the house of Jacob who went to Egypt were seventy.

28 Then he sent Judah before him to Joseph, to point out before him the way to Goshen. And they came to the land of Goshen. 29 So Joseph made ready his chariot and went up to

Pharaoh's Speech to the Nation

ENBC (Egyptian National Broadcasting Corporation)—Following is the speech of our Pharaoh, king of Egypt, which is being carried live on all Egyptian television networks:

"My dear citizens of Egypt: I know there have been many questions about our Hebrew friends from the north. Some of you object to their coming into our land.

"As you know, Joseph the Hebrew has saved our nation from a great famine. Without Joseph's help, many of us would have died. Our debt to his kindness is very great indeed.

"Joseph's family now needs grazing land for their flocks and herds. We are not keepers of sheep, goats, or cattle, but there is a large grassy area in Goshen. There the Hebrews may raise their families and livestock in peace and plenty.

"Let us stop our grumbling about the Hebrews. Let us treat them as neighbors. Thanks to Joseph and Joseph's God, there is plenty for all of us."

Goshen to meet his father Israel; and he presented himself to him, and fell on his neck and wept on his neck a good while.

30 And Israel said to Joseph, "Now let me die, since I have seen your face, because you *are* still alive."

31 Then Joseph said to his brothers and to his father's household, "I will go up and tell Pharaoh, and say to him, 'My brothers and those of my father's house, who *were* in the land of Canaan, have come to me. 32 And the men *are* shepherds, for their occupation has been to feed livestock; and they have brought their flocks, their herds, and all that they have.' 33 So it shall be, when Pharaoh calls you and says, 'What is your occupation?' 34 that you shall say, 'Your servants' occupation has been with livestock from our youth even till now, both we *and* also our fathers,' that you may dwell in the land of Goshen; for *every* shepherd *is* an abomination to the Egyptians."

Pharaoh honors Jacob's family

47 Then Joseph went and told Pharaoh, and said, "My father and my brothers, their flocks and their herds and all that they possess, have come from the land of Canaan; and indeed they *are* in the land of Goshen." 2 And he took five men from among his brothers and presented them to Pharaoh. 3 Then Pharaoh said to his brothers, "What *is* your occupation?"

And they said to Pharaoh, "Your servants *are* shepherds, both we *and* also our fathers." 4 And they said to Pharaoh, "We have come to dwell in the land, because your servants have no pasture for their flocks, for the famine *is* severe in the land of Canaan. Now therefore, please let your servants dwell in the land of Goshen."

5 Then Pharaoh spoke to Joseph, saying, "Your father and your brothers have come to you. 6 The land of Egypt *is* before you. Have your father and brothers dwell in the best of the land; let them dwell in the land of Goshen. And if you know *any* competent men among them, then make them chief herdsmen over my livestock."

7 Then Joseph brought in his father Jacob and set him before Pharaoh; and Jacob blessed Pharaoh. 8 Pharaoh said to Jacob, "How old *are* you?"

9 And Jacob said to Pharaoh, "The days of the years of my pilgrimage *are* one hundred and thirty years; few and evil have been the days of the years of my life, and they have not attained to the days of the years of the life of my fathers in the days of their pilgrimage." 10 So Jacob blessed Pharaoh, and went out from before Pharaoh.

11 And Joseph situated his father and his brothers, and gave them a

possession in the land of Egypt, in the best of the land, in the land of Rameses, as Pharaoh had commanded. 12 Then Joseph provided his father, his brothers, and all his father's household with bread, according to the number in *their* families.

13 Now *there was* no bread in all the land; for the famine *was* very severe, so that the land of Egypt and the land of Canaan languished because of the famine. 14 And Joseph gathered up all the money that was found in the land of Egypt and in the land of Canaan, for the grain which they bought; and Joseph brought the money into Pharaoh's house.

15 So when the money failed in the land of Egypt and in the land of Canaan, all the Egyptians came to Joseph and said, "Give us bread, for why should we die in your presence? For the money has failed."

16 Then Joseph said, "Give your livestock, and I will give you *bread* for your livestock, if the money is gone." 17 So they brought their livestock to Joseph, and Joseph gave them bread in *exchange* for the horses, the flocks, the cattle of the herds, and for the donkeys. Thus he fed them with bread in *exchange* for all their livestock that year.

18 When that year had ended, they came to him the next year and said to him, "We will not hide from my lord that our money is gone; my lord also has our herds of livestock. There is nothing left in the sight of my lord but our bodies and our lands. 19 Why should we die before your eyes, both we and our land? Buy us and our land for bread, and we and our land will be servants of Pharaoh; give *us* seed, that we may live and not die, that the land may not be desolate."

20 Then Joseph bought all the land of Egypt for Pharaoh; for every man of the Egyptians sold his field, because the famine was severe upon them. So the land became Pharaoh's. 21 And as for the people, he moved them into the cities, from *one* end of the borders of Egypt to the *other* end. 22 Only the

land of the priests he did not buy; for the priests had rations *allotted to them* by Pharaoh, and they ate their rations which Pharaoh gave them; therefore they did not sell their lands.

23 Then Joseph said to the people, "Indeed I have bought you and your land this day for Pharaoh. Look, *here is* seed for you, and you shall sow the land. 24 And it shall come to pass in the harvest that you shall give one-fifth to Pharaoh. Four-fifths shall be your own, as seed for the field and for your food, for those of your households and as food for your little ones."

25 So they said, "You have saved our lives; let us find favor in the sight of my lord, and we will be Pharaoh's servants." 26 And Joseph made it a law over the land of Egypt to this day, *that* Pharaoh should have one-fifth, except for the land of the priests only, *which* did not become Pharaoh's.

27 So Israel dwelt in the land of Egypt, in the country of Goshen; and they had possessions there and grew and multiplied exceedingly. 28 And Jacob lived in the land of Egypt seventeen years. So the length of Jacob's life was one hundred and forty-seven years. 29 When the time drew near that Israel must die, he called his son Joseph and said to him, "Now if I have found favor in your sight, please put your hand under my thigh, and deal kindly and truly with me. Please do not bury me in Egypt, 30 but let me lie with my fathers; you shall carry me out of Egypt and bury me in their burial place."

And he said, "I will do as you have said."

31 Then he said, "Swear to me." And he swore to him. So Israel bowed himself on the head of the bed.

Jacob blesses Joseph's sons

48 Now it came to pass after these things that Joseph was told, "Indeed your father *is* sick"; and he took with him his two sons, Manasseh and Ephraim. 2 And Jacob was told, "Look, your son Joseph is coming to you"; and Israel strengthened himself and sat up on the bed. ³ Then Jacob said to Joseph: "God Almighty appeared to me at Luz in the land of Canaan and blessed me, ⁴ and said to me, 'Behold, I will make you fruitful and multiply you, and I will make of you a multitude of people, and give this land to your descendants after you *as* an everlasting possession.' ⁵ And now your two sons, Ephraim and Manasseh, who were born to you in the land of Egypt before I came to you in Egypt, *are* mine; as Reuben and Simeon, they shall be mine. ⁶ Your offspring whom you beget after them shall be yours; they will be called by the name of their brothers in their inheritance. ⁷ But as for me, when I came from Padan, Rachel died beside me in the land of Canaan on the way, when *there was* but a little distance to go to Ephrath; and I buried her there on the way to Ephrath (that is, Bethlehem)."

⁸ Then Israel saw Joseph's sons, and said, "Who *are* these?"

⁹ Joseph said to his father, "They *are* my sons, whom God has given me in this *place*."

And he said, "Please bring them to me, and I will bless them." ¹⁰ Now the eyes of Israel were dim with age, *so that* he could not see. Then Joseph brought them near him, and he kissed them and embraced them. ¹¹ And Israel said to Joseph, "I had not thought to see your face; but in fact, God has also shown me your offspring!"

¹² So Joseph brought them from beside his knees, and he bowed down with his face to the earth. ¹³ And Joseph took them both, Ephraim with his right hand toward Israel's left hand, and Manasseh with his left hand toward Israel's right hand, and brought *them* near him. ¹⁴ Then Israel stretched out his right hand and laid *it* on Ephraim's head, who *was* the younger, and his left hand on Manasseh's head, guiding his hands knowingly, for Manasseh *was* the firstborn. ¹⁵ And he blessed Joseph, and said:

"God, before whom my fathers
    Abraham and Isaac walked,
  The God who has fed me all my
    life long to this day,
¹⁶ The Angel who has redeemed
    me from all evil,
  Bless the lads;

Jacob's wife, Rachel, was buried in this tomb near Bethlehem.

Let my name be named upon
    them,
And the name of my fathers
    Abraham and Isaac;
And let them grow into a
    multitude in the midst of the
    earth.''

17 Now when Joseph saw that his father laid his right hand on the head of Ephraim, it displeased him; so he took hold of his father's hand to remove it from Ephraim's head to Manasseh's head. 18 And Joseph said to his father, ''Not so, my father, for this *one is* the firstborn; put your right hand on his head.''

19 But his father refused and said, ''I know, my son, I know. He also shall become a people, and he also shall be great; but truly his younger brother shall be greater than he, and his descendants shall become a multitude of nations.''

20 So he blessed them that day, saying, ''By you Israel will bless, saying, 'May God make you as Ephraim and as Manasseh!' '' And thus he set Ephraim before Manasseh.

21 Then Israel said to Joseph, ''Behold, I am dying, but God will be with you and bring you back to the land of your fathers. 22 Moreover I have given to you one portion above your brothers, which I took from the hand of the Amorite with my sword and my bow.''

Jacob tells what will happen to his sons

49 And Jacob called his sons and said, ''Gather together, that I may tell you what shall befall you in the last days:

2 ''Gather together and hear, you
        sons of Jacob,
    And listen to Israel your father.

3 ''Reuben, you are my firstborn,
    My might and the beginning of
        my strength,
    The excellency of dignity and
        the excellency of power.

4 Unstable as water, you shall not
        excel,
    Because you went up to your
        father's bed;
    Then you defiled *it*—
    He went up to my couch.

5 ''Simeon and Levi *are* brothers;
    Instruments of cruelty *are in* their
        dwelling place.
6 Let not my soul enter their
        council;
    Let not my honor be united to
        their assembly;
    For in their anger they slew a
        man,
    And in their self-will they
        hamstrung an ox.
7 Cursed *be* their anger, for *it is*
        fierce;
    And their wrath, for it is cruel!
    I will divide them in Jacob
    And scatter them in Israel.

8 ''Judah, you *are he* whom your
        brothers shall praise;
    Your hand *shall be* on the neck
        of your enemies;
    Your father's children shall bow
        down before you.
9 Judah *is* a lion's whelp;
    From the prey, my son, you
        have gone up.
    He bows down, he lies down as
        a lion;
    And as a lion, who shall rouse
        him?
10 The scepter shall not depart
        from Judah,
    Nor a lawgiver from between his
        feet,
    Until Shiloh comes;
    And to Him *shall be* the
        obedience of the people.
11 Binding his donkey to the vine,
    And his donkey's colt to the
        choice vine,
    He washed his garments in wine,
    And his clothes in the blood of
        grapes.
12 His eyes *are* darker than wine,
    And his teeth whiter than milk.

13 ''Zebulun shall dwell by the haven
        of the sea;

He *shall become* a haven for
ships,
And his border shall adjoin
Sidon.

14 "Issachar is a strong donkey,
Lying down between two
burdens;
15 He saw that rest *was* good,
And that the land *was* pleasant;
He bowed his shoulder to bear
a burden,
And became a band of slaves.

16 "Dan shall judge his people
As one of the tribes of Israel.
17 Dan shall be a serpent by the
way,
A viper by the path,
That bites the horse's heels
So that its rider shall fall
backward.

18 I have waited for your salvation,
O Lord!

19 "Gad, a troop shall tramp upon
him,
But he shall triumph at last.

20 "Bread from Asher *shall be*
rich,
And he shall yield royal dainties.

21 "Naphtali *is* a deer let loose;
He uses beautiful words.

22 "Joseph *is* a fruitful bough,
A fruitful bough by a well;
His branches run over the wall.
23 The archers have bitterly grieved
him,
Shot *at him* and hated him.
24 But his bow remained in
strength,
And the arms of his hands were
made strong
By the hands of the Mighty *God*
of Jacob
(From there *is* the Shepherd, the
Stone of Israel),
25 By the God of your father who
will help you,
And by the Almighty who will
bless you

With blessings of heaven above,
Blessings of the deep that lies
beneath,
Blessings of the breasts and of
the womb.
26 The blessings of your father
Have excelled the blessings of
my ancestors,
Up to the utmost bound of the
everlasting hills.
They shall be on the head of
Joseph,
And on the crown of the head
of him who was separate from
his brothers.

27 "Benjamin is a ravenous wolf;
In the morning he shall devour
the prey,
And at night he shall divide the
spoil."

28 All these *are* the twelve tribes of
Israel, and this *is* what their father
spoke to them. And he blessed them;
he blessed each one according to his
own blessing.

29 Then he charged them and said
to them: "I am to be gathered to my
people; bury me with my fathers in the
cave that *is* in the field of Ephron the
Hittite, 30 in the cave that *is* in the field
of Machpelah, which *is* before Mamre
in the land of Canaan, which Abraham
bought with the field of Ephron the Hittite as a possession for a burial place.
31 There they buried Abraham and
Sarah his wife, there they buried Isaac
and Rebekah his wife, and there I buried Leah. 32 The field and the cave that
is there *were* purchased from the sons
of Heth." 33 And when Jacob had finished commanding his sons, he drew
his feet up into the bed and breathed
his last, and was gathered to his people.

Jacob dies and is buried

50 Then Joseph fell on his father's
face and wept over him, and kissed
him. 2 And Joseph commanded his
servants the physicians to embalm his
father. So the physicians embalmed

You should have seen my brothers when I told them who I really was: "I am Joseph, your brother, whom you sold into Egypt" (Genesis 45:4). For a long time they didn't recognize me in my official Egyptian robes.

Years before, they had even told my poor father, Jacob, that I was dead. But all the time I was in Egypt, God gave me higher and higher positions in Pharaoh's government. I had stored enough grain for seven years of famine, and when my father and brothers were hungry, I was able to feed them. Then Pharaoh allowed my family to come and live in Egypt.

Wasn't it a beautiful thing God did for my brothers? They meant to hurt me, but God used me to help them. That is how Jesus loves you and me: Our sins put Him to death, but He gives us life that never ends.

Israel. 3 Forty days were required for him, for such are the days required for those who are embalmed; and the Egyptians mourned for him seventy days.

4 Now when the days of his mourning were past, Joseph spoke to the household of Pharaoh, saying, "If now I have found favor in your eyes, please speak in the hearing of Pharaoh, saying, 5 'My father made me swear, saying, "Behold, I am dying; in my grave which I dug for myself in the land of Canaan, there you shall bury me."' Now therefore, please let me go up and bury my father, and I will come back.'"

6 And Pharaoh said, "Go up and bury your father, as he made you swear."

7 So Joseph went up to bury his father; and with him went up all the servants of Pharaoh, the elders of his house, and all the elders of the land of Egypt, 8 as well as all the house of Joseph, his brothers, and his father's house. Only their little ones, their flocks, and their herds they left in the land of Goshen. 9 And there went up with him both chariots and horsemen, and it was a very great gathering.

10 Then they came to the threshing floor of Atad, which is beyond the Jordan, and they mourned there with a great and very solemn lamentation. He observed seven days of mourning for his father. 11 And when the inhabitants of the land, the Canaanites, saw the mourning at the threshing floor of Atad, they said, "This is a deep mourning of the Egyptians." Therefore its name was called Abel Mizraim, which is beyond the Jordan.

12 So his sons did for him just as he had commanded them. 13 For his sons carried him to the land of Canaan, and buried him in the cave of the field of Machpelah, before Mamre, which Abraham bought with the field from Ephron the Hittite as property for a burial place. 14 And after he had buried his father, Joseph returned to Egypt, he and his brothers and all who went up with him to bury his father.

15 When Joseph's brothers saw that their father was dead, they said, "Perhaps Joseph will hate us, and may actually repay us for all the evil which we did to him." 16 So they sent messengers to Joseph, saying, "Before your father died he commanded, saying, 17 'Thus you shall say to Joseph: "I beg you, please forgive the trespass of your brothers and their sin; for they did evil to you."' Now, please, forgive the trespass of the servants of the God of your father." And Joseph wept when they spoke to him.

18 Then his brothers also went and fell down before his face, and they said, "Behold, we are your servants."

19 Joseph said to them, "Do not be

What Joseph's Brothers Learned

We will always thank God for our brother Reuben. He didn't let us kill our little brother Joseph, although we did sell him to some traders (see Genesis 27). We hated Joseph because he had dreamed that he would be a great man someday and we would all bow down to him.

Years later there was a great famine, and our family was hungry. When we heard Egypt had food, we went down to buy some. Can you imagine how terrified we were when the great man we met in Egypt turned out to be Joseph? Naturally, we thought he would be angry.

But Joseph forgave us, and we learned that day about God's amazing love. Even our cruelty to Joseph was used by the Lord to save our family.

---

afraid, for *am* I in the place of God? **20** But as for you, you meant evil against me; *but* God meant it for good, in order to bring it about as *it is* this day, to save many people alive. **21** Now therefore, do not be afraid; I will provide for you and your little ones." And he comforted them and spoke kindly to them.

22 So Joseph dwelt in Egypt, he and his father's household. And Joseph lived one hundred and ten years. **23** Joseph saw Ephraim's children to the third *generation.* The children of Machir, the son of Manasseh, were also brought up on Joseph's knees.

24 And Joseph said to his brethren, "I am dying; but God will surely visit you, and bring you out of this land to the land of which He swore to Abraham, to Isaac, and to Jacob." **25** Then Joseph took an oath from the children of Israel, saying, "God will surely visit you, and you shall carry up my bones from here." **26** So Joseph died, *being* one hundred and ten years old; and they embalmed him, and he was put in a coffin in Egypt.

The Book of
EXODUS

Pronounce my name *MO-zez*. The name is connected with a Hebrew word meaning "Drawn Out," because I was drawn out of the Nile River.

I wrote Genesis, Exodus, Leviticus, Numbers, and Deuteronomy, but you don't meet me until the Book of Exodus where you read that I was born in Egypt (Exodus 2:2).

Although I am really a Hebrew, I grew up as an Egyptian prince (Exodus 2:1–10). Because I am a Hebrew, I became angry when I saw an Egyptian slave driver beating one of my people. I killed the Egyptian, and I had to run away into the desert where I became a hired shepherd (Exodus 2:11–25).

One day God spoke to me from a bush that seemed to be burning but didn't actually burn up (Exodus 3:1–6). He commanded me to go back to Egypt and lead my Hebrew people out of slavery and back to the land that God promised them.

In the end, the Lord didn't let me go into the Promised Land because I lost my temper with the people in a way that displeased Him (Numbers 20:1–12).

Always remember that you must ask for self-control if you are going to be a leader for God.

Israel suffers in Egypt

NOW these *are* the names of the children of Israel who came to Egypt; each man and his household came with Jacob: 2 Reuben, Simeon, Levi, and Judah; 3 Issachar, Zebulun, and Benjamin; 4 Dan, Naphtali, Gad, and Asher. 5 All those who were descendants of Jacob were seventy persons (for Joseph was in Egypt *already*). 6 And Joseph died, all his brothers, and all that generation. 7 But the children of Israel were fruitful and increased abundantly, multiplied and grew exceedingly mighty; and the land was filled with them.

8 Now there arose a new king over

DIGGING IN

1:8–13 The Nation of Egypt You can see on the map on page 99 where Israel once lived in the land of Egypt.

The history of the people of Egypt begins about two thousand years before the birth of Christ (B.C.), and Abraham made a trip to Egypt in about 2000 B.C. (see Genesis 12:10).

Genesis 46 tells how Jacob and his family came to live in Egypt soon after the time of Abraham. The people of Jacob (called Israel) lived in Egypt for 430 years. Then the Egyptians began to make slaves of Israel. At that time, (about 1500 B.C.), God commanded Moses to lead Israel back to the Promised Land. An Egyptian stone tablet tells about Israel leaving Egypt.

Israel's God was the Creator of all nature, but Egypt's gods were part of nature. The stone images of these gods were animals like the bull, the crocodile, the falcon, the ram, and the jackal. The king, or Pharaoh (pronounced *FAY-row*), was also worshiped as a god.

Egypt, who did not know Joseph. 9 And he said to his people, "Look, the people of the children of Israel *are* more and mightier than we; 10 come, let us deal shrewdly with them, lest they multiply, and it happen, in the event of war, that they also join our enemies and fight against us, and *so* go up out of the land." 11 Therefore they set taskmasters over them to afflict them with their burdens. And they built for Pharaoh supply cities, Pithom and Raamses. 12 But the more they afflicted them, the more they multiplied and grew. And they were in dread of the children of Israel. 13 So the Egyptians made the children of Israel serve with rigor. 14 And they made their lives bitter with hard bondage—in mortar, in brick, and in all manner of service in the field. All their service in which they made them serve *was* with rigor.

15 Then the king of Egypt spoke to the Hebrew midwives, of whom the name of one *was* Shiphrah and the name of the other Puah; 16 and he said, "When you do the duties of a midwife for the Hebrew women, and see *them* on the birthstools, if it *is* a son, then you shall kill him; but if it *is* a daughter, then she shall live." 17 But the midwives feared God, and did not do as the king of Egypt commanded them, but saved the male children alive. 18 So the king of Egypt called for the midwives and said to them, "Why have you done this thing, and saved the male children alive?"

19 And the midwives said to Pharaoh, "Because the Hebrew women *are* not like the Egyptian women; for they *are* lively and give birth before the midwives come to them."

20 Therefore God dealt well with the midwives, and the people multiplied and grew very mighty. 21 And so it was, because the midwives feared God, that He provided households for them.

22 So Pharaoh commanded all his people, saying, "Every son who is born you shall cast into the river, and every daughter you shall save alive."

Moses is born

2 And a man of the house of Levi went and took *as wife* a daughter of Levi. 2 So the woman conceived and bore a son. And when she saw that he *was* a beautiful *child,* she hid him three months. 3 But when she could no longer hide him, she took an ark of bulrushes for him, daubed it with asphalt and pitch, put the child in it, and laid *it* in the reeds by the river's bank. 4 And his sister stood afar off, to know what would be done to him.

5 Then the daughter of Pharaoh came down to bathe at the river. And her maidens walked along the riverside; and when she saw the ark among the reeds, she sent her maid to get it. 6 And when she opened *it,* she saw the child, and behold, the baby wept. So she had compassion on him, and said, "This is one of the Hebrews' children."

7 Then his sister said to Pharaoh's

Midwives help mothers when they are giving birth. We are the midwives who trusted God and refused to kill the Hebrew boy babies when they were born, as the cruel Pharaoh of Egypt commanded us to do.

Because we obeyed God, Moses was saved and grew up to be a great man of God who led his people out of Egypt and gave them God's laws.

People don't remember us much because we weren't Hebrews, but we are proof that God has people who obey Him even among His enemies. You don't have to be Jewish, or American, or African, or European, or Australian. God does not honor or dishonor people because of where they were born, but He cares for all people and calls all kinds of people to serve Him.

It was frightening to be a mother in Egypt when Moses was born.

Earlier, the government of Egypt had been good to Jews. They even gave us a large area called Goshen in northern Egypt to live in. There we raised our sheep and cattle. But now that Joseph was dead, we had been made slaves and the Egyptians treated us very harshly.

I knew that Pharaoh had ordered all male Hebrew babies killed, so when Moses was born, I hid him as long as I could. Finally, though, we had to do a terrible thing. We made a little waterproof box and floated Moses among the reeds growing along the Nile River.

We were sad when we gave up Moses, but Miriam, our daughter, stood watch over the little boy to see that no harm came to him.

daughter, "Shall I go and call a nurse for you from the Hebrew women, that she may nurse the child for you?"

8 And Pharaoh's daughter said to her, "Go." So the maiden went and called the child's mother. 9 Then Pharaoh's daughter said to her, "Take this child away and nurse him for me, and I will give you your wages." So the woman took the child and nursed him. 10 And the child grew, and she brought him to Pharaoh's daughter, and he became her son. So she called his name Moses, saying, "Because I drew him out of the water."

11 Now it came to pass in those days, when Moses was grown, that he went out to his brethren and looked at their burdens. And he saw an Egyptian beating a Hebrew, one of his brethren. 12 So he looked this way and that way, and when he saw no one, he killed the Egyptian and hid him in the sand. 13 And when he went out the second day, behold, two Hebrew men were fighting, and he said to the one who did the wrong, "Why are you striking your companion?"

14 Then he said, "Who made you a prince and a judge over us? Do you intend to kill me as you killed the Egyptian?"

So Moses feared and said, "Surely this thing is known!" 15 When Pharaoh heard of this matter, he sought to kill Moses. But Moses fled from the face of Pharaoh and dwelt in the land of Midian; and he sat down by a well.

Pharaoh's Daughter—My friends and I used to love swimming in the beautiful Nile River every day. But one special day, one of the most important events of my life happened—I found Moses.

He was in a little box that was floating among the Nile reeds. Curious, I opened the box, and there was the most beautiful little boy I had ever seen!

A young girl was standing nearby so I sent her to find me a Hebrew nurse for the baby. The surprise was that the nurse turned out to be Moses' *real mother.*

So I took Moses home with me, and he became my very own son. When Moses became a young man, his mother and father were thankful that he had been brought up in our palace. Moses grew up to be the greatest man in all the world of that time.

16 Now the priest of Midian had seven daughters. And they came and drew water, and they filled the troughs to water their father's flock. 17 Then the shepherds came and drove them away; but Moses stood up and helped them, and watered their flock.

18 When they came to Reuel their father, he said, "How is it that you have come so soon today?"

19 And they said, "An Egyptian delivered us from the hand of the shepherds, and he also drew enough water for us and watered the flock."

20 So he said to his daughters, "And where is he? Why is it that you have left the man? Call him, that he may eat bread."

21 Then Moses was content to live with the man, and he gave Zipporah his daughter to Moses. 22 And she bore him a son. He called his name Gershom, for he said, "I have been a stranger in a foreign land."

23 Now it happened in the process of time that the king of Egypt died. Then the children of Israel groaned because of the bondage, and they cried out; and their cry came up to God because of the bondage. 24 So God heard their groaning, and God remembered His covenant with Abraham, with Isaac, and with Jacob. 25 And God looked upon the children of Israel, and God acknowledged them.

God speaks from a burning bush

3 Now Moses was tending the flock of Jethro his father-in-law, the priest of Midian. And he led the flock to the back of the desert, and came to Horeb, the mountain of God. 2 And the Angel of the Lord appeared to him in a flame of fire from the midst of a bush. So he looked, and behold, the bush was burning with fire, but the bush was not consumed. 3 Then Moses said, "I will now turn aside and see this great sight, why the bush does not burn."

4 So when the Lord saw that he turned aside to look, God called to him from the midst of the bush and said, "Moses, Moses!"

And he said, "Here I am."

5 Then He said, "Do not draw near this place. Take your sandals off your feet, for the place where you stand is holy ground." 6 Moreover He said, "I am the God of your father—the God of Abraham, the God of Isaac, and the God of Jacob." And Moses hid his face, for he was afraid to look upon God.

7 And the Lord said: "I have surely seen the oppression of My people who are in Egypt, and have heard their cry because of their taskmasters, for I know their sorrows. 8 So I have come down to deliver them out of the hand of the Egyptians, and to bring them up from that land to a good and large land, to a land flowing with milk and honey, to the place of the Canaanites and the Hittites and the Amorites and the Perizzites and the Hivites and the Jebusites. 9 Now therefore, behold, the cry of the children of Israel has come to Me, and I have also seen the oppression with which the Egyptians oppress

DIGGING IN

3:1–14 Moses Meets God Moses had what it took to be a great hero of his people. He wasn't afraid to stand up for what was right.

But God could not use a man of anger. Moses murdered an Egyptian who was beating a Hebrew slave. This showed Moses that he had to learn patience and self-control. So God sent him into the desert of Sinai (pronounced SIGH-nigh) for 40 years. There he served as a shepherd for a wealthy sheep owner named Jethro.

This was a hard thing for Moses, who had been a prince in Egypt.

Then one day God appeared to Moses in a burning bush that didn't burn up. God sent Moses back to Egypt to save His people from slavery. He also told Moses that His true name is I AM. So Moses met the true God who is not a part of nature like Egypt's gods. The Lord is God, who is above everything He created. Do you know the I AM?

God spoke to Moses from a bush that did not burn up.

them. **10** Come now, therefore, and I will send you to Pharaoh that you may bring My people, the children of Israel, out of Egypt."

11 But Moses said to God, "Who *am* I that I should go to Pharaoh, and that I should bring the children of Israel out of Egypt?"

12 So He said, "I will certainly be with you. And this *shall be* a sign to you that I have sent you: When you have brought the people out of Egypt, you shall serve God on this mountain."

13 Then Moses said to God, "Indeed, *when* I come to the children of Israel and say to them, 'The God of your fathers has sent me to you,' and they say to me, 'What *is* His name?' what shall I say to them?"

14 And God said to Moses, **"I AM WHO I AM."** And He said, "Thus you shall say to the children of Israel, 'I AM

WORDFINDER

3:14 I AM WHO I AM The name God gives Himself. The name means that He always existed, even before time, and He always will exist. He depends on nothing outside Himself for His existence.

DIGGING IN

3:7 Israel in Egypt The pharaohs of Egypt at first welcomed Israel to their country. But after four hundred years, Israel grew into a great people. So the Egyptians began to see Israel as a danger to their nation. This is why they made slaves out of the Israelites.

They were still God's people, and He loved them. He remembered His promise to Abraham that His people were going to live in the land of Canaan forever (see Genesis 12). So Egypt was really no place for the Hebrews. Also, the slavery

had become very cruel. The Israelites were put to work building the cities of Rameses and Pithom (pronounced *RAM-uh-sees* and *PIE-thum*). If the Lord had not rescued His people, they would have died there and been forgotten.

But God had plans for Israel that would change the world for all time to come. So He would now bring them back to their own land.

Can you now see how God keeps working out His great plan of salvation?

has sent me to you.' " ¹⁵ Moreover God said to Moses, "Thus you shall say to the children of Israel: 'The LORD God of your fathers, the God of Abraham, the God of Isaac, and the God of Jacob, has sent me to you. This *is* My name forever, and this *is* My memorial to all generations.' ¹⁶ Go and gather the elders of Israel together, and say to them, 'The LORD God of your fathers, the God of Abraham, of Isaac, and of Jacob, appeared to me, saying, "I have surely visited you and *seen* what is done to you in Egypt; ¹⁷ and I have said I will bring you up out of the affliction of Egypt to the land of the Canaanites and the Hittites and the Amorites and the Perizzites and the Hivites and the Jebusites, to a land flowing with milk and honey." ' ¹⁸ Then they will heed your voice; and you shall come, you and the elders of Israel, to the king of Egypt; and you shall say to him, 'The LORD God of the Hebrews has met with us; and now, please, let us go three days' journey into the wilderness, that we may sacrifice to the LORD our God.' ¹⁹ But I am sure that the king of Egypt will not let you go, no, not even by a mighty hand. ²⁰ So I will stretch out My hand and strike Egypt with all My wonders which I will do in its midst; and after that he will let you go. ²¹ And I will give this people favor in the sight of the Egyptians; and it shall be, when you go, that you shall not go empty-handed. ²² But every woman shall ask of her neighbor, namely, of her who dwells near her house, articles of silver, articles of gold, and clothing; and you shall put *them* on your sons and on your daughters. So you shall plunder the Egyptians."

Moses returns to Egypt

4 Then Moses answered and said, "But suppose they will not believe me or listen to my voice; suppose they say, 'The LORD has not appeared to you.' "

² So the LORD said to him, "What *is* that in your hand?"

He said, "A rod."

³ And He said, "Cast it on the ground." So he cast it on the ground, and it became a serpent; and Moses fled from it. ⁴ Then the LORD said to Moses, "Reach out your hand and take *it* by the tail" (and he reached out his hand and caught it, and it became a rod in his hand), ⁵ "that they may believe that the LORD God of their fathers, the God of Abraham, the God of Isaac, and the God of Jacob, has appeared to you."

⁶ Furthermore the LORD said to him, "Now put your hand in your bosom." And he put his hand in his bosom, and when he took it out, behold, his hand *was* leprous, like snow. ⁷ And He said, "Put your hand in your bosom again." So he put his hand in his bosom again, and drew it out of his bosom, and behold, it was restored like his *other* flesh. ⁸ "Then it will be, if they do not believe you, nor heed the message of the first sign, that they may believe the message of the latter sign. ⁹ And it shall be, if they do not believe even these two signs, or listen to your voice, that you shall take water from the river and pour *it* on the dry *land*. The water which you take from the river will become blood on the dry *land*."

¹⁰ Then Moses said to the LORD, "O my Lord, I *am* not eloquent, neither before nor since You have spoken to Your servant; but I *am* slow of speech and slow of tongue."

¹¹ So the LORD said to him, "Who has made man's mouth? Or who makes the mute, the deaf, the seeing, or the blind? *Have* not I, the LORD? ¹² Now therefore, go, and I will be with your mouth and teach you what you shall say."

¹³ But he said, "O my Lord, please send by the hand of whomever *else* You may send."

¹⁴ So the anger of the LORD was kindled against Moses, and He said: "Is not Aaron the Levite your brother? I know that he can speak well. And look, he is also coming out to meet you. When he sees you, he will be glad in his heart. ¹⁵ Now you shall speak to him and put the words in his mouth.

And I will be with your mouth and with his mouth, and I will teach you what you shall do. 16 So he shall be your spokesman to the people. And he himself shall be as a mouth for you, and you shall be to him as God. 17 And you shall take this rod in your hand, with which you shall do the signs."

18 So Moses went and returned to Jethro his father-in-law, and said to him, "Please let me go and return to my brethren who *are* in Egypt, and see whether they are still alive."

And Jethro said to Moses, "Go in peace."

19 Now the LORD said to Moses in Midian, "Go, return to Egypt; for all the men who sought your life are dead." 20 Then Moses took his wife and his sons and set them on a donkey, and he returned to the land of Egypt. And Moses took the rod of God in his hand.

21 And the LORD said to Moses, "When you go back to Egypt, see that you do all those wonders before Pharaoh which I have put in your hand. But I will harden his heart, so that he will not let the people go. 22 Then you shall say to Pharaoh, 'Thus says the LORD: "Israel *is* My son, My firstborn. 23 So I say to you, let My son go that he may serve Me. But if you refuse to let him go, indeed I will kill your son, your firstborn." ' "

24 And it came to pass on the way, at the encampment, that the LORD met him and sought to kill him. 25 Then Zipporah took a sharp stone and cut off the foreskin of her son and cast *it* at *Moses'* feet, and said, "Surely you *are* a husband of blood to me!" 26 So He let him go. Then she said, "*You are* a husband of blood!"—because of the circumcision.

27 And the LORD said to Aaron, "Go into the wilderness to meet Moses." So he went and met him on the mountain of God, and kissed him. 28 So Moses told Aaron all the words of the LORD who had sent him, and all the signs which He had commanded him. 29 Then Moses and Aaron went and gathered together all the elders of the

children of Israel. 30 And Aaron spoke all the words which the LORD had spoken to Moses. Then he did the signs in the sight of the people. 31 So the people believed; and when they heard that the LORD had visited the children of Israel and that He had looked on their affliction, then they bowed their heads and worshiped.

"Let My people go"

5 Afterward Moses and Aaron went in and told Pharaoh, "Thus says the LORD God of Israel: 'Let My people go, that they may hold a feast to Me in the wilderness.' "

Who Was Pharaoh?

Pharaoh is pronounced *FAY-row*. This was the title of Egyptian kings for many hundreds of years. The word means "Great House." The Pharaoh was considered to be the son of Ra, the sun god. So the Pharaoh was also worshiped as a god. His word was absolute law.

2 And Pharaoh said, "Who *is* the LORD, that I should obey His voice to let Israel go? I do not know the LORD, nor will I let Israel go."

Pharaoh Rameses II may have been on the throne when the Israelites left Egypt.

3 So they said, "The God of the Hebrews has met with us. Please, let us go three days' journey into the desert and sacrifice to the LORD our God, lest He fall upon us with pestilence or with the sword."

4 Then the king of Egypt said to them, "Moses and Aaron, why do you take the people from their work? Get *back* to your labor." 5 And Pharaoh said, "Look, the people of the land *are* many now, and you make them rest from their labor!"

6 So the same day Pharaoh commanded the taskmasters of the people and their officers, saying, 7 "You shall no longer give the people straw to make brick as before. Let them go and gather straw for themselves. 8 And you shall lay on them the quota of bricks which they made before. You shall not reduce it. For they are idle; therefore they cry out, saying, 'Let us go *and* sacrifice to our God.' 9 Let more work be laid on the men, that they may labor in it, and let them not regard false words."

10 And the taskmasters of the people and their officers went out and spoke to the people, saying, "Thus says Pharaoh: 'I will not give you straw. 11 Go, get yourselves straw where you can find it; yet none of your work will be reduced.' " 12 So the people were scattered abroad throughout all the land of Egypt to gather stubble instead of straw. 13 And the taskmasters forced *them* to hurry, saying, "Fulfill your work, *your* daily quota, as when there was straw." 14 Also the officers of the children of Israel, whom Pharaoh's taskmasters had set over them, were beaten *and* were asked, "Why have you not fulfilled your task in making brick both yesterday and today, as before?"

15 Then the officers of the children of Israel came and cried out to Pharaoh, saying, "Why are you dealing thus with your servants? 16 There is no straw given to your servants, and they say to us, 'Make brick!' And indeed your servants *are* beaten, but the fault *is* in your *own* people."

17 But he said, "You *are* idle! Idle! Therefore you say, 'Let us go *and* sacrifice to the LORD.' 18 Therefore go now *and* work; for no straw shall be given you, yet you shall deliver the quota of bricks." 19 And the officers of the children of Israel saw *that* they *were* in trouble after it was said, "You shall

Cruel Egyptian taskmasters forced God's people to make bricks without straw.

not reduce *any* bricks from your daily quota.''

20 Then, as they came out from Pharaoh, they met Moses and Aaron who stood there to meet them. 21 And they said to them, ''Let the LORD look on you and judge, because you have made us abhorrent in the sight of Pharaoh and in the sight of his servants, to put a sword in their hand to kill us.''

22 So Moses returned to the LORD and said, ''Lord, why have You brought trouble on this people? Why *is* it You have sent me? 23 For since I came to Pharaoh to speak in Your name, he has done evil to this people; neither have You delivered Your people at all.''

Israel will not listen to God

6 Then the LORD said to Moses, ''Now you shall *see* what I will do to Pharaoh. For with a strong hand he will let them go, and with a strong hand he will drive them out of his land.''

2 And God spoke to Moses and said to him: ''I *am* the LORD. 3 I appeared to Abraham, to Isaac, and to Jacob, as God Almighty, but *by* My name LORD I was not known to them. 4 I have also established My **covenant** with them, to give them the land of Canaan, the land of their pilgrimage, in which they were strangers. 5 And I have also heard the groaning of the children of Israel whom the Egyptians keep in bondage, and I have remembered My covenant. 6 Therefore say to the children of Israel: 'I *am* the LORD; I will bring you out from under the burdens of the Egyptians, I will rescue you from their bondage, and I will **redeem** you with an outstretched arm and with great judgments. 7 I will take you as

My people, and I will be your God. Then you shall know that I *am* the LORD your God who brings you out from under the burdens of the Egyptians. 8 And I will bring you into the land which I swore to give to Abraham, Isaac, and Jacob; and I will give it to you *as* a heritage: I *am* the LORD.' ''
9 So Moses spoke thus to the children of Israel; but they did not heed Moses, because of anguish of spirit and cruel bondage.

10 And the LORD spoke to Moses, saying, 11 ''Go in, tell Pharaoh king of Egypt to let the children of Israel go out of his land.''

12 And Moses spoke before the LORD, saying, ''The children of Israel have not heeded me. How then shall Pharaoh heed me, for I *am* of uncircumcised lips?''

13 Then the LORD spoke to Moses and Aaron, and gave them a command for the children of Israel and for Pharaoh king of Egypt, to bring the children of Israel out of the land of Egypt.

14 These *are* the heads of their fathers' houses: The sons of Reuben, the firstborn of Israel, *were* Hanoch, Pallu, Hezron, and Carmi. These are the families of Reuben. 15 And the sons of Simeon *were* Jemuel, Jamin, Ohad, Jachin, Zohar, and Shaul the son of a Canaanite woman. These *are* the families of Simeon. 16 These *are* the names of the sons of Levi according to their generations: Gershon, Kohath, and Merari. And the years of the life of Levi *were* one hundred and thirty-seven. 17 The sons of Gershon *were* Libni and Shimi according to their families. 18 And the sons of Kohath *were* Amram, Izhar, Hebron, and Uzziel. And the years of the life of Kohath *were* one hundred and thirty-three. 19 The sons of Merari *were* Mahli and Mushi.

WORDFINDER

6:4 Covenant A legal agreement. God made a covenant with Abraham to give the land of Canaan to his descendants and to make Abraham a blessing to the whole world.

6:6 Redeem To buy something back from someone. Jesus bought back believers from the slavery of sin.

These *are* the families of Levi according to their generations. 20 Now Amram took for himself Jochebed, his father's sister, as wife; and she bore him Aaron and Moses. And the years of the life of Amram *were* one hundred and thirty-seven. 21 The sons of Izhar *were* Korah, Nepheg, and Zichri. 22 And the sons of Uzziel *were* Mishael, Elzaphan, and Zithri. 23 Aaron took to himself Elisheba, daughter of Amminadab, sister of Nahshon, as wife; and she bore him Nadab, Abihu, Eleazar, and Ithamar. 24 And the sons of Korah *were* Assir, Elkanah, and Abiasaph. These are the families of the Korahites. 25 Eleazar, Aaron's son, took for himself one of the daughters of Putiel as wife; and she bore him Phinehas. These *are* the heads of the fathers' houses of the Levites according to their families.

26 These *are the same* Aaron and Moses to whom the LORD said, "Bring out the children of Israel from the land of Egypt according to their armies." 27 These *are* the ones who spoke to Pharaoh king of Egypt, to bring out the children of Israel from Egypt. These *are the same* Moses and Aaron.

28 And it came to pass, on the day the LORD spoke to Moses in the land of Egypt, 29 that the LORD spoke to Moses, saying, "I *am* the LORD. Speak to Pharaoh king of Egypt all that I say to you."

30 But Moses said before the LORD, "Behold, I *am* of uncircumcised lips, and how shall Pharaoh heed me?"

Moses speaks to Pharaoh

7 So the LORD said to Moses: "See, I have made you *as* God to Pharaoh, and Aaron your brother shall be your prophet. 2 You shall speak all that I command you. And Aaron your brother shall tell Pharaoh to send the children of Israel out of his land. 3 And I will harden Pharaoh's heart, and multiply My signs and My wonders in the land of Egypt. 4 But Pharaoh will not heed you, so that I may lay My hand on Egypt and bring My armies *and* My people, the children of Israel, out of the land of Egypt by great judgments. 5 And the Egyptians shall know that I *am* the LORD, when I stretch out My hand on Egypt and bring out the children of Israel from among them."

6 Then Moses and Aaron did *so;* just as the LORD commanded them, so they did. 7 And Moses *was* eighty years old and Aaron eighty-three years old when they spoke to Pharaoh.

8 Then the LORD spoke to Moses and Aaron, saying, 9 "When Pharaoh speaks to you, saying, 'Show a miracle for yourselves,' then you shall say to Aaron, 'Take your rod and cast *it* before Pharaoh, *and* let it become a serpent.' " 10 So Moses and Aaron went in to Pharaoh, and they did so, just as the LORD commanded. And Aaron cast down his rod before Pharaoh and before his servants, and it became a serpent. 11 But Pharaoh also called the wise men and the sorcerers; so the magicians of Egypt, they also did in like manner with their enchantments. 12 For every man threw down his rod, and they became serpents. But Aaron's rod swallowed up their rods. 13 And Pharaoh's heart grew hard, and he did not heed them, as the LORD had said.

14 So the LORD said to Moses: "Pharaoh's heart *is* hard; he refuses to let the people go. 15 Go to Pharaoh in the morning, when he goes out to the water, and you shall stand by the river's bank to meet him; and the rod which was turned to a serpent you shall take in your hand. 16 And you shall say to him, 'The LORD God of the Hebrews has sent me to you, saying, "Let My people go, that they may serve Me in the wilderness"; but indeed, until now you would not hear! 17 Thus says the LORD: "By this you shall know that I *am* the LORD. Behold, I will strike the waters which *are* in the river with the rod that *is* in my hand, and they shall be turned to blood. 18 And the fish that *are* in the river shall die, the river shall stink, and the Egyptians will loathe to drink the water of the river." ' "

19 Then the LORD spoke to Moses, "Say to Aaron, 'Take your rod and stretch out your hand over the waters of Egypt, over their streams, over their rivers, over their ponds, and over all their pools of water, that they may become blood. And there shall be blood throughout all the land of Egypt, both in *buckets of* wood and *pitchers of* stone.' " 20 And Moses and Aaron did so, just as the LORD commanded. So he lifted up the rod and struck the waters that *were* in the river, in the sight of Pharaoh and in the sight of his servants. And all the waters that *were* in the river were turned to blood. 21 The fish that *were* in the river died, the river stank, and the Egyptians could not drink the water of the river. So there was blood throughout all the land of Egypt.

22 Then the magicians of Egypt did so with their enchantments; and Pharaoh's heart grew hard, and he did not heed them, as the LORD had said. 23 And Pharaoh turned and went into his house. Neither was his heart moved by this. 24 So all the Egyptians dug all around the river for water to drink, because they could not drink the

DIGGING IN

7:14—11:10 God Judges the Egyptians The verb *judge* has two meanings. Sometimes it means to make a choice. We judge some basketball players to be better than others.

But the word *judge* also means to punish. God judged the Egyptians because they were cruel to the people of Israel and refused to let them go. You can read how God punished the Egyptians ten times before Pharaoh of Egypt sent Israel away. Then he was glad to let them go!

God does not enjoy judging us. But sometimes that's the only way He can get our attention. (Often it is not enough to *tell* somebody he's wrong. We have to *show* him.) That means we have to learn by being punished when no other way can help. Nobody likes punishment. But punishment is sometimes the kindest thing to do because it stops us from doing things that ruin our lives.

The sad truth is that some people never seem to learn. Pharaoh of Egypt seems to be one of those people.

The Nile River, which God turned to blood.

water of the river. 25 And seven days passed after the LORD had struck the river.

Plagues of frogs, lice, and flies

8 And the LORD spoke to Moses, "Go to Pharaoh and say to him, 'Thus says the LORD: "Let My people go, that they may serve Me. 2 But if you refuse to let *them* go, behold, I will smite all your territory with frogs. 3 So the river shall bring forth frogs abundantly, which shall go up and come into your house, into your bedroom, on your bed, into the houses of your servants, on your people, into your ovens, and into your kneading bowls. 4 And the frogs shall come up on you, on your people, and on all your servants." ' "

5 Then the LORD spoke to Moses, "Say to Aaron, 'Stretch out your hand with your rod over the streams, over the rivers, and over the ponds, and cause frogs to come up on the land of Egypt.' " 6 So Aaron stretched out his hand over the waters of Egypt, and the frogs came up and covered the land of Egypt. 7 And the magicians did so with their enchantments, and brought up frogs on the land of Egypt.

8 Then Pharaoh called for Moses and Aaron, and said, "Entreat the LORD that He may take away the frogs from me and from my people; and I will let the people go, that they may sacrifice to the LORD."

9 And Moses said to Pharaoh, "Accept the honor of saying when I shall intercede for you, for your servants, and for your people, to destroy the frogs from you and your houses, *that* they may remain in the river only."

10 So he said, "Tomorrow." And he said, "*Let it be* according to your word, that you may know that *there is* no one like the LORD our God. 11 And the frogs shall depart from you, from your houses, from your servants, and from your people. They shall remain in the river only."

12 Then Moses and Aaron went out from Pharaoh. And Moses cried out to the LORD concerning the frogs which He had brought against Pharaoh. 13 So the LORD did according to the word of Moses. And the frogs died out of the houses, out of the courtyards, and out of the fields. 14 They gathered them together in heaps, and the land stank. 15 But when Pharaoh saw that there was relief, he hardened his heart and did not heed them, as the LORD had said.

16 So the LORD said to Moses, "Say to Aaron, 'Stretch out your rod, and strike the dust of the land, so that it may become lice throughout all the land of Egypt.' " 17 And they did so. For Aaron stretched out his hand with his rod and struck the dust of the earth, and it became lice on man and beast. All the dust of the land became lice throughout all the land of Egypt.

18 Now the magicians so worked with their enchantments to bring forth lice, but they could not. So there were lice on man and beast. 19 Then the magicians said to Pharaoh, "This *is* the finger of God." But Pharaoh's heart grew hard, and he did not heed them, just as the LORD had said.

20 And the LORD said to Moses, "Rise early in the morning and stand before Pharaoh as he comes out to the water. Then say to him, 'Thus says the LORD: "Let My people go, that they may serve Me. 21 Or else, if you will not let My people go, behold, I will send swarms *of flies* on you and your servants, on your people and into your houses. The houses of the Egyptians shall be full of swarms *of flies,* and also the ground on which they *stand.* 22 And in that day I will set apart the land of Goshen, in which My people dwell, that no swarms *of flies* shall be there, in order that you may know that I *am* the LORD in the midst of the land. 23 I will make a difference between My people and your people. Tomorrow this sign shall be." ' " 24 And the LORD did so. Thick swarms *of flies* came into the house of Pharaoh, *into* his servants' houses, and into all the land of Egypt. The land was corrupted because of the swarms *of flies.*

25 Then Pharaoh called for Moses

and Aaron, and said, "Go, sacrifice to your God in the land."

26 And Moses said, "It is not right to do so, for we would be sacrificing the abomination of the Egyptians to the LORD our God. If we sacrifice the abomination of the Egyptians before their eyes, then will they not stone us? 27 We will go three days' journey into the wilderness and sacrifice to the LORD our God as He will command us."

28 So Pharaoh said, "I will let you go, that you may sacrifice to the LORD your God in the wilderness; only you shall not go very far away. Intercede for me."

29 Then Moses said, "Indeed I am going out from you, and I will entreat the LORD, that the swarms *of flies* may depart tomorrow from Pharaoh, from his servants, and from his people. But let Pharaoh not deal deceitfully anymore in not letting the people go to sacrifice to the LORD."

30 So Moses went out from Pharaoh and entreated the LORD. 31 And the LORD did according to the word of Moses; He removed the swarms *of flies* from Pharaoh, from his servants, and from his people. Not one remained. 32 But Pharaoh hardened his heart at this time also; neither would he let the people go.

The plague on the cattle; the plagues of boils and hail

9 Then the LORD said to Moses, "Go in to Pharaoh and tell him, 'Thus says the LORD God of the Hebrews: "Let My people go, that they may serve Me. 2 For if you refuse to let *them* go, and still hold them, 3 behold, the hand of the LORD will be on your cattle in the field, on the horses, on the donkeys, on the camels, on the oxen, and on the sheep—a very severe pestilence. 4 And the LORD will make a difference between the livestock of Israel and the livestock of Egypt. So nothing shall die of all *that* belongs to the children of Israel." ' " 5 Then the LORD appointed a set time, saying, "Tomorrow the LORD will do this thing in the land."

6 So the LORD did this thing on the next day, and all the livestock of Egypt died; but of the livestock of the children of Israel, not one died. 7 Then Pharaoh sent, and indeed, not even one of the livestock of the Israelites was dead. But the heart of Pharaoh became hard, and he did not let the people go.

8 So the LORD said to Moses and Aaron, "Take for yourselves handfuls of ashes from a furnace, and let Moses scatter it toward the heavens in the sight of Pharaoh. 9 And it will become fine dust in all the land of Egypt, and it will cause boils that break out in sores on man and beast throughout all the land of Egypt." 10 Then they took ashes from the furnace and stood before Pharaoh, and Moses scattered *them* toward heaven. And *they* caused boils that break out in sores on man and beast. 11 And the magicians could not stand before Moses because of the boils, for the boils were on the magicians and on all the Egyptians. 12 But the LORD hardened the heart of Pharaoh; and he did not heed them, just as the LORD had spoken to Moses.

13 Then the LORD said to Moses, "Rise early in the morning and stand before Pharaoh, and say to him, 'Thus says the LORD God of the Hebrews: "Let My people go, that they may serve Me, 14 for at this time I will send all My plagues to your very heart, and on your servants and on your people, that you may know that *there is* none like Me in all the earth. 15 Now if I had stretched out My hand and struck you and your people with pestilence, then you would have been cut off from the earth. 16 But indeed for this *purpose* I have raised you up, that I may show My power *in* you, and that My name may be declared in all the earth. 17 As yet you exalt yourself against My people in that you will not let them go. 18 Behold, tomorrow about this time I will cause very heavy hail to rain down, such as has not been in Egypt since its founding until now. 19 Therefore send now *and* gather your livestock and all that you have in the field, for the hail shall come down on

every man and every animal which is found in the field and is not brought home; and they shall die." ' "

20 He who feared the word of the LORD among the servants of Pharaoh made his servants and his livestock flee to the houses. 21 But he who did not regard the word of the LORD left his servants and his livestock in the field.

22 Then the LORD said to Moses, "Stretch out your hand toward heaven, that there may be hail in all the land of Egypt—on man, on beast, and on every herb of the field, throughout the land of Egypt." 23 And Moses stretched out his rod toward heaven; and the LORD sent thunder and hail, and fire darted to the ground. And the LORD rained hail on the land of Egypt. 24 So there was hail, and fire mingled with the hail, so very heavy that there was none like it in all the land of Egypt since it became a nation. 25 And the hail struck throughout the whole land of Egypt, all that *was* in the field, both man and beast; and the hail struck every herb of the field and broke every tree of the field. 26 Only in the land of Goshen, where the children of Israel *were*, there was no hail.

27 And Pharaoh sent and called for Moses and Aaron, and said to them, "I have sinned this time. The LORD *is* righteous, and my people and I *are* wicked. 28 Entreat the LORD, that there may be no *more* mighty thundering and hail, for *it is* enough. I will let you go, and you shall stay no longer."

29 So Moses said to him, "As soon as I have gone out of the city, I will spread out my hands to the LORD; the thunder will cease, and there will be no more hail, that you may know that the earth *is* the LORD's. 30 But as for you and your servants, I know that you will not yet fear the LORD God."

31 Now the flax and the barley were struck, for the barley *was* in the head and the flax *was* in bud. 32 But the wheat and the spelt were not struck, for they *are* late crops.

33 So Moses went out of the city from Pharaoh and spread out his hands to the LORD; then the thunder and the hail ceased, and the rain was not poured on the earth. 34 And when Pharaoh saw that the rain, the hail, and the thunder had ceased, he sinned yet more; and he hardened his heart, he and his servants. 35 So the heart of Pharaoh was hard; neither would he let the children of Israel go, as the LORD had spoken by Moses.

The plagues of locusts and darkness

10 Now the LORD said to Moses, "Go in to Pharaoh; for I have hardened his heart and the hearts of his servants, that I may show these signs of Mine before him, 2 and that you may tell in the hearing of your son and your son's son the mighty things I have done in Egypt, and My signs which I have done among them, that you may know that I *am* the LORD."

3 So Moses and Aaron came in to Pharaoh and said to him, "Thus says the LORD God of the Hebrews: 'How long will you refuse to humble yourself before Me? Let My people go, that they may serve Me. 4 Or else, if you refuse to let My people go, behold, tomorrow I will bring locusts into your territory. 5 And they shall cover the face of the earth, so that no one will be able to see the earth; and they shall eat the residue of what is left, which remains to you from the hail, and they shall eat every tree which grows up for you out of the field. 6 They shall fill your houses, the houses of all your servants, and the houses of all the Egyptians—which neither your fathers nor your fathers' fathers have seen, since the day that they were on the earth to this day.' " And he turned and went out from Pharaoh.

7 Then Pharaoh's servants said to him, "How long shall this man be a snare to us? Let the men go, that they may serve the LORD their God. Do you not yet know that Egypt is destroyed?"

8 So Moses and Aaron were brought again to Pharaoh, and he said to them, "Go, serve the LORD your God. Who *are* the ones that are going?"

9 And Moses said, "We will go with our young and our old; with our sons and our daughters, with our flocks and our herds we will go, for we must hold a feast to the LORD."

10 Then he said to them, "The LORD had better be with you when I let you and your little ones go! Beware, for evil is ahead of you. 11 Not so! Go now, you *who are* men, and serve the LORD, for that is what you desired." And they were driven out from Pharaoh's presence.

12 Then the LORD said to Moses, "Stretch out your hand over the land of Egypt for the locusts, that they may come upon the land of Egypt, and eat every herb of the land—all that the hail has left." 13 So Moses stretched out his rod over the land of Egypt, and the LORD brought an east wind on the land all that day and all *that* night. When it was morning, the east wind brought the locusts. 14 And the locusts went up over all the land of Egypt and rested on all the territory of Egypt. *They were* very severe; previously there had been no such locusts as they, nor shall there be such after them. 15 For they covered the face of the whole earth, so that the land was darkened; and they ate every herb of the land and all the fruit of the trees which the hail had left. So there remained nothing green on the trees or on the plants of the field throughout all the land of Egypt.

16 Then Pharaoh called for Moses and Aaron in haste, and said, "I have sinned against the LORD your God and against you. 17 Now therefore, please forgive my sin only this once, and entreat the LORD your God, that He may take away from me this death only." 18 So he went out from Pharaoh and entreated the LORD. 19 And the LORD turned a very strong west wind, which took the locusts away and blew them into the Red Sea. There remained not one locust in all the territory of Egypt. 20 But the LORD hardened Pharaoh's heart, and he did not let the children of Israel go.

21 Then the LORD said to Moses, "Stretch out your hand toward heaven, that there may be darkness over the land of Egypt, darkness *which may even be felt*." 22 So Moses stretched out his hand toward heaven, and there was thick darkness in all the land of Egypt three days. 23 They did not see one another; nor did anyone rise from his place for three days. But all the children of Israel had light in their dwellings.

Pharaoh worshiped idols instead of the one true God.

24 Then Pharaoh called to Moses and said, "Go, serve the LORD; only let your flocks and your herds be kept back. Let your little ones also go with you."

25 But Moses said, "You must also give us sacrifices and burnt offerings, that we may sacrifice to the LORD our God. 26 Our livestock also shall go with us; not a hoof shall be left behind. For we must take some of them to serve the LORD our God, and even we do not know with what we must serve the LORD until we arrive there."

27 But the LORD hardened Pharaoh's heart, and he would not let them go. 28 Then Pharaoh said to him, "Get away from me! Take heed to yourself and see my face no more! For in the day you see my face you shall die!"

29 So Moses said, "You have spoken well. I will never see your face again."

Egypt's firstborn will die

11 And the LORD said to Moses, "I will bring one more plague on Pharaoh and on Egypt. Afterward he will let you go from here. When he lets you go, he will surely drive you out of here altogether. 2 Speak now in the hearing of the people, and let every man ask from his neighbor and every woman from her neighbor, articles of silver and articles of gold." 3 And the LORD gave the people favor in the sight of the Egyptians. Moreover the man Moses was very great in the land of Egypt, in the sight of Pharaoh's servants and in the sight of the people.

4 Then Moses said, "Thus says the LORD: 'About midnight I will go out into the midst of Egypt; 5 and all the first-born in the land of Egypt shall die, from the firstborn of Pharaoh who sits on his throne, even to the firstborn of the female servant who is behind the handmill, and all the firstborn of the animals. 6 Then there shall be a great cry throughout all the land of Egypt, such as was not like it before, nor shall be like it again. 7 But against none of the children of Israel shall a dog move its tongue, against man or beast, that

you may know that the LORD does make a difference between the Egyptians and Israel.' 8 And all these your servants shall come down to me and bow down to me, saying, 'Get out, and all the people who follow you!' After that I will go out." Then he went out from Pharaoh in great anger.

9 But the LORD said to Moses, "Pharaoh will not heed you, so that My wonders may be multiplied in the land of Egypt." 10 So Moses and Aaron did all these wonders before Pharaoh; and the LORD hardened Pharaoh's heart, and he did not let the children of Israel go out of his land.

God begins the Passover

12 Now the LORD spoke to Moses and Aaron in the land of Egypt, saying, 2 "This month shall be your beginning of months; it shall be the first month of the year to you. 3 Speak to all the congregation of Israel, saying: 'On the tenth of this month every man shall take for himself a lamb, according to the house of his father, a lamb for a household. 4 And if the household is too small for the lamb, let him and his neighbor next to his house take it according to the number of the persons; according to each man's need you shall make your count for the lamb. 5 Your lamb shall be without blemish, a male of the first year. You may take it from the sheep or from the goats. 6 Now you shall keep it until the four-teenth day of the same month. Then the whole assembly of the congregation of Israel shall kill it at twilight. 7 And they shall take some of the blood and put it on the two doorposts and on the lintel of the houses where they eat it. 8 Then they shall eat the flesh on that night; roasted in fire, with un-leavened bread and with bitter herbs they shall eat it. 9 Do not eat it raw, nor boiled at all with water, but roasted in fire—its head with its legs and its entrails. 10 You shall let none of it re-main until morning, and what remains of it until morning you shall burn with fire. 11 And thus you shall eat it: with

n your waist, your sandals on
eet, and your staff in your hand.
ou shall eat it in haste. It *is* the
ᴅ's **Passover.**

¹²'For I will pass through the land
f Egypt on that night, and will strike
all the firstborn in the land of Egypt,
both man and beast; and against all
the gods of Egypt I will execute judgment: I *am* the Lᴏʀᴅ. ¹³ Now the blood
shall be a sign for you on the houses
where you *are.* And when I see the
blood, I will pass over you; and the
plague shall not be on you to destroy
you when I strike the land of Egypt.

¹⁴ 'So this day shall be to you a
memorial; and you shall keep it as a
feast to the Lᴏʀᴅ throughout your generations. You shall keep it as a feast
by an everlasting ordinance. ¹⁵ Seven
days you shall eat unleavened bread.

On the first day you shall remove
leaven from your houses. For whoever
eats leavened bread from the first day
until the seventh day, that person shall
be cut off from Israel. ¹⁶ On the first
day *there shall be* a holy convocation,
and on the seventh day there shall be
a holy convocation for you. No manner of work shall be done on them;
but *that* which everyone must eat—
that only may be prepared by you.
¹⁷ So you shall observe *the Feast of*
Unleavened Bread, for on this same
day I will have brought your armies
out of the land of Egypt. Therefore you
shall observe this day throughout your
generations as an everlasting ordinance. ¹⁸ In the first *month,* on the
fourteenth day of the month at evening, you shall eat unleavened bread,
until the twenty-first day of the month

WORDFINDER

12:11 Passover The greatest Hebrew celebration. The people remember that the
Lord "passed over" their homes in Egypt because a lamb's blood was applied to
their doorways (see Exodus 12). After the death of the firstborn in Egypt, Pharaoh
freed God's people.

DIGGING IN

12:1–28 The Passover Passover was
the first great ceremony of the Jews when
they left Egypt. Passover was kept on the
fourteenth day of the first Hebrew month,
called Nisan (pronounced *NIGH-san*).

You already know that God judged the
Egyptians. The tenth judgment in Egypt
was the death of all the firstborn of the
land—both people and animals. But God
commanded each family of Israel to kill
a lamb and paint the blood of that lamb
on the sides and top of the doorway of
their home. When God saw the blood, He
"passed over" that home and no one died
there. That was the terrible night when
Pharaoh begged Moses to take Israel out
of Egypt. So Israel remembers Passover
to this day as the night when the Lord
passed over Israel, saving their children
and setting them all free.

Jesus is our Passover Lamb who was
killed for us. When God sees that we have
accepted the blood of Jesus as His sacrifice for us, He passes over us, and we
escape His judgment.

Passover was a happy time when God's
people remembered how He spared their lives
by passing over every home marked with
blood.

at evening. 19 For seven days no leaven shall be found in your houses, since whoever eats what is leavened, that same person shall be cut off from the congregation of Israel, whether *he is* a stranger or a native of the land. 20 You shall eat nothing leavened; in all your dwellings you shall eat unleavened bread.' "

21 Then Moses called for all the elders of Israel and said to them, "Pick out and take lambs for yourselves according to your families, and kill the Passover *lamb*. 22 And you shall take a bunch of hyssop, dip *it* in the blood that *is* in the basin, and strike the lintel and the two doorposts with the blood that *is* in the basin. And none of you shall go out of the door of his house until morning. 23 For the LORD will pass through to strike the Egyptians; and when He sees the blood on the lintel and on the two doorposts, the LORD will pass over the door and not allow the destroyer to come into your houses to strike *you*. 24 And you shall observe this thing as an ordinance for you and your sons forever. 25 It will come to pass when you come to the land which the LORD will give you, just as He promised, that you shall keep this service. 26 And it shall be, when your children say to you, 'What do you mean by this service?' 27 that you shall say, 'It *is* the Passover sacrifice of the LORD, who passed over the houses of the children of Israel in Egypt when He struck the Egyptians and delivered our households.' " So the people bowed their heads and worshiped. 28 Then the children of Israel went away and did *so;* just as the LORD had commanded Moses and Aaron, so they did.

29 And it came to pass at midnight that the LORD struck all the firstborn in the land of Egypt, from the firstborn of Pharaoh who sat on his throne to the firstborn of the captive who *was* in the dungeon, and all the firstborn of livestock. 30 So Pharaoh rose in the night, he, all his servants, and all the Egyptians; and there was a great cry in Egypt, for *there was* not a house where *there was* not one dead.

31 Then he called for Moses an Aaron by night, and said, "Rise, g out from among my people, both you and the children of Israel. And go serve the LORD as you have said. 32 Also take your flocks and your herds, as you have said, and be gone; and bless me also."

33 And the Egyptians urged the people, that they might send them out of the land in haste. For they said, "We *shall* all *be* dead." 34 So the people took their dough before it was leavened, having their kneading bowls bound up in their clothes on their shoulders. 35 Now the children of Israel had done according to the word of Moses, and they had asked from the Egyptians articles of silver, articles of gold, and clothing. 36 And the LORD had given the people favor in the sight of the Egyptians, so that they granted

An Egyptian scribe writes with strange "pencils."

hat they requested. Thus they *red the Egyptians.*

Then the children of Israel joured from Rameses to Succoth, out six hundred thousand men on ot, besides children. ³⁸ A mixed mulitude went up with them also, and flocks and herds—a great deal of livestock. ³⁹ And they baked unleavened cakes of the dough which they had brought out of Egypt; for it was not leavened, because they were driven out of Egypt and could not wait, nor had they prepared provisions for themselves.

⁴⁰ Now the sojourn of the children of Israel who lived in Egypt *was* four hundred and thirty years. ⁴¹ And it came to pass at the end of the four hundred and thirty years—on that very same day—it came to pass that all the armies of the LORD went out from the land of Egypt. ⁴² It *is* a night of solemn observance to the LORD for bringing them out of the land of Egypt. This *is* that night of the LORD, a solemn observance for all the children of Israel throughout their generations.

⁴³ And the LORD said to Moses and Aaron, "This *is* the ordinance of the Passover: No foreigner shall eat it. ⁴⁴ But every man's servant who is bought for money, when you have circumcised him, then he may eat it. ⁴⁵ A sojourner and a hired servant shall not eat it. ⁴⁶ In one house it shall be eaten; you shall not carry any of the flesh outside the house, nor shall you break one of its bones. ⁴⁷ All the congregation of Israel shall keep it. ⁴⁸ And

DIGGING IN

12:31–42 God's People Leave Egypt
Pharaoh was in a hurry to get Israel out of Egypt, and the people of Israel were also anxious to leave. So the Lord commanded them to eat the Passover lamb in their homes that night. Also they prepared bread that was "unleavened" (pronounced *un-LEV-und*). This is bread that has not been given time to rise before it is baked. There was no time for the bread to rise that night. So the people took the unbaked bread dough with them.

This was an exciting time in the history of Israel. But leaving Egypt is also a picture of how God wants *you* to follow Him—QUICKLY!

Israel had lost 430 years serving in Egypt. Now they were going out to serve God. You too must act quickly to leave everything that keeps you from serving Jesus. Now is the time to make that choice.

The people of Israel crossed the Red Sea near this spot.

when a stranger dwells with you *and wants* to keep the Passover to the LORD, let all his males be circumcised, and then let him come near and keep it; and he shall be as a native of the land. For no uncircumcised person shall eat it. 49 One law shall be for the native-born and for the stranger who dwells among you."

50 Thus all the children of Israel did; as the LORD commanded Moses and Aaron, so they did. 51 And it came to pass, on that very same day, that the LORD brought the children of Israel out of the land of Egypt according to their armies.

Israel is to remember the Exodus

13 Then the LORD spoke to Moses, saying, 2 "Consecrate to Me all the firstborn, whatever opens the womb among the children of Israel, *both* of man and beast; it is Mine."

3 And Moses said to the people: "Remember this day in which you went out of Egypt, out of the house of bondage; for by strength of hand the LORD brought you out of this *place.* No leavened bread shall be eaten. 4 On this day you are going out, in the month Abib. 5 And it shall be, when the LORD brings you into the land of the Canaanites and the Hittites and the Amorites and the Hivites and the Jebusites, which He swore to your fathers to give you, a land flowing with milk and honey, that you shall keep this service in this month. 6 Seven days you shall eat unleavened bread, and on the seventh day *there shall be* a feast to the LORD. 7 Unleavened bread shall be eaten seven days. And no leavened bread shall be seen among you, nor shall leaven be seen among you in all your quarters. 8 And you shall tell your son in that day, saying, 'This is done because of what the LORD did for me when I came up from Egypt.' 9 It shall be as a sign to you on your hand and as a memorial between your eyes, that the LORD's law may be in your mouth; for with a strong hand the LORD has brought you out of Egypt. 10 You shall

therefore keep this ordinance in its season from year to year.

11 "And it shall be, when the LORD brings you into the land of the Canaanites, as He swore to you and your fathers, and gives it to you, 12 that you shall set apart to the LORD all that open the womb, that is, every firstborn that comes from an animal which you have; the males *shall be* the LORD's. 13 But every firstborn of a donkey you shall redeem with a lamb; and if you will not redeem *it,* then you shall break its neck. And all the firstborn of man among your sons you shall redeem. 14 So it shall be, when your son asks you in time to come, saying, 'What *is* this?' that you shall say to him, 'By strength of hand the LORD brought us out of Egypt, out of the house of bondage. 15 And it came to pass, when Pharaoh was stubborn about letting us go, that the LORD killed all the firstborn in the land of Egypt, both the firstborn of man and the firstborn of beast. Therefore I sacrifice to the LORD all males that open the womb, but all the firstborn of my sons I redeem.' 16 It shall be as a sign on your hand and as frontlets between your eyes, for by strength of hand the LORD brought us out of Egypt."

17 Then it came to pass, when Pharaoh had let the people go, that God did not lead them *by* way of the land of the Philistines, although that *was* near; for God said, "Lest perhaps the people change their minds when they see war, and return to Egypt." 18 So God led the people around *by* way of the wilderness of the Red Sea. And the children of Israel went up in orderly ranks out of the land of Egypt.

19 And Moses took the bones of Joseph with him, for he had placed the children of Israel under solemn oath, saying, "God will surely visit you, and you shall carry up my bones from here with you."

20 So they took their journey from Succoth and camped in Etham at the edge of the wilderness. 21 And the LORD went before them by day in a pillar of cloud to lead the way, and

. . . . in a pillar of fire to give them
. . .o as to go by day and night.
. . . did not take away the pillar of
. .d by day or the pillar of fire by
. .ght *from* before the people.

Israel crosses the Red Sea

14 Now the LORD spoke to Moses, saying: 2 "Speak to the children of Israel, that they turn and camp before Pi Hahiroth, between Migdol and the sea, opposite Baal Zephon; you shall camp before it by the sea. 3 For Pharaoh will say of the children of Israel, 'They *are* bewildered by the land; the wilderness has closed them in.' 4 Then I will harden Pharaoh's heart, so that he will pursue them; and I will gain honor over Pharaoh and over all his army, that the Egyptians may know that I *am* the LORD." And they did so.

5 Now it was told the king of Egypt that the people had fled, and the heart of Pharaoh and his servants was turned against the people; and they said, "Why have we done this, that we have let Israel go from serving us?" 6 So he made ready his chariot and took his people with him. 7 Also, he took six hundred choice chariots, and all the chariots of Egypt with captains over every one of them. 8 And the LORD hardened the heart of Pharaoh king of Egypt, and he pursued the children of Israel; and the children of Israel went out with boldness. 9 So the Egyptians pursued them, all the horses *and* chariots of Pharaoh, his horsemen and his army, and overtook them camping by the sea beside Pi Hahiroth, before Baal Zephon.

10 And when Pharaoh drew near, the children of Israel lifted their eyes, and behold, the Egyptians marched after them. So they were very afraid, and the children of Israel cried out to the LORD. 11 Then they said to Moses, "Because *there were* no graves in Egypt, have you taken us away to die in the wilderness? Why have you so dealt with us, to bring us up out of Egypt? 12 *Is* this not the word that we told you in Egypt, saying, 'Let us alone that we

may serve the Egyptians'? For *it would have been* better for us to serve the Egyptians than that we should die in the wilderness."

13 And Moses said to the people, "Do not be afraid. Stand still, and see the salvation of the LORD, which He will accomplish for you today. For the Egyptians whom you see today, you shall see again no more forever. 14 The LORD will fight for you, and you shall hold your peace."

15 And the LORD said to Moses, "Why do you cry to Me? Tell the children of Israel to go forward. 16 "But lift up your rod, and stretch out your hand over the sea and divide it. And the children of Israel shall go on dry *ground* through the midst of the sea. 17 And I indeed will harden the hearts of the Egyptians, and they shall follow them. So I will gain honor over Pharaoh and over all his army, his chariots, and his horsemen. 18 Then the Egyptians shall know that I *am* the LORD, when I have gained honor for Myself over Pharaoh, his chariots, and his horsemen."

19 And the Angel of God, who went before the camp of Israel, moved and went behind them; and the pillar of cloud went from before them and stood behind them. 20 So it came between the camp of the Egyptians and the camp of Israel. Thus it was a cloud and darkness *to the one*, and it gave light by night *to the other*, so that the one did not come near the other all that night.

21 Then Moses stretched out his hand over the sea; and the LORD caused the sea to go *back* by a strong east wind all that night, and made the sea into dry *land*, and the waters were divided. 22 So the children of Israel went into the midst of the sea on the dry *ground*, and the waters *were* a wall to them on their right hand and on their left. 23 And the Egyptians pursued and went after them into the midst of the sea, all Pharaoh's horses, his chariots, and his horsemen.

24 Now it came to pass, in the morning watch, that the LORD looked down

The Exodus

Jordan River

CANAAN

The Great Sea (Mediterranean)

Dead Sea

LAND OF GOSHEN

Beersheba

Rameses?

Etham?

Migdol?

Kadesh-Barnea

Succoth?

EGYPT

SINAI

Nile River

Elath

Marah?

Gulf of Suez

Rephidim?

Gulf of Aqaba

Mount Sinai

RED SEA

It is moving day for Moses and more than 600,000 people with all their belongings! For four hundred years, God's people have been slaves in Egypt. Now, after ten awful plagues sent by God on the Egyptians, Pharaoh (FAY-row) has agreed to let His people go.

What are the first two stops on the long journey to the Promised Land? (12:37; 13:20) Why has God chosen this route? (13:18) Where does God tell Moses to set up camp? (14:2)

It looks as if God's people are trapped between the desert and the deep blue sea! Pharaoh's army is close on their heels. They must be scared to death! What great miracle takes place here? (14:13–28) Can you imagine how the people feel when God saves them from their enemies?

Moving south, the people are hot and thirsty. What happens at Marah (MARR-ah) and Rephidim (REFF-ih-dim)? (15:23–25; 17:1–6). At last Moses brings the tired travelers to the base of Mount Sinai (SIGH-nigh). What happens next changes everything for God's people, then and now! (20:1–17)

Jews Escape—Army Drowned!

Old Testament News Service

RED SEA—The Hebrew slaves who have made so much trouble for Egypt have escaped! Pharaoh led his army in hot pursuit of the fleeing Hebrews. When the army caught up to them, a blinding sandstorm or cloud confused the troops, and the Jews got away.

Eyewitnesses insist that the Red Sea parted, and the Jews crossed on dry land to the other side! Moses is reported to have held up his famous rod while the waters opened up.

Pharaoh's army, which chased the slaves into the dry seabed, was completely destroyed. Just as the troops reached the middle of the sea, the water fell back and drowned every last man. Without its army, the nation of Egypt is helpless.

upon the army of the Egyptians through the **pillar of fire and cloud,** and He troubled the army of the Egyptians. 25 And He took off their chariot wheels, so that they drove them with difficulty; and the Egyptians said, "Let us flee from the face of Israel, for the LORD fights for them against the Egyptians."

26 Then the LORD said to Moses, "Stretch out your hand over the sea, that the waters may come back upon the Egyptians, on their chariots, and on their horsemen." 27 And Moses stretched out his hand over the sea; and when the morning appeared, the sea returned to its full depth, while the Egyptians were fleeing into it. So the LORD overthrew the Egyptians in the midst of the sea. 28 Then the waters returned and covered the chariots, the horsemen, *and* all the army of Pharaoh that came into the sea after them. Not so much as one of them remained. 29 But the children of Israel had walked on dry *land* in the midst of the sea, and the waters *were* a wall to them on their right hand and on their left.

30 So the LORD saved Israel that day out of the hand of the Egyptians, and Israel saw the Egyptians dead on the seashore. 31 Thus Israel saw the great work which the LORD had done in Egypt; so the people feared the LORD, and believed the LORD and His servant Moses.

Moses sings a song to the Lord

15 Then Moses and the children of Israel sang this song to the LORD, and spoke, saying:

"I will sing to the LORD,
For He has triumphed
    gloriously!
The horse and its rider
He has thrown into the sea!
2 The LORD *is* my strength and
    song,
And He has become my
    salvation;
He *is* my God, and I will praise
    Him;
My father's God, and I will exalt
    Him.
3 The LORD *is* a man of war;
The LORD *is* His name.
4 Pharaoh's chariots and his army
    He has cast into the sea;
His chosen captains also are
    drowned in the Red Sea.

🌐 WORDFINDER

14:24 Pillar of Fire and Cloud A special appearance of God. This was one of the ways the invisible God once showed Himself to human eyes.

What Pharaoh Learned

I thought I had trapped Moses and his people that day on the edge of the Red Sea. Then the east wind blew all night and divided the water. Before long, the Jews were crossing on dry land to the other side.

So I sent my troops to chase them. That was my big mistake. I should have learned after my son's death that God meant to save those Jews at any cost. This time it cost the lives of my whole army. The sea fell back on my soldiers, and they all drowned.

I've learned too late that there is one true God. To obey Him is the only way that makes sense.

5   The depths have covered them;
    They sank to the bottom like a
       stone.

6   "Your right hand, O LORD, has
       become glorious in power;
    Your right hand, O LORD, has
       dashed the enemy in pieces.
7   And in the greatness of Your
       excellence
    You have overthrown those who
       rose against You;
    You sent forth Your wrath;
    It consumed them like stubble.
8   And with the blast of Your
       nostrils
    The waters were gathered
       together;
    The floods stood upright like a
       heap;
    The depths congealed in the
       heart of the sea.
9   The enemy said, 'I will pursue,
    I will overtake,
    I will divide the spoil;
    My desire shall be satisfied on
       them.
    I will draw my sword,
    My hand shall destroy them.'
10 You blew with Your wind,
    The sea covered them;
    They sank like lead in the mighty
       waters.

11 "Who is like You, O LORD, among
       the gods?
    Who is like You, glorious in
       holiness,
    Fearful in praises, doing
       wonders?

12 You stretched out Your right
       hand;
    The earth swallowed them.
13 You in Your mercy have led
       forth
    The people whom You have
       redeemed;
    You have guided them in Your
       strength
    To Your holy habitation.

14 "The people will hear and be
       afraid;
    Sorrow will take hold of the
       inhabitants of Philistia.
15 Then the chiefs of Edom will be
       dismayed;
    The mighty men of Moab,
    Trembling will take hold of
       them;
    All the inhabitants of Canaan will
       melt away.
16 Fear and dread will fall on
       them;
    By the greatness of Your
       arm
    They will be as still as a stone,
    Till Your people pass over, O
       LORD,
    Till the people pass over
    Whom You have purchased.
17 You will bring them in and plant
       them
    In the mountain of Your
       inheritance,
    In the place, O LORD, which You
       have made
    For Your own dwelling,
    The sanctuary, O LORD, which
       Your hands have established.

18 "The LORD shall reign forever and ever."

19 For the horses of Pharaoh went with his chariots and his horsemen into the sea, and the LORD brought back the waters of the sea upon them. But the children of Israel went on dry *land* in the midst of the sea.

20 Then Miriam the prophetess, the sister of Aaron, took the timbrel in her hand; and all the women went out after her with timbrels and with dances. 21 And Miriam answered them:

> "Sing to the LORD,
> For He has triumphed
>   gloriously!
> The horse and its rider
> He has thrown into the
>   sea!"

22 So Moses brought Israel from the Red Sea; then they went out into the Wilderness of Shur. And they went three days in the wilderness and found no water. 23 Now when they came to Marah, they could not drink the waters of Marah, for they *were* bitter. Therefore the name of it was called Marah. 24 And the people complained against Moses, saying, "What shall we drink?" 25 So he cried out to the LORD, and the LORD showed him a tree. When he cast *it* into the waters, the waters were made sweet.

There He made a statute and an ordinance for them, and there He tested them, 26 and said, "If you diligently heed the voice of the LORD your God and do what is right in His sight, give ear to His commandments and keep all His statutes, I will put none of the diseases on you which I have brought

When God rolled back the waters, the children of Israel walked across the Red Sea on dry ground.

on the Egyptians. For I *am* the Lᴏʀᴅ who heals you."

²⁷ Then they came to Elim, where there *were* twelve wells of water and seventy palm trees; so they camped there by the waters.

God sends manna and quails for food

16 And they journeyed from Elim, and all the congregation of the children of Israel came to the Wilderness of Sin, which is between Elim and Sinai, on the fifteenth day of the second month after they departed from the land of Egypt. ² Then the whole congregation of the children of Israel complained against Moses and Aaron in the wilderness. ³ And the children of Israel said to them, "Oh, that we had died by the hand of the Lᴏʀᴅ in the land of Egypt, when we sat by the pots of meat *and* when we ate bread to the full! For you have brought us out into this wilderness to kill this whole assembly with hunger."

⁴ Then the Lᴏʀᴅ said to Moses, "Behold, I will rain bread from heaven for you. And the people shall go out and gather a certain quota every day, that I may test them, whether they will walk in My law or not. ⁵ And it shall be on the sixth day that they shall prepare what they bring in, and it shall be twice as much as they gather daily."

⁶ Then Moses and Aaron said to all the children of Israel, "At evening you shall know that the Lᴏʀᴅ has brought you out of the land of Egypt. ⁷ And in the morning you shall *see* the glory of the Lᴏʀᴅ; for He hears your complaints against the Lᴏʀᴅ. But what *are* we, that you complain against us?" ⁸ Also Moses said, "*This shall be seen* when the Lᴏʀᴅ gives you meat to eat in the evening, and in the morning bread to the full; for the Lᴏʀᴅ hears your complaints which you make against Him. And what *are* we? Your complaints *are* not against us but against the Lᴏʀᴅ."

⁹ Then Moses spoke to Aaron, "Say to all the congregation of the children of Israel, 'Come near before the Lᴏʀᴅ, for He has heard your complaints.' " ¹⁰ Now it came to pass, as Aaron spoke to the whole congregation of the children of Israel, that they looked toward the wilderness, and behold, the glory of the Lᴏʀᴅ appeared in the cloud.

¹¹ And the Lᴏʀᴅ spoke to Moses, saying, ¹² "I have heard the complaints of the children of Israel. Speak to them, saying, 'At twilight you shall eat meat, and in the morning you shall be filled with bread. And you shall know that I *am* the Lᴏʀᴅ your God.' "

¹³ So it was that quails came up at evening and covered the camp, and in the morning the dew lay all around the camp. ¹⁴ And when the layer of dew lifted, there, on the surface of the wilderness, was a small round substance, *as* fine as frost on the ground. ¹⁵ So when the children of Israel saw *it*, they said to one another, "What is it?" For they did not know what it *was*.

And Moses said to them, "This *is* the bread which the Lᴏʀᴅ has given

DIGGING IN

16:4 Bread from Heaven From the skies, the Lord sent Israel a special nourishing food called manna, which means "What is it?" and looked like frost on the ground. There was enough of this food for every day's need in the desert. Manna could be boiled, baked, ground up, baked in pans, and made into cakes.

There was a special lesson in the manna for the Hebrew people—they could trust God for their daily needs. The only time their daily needs failed to be met was when the people stopped trusting God.

Jesus taught us to pray, "Give us this day our daily bread." You can learn from the manna: (1) God wants you to trust Him for your needs; (2) Jesus is the *true Bread* from heaven. In fact, He called Himself the "bread of life" (John 6:35). You need the life that only Jesus gives.

you to eat. ¹⁶ This is the thing which the LORD has commanded: 'Let every man gather it according to each one's need, one omer for each person; *according to the* number of persons; let every man take for *those* who *are* in his tent.' "

¹⁷ Then the children of Israel did so and gathered, some more, some less. ¹⁸ So when they measured *it* by omers, he who gathered much had nothing left over, and he who gathered little had no lack. Every man had gathered according to each one's need. ¹⁹ And Moses said, "Let no one leave any of it till morning." ²⁰ Notwithstanding they did not heed Moses. But some of them left part of it until morning, and it bred worms and stank. And Moses was angry with them. ²¹ So they gathered it every morning, every man according to his need. And when the sun became hot, it melted.

²² And so it was, on the sixth day, *that* they gathered twice as much bread, two omers for each one. And all the rulers of the congregation came and told Moses. ²³ Then he said to them, "This *is what* the LORD has said: 'Tomorrow *is* a Sabbath rest, a holy Sabbath to the LORD. Bake what you will bake *today,* and boil what you will boil; and lay up for yourselves all that remains, to be kept until morning.' " ²⁴ So they laid it up till morning, as Moses commanded; and it did not stink, nor were there any worms in it. ²⁵ Then Moses said, "Eat that today, for today *is* a Sabbath to the LORD; today you will not find it in the field. ²⁶ Six days you shall gather it, but on the seventh day, the Sabbath, there will be none."

²⁷ Now it happened *that some* of the people went out on the seventh day to gather, but they found none. ²⁸ And the LORD said to Moses, "How long do you refuse to keep My commandments and My laws? ²⁹ See! For the LORD has given you the Sabbath; therefore He gives you on the sixth day bread for two days. Let every man remain in his place; let no man go out of his place on the seventh day."

³⁰ So the people rested on the seventh day.

³¹ And the house of Israel called its name Manna. And it *was* like white coriander seed, and the taste of it *was* like wafers *made* with honey.

³² Then Moses said, "This *is* the thing which the LORD has commanded: 'Fill an omer with it, to be kept for your generations, that they may see the bread with which I fed you in the wilderness, when I brought you out of the land of Egypt.' " ³³ And Moses said to Aaron, "Take a pot and put an omer of manna in it, and lay it up before the LORD, to be kept for your generations." ³⁴ As the LORD commanded Moses, so Aaron laid it up before the Testimony, to be kept. ³⁵ And the children of Israel ate manna forty years, until they came to an inhabited land; they ate manna until they came to the border of the land of Canaan. ³⁶ Now an omer *is* one-tenth of an ephah.

God gives the people water

17 Then all the congregation of the children of Israel set out on their journey from the Wilderness of Sin, according to the commandment of the LORD, and camped in Rephidim; but *there was* no water for the people to drink. ² Therefore the people contended with Moses, and said, "Give us water, that we may drink."

So Moses said to them, "Why do you contend with me? Why do you tempt the LORD?"

³ And the people thirsted there for water, and the people complained against Moses, and said, "Why *is* it you have brought us up out of Egypt, to kill us and our children and our livestock with thirst?"

⁴ So Moses cried out to the LORD, saying, "What shall I do with this people? They are almost ready to stone me!"

⁵ And the LORD said to Moses, "Go on before the people, and take with you some of the elders of Israel. Also take in your hand your rod with which you struck the river, and go. ⁶ Behold,

Can You Get Water Out of the Rock?

The desert of Sinai (pronounced *SIGH-nigh*) was a very dry place, as it still is today, but God supplied water for the people to drink. Moses struck the rock, and the water came out. Jesus is the true Rock. He said, "Whoever believes in Me shall never thirst" (see John 6:35).

I will stand before you there on the rock in Horeb; and you shall strike the rock, and water will come out of it, that the people may drink."

And Moses did so in the sight of the elders of Israel. 7 So he called the name of the place Massah and Meribah, because of the contention of the children of Israel, and because they tempted the LORD, saying, "Is the LORD among us or not?"

8 Now Amalek came and fought with Israel in Rephidim. 9 And Moses said to Joshua, "Choose us some men and go out, fight with Amalek. Tomorrow I will stand on the top of the hill with the rod of God in my hand." 10 So Joshua did as Moses said to him, and fought with Amalek. And Moses, Aaron, and Hur went up to the top of the hill. 11 And so it was, when Moses held up his hand, that Israel prevailed; and when he let down his hand, Amalek prevailed. 12 But Moses' hands *became* heavy; so they took a stone and put *it* under him, and he sat on it. And Aaron and Hur supported his hands, one on one side, and the other on the other side; and his hands were steady until the going down of the sun. 13 So Joshua defeated Amalek and his people with the edge of the sword.

14 Then the LORD said to Moses, "Write this *for* a memorial in the book and recount *it* in the hearing of Joshua, that I will utterly blot out the remembrance of Amalek from under heaven." 15 And Moses built an altar and called its name, The-LORD-Is-My-Banner; 16 for he said, "Because

the LORD has sworn: the LORD *will have* war with Amalek from generation to generation."

Moses chooses judges

18 And Jethro, the priest of Midian, Moses' father-in-law, heard of all that God had done for Moses and for Israel His people—that the LORD had brought Israel out of Egypt. 2 Then Jethro, Moses' father-in-law, took Zipporah, Moses' wife, after he had sent her back, 3 with her two sons, of whom the name of one *was* Gershom (for he said, "I have been a stranger in a foreign land") 4 and the name of the other *was* Eliezer (for *he said,* "The God of my father *was* my help, and delivered me from the sword of Pharaoh"); 5 and Jethro, Moses' father-in-law, came with his sons and his wife to Moses in the wilderness, where he was encamped at the mountain of God. 6 Now he had said to Moses, "I, your father-in-law Jethro, am coming to you with your wife and her two sons with her."

7 So Moses went out to meet his father-in-law, bowed down, and kissed him. And they asked each other about *their* well-being, and they went into the tent. 8 And Moses told his father-in-law all that the LORD had done to Pharaoh and to the Egyptians for Israel's sake, all the hardship that had come upon them on the way, and *how* the LORD had delivered them. 9 Then Jethro rejoiced for all the good which the LORD had done for Israel, whom He had delivered out of the hand of the Egyptians. 10 And Jethro said, "Blessed *be* the LORD, who has delivered you out of the hand of the Egyptians and out of the hand of Pharaoh, *and* who has delivered the people from under the hand of the Egyptians. 11 Now I know that the LORD *is* greater than all the gods; for in the very thing in which they behaved proudly, *He was* above them." 12 Then Jethro, Moses' father-in-law, took a burnt offering and *other* sacrifices *to offer* to God. And Aaron came with all the elders of Israel to eat

bread with Moses' father-in-law before God.

13 And so it was, on the next day, that Moses sat to judge the people; and the people stood before Moses from morning until evening. 14 So when Moses' father-in-law saw all that he did for the people, he said, "What is this thing that you are doing for the people? Why do you alone sit, and all the people stand before you from morning until evening?"

15 And Moses said to his father-in-law, "Because the people come to me to inquire of God. 16 When they have a difficulty, they come to me, and I judge between one and another; and I make known the statutes of God and His laws."

17 So Moses' father-in-law said to him, "The thing that you do is not good. 18 Both you and these people who are with you will surely wear yourselves out. For this thing is too much for you; you are not able to perform it by yourself. 19 Listen now to my voice; I will give you counsel, and God will be with you: Stand before God for the people, so that you may bring the difficulties to God. 20 And you shall teach them the statutes and the laws, and show them the way in which they must walk and the work they must do. 21 Moreover you shall select from all the people able men, such as fear God, men of truth, hating covetousness; and place such over them to be rulers of thousands, rulers of hundreds, rulers of fifties, and rulers of tens. 22 And let them judge the people at all times.

Then it will be that every great matter they shall bring to you, but every small matter they themselves shall judge. So it will be easier for you, for they will bear the burden with you. 23 If you do this thing, and God so commands you, then you will be able to endure, and all this people will also go to their place in peace."

24 So Moses heeded the voice of his father-in-law and did all that he had said. 25 And Moses chose able men out of all Israel, and made them heads over the people: rulers of thousands, rulers of hundreds, rulers of fifties, and rulers of tens. 26 So they judged the people at all times; the hard cases they brought to Moses, but they judged every small case themselves.

27 Then Moses let his father-in-law depart, and he went his way to his own land.

God speaks to Moses at Mount Sinai

19 In the third month after the children of Israel had gone out of the land of Egypt, on the same day, they came to the Wilderness of Sinai. 2 For they had departed from Rephidim, had come to the Wilderness of Sinai, and camped in the wilderness. So Israel camped there before the mountain.

3 And Moses went up to God, and the LORD called to him from the mountain, saying, "Thus you shall say to the house of Jacob, and tell the children of Israel: 4 'You have seen what I did

DIGGING IN

18:13-24 Good Advice for Moses Moses was the only leader the people had. Then his father-in-law, Jethro (pronounced JETH-row), gave Moses some good advice: "Don't try to do everything yourself. You need others to help you care for the needs of the people."

So Moses selected leaders for groups beginning with a leader for each one thousand people, then for each one hundred people, for each fifty people, and for each

ten people. This idea for leaders is still followed today by most large groups, including your church.

God doesn't want us to be loners. We need one another. Sometimes God is the only One we need. But we also need to help each other get God's work done in the world. We need the wisdom of others to help us follow God's pathway. "In the multitude of counselors there is safety" (Proverbs 11:14).

A New Religion in the Sinai Desert?

CBN (Canaan Broadcasting Network)—The desert seems to be the last place in the world to begin a new religion. But, as you can see, our camera crews are showing you this amazing event.

Moses has gone up to the top of Mount Sinai, which is now covered by a thick cloud of smoke. Lightning flashes are darting from the clouds. There is loud thundering, and the earth is shaking. Some members of our news crew are afraid to stay here. The people of Israel are all standing at the foot of the mountain, waiting for Moses to come down.

Now you can hear a loud trumpet and the sound of a voice like thunder. The Lord of the Hebrews is announcing His Ten Commandments to Moses. The voice is frightening, and the people are terrified!

Is this how a whole new religion begins? The Hebrews believe these Ten Commandments are what God expects of all people everywhere. Maybe they're right. We have never seen anything like this display of power!

to the Egyptians, and *how* I bore you on eagles' wings and brought you to Myself. 5 Now therefore, if you will indeed obey My voice and keep My covenant, then you shall be a special treasure to Me above all people; for all the earth *is* Mine. 6 And you shall be to Me a kingdom of priests and a holy nation.' These *are* the words which you shall speak to the children of Israel."

7 So Moses came and called for the elders of the people, and laid before

them all these words which the Lord commanded him. 8 Then all the people answered together and said, "All that the Lord has spoken we will do." So Moses brought back the words of the people to the Lord. 9 And the Lord said to Moses, "Behold, I come to you in the thick cloud, that the people may hear when I speak with you, and believe you forever."

So Moses told the words of the people to the Lord.

10 Then the Lord said to Moses,

God spoke to Moses from the top of Mount Sinai, then gave him the Ten Commandments.

"Go to the people and consecrate them today and tomorrow, and let them wash their clothes. ¹¹ And let them be ready for the third day. For on the third day the LORD will come down upon Mount Sinai in the sight of all the people. ¹² You shall set bounds for the people all around, saying, 'Take heed to yourselves that you do not go up to the mountain or touch its base. Whoever touches the mountain shall surely be put to death. ¹³ Not a hand shall touch him, but he shall surely be stoned or shot with an arrow; whether man or beast, he shall not live.' When the trumpet sounds long, they shall come near the mountain."

¹⁴ So Moses went down from the mountain to the people and sanctified the people, and they washed their clothes. ¹⁵ And he said to the people, "Be ready for the third day; do not come near your wives."

¹⁶ Then it came to pass on the third day, in the morning, that there were thunderings and lightnings, and a thick cloud on the mountain; and the sound of the trumpet was very loud, so that all the people who were in the camp trembled. ¹⁷ And Moses brought the people out of the camp to meet with God, and they stood at the foot of the mountain. ¹⁸ Now Mount Sinai was completely in smoke, because the LORD descended upon it in fire. Its smoke ascended like the smoke of a furnace, and the whole mountain quaked greatly. ¹⁹ And when the blast of the trumpet sounded long and be-

came louder and louder, Moses spoke, and God answered him by voice. ²⁰ Then the LORD came down upon Mount Sinai, on the top of the mountain. And the LORD called Moses to the top of the mountain, and Moses went up.

²¹ And the LORD said to Moses, "Go down and warn the people, lest they break through to gaze at the LORD, and many of them perish. ²² Also let the priests who come near the LORD consecrate themselves, lest the LORD break out against them."

²³ But Moses said to the LORD, "The people cannot come up to Mount Sinai; for You warned us, saying, 'Set bounds around the mountain and consecrate it.'"

²⁴ Then the LORD said to him, "Away! Get down and then come up, you and Aaron with you. But do not let the priests and the people break through to come up to the LORD, lest He break out against them." ²⁵ So Moses went down to the people and spoke to them.

God gives Moses the Ten Commandments

20 And God spoke all these words, saying:

2 "I am the LORD your God, who brought you out of the land of Egypt, out of the house of bondage.

3 "You shall have no other gods before Me.

⚒ DIGGING IN

19:18 Love Your Neighbor Some people think Jesus is the One who first spoke God's commandment to love your neighbor as yourself (see Mark 12:31). But Jesus was quoting the very words that God spoke to Moses hundreds of years before. God has always wanted His people to love one another. If we don't love others, then we don't love God either (see 1 John 4:10.)

God has given us many clues about what love is like. Have you read what God

says about love in 1 Corinthians 13? That chapter describes exactly how love works.

Love can't be just nice words. The real proof of love is kind deeds. The best examples of love are people who think of others before they think of themselves. That's what Jesus did when He went to the Cross for you. He made Himself poor so you could be rich in heavenly treasure.

20:1–3 Who Is God? You hear the word God used a lot. Often the word is

4 "You shall not make for yourself a carved image—any likeness *of anything* that *is* in heaven above, or that *is* in the earth beneath, or that *is* in the water under the earth; 5 you shall not bow down to them nor serve them. For I, the LORD your God, *am* a jealous God, visiting the iniquity of the fathers upon the children to the third and fourth *generations* of those who hate Me, 6 but showing mercy to thousands, to those who love Me and keep My commandments.

7 "You shall not take the name of the LORD your God in vain, for the LORD will not hold *him* guiltless who takes His name in vain.

8 "Remember the Sabbath day, to keep it holy. 9 Six days you

⚒ DIGGING IN

used as a curse word. When you think about it, doesn't it seem strange that people use that word to express their anger?

Who are we talking about when we say "God"? Earlier we talked about God as Moses first met Him in the desert (Exodus 3). Then God said, "I AM WHO I AM." Does that sound strange to you?

Let's try to understand what God is saying. He is telling us that He is the One who is always present even though we can't see Him. This means we can't get away from God.

Some people like to say, "God has nothing to do with me!" That can't be true. Otherwise, they wouldn't be using His name whenever they curse. God is always speaking to us *inside,* and He is always demanding our attention and our obedience.

20:4–6 Worship God Only The greatest foolishness of sin is that we worship something or someone God made instead of God Himself. In Romans 1:25, the apostle Paul says we worship and serve the creation instead of the Creator. That is great foolishness.

We think it's funny that some peoples in the world worship images of animals or other objects. We know that such things can't answer prayers. People everywhere need the true God.

In an earlier note we spoke about the true God and how He is always demanding our attention and obedience. Man's greatest sin is that he prefers to worship something less than his Creator.

We have no excuse now, because Jesus came and showed us exactly what God is like. Let's worship only the God who made us so we can enjoy Him forever.

20:7 Honor God's Name We have already partly explained why people curse God when they're angry.

This is a big reason why those who love God must be careful about using His name. Jesus said, "Hallowed be Your name." When we talk about God, or talk to Him silently or out loud, we should be careful what we say.

Sometimes we may pray out loud where other people are listening. At those times, people should know by the way we talk to Him that we love Him. So don't use His name in an insulting or even in a careless way. God truly is your Friend, but He is not your "old buddy"!

If you were invited to the White House to see the President, how would you speak to him? What would you be thinking about? You would think, "What a great privilege to talk to my president!" You would say, "Sir, thank you for inviting me." When we talk to God, we should be thinking, "Thank You, Lord, for making me Your child."

20:8 Keep the Lord's Day God worked six days to make the heavens and the earth. He rested on the seventh day. That was a good example.

In olden days our ancestors had to work so hard they were glad when Sunday came and they could rest. Now that we have machines to do a lot of our work, we have more free time. So many people spend the Lord's Day just having a good time at the beach or at a ball game.

To know God, His people have to spend time with Him. If they don't spend shall labor and do all your work, ¹⁰ but the seventh day *is* the Sabbath of the LORD your God. *In it* you shall do no work: you, nor your son, nor your daughter, nor your male servant, nor your female servant, nor your cattle, nor your stranger who *is* within your gates. ¹¹ For *in* six days the LORD made the heavens and the earth, the sea, and all that *is* in them, and rested the seventh day. Therefore the LORD blessed the Sabbath day and hallowed it.

¹² "Honor your father and your mother, that your days may be long upon the land which the LORD your God is giving you.

¹³ "You shall not murder.

¹⁴ "You shall not commit adultery.

¹⁵ "You shall not steal.

DIGGING IN

time with God, He will become a stranger. Do you want to know God as He planned you should know Him? Then keep the Lord's Day. Be able to say, "I was glad when they said to me, 'Let us go into the house of the Lord' " (Psalm 122:1).

20:12 Honor Your Elders The commandment God gave to Moses is, "Honor your father and your mother." But some of us don't have both a father and a mother. Many of us have only one parent. And some of us have part-time parents who come home at different times of the day and night.

Sometimes you're lonely, and you have no one to talk to. Keep asking God, and He will send someone who will listen and talk to you. God cares very much for you, and He hears your prayers to Him. God wants to be like a great Father and Mother to you.

If you do have a mother and dad who love God and love you, we say, "Honor your father and your mother." Put them first on the list of people you admire. People who honor their parents are people who please God. God even promises that you will "live long upon the land which the Lord your God is giving you."

20:13 Be Careful for the Lives of Others All life is precious just because God created it. And He made all life beautiful. If you watch animals carefully, you realize how wonderful life is.

But God did something special when He created people. He made us in His image. (See the note on Genesis 1.) That is why God has warned us not to kill others. When we hurt people, we also hurt God.

You can best understand this commandment by looking at God's command to love your neighbor as yourself (see Leviticus 19:18). When you love people, you look for ways to make their lives better. God created life; He loves life. We can be part of God's desire to improve life for those around us.

Some people have never heard and understood the gospel of Jesus that promises them life: "I have come that they may have life, and that they may have it more abundantly" (John 10:10).

20:14 Be Faithful When You Marry God created us male and female. He knew that we would need the love of a special companion in life. That's why God created Eve for Adam. God meant this to be a truly beautiful arrangement.

Love best describes what God is like. God loves everything He made, and He also meant us to love each other, especially our partners in marriage. But love fails when sin comes into our lives. That is why so many marriages break up.

Being faithful to the one you marry makes good sense. Your husband or wife is God's special gift to you and should be your best earthly friend. No one else should ever take that person's place. We hope you will think a lot about this important commandment while you're still young.

20:15 Stealing Is a Sin It's an unhappy fact that some people steal the things that belong to others. Sin breaks God's loving arrangements for our lives, and the sin of stealing causes special suffering. If you love someone, you care

16 "You shall not bear false witness against your neighbor.

17 "You shall not covet your neighbor's house; you shall not covet your neighbor's wife, nor his male servant, nor his female servant, nor his ox, nor his donkey, nor anything that *is* your neighbor's."

18 Now all the people witnessed the thunderings, the lightning flashes, the sound of the trumpet, and the mountain smoking; and when the people saw *it,* they trembled and stood afar off. 19 Then they said to Moses, "You speak with us, and we will hear; but let not God speak with us, lest we die."

20 And Moses said to the people, "Do not fear; for God has come to test you, and that His fear may be be-fore you, so that you may not sin."

21 So the people stood afar off, but Moses drew near the thick darkness where God *was.*

22 Then the LORD said to Moses, "Thus you shall say to the children of Israel: 'You have seen that I have talked with you from heaven. 23 You shall not make *anything to be* with Me—gods of silver or gods of gold you shall not make for yourselves. 24 An altar of earth you shall make for Me, and you shall sacrifice on it your burnt of-ferings and your peace offerings, your sheep and your oxen. In every place where I record My name I will come to you, and I will bless you. 25 And if you make Me an altar of stone, you shall not build it of hewn stone; for if you use your tool on it, you have

✦ DIGGING IN

about everything in that person's life, in-cluding his belongings.

God has given us the privilege of hav-ing property, whether it be a little or a lot. If you love your next-door neighbor, you are careful not to dump trash on the lawn or do other things that take away the privilege of enjoying that home. To do such things is a kind of stealing. The less people love God, the less they love their neighbors, and the less they care about their neighbors' property.

Wouldn't it be a wonderful world if we all cared as much about our neighbors' things as we care about our own things? That's what God really means when He says, "You shall not steal."

20:16 Lying Is a Sin God Himself is the greatest Truth. So God also loves the truth.

Lies bring confusion and pain. When people no longer care about the truth, they stop being like God, and they make God's world an unhappy place to live in.

Lying about a neighbor is especially wrong. Such lies can ruin one's good name, and no one will trust that person anymore. Think what happens when someone accuses an innocent person of murder or some other crime. Even though that person is innocent, he may suffer just as much as if he is guilty. Lies have great power to destroy people. The old saying, "Sticks and stones may break my bones, but names can never hurt me" just isn't true!

The greatest guard against lying is to love the truth and to tell the truth as often as we can. Be quick to praise someone when he or she does something good. Always be ready to tell people the truth about Jesus. In fact, Jesus said, "I am . . . the truth" (John 14:6).

20:17 Envy Is a Sin Some people may not take things that belong to others, but they may do something just as bad as they *want* the things that others have.

Of course, just wanting things may not hurt anyone. But when the desire be-comes *envy,* then it often does great harm. First, envy is a bad attitude that wastes our time and strength. People can make themselves sick by envying others. Envy also usually causes evil actions. If you envy someone long enough, then you will find ways to hurt that person. You may tell lies about people because you envy them. Or you may actually steal from them the things you wish you had.

There is a cure for envy: Be thankful for all that God has given you. None of us can truly say God has been unkind to us. He has given us much more than we deserve.

profaned it. ²⁶ Nor shall you go up by steps to My altar, that your nakedness may not be exposed on it.'

How to treat servants

21 "Now these *are* the judgments which you shall set before them: ² If you buy a Hebrew servant, he shall serve six years; and in the seventh he shall go out free and pay nothing. ³ If he comes in by himself, he shall go out by himself; if he *comes in* married, then his wife shall go out with him. ⁴ If his master has given him a wife, and she has borne him sons or daughters, the wife and her children shall be her master's, and he shall go out by himself. ⁵ But if the servant plainly says, 'I love my master, my wife, and my children; I will not go out free,' ⁶ then his master shall bring him to the judges. He shall also bring him to the door, or to the doorpost, and his master shall pierce his ear with an awl; and he shall serve him forever.

⁷ "And if a man sells his daughter to be a female slave, she shall not go out as the male slaves do. ⁸ If she does not please her master, who has betrothed her to himself, then he shall let her be redeemed. He shall have no right to sell her to a foreign people, since he has dealt deceitfully with her. ⁹ And if he has betrothed her to his son, he shall deal with her according to the custom of daughters. ¹⁰ If he takes another *wife,* he shall not diminish her food, her clothing, and her marriage rights. ¹¹ And if he does not do these three for her, then she shall go out free, without *paying* money.

¹² "He who strikes a man so that he dies shall surely be put to death. ¹³ However, if he did not lie in wait, but God delivered *him* into his hand, then I will appoint for you a place where he may flee.

¹⁴ "But if a man acts with premeditation against his neighbor, to kill him by treachery, you shall take him from My altar, that he may die.

¹⁵ "And he who strikes his father or his mother shall surely be put to death.

¹⁶ "He who kidnaps a man and sells him, or if he is found in his hand, shall surely be put to death.

¹⁷ "And he who curses his father or his mother shall surely be put to death.

¹⁸ "If men contend with each other, and one strikes the other with a stone or with *his* fist, and he does not die but is confined to *his* bed, ¹⁹ if he rises again and walks about outside with his staff, then he who struck *him* shall be acquitted. He shall only pay *for* the loss of his time, and shall provide *for him* to be thoroughly healed.

²⁰ "And if a man beats his male or female servant with a rod, so that he dies under his hand, he shall surely be punished. ²¹ Notwithstanding, if he remains alive a day or two, he shall not be punished; for he *is* his property.

²² "If men fight, and hurt a woman with child, so that she gives birth prematurely, yet no harm follows, he shall surely be punished accordingly as the woman's husband imposes on him; and he shall pay as the judges *determine.* ²³ But if *any* harm follows, then you shall give life for life, ²⁴ eye for eye, tooth for tooth, hand for hand, foot for foot, ²⁵ burn for burn, wound for wound, stripe for stripe.

²⁶ "If a man strikes the eye of his male or female servant, and destroys it, he shall let him go free for the sake of his eye. ²⁷ And if he knocks out the tooth of his male or female servant, he shall let him go free for the sake of his tooth.

²⁸ "If an ox gores a man or a woman to death, then the ox shall surely be stoned, and its flesh shall not be eaten; but the owner of the ox *shall be* acquitted. ²⁹ But if the ox tended to thrust with its horn in times past, and it has been made known to his owner, and he has not kept it confined, so that it has killed a man or a woman, the ox shall be stoned and its owner also shall be put to death. ³⁰ If there is imposed on him a sum of money, then he shall pay to redeem his life, whatever is imposed on him. ³¹ Whether it has gored a son or gored a daughter, according

to this judgment it shall be done to him. ³² If the ox gores a male or female servant, he shall give to their master thirty shekels of silver, and the ox shall be stoned.

³³ "And if a man opens a pit, or if a man digs a pit and does not cover it, and an ox or a donkey falls in it, ³⁴ the owner of the pit shall make *it* good; he shall give money to their owner, but the dead *animal* shall be his.

³⁵ "If one man's ox hurts another's, so that it dies, then they shall sell the live ox and divide the money from it; and the dead ox they shall also divide. ³⁶ Or if it was known that the ox tended to thrust in time past, and its owner has not kept it confined, he shall surely pay ox for ox, and the dead animal shall be his own.

How to take care of property

22 "If a man steals an ox or a sheep, and slaughters it or sells it, he shall restore five oxen for an ox and four sheep for a sheep. ² If the thief is found breaking in, and he is struck so that he dies, *there shall be* no guilt for his bloodshed. ³ If the sun has risen on him, *there shall be* guilt for his bloodshed. He should make full restitution; if he has nothing, then he shall be sold for his theft. ⁴ If the theft is certainly found alive in his hand, whether it is an ox or donkey or sheep, he shall restore double.

⁵ "If a man causes a field or vineyard to be grazed, and lets loose his animal, and it feeds in another man's field, he shall make restitution from the best of his own field and the best of his own vineyard.

⁶ "If fire breaks out and catches in thorns, so that stacked grain, standing grain, or the field is consumed, he who kindled the fire shall surely make restitution.

⁷ "If a man delivers to his neighbor money or articles to keep, and it is stolen out of the man's house, if the thief is found, he shall pay double. ⁸ If the

thief is not found, then the master of the house shall be brought to the judges *to see* whether he has put his hand into his neighbor's goods.

⁹ "For any kind of trespass, *whether it concerns* an ox, a donkey, a sheep, or clothing, *or* for any kind of lost thing which *another* claims to be his, the cause of both parties shall come before the judges; *and* whomever the judges condemn shall pay double to his neighbor. ¹⁰ If a man delivers to his neighbor a donkey, an ox, a sheep, or any animal to keep, and it dies, is hurt, or driven away, no one seeing *it,* ¹¹ *then* an oath of the LORD shall be between them both, that he has not put his hand into his neighbor's goods; and the owner of it shall accept *that,* and he shall not make *it* good. ¹² But if, in fact, it is stolen from him, he shall make restitution to the owner of it. ¹³ If it is torn to pieces *by a beast, then* he shall bring it as evidence, *and* he shall not make good what was torn.

¹⁴ "And if a man borrows *anything* from his neighbor, and it becomes injured or dies, the owner of it not *being* with it, he shall surely make *it* good. ¹⁵ If its owner *was* with it, he shall not make *it* good; if it *was* hired, it came for its hire.

¹⁶ "If a man entices a virgin who is not betrothed, and lies with her, he shall surely pay the bride-price for her *to be* his wife. ¹⁷ If her father utterly refuses to give her to him, he shall pay money according to the bride-price of virgins.

¹⁸ "You shall not permit a sorceress to live.

¹⁹ "Whoever lies with an animal shall surely be put to death.

²⁰ "He who sacrifices to *any* god, except to the LORD only, he shall be utterly destroyed.

²¹ "You shall neither mistreat a stranger nor oppress him, for you were strangers in the land of Egypt.

²² "You shall not afflict any widow or fatherless child. ²³ If you afflict them in any way, *and* they cry at all to Me, I will surely hear their cry; ²⁴ and My wrath will become hot, and I will kill

you with the sword; your wives shall be widows, and your children fatherless.

25 "If you lend money to *any of* My people *who are* poor among you, you shall not be like a moneylender to him; you shall not charge him interest. 26 If you ever take your neighbor's garment as a pledge, you shall return it to him before the sun goes down. 27 For that *is* his only covering, it *is* his garment for his skin. What will he sleep in? And it will be that when he cries to Me, I will hear, for I *am* gracious.

28 "You shall not revile God, nor curse a ruler of your people.

29 "You shall not delay *to offer* the first of your ripe produce and your juices. The firstborn of your sons you shall give to Me. 30 Likewise you shall do with your oxen *and* your sheep. It shall be with its mother seven days; on the eighth day you shall give it to Me.

31 "And you shall be holy men to Me: you shall not eat meat torn *by beasts* in the field; you shall throw it to the dogs.

The Angel of the Lord leads Israel

23 "You shall not circulate a false report. Do not put your hand with the wicked to be an unrighteous witness. 2 You shall not follow a crowd to do evil; nor shall you testify in a dispute so as to turn aside after many to pervert *justice.* 3 You shall not show partiality to a poor man in his dispute.

4 "If you meet your enemy's ox or his donkey going astray, you shall surely bring it back to him again. 5 If you see the donkey of one who hates you lying under its burden, and you would refrain from helping it, you shall surely help him with it.

6 "You shall not pervert the judgment of your poor in his dispute. 7 Keep yourself far from a false matter; do not kill the innocent and righteous. For I will not justify the wicked. 8 And you shall take no bribe, for a bribe blinds the discerning and perverts the words of the righteous.

9 "Also you shall not oppress a stranger, for you know the heart of a stranger, because you were strangers in the land of Egypt.

10 "Six years you shall sow your land and gather in its produce, 11 but the seventh *year* you shall let it rest and lie fallow, that the poor of your people may eat; and what they leave, the beasts of the field may eat. In like manner you shall do with your vineyard *and* your olive grove. 12 Six days you shall do your work, and on the seventh day you shall rest, that your ox and your donkey may rest, and the son of your female servant and the stranger may be refreshed.

13 "And in all that I have said to you, be circumspect and make no mention of the name of other gods, nor let it be heard from your mouth.

14 "Three times you shall keep a feast to Me in the year: 15 You shall keep the Feast of Unleavened Bread (you shall eat unleavened bread seven days, as I commanded you, at the time appointed in the month of Abib, for in it you came out of Egypt; none shall appear before Me empty); 16 and the Feast of Harvest, the **firstfruits** of your labors which you have sown in the field; and the Feast of Ingathering at the end of the year, when you have gathered in *the fruit of* your labors from the field.

17 "Three times in the year all your males shall appear before the Lord God.

18 "You shall not offer the blood of My sacrifice with leavened bread; nor

---

WORDFINDER

23:16 Firstfruits Israel's offering to God at the Feast of Harvest. They gave God the first and best of their work. Our first and best also belong to God.

shall the fat of My sacrifice remain until morning. 19 The first of the firstfruits of your land you shall bring into the house of the LORD your God. You shall not boil a young goat in its mother's milk.

20 "Behold, I send an Angel before you to keep you in the way and to bring you into the place which I have prepared. 21 Beware of Him and obey His voice; do not provoke Him, for He will not pardon your transgressions; for My name is in Him. 22 But if you indeed obey His voice and do all that I speak, thenI will be an enemy to your enemies and an adversary to your adversaries. 23 For My Angel will go before you and bring you in to the Amorites and the Hittites and the Perizzites and the Canaanites and the Hivites and the Jebusites; and I will cut them off. 24 You shall not bow down to their gods, nor serve them, nor do according to their works; but you shall utterly overthrow them and completely break down their sacred pillars.

25 "So you shall serve the LORD your God, and He will bless your bread and your water. And I will take sickness away from the midst of you. 26 No one shall suffer miscarriage or be barren in your land; I will fulfill the number of your days.

27 "I will send My fear before you, I will cause confusion among all the people to whom you come, and will make all your enemies turn their backs to you. 28 And I will send hornets before you, which shall drive out the Hivite, the Canaanite, and the Hittite from before you. 29 I will not drive them out from before you in one year, lest the land become desolate and the beasts of the field become too numerous for you. 30 Little by little I will drive them out from before you, until you have increased, and you inherit the land. 31 And I will set your bounds from the Red Sea to the sea, Philistia, and from the desert to the River. For I will deliver the inhabitants of the land into your hand, and you shall drive them out before you. 32 You shall make no covenant with them, nor with their gods.

33 They shall not dwell in your land, lest they make you sin against Me. For if you serve their gods, it will surely be a snare to you."

Israel promises to obey God

24 Now He said to Moses, "Come up to the LORD, you and Aaron, Nadab and Abihu, and seventy of the elders of Israel, and worship from afar. 2 And Moses alone shall come near the LORD, but they shall not come near; nor shall the people go up with him."

3 So Moses came and told the people all the words of the LORD and all the judgments. And all the people answered with one voice and said, "All the words which the LORD has said we will do." 4 And Moses wrote all the words of the LORD. And he rose early in the morning, and built an altar at the foot of the mountain, and twelve pillars according to the twelve tribes of Israel. 5 Then he sent young men of the children of Israel, who offered burnt offerings and sacrificed peace offerings of oxen to the LORD. 6 And Moses took half the blood and put it in basins, and half the blood he sprinkled on the altar. 7 Then he took the Book of the Covenant and read in the hearing of the people. And they said, "All that the LORD has said we will do, and be obedient." 8 And Moses took the blood, sprinkled it on the people, and said, "This is the blood of the covenant which the LORD has made with you according to all these words."

9 Then Moses went up, also Aaron, Nadab, and Abihu, and seventy of the elders of Israel, 10 and they saw the God of Israel. And there was under His feet as it were a paved work of sapphire stone, and it was like the very heavens in its clarity. 11 But on the nobles of the children of Israel He did not lay His hand. So they saw God, and they ate and drank.

12 Then the LORD said to Moses, "Come up to Me on the mountain and be there; and I will give you tablets of

stone, and the **law** and commandments which I have written, that you may teach them."

13 So Moses arose with his assistant Joshua, and Moses went up to the mountain of God. 14 And he said to the elders, "Wait here for us until we come back to you. Indeed, Aaron and Hur *are* with you. If any man has a difficulty, let him go to them." 15 Then Moses went up into the mountain, and a cloud covered the mountain.

16 Now the glory of the LORD rested on Mount Sinai, and the cloud covered it six days. And on the seventh day He called to Moses out of the midst of the cloud. 17 The sight of the glory of the LORD *was* like a consuming fire on the top of the mountain in the eyes of the children of Israel. 18 So Moses went into the midst of the cloud and went up into the mountain. And Moses was on the mountain forty days and forty nights.

How to make the ark of the Testimony

25 Then the LORD spoke to Moses, saying: 2 "Speak to the children of Israel, that they bring Me an offering. From everyone who gives it willingly with his heart you shall take My offering. 3 And this *is* the offering which you shall take from them: gold, silver, and bronze; 4 blue, purple, and scarlet *thread,* fine linen, and goats' *hair;* 5 ram skins dyed red, badger skins, and acacia wood; 6 oil for the light, and spices for the anointing oil and for the sweet incense; 7 onyx stones, and stones to be set in the ephod and in the breastplate. 8 And let them make Me a sanctuary, that I may dwell among them. 9 According to all that I show you, *that is,* the pattern of the

The ark of the covenant contained the stone tablets on which the Ten Commandments were written.

tabernacle and the pattern of all its furnishings, just so you shall make *it.*

10 "And they shall make an ark of acacia wood; two and a half cubits *shall be* its length, a cubit and a half its width, and a cubit and a half its height. 11 And you shall overlay it with pure gold, inside and out you shall overlay it, and shall make on it a molding of gold all around. 12 You shall cast four rings of gold for it, and put *them* in its four corners; two rings *shall be* on one side, and two rings on the other side. 13 And you shall make poles *of* acacia wood, and overlay them with gold. 14 You shall put the poles into the rings on the sides of the ark, that the ark may be carried by them. 15 The poles shall be in the rings of the ark; they shall not be taken from it. 16 And you shall put into the ark the Testimony which I will give you.

17 "You shall make a **mercy seat** of

pure gold; two and a half cubits *shall be* its length and a cubit and a half its width. ¹⁸ And you shall make two cherubim of gold; of hammered work you shall make them at the two ends of the mercy seat. ¹⁹ Make one cherub at one end, and the other cherub at the other end; you shall make the cherubim at the two ends of it *of one piece* with the mercy seat. ²⁰ And the cherubim shall stretch out *their* wings above, covering the mercy seat with their wings, and they shall face one another; the faces of the cherubim *shall be* toward the mercy seat. ²¹ You shall put the mercy seat on top of the ark, and in the ark you shall put the Testimony that I will give you. ²² And there I will meet with you, and I will speak with you from above the mercy seat, from between the two cherubim which *are* on the **ark of the Testimony,** about everything which I will give you in commandment to the children of Israel.

A lampstand with seven branches was the symbol of God's presence in the Holy Place.

²³ "You shall also make a **table** of acacia wood; two cubits *shall be* its length, a cubit its width, and a cubit and a half its height. ²⁴ And you shall overlay it with pure gold, and make a molding of gold all around. ²⁵ You shall make for it a frame of a handbreadth all around, and you shall make a gold molding for the frame all around. ²⁶ And you shall make for it four rings of gold, and put the rings on the four corners that *are* at its four legs. ²⁷ The rings shall be close to the frame, as holders for the poles to bear the table. ²⁸ And you shall make the poles of acacia wood, and overlay them with gold, that the table may be carried with them. ²⁹ You shall make its dishes, its pans, its pitchers, and its bowls for pouring. You shall make them of pure gold. ³⁰ And you shall set the showbread on the table before Me always.

³¹ "You shall also make a **lampstand** of pure gold; the lampstand shall be of hammered work. Its shaft, its branches, its bowls, its *ornamental* knobs, and flowers shall be *of one piece.* ³² And six branches shall come out of its sides: three branches of the lampstand out of one side, and three branches of the lampstand out of the other side. ³³ Three bowls *shall be* made like almond *blossoms* on one branch, *with* an *ornamental* knob and a flower, and three bowls made like almond *blossoms* on the other branch, *with* an *ornamental* knob and a flower—and so for the six branches that come out of the lampstand. ³⁴ On the lampstand itself four bowls

---

🌐 WORDFINDER

25:22 Ark of the Testimony A gold-covered wooden chest about 45 inches long by 27 inches wide by 27 inches high. The chest first contained the Ten Commandments, but later also contained some manna and Aaron's wooden staff (see Numbers 11:6).

25:23 Table of Showbread A table about 36 inches long by 18 inches wide by 27 inches high. Every Sabbath 12 loaves of bread were arranged on the table. They were a symbol of God's presence and supply.

25:31 Lampstand An ornate, gold lamp of seven branches. It was a symbol of God's presence in what was called the Holy Place of Israel's place of worship.

shall be made like almond *blossoms, each with* its *ornamental* knob and flower. 35 And *there shall be* a knob under the *first* two branches of the same, a knob under the *second* two branches of the same, and a knob under the *third* two branches of the same, according to the six branches that extend from the lampstand. 36 Their knobs and their branches *shall be of one piece;* all of it *shall be* one hammered piece of pure gold. 37 You shall make seven lamps for it, and they shall arrange its lamps so that they give light in front of it. 38 And its wick-trimmers and their trays *shall be* of pure gold. 39 It shall be made of a talent of pure gold, with all these utensils. 40 And see to it that you make *them* according to the pattern which was shown you on the mountain.

How to make the tabernacle

26 "Moreover you shall make the tabernacle *with* ten curtains *of* fine woven linen and blue, purple, and scarlet *thread;* with artistic designs of cherubim you shall weave them. 2 The length of each curtain *shall be* twenty-eight cubits, and the width of each curtain four cubits. And every one of the curtains shall have the same measurements. 3 Five curtains shall be coupled to one another, and *the other* five curtains *shall be* coupled to one another. 4 And you shall make loops of blue *yarn* on the edge of the curtain on the selvedge of *one* set, and likewise you shall do on the outer edge of *the other* curtain of the second set. 5 Fifty loops you shall make in the one curtain, and fifty loops you shall make on the edge of the curtain that *is* on the end of the second set, that the loops may be clasped to one another. 6 And you shall make fifty clasps of gold, and couple the curtains together with the clasps, so that it may be one tabernacle.

7 "You shall also make curtains of goats' *hair,* to be a tent over the tabernacle. You shall make eleven curtains. 8 The length of each curtain *shall be*

thirty cubits, and the width of each curtain four cubits; and the eleven curtains shall all have the same measurements. 9 And you shall couple five curtains by themselves and six curtains by themselves, and you shall double over the sixth curtain at the forefront of the tent. 10 You shall make fifty loops on the edge of the curtain that is outermost in *one* set, and fifty loops on the edge of the curtain of the second set. 11 And you shall make fifty bronze clasps, put the clasps into the loops, and couple the tent together, that it may be one. 12 The remnant that remains of the curtains of the tent, the half curtain that remains, shall hang over the back of the tabernacle. 13 And a cubit on one side and a cubit on the other side, of what remains of the length of the curtains of the tent, shall hang over the sides of the tabernacle, on this side and on that side, to cover it.

14 "You shall also make a covering of ram skins dyed red for the tent, and a covering of badger skins above that.

15 "And for the tabernacle you shall make the boards of acacia wood, standing upright. 16 Ten cubits *shall be* the length of a board, and a cubit and a half *shall be* the width of each board. 17 Two tenons *shall be* in each board for binding one to another. Thus you shall make for all the boards of the tabernacle. 18 And you shall make the boards for the tabernacle, twenty boards for the south side. 19 You shall make forty sockets of silver under the twenty boards: two sockets under each of the boards for its two tenons. 20 And for the second side of the tabernacle, the north side, *there shall be* twenty boards 21 and their forty sockets of silver: two sockets under each of the boards. 22 For the far side of the tabernacle, westward, you shall make six boards. 23 And you shall also make two boards for the two back corners of the tabernacle. 24 They shall be coupled together at the bottom and they shall be coupled together at the top by one ring. Thus it shall be for both of them. They shall be for the two corners.

25 So there shall be eight boards with their sockets of silver—sixteen sockets—two sockets under each of the boards.

26 "And you shall make bars of acacia wood: five for the boards on one side of the tabernacle, 27 five bars for the boards on the other side of the tabernacle, and five bars for the boards of the side of the tabernacle, for the far side westward. 28 The middle bar shall pass through the midst of the boards from end to end. 29 You shall overlay the boards with gold, make their rings of gold as holders for the bars, and overlay the bars with gold. 30 And you shall raise up the tabernacle according to its pattern which you were shown on the mountain.

31 "You shall make a veil woven of blue, purple, and scarlet thread, and fine woven linen. It shall be woven with an artistic design of cherubim. 32 You shall hang it upon the four pillars of acacia wood overlaid with gold. Their hooks shall be gold, upon four sockets of silver. 33 And you shall hang the veil from the clasps. Then you shall bring the ark of the Testimony in there, behind the veil. The veil shall be a divider for you between the holy place and the Most Holy. 34 You shall put the mercy seat upon the ark of the Testimony in the Most Holy. 35 You shall set the table outside the veil, and the lampstand across from the table on the side of the tabernacle toward the south; and you shall put the table on the north side.

36 "You shall make a screen for the door of the tabernacle, woven of blue, purple, and scarlet thread, and fine woven linen, made by a weaver. 37 And you shall make for the screen five pillars of acacia wood, and overlay them with gold; their hooks shall be gold, and you shall cast five sockets of bronze for them.

How to make the altar of burnt offering

27 "You shall make an **altar** of acacia wood, five cubits long and five cubits wide—the altar shall be square—and its height shall be three cubits. 2 You shall make its horns on its four corners; its horns shall be of one piece with it. And you shall overlay it with bronze. 3 Also you shall make its pans to receive its ashes, and its shovels and its basins and its forks and its firepans; you shall make all its utensils of bronze. 4 You shall make a grate for it, a network of bronze; and on the network you shall make four bronze rings at its four corners. 5 You shall put it under the rim of the altar beneath, that the network may be midway up the altar. 6 And you shall make poles for the altar, poles of acacia wood, and overlay them with bronze. 7 The poles shall be put in the rings, and the poles shall be on the two sides of the altar to bear it. 8 You shall make it hollow with boards; as it was shown you on the mountain, so shall they make it.

9 "You shall also make the court of the tabernacle. For the south side there shall be hangings for the court made of fine woven linen, one hundred cubits long for one side. 10 And its twenty pillars and their twenty sockets shall be bronze. The hooks of the pillars and their bands shall be silver. 11 Likewise along the length of the north side there shall be hangings one hundred cubits long, with its twenty pillars and their twenty sockets of bronze, and the hooks of the pillars and their bands of silver.

12 "And along the width of the court on the west side shall be hangings of fifty cubits, with their ten pillars and their ten sockets. 13 The width of the court on the east side shall be fifty cubits. 14 The hangings on one side of

---

WORDFINDER

27:1 Altar of Burnt Offering An altar about 90 by 90 by 54 inches high, used for burnt offerings. The people brought animals to the altar. The animals were killed, then sacrificed by fire to pay for the people's sins.

the gate shall be fifteen cubits, with their three pillars and their three sockets. ¹⁵ And on the other side shall be hangings of fifteen cubits, with their three pillars and their three sockets.

¹⁶ "For the gate of the court there shall be a screen twenty cubits long, woven of blue, purple, and scarlet thread, and fine woven linen, made by a weaver. It shall have four pillars and four sockets. ¹⁷ All the pillars around the court shall have bands of silver; their hooks shall be of silver and their sockets of bronze. ¹⁸ The length of the court shall be one hundred cubits, the width fifty throughout, and the height five cubits, made of fine woven linen, and its sockets of bronze. ¹⁹ All the utensils of the tabernacle for all its service, all its pegs, and all the pegs of the court, shall be of bronze.

²⁰ "And you shall command the children of Israel that they bring you pure oil of pressed olives for the light, to cause the lamp to burn continually. ²¹ In the tabernacle of meeting, outside the veil which is before the Testimony, Aaron and his sons shall tend it from evening until morning before the LORD. It shall be a statute forever to their generations on behalf of the children of Israel.

How to make the priests' clothing

28 "Now take Aaron your brother, and his sons with him, from among the children of Israel, that he may minister to Me as priest, Aaron and Aaron's sons: Nadab, Abihu, Eleazar, and Itha-

The priests wore a breastplate on which 12 precious stones were engraved with the names of the 12 tribes of Israel. In this way the priests kept all the people over their hearts when they worshiped the Lord.

mar. ² And you shall make holy garments for Aaron your brother, for glory and for beauty. ³ So you shall speak to all who are gifted artisans, whom I have filled with the spirit of wisdom, that they may make Aaron's garments, to consecrate him, that he may minister to Me as priest. ⁴ And these are the garments which they shall make: a breastplate, an ephod, a robe, a skillfully woven tunic, a turban, and a sash. So they shall make holy garments for Aaron your brother and his sons, that he may minister to Me as priest.

⁵ "They shall take the gold, blue, purple, and scarlet thread, and the fine linen, ⁶ and they shall make the ephod of gold, blue, purple, and scarlet thread, and fine woven linen,

---

What Is a Priest?

A priest is someone who comes before God and prays for the people. In the Old Testament, the people could not worship God unless the priest made sacrifices for them. Aaron's family were priests. In the New Testament, Jesus is our Priest forever, and His crucified body is our sacrifice.

artistically worked. [7] It shall have two shoulder straps joined at its two edges, and *so* it shall be joined together. [8] And the intricately woven band of the ephod, which *is* on it, shall be of the same workmanship, *made of* gold, blue, purple, and scarlet *thread,* and fine woven linen.

[9] "Then you shall take two onyx stones and engrave on them the names of the sons of Israel: [10] six of their names on one stone and six names on the other stone, in order of their birth. [11] With the work of an engraver in stone, *like* the engravings of a signet, you shall engrave the two stones with the names of the sons of Israel. You shall set them in settings of gold. [12] And you shall put the two stones on the shoulders of the ephod *as* memorial stones for the sons of Israel. So Aaron shall bear their names before the LORD on his two shoulders as a memorial. [13] You shall also make settings of gold, [14] and you shall make two chains of pure gold like braided cords, and fasten the braided chains to the settings.

[15] "You shall make the breastplate of judgment. Artistically woven according to the workmanship of the ephod you shall make it: of gold, blue, purple, and scarlet *thread,* and fine woven linen, you shall make it. [16] It shall be doubled into a square: a span *shall be* its length, and a span *shall be* its width. [17] And you shall put settings of stones in it, four rows of stones: *The first* row *shall be* a sardius, a topaz, and an emerald; *this shall be* the first row; [18] the second row *shall be* a turquoise, a sapphire, and a diamond; [19] the third row, a jacinth, an agate, and an amethyst; [20] and the fourth row, a beryl, an onyx, and a jasper. They shall be set in gold settings. [21] And the stones shall have the names of the sons of Israel, twelve according to their names, *like* the engravings of a signet, each one with its own name; they shall be according to the twelve tribes.

[22] "You shall make chains for the breastplate at the end, like braided cords of pure gold. [23] And you shall make two rings of gold for the breastplate, and put the two rings on the two ends of the breastplate. [24] Then you shall put the two braided *chains* of gold in the two rings which are on the ends of the breastplate; [25] and the *other* two ends of the two braided *chains* you shall fasten to the two settings, and put them on the shoulder straps of the ephod in the front.

[26] "You shall make two rings of gold, and put them on the two ends of the breastplate, on the edge of it, which is on the inner side of the ephod. [27] And two *other* rings of gold you shall make, and put them on the two shoulder straps, underneath the ephod toward its front, right at the seam above the intricately woven band of the ephod. [28] They shall bind the breastplate by means of its rings to the rings of the ephod, using a blue cord, so that it is above the intricately woven band of the ephod, and so that the breastplate does not come loose from the ephod.

[29] "So Aaron shall bear the names of the sons of Israel on the breastplate of judgment over his heart, when he goes into the holy *place,* as a memorial before the LORD continually. [30] And you shall put in the breastplate of judgment the Urim and the Thummim, and they shall be over Aaron's heart when he goes in before the LORD. So Aaron shall bear the judgment of the children of Israel over his heart before the LORD continually.

[31] "You shall make the robe of the ephod all of blue. [32] There shall be an opening for his head in the middle of it; it shall have a woven binding all around its opening, like the opening in a coat of mail, so that it does not tear. [33] And upon its hem you shall make pomegranates of blue, purple, and scarlet, all around its hem, and bells of gold between them all around: [34] a golden bell and a pomegranate, a golden bell and a pomegranate, upon the hem of the robe all around. [35] And it shall be upon Aaron when he ministers, and its sound will be heard when he goes into the holy *place*

before the LORD and when he comes out, that he may not die.

36 "You shall also make a plate of pure gold and engrave on it, *like* the engraving of a signet:

HOLINESS TO THE LORD.

37 And you shall put it on a blue cord, that it may be on the turban; it shall be on the front of the turban. 38 So it shall be on Aaron's forehead, that Aaron may bear the iniquity of the holy things which the children of Israel hallow in all their holy gifts; and it shall always be on his forehead, that they may be accepted before the LORD.

39 "You shall skillfully weave the tunic of fine linen *thread,* you shall make the turban of fine linen, and you shall make the sash of woven work.

40 "For Aaron's sons you shall make tunics, and you shall make sashes for them. And you shall make hats for them, for glory and beauty. 41 So you shall put them on Aaron your brother and on his sons with him. You shall anoint them, **consecrate** them, and sanctify them, that they may minister to Me as priests. 42 And you shall make for them linen trousers to cover their nakedness; they shall reach from the waist to the thighs. 43 They shall be on Aaron and on his sons when they come into the tabernacle of meeting, or when they come near the altar to minister in the holy *place,* that they do not incur iniquity and die. *It shall be* a statute forever to him and his descendants after him.

How to offer sacrifices

29 "And this is what you shall do to them to hallow them for ministering to Me as priests: Take one young bull and two rams without blemish, 2 and unleavened bread, unleavened cakes mixed with oil, and unleavened wafers anointed with oil (you shall make them of wheat flour). 3 You shall put them in one basket and bring them in the basket, with the bull and the two rams.

4 "And Aaron and his sons you shall bring to the door of the tabernacle of meeting, and you shall wash them with water. 5 Then you shall take the garments, put the tunic on Aaron, and the robe of the ephod, the ephod, and the breastplate, and gird him with the intricately woven band of the ephod. 6 You shall put the turban on his head, and put the holy crown on the turban. 7 And you shall take the anointing oil, pour *it* on his head, and anoint him. 8 Then you shall bring his sons and put tunics on them. 9 And you shall gird them with sashes, Aaron and his sons, and put the hats on them. The priesthood shall be theirs for a perpetual statute. So you shall consecrate Aaron and his sons.

10 "You shall also have the bull brought before the tabernacle of meeting, and Aaron and his sons shall put their hands on the head of the bull. 11 Then you shall kill the bull before the LORD, *by* the door of the tabernacle of meeting. 12 You shall take *some* of the blood of the bull and put *it* on the horns of the altar with your finger, and pour all the blood beside the base of the altar. 13 And you shall take all the fat that covers the entrails, the fatty lobe *attached* to the liver, and the two kidneys and the fat that *is* on them, and burn *them* on the altar. 14 But the flesh of the bull, with its skin and its offal, you shall burn with fire outside the camp. It *is* a sin offering.

15 "You shall also take one ram, and Aaron and his sons shall put their hands on the head of the ram; 16 and you shall kill the ram, and you shall take its blood and sprinkle *it* all around on the altar. 17 Then you shall cut the ram in pieces, wash its entrails and its legs, and put *them* with its pieces and with its head. 18 And you shall burn

WORDFINDER

28:41 Consecrate Pronounced *KON-see-krate.* A verb meaning "set apart" for God's use. Holy places and holy objects are consecrated, but people also must be consecrated.

the whole ram on the altar. It *is* a burnt offering to the LORD; it *is* a sweet aroma, an offering made by fire to the LORD.

19 "You shall also take the other ram, and Aaron and his sons shall put their hands on the head of the ram. 20 Then you shall kill the ram, and take some of its blood and put *it* on the tip of the right ear of Aaron and on the tip of the right ear of his sons, on the thumb of their right hand and on the big toe of their right foot, and sprinkle the blood all around on the altar. 21 And you shall take some of the blood that is on the altar, and some of the anointing oil, and sprinkle *it* on Aaron and on his garments, on his sons and on the garments of his sons with him; and he and his garments shall be hallowed, and his sons and his sons' garments with him.

22 "Also you shall take the fat of the ram, the fat tail, the fat that covers the entrails, the fatty lobe *attached to* the liver, the two kidneys and the fat on them, the right thigh (for it *is* a ram of consecration), 23 one loaf of bread, one cake *made with* oil, and one wafer from the basket of the unleavened bread that *is* before the LORD; 24 and you shall put all these in the hands of Aaron and in the hands of his sons, and you shall wave them *as* a wave offering before the LORD. 25 You shall receive them back from their hands and burn *them* on the altar as a burnt offering, as a sweet aroma before the LORD. It *is* an offering made by fire to the LORD.

26 "Then you shall take the breast of the ram of Aaron's consecration and wave it *as* a wave offering before the LORD; and it shall be your portion. 27 And from the ram of the consecration you shall consecrate the breast of the wave offering which is waved, and the thigh of the heave offering which

is raised, of *that* which *is* for Aaron and of *that* which is for his sons. 28 It shall be from the children of Israel *for* Aaron and his sons by a statute forever. For it is a heave offering; it shall be a heave offering from the children of Israel from the sacrifices of their peace offerings, *that is,* their heave offering to the LORD.

29 "And the holy garments of Aaron shall be his sons' after him, to be anointed in them and to be consecrated in them. 30 That son who becomes priest in his place shall put them on for seven days, when he enters the tabernacle of meeting to minister in the holy *place.*

31 "And you shall take the ram of the consecration and boil its flesh in the holy place. 32 Then Aaron and his sons shall eat the flesh of the ram, and the bread that *is* in the basket, by the door of the tabernacle of meeting. 33 They shall eat those things with which the atonement was made, to consecrate *and* to sanctify them; but an outsider shall not eat *them,* because they *are* holy. 34 And if any of the flesh of the consecration offerings, or of the bread, remains until the morning, then you shall burn the remainder with fire. It shall not be eaten, because it *is* holy.

35 "Thus you shall do to Aaron and his sons, according to all that I have commanded you. Seven days you shall consecrate them. 36 And you shall offer a bull every day *as* a sin offering for **atonement.** You shall cleanse the altar when you make atonement for it, and you shall anoint it to sanctify it. 37 Seven days you shall make atonement for the altar and sanctify it. And the altar shall be most holy. Whatever touches the altar must be holy.

38 "Now this *is* what you shall offer on the altar: two lambs of the first year, day by day continually. 39 One lamb you shall offer in the morning, and the other lamb you shall offer at twilight.

WORDFINDER

29:36 Atonement The act of paying God what we owe for our sins. In the Old Testament, the sacrificed animal was a symbol of atonement, but Christ is now our true Atonement.

40 With the one lamb shall be one-tenth *of an ephah* of flour mixed with one-fourth of a hin of pressed oil, and one-fourth of a hin of wine *as* a drink offering. 41 And the other lamb you shall offer at twilight; and you shall offer with it the grain offering and the drink offering, as in the morning, for a sweet aroma, an offering made by fire to the LORD. 42 *This shall be* a continual burnt offering throughout your generations *at* the door of the tabernacle of meeting before the LORD, where I will meet you to speak with you. 43 And there I will meet with the children of Israel, and *the tabernacle* shall be sanctified by My glory. 44 So I will consecrate the tabernacle of meeting and the altar. I will also consecrate both Aaron and his sons to minister to Me as priests. 45 I will dwell among the children of Israel and will be their God. 46 And they shall know that I *am* the LORD their God, who brought them up out of the land of Egypt, that I may dwell among them. I *am* the LORD their God.

How to make the altar of incense

30 "You shall make an altar to burn incense on; you shall make it of acacia wood. 2 A cubit *shall be* its length and a cubit its width—it shall be square—and two cubits *shall be* its height. Its horns *shall be* of one piece with it. 3 And you shall overlay its top, its sides all around, and its horns with pure gold; and you shall make for it a molding of gold all around. 4 Two gold rings you shall make for it, under the molding on both its sides. You shall place *them* on its two sides, and they will be holders for the poles with which to bear it. 5 You shall make the poles of acacia wood, and overlay them with gold. 6 And you shall put it before the veil that *is* before the ark of the Testi-

mony, before the mercy seat that *is* over the Testimony, where I will meet with you.

7 "Aaron shall burn on it sweet incense every morning; when he tends the lamps, he shall burn incense on it. 8 And when Aaron lights the lamps at twilight, he shall burn incense on it, a perpetual incense before the LORD throughout your generations. 9 You shall not offer strange incense on it, or a burnt offering, or a grain offering; nor shall you pour a drink offering on it. 10 And Aaron shall make atonement upon its horns once a year with the blood of the sin offering of atonement; once a year he shall make atonement upon it throughout your generations. It *is* most holy to the LORD."

11 Then the LORD spoke to Moses, saying: 12 "When you take the census of the children of Israel for their number, then every man shall give a ransom for himself to the LORD, when you number them, that there may be no plague among them when *you* number them. 13 This is what everyone among those who are numbered shall give: half a shekel according to the shekel of the sanctuary (a shekel *is* twenty gerahs). The half-shekel *shall be* an offering to the LORD. 14 Everyone included among those who are numbered, from twenty years old and above, shall give an offering to the LORD. 15 The rich shall not give more and the poor shall not give less than half a shekel, when *you* give an offering to the LORD, to make atonement for yourselves. 16 And you shall take the atonement money of the children of Israel, and shall appoint it for the service of the tabernacle of meeting, that it may be a memorial for the children of Israel before the LORD, to make atonement for yourselves."

17 Then the LORD spoke to Moses, saying: 18 "You shall also make a **laver**

WORDFINDER

30:18 Laver Pronounced *LAY-ver.* A special washstand made of bronze. The laver stood between the altar of burnt offering and the door of the Old Testament worship place. The priests washed their hands there as an act of purifying themselves.

The bronze laver (or washstand) where the priests washed their hands as an act of purifying themselves.

an ointment compounded according to the art of the perfumer. It shall be a holy anointing oil. 26 With it you shall anoint the tabernacle of meeting and the ark of the Testimony; 27 the table and all its utensils, the lampstand and its utensils, and the **altar of incense;** 28 the altar of burnt offering with all its utensils, and the laver and its base. 29 You shall consecrate them, that they may be most holy; whatever touches them must be holy. 30 And you shall anoint Aaron and his sons, and consecrate them, that *they* may minister to Me as priests.

31 "And you shall speak to the children of Israel, saying: 'This shall be a holy anointing oil to Me throughout your generations. 32 It shall not be poured on man's flesh; nor shall you make *any other* like it, according to its composition. It *is* holy, *and* it shall be holy to you. 33 Whoever compounds *any* like it, or whoever puts

of bronze, with its base also of bronze, for washing. You shall put it between the tabernacle of meeting and the altar. And you shall put water in it, 19 for Aaron and his sons shall wash their hands and their feet in water from it. 20 When they go into the tabernacle of meeting, or when they come near the altar to minister, to burn an offering made by fire to the LORD, they shall wash with water, lest they die. 21 So they shall wash their hands and their feet, lest they die. And it shall be a statute forever to them—to him and his descendants throughout their generations."

22 Moreover the LORD spoke to Moses, saying: 23 "Also take for yourself quality spices—five hundred *shekels* of liquid myrrh, half as much sweet-smelling cinnamon (two hundred and fifty *shekels*), two hundred and fifty *shekels* of sweet-smelling cane, 24 five hundred *shekels* of cassia, according to the shekel of the sanctuary, and a hin of olive oil. 25 And you shall make from these a holy anointing oil,

The altar of incense where offerings were made to God every morning and every evening.

WORDFINDER

30:27 Altar of Incense A gold-covered altar about 18 inches long by 18 inches wide by 36 inches high. Every morning the high priest burned incense on the altar as a symbol of the prayers of the people.

any of it on an outsider, shall be cut off from his people.' "

34 And the LORD said to Moses: "Take sweet spices, stacte and onycha and galbanum, and pure frankincense with *these* sweet spices; there shall be equal amounts of each. 35 You shall make of these an incense, a compound according to the art of the perfumer, salted, pure, *and* holy. 36 And you shall beat *some* of it very fine, and put some of it before the Testimony in the tabernacle of meeting where I will meet with you. It shall be most holy to you. 37 But *as for* the incense which you shall make, you shall not make any for yourselves, according to its composition. It shall be to you holy for the LORD. 38 Whoever makes *any* like it, to smell it, he shall be cut off from his people."

Why the Sabbath is important

31 Then the LORD spoke to Moses, saying: 2 "See, I have called by name Bezalel the son of Uri, the son of Hur, of the tribe of Judah. 3 And I have filled him with the Spirit of God, in wisdom, in understanding, in knowledge, and in all *manner of* workmanship, 4 to design artistic works, to work in gold, in silver, in bronze, 5 in cutting jewels for setting, in carving wood, and to work in all *manner of* workmanship.

6 "And I, indeed I, have appointed with him Aholiab the son of Ahisa-mach, of the tribe of Dan; and I have put wisdom in the hearts of all the gifted artisans, that they may make all that I have commanded you: 7 the tabernacle of meeting, the ark of the Testimony and the mercy seat that *is* on it, and all the furniture of the tabernacle— 8 the table and its utensils, the pure *gold* lampstand with all its utensils, the altar of incense, 9 the altar of burnt offering with all its utensils, and the laver and its base— 10 the garments of ministry, the holy garments for Aaron the priest and the garments of his sons, to minister as priests, 11 and the anointing oil and sweet incense for the holy *place*. According to all that I have commanded you they shall do."

12 And the LORD spoke to Moses, saying, 13 "Speak also to the children of Israel, saying: 'Surely My Sabbaths you shall keep, for it *is* a sign between Me and you throughout your generations, that *you* may know that I *am* the LORD who sanctifies you. 14 You shall keep the Sabbath, therefore, for *it is* holy to you. Everyone who profanes it shall surely be put to death; for whoever does *any* work on it, that person shall be cut off from among his people. 15 Work shall be done for six days, but the seventh *is* the Sabbath of rest, holy to the LORD. Whoever does *any* work on the Sabbath day, he shall surely be put to death. 16 Therefore the children of Israel shall keep the Sabbath, to observe the

---

Bezalel and Aholiab—My name is pronounced *BEZ-ah-lell*. My partner's name is Aholiab (pronounced *ah-HOLY-ab*). He and I always enjoyed making nice things with our hands. We learned our skills from the Egyptian artisans.

When Moses needed men skilled in working with gold, silver, and bronze, in jewel cutting and in wood carving for the new worship place, we really didn't feel we were good enough to make the beautiful things he needed.

Then something wonderful happened, just as Moses promised. As soon as we agreed to help him, we were surprised to find that the articles we made seemed more beautiful than ever. We could hardly believe the marvelous things that came from our hands—the tabernacle (pronounced *TAB-er-nak-kel*), the ark, the golden mercy seat, and all the other articles!

So just give your abilities to God, and He will do the rest.

Jews Worship Gold Calf

Old Testament News Service

MOUNT SINAI—To those who have followed earlier news releases (Exodus 19 and 20) telling about the great new religion at Mount Sinai, this report will come as a surprise.

When Moses climbed the mountain to speak with God, he left his brother Aaron in charge of the people in the valley below. Our own sources at the scene say the Hebrews believed Moses had deserted them. The people then demanded that Aaron make a new god for them.

Gold was collected from all the campers, and Aaron made an idol in the shape of a calf. There was a worship service followed by a wild party. From all reports, the people behaved in a disgraceful way, disturbing the peace.

The Jews have clearly broken their promises to God. We will be standing by to cover further developments among these strange people.

Sabbath throughout their generations *as* a perpetual covenant. 17 It *is* a sign between Me and the children of Israel forever; for *in* six days the LORD made the heavens and the earth, and on the seventh day He rested and was refreshed.' "

18 And when He had made an end of speaking with him on Mount Sinai, He gave Moses two tablets of the Testimony, tablets of stone, written with the finger of God.

The people worship a golden calf

32 Now when the people saw that Moses delayed coming down from the mountain, the people gathered together to Aaron, and said to him, "Come, make us gods that shall go before us; for *as for* this Moses, the man who brought us up out of the land of Egypt, we do not know what has become of him."

2 And Aaron said to them, "Break

While Moses was on the mountain with God, the people made a golden calf and worshiped it.

off the golden earrings which *are* in the ears of your wives, your sons, and your daughters, and bring *them* to me." 3 So all the people broke off the golden earrings which *were* in their ears, and brought *them* to Aaron. 4 And he received *the* gold from their hand, and he fashioned it with an engraving tool, and made a molded calf.

Then they said, "This *is* your god, O Israel, that brought you out of the land of Egypt!"

5 So when Aaron saw *it*, he built an altar before it. And Aaron made a proclamation and said, "Tomorrow *is* a feast to the LORD." 6 Then they rose early on the next day, offered burnt offerings, and brought peace offerings; and the people sat down to eat and drink, and rose up to play.

7 And the LORD said to Moses, "Go, get down! For your people whom you brought out of the land of Egypt have corrupted *themselves*. 8 They have turned aside quickly out of the way which I commanded them. They have made themselves a molded calf, and worshiped it and sacrificed to it, and said, 'This *is* your god, O Israel, that brought you out of the land of Egypt!' " 9 And the LORD said to Moses, "I have seen this people, and indeed it *is* a stiff-necked people! 10 Now therefore, let Me alone, that My wrath may burn hot against them and I may consume them. And I will make of you a great nation."

11 Then Moses pleaded with the LORD his God, and said: "LORD, why does Your wrath burn hot against Your people whom You have brought out of the land of Egypt with great power and with a mighty hand? 12 Why should the Egyptians speak, and say, 'He brought them out to harm them, to kill them in the mountains, and to consume them from the face of the earth'? Turn from Your fierce wrath, and relent from this harm to Your people. 13 Remember Abraham, Isaac, and Israel, Your servants, to whom You swore by Your own self, and said to them, 'I will multiply your descendants as the stars of heaven; and all this land

that I have spoken of I give to your descendants, and they shall inherit *it* forever.' " 14 So the LORD relented from the harm which He said He would do to His people.

15 And Moses turned and went down from the mountain, and the two tablets of the Testimony *were* in his hand. The tablets *were* written on both sides; on the one *side* and on the other they were written. 16 Now the tablets *were* the work of God, and the writing *was* the writing of God engraved on the tablets.

17 And when Joshua heard the noise of the people as they shouted, he said to Moses, "*There is* a noise of war in the camp."

18 But he said:

> "*It is* not the noise of the shout
>   of victory,
> Nor the noise of the cry of
>   defeat,
> *But* the sound of singing I hear."

19 So it was, as soon as he came near the camp, that he saw the calf *and* the dancing. So Moses' anger became hot, and he cast the tablets out of his hands and broke them at the foot of the mountain. 20 Then he took the calf which they had made, burned *it* in the fire, and ground *it* to powder; and he scattered *it* on the water and made the children of Israel drink *it*. 21 And Moses said to Aaron, "What did this people do to you that you have brought *so* great a sin upon them?"

22 So Aaron said, "Do not let the anger of my lord become hot. You know the people, that they *are set* on evil. 23 For they said to me, 'Make us gods that shall go before us; *as for* this Moses, the man who brought us out of the land of Egypt, we do not know what has become of him.' 24 And I said to them, 'Whoever has any gold, let them break *it* off.' So they gave *it* to me, and I cast it into the fire, and this calf came out."

25 Now when Moses saw that the people *were* unrestrained (for Aaron had not restrained them, to *their*

shame among their enemies), 26 then Moses stood in the entrance of the camp, and said, "Whoever is on the LORD's side—come to me!" And all the sons of Levi gathered themselves together to him. 27 And he said to them, "Thus says the LORD God of Israel: 'Let every man put his sword on his side, and go in and out from entrance to entrance throughout the camp, and let every man kill his brother, every man his companion, and every man his neighbor.' " 28 So the sons of Levi did according to the word of Moses. And about three thousand men of the people fell that day. 29 Then Moses said, "Consecrate yourselves today to the LORD, that He may bestow on you a blessing this day, for every man has opposed his son and his brother."

30 Now it came to pass on the next day that Moses said to the people, "You have committed a great sin. So now I will go up to the LORD; perhaps I can make atonement for your sin." 31 Then Moses returned to the LORD and said, "Oh, these people have committed a great sin, and have made for themselves a god of gold! 32 Yet now, if You will forgive their sin—but if not, I pray, blot me out of Your book which You have written."

33 And the LORD said to Moses, "Whoever has sinned against Me, I will blot him out of My book. 34 Now therefore, go, lead the people to the place of which I have spoken to you. Behold, My Angel shall go before you. Nevertheless, in the day when I visit for punishment, I will visit punishment upon them for their sin."

35 So the LORD plagued the people because of what they did with the calf which Aaron made.

Moses prays for God's presence

33 Then the LORD said to Moses, "Depart and go up from here, you and the people whom you have brought out of the land of Egypt, to the land of which I swore to Abraham, Isaac, and Jacob, saying, 'To your descendants I will give it.' 2 And I will send

My Angel before you, and I will drive out the Canaanite and the Amorite and the Hittite and the Perizzite and the Hivite and the Jebusite. 3 Go up to a land flowing with milk and honey; for I will not go up in your midst, lest I consume you on the way, for you are a stiff-necked people."

4 And when the people heard this bad news, they mourned, and no one put on his ornaments. 5 For the LORD had said to Moses, "Say to the children of Israel, 'You are a stiff-necked people. I could come up into your midst in one moment and consume you. Now therefore, take off your ornaments, that I may know what to do to you.' " 6 So the children of Israel stripped themselves of their ornaments by Mount Horeb.

7 Moses took his tent and pitched it outside the camp, far from the camp, and called it the tabernacle of meeting. And it came to pass that everyone who sought the LORD went out to the tabernacle of meeting which was outside the camp. 8 So it was, whenever Moses went out to the tabernacle, that all the people rose, and each man stood at his tent door and watched Moses until he had gone into the tabernacle. 9 And it came to pass, when Moses entered the tabernacle, that the pillar of cloud descended and stood at the door of the tabernacle, and the LORD talked with Moses. 10 All the people saw the pillar of cloud standing at the tabernacle door, and all the people rose and worshiped, each man in his tent door. 11 So the LORD spoke to Moses face to face, as a man speaks to his friend. And he would return to the camp, but his servant Joshua the son of Nun, a young man, did not depart from the tabernacle.

12 Then Moses said to the LORD, "See, You say to me, 'Bring up this people.' But You have not let me know whom You will send with me. Yet You have said, 'I know you by name, and you have also found grace in My sight.' 13 Now therefore, I pray, if I have found grace in Your sight, show me now Your way, that I may know You

For 40 years, while they wandered in the wilderness, the people lived in tents that they could pack up and carry with them.

and that I may find grace in Your sight. And consider that this nation *is* Your people."

14 And He said, "My Presence will go *with you,* and I will give you rest."

15 Then he said to Him, "If Your Presence does not go *with us,* do not bring us up from here. 16 For how then will it be known that Your people and I have found grace in Your sight, except You go with us? So we shall be separate, Your people and I, from all the people who *are* upon the face of the earth."

17 So the LORD said to Moses, "I will also do this thing that you have spoken; for you have found grace in My sight, and I know you by name."

18 And he said, "Please, show me Your glory."

19 Then He said, "I will make all My goodness pass before you, and I will proclaim the name of the LORD before you. I will be gracious to whom I will be gracious, and I will have compassion on whom I will have compassion."

20 But He said, "You cannot see My face; for no man shall see Me, and live." 21 And the LORD said, "Here is a place by Me, and you shall stand on the rock. 22 So it shall be, while My glory passes by, that I will put you in the cleft of the rock, and will cover you with My hand while I pass by. 23 Then I will take away My hand, and you shall see My back; but My face shall not be seen."

God writes the Law again

34 And the LORD said to Moses, "Cut two tablets of stone like the first *ones,* and I will write on *these* tablets the words that were on the first tablets which you broke. 2 So be ready in the morning, and come up in the morning to Mount Sinai, and present yourself to Me there on the top of the mountain. 3 And no man shall come up with you, and let no man be seen throughout all the mountain; let neither flocks nor herds feed before that mountain."

4 So he cut two tablets of stone like the first *ones.* Then Moses rose early in the morning and went up Mount Sinai, as the LORD had commanded him; and he took in his hand the two tablets of stone.

5 Now the LORD descended in the cloud and stood with him there, and proclaimed the name of the LORD. 6 And the LORD passed before him and

proclaimed, "The Lord, the Lord God, merciful and gracious, longsuffer- ing, and abounding in goodness and truth, 7 keeping mercy for thousands, forgiving iniquity and transgression and **sin,** by no means clearing *the guilty,* visiting the iniquity of the fathers upon the children and the children's children to the third and the fourth genera- tion."

8 So Moses made haste and bowed his head toward the earth, and wor- shiped. 9 Then he said, "If now I have found grace in Your sight, O Lord, let my Lord, I pray, go among us, even though we *are* a stiff-necked people; and pardon our iniquity and our sin, and take us as Your inheritance."

10 And He said: "Behold, I make a covenant. Before all your people I will do marvels such as have not been done in all the earth, nor in any nation; and all the people among whom you *are* shall see the work of the Lord. For it *is* an awesome thing that I will do with you. 11 Observe what I command you this day. Behold, I am driving out from before you the Amorite and the Canaanite and the Hittite and the Per- izzite and the Hivite and the Jebusite. 12 Take heed to yourself, lest you make a covenant with the inhabitants of the land where you are going, lest it be a snare in your midst. 13 But you shall destroy their altars, break their *sacred* pillars, and cut down their wooden im- ages 14 (for you shall worship no other god, for the Lord, whose name *is* Jeal- ous, *is* a jealous God), 15 lest you make a covenant with the inhabitants of the land, and they play the harlot with their gods and make sacrifice to their gods, and *one of them* invites you and you eat of his sacrifice, 16 and you take of his daughters for your sons, and his daughters play the harlot with their gods and make your sons play the har- lot with their gods.

17 "You shall make no molded gods for yourselves.

18 "The Feast of Unleavened Bread you shall keep. Seven days you shall eat unleavened bread, as I com- manded you, in the appointed time of the month of Abib; for in the month of Abib you came out from Egypt.

19 "All that open the womb *are* Mine, and every male firstborn among your livestock, *whether* ox or sheep. 20 But the firstborn of a donkey you shall redeem with a lamb. And if you will not redeem *him,* then you shall break his neck. All the firstborn of your sons you shall redeem.

"And none shall appear before Me empty-handed.

21 "Six days you shall work, but on the seventh day you shall rest; in plow- ing time and in harvest you shall rest.

22 "And you shall observe the Feast of Weeks, of the firstfruits of wheat har- vest, and the Feast of Ingathering at the year's end.

23 "Three times in the year all your men shall appear before the Lord, the Lord God of Israel. 24 For I will cast out the nations before you and enlarge your borders; neither will any man covet your land when you go up to appear before the Lord your God three times in the year.

25 "You shall not offer the blood of My sacrifice with leaven, nor shall the sacrifice of the Feast of the Passover be left until morning.

26 "The first of the firstfruits of your land you shall bring to the house of the Lord your God. You shall not boil a young goat in its mother's milk."

27 Then the Lord said to Moses, "Write these words, for according to the tenor of these words I have made a covenant with you and with Israel." 28 So he was there with the Lord forty days and forty nights; he neither ate

WORDFINDER

34:7 Sin Disobedience of God's law or rebellion against His will. All people sin, but Christ died to take sin away.

bread nor drank water. And He wrote on the tablets the words of the covenant, the Ten Commandments.

29 Now it was so, when Moses came down from Mount Sinai (and the two tablets of the Testimony *were* in Moses' hand when he came down from the mountain), that Moses did not know that the skin of his face shone while he talked with Him. 30 So when Aaron and all the children of Israel saw Moses, behold, the skin of his face shone, and they were afraid to come near him. 31 Then Moses called to them, and Aaron and all the rulers of the congregation returned to him; and Moses talked with them. 32 Afterward all the children of Israel came near, and he gave them as commandments all that the LORD had spoken with him on Mount Sinai. 33 And when Moses had finished speaking with them, he put a veil on his face. 34 But whenever Moses went in before the LORD to speak with Him, he would take the veil off until he came out; and he would come out and speak to the children of Israel whatever he had been commanded. 35 And whenever the children of Israel saw the face of Moses, that the skin of Moses' face shone, then Moses would put the veil on his face again, until he went in to speak with Him.

Laws about the Sabbath

35 Then Moses gathered all the congregation of the children of Israel together, and said to them, "These *are* the words which the LORD has commanded *you* to do: 2 Work shall be done for six days, but the seventh day shall be a holy day for you, a Sabbath of rest to the LORD. Whoever does any work on it shall be put to death. 3 You shall kindle no fire throughout your dwellings on the Sabbath day."

4 And Moses spoke to all the congregation of the children of Israel, saying, "This *is* the thing which the LORD commanded, saying: 5 'Take from among you an offering to the LORD. Whoever *is* of a willing heart, let him bring it as an offering to the LORD: gold, silver,

and bronze; 6 blue, purple, and scarlet *thread,* fine linen, and goats' *hair;* 7 ram skins dyed red, badger skins, and acacia wood; 8 oil for the light, and spices for the anointing oil and for the sweet incense; 9 onyx stones, and stones to be set in the ephod and in the breastplate.

10 'All *who are* gifted artisans among you shall come and make all that the LORD has commanded: 11 the tabernacle, its tent, its covering, its clasps, its boards, its bars, its pillars, and its sockets; 12 the ark and its poles, *with* the mercy seat, and the veil of the covering; 13 the table and its poles, all its utensils, and the showbread; 14 also the lampstand for the light, its utensils, its lamps, and the oil for the light; 15 the incense altar, its poles, the anointing oil, the sweet incense, and the screen for the door at the entrance of the tabernacle; 16 the altar of burnt offering with its bronze grating, its poles, all its utensils, *and* the laver and its base; 17 the hangings of the court, its pillars, their sockets, and the screen for the gate of the court; 18 the pegs of the tabernacle, the pegs of the court, and their cords; 19 the garments of ministry, for ministering in the holy *place*—the holy garments for Aaron the priest and the garments of his sons, to minister as priests.' "

20 And all the congregation of the children of Israel departed from the presence of Moses. 21 Then everyone came whose heart was stirred, and everyone whose spirit was willing, *and* they brought the LORD's offering for the work of the tabernacle of meeting, for all its service, and for the holy garments. 22 They came, both men and women, as many as had a willing heart, *and* brought earrings and nose rings, rings and necklaces, all jewelry of gold, that is, every man who *made* an offering of gold to the LORD. 23 And every man, with whom was found blue, purple, and scarlet *thread,* fine linen, goats' *hair,* red skins of rams, and badger skins, brought *them.* 24 Everyone who offered an offering of silver or bronze brought the LORD's

Wool, flax, and goats' hair were spun into thread, then woven into cloth for making garments and tents.

offering. And everyone with whom was found acacia wood for any work of the service, brought *it.* 25 All the women *who were* gifted artisans spun yarn with their hands, and brought what they had spun, of blue, purple, *and* scarlet, and fine linen. 26 And all the women whose hearts stirred with wisdom spun yarn of goats' *hair.* 27 The rulers brought onyx stones, and the stones to be set in the ephod and in the breastplate, 28 and spices and oil for the light, for the anointing oil, and for the sweet incense. 29 The children of Israel brought a freewill offering to the LORD, all the men and women whose hearts were willing to bring *material* for all kinds of work which the LORD, by the hand of Moses, had commanded to be done.

30 And Moses said to the children of Israel, "See, the LORD has called by name Bezalel the son of Uri, the son of Hur, of the tribe of Judah; 31 and He has filled him with the Spirit of God, in wisdom and understanding, in knowledge and all manner of workmanship, 32 to design artistic works, to work in gold and silver and bronze, 33 in cutting jewels for setting, in carving wood, and to work in all manner of artistic workmanship.

34 "And He has put in his heart the ability to teach, *in* him and Aholiab the son of Ahisamach, of the tribe of Dan. 35 He has filled them with skill to do all manner of work of the engraver and the designer and the tapestry maker, in blue, purple, and scarlet *thread,* and fine linen, and of the weaver—those who do every work and those who design artistic works.

The people build the tabernacle

36 "And Bezalel and Aholiab, and every gifted artisan in whom the LORD has put wisdom and understanding, to know how to do all manner of work for the service of the sanctuary, shall do according to all that the LORD has commanded."

2 Then Moses called Bezalel and Aholiab, and every gifted artisan in whose heart the LORD had put wisdom, everyone whose heart was stirred, to come and do the work. 3 And they received from Moses all the offering which the children of Israel had brought for the work of the service of making the sanctuary. So they continued bringing to him freewill offerings every morning. 4 Then all the craftsmen who were doing all the work of the sanctuary came, each from the work he was doing, 5 and they spoke to Moses, saying, "The people bring much more than enough for the service of the work which the LORD commanded *us* to do."

6 So Moses gave a commandment, and they caused it to be proclaimed throughout the camp, saying, "Let neither man nor woman do any more work for the offering of the sanctuary."

And the people were restrained from bringing, 7 for the material they had was sufficient for all the work to be done—indeed too much.

8 Then all the gifted artisans among them who worked on the tabernacle made ten curtains woven of fine linen, and of blue, purple, and scarlet thread; *with* artistic designs of cherubim they made them. 9 The length of each curtain *was* twenty-eight cubits, and the width of each curtain four cubits; the curtains *were* all the same size. 10 And he coupled five curtains to one another, and *the other* five curtains he coupled to one another. 11 He made loops of blue *yarn* on the edge of the curtain on the selvedge of one set; likewise he did on the outer edge of *the other* curtain of the second set. 12 Fifty loops he made on one curtain, and fifty loops he made on the edge of the curtain on the end of the second set; the loops held one *curtain* to another. 13 And he made fifty clasps of gold, and coupled the curtains to one another with the clasps, that it might be one tabernacle.

14 He made curtains of goats' *hair* for the tent over the tabernacle; he made eleven curtains. 15 The length of each curtain *was* thirty cubits, and the width of each curtain four cubits; the eleven curtains *were* the same size. 16 He coupled five curtains by themselves and six curtains by themselves. 17 And he made fifty loops on the edge of the curtain that is outermost in one set, and fifty loops he made on the edge of the curtain of the second set. 18 He also made fifty bronze clasps to couple the tent together, that it might be one. 19 Then he made a covering for the tent of ram skins dyed red, and a covering of badger skins above *that.*

20 For the tabernacle he made boards of acacia wood, standing upright. 21 The length of each board *was* ten cubits, and the width of each board a cubit and a half. 22 Each board had two tenons for binding one to another. Thus he made for all the boards of the tabernacle. 23 And he made boards for the tabernacle, twenty boards for the south side. 24 Forty sockets of silver he made to go under the twenty boards: two sockets under each of the boards for its two tenons. 25 And for the other side of the tabernacle, the north side, he made twenty boards 26 and their forty sockets of silver: two sockets under each of the boards. 27 For the west side of the tabernacle he made six boards. 28 He also made two boards for the two back corners of the tabernacle. 29 And they were coupled at the bottom and coupled together at the top by one ring. Thus he made both of them for the two corners. 30 So there were eight boards and their sockets—sixteen sockets of silver—two sockets under each of the boards.

31 And he made bars of acacia wood: five for the boards on one side of the tabernacle, 32 five bars for the boards on the other side of the tabernacle, and five bars for the boards of the tabernacle on the far side westward. 33 And he made the middle bar to pass through the boards from one end to the other. 34 He overlaid the boards with gold, made their rings of gold *to be* holders for the bars, and overlaid the bars with gold.

35 And he made a veil of blue, purple, and scarlet *thread,* and fine woven linen; it was worked *with* an artistic design of cherubim. 36 He made for it four pillars of acacia *wood,* and overlaid them with gold, with their hooks of gold; and he cast four sockets of silver for them.

37 He also made a screen for the tabernacle door, of blue, purple, and scarlet *thread,* and fine woven linen, made by a weaver, 38 and its five pillars with their hooks. And he overlaid their capitals and their rings with gold, but their five sockets *were* bronze.

The furniture of the tabernacle

37 Then Bezalel made the ark of acacia wood; two and a half cubits *was* its length, a cubit and a half its width, and a cubit and a half its height. 2 He overlaid it with pure gold inside and outside, and made a molding of gold all around it. ³ And he cast for it four rings of gold *to be set* in its four corners: two rings on one side, and two rings on the other side of it. ⁴ He made poles of acacia wood, and overlaid them with gold. ⁵ And he put the poles into the rings at the sides of the ark, to bear the ark. ⁶ He also made the mercy seat of pure gold; two and a half cubits *was* its length and a cubit and a half its width. ⁷ He made two cherubim of beaten gold; he made them of one piece at the two ends of the mercy seat: ⁸ one cherub at one end on this side, and the other cherub at the *other* end on that side. He made the cherubim at the two ends *of one piece* with the mercy seat. ⁹ The cherubim spread out *their* wings above, *and* covered the mercy seat with their wings. They faced one another; the faces of the cherubim were toward the mercy seat.

¹⁰ He made the table of acacia wood; two cubits *was* its length, a cubit its width, and a cubit and a half its height. ¹¹ And he overlaid it with pure gold, and made a molding of gold all around it. ¹² Also he made a frame of a handbreadth all around it, and made a molding of gold for the frame all

around it. ¹³ And he cast for it four rings of gold, and put the rings on the four corners that *were* at its four legs. ¹⁴ The rings were close to the frame, as holders for the poles to bear the table. ¹⁵ And he made the poles of acacia wood to bear the table, and overlaid them with gold. ¹⁶ He made of pure gold the utensils which were on the table: its dishes, its cups, its bowls, and its pitchers for pouring.

¹⁷ He also made the lampstand of pure gold; of hammered work he made the lampstand. Its shaft, its branches, its bowls, its *ornamental* knobs, and its flowers were of the same piece. ¹⁸ And six branches came out of its sides: three branches of the lampstand out of one side, and three branches of the lampstand out of the other side. ¹⁹ There were three bowls made like almond *blossoms* on one branch, with an *ornamental* knob and a flower, and three bowls made like almond *blossoms* on the other branch, with an *ornamental* knob and a flower—and so for the six branches coming out of the lampstand. ²⁰ And on the lampstand itself *were* four bowls made like almond *blossoms, each with* its *ornamental* knob and flower. ²¹ *There was*

Hebrew priests make sacrifices at the altar of burnt offering.

a knob under the *first* two branches of the same, a knob under the *second* two branches of the same, and a knob under the *third* two branches of the same, according to the six branches extending from it. 22 Their knobs and their branches were of one piece; all of it *was* one hammered piece of pure gold. 23 And he made its seven lamps, its wick-trimmers, and its trays of pure gold. 24 Of a talent of pure gold he made it, with all its utensils.

25 He made the incense altar of acacia wood. Its length *was* a cubit and its width a cubit—*it was* square—and two cubits *was* its height. Its horns were *of one piece* with it. 26 And he overlaid it with pure gold: its top, its sides all around, and its horns. He also made for it a molding of gold all around it. 27 He made two rings of gold for it under its molding, by its two corners on both sides, as holders for the poles with which to bear it. 28 And he made the poles of acacia wood, and overlaid them with gold.

29 He also made the holy anointing oil and the pure incense of sweet spices, according to the work of the perfumer.

The court of the tabernacle

38 He made the altar of burnt offering of acacia wood; five cubits *was* its length and five cubits its width—*it was* square—and its height *was* three cubits. 2 He made its horns on its four corners; the horns were *of one piece* with it. And he overlaid it with bronze. 3 He made all the utensils for the altar: the pans, the shovels, the basins, the forks, and the firepans; all its utensils he made of bronze. 4 And he made a grate of bronze network for the altar, under its rim, midway from the bottom. 5 He cast four rings for the four corners of the bronze grating, *as* holders for the poles. 6 And he made the poles of acacia wood, and overlaid them with bronze. 7 Then he put the poles into the rings on the sides of the altar, with which to bear it. He made the altar hollow with boards.

8 He made the laver of bronze and its base of bronze, from the bronze mirrors of the serving women who assembled at the door of the **tabernacle of meeting.**

9 Then he made the court on the south side; the hangings of the court

---

🌐 WORDFINDER

38:8 Tabernacle of Meeting   Israel's worship place in the desert. It was a special tent divided into two rooms—a Holy Place and a Most Holy Place. Only the priests were allowed in the tabernacle.

⛏ DIGGING IN

38:1—40:38 What Old Testament Worship Means for Us You may be puzzled when you read about all the things people needed for worship in the Old Testament. You read the instructions for making all the strange furniture for the worship place, or tabernacle (pronounced *TAB-er-nak-kel*). Then you read about the priests and how they dressed. There are so many details about how and when to make sacrifices. What do all these parts of Old Testament worship mean for you?

The main thing to remember is that Old Testament worship was the way God was *teaching* the people about sin and how much sin costs. Sin caused separation from God. The daily animal sacrifices the people had to make showed that sin costs life that is precious. But someday the real cost of sin would be paid for by Someone very dear to God—*His own Son!*

So Old Testament worship points to the coming of Jesus and shows how He would die in the place of sinful people. We don't need the animal sacrifices now because Jesus took away our sins by sacrificing Himself.

were of fine woven linen, one hundred cubits long. 10 There *were* twenty pillars for them, with twenty bronze sockets. The hooks of the pillars and their bands *were* silver. 11 On the north side *the hangings were* one hundred cubits *long,* with twenty pillars and their twenty bronze sockets. The hooks of the pillars and their bands *were* silver. 12 And on the west side *there were* hangings of fifty cubits, with ten pillars and their ten sockets. The hooks of the pillars and their bands *were* silver. 13 For the east side *the hangings were* fifty cubits. 14 The hangings of one side *of the gate were* fifteen cubits *long,* *with* their three pillars and their three sockets, 15 and the same for the other side of the court gate; on this side and that *were* hangings of fifteen cubits, *with* their three pillars and their three sockets. 16 All the hangings of the court all around *were of* fine woven linen. 17 The sockets for the pillars *were* bronze, the hooks of the pillars and their bands *were* silver, and the overlay of their capitals *was* silver; and all the pillars of the court had bands of silver. 18 The screen for the gate of the court *was* woven of blue, purple, and scarlet *thread,* and of fine woven linen. The length *was* twenty cubits, and the height along its width *was* five cubits, corresponding to the hangings of the court. 19 And *there were* four pillars *with* their four sockets of bronze; their hooks *were* silver, and the overlay of their capitals and their bands *was* silver. 20 All the pegs of the tabernacle, and of the court all around, *were* bronze.

21 This is the inventory of the tabernacle, the tabernacle of the Testimony, which was counted according to the commandment of Moses, for the service of the Levites, by the hand of Ithamar, son of Aaron the priest.

22 Bezalel the son of Uri, the son of Hur, of the tribe of Judah, made all that the LORD had commanded Moses. 23 And with him *was* Aholiab the son of Ahisamach, of the tribe of Dan, an engraver and designer, a weaver of

blue, purple, and scarlet *thread,* and of fine linen.

24 All the gold that was used in all the work of the holy *place,* that is, the gold of the offering, was twenty-nine talents and seven hundred and thirty shekels, according to the shekel of the sanctuary. 25 And the silver from those who were numbered of the congregation *was* one hundred talents and one thousand seven hundred and seventy-five shekels, according to the shekel of the sanctuary: 26 a bekah for each man (*that is,* half a shekel, according to the shekel of the sanctuary), for everyone included in the numbering from twenty years old and above, for six hundred and three thousand, five hundred and fifty *men.* 27 And from the hundred talents of silver were cast the sockets of the sanctuary and the bases of the veil: one hundred sockets from the hundred talents, one talent for each socket. 28 Then from the one thousand seven hundred and seventy-five *shekels* he made hooks for the pillars, overlaid their capitals, and made bands for them.

29 The offering of bronze *was* seventy talents and two thousand four hundred shekels. 30 And with it he made the sockets for the door of the tabernacle of meeting, the bronze altar, the bronze grating for it, and all the utensils for the altar, 31 the sockets for the court all around, the bases for the court gate, all the pegs for the tabernacle, and all the pegs for the court all around.

What the priests wear

39 Of the blue, purple, and scarlet *thread* they made garments of ministry, for ministering in the holy *place,* and made the holy garments for Aaron, as the LORD had commanded Moses.

2 He made the ephod of gold, blue, purple, and scarlet *thread,* and of fine woven linen. 3 And they beat the gold into thin sheets and cut *it into* threads, to work *it in with* the blue, purple, and scarlet *thread,* and the fine linen, *into* artistic designs. 4 They made shoulder

straps for it to couple *it* together; it was coupled together at its two edges. 5 And the intricately woven band of his ephod that *was* on it *was* of the same workmanship, *woven of* gold, blue, purple, and scarlet *thread,* and of fine woven linen, as the Lord had commanded Moses.

6 And they set onyx stones, enclosed in settings of gold; they were engraved, as signets are engraved, with the names of the sons of Israel. 7 He put them on the shoulders of the ephod *as* memorial stones for the sons of Israel, as the Lord had commanded Moses.

8 And he made the breastplate, artistically woven like the workmanship of the ephod, of gold, blue, purple, and scarlet *thread,* and of fine woven linen. 9 They made the breastplate square by doubling it; a span *was* its length and a span its width when doubled. 10 And they set in it four rows of stones: a row with a sardius, a topaz, and an emerald was the first row; 11 the second row, a turquoise, a sapphire, and a diamond; 12 the third row, a jacinth, an agate, and an amethyst; 13 the fourth row, a beryl, an onyx, and a jasper. *They were* enclosed in settings of gold in their mountings. 14 *There were* twelve stones according to the names of the sons of Israel: according to their names, *engraved like* a signet, each one with its own name according to the twelve tribes. 15 And they made chains for the breastplate at the ends, like braided cords of pure gold. 16 They also made two settings of gold and two gold rings, and put the two rings on the two ends of the breastplate. 17 And they put the two braided *chains* of gold in the two rings on the ends of the breastplate. 18 The two ends of the two braided *chains* they fastened in the two settings, and put them on the shoulder straps of the ephod in the front. 19 And they made two rings of gold and put *them* on the two ends of the breastplate, on the edge of it, which *was* on the inward side of the ephod. 20 They made two *other* gold rings and put them on the two shoulder straps, underneath the ephod toward

its front, right at the seam above the intricately woven band of the ephod. 21 And they bound the breastplate by means of its rings to the rings of the ephod with a blue cord, so that it would be above the intricately woven band of the ephod, and that the breastplate would not come loose from the ephod, as the Lord had commanded Moses.

22 He made the robe of the ephod of woven work, all of blue. 23 And *there was* an opening in the middle of the robe, like the opening in a coat of mail, *with* a woven binding all around the opening, so that it would not tear. 24 They made on the hem of the robe pomegranates of blue, purple, and scarlet, and of fine woven *linen.* 25 And they made bells of pure gold, and put the bells between the pomegranates on the hem of the robe all around between the pomegranates: 26 a bell and a pomegranate, a bell and a pomegranate, all around the hem of the robe to minister in, as the Lord had commanded Moses.

27 They made tunics, artistically woven of fine linen, for Aaron and his sons, 28 a turban of fine linen, exquisite hats of fine linen, short trousers of fine woven linen, 29 and a sash of fine woven linen with blue, purple, and scarlet *thread,* made by a weaver, as the Lord had commanded Moses.

30 Then they made the plate of the holy crown of pure gold, and wrote on it an inscription *like* the engraving of a signet:

HOLINESS TO THE LORD.

31 And they tied to it a blue cord, to fasten *it* above on the turban, as the Lord had commanded Moses.

32 Thus all the work of the tabernacle of the tent of meeting was finished. And the children of Israel did according to all that the Lord had commanded Moses; so they did. 33 And they brought the tabernacle to Moses, the tent and all its furnishings: its clasps, its boards, its bars, its pillars, and its sockets; 34 the covering of ram skins dyed red, the covering of badger skins,

and the veil of the covering; 35 the ark of the Testimony with its poles, and the mercy seat; 36 the table, all its utensils, and the showbread; 37 the pure *gold* lampstand with its lamps (the lamps set in order), all its utensils, and the oil for light; 38 the gold altar, the anointing oil, and the sweet incense; the screen for the tabernacle door; 39 the bronze altar, its grate of bronze, its poles, and all its utensils; the laver with its base; 40 the hangings of the court, its pillars and its sockets, the screen for the court gate, its cords, and its pegs; all the utensils for the service of the tabernacle, for the tent of meeting; 41 and the garments of ministry, to minister in the holy *place:* the holy garments for Aaron the priest, and his sons' garments, to minister as priests.

42 According to all that the LORD had commanded Moses, so the children of Israel did all the work. 43 Then Moses looked over all the work, and indeed they had done it; as the LORD had commanded, just so they had done it. And Moses blessed them.

The tabernacle is finished

40 Then the LORD spoke to Moses, saying: 2 "On the first day of the first month you shall set up the tabernacle of the tent of meeting. 3 You shall put in it the ark of the Testimony, and partition off the ark with the veil. 4 You shall bring in the table and arrange the things that are to be set in order on

---

What Was the Worship Place Like in the Desert?

The "tabernacle" (pronounced *TAB-er-nak-kel*) was a special kind of tent. Only the priests could go in there to worship for the people. It consisted of an altar for sacrifice, a place for the priests to wash, a lampstand, an altar for burning incense, a table for the holy bread, curtains (veil), and a Most Holy Place where the ark of the covenant was placed (see Exodus 26:31–36).

---

it; and you shall bring in the lampstand and light its lamps. 5 You shall also set the altar of gold for the incense before the ark of the Testimony, and put up the screen for the door of the tabernacle. 6 Then you shall set the altar of the burnt offering before the door of the tabernacle of the tent of meeting. 7 And you shall set the laver between the tabernacle of meeting and the altar, and put water in it. 8 You shall set up the court all around, and hang up the screen at the court gate.

9 "And you shall take the anointing oil, and anoint the tabernacle and all that *is* in it; and you shall hallow it and all its utensils, and it shall be holy. 10 You shall anoint the altar of the burnt offering and all its utensils, and consecrate the altar. The altar shall be most holy. 11 And you shall anoint the laver and its base, and consecrate it.

12 "Then you shall bring Aaron and his sons to the door of the tabernacle of meeting and wash them with water. 13 You shall put the holy garments on Aaron, and anoint him and consecrate him, that he may minister to Me as priest. 14 And you shall bring his sons and clothe them with tunics. 15 You shall anoint them, as you anointed their father, that they may minister to Me as priests; for their anointing shall surely be an everlasting priesthood throughout their generations."

16 Thus Moses did; according to all that the LORD had commanded him, so he did.

17 And it came to pass in the first month of the second year, on the first *day* of the month, *that* the tabernacle was raised up. 18 So Moses raised up the tabernacle, fastened its sockets, set up its boards, put in its bars, and raised up its pillars. 19 And he spread out the tent over the tabernacle and put the covering of the tent on top of it, as the LORD had commanded Moses. 20 He took the Testimony and put *it* into the ark, inserted the poles through the rings of the ark, and put the mercy seat on top of the ark. 21 And he brought the ark into the tabernacle,

hung up the veil of the covering, and partitioned off the ark of the Testimony, as the LORD had commanded Moses.

22 He put the table in the tabernacle of meeting, on the north side of the tabernacle, outside the veil; 23 and he set the bread in order upon it before the LORD, as the LORD had commanded Moses. 24 He put the lampstand in the tabernacle of meeting, across from the table, on the south side of the tabernacle; 25 and he lit the lamps before the LORD, as the LORD had commanded Moses. 26 He put the gold altar in the tabernacle of meeting in front of the veil; 27 and he burned sweet incense on it, as the LORD had commanded Moses. 28 He hung up the screen *at* the door of the tabernacle. 29 And he put the altar of burnt offering *before* the door of the tabernacle of the tent of meeting, and offered upon it the burnt offering and the grain offering, as the LORD had commanded Moses. 30 He set the laver between the tabernacle of meeting and the altar, and put water there for washing;

31 and Moses, Aaron, and his sons would wash their hands and their feet *with water* from it. 32 Whenever they went into the tabernacle of meeting, and when they came near the altar, they washed, as the LORD had commanded Moses. 33 And he raised up the court all around the tabernacle and the altar, and hung up the screen of the court gate. So Moses finished the work.

34 Then the cloud covered the tabernacle of meeting, and the glory of the LORD filled the tabernacle. 35 And Moses was not able to enter the tabernacle of meeting, because the cloud rested above it, and the glory of the LORD filled the tabernacle. 36 Whenever the cloud was taken up from above the tabernacle, the children of Israel would go onward in all their journeys. 37 But if the cloud was not taken up, then they did not journey till the day that it was taken up. 38 For the cloud of the LORD *was* above the tabernacle by day, and fire was over it by night, in the sight of all the house of Israel, throughout all their journeys.

The Book of
LEVITICUS

My name is pronounced *AIR-un*. I am the brother of Moses, and I was honored when the Lord ordered me to speak for Moses to the king of Egypt. My brother was never a good public speaker, so he was afraid to speak face to face with the king (see Exodus 4).

I was always sorry for one thing though. One day I gave in to the sinful wishes of the people and made a golden idol (Exodus 31:1–4). This nearly caused the end of our great dream of living in the new land that God had promised us. But my brother Moses prayed for us, and God forgave me and the people.

After this, I became the high priest of Israel. In addition to offering the regular sacrifice to God, I came before the Lord in the Most Holy Place once a year.

The burnt offering

NOW the LORD called to Moses, and spoke to him from the tabernacle of meeting, saying, 2 "Speak to the children of Israel, and say to them: 'When any one of you brings an offering to the LORD, you shall bring your offering of the livestock—of the herd and of the flock.

3 'If his offering is a burnt sacrifice of the herd, let him offer a male without blemish; he shall offer it of his own free will at the door of the tabernacle of meeting before the LORD. 4 Then he shall put his hand on the head of the burnt offering, and it will be accepted

What Is an Atonement?

In Old Testament times, people brought animal sacrifices to the priest. This was to make "atonement" for their sins (pronounced *ah-TONE-ment*). An atonement is a price paid for a person's sins. We put people in jail to "atone" for crimes. Only Jesus could pay the price we owe to God for our sins.

on his behalf to make atonement for him. 5 He shall kill the bull before the LORD; and the priests, Aaron's sons, shall bring the blood and sprinkle the blood all around on the altar that is by the door of the tabernacle of meeting. 6 And he shall skin the burnt offering and cut it into its pieces. 7 The sons of Aaron the priest shall put fire on the altar, and lay the wood in order on the fire. 8 Then the priests, Aaron's sons, shall lay the parts, the head, and the fat in order on the wood that is on the fire upon the altar; 9 but he shall wash its entrails and its legs with water. And the priest shall burn all on the altar as a burnt sacrifice, an offering made by fire, a sweet aroma to the LORD.

10 'If his offering is of the flocks—of the sheep or of the goats—as a burnt sacrifice, he shall bring a male without blemish. 11 He shall kill it on the north side of the altar before the LORD; and the priests, Aaron's sons, shall sprinkle its blood all around on the altar. 12 And he shall cut it into its pieces, with its head and its fat; and the priest shall lay them in order on the wood that is on the fire upon the altar; 13 but he shall wash the entrails and the legs with water. Then the priest

shall bring *it* all and burn *it* on the altar; it *is* a burnt sacrifice, an offering made by fire, a sweet aroma to the LORD.

14 'And if the burnt sacrifice of his offering to the LORD *is* of birds, then he shall bring his offering of turtledoves or young pigeons. 15 The priest shall bring it to the altar, wring off its head, and burn *it* on the altar; its blood shall be drained out at the side of the altar. 16 And he shall remove its crop with its feathers and cast it beside the altar on the east side, into the place for ashes. 17 Then he shall split it at its wings, *but* shall not divide *it* completely; and the priest shall burn it on the altar, on the wood that *is* on the fire. It *is* a burnt sacrifice, an offering made by fire, a sweet aroma to the LORD.

The grain offering

2 'When anyone offers a grain offering to the LORD, his offering shall be *of* fine flour. And he shall pour oil on it, and put frankincense on it. 2 He shall bring it to Aaron's sons, the priests, one of whom shall take from it his handful of fine flour and oil with all the frankincense. And the priest shall burn *it as* a memorial on the altar, an offering made by fire, a sweet aroma to the LORD. 3 The rest of the grain offering *shall be* Aaron's and his sons'. *It is* most holy of the offerings to the LORD made by fire.

4 'And if you bring as an offering a grain offering baked in the oven, *it shall be* unleavened cakes of fine flour mixed with oil, or unleavened wafers anointed with oil. 5 But if your offering *is* a grain offering *baked* in a pan, *it shall be of* fine flour, unleavened, mixed with oil. 6 You shall break it in pieces and pour oil on it; it *is* a grain offering.

7 'If your offering *is* a grain offering *baked* in a covered pan, it shall be made *of* fine flour with oil. 8 You shall bring the grain offering that is made of these things to the LORD. And when it is presented to the priest, he shall bring it to the altar. 9 Then the priest shall take from the grain offering a memorial portion, and burn *it* on the altar. It *is* an offering made by fire, a sweet aroma to the LORD. 10 And what is left of the grain offering *shall be* Aaron's and his sons'. *It is* most holy of the offerings to the LORD made by fire.

11 'No grain offering which you bring to the LORD shall be made with **leaven**, for you shall burn no leaven nor any honey in any offering to the LORD made by fire. 12 As for the offering of the firstfruits, you shall offer them to the LORD, but they shall not be burned on the altar for a sweet aroma. 13 And every offering of your grain offering you shall season with salt; you shall not allow the salt of the covenant of your God to be lacking from your grain offering. With all your offerings you shall offer salt.

14 'If you offer a grain offering of your firstfruits to the LORD, you shall offer for the grain offering of your firstfruits green heads of grain roasted on the fire, grain beaten from full heads. 15 And you shall put oil on it, and lay frankincense on it. It *is* a grain offering. 16 Then the priest shall burn the memorial portion: *part* of its beaten grain and *part* of its oil, with all the frankincense, as an offering made by fire to the LORD.

The peace offering

3 'When his offering *is* a sacrifice of a peace offering, if he offers *it* of the herd, whether male or female, he shall offer it without blemish before the LORD. 2 And he shall lay his hand on the head of his offering, and kill it *at*

WORDFINDER

2:11 Leaven Pronounced *LEV-in.* A substance used in ancient times to make bread dough rise. Today bakers use yeast to do this. Jesus compared the growth of God's kingdom to the slow work of leaven.

This "portable" worship place of the Israelites was a special tent called the tabernacle.

the door of the tabernacle of meeting; and Aaron's sons, the priests, shall sprinkle the blood all around on the altar. ³ Then he shall offer from the sacrifice of the peace offering an offering made by fire to the LORD. The fat that covers the entrails and all the fat that *is* on the entrails, ⁴ the two kidneys and the fat that *is* on them by the flanks, and the fatty lobe *attached* to the liver above the kidneys, he shall remove; ⁵ and Aaron's sons shall burn it on the altar upon the burnt sacrifice, which *is* on the wood that *is* on the fire, *as* an offering made by fire, a sweet aroma to the LORD.

⁶ 'If his offering as a sacrifice of a peace offering to the LORD *is* of the flock, *whether* male or female, he shall offer it without blemish. ⁷ If he offers a lamb as his offering, then he shall offer it before the LORD. ⁸ And he shall lay his hand on the head of his offering, and kill it before the tabernacle of meeting; and Aaron's sons shall sprinkle its blood all around on the altar.

⁹ 'Then he shall offer from the sacrifice of the peace offering, as an offering made by fire to the LORD, its fat *and* the whole fat tail which he shall remove close to the backbone. And the fat that covers the entrails and all the fat that

is on the entrails, ¹⁰ the two kidneys and the fat that *is* on them by the flanks, and the fatty lobe *attached* to the liver above the kidneys, he shall remove; ¹¹ and the priest shall burn *them* on the altar *as* food, an offering made by fire to the LORD.

¹² 'And if his offering *is* a goat, then he shall offer it before the LORD. ¹³ He shall lay his hand on its head and kill it before the tabernacle of meeting; and the sons of Aaron shall sprinkle its blood all around on the altar. ¹⁴ Then he shall offer from it his offering, as an offering made by fire to the LORD. The fat that covers the entrails and all the fat that *is* on the entrails, ¹⁵ the two kidneys and the fat that *is* on them by the flanks, and the fatty lobe *attached* to the liver above the kidneys, he shall remove; ¹⁶ and the priest shall burn them on the altar *as* food, an offering made by fire for a sweet aroma; all the fat *is* the LORD's.

¹⁷ 'This shall *be* a perpetual statute throughout your generations in all your dwellings: you shall eat neither fat nor blood.' "

The sin offering

4 Now the LORD spoke to Moses, saying, ² "Speak to the children of Israel,

saying: 'If a person sins unintentionally against any of the commandments of the LORD *in anything* which ought not to be done, and does any of them, 3 if the anointed priest sins, bringing guilt on the people, then let him offer to the LORD for his sin which he has sinned a young bull without blemish as a sin offering. 4 He shall bring the bull to the door of the tabernacle of meeting before the LORD, lay his hand on the bull's head, and kill the bull before the LORD. 5 Then the anointed priest shall take some of the bull's blood and bring it to the tabernacle of meeting. 6 The priest shall dip his finger in the blood and sprinkle some of the blood seven times before the LORD, in front of the veil of the sanctuary. 7 And the priest shall put some of the blood on the horns of the altar of sweet incense before the LORD, which is in the tabernacle of meeting; and he shall pour the remaining blood of the bull at the base of the altar of the burnt offering, which is at the door of the tabernacle of meeting. 8 He shall take from it all the fat of the bull as the sin offering. The fat that covers the entrails and all the fat which *is* on the entrails, 9 the two kidneys and the fat that *is* on them by the flanks, and the fatty lobe *attached* to the liver above the kidneys, he shall remove, 10 as it was taken from the bull of the sacrifice of the peace offering; and the priest shall burn them on the altar of the burnt offering. 11 But the bull's hide and all its flesh, with its head and legs, its entrails and offal— 12 the whole bull he shall carry outside the camp to a clean place, where the ashes are poured out, and burn it on wood with fire; where the ashes are poured out it shall be burned.

13 'Now if the whole congregation of Israel sins unintentionally, and the thing is hidden from the eyes of the assembly, and they have done *something against* any of the commandments of the LORD *in anything* which should not be done, and are guilty; 14 when the sin which they have committed becomes known, then the assembly shall offer a young bull for the sin, and bring it before the tabernacle of meeting. 15 And the elders of the congregation shall lay their hands on the head of the bull before the LORD. Then the bull shall be killed before the LORD. 16 The anointed priest shall bring some of the bull's blood to the tabernacle of meeting. 17 Then the priest shall dip his finger in the blood and sprinkle *it* seven times before the LORD, in front of the veil. 18 And he shall put *some* of the blood on the horns of the altar which *is* before the LORD, which *is* in the tabernacle of meeting; and he shall pour the remaining blood at the base of the altar of burnt offering, which is at the door of the tabernacle of meeting. 19 He shall take all the fat from it and burn *it* on the altar. 20 And he shall do with the bull as he did with the bull as a sin offering; thus he shall do with it. So the priest shall make atonement for them, and it shall be forgiven them. 21 Then he shall carry the bull outside the camp, and burn it as he burned the first bull. It *is* a sin offering for the assembly.

22 'When a ruler has sinned, and done *something* unintentionally *against* any of the commandments of the LORD his God *in anything* which should not be done, and is guilty, 23 or if his sin which he has committed comes to his knowledge, he shall bring as his offering a kid of the goats, a male without blemish. 24 And he shall lay his hand on the head of the goat, and kill it at the place where they kill the burnt offering before the LORD. It *is* a sin offering. 25 The priest shall take some of the blood of the sin offering with his finger, put *it* on the horns of the altar of burnt offering, and pour its blood at the base of the altar of burnt offering. 26 And he shall burn all its fat on the altar, like the fat of the sacrifice of the peace offering. So the priest shall make atonement for him concerning his sin, and it shall be forgiven him.

27 'If anyone of the common people sins unintentionally by doing *something against* any of the commandments of the LORD *in anything* which

ought not to be done, and is guilty, 28 or if his sin which he has committed comes to his knowledge, then he shall bring as his offering a kid of the goats, a female without blemish, for his sin which he has committed. 29 And he shall lay his hand on the head of the sin offering, and kill the sin offering at the place of the burnt offering. 30 Then the priest shall take *some* of its blood with his finger, put *it* on the horns of the altar of burnt offering, and pour all *the remaining* blood at the base of the altar. 31 He shall remove all its fat, as fat is removed from the sacrifice of the peace offering; and the priest shall burn it on the altar for a sweet aroma to the LORD. So the priest shall make atonement for him, and it shall be forgiven him.

32 'If he brings a lamb as his sin offering, he shall bring a female without blemish. 33 Then he shall lay his hand on the head of the sin offering, and kill it as a sin offering at the place where they kill the burnt offering. 34 The priest shall take *some* of the blood of the sin offering with his finger, put *it* on the horns of the altar of burnt offering, and pour all *the remaining* blood at the base of the altar. 35 He shall remove all its fat, as the fat of the lamb is removed from the sacrifice of the peace offering. Then the priest shall burn it on the altar, according to the offerings made by fire to the LORD. So the priest shall make atonement for his sin that he has committed, and it shall be forgiven him.

The trespass offering

5 'If a person sins in hearing the utterance of an oath, and *is* a witness, whether he has seen or known *of the matter*—if he does not tell *it*, he bears guilt.

2 'Or if a person touches any unclean thing, whether *it is* the carcass of an unclean beast, or the carcass of unclean livestock, or the carcass of unclean creeping things, and he is unaware of it, he also shall be unclean and guilty. 3 Or if he touches human

uncleanness—whatever uncleanness with which a man may be defiled, and he is unaware of it—when he realizes *it*, then he shall be guilty.

4 'Or if a person swears, speaking thoughtlessly with *his* lips to do evil or to do good, whatever *it is* that a man may pronounce by an oath, and he is unaware of it—when he realizes *it*, then he shall be guilty in any of these *matters*.

5 'And it shall be, when he is guilty in any of these *matters*, that he shall confess that he has sinned in that *thing*; 6 and he shall bring his trespass offering to the LORD for his sin which he has committed, a female from the flock, a lamb or a kid of the goats as a sin offering. So the priest shall make atonement for him concerning his sin.

7 'If he is not able to bring a lamb, then he shall bring to the LORD, for his trespass which he has committed, two turtledoves or two young pigeons: one as a sin offering and the other as a burnt offering. 8 And he shall bring them to the priest, who shall offer *that* which is for the sin offering first, and wring off its head from its neck, but shall not divide *it* completely. 9 Then he shall sprinkle *some* of the blood of the sin offering on the side of the altar, and the rest of the blood shall be drained out at the base of the altar. It *is* a sin offering. 10 And he shall offer the second *as* a burnt offering according to the prescribed manner. So the priest shall make atonement on his behalf for his sin which he has committed, and it shall be forgiven him.

11 'But if he is not able to bring two turtledoves or two young pigeons, then he who sinned shall bring for his offering one-tenth of an ephah of fine flour as a sin offering. He shall put no oil on it, nor shall he put frankincense on it, for it *is* a sin offering. 12 Then he shall bring it to the priest, and the priest shall take his handful of it as a memorial portion, and burn *it* on the altar according to the offerings made by fire to the LORD. It *is* a sin offering. 13 The priest shall make atonement for him, for his sin that he has committed in

any of these matters; and it shall be forgiven him. *The rest* shall be the priest's as a grain offering.' "

14 Then the LORD spoke to Moses, saying: 15 "If a person commits a trespass, and sins unintentionally in regard to the holy things of the LORD, then he shall bring to the LORD as his trespass offering a ram without blemish from the flocks, with your valuation in shekels of silver according to the shekel of the sanctuary, as a trespass offering. 16 And he shall make restitution for the harm that he has done in regard to the holy thing, and shall add one-fifth to it and give it to the priest. So the priest shall make atonement for him with the ram of the trespass offering, and it shall be forgiven him.

17 "If a person sins, and commits any of these things which are forbidden to be done by the commandments of the LORD, though he does not know *it,* yet he is guilty and shall bear his iniquity. 18 And he shall bring to the priest a ram without blemish from the flock, with your valuation, as a trespass offering. So the priest shall make atonement for him regarding his ignorance in which he erred and did not know *it,* and it shall be forgiven him. 19 It is a trespass offering; he has certainly trespassed against the LORD."

Laws about the burnt offering, the grain offering, and the sin offering

6 And the LORD spoke to Moses, saying: 2 "If a person sins and commits a trespass against the LORD by lying to his neighbor about what was delivered to him for safekeeping, or about a pledge, or about a robbery, or if he has extorted from his neighbor, 3 or if he has found what was lost and lies concerning it, and swears falsely—in any one of these things that a man may do in which he sins: 4 then it shall be, because he has sinned and is guilty, that he shall restore what he has stolen, or the thing which he has extorted, or what was delivered to him for safekeeping, or the lost thing which he found, 5 or all that about which he has

sworn falsely. He shall restore its full value, add one-fifth more to it, *and* give it to whomever it belongs, on the day of his trespass offering. 6 And he shall bring his trespass offering to the LORD, a ram without blemish from the flock, with your valuation, as a trespass offering, to the priest. 7 So the priest shall make atonement for him before the LORD, and he shall be forgiven for any one of these things that he may have done in which he trespasses."

8 Then the LORD spoke to Moses, saying, 9 "Command Aaron and his sons, saying, 'This *is* the law of the burnt offering: The burnt offering *shall be* on the hearth upon the altar all night until morning, and the fire of the altar shall be kept burning on it. 10 And the priest shall put on his linen garment, and his linen trousers he shall put on his body, and take up the ashes of the burnt offering which the fire has consumed on the altar, and he shall put them beside the altar. 11 Then he shall take off his garments, put on other garments, and carry the ashes outside the camp to a clean place. 12 And the fire on the altar shall be kept burning on it; it shall not be put out. And the priest shall burn wood on it every morning, and lay the burnt offering in order on it; and he shall burn on it the fat of the peace offerings. 13 A fire shall always be burning on the altar; it shall never go out.

14 'This *is* the law of the grain offering: The sons of Aaron shall offer it on the altar before the LORD. 15 He shall take from it his handful of the fine flour of the grain offering, with its oil, and all the frankincense which *is* on the grain offering, and shall burn *it* on the altar *for* a sweet aroma, as a memorial to the LORD. 16 And the remainder of it Aaron and his sons shall eat; with unleavened bread it shall be eaten in a holy place; in the court of the tabernacle of meeting they shall eat it. 17 It shall not be baked with leaven. I have given it *as* their portion of My offerings made by fire; it *is* most holy, like the sin offering and the trespass offering. 18 All the males among the

children of Aaron may eat it. *It shall be* a statute forever in your generations concerning the offerings made by fire to the LORD. Everyone who touches them must be holy.' "

19 And the LORD spoke to Moses, saying, 20 "This *is* the offering of Aaron and his sons, which they shall offer to the LORD, *beginning* on the day when he is anointed: one-tenth of an ephah of fine flour as a daily grain offering, half of it in the morning and half of it at night. 21 It shall be made in a pan with oil. *When it is* mixed, you shall bring it in. The baked pieces of the grain offering you shall offer *for* a sweet aroma to the LORD. 22 The priest from among his sons, who is anointed in his place, shall offer it. *It is* a statute forever to the LORD. It shall be wholly burned. 23 For every grain offering for the priest shall be wholly burned. It shall not be eaten."

24 Also the LORD spoke to Moses, saying, 25 "Speak to Aaron and to his sons, saying, 'This *is* the law of the sin offering: In the place where the burnt offering is killed, the sin offering shall be killed before the LORD. It *is* most holy. 26 The priest who offers it for sin shall eat it. In a holy place it shall be eaten, in the court of the tabernacle of meeting. 27 Everyone who touches its flesh must be holy. And when its blood is sprinkled on any garment, you shall wash that on which it was sprinkled, in a holy place. 28 But the earthen vessel in which it is boiled shall be broken. And if it is boiled in a bronze pot, it shall be both scoured and rinsed in water. 29 All the males among the priests may eat it. It *is* most holy. 30 But no sin offering from which *any* of the blood is brought into the tabernacle of meeting, to make atonement in the holy *place,* shall be eaten. It shall be burned in the fire.

Laws about the trespass offering and the peace offering

7 'Likewise this *is* the law of the trespass offering (it *is* most holy): 2 In the place where they kill the burnt offering they shall kill the trespass offering. And its blood he shall sprinkle all around on the altar. 3 And he shall offer from it all its fat. The fat tail and the fat that covers the entrails, 4 the two kidneys and the fat that *is* on them by the flanks, and the fatty lobe *attached* to the liver above the kidneys, he shall remove; 5 and the priest shall burn them on the altar *as* an offering made by fire to the LORD. It *is* a trespass offering. 6 Every male among the priests may eat it. It shall be eaten in a holy place. It *is* most holy. 7 The trespass offering *is* like the sin offering; *there is* one law for them both: the priest who makes atonement with it shall have *it*. 8 And the priest who offers anyone's burnt offering, that priest shall have for himself the skin of the burnt offering which he has offered. 9 Also every grain offering that is baked in the oven and all that is prepared in the covered pan, or in a pan, shall be the priest's who offers it. 10 Every grain offering, *whether* mixed with oil or dry, shall belong to all the sons of Aaron, to one as much as the other.

11 'This *is* the law of the sacrifice of peace offerings which he shall offer to the LORD: 12 If he offers it for a thanksgiving, then he shall offer, with the sacrifice of thanksgiving, unleavened cakes mixed with oil, unleavened wafers anointed with oil, or cakes of blended flour mixed with oil. 13 Besides the cakes, *as* his offering he shall offer leavened bread with the sacrifice of thanksgiving of his peace offering. 14 And from it he shall offer one cake from each offering *as* a heave offering to the LORD. It shall belong to the priest who sprinkles the blood of the peace offering.

15 'The flesh of the sacrifice of his peace offering for thanksgiving shall be eaten the same day it is offered. He shall not leave any of it until morning. 16 But if the sacrifice of his offering *is* a vow or a voluntary offering, it shall be eaten the same day that he offers his sacrifice; but on the next day the remainder of it also may be eaten; 17 the remainder of the flesh of the

sacrifice on the third day must be burned with fire. 18 And if *any* of the flesh of the sacrifice of his peace offering is eaten at all on the third day, it shall not be accepted, nor shall it be imputed to him; it shall be an abomination *to* him who offers it, and the person who eats of it shall bear guilt.

19 'The flesh that touches any unclean thing shall not be eaten. It shall be burned with fire. And as for the *clean* flesh, all who are clean may eat of it. 20 But the person who eats the flesh of the sacrifice of the peace offering that *belongs* to the LORD, while he is unclean, that person shall be cut off from his people. 21 Moreover the person who touches any unclean thing, *such as* human uncleanness, *an* unclean animal, or any abominable unclean thing, and who eats the flesh of the sacrifice of the peace offering that *belongs* to the LORD, that person shall be cut off from his people.' ''

22 And the LORD spoke to Moses, saying, 23 ''Speak to the children of Israel, saying: 'You shall not eat any fat, of ox or sheep or goat. 24 And the fat of an animal that dies *naturally,* and the fat of what is torn by wild beasts, may be used in any other way; but you shall by no means eat it. 25 For whoever eats the fat of the animal of which men offer an offering made by fire to the LORD, the person who eats *it* shall be cut off from his people. 26 Moreover you shall not eat any blood in any of your dwellings, *whether* of bird or beast. 27 Whoever eats any blood, that person shall be cut off from his people.' ''

28 Then the LORD spoke to Moses, saying, 29 ''Speak to the children of Israel, saying: 'He who offers the sacrifice of his peace offering to the LORD shall bring his offering to the LORD from the sacrifice of his peace offering. 30 His own hands shall bring the offerings made by fire to the LORD. The fat with the breast he shall bring, that the breast may be waved *as* a wave offering before the LORD. 31 And the priest shall burn the fat on the altar, but the breast shall be Aaron's and his

sons'. 32 Also the right thigh you shall give to the priest *as* a heave offering from the sacrifices of your peace offerings. 33 He among the sons of Aaron, who offers the blood of the peace offering and the fat, shall have the right thigh for *his* part. 34 For the breast of the wave offering and the thigh of the heave offering I have taken from the children of Israel, from the sacrifices of their peace offerings, and I have given them to Aaron the priest and to his sons from the children of Israel by a statute forever.' ''

35 This *is* the consecrated portion for Aaron and his sons, from the offerings made by fire to the LORD, on the day when *Moses* presented them to minister to the LORD as priests. 36 The LORD commanded this to be given to them by the children of Israel, on the day that He anointed them, *by* a statute forever throughout their generations.

37 This *is* the law of the burnt offering, the grain offering, the sin offering, the trespass offering, the consecrations, and the sacrifice of the peace offering, 38 which the LORD commanded Moses on Mount Sinai, on the day when He commanded the children of Israel to offer their offerings to the LORD in the Wilderness of Sinai.

The priests' offerings

8 And the LORD spoke to Moses, saying: 2 ''Take Aaron and his sons with him, and the garments, the anointing oil, a bull as the sin offering, two rams, and a basket of unleavened bread; 3 and gather all the congregation together at the door of the tabernacle of meeting.''

4 So Moses did as the LORD commanded him. And the congregation was gathered together at the door of the tabernacle of meeting. 5 And Moses said to the congregation, ''This *is* what the LORD commanded to be done.''

6 Then Moses brought Aaron and his sons and washed them with water. 7 And he put the tunic on him, girded him with the sash, clothed him with the robe, and put the ephod on him;

and he girded him with the intricately woven band of the ephod, and with it tied *the ephod* on him. 8 Then he put the breastplate on him, and he put the Urim and the Thummim in the breastplate. 9 And he put the turban on his head. Also on the turban, on its front, he put the golden plate, the holy crown, as the LORD had commanded Moses.

10 Also Moses took the anointing oil, and anointed the tabernacle and all that *was* in it, and consecrated them. 11 He sprinkled some of it on the altar seven times, anointed the altar and all its utensils, and the laver and its base, to consecrate them. 12 And he poured some of the anointing oil on Aaron's head and anointed him, to consecrate him.

13 Then Moses brought Aaron's sons and put tunics on them, girded them with sashes, and put hats on them, as the LORD had commanded Moses.

14 And he brought the bull for the sin offering. Then Aaron and his sons laid their hands on the head of the bull for the sin offering, 15 and Moses killed *it*. Then he took the blood, and put *some* on the horns of the altar all around with his finger, and purified the altar. And he poured the blood at the base of the altar, and consecrated it, to make atonement for it. 16 Then he took all the fat that *was* on the entrails, the fatty lobe *attached to* the liver, and the two kidneys with their fat, and Moses burned *them* on the altar. 17 But the bull, its hide, its flesh, and its offal, he burned with fire outside the camp, as the LORD had commanded Moses.

18 Then he brought the ram as the burnt offering. And Aaron and his sons laid their hands on the head of the ram, 19 and Moses killed *it*. Then he sprinkled the blood all around on the altar. 20 And he cut the ram into pieces; and Moses burned the head, the pieces, and the fat. 21 Then he washed the entrails and the legs in water. And Moses burned the whole ram on the altar. It *was* a burnt sacrifice for a sweet aroma, an offering made by fire to the LORD, as the LORD had commanded Moses.

22 And he brought the second ram, the ram of consecration. Then Aaron and his sons laid their hands on the head of the ram, 23 and Moses killed *it*. Also he took *some* of its blood and put it on the tip of Aaron's right ear, on the thumb of his right hand, and on the big toe of his right foot. 24 Then he brought Aaron's sons. And Moses put *some* of the blood on the tips of their right ears, on the thumbs of their right hands, and on the big toes of their right feet. And Moses sprinkled blood all around on the altar. 25 Then he took the fat and the fat tail, all the fat that *was* on the entrails, the fatty lobe *attached to* the liver, the two kidneys and their fat, and the right thigh; 26 and from the basket of unleavened bread that was before the LORD he took one unleavened cake, a cake of bread *anointed with* oil, and one wafer, and put *them* on the fat and on the right thigh; 27 and he put all *these* in Aaron's hands and in his sons' hands, and waved them *as* a wave offering before the LORD. 28 Then Moses took them from their hands and burned *them* on the altar, on the burnt offering. They *were* consecration offerings for a sweet aroma. That *was* an offering made by fire to the LORD. 29 And Moses took the breast and waved it *as* a wave offering before the LORD. It was Moses' part of the ram of consecration, as the LORD had commanded Moses.

30 Then Moses took some of the anointing oil and some of the blood which *was* on the altar, and sprinkled *it* on Aaron, on his garments, on his sons, and on the garments of his sons with him; and he consecrated Aaron, his garments, his sons, and the garments of his sons with him.

31 And Moses said to Aaron and his sons, "Boil the flesh *at* the door of the tabernacle of meeting, and eat it there with the bread that *is* in the basket of consecration offerings, as I commanded, saying, 'Aaron and his sons shall eat it.' 32 What remains of the flesh and of the bread you shall burn with fire. 33 And you shall not go outside the door of the tabernacle of

meeting *for* seven days, until the days of your consecration are ended. For seven days he shall consecrate you. 34 As he has done this day, *so* the LORD has commanded to do, to make atonement for you. 35 Therefore you shall stay *at* the door of the tabernacle of meeting day and night for seven days, and keep the charge of the LORD, so that you may not die; for so I have been commanded." 36 So Aaron and his sons did all the things that the LORD had commanded by the hand of Moses.

Aaron's first offerings

9 It came to pass on the eighth day that Moses called Aaron and his sons and the elders of Israel. 2 And he said to Aaron, "Take for yourself a young bull as a sin offering and a ram as a burnt offering, without blemish, and offer *them* before the LORD. 3 And to the children of Israel you shall speak, saying, 'Take a kid of the goats as a sin offering, and a calf and a lamb, *both* of the first year, without blemish, as a burnt offering, 4 also a bull and a ram as peace offerings, to sacrifice before the LORD, and a grain offering mixed with oil; for today the LORD will appear to you.' "

5 So they brought what Moses commanded before the tabernacle of meeting. And all the congregation drew near and stood before the LORD. 6 Then Moses said, "This *is* the thing which the LORD commanded you to do, and the glory of the LORD will appear to you." 7 And Moses said to Aaron, "Go to the altar, offer your sin offering and your burnt offering, and make atonement for yourself and for the people. Offer the offering of the people, and make atonement for them, as the LORD commanded."

8 Aaron therefore went to the altar and killed the calf of the sin offering, which *was* for himself. 9 Then the sons of Aaron brought the blood to him. And he dipped his finger in the blood, put *it* on the horns of the altar, and

poured the blood at the base of the altar. 10 But the fat, the kidneys, and the fatty lobe from the liver of the sin offering he burned on the altar, as the LORD had commanded Moses. 11 The flesh and the hide he burned with fire outside the camp.

12 And he killed the burnt offering; and Aaron's sons presented to him the blood, which he sprinkled all around on the altar. 13 Then they presented the burnt offering to him, with its pieces and head, and he burned *them* on the altar. 14 And he washed the entrails and the legs, and burned *them* with the burnt offering on the altar.

15 Then he brought the people's offering, and took the goat, which *was* the sin offering for the people, and killed it and offered it for sin, like the first one. 16 And he brought the burnt offering and offered it according to the prescribed manner. 17 Then he brought the grain offering, took a handful of it, and burned *it* on the altar, besides the burnt sacrifice of the morning.

18 He also killed the bull and the ram *as* sacrifices of peace offerings, which *were* for the people. And Aaron's sons presented to him the blood, which he sprinkled all around on the altar, 19 and the fat from the bull and the ram—the fatty tail, what covers *the entrails* and the kidneys, and the fatty lobe *attached to* the liver; 20 and they put the fat on the breasts. Then he burned the fat on the altar; 21 but the breasts and the right thigh Aaron waved *as* a wave offering before the LORD, as Moses had commanded.

22 Then Aaron lifted his hand toward the people, blessed them, and came down from offering the sin offering, the burnt offering, and peace offerings. 23 And Moses and Aaron went into the tabernacle of meeting, and came out and blessed the people. Then the glory of the LORD appeared to all the people, 24 and fire came out from before the LORD and consumed the burnt offering and the fat on the altar. When all the people saw *it,* they shouted and fell on their faces.

How priests should act

10 Then Nadab and Abihu, the sons of Aaron, each took his censer and put fire in it, put incense on it, and offered profane fire before the LORD, which He had not commanded them. 2 So fire went out from the LORD and devoured them, and they died before the LORD. 3 And Moses said to Aaron, "This is what the LORD spoke, saying:

'By those who come near Me
I must be regarded as holy;
And before all the people
I must be glorified.' "

So Aaron held his peace.

4 Then Moses called Mishael and Elzaphan, the sons of Uzziel the uncle of Aaron, and said to them, "Come near, carry your brethren from before the sanctuary out of the camp." 5 So they went near and carried them by their tunics out of the camp, as Moses had said.

6 And Moses said to Aaron, and to Eleazar and Ithamar, his sons, "Do not uncover your heads nor tear your clothes, lest you die, and wrath come upon all the people. But let your brethren, the whole house of Israel, bewail the burning which the LORD has kindled. 7 You shall not go out from the door of the tabernacle of meeting, lest you die, for the anointing oil of the LORD is upon you." And they did according to the word of Moses.

8 Then the LORD spoke to Aaron, saying: 9 "Do not drink wine or intoxicating drink, you, nor your sons with you, when you go into the tabernacle of meeting, lest you die. It shall be a statute forever throughout your generations, 10 that you may distinguish between holy and unholy, and between unclean and clean, 11 and that you may teach the children of Israel all the statutes which the LORD has spoken to them by the hand of Moses."

12 And Moses spoke to Aaron, and to Eleazar and Ithamar, his sons who were left: "Take the grain offering that remains of the offerings made by fire to the LORD, and eat it without leaven beside the altar; for it is most holy. 13 You shall eat it in a holy place, because it is your due and your sons' due, of the sacrifices made by fire to the LORD; for so I have been commanded. 14 The breast of the wave offering and the thigh of the heave offering you shall eat in a clean place, you, your sons, and your daughters with you; for they are your due and your sons' due, which are given from the sacrifices of peace offerings of the children of Israel. 15 The thigh of the heave offering and the breast of the wave offering they shall bring with the offerings of fat made by fire, to offer as a wave offering before the LORD. And it shall be yours and your sons' with you, by a statute forever, as the LORD has commanded."

16 Then Moses made careful inquiry about the goat of the sin offering, and there it was—burned up. And he was angry with Eleazar and Ithamar, the sons of Aaron who were left, saying, 17 "Why have you not eaten the sin offering in a holy place, since it is most holy, and God has given it to you to bear the guilt of the congregation, to make atonement for them before the LORD? 18 See! Its blood was not brought inside the holy place; indeed you should have eaten it in a holy place, as I commanded."

19 And Aaron said to Moses, "Look, this day they have offered their sin offering and their burnt offering before the LORD, and such things have befallen me! If I had eaten the sin offering today, would it have been accepted in the sight of the LORD?" 20 So when Moses heard that, he was content.

Clean and unclean animals

11 Now the LORD spoke to Moses and Aaron, saying to them, 2 "Speak to the children of Israel, saying, 'These are the animals which you may eat among all the animals that are on the earth: 3 Among the animals, whatever divides the hoof, having cloven hooves and chewing the cud—that you may eat. 4 Nevertheless these you shall not eat among those that chew the cud or those that have cloven hooves: the camel, because it chews the cud but does not have cloven hooves, is unclean to you; 5 the rock hyrax, because it chews the cud but does not have cloven hooves, is unclean to you; 6 the hare, because it chews the cud but does not have cloven hooves, is unclean to you; 7 and the swine, though it divides the hoof, having cloven hooves, yet does not chew the cud, is unclean to you. 8 Their flesh you shall not eat, and their carcasses you shall not touch. They are unclean to you.

9 'These you may eat of all that are in the water: whatever in the water has fins and scales, whether in the seas or in the rivers—that you may eat. 10 But all in the seas or in the rivers that do not have fins and scales, all that move in the water or any living thing which is in the water, they are an abomination to you. 11 They shall be an abomination to you; you shall not eat their flesh, but you shall regard their carcasses as an abomination. 12 Whatever in the water does not have fins or scales—that shall be an abomination to you.

13 'And these you shall regard as an abomination among the birds; they shall not be eaten, they are an abomination: the eagle, the vulture, the buzzard, 14 the kite, and the falcon after its kind; 15 every raven after its kind, 16 the ostrich, the short-eared owl, the sea gull, and the hawk after its kind; 17 the little owl, the fisher owl, and the screech owl; 18 the white owl, the jackdaw, and the carrion vulture; 19 the stork, the heron after its kind, the hoopoe, and the bat.

20 'All flying insects that creep on all fours shall be an abomination to you. 21 Yet these you may eat of every flying insect that creeps on all fours: those which have jointed legs above their feet with which to leap on the earth. 22 These you may eat: the locust after its kind, the destroying locust after its kind, the cricket after its kind, and the grasshopper after its kind. 23 But all other flying insects which have four feet shall be an abomination to you.

24 'By these you shall become unclean; whoever touches the carcass of any of them shall be unclean until evening; 25 whoever carries part of the carcass of any of them shall wash his clothes and be unclean until evening: 26 The carcass of any animal which divides the foot, but is not cloven-hoofed or does not chew the cud, is unclean to you. Everyone who touches it shall be unclean. 27 And whatever goes on its paws, among all kinds of animals that go on all fours, those are unclean to you. Whoever touches any such carcass shall be unclean until evening. 28 Whoever carries any such carcass shall wash his clothes and be unclean until evening. It is unclean to you.

29 'These also shall be unclean to you among the creeping things that creep on the earth: the mole, the mouse, and the large lizard after its kind; 30 the gecko, the monitor lizard, the sand reptile, the sand lizard, and the chameleon. 31 These are unclean to you among all that creep. Whoever touches them when they are dead shall be unclean until evening. 32 Anything on which any of them falls, when they are dead shall be unclean, whether it is any item of wood or clothing or skin

Because vultures feed on dead animals, God calls them an "abomination."

or sack, whatever item *it is,* in which *any* work is done, it must be put in water. And it shall be unclean until evening; then it shall be clean. ³³ Any earthen vessel into which *any* of them falls you shall break; and whatever *is* in it shall be unclean: ³⁴ in such a vessel, any edible food upon which water falls becomes unclean, and any drink that may be drunk from it becomes unclean. ³⁵ And everything on which *a part* of *any such* carcass falls shall be unclean; *whether it is* an oven or cooking stove, it shall be broken down; *for* they *are* unclean, and shall be unclean to you. ³⁶ Nevertheless a spring or a cistern, *in which there is* plenty of water, shall be clean, but whatever touches any such carcass becomes unclean. ³⁷ And if a part of *any such* carcass falls on any planting seed which is to be sown, it *remains* clean. ³⁸ But if water is put on the seed, and if *a part* of *any such* carcass falls on it, it *becomes* unclean to you.

³⁹ 'And if any animal which you may eat dies, he who touches its carcass shall be unclean until evening. ⁴⁰ He who eats of its carcass shall wash his clothes and be unclean until evening. He also who carries its carcass shall wash his clothes and be unclean until evening.

⁴¹ 'And every creeping thing that creeps on the earth *shall be* an abomination. It shall not be eaten. ⁴² Whatever crawls on its belly, whatever goes on *all* fours, or whatever has many feet among all creeping things that creep on the earth—these you shall not eat, for they *are* an abomination. ⁴³ You shall not make yourselves abominable with any creeping thing that creeps; nor shall you make yourselves unclean with them, lest you be defiled by them. ⁴⁴ For I *am* the LORD your God. You shall therefore consecrate yourselves, and you shall be holy; for I *am* holy. Neither shall you defile yourselves with any creeping thing that creeps on the earth. ⁴⁵ For I *am* the LORD who brings you up out of the land of Egypt, to be your God. You shall therefore be holy, for I *am* holy.

⁴⁶ 'This *is* the law of the animals and the birds and every living creature that moves in the waters, and of every creature that creeps on the earth, ⁴⁷ to distinguish between the unclean and the clean, and between the animal that may be eaten and the animal that may not be eaten.' "

What mothers are to do after childbirth

12 Then the LORD spoke to Moses, saying, ² "Speak to the children of Israel, saying: 'If a woman has conceived, and borne a male child, then she shall be unclean seven days; as in the days of her customary impurity she shall be unclean. ³ And on the eighth day the flesh of his foreskin shall be circumcised. ⁴ She shall then continue in the blood of *her* purification thirty-three days. She shall not touch any hallowed thing, nor come into the sanctuary until the days of her purification are fulfilled.

⁵ 'But if she bears a female child, then she shall be unclean two weeks, as in her customary impurity, and she shall continue in the blood of *her* purification sixty-six days.

⁶ 'When the days of her purification are fulfilled, whether for a son or a daughter, she shall bring to the priest a lamb of the first year as a burnt offering, and a young pigeon or a turtledove as a sin offering, to the door of the tabernacle of meeting. ⁷ Then he shall offer it before the LORD, and make atonement for her. And she shall be clean from the flow of her blood. This *is* the law for her who has borne a male or a female.

⁸ 'And if she is not able to bring a lamb, then she may bring two turtledoves or two young pigeons—one as a burnt offering and the other as a sin offering. So the priest shall make atonement for her, and she will be clean.' "

How to control skin diseases

13 And the LORD spoke to Moses and Aaron, saying: ² "When a man has on the skin of his body a swelling, a scab, or a bright spot, and it becomes on the skin of his body *like* a leprous sore, then he shall be brought to Aaron the priest or to one of his sons the priests. 3 The priest shall examine the sore on the skin of the body; and if the hair on the sore has turned white, and the sore appears *to be* deeper than the skin of his body, it *is* a leprous sore. Then the priest shall examine him, and pronounce him unclean. 4 But if the bright spot *is* white on the skin of his body, and does not appear *to be* deeper than the skin, and its hair has not turned white, then the priest shall isolate *the one who has* the sore seven days. 5 And the priest shall examine him on the seventh day; and indeed *if* the sore appears to be as it was, *and* the sore has not spread on the skin, then the priest shall isolate him another seven days. 6 Then the priest shall examine him again on the seventh day; and indeed *if* the sore has faded, *and* the sore has not spread on the skin, then the priest shall pronounce him clean; it *is only* a scab, and he shall wash his clothes and be clean. 7 But if the scab should at all spread over the skin, after he has been seen by the priest for his cleansing, he shall be seen by the priest again. 8 And *if* the priest sees that the scab has indeed spread on the skin, then the priest shall pronounce him unclean. It *is* leprosy.

9 "When the leprous sore is on a person, then he shall be brought to the priest. 10 And the priest shall examine *him;* and indeed *if* the swelling on the skin *is* white, and it has turned the hair white, and *there is* a spot of raw flesh in the swelling, 11 it *is* an old leprosy on the skin of his body. The priest shall pronounce him unclean, and shall not isolate him, for he *is* unclean.

12 "And if leprosy breaks out all over the skin, and the leprosy covers all the skin of *the one who has* the sore, from his head to his foot, wherever the priest looks, 13 then the priest shall consider; and indeed *if* the leprosy has covered all his body, he shall pronounce *him* clean *who has* the sore. It has all turned white. He *is* clean. 14 But when raw flesh appears on him, he shall be unclean. 15 And the priest shall examine the raw flesh and pronounce him to be unclean; *for* the raw flesh *is* unclean. It *is* leprosy. 16 Or if the raw flesh changes and turns white again, he shall come to the priest. 17 And the priest shall examine him; and indeed *if* the sore has turned white, then the priest shall pronounce *him* clean *who has* the sore. He *is* clean.

18 "If the body develops a boil in the skin, and it is healed, 19 and in the place of the boil there comes a white swelling or a bright spot, reddish-white, then it shall be shown to the priest; 20 and *if,* when the priest sees it, it indeed *appears* deeper than the skin, and its hair has turned white, the priest shall pronounce him unclean. It *is* a leprous sore which has broken out of the boil. 21 But if the priest examines it, and indeed *there are* no white hairs in it, and it *is* not deeper than the skin, but has faded, then the priest shall isolate him seven days; 22 and if it should at all spread over the skin, then the priest shall pronounce him unclean. It *is* a leprous sore. 23 But if the bright spot stays in one place, *and* has not spread, it *is* the scar of the boil; and the priest shall pronounce him clean.

24 "Or if the body receives a burn on its skin by fire, and the raw *flesh* of the burn becomes a bright spot, reddish-white or white, 25 then the priest shall examine it; and indeed *if* the hair of the bright spot has turned white, and it appears deeper than the skin, it *is* leprosy broken out in the burn. Therefore the priest shall pronounce him unclean. It *is* a leprous sore. 26 But if the priest examines it, and indeed *there are* no white hairs in the bright spot, and it *is* not deeper than the skin, but has faded, then the priest shall isolate him seven days. 27 And the priest shall examine him on the seventh day. If it has at all spread over the skin, then the priest shall pronounce him unclean. It *is* a leprous sore. 28 But if the bright spot stays in one place, *and* has not spread on the skin, but has faded,

it *is* a swelling from the burn. The priest shall pronounce him clean, for it *is* the scar from the burn.

29 "If a man or woman has a sore on the head or the beard, 30 then the priest shall examine the sore; and indeed if it appears deeper than the skin, *and there is* in it thin yellow hair, then the priest shall pronounce him unclean. It *is* a scaly leprosy of the head or beard. 31 But if the priest examines the scaly sore, and indeed it does not appear deeper than the skin, and *there is* no black hair in it, then the priest shall isolate *the one who has* the scale seven days. 32 And on the seventh day the priest shall examine the sore; and indeed *if* the scale has not spread, and there is no yellow hair in it, and the scale does not appear deeper than the skin, 33 he shall shave himself, but the scale he shall not shave. And the priest shall isolate *the one who has* the scale another seven days. 34 On the seventh day the priest shall examine the scale; and indeed *if* the scale has not spread over the skin, and does not appear deeper than the skin, then the priest shall pronounce him clean. He shall wash his clothes and be clean. 35 But if the scale should at all spread over the skin after his cleansing, 36 then the priest shall examine him; and indeed *if* the scale has spread over the skin, the priest need not seek for yellow hair. He *is* unclean. 37 But if the scale appears to be at a standstill, and there is black hair grown up in it, the scale has healed. He *is* clean, and the priest shall pronounce him clean.

38 "If a man or a woman has bright spots on the skin of the body, *specifically* white bright spots, 39 then the priest shall look; and indeed *if* the bright spots on the skin of the body *are* dull white, it *is* a white spot *that* grows on the skin. He *is* clean.

40 "As for the man whose hair has fallen from his head, he *is* bald, *but* he *is* clean. 41 He whose hair has fallen from his forehead, he *is* bald on the forehead, *but* he *is* clean. 42 And if there is on the bald head or bald forehead a reddish-white sore, it *is* leprosy breaking out on his bald head or his bald forehead. 43 Then the priest shall examine it; and indeed *if* the swelling of the sore *is* reddish-white on his bald head or on his bald forehead, as the appearance of leprosy on the skin of the body, 44 he is a leprous man. He *is* unclean. The priest shall surely pronounce him unclean; his sore *is* on his head.

45 "Now the leper on whom the sore is, his clothes shall be torn and his head bare; and he shall cover his mustache, and cry, 'Unclean! Unclean!' 46 He shall be unclean. All the days he has the sore he shall be unclean. He *is* unclean, and he shall dwell alone; his dwelling *shall be* outside the camp.

47 "Also, if a garment has a leprous plague in it, *whether it is* a woolen garment or a linen garment, 48 whether *it is* in the warp or woof of linen or wool, whether in leather or in anything made of leather, 49 and if the plague is greenish or reddish in the garment or in the leather, whether in the warp or in the woof, or in anything made of leather, it *is* a leprous plague and shall be shown to the priest. 50 The priest shall examine the plague and isolate *that which has* the plague seven days. 51 And he shall examine the plague on the seventh day. If the plague has spread in the garment, either in the warp or in the woof, in the leather *or* in anything made of leather, the plague *is* an active leprosy. It *is* unclean. 52 He shall therefore burn that garment in which is the plague, whether warp or woof, in wool or in linen, or anything of leather, for it *is* an active leprosy; *the garment* shall be burned in the fire.

53 "But if the priest examines *it,* and indeed the plague has not spread in the garment, either in the warp or in the woof, or in anything made of leather, 54 then the priest shall command that they wash *the thing* in which is the plague; and he shall isolate it another seven days. 55 Then the priest shall examine the plague after it has been washed; and indeed *if* the plague has not changed its color, though the

plague has not spread, it *is* unclean, and you shall burn it in the fire; it continues eating away, *whether* the damage *is* outside or inside. 56 If the priest examines *it,* and indeed the plague has faded after washing it, then he shall tear it out of the garment, whether out of the warp or out of the woof, or out of the leather. 57 But if it appears again in the garment, either in the warp or in the woof, or in anything made of leather, it *is* a spreading *plague;* you shall burn with fire that in which is the plague. 58 And if you wash the garment, either warp or woof, or whatever is made of leather, if the plague has disappeared from it, then it shall be washed a second time, and shall be clean.

59 "This *is* the law of the leprous plague in a garment of wool or linen, either in the warp or woof, or in anything made of leather, to pronounce it clean or to pronounce it unclean."

Cleansing from leprosy

14 Then the LORD spoke to Moses, saying, 2 "This shall be the law of the leper for the day of his cleansing: He shall be brought to the priest. 3 And the priest shall go out of the camp, and the priest shall examine *him*; and indeed, *if* the leprosy is healed in the leper, 4 then the priest shall command to take for him who is to be cleansed two living *and* clean birds, cedar wood, scarlet, and hyssop. 5 And the priest shall command that one of the birds be killed in an earthen vessel over running water. 6 As for the living bird, he shall take it, the cedar wood and the scarlet and the hyssop, and dip them and the living bird in the blood of the bird *that was* killed over the running water. 7 And he shall sprinkle it *seven* times on him who is to be cleansed from the leprosy, and shall pronounce him clean, and shall let the living bird loose in the open field. 8 He who is to be cleansed shall wash his clothes, shave off all his hair, and wash himself in water, that he may be clean. After that he shall come into the camp, and

shall stay outside his tent seven days. 9 But on the seventh day he shall shave all the hair off his head and his beard and his eyebrows—all his hair he shall shave off. He shall wash his clothes and wash his body in water, and he shall be clean.

10 "And on the eighth day he shall take two male lambs without blemish, one ewe lamb of the first year without blemish, three-tenths *of an ephah* of fine flour mixed with oil as a grain offering, and one log of oil. 11 Then the priest who makes *him* clean shall present the man who is to be made clean, and those things, before the LORD, *at* the door of the tabernacle of meeting. 12 And the priest shall take one male lamb and offer it as a trespass offering, and the log of oil, and wave them *as* a wave offering before the LORD. 13 Then he shall kill the lamb in the place where he kills the sin offering and the burnt offering, in a holy place; for as the sin offering *is* the priest's, so *is* the trespass offering. It *is* most holy. 14 The priest shall take *some* of the blood of the trespass offering, and the priest shall put *it* on the tip of the right ear of him who is to be cleansed, on the thumb of his right hand, and on the big toe of his right foot. 15 And the priest shall take *some* of the log of oil, and pour *it* into the palm of his own left hand. 16 Then the priest shall dip his right finger in the oil that *is* in his left hand, and shall sprinkle some of the oil with his finger seven times before the LORD. 17 And of the rest of the oil in his hand, the priest shall put *some* on the tip of the right ear of him who is to be cleansed, on the thumb of his right hand, and on the big toe of his right foot, on the blood of the trespass offering. 18 The rest of the oil that *is* in the priest's hand he shall put on the head of him who is to be cleansed. So the priest shall make atonement for him before the LORD.

19 "Then the priest shall offer the sin offering, and make atonement for him who is to be cleansed from his uncleanness. Afterward he shall kill the burnt offering. 20 And the priest shall offer the

burnt offering and the grain offering on the altar. So the priest shall make atonement for him, and he shall be clean.

21 "But if he *is* poor and cannot afford it, then he shall take one male lamb *as* a trespass offering to be waved, to make atonement for him, one-tenth *of an ephah* of fine flour mixed with oil as a grain offering, a log of oil, 22 and two turtledoves or two young pigeons, such as he is able to afford: one shall be a sin offering and the other a burnt offering. 23 He shall bring them to the priest on the eighth day for his cleansing, to the door of the tabernacle of meeting, before the Lord. 24 And the priest shall take the lamb of the trespass offering and the log of oil, and the priest shall wave them *as* a wave offering before the Lord. 25 Then he shall kill the lamb of the trespass offering, and the priest shall take *some* of the blood of the trespass offering and put *it* on the tip of the right ear of him who is to be cleansed, on the thumb of his right hand, and on the big toe of his right foot. 26 And the priest shall pour some of the oil into the palm of his own left hand. 27 Then the priest shall sprinkle with his right finger *some* of the oil that *is* in his left hand seven times before the Lord. 28 And the priest shall put *some* of the oil that *is* in his hand on the tip of the right ear of him who is to be cleansed, on the thumb of the right hand, and on the big toe of his right foot, on the place of the blood of the trespass offering. 29 The rest of the oil that *is* in the priest's hand he shall put on the head of him who is to be cleansed, to make atonement for him before the Lord. 30 And he shall offer one of the turtledoves or young pigeons, such as he can afford— 31 such as he is able to afford, the one *as* a sin offering and the other *as* a burnt offering, with the grain offering. So the priest shall make atonement for him who is to be cleansed before the Lord. 32 This *is* the law *for one* who had a leprous sore, who cannot afford the usual cleansing."

33 And the Lord spoke to Moses and Aaron, saying: 34 "When you have come into the land of Canaan, which I give you as a possession, and I put the leprous plague in a house in the land of your possession, 35 and he who owns the house comes and tells the priest, saying, 'It seems to me that *there is* some plague in the house,' 36 then the priest shall command that they empty the house, before the priest goes *into it* to examine the plague, that all that *is* in the house may not be made unclean; and afterward the priest shall go in to examine the house. 37 And he shall examine the plague; and indeed *if* the plague *is* on the walls of the house with ingrained streaks, greenish or reddish, which appear to be deep in the wall, 38 then the priest shall go out of the house, to the door of the house, and shut up the house seven days. 39 And the priest shall come again on the seventh day and look; and indeed *if* the plague has spread on the walls of the house, 40 then the priest shall command that they take away the stones in which *is* the plague, and they shall cast them into an unclean place outside the city. 41 And he shall cause the house to be scraped inside, all around, and the dust that they scrape off they shall pour out in an unclean place outside the city. 42 Then they shall take other stones and put *them* in the place of *those* stones, and he shall take other mortar and plaster the house.

43 "Now if the plague comes back and breaks out in the house, after he has taken away the stones, after he has scraped the house, and after it is plastered, 44 then the priest shall come and look; and indeed *if* the plague has spread in the house, it *is* an active leprosy in the house. It *is* unclean. 45 And he shall break down the house, its stones, its timber, and all the plaster of the house, and he shall carry *them* outside the city to an unclean place. 46 Moreover he who goes into the house at all while it is shut up shall be unclean until evening. 47 And he who lies down in the house shall wash

his clothes, and he who eats in the house shall wash his clothes.

48 "But if the priest comes in and examines *it,* and indeed the plague has not spread in the house after the house was plastered, then the priest shall pronounce the house clean, because the plague is healed. 49 And he shall take, to cleanse the house, two birds, cedar wood, scarlet, and hyssop. 50 Then he shall kill one of the birds in an earthen vessel over running water; 51 and he shall take the cedar wood, the hyssop, the scarlet, and the living bird, and dip them in the blood of the slain bird and in the running water, and sprinkle the house seven times. 52 And he shall cleanse the house with the blood of the bird and the running water and the living bird, with the cedar wood, the hyssop, and the scarlet. 53 Then he shall let the living bird loose outside the city in the open field, and make atonement for the house, and it shall be clean.

54 "This *is* the law for any leprous sore and scale, 55 for the leprosy of a garment and of a house, 56 for a swelling and a scab and a bright spot, 57 to teach when *it is* unclean and when *it is* clean. This *is* the law of leprosy."

Laws about the human body

15 And the LORD spoke to Moses and Aaron, saying, 2 "Speak to the children of Israel, and say to them: 'When any man has a discharge from his body, his discharge *is* unclean. 3 And this shall be his uncleanness in regard to his discharge—whether his body runs with his discharge, or his body is stopped up by his discharge, it *is* his uncleanness. 4 Every bed is unclean on which he who has the discharge lies, and everything on which he sits shall be unclean. 5 And whoever touches his bed shall wash his clothes and bathe in water, and be unclean until evening. 6 He who sits on anything on which he who has the discharge sat shall wash his clothes and bathe in water, and be unclean until evening. 7 And he who touches the

body of him who has the discharge shall wash his clothes and bathe in water, and be unclean until evening. 8 If he who has the discharge spits on him who is clean, then he shall wash his clothes and bathe in water, and be unclean until evening. 9 Any saddle on which he who has the discharge rides shall be unclean. 10 Whoever touches anything that was under him shall be unclean until evening. He who carries *any of* those things shall wash his clothes and bathe in water, and be unclean until evening. 11 And whomever the one who has the discharge touches, and has not rinsed his hands in water, he shall wash his clothes and bathe in water, and be unclean until evening. 12 The vessel of earth that he who has the discharge touches shall be broken, and every vessel of wood shall be rinsed in water.

13 'And when he who has a discharge is cleansed of his discharge, then he shall count for himself seven days for his cleansing, wash his clothes, and bathe his body in running water; then he shall be clean. 14 On the eighth day he shall take for himself two turtledoves or two young pigeons, and come before the LORD, to the door of the tabernacle of meeting, and give them to the priest. 15 Then the priest shall offer them, the one *as* a sin offering and the other *as* a burnt offering. So the priest shall make atonement for him before the LORD because of his discharge.

16 'If any man has an emission of semen, then he shall wash all his body in water, and be unclean until evening. 17 And any garment and any leather on which there is semen, it shall be washed with water, and be unclean until evening. 18 Also, when a woman lies with a man, and *there is* an emission of semen, they shall bathe in water, and be unclean until evening.

19 'If a woman has a discharge, *and* the discharge from her body is blood, she shall be set apart seven days; and whoever touches her shall be unclean until evening. 20 Everything that she lies on during her impurity shall be

unclean; also everything that she sits on shall be unclean. ²¹ Whoever touches her bed shall wash his clothes and bathe in water, and be unclean until evening. ²² And whoever touches anything that she sat on shall wash his clothes and bathe in water, and be unclean until evening. ²³ If *anything* is on her bed or on anything on which she sits, when he touches it, he shall be unclean until evening. ²⁴ And if any man lies with her at all, so that her impurity is on him, he shall be unclean seven days; and every bed on which he lies shall be unclean.

²⁵ 'If a woman has a discharge of blood for many days, other than at the time of her *customary* impurity, or if it runs beyond her *usual time of* impurity, all the days of her unclean discharge shall be as the days of her *customary* impurity. She *shall be* unclean. ²⁶ Every bed on which she lies all the days of her discharge shall be to her as the bed of her impurity; and whatever she sits on shall be unclean, as the uncleanness of her impurity. ²⁷ Whoever touches those things shall be unclean; he shall wash his clothes and bathe in water, and be unclean until evening.

²⁸ 'But if she is cleansed of her discharge, then she shall count for herself seven days, and after that she shall be clean. ²⁹ And on the eighth day she shall take for herself two turtledoves or two young pigeons, and bring them to the priest, to the door of the tabernacle of meeting. ³⁰ Then the priest shall offer the one *as* a sin offering and the other *as* a burnt offering, and the priest shall make atonement for her before the LORD for the discharge of her uncleanness.

³¹ 'Thus you shall separate the children of Israel from their uncleanness, lest they die in their uncleanness when they defile My tabernacle that *is* among them. ³² This *is* the law for one who has a discharge, and *for him* who emits semen and is unclean thereby, ³³ and for her who is indisposed because of her *customary* impurity, and for one who has a discharge, either man or woman, and for him who lies with her who is unclean.' "

The Day of Atonement

16 Now the LORD spoke to Moses after the death of the two sons of Aaron, when they offered *profane fire* before the LORD, and died; ² and the LORD said to Moses: "Tell Aaron your brother not to come at *just* any time into the Holy *Place* inside the veil, before the mercy seat which *is* on the ark, lest he die; for I will appear in the cloud above the mercy seat.

³ "Thus Aaron shall come into the Holy *Place:* with *the blood of* a young bull as a sin offering, and *of* a ram as a burnt offering. ⁴ He shall put the holy linen tunic and the linen trousers on his body; he shall be girded with a linen sash, and with the linen turban he shall be attired. These *are* holy garments. Therefore he shall wash his body in

DIGGING IN

16:1–34 The Day of Atonement Because God loves you, He takes away your sins. God taught the Old Testament people this truth in a special ceremony called the Day of Atonement. On this day, which came only once a year, the high priest would take the blood of the sacrifice and sprinkle it in the Most Holy Place of the tabernacle. (See the plan of the worship place in Leviticus 2.) The sacrifice was a bull and a goat. Then the high priest would lay his hands on another goat and send it away into the desert. By laying his hands on this goat, the high priest showed that the sins of the people were being carried away.

This Old Testament ceremony is just a picture of what Jesus has done for you. He is your real High Priest, and He has carried the blood of His sacrifice into heaven for you. He also has carried away your sins forever.

water, and put them on. ⁵ And he shall take from the congregation of the children of Israel two kids of the goats as a sin offering, and one ram as a burnt offering.

⁶ "Aaron shall offer the bull as a sin offering, which is for himself, and make atonement for himself and for his house. ⁷ He shall take the two goats and present them before the LORD at the door of the tabernacle of meeting. ⁸ Then Aaron shall cast lots for the two goats: one lot for the LORD and the other lot for the **scapegoat.** ⁹ And Aaron shall bring the goat on which the LORD's lot fell, and offer it as a sin offering. ¹⁰ But the goat on which the lot fell to be the scapegoat shall be presented alive before the LORD, to make atonement upon it, and to let it go as the scapegoat into the wilderness.

¹¹ "And Aaron shall bring the bull of the sin offering, which is for himself, and make atonement for himself and for his house, and shall kill the bull as the sin offering which is for himself. ¹² Then he shall take a censer full of burning coals of fire from the altar before the LORD, with his hands full of sweet incense beaten fine, and bring it inside the veil. ¹³ And he shall put the incense on the fire before the LORD, that the cloud of incense may cover the mercy seat that is on the Testimony, lest he die. ¹⁴ He shall take some of the blood of the bull and sprinkle it with his finger on the **mercy seat** on the east side; and before the mercy seat he shall sprinkle some of the blood with his finger seven times.

¹⁵ "Then he shall kill the goat of the sin offering, which is for the people, bring its blood inside the veil, do with that blood as he did with the blood of the bull, and sprinkle it on the mercy seat and before the mercy seat. ¹⁶ So

he shall make atonement for the Holy Place, because of the uncleanness of the children of Israel, and because of their transgressions, for all their sins; and so he shall do for the tabernacle of meeting which remains among them in the midst of their uncleanness. ¹⁷ There shall be no man in the tabernacle of meeting when he goes in to make atonement in the Holy Place, until he comes out, that he may make atonement for himself, for his household, and for all the assembly of Israel. ¹⁸ And he shall go out to the altar that is before the LORD, and make atonement for it, and shall take some of the blood of the bull and some of the blood of the goat, and put it on the horns of the altar all around. ¹⁹ Then he shall sprinkle some of the blood on it with his finger seven times, cleanse it, and consecrate it from the uncleanness of the children of Israel.

²⁰ "And when he has made an end of atoning for the Holy Place, the tabernacle of meeting, and the altar, he shall bring the live goat. ²¹ Aaron shall lay both his hands on the head of the live goat, confess over it all the iniquities of the children of Israel, and all their transgressions, concerning all their sins, putting them on the head of the goat, and shall send it away into the wilderness by the hand of a suitable man. ²² The goat shall bear on itself all their iniquities to an uninhabited land; and he shall release the goat in the wilderness.

²³ "Then Aaron shall come into the tabernacle of meeting, shall take off the linen garments which he put on when he went into the Holy Place, and shall leave them there. ²⁴ And he shall wash his body with water in a holy place, put on his garments, come out and offer his burnt offering and the burnt

---

⚜ WORDFINDER

16:8 Scapegoat A goat over whose head the high priest confessed the people's sins on the Day of Atonement. Goats were unclean animals because they have cloven hooves but do not chew the cud like cows (Lev. 11:3, 4).

16:14 Mercy Seat A flat gold seat that covered the top of the ark of the covenant. God revealed Himself in a cloud and fire over the mercy seat.

offering of the people, and make atonement for himself and for the people. 25 The fat of the sin offering he shall burn on the altar. 26 And he who released the goat as the scapegoat shall wash his clothes and bathe his body in water, and afterward he may come into the camp. 27 The bull *for* the sin offering and the goat *for* the sin offering, whose blood was brought in to make atonement in the Holy *Place,* shall be carried outside the camp. And they shall burn in the fire their skins, their flesh, and their offal. 28 Then he who burns them shall wash his clothes and bathe his body in water, and afterward he may come into the camp.

29 "*This* shall be a statute forever for you: In the seventh month, on the tenth *day* of the month, you shall afflict your souls, and do no work at all, *whether* a native of your own country or a stranger who dwells among you. 30 For on that day *the priest* shall make atonement for you, to cleanse you, *that* you may be clean from all your sins before the LORD. 31 It *is* a sabbath of solemn rest for you, and you shall afflict your souls. *It is* a statute forever. 32 And the priest, who is anointed and consecrated to minister as priest in his father's place, shall make atonement, and put on the linen clothes, the holy garments; 33 then he shall make atonement for the Holy Sanctuary, and he shall make atonement for the tabernacle of meeting and for the altar, and he shall make atonement for the priests and for all the people of the assembly. 34 This shall be an everlasting statute for you, to make atonement for the children of Israel, for all their sins, once a year." And he did as the LORD commanded Moses.

God commands one place of sacrifice

17 And the LORD spoke to Moses, saying, 2 "Speak to Aaron, to his sons, and to all the children of Israel, and say to them, 'This *is* the thing which the LORD has commanded, saying: 3 "Whatever man of the house of Israel who kills an ox or lamb or goat in the camp, or who kills *it* outside the camp, 4 and does not bring it to the door of the tabernacle of meeting to offer an offering to the LORD before the tabernacle of the LORD, the guilt of bloodshed shall be imputed to that man. He has shed blood; and that man shall be cut off from among his people, 5 to the end that the children of Israel may bring their sacrifices which they offer in the open field, that they may bring them to the LORD at the door of the tabernacle of meeting, to the priest, and offer them *as* peace offerings to the LORD. 6 And the priest shall sprinkle the blood on the altar of the LORD *at* the door of the tabernacle of meeting, and burn the fat for a sweet aroma to the LORD. 7 They shall no more offer their sacrifices to demons, after whom they have played the harlot. This shall be a statute forever for them throughout their generations." '

8 "Also you shall say to them: 'Whatever man of the house of Israel, or of the strangers who dwell among you, who offers a burnt offering or sacrifice, 9 and does not bring it to the door of the tabernacle of meeting, to offer it to the LORD, that man shall be cut off from among his people.

10 'And whatever man of the house of Israel, or of the strangers who dwell among you, who eats any blood, I will set My face against that person who eats blood, and will cut him off from among his people. 11 For the life of the flesh *is* in the blood, and I have given it to you upon the altar to make atonement for your souls; for it *is* the blood *that* makes atonement for the soul.' 12 Therefore I said to the children of Israel, 'No one among you shall eat blood, nor shall any stranger who dwells among you eat blood.'

13 "Whatever man of the children of Israel, or of the strangers who dwell among you, who hunts and catches any animal or bird that may be eaten, he shall pour out its blood and cover it with dust; 14 for *it is* the life of all flesh. Its blood sustains its life. Therefore I said to the children of Israel, 'You

shall not eat the blood of any flesh, for the life of all flesh is its blood. Whoever eats it shall be cut off.'

15 "And every person who eats what died *naturally* or what was torn *by beasts, whether he is* a native of your own country or a stranger, he shall both wash his clothes and bathe in water, and be unclean until evening. Then he shall be clean. 16 But if he does not wash *them* or bathe his body, then he shall bear his guilt."

God forbids immoral behavior

18 Then the LORD spoke to Moses, saying, 2 "Speak to the children of Israel, and say to them: 'I am the LORD your God. 3 According to the doings of the land of Egypt, where you dwelt, you shall not do; and according to the doings of the land of Canaan, where I am bringing you, you shall not do; nor shall you walk in their ordinances. 4 You shall observe My judgments and keep My ordinances, to walk in them: I *am* the LORD your God. 5 You shall therefore keep My statutes and My judgments, which if a man does, he shall live by them: I *am* the LORD.

6 'None of you shall approach anyone who is near of kin to him, to uncover his nakedness: I *am* the LORD. 7 The nakedness of your father or the nakedness of your mother you shall not uncover. She *is* your mother; you shall not uncover her nakedness. 8 The nakedness of your father's wife you shall not uncover; it *is* your father's nakedness. 9 The nakedness of your sister, the daughter of your father, or the daughter of your mother, *whether* born at home or elsewhere, their nakedness you shall not uncover. 10 The nakedness of your son's daughter or your daughter's daughter, their nakedness you shall not uncover; for theirs *is* your own nakedness. 11 The nakedness of your father's wife's daughter, begotten by your father—she *is* your sister—you shall not uncover her nakedness. 12 You shall not uncover the nakedness of your father's sister; she *is* near of kin to your father.

13 You shall not uncover the nakedness of your mother's sister, for she *is* near of kin to your mother. 14 You shall not uncover the nakedness of your father's brother. You shall not approach his wife; she *is* your aunt. 15 You shall not uncover the nakedness of your daughter-in-law—she *is* your son's wife—you shall not uncover her nakedness. 16 You shall not uncover the nakedness of your brother's wife; it *is* your brother's nakedness. 17 You shall not uncover the nakedness of a woman and her daughter, nor shall you take her son's daughter or her daughter's daughter, to uncover her nakedness. They *are* near of kin to her. It *is* wickedness. 18 Nor shall you take a woman as a rival to her sister, to uncover her nakedness while the other is alive.

19 'Also you shall not approach a woman to uncover her nakedness as long as she is in her *customary* impurity. 20 Moreover you shall not lie carnally with your neighbor's wife, to defile yourself with her. 21 And you shall not let any of your descendants pass through *the fire* to Molech, nor shall you profane the name of your God: I *am* the LORD. 22 You shall not lie with a male as with a woman. It *is* an abomination. 23 Nor shall you mate with any animal, to defile yourself with it. Nor shall any woman stand before an animal to mate with it. It *is* perversion.

24 'Do not defile yourselves with any of these things; for by all these the nations are defiled, which I am casting out before you. 25 For the land is defiled; therefore I visit the punishment of its iniquity upon it, and the land vomits out its inhabitants. 26 You shall therefore keep My statutes and My judgments, and shall not commit *any* of these abominations, *either* any of your own nation or any stranger who dwells among you 27 (for all these abominations the men of the land have done, who *were* before you, and thus the land is defiled); 28 lest the land vomit you out also when you defile it, as it vomited out the nations that *were* before you. 29 For whoever commits any of these abominations, the persons

who commit *them* shall be cut off from among their people.

30 'Therefore you shall keep My ordinance, so that *you* do not commit *any* of these abominable customs which were committed before you, and that you do not defile yourselves by them: I *am* the LORD your God.' "

God gives moral and ceremonial laws

19 And the LORD spoke to Moses, saying, 2 "Speak to all the congregation of the children of Israel, and say to them: 'You shall be **holy,** for I the LORD your God *am* holy.

3 'Every one of you shall revere his mother and his father, and keep My Sabbaths: I *am* the LORD your God.

4 'Do not turn to idols, nor make for yourselves molded gods: I *am* the LORD your God.

5 'And if you offer a sacrifice of a peace offering to the LORD, you shall offer it of your own free will. 6 It shall be eaten the same day you offer *it,* and on the next day. And if any remains until the third day, it shall be burned in the fire. 7 And if it is eaten at all on the third day, it *is* an abomination. It shall not be accepted. 8 Therefore *everyone* who eats it shall bear his iniquity, because he has profaned the hallowed *offering* of the LORD; and that person shall be cut off from his people.

9 'When you reap the harvest of your land, you shall not wholly reap the corners of your field, nor shall you gather the gleanings of your harvest. 10 And you shall not glean your vineyard, nor shall you gather *every* grape of your vineyard; you shall leave them for the poor and the stranger: I *am* the LORD your God.

11 'You shall not steal, nor deal falsely, nor lie to one another. 12 And you shall not swear by My name

falsely, nor shall you profane the name of your God: I *am* the LORD.

13 'You shall not cheat your neighbor, nor rob *him.* The wages of him who is hired shall not remain with you all night until morning. 14 You shall not curse the deaf, nor put a stumbling block before the blind, but shall fear your God: I *am* the LORD.

15 'You shall do no injustice in judgment. You shall not be partial to the poor, nor honor the person of the mighty. In righteousness you shall judge your neighbor. 16 You shall not go about *as* a talebearer among your people; nor shall you take a stand against the life of your neighbor: I *am* the LORD.

17 'You shall not hate your brother in your heart. You shall surely rebuke your neighbor, and not bear sin because of him. 18 You shall not take vengeance, nor bear any grudge against the children of your people, but you shall love your neighbor as yourself: I *am* the LORD.

19 'You shall keep My statutes. You shall not let your livestock breed with another kind. You shall not sow your field with mixed seed. Nor shall a garment of mixed linen and wool come upon you.

20 'Whoever lies carnally with a woman who *is* betrothed to a man as a concubine, and who has not at all been redeemed nor given her freedom, for this there shall be scourging; *but* they shall not be put to death, because she was not free. 21 And he shall bring his trespass offering to the LORD, to the door of the tabernacle of meeting, a ram as a trespass offering. 22 The priest shall make atonement for him with the ram of the trespass offering before the LORD for his sin which he has committed. And the sin which he has committed shall be forgiven him.

23 'When you come into the land,

WORDFINDER

19:2 Holy An adjective meaning "separate," but includes the idea of moral purity and being like God.

and have planted all kinds of trees for food, then you shall count their fruit as uncircumcised. Three years it shall be as uncircumcised to you. *It shall not be eaten.* 24 But in the fourth year all its fruit shall be holy, a praise to the LORD. 25 And in the fifth year you may eat its fruit, that it may yield to you its increase: I *am* the LORD your God.

26 'You shall not eat *anything* with the blood, nor shall you practice divination or soothsaying. 27 You shall not shave around the sides of your head, nor shall you disfigure the edges of your beard. 28 You shall not make any cuttings in your flesh for the dead, nor tattoo any marks on you: I *am* the LORD.

29 'Do not prostitute your daughter, to cause her to be a harlot, lest the land fall into harlotry, and the land become full of wickedness.

30 'You shall keep My Sabbaths and **reverence** My sanctuary: I *am* the LORD.

31 'Give no regard to mediums and familiar spirits; do not seek after them, to be defiled by them: I *am* the LORD your God.

32 'You shall rise before the gray headed and honor the presence of an old man, and fear your God: I *am* the LORD.

33 'And if a stranger dwells with you in your land, you shall not mistreat him. 34 The stranger who dwells among you shall be to you as one born among you, and you shall love him as yourself; for you were strangers in the land of Egypt: I *am* the LORD your God.

35 'You shall do no injustice in judgment, in measurement of length, weight, or volume. 36 You shall have honest scales, honest weights, an honest ephah, and an honest hin: I *am* the LORD your God, who brought you out of the land of Egypt.

37 'Therefore you shall observe all My statutes and all My judgments, and perform them: I *am* the LORD.' "

Punishments for breaking laws

20 Then the LORD spoke to Moses, saying, 2 "Again, you shall say to the children of Israel: 'Whoever of the children of Israel, or of the strangers who dwell in Israel, who gives *any* of his descendants to Molech, he shall surely be put to death. The people of the land shall stone him with stones. 3 I will set My face against that man, and will cut him off from his people, because he has given *some* of his descendants to Molech, to defile My sanctuary and profane My holy name. 4 And if the people of the land should in any way hide their *eyes* from the man, when he gives *some* of his descendants to Molech, and they do not kill him, 5 then I will set My face against that man and against his family; and I will cut him off from his people, and all who prostitute themselves with him to commit harlotry with Molech.

6 'And the person who turns to mediums and familiar spirits, to prostitute himself with them, I will set My face against that person and cut him off from his people. 7 Consecrate yourselves therefore, and be holy, for I *am* the LORD your God. 8 And you shall keep My statutes, and perform them: I *am* the LORD who sanctifies you.

9 'For everyone who curses his father or his mother shall surely be put to death. He has cursed his father or his mother. His blood *shall be* upon him.

10 'The man who commits adultery with *another* man's wife, *he* who commits adultery with his neighbor's wife, the adulterer and the adulteress, shall surely be put to death. 11 The man who lies with his father's wife has uncovered his father's nakedness; both of them shall surely be put to death. Their

---

WORDFINDER

19:30 Reverence Pronounced *REV-er-ents.* An attitude of respect and awe. Reverence is an attitude we should have for God in worship and in serving Him.

blood *shall be* upon them. ¹²If a man lies with his daughter-in-law, both of them shall surely be put to death. They have committed perversion. Their blood *shall be* upon them. ¹³If a man lies with a male as he lies with a woman, both of them have committed an abomination. They shall surely be put to death. Their blood *shall be* upon them. ¹⁴If a man marries a woman and her mother, it *is* wickedness. They shall be burned with fire, both he and they, that there may be no wickedness among you. ¹⁵If a man mates with an animal, he shall surely be put to death, and you shall kill the animal. ¹⁶If a woman approaches any animal and mates with it, you shall kill the woman and the animal. They shall surely be put to death. Their blood *is* upon them.

¹⁷'If a man takes his sister, his father's daughter or his mother's daughter, and sees her nakedness and she sees his nakedness, it *is* a wicked thing. And they shall be cut off in the sight of their people. He has uncovered his sister's nakedness. He shall bear his guilt. ¹⁸If a man lies with a woman during her sickness and uncovers her nakedness, he has exposed her flow, and she has uncovered the flow of her blood. Both of them shall be cut off from their people.

¹⁹'You shall not uncover the nakedness of your mother's sister nor of your father's sister, for that would uncover his near of kin. They shall bear their guilt. ²⁰If a man lies with his uncle's wife, he has uncovered his uncle's nakedness. They shall bear their sin; they shall die childless. ²¹If a man takes his brother's wife, it *is* an unclean thing. He has uncovered his brother's nakedness. They shall be childless.

²²'You shall therefore keep all My statutes and all My judgments, and perform them, that the land where I am bringing you to dwell may not vomit you out. ²³And you shall not walk in the statutes of the nation which I am casting out before you; for they commit all these things, and therefore I abhor them. ²⁴But I have said to you, "You shall inherit their land, and I will give

it to you to possess, a land flowing with milk and honey." I *am* the LORD your God, who has separated you from the peoples. ²⁵You shall therefore distinguish between clean animals and unclean, between unclean birds and clean, and you shall not make yourselves abominable by beast or by bird, or by any kind of living thing that creeps on the ground, which I have separated from you as unclean. ²⁶And you shall be holy to Me, for I the LORD *am* holy, and have separated you from the peoples, that you should be Mine.

²⁷'A man or a woman who is a medium, or who has familiar spirits, shall surely be put to death; they shall stone them with stones. Their blood *shall be* upon them.' "

Priests must be pure

21 And the LORD said to Moses, "Speak to the priests, the sons of Aaron, and say to them: 'None shall defile himself for the dead among his people, ²except for his relatives who are nearest to him: his mother, his father, his son, his daughter, and his brother; ³also his virgin sister who is near to him, who has had no husband, for her he may defile himself. ⁴*Otherwise* he shall not defile himself, *being* a chief man among his people, to profane himself.

⁵'They shall not make any bald *place* on their heads, nor shall they shave the edges of their beards nor make any cuttings in their flesh. ⁶They shall be holy to their God and not profane the name of their God, for they offer the offerings of the LORD made by fire, *and* the bread of their God; therefore they shall be holy. ⁷They shall not take a wife *who is* a harlot or a defiled woman, nor shall they take a woman divorced from her husband; for *the priest* is holy to his God. ⁸Therefore you shall consecrate him, for he offers the bread of your God. He shall be holy to you, for I the LORD, who sanctify you, *am* holy. ⁹The daughter of any priest, if she profanes herself by playing the harlot, she

profanes her father. She shall be burned with fire.

10 'He who is the **high priest** among his brethren, on whose head the anointing oil was poured and who is consecrated to wear the garments, shall not uncover his head nor tear his clothes; 11 nor shall he go near any dead body, nor defile himself for his father or his mother; 12 nor shall he go out of the sanctuary, nor profane the sanctuary of his God; for the consecration of the anointing oil of his God is upon him: I am the LORD. 13 And he shall take a wife in her virginity. 14 A widow or a divorced woman or a defiled woman or a harlot—these he shall not marry; but he shall take a virgin of his own people as wife. 15 Nor shall he profane his posterity among his people, for I the LORD sanctify him.' "

16 And the LORD spoke to Moses, saying, 17 "Speak to Aaron, saying: 'No man of your descendants in succeeding generations, who has any defect, may approach to offer the bread

of his God. 18 For any man who has a defect shall not approach: a man blind or lame, who has a marred face or any limb too long, 19 a man who has a broken foot or broken hand, 20 or is a hunchback or a dwarf, or a man who has a defect in his eye, or eczema or scab, or is a eunuch. 21 No man of the descendants of Aaron the priest, who has a defect, shall come near to offer the offerings made by fire to the LORD. He has a defect; he shall not come near to offer the bread of his God. 22 He may eat the bread of his God, both the most holy and the holy; 23 only he shall not go near the veil or approach the altar, because he has a defect, lest he profane My sanctuaries; for I the LORD sanctify them.' "

24 And Moses told it to Aaron and his sons, and to all the children of Israel.

Offerings must be pure

22 Then the LORD spoke to Moses, saying, 2 "Speak to Aaron and his

---

WORDFINDER

21:10 High Priest The priest who was over the other priests in Old Testament worship. Aaron, Moses' brother, was the first. Christ is now our High Priest.

On the Day of Atonement, the high priest was to enter the Most Holy Place and pray for the people. Jesus is now our only High Priest.

sons, that they separate themselves from the holy things of the children of Israel, and that they do not profane My holy name *by* what they dedicate to Me: I *am* the LORD. 3 Say to them: 'Whoever of all your descendants throughout your generations, who goes near the holy things which the children of Israel dedicate to the LORD, while he has uncleanness upon him, that person shall be cut off from My presence: I *am* the LORD.

4 'Whatever man of the descendants of Aaron, who *is* a leper or has a discharge, shall not eat the holy offerings until he is clean. And whoever touches anything made unclean *by* a corpse, or a man who has had an emission of semen, 5 or whoever touches any creeping thing by which he would be made unclean, or any person by whom he would become unclean, whatever his uncleanness may be— 6 the person who has touched any such thing shall be unclean until evening, and shall not eat the holy *offerings* unless he washes his body with water. 7 And when the sun goes down he shall be clean; and afterward he may eat the holy *offerings,* because it *is* his food. 8 Whatever dies *naturally* or is torn *by beasts* he shall not eat, to defile himself with it: I *am* the LORD.

9 'They shall therefore keep My ordinance, lest they bear sin for it and die thereby, if they profane it: I the LORD sanctify them.

10 'No outsider shall eat the holy *offering;* one who dwells with the priest, or a hired servant, shall not eat the holy thing. 11 But if the priest buys a person with his money, he may eat it; and one who is born in his house may eat his food. 12 If the priest's daughter is married to an outsider, she may not eat of the holy offerings. 13 But if the priest's daughter is a widow or divorced, and has no child, and has returned to her father's house as in her youth, she may eat her father's food; but no outsider shall eat it.

14 'And if a man eats the holy *offering* unintentionally, then he shall restore a holy *offering* to the priest, and add one-fifth to it. 15 They shall not profane the holy *offerings* of the children of Israel, which they offer to the LORD, 16 or allow them to bear the guilt of trespass when they eat their holy *offerings;* for I the LORD sanctify them.' "

17 And the LORD spoke to Moses, saying, 18 "Speak to Aaron and his sons, and to all the children of Israel, and say to them: 'Whatever man of the house of Israel, or of the strangers in Israel, who offers his sacrifice for any of his vows or for any of his freewill offerings, which they offer to the LORD as a burnt offering— 19 *you shall offer* of your own free will a male without blemish from the cattle, from the sheep, or from the goats. 20 Whatever has a defect, you shall not offer, for it shall not be acceptable on your behalf. 21 And whoever offers a sacrifice of a peace offering to the LORD, to fulfill *his* vow, or a freewill offering from the cattle or the sheep, it must be perfect to be accepted; there shall be no defect in it. 22 Those *that are* blind or broken or maimed, or have an ulcer or eczema or scabs, you shall not offer to the LORD, nor make an offering by fire of them on the altar to the LORD. 23 Either a bull or a lamb that has any limb too long or too short you may offer *as* a freewill offering, but for a vow it shall not be accepted.

24 'You shall not offer to the LORD what is bruised or crushed, or torn or cut; nor shall you make *any offering of them* in your land. 25 Nor from a foreigner's hand shall you offer any of these as the bread of your God, because their corruption *is* in them, *and* defects *are* in them. They shall not be accepted on your behalf.' "

26 And the LORD spoke to Moses, saying: 27 "When a bull or a sheep or a goat is born, it shall be seven days with its mother; and from the eighth day and thereafter it shall be accepted as an offering made by fire to the LORD. 28 *Whether it is* a cow or ewe, do not kill both her and her young on the same day. 29 And when you offer a sacrifice of thanksgiving to the LORD, offer

it of your own free will. 30 On the same day it shall be eaten; you shall leave none of it until morning: I am the LORD.

31 "Therefore you shall keep My commandments, and perform them: I am the LORD. 32 You shall not profane My holy name, but I will be hallowed among the children of Israel. I am the LORD who sanctifies you, 33 who brought you out of the land of Egypt, to be your God: I am the LORD."

God describes the feasts

23 And the LORD spoke to Moses, saying, 2 "Speak to the children of Israel, and say to them: 'The feasts of the LORD, which you shall proclaim to be holy convocations, these are My feasts.

3 'Six days shall work be done, but the seventh day is a Sabbath of solemn rest, a holy convocation. You shall do no work on it; it is the Sabbath of the LORD in all your dwellings.

4 'These are the feasts of the LORD, holy convocations which you shall proclaim at their appointed times. 5 On the fourteenth day of the first month at twilight is the LORD's Passover. 6 And on the fifteenth day of the same month is the Feast of Unleavened Bread to the LORD; seven days you must eat unleavened bread. 7 On the first day you shall have a holy convocation; you shall do no customary work on it. 8 But you shall offer an offering made by fire to the LORD for seven days. The seventh day shall be a holy convocation; you shall do no customary work on it.' "

9 And the LORD spoke to Moses, saying, 10 "Speak to the children of Israel, and say to them: 'When you come into the land which I give to you, and reap its harvest, then you shall bring a sheaf of the firstfruits of your harvest to the priest. 11 He shall wave the sheaf before the LORD, to be accepted on your behalf; on the day after the Sabbath the priest shall wave it. 12 And you shall offer on that day, when you wave the sheaf, a male lamb of the first year, without blemish, as a burnt offering to the LORD. 13 Its grain offering shall be two-tenths of an ephah of fine flour mixed with oil, an offering made by fire to the LORD, for a sweet aroma; and its drink offering shall be of wine, one-fourth of a hin. 14 You shall eat neither bread nor parched grain nor fresh grain until the same day that you

DIGGING IN

23:2 Important Old Testament Feasts The following are important feast times practiced by the people of the Old Testament:

* Passover and Unleavened Bread, beginning on the fourteenth day of the first Jewish month, our April. The people remembered how God passed over them in Egypt when the Egyptians' firstborn died. (See Exodus 12:1–28.)

* Day of Atonement, on the tenth day of the seventh Jewish month, our month of August. (See Leviticus 16:1–31.)

* Feast of Booths, on the fifteenth of the seventh month, also called the Feast of Tabernacles. The people lived in booths or tents to remember how they once lived in the desert after they left Egypt. (See Leviticus 23:33–36.)

* Feast of Weeks, also called the Harvest Feast and Pentecost, on the fiftieth day after Passover. (See Leviticus 23:15–21.)

* Sabbatical Year, every seventh year. The land was not farmed and debts were canceled. (See Leviticus 25:3–7.)

* Jubilee Year, every fiftieth year. The land was not farmed, debts were canceled, and slaves were set free. (See Leviticus 25:8–55.)

* Purim (pronounced PEW-reem), on the fourteenth and fifteenth days of the twelfth Jewish month, February and March of our year. This feast recalls how God saved Israel from Persian enemies during the time of Esther. (See Esther 9.)

* Hanukkah (pronounced HAH-nuh-kuh), also called the Feast of Lights. This feast was added after the close of the Old Testament to remember the Jews' victory over their Greek enemies.

have brought an offering to your God; *it shall be* a statute forever throughout your generations in all your dwellings.

15 'And you shall count for yourselves from the day after the Sabbath, from the day that you brought the sheaf of the wave offering: seven Sabbaths shall be completed. 16 Count fifty days to the day after the seventh Sabbath; then you shall offer a new grain offering to the LORD. 17 You shall bring from your dwellings two wave *loaves* of two-tenths *of an ephah*. They shall be of fine flour; they shall be baked with leaven. *They are* the firstfruits to the LORD. 18 And you shall offer with the bread seven lambs of the first year, without blemish, one young bull, and two rams. They shall be *as* a burnt offering to the LORD, with their grain offering and their drink offerings, an offering made by fire for a sweet aroma to the LORD. 19 Then you shall sacrifice one kid of the goats as a sin offering, and two male lambs of the first year as a sacrifice of a peace offering. 20 The priest shall wave them with the bread of the firstfruits *as* a wave offering before the LORD, with the two lambs. They shall be holy to the LORD for the priest. 21 And you shall proclaim on the same day *that* it is a holy convocation to you. You shall do no customary work *on it*. *It shall be* a statute forever in all your dwellings throughout your generations.

22 'When you reap the harvest of your land, you shall not wholly reap the corners of your field when you reap, nor shall you gather any gleaning from your harvest. You shall leave them for the poor and for the stranger: I *am* the LORD your God.' "

23 Then the LORD spoke to Moses, saying, 24 "Speak to the children of Israel, saying: 'In the seventh month, on the first *day* of the month, you shall have a sabbath-*rest,* a memorial of blowing of trumpets, a holy convocation. 25 You shall do no customary work *on it;* and you shall offer an offering made by fire to the LORD.' "

26 And the LORD spoke to Moses, saying: 27 "Also the tenth *day* of this seventh month *shall be* the Day of Atonement. It shall be a holy convocation for you; you shall afflict your souls, and offer an offering made by fire to the LORD. 28 And you shall do no work on that same day, for it *is* the Day of Atonement, to make atonement for you before the LORD your God. 29 For any person who is not afflicted *in soul* on that same day shall be cut off from his people. 30 And any person who does any work on that same day, that person I will destroy from among his people. 31 You shall do no manner of work; *it shall be* a statute forever throughout your generations in all your dwellings. 32 It *shall be* to you a sabbath of *solemn* rest, and you shall afflict your souls; on the ninth *day* of the month at evening, from evening to evening, you shall celebrate your sabbath."

33 Then the LORD spoke to Moses, saying, 34 "Speak to the children of Israel, saying: 'The fifteenth day of this seventh month *shall be* the Feast of Tabernacles *for* seven days to the LORD. 35 On the first day *there shall be* a holy convocation. You shall do no customary work *on it.* 36 *For* seven days you shall offer an offering made by fire to the LORD. On the eighth day you shall have a holy convocation, and you shall offer an offering made by fire to the LORD. It *is* a sacred assembly, *and* you shall do no customary work *on it.*

37 'These *are* the feasts of the LORD which you shall proclaim *to be* holy convocations, to offer an offering made by fire to the LORD, a burnt offering and a grain offering, a sacrifice and drink offerings, *everything* on its day— 38 besides the Sabbaths of the LORD, besides your gifts, besides all your vows, and besides all your freewill offerings which you give to the LORD.

39 'Also on the fifteenth day of the seventh month, when you have gathered in the fruit of the land, you shall keep the feast of the LORD *for* seven days; on the first day *there shall be* a sabbath-*rest,* and on the eighth day a sabbath-*rest.* 40 And you shall take for

yourselves on the first day the fruit of beautiful trees, branches of palm trees, the boughs of leafy trees, and willows of the brook; and you shall rejoice before the LORD your God for seven days. 41 You shall keep it as a feast to the LORD for seven days in the year. *It shall be* a statute forever in your generations. You shall celebrate it in the seventh month. 42 You shall dwell in booths for seven days. All who are native Israelites shall dwell in booths, 43 that your generations may know that I made the children of Israel dwell in booths when I brought them out of the land of Egypt: I *am* the LORD your God.' "

44 So Moses declared to the children of Israel the feasts of the LORD.

Punishment for dishonoring God

24 Then the LORD spoke to Moses, saying: 2 "Command the children of Israel that they bring to you pure oil of pressed olives for the light, to make the lamps burn continually. 3 Outside the veil of the Testimony, in the tabernacle of meeting, Aaron shall be in charge of it from evening until morning before the LORD continually; *it shall be* a statute forever in your generations. 4 He shall be in charge of the lamps on the pure *gold* lampstand before the LORD continually.

5 "And you shall take fine flour and bake twelve cakes with it. Two-tenths *of an ephah* shall be in each cake. 6 You shall set them in two rows, six in a row, on the pure *gold* table before the LORD. 7 And you shall put pure frankincense on *each* row, that it may be on the bread for a memorial, an offering made by fire to the LORD. 8 Every Sabbath he shall set it in order before the LORD continually, *being taken* from the children of Israel by an everlasting covenant. 9 And it shall be for Aaron and his sons, and they shall eat it in a holy place; for it *is* most holy to him from the offerings of the LORD made by fire, by a perpetual statute."

10 Now the son of an Israelite woman, whose father *was* an Egyptian, went out among the children of Israel; and this Israelite *woman's* son and a man of Israel fought each other in the camp. 11 And the Israelite woman's son blasphemed the name *of the LORD* and cursed; and so they brought him to Moses. (His mother's name *was* Shelomith the daughter of Dibri, of the tribe of Dan.) 12 Then they put him in custody, that the mind of the LORD might be shown to them.

13 And the LORD spoke to Moses, saying, 14 "Take outside the camp him who has cursed; then let all who heard *him* lay their hands on his head, and let all the congregation stone him.

15 "Then you shall speak to the children of Israel, saying: 'Whoever curses his God shall bear his sin. 16 And whoever blasphemes the name of the LORD shall surely be put to death. All the congregation shall certainly stone him, the stranger as well as him who is born in the land. When he blasphemes the name *of the LORD,* he shall be put to death.

17 'Whoever kills any man shall surely be put to death. 18 Whoever kills an animal shall make it good, animal for animal.

19 'If a man causes disfigurement of his neighbor, as he has done, so shall it be done to him— 20 fracture for fracture, eye for eye, tooth for tooth; as he has caused disfigurement of a man, so shall it be done to him. 21 And whoever kills an animal shall restore it; but whoever kills a man shall be put to death. 22 You shall have the same law for the stranger and for one from your own country; for I *am* the LORD your God.' "

23 Then Moses spoke to the children of Israel; and they took outside the camp him who had cursed, and stoned him with stones. So the children of Israel did as the LORD commanded Moses.

The seventh year and the Year of Jubilee

25 And the LORD spoke to Moses on Mount Sinai, saying, 2 "Speak to

the children of Israel, and say to them: 'When you come into the land which I give you, then the land shall keep a sabbath to the LORD. 3 Six years you shall sow your field, and six years you shall prune your vineyard, and gather its fruit; 4 but in the seventh year there shall be a sabbath of solemn rest for the land, a sabbath to the LORD. You shall neither sow your field nor prune your vineyard. 5 What grows of its own accord of your harvest you shall not reap, nor gather the grapes of your untended vine, *for* it is a year of rest for the land. 6 And the sabbath *produce* of the land shall be food for you: for you, your male and female servants, your hired man, and the stranger who dwells with you, 7 for your livestock and the beasts that *are* in your land— all its produce shall be for food.

8 'And you shall count seven sabbaths of years for yourself, seven times seven years; and the time of the seven sabbaths of years shall be to you forty-nine years. 9 Then you shall cause the trumpet of the Jubilee to sound on the tenth *day* of the seventh month; on the Day of Atonement you shall make the trumpet to sound throughout all your land. 10 And you shall consecrate the fiftieth year, and proclaim liberty throughout *all* the land to all its inhabitants. It shall be a Jubilee for you; and each of you shall return to his possession, and each of you shall return to his family. 11 That fiftieth year shall be a Jubilee to you; in it you shall neither

sow nor reap what grows of its own accord, nor gather *the grapes* of your untended vine. 12 For it *is* the Jubilee; it shall be holy to you; you shall eat its produce from the field.

13 'In this Year of Jubilee, each of you shall return to his possession. 14 And if you sell anything to your neighbor or buy from your neighbor's hand, you shall not oppress one another. 15 According to the number of years after the Jubilee you shall buy from your neighbor, and according to the number of years of crops he shall sell to you. 16 According to the multitude of years you shall increase its price, and according to the fewer number of years you shall diminish its price; for he sells to you *according* to the number *of the years* of the crops. 17 Therefore you shall not oppress one another, but you shall fear your God; for I *am* the LORD your God.

18 'So you shall observe My statutes and keep My judgments, and perform them; and you will dwell in the land in safety. 19 Then the land will yield its fruit, and you will eat your fill, and dwell there in safety.

20 'And if you say, "What shall we eat in the seventh year, since we shall not sow nor gather in our produce?" 21 Then I will command My blessing on you in the sixth year, and it will bring forth produce enough for three years. 22 And you shall sow in the eighth year, and eat old produce until the ninth year; until its produce comes in, you shall eat *of* the old *harvest*.

23 'The land shall not be sold permanently, for the land *is* Mine; for you *are* strangers and sojourners with Me. 24 And in all the land of your possession you shall grant redemption of the land.

25 'If one of your brethren becomes poor, and has sold *some* of his possession, and if his redeeming relative comes to redeem it, then he may redeem what his brother sold. 26 Or if the man has no one to redeem it, but he himself becomes able to redeem it, 27 then let him count the years since its sale, and restore the remainder to

The Hebrew trumpet was a ram's horn.

the man to whom he sold it, that he may return to his possession. 28 But if he is not able to have *it* restored to himself, then what was sold shall remain in the hand of him who bought it until the Year of Jubilee; and in the Jubilee it shall be released, and he shall return to his possession.

29 'If a man sells a house in a walled city, then he may redeem it within a whole year after it is sold; *within* a full year he may redeem it. 30 But if it is not redeemed within the space of a full year, then the house in the walled city shall belong permanently to him who bought it, throughout his generations. It shall not be released in the Jubilee. 31 However the houses of villages which have no wall around them shall be counted as the fields of the country. They may be redeemed, and they shall be released in the Jubilee. 32 Nevertheless the cities of the Levites, *and* the houses in the cities of their possession, the Levites may redeem at any time. 33 And if a man purchases a house from the Levites, then the house that was sold in the city of his possession shall be released in the Jubilee; for the houses in the cities of the Levites *are* their possession among the children of Israel. 34 But the field of the common-land of their cities may not be sold, for it *is* their perpetual possession.

35 'If one of your brethren becomes poor, and falls into poverty among you, then you shall help him, like a stranger or a sojourner, that he may live with you. 36 Take no usury or interest from him; but fear your God, that your brother may live with you. 37 You shall not lend him your money for usury, nor lend him your food at a profit. 38 I *am* the LORD your God, who brought you out of the land of Egypt, to give you the land of Canaan *and* to be your God.

39 'And if *one of* your brethren *who dwells* by you becomes poor, and sells himself to you, you shall not compel him to serve as a slave. 40 As a hired servant *and* a sojourner he shall be with you, *and* shall serve you until the Year of Jubilee. 41 And *then* he shall depart from you—he and his children with him—and shall return to his own family. He shall return to the possession of his fathers. 42 For they *are* My servants, whom I brought out of the land of Egypt; they shall not be sold as slaves. 43 You shall not rule over him with rigor, but you shall fear your God. 44 And as for your male and female slaves whom you may have—from the nations that are around you, from them you may buy male and female slaves. 45 Moreover you may buy the children of the strangers who dwell among you, and their families who are with you, which they beget in your land; and they shall become your property. 46 And you may take them as an inheritance for your children after you, to inherit *them as* a possession; they shall be your permanent slaves. But regarding your brethren, the children of Israel, you shall not rule over one another with rigor.

47 'Now if a sojourner or stranger close to you becomes rich, and *one of* your brethren *who dwells* by him becomes poor, and sells himself to the stranger *or* sojourner close to you, or to a member of the stranger's family, 48 after he is sold he may be redeemed again. One of his brothers may redeem him; 49 or his uncle or his uncle's son may redeem him; or *anyone* who is near of kin to him in his family may redeem him; or if he is able he may redeem himself. 50 Thus he shall reckon with him who bought him: The price of his release shall be according to the number of years, from the year that he was sold to him until the Year of Jubilee; *it shall be* according to the time of a hired servant for him. 51 If *there are* still many years *remaining,* according to them he shall repay the price of his redemption from the money with which he was bought. 52 And if there remain but a few years until the Year of Jubilee, then he shall reckon with him, *and* according to his years he shall repay him the price of his redemption. 53 He shall be with him as a yearly hired servant, and he shall

not rule with rigor over him in your sight. 54 And if he is not redeemed in these *years*, then he shall be released in the Year of Jubilee—he and his children with him. 55 For the children of Israel *are* servants to Me; they *are* My servants whom I brought out of the land of Egypt: I *am* the LORD your God.

God promises blessing and judgment

26 'You shall not make idols for yourselves;
neither a carved image nor a *sacred* pillar shall you rear up for yourselves;
nor shall you set up an engraved stone in your land, to bow down to it;
for I *am* the LORD your God.
2 You shall keep My Sabbaths and reverence My sanctuary:
I *am* the LORD.

3 'If you walk in My statutes and keep My commandments, and perform them,
4 then I will give you rain in its season, the land shall yield its produce, and the trees of the field shall yield their fruit.
5 Your threshing shall last till the time of vintage, and the vintage shall last till the time of sowing;
you shall eat your bread to the full, and dwell in your land safely.
6 I will give peace in the land, and you shall lie down, and none will make *you* afraid;
I will rid the land of evil beasts, and the sword will not go through your land.
7 You will chase your enemies, and they shall fall by the sword before you.
8 Five of you shall chase a hundred, and a hundred of you shall put ten thousand to flight;

your enemies shall fall by the sword before you.

9 'For I will look on you favorably and make you fruitful, multiply you and confirm My covenant with you.
10 You shall eat the old harvest, and clear out the old because of the new.
11 I will set My tabernacle among you, and My soul shall not abhor you.
12 I will walk among you and be your God, and you shall be My people.
13 I *am* the LORD your God, who brought you out of the land of Egypt, that *you* should not be their slaves;
I have broken the bands of your yoke and made you walk upright.

14 'But if you do not obey Me, and do not observe all these commandments,
15 and if you despise My statutes, or if your soul abhors My judgments, so that you do not perform all My commandments, *but* break My covenant,
16 I also will do this to you:
I will even appoint terror over you, wasting disease and fever which shall consume the eyes and cause sorrow of heart.
And you shall sow your seed in vain, for your enemies shall eat it.
17 I will set My face against you, and you shall be defeated by your enemies.
Those who hate you shall reign over you, and you shall flee when no one pursues you.

18 'And after all this, if you do not obey Me, then I will punish you seven times more for your sins.
19 I will break the pride of your power;

I will make your heavens like iron and your earth like bronze.

20 And your strength shall be spent in vain;

for your land shall not yield its produce, nor shall the trees of the land yield their fruit.

21 'Then, if you walk contrary to Me, and are not willing to obey Me, I will bring on you seven times more plagues, according to your sins.

22 I will also send wild beasts among you, which shall rob you of your children, destroy your livestock, and make you few in number;

and your highways shall be desolate.

23 'And if by these things you are not reformed by Me, but walk contrary to Me,

24 then I also will walk contrary to you, and I will punish you yet seven times for your sins.

25 And I will bring a sword against you that will execute the vengeance of the covenant;

when you are gathered together within your cities I will send pestilence among you;

and you shall be delivered into the hand of the enemy.

26 When I have cut off your supply of bread, ten women shall bake your bread in one oven, and they shall bring back your bread by weight, and you shall eat and not be satisfied.

27 'And after all this, if you do not obey Me, but walk contrary to Me,

28 then I also will walk contrary to you in fury;

and I, even I, will chastise you seven times for your sins.

29 You shall eat the flesh of your sons, and you shall eat the flesh of your daughters.

30 I will destroy your high places,

cut down your incense altars, and cast your carcasses on the lifeless forms of your idols;

and My soul shall abhor you.

31 I will lay your cities waste and bring your sanctuaries to desolation, and I will not smell the fragrance of your sweet aromas.

32 I will bring the land to desolation, and your enemies who dwell in it shall be astonished at it.

33 I will scatter you among the nations and draw out a sword after you;

your land shall be desolate and your cities waste.

34 Then the land shall enjoy its sabbaths as long as it lies desolate and you *are* in your enemies' land;

then the land shall rest and enjoy its sabbaths.

35 As long as *it* lies desolate it shall rest—

for the time it did not rest on your sabbaths when you dwelt in it.

36 'And as for those of you who are left, I will send faintness into their hearts in the lands of their enemies;

the sound of a shaken leaf shall cause them to flee;

they shall flee as though fleeing from a sword, and they shall fall when no one pursues.

37 They shall stumble over one another, as it *were* before a sword, when no one pursues;

and you shall have no *power* to stand before your enemies.

38 You shall perish among the nations, and the land of your enemies shall eat you up.

39 And those of you who are left shall waste away in their iniquity in your enemies' lands;

also in their fathers' iniquities, which are with them, they shall waste away.

40 'But if they confess their iniquity and the iniquity of their fathers, with their unfaithfulness in which they were unfaithful to Me, and that they also have walked contrary to Me,

41 and *that* I also have walked contrary to them and have brought them into the land of their enemies;

if their uncircumcised hearts are humbled, and they accept their guilt—

42 then I will remember My covenant with Jacob, and My covenant with Isaac and My covenant with Abraham I will remember;

I will remember the land.

43 The land also shall be left empty by them, and will enjoy its sabbaths while it lies desolate without them;

they will accept their guilt, because they despised My judgments and because their soul abhorred My statutes.

44 Yet for all that, when they are in the land of their enemies, I will not cast them away, nor shall I abhor them, to utterly destroy them and break My covenant with them;

for I *am* the LORD their God.

45 But for their sake I will remember the covenant of their ancestors, whom I brought out of the land of Egypt in the sight of the nations, that I might be their God:

I *am* the LORD.' "

46 These *are* the statutes and judgments and laws which the LORD made between Himself and the children of Israel on Mount Sinai by the hand of Moses.

People and belongings are dedicated to God

27 Now the LORD spoke to Moses, saying, 2 "Speak to the children of Israel, and say to them: 'When a man consecrates by a vow certain persons to the LORD, according to your valuation, 3 if your valuation is of a male from twenty years old up to sixty years old, then your valuation shall be fifty shekels of silver, according to the shekel of the sanctuary. 4 If it *is* a female, then your valuation shall be thirty shekels; 5 and if from five years old up to twenty years old, then your valuation for a male shall be twenty shekels, and for a female ten shekels; 6 and if from a month old up to five years old, then your valuation for a male shall be five shekels of silver, and for a female your valuation shall be three shekels of silver; 7 and if from sixty years old and above, if *it* is a male, then your valuation shall be fifteen shekels, and for a female ten shekels.

8 'But if he is too poor to pay your valuation, then he shall present himself before the priest, and the priest shall set a value for him; according to the ability of him who vowed, the priest shall value him.

9 'If *it* is an animal that men may bring as an offering to the LORD, all that *anyone* gives to the LORD shall be holy. 10 He shall not substitute it or exchange it, good for bad or bad for good; and if he at all exchanges animal for animal, then both it and the one exchanged for it shall be holy. 11 If *it* is an unclean animal which they do not offer as a sacrifice to the LORD, then he shall present the animal before the priest; 12 and the priest shall set a value for it, whether it is good or bad; as you, the priest, value it, so it shall be. 13 But if he *wants* at all *to* redeem it, then he must add one-fifth to your valuation.

14 'And when a man dedicates his house *to be* holy to the LORD, then the priest shall set a value for it, whether it is good or bad; as the priest values it, so it shall stand. 15 If he who dedicated it *wants to* redeem his house, then he must add one-fifth of the money of your valuation to it, and it shall be his.

16 'If a man dedicates to the LORD *part* of a field of his possession, then

your valuation shall be according to the seed for it. A homer of barley seed *shall be valued* at fifty shekels of silver. 17 If he dedicates his field from the Year of Jubilee, according to your valuation it shall stand. 18 But if he dedicates his field after the Jubilee, then the priest shall reckon to him the money due according to the years that remain till the Year of Jubilee, and it shall be deducted from your valuation. 19 And if he who dedicates the field ever wishes to redeem it, then he must add one-fifth of the money of your valuation to it, and it shall belong to him. 20 But if he does not want to redeem the field, or if he has sold the field to another man, it shall not be redeemed anymore; 21 but the field, when it is released in the Jubilee, shall be holy to the Lord, as a devoted field; it shall be the possession of the priest.

22 'And if a man dedicates to the Lord a field which he has bought, which is not the field of his possession, 23 then the priest shall reckon to him the worth of your valuation, up to the Year of Jubilee, and he shall give your valuation on that day *as* a holy *offering* to the Lord. 24 In the Year of Jubilee the field shall return to him from whom it was bought, to the one who *owned* the land as a possession. 25 And all your valuations shall be according to the shekel of the sanctuary: twenty gerahs to the shekel.

26 'But the firstborn of the animals, which should be the Lord's firstborn, no man shall dedicate; whether *it is* an ox or sheep, it *is* the Lord's. 27 And if *it is* an unclean animal, then he shall redeem *it* according to your valuation, and shall add one-fifth to it; or if it is not redeemed, then it shall be sold according to your valuation.

28 'Nevertheless no devoted *offering* that a man may devote to the Lord of all that he has, *both* man and beast, or the field of his possession, shall be sold or redeemed; every devoted *offering is* most holy to the Lord. 29 No person under the ban, who may become doomed to destruction among men, shall be redeemed, *but* shall surely be put to death. 30 And all the tithe of the land, *whether* of the seed of the land *or* of the fruit of the tree, *is* the Lord's. It *is* holy to the Lord. 31 If a man wants at all to redeem *any* of his tithes, he shall add one-fifth to it. 32 And concerning the tithe of the herd or the flock, of whatever passes under the rod, the tenth one shall be holy to the Lord. 33 He shall not inquire whether it is good or bad, nor shall he exchange it; and if he exchanges it at all, then both it and the one exchanged for it shall be holy; it shall not be redeemed.' "

34 These *are* the commandments which the Lord commanded Moses for the children of Israel on Mount Sinai.

The Book of
NUMBERS

Israel—You may remember that God changed Jacob's name to Israel (pronounced *IZ-ray-el*), which means "Prince with God." Jacob (or Israel) had 12 sons who became the fathers of the 12 tribes of the nation of Israel.

God called us to be His special people, not because we were better than other people, but because He wanted us to carry His great message to the other nations of the world. This is what God promised Abraham, Israel's great-grandfather, He would do.

The story of our nation is the story of God's great love and patience. We were often disobedient to the Lord, as you will read all through the Old Testament, but God was kind to us and never left us alone.

His greatest kindness was to send us the Messiah, Jesus Christ, who died for the sins of the world.

Moses counts the people of Israel

NOW the LORD spoke to Moses in the Wilderness of Sinai, in the tabernacle of meeting, on the first *day* of the second month, in the second year after they had come out of the land of Egypt, saying: 2 "Take a census of all the congregation of the children of Israel, by their families, by their fathers' houses, according to the number of names, every male individually, 3 from twenty years old and above—all who *are able to* go to war in Israel. You and Aaron shall number them by their armies. 4 And with you there shall be a man from every tribe, each one the head of his father's house.

5 "These are the names of the men who shall stand with you: from Reuben, Elizur the son of Shedeur; 6 from Simeon, Shelumiel the son of Zurishaddai; 7 from Judah, Nahshon the son of Amminadab; 8 from Issachar, Nethanel the son of Zuar; 9 from Zebulun, Eliab the son of Helon; 10 from the sons of Joseph: from Ephraim, Elishama the son of Ammihud; from Manasseh, Gamaliel the son of Pedahzur; 11 from Benjamin, Abidan the son of Gideoni; 12 from Dan, Ahiezer the son of Ammishaddai; 13 from Asher,

Pagiel the son of Ocran; 14 from Gad, Eliasaph the son of Deuel; 15 from Naphtali, Ahira the son of Enan."
16 These *were* chosen from the congregation, leaders of their fathers' tribes, heads of the divisions in Israel.

17 Then Moses and Aaron took these men who had been mentioned by name, 18 and they assembled all the congregation together on the first *day* of the second month; and they recited their ancestry by families, by their fathers' houses, according to the number of names, from twenty years old and above, each one individually. 19 As the LORD commanded Moses, so he numbered them in the Wilderness of Sinai.

20 Now the children of Reuben, Israel's oldest son, their genealogies by their families, by their fathers' house, according to the number of names, every male individually, from twenty years old and above, all who *were able to* go to war: 21 those who were numbered of the tribe of Reuben *were* forty-six thousand five hundred.

22 From the children of Simeon, their genealogies by their families, by their fathers' house, of those who were numbered, according to the number of names, every male individually, from twenty years old and above, all who *were able to* go to war: 23 those

who were numbered of the tribe of Simeon *were* fifty-nine thousand three hundred.

24 From the children of Gad, their genealogies by their families, by their fathers' house, according to the number of names, from twenty years old and above, all who *were able to* go to war: 25 those who were numbered of the tribe of Gad *were* forty-five thousand six hundred and fifty.

26 From the children of Judah, their genealogies by their families, by their fathers' house, according to the number of names, from twenty years old and above, all who *were able to* go to war: 27 those who were numbered of the tribe of Judah *were* seventy-four thousand six hundred.

28 From the children of Issachar, their genealogies by their families, by their fathers' house, according to the number of names, from twenty years old and above, all who *were able to* go to war: 29 those who were numbered of the tribe of Issachar *were* fifty-four thousand four hundred.

30 From the children of Zebulun, their genealogies by their families, by their fathers' house, according to the number of names, from twenty years old and above, all who *were able to* go to war: 31 those who were numbered of the tribe of Zebulun *were* fifty-seven thousand four hundred.

32 From the sons of Joseph, the children of Ephraim, their genealogies by their families, by their fathers' house, according to the number of names, from twenty years old and above, all who *were able to* go to war: 33 those who were numbered of the tribe of Ephraim *were* forty thousand five hundred.

34 From the children of Manasseh, their genealogies by their families, by their fathers' house, according to the number of names, from twenty years old and above, all who *were able to* go to war: 35 those who were numbered of the tribe of Manasseh *were* thirty-two thousand two hundred.

36 From the children of Benjamin, their genealogies by their families, by their fathers' house, according to the number of names, from twenty years old and above, all who *were able to* go to war: 37 those who were numbered of the tribe of Benjamin *were* thirty-five thousand four hundred.

38 From the children of Dan, their genealogies by their families, by their fathers' house, according to the number of names, from twenty years old and above, all who *were able to* go to war: 39 those who were numbered of the tribe of Dan *were* sixty-two thousand seven hundred.

40 From the children of Asher, their genealogies by their families, by their fathers' house, according to the number of names, from twenty years old and above, all who *were able to* go to war: 41 those who were numbered of the tribe of Asher *were* forty-one thousand five hundred.

42 From the children of Naphtali, their genealogies by their families, by their fathers' house, according to the number of names, from twenty years old and above, all who *were able to* go to war: 43 those who were numbered of the tribe of Naphtali *were* fifty-three thousand four hundred.

44 These are the ones who were numbered, whom Moses and Aaron numbered, with the leaders of Israel, twelve men, each one representing his father's house. 45 So all who were numbered of the children of Israel, by their fathers' houses, from twenty years old and above, all who *were able to* go to war in Israel— 46 all who were numbered were six hundred and three thousand five hundred and fifty.

47 But the Levites were not numbered among them by their fathers' tribe; 48 for the LORD had spoken to Moses, saying: 49 "Only the tribe of Levi you shall not number, nor take a census of them among the children of Israel; 50 but you shall appoint the Levites over the tabernacle of the Testimony, over all its furnishings, and over all things that belong to it; they shall carry the tabernacle and all its furnishings; they shall attend to it and camp around the tabernacle. 51 And when

the tabernacle is to go forward, the Levites shall take it down; and when the tabernacle is to be set up, the Levites shall set it up. The outsider who comes near shall be put to death. [52] The children of Israel shall pitch their tents, everyone by his own camp, everyone by his own standard, according to their armies; [53] but the Levites shall camp around the tabernacle of the Testimony, that there may be no wrath on the congregation of the children of Israel; and the Levites shall keep charge of the tabernacle of the Testimony."

[54] Thus the children of Israel did; according to all that the LORD commanded Moses, so they did.

How Israel is to camp

2 And the LORD spoke to Moses and Aaron, saying: [2] "Everyone of the children of Israel shall camp by his own standard, beside the emblems of his father's house; they shall camp some distance from the tabernacle of meeting. [3] On the east side, toward the rising of the sun, those of the standard of the forces with Judah shall camp according to their armies; and Nahshon the son of Amminadab *shall be* the leader of the children of Judah." [4] And his army was numbered at seventy-four thousand six hundred.

[5] "Those who camp next to him *shall be* the tribe of Issachar, and Nethanel the son of Zuar *shall be* the leader of the children of Issachar." [6] And his army was numbered at fifty-four thousand four hundred.

[7] "Then *comes* the tribe of Zebulun, and Eliab the son of Helon *shall be* the leader of the children of Zebulun." [8] And his army was numbered at fifty-seven thousand four hundred. [9] "All who were numbered according to their armies of the forces with Judah, one hundred and eighty-six thousand four hundred—these shall break camp first.

[10] "On the south side *shall be* the standard of the forces with Reuben according to their armies, and the leader

of the children of Reuben *shall be* Elizur the son of Shedeur." [11] And his army was numbered at forty-six thousand five hundred.

[12] "Those who camp next to him *shall be* the tribe of Simeon, and the leader of the children of Simeon *shall be* Shelumiel the son of Zurishaddai." [13] And his army was numbered at fifty-nine thousand three hundred.

[14] "Then *comes* the tribe of Gad, and the leader of the children of Gad *shall be* Eliasaph the son of Reuel." [15] And his army was numbered at forty-five thousand six hundred and fifty. [16] "All who were numbered according to their armies of the forces with Reuben, one hundred and fifty-one thousand four hundred and fifty—they shall be the second to break camp.

[17] "And the tabernacle of meeting shall move out with the camp of the Levites in the middle of the camps; as they camp, so they shall move out, everyone in his place, by their standards.

[18] "On the west side *shall be* the standard of the forces with Ephraim according to their armies, and the leader of the children of Ephraim *shall be* Elishama the son of Ammihud." [19] And his army was numbered at forty thousand five hundred.

[20] "Next to him *comes* the tribe of Manasseh, and the leader of the children of Manasseh *shall be* Gamaliel the son of Pedahzur." [21] And his army was numbered at thirty-two thousand two hundred.

[22] "Then *comes* the tribe of Benjamin, and the leader of the children of Benjamin *shall be* Abidan the son of Gideoni." [23] And his army was numbered at thirty-five thousand four hundred. [24] "All who were numbered according to their armies of the forces with Ephraim, one hundred and eight thousand one hundred—they shall be the third to break camp.

[25] "The standard of the forces with Dan *shall be* on the north side according to their armies, and the leader of the children of Dan *shall be* Ahiezer

the son of Ammishaddai." 26 And his army was numbered at sixty-two thousand seven hundred.

27 "Those who camp next to him *shall be* the tribe of Asher, and the leader of the children of Asher *shall be* Pagiel the son of Ocran." 28 And his army was numbered at forty-one thousand five hundred.

29 "Then *comes* the tribe of Naphtali, and the leader of the children of Naphtali *shall be* Ahira the son of Enan." 30 And his army was numbered at fifty-three thousand four hundred. 31 "All who *were* numbered of the forces with Dan, one hundred and fifty-seven thousand six hundred—they shall break camp last, with their standards."

32 These *are* the ones who were numbered of the children of Israel by their fathers' houses. All who were numbered according to their armies of the forces *were* six hundred and three thousand five hundred and fifty. 33 But the Levites were not numbered among the children of Israel, just as the LORD commanded Moses.

34 Thus the children of Israel did according to all that the LORD commanded Moses; so they camped by their standards and so they broke camp, each one by his family, according to their fathers' houses.

What the Levites are to do

3 Now these *are* the records of Aaron and Moses when the LORD spoke with Moses on Mount Sinai. 2 And these *are* the names of the sons of Aaron: Nadab, the firstborn, and Abihu, Eleazar, and Ithamar. 3 These *are* the names of the sons of Aaron, the anointed priests, whom he consecrated to minister as priests. 4 Nadab and Abihu had died before the LORD when they offered profane fire before the LORD in the Wilderness of Sinai; and they had no children. So Eleazar and Ithamar ministered as priests in the presence of Aaron their father.

5 And the LORD spoke to Moses, saying: 6 "Bring the tribe of Levi near, and present them before Aaron the priest, that they may serve him. 7 And they shall attend to his needs and the needs of the whole congregation before the tabernacle of meeting, to do the work of the tabernacle. 8 Also they shall attend to all the furnishings of the tabernacle of meeting, and to the needs of the children of Israel, to do the work of the tabernacle. 9 And you shall give

The tribes of Israel camped by tribe all around the tabernacle.

the Levites to Aaron and his sons; they *are* given entirely to him from among the children of Israel. ¹⁰ So you shall appoint Aaron and his sons, and they shall attend to their priesthood; but the outsider who comes near shall be put to death."

¹¹ Then the LORD spoke to Moses, saying: ¹² "Now behold, I Myself have taken the Levites from among the children of Israel instead of *every* firstborn who opens the womb among the children of Israel. Therefore the Levites shall be Mine, ¹³ because all the firstborn *are* Mine. On the day that I struck all the firstborn in the land of Egypt, I sanctified to Myself all the firstborn in Israel, both man and beast. They shall be Mine: I *am* the LORD."

¹⁴ Then the LORD spoke to Moses in the Wilderness of Sinai, saying: ¹⁵ "Number the children of Levi by their fathers' houses, by their families; you shall number every male from a month old and above."

¹⁶ So Moses numbered them according to the word of the LORD, as he was commanded. ¹⁷ These were the sons of Levi by their names: Gershon, Kohath, and Merari. ¹⁸ And these *are* the names of the sons of Gershon by their families: Libni and Shimei. ¹⁹ And the sons of Kohath by their families: Amram, Izehar, Hebron, and Uzziel. ²⁰ And the sons of Merari by their families: Mahli and Mushi. These *are* the families of the Levites by their fathers' houses.

²¹ From Gershon *came* the family of the Libnites and the family of the Shimites; these *were* the families of the Gershonites. ²² Those who were numbered, according to the number of all the males from a month old and above—of those who were numbered *there were* seven thousand five hundred. ²³ The families of the Gershonites were to camp behind the tabernacle westward. ²⁴ And the leader of the father's house of the Gershonites *was* Eliasaph the son of Lael. ²⁵ The duties of the children of Gershon in the tabernacle of meeting *included* the tabernacle, the tent with its covering, the

screen for the door of the tabernacle of meeting, ²⁶ the screen for the door of the court, the hangings of the court which *are* around the tabernacle and the altar, and their cords, according to all the work relating to them.

²⁷ From Kohath *came* the family of the Amramites, the family of the Izharites, the family of the Hebronites, and the family of the Uzzielites; these *were* the families of the Kohathites. ²⁸ According to the number of all the males, from a month old and above, *there were* eight thousand six hundred keeping charge of the sanctuary. ²⁹ The families of the children of Kohath were to camp on the south side of the tabernacle. ³⁰ And the leader of the fathers' house of the families of the Kohathites *was* Elizaphan the son of Uzziel. ³¹ Their duty *included* the ark, the table, the lampstand, the altars, the utensils of the sanctuary with which they ministered, the screen, and all the work relating to them.

³² And Eleazar the son of Aaron the priest *was to be* chief over the leaders of the Levites, *with* oversight of those who kept charge of the sanctuary.

³³ From Merari *came* the family of the Mahlites and the family of the Mushites; these *were* the families of Merari. ³⁴ And those who were numbered, according to the number of all the males from a month old and above, *were* six thousand two hundred. ³⁵ The leader of the fathers' house of the families of Merari *was* Zuriel the son of Abihail. These *were* to camp on the north side of the tabernacle. ³⁶ And the appointed duty of the children of Merari *included* the boards of the tabernacle, its bars, its pillars, its sockets, its utensils, all the work relating to them, ³⁷ and the pillars of the court all around, with their sockets, their pegs, and their cords.

³⁸ Moreover those who were to camp before the tabernacle on the east, before the tabernacle of meeting, *were* Moses, Aaron, and his sons, keeping charge of the sanctuary, to meet the needs of the children of Israel; but the outsider who came near was

to be put to death. 39 All who were numbered of the Levites, whom Moses and Aaron numbered at the commandment of the LORD, by their families, all the males from a month old and above, were twenty-two thousand.

40 Then the LORD said to Moses: "Number all the firstborn males of the children of Israel from a month old and above, and take the number of their names. 41 And you shall take the Levites for Me—I am the LORD—instead of all the firstborn among the children of Israel, and the livestock of the Levites instead of all the firstborn among the livestock of the children of Israel." 42 So Moses numbered all the firstborn among the children of Israel, as the LORD commanded him. 43 And all the firstborn males, according to the number of names from a month old and above, of those who were numbered of them, were twenty-two thousand two hundred and seventy-three.

44 Then the LORD spoke to Moses, saying: 45 "Take the Levites instead of all the firstborn among the children of Israel, and the livestock of the Levites instead of their livestock. The Levites shall be Mine: I am the LORD. 46 And for the redemption of the two hundred and seventy-three of the firstborn of the children of Israel, who are more than the number of the Levites, 47 you shall take five shekels for each one individually; you shall take them in the currency of the shekel of the sanctuary, the shekel of twenty gerahs. 48 And you shall give the money, with which the excess number of them is redeemed, to Aaron and his sons."

49 So Moses took the redemption money from those who were over and above those who were redeemed by the Levites. 50 From the firstborn of the children of Israel he took the money, one thousand three hundred and sixty-five shekels, according to the shekel of the sanctuary. 51 And Moses gave their redemption money to Aaron and his sons, according to the word of the LORD, as the LORD commanded Moses.

The groups of Levites are given different jobs

4 Then the LORD spoke to Moses and Aaron, saying: 2 "Take a census of the sons of Kohath from among the children of Levi, by their families, by their fathers' house, 3 from thirty years old and above, even to fifty years old, all who enter the service to do the work in the tabernacle of meeting.

4 "This is the service of the sons of Kohath in the tabernacle of meeting, relating to the most holy things: 5 When the camp prepares to journey, Aaron and his sons shall come, and they shall take down the covering veil and cover the ark of the Testimony with it. 6 Then they shall put on it a covering of badger skins, and spread over that a cloth entirely of blue; and they shall insert its poles.

7 "On the table of showbread they shall spread a blue cloth, and put on it the dishes, the pans, the bowls, and the pitchers for pouring; and the showbread shall be on it. 8 They shall spread over them a scarlet cloth, and cover the same with a covering of badger

Every Sabbath, 12 loaves of bread were arranged on the table of showbread, showing how God would always take care of His people.

skins; and they shall insert its poles.
9 And they shall take a blue cloth and
cover the lampstand of the light, with
its lamps, its wick-trimmers, its trays,
and all its oil vessels, with which they
service it. 10 Then they shall put it with
all its utensils in a covering of badger
skins, and put it on a carrying beam.

11 "Over the golden altar they shall
spread a blue cloth, and cover it with
a covering of badger skins; and they
shall insert its poles. 12 Then they shall
take all the utensils of service with
which they minister in the sanctuary,
put them in a blue cloth, cover them
with a covering of badger skins, and
put them on a carrying beam. 13 Also
they shall take away the ashes from
the altar, and spread a purple cloth
over it. 14 They shall put on it all its
implements with which they minister
there—the firepans, the forks, the
shovels, the basins, and all the utensils
of the altar—and they shall spread on
it a covering of badger skins, and insert
its poles. 15 And when Aaron and his
sons have finished covering the sanctuary and all the furnishings of the sanctuary, when the camp is set to go, then
the sons of Kohath shall come to carry
them; but they shall not touch any holy
thing, lest they die.

"These are the things in the tabernacle of meeting which the sons of Kohath are to carry.

16 "The appointed duty of Eleazar
the son of Aaron the priest is the oil
for the light, the sweet incense, the
daily grain offering, the anointing oil,
the oversight of all the tabernacle, of
all that is in it, with the sanctuary and
its furnishings."

17 Then the LORD spoke to Moses
and Aaron, saying: 18 "Do not cut off
the tribe of the families of the Kohathites from among the Levites; 19 but do
this in regard to them, that they may
live and not die when they approach
the most holy things: Aaron and his
sons shall go in and appoint each of
them to his service and his task.
20 But they shall not go in to watch
while the holy things are being covered, lest they die."

21 Then the LORD spoke to Moses,
saying: 22 "Also take a census of the
sons of Gershon, by their fathers'
house, by their families. 23 From thirty
years old and above, even to fifty years
old, you shall number them, all who
enter to perform the service, to do the
work in the tabernacle of meeting.
24 This is the service of the families of
the Gershonites, in serving and carrying: 25 They shall carry the curtains of
the tabernacle and the tabernacle of
meeting with its covering, the covering
of badger skins that is on it, the screen
for the door of the tabernacle of meeting, 26 the screen for the door of the
gate of the court, the hangings of the
court which are around the tabernacle
and altar, and their cords, all the furnishings for their service and all that
is made for these things: so shall they
serve.

27 "Aaron and his sons shall assign
all the service of the sons of the Gershonites, all their tasks and all their service. And you shall appoint to them
all their tasks as their duty. 28 This is
the service of the families of the sons
of Gershon in the tabernacle of meeting. And their duties shall be under the
authority of Ithamar the son of Aaron
the priest.

29 "As for the sons of Merari, you
shall number them by their families
and by their fathers' house. 30 From
thirty years old and above, even to fifty
years old, you shall number them, everyone who enters the service to do
the work of the tabernacle of meeting.
31 And this is what they must carry as
all their service for the tabernacle of
meeting: the boards of the tabernacle,
its bars, its pillars, its sockets, 32 and
the pillars around the court with their
sockets, pegs, and cords, with all their
furnishings and all their service; and
you shall assign to each man by name
the items he must carry. 33 This is the
service of the families of the sons of
Merari, as all their service for the tabernacle of meeting, under the authority of Ithamar the son of Aaron the
priest."

34 And Moses, Aaron, and the

leaders of the congregation numbered the sons of the Kohathites by their families and by their fathers' house, 35 from thirty years old and above, even to fifty years old, everyone who entered the service for work in the tabernacle of meeting; 36 and those who were numbered by their families were two thousand seven hundred and fifty. 37 These *were* the ones who were numbered of the families of the Kohathites, all who might serve in the tabernacle of meeting, whom Moses and Aaron numbered according to the commandment of the LORD by the hand of Moses.

38 And those who were numbered of the sons of Gershon, by their families and by their fathers' house, 39 from thirty years old and above, even to fifty years old, everyone who entered the service for work in the tabernacle of meeting— 40 those who were numbered by their families, by their fathers' house, were two thousand six hundred and thirty. 41 These *are* the ones who were numbered of the families of the sons of Gershon, of all who might serve in the tabernacle of meeting, whom Moses and Aaron numbered according to the commandment of the LORD.

42 Those of the families of the sons of Merari who were numbered, by their families, by their fathers' house, 43 from thirty years old and above, even to fifty years old, everyone who entered the service for work in the tabernacle of meeting— 44 those who were numbered by their families were three thousand two hundred. 45 These *are* the ones who were numbered of the families of the sons of Merari, whom Moses and Aaron numbered according to the word of the LORD by the hand of Moses.

46 All who were numbered of the Levites, whom Moses, Aaron, and the leaders of Israel numbered, by their families and by their fathers' houses, 47 from thirty years old and above, even to fifty years old, everyone who came to do the work of service and the work of bearing burdens in the tabernacle of meeting— 48 those who were numbered were eight thousand five hundred and eighty.

49 According to the commandment of the LORD they were numbered by the hand of Moses, each according to his service and according to his task; thus were they numbered by him, as the LORD commanded Moses.

God's law about jealousy

5 And the LORD spoke to Moses, saying: 2 "Command the children of Israel that they put out of the camp every leper, everyone who has a discharge, and whoever becomes defiled by a corpse. 3 You shall put out both male and female; you shall put them outside the camp, that they may not defile their camps in the midst of which I dwell." 4 And the children of Israel did so, and put them outside the camp; as the LORD spoke to Moses, so the children of Israel did.

5 Then the LORD spoke to Moses, saying, 6 "Speak to the children of Israel: 'When a man or woman commits any sin that men commit in unfaithfulness against the LORD, and that person is guilty, 7 then he shall confess the sin which he has committed. He shall make restitution for his trespass in full, plus one-fifth of it, and give *it* to the one he has wronged. 8 But if the man has no relative to whom restitution may be made for the wrong, the restitution for the wrong *must go* to the LORD for the priest, in addition to the ram of the atonement with which atonement is made for him. 9 Every offering of all the holy things of the children of Israel, which they bring to the priest, shall be his. 10 And every man's holy things shall be his; whatever any man gives the priest shall be his.' "

11 And the LORD spoke to Moses, saying, 12 "Speak to the children of Israel, and say to them: 'If any man's wife goes astray and behaves unfaithfully toward him, 13 and a man lies with her carnally, and it is hidden from the eyes of her husband, and it is concealed that she has defiled herself, and *there was* no witness against her, nor

was she caught— ¹⁴ if the spirit of jealousy comes upon him and he becomes jealous of his wife, who has defiled herself; or if the spirit of jealousy comes upon him and he becomes jealous of his wife, although she has not defiled herself— ¹⁵ then the man shall bring his wife to the priest. He shall bring the offering required for her, one-tenth of an ephah of barley meal; he shall pour no oil on it and put no frankincense on it, because it *is* a grain offering of jealousy, an offering for remembering, for bringing iniquity to remembrance.

¹⁶ 'And the priest shall bring her near, and set her before the Lord. ¹⁷ The priest shall take holy water in an earthen vessel, and take some of the dust that is on the floor of the tabernacle and put *it* into the water. ¹⁸ Then the priest shall stand the woman before the Lord, uncover the woman's head, and put the offering for remembering in her hands, which *is* the grain offering of jealousy. And the priest shall have in his hand the bitter water that brings a curse. ¹⁹ And the priest shall put her under oath, and say to the woman, "If no man has lain with you, and if you have not gone astray to uncleanness *while* under your husband's *authority,* be free from this bitter water that brings a curse. ²⁰ But if you have gone astray *while* under your husband's *authority,* and if you have defiled yourself and some man other than your husband has lain with you"— ²¹ then the priest shall put the woman under the oath of the curse, and he shall say to the woman—"the Lord make you a curse and an oath among your people, when the Lord makes your thigh rot and your belly swell; ²² and may this water that causes the curse go into your stomach, and make *your* belly swell and *your* thigh rot."

'Then the woman shall say, "Amen, so be it."

²³ 'Then the priest shall write these curses in a book, and he shall scrape *them* off into the bitter water. ²⁴ And he shall make the woman drink the bitter water that brings a curse, and

the water that brings the curse shall enter her *to become* bitter. ²⁵ Then the priest shall take the grain offering of jealousy from the woman's hand, shall wave the offering before the Lord, and bring it to the altar; ²⁶ and the priest shall take a handful of the offering, as its memorial portion, burn *it* on the altar, and afterward make the woman drink the water. ²⁷ When he has made her drink the water, then it shall be, if she has defiled herself and behaved unfaithfully toward her husband, that the water that brings a curse will enter her *and become* bitter, and her belly will swell, her thigh will rot, and the woman will become a curse among her people. ²⁸ But if the woman has not defiled herself, and is clean, then she shall be free and may conceive children.

²⁹ 'This *is* the law of jealousy, when a wife, *while* under her husband's *authority,* goes astray and defiles herself, ³⁰ or when the spirit of jealousy comes upon a man, and he becomes jealous of his wife; then he shall stand the woman before the Lord, and the priest shall execute all this law upon her. ³¹ Then the man shall be free from iniquity, but that woman shall bear her guilt.' "

Laws for Nazirites

6 Then the Lord spoke to Moses, saying, ² "Speak to the children of Israel, and say to them: 'When either a man or woman consecrates an offering to take the vow of a Nazirite, to separate himself to the Lord, ³ he shall separate himself from wine and *similar* drink; he shall drink neither vinegar made from wine nor vinegar made from *similar* drink; neither shall he drink any grape juice, nor eat fresh grapes or raisins. ⁴ All the days of his separation he shall eat nothing that is produced by the grapevine, from seed to skin.

⁵ 'All the days of the vow of his separation no razor shall come upon his head; until the days are fulfilled for which he separated himself to the

LORD, he shall be holy. *Then* he shall let the locks of the hair of his head grow. ⁶ All the days that he separates himself to the LORD he shall not go near a dead body. ⁷ He shall not make himself unclean even for his father or his mother, for his brother or his sister, when they die, because his separation to God *is* on his head. ⁸ All the days of his separation he shall be holy to the LORD.

⁹ 'And if anyone dies very suddenly beside him, and he defiles his consecrated head, then he shall shave his head on the day of his cleansing; on the seventh day he shall shave it. ¹⁰ Then on the eighth day he shall bring two turtledoves or two young pigeons to the priest, to the door of the tabernacle of meeting; ¹¹ and the priest shall offer one as a sin offering and *the* other as a burnt offering, and make atonement for him, because he sinned in regard to the corpse; and he shall sanctify his head that same day. ¹² He shall consecrate to the LORD the days of his separation, and bring a male lamb in its first year as a trespass offering; but the former days shall be lost, because his separation was defiled.

¹³ 'Now this *is* the law of the Nazirite: When the days of his separation are fulfilled, he shall be brought to the door of the tabernacle of meeting. ¹⁴ And he shall present his offering to the LORD: one male lamb in its first year without blemish as a burnt offering, one ewe lamb in its first year without blemish as a sin offering, one ram without blemish as a peace offering, ¹⁵ a basket of unleavened bread, cakes of fine flour mixed with oil, unleavened wafers anointed with oil, and their grain offering with their drink offerings. ¹⁶ 'Then the priest shall bring *them* before the LORD and offer his sin offering and his burnt offering; ¹⁷ and he shall offer the ram as a sacrifice of a peace offering to the LORD, with the basket of unleavened bread; the priest shall also offer its grain offering and its drink offering. ¹⁸ Then the Nazirite shall shave his consecrated head *at* the door of the tabernacle of meeting, and shall take the hair from his consecrated head and put *it* on the fire which is under the sacrifice of the peace offering.

¹⁹ 'And the priest shall take the boiled shoulder of the ram, one unleavened cake from the basket, and one unleavened wafer, and put *them* upon the hands of the Nazirite after he has shaved his consecrated *hair,* ²⁰ and the priest shall wave them as a wave offering before the LORD; they *are* holy for the priest, together with the breast of the wave offering and the thigh of the heave offering. After that the Nazirite may drink wine.'

²¹ "This is the law of the Nazirite who vows to the LORD the offering for his separation, and besides that, whatever else his hand is able to provide; according to the vow which he takes, so he must do according to the law of his separation."

²² And the LORD spoke to Moses, saying: ²³ "Speak to Aaron and his sons, saying, 'This is the way you shall bless the children of Israel. Say to them:

²⁴ "The LORD bless you and keep
     you;
²⁵   The LORD make His face shine
     upon you,
     And be gracious to you;
²⁶   The LORD lift up His
     countenance upon you,
     And give you peace." '

²⁷ "So they shall put My name on the children of Israel, and I will bless them."

The altar is dedicated with offerings

7 Now it came to pass, when Moses had finished setting up the tabernacle, that he anointed it and consecrated it and all its furnishings, and the altar and all its utensils; so he anointed them and consecrated them. ² Then the leaders of Israel, the heads of their fathers' houses, who *were* the leaders of the tribes and over those who were numbered, made an offering. 3 And they brought their offering before the LORD, six covered carts and twelve oxen, a cart for *every* two of the leaders, and for each one an ox; and they presented them before the tabernacle.

4 Then the LORD spoke to Moses, saying, 5 "Accept *these* from them, that they may be used in doing the work of the tabernacle of meeting; and you shall give them to the Levites, *to every* man according to his service." 6 So Moses took the carts and the oxen, and gave them to the Levites. 7 Two carts and four oxen he gave to the sons of Gershon, according to their service; 8 and four carts and eight oxen he gave to the sons of Merari, according to their service, under the authority of Ithamar the son of Aaron the priest. 9 But to the sons of Kohath he gave none, because theirs *was* the service of the holy things, *which* they carried on their shoulders.

10 Now the leaders offered the dedication *offering* for the altar when it was anointed; so the leaders offered their offering before the altar. 11 For the LORD said to Moses, "They shall offer their offering, one leader each day, for the dedication of the altar."

12 And the one who offered his offering on the first day *was* Nahshon the son of Amminadab, from the tribe of Judah. 13 His offering *was* one silver platter, the weight of which *was* one hundred and thirty *shekels,* and one silver bowl of seventy shekels, according to the shekel of the sanctuary, both of them full of fine flour mixed with oil as a grain offering; 14 one gold pan of ten *shekels,* full of incense; 15 one young bull, one ram, and one male lamb in its first year, as a burnt offering; 16 one kid of the goats as a sin offering; 17 and for the sacrifice of peace offerings: two oxen, five rams, five male goats, and five male lambs in their first year. This *was* the offering of Nahshon the son of Amminadab.

18 On the second day Nethanel the son of Zuar, leader of Issachar, presented *an offering.* 19 For his offering he offered one silver platter, the weight of which *was* one hundred and thirty *shekels,* and one silver bowl of seventy shekels, according to the shekel of the sanctuary, both of them full of fine flour mixed with oil as a grain offering; 20 one gold pan of ten *shekels,* full of incense; 21 one young bull, one ram, and one male lamb in its first year, as a burnt offering; 22 one kid of the goats as a sin offering; 23 and as the sacrifice of peace offerings: two oxen, five rams, five male goats, and five male lambs in their first year. This *was* the offering of Nethanel the son of Zuar.

24 On the third day Eliab the son of Helon, leader of the children of Zebulun, *presented an offering.* 25 His offering *was* one silver platter, the weight of which *was* one hundred and thirty *shekels,* and one silver bowl of seventy shekels, according to the shekel of the sanctuary, both of them full of fine flour mixed with oil as a grain offering; 26 one gold pan of ten *shekels,* full of incense; 27 one young bull, one ram, and one male lamb in its first year, as a burnt offering; 28 one kid of the goats as a sin offering; 29 and for the sacrifice of peace offerings: two oxen, five rams, five male goats, and five male lambs in their first year. This *was* the offering of Eliab the son of Helon.

30 On the fourth day Elizur the son of Shedeur, leader of the children of Reuben, *presented an offering.* 31 His offering *was* one silver platter, the weight of which *was* one hundred and thirty *shekels,* and one silver bowl of seventy shekels, according to the shekel of the sanctuary, both of them full of fine flour mixed with oil as a grain offering; 32 one gold pan of ten *shekels,* full of incense; 33 one young bull, one ram, and one male lamb in its first year, as a burnt offering; 34 one kid of the goats as a sin offering; 35 and as the sacrifice of peace offerings: two oxen, five rams, five male goats, and five male lambs in their first year. This *was* the offering of Elizur the son of Shedeur.

36 On the fifth day Shelumiel the son of Zurishaddai, leader of the children

of Simeon, *presented an offering*.
37 His offering *was* one silver platter, the weight of which *was* one hundred and thirty *shekels,* and one silver bowl of seventy shekels, according to the shekel of the sanctuary, both of them full of fine flour mixed with oil as a grain offering; 38 one gold pan of ten *shekels,* full of incense; 39 one young bull, one ram, and one male lamb in its first year, as a burnt offering; 40 one kid of the goats as a sin offering; 41 and as the sacrifice of peace offerings: two oxen, five rams, five male goats, and five male lambs in their first year. This *was* the offering of Shelumiel the son of Zurishaddai.

42 On the sixth day Eliasaph the son of Deuel, leader of the children of Gad, *presented an offering*. 43 His offering *was* one silver platter, the weight of which *was* one hundred and thirty *shekels,* and one silver bowl of seventy shekels, according to the shekel of the sanctuary, both of them full of fine flour mixed with oil as a grain offering; 44 one gold pan of ten *shekels,* full of incense; 45 one young bull, one ram, and one male lamb in its first year, as a burnt offering; 46 one kid of the goats as a sin offering; 47 and as the sacrifice of peace offerings: two oxen, five rams, five male goats, and five male lambs in their first year. This *was* the offering of Eliasaph the son of Deuel.

48 On the seventh day Elishama the son of Ammihud, leader of the children of Ephraim, *presented an offering*. 49 His offering *was* one silver platter, the weight of which *was* one hundred and thirty *shekels,* and one silver bowl of seventy shekels, according to the shekel of the sanctuary, both of them full of fine flour mixed with oil as a grain offering; 50 one gold pan of ten *shekels,* full of incense; 51 one young bull, one ram, and one male lamb in its first year, as a burnt offering; 52 one kid of the goats as a sin offering; 53 and as the sacrifice of peace offerings: two oxen, five rams, five male goats, and five male lambs in their first year. This *was* the offering of Elishama the son of Ammihud.

54 On the eighth day Gamaliel the son of Pedahzur, leader of the children of Manasseh, *presented an offering*. 55 His offering *was* one silver platter, the weight of which *was* one hundred and thirty *shekels,* and one silver bowl of seventy shekels, according to the shekel of the sanctuary, both of them full of fine flour mixed with oil as a grain offering; 56 one gold pan of ten *shekels,* full of incense; 57 one young bull, one ram, and one male lamb in its first year, as a burnt offering; 58 one kid of the goats as a sin offering; 59 and as the sacrifice of peace offerings: two oxen, five rams, five male goats, and five male lambs in their first year. This *was* the offering of Gamaliel the son of Pedahzur.

60 On the ninth day Abidan the son of Gideoni, leader of the children of Benjamin, *presented an offering*. 61 His offering *was* one silver platter, the weight of which *was* one hundred and thirty *shekels,* and one silver bowl of seventy shekels, according to the shekel of the sanctuary, both of them full of fine flour mixed with oil as a grain offering; 62 one gold pan of ten *shekels,* full of incense; 63 one young bull, one ram, and one male lamb in its first year, as a burnt offering; 64 one kid of the goats as a sin offering; 65 and as the sacrifice of peace offerings: two oxen, five rams, five male goats, and five male lambs in their first year. This *was* the offering of Abidan the son of Gideoni.

66 On the tenth day Ahiezer the son of Ammishaddai, leader of the children of Dan, *presented an offering*. 67 His offering *was* one silver platter, the weight of which *was* one hundred and thirty *shekels,* and one silver bowl of seventy shekels, according to the shekel of the sanctuary, both of them full of fine flour mixed with oil as a grain offering; 68 one gold pan of ten *shekels,* full of incense; 69 one young bull, one ram, and one male lamb in its first year, as a burnt offering; 70 one kid of the goats as a sin offering; 71 and as the sacrifice of peace offerings: two oxen, five rams, five male

goats, and five male lambs in their first year. This *was* the offering of Ahiezer the son of Ammishaddai.

72 On the eleventh day Pagiel the son of Ocran, leader of the children of Asher, *presented an offering.* 73 His offering *was* one silver platter, the weight of which *was* one hundred and thirty *shekels,* and one silver bowl of seventy shekels, according to the shekel of the sanctuary, both of them full of fine flour mixed with oil as a grain offering; 74 one gold pan of ten *shekels,* full of incense; 75 one young bull, one ram, and one male lamb in its first year, as a burnt offering; 76 one kid of the goats as a sin offering; 77 and as the sacrifice of peace offerings: two oxen, five rams, five male goats, and five male lambs in their first year. This *was* the offering of Pagiel the son of Ocran.

78 On the twelfth day Ahira the son of Enan, leader of the children of Naphtali, *presented an offering.* 79 His offering *was* one silver platter, the weight of which *was* one hundred and thirty *shekels,* and one silver bowl of seventy shekels, according to the shekel of the sanctuary, both of them full of fine flour mixed with oil as a grain offering; 80 one gold pan of ten *shekels,* full of incense; 81 one young bull, one ram, and one male lamb in its first year, as a burnt offering; 82 one kid of the goats as a sin offering; 83 and as the sacrifice of peace offerings: two oxen, five rams, five male goats, and five male lambs in their first year. This *was* the offering of Ahira the son of Enan.

84 This *was* the dedication *offering* for the altar from the leaders of Israel, when it was anointed: twelve silver platters, twelve silver bowls, and twelve gold pans. 85 Each silver platter *weighed* one hundred and thirty *shekels* and each bowl seventy *shekels.* All the silver of the vessels *weighed* two thousand four hundred *shekels,* according to the shekel of the sanctuary. 86 The twelve gold pans full of incense *weighed* ten *shekels* apiece, according to the shekel of the sanctuary; all the

gold of the pans *weighed* one hundred and twenty *shekels.* 87 All the oxen for the burnt offering *were* twelve young bulls, the rams twelve, the male lambs in their first year twelve, with their grain offering, and the kids of the goats as a sin offering twelve. 88 And all the oxen for the sacrifice of peace offerings were twenty-four bulls, the rams sixty, the male goats sixty, and the lambs in their first year sixty. This *was* the dedication *offering* for the altar after it was anointed.

89 Now when Moses went into the tabernacle of meeting to speak with Him, he heard the voice of One speaking to him from above the mercy seat that *was* on the ark of the Testimony, from between the two cherubim; thus He spoke to him.

How the Levites are dedicated

8 And the LORD spoke to Moses, saying: 2 "Speak to Aaron, and say to him, 'When you arrange the lamps, the seven lamps shall give light in front of the lampstand.' " 3 And Aaron did so; he arranged the lamps to face toward the front of the lampstand, as the LORD commanded Moses. 4 Now this workmanship of the lampstand *was* hammered gold; from its shaft to its flowers it *was* hammered work. According to the pattern which the LORD had shown Moses, so he made the lampstand.

5 Then the LORD spoke to Moses, saying: 6 "Take the Levites from among the children of Israel and cleanse them *ceremonially.* 7 Thus you shall do to them to cleanse them: Sprinkle water of purification on them, and let them shave all their body, and let them wash their clothes, and *so* make themselves clean. 8 Then let them take a young bull with its grain offering of fine flour mixed with oil, and you shall take another young bull as a sin offering. 9 And you shall bring the Levites before the tabernacle of meeting, and you shall gather together the whole congregation of the children of Israel. 10 So you shall bring the Levites before the LORD, and the children of

Israel shall lay their hands on the Levites; 11 and Aaron shall offer the Levites before the LORD *like* a wave offering from the children of Israel, that they may perform the work of the LORD. 12 Then the Levites shall lay their hands on the heads of the young bulls, and you shall offer one as a sin offering and the other as a burnt offering to the LORD, to make atonement for the Levites.

13 "And you shall stand the Levites before Aaron and his sons, and then offer them *like* a wave offering to the LORD. 14 Thus you shall separate the Levites from among the children of Israel, and the Levites shall be Mine. 15 After that the Levites shall go in to service the tabernacle of meeting. So you shall cleanse them and offer them *like* a wave offering. 16 For they *are* wholly given to Me from among the children of Israel; I have taken them for Myself instead of all who open the womb, the firstborn of all the children of Israel. 17 For all the firstborn among the children of Israel *are* Mine, *both* man and beast; on the day that I struck all the firstborn in the land of Egypt I sanctified them to Myself. 18 I have taken the Levites instead of all the firstborn of the children of Israel. 19 And I have given the Levites as a gift to Aaron and his sons from among the children of Israel, to do the work for the children of Israel in the tabernacle of meeting, and to make atonement for the children of Israel, that there be no plague among the children of Israel when the children of Israel come near the sanctuary."

20 Thus Moses and Aaron and all the congregation of the children of Israel did to the Levites; according to all that the LORD commanded Moses concerning the Levites, so the children of Israel did to them. 21 And the Levites purified themselves and washed their clothes; then Aaron presented them *like* a wave offering before the LORD, and Aaron made atonement for them to cleanse them. 22 After that the Levites went in to do their work in the tabernacle of meeting before Aaron and his sons; as

Who Were the Levites?

The word *Levite* (pronounced *LEE-vight*) comes from the name of Jacob's son, Levi. Levi's descendants were divided into two groups—priests and Levites. The priests made sacrifices for the people. The Levites carried and took care of the furniture in the tabernacle, or worship place.

the LORD commanded Moses concerning the Levites, so they did to them.

23 Then the LORD spoke to Moses, saying, 24 "This *is* what *pertains* to the Levites: From twenty-five years old and above one may enter to perform service in the work of the tabernacle of meeting; 25 and at the age of fifty years they must cease performing this work, and shall work no more. 26 They may minister with their brethren in the tabernacle of meeting, to attend to needs, but they *themselves* shall do no work. Thus you shall do to the Levites regarding their duties."

How to keep the Passover

9 Now the LORD spoke to Moses in the Wilderness of Sinai, in the first

Levites, Hebrews from the tribe of Levi, helped the priests and took care of the sanctuary.

month of the second year after they had come out of the land of Egypt, saying: 2 "Let the children of Israel keep the Passover at its appointed time. 3 On the fourteenth day of this month, at twilight, you shall keep it at its appointed time. According to all its rites and ceremonies you shall keep it." 4 So Moses told the children of Israel that they should keep the Passover. 5 And they kept the Passover on the fourteenth day of the first month, at twilight, in the Wilderness of Sinai; according to all that the LORD commanded Moses, so the children of Israel did.

6 Now there were certain men who were defiled by a human corpse, so that they could not keep the Passover on that day; and they came before Moses and Aaron that day. 7 And those men said to him, "We became defiled by a human corpse. Why are we kept from presenting the offering of the LORD at its appointed time among the children of Israel?"

8 And Moses said to them, "Stand still, that I may hear what the LORD will command concerning you."

9 Then the LORD spoke to Moses, saying, 10 "Speak to the children of Israel, saying: 'If anyone of you or your posterity is unclean because of a corpse, or is far away on a journey, he may still keep the LORD's Passover. 11 On the fourteenth day of the second month, at twilight, they may keep it. They shall eat it with unleavened bread

and bitter herbs. 12 They shall leave none of it until morning, nor break one of its bones. According to all the ordinances of the Passover they shall keep it. 13 But the man who is clean and is not on a journey, and ceases to keep the Passover, that same person shall be cut off from among his people, because he did not bring the offering of the LORD at its appointed time; that man shall bear his sin.

14 'And if a stranger dwells among you, and would keep the LORD's Passover, he must do so according to the rite of the Passover and according to its ceremony; you shall have one ordinance, both for the stranger and the native of the land.' "

15 Now on the day that the tabernacle was raised up, the cloud covered the tabernacle, the tent of the Testimony; from evening until morning it was above the tabernacle like the appearance of fire. 16 So it was always: the cloud covered it by day, and the appearance of fire by night. 17 Whenever the cloud was taken up from above the tabernacle, after that the children of Israel would journey; and in the place where the cloud settled, there the children of Israel would pitch their tents. 18 At the command of the LORD the children of Israel would journey, and at the command of the LORD they would camp; as long as the cloud stayed above the tabernacle they remained encamped. 19 Even when the cloud continued long, many days

What the Desert Wanderers Learned

After we escaped from the Egyptians and crossed the Red Sea, we started into the Desert of Sinai (pronounced SIGH-nigh).

The Sinai Desert was a big place, and little lived there. We wondered how we would stay alive and find our way through that hot, dry desert.

While we were at Mount Sinai, God gave us His laws. Then we had to be on our way to the Promised Land. The Lord sent an unusual cloud to lead us by day. At night the cloud became a bright, fiery mass that stood above the place of meeting. This cloud and fire was the presence of the Lord Himself. God always lives and remains with those who love Him. Jesus said, "I will never leave you."

above the tabernacle, the children of Israel kept the charge of the Lord and did not journey. 20 So it was, when the cloud was above the tabernacle a few days: according to the command of the Lord they would remain encamped, and according to the command of the Lord they would journey. 21 So it was, when the cloud remained only from evening until morning: when the cloud was taken up in the morning, then they would journey; whether by day or by night, whenever the cloud was taken up, they would journey. 22 *Whether it was* two days, a month, or a year that the cloud remained above the tabernacle, the children of Israel would remain encamped and not journey; but when it was taken up, they would journey. 23 At the command of the Lord they remained encamped, and at the command of the Lord they journeyed; they kept the charge of the Lord, at the command of the Lord by the hand of Moses.

The Israelites leave Mount Sinai

10 And the Lord spoke to Moses, saying: 2 "Make two silver trumpets for yourself; you shall make them of hammered work; you shall use them for calling the congregation and for directing the movement of the camps. 3 When they blow both of them, all the congregation shall gather before you at the door of the tabernacle of meeting. 4 But if they blow *only* one, then the leaders, the heads of the divisions of Israel, shall gather to you. 5 When you sound the advance, the camps that lie on the east side shall then begin their journey. 6 When you sound the advance the second time, then the camps that lie on the south side shall begin their journey; they shall sound the call for them to begin their journeys. 7 And when the assembly is to be gathered together, you shall blow, but not sound the advance. 8 The sons of Aaron, the priests, shall blow the trumpets; and these shall be to you as an ordinance forever throughout your generations.

9 "When you go to war in your land against the enemy who oppresses you, then you shall sound an alarm with the trumpets, and you will be remembered before the Lord your God, and you will be saved from your enemies. 10 Also in the day of your gladness, in your appointed feasts, and at the beginning of your months, you shall blow the trumpets over your burnt offerings and over the sacrifices of your peace offerings; and they shall be a memorial for you before your God: I *am* the Lord your God."

11 Now it came to pass on the twentieth *day* of the second month, in the second year, that the cloud was taken up from above the tabernacle of the Testimony. 12 And the children of Israel set out from the Wilderness of Sinai on their journeys; then the cloud settled down in the Wilderness of Paran. 13 So they started out for the first time according to the command of the Lord by the hand of Moses.

14 The standard of the camp of the children of Judah set out first according to their armies; over their army was Nahshon the son of Amminadab. 15 Over the army of the tribe of the children of Issachar *was* Nethanel the son of Zuar. 16 And over the army of the tribe of the children of Zebulun *was* Eliab the son of Helon.

17 Then the tabernacle was taken down; and the sons of Gershon and the sons of Merari set out, carrying the tabernacle.

18 And the standard of the camp of Reuben set out according to their armies; over their army *was* Elizur the son of Shedeur. 19 Over the army of the tribe of the children of Simeon *was* Shelumiel the son of Zurishaddai. 20 And over the army of the tribe of the children of Gad *was* Eliasaph the son of Deuel.

21 Then the Kohathites set out, carrying the holy things. (The tabernacle would be prepared for their arrival.)

22 And the standard of the camp of the children of Ephraim set out according to their armies; over their army *was* Elishama the son of Ammihud. 23 Over

the army of the tribe of the children of Manasseh *was* Gamaliel the son of Pedahzur. 24 And over the army of the tribe of the children of Benjamin *was* Abidan the son of Gideoni.

25 Then the standard of the camp of the children of Dan (the rear guard of all the camps) set out according to their armies; over their army *was* Ahiezer the son of Ammishaddai. 26 Over the army of the tribe of the children of Asher *was* Pagiel the son of Ocran. 27 And over the army of the tribe of the children of Naphtali *was* Ahira the son of Enan.

28 Thus *was* the order of march of the children of Israel, according to their armies, when they began their journey.

29 Now Moses said to Hobab the son of Reuel the Midianite, Moses' father-in-law, "We are setting out for the place of which the Lord said, 'I will give it to you.' Come with us, and we will treat you well; for the Lord has promised good things to Israel."

30 And he said to him, "I will not go, but I will depart to my *own* land and to my relatives."

31 So *Moses* said, "Please do not leave, inasmuch as you know how we are to camp in the wilderness, and you can be our eyes. 32 And it shall be, if you go with us—indeed it shall be— that whatever good the Lord will do to us, the same we will do to you."

33 So they departed from the mountain of the Lord on a journey of three days; and the ark of the covenant of the Lord went before them for the three days' journey, to search out a resting place for them. 34 And the cloud of the Lord *was* above them by day when they went out from the camp.

35 So it was, whenever the ark set out, that Moses said:

> "Rise up, O Lord!
> Let Your enemies be scattered,
> And let those who hate You flee
> before You."

36 And when it rested, he said:

> "Return, O Lord,
> *To* the many thousands of
> Israel."

Seventy men are chosen to help Moses

11 Now *when* the people complained, it displeased the Lord; for the Lord heard *it,* and His anger was aroused. So the fire of the Lord burned among them, and consumed *some* in the outskirts of the camp. 2 Then the people cried out to Moses, and when Moses prayed to the Lord, the fire was quenched. 3 So he called the name of the place Taberah, because the fire of the Lord had burned among them.

4 Now the mixed multitude who were among them yielded to intense craving; so the children of Israel also wept again and said: "Who will give us meat to eat? 5 We remember the fish which we ate freely in Egypt, the cucumbers, the melons, the leeks, the onions, and the garlic; 6 but now our whole being *is* dried up; *there is* nothing at all except this **manna** *before* our eyes!"

7 Now the manna *was* like coriander seed, and its color like the color of bdellium. 8 The people went about and gathered *it,* ground *it* on millstones or beat *it* in the mortar, cooked *it* in pans, and made cakes of it; and its taste was like the taste of pastry prepared with oil. 9 And when the dew fell on the camp in the night, the manna fell on it.

10 Then Moses heard the people weeping throughout their families, everyone at the door of his tent; and the anger of the Lord was greatly aroused; Moses also was displeased. 11 So Moses said to the Lord, "Why have You afflicted Your servant? And why have

WORDFINDER
_____

11:6 Manna The miraculous food God gave Israel in the desert. It looked like frost, and when cooked, tasted like pastry. The Hebrew word means "What Is It?".

I not found favor in Your sight, that You have laid the burden of all these people on me? 12 Did I conceive all these people? Did I beget them, that You should say to me, 'Carry them in your bosom, as a guardian carries a nursing child,' to the land which You swore to their fathers? 13 Where am I to get meat to give to all these people? For they weep all over me, saying, 'Give us meat, that we may eat.' 14 I am not able to bear all these people alone, because the burden is too heavy for me. 15 If You treat me like this, please kill me here and now—if I have found favor in Your sight—and do not let me see my wretchedness!"

16 So the LORD said to Moses: "Gather to Me seventy men of the elders of Israel, whom you know to be the elders of the people and officers over them; bring them to the tabernacle of meeting, that they may stand there with you. 17 Then I will come down and talk with you there. I will take of the Spirit that is upon you and will put the same upon them; and they shall bear the burden of the people with you, that you may not bear it yourself alone. 18 Then you shall say to the people, 'Consecrate yourselves for tomorrow, and you shall eat meat; for you have wept in the hearing of the LORD, saying, "Who will give us meat to eat? For it was well with us in Egypt." Therefore the LORD will give you meat, and you shall eat. 19 You shall eat, not one day, nor two days, nor five days, nor ten days, nor twenty days, 20 but for a whole month, until it comes out of your nostrils and becomes loathsome to you, because you have despised the LORD who is among you, and have wept before Him, saying, "Why did we ever come up out of Egypt?" ' "

21 And Moses said, "The people whom I am among are six hundred thousand men on foot; yet You have said, 'I will give them meat, that they may eat for a whole month.' 22 Shall flocks and herds be slaughtered for them, to provide enough for them? Or shall all the fish of the sea be gathered together for them, to provide enough for them?"

23 And the LORD said to Moses, "Has the LORD's arm been shortened? Now you shall see whether what I say will happen to you or not."

24 So Moses went out and told the people the words of the LORD, and he gathered the seventy men of the elders of the people and placed them around the tabernacle. 25 Then the LORD came down in the cloud, and spoke to him, and took of the Spirit that was upon him, and placed the same upon the seventy elders; and it happened, when the Spirit rested upon them, that they prophesied, although they never did so again.

26 But two men had remained in the camp: the name of one was Eldad, and the name of the other Medad. And the Spirit rested upon them. Now they were among those listed, but who had not gone out to the tabernacle; yet they prophesied in the camp. 27 And a young man ran and told Moses, and said, "Eldad and Medad are prophesying in the camp."

28 So Joshua the son of Nun, Moses' assistant, one of his choice men, answered and said, "Moses my lord, forbid them!"

29 Then Moses said to him, "Are you zealous for my sake? Oh, that all the LORD's people were prophets and that the LORD would put His Spirit upon them!" 30 And Moses returned to the camp, he and the elders of Israel.

31 Now a wind went out from the LORD, and it brought quail from the sea and left them fluttering near the camp, about a day's journey on this side and about a day's journey on the other side, all around the camp, and about two cubits above the surface of the ground. 32 And the people stayed up all that day, all night, and all the next day, and gathered the quail (he who gathered least gathered ten homers); and they spread them out for themselves all around the camp. 33 But while the meat was still between their teeth, before it was chewed, the wrath of the LORD was aroused against

What Aaron and Miriam Learned

Miriam and I were the sister and brother of Moses. This made us feel important. We thought we should be leaders of Israel, too. We also thought Moses should have asked our advice about the person he married.

Our attitude was all wrong. Moses didn't make himself the leader of Israel. He was God's own choice. Besides, it was none of our business whom Moses married.

So the Lord had to teach us a lesson. Miriam nearly died from the disease of leprosy, and for a while she was not allowed to live with the rest of us.

So don't try to be the most important person in your family or group. God chooses His own leaders in His own way.

the people, and the LORD struck the people with a very great plague. 34 So he called the name of that place Kibroth Hattaavah, because there they buried the people who had yielded to craving.

35 From Kibroth Hattaavah the people moved to Hazeroth, and camped at Hazeroth.

Miriam and Aaron speak against Moses

12 Then Miriam and Aaron spoke against Moses because of the Ethiopian woman whom he had married; for he had married an Ethiopian woman. 2 So they said, "Has the LORD indeed spoken only through Moses? Has He not spoken through us also?" And the LORD heard it. 3 (Now the man Moses was very humble, more than all men who were on the face of the earth.)

4 Suddenly the LORD said to Moses, Aaron, and Miriam, "Come out, you three, to the tabernacle of meeting!" So the three came out. 5 Then the LORD came down in the pillar of cloud and stood in the door of the tabernacle, and called Aaron and Miriam. And they both went forward. 6 Then He said,

"Hear now My words:
If there is a prophet among you,
I, the LORD, make Myself known
    to him in a vision;
I speak to him in a dream.
7 Not so with My servant Moses;
He is faithful in all My house.
8 I speak with him face to face,
Even plainly, and not in dark
    sayings;
And he sees the form of the
    LORD.
Why then were you not afraid
To speak against My servant
    Moses?"

9 So the anger of the LORD was aroused against them, and He departed. 10 And when the cloud departed from above the tabernacle, suddenly Miriam became leprous, as white as snow. Then Aaron turned toward Miriam, and there she was, a leper. 11 So Aaron said to Moses, "Oh, my lord! Please do not lay this sin on us,

WORDFINDER

12:11 Sin Disobedience of God's law or rebellion against His will. All people sin, but Christ died to take sin away.

Giants Seen Across River?

Old Testament News Service

KADESH BARNEA—A huge number of Jews are camped south of Kadesh Barnea, poised and ready to cross over and take possession of the land God promised Abraham (see Genesis 1:7, 8).

The spies Moses sent to scout the land have returned with mixed reports. Two of them, Joshua (pronounced *JOSH-you-uh*) and Caleb (pronounced *KAY-lub*), say the land is open and ready for the Jews to take. "This is some of the richest and most fertile land we have ever seen," report the two spies. "It is literally flowing with milk and honey."

As evidence, Joshua and Caleb brought back one cluster of grapes so large that it took two men to carry it!

Most of the spies disagree, however, and urge Moses not to proceed. "There were giants over there!" they insist. "We felt like grasshoppers compared to them. They are much too strong for us!"

If the Jews do not move into Canaan, they will have no place to live but the desert. They will be a people without a homeland, since they will surely not return to Egypt.

Some of the people of Canaan were so big that Moses' spies felt like grasshoppers!

in which we have done foolishly and in which we have sinned. 12 "Please do not let her be as one dead, whose flesh is half consumed when he comes out of his mother's womb!"

13 So Moses cried out to the LORD, saying, "Please heal her, O God, I pray!"

14 Then the LORD said to Moses, "If her father had but spit in her face, would she not be shamed seven days? Let her be shut out of the camp seven days, and afterward she may be received *again*." 15 So Miriam was shut out of the camp seven days, and the people did not journey till Miriam was brought in *again*. 16 And afterward the people moved from Hazeroth and camped in the Wilderness of Paran.

Twelve Israelites spy out Canaan

13 And the LORD spoke to Moses, saying, 2 "Send men to spy out the land of Canaan, which I am giving to the children of Israel; from each tribe of their fathers you shall send a man, every one a leader among them."

3 So Moses sent them from the Wilderness of Paran according to the command of the LORD, all of them men who *were* heads of the children of Israel. 4 Now these *were* their names:

from the tribe of Reuben, Shammua the son of Zaccur; 5 from the tribe of Simeon, Shaphat the son of Hori; 6 from the tribe of Judah, Caleb the son of Jephunneh; 7 from the tribe of Issachar, Igal the son of Joseph; 8 from the tribe of Ephraim, Hoshea the son of Nun; 9 from the tribe of Benjamin, Palti the son of Raphu; 10 from the tribe of Zebulun, Gaddiel the son of Sodi; 11 from the tribe of Joseph, *that is,* from the tribe of Manasseh, Gaddi the son of Susi; 12 from the tribe of Dan, Ammiel the son of Gemalli; 13 from the tribe of Asher, Sethur the son of Michael; 14 from the tribe of Naphtali, Nahbi the son of Vophsi; 15 from the tribe of Gad, Geuel the son of Machi.

16 These *are* the names of the men whom Moses sent to spy out the land. And Moses called Hoshea the son of Nun, Joshua.

17 Then Moses sent them to spy out the land of Canaan, and said to them, "Go up this *way* into the South, and go up to the mountains, 18 and see what the land is like: whether the people who dwell in it *are* strong or weak, few or many; 19 whether the land they dwell in *is* good or bad; whether the cities they inhabit *are* like camps or strongholds; 20 whether the land *is* rich or poor; and whether there are forests there or not. Be of good courage. And bring some of the fruit of the land." Now the time *was* the season of the first ripe grapes.

⚒ DIGGING IN

13:26–32 The Report of the Spies Usually there are two sides to the news. There is the good news and the bad news. Most of the spies Moses sent ahead to the Promised Land brought back only the bad news: "There we saw the giants."

Only two of the spies came back with good news: The land "flows with milk and honey." They meant that there was plenty of food and water there. They also had a different attitude: "We are well able to overcome it."

Which side of the news do you look at? God has promised to overcome all your troubles now or in the future. That is the good news, and it really is the only news that matters. Who cares about giants if the God who made giants is on our side?

It took two men to carry one cluster of grapes from the Valley of Eschol in the Promised Land!

21 So they went up and spied out the land from the Wilderness of Zin as far as Rehob, near the entrance of Hamath. 22 And they went up through the South and came to Hebron; Ahiman, Sheshai, and Talmai, the descendants of Anak, *were* there. (Now Hebron was built seven years before Zoan in Egypt.) 23 Then they came to the Valley of Eshcol, and there cut down a branch with one cluster of grapes; they carried it between two of them on a pole. *They* also *brought* some of the pomegranates and figs. 24 The place was called the Valley of Eshcol, because of the cluster which the men of Israel cut down there. 25 And they returned from spying out the land after forty days.

26 Now they departed and came back to Moses and Aaron and all the congregation of the children of Israel in the Wilderness of Paran, at Kadesh; they brought back word to them and to all the congregation, and showed them the fruit of the land. 27 Then they told him, and said: "We went to the land where you sent us. It truly flows with milk and honey, and this *is* its fruit. 28 Nevertheless the people who dwell in the land *are* strong; the cities *are* fortified *and* very large; moreover we saw the descendants of Anak there. 29 The Amalekites dwell in the land of the South; the Hittites, the Jebusites, and the Amorites dwell in the mountains; and the Canaanites dwell by the sea and along the banks of the Jordan."

30 Then Caleb quieted the people before Moses, and said, "Let us go up at once and take possession, for we are well able to overcome it."

31 But the men who had gone up with him said, "We are not able to go up against the people, for they *are* stronger than we." 32 And they gave the children of Israel a bad report of the land which they had spied out, saying, "The land through which we have gone as spies *is* a land that devours its inhabitants, and all the people whom we saw in it *are* men of *great* stature. 33 There we saw the giants (the descendants of Anak came from the giants); and we were like grasshoppers in our own sight, and so we were in their sight."

God punishes Israel for their unbelief

14 So all the congregation lifted up their voices and cried, and the people wept that night. 2 And all the children of Israel complained against Moses and Aaron, and the whole congregation said to them, "If only we had died in the land of Egypt! Or if only we had died in this wilderness! 3 Why has the LORD brought us to this land to fall by the sword, that our wives and children should become victims? Would it not be better for us to return to Egypt?" 4 So they said to one another, "Let us select a leader and return to Egypt."

5 Then Moses and Aaron fell on their faces before all the assembly of the congregation of the children of Israel.

6 But Joshua the son of Nun and Caleb the son of Jephunneh, *who were* among those who had spied out the land, tore their clothes; 7 and they spoke to all the congregation of the children of Israel, saying: "The land we passed through to spy out *is* an exceedingly good land. 8 If the LORD delights in us, then He will bring us into this land and give it to us, 'a land which flows with milk and honey.' 9 Only do not rebel against the LORD, nor fear the people of the land, for they *are* our bread; their protection has departed from them, and the LORD *is* with us. Do not fear them."

10 And all the congregation said to stone them with stones. Now the glory of the LORD appeared in the tabernacle of meeting before all the children of Israel.

11 Then the LORD said to Moses: "How long will these people reject Me? And how long will they not believe Me, with all the signs which I have performed among them? 12 I will strike them with the pestilence and disinherit them, and I will make of you a nation greater and mightier than they."

Hebrews Refuse to Enter Canaan

Old Testament News Service

KADESH BARNEA—The decision is now final. At first, there was doubt whether the people would, in fact, make the crossing to Canaan. Joshua, Caleb and Moses wanted to go, but the people threatened to kill Caleb and Joshua if they tried to lead the people at this time.

The Lord appeared once again, threatening to destroy the whole Jewish nation for their lack of faith. At that point, Moses began to pray for the people. Moses reminded God that He would be disgraced among the other nations if the people died. God could not break His own promises.

The Lord has agreed to pardon the sins of the people. However, He has also said that only Joshua and Caleb will ever see the land of Canaan. The others are all predicted to die during 40 years of wandering in the Sinai desert.

13 And Moses said to the LORD: "Then the Egyptians will hear *it*, for by Your might You brought these people up from among them, 14 and they will tell *it* to the inhabitants of this land. They have heard that You, LORD, *are* among these people; that You, LORD, are seen face to face and Your cloud stands above them, and You go before them in a **pillar of cloud** by day and in a **pillar of fire** by night. 15 Now *if* You kill these people as one man, then the nations which have heard of Your fame will speak, saying, 16 'Because the LORD was not able to bring this people to the land which He swore to give them, therefore He killed them in the wilderness.' 17 And now, I pray, let the power of my Lord be great, just as You have spoken, saying, 18 'The LORD is longsuffering and abundant in mercy, forgiving iniquity and transgression; but He by no means clears *the guilty,* visiting the iniquity of the fathers on the children to the third and fourth *generation.*' 19 Pardon the iniquity of this people, I pray, according to the greatness of Your mercy, just as You have forgiven this people, from Egypt even until now."

WORDFINDER

14:14 Pillar of Fire and Cloud A special appearance of God. This was one of the ways the invisible God once showed Himself to human eyes.

What the People of God Learned

God had led us out of Egypt and provided all our needs. He had formed us into His own special people and promised us a good land.

Then we refused to go when the Lord wanted us to go in and take the land He was giving us. We didn't believe His promises. We even wanted to kill those who did want to enter the new land. This was the tenth time we had gone against God's will for us. We would have died right then if Moses hadn't prayed for us.

Except for Joshua and Caleb, our whole generation died in the desert during 40 years of our wandering there. We hope you trust God more than we did when He offers you His good things.

20 Then the LORD said: "I have pardoned, according to your word; 21 but truly, as I live, all the earth shall be filled with the glory of the LORD— 22 because all these men who have seen My glory and the signs which I did in Egypt and in the wilderness, and have put Me to the test now these ten times, and have not heeded My voice, 23 they certainly shall not see the land of which I swore to their fathers, nor shall any of those who rejected Me see it. 24 But My servant Caleb, because he has a different spirit in him and has followed Me fully, I will bring into the land where he went, and his descendants shall inherit it. 25 Now the Amalekites and the Canaanites dwell in the valley; tomorrow turn and move out into the wilderness by the Way of the Red Sea."

26 And the LORD spoke to Moses and Aaron, saying, 27 "How long *shall I bear with* this evil congregation who complain against Me? I have heard the complaints which the children of Israel make against Me. 28 Say to them, 'As I live,' says the LORD, 'just as you have spoken in My hearing, so I will do to you: 29 The carcasses of you who have complained against Me shall fall in this wilderness, all of you who were numbered, according to your entire number, from twenty years old and above. 30 Except for Caleb the son of Jephunneh and Joshua the son of Nun, you shall by no means enter the land which I swore I would make you dwell in. 31 But your little ones, whom you said would be victims, I will bring in, and they shall know the land which you have despised. 32 But *as for* you, your carcasses shall fall in this wilderness. 33 And your sons shall be shepherds in the wilderness forty years, and bear the brunt of your infidelity, until your carcasses are consumed in the wilderness. 34 According to the number of the days in which you spied out the land, forty days, for each day you shall bear your guilt one year, *namely* forty years, and you shall know My rejection. 35 I the LORD have spoken this. I will surely do so to all this evil congregation who are gathered together against Me. In this wilderness they shall be consumed, and there they shall die.' "

36 Now the men whom Moses sent to spy out the land, who returned and made all the congregation complain against him by bringing a bad report of the land, 37 those very men who brought the evil report about the land, died by the plague before the LORD. 38 But Joshua the son of Nun and Caleb the son of Jephunneh remained alive, of the men who went to spy out the land.

39 Then Moses told these words to all the children of Israel, and the people mourned greatly. 40 And they rose early in the morning and went up to the top of the mountain, saying, "Here we are, and we will go up to the place which the LORD has promised, for we have sinned!"

41 And Moses said, "Now why do you transgress the command of the LORD? For this will not succeed. 42 Do not go up, lest you be defeated by your enemies, for the LORD *is* not among you. 43 For the Amalekites and the Canaanites *are* there before you, and you shall fall by the sword; because you have turned away from the LORD, the LORD will not be with you."

44 But they presumed to go up to the mountaintop. Nevertheless, neither the ark of the covenant of the LORD nor Moses departed from the camp. 45 Then the Amalekites and the Canaanites who dwelt in that mountain came down and attacked them, and drove them back as far as Hormah.

Laws about offerings

15 And the LORD spoke to Moses, saying, 2 "Speak to the children of Israel, and say to them: 'When you have come into the land you are to inhabit, which I am giving to you, 3 and you make an offering by fire to the LORD, a burnt offering or a sacrifice, to fulfill a vow or as a freewill offering or in your appointed feasts, to make a sweet aroma to the LORD, from the herd or the flock, 4 then he who presents his

offering to the LORD shall bring a grain offering of one-tenth *of an ephah* of fine flour mixed with one-fourth of a hin of oil; 5 and one-fourth of a hin of wine as a drink offering you shall prepare with the burnt offering or the sacrifice, for each lamb. 6 Or for a ram you shall prepare as a grain offering two-tenths *of an ephah* of fine flour mixed with one-third of a hin of oil; 7 and as a drink offering you shall offer one-third of a hin of wine as a sweet aroma to the LORD. 8 And when you prepare a young bull as a burnt offering, or as a sacrifice to fulfill a vow, or as a peace offering to the LORD, 9 then shall be offered with the young bull a grain offering of three-tenths *of an ephah* of fine flour mixed with half a hin of oil; 10 and you shall bring as the drink offering half a hin of wine as an offering made by fire, a sweet aroma to the LORD.

11 'Thus it shall be done for each young bull, for each ram, or for each lamb or young goat. 12 According to the number that you prepare, so you shall do with everyone according to their number. 13 All who are native-born shall do these things in this manner, in presenting an offering made by fire, a sweet aroma to the LORD. 14 And if a stranger dwells with you, or whoever *is* among you throughout your generations, and would present an offering made by fire, a sweet aroma to the LORD, just as you do, so shall he do. 15 One ordinance *shall be* for you of the assembly and for the stranger who dwells *with you,* an ordinance forever throughout your generations; as you are, so shall the stranger be before the LORD. 16 One law and one custom shall be for you and for the stranger who dwells with you.' "

17 Again the LORD spoke to Moses, saying, 18 "Speak to the children of Israel, and say to them: 'When you come into the land to which I bring you, 19 then it will be, when you eat of the bread of the land, that you shall offer up a heave offering to the LORD. 20 You shall offer up a cake of the first of your ground meal *as* a heave offer-

ing; as a heave offering of the threshing floor, so shall you offer it up. 21 Of the first of your ground meal you shall give to the LORD a heave offering throughout your generations.

22 'If you sin unintentionally, and do not observe all these commandments which the LORD has spoken to Moses— 23 all that the LORD has commanded you by the hand of Moses, from the day the LORD gave commandment and onward throughout your generations— 24 then it will be, if it is unintentionally committed, without the knowledge of the congregation, that the whole congregation shall offer one young bull as a burnt offering, as a sweet aroma to the LORD, with its grain offering and its drink offering, according to the ordinance, and one kid of the goats as a sin offering. 25 So the priest shall make atonement for the whole congregation of the children of Israel, and it shall be forgiven them, for it was unintentional; they shall bring their offering, an offering made by fire to the LORD, and their sin offering before the LORD, for their unintended sin. 26 It shall be forgiven the whole congregation of the children of Israel and the stranger who dwells among them, because all the people *did it* unintentionally.

27 'And if a person sins unintentionally, then he shall bring a female goat in its first year as a sin offering. 28 So the priest shall make atonement for the person who sins unintentionally, when he sins unintentionally before the LORD, to make atonement for him; and it shall be forgiven him. 29 You shall have one law for him who sins unintentionally, *for* him who is native-born among the children of Israel and for the stranger who dwells among them.

30 'But the person who does *any-thing* presumptuously, *whether he is* native-born or a stranger, that one brings reproach on the LORD, and he shall be cut off from among his people. 31 Because he has despised the word of the LORD, and has broken His commandment, that person shall be

completely cut off; his guilt *shall be* upon him.' "

32 Now while the children of Israel were in the wilderness, they found a man gathering sticks on the Sabbath day. 33 And those who found him gathering sticks brought him to Moses and Aaron, and to all the congregation. 34 They put him under guard, because it had not been explained what should be done to him.

35 Then the LORD said to Moses, "The man must surely be put to death; all the congregation shall stone him with stones outside the camp." 36 So, as the LORD commanded Moses, all the congregation brought him outside the camp and stoned him with stones, and he died.

37 Again the LORD spoke to Moses, saying, 38 "Speak to the children of Israel: Tell them to make tassels on the corners of their garments throughout their generations, and to put a blue thread in the tassels of the corners. 39 And you shall have the tassel, that you may look upon it and remember all the commandments of the LORD and do them, and that you *may* not follow the harlotry to which your own heart and your own *eyes* are inclined, 40 and that you may remember and do all My commandments, and be holy for your God. 41 I *am* the LORD your God, who brought you out of the land of Egypt, to be your God: I *am* the LORD your God."

Korah rebels against Moses

16 Now Korah the son of Izhar, the son of Kohath, the son of Levi, with Dathan and Abiram the sons of Eliab, and On the son of Peleth, sons of Reuben, took *men;* 2 and they rose up before Moses with some of the children of Israel, two hundred and fifty leaders of the congregation, representatives of the congregation, men of renown. 3 They gathered together against Moses and Aaron, and said to them, "*You take* too much upon yourselves, for all the congregation *is* **holy,** every one of them, and the LORD *is* among them. Why then do you exalt yourselves above the assembly of the LORD?"

4 So when Moses heard *it,* he fell on his face; 5 and he spoke to Korah and all his company, saying, "Tomorrow morning the LORD will show who *is* His and *who is* holy, and will cause *him* to come near to Him. That one whom He chooses He will cause to come near to Him. 6 Do this: Take censers, Korah and all your company; 7 put fire in them and put incense in them before the LORD tomorrow, and it shall be *that* the man whom the LORD chooses *is* the holy one. *You take* too much upon yourselves, you sons of Levi!"

8 Then Moses said to Korah, "Hear now, you sons of Levi: 9 *Is it* a small thing to you that the God of Israel has separated you from the congregation of Israel, to bring you near to Himself, to do the work of the tabernacle of the LORD, and to stand before the congregation to serve them; 10 and that He has brought you near *to Himself,* you and all your brethren, the sons of Levi, with you? And are you seeking the priesthood also? 11 Therefore you and all your company *are* gathered together against the LORD. And what *is* Aaron that you complain against him?"

12 And Moses sent to call Dathan and Abiram the sons of Eliab, but they said, "We will not come up! 13 *Is it* a small thing that you have brought us up out of a land flowing with milk and honey, to kill us in the wilderness, that you should keep acting like a prince over us? 14 Moreover you have not brought us into a land flowing with milk and honey, nor given us inheritance of fields and vineyards. Will you put

---

Revolt in the Jewish Camp

ENBC (Egyptian National Broadcasting Service)—The newsrooms of Egypt are buzzing with the latest shocking reports. The God of Israel has just destroyed 250 Jewish leaders along with Dathan (pronounced *DAY-thun*), Abiram (pronounced *uh-BIGH-rum*), Korah (pronounced *KOH-ruh*), and all their families!

These men led a rebellion against Moses and Aaron, complaining that the two leaders had no right to set themselves up over the whole nation of Israel.

The Lord of Israel appeared again to the people and was ready to destroy all of them except Moses and Aaron. Once again, Moses prayed for the people, and they were spared.

But eyewitnesses report that a terrible thing happened! The earth actually opened up and swallowed all the rebels.

One thing has become very clear: Bargaining with the God of Israel is a dangerous business.

out the eyes of these men? We will not come up!"

15 Then Moses was very angry, and said to the LORD, "Do not respect their offering. I have not taken one donkey from them, nor have I hurt one of them."

16 And Moses said to Korah, "Tomorrow, you and all your company be present before the LORD—you and

The earth opened up and swallowed the men who led a rebellion against Moses and Aaron.

they, as well as Aaron. ¹⁷ Let each take
his censer and put incense in it, and
each of you bring his censer before the
Lord, two hundred and fifty censers;
both you and Aaron, each *with* his censer." ¹⁸ So every man took his censer,
put fire in it, laid incense on it, and
stood at the door of the tabernacle of
meeting with Moses and Aaron.
¹⁹ And Korah gathered all the congre-
gation against them at the door of the
tabernacle of meeting. Then the glory
of the Lord appeared to all the congregation.

²⁰ And the Lord spoke to Moses and
Aaron, saying, ²¹ "Separate yourselves
from among this congregation, that I
may consume them in a moment."

²² Then they fell on their faces, and
said, "O God, the God of the spirits
of all flesh, shall one man sin, and You
be angry with all the congregation?"

²³ So the Lord spoke to Moses, say-
ing, ²⁴ "Speak to the congregation,
saying, 'Get away from the tents of Korah, Dathan, and Abiram.' "

²⁵ Then Moses rose and went to Da-
than and Abiram, and the elders of Israel followed him. ²⁶ And he spoke to
the congregation, saying, "Depart now
from the tents of these wicked men!
Touch nothing of theirs, lest you be
consumed in all their sins." ²⁷ So they
got away from around the tents of Ko-
rah, Dathan, and Abiram; and Dathan
and Abiram came out and stood at the
door of their tents, with their wives,
their sons, and their little children.

²⁸ And Moses said: "By this you shall
know that the Lord has sent me to
do all these works, for *I have* not *done
them* of my own will. ²⁹ If these men
die naturally like all men, or if they are
visited by the common fate of all men,
then the Lord has not sent me.
³⁰ But if the Lord creates a new thing,
and the earth opens its mouth and
swallows them up with all that belongs
to them, and they go down alive into
the pit, then you will understand that
these men have rejected the Lord."

³¹ Now it came to pass, as he fin-
ished speaking all these words, that the
ground split apart under them, ³² and

the earth opened its mouth and swallowed them up, with their households
and all the men with Korah, with all
their goods. ³³ So they and all those
with them went down alive into the
pit; the earth closed over them, and
they perished from among the assem-
bly. ³⁴ Then all Israel who *were* around
them fled at their cry, for they said,
"Lest the earth swallow us up *also!*"

³⁵ And a fire came out from the Lord
and consumed the two hundred and
fifty men who were offering incense.

³⁶ Then the Lord spoke to Moses,
saying: ³⁷ "Tell Eleazar, the son of
Aaron the priest, to pick up the censers
out of the blaze, for they are holy, and
scatter the fire some distance away.
³⁸ The censers of these men who
sinned against their own souls, let them
be made into hammered plates as a
covering for the altar. Because they
presented them before the Lord,
therefore they are holy; and they shall
be a sign to the children of Israel."
³⁹ So Eleazar the priest took the bronze
censers, which those who were burned
up had presented, and they were hammered out as a covering on the altar,
⁴⁰ *to be* a memorial to the children of
Israel that no outsider, who *is* not a
descendant of Aaron, should come
near to offer incense before the Lord,
that he might not become like Korah
and his companions, just as the Lord
had said to him through Moses.

⁴¹ On the next day all the congrega-
tion of the children of Israel complained against Moses and Aaron, saying, "You have killed the people of the
Lord." ⁴² Now it happened, when the
congregation had gathered against Moses and Aaron, that they turned toward
the tabernacle of meeting; and suddenly the cloud covered it, and the
glory of the Lord appeared. ⁴³ Then
Moses and Aaron came before the tabernacle of meeting.

⁴⁴ And the Lord spoke to Moses,
saying, ⁴⁵ "Get away from among this
congregation, that I may consume
them in a moment."

And they fell on their faces.

⁴⁶ So Moses said to Aaron, "Take a

censer and put fire in it from the altar, put incense *on it,* and take it quickly to the congregation and make atonement for them; for wrath has gone out from the LORD. The plague has begun." 47 Then Aaron took *it* as Moses commanded, and ran into the midst of the assembly; and already the plague had begun among the people. So he put in the incense and made atonement for the people. 48 And he stood between the dead and the living; so the plague was stopped. 49 Now those who died in the plague were fourteen thousand seven hundred, besides those who died in the Korah incident. 50 So Aaron returned to Moses at the door of the tabernacle of meeting, for the plague had stopped.

Aaron's rod bears fruit

17 And the LORD spoke to Moses, saying: 2 "Speak to the children of Israel, and get from them a rod from each father's house, all their leaders according to their fathers' houses— twelve rods. Write each man's name on his rod. 3 And you shall write Aaron's name on the rod of Levi. For there shall be one rod for the head of *each* father's house. 4 Then you shall place them in the tabernacle of meeting before the Testimony, where I meet with you. 5 And it shall be *that* the rod of the man whom I choose will blossom; thus I will rid Myself of the complaints of the children of Israel, which they make against you."

6 So Moses spoke to the children of Israel, and each of their leaders gave him a rod apiece, for each leader according to their fathers' houses, twelve rods; and the rod of Aaron *was* among their rods. 7 And Moses placed the rods before the LORD in the tabernacle of witness.

8 Now it came to pass on the next day that Moses went into the tabernacle of witness, and behold, the rod of Aaron, of the house of Levi, had sprouted and put forth buds, had produced blossoms and yielded ripe almonds. 9 Then Moses brought out all the rods from before the LORD to all the children of Israel; and they looked, and each man took his rod.

10 And the LORD said to Moses, "Bring Aaron's rod back before the Testimony, to be kept as a sign against the rebels, that you may put their complaints away from Me, lest they die." 11 Thus did Moses; just as the LORD had commanded him, so he did.

12 So the children of Israel spoke to Moses, saying, "Surely we die, we perish, we all perish! 13 Whoever even comes near the tabernacle of the LORD must die. Shall we all utterly die?"

How the priests are supported

18 Then the LORD said to Aaron: "You and your sons and your father's house with you shall bear the iniquity *related to* the sanctuary, and you and your sons with you shall bear the iniquity *associated with* your priesthood. 2 Also bring with you your brethren of the tribe of Levi, the tribe of your father, that they may be joined with you and serve you while you and your sons *are* with you before the tabernacle of witness. 3 They shall attend to your needs and all the needs of the tabernacle; but they shall not come near the articles of the sanctuary and the altar, lest they die—they and you also. 4 They shall be joined with you and attend to the needs of the tabernacle of meeting, for all the work of the tabernacle; but an outsider shall not come near you. 5 And you shall attend to the duties of the sanctuary and the duties of the altar, that there *may* be no more wrath on the children of Israel. 6 Behold, I Myself have taken your brethren the Levites from among the children of Israel; *they are* a gift to you, given by the LORD, to do the work of the tabernacle of meeting. 7 Therefore you and your sons with you shall attend to your priesthood for everything at the altar and behind the veil; and you shall serve. I give your priesthood *to you* as a gift for service, but the outsider who comes near shall be put to death."

8 And the LORD spoke to Aaron: "Here, I Myself have also given you charge of My heave offerings, all the holy gifts of the children of Israel; I have given them as a portion to you and your sons, as an ordinance forever. 9 This shall be yours of the most holy things *reserved* from the fire: every offering of theirs, every grain offering and every sin offering and every trespass offering which they render to Me, *shall be* most holy for you and your sons. 10 In a most holy *place* you shall eat it; every male shall eat it. It shall be holy to you.

11 "This also *is* yours: the heave offering of their gift, with all the wave offerings of the children of Israel; I have given them to you, and your sons and daughters with you, as an ordinance forever. Everyone who is clean in your house may eat it.

12 "All the best of the oil, all the best of the new wine and the grain, their firstfruits which they offer to the LORD, I have given them to you. 13 Whatever first ripe fruit is in their land, which they bring to the LORD, shall be yours. Everyone who is clean in your house may eat it.

14 "Every devoted thing in Israel shall be yours.

15 "Everything that first opens the womb of all flesh, which they bring to the LORD, whether man or beast, shall be yours; nevertheless the firstborn of man you shall surely redeem, and the firstborn of unclean animals you shall redeem. 16 And those redeemed of the devoted things you shall redeem when one month old, according to your valuation, for five shekels of silver, according to the shekel of the sanctuary, which *is* twenty gerahs. 17 But the firstborn of a cow, the firstborn of a sheep, or the firstborn of a goat you shall not redeem; they *are* holy. You shall sprinkle their blood on the altar, and burn their fat *as* an offering made by fire for a sweet aroma to the LORD. 18 And their flesh shall be yours, just as the wave breast and the right thigh are yours.

19 "All the heave offerings of the holy things, which the children of Israel offer to the LORD, I have given to you and your sons and daughters with you as an ordinance forever; it *is* a covenant of salt forever before the LORD with you and your descendants with you."

20 Then the LORD said to Aaron: "You shall have no inheritance in their land, nor shall you have any portion among them; I *am* your portion and your inheritance among the children of Israel.

21 "Behold, I have given the children of Levi all the tithes in Israel as an inheritance in return for the work which they perform, the work of the tabernacle of meeting. 22 Hereafter the children of Israel shall not come near the tabernacle of meeting, lest they bear sin and die. 23 But the Levites shall perform the work of the tabernacle of meeting, and they shall bear their iniquity; *it shall be* a statute forever, throughout your generations, that among the children of Israel they shall have no inheritance. 24 For the tithes of the children of Israel, which they offer up *as* a heave offering to the LORD, I have given to the Levites as an inheritance; therefore I have said to them, 'Among the children of Israel they shall have no inheritance.' "

25 Then the LORD spoke to Moses, saying, 26 "Speak thus to the Levites, and say to them: 'When you take from the children of Israel the tithes which I have given you from them as your inheritance, then you shall offer up a heave offering of it to the LORD, a tenth of the tithe. 27 And your heave offering shall be reckoned to you as though *it were* the grain of the threshing floor and as the fullness of the winepress. 28 Thus you shall also offer a heave offering to the LORD from all your tithes which you receive from the children of Israel, and you shall give the LORD's heave offering from it to Aaron the priest. 29 Of all your gifts you shall offer up *every* heave offering due to the LORD, from all the best of them, the consecrated part of them.' 30 Therefore you shall say to them: 'When you have

lifted up the best of it, then *the rest* shall be accounted to the Levites as the produce of the threshing floor and as the produce of the winepress. 31 You may eat it in any place, you and your households, for it *is* your reward for your work in the tabernacle of meeting. 32 And you shall bear no sin because of it, when you have lifted up the best of it. But you shall not profane the holy gifts of the children of Israel, lest you die.' ''

How the unclean is made clean

19 Now the Lord spoke to Moses and Aaron, saying, 2 "This *is* the ordinance of the law which the Lord has commanded, saying: 'Speak to the children of Israel, that they bring you a red heifer without blemish, in which there *is* no defect *and* on which a yoke has never come. 3 You shall give it to Eleazar the priest, that he may take it outside the camp, and it shall be slaughtered before him; 4 and Eleazar the priest shall take some of its blood with his finger, and sprinkle some of its blood seven times directly in front of the tabernacle of meeting. 5 Then the heifer shall be burned in his sight: its hide, its flesh, its blood, and its offal shall be burned. 6 And the priest shall take cedar wood and hyssop and scarlet, and cast *them* into the midst of the fire burning the heifer. 7 Then the priest shall wash his clothes, he shall bathe in water, and afterward he shall come into the camp; the priest shall be unclean until evening. 8 And the one who burns it shall wash his clothes in water, bathe in water, and shall be unclean until evening. 9 Then a man *who is* clean shall gather up the ashes of the heifer, and store *them* outside the camp in a clean place; and they shall be kept for the congregation of the children of Israel for the water of purification; it *is* for purifying from sin. 10 And the one who gathers the ashes of the heifer shall wash his clothes, and be unclean until evening. It shall be a statute forever to the children of Israel and

to the stranger who dwells among them.

11 'He who touches the dead body of anyone shall be unclean seven days. 12 He shall purify himself with the water on the third day and on the seventh day; *then* he will be clean. But if he does not purify himself on the third day and on the seventh day, he will not be clean. 13 Whoever touches the body of anyone who has died, and does not purify himself, defiles the tabernacle of the Lord. That person shall be cut off from Israel. He shall be unclean, because the water of purification was not sprinkled on him; his uncleanness *is* still on him.

14 'This *is* the law when a man dies in a tent: All who come into the tent and all who *are* in the tent shall be unclean seven days; 15 and *every* open vessel, which has no cover fastened on it, *is* unclean. 16 Whoever in the open field touches one who is slain by a sword or who has died, or a bone of a man, or a grave, shall be unclean seven days.

17 'And for an unclean *person* they shall take some of the ashes of the heifer burnt for purification from sin, and running water shall be put on them in a vessel. 18 A clean person shall take hyssop and dip *it* in the water, sprinkle *it* on the tent, on all the vessels, on the persons who were there, or on the one who touched a bone, the slain, the dead, or a grave. 19 The clean *person* shall sprinkle the unclean on the third day and on the seventh day; and on the seventh day he shall purify himself, wash his clothes, and bathe in water; and at evening he shall be clean.

20 'But the man who is unclean and does not purify himself, that person shall be cut off from among the assembly, because he has defiled the sanctuary of the Lord. The water of purification has not been sprinkled on him; he *is* unclean. 21 It shall be a perpetual statute for them. He who sprinkles the water of purification shall wash his clothes; and he who touches the water of purification shall be unclean until evening. 22 Whatever the unclean

person touches shall be unclean; and the person who touches *it* shall be unclean until evening.' "

Moses disobeys God

20 Then the children of Israel, the whole congregation, came into the Wilderness of Zin in the first month, and the people stayed in Kadesh; and Miriam died there and was buried there.

2 Now there was no water for the congregation; so they gathered together against Moses and Aaron. 3 And the people contended with Moses and spoke, saying: "If only we had died when our brethren died before the LORD! 4 Why have you brought up the assembly of the LORD into this wilderness, that we and our animals should die here? 5 And why have you made us come up out of Egypt, to bring us to this evil place? It *is* not a place of grain or figs or vines or pomegranates; nor *is* there any water to drink." 6 So Moses and Aaron went from the presence of the assembly to the door of the tabernacle of meeting, and they fell on their faces. And the glory of the LORD appeared to them.

7 Then the LORD spoke to Moses, saying, 8 "Take the rod; you and your brother Aaron gather the congregation together. Speak to the rock before their eyes, and it will yield its water; thus you shall bring water for them out of the rock, and give drink to the congregation and their animals." 9 So Moses took the rod from before the LORD as He commanded him.

10 And Moses and Aaron gathered the assembly together before the rock; and he said to them, "Hear now, you rebels! Must we bring water for you out of this rock?" 11 Then Moses lifted his hand and struck the rock twice with his rod; and water came out abundantly, and the congregation and their animals drank.

12 Then the LORD spoke to Moses and Aaron, "Because you did not believe Me, to hallow Me in the eyes of the children of Israel, therefore you shall not bring this assembly into the land which I have given them."

13 This *was* the water of Meribah, because the children of Israel contended with the LORD, and He was hallowed among them.

14 Now Moses sent messengers from Kadesh to the king of Edom. "Thus says your brother Israel: 'You know all the hardship that has befallen us, 15 how our fathers went down to Egypt, and we dwelt in Egypt a long time, and the Egyptians afflicted us and our fathers. 16 When we cried out to the LORD, He heard our voice and sent the Angel and brought us up out of Egypt; now here we are in Kadesh, a city on the edge of your border. 17 Please let us pass through your country. We will not pass through fields or vineyards, nor will we drink water from wells; we will go along the King's Highway; we will not turn aside to the right hand or to the left until we have passed through your territory.' "

18 Then Edom said to him, "You shall not pass through my *land,* lest I

🔨 DIGGING IN

20:10–12 Moses Disobeys God You can be thankful that God always tells you the whole truth—even about great heroes like Moses. Moses was not perfect. He did a good job, and he was faithful to God. But only TV heroes are perfect.

You will remember that Moses in early life was a man of anger. In anger he killed an Egyptian (see Exodus 2). After that God spent 40 years teaching Moses patience while he tended sheep. And Moses did learn to be patient. In fact, he showed

more than once that he was even willing to die for Israel his people.

But we all get tired, and when we're tired, we're sometimes impatient. Moses got tired of listening to people complain, so he became angry. The Lord did forgive Moses, *but* the Lord must be tougher with leaders than with the rest of us. So Moses was not allowed to enter the Promised Land. Someday you, too, may be a leader. Remember Moses!

Hebrew Religious Leader Dies

Sinai Sun Times

SINAI DESERT—Moses, the lawgiver of Israel, makes this special announcement:

"I am sorry to announce the death of my brother, Aaron. We have just come from his funeral on Mount Hor. As you know, Aaron was our first high priest. Except for his sin of making the gold calf (see Exodus 32), Aaron was a faithful minister of God. I am thankful the Lord forgave him that earlier sin. If I had been in his place, I fear I might have done the same.

"Aaron tried to keep all of God's commands about the sacrifice and how the people should worship. His family also has been an example of godly and joyful living.

"As the Lord has commanded me, I have given Aaron's position of high priest to his son, Eleazar (pronounced el-ee-AY-zer). We believe Eleazar will follow in his father's footsteps as a good and faithful servant of the Lord."

come out against you with the sword."

19 So the children of Israel said to him, "We will go by the Highway, and if I or my livestock drink any of your water, then I will pay for it; let me only pass through on foot, nothing *more*."

20 Then he said, "You shall not pass through." So Edom came out against them with many men and with a strong hand. 21 Thus Edom refused to give Israel passage through his territory; so Israel turned away from him.

22 Now the children of Israel, the whole congregation, journeyed from Kadesh and came to Mount Hor. 23 And the LORD spoke to Moses and Aaron in Mount Hor by the border of the land of Edom, saying: 24 "Aaron shall be gathered to his people, for he shall not enter the land which I have given to the children of Israel, because you rebelled against My word at the water of Meribah. 25 Take Aaron and Eleazar his son, and bring them up to Mount Hor; 26 and strip Aaron of his garments and put them on Eleazar his son; for Aaron shall be gathered to his people and die there." 27 So Moses did just as the LORD commanded, and they went up to Mount Hor in the sight of all the congregation. 28 Moses stripped Aaron of his garments and put them on Eleazar his son; and Aaron died there on the top of the mountain. Then Moses and Eleazar came down from the mountain. 29 Now when all the congregation saw that Aaron was dead, all the house of Israel mourned for Aaron thirty days.

God sends poisonous snakes to punish Israel

21 The king of Arad, the Canaanite, who dwelt in the South, heard that Israel was coming on the road to

When poisonous snakes bit many of the Israelites, God told Moses to make a bronze serpent. All who looked at it would live.

What Did the Bronze Serpent Mean?

God told Moses to make a bronze serpent and put it on a pole. When the people looked at the bronze serpent, they were healed from the deadly bite of real serpents. Now we can look to Jesus who heals us from the sting of sin. Jesus was raised on the Cross so we could live forever.

Atharim. Then he fought against Israel and took *some* of them prisoners. 2 So Israel made a vow to the LORD, and said, "If You will indeed deliver this people into my hand, then I will utterly destroy their cities." 3 And the LORD listened to the voice of Israel and delivered up the Canaanites, and they utterly destroyed them and their cities. So the name of that place was called Hormah.

4 Then they journeyed from Mount Hor by the Way of the Red Sea, to go around the land of Edom; and the soul of the people became very discouraged on the way. 5 And the people spoke against God and against Moses: "Why have you brought us up out of Egypt to die in the wilderness? For *there is* no food and no water, and our soul loathes this worthless bread." 6 So the LORD sent fiery serpents among the people, and they bit the people; and many of the people of Israel died.

7 Therefore the people came to Moses, and said, "We have sinned, for we have spoken against the LORD and against you; pray to the LORD that He take away the serpents from us." So Moses prayed for the people.

8 Then the LORD said to Moses, "Make a fiery *serpent,* and set it on a pole; and it shall be that everyone who is bitten, when he looks at it, shall live." 9 So Moses made a bronze serpent, and put it on a pole; and so it was, if a serpent had bitten anyone, when he looked at the bronze serpent, he lived.

10 Now the children of Israel moved on and camped in Oboth. 11 And they journeyed from Oboth and camped at Ije Abarim, in the wilderness which *is* east of Moab, toward the sunrise. 12 From there they moved and camped in the Valley of Zered. 13 From there they moved and camped on the other side of the Arnon, which *is* in the wilderness that extends from the border of the Amorites; for the Arnon *is* the border of Moab, between Moab and the Amorites. 14 Therefore it is said in the Book of the Wars of the LORD:

"Waheb in Suphah,
The brooks of the Arnon,
15 And the slope of the brooks
That reaches to the dwelling of Ar,
And lies on the border of Moab."

16 From there *they went* to Beer, which *is* the well where the LORD said to Moses, "Gather the people together, and I will give them water." 17 Then Israel sang this song:

"Spring up, O well!
All of you sing to it—
18 The well the leaders sank,
Dug by the nation's nobles,
By the lawgiver, with their staves."

And from the wilderness *they went* to Mattanah, 19 from Mattanah to Nahaliel, from Nahaliel to Bamoth, 20 and from Bamoth, *in* the valley that is in the country of Moab, to the top of Pisgah which looks down on the wasteland.

21 Then Israel sent messengers to Sihon king of the Amorites, saying, 22 "Let me pass through your land. We will not turn aside into fields or vineyards; we will not drink water from wells. We will go by the King's Highway until we have passed through your territory." 23 But Sihon would not allow Israel to pass through his territory. So Sihon gathered all his people together and went out against Israel in the wilderness, and he came to Jahaz

and fought against Israel. 24 Then Israel defeated him with the edge of the sword, and took possession of his land from the Arnon to the Jabbok, as far as the people of Ammon; for the border of the people of Ammon *was* fortified. 25 So Israel took all these cities, and Israel dwelt in all the cities of the Amorites, in Heshbon and in all its villages. 26 For Heshbon *was* the city of Sihon king of the Amorites, who had fought against the former king of Moab, and had taken all his land from his hand as far as the Arnon. 27 Therefore those who speak in proverbs say:

"Come to Heshbon, let it be built;
Let the city of Sihon be repaired.

28 "For fire went out from Heshbon,
A flame from the city of Sihon;
It consumed Ar of Moab,
The lords of the heights of the
     Arnon.
29 Woe to you, Moab!
You have perished, O people of
     Chemosh!
He has given his sons as
     fugitives,
And his daughters into captivity,
To Sihon king of the Amorites.

30 "But we have shot at them;
Heshbon has perished as far as
     Dibon.
Then we laid waste as far as
     Nophah,
Which *reaches* to Medeba."

31 Thus Israel dwelt in the land of the Amorites. 32 Then Moses sent to spy out Jazer; and they took its villages and drove out the Amorites who *were* there.

33 And they turned and went up by the way to Bashan. So Og king of Bashan went out against them, he and all his people, to battle at Edrei. 34 Then the LORD said to Moses, "Do not fear him, for I have delivered him into your hand, with all his people and his land; and you shall do to him as you did to Sihon king of the Amorites,

who dwelt at Heshbon." 35 So they defeated him, his sons, and all his people, until there was no survivor left him; and they took possession of his land.

Balak sends for Balaam

22 Then the children of Israel moved, and camped in the plains of Moab on the side of the Jordan *across from* Jericho.

2 Now Balak the son of Zippor saw all that Israel had done to the Amorites. 3 And Moab was exceedingly afraid of the people because they *were* many, and Moab was sick with dread because of the children of Israel. 4 So Moab said to the elders of Midian, "Now this company will lick up everything around us, as an ox licks up the grass of the field." And Balak the son of Zippor *was* king of the Moabites at that time. 5 Then he sent messengers to Balaam the son of Beor at Pethor, which *is* near the River in the land of the sons of his people, to call him, saying: "Look, a people has come from Egypt. See, they cover the face of the earth, and are settling next to me! 6 Therefore please come at once, curse this people for me, for they *are* too mighty for me. Perhaps I shall be able to defeat them and drive them out of the land, for I know that he whom you bless *is* blessed, and he whom you curse is cursed."

7 So the elders of Moab and the elders of Midian departed with the diviner's *fee* in their hand, and they came to Balaam and spoke to him the words of Balak. 8 And he said to them, "Lodge here tonight, and I will bring back word to you, as the LORD speaks to me." So the princes of Moab stayed with Balaam.

9 Then God came to Balaam and said, "Who *are* these men with you?"

10 So Balaam said to God, "Balak the son of Zippor, king of Moab, has sent to me, *saying,* 11 'Look, a people has come out of Egypt, and they cover the face of the earth. Come now, curse them for me; perhaps I shall be able to overpower them and drive them out.' "

¹² And God said to Balaam, "You shall not go with them; you shall not curse the people, for they *are* blessed."

¹³ So Balaam rose in the morning and said to the princes of Balak, "Go back to your land, for the LORD has refused to give me permission to go with you."

¹⁴ And the princes of Moab rose and went to Balak, and said, "Balaam refuses to come with us."

¹⁵ Then Balak again sent princes, more numerous and more honorable than they. ¹⁶ And they came to Balaam and said to him, "Thus says Balak the son of Zippor: 'Please let nothing hinder you from coming to me; ¹⁷ for I will certainly honor you greatly, and I

🔨 DIGGING IN

22:1–38 Balaam and Money Poor Balaam! He just couldn't decide which side to be on. But money helped him make up his mind. Balaam (pronounced *BAYlum*) was willing to sell God's gift of prophecy for money. Of course, we're thankful that the Lord had better plans. Just as Balaam himself said, "The word that God puts in my mouth, that I must speak."

As you get older, some people will tell you that "money makes the world go round." What's wrong with that? Everybody needs money to live in the world. The trap is that money can become *the most important thing* in life. That was Balaam's trap, too. You must pray that God will give you clear vision to see what's really important. You aren't going to be in this world long, and your time here must be spent in doing what God commands you to do. Then God will also supply all your needs.

God used a donkey to teach a pagan prophet, Balaam, about Jesus.

will do whatever you say to me. Therefore please come, curse this people for me.' "

18 Then Balaam answered and said to the servants of Balak, "Though Balak were to give me his house full of silver and gold, I could not go beyond the word of the LORD my God, to do less or more. 19 Now therefore, please, you also stay here tonight, that I may know what more the LORD will say to me."

20 And God came to Balaam at night and said to him, "If the men come to call you, rise *and* go with them; but only the word which I speak to you— that you shall do." 21 So Balaam rose in the morning, saddled his donkey, and went with the princes of Moab. 22 Then God's anger was aroused because he went, and the Angel of the LORD took His stand in the way as an adversary against him. And he was riding on his donkey, and his two servants *were* with him. 23 Now the donkey saw the Angel of the LORD standing in the way with His drawn sword in His hand, and the donkey turned aside out of the way and went into the field. So Balaam struck the donkey to turn her back onto the road. 24 Then the Angel of the LORD stood in a narrow path between the vineyards, *with* a wall on this side and a wall on that side. 25 And when the donkey saw the Angel of the LORD, she pushed herself against the wall and crushed Balaam's foot against the wall; so he struck her again. 26 Then the Angel of the LORD went further, and stood in a narrow place where there *was* no way to turn either to the right hand or to the left. 27 And when the donkey saw the Angel of the LORD, she lay down under Balaam; so Balaam's anger was aroused, and he struck the donkey with his staff.

28 Then the LORD opened the mouth of the donkey, and she said to Balaam, "What have I done to you, that you have struck me these three times?"

29 And Balaam said to the donkey, "Because you have abused me. I wish there were a sword in my hand, for now I would kill you!"

30 So the donkey said to Balaam, "*Am* I not your donkey on which you have ridden, ever since *I became* yours, to this day? Was I ever disposed to do this to you?"

And he said, "No."

31 Then the LORD opened Balaam's eyes, and he saw the Angel of the LORD standing in the way with His drawn sword in His hand; and he bowed his head and fell flat on his face. 32 And the Angel of the LORD said to him, "Why have you struck your donkey these three times? Behold, I have come out to stand against you, because *your* way is perverse before Me. 33 The donkey saw Me and turned aside from Me these three times. If she had not turned aside from Me, surely I would also have killed you by now, and let her live."

34 And Balaam said to the Angel of the LORD, "I have sinned, for I did not know You stood in the way against me. Now therefore, if it displeases You, I will turn back."

35 Then the Angel of the LORD said to Balaam, "Go with the men, but only the word that I speak to you, that you shall speak." So Balaam went with the princes of Balak.

36 Now when Balak heard that Balaam was coming, he went out to meet him at the city of Moab, which *is* on the border at the Arnon, the boundary of the territory. 37 Then Balak said to Balaam, "Did I not earnestly send to you, calling for you? Why did you not come to me? Am I not able to honor you?"

38 And Balaam said to Balak, "Look, I have come to you! Now, have I any power at all to say anything? The word that God puts in my mouth, that I must speak." 39 So Balaam went with Balak, and they came to Kirjath Huzoth. 40 Then Balak offered oxen and sheep, and he sent *some* to Balaam and to the princes who *were* with him.

41 So it was, the next day, that Balak took Balaam and brought him up to the high places of Baal, that from there he might observe the extent of the people.

Balaam tells the future

23 Then Balaam said to Balak, "Build seven altars for me here, and prepare for me here seven bulls and seven rams."

2 And Balak did just as Balaam had spoken, and Balak and Balaam offered a bull and a ram on *each* altar. 3 Then Balaam said to Balak, "Stand by your burnt offering, and I will go; perhaps the LORD will come to meet me, and whatever He shows me I will tell you." So he went to a desolate height. 4 And God met Balaam, and he said to Him, "I have prepared the seven altars, and I have offered on *each* altar a bull and a ram."

5 Then the LORD put a word in Balaam's mouth, and said, "Return to Balak, and thus you shall speak." 6 So he returned to him, and there he was, standing by his burnt offering, he and all the princes of Moab.

7 And he took up his oracle and said:

"Balak the king of Moab has
   brought me from Aram,
From the mountains of the east.
'Come, curse Jacob for me,
And come, denounce Israel!'

8 "How shall I curse whom God
   has not cursed?
And how shall I denounce
   whom the LORD has not
   denounced?
9 For from the top of the rocks I
   see him,
And from the hills I behold him;
There! A people dwelling alone,
Not reckoning itself among the
   nations.

10 "Who can count the dust of
   Jacob,
Or number one-fourth of Israel?
Let me die the death of the
   righteous,
And let my end be like his!"

11 Then Balak said to Balaam, "What have you done to me? I took you to curse my enemies, and look, you have blessed *them* bountifully!"

12 So he answered and said, "Must I not take heed to speak what the LORD has put in my mouth?"

13 Then Balak said to him, "Please come with me to another place from which you may see them; you shall see only the outer part of them, and shall not see them all; curse them for me from there." 14 So he brought him to the field of Zophim, to the top of Pisgah, and built seven altars, and offered a bull and a ram on *each* altar.

15 And he said to Balak, "Stand here by your burnt offering while I meet *the* LORD over there."

16 Then the LORD met Balaam, and put a word in his mouth, and said, "Go back to Balak, and thus you shall speak." 17 So he came to him, and there he was, standing by his burnt offering, and the princes of Moab were with him. And Balak said to him, "What has the LORD spoken?"

18 Then he took up his oracle and said:

"Rise up, Balak, and hear!
Listen to me, son of Zippor!

19 "God *is* not a man, that He
   should lie,
Nor a son of man, that He
   should repent.
Has He said, and will He not do?
Or has He spoken, and will He
   not make it good?
20 Behold, I have received *a*
   command to bless;
He has blessed, and I cannot
   reverse it.

21 "He has not observed iniquity in
   Jacob,
Nor has He seen wickedness in
   Israel.
The LORD his God *is* with him,
And the shout of a King *is*
   among them.
22 God brings them out of Egypt;
He has strength like a wild ox.

23 "For *there is* no sorcery against
   Jacob,

Nor any divination against Israel.
It now must be said of Jacob
And of Israel, 'Oh, what God has
    done!'
24 Look, a people rises like a
    lioness,
And lifts itself up like a lion;
It shall not lie down until it
    devours the prey,
And drinks the blood of the
    slain."

25 Then Balak said to Balaam, "Neither curse them at all, nor bless them at all!"
26 So Balaam answered and said to Balak, "Did I not tell you, saying, 'All that the LORD speaks, that I must do'?"
27 Then Balak said to Balaam, "Please come, I will take you to another place; perhaps it will please God that you may curse them for me from there." 28 So Balak took Balaam to the top of Peor, that overlooks the wasteland. 29 Then Balaam said to Balak, "Build for me here seven altars, and prepare for me here seven bulls and seven rams." 30 And Balak did as Balaam had said, and offered a bull and a ram on *every* altar.

Balaam foretells the happiness of Israel

24 Now when Balaam saw that it pleased the LORD to bless Israel, he did not go as at other times, to seek to use sorcery, but he set his face toward the wilderness. 2 And Balaam raised his eyes, and saw Israel encamped according to their tribes; and the Spirit of God came upon him.
3 Then he took up his oracle and said:

"The utterance of Balaam the son
    of Beor,
The utterance of the man whose
    eyes are opened,
4 The utterance of him who hears
    the words of God,
Who sees the vision of the
    Almighty,

Who falls down, with eyes wide
    open:

5 "How lovely are your tents, O
    Jacob!
Your dwellings, O Israel!
6 Like valleys that stretch out,
Like gardens by the riverside,
Like aloes planted by the LORD,
Like cedars beside the waters.
7 He shall pour water from his
    buckets,
And his seed *shall be* in many
    waters.

"His king shall be higher than
    Agag,
And his kingdom shall be
    exalted.

8 "God brings him out of Egypt;
He has strength like a wild ox;
He shall consume the nations,
    his enemies;
He shall break their bones
And pierce *them* with his arrows.
9 'He bows down, he lies down as
    a lion;
And as a lion, who shall rouse
    him?'

"Blessed *is* he who blesses you,
And cursed *is* he who curses
    you."

10 Then Balak's anger was aroused against Balaam, and he struck his hands together; and Balak said to Balaam, "I called you to curse my enemies, and look, you have bountifully blessed *them* these three times! 11 Now therefore, flee to your place. I said I would greatly honor you, but in fact, the LORD has kept you back from honor."
12 So Balaam said to Balak, "Did I not also speak to your messengers whom you sent to me, saying, 13 'If Balak were to give me his house full of silver and gold, I could not go beyond the word of the LORD, to do good or bad of my own will. What the LORD says, that I must speak'? 14 And now, indeed, I am going to my people.

Come, I will advise you what this people will do to your people in the latter days."

15 So he took up his oracle and said:

"The utterance of Balaam the son of Beor,
And the utterance of the man whose eyes are opened;
16 The utterance of him who hears the words of God,
And has the knowledge of the Most High,
Who sees the vision of the Almighty,
Who falls down, with eyes wide open:

17 "I see Him, but not now;
I behold Him, but not near;
A Star shall come out of Jacob;
A Scepter shall rise out of Israel,
And batter the brow of Moab,
And destroy all the sons of tumult.

18 "And Edom shall be a possession;
Seir also, his enemies, shall be a possession,
While Israel does valiantly.
19 Out of Jacob One shall have dominion,
And destroy the remains of the city."

20 Then he looked on Amalek, and he took up his oracle and said:

"Amalek was first among the nations,
But shall be last until he perishes."

21 Then he looked on the Kenites, and he took up his oracle and said:

"Firm is your dwelling place,
And your nest is set in the rock;
22 Nevertheless Kain shall be burned.
How long until Asshur carries you away captive?"

23 Then he took up his oracle and said:

"Alas! Who shall live when God does this?
24 But ships shall come from the coasts of Cyprus,
And they shall afflict Asshur and afflict Eber,
And so shall Amalek, until he perishes."

25 So Balaam rose and departed and returned to his place; Balak also went his way.

Phinehas acts to save the children of Israel

25 Now Israel remained in Acacia Grove, and the people began to commit harlotry with the women of Moab. 2 They invited the people to the sacrifices of their gods, and the people ate and bowed down to their gods. 3 So Israel was joined to Baal of Peor, and the anger of the LORD was aroused against Israel.

4 Then the LORD said to Moses, "Take all the leaders of the people and

---

DIGGING IN

24:17 Balaam Tells Barak About Christ We saw in Numbers 22 that Balaam was willing to sell out to the enemies of God. But did you notice the funny way God made Balaam do the right thing in the end?

Balaam's donkey told his master off. Balaam didn't even stop to think how odd it was for a donkey to speak the words of God! But that's exactly what happened

(see Numbers 22:28). It took a donkey to teach a prophet how to act!

Finally, in spite of himself, Balaam does a beautiful thing. He was hired to serve God's enemies, but Balaam tells about the coming of Christ instead (see Numbers 24:17). The "Star" and the "Scepter" refer to Jesus who would be born hundreds of years after Balaam.

hang the offenders before the LORD, out in the sun, that the fierce anger of the LORD may turn away from Israel.''

5 So Moses said to the judges of Israel, "Every one of you kill his men who were joined to Baal of Peor.''

6 And indeed, one of the children of Israel came and presented to his brethren a Midianite woman in the sight of Moses and in the sight of all the congregation of the children of Israel, who *were* weeping at the door of the tabernacle of meeting. 7 Now when Phinehas the son of Eleazar, the son of Aaron the priest, saw *it,* he rose from among the congregation and took a javelin in his hand; 8 and he went after the man of Israel into the tent and thrust both of them through, the man of Israel, and the woman through her body. So the plague was stopped among the children of Israel. 9 And those who died in the plague were twenty-four thousand.

10 Then the LORD spoke to Moses, saying: 11 "Phinehas the son of Eleazar, the son of Aaron the priest, has turned back My wrath from the children of Israel, because he was zealous with My zeal among them, so that I did not consume the children of Israel in My zeal. 12 Therefore say, 'Behold, I give to him My covenant of peace; 13 and it shall be to him and his descendants after him a covenant of an everlasting priesthood, because he was zealous for his God, and made atonement for the children of Israel.' ''

14 Now the name of the Israelite who was killed, who was killed with the Midianite woman, *was* Zimri the son of Salu, a leader of a father's house among the Simeonites. 15 And the name of the Midianite woman who was killed *was* Cozbi the daughter of Zur; he *was* head of the people of a father's house in Midian.

16 Then the LORD spoke to Moses, saying: 17 "Harass the Midianites, and attack them; 18 for they harassed you with their schemes by which they seduced you in the matter of Peor and in the matter of Cozbi, the daughter of a leader of Midian, their sister, who

was killed in the day of the plague because of Peor.''

Moses counts the children of Israel again

26 And it came to pass, after the plague, that the LORD spoke to Moses and Eleazar the son of Aaron the priest, saying: 2 "Take a census of all the congregation of the children of Israel from twenty years old and above, by their fathers' houses, all who are able to go to war in Israel.'' 3 So Moses and Eleazar the priest spoke with them in the plains of Moab by the Jordan, *across from* Jericho, saying: 4 *"Take a census of the people* from twenty years old and above, just as the LORD commanded Moses and the children of Israel who came out of the land of Egypt.''

5 Reuben *was* the firstborn of Israel. The children of Reuben *were: of* Hanoch, the family of the Hanochites; *of* Pallu, the family of the Palluites; 6 *of* Hezron, the family of the Hezronites; *of* Carmi, the family of the Carmites. 7 These *are* the families of the Reubenites: those who were numbered of them were forty-three thousand seven hundred and thirty. 8 And the son of Pallu *was* Eliab. 9 The sons of Eliab *were* Nemuel, Dathan, and Abiram. These *are* the Dathan and Abiram, representatives of the congregation, who contended against Moses and Aaron in the company of Korah, when they contended against the LORD; 10 and the earth opened its mouth and swallowed them up together with Korah when that company died, when the fire devoured two hundred and fifty men; and they became a sign. 11 Nevertheless the children of Korah did not die.

12 The sons of Simeon according to their families *were: of* Nemuel, the family of the Nemuelites; *of* Jamin, the family of the Jaminites; *of* Jachin, the family of the Jachinites; 13 *of* Zerah, the family of the Zarhites; *of* Shaul, the family of the Shaulites. 14 These *are* the

families of the Simeonites: twenty-two thousand two hundred.

15 The sons of Gad according to their families *were: of* Zephon, the family of the Zephonites; *of* Haggi, the family of the Haggites; *of* Shuni, the family of the Shunites; 16 *of* Ozni, the family of the Oznites; *of* Eri, the family of the Erites; 17 *of* Arod, the family of the Arodites; *of* Areli, the family of the Arelites. 18 These *are* the families of the sons of Gad according to those who were numbered of them: forty thousand five hundred.

19 The sons of Judah *were* Er and Onan; and Er and Onan died in the land of Canaan. 20 And the sons of Judah according to their families were: *of* Shelah, the family of the Shelanites; *of* Perez, the family of the Parzites; *of* Zerah, the family of the Zarhites. 21 And the sons of Perez were: *of* Hezron, the family of the Hezronites; *of* Hamul, the family of the Hamulites. 22 These *are* the families of Judah according to those who were numbered of them: seventy-six thousand five hundred.

23 The sons of Issachar according to their families *were: of* Tola, the family of the Tolaites; of Puah, the family of the Punites; 24 of Jashub, the family of the Jashubites; of Shimron, the family of the Shimronites. 25 These *are* the families of Issachar according to those who were numbered of them: sixty-four thousand three hundred.

26 The sons of Zebulun according to their families *were:* of Sered, the family of the Sardites; of Elon, the family of the Elonites; of Jahleel, the family of the Jahleelites. 27 These *are* the families of the Zebulunites according to those who were numbered of them: sixty thousand five hundred.

28 The sons of Joseph according to their families, by Manasseh and Ephraim, *were:* 29 The sons of Manasseh: of Machir, the family of the Machirites; and Machir begot Gilead; of Gilead, the family of the Gileadites. 30 These *are* the sons of Gilead: *of* Jeezer, the family of the Jeezerites; of Helek, the family of the Helekites;

31 *of* Asriel, the family of the Asrielites; *of* Shechem, the family of the Shechemites; 32 *of* Shemida, the family of the Shemidaites; *of* Hepher, the family of the Hepherites. 33 Now Zelophehad the son of Hepher had no sons, but daughters; and the names of the daughters of Zelophehad *were* Mahlah, Noah, Hoglah, Milcah, and Tirzah. 34 These *are* the families of Manasseh; and those who were numbered of them *were* fifty-two thousand seven hundred.

35 These *are* the sons of Ephraim according to their families: of Shuthelah, the family of the Shuthalhites; of Becher, the family of the Bachrites; of Tahan, the family of the Tahanites. 36 And these *are* the sons of Shuthelah: of Eran, the family of the Eranites. 37 These *are* the families of the sons of Ephraim according to those who were numbered of them: thirty-two thousand five hundred.

These *are* the sons of Joseph according to their families.

38 The sons of Benjamin according to their families were: of Bela, the family of the Belaites; of Ashbel, the family of the Ashbelites; of Ahiram, the family of the Ahiramites; 39 of Shupham, the family of the Shuphamites; of Hupham, the family of the Huphamites. 40 And the sons of Bela were Ard and Naaman: *of* Ard, the family of the Ardites; of Naaman, the family of the Naamites. 41 These *are* the sons of Benjamin according to their families; and those who were numbered of them *were* forty-five thousand six hundred.

42 These *are* the sons of Dan according to their families: of Shuham, the family of the Shuhamites. These *are* the families of Dan according to their families. 43 All the families of the Shuhamites, according to those who were numbered of them, *were* sixty-four thousand four hundred.

44 The sons of Asher according to their families *were:* of Jimna, the family of the Jimnites; of Jesui, the family of the Jesuites; of Beriah, the family of the Beriites. 45 Of the sons of Beriah:

of Heber, the family of the Heberites; of Malchiel, the family of the Malchielites. 46 And the name of the daughter of Asher *was* Serah. 47 These *are* the families of the sons of Asher according to those who were numbered of them: fifty-three thousand four hundred.

48 The sons of Naphtali according to their families *were:* of Jahzeel, the family of the Jahzeelites; of Guni, the family of the Gunites; 49 of Jezer, the family of the Jezerites; of Shillem, the family of the Shillemites. 50 These *are* the families of Naphtali according to their families; and those who were numbered of them *were* forty-five thousand four hundred.

51 These *are* those who were numbered of the children of Israel: six hundred and one thousand seven hundred and thirty.

52 Then the LORD spoke to Moses, saying: 53 "To these the land shall be divided as an inheritance, according to the number of names. 54 To a large *tribe* you shall give a larger inheritance, and to a small *tribe* you shall give a smaller inheritance. Each shall be given its inheritance according to those who were numbered of them. 55 But the land shall be divided by lot; they shall inherit according to the names of the tribes of their fathers. 56 According to the lot their inheritance shall be divided between the larger and the smaller."

57 And these *are* those who were numbered of the Levites according to their families: of Gershon, the family of the Gershonites; of Kohath, the family of the Kohathites; of Merari, the family of the Merarites. 58 These *are* the families of the Levites: the family of the Libnites, the family of the Hebronites, the family of the Mahlites, the family of the Mushites, and the family of the Korathites. And Kohath begot Amram. 59 The name of Amram's wife *was* Jochebed the daughter of Levi, who was born to Levi in Egypt; and to Amram she bore Aaron and Moses and their sister Miriam. 60 To Aaron were born Nadab and Abihu, Eleazar and Ithamar. 61 And Nadab and Abihu

died when they offered profane fire before the LORD.

62 Now those who were numbered of them were twenty-three thousand, every male from a month old and above; for they were not numbered among the other children of Israel, because there was no inheritance given to them among the children of Israel.

63 These *are* those who were numbered by Moses and Eleazar the priest, who numbered the children of Israel in the plains of Moab by the Jordan, *across from* Jericho. 64 But among these there was not a man of those who were numbered by Moses and Aaron the priest when they numbered the children of Israel in the Wilderness of Sinai. 65 For the LORD had said of them, "They shall surely die in the wilderness." So there was not left a man of them, except Caleb the son of Jephunneh and Joshua the son of Nun.

Joshua is dedicated as Israel's new leader

27 Then came the daughters of Zelophehad the son of Hepher, the son of Gilead, the son of Machir, the son of Manasseh, from the families of Manasseh the son of Joseph; and these *were* the names of his daughters: Mahlah, Noah, Hoglah, Milcah, and Tirzah. 2 And they stood before Moses, before Eleazar the priest, and before the leaders and all the congregation, *by* the doorway of the tabernacle of meeting, saying: 3 "Our father died in the wilderness; but he was not in the company of those who gathered together against the LORD, in company with Korah, but he died in his own sin; and he had no sons. 4 Why should the name of our father be removed from among his family because he had no son? Give us a possession among our father's brothers."

5 So Moses brought their case before the LORD.

6 And the LORD spoke to Moses, saying: 7 "The daughters of Zelophehad speak *what* is right; you shall surely give them a possession of inheritance

among their father's brothers, and cause the inheritance of their father to pass to them. 8 And you shall speak to the children of Israel, saying: 'If a man dies and has no son, then you shall cause his inheritance to pass to his daughter. 9 If he has no daughter, then you shall give his inheritance to his brothers. 10 If he has no brothers, then you shall give his inheritance to his father's brothers. 11 And if his father has no brothers, then you shall give his inheritance to the relative closest to him in his family, and he shall possess it.' " And it shall be to the children of Israel a statute of judgment, just as the LORD commanded Moses.

12 Now the LORD said to Moses: "Go up into this Mount Abarim, and see the land which I have given to the children of Israel. 13 And when you have seen it, you also shall be gathered to your people, as Aaron your brother was gathered. 14 For in the Wilderness of Zin, during the strife of the congregation, you rebelled against My command to hallow Me at the waters before their eyes." (These are the waters of Meribah, at Kadesh in the Wilderness of Zin.)

15 Then Moses spoke to the LORD, saying: 16 "Let the LORD, the God of the spirits of all flesh, set a man over the congregation, 17 who may go out before them and go in before them, who may lead them out and bring them in, that the congregation of the LORD may not be like sheep which have no shepherd."

18 And the LORD said to Moses: "Take Joshua the son of Nun with you, a man in whom is the Spirit, and lay your hand on him; 19 set him before Eleazar the priest and before all the congregation, and inaugurate him in their sight. 20 And you shall give some of your authority to him, that all the congregation of the children of Israel may be obedient. 21 He shall stand before Eleazar the priest, who shall inquire before the LORD for him by the judgment of the Urim. At his word they shall go out, and at his word they shall come in, he and all the children of Israel with him—all the congregation."

22 So Moses did as the LORD commanded him. He took Joshua and set him before Eleazar the priest and before all the congregation. 23 And he laid his hands on him and inaugurated him, just as the LORD commanded by the hand of Moses.

The daily, Sabbath, and monthly offerings

28 Now the LORD spoke to Moses, saying, 2 "Command the children of Israel, and say to them, 'My offering, My food for My offerings made by fire as a sweet aroma to Me, you shall be careful to offer to Me at their appointed time.'

3 "And you shall say to them, 'This is the offering made by fire which you shall offer to the LORD: two male lambs in their first year without blemish, day by day, as a regular burnt offering. 4 The one lamb you shall offer in the morning, the other lamb you shall offer in the evening, 5 and one-tenth of an ephah of fine flour as a grain offering mixed with one-fourth of a hin of pressed oil. 6 It is a regular burnt offering which was ordained at Mount Sinai for a sweet aroma, an offering made by fire to the LORD. 7 And its drink offering shall be one-fourth of a hin for each lamb; in a holy place you shall pour out the drink to the LORD as an offering. 8 The other lamb you shall offer in the evening; as the morning grain offering and its drink offering, you shall offer it as an offering made by fire, a sweet aroma to the LORD.

9 'And on the Sabbath day two lambs in their first year, without blemish, and two-tenths of an ephah of fine flour as a grain offering, mixed with oil, with its drink offering— 10 this is the burnt offering for every Sabbath, besides the regular burnt offering with its drink offering.

11 'At the beginnings of your months you shall present a burnt offering to the LORD: two young bulls, one ram, and seven lambs in their first year,

without blemish; 12 three-tenths *of an ephah* of fine flour as a grain offering, mixed with oil, for each bull; two-tenths *of an ephah* of fine flour as a grain offering, mixed with oil, for the one ram; 13 and one-tenth *of an ephah* of fine flour, mixed with oil, as a grain offering for each lamb, as a burnt offering of sweet aroma, an offering made by fire to the LORD. 14 Their drink offering shall be half a hin of wine for a bull, one-third of a hin for a ram, and one-fourth of a hin for a lamb; this *is* the burnt offering for each month throughout the months of the year. 15 Also one kid of the goats as a sin offering to the LORD shall be offered, besides the regular burnt offering and its drink offering.

16 'On the fourteenth day of the first month *is* the Passover of the LORD. 17 And on the fifteenth day of this month *is* the feast; unleavened bread shall be eaten for seven days. 18 On the first day *you shall have* a holy convocation. You shall do no customary work. 19 And you shall present an offering made by fire as a burnt offering to the LORD: two young bulls, one ram, and seven lambs in their first year. Be sure they are without blemish. 20 Their grain offering shall be of fine flour mixed with oil: three-tenths *of an ephah* you shall offer for a bull, and two-tenths for a ram; 21 you shall offer one-tenth *of an ephah* for each of the seven lambs; 22 also one goat *as* a sin offering, to make atonement for you. 23 You shall offer these besides the burnt offering of the morning, which *is* for a regular burnt offering. 24 In this manner you shall offer the food of the offering made by fire daily for seven days, as a sweet aroma to the LORD; it shall be offered besides the regular burnt offering and its drink offering. 25 And on the seventh day you shall have a holy convocation. You shall do no customary work.

26 'Also on the day of the firstfruits, when you bring a new grain offering to the LORD at your *Feast* of Weeks, you shall have a holy convocation. You shall do no customary work.

The Feast of Weeks was a special time of thanksgiving to God for a good harvest.

27 You shall present a burnt offering as a sweet aroma to the LORD: two young bulls, one ram, and seven lambs in their first year, 28 with their grain offering of fine flour mixed with oil: three-tenths *of an ephah* for each bull, two-tenths for the one ram, 29 and one-tenth for each of the seven lambs; 30 *also* one kid of the goats, to make atonement for you. 31 Be sure they are without blemish. You shall present *them* with their drink offerings, besides the regular burnt offering with its grain offering.

Offerings to be made at feasts

29 'And in the seventh month, on the first *day* of the month, you shall have a holy convocation. You shall do no customary work. For you it is a day of blowing the trumpets. 2 You shall offer a burnt offering as a sweet aroma to the LORD: one young bull, one ram, *and* seven lambs in their first year, without blemish. 3 Their grain offering *shall be* fine flour mixed with oil: three-tenths *of an ephah* for the bull, two-tenths for the ram, 4 and one-tenth for each of the seven lambs; 5 also one

kid of the goats *as* a sin offering, to make atonement for you; 6 besides the burnt offering with its grain offering for the New Moon, the regular burnt offering with its grain offering, and their drink offerings, according to their ordinance, as a sweet aroma, an offering made by fire to the LORD.

7 'On the tenth *day* of this seventh month you shall have a holy convocation. You shall afflict your souls; you shall not do any work. 8 You shall present a burnt offering to the LORD *as* a sweet aroma: one young bull, one ram, *and* seven lambs in their first year. Be sure they are without blemish. 9 Their grain offering *shall be of* fine flour mixed with oil: three-tenths *of an ephah* for the bull, two-tenths for the one ram, 10 and one-tenth for each of the seven lambs; 11 also one kid of the goats *as* a sin offering, besides the sin offering for **atonement,** the regular burnt offering with its grain offering, and their drink offerings.

12 'On the fifteenth day of the seventh month you shall have a holy convocation. You shall do no customary work, and you shall keep a feast to the LORD seven days. 13 You shall present a burnt offering, an offering made by fire as a sweet aroma to the LORD: thirteen young bulls, two rams, *and* fourteen lambs in their first year. They shall be without blemish. 14 Their grain offering *shall be of* fine flour mixed with oil: three-tenths *of an ephah* for each of the thirteen bulls, two-tenths for each of the two rams, 15 and one-tenth for each of the fourteen lambs; 16 also one kid of the goats *as* a sin offering, besides the regular burnt offering, its grain offering, and its drink offering.

17 'On the second day *present* twelve young bulls, two rams, fourteen lambs in their first year without blemish, 18 and their grain offering and their drink offerings for the bulls, for the

rams, and for the lambs, by their number, according to the ordinance; 19 also one kid of the goats *as* a sin offering, besides the regular burnt offering with its grain offering, and their drink offerings.

20 'On the third day *present* eleven bulls, two rams, fourteen lambs in their first year without blemish, 21 and their grain offering and their drink offerings for the bulls, for the rams, and for the lambs, by their number, according to the ordinance; 22 also one goat *as* a sin offering, besides the regular burnt offering, its grain offering, and its drink offering.

23 'On the fourth day *present* ten bulls, two rams, *and* fourteen lambs in their first year, without blemish, 24 and their grain offering and their drink offerings for the bulls, for the rams, and for the lambs, by their number, according to the ordinance; 25 also one kid of the goats *as* a sin offering, besides the regular burnt offering, its grain offering, and its drink offering.

26 'On the fifth day *present* nine bulls, two rams, *and* fourteen lambs in their first year without blemish, 27 and their grain offering and their drink offerings for the bulls, for the rams, and for the lambs, by their number, according to the ordinance; 28 also one goat *as* a sin offering, besides the regular burnt offering, its grain offering, and its drink offering.

29 'On the sixth day *present* eight bulls, two rams, *and* fourteen lambs in their first year without blemish, 30 and their grain offering and their drink offerings for the bulls, for the rams, and for the lambs, by their number, according to the ordinance; 31 also one goat *as* a sin offering, besides the regular burnt offering, its grain offering, and its drink offering.

32 'On the seventh day *present*

WORDFINDER

29:11 Atonement The act of paying God what we owe for our sins. In the Old Testament, the sacrificed animal was a symbol of atonement, but Christ is now our true Atonement.

seven bulls, two rams, *and* fourteen lambs in their first year without blemish, 33 and their grain offering and their drink offerings for the bulls, for the rams, and for the lambs, by their number, according to the ordinance; 34 also one goat *as* a sin offering, besides the regular burnt offering, its grain offering, and its drink offering.

35 'On the eighth day you shall have a sacred assembly. You shall do no customary work. 36 You shall present a burnt offering, an offering made by fire as a sweet aroma to the LORD: one bull, one ram, seven lambs in their first year without blemish, 37 and their grain offering and their drink offerings for the bull, for the ram, and for the lambs, by their number, according to the ordinance; 38 also one goat *as* a sin offering, besides the regular burnt offering, its grain offering, and its drink offering.

39 'These you shall present to the LORD at your appointed feasts (besides your vowed offerings and your freewill offerings) as your burnt offerings and your grain offerings, as your drink offerings and your peace offerings.' "

40 So Moses told the children of Israel everything, just as the LORD commanded Moses.

Laws about vows

30 Then Moses spoke to the heads of the tribes concerning the children of Israel, saying, "This *is* the thing which the LORD has commanded: 2 If a man makes a vow to the LORD, or swears an oath to bind himself by some agreement, he shall not break his word; he shall do according to all that proceeds out of his mouth.

3 "Or if a woman makes a vow to the LORD, and binds *herself* by some agreement while in her father's house in her youth, 4 and her father hears her vow and the agreement by which she has bound herself, and her father holds his peace, then all her vows shall stand, and every agreement with which she has bound herself shall stand. 5 But if her father overrules her on the day that

he hears, then none of her vows nor her agreements by which she has bound herself shall stand; and the LORD will release her, because her father overruled her.

6 "If indeed she takes a husband, while bound by her vows or by a rash utterance from her lips by which she bound herself, 7 and her husband hears *it,* and makes no response to her on the day that he hears, then her vows shall stand, and her agreements by which she bound herself shall stand. 8 But if her husband overrules her on the day that he hears *it,* he shall make void her vow which she took and what she uttered with her lips, by which she bound herself, and the LORD will release her.

9 "Also any vow of a widow or a divorced woman, by which she has bound herself, shall stand against her.

10 "If she vowed in her husband's house, or bound herself by an agreement with an oath, 11 and her husband heard *it,* and made no response to her *and* did not overrule her, then all her vows shall stand, and every agreement by which she bound herself shall stand. 12 But if her husband truly made them void on the day he heard *them,* then whatever proceeded from her lips concerning her vows or concerning the agreement binding her, it shall not stand; her husband has made them void, and the LORD will release her. 13 Every vow and every binding oath to afflict her soul, her husband may confirm it, or her husband may make it void. 14 Now if her husband makes no response whatever to her from day to day, then he confirms all her vows or all the agreements that bind her; he confirms them, because he made no response to her on the day that he heard *them.* 15 But if he does make them void after he has heard *them,* then he shall bear her guilt."

16 These *are* the statutes which the LORD commanded Moses, between a man and his wife, and between a father and his daughter in her youth in her father's house.

Israel conquers the Midianites

31 And the LORD spoke to Moses, saying: 2 "Take vengeance on the Midianites for the children of Israel. Afterward you shall be gathered to your people."

3 So Moses spoke to the people, saying, "Arm some of yourselves for war, and let them go against the Midianites to take vengeance for the LORD on Midian. 4 A thousand from each tribe of all the tribes of Israel you shall send to the war."

5 So there were recruited from the divisions of Israel one thousand from *each* tribe, twelve thousand armed for war. 6 Then Moses sent them to the war, one thousand from *each* tribe; he sent them to the war with Phinehas the son of Eleazar the priest, with the holy articles and the signal trumpets in his hand. 7 And they warred against the Midianites, just as the LORD commanded Moses, and they killed all the males. 8 They killed the kings of Midian with *the rest of* those who were killed—Evi, Rekem, Zur, Hur, and Reba, the five kings of Midian. Balaam the son of Beor they also killed with the sword.

9 And the children of Israel took the women of Midian captive, with their little ones, and took as spoil all their cattle, all their flocks, and all their goods. 10 They also burned with fire all the cities where they dwelt, and all their forts. 11 And they took all the spoil and all the booty—of man and beast.

12 Then they brought the captives, the booty, and the spoil to Moses, to Eleazar the priest, and to the congregation of the children of Israel, to the camp in the plains of Moab by the Jordan, *across from* Jericho. 13 And Moses, Eleazar the priest, and all the leaders of the congregation, went to meet them outside the camp. 14 But Moses was angry with the officers of the army, *with* the captains over thousands and captains over hundreds, who had come from the battle.

15 And Moses said to them: "Have you kept all the women alive? 16 Look, these *women* caused the children of Israel, through the counsel of Balaam, to trespass against the LORD in the incident of Peor, and there was a plague among the congregation of the LORD. 17 Now therefore, kill every male among the little ones, and kill every woman who has known a man intimately. 18 But keep alive for yourselves all the young girls who have not known a man intimately. 19 And as for you, remain outside the camp seven days; whoever has killed any person, and whoever has touched any slain, purify yourselves and your captives on the third day and on the seventh day. 20 Purify every garment, everything made of leather, everything woven of goats' *hair,* and everything made of wood."

21 Then Eleazar the priest said to the men of war who had gone to the battle, "This *is* the ordinance of the law which the LORD commanded Moses: 22 "Only the gold, the silver, the bronze, the iron, the tin, and the lead, 23 everything that can endure fire, you shall put through the fire, and it shall be clean; and it shall be purified with the water of purification. But all that cannot endure fire you shall put through water. 24 And you shall wash your clothes on the seventh day and be clean, and afterward you may come into the camp."

25 Now the LORD spoke to Moses, saying: 26 "Count up the plunder that was taken—of man and beast—you and Eleazar the priest and the chief fathers of the congregation; 27 and divide the plunder into two parts, between those who took part in the war, who went out to battle, and all the congregation. 28 And levy a tribute for the LORD on the men of war who went out to battle: one of every five hundred of the persons, the cattle, the donkeys, and the sheep; 29 take *it* from their half, and give *it* to Eleazar the priest as a heave offering to the LORD. 30 And from the children of Israel's half you shall take one of every fifty, drawn from the persons, the cattle, the donkeys, and the sheep, from all the livestock, and give them to the Levites

who keep charge of the tabernacle of the LORD." 31 So Moses and Eleazar the priest did as the LORD commanded Moses.

32 The booty remaining from the plunder, which the men of war had taken, was six hundred and seventy-five thousand sheep, 33 seventy-two thousand cattle, 34 sixty-one thousand donkeys, 35 and thirty-two thousand persons in all, of women who had not known a man intimately. 36 And the half, the portion for those who had gone out to war, was in number three hundred and thirty-seven thousand five hundred sheep; 37 and the LORD's tribute of the sheep was six hundred and seventy-five. 38 The cattle *were* thirty-six thousand, of which the LORD's tribute *was* seventy-two. 39 The donkeys *were* thirty thousand five hundred, of which the LORD's tribute *was* sixty-one. 40 The persons *were* sixteen thousand, of which the LORD's tribute *was* thirty-two persons. 41 So Moses gave the tribute *which was* the LORD's heave offering to Eleazar the priest, as the LORD commanded Moses.

42 And from the children of Israel's half, which Moses separated from the men who fought— 43 now the half belonging to the congregation was three hundred and thirty-seven thousand five hundred sheep, 44 thirty-six thousand cattle, 45 thirty thousand five hundred donkeys, 46 and sixteen thousand persons— 47 and from the children of Israel's half Moses took one of every fifty, drawn from man and beast, and gave them to the Levites, who kept charge of the tabernacle of the LORD, as the LORD commanded Moses.

48 Then the officers who *were* over thousands of the army, the captains of thousands and captains of hundreds, came near to Moses; 49 and they said to Moses, "Your servants have taken a count of the men of war who *are* under our command, and not a man of us is missing. 50 Therefore we have brought an offering for the LORD, what every man found of ornaments of gold: armlets and bracelets and signet rings and earrings and necklaces, to make

atonement for ourselves before the LORD." 51 So Moses and Eleazar the priest received the gold from them, all the fashioned ornaments. 52 And all the gold of the offering that they offered to the LORD, from the captains of thousands and captains of hundreds, was sixteen thousand seven hundred and fifty shekels. 53 (The men of war had taken spoil, every man for himself.) 54 And Moses and Eleazar the priest received the gold from the captains of thousands and of hundreds, and brought it into the tabernacle of meeting as a memorial for the children of Israel before the LORD.

Reuben and Gad settle their land

32 Now the children of Reuben and the children of Gad had a very great multitude of livestock; and when they saw the land of Jazer and the land of Gilead, that indeed the region *was* a place for livestock, 2 the children of Gad and the children of Reuben came and spoke to Moses, to Eleazar the priest, and to the leaders of the congregation, saying, 3 "Ataroth, Dibon, Jazer, Nimrah, Heshbon, Elealeh, Shebam, Nebo, and Beon, 4 the country which the LORD defeated before the congregation of Israel, is a land for livestock, and your servants have livestock." 5 Therefore they said, "If we have found favor in your sight, let this land be given to your servants as a possession. Do not take us over the Jordan."

6 And Moses said to the children of Gad and to the children of Reuben: "Shall your brethren go to war while you sit here? 7 Now why will you discourage the heart of the children of Israel from going over into the land which the LORD has given them? 8 Thus your fathers did when I sent them away from Kadesh Barnea to see the land. 9 For when they went up to the Valley of Eshcol and saw the land, they discouraged the heart of the children of Israel, so that they did not go into the land which the LORD had given them. 10 So the LORD's anger was

aroused on that day, and He swore an oath, saying, 11 'Surely none of the men who came up from Egypt, from twenty years old and above, shall see the land of which I swore to Abraham, Isaac, and Jacob, because they have not wholly followed Me, 12 except Caleb the son of Jephunneh, the Kenizzite, and Joshua the son of Nun, for they have wholly followed the LORD.' 13 So the LORD's anger was aroused against Israel, and He made them wander in the wilderness forty years, until all the generation that had done evil in the sight of the LORD was gone. 14 And look! You have risen in your fathers' place, a brood of sinful men, to increase still more the fierce anger of the LORD against Israel. 15 For if you turn away from following Him, He will once again leave them in the wilderness, and you will destroy all these people."

16 Then they came near to him and said: "We will build sheepfolds here for our livestock, and cities for our little ones, 17 but we ourselves will be armed, ready *to go* before the children of Israel until we have brought them to their place; and our little ones will dwell in the fortified cities because of the inhabitants of the land. 18 We will not return to our homes until every one of the children of Israel has received his inheritance. 19 For we will not inherit with them on the other side of the Jordan and beyond, because our inheritance has fallen to us on this eastern side of the Jordan."

20 Then Moses said to them: "If you do this thing, if you arm yourselves before the LORD for the war, 21 and all your armed men cross over the Jordan before the LORD until He has driven out His enemies from before Him, 22 and the land is subdued before the LORD, then afterward you may return and be blameless before the LORD and before Israel; and this land shall be your possession before the LORD. 23 But if you do not do so, then take note, you have sinned against the LORD; and be sure your sin will find you out. 24 Build cities for your little

ones and folds for your sheep, and do what has proceeded out of your mouth."

25 And the children of Gad and the children of Reuben spoke to Moses, saying: "Your servants will do as my lord commands. 26 Our little ones, our wives, our flocks, and all our livestock will be there in the cities of Gilead; 27 but your servants will cross over, every man armed for war, before the LORD to battle, just as my lord says."

28 So Moses gave command concerning them to Eleazar the priest, to Joshua the son of Nun, and to the chief fathers of the tribes of the children of Israel. 29 And Moses said to them: "If the children of Gad and the children of Reuben cross over the Jordan with you, every man armed for battle before the LORD, and the land is subdued before you, then you shall give them the land of Gilead as a possession. 30 But if they do not cross over armed with you, they shall have possessions among you in the land of Canaan."

31 Then the children of Gad and the children of Reuben answered, saying: "As the LORD has said to your servants, so we will do. 32 We will cross over armed before the LORD into the land of Canaan, but the possession of our inheritance *shall remain* with us on this side of the Jordan."

33 So Moses gave to the children of Gad, to the children of Reuben, and to half the tribe of Manasseh the son of Joseph, the kingdom of Sihon king of the Amorites and the kingdom of Og king of Bashan, the land with its cities within the borders, the cities of the surrounding country. 34 And the children of Gad built Dibon and Ataroth and Aroer, 35 Atroth and Shophan and Jazer and Jogbehah, 36 Beth Nimrah and Beth Haran, fortified cities, and folds for sheep. 37 And the children of Reuben built Heshbon and Elealeh and Kirjathaim, 38 Nebo and Baal Meon (*their* names being changed) and Shibmah; and they gave *other* names to the cities which they built.

39 And the children of Machir the son of Manasseh went to Gilead and took

it, and dispossessed the Amorites who *were* in it. 40 So Moses gave Gilead to Machir the son of Manasseh, and he dwelt in it. 41 Also Jair the son of Manasseh went and took its small towns, and called them Havoth Jair. 42 Then Nobah went and took Kenath and its villages, and he called it Nobah, after his own name.

Israel travels to Canaan

33 These *are* the journeys of the children of Israel, who went out of the land of Egypt by their armies under the hand of Moses and Aaron. 2 Now Moses wrote down the starting points of their journeys at the command of the LORD. And these *are* their journeys according to their starting points:

3 They departed from Rameses in the first month, on the fifteenth day of the first month; on the day after the Passover the children of Israel went out with boldness in the sight of all the Egyptians. 4 For the Egyptians were burying all *their* firstborn, whom the LORD had killed among them. Also on their gods the LORD had executed judgments.

5 Then the children of Israel moved from Rameses and camped at Succoth. 6 They departed from Succoth and camped at Etham, which *is* on the edge of the wilderness. 7 They moved from Etham and turned back to Pi Hahiroth, which *is* east of Baal Zephon; and they camped near Migdol. 8 They departed from before Hahiroth and passed through the midst of the sea into the wilderness, went three days' journey in the Wilderness of Etham, and camped at Marah. 9 They moved from Marah and came to Elim. At Elim *were* twelve springs of water and seventy palm trees; so they camped there.

10 They moved from Elim and camped by the Red Sea. 11 They moved from the Red Sea and camped in the Wilderness of Sin. 12 They journeyed from the Wilderness of Sin and camped at Dophkah. 13 They departed from Dophkah and camped at Alush. 14 They moved from Alush and camped at Rephidim, where there was no water for the people to drink.

15 They departed from Rephidim and camped in the Wilderness of Sinai. 16 They moved from the Wilderness of Sinai and camped at Kibroth Hattaavah. 17 They departed from Kibroth Hattaavah and camped at Hazeroth. 18 They departed from Hazeroth and camped at Rithmah. 19 They departed from Rithmah and camped at Rimmon Perez. 20 They departed from Rimmon Perez and camped at Libnah. 21 They moved from Libnah and camped at Rissah. 22 They journeyed from Rissah and camped at Kehelathah. 23 They went from Kehelathah and camped at Mount Shepher. 24 They moved from Mount Shepher and camped at Haradah. 25 They moved from Haradah and camped at Makheloth. 26 They moved from Makheloth and camped at Tahath. 27 They departed from Tahath and camped at Terah. 28 They moved from Terah and camped at Mithkah. 29 They went from Mithkah and camped at Hashmonah. 30 They departed from Hashmonah and camped at Moseroth. 31 They departed from Moseroth and camped at Bene Jaakan. 32 They moved from Bene Jaakan and camped at Hor Hagidgad. 33 They went from Hor Hagidgad and camped at Jotbathah. 34 They moved from Jotbathah and camped at Abronah. 35 They departed from Abronah and camped at Ezion Geber. 36 They moved from Ezion Geber and camped in the Wilderness of Zin, which *is* Kadesh. 37 They moved from Kadesh and camped at Mount Hor, on the boundary of the land of Edom.

38 Then Aaron the priest went up to Mount Hor at the command of the LORD, and died there in the fortieth year after the children of Israel had come out of the land of Egypt, on the first *day* of the fifth month. 39 Aaron *was* one hundred and twenty-three years old when he died on Mount Hor.

40 Now the king of Arad, the Canaanite, who dwelt in the South in the land of Canaan, heard of the coming of the children of Israel.

41 So they departed from Mount Hor and camped at Zalmonah. 42 They departed from Zalmonah and camped at Punon. 43 They departed from Punon and camped at Oboth. 44 They departed from Oboth and camped at Ije Abarim, at the border of Moab. 45 They departed from Ijim and camped at Dibon Gad. 46 They moved from Dibon Gad and camped at Almon Diblathaim. 47 They moved from Almon Diblathaim and camped in the mountains of Abarim, before Nebo. 48 They departed from the mountains of Abarim and camped in the plains of Moab by the Jordan, *across from* Jericho. 49 They camped by the Jordan, from Beth Jesimoth as far as the Abel Acacia Grove in the plains of Moab.

50 Now the LORD spoke to Moses in the plains of Moab by the Jordan, *across from* Jericho, saying, 51 "Speak to the children of Israel, and say to them: 'When you have crossed the Jordan into the land of Canaan, 52 then you shall drive out all the inhabitants of the land from before you, destroy all their engraved stones, destroy all their molded images, and demolish all their high places; 53 you shall dispossess *the inhabitants of* the land and dwell in it, for I have given you the land to possess. 54 And you shall divide the land by lot as an inheritance among your families; to the larger you shall give a larger inheritance, and to the smaller you shall give a smaller inheritance; there everyone's *inheritance* shall be whatever falls to him by lot. You shall inherit according to the tribes of your fathers. 55 But if you do not drive out the inhabitants of the land from before you, then it shall be that those whom you let remain *shall be* irritants in your eyes and thorns in your sides, and they shall harass you in the land where you dwell. 56 Moreover it shall be *that* I will do to you as I thought to do to them.' "

The borders of Canaan

34 Then the LORD spoke to Moses, saying, 2 "Command the children of Is-rael, and say to them: 'When you come into the land of Canaan, this *is* the land that shall fall to you as an inheritance—the land of Canaan to its boundaries. 3 Your southern border shall be from the Wilderness of Zin along the border of Edom; then your southern border shall extend eastward to the end of the Salt Sea; 4 your border shall turn from the southern side of the Ascent of Akrabbim, continue to Zin, and be on the south of Kadesh Barnea; then it shall go on to Hazar Addar, and continue to Azmon; 5 the border shall turn from Azmon to the Brook of Egypt, and it shall end at the Sea.

6 'As for the western border, you shall have the Great Sea for a border; this shall be your western border.

7 'And this shall be your northern border: From the Great Sea you shall mark out your *border* line to Mount Hor; 8 from Mount Hor you shall mark out *your border* to the entrance of Hamath; then the direction of the border shall be toward Zedad; 9 the border shall proceed to Ziphron, and it shall end at Hazar Enan. This shall be your northern border.

10 'You shall mark out your eastern border from Hazar Enan to Shepham; 11 the border shall go down from Shepham to Riblah on the east side of Ain; the border shall go down and reach to the eastern side of the Sea of Chinnereth; 12 the border shall go down along the Jordan, and it shall end at the Salt Sea. This shall be your land with its surrounding boundaries.' "

13 Then Moses commanded the children of Israel, saying: "This *is* the land which you shall inherit by lot, which the LORD has commanded to give to the nine tribes and to the half-tribe. 14 For the tribe of the children of Reuben according to the house of their fathers, and the tribe of the children of Gad according to the house of their fathers, have received *their inheritance;* and the half-tribe of Manasseh has received its inheritance. 15 The two tribes and the half-tribe have received their inheritance on this side of the

Jordan, *across from* Jericho eastward, toward the sunrise."

16 And the LORD spoke to Moses, saying, 17 "These *are* the names of the men who shall divide the land among you as an inheritance: Eleazar the priest and Joshua the son of Nun. 18 And you shall take one leader of every tribe to divide the land for the inheritance. 19 These *are* the names of the men: from the tribe of Judah, Caleb the son of Jephunneh; 20 from the tribe of the children of Simeon, Shemuel the son of Ammihud; 21 from the tribe of Benjamin, Elidad the son of Chislon; 22 a leader from the tribe of the children of Dan, Bukki the son of Jogli; 23 from the sons of Joseph: a leader from the tribe of the children of Manasseh, Hanniel the son of Ephod, 24 and a leader from the tribe of the children of Ephraim, Kemuel the son of Shiphtan; 25 a leader from the tribe of the children of Zebulun, Elizaphan the son of Parnach; 26 a leader from the tribe of the children of Issachar, Paltiel the son of Azzan; 27 a leader from the tribe of the children of Asher, Ahihud the son of Shelomi; 28 and a leader from the tribe of the children of Naphtali, Pedahel the son of Ammihud."

29 These *are* the ones the LORD commanded to divide the inheritance among the children of Israel in the land of Canaan.

Laws about violence and murder

35 And the LORD spoke to Moses in the plains of Moab by the Jordan *across from* Jericho, saying: 2 "Command the children of Israel that they give the Levites cities to dwell in from the inheritance of their possession, and you shall *also* give the Levites common-land around the cities. 3 They shall have the cities to dwell in; and their common-land shall be for their cattle, for their herds, and for all their animals. 4 The common-land of the cities which you will give the Levites *shall extend* from the wall of the city outward a thousand cubits all around.

5 And you shall measure outside the city on the east side two thousand cubits, on the south side two thousand cubits, on the west side two thousand cubits, and on the north side two thousand cubits. The city *shall be* in the middle. This shall belong to them as common-land for the cities.

6 "Now among the cities which you will give to the Levites *you shall appoint* six cities of refuge, to which a manslayer may flee. And to these you shall add forty-two cities. 7 So all the cities you will give to the Levites *shall be* forty-eight; these *you shall give* with their common-land. 8 And the cities which you will give *shall be* from the possession of the children of Israel; from the larger *tribe* you shall give many, from the smaller you shall give few. Each shall give some of its cities to the Levites, in proportion to the inheritance that each receives."

9 Then the LORD spoke to Moses, saying, 10 "Speak to the children of Israel, and say to them: 'When you cross the Jordan into the land of Canaan, 11 then you shall appoint cities to be cities of refuge for you, that the manslayer who kills any person accidentally may flee there. 12 They shall be cities of refuge for you from the avenger, that the manslayer may not die until he stands before the congregation in judgment. 13 And of the cities which you give, you shall have six cities of refuge. 14 You shall appoint three cities on this side of the Jordan, and three cities you shall appoint in the land of Canaan, *which* will be cities of refuge. 15 These six cities shall be for refuge for the children of Israel, for the stranger, and for the sojourner among them, that anyone who kills a person accidentally may flee there.

16 'But if he strikes him with an iron implement, so that he dies, he *is* a murderer; the murderer shall surely be put to death. 17 And if he strikes him with a stone in the hand, by which one could die, and he does die, he *is* a murderer; the murderer shall surely be put to death. 18 Or *if* he strikes him with a wooden hand weapon, by

which one could die, and he does die, he *is* a murderer; the murderer shall surely be put to death. 19 The avenger of blood himself shall put the murderer to death; when he meets him, he shall put him to death. 20 If he pushes him out of hatred or, while lying in wait, hurls something at him so that he dies, 21 or in enmity he strikes him with his hand so that he dies, the one who struck *him* shall surely be put to death. He *is* a murderer. The avenger of blood shall put the murderer to death when he meets him.

22 'However, if he pushes him suddenly without enmity, or throws anything at him without lying in wait, 23 or uses a stone, by which a man could die, throwing *it* at him without seeing *him,* so that he dies, while he was not his enemy or seeking his harm, 24 then the congregation shall judge between the manslayer and the avenger of blood according to these judgments. 25 So the congregation shall deliver the manslayer from the hand of the avenger of blood, and the congregation shall return him to the city of refuge where he had fled, and he shall remain there until the death of the high priest who was anointed with the holy oil. 26 But if the manslayer at any time goes outside the limits of the city of refuge where he fled, 27 and the avenger of blood finds him outside the limits of his city of refuge, and the avenger of blood kills the manslayer, he shall not be guilty of blood, 28 because he should have remained in his city of refuge until the death of the high priest. But after the death of the high priest the manslayer may return to the land of his possession.

29 'And these *things* shall be a statute of judgment to you throughout your generations in all your dwellings. 30 Whoever kills a person, the murderer shall be put to death on the testimony of witnesses; but one witness is not *sufficient* testimony against a person for the death *penalty.* 31 Moreover you shall take no ransom for the life of a murderer who *is* guilty of death, but he shall surely be put to death.

32 And you shall take no ransom for him who has fled to his city of refuge, that he may return to dwell in the land before the death of the priest. 33 So you shall not pollute the land where you *are;* for blood defiles the land, and no atonement can be made for the land, for the blood that is shed on it, except by the blood of him who shed it. 34 Therefore do not defile the land which you inhabit, in the midst of which I dwell; for I the LORD dwell among the children of Israel.' "

Israelites are to marry within their tribes

36 Now the chief fathers of the families of the children of Gilead the son of Machir, the son of Manasseh, of the families of the sons of Joseph, came near and spoke before Moses and before the leaders, the chief fathers of the children of Israel. 2 And they said: "The LORD commanded my lord *Moses* to give the land as an inheritance by lot to the children of Israel, and my lord was commanded by the LORD to give the inheritance of our brother Zelophehad to his daughters. 3 Now if they are married to any of the sons of the *other* tribes of the children of Israel, then their inheritance will be taken from the inheritance of our fathers, and it will be added to the inheritance of the tribe into which they marry; so it will be taken from the lot of our inheritance. 4 And when the Jubilee of the children of Israel comes, then their inheritance will be added to the inheritance of the tribe into which they marry; so their inheritance will be taken away from the inheritance of the tribe of our fathers."

5 Then Moses commanded the children of Israel according to the word of the LORD, saying: "What the tribe of the sons of Joseph speaks is right. 6 This *is* what the LORD commands concerning the daughters of Zelophehad, saying, 'Let them marry whom they think best, but they may marry only within the family of their father's tribe.' 7 So the inheritance of the

children of Israel shall not change hands from tribe to tribe, for every one of the children of Israel shall keep the inheritance of the tribe of his fathers. [8] And every daughter who possesses an inheritance in any tribe of the children of Israel shall be the wife of one of the family of her father's tribe, so that the children of Israel each may possess the inheritance of his fathers. [9] Thus no inheritance shall change hands from one tribe to another, but every tribe of the children of Israel shall keep its own inheritance."

[10] Just as the LORD commanded Moses, so did the daughters of Zelophehad; [11] for Mahlah, Tirzah, Hoglah, Milcah, and Noah, the daughters of Zelophehad, were married to the sons of their father's brothers. [12] They were married into the families of the children of Manasseh the son of Joseph, and their inheritance remained in the tribe of their father's family.

[13] These are the commandments and the judgments which the LORD commanded the children of Israel by the hand of Moses in the plains of Moab by the Jordan, across from Jericho.

The Book of
DEUTERONOMY

A Hebrew Family—Our family has been in the desert of Sinai (pronounced *SIGH-nigh*) for 40 years. Moses led our fathers and mothers out of Egypt, but when the whole nation refused to enter the Promised Land, our parents had to live in the desert until their whole generation died.

Now we are going to have a second chance to enjoy God's promise. We have never seen the Promised Land of Canaan (pronounced *KAY-nun*) that God gave to our great ancestor Abraham. But we have taught our sons and daughters all of the laws that God commanded Moses.

So our children are now looking forward to a new life in the land where grapes grow as big as tomatoes, a land that flows with milk and honey.

We are also living for an even better land that God has prepared for everyone who loves Him.

Moses reviews Israel's disobedience

THESE *are* the words which Moses spoke to all Israel on this side of the Jordan in the wilderness, in the plain opposite Suph, between Paran, Tophel, Laban, Hazeroth, and Dizahab. 2 *It is* eleven days' *journey* from Horeb by way of Mount Seir to Kadesh Barnea. 3 Now it came to pass in the fortieth year, in the eleventh month, on the first *day* of the month, *that* Moses spoke to the children of Israel according to all that the LORD had given him as commandments to them, 4 after he had killed Sihon king of the Amorites, who dwelt in Heshbon, and Og king of Bashan, who dwelt at Ashtaroth in Edrei.

5 On this side of the Jordan in the land of Moab, Moses began to explain this law, saying, 6 "The LORD our God spoke to us in Horeb, saying: 'You have dwelt long enough at this mountain. 7 Turn and take your journey, and go to the mountains of the Amorites, to all the neighboring *places* in the plain, in the mountains and in the lowland, in the South and on the seacoast, to the land of the Canaanites and to Lebanon, as far as the great river, the River Euphrates. 8 See, I have set the land before you; go in and possess the land which the LORD swore to your fathers—to Abraham, Isaac, and Jacob—to give to them and their descendants after them.'

9 "And I spoke to you at that time, saying: 'I alone am not able to bear you. 10 The LORD your God has multiplied you, and here you *are* today, as the stars of heaven in multitude. 11 May the LORD God of your fathers make you a thousand times more numerous than you are, and bless you as He has promised you! 12 How can I alone bear your problems and your burdens and your complaints? 13 Choose wise, understanding, and knowledgeable men from among your tribes, and I will make them heads over you.' 14 And you answered me and said, 'The thing which you have told *us* to do *is* good.' 15 So I took the heads of your tribes, wise and knowledgeable men, and made them heads over you, leaders of thousands, leaders of hundreds, leaders of fifties, leaders of tens, and officers for your tribes.

16 "Then I commanded your judges at that time, saying, 'Hear *the cases* between your brethren, and judge

righteously between a man and his brother or the stranger who is with him. 17 You shall not show partiality in judgment; you shall hear the small as well as the great; you shall not be afraid in any man's presence, for the judgment *is* God's. The case that is too hard for you, bring to me, and I will hear it.' 18 And I commanded you at that time all the things which you should do.

19 "So we departed from Horeb, and went through all that great and terrible wilderness which you saw on the way to the mountains of the Amorites, as the LORD our God had commanded us. Then we came to Kadesh Barnea. 20 And I said to you, 'You have come to the mountains of the Amorites, which the LORD our God is giving us. 21 Look, the LORD your God has set the land before you; go up *and* possess *it,* as the LORD God of your fathers has spoken to you; do not fear or be discouraged.'

22 "And every one of you came near to me and said, 'Let us send men before us, and let them search out the land for us, and bring back word to us of the way by which we should go up, and of the cities into which we shall come.'

23 "The plan pleased me well; so I took twelve of your men, one man from *each* tribe. 24 And they departed and went up into the mountains, and came to the Valley of Eshcol, and spied it out. 25 They also took *some* of the fruit of the land in their hands and brought *it* down to us; and they brought back word to us, saying, 'It is a good land which the LORD our God is giving us.'

26 "Nevertheless you would not go up, but rebelled against the command of the LORD your God; 27 and you complained in your tents, and said, 'Because the LORD hates us, He has brought us out of the land of Egypt to deliver us into the hand of the Amorites, to destroy us. 28 Where can we go up? Our brethren have discouraged our hearts, saying, "The people *are* greater and taller than we; the cities *are* great and fortified up to heaven; moreover we have seen the sons of the Anakim there."'

29 "Then I said to you, 'Do not be terrified, or afraid of them. 30 The LORD your God, who goes before you, He will fight for you, according to all He did for you in Egypt before your eyes, 31 and in the wilderness where you saw how the LORD your God carried you, as a man carries his son, in all the way that you went until you came to this place.' 32 Yet, for all that, you did not believe the LORD your God, 33 who went in the way before you to search out a place for you to pitch your tents, to show you the way you should go, in the fire by night and in the cloud by day.

34 "And the LORD heard the sound of your words, and was angry, and took an oath, saying, 35 'Surely not one of these men of this evil generation shall see that good land of which I swore to give to your fathers, 36 except Caleb the son of Jephunneh; he shall see it, and to him and his children I am giving the land on which he walked, because he wholly followed the LORD.' 37 The LORD was also angry with me for your sakes, saying, 'Even you shall not go in there. 38 Joshua the son of Nun, who stands before you, he shall go in there. Encourage him, for he shall cause Israel to inherit it.

39 'Moreover your little ones and your children, who you say will be victims, who today have no knowledge of good and evil, they shall go in there; to them I will give it, and they shall possess it. 40 But *as for* you, turn and take your journey into the wilderness by the Way of the Red Sea.'

41 "Then you answered and said to me, 'We have sinned against the LORD; we will go up and fight, just as the LORD our God commanded us.' And when everyone of you had girded on his weapons of war, you were ready to go up into the mountain.

42 "And the LORD said to me, 'Tell them, "Do not go up nor fight, for I *am* not among you; lest you be defeated before your enemies."' 43 So I

Moses Speaks at Jordan River Crossing

World Press Wire Service

JORDAN RIVER—World Press reporters are at the Jordan River where Moses is delivering the first of several planned speeches to Israel. Following these speeches, the Hebrew people will at last cross over to the Promised Land of Canaan.

Today, Moses has given a history lesson to the people of Israel. He has reminded the people how they left Mount Sinai (or Mount Horeb) to continue their journey to Canaan. Since the people had multiplied in the 40 years of wandering through the wilderness, Moses had organized them into groups of thousands, hundreds, fifties, tens, and had appointed officers over them.

Moses has also reminded the people of how they failed to trust the Lord for protection, and refused to enter Canaan the first time. As a result, they have spent 40 years wandering in the Sinai Desert. Strangely, though, the people of Israel have never lacked for anything and have even defeated enemies during those years.

Finally, Moses has repeated the Ten Commandments for those who were not old enough to hear them when they were given at Mount Sinai 40 years ago.

spoke to you; yet you would not listen, but rebelled against the command of the LORD, and presumptuously went up into the mountain. 44 And the Amorites who dwelt in that mountain came out against you and chased you as bees do, and drove you back from Seir to Hormah. 45 Then you returned and wept before the LORD, but the LORD would not listen to your voice nor give ear to you.

46 "So you remained in Kadesh many days, according to the days that you spent *there*.

Israel wanders in the wilderness

2 "Then we turned and journeyed into the wilderness of the Way of the Red Sea, as the LORD spoke to me, and we skirted Mount Seir for many days.

2 "And the LORD spoke to me, saying: 3 'You have skirted this mountain long enough; turn northward. 4 And command the people, saying, "You *are about to* pass through the territory of your brethren, the descendants of Esau, who live in Seir; and they will be afraid of you. Therefore watch yourselves carefully. 5 Do not meddle with them, for I will not give you *any* of their land, no, not so much as one footstep, because I have given Mount Seir to Esau *as* a possession. 6 You shall buy food from them with money, that you may eat; and you shall also buy water from them with money, that you may drink.

7 "For the LORD your God has blessed you in all the work of your hand. He knows your trudging through this great wilderness. These forty years the LORD your God *has been* with you; you have lacked nothing." '

8 "And when we passed beyond our brethren, the descendants of Esau who dwell in Seir, away from the road of the plain, away from Elath and Ezion Geber, we turned and passed by way of the Wilderness of Moab. 9 Then the LORD said to me, 'Do not harass Moab, nor contend with them in battle, for I will not give you *any* of their land *as* a possession, because I have given Ar to the descendants of Lot *as* a possession.' "

10 (The Emim had dwelt there in times past, a people as great and numerous and tall as the Anakim. 11 They were also regarded as giants, like the Anakim, but the Moabites call them Emim. 12 The Horites formerly dwelt in Seir, but the descendants of Esau

dispossessed them and destroyed them from before them, and dwelt in their place, just as Israel did to the land of their possession which the LORD gave them.)

13 " 'Now rise and cross over the Valley of the Zered.' So we crossed over the Valley of the Zered. 14 And the time we took to come from Kadesh Barnea until we crossed over the Valley of the Zered *was* thirty-eight years, until all the generation of the men of war was consumed from the midst of the camp, just as the LORD had sworn to them. 15 For indeed the hand of the LORD was against them, to destroy them from the midst of the camp until they were consumed.

16 "So it was, when all the men of war had finally perished from among the people, 17 that the LORD spoke to me, saying: 18 'This day you are to cross over at Ar, the boundary of Moab. 19 And *when* you come near the people of Ammon, do not harass them or meddle with them, for I will not give you *any* of the land of the people of Ammon *as* a possession, because I have given it to the descendants of Lot *as* a possession.' "

20 (That was also regarded as a land of giants; giants formerly dwelt there. But the Ammonites call them Zamzummim, 21 a people as great and numerous and tall as the Anakim. But the LORD destroyed them before them, and they dispossessed them and dwelt in their place, 22 just as He had done for the descendants of Esau, who dwelt in Seir, when He destroyed the Horites from before them. They dispossessed them and dwelt in their place, even to this day. 23 And the Avim, who dwelt in villages as far as Gaza—the Caphtorim, who came from Caphtor, destroyed them and dwelt in their place.)

24 " 'Rise, take your journey, and cross over the River Arnon. Look, I have given into your hand Sihon the Amorite, king of Heshbon, and his land. Begin to possess *it*, and engage him in battle. 25 This day I will begin to put the dread and fear of you upon the nations under the whole heaven,

who shall hear the report of you, and shall tremble and be in anguish because of you.'

26 "And I sent messengers from the Wilderness of Kedemoth to Sihon king of Heshbon, with words of peace, saying, 27 'Let me pass through your land; I will keep strictly to the road, and I will turn neither to the right nor to the left. 28 You shall sell me food for money, that I may eat, and give me water for money, that I may drink; only let me pass through on foot, 29 just as the descendants of Esau who dwell in Seir and the Moabites who dwell in Ar did for me, until I cross the Jordan to the land which the LORD our God is giving us.'

30 "But Sihon king of Heshbon would not let us pass through, for the LORD your God hardened his spirit and made his heart obstinate, that He might deliver him into your hand, as *it is* this day.

31 "And the LORD said to me, 'See, I have begun to give Sihon and his land over to you. Begin to possess *it*, that you may inherit his land.' 32 Then Sihon and all his people came out against us to fight at Jahaz. 33 And the LORD our God delivered him over to us; so we defeated him, his sons, and all his people. 34 We took all his cities at that time, and we utterly destroyed the men, women, and little ones of every city; we left none remaining. 35 We took only the livestock as plunder for ourselves, with the spoil of the cities which we took. 36 From Aroer, which *is* on the bank of the River Arnon, and *from* the city that *is* in the ravine, as far as Gilead, there was not one city too strong for us; the LORD our God delivered all to us. 37 Only you did not go near the land of the people of Ammon—anywhere along the River Jabbok, or to the cities of the mountains, or wherever the LORD our God had forbidden us.

Israel conquers Og of Bashan

3 "Then we turned and went up the road to Bashan; and Og king of

Bashan came out against us, he and all his people, to battle at Edrei. 2 And the LORD said to me, 'Do not fear him, for I have delivered him and all his people and his land into your hand; you shall do to him as you did to Sihon king of the Amorites, who dwelt at Heshbon.'

3 "So the LORD our God also delivered into our hands Og king of Bashan, with all his people, and we attacked him until he had no survivors remaining. 4 And we took all his cities at that time; there was not a city which we did not take from them: sixty cities, all the region of Argob, the kingdom of Og in Bashan. 5 All these cities were fortified with high walls, gates, and bars, besides a great many rural towns. 6 And we utterly destroyed them, as we did to Sihon king of Heshbon, utterly destroying the men, women, and children of every city. 7 But all the livestock and the spoil of the cities we took as booty for ourselves.

8 "And at that time we took the land from the hand of the two kings of the Amorites who were on this side of the Jordan, from the River Arnon to Mount Hermon 9 (the Sidonians call Hermon Sirion, and the Amorites call it Senir), 10 all the cities of the plain, all Gilead, and all Bashan, as far as Salcah and Edrei, cities of the kingdom of Og in Bashan.

11 "For only Og king of Bashan remained of the remnant of the giants. Indeed his bedstead was an iron bedstead. (Is it not in Rabbah of the people of Ammon?) Nine cubits is its length and four cubits its width, according to the standard cubit.

12 "And this land, which we possessed at that time, from Aroer, which is by the River Arnon, and half the mountains of Gilead and its cities, I gave to the Reubenites and the Gadites. 13 The rest of Gilead, and all Bashan, the kingdom of Og, I gave to half the tribe of Manasseh. (All the region of Argob, with all Bashan, was called the land of the giants. 14 Jair the son of Manasseh took all the region of Argob, as far as the border of the Geshurites and the Maachathites, and called Bashan after his own name, Havoth Jair, to this day.)

15 "Also I gave Gilead to Machir. 16 And to the Reubenites and the Gadites I gave from Gilead as far as the River Arnon, the middle of the river as the border, as far as the River Jabbok, the border of the people of Ammon; 17 the plain also, with the Jordan as the border, from Chinnereth as far as the east side of the Sea of the Arabah (the Salt Sea), below the slopes of Pisgah.

18 "Then I commanded you at that time, saying: 'The LORD your God has given you this land to possess. All you men of valor shall cross over armed before your brethren, the children of Israel. 19 But your wives, your little ones, and your livestock (I know that you have much livestock) shall stay in your cities which I have given you, 20 until the LORD has given rest to your brethren as to you, and they also possess the land which the LORD your God is giving them beyond the Jordan. Then each of you may return to his possession which I have given you.'

21 "And I commanded Joshua at that time, saying, 'Your eyes have seen all that the LORD your God has done to these two kings; so will the LORD do to all the kingdoms through which you pass. 22 You must not fear them, for the LORD your God Himself fights for you.'

23 "Then I pleaded with the LORD at that time, saying: 24 'O Lord GOD, You have begun to show Your servant Your greatness and Your mighty hand, for what god is there in heaven or on earth who can do anything like Your works and Your mighty deeds? 25 I pray, let me cross over and see the good land beyond the Jordan, those pleasant mountains, and Lebanon.'

26 "But the LORD was angry with me on your account, and would not listen to me. So the LORD said to me: 'Enough of that! Speak no more to Me of this matter. 27 Go up to the top of Pisgah, and lift your eyes toward the west, the north, the south, and the

east; behold *it* with your eyes, for you shall not cross over this Jordan. 28 But command Joshua, and encourage him and strengthen him; for he shall go over before this people, and he shall cause them to inherit the land which you will see.'

29 "So we stayed in the valley opposite Beth Peor.

God warns against serving other gods

4 "Now, O Israel, listen to the statutes and the judgments which I teach you to observe, that you may live, and go in and possess the land which the LORD God of your fathers is giving you. 2 You shall not add to the word which I command you, nor take from it, that you may keep the commandments of the LORD your God which I command you. 3 Your eyes have seen what the LORD did at Baal Peor; for the LORD your God has destroyed from among you all the men who followed Baal of Peor. 4 But you who held fast to the LORD your God *are* alive today, *every* one of you.

5 "Surely I have taught you statutes and judgments, just as the LORD my God commanded me, that you should act according *to them* in the land which you go to possess. 6 Therefore be careful to observe *them;* for this *is* your wisdom and your understanding in the sight of the peoples who will hear all these statutes, and say, 'Surely this great nation *is* a wise and understanding people.'

7 "For what great nation *is there* that has God *so* near to it, as the LORD our God *is* to us, for whatever *reason* we may call upon Him? 8 And what great nation *is there* that has *such* statutes and righteous judgments as are in all this law which I set before you this day? 9 Only take heed to yourself, and diligently keep yourself, lest you forget the things your eyes have seen, and lest they depart from your heart all the days of your life. And teach them to your children and your grandchildren,

10 *especially concerning* the day you stood before the LORD your God in Horeb, when the LORD said to me, 'Gather the people to Me, and I will let them hear My words, that they may learn to fear Me all the days they live on the earth, and *that* they may teach their children.'

11 "Then you came near and stood at the foot of the mountain, and the mountain burned with fire to the midst of heaven, with darkness, cloud, and thick darkness. 12 And the LORD spoke to you out of the midst of the fire. You heard the sound of the words, but saw no form; *you* only *heard* a voice. 13 So He declared to you His covenant which He commanded you to perform, the Ten Commandments; and He wrote them on two tablets of stone. 14 And the LORD commanded me at that time to teach you statutes and judgments, that you might observe them in the land which you cross over to possess.

15 "Take careful heed to yourselves, for you saw no form when the LORD spoke to you at Horeb out of the midst of the fire, 16 lest you act corruptly and make for yourselves a carved image in the form of any figure: the likeness of male or female, 17 the likeness of any animal that *is* on the earth or the likeness of any winged bird that flies in the air, 18 the likeness of anything that creeps on the ground or the likeness of any fish that *is* in the water beneath the earth. 19 And *take heed,* lest you lift your eyes to heaven, and *when* you see the sun, the moon, and the stars, all the host of heaven, you feel driven to worship them and serve them, which the LORD your God has given to all the peoples under the whole heaven as a heritage. 20 But the LORD has taken you and brought you out of the iron furnace, out of Egypt, to be His people, an inheritance, as you are this day. 21 Furthermore the LORD was angry with me for your sakes, and swore that I would not cross over the Jordan, and that I would not enter the good land which the LORD your God is giving you as an

inheritance. 22 But I must die in this land, I must not cross over the Jordan; but you shall cross over and possess that good land. 23 Take heed to yourselves, lest you forget the covenant of the LORD your God which He made with you, and make for yourselves a carved image in the form of anything which the LORD your God has forbidden you. 24 For the LORD your God *is* a consuming fire, a jealous God.

25 "When you beget children and grandchildren and have grown old in the land, and act corruptly and make a carved image in the form of anything, and do evil in the sight of the LORD your God to provoke Him to anger, 26 I call heaven and earth to witness against you this day, that you will soon utterly perish from the land which you cross over the Jordan to possess; you will not prolong *your* days in it, but will be utterly destroyed. 27 And the LORD will scatter you among the peoples, and you will be left few in number among the nations where the LORD will drive you. 28 And there you will serve gods, the work of men's hands, wood and stone, which neither see nor hear nor eat nor smell. 29 But from there you will seek the LORD your God, and you will find *Him* if you seek Him with all your heart and with all your soul. 30 When you are in distress, and all these things come upon you in the latter days, when you turn to the LORD your God and obey His voice 31 (for the LORD your God *is* a merciful God), He will not forsake you nor destroy you, nor forget the covenant of your fathers which He swore to them.

32 "For ask now concerning the days that are past, which were before you, since the day that God created man on the earth, and *ask* from one end of heaven to the other, whether *any* great *thing* like this has happened, or *anything* like it has been heard. 33 Did *any* people *ever* hear the voice of God speaking out of the midst of the fire, as you have heard, and live? 34 Or did God *ever* try to go *and* take for Himself a nation from the midst of *another* nation, by trials, by signs, by wonders, by war, by a mighty hand and an outstretched arm, and by great terrors, according to all that the LORD your God did for you in Egypt before your eyes? 35 To you it was shown, that you might know that the LORD Himself *is* God; *there is* none other besides Him. 36 Out of heaven He let you hear His voice, that He might instruct you; on earth He showed you His great fire, and you heard His words out of the midst of the fire. 37 And because He loved your fathers, therefore He chose their descendants after them; and He brought you out of Egypt with His Presence, with His mighty power, 38 driving out from before you nations greater and mightier than you, to bring you in, to give you their land *as* an inheritance, as *it is* this day. 39 Therefore know this day, and consider *it* in your heart, that the LORD Himself *is* God in heaven above and on the earth beneath; *there is* no other. 40 You shall therefore keep His statutes and His commandments which I command you today, that it may go well with you and with your children after you, and that you may prolong *your* days in the land which the LORD your God is giving you for all time."

41 Then Moses set apart three cities on this side of the Jordan, toward the rising of the sun, 42 that the manslayer might flee there, who kills his neighbor unintentionally, without having hated him in time past, and that by fleeing to one of these cities he might live: 43 Bezer in the wilderness on the plateau for the Reubenites, Ramoth in Gilead for the Gadites, and Golan in Bashan for the Manassites.

44 Now this *is* the law which Moses set before the children of Israel. 45 These *are* the testimonies, the statutes, and the judgments which Moses spoke to the children of Israel after they came out of Egypt, 46 on this side of the Jordan, in the valley opposite Beth Peor, in the land of Sihon king of the Amorites, who dwelt at Heshbon, whom Moses and the children of Israel defeated after they came out of Egypt. 47 And they took possession of his land

and the land of Og king of Bashan, two kings of the Amorites, who *were* on this side of the Jordan, toward the rising of the sun, [48] from Aroer, which *is* on the bank of the River Arnon, *even* to Mount Sion (that is, Hermon), [49] and all the plain on the east side of the Jordan as far as the Sea of the Arabah, below the slopes of Pisgah.

God gives the Ten Commandments

5 And Moses called all Israel, and said to them: "Hear, O Israel, the statutes and judgments which I speak in your hearing today, that you may learn them and be careful to observe them. [2] The LORD our God made a covenant with us in Horeb. [3] The LORD did not make this covenant with our fathers, but with us, those who *are* here today, all of us who *are* alive. [4] The LORD talked with you face to face on the mountain from the midst of the fire. [5] I stood between the LORD and you at that time, to declare to you the word

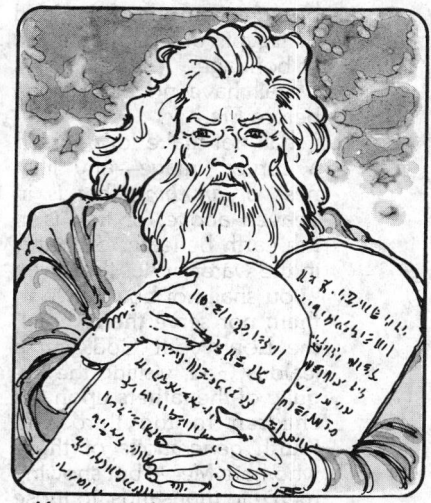

Moses gets the people ready to enter the Promised Land at last by reviewing all that God has done for them.

of the LORD; for you were afraid because of the fire, and you did not go up the mountain. *He* said:
[6] 'I *am* the LORD your God who

DIGGING IN

5:1 Why Moses Wrote Deuteronomy The word *Deuteronomy* (pronounced *dew-ter-ONN-oh-mee*) comes from a Greek word meaning "second law."

But Deuteronomy is not a new law. Remember that the people who heard the Law the first time were now all dead, except for Caleb, Joshua, Moses, and their families. (See Numbers 14:28–33.) The new generation had not heard a public reading of the Law, so Moses now reads the Ten Commandments to them just as He received them from the Lord in Exodus 20.

Besides a review of the laws God had given to Moses earlier, the Book of Deuteronomy is also a series of speeches by Moses. In these speeches, Moses reviews what has happened since the Hebrews left Egypt. He also explains how God expects the people to live from now on as they enter the Promised Land.

Moses blesses the people after warning them about the danger of disobedience. Then he appoints Joshua the next leader of Israel.

5:32, 33 Why God Gave Us the Ten Commandments *RED LIGHT AHEAD!* says the sign. Without good warning signs, our lives can be ruined. Good rules of the road show us the way around the places we can be hurt.

As you study God's Ten Rules (or Commandments) you will see that they aren't just ten separate rules. They are all linked together by one goal—that we may enjoy God and the world that God made. If you think carefully, you can see that people who break God's laws get into a lot of trouble.

When you make something with your hands, you know that you made it to bring you joy. If what you make doesn't make you happy, you throw it away.

God also made you so you could bring Him joy. When you keep God's commands, you are being the person God planned you to be. That pleases Him, and then you are happy, too.

brought you out of the land of Egypt, out of the house of bondage.

7 'You shall have no other gods before Me.

8 'You shall not make for yourself a carved image—any likeness *of anything* that *is* in heaven above, or that *is* in the earth beneath, or that *is* in the water under the earth; 9 you shall not bow down to them nor *serve* them. For I, the LORD your God, *am* a jealous God, visiting the iniquity of the fathers upon the children to the third and fourth *generations* of those who hate Me, 10 but showing mercy to thousands, to those who love Me and keep My commandments.

11 'You shall not take the name of the LORD your God in vain, for the LORD will not hold *him* guiltless who takes His name in vain.

12 'Observe the Sabbath day, to keep it holy, as the LORD your God commanded you. 13 Six days you shall labor and do all your work, 14 but the seventh day *is* the Sabbath of the LORD your God. *In it* you shall do no work: you, nor your son, nor your daughter, nor your male servant, nor your female servant, nor your ox, nor your donkey, nor any of your cattle, nor your stranger who *is* within your gates, that your male servant and your female servant may rest as well as you. 15 And remember that you were a slave in the land of Egypt, and the LORD your God brought you out from there by a mighty hand and by an outstretched arm; therefore the LORD your God commanded you to keep the Sabbath day.

16 'Honor your father and your mother, as the LORD your God has commanded you, that your days may be long, and that it may be well with you in the land which the LORD your God is giving you.

17 'You shall not murder.

18 'You shall not commit adultery.

19 'You shall not steal.

20 'You shall not bear false witness against your neighbor.

21 'You shall not covet your neighbor's *wife*; and you shall not desire your neighbor's house, his field, his male servant, his female servant, his ox, his donkey, or anything that *is* your neighbor's.'

22 "These words the LORD spoke to all your assembly, in the mountain from the midst of the fire, the cloud, and the thick darkness, with a loud voice; and He added no more. And He wrote them on two tablets of stone and gave them to me.

23 "So it was, when you heard the voice from the midst of the darkness, while the mountain was burning with fire, that you came near to me, all the heads of your tribes and your elders. 24 And you said: 'Surely the LORD our God has shown us His glory and His greatness, and we have heard His voice from the midst of the fire. We have seen this day that God speaks with man; yet he *still* lives. 25 Now therefore, why should we die? For this great fire will consume us; if we hear the voice of the LORD our God anymore, then we shall die. 26 For who *is there* of all flesh who has heard the voice of the living God speaking from the midst of the fire, as we *have,* and lived? 27 You go near and hear all that the LORD our God may say, and tell us all that the LORD our God says to you, and we will hear and do *it.*'

28 "Then the LORD heard the voice of your words when you spoke to me, and the LORD said to me: 'I have heard the voice of the words of this people which they have spoken to you. They are right *in* all that they have spoken. 29 Oh, that they had such a heart in

The Ten Commandments For Young Explorers

(Exodus 20:1-17, adapted)

God knows so much more about us than we know about ourselves that He gave us a special set of rules to guarantee the most joyful life we can live. We call these rules the Ten Commandments.

I.

I am your Lord and your God. There is no other God but Me. Do not worship false gods, and do not even make people such as sports heroes, movie stars, and musicians more important to you than I am.

II.

Do not worship any object—pictures, books, crystals—as if it is I.

III.

Remember to use My name only in ways that show Me that you love and respect Me.

IV.

Remember to keep one special day a week just for you and Me. Think about how much I love you and care for you.

V.

Remember to respect your father and mother so you will enjoy a longer and happier life.

VI.

Do not deliberately take away the life I have given someone else. Begin now to learn how to control your temper.

VII.

Do not share your body with anyone except · the person you marry.

VIII.

Do not take anything that does not belong to you—toys, games, clothes, candy, or anything else.

IX.

Do not tell lies. Remember that Satan is the father of lies.

X.

Do not even *wish* for something that belongs to others—your neighbor's big house, your friend's fancy ten-speed bike. Be glad God has blessed them.

Jesus summed up all these rules in one word: LOVE. He said, "Love the Lord your God with all your heart, with all your soul, and with all your mind...and your neighbor as yourself." (Matthew 22: 34–39)

If we love God and others as much as we love ourselves, we will want the very best for them.

them that they would fear Me and always keep all My commandments, that it might be well with them and with their children forever! [30] Go and say to them, "Return to your tents." [31] But as for you, stand here by Me, and I will speak to you all the commandments, the statutes, and the judgments which you shall teach them, that they may observe *them* in the land which I am giving them to possess.'

[32] "Therefore you shall be careful to do as the LORD your God has commanded you; you shall not turn aside to the right hand or to the left. [33] You shall walk in all the ways which the LORD your God has commanded you, that you may live and *that it may be* well with you, and *that* you may prolong *your* days in the land which you shall possess.

God names the greatest commandment

6 "Now this *is* the commandment, *and these are* the statutes and judgments which the LORD your God has commanded to teach you, that you may observe *them* in the land which you are crossing over to possess, [2] that you may fear the LORD your God, to keep all His statutes and His commandments which I command

you, you and your son and your grandson, all the days of your life, and that your days may be prolonged. [3] Therefore hear, O Israel, and be careful to observe *it*, that it may be well with you, and that you may multiply greatly as the LORD God of your fathers has promised you—'a land flowing with milk and honey.'

[4] "Hear, O Israel: The LORD our God, the LORD *is* one! [5] You shall **love** the LORD your God with all your heart, with all your soul, and with all your strength.

[6] "And these words which I command you today shall be in your heart. [7] You shall teach them diligently to your children, and shall talk of them when you sit in your house, when you walk by the way, when you lie down, and when you rise up. [8] You shall bind them as a sign on your hand, and they shall be as frontlets between your eyes. [9] You shall write them on the doorposts of your house and on your gates.

[10] "So it shall be, when the LORD your God brings you into the land of which He swore to your fathers, to Abraham, Isaac, and Jacob, to give you large and beautiful cities which you did not build, [11] houses full of all good things, which you did not fill, hewn-out wells which you did not dig, vineyards and olive trees which you

WORDFINDER

6:5 Love An attitude that leads to the behavior Paul describes in 1 Corinthians 13. Christian love is not selfish but always seeks the best for everybody. Such love is the greatest gift of God.

DIGGING IN

6:5 The Great Commandment When Jesus was asked about the greatest commandment, He used the words of Deuteronomy 6:5: "You shall love the Lord your God with all your heart, with all your soul, and with all your strength."

Don't miss the best in life. You will miss the best if you don't obey this great commandment. Knowing and loving God is worth more than the greatest treasure you can think of. Why is this true? Because

God Himself is the Author and Giver of everything you now have or ever will have. Nothing you own can bring you happiness if you do not love God.

Decide now to love God "with all your heart"—that is, with all your mind, feelings, and decisions. Also, love Him "with all your life"—that is, with all your actions. Finally, love God with "all your might"—that is, with all the strength you have.

did not plant—when you have eaten and are full— 12 then beware, lest you forget the LORD who brought you out of the land of Egypt, from the house of bondage. 13 You shall fear the LORD your God and serve Him, and shall take oaths in His name. 14 You shall not go after other gods, the gods of the peoples who are all around you 15 (for the LORD your God is a jealous God among you), lest the anger of the LORD your God be aroused against you and destroy you from the face of the earth.

16 "You shall not tempt the LORD your God as you tempted Him in Massah. 17 You shall diligently keep the commandments of the LORD your God, His testimonies, and His statutes which He has commanded you. 18 And you shall do what is right and good in the sight of the LORD, that it may be well with you, and that you may go in and possess the good land of which the LORD swore to your fathers, 19 to cast out all your enemies from before you, as the LORD has spoken.

20 "When your son asks you in time to come, saying, 'What is the meaning of the testimonies, the statutes, and the judgments which the LORD our God has commanded you?' 21 then you shall say to your son: 'We were slaves of Pharaoh in Egypt, and the LORD brought us out of Egypt with a mighty hand; 22 and the LORD showed signs and wonders before our eyes, great and severe, against Egypt, Pharaoh, and all his household. 23 Then He brought us out from there, that He might bring us in, to give us the land of which He swore to our fathers. 24 And the LORD commanded us to observe all these statutes, to fear the LORD our God, for our good always, that He might preserve us alive, as it is this day. 25 Then it will be righteousness for us, if we are careful to observe all these commandments before the LORD our God, as He has commanded us.'

The blessings of obedience

7 "When the LORD your God brings you into the land which you go to possess, and has cast out many nations before you, the Hittites and the Girgashites and the Amorites and the Canaanites and the Perizzites and the Hivites and the Jebusites, seven nations greater and mightier than you, 2 and when the LORD your God delivers them over to you, you shall conquer them and utterly destroy them. You shall make no covenant with them nor show mercy to them. 3 Nor shall you make marriages with them. You shall not give your daughter to their son, nor take their daughter for your son. 4 For they will turn your sons away from following Me, to serve other gods; so the anger of the LORD will be aroused against you and destroy you suddenly. 5 But thus you shall deal with them: you shall destroy their altars, and

---

DIGGING IN

7:1,2 Why God Ordered Some Nations to Be Destroyed God promised the land of Canaan (pronounced KAY-nun) to Abraham hundreds of years before Israel conquered it (see Genesis 12, 15, and 17). But since Abraham's time, some very wicked people had lived in the land. They were called Canaanites (pronounced KAY-nuh-nights).

You don't have to read very far in the Bible before you learn that God is also a Judge. As a Judge, He must condemn the wicked. That is what He had to do with those who lived in Canaan when the armies of Israel came.

There can be no kingdom of God where the kingdom of evil is not destroyed.

The people of Canaan were not just living a quiet life and quietly worshiping false gods. They were actually sacrificing their infant children to their gods, and they were doing other kinds of horrible evil. The people there had proved for a long time that they were no longer fit to live in God's world.

Let us pray that we may not become like the Canaanites.

break down their *sacred* pillars, and cut down their wooden images, and burn their carved images with fire.

6 "For you *are* a holy people to the LORD your God; the LORD your God has chosen you to be a people for Himself, a special treasure above all the peoples on the face of the earth. 7 The LORD did not set His love on you nor choose you because you were more in number than any other people, for you were the least of all peoples; 8 but because the LORD loves you, and because He would keep the oath which He swore to your fathers, the LORD has brought you out with a mighty hand, and redeemed you from the house of bondage, from the hand of Pharaoh king of Egypt.

9 "Therefore know that the LORD your God, He *is* God, the faithful God who keeps covenant and mercy for a thousand generations with those who love Him and keep His commandments; 10 and He repays those who hate Him to their face, to destroy them. He will not be slack with him who hates Him; He will repay him to his face. 11 Therefore you shall keep the commandment, the statutes, and the judgments which I command you today, to observe them.

12 "Then it shall come to pass, because you listen to these judgments, and keep and do them, that the LORD your God will keep with you the covenant and the mercy which He swore to your fathers. 13 And He will love you and bless you and multiply you; He will also bless the fruit of your womb and the fruit of your land, your grain and your new wine and your oil, the increase of your cattle and the offspring of your flock, in the land of which He swore to your fathers to give you. 14 You shall be blessed above all peoples; there shall not be a male or female barren among you or among your livestock. 15 And the LORD will take away from you all sickness, and will afflict you with none of the terrible diseases of Egypt which you have known, but will lay *them* on all those who hate you. 16 Also you shall destroy

all the peoples whom the LORD your God delivers over to you; your eye shall have no pity on them; nor shall you serve their gods, for that *will be* a snare to you.

17 "If you should say in your heart, 'These nations are greater than I; how can I dispossess them?'— 18 you shall not be afraid of them, *but* you shall remember well what the LORD your God did to Pharaoh and to all Egypt: 19 the great trials which your eyes saw, the signs and the wonders, the mighty hand and the outstretched arm, by which the LORD your God brought you out. So shall the LORD your God do to all the peoples of whom you are afraid. 20 Moreover the LORD your God will send the hornet among them until those who are left, who hide themselves from you, are destroyed. 21 You shall not be terrified of them; for the LORD your God, the great and awesome God, *is* among you. 22 And the LORD your God will drive out those nations before you little by little; you will be unable to destroy them at once, lest the beasts of the field become *too* numerous for you. 23 But the LORD your God will deliver them over to you, and will inflict defeat upon them until they are destroyed. 24 And He will deliver their kings into your hand, and you will destroy their name from under heaven; no one shall be able to stand against you until you have destroyed them. 25 You shall burn the carved images of their gods with fire; you shall not covet the silver or gold *that is* on them, nor take *it* for yourselves, lest you be snared by it; for it *is* an abomination to the LORD your God. 26 Nor shall you bring an abomination into your house, lest you be doomed to destruction like it. You shall utterly detest it and utterly abhor it, for it *is* an accursed thing.

Remember and obey the Lord

8 "Every commandment which I command you today you must be careful to observe, that you may live and multiply, and go in and possess

Why Did Israel Spend Forty Years in the Desert?

Israel could have entered the Promised Land a short time after leaving Egypt, but they refused to go into the land at first. So the Lord made them stay in the desert for 40 years. During that time nearly a whole generation of people died. But Israel learned to obey the Lord.

the land of which the LORD swore to your fathers. 2 And you shall remember that the LORD your God led you all the way these forty years in the wilderness, to humble you *and* test you, to know what *was* in your heart, whether you would keep His commandments or not. 3 So He humbled you, allowed you to hunger, and fed you with **manna** which you did not know nor did your fathers know, that He might make you know that man shall not live by bread alone; but man lives by every *word* that proceeds from the mouth of the LORD. 4 Your garments did not wear out on you, nor did your foot swell these forty years. 5 You should know in your heart that as a man chastens his son, *so* the LORD your God chastens you.

6 "Therefore you shall keep the commandments of the LORD your God, to walk in His ways and to fear Him. 7 For the LORD your God is bringing you into a good land, a land of brooks of water, of fountains and springs, that flow out of valleys and hills; 8 a land of wheat and barley, of vines and fig trees and pomegranates, a land of olive oil and honey; 9 a land in which you will eat bread without scarcity, in which you will lack nothing; a land whose stones *are* iron and out of whose hills you can dig copper. 10 When you have eaten and are full,

then you shall bless the LORD your God for the good land which He has given you.

11 "Beware that you do not forget the LORD your God by not keeping His commandments, His judgments, and His statutes which I command you today, 12 lest—*when* you have eaten and are full, and have built beautiful houses and dwell *in them;* 13 and *when* your herds and your flocks multiply, and your silver and your gold are multiplied, and all that you have is multiplied; 14 when your heart is lifted up, and you forget the LORD your God who brought you out of the land of Egypt, from the house of bondage; 15 who led you through that great and terrible wilderness, *in which were* fiery serpents and scorpions and thirsty land where there was no water; who brought water for you out of the flinty rock; 16 who fed you in the wilderness with manna, which your fathers did not know, that He might humble you and that He might test you, to do you good in the end— 17 then you say in your heart, 'My power and the might of my hand have gained me this wealth.' 18 "And you shall remember the LORD your God, for *it is* He who gives you power to get wealth, that He may establish His covenant which He swore to your fathers, as *it is* this day. 19 Then it shall be, if you by any means forget the LORD your God, and follow other gods, and serve them and worship them, I testify against you this day that you shall surely perish. 20 As the nations which the LORD destroys before you, so you shall perish, because you would not be obedient to the voice of the LORD your God.

Remember the rebellion at Mount Horeb

9 "Hear, O Israel: You *are* to cross over the Jordan today, and go in to

WORDFINDER

8:3 Manna The miraculous food God gave Israel in the desert. It looked like frost, and when cooked, tasted like pastry. The Hebrew word means "What Is It?".

dispossess nations greater and mightier than yourself, cities great and fortified up to heaven, 2 a people great and tall, the descendants of the Anakim, whom you know, and *of whom* you heard *it* said, 'Who can stand before the descendants of Anak?' 3 Therefore understand today that the LORD your God *is* He who goes over before you *as* a consuming fire. He will destroy them and bring them down before you; so you shall drive them out and destroy them quickly, as the LORD has said to you.

4 "Do not think in your heart, after the LORD your God has cast them out before you, saying, 'Because of my righteousness the LORD has brought me in to possess this land'; but *it is* because of the wickedness of these nations *that* the LORD is driving them out from before you. 5 *It is* not because of your righteousness or the uprightness of your heart *that* you go in to possess their land, but because of the wickedness of these nations *that* the LORD your God drives them out from before you, and that He may fulfill the word which the LORD swore to your fathers, to Abraham, Isaac, and Jacob. 6 Therefore understand that the LORD your God is not giving you this good land to possess because of your righteousness, for you *are* a stiff-necked people.

7 "Remember! Do not forget how you provoked the LORD your God to wrath in the wilderness. From the day that you departed from the land of Egypt until you came to this place, you have been rebellious against the LORD. 8 Also in Horeb you provoked the LORD to wrath, so that the LORD was angry *enough* with you to have destroyed you. 9 When I went up into the mountain to receive the tablets of stone, the tablets of the covenant which the LORD made with you, then I stayed on the mountain forty days and forty nights. I neither ate bread nor drank water. 10 Then the LORD delivered to me two tablets of stone written with the finger of God, and on them *were* all the words which the LORD had spoken to you on the mountain from the midst of the fire in the day of the assembly. 11 And it came to pass, at the end of forty days and forty nights, *that* the LORD gave me the two tablets of stone, the tablets of the covenant.

12 "Then the LORD said to me, 'Arise, go down quickly from here, for your people whom you brought out of Egypt have acted corruptly; they have quickly turned aside from the way which I commanded them; they have made themselves a molded image.'

13 "Furthermore the LORD spoke to me, saying, 'I have seen this people, and indeed they are a stiff-necked people. 14 Let Me alone, that I may destroy them and blot out their name from under heaven; and I will make of you a nation mightier and greater than they.'

15 "So I turned and came down from the mountain, and the mountain burned with fire; and the two tablets

---

⛏ DIGGING IN

9:7–29 We Can Learn from Our Failures Learning from our failures is not the best way to learn, but sometimes it's the only way.

One day a father got tired of correcting his son. So he got a board, a hammer, and some nails and told his son to drive a nail in the board every time he did something wrong. "Then bring the board to me," the father said.

When the board was full of nails, the father told his boy, "That's a sad sight, son, but I'll tell you what—every time you do a good deed, you can pull out a nail."

After many days the boy brought the board back to his father. Sure enough, it was empty. "That's good, son," said the boy's dad, "but look—*the board is full of nail holes!* We'll just hang this board in your bedroom as a reminder of what you've learned."

Israel needed to be reminded of its nail holes, and so do we. But the nail holes we made are in our Savior's hands.

of the covenant *were* in my two hands. 16 And I looked, and behold, you had sinned against the LORD your God— had made for yourselves a molded calf! You had turned aside quickly from the way which the LORD had commanded you. 17 Then I took the two tablets and threw them out of my two hands and broke them before your eyes. 18 And I fell down before the LORD, as at the first, forty days and forty nights; I neither ate bread nor drank water, because of all your sin which you committed in doing wickedly in the sight of the LORD, to provoke Him to anger. 19 For I was afraid of the anger and hot displeasure with which the LORD was angry with you, to destroy you. But the LORD listened to me at that time also. 20 And the LORD was very angry with Aaron *and* would have destroyed him; so I prayed for Aaron also at the same time. 21 Then I took your sin, the calf which you had made, and burned it with fire and crushed it *and* ground *it* very small, until it was as fine as dust; and I threw its dust into the brook that descended from the mountain.

22 "Also at Taberah and Massah and Kibroth Hattaavah you provoked the LORD to wrath. 23 Likewise, when the LORD sent you from Kadesh Barnea, saying, 'Go up and possess the land which I have given you,' then you rebelled against the commandment of the LORD your God, and you did not believe Him nor obey His voice. 24 You have been rebellious against the LORD from the day that I knew you.

25 "Thus I prostrated myself before the LORD; forty days and forty nights I kept prostrating myself, because the LORD had said He would destroy you. 26 Therefore I prayed to the LORD, and said: 'O Lord GOD, do not destroy Your people and Your inheritance whom You have redeemed through Your greatness, whom You have brought out of Egypt with a mighty hand. 27 Remember Your servants, Abraham, Isaac, and Jacob; do not look on the stubbornness of this people, or on their wickedness or their sin,

28 lest the land from which You brought us should say, "Because the LORD was not able to bring them to the land which He promised them, and because He hated them, He has brought them out to kill them in the wilderness." 29 Yet they *are* Your people and Your inheritance, whom You brought out by Your mighty power and by Your outstretched arm.'

Moses receives a second pair of stone tablets

10 "At that time the LORD said to me, 'Hew for yourself two tablets of stone like the first, and come up to Me on the mountain and make yourself an ark of wood. 2 And I will write on the tablets the words that were on the first tablets, which you broke; and you shall put them in the ark.'

3 "So I made an ark of acacia wood, hewed two tablets of stone like the first, and went up the mountain, having the two tablets in my hand. 4 And He wrote on the tablets according to the first writing, the Ten Commandments, which the LORD had spoken to you in the mountain from the midst of the fire in the day of the assembly; and the LORD gave them to me. 5 Then I turned and came down from the mountain, and put the tablets in the ark which I had made; and there they are, just as the LORD commanded me."

6 (Now the children of Israel journeyed from the wells of Bene Jaakan to Moserah, where Aaron died, and where he was buried; and Eleazar his son ministered as priest in his stead. 7 From there they journeyed to Gudgodah, and from Gudgodah to Jotbathah, a land of rivers of water. 8 At that time the LORD separated the tribe of Levi to bear the ark of the covenant of the LORD, to stand before the LORD to minister to Him and to bless in His name, to this day. 9 Therefore Levi has no portion nor inheritance with his brethren; the LORD *is* his inheritance, just as the LORD your God promised him.)

10 "As at the first time, I stayed in the mountain forty days and forty nights; the LORD also heard me at that time, *and* the LORD chose not to destroy you. 11 Then the LORD said to me, 'Arise, begin *your* journey before the people, that they may go in and possess the land which I swore to their fathers to give them.'

12 "And now, Israel, what does the LORD your God require of you, but to fear the LORD your God, to walk in all His ways and to love Him, to serve the LORD your God with all your heart and with all your soul, 13 *and* to keep the commandments of the LORD and His statutes which I command you today for your good? 14 Indeed heaven and the highest heavens belong to the LORD your God, *also* the earth with all that *is* in it. 15 The LORD delighted only in your fathers, to love them; and He chose their descendants after them, you above all peoples, as *it is* this day. 16 Therefore circumcise the foreskin of your heart, and be stiff-necked no longer. 17 For the LORD your God *is* God of gods and Lord of lords, the great God, mighty and awesome, who shows no partiality nor takes a bribe. 18 He administers justice for the fatherless and the widow, and loves the stranger, giving him food and clothing. 19 Therefore love the stranger, for you were strangers in the land of Egypt. 20 You shall fear the LORD your God; you shall serve Him, and to Him you shall hold fast, and take oaths in His name. 21 He *is* your praise, and He *is* your God, who has done for you these great and awesome things which your eyes have seen. 22 Your fathers went down to Egypt with seventy persons, and now the LORD your God has made you as the stars of heaven in multitude.

The blessings of the Promised Land

11 "Therefore you shall love the LORD your God, and keep His charge, His statutes, His judgments, and His commandments always. 2 Know today that *I do* not *speak* with your children, who have not known and who have not seen the chastening of the LORD your God, His greatness and His mighty hand and His outstretched arm— 3 His signs and His acts which He did in the midst of Egypt, to Pharaoh king of Egypt, and to all his land; 4 what He did to the army of Egypt, to their horses and their chariots: how He made the waters of the Red Sea overflow them as they pursued you, and *how* the LORD has destroyed them to this day; 5 what He did for you in the wilderness until you came to this place; 6 and what He did to Dathan and Abiram the sons of Eliab, the son of Reuben: how the earth opened its mouth and swallowed them up, their households, their tents, and all the substance that *was* in their possession, in the midst of all Israel— 7 but your eyes have seen every great act of the LORD which He did.

8 "Therefore you shall keep every commandment which I command you today, that you may be strong, and go in and possess the land which you cross over to possess, 9 and that you may prolong *your* days in the land which the LORD swore to give your fathers, to them and their descendants, 'a land flowing with milk and honey.' 10 For the land which you go to possess *is* not like the land of Egypt from which you have come, where you sowed your seed and watered *it* by foot, as a vegetable garden; 11 but the land which you cross over to possess *is* a land of hills and valleys, which drinks water from the rain of heaven, 12 a land for which the LORD your God cares; the eyes of the LORD your God *are* always on it, from the beginning of the year to the very end of the year.

13 'And it shall be that if you earnestly obey My commandments which I command you today, to love the LORD your God and serve Him with all your heart and with all your soul, 14 then I will give *you* the rain for your land in its season, the early rain and the latter rain, that you may gather in your grain, your new wine, and your oil. 15 And I will send grass in your

fields for your livestock, that you may eat and be filled.' 16 Take heed to yourselves, lest your heart be deceived, and you turn aside and serve other gods and worship them, 17 lest the LORD's anger be aroused against you, and He shut up the heavens so that there be no rain, and the land yield no produce, and you perish quickly from the good land which the LORD is giving you.

18 "Therefore you shall lay up these words of mine in your heart and in your soul, and bind them as a sign on your hand, and they shall be as frontlets between your eyes. 19 You shall teach them to your children, speaking of them when you sit in your house, when you walk by the way, when you lie down, and when you rise up. 20 And you shall write them on the doorposts of your house and on your gates, 21 that your days and the days of your children may be multiplied in the land of which the LORD swore to your fathers to give them, like the days of the heavens above the earth.

22 "For if you carefully keep all these commandments which I command you to do—to love the LORD your God, to walk in all His ways, and to hold fast to Him— 23 then the LORD will drive out all these nations from before you, and you will dispossess greater and mightier nations than yourselves. 24 Every place on which the sole of your foot treads shall be yours: from the wilderness and Lebanon, from the river, the River Euphrates, even to the Western Sea, shall be your territory. 25 No man shall be able to stand against you; the LORD your God will put the dread of you and the fear of you upon all the land where you tread, just as He has said to you.

26 "Behold, I set before you today a blessing and a curse: 27 the blessing, if you obey the commandments of the LORD your God which I command you today; 28 and the curse, if you do not obey the commandments of the LORD your God, but turn aside from the way which I command you today, to go after other gods which you have not known. 29 Now it shall be, when the

LORD your God has brought you into the land which you go to possess, that you shall put the blessing on Mount Gerizim and the curse on Mount Ebal. 30 Are they not on the other side of the Jordan, toward the setting sun, in the land of the Canaanites who dwell in the plain opposite Gilgal, beside the terebinth trees of Moreh? 31 For you will cross over the Jordan and go in to possess the land which the LORD your God is giving you, and you will possess it and dwell in it. 32 And you shall be careful to observe all the statutes and judgments which I set before you today.

God demands loyalty and worship

12 "These are the statutes and judgments which you shall be careful to observe in the land which the LORD God of your fathers is giving you to possess, all the days that you live on the earth. 2 You shall utterly destroy all the places where the nations which you shall dispossess served their gods, on the high mountains and on the hills and under every green tree. 3 And you shall destroy their altars, break their sacred pillars, and burn their wooden images with fire; you shall cut down the carved images of their gods and destroy their names from that place. 4 You shall not worship the LORD your God with such things.

5 "But you shall seek the place where the LORD your God chooses, out of all your tribes, to put His name for His dwelling place; and there you shall go. 6 There you shall take your burnt offerings, your sacrifices, your tithes, the heave offerings of your hand, your vowed offerings, your freewill offerings, and the firstborn of your herds and flocks. 7 And there you shall eat before the LORD your God, and you shall rejoice in all to which you have put your hand, you and your households, in which the LORD your God has blessed you.

8 "You shall not at all do as we are doing here today—every man doing whatever is right in his own eyes—

9 for as yet you have not come to the rest and the inheritance which the LORD your God is giving you. 10 But *when* you cross over the Jordan and dwell in the land which the LORD your God is giving you to inherit, and He gives you rest from all your enemies round about, so that you dwell in safety, 11 then there will be the place where the LORD your God chooses to make His name abide. There you shall bring all that I command you: your burnt offerings, your sacrifices, your tithes, the heave offerings of your hand, and all your choice offerings which you vow to the LORD. 12 And you shall rejoice before the LORD your God, you and your sons and your daughters, your male and female servants, and the Levite who *is* within your gates, since he has no portion nor inheritance with you. 13 Take heed to yourself that you do not offer your burnt offerings in *every* place that you see; 14 but in the place which the LORD chooses, in one of your tribes, there you shall offer your burnt offerings, and there you shall do all that I command you.

15 "However, you may slaughter and eat meat within all your gates, whatever your heart desires, according to the blessing of the LORD your God which He has given you; the unclean and the clean may eat of it, of the gazelle and the deer alike. 16 Only you shall not eat the blood; you shall pour it on the earth like water. 17 You may not eat within your gates the tithe of your grain or your new wine or your oil, of the firstborn of your herd or your flock, of any of your offerings which you vow, of your freewill offerings, or of the heave offering of your hand. 18 But you must eat them before the LORD your God in the place which the LORD your God chooses, you and your son and your daughter, your male servant and your female servant, and the Levite who *is* within your gates; and you shall rejoice before the LORD your God in all to which you put your hands. 19 Take heed to yourself that you do not forsake the Levite as long as you live in your land.

20 "When the LORD your God enlarges your border as He has promised you, and you say, 'Let me eat meat,' because you long to eat meat, you may eat as much meat as your heart desires. 21 If the place where the LORD your God chooses to put His name is too far from you, then you may slaughter from your herd and from your flock which the LORD has given you, just as I have commanded you, and you may eat within your gates as much as your heart desires. 22 Just as the gazelle and the deer are eaten, so you may eat them; the unclean and the clean alike may eat them. 23 Only be sure that you do not eat the blood, for the blood *is* the life; you may not eat the life with the meat. 24 You shall not eat it; you shall pour it on the earth like water. 25 You shall not eat it, that it may go well with you and your children after you, when you do *what is* right in the sight of the LORD. 26 Only the holy things which you have, and your vowed offerings, you shall take and go to the place which the LORD chooses.

⚒ DIGGING IN

12:11 Giving to God By now you may have heard someone speak about tithing (pronounced *TIE-thing*). A tithe is one-tenth of one's possessions.

Of course everything you are and everything you have comes from God. You may say, "Yes, but I worked for it!" But you couldn't work at all if God didn't give you the strength and the chance to work. So you really owe God everything. But God is practical, and He knows what we need to live. So He says, "You can keep most of it; I only want a tenth." God is very generous to ask us for only a tenth of our money. It costs a lot to send a missionary across the sea.

The time to start tithing is *now*. Then, as you grow up, tithing will be a habit of life. People who tithe say, "It seems like the more I give to God, the more He gives back to me."

27 And you shall offer your burnt offerings, the meat and the blood, on the altar of the LORD your God; and the blood of your sacrifices shall be poured out on the altar of the LORD your God, and you shall eat the meat. 28 Observe and obey all these words which I command you, that it may go well with you and your children after you forever, when you do *what is* good and right in the sight of the LORD your God.

29 "When the LORD your God cuts off from before you the nations which you go to dispossess, and you displace them and dwell in their land, 30 take heed to yourself that you are not ensnared to follow them, after they are destroyed from before you, and that you do not inquire after their gods, saying, 'How did these nations serve their gods? I also will do likewise.' 31 You shall not worship the LORD your God in that way; for every abomination to the LORD which He hates they have done to their gods; for they burn even their sons and daughters in the fire to their gods.

32 "Whatever I command you, be careful to observe it; you shall not add to it nor take away from it.

Worshipers of false gods will be punished

13 "If there arises among you a prophet or a dreamer of dreams, and he gives you a sign or a wonder, 2 and the sign or the wonder comes to pass, of which he spoke to you, saying, 'Let us go after other gods'— which you have not known—'and let us serve them,' 3 you shall not listen to the words of that prophet or that dreamer of dreams, for the LORD your God is testing you to know whether you love the LORD your God with all your heart and with all your soul. 4 You shall walk after the LORD your God and fear Him, and keep His commandments and obey His voice; you shall serve Him and hold fast to Him. 5 But that prophet or that dreamer of dreams shall be put to death, because he has spoken in order to turn *you*

away from the LORD your God, who brought you out of the land of Egypt and redeemed you from the house of bondage, to entice you from the way in which the LORD your God commanded you to walk. So you shall put away the evil from your midst.

6 "If your brother, the son of your mother, your son or your daughter, the wife of your bosom, or your friend who is as your own soul, secretly entices you, saying, 'Let us go and serve other gods,' which you have not known, neither you nor your fathers, 7 of the gods of the people which *are* all around you, near to you or far off from you, from *one* end of the earth to the *other* end of the earth, 8 you shall not consent to him or listen to him, nor shall your eye pity him, nor shall you spare him or conceal him; 9 but you shall surely kill him; your hand shall be first against him to put him to death, and afterward the hand of all the people. 10 And you shall stone him with stones until he dies, because he sought to entice you away from the LORD your God, who brought you out of the land of Egypt, from the house of bondage. 11 So all Israel shall hear and fear, and not again do such wickedness as this among you.

12 "If you hear someone in one of your cities, which the LORD your God gives you to dwell in, saying, 13 'Corrupt men have gone out from among you and enticed the inhabitants of their city, saying, "Let us go and serve other gods" '—which you have not known— 14 then you shall inquire, search out, and ask diligently. And *if it is* indeed true *and* certain *that* such an abomination was committed among you, 15 you shall surely strike the inhabitants of that city with the edge of the sword, utterly destroying it, all that is in it and its livestock—with the edge of the sword. 16 And you shall gather all its plunder into the middle of the street, and completely burn with fire the city and all its plunder, for the LORD your God. It shall be a heap forever; it shall not be built again. 17 So none of the accursed things shall remain in your hand, that the LORD may turn from the

fierceness of His anger and show you mercy, have compassion on you and multiply you, just as He swore to your fathers, 18 because you have listened to the voice of the LORD your God, to keep all His commandments which I command you today, to do *what is* right in the eyes of the LORD your God.

Clean and unclean food

14 "You *are* the children of the LORD your God; you shall not cut yourselves nor shave the front of your head for the dead. 2 For you *are* a holy people to the LORD your God, and the LORD has chosen you to be a people for Himself, a special treasure above all the peoples who *are* on the face of the earth.

3 "You shall not eat any detestable thing. 4 These *are* the animals which you may eat: the ox, the sheep, the goat, 5 the deer, the gazelle, the roe deer, the wild goat, the mountain goat, the antelope, and the mountain sheep. 6 And you may eat *every* animal with cloven hooves, having the hoof split into two parts, *and that* chews the cud, among the animals. 7 Nevertheless, of those that chew the cud or have cloven hooves, you shall not eat, *such as* these: the camel, the hare, and the rock hyrax; for they chew the cud but do not have cloven hooves; they *are* unclean for you. 8 Also the swine is unclean for you, because it has cloven hooves, yet *does* not *chew* the cud; you shall not eat their flesh or touch their dead carcasses.

9 "These you may eat of all that *are* in the waters: you may eat all that have fins and scales. 10 And whatever does not have fins and scales you shall not eat; it *is* unclean for you.

11 "All clean birds you may eat. 12 But these you shall not eat: the eagle, the vulture, the buzzard, 13 the red kite, the falcon, and the kite after their kinds; 14 every raven after its kind; 15 the ostrich, the short-eared owl, the sea gull, and the hawk after their kinds; 16 the little owl, the screech owl, the white owl, 17 the jackdaw, the carrion vulture, the fisher owl, 18 the stork, the heron after its kind, and the hoopoe and the bat.

19 "Also every creeping thing that flies is unclean for you; they shall not be eaten.

20 "You may eat all clean birds.

21 "You shall not eat anything that dies *of itself;* you may give it to the alien who is within your gates, that he may eat it, or you may sell it to a foreigner; for you *are* a holy people to the LORD your God.

"You shall not boil a young goat in its mother's milk.

22 "You shall truly tithe all the increase of your grain that the field produces year by year. 23 And you shall eat before the LORD your God, in the place where He chooses to make His name abide, the tithe of your grain and your new wine and your oil, of the firstborn of your herds and your flocks, that you may learn to fear the LORD your God always. 24 But if the journey is too long for you, so that you are not able to carry *the tithe, or* if the place where the LORD your God chooses to put His name is too far from you, when the LORD your God has blessed you, 25 then you shall exchange *it* for money, take the money in your hand, and go to the place which the LORD your God chooses. 26 And you shall spend that money for whatever your heart desires: for oxen or sheep, for wine or similar drink, for whatever your heart desires; you shall eat there before the LORD your God, and you shall rejoice, you and your household. 27 You shall not forsake the Levite who *is* within your gates, for he has no part nor inheritance with you.

28 "At the end of *every* third year you shall bring out the tithe of your produce of that year and store *it* up within your gates. 29 And the Levite, because he has no portion nor inheritance with you, and the stranger and the fatherless and the widow who *are* within your gates, may come and eat and be satisfied, that the LORD your God may bless you in all the work of your hand which you do.

The law about the year of release

15 "At the end of *every* seven years you shall grant a release *of debts*. ² And this *is* the form of the release: Every creditor who has lent *anything* to his neighbor shall release *it;* he shall not require *it* of his neighbor or his brother, because it is called the Lord's release. ³ Of a foreigner you may require *it;* but you shall give up your claim to what is owed by your brother, ⁴ except when there may be no poor among you; for the Lord will greatly bless you in the land which the Lord your God is giving you to possess *as* an inheritance— ⁵ only if you carefully obey the voice of the Lord your God, to observe with care all these commandments which I command you today. ⁶ For the Lord your God will bless you just as He promised you; you shall lend to many nations, but you shall not borrow; you shall reign over many nations, but they shall not reign over you.

⁷ "If there is among you a poor man of your brethren, within any of the gates in your land which the Lord your God is giving you, you shall not harden your heart nor shut your hand from your poor brother, ⁸ but you shall open your hand wide to him and willingly lend him sufficient for his need, whatever he needs. ⁹ Beware lest there be a wicked thought in your heart, saying, 'The seventh year, the year of release, is at hand,' and your eye be evil against your poor brother and you give him nothing, and he cry out to the Lord against you, and it become sin among

you. ¹⁰ You shall surely give to him, and your heart should not be grieved when you give to him, because for this thing the Lord your God will bless you in all your works and in all to which you put your hand. ¹¹ For the poor will never cease from the land; therefore I command you, saying, 'You shall open your hand wide to your brother, to your poor and your needy, in your land.'

¹² "If your brother, a Hebrew man, or a Hebrew woman, is sold to you and serves you six years, then in the seventh year you shall let him go free from you. ¹³ And when you send him away free from you, you shall not let him go away empty-handed; ¹⁴ you shall supply him liberally from your flock, from your threshing floor, and from your winepress. *From what* the Lord has blessed you with, you shall give to him. ¹⁵ You shall remember that you were a slave in the land of Egypt, and the Lord your God redeemed you; therefore I command you this thing today. ¹⁶ And if it happens that he says to you, 'I will not go away from you,' because he loves

Does God Care for the Poor?

God never changes. He has always loved His people even when they were disobedient. So he cared for poor people in Old Testament times. Christians should be leaders in caring for poor people. Then we will be known as people who are like God.

DIGGING IN

15:1–6 Be Generous to Your Neighbors The real proof that someone loves God is that he loves others, too. Love is not just a warm fuzzy, or a kind feeling. Love *works*.

Being kind to nice people is easy. But you may know some people who are not always nice. That fact doesn't allow you to act in an unkind way. You aren't expected to give away everything you own, but sharing with others in need is a

mark of love.

A little boy lived across the fence from a little girl. The boy had a tricycle, but the girl had none. So the little boy took apart his tricycle and gave half of it to the little girl! Of course, neither the boy nor the girl had much to play with. But the idea in the boy's heart was right.

Generous actions send a message to hopeless people that God still lives.

you and your house, since he prospers with you, 17 then you shall take an awl and thrust *it* through his ear to the door, and he shall be your servant forever. Also to your female servant you shall do likewise. 18 It shall not seem hard to you when you send him away free from you; for he has been worth a double hired servant in serving you six years. Then the LORD your God will bless you in all that you do.

19 "All the firstborn males that come from your herd and your flock you shall **sanctify** to the LORD your God; you shall do no work with the firstborn of your herd, nor shear the firstborn of your flock. 20 You and your household shall eat *it* before the LORD your God year by year in the place which the LORD chooses. 21 But if there is a defect in it, *if it is* lame or blind *or has* any serious defect, you shall not sacrifice it to the LORD your God. 22 You may eat it within your gates; the unclean and the clean *person* alike *may eat it,* as *if it were* a gazelle or a deer. 23 Only you shall not eat its blood; you shall pour it on the ground like water.

The three main feasts

16 "Observe the month of Abib, and keep the Passover to the LORD your God, for in the month of Abib the LORD your God brought you out of Egypt by night. 2 Therefore you shall sacrifice the Passover to the LORD your God, from the flock and the herd, in the place where the LORD chooses to put His name. 3 You shall eat no leavened bread with it; seven days you shall eat unleavened bread with it, *that is,* the bread of affliction (for you came out of the land of Egypt in haste), that you may remember the day in which you came out of the land of Egypt all the days of your life. 4 And no leaven shall be seen among you in all your territory for seven days, nor shall *any*

of the meat which you sacrifice the first day at twilight remain overnight until morning.

5 "You may not sacrifice the Passover within any of your gates which the LORD your God gives you; 6 but at the place where the LORD your God chooses to make His name abide, there you shall sacrifice the Passover at twilight, at the going down of the sun, at the time you came out of Egypt. 7 And you shall roast and eat *it* in the place which the LORD your God chooses, and in the morning you shall turn and go to your tents. 8 Six days you shall eat unleavened bread, and on the seventh day there *shall be* a sacred assembly to the LORD your God. You shall do no work *on it.*

9 "You shall count seven weeks for yourself; begin to count the seven weeks from *the time* you begin *to put* the sickle to the grain. 10 Then you shall keep the Feast of Weeks to the LORD your God with the tribute of a freewill offering from your hand, which you shall give as the LORD your God blesses you. 11 You shall rejoice before the LORD your God, you and your son and your daughter, your male servant and your female servant, the Levite who *is* within your gates, the stranger and the fatherless and the widow who *are* among you, at the place where the LORD your God chooses to make His name abide. 12 And you shall remember that you were a slave in Egypt, and you shall be careful to observe these statutes.

13 "You shall observe the Feast of Tabernacles seven days, when you have gathered from your threshing floor and from your winepress. 14 And you shall rejoice in your feast, you and your son and your daughter, your male servant and your female servant and the Levite, the stranger and the fatherless and the widow, who *are* within your gates. 15 Seven days you shall

keep a sacred feast to the LORD your God in the place which the LORD chooses, because the LORD your God will bless you in all your produce and in all the work of your hands, so that you surely rejoice.

16 "Three times a year all your males shall appear before the LORD your God in the place which He chooses: at the Feast of Unleavened Bread, at the Feast of Weeks, and at the Feast of Tabernacles; and they shall not appear before the LORD empty-handed. 17 Every man *shall give* as he is able, according to the blessing of the LORD your God which He has given you.

18 "You shall appoint judges and officers in all your gates, which the LORD your God gives you, according to your tribes, and they shall judge the people with just judgment. 19 You shall not pervert justice; you shall not show partiality, nor take a bribe, for a bribe blinds the eyes of the wise and twists the words of the righteous. 20 You shall follow what is altogether just, that you may live and inherit the land which the LORD your God is giving you.

21 "You shall not plant for yourself any tree, as a wooden image, near the altar which you build for yourself to the LORD your God. 22 You shall not set up a sacred pillar, which the LORD your God hates.

Various instructions

17 "You shall not sacrifice to the LORD your God a bull or sheep which has any blemish *or* defect, for that *is* an abomination to the LORD your God.

2 "If there is found among you, within any of your gates which the LORD your God gives you, a man or a woman who has been wicked in the sight of the LORD your God, in transgressing His covenant, 3 who has gone and served other gods and worshiped them, either the sun or moon or any of the host of heaven, which I have not commanded, 4 and it is told you, and you hear *of it,* then you shall inquire diligently. And if *it is* indeed true *and* certain that such an abomination

has been committed in Israel, 5 then you shall bring out to your gates that man or woman who has committed that wicked thing, and shall stone to death that man or woman with stones. 6 Whoever is deserving of death shall be put to death on the testimony of two or three witnesses; he shall not be put to death on the testimony of one witness. 7 The hands of the witnesses shall be the first against him to put him to death, and afterward the hands of all the people. So you shall put away the evil from among you.

8 "If a matter arises which is too hard for you to judge, between degrees of guilt for bloodshed, between one judgment or another, or between one punishment or another, matters of controversy within your gates, then you shall arise and go up to the place which the LORD your God chooses. 9 And you shall come to the priests, the Levites, and to the judge *there* in those days, and inquire *of them;* they shall pronounce upon you the sentence of judgment. 10 You shall do according to the sentence which they pronounce upon you in that place which the LORD chooses. And you shall be careful to do according to all that they order you. 11 According to the sentence of the law in which they instruct you, according to the judgment which they tell you, you shall do; you shall not turn aside *to* the right hand or *to* the left from the sentence which they pronounce upon you. 12 Now the man who acts presumptuously and will not heed the priest who stands to minister there before the LORD your God, or the judge, that man shall die. So you shall put away the evil from Israel. 13 And all the people shall hear and fear, and no longer act presumptuously.

14 "When you come to the land which the LORD your God is giving you, and possess it and dwell in it, and say, 'I will set a king over me like all the nations that *are* around me,' 15 you shall surely set a king over you whom the LORD your God chooses; *one* from among your brethren you shall set as king over you; you may

not set a foreigner over you, who is not your brother. 16 But he shall not multiply horses for himself, nor cause the people to return to Egypt to multiply horses, for the LORD has said to you, 'You shall not return that way again.' 17 Neither shall he multiply wives for himself, lest his heart turn away; nor shall he greatly multiply silver and gold for himself.

18 "Also it shall be, when he sits on the throne of his kingdom, that he shall write for himself a copy of this law in a book, from the one before the priests, the Levites. 19 And it shall be with him, and he shall read it all the days of his life, that he may learn to fear the LORD his God and be careful to observe all the words of this law and these statutes, 20 that his heart may not be lifted above his brethren, that he may not turn aside from the commandment to the right hand or to the left, and that he may prolong his days in his kingdom, he and his children in the midst of Israel.

The Levites' share; a new prophet is coming

18 "The priests, the Levites—all the tribe of Levi—shall have no part nor inheritance with Israel; they shall eat the offerings of the LORD made by fire, and His portion. 2 Therefore they shall have no inheritance among their brethren; the LORD is their inheritance, as He said to them.

3 "And this shall be the priest's due from the people, from those who offer a sacrifice, whether it is bull or sheep: they shall give to the priest the shoulder, the cheeks, and the stomach. 4 The firstfruits of your grain and your new wine and your oil, and the first of the fleece of your sheep, you shall give him. 5 For the LORD your God has chosen him out of all your tribes to stand to minister in the name of the LORD, him and his sons forever.

6 "So if a Levite comes from any of your gates, from where he dwells among all Israel, and comes with all the desire of his mind to the place which the LORD chooses, 7 then he may serve in the name of the LORD his God as all his brethren the Levites do, who stand there before the LORD. 8 They shall have equal portions to eat, besides what comes from the sale of his inheritance.

9 "When you come into the land which the LORD your God is giving you, you shall not learn to follow the abominations of those nations. 10 There shall not be found among you anyone who makes his son or his daughter pass through the fire, or one who practices witchcraft, or a soothsayer, or one who interprets omens, or a sorcerer, 11 or one who conjures spells, or a medium, or a spiritist, or one who calls up the dead. 12 For all who do these things are an abomination to the LORD, and because of these abominations the LORD your God drives them out from before you. 13 You shall be blameless before the LORD your God. 14 For these nations which you will dispossess listened to soothsayers and diviners; but

🪓 DIGGING IN

18:9–14 Beware of the Occult Even today some people in our land are practicing evil magic and witchcraft. Others even sacrifice children to Satan. You don't have to be very smart to know that God hates these things. Such practices are part of the "occult" (pronounced oh-KULT).

Many people who don't worship God become curious about magic and the world of unseen spirits. Such people often find themselves trapped into doing things that destroy themselves and others. Illegal drugs often play a part in occult activities.

When you know Jesus, you realize how sad such people are. Jesus is the Head of all unseen spirits, and He has overcome Satan. To know Jesus is to be free from the occult. Jesus is the Truth who makes you free from all slavery to Satan (see John 8:36).

Did Moses Tell About Christ's Coming?

We are the people who look back two thousand years to the time when Christ came. Moses, however, looked forward fifteen hundred years to the coming of "a Prophet like me." That Prophet was Christ. You can see that people in Moses' time believed in Jesus even though they never saw Him.

as for you, the LORD your God has not appointed such for you.

15 "The LORD your God will raise up for you a Prophet like me from your midst, from your brethren. Him you shall hear, 16 according to all you desired of the LORD your God in Horeb in the day of the assembly, saying, 'Let me not hear again the voice of the LORD my God, nor let me see this great fire anymore, lest I die.'

17 "And the LORD said to me: 'What they have spoken is good. 18 I will raise up for them a Prophet like you from among their brethren, and will put My words in His mouth, and He shall speak to them all that I command Him. 19 And it shall be that whoever will not hear My words, which He speaks in My name, I will require it of him. 20 But the prophet who presumes to speak a word in My name, which I have not commanded him to speak, or who speaks in the name of other gods, that prophet shall die.' 21 And if you say in your heart, 'How shall we know the word which the LORD has not spoken?'— 22 when a prophet speaks in the name of the LORD, if the thing does not happen or come to pass, that is the thing which the LORD has not spoken; the prophet has spoken it presumptuously; you shall not be afraid of him.

Cities of safety

19 "When the LORD your God has cut off the nations whose land the LORD

your God is giving you, and you dispossess them and dwell in their cities and in their houses, 2 you shall separate three cities for yourself in the midst of your land which the LORD your God is giving you to possess. 3 You shall prepare roads for yourself, and divide into three parts the territory of your land which the LORD your God is giving you to inherit, that any manslayer may flee there.

4 "And this is the case of the manslayer who flees there, that he may live: Whoever kills his neighbor unintentionally, not having hated him in time past— 5 as when a man goes to the woods with his neighbor to cut timber, and his hand swings a stroke with the ax to cut down the tree, and the head slips from the handle and strikes his neighbor so that he dies—he shall flee to one of these cities and live; 6 lest the avenger of blood, while his anger is hot, pursue the manslayer and overtake him, because the way is long, and kill him, though he was not deserving of death, since he had not hated the victim in time past. 7 Therefore I command you, saying, 'You shall separate three cities for yourself.'

8 "Now if the LORD your God enlarges your territory, as He swore to your fathers, and gives you the land which He promised to give to your fathers, 9 and if you keep all these commandments and do them, which I command you today, to love the LORD your God and to walk always in His ways, then you shall add three more cities for yourself besides these three, 10 lest innocent blood be shed in the midst of your land which the LORD your God is giving you as an inheritance, and thus guilt of bloodshed be upon you.

11 "But if anyone hates his neighbor, lies in wait for him, rises against him and strikes him mortally, so that he dies, and he flees to one of these cities, 12 then the elders of his city shall send and bring him from there, and deliver him over to the hand of the avenger of blood, that he may die. 13 Your eye shall not pity him, but you shall put

away *the guilt of* innocent blood from Israel, that it may go well with you.

14 "You shall not remove your neighbor's landmark, which the men of old have set, in your inheritance which you will inherit in the land that the LORD your God is giving you to possess.

15 "One witness shall not rise against a man concerning any iniquity or any sin that he commits; by the mouth of two or three witnesses the matter shall be established. 16 If a false witness rises against any man to testify against him of wrongdoing, 17 then both men in the controversy shall stand before the LORD, before the priests and the judges who serve in those days. 18 And the judges shall make careful inquiry, and indeed, *if* the witness *is* a false witness, who has testified falsely against his brother, 19 then you shall do to him as he thought to have done to his brother; so you shall put away the evil from among you. 20 And those who remain shall hear and fear, and hereafter they shall not again commit such evil among you. 21 Your eye shall not pity: life *shall be* for life, eye for eye, tooth for tooth, hand for hand, foot for foot.

Laws about war

20 "When you go out to battle against your enemies, and see horses and chariots *and* people more numerous than you, do not be afraid of them; for the LORD your God *is* with you, who brought you up from the land of Egypt. 2 So it shall be, when you are on the verge of battle, that the priest shall approach and speak to the people. 3 And he shall say to them, 'Hear, O Israel: Today you are on the verge of battle with your enemies. Do not

Don't be afraid of your enemies, no matter how fierce they look.

DIGGING IN

20:1–4 Are You a Soldier for Jesus?
The fact of war should tell us that we still live in a sinful world. If God could have given Israel the Promised Land of Canaan without war, He would have done so. We have seen before that God sent His armies into Canaan to judge that nation for its horrible sins (see Deuteronomy 7 and the note there).

Now Jesus calls us to a new kind of war. It is not a war of physical combat and bloodshed. Jesus is leading His people in a *spiritual* war against the unseen kingdom of Satan. Our main weapon in this war is the Word of God. The Holy Spirit gives us power to fight and win the Christian war.

Christ's method or strategy is to send His army of people into all the world to proclaim the gospel of free salvation to all who will trust Jesus.

You, too, may have a part in Christ's war. Ask the Lord to show you how He wants you to serve in His army.

let your heart faint, do not be afraid, and do not tremble or be terrified because of them; 4 for the Lord your God *is* He who goes with you, to fight for you against your enemies, to save you.'

5 "Then the officers shall speak to the people, saying: 'What man *is there* who has built a new house and has not dedicated it? Let him go and return to his house, lest he die in the battle and another man dedicate it. 6 Also what man *is there* who has planted a vineyard and has not eaten of it? Let him go and return to his house, lest he die in the battle and another man eat of it. 7 And what man *is there* who is betrothed to a woman and has not married her? Let him go and return to his house, lest he die in the battle and another man marry her.'

8 "The officers shall speak further to the people, and say, 'What man *is there who is* fearful and fainthearted? Let him go and return to his house, lest the heart of his brethren faint like his heart.' 9 And so it shall be, when the officers have finished speaking to the people, that they shall make captains of the armies to lead the people.

10 "When you go near a city to fight against it, then proclaim an offer of peace to it. 11 And it shall be that if they accept your offer of peace, and open to you, then all the people *who are* found in it shall be placed under tribute to you, and serve you. 12 Now if *the city* will not make peace with you, but war against you, then you shall besiege it. 13 And when the Lord your God delivers it into your hands, you shall strike every male in it with the edge of the sword. 14 But the women, the little ones, the livestock, and all that is in the city, all its spoil, you shall plunder for yourself; and you shall eat the enemies' plunder which the Lord your God gives you. 15 Thus you shall do to all the cities *which are* very far from you, which *are* not of the cities of these nations.

16 "But of the cities of these peoples which the Lord your God gives you *as* an inheritance, you shall let nothing that breathes remain alive, 17 but you shall utterly destroy them: the Hittite and the Amorite and the Canaanite and the Perizzite and the Hivite and the Jebusite, just as the Lord your God has commanded you, 18 lest they teach you to do according to all their abominations which they have done for their gods, and you sin against the Lord your God.

19 "When you besiege a city for a long time, while making war against it to take it, you shall not destroy its trees by wielding an ax against them; if you can eat of them, do not cut them down to use in the siege, for the tree of the field *is* man's *food.* 20 Only the trees which you know *are* not trees for food you may destroy and cut down, to build siegeworks against the city that makes war with you, until it is subdued.

Laws about unsolved murder; other laws

21 "If *anyone* is found slain, lying in the field in the land which the Lord your God is giving you to possess, *and* it is not known who killed him, 2 then your elders and your judges shall go out and measure *the distance* from the slain man to the surrounding cities. 3 And it shall be *that* the elders of the city nearest to the slain man will take a heifer which has not been worked *and* which has not pulled with a yoke. 4 The elders of that city shall bring the heifer down to a valley with flowing water, which is neither plowed nor sown, and they shall break the heifer's neck there in the valley. 5 Then the priests, the sons of Levi, shall come near, for the Lord your God has chosen them to minister to Him and to bless in the name of the Lord; by their word every controversy and every assault shall be *settled.* 6 And all the elders of that city nearest to the slain *man* shall wash their hands over the heifer whose neck was broken in the valley. 7 Then they shall answer and say, 'Our hands have not shed this blood, nor have our eyes seen *it.* 8 Provide atonement, O Lord, for Your

people Israel, whom You have redeemed, and do not lay innocent blood to the charge of Your people Israel.' And atonement shall be provided on their behalf for the blood. 9 So you shall put away the *guilt of* innocent blood from among you when you do *what is* right in the sight of the LORD.

10 "When you go out to war against your enemies, and the LORD your God delivers them into your hand, and you take them captive, 11 and you *see* among the captives a beautiful woman, and desire her and would take her for your wife, 12 then you shall bring her home to your house, and she shall shave her head and trim her nails. 13 She shall put off the clothes of her captivity, remain in your house, and mourn her father and her mother a full month; after that you may go in to her and be her husband, and she shall be your wife. 14 And it shall be, if you have no delight in her, then you shall set her free, but you certainly shall not sell her for money; you shall not treat her brutally, because you have humbled her.

15 "If a man has two wives, one loved and the other unloved, and they have borne him children, *both* the loved and the unloved, and *if* the firstborn son is of her who is unloved, 16 then it shall be, on the day he bequeaths his possessions to his sons, *that* he must not bestow firstborn status on the son of the loved wife in preference to the son of the unloved, the *true* firstborn. 17 But he shall acknowledge the son of the unloved wife *as* the firstborn by giving him a double portion of all that he has, for he *is* the beginning of his strength; the right of the firstborn *is* his.

18 "If a man has a stubborn and rebellious son who will not obey the voice of his father or the voice of his mother, and *who,* when they have chastened him, will not heed them, 19 then his father and his mother shall take hold of him and bring him out to the elders of his city, to the gate of his city. 20 And they shall say to the

elders of his city, 'This son of ours is stubborn and rebellious; he will not obey our voice; he is a glutton and a drunkard.' 21 Then all the men of his city shall stone him to death with stones; so you shall put away the evil from among you, and all Israel shall hear and fear.

22 "If a man has committed a sin deserving of death, and he is put to death, and you hang him on a tree, 23 his body shall not remain overnight on the tree, but you shall surely bury him that day, so that you do not defile the land which the LORD your God is giving you *as* an inheritance; for he who is hanged *is* accursed of God.

Marriage laws

22 "You shall not see your brother's ox or his sheep going astray, and hide yourself from them; you shall certainly bring them back to your brother. 2 And if your brother *is* not near you, or if you do not know him, then you shall bring it to your own house, and it shall remain with you until your brother seeks it; then you shall restore it to him. 3 You shall do the same with his donkey, and so shall you do with his garment; with any lost thing of your brother's, which he has lost and you have found, you shall do likewise; you must not hide yourself.

4 "You shall not see your brother's donkey or his ox fall down along the road, and hide yourself from them; you shall surely help him lift *them* up again.

5 "A woman shall not wear anything that pertains to a man, nor shall a man put on a woman's garment, for all who do so *are* an abomination to the LORD your God.

6 "If a bird's nest happens to be before you along the way, in any tree or on the ground, with young ones or eggs, with the mother sitting on the young or on the eggs, you shall not take the mother with the young; 7 you shall surely let the mother go, and take the young for yourself, that it may be well with you and *that* you may prolong *your* days.

8 "When you build a new house, then you shall make a parapet for your roof, that you may not bring guilt of bloodshed on your household if anyone falls from it.

9 "You shall not sow your vineyard with different kinds of seed, lest the yield of the seed which you have sown and the fruit of your vineyard be defiled.

10 "You shall not plow with an ox and a donkey together.

11 "You shall not wear a garment of different sorts, *such as* wool and linen mixed together.

12 "You shall make tassels on the four corners of the clothing with which you cover *yourself*.

13 "If any man takes a wife, and goes in to her, and detests her, 14 and charges her with shameful conduct, and brings a bad name on her, and says, 'I took this woman, and when I came to her I found she *was* not a virgin,' 15 then the father and mother of the young woman shall take and bring out *the evidence of* the young woman's virginity to the elders of the city at the gate. 16 And the young woman's father shall say to the elders, 'I gave my daughter to this man as wife, and he detests her. 17 Now he has charged her with shameful conduct, saying, "I found your daughter *was* not a virgin," and yet these *are the evidences of* my daughter's virginity.' And they shall spread the cloth before the elders of the city. 18 Then the elders of that city shall take that man and punish him; 19 and they shall fine him one hundred *shekels* of silver and give *them* to the father of the young woman, because he has brought a bad name on a virgin of Israel. And she shall be his wife; he cannot divorce her all his days.

20 "But if the thing is true, *and evidences of* virginity are not found for the young woman, 21 then they shall bring out the young woman to the door of her father's house, and the men of her city shall stone her to death with stones, because she has done a disgraceful thing in Israel, to play the harlot in her father's house. So you

shall put away the evil from among you.

22 "If a man is found lying with a woman married to a husband, then both of them shall die—the man that lay with the woman, and the woman; so you shall put away the evil from Israel.

23 "If a young woman *who is* a virgin is betrothed to a husband, and a man finds her in the city and lies with her, 24 then you shall bring them both out to the gate of that city, and you shall stone them to death with stones, the young woman because she did not cry out in the city, and the man because he humbled his neighbor's wife; so you shall put away the evil from among you.

25 "But if a man finds a betrothed young woman in the countryside, and the man forces her and lies with her, then only the man who lay with her shall die. 26 But you shall do nothing to the young woman; *there is* in the young woman no sin *deserving* of death, for just as when a man rises against his neighbor and kills him, *even* so *is* this matter. 27 For he found her in the countryside, *and* the betrothed young woman cried out, but *there was* no one to save her.

28 "If a man finds a young woman *who is* a virgin, who is not betrothed, and he seizes her and lies with her, and they are found out, 29 then the man who lay with her shall give to the young woman's father fifty *shekels* of silver, and she shall be his wife because he has humbled her; he shall not be permitted to divorce her all his days.

30 "A man shall not take his father's wife, nor uncover his father's bed.

Who will be kept out of the congregation

23 "He who is emasculated by crushing or mutilation shall not enter the assembly of the LORD.

2 "One of illegitimate birth shall not enter the assembly of the LORD; even to the tenth generation none of his

descendants shall enter the assembly of the LORD.

3 "An **Ammonite** or **Moabite** shall not enter the assembly of the LORD; even to the tenth generation none of his *descendants* shall enter the assembly of the LORD forever, 4 because they did not meet you with bread and water on the road when you came out of Egypt, and because they hired against you Balaam the son of Beor from Pethor of Mesopotamia, to curse you. 5 Nevertheless the LORD your God would not listen to Balaam, but the LORD your God turned the curse into a blessing for you, because the LORD your God loves you. 6 You shall not seek their peace nor their prosperity all your days forever.

7 "You shall not abhor an Edomite, for he *is* your brother. You shall not abhor an Egyptian, because you were an alien in his land. 8 The children of the third generation born to them may enter the assembly of the LORD.

9 "When the army goes out against your enemies, then keep yourself from every wicked thing. 10 If there is any man among you who becomes unclean by some occurrence in the night, then he shall go outside the camp; he shall not come inside the camp. 11 But it shall be, when evening comes, that he shall wash with water; and when the sun sets, he may come into the camp.

12 "Also you shall have a place outside the camp, where you may go out; 13 and you shall have an implement among your equipment, and when you sit down outside, you shall dig with it and turn and cover your refuse. 14 For the LORD your God walks in the midst of your camp, to deliver you and give your enemies over to you; therefore your camp shall be holy, that He may see no unclean thing among you, and turn away from you.

15 "You shall not give back to his master the slave who has escaped from his master to you. 16 He may dwell with you in your midst, in the place which he chooses within one of your gates, where it seems best to him; you shall not oppress him.

17 "There shall be no *ritual* harlot of the daughters of Israel, or a perverted one of the sons of Israel. 18 You shall not bring the wages of a harlot or the price of a dog to the house of the LORD your God for any vowed offering, for both of these *are* an abomination to the LORD your God.

19 "You shall not charge interest to your brother—interest on money *or* food *or* anything that is lent out at interest. 20 To a foreigner you may charge interest, but to your brother you shall not charge interest, that the LORD your God may bless you in all to which you set your hand in the land which you are entering to possess.

Have You Made a Promise to God?

Sometimes we break our promises. But it's very dangerous to break your promises to God. In fact, it's better not to promise at all than to break your promise. God wants you to promise Him your life. That's the best promise you can make.

---

21 "When you make a vow to the LORD your God, you shall not delay to pay it; for the LORD your God will surely require it of you, and it would be sin to you. 22 But if you abstain from vowing, it shall not be sin to you. 23 That which has gone from your lips you shall keep and perform, for you voluntarily vowed to the LORD your God what you have promised with your mouth.

WORDFINDER

23:3 Ammonites and Moabites The nations that descended from Ammon and Moab, two sons of Lot. (See Genesis 19:30–38.)

When you make a promise to God, be sure to keep it!

24 "When you come into your neighbor's vineyard, you may eat your fill of grapes at your pleasure, but you shall not put *any* in your container. 25 When you come into your neighbor's standing grain, you may pluck the heads with your hand, but you shall not use a sickle on your neighbor's standing grain.

Laws about the family

24 "When a man takes a wife and marries her, and it happens that she finds no favor in his eyes because he has found some uncleanness in her, and he writes her a certificate of divorce, puts *it* in her hand, and sends her out of his house, 2 when she has departed from his house, and goes and becomes another man's *wife,* 3 if the latter husband detests her and writes her a certificate of divorce, puts *it* in her hand, and sends her out of his house, or if the latter husband dies who took her as his wife, 4 *then* her former husband who divorced her must not take her back to be his wife after she has been defiled; for that *is* an abomination before the Lord, and you shall not bring sin on the land which the

Lord your God is giving you *as* an inheritance.

5 "When a man has taken a new wife, he shall not go out to war or be charged with any business; he shall be free at home one year, and bring happiness to his wife whom he has taken.

6 "No man shall take the lower or the upper millstone in pledge, for he takes *one's* living in pledge.

7 "If a man is found kidnapping any of his brethren of the children of Israel, and mistreats him or sells him, then that kidnapper shall die; and you shall put away the evil from among you.

8 "Take heed in an outbreak of leprosy, that you carefully observe and do according to all that the priests, the Levites, shall teach you; just as I commanded them, *so* you shall be careful to do. 9 Remember what the Lord your God did to Miriam on the way when you came out of Egypt!

10 "When you lend your brother anything, you shall not go into his house to get his pledge. 11 You shall stand outside, and the man to whom you lend shall bring the pledge out to you. 12 And if the man *is* poor, you shall not keep his pledge overnight. 13 You shall in any case return the pledge to him again when the sun goes down, that he may sleep in his own garment and bless you; and it shall be righteousness to you before the Lord your God.

14 "You shall not oppress a hired servant *who is* poor and needy, *whether* one of your brethren or one of the aliens who *is* in your land within your gates. 15 Each day you shall give *him* his wages, and not let the sun go down on it, for he *is* poor and has set his heart on it; lest he cry out against you to the Lord, and it be sin to you.

16 "Fathers shall not be put to death for *their* children, nor shall children be put to death for *their* fathers; a person shall be put to death for his own sin.

17 "You shall not pervert justice due the stranger or the fatherless, nor take a widow's garment as a pledge. 18 But you shall remember that you were a slave in Egypt, and the Lord

your God redeemed you from there; therefore I command you to do this thing.

19 "When you reap your harvest in your field, and forget a sheaf in the field, you shall not go back to get it; it shall be for the stranger, the fatherless, and the widow, that the LORD your God may bless you in all the work of your hands. 20 When you beat your olive trees, you shall not go over the boughs again; it shall be for the stranger, the fatherless, and the widow. 21 When you gather the grapes of your vineyard, you shall not glean it afterward; it shall be for the stranger, the fatherless, and the widow. 22 And you shall remember that you were a slave in the land of Egypt; therefore I command you to do this thing.

Social duties

25 "If there is a dispute between men, and they come to court, that the judges may judge them, and they justify the righteous and condemn the wicked, 2 then it shall be, if the wicked man deserves to be beaten, that the judge will cause him to lie down and be beaten in his presence, according to his guilt, with a certain number of blows. 3 Forty blows he may give him and no more, lest he should exceed this and beat him with many blows above these, and your brother be humiliated in your sight.

4 "You shall not muzzle an ox while it treads out the grain.

5 "If brothers dwell together, and one of them dies and has no son, the widow of the dead man shall not be married to a stranger outside the family; her husband's brother shall go in to her, take her as his wife, and perform the duty of a husband's brother to her. 6 And it shall be that the firstborn son which she bears will succeed to the name of his dead brother, that his name may not be blotted out of Israel. 7 But if the man does not want to take his brother's wife, then let his brother's wife go up to the gate to the elders, and say, 'My husband's brother refuses to raise up a name to his brother in Israel; he will not perform the duty of my husband's brother.' 8 Then the elders of his city shall call him and speak to him. But if he stands firm and says, 'I do not want to take her,' 9 then his brother's wife shall come to him in the presence of the elders, remove his sandal from his foot, spit in his face, and answer and say, 'So shall it be done to the man who will not build up his brother's house.' 10 And his name shall be called in Israel, 'The house of him who had his sandal removed.'

11 "If two men fight together, and the wife of one draws near to rescue her husband from the hand of the one attacking him, and puts out her hand and seizes him by the genitals, 12 then you shall cut off her hand; your eye shall not pity her.

13 "You shall not have in your bag differing weights, a heavy and a light. 14 You shall not have in your house differing measures, a large and a small. 15 You shall have a perfect and just weight, a perfect and just measure, that your days may be lengthened in the land which the LORD your God is giving you. 16 For all who do such things, all who behave unrighteously, are an abomination to the LORD your God.

17 "Remember what Amalek did to you on the way as you were coming out of Egypt, 18 how he met you on the way and attacked your rear ranks, all the stragglers at your rear, when you were tired and weary; and he did not fear God. 19 Therefore it shall be, when the LORD your God has given you rest from your enemies all around, in the land which the LORD your God is giving you to possess as an inheritance, that you will blot out the remembrance of Amalek from under heaven. You shall not forget.

The offerings of firstfruits and tithes

26 "And it shall be, when you come into the land which the LORD your God is giving you as an inheritance, and you

possess it and dwell in it, 2 that you shall take some of the first of all the produce of the ground, which you shall bring from your land that the LORD your God is giving you, and put *it* in a basket and go to the place where the LORD your God chooses to make His name abide. 3 And you shall go to the one who is priest in those days, and say to him, 'I declare today to the LORD your God that I have come to the country which the LORD swore to our fathers to give us.'

4 "Then the priest shall take the basket out of your hand and set it down before the altar of the LORD your God. 5 And you shall answer and say before the LORD your God: 'My father *was* a Syrian, about to perish, and he went down to Egypt and dwelt there, few in number; and there he became a nation, great, mighty, and populous. 6 But the Egyptians mistreated us, afflicted us, and laid hard bondage on us. 7 Then we cried out to the LORD God of our fathers, and the LORD heard our voice and looked on our affliction and our labor and our oppression. 8 So the LORD brought us out of Egypt with a mighty hand and with an outstretched arm, with great terror and with signs and wonders. 9 He has brought us to this place and has given us this land, "a land flowing with milk and honey"; 10 and now, behold, I have brought the firstfruits of the land which you, O LORD, have given me.'

"Then you shall set it before the LORD your God, and worship before the LORD your God. 11 So you shall rejoice in *every* good *thing* which the LORD your God has given to you and your house, you and the Levite and the stranger who *is* among you.

12 "When you have finished laying aside all the tithe of your increase in the third year—the year of tithing— and have given *it* to the Levite, the stranger, the fatherless, and the widow, so that they may eat within your gates and be filled, 13 then you shall say before the LORD your God: 'I have removed the holy *tithe* from *my* house, and also have given them to the Levite,

the stranger, the fatherless, and the widow, according to all Your commandments which You have commanded me; I have not transgressed Your commandments, nor have I forgotten *them.* 14 I have not eaten any of it when in mourning, nor have I removed *any* of it for an unclean *use,* nor given *any* of it for the dead. I have obeyed the voice of the LORD my God, and have done according to all that You have commanded me. 15 Look down from Your holy habitation, from heaven, and bless Your people Israel and the land which You have given us, just as You swore to our fathers, "a land flowing with milk and honey."'

16 "This day the LORD your God commands you to observe these statutes and judgments; therefore you shall be careful to observe them with all your heart and with all your soul. 17 Today you have proclaimed the LORD to be your God, and that you will walk in His ways and keep His statutes, His commandments, and His judgments, and that you will obey His voice. 18 Also today the LORD has proclaimed you to be His special people, just as He promised you, that *you* should keep all His commandments, 19 and that He will set you high above all nations which He has made, in praise, in name, and in honor, and that you may be a holy people to the LORD your God, just as He has spoken."

Moses pronounces curses at Mount Ebal

27 Now Moses, with the elders of Israel, commanded the people, saying: "Keep all the commandments which I command you today. 2 And it shall be, on the day when you cross over the Jordan to the land which the LORD your God is giving you, that you shall set up for yourselves large stones, and whitewash them with lime. 3 You shall write on them all the words of this law, when you have crossed over, that you may enter the land which the LORD your God is giving you, 'a land flowing

with milk and honey,' just as the LORD God of your fathers promised you. 4 Therefore it shall be, when you have crossed over the Jordan, *that* on Mount Ebal you shall set up these stones, which I command you today, and you shall whitewash them with lime. 5 And there you shall build an altar to the LORD your God, an altar of stones; you shall not use an iron *tool* on them. 6 You shall build with whole stones the altar of the LORD your God, and offer burnt offerings on it to the LORD your God. 7 You shall offer peace offerings, and shall eat there, and rejoice before the LORD your God. 8 And you shall write very plainly on the stones all the words of this law."

9 Then Moses and the priests, the Levites, spoke to all Israel, saying, "Take heed and listen, O Israel: This day you have become the people of the LORD your God. 10 Therefore you shall obey the voice of the LORD your God, and observe His commandments and His statutes which I command you today."

11 And Moses commanded the people on the same day, saying, 12 "These shall stand on Mount Gerizim to bless the people, when you have crossed over the Jordan: Simeon, Levi, Judah, Issachar, Joseph, and Benjamin; 13 and these shall stand on Mount Ebal to curse: Reuben, Gad, Asher, Zebulun, Dan, and Naphtali.

14 "And the Levites shall speak with a loud voice and say to all the men of Israel: 15 'Cursed *is* the one who makes a carved or molded image, an abomination to the LORD, the work of the hands of the craftsman, and sets *it* up in secret.'

"And all the people shall answer and say, 'Amen!'

16 'Cursed *is* the one who treats his father or his mother with contempt.'

"And all the people shall say, 'Amen!'

17 'Cursed *is* the one who moves his neighbor's landmark.'

"And all the people shall say, 'Amen!'

18 'Cursed *is* the one who makes the blind to wander off the road.'

"And all the people shall say, 'Amen!'

19 'Cursed *is* the one who perverts the justice due the stranger, the fatherless, and widow.'

"And all the people shall say, 'Amen!'

20 'Cursed *is* the one who lies with his father's wife, because he has uncovered his father's bed.'

"And all the people shall say, 'Amen!'

21 'Cursed *is* the one who lies with any kind of animal.'

"And all the people shall say, 'Amen!'

22 'Cursed *is* the one who lies with his sister, the daughter of his father or the daughter of his mother.'

"And all the people shall say, 'Amen!'

23 'Cursed *is* the one who lies with his mother-in-law.'

"And all the people shall say, 'Amen!'

24 'Cursed *is* the one who attacks his neighbor secretly.'

"And all the people shall say, 'Amen!'

25 'Cursed *is* the one who takes a bribe to slay an innocent person.'

"And all the people shall say, 'Amen!'

26 'Cursed *is* the one who does not confirm *all* the words of this law.'

"And all the people shall say, 'Amen!' "

The results of obeying or disobeying God

28 "Now it shall come to pass, if you diligently obey the voice of the LORD your God, to observe carefully all His commandments which I command you today, that the LORD your God will set you high above all nations of the earth. 2 And all these blessings shall come upon you and overtake you, because you obey the voice of the LORD your God:

3 "Blessed *shall* you *be* in the city,

and blessed *shall* you *be* in the country.

4 "Blessed *shall be* the fruit of your body, the produce of your ground and the increase of your herds, the increase of your cattle and the offspring of your flocks.

5 "Blessed *shall be* your basket and your kneading bowl.

6 "Blessed *shall* you *be* when you come in, and blessed *shall* you *be* when you go out.

7 "The LORD will cause your enemies who rise against you to be defeated before your face; they shall come out against you one way and flee before you seven ways.

8 "The LORD will command the blessing on you in your storehouses and in all to which you set your hand, and He will bless you in the land which the LORD your God is giving you.

9 "The LORD will establish you as a holy people to Himself, just as He has sworn to you, if you keep the commandments of the LORD your God and walk in His ways. 10 Then all peoples of the earth shall see that you are called by the name of the LORD, and they shall be afraid of you. 11 And the LORD will grant you plenty of goods, in the fruit of your body, in the increase of your livestock, and in the produce of your ground, in the land of which the LORD swore to your fathers to give you. 12 The LORD will open to you His good treasure, the heavens, to give the rain to your land in its season, and to bless all the work of your hand. You shall lend to many nations, but you shall not borrow. 13 And the LORD will make you the head and not the tail; you shall be above only, and not be beneath, if you heed the commandments of the LORD your God, which I command you today, and are careful to observe *them*. 14 So you shall not turn aside from any of the words which I command you this day, *to* the right or the left, to go after other gods to serve them.

15 "But it shall come to pass, if you do not obey the voice of the LORD your God, to observe carefully all His commandments and His statutes which I

command you today, that all these curses will come upon you and overtake you:

16 "Cursed *shall* you *be* in the city, and cursed *shall* you *be* in the country.

17 "Cursed *shall be* your basket and your kneading bowl.

18 "Cursed *shall be* the fruit of your body and the produce of your land, the increase of your cattle and the offspring of your flocks.

19 "Cursed *shall* you *be* when you come in, and cursed *shall* you *be* when you go out.

20 "The LORD will send on you cursing, confusion, and rebuke in all that you set your hand to do, until you are destroyed and until you perish quickly, because of the wickedness of your doings in which you have forsaken Me. 21 The LORD will make the plague cling to you until He has consumed you from the land which you are going to possess. 22 The LORD will strike you with consumption, with fever, with inflammation, with severe burning fever, with the sword, with scorching, and with mildew; they shall pursue you until you perish. 23 And your heavens which *are* over your head shall be bronze, and the earth which is under you *shall be* iron. 24 The LORD will change the rain of your land to powder and dust; from the heaven it shall come down on you until you are destroyed.

25 "The LORD will cause you to be defeated before your enemies; you shall go out one way against them and flee seven ways before them; and you shall become troublesome to all the kingdoms of the earth. 26 Your carcasses shall be food for all the birds of the air and the beasts of the earth, and no one shall frighten *them* away. 27 The LORD will strike you with the boils of Egypt, with tumors, with the scab, and with the itch, from which you cannot be healed. 28 The LORD will strike you with madness and blindness and confusion of heart. 29 And you shall grope at noonday, as a blind man gropes in darkness; you shall not prosper in your ways; you shall be only

oppressed and plundered continually, and no one shall save *you.*

30 "You shall betroth a wife, but another man shall lie with her; you shall build a house, but you shall not dwell in it; you shall plant a vineyard, but shall not gather its grapes. 31 Your ox *shall be* slaughtered before your eyes, but you shall not eat of it; your donkey *shall be* violently taken away from before you, and shall not be restored to you; your sheep *shall be* given to your enemies, and you shall have no one to rescue *them.* 32 Your sons and your daughters *shall be* given to another people, and your eyes shall look and fail *with longing* for them all day long; and *there shall be* no strength in your hand. 33 A nation whom you have not known shall eat the fruit of your land and the produce of your labor, and you shall be only oppressed and crushed continually. 34 So you shall be driven mad because of the sight which your eyes see. 35 The Lord will strike you in the knees and on the legs with severe boils which cannot be healed, and from the sole of your foot to the top of your head.

36 "The Lord will bring you and the king whom you set over you to a nation which neither you nor your fathers have known, and there you shall serve other gods—wood and stone. 37 And you shall become an astonishment, a proverb, and a byword among all nations where the Lord will drive you.

38 "You shall carry much seed out to the field but gather little in, for the locust shall consume it. 39 You shall plant vineyards and tend *them,* but you shall neither drink *of* the wine nor gather the *grapes;* for the worms shall eat them. 40 You shall have olive trees throughout all your territory, but you shall not anoint *yourself* with the oil; for your olives shall drop off. 41 You shall beget sons and daughters, but they shall not be yours; for they shall go into captivity. 42 Locusts shall consume all your trees and the produce of your land.

43 "The alien who *is* among you shall rise higher and higher above you,

and you shall come down lower and lower. 44 He shall lend to you, but you shall not lend to him; he shall be the head, and you shall be the tail.

45 "Moreover all these curses shall come upon you and pursue and overtake you, until you are destroyed, because you did not obey the voice of the Lord your God, to keep His commandments and His statutes which He commanded you. 46 And they shall be upon you for a sign and a wonder, and on your descendants forever.

47 "Because you did not serve the Lord your God with joy and gladness of heart, for the abundance of everything, 48 therefore you shall serve your enemies, whom the Lord will send against you, in hunger, in thirst, in nakedness, and in need of everything; and He will put a yoke of iron on your neck until He has destroyed you. 49 The Lord will bring a nation against you from afar, from the end of the earth, *as swift* as the eagle flies, a nation whose language you will not understand, 50 a nation of fierce countenance, which does not respect the elderly nor show favor to the young. 51 And they shall eat the increase of your livestock and the produce of your land, until you are destroyed; they shall not leave you grain or new wine or oil, *or* the increase of your cattle or the offspring of your flocks, until they have destroyed you.

52 "They shall besiege you at all your gates until your high and fortified walls, in which you trust, come down throughout all your land; and they shall besiege you at all your gates throughout all your land which the Lord your God has given you. 53 You shall eat the fruit of your own body, the flesh of your sons and your daughters whom the Lord your God has given you, in the siege and desperate straits in which your enemy shall distress you. 54 The sensitive and very refined man among you will be hostile toward his brother, toward the wife of his bosom, and toward the rest of his children whom he leaves behind, 55 so that he will not give any of them the flesh of his

children whom he will eat, because he has nothing left in the siege and desperate straits in which your enemy shall distress you at all your gates. 56 The tender and delicate woman among you, who would not venture to set the sole of her foot on the ground because of her delicateness and sensitivity, will refuse, to the husband of her bosom, and to her son and her daughter, 57 her placenta which comes out from between her feet and her children whom she bears; for she will eat them secretly for lack of everything in the siege and desperate straits in which your enemy shall distress you at all your gates.

58 "If you do not carefully observe all the words of this law that are written in this book, that you may fear this glorious and awesome name, THE LORD YOUR GOD, 59 then the LORD will bring upon you and your descendants extraordinary plagues—great and prolonged plagues—and serious and prolonged sicknesses. 60 Moreover He will bring back on you all the diseases of Egypt, of which you were afraid, and they shall cling to you. 61 Also every sickness and every plague, which is not written in this Book of the Law, will the LORD bring upon you until you are destroyed. 62 You shall be left few in number, whereas you were as the stars of heaven in multitude, because you would not obey the voice of the LORD your God. 63 And it shall be, that just as the LORD rejoiced over you to do you good and multiply you, so the LORD will rejoice over you to destroy you and bring you to nothing; and you shall be plucked from off the land which you go to possess.

64 "Then the LORD will scatter you among all peoples, from one end of the earth to the other, and there you shall serve other gods, which neither you nor your fathers have known—wood and stone. 65 And among those nations you shall find no rest, nor shall the sole of your foot have a resting place; but there the LORD will give you a trembling heart, failing eyes, and anguish of soul. 66 Your life shall hang in doubt before you; you shall fear day and night, and have no assurance of life. 67 In the morning you shall say, 'Oh, that it were evening!' And at evening you shall say, 'Oh, that it were morning!' because of the fear which terrifies your heart, and because of the sight which your eyes see.

68 "And the LORD will take you back to Egypt in ships, by the way of which I said to you, 'You shall never see it again.' And there you shall be offered for sale to your enemies as male and female slaves, but no one will buy you."

God gives His promise to Israel again

29 These are the words of the covenant which the LORD commanded Moses to make with the children of Israel in the land of Moab, besides the covenant which He made with them in Horeb.

2 Now Moses called all Israel and said to them: "You have seen all that the LORD did before your eyes in the land of Egypt, to Pharaoh and to all his servants and to all his land— 3 the great trials which your eyes have seen, the signs, and those great wonders. 4 Yet the LORD has not given you a heart to perceive and eyes to see and ears to hear, to this very day. 5 And I have led you forty years in the wilderness. Your clothes have not worn out on you, and your sandals have not worn out on your feet. 6 You have not eaten bread, nor have you drunk wine or similar drink, that you may know that I am the LORD your God. 7 And when you came to this place, Sihon king of Heshbon and Og king of Bashan came out against us to battle, and we conquered them. 8 We took their land and gave it as an inheritance to the Reubenites, to the Gadites, and to half the tribe of Manasseh. 9 Therefore keep the words of this covenant, and do them, that you may prosper in all that you do.

10 "All of you stand today before the LORD your God: your leaders and your

tribes and your elders and your officers, all the men of Israel, 11 your little ones and your wives—also the stranger who is in your camp, from the one who cuts your wood to the one who draws your water— 12 that you may enter into covenant with the LORD your God, and into His oath, which the LORD your God makes with you today, 13 that He may establish you today as a people for Himself, and *that* He may be God to you, just as He has spoken to you, and just as He has sworn to your fathers, to Abraham, Isaac, and Jacob.

14 "I make this covenant and this oath, not with you alone, 15 but with *him* who stands here with us today before the LORD our God, as well as with *him* who is not here with us today 16 (for you know that we dwelt in the land of Egypt and that we came through the nations which you passed by, 17 and you saw their abominations and their idols which *were* among them—wood and stone and silver and gold); 18 so that there may not be among you man or woman or family or tribe, whose heart turns away today from the LORD our God, to go *and* serve the gods of these nations, and that there may not be among you a root bearing bitterness or wormwood; 19 and so it may not happen, when he hears the words of this curse, that he blesses himself in his heart, saying, 'I shall have peace, even though I follow the dictates of my heart'—as though the drunkard could be included with the sober.

20 "The LORD would not spare him; for then the anger of the LORD and His jealousy would burn against that man, and every curse that is written in this book would settle on him, and the LORD would blot out his name from under heaven. 21 And the LORD would separate him from all the tribes of Israel for adversity, according to all the curses of the covenant that are written in this Book of the Law, 22 so that the coming generation of your children who rise up after you, and the foreigner who comes from a far land, would say, when they see the plagues of that land

and the sicknesses which the LORD has laid on it:

23 'The whole land *is* brimstone, salt, and burning; it is not sown, nor does it bear, nor does any grass grow there, like the overthrow of Sodom and Gomorrah, Admah, and Zeboiim, which the LORD overthrew in His anger and His wrath.' 24 All nations would say, 'Why has the LORD done so to this land? What does the heat of this great anger mean?' 25 Then *people* would say: 'Because they have forsaken the covenant of the LORD God of their fathers, which He made with them when He brought them out of the land of Egypt; 26 for they went and served other gods and worshiped them, gods that they did not know and that He had not given to them. 27 Then the anger of the LORD was aroused against this land, to bring on it every curse that is written in this book. 28 And the LORD uprooted them from their land in anger, in wrath, and in great indignation, and cast them into another land, as *it is* this day.'

29 "The secret *things belong* to the LORD our God, but those *things which are* revealed *belong* to us and to our children forever, that *we* may do all the words of this law.

God blesses those who return to Him

30 "Now it shall come to pass, when all these things come upon you, the blessing and the curse which I have set before you, and you call *them* to mind among all the nations where the LORD your God drives you, 2 and you return to the LORD your God and obey His voice, according to all that I command you today, you and your children, with all your heart and with all your soul, 3 that the LORD your God will bring you back from captivity, and have compassion on you, and gather you again from all the nations where the LORD your God has scattered you. 4 If *any* of you are driven out to the farthest *parts* under heaven, from there the LORD your God will gather you,

and from there He will bring you. 5 Then the LORD your God will bring you to the land which your fathers possessed, and you shall possess it. He will prosper you and multiply you more than your fathers. 6 And the LORD your God will circumcise your heart and the heart of your descendants, to love the LORD your God with all your heart and with all your soul, that you may live.

7 "Also the LORD your God will put all these curses on your enemies and on those who hate you, who persecuted you. 8 And you will again obey the voice of the LORD and do all His commandments which I command you today. 9 The LORD your God will make you abound in all the work of your hand, in the fruit of your body, in the increase of your livestock, and in the produce of your land for good. For the LORD will again rejoice over you for good as He rejoiced over your fathers, 10 if you obey the voice of the LORD your God, to keep His commandments and His statutes which are written in this Book of the Law, and if you turn to the LORD your God with all your heart and with all your soul.

11 "For this commandment which I command you today is not too mysterious for you, nor is it far off. 12 It is not in heaven, that you should say, 'Who will ascend into heaven for us and bring it to us, that we may hear it and do it?' 13 Nor is it beyond the sea, that you should say, 'Who will go over the sea for us and bring it to us, that we may hear it and do it?' 14 But the word is very near you, in your mouth and in your heart, that you may do it.

15 "See, I have set before you today life and good, death and evil, 16 in that I command you today to love the LORD your God, to walk in His ways, and to keep His commandments, His statutes, and His judgments, that you may live and multiply; and the LORD your God will bless you in the land which you go to possess. 17 But if your heart turns away so that you do not hear, and are drawn away, and worship other gods and serve them, 18 I announce to you today that you shall surely perish; you shall not prolong your days in the land which you cross over the Jordan to go in and possess. 19 I call heaven and earth as witnesses today against you, that I have set before you life and death, blessing and cursing; therefore choose life, that both you and your descendants may live; 20 that you may love the LORD your God, that you may obey His voice, and that you may cling to Him, for He is your life and the length of your days; and that you may dwell in the land which the LORD swore to your fathers, to Abraham, Isaac, and Jacob, to give them."

Joshua takes over as Israel's new leader

31 Then Moses went and spoke these words to all Israel. 2 And he said to them: "I am one hundred and twenty years old today. I can no longer go out and come in. Also the LORD has said to me, 'You shall not cross over this Jordan.' 3 The LORD your

---

⚒ DIGGING IN

30:18–20 Choose Life Moses had to say some tough things to Israel before they crossed the Jordan into the Promised Land of Canaan. Israel still had a lot of hard lessons to learn. Their biggest lesson: "Choose life, that both you and your descendants may live."

This is a very simple lesson, but it's very hard for people to learn. Many say they want to live, but they act like they want to die. On busy streets and high-

ways, you see this every day. People drive as if they want to die. Alcohol and drugs have ruined their wish to live. But God is always there, even if we can't see Him. He keeps saying, "Choose life!"

You have to make that choice for yourself. You must say to God, "I'm turning my back on the ways of death, and I'm going to live because Jesus gives me His power to live."

God Himself crosses over before you; He will destroy these nations from before you, and you shall dispossess them. Joshua himself crosses over before you, just as the Lord has said. ⁴ And the Lord will do to them as He did to Sihon and Og, the kings of the Amorites and their land, when He destroyed them. ⁵ The Lord will give them over to you, that you may do to them according to every commandment which I have commanded you. ⁶ Be strong and of good courage, do not fear nor be afraid of them; for the Lord your God, He is the One who goes with you. He will not leave you nor forsake you."

⁷ Then Moses called Joshua and said to him in the sight of all Israel, "Be strong and of good courage, for you must go with this people to the land which the Lord has sworn to their fathers to give them, and you shall cause them to inherit it. ⁸ And the Lord, He is the One who goes before you. He will be with you, He will not leave you nor forsake you; do not fear nor be dismayed."

⁹ So Moses wrote this law and deliv- ered it to the priests, the sons of Levi, who bore the ark of the covenant of the Lord, and to all the elders of Israel. ¹⁰ And Moses commanded them, saying: "At the end of every seven years, at the appointed time in the year of release, at the Feast of Tabernacles, ¹¹ when all Israel comes to appear before the Lord your God in the place which He chooses, you shall read this law before all Israel in their hearing. ¹² Gather the people together, men and women and little ones, and the stranger who is within your gates, that they may hear and that they may learn to fear the Lord your God and carefully observe all the words of this law, ¹³ and that their children, who have not known it, may hear and learn to fear the Lord your God as long as you live in the land which you cross the Jordan to possess."

¹⁴ Then the Lord said to Moses, "Behold, the days approach when you must die; call Joshua, and present yourselves in the tabernacle of meeting, that I may inaugurate him."

So Moses and Joshua went and presented themselves in the tabernacle of

⚒ DIGGING IN

31:9–13 The Five Books of Moses
The five books of Moses were the first books of the Old Testament, called the Law—Genesis, Exodus, Leviticus, Numbers, and Deuteronomy.

You can see that not all of the five books of Moses contained laws. Some of the things Moses wrote were about the history of man and the Jewish nation. Genesis shows us where we come from and God's early plan of salvation.

Some people used to say that Moses didn't know enough to write the five books in his time. But now we have discovered lots of books that were written on clay and stone long before the time of Moses. This proves that people were smarter in ancient times than we thought they were.

You can understand the rest of the Bible only if you study the five books of Moses first.

Every seven years, the priests read the law to all the people.

meeting. 15 Now the LORD appeared at the tabernacle in a pillar of cloud, and the pillar of cloud stood above the door of the tabernacle.

16 And the LORD said to Moses: "Behold, you will rest with your fathers; and this people will rise and play the harlot with the gods of the foreigners of the land, where they go to be among them, and they will forsake Me and break My covenant which I have made with them. 17 Then My anger shall be aroused against them in that day, and I will forsake them, and I will hide My face from them, and they shall be devoured. And many evils and troubles shall befall them, so that they will say in that day, 'Have not these evils come upon us because our God is not among us?' 18 And I will surely hide My face in that day because of all the evil which they have done, in that they have turned to other gods.

19 "Now therefore, write down this song for yourselves, and teach it to the children of Israel; put it in their mouths, that this song may be a witness for Me against the children of Israel. 20 When I have brought them to the land flowing with milk and honey, of which I swore to their fathers, and they have eaten and filled themselves and grown fat, then they will turn to other gods and serve them; and they will provoke Me and break My covenant. 21 Then it shall be, when many evils and troubles have come upon them, that this song will testify against them as a witness; for it will not be forgotten in the mouths of their descendants, for I know the inclination of their behavior today, even before I have brought them to the land of which I swore to give them."

22 Therefore Moses wrote this song the same day, and taught it to the children of Israel. 23 Then He inaugurated Joshua the son of Nun, and said, "Be strong and of good courage; for you shall bring the children of Israel into the land of which I swore to them, and I will be with you."

24 So it was, when Moses had completed writing the words of this law in a book, when they were finished, 25 that Moses commanded the Levites, who bore the ark of the covenant of the LORD, saying: 26 "Take this Book of the Law, and put it beside the ark of the covenant of the LORD your God, that it may be there as a witness against you; 27 for I know your rebellion and your stiff neck. If today, while I am yet alive with you, you have been rebellious against the LORD, then how much more after my death? 28 Gather to me all the elders of your tribes, and your officers, that I may speak these words in their hearing and call heaven and earth to witness against them. 29 For I know that after my death you will become utterly corrupt, and turn aside from the way which I have commanded you. And evil will befall you in the latter days, because you will do evil in the sight of the LORD, to provoke Him to anger through the work of your hands."

30 Then Moses spoke in the hearing of all the assembly of Israel the words of this song until they were ended:

Moses sings a song

32 "Give ear, O heavens, and I will speak;
And hear, O earth, the words of my mouth.

2 Let my teaching drop as the rain,
My speech distill as the dew,
As raindrops on the tender herb,
And as showers on the grass.

3 For I proclaim the name of the LORD:
Ascribe greatness to our God.

4 He is the Rock, His work is perfect;
For all His ways are justice,
A God of truth and without injustice;
Righteous and upright is He.

5 "They have corrupted themselves;
They are not His children,
Because of their blemish:
A perverse and crooked generation.

6 Do you thus deal with the LORD,
  O foolish and unwise people?
  Is He not your Father, *who*
    bought you?
  Has He not made you and
    established you?

7 "Remember the days of old,
  Consider the years of many
    generations.
  Ask your father, and he will
    show you;
  Your elders, and they will tell
    you:
8 When the Most High divided
    their inheritance to the
    nations,
  When He separated the sons of
    Adam,
  He set the boundaries of the
    peoples
  According to the number of the
    children of Israel.
9 For the LORD's portion *is* His
    people;
  Jacob *is* the place of His
    inheritance.

10 "He found him in a desert land
   And in the wasteland, a howling
     wilderness;
   He encircled him, He instructed
     him,
   He kept him as the apple of His
     eye.
11 As an eagle stirs up its nest,
   Hovers over its young,
   Spreading out its wings, taking
     them up,
   Carrying them on its wings,
12 *So* the LORD alone led him,
   And *there was* no foreign god
     with him.

13 "He made him ride in the heights
     of the earth,
   That he might eat the produce
     of the fields;
   He made him draw honey from
     the rock,
   And oil from the flinty rock;
14 Curds from the cattle, and milk
     of the flock,
   With fat of lambs;

And rams of the breed of
  Bashan, and goats,
With the choicest wheat;
And you drank wine, the blood
  of the grapes.

15 "But Jeshurun grew fat and
     kicked;
   You grew fat, you grew thick,
   You are obese!
   Then he forsook God *who* made
     him,
   And scornfully esteemed the
     Rock of his salvation.
16 They provoked Him to jealousy
     with foreign *gods;*
   With abominations they
     provoked Him to anger.
17 They sacrificed to demons, not
     to God,
   To gods they did not know,
   To new *gods,* new arrivals
   That your fathers did not fear.
18 Of the Rock *who* begot you, you
     are unmindful,
   And have forgotten the God
     who fathered you.

19 "And when the LORD saw *it,* He
     spurned *them,*
   Because of the provocation of
     His sons and His daughters.
20 And He said: 'I will hide My face
     from them,
   I will see what their end *will be,*
   For they *are* a perverse
     generation,
   Children in whom *is* no faith.
21 They have provoked Me to
     jealousy by *what* is not God;
   They have moved Me to anger
     by their foolish idols.
   But I will provoke them to
     jealousy by *those who are* not
     a nation;
   I will move them to anger by a
     foolish nation.
22 For a fire is kindled in My anger,
   And shall burn to the lowest hell;
   It shall consume the earth with
     her increase,
   And set on fire the foundations
     of the mountains.

23 'I will heap disasters on them;
  I will spend My arrows on them.
24 They shall be wasted with
    hunger,
  Devoured by pestilence and
    bitter destruction;
  I will also send against them the
    teeth of beasts,
  With the poison of serpents of
    the dust.
25 The sword shall destroy outside;
  There shall be terror within
  For the young man and virgin,
  The nursing child with the man
    of gray hairs.
26 I would have said, "I will dash
    them in pieces,
  I will make the memory of them
    to cease from among men,"
27 Had I not feared the wrath of
    the enemy,
  Lest their adversaries should
    misunderstand,
  Lest they should say, "Our hand
    is high;
  And it is not the LORD who has
    done all this." '

28 "For they are a nation void of
    counsel,
  Nor is there any understanding
    in them.
29 Oh, that they were wise, that
    they understood this,
  That they would consider their
    latter end!
30 How could one chase a
    thousand,
  And two put ten thousand to
    flight,
  Unless their Rock had sold them,
  And the LORD had surrendered
    them?
31 For their rock is not like our
    Rock,
  Even our enemies themselves
    being judges.
32 For their vine is of the vine of
    Sodom
  And of the fields of Gomorrah;
  Their grapes are grapes of gall,
  Their clusters are bitter.
33 Their wine is the poison of
    serpents,

And the cruel venom of
  cobras.
34 'Is this not laid up in store with
    Me,
  Sealed up among My treasures?
35 Vengeance is Mine, and
    recompense;
  Their foot shall slip in due time;
  For the day of their calamity is
    at hand,
  And the things to come hasten
    upon them.'

36 "For the LORD will judge His
    people
  And have compassion on His
    servants,
  When He sees that their power
    is gone,
  And there is no one remaining,
    bond or free.
37 He will say: 'Where are their
    gods,
  The rock in which they sought
    refuge?
38 Who ate the fat of their
    sacrifices,
  And drank the wine of their
    drink offering?
  Let them rise and help you,
  And be your refuge.
39 'Now see that I, even I, am He,
  And there is no God besides Me;
  I kill and I make alive;
  I wound and I heal;
  Nor is there any who can deliver
    from My hand.
40 For I raise My hand to heaven,
  And say, "As I live forever,
41 If I whet My glittering sword,
  And My hand takes hold on
    judgment,
  I will render vengeance to My
    enemies,
  And repay those who hate Me.
42 I will make My arrows drunk
    with blood,
  And My sword shall devour
    flesh,
  With the blood of the slain and
    the captives,
  From the heads of the leaders
    of the enemy." '

43 "Rejoice, O Gentiles, *with* His people;
For He will avenge the blood of His servants,
And render vengeance to His adversaries;
He will provide atonement for His land *and* His people."

44 So Moses came with Joshua the son of Nun and spoke all the words of this song in the hearing of the people. 45 Moses finished speaking all these words to all Israel, 46 and he said to them: "Set your hearts on all the words which I testify among you today, which you shall command your children to be careful to observe—all the words of this law. 47 For it *is* not a futile thing for you, because it *is* your life, and by this word you shall prolong *your* days in the land which you cross over the Jordan to possess."

48 Then the LORD spoke to Moses that very same day, saying: 49 "Go up this mountain of the Abarim, Mount Nebo, which *is* in the land of Moab, across from Jericho; view the land of Canaan, which I give to the children of Israel as a possession; 50 and die on the mountain which you ascend, and be gathered to your people, just as Aaron your brother died on Mount Hor and was gathered to his people; 51 because you trespassed against Me among the children of Israel at the waters of Meribah Kadesh, in the Wilderness of Zin, because you did not hallow Me in the midst of the children of Israel. 52 Yet you shall see the land before *you,* though you shall not go there, into the land which I am giving to the children of Israel."

Moses gives a final blessing on Israel

33 Now this *is* the blessing with which Moses the man of God blessed the children of Israel before his death. 2 And he said:

"The LORD came from Sinai,
And dawned on them from Seir;
He shone forth from Mount Paran,
And He came with ten thousands of saints;
From His right hand Came a fiery law for them.
3 Yes, He loves the people;
All His saints *are* in Your hand;
They sit down at Your feet;
Everyone receives Your words.
4 Moses commanded a law for us,
A heritage of the congregation of Jacob.
5 And He was King in Jeshurun,
When the leaders of the people were gathered,
All the tribes of Israel together.

6 "Let Reuben live, and not die,
Nor let his men be few."

7 And this he said of Judah:

"Hear, LORD, the voice of Judah,
And bring him to his people;
Let his hands be sufficient for him,
And may You be a help against his enemies."

8 And of Levi he said:

"*Let* Your Thummim and Your Urim *be* with Your holy one,
Whom You tested at Massah,
And with whom You contended at the waters of Meribah,
9 Who says of his father and mother,
'I have not seen them';
Nor did he acknowledge his brothers,
Or know his own children;
For they have observed Your word
And kept Your covenant.
10 They shall teach Jacob Your judgments,
And Israel Your law.
They shall put incense before You,
And a whole burnt sacrifice on Your altar.
11 Bless his substance, LORD,

And accept the work of his
hands;
Strike the loins of those who rise
against him,
And of those who hate him, that
they rise not again."

12 Of Benjamin he said:

"The beloved of the LORD shall
dwell in safety by Him,
Who shelters him all the day
long;
And he shall dwell between His
shoulders."

13 And of Joseph he said:

"Blessed of the LORD *is* his land,
With the precious things of
heaven, with the dew,
And the deep lying beneath,
14 With the precious fruits of the
sun,
With the precious produce of the
months,
15 With the best things of the
ancient mountains,
With the precious things of the
everlasting hills,
16 With the precious things of the
earth and its fullness,
And the favor of Him who dwelt
in the bush.
Let *the blessing* come 'on the
head of Joseph,
And on the crown of the head
of him *who was* separate from
his brothers.'
17 His glory *is like* a firstborn bull,
And his horns *like* the horns of
the wild ox;
Together with them
He shall push the peoples
To the ends of the earth;
They *are* the ten thousands of
Ephraim,
And they *are* the thousands of
Manasseh."

18 And of Zebulun he said:

"Rejoice, Zebulun, in your going
out,
And Issachar in your tents!

19 They shall call the peoples *to* the
mountain;
There they shall offer sacrifices
of righteousness;
For they shall partake *of* the
abundance of the seas
And *of* treasures hidden in the
sand."

20 And of Gad he said:

"Blessed *is* he who enlarges Gad;
He dwells as a lion,
And tears the arm and the crown
of his head.
21 He provided the first *part* for
himself,
Because a lawgiver's portion
was reserved there.
He came *with* the heads of the
people;
He administered the justice of
the LORD,
And His judgments with Israel."

22 And of Dan he said:

"Dan *is* a lion's whelp;
He shall leap from Bashan."

23 And of Naphtali he said:

"O Naphtali, satisfied with favor,
And full of the blessing of the
LORD,
Possess the west and the south."

24 And of Asher he said:

"Asher *is* most blessed of sons;
Let him be favored by his
brothers,
And let him dip his foot in oil.
25 Your sandals *shall be* iron and
bronze;
As your days, *so shall* your
strength *be*.

26 "*There is* no one like the God of
Jeshurun,
Who rides the heavens to help
you,
And in His excellency on the
clouds.
27 The eternal God *is your* refuge,

Greatest Jewish Leader Dies

The Mount Nebo Messenger

MOUNT NEBO—No one was present last week when Moses, the man of God, died on Mount Nebo. It is reported that he spent his last hours alone with God, viewing the beauty of the Promised Land he was forbidden to enter.

Moses' great dream was to cross the Jordan River into Canaan with his people. But he was not permitted to do so because of an earlier disobedience. This was his punishment for forgetting that he was just a servant of God and not a master. (See Numbers 20:10–12.) Apparently God had to make an example of Moses since he was supposed to set the pattern for all Hebrews.

Moses' funeral was conducted by God Himself. He buried Moses in a valley in Moab, near Beth Peor, though the exact location is unknown. Friends and relatives of Moses will mourn for thirty days.

And underneath *are* the
  everlasting arms;
He will thrust out the enemy
  from before you,
And will say, 'Destroy!'
28 Then Israel shall dwell in safety,
The fountain of Jacob alone,
In a land of grain and new wine;
His heavens shall also drop dew.
29 Happy *are* you, O Israel!
Who *is* like you, a people saved
  by the LORD,
The shield of your help
And the sword of your majesty!
Your enemies shall submit to
  you,
And you shall tread down their
  high places."

Moses dies on Mount Nebo

34 Then Moses went up from the plains of Moab to Mount Nebo, to the top of Pisgah, which is across from Jericho. And the LORD showed him all the land of Gilead as far as Dan, 2 all Naphtali and the land of Ephraim and Manasseh, all the land of Judah as far as the Western Sea, 3 the South, and the plain of the Valley of Jericho, the city of palm trees, as far as Zoar. 4 Then the LORD said to him, "This *is* the land of which I swore to give Abraham, Isaac, and Jacob, saying, 'I will give it to your descendants.' I have caused you to see *it* with your eyes, but you shall not cross over there."

5 So Moses the servant of the LORD died there in the land of Moab, according to the word of the LORD. 6 And He buried him in a valley in the land of Moab, opposite Beth Peor; but no one knows his grave to this day. 7 Moses *was* one hundred and twenty years old when he died. His eyes were not dim nor his natural vigor diminished. 8 And the children of Israel wept for Moses in the plains of Moab thirty days. So the days of weeping *and* mourning for Moses ended.

9 Now Joshua the son of Nun was full of the spirit of wisdom, for Moses had laid his hands on him; so the children of Israel heeded him, and did as the LORD had commanded Moses.

10 But since then there has not arisen in Israel a prophet like Moses, whom the LORD knew face to face, 11 in all the signs and wonders which the LORD sent him to do in the land of Egypt, before Pharaoh, before all his servants, and in all his land, 12 and by all that mighty power and all the great terror which Moses performed in the sight of all Israel.

The Book of

JOSHUA

My name is pronounced *JOSH-you-uh* and means "Savior." God really did lead me to save my people from their enemies.

I brought God's people across the Jordan River into the land of Canaan, which God long ago promised to Abraham. There the Commander of the Army of the Lord—who was really God Himself—led us in battle.

Since Abraham's time, the land of Canaan was filled with evil people who even sacrificed little children to their false gods. So the Lord decided to clear the land of such people and give the land back to us for as long as we obeyed His laws.

You also live in a country where God has blessed you because your ancestors have obeyed His laws. The Lord will bless people with a good land when they honor Him.

My name means the same as the name of the great Savior from heaven—Jesus.

God commands Joshua to cross the Jordan

AFTER the death of Moses the servant of the LORD, it came to pass that the LORD spoke to Joshua the son of Nun, Moses' assistant, saying: 2 "Moses My servant is dead. Now therefore, arise, go over this Jordan, you and all this people, to the land which I am giving to them— the children of Israel. 3 Every place that the sole of your foot will tread upon I have given you, as I said to Moses. 4 From the wilderness and this Lebanon as far as the great river, the River Euphrates, all the land of the Hittites, and to the Great Sea toward the going down of the sun, shall be your territory. 5 No man shall *be able to* stand before you all the days of your life; as I was with Moses, *so* I will be with you. I will not leave you nor forsake you. 6 Be strong and of good courage, for to this people you shall divide as an inheritance the land which I swore to their fathers to give them. 7 Only be strong and very courageous, that you

may observe to do according to all the law which Moses My servant commanded you; do not turn from it to the right hand or to the left, that you may prosper wherever you go. 8 This Book of the Law shall not depart from your mouth, but you shall meditate in it day and night, that you may observe to do according to all that is written in it. For then you will make your way prosperous, and then you will have good success. 9 Have I not commanded you? Be strong and of good courage; do not be afraid, nor be dismayed, for the LORD your God *is* with you wherever you go."

10 Then Joshua commanded the officers of the people, saying, 11 "Pass through the camp and command the people, saying, 'Prepare provisions for yourselves, for within three days you will cross over this Jordan, to go in to possess the land which the LORD your God is giving you to possess.' "

12 And to the Reubenites, the Gadites, and half the tribe of Manasseh

> I, Rahab, was terrified when the Hebrew spies came to my home. I was a very wicked person living in Jericho (pronounced *JERRY-ko*), and I had heard that Joshua's Hebrew army was going to destroy our city.
>
> When the spies told me what was going to happen, I agreed that God was right to judge our sinful country. I confessed my sins and became a new person. God saved me that day, not because I was a good woman (I wasn't), but because I was sorry and gave my life to Him. You might say I joined God's army. When the Hebrew troops came into Jericho, they didn't harm me. I left a scarlet cord in my window to remind them that I had hidden their spies.
>
> Someday God is going to destroy the whole world for its wickedness. If you receive Jesus as your Savior, the scarlet sign of His blood will save you from that awful judgment.

Joshua spoke, saying, 13 "Remember the word which Moses the servant of the LORD commanded you, saying, 'The LORD your God is giving you rest and is giving you this land.' 14 Your wives, your little ones, and your livestock shall remain in the land which Moses gave you on this side of the Jordan. But you shall pass before your brethren armed, all your mighty men of valor, and help them, 15 until the LORD has given your brethren rest, as He *gave* you, and they also have taken possession of the land which the LORD your God is giving them. Then you shall return to the land of your possession and enjoy it, which Moses the LORD's servant gave you on this side of the Jordan toward the sunrise."

16 So they answered Joshua, saying, "All that you command us we will do, and wherever you send us we will go. 17 Just as we heeded Moses in all things, so we will heed you. Only the LORD your God be with you, as He was with Moses. 18 Whoever rebels against your command and does not heed your words, in all that you command him, shall be put to death. Only be strong and of good courage."

Rahab hides the spies

2 Now Joshua the son of Nun sent out two men from Acacia Grove to spy secretly, saying, "Go, view the land, especially Jericho."

So they went, and came to the house of a harlot named Rahab, and lodged there. 2 And it was told the king of Jericho, saying, "Behold, men have come here tonight from the children of Israel to search out the country."

3 So the king of Jericho sent to Rahab, saying, "Bring out the men who have come to you, who have entered

DIGGING IN

1:8, 9 A Command and a Promise We have the wrong idea if we think God's orders are harsh or unpleasant. He gives us His commands so we will be happy and succeed at living in the world.

Right now you might say, "I don't need orders because I'm happy just the way I am." Maybe you're happy today, and you may even be happy for many days to come. But what will happen when you have a really bad day? Such days come

to everyone who lives in the world. Where will you turn? If you haven't been listening to God, then you won't know God's way of solving your problem.

In fact, God says to Joshua, "Don't worry, I'm going to be with you wherever you go!" All Joshua had to do was obey what God told him, and God would always be right there to help Him. God wants to be there always to help you, too.

your house, for they have come to search out all the country."

4 Then the woman took the two men and hid them. So she said, "Yes, the men came to me, but I did not know where they *were* from. 5 And it happened as the gate was being shut, when it was dark, that the men went out. Where the men went I do not know; pursue them quickly, for you may overtake them." 6 (But she had brought them up to the roof and hidden them with the stalks of flax, which she had laid in order on the roof.) 7 Then the men pursued them by the road to the Jordan, to the fords. And as soon as those who pursued them had gone out, they shut the gate.

8 Now before they lay down, she came up to them on the roof, 9 and said to the men: "I know that the LORD has given you the land, that the terror of you has fallen on us, and that all the inhabitants of the land are faint-hearted because of you. 10 For we have heard how the LORD dried up the water of the Red Sea for you when you came out of Egypt, and what you did to the two kings of the Amorites who *were* on the other side of the Jordan, Sihon and Og, whom you utterly destroyed. 11 And as soon as we heard *these things,* our hearts melted; neither did there remain any more courage in anyone because of you, for the LORD your God, He *is* God in heaven above and on earth beneath. 12 Now therefore, I beg you, swear to me by the LORD, since I have shown you kindness, that you also will show kindness

to my father's house, and give me a true token, 13 and spare my father, my mother, my brothers, my sisters, and all that they have, and deliver our lives from death."

14 So the men answered her, "Our lives for yours, if none of you tell this business of ours. And it shall be, when the LORD has given us the land, that we will deal kindly and truly with you."

15 Then she let them down by a rope through the window, for her house *was* on the city wall; she dwelt on the wall. 16 And she said to them, "Get to the mountain, lest the pursuers meet you. Hide there three days, until the pursuers have returned. Afterward you may go your way."

17 So the men said to her: "We *will be* blameless of this oath of yours which you have made us swear, 18 unless, *when* we come into the land, you bind this line of scarlet cord in the window through which you let us down, and unless you bring your father, your mother, your brothers, and all your father's household to your own home. 19 So it shall be *that* whoever goes outside the doors of your house into the street, his blood *shall be* on his own head, and we *will be* guiltless. And whoever is with you in the house, his blood *shall be* on our head if a hand is laid on him. 20 And if you tell this business of ours, then we will be free from your oath which you made us swear."

21 Then she said, "According to your words, so *be* it." And she sent them away, and they departed. And she

---

⚒ DIGGING IN

2:17, 18 The Scarlet Cord You have seen how Rahab helped Joshua's spies in Joshua 2. The sign that saved Rahab when the army of Israel came was the sign of the scarlet cord in her window. The scarlet cord was easy to see, but isn't it interesting that the cord was also the color of blood?

On the night of Passover in Egypt (see Exodus 12), God "passed over" the Hebrew homes when He saw the scarlet blood of the Passover lamb on their

doors. So they were saved from death.

As time passed, God taught His Old Testament people that their sins had to be paid for by the life of Someone else. At first He taught them to sacrifice sheep, goats, cattle, and birds. But their beloved animals couldn't pay the awful cost of sin. That was only a way of teaching the people that sin *costs death.*

But this *scarlet line* of death points to the beloved Son of God whose blood takes away the sin of the world.

bound the scarlet cord in the window. 22 They departed and went to the mountain, and stayed there three days until the pursuers returned. The pursuers sought *them* all along the way, but did not find *them*. 23 So the two men returned, descended from the mountain, and crossed over; and they came to Joshua the son of Nun, and told him all that had befallen them. 24 And they said to Joshua, "Truly the LORD has delivered all the land into our hands, for indeed all the inhabitants of the country are fainthearted because of us."

Israel crosses the Jordan

3 Then Joshua rose early in the morning; and they set out from Acacia Grove and came to the Jordan, he and all the children of Israel, and lodged there before they crossed over. 2 So it was, after three days, that the officers went through the camp; 3 and they commanded the people, saying, "When you see the ark of the covenant of the LORD your God, and the priests, the Levites, bearing it, then you shall set out from your place and go after it. 4 Yet there shall be a space between you and it, about two thousand cubits by measure. Do not come near it, that you may know the way by which you must go, for you have not passed *this* way before."

5 And Joshua said to the people, "Sanctify yourselves, for tomorrow the LORD will do wonders among you." 6 Then Joshua spoke to the priests, saying, "Take up the ark of the covenant and cross over before the people."

So they took up the ark of the covenant and went before the people.

7 And the LORD said to Joshua, "This day I will begin to exalt you in the sight of all Israel, that they may know that,

as I was with Moses, *so* I will be with you. 8 You shall command the priests who bear the ark of the covenant, saying, 'When you have come to the edge of the water of the Jordan, you shall stand in the Jordan.' "

9 So Joshua said to the children of Israel, "Come here, and hear the words of the LORD your God." 10 And Joshua said, "By this you shall know that the living God *is* among you, and *that* He will without fail drive out from before you the **Canaanites** and the Hittites and the Hivites and the Perizzites and the Girgashites and the Amorites and the Jebusites: 11 Behold, the ark of the covenant of the Lord of all the earth is crossing over before you into the Jordan. 12 Now therefore, take for yourselves twelve men from the tribes of Israel, one man from every tribe. 13 And it shall come to pass, as soon as the soles of the feet of the priests who bear the ark of the LORD, the Lord of all the earth, shall rest in the waters of the Jordan, *that* the waters of the Jordan shall be cut off, the waters that come down from upstream, and they shall stand as a heap."

14 So it was, when the people set out from their camp to cross over the Jordan, with the priests bearing the ark of the covenant before the people, 15 and as those who bore the ark came to the Jordan, and the feet of the priests who bore the ark dipped in the edge of the water (for the Jordan overflows all its banks during the whole time of harvest), 16 that the waters which came down from upstream stood *still, and* rose in a heap very far away at Adam, the city that *is* beside Zaretan. So the waters that went down into the Sea of the Arabah, the Salt Sea, failed, *and* were cut off; and the people crossed over opposite Jericho. 17 Then the priests who bore the ark of the covenant of the LORD stood firm

---

WORDFINDER

3:10 Canaanites Pronounced *KAY-nuh-nights*. Descendants of Noah's grandson, Canaan. When Jacob and his family moved to Egypt, the dwellers in Palestine became known as Canaanites. Then Palestine was called Canaan.

Hebrews Cross River Jordan

CBN (Canaan Broadcasting Network)—The greatest news of the day reaches us from the Jordan River. The Jews are camped by the river, ready to cross over into Canaan, the Promised Land. (See Numbers 14.) This time it looks as if the Jews are really going to go through with it!

Our camera crews will remain on the scene throughout the day to bring you the events as they unfold. Here come the priests, carrying the ark of the covenant, containing the sacred Law of God. They are approaching the water's edge. Now they are standing, ankle-deep, in the water.

Something unusual is happening! The water has been blocked upstream in some way, and the riverbed seems to be drying out! It appears that forty thousand troops, plus all the people, will be able to cross on dry land! Not since the parting of the Red Sea has such a thing been seen!

Now the last of the people have crossed, and the priests are bringing the ark to the bank of the Jordan. As soon as they reach the other side . . . yes! The water is beginning to flow again!

on dry ground in the midst of the Jordan; and all Israel crossed over on dry ground, until all the people had crossed completely over the Jordan.

Twelve stones help the people remember

4 And it came to pass, when all the people had completely crossed over the Jordan, that the LORD spoke to Joshua, saying: 2 "Take for yourselves twelve men from the people, one man from every tribe, 3 and command them, saying, 'Take for yourselves twelve stones from here, out of the midst of the Jordan, from the place where the priests' feet stood firm. You shall carry them over with you and leave them in the lodging place where you lodge tonight.'"

When the priests carrying the ark of the covenant stepped into the Jordan River, the water was dammed up and the people crossed over on dry land.

4 Then Joshua called the twelve men whom he had appointed from the children of Israel, one man from every tribe; 5 and Joshua said to them: "Cross over before the ark of the LORD your God into the midst of the Jordan, and each one of you take up a stone on his shoulder, according to the number of the tribes of the children of Israel, 6 that this may be a sign among you when your children ask in time to come, saying, 'What do these stones *mean* to you?' 7 Then you shall answer them that the waters of the Jordan were cut off before the ark of the covenant of the LORD; when it crossed over the Jordan, the waters of the Jordan were cut off. And these stones shall be for a memorial to the children of Israel forever."

8 And the children of Israel did so, just as Joshua commanded, and took up twelve stones from the midst of the Jordan, as the LORD had spoken to Joshua, according to the number of the tribes of the children of Israel, and carried them over with them to the place where they lodged, and laid them down there. 9 Then Joshua set up twelve stones in the midst of the Jordan, in the place where the feet of the priests who bore the ark of the covenant stood; and they are there to this day.

10 So the priests who bore the ark stood in the midst of the Jordan until everything was finished that the LORD had commanded Joshua to speak to the people, according to all that Moses had commanded Joshua; and the people hurried and crossed over. 11 Then it came to pass, when all the people had completely crossed over, that the ark of the LORD and the priests crossed over in the presence of the people. 12 And the men of Reuben, the men of Gad, and half the tribe of Manasseh crossed over armed before the children of Israel, as Moses had spoken to them. 13 About forty thousand prepared for war crossed over before the LORD for battle, to the plains of Jericho. 14 On that day the LORD exalted Joshua in the sight of all Israel; and they feared him, as they had feared Moses, all the days of his life.

15 Then the LORD spoke to Joshua, saying, 16 "Command the priests who bear the ark of the Testimony to come up from the Jordan." 17 Joshua therefore commanded the priests, saying, "Come up from the Jordan." 18 And it came to pass, when the priests who bore the ark of the covenant of the LORD had come from the midst of the Jordan, *and* the soles of the priests' feet touched the dry land, that the waters of the Jordan returned to their place and overflowed all its banks as before.

19 Now the people came up from the Jordan on the tenth *day* of the first month, and they camped in Gilgal on the east border of Jericho. 20 And those twelve stones which they took out of the Jordan, Joshua set up in Gilgal. 21 Then he spoke to the children of Israel, saying: "When your children ask their fathers in time to come, saying, 'What *are* these stones?' 22 then you shall let your children know, saying, 'Israel crossed over this Jordan on dry land'; 23 for the LORD your God dried up the waters of the Jordan before you until you had crossed over, as the LORD your God did to the Red Sea, which He dried up before us until we had crossed over, 24 that all the peoples of the earth may know the hand of the LORD, that it *is* mighty, that you may fear the LORD your God forever."

Circumcision and Passover at Gilgal

5 So it was, when all the kings of the Amorites who *were* on the west side of the Jordan, and all the kings of the Canaanites who *were* by the sea, heard that the LORD had dried up the waters of the Jordan from before the children of Israel until we had crossed over, that their heart melted; and there was no spirit in them any longer because of the children of Israel.

2 At that time the LORD said to Joshua, "Make flint knives for yourself, and circumcise the sons of Israel again

the second time." ³So Joshua made flint knives for himself, and circumcised the sons of Israel at the hill of the foreskins. ⁴And this *is* the reason why Joshua circumcised them: All the people who came out of Egypt *who were* males, all the men of war, had died in the wilderness on the way, after they had come out of Egypt. ⁵For all the people who came out had been circumcised, but all the people born in the wilderness, on the way as they came out of Egypt, had not been circumcised. ⁶For the children of Israel walked forty years in the wilderness, till all the people *who were* men of war, who came out of Egypt, were consumed, because they did not obey the voice of the LORD—to whom the LORD swore that He would not show them the land which the LORD had sworn to their fathers that He would give us, "a land flowing with milk and honey."

⁷Then Joshua circumcised their sons *whom* He raised up in their place; for they were uncircumcised, because they had not been circumcised on the way.

⁸So it was, when they had finished circumcising all the people, that they stayed in their places in the camp till they were healed. ⁹Then the LORD said to Joshua, "This day I have rolled away the reproach of Egypt from you." Therefore the name of the place is called Gilgal to this day.

¹⁰Now the children of Israel camped in Gilgal, and kept the Passover on the fourteenth day of the month at twilight on the plains of Jericho. ¹¹And they ate of the produce of the land on the day after the Passover, unleavened bread and parched grain, on the very same day. ¹²Then the manna ceased on the day after they had eaten the produce of the land; and the children of Israel no longer had manna, but they ate the food of the land of Canaan that year.

¹³And it came to pass, when Joshua was by Jericho, that he lifted his eyes and looked, and behold, a Man stood opposite him with His sword drawn in His hand. And Joshua went to Him and said to Him, "Are You for us or for our adversaries?"

¹⁴So He said, "No, but *as* Commander of the army of the LORD I have now come."

And Joshua fell on his face to the earth and worshiped, and said to Him, "What does my Lord say to His servant?"

¹⁵Then the Commander of the LORD's army said to Joshua, "Take your sandal off your foot, for the place where you stand *is* holy." And Joshua did so.

Jericho falls

6 Now Jericho was securely shut up because of the children of Israel; none went out, and none came in. ²And the LORD said to Joshua: "See! I have given Jericho into your hand, its king, *and* the mighty men of valor. ³You shall march around the city, all *you* men of war; you shall go all around

---

⚒ DIGGING IN

5:13–15 The Soldier from Heaven Will Help You Do you ever feel all alone with your troubles? As you get older, the world seems to become a harder place to live in, and you have to get along by yourself many times.

Joshua, the general of Israel's army, may have felt this way, too. Until now, he had always had Moses to guide him. Moses was like a father to Joshua. But now Moses was gone, and Joshua was in charge all alone.

Joshua was wondering how he would fight the battle of Jericho (pronounced *JERRY-ko*) when a mighty Soldier appeared to him with a sword in His hand. At first Joshua must have thought he was going to be killed! But the strange Soldier told Joshua that He was the "Commander of the army of the Lord."

Can you guess who this mighty Soldier was? It was the Lord Himself who appeared to remind Joshua that his battles were really God's battles. As you will see, the Lord Himself did defeat Jericho.

You are *never* alone.

Hebrew Invaders Conquer Jericho

CBN (Canaan Broadcasting Network)—When the Hebrews crossed the Jordan River, our news team crossed over with them.

We are now watching the conquest of Jericho (pronounced *JERRY-ko*), a city of Canaan. The city is surrounded by a high, thick wall. So we are wondering how the Hebrews can possibly win this battle.

What the Jews are doing is a great mystery to us. We have never seen anything like it. They have marched around the city wall once a day for six days, blowing horns as they go. Today, on the seventh day, they have marched around the city seven times.

Now something is happening that makes our hair stand on end. The priests have just blown their horns hard and long. Will you believe it? The walls of Jericho are actually falling down! The Hebrew troops have only to walk in and take over the city!

the city once. This you shall do six days. ⁴ And seven priests shall bear seven trumpets of rams' horns before the ark. But the seventh day you shall march around the city seven times, and the priests shall blow the trumpets. ⁵ It shall come to pass, when they make a long *blast* with the ram's horn, *and* when you hear the sound of the trumpet, that all the people shall shout with a great shout; then the wall of the city will fall down flat. And the people shall go up every man straight before him.''

⁶ Then Joshua the son of Nun called the priests and said to them, ''Take up the ark of the covenant, and let seven priests bear seven trumpets of rams' horns before the ark of the LORD.'' ⁷ And he said to the people, ''Proceed, and march around the city, and let him who is armed advance before the ark of the LORD.''

⁸ So it was, when Joshua had spoken to the people, that the seven priests bearing the seven trumpets of rams' horns before the LORD advanced

The walls of Jericho fell down flat when the priests blew their trumpets and all the people shouted.

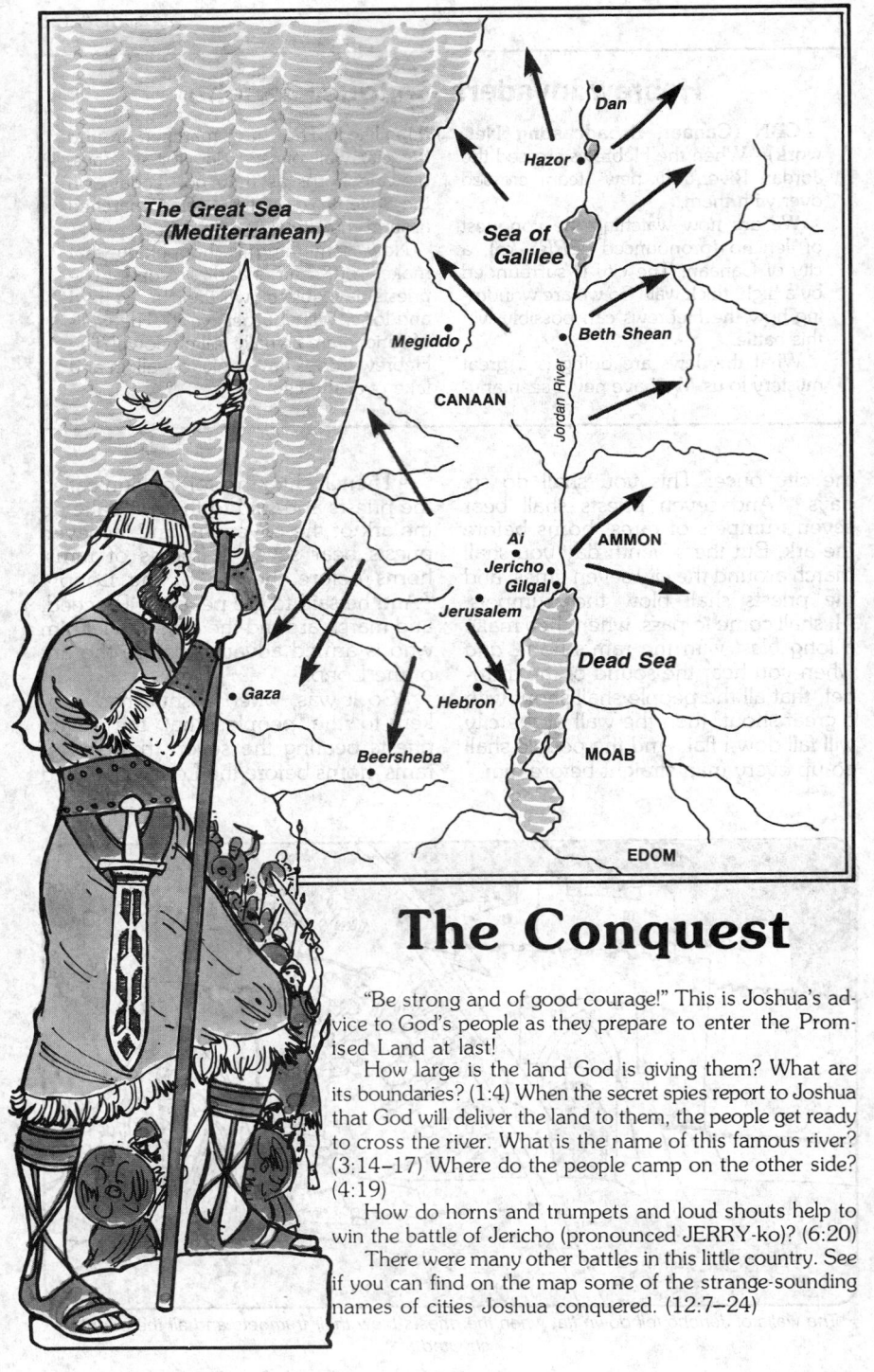

The Great Sea (Mediterranean)

Dan
Hazor
Sea of Galilee
Megiddo
Beth Shean
CANAAN
Jordan River
Ai
Jericho
Gilgal
AMMON
Jerusalem
Dead Sea
Gaza
Hebron
MOAB
Beersheba
EDOM

The Conquest

"Be strong and of good courage!" This is Joshua's advice to God's people as they prepare to enter the Promised Land at last!

How large is the land God is giving them? What are its boundaries? (1:4) When the secret spies report to Joshua that God will deliver the land to them, the people get ready to cross the river. What is the name of this famous river? (3:14–17) Where do the people camp on the other side? (4:19)

How do horns and trumpets and loud shouts help to win the battle of Jericho (pronounced JERRY-ko)? (6:20)

There were many other battles in this little country. See if you can find on the map some of the strange-sounding names of cities Joshua conquered. (12:7–24) and blew the trumpets, and the ark of the covenant of the LORD followed them. 9 The armed men went before the priests who blew the trumpets, and the rear guard came after the ark, while *the priests* continued blowing the trumpets. 10 Now Joshua had commanded the people, saying, "You shall not shout or make any noise with your voice, nor shall a word proceed out of your mouth, until the day I say to you, 'Shout!' Then you shall shout." 11 So he had the ark of the LORD circle the city, going around *it* once. Then they came into the camp and lodged in the camp.

12 And Joshua rose early in the morning, and the priests took up the ark of the LORD. 13 Then seven priests bearing seven trumpets of rams' horns before the ark of the LORD went on continually and blew with the trumpets. And the armed men went before them. But the rear guard came after the ark of the LORD, while *the priests* continued blowing the trumpets. 14 And the second day they marched around the city once and returned to the camp. So they did six days.

15 But it came to pass on the seventh day that they rose early, about the dawning of the day, and marched around the city seven times in the same manner. On that day only they marched around the city seven times. 16 And the seventh time it happened, when the priests blew the trumpets, that Joshua said to the people: "Shout, for the LORD has given you the city! 17 Now the city shall be doomed by the LORD to destruction, it and all who *are* in it. Only Rahab the harlot shall live, she and all who *are* with her in the house, because she hid the messengers that we sent. 18 And you, by all means abstain from the accursed things, lest you become accursed when you take of the accursed things, and make the camp of Israel a curse, and trouble it. 19 But all the silver and gold, and vessels of bronze and iron, *are* consecrated to the LORD; they shall come into the treasury of the LORD."

20 So the people shouted when *the priests* blew the trumpets. And it happened when the people heard the sound of the trumpet, and the people shouted with a great shout, that the wall fell down flat. Then the people went up into the city, *every* man straight before him, and they took the city. 21 And they utterly destroyed all that *was* in the city, both man and woman, young and old, ox and sheep and donkey, with the edge of the sword.

22 But Joshua had said to the two men who had spied out the country, "Go into the harlot's house, and from there bring out the woman and all that she has, as you swore to her." 23 And the young men who had been spies went in and brought out Rahab, her father, her mother, her brothers, and all that she had. So they brought out all her relatives and left them outside the camp of Israel. 24 But they burned the city and all that *was* in it with fire. Only the silver and gold, and the vessels of bronze and iron, they put into the treasury of the house of the LORD. 25 And Joshua spared Rahab the harlot, her father's household, and all that she had. So she dwells in Israel to this day, because she hid the messengers whom Joshua sent to spy out Jericho.

26 Then Joshua charged *them* at that time, saying, "Cursed *be* the man before the LORD who rises up and builds this city Jericho; he shall lay its foundation with his firstborn, and with his youngest he shall set up its gates."

27 So the LORD was with Joshua, and his fame spread throughout all the country.

Achan disobeys God

7 But the children of Israel committed a trespass regarding the accursed things, for Achan the son of Carmi, the son of Zabdi, the son of Zerah, of the tribe of Judah, took of the accursed things; so the anger of the LORD burned against the children of Israel.

2 Now Joshua sent men from Jericho to Ai, which *is* beside Beth Aven, on the east side of Bethel, and spoke to

them, saying, "Go up and spy out the country." So the men went up and spied out Ai. ³ And they returned to Joshua and said to him, "Do not let all the people go up, but let about two or three thousand men go up and attack Ai. Do not weary all the people there, for *the people of Ai are few*." ⁴ So about three thousand men went up there from the people, but they fled before the men of Ai. ⁵ And the men of Ai struck down about thirty-six men, for they chased them *from* before the gate as far as Shebarim, and struck them down on the descent; therefore the hearts of the people melted and became like water.

⁶ Then Joshua tore his clothes, and fell to the earth on his face before the ark of the LORD until evening, he and the elders of Israel; and they put dust on their heads. ⁷ And Joshua said, "Alas, Lord GOD, why have You brought this people over the Jordan at all—to deliver us into the hand of the Amorites, to destroy us? Oh, that we had been content, and dwelt on the other side of the Jordan! ⁸ O Lord, what shall I say when Israel turns its back before its enemies? ⁹ For the Canaanites and all the inhabitants of the land will hear *it*, and surround us, and cut off our name from the earth. Then what will You do for Your great name?"

¹⁰ So the LORD said to Joshua: "Get up! Why do you lie thus on your face? ¹¹ Israel has sinned, and they have also transgressed My covenant which I

commanded them. For they have even taken some of the accursed things, and have both stolen and deceived; and they have also put *it* among their own stuff. ¹² Therefore the children of Israel could not stand before their enemies, *but* turned *their* backs before their enemies, because they have become doomed to destruction. Neither will I be with you anymore, unless you destroy the accursed from among you. ¹³ Get up, sanctify the people, and say, 'Sanctify yourselves for tomorrow, because thus says the LORD God of Israel: "*There is* an accursed thing in your midst, O Israel; you cannot stand before your enemies until you take away the accursed thing from among you." ¹⁴ In the morning therefore you shall be brought according to your tribes. And it shall be *that* the tribe which the LORD takes shall come according to families; and the family which the LORD takes shall come by households; and the household which the LORD takes shall come man by man. ¹⁵ Then it shall be *that* he who is taken with the accursed thing shall be burned with fire, he and all that he has, because he has transgressed the covenant of the LORD, and because he has done a disgraceful thing in Israel.' "

¹⁶ So Joshua rose early in the morning and brought Israel by their tribes, and the tribe of Judah was taken. ¹⁷ He brought the clan of Judah, and he took the family of the Zarhites; and he brought the family of the Zarhites man by man, and Zabdi was taken.

⚒ DIGGING IN

7:10–12 One Reason We Don't Always Win Everyone likes to be a winner. And after the battle of Jericho, the people of Israel and Joshua felt they couldn't lose. But they did.

You know what happened at Ai (pronounced *AY-eye*). See the news article, "Joshua Conquers Ai."

God has promised to help us overcome our hard places in life, but if we're not honest with God, He can't help us. He can't help us because He would be sharing our disobedience if He did.

If you try to go out into the battle of life without a careful look at your heart and life, you can be sure your plans will fall flat!

Nobody is completely free from sin. Achan's sin should have been confessed before the first battle for Ai. This is a good example for us.

Always play fair with God. Tell him about the disobedience in your heart. Ask Him to forgive and take away your sins. Then you can't lose the battle.

Joshua Conquers Ai

CBN (Canaan Broadcasting Network)—Israel's conquest of Canaan has been quite an experience for our Egyptian news team. We had never seen a battle like the one at Jericho. Then we saw the fall of the city Ai (pronounced *AY-eye*).

Things didn't go as well for the Jews at Ai as at Jericho. The first try failed badly, and a number of Israel's soldiers were killed. Our sources report that the Lord told Joshua that this defeat was the result of secret sin in the Hebrew camp. One of their soldiers, a man named Achan (pronounced *AY-kin*), kept a forbidden article that he had taken from Jericho. That man has reportedly come to a bad end (see verse 25).

The next attack on Ai was a success. The Hebrew army under Joshua pretended to run from the army of Ai. But that was a trick. Other Hebrew soldiers were waiting in ambush for the enemy troops. So Ai has fallen to the Jews.

18 Then he brought his household man by man, and Achan the son of Carmi, the son of Zabdi, the son of Zerah, of the tribe of Judah, was taken. 19 Now Joshua said to Achan, "My son, I beg you, give glory to the Lord God of Israel, and make confession to Him, and tell me now what you have done; do not hide *it* from me."

20 And Achan answered Joshua and said, "Indeed I have sinned against the Lord God of Israel, and this is what I have done: 21 When I saw among the spoils a beautiful Babylonian garment, two hundred shekels of silver, and a wedge of gold weighing fifty shekels, I coveted them and took them. And there they are, hidden in the earth in the midst of my tent, with the silver under it."

22 So Joshua sent messengers, and they ran to the tent; and there it was, hidden in his tent, with the silver under it. 23 And they took them from the midst of the tent, brought them to Joshua and to all the children of Israel, and laid them out before the Lord. 24 Then Joshua, and all Israel with him, took Achan the son of Zerah, the silver, the garment, the wedge of gold, his sons, his daughters, his oxen, his donkeys, his sheep, his tent, and all that he had, and they brought them to the Valley of Achor. 25 And Joshua said, "Why have you troubled us? The Lord will trouble you this day." So all Israel stoned him with stones; and they burned them with fire after they had stoned them with stones.

26 Then they raised over him a great heap of stones, still there to this day. So the Lord turned from the fierceness of His anger. Therefore the name of that place has been called the Valley of Achor to this day.

What Does Achan Mean to You?

Achan (pronounced *AY-kin*) caused the failure of Joshua's first try to conquer Ai (pronounced *AY-eye*). The Lord had warned the army of Israel to destroy all their enemies' goods, but Achan stole something for himself. The lesson here is that we must not try to hide our sins from God.

Israel captures and destroys Ai

8 Now the Lord said to Joshua: "Do not be afraid, nor be dismayed; take all the people of war with you, and arise, go up to Ai. See, I have given into your hand the king of Ai, his people, his city, and his land. 2 And you shall do to Ai and its king as you did to Jericho and its king. Only its spoil and its cattle you shall take as booty

for yourselves. Lay an ambush for the city behind it.''

3 So Joshua arose, and all the people of war, to go up against Ai; and Joshua chose thirty thousand mighty men of valor and sent them away by night. 4 And he commanded them, saying: "Behold, you shall lie in ambush against the city, behind the city. Do not go very far from the city, but all of you be ready. 5 Then I and all the people who are with me will approach the city; and it will come about, when they come out against us as at the first, that we shall flee before them. 6 For they will come out after us till we have drawn them from the city, for they will say, 'They are fleeing before us as at the first.' Therefore we will flee before them. 7 Then you shall rise from the ambush and seize the city, for the LORD your God will deliver it into your hand. 8 And it will be, when you have taken the city, that you shall set the city on fire. According to the commandment of the LORD you shall do. See, I have commanded you.''

9 Joshua therefore sent them out; and they went to lie in ambush, and stayed between Bethel and Ai, on the west side of Ai; but Joshua lodged that night among the people. 10 Then Joshua rose up early in the morning and mustered the people, and went up, he and the elders of Israel, before the people to Ai. 11 And all the people of war who were with him went up and drew near; and they came before the city and camped on the north side of Ai. Now a valley lay between them and Ai. 12 So he took about five thousand men and set them in ambush between Bethel and Ai, on the west side of the city. 13 And when they had set the people, all the army that was on the north of the city, and its rear guard on the west of the city, Joshua went that night into the midst of the valley.

14 Now it happened, when the king of Ai saw it, that the men of the city hurried and rose early and went out against Israel to battle, he and all his people, at an appointed place before the plain. But he did not know that there was an ambush against him behind the city. 15 And Joshua and all Israel made as if they were beaten before them, and fled by the way of the wilderness. 16 So all the people who were in Ai were called together to pursue them. And they pursued Joshua and were drawn away from the city. 17 There was not a man left in Ai or Bethel who did not go out after Israel. So they left the city open and pursued Israel.

18 Then the LORD said to Joshua, "Stretch out the spear that is in your hand toward Ai, for I will give it into your hand." And Joshua stretched out the spear that was in his hand toward the city. 19 So those in ambush arose quickly out of their place; they ran as soon as he had stretched out his hand, and they entered the city and took it, and hurried to set the city on fire. 20 And when the men of Ai looked behind them, they saw, and behold, the smoke of the city ascended to heaven. So they had no power to flee this way or that way, and the people who had fled to the wilderness turned back on the pursuers.

21 Now when Joshua and all Israel saw that the ambush had taken the city and that the smoke of the city ascended, they turned back and struck down the men of Ai. 22 Then the others came out of the city against them; so they were caught in the midst of Israel, some on this side and some on that side. And they struck them down, so that they let none of them remain or escape. 23 But the king of Ai they took alive, and brought him to Joshua.

24 And it came to pass when Israel had made an end of slaying all the inhabitants of Ai in the field, in the wilderness where they pursued them, and when they all had fallen by the edge of the sword until they were consumed, that all the Israelites returned to Ai and struck it with the edge of the sword. 25 So it was that all who fell that day, both men and women, were twelve thousand—all the people of Ai. 26 For Joshua did not draw back his hand, with which he stretched out

the spear, until he had utterly destroyed all the inhabitants of Ai. [27] Only the livestock and the spoil of that city Israel took as booty for themselves, according to the word of the LORD which He had commanded Joshua. [28] So Joshua burned Ai and made it a heap forever, a desolation to this day. [29] And the king of Ai he hanged on a tree until evening. And as soon as the sun was down, Joshua commanded that they should take his corpse down from the tree, cast it at the entrance of the gate of the city, and raise over it a great heap of stones *that remains* to this day.

[30] Now Joshua built an altar to the LORD God of Israel in Mount Ebal, [31] as Moses the servant of the LORD had commanded the children of Israel, as it is written in the Book of the Law of Moses: "an altar of whole stones over which no man has wielded an iron *tool*." And they offered on it burnt offerings to the LORD, and sacrificed peace offerings. [32] And there, in the presence of the children of Israel, he wrote on the stones a copy of the law of Moses, which he had written. [33] Then all Israel, with their elders and officers and judges, stood on either side of the ark before the priests, the Levites, who bore the ark of the covenant of the LORD, the stranger as well as he who was born among them. Half of them *were* in front of Mount Gerizim and half of them in front of Mount Ebal, as Moses the servant of the LORD had commanded before, that they should bless the people of Israel. [34] And afterward he read all the words of the law, the blessings and the cursings, according to all that is written in the Book of the Law. [35] There was not a word of all that Moses had commanded which Joshua did not read before all the assembly of Israel, with the women, the little ones, and the strangers who were living among them.

The Gibeonites deceive Israel

9 And it came to pass when all the kings who *were* on this side of the Jordan, in the hills and in the lowland and in all the coasts of the Great Sea toward Lebanon—the Hittite, the Amorite, the Canaanite, the Perizzite, the Hivite, and the Jebusite—heard *about it*, [2] that they gathered together to fight with Joshua and Israel with one accord.

[3] But when the inhabitants of Gibeon heard what Joshua had done to Jericho and Ai, [4] they worked craftily, and went and pretended to be ambassadors. And they took old sacks on their donkeys, old wineskins torn and mended, [5] old and patched sandals on their feet, and old garments on themselves; and all the bread of their provision was dry *and* moldy. [6] And they went to Joshua, to the camp at Gilgal, and said to him and to the men of Israel, "We have come from a far country; now therefore, make a covenant with us."

[7] Then the men of Israel said to the Hivites, "Perhaps you dwell among us; so how can we make a covenant with you?"

[8] But they said to Joshua, "We *are* your servants."

And Joshua said to them, "Who *are* you, and where do you come from?"

[9] So they said to him: "From a very far country your servants have come, because of the name of the LORD your God; for we have heard of His fame, and all that He did in Egypt, [10] and all that He did to the two kings of the Amorites who *were* beyond the Jordan—to Sihon king of Heshbon, and Og king of Bashan, who was at Ashtaroth. [11] Therefore our elders and all the inhabitants of our country spoke to us, saying, 'Take provisions with you for the journey, and go to meet them, and say to them, "We *are* your servants; now therefore, make a covenant with us." ' [12] This bread of ours we took hot *for* our provision from our houses on the day we departed to come to you. But now look, it is dry and moldy. [13] And these wineskins which we filled *were* new, and see, they are torn; and these our garments and our sandals

Israel Makes Treaty with Gibeon

Canaan Wire Service

GIBEON—Our news reporters are shocked by the speed with which the Jews are taking the land of Canaan. Joshua's army can't be stopped!

A recent report from Gibeon (pronounced *GIB-ee-un*) describes the people's plan to escape the Hebrew army. The story is that the people of Gibeon sent a few men in worn-out clothes and with old food supplies to Israel. They told Joshua they were from a faraway country and wanted to make a treaty with Israel. Joshua agreed.

Later, the Jews found they had been fooled, but it was too late. The treaty had been made, and the Jews had to keep their agreement with Gibeon.

The Hebrews had the last word anyway—the people from Gibeon were made slaves. But we think Gibeon played a smart trick on the Jews. At least the people of Gibeon escaped with their lives!

have become old because of the very long journey.''

14 Then the men of Israel took some of their provisions; but they did not ask counsel of the LORD. 15 So Joshua made peace with them, and made a covenant with them to let them live; and the rulers of the congregation swore to them.

16 And it happened at the end of three days, after they had made a covenant with them, that they heard that they *were* their neighbors who dwelt near them. 17 Then the children of Israel journeyed and came to their cities on the third day. Now their cities *were* Gibeon, Chephirah, Beeroth, and Kirjath Jearim. 18 But the children of Israel did not attack them, because the rulers of the congregation had sworn to them by the LORD God of Israel. And all the congregation complained against the rulers.

19 Then all the rulers said to all the congregation, ''We have sworn to them by the LORD God of Israel; now therefore, we may not touch them. 20 This we will do to them: We will let them live, lest wrath be upon us because of the oath which we swore to them.'' 21 And the rulers said to them, ''Let them live, but let them be woodcutters and water carriers for all the congregation, as the rulers had promised them.''

22 Then Joshua called for them, and he spoke to them, saying, ''Why have you deceived us, saying, 'We *are* very far from you,' when you dwell near us? 23 Now therefore, you *are* cursed, and none of you shall be freed from being slaves—woodcutters and water carriers for the house of my God.''

24 So they answered Joshua and said, ''Because your servants were clearly told that the LORD your God commanded His servant Moses to give you all the land, and to destroy all the inhabitants of the land from before you; therefore we were very much afraid for our lives because of you, and have done this thing. 25 And now, here we are, in your hands; do with us as it seems good and right to do to us.'' 26 So he did to them, and delivered them out of the hand of the children of Israel, so that they did not kill them. 27 And that day Joshua made them woodcutters and water carriers for the congregation and for the altar of the LORD, in the place which He would choose, even to this day.

The sun and moon stand still

10 Now it came to pass when Adoni-Zedek king of Jerusalem heard how Joshua had taken Ai and had utterly destroyed it—as he had done to

Jericho and its king, so he had done to Ai and its king—and how the inhabitants of Gibeon had made peace with Israel and were among them, 2 that they feared greatly, because Gibeon was a great city, like one of the royal cities, and because it was greater than Ai, and all its men were mighty. 3 Therefore Adoni-Zedek king of Jerusalem sent to Hoham king of Hebron, Piram king of Jarmuth, Japhia king of Lachish, and Debir king of Eglon, saying, 4 "Come up to me and help me, that we may attack Gibeon, for it has made peace with Joshua and with the children of Israel." 5 Therefore the five kings of the Amorites, the king of Jerusalem, the king of Hebron, the king of Jarmuth, the king of Lachish, and the king of Eglon, gathered together and went up, they and all their armies, and camped before Gibeon and made war against it.

6 And the men of Gibeon sent to Joshua at the camp at Gilgal, saying, "Do not forsake your servants; come up to us quickly, save us and help us, for all the kings of the Amorites who dwell in the mountains have gathered together against us."

7 So Joshua ascended from Gilgal, he and all the people of war with him, and all the mighty men of valor. 8 And the LORD said to Joshua, "Do not fear them, for I have delivered them into your hand; not a man of them shall stand before you." 9 Joshua therefore came upon them suddenly, having marched all night from Gilgal. 10 So the LORD routed them before Israel, killed them with a great slaughter at Gibeon, chased them along the road that goes to Beth Horon, and struck them down as far as Azekah and Makkedah. 11 And it happened, as they fled before Israel and were on the descent of Beth Horon, that the LORD cast down large hailstones from heaven on them as far as Azekah, and they died. There were more who died from the hailstones than the children of Israel killed with the sword.

12 Then Joshua spoke to the LORD in the day when the LORD delivered up the Amorites before the children of Israel, and he said in the sight of Israel:

"Sun, stand still over Gibeon;
And Moon, in the Valley of Aijalon."
13 So the sun stood still,
And the moon stopped,
Till the people had revenge
Upon their enemies.

Is this not written in the Book of Jasher? So the sun stood still in the midst of heaven, and did not hasten to go down for about a whole day. 14 And there has been no day like that, before it or after it, that the LORD heeded the voice of a man; for the LORD fought for Israel.

15 Then Joshua returned, and all Israel with him, to the camp at Gilgal.

16 But these five kings had fled and hidden themselves in a cave at Makkedah. 17 And it was told Joshua, saying, "The five kings have been found hidden in the cave at Makkedah."

18 So Joshua said, "Roll large stones against the mouth of the cave, and set men by it to guard them. 19 And do not stay there yourselves, but pursue your enemies, and attack their rear guard. Do not allow them to enter their cities, for the LORD your God has delivered them into your hand." 20 Then it happened, while Joshua and the children of Israel made an end of slaying them with a very great slaughter, till they had finished, that those who escaped entered fortified cities. 21 And all the people returned to the camp, to Joshua at Makkedah, in peace.

No one moved his tongue against any of the children of Israel.

22 Then Joshua said, "Open the mouth of the cave, and bring out those five kings to me from the cave." 23 And they did so, and brought out those five kings to him from the cave: the king of Jerusalem, the king of Hebron, the king of Jarmuth, the king of Lachish, and the king of Eglon. 24 So it was, when they brought out those kings to Joshua, that Joshua called for all the men of Israel, and said

What Was the Longest Day in History?

The day our army landed in France in World War II was called "the longest day of the war." Because no one was sure the invasion would succeed, that day seemed to last forever. These verses, however, tell about a day that really *was* longer! Joshua needed more daylight hours to fight his battle, so the Lord made the day longer.

to the captains of the men of war who went with him, "Come near, put your feet on the necks of these kings." And they drew near and put their feet on their necks. 25 Then Joshua said to them, "Do not be afraid, nor be dismayed; be strong and of good courage, for thus the LORD will do to all your enemies against whom you

fight." 26 And afterward Joshua struck them and killed them, and hanged them on five trees; and they were hanging on the trees until evening. 27 So it was at the time of the going down of the sun *that* Joshua commanded, and they took them down from the trees, cast them into the cave where they had been hidden, and laid large stones against the cave's mouth, *which remain* until this very day.

28 On that day Joshua took Makkedah, and struck it and its king with the edge of the sword. He utterly destroyed them—all the people who *were* in it. He let none remain. He also did to the king of Makkedah as he had done to the king of Jericho.

29 Then Joshua passed from Makkedah, and all Israel with him, to Libnah; and they fought against Libnah. 30 And the LORD also delivered it and its king into the hand of Israel; he

God caused the sun and moon to stand still while He fought for Israel.

struck it and all the people who *were* in it with the *edge* of the sword. He let none remain in it, but did to its king as he had done to the king of Jericho.

31 Then Joshua passed from Libnah, and all Israel with him, to Lachish; and they encamped against it and fought against it. 32 And the LORD delivered Lachish into the hand of Israel, who took it on the second day, and struck it and all the people who *were* in it with the edge of the sword, according to all that he had done to Libnah. 33 Then Horam king of Gezer came up to help Lachish; and Joshua struck him and his people, until he left him none remaining.

34 From Lachish Joshua passed to Eglon, and all Israel with him; and they encamped against it and fought against it. 35 They took it on that day and struck it with the edge of the sword; all the people who *were* in it he utterly destroyed that day, according to all that he had done to Lachish.

36 So Joshua went up from Eglon, and all Israel with him, to Hebron; and they fought against it. 37 And they took it and struck it with the edge of the sword—its king, all its cities, and all the people who *were* in it; he left none remaining, according to all that he had done to Eglon, but utterly destroyed it and all the people who *were* in it.

38 Then Joshua returned, and all Israel with him, to Debir; and they fought against it. 39 And he took it and its king and all its cities; they struck them with the edge of the sword and utterly destroyed all the people who *were* in it. He left none remaining; as he had done to Hebron, so he did to Debir and its king, as he had done also to Libnah and its king.

40 So Joshua conquered all the land: the mountain country and the South and the lowland and the wilderness slopes, and all their kings; he left none remaining, but utterly destroyed all that breathed, as the LORD God of Israel had commanded. 41 And Joshua conquered them from Kadesh Barnea as far as Gaza, and all the country of Goshen, even as far as Gibeon.

42 All these kings and their land Joshua took at one time, because the LORD God of Israel fought for Israel. 43 Then Joshua returned, and all Israel with him, to the camp at Gilgal.

Joshua conquers all the land

11 And it came to pass, when Jabin king of Hazor heard *these things,* that he sent to Jobab king of Madon, to the king of Shimron, to the king of Achshaph, 2 and to the kings who *were* from the north, in the mountains, in the plain south of Chinneroth, in the lowland, and in the heights of Dor on the west, 3 to the Canaanites in the east and in the west, the Amorite, the Hittite, the Perizzite, the Jebusite in the mountains, and the Hivite below Hermon in the land of Mizpah. 4 So they went out, they and all their armies with them, *as* many people *as* the sand that *is* on the seashore in multitude, with very many horses and chariots. 5 And when all these kings had met together, they came and camped together at the waters of Merom to fight against Israel.

6 But the LORD said to Joshua, "Do not be afraid because of them, for tomorrow about this time I will deliver all of them slain before Israel. You shall hamstring their horses and burn their chariots with fire." 7 So Joshua and all the people of war with him came against them suddenly by the waters of Merom, and they attacked them. 8 And the LORD delivered them into the hand of Israel, who defeated them and chased them to Greater Sidon, to the Brook Misrephoth, and to the Valley of Mizpah eastward; they attacked them until they left none of them remaining. 9 So Joshua did to them as the LORD had told him: he hamstrung their horses and burned their chariots with fire.

10 Joshua turned back at that time and took Hazor, and struck its king with the sword; for Hazor was formerly the head of all those kingdoms. 11 And they struck all the people who *were* in it with the edge of the sword, utterly destroying *them.* There was none left

How Did Joshua's Army Conquer Canaan?

The army of Joshua conquered nearly the whole land of Canaan. This included the enemies Israel was afraid of when they refused to enter the Promised Land the first time (see Numbers 13:31). Some of these enemies were giants. We learn from this that God fights all our battles of life if we will just do what He says.

breathing. Then he burned Hazor with fire.

12 So all the cities of those kings, and all their kings, Joshua took and struck with the edge of the sword. He utterly destroyed them, as Moses the servant of the LORD had commanded. 13 But *as for* the cities that stood on their mounds, Israel burned none of them, except Hazor only, *which* Joshua burned. 14 And all the spoil of these cities and the livestock, the children of Israel took as booty for themselves; but they struck every man with the edge of the sword until they had destroyed them, and they left none breathing. 15 As the LORD had commanded Moses his servant, so Moses commanded Joshua, and so Joshua did. He left nothing undone of all that the LORD had commanded Moses.

16 Thus Joshua took all this land: the mountain country, all the South, all the land of Goshen, the lowland, and the Jordan plain—the mountains of Israel and its lowlands, 17 from Mount Halak and the ascent to Seir, even as far as Baal Gad in the Valley of Lebanon below Mount Hermon. He captured all their kings, and struck them down and killed them. 18 Joshua made war a long time with all those kings. 19 There was not a city that made peace with the children of Israel, except the Hivites, the inhabitants of Gibeon. All *the others* they took in battle. 20 For it was of the LORD to harden their hearts, that they should come against Israel in battle, that He might utterly destroy them, *and* that they might receive no mercy, but that He might destroy them, as the LORD had commanded Moses.

21 And at that time Joshua came and cut off the Anakim from the mountains: from Hebron, from Debir, from Anab, from all the mountains of Judah, and from all the mountains of Israel; Joshua utterly destroyed them with their cities. 22 None of the Anakim were left in the

Joshua obeyed God and destroyed the city of Hazor.

land of the children of Israel; they remained only in Gaza, in Gath, and in Ashdod.

23 So Joshua took the whole land, according to all that the LORD had said to Moses; and Joshua gave it as an inheritance to Israel according to their divisions by their tribes. Then the land rested from war.

Joshua conquers a number of kings

12 These *are* the kings of the land whom the children of Israel defeated, and whose land they possessed on the other side of the Jordan toward the rising of the sun, from the River Arnon to Mount Hermon, and all the eastern Jordan plain: 2 *One king was* Sihon king of the Amorites, who dwelt in Heshbon *and* ruled half of Gilead, from Aroer, which is on the bank of the River Arnon, from the middle of that river, even as far as the River Jabbok, *which is* the border of the Ammonites, 3 and the eastern Jordan plain from the Sea of Chinneroth as far as the Sea of the Arabah (the Salt Sea), the road to Beth Jeshimoth, and southward below the slopes of Pisgah. 4 *The other king was* Og king of Bashan and his territory, *who was* of the remnant of the giants, who dwelt at Ashtaroth and at Edrei, 5 and reigned over Mount Hermon, over Salcah, over all Bashan, as far as the border of the Geshurites and the Maachathites, and over half of Gilead *to* the border of Sihon king of Heshbon.

6 These Moses the servant of the LORD and the children of Israel had conquered; and Moses the servant of the LORD had given it *as* a possession to the Reubenites, the Gadites, and half the tribe of Manasseh.

7 And these *are* the kings of the country which Joshua and the children of Israel conquered on this side of the Jordan, on the west, from Baal Gad in the Valley of Lebanon as far as Mount Halak and the ascent to Seir, which Joshua gave to the tribes of Israel *as* a possession according to their

divisions, 8 in the mountain country, in the lowlands, in the *Jordan* plain, in the slopes, in the wilderness, and in the South—the Hittites, the Amorites, the Canaanites, the Perizzites, the Hivites, and the Jebusites: 9 the king of Jericho, one; the king of Ai, which *is* beside Bethel, one; 10 the king of Jerusalem, one; the king of Hebron, one; 11 the king of Jarmuth, one; the king of Lachish, one; 12 the king of Eglon, one; the king of Gezer, one; 13 the king of Debir, one; the king of Geder, one; 14 the king of Hormah, one; the king of Arad, one; 15 the king of Libnah, one; the king of Adullam, one; 16 the king of Makkedah, one; the king of Bethel, one; 17 the king of Tappuah, one; the king of Hepher, one; 18 the king of Aphek, one; the king of Lasharon, one; 19 the king of Madon, one; the king of Hazor, one; 20 the king of Shimron Meron, one; the king of Achshaph, one; 21 the king of Taanach, one; the king of Megiddo, one; 22 the king of Kedesh, one; the king of Jokneam in Carmel, one; 23 the king of Dor in the heights of Dor, one; the king of the people of Gilgal, one; 24 the king of Tirzah, one—all the kings, thirty-one.

The land east of the Jordan River

13 Now Joshua was old, advanced in years. And the LORD said to him: "You are old, advanced in years, and there remains very much land yet to be possessed. 2 This is the land that yet remains: all the territory of the Philistines and all *that of* the Geshurites, 3 from Sihor, which *is* east of Egypt, as far as the border of Ekron northward (*which* is counted as Canaanite); the five lords of the Philistines—the Gazites, the Ashdodites, the Ashkelonites, the Gittites, and the Ekronites; also the Avites; 4 from the south, all the land of the Canaanites, and Mearah that belongs to the Sidonians as far as Aphek, to the border of the Amorites; 5 the land of the Gebalites, and all Lebanon, toward the sunrise, from Baal Gad below Mount Hermon as far as the

Ruins of Aphek, a Philistine city conquered by Joshua.

entrance to Hamath; 6 all the inhabitants of the mountains from Lebanon as far as the Brook Misrephoth, *and* all the Sidonians—them I will drive out from before the children of Israel; only divide it by lot to Israel as an inheritance, as I have commanded you. 7 Now therefore, divide this land as an inheritance to the nine tribes and half the tribe of Manasseh."

8 With the other half-tribe the Reubenites and the Gadites received their inheritance, which Moses had given them, beyond the Jordan eastward, as Moses the servant of the LORD had given them: 9 from Aroer which *is* on the bank of the River Arnon, and the town that *is* in the midst of the ravine, and all the plain of Medeba as far as Dibon; 10 all the cities of Sihon king of the Amorites, who reigned in Heshbon, as far as the border of the children of Ammon; 11 Gilead, and the border of the Geshurites and Maachathites, all Mount Hermon, and all Bashan as far as Salcah; 12 all the kingdom of Og in Bashan, who reigned in Ashtaroth and Edrei, who remained of the remnant

of the giants; for Moses had defeated and cast out these.

13 Nevertheless the children of Israel did not drive out the Geshurites or the Maachathites, but the Geshurites and the Maachathites dwell among the Israelites until this day.

14 Only to the tribe of Levi he had given no inheritance; the sacrifices of the LORD God of Israel made by fire *are* their inheritance, as He said to them.

15 And Moses had given to the tribe of the children of Reuben *an inheritance* according to their families. 16 Their territory was from Aroer, which *is* on the bank of the River Arnon, and the city that *is* in the midst of the ravine, and all the plain by Medeba; 17 Heshbon and all its cities that *are* in the plain: Dibon, Bamoth Baal, Beth Baal Meon, 18 Jahaza, Kedemoth, Mephaath, 19 Kirjathaim, Sibmah, Zereth Shahar on the mountain of the valley, 20 Beth Peor, the slopes of Pisgah, and Beth Jeshimoth— 21 all the cities of the plain and all the kingdom of Sihon king of the Amorites, who

reigned in Heshbon, whom Moses had struck with the princes of Midian: Evi, Rekem, Zur, Hur, and Reba, who *were* princes of Sihon dwelling in the country. 22 The children of Israel also killed with the sword Balaam the son of Beor, the soothsayer, among those who were killed by them. 23 And the border of the children of Reuben was the bank of the Jordan. This *was* the inheritance of the children of Reuben according to their families, the cities and their villages.

24 Moses also had given *an inheritance* to the tribe of Gad, to the children of Gad according to their families. 25 Their territory was Jazer, and all the cities of Gilead, and half the land of the Ammonites as far as Aroer, which *is* before Rabbah, 26 and from Heshbon to Ramath Mizpah and Betonim, and from Mahanaim to the border of Debir, 27 and in the valley Beth Haram, Beth Nimrah, Succoth, and Zaphon, the rest of the kingdom of Sihon king of Heshbon, with the Jordan as *its* border, as far as the edge of the Sea of Chinnereth, on the other side of the Jordan eastward. 28 This *is* the inheritance of the children of Gad according to their families, the cities and their villages.

29 Moses also had given *an inheritance* to half the tribe of Manasseh; it was for half the tribe of the children of Manasseh according to their families: 30 Their territory was from Mahanaim, all Bashan, all the kingdom of Og king of Bashan, and all the towns of Jair which are in Bashan, sixty cities; 31 half of Gilead, and Ashtaroth and Edrei, cities of the kingdom of Og in Bashan, *were* for the children of Machir the son of Manasseh, for half of the children of Machir according to their families.

32 These *are the areas* which Moses had distributed as an inheritance in the plains of Moab on the other side of the Jordan, by Jericho eastward. 33 But to the tribe of Levi Moses had given no inheritance; the LORD God of Israel *was* their inheritance, as He had said to them.

The land west of the Jordan River; Caleb is given Hebron

14 These *are the areas* which the children of Israel inherited in the land of Canaan, which Eleazar the priest, Joshua the son of Nun, and the heads of the fathers of the tribes of the children of Israel distributed as an inheritance to them. 2 Their inheritance *was* by lot, as the LORD had commanded by the hand of Moses, for the nine tribes and the half-tribe. 3 For Moses had given the inheritance of the two tribes and the half-tribe on the other side of the Jordan; but to the Levites he had given no inheritance among them. 4 For the children of Joseph were two tribes: Manasseh and Ephraim. And they gave no part to the Levites in the land, except cities to dwell *in*, with their common-lands for their livestock and their property. 5 As the LORD had commanded Moses, so the children of Israel did; and they divided the land.

6 Then the children of Judah came to Joshua in Gilgal. And Caleb the son of Jephunneh the Kenizzite said to him: "You know the word which the LORD said to Moses the man of God concerning you and me in Kadesh Barnea. 7 I *was* forty years old when Moses the servant of the LORD sent me from Kadesh Barnea to spy out the land, and I brought back word to him as *it was* in my heart. 8 Nevertheless my brethren who went up with me made the heart of the people melt, but I wholly followed the LORD my God. 9 So Moses swore on that day, saying, 'Surely the land where your foot has trodden shall be your inheritance and your children's forever, because you have wholly followed the LORD my God.' 10 And now, behold, the LORD has kept me alive, as He said, these forty-five years, *ever* since the LORD spoke this word to Moses while Israel wandered in the wilderness; and now, here I am this day, eighty-five years old. 11 As yet I *am as* strong this day as on the day that Moses sent me; just as my strength *was* then, so now *is* my strength for

war, both for going out and for coming in. ¹²Now therefore, give me this mountain of which the LORD spoke in that day; for you heard in that day how the Anakim *were* there, and *that* the cities *were* great *and* fortified. It may be that the LORD *will be* with me, and I shall be able to drive them out as the LORD said."

¹³And Joshua blessed him, and gave Hebron to Caleb the son of Jephunneh as an inheritance. ¹⁴Hebron therefore became the inheritance of Caleb the son of Jephunneh the Kenizzite to this day, because he wholly followed the LORD God of Israel. ¹⁵And the name of Hebron formerly was Kirjath Arba (*Arba was* the greatest man among the Anakim).

Then the land had rest from war.

The cities of Judah

15 So *this* was the lot of the tribe of the children of Judah according to their families:

The border of Edom at the Wilderness of Zin southward *was* the extreme southern boundary. ²And their southern border began at the shore of the Salt Sea, from the bay that faces southward. ³Then it went out to the southern side of the Ascent of Akrabbim, passed along to Zin, ascended on the south side of Kadesh Barnea, passed along to Hezron, went up to Adar, and went around to Karkaa. ⁴*From there* it passed toward Azmon and went out to the Brook of Egypt; and the border ended at the sea. This shall be your southern border.

⁵The east border *was* the Salt Sea as far as the mouth of the Jordan.

And the border on the northern quarter *began* at the bay of the sea at the mouth of the Jordan. ⁶The border went up to Beth Hoglah and passed north of Beth Arabah; and the border went up to the stone of Bohan the son of Reuben. ⁷Then the border went up toward Debir from the Valley of Achor, and it turned northward toward Gilgal, which *is* before the Ascent of Adummim, which *is* on the south side of the valley. The border continued toward the waters of En Shemesh and ended at En Rogel. ⁸And the border went up by the Valley of the Son of Hinnom to the southern slope of the Jebusite *city* (which *is* Jerusalem). The border went up to the top of the mountain that *lies* before the Valley of Hinnom westward, which *is* at the end of the Valley of Rephaim northward. ⁹Then the border went around from the top of the hill to the fountain of the water of Nephtoah, and extended to the cities of Mount Ephron. And the border went around to Baalah (which *is* Kirjath Jearim). ¹⁰Then the border turned westward from Baalah to Mount Seir, passed along to the side of Mount Jearim on the north (which *is* Chesalon), went down to Beth Shemesh, and passed on to Timnah. ¹¹And the border went out to the side of Ekron northward. Then the border went around to Shicron, passed along to Mount Baalah, and extended to Jabneel; and the border ended at the sea.

¹²The west border *was* the coastline of the Great Sea. This *is* the boundary of the children of Judah all around according to their families.

¹³Now to Caleb the son of Jephunneh he gave a share among the children of Judah, according to the commandment of the LORD to Joshua, *namely,* Kirjath Arba, which *is* Hebron (*Arba was* the father of Anak). ¹⁴Caleb drove out the three sons of Anak from there: Sheshai, Ahiman, and Talmai, the children of Anak. ¹⁵Then he went up from there to the inhabitants of Debir (formerly the name of Debir *was* Kirjath Sepher).

¹⁶And Caleb said, "He who attacks Kirjath Sepher and takes it, to him I will give Achsah my daughter as wife." ¹⁷So Othniel the son of Kenaz, the brother of Caleb, took it; and he gave him Achsah his daughter as wife. ¹⁸Now it was so, when she came *to him,* that she persuaded him to ask her father for a field. So she dismounted from *her* donkey, and Caleb said to her, "What do you wish?" ¹⁹She answered, "Give me a blessing; since you

have given me land in the South, give me also springs of water." So he gave her the upper springs and the lower springs.

20 This *was* the inheritance of the tribe of the children of Judah according to their families:

21 The cities at the limits of the tribe of the children of Judah, toward the border of Edom in the South, were Kabzeel, Eder, Jagur, 22 Kinah, Dimonah, Adadah, 23 Kedesh, Hazor, Ithnan, 24 Ziph, Telem, Bealoth, 25 Hazor, Hadattah, Kerioth, Hezron (which *is* Hazor), 26 Amam, Shema, Moladah, 27 Hazar Gaddah, Heshmon, Beth Pelet, 28 Hazar Shual, Beersheba, Bizjothjah, 29 Baalah, Ijim, Ezem, 30 Eltolad, Chesil, Hormah, 31 Ziklag, Madmannah, Sansannah, 32 Lebaoth, Shilhim, Ain, and Rimmon: all the cities *are* twenty-nine, with their villages.

33 In the lowland: Eshtaol, Zorah, Ashnah, 34 Zanoah, En Gannim, Tappuah, Enam, 35 Jarmuth, Adullam, Socoh, Azekah, 36 Sharaim, Adithaim, Gederah, and Gederothaim: fourteen cities with their villages; 37 Zenan, Hadashah, Migdal Gad, 38 Dilean, Mizpah, Joktheel, 39 Lachish, Bozkath, Eglon, 40 Cabbon, Lahmas, Kithlish, 41 Gederoth, Beth Dagon, Naamah, and Makkedah: sixteen cities with their villages; 42 Libnah, Ether, Ashan, 43 Jiphtah, Ashnah, Nezib, 44 Keilah, Achzib, and Mareshah: nine cities with their villages; 45 Ekron, with its towns and villages; 46 from Ekron to the sea, all that *lay* near Ashdod, with their villages; 47 Ashdod with its towns and villages, Gaza with its towns and villages—as far as the Brook of Egypt and the Great Sea with *its* coastline.

48 And in the mountain country: Shamir, Jattir, Sochoh, 49 Dannah, Kirjath Sannah (which *is* Debir), 50 Anab, Eshtemoh, Anim, 51 Goshen, Holon, and Giloh: eleven cities with their villages; 52 Arab, Dumah, Eshean, 53 Janum, Beth Tappuah, Aphekah, 54 Humtah, Kirjath Arba (which *is* Hebron), and Zior: nine cities with their villages; 55 Maon, Carmel, Ziph, Juttah, 56 Jezreel, Jokdeam, Zanoah, 57 Kain,

Gibeah, and Timnah: ten cities with their villages; 58 Halhul, Beth Zur, Gedor, 59 Maarath, Beth Anoth, and Eltekon: six cities with their villages; 60 Kirjath Baal (which *is* Kirjath Jearim) and Rabbah: two cities with their villages.

61 In the wilderness: Beth Arabah, Middin, Secacah, 62 Nibshan, the City of Salt, and En Gedi: six cities with their villages.

63 As for the Jebusites, the inhabitants of Jerusalem, the children of Judah could not drive them out; but the Jebusites dwell with the children of Judah at Jerusalem to this day.

The borders of Ephraim

16 The lot fell to the children of Joseph from the Jordan, by Jericho, to the waters of Jericho on the east, to the wilderness that goes up from Jericho through the mountains to Bethel, 2 then went out from Bethel to Luz, passed along to the border of the Archites at Ataroth, 3 and went down westward to the boundary of the Japhletites, as far as the boundary of Lower Beth Horon to Gezer; and it ended at the sea.

4 So the children of Joseph, Manasseh and Ephraim, took their inheritance.

5 The border of the children of Ephraim, according to their families, was *thus:* The border of their inheritance on the east side was Ataroth Addar as far as Upper Beth Horon.

6 And the border went out toward the sea on the north side of Michmethath; then the border went around eastward to Taanath Shiloh, and passed by it on the east of Janohah. 7 Then it went down from Janohah to Ataroth and Naarah, reached to Jericho, and came out at the Jordan.

8 The border went out from Tappuah westward to the Brook Kanah, and it ended at the sea. This *was* the inheritance of the tribe of the children of Ephraim according to their families. 9 The separate cities for the children of Ephraim *were* among the

inheritance of the children of Manasseh, all the cities with their villages.

10 And they did not drive out the Canaanites who dwelt in Gezer; but the Canaanites dwell among the Ephraimites to this day and have become forced laborers.

Manasseh's territory

17 There was also a lot for the tribe of Manasseh, for he *was* the firstborn of Joseph: *namely* for Machir the firstborn of Manasseh, the father of Gilead, because he was a man of war; therefore he was given Gilead and Bashan. 2 And there was *a lot* for the rest of the children of Manasseh according to their families: for the children of Abiezer, the children of Helek, the children of Asriel, the children of Shechem, the children of Hepher, and the children of Shemida; these *were* the male children of Manasseh the son of Joseph according to their families.

3 But Zelophehad the son of Hepher, the son of Gilead, the son of Machir, the son of Manasseh, had no sons, but only daughters. And these *are* the names of his daughters: Mahlah, Noah, Hoglah, Milcah, and Tirzah. 4 And they came near before Eleazar the priest, before Joshua the son of Nun, and before the rulers, saying, "The LORD commanded Moses to give us an inheritance among our brothers." Therefore, according to the commandment of the LORD, he gave them an inheritance among their father's brothers. 5 Ten shares fell to Manasseh, besides the land of Gilead and Bashan, which *were* on the other side of the Jordan, 6 because the daughters of Manasseh received an inheritance among his sons; and the rest of Manasseh's sons had the land of Gilead.

7 And the territory of Manasseh was from Asher to Michmethath, that *lies* east of Shechem; and the border went along south to the inhabitants of En Tappuah. 8 Manasseh had the land of Tappuah, but Tappuah on the border of Manasseh *belonged* to the children of Ephraim. 9 And the border descended to the Brook Kanah, southward to the brook. These cities of Ephraim *are* among the cities of Manasseh. The border of Manasseh *was* on the north side of the brook; and it ended at the sea.

10 Southward *it was* Ephraim's, northward *it was* Manasseh's, and the sea was its border. Manasseh's territory was adjoining Asher on the north and Issachar on the east. 11 And in Issachar and in Asher, Manasseh had Beth Shean and its towns, Ibleam and its towns, the inhabitants of Dor and its towns, the inhabitants of En Dor and its towns, the inhabitants of Taanach and its towns, and the inhabitants of Megiddo and its towns—three hilly regions. 12 Yet the children of Manasseh could not drive out *the inhabitants of* those cities, but the Canaanites were determined to dwell in that land. 13 And it happened, when the children of Israel grew strong, that they put the Canaanites to forced labor, but did not utterly drive them out.

14 Then the children of Joseph spoke to Joshua, saying, "Why have you given us *only* one lot and one share to inherit, since we *are* a great people, inasmuch as the LORD has blessed us until now?"

15 So Joshua answered them, "If you *are* a great people, *then* go up to the forest *country* and clear a place for yourself there in the land of the Perizzites and the giants, since the mountains of Ephraim are too confined for you."

16 But the children of Joseph said, "The mountain country is not enough for us; and all the Canaanites who dwell in the land of the valley have chariots of iron, *both those* who *are* of Beth Shean and its towns and *those* who *are* of the Valley of Jezreel."

17 And Joshua spoke to the house of Joseph—to Ephraim and Manasseh—saying, "You *are* a great people and have great power; you shall not have *only* one lot, 18 but the mountain country shall be yours. Although it *is* wooded, you shall cut it down, and its farthest extent shall be yours; for

you shall drive out the Canaanites, though they have iron chariots *and* are strong."

The land is described and divided

18 Now the whole congregation of the children of Israel assembled together at Shiloh, and set up the tabernacle of meeting there. And the land was subdued before them. 2 But there remained among the children of Israel seven tribes which had not yet received their inheritance.

3 Then Joshua said to the children of Israel: "How long will you neglect to go and possess the land which the LORD God of your fathers has given you? 4 Pick out from among you three men for *each* tribe, and I will send them; they shall rise and go through the land, survey it according to their inheritance, and come *back* to me. 5 And they shall divide it into seven parts. Judah shall remain in their territory on the south, and the house of Joseph shall remain in their territory on the north. 6 You shall therefore survey the land in seven parts and bring *the survey* here to me, that I may cast lots for you here before the LORD our God. 7 But the Levites have no part among you, for the priesthood of the LORD *is* their inheritance. And Gad, Reuben, and half the tribe of Manasseh have received their inheritance beyond the Jordan on the east, which Moses the servant of the LORD gave them."

8 Then the men arose to go away; and Joshua charged those who went to survey the land, saying, "Go, walk through the land, survey it, and come back to me, that I may cast lots for you here before the LORD in Shiloh." 9 So the men went, passed through the land, and wrote the survey in a book in seven parts by cities; and they came to Joshua at the camp in Shiloh. 10 Then Joshua cast lots for them in Shiloh before the LORD, and there Joshua divided the land to the children of Israel according to their divisions.

11 Now the lot of the tribe of the children of Benjamin came up according to their families, and the territory of their lot came out between the children of Judah and the children of Joseph. 12 Their border on the north side began at the Jordan, and the border went up to the side of Jericho on the north, and went up through the mountains westward; it ended at the Wilderness of Beth Aven. 13 The border went over from there toward Luz, to the side of Luz (which *is* Bethel) southward; and the border descended to Ataroth Addar, near the hill that *lies* on the south side of Lower Beth Horon.

14 Then the border extended around the west side to the south, from the hill that *lies* before Beth Horon southward; and it ended at Kirjath Baal (which *is* Kirjath Jearim), a city of the children of Judah. This *was* the west side.

15 The south side *began* at the end of Kirjath Jearim, and the border extended on the west and went out to the spring of the waters of Nephtoah. 16 Then the border came down to the end of the mountain that *lies* before the Valley of the Son of Hinnom, which *is* in the Valley of the Rephaim on the north, descended to the Valley of Hinnom, to the side of the Jebusite *city* on the south, and descended to En Rogel. 17 And it went around from the north, went out to En Shemesh, and *extended* toward Geliloth, which is before the Ascent of Adummim, and descended to the stone of Bohan the son of Reuben. 18 Then it passed along toward the north side of Arabah, and went down to Arabah. 19 And the border passed along to the north side of Beth Hoglah; then the border ended at the north bay at the Salt Sea, at the south end of the Jordan. This *was* the southern boundary.

20 The Jordan was its border on the east side. This *was* the inheritance of the children of Benjamin, according to its boundaries all around, according to their families.

21 Now the cities of the tribe of the children of Benjamin, according to their families, were Jericho, Beth Hoglah, Emek Keziz, 22 Beth Arabah,

Zemaraim, Bethel, 23 Avim, Parah, Ophrah, 24 Chephar Haammoni, Ophni, and Gaba: twelve cities with their villages; 25 Gibeon, Ramah, Beeroth, 26 Mizpah, Chephirah, Mozah, 27 Rekem, Irpeel, Taralah, 28 Zelah, Eleph, Jebus (which *is* Jerusalem), Gibeath, *and* Kirjath: fourteen cities with their villages. This was the inheritance of the children of Benjamin according to their families.

The rest of the land is divided

19 The second lot came out for Simeon, for the tribe of the children of Simeon according to their families. And their inheritance was within the inheritance of the children of Judah. 2 They had in their inheritance Beersheba (Sheba), Moladah, 3 Hazar Shual, Balah, Ezem, 4 Eltolad, Bethul, Hormah, 5 Ziklag, Beth Marcaboth, Hazar Susah, 6 Beth Lebaoth, and Sharuhen: thirteen cities and their villages; 7 Ain, Rimmon, Ether, and Ashan: four cities and their villages; 8 and all the villages that *were* all around these cities as far as Baalath Beer, Ramah of the South. This *was* the inheritance of the tribe of the children of Simeon according to their families.

9 The inheritance of the children of Simeon *was included* in the share of the children of Judah, for the share of the children of Judah was too much for them. Therefore the children of Simeon had *their* inheritance within the inheritance of that people.

10 The third lot came out for the children of Zebulun according to their families, and the border of their inheritance was as far as Sarid. 11 Their border went toward the west and to Maralah, went to Dabbasheth, and extended along the brook that is east of Jokneam. 12 Then from Sarid it went eastward toward the sunrise along the border of Chisloth Tabor, and went out toward Daberath, bypassing Japhia. 13 And from there it passed along on the east of Gath Hepher, toward Eth

Kazin, and extended to Rimmon, which borders on Neah. 14 Then the border went around it on the north side of Hannathon, and it ended in the Valley of Jiphthah El. 15 Included were Kattath, Nahallal, Shimron, Idalah, and Bethlehem: twelve cities with their villages. 16 This *was* the inheritance of the children of Zebulun according to their families, these cities with their villages.

17 The fourth lot came out to Issachar, for the children of Issachar according to their families. 18 And their territory went to Jezreel, and *included* Chesulloth, Shunem, 19 Haphraim, Shion, Anaharath, 20 Rabbith, Kishion, Abez, 21 Remeth, En Gannim, En Haddah, and Beth Pazzez. 22 And the border reached to Tabor, Shahazimah, and Beth Shemesh; their border ended at the Jordan: sixteen cities with their villages. 23 This *was* the inheritance of the tribe of the children of Issachar according to their families, the cities and their villages.

24 The fifth lot came out for the tribe of the children of Asher according to their families. 25 And their territory included Helkath, Hali, Beten, Achshaph, 26 Alammelech, Amad, and Mishal; it reached to Mount Carmel westward, along *the Brook* Shihor Libnath. 27 It turned toward the sunrise to Beth Dagon; and it reached to Zebulun and to the Valley of Jiphthah El, then northward beyond Beth Emek and Neiel, bypassing Cabul *which was* on the left, 28 including Ebron, Rehob, Hammon, and Kanah, as far as Greater Sidon. 29 And the border turned to Ramah and to the fortified city of Tyre; then the border turned to Hosah, and ended at the sea by the region of Achzib. 30 Also Ummah, Aphek, and Rehob *were included*: twenty-two cities with their villages. 31 This *was* the inheritance of the tribe of the children of Asher according to their families, these cities with their villages.

32 The sixth lot came out to the children of Naphtali, for the children of Naphtali according to their families.

33 And their border began at Heleph, enclosing the territory from the terebinth tree in Zaanannim, Adami Nekeb, and Jabneel, as far as Lakkum; it ended at the Jordan. 34 From Heleph the border extended westward to Aznoth Tabor, and went out from there toward Hukkok; it adjoined Zebulun on the south side and Asher on the west side, and ended at Judah by the Jordan toward the sunrise. 35 And the fortified cities are Ziddim, Zer, Hammath, Rakkath, Chinnereth, 36 Adamah, Ramah, Hazor, 37 Kedesh, Edrei, En Hazor, 38 Iron, Migdal El, Horem, Beth Anath, and Beth Shemesh: nineteen cities with their villages. 39 This was the inheritance of the tribe of the children of Naphtali according to their families, the cities and their villages.

40 The seventh lot came out for the tribe of the children of Dan according to their families. 41 And the territory of their inheritance was Zorah, Eshtaol, Ir Shemesh, 42 Shaalabbin, Aijalon, Jethlah, 43 Elon, Timnah, Ekron, 44 Eltekeh, Gibbethon, Baalath, 45 Jehud, Bene Berak, Gath Rimmon, 46 Me Jarkon, and Rakkon, with the region near Joppa. 47 And the border of the children of Dan went beyond these, because the children of Dan went up to fight against Leshem and took it; and they struck it with the edge of the sword, took possession of it, and dwelt in it. They called Leshem, Dan, after the name of Dan their father. 48 This is the inheritance of the tribe of the children of Dan according to their families, these cities with their villages.

49 When they had made an end of dividing the land as an inheritance according to their borders, the children of Israel gave an inheritance among them to Joshua the son of Nun. 50 According to the word of the LORD they gave him the city which he asked for, Timnath Serah in the mountains of Ephraim; and he built the city and dwelt in it.

51 These were the inheritances which Eleazar the priest, Joshua the son of Nun, and the heads of the fathers of the tribes of the children of Israel divided as an inheritance by lot in Shiloh before the LORD, at the door of the tabernacle of meeting. So they made an end of dividing the country.

The Lord names six cities of safety

20 The LORD also spoke to Joshua, saying, 2 "Speak to the children of Israel, saying: 'Appoint for yourselves cities of refuge, of which I spoke to you through Moses, 3 that the slayer who kills a person accidentally or unintentionally may flee there; and they shall be your refuge from the avenger of blood. 4 And when he flees to one of those cities, and stands at the entrance of the gate of the city, and declares his case in the hearing of the elders of that city, they shall take him into the city as one of them, and give him a place, that he may dwell among them. 5 Then if the avenger of blood pursues him, they shall not deliver the slayer into his hand, because he struck his neighbor unintentionally, but did not hate him beforehand. 6 And he shall dwell in that city until he stands before the congregation for judgment, and until the death of the one who is high priest in those days. Then the slayer may return and come to his own city and his own house, to the city from which he fled.' "

7 So they appointed Kedesh in Galilee, in the mountains of Naphtali, Shechem in the mountains of Ephraim, and Kirjath Arba (which is Hebron) in the mountains of Judah. 8 And on the other side of the Jordan, by Jericho eastward, they assigned Bezer in the wilderness on the plain, from the tribe of Reuben, Ramoth in Gilead, from the tribe of Gad, and Golan in Bashan, from the tribe of Manasseh. 9 These were the cities appointed for all the children of Israel and for the stranger who dwelt among them, that whoever killed a person accidentally might flee there, and not die by the hand of the avenger of blood until he stood before the congregation.

The cities of the Levites

21 Then the heads of the fathers' *houses* of the Levites came near to Eleazar the priest, to Joshua the son of Nun, and to the heads of the fathers' *houses* of the tribes of the children of Israel. 2 And they spoke to them at Shiloh in the land of Canaan, saying, "The LORD commanded through Moses to give us cities to dwell in, with their common-lands for our livestock." 3 So the children of Israel gave to the Levites from their inheritance, at the commandment of the LORD, these cities and their common-lands:

4 Now the lot came out for the families of the Kohathites. And the children of Aaron the priest, *who were* of the Levites, had thirteen cities by lot from the tribe of Judah, from the tribe of Simeon, and from the tribe of Benjamin. 5 The rest of the children of Kohath had ten cities by lot from the families of the tribe of Ephraim, from the tribe of Dan, and from the half-tribe of Manasseh.

6 And the children of Gershon had thirteen cities by lot from the families of the tribe of Issachar, from the tribe of Asher, from the tribe of Naphtali, and from the half-tribe of Manasseh in Bashan.

7 The children of Merari according to their families had twelve cities from the tribe of Reuben, from the tribe of Gad, and from the tribe of Zebulun.

8 And the children of Israel gave these cities with their common-lands by lot to the Levites, as the LORD had commanded by the hand of Moses.

9 So they gave from the tribe of the children of Judah and from the tribe of the children of Simeon these cities which are designated by name, 10 which were for the children of Aaron, one of the families of the Kohathites, *who were* of the children of Levi; for the lot was theirs first. 11 And they gave them Kirjath Arba (*Arba was* the father of Anak), which *is* Hebron, in the mountains of Judah, with the common-land surrounding it. 12 But the fields of the city and its villages they gave to Caleb the son of Jephunneh as his possession.

13 Thus to the children of Aaron the priest they gave Hebron with its common-land (a city of refuge for the slayer), Libnah with its common-land, 14 Jattir with its common-land, Eshtemoa with its common-land, 15 Holon with its common-land, Debir with its common-land, 16 Ain with its common-land, Juttah with its common-land, and Beth Shemesh with its common-land: nine cities from those two tribes; 17 and from the tribe of Benjamin, Gibeon with its common-land, Geba with its common-land, 18 Anathoth with its common-land, and Almon with its common-land: four cities. 19 All the cities of the children of Aaron, the priests, *were* thirteen cities with their common-lands.

20 And the families of the children of Kohath, the Levites, the rest of the children of Kohath, even they had the cities of their lot from the tribe of Ephraim. 21 For they gave them Shechem with its common-land in the mountains of Ephraim (a city of refuge for the slayer), Gezer with its common-land, 22 Kibzaim with its common-land, and Beth Horon with its common-land: four cities; 23 and from the tribe of Dan, Eltekeh with its common-land, Gibbethon with its common-land, 24 Aijalon with its common-land, *and* Gath Rimmon with its common-land: four cities; 25 and from the half-tribe of Manasseh, Tanach with its common-land and Gath Rimmon with its common-land: two cities. 26 All the ten cities with their common-lands were for the rest of the families of the children of Kohath.

27 Also to the children of Gershon, of the families of the Levites, from the *other* half-tribe of Manasseh, *they gave* Golan in Bashan with its common-land (a city of refuge for the slayer), and Be Eshterah with its common-land: two cities; 28 and from the tribe of Issachar, Kishion with its common-land, Daberath with its common-land, 29 Jarmuth with its common-land, *and* En Gannim with its common-land: four cities; 30 and from the tribe of Asher,

Mishal with its common-land, Abdon with its common-land, 31 Helkath with its common-land, and Rehob with its common-land: four cities; 32 and from the tribe of Naphtali, Kedesh in Galilee with its common-land (a city of refuge for the slayer), Hammoth Dor with its common-land, and Kartan with its common-land: three cities. 33 All the cities of the Gershonites according to their families *were* thirteen cities with their common-lands.

34 And to the families of the children of Merari, the rest of the Levites, from the tribe of Zebulun, Jokneam with its common-land, Kartah with its common-land, 35 Dimnah with its common-land, *and* Nahalal with its common-land: four cities; 36 and from the tribe of Reuben, Bezer with its common-land, Jahaz with its common-land, 37 Kedemoth with its common-land, and Mephaath with its common-land: four cities; 38 and from the tribe of Gad, Ramoth in Gilead with its common-land (a city of refuge for the slayer), Mahanaim with its common-land, 39 Heshbon with its common-land, *and* Jazer with its common-land: four cities in all. 40 So all the cities for the children of Merari according to their families, the rest of the families of the Levites, were *by* their lot twelve cities.

41 All the cities of the Levites within the possession of the children of Israel *were* forty-eight cities with their common-lands. 42 Every one of these cities had its common-land surrounding it; thus *were* all these cities.

43 So the LORD gave to Israel all the land of which He had sworn to give to their fathers, and they took possession of it and dwelt in it. 44 The LORD gave them rest all around, according to all that He had sworn to their fathers. And not a man of all their enemies stood against them; the LORD delivered all their enemies into their hand. 45 Not a word failed of any good thing which the LORD had spoken to the house of Israel. All came to pass.

An altar by the Jordan River

22 Then Joshua called the Reubenites, the Gadites, and half the tribe of Manasseh, 2 and said to them: "You have kept all that Moses the servant of the LORD commanded you, and have obeyed my voice in all that I commanded you. 3 You have not left your brethren these many days, up to this day, but have kept the charge of the commandment of the LORD your God. 4 And now the LORD your God has given rest to your brethren, as He promised them; now therefore, return and go to your tents *and* to the land of your possession, which Moses the servant of the LORD gave you on the other side of the Jordan. 5 But take careful heed to do the commandment and the law which Moses the servant of the LORD commanded you, to love the LORD your God, to walk in all His ways, to keep His commandments, to hold fast to Him, and to serve Him with all your heart and with all your soul." 6 So Joshua blessed them and sent them away, and they went to their tents.

DIGGING IN

21:43–55 God Is True to His Promises Take time to talk to older people who have known God for a long time. It can save you a lot of learning from hard knocks. It is wise to learn from experience, but it's even wiser to learn from the experience of others.

There's another great reason for asking older believers to share with you. They have proven what Joshua found out at the end of his wars in Canaan. God doesn't just keep His promises—He keeps *all* of His promises to the letter.

It's really neat as you get a little older to look back in memory and see how good God has been. There will be times when your faith almost failed, and you were scared because you thought God would not come through. But He always did!

The more times you see God working like that, the more you trust Him.

7 Now to half the tribe of Manasseh Moses had given a possession in Bashan, but to the *other* half of it Joshua gave *a possession* among their brethren on this side of the Jordan, westward. And indeed, when Joshua sent them away to their tents, he blessed them, 8 and spoke to them, saying, "Return with much riches to your tents, with very much livestock, with silver, with gold, with bronze, with iron, and with very much clothing. Divide the spoil of your enemies with your brethren."

9 So the children of Reuben, the children of Gad, and half the tribe of Manasseh returned, and departed from the children of Israel at Shiloh, which *is* in the land of Canaan, to go to the country of Gilead, to the land of their possession, which they had obtained according to the word of the LORD by the hand of Moses.

10 And when they came to the region of the Jordan which *is* in the land of Canaan, the children of Reuben, the children of Gad, and half the tribe of Manasseh built an altar there by the Jordan—a great, impressive altar. 11 Now the children of Israel heard *someone* say, "Behold, the children of Reuben, the children of Gad, and half the tribe of Manasseh have built an altar on the frontier of the land of Canaan, in the region of the Jordan—on the children of Israel's side." 12 And when the children of Israel heard *of it,* the whole congregation of the children of Israel gathered together at Shiloh to go to war against them.

13 Then the children of Israel sent Phinehas the son of Eleazar the priest to the children of Reuben, to the children of Gad, and to half the tribe of Manasseh, into the land of Gilead, 14 and with him ten rulers, one ruler each from the chief house of every tribe of Israel; and each one *was* the head of the house of his father among the divisions of Israel. 15 Then they came to the children of Reuben, to the children of Gad, and to half the tribe of Manasseh, to the land of Gilead, and they spoke with them, saying, 16 "Thus says the whole congregation of the LORD: 'What treachery *is* this that you have committed against the God of Israel, to turn away this day from following the LORD, in that you have built for yourselves an altar, that you might rebel this day against the LORD? 17 *Is* the iniquity of Peor not enough for us, from which we are not cleansed till this day, although there was a plague in the congregation of the LORD, 18 but that you must turn away this day from following the LORD? And it shall be, if you rebel today against the LORD, that tomorrow He will be angry with the whole congregation of Israel. 19 Nevertheless, if the land of your possession *is* unclean, *then* cross over to the land of the possession of the LORD, where the LORD's tabernacle stands, and take possession among us; but do not rebel against the LORD, nor rebel against us, by building yourselves an altar besides the altar of the LORD our God. 20 Did not Achan the son of Zerah commit a trespass in the accursed thing, and wrath fell on all the congregation of Israel? And that man did not perish alone in his iniquity.'"

21 Then the children of Reuben, the children of Gad, and half the tribe of Manasseh answered and said to the heads of the divisions of Israel: 22 "The LORD God of gods, the LORD God of gods, He knows, and let Israel itself know—if *it is* in rebellion, or if in treachery against the LORD, do not save us this day. 23 If we have built ourselves an altar to turn from following the LORD, or if to offer on it burnt offerings or grain offerings, or if to offer peace offerings on it, let the LORD Himself require *an account.* 24 But in fact we have done it for fear, for a reason, saying, 'In time to come your descendants may speak to our descendants, saying, "What have you to do with the LORD God of Israel? 25 For the LORD has made the Jordan a border between you and us, *you* children of Reuben and children of Gad. You have no part in the LORD." So your descendants would make our descendants cease fearing the LORD.' 26 Therefore we

said, 'Let us now prepare to build ourselves an altar, not for burnt offering nor for sacrifice, 27 but *that* it *may be* a witness between you and us and our generations after us, that we may perform the service of the LORD before Him with our burnt offerings, with our sacrifices, and with our peace offerings; that your descendants may not say to our descendants in time to come, "You have no part in the LORD." ' 28 Therefore we said that it will be, when they say *this* to us or to our generations in time to come, that we may say, 'Here is the replica of the altar of the LORD which our fathers made, though not for burnt offerings nor for sacrifices; but it *is* a witness between us and you.' 29 Far be it from us that we should rebel against the LORD, and turn from following the LORD this day, to build an altar for burnt offerings, for grain offerings, or for sacrifices, besides the altar of the LORD our God which *is* before His tabernacle."

30 Now when Phinehas the priest and the rulers of the congregation, the heads of the divisions of Israel who *were* with him, heard the words that the children of Reuben, the children of Gad, and the children of Manasseh spoke, it pleased them. 31 Then Phinehas the son of Eleazar the priest said to the children of Reuben, the children of Gad, and the children of Manasseh, "This day we perceive that the LORD *is* among us, because you have not committed this treachery against the LORD. Now you have delivered the children of Israel out of the hand of the LORD."

32 And Phinehas the son of Eleazar the priest, and the rulers, returned from the children of Reuben and the children of Gad, from the land of Gilead to the land of Canaan, to the children of Israel, and brought back word to them. 33 So the thing pleased the children of Israel, and the children of Israel blessed God; they spoke no more of going against them in battle, to destroy the land where the children of Reuben and Gad dwelt.

34 The children of Reuben and the children of Gad called the altar, *Witness,* "For *it is* a witness between us that the LORD *is* God."

Joshua's last words to Israel

23 Now it came to pass, a long time after the LORD had given rest to Israel from all their enemies round about, that Joshua was old, advanced in age. 2 And Joshua called for all Israel, for their elders, for their heads, for their judges, and for their officers, and said to them:

"I am old, advanced in age. 3 You have seen all that the LORD your God has done to all these nations because of you, for the LORD your God *is* He who has fought for you. 4 See, I have divided to you by lot these nations that remain, to be an inheritance for your tribes, from the Jordan, with all the nations that I have cut off, as far as the Great Sea westward. 5 And the LORD your God will expel them from before you and drive them out of your sight. So you shall possess their land, as the LORD your God promised you. 6 Therefore be very courageous to keep and to do all that is written in the Book of the Law of Moses, lest you turn aside from it to the right hand or to the left, 7 *and* lest you go among these nations, these who remain among you. You shall not make mention of the name of their gods, nor cause *anyone* to swear *by them;* you shall not serve them nor bow down to them, 8 but you shall hold fast to the LORD your God, as you have done to this day. 9 For the LORD has driven out from before you great and strong nations; but *as for* you, no one has been able to stand against you to this day. 10 One man of you shall chase a thousand, for the LORD your God *is* He who fights for you, as He promised you. 11 Therefore take careful heed to yourselves, that you love the LORD your God. 12 Or else, if indeed you do go back, and cling to the remnant of these nations— these that remain among you—and make marriages with them, and go in to them and they to you, 13 know for

What Joshua Learned

For many years after Moses died, I was the leader of God's people. I brought them into the land God had promised Abraham long ago, and I helped them fight their wars against enemies. Now I, too, am going to die.

I have learned that God keeps every word of all His promises. I know this because I was just a young man when I left Egypt with my family. I have seen how God blesses and sometimes punishes His people. I was there when they refused to enter the land God wanted to give them.

"Joshua" is the Old Testament way of spelling "Jesus" in the New Testament. I was God's man to save our people in the Old Testament, but Jesus is your true Savior from heaven. Do you trust Him?

certain that the LORD your God will no longer drive out these nations from before you. But they shall be snares and traps to you, and scourges on your sides and thorns in your eyes, until you perish from this good land which the LORD your God has given you.

14 "Behold, this day I *am* going the way of all the earth. And you know in all your hearts and in all your souls that not one thing has failed of all the good things which the LORD your God spoke concerning you. All have come to pass for you; not one word of them has failed. 15 Therefore it shall come to pass, that as all the good things have come upon you which the LORD your God promised you, so the LORD will bring upon you all harmful things, until He has destroyed you from this good land which the LORD your God has given you. 16 When you have transgressed the covenant of the LORD your God, which He commanded you, and have gone and served other gods, and bowed down to them, then the anger of the LORD will burn against you, and you shall perish quickly from the good land which He has given you."

The covenant at Shechem

24 Then Joshua gathered all the tribes of Israel to Shechem and called for the elders of Israel, for their heads, for their judges, and for their officers; and they presented themselves before God. 2 And Joshua said to all the people, "Thus says the LORD God of Israel: 'Your fathers, *including* Terah, the father of Abraham and the father of Nahor, dwelt on the other side of the River in old times; and they served other gods. 3 Then I took your father Abraham from the other side of the River, led him throughout all the land of Canaan, and multiplied his descendants and gave him Isaac. 4 To Isaac I gave Jacob and Esau. To Esau I gave the mountains of Seir to possess, but Jacob and his children went down to Egypt. 5 Also I sent Moses and Aaron, and I plagued Egypt, according to what I did among them. Afterward I brought you out.

6 'Then I brought your fathers out of Egypt, and you came to the sea; and the Egyptians pursued your fathers with chariots and horsemen to the Red Sea. 7 So they cried out to the LORD; and He put darkness between you and the Egyptians, brought the sea upon them, and covered them. And your eyes saw what I did in Egypt. Then you dwelt in the wilderness a long time. 8 And I brought you into the land of the Amorites, who dwelt on the other side of the Jordan, and they fought with you. But I gave them into your hand, that you might possess their

land, and I destroyed them from before you. ⁹ Then Balak the son of Zippor, king of Moab, arose to make war against Israel, and sent and called Balaam the son of Beor to curse you. ¹⁰ But I would not listen to Balaam; therefore he continued to bless you. So I delivered you out of his hand. ¹¹ Then you went over the Jordan and came to Jericho. And the men of Jericho fought against you—*also* the Amorites, the Perizzites, the Canaanites, the Hittites, the Girgashites, the Hivites, and the Jebusites. But I delivered them into your hand. ¹² I sent the hornet before you which drove them out from before you, *also* the two kings of the Amorites, *but* not with your sword or with your bow. ¹³ I have given you a land for which you did not labor, and cities which you did not build, and you dwell in them; you eat of the vineyards and olive groves which you did not plant.'

¹⁴ "Now therefore, fear the Lord, serve Him in sincerity and in truth, and put away the gods which your fathers served on the other side of the River and in Egypt. Serve the Lord! ¹⁵ And if it seems evil to you to serve the Lord, choose for yourselves this day whom you will serve, whether the gods which your fathers served that *were* on the other side of the River, or the gods of the Amorites, in whose land you dwell. But as for me and my house, we will serve the Lord."

¹⁶ So the people answered and said: "Far be it from us that we should forsake the Lord to serve other gods; ¹⁷ for the Lord our God *is* He who brought us and our fathers up out of the land of Egypt, from the house of bondage, who did those great signs in our sight, and preserved us in all the way that we went and among all the people through whom we passed. ¹⁸ And the Lord drove out from before us all the people, including the Amorites who dwelt in the land. We also will serve the Lord, for He *is* our God."

¹⁹ But Joshua said to the people, "You cannot serve the Lord, for He

is a holy God. He *is* a jealous God; He will not forgive your transgressions nor your sins. ²⁰ If you forsake the Lord and serve foreign gods, then He will turn and do you harm and consume you, after He has done you good."

²¹ And the people said to Joshua, "No, but we will serve the Lord!"

²² So Joshua said to the people, "You *are* witnesses against yourselves that you have chosen the Lord for yourselves, to serve Him."

And they said, "*We are* witnesses!"

²³ "Now therefore," *he said,* "put away the foreign gods which *are* among you, and incline your heart to the Lord God of Israel."

²⁴ And the people said to Joshua, "The Lord our God we will serve, and His voice we will obey!"

²⁵ So Joshua made a covenant with the people that day, and made for them a statute and an ordinance in Shechem. ²⁶ Then Joshua wrote these words in the Book of the Law of God. And he took a large stone, and set it up there under the oak that *was* by the sanctuary of the Lord. ²⁷ And Joshua said to all the people, "Behold, this stone shall be a witness to us, for it has heard all the words of the Lord which He spoke to us. It shall therefore be a witness to you, lest you deny your God." ²⁸ So Joshua let the people depart, each to his own inheritance.

²⁹ Now it came to pass after these things that Joshua the son of Nun, the servant of the Lord, died, *being* one hundred and ten years old. ³⁰ And they buried him within the border of his inheritance at Timnath Serah, which *is* in the mountains of Ephraim, on the north side of Mount Gaash.

³¹ Israel served the Lord all the days of Joshua, and all the days of the elders who outlived Joshua, who had known all the works of the Lord which He had done for Israel.

³² The bones of Joseph, which the children of Israel had brought up out of Egypt, they buried at Shechem, in the plot of ground which Jacob had

bought from the sons of Hamor the father of Shechem for one hundred pieces of silver, and which had become an inheritance of the children of Joseph.

33 And Eleazar the son of Aaron died. They buried him in a hill *belonging to* Phinehas his son, which was given to him in the mountains of Ephraim.

The Book of
JUDGES

A Judge—I'm not the same kind of judge you can see in a law court in your land. Oh, yes, I do decide arguments that are brought to me, but that is only one of my smaller duties.

When Israel disobeys God, then our enemies attack us. But when our people are sorry for their sins, God commands judges to save them. My great task as a judge is to lead and defend my people Israel against their enemies. Sometimes I have to lead them in battle. I am a good judge if I save the people from those who attack them.

You will read about many judges like me in this book. Some of the leading judges will tell you the story of how God used them to save His people.

God helps His people fight

Now after the death of Joshua it came to pass that the children of Israel asked the LORD, saying, "Who shall be first to go up for us against the Canaanites to fight against them?"

2 And the LORD said, "Judah shall go up. Indeed I have delivered the land into his hand."

3 So Judah said to Simeon his brother, "Come up with me to my allotted territory, that we may fight against the Canaanites; and I will likewise go with you to your allotted territory." And Simeon went with him.

4 Then Judah went up, and the LORD delivered the Canaanites and the Perizzites into their hand; and they killed ten thousand men at Bezek. 5 And they found Adoni-Bezek in Bezek, and fought against him; and they defeated the Canaanites and the Perizzites.

6 Then Adoni-Bezek fled, and they pursued him and caught him and cut off his thumbs and big toes. 7 And Adoni-Bezek said, "Seventy kings with their thumbs and big toes cut off used to gather scraps under my table; as I have done, so God has repaid me." Then they brought him to Jerusalem, and there he died.

8 Now the children of Judah fought against Jerusalem and took it; they struck it with the edge of the sword and set the city on fire. 9 And afterward the children of Judah went down to fight against the Canaanites who dwelt in the mountains, in the South, and in the lowland. 10 Then Judah went against the Canaanites who dwelt in Hebron. (Now the name of Hebron was formerly Kirjath Arba.) And they killed Sheshai, Ahiman, and Talmai.

11 From there they went against the inhabitants of Debir. (The name of Debir was formerly Kirjath Sepher.)

12 Then Caleb said, "Whoever attacks Kirjath Sepher and takes it, to him I will give my daughter Achsah as wife." 13 And Othniel the son of Kenaz, Caleb's younger brother, took it; so he gave him his daughter Achsah as wife. 14 Now it happened, when she came to him, that she urged him to ask her father for a field. And she dismounted from her donkey, and Caleb said to her, "What do you wish?" 15 So she said to him, "Give me a blessing; since you have given me land in the South, give me also springs of water."

And Caleb gave her the upper springs and the lower springs.

16 Now the children of the Kenite, Moses' father-in-law, went up from the

City of Palms with the children of Judah into the Wilderness of Judah, which *lies* in the South *near* Arad; and they went and dwelt among the people. 17 And Judah went with his brother Simeon, and they attacked the Canaanites who inhabited Zephath, and utterly destroyed it. So the name of the city was called Hormah. 18 Also Judah took Gaza with its territory, Ashkelon with its territory, and Ekron with its territory. 19 So the LORD was with Judah. And they drove out the mountaineers, but they could not drive out the inhabitants of the lowland, because they had chariots of iron. 20 And they gave Hebron to Caleb, as Moses had said. Then he expelled from there the three sons of Anak. 21 But the children of Benjamin did not drive out the Jebusites who inhabited Jerusalem; so the Jebusites dwell with the children of Benjamin in Jerusalem to this day.

22 And the house of Joseph also went up against Bethel, and the LORD *was* with them. 23 So the house of Joseph sent men to spy out Bethel. (The name of the city *was* formerly Luz.) 24 And when the spies saw a man coming out of the city, they said to him, "Please show us the entrance to the city, and we will show you mercy." 25 So he showed them the entrance to the city, and they struck the city with the edge of the sword; but they let the man and all his family go. 26 And the man went to the land of the Hittites, built a city, and called its name Luz, which *is* its name to this day.

27 However, Manasseh did not drive out *the inhabitants of* Beth Shean and its villages, or Taanach and its villages, or the inhabitants of Dor and its villages, or the inhabitants of Ibleam and its villages, or the inhabitants of Megiddo and its villages; for the Canaanites were determined to dwell in that land. 28 And it came to pass, when Israel was strong, that they put the Canaanites under tribute, but did not completely drive them out.

29 Nor did Ephraim drive out the Canaanites who dwelt in Gezer; so the Canaanites dwelt in Gezer among them.

30 Nor did Zebulun drive out the inhabitants of Kitron or the inhabitants of Nahalol; so the Canaanites dwelt among them, and were put under tribute.

31 Nor did Asher drive out the inhabitants of Acco or the inhabitants of Sidon, or of Ahlab, Achzib, Helbah, Aphik, or Rehob. 32 So the Asherites dwelt among the Canaanites, the inhabitants of the land; for they did not drive them out.

33 Nor did Naphtali drive out the inhabitants of Beth Shemesh or the inhabitants of Beth Anath; but they dwelt among the Canaanites, the inhabitants of the land. Nevertheless the inhabitants of Beth Shemesh and Beth Anath were put under tribute to them.

34 And the Amorites forced the children of Dan into the mountains, for they would not allow them to come down to the valley; 35 and the Amorites were determined to dwell in Mount Heres, in Aijalon, and in Shaalbim; yet when the strength of the house of Joseph became greater, they were put under tribute.

36 Now the boundary of the Amorites *was* from the Ascent of Akrabbim, from Sela, and upward.

Israel disobeys God

2 Then the Angel of the LORD came up from Gilgal to Bochim, and said: "I led you up from Egypt and brought you to the land of which I swore to your fathers; and I said, 'I will never break My covenant with you. 2 And you shall make no covenant with the inhabitants of this land; you shall tear down their altars.' But you have not obeyed My voice. Why have you done this? 3 Therefore I also said, 'I will not drive them out before you; but they shall be *thorns* in your side, and their gods shall be a snare to you.'" 4 So it was, when the Angel of the LORD spoke these words to all the children

of Israel, that the people lifted up their voices and wept.

5 Then they called the name of that place Bochim; and they sacrificed there to the LORD. 6 And when Joshua had dismissed the people, the children of Israel went each to his own inheritance to possess the land.

7 So the people served the LORD all the days of Joshua, and all the days of the elders who outlived Joshua, who had seen all the great works of the LORD which He had done for Israel. 8 Now Joshua the son of Nun, the servant of the LORD, died *when he was* one hundred and ten years old. 9 And they buried him within the border of his inheritance at Timnath Heres, in the mountains of Ephraim, on the north side of Mount Gaash. 10 When all that generation had been gathered to their fathers, another generation arose after them who did not know the LORD nor the work which He had done for Israel.

11 Then the children of Israel did evil in the sight of the LORD, and served the Baals; 12 and they forsook the LORD God of their fathers, who had brought them out of the land of Egypt; and they followed other gods from *among* the gods of the people who *were* all around them, and they bowed down to them; and they provoked the LORD to anger. 13 They forsook the LORD and served Baal and the Ashtoreths. 14 And the anger of the LORD was hot against Israel. So He delivered them

---

⚒ DIGGING IN

2:14 Follow the God of Your Elders Not much time had passed since the nation of Israel had escaped from Egypt and settled in the Promised Land of Canaan. Joshua came after Moses as Israel's leader. Under Joshua, Israel had conquered most of Canaan. But Israel disobeyed the Lord by making treaties with some of the wicked nations in Canaan.

Later, the people of Israel began to worship the false gods of those wicked nations. They stopped following the God of Moses and Joshua. Then God had to punish Israel.

The time of the Judges was an unhappy time for Israel. Their enemies often defeated them. All this was the result of not obeying the God of their elders, Moses and Joshua.

Disobedience is always followed by suffering. Sometimes the suffering doesn't happen right away, but it always comes. So, learn the lesson that Israel should have learned. Those who have lived long and walked with God should be your pattern for living.

Baal, a nature god, was the chief false god worshiped by the Canaanites and, later, by some Israelites.

into the hands of plunderers who de-spoiled them; and He sold them into the hands of their enemies all around, so that they could no longer stand be-fore their enemies. 15 Wherever they went out, the hand of the LORD was against them for calamity, as the LORD had said, and as the LORD had sworn to them. And they were greatly dis-tressed.

16 Nevertheless, the LORD raised up judges who delivered them out of the hand of those who plundered them. 17 Yet they would not listen to their judges, but they played the harlot with other gods, and bowed down to them. They turned quickly from the way in which their fathers walked, in obeying the commandments of the LORD; they did not do so. 18 And when the LORD raised up judges for them, the LORD was with the judge and delivered them out of the hand of their enemies all the days of the judge; for the LORD was moved to pity by their groaning because of those who oppressed them and harassed them. 19 And it came to pass, when the judge was dead, that they reverted and behaved more cor-ruptly than their fathers, by following other gods, to serve them and bow down to them. They did not cease from their own doings nor from their stubborn way.

20 Then the anger of the LORD was hot against Israel; and He said, "Be-cause this nation has transgressed My covenant which I commanded their fa-thers, and has not heeded My voice, 21 I also will no longer drive out before them any of the nations which Joshua left when he died, 22 so that through them I may test Israel, whether they will keep the ways of the LORD, to walk in them as their fathers kept them, or not." 23 Therefore the LORD left those nations, without driving them out im-mediately; nor did He deliver them into the hand of Joshua.

Israel saved from a wicked king

3 Now these are the nations which the LORD left, that He might test Israel by them, that is, all who had not known any of the wars in Canaan 2 (this was only so that the generations of the children of Israel might be taught to know war, at least those who had not formerly known it), 3 namely, five lords of the Philistines, all the Canaan-ites, the Sidonians, and the Hivites who dwelt in Mount Lebanon, from Mount Baal Hermon to the entrance of Hamath. 4 And they were left, that He might test Israel by them, to know whether they would obey the com-mandments of the LORD, which He had commanded their fathers by the hand of Moses.

5 Thus the children of Israel dwelt among the Canaanites, the Hittites, the Amorites, the Perizzites, the Hivites, and the Jebusites. 6 And they took their daughters to be their wives, and gave their daughters to their sons; and they served their gods.

7 So the children of Israel did evil in the sight of the LORD. They forgot the LORD their God, and served the Baals and **Asherahs.** 8 Therefore the anger of the LORD was hot against Is-rael, and He sold them into the hand of Cushan-Rishathaim king of Mesopo-tamia; and the children of Israel served Cushan-Rishathaim eight years. 9 When the children of Israel cried out to the LORD, the LORD raised up a de-liverer for the children of Israel, who delivered them: Othniel the son of Kenaz, Caleb's younger brother. 10 The Spirit of the LORD came upon him, and he judged Israel. He went out to war, and the LORD delivered

WORDFINDER

3:7 Asherah Pronounced *ah-SHE-rah.* A goddess of the Phoenicians and Syrians (pronounced *fe-NISH-she-uns* and *SEER-ih-uns*). The people of Israel also worshiped her when they later served idols. She was worshiped along with Baal (see 1 Kings 18:19).

Cushan-Rishathaim king of Mesopotamia into his hand; and his hand prevailed over Cushan-Rishathaim. 11 So the land had rest for forty years. Then Othniel the son of Kenaz died.

12 And the children of Israel again did evil in the sight of the LORD. So the LORD strengthened Eglon king of Moab against Israel, because they had done evil in the sight of the LORD. 13 Then he gathered to himself the people of Ammon and Amalek, went and defeated Israel, and took possession of the City of Palms. 14 So the children of Israel served Eglon king of Moab eighteen years.

15 But when the children of Israel cried out to the LORD, the LORD raised up a deliverer for them: Ehud the son of Gera, the Benjamite, a left-handed man. By him the children of Israel sent tribute to Eglon king of Moab. 16 Now Ehud made himself a dagger (it was double-edged and a cubit in length) and fastened it under his clothes on his right thigh. 17 So he brought the tribute to Eglon king of Moab. (Now Eglon *was* a very fat man.) 18 And when he had finished presenting the tribute, he sent away the people who had carried the tribute. 19 But he himself turned back from the stone images that *were* at Gilgal, and said, "I have a secret message for you, O king."

He said, "Keep silence!" And all who attended him went out from him.

20 So Ehud came to him (now he was sitting upstairs in his cool private chamber). Then Ehud said, "I have a message from God for you." So he arose from *his* seat. 21 Then Ehud reached with his left hand, took the dagger from his right thigh, and thrust it into his belly. 22 Even the hilt went in after the blade, and the fat closed over the blade, for he did not draw the dagger out of his belly; and his entrails came out. 23 Then Ehud went out through the porch and shut the doors of the upper room behind him and locked them.

24 When he had gone out, *Eglon's* servants came to look, and *to their* surprise, the doors of the upper room were locked. So they said, "He is probably attending to his needs in the cool chamber." 25 So they waited till they were embarrassed, and still he had not opened the doors of the upper room. Therefore they took the key and opened *them*. And there was their master, fallen dead on the floor.

26 But Ehud had escaped while they delayed, and passed beyond the stone images and escaped to Seirah. 27 And it happened, when he arrived, that he blew the trumpet in the mountains of Ephraim, and the children of Israel went down with him from the mountains; and he led them. 28 Then he said to them, "Follow *me,* for the LORD has delivered your enemies the Moabites into your hand." So they went down after him, seized the fords of the Jordan leading to Moab, and did not allow anyone to cross over. 29 And at that time they killed about ten thousand men of Moab, all stout men of valor; not a man escaped. 30 So Moab was subdued that day under the hand of Israel. And the land had rest for eighty years.

31 After him was Shamgar the son of Anath, who killed six hundred men of the Philistines with an ox goad; and he also delivered Israel.

Deborah and Barak

4 When Ehud was dead, the children of Israel again did evil in the sight of the LORD. 2 So the LORD sold them into the hand of Jabin king of Canaan, who reigned in Hazor. The commander of his army *was* Sisera, who dwelt in Harosheth Hagoyim. 3 And the children of Israel cried out to the LORD; for Jabin had nine hundred chariots of iron, and for twenty years he had harshly oppressed the children of Israel.

4 Now Deborah, a prophetess, the wife of Lapidoth, was judging Israel at that time. 5 And she would sit under the palm tree of Deborah between Ramah and Bethel in the mountains of Ephraim. And the children of Israel came up to her for judgment. 6 Then she sent and called for Barak the son

I, Deborah, was a prophetess in Israel when Barak was ordered to defend us against the king of Canaan (pronounced *KAY-nun*). The Lord showed me that Barak should take ten thousand men to fight against the army of General Sisera of Canaan.

Although I didn't take part in the battle, I kept my promise to go to the battlefield with Barak and his troops. Barak was encouraged by my advice, and that day he and his army defeated the army of the king of Canaan. So we celebrated by singing our victory duet together (see Judges 5).

Barak won the victory that day because he was willing to listen to good advice and because I was willing to take my place beside him as an encourager.

Learn to respect one another's God-given abilities while you are growing up. Respect, or honor, is the basis of the love God commands you to have for others.

of Abinoam from Kedesh in Naphtali, and said to him, "Has not the LORD God of Israel commanded, 'Go and deploy *troops* at Mount Tabor; take with you ten thousand men of the sons of Naphtali and of the sons of Zebulun; 7 and against you I will deploy Sisera, the commander of Jabin's army, with his chariots and his multitude at the River Kishon; and I will deliver him into your hand'?"

8 And Barak said to her, "If you will go with me, then I will go; but if you will not go with me, I will not go!"

9 So she said, "I will surely go with you; nevertheless there will be no glory for you in the journey you are taking, for the LORD will sell Sisera into the

The walls of the city where Barak defeated the Canaanites.

hand of a woman." Then Deborah arose and went with Barak to Kedesh. [10] And Barak called Zebulun and Naphtali to Kedesh; he went up with ten thousand men under his command, and Deborah went up with him.

[11] Now Heber the Kenite, of the children of Hobab the father-in-law of Moses, had separated himself from the Kenites and pitched his tent near the terebinth tree at Zaanaim, which is beside Kedesh.

[12] And they reported to Sisera that Barak the son of Abinoam had gone up to Mount Tabor. [13] So Sisera gathered together all his chariots, nine hundred chariots of iron, and all the people who were with him, from Harosheth Hagoyim to the River Kishon.

[14] Then Deborah said to Barak, "Up! For this is the day in which the LORD has delivered Sisera into your hand. Has not the LORD gone out before you?" So Barak went down from Mount Tabor with ten thousand men following him. [15] And the LORD routed Sisera and all his chariots and all his army with the edge of the sword before Barak; and Sisera alighted from his chariot and fled away on foot. [16] But Barak pursued the chariots and the army as far as Harosheth Hagoyim, and all the army of Sisera fell by the edge of the sword; not a man was left.

[17] However, Sisera had fled away on foot to the tent of Jael, the wife of Heber the Kenite; for there was peace between Jabin king of Hazor and the house of Heber the Kenite. [18] And Jael went out to meet Sisera, and said to him, "Turn aside, my lord, turn aside to me; do not fear." And when he had turned aside with her into the tent, she covered him with a blanket.

[19] Then he said to her, "Please give me a little water to drink, for I am thirsty." So she opened a jug of milk, gave him a drink, and covered him. [20] And he said to her, "Stand at the door of the tent, and if any man comes and inquires of you, and says, 'Is there any man here?' you shall say, 'No.' "

[21] Then Jael, Heber's wife, took a tent peg and took a hammer in her hand, and went softly to him and drove the peg into his temple, and it went down into the ground; for he was fast asleep and weary. So he died. [22] And then, as Barak pursued Sisera, Jael came out to meet him, and said to him, "Come, I will show you the man whom you seek." And when he went into her tent, there lay Sisera, dead with the peg in his temple.

[23] So on that day God subdued Jabin king of Canaan in the presence of the children of Israel. [24] And the hand of the children of Israel grew stronger and stronger against Jabin king of Canaan, until they had destroyed Jabin king of Canaan.

Deborah sings a song of victory

5 Then Deborah and Barak the son of Abinoam sang on that day, saying:

2 "When leaders lead in Israel,
   When the people willingly offer
      themselves,
   Bless the LORD!

3 "Hear, O kings! Give ear, O
      princes!
   I, even I, will sing to the LORD;
   I will sing praise to the LORD God
      of Israel.

4 "LORD, when You went out from
      Seir,
   When You marched from the
      field of Edom,
   The earth trembled and the
      heavens poured,
   The clouds also poured water;
5 The mountains gushed before
      the LORD,
   This Sinai, before the LORD God
      of Israel.

6 "In the days of Shamgar, son of
      Anath,
   In the days of Jael,
   The highways were deserted,
   And the travelers walked along
      the byways.
7 Village life ceased, it ceased in
      Israel,

Until I, Deborah, arose,
Arose a mother in Israel.
8 They chose new gods;
Then *there was* war in the gates;
Not a shield or spear was seen
among forty thousand in
Israel.
9 My heart *is* with the rulers of
Israel
Who offered themselves
willingly with the people.
Bless the Lord!

10 "Speak, you who ride on white
donkeys,
Who sit in judges' attire,
And who walk along the road.
11 Far from the noise of the
archers, among the watering
places,
There they shall recount the
righteous acts of the Lord,
The righteous acts *for* His
villagers in Israel;
Then the people of the Lord
shall go down to the gates.

12 "Awake, awake, Deborah!
Awake, awake, sing a song!
Arise, Barak, and lead your
captives away,
O son of Abinoam!

13 "Then the survivors came down,
the people against the nobles;
The Lord came down for me
against the mighty.
14 From Ephraim *were* those
whose roots were in Amalek.
After you, Benjamin, with your
peoples,
From Machir rulers came down,
And from Zebulun those who
bear the recruiter's staff.
15 And the princes of Issachar *were*
with Deborah;
As Issachar, so *was* Barak
Sent into the valley under his
command;
Among the divisions of Reuben
There were great resolves of
heart.
16 Why did you sit among the
sheepfolds,

To hear the pipings for the
flocks?
The divisions of Reuben have
great searchings of heart.
17 Gilead stayed beyond the
Jordan,
And why did Dan remain on
ships?
Asher continued at the seashore,
And stayed by his inlets.
18 Zebulun *is* a people *who*
jeopardized their lives to the
point of death,
Naphtali also, on the heights of
the battlefield.

19 "The kings came *and* fought,
Then the kings of Canaan fought
In Taanach, by the waters of
Megiddo;
They took no spoils of silver.
20 They fought from the heavens;
The stars from their courses
fought against Sisera.
21 The torrent of Kishon swept
them away,
That ancient torrent, the torrent
of Kishon.
O my soul, march on in strength!
22 Then the horses' hooves
pounded,
The galloping, galloping of his
steeds.
23 'Curse Meroz,' said the angel of
the Lord,
'Curse its inhabitants bitterly,
Because they did not come to
the help of the Lord,
To the help of the Lord against
the mighty.'

24 "Most blessed among women is
Jael,
The wife of Heber the Kenite;
Blessed is she among women in
tents.
25 He asked for water, she gave
milk;
She brought out cream in a
lordly bowl.
26 She stretched her hand to the
tent peg,
Her right hand to the workmen's
hammer;

My name is pronounced *GID-ee-un* and means "Warrior." Since my nation, Israel, had sinned so badly, I doubted that God would defend us any longer against our enemies. But then the Angel of the Lord visited me and told me that I was going to save Israel from Midian (pronounced *MID-ih-un*).

At first I didn't believe the Angel, and I kept asking for proof that God would be with me. The Lord was very patient and performed two miracles: the fire out of the rock (see Judges 6:20, 21) and the fleece (see Judges 6:36–40).

The greatest test came when God asked me to reduce my army from twenty-two thousand to three hundred men! I thought it would be impossible to fight the huge army of Midian with so few, but we defeated them that day.

When the Lord promises you something, you can expect Him to do it.

She pounded Sisera, she
   pierced his head,
She split and struck through his
   temple.
27 At her feet he sank, he fell, he
   lay still;
At her feet he sank, he fell;
Where he sank, there he fell
   dead.

28 "The mother of Sisera looked
   through the window,
And cried out through the lattice,
'Why is his chariot *so* long in
   coming?
Why tarries the clatter of his
   chariots?'
29 Her wisest ladies answered her,
Yes, she answered herself,
30 'Are they not finding and dividing
   the spoil:
To *every* man a girl *or* two;
For Sisera, plunder of dyed
   garments,
Plunder of garments
   embroidered and dyed,
Two pieces of dyed embroidery
   for the neck of the looter?'

31 "Thus let all Your enemies perish,
   O LORD!
But *let* those who love Him *be*
   like the sun

When it comes out in full
   strength."

So the land had rest for forty years.

God calls Gideon

6 Then the children of Israel did evil in the sight of the LORD. So the LORD delivered them into the hand of Midian for seven years, 2 and the hand of Midian prevailed against Israel. Because of the Midianites, the children of Israel made for themselves the dens, the caves, and the strongholds which *are* in the mountains. 3 So it was, whenever Israel had sown, Midianites would come up; also Amalekites and the people of the East would come up against them. 4 Then they would encamp against them and destroy the produce of the earth as far as Gaza, and leave no sustenance for Israel, neither sheep nor ox nor donkey. 5 For they would come up with their livestock and their tents, coming in as numerous as locusts; both they and their camels were without number; and they would enter the land to destroy it. 6 So Israel was greatly impoverished because of the Midianites, and the children of Israel cried out to the LORD.

7 And it came to pass, when the

children of Israel cried out to the LORD because of the Midianites, 8 that the LORD sent a prophet to the children of Israel, who said to them, "Thus says the LORD God of Israel: 'I brought you up from Egypt and brought you out of the house of bondage; 9 and I delivered you out of the hand of the Egyptians and out of the hand of all who oppressed you, and drove them out before you and gave you their land. 10 Also I said to you, "I am the LORD your God; do not fear the gods of the Amorites, in whose land you dwell." But you have not obeyed My voice.'"

11 Now the Angel of the LORD came and sat under the terebinth tree which was in Ophrah, which belonged to Joash the Abiezrite, while his son Gideon threshed wheat in the winepress, in order to hide it from the Midianites. 12 And the Angel of the LORD appeared to him, and said to him, "The LORD is with you, you mighty man of valor!"

13 Gideon said to Him, "O my lord, if the LORD is with us, why then has all this happened to us? And where are all His miracles which our fathers told us about, saying, 'Did not the LORD bring us up from Egypt?' But now the LORD has forsaken us and delivered us into the hands of the Midianites."

14 Then the LORD turned to him and said, "Go in this might of yours, and you shall save Israel from the hand of the Midianites. Have I not sent you?"

15 So he said to Him, "O my Lord, how can I save Israel? Indeed my clan is the weakest in Manasseh, and I am the least in my father's house."

16 And the LORD said to him, "Surely I will be with you, and you shall defeat the Midianites as one man."

17 Then he said to Him, "If now I have found favor in Your sight, then show me a sign that it is You who talk with me. 18 Do not depart from here, I pray, until I come to You and bring out my offering and set it before You."

And He said, "I will wait until you come back."

19 So Gideon went in and prepared a young goat, and unleavened bread from an ephah of flour. The meat he put in a basket, and he put the broth in a pot; and he brought them out to Him under the terebinth tree and presented them. 20 The Angel of God said to him, "Take the meat and the unleavened bread and lay them on this rock, and pour out the broth." And he did so.

21 Then the Angel of the LORD put out the end of the staff that was in His hand, and touched the meat and the unleavened bread; and fire rose out of the rock and consumed the meat and the unleavened bread. And the Angel of the LORD departed out of his sight.

22 Now Gideon perceived that He was the Angel of the LORD. So Gideon said, "Alas, O Lord GOD! For I have seen the Angel of the LORD face to face."

23 Then the LORD said to him, "Peace be with you; do not fear, you shall not die." 24 So Gideon built an altar there to the LORD, and called it The-LORD-Is-Peace. To this day it is still in Ophrah of the Abiezrites.

25 Now it came to pass the same

⚒ DIGGING IN

6:11–24 You Can Know God's Peace
The Lord sent enemies against Israel when they sinned, but He also sent leaders to save His people when they were sorry for their sins. Gideon was one of those leaders, called judges. Such judges did not judge as modern judges do in trial courts. These judges were usually military commanders.

God sent His special Angel to call Gid-eon to his work as a judge for Israel. But Gideon was afraid when he saw the Angel of the Lord. Gideon thought this meant that he would die. But the Lord said to Gideon, "Peace be with you." So Gideon called that place, "The Lord Is Peace." Such peace is the gift of God, and you can have that wonderful peace of God if you are sorry for your sins. Ask God for His peace every day.

night that the LORD said to him, "Take your father's young bull, the second bull of seven years old, and tear down the altar of Baal that your father has, and cut down the wooden image that *is* beside it; 26 and build an altar to the LORD your God on top of this rock in the proper arrangement, and take the second bull and offer a burnt sacrifice with the wood of the image which you shall cut down." 27 So Gideon took ten men from among his servants and did as the LORD had said to him. But because he feared his father's household and the men of the city too much to do *it* by day, he did *it* by night.

28 And when the men of the city arose early in the morning, there was the altar of Baal, torn down; and the wooden image that *was* beside it was cut down, and the second bull was being offered on the altar *which had been* built. 29 So they said to one another, "Who has done this thing?" And when they had inquired and asked, they said, "Gideon the son of Joash has done this thing." 30 Then the men of the city said to Joash, "Bring out your son, that he may die, because he has torn down the altar of Baal, and because he has cut down the wooden image that *was* beside it."

31 But Joash said to all who stood against him, "Would you plead for Baal? Would you save him? Let the one who would plead for him be put to death by morning! If he *is* a god, let him plead for himself, because his altar has been torn down!" 32 Therefore on that day he called him Jerubbaal, saying, "Let Baal plead against him, because he has torn down his altar."

33 Then all the Midianites and Amalekites, the people of the East, gathered together; and they crossed over and encamped in the Valley of Jezreel. 34 But the Spirit of the LORD came upon Gideon; then he blew the trumpet, and the Abiezrites gathered behind him. 35 And he sent messengers throughout all Manasseh, who also gathered behind him. He also sent messengers to Asher, Zebulun, and Naphtali; and they came up to meet them.

36 So Gideon said to God, "If You will save Israel by my hand as You have said— 37 look, I shall put a fleece of wool on the threshing floor; if there is dew on the fleece only, and *it is* dry on all the ground, then I shall know that You will save Israel by my hand, as You have said." 38 And it was so. When he rose early the next morning and squeezed the fleece together, he wrung the dew out of the fleece, a bowlful of water. 39 Then Gideon said to God, "Do not be angry with me, but let me speak just once more: Let me test, I pray, just once more with the fleece; let it now be dry only on the fleece, but on all the ground let there be dew." 40 And God did so that night. It was dry on the fleece only, but there was dew on all the ground.

Gideon's small army

7 Then Jerubbaal (that *is,* Gideon) and all the people who *were* with him rose early and encamped beside the well of Harod, so that the camp of the Midianites was on the north side of them by the hill of Moreh in the valley. 2 And the LORD said to Gideon, "The people who *are* with you *are* too many for Me to give the Midianites into their hands, lest Israel claim glory for itself against Me, saying, 'My own hand has saved me.' 3 Now therefore, proclaim in the hearing of the people, saying, 'Whoever *is* fearful and afraid, let him turn and depart at once from Mount Gilead.' " And twenty-two thousand of the people returned, and ten thousand remained.

4 But the LORD said to Gideon, "The people *are* still *too* many; bring them down to the water, and I will test them for you there. Then it will be, *that* of whom I say to you, 'This one shall go with you,' the same shall go with you; and of whomever I say to you, 'This one shall not go with you,' the same shall not go." 5 So he brought the people down to the water. And the LORD said to Gideon, "Everyone who laps

Can Small Be Great?

We often think *bigness* is what matters. But God proves over and over that He likes to use very *small* things to do His great works. Remember David and Goliath? (See 1 Samuel 17.) God also used Gideon's army of three hundred men to show us we win only because God helps us.

from the water with his tongue, as a dog laps, you shall set apart by himself; likewise everyone who gets down on his knees to drink." 6 And the number of those who lapped, *putting* their hand to their mouth, was three hundred men; but all the rest of the people got down on their knees to drink water. 7 Then the LORD said to Gideon, "By the three hundred men who lapped I will save you, and deliver the Midianites into your hand. Let all the *other* people go, every man to his place." 8 So the people took provisions and their trumpets in their hands. And he sent away all *the rest of* Israel, every man to his tent, and retained those three hundred men. Now the camp of Midian was below him in the valley.

9 It happened on the same night that the LORD said to him, "Arise, go down against the camp, for I have delivered it into your hand. 10 But if you are afraid to go down, go down to the camp with Purah your servant, 11 and you shall hear what they say; and afterward your hands shall be strengthened to go down against the camp." Then he went down with Purah his servant to the outpost of the armed men who *were* in the camp. 12 Now the Midianites and Amalekites, all the people of the East, were lying in the valley as numerous as locusts; and their camels *were* without number, as the sand by the seashore in multitude.

13 And when Gideon had come, there was a man telling a dream to his companion. He said, "I have had a dream: *To my* surprise, a loaf of barley bread tumbled into the camp of Mid-

ian; it came to a tent and struck it so that it fell and overturned, and the tent collapsed."

14 Then his companion answered and said, "This *is* nothing else but the sword of Gideon the son of Joash, a man of Israel! Into his hand God has delivered Midian and the whole camp."

15 And so it was, when Gideon heard the telling of the dream and its interpretation, that he worshiped. He returned to the camp of Israel, and said, "Arise, for the LORD has delivered the camp of Midian into your hand." 16 Then he divided the three hundred men *into* three companies, and he put a trumpet into every man's hand, with empty pitchers, and torches inside the pitchers. 17 And he said to them, "Look at me and do likewise; watch, and when I come to the edge of the camp you shall do as I do: 18 When I blow the trumpet, I and all who *are* with me, then you also blow the trumpets on every side of the whole camp, and say, '*The sword of* the LORD and of Gideon!'"

19 So Gideon and the hundred men who *were* with him came to the outpost of the camp at the beginning of the middle watch, just as they had posted the watch; and they blew the trumpets and broke the pitchers that *were* in their hands. 20 Then the three companies blew the trumpets and broke the pitchers—they held the torches in their left hands and the trumpets in their right hands for blowing—and they cried, "The sword of the LORD and of Gideon!" 21 And every man stood in his place all around the camp; and the whole army ran and cried out and fled. 22 When the three hundred blew the trumpets, the LORD set every man's sword against his companion throughout the whole camp; and the army fled to Beth Acacia, toward Zererah, as far as the border of Abel Meholah, by Tabbath.

23 And the men of Israel gathered together from Naphtali, Asher, and all Manasseh, and pursued the Midianites. 24 Then Gideon sent messengers

throughout all the mountains of Ephraim, saying, "Come down against the Midianites, and seize from them the watering places as far as Beth Barah and the Jordan." Then all the men of Ephraim gathered together and seized the watering places as far as Beth Barah and the Jordan. 25 And they captured two princes of the Midianites, Oreb and Zeeb. They killed Oreb at the rock of Oreb, and Zeeb they killed at the winepress of Zeeb. They pursued Midian and brought the heads of Oreb and Zeeb to Gideon on the other side of the Jordan.

Gideon wins the battle

8 Now the men of Ephraim said to him, "Why have you done this to us by not calling us when you went to fight with the Midianites?" And they reprimanded him sharply.

2 So he said to them, "What have I done now in comparison with you? Is not the gleaning of the grapes of Ephraim better than the vintage of Abiezer? 3 God has delivered into your hands the princes of Midian, Oreb and Zeeb. And what was I able to do in comparison with you?" Then their anger toward him subsided when he said that.

4 When Gideon came to the Jordan, he and the three hundred men who were with him crossed over, exhausted but still in pursuit. 5 Then he said to the men of Succoth, "Please give loaves of bread to the people who follow me, for they are exhausted, and I am pursuing Zebah and Zalmunna, kings of Midian."

6 And the leaders of Succoth said, "Are the hands of Zebah and Zalmunna now in your hand, that we should give bread to your army?"

7 So Gideon said, "For this cause, when the LORD has delivered Zebah and Zalmunna into my hand, then I will tear your flesh with the thorns of the wilderness and with briers!" 8 Then he went up from there to Penuel and spoke to them in the same way. And the men of Penuel answered him as the men of Succoth had answered. 9 So he also spoke to the men of Penuel, saying, "When I come back in peace, I will tear down this tower!"

10 Now Zebah and Zalmunna were at Karkor, and their armies with them, about fifteen thousand, all who were left of all the army of the people of the East; for one hundred and twenty thousand men who drew the sword had fallen. 11 Then Gideon went up by the road of those who dwell in tents on the east of Nobah and Jogbehah; and he attacked the army while the camp felt secure. 12 When Zebah and Zalmunna fled, he pursued them; and he took the two kings of Midian, Zebah and Zalmunna, and routed the whole army.

13 Then Gideon the son of Joash returned from battle, from the Ascent of Heres. 14 And he caught a young man of the men of Succoth and interrogated him; and he wrote down for him the leaders of Succoth and its elders, seventy-seven men. 15 Then he came to the men of Succoth and said, "Here are Zebah and Zalmunna, about whom you ridiculed me, saying, 'Are the hands of Zebah and Zalmunna now in your hand, that we should give bread to your weary men?'" 16 And he took the elders of the city, and thorns of the wilderness and briers, and with them he taught the men of Succoth. 17 Then he tore down the tower of Penuel and killed the men of the city.

18 And he said to Zebah and Zalmunna, "What kind of men were they whom you killed at Tabor?"

So they answered, "As you are, so were they; each one resembled the son of a king."

19 Then he said, "They were my brothers, the sons of my mother. As the LORD lives, if you had let them live, I would not kill you." 20 And he said to Jether his firstborn, "Rise, kill them!" But the youth would not draw his sword; for he was afraid, because he was still a youth.

21 So Zebah and Zalmunna said, "Rise yourself, and kill us; for as a man

is, so is his strength." So Gideon arose and killed Zebah and Zalmunna, and took the crescent ornaments that *were* on their camels' necks.

22 Then the men of Israel said to Gideon, "Rule over us, both you and your son, and your grandson also; for you have delivered us from the hand of Midian."

23 But Gideon said to them, "I will not rule over you, nor shall my son rule over you; the LORD shall rule over you." 24 Then Gideon said to them, "I would like to make a request of you, that each of you would give me the earrings from his plunder." For they had golden earrings, because they *were* Ishmaelites.

25 So they answered, "We will gladly give *them*." And they spread out a garment, and each man threw into it the earrings from his plunder. 26 Now the weight of the gold earrings that he requested was one thousand seven hundred *shekels* of gold, besides the crescent ornaments, pendants, and purple robes which *were* on the kings of Midian, and besides the chains that *were* around their camels' necks. 27 Then Gideon made it into an ephod and set it up in his city, Ophrah. And all Israel played the harlot with it there. It became a snare to Gideon and to his house.

28 Thus Midian was subdued before the children of Israel, so that they lifted their heads no more. And the country was quiet for forty years in the days of Gideon.

29 Then Jerubbaal the son of Joash went and dwelt in his own house. 30 Gideon had seventy sons who were his own offspring, for he had many wives. 31 And his concubine who *was* in Shechem also bore him a son, whose name he called Abimelech. 32 Now Gideon the son of Joash died at a good old age, and was buried in the tomb of Joash his father, in Ophrah of the Abiezrites.

33 So it was, as soon as Gideon was dead, that the children of Israel again played the harlot with the Baals, and made Baal-Berith their god. 34 Thus the children of Israel did not remember the LORD their God, who had delivered them from the hands of all their enemies on every side; 35 nor did they show kindness to the house of Jerubbaal (Gideon) in accordance with the good he had done for Israel.

Abimelech is punished

9 Then Abimelech the son of Jerubbaal went to Shechem, to his mother's brothers, and spoke with them and with all the family of the house of his mother's father, saying, 2 "Please speak in the hearing of all the men of Shechem: 'Which is better for you, that all seventy of the sons of Jerubbaal reign over you, or that one reign over you?' Remember that I *am* your own flesh and bone."

3 And his mother's brothers spoke all these words concerning him in the hearing of all the men of Shechem; and their heart was inclined to follow Abimelech, for they said, "He is our brother." 4 So they gave him seventy *shekels* of silver from the temple of Baal-Berith, with which Abimelech hired worthless and reckless men; and they followed him. 5 Then he went to his father's house at Ophrah and killed his brothers, the seventy sons of Jerubbaal, on one stone. But Jotham the youngest son of Jerubbaal was left, because he hid himself. 6 And all the men of Shechem gathered together, all of Beth Millo, and they went and made Abimelech king beside the terebinth tree at the pillar that *was* in Shechem.

7 Now when they told Jotham, he went and stood on top of Mount Gerizim, and lifted his voice and cried out. And he said to them:

> "Listen to me, you men of
>   Shechem,
> That God may listen to you!

8 "The trees once went forth to
>   anoint a king over them.
> And they said to the olive tree,
>   'Reign over us!'
9 But the olive tree said to them,

'Should I cease giving my oil,
With which they honor God and
men,
And go to sway over trees?'

10 "Then the trees said to the fig
tree,
'You come *and* reign over us!'
11 But the fig tree said to them,
'Should I cease my sweetness
and my good fruit,
And go to sway over trees?'

12 "Then the trees said to the vine,
'You come *and* reign over us!'
13 But the vine said to them,
'Should I cease my new wine,
Which cheers *both* God and
men,
And go to sway over trees?'

14 "Then all the trees said to the
bramble,
'You come *and* reign over us!'
15 And the bramble said to the
trees,
'If in truth you anoint me as king
over you,
Then come *and* take shelter in
my shade;
But if not, let fire come out of
the bramble
And devour the cedars of
Lebanon!'

16 "Now therefore, if you have acted in truth and sincerity in making Abimelech king, and if you have dealt well with Jerubbaal and his house, and have done to him as he deserves— 17 for my father fought for you, risked his life, and delivered you out of the hand of Midian; 18 but you have risen up against my father's house this day, and killed his seventy sons on one stone, and made Abimelech, the son of his female servant, king over the men of Shechem, because he is your brother— 19 if then you have acted in truth and sincerity with Jerubbaal and with his house this day, *then* rejoice in Abimelech, and let him also rejoice in you. 20 But if not, let fire come from Abimelech and devour the men of Shechem and Beth Millo; and let fire come from the men of Shechem and from Beth Millo and devour Abimelech!" 21 And Jotham ran away and fled; and he went to Beer and dwelt there, for fear of Abimelech his brother.

22 After Abimelech had reigned over Israel three years, 23 God sent a spirit of ill will between Abimelech and the men of Shechem; and the men of Shechem dealt treacherously with Abimelech, 24 that the crime *done* to the seventy sons of Jerubbaal might be settled and their blood be laid on Abimelech their brother, who killed them, and on the men of Shechem, who aided him in the killing of his brothers. 25 And the men of Shechem set men in ambush against him on the tops of the mountains, and they robbed all who passed by them along that way; and it was told Abimelech.

26 Now Gaal the son of Ebed came with his brothers and went over to Shechem; and the men of Shechem put their confidence in him. 27 So they went out into the fields, and gathered grapes from their vineyards and trod *them,* and made merry. And they went into the house of their god, and ate and drank, and cursed Abimelech. 28 Then Gaal the son of Ebed said, "Who *is* Abimelech, and who *is* Shechem, that we should serve him? *Is he* not the son of Jerubbaal, and *is not* Zebul his officer? Serve the men of Hamor the father of Shechem; but why should we serve him? 29 If only this people were under my authority! Then I would remove Abimelech." So he said to Abimelech, "Increase your army and come out!"

30 When Zebul, the ruler of the city, heard the words of Gaal the son of Ebed, his anger was aroused. 31 And he sent messengers to Abimelech secretly, saying, "Take note! Gaal the son of Ebed and his brothers have come to Shechem; and here they are, fortifying the city against you. 32 Now therefore, get up by night, you and the people who *are* with you, and lie in

wait in the field. 33 And it shall be, as soon as the sun is up in the morning, *that* you shall rise early and rush upon the city; and *when* he and the people who are with him come out against you, you may then do to them as you find opportunity."

34 So Abimelech and all the people who *were* with him rose by night, and lay in wait against Shechem in four companies. 35 When Gaal the son of Ebed went out and stood in the entrance to the city gate, Abimelech and the people who *were* with him rose from lying in wait. 36 And when Gaal saw the people, he said to Zebul, "Look, people are coming down from the tops of the mountains!"

But Zebul said to him, "You see the shadows of the mountains as *if they were* men."

37 So Gaal spoke again and said, "See, people are coming down from the center of the land, and another company is coming from the Diviners' Terebinth Tree."

38 Then Zebul said to him, "Where indeed *is* your mouth now, with which you said, 'Who is Abimelech, that we should serve him?' *Are* not these the people whom you despised? Go out, if you will, and fight with them now."

39 So Gaal went out, leading the men of Shechem, and fought with Abimelech. 40 And Abimelech chased him, and he fled from him; and many fell wounded, to the *very* entrance of the gate. 41 Then Abimelech dwelt at Arumah, and Zebul drove out Gaal and his brothers, so that they would not dwell in Shechem.

42 And it came about on the next day that the people went out into the field, and they told Abimelech. 43 So he took his people, divided them into three companies, and lay in wait in the field. And he looked, and there *were* the people, coming out of the city; and he rose against them and attacked them. 44 Then Abimelech and the company that *was* with him rushed forward and stood at the entrance of the gate of the city; and the *other* two companies rushed upon all who *were* in the

fields and killed them. 45 So Abimelech fought against the city all that day; he took the city and killed the people who *were* in it; and he demolished the city and sowed it with salt.

46 Now when all the men of the tower of Shechem had heard *that,* they entered the stronghold of the temple of the god Berith. 47 And it was told Abimelech that all the men of the tower of Shechem were gathered together. 48 Then Abimelech went up to Mount Zalmon, he and all the people who *were* with him. And Abimelech took an ax in his hand and cut down a bough from the trees, and took it and laid *it* on his shoulder; then he said to the people who were with him, "What you have seen me do, make haste *and* do as I *have done.*" 49 So each of the people likewise cut down his own bough and followed Abimelech, put *them* against the stronghold, and set the stronghold on fire above them, so that all the people of the tower of Shechem died, about a thousand men and women.

50 Then Abimelech went to Thebez, and he encamped against Thebez and took it. 51 But there was a strong tower in the city, and all the men and women—all the people of the city—fled there and shut themselves in; then they went up to the top of the tower. 52 So Abimelech came as far as the tower and fought against it; and he drew near the door of the tower to burn it with fire. 53 But a certain woman dropped an upper millstone on Abimelech's head and crushed his skull. 54 Then he called quickly to the young man, his armorbearer, and said to him, "Draw your sword and kill me, lest men say of me, 'A woman killed him.' " So his young man thrust him through, and he died. 55 And when the men of Israel saw that Abimelech was dead, they departed, every man to his place.

56 Thus God repaid the wickedness of Abimelech, which he had done to his father by killing his seventy brothers. 57 And all the evil of the men of Shechem God returned on their

own heads, and on them came the curse of Jotham the son of Jerubbaal.

God is unhappy with Israel

10 After Abimelech there arose to save Israel Tola the son of Puah, the son of Dodo, a man of Issachar; and he dwelt in Shamir in the mountains of Ephraim. 2 He judged Israel twenty-three years; and he died and was buried in Shamir.

3 After him arose Jair, a Gileadite; and he judged Israel twenty-two years. 4 Now he had thirty sons who rode on thirty donkeys; they also had thirty towns, which are called "Havoth Jair" to this day, which *are* in the land of Gilead. 5 And Jair died and was buried in Camon.

6 Then the children of Israel again did evil in the sight of the LORD, and served the Baals and the Ashtoreths, the gods of Syria, the gods of Sidon, the gods of Moab, the gods of the people of Ammon, and the gods of the Philistines; and they forsook the LORD and did not serve Him. 7 So the anger of the LORD was hot against Israel; and He sold them into the hands of the Philistines and into the hands of the people of Ammon. 8 From that year they harassed and oppressed the children of Israel for eighteen years—all the children of Israel who *were* on the other side of the Jordan in the land of the Amorites, in Gilead. 9 Moreover the people of Ammon crossed over the Jordan to fight against Judah also, against Benjamin, and against the house of Ephraim, so that Israel was severely distressed.

10 And the children of Israel cried out to the LORD, saying, "We have sinned against You, because we have both forsaken our God and served the Baals!"

11 So the LORD said to the children of Israel, "*Did I* not *deliver you* from the Egyptians and from the Amorites and from the people of Ammon and from the Philistines? 12 Also the Sidonians and Amalekites and Maonites oppressed you; and you cried out to Me,

and I delivered you from their hand. 13 Yet you have forsaken Me and served other gods. Therefore I will deliver you no more. 14 Go and cry out to the gods which you have chosen; let them deliver you in your time of distress."

15 And the children of Israel said to the LORD, "We have sinned! Do to us whatever seems best to You; only deliver us this day, we pray." 16 So they put away the foreign gods from among them and served the LORD. And His soul could no longer endure the misery of Israel.

17 Then the people of Ammon gathered together and encamped in Gilead. And the children of Israel assembled together and encamped in Mizpah. 18 And the people, the leaders of Gilead, said to one another, "Who is the man who will begin the fight against the people of Ammon? He shall be head over all the inhabitants of Gilead."

Jephthah—God's mighty man

11 Now Jephthah the Gileadite was a mighty man of valor, but he *was* the son of a harlot; and Gilead begot Jephthah. 2 Gilead's wife bore sons; and when his wife's sons grew up, they drove Jephthah out, and said to him, "You shall have no inheritance in our father's house, for you *are* the son of another woman." 3 Then Jephthah fled from his brothers and dwelt in the land of Tob; and worthless men banded together with Jephthah and went out *raiding* with him.

4 It came to pass after a time that the people of Ammon made war against Israel. 5 And so it was, when the people of Ammon made war against Israel, that the elders of Gilead went to get Jephthah from the land of Tob. 6 Then they said to Jephthah, "Come and be our commander, that we may fight against the people of Ammon."

7 So Jephthah said to the elders of Gilead, "Did you not hate me, and expel me from my father's house? Why

have you come to me now when you are in distress?"

8 And the elders of Gilead said to Jephthah, "That is why we have turned again to you now, that you may go with us and fight against the people of Ammon, and be our head over all the inhabitants of Gilead."

9 So Jephthah said to the elders of Gilead, "If you take me back home to fight against the people of Ammon, and the LORD delivers them to me, shall I be your head?"

10 And the elders of Gilead said to Jephthah, "The LORD will be a witness between us, if we do not do according to your words." 11 Then Jephthah went with the elders of Gilead, and the people made him head and commander over them; and Jephthah spoke all his words before the LORD in Mizpah.

12 Now Jephthah sent messengers to the king of the people of Ammon, saying, "What do you have against me, that you have come to fight against me in my land?"

13 And the king of the people of Ammon answered the messengers of Jephthah, "Because Israel took away my land when they came up out of Egypt, from the Arnon as far as the Jabbok, and to the Jordan. Now therefore, restore those lands peaceably."

14 So Jephthah again sent messengers to the king of the people of Ammon, 15 and said to him, "Thus says Jephthah: 'Israel did not take away the land of Moab, nor the land of the people of Ammon; 16 for when Israel came up from Egypt, they walked through the wilderness as far as the Red Sea and came to Kadesh. 17 Then Israel sent messengers to the king of Edom, saying, "Please let me pass through your land." But the king of Edom would not heed. And in like manner they sent to the king of Moab, but he would not consent. So Israel remained in Kadesh. 18 And they went along through the wilderness and bypassed the land of Edom and the land of Moab, came to the east side of the land of Moab, and encamped on the other side of the Arnon. But they did not

enter the border of Moab, for the Arnon was the border of Moab. 19 Then Israel sent messengers to Sihon king of the Amorites, king of Heshbon; and Israel said to him, "Please let us pass through your land into our place." 20 But Sihon did not trust Israel to pass through his territory. So Sihon gathered all his people together, encamped in Jahaz, and fought against Israel. 21 And the LORD God of Israel delivered Sihon and all his people into the hand of Israel, and they defeated them. Thus Israel gained possession of all the land of the Amorites, who inhabited that country. 22 They took possession of all the territory of the Amorites, from the Arnon to the Jabbok and from the wilderness to the Jordan.

23 'And now the LORD God of Israel has dispossessed the Amorites from before His people Israel; should you then possess it? 24 Will you not possess whatever Chemosh your god gives you to possess? So whatever the LORD our God takes possession of before us, we will possess. 25 And now, are you any better than Balak the son of Zippor, king of Moab? Did he ever strive against Israel? Did he ever fight against them? 26 While Israel dwelt in Heshbon and its villages, in Aroer and its villages, and in all the cities along the banks of the Arnon, for three hundred years, why did you not recover them within that time? 27 Therefore I have not sinned against you, but you wronged me by fighting against me. May the LORD, the Judge, render judgment this day between the children of Israel and the people of Ammon.' " 28 However, the king of the people of Ammon did not heed the words which Jephthah sent him.

29 Then the Spirit of the LORD came upon Jephthah, and he passed through Gilead and Manasseh, and passed through Mizpah of Gilead; and from Mizpah of Gilead he advanced toward the people of Ammon. 30 And Jephthah made a vow to the LORD, and said, "If You will indeed deliver the people of Ammon into my hands, 31 then it will be that whatever comes

out of the doors of my house to meet me, when I return in peace from the people of Ammon, shall surely be the LORD's, and I will offer it up as a burnt offering."

³² So Jephthah advanced toward the people of Ammon to fight against them, and the LORD delivered them into his hands. ³³ And he defeated them from Aroer as far as Minnith— twenty cities—and to Abel Keramim, with a very great slaughter. Thus the people of Ammon were subdued before the children of Israel.

³⁴ When Jephthah came to his house at Mizpah, there was his daughter, coming out to meet him with timbrels and dancing; and she *was his* only child. Besides her he had neither son nor daughter. ³⁵ And it came to pass, when he saw her, that he tore his clothes, and said, "Alas, my daughter! You have brought me very low! You are among those who trouble me! For I have given my word to the LORD, and I cannot go back on it."

³⁶ So she said to him, "My father, *if* you have given your word to the LORD, do to me according to what has gone out of your mouth, because the LORD has avenged you of your enemies, the people of Ammon." ³⁷ Then she said to her father, "Let this thing be done for me: let me alone for two months, that I may go and wander on the mountains and bewail my virginity, my friends and I."

³⁸ So he said, "Go." And he sent her away *for* two months; and she went with her friends, and bewailed her virginity on the mountains. ³⁹ And it was so at the end of two months that she returned to her father, and he carried out his vow with her which he had vowed. She knew no man.

And it became a custom in Israel ⁴⁰ *that* the daughters of Israel went four days each year to lament the daughter of Jephthah the Gileadite.

Jephthah judges Israel

12 Then the men of Ephraim gathered together, crossed over toward Zaphon, and said to Jephthah, "Why did you cross over to fight against the people of Ammon, and did not call us to go with you? We will burn your house down on you with fire!"

² And Jephthah said to them, "My people and I were in a great struggle with the people of Ammon; and when I called you, you did not deliver me out of their hands. ³ So when I saw that you would not deliver *me,* I took my life in my hands and crossed over against the people of Ammon; and the LORD delivered them into my hand. Why then have you come up to me this day to fight against me?" ⁴ Now Jephthah gathered together all the men of Gilead and fought against Ephraim. And the men of Gilead defeated Ephraim, because they said, "You Gileadites *are* fugitives of Ephraim among the Ephraimites *and* among the Manassites." ⁵ The Gileadites seized the fords of the Jordan before the Ephraimites *arrived.* And when *any* Ephraimite who escaped said, "Let me cross over," the men of Gilead would say to him, "*Are* you an Ephraimite?" If he said, "No," ⁶ then they would say to him, "Then say, 'Shibboleth'!" And he would say, "Sibboleth," for he could not pronounce *it* right. Then they would take him and kill him at the fords of the Jordan. There fell at that time forty-two thousand Ephraimites.

⁷ And Jephthah judged Israel six years. Then Jephthah the Gileadite died and was buried among the cities of Gilead.

⁸ After him, Ibzan of Bethlehem judged Israel. ⁹ He had thirty sons. And he gave away thirty daughters in marriage, and brought in thirty daughters from elsewhere for his sons. He judged Israel seven years. ¹⁰ Then Ibzan died and was buried at Bethlehem.

¹¹ After him, Elon the Zebulunite judged Israel. He judged Israel ten years. ¹² And Elon the Zebulunite died and was buried at Aijalon in the country of Zebulun.

¹³ After him, Abdon the son of Hillel the Pirathonite judged Israel. ¹⁴ He had

forty sons and thirty grandsons, who rode on seventy young donkeys. He judged Israel eight years. [15] Then Abdon the son of Hillel the Pirathonite died and was buried in Pirathon in the land of Ephraim, in the mountains of the Amalekites.

Samson is born

13 Again the children of Israel did evil in the sight of the LORD, and the LORD delivered them into the hand of the Philistines for forty years.

[2] Now there was a certain man from Zorah, of the family of the Danites, whose name *was* Manoah; and his wife *was* barren and had no children. [3] And the Angel of the LORD appeared to the woman and said to her, "Indeed now, you are barren and have borne no children, but you shall conceive and bear a son. [4] Now therefore, please be careful not to drink wine or *similar* drink, and not to eat anything unclean. [5] For behold, you shall conceive and bear a son. And no razor shall come upon his head, for the child shall be a Nazirite to God from the womb; and he shall begin to deliver Israel out of the hand of the Philistines."

[6] So the woman came and told her husband, saying, "A Man of God came to me, and His countenance *was* like the countenance of the Angel of God, very awesome; but I did not ask Him where He *was* from, and He did not tell me His name. [7] And He said to me, 'Behold, you shall conceive and bear a son. Now drink no wine or *similar* drink, nor eat anything unclean, for the child shall be a Nazirite to God from the womb to the day of his death.'"

[8] Then Manoah prayed to the LORD, and said, "O my Lord, please let the Man of God whom You sent come to us again and teach us what we shall do for the child who will be born."

[9] And God listened to the voice of Manoah, and the Angel of God came to the woman again as she was sitting in the field; but Manoah her husband *was* not with her. [10] Then the woman ran in haste and told her husband, and said to him, "Look, the Man who came to me the *other* day has just now appeared to me!"

[11] So Manoah arose and followed his wife. When he came to the Man, he said to Him, "Are You the Man who spoke to this woman?"

And He said, "I *am*."

[12] Manoah said, "Now let Your words come *to pass*! What will be the boy's rule of life, and his work?"

[13] So the Angel of the LORD said to Manoah, "Of all that I said to the woman let her be careful. [14] She may not eat anything that comes from the vine, nor may she drink wine or *similar* drink, nor eat anything unclean. All that I commanded her let her observe."

[15] Then Manoah said to the Angel of the LORD, "Please let us detain You, and we will prepare a young goat for You."

[16] And the Angel of the LORD said to Manoah, "Though you detain Me, I will not eat your food. But if you offer a burnt offering, you must offer it to the LORD." (For Manoah did not know He *was* the Angel of the LORD.)

[17] Then Manoah said to the Angel of the LORD, "What *is* Your name, that when Your words come *to pass* we may honor You?"

[18] And the Angel of the LORD said to him, "Why do you ask My name, seeing it *is* wonderful?"

[19] So Manoah took the young goat with the grain offering, and offered it upon the rock to the LORD. And He did a wondrous thing while Manoah and his wife looked on— [20] it happened as the flame went up toward heaven from the altar—the Angel of the LORD ascended in the flame of the altar! When Manoah and his wife saw *this*, they fell on their faces to the ground. [21] When the Angel of the LORD appeared no more to Manoah and his wife, then Manoah knew that He *was* the Angel of the LORD.

[22] And Manoah said to his wife, "We shall surely die, because we have seen God!"

23 But his wife said to him, "If the LORD had desired to kill us, He would not have accepted a burnt offering and a grain offering from our hands, nor would He have shown us all these *things*, nor would He have told us *such things* as these at this time."

24 So the woman bore a son and called his name Samson; and the child grew, and the LORD blessed him. 25 And the Spirit of the LORD began to move upon him at Mahaneh Dan between Zorah and Eshtaol.

Samson asks a riddle

14 Now Samson went down to Timnah, and saw a woman in Timnah of the daughters of the Philistines. 2 So he went up and told his father and mother, saying, "I have seen a woman in Timnah of the daughters of the Philistines; now therefore, get her for me as a wife."

3 Then his father and mother said to him, "*Is there* no woman among the daughters of your brethren, or among all my people, that you must go and get a wife from the uncircumcised Philistines?"

And Samson said to his father, "Get her for me, for she pleases me well."

4 But his father and mother did not know that it was of the LORD—that He was seeking an occasion to move against the Philistines. For at that time the Philistines had dominion over Israel.

5 So Samson went down to Timnah with his father and mother, and came to the vineyards of Timnah.

Now *to his* surprise, a young lion *came* roaring against him. 6 And the Spirit of the LORD came mightily upon him, and he tore the lion apart as one would have torn apart a young goat, though *he had* nothing in his hand. But he did not tell his father or his mother what he had done.

7 Then he went down and talked with the woman; and she pleased Samson well. 8 After some time, when he returned to get her, he turned aside to see the carcass of the lion. And be-

Samson, the strongest man in the Bible, often fought and killed wild animals.

hold, a swarm of bees and honey *were* in the carcass of the lion. 9 He took some of it in his hands and went along, eating. When he came to his father and mother, he gave *some* to them, and they also ate. But he did not tell them that he had taken the honey out of the carcass of the lion.

10 So his father went down to the woman. And Samson gave a feast there, for young men used to do so. 11 And it happened, when they saw him, that they brought thirty companions to be with him.

12 Then Samson said to them, "Let me pose a riddle to you. If you can correctly solve and explain it to me within the seven days of the feast, then I will give you thirty linen garments and thirty changes of clothing. 13 But if you cannot explain *it* to me, then you shall

give me thirty linen garments and thirty changes of clothing.''

And they said to him, "Pose your riddle, that we may hear it.''

14 So he said to them:

> "Out of the eater came something to eat,
> And out of the strong came something sweet.''

Now for three days they could not explain the riddle.

15 But it came to pass on the seventh day that they said to Samson's wife, "Entice your husband, that he may explain the riddle to us, or else we will burn you and your father's house with fire. Have you invited us in order to take what is ours? Is that not so?''

16 Then Samson's wife wept on him, and said, "You only hate me! You do not love me! You have posed a riddle to the sons of my people, but you have not explained it to me.''

And he said to her, "Look, I have not explained it to my father or my mother; so should I explain it to you?''

17 Now she had wept on him the seven days while their feast lasted. And it happened on the seventh day that he told her, because she pressed him so much. Then she explained the riddle to the sons of her people. 18 So the men of the city said to him on the seventh day before the sun went down:

> "What is sweeter than honey?
> And what is stronger than a lion?''

And he said to them:

> "If you had not plowed with my heifer,
> You would not have solved my riddle!''

19 Then the Spirit of the LORD came upon him mightily, and he went down to Ashkelon and killed thirty of their men, took their apparel, and gave the changes of clothing to those who had explained the riddle. So his anger was aroused, and he went back up to his father's house. 20 And Samson's wife was given to his companion, who had been his best man.

Samson burns the Philistines' corn

15 After a while, in the time of wheat harvest, it happened that Samson visited his wife with a young goat. And he said, "Let me go in to my wife, into her room.'' But her father would not permit him to go in.

2 Her father said, "I really thought that you thoroughly hated her; therefore I gave her to your companion. Is not her younger sister better than she? Please, take her instead.''

3 And Samson said to them, "This time I shall be blameless regarding the Philistines if I harm them!'' 4 Then Samson went and caught three hundred foxes; and he took torches, turned the foxes tail to tail, and put a torch between each pair of tails. 5 When he had set the torches on fire, he let the foxes go into the standing grain of the Philistines, and burned up both the shocks and the standing grain, as well as the vineyards and olive groves.

6 Then the Philistines said, "Who has done this?''

And they answered, "Samson, the son-in-law of the Timnite, because he has taken his wife and given her to his companion.'' So the Philistines came up and burned her and her father with fire.

7 Samson said to them, "Since you would do a thing like this, I will surely take revenge on you, and after that I will cease.'' 8 So he attacked them hip and thigh with a great slaughter; then he went down and dwelt in the cleft of the rock of Etam.

9 Now the Philistines went up, encamped in Judah, and deployed themselves against Lehi. 10 And the men of Judah said, "Why have you come up against us?''

So they answered, "We have come

My birth was a miracle because everybody thought my mother could not have children. But the Angel of God told my mother and my father, Manoah, that they would have a son. They named me Samson.

God also told Manoah that I would be a Nazirite (pronounced *NAZ-uh-right*). A Nazirite was someone whose life was especially given to God. One of the signs of a Nazirite was that he didn't cut his hair.

When I was born, the Holy Spirit gave me unusual physical strength. At that time, the Philistines (pronounced *fih-LIS-teens*) were our enemies. When I fought against them, they came to arrest me, but I broke the ropes they tied me with and killed a thousand of their troops with only the jawbone of a donkey!

This is just one of the miracles of strength I performed against our enemies. The truth to remember is that you and God are a winning team in all the tests of life.

up to arrest Samson, to do to him as he has done to us."

11 Then three thousand men of Judah went down to the cleft of the rock of Etam, and said to Samson, "Do you not know that the Philistines rule over us? What is this you have done to us?"

And he said to them, "As they did to me, so I have done to them."

12 But they said to him, "We have come down to arrest you, that we may deliver you into the hand of the Philistines."

Then Samson said to them, "Swear to me that you will not kill me yourselves."

13 So they spoke to him, saying, "No, but we will tie you securely and deliver you into their hand; but we will surely not kill you." And they bound him with two new ropes and brought him up from the rock.

14 When he came to Lehi, the Philistines came shouting against him. Then the Spirit of the LORD came mightily upon him; and the ropes that *were* on his arms became like flax that is burned with fire, and his bonds broke loose from his hands. 15 He found a fresh jawbone of a donkey, reached out his hand and took it, and killed a thousand men with it. 16 Then Samson said:

"With the jawbone of a donkey,
Heaps upon heaps,
With the jawbone of a donkey
I have slain a thousand men!"

17 And so it was, when he had finished speaking, that he threw the jawbone from his hand, and called that place Ramath Lehi.

18 Then he became very thirsty; so he cried out to the LORD and said, "You have given this great deliverance by the hand of Your servant; and now shall I die of thirst and fall into the hand of the uncircumcised?" 19 So God split the hollow place that *is* in Lehi, and water came out, and he drank; and his spirit returned, and he revived. Therefore he called its name En Hakkore, which is in Lehi to this day. 20 And he judged Israel twenty years in the days of the Philistines.

Delilah tricks Samson

16 Now Samson went to Gaza and saw a harlot there, and went in to her. 2 *When* the Gazites *were told,* "Samson has come here!" they surrounded *the place* and lay in wait for him all night at the gate of the city. They were quiet all night, saying, "In the morning,

when it is daylight, we will kill him."
3 And Samson lay *low* till midnight; then he arose at midnight, took hold of the doors of the gate of the city and the two gateposts, pulled them up, bar and all, put *them* on his shoulders, and carried them to the top of the hill that faces Hebron.

4 Afterward it happened that he loved a woman in the Valley of Sorek, whose name *was* Delilah. 5 And the lords of the Philistines came up to her and said to her, "Entice him, and find out where his great strength *lies,* and by what *means* we may overpower him, that we may bind him to afflict him; and every one of us will give you eleven hundred *pieces* of silver."

6 So Delilah said to Samson, "Please tell me where your great strength *lies,* and with what you may be bound to afflict you."

7 And Samson said to her, "If they bind me with seven fresh bowstrings, not yet dried, then I shall become weak, and be like any *other* man."

8 So the lords of the Philistines brought up to her seven fresh bowstrings, not yet dried, and she bound him with them. 9 Now *men were* lying in wait, staying with her in the room. And she said to him, "The Philistines *are* upon you, Samson!" But he broke

the bowstrings as a strand of yarn breaks when it touches fire. So the secret of his strength was not known.

10 Then Delilah said to Samson, "Look, you have mocked me and told me lies. Now, please tell me what you may be bound with."

11 So he said to her, "If they bind me securely with new ropes that have never been used, then I shall become weak, and be like any *other* man."

12 Therefore Delilah took new ropes and bound him with them, and said to him, "The Philistines *are* upon you, Samson!" And *men were* lying in wait, staying in the room. But he broke them off his arms like a thread.

13 Delilah said to Samson, "Until now you have mocked me and told me lies. Tell me what you may be bound with."

And he said to her, "If you weave the seven locks of my head into the web of the loom"—

14 So she wove *it* tightly with the batten of the loom, and said to him, "The Philistines *are* upon you, Samson!" But he awoke from his sleep, and pulled out the batten and the web from the loom.

15 Then she said to him, "How can you say, 'I love you,' when your heart is not with me? You have mocked me

---

What Samson Learned

I was the strongest man you will meet in the Bible, but my strength was not my own. The Lord gave me physical power to defend my people against our enemies.

Then I forgot I was God's man. I allowed a pretty girl to tease me into telling her the secret of my strength.

I was a Nazirite (pronounced *NAZ-uh-right*), and as a Nazirite, I promised God I would not cut my hair. When I told my girl friend Delilah (pronounced *de-LIE-luh*) my secret, she let my enemies cut my hair while I slept.

I learned too late that God's servants must always remember they belong to Him. God alone makes us all we can ever become for Him. Use your abilities to serve God in everything you do.

Strong Man Shatters Building with Bare Hands

The Philistia Daily News

GAZA—Samson, the strong man and an enemy of the state, is dead, along with many of the leading citizens of Gaza (pronounced *GAY-zuh*). While performing feats of strength for a temple audience, he reached out with both hands and pushed on the pillars that supported the building. Before anyone could stop him, the whole building had collapsed, killing Samson and everyone in the temple.

Samson had recently been arrested by city police with the help of his girl friend, Delilah. While serving time in Gaza Prison, Samson ground grain as a community service project.

Shortly afterward, he was brought to the temple of Dagon (pronounced *DAY-gun*) to entertain the temple crowd who had gathered to worship their god. Apparently Samson, a believer in the God of the Hebrews, was willing to die for his beliefs.

---

these three times, and have not told me where your great strength *lies*." ¹⁶ And it came to pass, when she pestered him daily with her words and pressed him, so that his soul was vexed to death, ¹⁷ that he told her all his heart, and said to her, "No razor has ever come upon my head, for I *have been* a Nazirite to God from my mother's womb. If I am shaven, then my strength will leave me, and I shall become weak, and be like any *other* man."

¹⁸ When Delilah saw that he had told her all his heart, she sent and called for the lords of the Philistines, saying, "Come up once more, for he has told me all his heart." So the lords of the Philistines came up to her and brought the money in their hand. ¹⁹ Then she

Samson destroys the temple of Dagon with his bare hands.

lulled him to sleep on her knees, and called for a man and had him shave off the seven locks of his head. Then she began to torment him, and his strength left him. 20 And she said, "The Philistines *are* upon you, Samson!" So he awoke from his sleep, and said, "I will go out as before, at other times, and shake myself free!" But he did not know that the LORD had departed from him.

21 Then the Philistines took him and put out his eyes, and brought him down to Gaza. They bound him with bronze fetters, and he became a grinder in the prison. 22 However, the hair of his head began to grow again after it had been shaven.

23 Now the lords of the Philistines gathered together to offer a great sacrifice to Dagon their god, and to rejoice. And they said:

> "Our god has delivered into our
> hands
> Samson our enemy!"

24 When the people saw him, they praised their god; for they said:

> "Our god has delivered into our
> hands our enemy,
> The destroyer of our land,
> And the one who multiplied our
> dead."

25 So it happened, when their hearts were merry, that they said, "Call for Samson, that he may perform for us." So they called for Samson from the prison, and he performed for them. And they stationed him between the pillars. 26 Then Samson said to the lad who held him by the hand, "Let me feel the pillars which support the temple, so that I can lean on them." 27 Now the temple was full of men and women. All the lords of the Philistines *were* there—about three thousand men and women on the roof watching while Samson performed.

28 Then Samson called to the LORD, saying, "O Lord GOD, remember me, I pray! Strengthen me, I pray, just this once, O God, that I may with one *blow* take vengeance on the Philistines for my two eyes!" 29 And Samson took hold of the two middle pillars which supported the temple, and he braced himself against them, one on his right and the other on his left. 30 Then Samson said, "Let me die with the Philistines!" And he pushed with *all his* might, and the temple fell on the lords and all the people who *were* in it. So the dead that he killed at his death were more than he had killed in his life.

31 And his brothers and all his father's household came down and took him, and brought *him* up and buried him between Zorah and Eshtaol in the tomb of his father Manoah. He had judged Israel twenty years.

Micah worships idols

17 Now there was a man from the mountains of Ephraim, whose name *was* Micah. 2 And he said to his mother, "The eleven hundred *shekels* of silver that were taken from you, and on which you put a curse, *even saying* it in my ears—here *is* the silver with me; I took it."

And his mother said, "*May you be* blessed by the LORD, my son!" 3 So when he had returned the eleven hundred *shekels* of silver to his mother, his mother said, "I had wholly dedicated the silver from my hand to the LORD for my son, to make a carved image and a molded image; now therefore, I will return it to you." 4 Thus he returned the silver to his mother. Then his mother took two hundred *shekels* of silver and gave them to the silversmith, and he made it into a carved image and a molded image; and they were in the house of Micah.

5 The man Micah had a shrine, and made an ephod and household idols; and he consecrated one of his sons, who became his priest. 6 In those days *there was* no king in Israel; everyone did *what was* right in his own eyes.

7 Now there was a young man from Bethlehem in Judah, of the family of

Judah; he *was* a Levite, and was staying there. 8 The man departed from the city of Bethlehem in Judah to stay wherever he could find *a place*. Then he came to the mountains of Ephraim, to the house of Micah, as he journeyed. 9 And Micah said to him, "Where do you come from?"

So he said to him, "I *am* a Levite from Bethlehem in Judah, and I am on my way to find *a place* to stay."

10 Micah said to him, "Dwell with me, and be a father and a priest to me, and I will give you ten *shekels* of silver per year, a suit of clothes, and your sustenance." So the Levite went in. 11 Then the Levite was content to dwell with the man; and the young man became like one of his sons to him. 12 So Micah consecrated the Levite, and the young man became his priest, and lived in the house of Micah. 13 Then Micah said, "Now I know that the LORD will be good to me, since I have a Levite as priest!"

The Danites follow Micah's example

18 In those days *there was* no king in Israel. And in those days the tribe of the Danites was seeking an inheritance for itself to dwell in; for until that day *their* inheritance among the tribes of Israel had not fallen to them. 2 So the children of Dan sent five men of their family from their territory, men of valor from Zorah and Eshtaol, to spy out the land and search it. They said to them, "Go, search the land." So they went to the mountains of Ephraim, to the house of Micah, and lodged there. 3 While they *were* at the house of Micah, they recognized the voice of the young Levite. They turned aside and said to him, "Who brought you here? What are you doing in this *place?* What do you have here?"

4 He said to them, "Thus and so Micah did for me. He has hired me, and I have become his priest."

5 So they said to him, "Please inquire of God, that we may know whether the journey on which we go will be prosperous."

6 And the priest said to them, "Go in peace. The presence of the LORD *be* with you on your way."

7 So the five men departed and went to Laish. They saw the people who *were* there, how they dwelt safely, in the manner of the Sidonians, quiet and secure. *There were* no rulers in the land who might put *them* to shame for anything. They *were* far from the Sidonians, and they had no ties with anyone.

8 Then *the spies* came back to their brethren at Zorah and Eshtaol, and their brethren said to them, "What *is* your *report?*"

9 So they said, "Arise, let us go up against them. For we have seen the land, and indeed it *is* very good. *Would* you *do* nothing? Do not hesitate to go, *and* enter to possess the land. 10 When you go, you will come to a secure people and a large land. For God has given it into your hands, a place where *there is* no lack of anything that *is* on the earth."

11 And six hundred men of the family of the Danites went from there, from Zorah and Eshtaol, armed with weapons of war. 12 Then they went up and encamped in Kirjath Jearim in Judah. (Therefore they call that place Mahaneh Dan to this day. There *it is,* west of Kirjath Jearim.) 13 And they passed from there to the mountains of Ephraim, and came to the house of Micah.

14 Then the five men who had gone to spy out the country of Laish answered and said to their brethren, "Do you know that there are in these houses an ephod, household idols, a carved image, and a molded image? Now therefore, consider what you should do." 15 So they turned aside there, and came to the house of the young Levite man—to the house of Micah—and greeted him. 16 The six hundred men armed with their weapons of war, who *were* of the children of Dan, stood by the entrance of the gate. 17 Then the five men who had

gone to spy out the land went up. Entering there, they took the carved image, the ephod, the household idols, and the molded image. The priest stood at the entrance of the gate with the six hundred men *who were* armed with weapons of war.

18 When these went into Micah's house and took the carved image, the ephod, the household idols, and the molded image, the priest said to them, "What are you doing?"

19 And they said to him, "Be quiet, put your hand over your mouth, and come with us; be a father and a priest to us. *Is it* better for you to be a priest to the household of one man, or that you be a priest to a tribe and a family in Israel?" 20 So the priest's heart was glad; and he took the ephod, the household idols, and the carved image, and took his place among the people.

21 Then they turned and departed, and put the little ones, the livestock, and the goods in front of them. 22 When they were a good way from the house of Micah, the men who *were* in the houses near Micah's house gathered together and overtook the children of Dan. 23 And they called out to the children of Dan. So they turned around and said to Micah, "What ails you, that you have gathered such a company?"

24 So he said, "You have taken away my gods which I made, and the priest, and you have gone away. Now what more do I have? How can you say to me, 'What ails you?' "

25 And the children of Dan said to him, "Do not let your voice be heard among us, lest angry men fall upon you, and you lose your life, with the lives of your household!" 26 Then the children of Dan went their way. And when Micah saw that they *were* too strong for him, he turned and went back to his house.

27 So they took *the things* Micah had made, and the priest who had belonged to him, and went to Laish, to a people quiet and secure; and they struck them with the edge of the sword and burned the city with fire. 28 *There*

was no deliverer, because it *was* far from Sidon, and they had no ties with anyone. It was in the valley that belongs to Beth Rehob. So they rebuilt the city and dwelt there. 29 And they called the name of the city Dan, after the name of Dan their father, who was born to Israel. However, the name of the city formerly *was* Laish.

30 Then the children of Dan set up for themselves the carved image; and Jonathan the son of Gershom, the son of Manasseh, and his sons were priests to the tribe of Dan until the day of the captivity of the land. 31 So they set up for themselves Micah's carved image which he made, all the time that the house of God was in Shiloh.

The Levite's wife

19 And it came to pass in those days, when *there was* no king in Israel, that there was a certain Levite staying in the remote mountains of Ephraim. He took for himself a concubine from Bethlehem in Judah. 2 But his concubine played the harlot against him, and went away from him to her father's house at Bethlehem in Judah, and was there four whole months. 3 Then her husband arose and went after her, to speak kindly to her *and* bring her back, having his servant and a couple of donkeys with him. So she brought him into her father's house; and when the father of the young woman saw him, he was glad to meet him. 4 Now his father-in-law, the young woman's father, detained him; and he stayed with him three days. So they ate and drank and lodged there.

5 Then it came to pass on the fourth day that they arose early in the morning, and he stood to depart; but the young woman's father said to his son-in-law, "Refresh your heart with a morsel of bread, and afterward go your way."

6 So they sat down, and the two of them ate and drank together. Then the young woman's father said to the man, "Please be content to stay all night, and let your heart be merry." 7 And

when the man stood to depart, his father-in-law urged him; so he lodged there again. 8 Then he arose early in the morning on the fifth day to depart, but the young woman's father said, "Please refresh your heart." So they delayed until afternoon; and both of them ate.

9 And when the man stood to depart—he and his concubine and his servant—his father-in-law, the young woman's father, said to him, "Look, the day is now drawing toward evening; please spend the night. See, the day is coming to an end; lodge here, that your heart may be merry. Tomorrow go your way early, so that you may get home."

10 However, the man was not willing to spend that night; so he rose and departed, and came opposite Jebus (that is, Jerusalem). With him were the two saddled donkeys; his concubine was also with him. 11 They were near Jebus, and the day was far spent; and the servant said to his master, "Come, please, and let us turn aside into this city of the Jebusites and lodge in it."

12 But his master said to him, "We will not turn aside here into a city of foreigners, who are not of the children of Israel; we will go on to Gibeah." 13 So he said to his servant, "Come, let us draw near to one of these places, and spend the night in Gibeah or in Ramah." 14 And they passed by and went their way; and the sun went down on them near Gibeah, which belongs to Benjamin. 15 They turned aside there to go in to lodge in Gibeah. And when he went in, he sat down in the open square of the city, for no one would take them into his house to spend the night.

16 Just then an old man came in from his work in the field at evening, who also was from the mountains of Ephraim; he was staying in Gibeah, whereas the men of the place were Benjamites. 17 And when he raised his eyes, he saw the traveler in the open square of the city; and the old man said, "Where are you going, and where do you come from?"

18 So he said to him, "We are passing from Bethlehem in Judah toward the remote mountains of Ephraim; I am from there. I went to Bethlehem in Judah; now I am going to the house of the LORD. But there is no one who will take me into his house, 19 although we have both straw and fodder for our donkeys, and bread and wine for myself, for your female servant, and for the young man who is with your servant; there is no lack of anything."

20 And the old man said, "Peace be with you! However, let all your needs be my responsibility; only do not spend the night in the open square." 21 So he brought him into his house, and gave fodder to the donkeys. And they washed their feet, and ate and drank.

22 As they were enjoying themselves, suddenly certain men of the city, perverted men, surrounded the house and beat on the door. They spoke to the master of the house, the old man, saying, "Bring out the man who came to your house, that we may know him carnally!"

23 But the man, the master of the house, went out to them and said to them, "No, my brethren! I beg you, do not act so wickedly! Seeing this man has come into my house, do not commit this outrage. 24 Look, here is my virgin daughter and the man's concubine; let me bring them out now. Humble them, and do with them as you please; but to this man do not do such a vile thing!" 25 But the men would not heed him. So the man took his concubine and brought her out to them. And they knew her and abused her all night until morning; and when the day began to break, they let her go.

26 Then the woman came as the day was dawning, and fell down at the door of the man's house where her master was, till it was light.

27 When her master arose in the morning, and opened the doors of the house and went out to go his way, there was his concubine, fallen at the door of the house with her hands on the threshold. 28 And he said to her, "Get up and let us be going." But

there was no answer. So the man lifted her onto the donkey; and the man got up and went to his place.

29 When he entered his house he took a knife, laid hold of his concubine, and divided her into twelve pieces, limb by limb, and sent her throughout all the territory of Israel. 30 And so it was that all who saw it said, "No such deed has been done or seen from the day that the children of Israel came up from the land of Egypt until this day. Consider it, confer, and speak up!"

The Israelites win the war

20 So all the children of Israel came out, from Dan to Beersheba, as well as from the land of Gilead, and the congregation gathered together as one man before the LORD at Mizpah. 2 And the leaders of all the people, all the tribes of Israel, presented themselves in the assembly of the people of God, four hundred thousand foot soldiers who drew the sword. 3 (Now the children of Benjamin heard that the children of Israel had gone up to Mizpah.)

Then the children of Israel said, "Tell us, how did this wicked deed happen?"

4 So the Levite, the husband of the woman who was murdered, answered and said, "My concubine and I went into Gibeah, which belongs to Benjamin, to spend the night. 5 And the men of Gibeah rose against me, and surrounded the house at night because of me. They intended to kill me, but instead they ravished my concubine so that she died. 6 So I took hold of my concubine, cut her in pieces, and sent her throughout all the territory of the inheritance of Israel, because they committed lewdness and outrage in Israel. 7 Look! All of you are children of Israel; give your advice and counsel here and now!"

8 So all the people arose as one man, saying, "None of us will go to his tent, nor will any turn back to his house; 9 but now this is the thing which we will do to Gibeah: We will go up

against it by lot. 10 We will take ten men out of every hundred throughout all the tribes of Israel, a hundred out of every thousand, and a thousand out of every ten thousand, to make provisions for the people, that when they come to Gibeah in Benjamin, they may repay all the vileness that they have done in Israel." 11 So all the men of Israel were gathered against the city, united together as one man.

12 Then the tribes of Israel sent men through all the tribe of Benjamin, saying, "What is this wickedness that has occurred among you? 13 Now therefore, deliver up the men, the perverted men who are in Gibeah, that we may put them to death and remove the evil from Israel!" But the children of Benjamin would not listen to the voice of their brethren, the children of Israel. 14 Instead, the children of Benjamin gathered together from their cities to Gibeah, to go to battle against the children of Israel. 15 And from their cities at that time the children of Benjamin numbered twenty-six thousand men who drew the sword, besides the inhabitants of Gibeah, who numbered seven hundred select men. 16 Among all this people were seven hundred select men who were left-handed; every one could sling a stone at a hair's breadth and not miss. 17 Now besides Benjamin, the men of Israel numbered four hundred thousand men who drew the sword; all of these were men of war.

18 Then the children of Israel arose and went up to the house of God to inquire of God. They said, "Which of us shall go up first to battle against the children of Benjamin?"

The LORD said, "Judah first!"

19 So the children of Israel rose in the morning and encamped against Gibeah. 20 And the men of Israel went out to battle against Benjamin, and the men of Israel put themselves in battle array to fight against them at Gibeah. 21 Then the children of Benjamin came out of Gibeah, and on that day cut down to the ground twenty-two thousand men of the Israelites. 22 And the

people, that is, the men of Israel, encouraged themselves and again formed the battle line at the place where they had put themselves in array on the first day. 23 Then the children of Israel went up and wept before the LORD until evening, and asked counsel of the LORD, saying, "Shall I again draw near for battle against the children of my brother Benjamin?"

And the LORD said, "Go up against him."

24 So the children of Israel approached the children of Benjamin on the second day. 25 And Benjamin went out against them from Gibeah on the second day, and cut down to the ground eighteen thousand more of the children of Israel; all these drew the sword.

26 Then all the children of Israel, that is, all the people, went up and came to the house of God and wept. They sat there before the LORD and fasted that day until evening; and they offered burnt offerings and peace offerings before the LORD. 27 So the children of Israel inquired of the LORD (the ark of the covenant of God *was* there in those days, 28 and Phinehas the son of Eleazar, the son of Aaron, stood before it in those days), saying, "Shall I yet again go out to battle against the children of my brother Benjamin, or shall I cease?"

And the LORD said, "Go up, for tomorrow I will deliver them into your hand."

29 Then Israel set men in ambush all around Gibeah. 30 And the children of Israel went up against the children of Benjamin on the third day, and put themselves in battle array against Gibeah as at the other times. 31 So the children of Benjamin went out against the people, *and* were drawn away from the city. They began to strike down *and* kill some of the people, as at the other times, in the highways (one of which goes up to Bethel and the other to Gibeah) and in the field, about thirty men of Israel. 32 And the children of Benjamin said, "They *are* defeated before us, as at first."

But the children of Israel said, "Let us flee and draw them away from the city to the highways." 33 So all the men of Israel rose from their place and put themselves in battle array at Baal Tamar. Then Israel's men in ambush burst forth from their position in the plain of Geba. 34 And ten thousand select men from all Israel came against Gibeah, and the battle was fierce. But *the Benjamites* did not know that disaster *was* upon them. 35 The LORD defeated Benjamin before Israel. And the children of Israel destroyed that day twenty-five thousand one hundred Benjamites; all these drew the sword.

36 So the children of Benjamin saw that they *were* defeated. The men of Israel had given ground to the Benjamites, because they relied on the men in ambush whom they had set against Gibeah. 37 And the men in ambush quickly rushed upon Gibeah; the men in ambush spread out and struck the whole city with the edge of the sword. 38 Now the appointed signal between the men of Israel and the men in ambush was that they would make a great cloud of smoke rise up from the city, 39 whereupon the men of Israel would turn in battle. Now Benjamin had begun to strike *and* kill about thirty of the men of Israel. For they said, "Surely they are defeated before us, as *in* the first battle." 40 But when the cloud began to rise from the city in a column of smoke, the Benjamites looked behind them, and there was the whole city going up *in smoke* to heaven. 41 And when the men of Israel turned back, the men of Benjamin panicked, for they saw that disaster had come upon them. 42 Therefore they turned *their backs* before the men of Israel in the direction of the wilderness; but the battle overtook them, and whoever *came* out of the cities they destroyed in their midst. 43 They surrounded the Benjamites, chased them, *and* easily trampled them down as far as the front of Gibeah toward the east. 44 And eighteen thousand men of Benjamin fell; all these *were* men of valor. 45 Then they turned and fled toward

the wilderness to the rock of Rimmon;
and they cut down five thousand of
them on the highways. Then they pursued them relentlessly up to Gidom,
and killed two thousand of them.
46 So all who fell of Benjamin that day
were twenty-five thousand men who
drew the sword; all these were men
of valor.

47 But six hundred men turned and
fled toward the wilderness to the rock
of Rimmon, and they stayed at the
rock of Rimmon for four months.
48 And the men of Israel turned back
against the children of Benjamin, and
struck them down with the edge of the
sword—from every city, men and
beasts, all who were found. They also
set fire to all the cities they came to.

The Benjamites find wives

21 Now the men of Israel had sworn
an oath at Mizpah, saying, "None of
us shall give his daughter to Benjamin
as a wife." 2 Then the people came
to the house of God, and remained
there before God till evening. They
lifted up their voices and wept bitterly,
3 and said, "O LORD God of Israel, why
has this come to pass in Israel, that
today there should be one tribe missing
in Israel?"

4 So it was, on the next morning,
that the people rose early and built an
altar there, and offered burnt offerings
and peace offerings. 5 The children of
Israel said, "Who is there among all
the tribes of Israel who did not come
up with the assembly to the LORD?"
For they had made a great oath concerning anyone who had not come up
to the LORD at Mizpah, saying, "He
shall surely be put to death." 6 And
the children of Israel grieved for Benjamin their brother, and said, "One tribe
is cut off from Israel today. 7 What shall
we do for wives for those who remain,
seeing we have sworn by the LORD that
we will not give them our daughters
as wives?"

8 And they said, "What one is there
from the tribes of Israel who did not
come up to Mizpah to the LORD?" And,

in fact, no one had come to the camp
from Jabesh Gilead to the assembly.
9 For when the people were counted,
indeed, not one of the inhabitants of
Jabesh Gilead was there. 10 So the
congregation sent out there twelve
thousand of their most valiant men,
and commanded them, saying, "Go
and strike the inhabitants of Jabesh
Gilead with the edge of the sword, including the women and children.
11 And this is the thing that you shall
do: You shall utterly destroy every
male, and every woman who has
known a man intimately." 12 So they
found among the inhabitants of Jabesh
Gilead four hundred young virgins
who had not known a man intimately;
and they brought them to the camp
at Shiloh, which is in the land of Canaan.

13 Then the whole congregation sent
word to the children of Benjamin who
were at the rock of Rimmon, and announced peace to them. 14 So Benjamin came back at that time, and they
gave them the women whom they had
saved alive of the women of Jabesh
Gilead; and yet they had not found
enough for them.

15 And the people grieved for Benjamin, because the LORD had made a
void in the tribes of Israel.

16 Then the elders of the congregation said, "What shall we do for wives
for those who remain, since the
women of Benjamin have been destroyed?" 17 And they said, "There
must be an inheritance for the survivors of Benjamin, that a tribe may not
be destroyed from Israel. 18 However,
we cannot give them wives from our
daughters, for the children of Israel
have sworn an oath, saying, 'Cursed
be the one who gives a wife to Benjamin.' " 19 Then they said, "In fact,
there is a yearly feast of the LORD in
Shiloh, which is north of Bethel, on
the east side of the highway that goes
up from Bethel to Shechem, and south
of Lebonah."

20 Therefore they instructed the children of Benjamin, saying, "Go, lie in
wait in the vineyards, 21 and watch;

What Israel Learned

We have come a long way in the hundreds of years since God brought us out of Egypt to our new land. But the sad truth is that our journey has been in the wrong direction. We have been moving away from God all the way.

Most stories in history will tell you how other nations became great, but in the Book of Judges you can see that we only became a very wicked people. We proved we didn't have what it took to be a great people for God.

What can you learn from our failure? God was teaching us that we couldn't be good by ourselves. We needed someone to save us from our sins. That is why God would one day send His only Son, Jesus. This same Jesus wants to be your Savior, too.

---

and just when the daughters of Shiloh come out to perform their dances, then come out from the vineyards, and every man catch a wife for himself from the daughters of Shiloh; then go to the land of Benjamin. 22 Then it shall be, when their fathers or their brothers come to us to complain, that we will say to them, 'Be kind to them for our sakes, because we did not take a wife for any of them in the war; for *it is* not *as though* you have given the *women* to them at this time, making yourselves guilty of your oath.' "

23 And the children of Benjamin did so; they took enough wives for their number from those who danced, whom they caught. Then they went and returned to their inheritance, and they rebuilt the cities and dwelt in them. 24 So the children of Israel departed from there at that time, every man to his tribe and family; they went out from there, every man to his inheritance.

25 In those days *there was* no king in Israel; everyone did *what was* right in his own eyes.

The Book of
RUTH

 Mine is one of the most amazing stories of the Bible. Like Rahab, whom you read about in Joshua 2, I was not even a Hebrew. I was from Moab, which was an enemy nation of Israel. Another wonderful fact is that my husband Boaz was from the family of Rahab!

But the most exciting truth of all is that Boaz and I were the great-grandparents of King David. David was that great ancestor of Jesus the Savior, who was born a thousand years later.

Why is my story so amazing? Because it was the last thing anybody would expect—that a young girl from Moab would be accepted as the wife of one of the leading citizens of Bethlehem. And we would live right where Jesus Himself would be born!

Ruth decides to stay with Naomi

Now it came to pass, in the days when the judges ruled, that there was a famine in the land. And a certain man of Bethlehem, Judah, went to dwell in the country of Moab, he and his wife and his two sons. 2 The name of the man *was* Elimelech, the name of his wife *was* Naomi, and the names of his two sons *were* Mahlon and Chilion—Ephrathites of Bethlehem, Judah. And they went to the country of Moab and remained there. 3 Then Elimelech, Naomi's husband, died; and she was left, and her two sons. 4 Now they took wives of the women of Moab: the name of the one *was* Orpah, and the name of the other Ruth. And they dwelt there about ten years. 5 Then both Mahlon and Chilion also died; so the woman survived her two sons and her husband.

6 Then she arose with her daughters-in-law that she might return from the country of Moab, for she had heard in the country of Moab that the LORD had visited His people by giving them bread. 7 Therefore she went out from the place where she was, and her two daughters-in-law with her; and they went on the way to return to the land of Judah. 8 And Naomi said to her two daughters-in-law, "Go, return each to her mother's house. The LORD deal kindly with you, as you have dealt with the dead and with me. 9 The LORD grant that you may find rest, each in the house of her husband."

So she kissed them, and they lifted up their voices and wept. 10 And they said to her, "Surely we will return with you to your people."

11 But Naomi said, "Turn back, my daughters; why will you go with me? *Are* there still sons in my womb, that they may be your husbands? 12 Turn back, my daughters, go—for I am too old to have a husband. If I should say I have hope, *if* I should have a husband tonight and should also bear sons, 13 would you wait for them till they were grown? Would you restrain yourselves from having husbands? No, my daughters; for it grieves me very much for your sakes that the hand of the LORD has gone out against me!"

14 Then they lifted up their voices and wept again; and Orpah kissed her mother-in-law, but Ruth clung to her.

15 And she said, "Look, your sister-in-law has gone back to her people and to her gods; return after your sister-in-law."

16 But Ruth said:

"Entreat me not to leave you,
     Or to turn back from following
         after you;
     For wherever you go, I will
         go;
     And wherever you lodge, I will
         lodge;
     Your people *shall be* my people,
     And your God, my God.
17 Where you die, I will die,
     And there will I be buried.
     The LORD do so to me, and
         more also,
     If *anything but* death parts you
         and me."

18 When she saw that she was determined to go with her, she stopped speaking to her.

19 Now the two of them went until they came to Bethlehem. And it happened, when they had come to Bethlehem, that all the city was excited because of them; and the women said, "*Is* this Naomi?"

20 But she said to them, "Do not call me Naomi; call me Mara, for the Almighty has dealt very bitterly with me. 21 I went out full, and the LORD has brought me home again empty. Why do you call me Naomi, since the LORD has testified against me, and the Almighty has afflicted me?"

22 So Naomi returned, and Ruth the Moabitess her daughter-in-law with her, who returned from the country of Moab. Now they came to Bethlehem at the beginning of barley harvest.

Ruth meets Boaz

2 There was a relative of Naomi's husband, a man of great wealth, of the family of Elimelech. His name *was* Boaz. 2 So Ruth the Moabitess said to Naomi, "Please let me go to the field, and glean heads of grain after *him* in whose sight I may find favor."

And she said to her, "Go, my daughter."

3 Then she left, and went and gleaned in the field after the reapers. And she happened to come to the part of the field *belonging* to Boaz, who *was* of the family of Elimelech.

4 Now behold, Boaz came from Bethlehem, and said to the reapers, "The LORD *be* with you!"

And they answered him, "The LORD bless you!"

5 Then Boaz said to his servant who was in charge of the reapers, "Whose young woman *is* this?"

6 So the servant who was in charge of the reapers answered and said, "It *is* the young Moabite woman who came back with Naomi from the country of Moab. 7 And she said, 'Please let me glean and gather after the reapers among the sheaves.' So she came and has continued from morning until now, though she rested a little in the house."

8 Then Boaz said to Ruth, "You will listen, my daughter, will you not? Do not go to glean in another field, nor go from here, but stay close by my young women. 9 *Let* your eyes *be* on the field which they reap, and go after them. Have I not commanded the young men not to touch you? And when you are thirsty, go to the vessels and drink from what the young men have drawn."

10 So she fell on her face, bowed down to the ground, and said to him, "Why have I found favor in your eyes, that you should take notice of me, since I *am* a foreigner?"

11 And Boaz answered and said to her, "It has been fully reported to me, all that you have done for your mother-in-law since the death of your husband, and *how* you have left your father and your mother and the land of your birth, and have come to a people whom you did not know before. 12 The LORD repay your work, and a full reward be given you by the LORD God of Israel, under whose wings you have come for refuge."

13 Then she said, "Let me find favor

Naomi—My name means "Pleasant," but at one time I wanted to be called "Mara," which is a Hebrew word meaning "Bitter."

When our family moved to Moab, we were filled with hope. In our own land of Israel there was only famine and hunger, but in Moab there was plenty.

Then everything went wrong. First my husband died, and then my two sons. My sons had married two of the girls from Moab—Ruth and Orpah.

When I decided to go back to Israel, the girls wanted to come with me. But I warned them that people from Moab were not welcome in our land.

Orpah did go back home, but Ruth was determined to come with me. Her faith was strong, for she said, "Your God shall be my God."

To my surprise, God did supply a wonderful new husband to care for Ruth, so my life became truly pleasant again—just like my name.

in your sight, my lord; for you have comforted me, and have spoken kindly to your maidservant, though I am not like one of your maidservants."

14 Now Boaz said to her at mealtime, "Come here, and eat of the bread, and dip your piece of bread in the vinegar." So she sat beside the reapers, and he passed parched *grain* to her; and she ate and was satisfied, and kept some back. 15 And when she rose up to glean, Boaz commanded his young

men, saying, "Let her glean even among the sheaves, and do not reproach her. 16 Also let *grain* from the bundles fall purposely for her; leave *it* that she may glean, and do not rebuke her."

17 So she gleaned in the field until evening, and beat out what she had gleaned, and it was about an ephah of barley. 18 Then she took *it* up and went into the city, and her mother-in-law saw what she had gleaned. So she

Ruth gathers grain left for the poor by kind Boaz.

brought out and gave to her what she had kept back after she had been satisfied.

19 And her mother-in-law said to her, "Where have you gleaned today? And where did you work? Blessed be the one who took notice of you."

So she told her mother-in-law with whom she had worked, and said, "The man's name with whom I worked today is Boaz."

20 Then Naomi said to her daughter-in-law, "Blessed be he of the Lord, who has not forsaken His kindness to the living and the dead!" And Naomi said to her, "This man is a relation of ours, one of our close relatives."

21 Ruth the Moabitess said, "He also said to me, 'You shall stay close by my young men until they have finished all my harvest.' "

22 And Naomi said to Ruth her daughter-in-law, "It is good, my daughter, that you go out with his young women, and that people do not meet you in any other field." 23 So she stayed close by the young women of Boaz, to glean until the end of barley harvest and wheat harvest; and she dwelt with her mother-in-law.

Boaz is kind to Ruth

3 Then Naomi her mother-in-law said to her, "My daughter, shall I not seek security for you, that it may be well with you? 2 Now Boaz, whose young women you were with, is he not our relative? In fact, he is winnowing barley tonight at the threshing floor. 3 Therefore wash yourself and anoint yourself, put on your best garment and go down to the threshing floor; but do not make yourself known to the man until he has finished eating and drinking. 4 Then it shall be, when he lies down, that you shall notice the place where he lies; and you shall go in, uncover his feet, and lie down; and he will tell you what you should do."

5 And she said to her, "All that you say to me I will do."

6 So she went down to the threshing floor and did according to all that her mother-in-law instructed her. 7 And after Boaz had eaten and drunk, and his heart was cheerful, he went to lie down at the end of the heap of grain; and she came softly, uncovered his feet, and lay down.

8 Now it happened at midnight that the man was startled, and turned himself; and there, a woman was lying at his feet. 9 And he said, "Who are you?"

So she answered, "I am Ruth, your maidservant. Take your maidservant under your wing, for you are a close relative."

10 Then he said, "Blessed are you of the Lord, my daughter! For you have shown more kindness at the end than at the beginning, in that you did not go after young men, whether poor or rich. 11 And now, my daughter, do not fear. I will do for you all that you request, for all the people of my town know that you are a virtuous woman. 12 Now it is true that I am a close relative; however, there is a relative closer than I. 13 Stay this night, and in the morning it shall be that if he will perform the duty of a close relative for you—good; let him do it. But if he does not want to perform the duty for you, then I will perform the duty for you, as the Lord lives! Lie down until morning."

14 So she lay at his feet until morning, and she arose before one could recognize another. Then he said, "Do not let it be known that the woman came to the threshing floor." 15 Also he said, "Bring the shawl that is on you and hold it." And when she held it, he measured six ephahs of barley, and laid it on her. Then she went into the city.

16 When she came to her mother-in-law, she said, "Is that you, my daughter?"

Then she told her all that the man had done for her. 17 And she said, "These six ephahs of barley he gave me; for he said to me, 'Do not go empty-handed to your mother-in-law.' "

18 Then she said, "Sit still, my

daughter, until you know how the matter will turn out; for the man will not rest until he has concluded the matter this day.''

Ruth and Boaz are married

4 Now Boaz went up to the gate and sat down there; and behold, the close relative of whom Boaz had spoken came by. So Boaz said, ''Come aside, friend, sit down here.'' So he came aside and sat down. ²And he took ten men of the elders of the city, and said, ''Sit down here.'' So they sat down. ³Then he said to the close relative, ''Naomi, who has come back from the country of Moab, sold the piece of land which *belonged* to our brother Elimelech. ⁴And I thought to inform you, saying, 'Buy *it* back in the presence of the inhabitants and the elders of my people. If you will redeem *it,* redeem *it;* but if you will not redeem *it, then* tell me, that I may know; for *there is* no one but you to redeem *it,* and I *am* next after you.' ''

And he said, ''I will redeem *it.*''

⁵Then Boaz said, ''On the day you buy the field from the hand of Naomi, you must also buy *it* from Ruth the Moabitess, the wife of the dead, to perpetuate the name of the dead through his inheritance.''

⁶And the close relative said, ''I cannot redeem *it* for myself, lest I ruin my own inheritance. You redeem my right of redemption for yourself, for I cannot redeem *it.*''

⁷Now this *was the custom* in former times in Israel concerning redeeming and exchanging, to confirm anything: one man took off his sandal and gave *it* to the other, and this *was* a confirmation in Israel.

⁸Therefore the close relative said to Boaz, ''Buy *it* for yourself.'' So he took off his sandal. ⁹And Boaz said to the elders and all the people, ''You *are* witnesses this day that I have bought all that was Elimelech's, and all that *was* Chilion's and Mahlon's, from the hand of Naomi. ¹⁰Moreover, Ruth the Mo-

abitess, the widow of Mahlon, I have acquired as my wife, to perpetuate the name of the dead through his inheritance, that the name of the dead may not be cut off from among his brethren and from his position at the gate. You *are* witnesses this day.''

¹¹And all the people who *were* at the gate, and the elders, said, ''*We are* witnesses. The LORD make the woman who is coming to your house like Rachel and Leah, the two who built the house of Israel; and may you prosper in Ephrathah and be famous in Bethlehem. ¹²May your house be like the house of Perez, whom Tamar bore to Judah, because of the offspring which the LORD will give you from this young woman.''

¹³So Boaz took Ruth and she became his wife; and when he went in to her, the LORD gave her conception, and she bore a son. ¹⁴Then the women said to Naomi, ''Blessed *be* the LORD, who has not left you this day without a close relative; and may his name be famous in Israel! ¹⁵And may he be to you a *restorer* of life and a nourisher of your old age; for your daughter-in-law, who loves you, who is better to you than seven sons, has borne him.'' ¹⁶Then Naomi took the child and laid him on her bosom, and became a nurse to him. ¹⁷Also the neighbor women gave him a name,

What Was the Law of the Kinsman?

If a woman's husband died in Old Testament times, then her husband's nearest male relative was supposed to marry her. This was the law of the kinsman or relative. In this case, the closest relative *did not* marry Ruth. When the man who should have married Ruth chose not to, Boaz, who was next in line, married her. This law also made it possible for Ruth and Boaz to be ancestors of King David. Jesus came from David's family a thousand years later.

saying, "There is a son born to Naomi." And they called his name Obed. He *is* the father of Jesse, the father of David.

¹⁸ Now this *is* the genealogy of Perez: Perez begot Hezron; ¹⁹ Hezron begot Ram, and Ram begot Amminadab; ²⁰ Amminadab begot Nahshon, and Nahshon begot Salmon; ²¹ Salmon begot Boaz, and Boaz begot Obed; ²² Obed begot Jesse, and Jesse begot David.

The Book of
1 SAMUEL

Hannah—At first my husband Elkanah (pronounced *el-KAY-nuh*) and I were sad because I could have no children. Like all the women of Israel, I wanted to have a son. We all hoped our sons might be the promised Messiah who was to be born much later. (*See* Matthew 2 and Luke 2 in the New Testament.)

One day my husband and I went to the place of worship, and there I prayed that God would give me a son. Eli (pronounced *EE-lie*), who was priest in those days, thought I was drunk because he saw my lips moving. But when he realized I was praying, he blessed me and prayed that God would answer my prayer.

God was wonderful to us. Elkanah and I did have a son, and I called his name Samuel, which means "Heard by God," because God heard my prayer. Samuel grew up to be one of Israel's greatest leaders.

Samuel is born

Now there was a certain man of Ramathaim Zophim, of the mountains of Ephraim, and his name *was* Elkanah the son of Jeroham, the son of Elihu, the son of Tohu, the son of Zuph, an Ephraimite. ²And he had two wives: the name of one *was* Hannah, and the name of the other Peninnah. Peninnah had children, but Hannah had no children. ³This man went up from his city yearly to worship and sacrifice to the **Lord of hosts** in Shiloh. Also the two sons of Eli, Hophni and Phinehas, the priests of the Lord, *were* there. ⁴And whenever the time came for Elkanah to make an offering, he would give portions to Peninnah his wife and to all her sons and daughters. ⁵But to Hannah he would give a double portion, for he loved Hannah, although the Lord had closed her womb. ⁶And her rival also provoked her severely, to make her miserable, because the Lord had closed her womb. ⁷So it was, year by year, when she went up to the house of the Lord, that she provoked her; therefore she wept and did not eat.

⁸Then Elkanah her husband said to her, "Hannah, why do you weep? Why do you not eat? And why is your heart grieved? *Am* I not better to you than ten sons?"

⁹So Hannah arose after they had finished eating and drinking in Shiloh. Now Eli the priest was sitting on the seat by the doorpost of the tabernacle of the Lord. ¹⁰And she *was* in bitterness of soul, and prayed to the Lord and wept in anguish. ¹¹Then she made a vow and said, "O Lord of hosts, if You will indeed look on the affliction of Your maidservant and remember me, and not forget Your maidservant, but will give Your maidservant a male child, then I will give him to the Lord all the days of his life, and no razor shall come upon his head."

¹²And it happened, as she contin-

WORDFINDER

1:3 Lord of Hosts A name for God as the leader of His heavenly armies. Lord Sabaoth (pronounced *SAB-ay-oth*), from the Hebrew, means the same.

ued praying before the LORD, that Eli watched her mouth. 13 Now Hannah spoke in her heart; only her lips moved, but her voice was not heard. Therefore Eli thought she was drunk. 14 So Eli said to her, "How long will you be drunk? Put your wine away from you!"

15 But Hannah answered and said, "No, my lord, I *am* a woman of sorrowful spirit. I have drunk neither wine nor intoxicating drink, but have poured out my soul before the LORD. 16 Do not consider your maidservant a wicked woman, for out of the abundance of my complaint and grief I have spoken until now."

17 Then Eli answered and said, "Go in peace, and the God of Israel grant your petition which you have asked of Him."

18 And she said, "Let your maidservant find favor in your sight." So the woman went her way and ate, and her face was no longer *sad.*

19 Then they rose early in the morning and worshiped before the LORD, and returned and came to their house at Ramah. And Elkanah knew Hannah his wife, and the LORD remembered her. 20 So it came to pass in the process of time that Hannah conceived and bore a son, and called his name Samuel, *saying,* "Because I have asked for him from the LORD."

21 Now the man Elkanah and all his house went up to offer to the LORD the yearly sacrifice and his vow. 22 But Hannah did not go up, for she said to her husband, "*Not* until the child is weaned; then I will take him, that he may appear before the LORD and remain there forever."

23 So Elkanah her husband said to her, "Do what seems best to you; wait until you have weaned him. Only let the LORD establish His word." Then the woman stayed and nursed her son until she had weaned him.

24 Now when she had weaned him, she took him up with her, with three bulls, one ephah of flour, and a skin of wine, and brought him to the house of the LORD in Shiloh. And the child

was young. 25 Then they slaughtered a bull, and brought the child to Eli. 26 And she said, "O my lord! As your soul lives, my lord, I *am* the woman who stood by you here, praying to the LORD. 27 For this child I prayed, and the LORD has granted me my petition which I asked of Him. 28 Therefore I also have lent him to the LORD; as long as he lives he shall be lent to the LORD." So they worshiped the LORD there.

Eli's sons disappoint God

2 And Hannah prayed and said:

"My heart rejoices in the LORD;
My horn is exalted in the LORD.
I smile at my enemies,
Because I rejoice in Your
salvation.

2 "No one is holy like the LORD,
For *there is* none besides You,
Nor *is there* any rock like our
God.

3 "Talk no more so very proudly;
Let no arrogance come from
your mouth,
For the LORD *is* the God of
knowledge;
And by Him actions are
weighed.

4 "The bows of the mighty men *are*
broken,
And those who stumbled are
girded with strength.
5 *Those who were* full have hired
themselves out for bread,
And the hungry have ceased *to*
hunger.
Even the barren has borne
seven,
And she who has many children
has become feeble.

6 "The LORD kills and makes alive;
He brings down to the grave and
brings up.
7 The LORD makes poor and
makes rich;
He brings low and lifts up.

The village of Ramah, where Samuel was born and later buried.

8   He raises the poor from the dust
And lifts the beggar from the ash
     heap,
To set *them* among princes
And make them inherit the
     throne of glory.

"For the pillars of the earth *are*
     the LORD's,
And He has set the world upon
     them.
9   He will guard the feet of His
     saints,
But the wicked shall be silent in
     darkness.

"For by strength no man shall
     prevail.
10   The adversaries of the LORD
     shall be broken in pieces;
From heaven He will thunder
     against them.
The LORD will judge the ends of
     the earth.

"He will give strength to His king,
And exalt the horn of His
     anointed."

11 Then Elkanah went to his house at Ramah. But the child ministered to the LORD before Eli the priest.

12 Now the sons of Eli *were* corrupt; they did not know the LORD. 13 And the priests' custom with the people *was that* when any man offered a sacrifice, the priest's servant would come with a three-pronged fleshhook in his hand while the meat was boiling. 14 Then he would thrust *it* into the pan, or kettle, or caldron, or pot; and the priest would take for himself all that the fleshhook brought up. So they did in Shiloh to all the Israelites who came there. 15 Also, before they burned the fat, the priest's servant would come and say to the man who sacrificed, "Give meat for roasting to the priest, for he will not take boiled meat from you, but raw."

16 And *if* the man said to him, "They should really burn the fat first; *then* you may take *as much* as your heart desires," he would then answer him, "*No,* but you must give *it* now; and if not, I will take *it* by force."

17 Therefore the sin of the young men was very great before the LORD, for men abhorred the offering of the LORD.

18 But Samuel ministered before the LORD, *even as* a child, wearing a linen ephod. 19 Moreover his mother used to make him a little robe, and bring *it* to him year by year when she came up with her husband to offer the yearly sacrifice. 20 And Eli would bless Elkanah and his wife, and say, "The LORD give you descendants from this woman for the loan that was given to the LORD." Then they would go to their own home.

21 And the LORD visited Hannah, so that she conceived and bore three sons

and two daughters. Meanwhile the child Samuel grew before the LORD.

22 Now Eli was very old; and he heard everything his sons did to all Israel, and how they lay with the women who assembled at the door of the tabernacle of meeting. 23 So he said to them, "Why do you do such things? For I hear of your evil dealings from all the people. 24 No, my sons! For it is not a good report that I hear. You make the LORD's people transgress. 25 If one man sins against another, God will judge him. But if a man sins against the LORD, who will intercede for him?" Nevertheless they did not heed the voice of their father, because the LORD desired to kill them.

26 And the child Samuel grew in stature, and in favor both with the LORD and men.

27 Then a man of God came to Eli and said to him, "Thus says the LORD: 'Did I not clearly reveal Myself to the house of your father when they were in Egypt in Pharaoh's house? 28 Did I not choose him out of all the tribes of Israel to be My priest, to offer upon My altar, to burn incense, and to wear an ephod before Me? And did I not give to the house of your father all the offerings of the children of Israel made by fire? 29 Why do you kick at My sacrifice and My offering which I have commanded in My dwelling place, and honor your sons more than Me, to make yourselves fat with the best of all the offerings of Israel My people?' 30 Therefore the LORD God of Israel says: 'I said indeed that your house and the house of your father would walk before Me forever.' But now the LORD says: 'Far be it from Me; for those who honor Me I will honor, and those who despise Me shall be lightly esteemed. 31 Behold, the days are coming that I will cut off your arm and the arm of your father's house, so that there will not be an old man in your house. 32 And you will see an enemy in My dwelling place, despite all the good which God does for Israel. And there shall not be an old man in your house forever. 33 But any of your men

whom I do not cut off from My altar shall consume your eyes and grieve your heart. And all the descendants of your house shall die in the flower of their age. 34 Now this shall be a sign to you that will come upon your two sons, on Hophni and Phinehas: in one day they shall die, both of them. 35 Then I will raise up for Myself a faithful priest who shall do according to what is in My heart and in My mind. I will build him a sure house, and he shall walk before My anointed forever. 36 And it shall come to pass that everyone who is left in your house will come and bow down to him for a piece of silver and a morsel of bread, and say, "Please, put me in one of the priestly positions, that I may eat a piece of bread." ' "

Samuel warns Eli, the priest

3 Now the boy Samuel ministered to the LORD before Eli. And the word of the LORD was rare in those days; there was no widespread revelation. 2 And it came to pass at that time, while Eli was lying down in his place, and when his eyes had begun to grow so dim that he could not see, 3 and before the lamp of God went out in the tabernacle of the LORD where the ark of God was, and while Samuel was lying down, 4 that the LORD called Samuel. And he answered, "Here I am!" 5 So he ran to Eli and said, "Here I am, for you called me."

And he said, "I did not call; lie down again." And he went and lay down.

6 Then the LORD called yet again, "Samuel!"

So Samuel arose and went to Eli, and said, "Here I am, for you called me." He answered, "I did not call, my son; lie down again." 7 (Now Samuel did not yet know the LORD, nor was the word of the LORD yet revealed to him.)

8 And the LORD called Samuel again the third time. So he arose and went to Eli, and said, "Here I am, for you did call me."

Then Eli perceived that the LORD

Some people think God calls only older people to serve Him. That isn't true, because I was helping Eli the priest in his ministry when I was even younger than you.

Then one night after I went to bed, God spoke to me. He told me He was angry with Eli because his sons were priests who did not respect God or God's house. When Eli asked me, I told him what God said to me, and Eli believed that what I told him was God's message. As I was growing up, the Lord revealed Himself to me, and I spoke God's words to Israel, my people.

God finally became so angry with our nation that He even allowed the Philistines to capture our most precious possession, which was the *ark of the covenant* (see Exodus 25:10–22). At that time, Eli fell over and died, and I became Israel's new leader.

had called the boy. ⁹ Therefore Eli said to Samuel, "Go, lie down; and it shall be, if He calls you, that you must say, 'Speak, Lord, for Your servant hears.'" So Samuel went and lay down in his place.

¹⁰ Now the Lord came and stood and called as at other times, "Samuel! Samuel!"

And Samuel answered, "Speak, for Your servant hears."

¹¹ Then the Lord said to Samuel: "Behold, I will do something in Israel at which both ears of everyone who hears it will tingle. ¹² In that day I will perform against Eli all that I have spoken concerning his house, from beginning to end. ¹³ For I have told him that I will judge his house forever for the iniquity which he knows, because his sons made themselves vile, and he did not restrain them. ¹⁴ And therefore I have sworn to the house of Eli that the iniquity of Eli's house shall not be atoned for by sacrifice or offering forever."

¹⁵ So Samuel lay down until morning, and opened the doors of the house of the Lord. And Samuel was afraid to tell Eli the vision. ¹⁶ Then Eli called Samuel and said, "Samuel, my son!"

He answered, "Here I am."

¹⁷ And he said, "What is the word

that *the Lord* spoke to you? Please do not hide *it* from me. God do so to you, and more also, if you hide anything from me of all the things that He said to you." ¹⁸ Then Samuel told him everything, and hid nothing from him. And he said, "It *is* the Lord. Let Him do what seems good to Him."

¹⁹ So Samuel grew, and the Lord was with him and let none of his words fall to the ground. ²⁰ And all Israel from Dan to Beersheba knew that Samuel *had been* established as a prophet of the Lord. ²¹ Then the Lord appeared again in Shiloh. For the Lord revealed Himself to Samuel in Shiloh by the word of the Lord.

Old Eli dies

4 And the word of Samuel came to all Israel.

Now Israel went out to battle against the Philistines, and encamped beside Ebenezer; and the Philistines encamped in Aphek. ² Then the Philistines put themselves in battle array against Israel. And when they joined battle, Israel was defeated by the Philistines, who killed about four thousand men of the army in the field. ³ And when the people had come into the camp, the elders of Israel said, "Why has the LORD defeated us today before the Philistines? Let us bring the ark of the covenant of the LORD from Shiloh to us, that when it comes among us it may save us from the hand of our enemies." 4 So the people sent to Shiloh, that they might bring from there the ark of the covenant of the LORD of hosts, who dwells *between* the cherubim. And the two sons of Eli, Hophni and Phinehas, *were* there with the ark of the covenant of God.

5 And when the ark of the covenant of the LORD came into the camp, all Israel shouted so loudly that the earth shook. 6 Now when the Philistines heard the noise of the shout, they said, "What *does* the sound of this great shout in the camp of the Hebrews *mean?*" Then they understood that the ark of the LORD had come into the camp. 7 So the Philistines were afraid, for they said, "God has come into the camp!" And they said, "Woe to us! For such a thing has never happened before. 8 Woe to us! Who will deliver us from the hand of these mighty gods? These *are* the gods who struck the Egyptians with all the plagues in the wilderness. 9 Be strong and conduct yourselves like men, you Philistines, that you do not become servants of the Hebrews, as they have been to you. Conduct yourselves like men, and fight!"

10 So the Philistines fought, and Israel was defeated, and every man fled to his tent. There was a very great slaughter, and there fell of Israel thirty thousand foot soldiers. 11 Also the ark of God was captured; and the two sons of Eli, Hophni and Phinehas, died.

12 Then a man of Benjamin ran from the battle line the same day, and came to Shiloh with his clothes torn and dirt on his head. 13 Now when he came, there was Eli, sitting on a seat by the wayside watching, for his heart trembled for the ark of God. And when the man came into the city and told *it,* all the city cried out. 14 When Eli heard the noise of the outcry, he said, "What *does* the sound of this tumult *mean?*" And the man came quickly and told Eli. 15 Eli was ninety-eight years old, and his eyes were so dim that he could not see.

16 Then the man said to Eli, "I *am* he who came from the battle. And I fled today from the battle line."

And he said, "What happened, my son?"

17 So the messenger answered and said, "Israel has fled before the Philistines, and there has been a great slaughter among the people. Also your two sons, Hophni and Phinehas, are dead; and the ark of God has been captured."

18 Then it happened, when he made mention of the ark of God, that Eli fell off the seat backward by the side of the gate; and his neck was broken and he died, for the man was old and heavy. And he had judged Israel forty years.

19 Now his daughter-in-law, Phinehas' wife, was with child, *due* to be

🪓 DIGGING IN

4:18 The Sad Death of a Good Man Eli the priest was a godly man who lived during the time of the judges. We read about him in 1 Samuel.

But this man had one serious fault. He failed to train his sons to be godly like himself. These two boys, Hophni and Phinehas, were priests like their father. (Pronounce their names *HOF-nigh* and *FIN-ee-us.*) But they stole from the sacrifices brought by the people.

God can't allow such sin in His ministers. So God used the Philistine (pronounced *fih-LIS-teen*) nation to punish all Israel for the sins of Hophni and Phinehas. The worst thing the Philistines did was to capture the ark of the Lord. Remember that the ark contained the Law of God (see Exodus 25:10–22). Poor Eli fell over dead when he heard that the ark had been captured.

The Old Testament ark was made of wood and metal. Now God wants you to be a *living ark* in which God's Word dwells.

delivered; and when she heard the news that the ark of God was captured, and that her father-in-law and her husband were dead, she bowed herself and gave birth, for her labor pains came upon her. 20 And about the time of her death the women who stood by her said to her, "Do not fear, for you have borne a son." But she did not answer, nor did she regard it. 21 Then she named the child Ichabod, saying, "The glory has departed from Israel!" because the ark of God had been captured and because of her father-in-law and her husband. 22 And she said, "The glory has departed from Israel, for the ark of God has been captured."

The Philistines move the ark of God

5 Then the Philistines took the ark of God and brought it from Ebenezer to Ashdod. 2 When the Philistines took the ark of God, they brought it into the house of Dagon and set it by Dagon. 3 And when the people of Ashdod arose early in the morning, there was Dagon, fallen on its face to the earth before the ark of the LORD. So they took Dagon and set it in its place again. 4 And when they arose early the next morning, there was Dagon, fallen on its face to the ground before the ark of the LORD. The head of Dagon and both the palms of its hands were broken off on the threshold; only Dagon's torso was left of it. 5 Therefore neither the priests of Dagon nor any who come into Dagon's house tread on the threshold of Dagon in Ashdod to this day.

6 But the hand of the LORD was heavy on the people of Ashdod, and He ravaged them and struck them with tumors, both Ashdod and its territory. 7 And when the men of Ashdod saw how it was, they said, "The ark of the God of Israel must not remain with us, for His hand is harsh toward us and Dagon our god." 8 Therefore they sent and gathered to themselves all the lords of the Philistines, and said, "What shall we do with the ark of the God of Israel?"

And they answered, "Let the ark of the God of Israel be carried away to Gath." So they carried the ark of the God of Israel away. 9 So it was, after they had carried it away, that the hand of the LORD was against the city with

⛏ DIGGING IN

5:1–5 God and Idols In 1 Samuel 4, you read that the Philistines (pronounced *fih-LIS-teens*) captured the ark of the Lord, the most holy possession of the Jews.

Then the Philistines placed the ark in the temple of their metal idol named Dagon (pronounced *DAY-gon*), which was half man and half fish. The Philistines were frightened when Dagon fell over twice before the ark of the Lord. So they kept trying to find ways to get rid of the ark.

People today worship all kinds of false gods. Not all these gods are wood, metal, or stone statues like Dagon. Some people worship money, and others worship power. The Word of God says that "the love of money is a root of all kinds of evil" (1 Timothy 6:10).

To put anything or anyone before the true God is idolatry (pronounced *eye-DOLL-uh-tree*). God, your Creator, is before all things, and He alone deserves your worship.

Dagon, the chief idol-god of the Philistines.

a very great destruction; and He struck the men of the city, both small and great, and tumors broke out on them.

10 Therefore they sent the ark of God to Ekron. So it was, as the ark of God came to Ekron, that the Ekronites cried out, saying, "They have brought the ark of the God of Israel to us, to kill us and our people!" 11 So they sent and gathered together all the lords of the Philistines, and said, "Send away the ark of the God of Israel, and let it go back to its own place, so that it does not kill us and our people." For there was a deadly destruction throughout all the city; the hand of God was very heavy there. 12 And the men who did not die were stricken with the tumors, and the cry of the city went up to heaven.

The ark of God is returned

6 Now the ark of the LORD was in the country of the Philistines seven months. 2 And the Philistines called for the priests and the diviners, saying, "What shall we do with the ark of the LORD? Tell us how we should send it to its place."

3 So they said, "If you send away the ark of the God of Israel, do not send it empty; but by all means return it to Him with a trespass offering. Then you will be healed, and it will be known to you why His hand is not removed from you."

4 Then they said, "What is the trespass offering which we shall return to Him?"

They answered, "Five golden tumors and five golden rats, according to the number of the lords of the Philistines. For the same plague was on all of you and on your lords. 5 Therefore you shall make images of your tumors and images of your rats that ravage the land, and you shall give glory to the God of Israel; perhaps He will lighten His hand from you, from your gods, and from your land. 6 Why then do you harden your hearts as the Egyptians and Pharaoh hardened their hearts? When He did mighty things among them, did they not let the people go, that they might depart? 7 Now therefore, make a new cart, take two milk cows which have never been yoked, and hitch the cows to the cart; and take their calves home, away from them. 8 Then take the ark of the LORD and set it on the cart; and put the articles of gold which you are returning to Him as a trespass offering in a chest by its side. Then send it away, and let it go. 9 And watch: if it goes up the road to its own territory, to Beth Shemesh, then He has done us this great evil. But if not, then we shall know that it is not His hand that struck us—it happened to us by chance."

10 Then the men did so; they took two milk cows and hitched them to the cart, and shut up their calves at home. 11 And they set the ark of the LORD on the cart, and the chest with the gold rats and the images of their tumors. 12 Then the cows headed straight for the road to Beth Shemesh, and went along the highway, lowing as they went, and did not turn aside to the right hand or the left. And the lords of the Philistines went after them to the border of Beth Shemesh.

13 Now the people of Beth Shemesh were reaping their wheat harvest in the valley; and they lifted their eyes and saw the ark, and rejoiced to see it. 14 Then the cart came into the field of Joshua of Beth Shemesh, and stood there; a large stone was there. So they split the wood of the cart and offered the cows as a burnt offering to the LORD. 15 The Levites took down the ark of the LORD and the chest that was with it, in which were the articles of gold, and put them on the large stone. Then the men of Beth Shemesh offered burnt offerings and made sacrifices the same day to the LORD. 16 So when the five lords of the Philistines had seen it, they returned to Ekron the same day.

17 These are the golden tumors which the Philistines returned as a trespass offering to the LORD: one for Ashdod, one for Gaza, one for Ashkelon, one for Gath, one for Ekron; 18 and

the golden rats, *according to* the number of all the cities of the Philistines *belonging* to the five lords, *both* fortified cities and country villages, even as far as the large *stone of* Abel on which they set the ark of the LORD, *which stone remains* to this day in the field of Joshua of Beth Shemesh.

19 Then He struck the men of Beth Shemesh, because they had looked into the ark of the LORD. He struck fifty thousand and seventy men of the people, and the people lamented because the LORD had struck the people with a great slaughter.

20 And the men of Beth Shemesh said, "Who is able to stand before this holy LORD God? And to whom shall it go up from us?" 21 So they sent messengers to the inhabitants of Kirjath Jearim, saying, "The Philistines have brought back the ark of the LORD; come down *and* take it up with you."

Samuel tells Israel to repent

7 Then the men of Kirjath Jearim came and took the ark of the LORD, and brought it into the house of Abinadab on the hill, and consecrated Eleazar his son to keep the ark of the LORD.

2 So it was that the ark remained in Kirjath Jearim a long time; it was there twenty years. And all the house of Israel lamented after the LORD.

3 Then Samuel spoke to all the house of Israel, saying, "If you return to the LORD with all your hearts, *then* put away the foreign gods and the Ashtoreths from among you, and prepare your hearts for the LORD, and serve Him only; and He will deliver you from the hand of the Philistines." 4 So the children of Israel put away the Baals and the Ashtoreths, and served the LORD only.

5 And Samuel said, "Gather all Israel to Mizpah, and I will pray to the LORD for you." 6 So they gathered together at Mizpah, drew water, and poured *it* out before the LORD. And they fasted that day, and said there, "We have sinned against the LORD." And Samuel judged the children of Israel at Mizpah.

7 Now when the Philistines heard that the children of Israel had gathered together at Mizpah, the lords of the Philistines went up against Israel. And when the children of Israel heard *of* it, they were afraid of the Philistines. 8 So the children of Israel said to Samuel, "Do not cease to cry out to the LORD our God for us, that He may save us from the hand of the Philistines."

9 And Samuel took a suckling lamb and offered *it as* a whole burnt offering to the LORD. Then Samuel cried out to the LORD for Israel, and the LORD answered him. 10 Now as Samuel was offering up the burnt offering, the Philistines drew near to battle against Israel. But the LORD thundered with a loud thunder upon the Philistines that day, and so confused them that they were overcome before Israel. 11 And the men of Israel went out of Mizpah and pursued the Philistines, and drove them back as far as below Beth Car. 12 Then Samuel took a stone and set *it* up between Mizpah and Shen, and called its name Ebenezer, saying, "Thus far the LORD has helped us."

13 So the Philistines were subdued, and they did not come anymore into the territory of Israel. And the hand of the LORD was against the Philistines all the days of Samuel. 14 Then the cities which the Philistines had taken from Israel were restored to Israel, from Ekron to Gath; and Israel recovered its territory from the hands of the Philistines. Also there was peace between Israel and the Amorites.

15 And Samuel judged Israel all the days of his life. 16 He went from year to year on a circuit to Bethel, Gilgal, and Mizpah, and judged Israel in all those places. 17 But he always returned to Ramah, for his home *was* there. There he judged Israel, and there he built an altar to the LORD.

Israel wants a king

8 Now it came to pass when Samuel was old that he made his sons judges over Israel. 2 The name of his firstborn was Joel, and the name of his second,

Abijah; *they were* judges in Beersheba. ³ But his sons did not walk in his ways; they turned aside after dishonest gain, took bribes, and perverted justice.

⁴ Then all the elders of Israel gathered together and came to Samuel at Ramah, ⁵ and said to him, "Look, you are old, and your sons do not walk in your ways. Now make us a king to judge us like all the nations."

⁶ But the thing displeased Samuel when they said, "Give us a king to judge us." So Samuel prayed to the LORD. ⁷ And the LORD said to Samuel, "Heed the voice of the people in all that they say to you; for they have not rejected you, but they have rejected Me, that I should not reign over them. ⁸ According to all the works which they have done since the day that I brought them up out of Egypt, even to this day—with which they have forsaken Me and served other gods—so they are doing to you also. ⁹ Now therefore, heed their voice. However, you shall solemnly forewarn them, and show them the behavior of the king who will reign over them."

¹⁰ So Samuel told all the words of the LORD to the people who asked him for a king. ¹¹ And he said, "This will be the behavior of the king who will reign over you: He will take your sons and appoint *them* for his own chariots and *to be* his horsemen, and *some* will run before his chariots. ¹² He will appoint captains over his thousands and captains over his fifties, *will set some* to plow his ground and reap his harvest, and *some* to make his weapons of war and equipment for his chariots. ¹³ He will take your daughters *to be* perfumers, cooks, and bakers. ¹⁴ And he will take the best of your fields, your vineyards, and your olive groves, and give *them* to his servants. ¹⁵ He will take a tenth of your grain and your vintage, and give it to his officers and servants. ¹⁶ And he will take your male servants, your female servants, your finest young men, and your donkeys, and put *them* to his work. ¹⁷ He will take a tenth of your sheep. And you will be his servants. ¹⁸ And you will cry

out in that day because of your king whom you have chosen for yourselves, and the LORD will not hear you in that day."

¹⁹ Nevertheless the people refused to obey the voice of Samuel; and they said, "No, but we will have a king over us, ²⁰ that we also may be like all the nations, and that our king may judge us and go out before us and fight our battles."

²¹ And Samuel heard all the words of the people, and he repeated them in the hearing of the LORD. ²² So the LORD said to Samuel, "Heed their voice, and make them a king."

And Samuel said to the men of Israel, "Every man go to his city."

Saul is named king

9 There was a man of Benjamin whose name *was* Kish the son of Abiel, the son of Zeror, the son of Bechorath, the son of Aphiah, a Benjamite, a mighty man of power. ² And he had a choice and handsome son whose name *was* Saul. *There was* not a more handsome person than he among the children of Israel. From his shoulders upward *he was* taller than any of the people.

³ Now the donkeys of Kish, Saul's father, were lost. And Kish said to his son Saul, "Please take one of the servants with you, and arise, go and look for the donkeys." ⁴ So he passed through the mountains of Ephraim and through the land of Shalisha, but they did not find *them*. Then they passed through the land of Shaalim, and *they were* not *there*. Then he passed through the land of the Benjamites, but they did not find *them*.

⁵ When they had come to the land of Zuph, Saul said to his servant who *was* with him, "Come, let us return, lest my father cease *caring* about the donkeys and become worried about us."

⁶ And he said to him, "Look now, *there is* in this city a man of God, and *he is* an honorable man; all that he

King Saul—Israel had grown tired of having only God as their King. Since other nations had kings who dressed up and strutted like peacocks and wore crowns on their heads, Israel wanted a king, too. As I look back now, I wish I had never been king of Israel.

My father, Kish, was a leading citizen, and people said I was the tallest and most handsome young man in our nation. They wanted me to be their king because they thought I *looked* like a king and because of my good name.

At first everything seemed to go well. We won a great battle against the nation of Ammon. Then Samuel the prophet made a fine speech when I was crowned king of Israel. He also reminded Israel that they were wrong in demanding a king. But if they obeyed God's laws, they could still be a happy and prosperous nation.

Now I realize I should never have let them make me a king. There is a lot more to being a leader than looks and family connections.

Samuel anoints Saul

10 Then Samuel took a flask of oil and poured *it* on his head, and kissed him and said: "*Is it* not because the LORD has anointed you commander over His inheritance? 2 When you have departed from me today, you will find two men by Rachel's tomb in the territory of Benjamin at Zelzah; and they will say to you, 'The donkeys which you went to look for have been found. And now your father has ceased caring about the donkeys and is worrying about you, saying, "What shall I do about my son?"' 3 Then you shall go on forward from there and come to the terebinth tree of Tabor. There three men going up to God at Bethel will meet you, one carrying three young goats, another carrying three loaves of bread, and another carrying a skin of wine. 4 And they will greet you and give you two *loaves* of bread, which you shall receive from their hands. 5 After that you shall come to the hill of God where the Philistine garrison is. And it will happen, when you have come there to the city, that you will meet a group of prophets coming down from the high place with a stringed instrument, a tambourine, a flute, and a harp before them; and they will be prophesying. 6 Then the Spirit of the LORD will come upon you, and

you will prophesy with them and be turned into another man. 7 And let it be, when these signs come to you, *that* you do as the occasion demands; for God *is* with you. 8 You shall go down before me to Gilgal; and surely I will come down to you to offer burnt offerings *and* make sacrifices of peace offerings. Seven days you shall wait, till I come to you and show you what you should do."

9 So it was, when he had turned his back to go from Samuel, that God gave him another heart; and all those signs came to pass that day. 10 When they came there to the hill, there was a group of prophets to meet him; then the Spirit of God came upon him, and he prophesied among them. 11 And it happened, when all who knew him formerly saw that he indeed prophesied among the prophets, that the people said to one another, "What *is* this *that* has come upon the son of Kish? *Is* Saul also among the prophets?" 12 Then a man from there answered and said, "But who *is* their father?" Therefore it became a proverb: "*Is* Saul also among the prophets?" 13 And when he had finished prophesying, he went to the high place.

14 Then Saul's uncle said to him and his servant, "Where did you go?"

So he said, "To look for the donkeys. When we saw that *they were*

Samuel—Being a prophet is a great honor. But I can tell you it isn't a lot of fun! As you read the lives of the great prophets of God, you will probably agree with me.

People usually don't like prophets because most of the time the people only want to hear how good they are. The prophet's job is to tell people the truth. If a prophet isn't truthful, he will be part of the cause for the unhappiness that comes when we no longer please God.

I almost hated my work on the day I had to make Saul the king of Israel, but the Lord and I knew it was the only way Israel could learn their lesson. Only God can be the true King of our lives.

nowhere *to be found,* we went to Samuel."

15 And Saul's uncle said, "Tell me, please, what Samuel said to you."

16 So Saul said to his uncle, "He told us plainly that the donkeys had been found." But about the matter of the kingdom, he did not tell him what Samuel had said.

17 Then Samuel called the people together to the Lord at Mizpah, 18 and said to the children of Israel, "Thus says the Lord God of Israel: 'I brought up Israel out of Egypt, and delivered you from the hand of the Egyptians *and* from the hand of all kingdoms and from those who oppressed you.' 19 But you have today rejected your God, who Himself saved you from all your adversities and your tribulations; and you have said to Him, 'No, set a

king over us!' Now therefore, present yourselves before the Lord by your tribes and by your clans."

20 And when Samuel had caused all the tribes of Israel to come near, the tribe of Benjamin was chosen. 21 When he had caused the tribe of Benjamin to come near by their families, the family of Matri was chosen. And Saul the son of Kish was chosen. But when they sought him, he could not be found. 22 Therefore they inquired of the Lord further, "Has the man come here yet?"

And the Lord answered, "There he is, hidden among the equipment."

23 So they ran and brought him from there; and when he stood among the people, he was taller than any of the people from his shoulders upward. 24 And Samuel said to all the people, "Do you see him whom the Lord has

Hebrews Choose a King

World Press Wire Service

MIZPAH—News has just arrived that Saul has been made king of the nation of Israel.

This is a new thing for the Hebrews. The Jews have never had any king except their God, the Lord. Now we are told that Judge Samuel has proclaimed Saul king. But Samuel isn't happy about the idea. He has told our reporters that he did this against his will and only because the Lord ordered him to do it.

Now it seems that God has allowed the Jews to choose a king to teach them a lesson. It may be a very bitter lesson. We have noticed that kings and dictators become hard masters. No doubt the Jews will regret their decision as time goes by.

In the meantime, this news office is watching to see how the Jews get along with King Saul.

chosen, that *there is* no one like him among all the people?"

So all the people shouted and said, "Long live the king!"

25 Then Samuel explained to the people the behavior of royalty, and wrote *it* in a book and laid *it* up before the LORD. And Samuel sent all the people away, every man to his house. 26 And Saul also went home to Gibeah; and valiant *men* went with him, whose hearts God had touched. 27 But some rebels said, "How can this man save us?" So they despised him, and brought him no presents. But he held his peace.

Saul wins a battle

11 Then Nahash the Ammonite came up and encamped against Jabesh Gilead; and all the men of Jabesh said to Nahash, "Make a covenant with us, and *we* will serve you."

2 And Nahash the Ammonite answered them, "On this *condition* I will make *a covenant* with you, that I may put out all your right eyes, and bring reproach on all Israel."

3 Then the elders of Jabesh said to him, "Hold off for seven days, that we may send messengers to all the territory of Israel. And then, if *there is* no one to save us, we will come out to you."

4 So the messengers came to Gibeah of Saul and told the news in the hearing of the people. And all the people lifted up their voices and wept. 5 Now there was Saul, coming behind the herd from the field; and Saul said, "What *troubles* the people, that they weep?" And they told him the words of the men of Jabesh. 6 Then the Spirit of God came upon Saul when he heard this news, and his anger was greatly aroused. 7 So he took a yoke of oxen and cut them in pieces, and sent *them* throughout all the territory of Israel by the hands of messengers, saying, "Whoever does not go out with Saul and Samuel to battle, so it shall be done to his oxen."

And the fear of the LORD fell on the people, and they came out with one consent. 8 When he numbered them in Bezek, the children of Israel were three hundred thousand, and the men of Judah thirty thousand. 9 And they said to the messengers who came, "Thus you shall say to the men of Jabesh Gilead: 'Tomorrow, by *the time* the sun is hot, you shall have help.' " Then the messengers came and reported *it* to the men of Jabesh, and they were glad. 10 Therefore the men of Jabesh said, "Tomorrow we will come out to you, and you may do with us whatever seems good to you."

11 So it was, on the next day, that Saul put the people in three companies; and they came into the midst of the camp in the morning watch, and killed Ammonites until the heat of the day. And it happened that those who survived were scattered, so that no two of them were left together.

12 Then the people said to Samuel, "Who *is* he who said, 'Shall Saul reign over us?' Bring the men, that we may put them to death."

13 But Saul said, "Not a man shall be put to death this day, for today the LORD has accomplished salvation in Israel."

14 Then Samuel said to the people, "Come, let us go to Gilgal and renew the kingdom there." 15 So all the people went to Gilgal, and there they made Saul king before the LORD in Gilgal. There they made sacrifices of peace offerings before the LORD, and there Saul and all the men of Israel rejoiced greatly.

Samuel speaks to God's people

12 Now Samuel said to all Israel: "Indeed I have heeded your voice in all that you said to me, and have made a king over you. 2 And now here is the king, walking before you; and I am old and grayheaded, and look, my sons *are* with you. I have walked before you from my childhood to this day. 3 Here I am. Witness against me before the LORD and before His anointed: Whose ox have I taken, or whose donkey have I taken, or whom have I cheated? Whom have I oppressed, or from whose hand have I received *any* bribe with which to blind my eyes? I will restore *it* to you."

4 And they said, "You have not cheated us or oppressed us, nor have you taken anything from any man's hand."

5 Then he said to them, "The LORD *is* witness against you, and His anointed *is* witness this day, that you have not found anything in my hand."

And they answered, "*He is* witness."

6 Then Samuel said to the people, "*It is* the LORD who raised up Moses and Aaron, and who brought your fathers up from the land of Egypt. 7 Now therefore, stand still, that I may reason with you before the LORD concerning all the righteous acts of the LORD which He did to you and your fathers: 8 When Jacob had gone into Egypt, and your fathers cried out to the LORD, then the LORD sent Moses and Aaron, who brought your fathers out of Egypt and made them dwell in this place. 9 And when they forgot the LORD their God, He sold them into the hand of Sisera, commander of the army of Hazor, into the hand of the Philistines, and into the hand of the king of Moab; and they fought against them. 10 Then they cried out to the LORD, and said, 'We have sinned, because we have forsaken the LORD and served the Baals and Ashtoreths; but now deliver us from the hand of our enemies, and we will serve You.' 11 And the LORD sent Jerubbaal, Bedan, Jephthah, and Samuel, and delivered you out of the hand of your enemies on every side; and you dwelt in safety. 12 And when you saw that Nahash king of the Ammonites came against you, you said to me, 'No, but a king shall reign over us,' when the LORD your God *was* your king. 13 "Now therefore, here is the king whom you have chosen *and* whom you have desired. And take note, the LORD has set a king over you. 14 If you fear the LORD and serve Him and obey

His voice, and do not rebel against the commandment of the LORD, then both you and the king who reigns over you will continue following the LORD your God. 15 However, if you do not obey the voice of the LORD, but rebel against the commandment of the LORD, then the hand of the LORD will be against you, as *it was* against your fathers.

16 "Now therefore, stand and see this great thing which the LORD will do before your eyes: 17 *Is* today not the wheat harvest? I will call to the LORD, and He will send thunder and rain, that you may perceive and see that your wickedness *is* great, which you have done in the sight of the LORD, in asking a king for yourselves."

18 So Samuel called to the LORD, and the LORD sent thunder and rain that day; and all the people greatly feared the LORD and Samuel.

19 And all the people said to Samuel, "Pray for your servants to the LORD your God, that we may not die; for we have added to all our sins the evil of asking a king for ourselves."

20 Then Samuel said to the people, "Do not fear. You have done all this wickedness; yet do not turn aside from following the LORD, but serve the LORD with all your heart. 21 And do not turn aside; for *then you would go* after empty things which cannot profit or deliver, for they *are* nothing. 22 For the LORD will not forsake His people, for His great name's sake, because it has pleased the LORD to make you His people. 23 Moreover, as for me, far be it from me that I should sin against the LORD in ceasing to pray for you; but I will teach you the good and the right way. 24 Only fear the LORD, and serve Him in truth with all your heart; for consider what great things He has done for you. 25 But if you still do wickedly, you shall be swept away, both you and your king."

Israel is in trouble

13 Saul reigned one year; and when he had reigned two years over Israel,

2 Saul chose for himself three thousand *men* of Israel. Two thousand were with Saul in Michmash and in the mountains of Bethel, and a thousand were with Jonathan in Gibeah of Benjamin. The rest of the people he sent away, every man to his tent.

3 And Jonathan attacked the garrison of the Philistines that *was* in Geba, and the Philistines heard *of it.* Then Saul blew the trumpet throughout all the land, saying, "Let the Hebrews hear!" 4 Now all Israel heard it said *that* Saul had attacked a garrison of the Philistines, and *that* Israel had also become an abomination to the Philistines. And the people were called together to Saul at Gilgal.

5 Then the Philistines gathered together to fight with Israel, thirty thousand chariots and six thousand horsemen, and people as the sand which *is* on the seashore in multitude. And they came up and encamped in Michmash, to the east of Beth Aven. 6 When the men of Israel saw that they were in danger (for the people were distressed), then the people hid in caves, in thickets, in rocks, in holes, and in pits. 7 And *some of* the Hebrews crossed over the Jordan to the land of Gad and Gilead.

As for Saul, he *was* still in Gilgal, and all the people followed him trembling. 8 Then he waited seven days, according to the time set by Samuel. But Samuel did not come to Gilgal; and the people were scattered from him. 9 So Saul said, "Bring a burnt offering and peace offerings here to me." And he offered the burnt offering. 10 Now it happened, as soon as he had finished presenting the burnt offering, that Samuel came; and Saul went out to meet him, that he might greet him.

11 And Samuel said, "What have you done?"

Saul said, "When I saw that the people were scattered from me, and *that* you did not come within the days appointed, and *that* the Philistines gathered together at Michmash, 12 then I said, 'The Philistines will now come down on me at Gilgal, and I have not made supplication to the LORD.' Therefore I felt compelled, and offered a burnt offering."

13 And Samuel said to Saul, "You have done foolishly. You have not kept the commandment of the LORD your God, which He commanded you. For now the LORD would have established your kingdom over Israel forever. 14 But now your kingdom shall not continue. The LORD has sought for Himself a man after His own heart, and the LORD has commanded him *to be* commander over His people, because you have not kept what the LORD commanded you."

15 Then Samuel arose and went up from Gilgal to Gibeah of Benjamin. And Saul numbered the people present with him, about six hundred men.

16 Saul, Jonathan his son, and the people present with them remained in Gibeah of Benjamin. But the Philistines encamped in Michmash. 17 Then raiders came out of the camp of the Philistines in three companies. One company turned onto the road to Ophrah, to the land of Shual, 18 another company turned to the road *to* Beth Horon, and another company turned *to* the road of the border that overlooks the Valley of Zeboim toward the wilderness.

19 Now there was no blacksmith to be found throughout all the land of Israel, for the Philistines said, "Lest the Hebrews make swords or spears." 20 But all the Israelites would go down to the Philistines to sharpen each man's plowshare, his mattock, his ax, and his sickle; 21 and the charge for a sharpening was a pim for the plowshares, the mattocks, the forks, and the axes, and to set the points of the goads. 22 So it came about, on the day of battle, that there was neither sword nor spear found in the hand of any of the people who *were* with Saul and Jonathan. But they were found with Saul and Jonathan his son.

23 And the garrison of the Philistines went out to the pass of Michmash.

Saul's curse

14 Now it happened one day that Jonathan the son of Saul said to the young man who bore his armor, "Come, let us go over to the Philistines' garrison that *is* on the other side." But he did not tell his father. ² And Saul was sitting in the outskirts of Gibeah under a pomegranate tree which *is* in Migron. The people who *were* with him *were* about six hundred men. ³ Ahijah the son of Ahitub, Ichabod's brother, the son of Phinehas, the son of Eli, the LORD's priest in Shiloh, was wearing an ephod. But the people did not know that Jonathan had gone.

⁴ Between the passes, by which Jonathan sought to go over to the Philistines' garrison, *there was* a sharp rock on one side and a sharp rock on the other side. And the name of one *was* Bozez, and the name of the other Seneh. ⁵ The front of one faced northward opposite Michmash, and the other southward opposite Gibeah.

⁶ Then Jonathan said to the young man who bore his armor, "Come, let us go over to the garrison of these uncircumcised; it may be that the LORD will work for us. For nothing restrains the LORD from saving by many or by few."

⁷ So his armorbearer said to him, "Do all that is in your heart. Go then; here I am with you, according to your heart."

⁸ Then Jonathan said, "Very well, let us cross over to *these* men, and we will show ourselves to them. ⁹ If they say thus to us, 'Wait until we come to you,' then we will stand still in our place and not go up to them. ¹⁰ But if they say thus, 'Come up to us,' then we will go up. For the LORD has delivered them into our hand, and this *will be* a sign to us."

¹¹ So both of them showed themselves to the garrison of the Philistines. And the Philistines said, "Look, the Hebrews are coming out of the holes where they have hidden." ¹² Then the men of the garrison called to Jonathan and his armorbearer, and said, "Come up to us, and we will show you something."

Jonathan said to his armorbearer, "Come up after me, for the LORD has delivered them into the hand of Israel." ¹³ And Jonathan climbed up on his hands and knees with his armorbearer after him; and they fell before Jonathan. And as he came after him, his armorbearer killed them. ¹⁴ That first slaughter which Jonathan and his armorbearer made was about twenty men within about half an acre of land.

¹⁵ And there was trembling in the camp, in the field, and among all the people. The garrison and the raiders also trembled; and the earth quaked, so that it was a very great trembling. ¹⁶ Now the watchmen of Saul in Gibeah of Benjamin looked, and *there* was the multitude, melting away; and they went here and there. ¹⁷ Then Saul said to the people who *were* with him, "Now call the roll and see who has gone from us." And when they had called the roll, surprisingly, Jonathan and his armorbearer *were* not *there*. ¹⁸ And Saul said to Ahijah, "Bring the ark of God here" (for at that time the ark of God was with the children of Israel). ¹⁹ Now it happened, while Saul talked to the priest, that the noise which *was* in the camp of the Philistines continued to increase; so Saul said to the priest, "Withdraw your hand." ²⁰ Then Saul and all the people who *were* with him assembled, and they went to the battle; and indeed every man's sword was against his neighbor, *and there was* very great confusion. ²¹ Moreover the Hebrews *who* were with the Philistines before that time, who went up with them into the camp *from* the surrounding *country,* they also joined the Israelites who *were* with Saul and Jonathan. ²² Likewise all the men of Israel who had hidden in the mountains of Ephraim, *when* they heard that the Philistines fled, they also followed hard after them in the battle. ²³ So the LORD saved Israel that day, and the battle shifted to Beth Aven.

²⁴ And the men of Israel were dis-

tressed that day, for Saul had placed the people under oath, saying, "Cursed is the man who eats any food until evening, before I have taken vengeance on my enemies." So none of the people tasted food. 25 Now all the people of the land came to a forest; and there was honey on the ground. 26 And when the people had come into the woods, there was the honey, dripping; but no one put his hand to his mouth, for the people feared the oath. 27 But Jonathan had not heard his father charge the people with the oath; therefore he stretched out the end of the rod that was in his hand and dipped it in a honeycomb, and put his hand to his mouth; and his countenance brightened. 28 Then one of the people said, "Your father strictly charged the people with an oath, saying, 'Cursed is the man who eats food this day.' " And the people were faint.

29 But Jonathan said, "My father has troubled the land. Look now, how my countenance has brightened because I tasted a little of this honey. 30 How much better if the people had eaten freely today of the spoil of their enemies which they found! For now would there not have been a much greater slaughter among the Philistines?"

31 Now they had driven back the Philistines that day from Michmash to Aijalon. So the people were very faint. 32 And the people rushed on the spoil, and took sheep, oxen, and calves, and slaughtered them on the ground; and the people ate them with the blood. 33 Then they told Saul, saying, "Look, the people are sinning against the LORD by eating with the blood!"

So he said, "You have dealt treacherously; roll a large stone to me this day." 34 Then Saul said, "Disperse yourselves among the people, and say to them, 'Bring me here every man's ox and every man's sheep, slaughter them here, and eat; and do not sin against the LORD by eating with the blood.' " So every one of the people brought his ox with him that night, and slaughtered it there. 35 Then Saul built

an altar to the LORD. This was the first altar that he built to the LORD.

36 Now Saul said, "Let us go down after the Philistines by night, and plunder them until the morning light; and let us not leave a man of them."

And they said, "Do whatever seems good to you."

Then the priest said, "Let us draw near to God here."

37 So Saul asked counsel of God, "Shall I go down after the Philistines? Will You deliver them into the hand of Israel?" But He did not answer him that day. 38 And Saul said, "Come over here, all you chiefs of the people, and know and see what this sin was today. 39 For as the LORD lives, who saves Israel, though it be in Jonathan my son, he shall surely die." But not a man among all the people answered him. 40 Then he said to all Israel, "You be on one side, and my son Jonathan and I will be on the other side."

And the people said to Saul, "Do what seems good to you."

41 Therefore Saul said to the LORD God of Israel, "Give a perfect lot." So Saul and Jonathan were taken, but the people escaped. 42 And Saul said, "Cast lots between my son Jonathan and me." So Jonathan was taken. 43 Then Saul said to Jonathan, "Tell me what you have done."

And Jonathan told him, and said, "I only tasted a little honey with the end of the rod that was in my hand. So now I must die!"

44 Saul answered, "God do so and more also; for you shall surely die, Jonathan."

45 But the people said to Saul, "Shall Jonathan die, who has accomplished this great deliverance in Israel? Certainly not! As the LORD lives, not one hair of his head shall fall to the ground, for he has worked with God this day." So the people rescued Jonathan, and he did not die.

46 Then Saul returned from pursuing the Philistines, and the Philistines went to their own place.

47 So Saul established his sovereignty over Israel, and fought against

all his enemies on every side, against Moab, against the people of Ammon, against Edom, against the kings of Zobah, and against the Philistines. Wherever he turned, he harassed *them.* 48 And he gathered an army and attacked the Amalekites, and delivered Israel from the hands of those who plundered them.

49 The sons of Saul *were* Jonathan, Jishui, and Malchishua. And the names of his two daughters *were these:* the name of the firstborn Merab, and the name of the younger Michal. 50 The name of Saul's wife *was* Ahinoam the daughter of Ahimaaz. And the name of the commander of his army *was* Abner the son of Ner, Saul's uncle. 51 Kish *was* the father of Saul, and Ner the father of Abner *was* the son of Abiel.

52 Now there was fierce war with the Philistines all the days of Saul. And when Saul saw any strong man or any valiant man, he took him for himself.

God is displeased with Saul

15 Samuel also said to Saul, "The LORD sent me to anoint you king over His people, over Israel. Now therefore, heed the voice of the words of the LORD. 2 Thus says the LORD of hosts: 'I will punish Amalek *for* what he did to Israel, how he ambushed him on the way when he came up from Egypt. 3 Now go and attack Amalek, and utterly destroy all that they have, and do not spare them. But kill both man and woman, infant and nursing child,

ox and sheep, camel and donkey.' "

4 So Saul gathered the people together and numbered them in Telaim, two hundred thousand foot soldiers and ten thousand men of Judah. 5 And Saul came to a city of Amalek, and lay in wait in the valley.

6 Then Saul said to the Kenites, "Go, depart, get down from among the Amalekites, lest I destroy you with them. For you showed kindness to all the children of Israel when they came up out of Egypt." So the Kenites departed from among the Amalekites. 7 And Saul attacked the Amalekites, from Havilah all the way to Shur, which is east of Egypt. 8 He also took Agag king of the Amalekites alive, and utterly destroyed all the people with the edge of the sword. 9 But Saul and the people spared Agag and the best of the sheep, the oxen, the fatlings, the lambs, and all *that was* good, and were unwilling to utterly destroy them. But everything despised and worthless, that they utterly destroyed.

10 Now the word of the LORD came to Samuel, saying, 11 "I greatly regret that I have set up Saul *as* king, for he has turned back from following Me, and has not performed My commandments." And it grieved Samuel, and he cried out to the LORD all night. 12 So when Samuel rose early in the morning to meet Saul, it was told Samuel, saying, "Saul went to Carmel, and indeed, he set up a monument for himself; and he has gone on around, passed by, and gone down to Gilgal." 13 Then Samuel went to Saul, and Saul said to him, "Blessed *are* you of the

---

⚒ DIGGING IN

15:10–23 The People's King Fails You have read in 1 Samuel 9 that Saul was chosen to be king of Israel. The people loved Saul because he seemed like a real king. He was tall, handsome, and a good soldier. What more could they want in a leader?

God really didn't want a king at all, but he let the people have their king to teach them a hard lesson. See 1 Samuel 8:7–9, where God says, "They have rejected

Me, that I should not reign over them." No wonder Saul failed as king!

Saul failed, too, when the test came for him to obey God. Saul didn't completely destroy the people of Amalek (pronounced *AM-uh-lek*). At that time Saul proved he was a coward because he blamed his people for disobeying the Lord (see verse 21). God's leaders must be ready to obey Him.

Are you ready to be a leader for God?

LORD! I have performed the commandment of the LORD.''

14 But Samuel said, "What then *is* this bleating of the sheep in my ears, and the lowing of the oxen which I hear?"

15 And Saul said, "They have brought them from the Amalekites; for the people spared the best of the sheep and the oxen, to sacrifice to the LORD your God; and the rest we have utterly destroyed.''

16 Then Samuel said to Saul, "Be quiet! And I will tell you what the LORD said to me last night.''

And he said to him, "Speak on.''

17 So Samuel said, "When you *were* little in your own eyes, *were* you not head of the tribes of Israel? And did not the LORD anoint you king over Israel? 18 Now the LORD sent you on a mission, and said, 'Go, and utterly destroy the sinners, the Amalekites, and fight against them until they are consumed.' 19 Why then did you not obey the voice of the LORD? Why did you swoop down on the spoil, and do evil in the sight of the LORD?''

20 And Saul said to Samuel, "But I have obeyed the voice of the LORD, and gone on the mission on which the LORD sent me, and brought back Agag king of Amalek; I have utterly destroyed the Amalekites. 21 But the people took of the plunder, sheep and oxen, the best of the things which should have been utterly destroyed, to sacrifice to the LORD your God in Gilgal.''

22 So Samuel said:

"Has the LORD *as great* delight in burnt offerings and **sacrifices,**
As in obeying the voice of the LORD?

Behold, to obey is better than sacrifice,
And to heed than the fat of rams.
23 For rebellion *is as* the sin of witchcraft,
And stubbornness *is as* iniquity and **idolatry.**
Because you have rejected the word of the LORD,
He also has rejected you from *being* king.''

24 Then Saul said to Samuel, "I have sinned, for I have transgressed the commandment of the LORD and your words, because I feared the people and obeyed their voice. 25 Now therefore, please pardon my sin, and return with me, that I may worship the LORD.''

26 But Samuel said to Saul, "I will not return with you, for you have rejected the word of the LORD, and the LORD has rejected you from being king over Israel.''

27 And as Samuel turned around to go away, *Saul* seized the edge of his robe, and it tore. 28 So Samuel said to him, "The LORD has torn the kingdom of Israel from you today, and has given it to a neighbor of yours, *who is* better than you. 29 And also the Strength of Israel will not lie nor relent. For He *is* not a man, that He should relent.''

30 Then he said, "I have sinned; *yet* honor me now, please, before the elders of my people and before Israel, and return with me, that I may worship the LORD your God.'' 31 So Samuel turned back after Saul, and Saul worshiped the LORD.

32 Then Samuel said, "Bring Agag king of the Amalekites here to me.'' So Agag came to him cautiously.

WORDFINDER

15:22 Sacrifice Pronounced *SACK-rih-fyce.* An offering to God. In the Old Testament, the people sacrificed the blood of animals for sin. In the New Testament, Christ is our only sacrifice for sin.

15:23 Idolatry Pronounced *eye-DOLL-uh-tree.* The worship of idols and false gods. Unless you work or serve God, you will serve something or someone less than God.

> **David**—I was very happy as a shepherd, but one day the prophet Samuel came to our home and called me out of the fields from tending my sheep. Next thing I knew, Samuel had poured oil on my head and said I was going to be king of Israel. It was the custom to pour holy oil on a new priest or king in those times. Right away the Spirit of God filled me, and I knew I would really be king one day.
>
> But I was always sad for King Saul. He seemed to fail at everything he tried, while everything I did turned out well. Because I killed the Philistine giant, Goliath, with just a sling, I became a national hero overnight.
>
> One day poor Saul killed himself when he was losing a battle with the Philistines. So I wrote a song about him and Jonathan, his son. (See 2 Samuel 1:19–27.)

And Agag said, "Surely the bitterness of death is past."

33 But Samuel said, "As your sword has made women childless, so shall your mother be childless among women." And Samuel hacked Agag in pieces before the LORD in Gilgal.

34 Then Samuel went to Ramah, and Saul went up to his house at Gibeah of Saul. 35 And Samuel went no more to see Saul until the day of his death. Nevertheless Samuel mourned for Saul, and the LORD regretted that He had made Saul king over Israel.

David becomes king

16 Now the LORD said to Samuel, "How long will you mourn for Saul, seeing I have rejected him from reigning over Israel? Fill your horn with oil, and go; I am sending you to Jesse the Bethlehemite. For I have provided Myself a king among his sons."

2 And Samuel said, "How can I go? If Saul hears it, he will kill me."

But the LORD said, "Take a heifer with you, and say, 'I have come to sacrifice to the LORD.' 3 Then invite Jesse to the sacrifice, and I will show you what you shall do; you shall anoint for Me the one I name to you."

4 So Samuel did what the LORD said, and went to Bethlehem. And the elders of the town trembled at his coming, and said, "Do you come peaceably?"

5 And he said, "Peaceably; I have come to sacrifice to the LORD. Sanctify yourselves, and come with me to the sacrifice." Then he consecrated Jesse and his sons, and invited them to the sacrifice.

6 So it was, when they came, that he looked at Eliab and said, "Surely the LORD's anointed is before Him!"

7 But the LORD said to Samuel, "Do not look at his appearance or at his physical stature, because I have refused him. For the LORD does not see as man sees; for man looks at the outward appearance, but the LORD looks at the heart."

8 So Jesse called Abinadab, and made him pass before Samuel. And he said, "Neither has the LORD chosen this one." 9 Then Jesse made Shammah pass by. And he said, "Neither has the LORD chosen this one." 10 Thus Jesse made seven of his sons pass before Samuel. And Samuel said to Jesse, "The LORD has not chosen these." 11 And Samuel said to Jesse, "Are all the young men here?" Then he said, "There remains yet the youngest, and there he is, keeping the sheep."

And Samuel said to Jesse, "Send and bring him. For we will not sit down till he comes here." 12 So he sent and brought him in. Now he was ruddy, with bright eyes, and good-looking. And the LORD said, "Arise, anoint him; for this is the one!" 13 Then Samuel took the horn of oil and anointed him in the midst of his brothers; and the Spirit of the LORD came upon David

What Samuel Learned

It has been a hard lesson for me that God's view of things is often different from mine.

First, I wasted too much time being sorry for King Saul. Instead, God wanted me to get on with His work. God's time is always *right now!*

Then I was wrong about God's man who should be the next king of Israel. I thought God would want a tall, strong, grown-up man to replace Saul. After all, King Saul had been the tallest man in Israel. So I was sure that one of Jesse's older sons was the right man, but the Lord told me that He "looks at the heart"—the way we really think.

So who would be king, I wondered? You can imagine my surprise when it was David, the *youngest* son of Jesse! Then I learned that I can never know God's will by guessing.

from that day forward. So Samuel arose and went to Ramah.

14 But the Spirit of the Lord departed from Saul, and a distressing spirit from the Lord troubled him. 15 And Saul's servants said to him, "Surely, a distressing spirit from God is troubling you. 16 Let our master now command your servants, *who are* before you, to seek out a man *who is* a skillful player on the harp. And it shall be that he will play it with his hand when the distressing spirit from God is upon you, and you shall be well."

17 So Saul said to his servants, "Provide me now a man who can play well, and bring *him* to me."

18 Then one of the servants answered and said, "Look, I have seen a son of Jesse the Bethlehemite, *who is* skillful in playing, a mighty man of valor, a man of war, prudent in speech, and a handsome person; and the Lord *is* with him."

19 Therefore Saul sent messengers to Jesse, and said, "Send me your son David, who *is* with the sheep." 20 And Jesse took a donkey loaded *with* bread, a skin of wine, and a young goat, and sent *them* by his son David to Saul. 21 So David came to Saul and stood before him. And he loved him greatly, and he became his armorbearer. 22 Then Saul sent to Jesse, saying, "Please let David stand before me, for he has found favor in my sight."

23 And so it was, whenever the spirit from God was upon Saul, that David would take a harp and play *it* with his hand. Then Saul would become refreshed and well, and the distressing spirit would depart from him.

David kills Goliath

17 Now the Philistines gathered their armies together to battle, and were gathered at Sochoh, which *belongs* to Judah; they encamped between Sochoh and Azekah, in Ephes Dammim. 2 And Saul and the men of Israel were gathered together, and they encamped in the Valley of Elah, and drew up in battle array against the Philistines. 3 The Philistines stood on a mountain on one side, and Israel stood on a mountain on the other side, with a valley between them.

4 And a champion went out from the camp of the Philistines, named Goliath, from Gath, whose height *was* six cubits and a span. 5 *He had* a bronze helmet on his head, and he *was* armed with a coat of mail, and the weight of the coat *was* five thousand shekels of bronze. 6 And *he had* bronze armor on his legs and a bronze javelin between his shoulders. 7 Now the staff of his spear *was* like a weaver's beam, and his iron spearhead *weighed* six hundred shekels; and a shield-bearer went before him. 8 Then he stood and cried

out to the armies of Israel, and said to them, "Why have you come out to line up for battle? *Am* I not a Philistine, and you the servants of Saul? Choose a man for yourselves, and let him come down to me. ⁹ If he is able to fight with me and kill me, then we will be your servants. But if I prevail against him and kill him, then you shall be our servants and serve us." ¹⁰ And the Philistine said, "I defy the armies of Israel this day; give me a man, that we may fight together." ¹¹ When Saul and all Israel heard these words of the Philistine, they were dismayed and greatly afraid.

¹² Now David *was* the son of that Ephrathite of Bethlehem Judah, whose name *was* Jesse, and who had eight sons. And the man was old, advanced *in years,* in the days of Saul. ¹³ The three oldest sons of Jesse had gone to follow Saul to the battle. The names of his three sons who went to the battle *were* Eliab the firstborn, next to him Abinadab, and the third Shammah. ¹⁴ David *was* the youngest. And the three oldest followed Saul. ¹⁵ But David occasionally went and returned from Saul to feed his father's sheep at Bethlehem.

¹⁶ And the Philistine drew near and presented himself forty days, morning and evening.

¹⁷ Then Jesse said to his son David, "Take now for your brothers an ephah of this dried *grain* and these ten loaves, and run to your brothers at the camp. ¹⁸ And carry these ten cheeses to the captain of *their* thousand, and see how your brothers fare, and bring back news of them." ¹⁹ Now Saul and they and all the men of Israel *were* in the Valley of Elah, fighting with the Philistines.

²⁰ So David rose early in the morning, left the sheep with a keeper, and took *the things* and went as Jesse had commanded him. And he came to the camp as the army was going out to the fight and shouting for the battle. ²¹ For Israel and the Philistines had drawn up in battle array, army against army. ²² And David left his supplies in the hand of the supply keeper, ran to the army, and came and greeted his brothers. ²³ Then as he talked with them, there was the champion, the Philistine of Gath, Goliath by name, coming up from the armies of the Philistines; and he spoke according to the same words. So David heard *them.* ²⁴ And all the men of Israel, when they saw the man, fled from him and were dreadfully afraid. ²⁵ So the men of Israel said, "Have you seen this man who has come up? Surely he has come up to defy Israel; and it shall be *that* the man who kills him the king will enrich with great riches, will give him his daughter, and give his father's house exemption *from taxes* in Israel."

²⁶ Then David spoke to the men who stood by him, saying, "What shall be done for the man who kills this Philistine and takes away the reproach from Israel? For who *is* this uncircumcised Philistine, that he should defy the armies of the living God?"

²⁷ And the people answered him in this manner, saying, "So shall it be done for the man who kills him."

²⁸ Now Eliab his oldest brother heard when he spoke to the men; and Eliab's anger was aroused against David, and he said, "Why did you come down here? And with whom have you left those few sheep in the wilderness? I know your pride and the insolence of your heart, for you have come down to see the battle."

²⁹ And David said, "What have I done now? *Is there* not a cause?" ³⁰ Then he turned from him toward another and said the same thing; and these people answered him as the first ones *did.*

³¹ Now when the words which David spoke were heard, they reported *them* to Saul; and he sent for him. ³² Then David said to Saul, "Let no man's heart fail because of him; your servant will go and fight with this Philistine." ³³ And Saul said to David, "You are not able to go against this Philistine to fight with him; for you *are* a youth, and he a man of war from his youth." ³⁴ But David said to Saul, "Your ser-

vant used to keep his father's sheep, and when a lion or a bear came and took a lamb out of the flock, 35 I went out after it and struck it, and delivered *the lamb* from its mouth; and when it arose against me, I caught *it* by its beard, and struck and killed it. 36 Your servant has killed both lion and bear; and this uncircumcised Philistine will be like one of them, seeing he has defied the armies of the living God." 37 Moreover David said, "The LORD, who delivered me from the paw of the lion and from the paw of the bear, He will deliver me from the hand of this Philistine."

And Saul said to David, "Go, and the LORD be with you!"

38 So Saul clothed David with his armor, and he put a bronze helmet on his head; he also clothed him with a coat of mail. 39 David fastened his sword to his armor and tried to walk, for he had not tested *them.* And David said to Saul, "I cannot walk with these, for I have not tested *them.*" So David took them off.

40 Then he took his staff in his hand; and he chose for himself five smooth stones from the brook, and put them in a shepherd's bag, in a pouch which he had, and his sling was in his hand. And he drew near to the Philistine. 41 So the Philistine came, and began drawing near to David, and the man who bore the shield *went* before him. 42 And when the Philistine looked about and saw David, he disdained him; for he was *only* a youth, ruddy and good-looking. 43 So the Philistine said to David, "Am I a dog, that you come to me with sticks?" And the Philistine cursed David by his gods. 44 And the Philistine said to David, "Come to me, and I will give your flesh to the birds of the air and the beasts of the field!"

45 Then David said to the Philistine, "You come to me with a sword, with a spear, and with a javelin. But I come to you in the name of the LORD of hosts, the God of the armies of Israel, whom you have defied. 46 This day the LORD will deliver you into my hand, and I will strike you and take your head from you. And this day I will give the carcasses of the camp of the Philistines to the birds of the air and the wild beasts of the earth, that all the earth may know that there is a God in Israel. 47 Then all this assembly shall know that the LORD does not save with sword and spear; for the battle *is* the LORD's, and He will give you into our hands."

48 So it was, when the Philistine arose and came and drew near to meet David, that David hurried and ran toward the army to meet the Philistine. 49 Then David put his hand in his bag and took out a stone; and he slung *it*

What Goliath Learned

Those Hebrews were really getting on our nerves, and we Philistines (pronounced *fih-LIS-teens*) were determined to finish them once and for all!

Since I was nearly 10 feet tall, I was sure I could make a quick end of any Hebrew soldier they chose. So I challenged them to send me a man for a battle. Whichever one of us killed the other would decide the war between the Hebrews and the Philistines.

Can you imagine my shock when those Jews sent out a young boy? I nearly rolled on the ground laughing at the little fellow. There he stood— no bow, no arrows, no sword, no spear!

Just as I started toward him, the young fool came running at me whirling a shepherd's sling around his head! The next thing I knew, I was lying on the ground dying from a stone that had struck me between the eyes.

God isn't impressed with our size or how strong we think we are. He wants people like David, who trust in God's strength.

Young David topples the giant Goliath with a slingshot and the "name of the Lord of hosts!"

and struck the Philistine in his forehead, so that the stone sank into his forehead, and he fell on his face to the earth. ⁵⁰ So David prevailed over the Philistine with a sling and a stone, and struck the Philistine and killed him. But *there was* no sword in the hand of David. ⁵¹ Therefore David ran and stood over the Philistine, took his sword and drew it out of its sheath and killed him, and cut off his head with it.

And when the Philistines saw that their champion was dead, they fled. ⁵² Now the men of Israel and Judah arose and shouted, and pursued the Philistines as far as the entrance of the valley and to the gates of Ekron. And the wounded of the Philistines fell along the road to Shaaraim, even as

---

⛏ DIGGING IN

17:51 You Can Conquer Giants Not all giants look like Goliath. In fact, some of them aren't real people at all.

Some giants are the hard places we have to face in our lives—like that math exam you have to take. Right now, it seems as big as a mountain, but God can help you cut it down to the size of a pea!

It's wonderful to learn as you go along in life that no problem is too big for God.

Satan tries to tell you that you have to fight your battles all alone. But that's a big lie. When you make a habit of turning your giant problems over to God in prayer, you will find out that God is fighting right beside you. Then you become as brave as David. Just as David said when he met Goliath: "The Lord does not save with sword and spear; for the battle is the Lord's" (1 Samuel 17:47).

As you know by now, my father Saul was the king of Israel, but I knew my father's heart was not right with God. If only he had gone to Samuel and confessed his sins to God, our family might have been spared.

I could see that David was a good man at heart and that God was preparing him to be king instead of Saul. I warned David when my father plotted to kill him. So David ran away and had to live like an outlaw, even hiding out for a time with our enemies.

Later, I was killed in battle, but David promised me he would always be kind to my family when he became king. And he kept his promise! King David invited my crippled son, Mephibosheth (pronounced *meh-FIB-oh-sheth*), to live with him in the palace for the rest of his life!

far as Gath and Ekron. 53 Then the children of Israel returned from chasing the Philistines, and they plundered their tents. 54 And David took the head of the Philistine and brought it to Jerusalem, but he put his armor in his tent.

55 When Saul saw David going out against the Philistine, he said to Abner, the commander of the army, "Abner, whose son *is* this youth?"

And Abner said, "As your soul lives, O king, I do not know."

56 So the king said, "Inquire whose son this young man *is*."

57 Then, as David returned from the slaughter of the Philistine, Abner took him and brought him before Saul with the head of the Philistine in his hand. 58 And Saul said to him, "Whose son *are* you, young man?"

So David answered, "*I am* the son of your servant Jesse the Bethlehemite."

Saul is jealous of David

18 Now when he had finished speaking to Saul, the soul of Jonathan was knit to the soul of David, and Jonathan loved him as his own soul. 2 Saul took him that day, and would not let him go home to his father's house anymore. 3 Then Jonathan and David made a covenant, because he loved him as his own soul. 4 And Jonathan took off the robe that *was* on him

and gave it to David, with his armor, even to his sword and his bow and his belt.

5 So David went out wherever Saul sent him, *and* behaved wisely. And Saul set him over the men of war, and he was accepted in the sight of all the people and also in the sight of Saul's servants. 6 Now it had happened as they were coming *home*, when David was returning from the slaughter of the Philistine, that the women had come out of all the cities of Israel, singing and dancing, to meet King Saul, with tambourines, with joy, and with musical instruments. 7 So the women sang as they danced, and said:

"Saul has slain his thousands,
And David his ten thousands."

8 Then Saul was very angry, and the saying displeased him; and he said, "They have ascribed to David ten thousands, and to me they have ascribed *only* thousands. Now *what* more can he have but the kingdom?" 9 So Saul eyed David from that day forward.

10 And it happened on the next day that the distressing spirit from God came upon Saul, and he prophesied inside the house. So David played *music* with his hand, as at other times; but *there was* a spear in Saul's hand. 11 And Saul cast the spear, for he said,

---

Can Young David Take Saul's Throne?

The Jebus Times

JEBUS—A near riot in city streets across the land was caused by a recent political upset when Judge Samuel declared young David king while King Saul was still in office (see 1 Samuel 16:13).

David, the military hero who killed Goliath the giant (pronounced *go-LIE-uth*), is a popular favorite in this area. Now women are dancing and singing in the streets: "Saul has slain his thousands, and David his ten thousands."

It is reported that King Saul has tried several times to kill the young man, because Saul thinks David will try to take over the throne. David denies all such rumors. He continues to be a loyal officer in Saul's army.

Reports have now been confirmed that David is hiding out in Gath (rhymes with BATH) with our Philistine enemy, King Achish (pronounced *AY-kish*). (See 1 Samuel 21:10.)

"I will pin David to the wall!" But David escaped his presence twice.

12 Now Saul was afraid of David, because the Lord was with him, but had departed from Saul. 13 Therefore Saul removed him from his presence, and made him his captain over a thousand; and he went out and came in before the people. 14 And David behaved wisely in all his ways, and the Lord *was* with him. 15 Therefore, when Saul saw that he behaved very wisely, he was afraid of him. 16 But all Israel and Judah loved David, because he went out and came in before them.

17 Then Saul said to David, "Here is my older daughter Merab; I will give her to you as a wife. Only be valiant for me, and fight the Lord's battles." For Saul thought, "Let my hand not be against him, but let the hand of the Philistines be against him."

18 So David said to Saul, "Who *am* I, and what *is* my life *or* my father's family in Israel, that I should be son-in-law to the king?" 19 But it happened at the time when Merab, Saul's daughter, should have been given to David, that she was given to Adriel the Meholathite as a wife.

20 Now Michal, Saul's daughter, loved David. And they told Saul, and the thing pleased him. 21 So Saul said, "I will give her to him, that she may be a snare to him, and that the hand of the Philistines may be against him."

Therefore Saul said to David a second time, "You shall be my son-in-law today."

22 And Saul commanded his servants, "Communicate with David secretly, and say, 'Look, the king has delight in you, and all his servants love you. Now therefore, become the king's son-in-law.' "

23 So Saul's servants spoke those words in the hearing of David. And David said, "Does it seem to you *a* light *thing* to be a king's son-in-law, seeing I *am* a poor and lightly esteemed man?" 24 And the servants of Saul told him, saying, "In this manner David spoke."

25 Then Saul said, "Thus you shall say to David: 'The king does not desire any dowry but one hundred foreskins of the Philistines, to take vengeance on the king's enemies.' " But Saul thought to make David fall by the hand of the Philistines. 26 So when his servants told David these words, it pleased David well to become the king's son-in-law. Now the days had not expired; 27 therefore David arose and went, he and his men, and killed two hundred men of the Philistines. And David brought their foreskins, and they gave them in full count to the king, that he might become the king's son-in-law. Then Saul gave him Michal his daughter as a wife.

28 Thus Saul saw and knew that the

LORD *was* with David, and *that* Michal, Saul's daughter, loved him; 29 and Saul was still more afraid of David. So Saul became David's enemy continually. 30 Then the princes of the Philistines went out *to war.* And so it was, whenever they went out, *that* David behaved more wisely than all the servants of Saul, so that his name became highly esteemed.

Saul tries to kill David

19 Now Saul spoke to Jonathan his son and to all his servants, that they should kill David; but Jonathan, Saul's son, delighted greatly in David. 2 So Jonathan told David, saying, "My father Saul seeks to kill you. Therefore please be on your guard until morning, and stay in a secret *place* and hide. 3 And I will go out and stand beside my father in the field where you *are,* and I will speak with my father about you. Then what I observe, I will tell you."

4 Thus Jonathan spoke well of David to Saul his father, and said to him, "Let not the king sin against his servant, against David, because he has not sinned against you, and because his works *have been* very good toward you. 5 For he took his life in his hands and killed the Philistine, and the LORD brought about a great deliverance for all Israel. You saw *it* and rejoiced. Why then will you sin against innocent blood, to kill David without a cause?"

6 So Saul heeded the voice of Jona-than, and Saul swore, "As the LORD lives, he shall not be killed." 7 Then Jonathan called David, and Jonathan told him all these things. So Jonathan brought David to Saul, and he was in his presence as in times past.

8 And there was war again; and David went out and fought with the Philistines, and struck them with a mighty blow, and they fled from him.

9 Now the distressing spirit from the LORD came upon Saul as he sat in his house with his spear in his hand. And David was playing *music* with *his* hand. 10 Then Saul sought to pin David to the wall with the spear, but he slipped away from Saul's presence; and he drove the spear into the wall. So David fled and escaped that night.

11 Saul also sent messengers to David's house to watch him and to kill him in the morning. And Michal, David's wife, told him, saying, "If you do not save your life tonight, tomorrow you will be killed." 12 So Michal let David down through a window. And he went and fled and escaped. 13 And Michal took an image and laid *it* in the bed, put a cover of goats' *hair* for his head, and covered *it* with clothes. 14 So when Saul sent messengers to take David, she said, "He *is* sick."

15 Then Saul sent the messengers *back* to see David, saying, "Bring him up to me in the bed, that I may kill him." 16 And when the messengers had come in, there *was* the image in the bed, with a cover of goats' *hair* for his head. 17 Then Saul said to

⚒ DIGGING IN

19:11 King Saul Plots Against David
David probably was King Saul's most loyal and useful subject. David had killed Goliath, and he led his troops to defeat Saul's enemies.

But Saul didn't trust young David. He saw David as the one who would someday take over his throne. So Saul tried to kill David even as he was singing to calm Saul's fears.

What can you learn from Saul's treatment of David? You can learn that the world isn't always fair, just as Saul was not fair to David. But it is more important to learn that it doesn't matter as long as God is on your side. "A thousand may fall at your side, and ten thousand at your right hand; but it [harm] shall not come near you," wrote David (Psalm 91:7).

David escaped from Saul because God took care of him. If you will just put your trust in God as David did, your enemies cannot hurt you.

Michal, "Why have you deceived me like this, and sent my enemy away, so that he has escaped?"

And Michal answered Saul, "He said to me, 'Let me go! Why should I kill you?'"

18 So David fled and escaped, and went to Samuel at Ramah, and told him all that Saul had done to him. And he and Samuel went and stayed in Naioth. 19 Now it was told Saul, saying, "Take note, David is at Naioth in Ramah!" 20 Then Saul sent messengers to take David. And when they saw the group of prophets prophesying, and Samuel standing as leader over them, the Spirit of God came upon the messengers of Saul, and they also prophesied. 21 And when Saul was told, he sent other messengers, and they prophesied likewise. Then Saul sent messengers again the third time, and they prophesied also. 22 Then he also went to Ramah, and came to the great well that is at Sechu. So he asked, and said, "Where are Samuel and David?"

And someone said, "Indeed they are at Naioth in Ramah." 23 So he went there to Naioth in Ramah. Then the Spirit of God was upon him also, and he went on and prophesied until he came to Naioth in Ramah. 24 And he also stripped off his clothes and prophesied before Samuel in like manner, and lay down naked all that day and all that night. Therefore they say, "Is Saul also among the prophets?"

Jonathan's promise to David

20 Then David fled from Naioth in Ramah, and went and said to Jonathan, "What have I done? What is my iniquity, and what is my sin before your father, that he seeks my life?"

2 So Jonathan said to him, "By no means! You shall not die! Indeed, my father will do nothing either great or small without first telling me. And why should my father hide this thing from me? It is not so!"

3 Then David took an oath again, and said, "Your father certainly knows that I have found favor in your eyes, and he has said, 'Do not let Jonathan know this, lest he be grieved.' But truly, as the LORD lives and as your soul lives, there is but a step between me and death."

4 So Jonathan said to David, "Whatever you yourself desire, I will do it for you."

5 And David said to Jonathan, "Indeed tomorrow is the New Moon, and I should not fail to sit with the king to eat. But let me go, that I may hide in the field until the third day at evening. 6 If your father misses me at all, then say, 'David earnestly asked permission of me that he might run over to Bethlehem, his city, for there is a yearly sacrifice there for all the family.' 7 If he says thus: 'It is well,' your servant will be safe. But if he is very angry, be sure that evil is determined by him. 8 Therefore you shall deal kindly with your servant, for you have brought your servant into a covenant of the LORD with you. Nevertheless, if there is iniquity in me, kill me yourself, for why should you bring me to your father?"

9 But Jonathan said, "Far be it from you! For if I knew certainly that evil was determined by my father to come upon you, then would I not tell you?"

10 Then David said to Jonathan, "Who will tell me, or what if your father answers you roughly?"

11 And Jonathan said to David, "Come, let us go out into the field." So both of them went out into the field. 12 Then Jonathan said to David: "The LORD God of Israel is witness! When I have sounded out my father sometime tomorrow, or the third day, and indeed there is good toward David, and I do not send to you and tell you, 13 may the LORD do so and much more to Jonathan. But if it pleases my father to do you evil, then I will report it to you and send you away, that you may go in safety. And the LORD be with you as He has been with my father. 14 And you shall not only show me the kindness of the LORD while I still live, that I may not die; 15 but you shall not cut off your kindness from my house for-

ever, no, not when the LORD has cut off every one of the enemies of David from the face of the earth." 16 So Jonathan made *a covenant* with the house of David, *saying,* "Let the LORD require *it* at the hand of David's enemies."

17 Now Jonathan again caused David to vow, because he loved him; for he loved him as he loved his own soul. 18 Then Jonathan said to David, "Tomorrow *is* the New Moon; and you will be missed, because your seat will be empty. 19 And *when* you have stayed three days, go down quickly and come to the place where you hid on the day of the deed; and remain by the stone Ezel. 20 Then I will shoot three arrows to the side, as though I shot at a target; 21 and there I will send a lad, *saying,* 'Go, find the arrows.' If I expressly say to the lad, 'Look, the arrows *are* on this side of you; get them and come'— then, as the LORD lives, *there is* safety for you and no harm. 22 But if I say thus to the young man, 'Look, the arrows *are* beyond you'—go your way, for the LORD has sent you away. 23 And as for the matter which you and I have spoken of, indeed the LORD *be* between you and me forever."

24 Then David hid in the field. And when the New Moon had come, the king sat down to eat the feast. 25 Now the king sat on his seat, as at other times, on a seat by the wall. And Jonathan arose, and Abner sat by Saul's side, but David's place was empty. 26 Nevertheless Saul did not say anything that day, for he thought, "Something has happened to him; he *is* unclean, surely he *is* unclean." 27 And it happened the next day, the second *day* of the month, that David's place was empty. And Saul said to Jonathan his son, "Why has the son of Jesse not come to eat, either yesterday or today?"

28 So Jonathan answered Saul, "David earnestly asked *permission* of me *to go* to Bethlehem. 29 And he said, 'Please let me go, for our family has a sacrifice in the city, and my brother has commanded me *to be there.* And now, if I have found favor in your eyes, please let me get away and see my brothers.' Therefore he has not come to the king's table."

30 Then Saul's anger was aroused against Jonathan, and he said to him, "You son of a perverse, rebellious *woman!* Do I not know that you have chosen the son of Jesse to your own

Jonathan signals his friend David that danger is coming by shooting three arrows into the air.

shame and to the shame of your mother's nakedness? 31 For as long as the son of Jesse lives on the earth, you shall not be established, nor your kingdom. Now therefore, send and bring him to me, for he shall surely die."

32 And Jonathan answered Saul his father, and said to him, "Why should he be killed? What has he done?" 33 Then Saul cast a spear at him to kill him, by which Jonathan knew that it was determined by his father to kill David.

34 So Jonathan arose from the table in fierce anger, and ate no food the second day of the month, for he was grieved for David, because his father had treated him shamefully.

35 And so it was, in the morning, that Jonathan went out into the field at the time appointed with David, and a little lad was with him. 36 Then he said to his lad, "Now run, find the arrows which I shoot." As the lad ran, he shot an arrow beyond him. 37 When the lad had come to the place where the arrow was which Jonathan had shot, Jonathan cried out after the lad and said, "Is not the arrow beyond you?" 38 And Jonathan cried out after the lad, "Make haste, hurry, do not delay!" So Jonathan's lad gathered up the arrows and came back to his master. 39 But the lad did not know anything. Only Jonathan and David knew of the matter. 40 Then Jonathan gave his weapons to his lad, and said to him, "Go, carry them to the city."

41 As soon as the lad had gone, David arose from a place toward the south, fell on his face to the ground, and bowed down three times. And they kissed one another; and they wept together, but David more so. 42 Then Jonathan said to David, "Go in peace, since we have both sworn in the name of the LORD, saying, 'May the LORD be between you and me, and between your descendants and my descendants, forever.'" So he arose and departed, and Jonathan went into the city.

David runs from Saul

21 Now David came to Nob, to Ahimelech the priest. And Ahimelech was afraid when he met David, and said to him, "Why are you alone, and no one is with you?"

2 So David said to Ahimelech the priest, "The king has ordered me on some business, and said to me, 'Do not let anyone know anything about the business on which I send you, or what I have commanded you.' And I have directed my young men to such and such a place. 3 Now therefore, what have you on hand? Give me five loaves of bread in my hand, or whatever can be found."

4 And the priest answered David and said, "There is no common bread on hand; but there is holy bread, if the young men have at least kept themselves from women."

5 Then David answered the priest, and said to him, "Truly, women have been kept from us about three days since I came out. And the vessels of

---

⚒ DIGGING IN

21:1–6 Put First Things First In Matthew 12 you can read that Jesus liked what David did. When David and his soldiers were hungry, the priest gave them holy bread that was kept only for the priests.

We have a lot to learn from David here. Some people think serving God is mostly beautiful ceremonies in handsome buildings. They also imagine God is pleased by how nice our prayers sound to people around us.

But David had to feed his hungry men. That was more important than keeping the holy bread separate in the worship place. Jesus also warned about praying just so people will think we're holy. To Jesus, what we do is more important than what we say. As Samuel said to Saul, "To obey is better than sacrifice" (1 Samuel 15:22).

the young men are holy, and *the bread is* in effect common, even though it was consecrated in the vessel this day."

6 So the priest gave him holy *bread;* for there was no bread there but the showbread which had been taken from before the LORD, in order to put hot bread *in its place* on the day when it was taken away.

7 Now a certain man of the servants of Saul *was* there that day, detained before the LORD. And his name *was* Doeg, an Edomite, the chief of the herdsmen who *belonged* to Saul.

8 And David said to Ahimelech, "Is there not here on hand a spear or a sword? For I have brought neither my sword nor my weapons with me, because the king's business required haste."

9 So the priest said, "The sword of Goliath the Philistine, whom you killed in the Valley of Elah, there it is, wrapped in a cloth behind the ephod. If you will take that, take *it.* For *there is* no other except that one here."

And David said, "*There is* none like it; give it to me."

10 Then David arose and fled that day from before Saul, and went to Achish the king of Gath. 11 And the servants of Achish said to him, "*Is* this not David the king of the land? Did they not sing of him to one another in dances, saying:

'Saul has slain his thousands,
And David his ten thousands'?"

12 Now David took these words to heart, and was very much afraid of Achish the king of Gath. 13 So he changed his behavior before them, pretended madness in their hands, scratched on the doors of the gate, and let his saliva fall down on his beard. 14 Then Achish said to his servants, "Look, you see the man is insane. Why have you brought him to me? 15 Have I need of madmen, that you have brought this *fellow* to play the madman in my presence? Shall this *fellow* come into my house?"

David kills his enemies

22 David therefore departed from there and escaped to the cave of Adullam. So when his brothers and all his father's house heard *it,* they went down there to him. 2 And everyone *who was* in distress, everyone who *was* in debt, and everyone *who was* discontented gathered to him. So he became captain over them. And there were about four hundred men with him.

3 Then David went from there to Mizpah of Moab; and he said to the king of Moab, "Please let my father and mother come here with you, till I know what God will do for me." 4 So he brought them before the king of Moab, and they dwelt with him all the time that David was in the stronghold.

5 Now the prophet Gad said to David, "Do not stay in the stronghold; depart, and go to the land of Judah." So David departed and went into the forest of Hereth.

6 When Saul heard that David and the men who *were* with him had been discovered—now Saul was staying in Gibeah under a tamarisk tree in Ramah, with his spear in his hand, and all his servants standing about him— 7 then Saul said to his servants who stood about him, "Hear now, you Benjamites! Will the son of Jesse give every one of you fields and vineyards, *and* make you all captains of thousands and captains of hundreds? 8 All of you have conspired against me, and *there is* no one who reveals to me that my son has made a covenant with the son of Jesse; and *there is* not one of you who is sorry for me or reveals to me that my son has stirred up my servant against me, to lie in wait, as *it is* this day."

9 Then answered Doeg the Edomite, who was set over the servants of Saul, and said, "I saw the son of Jesse going to Nob, to Ahimelech the son of Ahitub. 10 And he inquired of the LORD for him, gave him provisions, and gave him the sword of Goliath the Philistine."

11 So the king sent to call Ahimelech the priest, the son of Ahitub, and all his father's house, the priests who *were* in Nob. And they all came to the king. 12 And Saul said, "Hear now, son of Ahitub!"

He answered, "Here I am, my lord."

13 Then Saul said to him, "Why have you conspired against me, you and the son of Jesse, in that you have given him bread and a sword, and have inquired of God for him, that he should rise against me, to lie in wait, as it is this day?"

14 So Ahimelech answered the king and said, "And who among all your servants *is as* faithful as David, who is the king's son-in-law, who goes at your bidding, and is honorable in your house? 15 Did I then begin to inquire of God for him? Far be it from me! Let not the king **impute** anything to his servant, *or* to any in the house of my father. For your servant knew nothing of all this, little or much."

16 And the king said, "You shall surely die, Ahimelech, you and all your father's house!" 17 Then the king said to the guards who stood about him, "Turn and kill the priests of the LORD, because their hand also *is* with David, and because they knew when he fled and did not tell it to me." But the servants of the king would not lift their hands to strike the priests of the LORD. 18 And the king said to Doeg, "You turn and kill the priests!" So Doeg the Edomite turned and struck the priests, and killed on that day eighty-five men who wore a linen ephod. 19 Also Nob, the city of the priests, he struck with the edge of the sword, both men and women, children and nursing infants, oxen and donkeys and sheep—with the edge of the sword.

20 Now one of the sons of Ahimelech the son of Ahitub, named Abiathar, escaped and fled after David. 21 And Abi-athar told David that Saul had killed the LORD's priests. 22 So David said to Abiathar, "I knew that day, when Doeg the Edomite *was* there, that he would surely tell Saul. I have caused *the death* of all the persons of your father's house. 23 Stay with me; do not fear. For he who seeks my life seeks your life, but with me you *shall be* safe."

David hides in the wilderness

23 Then they told David, saying, "Look, the Philistines are fighting against Keilah, and they are robbing the threshing floors."

2 Therefore David inquired of the LORD, saying, "Shall I go and attack these Philistines?"

And the LORD said to David, "Go and attack the Philistines, and save Keilah."

3 But David's men said to him, "Look, we are afraid here in Judah. How much more then if we go to Keilah against the armies of the Philistines?" 4 Then David inquired of the LORD once again.

And the LORD answered him and said, "Arise, go down to Keilah. For I will deliver the Philistines into your hand." 5 And David and his men went to Keilah and fought with the Philistines, struck them with a mighty blow, and took away their livestock. So David saved the inhabitants of Keilah.

6 Now it happened, when Abiathar the son of Ahimelech fled to David at Keilah, *that* he went down *with* an ephod in his hand.

7 And Saul was told that David had gone to Keilah. So Saul said, "God has delivered him into my hand, for he has shut himself in by entering a town that has gates and bars." 8 Then Saul called all the people together for war, to go down to Keilah to besiege David and his men.

WORDFINDER

22:15 Impute Pronounced *im-PYOOT*. To consider a person guilty or not guilty. God *imputes* the goodness of Christ to people who believe the gospel. He no longer *imputes* sin to them (no longer considers them guilty).

David hid from King Saul here in this oasis at En Gedi.

9 When David knew that Saul plotted evil against him, he said to Abiathar the priest, "Bring the ephod here." 10 Then David said, "O LORD God of Israel, Your servant has certainly heard that Saul seeks to come to Keilah to destroy the city for my sake. 11 Will the men of Keilah deliver me into his hand? Will Saul come down, as Your servant has heard? O LORD God of Israel, I pray, tell Your servant."

And the LORD said, "He will come down."

12 Then David said, "Will the men of Keilah deliver me and my men into the hand of Saul?"

And the LORD said, "They will deliver you."

13 So David and his men, about six hundred, arose and departed from Keilah and went wherever they could go. Then it was told Saul that David had escaped from Keilah; so he halted the expedition.

14 And David stayed in strongholds in the wilderness, and remained in the mountains in the Wilderness of Ziph. Saul sought him every day, but God did not deliver him into his hand. 15 So David saw that Saul had come out to seek his life. And David was in the Wilderness of Ziph in a forest.

16 Then Jonathan, Saul's son, arose and went to David in the woods and strengthened his hand in God. 17 And he said to him, "Do not fear, for the hand of Saul my father shall not find you. You shall be king over Israel, and I shall be next to you. Even my father Saul knows that." 18 So the two of them made a covenant before the LORD. And David stayed in the woods, and Jonathan went to his own house.

19 Then the Ziphites came up to Saul at Gibeah, saying, "Is David not hiding with us in strongholds in the woods, in the hill of Hachilah, which is on the south of Jeshimon? 20 Now therefore, O king, come down according to all the desire of your soul to come down; and our part shall be to deliver him into the king's hand."

21 And Saul said, "Blessed are you of the LORD, for you have compassion on me. 22 Please go and find out for sure, and see the place where his hideout is, and who has seen him there. For I am told he is very crafty. 23 See therefore, and take knowledge of all the lurking places where he hides; and come back to me with certainty, and I will go with you. And it shall be, if he is in the land, that I will search for him throughout all the clans of Judah."

24 So they arose and went to Ziph before Saul. But David and his men *were* in the Wilderness of Maon, in the plain on the south of Jeshimon. 25 When Saul and his men went to seek *him,* they told David. Therefore he went down to the rock, and stayed in the Wilderness of Maon. And when Saul heard *that,* he pursued David in the Wilderness of Maon. 26 Then Saul went on one side of the mountain, and David and his men on the other side of the mountain. So David made haste to get away from Saul, for Saul and his men were encircling David and his men to take them.

27 But a messenger came to Saul, saying, "Hurry and come, for the Philistines have invaded the land!" 28 Therefore Saul returned from pursuing David, and went against the Philistines; so they called that place the Rock of Escape. 29 Then David went up from there and dwelt in strongholds at En Gedi.

David lets Saul live

24 Now it happened, when Saul had returned from following the Philistines, that it was told him, saying, "Take note! David *is* in the Wilderness of En Gedi." 2 Then Saul took three thousand chosen men from all Israel, and went to seek David and his men on the Rocks of the Wild Goats. 3 So he came to the sheepfolds by the road, where there *was* a cave; and Saul went in to attend to his needs. (David and his men were staying in the recesses of the cave.) 4 Then the men of David said to him, "This is the day of which the LORD said to you, 'Behold, I will deliver your enemy into your hand, that you may do to him as it seems good to you.' " And David arose and secretly cut off a corner of Saul's robe. 5 Now it happened afterward that David's heart troubled him because he had cut Saul's *robe.* 6 And he said to his men, "The LORD forbid that I should do this thing to my master, the LORD's anointed, to stretch out my hand against him, seeing he *is* the anointed of the LORD." 7 So David restrained his servants with *these* words, and did not allow them to rise against Saul. And Saul got up from the cave and went on *his* way.

8 David also arose afterward, went

🔨 DIGGING IN

24:1–22 Honor God's Leaders You can read in 1 Samuel 19 how King Saul began to plot against David. David had to live like an outlaw with his four hundred men, hiding out from Saul and his soldiers in the hills and caves. But one day Saul fell into David's hands. Saul went to rest in a cave, but he didn't know David and his men were already there. Although David had the chance to kill Saul, he played a joke on Saul instead by cutting off a corner of his robe when he wasn't looking!

Then David was ashamed of what he did and begged Saul to believe that he meant him no harm. For just a moment, even King Saul could see how wrong he was by trying to kill his young friend. David had proved his loyalty to Saul.

Don't you think David became a greater person when he honored his king like that?

David spares King Saul's life, but cuts the corner of his robe as a warning.

out of the cave, and called out to Saul, saying, "My lord the king!" And when Saul looked behind him, David stooped with his face to the earth, and bowed down. 9 And David said to Saul: "Why do you listen to the words of men who say, 'Indeed David seeks your harm'? 10 Look, this day your eyes have seen that the LORD delivered you today into my hand in the cave, and *someone* urged *me* to kill you. But *my eye* spared you, and I said, 'I will not stretch out my hand against my lord, for he *is* the LORD's anointed.' 11 Moreover, my father, see! Yes, see the corner of your robe in my hand! For in that I cut off the corner of your robe, and did not kill you, know and see that *there is* neither evil nor rebellion in my hand, and I have not sinned against you. Yet you hunt my life to take it. 12 Let the LORD judge between you and me, and let the LORD avenge me on you. But my hand shall not be against you. 13 As the proverb of the ancients says, 'Wickedness proceeds from the wicked.' But my hand shall not be against you. 14 After whom has the king of Israel come out? Whom do you pursue? A dead dog? A flea? 15 Therefore let the LORD be judge, and judge between you and me, and see and plead my case, and deliver me out of your hand."

16 So it was, when David had finished speaking these words to Saul, that Saul said, "Is this your voice, my son David?" And Saul lifted up his voice and wept. 17 Then he said to David: "You *are* more righteous than I; for you have rewarded me with good, whereas I have rewarded you with evil. 18 And you have shown this day how you have dealt well with me; for when the LORD delivered me into your hand, you did not kill me. 19 For if a man finds his enemy, will he let him get away safely? Therefore may the LORD reward you with good for what you have done to me this day. 20 And now I know indeed that you shall surely be king, and that the kingdom of Israel shall be established in your hand. 21 Therefore swear now to me by the LORD that you will not cut off my descendants after me, and that you will not destroy my name from my father's house."

22 So David swore to Saul. And Saul went home, but David and his men went up to the stronghold.

Abigail—David's wife

25 Then Samuel died; and the Israelites gathered together and lamented for him, and buried him at his home in Ramah. And David arose and went down to the Wilderness of Paran.

2 Now *there was* a man in Maon whose business *was* in Carmel, and the man *was* very rich. He had three thousand sheep and a thousand goats. And he was shearing his sheep in Carmel. 3 The name of the man *was* Nabal, and the name of his wife Abigail. And *she was* a woman of good understanding and beautiful appearance; but the man *was* harsh and evil in *his* doings. He *was of the house of* Caleb.

4 When David heard in the wilderness that Nabal was shearing his sheep, 5 David sent ten young men; and David said to the young men, "Go up to Carmel, go to Nabal, and greet him in my name. 6 And thus you shall say to him who lives *in prosperity:* 'Peace *be* to you, peace to your house, and peace to all that you have! 7 Now I have heard that you have shearers. Your shepherds were with us, and we did not hurt them, nor was there anything missing from them all the while they were in Carmel. 8 Ask your young men, and they will tell you. Therefore let *my* young men find favor in your eyes, for we come on a feast day. Please give whatever comes to your hand to your servants and to your son David.' "

9 So when David's young men came, they spoke to Nabal according to all these words in the name of David, and waited.

10 Then Nabal answered David's servants, and said, "Who is David, and who *is* the son of Jesse? There are many servants nowadays who break

> **Abigail**—It is hard for me to hold back tears of thanksgiving as I tell you about David's goodness to me.
>
> I was married to a man called Nabal. He was well named because his name means "Fool." Nabal was a wealthy businessman, but he proved he was a fool by the way he treated David. One day David came, asking Nabal for food for his young men and himself, but Nabal answered him with insults.
>
> Right away David wanted to kill Nabal, but I took a load of food on my donkeys to David and asked him to forgive my foolish husband. I admitted that Nabal was no good and begged David not to become guilty of the man's murder.
>
> How thankful I am that David listened to me! Not long afterward Nabal died, and David asked me to marry him. So I have been David's happy wife since that day.

away each one from his master. 11 Shall I then take my bread and my water and my meat that I have killed for my shearers, and give *it* to men when I do not know where they *are* from?"

12 So David's young men turned on their heels and went back; and they came and told him all these words. 13 Then David said to his men, "Every man gird on his sword." So every man girded on his sword, and David also girded on his sword. And about four hundred men went with David, and two hundred stayed with the supplies.

14 Now one of the young men told Abigail, Nabal's wife, saying, "Look, David sent messengers from the wilderness to greet our master; and he reviled them. 15 But the men *were* very good to us, and we were not hurt, nor did we miss anything as long as we accompanied them, when we were in the fields. 16 They were a wall to us both by night and day, all the time we were with them keeping the sheep. 17 Now therefore, know and consider what you will do, for harm is determined against our master and against all his household. For he *is such* a scoundrel that *one* cannot speak to him."

18 Then Abigail made haste and took two hundred *loaves* of bread, two skins of wine, five sheep already dressed, five seahs of roasted *grain,* one hun-

dred clusters of raisins, and two hundred cakes of figs, and loaded *them* on donkeys. 19 And she said to her servants, "Go on before me; see, I am coming after you." But she did not tell her husband Nabal.

20 So it was, *as* she rode on the donkey, that she went down under cover of the hill; and there were David and his men, coming down toward her, and she met them. 21 Now David had said, "Surely in vain I have protected all that this *fellow* has in the wilderness, so that nothing was missed of all that *belongs* to him. And he has repaid me evil for good. 22 May God do so, and more also, to the enemies of David, if I leave one male of all who *belong* to him by morning light."

23 Now when Abigail saw David, she dismounted quickly from the donkey, fell on her face before David, and bowed down to the ground. 24 So she fell at his feet and said: "On me, my lord, *on me let* this iniquity *be!* And please let your maidservant speak in your ears, and hear the words of your maidservant. 25 Please, let not my lord regard this scoundrel Nabal. For as his name *is, so is* he: Nabal *is* his name, and folly *is* with him! But I, your maidservant, did not see the young men of my lord whom you sent. 26 Now therefore, my lord, *as* the LORD lives and *as* your soul lives, since the LORD has held you back from coming to

bloodshed and from avenging yourself with your own hand, now then, let your enemies and those who seek harm for my lord be as Nabal. 27 And now this present which your maidservant has brought to my lord, let it be given to the young men who follow my lord. 28 Please forgive the trespass of your maidservant. For the LORD will certainly make for my lord an enduring house, because my lord fights the battles of the LORD, and evil is not found in you throughout your days. 29 Yet a man has risen to pursue you and seek your life, but the life of my lord shall be bound in the bundle of the living with the LORD your God; and the lives of your enemies He shall sling out, *as from* the pocket of a sling. 30 And it shall come to pass, when the LORD has done for my lord according to all the good that He has spoken concerning you, and has appointed you ruler over Israel, 31 that this will be no grief to you, nor offense of heart to my lord, either that you have shed blood without cause, or that my lord has avenged himself. But when the LORD has dealt well with my lord, then remember your maidservant."

32 Then David said to Abigail: "Blessed *is* the LORD God of Israel, who sent you this day to meet me! 33 And blessed *is* your advice and blessed *are* you, because you have kept me this day from coming to bloodshed and from avenging myself with my own hand. 34 For indeed, *as* the LORD God of Israel lives, who has kept me back from hurting you, unless you had hurried and come to meet me, surely by morning light no males would have been left to Nabal!" 35 So David received from her hand what she had brought him, and said to her, "Go up in peace to your house. See, I have heeded your voice and respected your person."

36 Now Abigail went to Nabal, and there he was, holding a feast in his house, like the feast of a king. And Nabal's heart *was* merry within him, for he *was* very drunk; therefore she told him nothing, little or much, until morn-

ing light. 37 So it was, in the morning, when the wine had gone from Nabal, and his wife had told him these things, that his heart died within him, and he became *like* a stone. 38 Then it happened, *after* about ten days, that the LORD struck Nabal, and he died.

39 So when David heard that Nabal was dead, he said, "Blessed *be* the LORD, who has pleaded the cause of my reproach from the hand of Nabal, and has kept His servant from evil! For the LORD has returned the wickedness of Nabal on his own head."

And David sent and proposed to Abigail, to take her as his wife. 40 When the servants of David had come to Abigail at Carmel, they spoke to her saying, "David sent us to you, to ask you to become his wife."

41 Then she arose, bowed her face to the earth, and said, "Here is your maidservant, a servant to wash the feet of the servants of my lord." 42 So Abigail rose in haste and rode on a donkey, attended by five of her maidens; and she followed the messengers of David, and became his wife. 43 David also took Ahinoam of Jezreel, and so both of them were his wives.

44 But Saul had given Michal his daughter, David's wife, to Palti the son of Laish, who *was* from Gallim.

David spares Saul again

26 Now the Ziphites came to Saul at Gibeah, saying, "Is David not hiding in the hill of Hachilah, opposite Jeshimon?" 2 Then Saul arose and went down to the Wilderness of Ziph, having three thousand chosen men of Israel with him, to seek David in the Wilderness of Ziph. 3 And Saul encamped in the hill of Hachilah, which *is* opposite Jeshimon, by the road. But David stayed in the wilderness, and he saw that Saul came after him into the wilderness. 4 David therefore sent out spies, and understood that Saul had indeed come.

5 So David arose and came to the place where Saul had encamped. And

David saw the place where Saul lay, and Abner the son of Ner, the commander of his army. Now Saul lay within the camp, with the people encamped all around him. 6 Then David answered, and said to Ahimelech the Hittite and to Abishai the son of Zeruiah, brother of Joab, saying, "Who will go down with me to Saul in the camp?"

And Abishai said, "I will go down with you."

7 So David and Abishai came to the people by night; and there Saul lay sleeping within the camp, with his spear stuck in the ground by his head. And Abner and the people lay all around him. 8 Then Abishai said to David, "God has delivered your enemy into your hand this day. Now therefore, please, let me strike him at once with the spear, right to the earth; and I will not *have to strike* him a second time!"

9 But David said to Abishai, "Do not destroy him; for who can stretch out his hand against the LORD's anointed, and be guiltless?" 10 David said furthermore, "As the LORD lives, the LORD shall strike him, or his day shall come to die, or he shall go out to battle and perish. 11 The LORD forbid that I should stretch out my hand against the LORD's anointed. But please, take now the spear and the jug of water that *are* by his head, and let us go." 12 So David took the spear and the jug of water *by* Saul's head, and they got away; and no man saw or knew *it* or awoke. For they *were* all asleep, because a deep sleep from the LORD had fallen on them.

13 Now David went over to the other side, and stood on the top of a hill afar off, a great distance *being* between them. 14 And David called out to the people and to Abner the son of Ner, saying, "Do you not answer, Abner?"

Then Abner answered and said, "Who *are* you, calling out to the king?"

15 So David said to Abner, "*Are* you not a man? And who *is* like you in Israel? Why then have you not guarded your lord the king? For one

of the people came in to destroy your lord the king. 16 This thing that you have done *is* not good. As the LORD lives, you deserve to die, because you have not guarded your master, the LORD's anointed. And now see where the king's spear *is*, and the jug of water that *was* by his head."

17 Then Saul knew David's voice, and said, "*Is* that your voice, my son David?"

David said, "*It is* my voice, my lord, O king." 18 And he said, "Why does my lord thus pursue his servant? For what have I done, or what evil *is* in my hand? 19 Now therefore, please, let my lord the king hear the words of his servant: If the LORD has stirred you up against me, let Him accept an offering. But if *it is* the children of men, *may* they *be* cursed before the LORD, for they have driven me out this day from sharing in the inheritance of the LORD, saying, 'Go, serve other gods.' 20 So now, do not let my blood fall to the earth before the face of the LORD. For the king of Israel has come out to seek a flea, as when one hunts a partridge in the mountains."

21 Then Saul said, "I have sinned. Return, my son David. For I will harm you no more, because my life was precious in your eyes this day. Indeed I have played the fool and erred exceedingly."

22 And David answered and said, "Here is the king's spear. Let one of the young men come over and get it. 23 May the LORD repay every man *for* his righteousness and his faithfulness; for the LORD delivered you into *my* hand today, but I would not stretch out my hand against the LORD's anointed. 24 And indeed, as your life was valued much this day in my eyes, so let my life be valued much in the eyes of the LORD, and let Him deliver me out of all tribulation."

25 Then Saul said to David, "*May* you *be* blessed, my son David! You shall both do great things and also still prevail."

So David went on his way, and Saul returned to his place.

David and Achish

27 And David said in his heart, "Now I shall perish someday by the hand of Saul. *There is* nothing better for me than that I should speedily escape to the land of the Philistines; and Saul will despair of me, to seek me anymore in any part of Israel. So I shall escape out of his hand." ² Then David arose and went over with the six hundred men who *were* with him to Achish the son of Maoch, king of Gath. ³ So David dwelt with Achish at Gath, he and his men, each man with his household, *and* David with his two wives, Ahinoam the Jezreelitess, and Abigail the Carmelitess, Nabal's widow. ⁴ And it was told Saul that David had fled to Gath; so he sought him no more.

⁵ Then David said to Achish, "If I have now found favor in your eyes, let them give me a place in some town in the country, that I may dwell there. For why should your servant dwell in the royal city with you?" ⁶ So Achish gave him Ziklag that day. Therefore Ziklag has belonged to the kings of Judah to this day. ⁷ Now the time that David dwelt in the country of the Philistines was one full year and four months.

⁸ And David and his men went up and raided the Geshurites, the Girzites, and the Amalekites. For those nations were the inhabitants of the land from of old, as you go to Shur, *even* as far as the land of Egypt. ⁹ Whenever David attacked the land, he left neither man nor woman alive, but took away the sheep, the oxen, the donkeys, the camels, and the apparel, and returned and came to Achish. ¹⁰ Then Achish would say, "Where have you made a raid today?" And David would say, "Against the southern *area* of Judah, or against the southern *area* of the Jerahmeelites, or against the southern *area* of the Kenites." ¹¹ David would save neither man nor woman alive, to bring *news* to Gath, saying, "Lest they should inform on us, saying, 'Thus David did.'" And thus *was* his behavior all the time he dwelt in the country of the Philistines. ¹² So Achish believed David, saying, "He has made his people Israel utterly abhor him; therefore he will be my servant forever."

Saul and the witch of En Dor

28 Now it happened in those days that the Philistines gathered their armies together for war, to fight with Israel. And Achish said to David, "You assuredly know that you will go out with me to battle, you and your men."

² So David said to Achish, "Surely you know what your servant can do."

And Achish said to David, "Therefore I will make you one of my chief guardians forever."

³ Now Samuel had died, and all Israel had lamented for him and buried him in Ramah, in his own city. And Saul had put the mediums and the spiritists out of the land.

⁴ Then the Philistines gathered together, and came and encamped at Shunem. So Saul gathered all Israel together, and they encamped at Gilboa. ⁵ When Saul saw the army of the Philistines, he was afraid, and his heart trembled greatly. ⁶ And when Saul inquired of the LORD, the LORD did not answer him, either by dreams or by Urim or by the prophets.

⁷ Then Saul said to his servants, "Find me a woman who is a medium, that I may go to her and inquire of her."

And his servants said to him, "In fact, *there is* a woman who is a medium at En Dor."

⁸ So Saul disguised himself and put on other clothes, and he went, and two men with him; and they came to the woman by night. And he said, "Please conduct a séance for me, and bring up for me the one I shall name to you."

⁹ Then the woman said to him, "Look, you know what Saul has done, how he has cut off the mediums and the spiritists from the land. Why then do you lay a snare for my life, to cause me to die?"

¹⁰ And Saul swore to her by the

What Are Mediums?

Today we sometimes call mediums, "spiritists." Such people say they talk with the spirits of people who have died. Some people make money by being mediums. God forbids His people to deal with spirit mediums. So what Saul did, proved he was not living in obedience to God.

LORD, saying, "As the LORD lives, no punishment shall come upon you for this thing."

11 Then the woman said, "Whom shall I bring up for you?"

And he said, "Bring up Samuel for me."

12 When the woman saw Samuel, she cried out with a loud voice. And the woman spoke to Saul, saying, "Why have you deceived me? For you are Saul!"

13 And the king said to her, "Do not be afraid. What did you see?"

And the woman said to Saul, "I saw a spirit ascending out of the earth."

14 So he said to her, "What is his form?"

And she said, "An old man is com-ing up, and he is covered with a mantle." And Saul perceived that it was Samuel, and he stooped with his face to the ground and bowed down.

15 Now Samuel said to Saul, "Why have you disturbed me by bringing me up?"

And Saul answered, "I am deeply distressed; for the Philistines make war against me, and God has departed from me and does not answer me anymore, neither by prophets nor by dreams. Therefore I have called you, that you may reveal to me what I should do."

16 Then Samuel said: "So why do you ask me, seeing the LORD has departed from you and has become your enemy? 17 And the LORD has done for Himself as He spoke by me. For the LORD has torn the kingdom out of your hand and given it to your neighbor, David. 18 Because you did not obey the voice of the LORD nor execute His fierce wrath upon Amalek, therefore the LORD has done this thing to you this day. 19 Moreover the LORD will also deliver Israel with you into the hand of the Philistines. And tomorrow you and your sons will be with me. The LORD will also deliver the army of Israel into the hand of the Philistines."

King Saul asks the witch of En Dor to predict a battle with the Philistines.

What Saul Learned

I'm not worried so much about what I learned. It's what I *didn't learn* that bothers me now.

You see, I should have asked the Lord to show me His way in everything. Instead, I just stupidly kept trying to go around the Lord to get things done.

Probably the worst and most foolish thing I ever did was to visit that witch over in En Dor. I needed advice about how to make war against our enemies. Can you imagine? I even thought that evil woman could bring old Samuel back from the dead to advise me!

The witch was terrified when the Lord Himself did send Samuel. But Samuel only cursed me. Because I failed to trust God, I was finished forever. Soon after that, I was killed in battle.

---

20 Immediately Saul fell full length on the ground, and was dreadfully afraid because of the words of Samuel. And there was no strength in him, for he had eaten no food all day or all night.

21 And the woman came to Saul and saw that he was severely troubled, and said to him, "Look, your maidservant has obeyed your voice, and I have put my life in my hands and heeded the words which you spoke to me. 22 Now therefore, please, heed also the voice of your maidservant, and let me set a piece of bread before you; and eat, that you may have strength when you go on *your* way."

23 But he refused and said, "I will not eat."

So his servants, together with the woman, urged him; and he heeded their voice. Then he arose from the ground and sat on the bed. 24 Now the woman had a fatted calf in the house, and she hastened to kill it. And she took flour and kneaded *it,* and baked unleavened bread from it. 25 So she brought *it* before Saul and his servants, and they ate. Then they rose and went away that night.

Achish sends David away

29 Then the Philistines gathered together all their armies at Aphek, and the Israelites encamped by a fountain which is in Jezreel. 2 And the lords of the Philistines passed in review by hundreds and by thousands, but David and his men passed in review at the rear with Achish. 3 Then the princes of the Philistines said, "What *are* these Hebrews *doing here?*"

And Achish said to the princes of the Philistines, "*Is* this not David, the servant of Saul king of Israel, who has been with me these days, or these years? And to this day I have found no fault in him since he defected *to me.*"

4 But the princes of the Philistines were angry with him; so the princes of the Philistines said to him, "Make this fellow return, that he may go back to the place which you have appointed for him, and do not let him go down with us to battle, lest in the battle he become our adversary. For with what could he reconcile himself to his master, if not with the heads of these men? 5 *Is* this not David, of whom they sang to one another in dances, saying:

'Saul has slain his thousands,
And David his ten thousands'?"

6 Then Achish called David and said to him, "Surely, *as* the LORD lives, you have been upright, and your going out and your coming in with me in the army is good in my sight. For to this day I have not found evil in you since

the day of your coming to me. Nevertheless the lords do not favor you. 7 Therefore return now, and go in peace, that you may not displease the lords of the Philistines."

8 So David said to Achish, "But what have I done? And to this day what have you found in your servant as long as I have been with you, that I may not go and fight against the enemies of my lord the king?"

9 Then Achish answered and said to David, "I know that you *are* as good in my sight as an angel of God; nevertheless the princes of the Philistines have said, 'He shall not go up with us to the battle.' 10 Now therefore, rise early in the morning with your master's servants who have come with you. And as soon as you are up early in the morning and have light, depart."

11 So David and his men rose early to depart in the morning, to return to the land of the Philistines. And the Philistines went up to Jezreel.

David attacks his enemies

30 Now it happened, when David and his men came to Ziklag, on the third day, that the Amalekites had invaded the South and Ziklag, attacked Ziklag and burned it with fire, 2 and had taken captive the women and those who *were* there, from small to great; they did not kill anyone, but carried *them* away and went their way. 3 So David and his men came to the city, and there it was, burned with fire; and their wives, their sons, and their daughters had been taken captive. 4 Then David and the people who *were* with him lifted up their voices and wept, until they had no more power to weep. 5 And David's two wives, Ahinoam the Jezreelitess, and Abigail the widow of Nabal the Carmelite, had been taken captive. 6 Now David was greatly distressed, for the people spoke of stoning him, because the soul of all the people was grieved, every man for his sons and his daughters. But David strengthened himself in the LORD his God.

7 Then David said to Abiathar the priest, Ahimelech's son, "Please bring the ephod here to me." And Abiathar brought the ephod to David. 8 So David inquired of the LORD, saying, "Shall I pursue this troop? Shall I overtake them?"

And He answered him, "Pursue, for you shall surely overtake *them* and without fail recover *all*."

9 So David went, he and the six hundred men who *were* with him, and came to the Brook Besor, where those stayed who were left behind. 10 But David pursued, he and four hundred men; for two hundred stayed *behind,* who were so weary that they could not cross the Brook Besor.

11 Then they found an Egyptian in the field, and brought him to David; and they gave him bread and he ate, and they let him drink water. 12 And they gave him a piece of a cake of figs and two clusters of raisins. So when he had eaten, his strength came back to him; for he had eaten no bread nor drunk water for three days and three nights. 13 Then David said to him, "To whom do you *belong,* and where *are* you from?"

And he said, "I *am* a young man from Egypt, servant of an Amalekite; and my master left me behind, because three days ago I fell sick. 14 We made an invasion of the southern *area* of the Cherethites, in the *territory* which *belongs* to Judah, and of the southern *area* of Caleb; and we burned Ziklag with fire."

15 And David said to him, "Can you take me down to this troop?"

So he said, "Swear to me by God that you will neither kill me nor deliver me into the hands of my master, and I will take you down to this troop."

16 And when he had brought him down, there they were, spread out over all the land, eating and drinking and dancing, because of all the great spoil which they had taken from the land of the Philistines and from the land of Judah. 17 Then David attacked them from twilight until the evening of the next day. Not a man of them

escaped, except four hundred young men who rode on camels and fled. 18 So David recovered all that the Amalekites had carried away, and David rescued his two wives. 19 And nothing of theirs was lacking, either small or great, sons or daughters, spoil or anything which they had taken from them; David recovered all. 20 Then David took all the flocks and herds they had driven before those *other* livestock, and said, "This *is* David's spoil."

21 Now David came to the two hundred men who had been so weary that they could not follow David, whom they also had made to stay at the Brook Besor. So they went out to meet David and to meet the people who *were* with him. And when David came near the people, he greeted them. 22 Then all the wicked and worthless men of those who went with David answered and said, "Because they did not go with us, we will not give them *any* of the spoil that we have recovered, except for every man's wife and children, that they may lead *them* away and depart."

23 But David said, "My brethren, you shall not do so with what the LORD has given us, who has preserved us and delivered into our hand the troop that came against us. 24 For who will heed you in this matter? But as his part *is* who goes down to the battle, so *shall* his part *be* who stays by the supplies; they shall share alike." 25 So it was, from that day forward; he made it a statute and an ordinance for Israel to this day.

26 Now when David came to Ziklag, he sent *some* of the spoil to the elders of Judah, to his friends, saying, "Here is a present for you from the spoil of the enemies of the LORD"— 27 to those who *were* in Bethel, *those* who *were* in Ramoth of the South, *those* who *were* in Jattir, 28 *those* who *were* in Aroer, *those* who *were* in Siphmoth, *those* who *were* in Eshtemoa, 29 *those* who *were* in Rachal, *those* who *were* in the cities of the Jerahmeelites, *those* who *were* in the cities of the Kenites, 30 *those* who *were* in Hormah, *those*

who *were* in Chorashan, *those* who *were* in Athach, 31 *those* who *were* in Hebron, and to all the places where David himself and his men were accustomed to rove.

Saul and Jonathan die

31 Now the Philistines fought against Israel; and the men of Israel fled from before the Philistines, and fell slain on Mount Gilboa. 2 Then the Philistines followed hard after Saul and his sons. And the Philistines killed Jonathan, Abinadab, and Malchishua, Saul's sons. 3 The battle became fierce against Saul. The archers hit him, and he was severely wounded by the archers.

4 Then Saul said to his armorbearer, "Draw your sword, and thrust me through with it, lest these uncircumcised men come and thrust me through and abuse me."

But his armorbearer would not, for he was greatly afraid. Therefore Saul took a sword and fell on it. 5 And when his armorbearer saw that Saul was dead, he also fell on his sword, and died with him. 6 So Saul, his three sons, his armorbearer, and all his men died together that same day.

7 And when the men of Israel who *were* on the other side of the valley, and *those* who *were* on the other side of the Jordan, saw that the men of Israel had fled and that Saul and his sons were dead, they forsook the cities and fled; and the Philistines came and dwelt in them. 8 So it happened the next day, when the Philistines came to strip the slain, that they found Saul and his three sons fallen on Mount Gilboa. 9 And they cut off his head and stripped off his armor, and sent *word* throughout the land of the Philistines, to proclaim *it in* the temple of their idols and among the people. 10 Then they put his armor in the temple of the Ashtoreths, and they fastened his body to the wall of Beth Shan.

11 Now when the inhabitants of Jabesh Gilead heard what the Philistines had done to Saul, 12 all the valiant men

King Saul Defeated, Takes Own Life

The Promised Land Gazette

MOUNT GILBOA—King Saul, stunned by his defeat at the hands of the Philistines (pronounced *fih-LIS-teens*), has taken his own life on the battlefield on Mount Gilboa.

It is reported that Saul, seriously wounded, ordered the soldier who carried his weapon to kill him. When the man refused, the king fell on his own sword. Saul's three sons, including Jonathan, David's special friend, are dead as well.

This is a tragic defeat for Israel. The Philistines have placed the bodies of King Saul and his sons on public display. Efforts will be made to claim the bodies.

In the next few days this newspaper will publish an official song of mourning written by David in tribute to the fallen king and Prince Jonathan. (See 2 Samuel 1:17.)

arose and traveled all night, and took the body of Saul and the bodies of his sons from the wall of Beth Shan; and they came to Jabesh and burned them there. ¹³ Then they took their bones and buried *them* under the tamarisk tree at Jabesh, and fasted seven days.

The Book of
2 SAMUEL

God called me, David, as a shepherd boy to replace disobedient King Saul. But I learned that no man—not even a man who truly loves God—is good enough to rule God's people! As soon as I was free to enjoy some rest, I fell into a terrible sin. I even had a man killed so that I could take his wife for myself. Since that time there has been no peace in my family.

To begin with, my son Absalom (pronounced AB-sah-lum) killed his brother Amnon (pronounced AM-non). Then Absalom stole my throne for a short time. Finally, Absalom himself was killed. My heart was broken that day.

One day, a far greater Son of mine will rule on my throne forever and ever. That greater Son is Jesus Christ. Psalm 72 is one of the many beautiful songs I wrote about Jesus. But above all—He is also the Son of God!

David weeps for Saul

Now it came to pass after the death of Saul, when David had returned from the slaughter of the Amalekites, and David had stayed two days in Ziklag, 2 on the third day, behold, it happened that a man came from Saul's camp with his clothes torn and dust on his head. So it was, when he came to David, that he fell to the ground and prostrated himself.

3 And David said to him, "Where have you come from?"

So he said to him, "I have escaped from the camp of Israel."

4 Then David said to him, "How did the matter go? Please tell me."

And he answered, "The people have fled from the battle, many of the people are fallen and dead, and Saul and Jonathan his son are dead also."

5 So David said to the young man who told him, "How do you know that Saul and Jonathan his son are dead?"

6 Then the young man who told him said, "As I happened by chance to be on Mount Gilboa, there was Saul, leaning on his spear; and indeed the chariots and horsemen followed hard after

him. 7 Now when he looked behind him, he saw me and called to me. And I answered, 'Here I am.' 8 And he said to me, 'Who are you?' So I answered him, 'I am an Amalekite.' 9 He said to me again, 'Please stand over me and kill me, for anguish has come upon me, but my life still remains in me.' 10 So I stood over him and killed him, because I was sure that he could not live after he had fallen. And I took the crown that was on his head and the bracelet that was on his arm, and have brought them here to my lord."

11 Therefore David took hold of his own clothes and tore them, and so did all the men who were with him. 12 And they mourned and wept and fasted until evening for Saul and for Jonathan his son, for the people of the LORD and for the house of Israel, because they had fallen by the sword.

13 Then David said to the young man who told him, "Where are you from?"

And he answered, "I am the son of an alien, an Amalekite."

14 So David said to him, "How was it you were not afraid to put forth your hand to destroy the LORD's anointed?"

What a Young Man Learned

I learned I had the wrong idea about David. I thought he wanted Saul dead. So I ran to David with the news that I had killed King Saul.

But David wasn't glad at all that Saul was dead. I had never seen anyone like David. He was actually sorry for his enemy, Saul.

How can you understand someone like David? He was always a good friend and servant of King Saul, and he even fought Saul's wars for him. But time after time, David was nearly killed by Saul.

Now David was angry because I had killed his enemy! So I lost my own life that day.

Be careful how you treat God's enemies. Like David, the Lord loves people who hate Him. Can you understand love like that?

---

15 Then David called one of the young men and said, "Go near, *and* execute him!" And he struck him so that he died. 16 So David said to him, "Your blood *is* on your own head, for your own mouth has testified against you, saying, 'I have killed the LORD's anointed.'"

17 Then David lamented with this lamentation over Saul and over Jonathan his son, 18 and he told *them* to teach the children of Judah *the Song of* the Bow; indeed *it is* written in the Book of Jasher:

19 "The beauty of Israel is slain on
  your high places!
  How the mighty have fallen!

20 Tell *it* not in Gath,
  Proclaim *it* not in the streets of
    Ashkelon—
  Lest the daughters of the
    Philistines rejoice,
  Lest the daughters of the
    uncircumcised triumph.

21 "O mountains of Gilboa,
  Let there be no dew nor rain
    upon you,
  Nor fields of offerings.
  For the shield of the mighty is
    cast away there!
  The shield of Saul, not anointed
    with oil.

22 From the blood of the slain,
  From the fat of the mighty,
  The bow of Jonathan did not
    turn back,

And the sword of Saul did not
  return empty.

23 "Saul and Jonathan *were*
    beloved and pleasant in their
    lives,
  And in their death they were not
    divided;
  They *were* swifter than eagles,
  They *were* stronger than lions.

24 "O daughters of Israel, weep over
    Saul,
  Who clothed you in scarlet, with
    luxury;
  Who put ornaments of gold on
    your apparel.

25 "How the mighty have fallen in
    the midst of the battle!
  Jonathan *was* slain in your high
    places.

26 I am distressed for you, my
    brother Jonathan;
  You have been very pleasant to
    me;
  Your love to me was wonderful,
  Surpassing the love of women.

27 "How the mighty have fallen,
  And the weapons of war
    perished!"

Israel and Judah go to war

2 It happened after this that David inquired of the LORD, saying, "Shall I

go up to any of the cities of Judah?"

And the LORD said to him, "Go up."

David said, "Where shall I go up?"

And He said, "To Hebron."

2 So David went up there, and his two wives also, Ahinoam the Jezreelitess, and Abigail the widow of Nabal the Carmelite. 3 And David brought up the men who *were* with him, every man with his household. So they dwelt in the cities of Hebron.

4 Then the men of Judah came, and there they anointed David king over the house of Judah. And they told David, saying, "The men of Jabesh Gilead *were the ones* who buried Saul." 5 So David sent messengers to the men of Jabesh Gilead, and said to them, "You *are* blessed of the LORD, for you have shown this kindness to your lord, to Saul, and have buried him. 6 And now may the LORD show kindness and truth to you. I also will repay you this kindness, because you have done this thing. 7 Now therefore, let your hands be strengthened, and be valiant; for your master Saul is dead, and also the house of Judah has anointed me king over them."

8 But Abner the son of Ner, commander of Saul's army, took Ishbosheth the son of Saul and brought him over to Mahanaim; 9 and he made him king over Gilead, over the Ashurites, over Jezreel, over Ephraim, over Benjamin, and over all Israel. 10 Ishbosheth, Saul's son, *was* forty years old when he began to reign over Israel, and he reigned two years. Only the house of Judah followed David. 11 And the time that David was king in Hebron over the house of Judah was seven years and six months.

12 Now Abner the son of Ner, and the servants of Ishbosheth the son of Saul, went out from Mahanaim to Gibeon. 13 And Joab the son of Zeruiah, and the servants of David, went out and met them by the pool of Gibeon. So they sat down, one on one side of the pool and the other on the other side of the pool. 14 Then Abner said to Joab, "Let the young men now arise and compete before us."

And Joab said, "Let them arise."

15 So they arose and went over by number, twelve from Benjamin, *followers* of Ishbosheth the son of Saul, and twelve from the servants of David. 16 And each one grasped his opponent by the head and *thrust* his sword in his opponent's side; so they fell down together. Therefore that place was called the Field of Sharp Swords, which *is* in Gibeon. 17 So there was a very fierce battle that day, and Abner and the men of Israel were beaten before the servants of David.

18 Now the three sons of Zeruiah were there: Joab and Abishai and Asahel. And Asahel *was as* fleet of foot as a wild gazelle. 19 So Asahel pursued Abner, and in going he did not turn to the right hand or to the left from following Abner.

20 Then Abner looked behind him and said, "*Are* you Asahel?"

He answered, "I *am*."

21 And Abner said to him, "Turn aside to your right hand or to your left, and lay hold on one of the young men and take his armor for yourself." But Asahel would not turn aside from following him. 22 So Abner said again to Asahel, "Turn aside from following me. Why should I strike you to the ground? How then could I face your brother Joab?" 23 However, he refused to turn aside. Therefore Abner struck him in the stomach with the blunt end of the spear, so that the spear came out of his back; and he fell down there and died on the spot. So it was *that* as many as came to the place where Asahel fell down and died, stood still.

24 Joab and Abishai also pursued Abner. And the sun was going down when they came to the hill of Ammah, which *is* before Giah by the road to the Wilderness of Gibeon. 25 Now the children of Benjamin gathered together behind Abner and became a unit, and took their stand on top of a hill. 26 Then Abner called to Joab and said, "Shall the sword devour forever? Do you not know that it will be bitter in the latter end? How long will it be then

until you tell the people to return from pursuing their brethren?''

27 And Joab said, ''As God lives, unless you had spoken, surely then by morning all the people would have given up pursuing their brethren.'' 28 So Joab blew a trumpet; and all the people stood still and did not pursue Israel anymore, nor did they fight anymore. 29 Then Abner and his men went on all that night through the plain, crossed over the Jordan, and went through all Bithron; and they came to Mahanaim.

30 So Joab returned from pursuing Abner. And when he had gathered all the people together, there were missing of David's servants nineteen men and Asahel. 31 But the servants of David had struck down, of Benjamin and Abner's men, three hundred and sixty men who died. 32 Then they took up Asahel and buried him in his father's tomb, which was in Bethlehem. And Joab and his men went all night, and they came to Hebron at daybreak.

Abner is killed

3 Now there was a long war between the house of Saul and the house of David. But David grew stronger and stronger, and the house of Saul grew weaker and weaker.

2 Sons were born to David in Hebron: His firstborn was Amnon by Ahinoam the Jezreelitess; 3 his second, Chileab, by Abigail the widow of Nabal the Carmelite; the third, Absalom the son of Maacah, the daughter of Talmai, king of Geshur; 4 the fourth, Adonijah the son of Haggith; the fifth, Shephatiah the son of Abital; 5 and the sixth, Ithream, by David's wife Eglah. These were born to David in Hebron.

6 Now it was so, while there was war between the house of Saul and the house of David, that Abner was strengthening his hold on the house of Saul.

7 And Saul had a concubine, whose name was Rizpah, the daughter of Aiah. So Ishbosheth said to Abner,

''Why have you gone in to my father's concubine?''

8 Then Abner became very angry at the words of Ishbosheth, and said, ''Am I a dog's head that belongs to Judah? Today I show loyalty to the house of Saul your father, to his brothers, and to his friends, and have not delivered you into the hand of David; and you charge me today with a fault concerning this woman? 9 May God do so to Abner, and more also, if I do not do for David as the LORD has sworn to him— 10 to transfer the kingdom from the house of Saul, and set up the throne of David over Israel and over Judah, from Dan to Beersheba.'' 11 And he could not answer Abner another word, because he feared him.

12 Then Abner sent messengers on his behalf to David, saying, ''Whose is the land?'' saying also, ''Make your covenant with me, and indeed my hand shall be with you to bring all Israel to you.''

13 And David said, ''Good, I will make a covenant with you. But one thing I require of you: you shall not see my face unless you first bring Michal, Saul's daughter, when you come to see my face.'' 14 So David sent messengers to Ishbosheth, Saul's son, saying, ''Give me my wife Michal, whom I betrothed to myself for a hundred foreskins of the Philistines.'' 15 And Ishbosheth sent and took her from her husband, from Paltiel the son of Laish. 16 Then her husband went along with her to Bahurim, weeping behind her. So Abner said to him, ''Go, return!'' And he returned.

17 Now Abner had communicated with the elders of Israel, saying, ''In time past you were seeking for David to be king over you. 18 Now then, do it! For the LORD has spoken of David, saying, 'By the hand of My servant David, I will save My people Israel from the hand of the Philistines and the hand of all their enemies.' '' 19 And Abner also spoke in the hearing of Benjamin. Then Abner also went to speak in the hearing of David in Hebron all

that seemed good to Israel and the whole house of Benjamin.

20 So Abner and twenty men with him came to David at Hebron. And David made a feast for Abner and the men who *were* with him. 21 Then Abner said to David, "I will arise and go, and gather all Israel to my lord the king, that they may make a covenant with you, and that you may reign over all that your heart desires." So David sent Abner away, and he went in peace.

22 At that moment the servants of David and Joab came from a raid and brought much spoil with them. But Abner *was* not with David in Hebron, for he had sent him away, and he had gone in peace. 23 When Joab and all the troops that *were* with him had come, they told Joab, saying, "Abner the son of Ner came to the king, and he sent him away, and he has gone in peace." 24 Then Joab came to the king and said, "What have you done? Look, Abner came to you; why *is* it *that* you sent him away, and he has already gone? 25 Surely you realize that Abner the son of Ner came to deceive you, to know your going out and your coming in, and to know all that you are doing."

26 And when Joab had gone from David's presence, he sent messengers after Abner, who brought him back from the well of Sirah. But David did not know *it.* 27 Now when Abner had returned to Hebron, Joab took him aside in the gate to speak with him privately, and there stabbed him in the stomach, so that he died for the blood of Asahel his brother.

28 Afterward, when David heard *it,* he said, "My kingdom and I *are* guiltless before the LORD forever of the blood of Abner the son of Ner. 29 Let it rest on the head of Joab and on all his father's house; and let there never fail to be in the house of Joab one who has a discharge or is a leper, who leans on a staff or falls by the sword, or who lacks bread." 30 So Joab and Abishai his brother killed Abner, be-

cause he had killed their brother Asahel at Gibeon in the battle.

31 Then David said to Joab and to all the people who were with him, "Tear your clothes, gird yourselves with sackcloth, and mourn for Abner." And King David followed the coffin. 32 So they buried Abner in Hebron; and the king lifted up his voice and wept at the grave of Abner, and all the people wept. 33 And the king sang *a lament* over Abner and said:

"Should Abner die as a fool dies?
34   Your hands were not bound
      Nor your feet put into fetters;
      As a man falls before wicked
          men, *so* you fell."

Then all the people wept over him again.

35 And when all the people came to persuade David to eat food while it was still day, David took an oath, saying, "God do so to me, and more also, if I taste bread or anything else till the sun goes down!" 36 Now all the people took note *of it,* and it pleased them, since whatever the king did pleased all the people. 37 For all the people and all Israel understood that day that it had not been the king's *intent* to kill Abner the son of Ner. 38 Then the king said to his servants, "Do you not know that a prince and a great man has fallen this day in Israel? 39 And I *am* weak today, though anointed king; and these men, the sons of Zeruiah, *are* too harsh for me. The LORD shall repay the evildoer according to his wickedness."

Jonathan's little son

4 When Saul's son heard that Abner had died in Hebron, he lost heart, and all Israel was troubled. 2 Now Saul's son *had* two men *who were* captains of troops. The name of one *was* Baanah and the name of the other Rechab, the sons of Rimmon the Beerothite, of the children of Benjamin. (For Beeroth also was *part* of Benjamin, 3 because the Beerothites fled to

Gittaim and have been sojourners there until this day.)

⁴ Jonathan, Saul's son, had a son *who was* lame in *his* feet. He was five years old when the news about Saul and Jonathan came from Jezreel; and his nurse took him up and fled. And it happened, as she made haste to flee, that he fell and became lame. His name *was* Mephibosheth.

⁵ Then the sons of Rimmon the Beerothite, Rechab and Baanah, set out and came at about the heat of the day to the house of Ishbosheth, who was lying on his bed at noon. ⁶ And they came there, all the way into the house, *as though* to get wheat, and they stabbed him in the stomach. Then Rechab and Baanah his brother escaped. ⁷ For when they came into the house, he was lying on his bed in his bedroom; then they struck him and killed him, beheaded him and took his head, and were all night escaping through the plain. ⁸ And they brought the head of Ishbosheth to David at Hebron, and said to the king, "Here is the head of Ishbosheth, the son of Saul your enemy, who sought your life; and the LORD has avenged my lord the king this day of Saul and his descendants."

⁹ But David answered Rechab and Baanah his brother, the sons of Rimmon the Beerothite, and said to them, "As the LORD lives, who has redeemed my life from all adversity, ¹⁰ when someone told me, saying, 'Look, Saul is dead,' thinking to have brought good news, I arrested him and had him executed in Ziklag—the one who *thought* I would give him a reward for *his* news. ¹¹ How much more, when wicked men have killed a righteous person in his own house on his bed? Therefore, shall I not now require his blood at your hand and remove you from the earth?" ¹² So David commanded his young men, and they executed them, cut off their hands and feet, and hanged *them* by the pool in Hebron. But they took the head of Ishbosheth and buried *it* in the tomb of Abner in Hebron.

David, king of all Israel

5 Then all the tribes of Israel came to David at Hebron and spoke, saying, "Indeed we *are* your bone and your flesh. ² Also, in time past, when Saul was king over us, you were the one who led Israel out and brought them in; and the LORD said to you, 'You shall shepherd My people Israel, and be ruler over Israel.' " ³ Therefore all the elders of Israel came to the king at Hebron, and King David made a covenant with them at Hebron before the LORD. And they anointed David king over Israel. ⁴ David *was* thirty years old when he began to reign, *and* he reigned forty years. ⁵ In Hebron he reigned over Judah seven years and six months, and in Jerusalem he reigned thirty-three years over all Israel and Judah.

⁶ And the king and his men went to Jerusalem against the Jebusites, the inhabitants of the land, who spoke to David, saying, "You shall not come in here; but the blind and the lame will repel you," thinking, "David cannot come in here." ⁷ Nevertheless David

---

⛏ DIGGING IN

5:5 David Rules Over All Israel There were 12 tribes, or nations, in the greater nation of Israel. David came from the tribe of Judah, and for seven years, he ruled over that tribe. Then there was a long war between David and the rest of Israel, which was led by the tribe of Benjamin.

At last the other tribes of Israel came and asked David to be their king, too. So David ruled over all 12 tribes of Israel for 33 years. David was a king for 40 years, beginning at about a thousand years before Jesus was born. God called David the man with a heart like His.

As you go through life, you also can have a heart like God's. You can still please Him, even though sometimes you fail as David did.

Young Hebrew King Conquers Jerusalem

ITN (Israel Television Network) (outside the city of Jebus, with King David and the troops)—This city on Mount Zion will soon be a bloody battlefield. David plans to begin his attack at any moment. But the people of Jebus are laughing at him and mocking: "Our lame and blind people will drive you back!"

David has taken the dare! The attack has begun. The air is thick with arrows.

But David's men climb up the wall and break into the city of Jebus. David himself leads the attack. His sword is flashing and darting everywhere.

In less than an hour, David and his soldiers have defeated the army of Jebus. David will rename the place the "City of David," and plans to make it the capital city of Israel. (Today Jebus is called Jerusalem.)

took the stronghold of Zion (that *is,* the City of David).

8 Now David said on that day, "Whoever climbs up by way of the water shaft and defeats the Jebusites (the lame and the blind, *who are* hated by David's soul), *he shall be chief and captain.*" Therefore they say, "The blind and the lame shall not come into the house."

9 Then David dwelt in the stronghold, and called it the City of David. And David built all around from the Millo and inward. 10 So David went on and became great, and the LORD God of hosts *was* with him.

11 Then Hiram king of Tyre sent messengers to David, and cedar trees, and carpenters and masons. And they built David a house. 12 So David knew that the LORD had established him as king over Israel, and that He had exalted His kingdom for the sake of His people Israel.

13 And David took more concubines and wives from Jerusalem, after he had come from Hebron. Also more sons and daughters were born to David. 14 Now these *are* the names of those who were born to him in Jerusalem: Shammua, Shobab, Nathan, Solomon, 15 Ibhar, Elishua, Nepheg, Japhia, 16 Elishama, Eliada, and Eliphelet.

17 Now when the Philistines heard that they had anointed David king over Israel, all the Philistines went up to search for David. And David heard *of it* and went down to the stronghold. 18 The Philistines also went and deployed themselves in the Valley of Rephaim. 19 So David inquired of the LORD, saying, "Shall I go up against the Philistines? Will You deliver them into my hand?"

And the LORD said to David, "Go

The Gihon Spring empties into a tunnel through which David climbed up to conquer Jebus, now called Jerusalem.

up, for I will doubtless deliver the Philistines into your hand."

20 So David went to Baal Perazim, and David defeated them there; and he said, "The LORD has broken through my enemies before me, like a breakthrough of water." Therefore he called the name of that place Baal Perazim. 21 And they left their images there, and David and his men carried them away.

22 Then the Philistines went up once again and deployed themselves in the Valley of Rephaim. 23 Therefore David inquired of the LORD, and He said, "You shall not go up; circle around behind them, and come upon them in front of the mulberry trees. 24 And it shall be, when you hear the sound of marching in the tops of the mulberry trees, then you shall advance quickly. For then the LORD will go out before you to strike the camp of the Philistines." 25 And David did so, as the LORD commanded him; and he drove back the Philistines from Geba as far as Gezer.

David brings back the ark

6 Again David gathered all *the* choice *men* of Israel, thirty thousand. 2 And David arose and went with all the people who *were* with him from Baale Judah to bring up from there the ark of God, whose name is called by the Name, the LORD of Hosts, who dwells *between* the cherubim. 3 So they set the ark of God on a new cart, and brought it out of the house of Abinadab, which *was* on the hill; and Uzzah and Ahio, the sons of Abinadab, drove the new cart. 4 And they brought it out of the house of Abinadab, which *was* on the hill, accompanying the ark of God; and Ahio went before the ark. 5 Then David and all the house of Israel played *music* before the LORD on all kinds of *instruments of* fir wood, on harps, on stringed instruments, on tambourines, on sistrums, and on cymbals.

6 And when they came to Nachon's threshing floor, Uzzah put out *his* hand to the ark of God and took hold of it,

for the oxen stumbled. 7 Then the anger of the LORD was aroused against Uzzah, and God struck him there for *his* error; and he died there by the ark of God. 8 And David became angry because of the LORD's outbreak against Uzzah; and he called the name of the place Perez Uzzah to this day.

9 David was afraid of the LORD that day; and he said, "How can the ark of the LORD come to me?" 10 So David would not move the ark of the LORD with him into the City of David; but David took it aside into the house of Obed-Edom the Gittite. 11 The ark of the LORD remained in the house of Obed-Edom the Gittite three months. And the LORD blessed Obed-Edom and all his household.

12 Now it was told King David, saying, "The LORD has blessed the house of Obed-Edom and all that *belongs* to him, because of the ark of God." So David went and brought up the ark of God from the house of Obed-Edom to the City of David with gladness. 13 And so it was, when those bearing the ark of the LORD had gone six paces, that he sacrificed oxen and fatted sheep. 14 Then David danced before the LORD with all *his* might; and David *was* wearing a linen ephod. 15 So David and all the house of Israel brought up the ark of the LORD with shouting and with the sound of the trumpet.

16 Now as the ark of the LORD came into the City of David, Michal, Saul's daughter, looked through a window and saw King David leaping and whirling before the LORD; and she despised him in her heart. 17 So they brought the ark of the LORD, and set it in its place in the midst of the tabernacle that David had erected for it. Then David offered burnt offerings and peace offerings before the LORD. 18 And when David had finished offering burnt offerings and peace offerings, he blessed the people in the name of the LORD of hosts. 19 Then he distributed among all the people, among the whole multitude of Israel, both the women and the men, to everyone a loaf of bread, a piece *of meat,* and a cake of raisins.

So all the people departed, everyone to his house.

20 Then David returned to bless his household. And Michal the daughter of Saul came out to meet David, and said, "How glorious was the king of Israel today, uncovering himself today in the eyes of the maids of his servants, as one of the base fellows shamelessly uncovers himself!"

21 So David said to Michal, "It was before the LORD, who chose me instead of your father and all his house, to appoint me ruler over the people of the LORD, over Israel. Therefore I will play music before the LORD. 22 And I will be even more undignified than this, and will be humble in my own sight. But as for the maidservants of whom you have spoken, by them I will be held in honor."

23 Therefore Michal the daughter of Saul had no children to the day of her death.

God makes a promise to David

7 Now it came to pass when the king was dwelling in his house, and the LORD had given him rest from all his enemies all around, 2 that the king said to Nathan the prophet, "See now, I dwell in a house of cedar, but the ark of God dwells inside tent curtains."

3 Then Nathan said to the king, "Go, do all that is in your heart, for the LORD is with you."

4 But it happened that night that the word of the LORD came to Nathan, saying, 5 "Go and tell My servant David, 'Thus says the LORD: "Would you build a house for Me to dwell in? 6 For I have not dwelt in a house since the time that I brought the children of Israel up from Egypt, even to this day, but have moved about in a tent and in a tabernacle. 7 Wherever I have moved about with all the children of Israel, have I ever spoken a word to anyone from the tribes of Israel, whom I commanded to shepherd My people Israel, saying, 'Why have you not built Me a house of cedar?' "' 8 Now therefore, thus shall you say to My servant David, 'Thus says the LORD of hosts: "I took you from the sheepfold, from following the sheep, to be ruler over My people, over Israel. 9 And I have been with you wherever you have gone, and have cut off all your enemies from before you, and have made you a great name, like the name of the great men who are on the earth. 10 Moreover I will appoint a place for My people Israel, and will plant them, that they may dwell in a place of their own and move no more; nor shall the sons of wickedness oppress them anymore, as previously, 11 since the time that I commanded judges to be over My people Israel, and have caused you to rest from all your enemies. Also the LORD tells you that He will make you a house.

12 "When your days are fulfilled and you rest with your fathers, I will set up your seed after you, who will come from your body, and I will establish his kingdom. 13 He shall build a house for My name, and I will establish the

DIGGING IN

7:12–15 God's Promise to David David couldn't have dreamed of all that God had planned for him. It was just too much to imagine. Someday—a thousand years later—Jesus would be born to a couple who came from David's family. Saul's throne and David's throne only lasted a while, but the throne of David's great Son would last "forever"! That was God's great promise to David.

As you study your Bible, you will see that this had been God's wonderful idea since the time of Adam and Eve. God would send a Savior who would take away all our sins. But this Savior would be more than just the son of Adam and Eve. He would be more than the son of Abraham and Sarah. He would be more than the son of David. He would be the Son of God. The Son of God Himself, who had lived forever in heaven, would reign from a throne that would last forever and ever. That was God's master plan.

throne of his kingdom forever. 14 I will be his Father, and he shall be My son. If he commits iniquity, I will chasten him with the rod of men and with the blows of the sons of men. 15 But My mercy shall not depart from him, as I took *it* from Saul, whom I removed from before you. 16 And your house and your kingdom shall be established forever before you. Your throne shall be established forever." ' "

17 According to all these words and according to all this vision, so Nathan spoke to David.

18 Then King David went in and sat before the LORD; and he said: "Who *am* I, O Lord GOD? And what is my house, that You have brought me this far? 19 And yet this was a small thing in Your sight, O Lord GOD; and You have also spoken of Your servant's house for a great while to come. *Is* this the manner of man, O Lord GOD? 20 Now what more can David say to You? For You, Lord GOD, know Your servant. 21 For Your word's sake, and according to Your own heart, You have done all these great things, to make Your servant know *them*. 22 Therefore You are great, O Lord GOD. For *there is* none like You, nor *is there any* God besides You, according to all that we have heard with our ears. 23 And who *is* like Your people, like Israel, the one nation on the earth whom God went to redeem for Himself as a people, to make for Himself a name—and to do for Yourself great and awesome deeds for Your land— before Your people whom You redeemed for Yourself from Egypt, the nations, and their gods? 24 For You have made Your people Israel Your very own people forever; and You, LORD, have become their God.

25 "Now, O LORD God, the word which You have spoken concerning Your servant and concerning his house, establish *it* forever and do as You have said. 26 So let Your name be magnified forever, saying, 'The LORD of hosts *is* the God over Israel.' And let the house of Your servant David be established before You. 27 For

You, O LORD of hosts, God of Israel, have revealed *this* to Your servant, saying, 'I will build you a house.' Therefore Your servant has found it in his heart to pray this prayer to You.

28 "And now, O Lord GOD, You are God, and Your words are true, and You have promised this goodness to Your servant. 29 Now therefore, let it please You to bless the house of Your servant, that it may continue before You forever; for You, O Lord GOD, have spoken *it,* and with Your blessing let the house of Your servant be blessed forever."

David adds to his kingdom

8 After this it came to pass that David attacked the Philistines and subdued them. And David took Metheg Ammah from the hand of the Philistines.

2 Then he defeated Moab. Forcing them down to the ground, he measured them off with a line. With two lines he measured off those to be put to death, and with one full line those to be kept alive. So the Moabites became David's servants, *and* brought tribute.

3 David also defeated Hadadezer the son of Rehob, king of Zobah, as he went to recover his territory at the River Euphrates. 4 David took from him one thousand *chariots,* seven hundred horsemen, and twenty thousand foot soldiers. Also David hamstrung all the chariot horses, *except* that he spared *enough* of them for one hundred chariots.

5 When the Syrians of Damascus came to help Hadadezer king of Zobah, David killed twenty-two thousand of the Syrians. 6 Then David put garrisons in Syria of Damascus; and the Syrians became David's servants, *and* brought tribute. So the LORD preserved David wherever he went. 7 And David took the shields of gold that had belonged to the servants of Hadadezer, and brought them to Jerusalem. 8 Also from Betah and from Berothai, cities of Hadadezer, King David took a large amount of bronze.

I was five years old when my father Jonathan and my grandfather Saul were killed in battle. When my nurse was trying to save me, I fell and became lame for the rest of my life. My name is pronounced *meh-FIB-oh-sheth*.

Long before this, David had promised he would always take care of my father's family. (See 1 Samuel 20:14, 15.) David and my father had loved each other like brothers.

David kept his promise. He gave me all of my grandfather's property. Saul's servants would now farm the family's land for me while I lived at King David's palace like one of his own sons.

King David was not always right in what he did, but he truly loved God. Sometimes you can see that he is like his greater Son Jesus. Like Jesus, David forgave his enemies and was kind to them. (See Luke 23:34.) David was kind to me, too.

9 When Toi king of Hamath heard that David had defeated all the army of Hadadezer, 10 then Toi sent Joram his son to King David, to greet him and bless him, because he had fought against Hadadezer and defeated him (for Hadadezer had been at war with Toi); and *Joram* brought with him articles of silver, articles of gold, and articles of bronze. 11 King David also dedicated these to the LORD, along with the silver and gold that he had dedicated from all the nations which he had subdued— 12 from Syria, from Moab, from the people of Ammon, from the Philistines, from Amalek, and from the spoil of Hadadezer the son of Rehob, king of Zobah.

13 And David made *himself* a name when he returned from killing eighteen thousand Syrians in the Valley of Salt. 14 He also put garrisons in Edom; throughout all Edom he put garrisons, and all the Edomites became David's servants. And the LORD preserved David wherever he went.

15 So David reigned over all Israel; and David administered judgment and justice to all his people. 16 Joab the son of Zeruiah *was* over the army; Jehoshaphat the son of Ahilud *was* recorder; 17 Zadok the son of Ahitub and Ahimelech the son of Abiathar *were* the priests; Seraiah *was* the scribe; 18 Benaiah the son of Jehoiada *was* over both the Cherethites and the Pe-

lethites; and David's sons were chief ministers.

David is kind to Jonathan's lame son

9 Now David said, "Is there still anyone who is left of the house of Saul, that I may show him kindness for Jonathan's sake?"

2 And *there was* a servant of the house of Saul whose name *was* Ziba. So when they had called him to David, the king said to him, "*Are* you Ziba?"

He said, "At your service!"

3 Then the king said, "*Is* there not still someone of the house of Saul, to whom I may show the kindness of God?"

And Ziba said to the king, "There is still a son of Jonathan *who is* lame in *his* feet."

4 So the king said to him, "Where *is* he?"

And Ziba said to the king, "Indeed he *is* in the house of Machir the son of Ammiel, in Lo Debar."

5 Then King David sent and brought him out of the house of Machir the son of Ammiel, from Lo Debar.

6 Now when Mephibosheth the son of Jonathan, the son of Saul, had come to David, he fell on his face and prostrated himself. Then David said, "Mephibosheth?"

And he answered, "Here is your servant!"

7 So David said to him, "Do not fear, for I will surely show you kindness for Jonathan your father's sake, and will restore to you all the land of Saul your grandfather; and you shall eat bread at my table continually."

8 Then he bowed himself, and said, "What is your servant, that you should look upon such a dead dog as I?"

9 And the king called to Ziba, Saul's servant, and said to him, "I have given to your master's son all that belonged to Saul and to all his house. 10 You therefore, and your sons and your servants, shall work the land for him, and you shall bring in the harvest, that your master's son may have food to eat. But Mephibosheth your master's son shall eat bread at my table always." Now Ziba had fifteen sons and twenty servants.

11 Then Ziba said to the king, "According to all that my lord the king has commanded his servant, so will your servant do."

"As for Mephibosheth," said the king, "he shall eat at my table like one of the king's sons." 12 Mephibosheth had a young son whose name was Micha. And all who dwelt in the house of Ziba were servants of Mephibosheth. 13 So Mephibosheth dwelt in Jerusalem, for he ate continually at the king's table. And he was lame in both his feet.

David defeats his enemies

10 It happened after this that the king of the people of Ammon died, and Hanun his son reigned in his place. 2 Then David said, "I will show kindness to Hanun the son of Nahash, as his father showed kindness to me."

So David sent by the hand of his servants to comfort him concerning his father. And David's servants came into the land of the people of Ammon. 3 And the princes of the people of Ammon said to Hanun their lord, "Do you think that David really honors your father because he has sent comforters

to you? Has David not rather sent his servants to you to search the city, to spy it out, and to overthrow it?"

4 Therefore Hanun took David's servants, shaved off half of their beards, cut off their garments in the middle, at their buttocks, and sent them away. 5 When they told David, he sent to meet them, because the men were greatly ashamed. And the king said, "Wait at Jericho until your beards have grown, and then return."

6 When the people of Ammon saw that they had made themselves repulsive to David, the people of Ammon sent and hired the Syrians of Beth Rehob and the Syrians of Zoba, twenty thousand foot soldiers; and from the king of Maacah one thousand men, and from Ish-Tob twelve thousand men. 7 Now when David heard of it, he sent Joab and all the army of the mighty men. 8 Then the people of Ammon came out and put themselves in battle array at the entrance of the gate. And the Syrians of Zoba, Beth Rehob, Ish-Tob, and Maacah were by themselves in the field.

9 When Joab saw that the battle line was against him before and behind, he chose some of Israel's best and put them in battle array against the Syrians. 10 And the rest of the people he put under the command of Abishai his brother, that he might set them in battle array against the people of Ammon. 11 Then he said, "If the Syrians are too strong for me, then you shall help me; but if the people of Ammon are too strong for you, then I will come and help you. 12 Be of good courage, and let us be strong for our people and for the cities of our God. And may the LORD do what is good in His sight."

13 So Joab and the people who were with him drew near for the battle against the Syrians, and they fled before him. 14 When the people of Ammon saw that the Syrians were fleeing, they also fled before Abishai, and entered the city. So Joab returned from the people of Ammon and went to Jerusalem.

15 When the Syrians saw that they

Bathsheba—My name is pronounced *bath-SHE-bah*. I was the wife of Uriah (pronounced *you-RIGH-uh*), a soldier in King David's army. I was all that poor Uriah had, but David stole me from him. David also arranged to have Uriah killed in battle, so that he could feel free to take me as his own wife.

The prophet Nathan (pronounced *NAY-thun*) finally accused David of his great sin (see 2 Samuel 12), and David had to confess, "I have sinned." Our innocent infant son died because of what David had done. A thousand years later, David's greater Son, Jesus, would die for the sins of the whole world.

David was sorry for his sins. Then God gave us a new son, whose name was Solomon, meaning "Peaceful." Yes, the Lord did make peace with David. Solomon grew up to be king of Israel, the greatest country in the world of that day.

had been defeated by Israel, they gathered together. 16 Then Hadadezer sent and brought out the Syrians who *were* beyond the River, and they came to Helam. And Shobach the commander of Hadadezer's army *went* before them. 17 When it was told David, he gathered all Israel, crossed over the Jordan, and came to Helam. And the Syrians set themselves in battle array against David and fought with him. 18 Then the Syrians fled before Israel; and David killed seven hundred charioteers and forty thousand horsemen of the Syrians, and struck Shobach the commander of their army, who died there. 19 And when all the kings *who were* servants to Hadadezer saw that they were defeated by Israel, they made peace with Israel and served them. So the Syrians were afraid to help the people of Ammon anymore.

David and Bathsheba

11 It happened in the spring of the year, at the time when kings go out *to battle*, that David sent Joab and his servants with him, and all Israel; and they destroyed the people of Ammon and besieged Rabbah. But David remained at Jerusalem.

2 Then it happened one evening that David arose from his bed and walked on the roof of the king's house. And from the roof he saw a woman bathing, and the woman *was* very beautiful to behold. 3 So David sent and inquired about the woman. And *someone* said, "*Is* this not Bathsheba, the daughter of Eliam, the wife of Uriah the Hittite?" 4 Then David sent messengers, and took her; and she came to him, and he lay with her, for she was cleansed from her impurity; and she returned to her house. 5 And the woman conceived; so she sent and told David, and said, "I *am* with child."

6 Then David sent to Joab, *saying,* "Send me Uriah the Hittite." And Joab sent Uriah to David. 7 When Uriah had come to him, David asked how Joab was doing, and how the people were doing, and how the war prospered. 8 And David said to Uriah, "Go down to your house and wash your feet." So Uriah departed from the king's house, and a gift *of food* from the king followed him. 9 But Uriah slept at the door of the king's house with all the servants of his lord, and did not go down to his house. 10 So when they told David, saying, "Uriah did not go down to his house," David said to Uriah, "Did you not come from a journey? Why did you not go down to your house?"

11 And Uriah said to David, "The ark and Israel and Judah are dwelling in tents, and my lord Joab and the

servants of my lord are encamped in the open fields. Shall I then go to my house to eat and drink, and to lie with my wife? As you live, and as your soul lives, I will not do this thing."

12 Then David said to Uriah, "Wait here today also, and tomorrow I will let you depart." So Uriah remained in Jerusalem that day and the next. 13 Now when David called him, he ate and drank before him; and he made him drunk. And at evening he went out to lie on his bed with the servants of his lord, but he did not go down to his house.

14 In the morning it happened that David wrote a letter to Joab and sent it by the hand of Uriah. 15 And he wrote in the letter, saying, "Set Uriah in the forefront of the hottest battle, and retreat from him, that he may be struck down and die." 16 So it was, while Joab besieged the city, that he assigned Uriah to a place where he knew there were valiant men. 17 Then the men of the city came out and fought with Joab. And some of the people of the servants of David fell; and Uriah the Hittite died also.

18 Then Joab sent and told David all the things concerning the war, 19 and charged the messenger, saying, "When you have finished telling the matters of the war to the king, 20 if it happens that the king's wrath rises, and he says to you: 'Why did you approach so near to the city when you fought? Did you not know that they would shoot from the wall? 21 Who struck Abimelech the son of Jerubbesheth? Was it not a woman who cast a piece of a millstone on him from the wall, so that he died in Thebez? Why did you go near the wall?'—then you shall say, 'Your servant Uriah the Hittite is dead also.'"

22 So the messenger went, and came and told David all that Joab had sent by him. 23 And the messenger said to David, "Surely the men prevailed against us and came out to us in the field; then we drove them back as far as the entrance of the gate. 24 The archers shot from the wall at your ser-

vants; and some of the king's servants are dead, and your servant Uriah the Hittite is dead also."

25 Then David said to the messenger, "Thus you shall say to Joab: 'Do not let this thing displease you, for the sword devours one as well as another. Strengthen your attack against the city, and overthrow it.' So encourage him."

26 When the wife of Uriah heard that Uriah her husband was dead, she mourned for her husband. 27 And when her mourning was over, David sent and brought her to his house, and she became his wife and bore him a son. But the thing that David had done displeased the LORD.

Nathan accuses David

12 Then the LORD sent Nathan to David. And he came to him, and said to him: "There were two men in one city, one rich and the other poor. 2 The rich man had exceedingly many flocks and herds. 3 But the poor man had nothing, except one little ewe lamb which he had bought and nourished; and it grew up together with him and with his children. It ate of his own food and drank from his own cup and lay in his bosom; and it was like a daughter to him. 4 And a traveler came to the rich man, who refused to take from his own flock and from his own herd to prepare one for the wayfaring man who had come to him; but he took the poor man's lamb and prepared it for the man who had come to him."

5 So David's anger was greatly aroused against the man, and he said to Nathan, "As the LORD lives, the man who has done this shall surely die! 6 And he shall restore fourfold for the lamb, because he did this thing and because he had no pity."

7 Then Nathan said to David, "You are the man! Thus says the LORD God of Israel: 'I anointed you king over Israel, and I delivered you from the hand of Saul. 8 I gave you your master's house and your master's wives into your keeping, and gave you the house of Israel and Judah. And if that had

What King David Learned

The Lord had shown me every kindness. He had taken me from being a poor shepherd boy to make me king of Israel. Then I began to imagine I should have anything I wanted. I already had too many wives. I should have made peace with my wife Michal (pronounced *MY-kul*), Saul's daughter.

Instead, I took another man's wife as well. For a long time I thought nobody knew I had also arranged her husband's death. Then the prophet Nathan told me the truth about myself. I was a murderer and an adulterer! How could God forgive me?

Because of this, I wrote the prayer in Psalm 51. Although I didn't deserve it, the Lord actually forgave me. If He could forgive me, He will forgive all who truly confess their sins.

been too little, I also would have given you much more! 9 Why have you despised the commandment of the Lord, to do evil in His sight? You have killed Uriah the Hittite with the sword; you have taken his wife *to be* your wife, and have killed him with the sword of the people of Ammon. 10 Now therefore, the sword shall never depart from your house, because you have despised Me, and have taken the wife of Uriah the Hittite to be your wife.' 11 Thus says the Lord: 'Behold, I will raise up adversity against you from your own house; and I will take your wives before your eyes and give *them* to your neighbor, and he shall lie with your wives in the sight of this sun. 12 For you did *it* secretly, but I will do this thing before all Israel, before the sun.' "

13 So David said to Nathan, "I have sinned against the Lord."

And Nathan said to David, "The Lord also has put away your sin; you shall not die. 14 However, because by this deed you have given great occasion to the enemies of the Lord to blaspheme, the child also *who is* born to you shall surely die." 15 Then Nathan departed to his house.

And the Lord struck the child that Uriah's wife bore to David, and it became ill. 16 David therefore pleaded with God for the child, and David fasted and went in and lay all night on the ground. 17 So the elders of his house arose *and went* to him, to raise him up from the ground. But he would not, nor did he eat food with them. 18 Then on the seventh day it came to pass that the child died. And the servants of David were afraid to tell him that the child was dead. For they said, "Indeed, while the child was alive, we spoke to him, and he would not heed our voice. How can we tell him that the child is dead? He may do some harm!"

19 When David saw that his servants were whispering, David perceived that the child was dead. Therefore David said to his servants, "Is the child dead?"

And they said, "He is dead."

20 So David arose from the ground, washed and anointed himself, and changed his clothes; and he went into the house of the Lord and worshiped. Then he went to his own house; and when he requested, they set food before him, and he ate. 21 Then his servants said to him, "What *is* this that you have done? You fasted and wept for the child *while he was* alive, but when the child died, you arose and ate food."

22 And he said, "While the child was

alive, I fasted and wept; for I said, 'Who can tell *whether* the LORD will be gracious to me, that the child may live?' 23 But now he is dead; why should I fast? Can I bring him back again? I shall go to him, but he shall not return to me."

24 Then David comforted Bathsheba his wife, and went in to her and lay with her. So she bore a son, and he called his name Solomon. Now the LORD loved him, 25 and He sent *word* by the hand of Nathan the prophet: So he called his name Jedidiah, because of the LORD.

26 Now Joab fought against Rabbah of the people of Ammon, and took the royal city. 27 And Joab sent messengers to David, and said, "I have fought against Rabbah, and I have taken the city's water *supply.* 28 Now therefore, gather the rest of the people together and encamp against the city and take it, lest I take the city and it be called after my name." 29 So David gathered all the people together and went to Rabbah, fought against it, and took it. 30 Then he took their king's crown from his head. Its weight *was* a talent of gold, with precious stones. And it was *set* on David's head. Also he brought out the spoil of the city in great abundance. 31 And he brought out the people who *were* in it, and put *them to work* with saws and iron picks and iron axes, and made them cross over to the brick works. So he did to all the cities of the people of Ammon. Then David and all the people returned to Jerusalem.

Amnon sins against Tamar

13 After this Absalom the son of David had a lovely sister, whose name *was* Tamar; and Amnon the son of David loved her. 2 Amnon was so distressed over his sister Tamar that he became sick; for she *was* a virgin. And it was improper for Amnon to do anything to her. 3 But Amnon had a friend whose name *was* Jonadab the son of Shimeah, David's brother. Now Jonadab *was* a very crafty man. 4 And he

said to him, "Why *are* you, the king's son, becoming thinner day after day? Will you not tell me?"

Amnon said to him, "I love Tamar, my brother Absalom's sister."

5 So Jonadab said to him, "Lie down on your bed and pretend to be ill. And when your father comes to see you, say to him, 'Please let my sister Tamar come and give me food, and prepare the food in my sight, that I may *see it* and eat it from her hand.' " 6 Then Amnon lay down and pretended to be ill; and when the king came to see him, Amnon said to the king, "Please let Tamar my sister come and make a couple of cakes for me in my sight, that I may eat from her hand."

7 And David sent home to Tamar, saying, "Now go to your brother Amnon's house, and prepare food for him." 8 So Tamar went to her brother Amnon's house; and he was lying down. Then she took flour and kneaded *it,* made cakes in his sight, and baked the cakes. 9 And she took the pan and placed *them* out before him, but he refused to eat. Then Amnon said, "Have everyone go out from me." And they all went out from him. 10 Then Amnon said to Tamar, "Bring the food into the bedroom, that I may eat from your hand." And Tamar took the cakes which she had made, and brought *them* to Amnon her brother in the bedroom. 11 Now when she had brought *them* to him to eat, he took hold of her and said to her, "Come, lie with me, my sister."

12 But she answered him, "No, my brother, do not force me, for no such thing should be done in Israel. Do not do this disgraceful thing! 13 And I, where could I take my shame? And as for you, you would be like one of the fools in Israel. Now therefore, please speak to the king; for he will not withhold me from you." 14 However, he would not heed her voice; and being stronger than she, he forced her and lay with her.

15 Then Amnon hated her exceedingly, so that the hatred with which he

---

King's Son Murdered!

The Jerusalem Times

JERUSALEM—King David is reeling in the face of several tragedies that have struck him and his family in a matter of weeks.

Some years ago, the king was accused of a serious sin with the wife of a well-known officer. Now, two of King David's sons are dead.

Reports have trickled in that Absalom (pronounced *AB-sah-lum*) led his brother, Amnon (pronounced *AM-non*), into a trap and killed him. Revenge is the suspected motive, since Amnon is known to have mistreated their sister, Tamar (pronounced *TAY-mer*).

Heartbroken over Amnon's death, King David had been hoping to make peace with his remaining son. Later, however, Absalom made war against David and was killed in a bizarre accident on horseback.

Despite reports that he is far from perfect, King David's popularity has increased. He is loved by his people and by God alike.

---

hated her *was* greater than the love with which he had loved her. And Amnon said to her, "Arise, be gone!"

16 So she said to him, "No, indeed! This evil of sending me away *is* worse than the other that you did to me."

But he would not listen to her. 17 Then he called his servant who attended him, and said, "Here! Put this *woman* out, away from me, and bolt the door behind her." 18 Now she had on a robe of many colors, for the king's virgin daughters wore such apparel. And his servant put her out and bolted the door behind her.

19 Then Tamar put ashes on her head, and tore her robe of many colors that *was* on her, and laid her hand on her head and went away crying bitterly. 20 And Absalom her brother said to her, "Has Amnon your brother been with you? But now hold your peace, my sister. He *is* your brother; do not take this thing to heart." So Tamar remained desolate in her brother Absalom's house.

21 But when King David heard of all these things, he was very angry. 22 And Absalom spoke to his brother Amnon neither good nor bad. For Absalom hated Amnon, because he had forced his sister Tamar.

23 And it came to pass, after two full years, that Absalom had sheepshearers in Baal Hazor, which *is* near Ephraim; so Absalom invited all the king's sons. 24 Then Absalom came to the king and said, "Kindly note, your servant has sheepshearers; please, let the king and his servants go with your servant."

25 But the king said to Absalom, "No, my son, let us not all go now, lest we be a burden to you." Then he urged him, but he would not go; and he blessed him.

26 Then Absalom said, "If not, please let my brother Amnon go with us."

And the king said to him, "Why should he go with you?" 27 But Absalom urged him; so he let Amnon and all the king's sons go with him.

28 Now Absalom had commanded his servants, saying, "Watch now, when Amnon's heart is merry with wine, and when I say to you, 'Strike Amnon!' then kill him. Do not be afraid. Have I not commanded you? Be courageous and valiant." 29 So the servants of Absalom did to Amnon as Absalom had commanded. Then all the king's sons arose, and each one got on his mule and fled.

30 And it came to pass, while they were on the way, that news came to David, saying, "Absalom has killed all

the king's sons, and not one of them is left!'' 31 So the king arose and tore his garments and lay on the ground, and all his servants stood by with their clothes torn. 32 Then Jonadab the son of Shimeah, David's brother, answered and said, "Let not my lord suppose they have killed all the young men, the king's sons, for only Amnon is dead. For by the command of Absalom this has been determined from the day that he forced his sister Tamar. 33 Now therefore, let not my lord the king take the thing to his heart, to think that all the king's sons are dead. For only Amnon is dead.''

34 Then Absalom fled. And the young man who was keeping watch lifted his eyes and looked, and there, many people were coming from the road on the hillside behind him. 35 And Jonadab said to the king, "Look, the king's sons are coming; as your servant said, so it is.'' 36 So it was, as soon as he had finished speaking, that the king's sons indeed came, and they lifted up their voice and wept. Also the king and all his servants wept very bitterly.

37 But Absalom fled and went to Talmai the son of Ammihud, king of Geshur. And *David* mourned for his son every day. 38 So Absalom fled and went to Geshur, and was there three years. 39 And King David longed to go to Absalom. For he had been comforted concerning Amnon, because he was dead.

Joab has a plan

14 So Joab the son of Zeruiah perceived that the king's heart *was* concerned about Absalom. 2 And Joab sent to Tekoa and brought from there a wise woman, and said to her, "Please pretend to be a mourner, and put on mourning apparel; do not anoint yourself with oil, but act like a woman who has been mourning a long time for the dead. 3 Go to the king and speak to him in this manner.'' So Joab put the words in her mouth.

4 And when the woman of Tekoa spoke to the king, she fell on her face to the ground and prostrated herself, and said, "Help, O king!''

5 Then the king said to her, "What troubles you?''

And she answered, "Indeed I *am* a widow, my husband is dead. 6 Now your maidservant had two sons; and the two fought with each other in the field, and *there was* no one to part them, but the one struck the other and killed him. 7 And now the whole family has risen up against your maidservant, and they said, 'Deliver him who struck his brother, that we may execute him for the life of his brother whom he killed; and we will destroy the heir also.' So they would extinguish my ember that is left, and leave to my husband *neither* name nor remnant on the earth.''

8 Then the king said to the woman, "Go to your house, and I will give orders concerning you.''

9 And the woman of Tekoa said to the king, "My lord, O king, *let* the iniquity *be* on me and on my father's house, and the king and his throne *be* guiltless.''

10 So the king said, "Whoever says *anything* to you, bring him to me, and he shall not touch you anymore.''

11 Then she said, "Please let the king remember the LORD your God, and do not permit the avenger of blood to destroy anymore, lest they destroy my son.''

And he said, "As the LORD lives, not one hair of your son shall fall to the ground.''

12 Therefore the woman said, "Please, let your maidservant speak *another* word to my lord the king.''

And he said, "Say on.''

13 So the woman said: "Why then have you schemed such a thing against the people of God? For the king speaks this thing as one who is guilty, *in that* the king does not bring his banished one home again. 14 For we will surely die and *become* like water spilled on the ground, which cannot be gathered up again. Yet God does not take away a life; but He devises means, so that

His banished ones are not expelled from Him. 15 Now therefore, I have come to speak of this thing to my lord the king because the people have made me afraid. And your maidservant said, 'I will now speak to the king; it may be that the king will perform the request of his maidservant. 16 For the king will hear and deliver his maidservant from the hand of the man *who would* destroy me and my son together from the inheritance of God.' 17 Your maidservant said, 'The word of my lord the king will now be comforting; for as the angel of God, so *is* my lord the king in discerning good and evil. And may the Lord your God be with you.' "

18 Then the king answered and said to the woman, "Please do not hide from me anything that I ask you."

And the woman said, "Please, let my lord the king speak."

19 So the king said, "*Is* the hand of Joab with you in all this?" And the woman answered and said, "*As* you live, my lord the king, no one can turn to the right hand or to the left from anything that my lord the king has spoken. For your servant Joab commanded me, and he put all these words in the mouth of your maidservant. 20 To bring about this change of affairs your servant Joab has done this thing; but my lord *is* wise, according to the wisdom of the angel of God, to know everything that *is* in the earth."

21 And the king said to Joab, "All right, I have granted this thing. Go therefore, bring back the young man Absalom."

22 Then Joab fell to the ground on his face and bowed himself, and thanked the king. And Joab said, "Today your servant knows that I have found favor in your sight, my lord, O king, in that the king has fulfilled the request of his servant." 23 So Joab arose and went to Geshur, and brought Absalom to Jerusalem. 24 And the king said, "Let him return to his own house, but do not let him *see* my face." So Absalom returned to his own house, but did not *see* the king's face.

25 Now in all Israel there was no one who was praised as much as Absalom for his good looks. From the sole of his foot to the crown of his head there was no blemish in him. 26 And when he cut the hair of his head—at the end of *every* year he cut *it* because it was heavy on him—when he cut it, he weighed the hair of his head at two hundred shekels according to the king's standard. 27 To Absalom were born three sons, and one daughter whose name *was* Tamar. She was a woman of beautiful appearance.

28 And Absalom dwelt two full years in Jerusalem, but did not see the king's face. 29 Therefore Absalom sent for Joab, to send him to the king, but he would not come to him. And when he sent again the second time, he would not come. 30 So he said to his servants, "See, Joab's field is near mine, and he has barley there; go and set it on fire." And Absalom's servants set the field on fire.

31 Then Joab arose and came to Absalom's house, and said to him, "Why have your servants set my field on fire?"

32 And Absalom answered Joab, "Look, I sent to you, saying, 'Come here, so that I may send you to the king, to say, "Why have I come from Geshur? *It would be* better for me *to be* there still." ' Now therefore, let me see the king's face; but if there is iniquity in me, let him execute me."

33 So Joab went to the king and told him. And when he had called for Absalom, he came to the king and bowed himself on his face to the ground before the king. Then the king kissed Absalom.

David leaves Jerusalem

15 After this it happened that Absalom provided himself with chariots and horses, and fifty men to run before him. 2 Now Absalom would rise early and stand beside the way to the gate. *So* it was, whenever anyone who had a lawsuit came to the king for a

decision, that Absalom would call to him and say, "What city *are* you from?" And he would say, "Your servant *is* from such and such a tribe of Israel." ³ Then Absalom would say to him, "Look, your case *is* good and right; but *there is* no deputy of the king to hear you." ⁴ Moreover Absalom would say, "Oh, that I were made judge in the land, and everyone who has any suit or cause would come to me; then I would give him justice." ⁵ And *so* it was, whenever anyone came near to bow down to him, that he would put out his hand and take him and kiss him. ⁶ In this manner Absalom acted toward all Israel who came to the king for judgment. So Absalom stole the hearts of the men of Israel.

⁷ Now it came to pass after forty years that Absalom said to the king, "Please, let me go to Hebron and pay the vow which I made to the LORD. ⁸ For your servant took a vow while I dwelt at Geshur in Syria, saying, 'If the LORD indeed brings me back to Jerusalem, then I will serve the LORD.'"

⁹ And the king said to him, "Go in peace." So he arose and went to Hebron.

¹⁰ Then Absalom sent spies throughout all the tribes of Israel, saying, "As soon as you hear the sound of the trumpet, then you shall say, 'Absalom reigns in Hebron!'" ¹¹ And with Absalom went two hundred men invited from Jerusalem, and they went along innocently and did not know anything. ¹² Then Absalom sent for Ahithophel the Gilonite, David's counselor, from his city—from Giloh—while he offered sacrifices. And the conspiracy grew strong, for the people with Absalom continually increased in number.

¹³ Now a messenger came to David, saying, "The hearts of the men of Israel are with Absalom."

¹⁴ So David said to all his servants who *were* with him at Jerusalem, "Arise, and let us flee, or we shall not escape from Absalom. Make haste to depart, lest he overtake us suddenly and bring disaster upon us, and strike the city with the edge of the sword."

¹⁵ And the king's servants said to the king, "We *are* your servants, *ready to do* whatever my lord the king commands." ¹⁶ Then the king went out with all his household after him. But the king left ten women, concubines, to keep the house. ¹⁷ And the king went out with all the people after him, and stopped at the outskirts. ¹⁸ Then all his servants passed before him; and all the Cherethites, all the Pelethites, and all the Gittites, six hundred men who had followed him from Gath, passed before the king.

¹⁹ Then the king said to Ittai the Gittite, "Why are you also going with us? Return and remain with the king. For you *are* a foreigner and also an exile from your own place. ²⁰ In fact, you came *only* yesterday. Should I make you wander up and down with us today, since I go I know not where? Return, and take your brethren back. Mercy and truth *be* with you."

²¹ But Ittai answered the king and said, "As the LORD lives, and *as* my lord the king lives, surely in whatever place my lord the king shall be, whether in death or life, even there also your servant will be."

²² So David said to Ittai, "Go, and cross over." Then Ittai the Gittite and all his men and all the little ones who *were* with him crossed over. ²³ And all the country wept with a loud voice, and all the people crossed over. The king himself also crossed over the Brook Kidron, and all the people crossed over toward the way of the wilderness.

²⁴ There was Zadok also, and all the Levites with him, bearing the ark of the covenant of God. And they set down the ark of God, and Abiathar went up until all the people had finished crossing over from the city. ²⁵ Then the king said to Zadok, "Carry the ark of God back into the city. If I find favor in the eyes of the LORD, He will bring me back and show me *both* it and His dwelling place. ²⁶ But if He says thus: 'I have no delight in you,' here I am, let Him do to me as seems good to Him." ²⁷ The king also said

to Zadok the priest, "*Are* you *not* a seer? Return to the city in peace, and your two sons with you, Ahimaaz your son, and Jonathan the son of Abiathar. 28 See, I will wait in the plains of the wilderness until word comes from you to inform me." 29 Therefore Zadok and Abiathar carried the ark of God back to Jerusalem. And they remained there.

30 So David went up by the Ascent of the *Mount of* Olives, and wept as he went up; and he had his head covered and went barefoot. And all the people who *were* with him covered their heads and went up, weeping as they went up. 31 Then *someone* told David, saying, "Ahithophel *is* among the conspirators with Absalom." And David said, "O Lord, I pray, turn the counsel of Ahithophel into foolishness!"

32 Now it happened when David had come to the top *of the mountain,* where he worshiped God—there was Hushai the Archite coming to meet him with his robe torn and dust on his head. 33 David said to him, "If you go on with me, then you will become a burden to me. 34 But if you return to the city, and say to Absalom, 'I will be your servant, O king; *as* I *was* your father's servant previously, so I *will* now also *be* your servant,' then you may defeat the counsel of Ahithophel for me. 35 And *do* you not *have* Zadok and Abiathar the priests with you there? Therefore it will be *that* whatever you hear from the king's house, you shall tell to Zadok and Abiathar the priests. 36 Indeed *they have* there with them their two sons, Ahimaaz, Zadok's *son,* and Jonathan, Abiathar's *son;* and by them you shall *send* me everything you hear."

37 So Hushai, David's friend, went into the city. And Absalom came into Jerusalem.

Absalom enters Jerusalem

16 When David was a little past the top *of the mountain,* there was Ziba the servant of Mephibosheth, who met him with a couple of saddled donkeys, and on them two hundred *loaves* of bread, one hundred clusters of raisins, one hundred summer fruits, and a skin of wine. 2 And the king said to Ziba, "What do you mean to do with these?"

So Ziba said, "The donkeys *are* for the king's household to ride on, the bread and summer fruit for the young men to eat, and the wine for those who are faint in the wilderness to drink."

3 Then the king said, "And where *is* your master's son?"

And Ziba said to the king, "Indeed he is staying in Jerusalem, for he said, 'Today the house of Israel will restore the kingdom of my father to me.' "

4 So the king said to Ziba, "Here, all that *belongs* to Mephibosheth *is* yours."

And Ziba said, "I humbly bow before you, *that* I may find favor in your sight, my lord, O king!"

5 Now when King David came to Bahurim, there was a man from the family of the house of Saul, whose name *was* Shimei the son of Gera, coming from there. He came out, cursing continuously as he came. 6 And he threw stones at David and at all the servants of King David. And all the people and all the mighty men *were* on his right hand and on his left. 7 Also Shimei said thus when he cursed: "Come out! Come out! You bloodthirsty man, you rogue! 8 The Lord has brought upon you all the blood of the house of Saul, in whose place you have reigned; and the Lord has delivered the kingdom into the hand of Absalom your son. So now you *are caught* in your own evil, because you are a bloodthirsty man!"

9 Then Abishai the son of Zeruiah said to the king, "Why should this dead dog curse my lord the king? Please, let me go over and take off his head!"

10 But the king said, "What have I to do with you, you sons of Zeruiah? So let him curse, because the Lord has said to him, 'Curse David.' Who then shall say, 'Why have you done so?' "

11 And David said to Abishai and all his servants, "See how my son who came from my own body seeks my life. How much more now *may this* Benjamite? Let him alone, and let him curse; for so the LORD has ordered him. 12 It may be that the LORD will look on my affliction, and that the LORD will repay me with good for his cursing this day." 13 And as David and his men went along the road, Shimei went along the hillside opposite him and cursed as he went, threw stones at him and kicked up dust. 14 Now the king and all the people who *were* with him became weary; so they refreshed themselves there.

15 Meanwhile Absalom and all the people, the men of Israel, came to Jerusalem; and Ahithophel *was* with him. 16 And so it was, when Hushai the Archite, David's friend, came to Absalom, that Hushai said to Absalom, "*Long* live the king! *Long* live the king!"

17 So Absalom said to Hushai, "*Is* this your loyalty to your friend? Why did you not go with your friend?"

18 And Hushai said to Absalom, "No, but whom the LORD and this people and all the men of Israel choose, his I will be, and with him I will remain. 19 "Furthermore, whom should I serve? *Should I* not *serve* in the presence of his son? As I have served in your father's presence, so will I be in your presence."

20 Then Absalom said to Ahithophel, "Give advice as to what we should do."

21 And Ahithophel said to Absalom, "Go in to your father's concubines, whom he has left to keep the house; and all Israel will hear that you are abhorred by your father. Then the hands of all who are with you will be strong." 22 So they pitched a tent for Absalom on the top of the house, and Absalom went in to his father's concubines in the sight of all Israel.

23 Now the advice of Ahithophel, which he gave in those days, *was* as if one had inquired at the oracle of God. So *was* all the advice of Ahitho-phel both with David and with Absalom.

David's friends plot against him

17 Moreover Ahithophel said to Absalom, "Now let me choose twelve thousand men, and I will arise and pursue David tonight. 2 I will come upon him while he *is* weary and weak, and make him afraid. And all the people who *are* with him will flee, and I will strike only the king. 3 Then I will bring back all the people to you. When all return except the man whom you seek, all the people will be at peace."

4 And the saying pleased Absalom and all the elders of Israel.

5 Then Absalom said, "Now call Hushai the Archite also, and let us hear what he says too." 6 And when Hushai came to Absalom, Absalom spoke to him, saying, "Ahithophel has spoken in this manner. Shall we do as he says? If not, speak up."

7 So Hushai said to Absalom: "The advice that Ahithophel has given *is* not good at this time. 8 For," said Hushai, "you know your father and his men, that they *are* mighty men, and they *are* enraged in their minds, like a bear robbed of her cubs in the field; and your father *is* a man of war, and will not camp with the people. 9 Surely by now he is hidden in some pit, or in some *other* place. And it will be, when some of them are overthrown at the first, that whoever hears *it* will say, 'There is a slaughter among the people who follow Absalom.' 10 And even he *who is* valiant, whose heart *is* like the heart of a lion, will melt completely. For all Israel knows that your father *is* a mighty man, and *those* who *are* with him *are* valiant men. 11 Therefore I advise that all Israel be fully gathered to you, from Dan to Beersheba, like the sand that *is* by the sea for multitude, and that you go to battle in person. 12 So we will come upon him in some place where he may be found, and we will fall on him as the dew falls on the ground. And of him and all the men who *are* with him there shall not be

left so much as one. ¹³ Moreover, if he has withdrawn into a city, then all Israel shall bring ropes to that city; and we will pull it into the river, until there is not one small stone found there."

¹⁴ So Absalom and all the men of Israel said, "The advice of Hushai the Archite *is* better than the advice of Ahithophel." For the LORD had purposed to defeat the good advice of Ahithophel, to the intent that the LORD might bring disaster on Absalom.

¹⁵ Then Hushai said to Zadok and Abiathar the priests, "Thus and so Ahithophel advised Absalom and the elders of Israel, and thus and so I have advised. ¹⁶ Now therefore, send quickly and tell David, saying, 'Do not spend this night in the plains of the wilderness, but speedily cross over, lest the king and all the people who *are* with him be swallowed up.' " ¹⁷ Now Jonathan and Ahimaaz stayed at En Rogel, for they dared not be seen coming into the city; so a female servant would come and tell them, and they would go and tell King David. ¹⁸ Nevertheless a lad saw them, and told Absalom. But both of them went away quickly and came to a man's house in Bahurim, who had a well in his court; and they went down into it. ¹⁹ Then the woman took and spread a covering over the well's mouth, and spread ground grain on it; and the thing was not known. ²⁰ And when Absalom's servants came to the woman at the house, they said, "Where *are* Ahimaaz and Jonathan?"

So the woman said to them, "They have gone over the water brook."

And when they had searched and could not find *them,* they returned to Jerusalem. ²¹ Now it came to pass, after they had departed, that they came up out of the well and went and told King David, and said to David, "Arise and cross over the water quickly. For thus has Ahithophel advised against you." ²² So David and all the people who *were* with him arose and crossed over the Jordan. By morning light not one of them was left who had not gone over the Jordan.

²³ Now when Ahithophel saw that his advice was not followed, he saddled a donkey, and arose and went home to his house, to his city. Then he put his household in order, and hanged himself, and died; and he was buried in his father's tomb.

²⁴ Then David went to Mahanaim. And Absalom crossed over the Jordan, he and all the men of Israel with him. ²⁵ And Absalom made Amasa captain of the army instead of Joab. This Amasa *was* the son of a man whose name *was* Jithra, an Israelite, who had gone in to Abigail the daughter of Nahash, sister of Zeruiah, Joab's mother. ²⁶ So Israel and Absalom encamped in the land of Gilead.

²⁷ Now it happened, when David had come to Mahanaim, that Shobi the son of Nahash from Rabbah of the people of Ammon, Machir the son of Ammiel from Lo Debar, and Barzillai the Gileadite from Rogelim, ²⁸ brought beds and basins, earthen vessels and wheat, barley and flour, parched *grain* and beans, lentils and parched *seeds,* ²⁹ honey and curds, sheep and cheese of the herd, for David and the people who *were* with him to eat. For they said, "The people are hungry and weary and thirsty in the wilderness."

Absalom hangs from a tree

18 And David numbered the people who *were* with him, and set captains of thousands and captains of hundreds over them. ² Then David sent out one third of the people under the hand of Joab, one third under the hand of Abishai the son of Zeruiah, Joab's brother, and one third under the hand of Ittai the Gittite. And the king said to the people, "I also will surely go out with you myself."

³ But the people answered, "You shall not go out! For if we flee away, they will not care about us; nor if half of us die, will they care about us. But *you are* worth ten thousand of us now. For you are now more help to us in the city."

⁴ Then the king said to them,

"Whatever seems best to you I will do." So the king stood beside the gate, and all the people went out by hundreds and by thousands. 5 Now the king had commanded Joab, Abishai, and Ittai, saying, "*Deal* gently for my sake with the young man Absalom." And all the people heard when the king gave all the captains orders concerning Absalom.

6 So the people went out into the field of battle against Israel. And the battle was in the woods of Ephraim. 7 The people of Israel were overthrown there before the servants of David, and a great slaughter of twenty thousand took place there that day. 8 For the battle there was scattered over the face of the whole countryside, and the woods devoured more people that day than the sword devoured.

9 Then Absalom met the servants of David. Absalom rode on a mule. The mule went under the thick boughs of a great terebinth tree, and his head caught in the terebinth; so he was left hanging between heaven and earth. And the mule which *was* under him went on. 10 Now a certain man saw *it* and told Joab, and said, "I just saw Absalom hanging in a terebinth tree!"

11 So Joab said to the man who told him, "You just saw *him!* And why did you not strike him there to the ground? I would have given you ten *shekels* of silver and a belt."

12 But the man said to Joab, "Though I were to receive a thousand *shekels* of silver in my hand, I would not raise my hand against the king's son. For in our hearing the king commanded you and Abishai and Ittai, saying, 'Beware lest anyone *touch* the young man Absalom!' 13 Otherwise I would have dealt falsely against my own life. For there is nothing hidden from the king, and you yourself would have set yourself against *me.*"

14 Then Joab said, "I cannot linger with you." And he took three spears in his hand and thrust them through Absalom's heart, while he was *still* alive in the midst of the terebinth tree. 15 And ten young men who bore Joab's armor surrounded Absalom, and struck and killed him.

16 So Joab blew the trumpet, and the people returned from pursuing Israel. For Joab held back the people. 17 And they took Absalom and cast him into a large pit in the woods, and laid a very large heap of stones over him.

David's son, Absalom, died when his long hair became entangled in the branch of a tree while he was riding horseback.

Then all Israel fled, everyone to his tent.

18 Now Absalom in his lifetime had taken and set up a pillar for himself, which *is* in the King's Valley. For he said, "I have no son to keep my name in remembrance." He called the pillar after his own name. And to this day it is called Absalom's Monument.

19 Then Ahimaaz the son of Zadok said, "Let me run now and take the news to the king, how the LORD has avenged him of his enemies."

20 And Joab said to him, "You shall not take the news this day, for you shall take the news another day. But today you shall take no news, because the king's son is dead." 21 Then Joab said to the Cushite, "Go, tell the king what you have seen." So the Cushite bowed himself to Joab and ran.

22 And Ahimaaz the son of Zadok said again to Joab, "But whatever happens, please let me also run after the Cushite."

So Joab said, "Why will you run, my son, since you have no news ready?"

23 "But whatever happens," *he said*, "let me run."

So he said to him, "Run." Then Ahimaaz ran by way of the plain, and outran the Cushite.

24 Now David was sitting between the two gates. And the watchman went up to the roof over the gate, to the wall, lifted his eyes and looked, and there was a man, running alone. 25 Then the watchman cried out and told the king. And the king said, "If he is alone, *there is* news in his mouth." And he came rapidly and drew near.

26 Then the watchman saw *another* man running, and the watchman called to the gatekeeper and said, "There is *another* man, running alone!"

And the king said, "He also brings news."

27 So the watchman said, "I think the running of the first is like the running of Ahimaaz the son of Zadok."

And the king said, "He *is* a good man, and comes with good news."

28 So Ahimaaz called out and said to the king, "All is well!" Then he bowed down with his face to the earth before the king, and said, "Blessed *be* the LORD your God, who has delivered up the men who raised their hand against my lord the king!"

29 The king said, "Is the young man Absalom safe?"

Ahimaaz answered, "When Joab sent the king's servant and *me* your servant, I saw a great tumult, but I did not know what *it was* about."

30 And the king said, "Turn aside *and* stand here." So he turned aside and stood still.

31 Just then the Cushite came, and the Cushite said, "There is good news, my lord the king! For the LORD has avenged you this day of all those who rose against you."

32 And the king said to the Cushite, "Is the young man Absalom safe?"

So the Cushite answered, "May the enemies of my lord the king, and all who rise against you to do harm, be like *that* young man!"

33 Then the king was deeply moved, and went up to the chamber over the gate, and wept. And as he went, he said thus: "O my son Absalom—my son, my son Absalom—if only I had died in your place! O Absalom my son, my son!"

King David returns to Jerusalem

19 And Joab was told, "Behold, the king is weeping and mourning for Absalom." 2 So the victory that day was *turned* into mourning for all the people. For the people heard it said that day, "The king is grieved for his son." 3 And the people stole back into the city that day, as people who are ashamed steal away when they flee in battle. 4 But the king covered his face, and the king cried out with a loud voice, "O my son Absalom! O Absalom, my son, my son!"

5 Then Joab came into the house to the king, and said, "Today you have disgraced all your servants who today have saved your life, the lives of your

Shimei—My name is pronounced *SHIM-ee-eye*. I am a man who doesn't deserve to be called King David's friend, even though he did forgive my unkindness to him.

When King David's son Absalom made war against David, the king had to run away. While poor, unhappy David was leaving Jerusalem, I came out and called him names and threw stones at him.

I was amazed that David was so calm. He never answered me or even allowed his men to stop me. Later, disobedient Absalom was killed and his army was defeated. What should I do now? I would go to the king and ask him to forgive me for being so mean to him!

Once again the king surprised me: He really did forgive me. I think God must be like David. Yes, God forgives people who are truly sorry for their sins.

sons and daughters, the lives of your wives and the lives of your concubines, 6 in that you love your enemies and hate your friends. For you have declared today that you regard neither princes nor servants; for today I perceive that if Absalom had lived and all of us had died today, then it would have pleased you well. 7 Now therefore, arise, go out and speak comfort to your servants. For I swear by the LORD, if you do not go out, not one will stay with you this night. And that will be worse for you than all the evil that has befallen you from your youth until now." 8 Then the king arose and sat in the gate. And they told all the people, saying, "There is the king, sitting in the gate." So all the people came before the king.

For everyone of Israel had fled to his tent.

9 Now all the people were in a dispute throughout all the tribes of Israel, saying, "The king saved us from the hand of our enemies, he delivered us from the hand of the Philistines, and now he has fled from the land because of Absalom. 10 But Absalom, whom we anointed over us, has died in battle. Now therefore, why do you say nothing about bringing back the king?"

11 So King David sent to Zadok and Abiathar the priests, saying, "Speak to the elders of Judah, saying, 'Why are you the last to bring the king back to his house, since the words of all Israel have come to the king, to his *very* house? 12 You *are* my brethren, you *are* my bone and my flesh. Why then are you the last to bring back the king?' 13 And say to Amasa, 'Are you not my bone and my flesh? God do so to me, and more also, if you are not commander of the army before me continually in place of Joab.' " 14 So he swayed the hearts of all the men of Judah, just as *the heart of* one man, so that they sent *this word* to the king: "Return, you and all your servants!"

15 Then the king returned and came to the Jordan. And Judah came to Gilgal, to go to meet the king, to escort the king across the Jordan. 16 And Shimei the son of Gera, a Benjamite, who *was* from Bahurim, hurried and came down with the men of Judah to meet King David. 17 *There were* a thousand men of Benjamin with him, and Ziba the servant of the house of Saul, and his fifteen sons and his twenty servants with him; and they went over the Jordan before the king. 18 Then a ferryboat went across to carry over the king's household, and to do what he thought good.

Now Shimei the son of Gera fell down before the king when he had crossed the Jordan. 19 Then he said to the king, "Do not let my lord impute iniquity to me, or remember what wrong your servant did on the day that my lord the king left Jerusalem, that the king should take *it* to heart. 20 For

I, your servant, know that I have sinned. Therefore here I am, the first to come today of all the house of Joseph to go down to meet my lord the king."

21 But Abishai the son of Zeruiah answered and said, "Shall not Shimei be put to death for this, because he cursed the LORD's anointed?"

22 And David said, "What have I to do with you, you sons of Zeruiah, that you should be adversaries to me today? Shall any man be put to death today in Israel? For do I not know that today I *am* king over Israel?"

23 Therefore the king said to Shimei, "You shall not die." And the king swore to him.

24 Now Mephibosheth the son of Saul came down to meet the king. And he had not cared for his feet, nor trimmed his mustache, nor washed his clothes, from the day the king departed until the day he returned in peace.

25 So it was, when he had come to Jerusalem to meet the king, that the king said to him, "Why did you not go with me, Mephibosheth?"

26 And he answered, "My lord, O king, my servant deceived me. For your servant said, 'I will saddle a donkey for myself, that I may ride on it and go to the king,' because your servant *is* lame. 27 And he has slandered your servant to my lord the king, but my lord the king *is* like the angel of God. Therefore do *what is* good in your eyes. 28 For all my father's house were but dead men before my lord the king. Yet you set your servant among those who eat at your own table. Therefore what right have I still to cry out anymore to the king?"

29 So the king said to him, "Why do you speak anymore of your matters? I have said, 'You and Ziba divide the land.'"

30 Then Mephibosheth said to the king, "Rather, let him take it all, inasmuch as my lord the king has come back in peace to his own house."

31 And Barzillai the Gileadite came down from Rogelim and went across the Jordan with the king, to escort him across the Jordan. 32 Now Barzillai was a very aged man, eighty years old. And he had provided the king with supplies while he stayed at Mahanaim, for he *was* a very rich man. 33 And the king said to Barzillai, "Come across with me, and I will provide for you while you are with me in Jerusalem."

34 But Barzillai said to the king, "How long have I to live, that I should go up with the king to Jerusalem? 35 I *am* today eighty years old. Can I discern between the good and bad? Can your servant taste what I eat or what I drink? Can I hear any longer the voice of singing men and singing women? Why then should your servant be a further burden to my lord the king? 36 Your servant will go a little way across the Jordan with the king. And why should the king repay me *with* such a reward? 37 Please let your servant turn back again, that I may die in my own city, near the grave of my father and mother. But here is your servant Chimham; let him cross over with my lord the king, and do for him what seems good to you."

38 And the king answered, "Chimham shall cross over with me, and I will do for him what seems good to you. Now whatever you request of me, I will do for you." 39 Then all the people went over the Jordan. And when the king had crossed over, the king kissed Barzillai and blessed him, and he returned to his own place.

40 Now the king went on to Gilgal, and Chimham went on with him. And all the people of Judah escorted the king, and also half the people of Israel. 41 Just then all the men of Israel came to the king, and said to the king, "Why have our brethren, the men of Judah, stolen you away and brought the king, his household, and all David's men with him across the Jordan?"

42 So all the men of Judah answered the men of Israel, "Because the king *is* a close relative of ours. Why then are you angry over this matter? Have we ever eaten at the king's *expense?* Or has he given us any gift?"

⁴³ And the men of Israel answered the men of Judah, and said, "We have ten shares in the king; therefore we also have more *right* to David than you. Why then do you despise us— were we not the first to advise bringing back our king?"

Yet the words of the men of Judah were fiercer than the words of the men of Israel.

Sheba rebels against David

20 And there happened to be there a rebel, whose name *was* Sheba the son of Bichri, a Benjamite. And he blew a trumpet, and said:

> "We have no share in David,
>   Nor do we have inheritance in
>   the son of Jesse;
> Every man to his tents, O
>   Israel!"

² So every man of Israel deserted David, *and* followed Sheba the son of Bichri. But the men of Judah, from the Jordan as far as Jerusalem, remained loyal to their king.

³ Now David came to his house at Jerusalem. And the king took the ten women, his concubines whom he had left to keep the house, and put them in seclusion and supported them, but did not go in to them. So they were shut up to the day of their death, living in widowhood.

⁴ And the king said to Amasa, "Assemble the men of Judah for me within three days, and be present here yourself." ⁵ So Amasa went to assemble *the men of* Judah. But he delayed longer than the set time which David had appointed him. ⁶ And David said to Abishai, "Now Sheba the son of Bichri will do us more harm than Absalom. Take your lord's servants and pursue him, lest he find for himself fortified cities, and escape us." ⁷ So Joab's men, with the Cherethites, the Pelethites, and all the mighty men, went out after him. And they went out of Jerusalem to pursue Sheba the son of Bichri. ⁸ When they *were* at the large stone which *is* in Gibeon, Amasa came before them. Now Joab was dressed in battle armor; on it was a belt *with* a sword fastened in its sheath at his hips; and as he was going forward, it fell out. ⁹ Then Joab said to Amasa, "*Are* you in health, my brother?" And Joab took Amasa by the beard with his right hand to kiss him. ¹⁰ But Amasa did not notice the sword that *was* in Joab's hand. And he struck him with it in the stomach, and his entrails poured out on the ground; and he did not *strike* him again. Thus he died.

Then Joab and Abishai his brother pursued Sheba the son of Bichri. ¹¹ Meanwhile one of Joab's men stood near Amasa, and said, "Whoever favors Joab and whoever *is* for David— follow Joab!" ¹² But Amasa wallowed in *his* blood in the middle of the highway. And when the man saw that all the people stood still, he moved Amasa from the highway to the field and threw a garment over him, when he saw that everyone who came upon him halted. ¹³ When he was removed from the highway, all the people went on after Joab to pursue Sheba the son of Bichri.

¹⁴ And he went through all the tribes of Israel to Abel and Beth Maachah and all the Berites. So they were gathered together and also went after *Sheba*. ¹⁵ Then they came and besieged him in Abel of Beth Maachah; and they cast up a siege mound against the city, and it stood by the rampart. And all the people who *were* with Joab battered the wall to throw it down.

¹⁶ Then a wise woman cried out from the city, "Hear, hear! Please say to Joab, 'Come nearby, that I may speak with you.'" ¹⁷ When he had come near to her, the woman said, "*Are* you Joab?"

He answered, "I *am*."

Then she said to him, "Hear the words of your maidservant."

And he answered, "I am listening."

¹⁸ So she spoke, saying, "They used to talk in former times, saying, 'They shall surely seek *guidance* at Abel,' and so they would end *disputes*. ¹⁹ I *am*

among the peaceable and faithful in
Israel. You seek to destroy a city and
a mother in Israel. Why would you
swallow up the inheritance of the
LORD?"

20 And Joab answered and said,
"Far be it, far be it from me, that I
should swallow up or destroy! 21 That
is not so. But a man from the mountains of Ephraim, Sheba the son of
Bichri by name, has raised his hand
against the king, against David. Deliver
him only, and I will depart from the
city."

So the woman said to Joab, "Watch,
his head will be thrown to you over
the wall." 22 Then the woman in her
wisdom went to all the people. And
they cut off the head of Sheba the son
of Bichri, and threw it out to Joab.
Then he blew a trumpet, and they
withdrew from the city, every man to
his tent. So Joab returned to the king
at Jerusalem.

23 And Joab was over all the army
of Israel; Benaiah the son of Jehoiada
was over the Cherethites and the Pelethites; 24 Adoram was in charge of
revenue; Jehoshaphat the son of Ahilud was recorder; 25 Sheva was scribe;
Zadok and Abiathar were the priests;
26 and Ira the Jairite was a chief minister under David.

The seven sons of Saul are hanged

21 Now there was a famine in the
days of David for three years, year after
year; and David inquired of the LORD.
And the LORD answered, "It is because
of Saul and his bloodthirsty house, because he killed the Gibeonites."
2 So the king called the Gibeonites and
spoke to them. Now the Gibeonites
were not of the children of Israel, but
of the remnant of the Amorites; the
children of Israel had sworn protection
to them, but Saul had sought to kill
them in his zeal for the children of Israel and Judah.

3 Therefore David said to the Gibeonites, "What shall I do for you?

And with what shall I make atonement,
that you may bless the inheritance of
the LORD?"

4 And the Gibeonites said to him,
"We will have no silver or gold from
Saul or from his house, nor shall you
kill any man in Israel for us."

So he said, "Whatever you say, I
will do for you."

5 Then they answered the king, "As
for the man who consumed us and
plotted against us, that we should be
destroyed from remaining in any of the
territories of Israel, 6 let seven men of
his descendants be delivered to us, and
we will hang them before the LORD in
Gibeah of Saul, whom the LORD
chose."

And the king said, "I will give them."
7 But the king spared Mephibosheth
the son of Jonathan, the son of Saul,
because of the LORD's oath that was
between them, between David and
Jonathan the son of Saul. 8 So the king
took Armoni and Mephibosheth, the
two sons of Rizpah the daughter of
Aiah, whom she bore to Saul, and the
five sons of Michal the daughter of
Saul, whom she brought up for Adriel
the son of Barzillai the Meholathite;
9 and he delivered them into the hands
of the Gibeonites, and they hanged
them on the hill before the LORD. So
they fell, all seven together, and were
put to death in the days of harvest, in
the first days, in the beginning of barley
harvest.

10 Now Rizpah the daughter of Aiah
took sackcloth and spread it for herself
on the rock, from the beginning of harvest until the late rains poured on them
from heaven. And she did not allow
the birds of the air to rest on them by
day nor the beasts of the field by night.

11 And David was told what Rizpah
the daughter of Aiah, the concubine
of Saul, had done. 12 Then David went
and took the bones of Saul, and the
bones of Jonathan his son, from the
men of Jabesh Gilead who had stolen
them from the street of Beth Shan,
where the Philistines had hung them
up, after the Philistines had struck
down Saul in Gilboa. 13 So he brought

up the bones of Saul and the bones of Jonathan his son from there; and they gathered the bones of those who had been hanged. 14 They buried the bones of Saul and Jonathan his son in the country of Benjamin in Zelah, in the tomb of Kish his father. So they performed all that the king commanded. And after that God heeded the prayer for the land.

15 When the Philistines were at war again with Israel, David and his servants with him went down and fought against the Philistines; and David grew faint. 16 Then Ishbi-Benob, who *was* one of the sons of the giant, the weight of whose bronze spear *was* three hundred *shekels,* who was bearing a new *sword,* thought he could kill David. 17 But Abishai the son of Zeruiah came to his aid, and struck the Philistine and killed him. Then the men of David swore to him, saying, "You shall go out no more with us to battle, lest you quench the lamp of Israel."

18 Now it happened afterward that there was again a battle with the Philistines at Gob. Then Sibbechai the Hushathite killed Saph, who *was* one of the sons of the giant. 19 Again there was war at Gob with the Philistines, where Elhanan the son of Jaare-Oregim the Bethlehemite killed *the brother of* Goliath the Gittite, the shaft of whose spear *was* like a weaver's beam.

20 Yet again there was war at Gath, where there was a man of *great* stature, who had six fingers on each hand and six toes on each foot, twenty-four in number; and he also was born to the giant. 21 So when he defied Israel, Jonathan the son of Shimea, David's brother, killed him.

22 These four were born to the giant in Gath, and fell by the hand of David and by the hand of his servants.

David sings a song of deliverance

22 Then David spoke to the LORD the words of this song, on the day when the LORD had delivered him from the hand of all his enemies, and from the hand of Saul. 2 And he said:

"The LORD *is* my rock and my
    fortress and my deliverer;
3 The God of my strength, in
    whom I will trust;
My shield and the horn of my
    salvation,
My stronghold and my refuge;
My Savior, You save me from
    violence.
4 I will call upon the LORD, *who
    is worthy* to be praised;
So shall I be saved from my
    enemies.

5 "When the waves of death
    surrounded me,
The floods of ungodliness made
    me afraid.
6 The sorrows of Sheol
    surrounded me;
The snares of death confronted
    me.
7 In my distress I called upon the
    LORD,

⚒ DIGGING IN

22:2—23:7 David the Songwriter Many people like to write songs, and some people are very good at songwriting. David was a great songwriter.

Some people say David couldn't write songs because he was only a rough soldier. That's really very silly. Some people think World War II General George Patton was a rough soldier, but General Patton also wrote good poetry.

David wrote the two songs or poems in 2 Samuel 22 and 23, and he also wrote many of the psalms. We know that David meant his poems and psalms to be sung because David was also a musician.

They didn't have pianos and guitars in David's time. David played his songs to the tune of a harp. Everybody should know Psalm 23. In that song, David the shepherd tells about the Lord who is David's own great Shepherd.

Would you like to write a song about Jesus?

And cried out to my God;
He heard my voice from His
   temple,
And my cry *entered* His ears.

8 "Then the earth shook and
      trembled;
The foundations of heaven
   quaked and were shaken,
Because He was angry.
9 Smoke went up from His
   nostrils,
And devouring fire from His
   mouth;
Coals were kindled by it.
10 He bowed the heavens also, and
   came down
With darkness under His feet.
11 He rode upon a cherub, and
   flew;
And He was seen upon the
   wings of the wind.
12 He made darkness canopies
   around Him,
Dark waters *and* thick clouds of
   the skies.
13 From the brightness before Him
Coals of fire were kindled.

14 "The LORD thundered from
      heaven,
And the Most High uttered His
   voice.
15 He sent out arrows and scattered
   them;
Lightning bolts, and He
   vanquished them.
16 Then the channels of the sea
   were seen,
The foundations of the world
   were uncovered,
At the rebuke of the LORD,
At the blast of the breath of His
   nostrils.

17 "He sent from above, He took
      me,
He drew me out of many waters.
18 He delivered me from my strong
   enemy,
From those who hated me;
For they were too strong for me.
19 They confronted me in the day
   of my calamity,

But the LORD was my support.
20 He also brought me out into a
   broad place;
He delivered me because He
   delighted in me.

21 "The LORD rewarded me
   according to my
   righteousness;
According to the cleanness of
   my hands
He has recompensed me.
22 For I have kept the ways of the
   LORD,
And have not wickedly departed
   from my God.
23 For all His judgments *were*
   before me;
And *as for* His statutes, I did not
   depart from them.
24 I was also blameless before Him,
And I kept myself from my
   iniquity.
25 Therefore the LORD has
   recompensed me according to
   my righteousness,
According to my cleanness in
   His eyes.

26 "With the merciful You will show
   Yourself merciful;
With a blameless man You will
   show Yourself blameless;
27 With the pure You will show
   Yourself pure;
And with the devious You will
   show Yourself shrewd.
28 You will save the humble
   people;
But Your *eyes are* on the
   haughty, *that* You may bring
   them down.

29 "For You *are* my lamp, O LORD;
The LORD shall enlighten my
   darkness.
30 For by You I can run against a
   troop;
By my God I can leap over a
   wall.
31 *As for* God, His way *is* perfect;
The word of the LORD *is* proven;
He *is* a shield to all who trust in
   Him.

32 "For who *is* God, except the
     LORD?
     And who *is* a rock, except our
     God?
33 God *is* my strength *and* power,
     And He makes my way perfect.
34 He makes my feet like the *feet*
     of deer,
     And sets me on my high places.
35 He teaches my hands to make
     war,
     So that my arms can bend a bow
     of bronze.

36 "You have also given me the
     shield of Your salvation;
     Your gentleness has made me
     great.
37 You enlarged my path under
     me;
     So my feet did not slip.

38 "I have pursued my enemies and
     destroyed them;
     Neither did I turn back again till
     they were destroyed.
39 And I have destroyed them and
     wounded them,
     So that they could not rise;
     They have fallen under my feet.
40 For You have armed me with
     strength for the battle;
     You have subdued under me
     those who rose against me.
41 You have also given me the
     necks of my enemies,
     So that I destroyed those who
     hated me.
42 They looked, but *there was*
     none to save;
     Even to the LORD, but He did
     not answer them.
43 Then I beat them as fine as the
     dust of the earth;
     I trod them like dirt in the streets,
     And I spread them out.

44 "You have also delivered me
     from the strivings of my
     people;
     You have kept me as the head
     of the nations.
     A people I have not known shall
     serve me.

45 The foreigners submit to me;
     As soon as they hear, they obey
     me.
46 The foreigners fade away,
     And come frightened from their
     hideouts.

47 "The LORD lives!
     Blessed *be* my Rock!
     Let God be exalted,
     The Rock of my salvation!
48 *It is* God who avenges me,
     And subdues the peoples under
     me;
49 He delivers me from my
     enemies.
     You also lift me up above those
     who rise against me;
     You have delivered me from the
     violent man.
50 Therefore I will give thanks to
     You, O LORD, among the
     Gentiles,
     And sing praises to Your name.

51 "*He is* the tower of salvation to
     His king,
     And shows mercy to His
     anointed,
     To David and his descendants
     forevermore."

David's last words

23 Now these *are* the last words of
David.

     Thus says David the son of
     Jesse;
     Thus says the man raised up on
     high,
     The anointed of the God of
     Jacob,
     And the sweet psalmist of Israel:

2 "The Spirit of the LORD spoke by
     me,
     And His word *was* on my
     tongue.
3 The God of Israel said,
     The Rock of Israel spoke to me:
     'He who rules over men *must*
     be just,
     Ruling in the fear of God.

4 And *he shall be* like the light of
   the morning *when* the sun
   rises,
   A morning without clouds,
   Like the tender grass *springing*
   out of the earth,
   By clear shining after rain.'

5 "Although my house *is* not so
   with God,
   Yet He has made with me an
   everlasting covenant,
   Ordered in all *things* and secure.
   For *this is* all my salvation and
   all *my* desire;
   Will He not make *it* increase?

6 But *the sons* of rebellion *shall*
   all *be* as thorns thrust away,
   Because they cannot be taken
   with hands.

7 But the man *who* touches them
   Must be armed with iron and the
   shaft of a spear,
   And they shall be utterly burned
   with fire in *their* place."

8 These *are* the names of the mighty
men whom David had: Josheb-Bas-
shebeth the Tachmonite, chief among
the captains. He was called Adino the
Eznite, because he had killed eight
hundred men at one time. 9 And after
him *was* Eleazar the son of Dodo, the
Ahohite, *one* of the three mighty men
with David when they defied the Philistines *who* were gathered there for battle, and the men of Israel had retreated.
10 He arose and attacked the Philistines
until his hand was weary, and his hand
stuck to the sword. The LORD brought
about a great victory that day; and the
people returned after him only to plun-

der. 11 And after him *was* Shammah
the son of Agee the Hararite. The Philistines had gathered together into a
troop where there was a piece of
ground full of lentils. So the people fled
from the Philistines. 12 But he stationed
himself in the middle of the field, defended it, and killed the Philistines. So
the LORD brought about a great victory.

13 Then three of the thirty chief men
went down at harvest time and came
to David at the cave of Adullam. And
the troop of Philistines encamped in
the Valley of Rephaim. 14 David *was*
then in the stronghold, and the garrison of the Philistines *was* then *in* Bethlehem. 15 And David said with longing,
"Oh, that someone would give me a
drink of the water from the well of
Bethlehem, which *is* by the gate!"
16 So the three mighty men broke
through the camp of the Philistines,
drew water from the well of Bethlehem
that *was* by the gate, and took it and
brought *it* to David. Nevertheless he
would not drink it, but poured it out
to the LORD. 17 And he said, "Far be
it from me, O LORD, that I should do
this! Is *this not* the blood of the men
who went in *jeopardy of* their lives?"
Therefore he would not drink it.
These things were done by the three
mighty men.

18 Now Abishai the brother of Joab,
the son of Zeruiah, was chief of *another* three. He lifted his spear against
three hundred *men,* killed *them,* and
won a name among *these* three.
19 Was he not the most honored of
three? Therefore he became their captain. However, he did not attain to the
first three.

20 Benaiah *was* the son of Jehoiada,
the son of a valiant man from Kabzeel,
who had done many deeds. He had
killed two lion-like heroes of Moab. He
also had gone down and killed a lion
in the midst of a pit on a snowy day.
21 And he killed an Egyptian, a spectac-
ular man. The Egyptian *had* a spear
in his hand; so he went down to him
with a staff, wrested the spear out of
the Egyptian's hand, and killed him
with his own spear. 22 These *things*

Who Are God's Heroes?

David was a soldier all his life, and
he called many young men to be his
fellow soldiers. These are called
"mighty men" in the Bible. At times
God's plan calls for special people
who are very strong in spirit to do great
works for Him. Will you be one of
God's heroes?

Benaiah the son of Jehoiada did, and won a name among three mighty men. 23 He was more honored than the thirty, but he did not attain to the *first* three. And David appointed him over his guard.

24 Asahel the brother of Joab *was* one of the thirty; Elhanan the son of Dodo of Bethlehem, 25 Shammah the Harodite, Elika the Harodite, 26 Helez the Paltite, Ira the son of Ikkesh the Tekoite, 27 Abiezer the Anathothite, Mebunnai the Hushathite, 28 Zalmon the Ahohite, Maharai the Netophathite, 29 Heleb the son of Baanah (the Netophathite), Ittai the son of Ribai from Gibeah of the children of Benjamin, 30 Benaiah a Pirathonite, Hiddai from the brooks of Gaash, 31 Abi-Albon the Arbathite, Azmaveth the Barhumite, 32 Eliahba the Shaalbonite (of the sons of Jashen), Jonathan, 33 Shammah the Hararite, Ahiam the son of Sharar the Hararite, 34 Eliphelet the son of Ahasbai, the son of the Maachathite, Eliam the son of Ahithophel the Gilonite, 35 Hezrai the Carmelite, Paarai the Arbite, 36 Igal the son of Nathan of Zobah, Bani the Gadite, 37 Zelek the Ammonite, Naharai the Beerothite (armorbearer of Joab the son of Zeruiah), 38 Ira the Ithrite, Gareb the Ithrite, 39 *and* Uriah the Hittite: thirty-seven in all.

God punishes David

24 Again the anger of the LORD was aroused against Israel, and He moved David against them to say, "Go, number Israel and Judah."

2 So the king said to Joab the commander of the army who *was* with him, "Now go throughout all the tribes of Israel, from Dan to Beersheba, and count the people, that I may know the number of the people."

3 And Joab said to the king, "Now may the LORD your God add to the people a hundred times more than there are, and may the eyes of my lord the king *see it.* But why does my lord the king desire this thing?" 4 Nevertheless the king's word prevailed against Joab and against the captains of the army. Therefore Joab and the captains of the army went out from the presence of the king to count the people of Israel.

5 And they crossed over the Jordan and camped in Aroer, on the right side of the town which *is* in the midst of the ravine of Gad, and toward Jazer. 6 Then they came to Gilead and to the land of Tahtim Hodshi; they came to Dan Jaan and around to Sidon; 7 and they came to the stronghold of Tyre and to all the cities of the Hivites and the Canaanites. Then they went out to South Judah *as far as* Beersheba. 8 So when they had gone through all the land, they came to Jerusalem at the end of nine months and twenty days. 9 Then Joab gave the sum of the number of the people to the king. And there *were* in Israel eight hundred thousand valiant men who drew the sword, and the men of Judah were five hundred thousand men.

10 And David's heart condemned him after he had numbered the people. So David said to the LORD, "I have sinned greatly in what I have done; but now, I pray, O LORD, take away the

⚔ DIGGING IN

24:1–16 Sin Costs Too Much God sent a great disease, or plague, because of the disobedience of King David and the people. Seventy thousand men died from the plague before the Lord stopped the disease.

What do we learn from this unhappy story? We know that many thousands of people die everyday all over the world. Why? The Word of God says, "The wages

of sin is death" (Romans 6:23). We shouldn't be dying at all, but we do die because we are all sinners.

This story is not told to scare you. You should learn that the plague of sin costs far too much. Let us learn to hate our sins and to love God, for He also said, "The gift of God is eternal life through Jesus Christ our Lord" (Romans 6:23).

iniquity of Your servant, for I have done very foolishly.''

11 Now when David arose in the morning, the word of the LORD came to the prophet Gad, David's seer, saying, 12 "Go and tell David, 'Thus says the LORD: "I offer you three *things*; choose one of them for yourself, that I may do *it* to you." ' " 13 So Gad came to David and told him; and he said to him, "Shall seven years of famine come to you in your land? Or shall you flee three months before your enemies, while they pursue you? Or shall there be three days' plague in your land? Now consider and see what answer I should take back to Him who sent me.''

14 And David said to Gad, "I am in great distress. Please let us fall into the hand of the LORD, for His mercies *are* great; but do not let me fall into the hand of man.''

15 So the LORD sent a plague upon Israel from the morning till the appointed time. From Dan to Beersheba seventy thousand men of the people died. 16 And when the angel stretched out His hand over Jerusalem to destroy it, the LORD relented from the destruction, and said to the angel who was destroying the people, "It is enough; now restrain your hand." And the angel of the LORD was by the threshing floor of Araunah the Jebusite.

17 Then David spoke to the LORD when he saw the angel who was striking the people, and said, "Surely I have sinned, and I have done wickedly; but these sheep, what have they done? Let Your hand, I pray, be against me and against my father's house.''

18 And Gad came that day to David and said to him, "Go up, erect an altar to the LORD on the threshing floor of Araunah the Jebusite.'' 19 So David, according to the word of Gad, went up as the LORD commanded. 20 Now Araunah looked, and saw the king and his servants coming toward him. So Araunah went out and bowed before the king with his face to the ground.

21 Then Araunah said, "Why has my lord the king come to his servant?''

And David said, "To buy the threshing floor from you, to build an altar to the LORD, that the plague may be withdrawn from the people.''

22 Now Araunah said to David, "Let my lord the king take and offer up whatever *seems* good to him. Look, *here are* oxen for burnt sacrifice, and threshing implements and the yokes of the oxen for wood. 23 All these, O king, Araunah has given to the king.''

And Araunah said to the king, "May the LORD your God accept you.''

24 Then the king said to Araunah, "No, but I will surely buy *it* from you for a price; nor will I offer burnt offerings to the LORD my God with that which costs me nothing.'' So David bought the threshing floor and the oxen for fifty shekels of silver. 25 And David built there an altar to the LORD, and offered burnt offerings and peace offerings. So the LORD heeded the prayers for the land, and the plague was withdrawn from Israel.

DIGGING IN

24:17–25 God Heals Sin David prayed for the people when they were dying from the plague. David even believed that his sin alone had caused the sickness, so he asked the Lord to punish him instead of Israel, his people. Then he built an altar and made a sacrifice for sin.

What do we learn from this strange story? First, we learn how much David loved his people. He was even ready to die for them, and he took the blame for their sins on himself. That was a very big kind of love.

What David did was really a little picture of what God planned to do about a thousand years after David's time. Then Jesus, the great Son of David, would also pray for us (see John 17). Finally, Jesus would take the blame for our sins and would allow Himself to be sacrificed on a cruel Roman cross. Only Jesus, who was also the Son of God, could take your place.

The Book of
1 KINGS

King Solomon—I almost didn't become king of Israel at all.

When my father, King David, was old and weak, my brother made himself king before my father knew it. Then Bathsheba, my mother, and Nathan, the prophet, told the king what my brother had done. So King David called Nathan and the priest, and they made me king right away!

When David died, Israel was the greatest nation in the world of that time—all the way from the River Euphrates (pronounced *you-FRAY-tees*) in the east to Egypt in the south.

We were the strongest nation in the world partly because I had many cargo ships. They carried our goods for sale to ports all over the world.

But the great reason we prospered was that our nation honored the Lord. God has always blessed those nations that honor Him and obey His laws.

Solomon is crowned king

NOW King David was old, advanced in years; and they put covers on him, but he could not get warm. 2 Therefore his servants said to him, "Let a young woman, a virgin, be sought for our lord the king, and let her stand before the king, and let her care for him; and let her lie in your bosom, that our lord the king may be warm." 3 So they sought for a lovely young woman throughout all the territory of Israel, and found Abishag the Shunammite, and brought her to the king. 4 The young woman *was* very lovely; and she cared for the king, and served him; but the king did not know her.

5 Then Adonijah the son of Haggith exalted himself, saying, "I will be king"; and he prepared for himself chariots and horsemen, and fifty men to run before him. 6 (And his father had not rebuked him at any time by saying, "Why have you done so?" He *was* also very good-looking. *His mother* had borne him after Absalom.) 7 Then he conferred with Joab the son of Zeruiah and with Abiathar the priest, and they followed and helped Adonijah.

8 But Zadok the priest, Benaiah the son of Jehoiada, Nathan the prophet, Shimei, Rei, and the mighty men who *belonged* to David were not with Adonijah.

9 And Adonijah sacrificed sheep and oxen and fattened cattle by the stone of Zoheleth, which *is* by En Rogel; he also invited all his brothers, the king's sons, and all the men of Judah, the king's servants. 10 But he did not invite Nathan the prophet, Benaiah, the mighty men, or Solomon his brother.

11 So Nathan spoke to Bathsheba the mother of Solomon, saying, "Have you not heard that Adonijah the son of Haggith has become king, and David our lord does not know *it?* 12 Come, please, let me now give you advice, that you may save your own life and the life of your son Solomon. 13 Go immediately to King David and say to him, 'Did you not, my lord, O king, swear to your maidservant, saying, "Assuredly your son Solomon shall reign after me, and he shall sit on my throne"? Why then has Adonijah become king?' 14 Then, while you are still talking there with the king, I also will come in after you and confirm your words."

Bible Bookshelf

God's Word is divided into two Testaments, or Covenants—
the Old and the New. Over a very long time,
God inspired (breathed into) special people He chose to write the
66 books you will find here. These books tell us all about God, His
creation of the world and mankind, how sin started, and God's plan
for sending His Son Jesus to save us and take us to
heaven to live with Him always.

OLD TESTAMENT
(39 Books)

LAW
Genesis
Exodus
Leviticus
Numbers
Deuteronomy

HISTORY
Joshua
Judges
Ruth
1, 2 Samuel
1, 2 Kings
1, 2 Chronicles
Ezra
Nehemiah
Esther

POETRY
Job
Psalms
Proverbs
Ecclesiastes
Song of Solomon
Lamentations

MAJOR PROPHETS
Isaiah
Jeremiah
Ezekiel
Daniel

MINOR PROPHETS
Hosea
Joel
Amos
Obadiah
Jonah
Micah
Nahum
Habakkuk
Zephaniah
Haggai
Zechariah
Malachi

Bible Bookshelf

The New Testament books tell about Jesus' birth and life,
His ministry, death, and resurrection; explain how the church began;
include letters from Paul and others to the people in those early
churches; and give John's vision of the end of the world.

NEW TESTAMENT
(27 Books)

THE GOSPELS

Matthew
Mark
Luke
John

CHURCH HISTORY

Acts

LETTERS

Romans
1, 2 Corinthians
Galatians
Ephesians

Philippians
Colossians
1, 2 Thessalonians
1, 2 Timothy
Titus
Philemon
Hebrews
James
1, 2 Peter
1, 2, 3 John
Jude

PROPHECY

Revelation

15 So Bathsheba went into the chamber to the king. (Now the king was very old, and Abishag the Shunammite was serving the king.) 16 And Bathsheba bowed and did homage to the king. Then the king said, "What is your wish?"

17 Then she said to him, "My lord, you swore by the LORD your God to your maidservant, *saying,* 'Assuredly Solomon your son shall reign after me, and he shall sit on my throne.' 18 So now, look! Adonijah has become king; and now, my lord the king, you do not know about *it.* 19 He has sacrificed oxen and fattened cattle and sheep in abundance, and has invited all the sons of the king, Abiathar the priest, and Joab the commander of the army; but Solomon your servant he has not invited. 20 And as for you, my lord, O king, the eyes of all Israel *are* on you, that you should tell them who will sit on the throne of my lord the king after him. 21 Otherwise it will happen, when my lord the king rests with his fathers, that I and my son Solomon will be counted as offenders."

22 And just then, while she was still talking with the king, Nathan the prophet also came in. 23 So they told the king, saying, "Here is Nathan the prophet." And when he came in before the king, he bowed down before the king with his face to the ground. 24 And Nathan said, "My lord, O king, have you said, 'Adonijah shall reign after me, and he shall sit on my throne'? 25 For he has gone down today, and has sacrificed oxen and fattened cattle and sheep in abundance, and has invited all the king's sons, and the commanders of the army, and Abiathar the priest; and look! They are eating and drinking before him; and they say, 'Long live King Adonijah!' 26 But he has not invited me—me your servant—nor Zadok the priest, nor Benaiah the son of Jehoiada, nor your servant Solomon. 27 Has this thing been done by my lord the king, and you have not told your servant who should sit on the throne of my lord the king after him?"

28 Then King David answered and said, "Call Bathsheba to me." So she came into the king's presence and stood before the king. 29 And the king took an oath and said, "As the LORD lives, who has redeemed my life from every distress, 30 just as I swore to you by the LORD God of Israel, saying, 'Assuredly Solomon your son shall be king after me, and he shall sit on my throne in my place,' so I certainly will do this day."

31 Then Bathsheba bowed with *her* face to the earth, and paid homage to the king, and said, "Let my lord King David live forever!"

32 And King David said, "Call to me Zadok the priest, Nathan the prophet, and Benaiah the son of Jehoiada." So they came before the king. 33 The king also said to them, "Take with you the servants of your lord, and have Solomon my son ride on my own mule, and take him down to Gihon. 34 There let Zadok the priest and Nathan the prophet anoint him king over Israel; and blow the horn, and say, 'Long live King Solomon!' 35 Then you shall come up after him, and he shall come and sit on my throne, and he shall be king in my place. For I have appointed him to be ruler over Israel and Judah."

36 Benaiah the son of Jehoiada answered the king and said, "Amen! May the LORD God of my lord the king say so *too.* 37 As the LORD has been with my lord the king, even so may He be with Solomon, and make his throne greater than the throne of my lord King David."

38 So Zadok the priest, Nathan the prophet, Benaiah the son of Jehoiada, the Cherethites, and the Pelethites went down and had Solomon ride on King David's mule, and took him to Gihon. 39 Then Zadok the priest took a horn of oil from the tabernacle and anointed Solomon. And they blew the horn, and all the people said, "Long live King Solomon!" 40 And all the people went up after him; and the people played the flutes and rejoiced with great joy, so that the earth *seemed to* split with their sound.

41 Now Adonijah and all the guests who *were* with him heard *it* as they finished eating. And when Joab heard the sound of the horn, he said, "Why *is* the city in such a noisy uproar?" 42 While he was still speaking, there came Jonathan, the son of Abiathar the priest. And Adonijah said to him, "Come in, for you *are* a prominent man, and bring good news."

43 Then Jonathan answered and said to Adonijah, "No! Our lord King David has made Solomon king. 44 The king has sent with him Zadok the priest, Nathan the prophet, Benaiah the son of Jehoiada, the Cherethites, and the Pelethites; and they have made him ride on the king's mule. 45 So Zadok the priest and Nathan the prophet have anointed him king at Gihon; and they have gone up from there rejoicing, so that the city is in an uproar. This *is* the noise that you have heard. 46 Also Solomon sits on the throne of the kingdom. 47 And moreover the king's servants have gone to bless our lord King David, saying, 'May God make the name of Solomon better than your name, and may He make his throne greater than your throne.' Then the king bowed himself on the bed. 48 Also the king said thus, 'Blessed *be* the LORD God of Israel, who has given *one* to sit on my throne this day, while my eyes see *it!*' "

49 So all the guests who were with Adonijah were afraid, and arose, and each one went his way.

50 Now Adonijah was afraid of Solomon; so he arose, and went and took hold of the horns of the altar. 51 And it was told Solomon, saying, "Indeed Adonijah is afraid of King Solomon; for look, he has taken hold of the horns of the altar, saying, 'Let King Solomon swear to me today that he will not put his servant to death with the sword.' "

52 Then Solomon said, "If he proves himself a worthy man, not one hair of him shall fall to the earth; but if wickedness is found in him, he shall die." 53 So King Solomon sent them to bring him down from the altar. And he came and fell down before King Solomon; and Solomon said to him, "Go to your house."

David instructs Solomon

2 Now the days of David drew near that he should die, and he charged Solomon his son, saying: 2 "I go the way of all the earth; be strong, therefore, and prove yourself a man. 3 And keep the charge of the LORD your God: to walk in His ways, to keep His statutes, His commandments, His judgments, and His testimonies, as it is written in the Law of Moses, that you may prosper in all that you do and wherever you turn; 4 that the LORD may fulfill His word which He spoke concerning me, saying, 'If your sons take heed to their way, to walk before Me in truth with all their heart and with all their soul,' He said, 'you shall not lack a man on the throne of Israel.'

5 "Moreover you know also what Joab the son of Zeruiah did to me, *and* what he did to the two commanders of the armies of Israel, to Abner the son of Ner and Amasa the son of Jether, whom he killed. And he shed the blood of war in peacetime, and put the blood of war on his belt that *was* around his waist, and on his sandals that *were* on his feet. 6 Therefore do according to your wisdom, and do not let his gray hair go down to the grave in peace.

7 "But show kindness to the sons of Barzillai the Gileadite, and let them be among those who eat at your table, for so they came to me when I fled from Absalom your brother.

8 "And see, *you have* with you Shimei the son of Gera, a Benjamite from Bahurim, who cursed me with a malicious curse in the day when I went to Mahanaim. But he came down to meet me at the Jordan, and I swore to him by the LORD, saying, 'I will not put you to death with the sword.' 9 Now therefore, do not hold him guiltless, for you *are* a wise man and know what you ought to do to him; but bring his gray hair down to the grave with blood."

¹⁰ So David rested with his fathers, and was buried in the City of David. ¹¹ The period that David reigned over Israel *was* forty years; seven years he reigned in Hebron, and in Jerusalem he reigned thirty-three years. ¹² Then Solomon sat on the throne of his father David; and his kingdom was firmly established.

¹³ Now Adonijah the son of Haggith came to Bathsheba the mother of Solomon. So she said, "Do you come peaceably?"

And he said, "Peaceably." ¹⁴ Moreover he said, "I have something *to say* to you."

And she said, "Say it."

¹⁵ Then he said, "You know that the kingdom was mine, and all Israel had set their expectations on me, that I should reign. However, the kingdom has been turned over, and has become my brother's; for it was his from the LORD. ¹⁶ Now I ask one petition of you; do not deny me."

And she said to him, "Say it."

¹⁷ Then he said, "Please speak to King Solomon, for he will not refuse you, that he may give me Abishag the Shunammite as wife."

¹⁸ So Bathsheba said, "Very well, I will speak for you to the king."

¹⁹ Bathsheba therefore went to King Solomon, to speak to him for Adonijah. And the king rose up to meet her and bowed down to her, and sat down on his throne and had a throne set for the king's mother; so she sat at his right hand. ²⁰ Then she said, "I desire one small petition of you; do not refuse me."

And the king said to her, "Ask it, my mother, for I will not refuse you."

²¹ So she said, "Let Abishag the Shunammite be given to Adonijah your brother as wife."

²² And King Solomon answered and said to his mother, "Now why do you ask Abishag the Shunammite for Adonijah? Ask for him the kingdom also—for he *is* my older brother—for him, and for Abiathar the priest, and for Joab the son of Zeruiah." ²³ Then King Solomon swore by the LORD, say-

ing, "May God do so to me, and more also, if Adonijah has not spoken this word against his own life! ²⁴ Now therefore, *as* the LORD lives, who has confirmed me and set me on the throne of David my father, and who has established a house for me, as He promised, Adonijah shall be put to death today!"

²⁵ So King Solomon sent by the hand of Benaiah the son of Jehoiada; and he struck him down, and he died.

²⁶ And to Abiathar the priest the king said, "Go to Anathoth, to your own fields, for you *are* deserving of death; but I will not put you to death at this time, because you carried the ark of the Lord GOD before my father David, and because you were afflicted every time my father was afflicted." ²⁷ So Solomon removed Abiathar from being priest to the LORD, that he might fulfill the word of the LORD which He spoke concerning the house of Eli at Shiloh.

²⁸ Then news came to Joab, for Joab had defected to Adonijah, though he had not defected to Absalom. So Joab fled to the tabernacle of the LORD, and took hold of the horns of the altar. ²⁹ And King Solomon was told, "Joab has fled to the tabernacle of the LORD; there *he is,* by the altar." Then Solomon sent Benaiah the son of Jehoiada, saying, "Go, strike him down." ³⁰ So Benaiah went to the tabernacle of the LORD, and said to him, "Thus says the king, 'Come out!' "

And he said, "No, but I will die here." And Benaiah brought back word to the king, saying, "Thus said Joab, and thus he answered me."

³¹ Then the king said to him, "Do as he has said, and strike him down and bury him, that you may take away from me and from the house of my father the innocent blood which Joab shed. ³² So the LORD will return his blood on his head, because he struck down two men more righteous and better than he, and killed them with the sword—Abner the son of Ner, the commander of the army of Israel, and Amasa the son of Jether, the

commander of the army of Judah—though my father David did not know it. ³³ Their blood shall therefore return upon the head of Joab and upon the head of his descendants forever. But upon David and his descendants, upon his house and his throne, there shall be peace forever from the LORD."

³⁴ So Benaiah the son of Jehoiada went up and struck and killed him; and he was buried in his own house in the wilderness. ³⁵ The king put Benaiah the son of Jehoiada in his place over the army, and the king put Zadok the priest in the place of Abiathar.

³⁶ Then the king sent and called for Shimei, and said to him, "Build yourself a house in Jerusalem and dwell there, and do not go out from there anywhere. ³⁷ For it shall be, on the day you go out and cross the Brook Kidron, know for certain you shall surely die; your blood shall be on your own head."

³⁸ And Shimei said to the king, "The saying is good. As my lord the king has said, so your servant will do." So Shimei dwelt in Jerusalem many days.

³⁹ Now it happened at the end of three years, that two slaves of Shimei ran away to Achish the son of Maachah, king of Gath. And they told Shimei, saying, "Look, your slaves are in Gath!" ⁴⁰ So Shimei arose, saddled his donkey, and went to Achish at Gath to seek his slaves. And Shimei went and brought his slaves from Gath. ⁴¹ And Solomon was told that Shimei had gone from Jerusalem to Gath and had come back. ⁴² Then the king sent and called for Shimei, and said to him, "Did I not make you swear by the LORD, and warn you, saying, 'Know for certain that on the day you go out and travel anywhere, you shall surely die'? And you said to me, 'The word I have heard is good.' ⁴³ Why then have you not kept the oath of the LORD and the commandment that I gave you?" ⁴⁴ The king said moreover to Shimei, "You know, as your heart acknowledges, all the wickedness that you did to my father David; therefore the LORD will return your wickedness on your own head. ⁴⁵ But King Solomon shall be blessed, and the throne of David shall be established before the LORD forever."

⁴⁶ So the king commanded Benaiah the son of Jehoiada; and he went out and struck him down, and he died. Thus the kingdom was established in the hand of Solomon.

Solomon prays for wisdom

3 Now Solomon made a treaty with Pharaoh king of Egypt, and married Pharaoh's daughter; then he brought her to the City of David until he had finished building his own house, and the house of the LORD, and the wall all around Jerusalem. ² Meanwhile the people sacrificed at the high places, because there was no house built for the name of the LORD until those days. ³ And Solomon loved the LORD, walking in the statutes of his father David, except that he sacrificed and burned incense at the high places.

⁴ Now the king went to Gibeon to sacrifice there, for that was the great high place: Solomon offered a thousand burnt offerings on that altar. ⁵ At Gibeon the LORD appeared to Solomon in a dream by night; and God said, "Ask! What shall I give you?"

⁶ And Solomon said: "You have shown great mercy to Your servant David my father, because he walked before You in truth, in righteousness, and in uprightness of heart with You; You have continued this great kindness for him, and You have given him a son to sit on his throne, as it is this day. ⁷ Now, O LORD my God, You have made Your servant king instead of my father David, but I am a little child; I do not know how to go out or come in. ⁸ And Your servant is in the midst of Your people whom You have chosen, a great people, too numerous to be numbered or counted. ⁹ Therefore give to Your servant an understanding heart to judge Your people, that I may discern between good and evil. For who is able to judge this great people of Yours?"

King Solomon pleased God when he prayed for wisdom rather than riches and long life.

15 Then Solomon awoke; and indeed it had been a dream. And he came to Jerusalem and stood before the ark of the covenant of the LORD, offered up burnt offerings, offered peace offerings, and made a feast for all his servants.

16 Now two women *who were* harlots came to the king, and stood before him. 17 And one woman said, "O my lord, this woman and I dwell in the same house; and I gave birth while she *was* in the house. 18 Then it happened, the third day after I had given birth, that this woman also gave birth. And we *were* together; no one *was* with us in the house, except the two of us in the house. 19 And this woman's son died in the night, because she lay on him. 20 So she arose in the middle of the night and took my son from my side, while your maidservant slept, and laid him in her bosom, and laid her dead child in my bosom. 21 And when I rose in the morning to nurse my son, there he was, dead. But when I had examined him in the morning, indeed, he was not my son whom I had borne."

22 Then the other woman said, "No! But the living one *is* my son, and the dead one *is* your son."

And the first woman said, "No! But the dead one *is* your son, and the living one *is* my son."

Thus they spoke before the king.

23 And the king said, "The one says, 'This *is* my son, who lives, and your son *is* the dead one'; and the other says, 'No! But your son *is* the dead one, and my son *is* the living one.' "

24 Then the king said, "Bring me a sword." So they brought a sword before the king. 25 And the king said, "Divide the living child in two, and give half to one, and half to the other."

26 Then the woman whose son *was* living spoke to the king, for she yearned with compassion for her son; and she said, "O my lord, give her the living child, and by no means kill him!"

But the other said, "Let him be neither mine nor yours, *but* divide *him*."

27 So the king answered and said,

10 The speech pleased the LORD, that Solomon had asked this thing. 11 Then God said to him: "Because you have asked this thing, and have not asked long life for yourself, nor have asked riches for yourself, nor have asked the life of your enemies, but have asked for yourself understanding to discern justice, 12 behold, I have done according to your words; see, I have given you a wise and understanding heart, so that there has not been anyone like you before you, nor shall any like you arise after you. 13 And I have also given you what you have not asked: both riches and honor, so that there shall not be anyone like you among the kings all your days. 14 So if you walk in My ways, to keep My statutes and My commandments, as your father David walked, then I will lengthen your days."

"Give the first woman the living child, and by no means kill him; she *is* his mother."

28 And all Israel heard of the judgment which the king had rendered; and they feared the king, for they saw that the **wisdom** of God *was* in him to administer justice.

A list of Solomon's officers

4 So King Solomon was king over all Israel. 2 And these *were* his officials: Azariah the son of Zadok, the priest; 3 Elihoreph and Ahijah, the sons of Shisha, scribes; Jehoshaphat the son of Ahilud, the recorder; 4 Benaiah the son of Jehoiada, over the army; Zadok and Abiathar, the priests; 5 Azariah the son of Nathan, over the officers; Zabud the son of Nathan, a priest *and* the king's friend; 6 Ahishar, over the household; and Adoniram the son of Abda, over the labor force.

7 And Solomon had twelve governors over all Israel, who provided food for the king and his household; each one made provision for one month of the year. 8 These *are* their names: Ben-Hur, in the mountains of Ephraim; 9 Ben-Deker, in Makaz, Shaalbim, Beth Shemesh, and Elon Beth Hanan; 10 Ben-Hesed, in Arubboth; to him *belonged* Sochoh and all the land of Hepher; 11 Ben-Abinadab, *in* all the regions of Dor; he had Taphath the daughter of Solomon as wife; 12 Baana the son of Ahilud, *in* Taanach, Megiddo, and all Beth Shean, which *is* beside Zaretan below Jezreel, from Beth Shean to Abel Meholah, as far as the other side of Jokneam; 13 Ben-Geber, in Ramoth Gilead; to him *belonged* the towns of Jair the son of Manasseh, in Gilead; to him *also belonged* the region of Argob in Bashan—sixty large cities with walls and bronze gate-bars; 14 Ahinadab the son of Iddo, *in* Mahanaim; 15 Ahimaaz, in Naphtali; he

also took Basemath the daughter of Solomon as wife; 16 Baanah the son of Hushai, in Asher and Aloth; 17 Jehoshaphat the son of Paruah, in Issachar; 18 Shimei the son of Elah, in Benjamin; 19 Geber the son of Uri, in the land of Gilead, *in* the country of Sihon king of the Amorites, and of Og king of Bashan. *He was* the only governor who *was* in the land.

20 Judah and Israel *were* as numerous as the sand by the sea in multitude, eating and drinking and rejoicing. 21 So Solomon reigned over all kingdoms from the River *to* the land of the Philistines, as far as the border of Egypt. *They* brought tribute and served Solomon all the days of his life.

22 Now Solomon's provision for one day was thirty kors of fine flour, sixty kors of meal, 23 ten fatted oxen, twenty oxen from the pastures, and one hundred sheep, besides deer, gazelles, roebucks, and fatted fowl.

24 For he had dominion over all *the region* on this side of the River from Tiphsah even to Gaza, namely over all the kings on this side of the River; and he had peace on every side all around him. 25 And Judah and Israel dwelt safely, each man under his vine and his fig tree, from Dan as far as Beersheba, all the days of Solomon.

26 Solomon had forty thousand stalls of horses for his chariots, and twelve thousand horsemen. 27 And these governors, each man in his month, provided food for King Solomon and for all who came to King Solomon's table. There was no lack in their supply. 28 They also brought barley and straw to the proper place, for the horses and steeds, each man according to his charge.

29 And God gave Solomon wisdom and exceedingly great understanding, and largeness of heart like the sand on the seashore. 30 Thus Solomon's wisdom excelled the wisdom of all the

---

WORDFINDER

3:28 Wisdom The ability to use facts to bring about good results. The so-called wisdom of this world could not do this. Jesus Christ is the source of true wisdom.

King Solomon Called World's Greatest Genius

JTN (Jerusalem Television Network)—It is not often that a nation is blessed with a king who is also a great scholar.

The whole world is astounded by the brilliance of King Solomon, the son who succeeded good King David. Scholars and students from all over the world are coming to visit our king and to hear his wisdom.

When our camera crew visited the palace last week, we were surprised to find that the throne room has become an actual classroom with lessons taught by King Solomon himself! There is standing room only for his lectures on history, geography, and astronomy.

When a reporter interviewing the king mentioned that he should open a school of higher learning, and charge tuition, King Solomon only laughed. He said he couldn't charge money for something God had given him—free!

---

men of the East and all the wisdom of Egypt. 31 For he was wiser than all men—than Ethan the Ezrahite, and Heman, Chalcol, and Darda, the sons of Mahol; and his fame was in all the surrounding nations. 32 He spoke three thousand proverbs, and his songs were one thousand and five. 33 Also he spoke of trees, from the cedar tree of Lebanon even to the hyssop that springs out of the wall; he spoke also of animals, of birds, of creeping things, and of fish. 34 And men of all nations, from all the kings of the earth who had heard of his wisdom, came to hear the wisdom of Solomon.

Solomon and Hiram sign a peace treaty

5 Now Hiram king of Tyre sent his servants to Solomon, because he heard that they had anointed him king in place of his father, for Hiram had always loved David. 2 Then Solomon sent to Hiram, saying:

3   You know how my father David could not build a house for the name of the LORD his God because of the wars which were fought against him on every side, until the LORD put his foes under the soles of his feet.

4   But now the LORD my God has given me rest on every side; there is neither adversary nor evil occurrence.

5   And behold, I propose to build a house for the name of the LORD my God, as the LORD spoke to my father David, saying, "Your son, whom I will set on your throne in your place, he shall build the house for My name."

6   Now therefore, command that they cut down cedars for me from Lebanon; and my servants will be with your servants, and I will pay you wages for your servants according to whatever you say. For you know there is none among us who has skill to cut timber like the Sidonians.

7 So it was, when Hiram heard the words of Solomon, that he rejoiced greatly and said,

Blessed be the LORD this day, for He has given David a wise son over this great people!

8 Then Hiram sent to Solomon, saying:

I have considered the message which you sent me, and I will do all you desire concerning the cedar and cypress logs.

9   My servants shall bring them down from Lebanon to the sea;

Great Temple Completed at Jerusalem

The Jerusalem Times

JERUSALEM—The great house of God that King David dreamed of building during his reign (see 2 Samuel 7 and 1 Chronicles 17) was completed early this week in Jerusalem. God had told King David that a worship place would be built during his son Solomon's administration. It has been the great work of King Solomon's career.

Until Solomon built the temple, the people of Israel had worshiped in a tent or tabernacle (pronounced *TAB-er-nak-kel*). Tourists who have seen the new temple are amazed at its beauty.

There is some confusion, however. When God made His agreement or "covenant" (pronounced *KUV-uh-nunt*) with David, He said the throne of David's Son would last forever. Due to recent political developments, we know that Solomon's throne and kingdom have come to an end.

We know of no other son of David who might inherit the throne. The mystery remains: Who is the "Son of David" who will rule someday?

I will float them in rafts by sea to the place you indicate to me, and will have them broken apart there; then you can take *them* away. And you shall fulfill my desire by giving food for my household.

¹⁰ Then Hiram gave Solomon cedar and cypress logs *according to* all his desire. ¹¹ And Solomon gave Hiram twenty thousand kors of wheat *as* food for his household, and twenty kors of pressed oil. Thus Solomon gave to Hiram year by year.

¹² So the LORD gave Solomon wisdom, as He had promised him; and there was peace between Hiram and Solomon, and the two of them made a treaty together.

¹³ Then King Solomon raised up a labor force out of all Israel; and the labor force was thirty thousand men. ¹⁴ And he sent them to Lebanon, ten thousand a month in shifts: they were one month in Lebanon *and* two months at home; Adoniram *was* in charge of the labor force. ¹⁵ Solomon had seventy thousand who carried burdens, and eighty thousand who quarried *stone* in the mountains, ¹⁶ besides three thousand three hundred from the chiefs of Solomon's deputies, who supervised the people who labored in the work. ¹⁷ And the king commanded them to quarry large stones, costly stones, *and* hewn stones, to lay the foundation of the **temple.** ¹⁸ So Solomon's builders, Hiram's builders, and the Gebalites quarried *them;* and they prepared timber and stones to build the temple.

Solomon builds the temple

6 And it came to pass in the four hundred and eightieth year after the children of Israel had come out of the land of Egypt, in the fourth year of Solomon's reign over Israel, in the month of Ziv, which *is* the second month, that he began to build the house of the LORD. ² Now the house which King Solomon built for the LORD, its length *was* sixty cubits, its width twenty, and its height thirty cubits. ³ The vestibule in front of the sanctuary of the house *was* twenty cubits long across the width

🌐 **WORDFINDER**

5:17 Temple   Israel's place of worship after they settled in Canaan. It was a building of finished stone. Worship in the temple was the same as it had been in the tabernacle.

of the house, *and* the width of *the vestibule extended* ten cubits from the front of the house. ⁴ And he made for the house windows with beveled frames.

⁵ Against the wall of the temple he built chambers all around, *against* the walls of the temple, all around the sanctuary and the inner sanctuary. Thus he made side chambers all around it. ⁶ The lowest chamber *was* five cubits wide, the middle *was* six cubits wide, and the third *was* seven cubits wide; for he made narrow ledges around the outside of the temple, so that *the support beams* would not be fastened into the walls of the temple. ⁷ And the temple, when it was being built, was built with stone finished at the quarry, so that no hammer or chisel *or* any iron tool was heard in the temple while it was being built. ⁸ The doorway for the middle story *was* on the right side of the temple. They went up by stairs to the middle *story,* and from the middle to the third.

⁹ So he built the temple and finished it, and he paneled the temple with beams and boards of cedar. ¹⁰ And he built side chambers against the entire temple, each five cubits high; they were attached to the temple with cedar beams.

¹¹ Then the word of the LORD came to Solomon, saying: ¹² "Concerning this temple which you are building, if you walk in My statutes, execute My judgments, keep all My commandments, and walk in them, then I will perform My word with you, which I spoke to your father David. ¹³ And I will dwell among the children of Israel, and will not forsake My people Israel."

¹⁴ So Solomon built the temple and finished it. ¹⁵ And he built the inside walls of the temple with cedar boards; from the floor of the temple to the ceiling he paneled the inside with wood; and he covered the floor of the temple with planks of cypress. ¹⁶ Then he built the twenty-cubit room at the rear of the temple, from floor to ceiling, with cedar boards; he built *it* inside as the inner sanctuary, as the Most Holy

Place. ¹⁷ And in front of it the temple sanctuary was forty cubits *long.* ¹⁸ The inside of the temple was cedar, carved with ornamental buds and open flowers. All *was* cedar; there was no stone *to be* seen.

¹⁹ And he prepared the inner sanctuary inside the temple, to set the ark of the covenant of the LORD there. ²⁰ The inner sanctuary *was* twenty cubits long, twenty cubits wide, and twenty cubits high. He overlaid it with pure gold, and overlaid the altar of cedar. ²¹ So Solomon overlaid the inside of the temple with pure gold. He stretched gold chains across the front of the inner sanctuary, and overlaid it with gold. ²² The whole temple he overlaid with gold, until he had finished all the temple; also he overlaid with gold the entire altar that *was* by the inner sanctuary.

²³ Inside the inner sanctuary he made two cherubim *of* olive wood, *each* ten cubits high. ²⁴ One wing of the cherub *was* five cubits, and the other wing of the cherub five cubits: ten cubits from the tip of one wing to the tip of the other. ²⁵ And the other cherub *was* ten cubits; both cherubim *were* of the same size and shape. ²⁶ The height of one cherub *was* ten cubits, and so *was* the other cherub. ²⁷ Then he set the cherubim inside the inner room; and they stretched out the wings of the cherubim so that the wing of the one touched *one* wall, and the wing of the other cherub touched the other wall. And their wings touched each other in the middle of the room. ²⁸ Also he overlaid the cherubim with gold.

²⁹ Then he carved all the walls of the temple all around, both the inner and outer *sanctuaries,* with carved figures of cherubim, palm trees, and open flowers. ³⁰ And the floor of the temple he overlaid with gold, both the inner and outer *sanctuaries.*

³¹ For the entrance of the inner sanctuary he made doors *of* olive wood; the lintel *and* doorposts *were* one-fifth *of the wall.* ³² The two doors *were of* olive wood; and he carved on them

figures of cherubim, palm trees, and open flowers, and overlaid *them* with gold; and he spread gold on the cherubim and on the palm trees. 33 So for the door of the sanctuary he also made doorposts *of* olive wood, one-fourth *of* the wall. 34 And the two doors *were of* cypress wood; two panels *comprised* one folding door, and two panels *comprised* the other folding door. 35 Then he carved cherubim, palm trees, and open flowers *on them*, and overlaid *them* with gold applied evenly on the carved work.

36 And he built the inner court with three rows of hewn stone and a row of cedar beams.

37 In the fourth year the foundation of the house of the LORD was laid, in the month of Ziv. 38 And in the eleventh year, in the month of Bul, which is the eighth month, the house was finished in all its details and according to all its plans. So he was seven years in building it.

The furniture of the temple

7 But Solomon took thirteen years to build his own house; so he finished all his house.

2 He also built the House of the Forest of Lebanon; its length *was* one hundred cubits, its width fifty cubits, and its height thirty cubits, with four rows of cedar pillars, and cedar beams on the pillars. 3 And *it was* paneled with cedar above the beams that *were* on forty-five pillars, fifteen *to* a row. 4 *There were* windows *with beveled frames in* three rows, and window *was* opposite window *in* three tiers. 5 And all the doorways and doorposts *had* rectangular frames; and window *was* opposite window *in* three tiers.

6 He also made the Hall of Pillars: its length *was* fifty cubits, and its width thirty cubits; and in front of them *was* a portico with pillars, and a canopy *was* in front of them.

7 Then he made a hall for the throne, the Hall of Judgment, where he might judge; and *it was* paneled with cedar from floor to ceiling.

8 And the house where he dwelt *had* another court inside the hall, of like workmanship. Solomon also made a house like this hall for Pharaoh's daughter, whom he had taken *as wife.*

9 All these *were of* costly stones cut to size, trimmed with saws, inside and out, from the foundation to the eaves, and also on the outside to the great court. 10 The foundation *was of* costly stones, large stones, some ten cubits and some eight cubits. 11 And above *were* costly stones, hewn to size, and cedar wood. 12 The great court *was* enclosed with three rows of hewn stones and a row of cedar beams. So were the inner court of the house of the LORD and the vestibule of the temple.

13 Now King Solomon sent and brought Huram from Tyre. 14 He *was* the son of a widow from the tribe of Naphtali, and his father *was* a man of Tyre, a bronze worker; he was filled with wisdom and understanding and skill in working with all kinds of bronze work. So he came to King Solomon and did all his work.

15 And he cast two pillars of bronze, each one eighteen cubits high, and a line of twelve cubits measured the circumference of each. 16 Then he made two capitals *of* cast bronze, to set on the tops of the pillars. The height of one capital *was* five cubits, and the height of the other capital *was* five cubits. 17 *He made* a lattice network, with wreaths of chainwork, for the capitals which *were* on top of the pillars: seven chains for one capital and seven for the other capital. 18 So he made the pillars, and two rows of pomegranates above the network all around to cover the capitals that *were* on top; and thus he did for the other capital.

19 The capitals which *were* on top of the pillars in the hall *were* in the shape of lilies, four cubits. 20 The capitals on the two pillars also *had* pomegranates above, by the convex surface which *was* next to the network; and there *were* two hundred such pomegranates in rows on each of the capitals all around.

21 Then he set up the pillars by the

vestibule of the temple; he set up the pillar on the right and called its name Jachin, and he set up the pillar on the left and called its name Boaz. 22 The tops of the pillars were in the shape of lilies. So the work of the pillars was finished.

23 And he made the Sea of cast bronze, ten cubits from one brim to the other; it was completely round. Its height was five cubits, and a line of thirty cubits measured its circumference.

24 Below its brim were ornamental buds encircling it all around, ten to a cubit, all the way around the Sea. The ornamental buds were cast in two rows when it was cast. 25 It stood on twelve oxen: three looking toward the north, three looking toward the west, three looking toward the south, and three looking toward the east; the Sea was set upon them, and all their back parts pointed inward. 26 It was a handbreadth thick; and its brim was shaped like the brim of a cup, like a lily blossom. It contained two thousand baths.

27 He also made ten carts of bronze; four cubits was the length of each cart, four cubits its width, and three cubits its height. 28 And this was the design of the carts: They had panels, and the panels were between frames; 29 on the panels that were between the frames were lions, oxen, and cherubim. And on the frames was a pedestal on top. Below the lions and oxen were wreaths of plaited work. 30 Every cart had four bronze wheels and axles of bronze, and its four feet had supports. Under the laver were supports of cast bronze beside each wreath. 31 Its opening inside the crown at the top was one cubit in diameter; and the opening was round, shaped like a pedestal, one and a half cubits in outside diameter; and also on the opening were engravings, but the panels were square, not round.

32 Under the panels were the four wheels, and the axles of the wheels were joined to the cart. The height of a wheel was one and a half cubits. 33 The workmanship of the wheels was like the workmanship of a chariot wheel; their axle pins, their rims, their spokes, and their hubs were all of cast bronze. 34 And there were four supports at the four corners of each cart; its supports were part of the cart itself. 35 On the top of the cart, at the height of half a cubit, it was perfectly round. And on the top of the cart, its flanges and its panels were of the same casting. 36 On the plates of its flanges and on its panels he engraved cherubim, lions, and palm trees, wherever there was a clear space on each, with wreaths all around. 37 Thus he made the ten carts. All of them were of the same mold, one measure, and one shape.

38 Then he made ten lavers of bronze; each **laver** contained forty baths, and each laver was four cubits. On each of the ten carts was a laver. 39 And he put five carts on the right side of the house, and five on the left side of the house. He set the Sea on the right side of the house, toward the southeast.

40 Huram made the lavers and the shovels and the bowls. So Huram finished doing all the work that he was to do for King Solomon for the house of the LORD: 41 the two pillars, the two bowl-shaped capitals that were on top of the two pillars; the two networks covering the two bowl-shaped capitals which were on top of the pillars; 42 four hundred pomegranates for the two networks (two rows of pomegranates for each network, to cover the two bowl-shaped capitals that were on top of the pillars); 43 the ten carts, and ten lavers on the carts; 44 one Sea, and twelve oxen under the Sea; 45 the pots, the shovels, and the bowls.

⬤WORDFINDER

7:38 Laver Pronounced *LAY-ver*. A special washstand made of bronze. The laver stood between the altar of burnt offering and the door of the Old Testament worship place. The priests washed their hands there as an act of purifying themselves.

All these articles which Huram made for King Solomon *for* the house of the LORD *were of* burnished bronze. 46 In the plain of Jordan the king had them cast in clay molds, between Succoth and Zaretan. 47 And Solomon did not weigh all the articles, because *there were* so many; the weight of the bronze was not determined.

48 Thus Solomon had all the furnishings made for the house of the LORD: the altar of gold, and the table of gold on which *was* the showbread; 49 the lampstands of pure gold, five on the right *side* and five on the left in front of the inner sanctuary, with the flowers and the lamps and the wick-trimmers of gold; 50 the basins, the trimmers, the bowls, the ladles, and the censers of pure gold; and the hinges of gold, *both* for the doors of the inner room (the Most Holy *Place*) *and* for the doors of the main hall of the temple.

51 So all the work that King Solomon had done for the house of the LORD was finished; and Solomon brought in the things which his father David had dedicated: the silver and the gold and the furnishings. He put them in the treasuries of the house of the LORD.

God comes to live in the temple

8 Now Solomon assembled the elders of Israel and all the heads of the tribes, the chief fathers of the children of Israel, to King Solomon in Jerusalem, that they might bring up the ark of the covenant of the LORD from the City of David, which *is* Zion. 2 Therefore all the men of Israel assembled with King Solomon at the feast in the month of Ethanim, which *is* the seventh month. 3 So all the elders of Israel came, and the priests took up the ark. 4 Then they brought up the ark of the LORD, the tabernacle of meeting, and all the holy furnishings that *were* in the tabernacle. The priests and the Levites brought them up. 5 Also King Solomon, and all the congregation of Israel who were assembled with him, *were* with him before the ark, sacrificing sheep and oxen that could not be counted or numbered for multitude. 6 Then the priests brought in the ark of the covenant of the LORD to its place, into the inner sanctuary of the temple, to the Most Holy *Place,* under the wings of the cherubim. 7 For the cherubim spread *their* two wings over the place of the ark, and the cherubim overshadowed the ark and its poles. 8 The poles extended so that the ends of the poles could be seen from the holy *place,* in front of the inner sanctuary; but they could not be seen from outside. And they are there to this day. 9 Nothing *was* in the ark except the two tablets of stone which Moses put there at Horeb, when the LORD made *a covenant* with the children of Israel, when they came out of the land of Egypt.

10 And it came to pass, when the priests came out of the holy *place,* that the cloud filled the house of the LORD, 11 so that the priests could not continue ministering because of the cloud; for the glory of the LORD filled the house of the LORD.

12 Then Solomon spoke:

"The LORD said He would dwell
    in the dark cloud.
13 I have surely built You an
    exalted house,
And a place for You to dwell in
    forever."

14 Then the king turned around and blessed the whole assembly of Israel, while all the assembly of Israel was standing. 15 And he said: "Blessed *be* the LORD God of Israel, who spoke with His mouth to my father David, and with His hand has fulfilled *it,* saying, 16 'Since the day that I brought My people Israel out of Egypt, I have chosen no city from any tribe of Israel *in which* to build a house, that My name might be there; but I chose David to be over My people Israel.' 17 Now it was in the heart of my father David to build a temple for the name of the LORD God of Israel. 18 But the LORD said to my father David, 'Whereas it was in your heart to build

a temple for My name, you did well that it was in your heart. 19 Nevertheless you shall not build the temple, but your son who will come from your body, he shall build the temple for My name.' 20 So the LORD has fulfilled His word which He spoke; and I have filled the position of my father David, and sit on the throne of Israel, as the LORD promised; and I have built a temple for the name of the LORD God of Israel. 21 And there I have made a place for the ark, in which is the covenant of the LORD which He made with our fathers, when He brought them out of the land of Egypt.''

22 Then Solomon stood before the altar of the LORD in the presence of all the assembly of Israel, and spread out his hands toward heaven; 23 and he said: ''LORD God of Israel, there is no God in heaven above or on earth below like You, who keep Your covenant and mercy with Your servants who walk before You with all their hearts. 24 You have kept what You promised Your servant David my father; You have both spoken with Your mouth and fulfilled it with Your hand, as it is this day. 25 Therefore, LORD God of Israel, now keep what You promised Your servant David my father, saying, 'You shall not fail to have a man sit before Me on the throne of Israel, only if your sons take heed to their way, that they walk before Me as you have walked before Me.' 26 And now I pray, O God of Israel, let Your word come true, which You have spoken to Your servant David my father.

27 ''But will God indeed dwell on the earth? Behold, heaven and the heaven of heavens cannot contain You. How much less this temple which I have built! 28 Yet regard the prayer of Your servant and his supplication, O LORD my God, and listen to the cry and the prayer which Your servant is praying before You today: 29 that Your eyes may be open toward this temple night and day, toward the place of which You said, 'My name shall be there,' that You may hear the prayer which Your servant makes toward this place.

30 And may You hear the supplication of Your servant and of Your people Israel, when they pray toward this place. Hear in heaven Your dwelling place; and when You hear, forgive.

31 ''When anyone sins against his neighbor, and is forced to take an oath, and comes and takes an oath before Your altar in this temple, 32 then hear in heaven, and act, and judge Your servants, condemning the wicked, bringing his way on his head, and justifying the righteous by giving him according to his righteousness.

33 ''When Your people Israel are defeated before an enemy because they have sinned against You, and when they turn back to You and confess Your name, and pray and make supplication to You in this temple, 34 then hear in heaven, and forgive the sin of Your people Israel, and bring them back to the land which You gave to their fathers.

35 ''When the heavens are shut up and there is no rain because they have sinned against You, when they pray toward this place and confess Your name, and turn from their sin because You afflict them, 36 then hear in heaven, and forgive the sin of Your servants, Your people Israel, that You may teach them the good way in which they should walk; and send rain on Your land which You have given to Your people as an inheritance.

37 ''When there is famine in the land, pestilence or blight or mildew, locusts or grasshoppers; when their enemy besieges them in the land of their cities; whatever plague or whatever sickness there is; 38 whatever prayer, whatever supplication is made by anyone, or by all Your people Israel, when each one knows the plague of his own heart, and spreads out his hands toward this temple: 39 then hear in heaven Your dwelling place, and forgive, and act, and give to everyone according to all his ways, whose heart You know (for You alone know the hearts of all the sons of men), 40 that they may fear You all the days that they live in the land which You gave to our fathers.

41 "Moreover, concerning a foreigner, who *is* not of Your people Israel, but has come from a far country for Your name's sake 42 (for they will hear of Your great name and Your strong hand and Your outstretched arm), when he comes and prays toward this temple, 43 hear in heaven Your dwelling place, and do according to all for which the foreigner calls to You, that all peoples of the earth may know Your name and fear You, as *do* Your people Israel, and that they may know that this temple which I have built is called by Your name.

44 "When Your people go out to battle against their enemy, wherever You send them, and when they pray to the LORD toward the city which You have chosen and the temple which I have built for Your name, 45 then hear in heaven their prayer and their supplication, and maintain their cause.

46 "When they sin against You (for *there is* no one who does not sin), and You become angry with them and deliver them to the enemy, and they take them captive to the land of the enemy, far or near; 47 *yet* when they come to themselves in the land where they were carried captive, and repent, and make supplication to You in the land of those who took them captive, saying, 'We have sinned and done wrong, we have committed wickedness'; 48 and *when* they return to You with all their heart and with all their soul in the land of their enemies who led them away captive, and pray to You toward their land which You gave to their fathers, the city which You have chosen and the temple which I have built for Your name: 49 then hear in heaven Your dwelling place their prayer and their supplication, and maintain their cause, 50 and forgive Your people who have sinned against You, and all their transgressions which they have transgressed against You; and grant them compassion before those who took them captive, that they may have compassion on them 51 (for they *are* Your people and Your inheritance, whom You brought out of Egypt, out of the iron furnace), 52 that Your *eyes* may be open to the supplication of Your servant and the supplication of Your people Israel, to listen to them whenever they call to You. 53 For You separated them from among all the peoples of the earth *to be* Your inheritance, as You spoke by Your servant Moses, when You brought our fathers out of Egypt, O Lord GOD."

54 And so it was, when Solomon had finished praying all this prayer and supplication to the LORD, that he arose from before the altar of the LORD, from kneeling on his knees with his hands spread up to heaven. 55 Then he stood and blessed all the assembly of Israel with a loud voice, saying: 56 "Blessed *be* the LORD, who has given rest to His people Israel, according to all that He promised. There has not failed one word of all His good promise, which He promised through His servant Moses. 57 May the LORD our God be with us, as He was with our fathers. May He not leave us nor forsake us, 58 that He may incline our hearts to Himself, to walk in all His ways, and to keep His commandments and His statutes and His judgments, which He commanded our fathers. 59 And may these words of mine, with which I have made supplication before the LORD, be near the LORD our God day and night, that He may maintain the cause of His servant and the cause of His people Israel, as each day may require, 60 that all the peoples of the earth may know that the LORD *is* God; *there* is no other. 61 Let your heart therefore be loyal to the LORD our God, to walk in His statutes and keep His commandments, as at this day."

62 Then the king and all Israel with him offered sacrifices before the LORD. 63 And Solomon offered a sacrifice of peace offerings, which he offered to the LORD, twenty-two thousand bulls and one hundred and twenty thousand sheep. So the king and all the children of Israel dedicated the house of the LORD. 64 On the same day the king consecrated the middle of the court that *was* in front of the house of the

LORD; for there he offered burnt offerings, grain offerings, and the fat of the peace offerings, because the bronze altar that *was* before the LORD *was* too small to receive the burnt offerings, the grain offerings, and the fat of the peace offerings.

65 At that time Solomon held a feast, and all Israel with him, a great assembly from the entrance of Hamath to the Brook of Egypt, before the LORD our God, seven days and seven *more* days—fourteen days. 66 On the eighth day he sent the people away; and they blessed the king, and went to their tents joyful and glad of heart for all the good that the LORD had done for His servant David, and for Israel His people.

God makes a promise to Solomon

9 And it came to pass, when Solomon had finished building the house of the LORD and the king's house, and all Solomon's desire which he wanted to do, 2 that the LORD appeared to Solomon the second time, as He had appeared to him at Gibeon. 3 And the LORD said to him: "I have heard your prayer and your supplication that you have made before Me; I have consecrated this house which you have built to put My name there forever, and My eyes and My heart will be there perpetually. 4 Now if you walk before Me as your father David walked, in integrity of heart and in uprightness, to do according to all that I have commanded you, *and* if you keep My statutes and My judgments, 5 then I will establish the throne of your kingdom over Israel forever, as I promised David your father, saying, 'You shall not fail to have a man on the throne of Israel.' 6 *But* if you or your sons at all turn from following Me, and do not keep My commandments *and* My statutes which

I have set before you, but go and serve other gods and worship them, 7 then I will cut off Israel from the land which I have given them; and this house which I have consecrated for My name I will cast out of My sight. Israel will be a proverb and a byword among all peoples. 8 And *as for* this house, *which* is exalted, everyone who passes by it will be astonished and will hiss, and say, 'Why has the LORD done thus to this land and to this house?' 9 Then they will answer, 'Because they forsook the LORD their God, who brought their fathers out of the land of Egypt, and have embraced other gods, and worshiped them and served them; therefore the LORD has brought all this calamity on them.' "

10 Now it happened at the end of twenty years, when Solomon had built the two houses, the house of the LORD and the king's house 11 (Hiram the king of Tyre had supplied Solomon with cedar and cypress and gold, as much as he desired), *that* King Solomon then gave Hiram twenty cities in the land of Galilee. 12 Then Hiram went from Tyre to see the cities which Solomon had given him, but they did not please him. 13 So he said, "What *kind of* cities *are* these which you have given me, my brother?" And he called them the land of Cabul, as they are to this day. 14 Then Hiram sent the king one hundred and twenty talents of gold.

15 And this *is* the reason for the labor force which King Solomon raised: to build the house of the LORD, his own house, the Millo, the wall of Jerusalem, Hazor, Megiddo, and Gezer. 16 (Pharaoh king of Egypt had gone up and taken Gezer and burned it with fire, had killed the **Canaanites** who dwelt in the city, and had given it *as* a dowry to his daughter, Solomon's wife.) 17 And Solomon built Gezer, Lower Beth Horon, 18 Baalath, and Tadmor

WORDFINDER
9:16 Canaanites Pronounced *KAY-nuh-nights*. Descendants of Noah's grandson, Canaan. When Jacob and his family moved to Egypt, the dwellers in Palestine became known as Canaanites. Then Palestine was called Canaan.

One of King Solomon's cargo ships, which carried gold, silver, ivory, and exotic animals from many parts of the world.

in the wilderness, in the land *of Judah,* ¹⁹ all the storage cities that Solomon had, cities for his chariots and cities for his cavalry, and whatever Solomon desired to build in Jerusalem, in Lebanon, and in all the land of his dominion.

²⁰ All the people *who were* left of the Amorites, Hittites, Perizzites, Hivites, and Jebusites, who *were* not of the children of Israel— ²¹ that is, their descendants who were left in the land after them, whom the children of Israel had not been able to destroy completely—from these Solomon raised forced labor, as it is to this day. ²² But of the children of Israel Solomon made no forced laborers, because they *were* men of war and his servants: his officers, his captains, commanders of his chariots, and his cavalry.

²³ Others *were* chiefs of the officials who *were* over Solomon's work: five hundred and fifty, who ruled over the people who did the work.

²⁴ But Pharaoh's daughter came up from the City of David to her house which *Solomon* had built for her. Then he built the Millo.

²⁵ Now three times a year Solomon offered burnt offerings and peace offerings on the altar which he had built for the LORD, and he burned incense with them *on the altar* that *was* before

the LORD. So he finished the temple.

²⁶ King Solomon also built a fleet of ships at Ezion Geber, which *is* near Elath on the shore of the Red Sea, in the land of Edom. ²⁷ Then Hiram sent his servants with the fleet, seamen who knew the sea, to work with the servants of Solomon. ²⁸ And they went to Ophir, and acquired four hundred and twenty talents of gold from there, and brought *it* to King Solomon.

God blesses Solomon with riches and fame

10 Now when the queen of Sheba heard of the fame of Solomon concerning the name of the LORD, she came to test him with hard questions. ² She came to Jerusalem with a very great retinue, with camels that bore spices, very much gold, and precious stones; and when she came to Solomon, she spoke with him about all that was in her heart. ³ So Solomon answered all her questions; there was nothing so difficult for the king that he could not explain *it* to her. ⁴ And when the queen of Sheba had seen all the wisdom of Solomon, the house that he had built, ⁵ the food on his table, the seating of his servants, the service of his waiters and their apparel, his

The Queen of Sheba—My little country, called Sheba (pronounced *SHEE-bah*), was southwest of Israel. We were a nation because Israel allowed us to be there.

I could hardly believe all the wonderful things I had heard about King Solomon, so I paid him a royal visit. Solomon's great knowledge amazed me. His thousands of proverbs with advice for everyday needs were known all over the world. When I asked him many questions, he answered me with greater wisdom than anyone I ever knew.

By the time my visit was over, I was also overwhelmed by the wealth and beauty of Solomon's great kingdom. I then realized that I had not heard even half of Solomon's greatness. So I confessed that the true God, the Creator of heaven and earth, was the One who made Israel and Solomon great. Then I worshiped the Lord, and I also gave Solomon so much gold that it took 120 strong men to carry it!

cupbearers, and his entryway by which he went up to the house of the Lord, there was no more spirit in her. 6 Then she said to the king: "It was a true report which I heard in my own land about your words and your wisdom. 7 However I did not believe the words until I came and saw with my own eyes; and indeed the half was not told me. Your wisdom and prosperity exceed the fame of which I heard. 8 Happy *are* your men and happy *are* these your servants, who stand continually before you *and* hear your wisdom! 9 Blessed be the Lord your God, who delighted in you, setting you on the throne of Israel! Because the Lord has loved Israel forever, therefore He made you king, to do justice and righteousness."

10 Then she gave the king one hundred and twenty talents of gold, spices in great quantity, and precious stones. There never again came such abundance of spices as the queen of Sheba gave to King Solomon. 11 Also, the ships of Hiram, which brought gold from Ophir, brought great *quantities* of almug wood and precious stones from Ophir. 12 And the king made steps of the almug wood for the house of the

Lord and for the king's house, also harps and stringed instruments for singers. There never again came such almug wood, nor has the like been seen to this day.

13 Now King Solomon gave the queen of Sheba all she desired, whatever she asked, besides what Solomon had given her according to the royal generosity. So she turned and went to her own country, she and her servants.

14 The weight of gold that came to Solomon yearly was six hundred and sixty-six talents of gold, 15 besides *that* from the traveling merchants, from the income of traders, from all the kings of Arabia, and from the governors of the country.

16 And King Solomon made two hundred large shields *of* hammered gold; six hundred *shekels* of gold went into each shield. 17 He also *made* three hundred shields *of* hammered gold; three minas of gold went into each shield. The king put them in the House of the Forest of Lebanon.

18 Moreover the king made a great throne of ivory, and overlaid it with pure gold. 19 The throne had six steps, and the top of the throne *was* round at the back; *there were* armrests on

WORDFINDER

10:5 Cupbearer An official in the palace who served wine to the king. He was also a trusted royal adviser.

either side of the place of the seat, and two lions stood beside the armrests. 20 Twelve lions stood there, one on each side of the six steps; nothing like *this* had been made for any *other* kingdom.

21 All King Solomon's drinking vessels *were* gold, and all the vessels of the House of the Forest of Lebanon *were* pure gold. Not *one was* silver, for this was accounted as nothing in the days of Solomon. 22 For the king had merchant ships at sea with the fleet of Hiram. Once *every* three years the merchant ships came bringing gold, silver, ivory, apes, and monkeys. 23 So King Solomon surpassed all the kings of the earth in riches and wisdom.

24 Now all the earth sought the presence of Solomon to hear his wisdom, which God had put in his heart. 25 Each man brought his present: articles of silver and gold, garments, armor, spices, horses, and mules, at a set rate year by year.

26 And Solomon gathered chariots and horsemen; he had one thousand four hundred chariots and twelve thousand horsemen, whom he stationed in the chariot cities and with the king at Jerusalem. 27 The king made silver *as common* in Jerusalem as stones, and he made cedar trees as abundant as the sycamores which *are* in the lowland.

28 Also Solomon had horses imported from Egypt and Keveh; the king's merchants bought them in Keveh at the *current* price. 29 Now a chariot that was imported from Egypt cost six hundred *shekels* of silver, and a horse one hundred and fifty; and thus, through their agents, they exported *them* to all the kings of the Hittites and the kings of Syria.

Solomon disobeys God

11 But King Solomon loved many foreign women, as well as the daughter of Pharaoh: women of the Moabites, Ammonites, Edomites, Sidonians, *and* Hittites— 2 from the nations of whom the LORD had said to the children of Israel, "You shall not intermarry with them, nor they with you. Surely they will turn away your hearts after their gods." Solomon clung to these in love. 3 And he had seven hundred wives, princesses, and three hundred concubines; and his wives turned away his heart. 4 For it was so, when Solomon was old, that his wives turned his heart after other gods; and his heart was not loyal to the LORD his God, as *was* the heart of his father David. 5 For Solomon went after Ashtoreth the goddess of the Sidonians, and after Milcom the abomination of the Ammonites. 6 Solomon did evil in the sight of the LORD, and did not fully follow the LORD, as *did* his father David. 7 Then Solomon built a high place for Chemosh the abomination of Moab, on the hill that *is* east of Jerusalem, and for Molech the abomination of the people of Ammon. 8 And he did likewise for all his foreign wives, who burned incense and sacrificed to their gods.

9 So the LORD became angry with

⚒ DIGGING IN

11:4 King Solomon Turns Away from God At first Solomon, the son of David and Bathsheba, seemed to be a great king. He even carried out God's command to build the temple at Jerusalem. David had been a soldier. But Solomon was a man of peace, and this was the meaning of his name. He received a very large kingdom from his father David, and he enjoyed great wealth. Solomon was known as the wisest man in the world of his time.

But Solomon was not wise about everything. He married many Gentile wives. Many of these wives didn't worship the true God, and they led Solomon to worship their false gods. Sad to say, Solomon turned out to be a "wise fool" in the end.

Sometimes people who are gifted by God in special ways become proud. Then such people think they don't need to obey the laws of God. Pride often ruins someone who is great in every other way.

Solomon, because his heart had turned from the LORD God of Israel, who had appeared to him twice, 10 and had commanded him concerning this thing, that he should not go after other gods; but he did not keep what the LORD had commanded. 11 Therefore the LORD said to Solomon, "Because you have done this, and have not kept My covenant and My statutes, which I have commanded you, I will surely tear the kingdom away from you and give it to your servant. 12 Nevertheless I will not do it in your days, for the sake of your father David; I will tear it out of the hand of your son. 13 However I will not tear away the whole kingdom; I will give one tribe to your son for the sake of my servant David, and for the sake of Jerusalem which I have chosen."

14 Now the LORD raised up an adversary against Solomon, Hadad the Edomite; he was a descendant of the king in Edom. 15 For it happened, when David was in Edom, and Joab the commander of the army had gone up to bury the slain, after he had killed every male in Edom 16 (because for six months Joab remained there with all Israel, until he had cut down every male in Edom), 17 that Hadad fled to go to Egypt, he and certain Edomites of his father's servants with him. Hadad was still a little child. 18 Then they arose from Midian and came to Paran; and they took men with them from Paran and came to Egypt, to Pharaoh king of Egypt, who gave him a house, apportioned food for him, and gave him land. 19 And Hadad found great favor in the sight of Pharaoh, so that he gave him as wife the sister of his own wife, that is, the sister of Queen Tahpenes. 20 Then the sister of Tahpenes bore him Genubath his son, whom Tahpenes weaned in Pharaoh's house. And Genubath was in Pharaoh's household among the sons of Pharaoh.

21 So when Hadad heard in Egypt that David rested with his fathers, and that Joab the commander of the army was dead, Hadad said to Pharaoh, "Let me depart, that I may go to my own country."

22 Then Pharaoh said to him, "But what have you lacked with me, that suddenly you seek to go to your own country?"

So he answered, "Nothing, but do let me go anyway."

23 And God raised up another adversary against him, Rezon the son of Eliadah, who had fled from his lord, Hadadezer king of Zobah. 24 So he gathered men to him and became captain over a band of raiders, when David killed those of Zobah. And they went to Damascus and dwelt there, and reigned in Damascus. 25 He was an adversary of Israel all the days of Solomon (besides the trouble that Hadad caused); and he abhorred Israel, and reigned over Syria.

26 Then Solomon's servant, Jeroboam the son of Nebat, an Ephraimite from Zereda, whose mother's name was Zeruah, a widow, also rebelled against the king.

27 And this is what caused him to rebel against the king: Solomon had built the Millo and repaired the damages to the City of David his father. 28 The man Jeroboam was a mighty man of valor; and Solomon, seeing that the young man was industrious, made him the officer over all the labor force of the house of Joseph.

29 Now it happened at that time, when Jeroboam went out of Jerusalem, that the prophet Ahijah the Shilonite met him on the way; and he had clothed himself with a new garment, and the two were alone in the field. 30 Then Ahijah took hold of the new garment that was on him, and tore it into twelve pieces. 31 And he said to Jeroboam, "Take for yourself ten pieces, for thus says the LORD, the God of Israel: 'Behold, I will tear the kingdom out of the hand of Solomon and will give ten tribes to you 32 (but he shall have one tribe for the sake of My servant David, and for the sake of Jerusalem, the city which I have chosen out of all the tribes of Israel), 33 because they have forsaken Me, and

worshiped Ashtoreth the goddess of the Sidonians, Chemosh the god of the Moabites, and Milcom the god of the people of Ammon, and have not walked in My ways to do *what is* right in My eyes and *keep* My statutes and My judgments, as *did* his father David. ³⁴ However I will not take the whole kingdom out of his hand, because I have made him ruler all the days of his life for the sake of My servant David, whom I chose because he kept My commandments and My statutes. ³⁵ But I will take the kingdom out of his son's hand and give it to you—ten tribes. ³⁶ And to his son I will give one tribe, that My servant David may always have a lamp before Me in Jerusalem, the city which I have chosen for Myself, to put My name there. ³⁷ So I will take you, and you shall reign over all your heart desires, and you shall be king over Israel. ³⁸ Then it shall be, if you heed all that I command you, walk in My ways, and do *what is* right in My sight, to keep My statutes and My commandments, as My servant David did, then I will be with you and build for you an enduring house, as I built for David, and will give Israel to you. ³⁹ And I will afflict the descendants of David because of this, but not forever.' "

⁴⁰ Solomon therefore sought to kill Jeroboam. But Jeroboam arose and fled to Egypt, to Shishak king of Egypt, and was in Egypt until the death of Solomon.

⁴¹ Now the rest of the acts of Solomon, all that he did, and his wisdom, *are* they not written in the book of the acts of Solomon? ⁴² And the period that Solomon reigned in Jerusalem over all Israel *was* forty years. ⁴³ Then Solomon rested with his fathers, and was buried in the City of David his father. And Rehoboam his son reigned in his place.

King Rehoboam rules

12 And Rehoboam went to Shechem, for all Israel had gone to Shechem to make him king. ² So it hap-

pened, when Jeroboam the son of Nebat heard *it* (he was still in Egypt, for he had fled from the presence of King Solomon and had been dwelling in Egypt), ³ that they sent and called him. Then Jeroboam and the whole assembly of Israel came and spoke to Rehoboam, saying, ⁴ "Your father made our yoke heavy; now therefore, lighten the burdensome service of your father, and his heavy yoke which he put on us, and we will serve you."

⁵ So he said to them, "Depart *for* three days, then come back to me." And the people departed.

⁶ Then King Rehoboam consulted the elders who stood before his father Solomon while he still lived, and he said, "How do you advise *me* to answer these people?"

⁷ And they spoke to him, saying, "If you will be a servant to these people today, and serve them, and answer them, and speak good words to them, then they will be your servants forever."

⁸ But he rejected the advice which the elders had given him, and consulted the young men who had grown up with him, who stood before him. ⁹ And he said to them, "What advice do you give? How should we answer this people who have spoken to me, saying, 'Lighten the yoke which your father put on us'?"

¹⁰ Then the young men who had grown up with him spoke to him, saying, "Thus you should speak to this people who have spoken to you, saying, 'Your father made our yoke heavy, but you make *it* lighter on us'— thus you shall say to them: 'My little *finger* shall be thicker than my father's waist! ¹¹ And now, whereas my father put a heavy yoke on you, I will add to your yoke; my father chastised you with whips, but I will chastise you with scourges!' "

¹² So Jeroboam and all the people came to Rehoboam the third day, as the king had directed, saying, "Come back to me the third day." ¹³ Then the king answered the people roughly, and rejected the advice which the elders

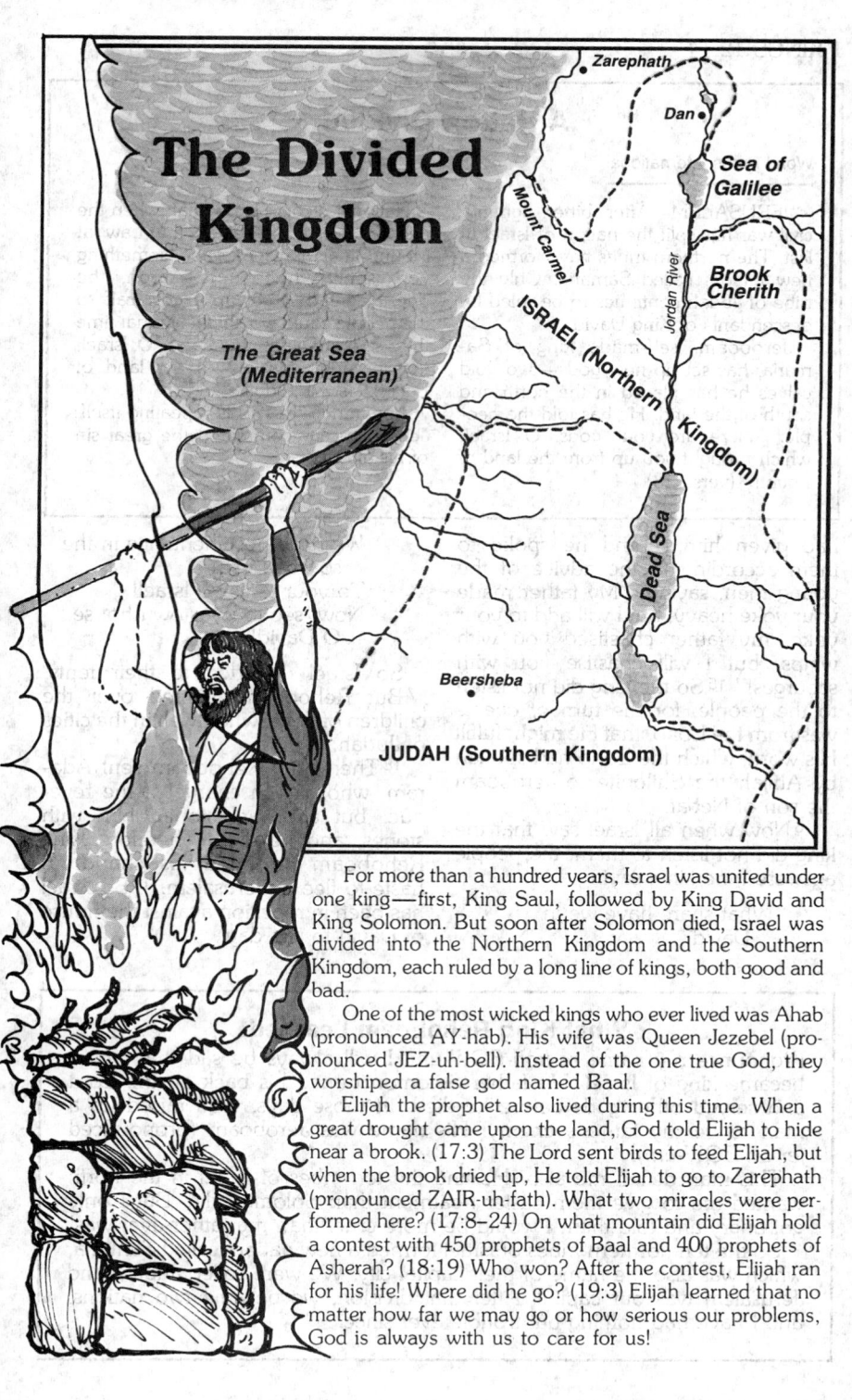

The Divided Kingdom

Zarephath

Dan

Sea of Galilee

Mount Carmel

Brook Cherith

ISRAEL (Northern Kingdom)

Jordan River

The Great Sea (Mediterranean)

Dead Sea

Beersheba

JUDAH (Southern Kingdom)

For more than a hundred years, Israel was united under one king—first, King Saul, followed by King David and King Solomon. But soon after Solomon died, Israel was divided into the Northern Kingdom and the Southern Kingdom, each ruled by a long line of kings, both good and bad.

One of the most wicked kings who ever lived was Ahab (pronounced AY-hab). His wife was Queen Jezebel (pronounced JEZ-uh-bell). Instead of the one true God, they worshiped a false god named Baal.

Elijah the prophet also lived during this time. When a great drought came upon the land, God told Elijah to hide near a brook. (17:3) The Lord sent birds to feed Elijah, but when the brook dried up, He told Elijah to go to Zarephath (pronounced ZAIR-uh-fath). What two miracles were performed here? (17:8–24) On what mountain did Elijah hold a contest with 450 prophets of Baal and 400 prophets of Asherah? (18:19) Who won? After the contest, Elijah ran for his life! Where did he go? (19:3) Elijah learned that no matter how far we may go or how serious our problems, God is always with us to care for us!

A Nation Divided

World Press International

JERUSALEM—After bitter fighting, civil war has split the nation of Israel at last. The northern tribes have formed a new nation, called Samaria. Only the tribe of Judah continues to be ruled by descendants of King David.

Jeroboam, self-made king of Samaria, has set up new gods—two gold calves he has placed in the north and south of the land. He has told the people: "Here are your gods, O Israel, which brought you up from the land of Egypt!" (verse 28).

National records show that, when the people of Israel received the Law at Mount Sinai many years ago, something very similar happened. Aaron, the priest, agreed to set up a gold calf so the people could worship it. At that time they said: "This is your god, O Israel, that brought you out of the land of Egypt!" (see Exodus 32:4).

Apparently, history is repeating itself. Jeroboam has committed the great sin of his ancestors!

had given him; 14 and he spoke to them according to the advice of the young men, saying, "My father made your yoke heavy, but I will add to your yoke; my father chastised you with whips, but I will chastise you with scourges!" 15 So the king did not listen to the people; for the turn *of events* was from the LORD, that He might fulfill His word, which the LORD had spoken by Ahijah the Shilonite to Jeroboam the son of Nebat.

16 Now when all Israel saw that the king did not listen to them, the people answered the king, saying:

"What share have we in David?
We have no inheritance in the son of Jesse.
To your tents, O Israel!
Now, see to your own house, O David!"

So Israel departed to their tents. 17 But Rehoboam reigned over the children of Israel who dwelt in the cities of Judah.

18 Then King Rehoboam sent Adoram, who *was* in charge of the revenue; but all Israel stoned him with stones, and he died. Therefore King Rehoboam mounted his chariot in haste to flee to Jerusalem. 19 So Israel has been in rebellion against the house of David to this day.

What King Rehoboam Learned

Pronounce my name *re-hoh-BOW-um*. I will always be sad that I ever became king of Israel. My father Solomon turned his back on the Lord and served other gods before he died. In those days, God raised up a man to be my father's enemy. His name was Jeroboam (pronounced *jer-oh-BOW-um*).

This man defied me also. He and the ten tribes of Israel in the north wanted me to give them easier treatment than Solomon did. But I only got angry and told them I would be more cruel than my father *ever* was!

So the ten northern tribes of Israel formed a new nation, called Samaria, which was also the name of their capital city. We were called Judah, and Jerusalem was our capital. After that division, we became two nations, and I have had nothing but trouble *ever* since.

20 Now it came to pass when all Israel heard that Jeroboam had come back, they sent for him and called him to the congregation, and made him king over all Israel. There was none who followed the house of David, but the tribe of Judah only.

21 And when Rehoboam came to Jerusalem, he assembled all the house of Judah with the tribe of Benjamin, one hundred and eighty thousand chosen *men* who were warriors, to fight against the house of Israel, that he might restore the kingdom to Rehoboam the son of Solomon. 22 But the word of God came to Shemaiah the man of God, saying, 23 "Speak to Rehoboam the son of Solomon, king of Judah, to all the house of Judah and Benjamin, and to the rest of the people, saying, 24 'Thus says the LORD: "You shall not go up nor fight against your brethren the children of Israel. Let every man return to his house, for this thing is from Me."'" Therefore they obeyed the word of the LORD, and turned back, according to the word of the LORD.

25 Then Jeroboam built Shechem in the mountains of Ephraim, and dwelt there. Also he went out from there and built Penuel. 26 And Jeroboam said in his heart, "Now the kingdom may return to the house of David: 27 If these people go up to offer sacrifices in the house of the LORD at Jerusalem, then the heart of this people will turn back to their lord, Rehoboam king of Judah, and they will kill me and go back to Rehoboam king of Judah."

28 Therefore the king asked advice, made two calves of gold, and said to the people, "It is too much for you to go up to Jerusalem. Here are your gods, O Israel, which brought you up from the land of Egypt!" 29 And he set up one in Bethel, and the other he put in Dan. 30 Now this thing became a sin, for the people went *to worship* before the one as far as Dan. 31 He made shrines on the high places, and made priests from *every* class of people, who were not of the sons of Levi.

32 Jeroboam ordained a feast on the fifteenth day of the eighth month, like the feast that *was* in Judah, and offered sacrifices on the altar. So he did at Bethel, sacrificing to the calves that he had made. And at Bethel he installed the priests of the high places which he had made. 33 So he made offerings on the altar which he had made at Bethel on the fifteenth day of the eighth month, in the month which he had devised in his own heart. And he ordained a feast for the children of Israel, and offered sacrifices on the altar and burned incense.

King Jeroboam is warned

13 And behold, a man of God went from Judah to Bethel by the word of the LORD, and Jeroboam stood by the altar to burn incense. 2 Then he cried out against the altar by the word of the LORD, and said, "O altar, altar! Thus says the LORD: 'Behold, a child, Josiah by name, shall be born to the house of David; and on you he shall sacrifice the priests of the high places who burn incense on you, and men's bones shall be burned on you.'" 3 And he gave a sign the same day, saying, "This *is* the sign which the LORD has spoken: Surely the altar shall split apart, and the ashes on it shall be poured out."

4 So it came to pass when King Jeroboam heard the saying of the man of God, who cried out against the altar in Bethel, that he stretched out his hand from the altar, saying, "Arrest him!" Then his hand, which he stretched out toward him, withered, so that he could not pull it back to himself. 5 The altar also was split apart, and the ashes poured out from the altar, according to the sign which the man of God had given by the word of the LORD. 6 Then the king answered and said to the man of God, "Please entreat the favor of the LORD your God, and pray for me, that my hand may be restored to me."

So the man of God entreated the LORD, and the king's hand was restored to him, and became as before.

7 Then the king said to the man of God, "Come home with me and refresh yourself, and I will give you a reward."

8 But the man of God said to the king, "If you were to give me half your house, I would not go in with you; nor would I eat bread nor drink water in this place. 9 For so it was commanded me by the word of the LORD, saying, 'You shall not eat bread, nor drink water, nor return by the same way you came.' " 10 So he went another way and did not return by the way he came to Bethel.

11 Now an old prophet dwelt in Bethel, and his sons came and told him all the works that the man of God had done that day in Bethel; they also told their father the words which he had spoken to the king. 12 And their father said to them, "Which way did he go?" For his sons had seen which way the man of God went who came from Judah. 13 Then he said to his sons, "Saddle the donkey for me." So they saddled the donkey for him; and he rode on it, 14 and went after the man of God, and found him sitting under an oak. Then he said to him, "Are you the man of God who came from Judah?"

And he said, "I am."

15 Then he said to him, "Come home with me and eat bread."

16 And he said, "I cannot return with you nor go in with you; neither can I eat bread nor drink water with you in this place. 17 For I have been told by the word of the LORD, 'You shall not eat bread nor drink water there, nor return by going the way you came.' "

18 He said to him, "I too am a prophet as you are, and an angel spoke to me by the word of the LORD, saying, 'Bring him back with you to your house, that he may eat bread and drink water.' " (He was lying to him.)

19 So he went back with him, and ate bread in his house, and drank water.

20 Now it happened, as they sat at the table, that the word of the LORD came to the prophet who had brought

him back; 21 and he cried out to the man of God who came from Judah, saying, "Thus says the LORD: 'Because you have disobeyed the word of the LORD, and have not kept the commandment which the LORD your God commanded you, 22 but you came back, ate bread, and drank water in the place of which the LORD said to you, "Eat no bread and drink no water," your corpse shall not come to the tomb of your fathers.' "

23 So it was, after he had eaten bread and after he had drunk, that he saddled the donkey for him, the prophet whom he had brought back. 24 When he was gone, a lion met him on the road and killed him. And his corpse was thrown on the road, and the donkey stood by it. The lion also stood by the corpse. 25 And there, men passed by and saw the corpse thrown on the road, and the lion standing by the corpse. Then they went and told it in the city where the old prophet dwelt.

26 Now when the prophet who had brought him back from the way heard it, he said, "It is the man of God who was disobedient to the word of the LORD. Therefore the LORD has delivered him to the lion, which has torn him and killed him, according to the word of the LORD which He spoke to him." 27 And he spoke to his sons, saying, "Saddle the donkey for me." So they saddled it. 28 Then he went and found his corpse thrown on the road, and the donkey and the lion standing by the corpse. The lion had not eaten the corpse nor torn the donkey. 29 And the prophet took up the corpse of the man of God, laid it on the donkey, and brought it back. So the old prophet came to the city to mourn, and to bury him. 30 Then he laid the corpse in his own tomb; and they mourned over him, saying, "Alas, my brother!" 31 So it was, after he had buried him, that he spoke to his sons, saying, "When I am dead, then bury me in the tomb where the man of God is buried; lay my bones beside his bones. 32 For the saying which he cried out

by the word of the LORD against the altar in Bethel, and against all the shrines on the high places which *are* in the cities of Samaria, will surely come to pass."

33 After this *event* Jeroboam did not turn from his evil way, but again he made priests from every class of people for the high places; whoever wished, he consecrated him, and he became *one* of the priests of the high places. 34 And this thing was the sin of the house of Jeroboam, so as to exterminate and destroy *it* from the face of the earth.

Ahijah's prophecy

14 At that time Abijah the son of Jeroboam became sick. 2 And Jeroboam said to his wife, "Please arise, and disguise yourself, that they may not recognize you as the wife of Jeroboam, and go to Shiloh. Indeed, Ahijah the prophet *is* there, who told me that *I would be* king over this people. 3 Also take with you ten loaves, *some* cakes, and a jar of honey, and go to him; he will tell you what will become of the child." 4 And Jeroboam's wife did so; she arose and went to Shiloh, and came to the house of Ahijah. But Ahijah could not see, for his eyes were glazed by reason of his age.

5 Now the LORD had said to Ahijah, "Here is the wife of Jeroboam, coming to ask you something about her son, for he *is* sick. Thus and thus you shall say to her; for it will be, when she comes in, that she will pretend *to be* another *woman*."

6 And so it was, when Ahijah heard the sound of her footsteps as she came through the door, he said, "Come in, wife of Jeroboam. Why do you pretend *to be* another *person*? For I *have been* sent to you *with* bad *news*. 7 Go, tell Jeroboam, 'Thus says the LORD God of Israel: "Because I exalted you from among the people, and made you ruler over My people Israel, 8 and tore the kingdom away from the house of David, and gave it to you;

and *yet* you have not been as My servant David, who kept My commandments and who followed Me with all his heart, to do only *what was* right in My eyes; 9 but you have done more evil than all who were before you, for you have gone and made for yourself other gods and molded images to provoke Me to anger, and have cast Me behind your back— 10 therefore behold! I will bring disaster on the house of Jeroboam, and will cut off from Jeroboam every male in Israel, bond and free; I will take away the remnant of the house of Jeroboam, as one takes away refuse until it is all gone. 11 The dogs shall eat whoever belongs to Jeroboam and dies in the city, and the birds of the air shall eat whoever dies in the field; for the LORD has spoken!" '

12 Arise therefore, go to your own house. When your feet enter the city, the child shall die. 13 And all Israel shall mourn for him and bury him, for he is the only one of Jeroboam who shall come to the grave, because in him there is found something good toward the LORD God of Israel in the house of Jeroboam.

14 "Moreover the LORD will raise up for Himself a king over Israel who shall cut off the house of Jeroboam; this is the day. What? Even now! 15 For the LORD will strike Israel, as a reed is shaken in the water. He will uproot Israel from this good land which He gave to their fathers, and will scatter them beyond the River, because they have made their wooden images, provoking the LORD to anger. 16 And He will give Israel up because of the sins of Jeroboam, who sinned and who made Israel sin."

17 Then Jeroboam's wife arose and departed, and came to Tirzah. When she came to the threshold of the house, the child died. 18 And they buried him; and all Israel mourned for him, according to the word of the LORD which He spoke through His servant Ahijah the prophet.

19 Now the rest of the acts of Jeroboam, how he made war and how he reigned, indeed they *are* written in the

book of the chronicles of the kings of Israel. 20 The period that Jeroboam reigned was twenty-two years. So he rested with his fathers. Then Nadab his son reigned in his place.

21 And Rehoboam the son of Solomon reigned in Judah. Rehoboam was forty-one years old when he became king. He reigned seventeen years in Jerusalem, the city which the LORD had chosen out of all the tribes of Israel, to put His name there. His mother's name was Naamah, an Ammonitess. 22 Now Judah did evil in the sight of the LORD, and they provoked Him to jealousy with their sins which they committed, more than all that their fathers had done. 23 For they also built for themselves high places, sacred pillars, and wooden images on every high hill and under every green tree. 24 And there were also perverted persons in the land. They did according to all the abominations of the nations which the LORD had cast out before the children of Israel.

25 It happened in the fifth year of King Rehoboam that Shishak king of Egypt came up against Jerusalem. 26 And he took away the treasures of the house of the LORD and the treasures of the king's house; he took away everything. He also took away all the gold shields which Solomon had made. 27 Then King Rehoboam made bronze shields in their place, and committed them to the hands of the captains of the guard, who guarded the doorway of the king's house. 28 And whenever the king entered the house of the LORD, the guards carried them, then brought them back into the guardroom.

29 Now the rest of the acts of Rehoboam, and all that he did, are they not written in the book of the chronicles of the kings of Judah? 30 And there was war between Rehoboam and Jeroboam all their days. 31 So Rehoboam rested with his fathers, and was buried with his fathers in the City of David. His mother's name was Naamah, an Ammonitess. Then Abijam his son reigned in his place.

Four wicked kings of Israel and Judah

15 In the eighteenth year of King Jeroboam the son of Nebat, Abijam became king over Judah. 2 He reigned three years in Jerusalem. His mother's name was Maachah the granddaughter of Abishalom. 3 And he walked in all the sins of his father, which he had done before him; his heart was not loyal to the LORD his God, as was the heart of his father David. 4 Nevertheless for David's sake the LORD his God gave him a lamp in Jerusalem, by setting up his son after him and by establishing Jerusalem; 5 because David did what was right in the eyes of the LORD, and had not turned aside from anything that He commanded him all the days of his life, except in the matter of Uriah the Hittite. 6 And there was war between Rehoboam and Jeroboam all the days of his life. 7 Now the rest of the acts of Abijam, and all that he did, are they not written in the book of the chronicles of the kings of Judah? And there was war between Abijam and Jeroboam.

8 So Abijam rested with his fathers, and they buried him in the City of David. Then Asa his son reigned in his place.

9 In the twentieth year of Jeroboam king of Israel, Asa became king over Judah. 10 And he reigned forty-one years in Jerusalem. His grandmother's name was Maachah the granddaughter of Abishalom. 11 Asa did what was right in the eyes of the LORD, as did his father David. 12 And he banished the perverted persons from the land, and removed all the idols that his fathers had made. 13 Also he removed Maachah his grandmother from being queen mother, because she had made an obscene image of Asherah. And Asa cut down her obscene image and burned it by the Brook Kidron. 14 But the high places were not removed. Nevertheless Asa's heart was loyal to the LORD all his days. 15 He also brought into the house of the LORD the

things which his father had dedicated, and the things which he himself had dedicated: silver and gold and utensils.

16 Now there was war between Asa and Baasha king of Israel all their days. 17 And Baasha king of Israel came up against Judah, and built Ramah, that he might let none go out or come in to Asa king of Judah. 18 Then Asa took all the silver and gold *that was* left in the treasuries of the house of the LORD and the treasuries of the king's house, and delivered them into the hand of his servants. And King Asa sent them to Ben-Hadad the son of Tabrimmon, the son of Hezion, king of Syria, who dwelt in Damascus, saying, 19 "*Let there be* a treaty between you and me, as there was between my father and your father. See, I have sent you a present of silver and gold. Come and break your treaty with Baasha king of Israel, so that he will withdraw from me."

20 So Ben-Hadad heeded King Asa, and sent the captains of his armies against the cities of Israel. He attacked Ijon, Dan, Abel Beth Maachah, and all Chinneroth, with all the land of Naphtali. 21 Now it happened, when Baasha heard *it,* that he stopped building Ramah, and remained in Tirzah.

22 Then King Asa made a proclamation throughout all Judah; none *was* exempted. And they took away the stones and timber of Ramah, which Baasha had used for building; and with them King Asa built Geba of Benjamin, and Mizpah.

23 The rest of all the acts of Asa, all his might, all that he did, and the cities which he built, *are* they not written in the book of the chronicles of the kings of Judah? But in the time of his old age he was diseased in his feet. 24 So Asa rested with his fathers, and was buried with his fathers in the City of David his father. Then Jehoshaphat his son reigned in his place.

25 Now Nadab the son of Jeroboam became king over Israel in the second year of Asa king of Judah, and he reigned over Israel two years. 26 And he did evil in the sight of the LORD,

and walked in the way of his father, and in his sin by which he had made Israel sin.

27 Then Baasha the son of Ahijah, of the house of Issachar, conspired against him. And Baasha killed him at Gibbethon, which *belonged* to the Philistines, while Nadab and all Israel laid siege to Gibbethon. 28 Baasha killed him in the third year of Asa king of Judah, and reigned in his place. 29 And it was so, when he became king, *that* he killed all the house of Jeroboam. He did not leave to Jeroboam anyone that breathed, until he had destroyed him, according to the word of the LORD which He had spoken by His servant Ahijah the Shilonite, 30 because of the sins of Jeroboam, which he had sinned and by which he had made Israel sin, because of his provocation with which he had provoked the LORD God of Israel to anger.

31 Now the rest of the acts of Nadab, and all that he did, *are* they not written in the book of the chronicles of the kings of Israel? 32 And there was war between Asa and Baasha king of Israel all their days.

33 In the third year of Asa king of Judah, Baasha the son of Ahijah became king over all Israel in Tirzah, and *reigned* twenty-four years. 34 He did evil in the sight of the LORD, and walked in the way of Jeroboam, and in his sin by which he had made Israel sin.

Four more kings of Israel

16 Then the word of the LORD came to Jehu the son of Hanani, against Baasha, saying: 2 "Inasmuch as I lifted you out of the dust and made you ruler over My people Israel, and you have walked in the way of Jeroboam, and have made My people Israel sin, to provoke Me to anger with their sins, 3 surely I will take away the posterity of Baasha and the posterity of his house, and I will make your house like the house of Jeroboam the son of Nebat. 4 The dogs shall eat whoever belongs to Baasha and dies in the city,

and the birds of the air shall eat whoever dies in the fields."

5 Now the rest of the acts of Baasha, what he did, and his might, *are* they not written in the book of the chronicles of the kings of Israel? 6 So Baasha rested with his fathers and was buried in Tirzah. Then Elah his son reigned in his place.

7 And also the word of the LORD came by the prophet Jehu the son of Hanani against Baasha and his house, because of all the evil that he did in the sight of the LORD in provoking Him to anger with the work of his hands, in being like the house of Jeroboam, and because he killed them.

8 In the twenty-sixth year of Asa king of Judah, Elah the son of Baasha became king over Israel, *and reigned* two years in Tirzah. 9 Now his servant Zimri, commander of half *his* chariots, conspired against him as he was in Tirzah drinking himself drunk in the house of Arza, steward of *his* house in Tirzah. 10 And Zimri went in and struck him and killed him in the twenty-seventh year of Asa king of Judah, and reigned in his place.

11 Then it came to pass, when he began to reign, as soon as he was seated on his throne, *that* he killed all the household of Baasha; he did not leave him one male, neither of his relatives nor of his friends. 12 Thus Zimri destroyed all the household of Baasha, according to the word of the LORD, which He spoke against Baasha by Jehu the prophet, 13 for all the sins of Baasha and the sins of Elah his son, by which they had sinned and by which they had made Israel sin, in provoking the LORD God of Israel to anger with their idols.

14 Now the rest of the acts of Elah, and all that he did, *are* they not written in the book of the chronicles of the kings of Israel?

15 In the twenty-seventh year of Asa king of Judah, Zimri had reigned in Tirzah seven days. And the people *were* encamped against Gibbethon, which *belonged* to the Philistines. 16 Now the people *who were* encamped heard it

said, "Zimri has conspired and also has killed the king." So all Israel made Omri, the commander of the army, king over Israel that day in the camp. 17 Then Omri and all Israel with him went up from Gibbethon, and they besieged Tirzah. 18 And it happened, when Zimri saw that the city was taken, that he went into the citadel of the king's house and burned the king's house down upon himself with fire, and died, 19 because of the sins which he had committed in doing evil in the sight of the LORD, in walking in the way of Jeroboam, and in his sin which he had committed to make Israel sin.

20 Now the rest of the acts of Zimri, and the treason he committed, *are* they not written in the book of the chronicles of the kings of Israel?

21 Then the people of Israel were divided into two parts: half of the people followed Tibni the son of Ginath, to make him king, and half followed Omri. 22 But the people who followed Omri prevailed over the people who followed Tibni the son of Ginath. So Tibni died and Omri reigned. 23 In the thirty-first year of Asa king of Judah, Omri became king over Israel, *and reigned* twelve years. Six years he reigned in Tirzah. 24 And he bought the hill of Samaria from Shemer for two talents of silver; then he built on the hill, and called the name of the city which he built, Samaria, after the name of Shemer, owner of the hill. 25 Omri did evil in the eyes of the LORD, and did worse than all who *were* before him. 26 For he walked in all the ways of Jeroboam the son of Nebat, and in his sin by which he had made Israel sin, provoking the LORD God of Israel to anger with their idols.

27 Now the rest of the acts of Omri which he did, and the might that he showed, *are* they not written in the book of the chronicles of the kings of Israel?

28 So Omri rested with his fathers and was buried in Samaria. Then Ahab his son reigned in his place.

29 In the thirty-eighth year of Asa king of Judah, Ahab the son of Omri

The hill on which King Omri built the city of Samaria.

became king over Israel; and Ahab the son of Omri reigned over Israel in Samaria twenty-two years. 30 Now Ahab the son of Omri did evil in the sight of the LORD, more than all who *were* before him. 31 And it came to pass, as though it had been a trivial thing for him to walk in the sins of Jeroboam the son of Nebat, that he took as wife Jezebel the daughter of Ethbaal, king of the Sidonians; and he went and served Baal and worshiped him. 32 Then he set up an altar for Baal in the temple of Baal, which he had built in Samaria. 33 And Ahab made a wooden image. Ahab did more to provoke the LORD God of Israel to anger than all the kings of Israel who were before him. 34 In his days Hiel of Bethel built Jericho. He laid its foundation with Abiram his firstborn, and with his youngest *son* Segub he set up its gates, according to the word of the LORD, which He had spoken through Joshua the son of Nun.

Elijah heals a little boy

17 And Elijah the Tishbite, of the inhabitants of Gilead, said to Ahab, "*As* the LORD God of Israel lives, before whom I stand, there shall not be dew nor rain these years, except at my word."

2 Then the word of the LORD came to him, saying, 3 "Get away from here and turn eastward, and hide by the Brook Cherith, which flows into the Jordan. 4 And it will be *that* you shall drink from the brook, and I have commanded the ravens to feed you there."

5 So he went and did according to the word of the LORD, for he went and stayed by the Brook Cherith, which flows into the Jordan. 6 The ravens brought him bread and meat in the morning, and bread and meat in the evening; and he drank from the brook. 7 And it happened after a while that the brook dried up, because there had been no rain in the land.

8 Then the word of the LORD came to him, saying, 9 "Arise, go to Zarephath, which *belongs* to Sidon, and dwell there. See, I have commanded a widow there to provide for you." 10 So he arose and went to Zarephath. And when he came to the gate of the city, indeed a widow *was* there gathering sticks. And he called to her and said, "Please bring me a little water in a cup, that I may drink." 11 And as she was going to get *it,* he called to her and said, "Please bring me a morsel of bread in your hand."

12 So she said, "As the LORD your God lives, I do not have bread, only a handful of flour in a bin, and a little

My name is pronounced *ih-LIE-jah* and means "The Lord Is My God." Israel's fame had passed away after Solomon was king, so God began to send prophets to warn the nation about the suffering that sin brings. Then God called me to announce a drought (pronounced *drowt*) in the land. There would be no rain for a long, long time.

I challenged the prophets of the false god Baal (pronounced *BAYL*) to a contest on Mount Carmel. If Baal could send fire, then he would be our god. But if my Lord sent fire, then He would be God.

I laughed to see those Baal-worshipers screaming and shouting all day at their god. But Baal couldn't answer them, because he was really nothing at all!

Finally, I built a simple altar, offered a sacrifice, and made a short prayer to the Lord. God's fire came from heaven and ate up my sacrifice, and the rain came at last.

oil in a jar; and see, I *am* gathering a couple of sticks that I may go in and prepare it for myself and my son, that we may eat it, and die."

13 And Elijah said to her, "Do not fear; go *and* do as you have said, but make me a small cake from it first, and bring *it* to me; and afterward make *some* for yourself and your son. 14 For thus says the LORD God of Israel: 'The bin of flour shall not be used up, nor shall the jar of oil run dry, until the day the LORD sends rain on the earth.' "

15 So she went away and did according to the word of Elijah; and she and he and her household ate for *many* days. 16 The bin of flour was not used up, nor did the jar of oil run dry, according to the word of the LORD which He spoke by Elijah.

17 Now it happened after these things *that* the son of the woman who owned the house became sick. And his sickness was so serious that there was no breath left in him. 18 So she said to Elijah, "What have I to do with you, O man of God? Have you come to me to bring my sin to remembrance, and to kill my son?"

19 And he said to her, "Give me your son." So he took him out of her arms and carried him to the upper room where he was staying, and laid him on his own bed. 20 Then he cried out to the LORD and said, "O LORD my God, have You also brought tragedy on the widow with whom I lodge, by killing her son?" 21 And he stretched himself out on the child three times, and cried out to the LORD and said, "O LORD my God, I pray, let this child's soul come back to him." 22 Then the LORD heard the voice of Elijah; and the soul of the child came back to him, and he revived.

23 And Elijah took the child and brought him down from the upper room into the house, and gave him to his mother. And Elijah said, "See, your son lives!"

24 Then the woman said to Elijah, "Now by this I know that you *are* a man of God, *and* that the word of the LORD in your mouth *is* the truth."

The contest on Mount Carmel

18 And it came to pass *after* many days that the word of the LORD came to Elijah, in the third year, saying, "Go, present yourself to Ahab, and I will send rain on the earth."

2 So Elijah went to present himself to Ahab; and *there was* a severe famine in Samaria. 3 And Ahab had called

What a Certain Widow Learned

In the beginning I didn't know what to think of Elijah the prophet. My little son and I were very poor, but Elijah wanted to come and live with us. I remember now that we always had plenty while Elijah was with us. Our food supply just never ran out!

Let me tell you something else. Once, while Elijah was staying with us, my son became very sick. I don't know whether he died or just nearly died. But Elijah stretched his body over my boy, and would you believe! My son revived and has been well to this day.

I have learned from this experience to listen when God speaks. I don't doubt the Lord's goodness, and I trust Him with my whole life.

Obadiah, who *was* in charge of *his* house. (Now Obadiah feared the LORD greatly. 4 For so it was, while Jezebel massacred the prophets of the LORD, that Obadiah had taken one hundred prophets and hidden them, fifty to a cave, and had fed them with bread and water.) 5 And Ahab had said to Obadiah, "Go into the land to all the springs of water and to all the brooks; perhaps we may find grass to keep the horses and mules alive, so that we will not have to kill any livestock." 6 So they divided the land between them to explore it; Ahab went one way by himself, and Obadiah went another way by himself.

7 Now as Obadiah was on his way, suddenly Elijah met him; and he recognized him, and fell on his face, and said, "*Is* that you, my lord Elijah?"

8 And he answered him, "*It is* I. Go, tell your master, 'Elijah *is here*.' "

9 So he said, "How have I sinned, that you are delivering your servant into the hand of Ahab, to kill me? 10 As the LORD your God lives, there is no nation or kingdom where my master has not sent someone to hunt for you; and when they said, 'He is not *here*,' he took an oath from the kingdom or nation that they could not find you. 11 And now you say, 'Go, tell your master, "Elijah *is here*" '! 12 And it shall come to pass, *as soon as* I am gone from you, that the Spirit of the LORD will carry you to a place I do not know; so when I go and tell Ahab, and he cannot find you, he will kill me. But I your servant have feared the LORD from my youth. 13 Was it not reported to my lord what I did when Jezebel killed the prophets of the LORD, how I hid one hundred men of the LORD's prophets, fifty to a cave, and fed them with bread and water? 14 And now you say, 'Go, tell your master, "Elijah *is here*." ' He will kill me!"

15 Then Elijah said, "As the LORD of hosts lives, before whom I stand, I will surely present myself to him today."

16 So Obadiah went to meet Ahab, and told him; and Ahab went to meet Elijah.

17 Then it happened, when Ahab saw Elijah, that Ahab said to him, "*Is that* you, O troubler of Israel?"

18 And he answered, "I have not troubled Israel, but you and your father's house *have,* in that you have forsaken the commandments of the LORD and have followed the Baals. 19 Now therefore, send *and* gather all Israel to me on Mount Carmel, the four hundred and fifty prophets of **Baal,**

WORDFINDER

18:19 Baal The chief false god of the Canaanites (pronounced *KAY-nuh-nights*) and Phoenicians (pronounced *fe-NISH-she-uns*). He was a nature god and was worshiped in immoral ceremonies forbidden to Israel.

God sends fire to consume Elijah's sacrifice on Mount Carmel before 450 prophets of Baal.

and the four hundred prophets of Asherah, who eat at Jezebel's table.''

20 So Ahab sent for all the children of Israel, and gathered the prophets together on Mount Carmel. 21 And Elijah came to all the people, and said, "How long will you falter between two opinions? If the LORD is God, follow Him; but if Baal, follow him.'' But the people answered him not a word. 22 Then Elijah said to the people, "I alone am left a prophet of the LORD; but Baal's prophets are four hundred and fifty men. 23 Therefore let them give us two bulls; and let them choose one bull for themselves, cut it in pieces, and lay it on the wood, but put no fire under it; and I will prepare the other bull, and lay it on the wood, but put no fire under it. 24 Then you call on the name of your gods, and I will call on the name of the LORD; and the God who answers by fire, He is God.''

So all the people answered and said, "It is well spoken.''

25 Now Elijah said to the prophets of Baal, "Choose one bull for yourselves and prepare it first, for you are many; and call on the name of your god, but put no fire under it.''

26 So they took the bull which was given them, and they prepared it, and called on the name of Baal from morning even till noon, saying, "O Baal, hear us!'' But there was no voice; no one answered. Then they leaped about the altar which they had made.

27 And so it was, at noon, that Elijah mocked them and said, "Cry aloud, for he is a god; either he is meditating, or he is busy, or he is on a journey, or perhaps he is sleeping and must be awakened.'' 28 So they cried aloud, and cut themselves, as was their custom, with knives and lances, until the blood gushed out on them. 29 And when midday was past, they prophesied until the time of the offering of the evening sacrifice. But there was no voice; no one answered, no one paid attention.

30 Then Elijah said to all the people, "Come near to me.'' So all the people came near to him. And he repaired the altar of the LORD that was broken down. 31 And Elijah took twelve stones, according to the number of the tribes of the sons of Jacob, to whom the word of the LORD had come, saying, "Israel shall be your name.'' 32 Then with the stones he built an altar in the name of the LORD; and he made a trench around the altar large enough to hold two seahs of seed. 33 And he

put the wood in order, cut the bull in pieces, and laid *it* on the wood, and said, "Fill four waterpots with water, and pour *it* on the burnt sacrifice and on the wood." 34 Then he said, "Do *it* a second time," and they did *it* a second time; and he said, "Do *it* a third time," and they did *it* a third time. 35 So the water ran all around the altar; and he also filled the trench with water.

36 And it came to pass, at *the time of* the offering of the *evening* sacrifice, that Elijah the prophet came near and said, "LORD God of Abraham, Isaac, and Israel, let it be known this day that You *are* God in Israel and I *am* Your servant, and *that* I have done all these things at Your word. 37 Hear me, O LORD, hear me, that this people may know that You *are* the LORD God, and *that* You have turned their hearts back *to You* again."

38 Then the fire of the LORD fell and consumed the burnt sacrifice, and the wood and the stones and the dust, and it licked up the water that *was* in the trench. 39 Now when all the people saw *it,* they fell on their faces; and they said, "The LORD, He *is* God! The LORD, He *is* God!"

40 And Elijah said to them, "Seize the prophets of Baal! Do not let one of them escape!" So they seized them; and Elijah brought them down to the Brook Kishon and executed them there.

41 Then Elijah said to Ahab, "Go up, eat and drink; for *there is* the sound of abundance of rain." 42 So Ahab went up to eat and drink. And Elijah went up to the top of Carmel; then he bowed down on the ground, and put his face between his knees, 43 and said to his servant, "Go up now, look toward the sea."

So he went up and looked, and said, "*There is* nothing." And *seven times* he said, "Go again."

44 Then it came to pass the seventh *time,* that he said, "There is a cloud, as small as a man's hand, rising out of the sea!" So he said, "Go up, say to Ahab, 'Prepare *your chariot,* and go down before the rain stops you.'"

45 Now it happened in the meantime that the sky became black with clouds and wind, and there was a heavy rain. So Ahab rode away and went to Jezreel. 46 Then the hand of the LORD came upon Elijah; and he girded up his loins and ran ahead of Ahab to the entrance of Jezreel.

Elijah runs for his life

19 And Ahab told Jezebel all that Elijah had done, also how he had executed all the prophets with the sword. 2 Then Jezebel sent a messenger to Elijah, saying, "So let the gods do *to me,* and more also, if I do not make your life as the life of one of them by tomorrow about this time." 3 And when he saw *that,* he arose and ran for his life, and went to Beersheba, which *belongs* to Judah, and left his servant there.

4 But he himself went a day's journey into the wilderness, and came and sat down under a broom tree. And he prayed that he might die, and said, "It is enough! Now, LORD, take my life, for I *am* no better than my fathers!"

5 Then as he lay and slept under a broom tree, suddenly an angel touched him, and said to him, "Arise

Elijah, fearing that Queen Jezebel is going to kill him, prays under a broom tree.

and eat." 6 Then he looked, and there by his head *was* a cake baked on coals, and a jar of water. So he ate and drank, and lay down again. 7 And the angel of the LORD came back the second time, and touched him, and said, "Arise *and* eat, because the journey is too great for you." 8 So he arose, and ate and drank; and he went in the strength of that food forty days and forty nights as far as Horeb, the mountain of God.

9 And there he went into a cave, and spent the night in that place; and behold, the word of the LORD *came* to him, and He said to him, "What are you doing here, Elijah?"

10 So he said, "I have been very zealous for the LORD God of hosts; for the children of Israel have forsaken Your covenant, torn down Your altars, and killed Your prophets with the sword. I alone am left; and they seek to take my life."

11 Then He said, "Go out, and stand on the mountain before the LORD." And behold, the LORD passed by, and a great and strong wind tore into the mountains and broke the rocks in pieces before the LORD, *but* the LORD *was* not in the wind; and after the wind an earthquake, *but* the LORD *was* not in the earthquake; 12 and after the earthquake a fire, *but* the LORD *was* not in the fire; and after the fire a still small voice.

13 So it was, when Elijah heard *it,* that he wrapped his face in his mantle and went out and stood in the entrance of the cave. Suddenly a voice *came* to him, and said, "What are you doing here, Elijah?"

14 And he said, "I have been very zealous for the LORD God of hosts; because the children of Israel have forsaken Your covenant, torn down Your altars, and killed Your prophets with the sword. I alone am left; and they seek to take my life."

15 Then the LORD said to him: "Go, return on your way to the Wilderness of Damascus; and when you arrive, anoint Hazael *as* king over Syria. 16 Also you shall anoint Jehu the son of Nimshi *as* king over Israel. And Elisha the son of Shaphat of Abel Meholah you shall anoint *as* prophet in your place. 17 It shall be *that* whoever escapes the sword of Hazael, Jehu will kill; and whoever escapes the sword of Jehu, Elisha will kill. 18 Yet I have reserved seven thousand in Israel, all whose knees have not bowed to Baal, and *every* mouth that has not kissed him."

19 So he departed from there, and found Elisha the son of Shaphat, who *was* plowing *with* twelve yoke *of* oxen before him, and he *was* with the twelfth. Then Elijah passed by him and threw his mantle on him. 20 And he left the oxen and ran after Elijah, and

---

What Elijah Learned

When the king's wife Jezebel said she was going to have me killed, I ran away. Then I imagined everybody was against me.

So I escaped and hid in a cave. There the Lord found me and asked, "What are you doing here, Elijah?" When He said this, I was very ashamed for running and hiding.

Then the Lord gave me a new job. I must make Jehu (pronounced *JAY-hu*) king, and make Elisha a prophet of the Lord. The Lord also told me there were still seven thousand people in Israel who worshiped Him!

I was a new man after that experience. I was never afraid of anyone again because I knew the Lord was always beside me.

said, "Please let me kiss my father and my mother, and *then* I will follow you."

And he said to him, "Go back again, for what have I done to you?"

21 So *Elisha* turned back from him, and took a yoke of oxen and slaughtered them and boiled their flesh, using the oxen's equipment, and gave it to the people, and they ate. Then he arose and followed Elijah, and became his servant.

God gives a victory to King Ahab

20 Now Ben-Hadad the king of Syria gathered all his forces together; thirty-two kings *were* with him, with horses and chariots. And he went up and besieged Samaria, and made war against it. 2 Then he sent messengers into the city to Ahab king of Israel, and said to him, "Thus says Ben-Hadad: 3 'Your silver and your gold *are* mine; your loveliest wives and children are mine.' "

4 And the king of Israel answered and said, "My lord, O king, just as you say, I and all that I have *are* yours."

5 Then the messengers came back and said, "Thus speaks Ben-Hadad, saying, 'Indeed I have sent to you, saying, "You shall deliver to me your silver and your gold, your wives and your children"; 6 but I will send my servants to you tomorrow about this time, and they shall search your house and the houses of your servants. And it shall be, *that* whatever is pleasant in your eyes, they will put *it* in their hands and take *it.*' "

7 So the king of Israel called all the elders of the land, and said, "Notice, please, and see how this *man* seeks trouble, for he sent to me for my wives, my children, my silver, and my gold; and I did not deny him."

8 And all the elders and all the people said to him, "Do not listen or consent."

9 Therefore he said to the messengers of Ben-Hadad, "Tell my lord the king, 'All that you sent for to your servant the first time I will do, but this thing I cannot do.' "

And the messengers departed and brought back word to him.

10 Then Ben-Hadad sent to him and said, "The gods do so to me, and more also, if enough dust is left of Samaria for a handful for each of the people who follow me."

11 So the king of Israel answered and said, "Tell *him,* 'Let not the one who puts on *his armor* boast like the one who takes *it off.*' "

12 And it happened when Ben-Hadad heard this message, as he and the kings *were* drinking at the command post, that he said to his servants, "Get ready." And they got ready to attack the city.

13 Suddenly a prophet approached Ahab king of Israel, saying, "Thus says the LORD: 'Have you seen all this great multitude? Behold, I will deliver it into your hand today, and you shall know that I *am* the LORD.' "

14 So Ahab said, "By whom?"

And he said, "Thus says the LORD: 'By the young leaders of the provinces.' "

Then he said, "Who will set the battle in order?"

And he answered, "You."

15 Then he mustered the young leaders of the provinces, and there were two hundred and thirty-two; and after them he mustered all the people, all the children of Israel—seven thousand.

16 So they went out at noon. Meanwhile Ben-Hadad and the thirty-two kings helping him were getting drunk at the command post. 17 The young leaders of the provinces went out first. And Ben-Hadad sent out *a patrol,* and they told him, saying, "Men are coming out of Samaria!" 18 So he said, "If they have come out for peace, take them alive; and if they have come out for war, take them alive."

19 Then these young leaders of the provinces went out of the city with the army which followed them. 20 And each one killed his man; so the Syrians fled, and Israel pursued them; and Ben-Hadad the king of Syria escaped on a horse with the cavalry. 21 Then

the king of Israel went out and attacked the horses and chariots, and killed the Syrians with a great slaughter.

22 And the prophet came to the king of Israel and said to him, "Go, strengthen yourself; take note, and see what you should do, for in the spring of the year the king of Syria will come up against you."

23 Then the servants of the king of Syria said to him, "Their gods *are* gods of the hills. Therefore they were stronger than we; but if we fight against them in the plain, surely we will be stronger than they. 24 So do this thing: Dismiss the kings, each from his position, and put captains in their places; 25 and you shall muster an army like the army that you have lost, horse for horse and chariot for chariot. Then we will fight against them in the plain; surely we will be stronger than they."

And he listened to their voice and did so.

26 So it was, in the spring of the year, that Ben-Hadad mustered the Syrians and went up to Aphek to fight against Israel. 27 And the children of Israel were mustered and given provisions, and they went against them. Now the children of Israel encamped before them like two little flocks of goats, while the Syrians filled the countryside.

28 Then a man of God came and spoke to the king of Israel, and said, "Thus says the LORD: 'Because the Syrians have said, "The LORD *is* God of the hills, but He *is* not God of the valleys," therefore I will deliver all this great multitude into your hand, and you shall know that I *am* the LORD.' "

29 And they encamped opposite each other for seven days. So it was that on the seventh day the battle was joined; and the children of Israel killed one hundred thousand foot soldiers *of* the Syrians in one day. 30 But the rest fled to Aphek, into the city; then a wall fell on twenty-seven thousand of the men *who were* left.

And Ben-Hadad fled and went into the city, into an inner chamber. 31 Then his servants said to him, "Look now, we have heard that the kings of the house of Israel *are* merciful kings. Please, let us put sackcloth around our waists and ropes around our heads, and go out to the king of Israel; perhaps he will spare your life."

32 So they wore sackcloth around their waists and *put* ropes around their heads, and came to the king of Israel and said, "Your servant Ben-Hadad says, 'Please let me live.' "

And he said, "*Is* he still alive? He *is* my brother."

33 Now the men were watching closely to see whether *any sign of mercy would come* from him; and they quickly grasped *at this word* and said, "Your brother Ben-Hadad."

So he said, "Go, bring him." Then Ben-Hadad came out to him; and he had him come up into the chariot.

34 So *Ben-Hadad* said to him, "The cities which my father took from your father I will restore; and you may set up marketplaces for yourself in Damascus, as my father did in Samaria."

Then *Ahab said,* "I will send you away with this treaty." So he made a treaty with him and sent him away.

35 Now a certain man of the sons of the prophets said to his neighbor by the word of the LORD, "Strike me, please." And the man refused to strike him. 36 Then he said to him, "Because you have not obeyed the voice of the LORD, surely, as soon as you depart from me, a lion shall kill you." And as soon as he left him, a lion found him and killed him.

37 And he found another man, and said, "Strike me, please." So the man struck him, inflicting a wound. 38 Then the prophet departed and waited for the king by the road, and disguised himself with a bandage over his eyes. 39 Now as the king passed by, he cried out to the king and said, "Your servant went out into the midst of the battle; and there, a man came over and brought a man to me, and said, 'Guard this man; if by any means he is missing, your life shall be for his life, or else you shall pay a talent of silver.' 40 While your servant was busy here and there, he was gone."

Why Was Naboth Killed?

The Jezreel Post

JEZREEL—The recent death of Naboth (pronounced *NAY-bahth*), of Jezreel (pronounced *JEZ-ree-ell*), owner of a local vineyard, remains an unsolved mystery in police files.

The official story is that Naboth was executed while at a banquet held in his honor. Two witnesses accused the man of blasphemy against God and the king. As you may know, blasphemy (pronounced *BLASS-fuh-mee*) means "abusing a person's name or character."

All reports indicate that Naboth was a good man who never spoke unkindly about anyone, especially the king. Nor was Naboth ever heard using God's name in vain!

We suspect other motives for Naboth's death. It is well known that King Ahab wanted Naboth's valuable property, and that he has already taken it over. It is thought that Queen Jezebel (pronounced *JEZ-uh-bell*) also played a part in this unhappy tale.

Then the king of Israel said to him, "So *shall* your judgment *be;* you yourself have decided *it.*"

41 And he hastened to take the bandage away from his eyes; and the king of Israel recognized him as one of the prophets. 42 Then he said to him, "Thus says the LORD: 'Because you have let slip out of *your* hand a man whom I appointed to utter destruction, therefore your life shall go for his life, and your people for his people.' "

43 So the king of Israel went to his house sullen and displeased, and came to Samaria.

Elijah gives Ahab bad news

21 And it came to pass after these things *that* Naboth the Jezreelite had a vineyard which *was* in Jezreel, next to the palace of Ahab king of Samaria. 2 So Ahab spoke to Naboth, saying, "Give me your vineyard, that I may have it for a vegetable garden, because it *is* near, next to my house; and for it I will give you a vineyard better than it. *Or,* if it seems good to you, I will give you its worth in money."

3 But Naboth said to Ahab, "The LORD forbid that I should give the inheritance of my fathers to you!"

4 So Ahab went into his house sullen and displeased because of the word

which Naboth the Jezreelite had spoken to him; for he had said, "I will not give you the inheritance of my fathers." And he lay down on his bed, and turned away his face, and would eat no food. 5 But Jezebel his wife came to him, and said to him, "Why is your spirit so sullen that you eat no food?"

6 He said to her, "Because I spoke to Naboth the Jezreelite, and said to him, 'Give me your vineyard for money; or else, if it pleases you, I will give you *another* vineyard for it.' And he answered, 'I will not give you my vineyard.' "

7 Then Jezebel his wife said to him, "You now exercise authority over Israel! Arise, eat food, and let your heart be cheerful; I will give you the vineyard of Naboth the Jezreelite."

8 And she wrote letters in Ahab's name, sealed *them* with his seal, and sent the letters to the elders and the nobles who *were* dwelling in the city with Naboth. 9 She wrote in the letters, saying,

Proclaim a fast, and seat Naboth with high honor among the people; 10 and seat two men, scoundrels, before him to bear witness against him, saying, You have blasphemed God and the

Ahab and Jezebel—We are the worst married couple you will meet in the Bible. I am Ahab, and my wife's name is Jezebel (pronounced *JEZ-uh-bell*). We were the king and queen of Israel when that troublemaker Elijah was the prophet. He's the one who stopped the rain and made fools of all our Baal priests on Mount Carmel.

Later, that nuisance Elijah came along and foretold that both my wife and I would die horribly for our evil deeds. See 1 Kings 22:34–38 for the story of my death, and see 2 Kings 9:30–37, for the story of how Jezebel's life ended.

It is very dark where Jezebel and I are now. We are constantly tormented by the everlasting memory of all our evil deeds. Worst of all, God is nowhere near to comfort us.

king. *Then* take him out, and stone him, that he may die.

11 So the men of his city, the elders and nobles who were inhabitants of his city, did as Jezebel had sent to them, as it *was* written in the letters which she had sent to them. 12 They proclaimed a fast, and seated Naboth with high honor among the people. 13 And two men, scoundrels, came in and sat before him; and the scoundrels witnessed against him, against Naboth, in the presence of the people, saying, "Naboth has blasphemed God and the king!" Then they took him outside the city and stoned him with stones, so that he died. 14 Then they sent to Jezebel, saying, "Naboth has been stoned and is dead."

15 And it came to pass, when Jezebel heard that Naboth had been stoned and was dead, that Jezebel said to Ahab, "Arise, take possession of the vineyard of Naboth the Jezreelite, which he refused to give you for money; for Naboth is not alive, but dead." 16 So it was, when Ahab heard that Naboth was dead, that Ahab got up and went down to take possession of the vineyard of Naboth the Jezreelite.

17 Then the word of the LORD came to Elijah the Tishbite, saying, 18 "Arise, go down to meet Ahab king of Israel, who *lives* in Samaria. There *he is*, in the vineyard of Naboth, where he has gone down to take possession of it.

19 You shall speak to him, saying, 'Thus says the LORD: "Have you murdered and also taken possession?" ' And you shall speak to him, saying, 'Thus says the LORD: "In the place where dogs licked the blood of Naboth, dogs shall lick your blood, even yours." ' "

20 So Ahab said to Elijah, "Have you found me, O my enemy?"

And he answered, "I have found *you*, because you have sold yourself to do evil in the sight of the LORD: 21 'Behold, I will bring calamity on you. I will take away your posterity, and will cut off from Ahab every male in Israel, both bond and free. 22 I will make your house like the house of Jeroboam the son of Nebat, and like the house of Baasha the son of Ahijah, because of the provocation with which you have provoked *Me* to anger, and made Israel sin.' 23 And concerning Jezebel the LORD also spoke, saying, 'The dogs shall eat Jezebel by the wall of Jezreel.' 24 The dogs shall eat whoever belongs to Ahab and dies in the city, and the birds of the air shall eat whoever dies in the field.' "

25 But there was no one like Ahab who sold himself to do wickedness in the sight of the LORD, because Jezebel his wife stirred him up. 26 And he behaved very abominably in following idols, according to all *that* the Amorites had done, whom the LORD had cast out before the children of Israel.

27 So it was, when Ahab heard those

words, that he tore his clothes and put sackcloth on his body, and fasted and lay in sackcloth, and went about mourning.

28 And the word of the LORD came to Elijah the Tishbite, saying, 29 "See how Ahab has humbled himself before Me? Because he has humbled himself before Me, I will not bring the calamity in his days. In the days of his son I will bring the calamity on his house."

Micaiah tells the truth

22 Now three years passed without war between Syria and Israel. 2 Then it came to pass, in the third year, that Jehoshaphat the king of Judah went down to *visit* the king of Israel.

3 And the king of Israel said to his servants, "Do you know that Ramoth in Gilead *is* ours, but we hesitate to take it out of the hand of the king of Syria?" 4 So he said to Jehoshaphat, "Will you go with me to fight at Ramoth Gilead?"

Jehoshaphat said to the king of Israel, "I *am* as you *are,* my people as your people, my horses as your horses." 5 Also Jehoshaphat said to the king of Israel, "Please inquire for the word of the LORD today."

6 Then the king of Israel gathered the prophets together, about four hundred men, and said to them, "Shall I go against Ramoth Gilead to fight, or shall I refrain?"

So they said, "Go up, for the Lord will deliver *it* into the hand of the king."

7 And Jehoshaphat said, "Is there not still a prophet of the LORD here, that we may inquire of Him?"

8 So the king of Israel said to Jehoshaphat, "There is still one man, Micaiah the son of Imlah, by whom we may inquire of the LORD; but I hate him, because he does not prophesy good concerning me, but evil."

And Jehoshaphat said, "Let not the king say such things!"

9 Then the king of Israel called an officer and said, "Bring Micaiah the son of Imlah quickly!"

10 The king of Israel and Jehosha-phat the king of Judah, having put on *their* robes, sat each on his throne, at a threshing floor at the entrance of the gate of Samaria; and all the prophets prophesied before them. 11 Now Zedekiah the son of Chenaanah had made horns of iron for himself; and he said, "Thus says the LORD: 'With these you shall gore the Syrians until they are destroyed.' " 12 And all the prophets prophesied so, saying, "Go up to Ramoth Gilead and prosper, for the LORD will deliver *it* into the king's hand."

13 Then the messenger who had gone to call Micaiah spoke to him, saying, "Now listen, the words of the prophets with one accord encourage the king. Please, let your word be like the word of one of them, and speak encouragement."

14 And Micaiah said, "As the LORD lives, whatever the LORD says to me, that I will speak."

15 Then he came to the king; and the king said to him, "Micaiah, shall we go to war against Ramoth Gilead, or shall we refrain?"

And he answered him, "Go and prosper, for the LORD will deliver *it* into the hand of the king!"

16 So the king said to him, "How many times shall I make you swear that you tell me nothing but the truth in the name of the LORD?"

17 Then he said, "I saw all Israel scattered on the mountains, as sheep that have no shepherd. And the LORD said, 'These have no master. Let each return to his house in peace.' "

18 And the king of Israel said to Jehoshaphat, "Did I not tell you he would not prophesy good concerning me, but evil?"

19 Then *Micaiah* said, "Therefore hear the word of the LORD: I saw the LORD sitting on His throne, and all the host of heaven standing by, on His right hand and on His left. 20 And the LORD said, 'Who will persuade Ahab to go up, that he may fall at Ramoth Gilead?' So one spoke in this manner, and another spoke in that manner. 21 Then a spirit came forward and stood before the LORD, and said, 'I will

persuade him.' 22 The LORD said to him, 'In what way?' So he said, 'I will go out and be a lying spirit in the mouth of all his prophets.' And the LORD said, 'You shall persuade *him*, and also prevail. Go out and do so.' 23 Therefore look! The LORD has put a lying spirit in the mouth of all these prophets of yours, and the LORD has declared disaster against you."

24 Now Zedekiah the son of Chenaanah went near and struck Micaiah on the cheek, and said, "Which way did the spirit from the LORD go from me to speak to you?"

25 And Micaiah said, "Indeed, you shall see on that day when you go into an inner chamber to hide!"

26 So the king of Israel said, "Take Micaiah, and return him to Amon the governor of the city and to Joash the king's son; 27 and say, 'Thus says the king: "Put this *fellow* in prison, and feed him with bread of affliction and water of affliction, until I come in peace." ' "

28 But Micaiah said, "If you ever return in peace, the LORD has not spoken by me." And he said, "Take heed, all you people!"

29 So the king of Israel and Jehoshaphat the king of Judah went up to Ramoth Gilead. 30 And the king of Israel said to Jehoshaphat, "I will disguise myself and go into battle; but you put on your robes." So the king of Israel disguised himself and went into battle.

31 Now the king of Syria had commanded the thirty-two captains of his chariots, saying, "Fight with no one small or great, but only with the king of Israel." 32 So it was, when the captains of the chariots saw Jehoshaphat, that they said, "Surely it *is* the king of Israel!" Therefore they turned aside to fight against him, and Jehoshaphat cried out. 33 And it happened, when the captains of the chariots saw that it *was* not the king of Israel, that they turned back from pursuing him. 34 Now a *certain* man drew a bow at random, and struck the king of Israel between the joints of his armor. So he said to the driver of his chariot, "Turn around and take me out of the battle, for I am wounded."

35 The battle increased that day; and the king was propped up in his chariot, facing the Syrians, and died at evening. The blood ran out from the wound onto the floor of the chariot. 36 Then, as the sun was going down, a shout went throughout the army, saying, "Every man to his city, and every man to his own country!"

37 So the king died, and was brought to Samaria. And they buried the king in Samaria. 38 Then *someone* washed the chariot at a pool in Samaria, and the dogs licked up his blood while the harlots bathed, according to the word of the LORD which He had spoken.

39 Now the rest of the acts of Ahab, and all that he did, the ivory house which he built and all the cities that he built, *are* they not written in the book of the chronicles of the kings of Israel? 40 So Ahab rested with his fathers. Then Ahaziah his son reigned in his place.

41 Jehoshaphat the son of Asa had become king over Judah in the fourth year of Ahab king of Israel. 42 Jehoshaphat *was* thirty-five years old when he became king, and he reigned twenty-five years in Jerusalem. His mother's name *was* Azubah the daughter of Shilhi. 43 And he walked in all the ways of his father Asa. He did not turn aside from them, doing *what was* right in the eyes of the LORD. Nevertheless the high places were not taken away, *for* the people offered sacrifices and burned incense on the high places. 44 Also Jehoshaphat made peace with the king of Israel.

45 Now the rest of the acts of Jehoshaphat, the might that he showed, and how he made war, *are* they not written in the book of the chronicles of the kings of Judah? 46 And the rest of the perverted persons, who remained in the days of his father Asa, he banished from the land. 47 *There was* then no king in Edom, only a deputy of the king.

48 Jehoshaphat made merchant

ships to go to Ophir for gold; but they never sailed, for the ships were wrecked at Ezion Geber. 49 Then Ahaziah the son of Ahab said to Jehoshaphat, "Let my servants go with your servants in the ships." But Jehoshaphat would not.

50 And Jehoshaphat rested with his fathers, and was buried with his fathers in the City of David his father. Then Jehoram his son reigned in his place.

51 Ahaziah the son of Ahab became king over Israel in Samaria in the seventeenth year of Jehoshaphat king of Judah, and reigned two years over Israel. 52 He did evil in the sight of the LORD, and walked in the way of his father and in the way of his mother and in the way of Jeroboam the son of Nebat, who had made Israel sin; 53 for he served Baal and worshiped him, and provoked the LORD God of Israel to anger, according to all that his father had done.

🪓 DIGGING IN

22:53 The Kings of North and South
All twenty of northern Israel's kings were wicked, and most of Judah's twenty kings were also wicked. Only a few, like Asa, Hezekiah, and Josiah, were good kings.

About two hundred years later, after Israel was split into two kingdoms, Israel in the north was destroyed by the nation of Assyria (pronounced ah-SEER-ih-uh). The southern kingdom of Judah was conquered by the army of Babylon (pronounced BAB-ih-lun) about two hundred years after that. The destruction of Israel and Judah was the result of disobeying God's laws.

Keep in mind that the gradual fall of Israel began with David. God told him that, because of his sins, "the sword shall never depart from your house" (2 Samuel 12:10).

The Book of
2 KINGS

The Nation of Israel—Our country is divided now. Ten of our tribes are the nation of Samaria (pronounced *suh-MARE-ee-ah*). Two of our tribes, Judah and Benjamin, formed the nation called Judah. Simeon joined us later. This breakup of our nation was caused by our sins. You can see how we sinned first by demanding a king in the time of Saul. Look at 1 Samuel 8:19–22.

After David, most of our kings disobeyed the Lord, and God would not accept our worship anymore because we didn't really love Him with all our hearts.

Sometimes it seemed that we would really return to God, like when King Hezekiah (pronounced *hez-uh-KIGH-uh*) and King Josiah (pronounced *jo-SIGH-uh*) prayed to God and asked Him to forgive our sins.

But we didn't honestly want to return to God. Now strangers are going to come and make us slaves in a foreign country.

King Ahaziah dies

MOAB rebelled against Israel after the death of Ahab.

2 Now Ahaziah fell through the lattice of his upper room in Samaria, and was injured; so he sent messengers and said to them, "Go, inquire of Baal-Zebub, the god of Ekron, whether I shall recover from this injury." 3 But the angel of the LORD said to Elijah the Tishbite, "Arise, go up to meet the messengers of the king of Samaria, and say to them, '*Is it because there is* no God in Israel *that* you are going to inquire of Baal-Zebub, the god of Ekron?' 4 Now therefore, thus says the LORD: 'You shall not come down from the bed to which you have gone up, but you shall surely die.' " So Elijah departed.

5 And when the messengers returned to him, he said to them, "Why have you come back?"

6 So they said to him, "A man came up to meet us, and said to us, 'Go, return to the king who sent you, and say to him, "Thus says the LORD: '*Is it because there is* no God in Israel *that* you are sending to inquire of Baal-Zebub, the god of Ekron? Therefore

you shall not come down from the bed to which you have gone up, but you shall surely die.' " ' "

7 Then he said to them, "What kind of man *was it* who came up to meet you and told you these words?"

8 So they answered him, "A hairy man wearing a leather belt around his waist."

And he said, "It *is* Elijah the Tishbite."

9 Then the king sent to him a captain of fifty with his fifty men. So he went up to him; and there he was, sitting on the top of a hill. And he spoke to him: "Man of God, the king has said, 'Come down!' "

10 So Elijah answered and said to the captain of fifty, "If I *am* a man of God, then let fire come down from heaven and consume you and your fifty men." And fire came down from heaven and consumed him and his fifty. 11 Then he sent to him another captain of fifty with his fifty men.

And he answered and said to him: "Man of God, thus has the king said, 'Come down quickly!' "

12 So Elijah answered and said to them, "If I *am* a man of God, let fire come down from heaven and consume

you and your fifty men." And the fire of God came down from heaven and consumed him and his fifty.

¹³ Again, he sent a third captain of fifty with his fifty men. And the third captain of fifty went up, and came and fell on his knees before Elijah, and pleaded with him, and said to him: "Man of God, please let my life and the life of these fifty servants of yours be precious in your sight. ¹⁴ Look, fire has come down from heaven and burned up the first two captains of fifties with their fifties. But let my life now be precious in your sight."

¹⁵ And the angel of the LORD said to Elijah, "Go down with him; do not be afraid of him." So he arose and went down with him to the king. ¹⁶ Then he said to him, "Thus says the LORD: 'Because you have sent messengers to inquire of Baal-Zebub, the god of Ekron, *is it* because *there is* no God in Israel to inquire of His word? Therefore you shall not come down from the bed to which you have gone up, but you shall surely die.'"

¹⁷ So *Ahaziah* died according to the word of the LORD which Elijah had spoken. Because he had no son, Jehoram became king in his place, in the second year of Jehoram the son of Jehoshaphat, king of Judah.

¹⁸ Now the rest of the acts of Ahaziah which he did, *are* they not written in the book of the chronicles of the kings of Israel?

Elijah and Elisha cross the Jordan

2 And it came to pass, when the LORD was about to take up Elijah into heaven by a whirlwind, that Elijah went with Elisha from Gilgal. ² Then Elijah said to Elisha, "Stay here, please, for the LORD has sent me on to Bethel."

But Elisha said, "As the LORD lives, and *as* your soul lives, I will not leave you!" So they went down to Bethel.

³ Now the sons of the prophets who *were* at Bethel came out to Elisha, and said to him, "Do you know that the LORD will take away your master from over you today?"

And he said, "Yes, I know; keep silent!"

⁴ Then Elijah said to him, "Elisha, stay here, please, for the LORD has sent me on to Jericho."

But he said, "As the LORD lives, and *as* your soul lives, I will not leave you!" So they came to Jericho.

⁵ Now the sons of the prophets who *were* at Jericho came to Elisha and said to him, "Do you know that the LORD will take away your master from over you today?"

So he answered, "Yes, I know; keep silent!"

⁶ Then Elijah said to him, "Stay

You should have been there! Horses and chariots of fire roared down from the skies, and I saw the prophet Elijah go up to heaven in a whirlwind!

But Elijah's outer covering, called a mantle, fell on me, Elisha. This was a sign that I would follow him in his work as a prophet. I also had twice as much power as he did to perform miracles.

Probably my best miracle was at the town of Shunem, where I told a childless couple that they would have a baby boy.

When their little son became sick and died, the mother was sorry that she had ever had a child. But God restored the boy's life, and the family was reunited and happy again, thankful to God for His gift. (My name is pronounced *ih-LIE-shuh* and means "His God Is the Lord.")

Elijah is taken up to heaven in a chariot of fire.

here, please, for the LORD has sent me on to the Jordan."

But he said, "As the LORD lives, and *as* your soul lives, I will not leave you!" So the two of them went on. 7 And fifty men of the sons of the prophets went and stood facing *them* at a distance, while the two of them stood by the Jordan. 8 Now Elijah took his mantle, rolled *it* up, and struck the water; and it was divided this way and that, so that the two of them crossed over on dry ground.

9 And so it was, when they had crossed over, that Elijah said to Elisha, "Ask! What may I do for you, before I am taken away from you?"

Elisha said, "Please let a double portion of your spirit be upon me."

10 So he said, "You have asked a hard thing. *Nevertheless,* if you see me *when I am* taken from you, it shall be so for you; but if not, it shall not be *so.*" 11 Then it happened, as they continued on and talked, that suddenly a chariot of fire *appeared* with horses of fire, and separated the two of them; and Elijah went up by a whirlwind into heaven.

12 And Elisha saw *it*, and he cried out, "My father, my father, the chariot of Israel and its horsemen!" So he saw him no more. And he took hold of his own clothes and tore them into two pieces. 13 He also took up the mantle of Elijah that had fallen from him, and went back and stood by the bank of the Jordan. 14 Then he took the mantle of Elijah that had fallen from him, and struck the water, and said, "Where *is* the LORD God of Elijah?" And when he also had struck the water, it was divided this way and that; and Elisha crossed over.

15 Now when the sons of the prophets who *were* from Jericho saw him, they said, "The spirit of Elijah rests on Elisha." And they came to meet him, and bowed to the ground before him. 16 Then they said to him, "Look now, there are fifty strong men with your servants. Please let them go and search for your master, lest perhaps the Spirit of the LORD has taken him up and cast him upon some mountain or into some valley."

And he said, "You shall not send anyone."

17 But when they urged him till he was ashamed, he said, "Send *them!*" Therefore they sent fifty men, and they searched for three days but did not find him. 18 And when they came back to him, for he had stayed in Jericho, he

said to them, "Did I not say to you, 'Do not go'?"

19 Then the men of the city said to Elisha, "Please notice, the situation of this city is pleasant, as my lord sees; but the water is bad, and the ground barren."

20 And he said, "Bring me a new bowl, and put salt in it." So they brought it to him. 21 Then he went out to the source of the water, and cast in the salt there, and said, "Thus says the LORD: 'I have healed this water; from it there shall be no more death or barrenness.'" 22 So the water remains healed to this day, according to the word of Elisha which he spoke.

23 Then he went up from there to Bethel; and as he was going up the road, some youths came from the city and mocked him, and said to him, "Go up, you baldhead! Go up, you baldhead!"

24 So he turned around and looked at them, and pronounced a curse on them in the name of the LORD. And two female bears came out of the woods and mauled forty-two of the youths.

25 Then he went from there to Mount Carmel, and from there he returned to Samaria.

Elisha predicts victory

3 Now Jehoram the son of Ahab became king over Israel at Samaria in the eighteenth year of Jehoshaphat king of Judah, and reigned twelve years. 2 And he did evil in the sight of the LORD, but not like his father and mother; for he put away the sacred pillar of Baal that his father had made. 3 Nevertheless he persisted in the sins of Jeroboam the son of Nebat, who had made Israel sin; he did not depart from them.

4 Now Mesha king of Moab was a sheepbreeder, and he regularly paid the king of Israel one hundred thousand lambs and the wool of one hundred thousand rams. 5 But it happened, when Ahab died, that the king

of Moab rebelled against the king of Israel.

6 So King Jehoram went out of Samaria at that time and mustered all Israel. 7 Then he went and sent to Jehoshaphat king of Judah, saying, "The king of Moab has rebelled against me. Will you go with me to fight against Moab?"

And he said, "I will go up; I am as you are, my people as your people, my horses as your horses." 8 Then he said, "Which way shall we go up?"

And he answered, "By way of the Wilderness of Edom."

9 So the king of Israel went with the king of Judah and the king of Edom, and they marched on that roundabout route seven days; and there was no water for the army, nor for the animals that followed them. 10 And the king of Israel said, "Alas! For the LORD has called these three kings together to deliver them into the hand of Moab."

11 But Jehoshaphat said, "Is there no prophet of the LORD here, that we may inquire of the LORD by him?"

So one of the servants of the king of Israel answered and said, "Elisha the son of Shaphat is here, who poured water on the hands of Elijah."

12 And Jehoshaphat said, "The word of the LORD is with him." So the king of Israel and Jehoshaphat and the king of Edom went down to him.

13 Then Elisha said to the king of Israel, "What have I to do with you? Go to the prophets of your father and the prophets of your mother."

But the king of Israel said to him, "No, for the LORD has called these three kings together to deliver them into the hand of Moab."

14 And Elisha said, "As the LORD of hosts lives, before whom I stand, surely were it not that I regard the presence of Jehoshaphat king of Judah, I would not look at you, nor see you. 15 But now bring me a musician."

Then it happened, when the musician played, that the hand of the LORD came upon him. 16 And he said, "Thus says the LORD: 'Make this valley full of ditches.' 17 For thus says the LORD:

'You shall not see wind, nor shall you see rain; yet that valley shall be filled with water, so that you, your cattle, and your animals may drink.' 18 And this is a simple matter in the sight of the LORD; He will also deliver the Moabites into your hand. 19 Also you shall attack every fortified city and every choice city, and shall cut down every good tree, and stop up every spring of water, and ruin every good piece of land with stones."

20 Now it happened in the morning, when the grain offering was offered, that suddenly water came by way of Edom, and the land was filled with water.

21 And when all the Moabites heard that the kings had come up to fight against them, all who were able to bear arms and older were gathered; and they stood at the border. 22 Then they rose up early in the morning, and the sun was shining on the water; and the Moabites saw the water on the other side as red as blood. 23 And they said, "This is blood; the kings have surely struck swords and have killed one another; now therefore, Moab, to the spoil!"

24 So when they came to the camp of Israel, Israel rose up and attacked the Moabites, so that they fled before them; and they entered their land, killing the Moabites. 25 Then they destroyed the cities, and each man threw a stone on every good piece of land and filled it; and they stopped up all the springs of water and cut down all the good trees. But they left the stones of Kir Haraseth intact. However the slingers surrounded and attacked it.

26 And when the king of Moab saw that the battle was too fierce for him, he took with him seven hundred men who drew swords, to break through to the king of Edom, but they could not. 27 Then he took his eldest son who would have reigned in his place, and offered him as a burnt offering upon the wall; and there was great indignation against Israel. So they departed from him and returned to their own land.

Elisha helps the woman from Shunem

4 A certain woman of the wives of the sons of the prophets cried out to Elisha, saying, "Your servant my husband is dead, and you know that your servant feared the LORD. And the creditor is coming to take my two sons to be his slaves."

2 So Elisha said to her, "What shall I do for you? Tell me, what do you have in the house?" And she said, "Your maidservant has nothing in the house but a jar of oil."

3 Then he said, "Go, borrow vessels from everywhere, from all your neighbors—empty vessels; do not gather just a few. 4 And when you have come in, you shall shut the door behind you and your sons; then pour it into all those vessels, and set aside the full ones."

5 So she went from him and shut the door behind her and her sons, who brought the vessels to her; and she poured it out. 6 Now it came to pass, when the vessels were full, that she said to her son, "Bring me another vessel."

And he said to her, "There is not another vessel." So the oil ceased. 7 Then she came and told the man of God. And he said, "Go, sell the oil and pay your debt; and you and your sons live on the rest."

8 Now it happened one day that Elisha went to Shunem, where there was a notable woman, and she persuaded him to eat some food. So it was, as often as he passed by, he would turn in there to eat some food. 9 And she said to her husband, "Look now, I know that this is a holy man of God, who passes by us regularly. 10 Please, let us make a small upper room on the wall; and let us put a bed for him there, and a table and a chair and a lampstand; so it will be, whenever he comes to us, he can turn in there."

11 And it happened one day that he came there, and he turned in to the upper room and lay down there. 12 Then he said to Gehazi his servant, "Call this Shunammite woman."

A good woman of Shunem prepared a guest room for the prophet Elisha.

When he had called her, she stood before him. 13 And he said to him, "Say now to her, 'Look, you have been concerned for us with all this care. What *can I* do for you? Do you want me to speak on your behalf to the king or to the commander of the army?' "

She answered, "I dwell among my own people."

14 So he said, "What then *is* to be done for her?"

And Gehazi answered, "Actually, she has no son, and her husband is old."

15 So he said, "Call her." When he had called her, she stood in the doorway. 16 Then he said, "About this time next year you shall embrace a son."

And she said, "No, my lord. Man of God, do not lie to your maidservant!"

17 But the woman conceived, and bore a son when the appointed time had come, of which Elisha had told her.

18 And the child grew. Now it happened one day that he went out to his father, to the reapers. 19 And he said to his father, "My head, my head!"

So he said to a servant, "Carry him to his mother." 20 When he had taken him and brought him to his mother, he sat on her knees till noon, and *then* died. 21 And she went up and laid him on the bed of the man of God, shut *the door* upon him, and went out. 22 Then she called to her husband, and said, "Please send me one of the young men and one of the donkeys, that I may run to the man of God and come back."

23 So he said, "Why are you going to him today? *It is* neither the New Moon nor the Sabbath."

And she said, "*It is* well." 24 Then she saddled a donkey, and said to her servant, "Drive, and go forward; do not slacken the pace for me unless I tell you." 25 And so she departed, and went to the man of God at Mount Carmel.

So it was, when the man of God saw her afar off, that he said to his servant Gehazi, "Look, the Shunammite woman! 26 Please run now to meet her, and say to her, 'Is it well with you? *Is it* well with your husband? *Is it* well with the child?' "

And she answered, "*It is* well." 27 Now when she came to the man of God at the hill, she caught him by the feet, but Gehazi came near to push her away. But the man of God said, "Let

What a Certain Mother Learned

My husband and I waited a long time for a son, but to our great sorrow, he died just a few years after he was born.

Elisha, the man of God, said our son would live again, but we wondered what he meant. Was he talking about life after death? And if so, would we have to wait until we died, too, to see our only child again?

But we found out that Elisha wasn't just talking about eternal life. Through the power of the same God who later raised His Son Jesus from the dead, Elisha gave us back our little son—alive! I learned that God is always the same. Someday He will call us all back from the grave, and we will never die again.

her alone; for her soul *is* in deep distress, and the LORD has hidden *it* from me, and has not told me.''

28 So she said, "Did I ask a son of my lord? Did I not say, 'Do not deceive me'?"

29 Then he said to Gehazi, "Get yourself ready, and take my staff in your hand, and be on your way. If you meet anyone, do not greet him; and if anyone greets you, do not answer him; but lay my staff on the face of the child."

30 And the mother of the child said, "*As* the LORD lives, and *as* your soul lives, I will not leave you." So he arose and followed her. 31 Now Gehazi went on ahead of them, and laid the staff on the face of the child; but *there was* neither voice nor hearing. Therefore he went back to meet him, and told him, saying, "The child has not awakened."

32 When Elisha came into the house, there was the child, lying dead on his bed. 33 He went in therefore, shut the door behind the two of them, and prayed to the LORD. 34 And he went up and lay on the child, and put his mouth on his mouth, his eyes on his eyes, and his hands on his hands; and he stretched himself out on the child, and the flesh of the child became warm. 35 He returned and walked back and forth in the house, and again went up and stretched himself out on him; then the child sneezed seven times, and the child opened his eyes. 36 And he called Gehazi and said, "Call this

Shunammite woman." So he called her. And when she came in to him, he said, "Pick up your son." 37 So she went in, fell at his feet, and bowed to the ground; then she picked up her son and went out.

38 And Elisha returned to Gilgal, and *there was* a famine in the land. Now the sons of the prophets *were* sitting before him; and he said to his servant, "Put on the large pot, and boil stew for the sons of the prophets." 39 So one went out into the field to gather herbs, and found a wild vine, and gathered from it a lapful of wild gourds, and came and sliced *them* into the pot of stew, though they did not know *what they were.* 40 Then they served it to the men to eat. Now it happened, as they were eating the stew, that they cried out and said, "Man of God, *there is* death in the pot!" And they could not eat *it.*

41 So he said, "Then bring some flour." And he put *it* into the pot, and said, "Serve *it* to the people, that they may eat." And there was nothing harmful in the pot.

42 Then a man came from Baal Shalisha, and brought the man of God bread of the firstfruits, twenty loaves of barley bread, and newly ripened grain in his knapsack. And he said, "Give *it* to the people, that they may eat."

43 But his servant said, "What? Shall I set this before one hundred men?" He said again, "Give it to the peo-

ple, that they may eat; for thus says the LORD: 'They shall eat and have *some* left over.' " 44 So he set *it* before them; and they ate and had *some* left over, according to the word of the LORD.

Elisha heals Captain Naaman

5 Now Naaman, commander of the army of the king of Syria, was a great and honorable man in the eyes of his master, because by him the LORD had given victory to Syria. He was also a mighty man of valor, *but* a leper. 2 And the Syrians had gone out on raids, and had brought back captive a young girl from the land of Israel. She waited on Naaman's wife. 3 Then she said to her mistress, "If only my master *were* with the prophet who *is* in Samaria! For he would heal him of his leprosy." 4 And *Naaman* went in and told his master, saying, "Thus and thus said the girl who *is* from the land of Israel."

5 Then the king of Syria said, "Go now, and I will send a letter to the king of Israel."

So he departed and took with him ten talents of silver, six thousand *shekels* of gold, and ten changes of clothing. 6 Then he brought the letter to the king of Israel, which said,

Now be advised, when this letter comes to you, that I have sent Naaman my servant to you, that you may heal him of his leprosy.

7 And it happened, when the king of Israel read the letter, that he tore his clothes and said, "*Am* I God, to kill and make alive, that this man sends a man to me to heal him of his leprosy? Therefore please consider, and see how he seeks a quarrel with me."

8 So it was, when Elisha the man of God heard that the king of Israel had torn his clothes, that he sent to the king, saying, "Why have you torn your clothes? Please let him come to me, and he shall know that there is a prophet in Israel."

9 Then Naaman went with his horses and chariot, and he stood at the door of Elisha's house. 10 And Elisha sent a messenger to him, saying, "Go and wash in the Jordan seven times, and your flesh shall be restored to you, and *you shall* be clean." 11 But Naaman became furious, and went away and said, "Indeed, I said to myself, 'He will surely come out *to me,* and stand and call on the name of the LORD his God, and wave his hand over the place, and heal the leprosy.' 12 *Are* not the Abanah and the Pharpar, the rivers of Damascus, better than all the waters of Israel? Could I not wash in them and be clean?" So he turned and went away in a rage. 13 And his servants came near and spoke to him, and said,

---

Naaman's Servant Girl—General Naaman (pronounced *NAY-uh-mun*) was an important officer in the King of Syria's army. But he had the disease of leprosy, and nobody could help him.

I was just a young servant girl in General Naaman's home, but I dared to tell his wife that there was a prophet in Israel who could heal her husband.

At first the king of Syria sent a large gift to the king of Israel, hoping Israel's king would heal my master. Of course, no ordinary king could do a miracle.

Then the prophet Elisha sent word to the general that he must bathe seven times in the River Jordan. General Naaman was furious, because he thought Elisha was playing a trick on him. The Syrian general finally went and bathed in the Jordan as Elisha told him. Sure enough, General Naaman was healed, and he believed in the true God.

"My father, *if* the prophet had told you *to do* something great, would you not have done *it?* How much more then, when he says to you, 'Wash, and be clean'?" ¹⁴ So he went down and dipped seven times in the Jordan, according to the saying of the man of God; and his flesh was restored like the flesh of a little child, and he was clean.

¹⁵ And he returned to the man of God, he and all his aides, and came and stood before him; and he said, "Indeed, now I know that *there is* no God in all the earth, except in Israel; now therefore, please take a gift from your servant."

¹⁶ But he said, "As the LORD lives, before whom I stand, I will receive nothing." And he urged him to take *it,* but he refused.

¹⁷ So Naaman said, "Then, if not, please let your servant be given two mule-loads of earth; for your servant will no longer offer either burnt offering or sacrifice to other gods, but to the LORD. ¹⁸ Yet in this thing may the LORD pardon your servant: when my master goes into the temple of Rimmon to worship there, and he leans on my hand, and I bow down in the temple of Rimmon—when I bow down in the temple of Rimmon, may the LORD please pardon your servant in this thing."

¹⁹ Then he said to him, "Go in peace." So he departed from him a short distance.

²⁰ But Gehazi, the servant of Elisha the man of God, said, "Look, my master has spared Naaman this Syrian, while not receiving from his hands what he brought; but *as* the LORD lives, I will run after him and take something from him." ²¹ So Gehazi pursued Naaman. When Naaman saw *him* running after him, he got down from the chariot to meet him, and said, "*Is* all well?"

²² And he said, "All *is* well. My master has sent me, saying, 'Indeed, just now two young men of the sons of the prophets have come to me from the mountains of Ephraim. Please give them a talent of silver and two changes of garments.' "

²³ So Naaman said, "Please, take two talents." And he urged him, and bound two talents of silver in two bags, with two changes of garments, and handed *them* to two of his servants; and they carried *them* on ahead of him. ²⁴ When he came to the citadel, he took *them* from their hand, and stored *them* away in the house; then he let the men go, and they departed. ²⁵ Now he went in and stood before his master. Elisha said to him, "Where did you go, Gehazi?"

And he said, "Your servant did not go anywhere."

²⁶ Then he said to him, "Did not my heart go *with you* when the man turned back from his chariot to meet you? *Is it* time to receive money and to receive clothing, olive groves and vineyards, sheep and oxen, male and female servants? ²⁷ Therefore the leprosy of Naaman shall cling to you and your descendants forever." And he went out from his presence leprous, *as white* as snow.

Elisha and the Syrians

6 And the sons of the prophets said to Elisha, "See now, the place where we dwell with you is too small for us. ² Please, let us go to the Jordan, and let every man take a beam from there, and let us make there a place where we may dwell."

So he answered, "Go."

³ Then one said, "Please consent to go with your servants."

And he answered, "I will go." ⁴ So he went with them. And when they came to the Jordan, they cut down trees. ⁵ But as one was cutting down a tree, the iron *ax head* fell into the water; and he cried out and said, "Alas, master! For it was borrowed."

⁶ So the man of God said, "Where did it fall?" And he showed him the place. So he cut off a stick, and threw *it* in there; and he made the iron float. ⁷ Therefore he said, "Pick *it* up for

Do Miracles Really Happen?

The Jericho Journal

JERICHO—This newspaper has never been in the habit of reporting miracles. Of course, we believe in miracles, as all good Hebrews should. But it has been some time since anyone has actually seen a miracle in our land.

An eyewitness account of a genuine miracle has now been submitted by our roving reporter.

While preparing to build a house for the prophet Elisha and themselves, several sons of the prophets were cutting down trees near the Jordan River. An ax head flew off the handle and into the water.

Elisha who was at the scene, asked the men to point out where the ax head had fallen. When they told him, he simply threw a stick into the water, and the heavy ax head came to the surface and floated.

The ax head was saved, which was a happy fact since the tool was borrowed!

---

yourself." So he reached out his hand and took it.

8 Now the king of Syria was making war against Israel; and he consulted with his servants, saying, "My camp *will be* in such and such a place." 9 And the man of God sent to the king of Israel, saying, "Beware that you do not pass this place, for the Syrians are coming down there." 10 Then the king of Israel sent *someone* to the place of which the man of God had told him. Thus he warned him, and he was watchful there, not just once or twice.

11 Therefore the heart of the king of Syria was greatly troubled by this thing; and he called his servants and said to them, "Will you not show me which of us *is* for the king of Israel?"

12 And one of his servants said, "None, my lord, O king; but Elisha, the prophet who *is* in Israel, tells the king of Israel the words that you speak in your bedroom."

13 So he said, "Go and see where he *is,* that I may send and get him." And it was told him, saying, "Surely *he is* in Dothan."

14 Therefore he sent horses and chariots and a great army there, and they came by night and surrounded the city. 15 And when the servant of the man of God arose early and went out, there was an army, surrounding the city with horses and chariots. And his servant said to him, "Alas, my master! What shall we do?"

16 So he answered, "Do not fear, for those who *are* with us *are* more than those who *are* with them." 17 And

---

🪓 DIGGING IN

6:8–17 God and You Are Enough
When Syria was making war against Israel, Elisha's servant went out one morning and saw the army of Syria surrounding the city of Dothan (pronounced *DOH-thun*). He was terrified. But the prophet Elisha asked God to open his servant's eyes. Then the servant could see horses and chariots of fire all around Elisha.

What can you learn from what Elisha's servant saw? Sometimes you think you are alone with all your problems. That is when you should remember Elisha. God's army was all around even though Elisha's servant couldn't see it.

God's army is always there to help His people. Like Elisha's servant, sometimes you need to ask God to open your eyes to see that you aren't really alone. Don't believe only what you see with your eyes. God is invisible, but you and He are enough to make you a winner over all your trials.

Elisha prayed, and said, "LORD, I pray, open his eyes that he may see." Then the LORD opened the eyes of the young man, and he saw. And behold, the mountain *was* full of horses and chariots of fire all around Elisha. 18 So when *the Syrians* came down to him, Elisha prayed to the LORD, and said, "Strike this people, I pray, with blindness." And He struck them with blindness according to the word of Elisha.

19 Now Elisha said to them, "This *is* not the way, nor *is* this the city. Follow me, and I will bring you to the man whom you seek." But he led them to Samaria.

20 So it was, when they had come to Samaria, that Elisha said, "LORD, open the eyes of these *men,* that they may see." And the LORD opened their eyes, and they saw; and there *they were,* inside Samaria!

21 Now when the king of Israel saw them, he said to Elisha, "My father, shall I kill *them?* Shall I kill *them?*"

22 But he answered, "You shall not kill *them.* Would you kill those whom you have taken captive with your sword and your bow? Set food and water before them, that they may eat and drink and go to their master."

23 Then he prepared a great feast for them; and after they ate and drank, he sent them away and they went to their master. So the bands of Syrian *raiders* came no more into the land of Israel.

24 And it happened after this that Ben-Hadad king of Syria gathered all his army, and went up and besieged Samaria. 25 And there was a great famine in Samaria; and indeed they besieged it until a donkey's head was *sold* for eighty *shekels* of silver, and one-fourth of a kab of dove droppings for five *shekels* of silver.

26 Then, as the king of Israel was passing by on the wall, a woman cried out to him, saying, "Help, my lord, O king!"

27 And he said, "If the LORD does not help you, where can I find help for you? From the threshing floor or from the winepress?" 28 Then the king

said to her, "What is troubling you?"

And she answered, "This woman said to me, 'Give your son, that we may eat him today, and we will eat my son tomorrow.' 29 So we boiled my son, and ate him. And I said to her on the next day, 'Give your son, that we may eat him'; but she has hidden her son."

30 Now it happened, when the king heard the words of the woman, that he tore his clothes; and as he passed by on the wall, the people looked, and there underneath *he had* sackcloth on his body. 31 Then he said, "God do so to me and more also, if the head of Elisha the son of Shaphat remains on him today!"

32 But Elisha was sitting in his house, and the elders were sitting with him. And *the king* sent a man ahead of him, but before the messenger came to him, he said to the elders, "Do you see how this son of a murderer has sent someone to take away my head? Look, when the messenger comes, shut the door, and hold him fast at the door. *Is* not the sound of his master's feet behind him?" 33 And while he was still talking with them, there *was* the messenger, coming down to him; and then *the king* said, "Surely this calamity *is* from the LORD; why should I wait for the LORD any longer?"

The Syrians run away

7 Then Elisha said, "Hear the word of the LORD. Thus says the LORD: 'Tomorrow about this time a seah of fine flour *shall be sold* for a shekel, and two seahs of barley for a shekel, at the gate of Samaria.' "

2 So an officer on whose hand the king leaned answered the man of God and said, "Look, *if* the LORD would make windows in heaven, could this thing be?"

And he said, "In fact, you shall see *it* with your eyes, but you shall not eat of it."

3 Now there were four leprous men at the entrance of the gate; and they said to one another, "Why are we sit-

ting here until we die? [4] If we say, 'We will enter the city,' the famine *is* in the city, and we shall die there. And if we sit here, we die also. Now therefore, come, let us surrender to the army of the Syrians. If they keep us alive, we shall live; and if they kill us, we shall only die." [5] And they rose at twilight to go to the camp of the Syrians; and when they had come to the outskirts of the Syrian camp, to their surprise no one *was* there. [6] For the LORD had caused the army of the Syrians to hear the noise of chariots and the noise of horses—the noise of a great army; so they said to one another, "Look, the king of Israel has hired against us the kings of the Hittites and the kings of the Egyptians to attack us!" [7] Therefore they arose and fled at twilight, and left the camp intact—their tents, their horses, and their donkeys—and they fled for their lives. [8] And when these lepers came to the outskirts of the camp, they went into one tent and ate and drank, and carried from it silver and gold and clothing, and went and hid *them;* then they came back and entered another tent, and carried *some* from there *also,* and went and hid *it.*

[9] Then they said to one another, "We are not doing right. This day *is* a day of good news, and we remain silent. If we wait until morning light, some punishment will come upon us. Now therefore, come, let us go and tell the king's household." [10] So they went and called to the gatekeepers of the city, and told them, saying, "We went to the Syrian camp, and surprisingly no one *was* there, not a human sound—only horses and donkeys tied, and the tents intact." [11] And the gatekeepers called out, and they told *it* to the king's household inside.

[12] So the king arose in the night and said to his servants, "Let me now tell you what the Syrians have done to us. They know that we *are* hungry; therefore they have gone out of the camp to hide themselves in the field, saying, 'When they come out of the city, we

shall catch them alive, and get into the city.' "

[13] And one of his servants answered and said, "Please, let several *men* take five of the remaining horses which are left in the city. Look, they *may either become* like all the multitude of Israel that are left in it; or indeed, *I say,* they *may become* like all the multitude of Israel left from those who are consumed; so let us send them and see." [14] Therefore they took two chariots with horses; and the king sent them in the direction of the Syrian army, saying, "Go and see." [15] And they went after them to the Jordan; and indeed all the road *was* full of garments and weapons which the Syrians had thrown away in their haste. So the messengers returned and told the king. [16] Then the people went out and plundered the tents of the Syrians. So a seah of fine flour was *sold* for a shekel, and two seahs of barley for a shekel, according to the word of the LORD.

[17] Now the king had appointed the officer on whose hand he leaned to have charge of the gate. But the people trampled him in the gate, and he died, just as the man of God had said, who spoke when the king came down to him. [18] So it happened just as the man of God had spoken to the king, saying, "Two seahs of barley for a shekel, and a seah of fine flour for a shekel, shall be *sold* tomorrow about this time in the gate of Samaria."

[19] Then that officer had answered the man of God, and said, "Now look, *if* the LORD would make windows in heaven, could such a thing be?"

And he had said, "In fact, you shall see *it* with your eyes, but you shall not eat of it." [20] And so it happened to him, for the people trampled him in the gate, and he died.

The king returns the Shunammite's land

8 Then Elisha spoke to the woman whose son he had restored to life, saying, "Arise and go, you and your household, and stay wherever you

Was the King of Syria Murdered?

The Syrian News Agency

DAMASCUS—The King of Syria is dead! King Ben-Hadad (pronounced *ben-HAY-dad*), who had been very ill for some time, had sent a trusted officer to ask Elisha (pronounced *ih-LIE-shuh*), the prophet in Israel, if he would get well. That officer's name was Hazael (pronounced *HAZ-ay-ell*).

The prophet told the king's officer that King Ben-Hadad surely would get better—but that he would die soon after!

Elisha's friends have also informed us that the prophet predicted that Hazael would be the next king of Syria. Elisha later revealed that Hazael would be a cruel enemy of Israel who would soon kill many Israelites.

SNA is unable to learn any more facts about the king's death at this time. But we understand that the writers of Bible history later discovered what Hazael did to the king (see 2 Kings 8:15).

can; for the LORD has called for a famine, and furthermore, it will come upon the land for seven years." 2 So the woman arose and did according to the saying of the man of God, and she went with her household and dwelt in the land of the Philistines seven years.

3 It came to pass, at the end of seven years, that the woman returned from the land of the Philistines; and she went to make an appeal to the king for her house and for her land. 4 Then the king talked with Gehazi, the servant of the man of God, saying, "Tell me, please, all the great things Elisha has done." 5 Now it happened, as he was telling the king how he had restored the dead to life, that there was the woman whose son he had restored to life, appealing to the king for her house and for her land. And Gehazi said, "My lord, O king, this *is* the woman, and this *is* her son whom Elisha restored to life." 6 And when the king asked the woman, she told him.

So the king appointed a certain officer for her, saying, "Restore all that *was* hers, and all the proceeds of the field from the day that she left the land until now."

7 Then Elisha went to Damascus, and Ben-Hadad king of Syria was sick; and it was told him, saying, "The man of God has come here." 8 And the king said to Hazael, "Take a present in your hand, and go to meet the man of God,

and inquire of the LORD by him, saying, 'Shall I recover from this disease?' " 9 So Hazael went to meet him and took a present with him, of every good thing of Damascus, forty camel-loads; and he came and stood before him, and said, "Your son Ben-Hadad king of Syria has sent me to you, saying, 'Shall I recover from this disease?' "

10 And Elisha said to him, "Go, say to him, 'You shall certainly recover.' However the LORD has shown me that he will really die." 11 Then he set his countenance in a stare until he was ashamed; and the man of God wept. 12 And Hazael said, "Why is my lord weeping?"

He answered, "Because I know the evil that you will do to the children of Israel: Their strongholds you will set on fire, and their young men you will kill with the sword; and you will dash their children, and rip open their women with child."

13 So Hazael said, "But what *is* your servant—a dog, that he should do this gross thing?"

And Elisha answered, "The LORD has shown me that you *will become* king over Syria."

14 Then he departed from Elisha, and came to his master, who said to him, "What did Elisha say to you?" And he answered, "He told me you would surely recover." 15 But it happened on the next day that he took a

thick cloth and dipped *it* in water, and spread *it* over his face so that he died; and Hazael reigned in his place.

16 Now in the fifth year of Joram the son of Ahab, king of Israel, Jehoshaphat *having been* king of Judah, Jehoram the son of Jehoshaphat began to reign as king of Judah. 17 He was thirty-two years old when he became king, and he reigned eight years in Jerusalem. 18 And he walked in the way of the kings of Israel, just as the house of Ahab had done, for the daughter of Ahab was his wife; and he did evil in the sight of the LORD. 19 Yet the LORD would not destroy Judah, for the sake of His servant David, as He promised him to give a lamp to him *and* his sons forever.

20 In his days Edom revolted against Judah's authority, and made a king over themselves. 21 So Joram went to Zair, and all his chariots with him. Then he rose by night and attacked the Edomites who had surrounded him and the captains of the chariots; and the troops fled to their tents. 22 Thus Edom has been in revolt against Judah's authority to this day. And Libnah revolted at that time.

23 Now the rest of the acts of Joram, and all that he did, *are* they not written in the book of the chronicles of the kings of Judah? 24 So Joram rested with his fathers, and was buried with his fathers in the City of David. Then Ahaziah his son reigned in his place.

25 In the twelfth year of Joram the son of Ahab, king of Israel, Ahaziah the son of Jehoram, king of Judah, began to reign. 26 Ahaziah *was* twenty-two years old when he became king, and he reigned one year in Jerusalem. His mother's name *was* Athaliah the granddaughter of Omri, king of Israel. 27 And he walked in the way of the house of Ahab, and did evil in the sight of the LORD, like the house of Ahab, for he *was* the son-in-law of the house of Ahab.

28 Now he went with Joram the son of Ahab to war against Hazael king of Syria at Ramoth Gilead; and the Syrians wounded Joram. 29 Then King Joram went back to Jezreel to recover from the wounds which the Syrians had inflicted on him at Ramah, when he fought against Hazael king of Syria. And Ahaziah the son of Jehoram, king of Judah, went down to see Joram the son of Ahab in Jezreel, because he was sick.

Joram, Ahaziah, and Jezebel die violently

9 And Elisha the prophet called one of the sons of the prophets, and said to him, "Get yourself ready, take this flask of oil in your hand, and go to Ramoth Gilead. 2 Now when you arrive at that place, look there for Jehu the son of Jehoshaphat, the son of Nimshi, and go in and make him rise up from among his associates, and take him to an inner room. 3 Then take the flask of oil, and pour *it* on his head, and say, 'Thus says the LORD: "I have anointed you king over Israel." ' Then open the door and flee, and do not delay."

4 So the young man, the servant of the prophet, went to Ramoth Gilead. 5 And when he arrived, there *were* the captains of the army sitting; and he said, "I have a message for you, Commander."

Jehu said, "For which *one* of us?"

And he said, "For you, Commander." 6 Then he arose and went into the house. And he poured the oil on his head, and said to him, "Thus says the LORD God of Israel: 'I have anointed you king over the people of the LORD, over Israel. 7 You shall strike down the house of Ahab your master, that I may avenge the blood of My servants the prophets, and the blood of all the servants of the LORD, at the hand of Jezebel. 8 For the whole house of Ahab shall perish; and I will cut off from Ahab all the males in Israel, both bond and free. 9 So I will make the house of Ahab like the house of Jeroboam the son of Nebat, and like the house of Baasha the son of Ahijah. 10 The dogs shall eat Jezebel on the plot *of ground* at Jezreel, and *there shall be* none to bury *her.*' " And he opened the door and fled.

11 Then Jehu came out to the servants of his master, and *one* said to him, "*Is* all well? Why did this madman come to you?"

And he said to them, "You know the man and his babble."

12 And they said, "A lie! Tell us now."

So he said, "Thus and thus he spoke to me, saying, 'Thus says the LORD: "I have anointed you king over Israel." ' "

13 Then each man hastened to take his garment and put *it* under him on the top of the steps; and they blew trumpets, saying, "Jehu is king!"

14 So Jehu the son of Jehoshaphat, the son of Nimshi, conspired against Joram. (Now Joram had been defending Ramoth Gilead, he and all Israel, against Hazael king of Syria. 15 But King Joram had returned to Jezreel to recover from the wounds which the Syrians had inflicted on him when he fought with Hazael king of Syria.) And Jehu said, "If you are so minded, let no one leave *or* escape from the city to go and tell *it* in Jezreel." 16 So Jehu rode in a chariot and went to Jezreel, for Joram was laid up there; and Ahaziah king of Judah had come down to see Joram.

17 Now a watchman stood on the tower in Jezreel, and he saw the company of Jehu as he came, and said, "I see a company of men."

And Joram said, "Get a horseman and send him to meet them, and let him say, '*Is it* peace?' "

18 So the horseman went to meet him, and said, "Thus says the king: '*Is it* peace?' "

And Jehu said, "What have you to do with peace? Turn around and follow me."

So the watchman reported, saying, "The messenger went to them, but is not coming back."

19 Then he sent out a second horseman who came to them, and said, "Thus says the king: '*Is it* peace?' "

And Jehu answered, "What have you to do with peace? Turn around and follow me."

20 So the watchman reported, saying, "He went up to them and is not coming back; and the driving *is* like the driving of Jehu the son of Nimshi, for he drives furiously!"

21 Then Joram said, "Make ready." And his chariot was made ready. Then Joram king of Israel and Ahaziah king of Judah went out, each in his chariot; and they went out to meet Jehu, and met him on the property of Naboth the Jezreelite. 22 Now it happened, when Joram saw Jehu, that he said, "*Is it* peace, Jehu?"

So he answered, "What peace, as long as the harlotries of your mother Jezebel and her witchcraft *are so* many?"

23 Then Joram turned around and fled, and said to Ahaziah, "Treachery, Ahaziah!" 24 Now Jehu drew his bow with full strength and shot Jehoram between his arms; and the arrow came out at his heart, and he sank down in his chariot. 25 Then *Jehu* said to Bidkar his captain, "Pick *him* up, *and* throw him into the tract of the field of Naboth the Jezreelite; for remember, when you and I were riding together behind Ahab his father, that the LORD laid this burden upon him: 26 'Surely I saw yesterday the blood of Naboth and the blood of his sons,' says the LORD, 'and I will repay you in this plot,' says the LORD. Now therefore, take *and* throw him on the plot *of ground,* according to the word of the LORD."

27 But when Ahaziah king of Judah saw *this,* he fled by the road to Beth Haggan. So Jehu pursued him, and said, "Shoot him also in the chariot." *And they shot him* at the Ascent of Gur, which is by Ibleam. Then he fled to Megiddo, and died there. 28 And his servants carried him in the chariot to Jerusalem, and buried him in his tomb with his fathers in the City of David. 29 In the eleventh year of Joram the son of Ahab, Ahaziah had become king over Judah.

30 Now when Jehu had come to Jezreel, Jezebel heard *of it;* and she

put paint on her *eyes* and adorned her head, and looked through a window. 31 Then, as Jehu entered at the gate, she said, "*Is it* peace, Zimri, murderer of your master?"

32 And he looked up at the window, and said, "Who *is* on my side? Who?" So two *or* three eunuchs looked out at him. 33 Then he said, "Throw her down." So they threw her down, and *some* of her blood spattered on the wall and on the horses; and he trampled her underfoot. 34 And when he had gone in, he ate and drank. Then he said, "Go now, see to this accursed *woman,* and bury her, for she was a king's daughter." 35 So they went to bury her, but they found no more of her than the skull and the feet and the palms of *her* hands. 36 Therefore they came back and told him. And he said, "This *is* the word of the Lord, which He spoke by His servant Elijah the Tishbite, saying, 'On the plot *of ground* at Jezreel dogs shall eat the flesh of Jezebel; 37 and the corpse of Jezebel shall be as refuse on the surface of the field, in the plot at Jezreel, so that they shall not say, "Here *lies* Jezebel." ' "

The seventy sons of Ahab

10 Now Ahab had seventy sons in Samaria. And Jehu wrote and sent letters to Samaria, to the rulers of Jezreel, to the elders, and to those who reared Ahab's *sons,* saying:

2   Now as soon as this letter comes to you, since your master's sons *are* with you, and you have chariots and horses, a fortified city also, and weapons, 3 choose the best qualified of your master's sons, set *him* on his father's throne, and fight for your master's house.

4 But they were exceedingly afraid, and said, "Look, two kings could not stand up to him; how then can we stand?" 5 And he who *was* in charge of the house, and he who *was* in charge of the city, the elders also, and those who reared *the sons,* sent to Jehu, saying, "We *are* your servants, we will do all you tell us; but we will not make anyone king. Do *what is* good in your sight." 6 Then he wrote a second letter to them, saying:

If you *are* for me and will obey my voice, take the heads of the men, your master's sons, and come to me at Jezreel by this time tomorrow.

Now the king's sons, seventy persons, *were* with the great men of the city, *who* were rearing them. 7 So it was, when the letter came to them, that they took the king's sons and slaughtered seventy persons, put their heads in baskets and sent *them* to him at Jezreel.

8 Then a messenger came and told him, saying, "They have brought the heads of the king's sons."

And he said, "Lay them in two heaps at the entrance of the gate until morning."

9 So it was, in the morning, that he went out and stood, and said to all the people, "You *are* righteous. Indeed I conspired against my master and killed him; but who killed all these? 10 Know now that nothing shall fall to the earth of the word of the Lord which the Lord spoke concerning the house of Ahab; for the Lord has done what He spoke by His servant Elijah." 11 So Jehu killed all who remained of the house of Ahab in Jezreel, and all his great men and his close acquaintances and his priests, until he left him none remaining.

12 And he arose and departed and went to Samaria. On the way, at Beth Eked of the Shepherds, 13 Jehu met with the brothers of Ahaziah king of Judah, and said, "Who *are* you?"

So they answered, "We *are* the brothers of Ahaziah; we have come down to greet the sons of the king and the sons of the queen mother."

14 And he said, "Take them alive!" So they took them alive, and killed them at the well of Beth Eked, forty-two men; and he left none of them.

15 Now when he departed from there, he met Jehonadab the son of Rechab, *coming* to meet him; and he greeted him and said to him, "Is your heart right, as my heart *is* toward your heart?"

And Jehonadab answered, "It is." *Jehu said,* "If it is, give *me* your hand." So he gave *him* his hand, and he took him up to him into the chariot. 16 Then he said, "Come with me, and see my zeal for the LORD." So they had him ride in his chariot. 17 And when he came to Samaria, he killed all who remained to Ahab in Samaria, till he had destroyed them, according to the word of the LORD which He spoke to Elijah.

18 Then Jehu gathered all the people together, and said to them, "Ahab served Baal a little, Jehu will serve him much. 19 Now therefore, call to me all the prophets of Baal, all his servants, and all his priests. Let no one be missing, for I have a great sacrifice for Baal. Whoever is missing shall not live." But Jehu acted deceptively, with the intent of destroying the worshipers of Baal. 20 And Jehu said, "Proclaim a solemn assembly for Baal." So they proclaimed *it.* 21 Then Jehu sent throughout all Israel; and all the worshipers of Baal came, so that there was not a man left who did not come. So they came into the temple of Baal, and the temple of Baal was full from one end to the other. 22 And he said to the one in charge of the wardrobe, "Bring out vestments for all the worshipers of Baal." So he brought out vestments for them. 23 Then Jehu and Jehonadab the son of Rechab went into the temple of Baal, and said to the worshipers of Baal, "Search and *see* that no servants of the LORD are here with you, but only the worshipers of Baal." 24 So they went in to offer sacrifices and burnt offerings. Now Jehu had appointed for himself eighty men on the outside, and had said, "*If* any of the men whom I have brought into your hands escapes, *whoever lets him escape, it shall be* his life for the life of the other."

25 Now it happened, as soon as he had made an end of offering the burnt offering, that Jehu said to the guard and to the captains, "Go in *and* kill them; let no one come out!" And they killed them with the edge of the sword; then the guards and the officers threw *them* out, and went into the inner room of the temple of Baal. 26 And they brought the *sacred* pillars out of the temple of Baal and burned them. 27 Then they broke down the *sacred* pillar of Baal, and tore down the temple of Baal and made it a refuse dump to this day. 28 Thus Jehu destroyed Baal from Israel.

29 However Jehu did not turn away from the sins of Jeroboam the son of Nebat, who had made Israel sin, *that is,* from the golden calves that *were* at Bethel and Dan. 30 And the LORD said to Jehu, "Because you have done well in doing *what is* right in My sight, *and* have done to the house of Ahab all that *was* in My heart, your sons shall sit on the throne of Israel to the fourth *generation.*" 31 But Jehu took no heed to walk in the law of the LORD God of Israel with all his heart; for he did not depart from the sins of Jeroboam, who had made Israel sin.

32 In those days the LORD began to cut off *parts* of Israel; and Hazael conquered them in all the territory of Israel 33 from the Jordan eastward: all the land of Gilead—Gad, Reuben, and Manasseh—from Aroer, which *is* by the River Arnon, including Gilead and Bashan.

34 Now the rest of the acts of Jehu, all that he did, and all his might, *are* they not written in the book of the chronicles of the kings of Israel? 35 So Jehu rested with his fathers, and they buried him in Samaria. Then Jehoahaz his son reigned in his place. 36 And the period that Jehu reigned over Israel in Samaria *was* twenty-eight years.

Joash—the boy king

11 When Athaliah the mother of Ahaziah saw that her son was dead,

Boy King Reigns in Judah

World Press International

JERUSALEM—There is shocking news from Jerusalem tonight. Seven-year-old Joash has been crowned king of Judah following the death of Queen Athaliah (pronounced ath-uh-LIE-uh) by order of Jehoiada the priest (pronounced *jeh-HOY-uh-duh*).

Seven years ago Athaliah murdered nearly all the heirs to Judah's throne, but young Joash (pronounced *JOE-ash*), son of King Ahaziah (pronounced *ay-huh-ZIGH-uh*), was rescued and hidden in the temple for six years. The child has been under an armed guard since that time. But his existence had been kept a secret until now.

In a quick ceremony attended by soldiers and bodyguards, young Joash was crowned king by Jehoiada the priest. Our sources report that there were shouts of "Long live the king!" and much rejoicing as the rightful heir took the throne.

Queen Athaliah heard the noise and rushed in, accusing the crowd of treason. She was arrested on the spot and executed outside the temple.

---

she arose and destroyed all the royal heirs. ² But Jehosheba, the daughter of King Joram, sister of Ahaziah, took Joash the son of Ahaziah, and stole him away from among the king's sons *who were* being murdered; and they hid him and his nurse in the bedroom, from Athaliah, so that he was not killed. ³ So he was hidden with her in the house of the LORD for six years, while Athaliah reigned over the land.

⁴ In the seventh year Jehoiada sent and brought the captains of hundreds—of the bodyguards and the escorts—and brought them into the house of the LORD to him. And he made a covenant with them and took an oath from them in the house of the LORD, and showed them the king's son. ⁵ Then he commanded them, saying, "This *is* what you shall do: One-third of you who come on duty on the Sabbath shall be keeping watch over the king's house, ⁶ one-third *shall be* at the gate of Sur, and one-third at the gate behind the escorts. You shall keep the watch of the house, lest it be broken down. ⁷ The two contingents of you who go off duty on the Sabbath shall keep the watch of the house of the LORD for the king. ⁸ But you shall surround the king on all sides, every man with his weapons in his hand; and whoever comes within range, let him be put to death. You are to be with the king as he goes out and as he comes in."

⁹ So the captains of the hundreds did according to all that Jehoiada the priest commanded. Each of them took his men who were to be on duty on the Sabbath, with those who were going off duty on the Sabbath, and came to

Joash was only seven years old when he was crowned king of Israel.

Jehoiada the priest. ¹⁰ And the priest gave the captains of hundreds the spears and shields which *had belonged* to King David, that were in the temple of the LORD. ¹¹ Then the escorts stood, every man with his weapons in his hand, all around the king, from the right side of the temple to the left side of the temple, by the altar and the house. ¹² And he brought out the king's son, put the crown on him, and *gave him* the Testimony; they made him king and anointed him, and they clapped their hands and said, "Long live the king!"

¹³ Now when Athaliah heard the noise of the escorts *and* the people, she came to the people *in* the temple of the LORD. ¹⁴ When she looked, there was the king standing by a pillar according to custom; and the leaders and the trumpeters were by the king. All the people of the land were rejoicing and blowing trumpets. So Athaliah tore her clothes and cried out, "Treason! Treason!"

¹⁵ And Jehoiada the priest commanded the captains of the hundreds, the officers of the army, and said to them, "Take her outside under guard, and slay with the sword whoever follows her." For the priest had said, "Do not let her be killed in the house of the LORD." ¹⁶ So they seized her; and she went by way of the horses' entrance *into* the king's house, and there she was killed.

¹⁷ Then Jehoiada made a covenant between the LORD, the king, and the people, that they should be the LORD's people, and *also* between the king and the people. ¹⁸ And all the people of the land went to the temple of Baal, and tore it down. They thoroughly broke in pieces its altars and images, and killed Mattan the priest of Baal before the altars. And the priest appointed officers over the house of the LORD. ¹⁹ Then he took the captains of hundreds, the bodyguards, the escorts, and all the people of the land; and they brought the king down from the house of the LORD, and went by way of the gate of the escorts to the king's house.

Then he sat on the throne of the kings. ²⁰ So all the people of the land rejoiced; and the city was quiet, for they had slain Athaliah with the sword *in* the king's house. ²¹ Jehoash *was* seven years old when he became king.

Young King Jehoash rules Judah

12 In the seventh year of Jehu, Jehoash became king, and he reigned forty years in Jerusalem. His mother's name *was* Zibiah of Beersheba. ² Jehoash did *what was* right in the sight of the LORD all the days in which Jehoiada the priest instructed him. ³ But the high places were not taken away; the people still sacrificed and burned incense on the high places.

⁴ And Jehoash said to the priests, "All the money of the dedicated gifts that are brought into the house of the LORD—each man's census money, each man's assessment money—*and* all the money that a man purposes in his heart to bring into the house of the LORD, ⁵ let the priests take *it* themselves, each from his constituency; and let them repair the damages of the temple, wherever any dilapidation is found."

⁶ Now it was so, by the twenty-third year of King Jehoash, *that* the priests had not repaired the damages of the temple. ⁷ So King Jehoash called Jehoiada the priest and the *other* priests, and said to them, "Why have you not repaired the damages of the temple? Now therefore, do not take *more* money from your constituency, but deliver it for repairing the damages of the temple." ⁸ And the priests agreed that they would neither receive *more* money from the people, nor repair the damages of the temple.

⁹ Then Jehoiada the priest took a chest, bored a hole in its lid, and set it beside the altar, on the right side as one comes into the house of the LORD; and the priests who kept the door put there all the money brought into the house of the LORD. ¹⁰ So it was, whenever they saw that *there was* much money in the chest, that the king's

scribe and the high priest came up and put it in bags, and counted the money that was found in the house of the LORD. ¹¹ Then they gave the money, which had been apportioned, into the hands of those who did the work, who had the oversight of the house of the LORD; and they paid it out to the carpenters and builders who worked on the house of the LORD, ¹² and to masons and stonecutters, and for buying timber and hewn stone, to repair the damage of the house of the LORD, and for all that was paid out to repair the temple. ¹³ However there were not made for the house of the LORD basins of silver, trimmers, sprinkling-bowls, trumpets, any articles of gold or articles of silver, from the money brought into the house of the LORD. ¹⁴ But they gave that to the workmen, and they repaired the house of the LORD with it. ¹⁵ Moreover they did not require an account from the men into whose hand they delivered the money to be paid to workmen, for they dealt faithfully. ¹⁶ The money from the trespass offerings and the money from the sin offerings was not brought into the house of the LORD. It belonged to the priests.

¹⁷ Hazael king of Syria went up and fought against Gath, and took it; then Hazael set his face to go up to Jerusalem. ¹⁸ And Jehoash king of Judah took all the sacred things that his fathers, Jehoshaphat and Jehoram and Ahaziah, kings of Judah, had dedicated, and his own sacred things, and all the gold found in the treasuries of the house of the LORD and in the king's house, and sent *them* to Hazael king of Syria. Then he went away from Jerusalem.

¹⁹ Now the rest of the acts of Joash, and all that he did, *are* they not written in the book of the chronicles of the kings of Judah?

²⁰ And his servants arose and formed a conspiracy, and killed Joash in the house of the Millo, which goes down to Silla. ²¹ For Jozachar the son of Shimeath and Jehozabad the son of Shomer, his servants, struck him. So he died, and they buried him with

his fathers in the City of David. Then Amaziah his son reigned in his place.

Elisha's last words

13 In the twenty-third year of Joash the son of Ahaziah, king of Judah, Jehoahaz the son of Jehu became king over Israel in Samaria, *and reigned* seventeen years. ² And he did evil in the sight of the LORD, and followed the sins of Jeroboam the son of Nebat, who had made Israel sin. He did not depart from them.

³ Then the anger of the LORD was aroused against Israel, and He delivered them into the hand of Hazael king of Syria, and into the hand of Ben-Hadad the son of Hazael, all *their* days. ⁴ So Jehoahaz pleaded with the LORD, and the LORD listened to him; for He saw the oppression of Israel, because the king of Syria oppressed them. ⁵ Then the LORD gave Israel a deliverer, so that they escaped from under the hand of the Syrians; and the children of Israel dwelt in their tents as before. ⁶ Nevertheless they did not depart from the sins of the house of Jeroboam, who had made Israel sin, *but* walked in them; and the wooden image also remained in Samaria. ⁷ For He left of the army of Jehoahaz only fifty horsemen, ten chariots, and ten thousand foot soldiers; for the king of Syria had destroyed them and made them like the dust at threshing.

⁸ Now the rest of the acts of Jehoahaz, all that he did, and his might, *are* they not written in the book of the chronicles of the kings of Israel? ⁹ So Jehoahaz rested with his fathers, and they buried him in Samaria. Then Joash his son reigned in his place.

¹⁰ In the thirty-seventh year of Joash king of Judah, Jehoash the son of Jehoahaz became king over Israel in Samaria, *and reigned* sixteen years. ¹¹ And he did evil in the sight of the LORD. He did not depart from all the sins of Jeroboam the son of Nebat, who made Israel sin, *but* walked in them.

¹² Now the rest of the acts of Joash,

all that he did, and his might with which he fought against Amaziah king of Judah, *are* they not written in the book of the chronicles of the kings of Israel? 13 So Joash rested with his fathers. Then Jeroboam sat on his throne. And Joash was buried in Samaria with the kings of Israel.

14 Elisha had become sick with the illness of which he would die. Then Joash the king of Israel came down to him, and wept over his face, and said, "O my father, my father, the chariots of Israel and their horsemen!"

15 And Elisha said to him, "Take a bow and some arrows." So he took himself a bow and some arrows. 16 Then he said to the king of Israel, "Put your hand on the bow." So he put his hand *on it,* and Elisha put his hands on the king's hands. 17 And he said, "Open the east window"; and he opened *it.* Then Elisha said, "Shoot"; and he shot. And he said, "The arrow of the LORD's deliverance and the arrow of deliverance from Syria; for you must strike the Syrians at Aphek till you have destroyed *them.*" 18 Then he said, "Take the arrows"; so he took *them.* And he said to the king of Israel, "Strike the ground"; so he struck three times, and stopped. 19 And the man of God was angry with him, and said, "You should have struck five or six times; then you would have struck Syria till you had destroyed *it!* But now you will strike Syria *only* three times."

20 Then Elisha died, and they buried him. And the *raiding* bands from Moab invaded the land in the spring of the year. 21 So it was, as they were burying a man, that suddenly they spied a band *of raiders;* and they put the man in the tomb of Elisha; and when the man was let down and touched the bones of Elisha, he revived and stood on his feet.

22 And Hazael king of Syria oppressed Israel all the days of Jehoahaz. 23 But the LORD was gracious to them, had compassion on them, and regarded them, because of His covenant with Abraham, Isaac, and Jacob, and would not yet destroy them or cast them from His presence.

24 Now Hazael king of Syria died. Then Ben-Hadad his son reigned in his place. 25 And Jehoash the son of Jehoahaz recaptured from the hand of Ben-Hadad, the son of Hazael, the cities which he had taken out of the hand of Jehoahaz his father by war. Three times Joash defeated him and recaptured the cities of Israel.

Amaziah rules Judah

14 In the second year of Joash the son of Jehoahaz, king of Israel, Amaziah the son of Joash, king of Judah, became king. 2 He was twenty-five years old when he became king, and he reigned twenty-nine years in Jerusalem. His mother's name was Jehoaddan of Jerusalem. 3 And he did *what was* right in the sight of the LORD, yet not like his father David; he did everything as his father Joash had done. 4 However the high places were not taken away, and the people still sacrificed and burned incense on the high places.

5 Now it happened, as soon as the kingdom was established in his hand, that he executed his servants who had murdered his father the king. 6 But the children of the murderers he did not execute, according to what is written in the Book of the Law of Moses, in which the LORD commanded, saying, "Fathers shall not be put to death for their children, nor shall children be put to death for their fathers; but a person shall be put to death for his own sin."

7 He killed ten thousand Edomites in the Valley of Salt, and took Sela by war, and called its name Joktheel to this day.

8 Then Amaziah sent messengers to Jehoash the son of Jehoahaz, the son of Jehu, king of Israel, saying, "Come, let us face one another *in battle.*" 9 And Jehoash king of Israel sent to Amaziah king of Judah, saying, "The thistle that *was* in Lebanon sent to the cedar that *was* in Lebanon, saying, 'Give your daughter to my son as wife';

and a wild beast that *was* in Lebanon passed by and trampled the thistle. [10] You have indeed defeated Edom, and your heart has lifted you up. Glory *in that,* and stay at home; for why should you meddle with trouble so that you fall—you and Judah with you?" [11] But Amaziah would not heed. Therefore Jehoash king of Israel went out; so he and Amaziah king of Judah faced one another at Beth Shemesh, which *belongs* to Judah. [12] And Judah was defeated by Israel, and every man fled to his tent. [13] Then Jehoash king of Israel captured Amaziah king of Judah, the son of Jehoash, the son of Ahaziah, at Beth Shemesh; and he went to Jerusalem, and broke down the wall of Jerusalem from the Gate of Ephraim to the Corner Gate—four hundred cubits. [14] And he took all the gold and silver, all the articles that *were* found in the house of the LORD and in the treasuries of the king's house, and hostages, and returned to Samaria.

[15] Now the rest of the acts of Jehoash which he did—his might, and how he fought with Amaziah king of Judah—*are* they not written in the book of the chronicles of the kings of Israel? [16] So Jehoash rested with his fathers, and was buried in Samaria with the kings of Israel. Then Jeroboam his son reigned in his place.

[17] Amaziah the son of Joash, king of Judah, lived fifteen years after the death of Jehoash the son of Jehoahaz, king of Israel. [18] Now the rest of the acts of Amaziah, *are* they not written in the book of the chronicles of the kings of Judah? [19] And they formed a conspiracy against him in Jerusalem, and he fled to Lachish; but they sent after him to Lachish and killed him there. [20] Then they brought him on horses, and he was buried at Jerusalem with his fathers in the City of David.

[21] And all the people of Judah took Azariah, who *was* sixteen years old, and made him king instead of his father Amaziah. [22] He built Elath and restored it to Judah, after the king rested with his fathers.

[23] In the fifteenth year of Amaziah the son of Joash, king of Judah, Jeroboam the son of Joash, king of Israel, became king in Samaria, *and reigned* forty-one years. [24] And he did evil in the sight of the LORD; he did not depart from all the sins of Jeroboam the son of Nebat, who had made Israel sin. [25] He restored the territory of Israel from the entrance of Hamath to the Sea of the Arabah, according to the word of the LORD God of Israel, which He had spoken through His servant Jonah the son of Amittai, the prophet who *was* from Gath Hepher. [26] For the LORD saw *that* the affliction of Israel *was* very bitter; and whether bond or free, there was no helper for Israel. [27] And the LORD did not say that He would blot out the name of Israel from under heaven; but He saved them by the hand of Jeroboam the son of Joash.

[28] Now the rest of the acts of Jeroboam, and all that he did—his might, how he made war, and how he recaptured for Israel, from Damascus and Hamath, *what had belonged* to Judah—*are* they not written in the book of the chronicles of the kings of Israel? [29] So Jeroboam rested with his fathers, the kings of Israel. Then Zechariah his son reigned in his place.

Good and evil kings of Israel and Judah

15 In the twenty-seventh year of Jeroboam king of Israel, Azariah the son of Amaziah, king of Judah, became king. [2] He was sixteen years old when he became king, and he reigned fifty-two years in Jerusalem. His mother's name *was* Jecholiah of Jerusalem. [3] And he did *what was* right in the sight of the LORD, according to all that his father Amaziah had done, [4] except that the high places were not removed; the people still sacrificed and burned incense on the high places. [5] Then the LORD struck the king, so that he was a leper until the day of his death; so he dwelt in an isolated house. And Jotham the king's son *was* over the *royal* house, judging the people of the land.

6 Now the rest of the acts of Azariah, and all that he did, *are* they not written in the book of the chronicles of the kings of Judah? 7 So Azariah rested with his fathers, and they buried him with his fathers in the City of David. Then Jotham his son reigned in his place.

8 In the thirty-eighth year of Azariah king of Judah, Zechariah the son of Jeroboam reigned over Israel in Samaria six months. 9 And he did evil in the sight of the LORD, as his fathers had done; he did not depart from the sins of Jeroboam the son of Nebat, who had made Israel sin. 10 Then Shallum the son of Jabesh conspired against him, and struck and killed him in front of the people; and he reigned in his place.

11 Now the rest of the acts of Zechariah, indeed they *are* written in the book of the chronicles of the kings of Israel.

12 This *was* the word of the LORD which He spoke to Jehu, saying, "Your sons shall sit on the throne of Israel to the fourth *generation*." And so it was.

13 Shallum the son of Jabesh became king in the thirty-ninth year of Uzziah king of Judah; and he reigned a full month in Samaria. 14 For Menahem the son of Gadi went up from Tirzah, came to Samaria, and struck Shallum the son of Jabesh in Samaria and killed him; and he reigned in his place.

15 Now the rest of the acts of Shallum, and the conspiracy which he led, indeed they *are* written in the book of the chronicles of the kings of Israel. 16 Then from Tirzah, Menahem attacked Tiphsah, all who *were* there, and its territory. Because they did not surrender, therefore he attacked *it*. All the women there who were with child he ripped open.

17 In the thirty-ninth year of Azariah king of Judah, Menahem the son of Gadi became king over Israel, *and* reigned ten years in Samaria. 18 And

he did evil in the sight of the LORD; he did not depart all his days from the sins of Jeroboam the son of Nebat, who had made Israel sin. 19 Pul king of Assyria came against the land; and Menahem gave Pul a thousand talents of silver, that his hand might be with him to strengthen the kingdom under his control. 20 And Menahem exacted the money from Israel, from all the very wealthy, from each man fifty shekels of silver, to give to the king of Assyria. So the king of Assyria turned back, and did not stay there in the land.

21 Now the rest of the acts of Menahem, and all that he did, *are* they not written in the book of the chronicles of the kings of Israel? 22 So Menahem rested with his fathers. Then Pekahiah his son reigned in his place.

23 In the fiftieth year of Azariah king of Judah, Pekahiah the son of Menahem became king over Israel in Samaria, *and reigned* two years. 24 And he did evil in the sight of the LORD; he did not depart from the sins of Jeroboam the son of Nebat, who had made Israel sin. 25 Then Pekah the son of Remaliah, an officer of his, conspired against him and killed him in Samaria, in the citadel of the king's house, along with Argob and Arieh; and with him were fifty men of Gilead. He killed him and reigned in his place.

26 Now the rest of the acts of Pekahiah, and all that he did, indeed they *are* written in the book of the chronicles of the kings of Israel.

27 In the fifty-second year of Azariah king of Judah, Pekah the son of Remaliah became king over Israel in Samaria, *and reigned* twenty years. 28 And he did evil in the sight of the LORD; he did not depart from the sins of Jeroboam the son of Nebat, who had made Israel sin. 29 In the days of Pekah king of Israel, Tiglath-Pileser king of Assyria came and took Ijon, Abel Beth Maachah, Janoah, Kedesh, Hazor, Gilead, and Galilee, all the land of Naphtali; and he carried them captive to Assyria. 30 Then Hoshea the son of Elah led a conspiracy against Pekah

the son of Remaliah, and struck and killed him; so he reigned in his place in the twentieth year of Jotham the son of Uzziah.

31 Now the rest of the acts of Pekah, and all that he did, indeed they *are* written in the book of the chronicles of the kings of Israel.

32 In the second year of Pekah the son of Remaliah, king of Israel, Jotham the son of Uzziah, king of Judah, began to reign. 33 He was twenty-five years old when he became king, and he reigned sixteen years in Jerusalem. His mother's name *was* Jerusha the daughter of Zadok. 34 And he did *what was* right in the sight of the LORD; he did according to all that his father Uzziah had done. 35 However the high places were not removed; the people still sacrificed and burned incense on the high places. He built the Upper Gate of the house of the LORD.

36 Now the rest of the acts of Jotham, and all that he did, *are* they not written in the book of the chronicles of the kings of Judah? 37 In those days the LORD began to send Rezin king of Syria and Pekah the son of Remaliah against Judah. 38 So Jotham rested with his fathers, and was buried with his fathers in the City of David his father. Then Ahaz his son reigned in his place.

Ahaz and Hezekiah rule Judah

16 In the seventeenth year of Pekah the son of Remaliah, Ahaz the son of Jotham, king of Judah, began to reign. 2 Ahaz *was* twenty years old when he became king, and he reigned sixteen years in Jerusalem; and he did not do *what was* right in the sight of the LORD his God, as his father David *had done.* 3 But he walked in the way of the kings of Israel; indeed he made his son pass through the fire, according to the abominations of the nations whom the LORD had cast out from before the children of Israel. 4 And he sacrificed and burned incense on the high places, on the hills, and under *every* green tree.

5 Then Rezin king of Syria and Pekah the son of Remaliah, king of Israel, came up to Jerusalem to *make* war; and they besieged Ahaz but could not overcome *him.* 6 At that time Rezin king of Syria captured Elath for Syria, and drove the men of Judah from Elath. Then the Edomites went to Elath, and dwell there to this day.

7 So Ahaz sent messengers to Tiglath-Pileser king of Assyria, saying, "I *am* your servant and your son. Come up and save me from the hand of the king of Syria and from the hand of the king of Israel, who rise up against me." 8 And Ahaz took the silver and gold that was found in the house of the LORD, and in the treasuries of the king's house, and sent *it as* a present to the king of Assyria. 9 So the king of Assyria heeded him; for the king of Assyria went up against Damascus and took it, carried *its people* captive to Kir, and killed Rezin.

10 Now King Ahaz went to Damascus to meet Tiglath-Pileser king of Assyria, and saw an altar that *was* at Damascus; and King Ahaz sent to Urijah the priest the design of the altar and its pattern, according to all its workmanship. 11 Then Urijah the priest built an altar according to all that King Ahaz had sent from Damascus. So Urijah the priest made *it* before King Ahaz came back from Damascus. 12 And when the king came back from Damascus, the king saw the altar; and the king approached the altar and made offerings on it. 13 So he burned his burnt offering and his grain offering; and he poured his drink offering and sprinkled the blood of his peace offerings on the altar. 14 He also brought the bronze altar which *was* before the LORD, from the front of the temple—from between the *new* altar and the house of the LORD—and put it on the north side of the *new* altar. 15 Then King Ahaz commanded Urijah the priest, saying, "On the great *new* altar burn the morning burnt offering, the evening grain offering, the king's burnt sacrifice, and his grain offering, with the burnt offering of all the people of the land, their grain offering, and their drink offerings; and sprinkle

on it all the blood of the burnt offering and all the blood of the sacrifice. And the bronze altar shall be for me to inquire by." 16 Thus did Urijah the priest, according to all that King Ahaz commanded.

17 And King Ahaz cut off the panels of the carts, and removed the lavers from them; and he took down the Sea from the bronze oxen that *were* under it, and put it on a pavement of stones. 18 Also he removed the Sabbath pavilion which they had built in the temple, and he removed the king's outer entrance from the house of the LORD, on account of the king of Assyria.

19 Now the rest of the acts of Ahaz which he did, *are* they not written in the book of the chronicles of the kings of Judah? 20 So Ahaz rested with his fathers, and was buried with his fathers in the City of David. Then Hezekiah his son reigned in his place.

Israel is invaded by Assyria

17 In the twelfth year of Ahaz king of Judah, Hoshea the son of Elah became king of Israel in Samaria, *and he reigned* nine years. 2 And he did evil in the sight of the LORD, but not as the kings of Israel who were before him. 3 Shalmaneser king of Assyria came up against him; and Hoshea became his vassal, and paid him tribute money. 4 And the king of Assyria uncovered a conspiracy by Hoshea; for he had sent messengers to So, king of Egypt, and brought no tribute to the king of Assyria, as *he had done* year by year. Therefore the king of Assyria shut him up, and bound him in prison.

5 Now the king of Assyria went throughout all the land, and went up to Samaria and besieged it for three years. 6 In the ninth year of Hoshea, the king of Assyria took Samaria and carried Israel away to Assyria, and placed them in Halah and by the Habor, the River of Gozan, and in the cities of the Medes.

7 For so it was that the children of Israel had sinned against the LORD their God, who had brought them up out of the land of Egypt, from under the hand of Pharaoh king of Egypt; and they had feared other gods, 8 and had walked in the statutes of the nations whom the LORD had cast out from before the children of Israel, and of the kings of Israel, which they had made. 9 Also the children of Israel secretly did against the LORD their God things that *were* not right, and they built for themselves high places in all their cities, from watchtower to fortified city. 10 They set up for themselves *sacred* pillars and wooden images on every high hill and under every green tree. 11 There they burned incense on all the high places, like the nations whom the LORD had carried away before them; and they did wicked things to provoke the LORD to anger, 12 for they served idols, of which the LORD had said to them, "You shall not do this thing."

13 Yet the LORD testified against Israel and against Judah, by all of His prophets, every seer, saying, "Turn from your evil ways, and keep My commandments *and* My statutes, according to all the law which I commanded your fathers, and which I sent to you by My servants the prophets." 14 Nevertheless they would not hear, but stiffened their necks, like the necks of their fathers, who did not believe in the LORD their God. 15 And they rejected His statutes and His covenant that He had made with their fathers, and His testimonies which He had testified against them; they followed idols, became idolaters, and *went* after the nations who *were* all around them, *concerning* whom the LORD had charged them that they should not do like them. 16 So they left all the commandments of the LORD their God, made for themselves a molded image *and* two calves, made a wooden image and worshiped all the host of heaven, and served Baal. 17 And they caused their sons and daughters to pass through the fire, practiced witchcraft and soothsaying, and sold themselves to do evil in the sight of the LORD, to provoke Him to anger. 18 Therefore the LORD was very angry with Israel,

Assyria Crushes Northern Kingdom

ITN (Israel Television Network)— Our crews are on hand to bring you firsthand reports of the end of the Northern Kingdom of Israel.

For three years King Shalmaneser (pronounced *shall-man-EE-zer*) of Assyria (pronounced *ah-SEER-ih-uh*) has been making war against Israel. King Hoshea (pronounced *ho-SHAY-uh*) of Israel was trying to get help from Egypt. But the king of Assyria heard about the plan and has put Hoshea in prison. Now

Israel is falling before the advancing army of Assyria.

The fall of Israel marks the end of a sad period in the history of God's Old Testament people. The Lord saved us all from slavery in Egypt, but our people have constantly rebelled against Him.

ITN expresses the hope that the same fate will not happen to our Southern Kingdom of Judah. But the signs are not good. (See 2 Kings 24 and 25.)

---

and removed them from His sight; there was none left but the tribe of Judah alone.

19 Also Judah did not keep the commandments of the LORD their God, but walked in the statutes of Israel which they made. 20 And the LORD rejected all the descendants of Israel, afflicted them, and delivered them into the hand of plunderers, until He had cast them from His sight. 21 For He tore Israel from the house of David, and they made Jeroboam the son of Nebat king. Then Jeroboam drove Israel from following the LORD, and made them commit a great sin. 22 For the children of Israel walked in all the sins of Jeroboam which he did; they did not depart from them, 23 until the LORD re-

moved Israel out of His sight, as He had said by all His servants the prophets. So Israel was carried away from their own land to Assyria, *as it is* to this day.

24 Then the king of Assyria brought *people* from Babylon, Cuthah, Ava, Hamath, and from Sepharvaim, and placed *them* in the cities of Samaria instead of the children of Israel; and they took possession of Samaria and dwelt in its cities. 25 And it was so, at the beginning of their dwelling there, *that* they did not fear the LORD; therefore the LORD sent lions among them, which killed *some* of them. 26 So they spoke to the king of Assyria, saying, "The nations whom you have removed and placed in the cities of

---

⚒ DIGGING IN

17:23 The Empire of Assyria The empire of Assyria (pronounced *ah-SEER-ih-uh*) is not the same as the country of Syria. They are two different countries in different places.

The Assyrian Empire existed over two thousand years before Jesus was born. Its original capital was Asshur (pronounced *ah-SURE*) but was later Nineveh (pronounced *NIN-uh-vuh*). Jonah the prophet preached in Nineveh. See his book.

Assyria at one time spread as far west as the Mediterranean Sea. Finally, it was limited to an area between the Tigris and

Euphrates rivers (pronounced *TIE-gris* and *you-FRAY-tees*). See the map on page 512. The Assyrians were the most powerful nation in the world between nine hundred and six hundred years before Jesus was born.

Northern Israel was conquered by the Assyrians 722 years before Jesus, and thousands of Jews were taken captive to Assyria. That empire was conquered by the Babylonians (pronounced *bab-ih-LOW-nih-uns*) 612 years before Christ. Nahum the prophet wrote about the fall of Nineveh. See his book.

Samaria do not know the rituals of the God of the land; therefore He has sent lions among them, and indeed, they are killing them because they do not know the rituals of the God of the land." 27 Then the king of Assyria commanded, saying, "Send there one of the priests whom you brought from there; let him go and dwell there, and let him teach them the rituals of the God of the land." 28 Then one of the priests whom they had carried away from Samaria came and dwelt in Bethel, and taught them how they should fear the LORD.

29 However every nation continued to make gods of its own, and put *them* in the shrines on the high places which the Samaritans had made, *every* nation in the cities where they dwelt. 30 The men of Babylon made Succoth Benoth, the men of Cuth made Nergal, the men of Hamath made Ashima, 31 and the Avites made Nibhaz and Tartak; and the Sepharvites burned their children in fire to Adrammelech and Anammelech, the gods of Sepharvaim. 32 So they feared the LORD, and from every class they appointed for themselves priests of the high places, who sacrificed for them in the shrines of the high places. 33 They feared the LORD, yet served their own gods—according to the rituals of the nations from among whom they were carried away.

34 To this day they continue practicing the former rituals; they do not fear the LORD, nor do they follow their statutes or their ordinances, or the law and commandment which the LORD had commanded the children of Jacob, whom He named Israel, 35 with whom the LORD had made a covenant and charged them, saying: "You shall not fear other gods, nor bow down to them nor serve them nor sacrifice to them; 36 but the LORD, who brought you up from the land of Egypt with great power and an outstretched arm, Him you shall fear, Him you shall worship, and to Him you shall offer sacrifice. 37 And the statutes, the ordinances, the law, and the commandment which He

wrote for you, you shall be careful to observe forever; you shall not fear other gods. 38 And the covenant that I have made with you, you shall not forget, nor shall you fear other gods. 39 But the LORD your God you shall fear; and He will deliver you from the hand of all your enemies." 40 However they did not obey, but they followed their former rituals. 41 So these nations feared the LORD, yet served their carved images; also their children and their children's children have continued doing as their fathers did, even to this day.

Sennacherib attacks Judah

18 Now it came to pass in the third year of Hoshea the son of Elah, king of Israel, *that* Hezekiah the son of Ahaz, king of Judah, began to reign. 2 He was twenty-five years old when he became king, and he reigned twenty-nine years in Jerusalem. His mother's name *was* Abi the daughter of Zechariah. 3 And he did *what was* right in the sight of the LORD, according to all that his father David had done.

4 He removed the high places and broke the *sacred* pillars, cut down the wooden image and broke in pieces the bronze serpent that Moses had made; for until those days the children of Israel burned incense to it, and called it Nehushtan. 5 He trusted in the LORD God of Israel, so that after him was none like him among all the kings of Judah, nor who were before him. 6 For he held fast to the LORD; he did not depart from following Him, but kept His commandments, which the LORD had commanded Moses. 7 The LORD was with him; he prospered wherever he went. And he rebelled against the king of Assyria and did not serve him. 8 He subdued the Philistines, as far as Gaza and its territory, from watchtower to fortified city.

9 Now it came to pass in the fourth year of King Hezekiah, which *was* the seventh year of Hoshea the son of Elah, king of Israel, *that* Shalmaneser king of Assyria came up against Sa-

maria and besieged it. 10 And at the end of three years they took it. In the sixth year of Hezekiah, that is, the ninth year of Hoshea king of Israel, Samaria was taken. 11 Then the king of Assyria carried Israel away captive to Assyria, and put them in Halah and by the Habor, the River of Gozan, and in the cities of the Medes, 12 because they did not obey the voice of the LORD their God, but transgressed His covenant and all that Moses the servant of the LORD had commanded; and they would neither hear nor do them.

13 And in the fourteenth year of King Hezekiah, Sennacherib king of Assyria came up against all the fortified cities of Judah and took them. 14 Then Hezekiah king of Judah sent to the king of Assyria at Lachish, saying, "I have done wrong; turn away from me; whatever you impose on me I will pay." And the king of Assyria assessed Hezekiah king of Judah three hundred talents of silver and thirty talents of gold. 15 So Hezekiah gave him all the silver that was found in the house of the LORD and in the treasuries of the king's house. 16 At that time Hezekiah stripped the gold from the doors of the temple of the LORD, and from the pillars which Hezekiah king of Judah had overlaid, and gave it to the king of Assyria.

17 Then the king of Assyria sent the Tartan, the Rabsaris, and the Rabshakeh from Lachish, with a great army against Jerusalem, to King Hezekiah. And they went up and came to Jerusalem. When they had come up, they went and stood by the aqueduct from the upper pool, which was on the highway to the Fuller's Field. 18 And when they had called to the king, Eliakim the son of Hilkiah, who was over the household, Shebna the scribe, and Joah the son of Asaph, the recorder, came out to them. 19 Then the Rabshakeh said to them, "Say now to Hezekiah, 'Thus says the great king, the king of Assyria: "What confidence is this in which you trust? 20 You speak of having plans and power for war; but they are mere words. And in whom do you

trust, that you rebel against me? 21 Now look! You are trusting in the staff of this broken reed, Egypt, on which if a man leans, it will go into his hand and pierce it. So is Pharaoh king of Egypt to all who trust in him. 22 But if you say to me, 'We trust in the LORD our God,' is it not He whose high places and whose altars Hezekiah has taken away, and said to Judah and Jerusalem, 'You shall worship before this altar in Jerusalem'?" ' 23 Now therefore, I urge you, give a pledge to my master the king of Assyria, and I will give you two thousand horses—if you are able on your part to put riders on them! 24 How then will you repel one captain of the least of my master's servants, and put your trust in Egypt for chariots and horsemen? 25 Have I now come up without the LORD against this place to destroy it? The LORD said to me, 'Go up against this land, and destroy it.' "

26 Then Eliakim the son of Hilkiah, Shebna, and Joah said to the Rabshakeh, "Please speak to your servants in Aramaic, for we understand it; and do not speak to us in Hebrew in the hearing of the people who are on the wall."

27 But the Rabshakeh said to them, "Has my master sent me to your master and to you to speak these words, and not to the men who sit on the wall, who will eat and drink their own waste with you?"

28 Then the Rabshakeh stood and called out with a loud voice in Hebrew, and spoke, saying, "Hear the word of the great king, the king of Assyria! 29 Thus says the king: 'Do not let Hezekiah deceive you, for he shall not be able to deliver you from his hand; 30 nor let Hezekiah make you trust in the LORD, saying, "The LORD will surely deliver us; this city shall not be given into the hand of the king of Assyria." ' 31 Do not listen to Hezekiah; for thus says the king of Assyria: 'Make peace with me by a present and come out to me; and every one of you eat from his own vine and every one from his own fig tree, and every one of you

drink the waters of his own cistern; 32 until I come and take you away to a land like your own land, a land of grain and new wine, a land of bread and vineyards, a land of olive groves and honey, that you may live and not die. But do not listen to Hezekiah, lest he persuade you, saying, "The LORD will deliver us." 33 Has any of the gods of the nations at all delivered its land from the hand of the king of Assyria? 34 Where *are* the gods of Hamath and Arpad? Where *are* the gods of Sepharvaim and Hena and Ivah? Indeed, have they delivered Samaria from my hand? 35 Who among all the gods of the lands have delivered their countries from my hand, that the LORD should deliver Jerusalem from my hand?' "

36 But the people held their peace and answered him not a word; for the king's commandment was, "Do not answer him." 37 Then Eliakim the son of Hilkiah, who *was* over the household, Shebna the scribe, and Joah the son of Asaph, the recorder, came to Hezekiah with *their* clothes torn, and told him the words of *the* Rabshakeh.

God delivers Judah

19 And so it was, when King Hezekiah heard *it*, that he tore his clothes, covered himself with sackcloth, and went into the house of the LORD. 2 Then he sent Eliakim, who *was* over the household, Shebna the scribe, and the elders of the priests, covered with sackcloth, to Isaiah the prophet, the son of Amoz. 3 And they said to him, "Thus says Hezekiah: 'This day *is* a day of trouble, and rebuke, and **blasphemy;** for the children have come to birth, but *there is* no strength to bring them forth. 4 It may be that the LORD your God will hear all the words of *the* Rabshakeh, whom his master the king of Assyria has sent to reproach the living God, and will rebuke the

words which the LORD your God has heard. Therefore lift up *your* prayer for the remnant that is left.' "

5 So the servants of King Hezekiah came to Isaiah. 6 And Isaiah said to them, "Thus you shall say to your master, 'Thus says the LORD: "Do not be afraid of the words which you have heard, with which the servants of the king of Assyria have blasphemed Me. 7 Surely I will send a spirit upon him, and he shall hear a rumor and return to his own land; and I will cause him to fall by the sword in his own land." ' "

8 Then *the* Rabshakeh returned and found the king of Assyria warring against Libnah, for he heard that he had departed from Lachish. 9 And the king heard concerning Tirhakah king of Ethiopia, "Look, he has come out to make war with you." So he again sent messengers to Hezekiah, saying, 10 "Thus you shall speak to Hezekiah king of Judah, saying: 'Do not let your God in whom you trust deceive you, saying, "Jerusalem shall not be given into the hand of the king of Assyria." 11 Look! You have heard what the kings of Assyria have done to all lands by utterly destroying them; and shall you be delivered? 12 Have the gods of the nations delivered those whom my fathers have destroyed, Gozan and Haran and Rezeph, and the people of Eden who *were* in Telassar? 13 Where *is* the king of Hamath, the king of Arpad, and the king of the city of Sepharvaim, Hena, and Ivah?' "

14 And Hezekiah received the letter from the hand of the messengers, and read it; and Hezekiah went up to the house of the LORD, and spread it before the LORD. 15 Then Hezekiah prayed before the LORD, and said: "O LORD God of Israel, *the One* who dwells *between* the cherubim, You are God, You alone, of all the kingdoms of the earth. You have made heaven and earth. 16 Incline Your ear, O LORD,

WORDFINDER

19:3 Blasphemy Pronounced *BLASS-fuh-mee*. Profanity, cursing, or insulting God.

and hear; open Your *eyes*, O LORD, and *see*; and hear the words of Sennacherib, which he has sent to reproach the living God. ¹⁷ Truly, LORD, the kings of Assyria have laid waste the nations and their lands, ¹⁸ and have cast their gods into the fire; for they *were* not gods, but the work of men's hands—wood and stone. Therefore they destroyed them. ¹⁹ Now therefore, O LORD our God, I pray, save us from his hand, that all the kingdoms of the earth may know that You *are* the LORD God, You alone.''

²⁰ Then Isaiah the son of Amoz sent to Hezekiah, saying, "Thus says the LORD God of Israel: 'Because you have prayed to Me against Sennacherib king of Assyria, I have heard.' ²¹ This *is* the word which the LORD has spoken concerning him:

'The virgin, the daughter of Zion,
Has despised you, laughed you
  to scorn;
The daughter of Jerusalem
Has shaken *her* head behind
  your back!

²² 'Whom have you reproached
  and blasphemed?
Against whom have you raised
  your voice,
And lifted up your eyes on high?
Against the Holy *One* of Israel.

²³ By your messengers you have
  reproached the Lord,
And said: "By the multitude of
  my chariots
I have come up to the height of
  the mountains,
To the limits of Lebanon;
I will cut down its tall cedars
And its choice cypress trees;
I will enter the extremity of its
  borders,
To its fruitful forest.

²⁴ I have dug and drunk strange
  water,
And with the soles of my feet I
  have dried up
All the brooks of defense.''

²⁵ 'Did you not hear long ago
How I made it,

From ancient times that I formed
  it?
Now I have brought it to pass,
That you should be
For crushing fortified cities *into*
  heaps of ruins.

²⁶ Therefore their inhabitants had
  little power;
They were dismayed and
  confounded;
They *were as* the grass of the
  field
And the green herb,
As the grass on the housetops
And *grain* blighted before it is
  grown.

²⁷ 'But I know your dwelling place,
Your going out and your coming
  in,
And your rage against Me.

²⁸ Because your rage against Me
  and your tumult
Have come up to My ears,
Therefore I will put My hook in
  your nose
And My bridle in your lips,
And I will turn you back
By the way which you came.

²⁹ 'This *shall be* a sign to you:

You shall eat this year such as
  grows of itself,
And in the second year what
  springs from the same;
Also in the third year sow and
  reap,
Plant vineyards and eat the fruit
  of them.

³⁰ And the remnant who have
  escaped of the house of Judah
Shall again take root downward,
And bear fruit upward.

³¹ For out of Jerusalem shall go a
  remnant,
And those who escape from
  Mount Zion.
The zeal of the LORD of hosts
  will do this.'

³² "Therefore thus says the LORD concerning the king of Assyria:

Esarhaddon became king of Assyria after his father, Sennacherib, was killed.

'He shall not come into this city,
Nor shoot an arrow there,
Nor come before it with shield,
Nor build a siege mound against
    it.
33 By the way that he came,
By the same shall he return;
And he shall not come into this
    city,'
Says the LORD.
34 'For I will defend this city, to save
    it
For My own sake and for My
    servant David's sake.' "

35 And it came to pass on a certain night that the **angel of the LORD** went out, and killed in the camp of the Assyrians one hundred and eighty-five thousand; and when *people* arose early in the morning, there were the corpses—all dead. 36 So Sennacherib king of Assyria departed and went away, returned *home,* and remained at Nineveh. 37 Now it came to pass, as he was worshiping in the temple of Nisroch his god, that his sons Adrammelech and Sharezer struck him down with the sword; and they escaped into the land of Ararat. Then Esarhaddon his son reigned in his place.

Hezekiah gets well

20 In those days Hezekiah was sick and near death. And Isaiah the prophet, the son of Amoz, went to him and said to him, "Thus says the LORD: 'Set your house in order, for you shall die, and not live.' "

2 Then he turned his face toward the wall, and prayed to the LORD, saying, 3 "Remember now, O LORD, I pray, how I have walked before You in truth and with a loyal heart, and have done *what was* good in Your sight." And Hezekiah wept bitterly.

4 And it happened, before Isaiah had gone out into the middle court, that the word of the LORD came to him, saying, 5 "Return and tell Hezekiah the leader of My people, 'Thus says the LORD, the God of David your father: "I have heard your prayer, I have seen your tears; surely I will heal you. On the third day you shall go up to the house of the LORD. 6 And I will add to your days fifteen years. I will deliver you and this city from the hand of the king of Assyria; and I will defend this city for My own sake, and for the sake of My servant David." ' "

7 Then Isaiah said, "Take a lump of figs." So they took and laid *it* on the boil, and he recovered.

WORDFINDER

19:35 Angel of the Lord   Sometimes called the Angel of the Presence. This Angel was really a way in which the Lord Himself was revealed to people.

8 And Hezekiah said to Isaiah, "What *is* the sign that the LORD will heal me, and that I shall go up to the house of the LORD the third day?"

9 Then Isaiah said, "This is the sign to you from the LORD, that the LORD will do the thing which He has spoken: *shall* the shadow go forward ten degrees or go backward ten degrees?"

10 And Hezekiah answered, "It is an easy thing for the shadow to go down ten degrees; no, but let the shadow go backward ten degrees."

11 So Isaiah the prophet cried out to the LORD, and He brought the shadow ten degrees backward, by which it had gone down on the sundial of Ahaz.

12 At that time Berodach-Baladan the son of Baladan, king of Babylon, sent letters and a present to Hezekiah, for he heard that Hezekiah had been sick. 13 And Hezekiah was attentive to them, and showed them all the house of his treasures—the silver and gold, the spices and precious ointment, and all his armory—all that was found among his treasures. There was nothing in his house or in all his dominion that Hezekiah did not show them.

14 Then Isaiah the prophet went to King Hezekiah, and said to him, "What did these men say, and from where did they come to you?"

So Hezekiah said, "They came from a far country, from Babylon."

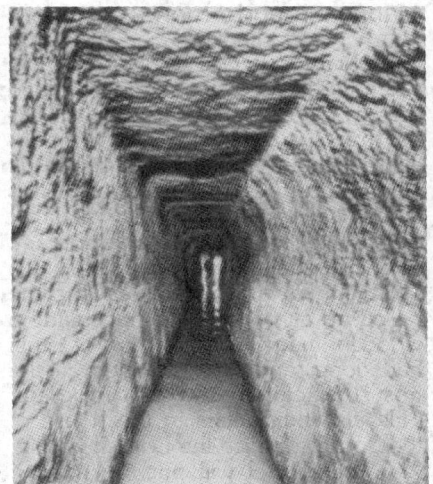

King Hezekiah built this tunnel so that Jerusalem could have water when under attack.

15 And he said, "What have they seen in your house?"

So Hezekiah answered, "They have seen all that *is* in my house; there is nothing among my treasures that I have not shown them."

16 Then Isaiah said to Hezekiah, "Hear the word of the LORD: 17 'Behold, the days are coming when all that *is* in your house, and what your fathers have accumulated until this day, shall be carried to Babylon; nothing shall be left,' says the LORD. 18 'And they shall take away some of your sons who will descend from you, whom you will beget; and they shall be eunuchs in the palace of the king of Babylon.' "

19 So Hezekiah said to Isaiah, "The word of the LORD which you have spoken *is* good!" For he said, "Will there not be peace and truth at least in my days?"

20 Now the rest of the acts of Hezekiah—all his might, and how he made a pool and a tunnel and brought water into the city—*are* they not written in the book of the chronicles of the kings of Judah? 21 So Hezekiah rested with his fathers. Then Manasseh his son reigned in his place.

How King Hezekiah Got Drinking Water

King Hezekiah (pronounced *hez-uh-KIGH-uh*) feared the Assyrians (pronounced *ah-SEER-ih-uns*) would attack Jerusalem and cut off their water supply. So he built a secret water tunnel from an underground reservoir into Jerusalem. Then Jerusalem had drinking water when the Assyrian army was outside the city. The tunnel was about 1,750 feet long.

Manasseh and Amon rule Judah

21 Manasseh *was* twelve years old when he became king, and he reigned fifty-five years in Jerusalem. His mother's name *was* Hephzibah. ²And he did evil in the sight of the LORD, according to the abominations of the nations whom the LORD had cast out before the children of Israel. ³For he rebuilt the high places which Hezekiah his father had destroyed; he raised up altars for Baal, and made a wooden image, as Ahab king of Israel had done; and he worshiped all the host of heaven and served them. ⁴He also built altars in the house of the LORD, of which the LORD had said, "In Jerusalem I will put My name." ⁵And he built altars for all the host of heaven in the two courts of the house of the LORD. ⁶Also he made his son pass through the fire, practiced soothsaying, used witchcraft, and consulted spiritists and mediums. He did much evil in the sight of the LORD, to provoke *Him* to anger. ⁷He even set a carved image of **Asherah** that he had made, in the house of which the LORD had said to David and to Solomon his son, "In this house and in Jerusalem, which I have chosen out of all the tribes of Israel, I will put My name forever; ⁸and I will not make the feet of Israel wander anymore from the land which I gave their fathers—only if they are careful to do according to all that I have commanded them, and according to all the law that My servant Moses commanded them." ⁹But they paid no attention, and Manasseh seduced them to do more evil than the nations whom the LORD had destroyed before the children of Israel.

¹⁰And the LORD spoke by His servants the prophets, saying, ¹¹"Because Manasseh king of Judah has done these abominations (he has acted more wickedly than all the Amorites who *were* before him, and has also made Judah sin with his idols), ¹²therefore thus says the LORD God of Israel: 'Behold, *I* am bringing *such* calamity upon Jerusalem and Judah, that whoever hears of it, both his ears will tingle. ¹³And I will stretch over Jerusalem the measuring line of Samaria and the plummet of the house of Ahab; I will wipe Jerusalem as *one* wipes a dish, wiping *it* and turning *it* upside down. ¹⁴So I will forsake the remnant of My inheritance and deliver them into the hand of their enemies; and they shall become victims of plunder to all

🜨 WORDFINDER

21:7 Asherah Pronounced *ah-SHE-rah*. A goddess of the Phoenicians and Syrians (pronounced *fe-NISH-she-uns* and *SEER-ih-uns*). The people of Israel also worshiped her when they later served idols. She was worshiped along with Baal (see 1 Kings 18:19).

⛏ DIGGING IN

21:1–17 The Great Sin of King Manasseh King Manasseh (pronounced *muh-NASS-uh*) came to the throne of Judah in Jerusalem when he was only 12 years old. He was the son of the good King Hezekiah, but Manasseh did more evil than any of the kings before him. Manasseh set up worship places to idols in the temple of the Lord. It's horrible to think, but he even sacrificed his own son by fire.

We used to believe that the things Manasseh did could not possibly happen today. But sometimes we hear reports of people sacrificing children. Much as we hate to think about it, Satan is alive and working today.

You need to set your mind and heart on learning God's Word. Like Manasseh, even a boy or girl may be destroyed by Satan's lies.

their enemies, ¹⁵ because they have done evil in My sight, and have provoked Me to anger since the day their fathers came out of Egypt, even to this day.' ''

¹⁶ Moreover Manasseh shed very much innocent blood, till he had filled Jerusalem from one end to another, besides his sin by which he made Judah sin, in doing evil in the sight of the Lord.

¹⁷ Now the rest of the acts of Manasseh—all that he did, and the sin that he committed—are they not written in the book of the chronicles of the kings of Judah? ¹⁸ So Manasseh rested with his fathers, and was buried in the garden of his own house, in the garden of Uzza. Then his son Amon reigned in his place.

¹⁹ Amon was twenty-two years old when he became king, and he reigned two years in Jerusalem. His mother's name was Meshullemeth the daughter of Haruz of Jotbah. ²⁰ And he did evil in the sight of the Lord, as his father Manasseh had done. ²¹ So he walked in all the ways that his father had walked; and he served the idols that his father had served, and worshiped them. ²² He forsook the Lord God of his fathers, and did not walk in the way of the Lord.

²³ Then the servants of Amon conspired against him, and killed the king in his own house. ²⁴ But the people of the land executed all those who had conspired against King Amon. Then the people of the land made his son Josiah king in his place.

²⁵ Now the rest of the acts of Amon which he did, are they not written in the book of the chronicles of the kings of Judah? ²⁶ And he was buried in his tomb in the garden of Uzza. Then Josiah his son reigned in his place.

Hilkiah finds the book of the Law

22 Josiah was eight years old when he became king, and he reigned thirty-one years in Jerusalem. His mother's

name was Jedidah the daughter of Adaiah of Bozkath. ² And he did what was right in the sight of the Lord, and walked in all the ways of his father David; he did not turn aside to the right hand or to the left.

³ Now it came to pass, in the eighteenth year of King Josiah, that the king sent Shaphan the scribe, the son of Azaliah, the son of Meshullam, to the house of the Lord, saying: ⁴ "Go up to Hilkiah the high priest, that he may count the money which has been brought into the house of the Lord, which the doorkeepers have gathered from the people. ⁵ And let them deliver it into the hand of those doing the work, who are the overseers in the house of the Lord; let them give it to those who are in the house of the Lord doing the work, to repair the damages of the house— ⁶ to carpenters and builders and masons—and to buy timber and hewn stone to repair the house. ⁷ However there need be no accounting made with them of the money delivered into their hand, because they deal faithfully."

⁸ Then Hilkiah the high priest said to Shaphan the scribe, "I have found the Book of the Law in the house of the Lord." And Hilkiah gave the book to Shaphan, and he read it. ⁹ So Shaphan the scribe went to the king, bringing the king word, saying, "Your servants have gathered the money that was found in the house, and have delivered it into the hand of those who do the work, who oversee the house of the Lord." ¹⁰ Then Shaphan the scribe showed the king, saying, "Hilkiah the priest has given me a book." And Shaphan read it before the king.

¹¹ Now it happened, when the king heard the words of the Book of the Law, that he tore his clothes. ¹² Then the king commanded Hilkiah the priest, Ahikam the son of Shaphan, Achbor the son of Michaiah, Shaphan the scribe, and Asaiah a servant of the king, saying, ¹³ "Go, inquire of the Lord for me, for the people and for

Young King Turns to God

ITN (Israel Television Network)—Following is an announcement by King Josiah (pronounced *jo-SIGH-uh*). This address is being carried live by all television stations:

"As you all know, I have been honored by the Lord to be your king for 18 years. When I came to the throne, I was only eight years old, and with God's help I have tried to rule our nation well.

"Now a frightening thing has happened. Our high priest has found the Book of the Law, which has been lost for many years. According to this Book, our people have been sinning against the Lord by worshiping false gods.

"Therefore, I have ordered that the idols and unfaithful priests be removed from the temple. The whole land will be made free from idolatry. I have also ordered that we will all gather at the temple while I read God's Book to you. We will also keep the Passover as in old times." (See Exodus 12:1–10.)

all Judah, concerning the words of this book that has been found; for great *is* the wrath of the LORD that is aroused against us, because our fathers have not obeyed the words of this book, to do according to all that is written concerning us."

14 So Hilkiah the priest, Ahikam, Achbor, Shaphan, and Asaiah went to Huldah the prophetess, the wife of Shallum the son of Tikvah, the son of Harhas, keeper of the wardrobe. (She dwelt in Jerusalem in the Second Quarter.) And they spoke with her. 15 Then she said to them, "Thus says the LORD God of Israel, 'Tell the man who sent you to Me, 16 "Thus says the LORD: 'Behold, I will bring calamity on this place and on its inhabitants—all the words of the book which the king of Judah has read— 17 because they have forsaken Me and burned incense to other gods, that they might provoke Me to anger with all the works of their hands. Therefore My wrath shall be aroused against this place and shall not be quenched.' " ' 18 But as for the king of Judah, who sent you to inquire of the LORD, in this manner you shall speak to him, 'Thus says the LORD God of Israel: "Concerning the words which you have heard— 19 because your heart was tender, and you humbled yourself before the LORD when you heard what I spoke against this place and against its inhabitants, that they

would become a desolation and a curse, and you tore your clothes and wept before Me, I also have heard *you*," says the LORD. 20 Surely, therefore, I will gather you to your fathers, and you shall be gathered to your grave in peace; and your eyes shall not see all the calamity which I will bring on this place." ' " So they brought back word to the king.

Good King Josiah restores true worship

23 Now the king sent them to gather all the elders of Judah and Jerusalem to him. 2 The king went up to the house of the LORD with all the men of Judah, and with him all the inhabitants of Jerusalem—the priests and the prophets and all the people, both small and great. And he read in their hearing all the words of the Book of the Covenant which had been found in the house of the LORD.

3 Then the king stood by a pillar and made a covenant before the LORD, to follow the LORD and to keep His commandments and His testimonies and His statutes, with all *his* heart and all *his* soul, to perform the words of this covenant that were written in this book. And all the people took a stand for the covenant. 4 And the king commanded Hilkiah the high priest, the

priests of the second order, and the doorkeepers, to bring out of the temple of the LORD all the articles that were made for Baal, for Asherah, and for all the host of heaven; and he burned them outside Jerusalem in the fields of Kidron, and carried their ashes to Bethel. 5 Then he removed the idolatrous priests whom the kings of Judah had ordained to burn incense on the high places in the cities of Judah and in the places all around Jerusalem, and those who burned incense to Baal, to the sun, to the moon, to the constellations, and to all the host of heaven. 6 And he brought out the wooden image from the house of the LORD, to the Brook Kidron outside Jerusalem, burned it at the Brook Kidron and ground it to ashes, and threw its ashes on the graves of the common people. 7 Then he tore down the *ritual* booths of the perverted persons that *were* in the house of the LORD, where the women wove hangings for the wooden image. 8 And he brought all the priests from the cities of Judah, and defiled the high places where the priests had burned incense, from Geba to Beersheba; also he broke down the high places at the gates which *were* at the entrance of the Gate of Joshua the governor of the city, which *were* to the left of the city gate. 9 Nevertheless the priests of the high places did not come up to the altar of the LORD in Jerusalem, but they ate unleavened bread among their brethren.

10 And he defiled Topheth, which *is* in the Valley of the Son of Hinnom, that no man might make his son or his daughter pass through the fire to Molech. 11 Then he removed the horses that the kings of Judah had dedicated to the sun, at the entrance to the house of the LORD, by the chamber of Nathan-Melech, the officer who *was* in the court; and he burned the chariots of the sun with fire. 12 The altars that *were* on the roof, the upper chamber of Ahaz, which the kings of Judah had made, and the altars which Manasseh had made in the two courts of the house of the LORD, the king broke down and pulverized there, and threw their dust into the Brook Kidron. 13 Then the king defiled the high places that *were* east of Jerusalem, which *were* on the south of the Mount of Corruption, which Solomon king of Israel had built for Ashtoreth the abomination of the Sidonians, for Chemosh the abomination of the Moabites, and for Milcom the abomination of the people of Ammon. 14 And he broke in pieces the *sacred* pillars and cut down the wooden images, and filled their places with the bones of men.

15 Moreover the altar that *was* at Bethel, *and* the high place which Jeroboam the son of Nebat, who made Israel sin, had made, both that altar and the high place he broke down; and he burned the high place *and* crushed *it* to powder, and burned the wooden image. 16 As Josiah turned, he saw the tombs that *were* there on the mountain. And he sent and took the bones out of the tombs and burned *them* on the altar, and defiled it according to the word of the LORD which the man of God proclaimed, who proclaimed these words. 17 Then he said, "What gravestone *is* this that I see?"

So the men of the city told him, "*It is* the tomb of the man of God who came from Judah and proclaimed these things which you have done against the altar of Bethel."

18 And he said, "Let him alone; let no one move his bones." So they let his bones alone, with the bones of the prophet who came from Samaria.

19 Now Josiah also took away all the shrines of the high places that *were* in the cities of Samaria, which the kings of Israel had made to provoke the LORD to anger; and he did to them according to all the deeds he had done in Bethel. 20 He executed all the priests of the high places who *were* there, on the altars, and burned men's bones on them; and he returned to Jerusalem.

21 Then the king commanded all the

people, saying, "Keep the **Passover** to the LORD your God, as *it is* written in this Book of the Covenant." 22 Such a Passover surely had never been held since the days of the judges who judged Israel, nor in all the days of the kings of Israel and the kings of Judah. 23 But in the eighteenth year of King Josiah this Passover was held before the LORD in Jerusalem. 24 Moreover Josiah put away those who consulted mediums and spiritists, the household gods and idols, all the abominations that were seen in the land of Judah and in Jerusalem, that he might perform the words of the law which were written in the book that Hilkiah the priest found in the house of the LORD. 25 Now before him there was no king like him, who turned to the LORD with all his heart, with all his soul, and with all his might, according to all the Law of Moses; nor after him did *any* arise like him.

26 Nevertheless the LORD did not turn from the fierceness of His great wrath, with which His anger was aroused against Judah, because of all the provocations with which Manasseh had provoked Him. 27 And the LORD said, "I will also remove Judah from My sight, as I have removed Israel, and will cast off this city Jerusalem which I have chosen, and the house of which I said, 'My name shall be there.'"

28 Now the rest of the acts of Josiah, and all that he did, *are* they not written in the book of the chronicles of the kings of Judah? 29 In his days Pharaoh Necho king of Egypt went to the aid of the king of Assyria, to the River Euphrates; and King Josiah went against him. And *Pharaoh Necho* killed him at Megiddo when he confronted him. 30 Then his servants moved his body in a chariot from Megiddo, brought him to Jerusalem, and buried

him in his own tomb. And the people of the land took Jehoahaz the son of Josiah, anointed him, and made him king in his father's place.

31 Jehoahaz *was* twenty-three years old when he became king, and he reigned three months in Jerusalem. His mother's name *was* Hamutal the daughter of Jeremiah of Libnah. 32 And he did evil in the sight of the LORD, according to all that his fathers had done. 33 Now Pharaoh Necho put him in prison at Riblah in the land of Hamath, that he might not reign in Jerusalem; and he imposed on the land a tribute of one hundred talents of silver and a talent of gold. 34 Then Pharaoh Necho made Eliakim the son of Josiah king in place of his father Josiah, and changed his name to Jehoiakim. And *Pharaoh* took Jehoahaz and went to Egypt, and he died there.

35 So Jehoiakim gave the silver and gold to Pharaoh; but he taxed the land to give money according to the command of Pharaoh; he exacted the silver and gold from the people of the land, from every one according to his assessment, to give *it* to Pharaoh Necho. 36 Jehoiakim *was* twenty-five years old when he became king, and he reigned eleven years in Jerusalem. His mother's name *was* Zebudah the daughter of Pedaiah of Rumah. 37 And he did evil in the sight of the LORD, according to all that his fathers had done.

The king of Judah is captured by Babylon

24 In his days Nebuchadnezzar king of Babylon came up, and Jehoiakim became his vassal *for* three years. Then he turned and rebelled against him. 2 And the LORD sent against him *raiding* bands of Chaldeans, bands of Syr-

---

WORDFINDER

23:21 Passover The greatest Hebrew celebration. The people remember that the Lord "passed over" their homes in Egypt because a lamb's blood was applied to their doorways (see Exodus 12). After the death of the firstborn in Egypt, Pharaoh freed God's people.

ians, bands of Moabites, and bands of the people of Ammon; He sent them against Judah to destroy it, according to the word of the LORD which He had spoken by His servants the prophets. ³ Surely at the commandment of the LORD *this* came upon Judah, to remove *them* from His sight because of the sins of Manasseh, according to all that he had done, ⁴ and also because of the innocent blood that he had shed; for he had filled Jerusalem with innocent blood, which the LORD would not pardon.

⁵ Now the rest of the acts of Jehoiakim, and all that he did, *are* they not written in the book of the chronicles of the kings of Judah? ⁶ So Jehoiakim rested with his fathers. Then Jehoiachin his son reigned in his place. ⁷ And the king of Egypt did not come out of his land anymore, for the king of Babylon had taken all that belonged to the king of Egypt from the Brook of Egypt to the River Euphrates.

⁸ Jehoiachin *was* eighteen years old when he became king, and he reigned in Jerusalem three months. His mother's name *was* Nehushta the daughter of Elnathan of Jerusalem. ⁹ And he did evil in the sight of the LORD, according to all that his father had done.

¹⁰ At that time the servants of Nebuchadnezzar king of Babylon came up against Jerusalem, and the city was besieged. ¹¹ And Nebuchadnezzar king of Babylon came against the city, as his servants were besieging it. ¹² Then Jehoiachin king of Judah, his mother, his servants, his princes, and his officers went out to the king of Babylon; and the king of Babylon, in the eighth year of his reign, took him prisoner. ¹³ And he carried out from there all the treasures of the house of the LORD and the treasures of the king's house, and he cut in pieces all the articles of gold which Solomon king of Israel had made in the temple of the LORD, as the LORD had said. ¹⁴ Also he carried into captivity all Jerusalem: all the captains and all the mighty men of valor, ten thousand captives, and all the craftsmen and smiths. None remained except the poorest people of the land. ¹⁵ And he carried Jehoiachin captive to Babylon. The king's mother, the king's wives, his officers, and the mighty of the land he carried into captivity from Jerusalem to Babylon. ¹⁶ All the valiant men, seven thousand, and craftsmen and smiths, one thousand, all *who were* strong *and* fit for war, these the king of Babylon brought captive to Babylon.

¹⁷ Then the king of Babylon made Mattaniah, *Jehoiachin's* uncle, king in his place, and changed his name to Zedekiah.

¹⁸ Zedekiah *was* twenty-one years old when he became king, and he reigned eleven years in Jerusalem. His mother's name *was* Hamutal the daughter of Jeremiah of Libnah. ¹⁹ He also did evil in the sight of the LORD, according to all that Jehoiakim had done. ²⁰ For because of the anger of the LORD *this* happened in Jerusalem and Judah, that He finally cast them out from His presence. Then Zedekiah rebelled against the king of Babylon.

Judah is carried into captivity

25 Now it came to pass in the ninth year of his reign, in the tenth month, on the tenth *day* of the month, *that* Nebuchadnezzar king of Babylon and all his army came against Jerusalem and encamped against it; and they built a siege wall against it all around. ² So the city was besieged until the eleventh year of King Zedekiah. ³ By the ninth *day* of the *fourth* month the famine had become so severe in the city that there was no food for the people of the land.

⁴ Then the city wall was broken through, and all the men of war *fled* at night by way of the gate between two walls, which was by the king's garden, even though the Chaldeans *were* still encamped all around against the city. And *the king* went by way of the plain. ⁵ But the army of the Chaldeans pursued the king, and they overtook

Daniel is a long way from home! When Jerusalem is captured by Nebuchadnezzar (pronounced neb-you-kad-NEZ-zer), Daniel and his three friends are among the Israelites brought to Babylon. (1:2) In this faraway land, they have some exciting adventures in which they learn how to trust God in everything.

First, the king sets up a golden image in the Plain of Dura (3:1), and commands all the people to fall down and worship it. Daniel's friends—Shadrach (SHAD-rack), Meshach (ME-shack), and Abednego (ah-BED-nee-go)—refuse. What happens to them? (3:19–22) How does God help? (3:25)

Later, another wicked king gives a party at the palace in Babylon. At the party a mysterious hand appears and writes on the wall. What strange words are written there? (5:25) The king is so scared that his knees knock together! Daniel explains the meaning to the king and later gets a big promotion! (5:26–28)

The Babylonian Empire

MEDIA

Carchemish

Nineveh
Haran
ASSYRIA

Asshur

Tigris

Euphrates

ELAM

Great Sea (Mediterranean)

Damascus

Babylon
Plain of Dura

Susa (Shushan)

Ur

Jerusalem

EGYPT

Babylon's Army Overruns Judah

World Press International

JERUSALEM—Jerusalem has fallen before the advancing armies of Babylon. For more than a year, this city has been surrounded. The people are starving, and no one has gone in or out.

Finally, the city wall was broken down, and the Hebrew troops have been escaping. King Zedekiah (pronounced zed-uh-KIGH-uh) has also fled. But late reports say the king is now a prisoner of the armed forces of Babylon.

Eyewitnesses report that the dead and those dying of starvation are everywhere. There are even rumors that human flesh is being eaten.

The flames of burning Jerusalem are leaping high above the city. The temple, the king's palace, and all the main buildings have been destroyed. All the wealth of the city is being looted by the invaders and carried away.

Able-bodied citizens are being organized as slave labor for transport to Babylon. Only the poor and disabled will be left behind to farm the land.

him in the plains of Jericho. All his army was scattered from him. ⁶ So they took the king and brought him up to the king of Babylon at Riblah, and they pronounced judgment on him. ⁷ Then they killed the sons of Zedekiah before his eyes, put out the eyes of Zedekiah, bound him with bronze fetters, and took him to Babylon.

⁸ And in the fifth month, on the seventh day of the month (which was the nineteenth year of King Nebuchadnezzar king of Babylon), Nebuzaradan the captain of the guard, a servant of the king of Babylon, came to Jerusalem. ⁹ He burned the house of the LORD and the king's house; all the houses of Jeru-salem, that is, all the houses of the great, he burned with fire. ¹⁰ And all the army of the Chaldeans who were with the captain of the guard broke down the walls of Jerusalem all around.

¹¹ Then Nebuzaradan the captain of the guard carried away captive the rest of the people who remained in the city and the defectors who had deserted to the king of Babylon, with the rest of the multitude. ¹² But the captain of the guard left some of the poor of the land as vinedressers and farmers. ¹³ The bronze pillars that were in the house of the LORD, and the carts and the bronze Sea that were in the house

DIGGING IN

25:21 The Empire of Babylonia You must remember that Abraham, the father of the Jews, came from Babylonia, usually called Chaldea (pronounced kal-DEE-uh) in the Bible. Now look at the map on page 512 showing Israel and the Babylonian Empire.

The empires of Assyria and Babylonia were at war for a long time. First, the Assyrians conquered the Babylonians 1,270 years before Jesus was born. About six hundred years later, the Babylonians defeated the Assyrians. Babylonia spread its empire as far west as Israel on the Mediterranean Sea about six hundred years before Jesus. About 20 years after that, the Babylonians burned Jerusalem and took many prisoners to Babylon. The Jews were in Babylon for a total of 70 years. The Persians came and set the Jews free 536 years before Christ.

The main fact you should remember is that although God's people of Israel have suffered, they have continued to exist all this time. The nation of Israel still exists today, but Assyria and Babylonia have long ago passed away. God remembers His promise to Abraham, the father of Israel. (See Genesis 12:1–3.)

of the LORD, the Chaldeans broke in pieces, and carried their bronze to Babylon. 14 They also took away the pots, the shovels, the trimmers, the spoons, and all the bronze utensils with which the priests ministered. 15 The firepans and the basins, the things of solid gold and solid silver, the captain of the guard took away. 16 The two pillars, one Sea, and the carts, which Solomon had made for the house of the LORD, the bronze of all these articles was beyond measure. 17 The height of one pillar *was* eighteen cubits, and the capital on it *was* of bronze. The height of the capital was three cubits, and the network and pomegranates all around the capital were all of bronze. The second pillar was the same, with a network.

18 And the captain of the guard took Seraiah the chief priest, Zephaniah the second priest, and the three doorkeepers. 19 He also took out of the city an officer who had charge of the men of war, five men of the king's close associates who were found in the city, the chief recruiting officer of the army, who mustered the people of the land, and sixty men of the people of the land *who were* found in the city. 20 So Nebuzaradan, captain of the guard, took these and brought them to the king of Babylon at Riblah. 21 Then the king of Babylon struck them and put them to death at Riblah in the land of Hamath. Thus Judah was carried away captive from its own land.

22 Then he made Gedaliah the son of Ahikam, the son of Shaphan, governor over the people who remained in the land of Judah, whom Nebuchadnezzar king of Babylon had left. 23 Now when all the captains of the armies, they and *their* men, heard that the king of Babylon had made Gedaliah governor, they came to Gedaliah at Mizpah—Ishmael the son of Nethaniah, Johanan the son of Careah, Seraiah the son of Tanhumeth the Netophathite, and Jaazaniah the son of a Maachathite, they and their men. 24 And Gedaliah took an oath before them and their men, and said to them,

Ancient Babylon's Main Street.

"Do not be afraid of the servants of the Chaldeans. Dwell in the land and serve the king of Babylon, and it shall be well with you."

25 But it happened in the seventh month that Ishmael the son of Nethaniah, the son of Elishama, of the royal family, came with ten men and struck and killed Gedaliah, the Jews, as well as the Chaldeans who were with him at Mizpah. 26 And all the people, small and great, and the captains of the armies, arose and went to Egypt; for they were afraid of the Chaldeans.

27 Now it came to pass in the thirty-seventh year of the captivity of Jehoiachin king of Judah, in the twelfth month, on the twenty-seventh *day* of the month, *that* Evil-Merodach king of Babylon, in the year that he began to reign, released Jehoiachin king of Judah from prison. 28 He spoke kindly to him, and gave him a more prominent seat than those of the kings who *were* with him in Babylon. 29 So Jehoiachin changed from his prison garments, and he ate bread regularly before the king all the days of his life. 30 And as for his provisions, *there was* a regular ration given him by the king, a portion for each day, all the days of his life.

The Book of
1 CHRONICLES

Adam's family

ADAM, Seth, Enosh, 2 Cainan, Mahalalel, Jared, 3 Enoch, Methuselah, Lamech, 4 Noah, Shem, Ham, and Japheth.

5 The sons of Japheth were Gomer, Magog, Madai, Javan, Tubal, Meshech, and Tiras. 6 The sons of Gomer were Ashkenaz, Diphath, and Togarmah. 7 The sons of Javan were Elishah, Tarshishah, Kittim, and Rodanim.

8 The sons of Ham were Cush, Mizraim, Put, and Canaan. 9 The sons of Cush were Seba, Havilah, Sabta, Raama, and Sabtecha. The sons of Raama were Sheba and Dedan. 10 Cush begot Nimrod; he began to be a mighty one on the earth. 11 Mizraim begot Ludim, Anamim, Lehabim, Naphtuhim, 12 Pathrusim, Casluhim (from whom came the Philistines and the Caphtorim). 13 Canaan begot Sidon, his firstborn, and Heth; 14 the Jebusite, the Amorite, and the Girgashite; 15 the Hivite, the Arkite, and the Sinite; 16 the Arvadite, the Zemarite, and the Hamathite.

17 The sons of Shem were Elam, Asshur, Arphaxad, Lud, Aram, Uz, Hul, Gether, and Meshech. 18 Arphaxad begot Shelah, and Shelah begot Eber. 19 To Eber were born two sons: the name of one was Peleg, for in his days the earth was divided; and his brother's name was Joktan. 20 Joktan begot Almodad, Sheleph, Hazarmaveth, Jerah, 21 Hadoram, Uzal, Diklah, 22 Ebal, Abimael, Sheba, 23 Ophir, Havilah, and Jobab. All these were the sons of Joktan.

24 Shem, Arphaxad, Shelah, 25 Eber, Peleg, Reu, 26 Serug, Nahor, Terah, 27 and Abram, who is Abraham.
28 The sons of Abraham were Isaac and Ishmael.

29 These are their genealogies: The firstborn of Ishmael was Nebajoth; then Kedar, Adbeel, Mibsam, 30 Mishma, Dumah, Massa, Hadad, Tema, 31 Jetur, Naphish, and Kedemah. These were the sons of Ishmael.

32 Now the sons born to Keturah, Abraham's concubine, were Zimran, Jokshan, Medan, Midian, Ishbak, and Shuah. The sons of Jokshan were Sheba and Dedan. 33 The sons of Midian were Ephah, Epher, Hanoch, Abida, and Eldaah. All these were the children of Keturah.

34 And Abraham begot Isaac. The sons of Isaac were Esau and Israel.
35 The sons of Esau were Eliphaz, Reuel, Jeush, Jaalam, and Korah.
36 And the sons of Eliphaz were Teman, Omar, Zephi, Gatam, and Kenaz; and by Timna, Amalek. 37 The sons of Reuel were Nahath, Zerah, Shammah, and Mizzah.

38 The sons of Seir were Lotan, Shobal, Zibeon, Anah, Dishon, Ezer, and Dishan. 39 And the sons of Lotan were

DIGGING IN

1:1 God Created the Family The next eight chapters of 1 Chronicles may seem very boring. They just list some of the descendants of Adam, leading to the nation of Israel. Right now most of these names don't mean very much to you. But they are really a wonderful book of memories, showing God's faithfulness to some ordinary people who lived during those early times.

The first thing you should notice is that God thinks the family is very important.

In fact, God created the family to be the way in which young people would learn the plan of salvation through Jesus. God meant us to have parents who would teach us the Bible and lead us to Christ.

You may not have a mother and father, or you may have only one parent. But please don't be sad. God cares for orphans in a special way. He knows how to send people who will love you and help you understand God's ways.

Hori and Homam; Lotan's sister *was* Timna. ⁴⁰ The sons of Shobal *were* Alian, Manahath, Ebal, Shephi, and Onam. The sons of Zibeon *were* Ajah and Anah. ⁴¹ The son of Anah *was* Dishon. The sons of Dishon *were* Hamran, Eshban, Ithran, and Cheran. ⁴² The sons of Ezer *were* Bilhan, Zaavan, *and* Jaakan. The sons of Dishon *were* Uz and Aran.

⁴³ Now these *were* the kings who reigned in the land of Edom before a king reigned over the children of Israel: Bela the son of Beor, and the name of his city was Dinhabah. ⁴⁴ And when Bela died, Jobab the son of Zerah of Bozrah reigned in his place. ⁴⁵ When Jobab died, Husham of the land of the Temanites reigned in his place. ⁴⁶ And when Husham died, Hadad the son of Bedad, who attacked Midian in the field of Moab, reigned in his place. The name of his city *was* Avith. ⁴⁷ When Hadad died, Samlah of Masrekah reigned in his place. ⁴⁸ And when Samlah died, Saul of Rehoboth-by-the-River reigned in his place. ⁴⁹ When Saul died, Baal-Hanan the son of Achbor reigned in his place. ⁵⁰ And when Baal-Hanan died, Hadad reigned in his place; and the name of his city was Pai. His wife's name was Mehetabel the daughter of Matred, the daughter of Mezahab. ⁵¹ Hadad died also. And the chiefs of Edom were Chief Timnah, Chief Aliah, Chief Jetheth, ⁵² Chief Aholibamah, Chief Elah, Chief Pinon, ⁵³ Chief Kenaz, Chief Teman, Chief Mibzar, ⁵⁴ Chief Magdiel, and Chief Iram. These *were* the chiefs of Edom.

Israel's family

2 These *were* the sons of Israel: Reuben, Simeon, Levi, Judah, Issachar, Zebulun, ² Dan, Joseph, Benjamin, Naphtali, Gad, and Asher.

³ The sons of Judah *were* Er, Onan, and Shelah. *These* three were born to him by the daughter of Shua, the Canaanitess. Er, the firstborn of Judah, was wicked in the sight of the LORD; so He killed him. ⁴ And Tamar, his daughter-in-law, bore him Perez and Zerah. All the sons of Judah *were* five.

⁵ The sons of Perez *were* Hezron and Hamul. ⁶ The sons of Zerah *were* Zimri, Ethan, Heman, Calcol, and Dara—five of them in all.

⁷ The son of Carmi *was* Achar, the troubler of Israel, who transgressed in the accursed thing.

⁸ The son of Ethan *was* Azariah.

⁹ Also the sons of Hezron who were born to him *were* Jerahmeel, Ram, and Chelubai. ¹⁰ Ram begot Amminadab, and Amminadab begot Nahshon, leader of the children of Judah; ¹¹ Nahshon begot Salma, and Salma begot Boaz; ¹² Boaz begot Obed, and Obed begot Jesse; ¹³ Jesse begot Eliab his firstborn, Abinadab the second, Shimea the third, ¹⁴ Nethanel the fourth, Raddai the fifth, ¹⁵ Ozem the sixth, *and* David the seventh.

¹⁶ Now their sisters *were* Zeruiah and Abigail. And the sons of Zeruiah *were* Abishai, Joab, and Asahel—three. ¹⁷ Abigail bore Amasa; and the father of Amasa *was* Jether the Ishmaelite.

¹⁸ Caleb the son of Hezron had children by Azubah, *his* wife, and by Jerioth. Now these were her sons: Jesher, Shobab, and Ardon. ¹⁹ When Azubah died, Caleb took Ephrath as his wife, who bore him Hur. ²⁰ And Hur begot Uri, and Uri begot Bezalel.

²¹ Now afterward Hezron went in to the daughter of Machir the father of Gilead, whom he married when he *was* sixty years old; and she bore him Segub. ²² Segub begot Jair, who had twenty-three cities in the land of Gilead. ²³ (Geshur and Syria took from them the towns of Jair, with Kenath and its towns—sixty towns.) All these *belonged to* the sons of Machir the father of Gilead. ²⁴ After Hezron died in Caleb Ephrathah, Hezron's wife Abijah bore him Ashhur the father of Tekoa.

²⁵ The sons of Jerahmeel, the firstborn of Hezron, *were* Ram, the firstborn, and Bunah, Oren, Ozem, *and* Ahijah. ²⁶ Jerahmeel had another wife, whose name was Atarah; she was the mother of Onam. ²⁷ The sons of Ram, the firstborn of Jerahmeel, were Maaz, Jamin, and Eker. ²⁸ The sons of Onam

The Book of
1 CHRONICLES

Adam's family

ADAM, Seth, Enosh, 2 Cainan, Mahalalel, Jared, 3 Enoch, Methuselah, Lamech, 4 Noah, Shem, Ham, and Japheth.

5 The sons of Japheth *were* Gomer, Magog, Madai, Javan, Tubal, Meshech, and Tiras. 6 The sons of Gomer *were* Ashkenaz, Diphath, and Togarmah. 7 The sons of Javan *were* Elishah, Tarshishah, Kittim, and Rodanim.

8 The sons of Ham *were* Cush, Mizraim, Put, and Canaan. 9 The sons of Cush *were* Seba, Havilah, Sabta, Raama, and Sabtecha. The sons of Raama *were* Sheba and Dedan. 10 Cush begot Nimrod; he began to be a mighty one on the earth. 11 Mizraim begot Ludim, Anamim, Lehabim, Naphtuhim, 12 Pathrusim, Casluhim (from whom came the Philistines and the Caphtorim). 13 Canaan begot Sidon, his firstborn, and Heth; 14 the Jebusite, the Amorite, and the Girgashite; 15 the Hivite, the Arkite, and the Sinite; 16 the Arvadite, the Zemarite, and the Hamathite.

17 The sons of Shem *were* Elam, Asshur, Arphaxad, Lud, Aram, Uz, Hul, Gether, and Meshech. 18 Arphaxad begot Shelah, and Shelah begot Eber. 19 To Eber were born two sons: the name of one *was* Peleg, for in his days the earth was divided; and his brother's name *was* Joktan. 20 Joktan begot Almodad, Sheleph, Hazarmaveth, Jerah, 21 Hadoram, Uzal, Diklah, 22 Ebal, Abimael, Sheba, 23 Ophir, Havilah, and Jobab. All these *were* the sons of Joktan.

24 Shem, Arphaxad, Shelah, 25 Eber, Peleg, Reu, 26 Serug, Nahor, Terah, 27 and Abram, who *is* Abraham. 28 The sons of Abraham *were* Isaac and Ishmael.

29 These *are* their genealogies: The firstborn of Ishmael *was* Nebajoth; then Kedar, Adbeel, Mibsam, 30 Mishma, Dumah, Massa, Hadad, Tema, 31 Jetur, Naphish, and Kedemah. These *were* the sons of Ishmael.

32 Now the sons born to Keturah, Abraham's concubine, *were* Zimran, Jokshan, Medan, Midian, Ishbak, and Shuah. The sons of Jokshan *were* Sheba and Dedan. 33 The sons of Midian *were* Ephah, Epher, Hanoch, Abida, and Eldaah. All these *were* the children of Keturah.

34 And Abraham begot Isaac. The sons of Isaac *were* Esau and Israel. 35 The sons of Esau *were* Eliphaz, Reuel, Jeush, Jaalam, and Korah. 36 And the sons of Eliphaz *were* Teman, Omar, Zephi, Gatam, *and* Kenaz; and *by* Timna, Amalek. 37 The sons of Reuel *were* Nahath, Zerah, Shammah, and Mizzah.

38 The sons of Seir *were* Lotan, Shobal, Zibeon, Anah, Dishon, Ezer, and Dishan. 39 And the sons of Lotan *were*

DIGGING IN

1:1 God Created the Family The next eight chapters of 1 Chronicles may seem very boring. They just list some of the descendants of Adam, leading to the nation of Israel. Right now most of these names don't mean very much to you. But they are really a wonderful book of memories, showing God's faithfulness to some ordinary people who lived during those early times.

The first thing you should notice is that God thinks the family is very important.

In fact, God created the family to be the way in which young people would learn the plan of salvation through Jesus. God meant us to have parents who would teach us the Bible and lead us to Christ.

You may not have a mother and father, or you may have only one parent. But please don't be sad. God cares for orphans in a special way. He knows how to send people who will love you and help you understand God's ways.

Hori and Homam; Lotan's sister *was* Timna. 40 The sons of Shobal *were* Alian, Manahath, Ebal, Shephi, and Onam. The sons of Zibeon *were* Ajah and Anah. 41 The son of Anah *was* Dishon. The sons of Dishon *were* Hamran, Eshban, Ithran, and Cheran. 42 The sons of Ezer *were* Bilhan, Zaavan, *and* Jaakan. The sons of Dishan *were* Uz and Aran.

43 Now these *were* the kings who reigned in the land of Edom before a king reigned over the children of Israel: Bela the son of Beor, and the name of his city was Dinhabah. 44 And when Bela died, Jobab the son of Zerah of Bozrah reigned in his place. 45 When Jobab died, Husham of the land of the Temanites reigned in his place. 46 And when Husham died, Hadad the son of Bedad, who attacked Midian in the field of Moab, reigned in his place. The name of his city *was* Avith. 47 When Hadad died, Samlah of Masrekah reigned in his place. 48 And when Samlah died, Saul of Rehoboth-by-the-River reigned in his place. 49 When Saul died, Baal-Hanan the son of Achbor reigned in his place. 50 And when Baal-Hanan died, Hadad reigned in his place; and the name of his city was Pai. His wife's name was Mehetabel the daughter of Matred, the daughter of Mezahab. 51 Hadad died also. And the chiefs of Edom were Chief Timnah, Chief Aliah, Chief Jetheth, 52 Chief Aholibamah, Chief Elah, Chief Pinon, 53 Chief Kenaz, Chief Teman, Chief Mibzar, 54 Chief Magdiel, and Chief Iram. These *were* the chiefs of Edom.

Israel's family

2 These *were* the sons of Israel: Reuben, Simeon, Levi, Judah, Issachar, Zebulun, 2 Dan, Joseph, Benjamin, Naphtali, Gad, and Asher.

3 The sons of Judah *were* Er, Onan, and Shelah. *These* three were born to him by the daughter of Shua, the Canaanitess. Er, the firstborn of Judah, was wicked in the sight of the LORD; so He killed him. 4 And Tamar, his daughter-in-law, bore him Perez and

Zerah. All the sons of Judah *were* five.

5 The sons of Perez *were* Hezron and Hamul. 6 The sons of Zerah *were* Zimri, Ethan, Heman, Calcol, and Dara—five of them in all.

7 The son of Carmi *was* Achar, the troubler of Israel, who transgressed in the accursed thing.

8 The son of Ethan *was* Azariah.

9 Also the sons of Hezron who were born to him *were* Jerahmeel, Ram, and Chelubai. 10 Ram begot Amminadab, and Amminadab begot Nahshon, leader of the children of Judah; 11 Nahshon begot Salma, and Salma begot Boaz; 12 Boaz begot Obed, and Obed begot Jesse; 13 Jesse begot Eliab his firstborn, Abinadab the second, Shimea the third, 14 Nethanel the fourth, Raddai the fifth, 15 Ozem the sixth, *and* David the seventh.

16 Now their sisters *were* Zeruiah and Abigail. And the sons of Zeruiah *were* Abishai, Joab, and Asahel—three. 17 Abigail bore Amasa; and the father of Amasa *was* Jether the Ishmaelite.

18 Caleb the son of Hezron had children by Azubah, *his* wife, and by Jerioth. Now these were her sons: Jesher, Shobab, and Ardon. 19 When Azubah died, Caleb took Ephrath as his wife, who bore him Hur. 20 And Hur begot Uri, and Uri begot Bezalel.

21 Now afterward Hezron went in to the daughter of Machir the father of Gilead, whom he married when he *was* sixty years old; and she bore him Segub. 22 Segub begot Jair, who had twenty-three cities in the land of Gilead. 23 (Geshur and Syria took from them the towns of Jair, with Kenath and its towns—sixty towns.) All these *belonged to* the sons of Machir the father of Gilead. 24 After Hezron died in Caleb Ephrathah, Hezron's wife Abijah bore him Ashhur the father of Tekoa.

25 The sons of Jerahmeel, the firstborn of Hezron, *were* Ram, the firstborn, and Bunah, Oren, Ozem, *and* Ahijah. 26 Jerahmeel had another wife, whose name was Atarah; she was the mother of Onam. 27 The sons of Ram, the firstborn of Jerahmeel, were Maaz, Jamin, and Eker. 28 The sons of Onam

were Shammai and Jada. The sons of Shammai were Nadab and Abishur.

29 And the name of the wife of Abishur was Abihail, and she bore him Ahban and Molid. 30 The sons of Nadab were Seled and Appaim; Seled died without children. 31 The son of Appaim was Ishi, the son of Ishi was Sheshan, and Sheshan's son was Ahlai. 32 The sons of Jada, the brother of Shammai, were Jether and Jonathan; Jether died without children. 33 The sons of Jonathan were Peleth and Zaza. These were the sons of Jerahmeel.

34 Now Sheshan had no sons, only daughters. And Sheshan had an Egyptian servant whose name was Jarha. 35 Sheshan gave his daughter to Jarha his servant as wife, and she bore him Attai. 36 Attai begot Nathan, and Nathan begot Zabad; 37 Zabad begot Ephlal, and Ephlal begot Obed; 38 Obed begot Jehu, and Jehu begot Azariah; 39 Azariah begot Helez, and Helez begot Eleasah; 40 Eleasah begot Sismai, and Sismai begot Shallum; 41 Shallum begot Jekamiah, and Jekamiah begot Elishama.

42 The descendants of Caleb the brother of Jerahmeel were Mesha, his firstborn, who was the father of Ziph, and the sons of Mareshah the father of Hebron. 43 The sons of Hebron were Korah, Tappuah, Rekem, and Shema. 44 Shema begot Raham the father of Jorkoam, and Rekem begot Shammai. 45 And the son of Shammai was Maon, and Maon was the father of Beth Zur.

46 Ephah, Caleb's concubine, bore Haran, Moza, and Gazez; and Haran begot Gazez. 47 And the sons of Jahdai were Regem, Jotham, Geshan, Pelet, Ephah, and Shaaph.

48 Maachah, Caleb's concubine, bore Sheber and Tirhanah. 49 She also bore Shaaph the father of Madmannah, Sheva the father of Machbenah and the father of Gibea. And the daughter of Caleb was Achsah.

50 These were the descendants of Caleb: The sons of Hur, the firstborn of Ephrathah, were Shobal the father of Kirjath Jearim, 51 Salma the father of Bethlehem, and Hareph the father of Beth Gader.

52 And Shobal the father of Kirjath Jearim had descendants: Haroeh, and half of the families of Manuhoth. 53 The families of Kirjath Jearim were the Ithrites, the Puthites, the Shumathites, and the Mishraites. From these came the Zorathites and the Eshtaolites.

54 The sons of Salma were Bethlehem, the Netophathites, Atroth Beth Joab, half of the Manahethites, and the Zorites.

55 And the families of the scribes who dwelt at Jabez were the Tirathites, the Shimeathites, and the Suchathites. These were the Kenites who came from Hammath, the father of the house of Rechab.

David's family

3 Now these were the sons of David who were born to him in Hebron: The firstborn was Amnon, by Ahinoam the Jezreelitess; the second, Daniel, by Abigail the Carmelitess; 2 the third, Absalom the son of Maacah, the daughter of Talmai, king of Geshur; the fourth, Adonijah the son of Haggith; 3 the fifth, Shephatiah, by Abital; the sixth, Ithream, by his wife Eglah.

4 These six were born to him in Hebron. There he reigned seven years and six months, and in Jerusalem he reigned thirty-three years. 5 And these were born to him in Jerusalem: Shimea, Shobab, Nathan, and Solomon—four by Bathshua the daughter of Ammiel. 6 Also there were Ibhar, Elishama, Eliphelet, 7 Nogah, Nepheg, Japhia, 8 Elishama, Eliada, and Eliphelet—nine in all. 9 These were all the sons of David, besides the sons of the concubines, and Tamar their sister.

10 Solomon's son was Rehoboam; Abijah was his son, Asa his son, Jehoshaphat his son, 11 Joram his son, Ahaziah his son, Joash his son, 12 Amaziah his son, Azariah his son, Jotham his son, 13 Ahaz his son, Hezekiah his son, Manasseh his son,

14 Amon his son, *and* Josiah his son.
15 The sons of Josiah *were* Johanan the firstborn, the second Jehoiakim, the third Zedekiah, and the fourth Shallum. 16 The sons of Jehoiakim *were* Jeconiah his son *and* Zedekiah his son.

17 And the sons of Jeconiah *were* Assir, Shealtiel his son, 18 *and* Malchiram, Pedaiah, Shenazzar, Jecamiah, Hoshama, and Nedabiah. 19 The sons of Pedaiah *were* Zerubbabel and Shimei. The sons of Zerubbabel *were* Meshullam, Hananiah, Shelomith their sister, 20 and Hashubah, Ohel, Berechiah, Hasadiah, and Jushab-Hesed—five *in all.*

21 The sons of Hananiah *were* Pelatiah and Jeshaiah, the sons of Rephaiah, the sons of Arnan, the sons of Obadiah, and the sons of Shechaniah. 22 The son of Shechaniah was Shemaiah. The sons of Shemaiah *were* Hattush, Igal, Bariah, Neariah, and Shaphat—six *in all.* 23 The sons of Neariah *were* Elioenai, Hezekiah, and Azrikam—three *in all.* 24 The sons of Elioenai *were* Hodaviah, Eliashib, Pelaiah, Akkub, Johanan, Delaiah, and Anani—seven *in all.*

Judah's family

4 The sons of Judah *were* Perez, Hezron, Carmi, Hur, and Shobal. 2 And Reaiah the son of Shobal begot Jahath, and Jahath begot Ahumai and Lahad. These *were* the families of the Zorathites. 3 These *were* the sons *of the father* of Etam: Jezreel, Ishma, and Idbash; and the name of their sister *was* Hazelelponi; 4 and Penuel *was* the father of Gedor, and Ezer *was the* father of Hushah.

These *were* the sons of Hur, the firstborn of Ephrathah the father of Bethlehem.

5 And Ashhur the father of Tekoa had two wives, Helah and Naarah. 6 Naarah bore him Ahuzzam, Hepher, Temeni, and Haahashtari. These *were* the sons of Naarah. 7 The sons of Helah *were* Zereth, Zohar, and Ethnan; 8 and Koz begot Anub, Zobebah, and the families of Aharhel the son of Harum.

9 Now Jabez was more honorable than his brothers, and his mother called his name Jabez, saying, "Because I bore *him* in pain." 10 And Jabez called on the God of Israel saying, "Oh, that You would bless me indeed, and enlarge my territory, that Your hand would be with me, and that You would keep *me* from evil, that I may not cause pain!" So God granted him what he requested.

11 Chelub the brother of Shuhah begot Mehir, who *was* the father of Eshton. 12 And Eshton begot Beth-Rapha, Paseah, and Tehinnah the father of Ir-Nahash. These *were* the men of Rechah.

13 The sons of Kenaz *were* Othniel and Seraiah. The sons of Othniel *were* Hathath, 14 and Meonothai *who* begot Ophrah. Seraiah begot Joab the father of Ge Harashim, for they were craftsmen. 15 The sons of Caleb the son of Jephunneh *were* Iru, Elah, and Naam. The son of Elah *was* Kenaz. 16 The sons of Jehallelel *were* Ziph, Ziphah, Tiria, and Asarel. 17 The sons of Ezrah *were* Jether, Mered, Epher, and Jalon. And *Mered's wife bore* Miriam, Shammai, and Ishbah the father of Eshtemoa. 18 (His wife Jehudijah bore Jered the father of Gedor, Heber the father of Sochoh, and Jekuthiel the father of Zanoah.) And these were the sons of Bithiah the daughter of Pharaoh, whom Mered took.

19 The sons of Hodiah's wife, the sister of Naham, *were* the fathers of Keilah the Garmite and of Eshtemoa the Maachathite. 20 And the sons of Shimon *were* Amnon, Rinnah, Ben-Hanan, and Tilon. And the sons of Ishi *were* Zoheth and Ben-Zoheth.

21 The sons of Shelah the son of Judah *were* Er the father of Lecah, Laadah the father of Mareshah, and the families of the house of the linen workers of the house of Ashbea; 22 also Jokim, the men of Chozeba, and Joash; Saraph, who ruled in Moab, and Jashubi-Lehem. Now the records are ancient. 23 These *were* the potters

and those who dwell at Netaim and Gederah; there they dwelt with the king for his work.

24 The sons of Simeon *were* Nemuel, Jamin, Jarib, Zerah, *and* Shaul, 25 Shallum his son, Mibsam his son, and Mishma his son. 26 And the sons of Mishma *were* Hamuel his son, Zacchur his son, and Shimei his son. 27 Shimei had sixteen sons and six daughters; but his brothers did not have many children, nor did any of their families multiply as much as the children of Judah.

28 They dwelt at Beersheba, Moladah, Hazar Shual, 29 Bilhah, Ezem, Tolad, 30 Bethuel, Hormah, Ziklag, 31 Beth Marcaboth, Hazar Susim, Beth Biri, and at Shaaraim. These *were* their cities until the reign of David. 32 And their villages *were* Etam, Ain, Rimmon, Tochen, and Ashan—five cities— 33 and all the villages that *were* around these cities as far as Baal. These *were* their dwelling places, and they maintained their genealogy: 34 Meshobab, Jamlech, and Joshah the son of Amaziah; 35 Joel, and Jehu the son of Joshibiah, the son of Seraiah, the son of Asiel; 36 Elioenai, Jaakobah, Jeshohaiah, Asaiah, Adiel, Jesimiel, and Benaiah; 37 Ziza the son of Shiphi, the son of Allon, the son of Jedaiah, the son of Shimri, the son of Shemaiah— 38 these mentioned by name *were* leaders in their families, and their father's house increased greatly.

39 So they went to the entrance of Gedor, as far as the east side of the valley, to seek pasture for their flocks. 40 And they found rich, good pasture, and the land *was* broad, quiet, and peaceful; for some Hamites formerly lived there.

41 These recorded by name came in the days of Hezekiah king of Judah; and they attacked their tents and the Meunites who were found there, and utterly destroyed them, as it is to this day. So they dwelt in their place, because *there was* pasture for their flocks there. 42 Now *some* of them, five hundred men of the sons of Simeon, went to Mount Seir, having as their captains

Pelatiah, Neariah, Rephaiah, and Uzziel, the sons of Ishi. 43 And they defeated the rest of the Amalekites who had escaped. They have dwelt there to this day.

The families of Reuben, Gad, and Manasseh

5 Now the sons of Reuben the firstborn of Israel—he *was* indeed the firstborn, but because he defiled his father's bed, his birthright was given to the sons of Joseph, the son of Israel, so that the genealogy is not listed according to the birthright; 2 yet Judah prevailed over his brothers, and from him *came* a ruler, although the birthright was Joseph's— 3 the sons of Reuben the firstborn of Israel were Hanoch, Pallu, Hezron, and Carmi.

4 The sons of Joel *were* Shemaiah his son, Gog his son, Shimei his son, 5 Micah his son, Reaiah his son, Baal his son, 6 and Beerah his son, whom Tiglath-Pileser king of Assyria carried into captivity. He *was* leader of the Reubenites. 7 And his brethren by their families, when the genealogy of their generations was registered: the chief, Jeiel, and Zechariah, 8 and Bela the son of Azaz, the son of Shema, the son of Joel, who dwelt in Aroer, as far as Nebo and Baal Meon. 9 Eastward they settled as far as the entrance of the wilderness this side of the River Euphrates, because their cattle had multiplied in the land of Gilead.

10 Now in the days of Saul they made war with the Hagrites, who fell by their hand; and they dwelt in their tents throughout the entire *area* east of Gilead.

11 And the children of Gad dwelt next to them in the land of Bashan as far as Salcah: 12 Joel *was* the chief, Shapham the next, then Jaanai and Shaphat in Bashan, 13 and their brethren of their father's house: Michael, Meshullam, Sheba, Jorai, Jachan, Zia, and Eber—seven *in all*. 14 These *were* the children of Abihail the son of Huri, the son of Jaroah, the son of Gilead, the son of Michael, the son of

Jeshishai, the son of Jahdo, the son of Buz; 15 Ahi the son of Abdiel, the son of Guni, *was* chief of their father's house. 16 And *the Gadites* dwelt in Gilead, in Bashan and in its villages, and in all the common-lands of Sharon within their borders. 17 All these were registered by genealogies in the days of Jotham king of Judah, and in the days of Jeroboam king of Israel.

18 The sons of Reuben, the Gadites, and half the tribe of Manasseh *had* forty-four thousand seven hundred and sixty valiant men, men able to bear shield and sword, to shoot with the bow, and skillful in war, who went to war. 19 They made war with the Hagrites, Jetur, Naphish, and Nodab. 20 And they were helped against them, and the Hagrites were delivered into their hand, and all who *were* with them, for they cried out to God in the battle. He heeded their prayer, because they put their trust in Him. 21 Then they took away their livestock—fifty thousand of their camels, two hundred and fifty thousand of their sheep, and two thousand of their donkeys—also one hundred thousand of their men; 22 for many fell dead, because the war *was* God's. And they dwelt in their place until the captivity.

23 So the children of the half-tribe of Manasseh dwelt in the land. Their *numbers* increased from Bashan to Baal Hermon, that is, to Senir, or Mount Hermon. 24 These *were* the heads of their fathers' houses: Epher, Ishi, Eliel, Azriel, Jeremiah, Hodaviah, and Jahdiel. They *were* mighty men of valor, famous men, *and* heads of their fathers' houses.

25 And they were unfaithful to the God of their fathers, and played the harlot after the gods of the peoples of the land, whom God had destroyed before them. 26 So the God of Israel stirred up the spirit of Pul king of Assyria, that is, Tiglath-Pileser king of Assyria. He carried the Reubenites, the Gadites, and the half-tribe of Manasseh into captivity. He took them to Halah, Habor, Hara, and the river of Gozan to this day.

Levi's family

6 The sons of Levi *were* Gershon, Kohath, and Merari. 2 The sons of Kohath *were* Amram, Izhar, Hebron, and Uzziel. 3 The children of Amram *were* Aaron, Moses, and Miriam. And the sons of Aaron *were* Nadab, Abihu, Eleazar, and Ithamar. 4 Eleazar begot Phinehas, *and* Phinehas begot Abishua; 5 Abishua begot Bukki, and Bukki begot Uzzi; 6 Uzzi begot Zerahiah, and Zerahiah begot Meraioth; 7 Meraioth begot Amariah, and Amariah begot Ahitub; 8 Ahitub begot Zadok, and Zadok begot Ahimaaz; 9 Ahimaaz begot Azariah, and Azariah begot Johanan; 10 Johanan begot Azariah (it was he who ministered as priest in the temple that Solomon built in Jerusalem); 11 Azariah begot Amariah, and Amariah begot Ahitub; 12 Ahitub begot Zadok, and Zadok begot Shallum; 13 Shallum begot Hilkiah, and Hilkiah begot Azariah; 14 Azariah begot Seraiah, and Seraiah begot Jehozadak. 15 Jehozadak went *into captivity* when the LORD carried Judah and Jerusalem into captivity by the hand of Nebuchadnezzar.

16 The sons of Levi *were* Gershon, Kohath, and Merari. 17 These are the names of the sons of Gershon: Libni and Shimei. 18 The sons of Kohath *were* Amram, Izhar, Hebron, and Uzziel. 19 The sons of Merari *were* Mahli and Mushi. Now these *are* the families of the Levites according to their fathers: 20 Of Gershon *were* Libni his son, Jahath his son, Zimmah his son, 21 Joah his son, Iddo his son, Zerah his son, *and* Jeatherai his son. 22 The sons of Kohath *were* Amminadab his son, Korah his son, Assir his son, 23 Elkanah his son, Ebiasaph his son, Assir his son, 24 Tahath his son, Uriel his son, Uzziah his son, and Shaul his son. 25 The sons of Elkanah *were* Amasai and Ahimoth. 26 *As for* Elkanah, the sons of Elkanah *were* Zophai his son, Nahath his son, 27 Eliab his son, Jeroham his son, *and* Elkanah his son. 28 The sons of Samuel *were Joel* the firstborn, and Abijah the second.

29 The sons of Merari *were* Mahli, Libni his son, Shimei his son, Uzzah his son, 30 Shimea his son, Haggiah his son, *and* Asaiah his son.

31 Now these are the men whom David appointed over the service of song in the house of the LORD, after the ark came to rest. 32 They were ministering with music before the dwelling place of the tabernacle of meeting, until Solomon had built the house of the LORD in Jerusalem, and they served in their office according to their order.

33 And these *are* the ones who ministered with their sons: Of the sons of the Kohathites *were* Heman the singer, the son of Joel, the son of Samuel, 34 the son of Elkanah, the son of Jeroham, the son of Eliel, the son of Toah, 35 the son of Zuph, the son of Elkanah, the son of Mahath, the son of Amasai, 36 the son of Elkanah, the son of Joel, the son of Azariah, the son of Zephaniah, 37 the son of Tahath, the son of Assir, the son of Ebiasaph, the son of Korah, 38 the son of Izhar, the son of Kohath, the son of Levi, the son of Israel. 39 And his brother Asaph, who stood at his right hand, *was* Asaph the son of Berachiah, the son of Shimea, 40 the son of Michael, the son of Baaseiah, the son of Malchijah, 41 the son of Ethni, the son of Zerah, the son of Adaiah, 42 the son of Ethan, the son of Zimmah, the son of Shimei, 43 the son of Jahath, the son of Gershon, the son of Levi.

44 Their brethren, the sons of Merari, on the left hand, *were* Ethan the son of Kishi, the son of Abdi, the son of Malluch, 45 the son of Hashabiah, the son of Amaziah, the son of Hilkiah, 46 the son of Amzi, the son of Bani, the son of Shamer, 47 the son of Mahli, the son of Mushi, the son of Merari, the son of Levi.

48 And their brethren, the Levites, *were* appointed to every kind of service of the tabernacle of the house of God.

49 But Aaron and his sons offered sacrifices on the altar of burnt offering and on the altar of incense, for all the work of the Most Holy *Place,* and to make atonement for Israel, according to all that Moses the servant of God had commanded. 50 Now these *are* the sons of Aaron: Eleazar his son, Phinehas his son, Abishua his son, 51 Bukki his son, Uzzi his son, Zerahiah his son, 52 Meraioth his son, Amariah his son, Ahitub his son, 53 Zadok his son, *and* Ahimaaz his son.

54 Now these *are* their dwelling places throughout their settlements in their territory, for they were *given* by lot to the sons of Aaron, of the family of the Kohathites: 55 They gave them Hebron in the land of Judah, with its surrounding common-lands. 56 But the fields of the city and its villages they gave to Caleb the son of Jephunneh. 57 And to the sons of Aaron they gave *one of* the cities of refuge, Hebron; also Libnah with its common-lands, Jattir, Eshtemoa with its common-lands, 58 Hilen with its common-lands, Debir with its common-lands, 59 Ashan with its common-lands, and Beth Shemesh with its common-lands. 60 And from the tribe of Benjamin: Geba with its common-lands, Alemeth with its common-lands, and Anathoth with its common-lands. All their cities among their families *were* thirteen.

61 To the rest of the family of the tribe of the Kohathites *they gave* by lot ten cities from half the tribe of Manasseh. 62 And to the sons of Gershon, throughout their families, *they gave* thirteen cities from the tribe of Issachar, from the tribe of Asher, from the tribe of Naphtali, and from the tribe of Manasseh in Bashan. 63 To the sons of Merari, throughout their families, *they gave* twelve cities from the tribe of Reuben, from the tribe of Gad, and from the tribe of Zebulun. 64 So the children of Israel gave *these* cities with their common-lands to the Levites. 65 And they gave by lot from the tribe of the children of Judah, from the tribe of the children of Simeon, and from the tribe of the children of Benjamin these cities which are called by *their* names.

66 Now some of the families of the sons of Kohath *were given* cities as their territory from the tribe of

Ephraim. 67 And they gave them *one of* the cities of refuge, Shechem with its common-lands, in the mountains of Ephraim, also Gezer with its common-lands, 68 Jokmeam with its common-lands, Beth Horon with its common-lands, 69 Aijalon with its common-lands, and Gath Rimmon with its common-lands. 70 And from the half-tribe of Manasseh: Aner with its common-lands and Bileam with its common-lands, for the rest of the family of the sons of Kohath.

71 From the family of the half-tribe of Manasseh the sons of Gershon *were given* Golan in Bashan with its common-lands and Ashtaroth with its common-lands. 72 And from the tribe of Issachar: Kedesh with its common-lands, Daberath with its common-lands, 73 Ramoth with its common-lands, and Anem with its common-lands. 74 And from the tribe of Asher: Mashal with its common-lands, Abdon with its common-lands, 75 Hukok with its common-lands, and Rehob with its common-lands. 76 And from the tribe of Naphtali: Kedesh in Galilee with its common-lands, Hammon with its common-lands, and Kirjathaim with its common-lands.

77 From the tribe of Zebulun the rest of the children of Merari *were given* Rimmon with its common-lands and Tabor with its common-lands. 78 And on the other side of the Jordan, across from Jericho, on the east side of the Jordan, *they were given* from the tribe of Reuben: Bezer in the wilderness with its common-lands, Jahzah with its common-lands, 79 Kedemoth with its common-lands, and Mephaath with its common-lands. 80 And from the tribe of Gad: Ramoth in Gilead with its common-lands, Mahanaim with its common-lands, 81 Heshbon with its common-lands, and Jazer with its common-lands.

The people who lived in Israel

7 The sons of Issachar *were* Tola, Puah, Jashub, and Shimron—four *in all.* 2 The sons of Tola *were* Uzzi, Re-

phaiah, Jeriel, Jahmai, Jibsam, and Shemuel, heads of their father's house. *The sons* of Tola *were* mighty men of valor in their generations; their number in the days of David *was* twenty-two thousand six hundred. 3 The son of Uzzi *was* Izrahiah, and the sons of Izrahiah *were* Michael, Obadiah, Joel, and Ishiah. All five of them *were* chief men. 4 And with them, by their generations, according to their fathers' houses, *were* thirty-six thousand troops ready for war; for they had many wives and sons.

5 Now their brethren among all the families of Issachar *were* mighty men of valor, listed by their genealogies, eighty-seven thousand in all.

6 *The sons* of Benjamin *were* Bela, Becher, and Jediael—three *in all.* 7 The sons of Bela *were* Ezbon, Uzzi, Uzziel, Jerimoth, and Iri—five *in all.* They *were* heads of *their* fathers' houses, and they were listed by their genealogies, twenty-two thousand and thirty-four mighty men of valor.

8 The sons of Becher *were* Zemirah, Joash, Eliezer, Elioenai, Omri, Jerimoth, Abijah, Anathoth, and Alemeth. All these *are* the sons of Becher. 9 And they were recorded by genealogy according to their generations, heads of their fathers' houses, twenty thousand two hundred mighty men of valor. 10 The son of Jediael *was* Bilhan, and the sons of Bilhan *were* Jeush, Benjamin, Ehud, Chenaanah, Zethan, Tharshish, and Ahishahar.

11 All these sons of Jediael *were* heads of their fathers' houses; *there were* seventeen thousand two hundred mighty men of valor fit to go out for war *and* battle. 12 Shuppim and Huppim *were* the sons of Ir, *and* Hushim *was* the son of Aher.

13 The sons of Naphtali *were* Jahziel, Guni, Jezer, and Shallum, the sons of Bilhah.

14 The descendants of Manasseh: his Syrian concubine bore him Machir the father of Gilead, the father of Asriel. 15 Machir took as his wife *the sister* of Huppim and Shuppim, whose name *was* Maachah. The name of *Gilead's*

grandson *was* Zelophehad, but Zelophehad begot only daughters. 16 (Maachah the wife of Machir bore a son, and she called his name Peresh. The name of his brother *was* Sheresh, and his sons *were* Ulam and Rakem. 17 The son of Ulam *was* Bedan.) These *were* the descendants of Gilead the son of Machir, the son of Manasseh.

18 His sister Hammoleketh bore Ishhod, Abiezer, and Mahlah.

19 And the sons of Shemida were Ahian, Shechem, Likhi, and Aniam.

20 The sons of Ephraim *were* Shuthelah, Bered his son, Tahath his son, Eladah his son, Tahath his son, 21 Zabad his son, Shuthelah his son, and Ezer and Elead. The men of Gath who were born in *that* land killed *them* because they came down to take away their cattle. 22 Then Ephraim their father mourned many days, and his brethren came to comfort him.

23 And when he went in to his wife, she conceived and bore a son; and he called his name Beriah, because tragedy had come upon his house. 24 Now his daughter *was* Sheerah, who built Lower and Upper Beth Horon and Uzzen Sheerah; 25 and Rephah *was* his son, *as well* as Resheph, and Telah his son, Tahan his son, 26 Laadan his son, Ammihud his son, Elishama his son, 27 Nun his son, and Joshua his son.

28 Now their possessions and dwelling places *were* Bethel and its towns: to the east Naaran, to the west Gezer and its towns, and Shechem and its towns, as far as Ayyah and its towns; 29 and by the borders of the children of Manasseh *were* Beth Shean and its towns, Taanach and its towns, Megiddo and its towns, Dor and its towns. In these dwelt the children of Joseph, the son of Israel.

30 The sons of Asher *were* Imnah, Ishvah, Ishvi, Beriah, and their sister Serah. 31 The sons of Beriah *were* Heber and Malchiel, who was the father of Birzaith. 32 And Heber begot Japhlet, Shomer, Hotham, and their sister Shua. 33 The sons of Japhlet *were* Pasach, Bimhal, and Ashvath. These *were* the children of Japhlet.

34 The sons of Shemer *were* Ahi, Rohgah, Jehubbah, and Aram. 35 And the sons of his brother Helem *were* Zophah, Imna, Shelesh, and Amal. 36 The sons of Zophah *were* Suah, Harnepher, Shual, Beri, Imrah, 37 Bezer, Hod, Shamma, Shilshah, Jithran, and Beera. 38 The sons of Jether *were* Jephunneh, Pispah, and Ara. 39 The sons of Ulla *were* Arah, Haniel, and Rizia.

40 All these *were* the children of Asher, heads of *their* fathers' houses, choice men, mighty men of valor, chief leaders. And they were recorded by genealogies among the army fit for battle; their number *was* twenty-six thousand.

King Saul's family tree

8 Now Benjamin begot Bela his firstborn, Ashbel the second, Aharah the third, 2 Nohah the fourth, and Rapha the fifth. 3 The sons of Bela *were* Addar, Gera, Abihud, 4 Abishua, Naaman, Ahoah, 5 Gera, Shephuphan, and Huram.

6 These *are* the sons of Ehud, who were the heads of the fathers' *houses* of the inhabitants of Geba, and who forced them to move to Manahath: 7 Naaman, Ahijah, and Gera who forced them to move. He begot Uzza and Ahihud.

8 Also Shaharaim had children in the country of Moab, after he had sent away Hushim and Baara his wives. 9 By Hodesh his wife he begot Jobab, Zibia, Mesha, Malcam, 10 Jeuz, Sachiah, and Mirmah. These *were* his sons, heads of their fathers' *houses*.

11 And by Hushim he begot Abitub and Elpaal. 12 The sons of Elpaal *were* Eber, Misham, and Shemed, who built Ono and Lod with its towns; 13 and Beriah and Shema, who *were* heads of their fathers' *houses* of the inhabitants of Aijalon, who drove out the inhabitants of Gath. 14 Ahio, Shashak, Jeremoth, 15 Zebadiah, Arad, Eder, 16 Michael, Ispah, and Joha *were* the sons of Beriah. 17 Zebadiah, Meshullam, Hizki, Heber, 18 Ishmerai, Jizliah,

and Jobab *were* the sons of Elpaal. ¹⁹ Jakim, Zichri, Zabdi, ²⁰ Elienai, Zillethai, Eliel, ²¹ Adaiah, Beraiah, and Shimrath *were* the sons of Shimei. ²² Ishpan, Eber, Eliel, ²³ Abdon, Zichri, Hanan, ²⁴ Hananiah, Elam, Antothijah, ²⁵ Iphdeiah, and Penuel *were* the sons of Shashak. ²⁶ Shamsherai, Shehariah, Athaliah, ²⁷ Jaareshiah, Elijah, and Zichri *were* the sons of Jeroham.

²⁸ These *were* heads of the fathers' *houses* by their generations, chief men. These dwelt in Jerusalem.

²⁹ Now the father of Gibeon, whose wife's name *was* Maacah, dwelt at Gibeon. ³⁰ And his firstborn son *was* Abdon, then Zur, Kish, Baal, Nadab, ³¹ Gedor, Ahio, Zecher, ³² and Mikloth, *who* begot Shimeah. They also dwelt alongside their relatives in Jerusalem, with their brethren. ³³ Ner begot Kish, Kish begot Saul, and Saul begot Jonathan, Malchishua, Abinadab, and Esh-Baal. ³⁴ The son of Jonathan *was* Merib-Baal, and Merib-Baal begot Micah. ³⁵ The sons of Micah *were* Pithon, Melech, Tarea, and Ahaz. ³⁶ And Ahaz begot Jehoaddah; Jehoaddah begot Alemeth, Azmaveth, and Zimri; and Zimri begot Moza. ³⁷ Moza begot Binea, Raphah his son, Eleasah his son, *and* Azel his son.

³⁸ Azel had six sons whose names *were* these: Azrikam, Bocheru, Ishmael, Sheariah, Obadiah, and Hanan. All these *were* the sons of Azel. ³⁹ And the sons of Eshek his brother *were* Ulam his firstborn, Jeush the second, and Eliphelet the third.

⁴⁰ The sons of Ulam were mighty men of valor—archers. *They* had many sons and grandsons, one hundred and fifty *in all*. These *were* all sons of Benjamin.

A list of priests and Levites in Jerusalem

9 So all Israel was recorded by genealogies, and indeed, they *were* inscribed in the book of the kings of Israel. But Judah was carried away captive to Babylon because of their unfaithfulness. ² And the first inhabitants who *dwelt* in their possessions in their cities *were* Israelites, priests, Levites, and the Nethinim.

³ Now in Jerusalem the children of Judah dwelt, and some of the children of Benjamin, and of the children of Ephraim and Manasseh: ⁴ Uthai the son of Ammihud, the son of Omri, the son of Imri, the son of Bani, of the descendants of Perez, the son of Judah. ⁵ Of the Shilonites: Asaiah the firstborn and his sons. ⁶ Of the sons of Zerah: Jeuel, and their brethren— six hundred and ninety. ⁷ Of the sons of Benjamin: Sallu the son of Meshullam, the son of Hodaviah, the son of Hassenuah; ⁸ Ibneiah the son of Jeroham; Elah the son of Uzzi, the son of Michri; Meshullam the son of Shephatiah, the son of Reuel, the son of Ibnijah; ⁹ and their brethren, according to their generations—nine hundred and fifty-six. All these men *were* heads of

---

⚒ DIGGING IN

9:1 God's Faithfulness to Unfaithful Israel We have seen that God sent Israel and Judah into slavery. Second Kings 17 tells about the slavery of Israel in the north, and 2 Kings 25 tells about the defeat of Judah in the south.

The northern kingdom of Israel was never rebuilt, but the southern kingdom of Judah rose again 536 years before Jesus was born.

In recent times, God has been gathering the Jews from all over the world to rebuild their nation. After all their suffering, Israel will be built again. God will keep His promises to Abraham (see Genesis 12, 15, and 17).

Although Israel was unfaithful, God was always faithful. God promised that people all over the world would be blessed through Abraham. That's why you're reading these words—God wants to bless you because of His promise to Abraham four thousand years ago!

a father's *house* in their fathers' houses.

¹⁰ Of the priests: Jedaiah, Jehoiarib, and Jachin; ¹¹ Azariah the son of Hilkiah, the son of Meshullam, the son of Zadok, the son of Meraioth, the son of Ahitub, the officer over the house of God; ¹² Adaiah the son of Jeroham, the son of Pashur, the son of Malchijah; Maasai the son of Adiel, the son of Jahzerah, the son of Meshullam, the son of Meshillemith, the son of Immer; ¹³ and their brethren, heads of their fathers' *houses*—one thousand seven hundred and sixty. *They were* very able men for the work of the service of the house of God.

¹⁴ Of the Levites: Shemaiah the son of Hasshub, the son of Azrikam, the son of Hashabiah, of the sons of Merari; ¹⁵ Bakbakkar, Heresh, Galal, and Mattaniah the son of Micah, the son of Zichri, the son of Asaph; ¹⁶ Obadiah the son of Shemaiah, the son of Galal, the son of Jeduthun; and Berechiah the son of Asa, the son of Elkanah, who lived in the villages of the Netophathites.

¹⁷ And the gatekeepers *were* Shallum, Akkub, Talmon, Ahiman, and their brethren. Shallum *was* the chief. ¹⁸ Until then *they had been* gatekeepers for the camps of the children of Levi at the King's Gate on the east. ¹⁹ Shallum the son of Kore, the son of Ebiasaph, the son of Korah, and his brethren, from his father's house, the Korahites, *were* in charge of the work of the service, gatekeepers of the tabernacle. Their fathers had been keepers of the entrance to the camp of the LORD. ²⁰ And Phinehas the son of Eleazar had been the officer over them in time past; the LORD *was* with him. ²¹ Zechariah the son of Meshelemiah *was* keeper of the door of the tabernacle of meeting.

²² All those chosen as gatekeepers *were* two hundred and twelve. They were recorded by their genealogy, in their villages. David and Samuel the seer had appointed them to their trusted office. ²³ So they and their children *were* in charge of the gates of the house of the LORD, the house of the tabernacle, by assignment. ²⁴ The gatekeepers were assigned to the four directions: the east, west, north, and south. ²⁵ And their brethren in their villages *had* to come with them from time to time for seven days. ²⁶ For in this trusted office *were* four chief gatekeepers; they were Levites. And they had charge over the chambers and treasuries of the house of God. ²⁷ And they lodged *all* around the house of God because they *had* the responsibility, and they *were* in charge of opening *it* every morning.

²⁸ Now *some* of them were in charge of the serving vessels, for they brought them in and took them out by count. ²⁹ *Some* of them *were* appointed over the furnishings and over all the implements of the sanctuary, and over the fine flour and the wine and the oil and the incense and the spices. ³⁰ And *some* of the sons of the priests made the ointment of the spices.

³¹ Mattithiah of the Levites, the firstborn of Shallum the Korahite, had the trusted office over the things that were baked in the pans. ³² And some of their brethren of the sons of the Kohathites *were* in charge of preparing the showbread for every Sabbath.

³³ These are the singers, heads of the fathers' *houses* of the Levites, *who* lodged in the chambers, *and were* free *from other duties;* for they were employed in *that* work day and night. ³⁴ These heads of the fathers' *houses* of the Levites *were* heads throughout their generations. They dwelt at Jerusalem.

³⁵ Jeiel the father of Gibeon, whose wife's name *was* Maacah, dwelt at Gibeon. ³⁶ His firstborn son *was* Abdon, then Zur, Kish, Baal, Ner, Nadab, ³⁷ Gedor, Ahio, Zechariah, and Mikloth. ³⁸ And Mikloth begot Shimeam. They also dwelt alongside their relatives in Jerusalem, with their brethren. ³⁹ Ner begot Kish, Kish begot Saul, and Saul begot Jonathan, Malchishua, Abinadab, and Esh-Baal. ⁴⁰ The son of Jonathan *was* Merib-Baal, and Merib-Baal begot Micah. ⁴¹ The sons of Micah

were Pithon, Melech, Tahrea, *and Ahaz.* 42 And Ahaz begot Jarah; Jarah begot Alemeth, Azmaveth, and Zimri; and Zimri begot Moza; 43 Moza begot Binea, Rephaiah his son, Eleasah his son, and Azel his son.

44 And Azel had six sons whose names *were* these: Azrikam, Bocheru, Ishmael, Sheariah, Obadiah, and Hanan; these *were* the sons of Azel.

Saul and his sons are killed

10 Now the Philistines fought against Israel; and the men of Israel fled from before the Philistines, and fell slain on Mount Gilboa. 2 Then the Philistines followed hard after Saul and his sons. And the Philistines killed Jonathan, Abinadab, and Malchishua, Saul's sons. 3 The battle became fierce against Saul. The archers hit him, and he was wounded by the archers. 4 Then Saul said to his armorbearer, "Draw your sword, and thrust me through with it, lest these uncircumcised men come and abuse me." But his armorbearer would not, for he was greatly afraid. Therefore Saul took a sword and fell on it. 5 And when his armorbearer saw that Saul was dead, he also fell on his sword and died. 6 So Saul and his three sons died, and all his house died together. 7 And when all the men of Israel who *were* in the valley saw that they had fled and that Saul and his sons were dead, they forsook their cities and fled; then the Philistines came and dwelt in them.

8 So it happened the next day, when the Philistines came to strip the slain, that they found Saul and his sons fallen on Mount Gilboa. 9 And they stripped him and took his head and his armor, and sent word *throughout* the land of the Philistines to proclaim the news *in the temple* of their idols and among the people. 10 Then they put his armor in the temple of their gods, and fastened his head in the temple of Dagon. 11 And when all Jabesh Gilead heard all that the Philistines had done to Saul, 12 all the valiant men arose and took the body of Saul and the bodies of his sons; and they brought them to Jabesh, and buried their bones under the tamarisk tree at Jabesh, and fasted seven days. 13 So Saul died for his unfaithfulness which he had committed against the LORD, because he did not keep the word of the LORD, and also because he consulted a medium for guidance. 14 But *he* did not inquire of the LORD; therefore He killed him, and turned the kingdom over to David the son of Jesse.

David is crowned king of Israel

11 Then all Israel came together to David at Hebron, saying, "Indeed we *are* your bone and your flesh. 2 Also, in time past, even when Saul was king, you *were* the one who led Israel out and brought them in; and the LORD your God said to you, 'You shall shepherd My people Israel, and be ruler

---

⚒ **DIGGING IN**

9:44 God Keeps Perfect Lists In 1 Chronicles 1, we saw how God uses the family in his plan of salvation.

Another fact we learn from the story of Israel is that God keeps perfect lists of His people and everything they do—and everything they *don't* do. We forget things, but God can remember everything!

Sometimes we do things that we like to hide. Then we imagine nobody knows, but we are only fooling ourselves. God

sees all, He knows all, and He never forgets. We should think hard about that.

But wait a minute! God also said, "Their sin I will remember no more" (Jeremiah 31:34). Can God remember and forget at the same time? Yes! When we remember our sins and tell Him we hate them, He forgives us. "The blood of Jesus Christ His Son cleanses us from all sin" (1 John 1:7). Then God doesn't remember our sins anymore.

over My people Israel.' " ³ Therefore all the elders of Israel came to the king at Hebron, and David made a covenant with them at Hebron before the LORD. And they anointed David king over Israel, according to the word of the LORD by Samuel.

⁴ And David and all Israel went to Jerusalem, which is Jebus, where the Jebusites were, the inhabitants of the land. ⁵ But the inhabitants of Jebus said to David, "You shall not come in here!" Nevertheless David took the stronghold of Zion (that is, the City of David). ⁶ Now David said, "Whoever attacks the Jebusites first shall be chief and captain." And Joab the son of Zeruiah went up first, and became chief. ⁷ Then David dwelt in the stronghold; therefore they called it the City of David. ⁸ And he built the city around it, from the Millo to the surrounding area. Joab repaired the rest of the city. ⁹ So David went on and became great, and the LORD of hosts was with him.

¹⁰ Now these were the heads of the mighty men whom David had, who strengthened themselves with him in his kingdom, with all Israel, to make him king, according to the word of the LORD concerning Israel.

¹¹ And this is the number of the mighty men whom David had: Jashobeam the son of a Hachmonite, chief of the captains; he had lifted up his spear against three hundred, killed by him at one time.

¹² After him was Eleazar the son of Dodo, the Ahohite, who was one of the three mighty men. ¹³ He was with David at Pasdammim. Now there the Philistines were gathered for battle, and there was a piece of ground full of barley. So the people fled from the Philistines. ¹⁴ But they stationed themselves in the middle of that field, defended it, and killed the Philistines. So the LORD brought about a great victory.

¹⁵ Now three of the thirty chief men went down to the rock to David, into the cave of Adullam; and the army of the Philistines encamped in the Valley of Rephaim. ¹⁶ David was then in the stronghold, and the garrison of the Philistines was then in Bethlehem. ¹⁷ And David said with longing, "Oh, that someone would give me a drink of water from the well of Bethlehem, which is by the gate!" ¹⁸ So the three broke through the camp of the Philistines, drew water from the well of Bethlehem that was by the gate, and took it and brought it to David. Nevertheless David would not drink it, but poured it out to the LORD. ¹⁹ And he said, "Far be it from me, O my God, that I should do this! Shall I drink the blood of these men who have put their lives in jeopardy? For at the risk of their lives they brought it." Therefore he would not drink it. These things were done by the three mighty men.

²⁰ Abishai the brother of Joab was chief of another three. He had lifted up his spear against three hundred men, killed them, and won a name among these three. ²¹ Of the three he was more honored than the other two men. Therefore he became their captain. However he did not attain to the first three.

²² Benaiah was the son of Jehoiada, the son of a valiant man from Kabzeel, who had done many deeds. He had killed two lion-like heroes of Moab. He also had gone down and killed a lion in the midst of a pit on a snowy day. ²³ And he killed an Egyptian, a man of great height, five cubits tall. In the Egyptian's hand there was a spear like a weaver's beam; and he went down to him with a staff, wrested the spear out of the Egyptian's hand, and killed him with his own spear. ²⁴ These things Benaiah the son of Jehoiada did, and won a name among three mighty men. ²⁵ Indeed he was more honored than the thirty, but he did not attain to the first three. And David appointed him over his guard.

²⁶ Also the mighty warriors were Asahel the brother of Joab, Elhanan the son of Dodo of Bethlehem, ²⁷ Shammoth the Harorite, Helez the Pelonite, ²⁸ Ira the son of Ikkesh the Tekoite, Abiezer the Anathothite, ²⁹ Sibbechai the Hushathite, Ilai the Ahohite, ³⁰ Maharai the Netophathite,

Heled the son of Baanah the Netophathite, 31 Ithai the son of Ribai of
Gibeah, of the sons of Benjamin, Benaiah the Pirathonite, 32 Hurai of the
brooks of Gaash, Abiel the Arbathite,
33 Azmaveth the Baharumite, Eliahba
the Shaalbonite, 34 the sons of Hashem
the Gizonite, Jonathan the son of Sha-
geh the Hararite, 35 Ahiam the son of
Sacar the Hararite, Eliphal the son of
Ur, 36 Hepher the Mecherathite, Ahijah
the Pelonite, 37 Hezro the Carmelite,
Naarai the son of Ezbai, 38 Joel the
brother of Nathan, Mibhar the son of
Hagri, 39 Zelek the Ammonite, Naharai
the Berothite (the armorbearer of Joab
the son of Zeruiah), 40 Ira the Ithrite,
Gareb the Ithrite, 41 Uriah the Hittite,
Zabad the son of Ahlai, 42 Adina the
son of Shiza the Reubenite (a chief of
the Reubenites) and thirty with him,
43 Hanan the son of Maachah, Joshaphat the Mithnite, 44 Uzzia the Ashte-
rathite, Shama and Jeiel the sons of
Hotham the Aroerite, 45 Jediael the son
of Shimri, and Joha his brother, the
Tizite, 46 Eliel the Mahavite, Jeribai and
Joshaviah the sons of Elnaam, Ithmah
the Moabite, 47 Eliel, Obed, and Jaasiel
the Mezobaite.

David's army

12 Now these *were* the men who
came to David at Ziklag while he was
still a fugitive from Saul the son of Kish;
and they *were* among the mighty men,
helpers in the war, 2 armed with bows,
using both the right hand and the left
in *hurling* stones and *shooting* arrows
with the bow. *They were* of Benjamin,
Saul's brethren.

3 The chief *was* Ahiezer, then Joash,
the sons of Shemaah the Gibeathite;
Jeziel and Pelet the sons of Azmaveth;
Berachah, and Jehu the Anathothite;
4 Ishmaiah the Gibeonite, a mighty
man among the thirty, and over the
thirty; Jeremiah, Jahaziel, Johanan,
and Jozabad the Gederathite; 5 Eluzai,
Jerimoth, Bealiah, Shemariah, and
Shephatiah the Haruphite; 6 Elkanah,
Jisshiah, Azarel, Joezer, and Jashobeam, the Korahites; 7 and Joelah and

Zebadiah the sons of Jeroham of Gedor.

8 *Some* Gadites joined David at the
stronghold in the wilderness, mighty
men of valor, men trained for battle,
who could handle shield and spear,
whose faces *were like* the faces of lions,
and *were* as swift as gazelles on the
mountains: 9 Ezer the first, Obadiah the
second, Eliab the third, 10 Mishmannah
the fourth, Jeremiah the fifth, 11 Attai
the sixth, Eliel the seventh, 12 Johanan
the eighth, Elzabad the ninth, 13 Jeremiah the tenth, and Machbanai the
eleventh. 14 These *were* from the sons
of Gad, captains of the army; the least
was over a hundred, and the greatest
was over a thousand. 15 These *are* the
ones who crossed the Jordan in the
first month, when it had overflowed all
its banks; and they put to flight all *those*
in the valleys, to the east and to the
west.

16 Then some of the sons of Benjamin and Judah came to David at the
stronghold. 17 And David went out to
meet them, and answered and said to
them, "If you have come peaceably
to me to help me, my heart will be
united with you; but if to betray me
to my enemies, since *there is* no wrong
in my hands, may the God of our fathers look and bring judgment."
18 Then the Spirit came upon Amasai,
chief of the captains, *and he said:*

> "*We are* yours, O David;
> We *are* on your side, O son of
>   Jesse!
> Peace, peace to you,
> And peace to your helpers!
> For your God helps you."

So David received them, and made
them captains of the troop.
19 And *some* from Manasseh defected to David when he was going
with the Philistines to battle against
Saul; but they did not help them, for
the lords of the Philistines sent him
away by agreement, saying, "He may
defect to his master Saul *and endanger*
our heads." 20 When he went to Ziklag,
those of Manasseh who defected to

him were Adnah, Jozabad, Jediael, Michael, Jozabad, Elihu, and Zillethai, captains of the thousands who *were* from Manasseh. 21 And they helped David against the bands *of raiders,* for they *were* all mighty men of valor, and they were captains in the army. 22 For at *that* time they came to David day by day to help him, until *it was* a great army, like the army of God.

23 Now these *were* the numbers of the divisions *that were* equipped for war, *and* came to David at Hebron to turn *over* the kingdom of Saul to him, according to the word of the LORD: 24 of the sons of Judah bearing shield and spear, six thousand eight hundred armed for war; 25 of the sons of Simeon, mighty men of valor fit for war, seven thousand one hundred; 26 of the sons of Levi four thousand six hundred; 27 Jehoiada, the leader of the Aaronites, and with him three thousand seven hundred; 28 Zadok, a young man, a valiant warrior, and from his father's house twenty-two captains; 29 of the sons of Benjamin, relatives of Saul, three thousand (until then the greatest part of them had remained loyal to the house of Saul); 30 of the sons of Ephraim twenty thousand eight hundred, mighty men of valor, famous men throughout their father's house; 31 of the half-tribe of Manasseh eighteen thousand, who were designated by name to come and make David king; 32 of the sons of Issachar who had understanding of the times, to know what Israel ought to do, their chiefs were two hundred; and all their brethren were at their command; 33 of Zebulun there were fifty thousand who went out to battle, expert in war with all weapons of war, stouthearted men who could keep ranks; 34 of Naphtali one thousand captains, and with them thirty-seven thousand with shield and spear; 35 of the Danites who could keep battle formation, twenty-eight thousand six hundred; 36 of Asher, those who could go out to war, able to keep battle formation, forty thousand; 37 of the Reubenites and the Gadites and the half-tribe of Manasseh,

from the other side of the Jordan, one hundred and twenty thousand armed for battle with every *kind* of weapon of war.

38 All these men of war, who could keep ranks, came to Hebron with a loyal heart, to make David king over all Israel; and all the rest of Israel *were* of one mind to make David king. 39 And they were there with David three days, eating and drinking, for their brethren had prepared for them. 40 Moreover those who were near to them, from as far away as Issachar and Zebulun and Naphtali, were bringing food on donkeys and camels, on mules and oxen—provisions of flour and cakes of figs and cakes of raisins, wine and oil and oxen and sheep abundantly, for *there was* joy in Israel.

David wants to bring back the ark

13 Then David consulted with the captains of thousands and hundreds, *and* with every leader. 2 And David said to all the assembly of Israel, "If *it seems* good to you, and if it is of the LORD our God, let us send out to our brethren everywhere *who are* left in all the land of Israel, and with them to the priests and Levites *who are* in their cities *and* their common-lands, that they may gather together to us; 3 and let us bring the ark of our God back to us, for we have not inquired at it since the days of Saul." 4 Then all the assembly said that they would do so, for the thing was right in the eyes of all the people.

5 So David gathered all Israel together, from Shihor in Egypt to as far as the entrance of Hamath, to bring the ark of God from Kirjath Jearim. 6 And David and all Israel went up to Baalah, to Kirjath Jearim, which belonged to Judah, to bring up from there the ark of God the LORD, who dwells *between* the cherubim, where *His* name is proclaimed. 7 So they carried the ark of God on a new cart from the house of Abinadab, and Uzza and Ahio drove the cart. 8 Then David and all Israel played *music* before God with

all *their* might, with singing, on harps, on stringed instruments, on tambourines, on cymbals, and with trumpets.

9 And when they came to Chidon's threshing floor, Uzza put out his hand to hold the ark, for the oxen stumbled. 10 Then the anger of the LORD was aroused against Uzza, and He struck him because he put his hand to the ark; and he died there before God. 11 And David became angry because of the LORD's outbreak against Uzza; therefore that place is called Perez Uzza to this day. 12 David was afraid of God that day, saying, "How can I bring the ark of God to me?"

13 So David would not move the ark with him into the City of David, but took it aside into the house of Obed-Edom the Gittite. 14 The ark of God remained with the family of Obed-Edom in his house three months. And the LORD blessed the house of Obed-Edom and all that he had.

David wins a battle

14 Now Hiram king of Tyre sent messengers to David, and cedar trees, with masons and carpenters, to build him a house. 2 So David knew that the LORD had established him as king over Israel, for his kingdom was highly exalted for the sake of His people Israel.

3 Then David took more wives in Jerusalem, and David begot more sons and daughters. 4 And these are the names of his children whom he had in Jerusalem: Shammua, Shobab, Nathan, Solomon, 5 Ibhar, Elishua, Elpelet, 6 Nogah, Nepheg, Japhia, 7 Elishama, Beeliada, and Eliphelet.

8 Now when the Philistines heard that David had been anointed king over all Israel, all the Philistines went up to search for David. And David heard *of it* and went out against them. 9 Then the Philistines went and made a raid on the Valley of Rephaim. 10 And David inquired of God, saying, "Shall I go up against the Philistines? Will You deliver them into my hand?"

The LORD said to him, "Go up, for I will deliver them into your hand."

Who Were the Philistines?

The Philistines (pronounced *fih-LIS-teens*) lived on the Mediterranean coast south of Israel. Their nation was one that Joshua had failed to conquer (see Joshua 13:2), and so they remained, causing trouble for Israel throughout their early history.

11 So they went up to Baal Perazim, and David defeated them there. Then David said, "God has broken through my enemies by my hand like a breakthrough of water." Therefore they called the name of that place Baal Perazim. 12 And when they left their gods there, David gave a commandment, and they were burned with fire.

13 Then the Philistines once again made a raid on the valley. 14 Therefore David inquired again of God, and God said to him, "You shall not go up after them; circle around them, and come upon them in front of the mulberry trees. 15 And it shall be, when you hear a sound of marching in the tops of the mulberry trees, then you shall go out to battle, for God has gone out before you to strike the camp of the Philistines." 16 So David did as God commanded him, and they drove back the army of the Philistines from Gibeon as far as Gezer. 17 Then the fame of David went out into all lands, and the LORD brought the fear of him upon all nations.

David brings the ark to Jerusalem

15 *David* built houses for himself in the City of David; and he prepared a place for the ark of God, and pitched a tent for it. 2 Then David said, "No one may carry the ark of God but the Levites, for the LORD has chosen them to carry the ark of God and to minister before Him forever." 3 And David gathered all Israel together at Jerusalem, to bring up the ark of the LORD to its place, which he had prepared for it. 4 Then David assembled the children of Aaron and the Levites: 5 of the sons of Kohath, Uriel the chief, and one hundred and twenty of his brethren; 6 of the sons of Merari, Asaiah the chief, and two hundred and twenty of his brethren; 7 of the sons of Gershom, Joel the chief, and one hundred and thirty of his brethren; 8 of the sons of Elizaphan, Shemaiah the chief, and two hundred of his brethren; 9 of the sons of Hebron, Eliel the chief, and eighty of his brethren; 10 of the sons of Uzziel, Amminadab the chief, and one hundred and twelve of his brethren.

11 And David called for Zadok and Abiathar the priests, and for the Levites: for Uriel, Asaiah, Joel, Shemaiah, Eliel, and Amminadab. 12 He said to them, "You *are* the heads of the fathers' *houses* of the Levites; sanctify yourselves, you and your brethren, that you may bring up the ark of the LORD God of Israel to *the place* I have prepared for it. 13 For because you *did* not *do it* the first *time,* the LORD our God broke out against us, because we did not consult Him about the proper order."

14 So the priests and the Levites sanctified themselves to bring up the ark of the LORD God of Israel. 15 And the children of the Levites bore the ark of God on their shoulders, by its poles, as Moses had commanded according to the word of the LORD.

16 Then David spoke to the leaders of the Levites to appoint their brethren *to be* the singers accompanied by instruments of music, stringed instruments, harps, and cymbals, by raising the voice with resounding joy. 17 So the Levites appointed Heman the son of Joel; and of his brethren, Asaph the son of Berechiah; and of their brethren, the sons of Merari, Ethan the son of Kushaiah; 18 and with them their brethren of the second *rank:* Zechariah, Ben, Jaaziel, Shemiramoth, Jehiel, Unni, Eliab, Benaiah, Maaseiah, Mattithiah, Elipheleh, Mikneiah, Obed-Edom, and Jeiel, the gatekeepers; 19 the singers, Heman, Asaph, and Ethan, *were* to sound the cymbals of

bronze; 20 Zechariah, Aziel, Shemiramoth, Jehiel, Unni, Eliab, Maaseiah, and Benaiah, with strings according to Alamoth; 21 Mattithiah, Elipheleh, Mikneiah, Obed-Edom, Jeiel, and Azaziah, to direct with harps on the Sheminith; 22 Chenaniah, leader of the Levites, was instructor *in charge of* the music, because he *was* skillful; 23 Berechiah and Elkanah *were* doorkeepers for the ark; 24 Shebaniah, Joshaphat, Nethanel, Amasai, Zechariah, Benaiah, and Eliezer, the priests, were to blow the trumpets before the ark of God; and Obed-Edom and Jehiah, doorkeepers for the ark.

25 So David, the elders of Israel, and the captains over thousands went to bring up the ark of the covenant of the LORD from the house of Obed-Edom with joy. 26 And so it was, when God helped the Levites who bore the ark of the covenant of the LORD, that they offered seven bulls and seven rams. 27 David was clothed with a robe of fine linen, as were all the Levites who bore the ark, the singers, and Chenaniah the music master *with* the singers. David also wore a linen ephod. 28 Thus all Israel brought up the ark of the covenant of the LORD with shouting and with the sound of the horn, with trumpets and with cymbals, making music with stringed instruments and harps.

29 And it happened, *as* the ark of the covenant of the LORD came to the City of David, that Michal, Saul's daughter, looked through a window and saw King David whirling and playing music; and she despised him in her heart.

David sings a song of thanksgiving

16 So they brought the ark of God, and set it in the midst of the tabernacle that David had erected for it. Then they offered burnt offerings and peace offerings before God. 2 And when David had finished offering the burnt offerings and the peace offerings, he blessed the people in the name of the LORD.

3 Then he distributed to everyone of Israel, both man and woman, to everyone a loaf of bread, a piece *of meat,* and a cake of raisins.

4 And he appointed some of the Levites to minister before the ark of the LORD, to commemorate, to thank, and to praise the LORD God of Israel: 5 Asaph the chief, and next to him Zechariah, *then* Jeiel, Shemiramoth, Jehiel, Mattithiah, Eliab, Benaiah, and Obed-Edom: Jeiel with stringed instruments and harps, but Asaph made music with cymbals; 6 Benaiah and Jahaziel the priests regularly *blew* the trumpets before the ark of the covenant of God.

7 On that day David first delivered *this psalm* into the hand of Asaph and his brethren, to thank the LORD:

8 Oh, give thanks to the LORD!
Call upon His name;
Make known His deeds among
the peoples!
9 Sing to Him, sing psalms to Him;
Talk of all His wondrous works!
10 Glory in His holy name;
Let the hearts of those rejoice
who seek the LORD!

⚒ DIGGING IN

16:5, 6 Music in Old Testament Times Music played a large part in Old Testament worship. You can read in Exodus 15 how Miriam and the other women sang before the Lord. The earliest song in the Bible is the song of Moses in the same chapter. Later, there was music at banquets, feasts, and at the crowning of kings. The Hebrew people were so musical that even the king of Assyria commanded Jewish musicians to play before him.

King David brought music into the Jewish temple service with a choir and orchestra of four thousand members. Asaph, Heman, and Jeduthun (pronounced *AY-saf, HE-man,* and *je-DEW-thun)* helped David set up this orchestra and choir. The psalms were written for singing.

At the end of Old Testament times, a Greek scholar wrote that Hebrew female singers were the most musical in the world.

Some musical instruments used were bagpipes, trumpets, bells, flutes, harps, drums, and tambourines.

These musical instruments—the harp, the cymbals, and the trumpet—were among those used in early worship services.

11 Seek the LORD and His strength;
   Seek His face evermore!
12 Remember His marvelous works
   which He has done,
   His wonders, and the judgments
   of His mouth,
13 O seed of Israel His servant,
   You children of Jacob, His
   chosen ones!

14 He *is* the LORD our God;
   His judgments *are* in all the
   earth.
15 Remember His covenant
   forever,
   The word which He
   commanded, for a thousand
   generations,
16 *The covenant which* He made
   with Abraham,
   And His oath to Isaac,
17 And confirmed it to Jacob for a
   statute,
   To Israel *for* an everlasting
   covenant,
18 Saying, "To you I will give the
   land of Canaan
   As the allotment of your
   inheritance,"
19 When you were few in number,
   Indeed very few, and strangers
   in it.

20 When they went from one
   nation to another,
   And from *one* kingdom to
   another people,
21 He permitted no man to do
   them wrong;
   Yes, He rebuked kings for their
   sakes,
22 *Saying,* "Do not touch My
   anointed ones,
   And do My prophets no harm."

23 Sing to the LORD, all the earth;
   Proclaim the good news of His
   salvation from day to day.
24 Declare His glory among the
   nations,
   His wonders among all peoples.

25 For the LORD *is* great and greatly
   to be praised;

He *is* also to be feared above
   all gods.
26 For all the gods of the peoples
   are idols,
   But the LORD made the heavens.
27 Honor and majesty *are* before
   Him;
   Strength and gladness are in His
   place.

28 Give to the LORD, O families of
   the peoples,
   Give to the LORD glory and
   strength.
29 Give to the LORD the glory *due*
   His name;
   Bring an offering, and come
   before Him.
   Oh, worship the LORD in the
   beauty of holiness!
30 Tremble before Him, all the
   earth.
   The world also is firmly
   established,
   It shall not be moved.

31 Let the heavens rejoice, and let
   the earth be glad;
   And let them say among the
   nations, "The LORD reigns."
32 Let the sea roar, and all its
   fullness;
   Let the field rejoice, and all that
   is in it.
33 Then the trees of the woods shall
   rejoice before the LORD,
   For He is coming to judge the
   earth.

34 Oh, give thanks to the LORD, for
   He is good!
   For His mercy *endures* forever.
35 And say, "Save us, O God of
   our salvation;
   Gather us together, and deliver
   us from the Gentiles,
   To give thanks to Your holy
   name,
   To triumph in Your praise."

36 Blessed *be* the LORD God of
   Israel
   From everlasting to
   everlasting!

And all the people said, "Amen!" and praised the LORD.

37 So he left Asaph and his brothers there before the ark of the covenant of the LORD to minister before the ark regularly, as every day's work required; 38 and Obed-Edom with his sixty-eight brethren, including Obed-Edom the son of Jeduthun, and Hosah, *to be* gatekeepers; 39 and Zadok the priest and his brethren the priests, before the tabernacle of the LORD at the high place that *was* at Gibeon, 40 to offer burnt offerings to the LORD on the **altar of burnt offering** regularly morning and evening, and *to do* according to all that is written in the Law of the LORD which He commanded Israel; 41 and with them Heman and Jeduthun and the rest who were chosen, who *were* designated by name, to give thanks to the LORD, because His mercy *endures* forever; 42 and with them Heman and Jeduthun, to sound aloud with trumpets and cymbals and the musical instruments of God. Now the sons of Jeduthun *were* gatekeepers.

43 Then all the people departed, every man to his house; and David returned to bless his house.

God makes a promise to David

17 Now it came to pass, when David was dwelling in his house, that David said to Nathan the prophet, "See now, I dwell in a house of cedar, but the ark of the covenant of the LORD *is* under tent curtains."

2 Then Nathan said to David, "Do all that *is* in your heart, for God *is* with you."

3 But it happened that night that the word of God came to Nathan, saying, 4 "Go and tell My servant David, 'Thus says the LORD: "You shall not build Me a house to dwell in. 5 For I have not dwelt in a house since the time that I brought up Israel, even to this day, but have gone from tent to tent, and from *one* tabernacle *to another*. 6 Wherever I have moved about with all Israel, have I ever spoken a word to any of the judges of Israel, whom I commanded to shepherd My people, saying, 'Why have you not built Me a house of cedar?' " ' 7 Now therefore, thus shall you say to My servant David, 'Thus says the LORD of hosts: "I took you from the sheepfold, from following the sheep, to be ruler over My people Israel. 8 And I have been with you wherever you have gone, and have cut off all your enemies from before you, and have made you a name like the name of the great men who *are* on the earth. 9 Moreover I will appoint a place for My people Israel, and will plant them, that they may dwell in a place of their own and move no more; nor shall the sons of wickedness oppress them anymore, as previously, 10 since the time that I commanded judges *to be* over My people Israel. Also I will subdue all your enemies. Furthermore I tell you that the LORD will build you a house. 11 And it shall be, when your days are fulfilled, when you must go *to be* with your fathers, that I will set up your seed after you, who will be of your sons; and I will establish his kingdom. 12 He shall build Me a house, and I will establish his throne forever. 13 I will be his Father, and he shall be My son; and I will not take My mercy away from him, as I took *it* from *him* who was before you. 14 And I will establish him in My house and in My kingdom forever; and his throne shall be established forever." ' "

15 According to all these words and

WORDFINDER

16:40 Altar of Burnt Offering   An altar about 90 by 90 by 54 inches high, used for burnt offerings. The people brought animals to the altar. The animals were killed, then sacrificed by fire to pay for the people's sins.

according to all this vision, so Nathan spoke to David.

16 Then King David went in and sat before the LORD; and he said: "Who *am* I, O LORD God? And what is my house, that You have brought me this far? 17 And *yet* this was a small thing in Your sight, O God; and You have *also* spoken of Your servant's house for a great while to come, and have regarded me according to the rank of a man of high degree, O LORD God. 18 What more can David *say* to You for the honor of Your servant? For You know Your servant. 19 O LORD, for Your servant's sake, and according to Your own heart, You have done all this greatness, in making known all these great things. 20 O LORD, *there is* none like You, nor *is there any* God besides You, according to all that *we* have heard with our ears. 21 And who *is* like Your people Israel, the one nation on the earth whom God went to redeem for Himself *as* a people—to make for Yourself a name by great and awesome deeds, by driving out nations from before Your people whom You redeemed from Egypt? 22 For You have made Your people Israel Your very own people forever; and You, LORD, have become their God.

23 "And now, O LORD, the word which You have spoken concerning Your servant and concerning his house, *let it* be established forever, and do as You have said. 24 So let it be established, that Your name may be magnified forever, saying, 'The LORD of hosts, the God of Israel, *is* Israel's God.' And let the house of Your servant David be established before You. 25 For You, O my God, have revealed to Your servant that You will build him a house. Therefore Your servant has found it *in his heart* to pray before You. 26 And now, LORD, You are God, and have promised this goodness to Your servant. 27 Now You have been pleased to bless the house of Your servant, that it may continue before You forever; for You have blessed it, O LORD, and *it shall be* blessed forever."

David's kingdom increases

18 After this it came to pass that David attacked the Philistines, subdued them, and took Gath and its towns from the hand of the Philistines. 2 Then he defeated Moab, and the Moabites became David's servants, *and* brought tribute.

3 And David defeated Hadadezer king of Zobah *as far as* Hamath, as he went to establish his power by the River Euphrates. 4 David took from him one thousand chariots, seven thousand horsemen, and twenty thousand foot soldiers. Also David hamstrung all the chariot *horses,* except that he spared enough of them for one hundred chariots.

5 When the Syrians of Damascus came to help Hadadezer king of Zobah, David killed twenty-two thousand of the Syrians. 6 Then David put *garrisons* in Syria of Damascus; and the Syrians became David's servants, *and* brought tribute. So the LORD preserved David wherever he went. 7 And David took the shields of gold that *were* on the servants of Hadadezer, and brought them to Jerusalem. 8 Also from Tibhath and from Chun, cities of Hadadezer, David brought a large amount of bronze, with which Solomon made the bronze Sea, the pillars, and the articles of bronze.

9 Now when Tou king of Hamath heard that David had defeated all the army of Hadadezer king of Zobah, 10 he sent Hadoram his son to King David, to greet him and bless him, because he had fought against Hadadezer and defeated him (for Hadadezer had been at war with Tou); and *Hadoram brought with him* all kinds of articles of gold, silver, and bronze. 11 King David also dedicated these to the LORD, along with the silver and gold that he had brought from all *these* nations—from Edom, from Moab, from the people of Ammon, from the Philistines, and from Amalek.

12 Moreover Abishai the son of Zeruiah killed eighteen thousand Edomites in the Valley of Salt. 13 He also

put garrisons in Edom, and all the Edomites became David's servants. And the LORD preserved David wherever he went.

14 So David reigned over all Israel, and administered judgment and justice to all his people. 15 Joab the son of Zeruiah *was* over the army; Jehoshaphat the son of Ahilud *was* recorder; 16 Zadok the son of Ahitub and Abimelech the son of Abiathar *were* the priests; Shavsha *was* the scribe; 17 Benaiah the son of Jehoiada *was* over the Cherethites and the Pelethites; and David's sons *were* chief ministers at the king's side.

David defeats the Syrians

19 It happened after this that Nahash the king of the people of Ammon died, and his son reigned in his place. 2 Then David said, "I will show kindness to Hanun the son of Nahash, because his father showed kindness to me." So David sent messengers to comfort him concerning his father. And David's servants came to Hanun in the land of the people of Ammon to comfort him.

3 And the princes of the people of Ammon said to Hanun, "Do you think that David really honors your father because he has sent comforters to you? Did his servants not come to you to search and to overthrow and to spy out the land?"

4 Therefore Hanun took David's servants, shaved them, and cut off their garments in the middle, at their buttocks, and sent them away. 5 Then *some* went and told David about the men; and he sent to meet them, because the men were greatly ashamed. And the king said, "Wait at Jericho until your beards have grown, and *then* return."

6 When the people of Ammon saw that they had made themselves repulsive to David, Hanun and the people of Ammon sent a thousand talents of silver to hire for themselves chariots and horsemen from Mesopotamia, from Syrian Maacah, and from Zobah.

7 So they hired for themselves thirty-two thousand chariots, with the king of Maacah and his people, who came and encamped before Medeba. Also the people of Ammon gathered together from their cities, and came to battle.

8 Now when David heard *of it,* he sent Joab and all the army of the mighty men. 9 Then the people of Ammon came out and put themselves in battle array before the gate of the city, and the kings who had come *were* by themselves in the field.

10 When Joab saw that the battle line was against him before and behind, he chose some of Israel's best, and put *them* in battle array against the Syrians. 11 And the rest of the people he put under the command of Abishai his brother, and they set *themselves* in battle array against the people of Ammon. 12 Then he said, "If the Syrians are too strong for me, then you shall help me; but if the people of Ammon are too strong for you, then I will help you. 13 Be of good courage, and let us be strong for our people and for the cities of our God. And may the LORD do *what is* good in His sight."

14 So Joab and the people who *were* with him drew near for the battle against the Syrians, and they fled before him. 15 When the people of Ammon saw that the Syrians were fleeing, they also fled before Abishai his brother, and entered the city. So Joab went to Jerusalem.

16 Now when the Syrians saw that they had been defeated by Israel, they sent messengers and brought the Syrians who were beyond the River, and Shophach the commander of Hadadezer's army *went* before them. 17 When it was told David, he gathered all Israel, crossed over the Jordan and came upon them, and set up in battle array against them. So when David had set up in *battle* array against the Syrians, they fought with him. 18 Then the Syrians fled before Israel; and David killed seven thousand charioteers and forty thousand foot soldiers of the Syrians, and killed Shophach the com-

mander of the army. ¹⁹ And when the servants of Hadadezer saw that they were defeated by Israel, they made peace with David and became his servants. So the Syrians were not willing to help the people of Ammon anymore.

David's men kill many giants

20 It happened in the spring of the year, at the time kings go out *to battle*, that Joab led out the armed forces and ravaged the country of the people of Ammon, and came and besieged Rabbah. But David stayed at Jerusalem. And Joab defeated Rabbah and overthrew it. ² Then David took their king's crown from his head, and found it to weigh a talent of gold, and *there were* precious stones in it. And it was set on David's head. Also he brought out the spoil of the city in great abundance. ³ And he brought out the people who *were* in it, and put *them* to work with saws, with iron picks, and with axes. So David did to all the cities of the people of Ammon. Then David and all the people returned *to* Jerusalem.

⁴ Now it happened afterward that war broke out at Gezer with the Philistines, at which time Sibbechai the Hushathite killed Sippai, *who was one* of the sons of the giant. And they were subdued.

⁵ Again there was war with the Philistines, and Elhanan the son of Jair killed Lahmi the brother of Goliath the Gittite, the shaft of whose spear *was* like a weaver's beam.

⁶ Yet again there was war at Gath, where there was a man of *great* stature, with twenty-four fingers and toes, six *on each hand* and six *on each foot;* and he also was born to the giant. ⁷ So when he defied Israel, Jonathan the son of Shimea, David's brother, killed him.

⁸ These were born to the giant in Gath, and they fell by the hand of David and by the hand of his servants.

David builds an altar to God

21 Now **Satan** stood up against Israel, and moved David to number Israel. ² So David said to Joab and to the leaders of the people, "Go, number Israel from Beersheba to Dan, and bring the number of them to me that I may know *it.*"

³ And Joab answered, "May the LORD make His people a hundred times more than they are. But, my lord the king, *are* they not all my lord's servants? Why then does my lord require this thing? Why should he be a cause of guilt in Israel?"

⁴ Nevertheless the king's word prevailed against Joab. Therefore Joab departed and went throughout all Israel and came to Jerusalem. ⁵ Then Joab gave the sum of the number of the people to David. All Israel *had* one million one hundred thousand men who drew the sword, and Judah *had* four hundred and seventy thousand men who drew the sword. ⁶ But he did not count Levi and Benjamin among them, for the king's word was abominable to Joab.

⁷ And God was displeased with this thing; therefore He struck Israel. ⁸ So David said to God, "I have sinned greatly, because I have done this thing; but now, I pray, take away the iniquity of Your servant, for I have done very foolishly."

⁹ Then the LORD spoke to Gad, David's seer, saying, ¹⁰ "Go and tell David, saying, 'Thus says the LORD: "I offer you three *things;* choose one of them for yourself, that I may do *it* to you."'"

¹¹ So Gad came to David and said to him, "Thus says the LORD: 'Choose

---

WORDFINDER ════════════════════════════

21:1 Satan Pronounced *SAY-tun.* The personal name of the Devil. The name means "Adversary" or "Enemy." Satan is the chief spiritual enemy of God. He is an angel who rebelled against the Lord.

What King David Learned

God made me succeed at everything I tried. But as time went by, I began to think I succeeded because I was so clever. I had a large army, and I defeated all my enemies.

Just how large was my army, anyway? I was determined to find out. By knowing the number of my troops, I could tell if we were strong enough to defeat any new enemy.

But the Lord told me I was wrong. Why?

I was wrong in numbering my troops because God wanted me to live the way I did when I first became king. God wanted me to trust *Him*, not *numbers*. I forgot it was always the Lord who won our battles, not really our army. That turned out to be a costly lesson, as you can read for yourself.

for yourself, 12 either three years of famine, or three months to be defeated by your foes with the sword of your enemies overtaking *you,* or else for three days the sword of the LORD—the plague in the land, with the angel of the LORD destroying throughout all the territory of Israel.' Now consider what answer I should take back to Him who sent me."

13 And David said to Gad, "I am in great distress. Please let me fall into the hand of the LORD, for His mercies *are* very great; but do not let me fall into the hand of man."

14 So the LORD sent a plague upon Israel, and seventy thousand men of Israel fell. 15 And God sent an **angel** to Jerusalem to destroy it. As he was destroying, the LORD looked and relented of the disaster, and said to the angel who was destroying, "It is enough; now restrain your hand." And the angel of the LORD stood by the threshing floor of Ornan the Jebusite.

16 Then David lifted his eyes and saw the angel of the LORD standing between earth and heaven, having in his hand a drawn sword stretched out over Jerusalem. So David and the elders, clothed in sackcloth, fell on their faces. 17 And David said to God, "Was it not I who commanded the people to be numbered? I am the one who has sinned and done evil indeed; but these sheep, what have they done? Let Your hand, I pray, O LORD my God, be against me and my father's house, but not against Your people that they should be plagued."

18 Therefore, the angel of the LORD commanded Gad to say to David that David should go and erect an altar to the LORD on the threshing floor of Ornan the Jebusite. 19 So David went up at the word of Gad, which he had spoken in the name of the LORD. 20 Now Ornan turned and saw the angel; and his four sons *who were* with him hid themselves, but Ornan continued threshing wheat. 21 So David came to Ornan, and Ornan looked and saw David. And he went out from the threshing floor, and bowed before David with *his* face to the ground. 22 Then David said to Ornan, "Grant me the place

🌐 WORDFINDER

21:15 Angel Means "messenger." The messenger is usually from heaven, but sometimes the messenger is human. For example, Malachi, the name of the Old Testament prophet, means "my angel" or "my messenger."

of *this* threshing floor, that I may build an altar on it to the LORD. You shall grant it to me at the full price, that the plague may be withdrawn from the people."

23 But Ornan said to David, "Take *it* to yourself, and let my lord the king do *what is* good in his eyes. Look, I *also* give *you* the oxen for burnt offerings, the threshing implements for wood, and the wheat for the grain offering; I give *it* all."

24 Then King David said to Ornan, "No, but I will surely buy *it* for the full price, for I will not take what is yours for the LORD, nor offer burnt offerings with *that which* costs *me* nothing." 25 So David gave Ornan six hundred shekels of gold by weight for the place. 26 And David built there an altar to the LORD, and offered burnt offerings and peace offerings, and called on the LORD; and He answered him from heaven by fire on the altar of burnt offering.

27 So the LORD commanded the angel, and he returned his sword to its sheath.

28 At that time, when David saw that the LORD had answered him on the threshing floor of Ornan the Jebusite, he sacrificed there. 29 For the tabernacle of the LORD and the altar of the burnt offering, which Moses had made in the wilderness, *were* at that time at the high place in Gibeon. 30 But David could not go before it to inquire of God, for he was afraid of the sword of the angel of the LORD.

David prepares to build the temple

22 Then David said, "This *is* the house of the LORD God, and this *is* the altar of burnt offering for Israel."

2 So David commanded to gather the aliens who *were* in the land of Israel; and he appointed masons to cut hewn stones to build the house of God. 3 And David prepared iron in abundance for the nails of the doors of the gates and for the joints, and bronze in abundance beyond measure, 4 and cedar trees in abundance; for the Sidonians and those from Tyre brought much cedar wood to David.

5 Now David said, "Solomon my son *is* young and inexperienced, and the house to be built for the LORD *must be* exceedingly magnificent, famous and glorious throughout all countries. I will now make preparation for it." So David made abundant preparations before his death.

6 Then he called for his son Solomon, and charged him to build a house for the LORD God of Israel. 7 And David said to Solomon: "My son, as for me, it was in my mind to build a house to the name of the LORD my God; 8 but the word of the LORD came to me, saying, 'You have shed much blood and have made great wars; you shall not build a house for My name, because you have shed much blood on the earth in My sight. 9 Behold, a son shall be born to you, who shall be a man of rest; and I will give him rest from all his enemies all around. His name shall be Solomon, for I will give peace and quietness to Israel in his days. 10 He shall build a house for My name, and he shall be My son, and I *will be* his Father; and I will establish the throne of his kingdom over Israel forever.' 11 Now, my son, may the LORD be with you; and may you prosper, and build the house of the LORD your God, as He has said to you. 12 Only may the LORD give you wisdom and understanding, and give you charge concerning Israel, that you may keep the law of the LORD your God. 13 Then you will prosper, if you take care to fulfill the statutes and judgments with which the LORD charged Moses concerning Israel. Be strong and of good courage; do not fear nor be dismayed. 14 Indeed I have taken much trouble to prepare for the house of the LORD one hundred thousand talents of gold and one million talents of silver, and bronze and iron beyond measure, for it is so abundant. I have prepared timber and stone also, and you may add to them. 15 Moreover *there are* workmen with you in

abundance: woodsmen and stone-cutters, and all types of skillful men for every kind of work. 16 Of gold and silver and bronze and iron *there is* no limit. Arise and begin working, and the LORD be with you."

17 David also commanded all the leaders of Israel to help Solomon his son, *saying,* 18 "*Is* not the LORD your God with you? And has He *not* given you rest on every side? For He has given the inhabitants of the land into my hand, and the land is subdued before the LORD and before His people. 19 Now set your heart and your soul to seek the LORD your God. Therefore arise and build the sanctuary of the LORD God, to bring the ark of the covenant of the LORD and the holy articles of God into the house that is to be built for the name of the LORD."

The Levites are given instructions

23 So when David was old and full of days, he made his son Solomon king over Israel.

2 And he gathered together all the leaders of Israel, with the priests and the Levites. 3 Now the Levites were numbered from the age of thirty years and above; and the number of individual males was thirty-eight thousand. 4 Of these, twenty-four thousand *were* to look after the work of the house of the LORD, six thousand *were* officers and judges, 5 four thousand *were* gatekeepers, and four thousand praised the LORD with *musical* instruments, "which I made," *said David,* "for giving praise."

6 Also David separated them into divisions among the sons of Levi: Gershon, Kohath, and Merari.

7 Of the Gershonites: Laadan and Shimei. 8 The sons of Laadan: the first Jehiel, then Zetham and Joel—three *in all.* 9 The sons of Shimei: Shelomith, Haziel, and Haran—three *in all.* These were the heads of the fathers' *houses* of Laadan. 10 And the sons of Shimei: Jahath, Zina, Jeush, and Beriah. These *were* the four sons of Shimei. 11 Jahath was the first and Zizah the second. But Jeush and Beriah did not have many sons; therefore they were assigned as one father's house.

12 The sons of Kohath: Amram, Izhar, Hebron, and Uzziel—four *in all.* 13 The sons of Amram: Aaron and Moses; and Aaron was set apart, he and his sons forever, that he should sanctify the most holy things, to burn incense before the LORD, to minister to Him, and to give the blessing in His name forever. 14 Now the sons of Moses the man of God were reckoned to the tribe of Levi. 15 The sons of Moses *were* Gershon and Eliezer. 16 Of the sons of Gershon, Shebuel *was* the first. 17 Of the descendants of Eliezer, Rehabiah was the first. And Eliezer had no other sons, but the sons of Rehabiah were very many. 18 Of the sons of Izhar, Shelomith *was* the first. 19 Of the sons of Hebron, Jeriah *was* the first, Amariah the second, Jahaziel the third, and Jekameam the fourth. 20 Of the sons of Uzziel, Michah *was* the first and Jesshiah the second.

21 The sons of Merari *were* Mahli and Mushi. The sons of Mahli *were* Eleazar and Kish. 22 And Eleazar died, and had no sons, but only daughters; and their brethren, the sons of Kish, took them *as wives.* 23 The sons of Mushi *were* Mahli, Eder, and Jeremoth—three *in all.*

24 These *were* the sons of Levi by their fathers' houses—the heads of the fathers' *houses* as they were counted individually by the number of their names, who did the work for the service of the house of the LORD, from the age of twenty years and above.

25 For David said, "The LORD God of Israel has given rest to His people, that they may dwell in Jerusalem forever"; 26 and also to the Levites, "They shall no longer carry the tabernacle, or any of the articles for its service." 27 For by the last words of David the Levites *were* numbered from twenty years old and above; 28 because their duty *was* to help the sons of Aaron in the service of the house of the LORD, in the courts and in the chambers, in the purifying of all holy things and the work of the service of

the house of God, 29 both with the showbread and the fine flour for the grain offering, with the unleavened cakes and *what is baked in* the pan, with what is mixed and with all kinds of measures and sizes; 30 to stand every morning to thank and praise the LORD, and likewise at evening; 31 and at every presentation of a burnt offering to the LORD on the Sabbaths and on the New Moons and on the set feasts, by number according to the ordinance governing them, regularly before the LORD; 32 and that they should attend to the needs of the tabernacle of meeting, the needs of the holy *place,* and the needs of the sons of Aaron their brethren in the work of the house of the LORD.

The priests are divided

24 Now *these are* the divisions of the sons of Aaron. The sons of Aaron *were* Nadab, Abihu, Eleazar, and Ithamar. 2 And Nadab and Abihu died before their father, and had no children; therefore Eleazar and Ithamar ministered as priests. 3 Then David with Zadok of the sons of Eleazar, and Ahimelech of the sons of Ithamar, divided them according to the schedule of their service.

4 There were more leaders found of the sons of Eleazar than of the sons of Ithamar, and *thus* they were divided. Among the sons of Eleazar *were* sixteen heads of *their* fathers' houses, and eight heads of their fathers' houses among the sons of Ithamar. 5 Thus they were divided by lot, one group as another, for there were officials of the sanctuary and officials *of the house* of God, from the sons of Eleazar and from the sons of Ithamar. 6 And the scribe, Shemaiah the son of Nethanel, *one of* the Levites, wrote them down before the king, the leaders, Zadok the priest, Ahimelech the son of Abiathar, and the heads of the fathers' *houses* of the priests and Levites, one father's house taken for Eleazar and *one* for Ithamar.

7 Now the first lot fell to Jehoiarib,

the second to Jedaiah, 8 the third to Harim, the fourth to Seorim, 9 the fifth to Malchijah, the sixth to Mijamin, 10 the seventh to Hakkoz, the eighth to Abijah, 11 the ninth to Jeshua, the tenth to Shecaniah, 12 the eleventh to Eliashib, the twelfth to Jakim, 13 the thirteenth to Huppah, the fourteenth to Jeshebeab, 14 the fifteenth to Bilgah, the sixteenth to Immer, 15 the seventeenth to Hezir, the eighteenth to Happizzez, 16 the nineteenth to Pethahiah, the twentieth to Jehezekel, 17 the twenty-first to Jachin, the twenty-second to Gamul, 18 the twenty-third to Delaiah, the twenty-fourth to Maaziah.

19 This *was* the schedule of their service for coming into the house of the LORD according to their ordinance by the hand of Aaron their father, as the LORD God of Israel had commanded him.

20 And the rest of the sons of Levi: of the sons of Amram, Shubael; of the sons of Shubael, Jehdeiah. 21 Concerning Rehabiah, of the sons of Rehabiah, the first *was* Isshiah. 22 Of the Izharites, Shelomoth; of the sons of Shelomoth, Jahath. 23 Of the sons *of Hebron,* Jeriah *was the first,* Amariah the second, Jahaziel the third, *and* Jekameam the fourth. 24 *Of* the sons of Uzziel, Michah; of the sons of Michah, Shamir. 25 The brother of Michah, Isshiah; of the sons of Isshiah, Zechariah. 26 The sons of Merari *were* Mahli and Mushi; the son of Jaaziah, Beno. 27 The sons of Merari by Jaaziah *were* Beno, Shoham, Zaccur, and Ibri. 28 Of Mahli: Eleazar, who had no sons. 29 Of Kish: the son of Kish, Jerahmeel.

30 Also the sons of Mushi *were* Mahli, Eder, and Jerimoth. These *were* the sons of the Levites according to their fathers' houses.

31 These also cast lots just as their brothers the sons of Aaron did, in the presence of King David, Zadok, Ahimelech, and the heads of the fathers' *houses* of the priests and Levites. The chief fathers *did* just as their younger brethren.

The musicians are divided

25 Moreover David and the captains of the army separated for the service *some* of the sons of Asaph, of Heman, and of Jeduthun, who *should* prophesy with harps, stringed instruments, and cymbals. And the number of the skilled men performing their service was: 2 Of the sons of Asaph: Zaccur, Joseph, Nethaniah, and Asharelah; the sons of Asaph *were* under the direction of Asaph, who prophesied according to the order of the king. 3 Of Jeduthun, the sons of Jeduthun: Gedaliah, Zeri, Jeshaiah, Shimei, Hashabiah, and Mattithiah, six, under the direction of their father Jeduthun, who prophesied with a harp to give thanks and to praise the LORD. 4 Of Heman, the sons of Heman: Bukkiah, Mattaniah, Uzziel, Shebuel, Jerimoth, Hananiah, Hanani, Eliathah, Giddalti, Romamti-Ezer, Joshbekashah, Mallothi, Hothir, *and* Mahazioth. 5 All these *were* the sons of Heman the king's seer in the words of God, to exalt his horn. For God gave Heman fourteen sons and three daughters.

6 All these *were* under the direction of their father for the music *in* the house of the LORD, with cymbals, stringed instruments, and harps, for the service of the house of God. Asaph, Jeduthun, and Heman *were* under the authority of the king. 7 So the number of them, with their brethren who were instructed in the songs of the LORD, all who were skillful, *was* two hundred and eighty-eight.

8 And they cast lots for their duty, the small as well as the great, the teacher with the student.

9 Now the first lot for Asaph came out for Joseph; the second for Gedaliah, him with his brethren and sons, twelve; 10 the third for Zaccur, his sons and his brethren, twelve; 11 the fourth for Jizri, his sons and his brethren, twelve; 12 the fifth for Nethaniah, his sons and his brethren, twelve; 13 the sixth for Bukkiah, his sons and his brethren, twelve; 14 the seventh for Jesharelah, his sons and his brethren, twelve; 15 the eighth for Jeshaiah, his sons and his brethren, twelve; 16 the ninth for Mattaniah, his sons and his brethren, twelve; 17 the tenth for Shimei, his sons and his brethren, twelve; 18 the eleventh for Azarel, his sons and his brethren, twelve; 19 the twelfth for Hashabiah, his sons and his brethren, twelve; 20 the thirteenth for Shubael, his sons and his brethren, twelve; 21 the fourteenth for Mattithiah, his sons and his brethren, twelve; 22 the fifteenth for Jeremoth, his sons and his brethren, twelve; 23 the sixteenth for Hananiah, his sons and his brethren, twelve; 24 the seventeenth for Joshbekashah, his sons and his brethren, twelve; 25 the eighteenth for Hanani, his sons and his brethren, twelve; 26 the nineteenth for Mallothi, his sons and his brethren, twelve; 27 the twentieth for Eliathah, his sons and his brethren, twelve; 28 the twenty-first for Hothir, his sons and his brethren, twelve; 29 the twenty-second for Giddalti, his sons and his brethren, twelve; 30 the twenty-third for Mahazioth, his sons and his brethren, twelve; 31 the twenty-fourth for Romamti-Ezer, his sons and his brethren, twelve.

A list of gatekeepers and overseers

26 Concerning the divisions of the gatekeepers: of the Korahites, Meshelemiah the son of Kore, of the sons of Asaph. 2 And the sons of Meshelemiah *were* Zechariah the firstborn, Jediael the second, Zebadiah the third, Jathniel the fourth, 3 Elam the fifth, Jehohanan the sixth, Eliehoenai the seventh.

4 Moreover the sons of Obed-Edom *were* Shemaiah the firstborn, Jehozabad the second, Joah the third, Sacar the fourth, Nethanel the fifth, 5 Ammiel the sixth, Issachar the seventh, Peulthai the eighth; for God blessed him.

6 Also to Shemaiah his son were sons born who governed their fathers' houses, because they *were* men of great ability. 7 The sons of Shemaiah *were* Othni, Rephael, Obed, and Elza-

bad, whose brothers Elihu and Semachiah *were* able men.

8 All these *were* of the sons of Obed-Edom, they and their sons and their brethren, able men with strength for the work: sixty-two of Obed-Edom.

9 And Meshelemiah had sons and brethren, eighteen able men.

10 Also Hosah, of the children of Merari, had sons: Shimri the first (for *though* he was not the firstborn, his father made him the first), 11 Hilkiah the second, Tebaliah the third, Zechariah the fourth; all the sons and brethren of Hosah *were* thirteen.

12 Among these *were* the divisions of the gatekeepers, among the chief men, *having* duties just like their brethren, to serve in the house of the LORD. 13 And they cast lots for each gate, the small as well as the great, according to their father's house. 14 The lot for the East *Gate* fell to Shelemiah. Then they cast lots *for* his son Zechariah, a wise counselor, and his lot came out for the North Gate; 15 to Obed-Edom the South Gate, and to his sons the storehouse. 16 To Shuppim and Hosah *the lot came out* for the West Gate, with the Shallecheth Gate on the ascending highway—watchman opposite watchman. 17 On the east were six Levites, on the north four each day, on the south four each day, and for the storehouse two by two. 18 As for the Parbar on the west, *there were* four on the highway *and* two at the Parbar. 19 These were the divisions of the gatekeepers among the sons of Korah and among the sons of Merari.

20 Of the Levites, Ahijah *was* over the treasuries of the house of God and over the treasuries of the dedicated things. 21 The sons of Laadan, the descendants of the Gershonites of Laadan, heads of their fathers' *houses,* of Laadan the Gershonite: Jehieli. 22 The sons of Jehieli, Zetham and Joel his brother, *were* over the treasuries of the house of the LORD. 23 Of the Amramites, the Izharites, the Hebronites, and the Uzzielites: 24 Shebuel the son of Gershom, the son of Moses, *was* overseer of the treasuries. 25 And his breth-

ren by Eliezer *were* Rehabiah his son, Jeshaiah his son, Joram his son, Zichri his son, and Shelomith his son.

26 This Shelomith and his brethren *were* over all the treasuries of the dedicated things which King David and the heads of fathers' *houses,* the captains over thousands and hundreds, and the captains of the army, had dedicated. 27 Some of the spoils won in battles they dedicated to maintain the house of the LORD. 28 And all that Samuel the seer, Saul the son of Kish, Abner the son of Ner, and Joab the son of Zeruiah had dedicated, *every* dedicated *thing,* was under the hand of Shelomith and his brethren.

29 Of the Izharites, Chenaniah and his sons *performed* duties as officials and judges over Israel outside Jerusalem. 30 Of the Hebronites, Hashabiah and his brethren, one thousand seven hundred able men, had the oversight of Israel on the west side of the Jordan for all the business of the LORD, and in the service of the king. 31 Among the Hebronites, Jerijah *was* head of the Hebronites according to his genealogy of the fathers. In the fortieth year of the reign of David they were sought, and there *were* found among them capable men at Jazer of Gilead. 32 And his brethren *were* two thousand seven hundred able men, heads of fathers' *houses,* whom King David made officials over the Reubenites, the Gadites, and the half-tribe of Manasseh, for every matter pertaining to God and the affairs of the king.

A list of kingdom officers

27 And the children of Israel, according to their number, the heads of fathers' *houses,* the captains of thousands and hundreds and their officers, served the king in every matter of the *military* divisions. *These divisions* came in and went out month by month throughout all the months of the year, each division *having* twenty-four thousand.

2 Over the first division for the first

month *was* Jashobeam the son of Zabdiel, and in his division *were* twenty-four thousand; ³ *he was* of the children of Perez, and the chief of all the captains of the army for the first month. ⁴ Over the division of the second month *was* Dodai an Ahohite, and of his division Mikloth also *was* the leader; in his division *were* twenty-four thousand. ⁵ The third captain of the army for the third month *was* Benaiah, the son of Jehoiada the priest, who was chief; in his division *were* twenty-four thousand. ⁶ This was the Benaiah *who was* mighty *among* the thirty, and was over the thirty; in his division *was* Ammizabad his son. ⁷ The fourth *captain* for the fourth month *was* Asahel the brother of Joab, and Zebadiah his son after him; in his division *were* twenty-four thousand. ⁸ The fifth *captain* for the fifth month *was* Shamhuth the Izrahite; in his division were twenty-four thousand. ⁹ The sixth *captain* for the sixth month *was* Ira the son of Ikkesh the Tekoite; in his division *were* twenty-four thousand. ¹⁰ The seventh *captain* for the seventh month *was* Helez the Pelonite, of the children of Ephraim; in his division *were* twenty-four thousand. ¹¹ The eighth *captain* for the eighth month *was* Sibbechai the Hushathite, of the Zarhites; in his division *were* twenty-four thousand. ¹² The ninth *captain* for the ninth month *was* Abiezer the Anathothite, of the Benjamites; in his division *were* twenty-four thousand. ¹³ The tenth *captain* for the tenth month *was* Maharai the Netophathite, of the Zarhites; in his division *were* twenty-four thousand. ¹⁴ The eleventh *captain* for the eleventh month *was* Benaiah the Pirathonite, of the children of Ephraim; in his division *were* twenty-four thousand. ¹⁵ The twelfth *captain* for the twelfth month *was* Heldai the Netophathite, of Othniel; in his division *were* twenty-four thousand.

¹⁶ Furthermore, over the tribes of Israel: the officer over the Reubenites *was* Eliezer the son of Zichri; over the Simeonites, Shephatiah the son of Maachah; ¹⁷ *over* the Levites, Hashabiah the son of Kemuel; over the Aaronites, Zadok; ¹⁸ *over* Judah, Elihu, *one* of David's brothers; *over* Issachar, Omri the son of Michael; ¹⁹ *over* Zebulun, Ishmaiah the son of Obadiah; *over* Naphtali, Jerimoth the son of Azriel; ²⁰ *over* the children of Ephraim, Hoshea the son of Azaziah; *over* the half-tribe of Manasseh, Joel the son of Pedaiah; ²¹ *over* the half-*tribe* of Manasseh in Gilead, Iddo the son of Zechariah; *over* Benjamin, Jaasiel the son of Abner; ²² *over* Dan, Azarel the son of Jeroham. These *were* the leaders of the tribes of Israel.

²³ But David did not take the number of those twenty years old and under, because the LORD had said He would multiply Israel like the stars of the heavens. ²⁴ Joab the son of Zeruiah began a census, but he did not finish, for wrath came upon Israel because of this census; nor was the number recorded in the account of the chronicles of King David.

²⁵ And Azmaveth the son of Adiel *was* over the king's treasuries; and Jehonathan the son of Uzziah was over the storehouses in the field, in the cities, in the villages, and in the fortresses. ²⁶ Ezri the son of Chelub *was* over those who did the work of the field for tilling the ground. ²⁷ And Shimei the Ramathite *was* over the vineyards, and Zabdi the Shiphmite was over the produce of the vineyards for the supply of wine. ²⁸ Baal-Hanan the Gederite was over the olive trees and the sycamore trees that *were* in the lowlands, and Joash *was* over the store of oil. ²⁹ And Shitrai the Sharonite *was* over the herds that fed in Sharon, and Shaphat the son of Adlai was over the herds *that were* in the valleys. ³⁰ Obil the Ishmaelite *was* over the camels, Jehdeiah the Meronothite *was* over the donkeys, ³¹ and Jaziz the Hagrite *was* over the flocks. All these *were* the officials over King David's property.

³² Also Jehonathan, David's uncle, *was* a counselor, a wise man, and a scribe; and Jehiel the son of Hachmoni *was* with the king's sons. ³³ Ahithophel

was the king's counselor, and Hushai the Archite *was* the king's companion. ³⁴ After Ahithophel *was* Jehoiada the son of Benaiah, then Abiathar. And the general of the king's army *was* Joab.

David tells Solomon to build the temple

28 Now David assembled at Jerusalem all the leaders of Israel: the officers of the tribes and the captains of the divisions who served the king, the captains over thousands and captains over hundreds, and the **stewards** over all the substance and possessions of the king and of his sons, with the officials, the valiant men, and all the mighty men of valor.

² Then King David rose to his feet and said, "Hear me, my brethren and my people: I *had* it in my heart to build a house of rest for the ark of the covenant of the LORD, and for the footstool of our God, and had made preparations to build it. ³ But God said to me, 'You shall not build a house for My name, because you *have been* a man of war and have shed blood.' ⁴ However the LORD God of Israel chose me above all the house of my father to be king over Israel forever, for He has chosen Judah *to be* the ruler. And of the house of Judah, the house of my father, and among the sons of my father, He was pleased with me to make *me* king over all Israel. ⁵ And of all my sons (for the LORD has given me many sons) He has chosen my son Solomon to sit on the throne of the kingdom of the LORD over Israel. ⁶ Now He said to me, 'It is your son Solomon *who* shall build My house and My courts; for I have chosen him *to be* My son, and I will be his Father. ⁷ Moreover I

will establish his kingdom forever, if he is steadfast to observe My commandments and My judgments, as it is this day.' ⁸ Now therefore, in the sight of all Israel, the assembly of the LORD, and in the hearing of our God, be careful to seek out all the commandments of the LORD your God, that you may possess this good land, and leave *it* as an inheritance for your children after you forever.

⁹ "As for you, my son Solomon, know the God of your father, and serve Him with a loyal heart and with a willing mind; for the LORD searches all hearts and understands all the intent of the thoughts. If you seek Him, He will be found by you; but if you forsake Him, He will cast you off forever. ¹⁰ Consider now, for the LORD has chosen you to build a house for the sanctuary; be strong, and do it."

¹¹ Then David gave his son Solomon the plans for the vestibule, its houses, its treasuries, its upper chambers, its inner chambers, and the place of the mercy seat; ¹² and the plans for all that he had by the Spirit, of the courts of the house of the LORD, of all the chambers all around, of the treasuries of the house of God, and of the treasuries for the dedicated things; ¹³ also for the division of the priests and the Levites, for all the work of the service of the house of the LORD, and for all the articles of service in the house of the LORD. ¹⁴ *He gave* gold by weight for *things* of gold, for all articles used in every kind of service; also *silver* for all articles of silver by weight, for all articles used in every kind of service; ¹⁵ the weight for the lampstands of gold, and their lamps of gold, by weight for each lampstand and its lamps; for the lampstands of silver by weight, for the lampstand and its lamps, according to the use of each lampstand. ¹⁶ And by

WORDFINDER

28:1 Stewards Those in charge of property or an area of work. The apostles of the New Testament were "stewards of the mysteries of God." They were in charge of the work of preaching the gospel.

weight *he gave* gold for the **tables of the showbread,** for each table, and silver for the tables of silver; ¹⁷ also pure gold for the forks, the basins, the pitchers of pure gold, and the golden bowls—*he gave gold* by weight for every bowl; and for the silver bowls, *silver* by weight for *every* bowl; ¹⁸ and refined gold by weight for the **altar of incense,** and for the construction of the chariot, that is, the gold cherubim that spread *their wings* and overshadowed the ark of the covenant of the LORD. ¹⁹ "All *this,*" said *David,* "the LORD made me understand in writing, by *His* hand upon me, all the works of these plans."

²⁰ And David said to his son Solomon, "Be strong and of good courage, and do *it;* do not fear nor be dismayed, for the LORD God—my God—*will be* with you. He will not leave you nor forsake you, until you have finished all the work for the service of the house of the LORD. ²¹ *Here are* the divisions of the priests and the Levites for all the service of the house of God; and *every* willing craftsman *will be* with you for all manner of workmanship, for *every* kind of service; also the leaders and all the people *will be* completely at your command."

The people are cheerful givers

29 Furthermore King David said to all the assembly: "My son Solomon, whom alone God has chosen, *is* young and inexperienced; and the work *is* great, because the temple *is* not for man but for the LORD God. ² Now for the house of my God I have prepared with all my might: gold for *things to be made of* gold, silver for *things of* silver, bronze for *things of* bronze, iron for *things of* iron, wood for *things of* wood, onyx stones, *stones* to be set, glistening stones of various colors, all kinds of precious stones, and marble slabs in abundance. ³ Moreover, because I have set my affection on the house of my God, I have given to the house of my God, over and above all that I have prepared for the holy house, my own special treasure of gold and silver: ⁴ three thousand talents of gold, of the gold of Ophir, and seven thousand talents of refined silver, to overlay the walls of the houses; ⁵ the gold for *things of* gold and the silver for *things of* silver, and for all kinds of work *to be done* by the hands of craftsmen. Who *then* is willing to consecrate himself this day to the LORD?"

⁶ Then the leaders of the fathers' *houses,* leaders of the tribes of Israel, the captains of thousands and of hundreds, with the officers over the king's work, offered willingly. ⁷ They gave for the work of the house of God five thousand talents and ten thousand darics of gold, ten thousand talents of silver, eighteen thousand talents of bronze, and one hundred thousand talents of iron. ⁸ And whoever had *precious* stones gave *them* to the treasury of the house of the LORD, into the hand of Jehiel the Gershonite. ⁹ Then the people rejoiced, for they had offered willingly, because with a loyal heart they had offered willingly to the LORD; and King David also rejoiced greatly.

¹⁰ Therefore David blessed the LORD before all the assembly; and David said:

"Blessed are You, LORD God of Israel, our Father, forever and ever.
¹¹ Yours, O LORD, *is the greatness,*

WORDFINDER

28:16 Table of Showbread   A table about 36 inches long by 18 inches wide by 27 inches high. Every Sabbath 12 loaves of bread were arranged on the table. They were a symbol of God's presence and supply.

28:18 Altar of Incense   A gold-covered altar about 18 inches long by 18 inches wide by 36 inches high. Every morning the high priest burned incense on the altar as a symbol of the prayers of the people.

King David Turns Government Over to Solomon

KDTV (King David Television Network)—KDTV news teams are on hand to bring you early coverage of King Solomon's rise to power.

Solomon, David's favorite son and heir to the throne of Israel, has taken his father's place after a reign of 40 years.

You have just heard the king explain his actions. The Lord had earlier told David that he could not build the temple of God. That work would be done by Solomon. David has warned Solomon to worship and serve the Lord faithfully.

The king has ended his speech by giving Solomon the plans for the temple. He has also ordered immense amounts of gold, silver, bronze, and iron for the temple and its furniture.

Finally, in a grand ceremony, Solomon has been made king and now sits on David's throne. We will follow Solomon's reign with great interest.

The power and the glory,
The victory and the majesty;
For all *that is* in heaven and in
    earth *is* Yours;
Yours *is* the kingdom, O Lord,
And You are exalted as head
    over all.

12 Both riches and honor *come*
    from You,
And You reign over all.
In Your hand *is* power and
    might;
In Your hand *it is* to make great
And to give strength to all.

13 "Now therefore, our God,
We thank You
And praise Your glorious name.
14 But who *am* I, and who *are* my
    people,
That we should be able to offer
    so willingly as this?
For all things *come* from You,
And of Your own we have given
    You.
15 For we *are* aliens and pilgrims
    before You,
As *were* all our fathers;
Our days on earth *are* as a
    shadow,
And without hope.

16 "O Lord our God, all this abundance that we have prepared to build You a house for Your holy name is from Your hand, and *is* all Your own.

17 I know also, my God, that You test the heart and have pleasure in uprightness. As for me, in the uprightness of my heart I have willingly offered all these *things;* and now with joy I have seen Your people, who are present here to offer willingly to You. 18 O Lord God of Abraham, Isaac, and Israel, our fathers, keep this forever in the intent of the thoughts of the heart of Your people, and fix their heart toward You. 19 And give my son Solomon a loyal heart to keep Your commandments and Your testimonies and Your statutes, to do all *these things,* and to build the temple for which I have made provision."

20 Then David said to all the assembly, "Now bless the Lord your God." So all the assembly blessed the Lord God of their fathers, and bowed their heads and prostrated themselves before the Lord and the king.

21 And they made sacrifices to the Lord and offered burnt offerings to the Lord on the next day: a thousand bulls, a thousand rams, a thousand lambs, with their drink offerings, and sacrifices in abundance for all Israel. 22 So they ate and drank before the Lord with great gladness on that day. And they made Solomon the son of David king the second time, and anointed *him* before the Lord *to be* the leader, and Zadok *to be* priest. 23 Then Solomon sat on the throne of the Lord as king instead of David his

father, and prospered; and all Israel obeyed him. 24 All the leaders and the mighty men, and also all the sons of King David, submitted themselves to King Solomon. 25 So the LORD exalted Solomon exceedingly in the sight of all Israel, and bestowed on him *such* royal majesty as had not been on any king before him in Israel.

26 Thus David the son of Jesse reigned over all Israel. 27 And the period that he reigned over Israel *was* forty years; seven years he reigned in Hebron, and thirty-three *years* he reigned in Jerusalem. 28 So he died in a good old age, full of days and riches and honor; and Solomon his son reigned in his place. 29 Now the acts of King David, first and last, indeed they *are* written in the book of Samuel the seer, in the book of Nathan the prophet, and in the book of Gad the seer, 30 with all his reign and his might, and the events that happened to him, to Israel, and to all the kingdoms of the lands.

The Book of
2 CHRONICLES

A Hebrew King—An earthly king has a lonely and hopeless road to walk. Many of the things I try to do fail. I just don't have the wisdom I need to rule over a nation. The whole idea of a king was a mistake since the time of Saul. God didn't want kings on the throne of Israel because He alone has the ability and the wisdom to govern the affairs of men.

I confess I'm a selfish man. How can a selfish man govern for the good of his fellowman?

Your history books will tell you that the forefathers of America knew kings were a mistake. They learned this from the Bible. No mere man can be trusted with the well-being of a nation. That is why it is written on your coins: "In God we trust." Every nation should be "one nation under God," just as your Pledge of Allegiance says.

Solomon prays for wisdom

NOW Solomon the son of David was strengthened in his kingdom, and the LORD his God *was* with him and exalted him exceedingly.

2 And Solomon spoke to all Israel, to the captains of thousands and of hundreds, to the judges, and to *every* leader in all Israel, the heads of the fathers' *houses*. 3 Then Solomon, and all the assembly with him, went to the high place that *was* at Gibeon; for the tabernacle of meeting with God was there, which Moses the servant of the LORD had made in the wilderness. 4 But David had brought up the ark of God from Kirjath Jearim to *the place* David had prepared for it, for he had pitched a tent for it at Jerusalem. 5 Now the bronze altar that Bezalel the son of Uri, the son of Hur, had made, he put before the tabernacle of the LORD; Solomon and the assembly sought Him *there*. 6 And Solomon went up there to the bronze altar before the LORD, which *was* at the tabernacle of meeting, and offered a thousand burnt offerings on it.

7 On that night God appeared to Solomon, and said to him, "Ask! What shall I give you?"

8 And Solomon said to God: "You have shown great mercy to David my father, and have made me king in his place. 9 Now, O LORD God, let Your promise to David my father be established, for You have made me king over a people like the dust of the earth in multitude. 10 Now give me wisdom and knowledge, that I may go out and come in before this people; for who can judge this great people of Yours?"

11 Then God said to Solomon: "Because this was in your heart, and you have not asked riches or wealth or honor or the life of your enemies, nor have you asked long life—but have asked wisdom and knowledge for yourself, that you may judge My people over whom I have made you king— 12 wisdom and knowledge *are* granted to you; and I will give you riches and wealth and honor, such as none of the kings have had who *were* before you, nor shall any after you have the like."

13 So Solomon came to Jerusalem from the high place that *was* at Gibeon, from before the tabernacle of meeting, and reigned over Israel. 14 And Solomon gathered chariots and horsemen; he had one thousand four hundred chariots and twelve thousand horsemen, whom he stationed in the chariot cities and with the king in Jerusalem. 15 Also the king made silver and

King of Tyre to Help Build Temple

The Jerusalem Times

JERUSALEM—King Solomon is preparing to build the long-expected temple, the fulfillment of King David's last command to his son.

We have also learned that King Hiram of Tyre (pronounced *HIGH-rum* of *TIRE*) agreed to give his full support to the work. Solomon has written to the king requesting aid in men and materials, and is happy with Hiram's promise to supply lumber for the building.

This is amazing news because Hiram doesn't worship the God of the Hebrews. So far, however, Hiram has proved to be a loyal friend to both King David and King Solomon.

gold as common in Jerusalem as stones, and he made cedars as abundant as the sycamores which *are* in the lowland. 16 And Solomon had horses imported from Egypt and Keveh; the king's merchants bought them in Keveh at the *current* price. 17 They also acquired and imported from Egypt a chariot for six hundred *shekels* of silver, and a horse for one hundred and fifty; thus, through their agents, they exported them to all the kings of the Hittites and the kings of Syria.

Solomon gets ready to build

2 Then Solomon determined to build a temple for the name of the LORD, and a royal house for himself. 2 Solomon selected seventy thousand men to bear burdens, eighty thousand to quarry *stone* in the mountains, and three thousand six hundred to oversee them. 3 Then Solomon sent to Hiram king of Tyre, saying:

As you have dealt with David my father, and sent him cedars to build himself a house to dwell in, *so deal with me.* 4 Behold, I am building a temple for the name of the LORD my God, to dedicate *it* to Him, to burn before Him sweet incense, for the continual showbread, for the burnt offerings morning and evening, on the Sabbaths, on the New Moons, and on the set feasts of the LORD our God. This *is an* ordinance forever to Israel.

5 And the temple which I build *will be* great, for our God is greater than all gods. 6 But who is able to build Him a temple, since heaven and the heaven of heavens cannot contain Him? Who *am* I then, that I should build Him a temple, except to burn sacrifice before Him?

7 Therefore send me at once a man skillful to work in gold and silver, in bronze and iron, in purple and crimson and blue, who has skill to engrave with the skillful men who are with me in

King Hiram of Tyre made a trade agreement with King Solomon.

Judah and Jerusalem, whom David my father provided. 8 Also send me cedar and cypress and algum logs from Lebanon, for I know that your servants have skill to cut timber in Lebanon; and indeed my servants *will be* with your servants, 9 to prepare timber for me in abundance, for the temple which I am about to build *shall be* great and wonderful.

10 And indeed I will give to your servants, the woodsmen who cut timber, twenty thousand kors of ground wheat, twenty thousand kors of barley, twenty thousand baths of wine, and twenty thousand baths of oil.

11 Then Hiram king of Tyre answered in writing, which he sent to Solomon:

Because the LORD loves His people, He has made you king over them.

12 Hiram also said:

Blessed *be* the LORD God of Israel, who made heaven and earth, for He has given King David a wise son, endowed with prudence and understanding, who will build a temple for the LORD and a royal house for himself!

13 And now I have sent a skillful man, endowed with understanding, Huram my master *craftsman* 14 (the son of a woman of the daughters of Dan, and his father was a man of Tyre), skilled to work in gold and silver, bronze and iron, stone and wood, purple and blue, fine linen and crimson, and to make any engraving and to accomplish any plan which may be given to him, with your skillful men and with the skillful men of my lord David your father.

15 Now therefore, the wheat, the barley, the oil, and the wine which my lord has spoken of, let him send to his servants. 16 And we will cut wood from Lebanon, as much as you need; we will bring it to you in rafts by sea to Joppa, and you will carry it up to Jerusalem.

17 Then Solomon numbered all the aliens who *were* in the land of Israel, after the census in which David his father had numbered them; and there were found to be one hundred and fifty-three thousand six hundred. 18 And he made seventy thousand of them bearers of burdens, eighty thousand stonecutters in the mountain, and three thousand six hundred overseers to make the people work.

Building materials for the temple

3 Now Solomon began to build the house of the LORD at Jerusalem on Mount Moriah, where *the LORD* had

DIGGING IN

3:1 The Temple in God's Plan The earliest place of worship was a special tent called a tabernacle (pronounced *TAB-er-nak-kel*). Later, God commanded Solomon to build the temple that was meant to be the permanent place of worship at Jerusalem. Both the tabernacle and the temple were the places where God revealed Himself to His people. Here also was the place where the people brought their offerings for sin and thanksgiving.

The stone temple didn't last forever. It was destroyed three times—first by the Babylonians, then by the Syrians, and finally by the Romans. Each time God allowed the temple to be destroyed because the people were not worshiping Him in their hearts. The heart is the real temple where God must be worshiped. Any other place of worship means nothing without the true worship of our hearts. Those who now truly worship God are themselves the real temple of God.

appeared to his father David, at the place that David had prepared on the threshing floor of Ornan the Jebusite. 2 And he began to build on the second *day* of the second month in the fourth year of his reign.

3 This is the foundation which Solomon laid for building the house of God: The length *was* sixty cubits (by cubits according to the former measure) and the width twenty cubits. 4 And the vestibule that *was* in front *of the sanctuary* was twenty cubits long across the width of the house, and the height *was* one hundred and twenty. He overlaid the inside with pure gold. 5 The larger room he paneled with cypress which he overlaid with fine gold, and he carved palm trees and chainwork on it. 6 And he decorated the house with precious stones for beauty, and the gold *was* gold from Parvaim. 7 He also overlaid the house—the beams and doorposts, its walls and doors—with gold; and he carved cherubim on the walls.

8 And he made the Most Holy Place. Its length was according to the width of the house, twenty cubits, and its width twenty cubits. He overlaid it with six hundred talents of fine gold. 9 The weight of the nails *was* fifty shekels of gold; and he overlaid the upper area with gold. 10 In the Most Holy Place he made two cherubim, fashioned by carving, and overlaid them with gold. 11 The wings of the cherubim *were* twenty cubits in *overall* length: one wing *of the one cherub was* five cubits, touching the wall of the room, and the other wing *was* five cubits, touching the wing of the other cherub; 12 *one* wing of the other cherub *was* five cubits, touching the wall of the room, and the other wing *also was* five cubits, touching the wing of the other cherub. 13 The wings of these cherubim spanned twenty cubits overall. They stood on their feet, and they faced inward. 14 And he made the veil of blue, purple, crimson, and fine linen, and wove cherubim into it.

15 Also he made in front of the temple two pillars thirty-five cubits high, and the capital that *was* on the top of each of *them* was five cubits. 16 He made wreaths of chainwork, as in the inner sanctuary, and put *them* on top of the pillars; and he made one hundred pomegranates, and put *them* on the wreaths of chainwork. 17 Then he set up the pillars before the temple, one on the right hand and the other on the left; he called the name of the one on the right hand Jachin, and the name of the one on the left Boaz.

The blueprint and furniture for the temple

4 Moreover he made a bronze altar: twenty cubits was its length, twenty cubits its width, and ten cubits its height.

2 Then he made the Sea of cast *bronze,* ten cubits from one brim to the other; *it was* completely round. Its height *was* five cubits, and a line of thirty cubits measured its circumference. 3 And under it *was* the likeness of oxen encircling it all around, ten to a cubit, all the way around the Sea. The oxen *were* cast in two rows, when it was cast. 4 It stood on twelve oxen:

In the new temple, this bronze basin was used by the priests for washing their hands as an act of purification.

three looking toward the north, three looking toward the west, three looking toward the south, and three looking toward the east; the Sea *was set* upon them, and all their back parts *pointed* inward. ⁵ It *was* a handbreadth thick; and its brim was shaped like the brim of a cup, *like* a lily blossom. It contained three thousand baths.

⁶ He also made ten lavers, and put five on the right side and five on the left, to wash in them; such things as they offered for the burnt offering they would wash in them, but the Sea *was* for the priests to wash in. ⁷ And he made ten lampstands of gold according to their design, and set *them* in the temple, five on the right side and five on the left. ⁸ He also made ten tables, and placed *them* in the temple, five on the right side and five on the left. And he made one hundred bowls of gold.

⁹ Furthermore he made the court of the priests, and the great court and doors for the court; and he overlaid these doors with bronze. ¹⁰ He set the Sea on the right side, toward the southeast.

¹¹ Then Huram made the pots and the shovels and the bowls. So Huram finished doing the work that he was to do for King Solomon for the house of God: ¹² the two pillars and the bowl-shaped capitals *that were* on top of the two pillars; the two networks covering the two bowl-shaped capitals which *were* on top of the pillars; ¹³ four hundred pomegranates for the two networks (two rows of pomegranates for each network, to cover the two bowl-shaped capitals that *were* on the pillars); ¹⁴ he also made carts and the lavers on the carts; ¹⁵ one Sea and twelve oxen under it; ¹⁶ also the pots, the shovels, the forks—and all their articles Huram his master *craftsman* made of burnished bronze for King Solomon for the house of the LORD.

¹⁷ In the plain of Jordan the king had them cast in clay molds, between Succoth and Zeredah. ¹⁸ And Solomon had all these articles made in such great abundance that the weight of the bronze was not determined.

¹⁹ Thus Solomon had all the furnishings made for the house of God: the altar of gold and the tables on which *was* the showbread; ²⁰ the lampstands with their lamps of pure gold, to burn in the prescribed manner in front of the inner sanctuary, ²¹ with the flowers and the lamps and the wick-trimmers of gold, of purest gold; ²² the trimmers, the bowls, the ladles, and the censers of pure gold. As for the entry of the sanctuary, its inner doors to the Most Holy *Place,* and the doors of the main hall of the temple, *were* gold.

The ark of God is brought to the temple

5 So all the work that Solomon had done for the house of the LORD was finished; and Solomon brought in the things which his father David had dedicated: the silver and the gold and all the furnishings. And he put *them* in the treasuries of the house of God.

² Now Solomon assembled the elders of Israel and all the heads of the tribes, the chief fathers of the children of Israel, in Jerusalem, that they might bring the ark of the covenant of the LORD up from the City of David, which is Zion. ³ Therefore all the men of Israel assembled with the king at the feast, which *was* in the seventh month. ⁴ So all the elders of Israel came, and the Levites took up the ark. ⁵ Then they brought up the ark, the tabernacle of meeting, and all the holy furnishings that *were* in the tabernacle. The priests and the Levites brought them up. ⁶ Also King Solomon, and all the congregation of Israel who were assembled with him before the ark, were sacrificing sheep and oxen that could not be counted or numbered for multitude. ⁷ Then the priests brought in the ark of the covenant of the LORD to its place, into the inner sanctuary of the temple, to the Most Holy *Place,* under the wings of the cherubim. ⁸ For the cherubim spread *their* wings over the

King Solomon built a beautiful temple and dedicated it to the worship of God.

place of the ark, and the cherubim overshadowed the ark and its poles. 9 The poles extended so that the ends of the poles of the ark could be seen from *the holy place,* in front of the inner sanctuary; but they could not be seen from outside. And they are there to this day. 10 Nothing was in the ark except the two tablets which Moses put *there* at Horeb, when the LORD made *a covenant* with the children of Israel, when they had come out of Egypt.

11 And it came to pass when the priests came out of the *Most* Holy *Place* (for all the priests who *were* present had sanctified themselves, without keeping to their divisions), 12 and the Levites *who were* the singers, all those of Asaph and Heman and Jeduthun, with their sons and their brethren, stood at the east end of the altar,

clothed in white linen, having cymbals, stringed instruments and harps, and with them one hundred and twenty priests sounding with trumpets— 13 indeed it came to pass, when the trumpeters and singers *were* as one, to make one sound to be heard in praising and thanking the LORD, and when they lifted up their voice with the trumpets and cymbals and instruments of music, and praised the LORD, *saying:*

"*For He is* good,
For His mercy *endures*
forever,"

that the house, the house of the LORD, was filled with a cloud, 14 so that the priests could not continue ministering because of the cloud; for the glory of the LORD filled the house of God.

DIGGING IN

5:14 The Glory of God in the Temple Sometimes God visited His people in the form of a bright cloud, called the "shekinah" (pronounced *shi-KIGH-nuh*). We first read about this cloud in Exodus 14, when the cloud of God's presence protected Israel from the army of Egypt. This same cloud led the people in the desert (Exodus 13:21). This is the cloud that covered the mountain when God gave Moses the Ten Commandments (Exodus 19:18).

Finally, the cloud of God's presence filled the tent of meeting (Exodus 40:34) and the temple (2 Chronicles 5:14).

In the New Testament, God's presence comes to us by the Holy Spirit. When you believe in Jesus, the Holy Spirit comes to live in your body. The Holy Spirit is God Himself. He is the same Spirit who visited the people in the cloud of the Old Testament.

Solomon dedicates the temple

6 Then Solomon spoke:

"The LORD said
He would dwell in the dark
cloud.
2 I have surely built You an
exalted house,
And a place for You to dwell
in forever."

3 Then the king turned around and blessed the whole assembly of Israel, while all the assembly of Israel was standing. 4 And he said: "Blessed be the LORD God of Israel, who has fulfilled with His hands what He spoke with His mouth to my father David, saying, 5 'Since the day that I brought My people out of the land of Egypt, I have chosen no city from any tribe of Israel in which to build a house, that My name might be there, nor did I choose any man to be a ruler over My people Israel. 6 Yet I have chosen Jerusalem, that My name may be there, and I have chosen David to be over My people Israel.' 7 Now it was in the heart of my father David to build a temple for the name of the LORD God of Israel. 8 But the LORD said to my father David, 'Whereas it was in your heart to build a temple for My name, you did well in that it was in your heart. 9 Nevertheless you shall not build the temple, but your son who will come from your body, he shall build the temple for My name.' 10 So the LORD has fulfilled His word which He spoke, and I have filled the position of my father David, and sit on the throne of Israel, as the LORD promised; and I have built the temple for the name of the LORD God of Israel. 11 And there I have put the ark, in which is the covenant of the LORD which He made with the children of Israel."

12 Then Solomon stood before the altar of the LORD in the presence of all the assembly of Israel, and spread out his hands 13 (for Solomon had made a bronze platform five cubits long, five cubits wide, and three cubits high, and had set it in the midst of the court; and he stood on it, knelt down on his knees before all the assembly of Israel, and spread out his hands toward heaven); 14 and he said: "LORD God of Israel, there is no God in heaven or on earth like You, who keep Your covenant and mercy with Your servants who walk before You with all their hearts. 15 You have kept what You promised Your servant David my father; You have both spoken with Your mouth and fulfilled it with Your hand, as it is this day. 16 Therefore, LORD God of Israel, now keep what You promised Your servant David my father, saying, 'You shall not fail to have a man sit before Me on the throne of Israel, only if your sons take heed to their way, that they walk in My law as you have walked before Me.' 17 And now, O LORD God of Israel, let Your word come true, which You have spoken to Your servant David.

18 "But will God indeed dwell with men on the earth? Behold, heaven and the heaven of heavens cannot contain You. How much less this temple which I have built! 19 Yet regard the prayer of Your servant and his supplication, O LORD my God, and listen to the cry and the prayer which Your servant is praying before You: 20 that Your eyes may be open toward this temple day and night, toward the place where You said You would put Your name, that You may hear the prayer which Your servant makes toward this place. 21 And may You hear the supplications of Your servant and of Your people Israel, when they pray toward this place. Hear from heaven Your dwelling place, and when You hear, forgive.

22 "If anyone sins against his neighbor, and is forced to take an oath, and comes and takes an oath before Your altar in this temple, 23 then hear from heaven, and act, and judge Your servants, bringing retribution on the wicked by bringing his way on his own head, and justifying the righteous by giving him according to his righteousness.

24 "Or if Your people Israel are defeated before an enemy because they

have sinned against You, and return and confess Your name, and pray and make supplication before You in this temple, 25 then hear from heaven and forgive the sin of Your people Israel, and bring them back to the land which You gave to them and their fathers.

26 "When the heavens are shut up and there is no rain because they have sinned against You, when they pray toward this place and confess Your name, and turn from their sin because You afflict them, 27 then hear *in* heaven, and forgive the sin of Your servants, Your people Israel, that You may teach them the good way in which they should walk; and send rain on Your land which You have given to Your people as an inheritance.

28 "When there is famine in the land, pestilence or blight or mildew, locusts or grasshoppers; when their enemies besiege them in the land of their cities; whatever plague or whatever sickness *there is;* 29 whatever prayer, whatever supplication is *made* by anyone, or by all Your people Israel, when each one knows his own burden and his own grief, and spreads out his hands to this temple: 30 then hear from heaven Your dwelling place, and forgive, and give to everyone according to all his ways, whose heart You know (for You alone know the hearts of the sons of men), 31 that they may fear You, to walk in Your ways as long as they live in the land which You gave to our fathers.

32 "Moreover, concerning a foreigner, who is not of Your people Israel, but has come from a far country for the sake of Your great name and Your mighty hand and Your outstretched arm, when they come and pray in this temple; 33 then hear from heaven Your dwelling place, and do according to all for which the foreigner calls to You, that all peoples of the earth may know Your name and fear You, as *do* Your people Israel, and that they may know that this temple which I have built is called by Your name.

34 "When Your people go out to battle against their enemies, wherever You send them, and when they pray to You toward this city which You have chosen and the temple which I have built for Your name, 35 then hear from heaven their prayer and their supplication, and maintain their cause.

36 "When they sin against You (for *there is* no one who does not sin), and You become angry with them and deliver them to the enemy, and they take them captive to a land far or near; 37 *yet* when they come to themselves in the land where they were carried captive, and repent, and make supplication to You in the land of their captivity, saying, 'We have sinned, we have done wrong, and have committed wickedness'; 38 and *when* they return to You with all their heart and with all their soul in the land of their captivity, where they have been carried captive, and pray toward their land which You gave to their fathers, the city which You have chosen, and toward the temple which I have built for Your name: 39 then hear from heaven Your dwelling place their prayer and their supplications, and maintain their cause, and forgive Your people who have sinned against You. 40 Now, my God, I pray, let Your eyes be open and *let* Your ears *be* attentive to the prayer *made* in this place.

41 "Now therefore,
Arise, O LORD God, to Your
 resting place,
You and the ark of Your
 strength.
Let Your priests, O LORD God,
 be clothed with salvation,
And let Your saints rejoice in
 goodness.

42 "O LORD God, do not turn away
 the face of Your Anointed;
Remember the mercies of Your
 servant David."

God makes a promise to Solomon

7 When Solomon had finished praying, fire came down from heaven and consumed the burnt offering and the sacrifices; and the glory of the LORD

What Israel Learned

Over 150,000 of us worked long and hard to build the temple of the Lord. King Hiram of Tyre (pronounced *HIGH-rum* of TIRE) lent us Huram, a skilled artisan, to make the temple beautiful. Hiram also gave us lumber from the forests in his country.

We were very proud of our work when it was completed. The building was beautifully finished with gold and ornaments of precious stones.

The temple was built at the place where David earlier made a burnt offering. And a thousand years before, Abraham had sacrificed at the same spot.

After all our work, though, the temple was still only a beautiful building. Then King Solomon prayed, and the temple was filled with God's glorious light. Also, God's fire came down from heaven and ate up the sacrifice. So we learned that only God's presence makes us able to worship Him truly.

---

filled the temple. 2 And the priests could not enter the house of the LORD, because the glory of the LORD had filled the LORD's house. 3 When all the children of Israel saw how the fire came down, and the glory of the LORD on the temple, they bowed their faces to the ground on the pavement, and worshiped and praised the LORD, *saying:*

"For *He is* good,
For His mercy *endures* forever."

4 Then the king and all the people offered sacrifices before the LORD. 5 King Solomon offered a sacrifice of twenty-two thousand bulls and one hundred and twenty thousand sheep. So the king and all the people dedicated the house of God. 6 And the priests attended to their services; the Levites also with instruments of the music of the LORD, which King David had made to praise the LORD, saying, "For His mercy *endures* forever," whenever David offered praise by their ministry. The priests sounded trumpets opposite them, while all Israel stood.

7 Furthermore Solomon consecrated the middle of the court that *was* in front of the house of the LORD; for there he offered burnt offerings and the fat of the peace offerings, because the bronze altar which Solomon had made was not able to receive the burnt offer-

ings, the grain offerings, and the fat.

8 At that time Solomon kept the feast seven days, and all Israel with him, a very great assembly from the entrance of Hamath to the Brook of Egypt. 9 And on the eighth day they held a sacred assembly, for they observed the dedication of the altar seven days, and the feast seven days. 10 On the twenty-third day of the seventh month he sent the people away to their tents, joyful and glad of heart for the good that the LORD had done for David, for Solomon, and for His people Israel. 11 Thus Solomon finished the house of the LORD and the king's house; and Solomon successfully accomplished all that came into his heart to make in the house of the LORD and in his own house.

12 Then the LORD appeared to Solomon by night, and said to him: "I have heard your prayer, and have chosen this place for Myself as a house of sacrifice. 13 When I shut up heaven and there is no rain, or command the locusts to devour the land, or send pestilence among My people, 14 if My people who are called by My name will humble themselves, and pray and seek My face, and turn from their wicked ways, then I will hear from heaven, and will forgive their sin and heal their land. 15 Now My eyes will be open and My ears attentive to prayer *made* in this

place. 16 For now I have chosen and sanctified this house, that My name may be there forever; and My eyes and My heart will be there perpetually. 17 As for you, if you walk before Me as your father David walked, and do according to all that I have commanded you, and if you keep My statutes and My judgments, 18 then I will establish the throne of your kingdom, as I covenanted with David your father, saying, 'You shall not fail *to have* a man as ruler in Israel.'

19 "But if you turn away and forsake My statutes and My commandments which I have set before you, and go and serve other gods, and worship them, 20 then I will uproot them from My land which I have given them; and this house which I have sanctified for My name I will cast out of My sight, and will make it a proverb and a byword among all peoples.

21 "And *as for* this house, which is exalted, everyone who passes by it will be astonished and say, 'Why has the LORD done thus to this land and this house?' 22 Then they will answer, 'Because they forsook the LORD God of their fathers, who brought them out of the land of Egypt, and embraced other gods, and worshiped them and served them; therefore He has brought all this calamity on them.' "

Solomon becomes world-famous

8 It came to pass at the end of twenty years, when Solomon had built the house of the LORD and his own house, 2 that the cities which Hiram had given to Solomon, Solomon built them; and he settled the children of Israel there. 3 And Solomon went to Hamath Zobah and seized it. 4 He also built Tadmor in the wilderness, and all the storage cities which he built in Hamath. 5 He built Upper Beth Horon and Lower Beth Horon, fortified cities *with* walls, gates, and bars, 6 also Baalath and all the storage cities that Solomon had, and all the chariot cities and the cities of the cavalry, and all that Solomon desired to build in Jerusalem,

in Lebanon, and in all the land of his dominion.

7 All the people *who were* left of the Hittites, Amorites, Perizzites, Hivites, and Jebusites, who *were* not of Israel— 8 that is, their descendants who were left in the land after them, whom the children of Israel did not destroy—from these Solomon raised forced labor, as it is to this day. 9 But Solomon did not make the children of Israel servants for his work. Some *were* men of war, captains of his officers, captains of his chariots, and his cavalry. 10 And others *were* chiefs of the officials of King Solomon: two hundred and fifty, who ruled over the people.

11 Now Solomon brought the daughter of Pharaoh up from the City of David to the house he had built for her, for he said, "My wife shall not dwell in the house of David king of Israel, because *the places* to which the ark of the LORD has come are holy."

12 Then Solomon offered burnt offerings to the LORD on the altar of the LORD which he had built before the vestibule, 13 according to the daily rate, offering according to the commandment of Moses, for the Sabbaths, the New Moons, and the three appointed yearly feasts—the Feast of Unleavened Bread, the Feast of Weeks, and the Feast of Tabernacles. 14 And, according to the order of David his father, he appointed the divisions of the priests for their service, the Levites for their duties (to praise and serve before the priests) as the duty of each day required, and the gatekeepers by their divisions at each gate; for so David the man of God had commanded. 15 They did not depart from the command of the king to the priests and Levites concerning any matter or concerning the treasuries.

16 Now all the work of Solomon was well-ordered from the day of the foundation of the house of the LORD until it was finished. So the house of the LORD was completed.

17 Then Solomon went to Ezion Geber and Elath on the seacoast, in the

land of Edom. ¹⁸And Hiram sent him ships by the hand of his servants, and servants who knew the sea. They went with the servants of Solomon to Ophir, and acquired four hundred and fifty talents of gold from there, and brought it to King Solomon.

The Queen of Sheba visits Solomon

9 Now when the queen of Sheba heard of the fame of Solomon, she came to Jerusalem to test Solomon with hard questions, *having* a very great retinue, camels that bore spices, gold in abundance, and precious stones; and when she came to Solomon, she spoke with him about all that was in her heart. ²So Solomon answered all her questions; there was nothing so difficult for Solomon that he could not explain it to her. ³And when the queen of Sheba had seen the wisdom of Solomon, the house that he had built, ⁴the food on his table, the seating of his servants, the service of his waiters and their apparel, his cupbearers and their apparel, and his entryway by which he went up to the house of the LORD, there was no more spirit in her.

⁵Then she said to the king: "*It was* a true report which I heard in my own land about your words and your wisdom. ⁶However I did not believe their words until I came and saw with my own eyes; and indeed the half of the greatness of your wisdom was not told me. You exceed the fame of which I heard. ⁷Happy *are* your men and happy *are* these your servants, who stand continually before you and hear your wisdom! ⁸Blessed be the LORD your God, who delighted in you, setting you on His throne *to be* king for the LORD your God! Because your God has loved Israel, to establish them forever, therefore He made you king over them, to do justice and righteousness."

⁹And she gave the king one hundred and twenty talents of gold, spices in great abundance, and precious stones; there never were any spices such as those the queen of Sheba gave to King Solomon.

¹⁰Also, the servants of Hiram and the servants of Solomon, who brought gold from Ophir, brought algum wood and precious stones. ¹¹And the king made walkways *of* the algum wood for the house of the LORD and for the king's house, also harps and stringed instruments for singers; and there were none such *as these* seen before in the land of Judah.

¹²Now King Solomon gave to the queen of Sheba all she desired, whatever she asked, *much more* than she had brought to the king. So she turned and went to her own country, she and her servants.

¹³The weight of gold that came to Solomon yearly was six hundred and sixty-six talents of gold, ¹⁴besides *what* the traveling merchants and traders brought. And all the kings of Arabia and governors of the country brought gold and silver to Solomon. ¹⁵And King Solomon made two hundred large shields of hammered gold; six hundred *shekels* of hammered gold went into each shield. ¹⁶He also *made* three hundred shields of hammered gold; three hundred *shekels* of gold went into each shield. The king put them in the House of the Forest of Lebanon.

¹⁷Moreover the king made a great throne of ivory, and overlaid it with pure gold. ¹⁸The throne *had* six steps, with a footstool of gold, *which were* fastened to the throne; there were armrests on either side of the place of the seat, and two lions stood beside the armrests. ¹⁹Twelve lions stood there, one on each side of the six steps; nothing like *this* had been made for any *other* kingdom.

²⁰All King Solomon's drinking vessels *were* gold, and all the vessels of the House of the Forest of Lebanon *were* pure gold. Not *one was* silver, for this was accounted as nothing in the days of Solomon. ²¹For the king's ships went to Tarshish with the servants of Hiram. Once every three years the merchant ships came, bringing

gold, silver, ivory, apes, and monkeys.
22 So King Solomon surpassed all the kings of the earth in riches and wisdom. 23 And all the kings of the earth sought the presence of Solomon to hear his wisdom, which God had put in his heart. 24 Each man brought his present: articles of silver and gold, garments, armor, spices, horses, and mules, at a set rate year by year.

25 Solomon had four thousand stalls for horses and chariots, and twelve thousand horsemen whom he stationed in the chariot cities and with the king at Jerusalem.

26 So he reigned over all the kings from the River to the land of the Philistines, as far as the border of Egypt. 27 The king made silver *as common* in Jerusalem as stones, and he made cedar trees as abundant as the sycamores which *are* in the lowland. 28 And they brought horses to Solomon from Egypt and from all lands.

29 Now the rest of the acts of Solomon, first and last, *are* they not written in the book of Nathan the prophet, in the prophecy of Ahijah the Shilonite, and in the visions of Iddo the seer concerning Jeroboam the son of Nebat? 30 Solomon reigned in Jerusalem over all Israel forty years. 31 Then Solomon rested with his fathers, and was buried in the City of David his father. And Rehoboam his son reigned in his place.

Solomon's son is crowned king

10 And Rehoboam went to Shechem, for all Israel had gone to Shechem to make him king. 2 So it happened, when Jeroboam the son of Nebat heard *it* (he was in Egypt, where he had fled from the presence of King Solomon), that Jeroboam returned from Egypt. 3 Then they sent for him and called him. And Jeroboam and all Israel came and spoke to Rehoboam, saying, 4 "Your father made our yoke heavy; now therefore, lighten the burdensome service of your father and his heavy yoke which he put on us, and we will serve you."

5 So he said to them, "Come back to me after three days." And the people departed.

6 Then King Rehoboam consulted the elders who stood before his father Solomon while he still lived, saying, "How do you advise *me* to answer these people?"

7 And they spoke to him, saying, "If you are kind to these people, and please them, and speak good words to them, they will be your servants forever."

8 But he rejected the advice which the elders had given him, and consulted the young men who had grown up with him, who stood before him. 9 And he said to them, "What advice do you give? How should we answer this people who have spoken to me, saying, 'Lighten the yoke which your father put on us'?"

10 Then the young men who had grown up with him spoke to him, saying, "Thus you should speak to the people who have spoken to you, saying, 'Your father made our yoke heavy, but you make *it* lighter on us'— thus you shall say to them: 'My little *finger* shall be thicker than my father's waist! 11 And now, whereas my father put a heavy yoke on you, I will add to your yoke; my father chastised you with whips, but I *will chastise you* with scourges!' "

12 So Jeroboam and all the people came to Rehoboam on the third day, as the king had directed, saying, "Come back to me the third day." 13 Then the king answered them roughly. King Rehoboam rejected the advice of the elders, 14 and he spoke to them according to the advice of the young men, saying, "My father made your yoke heavy, but I will add to it; my father chastised you with whips, but I *will chastise you* with scourges!" 15 So the king did not listen to the people; for the turn *of events* was from God, that the LORD might fulfill His word, which He had spoken by the hand of Ahijah the Shilonite to Jeroboam the son of Nebat.

16 Now when all Israel *saw* that the

king did not listen to them, the people answered the king, saying:

"What share have we in David?
We have no inheritance in the son of Jesse.
Every man to your tents, O Israel!
Now see to your own house, O David!"

So all Israel departed to their tents. 17 But Rehoboam reigned over the children of Israel who dwelt in the cities of Judah.
18 Then King Rehoboam sent Hadoram, who *was* in charge of revenue; but the children of Israel stoned him with stones, and he died. Therefore King Rehoboam mounted *his* chariot in haste to flee to Jerusalem. 19 So Israel has been in rebellion against the house of David to this day.

Rehoboam rules Judah

11 Now when Rehoboam came to Jerusalem, he assembled from the house of Judah and Benjamin one hundred and eighty thousand chosen *men* who were warriors, to fight against Israel, that he might restore the kingdom to Rehoboam.
2 But the word of the LORD came to Shemaiah the man of God, saying, 3 "Speak to Rehoboam the son of Solomon, king of Judah, and to all Israel in Judah and Benjamin, saying, 4 'Thus says the LORD: "You shall not go up or fight against your brethren! Let every man return to his house, for this thing is from Me." ' " Therefore they obeyed the words of the LORD, and turned back from attacking Jeroboam.
5 So Rehoboam dwelt in Jerusalem, and built cities for defense in Judah. 6 And he built Bethlehem, Etam, Tekoa, 7 Beth Zur, Sochoh, Adullam, 8 Gath, Mareshah, Ziph, 9 Adoraim, Lachish, Azekah, 10 Zorah, Aijalon, and Hebron, which are in Judah and Benjamin, fortified cities. 11 And he fortified the strongholds, and put captains in them, and stores of food, oil, and

wine. 12 Also in every city *he put* shields and spears, and made them very strong, having Judah and Benjamin on his side.
13 And from all their territories the priests and the Levites who *were* in all Israel took their stand with him. 14 For the Levites left their commonlands and their possessions and came to Judah and Jerusalem, for Jeroboam and his sons had rejected them from serving as priests to the LORD. 15 Then he appointed for himself priests for the high places, for the demons, and the calf idols which he had made. 16 And after *the Levites left,* those from all the tribes of Israel, such as set their heart to seek the LORD God of Israel, came to Jerusalem to sacrifice to the LORD God of their fathers. 17 So they strengthened the kingdom of Judah, and made Rehoboam the son of Solomon strong for three years, because they walked in the way of David and Solomon for three years.
18 Then Rehoboam took for himself as wife Mahalath the daughter of Jerimoth the son of David, *and of* Abihail the daughter of Eliah the son of Jesse. 19 And she bore him children: Jeush, Shamariah, and Zaham. 20 After her he took Maachah the granddaughter of Absalom; and she bore him Abijah, Attai, Ziza, and Shelomith. 21 Now Rehoboam loved Maachah the granddaughter of Absalom more than all his wives and his concubines; for he took eighteen wives and sixty concubines, and begot twenty-eight sons and sixty daughters. 22 And Rehoboam appointed Abijah the son of Maachah as chief, *to be* leader among his brothers; for he *intended* to make him king. 23 He dealt wisely, and dispersed some of his sons throughout all the territories of Judah and Benjamin, to every fortified city; and he gave them provisions in abundance. He also sought many wives *for them.*

Egypt conquers Judah

12 Now it came to pass, when Rehoboam had established the kingdom

and had strengthened himself, that he forsook the law of the LORD, and all Israel along with him. 2 And it happened in the fifth year of King Rehoboam *that* Shishak king of Egypt came up against Jerusalem, because they had transgressed against the LORD, 3 with twelve hundred chariots, sixty thousand horsemen, and people without number who came with him out of Egypt—the Lubim and the Sukkiim and the Ethiopians. 4 And he took the fortified cities of Judah and came to Jerusalem.

5 Then Shemaiah the prophet came to Rehoboam and the leaders of Judah, who were gathered together in Jerusalem because of Shishak, and said to them, "Thus says the LORD: 'You have forsaken Me, and therefore I also have left you in the hand of Shishak.'"

6 So the leaders of Israel and the king humbled themselves; and they said, "The LORD *is* righteous."

7 Now when the LORD saw that they humbled themselves, the word of the LORD came to Shemaiah, saying, "They have humbled themselves; *therefore* I will not destroy them, but I will grant them some deliverance. My wrath shall not be poured out on Jerusalem by the hand of Shishak. 8 Nevertheless they will be his servants, that they may distinguish My service from the service of the kingdoms of the nations."

9 So Shishak king of Egypt came up against Jerusalem, and took away the treasures of the house of the LORD and the treasures of the king's house; he took everything. He also carried away the gold shields which Solomon had made. 10 Then King Rehoboam made bronze shields in their place, and committed *them* to the hands of the captains of the guard, who guarded the doorway of the king's house. 11 And whenever the king entered the house of the LORD, the guard would go and bring them out; then they would take them back into the guardroom. 12 When he humbled himself, the wrath of the LORD turned from him,

so as not to destroy *him* completely; and things also went well in Judah.

13 Thus King Rehoboam strengthened himself in Jerusalem and reigned. Now Rehoboam *was* forty-one years old when he became king; and he reigned seventeen years in Jerusalem, the city which the LORD had chosen out of all the tribes of Israel, to put His name there. His mother's name *was* Naamah, an Ammonitess. 14 And he did evil, because he did not prepare his heart to seek the LORD.

15 The acts of Rehoboam, first and last, *are* they not written in the book of Shemaiah the prophet, and of Iddo the seer concerning genealogies? And *there were* wars between Rehoboam and Jeroboam all their days. 16 So Rehoboam rested with his fathers, and was buried in the City of David. Then Abijah his son reigned in his place.

Abijah and Jeroboam go to war

13 In the eighteenth year of King Jeroboam, Abijah became king over Judah. 2 He reigned three years in Jerusalem. His mother's name *was* Michaiah the daughter of Uriel of Gibeah.

And there was war between Abijah and Jeroboam. 3 Abijah set the battle in order with an army of valiant warriors, four hundred thousand choice men. Jeroboam also drew up in battle formation against him with eight hundred thousand choice men, mighty men of valor.

4 Then Abijah stood on Mount Zemaraim, which *is* in the mountains of Ephraim, and said, "Hear me, Jeroboam and all Israel: 5 Should you not know that the LORD God of Israel gave the dominion over Israel to David forever, to him and his sons, by a covenant of salt? 6 Yet Jeroboam the son of Nebat, the servant of Solomon the son of David, rose up and rebelled against his lord. 7 Then worthless rogues gathered to him, and strengthened themselves against Rehoboam the son of Solomon, when Rehoboam was young and inexperienced and could not withstand them. 8 And now

---

What King Jeroboam Learned

I was the king of Samaria, or Israel, in the north. In 2 Chronicles 10 you can read that I was the one who led Israel to rebel against Judah's King Rehoboam (pronounced *re-hoh-BOW-um*).

I was sure I did right in leading our ten tribes in the north to break away from Judah, God's people in the south. But then I made two gold calves as idols for my people to worship.

One day we trapped Rehoboam's army, but the Lord fought against me because of my idols, and the army of Judah won the battle.

So I learned too late that the only way to win in life is to be on God's side. Whose side are you on?

---

you think to withstand the kingdom of the LORD, which is in the hand of the sons of David; and you *are* a great multitude, and with you are the gold calves which Jeroboam made for you as gods. 9 Have you not cast out the priests of the LORD, the sons of Aaron, and the Levites, and made for yourselves priests, like the peoples of *other* lands, so that whoever comes to consecrate himself with a young bull and seven rams may be a priest of *things that are* not gods? 10 But as for us, the LORD *is* our God, and we have not forsaken Him; and the priests who minister to the LORD *are* the sons of Aaron, and the Levites *attend* to *their* duties. 11 And they burn to the LORD every morning and every evening burnt sacrifices and sweet incense; *they* also *set* the showbread *in order on* the pure *gold* table, and the lampstand of gold with its lamps to burn every evening; for we keep the command of the LORD our God, but you have forsaken Him. 12 Now look, God Himself is with us as *our* head, and His priests with sounding trumpets to sound the alarm against you. O children of Israel, do not fight against the LORD God of your fathers, for you shall not prosper!"

13 But Jeroboam caused an ambush to go around behind them; so they were in front of Judah, and the ambush *was* behind them. 14 And when Judah looked around, to their surprise the battle line *was* at both front and rear; and they cried out to the LORD, and the priests sounded the trumpets.

15 Then the men of Judah gave a shout; and as the men of Judah shouted, it happened that God struck Jeroboam and all Israel before Abijah and Judah. 16 And the children of Israel fled before Judah, and God delivered them into their hand. 17 Then Abijah and his people struck them with a great slaughter; so five hundred thousand choice men of Israel fell slain. 18 Thus the children of Israel were subdued at that time; and the children of Judah prevailed, because they relied on the LORD God of their fathers.

19 And Abijah pursued Jeroboam and took cities from him: Bethel with its villages, Jeshanah with its villages, and Ephrain with its villages. 20 So Jeroboam did not recover strength again in the days of Abijah; and the LORD struck him, and he died.

21 But Abijah grew mighty, married fourteen wives, and begot twenty-two sons and sixteen daughters. 22 Now the rest of the acts of Abijah, his ways, and his sayings *are* written in the annals of the prophet Iddo.

King Asa rules Judah

14 So Abijah rested with his fathers, and they buried him in the City of David. Then Asa his son reigned in his place. In his days the land was quiet for ten years.

2 Asa did *what was* good and right in the eyes of the LORD his God, 3 for he removed the altars of the foreign *gods* and the high places, and

broke down the *sacred* pillars and cut down the wooden images. 4 He commanded Judah to seek the LORD God of their fathers, and to observe the law and the commandment. 5 He also removed the high places and the incense altars from all the cities of Judah, and the kingdom was quiet under him. 6 And he built fortified cities in Judah, for the land had rest; he had no war in those years, because the LORD had given him rest. 7 Therefore he said to Judah, "Let us build these cities and make walls around *them,* and towers, gates, and bars, *while* the land *is* yet before us, because we have sought the LORD our God; we have sought *Him,* and He has given us rest on every side." So they built and prospered. 8 And Asa had an army of three hundred thousand from Judah who carried shields and spears, and from Benjamin two hundred and eighty thousand men who carried shields and drew bows; all these *were* mighty men of valor.

9 Then Zerah the Ethiopian came out against them with an army of a million men and three hundred chariots, and he came to Mareshah. 10 So Asa went out against him, and they set the troops in battle array in the Valley of Zephathah at Mareshah. 11 And Asa cried out to the LORD his God, and said, "LORD, *it is* nothing for You to help, whether with many or with those who have no power; help us, O LORD our God, for we rest on You, and in Your name we go against this multitude. O LORD, You *are* our God; do not let man prevail against You!"

12 So the LORD struck the Ethiopians before Asa and Judah, and the Ethiopians fled. 13 And Asa and the people who *were* with him pursued them to Gerar. So the Ethiopians were overthrown, and they could not recover, for they were broken before the LORD and His army. And they carried away very much spoil. 14 Then they defeated all the cities around Gerar, for the fear of the LORD came upon them; and they plundered all the cities, for there was exceedingly much spoil in them. 15 They also attacked the livestock enclosures, and carried off sheep and camels in abundance, and returned to Jerusalem.

Asa makes some good changes

15 Now the Spirit of God came upon Azariah the son of Oded. 2 And he went out to meet Asa, and said to him: "Hear me, Asa, and all Judah and Benjamin. The LORD *is* with you while you are with Him. If you seek Him, He will be found by you; but if you forsake Him, He will forsake you. 3 For a long time Israel *has been* without the true God, without a teaching priest, and without law; 4 but when in their trouble they turned to the LORD God of Israel, and sought Him, He was found by them. 5 And in those times *there was* no peace to the one who went out, nor to the one who came in, but great turmoil *was* on all the inhabitants of the lands. 6 So nation was destroyed by nation, and city by city, for God troubled them with every adversity. 7 But you, be strong and do not let your hands be weak, for your work shall be rewarded!"

8 And when Asa heard these words and the prophecy of Oded the prophet, he took courage, and removed the abominable idols from all the land of Judah and Benjamin and from the cities which he had taken in the mountains of Ephraim; and he restored the altar of the LORD that *was* before the vestibule of the LORD. 9 Then he gathered all Judah and Benjamin, and those who dwelt with them from Ephraim, Manasseh, and Simeon, for they came over to him in great numbers from Israel when they saw that the LORD his God was with him.

10 So they gathered together at Jerusalem in the third month, in the fifteenth year of the reign of Asa. 11 And they offered to the LORD at that time seven hundred bulls and seven thousand sheep from the spoil they had brought. 12 Then they entered into a covenant to seek the LORD God of their fathers with all their heart and with all

their soul; 13 and whoever would not seek the Lord God of Israel was to be put to death, whether small or great, whether man or woman. 14 Then they took an oath before the Lord with a loud voice, with shouting and trumpets and rams' horns. 15 And all Judah rejoiced at the oath, for they had sworn with all their heart and sought Him with all their soul; and He was found by them, and the Lord gave them rest all around.

16 Also he removed Maachah, the mother of Asa the king, from *being* queen mother, because she had made an obscene image of Asherah; and Asa cut down her obscene image, then crushed and burned *it* by the Brook Kidron. 17 But the high places were not removed from Israel. Nevertheless the heart of Asa was loyal all his days. 18 He also brought into the house of God the things that his father had dedicated and that he himself had dedicated: silver and gold and utensils. 19 And there was no war until the thirty-fifth year of the reign of Asa.

Asa signs a treaty with Syria and forgets God

16 In the thirty-sixth year of the reign of Asa, Baasha king of Israel came up against Judah and built Ramah, that he might let none go out or come in to Asa king of Judah. 2 Then Asa brought silver and gold from the treasuries of the house of the Lord and of the king's house, and sent to Ben-Hadad king of Syria, who dwelt in Damascus, saying, 3 *"Let there be* a treaty between you and me, as there was between my father and your father. See, I have sent you silver and gold; come, break your treaty with Baasha king of Israel, so that he will withdraw from me."

4 So Ben-Hadad heeded King Asa, and sent the captains of his armies against the cities of Israel. They attacked Ijon, Dan, Abel Maim, and all the storage cities of Naphtali. 5 Now it happened, when Baasha heard *it*, that he stopped building Ramah and ceased his work. 6 Then King Asa took all Judah, and they carried away the stones and timber of Ramah, which Baasha had used for building; and with them he built Geba and Mizpah.

7 And at that time Hanani the seer came to Asa king of Judah, and said to him: "Because you have relied on the king of Syria, and have not relied on the Lord your God, therefore the army of the king of Syria has escaped from your hand. 8 Were the Ethiopians and the Lubim not a huge army with very many chariots and horsemen? Yet, because you relied on the Lord, He delivered them into your hand. 9 For the eyes of the Lord run to and fro throughout the whole earth, to show Himself strong on behalf of *those* whose heart *is* loyal to Him. In this you

---

What King Asa Learned

Pronounce my name *AY-suh,* meaning "Healer." I learned too little too late. How could I be so stupid? I thought I could sell the treasures of the house of God to buy protection from a foreign army.

I also put our prophet in prison because he warned me what was going to happen. After that, I had nothing but war and suffering all my life. Finally, I died of a painful disease.

There is a great lesson in my life. I only wish I had learned it in time to help me become an obedient person. God was trying to tell me I must always put Him first.

In other words, don't sell your friendship with God in exchange for something less than God. That is the most terrible mistake you can make in your life.

have done foolishly; therefore from now on you shall have wars." [10] Then Asa was angry with the seer, and put him in prison, for *he was* enraged at him because of this. And Asa oppressed *some* of the people at that time.

[11] Note that the acts of Asa, first and last, are indeed written in the book of the kings of Judah and Israel. [12] And in the thirty-ninth year of his reign, Asa became diseased in his feet, and his malady was severe; yet in his disease he did not seek the LORD, but the physicians.

[13] So Asa rested with his fathers; he died in the forty-first year of his reign. [14] They buried him in his own tomb, which he had made for himself in the City of David; and they laid him in the bed which was filled with spices and various ingredients prepared in a mixture of ointments. They made a very great burning for him.

Jehoshaphat rules Judah

17 Then Jehoshaphat his son reigned in his place, and strengthened himself against Israel. [2] And he placed troops in all the fortified cities of Judah, and set garrisons in the land of Judah and in the cities of Ephraim which Asa his father had taken. [3] Now the LORD was with Jehoshaphat, because he walked in the former ways of his father David; he did not seek the Baals, [4] but sought the God of his father, and walked in His commandments and not according to the acts of Israel. [5] Therefore the LORD established the kingdom in his hand; and all Judah gave presents to Jehoshaphat, and he had riches and honor in abundance. [6] And his heart took delight in the ways of the LORD; moreover he removed the high places and wooden images from Judah.

[7] Also in the third year of his reign he sent his leaders, Ben-Hail, Obadiah, Zechariah, Nethanel, and Michaiah, to teach in the cities of Judah. [8] And with them *he sent* Levites: Shemaiah, Nethaniah, Zebadiah, Asahel, Shemira-

moth, Jehonathan, Adonijah, Tobijah, and Tobadonijah—the Levites; and with them Elishama and Jehoram, the priests. [9] So they taught in Judah, and *had* the Book of the Law of the LORD with them; they went throughout all the cities of Judah and taught the people.

[10] And the fear of the LORD fell on all the kingdoms of the lands that *were* around Judah, so that they did not make war against Jehoshaphat. [11] Also *some* of the Philistines brought Jehoshaphat presents and silver as tribute; and the Arabians brought him flocks, seven thousand seven hundred rams and seven thousand seven hundred male goats.

[12] So Jehoshaphat became increasingly powerful, and he built fortresses and storage cities in Judah. [13] He had much property in the cities of Judah; and the men of war, mighty men of valor, *were* in Jerusalem.

[14] These *are* their numbers, according to their fathers' houses. Of Judah, the captains of thousands: Adnah the captain, and with him three hundred thousand mighty men of valor; [15] and next to him *was* Jehohanan the captain, and with him two hundred and eighty thousand; [16] and next to him *was* Amasiah the son of Zichri, who willingly offered himself to the LORD, and with him two hundred thousand mighty men of valor. [17] Of Benjamin: Eliada a mighty man of valor, and with him two hundred thousand men armed with bow and shield; [18] and next to him *was* Jehozabad, and with him one hundred and eighty thousand prepared for war. [19] These served the king, besides those the king put in the fortified cities throughout all Judah.

Micaiah speaks God's word

18 Jehoshaphat had riches and honor in abundance; and by marriage he allied himself with Ahab. [2] After some years he went down to *visit* Ahab in Samaria; and Ahab killed sheep and oxen in abundance for him and the people who were with him, and persuaded him to go up *with him* to Ramoth Gilead. ³ So Ahab king of Israel said to Jehoshaphat king of Judah, "Will you go with me *against* Ramoth Gilead?"

And he answered him, "I *am* as you *are*, and my people as your people; *we will be* with you in the war."

⁴ Also Jehoshaphat said to the king of Israel, "Please inquire for the word of the Lord today."

⁵ Then the king of Israel gathered the prophets together, four hundred men, and said to them, "Shall we go to war against Ramoth Gilead, or shall I refrain?"

So they said, "Go up, for God will deliver it into the king's hand."

⁶ But Jehoshaphat said, "*Is there* not still a prophet of the Lord here, that we may inquire of Him?"

⁷ So the king of Israel said to Jehoshaphat, "*There is* still one man by whom we may inquire of the Lord; but I hate him, because he never prophesies good concerning me, but always evil. He *is* Micaiah the son of Imla."

And Jehoshaphat said, "Let not the king say such things!"

⁸ Then the king of Israel called one *of his* officers and said, "Bring Micaiah the son of Imla quickly!"

⁹ The king of Israel and Jehoshaphat king of Judah, clothed in *their* robes, sat each on his throne; and they sat at a threshing floor at the entrance of the gate of Samaria; and all the prophets prophesied before them. ¹⁰ Now Zedekiah the son of Chenaanah had made horns of iron for himself; and he said, "Thus says the Lord: 'With these you shall gore the Syrians until they are destroyed.'"

¹¹ And all the prophets prophesied so, saying, "Go up to Ramoth Gilead and prosper, for the Lord will deliver *it* into the king's hand."

¹² Then the messenger who had gone to call Micaiah spoke to him, saying, "Now listen, the words of the prophets with one accord encourage the king. Therefore please let your word be like *the word of* one of them, and speak encouragement."

¹³ And Micaiah said, "*As* the Lord lives, whatever my God says, that I will speak."

¹⁴ Then he came to the king; and the king said to him, "Micaiah, shall we go to war against Ramoth Gilead, or shall I refrain?"

And he said, "Go and prosper, and they shall be delivered into your hand!"

¹⁵ So the king said to him, "How many times shall I make you swear that you tell me nothing but the truth in the name of the Lord?"

¹⁶ Then he said, "I saw all Israel scattered on the mountains, as sheep that have no shepherd. And the Lord said, 'These have no master. Let each return to his house in peace.'"

¹⁷ And the king of Israel said to Jehoshaphat, "Did I not tell you he would not prophesy good concerning me, but evil?"

¹⁸ Then *Micaiah* said, "Therefore hear the word of the Lord: I saw the Lord sitting on His throne, and all the host of heaven standing on His right hand and His left. ¹⁹ And the Lord said, 'Who will persuade Ahab king of Israel to go up, that he may fall at Ramoth Gilead?' So one spoke in this manner, and another spoke in that manner. ²⁰ Then a spirit came forward and stood before the Lord, and said, 'I will persuade him.' The Lord said to him, 'In what way?' ²¹ So he said, 'I will go out and be a lying spirit in the mouth of all his prophets.' And *the* Lord said, 'You shall persuade *him* and also prevail; go out and do so.' ²² Therefore look! The Lord has put a lying spirit in the mouth of these prophets of yours, and the Lord has declared disaster against you."

²³ Then Zedekiah the son of Chenaanah went near and struck Micaiah on the cheek, and said, "Which way did the spirit from the Lord go from me to speak to you?"

²⁴ And Micaiah said, "Indeed you shall see on that day when you go into an inner chamber to hide!"

25 Then the king of Israel said, "Take Micaiah, and return him to Amon the governor of the city and to Joash the king's son; 26 and say, 'Thus says the king: "Put this *fellow* in prison, and feed him with bread of affliction and water of affliction, until I return in peace." ' "

27 But Micaiah said, "If you ever return in peace, the LORD has not spoken by me." And he said, "Take heed, all you people!"

28 So the king of Israel and Jehoshaphat the king of Judah went up to Ramoth Gilead. 29 And the king of Israel said to Jehoshaphat, "I will disguise myself and go into battle; but you put on your robes." So the king of Israel disguised himself, and they went into battle.

30 Now the king of Syria had commanded the captains of the chariots who *were* with him, saying, "Fight with no one small or great, but only with the king of Israel."

31 So it was, when the captains of the chariots saw Jehoshaphat, that they said, "It *is* the king of Israel!" Therefore they surrounded him to attack; but Jehoshaphat cried out, and the LORD helped him, and God diverted them from him. 32 For so it was, when the captains of the chariots saw that it was not the king of Israel, that they turned back from pursuing him. 33 Now a certain man drew a bow at random, and struck the king of Israel between the joints of his armor. So he said to the driver of his chariot, "Turn around and take me out of the battle, for I am wounded." 34 The battle increased that day, and the king of Israel propped *himself* up in *his* chariot facing the Syrians until evening; and about the time of sunset he died.

The king of Judah makes more changes

19 Then Jehoshaphat the king of Judah returned safely to his house in Jerusalem. 2 And Jehu the son of Hanani the seer went out to meet him, and said to King Jehoshaphat, "Should you help the wicked and love those who hate the LORD? Therefore the wrath of the LORD is upon you. 3 Nevertheless good things are found in you, in that you have removed the wooden images from the land, and have prepared your heart to seek God."

4 So Jehoshaphat dwelt at Jerusalem; and he went out again among the people from Beersheba to the mountains of Ephraim, and brought them back to the LORD God of their fathers. 5 Then he set judges in the land throughout all the fortified cities of Judah, city by city, 6 and said to the judges, "Take heed to what you are doing, for you do not judge for man but for the LORD, who is with you in the judgment. 7 Now therefore, let the fear of the LORD be upon you; take care and do *it,* for *there is* no iniquity with the LORD our God, no partiality, nor taking of bribes."

8 Moreover in Jerusalem, for the judgment of the LORD and for controversies, Jehoshaphat appointed some of the Levites and priests, and some of the chief fathers of Israel, when they returned to Jerusalem. 9 And he commanded them, saying, "Thus you shall act in the fear of the LORD, faithfully and with a loyal heart: 10 Whatever case comes to you from your brethren who dwell in their cities, whether of bloodshed or offenses against law or commandment, against statutes or ordinances, you shall warn them, lest they trespass against the LORD and wrath come upon you and your brethren. Do this, and you will not be guilty. 11 And take notice: Amariah the chief priest *is* over you in all matters of the LORD; and Zebadiah the son of Ishmael, the ruler of the house of Judah, for all the king's matters; also the Levites *will be* officials before you. Behave courageously, and the LORD will be with the good."

God fights a great battle

20 It happened after this *that* the people of Moab with the people of Ammon, and *others* with them besides the

Ammonites, came to battle against Jehoshaphat. 2 Then some came and told Jehoshaphat, saying, "A great multitude is coming against you from beyond the sea, from Syria; and they are in Hazazon Tamar" (which *is* En Gedi). 3 And Jehoshaphat feared, and set himself to seek the LORD, and proclaimed a fast throughout all Judah. 4 So Judah gathered together to ask *help* from the LORD; and from all the cities of Judah they came to seek the LORD.

5 Then Jehoshaphat stood in the assembly of Judah and Jerusalem, in the house of the LORD, before the new court, 6 and said: "O LORD God of our fathers, *are* You not God in heaven, and do You *not* rule over all the kingdoms of the nations, and in Your hand *is there not* power and might, so that no one is able to withstand You? 7 *Are* You not our God, *who* drove out the inhabitants of this land before Your people Israel, and gave it to the descendants of Abraham Your friend forever? 8 And they dwell in it, and have built You a sanctuary in it for Your name, saying, 9 'If disaster comes upon us—sword, judgment, pestilence, or famine—we will stand before this temple and in Your presence (for Your name *is* in this temple), and cry out to You in our affliction, and You will hear and save.' 10 And now, here are the people of Ammon, Moab, and Mount Seir—whom You would not let Israel invade when they came out of the land of Egypt, but they turned from them and did not destroy them— 11 here they are, rewarding us by coming to throw us out of Your possession which You have given us to inherit. 12 O our God, will You not judge them? For we have no power against this great multitude that is coming against us; nor do we know what to do, but our *eyes are* upon You."

13 Now all Judah, with their little ones, their wives, and their children, stood before the LORD.

14 Then the Spirit of the LORD came upon Jahaziel the son of Zechariah, the son of Benaiah, the son of Jeiel, the son of Mattaniah, a Levite of the sons of Asaph, in the midst of the assembly. 15 And he said, "Listen, all you of Judah and you inhabitants of Jerusalem, and you, King Jehoshaphat! Thus says the LORD to you: 'Do not be afraid nor dismayed because of this great multitude, for the battle *is* not yours, but God's. 16 Tomorrow go down against them. They will surely come up by the Ascent of Ziz, and you will find them at the end of the brook before the Wilderness of Jeruel. 17 You will not *need* to fight in this *battle.* Position yourselves, stand still and *see* the salvation of the LORD, who is with you, O Judah and Jerusalem!' Do not fear or be dismayed; tomorrow go out against them, for the LORD *is* with you."

18 And Jehoshaphat bowed his head with *his* face to the ground, and all Judah and the inhabitants of Jerusalem bowed before the LORD, worshiping the LORD. 19 Then the Levites of the children of the Kohathites and of the children of the Korahites stood up to praise the LORD God of Israel with voices loud and high.

20 So they rose early in the morning and went out into the Wilderness of Tekoa; and as they went out, Jehoshaphat stood and said, "Hear me, O Judah and you inhabitants of Jerusalem: Believe in the LORD your God, and you shall be established; believe His prophets, and you shall prosper." 21 And when he had consulted with the people, he appointed those who should sing to the LORD, and who should praise the beauty of holiness, as they went out before the army and were saying:

"Praise the LORD,
     For His mercy *endures* forever."

22 Now when they began to sing and to praise, the LORD set ambushes against the people of Ammon, Moab, and Mount Seir, who had come against Judah; and they were defeated. 23 For the people of Ammon and Moab stood up against the inhabitants of Mount Seir to utterly kill and destroy

them. And when they had made an end of the inhabitants of Seir, they helped to destroy one another.

24 So when Judah came to a place overlooking the wilderness, they looked toward the multitude; and there *were* their dead bodies, fallen on the earth. No one had escaped.

25 When Jehoshaphat and his people came to take away their spoil, they found among them an abundance of valuables on the dead bodies, and precious jewelry, which they stripped off for themselves, more than they could carry away; and they were three days gathering the spoil because there was so much. 26 And on the fourth day they assembled in the Valley of Berachah, for there they blessed the LORD; therefore the name of that place was called The Valley of Berachah until this day. 27 Then they returned, every man of Judah and Jerusalem, with Jehoshaphat in front of them, to go back to Jerusalem with joy, for the LORD had made them rejoice over their enemies. 28 So they came to Jerusalem, with stringed instruments and harps and trumpets, to the house of the LORD. 29 And the fear of God was on all the kingdoms of *those* countries when they heard that the LORD had fought against the enemies of Israel. 30 Then the realm of Jehoshaphat was quiet, for his God gave him rest all around.

31 So Jehoshaphat was king over Judah. *He was* thirty-five years old when he became king, and he reigned twenty-five years in Jerusalem. His mother's name *was* Azubah the daughter of Shilhi. 32 And he walked in the way of his father Asa, and did not turn aside from it, doing *what was* right in the sight of the LORD. 33 Nevertheless the high places *were* not taken away, for as yet the people had not directed their hearts to the God of their fathers.

34 Now the rest of the acts of Jehoshaphat, first and last, indeed they *are* written in the book of Jehu the son of Hanani, which *is* mentioned in the book of the kings of Israel.

35 After this Jehoshaphat king of Judah allied himself with Ahaziah king of Israel, who acted very wickedly. 36 And he allied himself with him to make ships to go to Tarshish, and they made the ships in Ezion Geber. 37 But Eliezer the son of Dodavah of Mareshah prophesied against Jehoshaphat, saying, "Because you have allied yourself with Ahaziah, the LORD has destroyed your works." Then the ships were wrecked, so that they were not able to go to Tarshish.

Jehoram does evil in God's sight

21 And Jehoshaphat rested with his fathers, and was buried with his fathers in the City of David. Then Jehoram his son reigned in his place. 2 He had brothers, the sons of Jehoshaphat: Azariah, Jehiel, Zechariah, Azaryahu, Michael, and Shephatiah; all these *were* the sons of Jehoshaphat king of Israel. 3 Their father gave them great gifts of silver and gold and precious things, with fortified cities in Judah; but he gave the kingdom to Jehoram, because he *was* the firstborn.

4 Now when Jehoram was established over the kingdom of his father, he strengthened himself and killed all his brothers with the sword, and also *others* of the princes of Israel.

5 Jehoram *was* thirty-two years old when he became king, and he reigned eight years in Jerusalem. 6 And he walked in the way of the kings of Israel, just as the house of Ahab had done, for he had the daughter of Ahab as a wife; and he did evil in the sight of the LORD. 7 Yet the LORD would not destroy the house of David, because of the covenant that He had made with David, and since He had promised to give a lamp to him and to his sons forever.

8 In his days Edom revolted against Judah's authority, and made a king over themselves. 9 So Jehoram went out with his officers, and all his chariots with him. And he rose by night and attacked the Edomites who had surrounded him and the captains of the chariots. 10 Thus Edom has been in revolt against Judah's authority to this

day. At that time Libnah revolted against his rule, because he had forsaken the LORD God of his fathers. 11 Moreover he made high places in the mountains of Judah, and caused the inhabitants of Jerusalem to commit harlotry, and led Judah astray.

12 And a letter came to him from Elijah the prophet, saying,

Thus says the LORD God of your
father David:
Because you have not walked
in the ways of Jehoshaphat your
father, or in the ways of Asa king
of Judah, 13 but have walked in
the way of the kings of Israel,
and have made Judah and the
inhabitants of Jerusalem to play
the harlot like the harlotry of the
house of Ahab, and also have
killed your brothers, those of
your father's household, who
were better than yourself,
14 behold, the LORD will strike
your people with a serious
affliction—your children, your
wives, and all your possessions;
15 and you will become very sick
with a disease of your intestines,
until your intestines come out by
reason of the sickness, day by
day.

16 Moreover the LORD stirred up against Jehoram the spirit of the Philistines and the Arabians who were near the Ethiopians. 17 And they came up into Judah and invaded it, and carried away all the possessions that were found in the king's house, and also his sons and his wives, so that there was not a son left to him except Jehoahaz, the youngest of his sons.

18 After all this the LORD struck him in his intestines with an incurable disease. 19 Then it happened in the course of time, after the end of two years, that his intestines came out because of his sickness; so he died in severe pain. And his people made no burning for him, like the burning for his fathers.

20 He was thirty-two years old when he became king. He reigned in Jerusa-

lem eight years and, to no one's sorrow, departed. However they buried him in the City of David, but not in the tombs of the kings.

Ahaziah rules Judah

22 Then the inhabitants of Jerusalem made Ahaziah his youngest son king in his place, for the raiders who came with the Arabians into the camp had killed all the older sons. So Ahaziah the son of Jehoram, king of Judah, reigned. 2 Ahaziah was forty-two years old when he became king, and he reigned one year in Jerusalem. His mother's name was Athaliah the granddaughter of Omri. 3 He also walked in the ways of the house of Ahab, for his mother advised him to do wickedly. 4 Therefore he did evil in the sight of the LORD, like the house of Ahab; for they were his counselors after the death of his father, to his destruction. 5 He also followed their advice, and went with Jehoram the son of Ahab king of Israel to war against Hazael king of Syria at Ramoth Gilead; and the Syrians wounded Joram. 6 Then he returned to Jezreel to recover from the wounds which he had received at Ramah, when he fought against Hazael king of Syria. And Azariah the son of Jehoram, king of Judah, went down to see Jehoram the son of Ahab in Jezreel, because he was sick.

7 His going to Joram was God's occasion for Ahaziah's downfall; for when he arrived, he went out with Jehoram against Jehu the son of Nimshi, whom the LORD had anointed to cut off the house of Ahab. 8 And it happened, when Jehu was executing judgment on the house of Ahab, and found the princes of Judah and the sons of Ahaziah's brothers who served Ahaziah, that he killed them. 9 Then he searched for Ahaziah; and they caught him (he was hiding in Samaria), and brought him to Jehu. When they had killed him, they buried him, "because," they said, "he is the son of Jehoshaphat, who sought the LORD with all his heart."

So the house of Ahaziah had no one

to assume power over the kingdom. 10 Now when Athaliah the mother of Ahaziah saw that her son was dead, she arose and destroyed all the royal heirs of the house of Judah. 11 But Jehoshabeath, the daughter of the king, took Joash the son of Ahaziah, and stole him away from among the king's sons who were being murdered, and put him and his nurse in a bedroom. So Jehoshabeath, the daughter of King Jehoram, the wife of Jehoiada the priest (for she was the sister of Ahaziah), hid him from Athaliah so that she did not kill him. 12 And he was hidden with them in the house of God for six years, while Athaliah reigned over the land.

Joash becomes king

23 In the seventh year Jehoiada strengthened himself, and made a covenant with the captains of hundreds: Azariah the son of Jeroham, Ishmael the son of Jehohanan, Azariah the son of Obed, Maaseiah the son of Adaiah, and Elishaphat the son of Zichri. 2 And they went throughout Judah and gathered the Levites from all the cities of Judah, and the chief fathers of Israel, and they came to Jerusalem. 3 Then all the assembly made a covenant with the king in the house of God. And he said to them, "Behold, the king's son shall reign, as the LORD has said of the sons of David. 4 This is what you shall do: One-third of you entering on the Sabbath, of the priests and the Levites, shall be keeping watch over the doors; 5 one-third shall be at the king's house; and one-third at the Gate of the Foundation. All the people shall be in the courts of the house of the LORD. 6 But let no one come into the house of the LORD except the priests and those of the Levites who serve. They may go in, for they are holy; but all the people shall keep the watch of the LORD. 7 And the Levites shall surround the king on all sides, every man with his weapons in his hand; and whoever comes into the house, let him be put to death. You

are to be with the king when he comes in and when he goes out."

8 So the Levites and all Judah did according to all that Jehoiada the priest commanded. And each man took his men who were to be on duty on the Sabbath, with those who were going off duty on the Sabbath; for Jehoiada the priest had not dismissed the divisions. 9 And Jehoiada the priest gave to the captains of hundreds the spears and the large and small shields which had belonged to King David, that were in the temple of God. 10 Then he set all the people, every man with his weapon in his hand, from the right side of the temple to the left side of the temple, along by the altar and by the temple, all around the king. 11 And they brought out the king's son, put the crown on him, gave him the Testimony, and made him king. Then Jehoiada and his sons anointed him, and said, "Long live the king!"

12 Now when Athaliah heard the noise of the people running and praising the king, she came to the people in the temple of the LORD. 13 When she looked, there was the king standing by his pillar at the entrance; and the leaders and the trumpeters were by the king. All the people of the land were rejoicing and blowing trumpets, also the singers with musical instruments, and those who led in praise. So Athaliah tore her clothes and said, "Treason! Treason!"

14 And Jehoiada the priest brought out the captains of hundreds who were set over the army, and said to them, "Take her outside under guard, and slay with the sword whoever follows her." For the priest had said, "Do not kill her in the house of the LORD."

15 So they seized her; and she went by way of the entrance of the Horse Gate into the king's house, and they killed her there.

16 Then Jehoiada made a covenant between himself, the people, and the king, that they should be the LORD's people. 17 And all the people went to the temple of Baal, and tore it down. They broke in pieces its altars and im-

ages, and killed Mattan the priest of Baal before the altars. ¹⁸ Also Jehoiada appointed the oversight of the house of the LORD to the hand of the priests, the Levites, whom David had assigned in the house of the LORD, to offer the burnt offerings of the LORD, as *it is* written in the Law of Moses, with rejoicing and with singing, *as it was established* by David. ¹⁹ And he set the gatekeepers at the gates of the house of the LORD, so that no one *who was* in any way unclean should enter.

²⁰ Then he took the captains of hundreds, the nobles, the governors of the people, and all the people of the land, and brought the king down from the house of the LORD; and they went through the Upper Gate to the king's house, and set the king on the throne of the kingdom. ²¹ So all the people of the land rejoiced; and the city was quiet, for they had slain Athaliah with the sword.

Joash repairs the temple

24 Joash *was* seven years old when he became king, and he reigned forty years in Jerusalem. His mother's name *was* Zibiah of Beersheba. ² Joash did *what was* right in the sight of the LORD all the days of Jehoiada the priest. ³ And Jehoiada took two wives for him, and he had sons and daughters.

⁴ Now it happened after this *that* Joash set his heart on repairing the house of the LORD. ⁵ Then he gathered the priests and the Levites, and said to them, "Go out to the cities of Judah, and gather from all Israel money to repair the house of your God from year to year, and see that you do it quickly."

However the Levites did not do it quickly. ⁶ So the king called Jehoiada the chief *priest,* and said to him, "Why have you not required the Levites to bring in from Judah and from Jerusalem the collection, *according to the commandment* of Moses the servant of the LORD and of the assembly of Israel, for the tabernacle of witness?" ⁷ For the sons of Athaliah, that wicked woman, had broken into the house of God, and had also presented all the dedicated things of the house of the LORD to the Baals.

⁸ Then at the king's command they made a chest, and set it outside at the gate of the house of the LORD. ⁹ And they made a proclamation throughout Judah and Jerusalem to bring to the LORD the collection *that* Moses the servant of God *had imposed* on Israel in the wilderness. ¹⁰ Then all the leaders and all the people rejoiced, brought their contributions, and put *them* into the chest until all had given. ¹¹ So it was, at that time, when the chest was brought to the king's official by the

---

King Joash—My name is pronounced *JO-ash* and means "The Lord Supports." I was only seven years old when I became king of Judah. Jehoiada (pronounced *jeh-HOY-uh-dah*), the priest, was like a father to me while he lived. He was a very good man.

The temple of the Lord had fallen into ruin and its costly furniture had been stolen. So Jehoiada and I collected money to restore the beauty of the temple. All of its furniture and implements were replaced, and all was well for us as long as Jehoiada lived.

After Jehoiada died, the leaders of Judah came and made me agree to allow false worship of idols in the land. Jehoiada's son, Zechariah (pronounced *zek-uh-RIGH-uh*), warned us about our wicked plans, but we killed him.

Soon after that, the Syrian army attacked us, and I was wounded. Then my own servants killed me. So I was at last punished for my great sin (see Numbers 32:23).

hand of the Levites, and when they saw that *there was* much money, that the king's scribe and the high priest's officer came and emptied the chest, and took it and returned it to its place. Thus they did day by day, and gathered money in abundance.

12 The king and Jehoiada gave it to those who did the work of the service of the house of the LORD; and they hired masons and carpenters to repair the house of the LORD, and also those who worked in iron and bronze to restore the house of the LORD. 13 So the workmen labored, and the work was completed by them; they restored the house of God to its original condition and reinforced it. 14 When they had finished, they brought the rest of the money before the king and Jehoiada; they made from it articles for the house of the LORD, articles for serving and offering, spoons and vessels of gold and silver. And they offered burnt offerings in the house of the LORD continually all the days of Jehoiada.

15 But Jehoiada grew old and was full of days, and he died; *he was* one hundred and thirty years old when he died. 16 And they buried him in the City of David among the kings, because he had done good in Israel, both toward God and His house.

17 Now after the death of Jehoiada the leaders of Judah came and bowed down to the king. And the king listened to them. 18 Therefore they left the house of the LORD God of their fathers, and served wooden images and idols; and wrath came upon Judah and Jerusalem because of their trespass. 19 Yet He sent prophets to them, to bring them back to the LORD; and they testified against them, but they would not listen.

20 Then the Spirit of God came upon Zechariah the son of Jehoiada the priest, who stood above the people, and said to them, "Thus says God: 'Why do you transgress the commandments of the LORD, so that you cannot prosper? Because you have forsaken the LORD, He also has forsaken you.' "
21 So they conspired against him, and

at the command of the king they stoned him with stones in the court of the house of the LORD. 22 Thus Joash the king did not remember the kindness which Jehoiada his father had done to him, but killed his son; and as he died, he said, "The LORD look on *it,* and repay!"

23 So it happened in the spring of the year *that* the army of Syria came up against him; and they came to Judah and Jerusalem, and destroyed all the leaders of the people from among the people, and sent all their spoil to the king of Damascus. 24 For the army of the Syrians came with a small company of men; but the LORD delivered a very great army into their hand, because they had forsaken the LORD God of their fathers. So they executed judgment against Joash. 25 And when they had withdrawn from him (for they left him severely wounded), his own servants conspired against him because of the blood of the sons of Jehoiada the priest, and killed him on his bed. So he died. And they buried him in the City of David, but they did not bury him in the tombs of the kings.

26 These are the ones who conspired against him: Zabad the son of Shimeath the Ammonitess, and Jehozabad the son of Shimrith the Moabitess. 27 Now *concerning* his sons, and the many oracles about him, and the repairing of the house of God, indeed they *are* written in the annals of the book of the kings. Then Amaziah his son reigned in his place.

Judah and Israel make war

25 Amaziah *was* twenty-five years old *when* he became king, and he reigned twenty-nine years in Jerusalem. His mother's name *was* Jehoaddan of Jerusalem. 2 And he did *what was* right in the sight of the LORD, but not with a loyal heart.

3 Now it happened, as soon as the kingdom was established for him, that he executed his servants who had murdered his father the king. 4 However he did not execute their children, but

did as *it is* written in the Law in the Book of Moses, where the LORD commanded, saying, "The fathers shall not be put to death for their children, nor shall the children be put to death for their fathers; but a person shall die for his own sin."

5 Moreover Amaziah gathered Judah together and set over them captains of thousands and captains of hundreds, according to *their* fathers' houses, throughout all Judah and Benjamin; and he numbered them from twenty years old and above, and found them to be three hundred thousand choice *men, able* to go to war, who could handle spear and shield. 6 He also hired one hundred thousand mighty men of valor from Israel for one hundred talents of silver. 7 But a man of God came to him, saying, "O king, do not let the army of Israel go with you, for the LORD *is* not with Israel— *not with* any of the children of Ephraim. 8 But if you go, be gone! Be strong in battle! *Even so,* God shall make you fall before the enemy; for God has power to help and to overthrow."

9 Then Amaziah said to the man of God, "But what *shall we* do about the hundred talents which I have given to the troops of Israel?"

And the man of God answered, "The LORD is able to give you much more than this." 10 So Amaziah discharged the troops that had come to him from Ephraim, to go back home. Therefore their anger was greatly aroused against Judah, and they returned home in great anger.

11 Then Amaziah strengthened himself, and leading his people, he went to the Valley of Salt and killed ten thousand of the people of Seir. 12 Also the children of Judah took captive ten thousand alive, brought them to the top of the rock, and cast them down from the top of the rock, so that they all were dashed in pieces.

13 But as for the soldiers of the army which Amaziah had discharged, so that they would not go with him to battle, they raided the cities of Judah from Samaria to Beth Horon, killed three thousand in them, and took much spoil.

14 Now it was so, after Amaziah came from the slaughter of the Edomites, that he brought the gods of the people of Seir, set them up *to be* his gods, and bowed down before them and burned incense to them. 15 Therefore the anger of the LORD was aroused against Amaziah, and He sent him a prophet who said to him, "Why have you sought the gods of the people, which could not rescue their own people from your hand?"

16 So it was, as he talked with him, that *the king* said to him, "Have we made you the king's counselor? Cease! Why should you be killed?"

Then the prophet ceased, and said, "I know that God has determined to destroy you, because you have done this and have not heeded my advice."

17 Now Amaziah king of Judah asked advice and sent to Joash the son of Jehoahaz, the son of Jehu, king of Israel, saying, "Come, let us face one another *in battle.*"

18 And Joash king of Israel sent to Amaziah king of Judah, saying, "The thistle that *was* in Lebanon sent to the cedar that was in Lebanon, saying, 'Give your daughter to my son as wife'; and a wild beast that *was* in Lebanon passed by and trampled the thistle. 19 Indeed you say that you have defeated the Edomites, and your heart is lifted up to boast. Stay at home now; why should you meddle with trouble, that you should fall—you and Judah with you?"

20 But Amaziah would not heed, for it *came* from God, that He might give them into the hand *of their enemies,* because they sought the gods of Edom. 21 So Joash king of Israel went out; and he and Amaziah king of Judah faced one another at Beth Shemesh, which *belongs* to Judah. 22 And Judah was defeated by Israel, and every man fled to his tent. 23 Then Joash the king of Israel captured Amaziah king of Judah, the son of Joash, the son of Jehoahaz, at Beth Shemesh; and he

brought him to Jerusalem, and broke down the wall of Jerusalem from the Gate of Ephraim to the Corner Gate— four hundred cubits. 24 And *he took* all the gold and silver, all the articles that were found in the house of God with Obed-Edom, the treasures of the king's house, and hostages, and returned to Samaria.

25 Amaziah the son of Joash, king of Judah, lived fifteen years after the death of Joash the son of Jehoahaz, king of Israel. 26 Now the rest of the acts of Amaziah, from first to last, indeed *are* they not written in the book of the kings of Judah and Israel? 27 After the time that Amaziah turned away from following the LORD, they made a conspiracy against him in Jerusalem, and he fled to Lachish; but they sent after him to Lachish and killed him there. 28 Then they brought him on horses and buried him with his fathers in the City of Judah.

A king becomes a leper

26 Now all the people of Judah took Uzziah, who *was* sixteen years old, and made him king instead of his father Amaziah. 2 He built Elath and restored it to Judah, after the king rested with his fathers.

3 Uzziah *was* sixteen years old when he became king, and he reigned fifty-two years in Jerusalem. His mother's name was Jecholiah of Jerusalem. 4 And he did *what was* right in the sight of the LORD, according to all that his father Amaziah had done. 5 He sought God in the days of Zechariah, who had understanding in the visions of God; and as long as he sought the LORD, God made him prosper.

6 Now he went out and made war against the Philistines, and broke down the wall of Gath, the wall of Jabneh, and the wall of Ashdod; and he built cities *around* Ashdod and among the Philistines. 7 God helped him against the Philistines, against the Arabians who lived in Gur Baal, and against the Meunites. 8 Also the Ammonites brought tribute to Uzziah. His fame spread as far as the entrance of Egypt, for he became exceedingly strong.

9 And Uzziah built towers in Jerusalem at the Corner Gate, at the Valley Gate, and at the corner buttress of the wall; then he fortified them. 10 Also he built towers in the desert. He dug many wells, for he had much livestock, both in the lowlands and in the plains; *he also had* farmers and vinedressers in the mountains and in Carmel, for he loved the soil.

11 Moreover Uzziah had an army of fighting men who went out to war by companies, according to the number on their roll as prepared by Jeiel the scribe and Maaseiah the officer, under the hand of Hananiah, *one* of the king's captains. 12 The total number of chief officers of the mighty men of valor *was* two thousand six hundred. 13 And under their authority *was* an army of three hundred and seven thousand five hundred, that made war with mighty power, to help the king against the enemy. 14 Then Uzziah prepared for

---

⚒ DIGGING IN

26:1—23 What Happens to Proud People? Uzziah (pronounced *uh-ZIGH-uh*) was a good king in most ways, and he also became strong in military power. But then something went wrong. Uzziah became proud, and he went into the temple and burned incense. This was something only the priests were allowed to do. It wasn't enough for Uzziah to be king. He wanted to be a priest also. In other words, Uzziah wanted to be able to do just as he pleased. He wanted to have everything his own way. That's how proud people act.

You'll notice that Uzziah's story has an unhappy ending. He was struck with the disease of leprosy and had to spend the rest of his life away from everybody else.

God says He resists the proud. He does not always use leprosy to deal with proud people, but they always suffer in the end because pride leads to destruction (see Proverbs 16:18).

them, for the entire army, shields, spears, helmets, body armor, bows, and slings *to cast* stones. ¹⁵ And he made devices in Jerusalem, invented by skillful men, to be on the towers and the corners, to shoot arrows and large stones. So his fame spread far and wide, for he was marvelously helped till he became strong.

¹⁶ But when he was strong his heart was lifted up, to *his* destruction, for he transgressed against the LORD his God by entering the temple of the LORD to burn incense on the altar of incense. ¹⁷ So Azariah the priest went in after him, and with him *were* eighty priests of the LORD—valiant men. ¹⁸ And they withstood King Uzziah, and said to him, "*It is* not for you, Uzziah, to burn incense to the LORD, but for the priests, the sons of Aaron, who are consecrated to burn incense. Get out of the sanctuary, for you have trespassed! You *shall have* no honor from the LORD God."

¹⁹ Then Uzziah became furious; and he *had* a censer in his hand to burn incense. And while he was angry with the priests, leprosy broke out on his forehead, before the priests in the house of the LORD, beside the incense altar. ²⁰ And Azariah the chief priest and all the priests looked at him, and there, on his forehead, he *was* leprous; so they thrust him out of that place. Indeed he also hurried to get out, because the LORD had struck him.

²¹ King Uzziah was a leper until the day of his death. He dwelt in an isolated house, because he was a leper; for he was cut off from the house of the LORD. Then Jotham his son *was* over the king's house, judging the people of the land.

²² Now the rest of the acts of Uzziah, from first to last, the prophet Isaiah the son of Amoz wrote. ²³ So Uzziah rested with his fathers, and they buried him with his fathers in the field of burial which *belonged* to the kings, for they said, "He is a leper." Then Jotham his son reigned in his place.

Uzziah rules Judah and sins

27 Jotham *was* twenty-five years old when he became king, and he reigned sixteen years in Jerusalem. His mother's name *was* Jerushah the daughter of Zadok. ² And he did *what was* right in the sight of the LORD, according to all that his father Uzziah had done (although he did not enter the temple of the LORD). But still the people acted corruptly.

³ He built the Upper Gate of the house of the LORD, and he built extensively on the wall of Ophel. ⁴ Moreover he built cities in the mountains of Judah, and in the forests he built fortresses and towers. ⁵ He also fought with the king of the Ammonites and defeated them. And the people of Ammon gave him in that year one hundred talents of silver, ten thousand kors of wheat, and ten thousand of barley. The people of Ammon paid this to him in the second and third years also. ⁶ So Jotham became mighty, because

---

🪓 DIGGING IN

27:6 How King Jotham Became Mighty "Jotham prepared his ways before the Lord his God." In other words Jotham talked to God about everything he did.

Sometimes we make big plans. But what seems like a good idea to us may not be what God has in mind at all. Some time ago the Ford Motor Company came up with a saying they used in television commercials: "Ford has a better idea." As time goes by, we begin to see that it is the same with God and us. We have great ideas. But then we find out that God always has a better idea.

As you prepare for a future career, remember that your time in this world will not really be very long. But life can be exciting and satisfying when you seek God's will in everything you plan. Then, like Jotham, you will become mighty because you prepared your ways before the Lord.

he prepared his ways before the LORD his God.

7 Now the rest of the acts of Jotham, and all his wars and his ways, indeed they *are* written in the book of the kings of Israel and Judah. 8 He was twenty-five years old when he became king, and he reigned sixteen years in Jerusalem. 9 So Jotham rested with his fathers, and they buried him in the City of David. Then Ahaz his son reigned in his place.

King Jotham obeys God

28 Ahaz *was* twenty years old when he became king, and he reigned sixteen years in Jerusalem; and he did not do *what was* right in the sight of the LORD, as his father David *had done.* 2 For he walked in the ways of the kings of Israel, and made molded images for the Baals. 3 He burned incense in the Valley of the Son of Hinnom, and burned his children in the fire, according to the abominations of the nations whom the LORD had cast out before the children of Israel. 4 And he sacrificed and burned incense on the high places, on the hills, and under every green tree.

5 Therefore the LORD his God delivered him into the hand of the king of Syria. They defeated him, and carried away a great multitude of them as captives, and brought *them* to Damascus. Then he was also delivered into the hand of the king of Israel, who defeated him with a great slaughter. 6 For Pekah the son of Remaliah killed one hundred and twenty thousand in Judah in one day, all valiant men, because they had forsaken the LORD God of their fathers. 7 Zichri, a mighty man of Ephraim, killed Maaseiah the king's son, Azrikam the officer over the house, and Elkanah *who was* second to the king. 8 And the children of Israel carried away captive of their brethren two hundred thousand women, sons, and daughters; and they also took away much spoil from them, and brought the spoil to Samaria.

9 But a prophet of the LORD was there, whose name *was* Oded; and he went out before the army that came to Samaria, and said to them: "Look, because the LORD God of your fathers was angry with Judah, He has delivered them into your hand; but you have killed them in a rage *that* reaches up to heaven. 10 And now you propose

The Valley of Hinnom, where Israel once sacrificed little children to pagan gods.

to force the children of Judah and Jerusalem to be your male and female slaves; *but are* you not also guilty before the LORD your God? 11 Now hear me, therefore, and return the captives, whom you have taken captive from your brethren, for the fierce wrath of the LORD is upon you."

12 Then some of the heads of the children of Ephraim, Azariah the son of Johanan, Berechiah the son of Meshillemoth, Jehizkiah the son of Shallum, and Amasa the son of Hadlai, stood up against those who came from the war, 13 and said to them, "You shall not bring the captives here, for we *already* have offended the LORD. You intend to add to our sins and to our guilt; for our guilt is great, and *there is* fierce wrath against Israel." 14 So the armed men left the captives and the spoil before the leaders and all the assembly. 15 Then the men who were designated by name rose up and took the captives, and from the spoil they clothed all who were naked among them, dressed them and gave them sandals, gave them food and drink, and anointed them; and they let all the feeble ones ride on donkeys. So they brought them to their brethren at Jericho, the city of palm trees. Then they returned to Samaria.

16 At the same time King Ahaz sent to the kings of Assyria to help him. 17 For again the Edomites had come, attacked Judah, and carried away captives. 18 The Philistines also had invaded the cities of the lowland and of the South of Judah, and had taken Beth Shemesh, Aijalon, Gederoth, Sochoh with its villages, Timnah with its villages, and Gimzo with its villages; and they dwelt there. 19 For the LORD brought Judah low because of Ahaz king of Israel, for he had encouraged moral decline in Judah and had been continually unfaithful to the LORD. 20 Also Tiglath-Pileser king of Assyria came to him and distressed him, and did not assist him. 21 For Ahaz took part *of the treasures* from the house of the LORD, from the house of the king, and from the leaders, and he gave *it* to the king of Assyria; but he did not help him.

22 Now in the time of his distress King Ahaz became increasingly unfaithful to the LORD. This *is that* King Ahaz. 23 For he sacrificed to the gods of Damascus which had defeated him, saying, "Because the gods of the kings of Syria help them, I will sacrifice to them that they may help me." But they were the ruin of him and of all Israel. 24 So Ahaz gathered the articles of the house of God, cut in pieces the articles of the house of God, shut up the doors of the house of the LORD, and made for himself altars in every corner of Jerusalem. 25 And in every single city of Judah he made high places to burn incense to other gods, and provoked to anger the LORD God of his fathers.

26 Now the rest of his acts and all his ways, from first to last, indeed they *are* written in the book of the kings of Judah and Israel. 27 So Ahaz rested with his fathers, and they buried him in the city, in Jerusalem; but they did not bring him into the tombs of the kings of Israel. Then Hezekiah his son reigned in his place.

Hezekiah opens the temple

29 Hezekiah became king *when he was* twenty-five years old, and he reigned twenty-nine years in Jerusalem. His mother's name *was* Abijah the daughter of Zechariah. 2 And he did *what was* right in the sight of the LORD, according to all that his father David had done.

3 In the first year of his reign, in the first month, he opened the doors of the house of the LORD and repaired them. 4 Then he brought in the priests and the Levites, and gathered them in the East Square, 5 and said to them: "Hear me, Levites! Now sanctify yourselves, sanctify the house of the LORD God of your fathers, and carry out the rubbish from the holy *place*. 6 For our fathers have trespassed and done evil in the eyes of the LORD our God; they have forsaken Him, have turned their faces away from the dwelling place of

the LORD, and turned *their* backs *on Him.* [7] They have also shut up the doors of the vestibule, put out the lamps, and have not burned incense or offered burnt offerings in the holy *place* to the God of Israel. [8] Therefore the wrath of the LORD fell upon Judah and Jerusalem, and He has given them up to trouble, to desolation, and to jeering, as you see with your eyes. [9] For indeed, because of this our fathers have fallen by the sword; and our sons, our daughters, and our wives *are* in captivity.

[10] "Now *it is* in my heart to make a covenant with the LORD God of Israel, that His fierce wrath may turn away from us. [11] My sons, do not be negligent now, for the LORD has chosen you to stand before Him, to serve Him, and that you should minister to Him and burn incense."

[12] Then these Levites arose: Mahath the son of Amasai and Joel the son of Azariah, of the sons of the Kohathites; of the sons of Merari, Kish the son of Abdi and Azariah the son of Jehallelel; of the Gershonites, Joah the son of Zimmah and Eden the son of Joah; [13] of the sons of Elizaphan, Shimri and Jeiel; of the sons of Asaph, Zechariah and Mattaniah; [14] of the sons of Heman, Jehiel and Shimei; and of the sons of Jeduthun, Shemaiah and Uzziel.

[15] And they gathered their brethren, sanctified themselves, and went according to the commandment of the king, at the words of the LORD, to cleanse the house of the LORD. [16] Then the priests went into the inner part of the house of the LORD to cleanse *it,* and brought out all the debris that they found in the temple of the LORD to the court of the house of the LORD. And the Levites took *it* out and carried *it* to the Brook Kidron.

[17] Now they began to sanctify on the first *day* of the first month, and on the eighth day of the month they came to the vestibule of the LORD. So they sanctified the house of the LORD in eight days, and on the sixteenth day of the first month they finished.

[18] Then they went in to King Hezekiah and said, "We have cleansed all the house of the LORD, the altar of burnt offerings with all its articles, and the table of the showbread with all its articles. [19] Moreover all the articles which King Ahaz in his reign had cast aside in his transgression we have prepared and sanctified; and there they *are,* before the altar of the LORD."

[20] Then King Hezekiah rose early, gathered the rulers of the city, and went up to the house of the LORD. [21] And they brought seven bulls, seven rams, seven lambs, and seven male goats for a sin offering for the kingdom, for the sanctuary, and for Judah. Then he commanded the priests, the sons of Aaron, to offer *them* on the altar of the LORD. [22] So they killed the bulls, and the priests received the blood and sprinkled *it* on the altar. Likewise they killed the rams and sprinkled the blood on the altar. They also killed the lambs and sprinkled the blood on the altar. [23] Then they brought out the male goats *for* the sin offering before the king and the assembly, and they laid their hands on them. [24] And the priests killed them; and they presented their blood on the altar as a sin offering to make an atonement for all Israel, for the king commanded *that* the burnt offering and the sin offering *be made* for all Israel.

[25] And he stationed the Levites in the house of the LORD with cymbals, with stringed instruments, and with harps, according to the commandment of David, of Gad the king's seer, and of Nathan the prophet; for thus *was* the commandment of the LORD by his prophets. [26] The Levites stood with the instruments of David, and the priests with the trumpets. [27] Then Hezekiah commanded *them* to offer the burnt offering on the altar. And when the burnt offering began, the song of the LORD *also* began, with the trumpets and with the instruments of David king of Israel. [28] So all the assembly worshiped, the singers sang, and the trumpeters sounded; all *this continued* until the burnt offering was finished. [29] And

when they had finished offering, the king and all who were present with him bowed and worshiped. 30 Moreover King Hezekiah and the leaders commanded the Levites to sing praise to the LORD with the words of David and of Asaph the seer. So they sang praises with gladness, and they bowed their heads and worshiped.

31 Then Hezekiah answered and said, "Now *that* you have consecrated yourselves to the LORD, come near, and bring sacrifices and thank offerings into the house of the LORD." So the assembly brought in sacrifices and thank offerings, and as many as were of a willing heart *brought* burnt offerings. 32 And the number of the burnt offerings which the assembly brought was seventy bulls, one hundred rams, *and* two hundred lambs; all these *were* for a burnt offering to the LORD. 33 The consecrated things *were* six hundred bulls and three thousand sheep. 34 But the priests were too few, so that they could not skin all the burnt offerings; therefore their brethren the Levites helped them until the work was ended and until the *other* priests had sanctified themselves, for the Levites were more diligent in sanctifying themselves than the priests. 35 Also the burnt offerings *were* in abundance, with the fat of the peace offerings and *with* the drink offerings for *every* burnt offering.

So the service of the house of the LORD was set in order. 36 Then Hezekiah and all the people rejoiced that God had prepared the people, since the events took place so suddenly.

The Passover is a happy time again

30 And Hezekiah sent to all Israel and Judah, and also wrote letters to Ephraim and Manasseh, that they should come to the house of the LORD at Jerusalem, to keep the Passover to the LORD God of Israel. 2 For the king and his leaders and all the assembly in Jerusalem had agreed to keep the Passover in the second month. 3 For they could not keep it at the regular time, because a sufficient number of priests had not consecrated themselves, nor had the people gathered together at Jerusalem. 4 And the matter pleased the king and all the assembly. 5 So they resolved to make a proclamation throughout all Israel, from Beersheba to Dan, that they should come to keep the Passover to the LORD God of Israel at Jerusalem, since they had not done *it* for a long *time* in the *prescribed* manner.

6 Then the runners went throughout all Israel and Judah with the letters from the king and his leaders, and spoke according to the command of the king: "Children of Israel, return to the LORD God of Abraham, Isaac, and Israel; then He will return to the remnant of you who have escaped from the hand of the kings of Assyria. 7 And do not be like your fathers and your brethren, who trespassed against the LORD God of their fathers, so that He gave them up to desolation, as you see. 8 Now do not be stiff-necked, as your fathers *were, but* yield yourselves to the LORD; and enter His sanctuary, which He has sanctified forever, and serve the LORD your God, that the fierceness of His wrath may turn away from you. 9 For if you return to the LORD, your brethren and your children *will be treated* with compassion by those who lead them captive, so that they may come back to this land; for the LORD your God *is* gracious and merciful, and will not turn His face from you if you return to Him."

10 So the runners passed from city to city through the country of Ephraim and Manasseh, as far as Zebulun; but they laughed at them and mocked them. 11 Nevertheless some from Asher, Manasseh, and Zebulun humbled themselves and came to Jerusalem. 12 Also the hand of God was on Judah to give them singleness of heart to obey the command of the king and the leaders, at the word of the LORD.

13 Now many people, a very great assembly, gathered at Jerusalem to keep the Feast of Unleavened Bread

King Hezekiah Brings Back Worship of God

The Jerusalem Times

JERUSALEM—Public worship of God has not existed in Judah for a long time, since King Ahaz (pronounced AY-haz) was an ungodly man who even sacrificed his children in fire to foreign gods.

But recent developments under his son, King Hezekiah, have been surprising. After confessing the great sins of our nation, the young king has commanded that the doors of the temple are to be opened for the first time in many years. He has also ordered that the inside of the temple and all its furniture be cleansed and used for the pure worship of the Lord.

In memory of the people's escape from Egypt nine hundred years ago, the king has also renewed the celebration of Passover (see Exodus 12). All parts of Old Testament worship have been restored as commanded by the laws God gave to Moses.

This day will long be remembered in the history of the people of Israel.

---

in the second month. 14 They arose and took away the altars that *were* in Jerusalem, and they took away all the incense altars and cast *them* into the Brook Kidron. 15 Then they slaughtered the Passover *lambs* on the fourteenth *day* of the second month. The priests and the Levites were ashamed, and sanctified themselves, and brought the burnt offerings to the house of the LORD. 16 They stood in their place according to their custom, according to the Law of Moses the man of God; the priests sprinkled the blood *received* from the hand of the Levites. 17 For *there were* many in the assembly who had not sanctified themselves; therefore the Levites had charge of the slaughter of the Passover *lambs* for everyone *who was* not clean, to sanctify *them* to the LORD. 18 For a multitude of the people, many from Ephraim, Manasseh, Issachar, and Zebulun, had not cleansed themselves, yet they ate the Passover contrary to what was written. But Hezekiah prayed for them, saying, "May the good LORD provide atonement for everyone 19 *who* prepares his heart to seek God, the LORD God of his fathers, though *he is* not *cleansed* according to the purification of the sanctuary." 20 And the LORD listened to Hezekiah and healed the people.

21 So the children of Israel who were present at Jerusalem kept the Feast of Unleavened Bread seven days with great gladness; and the Levites and the priests praised the LORD day by day, *singing* to the LORD, accompanied by loud instruments. 22 And Hezekiah gave encouragement to all the Levites who taught the good knowledge of the LORD; and they ate throughout the feast seven days, offering peace offerings and making confession to the LORD God of their fathers.

23 Then the whole assembly agreed to keep *the feast* another seven days, and they kept it *another* seven days with gladness. 24 For Hezekiah king of Judah gave to the assembly a thousand bulls and seven thousand sheep, and the leaders gave to the assembly a thousand bulls and ten thousand sheep; and a great number of priests sanctified themselves. 25 The whole assembly of Judah rejoiced, also the priests and Levites, all the assembly that came from Israel, the sojourners who came from the land of Israel, and those who dwelt in Judah. 26 So there was great joy in Jerusalem, for since the time of Solomon the son of David, king of Israel, *there had* been nothing like this in Jerusalem. 27 Then the priests, the Levites, arose and blessed the people, and their voice was heard; and their prayer came *up* to His holy dwelling place, to heaven.

Hezekiah takes care of the priests and Levites

31 Now when all this was finished, all Israel who were present went out to the cities of Judah and broke the sacred pillars in pieces, cut down the wooden images, and threw down the high places and the altars—from all Judah, Benjamin, Ephraim, and Manasseh—until they had utterly destroyed them all. Then all the children of Israel returned to their own cities, every man to his possession.

2 And Hezekiah appointed the divisions of the priests and the Levites according to their divisions, each man according to his service, the priests and Levites for burnt offerings and peace offerings, to serve, to give thanks, and to praise in the gates of the camp of the LORD. 3 The king also *appointed* a portion of his possessions for the burnt offerings: for the morning and evening burnt offerings, the burnt offerings for the Sabbaths and the New Moons and the set feasts, as *it is* written in the Law of the LORD.

4 Moreover he commanded the people who dwelt in Jerusalem to contribute support for the priests and the Levites, that they might devote themselves to the Law of the LORD.

5 As soon as the commandment was circulated, the children of Israel brought in abundance the firstfruits of grain and wine, oil and honey, and of all the produce of the field; and they brought in abundantly the tithe of everything. 6 And the children of Israel and Judah, who dwelt in the cities of Judah, brought the tithe of oxen and sheep; also the tithe of holy things which *were* consecrated to the LORD their God they laid in heaps.

7 In the third month they began laying them in heaps, and they finished in the seventh month. 8 And when Hezekiah and the leaders came and saw the heaps, they blessed the LORD and His people Israel. 9 Then Hezekiah questioned the priests and the Levites concerning the heaps. 10 And Azariah the chief priest, from the house of Za-

dok, answered him and said, "Since *the people* began to bring the offerings into the house of the LORD, we have had enough to eat and have plenty left, for the LORD has blessed His people; and what is left *is* this great abundance."

11 Now Hezekiah commanded *them* to prepare rooms in the house of the LORD, and they prepared them. 12 Then they faithfully brought in the offerings, the tithes, and the dedicated things; Cononiah the Levite had charge of them, and Shimei his brother *was* the next. 13 Jehiel, Azaziah, Nahath, Asahel, Jerimoth, Jozabad, Eliel, Ismachiah, Mahath, and Benaiah *were* overseers under the hand of Cononiah and Shimei his brother, at the commandment of Hezekiah the king and Azariah the ruler of the house of God. 14 Kore the son of Imnah the Levite, the keeper of the East Gate, *was* over the freewill offerings to God, to distribute the offerings of the LORD and the most holy things. 15 And under him *were* Eden, Miniamin, Jeshua, Shemaiah, Amariah, and Shecaniah, *his* faithful assistants in the cities of the priests, to distribute allotments to their brethren by divisions, to the great as well as the small.

16 Besides those males from three years old and up who were written in the genealogy, they distributed to everyone who entered the house of the LORD his daily portion for the work of his service, by his division, 17 and to the priests who were written in the genealogy according to their father's house, and to the Levites from twenty years old and up according to their work, by their divisions, 18 and to all who were written in the genealogy—their little ones and their wives, their sons and daughters, the whole company of them—for in their faithfulness they sanctified themselves in holiness.

19 Also for the sons of Aaron the priests, *who were* in the fields of the common-lands of their cities, in every single city, *there were* men who were designated by name to distribute portions to all the males among the priests

King Hezekiah—My name is pronounced *hez-uh-KIGH-uh* and means "The Lord Is Strength." I was one of the greatest kings of Judah. I reigned after my wicked father, Ahaz, who had even sacrificed his children to false gods.

During my reign, I destroyed all the idols that my father worshiped, and I caused the people to return to the true worship of the Lord.

Then the army of Sennacherib (pronounced *suh-NAK-er-rib*), king of Assyria, attacked us and took some of our cities. He also boasted that he would destroy Jerusalem, but Isaiah the prophet and I prayed to the Lord. Then one morning when we awoke, there was Sennacherib's army all lying dead on the ground!

At another time I was sick and nearly died, but Isaiah helped me in prayer again, and I was saved.

The underground water tunnel I built so that Jerusalem would be able to get water without going outside the city walls will last long after I am gone.

and to all who were listed by genealogies among the Levites.

20 Thus Hezekiah did throughout all Judah, and he did what *was* good and right and true before the LORD his God. 21 And in every work that he began in the service of the house of God, in the law and in the commandment, to seek his God, he did *it* with all his heart. So he prospered.

An angel fights Assyria

32 After these deeds of faithfulness, Sennacherib king of Assyria came and entered Judah; he encamped against the fortified cities, thinking to win them over to himself. 2 And when Hezekiah saw that Sennacherib had come, and that his purpose *was* to make war against Jerusalem, 3 he consulted with his leaders and commanders to stop the water from the springs which *were* outside the city; and they helped him. 4 Thus many people gathered together who stopped all the springs and the brook that ran through the land, saying, "Why should the kings of Assyria come and find much water?" 5 And he strengthened himself, built up all the wall that was broken, raised *it* up to the towers, and *built* another wall outside; also he repaired the Millo *in* the City of David, and made weapons and shields in abundance. 6 Then he set

military captains over the people, gathered them together to him in the open square of the city gate, and gave them encouragement, saying, 7 "Be strong and courageous; do not be afraid nor dismayed before the king of Assyria, nor before all the multitude that *is* with him; for *there are* more with us than with him. 8 With him *is* an arm of flesh; but with us *is* the LORD our God, to help us and to fight our battles." And the people were strengthened by the words of Hezekiah king of Judah.

9 After this Sennacherib king of Assyria sent his servants to Jerusalem (but he and all the forces with him *laid siege* against Lachish), to Hezekiah king of Judah, and to all Judah who *were* in Jerusalem, saying, 10 "Thus says Sennacherib king of Assyria: 'In what do you trust, that you remain under siege in Jerusalem? 11 Does not Hezekiah persuade you to give yourselves over to die by famine and by thirst, saying, "The LORD our God will deliver us from the hand of the king of Assyria"? 12 Has not the same Hezekiah taken away His high places and His altars, and commanded Judah and Jerusalem, saying, "You shall worship before one altar and burn incense on it"? 13 Do you not know what I and my fathers have done to all the peoples of *other* lands? Were the gods of the nations of those lands in any way able

to deliver their lands out of my hand? ¹⁴ Who *was there* among all the gods of those nations that my fathers utterly destroyed that could deliver his people from my hand, that your God should be able to deliver you from my hand? ¹⁵ Now therefore, do not let Hezekiah deceive you or persuade you like this, and do not believe him; for no god of any nation or kingdom was able to deliver his people from my hand or the hand of my fathers. How much less will your God deliver you from my hand?' "

¹⁶ Furthermore, his servants spoke against the LORD God and against His servant Hezekiah.

¹⁷ He also wrote letters to revile the LORD God of Israel, and to speak against Him, saying, "As the gods of the nations of *other* lands have not delivered their people from my hand, so the God of Hezekiah will not deliver His people from my hand." ¹⁸ Then they called out with a loud voice in Hebrew to the people of Jerusalem who *were* on the wall, to frighten them and trouble them, that they might take the city. ¹⁹ And they spoke against the God of Jerusalem, as against the gods of the people of the earth—the work of men's hands.

²⁰ Now because of this King Hezekiah and the prophet Isaiah, the son of Amoz, prayed and cried out to heaven. ²¹ Then the LORD sent an angel who cut down *every* mighty man of valor, leader, and captain in the camp of the king of Assyria. So he returned shamefaced to his own land. And when he had gone into the temple of his god, some of his own offspring struck him down with the sword there. ²² Thus the LORD saved Hezekiah and the inhabitants of Jerusalem from the hand of Sennacherib the king of Assyria, and from the hand of all *others,* and guided them on every side. ²³ And many brought gifts to the LORD at Jerusalem, and presents to Hezekiah king of Judah, so that he was exalted in the sight of all nations thereafter. ²⁴ In those days Hezekiah was sick and near death, and he prayed to the

LORD; and He spoke to him and gave him a sign. ²⁵ But Hezekiah did not repay according to the favor *shown* him, for his heart was lifted up; therefore wrath was looming over him and over Judah and Jerusalem. ²⁶ Then Hezekiah humbled himself for the pride of his heart, he and the inhabitants of Jerusalem, so that the wrath of the LORD did not come upon them in the days of Hezekiah.

²⁷ Hezekiah had very great riches and honor. And he made himself treasuries for silver, for gold, for precious stones, for spices, for shields, and for all kinds of desirable items; ²⁸ storehouses for the harvest of grain, wine, and oil; and stalls for all kinds of livestock, and folds for flocks. ²⁹ Moreover he provided cities for himself, and possessions of flocks and herds in abundance; for God had given him very much property. ³⁰ This same Hezekiah also stopped the water outlet of Upper Gihon, and brought the water by tunnel to the west side of the City of David. Hezekiah prospered in all his works.

³¹ However, *regarding* the ambassadors of the princes of Babylon, whom they sent to him to inquire about the wonder that was *done* in the land, God withdrew from him, in order to test him, that He might know all *that was* in his heart.

³² Now the rest of the acts of Hezekiah, and his goodness, indeed they *are* written in the vision of Isaiah the prophet, the son of Amoz, *and* in the book of the kings of Judah and Israel. ³³ So Hezekiah rested with his fathers, and they buried him in the upper tombs of the sons of David; and all Judah and the inhabitants of Jerusalem honored him at his death. Then Manasseh his son reigned in his place.

Wicked King Manasseh changes his mind

33 Manasseh *was* twelve years old when he became king, and he reigned fifty-five years in Jerusalem. ²But he did evil in the sight of the Lord, according to the abominations of the nations whom the Lord had cast out before the children of Israel. ³For he rebuilt the high places which Hezekiah his father had broken down; he raised up altars for the Baals, and made wooden images; and he worshiped all the host of heaven and served them. ⁴He also built altars in the house of the Lord, of which the Lord had said, "In Jerusalem shall My name be forever." ⁵And he built altars for all the host of heaven in the two courts of the house of the Lord. ⁶Also he caused his sons to pass through the fire in the Valley of the Son of Hinnom; he practiced soothsaying, used witchcraft and sorcery, and consulted mediums and spiritists. He did much evil in the sight of the Lord, to provoke Him to anger. ⁷He even set a carved image, the idol which he had made, in the house of God, of which God had said to David and to Solomon his son, "In this house and in Jerusalem, which I have chosen out of all the tribes of Israel, I will put My name forever; ⁸and I will not again remove the foot of Israel from the land which I have appointed for your fathers—only if they are careful to do all that I have commanded them, according to the whole law and the statutes and the ordinances by the hand of Moses." ⁹So Manasseh seduced Judah and the inhabitants of Jerusalem to do more evil than the nations whom the Lord had destroyed before the children of Israel.

¹⁰And the Lord spoke to Manasseh and his people, but they would not listen. ¹¹Therefore the Lord brought upon them the captains of the army of the king of Assyria, who took Manasseh with hooks, bound him with bronze *fetters,* and carried him off to Babylon. ¹²Now when he was in affliction, he implored the Lord his God, and humbled himself greatly before the God of his fathers, ¹³and prayed to Him; and He received his entreaty, heard his supplication, and brought him back to Jerusalem into his kingdom. Then Manasseh knew that the Lord *was* God.

¹⁴After this he built a wall outside the City of David on the west side of Gihon, in the valley, as far as the entrance of the Fish Gate; and *it* enclosed Ophel, and he raised it to a very great height. Then he put military captains in all the fortified cities of Judah. ¹⁵He took away the foreign gods and the idol from the house of the Lord, and all the altars that he had built in the mount of the house of the Lord and in Jerusalem; and he cast *them* out of the city. ¹⁶He also repaired the altar of the Lord, sacrificed peace offerings and thank offerings on it, and commanded Judah to serve the Lord God of Israel. ¹⁷Nevertheless the people still sacrificed on the high places, *but* only to the Lord their God.

¹⁸Now the rest of the acts of Manasseh, his prayer to his God, and the

---

⛏ DIGGING IN

33:21–25 The Sins of King Amon You can read about King Amon's father, Manasseh, in 2 Kings 21:1–18 and the note there. Amon is pronounced *AY-mun,* and Manasseh is pronounced *muh-NASS-uh.*

King Amon did all the evil things that his father Manasseh had done. But Amon was worse than his father because Amon never turned away from his sins. At the end of his life, King Manasseh did turn away from his sins (see 2 Chronicles 33:12). Amon's life came to a bad end when his own servants murdered him. He reigned two years and was only twenty-four years old when he was killed.

A nation's leaders are the people's example. Let us pray that God will always give us good leaders. God says that "the wages of sin is death" (Romans 6:23). We should learn this lesson from the unhappy lives of Manasseh and his son Amon.

words of the seers who spoke to him in the name of the LORD God of Israel, indeed they *are written* in the book of the kings of Israel. [19] Also his prayer and *how God* received his entreaty, and all his sin and trespass, and the sites where he built high places and set up wooden images and carved images, before he was humbled, indeed they *are* written among the sayings of Hozai. [20] So Manasseh rested with his fathers, and they buried him in his own house. Then his son Amon reigned in his place.

[21] Amon *was* twenty-two years old when he became king, and he reigned two years in Jerusalem. [22] But he did evil in the sight of the LORD, as his father Manasseh had done; for Amon sacrificed to all the carved images which his father Manasseh had made, and served them. [23] And he did not humble himself before the LORD, as his father Manasseh had humbled himself; but Amon trespassed more and more.

[24] Then his servants conspired against him, and killed him in his own house. [25] But the people of the land executed all those who had conspired against King Amon. Then the people of the land made his son Josiah king in his place.

Hilkiah solves a mystery

34 Josiah *was* eight years old when he became king, and he reigned thirty-one years in Jerusalem. [2] And he did *what was* right in the sight of the LORD, and walked in the ways of his father David; *he* did *not* turn aside to the right hand or to the left.

[3] For in the eighth year of his reign, while he was still young, he began to seek the God of his father David; and in the twelfth year he began to purge Judah and Jerusalem of the high places, the wooden images, the carved images, and the molded images. [4] They broke down the altars of the Baals in his presence, and the incense altars which *were* above them he cut down; and the wooden images, the carved images, and the molded images

he broke in pieces, and made dust of them and scattered *it* on the graves of those who had sacrificed to them. [5] He also burned the bones of the priests on their altars, and cleansed Judah and Jerusalem. [6] And *so he did* in the cities of Manasseh, Ephraim, and Simeon, as far as Naphtali and all around, with axes. [7] When he had broken down the altars and the wooden images, had beaten the carved images into powder, and cut down all the incense altars throughout all the land of Israel, he returned to Jerusalem.

[8] In the eighteenth year of his reign, when he had purged the land and the temple, he sent Shaphan the son of Azaliah, Maaseiah the governor of the city, and Joah the son of Joahaz the recorder, to repair the house of the LORD his God. [9] When they came to Hilkiah the high priest, they delivered the money that was brought into the house of God, which the Levites who kept the doors had gathered from the hand of Manasseh and Ephraim, from all the remnant of Israel, from all Judah and Benjamin, and *which* they had brought back to Jerusalem. [10] Then they put *it* in the hand of the foremen who had the oversight of the house of the LORD; and they gave it to the workmen who worked in the house of the LORD, to repair and restore the house. [11] They gave *it* to the craftsmen and builders to buy hewn stone and timber for beams, and to floor the houses which the kings of Judah had destroyed. [12] And the men did the work faithfully. Their overseers *were* Jahath and Obadiah the Levites, of the sons of Merari, and Zechariah and Meshullam, of the sons of the Kohathites, to supervise. *Others of* the Levites, all of whom were skillful with instruments of music, [13] *were* over the burden bearers and *were* overseers of all who did work in any kind of service. And *some* of the Levites *were* scribes, officers, and gatekeepers.

[14] Now when they brought out the money that was brought into the house of the LORD, Hilkiah the priest found the Book of the Law of the LORD *given*

How Important Is the Bible?

The Bible had been lost during the long time of Israel's kings. This is why the nation had not been following the Lord. Then one day Hilkiah, the priest, found God's Word hidden away in the temple. That was the beginning of a new and better time for Israel.

by Moses. 15 Then Hilkiah answered and said to Shaphan the scribe, "I have found the Book of the Law in the house of the LORD." And Hilkiah gave the book to Shaphan. 16 So Shaphan carried the book to the king, bringing the king word, saying, "All that was committed to your servants they are doing. 17 And they have gathered the money that was found in the house of the LORD, and have delivered it into the hand of the overseers and the workmen." 18 Then Shaphan the scribe told the king, saying, "Hilkiah the priest has given me a book." And Shaphan read it before the king.

19 Thus it happened, when the king heard the words of the Law, that he tore his clothes. 20 Then the king commanded Hilkiah, Ahikam the son of Shaphan, Abdon the son of Micah, Shaphan the scribe, and Asaiah a servant of the king, saying, 21 "Go, inquire of the LORD for me, and for those who are left in Israel and Judah, concerning the words of the book that is found; for great is the wrath of the LORD that is poured out on us, because our fathers have not kept the word of the LORD, to do according to all that is written in this book."

22 So Hilkiah and those the king had appointed went to Huldah the prophetess, the wife of Shallum the son of Tokhath, the son of Hasrah, keeper of the wardrobe. (She dwelt in Jerusalem in the Second Quarter.) And they spoke to her to that effect.

23 Then she answered them, "Thus says the LORD God of Israel, 'Tell the man who sent you to Me, 24 "Thus says the LORD: 'Behold, I will bring calamity on this place and on its inhab-

itants, all the curses that are written in the book which they have read before the king of Judah, 25 because they have forsaken Me and burned incense to other gods, that they might provoke Me to anger with all the works of their hands. Therefore My wrath will be poured out on this place, and not be quenched.' " ' 26 But as for the king of Judah, who sent you to inquire of the LORD, in this manner you shall speak to him, 'Thus says the LORD God of Israel: "Concerning the words which you have heard— 27 because your heart was tender, and you humbled yourself before God when you heard His words against this place and against its inhabitants, and you humbled yourself before Me, and you tore your clothes and wept before Me, I also have heard you," says the LORD. 28 "Surely I will gather you to your fathers, and you shall be gathered to your grave in peace; and your eyes shall not see all the calamity which I will bring on this place and its inhabitants." ' " So they brought back word to the king.

29 Then the king sent and gathered all the elders of Judah and Jerusalem. 30 The king went up to the house of the LORD, with all the men of Judah and the inhabitants of Jerusalem—the priests and the Levites, and all the people, great and small. And he read in their hearing all the words of the Book of the Covenant which had been found in the house of the LORD. 31 Then the king stood in his place and made a covenant before the LORD, to follow the LORD, and to keep His commandments and His testimonies and His statutes with all his heart and all his soul, to perform the words of the covenant that were written in this book. 32 And he made all who were present in Jerusalem and Benjamin take a stand. So the inhabitants of Jerusalem did according to the covenant of God, the God of their fathers. 33 Thus Josiah removed all the abominations from all the country that belonged to the children of Israel, and made all who were present in Israel diligently serve the

LORD their God. All his days they did not depart from following the LORD God of their fathers.

Josiah celebrates the Passover

35 Now Josiah kept a Passover to the LORD in Jerusalem, and they slaughtered the Passover *lambs* on the fourteenth *day* of the first month. ² And he set the priests in their duties and encouraged them for the service of the house of the LORD. ³ Then he said to the Levites who taught all Israel, who *were* holy to the LORD: "Put the holy ark in the house which Solomon the son of David, king of Israel, built. *It shall* no longer *be* a burden on *your* shoulders. Now serve the LORD your God and His people Israel. ⁴ Prepare *yourselves* according to your fathers' houses, according to your divisions, following the written instruction of David king of Israel and the written instruction of Solomon his son. ⁵ And stand in the holy *place* according to the divisions of the fathers' houses of your brethren the *lay* people, and *according to* the division of the father's house of the Levites. ⁶ So slaughter the Passover *offerings*, consecrate yourselves, and prepare *them* for your brethren, that *they* may do according to the word of the LORD by the hand of Moses."

⁷ Then Josiah gave the *lay* people lambs and young goats from the flock, all for Passover *offerings* for all who were present, to the number of thirty thousand, as well as three thousand cattle; these *were* from the king's possessions. ⁸ And his leaders gave willingly to the people, to the priests, and to the Levites. Hilkiah, Zechariah, and Jehiel, rulers of the house of God, gave to the priests for the Passover *offerings* two thousand six hundred *from the flock,* and three hundred cattle. ⁹ Also Conaniah, his brothers Shemaiah and Nethanel, and Hashabiah and Jeiel and Jozabad, chief of the Levites, gave to the Levites for Passover *offerings* five thousand *from the flock* and five hundred cattle.

¹⁰ So the service was prepared, and the priests stood in their places, and the Levites in their divisions, according to the king's command. ¹¹ And they slaughtered the Passover *offerings;* and the priests sprinkled *the blood* with their hands, while the Levites skinned *the animals.* ¹² Then they removed the burnt offerings that *they* might give them to the divisions of the fathers' houses of the *lay* people, to offer to the LORD, as *it is* written in the Book of Moses. And so *they did* with the cattle. ¹³ Also they roasted the Passover *offerings* with fire according to the ordinance; but the *other* holy *offerings* they boiled in pots, in caldrons, and in pans, and divided *them* quickly among all the *lay* people. ¹⁴ Then afterward they prepared portions for themselves and for the priests, because the priests, the sons of Aaron, *were busy* in offering burnt offerings and fat until night; therefore the Levites prepared portions for themselves and for the priests, the sons of Aaron. ¹⁵ And the singers, the sons of Asaph, *were* in their places, according to the command of David, Asaph, Heman, and Jeduthun the king's seer. Also the gatekeepers *were* at each gate; they did not have to leave their position, because their brethren the Levites prepared portions for them.

¹⁶ So all the service of the LORD was prepared the same day, to keep the Passover and to offer burnt offerings on the altar of the LORD, according to the command of King Josiah. ¹⁷ And the children of Israel who *were* present kept the Passover at that time, and the Feast of Unleavened Bread for seven days. ¹⁸ There had been no Passover kept in Israel like that since the days of Samuel the prophet; and none of the kings of Israel had kept such a Passover as Josiah kept, with the priests and the Levites, all Judah and Israel who were present, and the inhabitants of Jerusalem. ¹⁹ In the eighteenth year of the reign of Josiah this Passover was kept.

²⁰ After all this, when Josiah had prepared the temple, Necho king of Egypt

came up to fight against Carchemish by the Euphrates; and Josiah went out against him. 21 But he sent messengers to him, saying, "What have I to do with you, king of Judah? *I have* not *come* against you this day, but against the house with which I have war; for God commanded me to make haste. Refrain *from meddling with* God, who *is* with me, lest He destroy you." 22 Nevertheless Josiah would not turn his face from him, but disguised himself so that he might fight with him, and did not heed the words of Necho from the mouth of God. So he came to fight in the Valley of Megiddo.

23 And the archers shot King Josiah; and the king said to his servants, "Take me away, for I am severely wounded." 24 His servants therefore took him out of that chariot and put him in the second chariot that he had, and they brought him to Jerusalem. So he died, and was buried in *one of* the tombs of his fathers. And all Judah and Jerusalem mourned for Josiah.

25 Jeremiah also lamented for Josiah. And to this day all the singing men and the singing women speak of Josiah in their lamentations. They made it a custom in Israel; and indeed they *are* written in the Laments. 26 Now the rest of the acts of Josiah and his goodness, according to *what was* written in the Law of the LORD, 27 and his deeds from first to last, indeed they *are* written in the book of the kings of Israel and Judah.

Jerusalem is destroyed, but God has a plan

36 Then the people of the land took Jehoahaz the son of Josiah, and made him king in his father's place in Jerusalem. 2 Jehoahaz *was* twenty-three years old when he became king, and he reigned three months in Jerusalem. 3 Now the king of Egypt deposed him at Jerusalem; and he imposed on the land a tribute of one hundred talents of silver and a talent of gold. 4 Then the king of Egypt made *Jehoahaz's* brother Eliakim king over Judah and Jerusalem, and changed his name to Jehoiakim. And Necho took Jehoahaz his brother and carried him off to Egypt.

5 Jehoiakim *was* twenty-five years old when he became king, and he reigned eleven years in Jerusalem. And he did evil in the sight of the LORD his God. 6 Nebuchadnezzar king of Babylon came up against him, and bound him in bronze *fetters* to carry him off to Babylon. 7 Nebuchadnezzar also carried off *some* of the articles from the house of the LORD to Babylon, and put them in his temple at Babylon. 8 Now the rest of the acts of Jehoiakim, the abominations which he did, and what was found against him, indeed they *are* written in the book of the kings of Israel and Judah. Then Jehoiachin his son reigned in his place.

9 Jehoiachin *was* eight years old when he became king, and he reigned in Jerusalem three months and ten days. And he did evil in the sight of the LORD. 10 At the turn of the year King Nebuchadnezzar summoned *him* and took him to Babylon, with the costly articles from the house of the LORD, and made Zedekiah, *Jehoiakim's* brother, king over Judah and Jerusalem.

11 Zedekiah *was* twenty-one years old when he became king, and he reigned eleven years in Jerusalem. 12 He did evil in the sight of the LORD his God, *and* did not humble himself before Jeremiah the prophet, *who* spoke from the mouth of the LORD. 13 And he also rebelled against King Nebuchadnezzar, who had made him swear *an oath* by God; but he stiffened his neck and hardened his heart against turning to the LORD God of Israel. 14 Moreover all the leaders of the priests and the people transgressed more and more, *according* to all the abominations of the nations, and defiled the house of the LORD which He had consecrated in Jerusalem.

15 And the LORD God of their fathers sent *warnings* to them by His messengers, rising up early and sending *them,* because He had compassion on His

City of Jerusalem in Ruins

World Press International

JERUSALEM—This city, under attack for months, was recently surrounded by the army of Babylon led by Nebuzaradan (pronounced *neb-you-zar-AY-dan*). Following is an interview with General Nebuzaradan on the eve of Jerusalem's fall:

"In this year of 586 B.C., our troops are entering the city of Jerusalem. The Hebrew king and his army have made a run for it. Only the dead and dying remain.

"On the orders of our king, Nebu-chadnezzar (pronounced *neb-you-kad-NEZ-zar*), we are burning all public buildings. In a few hours, the entire city of Jerusalem will be a heap of ashes.

"It is heartbreaking to view the scenes of destruction I see all around me. A soldier's job is often bitter, and all of us hate our present duty. My only comfort in these smoking ruins is Jeremiah the prophet. He has told me this destruction is his God's judgment on this nation for many years of disobedience."

people and on His dwelling place. **16** But they mocked the messengers of God, despised His words, and scoffed at His prophets, until the wrath of the LORD arose against His people, till *there was* no remedy.

17 Therefore He brought against them the king of the Chaldeans, who killed their young men with the sword in the house of their sanctuary, and had no compassion on young man or virgin, on the aged or the weak; He gave *them* all into his hand. **18** And all the articles from the house of God, great and small, the treasures of the house of the LORD, and the treasures of the king and of his leaders, all *these* he took to Babylon. **19** Then they burned the house of God, broke down the wall of Jerusalem, burned all its palaces with fire, and destroyed all its precious possessions. **20** And those who escaped from the sword he carried away to Babylon, where they became servants to him and his sons until the rule of the kingdom of Persia, **21** to fulfill the word of the LORD by the mouth of Jeremiah, until the land had enjoyed her Sabbaths. As long as she lay desolate she kept Sabbath, to fulfill seventy years.

22 Now in the first year of Cyrus king of Persia, that the word of the LORD by the mouth of Jeremiah might be fulfilled, the LORD stirred up the spirit of Cyrus king of Persia, so that he made a proclamation throughout all his kingdom, and also *put it* in writing, saying,

23   Thus says Cyrus king of Persia:
All the kingdoms of the earth the
LORD God of heaven has given
me. And He has commanded
me to build Him a house at
Jerusalem which is in Judah.
Who *is* among you of all His
people? May the LORD his God
be with him, and let him go up!

The Book of
EZRA

My name is pronounced *EZ-ruh* and means "God Is a Help." For 70 years my people Israel were prisoners in Babylon (pronounced *BAB-ih-lun*), hundreds of miles from Jerusalem. I was a scribe. My job was to keep careful records of all that happened. So I wrote this book that bears my name.

When the Persians conquered Babylon, Cyrus (pronounced *SIGH-rus*), their king, decided to let my people go back home to Israel. At that time, Zerubbabel (pronounced *zeh-RUB-uh-bell*) was our leader. He became the first governor of Israel when our people returned to their own land to rebuild our temple.

About 458 years before Jesus was born, I, too, returned to Israel, a journey of four months. Then I had to teach my people all over again how to worship God and how to live for Him.

God's people return to Jerusalem

N OW in the first year of Cyrus king of Persia, that the word of the LORD by the mouth of Jeremiah might be fulfilled, the LORD stirred up the spirit of Cyrus king of Persia, so that he made a proclamation throughout all his kingdom, and also *put it* in writing, saying,

2 Thus says Cyrus king of Persia: All the kingdoms of the earth the LORD God of heaven has given me. And He has commanded me to build Him a house at Jerusalem which *is* in Judah. ³ Who *is* among you of all His

people? May his God be with him, and let him go up to Jerusalem which *is* in Judah, and build the house of the LORD God of Israel (He *is* God), which *is* in Jerusalem. ⁴ And whoever is left in any place where he dwells, let the men of his place help him with silver and gold, with goods and livestock, besides the freewill offerings for the house of God which *is* in Jerusalem.

⁵ Then the heads of the fathers' *houses* of Judah and Benjamin, and the priests and the Levites, with all whose spirits God had moved, arose

🪓 DIGGING IN

1:1–4 Good King Cyrus The prophet Isaiah (pronounced *eye-ZAY-uh*) told about King Cyrus two hundred years before that king lived. (See Isaiah 44:28—Isaiah 45:13.) We know that God had long planned to use King Cyrus in His service. God is in charge of everything that happens, and there are no surprises for Him.

For 70 years Israel had been a captive nation under Babylon (pronounced *BAB-ih-lun*). That was between 606 and 536

years before Jesus was born. At the end of that 70 years, Persia conquered Babylon. Then God caused King Cyrus of Persia to set the people of Israel free to return to Palestine. Cyrus sent a letter throughout his kingdom, proclaiming that God had given him the Persian Empire. He also ordered God's people to take all the wealth and goods they needed to rebuild the temple at Jerusalem.

to go up and build the house of the LORD which *is* in Jerusalem. 6 And all those who *were* around them encouraged them with articles of silver and gold, with goods and livestock, and with precious things, besides all *that* was willingly offered.

7 King Cyrus also brought out the articles of the house of the LORD, which Nebuchadnezzar had taken from Jerusalem and put in the temple of his gods; 8 and Cyrus king of Persia brought them out by the hand of Mithredath the treasurer, and counted them out to Sheshbazzar the prince of Judah. 9 This *is* the number of them: thirty gold platters, one thousand silver platters, twenty-nine knives, 10 thirty gold basins, four hundred and ten silver basins of a similar *kind, and* one thousand other articles. 11 All the articles of gold and silver *were* five thousand four hundred. All *these* Sheshbazzar took with the captives who *were* brought from Babylon to Jerusalem.

A list of the freed captives

2 Now these *are* the people of the province who came back from the captivity, of those who had been carried away, whom Nebuchadnezzar the king of Babylon had carried away to Babylon, and who returned to Jerusalem and Judah, everyone to his *own* city.

2 *Those* who came with Zerubbabel *were* Jeshua, Nehemiah, Seraiah, Reelaiah, Mordecai, Bilshan, Mispar, Bigvai, Rehum, *and* Baanah. The number of the men of the people of Israel: 3 the people of Parosh, two thousand one hundred and seventy-two; 4 the people of Shephatiah, three hundred and seventy-two; 5 the people of Arah, seven hundred and seventy-five; 6 the people of Pahath-Moab, of the people of Jeshua *and* Joab, two thousand eight hundred and twelve; 7 the people of Elam, one thousand two hundred and fifty-four; 8 the people of Zattu, nine hundred and forty-five; 9 the people of Zaccai, seven hundred and sixty; 10 the people of Bani, six hundred and forty-two; 11 the people of Bebai, six hundred and twenty-three; 12 the people of Azgad, one thousand two hundred and twenty-two; 13 the people of Adonikam, six hundred and sixty-six; 14 the people of Bigvai, two thousand and fifty-six; 15 the people of Adin, four hundred and fifty-four; 16 the people of Ater of Hezekiah, ninety-eight; 17 the people of Bezai, three hundred and twenty-three; 18 the people of Jorah, one hundred and twelve; 19 the people of Hashum, two hundred and twenty-three; 20 the people of Gibbar, ninety-five; 21 the people of Bethlehem, one hundred and twenty-three; 22 the men of Netophah, fifty-six; 23 the men of Anathoth, one hundred and twenty-eight; 24 the people of Azmaveth, forty-two; 25 the people of Kirjath Arim, Chephirah, and Beeroth, seven hundred and forty-three; 26 the people of Ramah and Geba, six hundred and twenty-one; 27 the men of Michmas, one

⛏ DIGGING IN

2:1–70 The Captives Return to Judah This chapter gives a long list of people who returned to Judah with Zerubbabel (pronounced *zeh-RUB-uh-bell*). Zerubbabel was the first governor of Judah when that nation was reborn after 70 years of captivity in Babylon. He was also an ancestor of Jesus, who lived over five hundred years later.

God has always wanted to set people free. We may not be in prisons of stone and steel. But many of us are prisoners in other ways. Some young people today are prisoners of *satanism,* which is the worship of the devil. A former young Satan worshiper writes from prison: "Listen to me. You can see where I am. I fell into the trap of the Devil. Jesus is the only way, and He loves you more than you ever can imagine." Don't be fooled by the Devil's promise of power. He only makes prisoners of people. But Jesus sets people free.

hundred and twenty-two; 28 the men of Bethel and Ai, two hundred and twenty-three; 29 the people of Nebo, fifty-two; 30 the people of Magbish, one hundred and fifty-six; 31 the people of the other Elam, one thousand two hundred and fifty-four; 32 the people of Harim, three hundred and twenty; 33 the people of Lod, Hadid, and Ono, seven hundred and twenty-five; 34 the people of Jericho, three hundred and forty-five; 35 the people of Senaah, three thousand six hundred and thirty.

36 The priests: the sons of Jedaiah, of the house of Jeshua, nine hundred and seventy-three; 37 the sons of Immer, one thousand and fifty-two; 38 the sons of Pashhur, one thousand two hundred and forty-seven; 39 the sons of Harim, one thousand and seventeen.

40 The Levites: the sons of Jeshua and Kadmiel, of the sons of Hodaviah, seventy-four.

41 The singers: the sons of Asaph, one hundred and twenty-eight.

42 The sons of the gatekeepers: the sons of Shallum, the sons of Ater, the sons of Talmon, the sons of Akkub, the sons of Hatita, and the sons of Shobai, one hundred and thirty-nine in all.

43 The Nethinim: the sons of Ziha, the sons of Hasupha, the sons of Tabbaoth, 44 the sons of Keros, the sons of Siaha, the sons of Padon, 45 the sons of Lebanah, the sons of Hagabah, the sons of Akkub, 46 the sons of Hagab, the sons of Shalmai, the sons of Hanan, 47 the sons of Giddel, the sons of Gahar, the sons of Reaiah, 48 the sons of Rezin, the sons of Nekoda, the sons of Gazzam, 49 the sons of Uzza, the sons of Paseah, the sons of Besai, 50 the sons of Asnah, the sons of Meunim, the sons of Nephusim, 51 the sons of Bakbuk, the sons of Hakupha, the sons of Harhur, 52 the sons of Bazluth, the sons of Mehida, the sons of Harsha, 53 the sons of Barkos, the sons of Sisera, the sons of Tamah, 54 the sons of Neziah, and the sons of Hatipha.

55 The sons of Solomon's servants: the sons of Sotai, the sons of Sophereth, the sons of Peruda, 56 the sons of Jaala, the sons of Darkon, the sons of Giddel, 57 the sons of Shephatiah, the sons of Hattil, the sons of Pochereth of Zebaim, and the sons of Ami. 58 All the Nethinim and the children of Solomon's servants were three hundred and ninety-two.

59 And these were the ones who came up from Tel Melah, Tel Harsha, Cherub, Addan, and Immer; but they could not identify their father's house or their genealogy, whether they were of Israel: 60 the sons of Delaiah, the sons of Tobiah, and the sons of Nekoda, six hundred and fifty-two; 61 and of the sons of the priests: the sons of Habaiah, the sons of Koz, and the sons of Barzillai, who took a wife of the daughters of Barzillai the Gileadite, and was called by their name. 62 These sought their listing among those who were registered by genealogy, but they were not found; therefore they were excluded from the priesthood as defiled. 63 And the governor said to them that they should not eat of the most holy things till a priest could consult with the **Urim and Thummim.**

64 The whole assembly together was forty-two thousand three hundred and sixty, 65 besides their male and female servants, of whom there were seven thousand three hundred and thirty-seven; and they had two hundred men and women singers. 66 Their horses were seven hundred and thirty-six, their mules two hundred and forty-five, 67 their camels four hundred and thirty-five, and their donkeys six thousand seven hundred and twenty.

68 Some of the heads of the fathers' houses, when they came to the house of the LORD which is in Jerusalem, of-

---

🌐 **WORDFINDER**

2:63 Urim and Thummim Stones or gems used by the high priest to learn the will of God.

fered freely for the house of God, to erect it in its place: 69 According to their ability, they gave to the treasury for the work sixty-one thousand gold drachmas, five thousand minas of silver, and one hundred priestly garments.

70 So the priests and the Levites, *some* of the people, the singers, the gatekeepers, and the Nethinim, dwelt in their cities, and all Israel in their cities.

The people joyfully worship God

3 And when the seventh month had come, and the children of Israel *were* in the cities, the people gathered together as one man to Jerusalem. 2 Then Jeshua the son of Jozadak and his brethren the priests, and Zerubbabel the son of Shealtiel and his brethren, arose and built the altar of the God of Israel, to offer burnt offerings on it, as *it is* written in the Law of Moses the man of God. 3 Though fear *had come* upon them because of the people of those countries, they set the altar on its bases; and they offered burnt offerings on it to the LORD, *both* the morning and evening burnt offerings. 4 They also kept the Feast of Tabernacles, as *it is* written, and *offered the* daily burnt offerings in the number required by ordinance for each day. 5 Afterwards *they offered* the regular burnt offering, and *those* for New Moons and for all the appointed feasts of the LORD that were consecrated, and *those* of everyone who willingly offered a freewill offering to the LORD. 6 From the first day of the seventh month they began to offer burnt offerings to the LORD, although the foundation of the temple of the LORD had not been laid. 7 They also gave money to the masons and the carpenters, and food, drink, and oil to the people of Sidon and Tyre to bring cedar logs from Lebanon to the sea, to Joppa, according to the permission which they had from Cyrus king of Persia.

8 Now in the second month of the second year of their coming to the house of God at Jerusalem, Zerubbabel the son of Shealtiel, Jeshua the son of Jozadak, and the rest of their brethren the priests and the Levites, and all those who had come out of the captivity to Jerusalem, began *work* and appointed the Levites from twenty years old and above to oversee the work of the house of the LORD. 9 Then Jeshua *with* his sons and brothers, Kadmiel *with* his sons, and the sons of Judah, arose as one to oversee those working on the house of God: the sons of Henadad *with* their sons and their brethren the Levites.

10 When the builders laid the foundation of the temple of the LORD, the priests stood in their apparel with trumpets, and the Levites, the sons of Asaph, with cymbals, to praise the LORD, according to the ordinance of David king of Israel. 11 And they sang responsively, praising and giving thanks to the LORD:

> "For *He is* good,
> For His mercy *endures* forever
>   toward Israel."

Then all the people shouted with a great shout, when they praised the LORD, because the foundation of the house of the LORD was laid.

12 But many of the priests and Levites and heads of the fathers' *houses,* old men who had seen the first temple, wept with a loud voice when the foundation of this temple was laid before their eyes. Yet many shouted aloud for joy, 13 so that the people could not discern the noise of the shout of joy from the noise of the weeping of the people, for the people shouted with a loud shout, and the sound was heard afar off.

Enemies try to stop the temple work

4 Now when the adversaries of Judah and Benjamin heard that the descendants of the captivity were building the temple of the LORD God of Israel, 2 they came to Zerubbabel and the

heads of the fathers' *houses*, and said to them, "Let us build with you, for we seek your God as you *do;* and we have sacrificed to Him since the days of Esarhaddon king of Assyria, who brought us here." ³ But Zerubbabel and Jeshua and the rest of the heads of the fathers' *houses* of Israel said to them, "You may do nothing with us to build a house for our God; but we alone will build to the LORD God of Israel, as King Cyrus the king of Persia has commanded us." ⁴ Then the people of the land tried to discourage the people of Judah. They troubled them in building, ⁵ and hired counselors against them to frustrate their purpose all the days of Cyrus king of Persia, even until the reign of Darius king of Persia.

⁶ In the reign of Ahasuerus, in the beginning of his reign, they wrote an accusation against the inhabitants of Judah and Jerusalem.

⁷ In the days of Artaxerxes also, Bishlam, Mithredath, Tabel, and the rest of their companions wrote to Artaxerxes king of Persia; and the letter *was* written in Aramaic script, and translated into the Aramaic language. ⁸ Rehum the commander and Shimshai the scribe wrote a letter against

DIGGING IN

4:1—6:12 Israel and the Persians
The treatment of the people of Israel by the Persians was a miracle. The Babylonians (pronounced *bab-ih-LOW-nih-uns*) had treated the Jews badly. But King Cyrus of Persia changed all that when he ordered the Jews to be set free.

All was not easy for the Jews who returned from Babylon to their home in Palestine. Other people had come to live there since the Jews were taken away as prisoners long ago. The enemies of

the Jews wrote a letter to the Persian king and demanded that the Jews be stopped. At first, the king made the Jews stop building the temple and the city. But Persian King Darius later ordered the building to continue. The prophets Haggai and Zechariah (pronounced *HAG-ay-eye* and *zek-uh-RIGH-uh*) also encouraged the Jews to build.

Remember, no one can stop what God decides to do.

Persian kings, including King Darius I, were buried in these tombs.

Jerusalem to King Artaxerxes in this fashion:

9 From Rehum the commander, Shimshai the scribe, and the rest of their companions— *representatives* of the Dinaites, the Apharsathchites, the Tarpelites, the people of Persia and Erech and Babylon and Shushan, the Dehavites, the Elamites, 10 and the rest of the nations whom the great and noble Osnapper took captive and settled in the cities of Samaria and the remainder beyond the River—and so forth.

11 (This *is* a copy of the letter that they sent him)

To King Artaxerxes from your servants, the men *of the region* beyond the River, and so forth:

12 Let it be known to the king that the Jews who came up from you have come to us at Jerusalem, and are building the rebellious and evil city, and are finishing *its* walls and repairing the foundations. 13 Let it now be known to the king that, if this city is built and the walls completed, they will not pay tax, tribute, or custom, and the king's treasury will be diminished. 14 Now because we receive support from the palace, it was not proper for us to see the king's dishonor; therefore we have sent and informed the king, 15 that search may be made in the book of the records of your fathers. And you will find in the book of the records and know that this city *is* a rebellious city, harmful to kings and provinces, and that they have incited sedition within the city in former times, for which cause this city was destroyed.

16 We inform the king that if this city is rebuilt and its walls are completed, the result will be that you will have no dominion beyond the River.

17 The king sent an answer:

To Rehum the commander, *to* Shimshai the scribe, *to* the rest of their companions who dwell in Samaria, and *to* the remainder beyond the River:

Peace, and so forth.

18 The letter which you sent to us has been clearly read before me. 19 And I gave the command, and a search has been made, and it was found that this city in former times has revolted against kings, and rebellion and sedition have been fostered in it. 20 There have also been mighty kings over Jerusalem, who have ruled over all *the region* beyond the River; and tax, tribute, and custom were paid to them. 21 Now give the command to make these men cease, that this city may not be built until the command is given by me.

22 Take heed now that you do not fail to do this. Why should damage increase to the hurt of the kings?

23 Now when the copy of King Artaxerxes' letter *was* read before Rehum, Shimshai the scribe, and their companions, they went up in haste to Jerusalem against the Jews, and by force of arms made them cease. 24 Thus the work of the house of God which *is* at Jerusalem ceased, and it was discontinued until the second year of the reign of Darius king of Persia.

The rebuilding goes on

5 Then the prophet Haggai and Zechariah the son of Iddo, prophets, prophesied to the Jews who *were* in Judah and Jerusalem, in the name of

the God of Israel, *who was* over them. ² So Zerubbabel the son of Shealtiel and Jeshua the son of Jozadak rose up and began to build the house of God which *is* in Jerusalem; and the prophets of God *were* with them, helping them.

³ At the same time Tattenai the governor of *the region* beyond the River and Shethar-Boznai and their companions came to them and spoke thus to them: "Who has commanded you to build this temple and finish this wall?" ⁴ Then, accordingly, we told them the names of the men who were constructing this building. ⁵ But the eye of their God was upon the elders of the Jews, so that they could not make them cease till a report could go to Darius. Then a written answer was returned concerning this *matter.* ⁶ This is a copy of the letter that Tattenai sent:

The governor of *the region* beyond the River, and Shethar-Boznai, and his companions, the Persians who *were in the region* beyond the River, to Darius the king.

⁷ (They sent a letter to him, in which was written thus)

To Darius the king:

All peace.

8   Let it be known to the king that we went into the province of Judea, to the temple of the great God, which is being built with heavy stones, and timber is being laid in the walls; and this work goes on diligently and prospers in their hands.

9   Then we asked those elders, *and* spoke thus to them: "Who commanded you to build this temple and to finish these walls?" ¹⁰ We also asked them their names to inform you, that we might write the names of the men who *were* chief among them.

11   And thus they returned us an answer, saying: "We are the servants of the God of heaven and earth, and we are rebuilding the temple that was built many years ago, which a great king of Israel built and completed. ¹² But because our fathers provoked the God of heaven to wrath, He gave them into the hand of Nebuchadnezzar king of Babylon, the Chaldean, *who* destroyed this temple and carried the people away to Babylon. ¹³ However, in the first year of Cyrus king of Babylon, King Cyrus issued a decree to build this house of God. ¹⁴ Also, the gold and silver articles of the house of God, which Nebuchadnezzar had taken from the temple that *was* in Jerusalem and carried into the temple of Babylon—those King Cyrus took from the temple of Babylon, and they were given to one named Sheshbazzar, whom he had made governor. ¹⁵ And he said to him, 'Take these articles; go, carry them to the temple *site* that *is* in Jerusalem, and let the house of God be rebuilt on its former site.' ¹⁶ Then the same Sheshbazzar came *and* laid the foundation of the house of God which *is* in Jerusalem; but from that time even until now it has been under construction, and it is not finished."

17   Now therefore, if *it seems* good to the king, let a search be made in the king's treasure house, which *is* there in Babylon, whether it is *so* that a decree was issued by King Cyrus to build this house of God at Jerusalem, and let the king send us his pleasure concerning this *matter.*

Jews Rebuild Temple at Jerusalem

Persian National Press

MEDIA—The temple at Jerusalem in the land of Israel is finally complete after years of lying in ruins since its fall in 586 B.C.

In 539 B.C., King Cyrus gave the order that the Jews were to be set free to return to their country and rebuild their beloved temple. Now, some twenty years later, the work has been completed.

Delays were caused by people living in that region who bitterly opposed the rebuilding. Some of those citizens hated the Jews and the temple. But when King Cyrus's written order was found again, the building was continued in spite of opposition. Builders have been encouraged by the preaching of the prophets Haggai and Zechariah (pronounced HAG-ay-eye and zek-uh-RIGH-uh).

A building permit is found

6 Then King Darius issued a decree, and a search was made in the archives, where the treasures were stored in Babylon. ²And at Achmetha, in the palace that is in the province of Media, a scroll was found, and in it a record was written thus:

³ In the first year of King Cyrus, King Cyrus issued a decree concerning the house of God at Jerusalem: "Let the house be rebuilt, the place where they offered sacrifices; and let the foundations of it be firmly laid, its height sixty cubits and its width sixty cubits, ⁴ with three rows of heavy stones and one row of new timber. Let the expenses be paid from the king's treasury. ⁵ Also let the gold and silver articles of the house of God, which Nebuchadnezzar took from the temple which is in Jerusalem and brought to Babylon, be restored and taken back to the temple which is in Jerusalem, each to its place; and deposit them in the house of God"—

⁶ Now therefore, Tattenai, governor of the region beyond the River, and Shethar-Boznai, and your companions the

Persians who are beyond the River, keep yourselves far from there. ⁷ Let the work of this house of God alone; let the governor of the Jews and the elders of the Jews build this house of God on its site.

⁸ Moreover I issue a decree as to what you shall do for the elders of these Jews, for the building of this house of God: Let the cost be paid at the king's expense from taxes on the region beyond the River; this is to be given immediately to these men, so that they are not hindered. ⁹ And whatever they need—young bulls, rams, and lambs for the burnt offerings of the God of heaven, wheat, salt, wine, and oil, according to the request of the priests who are in Jerusalem—let it be given them day by day without fail, ¹⁰ that they may offer sacrifices of sweet aroma to the God of heaven, and pray for the life of the king and his sons.

¹¹ Also I issue a decree that whoever alters this edict, let a timber be pulled from his house and erected, and let him be hanged on it; and let his house be made a refuse heap because of this. ¹² And may the God who

causes His name to dwell there destroy any king or people who put their hand to alter it, or to destroy this house of God which is in Jerusalem. I Darius issue a decree; let it be done diligently.

13 Then Tattenai, governor of *the region* beyond the River, Shethar-Boznai, and their companions diligently did according to what King Darius had sent. 14 So the elders of the Jews built, and they prospered through the prophesying of Haggai the prophet and Zechariah the son of Iddo. And they built and finished *it,* according to the commandment of the God of Israel, and according to the command of Cyrus, Darius, and Artaxerxes king of Persia. 15 Now the temple was finished on the third day of the month of Adar, which was in the sixth year of the reign of King Darius. 16 Then the children of Israel, the priests and the Levites and the rest of the descendants of the captivity, celebrated the dedication of this house of God with joy. 17 And they offered sacrifices at the dedication of this house of God, one hundred bulls, two hundred rams, four hundred lambs, and as a sin offering for all Israel twelve male goats, according to the number of the tribes of Israel. 18 They assigned the priests to their divisions and the Levites to their divisions, over the service of God in Jerusalem, as it is written in the Book of Moses.

19 And the descendants of the captivity kept the Passover on the fourteenth *day* of the first month. 20 For the priests and the Levites had purified themselves; all of them *were ritually* clean. And they slaughtered the Passover *lambs* for all the descendants of the captivity, for their brethren the priests, and for themselves. 21 Then the children of Israel who had returned from the captivity ate together with all who had separated themselves from the filth of the nations of the land in order to seek the LORD God of Israel. 22 And they kept the Feast of Unleavened Bread seven days with joy; for

the LORD made them joyful, and turned the heart of the king of Assyria toward them, to strengthen their hands in the work of the house of God, the God of Israel.

Ezra praises God in Jerusalem

7 Now after these things, in the reign of Artaxerxes king of Persia, Ezra the son of Seraiah, the son of Azariah, the son of Hilkiah, 2 the son of Shallum, the son of Zadok, the son of Ahitub, 3 the son of Amariah, the son of Azariah, the son of Meraioth, 4 the son of Zerahiah, the son of Uzzi, the son of Bukki, 5 the son of Abishua, the son of Phinehas, the son of Eleazar, the son of Aaron the chief priest— 6 this Ezra came up from Babylon; and he *was* a skilled scribe in the Law of Moses, which the LORD God of Israel had given. The king granted him all his request, according to the hand of the LORD his God upon him. 7 *Some* of the children of Israel, the priests, the Levites, the singers, the gatekeepers, and the Nethinim came up to Jerusalem in the seventh year of King Artaxerxes. 8 And Ezra came to Jerusalem in the fifth month, which *was* in the seventh year of the king. 9 On the first *day* of the first month he began *his* journey from Babylon, and on the first *day* of the fifth month he came to Jerusalem, according to the good hand of his God upon him. 10 For Ezra had prepared his heart to seek the Law of the LORD, and to do *it,* and to teach statutes and ordinances in Israel.

11 This *is* a copy of the letter that King Artaxerxes gave Ezra the priest, the scribe, expert in the words of the commandments of the LORD, and of His statutes to Israel:

12   Artaxerxes, king of kings,

     To Ezra the priest, a scribe of
     the Law of the God of heaven:

     Perfect *peace,* and so forth.

13   I issue a decree that all those of
     the people of Israel and the

The tomb of King Artaxerxes of Persia.

gold, do it according to the will of your God. 19 Also the articles that are given to you for the service of the house of your God, deliver in full before the God of Jerusalem. 20 And whatever more may be needed for the house of your God, which you may have occasion to provide, pay *for it* from the king's treasury.

21 And I, *even* I, Artaxerxes the king, issue a decree to all the treasurers who *are in the region* beyond the River, that whatever Ezra the priest, the scribe of the Law of the God of heaven, may require of you, let it be done diligently, 22 up to one hundred talents of silver, one hundred kors of wheat, one hundred baths of wine, one hundred baths of oil, and salt without prescribed limit. 23 Whatever is commanded by the God of heaven, let it diligently be done for the house of the God of heaven. For why should there be wrath against the realm of the king and his sons?

24 Also we inform you that it shall not be lawful to impose tax, tribute, or custom *on* any of the priests, Levites, singers, gatekeepers, Nethinim, or servants of this house of God. 25 And you, Ezra, according to your God-given wisdom, set magistrates and judges who may judge all the people who *are in the region* beyond the River, all such as know the laws of your God; and teach those who do not know *them.* 26 Whoever will not observe the law of your God and the law of the king, let judgment be executed speedily on him, whether *it be* death, or banishment, or confiscation of goods, or imprisonment.

priests and Levites in my realm, who volunteer to go up to Jerusalem, may go with you. 14 And whereas you are being sent by the king and his seven counselors to inquire concerning Judah and Jerusalem, with regard to the Law of your God which *is* in your hand; 15 and *whereas you are* to carry the silver and gold which the king and his counselors have freely offered to the God of Israel, whose dwelling *is* in Jerusalem; 16 and *whereas* all the silver and gold that you may find in all the province of Babylon, along with the freewill offering of the people and the priests, *are to be* freely offered for the house of their God in Jerusalem— 17 now therefore, be careful to buy with this money bulls, rams, and lambs, with their grain offerings and their drink offerings, and offer them on the altar of the house of your God in Jerusalem.

18 And whatever seems good to you and your brethren to do with the rest of the silver and the

27 Blessed *be* the LORD God of our fathers, who has put *such a thing* as

this in the king's heart, to beautify the house of the LORD which is in Jerusalem, 28 and has extended mercy to me before the king and his counselors, and before all the king's mighty princes.

So I was encouraged, as the hand of the LORD my God was upon me; and I gathered leading men of Israel to go up with me.

Ezra's friends

8 These are the heads of their fathers' houses, and this is the genealogy of those who went up with me from Babylon, in the reign of King Artaxerxes: 2 of the sons of Phinehas, Gershom; of the sons of Ithamar, Daniel; of the sons of David, Hattush; 3 of the sons of Shecaniah, of the sons of Parosh, Zechariah; and registered with him were one hundred and fifty males; 4 of the sons of Pahath-Moab, Eliehoenai the son of Zerahiah, and with him two hundred males; 5 of the sons of Shechaniah, Ben-Jahaziel, and with him three hundred males; 6 of the sons of Adin, Ebed the son of Jonathan, and with him fifty males; 7 of the sons of Elam, Jeshaiah the son of Athaliah, and with him seventy males; 8 of the sons of Shephatiah, Zebadiah the son of Michael, and with him eighty males; 9 of the sons of Joab, Obadiah the son of Jehiel, and with him two hundred and eighteen males; 10 of the sons of Shelomith, Ben-Josiphiah, and with him one hundred and sixty males; 11 of the sons of Bebai, Zechariah the

son of Bebai, and with him twenty-eight males; 12 of the sons of Azgad, Johanan the son of Hakkatan, and with him one hundred and ten males; 13 of the last sons of Adonikam, whose names are these—Eliphelet, Jeiel, and Shemaiah—and with them sixty males; 14 also of the sons of Bigvai, Uthai and Zabbud, and with them seventy males.

15 Now I gathered them by the river that flows to Ahava, and we camped there three days. And I looked among the people and the priests, and found none of the sons of Levi there. 16 Then I sent for Eliezer, Ariel, Shemaiah, Elnathan, Jarib, Elnathan, Nathan, Zechariah, and Meshullam, leaders; also for Joiarib and Elnathan, men of understanding. 17 And I gave them a command for Iddo the chief man at the place Casiphia, and I told them what they should say to Iddo and his brethren the Nethinim at the place Casiphia—that they should bring us servants for the house of our God. 18 Then, by the good hand of our God upon us, they brought us a man of understanding, of the sons of Mahli the son of Levi, the son of Israel, namely Sherebiah, with his sons and brothers, eighteen men; 19 and Hashabiah, and with him Jeshaiah of the sons of Merari, his brothers and their sons, twenty men; 20 also of the Nethinim, whom David and the leaders had appointed for the service of the Levites, two hundred and twenty Nethinim. All of them were designated by name.

21 Then I proclaimed a fast there at

DIGGING IN

7:28 Why You Should Be Encouraged Persian King Artaxerxes (pronounced are-tack-SURK-sees) lived over 450 years before Jesus was born. He was the king who came after King Cyrus. At first Artaxerxes discouraged the rebuilding work at Jerusalem. (See Ezra 4.) Now he sent Ezra the priest to organize the worship and government of Jerusalem and Judah.

Ezra said, "I was encouraged." Ezra

was encouraged because the king was with him in his desire to bring the Jews back to the true worship of God.

You, too, can be encouraged because the great King of the universe is with you in your desire to bring others to know Him. King Artaxerxes was only a man, but the Lord is the King of Kings. God moves the hands and minds of the rulers of this world to bring about His plans.

the river of Ahava, that we might humble ourselves before our God, to seek from Him the right way for us and our little ones and all our possessions. 22 For I was ashamed to request of the king an escort of soldiers and horsemen to help us against the enemy on the road, because we had spoken to the king, saying, "The hand of our God is upon all those for good who seek Him, but His power and His wrath are against all those who forsake Him." 23 So we fasted and entreated our God for this, and He answered our prayer.

24 And I separated twelve of the leaders of the priests—Sherebiah, Hashabiah, and ten of their brethren with them— 25 and weighed out to them the silver, the gold, and the articles, the offering for the house of our God which the king and his counselors and his princes, and all Israel who were present, had offered. 26 I weighed into their hand six hundred and fifty talents of silver, silver articles weighing one hundred talents, one hundred talents of gold, 27 twenty gold basins worth a thousand drachmas, and two vessels of fine polished bronze, precious as gold. 28 And I said to them, "You are holy to the LORD; the articles are holy also; and the silver and the gold are a freewill offering to the LORD God of your fathers. 29 Watch and keep them until you weigh them before the leaders of the priests and the Levites and heads of the fathers' houses of Israel in Jerusalem, in the chambers of the house of the LORD." 30 So the priests and the Levites received the silver and the gold and the articles by weight, to bring them to Jerusalem to the house of our God.

31 Then we departed from the river of Ahava on the twelfth day of the first month, to go to Jerusalem. And the hand of our God was upon us, and He delivered us from the hand of the enemy and from ambush along the road. 32 So we came to Jerusalem, and stayed there three days.

33 Now on the fourth day the silver and the gold and the articles were weighed in the house of our God by the hand of Meremoth the son of Uriah the priest, and with him was Eleazar the son of Phinehas; with them were the Levites, Jozabad the son of Jeshua and Noadiah the son of Binnui, 34 with the number and weight of everything. All the weight was written down at that time.

35 The children of those who had been carried away captive, who had come from the captivity, offered burnt offerings to the God of Israel: twelve bulls for all Israel, ninety-six rams, seventy-seven lambs, and twelve male goats as a sin offering. All this was a burnt offering to the LORD.

36 And they delivered the king's orders to the king's satraps and the governors in the region beyond the River. So they gave support to the people and the house of God.

Ezra confesses the people's sins

9 When these things were done, the leaders came to me, saying, "The people of Israel and the priests and the Levites have not separated themselves from the peoples of the lands, with respect to the abominations of the Canaanites, the Hittites, the Perizzites, the Jebusites, the Ammonites, the Moabites, the Egyptians, and the Amorites. 2 For they have taken some of their daughters as wives for themselves and their sons, so that the holy seed is mixed with the peoples of those lands. Indeed, the hand of the leaders and rulers has been foremost in this trespass." 3 So when I heard this thing, I tore my garment and my robe, and plucked out some of the hair of my head and beard, and sat down astonished. 4 Then everyone who trembled at the words of the God of Israel assembled to me, because of the transgression of those who had been carried away captive, and I sat astonished until the evening sacrifice.

5 At the evening sacrifice I arose from my fasting; and having torn my garment and my robe, I fell on my

knees and spread out my hands to the LORD my God. 6 And I said: "O my God, I am too ashamed and humiliated to lift up my face to You, my God; for our iniquities have risen higher than *our* heads, and our guilt has grown up to the heavens. 7 Since the days of our fathers to this day we *have been* very guilty, and for our iniquities we, our kings, *and* our priests have been delivered into the hand of the kings of the lands, to the sword, to captivity, to plunder, and to humiliation, as *it is* this day. 8 And now for a little while grace has been *shown* from the LORD our God, to leave us a remnant to escape, and to give us a peg in His holy place, that our God may enlighten our eyes and give us a measure of revival in our bondage. 9 For we *were* slaves. Yet our God did not forsake us in our bondage; but He extended mercy to us in the sight of the kings of Persia, to revive us, to repair the house of our God, to rebuild its ruins, and to give us a wall in Judah and Jerusalem. 10 And now, O our God, what shall we say after this? For we have forsaken Your commandments, 11 which You commanded by Your servants the prophets, saying, 'The land which you are entering to possess is an unclean land, with the uncleanness of the peoples of the lands, with their abominations which have filled it from one end to another with their impurity. 12 Now therefore, do not give your daughters

as wives for their sons, nor take their daughters to your sons; and never seek their peace or prosperity, that you may be strong and eat the good of the land, and leave *it* as an inheritance to your children forever.' 13 And after all that has come upon us for our evil deeds and for our great guilt, since You our God have punished us less than our iniquities *deserve,* and have given us *such* deliverance as this, 14 should we again break Your commandments, and join in marriage with the people *committing* these abominations? Would You not be angry with us until You had consumed *us,* so that *there would be* no remnant or survivor? 15 O LORD God of Israel, You *are* righteous, for we are left as a remnant, as *it is* this day. Here we *are* before You, in our guilt, though no one can stand before You because of this!"

The people, too, confess and God forgives them

10 Now while Ezra was praying, and while he was confessing, weeping, and bowing down before the house of God, a very large assembly of men, women, and children gathered to him from Israel; for the people wept very bitterly. 2 And Shechaniah the son of Jehiel, *one* of the sons of Elam, spoke up and said to Ezra, "We have trespassed against our God, and have

---

What the People Learned

When we came home from 70 years of slavery in Babylon, we found other people living in the land that God had given to our father Abraham centuries before.

At first, we didn't know how we should live among these strange people. Some of our sons and daughters began to marry the young people who were living in our land.

Our leader, Ezra, knew we had to keep our faith in God. If we married people of other nations, we might also learn to worship their false gods. So Ezra prayed for us, and we were sorry we had disobeyed the Lord. Then we promised we would marry only God's people.

When you marry someday, we hope you also will marry someone who shares your faith in Jesus.

taken **pagan** wives from the peoples of the land; yet now there is hope in Israel in spite of this. 3 Now therefore, let us make a covenant with our God to put away all these wives and those who have been born to them, according to the advice of my master and of those who tremble at the commandment of our God; and let it be done according to the law. 4 Arise, for *this* matter *is* your *responsibility.* We also *are* with you. Be of good courage, and do *it.*"

5 Then Ezra arose, and made the leaders of the priests, the Levites, and all Israel swear an oath that they would do according to this word. So they swore an oath. 6 Then Ezra rose up from before the house of God, and went into the chamber of Jehohanan the son of Eliashib; and *when* he came there, he ate no bread and drank no water, for he mourned because of the guilt of those from the captivity.

7 And they issued a proclamation throughout Judah and Jerusalem to all the descendants of the captivity, that they must gather at Jerusalem, 8 and that whoever would not come within three days, according to the instructions of the leaders and elders, all his property would be confiscated, and he himself would be separated from the assembly of those from the captivity.

9 So all the men of Judah and Benjamin gathered at Jerusalem within three days. It *was* the ninth month, on the twentieth of the month; and all the people sat in the open square of the house of God, trembling because of *this* matter and because of heavy rain. 10 Then Ezra the priest stood up and said to them, "You have transgressed and have taken pagan wives, adding to the guilt of Israel. 11 Now therefore, make confession to the LORD God of your fathers, and do His will; separate yourselves from the peoples of the land, and from the pagan wives."

12 Then all the assembly answered and said with a loud voice, "Yes! As you have said, so we must do. 13 But *there are* many people; *it is* the season for heavy rain, and we are not able to stand outside. Nor *is this* the work of one or two days, for *there are* many of us who have transgressed in this matter. 14 Please, let the leaders of our entire assembly stand; and let all those in our cities who have taken pagan wives come at appointed times, together with the elders and judges of their cities, until the fierce wrath of our God is turned away from us in this matter." 15 Only Jonathan the son of Asahel and Jahaziah the son of Tikvah opposed this, and Meshullam and Shabbethai the Levite gave them support.

16 Then the descendants of the captivity did so. And Ezra the priest, *with* certain heads of the fathers' *households,* were set apart by the fathers' *households,* each of them by name; and they sat down on the first day of the tenth month to examine the matter. 17 By the first day of the first month they finished *questioning* all the men who had taken pagan wives.

18 And among the sons of the priests who had taken pagan wives *the following* were found of the sons of Jeshua the son of Jozadak, and his brothers: Maaseiah, Eliezer, Jarib, and Gedaliah. 19 And they gave their promise that they would put away their wives; and *being* guilty, *they presented* a ram of the flock as their trespass offering.

20 Also of the sons of Immer: Hanani and Zebadiah; 21 of the sons of Harim: Maaseiah, Elijah, Shemaiah, Jehiel, and Uzziah; 22 of the sons of Pashhur: Elioenai, Maaseiah, Ishmael, Nethanel, Jozabad, and Elasah.

23 Also of the Levites: Jozabad, Shimei, Kelaiah (the same *is* Kelita), Pethahiah, Judah, and Eliezer.

24 Also of the singers: Eliashib; and

10:2 Pagan People who worship false gods or whose minds are mainly on material things, physical pleasure, and this present world.

of the gatekeepers: Shallum, Telem, and Uri.

25 And others of Israel: of the sons of Parosh: Ramiah, Jeziah, Malchiah, Mijamin, Eleazar, Malchijah, and Benaiah; 26 of the sons of Elam: Mattaniah, Zechariah, Jehiel, Abdi, Jeremoth, and Eliah; 27 of the sons of Zattu: Elioenai, Eliashib, Mattaniah, Jeremoth, Zabad, and Aziza; 28 of the sons of Bebai: Jehohanan, Hananiah, Zabbai, and Athlai; 29 of the sons of Bani: Meshullam, Malluch, Adaiah, Jashub, Sheal, and Ramoth; 30 of the sons of Pahath-Moab: Adna, Chelal, Benaiah, Maaseiah, Mattaniah, Bezalel, Binnui, and Manasseh; 31 of the sons of Harim: Eliezer, Ishijah, Malchijah, Shemaiah, Shimeon, 32 Benjamin, Malluch, and Shemariah; 33 of the sons of Hashum: Mattenai, Mattattah, Zabad, Eliphelet, Jeremai, Manasseh, and Shimei; 34 of the sons of Bani: Maadai, Amram, Uel, 35 Benaiah, Bedeiah, Cheluh, 36 Vaniah, Meremoth, Eliashib, 37 Mattaniah, Mattenai, Jaasai, 38 Bani, Binnui, Shimei, 39 Shelemiah, Nathan, Adaiah, 40 Machnadebai, Shashai, Sharai, 41 Azarel, Shelemiah, Shemariah, 42 Shallum, Amariah, and Joseph; 43 of the sons of Nebo: Jeiel, Mattithiah, Zabad, Zebina, Jaddai, Joel, and Benaiah.

44 All these had taken pagan wives, and some of them had wives by whom they had children.

The Book of
NEHEMIAH

The king of Persia allowed me, Nehemiah (pronounced *nee-huh-MY-uh*), to return to Israel 15 years after he sent Ezra back. The wall and the city of Jerusalem were in ruins, and I wanted to build them again. So the king gave me permission to go. My name means "God Is Comfort." God did comfort us when He brought us back to our land.

We had a good plan for rebuilding the wall. The city was divided up like a pie, so the people who lived in Jerusalem were divided into sections. Each group of people was responsible for building the part of the wall that protected that part of the city where they lived. Yes, our enemies opposed us, but half of us were armed while the other half worked on the wall. Even the workers carried swords.

With everybody working together according to this plan, we were able to finish the wall in 52 days. That was very fast work!

Nehemiah begs to return to Jerusalem

THE words of Nehemiah the son of Hachaliah.

It came to pass in the month of Chislev, *in* the twentieth year, as I was in Shushan the citadel, ² that Hanani one of my brethren came with men from Judah; and I asked them concerning the Jews who had escaped, who had survived the captivity, and concerning Jerusalem. ³ And they said to me, "The survivors who are left from the captivity in the province *are* there in great distress and reproach. The wall of Jerusalem *is* also broken down, and its gates *are* burned with fire."

⁴ So it was, when I heard these words, that I sat down and wept, and mourned *for many* days; I was fasting and praying before the God of heaven.

⁵ And I said: "I pray, LORD God of heaven, O great and awesome God, *You* who keep *Your* covenant and mercy with those who love You and observe Your commandments, ⁶ please let Your ear be attentive and Your eyes open, that You may hear

🪓 DIGGING IN

1:4–11 Caring About God's Work
Nehemiah (pronounced *nee-huh-MY-uh*) was one of the captives in Shushan, the capital of Persia, about 450 years before Christ was born.

Some of the people were left behind in Judah when the Jews were taken prisoners to Babylon. Nehemiah heard news that the people in Judah were suffering. He also heard that the wall and gates of Jerusalem were in ruins.

When Nehemiah heard these things, he began to pray and weep for the people and the city. Shortly after this, King Artaxerxes (pronounced *are-tack-SURK-sees*) gave Nehemiah permission to go back and repair the wall of the city.

We can only be part of God's work when we really care about God's plans. God now wants you to help build a kingdom that will last forever. Someday King Jesus is coming to rule over His kingdom. Will you pray like Nehemiah? Will you be a kingdom builder for God?

the prayer of Your servant which I pray before You now, day and night, for the children of Israel Your servants, and confess the sins of the children of Israel which we have sinned against You. Both my father's house and I have sinned. 7 We have acted very corruptly against You, and have not kept the commandments, the statutes, nor the ordinances which You commanded Your servant Moses. 8 Remember, I pray, the word that You commanded Your servant Moses, saying, 'If you are unfaithful, I will scatter you among the nations; 9 but if you return to Me, and keep My commandments and do them, though some of you were cast out to the farthest part of the heavens, yet I will gather them from there, and bring them to the place which I have chosen as a dwelling for My name.' 10 Now these are Your servants and Your people, whom You have redeemed by Your great power, and by Your strong hand. 11 O Lord, I pray, please let Your ear be attentive to the prayer of Your servant, and to the prayer of Your servants who desire to fear Your name; and let Your servant prosper this day, I pray, and grant him mercy in the sight of this man."

For I was the king's **cupbearer.**

Nehemiah goes home to rebuild the wall

2 And it came to pass in the month of Nisan, in the twentieth year of King Artaxerxes, when wine was before him, that I took the wine and gave it to the king. Now I had never been sad in his presence before. 2 Therefore the king said to me, "Why is your face sad, since you are not sick? This is nothing but sorrow of heart."

So I became dreadfully afraid, 3 and said to the king, "May the king live forever! Why should my face not be sad, when the city, the place of my fathers' tombs, lies waste, and its gates are burned with fire?"

4 Then the king said to me, "What do you request?"

So I prayed to the God of heaven. 5 And I said to the king, "If it pleases the king, and if your servant has found favor in your sight, I ask that you send me to Judah, to the city of my fathers' tombs, that I may rebuild it."

6 Then the king said to me (the queen also sitting beside him), "How long will your journey be? And when will you return?" So it pleased the king to send me; and I set him a time.

7 Furthermore I said to the king, "If it pleases the king, let letters be given to me for the governors of the region beyond the River, that they must permit me to pass through till I come to Judah, 8 and a letter to Asaph the keeper of the king's forest, that he must give me timber to make beams for the gates of the citadel which pertains to the temple, for the city wall, and for the house that I will occupy." And the king granted them to me according to the good hand of my God upon me.

9 Then I went to the governors in the region beyond the River, and gave them the king's letters. Now the king had sent captains of the army and horsemen with me. 10 When Sanballat the Horonite and Tobiah the Ammonite official heard of it, they were deeply disturbed that a man had come to seek the well-being of the children of Israel.

11 So I came to Jerusalem and was there three days. 12 Then I arose in the night, I and a few men with me; I told no one what my God had put in my heart to do at Jerusalem; nor was there any animal with me, except the one on which I rode. 13 And I went out by night through the Valley Gate to the Serpent Well and the Refuse Gate, and viewed the walls of Jerusalem which were broken down and its gates which were burned with fire. 14 Then I went

⊛WORDFINDER

1:11 Cupbearer An official in the palace who served wine to the king. He was also a trusted royal adviser.

King Gives Permission to Rebuild Jerusalem

Persian National Press

SHUSHAN—King Artaxerxes (pronounced *are-tack-SURK-sees*), now on the throne of Persia, has recently permitted Nehemiah the Jew (pronounced *nee-huh-MY-uh*) to go home to rebuild the city of Jerusalem, capital of Judah.

It has been 71 years since King Cyrus allowed other Jewish captives to return to their home country and rebuild the temple. Persians are amazed at the generosity of our king toward the foreigners. Before Persia conquered that nation,

our kings were known to be cruel to the Jews.

The only explanation for the king's action was stated by Nehemiah in a recent interview: "It was according to the good hand of God." The prophet insists that the Lord has softened the hearts of our kings toward His people.

We understand that Nehemiah's problems are not over. He is expected to face more trouble from enemies back in his own country.

---

on to the Fountain Gate and to the King's Pool, but *there was* no room for the animal under me to pass. [15] So I went up in the night by the valley, and viewed the wall; then I turned back and entered by the Valley Gate, and so returned. [16] And the officials did not know where I had gone or what I had done; I had not yet told the Jews,

the priests, the nobles, the officials, or the others who did the work.

[17] Then I said to them, "You see the distress that we *are* in, how Jerusalem *lies* waste, and its gates are burned with fire. Come and let us build the wall of Jerusalem, that we may no longer be a reproach." [18] And I told them of the hand of my God which had been good

King Artaxerxes, who gave Nehemiah permission to rebuild Jerusalem, had a palace in Persepolis, where these columns still stand.

upon me, and also of the king's words that he had spoken to me.

So they said, "Let us rise up and build." Then they set their hands to *this* good *work.*

19 But when Sanballat the Horonite, Tobiah the Ammonite official, and Geshem the Arab heard *of it,* they laughed at us and despised us, and said, "What *is* this thing that you are doing? Will you rebel against the king?"

20 So I answered them, and said to them, "The God of heaven Himself will prosper us; therefore we His servants will arise and build, but you have no heritage or right or memorial in Jerusalem."

The builders of the wall

3 Then Eliashib the high priest rose up with his brethren the priests and built the Sheep Gate; they consecrated it and hung its doors. They built as far as the Tower of the Hundred, *and* consecrated it, then as far as the Tower of Hananel. 2 Next to *Eliashib* the men of Jericho built. And next to them Zaccur the son of Imri built.

3 Also the sons of Hassenaah built the Fish Gate; they laid its beams and hung its doors with its bolts and bars. 4 And next to them Meremoth the son of Urijah, the son of Koz, made repairs. Next to them Meshullam the son of Berechiah, the son of Meshezabel, made repairs. Next to them Zadok the son of Baana made repairs. 5 Next to them the Tekoites made repairs; but their nobles did not put their shoulders to the work of their Lord.

6 Moreover Jehoiada the son of Paseah and Meshullam the son of Besodeiah repaired the Old Gate; they laid its beams and hung its doors, with its bolts and bars. 7 And next to them Melatiah the Gibeonite, Jadon the Meronothite, the men of Gibeon and Mizpah, repaired the residence of the governor *of the region* beyond the River. 8 Next to him Uzziel the son of Harhaiah, one of the goldsmiths, made repairs. Also next to him Hananiah,

one of the perfumers, made repairs; and they fortified Jerusalem as far as the Broad Wall. 9 And next to them Rephaiah the son of Hur, leader of half the district of Jerusalem, made repairs. 10 Next to them Jedaiah the son of Harumaph made repairs in front of his house. And next to him Hattush the son of Hashabniah made repairs.

11 Malchijah the son of Harim and Hashub the son of Pahath-Moab repaired another section, as well as the Tower of the Ovens. 12 And next to him was Shallum the son of Hallohesh, leader of half the district of Jerusalem; he and his daughters made repairs.

13 Hanun and the inhabitants of Zanoah repaired the Valley Gate. They built it, hung its doors with its bolts and bars, and *repaired* a thousand cubits of the wall as far as the Refuse Gate.

14 Malchijah the son of Rechab, leader of the district of Beth Haccerem, repaired the Refuse Gate; he built it and hung its doors with its bolts and bars.

15 Shallun the son of Col-Hozeh, leader of the district of Mizpah, repaired the Fountain Gate; he built it, covered it, hung its doors with its bolts and bars, and repaired the wall of the Pool of Shelah by the King's Garden, as far as the stairs that go down from the City of David. 16 After him Nehemiah the son of Azbuk, leader of half the district of Beth Zur, made repairs as far as *the place* in front of the tombs of David, to the man-made pool, and as far as the House of the Mighty.

17 After him the Levites, *under* Rehum the son of Bani, made repairs. Next to him Hashabiah, leader of half the district of Keilah, made repairs for his district. 18 After him their brethren, *under* Bavai the son of Henadad, leader of the *other* half of the district of Keilah, made repairs. 19 And next to him Ezer the son of Jeshua, the leader of Mizpah, repaired another section in front of the Ascent to the Armory at the buttress. 20 After him Baruch the son of Zabbai carefully repaired the other section, from the buttress to the door of the house of

Eliashib the high priest. 21 After him Meremoth the son of Urijah, the son of Koz, repaired another section, from the door of the house of Eliashib to the end of the house of Eliashib.

22 And after him the priests, the men of the plain, made repairs. 23 After him Benjamin and Hasshub made repairs opposite their house. After them Azariah the son of Maaseiah, the son of Ananiah, made repairs by his house. 24 After him Binnui the son of Henadad repaired another section, from the house of Azariah to the buttress, even as far as the corner. 25 Palal the son of Uzai *made repairs* opposite the buttress, and on the tower which projects from the king's upper house that *was* by the court of the prison. After him Pedaiah the son of Parosh *made repairs.*

26 Moreover the Nethinim who dwelt in Ophel *made repairs* as far as *the place* in front of the Water Gate toward the east, and on the projecting tower. 27 After them the Tekoites repaired another section, next to the great projecting tower, and as far as the wall of Ophel.

28 Beyond the Horse Gate the priests made repairs, each in front of his *own* house. 29 After them Zadok the son of

Immer made repairs in front of his *own* house. After him Shemaiah the son of Shechaniah, the keeper of the East Gate, made repairs. 30 After him Hananiah the son of Shelemiah, and Hanun, the sixth son of Zalaph, repaired another section. After him Meshullam the son of Berechiah made repairs in front of his dwelling. 31 After him Malchijah, one of the goldsmiths, made repairs as far as the house of the Nethinim and of the merchants, in front of the Miphkad Gate, and as far as the upper room at the corner. 32 And between the upper room at the corner, as far as the Sheep Gate, the goldsmiths and the merchants made repairs.

Some people make fun of Nehemiah

4 But it so happened, when Sanballat heard that we were rebuilding the wall, that he was furious and very indignant, and mocked the Jews. 2 And he spoke before his brethren and the army of Samaria, and said, "What are these feeble Jews doing? Will they fortify themselves? Will they offer sacrifices? Will they complete it in a day? Will they

Nehemiah and his workers rebuild the walls of Jerusalem.

revive the stones from the heaps of rubbish—*stones* that are burned?''

3 Now Tobiah the Ammonite *was* beside him, and he said, ''Whatever they build, if even a fox goes up *on it,* he will break down their stone wall.''

4 Hear, O our God, for we are despised; turn their reproach on their own heads, and give them as plunder to a land of captivity! 5 Do not cover their iniquity, and do not let their sin be blotted out from before You; for they have provoked *You* to anger before the builders.

6 So we built the wall, and the entire wall was joined together up to half its *height,* for the people had a mind to work.

7 Now it happened, when Sanballat, Tobiah, the Arabs, the Ammonites, and the Ashdodites heard that the walls of Jerusalem were being restored and the gaps were beginning to be closed, that they became very angry, 8 and all of them conspired together to come *and* attack Jerusalem and create confusion. 9 Nevertheless we made our prayer to our God, and because of them we set a watch against them day and night.

10 Then Judah said, ''The strength of the laborers is failing, and *there is* so much rubbish that we are not able to build the wall.''

11 And our adversaries said, ''They will neither know nor see anything, till we come into their midst and kill them and cause the work to cease.''

12 So it was, when the Jews who dwelt near them came, that they told us ten times, ''From whatever place you turn, *they will be* upon us.''

13 Therefore I positioned *men* behind the lower parts of the wall, at the openings; and I set the people according to their families, with their swords, their spears, and their bows. 14 And I looked, and arose and said to the nobles, to the leaders, and to the rest of the people, ''Do not be afraid of them. Remember the Lord, great and awesome, and fight for your brethren, your sons, your daughters, your wives, and your houses.''

15 And it happened, when our enemies heard that it was known to us, and *that* God had brought their plot to nothing, that all of us returned to the wall, everyone to his work. 16 So it was, from that time on, *that* half of my servants worked at construction, while the other half held the spears, the shields, the bows, and *wore* armor; and the leaders *were* behind all the house of Judah. 17 Those who built on the wall, and those who carried burdens, loaded themselves so that with one hand they worked at construction, and with the other held a weapon. 18 Every one of the builders had his sword girded at his side as he built. And the one who sounded the trumpet *was* beside me.

19 Then I said to the nobles, the rulers, and the rest of the people, ''The work *is* great and extensive, and we are separated far from one another on the wall. 20 Wherever you hear the sound of the trumpet, rally to us there. Our God will fight for us.''

21 So we labored in the work, and half of *the men* held the spears from daybreak until the stars appeared. 22 At the same time I also said to the people, ''Let each man and his servant stay at night in Jerusalem, that they may be our guard by night and a working party by day.'' 23 So neither I, my brethren, my servants, nor the men of the guard who followed me took off our clothes, *except* that everyone took them off for washing.

Nehemiah champions the poor

5 And there was a great outcry of the people and their wives against their Jewish brethren. 2 For there were those who said, ''We, our sons, and our daughters *are* many; therefore let us get grain, that we may eat and live.''

3 There were also *some* who said, ''We have mortgaged our lands and vineyards and houses, that we might buy grain because of the famine.''

4 There were also those who said, ''We have borrowed money for the king's tax *on* our lands and vineyards.

5 Yet now our flesh *is* as the flesh of our brethren, our children as their children; and indeed we are forcing our sons and our daughters to be slaves, and *some* of our daughters have been brought into slavery. *It is* not in our power *to redeem them,* for other men have our lands and vineyards."

6 And I became very angry when I heard their outcry and these words. 7 After serious thought, I rebuked the nobles and rulers, and said to them, "Each of you is exacting usury from his brother." So I called a great assembly against them. 8 And I said to them, "According to our ability we have redeemed our Jewish brethren who were sold to the nations. Now indeed, will you even sell your brethren? Or should they be sold to us?"

Then they were silenced and found nothing *to say.* 9 Then I said, "What you are doing *is* not good. Should you not walk in the fear of our God because of the reproach of the nations, our enemies? 10 I also, *with* my brethren and my servants, am lending them money and grain. Please, let us stop this usury! 11 Restore now to them, even this day, their lands, their vineyards, their olive groves, and their houses, also a hundredth of the money and the grain, the new wine and the oil, that you have charged them."

12 So they said, "We will restore *it,* and will require nothing from them; we will do as you say."

Then I called the priests, and required an oath from them that they would do according to this promise. 13 Then I shook out the fold of my garment and said, "So may God shake out each man from his house, and from his property, who does not perform this promise. Even thus may he be shaken out and emptied."

And all the assembly said, "Amen!" and praised the LORD. Then the people did according to this promise.

14 Moreover, from the time that I was appointed to be their governor in the land of Judah, from the twentieth year until the thirty-second year of King Artaxerxes, twelve years, neither I nor my brothers ate the governor's provisions. 15 But the former governors who *were* before me laid burdens on the people, and took from them bread and wine, besides forty shekels of silver. Yes, even their servants bore rule over the people, but I did not do so, because of the fear of God. 16 Indeed, I also continued the work on this wall, and we did not buy any land. All my servants *were* gathered there for the work.

17 And at my table *were* one hundred and fifty Jews and rulers, besides those who came to us from the nations around us. 18 Now *that* which was prepared daily *was* one ox *and* six choice sheep. Also fowl were prepared for me, and once every ten days an abundance of all kinds of wine. Yet in spite of this I did not demand the governor's provisions, because the bondage was heavy on this people.

19 Remember me, my God, for good, *according to* all that I have done for this people.

The plot to kill Nehemiah

6 Now it happened when Sanballat, Tobiah, Geshem the Arab, and the rest of our enemies heard that I had rebuilt the wall, and *that* there were no breaks left in it (though at that time I had not hung the doors in the gates), 2 that Sanballat and Geshem sent to me, saying, "Come, let us meet together among the villages in the plain of Ono." But they thought to do me harm.

3 So I sent messengers to them, saying, "I *am* doing a great work, so that I cannot come down. Why should the work cease while I leave it and go down to you?"

4 But they sent me this message four times, and I answered them in the same manner.

5 Then Sanballat sent his servant to me as before, the fifth time, with an open letter in his hand. 6 In it *was* written:

It is reported among the nations, and Geshem says, *that* you and the Jews plan to rebel; therefore, according to these rumors, you are rebuilding the wall, that you may be their king. 7 And you have also appointed prophets to proclaim concerning you at Jerusalem, saying, "There is a king in Judah!" Now these matters will be reported to the king. So come, therefore, and let us consult together.

8 Then I sent to him, saying, "No such things as you say are being done, but you invent them in your own heart."

9 For they all were trying to make us afraid, saying, "Their hands will be weakened in the work, and it will not be done."

Now therefore, O God, strengthen my hands.

10 Afterward I came to the house of Shemaiah the son of Delaiah, the son of Mehetabel, who was a secret informer; and he said, "Let us meet together in the house of God, within the temple, and let us close the doors of the temple, for they are coming to kill you; indeed, at night they will come to kill you."

11 And I said, "Should such a man as I flee? And who is there such as I who would go into the temple to save his life? I will not go in!" 12 Then I perceived that God had not sent him at all, but that he pronounced this **prophecy** against me because Tobiah and Sanballat had hired him. 13 For this reason he was hired, that I should be afraid and act that way and sin, so that they might have cause for an evil report, that they might reproach me.

14 My God, remember Tobiah and Sanballat, according to these their works, and the prophetess Noadiah and the rest of the prophets who would have made me afraid.

15 So the wall was finished on the twenty-fifth day of Elul, in fifty-two days. 16 And it happened, when all our enemies heard of it, and all the nations around us saw these things, that they were very disheartened in their own eyes; for they perceived that this work was done by our God.

17 Also in those days the nobles of Judah sent many letters to Tobiah, and the letters of Tobiah came to them. 18 For many in Judah were pledged to him, because he was the son-in-law of Shechaniah the son of Arah, and his son Jehohanan had married the daughter of Meshullam the son of Berechiah. 19 Also they reported his good deeds before me, and reported my words to him. Tobiah sent letters to frighten me.

Nehemiah finishes the wall

7 Then it was, when the wall was built and I had hung the doors, when the gatekeepers, the singers, and the Levites had been appointed, 2 that I gave the charge of Jerusalem to my brother Hanani, and Hananiah the leader of the citadel, for he was a faithful man and feared God more than many.

3 And I said to them, "Do not let the gates of Jerusalem be opened until the sun is hot; and while they stand guard, let them shut and bar the doors; and appoint guards from among the inhabitants of Jerusalem, one at his watch station and another in front of his own house."

4 Now the city was large and spacious, but the people in it were few, and the houses were not rebuilt. 5 Then my God put it into my heart to gather the nobles, the rulers, and the people, that they might be registered by genealogy. And I found a register of the genealogy of those who had come up in the first return, and found written in it:

WORDFINDER
6:12 Prophecy Pronounced PROFF-uh-see. A message or messages from God. Such messages in the Bible often tell about God's plans for the future.

6 These *are* the people of the province who came back from the captivity, of those who had been carried away, whom Nebuchadnezzar the king of Babylon had carried away, and who returned to Jerusalem and Judah, everyone to his city.

7 Those who came with Zerubbabel *were* Jeshua, Nehemiah, Azariah, Raamiah, Nahamani, Mordecai, Bilshan, Mispereth, Bigvai, Nehum, and Baanah.

The number of the men of the people of Israel: 8 the sons of Parosh, two thousand one hundred and seventy-two;

9 the sons of Shephatiah, three hundred and seventy-two;

10 the sons of Arah, six hundred and fifty-two;

11 the sons of Pahath-Moab, of the sons of Jeshua and Joab, two thousand eight hundred and eighteen;

12 the sons of Elam, one thousand two hundred and fifty-four;

13 the sons of Zattu, eight hundred and forty-five;

14 the sons of Zaccai, seven hundred and sixty;

15 the sons of Binnui, six hundred and forty-eight;

16 the sons of Bebai, six hundred and twenty-eight;

17 the sons of Azgad, two thousand three hundred and twenty-two;

18 the sons of Adonikam, six hundred and sixty-seven;

19 the sons of Bigvai, two thousand and sixty-seven;

20 the sons of Adin, six hundred and fifty-five;

21 the sons of Ater of Hezekiah, ninety-eight;

22 the sons of Hashum, three hundred and twenty-eight;

23 the sons of Bezai, three hundred and twenty-four;

24 the sons of Hariph, one hundred and twelve;

25 the sons of Gibeon, ninety-five;

26 the men of Bethlehem and Netophah, one hundred and eighty-eight;

27 the men of Anathoth, one hundred and twenty-eight;

28 the men of Beth Azmaveth, forty-two;

29 the men of Kirjath Jearim, Chephirah, and Beeroth, seven hundred and forty-three;

30 the men of Ramah and Geba, six hundred and twenty-one;

31 the men of Michmas, one hundred and twenty-two;

32 the men of Bethel and Ai, one hundred and twenty-three;

33 the men of the other Nebo, fifty-two;

34 the sons of the other Elam, one thousand two hundred and fifty-four;

35 the sons of Harim, three hundred and twenty;

36 the sons of Jericho, three hundred and forty-five;

37 the sons of Lod, Hadid, and Ono, seven hundred and twenty-one;

38 the sons of Senaah, three thousand nine hundred and thirty.

39 The priests: the sons of Jedaiah, of the house of Jeshua, nine hundred and seventy-three;

40 the sons of Immer, one thousand and fifty-two;

41 the sons of Pashhur, one thousand two hundred and forty-seven;

42 the sons of Harim, one thousand and seventeen.

43 The Levites: the sons of Jeshua, of Kadmiel, *and* of the sons of Hodevah, seventy-four.

44 The singers: the sons of Asaph, one hundred and forty-eight.

45 The gatekeepers: the sons of
Shallum,
the sons of Ater,
the sons of Talmon,
the sons of Akkub,
the sons of Hatita,
the sons of Shobai, one hundred
and thirty-eight.

46 The Nethinim: the sons of Ziha,
the sons of Hasupha,
the sons of Tabbaoth,
47 the sons of Keros,
the sons of Sia,
the sons of Padon,
48 the sons of Lebana,
the sons of Hagaba,
the sons of Salmai,
49 the sons of Hanan,
the sons of Giddel,
the sons of Gahar,
50 the sons of Reaiah,
the sons of Rezin,
the sons of Nekoda,
51 the sons of Gazzam,
the sons of Uzza,
the sons of Paseah,
52 the sons of Besai,
the sons of Meunim,
the sons of Nephishesim,
53 the sons of Bakbuk,
the sons of Hakupha,
the sons of Harhur,
54 the sons of Bazlith,
the sons of Mehida,
the sons of Harsha,
55 the sons of Barkos,
the sons of Sisera,
the sons of Tamah,
56 the sons of Neziah,
and the sons of Hatipha.

57 The sons of Solomon's servants:
the sons of Sotai,
the sons of Sophereth,
the sons of Perida,
58 the sons of Jaala,
the sons of Darkon,
the sons of Giddel,
59 the sons of Shephatiah,
the sons of Hattil,
the sons of Pochereth of
Zebaim,
and the children of Amon.
60 All the Nethinim, and the sons
of Solomon's servants, *were*
three hundred and ninety-two.

61 And these *were* the ones who
came up from Tel Melah, Tel
Harsha, Cherub, Addon, and
Immer, but they could not
identify their father's house nor
their lineage, whether they *were*
of Israel: 62 the sons of Delaiah,
the sons of Tobiah,
the sons of Nekoda, six hundred
and forty-two;
63 and of the priests: the sons of
Habaiah,
the sons of Koz,
the sons of Barzillai, who took
a wife of the daughters of
Barzillai the Gileadite, and was
called by their name.
64 These sought their **listing**
among those who were
registered by **genealogy,** but it
was not found; therefore they
were excluded from the
priesthood as defiled. 65 And the
governor said to them that they
should not eat of the most holy
things till a priest could consult
with the **Urim and Thummim.**

66 Altogether the whole assembly
was forty-two thousand three
hundred and sixty, 67 besides
their male and female servants,
of whom *there were* seven
thousand three hundred and
thirty-seven; and they had two
hundred and forty-five men and

WORDFINDER

7:64 Listing (Genealogy) The history of a family showing the family members of
each generation from the beginning.

7:65 Urim and Thummim Stones or gems used by the high priest to learn the
will of God.

women singers. 68 Their horses were seven hundred and thirty-six, their mules two hundred and forty-five, 69 their camels four hundred and thirty-five, and donkeys six thousand seven hundred and twenty.

70 And some of the heads of the fathers' houses gave to the work. The governor gave to the treasury one thousand gold drachmas, fifty basins, and five hundred and thirty priestly garments. 71 Some of the heads of the fathers' houses gave to the treasury of the work twenty thousand gold drachmas, and two thousand two hundred silver minas. 72 And that which the rest of the people gave was twenty thousand gold drachmas, two thousand silver minas, and sixty-seven priestly garments.

73 So the priests, the Levites, the gatekeepers, the singers, some of the people, the Nethinim, and all Israel dwelt in their cities.

When the seventh month came, the children of Israel were in their cities.

Ezra reads and explains the Law

8 Now all the people gathered together as one man in the open square

---

⚒ DIGGING IN

8:1–8 You Can Understand God's Word Nehemiah finished his assignment to build the wall of Jerusalem and then took a census of the people. Finally, all the people assembled to hear Ezra read God's Word in the open square of the city.

Ezra read the Scriptures, and others helped the people to understand what the Scriptures meant. God wants us to read His Word and ask Him to help us understand the meaning.

We not only have teachers to help us understand God's Word. We also have the Holy Spirit that Jesus promised us. Jesus said the Holy Spirit would lead us into all truth.

So you should never feel alone with the Scriptures. God Himself, the Holy Spirit, is your Helper. He has promised to give you understanding of His Word. Every time you read the Bible, listen as if the words were being spoken to you by the Holy Spirit. God will teach you what He wants you to learn.

When the work was completed, Ezra the priest read the Book of the Law to all the people.

that *was* in front of the Water Gate; and they told Ezra the scribe to bring the Book of the Law of Moses, which the LORD had commanded Israel. ² So Ezra the priest brought the Law before the assembly of men and women and all who *could* hear with understanding on the first day of the seventh month. ³ Then he read from it in the open square that *was* in front of the Water Gate from morning until midday, before the men and women and those who could understand; and the ears of all the people *were attentive* to the Book of the Law.

⁴ So Ezra the scribe stood on a platform of wood which they had made for the purpose; and beside him, at his right hand, stood Mattithiah, Shema, Anaiah, Urijah, Hilkiah, and Maaseiah; and at his left hand Pedaiah, Mishael, Malchijah, Hashum, Hashbadana, Zechariah, *and* Meshullam. ⁵ And Ezra opened the book in the sight of all the people, for he was *standing* above all the people; and when he opened it, all the people stood up. ⁶ And Ezra blessed the LORD, the great God.

Then all the people answered, "Amen, Amen!" while lifting up their hands. And they bowed their heads and worshiped the LORD with *their* faces to the ground.

⁷ Also Jeshua, Bani, Sherebiah, Jamin, Akkub, Shabbethai, Hodijah, Maaseiah, Kelita, Azariah, Jozabad, Hanan, Pelaiah, and the Levites, helped the people to understand the Law; and the people *stood* in their place. ⁸ So they read distinctly from the book, in the Law of God; and they gave the sense, and helped *them* to understand the reading.

⁹ And Nehemiah, who *was* the governor, Ezra the priest *and* scribe, and the Levites who taught the people said to all the people, "This day *is* holy to the LORD your God; do not mourn nor weep." For all the people wept, when they heard the words of the Law.

¹⁰ Then he said to them, "Go your way, eat the fat, drink the sweet, and send portions to those for whom nothing is prepared; for *this* day *is* holy to our Lord. Do not sorrow, for the joy of the LORD is your strength."

¹¹ So the Levites quieted all the people, saying, "Be still, for the day *is* holy; do not be grieved." ¹² And all the people went their way to eat and drink, to send portions and rejoice greatly, because they understood the words that *were* declared to them.

¹³ Now on the second day the heads of the fathers' *houses* of all the people, with the priests and Levites, were gathered to Ezra the scribe, in order to understand the words of the Law. ¹⁴ And they found written in the Law, which the LORD had commanded by Moses, that the children of Israel should dwell in booths during the feast of the seventh month, ¹⁵ and that they should announce and proclaim in all their cities and in Jerusalem, saying, "Go out to the mountain, and bring olive branches, branches of oil trees, myrtle branches, palm branches, and branches of leafy trees, to make booths, as *it is* written."

¹⁶ Then the people went out and brought *them* and made themselves booths, each one on the roof of his house, or in their courtyards or the courts of the house of God, and in the open square of the Water Gate and in the open square of the Gate of Ephraim. ¹⁷ So the whole assembly of those who had returned from the captivity made booths and sat under the booths; for since the days of Joshua the son of Nun until that day the children of Israel had not done so. And there was very great gladness. ¹⁸ Also day by day, from the first day until the last day, he read from the Book of the Law of God. And they kept the feast seven days; and on the eighth day *there was* a sacred assembly, according to the *prescribed* manner.

The people confess their sins

9 Now on the twenty-fourth day of this month the children of Israel were assembled with fasting, in sackcloth, and with dust on their heads. ² Then those of Israelite lineage separated

What Israel Learned

During the 70 years we were away from the land where we were born, we forgot how to worship the Lord in the right way. Then Ezra read God's Word to us, and we found out that ever since the time of Joshua, we had not been obeying God's plan for worship during the seventh month of our year. That time was called "the Feast of Booths." We would live in tents and remember that we had been tent-dwellers after we left Egypt in the time of Moses.

After we listened to Ezra reading God's Word, we knew we had broken God's Law. That's why we were not enjoying all of God's blessing. So we made up our minds to obey the Lord in everything.

Have you made up your mind to follow Jesus?

themselves from all foreigners; and they stood and confessed their sins and the iniquities of their fathers. ³ And they stood up in their place and read from the Book of the Law of the LORD their God *for one*-fourth of the day; and *for another* fourth they confessed and worshiped the LORD their God.

⁴ Then Jeshua, Bani, Kadmiel, Shebaniah, Bunni, Sherebiah, Bani, *and* Chenani stood on the stairs of the Levites and cried out with a loud voice to the LORD their God. ⁵ And the Levites, Jeshua, Kadmiel, Bani, Hashabniah, Sherebiah, Hodijah, Shebaniah, *and* Pethahiah, said:

"Stand up *and* bless the LORD
your God
Forever and ever!

"Blessed be Your glorious name,
Which is exalted above all
blessing and praise!
6 You alone *are* the LORD;
You have made heaven,
The heaven of heavens, with all
their host,
The earth and everything on it,
The seas and all that is in them,
And You preserve them all.
The host of heaven worships
You.

7 "You *are* the LORD God,
Who chose Abram,
And brought him out of Ur of
the Chaldeans,

And gave him the name
Abraham;
8 You found his heart faithful
before You,
And made a covenant with him
To give the land of the
Canaanites,
The Hittites, the Amorites,
The Perizzites, the Jebusites,
And the Girgashites—
To give *it* to his descendants.
You have performed Your
words,
For You *are* righteous.

A king and queen of the Hittites, whose land God promised to the Israelites.

9 "You saw the affliction of our fathers in Egypt,
And heard their cry by the Red Sea.
10 You showed signs and wonders against Pharaoh,
Against all his servants,
And against all the people of his land.
For You knew that they acted proudly against them.
So You made a name for Yourself, as *it is* this day.
11 And You divided the sea before them,
So that they went through the midst of the sea on the dry land;
And their persecutors You threw into the deep,
As a stone into the mighty waters.
12 Moreover You led them by day with a **cloudy pillar,**
And by night with a **pillar of fire,**
To give them light on the road Which they should travel.

13 "You came down also on Mount Sinai,
And spoke with them from heaven,
And gave them just ordinances and true laws,
Good statutes and commandments.
14 You made known to them Your holy Sabbath,
And commanded them precepts, statutes and laws,
By the hand of Moses Your servant.
15 You gave them bread from heaven for their hunger,
And brought them water out of the rock for their thirst,
And told them to go in to possess the land

Which You had sworn to give them.

16 "But they and our fathers acted proudly,
Hardened their necks,
And did not heed Your commandments.
17 They refused to obey,
And they were not mindful of Your wonders
That You did among them.
But they hardened their necks,
And in their rebellion
They appointed a leader
To return to their bondage.
But You *are* God,
Ready to pardon,
Gracious and merciful,
Slow to anger,
Abundant in kindness,
And did not forsake them.

18 "Even when they made a molded calf for themselves,
And said, 'This *is* your god That brought you up out of Egypt,'
And worked great provocations,
19 Yet in Your manifold mercies You did not forsake them in the wilderness.
The pillar of the cloud did not depart from them by day,
To lead them on the road;
Nor the pillar of fire by night,
To show them light,
And the way they should go.
20 You also gave Your good Spirit to instruct them,
And did not withhold Your manna from their mouth,
And gave them water for their thirst.
21 Forty years You sustained them in the wilderness;
They lacked nothing;
Their clothes did not wear out And their feet did not swell.

WORDFINDER

9:12 Pillar of Fire and Cloud   A special appearance of God. This was one of the ways the invisible God once showed Himself to human eyes.

22 "Moreover You gave them
      kingdoms and nations,
   And divided them into districts.
   So they took possession of the
      land of Sihon,
   The land of the king of
      Heshbon,
   And the land of Og king of
      Bashan.
23 You also multiplied their
      children as the stars of
      heaven,
   And brought them into the land
   Which You had told their fathers
   To go in and possess.
24 So the people went in
   And possessed the land;
   You subdued before them the
      inhabitants of the land,
   The Canaanites,
   And gave them into their hands,
   With their kings
   And the people of the land,
   That they might do with them
      as they wished.
25 And they took strong cities and
      a rich land,
   And possessed houses full of all
      goods,
   Cisterns *already* dug, vineyards,
      olive groves,
   And fruit trees in abundance.
   So they ate and were filled and
      grew fat,
   And delighted themselves in
      Your great goodness.

26 "Nevertheless they were
      disobedient
   And rebelled against You,
   Cast Your law behind their
      backs
   And killed Your prophets, who
      testified against them
   To turn them to Yourself;
   And they worked great
      provocations.
27 Therefore You delivered them
      into the hand of their
      enemies,
   Who oppressed them;
   And in the time of their trouble,
   When they cried to You,
   You heard from heaven;

   And according to Your
      abundant mercies
   You gave them deliverers who
      saved them
   From the hand of their enemies.

28 "But after they had rest,
   They again did evil before You.
   Therefore You left them in the
      hand of their enemies,
   So that they had dominion over
      them;
   Yet when they returned and
      cried out to You,
   You heard from heaven;
   And many times You delivered
      them according to Your
      mercies,
29 And testified against them,
   That You might bring them back
      to Your law.
   Yet they acted proudly,
   And did not heed Your
      commandments,
   But sinned against Your
      judgments,
   'Which if a man does, he shall
      live by them.'
   And they shrugged their
      shoulders,
   Stiffened their necks,
   And would not hear.
30 Yet for many years You had
      patience with them,
   And testified against them by
      Your Spirit in Your prophets.
   Yet they would not listen;
   Therefore You gave them into
      the hand of the peoples of the
      lands.
31 Nevertheless in Your great
      mercy
   You did not utterly consume
      them nor forsake them;
   For You *are* God, gracious and
      merciful.

32 "Now therefore, our God,
   The great, the mighty, and
      awesome God,
   Who keeps covenant and
      mercy:
   Do not let all the trouble seem
      small before You

That has come upon us,
Our kings and our princes,
Our priests and our prophets,
Our fathers and on all Your
    people,
From the days of the kings of
    Assyria until this day.
33 However You *are* just in all that
    has befallen us;
For You have dealt faithfully,
But we have done wickedly.
34 Neither our kings nor our
    princes,
Our priests nor our fathers,
Have kept Your law,
Nor heeded Your
    commandments and Your
    testimonies,
With which You testified against
    them.
35 For they have not served You
    in their kingdom,
Or in the many good *things* that
    You gave them,
Or in the large and rich land
    which You set before them;
Nor did they turn from their
    wicked works.

36 "Here we *are*, servants today!
And the land that You gave to
    our fathers,
To eat its fruit and its bounty,
Here we *are*, servants in it!
37 And it yields much increase to
    the kings
You have set over us,
Because of our sins;
Also they have dominion over
    our bodies and our cattle
At their pleasure;
And we *are* in great distress.

38 "And because of all this,
We make a sure *covenant* and
    write *it;*
Our leaders, our Levites, *and*
    our priests seal *it.*"

The people promise to obey God

10 Now those who placed *their* seal
on *the document were:*

Nehemiah the governor, the son
of Hacaliah, and Zedekiah,
2 Seraiah, Azariah, Jeremiah,
3 Pashhur, Amariah, Malchijah,
4 Hattush, Shebaniah, Malluch,
5 Harim, Meremoth, Obadiah,
6 Daniel, Ginnethon, Baruch,
7 Meshullam, Abijah, Mijamin,
8 Maaziah, Bilgai, *and*
Shemaiah. These *were* the
priests.

9 The Levites: Jeshua the son of
Azaniah, Binnui of the sons of
Henadad, *and* Kadmiel.

10 Their brethren: Shebaniah,
Hodijah, Kelita, Pelaiah, Hanan,
11 Micha, Rehob, Hashabiah,
12 Zaccur, Sherebiah,
Shebaniah, 13 Hodijah, Bani,
and Beninu.

14 The leaders of the people:
Parosh, Pahath-Moab, Elam,
Zattu, Bani, 15 Bunni, Azgad,
Bebai, 16 Adonijah, Bigvai, Adin,
17 Ater, Hezekiah, Azzur,
18 Hodijah, Hashum, Bezai,
19 Hariph, Anathoth, Nebai,
20 Magpiash, Meshullam, Hezir,
21 Meshezabel, Zadok, Jaddua,
22 Pelatiah, Hanan, Anaiah,
23 Hoshea, Hananiah, Hasshub,
24 Hallohesh, Pilha, Shobek,
25 Rehum, Hashabnah,
Maaseiah, 26 Ahijah, Hanan,
Anan, 27 Malluch, Harim, *and*
Baanah.

28 Now the rest of the people—the
priests, the Levites, the gatekeepers,
the singers, the Nethinim, and all those
who had separated themselves from
the peoples of the lands to the Law
of God, their wives, their sons, and
their daughters, everyone who had
knowledge and understanding—
29 these joined with their brethren, their
nobles, and entered into a curse and
an oath to walk in God's Law, which
was given by Moses the servant of
God, and to observe and do all the

commandments of the LORD our Lord, and His ordinances and His statutes: 30 We would not give our daughters as wives to the peoples of the land, nor take their daughters for our sons; 31 if the peoples of the land brought wares or any grain to sell on the Sabbath day, we would not buy it from them on the Sabbath, or on a holy day; and we would forego the seventh year's *produce* and the exacting of every debt.

32 Also we made ordinances for ourselves, to exact from ourselves yearly one-third of a shekel for the service of the house of our God: 33 for the showbread, for the regular grain offering, for the regular burnt offering of the Sabbaths, the New Moons, and the set feasts; for the holy things, for the sin offerings to make atonement for Israel, and all the work of the house of our God. 34 We cast lots among the priests, the Levites, and the people, for *bringing* the wood offering into the house of our God, according to our fathers' houses, at the appointed times year by year, to burn on the altar of the LORD our God as *it is* written in the Law.

35 And *we made ordinances* to bring the firstfruits of our ground and the firstfruits of all fruit of all trees, year by year, to the house of the LORD; 36 to bring the firstborn of our sons and our cattle, as *it is* written in the Law, and the firstborn of our herds and our flocks, to the house of our God, to the priests who minister in the house of our God; 37 to bring the firstfruits of

our dough, our offerings, the fruit from all kinds of trees, *the* new wine and oil, to the priests, to the storerooms of the house of our God; and to bring the tithes of our land to the Levites, for the Levites should receive the tithes in all our farming communities. 38 And the priest, the descendant of Aaron, shall be with the Levites when the Levites receive tithes; and the Levites shall bring up a tenth of the tithes to the house of our God, to the rooms of the storehouse.

39 For the children of Israel and the children of Levi shall bring the offering of the grain, of the new wine and the oil, to the storerooms where the articles of the sanctuary *are, where* the priests who minister and the gatekeepers and the singers *are;* and we will not neglect the house of our God.

The people chosen to live in the big city

11 Now the leaders of the people dwelt at Jerusalem; the rest of the people cast lots to bring one out of ten to dwell in Jerusalem, the holy city, and nine-tenths *were to dwell* in *other* cities. 2 And the people blessed all the men who willingly offered themselves to dwell at Jerusalem.

3 These *are* the heads of the province who dwelt in Jerusalem. (But in the cities of Judah everyone dwelt in his own possession in their cities—Israelites, priests, Levites, Nethinim, and descendants of Solomon's servants.) 4 Also in Jerusalem dwelt *some* of the

🪓 DIGGING IN

10:28–31 Make Your Promise to God
God kept His promise to bring the people of Israel from Babylon back to their land in Palestine. Then Ezra read the Scriptures to them. When the people heard God's Word, they realized it was God who had set them free. They made a promise to live for Him.

When anyone does a great kindness for you, do you feel thankful? Do you want to show that person how grateful you are for that kindness? Unthankful people are

usually very unhappy people, too.

You have heard often that God sent His Son Jesus to die for your sins and give you eternal life. If you believe this promise of God, then you know you have the gift of eternal life. This is God's great kindness to you. So it only makes sense to promise God your life. God wants to use your life to show His goodness and mercy to other people. Have you promised God your life?

children of Judah and of the children of Benjamin.

The children of Judah: Athaiah the son of Uzziah, the son of Zechariah, the son of Amariah, the son of Shephatiah, the son of Mahalalel, of the children of Perez; 5 and Maaseiah the son of Baruch, the son of Col-Hozeh, the son of Hazaiah, the son of Adaiah, the son of Joiarib, the son of Zechariah, the son of Shiloni. 6 All the sons of Perez who dwelt at Jerusalem *were* four hundred and sixty-eight valiant men.

7 And these are the sons of Benjamin: Sallu the son of Meshullam, the son of Joed, the son of Pedaiah, the son of Kolaiah, the son of Maaseiah, the son of Ithiel, the son of Jeshaiah; 8 and after him Gabbai *and* Sallai, nine hundred and twenty-eight. 9 Joel the son of Zichri *was* their overseer, and Judah the son of Senuah *was* second over the city.

10 Of the priests: Jedaiah the son of Joiarib, and Jachin; 11 Seraiah the son of Hilkiah, the son of Meshullam, the son of Zadok, the son of Meraioth, the son of Ahitub, *was* the leader of the house of God. 12 Their brethren who did the work of the house *were* eight hundred and twenty-two; and Adaiah the son of Jeroham, the son of Pelaliah, the son of Amzi, the son of Zechariah, the son of Pashhur, the son of Malchijah, 13 and his brethren, heads of the fathers' *houses, were* two hundred and forty-two; and Amashai the son of Azarel, the son of Ahzai, the son of Meshillemoth, the son of Immer, 14 and their brethren, mighty men of valor, *were* one hundred and twenty-eight. Their overseer *was* Zabdiel the son of *one of* the great men.

15 Also of the Levites: Shemaiah the son of Hasshub, the son of Azrikam, the son of Hashabiah, the son of Bunni; 16 Shabbethai and Jozabad, of the heads of the Levites, *had* the oversight of the business outside of the house of God; 17 Mattaniah the son of Micha, the son of Zabdi, the son of Asaph, the leader *who* began the thanksgiving with prayer; Bakbukiah,

the second among his brethren; and Abda the son of Shammua, the son of Galal, the son of Jeduthun. 18 All the Levites in the holy city *were* two hundred and eighty-four.

19 Moreover the gatekeepers, Akkub, Talmon, and their brethren who kept the gates, *were* one hundred and seventy-two.

20 And the rest of Israel, of the priests *and* Levites, *were* in all the cities of Judah, everyone in his inheritance. 21 But the Nethinim dwelt in Ophel. And Ziha and Gishpa *were* over the Nethinim.

22 Also the overseer of the Levites at Jerusalem *was* Uzzi the son of Bani, the son of Hashabiah, the son of Mattaniah, the son of Micha, of the sons of Asaph, the singers in charge of the service of the house of God. 23 For *it was* the king's command concerning them that a certain portion should be for the singers, a quota day by day. 24 Pethahiah the son of Meshezabel, of the children of Zerah the son of Judah, *was* the king's deputy in all matters concerning the people.

25 And as for the villages with their fields, *some* of the children of Judah dwelt in Kirjath Arba and its villages, Dibon and its villages, Jekabzeel and its villages; 26 in Jeshua, Moladah, Beth Pelet, 27 Hazar Shual, and Beersheba and its villages; 28 in Ziklag and Meconah and its villages; 29 in En Rimmon, Zorah, Jarmuth, 30 Zanoah, Adullam, and their villages; in Lachish and its fields; in Azekah and its villages. They dwelt from Beersheba to the Valley of Hinnom.

31 Also the children of Benjamin from Geba *dwelt* in Michmash, Aija, and Bethel, and their villages; 32 in Anathoth, Nob, Ananiah; 33 in Hazor, Ramah, Gittaim; 34 in Hadid, Zeboim, Neballat; 35 in Lod, Ono, *and* the Valley of Craftsmen. 36 Some of the Judean divisions of Levites *were* in Benjamin.

Leaders dedicate the city wall

12 Now these *are* the priests and the Levites who came up with Zerubbabel

Bible Heroes

Old Testament

Many long-ago Old Testament heroes were just like people we know today. Some were strong and others were weak. Some were old and others were young. Some were short and others were tall. Some were brave and others were fearful. See if you can guess the speaker in each of the riddles below:

I wish I hadn't listened
When the serpent called my name;
For ever since I ate that fruit
The world's not been the same!

WHO AM I?

___ ___ ___

(Look what happened when I disobeyed God! See Genesis 3:1–19.)

You've read about my animals
Parading two by two;
I used to be the keeper
Of the world's first floating zoo!

WHO AM I?

___ ___ ___ ___

(Read about the great Flood in Genesis 6:1–8:22.)

When God said I'd have a child,
I laughed so hard I cried!
I was so old at Isaac's birth
That God was glorified!

WHO AM I?

___ ___ ___ ___

(I learned that nothing is impossible with God. Read my amazing story in Genesis 21:1–7.)

Bible Heroes

The lions eyed me hungrily
But I escaped, unhurt.
An angel shut their mouths so I
Would not be their dessert!

WHO AM I?

— — — — — —

(Read about my narrow escape in Daniel 6:1–28.)

They sent a scrawny boy to fight;
I filled his heart with dread.
But when he aimed his slingshot,
I really lost my head!

WHO AM I?

— — — — — —

(David's weapons were better than mine, after all. Find out what they were in 1 Samuel 17:1–58, especially verse 45.)

I was the wisest man on earth;
I lived the best of lives.
But I'll admit it wasn't smart
To have so many wives!

WHO AM I?

— — — — — —

*(My seven hundred wives got me in big trouble!
Read about it in 1 Kings 11:1–13.)*

the son of Shealtiel, and Jeshua: Seraiah, Jeremiah, Ezra, 2 Amariah, Malluch, Hattush, 3 Shechaniah, Rehum,
Meremoth, 4 Iddo, Ginnethoi, Abijah,
5 Mijamin, Maadiah, Bilgah,
6 Shemaiah, Joiarib, Jedaiah, 7 Sallu,
Amok, Hilkiah, *and* Jedaiah.

These *were* the heads of the priests
and their brethren in the days of
Jeshua.

8 Moreover the Levites *were* Jeshua,
Binnui, Kadmiel, Sherebiah, Judah,
and Mattaniah *who led* the thanksgiving *psalms,* he and his brethren.
9 Also Bakbukiah and Unni, their
brethren, *stood* across from them in
their duties.

10 Jeshua begot Joiakim, Joiakim
begot Eliashib, Eliashib begot Joiada,
11 Joiada begot Jonathan, and Jonathan begot Jaddua.

12 Now in the days of Joiakim, the
priests, the heads of the fathers' *houses
were:* of Seraiah, Meraiah; of Jeremiah, Hananiah; 13 of Ezra, Meshullam; of Amariah, Jehohanan; 14 of
Melichu, Jonathan; of Shebaniah, Joseph; 15 of Harim, Adna; of Meraioth,
Helkai; 16 of Iddo, Zechariah; of Ginnethon, Meshullam; 17 of Abijah, Zichri;
the son of Minjamin; of Moadiah, Piltai;
18 of Bilgah, Shammua; of Shemaiah,
Jehonathan; 19 of Joiarib, Mattenai; of
Jedaiah, Uzzi; 20 of Sallai, Kallai; of
Amok, Eber; 21 of Hilkiah, Hashabiah;
and of Jedaiah, Nethanel.

22 During the reign of Darius the Persian, a record *was also kept* of the Levites and priests *who had been* heads
of their fathers' *houses* in the days of
Eliashib, Joiada, Johanan, and Jaddua. 23 The sons of Levi, the heads of
the fathers' *houses* until the days of
Johanan the son of Eliashib, *were* written in the book of the chronicles.

24 And the heads of the Levites *were*
Hashabiah, Sherebiah, and Jeshua the
son of Kadmiel, with their brothers
across from them, to praise *and* give
thanks, group alternating with group,
according to the command of David
the man of God. 25 Mattaniah, Bakbukiah, Obadiah, Meshullam, Talmon,
and Akkub *were* gatekeepers keeping

the watch at the storerooms of the
gates. 26 These *lived* in the days of
Joiakim the son of Jeshua, the son of
Jozadak, and in the days of Nehemiah
the governor, and of Ezra the priest,
the scribe.

27 Now at the dedication of the wall
of Jerusalem they sought out the Levites in all their places, to bring them
to Jerusalem to celebrate the dedication with gladness, both with thanksgivings and singing, *with* cymbals and
stringed instruments and harps. 28 And
the sons of the singers gathered together from the countryside around Jerusalem, from the villages of the Netophathites, 29 from the house of Gilgal, and from the fields of Geba and
Azmaveth; for the singers had built
themselves villages all around Jerusalem. 30 Then the priests and Levites
purified themselves, and purified the
people, the gates, and the wall.

31 So I brought the leaders of Judah
up on the wall, and appointed two
large thanksgiving choirs. *One* went to
the right hand on the wall toward the
Refuse Gate. 32 After them went Hoshaiah and half of the leaders of Judah,
33 and Azariah, Ezra, Meshullam,
34 Judah, Benjamin, Shemaiah, Jeremiah, 35 and some of the priests' sons
with trumpets—Zechariah the son of
Jonathan, the son of Shemaiah, the
son of Mattaniah, the son of Michaiah,
the son of Zaccur, the son of Asaph,
36 and his brethren, Shemaiah, Azarel,
Milalai, Gilalai, Maai, Nethanel, Judah,
and Hanani, with the musical instruments of David the man of God.
Ezra the scribe *went* before them.
37 By the Fountain Gate, in front of
them, they went up the stairs of the
City of David, on the stairway of the
wall, beyond the house of David, as
far as the Water Gate eastward.

38 The other thanksgiving choir went
the opposite *way,* and I *was* behind
them with half of the people on the
wall, going past the Tower of the
Ovens as far as the Broad Wall,
39 and above the Gate of Ephraim,
above the Old Gate, above the Fish
Gate, the Tower of Hananel, the

Tower of the Hundred, as far as the Sheep Gate; and they stopped by the Gate of the Prison.

40 So the two thanksgiving choirs stood in the house of God, likewise I and the half of the rulers with me; 41 and the priests, Eliakim, Maaseiah, Minjamin, Michaiah, Elioenai, Zechariah, *and* Hananiah, with trumpets; 42 also Maaseiah, Shemaiah, Eleazar, Uzzi, Jehohanan, Malchijah, Elam, and Ezer. The singers sang loudly with Jezrahiah the director.

43 Also that day they offered great sacrifices, and rejoiced, for God had made them rejoice with great joy; the women and the children also rejoiced, so that the joy of Jerusalem was heard afar off.

44 And at the same time some were appointed over the rooms of the storehouse for the offerings, the **firstfruits,** and the tithes, to gather into them from the fields of the cities the portions specified by the Law for the priests and Levites; for Judah rejoiced over the priests and Levites who ministered. 45 Both the singers and the gatekeepers kept the charge of their God and the charge of the purification, according to the command of David *and* Solomon his son. 46 For in the days of David and Asaph of old *there were* chiefs of the singers, and songs of praise and thanksgiving to God. 47 In the days of Zerubbabel and in the days of Nehemiah all Israel gave the portions for the singers and the gatekeepers, a portion for each day. They also consecrated *holy things* for the Levites, and the Levites consecrated *them* for the children of Aaron.

Nehemiah makes some tough changes

13 On that day they read from the Book of Moses in the hearing of the people, and in it was found written that no Ammonite or Moabite should ever come into the assembly of God, 2 because they had not met the children of Israel with bread and water, but hired Balaam against them to curse them. However, our God turned the curse into a blessing. 3 So it was, when they had heard the Law, that they separated all the mixed multitude from Israel.

4 Now before this, Eliashib the priest, having authority over the storerooms of the house of our God, *was* allied with Tobiah. 5 And he had prepared for him a large room, where previously they had stored the grain offerings, the frankincense, the articles, the tithes of grain, the new wine and oil, which were commanded *to be given* to the Levites and singers and gatekeepers, and the offerings for the priests. 6 But during all this I was not in Jerusalem, for in the thirty-second year of Artaxerxes king of Babylon I had returned to the king. Then after certain days I obtained leave from the king, 7 and I came to Jerusalem and discovered the evil that Eliashib had done for Tobiah, in preparing a room for him in the courts of the house of God. 8 And it grieved me bitterly; therefore I threw all the household goods of Tobiah out of the room. 9 Then I commanded them to cleanse the rooms; and I brought back into them the articles of the house of God, with the grain offering and the frankincense.

10 I also realized that the portions for the Levites had not been given *them;* for each of the Levites and the singers who did the work had gone back to his field. 11 So I contended with the rulers, and said, "Why is the house of God forsaken?" And I gathered them together and set them in their place. 12 Then all Judah brought the tithe of the grain and the new wine and the

oil to the storehouse. 13 And I appointed as treasurers over the storehouse Shelemiah the priest and Zadok the scribe, and of the Levites, Pedaiah; and next to them *was* Hanan the son of Zaccur, the son of Mattaniah; for they were considered faithful, and their task *was* to distribute to their brethren.

14 Remember me, O my God, concerning this, and do not wipe out my good deeds that I have done for the house of my God, and for its services!

15 In those days I saw *people* in Judah treading wine presses on the Sabbath, and bringing in sheaves, and loading donkeys with wine, grapes, figs, and all *kinds of* burdens, which they brought into Jerusalem on the Sabbath day. And I warned *them* about the day on which they were selling provisions. 16 Men of Tyre dwelt there also, who brought in fish and all kinds of goods, and sold *them* on the Sabbath to the children of Judah, and in Jerusalem.

17 Then I contended with the nobles of Judah, and said to them, "What evil thing *is* this that you do, by which you profane the Sabbath day? 18 Did not your fathers do thus, and did not our God bring all this disaster on us and on this city? Yet you bring added wrath on Israel by profaning the Sabbath."

19 So it was, at the gates of Jerusalem, as it began to be dark before the Sabbath, that I commanded the gates to be shut, and charged that they must not be opened till after the Sabbath. Then I posted *some* of my servants at the gates, *so that* no burdens would be brought in on the Sabbath day.

20 Now the merchants and sellers of all kinds of wares lodged outside Jerusalem once or twice.

21 Then I warned them, and said to them, "Why do you spend the night around the wall? If you do *so* again, I will lay hands on you!" From that time on they came no *more* on the Sabbath. 22 And I commanded the Levites that they should cleanse themselves, and that they should go and guard the gates, to sanctify the Sabbath day.

Remember me, O my God, concerning this also, and spare me according to the greatness of Your mercy!

23 In those days I also saw Jews *who* had married women of Ashdod, Ammon, *and* Moab. 24 And half of their children spoke the language of Ashdod, and could not speak the language of Judah, but spoke according to the language of one or the other people.

25 So I contended with them and cursed them, struck some of them and pulled out their hair, and made them swear by God, *saying,* "You shall not give your daughters as wives to their sons, nor take their daughters for your sons or yourselves. 26 Did not Solomon king of Israel sin by these things? Yet among many nations there was no king like him, who was beloved of his God; and God made him king over all Israel. Nevertheless pagan women caused even him to sin. 27 Should we then hear of your doing all this great evil, transgressing against our God by marrying pagan women?"

28 And *one* of the sons of Joiada, the son of Eliashib the high priest, *was*

⚒ DIGGING IN

13:12 Pay Your Tithe to God The word *tithe* means a "tenth." God commanded His people to give back to Him a tenth of their income.

Did you know that there would be no hungry people in the world if all Christians would just give a tenth of their income back to God? The Lord meant that what we give to Him should be used to preach the gospel and help the poor. People will listen to the gospel if only we act like Christians. How does a Christian act?

A Christian cares about people in need. It makes God angry when we meet a needy person and say, "God bless you," but do nothing for that person. God didn't just say nice words to us. He gave us the best He had when He gave His only begotten Son.

a son-in-law of Sanballat the Horonite; therefore I drove him from me.

29 Remember them, O my God, because they have defiled the priesthood and the covenant of the priesthood and the Levites.

30 Thus I cleansed them of every-thing pagan. I also assigned duties to the priests and the Levites, each to his service, 31 and *to bringing* the wood offering and the firstfruits at appointed times.

Remember me, O my God, for good!

⚒ DIGGING IN

13:30 Live a Pure Life You don't hear much about pure living. You do hear a lot about "doing your own thing." This often means doing things that are impure. How much sense would it make to go inside a house where every disease existed? You would soon get sick, and if you stayed there, you would die. God says, "The wages of sin is death" (Romans 6:23).

You can see that living a pure life makes a lot of sense. People who live impure lives catch terrible diseases that destroy themselves and other people, too. Such people not only get sick, but they often stop listening to God. Without God, they live in misery that can even last forever. That misery is called hell.

Nobody in his or her right mind wants to go to hell. But Satan blinds many, and they stop caring about what happens when they die.

Please care about your life. Keep yourself pure for God.

The Book of
ESTHER

My name is pronounced *ESS-ter* and means "A Star." Two of the books of your Bible are about famous women. You will remember that Ruth was the other one. I was an ordinary Jewish girl living among the captives in Persia. Mordecai, my older cousin, brought me up from childhood. Pronounce my cousin's name *MOR-duh-kigh.*

One day I was commanded to come to the palace of King Ahasuerus (pronounced *ah-haz-you-EAR-us*). That was when I learned that the king was looking for a new queen because his former wife had insulted him.

It all seemed very strange to me because I was only one of many young women that the king could choose from. It took a whole year just to make me beautiful enough to be seen by the king of Persia!

You can imagine how surprised I was when I, a Hebrew girl, was chosen to be queen! But this was only the beginning of a great adventure God was preparing for me and my nation Israel.

Queen Vashti is sent away

NOW it came to pass in the days of Ahasuerus (this *was* the Ahasuerus who reigned over one hundred and twenty-seven provinces, from India to Ethiopia), 2 in those days when King Ahasuerus sat on the throne of his kingdom, which *was* in Shushan the citadel, 3 *that* in the third year of his reign he made a feast for all his officials and servants— the powers of Persia and Media, the nobles, and the princes of the provinces *being* before him— 4 when he showed the riches of his glorious kingdom and the splendor of his excellent majesty for many days, one hundred and eighty days *in all.*

5 And when these days were completed, the king made a feast lasting seven days for all the people who were present in Shushan the citadel, from great to small, in the court of the garden of the king's palace. 6 *There were* white and blue linen *curtains* fastened with cords of fine linen and purple on silver rods and marble pillars; *and the* couches *were* of gold and silver on a *mosaic* pavement of alabaster, turquoise, and white and black marble. 7 And they served drinks in golden vessels, each vessel being different from the other, with royal wine in abundance, according to the generosity of the king. 8 In accordance with the law, the drinking was not compulsory; for so the king had ordered all the officers of his household, that they should do according to each man's pleasure.

9 Queen Vashti also made a feast for the women *in* the royal palace which *belonged* to King Ahasuerus.

10 On the seventh day, when the heart of the king was merry with wine, he commanded Mehuman, Biztha, Harbona, Bigtha, Abagtha, Zethar, and Carcas, seven eunuchs who served in the presence of King Ahasuerus, 11 to bring Queen Vashti before the king, *wearing* her royal crown, in order to show her beauty to the people and the officials, for she *was* beautiful to behold. 12 But Queen Vashti refused to come at the king's command brought by *his* eunuchs; therefore the

king was furious, and his anger burned within him.

13 Then the king said to the wise men who understood the times (for this *was* the king's manner toward all who knew law and justice, 14 those closest to him *being* Carshena, Shethar, Admatha, Tarshish, Meres, Marsena, and Memucan, the seven princes of Persia and Media, who had access to the king's presence, *and* who ranked highest in the kingdom): 15 "What *shall we* do to Queen Vashti, according to law, because she did not obey the command of King Ahasuerus *brought to her* by the eunuchs?"

16 And Memucan answered before the king and the princes: "Queen Vashti has not only wronged the king, but also all the princes, and all the people who *are* in all the provinces of King Ahasuerus. 17 For the queen's behavior will become known to all women, so that they will despise their husbands in their eyes, when they report, 'King Ahasuerus commanded Queen Vashti to be brought in before him, but she did not come.' 18 This very day the *noble* ladies of Persia and Media will say to all the king's officials that they have heard of the behavior of the queen. Thus *there will be* excessive contempt and wrath. 19 If it pleases the king, let a royal decree go out from him, and let it be recorded in the laws of the Persians and the Medes, so that it will not be altered, that Vashti shall come no more before King Ahasuerus; and let the king give her royal position to another who is better than she. 20 When the king's decree which he will make is proclaimed throughout all his empire (for it is great), all wives will honor their husbands, both great and small."

21 And the reply pleased the king and the princes, and the king did according to the word of Memucan. 22 Then he sent letters to all the king's provinces, to each province in its own script, and to every people in their own language, that each man should be master in his own house, and speak in the language of his own people.

Esther wins a beauty contest and becomes queen

2 After these things, when the wrath of King Ahasuerus subsided, he remembered Vashti, what she had done, and what had been decreed against her. 2 Then the king's servants who attended him said: "Let beautiful young virgins be sought for the king; 3 and let the king appoint officers in all the provinces of his kingdom, that they may gather all the beautiful young virgins to Shushan the citadel, into the women's quarters, under the custody of Hegai the king's eunuch, custodian of the women. And let beauty preparations be given *them*. 4 Then let the young woman who pleases the king be queen instead of Vashti."

This thing pleased the king, and he did so.

5 In Shushan the citadel there was a certain Jew whose name *was* Mordecai the son of Jair, the son of Shimei, the son of Kish, a Benjamite. 6 *Kish* had been carried away from Jerusalem with the captives who had been captured with Jeconiah king of Judah, whom Nebuchadnezzar the king of Babylon had carried away. 7 And *Mordecai* had brought up Hadassah, that *is,* Esther, his uncle's daughter, for she had neither father nor mother. The young woman *was* lovely and beautiful. When her father and mother died, Mordecai took her as his own daughter.

8 So it was, when the king's command and decree were heard, and when many young women were gathered at Shushan the citadel, *under* the custody of Hegai, that Esther also was taken to the king's palace, into the care of Hegai the custodian of the women. 9 Now the young woman pleased him, and she obtained his favor; so he readily gave beauty preparations to her, besides her allowance. Then seven choice maidservants were provided for her from the king's palace, and he moved her and her maidservants to the best *place* in the house of the women. 10 Esther had not revealed her peo-

As a royal beauty contestant, Esther spent a year using special oils and treatments before meeting the king.

ple or family, for Mordecai had charged her not to reveal *it.* ¹¹ And every day Mordecai paced in front of the court of the women's quarters, to learn of Esther's welfare and what was happening to her.

¹² Each young woman's turn came to go in to King Ahasuerus after she had completed twelve months' preparation, according to the regulations for the women, for thus were the days of their preparation apportioned: six months with oil of myrrh, and six months with perfumes and preparations for beautifying women. ¹³ Thus *prepared, each* young woman went to the king, and she was given whatever she desired to take with her from the women's quarters to the king's palace. ¹⁴ In the evening she went, and in the morning she returned to the second house of the women, to the custody

of Shaashgaz, the king's eunuch who kept the concubines. She would not go in to the king again unless the king delighted in her and called for her by name.

¹⁵ Now when the turn came for Esther the daughter of Abihail the uncle of Mordecai, who had taken her as his daughter, to go in to the king, she requested nothing but what Hegai the king's eunuch, the custodian of the women, advised. And Esther obtained favor in the sight of all who saw her. ¹⁶ So Esther was taken to King Ahasuerus, into his royal palace, in the tenth month, which *is* the month of Tebeth, in the seventh year of his reign. ¹⁷ The king loved Esther more than all the *other* women, and she obtained grace and favor in his sight more than all the virgins; so he set the royal crown upon her head and made her

queen instead of Vashti. 18 Then the king made a great feast, the Feast of Esther, for all his officials and servants; and he proclaimed a holiday in the provinces and gave gifts according to the generosity of a king.

19 When virgins were gathered together a second time, Mordecai sat within the king's gate. 20 Now Esther had not revealed her family and her people, just as Mordecai had charged her, for Esther obeyed the command of Mordecai as when she was brought up by him.

21 In those days, while Mordecai sat within the king's gate, two of the king's eunuchs, Bigthan and Teresh, doorkeepers, became furious and sought to lay hands on King Ahasuerus. 22 So the matter became known to Mordecai, who told Queen Esther, and Esther informed the king in Mordecai's name. 23 And when an inquiry was made into the matter, it was confirmed, and both were hanged on a gallows; and it was written in the book of the chronicles in the presence of the king.

Tricky Haman plans to destroy the Jews

3 After these things King Ahasuerus promoted Haman, the son of Hammedatha the Agagite, and advanced him and set his seat above all the princes who were with him. 2 And all the king's servants who were within the king's gate bowed and paid homage to Haman, for so the king had commanded concerning him. But Mordecai would not bow or pay homage. 3 Then the king's servants who were within the king's gate said to Mordecai, "Why do you transgress the king's command?" 4 Now it happened, when they spoke to him daily and he would not listen to them, that they told it to Haman, to see whether Mordecai's words would stand; for Mordecai had told them that he was a Jew. 5 When Haman saw that Mordecai did not bow or pay him homage, Haman was filled with wrath. 6 But he disdained to lay hands on Mordecai alone, for they had told him of the people of Mordecai. Instead, Haman sought to destroy all the Jews who were throughout the whole kingdom of Ahasuerus—the people of Mordecai.

7 In the first month, which is the month of Nisan, in the twelfth year of King Ahasuerus, they cast Pur (that is, the lot), before Haman to determine the day and the month, until it fell on the twelfth month, which is the month of Adar.

8 Then Haman said to King Ahasuerus, "There is a certain people scattered and dispersed among the people in all the provinces of your kingdom; their laws are different from all other people's, and they do not keep the king's laws. Therefore it is not fitting for the king to let them remain. 9 If it pleases the king, let a decree be written that they be destroyed, and I will pay ten thousand talents of silver into the hands of those who do the work, to bring it into the king's treasuries."

10 So the king took his signet ring from his hand and gave it to Haman, the son of Hammedatha the Agagite, the enemy of the Jews. 11 And the king said to Haman, "The money and the people are given to you, to do with them as seems good to you."

12 Then the king's scribes were called on the thirteenth day of the first month, and a decree was written according to all that Haman commanded—to the king's satraps, to the governors who were over each province, to the officials of all people, to every province according to its script, and to every people in their language. In the name of King Ahasuerus it was written, and sealed with the king's signet ring. 13 And the letters were sent by couriers into all the king's provinces, to destroy, to kill, and to annihilate all the Jews, both young and old, little children and women, in one day, on the thirteenth day of the twelfth month, which is the month of Adar, and to plunder their possessions. 14 A copy of the document was to be issued as law in every province, being published for all people, that they should be ready

for that day. 15 The couriers went out, hastened by the king's command; and the decree was proclaimed in Shushan the citadel. So the king and Haman sat down to drink, but the city of Shushan was perplexed.

The Jews fast and pray

4 When Mordecai learned all that had happened, he tore his clothes and put on sackcloth and ashes, and went out into the midst of the city. He cried out with a loud and bitter cry. 2 He went as far as the front of the king's gate, for no one *might* enter the king's gate clothed with sackcloth. 3 And in every province where the king's command and decree arrived, *there was* great mourning among the Jews, with fasting, weeping, and wailing; and many lay in sackcloth and ashes.

4 So Esther's maids and eunuchs came and told her, and the queen was deeply distressed. Then she sent garments to clothe Mordecai and take his sackcloth away from him, but he would not accept *them.* 5 Then Esther called Hathach, *one* of the king's eunuchs whom he had appointed to attend her, and she gave him a command concerning Mordecai, to learn what and why this *was.* 6 So Hathach went out to Mordecai in the city square that *was* in front of the king's gate. 7 And Mordecai told him all that had happened to him, and the sum of money that Haman had promised to pay into the king's treasuries to destroy the Jews. 8 He also gave him a copy of the written decree for their destruction, which was given at Shushan, that he might show it to Esther and explain it to her, and that he might command her to go in to the king to make supplication to him and plead before him for her people. 9 So Hathach returned and told Esther the words of Mordecai.

10 Then Esther spoke to Hathach, and gave him a command for Mordecai: 11 "All the king's servants and the people of the king's provinces know that any man or woman who goes into the inner court to the king, who has

not been called, *he has* but one law: put *all* to death, except the one to whom the king holds out the golden scepter, that he may live. Yet I myself have not been called to go in to the king these thirty days." 12 So they told Mordecai Esther's words.

13 And Mordecai told *them* to answer Esther: "Do not think in your heart that you will escape in the king's palace any more than all the other Jews. 14 For if you remain completely silent at this time, relief and deliverance will arise for the Jews from another place, but you and your father's house will perish. Yet who knows whether you have come to the kingdom for *such* a time as this?"

15 Then Esther told *them* to reply to Mordecai: 16 "Go, gather all the Jews who are present in Shushan, and fast for me; neither eat nor drink for three days, night or day. My maids and I will fast likewise. And so I will go to the king, which *is* against the law; and if I perish, I perish!"

17 So Mordecai went his way and did according to all that Esther commanded him.

Queen Esther risks her life

5 Now it happened on the third day that Esther put on *her* royal *robes* and stood in the inner court of the king's palace, across from the king's house, while the king sat on his royal throne in the royal house, facing the entrance of the house. 2 So it was, when the king saw Queen Esther standing in the court, *that* she found favor in his sight, and the king held out to Esther the golden scepter that *was* in his hand. Then Esther went near and touched the top of the scepter.

3 And the king said to her, "What do you wish, Queen Esther? What *is* your request? It shall be given to you—up to half the kingdom!"

4 So Esther answered, "If it pleases the king, let the king and Haman come today to the banquet that I have prepared for him."

5 Then the king said, "Bring Haman

quickly, that he may do as Esther has said." So the king and Haman went to the banquet that Esther had prepared.

6 At the banquet of wine the king said to Esther, "What *is* your petition? It shall be granted you. What *is* your request, up to half the kingdom? It shall be done!"

7 Then Esther answered and said, "My petition and request *is this:* 8 If I have found favor in the sight of the king, and if it pleases the king to grant my petition and fulfill my request, then let the king and Haman come to the banquet which I will prepare for them, and tomorrow I will do as the king has said."

9 So Haman went out that day joyful and with a glad heart; but when Haman saw Mordecai in the king's gate, and that he did not stand or tremble before him, he was filled with indignation against Mordecai. 10 Nevertheless Haman restrained himself and went home, and he sent and called for his friends and his wife Zeresh. 11 Then Haman told them of his great riches, the multitude of his children, everything in which the king had promoted him, and how he had advanced him above the officials and servants of the king.

12 Moreover Haman said, "Besides, Queen Esther invited no one but me to come in with the king to the banquet that she prepared; and tomorrow I am again invited by her, along with the king. 13 Yet all this avails me nothing, so long as I see Mordecai the Jew sitting at the king's gate."

14 Then his wife Zeresh and all his friends said to him, "Let a gallows be made, fifty cubits high, and in the morning suggest to the king that Mordecai be hanged on it; then go merrily with the king to the banquet."

And the thing pleased Haman; so he had the gallows made.

Haman gives Mordecai a royal robe and a horse

6 That night the king could not sleep. So one was commanded to bring the book of the records of the chronicles; and they were read before the king. 2 And it was found written that Mordecai had told of Bigthana and Teresh, two of the king's eunuchs, the doorkeepers who had sought to lay hands on King Ahasuerus. 3 Then the king said, "What honor or dignity has been bestowed on Mordecai for this?"

And the king's servants who attended him said, "Nothing has been done for him."

4 So the king said, "Who *is* in the court?" Now Haman had *just* entered the outer court of the king's palace to suggest that the king hang Mordecai on the gallows that he had prepared for him.

5 The king's servants said to him, "Haman is there, standing in the court."

And the king said, "Let him come in."

6 So Haman came in, and the king asked him, "What shall be done for the man whom the king delights to honor?"

Now Haman thought in his heart, "Whom would the king delight to honor more than me?" 7 And Haman answered the king, "*For* the man whom the king delights to honor, 8 let a royal robe be brought which the king has worn, and a horse on which the king has ridden, which has a royal crest placed on its head. 9 Then let this robe and horse be delivered to the hand of one of the king's most noble princes, that he may array the man whom the king delights to honor. Then parade him on horseback through the city square, and proclaim before him: 'Thus shall it be done to the man whom the king delights to honor!' "

10 Then the king said to Haman, "Hurry, take the robe and the horse, as you have suggested, and do so for Mordecai the Jew who sits within the king's gate! Leave nothing undone of all that you have spoken."

11 So Haman took the robe and the horse, arrayed Mordecai and led him on horseback through the city square, and proclaimed before him, "Thus

Queen Esther Saves Her People, Haman Hanged!

Persian National Press

SHUSHAN—The nation of Persia is in a state of shock today. Queen Esther, the Jewess, has accused Haman, a high state official, of plotting against her people.

Haman's plot to murder all Jews, including the queen's cousin, Mordecai (pronounced *MOR-duh-kigh*), was revealed at a banquet last month. At the banquet, Queen Esther told the king that Haman had sent a letter all over the land, ordering the Jews to be executed. She later asked the king to spare her people.

Not only did the king grant her request, but he had Haman hanged on the same gallows Haman had built for Mordecai! The Jews have been given permission to defend themselves against their enemies whenever necessary.

shall it be done to the man whom the king delights to honor!"

12 Afterward Mordecai went back to the king's gate. But Haman hurried to his house, mourning and with his head covered. 13 When Haman told his wife Zeresh and all his friends everything that had happened to him, his wise men and his wife Zeresh said to him, "If Mordecai, before whom you have begun to fall, is of Jewish descent, you will not prevail against him but will surely fall before him."

14 While they *were* still talking with him, the king's eunuchs came, and hastened to bring Haman to the banquet which Esther had prepared.

Haman goes to the gallows

7 So the king and Haman went to dine with Queen Esther. 2 And on the second day, at the banquet of wine, the king again said to Esther, "What *is* your petition, Queen Esther? It shall be granted you. And what *is* your request, up to half the kingdom? It shall be done!"

3 Then Queen Esther answered and said, "If I have found favor in your sight, O king, and if it pleases the king, let my life be given me at my petition, and my people at my request. 4 For we have been sold, my people and I, to be destroyed, to be killed, and to be annihilated. Had we been sold as male and female slaves, I would have held my tongue, although the enemy could never compensate for the king's loss."

5 So King Ahasuerus answered and said to Queen Esther, "Who is he, and

Wicked Haman was hanged on the very gallows he had built for Mordecai!

where is he, who would dare presume in his heart to do such a thing?"

6 And Esther said, "The adversary and enemy is this wicked Haman!"

So Haman was terrified before the king and queen.

7 Then the king arose in his wrath from the banquet of wine and went into the palace garden; but Haman stood before Queen Esther, pleading for his life, for he saw that evil was determined against him by the king. 8 When the king returned from the palace garden to the place of the banquet of wine, Haman had fallen across the couch where Esther was. Then the king said, "Will he also assault the queen while I am in the house?"

As the word left the king's mouth, they covered Haman's face. 9 Now Harbonah, one of the eunuchs, said to the king, "Look! The gallows, fifty cubits high, which Haman made for Mordecai, who spoke good on the king's behalf, is standing at the house of Haman."

Then the king said, "Hang him on it!"

10 So they hanged Haman on the gallows that he had prepared for Mordecai. Then the king's wrath subsided.

Esther saves her people

8 On that day King Ahasuerus gave Queen Esther the house of Haman, the enemy of the Jews. And Mordecai came before the king, for Esther had told how he was related to her. 2 So the king took off his signet ring, which he had taken from Haman, and gave it to Mordecai; and Esther appointed Mordecai over the house of Haman.

3 Now Esther spoke again to the king, fell down at his feet, and implored him with tears to counteract the evil of Haman the Agagite, and the scheme which he had devised against the Jews. 4 And the king held out the golden scepter toward Esther. So Esther arose and stood before the king, 5 and said, "If it pleases the king, and if I have found favor in his sight and the thing

seems right to the king and I am pleasing in his eyes, let it be written to revoke the letters devised by Haman, the son of Hammedatha the Agagite, which he wrote to annihilate the Jews who are in all the king's provinces. 6 For how can I endure to see the evil that will come to my people? Or how can I endure to see the destruction of my countrymen?"

7 Then King Ahasuerus said to Queen Esther and Mordecai the Jew, "Indeed, I have given Esther the house of Haman, and they have hanged him on the gallows because he tried to lay his hand on the Jews. 8 You yourselves write a decree concerning the Jews, as you please, in the king's name, and seal it with the king's signet ring; for whatever is written in the king's name and sealed with the king's signet ring no one can revoke."

9 So the king's scribes were called at that time, in the third month, which is the month of Sivan, on the twenty-third day; and it was written, according to all that Mordecai commanded, to the Jews, the satraps, the governors, and the princes of the provinces from India to Ethiopia, one hundred and twenty-seven provinces in all, to every province in its own script, to every people in their own language, and to the Jews in their own script and language. 10 And he wrote in the name of King Ahasuerus, sealed it with the king's signet ring, and sent letters by couriers on horseback, riding on royal horses bred from swift steeds.

11 By these letters the king permitted the Jews who were in every city to gather together and protect their lives—to destroy, kill, and annihilate all the forces of any people or province that would assault them, both little children and women, and to plunder their possessions, 12 on one day in all the provinces of King Ahasuerus, on the thirteenth day of the twelfth month, which is the month of Adar. 13 A copy of the document was to be issued as a decree in every province and published for all people, so that the Jews would be ready on that day to avenge

themselves on their enemies. ¹⁴ The couriers who rode on royal horses went out, hastened and pressed on by the king's command. And the decree was issued in Shushan the citadel.

¹⁵ So Mordecai went out from the presence of the king in royal apparel of blue and white, with a great crown of gold and a garment of fine linen and purple; and the city of Shushan rejoiced and was glad. ¹⁶ The Jews had light and gladness, joy and honor. ¹⁷ And in every province and city, wherever the king's command and decree came, the Jews had joy and gladness, a feast and a holiday. Then many of the people of the land became Jews, because fear of the Jews fell upon them.

The Jews are victorious

9 Now in the twelfth month, that is, the month of Adar, on the thirteenth day, the time came for the king's command and his decree to be executed. On the day that the enemies of the Jews had hoped to overpower them, the opposite occurred, in that the Jews themselves overpowered those who hated them. ² The Jews gathered together in their cities throughout all the provinces of King Ahasuerus to lay hands on those who sought their harm. And no one could withstand them, because fear of them fell upon all people. ³ And all the officials of the provinces, the satraps, the governors, and all those doing the king's work, helped the Jews, because the fear of Mordecai fell upon them. ⁴ For Mordecai was great in the king's palace, and his fame spread throughout all the provinces; for this man Mordecai became increasingly prominent. ⁵ Thus the Jews defeated all their enemies with the stroke of the sword, with slaughter and destruction, and did what they pleased with those who hated them.

⁶ And in Shushan the citadel the Jews killed and destroyed five hundred men. ⁷ Also Parshandatha, Dalphon, Aspatha, ⁸ Poratha, Adalia, Aridatha, ⁹ Parmashta, Arisai, Aridai, and Vajeza-tha— ¹⁰ the ten sons of Haman the son of Hammedatha, the enemy of the Jews—they killed; but they did not lay a hand on the plunder.

¹¹ On that day the number of those who were killed in Shushan the citadel was brought to the king. ¹² And the king said to Queen Esther, "The Jews have killed and destroyed five hundred men in Shushan the citadel, and the ten sons of Haman. What have they done in the rest of the king's provinces? Now what is your petition? It shall be granted to you. Or what is your further request? It shall be done."

¹³ Then Esther said, "If it pleases the king, let it be granted to the Jews who are in Shushan to do again tomorrow according to today's decree, and let Haman's ten sons be hanged on the gallows."

¹⁴ So the king commanded this to be done; the decree was issued in Shushan, and they hanged Haman's ten sons.

¹⁵ And the Jews who were in Shushan gathered together again on the fourteenth day of the month of Adar and killed three hundred men at Shushan; but they did not lay a hand on the plunder.

¹⁶ The remainder of the Jews in the king's provinces gathered together and protected their lives, had rest from their enemies, and killed seventy-five thousand of their enemies; but they did not lay a hand on the plunder. ¹⁷ This was on the thirteenth day of the month of Adar. And on the fourteenth of the month they rested and made it a day of feasting and gladness.

¹⁸ But the Jews who were at Shushan assembled together on the thirteenth day, as well as on the fourteenth; and on the fifteenth of the month they rested, and made it a day of feasting and gladness. ¹⁹ Therefore the Jews of the villages who dwelt in the unwalled towns celebrated the fourteenth day of the month of Adar with gladness and feasting, as a holiday, and for sending presents to one another.

²⁰ And Mordecai wrote these things

What Was the Feast of Purim?

The Hebrew word *purim* (pronounced *PEW-reem*) comes from the word *pur*, meaning "lot." To "cast lots" in helping to make a decision was like throwing dice nowadays. Haman had cast lots to decide the day when all Jews would be murdered (see Esther 3:7). The Feast of Purim celebrates Esther's work of saving the Jews.

and sent letters to all the Jews, near and far, who *were* in all the provinces of King Ahasuerus, 21 to establish among them that they should celebrate yearly the fourteenth and fifteenth days of the month of Adar, 22 as the days on which the Jews had rest from their enemies, as the month which was turned from sorrow to joy for them, and from mourning to a holiday; that they should make them days of feasting and joy, of sending presents to one another and gifts to the poor. 23 So the Jews accepted the custom which they had begun, as Mordecai had written to them, 24 because Haman, the son of Hammedatha the Agagite, the enemy of all the Jews, had plotted against the Jews to annihilate them, and had cast Pur (that *is*, the lot), to consume them and destroy them; 25 but when *Esther* came before the king, he commanded by letter that this

wicked plot which *Haman* had devised against the Jews should return on his own head, and that he and his sons should be hanged on the gallows.

26 So they called these days Purim, after the name Pur. Therefore, because of all the words of this letter, what they had seen concerning this matter, and what had happened to them, 27 the Jews established and imposed it upon themselves and their descendants and all who would join them, that without fail they should celebrate these two days every year, according to the written *instructions* and according to the prescribed time, 28 *that* these days *should be* remembered and kept throughout every generation, every family, every province, and every city, that these days of Purim should not fail *to be observed* among the Jews, and *that* the memory of them should not perish among their descendants.

29 Then Queen Esther, the daughter

Why Do We Have the Book of Esther?

Some people wonder why we have the Book of Esther because God is not even mentioned in the book. But the story is an important link in showing how the Lord preserved His people. The Jewish nation had to continue so the Messiah could come, just as God promised them.

What the Kings of Media and Persia Learned

We, the kings of Media and Persia came after King Ahasuerus (pronounced *ah-haz-you-EAR-us*). This was the king who married Esther, the relative of Mordecai.

God had marvelously arranged Esther's marriage to the king so that she would be able to save Israel, her people, from being murdered. Mordecai was also saved from death and was promoted to be next in rank to the king.

We no longer have the books of Media and Persia in which these happenings were written. But we kings of Media and Persia learned that the God of Esther and Mordecai is in charge of everything that happens.

of Abihail, with Mordecai the Jew, wrote with full authority to confirm this second letter about Purim. 30 And *Mordecai* sent letters to all the Jews, to the one hundred and twenty-seven provinces of the kingdom of Ahasuerus, *with* words of peace and truth, 31 to confirm these days of Purim at their *appointed* time, as Mordecai the Jew and Queen Esther had prescribed for them, and as they had decreed for themselves and their descendants concerning matters of their fasting and lamenting. 32 So the decree of Esther confirmed these matters of Purim, and it was written in the book.

Mordecai is promoted

10 And King Ahasuerus imposed tribute on the land and *on* the islands of the sea. 2 Now all the acts of his power and his might, and the account of the greatness of Mordecai, to which the king advanced him, *are* they not written in the book of the chronicles of the kings of Media and Persia? 3 For Mordecai the Jew *was* second to King Ahasuerus, and was great among the Jews and well received by the multitude of his brethren, seeking the good of his people and speaking peace to all his countrymen.

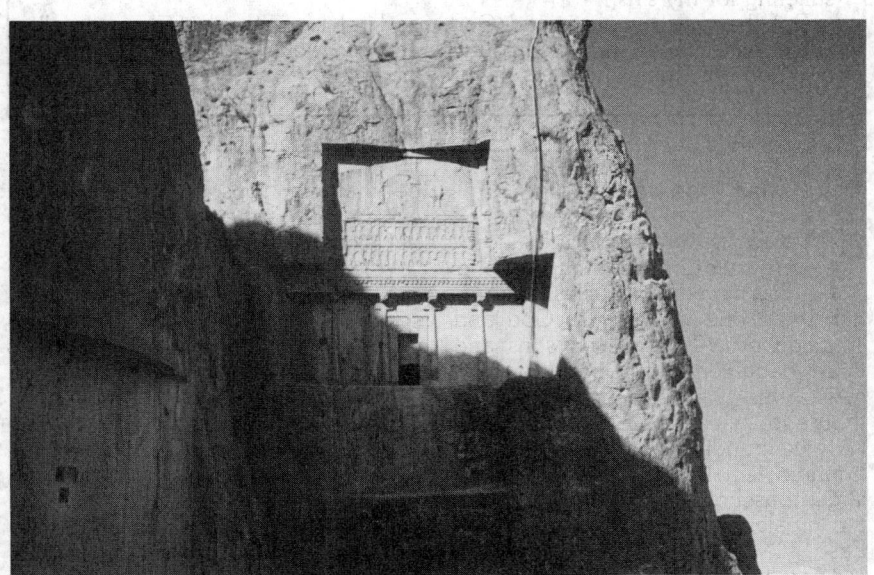

King Ahasuerus of Persia, who married Esther, was buried here.

The Book of
JOB

My name is pronounced *JOBE* and means "Enemy." The enemy in my book is Satan. I wasn't a Hebrew, but I worshiped the true God with my family in the land of Uz. I was very wealthy, and everybody in my country honored me.

I didn't understand why for a long time, but one day I lost everything I owned, including my children. Not long after that, I became very sick, and I was covered with boils.

As though that wasn't enough, three of my best friends visited me, but for seven days they didn't even speak to me. Then they said I must be suffering for my sins!

But that was not true, and God was kind to me and made me well again. As you read my story, you will realize that even good people suffer, but God only means to bless them in the end.

A rich man loses everything

THERE was a man in the land of Uz, whose name *was* Job; and that man was blameless and upright, and one who feared God and shunned evil. ² And seven sons and three daughters were born to him. ³ Also, his possessions were seven thousand sheep, three thousand camels, five hundred yoke of oxen, five hundred female donkeys, and a very large household, so that this man was the greatest of all the people of the East.

⁴ And his sons would go and feast *in their* houses, each on his *appointed* day, and would send and invite their three sisters to eat and drink with them. ⁵ So it was, when the days of feasting had run their course, that Job would send and sanctify them, and he would rise early in the morning and offer burnt offerings *according to* the number of them all. For Job said, "It may

be that my sons have sinned and cursed God in their hearts." Thus Job did regularly.

⁶ Now there was a day when the sons of God came to present themselves before the Lord, and **Satan** also came among them. ⁷ And the Lord said to Satan, "From where do you come?"

So Satan answered the Lord and said, "From going to and fro on the earth, and from walking back and forth on it."

⁸ Then the Lord said to Satan, "Have you considered My servant Job, that *there is* none like him on the earth, a blameless and upright man, one who fears God and shuns evil?"

⁹ So Satan answered the Lord and said, "Does Job fear God for nothing? ¹⁰ Have You not made a hedge around him, around his household, and around all that he has on every side? You have blessed the work of his hands, and his possessions have in-

Local Business Leader Is Bankrupt

The Arabian Times

UZ—A highly respected citizen of Uz, Job, has been reported bankrupt. Not only has Job lost his wealth and property, but his health has failed also.

In addition, Job's sons and daughters were killed last week when a house where they were eating dinner was blown down in a freak windstorm.

Job has always been honest in business, kind to the poor and afflicted, and has enjoyed a leading place in the community. No one has been able to explain why he has had so much suffering.

This newspaper joins the citizens of Uz in offering our brother Job our heartfelt sympathy, especially in the loss of his children. We trust that all our people will be as kind to Job as that godly man has been to all of us.

creased in the land. 11 But now, stretch out Your hand and touch all that he has, and he will surely curse You to Your face!"

12 And the LORD said to Satan, "Behold, all that he has *is* in your power; only do not lay a hand on his *person.*"

So Satan went out from the presence of the LORD.

13 Now there was a day when his sons and daughters *were* eating and drinking wine in their oldest brother's house; 14 and a messenger came to Job and said, "The oxen were plowing and the donkeys feeding beside them, 15 when the Sabeans raided *them* and took them away—indeed they have killed the servants with the edge of the sword; and I alone have escaped to tell you!"

16 While he *was* still speaking, another also came and said, "The fire of God fell from heaven and burned up the sheep and the servants, and consumed them; and I alone have escaped to tell you!"

17 While he *was* still speaking, another also came and said, "The Chaldeans formed three bands, raided the camels and took them away, yes, and killed the servants with the edge of the sword; and I alone have escaped to tell you!"

18 While he *was* still speaking, another also came and said, "Your sons and daughters *were* eating and drinking wine in their oldest brother's house,

19 and suddenly a great wind came from across the wilderness and struck the four corners of the house, and it fell on the young people, and they are dead; and I alone have escaped to tell you!"

20 Then Job arose, tore his robe, and shaved his head; and he fell to the ground and worshiped. 21 And he said:

"Naked I came from my mother's womb,
And naked shall I return there.
The LORD gave, and the LORD has taken away;
Blessed be the name of the LORD."

22 In all this Job did not sin nor charge God with wrong.

Satan gives Job a case of boils

2 Again there was a day when the sons of God came to present themselves before the LORD, and Satan came also among them to present himself before the LORD. 2 And the LORD said to Satan, "From where do you come?"

Satan answered the LORD and said, "From going to and fro on the earth, and from walking back and forth on it."

3 Then the LORD said to Satan, "Have you considered My servant Job, that *there is* none like him on the earth,

a blameless and upright man, one who fears God and shuns evil? And still he holds fast to his integrity, although you incited Me against him, to destroy him without cause.''

⁴ So Satan answered the LORD and said, ''Skin for skin! Yes, all that a man has he will give for his life. ⁵ But stretch out Your hand now, and touch his bone and his flesh, and he will surely curse You to Your face!''

⁶ And the LORD said to Satan, ''Behold, he *is* in your hand, but spare his life.''

⁷ So Satan went out from the presence of the LORD, and struck Job with painful boils from the sole of his foot to the crown of his head. ⁸ And he took for himself a potsherd with which to scrape himself while he sat in the midst of the ashes.

⁹ Then his wife said to him, ''Do you still hold fast to your integrity? Curse God and die!''

¹⁰ But he said to her, ''You speak as one of the foolish women speaks. Shall we indeed accept good from God, and shall we not accept adversity?'' In all this Job did not sin with his lips.

¹¹ Now when Job's three friends heard of all this adversity that had come upon him, each one came from his own place—Eliphaz the Temanite, Bildad the Shuhite, and Zophar the Naamathite. For they had made an appointment together to come and mourn with him, and to comfort him. ¹² And when they raised their eyes from afar, and did not recognize him, they lifted their voices and wept; and

each one tore his robe and sprinkled dust on his head toward heaven. ¹³ So they sat down with him on the ground seven days and seven nights, and no one spoke a word to him, for they saw that *his* grief was very great.

Job is sorry he was born!

3 After this Job opened his mouth and cursed the day of his *birth.* ² And Job spoke, and said:

3   ''May the day perish on which I
         was born,
      And the night *in which* it was
         said,
      'A male child is conceived.'
4   May that day be darkness;
      May God above not seek it,
      Nor the light shine upon it.
5   May darkness and the shadow
         of death claim it;
      May a cloud settle on it;
      May the blackness of the day
         terrify it.
6   *As for* that night, may darkness
         seize it;
      May it not rejoice among the
         days of the year,
      May it not come into the number
         of the months.
7   Oh, may that night be barren!
      May no joyful shout come into
         it!
8   May those curse it who curse the
         day,
      Those who are ready to arouse
         Leviathan.
9   May the stars of its morning be
         dark;

⚒ DIGGING IN

2:5 Satan the Enemy We first met Satan in Genesis 3. There we saw that he deceived Adam and Eve by making them think they could be gods. In Ezekiel 28:11–19, the Lord describes Satan as the great Enemy of God.

At first Satan was a chief angel, but he wanted to be equal with God, so he was thrown out of heaven. Satan is still trying to destroy God's work and God's

people, but the Bible says he will fail.

Some people worry about Satan's power. But Satan's power is never as great as God's. God is always in control, even though Satan deceives people who serve him.

Satan was defeated when Jesus died for His people on Calvary's cross. Now Satan cannot harm you if you trust in Jesus.

May it look for light, but *have* none,
And not see the dawning of the day;
10 Because it did not shut up the doors of my *mother's* womb,
Nor hide sorrow from my eyes.

11 "Why did I not die at birth?
Why did I *not* perish when I came from the womb?
12 Why did the knees receive me?
Or why the breasts, that I should nurse?
13 For now I would have lain still and been quiet,
I would have been asleep;
Then I would have been at rest
14 With kings and counselors of the earth,
Who built ruins for themselves,
15 Or with princes who had gold,
Who filled their houses *with* silver;
16 Or *why* was I not hidden like a stillborn child,
Like infants who never saw light?
17 There the wicked cease *from* troubling,
And there the weary are at rest.
18 *There* the prisoners rest together;
They do not hear the voice of the oppressor.
19 The small and great are there,
And the servant *is* free from his master.

20 "Why is light given to him who is in misery,
And life to the bitter of soul,
21 Who long for death, but it does not *come,*
And search for it more than hidden treasures;
22 Who rejoice exceedingly,
And are glad when they can find the grave?
23 *Why is light given* to a man whose way is hidden,
And whom God has hedged in?
24 For my sighing comes before I eat,

And my groanings pour out like water.
25 For the thing I greatly feared has come upon me,
And what I dreaded has happened to me.
26 I am not at ease, nor am I quiet;
I have no rest, for trouble comes."

Eliphaz scolds Job

4 Then Eliphaz the Temanite answered and said:

2 *"If* one attempts a word with you, will you become weary?
But who can withhold himself from speaking?
3 Surely you have instructed many,
And you have strengthened weak hands.
4 Your words have upheld him who was stumbling,
And you have strengthened the feeble knees;
5 But now it comes upon you, and you are weary;
It touches you, and you are troubled.
6 *Is* not your reverence your confidence?
And the integrity of your ways your hope?

7 "Remember now, who *ever* perished being innocent?
Or where were the upright *ever* cut off?
8 Even as I have seen,
Those who plow iniquity
And sow trouble reap the same.
9 By the blast of God they perish,
And by the breath of His anger they are consumed.
10 The roaring of the lion,
The voice of the fierce lion,
And the teeth of the young lions are broken.
11 The old lion perishes for lack of prey,
And the cubs of the lioness are scattered.

12 "Now a word was secretly
    brought to me,
And my ear received a whisper
    of it.
13 In disquieting thoughts from the
    visions of the night,
When deep sleep falls on men,
14 Fear came upon me, and
    trembling,
Which made all my bones
    shake.
15 Then a spirit passed before my
    face;
The hair on my body stood up.
16 It stood still,
But I could not discern its
    appearance.
A form *was* before my *eyes*;
There was silence;
Then I heard a voice *saying*:
17 'Can a **mortal** be more righteous
    than God?
Can a man be more pure than
    his Maker?
18 If He puts no trust in His
    servants,
If He charges His angels with
    error,
19 How much more those who
    dwell in houses of clay,
Whose foundation is in the dust,
Who are crushed before a
    moth?
20 They are broken in pieces from
    morning till evening;

They perish forever, with no one
    regarding.
21 Does not their own excellence
    go away?
They die, even without wisdom.'

Eliphaz continues his scolding

5   "Call out now;
Is there anyone who will answer
    you?
And to which of the holy ones
    will you turn?
2 For wrath kills a foolish man,
And envy slays a simple one.
3 I have seen the foolish taking
    root,
But suddenly I cursed his
    dwelling place.
4 His sons are far from safety,
They are crushed in the gate,
And *there is* no deliverer.
5 Because the hungry eat up his
    harvest,
Taking it even from the thorns,
And a snare snatches their
    substance.
6 For affliction does not come
    from the dust,
Nor does trouble spring from the
    ground;
7 Yet man is born to trouble,
As the sparks fly upward.
8 "But as for me, I would seek
    God,

⚙ WORDFINDER

4:17 Mortal   The opposite of immortal (see definition at Romans 2:7). Your present body will die, but your soul is *immortal* (cannot die). Someday believers will receive immortal bodies like Christ's body.

⛏ DIGGING IN

5:8 Boasting Is Dangerous Eliphaz (pronounced *EL-ih-faz*) was supposed to be a friend of Job when Job was suffering, but Eliphaz said Job was having trouble because he had sinned. That was not true.

Eliphaz also bragged about what he would do in Job's place: "I would seek God." Of course, this is exactly what Job was doing. So Eliphaz was not a very

good friend. All he did was say to Job, in other words, "I'm a better man than you, and I would ask God to forgive my sins."

Job didn't need to be told how wrong he was. Job was a far greater man than Eliphaz. What Job really needed was a friend who would comfort him in his trouble.

And to God I would commit my cause—

9 Who does great things, and unsearchable,
Marvelous things without number.

10 He gives rain on the earth,
And sends waters on the fields.

11 He sets on high those who are lowly,
And those who mourn are lifted to safety.

12 He frustrates the devices of the crafty,
So that their hands cannot carry out their plans.

13 He catches the wise in their own craftiness,
And the counsel of the cunning comes quickly upon them.

14 They meet with darkness in the daytime,
And grope at noontime as in the night.

15 But He saves the needy from the sword,
From the mouth of the mighty,
And from their hand.

16 So the poor have hope,
And injustice shuts her mouth.

17 "Behold, happy is the man whom God corrects;
Therefore do not despise the chastening of the Almighty.

18 For He bruises, but He binds up;
He wounds, but His hands make whole.

19 He shall deliver you in six troubles,
Yes, in seven no evil shall touch you.

20 In famine He shall redeem you from death,
And in war from the power of the sword.

21 You shall be hidden from the scourge of the tongue,
And you shall not be afraid of destruction when it comes.

22 You shall laugh at destruction and famine,
And you shall not be afraid of the beasts of the earth.

23 For you shall have a covenant with the stones of the field,
And the beasts of the field shall be at peace with you.

24 You shall know that your tent is in peace;
You shall visit your dwelling and find nothing amiss.

25 You shall also know that your descendants shall be many,
And your offspring like the grass of the earth.

26 You shall come to the grave at a full age,
As a sheaf of grain ripens in its season.

27 Behold, this we have searched out;
It is true.
Hear it, and know for yourself."

Job wonders why everything is going wrong

6 Then Job answered and said:

2 "Oh, that my grief were fully weighed,
And my calamity laid with it on the scales!

3 For then it would be heavier than the sand of the sea—
Therefore my words have been rash.

4 For the arrows of the Almighty are within me;
My spirit drinks in their poison;
The terrors of God are arrayed against me.

5 Does the wild donkey bray when it has grass,
Or does the ox low over its fodder?

6 Can flavorless food be eaten without salt?
Or is there any taste in the white of an egg?

7 My soul refuses to touch them;
They are as loathsome food to me.

8 "Oh, that I might have my request,

That God would grant *me* the thing that I long for!

9 That it would please God to crush me,
That He would loose His hand and cut me off!

10 Then I would still have comfort;
Though in anguish I would exult,
He will not spare;
For I have not concealed the words of the Holy One.

11 "What strength do I have, that I should hope?
And what *is* my end, that I should prolong my life?

12 *Is* my strength the strength of stones?
Or is my flesh bronze?

13 *Is* my help not within me?
And is success driven from me?

14 "To him who is afflicted, kindness *should be shown* by his friend,
Even though he forsakes the fear of the Almighty.

15 My brothers have dealt deceitfully like a brook,
Like the streams of the brooks that pass away,

16 Which are dark because of the ice,
And into which the snow vanishes.

17 When it is warm, they cease to flow;
When it is hot, they vanish from their place.

18 The paths of their way turn aside,
They go nowhere and perish.

19 The caravans of Tema look,
The travelers of Sheba hope for them.

20 They are disappointed because they were confident;
They come there and are confused.

21 For now you are nothing,
You see terror and are afraid.

22 Did I ever say, 'Bring *something* to me'?
Or, 'Offer a bribe for me from your wealth'?

23 Or, 'Deliver me from the enemy's hand'?
Or, 'Redeem me from the hand of oppressors'?

24 "Teach me, and I will hold my tongue;
Cause me to understand wherein I have erred.

25 How forceful are right words!
But what does your arguing prove?

26 Do you intend to rebuke *my* words,
And the speeches of a desperate one, *which are* as wind?

27 Yes, you overwhelm the fatherless,
And you undermine your friend.

28 Now therefore, be pleased to look at me;
For I would never lie to your face.

29 Yield now, let there be no injustice!
Yes, concede, my righteousness still stands!

30 Is there injustice on my tongue?

⛏ DIGGING IN

6:29, 30 A Self-satisfied Man Job was a good man. The Lord said so (see Job 1:8). Then Job made a mistake we all make too often. Job thought he had nothing more to learn: "My righteousness still stands," he said. Job's friends were wrong about Job, but Job still needed to learn that he was *nothing without God.* Can you learn that lesson?

Some of us are like Job. We do very well at everything we try. So we become self-satisfied. That's when God may have to remind us that we need Him. Perhaps you've been gifted with a sharp mind, or you're good at sports, or you can think or move faster than most of your friends. Does that make you feel smug? Look out! God may have to show you how weak you really are! But sometimes that's best. You can only be the kind of person God can use if you aren't self-satisfied.

Cannot my taste discern the
    unsavory?

Job asks for God's help

7 "Is there not a time of hard
    service for man on earth?
    Are not his days also like the
      days of a hired man?
2 Like a servant who earnestly
    desires the shade,
    And like a hired man who
      eagerly looks for his wages,
3 So I have been allotted months
    of futility,
    And wearisome nights have
      been appointed to me.
4 When I lie down, I say, 'When
    shall I arise,
    And the night be ended?'
    For I have had my fill of tossing
      till dawn.
5 My flesh is caked with worms
    and dust,
    My skin is cracked and breaks
      out afresh.

6 "My days are swifter than a
    weaver's shuttle,
    And are spent without hope.
7 Oh, remember that my life is a
    breath!
    My eye will never again see
      good.
8 The eye of him who sees me will
    see me no more;
    While your eyes are upon me, I
      shall no longer be.
9 As the cloud disappears and
    vanishes away,
    So he who goes down to the
      grave does not come up.
10 He shall never return to his
    house,
    Nor shall his place know him
      anymore.

11 "Therefore I will not restrain my
    mouth;
    I will speak in the anguish of my
      spirit;
    I will complain in the bitterness
      of my soul.

12 Am I a sea, or a sea serpent,
    That You set a guard over me?
13 When I say, 'My bed will comfort
    me,
    My couch will ease my
      complaint,'
14 Then You scare me with dreams
    And terrify me with visions,
15 So that my soul chooses
    strangling
    And death rather than my body.
16 I loathe my life;
    I would not live forever.
    Let me alone,
    For my days are but a breath.

17 "What is man, that You should
    exalt him,
    That You should set Your heart
      on him,
18 That You should visit him every
    morning,
    And test him every moment?
19 How long?
    Will You not look away from
    me,
    And let me alone till I swallow
      my saliva?
20 Have I sinned?
    What have I done to You, O
      watcher of men?
    Why have You set me as Your
      target,
    So that I am a burden to myself?
21 Why then do You not pardon
    my transgression,
    And take away my iniquity?
    For now I will lie down in the
      dust,
    And You will seek me diligently,
    But I will no longer be."

Bildad tells Job to repent

8 Then Bildad the Shuhite answered
and said:

2 "How long will you speak these
    things,
    And the words of your mouth
      be like a strong wind?
3 Does God subvert judgment?
    Or does the Almighty pervert
      justice?

4 If your sons have sinned against
   Him,
   He has cast them away for their
   transgression.
5 If you would earnestly seek
   God
   And make your supplication to
   the Almighty,
6 If you *were* pure and upright,
   Surely now He would awake for
   you,
   And prosper your rightful
   dwelling place.
7 Though your beginning was
   small,
   Yet your latter end would
   increase abundantly.

8 "For inquire, please, of the former
   age,
   And consider the things
   discovered by their fathers;
9 For we *were* born yesterday,
   and know nothing,
   Because our days on earth *are*
   a shadow.
10 Will they not teach you and tell
   you,
   And utter words from their
   heart?

11 "Can the **papyrus** grow up
   without a marsh?
   Can the reeds flourish without
   water?
12 While it *is* yet green *and* not cut
   down,
   It withers before any *other* plant.
13 So *are* the paths of all who forget
   God;
   And the hope of the hypocrite
   shall perish,
14 Whose confidence shall be cut
   off,
   And whose trust *is* a spider's
   web.
15 He leans on his house, but it
   does not stand.

   He holds it fast, but it does not
   endure.
16 He grows green in the sun,
   And his branches spread out in
   his garden.
17 His roots wrap around the rock
   heap,
   And look for a place in the
   stones.
18 If he is destroyed from his place,
   Then *it* will deny him, *saying,* 'I
   have not seen you.'

19 "Behold, this is the joy of His
   way,
   And out of the earth others will
   grow.
20 Behold, God will not cast away
   the blameless,
   Nor will He uphold the
   evildoers.
21 He will yet fill your mouth with
   laughing,
   And your lips with rejoicing.
22 Those who hate you will be
   clothed with shame,
   And the dwelling place of the
   wicked will come to nothing."

Job is not comforted

9 Then Job answered and said:

2 "Truly I know *it is* so,
   But how can a man be righteous
   before God?
3 If one wished to contend with
   Him,
   He could not answer Him one
   time out of a thousand.
4 *God is* wise in heart and mighty
   in strength.
   Who has hardened *himself*
   against Him and prospered?
5 He removes the mountains, and
   they do not know
   When He overturns them in His
   anger;

🦉 WORDFINDER ━━━━━━━━━━━━━━━━━━━━━

8:11 Papyrus Pronounced *puh-PIE-rus.* A reed that grows in northern Africa and southern Europe. In ancient times, these reeds were cut and pressed chiefly to make a kind of writing paper.

6 He shakes the earth out of its
   place,
   And its pillars tremble;
7 He commands the sun, and it
   does not rise;
   He seals off the stars;
8 He alone spreads out the
   heavens,
   And treads on the waves of the
   sea;
9 He made the Bear, Orion, and
   the Pleiades,
   And the chambers of the south;
10 He does great things past finding
   out,
   Yes, wonders without number.
11 If He goes by me, I do not see
   Him;
   If He moves past, I do not
   perceive Him;
12 If He takes away, who can
   hinder Him?
   Who can say to Him, 'What are
   You doing?'
13 God will not withdraw His anger,
   The allies of the proud lie
   prostrate beneath Him.

14 "How then can I answer Him,
   And choose my words *to reason*
   with Him?
15 For though I were righteous, I
   could not answer Him;
   I would beg mercy of my Judge.
16 If I called and He answered
   me,
   I would not believe that He was
   listening to my voice.
17 For He crushes me with a
   tempest,
   And multiplies my wounds
   without cause.
18 He will not allow me to catch
   my breath,
   But fills me with bitterness.
19 If *it is a matter* of strength,
   indeed *He is* strong;
   And if of justice, who will
   appoint my day *in court?*
20 Though I were righteous, my
   own mouth would condemn
   me;
   Though I *were* blameless, it
   would prove me perverse.

21 "I am blameless, yet I do not
   know myself;
   I despise my life.
22 It *is* all one *thing;*
   Therefore I say, 'He destroys the
   blameless and the wicked.'
23 If the scourge slays suddenly,
   He laughs at the plight of the
   innocent.
24 The earth is given into the hand
   of the wicked.
   He covers the faces of its judges.
   If it is not *He,* who else could it
   be?

25 "Now my days are swifter than a
   runner;
   They flee away, they see no
   good.
26 They pass by like swift ships,
   Like an eagle swooping on its
   prey.
27 If I say, 'I will forget my
   complaint,
   I will put off my sad face and
   wear a smile,'
28 I am afraid of all my sufferings;
   I know that You will not hold
   me innocent.
29 *If* I am condemned,
   Why then do I labor in vain?
30 If I wash myself with snow water,
   And cleanse my hands with
   soap,
31 Yet You will plunge me into the
   pit,
   And my own clothes will abhor
   me.

32 "For *He is* not a man, as I *am,*
   That I may answer Him,
   And that we should go to court
   together.
33 Nor is there any mediator
   between us,
   Who may lay his hand on us
   both.
34 Let Him take His rod away from
   me,
   And do not let dread of Him
   terrify me.
35 *Then* I would speak and not fear
   Him,
   But it is not so with me.

Job pleads with God

10 "My soul loathes my life;
I will give free course to my
complaint,
I will speak in the bitterness of
my soul.
2 I will say to God, 'Do not
condemn me;
Show me why You contend with
me.
3 *Does it* seem good to You that
You should oppress,
That You should despise the
work of Your hands,
And smile on the counsel of the
wicked?
4 Do You have *eyes* of flesh?
Or do You *see* as man *sees?*
5 *Are* Your days like the days of
a mortal man?
Are Your years like the days of
a mighty man,
6 That You should *seek* for my
iniquity
And search out my sin,
7 Although You know that I am
not wicked,
And *there is* no one who can
deliver from Your hand?

8 'Your hands have made me and
fashioned me,
An intricate unity;
Yet You would destroy me.
9 Remember, I pray, that You
have made me like clay.
And will You turn me into dust
again?
10 Did You not pour me out like
milk,
And curdle me like cheese,
11 Clothe me with skin and flesh,
And knit me together with bones
and sinews?
12 You have granted me life and
favor,
And Your care has preserved my
spirit.

13 'And these *things* You have
hidden in Your heart;
I know that this *was* with You:
14 If I sin, then You mark me,

And will not acquit me of my
iniquity.
15 If I am wicked, woe to me;
Even *if* I am righteous, I cannot
lift up my head.
I am full of disgrace;
See my misery!
16 If *my head* is exalted,
You hunt me like a fierce lion,
And again You show Yourself
awesome against me.
17 You renew Your witnesses
against me,
And increase Your indignation
toward me;
Changes and war are *ever* with
me.

18 'Why then have You brought me
out of the womb?
Oh, that I had perished and no
eye had seen me!
19 I would have been as though I
had not been.
I would have been carried from
the womb to the grave.
20 Are not my days few?
Cease! Leave me alone, that I
may take a little comfort,
21 Before I go *to the place from
which* I shall not return,
To the land of darkness and the
shadow of death,
22 A land as dark as darkness *itself,*
As the shadow of death, without
any order,
Where even the light *is* like
darkness.' "

Zophar also urges Job to repent

11 Then Zophar the Naamathite answered and said:

2 "Should not the multitude of
words be answered?
And should a man full of talk
be vindicated?
3 Should your empty talk make
men hold their peace?
And when you mock, should no
one rebuke you?
4 For you have said,

'My **doctrine** is pure,
And I am clean in your eyes.'
5 But oh, that God would speak,
And open His lips against you,
6 That He would show you the
secrets of wisdom!
For *they would* double *your*
prudence.
Know therefore that God exacts
from you
Less than your iniquity *deserves*.

7 "Can you search out the deep
things of God?
Can you find out the limits of
the Almighty?
8 *They are* higher than heaven—
what can you do?
Deeper than Sheol— what can
you know?
9 Their measure is longer than the
earth
And broader than the sea.

10 "If He passes by, imprisons, and
gathers *to judgment,*
Then who can hinder Him?
11 For He knows deceitful men;
He sees wickedness also.
Will He not then consider *it?*
12 For an empty-headed man will
be wise,
When a wild donkey's colt is
born a man.

13 "If you would prepare your
heart,
And stretch out your hands
toward Him;
14 If iniquity *were* in your hand,
and you put it far away,
And would not let wickedness
dwell in your tents;
15 Then surely you could lift up
your face without spot;
Yes, you could be steadfast, and
not fear;
16 Because you would forget *your*
misery,
And remember *it* as waters *that
have* passed away,
17 And *your* life would be brighter
than noonday.
Though you were dark, you
would be like the morning.
18 And you would be secure,
because there is hope;
Yes, you would dig *around
you, and* take your rest in
safety.
19 You would also lie down, and
no one would make *you*
afraid;
Yes, many would court your
favor.
20 But the eyes of the wicked will
fail,
And they shall not escape,
And their hope—loss of life!"

WORDFINDER

11:4 Doctrine Pronounced *DOK-trin.* The truth taught in the Bible. Christians believe all of God's doctrine or teaching as their foundation for salvation and living in the world.

DIGGING IN

11:1–6 A Man Without Mercy Zophar (pronounced *ZO-far*) was supposed to be a friend to Job. But he was no true friend! Listen to his hard words to Job: "Know therefore that God exacts from you less than your iniquity deserves" (verse 6). What Zophar didn't know was that God wasn't really punishing Job at all! God was only making Job a *better* man than he was. When good people suffer, they become better people.

Poor Zophar is the one to be pitied. He doesn't even know how to say a kind word to his suffering friend. What a small soul Zophar must have had!

Jesus once said, "Blessed are the merciful, for they shall obtain mercy" (Matthew 5:7). You may not believe it, but some people really don't know how to show mercy. So it is important for you to be a merciful person. Then people will see Jesus in you.

It is Job's turn to speak

12 Then Job answered and said:

2 "No doubt you *are* the people,
  And wisdom will die with you!
3 But I have understanding as well
    as you;
  I *am* not inferior to you.
  Indeed, who does not *know*
    such things as these?

4 "I am one mocked by his friends,
  Who called on God, and He
    answered him,
  The just and blameless *who is*
    ridiculed.
5 A lamp is despised in the
    thought of one who is at ease;
  It is made ready for those whose
    feet slip.
6 The tents of robbers prosper,
  And those who provoke God are
    secure—
  In what God provides by His
    hand.

7 "But now ask the beasts, and they
    will teach you;
  And the birds of the air, and they
    will tell you;
8 Or speak to the earth, and it will
    teach you;
  And the fish of the sea will
    explain to you.
9 Who among all these does not
    know
  That the hand of the Lord has
    done this,
10 In whose hand *is* the life of every
    living thing,
  And the breath of all mankind?
11 Does not the *ear* test words
  And the mouth taste its food?
12 Wisdom *is* with aged men,
  And with length of days,
    understanding.

13 "With Him *are* wisdom and
    strength,
  He has counsel and
    understanding.
14 If He breaks *a thing* down, it
    cannot be rebuilt;

If He imprisons a man, there can
    be no release.
15 If He withholds the waters, they
    dry up;
  If He sends them out, they
    overwhelm the earth.
16 With Him *are* strength and
    prudence.
  The deceived and the deceiver
    are His.
17 He leads counselors away
    plundered,
  And makes fools of the judges.
18 He loosens the bonds of kings,
  And binds their waist with a belt.
19 He leads princes away
    plundered,
  And overthrows the mighty.
20 He deprives the trusted ones of
    speech,
  And takes away the discernment
    of the elders.
21 He pours contempt on princes,
  And disarms the mighty.
22 He uncovers deep things out of
    darkness,
  And brings the shadow of death
    to light.
23 He makes nations great, and
    destroys them;
  He enlarges nations, and guides
    them.
24 He takes away the
    understanding of the chiefs of
    the people of the earth,
  And makes them wander in a
    pathless wilderness.
25 They grope in the dark without
    light,
  And He makes them stagger like
    a drunken *man.*

Job defends himself

13 "Behold, my eye has seen all *this,*
  My ear has heard and
    understood it.
2 What you know, I also know;
  I *am* not inferior to you.
3 But I would speak to the
    Almighty,
  And I desire to reason with God.
4 But you forgers of lies,
  You *are* all worthless physicians.

5 Oh, that you would be silent,
  And it would be your wisdom!
6 Now hear my reasoning,
  And heed the pleadings of my
    lips.
7 Will you speak wickedly for
    God,
  And talk deceitfully for Him?
8 Will you show partiality for Him?
  Will you contend for God?
9 Will it be well when He searches
    you out?
  Or can you mock Him as one
    mocks a man?
10 He will surely rebuke you
   If you secretly show partiality.
11 Will not His excellence make
     you afraid,
   And the dread of Him fall upon
     you?
12 Your platitudes *are* proverbs of
     ashes,
   Your defenses are defenses of
     clay.

13 "Hold your peace with me, and
     let me speak,
   Then let come on me what
     may!
14 Why do I take my flesh in my
     teeth,
   And put my life in my hands?
15 Though He slay me, yet will I
     trust Him.
   Even so, I will defend my own
     ways before Him.
16 He also *shall* be my salvation,
   For a **hypocrite** could not come
     before Him.
17 Listen carefully to my speech,
   And to my declaration with your
     ears.
18 See now, I have prepared *my*
     case,
   I know that I shall be vindicated.
19 Who *is* he *who* will contend with
     me?
   If now I hold my tongue, I
     perish.

20 "Only two *things* do not do to me,
   Then I will not hide myself from
     You:
21 Withdraw Your hand far from
     me,
   And let not the dread of You
     make me afraid.
22 Then call, and I will answer;
   Or let me speak, then You
     respond to me.
23 How many *are* my iniquities and
     sins?
   Make me know my transgression
     and my sin.
24 Why do You hide Your face,
   And regard me as Your enemy?
25 Will You frighten a leaf driven
     to and fro?
   And will You pursue dry
     stubble?
26 For You write bitter things
     against me,
   And make me inherit the
     iniquities of my youth.
27 You put my feet in the stocks,
   And watch closely all my paths.
   You set a limit for the soles of
     my feet.

28 "*Man* decays like a rotten thing,
   Like a garment that is moth-
     eaten.

Job talks about his troubles

14 "Man *who is* born of woman
   Is of few days and full of trouble.
2 He comes forth like a flower and
     fades away;
   He flees like a shadow and does
     not continue.
3 And do You open Your *eyes* on
     such a one,
   And bring me to judgment with
     Yourself?
4 Who can bring a clean *thing* out
     of an unclean?
   No one!
5 Since his days *are* determined,

13:16 Hypocrite Pronounced *HIP-puh-krit*. A person who pretends to be good or godly, but who actually is not. Jesus condemned hypocrites most of all.

The number of his months *is*
    with You;
You have appointed his limits,
    so that he cannot pass.
6 Look away from him that he
    may rest,
Till like a hired man he finishes
    his day.

7 "For there is hope for a tree,
If it is cut down, that it will sprout
    again,
And that its tender shoots will
    not cease.
8 Though its root may grow old
    in the earth,
And its stump may die in the
    ground,
9 *Yet* at the scent of water it will
    bud
And bring forth branches like a
    plant.
10 But man dies and is laid away;
Indeed he breathes his last
And where *is* he?
11 *As* water disappears from the
    sea,
And a river becomes parched
    and dries up,
12 So man lies down and does not
    rise.
Till the heavens *are* no more,
They will not awake
Nor be roused from their sleep.

13 "Oh, that You would hide me in
    the grave,
That You would conceal me
    until Your wrath is past,
That You would appoint me a
    set time, and remember me!
14 If a man dies, shall he live *again?*
All the days of my hard service
    I will wait,
Till my change comes.
15 You shall call, and I will answer
    You;
You shall desire the work of
    Your hands.
16 For now You number my steps,
But do not watch over my sin.
17 My transgression *is* sealed up in
    a bag,
And You cover my iniquity.

18 "But *as* a mountain falls *and*
    crumbles away,
And *as* a rock is moved from its
    place;
19 *As* water wears away stones,
And as torrents wash away the
    soil of the earth;
So You destroy the hope of
    man.
20 You prevail forever against him,
    and he passes on;
You change his countenance
    and send him away.
21 His sons come to honor, and he
    does not know *it;*
They are brought low, and he
    does not perceive *it.*
22 But his flesh will be in pain over
    it,
And his soul will mourn over it."

Eliphaz says Job is foolish

15 Then Eliphaz the Temanite answered and said:

2 "Should a wise man answer with
    empty knowledge,
And fill himself with the east
    wind?
3 Should he reason with
    unprofitable talk,
Or by speeches with which he
    can do no good?
4 Yes, you cast off fear,
And restrain prayer before God.
5 For your iniquity teaches your
    mouth,
And you choose the tongue of
    the crafty.
6 Your own mouth condemns
    you, and not I;
Yes, your own lips testify against
    you.

7 "*Are* you the first man *who* was
    born?
Or were you made before the
    hills?
8 Have you heard the counsel of
    God?
Do you limit wisdom to yourself?
9 What do you know that we do
    not know?

What do you understand that *is*
    not in us?
10 Both the gray-haired and the
    aged *are* among us,
    Much older than your father.
11 *Are* the consolations of God too
    small for you,
    And the word *spoken* gently
    with you?
12 Why does your heart carry you
    away,
    And what do your eyes wink at,
13 That you turn your spirit against
    God,
    And let *such* words go out of
    your mouth?

14 "What *is* man, that he could be
    pure?
    And *he who is* born of a woman,
    that he could be righteous?
15 If *God* puts no trust in His saints,
    And the heavens are not pure
    in His sight,
16 How much less man, *who is*
    abominable and filthy,
    Who drinks iniquity like water!

17 "I will tell you, hear me;
    What I have seen I will declare,
18 What wise men have told,
    Not hiding *anything received*
    from their fathers,
19 To whom alone the land was
    given,
    And no alien passed among
    them:
20 The wicked man writhes with
    pain all *his* days,
    And the number of years is
    hidden from the oppressor.
21 Dreadful sounds *are* in his ears;
    In prosperity the destroyer
    comes upon him.
22 He does not believe that he will
    return from darkness,
    For a sword is waiting for him.
23 He wanders about for bread,
    saying, 'Where *is it?*'
    He knows that a day of darkness
    is ready at his hand.
24 Trouble and anguish make him
    afraid;
    They overpower him, like a king
    ready for battle.

25 For he stretches out his hand
    against God,
    And acts defiantly against the
    Almighty,
26 Running stubbornly against Him
    With his strong, embossed
    shield.

27 "Though he has covered his face
    with his fatness,
    And made *his* waist heavy with
    fat,
28 He dwells in desolate cities,
    In houses which no one inhabits,
    Which are destined to become
    ruins.
29 He will not be rich,
    Nor will his wealth continue,
    Nor will his possessions
    overspread the earth.
30 He will not depart from
    darkness;
    The flame will dry out his
    branches,
    And by the breath of His mouth
    he will go away.
31 Let him not trust in futile *things,*
    deceiving himself,
    For futility will be his reward.
32 It will be accomplished before
    his time,
    And his branch will not be green.
33 He will shake off his unripe
    grape like a vine,
    And cast off his blossom like an
    olive tree.
34 For the company of hypocrites
    will be barren,
    And fire will consume the tents
    of bribery.
35 They conceive trouble and bring
    forth futility;
    Their womb prepares deceit."

Job complains about his so-called friends

16 Then Job answered and said:

2 "I have heard many such things;
    Miserable comforters *are* you all!
3 Shall words of wind have an
    end?

Or what provokes you that you
answer?
4 I also could speak as you *do*,
If your soul were in my soul's
place.
I could heap up words against
you,
And shake my head at you;
5 *But* I would strengthen you with
my mouth,
And the comfort of my lips
would relieve *your grief*.

6 "Though I speak, my grief is not
relieved;
And *if* I remain silent, how am I
eased?
7 But now He has worn me out;
You have made desolate all my
company.
8 You have shriveled me up,
And it is a witness *against me;*
My leanness rises up against
me
And bears witness to my face.
9 He tears *me* in His wrath, and
hates me;
He gnashes at me with His teeth;
My adversary sharpens His gaze
on me.
10 They gape at me with their
mouth,
They strike me reproachfully on
the cheek,
They gather together against
me.
11 God has delivered me to the
ungodly,
And turned me over to the
hands of the wicked.
12 I was at ease, but He has
shattered me;
He also has taken *me* by my
neck, and shaken me to
pieces;
He has set me up for His target,
13 His archers surround me.
He pierces my heart and does
not pity;
He pours out my gall on the
ground.
14 He breaks me with wound upon
wound;
He runs at me like a warrior.

15 "I have sewn sackcloth over my
skin,
And laid my head in the dust.
16 My face is flushed from weeping,
And on my eyelids *is* the shadow
of death;
17 Although no violence *is* in my
hands,
And my prayer *is* pure.

18 "O earth, do not cover my blood,
And let my cry have no *resting*
place!
19 Surely *even* now my witness *is*
in heaven,
And my evidence *is* on high.
20 My friends scorn me;
My eyes pour out *tears* to God.
21 Oh, that one might plead for a
man with God,
As a man *pleads* for his
neighbor!
22 For when a few years are
finished,
I shall go the way of no return.

Job prays for some relief

17 "My spirit is broken,
My days are extinguished,
The grave *is ready* for me.
2 *Are* not mockers with me?
And does not my eye dwell on
their provocation?

3 "Now put down a pledge for me
with Yourself.
Who *is he who* will shake hands
with me?
4 For You have hidden their heart
from understanding;
Therefore You will not exalt
them.
5 He who speaks flattery to *his*
friends,
Even the eyes of his children will
fail.

6 "But He has made me a byword
of the people,
And I have become one in
whose face men spit.
7 My eye has also grown dim
because of sorrow,

And all my members *are* like shadows.

8 Upright *men* are astonished at this,
And the innocent stirs himself up against the hypocrite.

9 Yet the righteous will hold to his way,
And he who has clean hands will be stronger and stronger.

10 "But please, come back again, all of you,
For I shall not find *one* wise *man* among you.

11 My days are past,
My purposes are broken off,
Even the thoughts of my heart.

12 They change the night into day;
'The light *is* near,' *they say,* in the face of darkness.

13 If I wait *for* the grave *as* my house,
If I make my bed in the darkness,

14 If I say to corruption, 'You *are* my father,'
And to the worm, 'You *are* my mother and my sister,'

15 Where then *is* my hope?
As for my hope, who can see it?

16 *Will* they go down to the gates of Sheol?
Shall *we have* rest together in the dust?"

Bildad says Job must deserve what he's getting

18 Then Bildad the Shuhite answered and said:

2 "How long *till* you put an end to words?
Gain understanding, and afterward we will speak.

3 Why are we counted as beasts,
And regarded as stupid in your sight?

4 You who tear yourself in anger,
Shall the earth be forsaken for you?

Or shall the rock be removed from its place?

5 "The light of the wicked indeed goes out,
And the flame of his fire does not shine.

6 The light is dark in his tent,
And his lamp beside him is put out.

7 The steps of his strength are shortened,
And his own counsel casts him down.

8 For he is cast into a net by his own feet,
And he walks into a snare.

9 The net takes *him* by the heel,
And a snare lays hold of him.

10 A noose *is* hidden for him on the ground,
And a trap for him in the road.

11 Terrors frighten him on every side,
And drive him to his feet.

12 His strength is starved,
And destruction *is* ready at his side.

13 It devours patches of his skin;
The firstborn of death devours his limbs.

14 He is uprooted from the shelter of his tent,
And they parade him before the king of terrors.

15 They dwell in his tent who are none of his;
Brimstone is scattered on his dwelling.

16 His roots are dried out below,
And his branch withers above.

17 The memory of him perishes from the earth,
And he has no name among the renowned.

18 He is driven from light into darkness,
And chased out of the world.

19 He has neither son nor posterity among his people,
Nor any remaining in his dwellings.

20 Those in the west are astonished at his day,

Job Says He Still Trusts in God

The Arabian Times

UZ—In a recent interview, Citizen Job, covered with painful boils from head to foot, described his suffering to a reporter of this newspaper: "Those whom I love have turned against me. . . . My bone clings to my skin and to my flesh" (verses 19, 20).

Three friends who were visiting were also interviewed. When asked his opinion of Job's suffering, Eliphaz said: "[He] has not given the weary water to drink, and [he has] withheld bread from the hungry" (Job 22: 7). Another friend reported: "[He] does not know God" (Job 18:21). But there is no evidence to support that Job is either unkind or an unbeliever.

What most surprised our reporter was a remark made by Job in the worst of his pain. Suddenly the good man lifted up his face to heaven and cried out: "I know that my Redeemer lives!"

Job's hope is not broken; his faith remains firm. He is a fine example of how to act when bad things happen to good people!

As those in the east are
    frightened.
21 Surely such *are* the dwellings of
    the wicked,
    And this *is* the place *of him who*
    does not know God."

Job puts his trust in God, not in his friends

19 Then Job answered and said:

2 "How long will you torment my
    soul,
    And break me in pieces with
    words?
3 These ten times you have
    reproached me;
    You are not ashamed *that* you
    have wronged me.
4 And if indeed I have erred,
    My error remains with me.
5 If indeed you exalt *yourselves*
    against me,
    And plead my disgrace against
    me,
6 Know then that God has
    wronged me,
    And has surrounded me with His
    net.

7 "If I cry out concerning wrong, I
    am not heard.
    If I cry aloud, *there is* no justice.

8 He has fenced up my way, so
    that I cannot pass;
    And He has set darkness in my
    paths.
9 He has stripped me of my glory,
    And taken the crown *from* my
    head.
10 He breaks me down on every
    side,
    And I am gone;
    My hope He has uprooted like
    a tree.
11 He has also kindled His wrath
    against me,
    And He counts me as *one of* His
    enemies.
12 His troops come together
    And build up their road against
    me;
    They encamp all around my
    tent.

13 "He has removed my brothers far
    from me,
    And my acquaintances are
    completely estranged from
    me.
14 My relatives have failed,
    And my close friends have
    forgotten me.
15 Those who dwell in my house,
    and my maidservants,
    Count me as a stranger;
    I am an alien in their sight.

16 I call my servant, but he gives
   no answer;
   I beg him with my mouth.
17 My breath is offensive to my
   wife,
   And I am repulsive to the
   children of my own body.
18 Even young children despise
   me;
   I arise, and they speak against
   me.
19 All my close friends abhor me,
   And those whom I love have
   turned against me.
20 My bone clings to my skin and
   to my flesh,
   And I have escaped by the skin
   of my teeth.

21 "Have pity on me, have pity on
   me, O you my friends,
   For the hand of God has struck
   me!
22 Why do you persecute me as
   God *does*,
   And are not satisfied with my
   flesh?

23 "Oh, that my words were written!
   Oh, that they *were* inscribed in
   a book!
24 That they *were* engraved on a
   rock
   With an iron pen and lead,
   forever!
25 For I know *that* my Redeemer
   lives,

And He shall stand at last on the
   earth;
26 And after my skin is destroyed,
   this *I know*,
   That in my flesh I shall *see* God,
27 Whom I shall see for myself,
   And my *eyes* shall behold, and
   not another.
   How my heart yearns within me!
28 If you should say, 'How shall we
   persecute him?'—
   Since the root of the matter is
   found in me,
29 Be afraid of the sword for
   yourselves;
   For wrath *brings* the punishment
   of the sword,
   That you may know *there is* a
   judgment."

Zophar preaches about wicked people

20 Then Zophar the Naamathite answered and said:

2 "Therefore my anxious thoughts
   make me answer,
   Because of the turmoil within
   me.
3 I have heard the rebuke that
   reproaches me,
   And the spirit of my
   understanding causes me to
   answer.

4 "Do you *not* know this of old,
   Since man was placed on earth,
5 That the triumphing of the
   wicked is short,
   And the joy of the hypocrite is
   but for a moment?
6 Though his haughtiness mounts
   up to the heavens,
   And his head reaches to the
   clouds,
7 *Yet* he will perish forever like his
   own refuse;
   Those who have seen him will
   say, 'Where is he?'
8 He will fly away like a dream,
   and not be found;
   Yes, he will be chased away like
   a vision of the night.

*Ancient writers formed characters on soft clay
tablets with a sharp tool (stylus).*

9 The *eye that* saw him will *see him* no more,
Nor will his place behold him anymore.
10 His children will seek the favor of the poor,
And his hands will restore his wealth.
11 His bones are full of his youthful vigor,
But it will lie down with him in the dust.

12 "Though *evil* is sweet in his mouth,
And he hides it under his tongue,
13 *Though* he spares it and does not forsake it,
But still *keeps* it in his mouth,
14 *Yet* his food in his stomach turns sour;
It becomes cobra venom within him.
15 He swallows down riches
And vomits them up again;
God casts them out of his belly.
16 He will suck the poison of cobras;
The viper's tongue will slay him.
17 He will not see the streams,
The rivers flowing with honey and cream.
18 He will restore that for which he labored,
And will not swallow *it* down;
From the proceeds of business He will get no enjoyment.
19 For he has oppressed *and* forsaken the poor,
He has violently seized a house which he did not build.

20 "Because he knows no quietness in his heart,
He will not save anything he desires.
21 Nothing is left for him to eat;
Therefore his well-being will not last.
22 In his self-sufficiency he will be in distress;
Every hand of misery will come against him.

23 *When* he is about to fill his stomach,
God will cast on him the fury of His wrath,
And will rain *it* on him while he is eating.
24 He will flee from the iron weapon;
A bronze bow will pierce him through.
25 It is drawn, and comes out of the body;
Yes, the glittering *point comes* out of his gall.
Terrors *come* upon him;
26 Total darkness *is* reserved for his treasures.
An unfanned fire will consume him;
It shall go ill with him who is left in his tent.
27 The heavens will reveal his iniquity,
And the earth will rise up against him.
28 The increase of his house will depart,
And his goods will flow away in the day of His wrath.
29 This *is* the portion from God for a wicked man,
The heritage appointed to him by God."

Job complains that the wicked do well

21 Then Job answered and said:

2 "Listen carefully to my speech,
And let this be your consolation.
3 Bear with me that I may speak,
And after I have spoken, keep mocking.

4 "As for me, *is* my complaint against man?
And if *it were,* why should I not be impatient?
5 Look at me and be astonished;
Put *your* hand over *your* mouth.
6 Even when I remember I am terrified,

And trembling takes hold of my
   flesh.
7 Why do the wicked live *and*
   become old,
   Yes, become mighty in power?
8 Their descendants are
   established with them in their
   sight,
   And their offspring before their
   eyes.
9 Their houses *are* safe from fear,
   Neither is the rod of God upon
   them.
10 Their bull breeds without failure;
   Their cow calves without
   miscarriage.
11 They send forth their little ones
   like a flock,
   And their children dance.
12 They sing to the tambourine and
   harp,
   And rejoice to the sound of the
   flute.
13 They spend their days in wealth,
   And in a moment go down to
   the grave.
14 Yet they say to God, 'Depart
   from us,
   For we do not desire the
   knowledge of Your ways.
15 Who is the Almighty, that we
   should serve Him?
   And what profit do we have if
   we pray to Him?'
16 Indeed their prosperity is not in
   their hand;
   The counsel of the wicked is far
   from me.

17 "How often is the lamp of the
   wicked put out?
   How often does their destruction
   come upon them,
   The sorrows God distributes in
   His anger?
18 They are like straw before the
   wind,
   And like chaff that a storm
   carries away.
19 *They say,* 'God lays up one's
   iniquity for his children';
   Let Him recompense him, that
   he may know *it.*
20 Let his eyes see his destruction,

And let him drink of the wrath
   of the Almighty.
21 For what does he care about his
   household after him,
   When the number of his months
   is cut in half?

22 "Can *anyone* teach God
   knowledge,
   Since He judges those on
   high?
23 One dies in his full strength,
   Being wholly at ease and secure;
24 His pails are full of milk,
   And the marrow of his bones is
   moist.
25 Another man dies in the
   bitterness of his soul,
   Never having eaten with
   pleasure.
26 They lie down alike in the dust,
   And worms cover them.

27 "Look, I know your thoughts,
   And the schemes *with which* you
   would wrong me.
28 For you say,
   'Where *is* the house of the
   prince?
   And where *is* the tent,
   The dwelling place of the
   wicked?'
29 Have you not asked those who
   travel the road?
   And do you not know their
   signs?
30 For the wicked are reserved for
   the day of doom;
   They shall be brought out on the
   day of wrath.
31 Who condemns his way to his
   face?
   And who repays him *for what*
   he has done?
32 Yet he shall be brought to the
   grave,
   And a vigil kept over the tomb.
33 The clods of the valley shall be
   sweet to him;
   Everyone shall follow him,
   As countless *have gone* before
   him.
34 How then can you comfort me
   with empty words,

Since falsehood remains in your
answers?''

Eliphaz accuses Job of sin

22 Then Eliphaz the Temanite answered and said:

2 "Can a man be profitable to God,
Though he who is wise may be
profitable to himself?
3 *Is it* any pleasure to the Almighty
that you are righteous?
Or *is it* gain *to Him* that you
make your ways blameless?

4 "Is it because of your fear of Him
that He corrects you,
And enters into judgment with
you?
5 *Is* not your wickedness great,
And your iniquity without end?
6 For you have taken pledges
from your brother for no
reason,
And stripped the naked of their
clothing.
7 You have not given the weary
water to drink,
And you have withheld bread
from the hungry.
8 But the mighty man possessed
the land,
And the honorable man dwelt
in it.
9 You have sent widows away
empty,
And the strength of the fatherless
was crushed.
10 Therefore snares *are* all around
you,
And sudden fear troubles you,
11 Or darkness *so that* you cannot
see;
And an abundance of water
covers you.

12 "Is not God in the height of
heaven?

And *see* the highest stars, how
lofty they are!
13 And you say, 'What does God
know?
Can He judge through the deep
darkness?
14 Thick clouds cover Him, so that
He cannot *see,*
And He walks above the circle
of heaven.'
15 Will you keep to the old way
Which wicked men have trod,
16 Who were cut down before their
time,
Whose foundations were swept
away by a flood?
17 They said to God, 'Depart from
us!
What can the Almighty do to
them?'
18 Yet He filled their houses with
good *things;*
But the counsel of the wicked
is far from me.

19 "The righteous see *it* and are
glad,
And the innocent laugh at them:
20 'Surely our adversaries are cut
down,
And the fire consumes their
remnant.'

21 "Now acquaint yourself with Him,
and be at peace;
Thereby good will come to you.
22 Receive, please, instruction from
His mouth,
And lay up His words in your
heart.
23 If you return to the Almighty,
you will be built up;
You will remove iniquity far from
your tents.
24 Then you will lay your gold in
the dust,
And the *gold* of Ophir among
the stones of the brooks.

WORDFINDER

22:12 Heaven The dwelling place of God, angels, and souls of the dead who belong to God. That heaven is not part of our universe, but sometimes the word just refers to the sky (see Genesis 1:8).

25 Yes, the Almighty will be your
   gold
   And your precious silver;
26 For then you will have your
   delight in the Almighty,
   And lift up your face to God.
27 You will make your prayer to
   Him,
   He will hear you,
   And you will pay your vows.
28 You will also declare a thing,
   And it will be established for
   you;
   So light will shine on your ways.
29 When they cast *you* down, and
   you say, 'Exaltation *will
   come!*'
   Then He will save the humble
   person.
30 He will *even* deliver one who is
   not innocent;
   Yes, he will be delivered by the
   purity of your hands."

God knows our ways

23 Then Job answered and said:

2 "Even today my complaint is
   bitter;
   My hand is listless because of my
   groaning.
3 Oh, that I knew where I might
   find Him,
   That I might come to His seat!
4 I would present *my* case before
   Him,
   And fill my mouth with
   arguments.
5 I would know the words *which*
   He would answer me,
   And understand what He would
   say to me.
6 Would He contend with me in
   His great power?
   No! But He would take *note* of
   me.
7 There the upright could reason
   with Him,
   And I would be delivered forever
   from my Judge.

8 "Look, I go forward, but He is
   not *there,*

And backward, but I cannot
   perceive Him;
9 When He works on the left
   hand, I cannot behold *Him;*
   When He turns to the right
   hand, I cannot see *Him.*
10 But He knows the way that I
   take;
   When He has tested me, I shall
   come forth as gold.
11 My foot has held fast to His
   steps;
   I have kept His way and not
   turned aside.
12 I have not departed from the
   commandment of His lips;
   I have treasured the words of His
   mouth
   More than my necessary *food.*

13 "But He *is* unique, and who can
   make Him change?
   And *whatever* His soul desires,
   that He does.
14 For He performs *what is*
   appointed for me,
   And many such *things are* with
   Him.
15 Therefore I am terrified at His
   presence;
   When I consider *this,* I am afraid
   of Him.
16 For God made my heart weak,
   And the Almighty terrifies me;
17 Because I was not cut off from
   the presence of darkness,
   And He did *not* hide deep
   darkness from my face.

Job speaks of violence on earth

24 "*Since* times are not hidden from
   the Almighty,
   Why do those who know Him
   see not His days?

2 "*Some* remove landmarks;
   They seize flocks violently and
   feed *on them;*
3 They drive away the donkey of
   the fatherless;
   They take the widow's ox as a
   pledge.

4 They push the needy off the road;
All the poor of the land are forced to hide.
5 Indeed, *like* wild donkeys in the desert,
They go out to their work, searching for food.
The wilderness *yields* food for them *and* for *their* children.
6 They gather their fodder in the field
And glean in the vineyard of the wicked.
7 They spend the night naked, without clothing,
And have no covering in the cold.
8 They are wet with the showers of the mountains,
And huddle around the rock for want of shelter.

9 "*Some* snatch the fatherless from the breast,
And take a pledge from the poor.
10 They cause *the poor* to go naked, without clothing;
And they take away the sheaves from the hungry.
11 They press out oil within their walls,
And tread winepresses, yet suffer thirst.
12 The dying groan in the city,
And the souls of the wounded cry out;
Yet God does not charge *them* with wrong.

13 "There are those who rebel against the light;
They do not know its ways Nor abide in its paths.
14 The murderer rises with the light;
He kills the poor and needy;
And in the night he is like a thief.
15 The eye of the adulterer waits for the twilight,
Saying, 'No eye will see me';
And he disguises *his* face.

16 In the dark they break into houses
Which they marked for themselves in the daytime;
They do not know the light.
17 For the morning is the same to them as the shadow of death;
If *someone* recognizes *them*,
They are in the terrors of the shadow of death.

18 "They *should be* swift on the face of the waters,
Their portion *should be* cursed in the earth,
So that no *one would* turn into the way of their vineyards.
19 As drought and heat consume the snow waters,
So the grave *consumes those who* have sinned.
20 The womb *should* forget him,
The worm *should* feed sweetly on him;
He *should* be remembered no more,
And wickedness *should* be broken like a tree.
21 For he preys on the barren *who* do not bear,
And does no good for the widow.

22 "But *God* draws the mighty away with His power;
He rises up, but no *man* is sure of life.
23 He gives them security, and they rely *on it*;
Yet His eyes *are* on their ways.
24 They are exalted for a little while,
Then they are gone.
They are brought low;
They are taken out of the way like all *others*;
They dry out like the heads of grain.

25 "Now if *it is* not *so*, who will prove me a liar,
And make my speech worth nothing?"

How can puny people face the Almighty?

25

Then Bildad the Shuhite answered and said:

2 "Dominion and fear *belong* to Him;
   He makes peace in His high places.
3 Is there any number to His armies?
   Upon whom does His light not rise?
4 How then can man be righteous before God?
   Or how can he be pure *who is* born of a woman?
5 If even the moon does not shine,
   And the stars are not pure in His sight,
6 How much less man, *who is* a maggot,
   And a son of man, *who is* a worm?"

Some friends *you* are! says Job

26

But Job answered and said:

2 "How have you helped *him who is* without power?
   How have you saved the arm *that has* no strength?
3 How have you counseled *one who has* no wisdom?
   And *how* have you declared sound advice to many?
4 To whom have you uttered words?

And whose spirit came from you?

5 "The dead tremble,
   Those under the waters and those inhabiting them.
6 Sheol *is* naked before Him,
   And Destruction has no covering.
7 He stretches out the north over empty space;
   He hangs the earth on nothing.
8 He binds up the water in His thick clouds,
   Yet the clouds are not broken under it.
9 He covers the face of *His* throne,
   And spreads His cloud over it.
10 He drew a circular horizon on the face of the waters,
   At the boundary of light and darkness.
11 The pillars of heaven tremble,
   And are astonished at His rebuke.
12 He stirs up the sea with His power,
   And by His understanding He breaks up the storm.
13 By His Spirit He adorned the heavens;
   His hand pierced the fleeing serpent.
14 Indeed these *are* the mere edges of His ways,
   And how small a whisper we hear of Him!
   But the thunder of His power who can understand?"

⛏ DIGGING IN

25:1–6 A Man Who Knew Too Much Can you know too much? You can if what you know never helps anybody. Bildad was like that. (Pronounce his name *BILL-dad*.)

Bildad was right about everything he said: "How then can man be righteous before God?" It is true that no one can be righteous before God. But Bildad didn't know that truth well enough. Bildad was taking God's place by judging Job. So what Bildad knew didn't help him, and it

didn't help his friend Job. His friend was in great pain, and all Bildad knew to do was preach to him.

How sad that Bildad knew so much, but did so little good for his friend! Bildad would have shown more sense if he had just sat quietly with Job. He might even have offered Job a cool drink of water. But Bildad only wanted to prove how wise he was. By doing so, he proved he was a fool.

Job takes the stand in his own defense

27 Moreover Job continued his discourse, and said:

2 "As God lives, *who* has taken
    away my justice,
    And the Almighty, *who* has
    made my **soul** bitter,
3 As long as my breath *is* in me,
    And the breath of God in my
    nostrils,
4 My lips will not speak
    wickedness,
    Nor my tongue utter deceit.
5 Far be it from me
    That I should say you are right;
    Till I die I will not put away my
    integrity from me.
6 My righteousness I hold fast, and
    will not let it go;
    My heart shall not reproach *me*
    as long as I live.

7 "May my enemy be like the
    wicked,
    And he who rises up against me
    like the unrighteous.
8 For what is the hope of the
    hypocrite,
    Though he may gain *much,*
    If God takes away his life?
9 Will God hear his cry
    When trouble comes upon
    him?
10 Will he delight himself in the
    Almighty?
    Will he always call on God?

11 "I will teach you about the hand
    of God;
    What *is* with the Almighty I will
    not conceal.
12 Surely all of you have seen *it;*
    Why then do you behave with
    complete nonsense?

13 "This is the portion of a wicked
    man with God,
    And the heritage of oppressors,
    received from the Almighty:
14 If his children are multiplied, *it
    is* for the sword;
    And his offspring shall not be
    satisfied with bread.
15 Those who survive him shall be
    buried in death,
    And their widows shall not
    weep,
16 Though he heaps up silver like
    dust,
    And piles up clothing like clay—
17 He may pile *it* up, but the just
    will wear *it,*
    And the innocent will divide the
    silver.
18 He builds his house like a moth,
    Like a booth *which* a watchman
    makes.
19 The rich man will lie down,
    But not be gathered *up;*
    He opens his eyes,
    And he *is* no more.
20 Terrors overtake him like a
    flood;
    A tempest steals him away in the
    night.
21 The east wind carries him away,
    and he is gone;
    It sweeps him out of his place.
22 It hurls against him and does not
    spare;
    He flees desperately from its
    power.
23 *Men* shall clap their hands at
    him,
    And shall hiss him out of his
    place.

Wisdom is God's gift

28 "Surely there is a mine for silver,
    And a place *where* gold is
    refined.

WORDFINDER

27:2 Soul The inner life of a person that cannot die. The soul of a believing person who dies goes to be with God in heaven. But the unbelieving person's soul is cut off from God.

2 Iron is taken from the earth,
   And copper *is* smelted *from* ore.
3 *Man* puts an end to darkness,
   And searches *every* recess
   For ore in the darkness and the
      shadow of death.
4 He breaks open a shaft away
      from people;
   In places forgotten by feet
   They hang far away from men;
   They swing to and fro.
5 *As for* the earth, from it comes
      bread,
   But underneath it is turned up
      as by fire;
6 Its stones *are* the source of
      sapphires,
   And it contains gold dust.
7 *That* path no bird knows,
   Nor has the falcon's eye seen it.
8 The proud lions have not
      trodden it,
   Nor has the fierce lion passed
      over it.
9 He puts his hand on the flint;
   He overturns the mountains at
      the roots.
10 He cuts out channels in the
      rocks,
   And his *eye* sees every precious
      thing.
11 He dams up the streams from
      trickling;
   What is hidden he brings forth
      to light.

12 "But where can wisdom be
      found?
   And where *is* the place of
      understanding?
13 Man does not know its value,
   Nor is it found in the land of the
      living.
14 The deep says, *'It is* not in me';
   And the sea says, *'It is* not with
      me.'
15 It cannot be purchased for gold,
   Nor can silver be weighed *for* its
      price.
16 It cannot be valued in the gold
      of Ophir,
   In precious onyx or sapphire.
17 Neither gold nor crystal can
      equal it,

Nor can it be exchanged for
   jewelry of fine gold.
18 No mention shall be made of
   coral or quartz,
   For the price of wisdom *is* above
      rubies.
19 The topaz of Ethiopia cannot
      equal it,
   Nor can it be valued in pure
      gold.

20 "From where then does wisdom
      come?
   And where *is* the place of
      understanding?
21 It is hidden from the eyes of all
      living,
   And concealed from the birds of
      the air.
22 Destruction and Death say,
   'We have heard a report about
      it with our ears.'
23 God understands its way,
   And He knows its place.
24 For He looks to the ends of the
      earth,
   And sees under the whole
      heavens,
25 To establish a weight for the
      wind,
   And apportion the waters by
      measure.
26 When He made a law for the
      rain,
   And a path for the thunderbolt,
27 Then He saw *wisdom* and
      declared it;
   He prepared it, indeed, He
      searched it out.
28 And to man He said,
   'Behold, the fear of the Lord, that
      is wisdom,
   And to depart from evil *is*
      understanding.' "

Job looks back on his past riches

29 Job further continued his discourse, and said:

2 "Oh, that I were as *in* months
      past,
   As *in* the days *when* God
      watched over me;

3   When His lamp shone upon my head,
And when by His light I walked through darkness;

4   Just as I was in the days of my prime,
When the friendly counsel of God was over my tent;

5   When the Almighty was yet with me,
When my children were around me;

6   When my steps were bathed with cream,
And the rock poured out rivers of oil for me!

7   "When I went out to the gate by the city,
When I took my seat in the open square,

8   The young men saw me and hid,
And the aged arose and stood;

9   The princes refrained from talking,
And put their hand on their mouth;

10   The voice of nobles was hushed,
And their tongue stuck to the roof of their mouth.

11   When the ear heard, then it blessed me,
And when the eye saw, then it approved me;

12   Because I delivered the poor who cried out,
The fatherless and the one who had no helper.

13   The blessing of a perishing man came upon me,
And I caused the widow's heart to sing for joy.

14   I put on righteousness, and it clothed me;
My justice was like a robe and a turban.

15   I was eyes to the blind,
And I was feet to the lame.

16   I was a father to the poor,
And I searched out the case that I did not know.

17   I broke the fangs of the wicked,
And plucked the victim from his teeth.

18   "Then I said, 'I shall die in my nest,
And multiply my days as the sand.

19   My root is spread out to the waters,
And the dew lies all night on my branch.

20   My glory is fresh within me,
And my bow is renewed in my hand.'

21   "Men listened to me and waited,
And kept silence for my counsel.

22   After my words they did not speak again,
And my speech settled on them as dew.

23   They waited for me as for the rain,
And they opened their mouth wide as for the spring rain.

24   If I mocked at them, they did not believe it,
And the light of my countenance they did not cast down.

25   I chose the way for them, and sat as chief;
So I dwelt as a king in the army,
As one who comforts mourners.

Job is at rock bottom

30 "But now they mock at me, men younger than I,
Whose fathers I disdained to put with the dogs of my flock.

2   Indeed, what profit is the strength of their hands to me?
Their vigor has perished.

3   They are gaunt from want and famine,
Fleeing late to the wilderness, desolate and waste,

4   Who pluck mallow by the bushes,
And broom tree roots for their food.

5   They were driven out from among men,
They shouted at them as at a thief.

6   They had to live in the clefts of the valleys,

In caves of the earth and the rocks.
7 Among the bushes they brayed,
Under the nettles they nestled.
8 *They were* sons of fools,
Yes, sons of vile men;
They *were* scourged from the land.

9 "And now I am their taunting song;
Yes, I am their byword.
10 They abhor me, they keep far from me;
They do not hesitate to spit in my face.
11 Because He has loosed my bowstring and afflicted me,
They have cast off restraint before me.
12 At *my* right *hand* the rabble arises;
They push away my feet,
And they raise against me their ways of destruction.
13 They break up my path,
They promote my calamity;
They have no helper.
14 They come as broad breakers;
Under the ruinous storm they roll along.
15 Terrors are turned upon me;
They pursue my honor as the wind,
And my prosperity has passed like a cloud.

16 "And now my soul is poured out because of my *plight;*
The days of affliction take hold of me.
17 My bones are pierced in me at night,
And my gnawing pains take no rest.
18 By great force my garment is disfigured;
It binds me about as the collar of my coat.
19 He has cast me into the mire,
And I have become like dust and ashes.

20 "I cry out to You, but You do not answer me;

I stand up, and You regard me.
21 *But* You have become cruel to me;
With the strength of Your hand You oppose me.
22 You lift me up to the wind and cause me to ride *on it;*
You spoil my success.
23 For I know *that* You will bring me *to* death,
And *to* the house appointed for all living.

24 "Surely He would not stretch out *His* hand against a heap of ruins,
If they cry out when He destroys *it.*
25 Have I not wept for him who was in trouble?
Has *not* my soul grieved for the poor?
26 But when I looked for good, evil came *to me;*
And when I waited for light, then came darkness.
27 My heart is in turmoil and cannot rest;
Days of affliction confront me.
28 I go about mourning, but not in the sun;
I stand up in the assembly *and* cry out for help.
29 I am a brother of jackals,
And a companion of ostriches.
30 My skin grows black and falls from me;
My bones burn with fever.
31 My harp is *turned* to mourning,
And my flute to the voice of those who weep.

Job claims to be a righteous man

31 "I have made a covenant with my eyes;
Why then should I look upon a young woman?
2 For what *is* the allotment of God from above,
And the inheritance of the Almighty from on high?
3 *Is* it not destruction for the wicked,

And disaster for the workers of
    iniquity?
4 Does He not see my ways,
    And count all my steps?

5 "If I have walked with falsehood,
    Or if my foot has hastened to
    deceit,
6 Let me be weighed on honest
    scales,
    That God may know my
    integrity.
7 If my step has turned from the
    way,
    Or my heart walked after my
    eyes,
    Or if any spot adheres to my
    hands,
8 *Then* let me sow, and another
    eat;
    Yes, let my harvest be rooted
    out.

9 "If my heart has been enticed by
    a woman,
    Or *if* I have lurked at my
    neighbor's door,
10 *Then* let my wife grind for
    another,
    And let others bow down over
    her.
11 For that *would be* wickedness;
    Yes, it *would be* iniquity
    deserving of judgment.
12 For that *would be* a fire *that*
    consumes to destruction,
    And would root out all my
    increase.

13 "If I have despised the cause of
    my male or female servant
    When they complained against
    me,
14 What then shall I do when God
    rises up?
    When He punishes, how shall I
    answer Him?
15 Did not He who made me in the
    womb make them?
    Did not the same One fashion
    us in the womb?

16 "If I have kept the poor from *their*
    desire,

Or caused the *eyes* of the widow
    to fail,
17 Or eaten my morsel by myself,
    So that the fatherless could not
    eat of it
18 (But from my youth I reared him
    as a father,
    And from my mother's womb I
    guided *the widow*);
19 If I have seen anyone perish for
    lack of clothing,
    Or any poor *man* without
    covering;
20 If his heart has not blessed me,
    And *if* he was *not* warmed with
    the fleece of my sheep;
21 If I have raised my hand against
    the fatherless,
    When I saw I had help in the
    gate;
22 *Then* let my arm fall from my
    shoulder,
    Let my arm be torn from the
    socket.
23 For destruction *from* God *is* a
    terror to me,
    And because of His
    magnificence I cannot endure.

24 "If I have made gold my hope,
    Or said to fine gold, '*You are*
    my confidence';
25 If I have rejoiced because my
    wealth *was* great,
    And because my hand had
    gained much;
26 If I have observed the sun when
    it shines,
    Or the moon moving *in*
    brightness,
27 So that my heart has been
    secretly enticed,
    And my mouth has kissed my
    hand;
28 This also *would be* an iniquity
    deserving of judgment,
    For I would have denied God
    who is above.

29 "If I have rejoiced at the
    destruction of him who hated
    me,
    Or lifted myself up when evil
    found him

30 (Indeed I have not allowed my
      mouth to sin
   By asking for a curse on his
      soul);
31 If the men of my tent have not
      said,
   'Who is there that has not been
      satisfied with his meat?'
32 (But no sojourner had to lodge
      in the street,
   For I have opened my doors to
      the traveler);
33 If I have covered my
      transgressions as Adam,
   By hiding my iniquity in my
      bosom,
34 Because I feared the great
      multitude,
   And dreaded the contempt of
      families,
   So that I kept silence
   And did not go out of the door—
35 Oh, that I had one to hear me!
   Here is my mark.
   Oh, that the Almighty would
      answer me,
   That my Prosecutor had written
      a book!
36 Surely I would carry it on my
      shoulder,
   And bind it on me like a crown;
37 I would declare to Him the
      number of my steps;
   Like a prince I would approach
      Him.

38 "If my land cries out against me,
   And its furrows weep together;

39 If I have eaten its fruit without
      money,
   Or caused its owners to lose their
      lives;
40 Then let thistles grow instead of
      wheat,
   And weeds instead of barley."

The words of Job are ended.

Elihu gives his opinion

32 So these three men ceased answering Job, because he was righteous in his own eyes. 2 Then the wrath of Elihu, the son of Barachel the Buzite, of the family of Ram, was aroused against Job; his wrath was aroused because he **justified** himself rather than God. 3 Also against his three friends his wrath was aroused, because they had found no answer, and yet had condemned Job.

4 Now because they were years older than he, Elihu had waited to speak to Job. 5 When Elihu saw that there was no answer in the mouth of these three men, his wrath was aroused.

6 So Elihu, the son of Barachel the Buzite, answered and said:

   "I am young in years, and you
      are very old;
   Therefore I was afraid,
   And dared not declare my
      opinion to you.
7 I said, 'Age should speak,
   And multitude of years should
      teach wisdom.'

WORDFINDER

32:2 Justified   Pronounced JUSS-tih-fyed. In the New Testament, to be considered righteous by God because you trust in Jesus Christ as your Savior from sin.

DIGGING IN

32:1—37:24 A Man of True Wisdom
After Job's so-called friends finished their foolish speeches, a young man named Elihu spoke up. (Pronounce his name ih-LIE-hew.) Elihu told Job's friends they had spoken foolishness, but Job said, "It profits a man nothing that he should delight in God" (Job 34:9). So Job also was not right in everything he said to his friends.

Elihu was wise because he didn't judge Job harshly. Instead, Elihu helped Job understand God's ways. He said, "Listen to this, O Job; stand still and consider the wondrous works of God" (Job 37:14).

We are thrilled as we read the wisdom of Elihu. Let us pray to be like this young man who spoke such wonderful things to Job. Wisdom is the gift of God.

Elihu—My name is Elihu (pronounced *ih-LIE-hue*) and means "He Is My God." I got tired of listening to Job arguing with his three friends for days. I decided I didn't agree with either Job or his nasty friends. So I tried to be a referee. I'm glad the Lord Himself finally spoke up and ended the long argument. It really did my heart good when God showed both Job and his friends that they had failed to understand the reason for Job's suffering.

The trouble was that Job began to doubt that God really loved him. Then the Lord showed Job that it makes good sense to trust God's wisdom, even when things go wrong for us.

But the Lord was very angry with Job's friends because they thought they knew so much. And they didn't comfort poor Job as they should have.

8 But *there is* a spirit in man,
And the breath of the Almighty
gives him understanding.
9 Great men are not *always* wise,
Nor do the aged *always*
understand justice.

10 "Therefore I say, 'Listen to me,
I also will declare my opinion.'
11 Indeed I waited for your words,
I listened to your reasonings,
while you searched out what
to say.
12 I paid close attention to you;
And surely not one of you
convinced Job,
Or answered his words—
13 Lest you say,
'We have found wisdom';
God will vanquish him, not man.
14 Now he has not directed *his*
words against me;
So I will not answer him with
your words.

15 "They are dismayed and answer
no more;
Words escape them.
16 And I have waited, because they
did not speak,
Because they stood still *and*
answered no more.
17 I also will answer my part,
I too will declare my opinion.
18 For I am full of words;
The spirit within me compels
me.

19 Indeed my belly *is* like wine *that*
has no vent;
It is ready to burst like new
wineskins.
20 I will speak, that I may find relief;
I must open my lips and answer.
21 Let me not, I pray, show
partiality to anyone;
Nor let me flatter any man.
22 For I do not know how to flatter,
Else my Maker would soon take
me away.

Elihu disagrees with Job

33 "But please, Job, hear my
speech,
And listen to all my words.
2 Now, I open my mouth;
My tongue speaks in my mouth.
3 My words *come* from my upright
heart;
My lips utter pure knowledge.
4 The Spirit of God has made
me,
And the breath of the Almighty
gives me life.
5 If you can answer me,
Set *your words* in order before
me;
Take your stand.
6 Truly I *am* as your spokesman
before God;
I also have been formed out of
clay.
7 Surely no fear of me will terrify
you,

Nor will my hand be heavy on
you.

8 "Surely you have spoken in my
hearing,
And I have heard the sound of
your words, *saying,*
9 'I *am* pure, without transgression;
I *am* innocent, and *there is* no
iniquity in me.
10 Yet He finds occasions against
me,
He counts me as His enemy;
11 He puts my feet in the stocks,
He watches all my paths.'

12 "Look, *in* this you are not
righteous.
I will answer you,
For God is greater than man.
13 Why do you contend with
Him?
For He does not give an
accounting of any of His
words.
14 For God may speak in one way,
or in another,
Yet man does not perceive it.
15 In a dream, in a vision of the
night,
When deep sleep falls upon
men,
While slumbering on their beds,
16 Then He opens the ears of men,
And seals their instruction.
17 In order to turn man *from his*
deed,
And conceal pride from man,
18 He keeps back his soul from the
Pit,
And his life from perishing by the
sword.

19 "*Man* is also chastened with pain
on his bed,
And with strong *pain* in many
of his bones,
20 So that his life abhors bread,
And his soul succulent food.
21 His flesh wastes away from sight,
And his bones stick out *which*
once were not seen.
22 Yes, his soul draws near the Pit,
And his life to the executioners.

23 "If there is a messenger for him,
A mediator, one among a
thousand,
To show man His uprightness,
24 Then He is gracious to him, and
says,
'Deliver him from going down to
the Pit;
I have found a ransom';
25 His flesh shall be young like a
child's,
He shall return to the days of
his youth.
26 He shall pray to God, and He
will delight in him,
He shall see His face with joy,
For He restores to man His
righteousness.
27 Then he looks at men and says,
'I have sinned, and perverted
what was right,
And it did not profit me.'
28 He will redeem his soul from
going down to the Pit,
And his life shall see the light.

29 "Behold, God works all these
things,
Twice, *in fact,* three *times* with
a man,
30 To bring back his soul from the
Pit,
That he may be enlightened with
the light of life.

31 "Give ear, Job, listen to me;
Hold your peace, and I will
speak.
32 If you have anything to say,
answer me;
Speak, for I desire to justify you.
33 If not, listen to me;
Hold your peace, and I will teach
you wisdom."

God cannot be unfair

34 Elihu further answered and said:

2 "Hear my words, you wise *men;*
Give ear to me, you who have
knowledge.
3 For the ear tests words
As the palate tastes food.

4   Let us choose justice for
     ourselves;
     Let us know among ourselves
     what *is* good.

5   "For Job has said, 'I am
     righteous,
     But God has taken away my
     justice;
6   Should I lie concerning my right?
     My wound *is* incurable, *though*
     I *am* without transgression.'
7   What man *is* like Job,
     Who drinks scorn like water,
8   Who goes in company with the
     workers of iniquity,
     And walks with wicked men?
9   For he has said, 'It profits a man
     nothing
     That he should delight in God.'

10   "Therefore listen to me, you men
     of understanding:
     Far be it from God *to do*
     wickedness,
     And *from* the Almighty to
     commit iniquity.
11   For He repays man *according to*
     his work,
     And makes man to find a reward
     according to *his* way.
12   Surely God will ne*ver* do
     wickedly,
     Nor will the Almighty pervert
     justice.
13   Who gave Him charge over the
     earth?
     Or who appointed *Him over* the
     whole world?
14   If He should set His heart on it,
     If He should gather to Himself
     His Spirit and His breath,
15   All flesh would perish together,
     And man would return to dust.

16   "If *you have* understanding, hear
     this;
     Listen to the sound of my words:
17   Should one who hates justice
     govern?
     Will you condemn *Him who is*
     most just?
18   *Is it fitting* to say to a king, 'You
     are worthless,'

     And to nobles, '*You are*
     wicked'?
19   Yet He is not partial to princes,
     Nor does He regard the rich
     more than the poor;
     For they *are* all the work of His
     hands.
20   In a moment they die, in the
     middle of the night;
     The people are shaken and pass
     away;
     The mighty are taken away
     without a hand.

21   "For His *eyes are* on the ways
     of man,
     And He sees all his steps.
22   There is no darkness nor
     shadow of death
     Where the workers of iniquity
     may hide themselves.
23   For He need not further consider
     a man,
     That he should go before God
     in judgment.
24   He breaks in pieces mighty men
     without inquiry,
     And sets others in their place.
25   Therefore He knows their works;
     He overthrows *them* in the
     night,
     And they are crushed.
26   He strikes them as wicked *men*
     In the open sight of others,
27   Because they turned back from
     Him,
     And would not consider any of
     His ways,
28   So that they caused the cry of
     the poor to come to Him;
     For He hears the cry of the
     afflicted.
29   When He gives quietness, who
     then can make trouble?
     And when He hides *His* face,
     who then can see Him,
     Whether *it is* against a nation or
     a man alone?—
30   That the hypocrite should not
     reign,
     Lest the people be ensnared.

31   "For has *anyone* said to God,
     'I have borne *chastening*;

I will offend no more;
32 Teach me *what* I do not *see*;
   If I have done iniquity, I will do
      no more'?
33 Should He repay *it* according to
      your *terms,*
   Just because you disavow it?
   You must choose, and not I;
   Therefore speak what you
      know.

34 "Men of understanding say to me,
   Wise men who listen to me:
35 'Job speaks without knowledge,
   His words *are* without wisdom.'
36 Oh, that Job *were* tried to the
      utmost,
   Because *his* answers *are like*
      those of wicked men!
37 For he adds rebellion to his sin;
   He claps *his hands* among us,
   And multiplies his words against
      God.''

Elihu thinks Job is speaking foolishly

35 Moreover Elihu answered and said:

2 "Do you think this is right?
   Do you say,
   'My righteousness is more than
      God's'?
3 For you say,
   'What advantage will it be to
      You?
   What profit shall I have, more
      than *if* I had sinned?'

4 "I will answer you,
   And your companions with you.
5 Look to the heavens and *see*;
   And behold the clouds—
   They are higher than you.
6 If you sin, what do you
      accomplish against Him?
   Or, *if* your transgressions are
      multiplied, what do you do to
      Him?
7 If you are righteous, what do
      you give Him?
   Or what does He receive from
      your hand?

8 Your wickedness affects a man
      such as you,
   And your righteousness a son of
      man.

9 "Because of the multitude of
      oppressions they cry out;
   They cry out for help because
      of the arm of the mighty.
10 But no one says, 'Where *is* God
      my Maker,
   Who gives songs in the night,
11 Who teaches us more than the
      beasts of the earth,
   And makes us wiser than the
      birds of heaven?'
12 There they cry out, but He does
      not answer,
   Because of the pride of evil
      men.
13 Surely God will not listen to
      empty *talk,*
   Nor will the Almighty regard it.
14 Although you say you do not *see*
      Him,
   Yet justice *is* before Him, and
      you must wait for Him.
15 And now, because He has not
      punished in His anger,
   Nor taken much notice of folly,
16 Therefore Job opens his mouth
      in vain;
   He multiplies words without
      knowledge.''

Elihu defends God's goodness

36 Elihu also proceeded and said:

2 "Bear with me a little, and I will
      show you
   That *there are* yet words to
      speak on God's behalf.
3 I will fetch my knowledge from
      afar;
   I will ascribe righteousness to my
      Maker.
4 For truly my words *are* not false;
   One who is perfect in knowledge
      is with you.

5 "Behold, God *is* mighty, but
      despises *no one;*

He is mighty in strength of understanding.

6 He does not preserve the life of the wicked,
But gives justice to the oppressed.

7 He does not withdraw His *eyes* from the righteous;
But *they are* on the throne with kings,
For He has seated them forever,
And they are exalted.

8 And if *they are* bound in fetters,
Held in the cords of affliction,

9 Then He tells them their work and their transgressions—
That they have acted defiantly.

10 He also opens their ear to instruction,
And commands that they turn from iniquity.

11 If they obey and serve *Him,*
They shall spend their days in prosperity,
And their years in pleasures.

12 But if they do not obey,
They shall perish by the sword,
And they shall die without knowledge.

13 "But the hypocrites in heart store up wrath;
They do not cry for help when He binds them.

14 They die in youth,
And their life *ends* among the perverted persons.

15 He delivers the poor in their affliction,
And opens their ears in oppression.

16 "Indeed He would have brought you out of dire distress,
Into a broad place where *there* is no restraint;
And what is set on your table *would be* full of richness.

17 But you are filled with the judgment due the wicked;
Judgment and justice take hold of you.

18 Because *there is* wrath, *beware* lest He take you away with *one* blow;

For a large ransom would not help you avoid *it.*

19 Will your riches,
Or all the mighty forces,
Keep you from distress?

20 Do not desire the night,
When people are cut off in their place.

21 Take heed, do not turn to iniquity,
For you have chosen this rather than affliction.

22 "Behold, God is exalted by His power;
Who teaches like Him?

23 Who has assigned Him His way,
Or who has said, 'You have done wrong'?

24 "Remember to magnify His work,
Of which men have sung.

25 Everyone has seen it;
Man looks on *it* from afar.

26 "Behold, God *is* great, and we do not know *Him;*
Nor can the number of His years *be* discovered.

27 For He draws up drops of water,
Which distill as rain from the mist,

28 Which the clouds drop down
And pour abundantly on man.

29 Indeed, can *anyone* understand the spreading of clouds,
The thunder from His canopy?

30 Look, He scatters His light upon it,
And covers the depths of the sea.

31 For by these He judges the peoples;
He gives food in abundance.

32 He covers *His* hands with lightning,
And commands it to strike.

33 His thunder declares it,
The cattle also, concerning the rising *storm.*

God does great things

37 "At this also my heart trembles,
And leaps from its place.

2 Hear attentively the thunder of
     His voice,
   And the rumbling *that* comes
     from His mouth.
3 He sends it forth under the
     whole heaven,
   His lightning to the ends of the
     earth.
4 After it a voice roars;
   He thunders with His majestic
     voice,
   And He does not restrain them
     when His voice is heard.
5 God thunders marvelously with
     His voice;
   He does great things which we
     cannot comprehend.
6 For He says to the snow, 'Fall
     on the earth';
   Likewise to the gentle rain and
     the heavy rain of His strength.
7 He seals the hand of every man,
   That all men may know His
     work.
8 The beasts go into dens,
   And remain in their lairs.
9 From the chamber *of the south*
     comes the whirlwind,
   And cold from the scattering
     winds *of the north.*
10 By the breath of God ice is
     given,
   And the broad waters are frozen.
11 Also with moisture He saturates
     the thick clouds;
   He scatters His bright clouds.
12 And they swirl about, being
     turned by His guidance,
   That they may do whatever He
     commands them
   On the face of the whole
     earth.
13 He causes it to come,
   Whether for correction,
   Or for His land,
   Or for mercy.

14 "Listen to this, O Job;
   Stand still and consider the
     wondrous works of God.
15 Do you know when God
     dispatches them,
   And causes the light of His cloud
     to shine?

16 Do you know how the clouds
     are balanced,
   Those wondrous works of
     Him who is perfect in
     knowledge?
17 Why *are* your garments hot,
   When He quiets the earth by the
     south *wind?*
18 With Him, have you spread out
     the skies,
   Strong as a cast metal mirror?

19 "Teach us what we should say to
     Him,
   For we can prepare nothing
     because of the darkness.
20 Should He be told that I *wish
     to* speak?
   If a man *were* to speak, surely
     he would be swallowed up.
21 Even now *men* cannot look at
     the light *when it is* bright in
     the skies,
   When the wind has passed and
     cleared them.
22 He comes from the north *as*
     golden *splendor;*
   With God *is* awesome majesty.
23 *As for* the Almighty, we cannot
     find Him;
   He is excellent in power,
   In judgment and abundant
     justice;
   He does not oppress.
24 Therefore men fear Him;
   He shows no partiality to any
     who are wise of heart."

God shows Job how little he knows

38 Then the LORD answered Job out
of the whirlwind, and said:

2 "Who *is* this who darkens counsel
     By words without knowledge?
3 Now prepare yourself like a
     man;
   I will question you, and you shall
     answer Me.

4 "Where were you when I laid the
     foundations of the earth?

Tell *Me,* if you have
understanding.

5 Who determined its
measurements?
Surely you know!
Or who stretched the line upon
it?

6 To what were its foundations
fastened?
Or who laid its cornerstone,

7 When the morning stars sang
together,
And all the sons of God shouted
for joy?

8 "Or *who* shut in the sea with
doors,
When it burst forth *and* issued
from the womb;

9 When I made the clouds its
garment,
And thick darkness its swaddling
band;

10 When I fixed My limit for it,
And set bars and doors;

11 When I said,
'This far you may come, but no
farther,
And here your proud waves
must stop!'

12 "Have you commanded the
morning since your days
began,
And caused the dawn to know
its place,

13 That it might take hold of the
ends of the earth,
And the wicked be shaken out
of it?

14 It takes on form like clay *under*
a seal,
And stands out like a garment.

15 From the wicked their light is
withheld,
And the upraised arm is broken.

16 "Have you entered the springs of
the sea?
Or have you walked in search
of the depths?

17 Have the gates of death been
revealed to you?

Or have you seen the doors of
the shadow of death?

18 Have you comprehended the
breadth of the earth?
Tell *Me,* if you know all this.

19 "Where *is* the way *to* the dwelling
of light?
And darkness, where *is* its place,

20 That you may take it to its
territory,
That you may know the paths
to its home?

21 Do you know *it,* because you
were born then,
Or *because* the number of your
days *is* great?

22 "Have you entered the treasury
of snow,
Or have you seen the treasury
of hail,

23 Which I have reserved for the
time of trouble,
For the day of battle and war?

24 By what way is light diffused,
Or the east wind scattered over
the earth?

25 "Who has divided a channel for
the overflowing *water,*
Or a path for the thunderbolt,

26 To cause it to rain on a land
where there is no one,
A wilderness in which *there is*
no man;

27 To satisfy the desolate waste,
And cause to spring forth the
growth of tender grass?

28 Has the rain a father?
Or who has begotten the drops
of dew?

29 From whose womb comes the
ice?
And the frost of heaven, who
gives it birth?

30 The waters harden like stone,
And the surface of the deep is
frozen.

31 "Can you bind the cluster of the
Pleiades,
Or loose the belt of Orion?

32 Can you bring out Mazzaroth in
    its season?
    Or can you guide the Great Bear
    with its cubs?
33 Do you know the ordinances of
    the heavens?
    Can you set their dominion over
    the earth?

34 "Can you lift up your voice to the
    clouds,
    That an abundance of water
    may cover you?
35 Can you send out lightnings,
    that they may go,
    And say to you, 'Here we are!'?
36 Who has put wisdom in the
    mind?
    Or who has given understanding
    to the heart?
37 Who can number the clouds by
    wisdom?
    Or who can pour out the bottles
    of heaven,
38 When the dust hardens in
    clumps,
    And the clods cling together?

39 "Can you hunt the prey for the
    lion,
    Or satisfy the appetite of the
    young lions,
40 When they crouch in *their* dens,
    Or lurk in their lairs to lie in wait?
41 Who provides food for the
    raven,
    When its young ones cry to God,
    And wander about for lack of
    food?

God continues to speak with Job

39 "Do you know the time when the
    wild mountain goats bear
    young?
    Or can you mark when the deer
    gives birth?
2 Can you number the months
    that they fulfill?
    Or do you know the time when
    they bear young?
3 They bow down,
    They bring forth their young,
    They deliver their offspring.
4 Their young ones are healthy,
    They grow strong with grain;
    They depart and do not return
    to them.

5 "Who set the wild donkey free?
    Who loosed the bonds of the
    onager,
6 Whose home I have made the
    wilderness,
    And the barren land his
    dwelling?
7 He scorns the tumult of the city;
    He does not heed the shouts of
    the driver.
8 The range of the mountains *is*
    his pasture,
    And he searches after *every*
    green thing.

9 "Will the wild ox be willing to
    serve you?
    Will he bed by your manger?
10 Can you bind the wild ox in the
    furrow with ropes?

DIGGING IN

38:1—41:34 Can You Answer God's Questions? When Job and his friends and the young man Elihu had finished talking, God Himself spoke up and answered everybody. He asked Job a long list of questions, like, "Where were you when I laid the foundations of the earth?" This is God's way of telling Job he isn't as smart as he thinks he is!

As you get older, you will begin to notice that the experts in science are always changing their minds. Human theories constantly contradict one another. The medicine for an illness this year will be thought bad for your health five years from now.

We're learning more and more that we know less and less about the world. What this adds up to is that people should trust God more than they trust people, even "experts." We need to keep studying the world around us, but we need even more to understand God's ways in His world.

Or will he plow the valleys
behind you?
11 Will you trust him because his
strength *is* great?
Or will you leave your labor to
him?
12 Will you trust him to bring home
your grain,
And gather it to your threshing
floor?

13 "The wings of the ostrich wave
proudly,
But are her wings and pinions
like the kindly stork's?
14 For she leaves her eggs on the
ground,
And warms them in the dust;
15 She forgets that a foot may crush
them,
Or that a wild beast may break
them.
16 She treats her young harshly, as
though *they were* not hers;
Her labor is in vain, without
concern,
17 Because God deprived her of
wisdom,
And did not endow her with
understanding.
18 When she lifts herself on high,
She scorns the horse and its
rider.

19 "Have you given the horse
strength?
Have you clothed his neck with
thunder?
20 Can you frighten him like a
locust?
His majestic snorting strikes
terror.
21 He paws in the valley, and
rejoices in *his* strength;
He gallops into the clash of
arms.
22 He mocks at fear, and is not
frightened;
Nor does he turn back from the
sword.
23 The quiver rattles against him,
The glittering spear and javelin.
24 He devours the distance with
fierceness and rage;

Nor does he come to a halt
because the trumpet *has*
sounded.
25 At *the blast of* the trumpet he
says, 'Aha!'
He smells the battle from afar,
The thunder of captains and
shouting.

26 "Does the hawk fly by your
wisdom,
And spread its wings toward the
south?
27 Does the eagle mount up at your
command,
And make its nest on high?
28 On the rock it dwells and resides,
On the crag of the rock and the
stronghold.
29 From there it spies out the prey;
Its eyes observe from afar.
30 Its young ones suck up blood;
And where the slain *are*, there
it *is*."

God speaks to Job from the whirlwind

40 Moreover the Lord answered
Job, and said:

2 "Shall the one who contends with
the Almighty correct *Him*?
He who rebukes God, let him
answer it."

3 Then Job answered the Lord and
said:

4 "Behold, I am vile;
What shall I answer You?
I lay my hand over my mouth.
5 Once I have spoken, but I will
not answer;

When Should You Be Quiet?

Job was a good man, but he sometimes talked too much. There's always the danger of saying something wrong when you talk too much. Job finally realized this when God appeared to him. God was much greater than Job's talk. So learn to be quiet in God's presence.

Yes, twice, but I will proceed no
further."

6 Then the LORD answered Job out
of the whirlwind, and said:

7 "Now prepare yourself like a
man;
I will question you, and you shall
answer Me:

8 "Would you indeed annul My
judgment?
Would you condemn Me that
you may be justified?
9 Have you an arm like God?
Or can you thunder with a voice
like His?
10 Then adorn yourself *with*
majesty and splendor,
And array yourself with glory
and beauty.

*The behemoth might have been a kind of
hippopotamus—a large water animal.*

11 Disperse the rage of your wrath;
Look on everyone *who is* proud,
and humble him.
12 Look on everyone *who is* proud,
and bring him low;
Tread down the wicked in their
place.
13 Hide them in the dust together,
Bind their faces in hidden
darkness.
14 Then I will also confess to
you
That your own right hand can
save you.

15 "Look now at the behemoth,
which I made *along* with you;
He eats grass like an ox.
16 See now, his strength *is* in his
hips,
And his power *is* in his stomach
muscles.
17 He moves his tail like a cedar;
The sinews of his thighs are
tightly knit.
18 His bones *are like* beams of
bronze,
His ribs like bars of iron.
19 He *is* the first of the ways of
God;
Only He who made him can
bring near His sword.

20 Surely the mountains yield food
for him,
And all the beasts of the field
play there.
21 He lies under the lotus trees,
In a covert of reeds and marsh.
22 The lotus trees cover him *with*
their shade;
The willows by the brook
surround him.
23 Indeed the river may rage,
Yet he is not disturbed;
He is confident, though the
Jordan gushes into his mouth,
24 *Though* he takes it in his eyes,
Or one pierces *his* nose with a
snare.

God asks Job if he can catch a crocodile

41 "Can you draw out Leviathan
with a hook,
Or *snare* his tongue with a line
which you lower?
2 Can you put a reed through his
nose,
Or pierce his jaw with a hook?
3 Will he make many supplications
to you?
Will he speak softly to you?

The leviathan was probably a form of crocodile—powerful and extremely dangerous!

4 Will he make a covenant with you?
Will you take him as a servant forever?

5 Will you play with him as *with* a bird,
Or will you leash him for your maidens?

6 Will *your* companions make a banquet of him?
Will they apportion him among the merchants?

7 Can you fill his skin with harpoons,
Or his head with fishing spears?

8 Lay your hand on him;
Remember the battle—
Never do it again!

9 Indeed, *any* hope of *overcoming* him is false;
Shall *one not* be overwhelmed at the sight of him?

10 No one *is so* fierce that he would dare stir him up.
Who then is able to stand against Me?

11 Who has preceded Me, that I should pay *him*?
Everything under heaven is Mine.

12 "I will not conceal his limbs,
His mighty power, or his graceful proportions.

13 Who can remove his outer coat?
Who can approach *him* with a double bridle?

14 Who can open the doors of his face,
With his terrible teeth all around?

15 *His* rows of scales are *his* pride,
Shut up tightly *as with* a seal;

16 One is so near another
That no air can come between them;

17 They are joined one to another,
They stick together and cannot be parted.

18 His sneezings flash forth light,
And his eyes *are* like the eyelids of the morning.

19 Out of his mouth go burning lights;
Sparks of fire shoot out.

20 Smoke goes out of his nostrils,
As *from* a boiling pot and burning rushes.

21 His breath kindles coals,
And a flame goes out of his mouth.

22 Strength dwells in his neck,
And sorrow dances before him.

23 The folds of his flesh are joined together;
They are firm on him and cannot be moved.

24 His heart is as hard as stone,
Even as hard as the lower *millstone.*

25 When he raises himself up, the mighty are afraid;
Because of his crashings they are beside themselves.

26 *Though* the sword reaches him, it cannot avail;
Nor does spear, dart, or javelin.

27 He regards iron as straw,
And bronze as rotten wood.

28 The arrow cannot make him flee;
Slingstones become like stubble to him.

29 Darts are regarded as straw;
He laughs at the threat of javelins.

What Job's Friends Learned

When we heard about Job's trouble, we traveled a long distance to visit him. We were not rich and famous like Job, and we realize now that we were jealous of him.

We came to watch the great man suffer. We were sure Job was just hiding what he was really like. So we asked him: "If you aren't an evil man, why are you suffering so much?" We were very smug in our opinion of Job.

Boy, were we wrong! The Lord was just making Job a better man, and we had only spoken a lot of nonsense. So we had to apologize to Job. Never be too sure of your opinions of others. God is the only true Judge.

30 His undersides *are* like sharp potsherds;
He spreads pointed *marks* in the mire.
31 He makes the deep boil like a pot;
He makes the sea like a pot of ointment.
32 He leaves a shining wake behind him;
One would think the deep had white hair.
33 On earth there is nothing like him,
Which is made without fear.
34 He beholds *every* high *thing;*
He *is* king over all the children of pride."

God blesses Job with more than before

42 Then Job answered the LORD and said:

2 "I know that You can do everything,
And that no purpose *of Yours* can be withheld from You.
3 *You asked,* 'Who *is* this who hides counsel without knowledge?'
Therefore I have uttered what I did not understand,
Things too wonderful for me, which I did not know.
4 Listen, please, and let me speak;
You said, 'I will question you, and you shall answer Me.'
5 "I have heard of You by the hearing of the ear,
But now my *eye sees* You.
6 Therefore I abhor *myself,*
And repent in dust and ashes."

7 And so it was, after the LORD had spoken these words to Job, that the LORD said to Eliphaz the Temanite,

DIGGING IN

42:1–17 God Cares When You Suffer Being brave when you're sick and in pain is hard. After a while, you can get downright angry with the whole thing. On the whole, Job was very patient. But sometimes the strain was too much, and he said things that were not true. See Job 16:11: "God has delivered me to the ungodly." In the end God had to correct Job (see Job 38—41). Then the Lord taught Job the real meaning of his suffering.

In times of suffering, we can grow closer to God. That is when we learn that we need God even more than we need health. The body becomes sick and dies. But we sing a hymn by George Robinson that says, "While God and I shall be, I am His and He is mine."

Job learned this lesson at last. Then God blessed Job with even more possessions than he had before.

Job's Family and Wealth Return

The Arabian Times

UZ—What has seemed like a long, dark night of suffering for a citizen of this town has become a morning of joy. "Weeping may endure for a night, but joy comes in the morning" (Psalm 30:5).

Job is now completely well. Not only that, but he has twice as many flocks and herds as before. Job also has been blessed with a whole new family. So we say, "Three cheers for Job, the man Satan couldn't destroy!"

Job's fault-finding friends have had to apologize for their foolish talk. It seems God was only proving to all of us that you can't keep a good man down when the Lord decides to make him stand!

Job is giving a garden party at his home on Saturday evening. The whole town is invited.

"My wrath is aroused against you and your two friends, for you have not spoken of Me *what is* right, as My servant Job *has.* 8 Now therefore, take for yourselves seven bulls and seven rams, go to My servant Job, and offer up for yourselves a burnt offering; and My servant Job shall pray for you. For I will accept him, lest I deal with you *according to your* folly; because you have not spoken of Me *what is* right, as My servant Job *has.*"

9 So Eliphaz the Temanite and Bildad the Shuhite *and* Zophar the Naamathite went and did as the LORD commanded them; for the LORD had accepted Job. 10 And the LORD restored Job's losses when he prayed for his friends. Indeed the LORD gave Job twice as much as he had before. 11 Then all his brothers, all his sisters, and all those who had been his acquaintances before, came to him and ate food with him in his house; and they consoled him and comforted him for all the adversity that the LORD had brought upon him. Each one gave him a piece of silver and each a ring of gold.

12 Now the LORD blessed the latter *days* of Job more than his beginning; for he had fourteen thousand sheep, six thousand camels, one thousand yoke of oxen, and one thousand female donkeys. 13 He also had seven sons and three daughters. 14 And he called the name of the first Jemimah, the name of the second Keziah, and the name of the third Keren-Happuch. 15 In all the land were found no women so beautiful as the daughters of Job; and their father gave them an inheritance among their brothers.

16 After this Job lived one hundred and forty years, and saw his children and grandchildren *for* four generations. 17 So Job died, old and full of days.

The Book of
PSALMS

The Singing People of God—Singing is one of our very favorite things to do when we love God. We may not always be where we can sing out loud, but God always puts a song in the hearts of His people. Did you know that about one-third of the Old Testament is poetry? A lot of the poems in the Bible have always been sung. We still sing the psalms.

In some of the psalms, the writer is singing his praise to God. Many psalms are prayers in which the singer pours out requests to God. Others tell of sorrow for sin. Still others are songs of thanks for God's gifts. We can always find a song that fits our need among the 150 psalms of the Bible.

Maybe you think you don't sing very well, but God listens to your heart to hear if you are singing to Him.

Book One: Psalms 1—41

PSALM 1

Two ways to live

BLESSED *is* the man
    Who walks not in the counsel
        of the ungodly,
      Nor stands in the path of
        sinners,
      Nor sits in the seat of the
        scornful;
2   But his delight *is* in the law of
      the LORD,
      And in His law he meditates
        day and night.
3   He shall be like a tree

Planted by the rivers of water,
    That brings forth its fruit in its
      season,
    Whose leaf also shall not
      wither;
    And whatever he does shall
      prosper.

Do You Enjoy God's Word?

Some people think the Bible is dull. Read the exciting Creation story and see how God made all things from nothing. Listen to the beautiful words of Jesus in the Sermon on the Mount. Look at the glorious descriptions of heaven in the Book of Revelation. God's Word is delightful.

 DIGGING IN

1:1 What Is the Book of Psalms? Psalms is the longest book in the Bible. There are 150 psalms. King David wrote 73 of them. The family of Asaph (pronounced *AY-saf*) wrote 12, the sons of Korah (pronounced *KO-rah*) wrote 11, Solomon wrote Psalms 72 and 127, Heman wrote Psalm 88, Ethan wrote Psalm 89, and Moses wrote Psalm 90. We don't know the authors of 50 of the psalms. Asaph, Korah, Heman, and Ethan provided music for temple worship in David's and Solomon's time.

The psalms were written to express deeply felt worship of God, and they were meant to be sung. Psalm 90 was written about 1400 B.C. by Moses. It is the oldest psalm. Psalm 137 is the newest psalm and was written during Israel's captivity in Babylon between the years 606 and 538 B.C.

The Psalms are divided into five smaller books: (1) Psalms 1—41; (2) Psalms 42—72; (3) Psalms 73—89; (4) Psalms 90—106; (5) Psalms 107—150.

4 The ungodly *are* not so,
But *are* like the chaff which the
     wind drives away.
5 Therefore the ungodly shall not
     stand in the judgment,
Nor sinners in the congregation
     of the righteous.
6 For the LORD knows the way of
     the righteous,
But the way of the ungodly shall
     perish.

PSALM 2

God is greater than earthly kings

WHY do the nations rage,
And the people plot a vain
     thing?
2 The kings of the earth set
     themselves,
And the rulers take counsel
     together,
Against the LORD and against His
     Anointed, *saying,*
3 "Let us break Their bonds in
     pieces
And cast away Their cords from
     us."

4 He who sits in the heavens shall
     laugh;
The LORD shall hold them in
     derision.
5 Then He shall speak to them in
     His wrath,
And distress them in His deep
     displeasure:
6 "Yet I have set My King
On My holy hill of Zion."

7 "I will declare the decree:
The LORD has said to Me,
'You *are* My Son,
Today I have begotten You.
8 Ask of Me, and I will give *You*
The nations *for* Your
     inheritance,
And the ends of the earth *for*
     Your possession.
9 You shall break them with a rod
     of iron;
You shall dash them to pieces
     like a potter's vessel.' "

10 Now therefore, be wise, O kings;
Be instructed, you judges of the
     earth.
11 Serve the LORD with fear,
And rejoice with trembling.
12 Kiss the Son, lest He be angry,
And you perish *in* the way,
When His wrath is kindled but
     a little.
Blessed *are* all those who put
     their trust in Him.

PSALM 3

We can pray when we are in trouble

A Psalm of David when he fled from Absalom his son.

LORD, how they have increased who
     trouble me!
Many *are* they who rise up
     against me.
2 Many *are* they who say of me,
"*There is* no help for him in
     God."   Selah

DIGGING IN

2:12 Put Your Trust in the Son of God In this wonderful psalm David tells about the coming Son of God. When David writes, "The Lord has said to Me, 'You are my Son' " (verse 7), He is referring to Jesus, who will be born a thousand years later.

Then David tells how God the Father promises to give the nations of the world to His great Son. Finally, David says we should put our trust in the Son of God.

Trusting Jesus means to depend on Him for everything. You stop counting on others or yourself to save you from all the bad effects of sin. To trust in Jesus means to start a whole new life with Him as your Friend and Savior. Whoever believes in Him shall not perish but have everlasting life (John 3:16). "Everlasting life" is the life that Jesus gives you right now as you trust Him with your whole being. That life will be spent with Him now and forever.

3 But You, O Lᴏʀᴅ, *are* a shield
    for me,
  My glory and the One who lifts
    up my head.
4 I cried to the Lᴏʀᴅ with my
    voice,
  And He heard me from His holy
    hill.   Selah

5 I lay down and slept;
  I awoke, for the Lᴏʀᴅ sustained
    me.
6 I will not be afraid of ten
    thousands of people
  Who have set *themselves*
    against me all around.

7 Arise, O Lᴏʀᴅ;
  Save me, O my God!
  For You have struck all my
    enemies on the cheekbone;
  You have broken the *teeth* of
    the ungodly.
8 Salvation *belongs* to the Lᴏʀᴅ.
  Your blessing *is* upon Your
    people.   Selah

PSALM 4

God takes care of us

To the Chief Musician. With stringed instruments. A
Psalm of David.

HEAR me when I call, O God of
    my righteousness!
  You have relieved me in *my*
    distress;
  Have mercy on me, and hear
    my prayer.

2 How long, O you sons of men,
  Will you turn my glory to shame?
  How long will you love
    worthlessness
  And seek falsehood?   Selah
3 But know that the Lᴏʀᴅ has set
    apart for Himself him who is
    godly;
  The Lᴏʀᴅ will hear when I call
    to Him.

4 Be angry, and do not sin.
  Meditate within your heart on
    your bed, and be still.   Selah
5 Offer the sacrifices of
    righteousness,
  And put your trust in the Lᴏʀᴅ.

6 *There are* many who say,
  "Who will show us *any* good?"
  Lᴏʀᴅ, lift up the light of Your
    countenance upon us.
7 You have put gladness in my
    heart,
  More than in the season that
    their grain and wine
    increased.
8 I will both lie down in peace, and
    sleep;
  For You alone, O Lᴏʀᴅ, make
    me dwell in safety.

PSALM 5

A morning prayer

To the Chief Musician. With flutes. A Psalm of David.

GIVE ear to my words, O Lᴏʀᴅ,
    Consider my meditation.

⛏ DIGGING IN

4:8 Going to Sleep in Jesus Some
people can't sleep because they worry.
When you have trusted Jesus, you stop
worrying. Then He gives you peace that
is beyond all understanding.

There are so many things in the world
that we can't understand. We don't know
what's going to happen tomorrow. Have
you ever heard the song, "Because He
lives, I can face tomorrow"? Yes, Jesus
is alive forever, and you can have His
peace. You may not know what the future

holds for you. *But you can know who
holds your future* in His hands—Jesus
does. And He never sleeps (see Psalm
121:4).

Learn to stop worrying by trusting Jesus
for all the things you can't understand.
Then you can sleep well.

Someday you will go to sleep for the
last time. But you needn't be afraid. Jesus
is with you even when you go through
the valley of death (Psalm 23:4).

2   Give heed to the voice of my
      cry,
    My King and my God,
    For to You I will pray.
3   My voice You shall hear in the
      morning, O LORD;
    In the morning I will direct it to
      You,
    And I will look up.

4   For You are not a God who
      takes pleasure in wickedness,
    Nor shall evil dwell with You.
5   The boastful shall not stand in
      Your sight;
    You hate all workers of iniquity.
6   You shall destroy those who
      speak falsehood;
    The LORD abhors the
      bloodthirsty and deceitful
      man.

7   But as for me, I will come into
      Your house in the multitude
      of Your mercy;
    In fear of You I will worship
      toward Your holy temple.
8   Lead me, O LORD, in Your
      righteousness because of my
      enemies;
    Make Your way straight before
      my face.

9   For there is no faithfulness in
      their mouth;
    Their inward part is destruction;
    Their throat is an open tomb;
    They flatter with their tongue.
10 Pronounce them guilty, O
      God!
    Let them fall by their own
      counsels;
    Cast them out in the multitude
      of their transgressions,
    For they have rebelled against
      You.

11 But let all those rejoice who put
      their trust in You;
    Let them ever shout for joy,
      because You defend them;
    Let those also who love Your
      name
    Be joyful in You.

12 For You, O LORD, will bless the
      righteous;
    With favor You will surround
      him as with a shield.

PSALM 6

God hears our prayers

To the Chief Musician. With stringed instruments.
On an eight-stringed harp. A Psalm of David.

O LORD, do not rebuke me in
      Your anger,
    Nor chasten me in Your hot
      displeasure.
2   Have mercy on me, O LORD, for
      I am weak;
    O LORD, heal me, for my bones
      are troubled.
3   My soul also is greatly troubled;
    But You, O LORD—how long?

4   Return, O LORD, deliver me!
    Oh, save me for Your mercies'
      sake!
5   For in death there is no
      remembrance of You;
    In the grave who will give You
      thanks?

6   I am weary with my groaning;
    All night I make my bed swim;
    I drench my couch with my
      tears.
7   My eye wastes away because of
      grief;
    It grows old because of all my
      enemies.

8   Depart from me, all you workers
      of iniquity;
    For the LORD has heard the
      voice of my weeping.
9   The LORD has heard my
      supplication;
    The LORD will receive my
      prayer.
10 Let all my enemies be ashamed
      and greatly troubled;
    Let them turn back and be
      ashamed suddenly.

PSALM 7

God is the perfect Judge

A Meditation of David, which he sang to the LORD
concerning the words of Cush, a Benjamite.

O LORD my God, in You I put
my trust;
Save me from all those who
persecute me;
And deliver me,

2 Lest they tear me like a lion,
Rending *me* in pieces, while
there is none to deliver.

3 O LORD my God, if I have done
this:
If there is iniquity in my hands,

4 If I have repaid evil to him who
was at peace with me,
Or have plundered my enemy
without cause,

5 Let the enemy pursue me and
overtake *me;*
Yes, let him trample my life to
the earth,
And lay my honor in the dust.
Selah

6 Arise, O LORD, in Your anger;
Lift Yourself up because of the
rage of my enemies;
Rise up for me *to* the judgment
You have commanded!

7 So the congregation of the
peoples shall surround You;
For their sakes, therefore, return
on high.

8 The LORD shall judge the
peoples;
Judge me, O LORD, according to
my righteousness,
And according to my integrity
within me.

9 Oh, let the wickedness of the
wicked come to an end,
But establish the just;
For the righteous God tests the
hearts and minds.

10 My defense *is* of God,
Who saves the upright in heart.

11 God *is* a just judge,
And God is angry *with the
wicked* every day.

12 If he does not turn back,
He will sharpen His sword;
He bends His bow and makes
it ready.

13 He also prepares for Himself
instruments of death;
He makes His arrows into fiery
shafts.

14 Behold, *the wicked* brings forth
iniquity;
Yes, he conceives trouble and
brings forth falsehood.

15 He made a pit and dug it out,
And has fallen into the ditch
which he made.

16 His trouble shall return upon his
own head,
And his violent dealing shall
come down on his own
crown.

17 I will praise the LORD according
to His righteousness,
And will sing praise to the name
of the LORD Most High.

PSALM 8

A song to God's glory

To the Chief Musician. On the instrument of Gath.
A Psalm of David.

O LORD, our Lord,
How excellent *is* Your name in
all the earth,
Who have set Your glory above
the heavens!

2 Out of the mouth of babes and
nursing infants
You have ordained strength,
Because of Your enemies,
That You may silence the enemy
and the avenger.

3 When I consider Your heavens,
the work of Your fingers,
The moon and the stars, which
You have ordained,

4 What is man that You are
mindful of him,
And the son of man that You
visit him?

5 For You have made him a little
   lower than the angels,
   And You have crowned him
   with glory and honor.

6 You have made him to have
   dominion over the works of
   Your hands;
   You have put all *things* under
   his *feet*,
7 All sheep and oxen—
   Even the beasts of the field,
8 The birds of the air,
   And the fish of the sea
   That pass through the paths of
   the seas.

9 O LORD, our Lord,
   How excellent *is* Your name in
   all the earth!

PSALM 9

God judges fairly

To the Chief Musician. To *the tune of* "Death of
the Son." A Psalm of David.

I WILL praise *You,* O LORD, with my
   whole heart;
   I will tell of all Your marvelous
   works.
2 I will be glad and rejoice in You;
   I will sing praise to Your name,
   O Most High.

3 When my enemies turn back,
   They shall fall and perish at Your
   presence.
4 For You have maintained my
   right and my cause;
   You sat on the throne judging
   in righteousness.
5 You have rebuked the nations,
   You have destroyed the wicked;
   You have blotted out their name
   forever and ever.

6 O enemy, destructions are
   finished forever!
   And you have destroyed cities;
   Even their memory has
   perished.
7 But the LORD shall endure
   forever;

He has prepared His throne for
   judgment.
8 He shall judge the world in
   righteousness,
   And He shall administer
   judgment for the peoples in
   uprightness.

9 The LORD also will be a refuge
   for the oppressed,
   A refuge in times of trouble.
10 And those who know Your
   name will put their trust in
   You;
   For You, LORD, have not
   forsaken those who seek You.

11 Sing praises to the LORD, who
   dwells in Zion!
   Declare His deeds among the
   people.
12 When He avenges blood, He
   remembers them;
   He does not forget the cry of the
   humble.

13 Have mercy on me, O LORD!
   Consider my trouble from those
   who hate me,
   You who lift me up from the
   gates of death,
14 That I may tell of all Your praise
   In the gates of the daughter of
   Zion.
   I will rejoice in Your salvation.

15 The nations have sunk down in
   the pit *which* they made;
   In the net which they hid, their
   own foot is caught.
16 The LORD is known *by the*
   judgment He executes;
   The wicked is snared in the work
   of his own hands.
              Meditation.   Selah

17 The wicked shall be turned into
   hell,
   And all the nations that forget
   God.
18 For the needy shall not always
   be forgotten;
   The expectation of the poor shall
   not perish forever.

19 Arise, O Lord,
   Do not let man prevail;
   Let the nations be judged in
      Your sight.
20 Put them in fear, O Lord,
   That the nations may know
      themselves *to be but* men.
                        Selah

PSALM 10

I sometimes wonder if the good guys will win

WHY do You stand afar off, O
   Lord?
   Why do You hide in times of
      trouble?
2 The wicked in *his* pride
      persecutes the poor;
   Let them be caught in the
      plots which they have
      devised.

3 For the wicked boasts of his
      heart's desire;
   He blesses the greedy *and*
      renounces the Lord.
4 The wicked in his proud
      countenance does not seek
      God;
   God *is* in none of his thoughts.

5 His ways are always prospering;
   Your judgments *are* far above,
      out of his sight;
   As for all his enemies, he sneers
      at them.
6 He has said in his heart, "I shall
      not be moved;
   I shall never be in adversity."

7 His mouth is full of cursing and
      deceit and oppression;
   Under his tongue *is* trouble and
      iniquity.

8 He sits in the lurking places of
      the villages;
   In the secret places he murders
      the innocent;
   His eyes are secretly fixed on the
      helpless.
9 He lies in wait secretly, as a lion
      in his den;
   He lies in wait to catch the poor;
   He catches the poor when he
      draws him into his net.
10 So he crouches, he lies low,
   That the helpless may fall by his
      strength.
11 He has said in his heart,
   "God has forgotten;
   He hides His face;
   He will never see."

12 Arise, O Lord!
   O God, lift up Your hand!
   Do not forget the humble.
13 Why do the wicked renounce
      God?
   He has said in his heart,
   "You will not require *an*
      account."

14 But You have seen, for You
      observe trouble and grief,
   To repay *it* by Your hand.
   The helpless commits himself to
      You;
   You are the helper of the
      fatherless.
15 Break the arm of the wicked and
      the evil *man;*

DIGGING IN

10:14 God Cares for Orphans Do you have a father and mother who love you and care for you? If so, you should be very thankful. God meant everybody to have a father and mother.

But in today's world, many young people have never known a father or a mother. Are you alone in the world? David, who wrote this psalm, wants you to know that God cares for orphans in spe-

cial ways. He hears them when they cry, and He helps them. David is telling you that you can call out to God wherever you are, and He will listen. He may not answer you right away, but He will visit you and make you know that He cares about you. He will fill all your needs.

As you grow up in the world, you will see more and more how God is guiding your steps in everything.

Seek out his wickedness *until*
    You find none.

16   The LORD *is* King forever and
        ever;
    The nations have perished out
        of His land.
17   LORD, You have heard the desire
        of the humble;
    You will prepare their heart;
    You will cause Your ear to hear,
18   To do justice to the fatherless
        and the oppressed,
    That the man of the earth may
        oppress no more.

PSALM 11

God sees everything

To the Chief Musician. A Psalm of David.

IN the LORD I put my trust;
    How can you say to my soul,
    "Flee *as* a bird to your
        mountain"?
2   For look! The wicked bend *their*
        bow,
    They make ready their arrow on
        the string,
    That they may shoot secretly at
        the upright in heart.
3   If the foundations are destroyed,
    What can the righteous do?

4   The LORD *is* in His holy temple,
    The LORD's throne *is* in heaven;
    His eyes behold,
    His eyelids test the sons of men.
5   The LORD tests the righteous,
    But the wicked and the one who
        loves violence His soul hates.
6   Upon the wicked He will rain
        coals;

Fire and brimstone and a
    burning wind
Shall be the portion of their cup.

7   For the LORD *is* righteous,
    He loves righteousness;
    His countenance beholds the
        upright.

PSALM 12

I trust God's promises

To the Chief Musician. On an eight-stringed harp.
A Psalm of David.

HELP, LORD, for the godly man
    ceases!
    For the faithful disappear from
        among the sons of men.
2   They speak idly everyone with
        his neighbor;
    With flattering lips *and* a double
        heart they speak.

3   May the LORD cut off all flattering
        lips,
    And the tongue that speaks
        proud things,
4   Who have said,
    "With our tongue we will prevail;
    Our lips *are* our own;
    Who *is* lord over us?"

5   "For the oppression of the poor,
        for the sighing of the needy,
    Now I will arise," says the LORD;
    "I will set *him* in the safety for
        which he yearns."

6   The words of the LORD *are* pure
        words,
    Like silver tried in a furnace of
        earth,

DIGGING IN

12:6, 7 God Keeps His Words Pure
When you write a letter to somebody, that letter will last for only a while. The person you wrote to may even keep your letter for a long time. But sooner or later, he throws your letter away. That's what happens to all human writing.

The Bible is God's letter to the world, and He has made sure that letter has never been lost. Some people think God couldn't keep His words pure for all these hundreds of years. But we know He has. We have many hundreds of copies of the Bible from ancient times. The message of the Bible has never changed. God created it for Himself. He loved you and died for you. He gives you everlasting life. So you owe your life to Him.

Jesus said, "My words will by no means pass away" (Matthew 24:35).

Purified seven times.
7 You shall keep them, O LORD,
You shall preserve them from
this generation forever.

8 The wicked prowl on every side,
When vileness is exalted among
the sons of men.

PSALM 13

I need God's help

To the Chief Musician. A Psalm of David.

HOW long, O LORD? Will You forget
me forever?
How long will You hide Your
face from me?
2 How long shall I take counsel in
my soul,
Having sorrow in my heart
daily?
How long will my enemy be
exalted over me?

3 Consider *and* hear me, O LORD
my God;
Enlighten my eyes,
Lest I sleep the *sleep of* death;
4 Lest my enemy say,
"I have prevailed against him";
Lest those who trouble me
rejoice when I am moved.

5 But I have trusted in Your
mercy;
My heart shall rejoice in Your
salvation.
6 I will sing to the LORD,
Because He has dealt bountifully
with me.

PSALM 14

Those who don't believe God are foolish

To the Chief Musician. A Psalm of David.

THE fool has said in his heart,
"*There is* no God."
They are corrupt,
They have done abominable
works,
There is none who does good.

2 The LORD looks down from
heaven upon the children of
men,
To see if there are any who
understand, who seek God.
3 They have all turned aside,
They have together become
corrupt;
There is none who does good,
No, not one.

4 Have all the workers of iniquity
no knowledge,
Who eat up my people *as* they
eat bread,
And do not call on the LORD?
5 There they are in great fear,
For God *is* with the generation
of the righteous.
6 You shame the counsel of the
poor,
But the LORD *is* his refuge.

7 Oh, that the salvation of Israel
would come out of Zion!
When the LORD brings back the
captivity of His people,
Let Jacob rejoice *and* Israel be
glad.

DIGGING IN

14:1 What A Fool Thinks Nobody wants to be a fool. A fool is somebody who makes his own life hard by thinking and doing things that hurt himself.

How does a fool start to be a fool? He begins by denying God. The Author of wisdom is God. But the fool often argues with God and says "I don't need you. I'm smart enough and strong enough to run my own life."

At first, the fool is proud and thinks he is getting along very well without God. Then one day he gets into trouble. He becomes very sick, and he is told he is going to die. Now he must face eternity without God. Since he never gave God a thought, he doesn't know how to pray. That fool is not a happy man at all. He is a very sad man because he left God out of his life. Start soon to make God your personal Friend. Then nothing can make you afraid.

PSALM 15

I want to be God's friend

A Psalm of David.

LORD, who may abide in Your
    tabernacle?
    Who may dwell in Your holy
        hill?

2 He who walks uprightly,
    And works righteousness,
    And speaks the truth in his
        heart;
3 He *who* does not backbite with
        his tongue,
    Nor does evil to his neighbor,
    Nor does he take up a
        reproach against his friend;
4 In whose eyes a vile person is
        despised,
    But he honors those who fear
        the LORD;
    He *who* swears to his own hurt
        and does not change;
5 He *who* does not put out his
        money at usury,
    Nor does he take a bribe
        against the innocent.

    He who does these *things* shall
        never be moved.

PSALM 16

I love to sing about God

A Michtam of David.

PRESERVE me, O God, for in You
    I put my trust.

2 *O my soul,* you have said to the
        LORD,
    "You *are* my Lord,
    My goodness is nothing apart
        from You."
3 As for the saints who *are* on the
        earth,
    "They are the excellent ones, in
        whom is all my delight."

4 Their sorrows shall be multiplied
        who hasten *after* another *god;*
    Their drink offerings of blood I
        will not offer,
    Nor take up their names on my
        lips.

5 O LORD, *You are* the portion of
        my inheritance and my cup;
    You maintain my lot.
6 The lines have fallen to me in
        pleasant *places;*
    Yes, I have a good inheritance.

7 I will bless the LORD who has
        given me counsel;
    My heart also instructs me in the
        night seasons.
8 I have set the LORD always
        before me;
    Because *He is* at my right hand
        I shall not be moved.

9 Therefore my heart is glad, and
        my glory rejoices;
    My flesh also will rest in hope.
10 For You will not leave my soul
        in Sheol,
    Nor will You allow Your Holy
        One to see corruption.

⚒ DIGGING IN

16:10, 11 David Sees the Savior We don't have to wait for the New Testament to find Jesus in the Bible. Jesus appears in different ways all through the Old Testament—long before He was born as a Baby at Bethlehem.

In Psalm 16 David sees Jesus as his Savior from death. Hundreds of years later, Jesus would rise from the grave and give His new life to David. Jesus also gives His new risen life to those of all time who believe in Him.

You can see that God's plan for conquering death was a very old plan. David knew about it, and even Job knew about it long before David lived. See where Job shouts the words, "I know that my Redeemer lives, and He shall stand at last on the earth!" (Job 19:25). Jesus can be your Savior because He overcame your great enemy—death.

2

11 You will show me the path of
     life;
    In Your presence *is* fullness of
     joy;
    At Your right hand *are* pleasures
     forevermore.

PSALM 17

We will see God face to face

A Prayer of David.

HEAR a just cause, O LORD,
    Attend to my cry;
    Give ear to my prayer *which is*
     not from deceitful lips.
2 Let my vindication come from
     Your presence;
    Let Your eyes look on the things
     that are upright.

3 You have tested my heart;
    You have visited *me* in the night;
    You have tried me and have
     found nothing;
    I have purposed that my mouth
     shall not transgress.
4 Concerning the works of men,
    By the word of Your lips,
    I have kept away from the paths
     of the destroyer.
5 Uphold my steps in Your paths,
    That my footsteps may not slip.

6 I have called upon You, for You
     will hear me, O God;
    Incline Your ear to me, *and* hear
     my speech.
7 Show Your marvelous
     lovingkindness by Your right
     hand,

O You who save those who trust
    in You
From those who rise up *against*
    them.
8 Keep me as the apple of Your
     eye;
    Hide me under the shadow of
     Your wings,
9 From the wicked who oppress
     me,
    From my deadly enemies who
     surround me.

10 They have closed up their fat
     hearts;
    With their mouths they speak
     proudly.
11 They have now surrounded us
     in our steps;
    They have set their eyes,
     crouching down to the earth,
12 As a lion is eager to tear his prey,
    And like a young lion lurking in
     secret places.

13 Arise, O LORD,
    Confront him, cast him down;
    Deliver my life from the wicked
     with Your sword,
14 With Your hand from men, O
     LORD,
    From men of the world *who
     have* their portion in *this* life,
    And whose belly You fill with
     Your hidden treasure.
    They are satisfied with children,
    And leave the rest of their
     possession for their babes.

15 As for me, I will see Your face
     in righteousness;
    I shall be satisfied when I awake
     in Your likeness.

⚒ DIGGING IN

17:15 When We Wake Up in Heaven
What is it like for a Christian to die? It's like going to sleep in the arms of Jesus. He has said to us, "I will never leave you," and He certainly will not leave us in the hour of death. Death is no longer the enemy of the Christian. We know that we will wake up and Jesus will be there. That will be heaven for us. Isn't it wonderful that David knew this, too? He said, "I will see Your face."

Some people are afraid to die because they don't know Jesus as their Savior. To be honest, we're all at least a little bit afraid of what we don't understand. God knows we don't understand all about dying. He just asks us to trust Him. If we have learned that Jesus never fails us in the other things of life, then we know we can also trust Him when we die.

PSALM 18

I love You, Lord

To the Chief Musician. A Psalm of David the servant of the LORD, who spoke to the LORD the words of this song on the day that the LORD delivered him from the hand of all his enemies and from the hand of Saul. And he said:

I WILL love You, O LORD, my
strength.
2 The LORD is my rock and my
fortress and my deliverer;
My God, my strength, in whom
I will trust;
My shield and the horn of my
salvation, my stronghold.
3 I will call upon the LORD, *who
is worthy* to be praised;
So shall I be saved from my
enemies.

4 The pangs of death surrounded
me,
And the floods of ungodliness
made me afraid.
5 The sorrows of Sheol
surrounded me;
The snares of death confronted
me.
6 In my distress I called upon the
LORD,
And cried out to my God;
He heard my voice from His
temple,
And my cry came before Him,
even to His ears.

7 Then the earth shook and
trembled;
The foundations of the hills also
quaked and were shaken,
Because He was angry.
8 Smoke went up from His
nostrils,
And devouring fire from His
mouth;
Coals *were* kindled by it.
9 He bowed the heavens also, and
came down
With darkness under His feet.
10 And He rode upon a cherub,
and flew;
He flew upon the wings of the
wind.

11 He made darkness His secret
place;
His canopy around Him *was*
dark waters
And thick clouds of the skies.
12 From the brightness before Him,
His thick clouds passed with
hailstones and coals of fire.
13 The LORD thundered from
heaven,
And the Most High uttered His
voice,
Hailstones and coals of fire.
14 He sent out His arrows and
scattered the foe,
Lightnings in abundance, and
He vanquished them.
15 Then the channels of the sea
were seen,
The foundations of the world
were uncovered
At Your rebuke, O LORD,
At the blast of the breath of Your
nostrils.

16 He sent from above, He took
me;
He drew me out of many waters.
17 He delivered me from my strong
enemy,
From those who hated me,
For they were too strong for me.
18 They confronted me in the day
of my calamity,
But the LORD was my support.
19 He also brought me out into a
broad place;
He delivered me because He
delighted in me.

20 The LORD rewarded me
according to my
righteousness;
According to the cleanness of
my hands
He has recompensed me.
21 For I have kept the ways of the
LORD,
And have not wickedly departed
from my God.
22 For all His judgments *were*
before me,
And I did not put away His
statutes from me.

23 I was also blameless before Him,
   And I kept myself from my
      iniquity.
24 Therefore the Lord has
      recompensed me according to
      my righteousness,
   According to the cleanness of
      my hands in His sight.

25 With the merciful You will show
      Yourself merciful;
   With a blameless man You will
      show Yourself blameless;
26 With the pure You will show
      Yourself pure;
   And with the devious You will
      show Yourself shrewd.
27 For You will save the humble
      people,
   But will bring down haughty
      looks.

28 For You will light my lamp;
   The Lord my God will enlighten
      my darkness.
29 For by You I can run against a
      troop,
   By my God I can leap over a
      wall.
30 As for God, His way is perfect;
   The word of the Lord is proven;
   He is a shield to all who trust in
      Him.

31 For who is God, except the
      Lord?
   And who is a rock, except our
      God?
32 It is God who arms me with
      strength,
   And makes my way perfect.
33 He makes my feet like the feet
      of deer,
   And sets me on my high places.
34 He teaches my hands to make
      war,
   So that my arms can bend a bow
      of bronze.

35 You have also given me the
      shield of Your salvation;
   Your right hand has held me up,
   Your gentleness has made me
      great.

36 You enlarged my path under
      me,
   So my feet did not slip.

37 I have pursued my enemies and
      overtaken them;
   Neither did I turn back again till
      they were destroyed.
38 I have wounded them,
   So that they could not rise;
   They have fallen under my feet.
39 For You have armed me with
      strength for the battle;
   You have subdued under me
      those who rose up against
      me.
40 You have also given me the
      necks of my enemies,
   So that I destroyed those who
      hated me.
41 They cried out, but there was
      none to save;
   Even to the Lord, but He did
      not answer them.
42 Then I beat them as fine as the
      dust before the wind;
   I cast them out like dirt in the
      streets.

43 You have delivered me from the
      strivings of the people;
   You have made me the head of
      the nations;
   A people I have not known shall
      serve me.
44 As soon as they hear of me they
      obey me;
   The foreigners submit to me.
45 The foreigners fade away,
   And come frightened from their
      hideouts.

46 The Lord lives!
   Blessed be my Rock!
   Let the God of my salvation be
      exalted.
47 It is God who avenges me,
   And subdues the peoples under
      me;
48 He delivers me from my
      enemies.
   You also lift me up above those
      who rise against me;

You have delivered me from the
violent man.
49 Therefore I will give thanks to
You, O LORD, among the
Gentiles,
And sing praises to Your name.

50 Great deliverance He gives to
His king,
And shows mercy to His
anointed,
To David and his descendants
forevermore.

PSALM 19

We see God in nature and in His Word

To the Chief Musician. A Psalm of David.

THE heavens declare the glory of
God;
And the firmament shows His
handiwork.
2 Day unto day utters speech,
And night unto night reveals
knowledge.

🪓 DIGGING IN

19:7–11 God's Word Is Your Best Guide Many people come to you and say they have the best advice for your life. On television you can see many ads for all kinds of gadgets and diets and even religious beliefs that are supposed to make your life better. Many of these television ads are false, and they deceive unthinking people. They don't really work, so they leave you disappointed.

God's Word never disappoints you. As you think about the words of Psalm 19,

you become stronger and wiser: "More to be desired are they than gold" (verse 10).

Start early to memorize God's Word. Psalm 19:17 is a good place to start. Then, wherever you are, you can always bring up God's words in your mind. Those words will fill you with strength as you face the battles of life. "Your word I have hidden in my heart, that I might not sin against You" (Psalm 119:11).

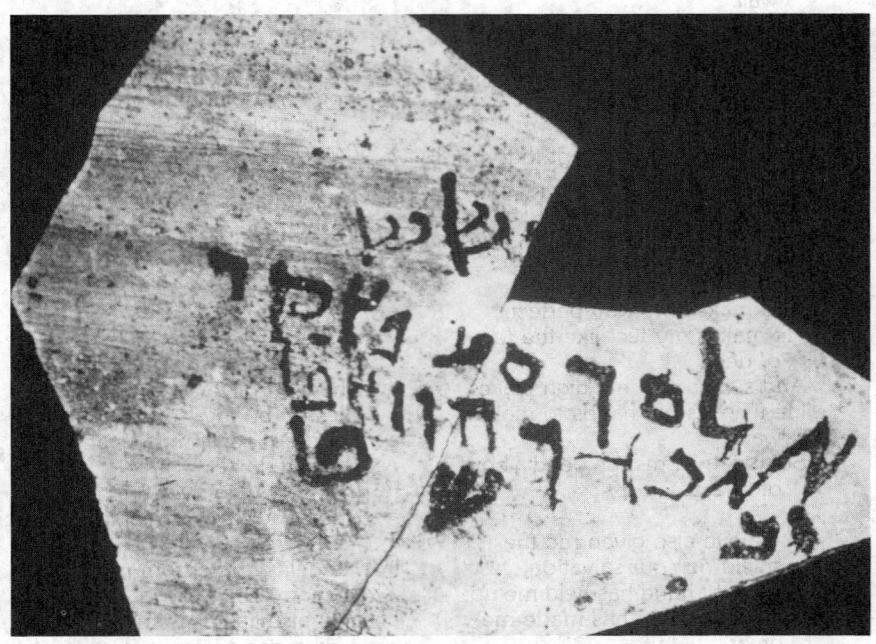

This Hebrew writing was the language in which God gave us most of the Old Testament.

3 There is no speech nor language
  Where their voice is not heard.
4 Their line has gone out through
  all the earth,
  And their words to the end of
  the world.

  In them He has set a tabernacle
  for the sun,
5 Which is like a bridegroom
  coming out of his chamber,
  And rejoices like a strong man
  to run its race.
6 Its rising is from one end of
  heaven,
  And its circuit to the other end;
  And there is nothing hidden
  from its heat.

7 The law of the LORD is perfect,
  converting the soul;
  The testimony of the LORD is
  sure, making wise the simple;
8 The statutes of the LORD are
  right, rejoicing the heart;
  The commandment of the LORD
  is pure, enlightening the eyes;
9 The fear of the LORD is clean,
  enduring forever;
  The judgments of the LORD are
  true and righteous altogether.
10 More to be desired are they than
  gold,
  Yea, than much fine gold;
  Sweeter also than honey and the
  honeycomb.
11 Moreover by them Your servant
  is warned,
  And in keeping them there is
  great reward.

12 Who can understand his errors?
  Cleanse me from secret faults.
13 Keep back Your servant also
  from presumptuous sins;
  Let them not have dominion
  over me.
  Then I shall be blameless,
  And I shall be innocent of great
  transgression.

14 Let the words of my mouth and
  the meditation of my heart
  Be acceptable in Your sight,
  O LORD, my strength and my
  Redeemer.

PSALM 20

God is always with us

To the Chief Musician. A Psalm of David.

MAY the LORD answer you in the
day of trouble;
May the name of the God of
Jacob defend you;
2 May He send you help from the
sanctuary,
And strengthen you out of Zion;
3 May He remember all your
offerings,
And accept your burnt sacrifice.
                              Selah

4 May He grant you according to
your heart's desire,
And fulfill all your purpose.
5 We will rejoice in your salvation,
And in the name of our God we
will set up our banners!

DIGGING IN

20:7 God Is Greater Than Anything He Made In 1990 some scientists sent a giant telescope into space. It cost billions of dollars. Some people joked that the telescope might even see God out there. The fact is the telescope couldn't see much of anything at all! We still hope it will be able to see many wonderful things in space, but it can never see God.

First, God is invisible. Second, God is far greater than anything He made. He is certainly greater than anything man can make—even greater than a giant telescope.

You see the world around you, and you can measure the size of everything in it—everything is so many pounds, so many feet long, and so many feet wide.

But God can't be measured. God is infinite. That means God is far greater than we can ever imagine. He has no beginning or ending, either in size or in time. We're limited and finite, but God is unlimited and eternal.

May the LORD fulfill all your
    petitions.

6   Now I know that the LORD saves
     His anointed;
     He will answer him from His
      holy heaven
     With the saving strength of His
      right hand.

7   Some *trust* in chariots, and some
     in horses;
     But *we* will remember the name
      of the LORD our God.
8   They have bowed down and
     fallen;
     But *we* have risen and stand
      upright.

9   Save, LORD!
     May the King answer us when
      we call.

PSALM 21

We thank God for His answers

To the Chief Musician. A Psalm of David.

THE king shall have joy in Your
     strength, O LORD;
     And in Your salvation how
      greatly shall he rejoice!
2   You have given him his heart's
     desire,
     And have not withheld the
      request of his lips.   Selah

3   For You meet him with the
     blessings of goodness;
     You set a crown of pure gold
      upon his head.
4   He asked life from You, *and* You
     gave *it* to him—
     Length of days forever and ever.
5   His glory *is* great in Your
     salvation;
     Honor and majesty You have
      placed upon him.
6   For You have made him most
     blessed forever;
     You have made him exceedingly
      glad with Your presence.
7   For the king trusts in the LORD,

And through the mercy of the
     Most High he shall not be
     moved.
8   Your hand will find all Your
     enemies;
     Your right hand will find those
      who hate You.
9   You shall make them as a fiery
     oven in the time of Your
     anger;
     The LORD shall swallow them up
      in His wrath,
     And the fire shall devour them.
10   Their offspring You shall destroy
     from the earth,
     And their descendants from
      among the sons of men.
11   For they intended evil against
     You;
     They devised a plot *which* they
      are not able *to perform.*
12   Therefore You will make them
     turn their back;
     You will make ready *Your*
      arrows on Your string toward
      their faces.

13   Be exalted, O LORD, in Your
     own strength!
     We will sing and praise Your
      power.

PSALM 22

Does God still love me?

To the Chief Musician. Set to "The Deer of the
Dawn." A Psalm of David.

MY God, My God, why have You
     forsaken Me?
     Why are You so far from helping
      Me,
     And from the words of My
      groaning?
2   O My God, I cry in the daytime,
     but You do not hear;
     And in the night season, and am
      not silent.

3   But You *are* holy,
     Enthroned in the praises of
      Israel.
4   Our fathers trusted in You;

They trusted, and You delivered them.
5 They cried to You, and were delivered;
They trusted in You, and were not ashamed.

6 But I *am* a worm, and no man;
A reproach of men, and despised by the people.
7 All those who *see* Me ridicule Me;
They shoot out the lip, they shake the head, *saying,*
8 "He trusted in the LORD, let Him rescue Him;
Let Him deliver Him, since He delights in Him!"

9 But You *are* He who took Me out of the womb;
You made Me trust *while* on My mother's breasts.
10 I was cast upon You from birth.
From My mother's womb You *have been* My God.
11 Be not far from Me,
For trouble *is* near;
For *there is* none to help.

12 Many bulls have surrounded Me;
Strong *bulls* of Bashan have encircled Me.
13 They gape at Me *with* their mouths,
Like a raging and roaring lion.

14 I am poured out like water,
And all My bones are out of joint;

My heart is like wax;
It has melted within Me.
15 My strength is dried up like a potsherd,
And My tongue clings to My jaws;
You have brought Me to the dust of death.

16 For dogs have surrounded Me;
The congregation of the wicked has enclosed Me.
They pierced My hands and My feet;
17 I can count all My bones.
They look *and* stare at Me.
18 They divide My garments among them,
And for My clothing they cast lots.

19 But You, O LORD, do not be far from Me;
O My Strength, hasten to help Me!
20 Deliver Me from the sword,
My precious *life* from the power of the dog.
21 Save Me from the lion's mouth
And from the horns of the wild oxen!

You have answered Me.

22 I will declare Your name to My brethren;
In the midst of the assembly I will praise You.
23 You who fear the LORD, praise Him!

DIGGING IN

22:1 David Sees the Suffering of Jesus The first words of Psalm 22 are the words Jesus cried out on the Cross hundreds of years after David wrote them. See Jesus' words in Matthew 27:46: "My God, My God, why have You forsaken Me?"

David goes on to describe all the pains of Jesus in Psalm 22:16, 18: "They pierced My hands and My feet . . . . They divide My garments among them, and for

My clothing they cast lots." David writes just as if he was right there when they crucified the Lord.

The New Testament tells us that the soldiers who crucified Jesus "cast lots" (threw dice) to see who would get his clothes. So you can see that even the smallest details of Jesus' death on the Cross were told long before the event happened.

All you descendants of Jacob,
   glorify Him,
And fear Him, all you offspring
   of Israel!
24 For He has not despised nor
   abhorred the affliction of the
   afflicted;
Nor has He hidden His face from
   Him;
But when He cried to Him, He
   heard.

25 My praise *shall be* of You in the
   great assembly;
I will pay My vows before those
   who fear Him.
26 The poor shall eat and be
   satisfied;
Those who seek Him will praise
   the Lord.
Let your heart live forever!

27 All the ends of the world
Shall remember and turn to the
   Lord,
And all the families of the
   nations
Shall worship before You.
28 For the kingdom *is* the Lord's,
And He rules over the nations.

29 All the prosperous of the earth
Shall eat and worship;
All those who go down to the
   dust
Shall bow before Him,
Even he who cannot keep
   himself alive.

30 A posterity shall serve Him.
It will be recounted of the Lord
   to the *next* generation,
31 They will come and declare His
   righteousness to a people who
   will be born,
That He has done *this.*

PSALM 23

The Good Shepherd

A Psalm of David.

THE Lord *is* my shepherd;
   I shall not want.

Who Is Your Shepherd?

You don't think of yourself as a sheep,
but in a way God does. When David
was a shepherd boy, he saw God as
his Shepherd. Jesus said, "I am the
good Shepherd." Shepherds knew all
their sheep by name in the times of
David and Jesus. God knows your
name, too.

2 He makes me to lie down in
   green pastures;
He leads me beside the still
   waters.
3 He restores my soul;
He leads me in the paths of
   righteousness
For His name's sake.

4 Yea, though I walk through the
   valley of the shadow of death,
I will fear no evil;
For You *are* with me;
Your rod and Your staff, they
   comfort me.

5 You prepare a table before me
   in the presence of my
   enemies;
You anoint my head with oil;
My cup runs over.

"The Lord is my Shepherd."

6 Surely goodness and mercy shall
     follow me
   All the days of my life;
   And I will dwell in the house of
     the LORD
   Forever.

PSALM 24

God owns the whole world

A Psalm of David.

THE earth is the LORD's, and all its
   fullness,
   The world and those who dwell
     therein.
2 For He has founded it upon the
     seas,
   And established it upon the
     waters.

3 Who may ascend into the hill of
     the LORD?
   Or who may stand in His holy
     place?
4 He who has clean hands and a
     pure heart,
   Who has not lifted up his soul
     to an idol,
   Nor sworn deceitfully.
5 He shall receive blessing from
     the LORD,
   And righteousness from the God
     of his salvation.
6 This is Jacob, the generation of
     those who seek Him,
   Who seek Your face.   Selah

7 Lift up your heads, O you gates!
   And be lifted up, you everlasting
     doors!
   And the King of glory shall come
     in.
8 Who is this King of glory?
   The LORD strong and mighty,
   The LORD mighty in battle.
9 Lift up your heads, O you gates!
   Lift up, you everlasting doors!
   And the King of glory shall come
     in.
10 Who is this King of glory?
   The LORD of hosts,
   He is the King of glory.   Selah

PSALM 25

ABCs for trouble

A Psalm of David.

TO You, O LORD, I lift up my
     soul.
2 O my God, I trust in You;
   Let me not be ashamed;
   Let not my enemies triumph
     over me.
3 Indeed, let no one who waits on
     You be ashamed;
   Let those be ashamed who deal
     treacherously without cause.

4 Show me Your ways, O LORD;
   Teach me Your paths.
5 Lead me in Your truth and teach
     me,
   For You are the God of my
     salvation;
   On You I wait all the day.

6 Remember, O LORD, Your
     tender mercies and Your
     lovingkindnesses,
   For they are from of old.
7 Do not remember the sins of my
     youth, nor my transgressions;
   According to Your mercy
     remember me,
   For Your goodness' sake, O
     LORD.

8 Good and upright is the LORD;
   Therefore He teaches sinners in
     the way.
9 The humble He guides in justice,
   And the humble He teaches His
     way.
10 All the paths of the LORD are
     mercy and truth,
   To such as keep His covenant
     and His testimonies.
11 For Your name's sake, O LORD,
   Pardon my iniquity, for it is
     great.

12 Who is the man that fears the
     LORD?
   Him shall He teach in the way
     He chooses.

13 He himself shall dwell in
   prosperity,
   And his descendants shall inherit
   the earth.
14 The secret of the LORD *is* with
   those who fear Him,
   And He will show them His
   covenant.
15 My eyes *are* ever toward the
   LORD,
   For He shall pluck my feet out
   of the net.

16 Turn Yourself to me, and have
   mercy on me,
   For I *am* desolate and afflicted.
17 The troubles of my heart have
   enlarged;
   Bring me out of my distresses!
18 Look on my affliction and my
   pain,
   And forgive all my sins.
19 Consider my enemies, for they
   are many;
   And they hate me with cruel
   hatred.
20 Keep my soul, and deliver me;
   Let me not be ashamed, for I
   put my trust in You.
21 Let integrity and uprightness
   preserve me,
   For I wait for You.

22 Redeem Israel, O God,
   Out of all their troubles!

PSALM 26

I want God to test my motives

A Psalm of David.

VINDICATE me, O LORD,
   For I have walked in my
   integrity.
   I have also trusted in the LORD;
   I shall not slip.
2 Examine me, O LORD, and
   prove me;
   Try my mind and my heart.
3 For Your lovingkindness *is*
   before my eyes,
   And I have walked in Your truth.
4 I have not sat with idolatrous
   mortals,
   Nor will I go in with hypocrites.

5 I have hated the assembly of
   evildoers,
   And will not sit with the wicked.
6 I will wash my hands in
   innocence;
   So I will go about Your altar, O
   LORD,
7 That I may proclaim with the
   voice of thanksgiving,
   And tell of all Your wondrous
   works.
8 LORD, I have loved the
   habitation of Your house,
   And the place where Your glory
   dwells.

9 Do not gather my soul with
   sinners,
   Nor my life with bloodthirsty
   men,
10 In whose hands *is* a sinister
   scheme,
   And whose right hand is full of
   bribes.

11 But as for me, I will walk in my
   integrity;
   Redeem me and be merciful to
   me.
12 My foot stands in an even place;
   In the congregations I will bless
   the LORD.

PSALM 27

I'm not afraid when God is near

A Psalm of David.

THE LORD *is* my light and my
   salvation;
   Whom shall I fear?
   The LORD *is* the strength of my
   life;
   Of whom shall I be afraid?
2 When the wicked came against
   me
   To eat up my flesh,
   My enemies and foes,
   They stumbled and fell.
3 Though an army may encamp
   against me,
   My heart shall not fear;

Though war may rise against
  me,
In this I *will be* confident.

4 One *thing* I have desired of the
    LORD,
  That will I seek:
  That I may dwell in the house
    of the LORD
  All the days of my life,
  To behold the beauty of the
    LORD,
  And to inquire in His temple.
5 For in the time of trouble
  He shall hide me in His pavilion;
  In the secret place of His
    tabernacle
  He shall hide me;
  He shall *set* me high upon a
    rock.

6 And now my head shall be lifted
    up above my enemies all
    around me;
  Therefore I will offer sacrifices of
    joy in His tabernacle;
  I will sing, yes, I will sing praises
    to the LORD.

7 Hear, O LORD, *when* I cry with
    my voice!
  Have mercy also upon me, and
    answer me.
8 *When You said,* "Seek My
    face,"
  My heart said to You, "Your
    face, LORD, I will seek."
9 Do not hide Your face from me;
  Do not turn Your servant away
    in anger;
  You have been my help;

Do not leave me nor forsake me,
  O God of my salvation.
10 When my father and my mother
    forsake me,
  Then the LORD will take care of
    me.

11 Teach me Your way, O LORD,
  And lead me in a smooth path,
    because of my enemies.
12 Do not deliver me to the will of
    my adversaries;
  For false witnesses have risen
    against me,
  And such as breathe out
    violence.
13 *I would have lost heart,* unless I
    had believed
  That I would see the goodness
    of the LORD
  In the land of the living.

14 Wait on the LORD;
  Be of good courage,
  And He shall strengthen your
    heart;
  Wait, I say, on the LORD!

PSALM 28

God hears those who love Him

A Psalm of David.

T O You I will cry, O LORD my Rock:
    Do not be silent to me,
  Lest, if You *are* silent to me,
  I become like those who go
    down to the pit.
2 Hear the voice of my
    supplications
  When I cry to You,

DIGGING IN

27:1 God Makes Us Unafraid Fear
can be a friend as well as an enemy. We
ought to be afraid to drive a hundred miles
an hour on the highway, and we ought
to fear going near a rattlesnake. But many
of our fears aren't necessary.

Some people are afraid of being in a
room alone. Others are afraid of the darkness. Many people are afraid of unseen
enemies. Most people are afraid to die.

God never planned that we should live
in fear of the world around us. He also
doesn't want us to be afraid of dying. The
Bible says, "The wages of sin is death"
(Romans 6:23). But that text goes on to
say, "The gift of God is eternal life in
Christ Jesus our Lord." If we have eternal
life with Jesus, we don't need to be afraid
anymore. "The Lord is the strength of my
life; of whom shall I be afraid?"

When I lift up my hands toward
Your holy sanctuary.

3 Do not take me away with the
wicked
And with the workers of iniquity,
Who speak peace to their
neighbors,
But evil *is* in their hearts.
4 Give them according to their
deeds,
And according to the wickedness
of their endeavors;
Give them according to the work
of their hands;
Render to them what they
deserve.
5 Because they do not regard the
works of the LORD,
Nor the operation of His hands,
He shall destroy them
And not build them up.

6 Blessed *be* the LORD,
Because He has heard the voice
of my supplications!
7 The LORD *is* my strength and my
shield;
My heart trusted in Him, and I
am helped;
Therefore my heart greatly
rejoices,
And with my song I will praise
Him.

8 The LORD *is* their strength,
And He *is* the saving refuge of
His anointed.
9 Save Your people,
And bless Your inheritance;
Shepherd them also,
And bear them up forever.

PSALM 29

I hear God's voice in the thunder

A Psalm of David.

GIVE unto the LORD, O you mighty
ones,
Give unto the LORD glory and
strength.
2 Give unto the LORD the glory
due to His name;

Worship the LORD in the beauty
of holiness.

3 The voice of the LORD *is* over
the waters;
The God of glory thunders;
The LORD *is* over many waters.
4 The voice of the LORD *is*
powerful;
The voice of the LORD *is* full of
majesty.

5 The voice of the LORD breaks the
cedars,
Yes, the LORD splinters the
cedars of Lebanon.
6 He makes them also skip like a
calf,
Lebanon and Sirion like a young
wild ox.
7 The voice of the LORD divides
the flames of fire.

8 The voice of the LORD shakes
the wilderness;
The LORD shakes the Wilderness
of Kadesh.
9 The voice of the LORD makes the
deer give birth,
And strips the forests bare;
And in His temple everyone
says, "Glory!"

10 The LORD sat *enthroned* at the
Flood,
And the LORD sits as King
forever.
11 The LORD will give strength to
His people;
The LORD will bless His people
with peace.

PSALM 30

I thank God for my health

A Psalm. A Song at the dedication of the house of
David.

I WILL extol You, O LORD, for You
have lifted me up,
And have not let my foes rejoice
over me.
2 O LORD my God, I cried out to
You,

And You healed me.
3 O Lord, You brought my soul
    up from the grave;
You have kept me alive, that I
    should not go down to the
    pit.

4 Sing praise to the Lord, you
    saints of His,
And give thanks at the
    remembrance of His holy
    name.
5 For His anger *is but for* a
    moment,
His favor *is for* life;
Weeping may endure for a
    night,
But joy *comes* in the morning.

6 Now in my prosperity I said,
    "I shall never be moved."
7 Lord, by Your favor You have
    made my mountain stand
    strong;
You hid Your face, *and* I was
    troubled.

8 I cried out to You, O Lord;
And to the Lord I made
    supplication:

9 "What profit *is there* in my blood,
When I go down to the pit?
Will the dust praise You?
Will it declare Your truth?
10 Hear, O Lord, and have mercy
    on me;
Lord, be my helper!"

11 You have turned for me my
    mourning into dancing;
You have put off my sackcloth
    and clothed me with gladness,
12 To the end that *my* glory may
    sing praise to You and not be
    silent.
O Lord my God, I will give
    thanks to You forever.

PSALM 31

I trust in You, O Lord

To the Chief Musician. A Psalm of David.

IN You, O Lord, I put my trust;
    Let me never be ashamed;
    Deliver me in Your
        righteousness.
2 Bow down Your ear to me,
    Deliver me speedily;

DIGGING IN

30:5 God Gives Joy After Sorrow We are all sad sometimes, and it isn't always wrong to be sad. Sometimes we're sad because we've made someone we love unhappy.

God is unhappy when we break His commandments. He gave us His laws to make us glad. When we break them, we also hurt ourselves. The Bible says you reap what you sow. Everything you do has a good or bad effect on you and on others around you.

You should be sad when you break God's laws by the way you talk, or by the way you act, or by the way you think. But God wants to be your Friend. He forgives you when you realize how much you have hurt Him by your sins. Then He gives you back your joy.

Whatever causes you to be sad today, God wants you to be glad tomorrow.

31:2 God Is Like the Rock of Gibraltar You've seen pictures of the great Rock of Gibraltar jutting out into the Mediterranean Sea, just at the tip of southern Spain. This great rock used to be an important sea fort to stop enemy ships from entering and leaving the Mediterranean Sea. Only friendly ships were allowed to pass through the narrow strait between Gibraltar and North Africa.

A modern insurance company uses the picture of the Rock of Gibraltar as its symbol. The company wants its customers to know their money is just as safe as if protected by that great rock.

In his psalm David asks God to be his Rock and his Fortress. God is like a fortress. He makes us feel safe in a world that gets more and more violent. Jesus is our Rock of Ages. He protects us from harm. We can rest safely in His care.

Be my rock of refuge,
A fortress of defense to save
me.

3 For You *are* my rock and my
fortress;
Therefore, for Your name's
sake,
Lead me and guide me.
4 Pull me out of the net which
they have secretly laid for
me,
For You *are* my strength.
5 Into Your hand I commit my
spirit;
You have redeemed me, O
LORD God of truth.

6 I have hated those who regard
useless idols;
But I trust in the LORD.
7 I will be glad and rejoice in Your
mercy,
For You have considered my
trouble;
You have known my soul in
adversities,
8 And have not shut me up into
the hand of the enemy;
You have set my feet in a wide
place.

9 Have mercy on me, O LORD, for
I am in trouble;
My eye wastes away with grief,
Yes, my soul and my body!
10 For my life is spent with grief,
And my years with sighing;
My strength fails because of my
iniquity,
And my bones waste away.
11 I am a reproach among all my
enemies,
But especially among my
neighbors,
And *am* repulsive to my
acquaintances;
Those who *see* me outside flee
from me.
12 I am forgotten like a dead man,
out of mind;
I am like a broken vessel.
13 For I hear the slander of many;
Fear *is* on every side;

While they take counsel together
against me,
They scheme to take away my
life.

14 But as for me, I trust in You, O
LORD;
I say, "You *are* my God."
15 My times *are* in Your hand;
Deliver me from the hand of my
enemies,
And from those who persecute
me.
16 Make Your face shine upon
Your servant;
Save me for Your mercies'
sake.
17 Do not let me be ashamed, O
LORD, for I have called upon
You;
Let the wicked be ashamed;
Let them be silent in the
grave.
18 Let the lying lips be put to
silence,
Which speak insolent things
proudly and contemptuously
against the righteous.

19 Oh, how great *is* Your goodness,
Which You have laid up for
those who fear You,
Which You have prepared for
those who trust in You
In the presence of the sons of
men!
20 You shall hide them in the secret
place of Your presence
From the plots of man;
You shall keep them secretly in
a pavilion
From the strife of tongues.

21 Blessed *be* the LORD,
For He has shown me His
marvelous kindness in a
strong city!
22 For I said in my haste,
"I am cut off from before Your
eyes";
Nevertheless You heard the
voice of my supplications
When I cried out to You.

23 Oh, love the LORD, all you His
   saints!
   For the LORD preserves the
      faithful,
   And fully repays the proud
      person.
24 Be of good courage,
   And He shall strengthen your
      heart,
   All you who hope in the LORD.

PSALM 32

God's forgiveness makes me happy

A Psalm of David. A Contemplation.

BLESSED *is he whose* transgression
   is forgiven,
   Whose sin *is* covered.
2 Blessed *is* the man to whom the
   LORD does not impute
      iniquity,
   And in whose spirit *there is* no
      deceit.

3 When I kept silent, my bones
      grew old
   Through my groaning all the day
      long.
4 For day and night Your hand
      was heavy upon me;
   My vitality was turned into the
      drought of summer.   Selah
5 I acknowledged my sin to You,
   And my iniquity I have not
      hidden.
   I said, "I will confess my
      transgressions to the LORD,"
   And You forgave the iniquity of
      my sin.   Selah

6 For this cause everyone who is
      godly shall pray to You
   In a time when You may be
      found;
   Surely in a flood of great waters
   They shall not come near him.

7 You *are* my hiding place;
   You shall preserve me from
      trouble;
   You shall surround me with
      songs of deliverance.   Selah

8 I will instruct you and teach you
      in the way you should go;
   I will guide you with My *eye*.
9 Do not be like the horse *or* like
      the mule,
   Which have no understanding,
   Which must be harnessed with
      bit and bridle,
   Else they will not come near
      you.

10 Many sorrows *shall be* to the
      wicked;
   But he who trusts in the LORD,
      mercy shall surround him.
11 Be glad in the LORD and rejoice,
      you righteous;
   And shout for joy, all *you* upright
      in heart!

PSALM 33

God is in charge

REJOICE in the LORD, O you
   righteous!
   For praise from the upright is
      beautiful.
2 Praise the LORD with the harp;
   Make melody to Him with an
      instrument of ten strings.
3 Sing to Him a new song;
   Play skillfully with a shout of joy.

4 For the word of the LORD *is* right,
   And all His work *is done* in truth.
5 He loves righteousness and
      justice;
   The earth is full of the goodness
      of the LORD.

WORDFINDER

31:23 Saints People who are set apart by God. The word comes from a Hebrew word meaning "holy" or "godly."

6   By the word of the LORD the
        heavens were made,
      And all the host of them by the
        breath of His mouth.
7   He gathers the waters of the sea
        together as a heap;
      He lays up the deep in
        storehouses.

8   Let all the earth fear the LORD;
      Let all the inhabitants of the
        world stand in awe of Him.
9   For He spoke, and it was *done;*
      He commanded, and it stood
        fast.

10   The LORD brings the counsel of
        the nations to nothing;
      He makes the plans of the
        peoples of no effect.
11   The counsel of the LORD stands
        forever,
      The plans of His heart to all
        generations.
12   Blessed *is* the nation whose God
        is the LORD,
      The people He has chosen as
        His own inheritance.

13   The LORD looks from heaven;
      He sees all the sons of men.
14   From the place of His dwelling
        He looks
      On all the inhabitants of the
        earth;
15   He fashions their hearts
        individually;
      He considers all their works.

16   No king *is* saved by the
        multitude of an army;

A mighty man is not delivered
  by great strength.
17   A horse *is* a vain hope for safety;
      Neither shall it deliver *any* by its
        great strength.

18   Behold, the eye of the LORD *is*
        on those who fear Him,
      On those who hope in His
        mercy,
19   To deliver their soul from death,
      And to keep them alive in
        famine.

20   Our soul waits for the LORD;
      He *is* our help and our shield.
21   For our heart shall rejoice in
        Him,
      Because we have trusted in His
        holy name.
22   Let Your mercy, O LORD, be
        upon us,
      Just as we hope in You.

PSALM 34

God cares about our troubles

A Psalm of David when he pretended madness
before Abimelech, who drove him away, and he
departed.

I WILL bless the LORD at all times;
      His praise *shall* continually *be* in
        my mouth.
2   My soul shall make its boast in
        the LORD;
      The humble shall hear *of it* and
        be glad.
3   Oh, magnify the LORD with me,
      And let us exalt His name
        together.

⚒ DIGGING IN

33:6 Praise God for His Wonderful Word Some people don't know who God is, so they can't praise Him. You feel like praising God when you know Him and know how much He has done for you.

God says He supports all things "by the word of His power" (Hebrews 1:3). It's hard to imagine anyone making something happen just by speaking. But did you know there are machines today that work when someone speaks to them? So

it isn't strange that God "spoke, and it was done" (verse 9).

God's words are not just noises or sounds. God's words make things happen. The Bible says we are "born again . . . through the word of God which lives and abides forever" (1 Peter 1:23). God's everlasting Word is the power by which He saves you from sin and makes you a new person. Then you can praise Him.

4   I sought the LORD, and He heard
    me,
    And delivered me from all my
    fears.
5   They looked to Him and were
    radiant,
    And their faces were not
    ashamed.
6   This poor man cried out, and the
    LORD heard *him*,
    And saved him out of all his
    troubles.
7   The angel of the LORD encamps
    all around those who fear
    Him,
    And delivers them.

8   Oh, taste and see that the LORD
    is good;
    Blessed *is* the man *who* trusts
    in Him!
9   Oh, fear the LORD, you His
    saints!
    There is no want to those who
    fear Him.
10 The young lions lack and suffer
    hunger;
    But those who seek the LORD
    shall not lack any good *thing*.

11 Come, you children, listen to
    me;
    I will teach you the fear of the
    LORD.
12 Who *is* the man *who* desires life,
    And loves *many* days, that he
    may see good?
13 Keep your tongue from evil,
    And your lips from speaking
    deceit.
14 Depart from evil and do good;
    Seek peace and pursue it.

15 The *eyes* of the LORD *are* on the
    righteous,
    And His ears *are open* to their
    cry.
16 The face of the LORD *is* against
    those who do evil,
    To cut off the remembrance of
    them from the earth.

17 *The righteous* cry out, and the
    LORD hears,
    And delivers them out of all their
    troubles.
18 The LORD *is* near to those who
    have a broken heart,
    And saves such as have a
    contrite spirit.

19 Many *are* the afflictions of the
    righteous,
    But the LORD delivers him out
    of them all.
20 He guards all his bones;
    Not one of them is broken.
21 Evil shall slay the wicked,
    And those who hate the
    righteous shall be
    condemned.
22 The LORD redeems the soul of
    His servants,
    And none of those who trust in
    Him shall be condemned.

PSALM 35

God loves to help His children

A Psalm of David.

PLEAD *my cause*, O LORD, with
    those who strive with me;
    Fight against those who fight
    against me.
2   Take hold of shield and buckler,
    And stand up for my help.
3   Also draw out the spear,
    And stop those who pursue me.
    Say to my soul,
    "I *am* your salvation."

4   Let those be put to shame and
    brought to dishonor
    Who seek after my life;
    Let those be turned back and
    brought to confusion
    Who plot my hurt.
5   Let them be like chaff before the
    wind,
    And let the angel of the LORD
    chase *them*.
6   Let their way be dark and
    slippery,
    And let the angel of the LORD
    pursue them.
7   For without cause they have

hidden their net for me *in* a pit,
Which they have dug without cause for my life.
8 Let destruction come upon him unexpectedly,
And let his net that he has hidden catch himself;
Into that very destruction let him fall.

9 And my soul shall be joyful in the LORD;
It shall rejoice in His salvation.
10 All my bones shall say,
"LORD, who *is* like You,
Delivering the poor from him who is too strong for him,
Yes, the poor and the needy from him who plunders him?"

11 Fierce witnesses rise up;
They ask me *things* that I do not know.
12 They reward me evil for good,
To the sorrow of my soul.
13 But as for me, when they were sick,
My clothing *was* sackcloth;
I humbled myself with fasting;
And my prayer would return to my own heart.
14 I paced about as though *he were* my friend *or* brother;
I bowed down heavily, as one who mourns *for his* mother.

15 But in my adversity they rejoiced
And gathered together;
Attackers gathered against me,
And I did not know *it;*
They tore *at me* and did not cease;
16 With ungodly mockers at feasts
They gnashed at me with their teeth.

17 Lord, how long will You look on?
Rescue me from their destructions,
My precious *life* from the lions.
18 I will give You thanks in the great assembly;

I will praise You among many people.

19 Let them not rejoice over me who are wrongfully my enemies;
Nor let them wink with the eye who hate me without a cause.
20 For they do not speak peace,
But they devise deceitful matters
Against *the* quiet ones in the land.
21 They also opened their mouth wide against me,
And said, "Aha, aha!
Our eyes have seen *it.*"

22 *This* You have seen, O LORD;
Do not keep silence.
O Lord, do not be far from me.
23 Stir up Yourself, and awake to my vindication,
To my cause, my God and my Lord.
24 Vindicate me, O LORD my God, according to Your righteousness;
And let them not rejoice over me.
25 Let them not say in their hearts, "Ah, so we would have it!"
Let them not say, "We have swallowed him up."

26 Let them be ashamed and brought to mutual confusion
Who rejoice at my hurt;
Let them be clothed with shame and dishonor
Who exalt themselves against me.

27 Let them shout for joy and be glad,
Who favor my righteous cause;
And let them say continually,
"Let the LORD be magnified,
Who has pleasure in the prosperity of His servant."
28 And my tongue shall speak of Your righteousness
And of Your praise all the day long.

PSALM 36

Look what happens to evildoers

To the Chief Musician. A Psalm of David the servant of the LORD.

AN oracle within my heart
　　concerning the transgression
　　of the wicked:
　There is no fear of God before
　　his eyes.
2　For he flatters himself in his own
　　eyes,
　When he finds out his iniquity
　　and when he hates.
3　The words of his mouth *are*
　　wickedness and deceit;
　He has ceased to be wise *and*
　　to do good.
4　He devises wickedness on his
　　bed;
　He sets himself in a way *that is*
　　not good;
　He does not abhor evil.

5　Your mercy, O LORD, *is* in the
　　heavens;
　Your faithfulness *reaches* to the
　　clouds.
6　Your righteousness *is* like the
　　great mountains;
　Your judgments *are* a great
　　deep;
　O LORD, You preserve man and
　　beast.

7　How precious *is* Your
　　lovingkindness, O God!
　Therefore the children of men
　　put their trust under the
　　shadow of Your wings.

8　They are abundantly satisfied
　　with the fullness of Your
　　house,
　And You give them drink from
　　the river of Your pleasures.
9　For with You *is* the fountain of
　　life;
　In Your light we see light.

10　Oh, continue Your
　　lovingkindness to those who
　　know You,
　And Your righteousness to the
　　upright in heart.
11　Let not the foot of pride come
　　against me,
　And let not the hand of the
　　wicked drive me away.
12　There the workers of iniquity
　　have fallen;
　They have been cast down and
　　are not able to rise.

PSALM 37

God helps me do good

A Psalm of David.

DO not fret because of evildoers,
　　Nor be envious of the workers
　　of iniquity.
2　For they shall soon be cut down
　　like the grass,
　And wither as the green herb.

3　Trust in the LORD, and do good;
　Dwell in the land, and feed on
　　His faithfulness.
4　Delight yourself also in the LORD,

DIGGING IN

36:9 God Is the Author of Life Life didn't begin when you were born. Life didn't even begin when God created the heavens and the earth. God had life in Himself forever and ever, before He made anything.

The life you have is a gift from God. When you know God is the Author of your life, then you are more careful about yourself. You should ask yourself questions like, "What does God want me to do with my life?" And, "How should I think about other people?" God gave them life, too.

But God is not only the Author of human life; He is also the Author of all life. God has placed us in charge of the world around us so that all life can be better. Are you a good caretaker of God's world?

God is also the Author of *eternal life.* We receive the gift of eternal life from Jesus who said, "I have come that they may have life" (John 10:10).

And He shall give you the
desires of your heart.

5 Commit your way to the LORD,
Trust also in Him,
And He shall bring *it* to pass.
6 He shall bring forth your
righteousness as the light,
And your justice as the noonday.

7 Rest in the LORD, and wait
patiently for Him;
Do not fret because of him who
prospers in his way,
Because of the man who brings
wicked schemes to pass.
8 Cease from anger, and forsake
wrath;
Do not fret—*it* only *causes*
harm.

9 For evildoers shall be cut off;
But those who wait on the LORD,
They shall inherit the earth.
10 For yet a little while and the
wicked *shall be* no *more;*
Indeed, you will look carefully
for his place,
But it *shall be* no *more.*
11 But the meek shall inherit the
earth,
And shall delight themselves in
the abundance of peace.

12 The wicked plots against the just,
And gnashes at him with his
teeth.
13 The Lord laughs at him,
For He sees that his day is
coming.

14 The wicked have drawn the
sword
And have bent their bow,
To cast down the poor and
needy,
To slay those who are of upright
conduct.
15 Their sword shall enter their own
heart,
And their bows shall be broken.

16 A little that a righteous man has
Is better than the riches of many
wicked.
17 For the arms of the wicked shall
be broken,
But the LORD upholds the
righteous.

18 The LORD knows the days of the
upright,
And their inheritance shall be
forever.
19 They shall not be ashamed in
the evil time,
And in the days of famine they
shall be satisfied.
20 But the wicked shall perish;
And the enemies of the LORD,
Like the splendor of the
meadows, shall vanish.
Into smoke they shall vanish
away.

21 The wicked borrows and does
not repay,
But the righteous shows mercy
and gives.
22 For *those* blessed by Him shall
inherit the earth,

DIGGING IN

37:7 Don't Worry, Wait for God Too often, the first thing we do when trouble comes is to worry. That really makes no sense because worry never helped anybody in trouble. In fact, worry can even make you sick. Then you're in worse trouble than before.

What can we do about our troubles? David says, "Wait patiently" for the Lord. That does make sense. After all, God already knows all about our problem, and He knows how to solve it.

We often want to get out of our troubles right away. But sometimes God doesn't work as fast as we'd like. God has His own time for doing everything, including answering our prayers.

Waiting is good training. Waiting gives us time to think calmly and pray. Often, after we calm down and pray, God comes quickly and solves our whole problem in a better way than we thought. God wants us to learn He is worth waiting for.

But *those* cursed by Him shall
    be cut off.

23 The steps of a *good* man are
    ordered by the LORD,
    And He delights in his way.
24 Though he fall, he shall not be
    utterly cast down;
    For the LORD upholds *him with*
    His hand.

25 I have been young, and *now* am
    old;
    Yet I have not seen the righteous
    forsaken,
    Nor his descendants begging
    bread.
26 *He is* ever merciful, and lends;
    And his descendants *are*
    blessed.

27 Depart from evil, and do good;
    And dwell forevermore.
28 For the LORD loves justice,
    And does not forsake His
    saints;
    They are preserved forever,
    But the descendants of the
    wicked shall be cut off.
29 The righteous shall inherit the
    land,
    And dwell in it forever.

30 The mouth of the righteous
    speaks wisdom,
    And his tongue talks of justice.
31 The law of his God *is* in his
    heart;
    None of his steps shall slide.

32 The wicked watches the
    righteous,
    And seeks to slay him.
33 The LORD will not leave him in
    his hand,
    Nor condemn him when he is
    judged.

34 Wait on the LORD,
    And keep His way,
    And He shall exalt you to inherit
    the land;
    When the wicked are cut off,
    you shall *see it.*

35 I have seen the wicked in great
    power,
    And spreading himself like a
    native green *tree.*
36 Yet he passed away, and
    behold, he *was* no *more;*
    Indeed I sought him, but he
    could not be found.

37 Mark the blameless *man,* and
    observe the upright;
    For the future of *that* man *is*
    peace.
38 But the transgressors shall be
    destroyed together;
    The future of the wicked shall
    be cut off.

39 But the salvation of the righteous
    is from the LORD;
    He is their strength in the time
    of trouble.
40 And the LORD shall help them
    and deliver them;
    He shall deliver them from the
    wicked,
    And save them,
    Because they trust in Him.

PSALM 38

I'm sorry for my sins

A Psalm of David. To bring to remembrance.

O LORD, do not rebuke me in
    Your wrath,
    Nor chasten me in Your hot
    displeasure!
2 For Your arrows pierce me
    deeply,
    And Your hand presses me
    down.

3 *There is* no soundness in my
    flesh
    Because of Your anger,
    Nor *any* health in my bones
    Because of my sin.
4 For my iniquities have gone over
    my head;
    Like a heavy burden they are
    too heavy for me.

5 My wounds are foul *and*
     festering
Because of my foolishness.

6 I am troubled, I am bowed down
     greatly;
I go mourning all the day long.
7 For my loins are full of
     inflammation,
And *there is* no soundness in my
     flesh.
8 I am feeble and severely broken;
I groan because of the turmoil
     of my heart.

9 Lord, all my desire *is* before
     You;
And my sighing is not hidden
     from You.
10 My heart pants, my strength fails
     me;
As for the light of my eyes, it
     also has gone from me.

11 My loved ones and my friends
     stand aloof from my plague,
And my relatives stand afar off.
12 Those also who seek my life lay
     snares *for me;*
Those who seek my hurt speak
     of destruction,
And plan deception all the day
     long.

13 But I, like a deaf *man,* do not
     hear;
And *I am* like a mute *who* does
     not open his mouth.
14 Thus I am like a man who does
     not hear,
And in whose mouth *is* no
     response.

15 For in You, O LORD, I hope;
You will hear, O Lord my
     God.
16 For I said, *"Hear me,* lest they
     rejoice over me,
Lest, when my foot slips, they
     exalt *themselves* against me."

17 For I *am* ready to fall,
And my sorrow *is* continually
     before me.

18 For I will declare my iniquity;
I will be in anguish over my sin.
19 But my enemies *are* vigorous,
     and they are strong;
And those who hate me
     wrongfully have multiplied.
20 Those also who render evil for
     good,
They are my adversaries,
     because I follow *what is* good.

21 Do not forsake me, O LORD;
O my God, be not far from me!
22 Make haste to help me,
O Lord, my salvation!

PSALM 39

God teaches me about life

To the Chief Musician. To Jeduthun. A Psalm of
David.

I SAID, "I will guard my ways,
     Lest I sin with my tongue;
I will restrain my mouth with a
     muzzle,
While the wicked are before
     me."
2 I was mute with silence,
I held my peace *even* from
     good;
And my sorrow was stirred up.
3 My heart was hot within me;
While I was musing, the fire
     burned.
Then I spoke with my tongue:

4 "LORD, make me to know my
     end,
And what *is* the measure of my
     days,
That I may know how frail I *am.*

How Long Is Your Life?

Most of us feel that we're going to live
a long time, but when we reach the
end of our lives, we will wonder where
all the time went. It will seem no time
at all. Be careful to spend your days
well. Now is the time to build things
for God that will last forever.

5 Indeed, You have made my
     days *as* handbreadths,
  And my age *is* as nothing before
     You;
  Certainly every man at his best
     state *is* but vapor.   Selah
6 Surely every man walks about
     like a shadow;
  Surely they busy themselves in
     vain;
  He heaps up *riches*,
  And does not know who will
     gather them.

7 "And now, Lord, what do I wait
     for?
  My hope *is* in You.
8 Deliver me from all my
     transgressions;
  Do not make me the reproach
     of the foolish.
9 I was mute, I did not open my
     mouth,
  Because it was You who did *it*.
10 Remove Your plague from me;
  I am consumed by the blow of
     Your hand.
11 When with rebukes You correct
     man for iniquity,
  You make his beauty melt away
     like a moth;
  Surely every man *is* vapor.
                            Selah

12 "Hear my prayer, O LORD,
  And give ear to my cry;
  Do not be silent at my tears;
  For I *am* a stranger with You,
  A sojourner, as all my fathers
     were.
13 Remove Your gaze from me,
     that I may regain strength,
  Before I go away and am no
     more."

PSALM 40

God never forgets us

To the Chief Musician. A Psalm of David.

I WAITED patiently for the LORD;
  And He inclined to me,
  And heard my cry.

2 He also brought me up out of
     a horrible pit,
  Out of the miry clay,
  And set my feet upon a rock,
  And established my steps.
3 He has put a new song in my
     mouth—
  Praise to our God;
  Many will see *it* and fear,
  And will trust in the LORD.

4 Blessed *is* that man who makes
     the LORD his trust,
  And does not respect the proud,
     nor such as turn aside to lies.
5 Many, O LORD my God, *are*
     Your wonderful works
  Which You have done;
  And Your thoughts toward us
  Cannot be recounted to You in
     order;
  If I would declare and speak *of
     them*,
  They are more than can be
     numbered.

6 Sacrifice and offering You did
     not desire;
  My ears You have opened.
  Burnt offering and sin offering
     You did not require.
7 Then I said, "Behold, I come;
  In the scroll of the book *it is*
     written of me.
8 I delight to do Your will, O my
     God,
  And Your law *is* within my
     heart.''

9 I have proclaimed the good
     news of righteousness
  In the great assembly;
  Indeed, I do not restrain my lips,
  O LORD, You Yourself know.
10 I have not hidden Your
     righteousness within my heart;
  I have declared Your faithfulness
     and Your salvation;
  I have not concealed Your
     lovingkindness and Your truth
  From the great assembly.

11 Do not withhold Your tender
     mercies from me, O LORD;

Let Your lovingkindness and
   Your truth continually
   preserve me.
12 For innumerable evils have
   surrounded me;
My iniquities have overtaken
   me, so that I am not able to
   look up;
They are more than the hairs of
   my head;
Therefore my heart fails me.

13 Be pleased, O LORD, to deliver
   me;
O LORD, make haste to help me!
14 Let them be ashamed and
   brought to mutual confusion
Who seek to destroy my life;
Let them be driven backward
   and brought to dishonor
Who wish me evil.
15 Let them be confounded
   because of their shame,
Who say to me, "Aha, aha!"

16 Let all those who seek You
   rejoice and be glad in You;
Let such as love Your salvation
   say continually,
"The LORD be magnified!"
17 But I *am* poor and needy;
Yet the LORD thinks upon me.
You *are* my help and my
   deliverer;
Do not delay, O my God.

PSALM 41

God is my best Friend

To the Chief Musician. A Psalm of David.

BLESSED *is* he who considers the
   poor;
   The LORD will deliver him in time
   of trouble.
2 The LORD will preserve him and
   keep him alive,
And he will be blessed on the
   earth;
You will not deliver him to the
   will of his enemies.
3 The LORD will strengthen him on
   his bed of illness;
You will sustain him on his
   sickbed.

4 I said, "LORD, be merciful to me;
Heal my soul, for I have sinned
   against You."
5 My enemies speak evil of me:
"When will he die, and his name
   perish?"
6 And if he comes to see *me,* he
   speaks lies;
His heart gathers iniquity to
   itself;
When he goes out, he tells *it.*

7 All who hate me whisper
   together against me;
Against me they devise my hurt.
8 "An evil disease," *they say,*
   "clings to him.
And *now* that he lies down, he
   will rise up no more."
9 Even my own familiar friend in
   whom I trusted,
Who ate my bread,
Has lifted up *his* heel against me.

10 But You, O LORD, be merciful
   to me, and raise me up,
That I may repay them.
11 By this I know that You are well
   pleased with me,
Because my enemy does not
   triumph over me.
12 As for me, You uphold me in
   my integrity,
And set me before Your face
   forever.

13 Blessed *be* the LORD God of
   Israel
From everlasting to everlasting!
Amen and Amen.

Book Two: Psalms 42—72

PSALM 42

I don't know why I'm sad

To the Chief Musician. A Contemplation of the sons
of Korah.

AS the deer pants for the water
   brooks,
   So pants my soul for You, O
   God.

2 My soul thirsts for God, for the living God.
When shall I come and appear before God?
3 My tears have been my food day and night,
While they continually say to me,
"Where *is* your God?"

4 When I remember these *things,*
I pour out my soul within me.
For I used to go with the multitude;
I went with them to the house of God,
With the voice of joy and praise,
With a multitude that kept a pilgrim feast.

5 Why are you cast down, O my soul?
And *why* are you disquieted within me?
Hope in God, for I shall yet praise Him
For the help of His countenance.

6 O my God, my soul is cast down within me;
Therefore I will remember You from the land of the Jordan,
And from the heights of Hermon,
From the Hill Mizar.
7 Deep calls unto deep at the noise of Your waterfalls;
All Your waves and billows have gone over me.
8 The LORD will command His lovingkindness in the daytime,

And in the night His song *shall be* with me—
A prayer to the God of my life.

9 I will say to God my Rock,
"Why have You forgotten me?
Why do I go mourning because of the oppression of the enemy?"
10 As with a breaking of my bones,
My enemies reproach me,
While they say to me all day long,
"Where *is* your God?"

11 Why are you cast down, O my soul?
And why are you disquieted within me?
Hope in God;
For I shall yet praise Him,
The help of my countenance and my God.

PSALM 43

God puts a smile on my face

VINDICATE me, O God,
And plead my cause against an ungodly nation;
Oh, deliver me from the deceitful and unjust man!
2 For You *are* the God of my strength;
Why do You cast me off?
Why do I go mourning because of the oppression of the enemy?

3 Oh, send out Your light and Your truth!

DIGGING IN

42:2 Seek God's Friendship We don't live very long in the world before we find out that friends can let us down. Sometimes they just move away and we never see them again. Others show, by the mean things they do, that they were never true friends in the first place.

Jesus knows what it means to lose your friends. His friends all ran away when His enemies took Him to be crucified.

We all need a Friend who never fails. God is that Friend. You can't see God, but He is always wherever you are, and He knows your needs. You need to spend a lot of time alone talking to God your Friend. As you spend time with God, you will come to know Him better. Then, as you grow up, He will prove to be your Friend forever. You will know you can trust Him with everything in your life.

Let them lead me;
Let them bring me to Your holy
hill
And to Your tabernacle.
4 Then I will go to the altar of God,
To God my exceeding joy;
And on the harp I will praise
You,
O God, my God.

5 Why are you cast down, O my
soul?
And why are you disquieted
within me?
Hope in God;
For I shall yet praise Him,
The help of my countenance
and my God.

PSALM 44

What happens to a nation without God

To the Chief Musician. A Contemplation of the sons of Korah.

WE have heard with our ears, O
God,
Our fathers have told us,
The deeds You did in their days,
In days of old:
2 You drove out the nations with
Your hand,
But them You planted;
You afflicted the peoples, and
cast them out.
3 For they did not gain possession
of the land by their own
sword,
Nor did their own arm save
them;
But it was Your right hand, Your
arm, and the light of Your
countenance,
Because You favored them.

4 You are my King, O God;
Command victories for Jacob.
5 Through You we will push down
our enemies;
Through Your name we will
trample those who rise up
against us.

6 For I will not trust in my bow,
Nor shall my sword save me.
7 But You have saved us from our
enemies,
And have put to shame those
who hated us.
8 In God we boast all day long,
And praise Your name forever.
Selah

9 But You have cast *us* off and
put us to shame,
And You do not go out with our
armies.
10 You make us turn back from the
enemy,
And those who hate us have
taken spoil for themselves.
11 You have given us up like sheep
intended for food,
And have scattered us among
the nations.
12 You sell Your people for *next
to* nothing,
And are not enriched by selling
them.

13 You make us a reproach to our
neighbors,
A scorn and a derision to those
all around us.
14 You make us a byword among
the nations,
A shaking of the head among
the peoples.
15 My dishonor *is* continually
before me,
And the shame of my face has
covered me,
16 Because of the voice of him who
reproaches and reviles,
Because of the enemy and the
avenger.

17 All this has come upon us;
But we have not forgotten You,
Nor have we dealt falsely with
Your covenant.
18 Our heart has not turned back,
Nor have our steps departed
from Your way;
19 But You have severely broken
us in the place of jackals,

And covered us with the shadow
of death.

20 If we had forgotten the name of
our God,
Or stretched out our hands to a
foreign god,
21 Would not God search this out?
For He knows the secrets of the
heart.
22 Yet for Your sake we are killed
all day long;
We are accounted as sheep for
the slaughter.

23 Awake! Why do You sleep, O
Lord?
Arise! Do not cast us off forever.
24 Why do You hide Your face,
And forget our affliction and our
oppression?
25 For our soul is bowed down to
the dust;
Our body clings to the ground.
26 Arise for our help,
And redeem us for Your
mercies' sake.

PSALM 45

King Messiah meets His bride

To the Chief Musician. Set to "The Lilies." A
Contemplation of the sons of Korah. A Song of Love.

MY heart is overflowing with a good
theme;
I recite my composition
concerning the King;
My tongue is the pen of a ready
writer.

2 You are fairer than the sons of
men;
Grace is poured upon Your lips;
Therefore God has blessed You
forever.
3 Gird Your sword upon Your
thigh, O Mighty One,
With Your glory and Your
majesty.
4 And in Your majesty ride
prosperously because of truth,
humility, and righteousness;
And Your right hand shall teach
You awesome things.
5 Your arrows are sharp in the
heart of the King's enemies;
The peoples fall under You.

6 Your throne, O God, is forever
and ever;
A scepter of righteousness is the
scepter of Your kingdom.
7 You love righteousness and hate
wickedness;
Therefore God, Your God, has
anointed You
With the oil of gladness more
than Your companions.
8 All Your garments are scented
with myrrh and aloes and
cassia,
Out of the ivory palaces, by
which they have made You
glad.
9 Kings' daughters are among
Your honorable women;
At Your right hand stands the
queen in gold from Ophir.

10 Listen, O daughter,
Consider and incline your ear;

⛏ DIGGING IN

45:6 God Is Forever and Ever Have
you thought about *eternity?* Eternity
means forever and ever—no beginning
and no ending. You had a beginning, and
someday your life in this world will end.
Even the world itself will come to an end.
In fact, we're so used to everything we
know having a beginning and an end, we
can hardly think of anything that doesn't
end.

God is forever and ever. He is different
from everything He made because He
never had a beginning and He will never
end. He has eternal life in Himself. Then
He shares His life with the people He
made in His image. So, even if we die in
this world, we will go on living somewhere. God wants you to share eternal
life with Him. You can live with Him forever if you give your life to Him now. Later
may be too late.

Forget your own people also,
and your father's house;

11 So the King will greatly desire
your beauty;
Because He *is* your Lord,
worship Him.

12 And the daughter of Tyre *will
come* with a gift;
The rich among the people will
seek your favor.

13 The royal daughter *is* all glorious
within *the palace;*
Her clothing *is* woven with
gold.

14 She shall be brought to the King
in robes of many colors;
The virgins, her companions
who follow her, shall be
brought to You.

15 With gladness and rejoicing they
shall be brought;
They shall enter the King's
palace.

16 Instead of Your fathers shall be
Your sons,
Whom You shall make princes
in all the earth.

17 I will make Your name to be
remembered in all
generations;
Therefore the people shall praise
You forever and ever.

PSALM 46

God helps when we are in trouble

To the Chief Musician. A Psalm of the sons of Korah.
A Song for Alamoth.

GOD *is* our refuge and strength,
A very present help in trouble.

2 Therefore we will not fear,
Even though the earth be
removed,
And though the mountains be
carried into the midst of the
sea;

3 *Though* its waters roar *and* be
troubled,
Though the mountains shake
with its swelling.   Selah

4 *There is* a river whose streams
shall make glad the city of
God,
The holy *place* of the tabernacle
of the Most High.

5 God *is* in the midst of her, she
shall not be moved;
God shall help her, just at the
break of dawn.

6 The nations raged, the kingdoms
were moved;
He uttered His voice, the earth
melted.

7 The LORD of hosts *is* with us;
The God of Jacob *is* our refuge.
   Selah

8 Come, behold the works of the
LORD,
Who has made desolations in
the earth.

9 He makes wars cease to the end
of the earth;
He breaks the bow and cuts the
spear in two;
He burns the chariot in the fire.

10 Be still, and know that I *am* God;
I will be exalted among the
nations,
I will be exalted in the earth!

11 The LORD of hosts *is* with us;
The God of Jacob *is* our refuge.
   Selah

PSALM 47

Celebrate the eternal King

To the Chief Musician. A Psalm of the sons of Korah.

OH, clap your hands, all you
peoples!
Shout to God with the voice of
triumph!

2 For the LORD Most High *is*
awesome;
He is a great King over all the
earth.

3 He will subdue the peoples
under us,
And the nations under our feet.

4 He will choose our inheritance
   for us,
   The excellence of Jacob whom
   He loves.   Selah

5 God has gone up with a shout,
   The LORD with the sound of a
   trumpet.
6 Sing praises to God, sing praises!
   Sing praises to our King, sing
   praises!
7 For God *is* the King of all the
   earth;
   Sing praises with understanding.

8 God reigns over the nations;
   God sits on His holy throne.
9 The princes of the people have
   gathered together,
   The people of the God of
   Abraham.
   For the shields of the earth
   belong to God;
   He is greatly exalted.

PSALM 48

God takes care of His city

A Song. A Psalm of the sons of Korah.

G REAT *is* the LORD, and greatly to
   be praised
   In the city of our God,
   In His holy mountain.
2 Beautiful in elevation,
   The joy of the whole earth,
   Is Mount Zion *on* the sides of
   the north,
   The city of the great King.

3 God *is* in her palaces;
   He is known as her refuge.
4 For behold, the kings
   assembled,
   They passed by together.
5 They saw *it, and* so they
   marveled;
   They were troubled, they
   hastened away.
6 Fear took hold of them there,
   And pain, as of a woman in birth
   pangs,
7 *As when* You break the ships of
   Tarshish
   With an east wind.

8 As we have heard,
   So we have seen
   In the city of the LORD of hosts,
   In the city of our God:
   God will establish it forever.
                               Selah

9 We have thought, O God, on
   Your lovingkindness,
   In the midst of Your temple.
10 According to Your name, O
   God,
   So *is* Your praise to the ends of
   the earth;
   Your right hand is full of
   righteousness.
11 Let Mount Zion rejoice,
   Let the daughters of Judah be
   glad,
   Because of Your judgments.

12 Walk about Zion,
   And go all around her.
   Count her towers;

⚒ DIGGING IN

47:8 God Rules the Nations Nearly every day the news reporters tell us about trouble in the world—war and hunger and murder. You may not see much trouble like this in your country, but because we hear and read about it so much, we often wonder how it will all end.

But you don't need to be afraid. God is in charge of the nations. He is leading us all to His final judgment. One day He will call all nations before Him and judge them by His Law. In the end, His perfect and everlasting kingdom will come, and the power of this world will pass away.

Have you made sure of your place in God's kingdom? Jesus said, "Come to Me, all you who labor and are heavy laden, and I will give you rest" (Matthew 11:28).

13 Mark well her bulwarks;
   Consider her palaces;
   That you may tell *it* to the
      generation following.
14 For this *is* God,
   Our God forever and ever;
   He will be our guide
   Even to death.

PSALM 49

Riches can't save us

To the Chief Musician. A Psalm of the sons of Korah.

HEAR this, all peoples;
   Give ear, all inhabitants of the
      world,
2 Both low and high,
   Rich and poor together.
3 My mouth shall speak wisdom,
   And the meditation of my heart
      shall give understanding.
4 I will incline my ear to a proverb;
   I will disclose my dark saying on
      the harp.

5 Why should I fear in the days
      of evil,
   When the iniquity at my heels
      surrounds me?
6 Those who trust in their wealth
   And boast in the multitude of
      their riches,
7 None *of them* can by any means
      redeem *his* brother,
   Nor give to God a ransom for
      him—
8 For the redemption of their souls
      is costly,
   And it shall cease forever—
9 That he should continue to live
      eternally,
   And not see the Pit.

10 For he sees wise men die;
   Likewise the fool and the
      senseless person perish,
   And leave their wealth to
      others.
11 Their inner thought *is that* their
      houses *will last* forever,
   Their dwelling places to all
      generations;

They call *their* lands after their
   own names.
12 Nevertheless man, *though* in
      honor, does not remain;
   He is like the beasts *that*
      perish.

13 This is the way of those who *are*
      foolish,
   And of their posterity who
      approve their sayings.   Selah
14 Like sheep they are laid in the
      grave;
   Death shall feed on them;
   The upright shall have dominion
      over them in the morning;
   And their beauty shall be
      consumed in the grave, far
      from their dwelling.
15 But God will redeem my soul
      from the power of the
      grave,
   For He shall receive me.   Selah

16 Do not be afraid when one
      becomes rich,
   When the glory of his house is
      increased;
17 For when he dies he shall carry
      nothing away;
   His glory shall not descend after
      him.
18 Though while he lives he blesses
      himself
   (For *men* will praise you when
      you do well for yourself),
19 He shall go to the generation of
      his fathers;
   They shall never see light.
20 A man *who is* in honor, yet does
      not understand,
   Is like the beasts *that* perish.

PSALM 50

How to worship God

A Psalm of Asaph.

THE Mighty One, God the LORD,
   Has spoken and called the earth
   From the rising of the sun to its
      going down.

2　Out of Zion, the perfection of
　　beauty,
　　God will shine forth.
3　Our God shall come, and shall
　　not keep silent;
　　A fire shall devour before Him,
　　And it shall be very tempestuous
　　all around Him.

4　He shall call to the heavens from
　　above,
　　And to the earth, that He may
　　judge His people:
5　"Gather My saints together to
　　Me,
　　Those who have made a
　　covenant with Me by
　　sacrifice."
6　Let the heavens declare His
　　righteousness,
　　For God Himself *is* Judge.
　　　　　　　　　　　　　Selah

7　"Hear, O My people, and I will
　　speak,
　　O Israel, and I will testify against
　　you;
　　I *am* God, your God!
8　I will not rebuke you for your
　　sacrifices
　　Or your burnt offerings,
　　Which are continually before
　　Me.
9　I will not take a bull from your
　　house,
　　Nor goats out of your folds.
10　For every beast of the forest *is*
　　Mine,
　　And the cattle on a thousand
　　hills.
11　I know all the birds of the
　　mountains,
　　And the wild beasts of the field
　　are Mine.

12　"If I were hungry, I would not tell
　　you;
　　For the world *is* Mine, and all
　　its fullness.
13　Will I eat the flesh of bulls,
　　Or drink the blood of goats?
14　Offer to God thanksgiving,
　　And pay your vows to the Most
　　High.

15　Call upon Me in the day of
　　trouble;
　　I will deliver you, and you shall
　　glorify Me."

16　But to the wicked God says:
　　"What *right* have you to declare
　　My statutes,
　　Or take My covenant in your
　　mouth,
17　Seeing you hate instruction
　　And cast My words behind
　　you?
18　When you saw a thief, you
　　consented with him,
　　And have been a partaker with
　　adulterers.
19　You give your mouth to evil,
　　And your tongue frames
　　deceit.
20　You sit *and* speak against your
　　brother;
　　You slander your own mother's
　　son.
21　These *things* you have done,
　　and I kept silent;
　　You thought that I was
　　altogether like you;
　　But I will rebuke you,
　　And set *them* in order before
　　your eyes.

22　"Now consider this, you who
　　forget God,
　　Lest I tear *you* in pieces,
　　And *there be* none to deliver:
23　Whoever offers praise glorifies
　　Me;
　　And to him who orders *his*
　　conduct *aright*
　　I will show the salvation of
　　God."

PSALM 51

I'm so sorry I did wrong

To the Chief Musician. A Psalm of David when
Nathan the prophet went to him, after he had gone
in to Bathsheba.

HAVE mercy upon me, O God,
　　According to Your
　　lovingkindness;

According to the multitude of
Your tender mercies,
Blot out my transgressions.
2 Wash me thoroughly from my
iniquity,
And cleanse me from my sin.

3 For I acknowledge my
transgressions,
And my sin *is* always before
me.
4 Against You, You only, have I
sinned,
And done *this* evil in Your
sight—
That You may be found just
when You speak,
And blameless when You
judge.

5 Behold, I was brought forth in
iniquity,
And in sin my mother conceived
me.
6 Behold, You desire truth in the
inward parts,
And in the hidden *part* You will
make me to know wisdom.

7 Purge me with hyssop, and I
shall be clean;
Wash me, and I shall be whiter
than snow.
8 Make me hear joy and gladness,
That the bones You have
broken may rejoice.
9 Hide Your face from my sins,
And blot out all my iniquities.

10 Create in me a clean heart, O
God,
And renew a steadfast spirit
within me.
11 Do not cast me away from Your
presence,
And do not take Your Holy
Spirit from me.

12 Restore to me the joy of Your
salvation,
And uphold me *by Your*
generous Spirit.
13 *Then* I will teach transgressors
Your ways,
And sinners shall be converted
to You.

14 Deliver me from the guilt of
bloodshed, O God,
The God of my salvation,
And my tongue shall sing aloud
of Your righteousness.
15 O Lord, open my lips,
And my mouth shall show forth
Your praise.
16 For You do not desire sacrifice,
or else I would give *it;*
You do not delight in burnt
offering.
17 The sacrifices of God *are* a
broken spirit,
A broken and a contrite heart—
These, O God, You will not
despise.

18 Do good in Your good pleasure
to Zion;
Build the walls of Jerusalem.
19 Then You shall be pleased
with the sacrifices of
righteousness,

⚒ DIGGING IN

51:2 Ask God to Forgive Your Sins
Sin is not a pleasant subject. But God
hates sin even more than we do. God
hates sin so much that He even sacrificed
His only Son to destroy sin.

If God hated sin that much, how can
we love our sins any longer? It makes
no sense at all for people to go on disobeying a God who loves them so much.
But even so, we still go on sinning in ways
that people can't see. God sees, though,
and He is hurt when His children sin
against Him. He gave us so much when
He gave His Son.

God accepts you when you say to Him,
"Here is my life; now I belong to You."
When you give your life to God, you're
also saying to Him, "I'm sorry for my sins;
please forgive me because Jesus died for
me." Then God hears you and He forgives you.

With burnt offering and whole
    burnt offering;
Then they shall offer bulls on
    Your altar.

PSALM 52

God will punish evil

To the Chief Musician. A Contemplation of David
when Doeg the Edomite went and told Saul, and
said to him, "David has gone to the house of
Ahimelech."

WHY do you boast in evil, O
        mighty man?
    The goodness of God *endures*
        continually.
2   Your tongue devises destruction,
    Like a sharp razor, working
        deceitfully.
3   You love evil more than good,
    Lying rather than speaking
        righteousness.   Selah
4   You love all devouring words,
    You deceitful tongue.

5   God shall likewise destroy you
        forever;
    He shall take you away, and
        pluck you out of *your* dwelling
        place,
    And uproot you from the land
        of the living.   Selah
6   The righteous also shall *see* and
        fear,
    And shall laugh at him, *saying,*
7   "Here is the man *who* did not
        make God his strength,
    But trusted in the abundance of
        his riches,
    And strengthened himself in his
        wickedness."

8   But I *am* like a green olive tree
        in the house of God;
    I trust in the mercy of God
        forever and ever.
9   I will praise You forever,
    Because You have done *it;*
    And in the presence of Your
        saints
    I will wait on Your name, for *it*
        is good.

PSALM 53

Our wrongdoing keeps us from God

To the Chief Musician. Set to "Mahalath." A
Contemplation of David.

THE fool has said in his heart,
        "*There is* no God."
    They are corrupt, and have
        done abominable iniquity;
    There is none who does good.

2   God looks down from heaven
        upon the children of men,
    To see if there are *any* who
        understand, who seek God.
3   Every one of them has turned
        aside;
    They have together become
        corrupt;
    There is none who does good,
    No, not one.

4   Have the workers of iniquity no
        knowledge,
    Who eat up my people *as* they
        eat bread,
    And do not call upon God?
5   There they are in great fear
    Where no fear was,
    For God has scattered the bones
        of him who encamps against
        you;
    You have put *them* to shame,
    Because God has despised
        them.

6   Oh, that the salvation of Israel
        would come out of Zion!
    When God brings back the
        captivity of His people,
    Let Jacob rejoice *and* Israel be
        glad.

PSALM 54

God is my Helper

To the Chief Musician. With stringed instruments. A
Contemplation of David when the Ziphites went and
said to Saul, "Is David not hiding with us?"

SAVE me, O God, by Your name,
    And vindicate me by Your
        strength.

2 Hear my prayer, O God;
Give ear to the words of my
mouth.
3 For strangers have risen up
against me,
And oppressors have sought
after my life;
They have not set God before
them.   Selah

4 Behold, God is my helper;
The Lord is with those who
uphold my life.
5 He will repay my enemies for
their evil.
Cut them off in Your truth.

6 I will freely sacrifice to You;
I will praise Your name, O LORD,
for it is good.
7 For He has delivered me out of
all trouble;
And my eye has seen its desire
upon my enemies.

PSALM 55

When my friends hurt my feelings

To the Chief Musician. With stringed instruments. A
Contemplation of David.

GIVE ear to my prayer, O God,
And do not hide Yourself from
my supplication.
2 Attend to me, and hear me;
I am restless in my complaint,
and moan noisily,
3 Because of the voice of the
enemy,
Because of the oppression of the
wicked;
For they bring down trouble
upon me,
And in wrath they hate me.

4 My heart is severely pained
within me,
And the terrors of death have
fallen upon me.
5 Fearfulness and trembling have
come upon me,
And horror has overwhelmed
me.

6 So I said, "Oh, that I had wings
like a dove!
I would fly away and be at rest.
7 Indeed, I would wander far off,
And remain in the wilderness.
                         Selah
8 I would hasten my escape
From the windy storm and
tempest."

9 Destroy, O Lord, and divide
their tongues,
For I have seen violence and
strife in the city.
10 Day and night they go around
it on its walls;
Iniquity and trouble are also in
the midst of it.
11 Destruction is in its midst;
Oppression and deceit do not
depart from its streets.

12 For it is not an enemy who
reproaches me;
Then I could bear it.
Nor is it one who hates me who
has exalted himself against
me;
Then I could hide from him.
13 But it was you, a man my equal,
My companion and my
acquaintance.
14 We took sweet counsel together,
And walked to the house of God
in the throng.

15 Let death seize them;
Let them go down alive into hell,
For wickedness is in their
dwellings and among them.

16 As for me, I will call upon God,
And the LORD shall save me.
17 Evening and morning and at
noon
I will pray, and cry aloud,
And He shall hear my voice.
18 He has redeemed my soul in
peace from the battle that was
against me,
For there were many against me.
19 God will hear, and afflict them,
Even He who abides from of
old.   Selah

Because they do not change,
Therefore they do not fear
God.

20 He has put forth his hands
against those who were at
peace with him;
He has broken his covenant.
21 *The words* of his mouth were
smoother than butter,
But war *was* in his heart;
His words were softer than oil,
Yet they *were* drawn swords.

22 Cast your burden on the Lord,
And He shall sustain you;
He shall never permit the
righteous to be moved.

23 But You, O God, shall bring
them down to the pit of
destruction;
Bloodthirsty and deceitful men
shall not live out half their
days;
But I will trust in You.

PSALM 56

I will trust God when I am afraid

To the Chief Musician. Set to ''The Silent Dove in
Distant Lands.'' A Michtam of David when the
Philistines captured him in Gath.

BE merciful to me, O God, for man
would swallow me up;
Fighting all day he oppresses
me.
2 My enemies would hound *me* all
day,
For *there are* many who fight
against me, O Most High.

3 Whenever I am afraid,
I will trust in You.
4 In God (I will praise His word),
In God I have put my trust;
I will not fear.
What can flesh do to me?

5 All day they twist my words;
All their thoughts *are* against me
for evil.
6 They gather together,

They hide, they mark my steps,
When they lie in wait for my life.
7 Shall they escape by iniquity?
In anger cast down the peoples,
O God!

8 You number my wanderings;
Put my tears into Your bottle;
Are they not in Your book?
9 When I cry out *to You,*
Then my enemies will turn back;
This I know, because God *is* for
me.
10 In God (I will praise *His* word),
In the Lord (I will praise *His*
word),
11 In God I have put my trust;
I will not be afraid.
What can man do to me?

12 Vows *made* to You *are binding*
upon me, O God;
I will render praises to You,
13 For You have delivered my soul
from death.
Have You not *kept* my feet from
falling,
That I may walk before God
In the light of the living?

PSALM 57

Singing in the dark

To the Chief Musician. Set to ''Do Not Destroy.'' A
Michtam of David when he fled from Saul into the
cave.

BE merciful to me, O God, be
merciful to me!
For my soul trusts in You;
And in the shadow of Your
wings I will make my refuge,
Until *these* calamities have
passed by.

2 I will cry out to God Most High,
To God who performs *all things*
for me.
3 He shall send from heaven and
save me;
He reproaches the one who
would swallow me up. Selah
God shall send forth His mercy
and His truth.

4 My soul is among lions;
I lie among the sons of men
Who are set on fire,
Whose teeth are spears and
arrows,
And their tongue a sharp sword.
5 Be exalted, O God, above the
heavens;
Let Your glory be above all the
earth.

6 They have prepared a net for my
steps;
My soul is bowed down;
They have dug a pit before
me;
Into the midst of it they
themselves have fallen.
Selah

7 My heart is steadfast, O God, my
heart is steadfast;
I will sing and give praise.
8 Awake, my glory!
Awake, lute and harp!
I will awaken the dawn.

9 I will praise You, O Lord, among
the peoples;
I will sing to You among the
nations.
10 For Your mercy reaches unto
the heavens,
And Your truth unto the clouds.

11 Be exalted, O God, above the
heavens;
Let Your glory be above all the
earth.

PSALM 58

God cares about right and wrong

To the Chief Musician. Set to "Do Not Destroy." A
Michtam of David.

D O you indeed speak righteousness,
you silent ones?
Do you judge uprightly, you
sons of men?
2 No, in heart you work
wickedness;
You weigh out the violence of
your hands in the earth.

3 The wicked are estranged from
the womb;
They go astray as soon as they
are born, speaking lies.
4 Their poison is like the poison
of a serpent;
They are like the deaf cobra that
stops its ear,
5 Which will not heed the voice
of charmers,
Charming ever so skillfully.

6 Break their teeth in their mouth,
O God!
Break out the fangs of the young
lions, O LORD!
7 Let them flow away as waters
which run continually;
When he bends his bow,
Let his arrows be as if cut in
pieces.
8 Let them be like a snail which
melts away as it goes,
Like a stillborn child of a
woman, that they may not see
the sun.

9 Before your pots can feel the
burning thorns,
He shall take them away as with
a whirlwind,
As in His living and burning
wrath.
10 The righteous shall rejoice when
he sees the vengeance;
He shall wash his feet in the
blood of the wicked,
11 So that men will say,
"Surely there is a reward for the
righteous;
Surely He is God who judges in
the earth."

PSALM 59

God protects us in the night

To the Chief Musician. Set to "Do Not Destroy." A
Michtam of David when Saul sent men, and they
watched the house in order to kill him.

D ELIVER me from my enemies, O
my God;
Defend me from those who rise
up against me.

2 Deliver me from the workers of
     iniquity,
   And save me from bloodthirsty
     men.

3 For look, they lie in wait for my
     life;
   The mighty gather against me,
   Not *for* my transgression nor *for*
     my sin, O LORD.
4 They run and prepare
     themselves through no fault *of*
     mine.

   Awake to help me, and behold!
5 You therefore, O LORD God of
     hosts, the God of Israel,
   Awake to punish all the nations;
   Do not be merciful to any
     wicked transgressors.   Selah

6 At evening they return,
   They growl like a dog,
   And go all around the city.
7 Indeed, they belch with their
     mouth;
   Swords *are* in their lips;
   For *they say,* "Who hears?"

8 But You, O LORD, shall laugh at
     them;
   You shall have all the nations in
     derision.
9 I will wait for You, O You his
     Strength;
   For God *is* my defense.
10 My God of mercy shall come to
     meet me;
   God shall let me *see my desire*
     on my enemies.

11 Do not slay them, lest my people
     forget;
   Scatter them by Your power,
   And bring them down,
   O Lord our shield.
12 *For* the sin of their mouth *and*
     the words of their lips,
   Let them even be taken in their
     pride,
   And for the cursing and lying
     which they speak.
13 Consume *them* in wrath,
   consume *them,*

That they *may* not *be;*
And let them know that God
  rules in Jacob
To the ends of the earth.
                              Selah

14 And at evening they return,
   They growl like a dog,
   And go all around the city.
15 They wander up and down for
     food,
   And howl if they are not
     satisfied.

16 But I will sing of Your power;
   Yes, I will sing aloud of Your
     mercy in the morning;
   For You have been my defense
   And refuge in the day of my
     trouble.
17 To You, O my Strength, I will
     sing praises;
   For God *is* my defense,
   My God of mercy.

PSALM 60

God is our only real help

To the Chief Musician. Set to "Lily of the
Testimony." A Michtam of David. For teaching.
When he fought against Mesopotamia and Syria
of Zobah, and Joab returned and killed twelve
thousand Edomites in the Valley of Salt.

O GOD, You have cast us off;
   You have broken us down;
   You have been displeased;
   Oh, restore us again!
2 You have made the earth
     tremble;
   You have broken it;
   Heal its breaches, for it is
     shaking.
3 You have shown Your people
     hard things;
   You have made us drink the
     wine of confusion.

4 You have given a banner to
     those who fear You,
   That it may be displayed
     because of the truth.   Selah
5 That Your beloved may be
     delivered,

Save *with* Your right hand, and
hear me.

6 God has spoken in His holiness:
"I will rejoice;
I will divide Shechem
And measure out the Valley of
Succoth.
7 Gilead *is* Mine, and Manasseh
is Mine;
Ephraim also *is* the helmet for
My head;
Judah *is* My lawgiver.
8 Moab *is* My washpot;
Over Edom I will cast My
shoe;
Philistia, shout in triumph
because of Me."

9 Who will bring me *to* the strong
city?
Who will lead me to Edom?
10 *Is it* not You, O God, *who* cast
us off?
And You, O God, *who* did not
go out with our armies?
11 Give us help from trouble,
For the help of man *is* useless.
12 Through God we will do
valiantly,
For *it is* He *who* shall tread down
our enemies.

PSALM 61

God never fails us

To the Chief Musician. On a stringed instrument. A
Psalm of David.

HEAR my cry, O God;
Attend to my prayer.
2 From the end of the earth I will
cry to You,
When my heart is overwhelmed;
Lead me to the rock that is
higher than I.

3 For You have been a shelter for
me,
A strong tower from the enemy.
4 I will abide in Your tabernacle
forever;

I will trust in the shelter of Your
wings.   Selah

5 For You, O God, have heard my
vows;
You have given *me* the heritage
of those who fear Your name.
6 You will prolong the king's life,
His years as many generations.
7 He shall abide before God
forever.
Oh, prepare mercy and truth,
which may preserve him!

8 So I will sing praise to Your
name forever,
That I may daily perform my
vows.

PSALM 62

God is my shelter

To the Chief Musician. To Jeduthun. A Psalm of
David.

TRULY my soul silently *waits* for
God;
From Him *comes* my salvation.
2 He only *is* my rock and my
salvation;
He is my defense;
I shall not be greatly moved.

3 How long will you attack a
man?
You shall be slain, all of you,
Like a leaning wall and a
tottering fence.
4 They only consult to cast *him*
down from his high position;
They delight in lies;
They bless with their mouth,
But they curse inwardly. Selah

5 My soul, wait silently for God
alone,
For my expectation *is* from Him.
6 He only *is* my rock and my
salvation;
He is my defense;
I shall not be moved.
7 In God *is* my salvation and my
glory;

The rock of my strength,
And my refuge, *is* in God.

8 Trust in Him at all times, you
    people;
  Pour out your heart before
    Him;
  God *is* a refuge for us.   Selah

9 Surely men of low degree *are* a
    vapor,
  Men of high degree *are* a lie;
  If they are weighed on the
    scales,
  They *are* altogether *lighter* than
    vapor.
10 Do not trust in oppression,
   Nor vainly hope in robbery;
   If riches increase,
   Do not set *your* heart *on*
     them.

11 God has spoken once,
   Twice I have heard this:
   That power *belongs* to God.
12 Also to You, O Lord, *belongs*
     mercy;
   For You render to each one
     according to his work.

PSALM 63

I want to be close to God

A Psalm of David when he was in the wilderness of
Judah.

O GOD, You *are* my God;
  Early will I seek You;
  My soul thirsts for You;
  My flesh longs for You

In a dry and thirsty land
  Where there is no water.
2 So I have looked for You in the
    sanctuary,
  To see Your power and Your
    glory.
3 Because Your lovingkindness *is*
    better than life,
  My lips shall praise You.
4 Thus I will bless You while I live;
  I will lift up my hands in Your
    name.
5 My soul shall be satisfied as with
    marrow and fatness,
  And my mouth shall praise You
    with joyful lips.

6 When I remember You on my
    bed,
  I meditate on You in the *night*
    watches.
7 Because You have been my
    help,
  Therefore in the shadow of Your
    wings I will rejoice.
8 My soul follows close behind
    You;
  Your right hand upholds me.

9 But those *who* seek my life, to
    destroy *it,*
  Shall go into the lower parts of
    the earth.
10 They shall fall by the sword;
   They shall be a portion for
     jackals.

11 But the king shall rejoice in God;
   Everyone who swears by Him
     shall glory;

 DIGGING IN

63:1 Are You Thirsty for God? Have you ever been so thirsty you thought you couldn't go another minute without a drink of water? Of course you have. That's the way God wants you to feel about *Him.* Life is weary and dry without God to be with you and lead you.

Not all people know how much they need God. That's very sad, because they really need Him even if they don't know they do. God wants you to desire Him more than everything else in life. After all, knowing God is worth more than anything you can ever own.

It's nice to have a home and friends and possessions. But without God, nothing in this world is worth living for. With God, life is exciting, and you will always be satisfied. He knows your needs better than you do. But God must come first in everything. He is always nearby, waiting for your invitation to come into your life.

But the mouth of those who
   speak lies shall be stopped.

PSALM 64

God can protect me from traps

To the Chief Musician. A Psalm of David.

HEAR my voice, O God, in my
   meditation;
   Preserve my life from fear of the
      enemy.
2   Hide me from the secret plots
      of the wicked,
   From the rebellion of the
      workers of iniquity,
3   Who sharpen their tongue like
      a sword,
   And bend *their bows to shoot*
      their arrows—bitter words,
4   That they may shoot in secret
      at the blameless;
   Suddenly they shoot at him and
      do not fear.

5   They encourage themselves *in*
      an evil matter;
   They talk of laying snares
      secretly;
   They say, "Who will see them?"
6   They devise iniquities:
   "We have perfected a shrewd
      scheme."
   Both the inward thought and the
      heart of man are deep.

7   But God shall shoot at them *with*
      an arrow;
   Suddenly they shall be
      wounded.
8   So He will make them stumble
      over their own tongue;
   All who see them shall flee away.
9   All men shall fear,
   And shall declare the work of
      God;
   For they shall wisely consider
      His doing.

10   The righteous shall be glad in the
      LORD, and trust in Him.
   And all the upright in heart shall
      glory.

PSALM 65

God is so great

To the Chief Musician. A Psalm of David. A Song.

PRAISE is awaiting You, O God, in
   Zion;
   And to You the vow shall be
      performed.
2   O You who hear prayer,
   To You all flesh will come.
3   Iniquities prevail against me;
   As for our transgressions,
   You will provide atonement for
      them.

4   Blessed *is the man* You choose,
   And cause to approach *You,*
   That he may dwell in Your
      courts.
   We shall be satisfied with the
      goodness of Your house,
   Of Your holy temple.

5   *By* awesome deeds in
      righteousness You will answer
      us,
   O God of our salvation,
   You who are the confidence of
      all the ends of the earth,
   And of the far-off seas;
6   Who established the mountains
      by His strength,
   Being clothed with power;
7   You who still the noise of the
      seas,
   The noise of their waves,
   And the tumult of the peoples.
8   They also who dwell in the
      farthest parts are afraid of
      Your signs;
   You make the outgoings of the
      morning and evening rejoice.

9   You visit the earth and water it,
   You greatly enrich it;
   The river of God is full of water;
   You provide their grain,
   For so You have prepared it.
10   You water its ridges abundantly,
   You settle its furrows;
   You make it soft with showers,
   You bless its growth.

11 You crown the year with Your
   goodness,
   And Your paths drip *with*
   abundance.
12 They drop *on* the pastures of the
   wilderness,
   And the little hills rejoice on
   every side.
13 The pastures are clothed with
   flocks;
   The valleys also are covered
   with grain;
   They shout for joy, they also
   sing.

PSALM 66

I like to remember what God has done

To the Chief Musician. A Song. A Psalm.

MAKE a joyful shout to God, all the
earth!
2 Sing out the honor of His name;
   Make His praise glorious.
3 Say to God,
   "How awesome are Your
   works!
   Through the greatness of Your
   power
   Your enemies shall submit
   themselves to You.
4 All the earth shall worship You
   And sing praises to You;
   They shall sing praises *to* Your
   name."   Selah

5 Come and see the works of
   God;

He is awesome *in His* doing
   toward the sons of men.
6 He turned the sea into dry *land;*
   They went through the river on
   foot.
   There we will rejoice in Him.
7 He rules by His power forever;
   His eyes observe the nations;
   Do not let the rebellious exalt
   themselves.   Selah

8 Oh, bless our God, you peoples!
   And make the voice of His praise
   to be heard,
9 Who keeps our soul among the
   living,
   And does not allow our feet to
   be moved.
10 For You, O God, have tested us;
   You have refined us as silver is
   refined.
11 You brought us into the net;
   You laid affliction on our backs.
12 You have caused men to ride
   over our heads;
   We went through fire and
   through water;
   But You brought us out to rich
   fulfillment.

13 I will go into Your house with
   burnt offerings;
   I will pay You my vows,
14 Which my lips have uttered
   And my mouth has spoken
   when I was in trouble.
15 I will offer You burnt sacrifices
   of fat animals,
   With the sweet aroma of rams;
   I will offer bulls with goats.
                       Selah

 DIGGING IN

66:3 God's Works Are Awesome!
Have you ever seen the great power of
a hurricane at sea? The waves rise up
like huge green mountains and tower over
your little ship. The wind screeches and
tears at every loose board, you are thrown
about like a rubber ball, and there is water
everywhere.

Have you looked out into space and
thought about its vastness? Consider how
the whole star system moves in exact
time like a perfect clock.

Think about your body and how it grows
and develops—more wonderful than any
machine. The whole order of nature is an
awesome scene of God at work.

None of these things came into being
by themselves. They are the work of a
brilliant Creator. He is the Master Designer of all we can see and of all we
can't see. The God we read about in the
Bible is the only One who could design
such a vast and complex universe.

16   Come *and* hear, all you who fear
     God,
     And I will declare what He has
     done for my soul.
17   I cried to Him with my mouth,
     And He was extolled with my
     tongue.
18   If I regard iniquity in my heart,
     The Lord will not hear.
19   *But* certainly God has heard *me;*
     He has attended to the voice of
     my prayer.

20   Blessed *be* God,
     Who has not turned away my
     prayer,
     Nor His mercy from me!

PSALM 67

A prayer for people in faraway lands

To the Chief Musician. On stringed instruments. A
Psalm. A Song.

GOD be merciful to us and bless
     us,
     And cause His face to shine
        upon us,   Selah
2   That Your way may be known
     on earth,
     Your salvation among all
     nations.

3   Let the peoples praise You, O
     God;
     Let all the peoples praise You.
4   Oh, let the nations be glad and
     sing for joy!
     For You shall judge the people
     righteously,
     And govern the nations on
     earth.   Selah

5   Let the peoples praise You, O
     God;
     Let all the peoples praise You.
6   *Then* the earth shall yield her
     increase;
     God, our own God, shall bless
     us.
7   God shall bless us,
     And all the ends of the earth
     shall fear Him.

PSALM 68

God gives us everything we need

To the Chief Musician. A Psalm of David. A Song.

LET God arise,
     Let His enemies be scattered;
     Let those also who hate Him flee
     before Him.
2   As smoke is driven away,
     So drive *them* away;
     As wax melts before the fire,
     So let the wicked perish at the
     presence of God.
3   But let the righteous be glad;
     Let them rejoice before God;
     Yes, let them rejoice
     exceedingly.

4   Sing to God, sing praises to His
     name;
     Extol Him who rides on the
     clouds,
     By His name YAH,
     And rejoice before Him.

5   A father of the fatherless, a
     defender of widows,
     Is God in His holy habitation.
6   God sets the solitary in families;
     He brings out those who are
     bound into prosperity;
     But the rebellious dwell in a dry
     land.

7   O God, when You went out
     before Your people,
     When You marched through the
     wilderness,   Selah
8   The earth shook;
     The heavens also dropped *rain*
     at the presence of God;
     Sinai itself *was moved* at the
     presence of God, the God of
     Israel.
9   You, O God, sent a plentiful
     rain,
     Whereby You confirmed Your
     inheritance,
     When it was weary.
10   Your congregation dwelt in it;
     You, O God, provided from
     Your goodness for the poor.

11 The Lord gave the word;
Great *was* the company of those
who proclaimed *it:*
12 "Kings of armies flee, they flee,
And she who remains at home
divides the spoil.
13 Though you lie down among the
sheepfolds,
You will be like the wings of a
dove covered with silver,
And her feathers with yellow
gold."
14 When the Almighty scattered
kings in it,
It was *white* as snow in Zalmon.

15 A mountain of God *is* the
mountain of Bashan;
A mountain *of many* peaks *is* the
mountain of Bashan.
16 Why do you fume with envy,
you mountains of *many*
peaks?
This is the mountain *which* God
desires to dwell in;
Yes, the LORD will dwell *in it*
forever.
17 The chariots of God *are* twenty
thousand,
Even thousands of thousands;
The Lord is among them *as in*
Sinai, in the Holy *Place.*
18 You have ascended on high,
You have led captivity captive;
You have received gifts among
men,
Even *from* the rebellious,
That the LORD God might dwell
there.

19 Blessed *be* the Lord,
Who daily loads us *with benefits,*
The God of our **salvation!**
                          Selah
20 Our God *is* the God of salvation;
And to GOD the Lord *belong*
escapes from death.

21 But God will wound the head
of His enemies,
The hairy scalp of the one who
still goes on in his trespasses.
22 The Lord said, "I will bring back
from Bashan,
I will bring *them* back from the
depths of the sea,
23 That your foot may crush *them*
in blood,
And the tongues of your dogs
may have their portion from
your enemies."
24 They have seen Your
procession, O God,
The procession of my God, my
King, into the sanctuary.
25 The singers went before, the
players on instruments
followed after;
Among *them were* the maidens
playing timbrels.
26 Bless God in the congregations,
The Lord, from the fountain of
Israel.
27 There *is* little Benjamin, their
leader,
The princes of Judah *and* their
company,
The princes of Zebulun *and* the
princes of Naphtali.
28 Your God has commanded your
strength;
Strengthen, O God, what You
have done for us.
29 Because of Your temple at
Jerusalem,
Kings will bring presents to You.
30 Rebuke the beasts of the reeds,
The herd of bulls with the calves
of the peoples,
Till everyone submits himself
with pieces of silver.
Scatter the peoples *who* delight
in war.
31 Envoys will come out of Egypt;

WORDFINDER

68:19 Salvation Pronounced *sal-VAY-shun.* A work of saving someone from danger or death. In the New Testament, salvation is Christ's work of dying to save us from sin and hell.

Ethiopia will quickly stretch out
her hands to God.

32 Sing to God, you kingdoms of
the earth;
Oh, sing praises to the Lord,
                      Selah
33 To Him who rides on the heaven
of heavens, *which were* of old!
Indeed, He sends out His voice,
a mighty voice.
34 Ascribe strength to God;
His excellence *is* over Israel,
And His strength *is* in the clouds.
35 O God, *You are* more awesome
than Your holy places.
The God of Israel *is* He who
gives strength and power to
His people.

Blessed *be* God!

PSALM 69

Those who look for God will live

To the Chief Musician. Set to "The Lilies." A Psalm
of David.

SAVE me, O God!
For the waters have come up to
my neck.
2 I sink in deep mire,
Where *there is* no standing;
I have come into deep waters,
Where the floods overflow me.
3 I am weary with my crying;
My throat is dry;
My eyes fail while I wait for my
God.

4 Those who hate me without a
cause
Are more than the hairs of my
head;
They are mighty who would
destroy me,
Being my enemies wrongfully;
Though I have stolen nothing,
I *still* must restore *it.*

5 O God, You know my
foolishness;
And my sins are not hidden from
You.

6 Let not those who wait for You,
O Lord GOD of hosts, be
ashamed because of me;
Let not those who *seek* You be
confounded because of me, O
God of Israel.
7 Because for Your sake I have
borne reproach;
Shame has covered my face.
8 I have become a stranger to my
brothers,
And an alien to my mother's
children;
9 Because zeal for Your house has
eaten me up,
And the reproaches of those
who reproach You have fallen
on me.
10 When I wept *and chastened* my
soul with fasting,
That became my reproach.
11 I also made sackcloth my
garment;
I became a byword to them.
12 Those who sit in the gate speak
against me,
And I *am* the song of the
drunkards.

13 But as for me, my prayer *is* to
You,
O LORD, *in* the acceptable time;
O God, in the multitude of Your
mercy,
Hear me in the truth of Your
salvation.
14 Deliver me out of the mire,
And let me not sink;
Let me be delivered from those
who hate me,
And out of the deep waters.
15 Let not the floodwater overflow
me,
Nor let the deep swallow me up;
And let not the pit shut its mouth
on me.

16 Hear me, O LORD, for Your
lovingkindness *is* good;
Turn to me according to the
multitude of Your tender
mercies.
17 And do not hide Your face from
Your servant,

For I am in trouble;
Hear me speedily.
18 Draw near to my soul, *and*
   redeem it;
   Deliver me because of my
   enemies.

19 You know my reproach, my
   shame, and my dishonor;
   My adversaries *are* all before
   You.
20 Reproach has broken my heart,
   And I am full of heaviness;
   I looked *for someone* to take
   pity, but *there was* none;
   And for comforters, but I found
   none.
21 They also gave me gall for my
   food,
   And for my thirst they gave me
   vinegar to drink.

22 Let their table become a snare
   before them,
   And their well-being a trap.
23 Let their eyes be darkened, so
   that they do not see;
   And make their loins shake
   continually.
24 Pour out Your indignation upon
   them,
   And let Your wrathful anger take
   hold of them.
25 Let their dwelling place be
   desolate;

Let no one live in their tents.
26 For they persecute the *ones* You
   have struck,
   And talk of the grief of those You
   have wounded.
27 Add iniquity to their iniquity,
   And let them not come into Your
   righteousness.
28 Let them be blotted out of the
   book of the living,
   And not be written with the
   righteous.

29 But I *am* poor and sorrowful;
   Let Your salvation, O God, set
   me up on high.
30 I will praise the name of God
   with a song,
   And will magnify Him with
   thanksgiving.
31 *This* also shall please the LORD
   better than an ox *or* bull,
   Which has horns and hooves.
32 The humble shall *see this and*
   be glad;
   And you who seek God, your
   hearts shall live.
33 For the LORD hears the poor,
   And does not despise His
   prisoners.

34 Let heaven and earth praise
   Him,
   The seas and everything that
   moves in them.

WORDFINDER

69:18 Redeem To buy something back from someone. In the New Testament, Jesus bought back believers from the slavery of sin.

DIGGING IN

69:17 God Cares When You Are in Trouble Do you sometimes feel all alone with troubles you can't help or understand? You may have no human person you can talk to, but there is a divine Person who cares very much about you. His name is Jesus, which means "Savior." A savior is someone who rescues from danger. Jesus is the great Savior who is always ready to rescue you from the things that trouble you most.

If you have a broken bicycle, you take it to someone who knows how to repair it. But Jesus knows all about you, and He wants you to come with all the broken pieces of your life and ask Him to mend them. Jesus can do that.

First, however, you must ask Jesus to help you. Go to a place alone and tell Him all about your trouble. He will show you the way out of it. He will lead you to somebody you can trust. Jesus knows you and cares about you more than you know.

35 For God will save Zion
And build the cities of Judah,
That they may dwell there and
possess it.
36 Also, the descendants of His
servants shall inherit it,
And those who love His name
shall dwell in it.

PSALM 70

God, help me now!

To the Chief Musician. *A Psalm* of David. To bring
to remembrance.

*M*AKE *haste,* O God, to deliver me!
Make haste to help me, O LORD!
2 Let them be ashamed and
confounded
Who seek my life;
Let them be turned back and
confused
Who desire my hurt.
3 Let them be turned back
because of their shame,
Who say, "Aha, aha!"

4 Let all those who seek You
rejoice and be glad in You;
And let those who love Your
salvation say continually,
"Let God be magnified!"

5 But I *am* poor and needy;
Make haste to me, O God!
You *are* my help and my
deliverer;
O LORD, do not delay.

PSALM 71

God cares for us all our lives

*I*N You, O LORD, I put my trust;
Let me never be put to shame.
2 Deliver me in Your
righteousness, and cause me
to escape;
Incline Your ear to me, and save
me.
3 Be my strong refuge,
To which I may resort
continually;
You have given the
commandment to save me,

For You *are* my rock and my
fortress.

4 Deliver me, O my God, out of
the hand of the wicked,
Out of the hand of the
unrighteous and cruel man.
5 For You are my hope, O Lord
GOD;
You are my trust from my youth.
6 By You I have been upheld from
birth;
You are He who took me out
of my mother's womb.
My praise *shall be* continually of
You.

7 I have become as a wonder to
many,
But You *are* my strong refuge.
8 Let my mouth be filled *with*
Your praise
And with Your glory all the day.

9 Do not cast me off in the time
of old age;
Do not forsake me when my
strength fails.
10 For my enemies speak against
me;
And those who lie in wait for my
life take counsel together,
11 Saying, "God has forsaken him;
Pursue and take him, for *there
is* none to deliver *him.*"

12 O God, do not be far from me;
O my God, make haste to help
me!
13 Let them be confounded *and*
consumed
Who are adversaries of my life;
Let them be covered *with*
reproach and dishonor
Who seek my hurt.

14 But I will hope continually,
And will praise You yet more
and more.
15 My mouth shall tell of Your
righteousness
And Your salvation all the day,
For I do not know *their* limits.
16 I will go in the strength of the
Lord GOD;

I will make mention of Your
   righteousness, of Yours only.

17 O God, You have taught me
   from my youth;
   And to this *day* I declare Your
     wondrous works.
18 Now also when *I am* old and
   grayheaded,
   O God, do not forsake me,
   Until I declare Your strength to
     this generation,
   Your power to everyone *who* is
     to come.

19 Also Your righteousness, O
   God, *is* very high,
   You who have done great
     things;
   O God, who *is* like You?
20 *You,* who have shown me great
   and severe troubles,
   Shall revive me again,
   And bring me up again from the
     depths of the earth.
21 You shall increase my greatness,
   And comfort me on every side.

22 Also with the lute I will praise
   You—
   And Your faithfulness, O my
     God!
   To You I will sing with the harp,
   O Holy One of Israel.
23 My lips shall greatly rejoice when
   I sing to You,
   And my soul, which You have
     redeemed.
24 My tongue also shall talk of Your
   righteousness all the day long;
   For they are confounded,

For they are brought to shame
   Who seek my hurt.

PSALM 72

The Messiah will rule

A Psalm of Solomon.

GIVE the king Your judgments, O
   God,
   And Your righteousness to the
     king's Son.
2 He will judge Your people with
   righteousness,
   And Your poor with justice.
3 The mountains will bring peace
   to the people,
   And the little hills, by
     righteousness.
4 He will bring justice to the poor
   of the people;
   He will save the children of the
     needy,
   And will break in pieces the
     oppressor.

5 They shall fear You
   As long as the sun and moon
     endure,
   Throughout all generations.
6 He shall come down like rain
   upon the grass before
     mowing,
   Like showers *that* water the
     earth.
7 In His days the righteous shall
   flourish,
   And abundance of peace,
   Until the moon is no more.

8 He shall have dominion also
   from sea to sea,

🪓 DIGGING IN

72:8 Jesus Shall Reign Over Everything Jesus was the kind Savior who grew up in a small town in Palestine. He went about doing good, healing the sick, and even raising the dead. He also had power over nature, as when He made the stormy sea calm. Then He was crucified and died. But on the third day, Jesus rose again, saying that He has the keys of death and hell (Revelation 1:18).

Right now we don't see Jesus anymore, and the world is ruled by human governments. But Jesus said, "I will come again." Someday He truly will come back, and He will rule over the whole world. Everyone will confess that He is Lord.

Life will be changed when Jesus is Ruler of all. There will be no more war or sickness or sin or death. Jesus will make everything beautiful. Are you looking for Jesus to come back?

And from the River to the ends
of the earth.
9 Those who dwell in the
wilderness will bow before
Him,
And His enemies will lick the
dust.
10 The kings of Tarshish and of the
isles
Will bring presents;
The kings of Sheba and Seba
Will offer gifts.
11 Yes, all kings shall fall down
before Him;
All nations shall serve Him.

12 For He will deliver the needy
when he cries,
The poor also, and *him* who has
no helper.
13 He will spare the poor and
needy,
And will save the souls of the
needy.
14 He will redeem their life from
oppression and violence;
And precious shall be their blood
in His sight.

15 And He shall live;
And the gold of Sheba will be
given to Him;
Prayer also will be made for Him
continually,
And daily He shall be praised.

16 There will be an abundance of
grain in the earth,
On the top of the mountains;
Its fruit shall wave like Lebanon;
And *those* of the city shall
flourish like grass of the earth.

17 His name shall endure forever;
His name shall continue as long
as the sun.
And *men* shall be blessed in
Him;
All nations shall call Him
blessed.

18 Blessed *be* the LORD God, the
God of Israel,

Who only does wondrous
things!
19 And blessed *be* His glorious
name forever!
And let the whole earth be filled
with His glory.
Amen and Amen.

20 The prayers of David the son of
Jesse are ended.

Book Three: Psalms 73—89

PSALM 73

God guides us when we pray

A Psalm of Asaph.

TRULY God *is* good to Israel,
To such as are pure in heart.
2 But as for me, my feet had
almost stumbled;
My steps had nearly slipped.
3 For I *was* envious of the boastful,
When I saw the prosperity of the
wicked.

4 For *there are* no pangs in their
death,
But their strength *is* firm.
5 They *are* not in trouble *as other*
men,
Nor are they plagued like *other*
men.
6 Therefore pride serves as their
necklace;
Violence covers them *like* a
garment.
7 Their eyes bulge with
abundance;
They have more than heart
could wish.
8 They scoff and speak wickedly
concerning oppression;
They speak loftily.
9 They set their mouth against the
heavens,
And their tongue walks through
the earth.
10 Therefore his people return
here,
And waters of a full *cup* are
drained by them.

11 And they say, "How does God
   know?
   And is there knowledge in the
   Most High?"
12 Behold, these *are* the ungodly,
   Who are always at ease;
   They increase *in* riches.
13 Surely I have cleansed my heart
   in vain,
   And washed my hands in
   innocence.
14 For all day long I have been
   plagued,
   And chastened *every* morning.

15 If I had said, "I will speak thus,"
   Behold, I would have been
   untrue to the generation of
   Your children.
16 When I thought *how* to
   understand this,
   It *was* too painful for me—
17 Until I went into the sanctuary
   of God;
   Then I understood their end.

18 Surely You set them in slippery
   places;
   You cast them down to
   destruction.
19 Oh, how they are *brought* to
   desolation, as in a moment!
   They are utterly consumed with
   terrors.
20 As a dream when *one* awakes,
   So, Lord, when You awake,
   You shall despise their image.

21 Thus my heart was grieved,
   And I was vexed in my mind.

22 I *was* so foolish and ignorant;
   I was *like* a beast before You.
23 Nevertheless I *am* continually
   with You;
   You hold *me* by my right hand.
24 You will guide me with Your
   counsel,
   And afterward receive me *to*
   glory.

25 Whom have I in heaven *but*
   You?
   And *there is* none upon earth
   that I desire besides You.
26 My flesh and my heart fail;
   But God *is* the strength of my
   heart and my portion forever.

27 For indeed, those who are far
   from You shall perish;
   You have destroyed all those
   who desert You for harlotry.
28 But *it is* good for me to draw
   near to God;
   I have put my trust in the Lord
   God,
   That I may declare all Your
   works.

PSALM 74

God keeps His promises

A Contemplation of Asaph.

O GOD, why have You cast *us* off
   forever?
   Why does Your anger smoke
   against the sheep of Your
   pasture?

⛏ DIGGING IN

73:24 God Is My Guide to Heaven A man named Asaph (pronounced *AY-saf*) wrote this psalm. Asaph was the head of a musical family in Israel. They provided the music for worship in the time of David and later.

Asaph was sure that God would guide him in this present life, and afterward take him to heaven (see verse 24). Asaph's heart was filled with the worship of God: "Whom have I in heaven but You? And there is none upon earth that I desire besides You" (verse 25).

The more you carefully think about life, the more you will see that nothing in this world is worth nearly as much as knowing God. And heaven is heaven only because God is there.

You do the best thing in life when you do as Asaph did. Trust God to lead you in this world. Then trust Him to bring you to heaven with Himself at last.

2 Remember Your congregation,
    which You have purchased of
    old,
The tribe of Your inheritance,
    which You have redeemed—
This Mount Zion where You
    have dwelt.
3 Lift up Your feet to the perpetual
    desolations.
The enemy has damaged
    everything in the sanctuary.
4 Your enemies roar in the midst
    of Your meeting place;
They set up their banners *for*
    signs.
5 They seem like men who lift up
Axes among the thick trees.
6 And now they break down its
    carved work, all at once,
With axes and hammers.
7 They have set fire to Your
    sanctuary;
They have defiled the dwelling
    place of Your name to the
    ground.
8 They said in their hearts,
"Let us destroy them altogether."
They have burned up all the
    meeting places of God in the
    land.

9 We do not see our signs;
There is no longer any prophet;
Nor *is there* any among us who
    knows how long.
10 O God, how long will the
    adversary reproach?
Will the enemy blaspheme Your
    name forever?
11 Why do You withdraw Your
    hand, *even* Your right hand?
Take it out of Your bosom and
    destroy *them.*
12 For God *is* my King from of
    old,
Working salvation in the midst
    of the earth.
13 You divided the sea by Your
    strength;
You broke the heads of the sea
    serpents in the waters.
14 You broke the heads of
    Leviathan in pieces,
And gave him *as* food to the

people inhabiting the
    wilderness.
15 You broke open the fountain
    and the flood;
You dried up mighty rivers.
16 The day *is* Yours, the night also
    is Yours;
You have prepared the light and
    the sun.
17 You have set all the borders of
    the earth;
You have made summer and
    winter.

18 Remember this, *that* the
    enemy has reproached, O
    LORD,
And *that* a foolish people has
    blasphemed Your name.
19 Oh, do not deliver the life of
    Your turtledove to the wild
    beast!
Do not forget the life of Your
    poor forever.
20 Have respect to the covenant;
For the dark places of the earth
    are full of the haunts of
    cruelty.
21 Oh, do not let the oppressed
    return ashamed!
Let the poor and needy praise
    Your name.

22 Arise, O God, plead Your own
    cause;
Remember how the foolish man
    reproaches You daily.
23 Do not forget the voice of Your
    enemies;
The tumult of those who rise up
    against You increases
    continually.

PSALM 75

God will judge the wicked

To the Chief Musician. Set to "Do Not Destroy." A
Psalm of Asaph. A Song.

WE give thanks to You, O God,
    we give thanks!
For Your wondrous works

declare *that* Your name is
near.

2   "When I choose the proper time,
    I will judge uprightly.
3   The earth and all its inhabitants
    are dissolved;
    I set up its pillars firmly.   Selah

4   "I said to the boastful, 'Do not
    deal boastfully,'
    And to the wicked, 'Do not lift
    up the horn.
5   Do not lift up your horn on
    high;
    Do *not* speak with a stiff neck.' "

6   For exaltation *comes* neither
    from the east
    Nor from the west nor from the
    south.
7   But God *is* the Judge:
    He puts down one,
    And exalts another.
8   For in the hand of the LORD
    there is a cup,
    And the wine is red;
    It is fully mixed, and He pours
    it out;
    Surely its dregs shall all the
    wicked of the earth
    Drain *and* drink down.

9   But I will declare forever,
    I will sing praises to the God of
    Jacob.

10 "All the horns of the wicked I will
    also cut off,
    But the horns of the righteous
    shall be exalted."

PSALM 76

God protects His people

To the Chief Musician. On stringed instruments. A
Psalm of Asaph. A Song.

IN Judah God *is* known;
    His name *is* great in Israel.
2   In Salem also is His tabernacle,
    And His dwelling place in Zion.
3   There He broke the arrows of
    the bow,
    The shield and sword of battle.
                                  Selah

4   You *are* more glorious and
    excellent
    Than the mountains of prey.
5   The stouthearted were
    plundered;
    They have sunk into their sleep;
    And none of the mighty men
    have found the use of their
    hands.
6   At Your rebuke, O God of
    Jacob,
    Both the chariot and horse were
    cast into a dead sleep.

7   You, Yourself, *are* to be feared;
    And who may stand in Your
    presence
    When once You are angry?
8   You caused judgment to be
    heard from heaven;
    The earth feared and was still,
9   When God arose to judgment,
    To deliver all the oppressed of
    the earth.   Selah

10 Surely the wrath of man shall
    praise You;

⛏ DIGGING IN

75:1 Always Give Thanks to God
Why should you give thanks to God? You
should always be thankful when anyone
is kind to you. But who has been nearly
so kind as God? He provides your home
and a free country to live in. He supplies
your daily food and clothing. You may
think you get these things by your own
work or by the work of others, but God
provides the opportunity to enjoy all these
good things and many, many more. He
even provides the air to breathe and gives
life moment by moment.

It is only right that you should be thankful to your parents and all who do good
things for you, but being thankful to God,
the One who gave you your parents and
all the good things you enjoy, makes even
more sense. If you aren't thankful, your
life will grow bitter and hateful. Then you
will be your own worst enemy.

With the remainder of wrath
You shall gird Yourself.

11 Make vows to the LORD your
God, and pay *them;*
Let all who are around Him
bring presents to Him who
ought to be feared.
12 He shall cut off the spirit of
princes;
He is awesome to the kings of
the earth.

PSALM 77

We think of God when we are in trouble

To the Chief Musician. To Jeduthun. A Psalm of Asaph.

I CRIED out to God with my voice—
To God with my voice;
And He gave ear to me.
2 In the day of my trouble I sought
the Lord;
My hand was stretched out in
the night without ceasing;
My soul refused to be
comforted.
3 I remembered God, and was
troubled;
I complained, and my spirit was
overwhelmed.   Selah

4 You hold my eyelids *open;*
I am so troubled that I cannot
speak.
5 I have considered the days of
old,
The years of ancient times.
6 I call to remembrance my song
in the night;
I meditate within my heart,
And my spirit makes diligent
search.

7 Will the Lord cast off forever?
And will He be favorable no
more?
8 Has His mercy ceased forever?
Has *His* promise failed
forevermore?
9 Has God forgotten to be
gracious?

Has He in anger shut up His
tender mercies?   Selah

10 And I said, "This *is* my anguish;
But I will remember the years
of the right hand of the Most
High."
11 I will remember the works of the
LORD;
Surely I will remember Your
wonders of old.
12 I will also meditate on all Your
work,
And talk of Your deeds.
13 Your way, O God, *is* in the
sanctuary;
Who *is* so great a God as *our*
God?
14 You *are* the God who does
wonders;
You have declared Your
strength among the peoples.
15 You have with *Your* arm
redeemed Your people,
The sons of Jacob and Joseph.
   Selah

16 The waters saw You, O God;
The waters saw You, they *were*
afraid;
The depths also trembled.
17 The clouds poured out water;
The skies sent out a sound;
Your arrows also flashed about.
18 The voice of Your thunder *was*
in the whirlwind;
The lightnings lit up the world;
The earth trembled and shook.
19 Your way *was* in the sea,
Your path in the great waters,
And Your footsteps were not
known.
20 You led Your people like a flock
By the hand of Moses and
Aaron.

PSALM 78

God is always faithful

A Contemplation of Asaph.

G IVE ear, O my people, *to* my law;
Incline your ears to the words
of my mouth.

2 I will open my mouth in a
parable;
I will utter dark sayings of old,
3 Which we have heard and
known,
And our fathers have told us.
4 We will not hide *them* from their
children,
Telling to the generation to
come the praises of the Lord,
And His strength and His
wonderful works that He has
done.

5 For He established a testimony
in Jacob,
And appointed a law in Israel,
Which He commanded our
fathers,
That they should make them
known to their children;
6 That the generation to come
might know *them,*
The children *who* would be
born,
That they may arise and declare
them to their children,
7 That they may set their hope in
God,
And not forget the works of
God,
But keep His commandments;
8 And may not be like their
fathers,
A stubborn and rebellious
generation,
A generation *that* did not set its
heart aright,
And whose spirit was not faithful
to God.

9 The children of Ephraim, *being*
armed *and* carrying bows,
Turned back in the day of battle.
10 They did not keep the covenant
of God;
They refused to walk in His
law,
11 And forgot His works
And His wonders that He had
shown them.

12 Marvelous things He did in the
sight of their fathers,

In the land of Egypt, *in* the field
of Zoan.
13 He divided the sea and caused
them to pass through;
And He made the waters stand
up like a heap.
14 In the daytime also He led them
with the cloud,
And all the night with a light of
fire.
15 He split the rocks in the
wilderness,
And gave *them* drink in
abundance like the depths.
16 He also brought streams out of
the rock,
And caused waters to run down
like rivers.

17 But they sinned even more
against Him
By rebelling against the Most
High in the wilderness.
18 And they tested God in their
heart
By asking for the food of their
fancy.
19 Yes, they spoke against God:
They said, "Can God prepare
a table in the wilderness?
20 Behold, He struck the rock,
So that the waters gushed out,
And the streams overflowed.
Can He give bread also?
Can He provide meat for His
people?"

21 Therefore the Lord heard *this*
and was furious;
So a fire was kindled against
Jacob,
And anger also came up against
Israel,
22 Because they did not believe in
God,
And did not trust in His
salvation.
23 Yet He had commanded the
clouds above,
And opened the doors of
heaven,
24 Had rained down manna on
them to eat,

And given them of the bread of
heaven.

25 Men ate angels' food;
He sent them food to the full.

26 He caused an east wind to blow
in the heavens;
And by His power He brought
in the south wind.

27 He also rained meat on them
like the dust,
Feathered fowl like the sand of
the seas;

28 And He let *them* fall in the midst
of their camp,
All around their dwellings.

29 So they ate and were well
filled,
For He gave them their own
desire.

30 They were not deprived of their
craving;
But while their food *was* still in
their mouths,

31 The wrath of God came against
them,
And slew the stoutest of them,
And struck down the choice *men*
of Israel.

32 In spite of this they still sinned,
And did not believe in His
wondrous works.

33 Therefore their days He
consumed in futility,
And their years in fear.

34 When He slew them, then they
sought Him;
And they returned and sought
earnestly for God.

35 Then they remembered that
God *was* their rock,
And the Most High God their
Redeemer.

36 Nevertheless they flattered Him
with their mouth,
And they lied to Him with their
tongue;

37 For their heart was not steadfast
with Him,
Nor were they faithful in His
covenant.

38 But He, *being* full of
compassion, forgave *their*
iniquity,
And did not destroy *them*.
Yes, many a time He turned His
anger away,
And did not stir up all His
wrath;

39 For He remembered that they
were but flesh,
A breath that passes away and
does not come again.

40 How often they provoked Him
in the wilderness,
And grieved Him in the
desert!

41 Yes, again and again they
tempted God,
And limited the Holy One of
Israel.

42 They did not remember His
power:
The day when He redeemed
them from the enemy,

43 When He worked His signs in
Egypt,
And His wonders in the field of
Zoan;

44 Turned their rivers into blood,
And their streams, that they
could not drink.

45 He sent swarms of flies among
them, which devoured
them,
And frogs, which destroyed
them.

46 He also gave their crops to the
caterpillar,
And their labor to the locust.

47 He destroyed their vines with
hail,
And their sycamore trees with
frost.

48 He also gave up their cattle to
the hail,
And their flocks to fiery lightning.

49 He cast on them the fierceness
of His anger,
Wrath, indignation, and trouble,
By sending angels of destruction
among them.

50 He made a path for His
anger;

He did not spare their soul from
death,
But gave their life over to the
plague,
51 And destroyed all the firstborn
in Egypt,
The first of *their* strength in the
tents of Ham.
52 But He made His own people
go forth like sheep,
And guided them in the
wilderness like a flock;
53 And He led them on safely, so
that they did not fear;
But the sea overwhelmed their
enemies.
54 And He brought them to His
holy border,
This mountain *which* His right
hand had acquired.
55 He also drove out the nations
before them,
Allotted them an inheritance by
survey,
And made the tribes of Israel
dwell in their tents.

56 Yet they tested and provoked
the Most High God,
And did not keep His
testimonies,
57 But turned back and acted
unfaithfully like their
fathers;
They were turned aside like a
deceitful bow.
58 For they provoked Him to
anger with their high
places,
And moved Him to jealousy with
their carved images.
59 When God heard *this,* He was
furious,
And greatly abhorred Israel,
60 So that He forsook the
tabernacle of Shiloh,
The tent He had placed among
men,
61 And delivered His strength into
captivity,
And His glory into the enemy's
hand.
62 He also gave His people over
to the sword,

And was furious with His
inheritance.
63 The fire consumed their young
men,
And their maidens were not
given in marriage.
64 Their priests fell by the sword,
And their widows made no
lamentation.

65 Then the Lord awoke as *from*
sleep,
Like a mighty man who shouts
because of wine.
66 And He beat back His enemies;
He put them to a perpetual
reproach.

67 Moreover He rejected the tent
of Joseph,
And did not choose the tribe of
Ephraim,
68 But chose the tribe of Judah,
Mount Zion which He loved.
69 And He built His sanctuary like
the heights,
Like the earth which He has
established forever.
70 He also chose David His servant,
And took him from the
sheepfolds;
71 From following the ewes that
had young He brought him,
To shepherd Jacob His people,
And Israel His inheritance.
72 So he shepherded them
according to the integrity of
his heart,
And guided them by the
skillfulness of his hands.

PSALM 79

A prayer for our nation

A Psalm of Asaph.

O GOD, the nations have come
into Your inheritance;
Your holy temple they have
defiled;
They have laid Jerusalem in
heaps.

2 The dead bodies of Your
servants
They have given as food for the
birds of the heavens,
The flesh of Your saints to the
beasts of the earth.
3 Their blood they have shed
like water all around
Jerusalem,
And there was no one to bury
them.
4 We have become a reproach to
our neighbors,
A scorn and derision to those
who are around us.

5 How long, LORD?
Will You be angry forever?
Will Your jealousy burn like
fire?
6 Pour out Your wrath on the
nations that do not know
You,
And on the kingdoms that do
not call on Your name.
7 For they have devoured Jacob,
And laid waste his dwelling
place.

8 Oh, do not remember former
iniquities against us!
Let Your tender mercies come
speedily to meet us,
For we have been brought very
low.
9 Help us, O God of our salvation,
For the glory of Your name;
And deliver us, and provide
atonement for our sins,
For Your name's sake!
10 Why should the nations say,
"Where is their God?"
Let there be known among the
nations in our sight
The avenging of the blood of
Your servants which has been
shed.

11 Let the groaning of the prisoner
come before You;
According to the greatness of
Your power
Preserve those who are
appointed to die;

12 And return to our neighbors
sevenfold into their bosom
Their reproach with which they
have reproached You,
O Lord.

13 So we, Your people and sheep
of Your pasture,
Will give You thanks forever;
We will show forth Your praise
to all generations.

PSALM 80

God will restore Israel

To the Chief Musician. Set to "The Lilies." A
Testimony of Asaph. A Psalm.

GIVE ear, O Shepherd of Israel,
You who lead Joseph like a
flock;
You who dwell between the
cherubim, shine forth!
2 Before Ephraim, Benjamin, and
Manasseh,
Stir up Your strength,
And come and save us!

3 Restore us, O God;
Cause Your face to shine,
And we shall be saved!

4 O LORD God of hosts,
How long will You be angry
Against the prayer of Your
people?
5 You have fed them with the
bread of tears,
And given them tears to drink
in great measure.
6 You have made us a strife to our
neighbors,
And our enemies laugh among
themselves.

7 Restore us, O God of hosts;
Cause Your face to shine,
And we shall be saved!

8 You have brought a vine out of
Egypt;
You have cast out the nations,
and planted it.
9 You prepared room for it,

And caused it to take deep root,
And it filled the land.
10 The hills were covered with its
    shadow,
And the mighty cedars with its
    boughs.
11 She sent out her boughs to the
    Sea,
And her branches to the River.

12 Why have You broken down her
    hedges,
So that all who pass by the way
    pluck her *fruit?*
13 The boar out of the woods
    uproots it,
And the wild beast of the field
    devours it.

14 Return, we beseech You, O God
    of hosts;
Look down from heaven and
    see,
And visit this vine
15 And the vineyard which Your
    right hand has planted,
And the branch *that* You made
    strong for Yourself.
16 *It is* burned with fire, *it is* cut
    down;
They perish at the rebuke of
    Your countenance.
17 Let Your hand be upon the man
    of Your right hand,
Upon the son of man *whom* You
    made strong for Yourself.
18 Then we will not turn back from
    You;
Revive us, and we will call upon
    Your name.

19 Restore us, O LORD God of
    hosts;
Cause Your face to shine,
And we shall be saved!

PSALM 81

I will listen to the Lord

To the Chief Musician. On an instrument of Gath.
A Psalm of Asaph.

SING aloud to God our strength;
    Make a joyful shout to the God
    of Jacob.

2 Raise a song and strike the
    timbrel,
The pleasant harp with the
    lute.

3 Blow the trumpet at the time of
    the New Moon,
At the full moon, on our solemn
    feast day.
4 For this *is* a statute for Israel,
A law of the God of Jacob.
5 This He established in Joseph *as*
    a testimony,
When He went throughout the
    land of Egypt,
Where I heard a language I did
    not understand.

6 "I removed his shoulder from the
    burden;
His hands were freed from the
    baskets.
7 You called in trouble, and I
    delivered you;
I answered you in the secret
    place of thunder;
I tested you at the waters of
    Meribah.   Selah

8 "Hear, O My people, and I will
    admonish you!
O Israel, if you will listen to
    Me!
9 There shall be no foreign god
    among you;
Nor shall you worship any
    foreign god.
10 I *am* the LORD your God,
Who brought you out of the land
    of Egypt;
Open your mouth wide, and I
    will fill it.

11 "But My people would not heed
    My voice,
And Israel would *have* none of
    Me.
12 So I gave them over to their own
    stubborn heart,
To walk in their own counsels.

13 "Oh, that My people would listen
    to Me,

That Israel would walk in My
ways!

14 I would soon subdue their
enemies,
And turn My hand against their
adversaries.

15 The haters of the LORD would
pretend submission to Him,
But their fate would endure
forever.

16 He would have fed them also
with the finest of wheat;
And with honey from the rock I
would have satisfied you."

PSALM 82

God alone judges fairly

A Psalm of Asaph.

GOD stands in the congregation of
the mighty;
He judges among the gods.

2 How long will you judge
unjustly,
And show partiality to the
wicked?   Selah

3 Defend the poor and fatherless;
Do justice to the afflicted and
needy.

4 Deliver the poor and needy;
Free *them* from the hand of the
wicked.

5 They do not know, nor do they
understand;
They walk about in darkness;
All the foundations of the earth
are unstable.

6 I said, "You *are* gods,
And all of you *are* children of
the Most High.

7 But you shall die like men,
And fall like one of the princes."

8 Arise, O God, judge the earth;
For You shall inherit all
nations.

PSALM 83

God will defeat His enemies

A Song. A Psalm of Asaph.

DO not keep silent, O God!
Do not hold Your peace,
And do not be still, O God!

2 For behold, Your enemies make
a tumult;

⚒ DIGGING IN

81:13 Have a Listening Heart Does your heart have ears? Not the kind of ears that are on your head. But your heart can hear in a way that your ears can't.

For example, some people may hear a siren warning them that a fire truck is coming, but they don't get out of the way. They aren't listening, so the fire truck runs into them and kills them. They may have heard the sound of the fire truck, but they paid no attention to its message.

God is also warning us that He is coming to judge the people of the world. Are you listening with your heart? Or are God's warnings just a lot of noise in your ears? God is always telling people that He wants to save them from sin. Are you listening to God with your heart, or are you just hearing with the ears of your head?

82:6 Are You a Child of God? Every-

one is somebody's child. You are the child of your parents. But if you ran away from home and refused to belong to your parents, you might not feel you were their child anymore.

In the same way, everybody is by nature a child of God. But not everybody wants God to be the Father. These people are really orphans of God.

You can only be a true child of God when you come to Him and say, "I want You to be my Father; I want to be Your child." Then God accepts you as a member of His family. Then Jesus is not only your Savior from sin, but He is also your older Brother.

Your earthly parents will die and leave you, but God can never die. He wants to be your Father always. Then Jesus will always be your Brother. Jesus said, "I will never leave you" (Hebrews 13:5).

And those who hate You have
lifted up their head.
3 They have taken crafty counsel
against Your people,
And consulted together against
Your sheltered ones.
4 They have said, "Come, and let
us cut them off from *being* a
nation,
That the name of Israel may be
remembered no more."

5 For they have consulted
together with one consent;
They form a confederacy against
You:
6 The tents of Edom and the
Ishmaelites;
Moab and the Hagrites;
7 Gebal, Ammon, and Amalek;
Philistia with the inhabitants of
Tyre;
8 Assyria also has joined with
them;
They have helped the children
of Lot.   Selah

9 Deal with them as *with* Midian,
As *with* Sisera,
As *with* Jabin at the Brook
Kishon,
10 Who perished at En Dor,
Who became *as* refuse on the
earth.
11 Make their nobles like Oreb and
like Zeeb,
Yes, all their princes like Zebah
and Zalmunna,
12 Who said, "Let us take for
ourselves
The pastures of God for a
possession."

13 O my God, make them like the
whirling dust,
Like the chaff before the wind!
14 As the fire burns the woods,
And as the flame sets the
mountains on fire,
15 So pursue them with Your
tempest,
And frighten them with Your
storm.
16 Fill their faces with shame,

That they may seek Your name,
O LORD.
17 Let them be confounded and
dismayed forever;
Yes, let them be put to shame
and perish,
18 That they may know that You,
whose name alone *is* the
LORD,
Are the Most High over all the
earth.

PSALM 84

Being in God's house makes me happy

To the Chief Musician. On an instrument of Gath.
A Psalm of the sons of Korah.

HOW lovely *is* Your tabernacle,
O LORD of hosts!
2 My soul longs, yes, even faints
For the courts of the LORD;
My heart and my flesh cry out
for the living God.

3 Even the sparrow has found a
home,
And the swallow a nest for
herself,
Where she may lay her young—
Even Your altars, O LORD of
hosts,
My King and my God.
4 Blessed *are* those who dwell in
Your house;
They will still be praising You.
Selah

5 Blessed *is* the man whose
strength *is* in You,
Whose heart *is* set on
pilgrimage.
6 *As they* pass through the Valley
of Baca,
They make it a spring;
The rain also covers it with
pools.
7 They go from strength to
strength;
Each one appears before God
in Zion.

8 O Lord God of hosts, hear my
    prayer;
  Give ear, O God of Jacob!
                              Selah
9 O God, behold our shield,
  And look upon the face of Your
    anointed.
10 For a day in Your courts *is* better
    than a thousand.
   I would rather be a doorkeeper
   in the house of my God
   Than dwell in the tents of
   wickedness.
11 For the Lord God *is* a sun and
    shield;
   The Lord will give grace and
    glory;
   No good *thing* will He withhold
   From those who walk uprightly.
12 O Lord of hosts,
   Blessed *is* the man who trusts
    in You!

PSALM 85

I pray for peace

To the Chief Musician. A Psalm of the sons of Korah.

LORD, You have been favorable to
    Your land;
  You have brought back the
    captivity of Jacob.
2 You have forgiven the iniquity
    of Your people;
  You have covered all their sin.
                              Selah
3 You have taken away all Your
    wrath;
  You have turned from the
    fierceness of Your anger.
4 Restore us, O God of our
    salvation,
  And cause Your anger toward
    us to cease.
5 Will You be angry with us
    forever?
  Will You prolong Your anger to
    all generations?
6 Will You not revive us again,
  That Your people may rejoice in
    You?

7 Show us Your mercy, Lord,
  And grant us Your salvation.
8 I will hear what God the Lord
    will speak,
  For He will speak peace
  To His people and to His saints;
  But let them not turn back to
    folly.
9 Surely His salvation *is* near to
    those who fear Him,
  That glory may dwell in our
    land.

10 Mercy and truth have met
    together;
   Righteousness and peace have
    kissed.
11 Truth shall spring out of the
    earth,
   And righteousness shall look
    down from heaven.
12 Yes, the Lord will give *what is*
    good;
   And our land will yield its
    increase.
13 Righteousness will go before
    Him,
   And shall make His footsteps *our*
    pathway.

PSALM 86

Teach us, O Lord

A Prayer of David.

BOW down Your ear, O Lord, hear
    me;
   For I *am* poor and needy.
2 Preserve my life, for I *am* holy;
  You are my God;
  Save Your servant who trusts in
    You!
3 Be merciful to me, O Lord,
  For I cry to You all day long.
4 Rejoice the soul of Your servant,
  For to You, O Lord, I lift up my
    soul.
5 For You, Lord, *are* good, and
    ready to forgive,
  And abundant in mercy to all
    those who call upon You.

6 Give ear, O LORD, to my prayer;
   And attend to the voice of my
      supplications.
7 In the day of my trouble I will
      call upon You,
   For You will answer me.

8 Among the gods *there is* none
      like You, O Lord;
   Nor *are there any works* like
      Your works.
9 All nations whom You have
      made
   Shall come and worship before
      You, O Lord,
   And shall glorify Your name.
10 For You *are* great, and do
      wondrous things;
   You alone *are* God.

11 Teach me Your way, O LORD;
   I will walk in Your truth;
   Unite my heart to fear Your
      name.
12 I will praise You, O Lord my
      God, with all my heart,
   And I will glorify Your name
      forevermore.
13 For great *is* Your mercy toward
      me,
   And You have delivered my soul
      from the depths of Sheol.

14 O God, the proud have risen
      against me,
   And a mob of violent *men* have
      sought my life,
   And have not set You before
      them.
15 But You, O Lord, *are* a God
      full of compassion, and
      gracious,
   Longsuffering and abundant in
      mercy and truth.

16 Oh, turn to me, and have mercy
      on me!
   Give Your strength to Your
      servant,
   And save the son of Your
      maidservant.
17 Show me a sign for good,
   That those who hate me may
      see it and be ashamed,

Because You, LORD, have
   helped me and comforted me.

PSALM 87

God loves His city

A Psalm of the sons of Korah. A Song.

HIS foundation *is* in the holy
      mountains.
2 The LORD loves the gates of Zion
   More than all the dwellings of
      Jacob.
3 Glorious things are spoken of
      you,
   O city of God!   Selah

4 "I will make mention of Rahab
      and Babylon to those who
      know Me;
   Behold, O Philistia and Tyre,
      with Ethiopia:
   'This *one* was born there.' "

5 And of Zion it will be said,
   "This *one* and that *one* were born
      in her;
   And the Most High Himself shall
      establish her."
6 The LORD will record,
   When He registers the peoples:
   "This *one* was born there."
                                       Selah

7 Both the singers and the players
      on instruments *say,*
   "All my springs *are* in you."

PSALM 88

God saves us from death

A Song. A Psalm of the sons of Korah. To the Chief
Musician. Set to "Mahalath Leannoth." A
Contemplation of Heman the Ezrahite.

O LORD, God of my salvation,
   I have cried out day and night
      before You.
2 Let my prayer come before You;
   Incline Your ear to my cry.

3 For my soul is full of troubles,
   And my life draws near to the
      grave.

4 I am counted with those who go
       down to the pit;
   I am like a man *who has* no
       strength,
5 Adrift among the dead,
   Like the slain who lie in the
       grave,
   Whom You remember no more,
   And who are cut off from Your
       hand.

6 You have laid me in the lowest
       pit,
   In darkness, in the depths.
7 Your wrath lies heavy upon
       me,
   And You have afflicted *me* with
       all Your waves.   Selah
8 You have put away my
       acquaintances far from me;
   You have made me an
       abomination to them;
   I am shut up, and I cannot get
       out;
9 My eye wastes away because of
       affliction.

   LORD, I have called daily upon
       You;
   I have stretched out my hands
       to You.
10 Will You work wonders for the
       dead?
   Shall the dead arise *and* praise
       You?   Selah
11 Shall Your lovingkindness be
       declared in the grave?
   Or Your faithfulness in the place
       of destruction?
12 Shall Your wonders be known
       in the dark?
   And Your righteousness in the
       land of forgetfulness?

13 But to You I have cried out,
       O LORD,
   And in the morning my prayer
       comes before You.
14 LORD, why do You cast off my
       soul?
   Why do You hide Your face
       from me?
15 I *have been* afflicted and ready
       to die from *my* youth;

   I suffer Your terrors;
   I am distraught.
16 Your fierce wrath has gone over
       me;
   Your terrors have cut me off.
17 They came around me all day
       long like water;
   They engulfed me altogether.
18 Loved one and friend You have
       put far from me,
   And my acquaintances into
       darkness.

PSALM 89

The Lord remembers those who serve Him

A Contemplation of Ethan the Ezrahite.

I WILL sing of the mercies of the
       LORD forever;
   With my mouth will I make
       known Your faithfulness to all
       generations.
2 For I have said, "Mercy shall be
       built up forever;
   Your faithfulness You shall
       establish in the very
       heavens."

3 "I have made a covenant with My
       chosen,
   I have sworn to My servant
       David:
4 'Your seed I will establish forever,
   And build up your throne to all
       generations.' "   Selah

5 And the heavens will praise Your
       wonders, O LORD;
   Your faithfulness also in the
       assembly of the saints.
6 For who in the heavens can be
       compared to the LORD?
   Who among the sons of the
       mighty can be likened to the
       LORD?
7 God is greatly to be feared in
       the assembly of the saints,
   And to be held in reverence by
       all *those* around Him.
8 O LORD God of hosts,

Who *is* mighty like You,
   O LORD?
Your faithfulness also surrounds
   You.
9 You rule the raging of the
      sea;
   When its waves rise, You still
      them.
10 You have broken Rahab in
      pieces, as one who is slain;
   You have scattered Your
      enemies with Your mighty
      arm.

11 The heavens *are* Yours, the
      earth also *is* Yours;
   The world and all its fullness,
      You have founded them.
12 The north and the south, You
      have created them;
   Tabor and Hermon rejoice in
      Your name.
13 You have a mighty arm;
   Strong is Your hand, *and* high
      is Your right hand.
14 Righteousness and justice *are*
      the foundation of Your
      throne;
   Mercy and truth go before Your
      face.
15 Blessed *are* the people who
      know the joyful sound!
   They walk, O LORD, in the light
      of Your countenance.
16 In Your name they rejoice all
      day long,
   And in Your righteousness they
      are exalted.
17 For You *are* the glory of their
      strength,
   And in Your favor our horn is
      exalted.
18 For our shield *belongs* to the
      LORD,
   And our king to the Holy One
      of Israel.

19 Then You spoke in a vision to
      Your holy one,
   And said: "I have given help to
      one who is mighty;
   I have exalted one chosen from
      the people.
20 I have found My servant David;

With My holy oil I have anointed
   him,
21 With whom My hand shall be
      established;
   Also My arm shall strengthen
      him.
22 The enemy shall not outwit him,
   Nor the son of wickedness afflict
      him.
23 I will beat down his foes before
      his face,
   And plague those who hate him.

24 "But My faithfulness and My
      mercy *shall be* with him,
   And in My name his horn shall
      be exalted.
25 Also I will set his hand over the
      sea,
   And his right hand over the
      rivers.
26 He shall cry to Me, 'You *are* my
      Father,
   My God, and the rock of my
      salvation.'
27 Also I will make him My
      firstborn,
   The highest of the kings of the
      earth.
28 My mercy I will keep for him
      forever,
   And My covenant shall stand
      firm with him.
29 His seed also I will make *to*
      endure forever,
   And his throne as the days of
      heaven.

30 "If his sons forsake My law
   And do not walk in My
      judgments,
31 If they break My statutes
   And do not keep My
      commandments,
32 Then I will punish their
      transgression with the rod,
   And their iniquity with stripes.
33 Nevertheless My lovingkindness
      I will not utterly take from
      him,
   Nor allow My faithfulness to fail.
34 My covenant I will not break,
   Nor alter the word that has gone
      out of My lips.

35 Once I have sworn by My
holiness;
I will not lie to David:
36 His seed shall endure forever,
And his throne as the sun before
Me;
37 It shall be established forever like
the moon,
Even *like* the faithful witness in
the sky.''   Selah

38 But You have cast off and
abhorred,
You have been furious with
Your anointed.
39 You have renounced the
covenant of Your servant;
You have profaned his crown *by
casting it* to the ground.
40 You have broken down all his
hedges;
You have brought his
strongholds to ruin.
41 All who pass by the way plunder
him;
He is a reproach to his
neighbors.
42 You have exalted the right hand
of his adversaries;
You have made all his enemies
rejoice.
43 You have also turned back the
edge of his sword,
And have not sustained him in
the battle.
44 You have made his glory
cease,
And cast his throne down to the
ground.
45 The days of his youth You have
shortened;
You have covered him with
shame.   Selah

46 How long, LORD?
Will You hide Yourself forever?
Will Your wrath burn like fire?
47 Remember how short my time
is;
For what futility have You
created all the children of
men?
48 What man can live and not see
death?

Can he deliver his life from the
power of the grave?   Selah
49 Lord, where *are* Your former
lovingkindnesses,
Which You swore to David in
Your truth?
50 Remember, Lord, the reproach
of Your servants—
How I bear in my bosom *the
reproach of* all the many
peoples,
51 With which Your enemies have
reproached, O LORD,
With which they have
reproached the footsteps of
Your anointed.

52 Blessed *be* the LORD
forevermore!
Amen and Amen.

Book Four: Psalms 90—106

PSALM 90

All our days come from God

A Prayer of Moses the man of God.

LORD, You have been our dwelling
place in all generations.
2 Before the mountains *were*
brought forth,
Or ever You had formed the
earth and the world,
Even from everlasting to
everlasting, You *are* God.

3 You turn man to destruction,
And say, "Return, O children of
men.''
4 For a thousand years in Your
sight
Are like yesterday when it is
past,
And *like* a watch in the night.
5 You carry them away *like* a
flood;
They are like a sleep.
In the morning they are like
grass *which* grows up:
6 In the morning it flourishes and
grows up;

In the evening it is cut down and withers.

7 For we have been consumed by Your anger,
And by Your wrath we are terrified.

8 You have set our iniquities before You,
Our secret *sins* in the light of Your countenance.

9 For all our days have passed away in Your wrath;
We finish our years like a sigh.

10 The days of our lives *are* seventy years;
And if by reason of strength *they are* eighty years,
Yet their boast *is* only labor and sorrow;
For it is soon cut off, and we fly away.

11 Who knows the power of Your anger?
For as the fear of You, *so is* Your wrath.

12 So teach *us* to number our days,
That *we* may gain a heart of wisdom.

13 Return, O Lord!
How long?
And have compassion on Your servants.

14 Oh, satisfy us early with Your mercy,
That *we* may rejoice and be glad all our days!

15 Make us glad according to the days *in which* You have afflicted us,

The years *in which* we have seen evil.

16 Let Your work appear to Your servants,
And Your glory to their children.

17 And let the beauty of the Lord our God be upon us,
And establish the work of our hands for us;
Yes, establish the work of our hands.

PSALM 91

God is our strong Protector

HE who dwells in the secret place of the Most High
Shall abide under the shadow of the Almighty.

2 I will say of the Lord, "He is my refuge and my fortress;
My God, in Him I will trust."

3 Surely He shall deliver you from the snare of the fowler
And from the perilous pestilence.

4 He shall cover you with His feathers,
And under His wings you shall take refuge;
His truth *shall be your* shield and buckler.

5 You shall not be afraid of the terror by night,
Nor of the arrow *that* flies by day,

6 *Nor* of the pestilence *that* walks in darkness,

⚒ DIGGING IN

90:12 Ask God for Wisdom Moses wrote these words. He realized his days on earth were few. So he prayed for wisdom. Next to love, the greatest gift of God is wisdom.

You need wisdom to live in the world. The world is getting more crowded, and there are many voices that claim to be the voices of truth. But many of these voices are lies. You need wisdom to know the difference between truth and falsehood.

The Devil came long ago and deceived Adam and Eve (see Genesis 3). He deceives people today in the same way. No matter how old you are, you need to ask God every day for wisdom to know right from wrong. Then you also need to spend time daily studying God's Word. As you follow these two rules, you will become wise.

Nor of the destruction *that* lays
waste at noonday.

7 A thousand may fall at your side,
And ten thousand at your right
hand;
But it shall not come near you.

8 Only with your eyes shall you
look,
And see the reward of the
wicked.

9 Because you have made the
LORD, *who is* my refuge,
Even the Most High, your
dwelling place,

10 No evil shall befall you,
Nor shall any plague come near
your dwelling;

11 For He shall give His angels
charge over you,
To keep you in all your ways.

12 In *their* hands they shall bear
you up,
Lest you dash your foot against
a stone.

13 You shall tread upon the lion
and the cobra,
The young lion and the serpent
you shall trample underfoot.

14 "Because he has set his love upon
Me, therefore I will deliver
him;
I will set him on high, because
he has known My name.

15 He shall call upon Me, and I will
answer him;
I *will be* with him in trouble;
I will deliver him and honor him.

16 With long life I will satisfy him,
And show him My salvation."

PSALM 92

We sing a song of praise

A Psalm. A Song for the Sabbath day.

*I*T is good to give thanks to the LORD,
And to sing praises to Your
name, O Most High;

2 To declare Your lovingkindness
in the morning,

And Your faithfulness every
night,

3 On an instrument of ten strings,
On the lute,
And on the harp,
With harmonious sound.

4 For You, LORD, have made me
glad through Your work;
I will triumph in the works of
Your hands.

5 O LORD, how great are Your
works!
Your thoughts are very deep.

6 A senseless man does not know,
Nor does a fool understand this.

7 When the wicked spring up like
grass,
And when all the workers of
iniquity flourish,
It is that they may be destroyed
forever.

8 But You, LORD, *are* on high
forevermore.

9 For behold, Your enemies,
O LORD,
For behold, Your enemies shall
perish;
All the workers of iniquity shall
be scattered.

10 But my horn You have exalted
like a wild ox;
I have been anointed with fresh
oil.

11 My eye also has seen *my desire*
on my enemies;
My ears hear *my desire* on the
wicked
Who rise up against me.

12 The righteous shall flourish like
a palm tree,
He shall grow like a cedar in
Lebanon.

13 Those who are planted in the
house of the LORD
Shall flourish in the courts of our
God.

14 They shall still bear fruit in old
age;
They shall be fresh and
flourishing,

*Big cedar trees from Lebanon provided lumber
for Solomon's temple.*

15 To declare that the LORD is
   upright;
   He is my rock, and *there is* no
   unrighteousness in Him.

PSALM 93

The Lord rules the earth

THE LORD reigns, He is clothed with
   majesty;
   The LORD is clothed,
   He has girded Himself with
   strength.
   Surely the world is established,
   so that it cannot be moved.
2 Your throne *is* established from
   of old;
   You *are* from everlasting.

3 The floods have lifted up,
   O LORD,
   The floods have lifted up their
   voice;
   The floods lift up their waves.
4 The LORD on high *is* mightier
   Than the noise of many waters,
   Than the mighty waves of the
   sea.

5 Your testimonies are very sure;
   Holiness adorns Your house,
   O LORD, forever.

PSALM 94

God's justice is sure

O LORD God, to whom vengeance
   belongs—
   O God, to whom vengeance
   belongs, shine forth!
2 Rise up, O Judge of the earth;
   Render punishment to the
   proud.
3 LORD, how long will the wicked,
   How long will the wicked
   triumph?

4 They utter speech, *and* speak
   insolent things;
   All the workers of iniquity boast
   in themselves.
5 They break in pieces Your
   people, O LORD,
   And afflict Your heritage.
6 They slay the widow and the
   stranger,
   And murder the fatherless.
7 Yet they say, "The LORD does
   not see,
   Nor does the God of Jacob
   understand."

8 Understand, you senseless
   among the people;
   And *you* fools, when will you be
   wise?
9 He who planted the ear, shall
   He not hear?
   He who formed the eye, shall
   He not see?
10 He who instructs the nations,
   shall He not correct,
   He who teaches man
   knowledge?
11 The LORD knows the thoughts
   of man,
   That they *are* futile.

12 Blessed *is* the man whom You
   instruct, O LORD,
   And teach out of Your law,

13 That You may give him rest from
   the days of adversity,
   Until the pit is dug for the
   wicked.
14 For the LORD will not cast off His
   people,
   Nor will He forsake His
   inheritance.
15 But judgment will return to
   righteousness,
   And all the upright in heart will
   follow it.

16 Who will rise up for me against
   the evildoers?
   Who will stand up for me against
   the workers of iniquity?
17 Unless the LORD *had been* my
   help,
   My soul would soon have settled
   in silence.
18 If I say, "My foot slips,"
   Your mercy, O LORD, will hold
   me up.
19 In the multitude of my anxieties
   within me,
   Your comforts delight my soul.

20 Shall the throne of iniquity,
   which devises evil by law,
   Have fellowship with You?
21 They gather together against the
   life of the righteous,
   And condemn innocent blood.
22 But the LORD has been my
   defense,
   And my God the rock of my
   refuge.
23 He has brought on them their
   own iniquity,
   And shall cut them off in their
   own wickedness;
   The LORD our God shall cut
   them off.

PSALM 95

We praise and obey God

OH come, let us sing to the LORD!
   Let us shout joyfully to the Rock
   of our salvation.
2 Let us come before His presence
   with thanksgiving;
   Let us shout joyfully to Him with
   psalms.
3 For the LORD *is* the great God,
   And the great King above all
   gods.
4 In His hand *are* the deep places
   of the earth;
   The heights of the hills *are* His
   also.
5 The sea *is* His, for He made it;
   And His hands formed the dry
   land.

6 Oh come, let us worship and
   bow down;
   Let us kneel before the LORD our
   Maker.
7 For He *is* our God,
   And *we are* the people of His
   pasture,
   And the sheep of His hand.

   Today, if you will hear His voice:
8 "Do not harden your hearts, as
   in the rebellion,
   As *in* the day of trial in the
   wilderness,
9 When your fathers tested Me;
   They tried Me, though they saw
   My work.
10 For forty years I was grieved with
   that generation,
   And said, 'It *is* a people who go
   astray in their hearts,
   And they do not know My
   ways.'
11 So I swore in My wrath,
   'They shall not enter My rest.' "

PSALM 96

God's power is above everything

OH, sing to the LORD a new song!
   Sing to the LORD, all the earth.
2 Sing to the LORD, bless His
   name;
   Proclaim the good news of His
   salvation from day to day.
3 Declare His glory among the
   nations,
   His wonders among all peoples.

4 For the LORD *is* great and greatly
   to be praised;

He *is* to be feared above all
gods.
5 For all the gods of the peoples
are idols,
But the LORD made the heavens.
6 Honor and majesty *are* before
Him;
Strength and beauty *are* in His
sanctuary.

7 Give to the LORD, O families of
the peoples,
Give to the LORD glory and
strength.
8 Give to the LORD the glory *due*
His name;
Bring an offering, and come into
His courts.
9 Oh, worship the LORD in the
beauty of holiness!
Tremble before Him, all the
earth.

10 Say among the nations, "The
LORD reigns;
The world also is firmly
established,
It shall not be moved;
He shall judge the peoples
righteously."

11 Let the heavens rejoice, and let
the earth be glad;
Let the sea roar, and all its
fullness;
12 Let the field be joyful, and all
that *is* in it.
Then all the trees of the woods
will rejoice before the LORD.
13 For He is coming, for He is
coming to judge the earth.
He shall judge the world with
righteousness,
And the peoples with His truth.

PSALM 97

We are happy because He is our King

THE LORD reigns;
Let the earth rejoice;
Let the multitude of isles be glad!

2 Clouds and darkness surround
Him;
Righteousness and justice *are*
the foundation of His throne.
3 A fire goes before Him,
And burns up His enemies
round about.
4 His lightnings light the world;
The earth sees and trembles.
5 The mountains melt like wax at
the presence of the LORD,
At the presence of the Lord of
the whole earth.
6 The heavens declare His
righteousness,
And all the peoples see His
glory.

7 Let all be put to shame who
serve carved images,
Who boast of idols.
Worship Him, all *you* gods.
8 Zion hears and is glad,
And the daughters of Judah
rejoice
Because of Your judgments,
O LORD.
9 For You, LORD, *are* most high
above all the earth;
You are exalted far above all
gods.

10 You who love the LORD, hate
evil!
He preserves the souls of His
saints;
He delivers them out of the hand
of the wicked.
11 Light is sown for the righteous,
And gladness for the upright in
heart.
12 Rejoice in the LORD, you
righteous,
And give thanks at the
remembrance of His holy
name.

PSALM 98

We sing a new song to the Lord

A Psalm.

OH, sing to the LORD a new
song!

For He has done marvelous
    things;
His right hand and His holy arm
    have gained Him the victory.
2 The LORD has made known His
    salvation;
His righteousness He has
    revealed in the sight of the
    nations.
3 He has remembered His mercy
    and His faithfulness to the
    house of Israel;
All the ends of the earth have
    seen the salvation of our
    God.

4 Shout joyfully to the LORD, all
    the earth;
Break forth in song, rejoice, and
    sing praises.
5 Sing to the LORD with the harp,
With the harp and the sound of
    a psalm,
6 With trumpets and the sound of
    a horn;
Shout joyfully before the LORD,
    the King.

7 Let the sea roar, and all its
    fullness,
The world and those who dwell
    in it;
8 Let the rivers clap *their* hands;
Let the hills be joyful together
    before the LORD,
9 For He is coming to judge the
    earth.
With righteousness He shall
    judge the world,
And the peoples with equity.

PSALM 99

The Lord our God is holy

THE LORD reigns;
    Let the peoples tremble!
He dwells *between* the
    cherubim;
Let the earth be moved!
2 The LORD *is* great in Zion,
And He *is* high above all the
    peoples.

What Does *Holy* Mean?

You often hear the word *holy*. What
does it mean? The word means, first
of all, that the holy person or object
is *separate*. God is separate from us
because He is our eternal Creator.
God is also *perfect* in righteousness
and love. We also can be holy as we
become like God.

3 Let them praise Your great and
    awesome name—
He *is* holy.

4 The King's strength also loves
    justice;
You have established equity;
You have executed justice and
    righteousness in Jacob.
5 Exalt the LORD our God,
And worship at His footstool—
He *is* holy.

6 Moses and Aaron were among
    His priests,
And Samuel was among those
    who called upon His name;
They called upon the LORD, and
    He answered them.
7 He spoke to them in the cloudy
    pillar;
They kept His testimonies and
    the ordinance He gave them.

8 You answered them, O LORD
    our God;
You were to them
    God-Who-Forgives,
Though You took vengeance on
    their deeds.
9 Exalt the LORD our God,
And worship at His holy hill;
For the LORD our God *is* holy.

PSALM 100

We come to the Lord with thanksgiving

A Psalm of Thanksgiving.

MAKE a joyful shout to the LORD,
    all you lands!

2 Serve the Lord with gladness;
   Come before His presence with
      singing.
3 Know that the Lord, He *is* God;
   It is He *who* has made us, and
      not we ourselves;
   We are His people and the
      sheep of His pasture.

4 Enter into His gates with
      thanksgiving,
   And into His courts with praise.
   Be thankful to Him, *and* bless
      His name.
5 For the Lord *is* good;
   His mercy *is* everlasting,
   And His truth *endures* to all
      generations.

PSALM 101

I want to be holy

A Psalm of David.

I WILL sing of mercy and justice;
   To You, O Lord, I will sing
      praises.

2 I will behave wisely in a perfect
      way.
   Oh, when will You come to me?
   I will walk within my house with
      a perfect heart.

3 I will set nothing wicked before
      my eyes;
   I hate the work of those who fall
      away;
   It shall not cling to me.

4 A perverse heart shall depart
      from me;
   I will not know wickedness.

5 Whoever secretly slanders his
      neighbor,
   Him I will destroy;
   The one who has a haughty look
      and a proud heart,
   Him I will not endure.

6 My eyes *shall be* on the faithful
      of the land,
   That they may dwell with me;
   He who walks in a perfect way,
   He shall serve me.
7 He who works deceit shall not
      dwell within my house;
   He who tells lies shall not
      continue in my presence.
8 Early I will destroy all the wicked
      of the land,
   That I may cut off all the
      evildoers from the city of the
      Lord.

PSALM 102

I really need the Lord

A Prayer of the afflicted, when he is overwhelmed
and pours out his complaint before the Lord.

H EAR my prayer, O Lord,
   And let my cry come to You.
2 Do not hide Your face from me
      in the day of my trouble;
   Incline Your ear to me;
   In the day that I call, answer me
      speedily.

⛏ DIGGING IN

100:3 God Made Us for Himself We have often said that God created all things, and He is your Creator, too. But we need to talk about *why* God created you.

Perhaps we could ask first why you "create" anything yourself. Have you ever made anything with your own hands like a boat, a model airplane, a doll, or a doll's house? Why did you make it? You created that thing to give you joy. If your cre-ation turned out badly, you fixed it so that you could still enjoy what you made.

God created you for the same reason. He created you for His enjoyment. Sad to say, we disappoint God by not being what He meant us to be. But God has made a way for us to come back and let Him make us new. In fact, He wants you and me to be born all over again. Have you asked your Creator to make you a "new creation"?

3 For my days are consumed like
     smoke,
   And my bones are burned like
     a hearth.
4 My heart is stricken and withered
     like grass,
   So that I forget to eat my bread.
5 Because of the sound of my
     groaning
   My bones cling to my skin.
6 I am like a pelican of the
     wilderness;
   I am like an owl of the desert.
7 I lie awake,
   And am like a sparrow alone on
     the housetop.
8 My enemies reproach me all day
     long;
   Those who deride me swear an
     oath against me.
9 For I have eaten ashes like
     bread,
   And mingled my drink with
     weeping,
10 Because of Your indignation and
     Your wrath;
   For You have lifted me up and
     cast me away.
11 My days *are* like a shadow that
     lengthens,
   And I wither away like grass.

12 But You, O Lord, shall endure
     forever,
   And the remembrance of Your
     name to all generations.
13 You will arise *and* have mercy
     on Zion;
   For the time to favor her,
   Yes, the set time, has come.
14 For Your servants take pleasure
     in her stones,
   And show favor to her dust.
15 So the nations shall fear the
     name of the Lord,
   And all the kings of the earth
     Your glory.
16 For the Lord shall build up Zion;
   He shall appear in His glory.
17 He shall regard the prayer of the
     destitute,
   And shall not despise their
     prayer.

18 This will be written for the
     generation to come,
   That a people yet to be created
     may praise the Lord.
19 For He looked down from the
     height of His sanctuary;
   From heaven the Lord viewed
     the earth,
20 To hear the groaning of the
     prisoner,
   To release those appointed to
     death,
21 To declare the name of the Lord
     in Zion,
   And His praise in Jerusalem,
22 When the peoples are gathered
     together,
   And the kingdoms, to serve the
     Lord.
23 He weakened my strength in the
     way;
   He shortened my days.
24 I said, "O my God,
   Do not take me away in the
     midst of my days;
   Your years *are* throughout all
     generations.
25 Of old You laid the foundation
     of the earth,
   And the heavens *are* the work
     of Your hands.
26 They will perish, but You will
     endure;
   Yes, they will all grow old like a
     garment;
   Like a cloak You will change
     them,
   And they will be changed.
27 But You *are* the same,
   And Your years will have no
     end.
28 The children of Your servants
     will continue,
   And their descendants will be
     established before You."

PSALM 103

God is so kind and loving

A Psalm of David.

BLESS the Lord, O my soul;
     And all that is within me, *bless*
       His holy name!

2 Bless the LORD, O my soul,
And forget not all His benefits:
3 Who forgives all your iniquities,
Who heals all your diseases,
4 Who redeems your life from
destruction,
Who crowns you with
lovingkindness and tender
mercies,
5 Who satisfies your mouth with
good *things,*
So that your youth is renewed
like the eagle's.

6 The LORD executes
righteousness
And justice for all who are
oppressed.
7 He made known His ways to
Moses,
His acts to the children of Israel.
8 The LORD *is* merciful and
gracious,
Slow to anger, and abounding
in mercy.
9 He will not always strive *with us,*
Nor will He keep *His anger*
forever.
10 He has not dealt with us
according to our sins,
Nor punished us according to
our iniquities.

11 For as the heavens are high
above the earth,
So great is His mercy toward
those who fear Him;
12 As far as the east is from the
west,
So far has He removed our
transgressions from us.
13 As a father pities *his* children,
So the LORD pities those who
fear Him.
14 For He knows our frame;
He remembers that we *are* dust.

15 *As for* man, his days *are* like
grass;
As a flower of the field, so he
flourishes.
16 For the wind passes over it, and
it is gone,
And its place remembers it no
more.

Wild flowers bloom near Jerusalem.

17 But the mercy of the LORD *is*
from everlasting to everlasting
On those who fear Him,
And His righteousness to
children's children,
18 To such as keep His covenant,
And to those who remember His
commandments to do them.

19 The LORD has established His
throne in heaven,
And His kingdom rules over all.

20 Bless the LORD, you His angels,
Who excel in strength, who do
His word,
Heeding the voice of His word.
21 Bless the LORD, all *you* His hosts,
You ministers of His, who do His
pleasure.
22 Bless the LORD, all His works,
In all places of His dominion.

Bless the LORD, O my soul!

PSALM 104

God cares for His creation

BLESS the LORD, O my soul!

O LORD my God, You are very
great:

You are clothed with honor and
   majesty,
2 Who cover *Yourself* with light as
   with a garment,
Who stretch out the heavens like
   a curtain.

3 He lays the beams of His upper
   chambers in the waters,
Who makes the clouds His
   chariot,
Who walks on the wings of the
   wind,
4 Who makes His angels spirits,
   His ministers a flame of fire.

5 *You who* laid the foundations of
   the earth,
So *that* it should not be moved
   forever,
6 You covered it with the deep as
   with a garment;
The waters stood above the
   mountains.
7 At Your rebuke they fled;
At the voice of Your thunder
   they hastened away.
8 They went up over the
   mountains;
They went down into the
   valleys,
To the place which You founded
   for them.
9 You have set a boundary that
   they may not pass over,
That they may not return to
   cover the earth.

10 He sends the springs into the
   valleys;
They flow among the hills.
11 They give drink to every beast
   of the field;
The wild donkeys quench their
   thirst.
12 By them the birds of the heavens
   have their home;
They sing among the branches.
13 He waters the hills from His
   upper chambers;
The earth is satisfied with the
   fruit of Your works.

14 He causes the grass to grow for
   the cattle,

And vegetation for the service of
   man,
That he may bring forth food
   from the earth,
15 And wine *that* makes glad the
   heart of man,
Oil to make *his* face shine,
And bread *which* strengthens
   man's heart.
16 The trees of the LORD are full
   of sap,
The cedars of Lebanon which
   He planted,
17 Where the birds make their
   nests;
The stork has her home in the
   fir trees.
18 The high hills *are* for the wild
   goats;
The cliffs are a refuge for the
   rock badgers.

19 He appointed the moon for
   seasons;
The sun knows its going down.
20 You make darkness, and it is
   night,
In which all the beasts of the
   forest creep about.
21 The young lions roar after their
   prey,
And seek their food from God.
22 *When* the sun rises, they gather
   together
And lie down in their dens.
23 Man goes out to his work
And to his labor until the
   evening.

24 O LORD, how manifold are Your
   works!
In wisdom You have made them
   all.
The earth is full of Your
   possessions—
25 This great and wide sea,
In which *are* innumerable
   teeming things,
Living things both small and
   great.
26 There the ships sail about;
There is that Leviathan
Which You have made to play
   there.

27 These all wait for You,
   That You may give *them* their
      food in due season.
28 *What* You give them they gather
      in;
   You open Your hand, they are
      filled with good.
29 You hide Your face, they are
      troubled;
   You take away their breath, they
      die and return to their dust.
30 You send forth Your Spirit, they
      are created;
   And You renew the face of the
      earth.

31 May the glory of the LORD
      endure forever;
   May the LORD rejoice in His
      works.
32 He looks on the earth, and it
      trembles;
   He touches the hills, and they
      smoke.

33 I will sing to the LORD as long
      as I live;
   I will sing praise to my God while
      I have my being.
34 May my meditation be sweet to
      Him;
   I will be glad in the LORD.
35 May sinners be consumed from
      the earth,
   And the wicked be no more.

   Bless the LORD, O my soul!
   Praise the LORD!

PSALM 105

God cares for His people

OH, give thanks to the LORD!
   Call upon His name;
   Make known His deeds among
      the peoples!
2 Sing to Him, sing psalms to
      Him;
   Talk of all His wondrous works!
3 Glory in His holy name;
   Let the hearts of those rejoice
      who seek the LORD!

4 Seek the LORD and His strength;
   Seek His face evermore!
5 Remember His marvelous works
      which He has done,
   His wonders, and the judgments
      of His mouth,
6 O seed of Abraham His servant,
   You children of Jacob, His
      chosen ones!

7 He *is* the LORD our God;
   His judgments *are* in all the
      earth.
8 He remembers His covenant
      forever,
   The word *which* He
      commanded, for a thousand
      generations,
9 *The covenant* which He made
      with Abraham,
   And His oath to Isaac,
10 And confirmed it to Jacob for a
      statute,
   To Israel *as* an everlasting
      covenant,
11 Saying, "To you I will give the
      land of Canaan
   As the allotment of your
      inheritance,"

12 When they were few in number,
   Indeed very few, and strangers
      in it.
13 When they went from one
      nation to another,
   From *one* kingdom to another
      people,
14 He permitted no one to do them
      wrong;
   Yes, He rebuked kings for their
      sakes,
15 *Saying,* "Do not touch My
      anointed ones,
   And do My prophets no harm."

16 Moreover He called for a famine
      in the land;
   He destroyed all the provision
      of bread.
17 He sent a man before them—
      Joseph—*who* was sold as a
      slave.
18 They hurt his feet with fetters,
   He was laid in irons.

19 Until the time that his word came
to pass,
The word of the LORD tested
him.
20 The king sent and released
him,
The ruler of the people let him
go free.
21 He made him lord of his house,
And ruler of all his possessions,
22 To bind his princes at his
pleasure,
And teach his elders wisdom.

23 Israel also came into Egypt,
And Jacob dwelt in the land of
Ham.
24 He increased His people greatly,
And made them stronger than
their enemies.
25 He turned their heart to hate His
people,
To deal craftily with His servants.

26 He sent Moses His servant,
And Aaron whom He had
chosen.
27 They performed His signs
among them,
And wonders in the land of
Ham.
28 He sent darkness, and made *it*
dark;
And they did not rebel against
His word.
29 He turned their waters into
blood,
And killed their fish.
30 Their land abounded with frogs,
Even in the chambers of their
kings.
31 He spoke, and there came
swarms of flies,
And lice in all their territory.
32 He gave them hail for rain,
And flaming fire in their land.
33 He struck their vines also, and
their fig trees,
And splintered the trees of their
territory.
34 He spoke, and locusts came,
Young locusts without number,
35 And ate up all the vegetation in
their land,

And devoured the fruit of their
ground.
36 He also destroyed all the
firstborn in their land,
The first of all their strength.

37 He also brought them out with
silver and gold,
And *there was* none feeble
among His tribes.
38 Egypt was glad when they
departed,
For the fear of them had fallen
upon them.
39 He spread a cloud for a
covering,
And fire to give light in the night.
40 *The people* asked, and He
brought quail,
And satisfied them with the
bread of heaven.
41 He opened the rock, and water
gushed out;
It ran in the dry places *like* a
river.

42 For He remembered His holy
promise,
And Abraham His servant.
43 He brought out His people with
joy,
His chosen ones with gladness.
44 He gave them the lands of the
Gentiles,
And they inherited the labor of
the nations,
45 That they might observe His
statutes
And keep His laws.

Praise the LORD!

PSALM 106

God is very patient

PRAISE the LORD!

Oh, give thanks to the LORD, for
He is good!
For His mercy *endures* forever.

2 Who can utter the mighty acts
of the LORD?

Who can declare all His praise?
3 Blessed *are* those who keep
    justice,
  And he who does righteousness
    at all times!

4 Remember me, O LORD, with
    the favor *You have toward*
    Your people.
  Oh, visit me with Your salvation,
5 That I may see the benefit of
    Your chosen ones,
  That I may rejoice in the
    gladness of Your nation,
  That I may glory with Your
    inheritance.

6 We have sinned with our fathers,
  We have committed iniquity,
  We have done wickedly.
7 Our fathers in Egypt did not
    understand Your wonders;
  They did not remember the
    multitude of Your mercies,
  But rebelled by the sea—the
    Red Sea.

8 Nevertheless He saved them for
    His name's sake,
  That He might make His mighty
    power known.
9 He rebuked the Red Sea also,
    and it dried up;
  So He led them through the
    depths,
  As through the wilderness.
10 He saved them from the hand
    of him who hated *them,*
  And redeemed them from the
    hand of the enemy.
11 The waters covered their
    enemies;
  There was not one of them left.
12 Then they believed His words;
  They sang His praise.

13 They soon forgot His works;
  They did not wait for His
    counsel,
14 But lusted exceedingly in the
    wilderness,
  And tested God in the desert.
15 And He gave them their request,
  But sent leanness into their soul.

16 When they envied Moses in the
    camp,
  And Aaron the saint of the
    LORD,
17 The earth opened up and
    swallowed Dathan,
  And covered the faction of
    Abiram.
18 A fire was kindled in their
    company;
  The flame burned up the
    wicked.

19 They made a calf in Horeb,
  And worshiped the molded
    image.
20 Thus they changed their glory
  Into the image of an ox that *eats*
    grass.
21 They forgot God their Savior,
  Who had done great things in
    Egypt,
22 Wondrous works in the land of
    Ham,
  Awesome things by the Red
    Sea.
23 Therefore He said that He would
    destroy them,
  Had not Moses His chosen one
    stood before Him in the
    breach,
  To turn away His wrath, lest He
    destroy *them.*

24 Then they despised the pleasant
    land;
  They did not believe His word,
25 But complained in their tents,
  And did not heed the voice of
    the LORD.
26 Therefore He raised His hand *in
    an oath* against them,
  To overthrow them in the
    wilderness,
27 To overthrow their descendants
    among the nations,
  And to scatter them in the lands.

28 They joined themselves also to
    Baal of Peor,
  And ate sacrifices made to the
    dead.
29 Thus they provoked *Him* to
    anger with their deeds,

And the plague broke out
  among them.
30 Then Phinehas stood up and
  intervened,
And the plague was stopped.
31 And that was accounted to him
  for righteousness
To all generations forevermore.

32 They angered *Him* also at the
  waters of strife,
So that it went ill with Moses on
  account of them;
33 Because they rebelled against
  His Spirit,
So that he spoke rashly with his
  lips.

34 They did not destroy the
  peoples,
Concerning whom the LORD had
  commanded them,
35 But they mingled with the
  Gentiles
And learned their works;
36 They served their idols,
Which became a snare to
  them.
37 They even sacrificed their sons
And their daughters to demons,
38 And shed innocent blood,
The blood of their sons and
  daughters,
Whom they sacrificed to the
  idols of Canaan;
And the land was polluted with
  blood.
39 Thus they were defiled by their
  own works,
And played the harlot by their
  own deeds.

40 Therefore the wrath of the LORD
  was kindled against His
  people,
So that He abhorred His own
  inheritance.
41 And He gave them into the hand
  of the Gentiles,

And those who hated them ruled
  over them.
42 Their enemies also oppressed
  them,
And they were brought into
  subjection under their hand.
43 Many times He delivered them;
But they rebelled in their
  counsel,
And were brought low for their
  iniquity.

44 Nevertheless He regarded their
  affliction,
When He heard their cry;
45 And for their sake He
  remembered His covenant,
And relented according to the
  multitude of His mercies.
46 He also made them to be pitied
By all those who carried them
  away captive.

47 Save us, O LORD our God,
And gather us from among the
  Gentiles,
To give thanks to Your holy
  name,
To triumph in Your praise.

48 Blessed *be* the LORD God of
  Israel
From everlasting to everlasting!
And let all the people say,
  "Amen!"

Praise the LORD!

Book Five: Psalms 107—150

PSALM 107

God brings the exiles back home

OH, give thanks to the LORD, for
  He is good!
For His mercy *endures* forever.

---

2 Let the redeemed of the LORD
   say *so*,
   Whom He has redeemed from
   the hand of the enemy,
3 And gathered out of the lands,
   From the east and from the
   west,
   From the north and from the
   south.

4 They wandered in the
   wilderness in a desolate way;
   They found no city to dwell in.
5 Hungry and thirsty,
   Their soul fainted in them.
6 Then they cried out to the LORD
   in their trouble,
   And He delivered them out of
   their distresses.
7 And He led them forth by the
   right way,
   That they might go to a city for
   a dwelling place.
8 Oh, that *men* would give thanks
   to the LORD *for* His goodness,
   And *for* His wonderful works to
   the children of men!
9 For He satisfies the longing soul,
   And fills the hungry soul with
   goodness.

10 Those who sat in darkness and
   in the shadow of death,
   Bound in affliction and irons—
11 Because they rebelled against
   the words of God,
   And despised the counsel of the
   Most High,
12 Therefore He brought down
   their heart with labor;
   They fell down, and *there was*
   none to help.
13 Then they cried out to the LORD
   in their trouble,
   And He saved them out of their
   distresses.
14 He brought them out of
   darkness and the shadow of
   death,
   And broke their chains in pieces.
15 Oh, that *men* would give thanks
   to the LORD *for* His goodness,
   And *for* His wonderful works to
   the children of men!

16 For He has broken the gates of
   bronze,
   And cut the bars of iron in two.

17 Fools, because of their
   transgression,
   And because of their iniquities,
   were afflicted.
18 Their soul abhorred all manner
   of food,
   And they drew near to the gates
   of death.
19 Then they cried out to the LORD
   in their trouble,
   And He saved them out of their
   distresses.
20 He sent His word and healed
   them,
   And delivered *them* from their
   destructions.
21 Oh, that *men* would give thanks
   to the LORD *for* His goodness,
   And *for* His wonderful works to
   the children of men!
22 Let them sacrifice the sacrifices
   of thanksgiving,
   And declare His works with
   rejoicing.

23 Those who go down to the sea
   in ships,
   Who do business on great
   waters,
24 They see the works of the
   LORD,
   And His wonders in the deep.
25 For He commands and raises
   the stormy wind,
   Which lifts up the waves of the
   sea.
26 They mount up to the heavens,
   They go down again to the
   depths;
   Their soul melts because of
   trouble.
27 They reel to and fro, and stagger
   like a drunken man,
   And are at their wits' end.
28 Then they cry out to the LORD
   in their trouble,
   And He brings them out of their
   distresses.
29 He calms the storm,
   So that its waves are still.

30 Then they are glad because they
   are quiet;
   So He guides them to their
   desired haven.
31 Oh, that *men* would give thanks
   to the LORD *for* His goodness,
   And *for* His wonderful works to
   the children of men!
32 Let them exalt Him also in the
   assembly of the people,
   And praise Him in the company
   of the elders.

33 He turns rivers into a wilderness,
   And the watersprings into dry
   ground;
34 A fruitful land into barrenness,
   For the wickedness of those who
   dwell in it.
35 He turns a wilderness into pools
   of water,
   And dry land into watersprings.
36 There He makes the hungry
   dwell,
   That they may establish a city
   for a dwelling place,
37 And sow fields and plant
   vineyards,
   That they may yield a fruitful
   harvest.
38 He also blesses them, and they
   multiply greatly;
   And He does not let their cattle
   decrease.

39 When they are diminished and
   brought low
   Through oppression, affliction
   and sorrow,
40 He pours contempt on princes,
   And causes them to wander in
   the wilderness *where there is*
   no way;
41 Yet He sets the poor on high,
   far from affliction,
   And makes *their* families like a
   flock.
42 The righteous see *it* and rejoice,
   And all iniquity stops its mouth.

43 Whoever *is* wise will observe
   these *things,*
   And they will understand the
   lovingkindness of the LORD.

PSALM 108

I pray to be strong

A Song. A Psalm of David.

O GOD, my heart is steadfast;
   I will sing and give praise, *even*
   with my glory.
2 Awake, lute and harp!
   I will awaken the dawn.
3 I will praise You, O LORD,
   among the peoples,
   And I will sing praises to You
   among the nations.
4 For Your mercy *is* great above
   the heavens,
   And Your truth *reaches* to the
   clouds.

5 Be exalted, O God, above the
   heavens,
   And Your glory above all the
   earth;
6 That Your beloved may be
   delivered,
   Save *with* Your right hand, and
   hear me.

7 God has spoken in His holiness:
   "I will rejoice;
   I will divide Shechem
   And measure out the Valley of
   Succoth.
8 Gilead *is* Mine; Manasseh *is*
   Mine;
   Ephraim also *is* the helmet for
   My head;
   Judah *is* My lawgiver.
9 Moab *is* My washpot;
   Over Edom I will cast My shoe;
   Over Philistia I will triumph."

10 Who will bring me *into* the
   strong city?
   Who will lead me to Edom?
11 *Is it* not *You,* O God, *who* cast
   us off?
   And *You,* O God, *who* did not
   go out with our armies?
12 Give us help from trouble,
   For the help of man is useless.
13 Through God we will do
   valiantly,

For *it is* He *who* shall tread down
our enemies.

PSALM 109

The Lord will plead our case

To the Chief Musician. A Psalm of David.

D O not keep silent,
   O God of my praise!
2   For the mouth of the wicked and
     the mouth of the deceitful
   Have opened against me;
   They have spoken against me
     with a lying tongue.
3   They have also surrounded me
     with words of hatred,
   And fought against me without
     a cause.
4   In return for my love they are
     my accusers,
   But I *give myself to* prayer.
5   Thus they have rewarded me
     evil for good,
   And hatred for my love.

6   Set a wicked man over him,
   And let an accuser stand at his
     right hand.
7   When he is judged, let him be
     found guilty,
   And let his prayer become sin.
8   Let his days be few,
   And let another take his office.
9   Let his children be fatherless,
   And his wife a widow.
10   Let his children continually be
     vagabonds, and beg;
   Let them seek *their bread* also
     from their desolate places.
11   Let the creditor seize all that he
     has,
   And let strangers plunder his
     labor.
12   Let there be none to extend
     mercy to him,
   Nor let there be any to favor his
     fatherless children.
13   Let his posterity be cut off,
   And in the generation following
     let their name be blotted out.
14   Let the iniquity of his fathers be
     remembered before the LORD,

And let not the sin of his mother
   be blotted out.
15   Let them be continually before
     the LORD,
   That He may cut off the memory
     of them from the earth;
16   Because he did not remember
     to show mercy,
   But persecuted the poor and
     needy man,
   That he might even slay the
     broken in heart.
17   As he loved cursing, so let it
     come to him;
   As he did not delight in blessing,
     so let it be far from him.
18   As he clothed himself with
     cursing as with his garment,
   So let it enter his body like
     water,
   And like oil into his bones.
19   Let it be to him like the garment
     which covers him,
   And for a belt with which he
     girds himself continually.
20   *Let* this *be* the LORD's reward to
     my accusers,
   And to those who speak evil
     against my person.

21   But You, O GOD the Lord,
   Deal with me for Your name's
     sake;
   Because Your mercy *is* good,
     deliver me.
22   For I *am* poor and needy,
   And my heart is wounded within
     me.
23   I am gone like a shadow when
     it lengthens;
   I am shaken off like a locust.
24   My knees are weak through
     fasting,
   And my flesh is feeble from lack
     of fatness.
25   I also have become a reproach
     to them;
   When they look at me, they
     shake their heads.

26   Help me, O LORD my God!
   Oh, save me according to Your
     mercy,

27 That they may know that this *is*
    Your hand—
    That You, LORD, have done it!
28 Let them curse, but You bless;
    When they arise, let them be
      ashamed,
    But let Your servant rejoice.
29 Let my accusers be clothed with
    shame,
    And let them cover themselves
      with their own disgrace as with
      a mantle.

30 I will greatly praise the LORD with
    my mouth;
    Yes, I will praise Him among the
      multitude.
31 For He shall stand at the right
    hand of the poor,
    To save *him* from those who
      condemn him.

PSALM 110

The Messiah is victorious

A Psalm of David.

THE LORD said to my Lord,
    "Sit at My right hand,
    Till I make Your enemies Your
      footstool."
2 The LORD shall send the rod of
    Your strength out of Zion.
    Rule in the midst of Your
      enemies!

3 Your people *shall be* volunteers
    In the day of Your power;
    In the beauties of holiness, from
      the womb of the morning,

    You have the dew of Your
      youth.
4 The LORD has sworn
    And will not relent,
    "You *are* a priest forever
    According to the order of
      Melchizedek."

5 The Lord *is* at Your right hand;
    He shall execute kings in the day
      of His wrath.
6 He shall judge among the
      nations,
    He shall fill *the places* with dead
      bodies,
    He shall execute the heads of
      many countries.
7 He shall drink of the brook by
    the wayside;
    Therefore He shall lift up the
      head.

PSALM 111

God does wonderful works

PRAISE the LORD!

    I will praise the LORD with *my*
      whole heart,
    In the assembly of the upright
      and *in* the congregation.

2 The works of the LORD *are* great,
    Studied by all who have
      pleasure in them.
3 His work *is* honorable and
      glorious,
    And His righteousness endures
      forever.

⛏ DIGGING IN

110:1 David Sees God's Son A thousand years before Jesus was born, David saw Him as the Son of God. David tells in Psalm 110 how he saw a vision of God the Father commanding His Son to "sit at My right hand, till I make Your enemies Your footstool."

In David's vision Jesus has risen from the dead and has gone up to heaven. There in God's throne room, His Father commands Jesus to sit and wait while all

His enemies are conquered.

Jesus later used these words to prove He was the Son of God. How could Jesus be only the "Son of David" if David also called Him "Lord"? (See Matthew 22:44.)

Jesus defeated Satan at the Cross. Now we, too, can wait and see all of God's enemies destroyed. Then Jesus will rule over the world He died to save. You can have peace because Jesus has already won the victory over death and sin.

4 He has made His wonderful
works to be remembered;
The Lord is gracious and full of
compassion.
5 He has given food to those who
fear Him;
He will ever be mindful of His
covenant.
6 He has declared to His people
the power of His works,
In giving them the heritage of the
nations.

7 The works of His hands are
verity and justice;
All His precepts are sure.
8 They stand fast forever and ever,
And are done in truth and
uprightness.
9 He has sent redemption to His
people;
He has commanded His
covenant forever:
Holy and awesome is His name.

10 The fear of the Lord is the
beginning of wisdom;
A good understanding have all
those who do His
commandments.
His praise endures forever.

PSALM 112

God takes care of His own

PRAISE the Lord!

Blessed is the man who fears the
Lord,
Who delights greatly in His
commandments.

2 His descendants will be mighty
on earth;
The generation of the upright
will be blessed.
3 Wealth and riches will be in his
house,
And his righteousness endures
forever.
4 Unto the upright there arises
light in the darkness;

He is gracious, and full of
compassion, and righteous.
5 A good man deals graciously
and lends;
He will guide his affairs with
discretion.
6 Surely he will never be shaken;
The righteous will be in
everlasting remembrance.
7 He will not be afraid of evil
tidings;
His heart is steadfast, trusting in
the Lord.
8 His heart is established;
He will not be afraid,
Until he sees his desire upon his
enemies.

9 He has dispersed abroad,
He has given to the poor;
His righteousness endures
forever;
His horn will be exalted with
honor.
10 The wicked will see it and be
grieved;
He will gnash his teeth and melt
away;
The desire of the wicked shall
perish.

PSALM 113

God takes care of the poor and hungry

PRAISE the Lord!

Praise, O servants of the Lord,
Praise the name of the Lord!
2 Blessed be the name of the Lord
From this time forth and
forevermore!
3 From the rising of the sun to its
going down
The Lord's name is to be
praised.

4 The Lord is high above all
nations,
His glory above the heavens.
5 Who is like the Lord our God,
Who dwells on high,

6   Who humbles Himself to behold
    The things that are in the
        heavens and in the earth?

7   He raises the poor out of the
        dust,
    And lifts the needy out of the
        ash heap,
8   That He may seat *him* with
        princes—
    With the princes of His people.
9   He grants the barren woman a
        home,
    Like a joyful mother of children.

    Praise the LORD!

PSALM 114

God is a miracle worker

WHEN Israel went out of Egypt,
    The house of Jacob from a
        people of strange language,
2   Judah became His sanctuary,
    And Israel His dominion.

3   The sea saw *it* and fled;
    Jordan turned back.
4   The mountains skipped like
        rams,
    The little hills like lambs.
5   What ails you, O sea, that you
        fled?
    O Jordan, *that* you turned back?
6   O mountains, *that* you skipped
        like rams?
    O little hills, like lambs?

7   Tremble, O earth, at the
        presence of the Lord,
    At the presence of the God of
        Jacob,
8   Who turned the rock *into* a pool
        of water,
    The flint into a fountain of
        waters.

PSALM 115

To God be the glory!

NOT unto us, O LORD, not unto us,
    But to Your name give glory,

    Because of Your mercy,
    Because of Your truth.
2   Why should the Gentiles say,
    "So where *is* their God?"

3   But our God *is* in heaven;
    He does whatever He pleases.
4   Their idols *are* silver and gold,
    The work of men's hands.
5   They have mouths, but they do
        not speak;
    Eyes they have, but they do not
        see;
6   They have ears, but they do not
        hear;
    Noses they have, but they do
        not smell;
7   They have hands, but they do
        not handle;
    Feet they have, but they do not
        walk;
    Nor do they mutter through their
        throat.
8   Those who make them are like
        them;
    So is everyone who trusts in
        them.

9   O Israel, trust in the LORD;
    He *is* their help and their shield.
10 O house of Aaron, trust in the
        LORD;
    He *is* their help and their shield.
11 You who fear the LORD, trust in
        the LORD;
    He *is* their help and their shield.

12 The LORD has been mindful of
        us;
    He will bless us;
    He will bless the house of Israel;
    He will bless the house of Aaron.
13 He will bless those who fear the
        LORD,
    Both small and great.

14 May the LORD give you increase
        more and more,
    You and your children.
15 *May* you *be* blessed by the
        LORD,
    Who made heaven and earth.

16 The heaven, *even* the heavens,
    are the LORD's;

But the earth He has given to
the children of men.
17 The dead do not praise the
Lᴏʀᴅ,
Nor any who go down into
silence.
18 But we will bless the Lᴏʀᴅ
From this time forth and
forevermore.

Praise the Lᴏʀᴅ!

PSALM 116

We thank God for saving our lives

I LOVE the Lᴏʀᴅ, because He has
heard
My voice *and* my supplications.
2 Because He has inclined His ear
to me,
Therefore I will call *upon Him*
as long as I live.

3 The pains of death surrounded
me,
And the pangs of Sheol laid hold
of me;
I found trouble and sorrow.
4 Then I called upon the name of
the Lᴏʀᴅ:
"O Lᴏʀᴅ, I implore You, deliver
my soul!"

5 Gracious *is* the Lᴏʀᴅ, and
righteous;
Yes, our God *is* merciful.
6 The Lᴏʀᴅ preserves the simple;
I was brought low, and He saved
me.
7 Return to your rest, O my soul,
For the Lᴏʀᴅ has dealt
bountifully with you.

8 For You have delivered my soul
from death,
My eyes from tears,
And my feet from falling.
9 I will walk before the Lᴏʀᴅ
In the land of the living.
10 I believed, therefore I spoke,
"I am greatly afflicted."
11 I said in my haste,
"All men *are* liars."

12 What shall I render to the Lᴏʀᴅ
For all His benefits toward me?
13 I will take up the cup of
salvation,
And call upon the name of the
Lᴏʀᴅ.
14 I will pay my vows to the Lᴏʀᴅ
Now in the presence of all His
people.

15 Precious in the sight of the Lᴏʀᴅ
Is the death of His saints.

16 O Lᴏʀᴅ, truly I *am* Your servant;
I *am* Your servant, the son of
Your maidservant;
You have loosed my bonds.
17 I will offer to You the sacrifice
of thanksgiving,
And will call upon the name of
the Lᴏʀᴅ.

18 I will pay my vows to the Lᴏʀᴅ
Now in the presence of all His
people,
19 In the courts of the Lᴏʀᴅ's
house,
In the midst of you,
O Jerusalem.

Praise the Lᴏʀᴅ!

PSALM 117

All people praise the Lord

PRAISE the Lᴏʀᴅ, all you Gentiles!
Laud Him, all you peoples!
2 For His merciful kindness is great
toward us,
And the truth of the Lᴏʀᴅ
endures forever.

Praise the Lᴏʀᴅ!

PSALM 118

We give thanks to God

OH, give thanks to the Lᴏʀᴅ, for
He is good!
For His mercy *endures* forever.

2 Let Israel now say,
"His mercy *endures* forever."
3 Let the house of Aaron now
   say,
"His mercy *endures* forever."
4 Let those who fear the LORD
   now say,
"His mercy *endures* forever."

5 I called on the LORD in distress;
The LORD answered me *and set*
   me in a broad place.
6 The LORD *is* on my side;
I will not fear.
What can man do to me?
7 The LORD is for me among those
   who help me;
Therefore I shall *see my desire*
   on those who hate me.
8 *It is* better to trust in the LORD
Than to put confidence in
   man.
9 *It is* better to trust in the LORD
Than to put confidence in
   princes.

10 All nations surrounded me,
But in the name of the LORD I
   will destroy them.
11 They surrounded me,
Yes, they surrounded me;
But in the name of the LORD I
   will destroy them.
12 They surrounded me like
   bees;
They were quenched like a fire
   of thorns;
For in the name of the LORD I
   will destroy them.
13 You pushed me violently, that I
   might fall,
But the LORD helped me.
14 The LORD *is* my strength and
   song,
And He has become my
   salvation.

15 The voice of rejoicing and
   salvation
Is in the tents of the righteous;
The right hand of the LORD does
   valiantly.
16 The right hand of the LORD is
   exalted;

The right hand of the LORD does
   valiantly.
17 I shall not die, but live,
And declare the works of the
   LORD.
18 The LORD has chastened me
   severely,
But He has not given me over
   to death.

19 Open to me the gates of
   righteousness;
I will go through them,
And I will praise the LORD.
20 This is the gate of the LORD,
Through which the righteous
   shall enter.

21 I will praise You,
For You have answered me,
And have become my salvation.

22 The stone *which* the builders
   rejected
Has become the chief
   cornerstone.
23 This was the LORD's doing;
It *is* marvelous in our eyes.
24 This *is* the day the LORD has
   made;
We will rejoice and be glad in
   it.

25 Save now, I pray, O LORD;
O LORD, I pray, send now
   prosperity.
26 Blessed *is* he who comes in the
   name of the LORD!
We have blessed you from the
   house of the LORD.
27 God *is* the LORD,
And He has given us light;
Bind the sacrifice with cords to
   the horns of the altar.
28 You *are* my God, and I will
   praise You;
You are my God, I will exalt
   You.

29 Oh, give thanks to the LORD, for
   He is good!
For His mercy *endures*
   forever.

PSALM 119

We thank God for His Word

א ALEPH

BLESSED *are* the undefiled in the
way,
Who walk in the law of the
LORD!
2 Blessed *are* those who keep His
testimonies,
Who seek Him with the whole
heart!
3 They also do no iniquity;
They walk in His ways.
4 You have commanded *us*
To keep Your precepts
diligently.
5 Oh, that my ways were directed
To keep Your statutes!
6 Then I would not be ashamed,
When I look into all Your
commandments.
7 I will praise You with uprightness
of heart,
When I learn Your righteous
judgments.
8 I will keep Your statutes;
Oh, do not forsake me utterly!

ב BETH

9 How can a young man cleanse
his way?
By taking heed according to
Your word.
10 With my whole heart I have
sought You;
Oh, let me not wander from
Your commandments!
11 Your **word** I have hidden in my
heart,
That I might not sin against You.
12 Blessed *are* You, O LORD!
Teach me Your statutes.
13 With my lips I have declared
All the judgments of Your
mouth.

Hide God's Word in your heart while you are young!

14 I have rejoiced in the way of
Your testimonies,
As *much as* in all riches.
15 I will meditate on Your precepts,
And contemplate Your ways.
16 I will delight myself in Your
statutes;
I will not forget Your word.

ג GIMEL

17 Deal bountifully with Your
servant,
That I may live and keep Your
word.
18 Open my eyes, that I may see
Wondrous things from Your law.
19 I *am* a stranger in the earth;
Do not hide Your
commandments from me.
20 My soul breaks with longing
For Your judgments at all times.
21 You rebuke the proud—the
cursed,
Who stray from Your
commandments.

WORDFINDER

119:11 Word (God's Word) God speaking in the Scriptures of the Old and New Testaments. In the New Testament, Jesus also is called "the Word" (John 1:1) because He is God's *personal* Word.

22 Remove from me reproach and
     contempt,
   For I have kept Your
     testimonies.
23 Princes also sit *and* speak against
     me,
   But Your servant meditates on
     Your statutes.
24 Your testimonies also *are* my
     delight
   And my counselors.

ד DALETH

25 My soul clings to the dust;
   Revive me according to Your
     word.
26 I have declared my ways, and
     You answered me;
   Teach me Your statutes.
27 Make me understand the way of
     Your precepts;
   So shall I meditate on Your
     wonderful works.
28 My soul melts from heaviness;
   Strengthen me according to
     Your word.
29 Remove from me the way of
     lying,
   And grant me Your law
     graciously.
30 I have chosen the way of truth;
   Your judgments I have laid
     before me.
31 I cling to Your testimonies;
   O LORD, do not put me to
     shame!
32 I will run the course of Your
     commandments,
   For You shall enlarge my heart.

ה HE

33 Teach me, O LORD, the way of
     Your statutes,
   And I shall keep it *to* the end.
34 Give me understanding, and I
     shall keep Your law;
   Indeed, I shall observe it with *my*
     whole heart.
35 Make me walk in the path of
     Your commandments,
   For I delight in it.
36 Incline my heart to Your
     testimonies,
   And not to covetousness.

37 Turn away my eyes from looking
     at worthless things,
   And revive me in Your way.
38 Establish Your word to Your
     servant,
   Who *is devoted* to fearing You.
39 Turn away my reproach which
     I dread,
   For Your judgments *are* good.
40 Behold, I long for Your precepts;
   Revive me in Your
     righteousness.

ו WAW

41 Let Your mercies come also to
     me, O LORD—
   Your salvation according to
     Your word.
42 So shall I have an answer for
     him who reproaches me,
   For I trust in Your word.
43 And take not the word of truth
     utterly out of my mouth,
   For I have hoped in Your
     ordinances.
44 So shall I keep Your law
     continually,
   Forever and ever.
45 And I will walk at liberty,
   For I seek Your precepts.
46 I will speak of Your testimonies
     also before kings,
   And will not be ashamed.
47 And I will delight myself in Your
     commandments,
   Which I love.
48 My hands also I will lift up to
     Your commandments,
   Which I love,
   And I will meditate on Your
     statutes.

ז ZAYIN

49 Remember the word to Your
     servant,
   Upon which You have caused
     me to hope.
50 This *is* my comfort in my
     affliction,
   For Your word has given me
     life.
51 The proud have me in great
     derision,

Yet I do not turn aside from
  Your law.
52 I remembered Your judgments
   of old, O Lord,
   And have comforted myself.
53 Indignation has taken hold of me
   Because of the wicked, who
   forsake Your law.
54 Your statutes have been my
   songs
   In the house of my pilgrimage.
55 I remember Your name in the
   night, O Lord,
   And I keep Your law.
56 This has become mine,
   Because I kept Your precepts.

Π HETH

57 *You are* my portion, O Lord;
   I have said that I would keep
   Your words.
58 I entreated Your favor with *my*
   whole heart;
   Be merciful to me according to
   Your word.
59 I thought about my ways,
   And turned my feet to Your
   testimonies.
60 I made haste, and did not
   delay
   To keep Your commandments.
61 The cords of the wicked have
   bound me,
   But I have not forgotten Your
   law.
62 At midnight I will rise to give
   thanks to You,
   Because of Your righteous
   judgments.
63 I *am* a companion of all who fear
   You,
   And of those who keep Your
   precepts.
64 The earth, O Lord, is full of
   Your mercy;
   Teach me Your statutes.

ט TETH

65 You have dealt well with Your
   servant,
   O Lord, according to Your
   word.
66 Teach me good judgment and
   knowledge,

For I believe Your
  commandments.
67 Before I was afflicted I went
   astray,
   But now I keep Your word.
68 You *are* good, and do good;
   Teach me Your statutes.
69 The proud have forged a lie
   against me,
   But I will keep Your precepts
   with *my* whole heart.
70 Their heart is as fat as grease,
   But I delight in Your law.
71 *It is* good for me that I have been
   afflicted,
   That I may learn Your statutes.
72 The law of Your mouth *is* better
   to me
   Than thousands of *coins of* gold
   and silver.

י YOD

73 Your hands have made me and
   fashioned me;
   Give me understanding, that I
   may learn Your
   commandments.
74 Those who fear You will be glad
   when they see me,
   Because I have hoped in Your
   word.
75 I know, O Lord, that Your
   judgments *are* right,
   And *that* in faithfulness You
   have afflicted me.
76 Let, I pray, Your merciful
   kindness be for my comfort,
   According to Your word to Your
   servant.
77 Let Your tender mercies come
   to me, that I may live;
   For Your law *is* my delight.
78 Let the proud be ashamed,
   For they treated me wrongfully
   with falsehood;
   But I will meditate on Your
   precepts.
79 Let those who fear You turn to
   me,
   Those who know Your
   testimonies.
80 Let my heart be blameless
   regarding Your statutes,
   That I may not be ashamed.

ᴋ KAPH

81 My soul faints for Your salvation,
But I hope in Your word.
82 My eyes fail *from searching* Your
word,
Saying, "When will You comfort
me?"
83 For I have become like a
wineskin in smoke,
Yet I do not forget Your statutes.
84 How many *are* the days of Your
servant?
When will You execute
judgment on those who
persecute me?
85 The proud have dug pits for me,
Which *is* not according to Your
law.
86 All Your commandments *are*
faithful;
They persecute me wrongfully;
Help me!
87 They almost made an end of me
on earth,
But I did not forsake Your
precepts.
88 Revive me according to Your
lovingkindness,
So that I may keep the testimony
of Your mouth.

ᴸ LAMED

89 Forever, O Lᴏʀᴅ,
Your word is settled in heaven.
90 Your faithfulness *endures* to all
generations;
You established the earth, and
it abides.
91 They continue this day
according to Your ordinances,
For all *are* Your servants.

92 Unless Your law *had been* my
delight,
I would then have perished in
my affliction.
93 I will never forget Your precepts,
For by them You have given me
life.
94 I *am* Yours, save me;
For I have sought Your precepts.
95 The wicked wait for me to
destroy me,
But I will consider Your
testimonies.
96 I have seen the consummation
of all perfection,
But Your commandment *is*
exceedingly broad.

ᴹ MEM

97 Oh, how I love Your law!
It *is* my meditation all the day.
98 You, through Your
commandments, make me
wiser than my enemies;
For they *are* ever with me.
99 I have more understanding than
all my teachers,
For Your testimonies *are* my
meditation.
100 I understand more than the
ancients,
Because I keep Your precepts.
101 I have restrained my feet from
every evil way,
That I may keep Your word.
102 I have not departed from Your
judgments,
For You Yourself have taught
me.
103 How sweet are Your words to
my taste,

🪓 DIGGING IN

119:97 Think God's Thoughts All Day Long The writer of this psalm tells how much he treasures the Word of God. He loves God's Word so much that he has fastened it in his memory. So, wherever he goes, the author thinks "all day" about the Word of God. He calls God's Word the "Law" of God. The "Law" and the "Word" mean the same thing.

We hope you fasten God's Word in your memory the way the psalm writer did.

When you make God's Word part of your mind, it's the same as thinking God's own thoughts. What a wonderful thing to stop thinking your own way and to start thinking God's way. Our minds are too easily filled with thoughts of hatred, sorrow, and anger. But God's mind is filled with love, joy, and peace. The apostle Paul later said we can have "the mind of Christ" (1 Corinthians 2:16).

Sweeter than honey to my mouth!

104 Through Your precepts I get understanding;
Therefore I hate *every* false way.

ⁿ NUN

105 Your word *is* a lamp to my feet
And a light to my path.
106 I have sworn and confirmed
That I will keep Your righteous judgments.
107 I am afflicted very much;
Revive me, O LORD, according to Your word.
108 Accept, I pray, the freewill offerings of my mouth, O LORD,
And teach me Your judgments.
109 My life *is* continually in my hand,
Yet I do not forget Your law.
110 The wicked have laid a snare for me,
Yet I have not strayed from Your precepts.
111 Your testimonies I have taken as a heritage forever,
For they *are* the rejoicing of my heart.
112 I have inclined my heart to perform Your statutes
Forever, to the very end.

ⁿ SAMEK

113 I hate the double-minded,
But I love Your law.
114 You *are* my hiding place and my shield;
I hope in Your word.
115 Depart from me, you evildoers,
For I will keep the commandments of my God!
116 Uphold me according to Your word, that I may live;
And do not let me be ashamed of my hope.
117 Hold me up, and I shall be safe,
And I shall observe Your statutes continually.
118 You reject all those who stray from Your statutes,
For their deceit *is* falsehood.
119 You put away all the wicked of the earth *like* dross;

Therefore I love Your testimonies.
120 My flesh trembles for fear of You,
And I am afraid of Your judgments.

ⁿ AYIN

121 I have done justice and righteousness;
Do not leave me to my oppressors.
122 Be surety for Your servant for good;
Do not let the proud oppress me.
123 My eyes fail *from seeking* Your salvation
And Your righteous word.
124 Deal with Your servant according to Your mercy,
And teach me Your statutes.
125 I *am* Your servant;
Give me understanding,
That I may know Your testimonies.
126 *It is* time for *You* to act, O LORD,
For they have regarded Your law as void.
127 Therefore I love Your commandments
More than gold, yes, than fine gold!
128 Therefore all *Your* precepts *concerning* all *things*
I consider *to be* right;
I hate every false way.

ⁿ PE

129 Your testimonies are wonderful;
Therefore my soul keeps them.
130 The entrance of Your words gives light;
It gives understanding to the simple.
131 I opened my mouth and panted,
For I longed for Your commandments.
132 Look upon me and be merciful to me,
As Your custom *is* toward those who love Your name.
133 Direct my steps by Your word,
And let no iniquity have dominion over me.

134 Redeem me from the oppression
of man,
That I may keep Your precepts.
135 Make Your face shine upon
Your servant,
And teach me Your statutes.
136 Rivers of water run down from
my eyes,
Because *men* do not keep Your
law.

צ TSADDE

137 Righteous *are* You, O LORD,
And upright *are* Your
judgments.
138 Your testimonies, *which* You
have commanded,
Are righteous and very faithful.
139 My zeal has consumed me,
Because my enemies have
forgotten Your words.
140 Your word *is* very pure;
Therefore Your servant
loves it.
141 I *am* small and despised,
Yet I do not forget Your
precepts.
142 Your righteousness *is* an
everlasting righteousness,
And Your law *is* truth.
143 Trouble and anguish have
overtaken me,
Yet Your commandments *are*
my delights.
144 The righteousness of Your
testimonies *is* everlasting;
Give me understanding, and I
shall live.

ק QOPH

145 I cry out with *my* whole heart;
Hear me, O LORD!
I will keep Your statutes.
146 I cry out to You;
Save me, and I will keep Your
testimonies.
147 I rise before the dawning of the
morning,
And cry for help;
I hope in Your word.
148 My eyes are awake through the
night watches,
That I may meditate on Your
word.

149 Hear my voice according to
Your lovingkindness;
O LORD, revive me according to
Your justice.
150 They draw near who follow after
wickedness;
They are far from Your law.
151 You *are* near, O LORD,
And all Your commandments
are truth.
152 Concerning Your testimonies,
I have known of old that You
have founded them forever.

ר RESH

153 Consider my affliction and
deliver me,
For I do not forget Your law.
154 Plead my cause and redeem me;
Revive me according to Your
word.
155 Salvation *is* far from the wicked,
For they do not seek Your
statutes.
156 Great *are* Your tender mercies,
O LORD;
Revive me according to Your
judgments.
157 Many *are* my persecutors and
my enemies,
Yet I do not turn from Your
testimonies.
158 I see the treacherous, and am
disgusted,
Because they do not keep Your
word.
159 Consider how I love Your
precepts;
Revive me, O LORD, according
to Your lovingkindness.
160 The entirety of Your word *is*
truth,
And *every* one of Your righteous
judgments *endures* forever.

ש SHIN

161 Princes persecute me without a
cause,
But my heart stands in awe of
Your word.
162 I rejoice at Your word
As one who finds great treasure.
163 I hate and abhor lying,
But I love Your law.

164 Seven times a day I praise You,
      Because of Your righteous
      judgments.
165 Great peace have those who
      love Your law,
      And nothing causes them to
      stumble.
166 LORD, I hope for Your salvation,
      And I do Your commandments.
167 My soul keeps Your testimonies,
      And I love them exceedingly.
168 I keep Your precepts and Your
      testimonies,
      For all my ways *are* before You.

Π TAU

169 Let my cry come before You,
      O LORD;
      Give me understanding
      according to Your word.
170 Let my supplication come before
      You;
      Deliver me according to Your
      word.
171 My lips shall utter praise,
      For You teach me Your statutes.
172 My tongue shall speak of Your
      word,
      For all Your commandments *are*
      righteousness.
173 Let Your hand become my help,
      For I have chosen Your
      precepts.
174 I long for Your salvation,
      O LORD,
      And Your law *is* my delight.
175 Let my soul live, and it shall
      praise You;
      And let Your judgments help
      me.
176 I have gone astray like a lost
      sheep;
      Seek Your servant,
      For I do not forget Your
      commandments.

PSALM 120

God always helps us when we ask Him

A Song of Ascents.

I N my distress I cried to the LORD,
      And He heard me.

2 Deliver my soul, O LORD, from
      lying lips
      And from a deceitful tongue.

3 What shall be given to you,
      Or what shall be done to you,
      You false tongue?
4 Sharp arrows of the warrior,
      With coals of the broom tree!

5 Woe is me, that I dwell in
      Meshech,
      That I dwell among the tents of
      Kedar!
6 My soul has dwelt too long
      With one who hates peace.
7 I *am for* peace;
      But when I speak, they *are* for
      war.

PSALM 121

God watches over us twenty-four hours a day

A Song of Ascents.

I WILL lift up my eyes to the hills—
      From whence comes my
      help?
2 My help *comes* from the
      LORD,
      Who made heaven and earth.

3 He will not allow your foot to
      be moved;
      He who keeps you will not
      slumber.
4 Behold, He who keeps Israel
      Shall neither slumber nor
      sleep.

5 The LORD *is* your keeper;
      The LORD *is* your shade at your
      right hand.
6 The sun shall not strike you by
      day,
      Nor the moon by night.

7 The LORD shall preserve you
      from all evil;
      He shall preserve your soul.

8 The LORD shall preserve your
   going out and your coming in
   From this time forth, and even
   forevermore.

PSALM 122

I love to worship in God's house

A Song of Ascents. Of David.

I WAS glad when they said to me,
   "Let us go into the house of the
   LORD."
2 Our feet have been standing
   Within your gates, O Jerusalem!

3 Jerusalem is built
   As a city that is compact
   together,
4 Where the tribes go up,
   The tribes of the LORD,
   To the Testimony of Israel,
   To give thanks to the name of
   the LORD.
5 For thrones are set there for
   judgment,
   The thrones of the house of
   David.

6 Pray for the peace of Jerusalem:
   "May they prosper who love you.
7 Peace be within your walls,
   Prosperity within your palaces."
8 For the sake of my brethren and
   companions,
   I will now say, "Peace be within
   you."

9 Because of the house of the
   LORD our God
   I will seek your good.

PSALM 123

We ask God for mercy

A Song of Ascents.

U NTO You I lift up my eyes,
   O You who dwell in the
   heavens.
2 Behold, as the eyes of servants
   look to the hand of their
   masters,
   As the eyes of a maid to the
   hand of her mistress,
   So our eyes look to the LORD
   our God,
   Until He has mercy on us.

3 Have mercy on us, O LORD,
   have mercy on us!
   For we are exceedingly filled
   with contempt.
4 Our soul is exceedingly filled
   With the scorn of those who are
   at ease,
   With the contempt of the proud.

PSALM 124

God is on our side

A Song of Ascents. Of David.

" I F it had not been the LORD who
   was on our side,"
   Let Israel now say—

⛏ DIGGING IN

121:8 God Will Keep You Safe Forever As the world becomes more and more crowded, life becomes less and less safe. Our streets are jammed with cars that often kill people. Horrible diseases are spreading. Living space becomes less available. Air and water are polluted.

So far, these problems may not affect you very much. Sooner or later, though, people will have to decide what they're going to do about these dangers. By then, it may be too late. God's Word says there is going to be great suffering on earth be-

cause of man's disobedience (see Revelation 16).

But you can be safe from all harm. Psalm 121:7 says, "The Lord shall preserve you from all evil." The psalm goes on to say, "He shall preserve your soul." Your body may die, but God will save that deeper part of you that can never die— your soul. Jesus died and rose so that your soul, that part of you that lives forever, will always live with Him (see John 3:16).

2 "If it had not been the LORD who
      was on our side,
   When men rose up against us,
3 Then they would have
      swallowed us alive,
   When their wrath was kindled
      against us;
4 Then the waters would have
      overwhelmed us,
   The stream would have gone
      over our soul;
5 Then the swollen waters
   Would have gone over our
      soul."

6 Blessed be the LORD,
   Who has not given us as prey
      to their teeth.
7 Our soul has escaped as a
      bird from the snare of the
      fowlers;
   The snare is broken, and we
      have escaped.
8 Our help is in the name of the
      LORD,
   Who made heaven and earth.

PSALM 125

We trust in the Lord

A Song of Ascents.

THOSE who trust in the LORD
   Are like Mount Zion,
   Which cannot be moved, but
      abides forever.
2 As the mountains surround
      Jerusalem,
   So the LORD surrounds His
      people
   From this time forth and
      forever.

3 For the scepter of wickedness
      shall not rest
   On the land allotted to the
      righteous,
   Lest the righteous reach out their
      hands to iniquity.

4 Do good, O LORD, to those who
      are good,

And to those who are upright in
   their hearts.

5 As for such as turn aside to their
      crooked ways,
   The LORD shall lead them away
   With the workers of iniquity.

   Peace be upon Israel!

PSALM 126

The Lord gives back what is lost

A Song of Ascents.

WHEN the LORD brought back the
      captivity of Zion,
   We were like those who dream.
2 Then our mouth was filled with
      laughter,
   And our tongue with singing.
   Then they said among the
      nations,
   "The LORD has done great things
      for them."
3 The LORD has done great things
      for us,
   And we are glad.

4 Bring back our captivity,
      O LORD,
   As the streams in the South.

5 Those who sow in tears
   Shall reap in joy.
6 He who continually goes forth
      weeping,
   Bearing seed for sowing,
   Shall doubtless come again with
      rejoicing,
   Bringing his sheaves with him.

PSALM 127

God makes our homes happy

A Song of Ascents. Of Solomon.

UNLESS the LORD builds the house,
   They labor in vain who build it;
   Unless the LORD guards the
      city,

The watchman stays awake in
vain.

2 *It is* vain for you to rise up early,
To sit up late,
To eat the bread of sorrows;
For so He gives His beloved
sleep.

3 Behold, children *are* a heritage
from the LORD,
The fruit of the womb *is* a
reward.
4 Like arrows in the hand of a
warrior,
So *are* the children of one's
youth.
5 Happy *is* the man who has his
quiver full of them;
They shall not be ashamed,
But shall speak with their
enemies in the gate.

PSALM 128

Trust in God brings family blessings

A Song of Ascents.

BLESSED *is* every one who fears
the LORD,
Who walks in His ways.

2 When you eat the labor of your
hands,
You *shall be* happy, and *it shall
be* well with you.
3 Your wife *shall be* like a fruitful
vine
In the very heart of your house,
Your children like olive plants
All around your table.
4 Behold, thus shall the man be
blessed
Who fears the LORD.

5 The LORD bless you out of Zion,
And may you see the good of
Jerusalem
All the days of your life.
6 Yes, may you see your
children's children.

Peace *be* upon Israel!

PSALM 129

I ask God to deal with my enemies

A Song of Ascents.

"MANY a time they have afflicted
me from my youth,"
Let Israel now say—
2 "Many a time they have afflicted
me from my youth;
Yet they have not prevailed
against me.
3 The plowers plowed on my
back;
They made their furrows long."
4 The LORD *is* righteous;
He has cut in pieces the cords
of the wicked.

5 Let all those who hate Zion
Be put to shame and turned
back.
6 Let them be as the grass *on* the
housetops,
Which withers before it grows
up,
7 With which the reaper does not
fill his hand,
Nor he who binds sheaves, his
arms.
8 Neither let those who pass by
them say,
"The blessing of the LORD *be*
upon you;
We bless you in the name of the
LORD!"

PSALM 130

I pray for forgiveness

A Song of Ascents.

OUT of the depths I have cried to
You, O LORD;
2 Lord, hear my voice!
Let Your ears be attentive
To the voice of my supplications.

3 If You, LORD, should mark
iniquities,
O Lord, who could stand?

4 But *there is* forgiveness with
  You,
  That You may be feared.

5 I wait for the LORD, my soul
  waits,
  And in His word I do hope.
6 My soul *waits* for the Lord
  More than those who watch for
  the morning—
  Yes, more than those who watch
  for the morning.

7 O Israel, hope in the LORD;
  For with the LORD *there is*
  mercy,
  And with Him *is* abundant
  redemption.
8 And He shall redeem Israel
  From all his iniquities.

PSALM 131

I pray to be humble

A Song of Ascents. Of David.

LORD, my heart is not haughty,
  Nor my eyes lofty.

Neither do I concern myself with
  great matters,
  Nor with things too profound for
  me.

2 Surely I have calmed and
  quieted my soul,
  Like a weaned child with his
  mother;
  Like a weaned child *is* my soul
  within me.

3 O Israel, hope in the LORD
  From this time forth and forever.

PSALM 132

I trust in David's God

A Song of Ascents.

LORD, remember David
  And all his afflictions;
2 How he swore to the LORD,
  And vowed to the Mighty One
  of Jacob:
3 "Surely I will not go into the
  chamber of my house,
  Or go up to the comfort of my
  bed;

DIGGING IN

130:1, 2 Talk to God When You're Afraid Sometimes you don't understand the world around you. It's like a crazy place where very little seems to make sense. Don't worry. You're probably right. The world is a confusing place much of the time. Every day we hear about horrible violence in the world. Husbands and wives kill each other, parents kill their babies, and innocent people are murdered in our streets. No wonder you're afraid at times.

Some people may foolishly say to you, "Don't worry, be happy!" That makes no sense either. If you're all alone in the world, it makes a lot of sense to worry sometimes. Only a fool could joke about it—like the ostrich who sticks his head in the sand!

But you aren't really alone! God says, "Take My hand and talk to Me." Everything will make sense when you reach out for Him.

132:3–5 Make your Heart God's Home We have said a lot about how great God is. But have you ever thought that God can also make Himself small? The great and eternal God made Himself very little when He was born as a baby at Bethlehem. Then He lived for more than thirty years in a human body like yours. God became Jesus.

Some people think they can only find God in big places—like the Grand Canyon, or Mount Everest, or a huge cathedral like Notre Dame. Although these places seem large to us, to God they're very small.

It's just as easy for God to live in you as it is for Him to live in a huge building. In fact, God told the prophet Isaiah (pronounced *eye-ZAY-uh*) that no one could build a place big enough for Him. But God also said He would live in ordinary people like us (see Isaiah 66:1, 2). God wants to live in you.

4 I will not give sleep to my eyes
   Or slumber to my eyelids,
5 Until I find a place for the LORD,
   A dwelling place for the Mighty
      One of Jacob.''

6 Behold, we heard of it in
      Ephrathah;
   We found it in the fields of the
      woods.
7 Let us go into His tabernacle;
   Let us worship at His footstool.
8 Arise, O LORD, to Your resting
      place,
   You and the ark of Your
      strength.
9 Let Your priests be clothed with
      righteousness,
   And let Your saints shout for joy.

10 For Your servant David's sake,
   Do not turn away the face of
      Your Anointed.

11 The LORD has sworn *in* truth to
      David;
   He will not turn from it:
   ''I will set upon your throne the
      fruit of your body.
12 If your sons will keep My
      covenant
   And My testimony which I shall
      teach them,
   Their sons also shall sit upon
      your throne forevermore.''

13 For the LORD has chosen Zion;
   He has desired *it* for His dwelling
      place:
14 ''This is My resting place forever;
   Here I will dwell, for I have
      desired it.
15 I will abundantly bless her
      provision;
   I will satisfy her poor with bread.
16 I will also clothe her priests with
      salvation,
   And her saints shall shout aloud
      for joy.
17 There I will make the horn of
      David grow;
   I will prepare a lamp for My
      Anointed.
18 His enemies I will clothe with
      shame,

But upon Himself His crown
   shall flourish.''

PSALM 133

We try to live together peacefully

A Song of Ascents. Of David.

BEHOLD, how good and how
      pleasant *it is*
   For brethren to dwell together
      in unity!

2 *It is* like the precious oil upon
      the head,
   Running down on the beard,
   The beard of Aaron,
   Running down on the edge of
      his garments.
3 *It is* like the dew of Hermon,
   Descending upon the mountains
      of Zion;
   For there the LORD commanded
      the blessing—
   Life forevermore.

PSALM 134

We bless the Lord

A Song of Ascents.

BEHOLD, bless the LORD,
   All *you* servants of the LORD,
   Who by night stand in the house
      of the LORD!
2 Lift up your hands *in* the
      sanctuary,
   And bless the LORD.

3 The LORD who made heaven
      and earth
   Bless you from Zion!

PSALM 135

God is real

PRAISE the LORD!

   Praise the name of the LORD;
   Praise *Him,* O you servants of
      the LORD!

2 You who stand in the house of
   the Lord,
   In the courts of the house of our
   God,
3 Praise the Lord, for the Lord *is*
   good;
   Sing praises to His name, for *it
   is* pleasant.
4 For the Lord has chosen Jacob
   for Himself,
   Israel for His special treasure.
5 For I know that the Lord *is*
   great,
   And our Lord *is* above all gods.
6 Whatever the Lord pleases He
   does,
   In heaven and in earth,
   In the seas and in all deep
   places.
7 He causes the vapors to ascend
   from the ends of the earth;
   He makes lightning for the rain;
   He brings the wind out of His
   treasuries.
8 He destroyed the firstborn of
   Egypt,
   Both of man and beast.
9 He sent signs and wonders into
   the midst of you, O Egypt,
   Upon Pharaoh and all his
   servants.
10 He defeated many nations
   And slew mighty kings—
11 Sihon king of the Amorites,
   Og king of Bashan,
   And all the kingdoms of
   Canaan—
12 And gave their land *as* a
   heritage,
   A heritage to Israel His people.

13 Your name, O Lord, *endures*
   forever,
   Your fame, O Lord, throughout
   all generations.
14 For the Lord will judge His
   people,
   And He will have compassion on
   His servants.
15 The idols of the nations *are* silver
   and gold,
   The work of men's hands.

16 They have mouths, but they do
   not speak;
   Eyes they have, but they do not
   see;
17 They have ears, but they do not
   hear;
   Nor is there *any* breath in their
   mouths.
18 Those who make them are like
   them;
   So is everyone who trusts in
   them.

19 Bless the Lord, O house of
   Israel!
   Bless the Lord, O house of
   Aaron!
20 Bless the Lord, O house of Levi!
   You who fear the Lord, bless
   the Lord!
21 Blessed be the Lord out of Zion,
   Who dwells in Jerusalem!

   Praise the Lord!

PSALM 136

God's love never ends

OH, give thanks to the Lord, for
   He is good!
   For His mercy *endures*
   forever.
2 Oh, give thanks to the God of
   gods!
   For His mercy *endures*
   forever.
3 Oh, give thanks to the Lord of
   lords!
   For His mercy *endures*
   forever:
4 To Him who alone does great
   wonders,
   For His mercy *endures*
   forever;
5 To Him who by wisdom made
   the heavens,
   For His mercy *endures*
   forever;
6 To Him who laid out the earth
   above the waters,
   For His mercy *endures*
   forever;

7 To Him who made great lights,
   For His mercy *endures*
      forever—
8 The sun to rule by day,
   For His mercy *endures*
      forever;
9 The moon and stars to rule by
      night,
   For His mercy *endures*
      forever.

10 To Him who struck Egypt in
      their firstborn,
   For His mercy *endures*
      forever;
11 And brought out Israel from
      among them,
   For His mercy *endures*
      forever;
12 With a strong hand, and with an
      outstretched arm,
   For His mercy *endures*
      forever;
13 To Him who divided the Red
      Sea in two,
   For His mercy *endures*
      forever;
14 And made Israel pass through
      the midst of it,
   For His mercy *endures*
      forever;
15 But overthrew Pharaoh and his
      army in the Red Sea,
   For His mercy *endures*
      forever;
16 To Him who led His people
      through the wilderness,
   For His mercy *endures*
      forever;
17 To Him who struck down great
      kings,
   For His mercy *endures*
      forever;
18 And slew famous kings,
   For His mercy *endures*
      forever—
19 Sihon king of the Amorites,
   For His mercy *endures*
      forever;
20 And Og king of Bashan,
   For His mercy *endures*
      forever—
21 And gave their land as a
      heritage,

   For His mercy *endures*
      forever;
22 A heritage to Israel His servant,
   For His mercy *endures*
      forever.

23 Who remembered us in our
      lowly state,
   For His mercy *endures*
      forever;
24 And rescued us from our
      enemies,
   For His mercy *endures*
      forever;
25 Who gives food to all flesh,
   For His mercy *endures*
      forever.

26 Oh, give thanks to the God of
      heaven!
   For His mercy *endures*
      forever.

PSALM 137

The captives want to go home

BY the rivers of Babylon,
   There we sat down, yea, we
      wept
   When we remembered Zion.
2 We hung our harps
   Upon the willows in the midst
      of it.
3 For there those who carried us
      away captive asked of us a
      song,
   And those who plundered us
      requested mirth,
   Saying, "Sing us *one* of the
      songs of Zion!"

4 How shall we sing the LORD's
      song
   In a foreign land?
5 If I forget you, O Jerusalem,
   Let my right hand forget *its*
      skill!
6 If I do not remember you,
   Let my tongue cling to the roof
      of my mouth—
   If I do not exalt Jerusalem
   Above my chief joy.

7 Remember, O Lord, against the
  sons of Edom
  The day of Jerusalem,
  Who said, "Raze it, raze it,
  To its very foundation!"

8 O daughter of Babylon, who are
  to be destroyed,
  Happy the one who repays you
  as you have served us!

9 Happy the one who takes and
  dashes
  Your little ones against the rock!

PSALM 138

A prayer of thanksgiving

A Psalm of David.

I WILL praise You with my whole
  heart;
  Before the gods I will sing praises
  to You.

2 I will worship toward Your holy
  temple,
  And praise Your name
  For Your lovingkindness and
  Your truth;
  For You have magnified Your
  word above all Your name.

3 In the day when I cried out, You
  answered me,
  And made me bold with strength
  in my soul.

4 All the kings of the earth shall
  praise You, O Lord,
  When they hear the words of
  Your mouth.

5 Yes, they shall sing of the ways
  of the Lord,
  For great is the glory of the
  Lord.

6 Though the Lord is on high,
  Yet He regards the lowly;
  But the proud He knows from
  afar.

7 Though I walk in the midst of
  trouble, You will revive me;
  You will stretch out Your hand
  Against the wrath of my
  enemies,
  And Your right hand will save
  me.

8 The Lord will perfect that which
  concerns me;
  Your mercy, O Lord, endures
  forever;
  Do not forsake the works of
  Your hands.

PSALM 139

God knows all about me

For the Chief Musician. A Psalm of David.

O LORD, You have searched me
  and known me.

2 You know my sitting down and
  my rising up;
  You understand my thought afar
  off.

3 You comprehend my path and
  my lying down,
  And are acquainted with all my
  ways.

4 For there is not a word on my
  tongue,
  But behold, O Lord, You know
  it altogether.

5 You have hedged me behind
  and before,
  And laid Your hand upon me.

6 Such knowledge is too
  wonderful for me;
  It is high, I cannot attain it.

7 Where can I go from Your
  Spirit?
  Or where can I flee from Your
  presence?

8 If I ascend into heaven, You are
  there;

How Much Does God Know About You?

You can have secrets from your parents or your friends, but you can't have secrets from God. God, your Creator, is a Person who knows everything. Right away you know you must make God your Friend. He can help you with those secret things that worry you.

If I make my bed in **hell,** behold,
You *are there*.

9 *If* I take the wings of the
   morning,
   And dwell in the uttermost parts
   of the sea,

10 Even there Your hand shall lead
   me,
   And Your right hand shall hold
   me.

11 If I say, "Surely the darkness
   shall fall on me,"
   Even the night shall be light
   about me;

12 Indeed, the darkness shall not
   hide from You,
   But the night shines as the day;
   The darkness and the light *are*
   both alike *to You*.

13 For You formed my inward
   parts;
   You covered me in my mother's
   womb.

14 I will praise You, for I am
   fearfully *and* wonderfully
   made;
   Marvelous are Your works,
   And *that* my soul knows very
   well.

15 My frame was not hidden from
   You,
   When I was made in secret,
   And skillfully wrought in the
   lowest parts of the earth.

16 Your eyes saw my substance,
   being yet unformed.
   And in Your book they all *were*
   written,
   The days fashioned for me,
   When *as yet there were* none
   of them.

17 How precious also are Your
   thoughts to me, O God!
   How great is the sum of them!

18 *If* I should count them, they
   would be more in number
   than the sand;

When I awake, I am still with
You.

19 Oh, that You would slay the
   wicked, O God!
   Depart from me, therefore, you
   bloodthirsty men.

20 For they speak against You
   wickedly;
   Your enemies take *Your name*
   in vain.

21 Do I not hate them, O Lord,
   who hate You?
   And do I not loathe those who
   rise up against You?

22 I hate them with perfect hatred;
   I count them my enemies.

23 Search me, O God, and know
   my heart;
   Try me, and know my anxieties;

24 And see if *there is any* wicked
   way in me,
   And lead me in the way
   everlasting.

PSALM 140

I ask God to keep me safe

To the Chief Musician. A Psalm of David.

DELIVER me, O Lord, from evil
   men;
   Preserve me from violent men,

2 Who plan evil things in *their*
   hearts;
   They continually gather together
   for war.

3 They sharpen their tongues like
   a serpent;
   The poison of asps *is* under their
   lips.   Selah

4 Keep me, O Lord, from the
   hands of the wicked;
   Preserve me from violent men,
   Who have purposed to make my
   steps stumble.

WORDFINDER

139:8 Hell A place of endless misery where ungodly people go when they die. It is translated from a word for the burning dumping ground outside Jerusalem in Jesus' time.

5 The proud have hidden a snare
    for me, and cords;
   They have spread a net by the
    wayside;
   They have set traps for me.
                                    Selah

6 I said to the LORD: "You *are* my
    God;
   Hear the voice of my
    supplications, O LORD.
7 O GOD the Lord, the strength of
    my salvation,
   You have covered my head in
    the day of battle.
8 Do not grant, O LORD, the
    desires of the wicked;
   Do not further his *wicked*
    scheme,
   Lest they be exalted.
                                    Selah

9 "*As for* the head of those who
    surround me,
   Let the evil of their lips cover
    them;
10 Let burning coals fall upon
    them;
   Let them be cast into the fire,
   Into deep pits, that they rise not
    up again.
11 Let not a slanderer be
    established in the earth;
   Let evil hunt the violent man to
    overthrow *him*."

12 I know that the LORD will
    maintain
   The cause of the afflicted,
   And justice for the poor.
13 Surely the righteous shall give
    thanks to Your name;
   The upright shall dwell in Your
    presence.

PSALM 141

The Lord is my hiding place

A Psalm of David.

LORD, I cry out to You;
    Make haste to me!
    Give ear to my voice when I cry
     out to You.

2 Let my prayer be set before You
    as incense,
   The lifting up of my hands *as*
    the evening sacrifice.

3 Set a guard, O LORD, over my
    mouth;
   Keep watch over the door of my
    lips.
4 Do not incline my heart to any
    evil thing,
   To practice wicked works
   With men who work iniquity;
   And do not let me eat of their
    delicacies.

5 Let the righteous strike me;
    It shall be a kindness.
   And let him rebuke me;
    It shall be as excellent oil;
   Let my head not refuse it.

   For still my prayer *is* against the
    deeds of the wicked.
6 Their judges are overthrown by
    the sides of the cliff,
   And they hear my words, for
    they are sweet.
7 Our bones are scattered at the
    mouth of the grave,
   As when one plows and breaks
    up the earth.

8 But my eyes *are* upon You,
    O GOD the Lord;
   In You I take refuge;
   Do not leave my soul destitute.
9 Keep me from the snares they
    have laid for me,
   And from the traps of the
    workers of iniquity.
10 Let the wicked fall into their own
    nets,
   While I escape safely.

PSALM 142

Someone is out to get me

A Contemplation of David. A Prayer when he was
in the cave.

I CRY out to the LORD with my voice;
    With my voice to the LORD I
     make my supplication.

2 I pour out my complaint before
      Him;
   I declare before Him my trouble.

3 When my spirit was
      overwhelmed within me,
   Then You knew my path.
   In the way in which I walk
   They have secretly set a snare
      for me.
4 Look on *my* right hand and see,
   For *there is* no one who
      acknowledges me;
   Refuge has failed me;
   No one cares for my soul.

5 I cried out to You, O LORD:
   I said, "You *are* my refuge,
   My portion in the land of the
      living.
6 Attend to my cry,
   For I am brought very low;
   Deliver me from my persecutors,
   For they are stronger than I.
7 Bring my soul out of prison,
   That I may praise Your name;
   The righteous shall surround
      me,
   For You shall deal bountifully
      with me."

PSALM 143

Sometimes I'm scared

A Psalm of David.

HEAR my prayer, O LORD,
   Give ear to my supplications!
   In Your faithfulness answer me,
   And in Your righteousness.

2 Do not enter into judgment with
      Your servant,
   For in Your sight no one living
      is righteous.

3 For the enemy has persecuted
      my soul;
   He has crushed my life to the
      ground;
   He has made me dwell in
      darkness,
   Like those who have long been
      dead.
4 Therefore my spirit is
      overwhelmed within me;
   My heart within me is distressed.

5 I remember the days of old;
   I meditate on all Your works;
   I muse on the work of Your
      hands.
6 I spread out my hands to You;
   My soul *longs* for You like a
      thirsty land.   Selah

7 Answer me speedily, O LORD;
   My spirit fails!
   Do not hide Your face from me,
   Lest I be like those who go down
      into the pit.
8 Cause me to hear Your
      lovingkindness in the
      morning,
   For in You do I trust;
   Cause me to know the way in
      which I should walk,
   For I lift up my soul to You.

9 Deliver me, O LORD, from my
      enemies;
   In You I take shelter.
10 Teach me to do Your will,

DIGGING IN

143:8 God Will Guide You A compass is the most valuable tool you can have when you're lost in a forest. Also, when you're at sea and can't see any land, you need a compass to lead you to a safe harbor.

Many people in the world are like sailors at sea without a compass. They have no guide to show them how to live, and they are soon led into danger by evil men.

You need a guide to show you how to live in happiness in the world. Some people would like you to think sin will make you happy. That is never true. Sin only makes people miserable after they're trapped in it.

God guides you in the way of wisdom, joy, and peace. His Spirit is like a living compass that always tells you when you're going the wrong way. Ask God to lead you "in the way everlasting" (Psalm 139:24).

For You *are* my God;
Your Spirit *is* good.
Lead me in the land of
    uprightness.

11 Revive me, O LORD, for Your
        name's sake!
    For Your righteousness' sake
        bring my soul out of trouble.
12 In Your mercy cut off my
        enemies,
    And destroy all those who afflict
        my soul;
    For I *am* Your servant.

PSALM 144

We sing about God's care

A Psalm of David.

BLESSED *be* the LORD my Rock,
    Who trains my hands for war,
    And my fingers for battle—
2   My lovingkindness and my
        fortress,
    My high tower and my deliverer,
    My shield and *the One* in whom
        I take refuge,
    Who subdues my people under
        me.

3   LORD, what *is* man, that You
        take knowledge of him?
    Or the son of man, that You are
        mindful of him?
4   Man is like a breath;
    His days *are* like a passing
        shadow.

5   Bow down Your heavens,
        O LORD, and come down;

Touch the mountains, and they
    shall smoke.
6   Flash forth lightning and scatter
        them;
    Shoot out Your arrows and
        destroy them.
7   Stretch out Your hand from
        above;
    Rescue me and deliver me out
        of great waters,
    From the hand of foreigners,
8   Whose mouth speaks lying
        words,
    And whose right hand *is* a right
        hand of falsehood.

9   I will sing a new song to You,
        O God;
    On a harp of ten strings I will
        sing praises to You,
10 *The One* who gives salvation to
        kings,
    Who delivers David His servant
    From the deadly sword.

11 Rescue me and deliver me from
        the hand of foreigners,
    Whose mouth speaks lying
        words,
    And whose right hand *is* a right
        hand of falsehood—
12 That our sons *may be* as plants
        grown up in their youth;
    That our daughters *may be* as
        pillars,
    Sculptured in palace style;
13 *That* our barns *may be* full,
    Supplying all kinds of produce;
    That our sheep may bring forth
        thousands
    And ten thousands in our fields;

⚒ DIGGING IN

144:15 Christians Are Happy People
"Happy are the people whose God is the
Lord." Not everybody who laughs or
smiles is happy. Sometimes people laugh
because they don't want others to see
how sad they really are.

Sometimes Christians are sad, too.
They're unhappy when they know they
have disobeyed the Lord. Also, it would
be very strange if we weren't sad when
our loved ones leave us or die. But Chris-

tians are usually happy people. They
know they belong to God and that He will
take care of them forever. Nothing in the
world can ever separate them from the
love of God. See Romans 8:38, 39.

God even *commands* you to be happy:
"Rejoice in the Lord always" (Philippians
4:4). God has good reason to tell you to
be happy. He gave His only Son for you,
and He loves you.

14 *That* our oxen *may be*
     well-laden;
     That there be no breaking in or
     going out;
     That there be no outcry in our
     streets.
15 Happy *are* the people who are
     in such a state;
     Happy *are* the people whose
     God *is* the LORD!

PSALM 145

Isn't God great?

A Praise of David.

I WILL extol You, my God, O King;
     And I will bless Your name
     forever and ever.
2 Every day I will bless You,
     And I will praise Your name
     forever and ever.
3 Great *is* the LORD, and greatly
     to be praised;
     And His greatness *is*
     unsearchable.

4 One generation shall praise Your
     works to another,
     And shall declare Your mighty
     acts.
5 I will meditate on the glorious
     splendor of Your majesty,
     And on Your wondrous works.
6 *Men* shall speak of the might of
     Your awesome acts,
     And I will declare Your
     greatness.
7 They shall utter the memory of
     Your great goodness,
     And shall sing of Your
     righteousness.

8 The LORD *is* gracious and full of
     compassion,
     Slow to anger and great in
     mercy.
9 The LORD *is* good to all,
     And His tender mercies *are* over
     all His works.

10 All Your works shall praise You,
     O LORD,
     And Your saints shall bless You.

11 They shall speak of the glory of
     Your kingdom,
     And talk of Your power,
12 To make known to the sons of
     men His mighty acts,
     And the glorious majesty of His
     kingdom.
13 Your kingdom *is* an everlasting
     kingdom,
     And Your dominion *endures*
     throughout all generations.

14 The LORD upholds all who fall,
     And raises up all *who are* bowed
     down.
15 The *eyes* of all look expectantly
     to You,
     And You give them their food
     in due season.
16 You open Your hand
     And satisfy the desire of every
     living thing.

17 The LORD *is* righteous in all His
     ways,
     Gracious in all His works.
18 The LORD *is* near to all who call
     upon Him,
     To all who call upon Him in
     truth.
19 He will fulfill the desire of those
     who fear Him;
     He also will hear their cry and
     save them.
20 The LORD preserves all who love
     Him,
     But all the wicked He will
     destroy.
21 My mouth shall speak the praise
     of the LORD,
     And all flesh shall bless His holy
     name
     Forever and ever.

PSALM 146

We praise God for all He does for us

PRAISE the LORD!

     Praise the LORD, O my soul!
2 While I live I will praise the LORD;

I will sing praises to my God
while I have my being.

3 Do not put your trust in princes,
Nor in a son of man, in whom
there is no help.
4 His spirit departs, he returns to
his earth;
In that very day his plans perish.

5 Happy *is he* who *has* the God
of Jacob for his help,
Whose hope *is* in the LORD his
God,
6 Who made heaven and earth,
The sea, and all that *is* in them;
Who keeps truth forever,
7 Who executes justice for the
oppressed,
Who gives food to the hungry.
The LORD gives freedom to the
prisoners.

8 The LORD opens *the eyes of* the
blind;
The LORD raises those who are
bowed down;
The LORD loves the righteous.
9 The LORD watches over the
strangers;
He relieves the fatherless and
widow;
But the way of the wicked He
turns upside down.

10 The LORD shall reign forever—
Your God, O Zion, to all
generations.

Praise the LORD!

PSALM 147

God is mighty

PRAISE the LORD!
For *it is* good to sing praises to
our God;
For *it is* pleasant, *and* praise is
beautiful.

2 The LORD builds up Jerusalem;
He gathers together the outcasts
of Israel.
3 He heals the brokenhearted
And binds up their wounds.
4 He counts the number of the
stars;
He calls them all by name.
5 Great *is* our Lord, and mighty
in power;
His understanding *is* infinite.
6 The LORD lifts up the humble;
He casts the wicked down to the
ground.

7 Sing to the LORD with
thanksgiving;
Sing praises on the harp to our
God,
8 Who covers the heavens with
clouds,
Who prepares rain for the earth,
Who makes grass to grow on the
mountains.
9 He gives to the beast its food,
And to the young ravens that
cry.

10 He does not delight in the
strength of the horse;

DIGGING IN

147:3 God Heals Broken Hearts
Sometimes you hear about people who have heart attacks. That isn't the same as a broken heart. A "broken heart" describes people who have lost the desire to go on living. We say they have "lost hope."

There are many brokenhearted people in the world. God cares about brokenhearted people. We ought to tell them that God wants to mend their broken hearts.

The reason many people are broken-hearted is that they don't know God as He truly is. All their lives they have been living as though they didn't need God. They may even become rich and important. Then one day they lose everything.

All the things they lived for are gone—their money, their importance, and their friends. Such people often kill themselves. But many also tell how God rescued them when they were brokenhearted. They prayed to Him and He saved them.

He takes no pleasure in the legs
of a man.
11 The LORD takes pleasure in
those who fear Him,
In those who hope in His mercy.

12 Praise the LORD, O Jerusalem!
Praise your God, O Zion!
13 For He has strengthened the
bars of your gates;
He has blessed your children
within you.
14 He makes peace *in* your
borders,
And fills you with the finest
wheat.

15 He sends out His command *to
the* earth;
His word runs very swiftly.
16 He gives snow like wool;
He scatters the frost like ashes;
17 He casts out His hail like
morsels;
Who can stand before His cold?
18 He sends out His word and
melts them;
He causes His wind to blow, *and*
the waters flow.

19 He declares His word to Jacob,
His statutes and His judgments
to Israel.
20 He has not dealt thus with any
nation;
And *as for His* judgments, they
have not known them.

Praise the LORD!

PSALM 148

All God's creatures praise Him

PRAISE the LORD!

Praise the LORD from the
heavens;
Praise Him in the heights!
2 Praise Him, all His angels;
Praise Him, all His hosts!
3 Praise Him, sun and moon;
Praise Him, all you stars of light!

4 Praise Him, you heavens of
heavens,
And you waters above the
heavens!

5 Let them praise the name of the
LORD,
For He commanded and they
were created.
6 He also established them forever
and ever;
He made a decree which shall
not pass away.

7 Praise the LORD from the earth,
You great sea creatures and all
the depths;
8 Fire and hail, snow and clouds;
Stormy wind, fulfilling His word;
9 Mountains and all hills;
Fruitful trees and all cedars;
10 Beasts and all cattle;
Creeping things and flying fowl;
11 Kings of the earth and all
peoples;
Princes and all judges of the
earth;
12 Both young men and maidens;
Old men and children.

13 Let them praise the name of the
LORD,
For His name alone is exalted;
His glory *is* above the earth and
heaven.
14 And He has exalted the horn of
His people,
The praise of all His saints—
Of the children of Israel,
A people near to Him.

Praise the LORD!

PSALM 149

The Lord is pleased with His people

PRAISE the LORD!

Sing to the LORD a new song,
And His praise in the assembly
of saints.

2 Let Israel rejoice in their Maker;
Let the children of Zion be joyful
in their King.
3 Let them praise His name with
the dance;
Let them sing praises to Him
with the timbrel and harp.
4 For the LORD takes pleasure in
His people;
He will beautify the humble with
salvation.

5 Let the saints be joyful in glory;
Let them sing aloud on their
beds.
6 *Let* the high praises of God *be*
in their mouth,
And a two-edged sword in their
hand,
7 To execute vengeance on the
nations,
And punishments on the
peoples;
8 To bind their kings with chains,
And their nobles with fetters of
iron;
9 To execute on them the written
judgment—
This honor have all His saints.

Praise the LORD!

PSALM 150

Praise the Lord

PRAISE the LORD!

Praise God in His sanctuary;
Praise Him in His mighty
firmament!

2 Praise Him for His mighty acts;
Praise Him according to His
excellent greatness!

3 Praise Him with the sound of the
trumpet;
Praise Him with the lute and
harp!
4 Praise Him with the timbrel and
dance;
Praise Him with stringed
instruments and flutes!
5 Praise Him with loud cymbals;
Praise Him with clashing
cymbals!

6 Let everything that has breath
praise the LORD.

Praise the LORD!

⛏ DIGGING IN

149:1 Christians Have a New Song
What is this new song? David talks about
it in Psalm 40:3: "He has put a new song
in my mouth—praise to our God." We
learn lots of songs in this world. Some
of them are great songs, like the national
anthem. Other songs tell of the evil that
lives in men's hearts. Hard rock music is
often like that.

The Christian's "new song" is praise
to God. Until God shows Himself to us,
we can't praise Him because we don't
know Him. Then we see what a great
thing He did for us when He saved us
from sin, and we can't help praising Him.
In Revelation 14:3, we see the saved people of Israel singing this "new song."

Wouldn't it be wonderful if everybody
could sing the new song of salvation? We
hope you can sing it, too, because God
loves you.

The Book of
PROVERBS

A Wise Young Man—Before I could act wisely, I had to find out what it means to be "wise."

I have learned that I may know many things, but I still may not be wise. Being wise means knowing how to *use* my knowledge to get good results. I may make perfect grades in school, but if I can't make the world around me a better place to live in, then all my learning is useless. God has taught me to think of the good of others. This is a great part of wisdom.

The greatest wisdom is to know that God has shown Himself to me in His Word. Then I am completely happy being the kind of person my wise Creator wants me to be in His world.

Why you need to read this book

THE proverbs of Solomon the son of David, king of Israel:

2 To know wisdom and
instruction,
To perceive the words of
understanding,
3 To receive the instruction of
wisdom,
Justice, judgment, and equity;
4 To give prudence to the simple,
To the young man knowledge
and discretion—
5 A wise *man* will hear and
increase learning,
And a man of understanding will
attain wise counsel,
6 To understand a proverb and an
enigma,
The words of the wise and their
riddles.

7 The fear of the LORD *is* the
beginning of knowledge,
But fools despise wisdom and
instruction.

8 My son, hear the instruction of
your father,
And do not forsake the law of
your mother;
9 For they *will be* a graceful
ornament on your head,
And chains about your neck.

10 My son, if sinners entice you,
Do not consent.
11 If they say, "Come with us,
Let us lie in wait to *shed* blood;
Let us lurk secretly for the
innocent without cause;

DIGGING IN

1:7 How Knowledge Begins Knowledge begins with "the fear of the Lord." This "fear" stands for the honor, love, and trust we owe to God. We also call such fear "reverence." Why must knowledge begin with *reverence* for God?

Unless we have a true measuring stick (ruler), we can't know how long a line is. If we don't have a speedometer, we don't know how fast our car is going.

In the same way, the human mind can-

not measure truth. Only God can show us the difference between truth and error. Many young people have a hard time knowing right from wrong because they don't know God. People's opinions, or even human laws, can't always tell you what is right. This is why Adam and Eve got in trouble (Genesis 3). They wouldn't let God govern their lives. Only God can really tell us what is right and true. So your knowledge must begin with God.

12 Let us swallow them alive like
  Sheol,
  And whole, like those who go
    down to the Pit;
13 We shall find all *kinds* of
    precious possessions,
  We shall fill our houses with
    spoil;
14 Cast in your lot among us,
  Let us all have one purse"—
15 My son, do not walk in the way
    with them,
  Keep your foot from their path;
16 For their feet run to evil,
  And they make haste to shed
    blood.
17 Surely, in vain the net is spread
  In the sight of any bird;
18 But they lie in wait for their *own*
    blood,
  They lurk secretly for their *own*
    lives.
19 So *are* the ways of everyone
    who is greedy for gain;
  It takes away the life of its
    owners.

20 Wisdom calls aloud outside;
  She raises her voice in the open
    squares.
21 She cries out in the chief
    concourses,
  At the openings of the gates in
    the city
  She speaks her words:
22 "How long, you simple ones, will
    you love simplicity?
  For scorners delight in their
    scorning,
  And fools hate knowledge.
23 Turn at my rebuke;
  Surely I will pour out my spirit
    on you;
  I will make my words known to
    you.
24 Because I have called and you
    refused,
  I have stretched out my hand
    and no one regarded,
25 Because you disdained all my
    counsel,
  And would have none of my
    rebuke,
26 I also will laugh at your calamity;

  I will mock when your terror
    comes,
27 When your terror comes like a
    storm,
  And your destruction comes like
    a whirlwind,
  When distress and anguish come
    upon you.

28 "Then they will call on me, but I
    will not answer;
  They will seek me diligently, but
    they will not find me.
29 Because they hated knowledge
  And did not choose the fear of
    the LORD,
30 They would have none of my
    counsel
  And despised my every rebuke.
31 Therefore they shall eat the fruit
    of their own way,
  And be filled to the full with their
    own fancies.
32 For the turning away of the
    simple will slay them,
  And the complacency of fools
    will destroy them;
33 But whoever listens to me will
    dwell safely,
  And will be secure, without fear
    of evil."

Wisdom keeps me out of trouble

2 My son, if you receive my words,
  And treasure my commands
    within you,
2 So that you incline your ear to
    wisdom,
  And apply your heart to
    understanding;
3 Yes, if you cry out for
    discernment,
  And lift up your voice for
    understanding,
4 If you seek her as silver,
  And search for her as *for* hidden
    treasures;
5 Then you will understand the
    fear of the LORD,
  And find the knowledge of God.
6 For the LORD gives wisdom;
  From His mouth *come*
    knowledge and
    understanding;

7   He stores up sound wisdom for
      the upright;
    He is a shield to those who walk
      uprightly;
8   He guards the paths of justice,
    And preserves the way of His
      saints.
9   Then you will understand
      righteousness and justice,
    Equity *and* every good path.

10 When wisdom enters your heart,
    And knowledge is pleasant to
      your soul,
11 Discretion will preserve you;
    Understanding will keep you,
12 To deliver you from the way of
      evil,
    From the man who speaks
      perverse things,
13 From those who leave the paths
      of uprightness
    To walk in the ways of darkness;
14 Who rejoice in doing evil,
    And delight in the perversity of
      the wicked;
15 Whose ways *are* crooked,
    And *who are* devious in their
      paths;
16 To deliver you from the immoral
      woman,
    From the seductress *who* flatters
      with her words,
17 Who forsakes the companion of
      her youth,
    And forgets the covenant of her
      God.
18 For her house leads down to
      death,
    And her paths to the dead;

19 None who go to her return,
    Nor do they regain the paths of
      life—
20 So you may walk in the way of
      goodness,
    And keep *to* the paths of
      righteousness.
21 For the upright will dwell in the
      land,
    And the blameless will remain in
      it;
22 But the wicked will be cut off
      from the earth,
    And the unfaithful will be
      uprooted from it.

Finding wisdom is like finding buried treasure

3 My son, do not forget my law,
    But let your heart keep my
      commands;
2   For length of days and long life
    And peace they will add to
      you.

3   Let not mercy and truth forsake
      you;
    Bind them around your neck,
    Write them on the tablet of your
      heart,
4   *And* so find favor and high
      esteem
    In the sight of God and man.

5   Trust in the LORD with all your
      heart,
    And lean not on your own
      understanding;

⚒ DIGGING IN

3:1, 2 Share Peace and Long Life with Others Many young people are getting sick and old long before they should. They smoke marijuana and use other drugs. Then their bodies waste away. Some boys and girls are even taking their own lives!

Too many people your age are sick because of their parents' sins. Babies are born with horrible diseases their parents gave to them. Some little children are even born with a drug habit they got from their mothers. Thank God if you haven't been born with these miseries.

God cares about all these unhappy children. You know that peace and long life come from trusting and obeying God's Word. God needs you to take the wonderful words of Jesus to other boys and girls. Ask Him to show you how He can use you to share His love with others.

Can You Trust God with Your Life?

Some people try to run their lives all by themselves. That never works. The reason is that God made us for Himself. Without God, we are not complete persons, and we fail. We're just tiny specks in God's universe. But He knows and understands your needs better than you do.

6 In all your ways acknowledge Him,
   And He shall direct your paths.

7 Do not be wise in your own eyes;
   Fear the LORD and depart from evil.
8 It will be health to your flesh,
   And strength to your bones.

9 Honor the LORD with your possessions,
   And with the firstfruits of all your increase;
10 So your barns will be filled with plenty,
   And your vats will overflow with new wine.

11 My son, do not despise the chastening of the LORD,

Nor detest His correction;
12 For whom the LORD loves He corrects,
   Just as a father the son in whom he delights.

13 Happy is the man who finds **wisdom,**
   And the man who gains understanding;
14 For her proceeds are better than the profits of silver,
   And her gain than fine gold.
15 She is more precious than rubies,
   And all the things you may desire cannot compare with her.
16 Length of days is in her right hand,
   In her left hand riches and honor.
17 Her ways are ways of pleasantness,
   And all her paths are peace.
18 She is a tree of life to those who take hold of her,
   And happy are all who retain her.

19 The LORD by wisdom founded the earth;
   By understanding He established the heavens;

WORDFINDER

3:13 Wisdom   The ability to use facts to bring about good results. The so-called wisdom of this world could not do this. Jesus Christ is the source of true wisdom.

DIGGING IN

3:5, 6 The Greatest Wisdom You should memorize this proverb: "Lean not on your own understanding." As you go through life, these words will make you strong when you have to make decisions. Some people might say, "You have to depend on yourself," and "God helps people who help themselves." But you don't have to depend on your own wisdom. The truth is that human wisdom very often fails. We don't understand our world as well as we

think we do. Only God has perfect understanding.

God urges you to count on Him when you have choices to make. He made you, and He knows all about you, so give your problems to Him. You will be surprised how clear your path becomes when God is choosing your way for you.

Remember, a tiny speck of a man knows very little about life. But God understands all about you and life.

20 By His knowledge the depths
      were broken up,
   And clouds drop down the dew.

21 My son, let them not depart from
      your eyes—
   Keep sound wisdom and
      discretion;
22 So they will be life to your soul
   And grace to your neck.
23 Then you will walk safely in your
      way,
   And your foot will not stumble.
24 When you lie down, you will not
      be afraid;
   Yes, you will lie down and your
      sleep will be sweet.
25 Do not be afraid of sudden
      terror,
   Nor of trouble from the wicked
      when it comes;
26 For the LORD will be your
      confidence,
   And will keep your foot from
      being caught.

27 Do not withhold good from
      those to whom it is due,
   When it is in the power of your
      hand to do so.
28 Do not say to your neighbor,
   "Go, and come back,
   And tomorrow I will give it,"
   When you have it with you.
29 Do not devise evil against your
      neighbor,
   For he dwells by you for safety's
      sake.
30 Do not strive with a man without
      cause,
   If he has done you no harm.

31 Do not envy the oppressor,
   And choose none of his ways;
32 For the perverse *person is* an
      abomination to the LORD,
   But His secret counsel *is* with the
      upright.
33 The curse of the LORD *is* on the
      house of the wicked,
   But He blesses the home of the
      just.
34 Surely He scorns the scornful,
   But gives grace to the humble.
35 The wise shall inherit glory,
   But shame shall be the legacy
      of fools.

Getting wisdom is the most important thing

4 Hear, *my* children, the
      instruction of a father,
   And give attention to know
      understanding;
2 For I give you good doctrine:
   Do not forsake my law.
3 When I was my father's son,
   Tender and the only one in the
      sight of my mother,
4 He also taught me, and said to
      me:
   "Let your heart retain my words;
   Keep my commands, and live.
5 Get wisdom! Get understanding!
   Do not forget, nor turn away
      from the words of my mouth.
6 Do not forsake her, and she will
      preserve you;
   Love her, and she will keep
      you.
7 Wisdom *is* the principal thing;
   Therefore get wisdom.

⛏ DIGGING IN

4:5, 6 Wisdom Is Safety This proverb compares wisdom to a wise lady—"She will preserve you." Therefore "get wisdom! Get understanding!"

As you grow up, you will hear lots of advice about how to be safe. Mostly it will be advice about how to get money. Believe it or not, some people will tell you to forget God and "do your own thing." They mean that you should live in the way that brings you the most money and gives you the most pleasure.

But money and pleasure come and go. As long as you are enjoying yourself, you may be satisfied *for a while.* But when you get sick or old, your money doesn't help you anymore. In fact, you'll feel lost because you never made God your Friend. After so long a time, you won't even be able to find God anymore. Get wisdom! Get hold of God while you're still young.

And in all your getting, get understanding.

8 Exalt her, and she will promote you;
She will bring you honor, when you embrace her.

9 She will place on your head an ornament of grace;
A crown of glory she will deliver to you."

10 Hear, my son, and receive my sayings,
And the years of your life will be many.

11 I have taught you in the way of wisdom;
I have led you in right paths.

12 When you walk, your steps will not be hindered,
And when you run, you will not stumble.

13 Take firm hold of instruction, do not let go;
Keep her, for she is your life.

14 Do not enter the path of the wicked,
And do not walk in the way of evil.

15 Avoid it, do not travel on it;
Turn away from it and pass on.

16 For they do not sleep unless they have done evil;
And their sleep is taken away unless they make someone fall.

17 For they eat the bread of wickedness,
And drink the wine of violence.

18 But the path of the just is like the shining sun,
That shines ever brighter unto the perfect day.

19 The way of the wicked is like darkness;
They do not know what makes them stumble.

20 My son, give attention to my words;
Incline your ear to my sayings.

21 Do not let them depart from your eyes;
Keep them in the midst of your heart;

22 For they are life to those who find them,
And health to all their flesh.

23 Keep your heart with all diligence,
For out of it spring the issues of life.

24 Put away from you a deceitful mouth,
And put perverse lips far from you.

25 Let your eyes look straight ahead,
And your eyelids look right before you.

26 Ponder the path of your feet,
And let all your ways be established.

27 Do not turn to the right or the left;
Remove your foot from evil.

When you are tempted, run for your life!

5 My son, pay attention to my wisdom;
Lend your ear to my understanding,

2 That you may preserve discretion,
And your lips may keep knowledge.

3 For the lips of an immoral woman drip honey,
And her mouth is smoother than oil;

4 But in the end she is bitter as wormwood,
Sharp as a two-edged sword.

5 Her feet go down to death,
Her steps lay hold of hell.

6 Lest you ponder her path of life—
Her ways are unstable;
You do not know them.

7 Therefore hear me now, my children,

And do not depart from the
words of my mouth.

8 Remove your way far from her,
And do not go near the door of
her house,

9 Lest you give your honor to
others,
And your years to the cruel *one*;

10 Lest aliens be filled with your
wealth,
And your labors *go* to the house
of a foreigner;

11 And you mourn at last,
When your flesh and your body
are consumed,

12 And say:
"How I have hated instruction,
And my heart despised
correction!

13 I have not obeyed the voice of
my teachers,
Nor inclined my ear to those
who instructed me!

14 I was on the verge of total ruin,
In the midst of the assembly and
congregation."

15 Drink water from your own
cistern,
And running water from your
own well.

16 Should your fountains be
dispersed abroad,
Streams of water in the streets?

17 Let them be only your own,
And not for strangers with you.

18 Let your fountain be blessed,
And rejoice with the wife of your
youth.

19 *As a* loving deer and a graceful
doe,
Let her breasts satisfy you at all
times;
And always be enraptured with
her love.

20 For why should you, my son, be
enraptured by an immoral
woman,
And be embraced in the arms
of a seductress?

21 For the ways of man *are* before
the eyes of the Lord,
And He ponders all his paths.

22 His own iniquities entrap the
wicked *man,*
And he is caught in the cords
of his sin.

23 He shall die for lack of
instruction,
And in the greatness of his folly
he shall go astray.

Seven sins that lead to big trouble

6 My son, if you become surety
for your friend,
If you have shaken hands in
pledge for a stranger,

2 You are snared by the words of
your mouth;
You are taken by the words of
your mouth.

3 So do this, my son, and deliver
yourself;
For you have come into the
hand of your friend:
Go and humble yourself;
Plead with your friend.

4 Give no sleep to your eyes,
Nor slumber to your eyelids.

5 Deliver yourself like a gazelle
from the hand *of the hunter,*
And like a bird from the hand
of the fowler.

6 Go to the ant, you sluggard!
Consider her ways and be wise,

7 Which, having no captain,
Overseer or ruler,

8 Provides her supplies in the
summer,
And gathers her food in the
harvest.

9 How long will you slumber, O
sluggard?
When will you rise from your
sleep?

10 A little sleep, a little slumber,
A little folding of the hands to
sleep—

11 So shall your poverty come on
you like a prowler,
And your need like an armed
man.

12 A worthless person, a wicked
man,
Walks with a perverse mouth;

13 He winks with his *eyes,*
   He shuffles his feet,
   He points with his fingers;
14 Perversity *is* in his heart,
   He devises evil continually,
   He sows discord.
15 Therefore his calamity shall
      come suddenly;
   Suddenly he shall be broken
      without remedy.

16 These six *things* the Lord hates,
   Yes, seven *are* an abomination
      to Him:
17 A proud look,
   A lying tongue,
   Hands that shed innocent blood,
18 A heart that devises wicked
      plans,
   Feet that are swift in running to
      evil,
19 A false witness *who* speaks lies,
   And one who sows discord
      among brethren.

20 My son, keep your father's
      command,
   And do not forsake the law of
      your mother.
21 Bind them continually upon
      your heart;
   Tie them around your neck.
22 When you roam, they will lead
      you;
   When you sleep, they will keep
      you;
   And *when* you awake, they will
      speak with you.
23 For the commandment *is* a
      lamp,
   And the law a light;

Reproofs of instruction *are* the
      way of life,
24 To keep you from the evil
      woman,
   From the flattering tongue of a
      seductress.
25 Do not lust after her beauty in
      your heart,
   Nor let her allure you with her
      eyelids.
26 For by means of a harlot
   A man is reduced to a crust of
      bread;
   And an adulteress will prey upon
      his precious life.
27 Can a man take fire to his
      bosom,
   And his clothes not be burned?
28 Can one walk on hot coals,
   And his feet not be seared?
29 So *is* he who goes in to his
      neighbor's wife;
   Whoever touches her shall not
      be innocent.

30 *People* do not despise a thief
   If he steals to satisfy himself
      when he is starving.
31 Yet *when* he is found, he must
      restore sevenfold;
   He may have to give up all the
      substance of his house.
32 Whoever commits adultery with
      a woman lacks understanding;
   He *who* does so destroys his
      own soul.
33 Wounds and dishonor he will
      get,
   And his reproach will not be
      wiped away.
34 For jealousy *is* a husband's fury;

DIGGING IN

6:9–11 Laziness Leads to Poverty
Not all people are poor because they're lazy. But a lazy person will nearly always be poor. God expects us to pray, but He also expects us to work.

You may think fun is pleasant and work is unpleasant. That's a false idea. Whatever work God gives you to do in life should also be fun. If your work isn't exciting, then that work wasn't meant for you.

There are many kinds of work that God gives His people to do. All work that is lawful is also good work. Start early to find out the work God wants to give you. School days will soon come to an end. Then comes a lifetime of work.

Life is God's gift and must not be wasted. Make up your mind to work in a way that pleases God, blesses others, and provides for your needs.

Therefore he will not spare in the
day of vengeance.
35 He will accept no recompense,
Nor will he be appeased though
you give many gifts.

Play keep away

7 My son, keep my words,
And treasure my commands
within you.
2 Keep my commands and live,
And my law as the apple of your
eye.
3 Bind them on your fingers;
Write them on the tablet of your
heart.
4 Say to wisdom, "You *are* my
sister,"
And call understanding *your*
nearest kin,
5 That they may keep you from
the immoral woman,
From the seductress *who* flatters
with her words.

6 For at the window of my house
I looked through my lattice,
7 And saw among the simple,
I perceived among the youths,
A young man devoid of
understanding,
8 Passing along the street near her
corner;
And he took the path to her
house
9 In the twilight, in the evening,
In the black and dark night.

10 And there a woman met him,
With the attire of a harlot, and
a crafty heart.
11 She *was* loud and rebellious,
Her *feet* would not stay at home.
12 At times *she was* outside, at
times in the open square,
Lurking at every corner.
13 So she caught him and kissed
him;
With an impudent face she said
to him:
14 "*I have* peace offerings with me;
Today I have paid my vows.
15 So I came out to meet you,

Diligently to seek your face,
And I have found you.
16 I have spread my bed with
tapestry,
Colored coverings of Egyptian
linen.
17 I have perfumed my bed
With myrrh, aloes, and
cinnamon.
18 Come, let us take our fill of love
until morning;
Let us delight ourselves with
love.
19 For my husband *is* not at home;
He has gone on a long journey;
20 He has taken a bag of money
with him,
And will come home on the
appointed day."

21 With her enticing speech she
caused him to yield,
With her flattering lips she
seduced him.
22 Immediately he went after her,
as an ox goes to the slaughter,
Or as a fool to the correction of
the stocks,
23 Till an arrow struck his liver.
As a bird hastens to the snare,
He did not know it *would cost*
his life.

24 Now therefore, listen to me, *my*
children;
Pay attention to the words of my
mouth:
25 Do not let your heart turn aside
to her ways,
Do not stray into her paths;
26 For she has cast down many
wounded,
And all who were slain by her
were strong *men*.
27 Her house *is* the way to hell,
Descending to the chambers of
death.

Being wise is the happy way to live

8 Does not wisdom cry out,
And understanding lift up her
voice?

2   She takes her stand on the top
      of the high hill,
    Beside the way, where the paths
      meet.
3   She cries out by the gates, at the
      entry of the city,
    At the entrance of the doors:
4   "To you, O men, I call,
    And my voice *is* to the sons of
      men.
5   O you simple ones, understand
      prudence,
    And you fools, be of an
      understanding heart.
6   Listen, for I will speak of
      excellent things,
    And from the opening of my lips
      will come right things;
7   For my mouth will speak truth;
    Wickedness *is* an abomination to
      my lips.
8   All the words of my mouth *are*
      with righteousness;
    Nothing crooked or perverse *is*
      in them.
9   They *are* all plain to him who
      understands,
    And right to those who find
      knowledge.
10 Receive my instruction, and not
      silver,
    And knowledge rather than
      choice gold;
11 For wisdom *is* better than rubies,
    And all the things one may
      desire cannot be compared
      with her.

12 "I, wisdom, dwell with prudence,
    And find out knowledge *and*
      discretion.

13 The fear of the LORD *is* to hate
      evil;
    Pride and arrogance and the evil
      way
    And the perverse mouth I hate.
14 Counsel *is* mine, and sound
      wisdom;
    I *am* understanding, I have
      strength.
15 By me kings reign,
    And rulers decree justice.
16 By me princes rule, and
      nobles,
    All the judges of the earth.
17 I love those who love me,
    And those who *seek* me
      diligently will find me.
18 Riches and honor *are* with me,
    Enduring riches and
      righteousness.
19 My fruit *is* better than gold, yes,
      than fine gold,
    And my revenue than choice
      silver.
20 I traverse the way of
      righteousness,
    In the midst of the paths of
      justice,
21 That I may cause those who love
      me to inherit wealth,
    That I may fill their treasuries.

22 "The LORD possessed me at the
      beginning of His way,
    Before His works of old.
23 I have been established from
      everlasting,
    From the beginning, before
      there was ever an earth.
24 When *there were* no depths I
      was brought forth,

 DIGGING IN

8:22–29 God Created the World by Wisdom Wisdom is not mere thoughts. God's wisdom is thoughts that *work*. God thought about the universe He was going to make, and then He put His "thoughts" to work. We have said before that God *spoke* and the worlds came into being.

These verses in Proverbs 8 could refer to the Lord Jesus Christ Himself as the Wisdom of God. In his Gospel, John says that Jesus is "the Word" of God (John 1:1).

Of course, Jesus isn't a word like the printing on a page. He is the *living* Word. Jesus is also the *Wisdom* of God. God's Son Jesus is the Wisdom that God spoke and caused the worlds to appear. (See Colossians 1:16.) God's wisdom can also help you do wonderful things that please Him.

God's wisdom is powerful thinking in action.

When *there were* no fountains
    abounding with water.
25 Before the mountains were
    settled,
    Before the hills, I was brought
    forth;
26 While as yet He had not made
    the earth or the fields,
    Or the primal dust of the world.
27 When He prepared the heavens,
    I *was* there,
    When He drew a circle on the
    face of the deep,
28 When He established the clouds
    above,
    When He strengthened the
    fountains of the deep,
29 When He assigned to the sea its
    limit,
    So that the waters would not
    transgress His command,
    When He marked out the
    foundations of the earth,
30 Then I was beside Him *as* a
    master craftsman;
    And I was daily *His* delight,
    Rejoicing always before Him,
31 Rejoicing in His inhabited world,
    And my delight *was* with the
    sons of men.

32 "Now therefore, listen to me, *my*
    children,
    For blessed *are those who* keep
    my ways.
33 Hear instruction and be wise,
    And do not disdain *it.*
34 Blessed is the man who listens
    to me,
    Watching daily at my gates,
    Waiting at the posts of my doors.
35 For whoever finds me finds life,
    And obtains favor from the
    Lord;
36 But he who sins against me
    wrongs his own soul;
    All those who hate me love
    death."

Respecting God leads to wisdom

9 Wisdom has built her house,
    She has hewn out her seven
    pillars;

2 She has slaughtered her meat,
    She has mixed her wine,
    She has also furnished her
    table.
3 She has sent out her maidens,
    She cries out from the highest
    places of the city,
4 "Whoever *is* simple, let him turn
    in here!"
    As for him who lacks
    understanding, she says to
    him,
5 "Come, eat of my bread
    And drink of the wine I have
    mixed.
6 Forsake foolishness and live,
    And go in the way of
    understanding.

7 "He who corrects a scoffer gets
    shame for himself,
    And he who rebukes a wicked
    man only harms himself.
8 Do not correct a scoffer, lest he
    hate you;
    Rebuke a wise *man,* and he will
    love you.
9 Give *instruction* to a wise *man,*
    and he will be still wiser;
    Teach a just *man,* and he will
    increase in learning.

10 "The fear of the Lord *is* the
    beginning of wisdom,
    And the knowledge of the Holy
    One *is* understanding.
11 For by me your days will be
    multiplied,
    And years of life will be added
    to you.
12 If you are wise, you are wise for
    yourself,
    And *if* you scoff, you will bear
    it alone."

13 A foolish woman is clamorous;
    She is simple, and knows
    nothing.
14 For she sits at the door of her
    house,
    On a seat *by* the highest places
    of the city,
15 To call to those who pass by,
    Who go straight on their way:

What Every Boy and Girl Should Learn

Are you ever afraid? Some people are afraid of the dark. Others fear being alone or in high places. Many people are ruled by all kinds of unnecessary fears.

There is one way to get rid of needless fear forever: "The fear of the Lord is the beginning of wisdom." Fear God and you will not fear anything else.

To fear God is to respect and honor Him. This means that you recognize how much power God has. God is in complete charge of the whole universe. Nothing ever happens in all creation that God does not control.

But God is also perfectly good, and He also limits what evil men can do. You will always be safe when you put yourself in God's hands.

---

16 "Whoever *is* simple, let him turn
     in here";
   And *as for* him who lacks
     understanding, she says to
     him,
17 "Stolen water is *sweet*,
   And bread *eaten* in secret is
     pleasant."
18 But he does not know that the
     dead *are* there,
   That her guests *are* in the depths
     of hell.

God's wisdom is an open invitation to all

10 The proverbs of Solomon:

A wise son makes a glad father,
But a foolish son *is* the grief of
  his mother.

2 Treasures of wickedness profit
    nothing,
   But righteousness delivers from
    death.
3 The LORD will not allow the
    righteous soul to famish,
   But He casts away the desire of
    the wicked.
4 He who has a slack hand
    becomes poor,
   But the hand of the diligent
    makes rich.
5 He who gathers in summer *is* a
    wise son;

He who sleeps in harvest *is* a
  son who causes shame.

6 Blessings *are* on the head of the
    righteous,
   But violence covers the mouth
    of the wicked.
7 The memory of the righteous *is*
    blessed,
   But the name of the wicked will
    rot.
8 The wise in heart will receive
    commands,
   But a prating fool will fall.
9 He who walks with integrity
    walks securely,
   But he who perverts his ways
    will become known.
10 He who winks with the *eye*
    causes trouble,
   But a prating fool will fall.
11 The mouth of the righteous *is* a
    well of life,
   But violence covers the mouth
    of the wicked.
12 Hatred stirs up strife,
   But love covers all sins.
13 Wisdom is found on the lips of
    him who has understanding,
   But a rod *is* for the back of him
    who is devoid of
    understanding.

14   Wise *people* store up
     knowledge,
     But the mouth of the foolish *is*
     near destruction.

15   The rich man's wealth *is* his
     strong city;
     The destruction of the poor *is*
     their poverty.

16   The labor of the righteous *leads*
     to life,
     The wages of the wicked to sin.

17   He who keeps instruction *is in*
     the way of life,
     But he who refuses correction
     goes astray.

18   Whoever hides hatred *has* lying
     lips,
     And whoever spreads slander *is*
     a fool.

19   In the multitude of words sin *is*
     not lacking,
     But he who restrains his lips *is*
     wise.

20   The tongue of the righteous *is*
     choice silver;
     The heart of the wicked *is worth*
     little.

21   The lips of the righteous feed
     many,
     But fools die for lack of wisdom.

22   The blessing of the LORD makes
     one rich,
     And He adds no sorrow with it.

23   To do evil *is* like sport to a fool,
     But a man of understanding has
     wisdom.

24   The fear of the wicked will come
     upon him,
     And the desire of the righteous
     will be granted.

25   When the whirlwind passes by,
     the wicked *is* no *more,*
     But the righteous *has* an
     everlasting foundation.

26   As vinegar to the teeth and
     smoke to the eyes,

So *is* the lazy *man* to those who
     send him.

27   The fear of the LORD prolongs
     days,
     But the years of the wicked will
     be shortened.

28   The hope of the righteous *will*
     be gladness,
     But the expectation of the
     wicked will perish.

29   The way of the LORD *is* strength
     for the upright,
     But destruction *will come* to the
     workers of iniquity.

30   The righteous will never be
     removed,
     But the wicked will not inhabit
     the earth.

31   The mouth of the righteous
     brings forth wisdom,
     But the perverse tongue will be
     cut out.

32   The lips of the righteous know
     what is acceptable,
     But the mouth of the wicked
     what is perverse.

God loves honesty, but hates cheating

11   Dishonest scales *are* an
     abomination to the LORD,
     But a just weight *is* His delight.

2   When pride comes, then comes
     shame;
     But with the humble *is* wisdom.

3   The integrity of the upright will
     guide them,
     But the perversity of the
     unfaithful will destroy them.

4   Riches do not profit in the day
     of wrath,
     But righteousness delivers from
     death.

5   The righteousness of the
     blameless will direct his way
     aright,
     But the wicked will fall by his
     own wickedness.

The Road To Heaven

(How To Be Saved)

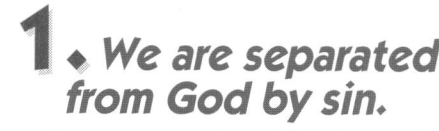

1. *We are separated from God by sin.*

"For all have sinned and fall short of the glory of God." (Romans 3:23)

2. *But He has taken the first step in rescuing us.*

"God demonstrates His own love toward us, in that while we were still sinners, Christ died for us." (Romans 5:8)

3. *God gives the gift of Forever Life.*

"The wages of sin is death, but the gift of God is eternal life in Christ Jesus our Lord." (Romans 6:23)

4. *Believe in Jesus' death and resurrection.*

"If you...believe in your heart that God has raised Him from the dead, you will be saved." (Romans 10:9)

5. *Just ask Him to be your Savior now.*

"For with the...mouth confession is made unto salvation." (Romans 10:10)

Exercise Your Spiritual Muscles

Your spiritual muscles—faith, hope, and love—need to be exercised before you can grow up to be spiritually strong and fit. Here's an exercise plan guaranteed to help you "work out" your salvation *(see Philippians 2:12):*

1. STUDY GOD'S WORD

BEGINNER: Once daily, 1 memory verse
INTERMEDIATE: Twice daily, 2 memory verses
ADVANCED: Twice daily, 3 memory verses

Psalm 119:11 (look up page 781)   Colossians 3:16 (look up page 1573)
Romans 10:8 (look up page 1499)   2 Timothy 2:15 (look up page 1593)
Ephesians 6:17b (look up page 1561)   Hebrews 4:12 (look up page 1605)

2. PRAY

BEGINNER, INTERMEDIATE, ADVANCED: Often!

Matthew 6:6-13 (look up page 1236)   Ephesians 6:18 (look up page 1561)
Matthew 7:7-11 (look up page 1238)   Philippians 4:6 (look up page 1566)
Matthew 18:19 (look up page 1258)   James 1:6 (look up page 1618)

3. MAKE CHRISTIAN FRIENDS

Sunday: Go to Church
Monday-Saturday: Be a Friend

Leviticus 19:18 (look up page 163)   John 13:34 (look up page 1406)
Proverbs 17:17 (look up page 827)   John 15:13 (look up page 1408)
Matthew 7:12 (look up page 1238)   Ephesians 5:19-20 (look up page 1559)

Staying "spiritually fit" takes lots of practice. But by following this exercise plan faithfully each day, you will learn that "loving the Lord your God with all your heart, with all your soul, and with all your strength" and loving your neighbor as yourself will keep you in great spiritual shape! (See Deuteronomy 6:5.)

6 The righteousness of the upright
will deliver them,
But the unfaithful will be caught
by *their* lust.

7 When a wicked man dies, *his*
expectation will perish,
And the hope of the unjust
perishes.

8 The righteous is delivered from
trouble,
And it comes to the wicked
instead.

9 The hypocrite with *his* mouth
destroys his neighbor,
But through knowledge the
righteous will be delivered.

10 When it goes well with the
righteous, the city rejoices;
And when the wicked perish,
there is jubilation.

11 By the blessing of the upright the
city is exalted,
But it is overthrown by the
mouth of the wicked.

12 He who is devoid of wisdom
despises his neighbor,
But a man of understanding
holds his peace.

13 A talebearer reveals secrets,
But he who is of a faithful spirit
conceals a matter.

14 Where *there is* no counsel, the
people fall;
But in the multitude of
counselors *there is* safety.

15 He who is surety for a stranger
will suffer,
But one who hates being surety
is secure.

16 A gracious woman retains
honor,
But ruthless *men* retain riches.

17 The merciful man does good for
his own soul,
But *he who is* cruel troubles his
own flesh.

18 The wicked *man* does deceptive
work,
But he who sows righteousness
will have a sure reward.

19 As righteousness *leads* to life,
So he who pursues evil *pursues
it* to his own death.

20 Those who are of a perverse
heart *are* an abomination to
the LORD,
But *the* blameless in their ways
are His delight.

21 *Though they join* forces, the
wicked will not go
unpunished;
But the posterity of the righteous
will be delivered.

22 As a ring of gold in a swine's
snout,
So is a lovely woman who lacks
discretion.

23 The desire of the righteous *is*
only good,
But the expectation of the
wicked *is* wrath.

DIGGING IN

11:1 God Loves Honesty Jesus said, "I am . . . the truth" (John 14:6). A compass always points north. God is Truth and always points to the truth. It is impossible for God not to tell the truth or to be dishonest. So God loves honesty in you because you are made in His image.

It isn't always easy to be honest. We're tempted to lie when we know that telling the truth is going to make us look bad to others. But if you love God sincerely, you will also love the truth. This will mean that you will be fair and honest in your dealings with others.

Someone without God has no reason to tell the truth. God is not in his thoughts. So he also cheats in business. Some time ago a lot of banks in the United States were found guilty of cheating. This will cause millions of people to suffer. When honesty fails, the nation fails.

24 There is *one* who scatters, yet
increases more;
And there is *one* who withholds
more than is right,
But it *leads* to poverty.
25 The generous soul will be made
rich,
And he who waters will also be
watered himself.
26 The people will curse him who
withholds grain,
But blessing *will be* on the head
of him who sells *it.*

27 He who earnestly seeks good
finds favor,
But trouble will come to him
who seeks *evil.*

28 He who trusts in his riches will
fall,
But the righteous will flourish
like foliage.

29 He who troubles his own house
will inherit the wind,
And the fool *will be* servant to
the wise of heart.

30 The fruit of the righteous *is a* tree
of life,
And he who wins souls *is* wise.

31 If the righteous will be
recompensed on the earth,
How much more the ungodly
and the sinner.

Wisdom helps you avoid mistakes

12 Whoever loves instruction loves
knowledge,
But he who hates correction *is*
stupid.

2 A good *man* obtains favor from
the LORD,
But a man of wicked intentions
He will condemn.

3 A man is not established by
wickedness,
But the root of the righteous
cannot be moved.

4 An excellent wife *is* the crown
of her husband,

🪓 DIGGING IN

11:25 God Blesses Generous People God is the most generous Person who exists. He *gave* the gift of life to all creatures, including you. He also *gave* His only begotten Son so that you could have eternal life.

Because God gives Himself, He also loves people who give themselves. Generous people are like God. A miser is an example of a selfish man. He thinks only of getting and keeping all the wealth he can get for himself. He doesn't even enjoy his money. Have you read or seen the story, *A Christmas Carol,* by Charles Dickens? In that story Scrooge was an unhappy miser before his life was changed. Then he found happiness in giving.

God wants you to have a generous heart. You don't have much time in the world, and your greatest happiness will come from spending your time and your money to help people in need. Remember, God gave His best for you, and you

can only give what He first gave to you.

12:1 Be a Wise Learner How boring to go on living in a world we refuse to learn about! The selfish man learns only enough to supply the needs of his body. But a wise learner tries to find out the meaning of all things.

God gave us the world so we could study it. This is what He means when He tells you to *subdue* the earth (see Genesis 1:28). In order to subdue or *manage* the world, you must first learn about it.

Hinduism, for example, teaches that the visible world doesn't matter, and we should ignore it. What an insult to the Creator who made everything very good! Our God wants you to grow in understanding the universe He created. But first you must come to know the One who created all His wonderful worlds. When you know the Creator, then you will also see His creation for what it is. All true learning begins with God and ends in understanding yourself and your world.

But she who causes shame *is* like
rottenness in his bones.

5   The thoughts of the righteous
    are right,
    But the counsels of the wicked
    are deceitful.
6   The words of the wicked *are,*
    "Lie in wait for blood,"
    But the mouth of the upright will
    deliver them.

7   The wicked are overthrown and
    are no more,
    But the house of the righteous
    will stand.

8   A man will be commended
    according to his wisdom,
    But he who is of a perverse heart
    will be despised.

9   Better *is the* one who is slighted
    but has a servant,
    Than he who honors himself but
    lacks bread.

10 A righteous *man* regards the life
    of his animal,
    But the tender mercies of the
    wicked *are* cruel.

11 He who tills his land will be
    satisfied with bread,
    But he who follows frivolity *is*
    devoid of understanding.

12 The wicked covet the catch of
    evil *men,*

But the root of the righteous
yields *fruit.*
13 The wicked is ensnared by the
    transgression of *his* lips,
    But the righteous will come
    through trouble.
14 A man will be satisfied with good
    by the fruit of *his* mouth,
    And the recompense of a man's
    hands will be rendered to him.

15 The way of a fool *is* right in his
    own eyes,
    But he who heeds counsel *is*
    wise.
16 A fool's wrath is known at once,
    But a prudent *man* covers
    shame.

17 He *who* speaks truth declares
    righteousness,
    But a false witness, deceit.
18 There is one who speaks like the
    piercings of a sword,
    But the tongue of the wise
    promotes health.
19 The truthful lip shall be
    established forever,
    But a lying tongue *is* but for a
    moment.
20 Deceit is in the heart of those
    who devise evil,
    But counselors of peace have
    joy.
21 No grave trouble will overtake
    the righteous,
    But the wicked shall be filled
    with evil.
22 Lying lips *are* an abomination to
    the LORD,

⛏ DIGGING IN

12:25 Worry Can Kill You Everybody who lives in this world has problems. There is a good way and a bad way to deal with your problems. Maybe you failed an exam, or maybe you are in trouble with somebody. What can you do? The first thing some people do when a problem comes is to worry. Not only that, but they *keep on worrying.* They hardly ever do anything to solve their problems.

The first thing to do when you have trouble is to ask God for wisdom and guidance. Then do whatever it takes to get rid of that problem. Study harder for the next exam. If you've done wrong to others, go and tell them the truth. God will stand by you. You will find that God's way of dealing with problems always works in the end. But lots of people get sick and even die because they made a lifelong habit of worrying.

But those who deal truthfully *are* His delight.

23 A prudent man conceals knowledge,
But the heart of fools proclaims foolishness.

24 The hand of the diligent will rule,
But the lazy *man* will be put to forced labor.

25 Anxiety in the heart of man causes depression,
But a good word makes it glad.

26 The righteous should choose his friends carefully,
For the way of the wicked leads them astray.

27 The lazy *man* does not roast what he took in hunting,
But diligence *is* man's precious possession.

28 In the way of righteousness *is* life,
And in *its* pathway *there is* no death.

How to be successful

13 A wise son *heeds* his father's instruction,
But a scoffer does not listen to rebuke.

2 A man shall eat well by the fruit of *his* mouth,

But the soul of the unfaithful feeds on violence.

3 He who guards his mouth preserves his life,
But he who opens wide his lips shall have destruction.

4 The soul of a lazy *man* desires, and *has* nothing;
But the soul of the diligent shall be made rich.

5 A righteous *man* hates lying,
But a wicked *man* is loathsome and comes to shame.

6 Righteousness guards *him* whose way is blameless,
But wickedness overthrows the sinner.

7 There is one who makes himself rich, yet *has* nothing;
And one who makes himself poor, yet *has* great riches.

8 The ransom of a man's life *is* his riches,
But the poor does not hear rebuke.

9 The light of the righteous rejoices,
But the lamp of the wicked will be put out.

10 By pride comes nothing but strife,
But with the well-advised *is* wisdom.

🔨 DIGGING IN

13:1 Growing Up God's Way You have begun to live in the world. Soon you'll be grown up. Right now you should pray for wisdom to grow up God's way.

Perhaps you've heard, "As the twig is bent, so the tree grows." Ever see a crooked tree? It's almost impossible to make a crooked tree straight. But if the tree had been straightened when it was young, it would never have grown crooked. Right now your mind and body are forming. You need help from older people to be sure you get off to a good start.

Wise teaching will help you make the right choices *now*. A lot of young people are making choices that will destroy their lives. They will never grow up well because they have chosen habits that will kill them or will ruin them for life. Give yourself a chance—grow up God's way and live!

11 Wealth *gained by* dishonesty will
be diminished,
But he who gathers by labor will
increase.

12 Hope deferred makes the heart
sick,
But *when* the desire comes, *it
is* a tree of life.

13 He who despises the word will
be destroyed,
But he who fears the
commandment will be
rewarded.

14 The law of the wise *is* a fountain
of life,
To turn *one* away from the
snares of death.

15 Good understanding gains
favor,
But *the* way of the unfaithful *is*
hard.

16 Every prudent *man* acts with
knowledge,
But a fool lays open *his* folly.

17 A wicked messenger falls into
trouble,
But a faithful ambassador *brings*
health.

18 Poverty and shame *will come* to
him who disdains correction,
But he who regards a rebuke will
be honored.

19 A desire accomplished is sweet
to the soul,
But *it is* an abomination to fools
to depart from evil.

20 He who walks with wise *men* will
be wise,
But the companion of fools will
be destroyed.

21 Evil pursues sinners,
But to the righteous, good shall
be repaid.

22 A good *man* leaves an
inheritance to his children's
children,

But the wealth of the sinner is
stored up for the righteous.

23 Much food *is in* the fallow
ground of the poor,
And for lack of justice there is
waste.

24 He who spares his rod hates his
son,
But he who loves him disciplines
him promptly.

25 The righteous eats to the
satisfying of his soul,
But the stomach of the wicked
shall be in want.

How to make wise choices

14 The wise woman builds her
house,
But the foolish pulls it down with
her hands.

2 He who walks in his uprightness
fears the LORD,
But *he who is* perverse in his
ways despises Him.

3 In the mouth of a fool *is* a rod
of pride,
But the lips of the wise will
preserve them.

4 Where no oxen *are,* the trough
is clean;
But much increase *comes* by the
strength of an ox.

5 A faithful witness does not lie,
But a false witness will utter lies.

6 A scoffer seeks wisdom and does
not *find it,*
But knowledge *is easy* to him
who understands.

7 Go from the presence of a
foolish man,
When you do not perceive *in
him* the lips of knowledge.

8 The wisdom of the prudent *is* to
understand his way,
But the folly of fools *is* deceit.

9 Fools mock at sin,
But among the upright *there is* favor.

10 The heart knows its own bitterness,
And a stranger does not share its joy.

11 The house of the wicked will be overthrown,
But the tent of the upright will flourish.

12 There is a way *that seems* right to a man,
But its end *is* the way of death.

13 Even in laughter the heart may sorrow,
And the end of mirth *may be* grief.

14 The backslider in heart will be filled with his own ways,
But a good man *will be satisfied* from above.

15 The simple believes *every* word,
But the prudent considers well his steps.

16 A wise *man* fears and departs from evil,
But a fool rages and is self-confident.

17 A quick-tempered *man* acts foolishly,
And a man of wicked intentions is hated.

18 The simple inherit folly,
But the prudent are crowned with knowledge.

19 The evil will bow before the good,
And the wicked at the gates of the righteous.

20 The poor *man* is hated even by his own neighbor,
But the rich *has* many friends.

21 He who despises his neighbor sins;
But he who has mercy on the poor, happy *is* he.

22 Do they not go astray who devise evil?
But mercy and truth *belong* to those who devise good.

23 In all labor there is profit,
But idle chatter *leads* only to poverty.

24 The crown of the wise is their riches,
But the foolishness of fools *is* folly.

25 A true witness delivers souls,
But a deceitful *witness* speaks lies.

26 In the fear of the LORD *there is* strong confidence,
And His children will have a place of refuge.

27 The fear of the LORD *is* a fountain of life,

⚒ DIGGING IN

14:17 Bad Temper Is Foolishness
You may feel strong sometimes when you lose your temper. That's because a chemical called adrenalin (pronounced *uh-DRENN-uh-lin*) is pouring into your bloodstream at that moment.

But you aren't really strong when you lose your temper. Later, you'll feel foolish and ashamed that you "flew off the handle." The strong people are those who stay cool when someone insults them.

God needs young people who trust Him in every hard spot. He gives them wisdom and guidance, so they know how to answer people who treat them badly.

See how Jesus acted in the Judgment Hall with Pilate: "But He answered him not one word, so that the governor marveled greatly" (Matthew 27:14). Pilate was amazed at Jesus' calm behavior. When you're calm, you're in charge of yourself and of every problem.

To turn *one* away from the
snares of death.

28 In a multitude of people *is* a
king's honor,
But in the lack of people *is* the
downfall of a prince.

29 *He who is* slow to wrath has
great understanding,
But *he who is* impulsive exalts
folly.

30 A sound heart *is* life to the body,
But envy *is* rottenness to the
bones.

31 He who oppresses the poor
reproaches his Maker,
But he who honors Him has
mercy on the needy.

32 The wicked is banished in his
wickedness,
But the righteous has a refuge
in his death.

33 Wisdom rests in the heart of him
who has understanding,
But *what is* in the heart of fools
is made known.

34 Righteousness exalts a nation,
But sin *is* a reproach to *any*
people.

35 The king's favor *is* toward a wise
servant,
But his wrath *is against* him who
causes shame.

What happens to the wise and foolish

15 A soft answer turns away wrath,
But a harsh word stirs up anger.
2 The tongue of the wise uses
knowledge rightly,
But the mouth of fools pours
forth foolishness.

3 The eyes of the LORD *are* in
every place,
Keeping watch on the evil and
the good.

4 A wholesome tongue *is* a tree
of life,
But perverseness in it breaks the
spirit.

5 A fool despises his father's
instruction,
But he who receives correction
is prudent.

6 *In* the house of the righteous
there is much treasure,
But in the revenue of the wicked
is trouble.

7 The lips of the wise disperse
knowledge,
But the heart of the fool *does*
not *do* so.

8 The sacrifice of the wicked *is* an
abomination to the LORD,
But the prayer of the upright *is*
His delight.

DIGGING IN

15:1 Learn Self-Control You will meet people who disagree with you. Sometimes you are right and sometimes you are wrong. Your goal must be to learn the truth, not to win an argument. The desire to win an argument is selfish. The sad thing is that *the truth* nearly always loses in an argument.

When someone disagrees with you, the first thing to do is to listen carefully to what that person says. As you take time to listen, your own feelings will calm down.

Then you'll be more concerned about learning the truth than about winning a fight.

As a Christian, you should be against false ideas. But in loving truth, you must first show your self-control. The real battle is not you against someone else. The real struggle is between the Lord, the God of truth, and Satan, the god of lies. People are more often led to the truth by a calm spirit than by anger.

9   The way of the wicked *is* an
    abomination to the Lord,
    But He loves him who follows
    righteousness.

10 Harsh discipline *is* for him who
    forsakes the way,
    And he who hates correction will
    die.

11 Hell and Destruction *are* before
    the Lord;
    So how much more the hearts
    of the sons of men.

12 A scoffer does not love one who
    corrects him,
    Nor will he go to the wise.

13 A merry heart makes a cheerful
    countenance,
    But by sorrow of the heart the
    spirit is broken.

14 The heart of him who has
    understanding *seeks*
    knowledge,
    But the mouth of fools feeds on
    foolishness.

15 All the days of the afflicted *are*
    evil,
    But he who is of a merry heart
    has a continual feast.

16 Better *is* a little with the fear of
    the Lord,
    Than great treasure with trouble.

17 Better *is* a dinner of herbs where
    love is,
    Than a fatted calf with hatred.

18 A wrathful man stirs up strife,
    But *he who is* slow to anger
    allays contention.

19 The way of the lazy *man is* like
    a hedge of thorns,
    But the way of the upright *is* a
    highway.

20 A wise son makes a father glad,
    But a foolish man despises his
    mother.

21 Folly *is* joy *to him who is*
    destitute of discernment,
    But a man of understanding
    walks uprightly.

22 Without counsel, plans go awry,
    But in the multitude of
    counselors they are
    established.

23 A man has joy by the answer
    of his mouth,
    And a word *spoken* in due
    season, how good *it is!*

24 The way of life *winds* upward
    for the wise,
    That he may turn away from hell
    below.

25 The Lord will destroy the house
    of the proud,
    But He will establish the
    boundary of the widow.

26 The thoughts of the wicked *are*
    an abomination to the Lord,
    But *the words* of the pure *are*
    pleasant.

27 He who is greedy for gain
    troubles his own house,
    But he who hates bribes will live.

28 The heart of the righteous
    studies how to answer,
    But the mouth of the wicked
    pours forth evil.

29 The Lord is far from the wicked,
    But He hears the prayer of the
    righteous.

30 The light of the *eyes* rejoices the
    heart,
    And a good report makes the
    bones healthy.

31 The ear that hears the rebukes
    of life
    Will abide among the wise.

32 He who disdains instruction
    despises his own soul,
    But he who heeds rebuke gets
    understanding.

33 The fear of the LORD is the
    instruction of wisdom,
    And before honor is humility.

It's better to be wise than wealthy

16 The preparations of the heart
    belong to man,
    But the answer of the tongue is
    from the LORD.

2   All the ways of a man are pure
    in his own eyes,
    But the LORD weighs the spirits.

3   Commit your works to the LORD,
    And your thoughts will be
    established.

4   The LORD has made all for
    Himself,
    Yes, even the wicked for the day
    of doom.

5   Everyone proud in heart is an
    abomination to the LORD;
    Though they join forces, none
    will go unpunished.

6   In mercy and truth
    Atonement is provided for
    iniquity;
    And by the fear of the LORD one
    departs from evil.

7   When a man's ways please the
    LORD,
    He makes even his enemies to
    be at peace with him.

8   Better is a little with
    righteousness,
    Than vast revenues without
    justice.

9   A man's heart plans his way,
    But the LORD directs his steps.

10 Divination is on the lips of the
    king;
    His mouth must not transgress
    in judgment.

11 Honest weights and scales are
    the LORD's;
    All the weights in the bag are
    His work.

12 It is an abomination for kings to
    commit wickedness,
    For a throne is established by
    righteousness.

13 Righteous lips are the delight of
    kings,
    And they love him who speaks
    what is right.

14 As messengers of death is the
    king's wrath,
    But a wise man will appease it.

15 In the light of the king's face is
    life,
    And his favor is like a cloud of
    the latter rain.

16 How much better to get wisdom
    than gold!
    And to get understanding is to
    be chosen rather than silver.

17 The highway of the upright is to
    depart from evil;
    He who keeps his way preserves
    his soul.

18 Pride goes before destruction,
    And a haughty spirit before a
    fall.

⚒ DIGGING IN

16:2 God Can Give You a Right Attitude A bad attitude is a self-righteous attitude: "I am right, and everybody else is wrong." That is the worst attitude of all.

God can change our opinion that we're good enough as we are. But "if we say we have no sin, we deceive ourselves, and the truth is not in us" (1 John 1:8). So God needs to change our attitudes and help us to see our sins. Then we will be kinder to others who fall into sin.

Think about Jesus dying on the Cross for your sins. He was perfect in every way. Although He never sinned, He let Himself be put to death like a sinner to pay for your sins and mine.

That really puts us in our place, doesn't it? We never deserve to be called "good." Only Jesus is good, and His Father loves us because Jesus died for us.

19 Better *to be* of a humble spirit
     with the lowly,
   Than to divide the spoil with the
     proud.

20 He who heeds the word wisely
     will find good,
   And whoever trusts in the LORD,
     happy *is* he.

21 The wise in heart will be called
     prudent,
   And sweetness of the lips
     increases learning.

22 Understanding *is* a wellspring of
     life to him who has it.
   But the correction of fools *is*
     folly.

23 The heart of the wise teaches his
     mouth,
   And adds learning to his lips.

24 Pleasant words *are like* a
     honeycomb,
   Sweetness to the soul and health
     to the bones.

25 There is a way *that seems* right
     to a man,
   But its end *is* the way of death.

26 The person who labors, labors
     for himself,
   For his *hungry* mouth drives him
     on.

27 An ungodly man digs up evil,
   And *it is* on his lips like a burning
     fire.

28 A perverse man sows strife,
   And a whisperer separates the
     best of friends.

29 A violent man entices his
     neighbor,
   And leads him in a way *that is*
     not good.

30 He winks his eye to devise
     perverse things;
   He purses his lips *and* brings
     about evil.

31 The silver-haired head *is* a
     crown of glory,

If it is found in the way of
     righteousness.

32 *He who is* slow to anger *is* better
     than the mighty,
   And he who rules his spirit than
     he who takes a city.

33 The lot is cast into the lap,
   But its *every* decision *is* from the
     LORD.

True friends are forever friends

17 Better *is* a dry morsel with
        quietness,
   Than a house full of feasting *with*
     strife.

2 A wise servant will rule over a
     son who causes shame,
   And will share an inheritance
     among the brothers.

3 The refining pot *is* for silver and
     the furnace for gold,
   But the LORD tests the hearts.

4 An evildoer gives heed to false
     lips;
   A liar listens eagerly to a spiteful
     tongue.

5 He who mocks the poor
     reproaches his Maker;
   He who is glad at calamity will
     not go unpunished.

6 Children's children *are* the
     crown of old men,
   And the glory of children *is* their
     father.

7 Excellent speech is not
     becoming to a fool,
   Much less lying lips to a prince.

8 A present *is* a precious stone in
     the eyes of its possessor;
   Wherever he turns, he prospers.

9 He who covers a transgression
     seeks love,
   But he who repeats a matter
     separates friends.

10 Rebuke is more effective for a
    wise *man*
    Than a hundred blows on a fool.

11 An evil *man* seeks only rebellion;
    Therefore a cruel messenger will
    be sent against him.

12 Let a man meet a bear robbed
    of her cubs,
    Rather than a fool in his folly.

13 Whoever rewards evil for good,
    Evil will not depart from his
    house.

14 The beginning of strife *is like*
    releasing water;
    Therefore stop contention
    before a quarrel starts.

15 He who justifies the wicked, and
    he who condemns the just,
    Both of them alike *are* an
    abomination to the Lord.

16 Why *is there* in the hand of a
    fool the purchase price of
    wisdom,
    Since *he has* no heart *for it?*

17 A friend loves at all times,
    And a brother is born for
    adversity.

18 A man devoid of understanding
    shakes hands in a pledge,
    And becomes surety for his
    friend.

19 He who loves transgression
    loves strife,
    And he who exalts his gate *seeks*
    destruction.

20 He who has a deceitful heart
    finds no good,
    And he who has a perverse
    tongue falls into evil.

21 He who begets a scoffer *does*
    so to his sorrow,
    And the father of a fool has no
    joy.

22 A merry heart does good, *like*
    medicine,
    But a broken spirit dries the
    bones.

23 A wicked *man* accepts a bribe
    behind the back
    To pervert the ways of justice.

24 Wisdom *is* in the sight of him
    who has understanding,
    But the eyes of a fool *are* on
    the ends of the earth.

25 A foolish son *is* a grief to his
    father,
    And bitterness to her who bore
    him.

26 Also, to punish the righteous *is*
    not good,
    Nor to strike princes for *their*
    uprightness.

27 He who has knowledge spares
    his words,
    And a man of understanding is
    of a calm spirit.

28 Even a fool is counted wise
    when he holds his peace;
    When he shuts his lips, *he is*
    considered perceptive.

How to get along with others

18 A man who isolates himself
    seeks his own desire;
    He rages against all wise
    judgment.

2 A fool has no delight in
    understanding,
    But in expressing his own heart.

3 When the wicked comes,
    contempt comes also;
    And with dishonor *comes*
    reproach.

4 The words of a man's mouth *are*
    deep waters;
    The wellspring of wisdom *is* a
    flowing brook.

5 *It is* not good to show partiality
    to the wicked,

Or to overthrow the righteous in judgment.

6 A fool's lips enter into contention,
And his mouth calls for blows.

7 A fool's mouth *is* his destruction,
And his lips *are* the snare of his soul.

8 The words of a talebearer *are* like tasty trifles,
And they go down into the inmost body.

9 He who is slothful in his work
Is a brother to him who is a great destroyer.

10 The name of the LORD *is* a strong tower;
The righteous run to it and are safe.

11 The rich man's wealth *is* his strong city,
And like a high wall in his own esteem.

12 Before destruction the heart of a man is haughty,
And before honor *is* humility.

13 He who answers a matter before he hears *it,*
It *is* folly and shame to him.

14 The spirit of a man will sustain him in sickness,
But who can bear a broken spirit?

15 The heart of the prudent acquires knowledge,
And the ear of the wise seeks knowledge.

16 A man's gift makes room for him,
And brings him before great men.

17 The first *one* to plead his cause *seems* right,
Until his neighbor comes and examines him.

18 Casting lots causes contentions to *cease,*
And keeps the mighty apart.

19 A brother offended *is harder to win* than a strong city,
And contentions *are* like the bars of a castle.

20 A man's stomach shall be satisfied from the fruit of his mouth;
From the produce of his lips he shall be filled.

21 Death and life *are* in the power of the tongue,
And those who love it will eat its fruit.

22 *He who* finds a wife finds a good *thing,*
And obtains favor from the LORD.

23 The poor *man* uses entreaties,
But the rich answers roughly.

24 A man *who has* friends must himself be friendly,

🪓 DIGGING IN

18:24 Be a Friend Some people complain because they have no friends, but to have friends, you must be a friend. Jesus went about doing good, so He had a great many friends. He had some important enemies, of course, but He also had a lot of friends. "The common people heard Him gladly" (Mark 12:37).

The most important thing for a Christian is to *be a friend.* This is what "love your neighbor" really means. Do you know someone who is poor and sick? Go and visit that person, and ask God to go with you. He will.

You need to know one thing—you always have a Friend. That Friend is Jesus, and He sticks closer than a brother. But you must be His friend, too. Then you and He will be together always, wherever you go.

But there is a friend *who* sticks closer than a brother.

Only God's plans will succeed

19 Better *is* the poor who walks in his integrity
Than *one who is* perverse in his lips, and is a fool.

2   Also it is not good *for* a soul *to be* without knowledge,
And he sins who hastens with *his* feet.

3   The foolishness of a man twists his way,
And his heart frets against the LORD.

4   Wealth makes many friends,
But the poor is separated from his friend.

5   A false witness will not go unpunished,
And *he who* speaks lies will not escape.

6   Many entreat the favor of the nobility,
And every man *is* a friend to one who gives gifts.

7   All the brothers of the poor hate him;
How much more do his friends go far from him!
He may pursue *them with* words, *yet* they abandon him.

8   He who gets wisdom loves his own soul;
He who keeps understanding will find good.

9   A false witness will not go unpunished,
And *he who* speaks lies shall perish.

10 Luxury is not fitting for a fool,
Much less for a servant to rule over princes.

11 The discretion of a man makes him slow to anger,
And his glory *is* to overlook a transgression.

12 The king's wrath *is* like the roaring of a lion,
But his favor *is* like dew on the grass.

13 A foolish son *is* the ruin of his father,
And the contentions of a wife *are* a continual dripping.

14 Houses and riches *are* an inheritance from fathers,
But a prudent wife *is* from the LORD.

15 Laziness casts *one* into a deep sleep,
And an idle person will suffer hunger.

16 He who keeps the commandment keeps his soul,
But he who is careless of his ways will die.

17 He who has pity on the poor lends to the LORD,
And He will pay back what he has given.

18 Chasten your son while there is hope,
And do not set your heart on his destruction.

19 *A man of* great wrath will suffer punishment;
For if you rescue *him,* you will have to do it again.

20 Listen to counsel and receive instruction,
That you may be wise in your latter days.

21 There are many plans in a man's heart,
Nevertheless the LORD's counsel—that will stand.

22 What is desired in a man is
    kindness,
    And a poor man is better than
    a liar.

23 The fear of the LORD *leads* to
    life,
    And *he who has it* will abide in
    satisfaction;
    He will not be visited with evil.

24 A lazy *man* buries his hand in
    the bowl,
    And will not so much as bring
    it to his mouth again.

25 Strike a scoffer, and the simple
    will become wary;
    Rebuke one who has
    understanding, *and* he will
    discern knowledge.

26 He who mistreats *his* father *and*
    chases away *his* mother
    Is a son who causes shame and
    brings reproach.

27 Cease listening to instruction,
    my son,
    And you will stray from the
    words of knowledge.

28 A disreputable witness scorns
    justice,
    And the mouth of the wicked
    devours iniquity.

29 Judgments are prepared for
    scoffers,
    And beatings for the backs of
    fools.

Your actions tell on you

20 Wine *is* a mocker,
    Strong drink *is* a brawler,
    And whoever is led astray by it
    is not wise.

2   The wrath of a king *is* like the
    roaring of a lion;
    Whoever provokes him to anger
    sins *against* his own life.

3   *It is* honorable for a man to stop
    striving,
    Since any fool can start a
    quarrel.

4   The lazy *man* will not plow
    because of winter;
    He will beg during harvest and
    have nothing.

5   Counsel in the heart of man *is*
    like deep water,
    But a man of understanding will
    draw it out.

6   Most men will proclaim each his
    own goodness,
    But who can find a faithful man?

7   The righteous *man* walks in his
    integrity;
    His children *are* blessed after
    him.

8   A king who sits on the throne
    of judgment
    Scatters all evil with his *eyes*.

DIGGING IN

19:23 The Fear of the Lord Brings Life How can fear bring life? The word *fear,* in Proverbs 19:23, means "reverence" or "respect." There is a right and a wrong way to treat different people. When you speak to a teacher at school, you possibly say "Ma'am" or "Sir." This means that you respect that person in a special way.

God also should be respected in a special way. When people insult God, He ignores them; but when we respect Him,

then He blesses us by giving us His very own life.

God's life is a special kind of life. It is beautiful, and it can't be destroyed. The Bible calls God's life "eternal" life. When you honor God as He really is, He gives you *eternal life* because His Son Jesus died to give you that life.

Who wouldn't want to have eternal life—the life of God Himself that neither man nor the Devil can destroy?

9 Who can say, "I have made my
   heart clean,
   I am pure from my sin"?

10 Diverse weights *and* diverse
   measures,
   They *are* both alike, an
   abomination to the LORD.

11 Even a child is known by his
   deeds,
   Whether what he does *is* pure
   and right.

12 The hearing ear and the seeing
   eye,
   The LORD has made them both.

13 Do not love sleep, lest you come
   to poverty;
   Open your eyes, *and* you will
   be satisfied with bread.

14 "*It is* good for nothing," cries the
   buyer;
   But when he has gone his way,
   then he boasts.

15 There is gold and a multitude of
   rubies,

But the lips of knowledge *are* a
precious jewel.

16 Take the garment of one who
   is surety *for* a stranger,
   And hold it as a pledge *when it*
   is for a seductress.

17 Bread gained by deceit *is* sweet
   to a man,
   But afterward his mouth will be
   filled with gravel.

18 Plans are established by counsel;
   By wise counsel wage war.

19 He who goes about *as* a
   talebearer reveals secrets;
   Therefore do not associate with
   one who flatters with his lips.

20 Whoever curses his father or his
   mother,
   His lamp will be put out in deep
   darkness.

21 An inheritance gained hastily at
   the beginning
   Will not be blessed at the end.

22 Do not say, "I will recompense
   evil";

⚒ DIGGING IN

20:9 Only God Can Make Us Pure
Some people don't want to steal, lie, or
swear, and they try not to. But "a man
made out of water can't climb out of the
water on a ladder of water." In the same
way, we can't make ourselves be good.
We will keep falling back into our old ways
of sin, like the man of water.

God can change your life. He will give
you a new desire to please Him in all your
ways. When you truly love God, you leave
your sins behind. Sometimes you will fail,
but God will give you a heart that sincerely
loves the things he loves.

You begin to please God when you
honestly tell Him you know you're a sinner. Then ask Him to forgive you and
make you able to please Him. God will
answer your prayer. "Blessed are the
pure in heart, for they shall see God"
(Matthew 5:8).

20:22 Revenge Doesn't Work When
somebody does something bad to you,

then you may feel you want to pay that
person back. We call that *revenge*. But
revenge never works.

Even the *desire* to hurt someone who
hurts you doesn't really pay. It only
causes you to feel bitter inside. You always hurt yourself by revenge at least as
much as you hurt that other person. You
harden your heart, and you stop being
able to love people. Love is God's way
of healing your hurts and the hurts of others.

God needs Christians who love Him
enough that they want to heal the hurts
of other people. Some people do unkind
things to you because they themselves
are hurting. God can help you to help people like that by saying something kind or
doing them a kind deed. Then you can
tell them about the God who loves them.
That is why Jesus said, "Do good to those
who hate you" (Matthew 5:44).

Wait for the LORD, and He will save you.

23 Diverse weights *are* an abomination to the LORD, And dishonest scales *are* not good.

24 A man's steps *are* of the LORD; How then can a man understand his own way?

25 *It is* a snare for a man to devote rashly *something as* holy, And afterward to reconsider *his* vows.

26 A wise king sifts out the wicked, And brings the threshing wheel over them.

27 The spirit of a man *is* the lamp of the LORD, Searching all the inner depths of his heart.

28 Mercy and truth preserve the king, And by lovingkindness he upholds his throne.

29 The glory of young men *is* their strength, And the splendor of old men *is* their gray head.

30 Blows that hurt cleanse away evil, As *do* stripes the inner depths of the heart.

God looks at our hearts

21 The king's heart *is* in the hand of the LORD, *Like* the rivers of water; He turns it wherever He wishes.

2 Every way of a man *is* right in his own eyes, But the LORD weighs the hearts.

3 To do righteousness and justice *Is* more acceptable to the LORD than sacrifice.

4 A haughty look, a proud heart, *And* the plowing of the wicked *are* sin.

5 The plans of the diligent *lead* surely to plenty, But *those of* everyone *who is* hasty, surely to poverty.

6 Getting treasures by a lying tongue *Is* the fleeting fantasy of those who seek death.

7 The violence of the wicked will destroy them, Because they refuse to do justice.

8 The way of a guilty man *is* perverse; But *as for* the pure, his work *is* right.

9 Better to dwell in a corner of a housetop, Than in a house shared with a contentious woman.

⚒ DIGGING IN

21:6 Lying Leads to Death We live in a world where lying is a way of life and death. When you see those slick television commercials, you know they're lying much of the time. Often the things they sell don't really work very well. If you bought an expensive bike that fell apart the next day, you wouldn't trust the people who sold it to you. That kind of lying to customers can cause unemployment, then hunger, and even death.

The truth is necessary for all of life. Truly successful business depends on people telling the truth. Your eternal salvation depends on God telling the truth, and God is always truthful. That is a strong foundation to build your life on.

10 The soul of the wicked desires
    evil;
    His neighbor finds no favor in
    his eyes.

11 When the scoffer is punished,
    the simple is made wise;
    But when the wise is instructed,
    he receives knowledge.

12 The righteous *God* wisely
    considers the house of the
    wicked,
    Overthrowing the wicked for
    their wickedness.

13 Whoever shuts his ears to the
    cry of the poor
    Will also cry himself and not be
    heard.

14 A gift in secret pacifies anger,
    And a bribe behind the back,
    strong wrath.

15 *It is* a joy for the just to do
    justice,
    But destruction *will come* to the
    workers of iniquity.

16 A man who wanders from the
    way of understanding
    Will rest in the assembly of the
    dead.

17 He who loves pleasure *will be*
    a poor man;
    He who loves wine and oil will
    not be rich.

18 The wicked *shall be* a ransom
    for the righteous,
    And the unfaithful for the
    upright.

19 Better to dwell in the
    wilderness,
    Than with a contentious and
    angry woman.

20 *There is* desirable treasure,
    And oil in the dwelling of the
    wise,
    But a foolish man squanders it.

21 He who follows righteousness
    and mercy
    Finds life, righteousness and
    honor.

22 A wise *man* scales the city of the
    mighty,
    And brings down the trusted
    stronghold.

23 Whoever guards his mouth and
    tongue
    Keeps his soul from troubles.

24 A proud *and* haughty *man*—
    "Scoffer" *is* his name;
    He acts with arrogant pride.

25 The desire of the lazy *man* kills
    him,
    For his hands refuse to labor.

26 He covets greedily all day
    long,
    But the righteous gives and does
    not spare.

27 The sacrifice of the wicked *is* an
    abomination;
    How much more *when* he brings
    it with wicked intent!

28 A false witness shall perish,
    But the man who hears *him* will
    speak endlessly.

29 A wicked man hardens his
    face,
    But *as for* the upright, he
    establishes his way.

30 *There is* no wisdom or
    understanding
    Or counsel against the LORD.

31 The horse *is* prepared for the
    day of battle,
    But deliverance *is* of the LORD.

Lessons for the young

22 A *good* name is to be chosen
      rather than great riches,
      Loving favor rather than silver
      and gold.

2 The rich and the poor have this
   in common,
   The Lord is the maker of them
   all.

3 A prudent *man* foresees evil and
   hides himself,
   But the simple pass on and are
   punished.

4 By humility *and* the fear of the
   Lord
   Are riches and honor and life.

5 Thorns *and* snares *are* in the
   way of the perverse;
   He who guards his soul will be
   far from them.

6 Train up a child in the way he
   should go,
   And when he is old he will not
   depart from it.

7 The rich rules over the poor,
   And the borrower *is* servant to
   the lender.

8 He who sows iniquity will reap
   sorrow,
   And the rod of his anger will fail.

9 He who has a generous eye will
   be blessed,
   For he gives of his bread to the
   poor.

10 Cast out the scoffer, and
   contention will leave;
   Yes, strife and reproach will
   cease.

11 He who loves purity of heart
   And has grace on his lips,
   The king *will be* his friend.

12 The eyes of the Lord preserve
   knowledge,
   But He overthrows the words of
   the faithless.

13 The lazy *man* says, "*There is* a
   lion outside!
   I shall be slain in the streets!"

14 The mouth of an immoral
   woman *is* a deep pit;
   He who is abhorred by the Lord
   will fall there.

15 Foolishness *is* bound up in the
   heart of a child;
   The rod of correction will drive
   it far from him.

16 He who oppresses the poor to
   increase his *riches,*
   And he who gives to the rich,
   will surely *come* to poverty.

17 Incline your ear and hear the
   words of the wise,
   And apply your heart to my
   knowledge;

18 For *it is* a pleasant thing if you
   keep them within you;
   Let them all be fixed upon your
   lips,

19 So that your trust may be in the
   Lord;
   I have instructed you today,
   even you.

🪓 DIGGING IN

22:1 Be Known as an Honest Person
Do you go to church and Sunday school?
Do you claim to be a Christian? Then you
must also be known as an honest person.
Someone who goes to church on Sunday
and cheats his neighbor on other days is
the worst kind of Christian. In fact, he
probably isn't a real Christian at all!

It's a terrible thing to *say* you're a Christian and not *act* like one. Soon people
will say, "That girl lied to me," or, "He
steals from people." That's what you call
a bad reputation.

What is even worse, you give Jesus a
bad reputation, too. Sometimes people
who tell the world they're Christians act
so bad that everybody laughs at them.
At the same time, the world begins to say,
"Jesus can't be a real Savior. Look at the
dishonest people who follow Him!"

20 Have I not written to you
     excellent things
Of counsels and knowledge,
21 That I may make you know the
     certainty of the words of truth,
That you may answer words of
     truth
To those who send to you?

22 Do not rob the poor because he
     is poor,
Nor oppress the afflicted at the
     gate;
23 For the LORD will plead their
     cause,
And plunder the soul of those
     who plunder them.

24 Make no friendship with an
     angry man,
And with a furious man do not
     go,
25 Lest you learn his ways
And set a snare for your soul.

26 Do not be one of those who
     shakes hands in a pledge,
One of those who is surety for
     debts;
27 If you have nothing *with which*
     to pay,
Why should he take away your
     bed from under you?

28 Do not remove the ancient
     landmark
Which your fathers have set.

29 Do you see a man *who* excels
     in his work?
He will stand before kings;

He will not stand before
     unknown *men.*

Listen to your dad

23 When you sit down to eat with
     a ruler,
Consider carefully what *is* before
     you;
2 And put a knife to your throat
If you *are* a man given to
     appetite.
3 Do not desire his delicacies,
For they *are* deceptive food.

4 Do not overwork to be rich;
Because of your own
     understanding, cease!
5 Will you set your eyes on that
     which is not?
For *riches* certainly make
     themselves wings;
They fly away like an eagle
     toward heaven.

6 Do not eat the bread of a miser,
Nor desire his delicacies;
7 For as he thinks in his heart, so
     is he.
"Eat and drink!" he says to you,
But his heart is not with you.
8 The morsel you have eaten, you
     will vomit up,
And waste your pleasant words.

9 Do not speak in the hearing of
     a fool,
For he will despise the wisdom
     of your words.

10 Do not remove the ancient
     landmark,

⚒ DIGGING IN

23:10, 11 Be Kind to Helpless People Jesus was rich, and He came to share His heavenly wealth with you. Jesus was strong, and He came to share His heavenly health with you.

Have you received wonderful life from Jesus? Then share that wonderful life with others. Jesus made the helpless lame man walk. You were crippled by your sins, but Jesus set you free. You, too, can visit helpless people and share Jesus' love with them. Sometimes it will cost you money to help people who are helpless. Jesus has promised to repay whatever it costs.

Jesus' main work when He came into the world was helping helpless people, and that is still His main work. He asks you to be His assistant. Perhaps someday you will go as a missionary to help people across the sea. But wherever you go, Jesus wants you to help the helpless.

Nor enter the fields of the
fatherless;

11 For their Redeemer is mighty;
He will plead their cause against
you.

12 Apply your heart to instruction,
And your ears to words of
knowledge.

13 Do not withhold correction from
a child,
For if you beat him with a rod,
he will not die.

14 You shall beat him with a rod,
And deliver his soul from **hell**.

15 My son, if your heart is wise,
My heart will rejoice—indeed, I
myself;

16 Yes, my inmost being will rejoice
When your lips speak right
things.

17 Do not let your heart envy
sinners,
But be zealous for the fear of
the LORD all the day;

18 For surely there is a hereafter,
And your hope will not be cut
off.

19 Hear, my son, and be wise;
And guide your heart in the way.

20 Do not mix with winebibbers,
Or with gluttonous eaters of
meat;

21 For the drunkard and the glutton
will come to poverty,
And drowsiness will clothe a
man with rags.

22 Listen to your father who begot
you,
And do not despise your mother
when she is old.

23 Buy the truth, and do not sell
it,

Also wisdom and instruction and
understanding.

24 The father of the righteous will
greatly rejoice,
And he who begets a wise child
will delight in him.

25 Let your father and your mother
be glad,
And let her who bore you
rejoice.

26 My son, give me your heart,
And let your eyes observe my
ways.

27 For a harlot is a deep pit,
And a seductress is a narrow
well.

28 She also lies in wait as for a
victim,
And increases the unfaithful
among men.

29 Who has woe?
Who has sorrow?
Who has contentions?
Who has complaints?
Who has wounds without
cause?
Who has redness of eyes?

30 Those who linger long at the
wine,
Those who go in search of
mixed wine.

31 Do not look on the wine when
it is red,
When it sparkles in the cup,
When it swirls around smoothly;

32 At the last it bites like a serpent,
And stings like a viper.

33 Your eyes will see strange things,
And your heart will utter
perverse things.

34 Yes, you will be like one who
lies down in the midst of the
sea,
Or like one who lies at the top
of the mast, saying:

WORDFINDER

23:14 Hell A place of endless misery where ungodly people go when they die. It is translated from a word for the burning dumping ground outside Jerusalem in Jesus' time.

35 "They have struck me, *but* I was
    not hurt;
They have beaten me, but I did
    not feel *it.*
When shall I awake, that I may
    seek another *drink?* "

God knows the heart

24 Do not be envious of evil
    men,
Nor desire to be with them;
2 For their heart devises violence,
    And their lips talk of
    troublemaking.

3 Through wisdom a house is
    built,
And by understanding it is
    established;
4 By knowledge the rooms are
    filled
With all precious and pleasant
    riches.

5 A wise man *is* strong,
Yes, a man of knowledge
    increases strength;
6 For by wise counsel you will
    wage your own war,
And in a multitude of counselors
    there is safety.

7 Wisdom *is* too lofty for a fool;
He does not open his mouth in
    the gate.

8 He who plots to do evil
Will be called a schemer.
9 The devising of foolishness *is* sin,

And the scoffer *is* an
    abomination to men.

10 *If* you faint in the day of
    adversity,
Your strength *is* small.

11 Deliver *those who* are drawn
    toward death,
And hold back *those* stumbling
    to the slaughter.
12 If you say, "Surely we did not
    know this,"
Does not He who weighs the
    hearts consider *it?*
He who keeps your soul, does
    He *not* know *it?*
And will He *not* render to *each*
    man according to his deeds?

13 My son, eat honey because *it is*
    good,
And the honeycomb *which is*
    sweet to your taste;
14 So *shall* the knowledge of
    wisdom *be* to your soul;
If you have found *it,* there is a
    prospect,
And your hope will not be cut
    off.

15 Do not lie in wait, O wicked
    man, against the dwelling of
    the righteous;
Do not plunder his resting place;
16 For a righteous *man* may fall
    seven times
And rise again,
But the wicked shall fall by
    calamity.

⚒ DIGGING IN

24:1 Choose Good Role Models
Since you will become like the people you admire, you should pick out people you want to be like. Maybe you have a favorite schoolteacher or scout leader, and you're saying to yourself, "I'd like to be like that person when I'm grown up."

It's always best if your role models (or examples) are your own parents. Let's pray that your parents will be the kind of folks you can look up to and say, "I want to be like you when I grow up, Dad," or "Mother, when I'm older, I'd like to be as kind as you."

But remember, earthly role models will sometimes disappoint you. You must pray to forgive the failures of those you admire. They're human, too. But it's good to know that Jesus never fails. He is the same yesterday, today, and forever (see Hebrews 13:8). What a great role model He is!

17 Do not rejoice when your enemy
     falls,
   And do not let your heart be
     glad when he stumbles;
18 Lest the LORD see *it,* and it
     displease Him,
   And He turn away His wrath
     from him.

19 Do not fret because of
     evildoers,
   Nor be envious of the wicked;
20 For there will be no prospect for
     the evil *man;*
   The lamp of the wicked will be
     put out.

21 My son, fear the LORD and the
     king;
   Do not associate with those
     given to change;
22 For their calamity will rise
     suddenly,
   And who knows the ruin those
     two can bring?

23 These *things* also *belong* to the
wise:

   It is not good to show partiality
     in judgment.
24 He who says to the wicked,
     "You *are* righteous,"
   Him the people will curse;
   Nations will abhor him.
25 But those who rebuke *the
     wicked* will have delight,
   And a good blessing will come
     upon them.

26 He who gives a right answer
     kisses the lips.

27 Prepare your outside work,
   Make it fit for yourself in the
     field;
   And afterward build your house.

28 Do not be a witness against your
     neighbor without cause,
   For would you deceive with your
     lips?
29 Do not say, "I will do to him
     just as he has done to me;

   I will render to the man
     according to his work."

30 I went by the field of the lazy
     man,
   And by the vineyard of the man
     devoid of understanding;
31 And there it was, all overgrown
     with thorns;
   Its surface was covered with
     nettles;
   Its stone wall was broken down.
32 When I saw *it,* I considered *it*
     well;
   I looked on *it and* received
     instruction:
33 A little sleep, a little slumber,
   A little folding of the hands to
     rest;
34 So shall your poverty come *like*
     a prowler,
   And your need like an armed
     man.

Always keep your promises

25 These also *are* proverbs of Solomon which the men of Hezekiah king
of Judah copied:

2 *It is* the glory of God to conceal
     a matter,
   But the glory of kings *is* to search
     out a matter.

3 As the heavens for height and
     the earth for depth,
   So the heart of kings *is*
     unsearchable.

4 Take away the dross from silver,
   And it will go to the silversmith
     for jewelry.
5 Take away the wicked from
     before the king,
   And his throne will be
     established in righteousness.

6 Do not exalt yourself in the
     presence of the king,
   And do not stand in the place
     of the great;
7 For *it is* better that he say to you,
     "Come up here,"

Than that you should be put
   lower in the presence of the
   prince,
Whom your eyes have seen.

8 Do not go hastily to court;
   For what will you do in the end,
   When your neighbor has put
      you to shame?
9 Debate your case with your
      neighbor,
   And do not disclose the secret
      to another;
10 Lest he who hears *it* expose your
      shame,
   And your reputation be ruined.

11 A word fitly spoken *is like* apples
      of gold
   In settings of silver.
12 *Like* an earring of gold and an
      ornament of fine gold
   Is a wise rebuker to an obedient
      ear.

13 Like the cold of snow in time
      of harvest
   Is a faithful messenger to those
      who send him,
   For he refreshes the soul of his
      masters.

14 Whoever falsely boasts of giving
   Is like clouds and wind without
      rain.

15 By long forbearance a ruler is
      persuaded,
   And a gentle tongue breaks a
      bone.

16 Have you found honey?
   Eat only as much as you need,
   Lest you be filled with it and
      vomit.

17 Seldom set foot in your
      neighbor's house,
   Lest he become weary of you
      and hate you.

18 A man who bears false witness
      against his neighbor
   Is like a club, a sword, and a
      sharp arrow.

19 Confidence in an unfaithful *man*
      in time of trouble
   Is like a bad tooth and a foot
      out of joint.

20 *Like* one who takes away a
      garment in cold weather,
   And like vinegar on soda,
   Is one who sings songs to a
      heavy heart.

21 If your enemy is hungry, give
      him bread to eat;
   And if he is thirsty, give him
      water to drink;
22 For *so* you will heap coals of fire
      on his head,
   And the LORD will reward you.

23 The north wind brings forth rain,
   And a backbiting tongue an
      angry countenance.

24 *It is* better to dwell in a corner
      of a housetop,

⛏ DIGGING IN

25:21 How Do You Treat Your Enemies? There are two ways to treat enemies. First, we must make sure that violent enemies can't hurt people anymore. That's why we put some of them in prison. But King Solomon's proverb says, "If your enemy is hungry, give him bread to eat; and if he is thirsty, give him water to drink." This saying by Solomon means that kindness is often the real key to hard hearts. At first, your enemies may not appreciate your kindness, but if you keep on being kind, there is always real hope they will trust you in the end. People in prison often tell how their lives began to change when a prison chaplain was kind to them.

To be kind does not mean to be "permissive." We are permissive when we allow people to go on being enemies of society without stopping them. But if you are unkind to your enemies, you are only showing them you are as bad as they are.

Than in a house shared with a
contentious woman.

25 As cold water to a weary soul,
So *is* good news from a far
country.

26 A righteous *man* who falters
before the wicked
Is like a murky spring and a
polluted well.

27 *It is* not good to eat much
honey;
So to seek one's own glory *is
not* glory.

28 Whoever *has* no rule over his
own spirit
Is like a city broken down,
without walls.

Honor and fools go together like snow in summer!

26 As snow in summer and rain in
harvest,
So honor is not fitting for a fool.

2 Like a flitting sparrow, like a
flying swallow,
So a curse without cause shall
not alight.

3 A whip for the horse,
A bridle for the donkey,
And a rod for the fool's back.

4 Do not answer a fool according
to his folly,
Lest you also be like him.

5 Answer a fool according to his
folly,
Lest he be wise in his own *eyes.*

6 He who sends a message by the
hand of a fool
Cuts off *his own* feet *and* drinks
violence.

7 *Like* the legs of the lame that
hang limp
Is a proverb in the mouth of
fools.

8 Like one who binds a stone in
a sling
Is he who gives honor to a fool.

9 *Like* a thorn *that* goes into the
hand of a drunkard
Is a proverb in the mouth of
fools.

10 The great *God* who formed
everything
Gives the fool *his* hire and the
transgressor *his* wages.

11 As a dog returns to his own
vomit,
So a fool repeats his folly.

12 Do you *see* a man wise in his
own eyes?
There is more hope for a fool
than for him.

13 The lazy *man* says, "*There is* a
lion in the road!
A fierce lion *is* in the streets!"

14 *As* a door turns on its hinges,
So *does* the lazy *man* on his
bed.

15 The lazy *man* buries his hand in
the bowl;
It wearies him to bring it back
to his mouth.

16 The lazy *man is* wiser in his own
eyes
Than seven men who can
answer sensibly.

17 He who passes by *and* meddles
in a quarrel not his own
Is like one who takes a dog by
the ears.

18 Like a madman who throws
firebrands, arrows, and death,

19 *Is* the man *who* deceives his
neighbor,
And says, "I was only joking!"

20 Where *there is* no wood, the fire
goes out;
And where *there is* no
talebearer, strife ceases.

21 As charcoal *is* to burning coals,
and wood to fire,
So *is* a contentious man to
kindle strife.

22 The words of a talebearer *are*
like tasty trifles,
And they go down into the
inmost body.

23 Fervent lips with a wicked heart
   Are like earthenware covered
   with silver dross.

24 He who hates, disguises *it* with
   his lips,
   And lays up deceit within
   himself;
25 When he speaks kindly, do not
   believe him,
   For *there are* seven
   abominations in his heart;
26 *Though his* hatred is covered
   by deceit,
   His wickedness will be revealed
   before the assembly.

27 Whoever digs a pit will fall into
   it,
   And he who rolls a stone will
   have it roll back on him.

28 A lying tongue hates *those who
   are* crushed by it,
   And a flattering mouth works
   ruin.

Don't brag about tomorrow

27 Do not boast about tomorrow,
   For you do not know what a day
   may bring forth.

2 Let another man praise you, and
   not your own mouth;
   A stranger, and not your own
   lips.

3 A stone *is* heavy and sand *is*
   weighty,

   But a fool's wrath *is* heavier than
   both of them.

4 Wrath *is* cruel and anger a
   torrent,
   But who *is* able to stand before
   jealousy?

5 Open rebuke *is* better
   Than love carefully concealed.

6 Faithful *are* the wounds of a
   friend,
   But the kisses of an enemy *are*
   deceitful.

7 A satisfied soul loathes the
   honeycomb,
   But to a hungry soul *every* bitter
   thing *is* sweet.

8 Like a bird that wanders from
   its nest
   Is a man who wanders from his
   place.

9 Ointment and perfume delight
   the heart,
   And the sweetness of a man's
   friend *gives delight* by hearty
   counsel.

10 Do not forsake your own friend
   or your father's friend,
   Nor go to your brother's house
   in the day of your calamity;
   Better *is* a neighbor nearby than
   a brother far away.

11 My son, be wise, and make my
   heart glad,

🪓 DIGGING IN

27:1 Trust God for Tomorrow We all
make plans for tomorrow, and we hope
to carry out our plans. But we really don't
know for sure what will happen tomorrow.
Tomorrow is God's time.

Perhaps you're planning a trip or a
party with your friends. Most often your
plans turn out OK. But sometimes things
happen that cause you to change your
plans. There is even a day coming when
everything you planned will come to an

end. You will not wake up on that morning
because you will be with God.

Put your plans in God's hands. He is
the One who is making your way. "A
man's heart plans his way, but the Lord
directs his steps" (Proverbs 16:9). It is
best to ask God to guide your plans each
day. You can trust Him to lead you in the
right paths. His way is always better than
your way because it leads to heaven at
last.

That I may answer him who
reproaches me.

12 A prudent *man* foresees evil *and*
hides himself;
The simple pass on *and* are
punished.

13 Take the garment of him who
is surety for a stranger,
And hold it in pledge *when* he
is surety for a seductress.

14 He who blesses his friend with
a loud voice, rising early in the
morning,
It will be counted a curse to
him.

15 A continual dripping on a very
rainy day
And a contentious woman are
alike;

16 Whoever restrains her restrains
the wind,
And grasps oil with his right
hand.

17 *As* iron sharpens iron,
So a man sharpens the
countenance of his friend.

18 Whoever keeps the fig tree will
eat its fruit;
So he who waits on his master
will be honored.

19 As in water face *reflects* face,
So a man's heart *reveals* the
man.

20 Hell and Destruction are never
full;
So the eyes of man are never
satisfied.

21 The refining pot *is* for silver and
the furnace for gold,
And a man *is valued* by what
others say of him.

22 Though you grind a fool in a
mortar with a pestle along
with crushed grain,

Yet his foolishness will not
depart from him.

23 Be diligent to know the state of
your flocks,
And attend to your herds;

24 For riches *are* not forever,
Nor does a crown *endure* to all
generations.

25 *When* the hay is removed, and
the tender grass shows itself,
And the herbs of the mountains
are gathered in,

26 The lambs *will provide* your
clothing,
And the goats the price of a
field;

27 *You shall have* enough goats'
milk for your food,
For the food of your household,
And the nourishment of your
maidservants.

Rich people may be the poorest of all

28 The wicked flee when no one
pursues,
But the righteous are bold as a
lion.

2   Because of the transgression of
a land, many *are* its princes;
But by a man of understanding
and knowledge
Right will be prolonged.

3   A poor man who oppresses the
poor
Is like a driving rain which leaves
no food.

4   Those who forsake the law
praise the wicked,
But such as keep the law
contend with them.

5   Evil men do not understand
justice,
But those who seek the LORD
understand all.

6   Better *is* the poor who walks in
his integrity

Than one perverse *in his* ways,
though he *be* rich.

7 Whoever keeps the law *is* a
discerning son,
But a companion of gluttons
shames his father.

8 One who increases his
possessions by usury and
extortion
Gathers it for him who will pity
the poor.

9 One who turns away his ear
from hearing the law,
Even his prayer *is* an
abomination.

10 Whoever causes the upright to
go astray in an evil way,
He himself will fall into his own
pit;
But the blameless will inherit
good.

11 The rich man *is* wise in his own
eyes,
But the poor who has
understanding searches him
out.

12 When the righteous rejoice,
there is great glory;
But when the wicked arise, men
hide themselves.

13 He who covers his sins will not
prosper,
But whoever confesses and
forsakes *them* will have
mercy.

14 Happy *is* the man who is always
reverent,
But he who hardens his heart
will fall into calamity.

15 *Like* a roaring lion and a
charging bear

Is a wicked ruler over poor
people.

16 A ruler who lacks understanding
is a great oppressor,
But he who hates **covetousness**
will prolong *his* days.

17 A man burdened with
bloodshed will flee into a pit;
Let no one help him.

18 Whoever walks blamelessly will
be saved,
But *he who is* perverse *in his*
ways will suddenly fall.

19 He who tills his land will have
plenty of bread,
But he who follows frivolity will
have poverty enough!

20 A faithful man will abound with
blessings,
But he who hastens to be rich
will not go unpunished.

21 To show partiality *is* not good,
Because for a piece of bread a
man will transgress.

22 A man with an evil eye hastens
after riches,
And does not consider that
poverty will come upon him.

23 He who rebukes a man will find
more favor afterward
Than he who flatters with the
tongue.

24 Whoever robs his father or his
mother,
And says, "*It is* no
transgression,"
The same *is* companion to a
destroyer.

25 He who is of a proud heart stirs
up strife,

⚜**WORDFINDER**

28:16 Covetousness Pronounced *KUV-ih-tuss-ness.* Envy or the extreme and
wrong desire to own what belongs to someone else.

But he who trusts in the LORD
will be prospered.

26 He who trusts in his own heart
is a fool,
But whoever walks wisely will be
delivered.

27 He who gives to the poor will
not lack,
But he who hides his eyes will
have many curses.

28 When the wicked arise, men
hide themselves;
But when they perish, the
righteous increase.

God honors fairness

29 He who is often rebuked, *and*
hardens *his* neck,
Will suddenly be destroyed, and
that without remedy.

2 When the righteous are in
authority, the people rejoice;
But when a wicked *man* rules,
the people groan.

3 Whoever loves wisdom makes
his father rejoice,
But a companion of harlots
wastes *his* wealth.

4 The king establishes the land by
justice,

But he who receives bribes
overthrows it.

5 A man who flatters his neighbor
Spreads a net for his feet.

6 By transgression an evil man is
snared,
But the righteous sings and
rejoices.

7 The righteous considers the
cause of the poor,
But the wicked does not
understand *such* knowledge.

8 Scoffers set a city aflame,
But wise *men* turn away wrath.

9 *If* a wise man contends with a
foolish man,
Whether *the fool* rages or
laughs, *there is* no peace.

10 The bloodthirsty hate the
blameless,
But the upright seek his
well-being.

11 A fool vents all his feelings,
But a wise *man* holds them
back.

12 If a ruler pays attention to lies,
All his servants *become*
wicked.

What King Solomon Learned

You can read about my life mostly in the first 11 chapters of the Book of
1 Kings. There you will learn that God gave me great gifts of wealth and
power. But my greatest gift was the wisdom to rule my country.

The sad thing was that I didn't use my wisdom to rule my own life. I
married many wives who led me to turn away from the Lord. What began
as my great career ended in my failure.

When God gave me so much wisdom, I should have known better
than to turn my back on Him. Though my wisdom corrected me many
times, I didn't learn the most important things about living.

Always meet God at the beginning of each day and give your life to
His care and plan. This good habit will keep you safe from making the
mistakes I made.

13 The poor *man* and the
    oppressor have this in
    common:
    The LORD gives light to the *eyes*
    of both.

14 The king who judges the poor
    with truth,
    His throne will be established
    forever.

15 The rod and rebuke give
    wisdom,
    But a child left *to himself* brings
    shame to his mother.

16 When the wicked are multiplied,
    transgression increases;
    But the righteous will see their
    fall.

17 Correct your son, and he will
    give you rest;
    Yes, he will give delight to your
    soul.

18 Where *there is* no revelation, the
    people cast off restraint;
    But happy *is* he who keeps the
    law.

19 A servant will not be corrected
    by mere words;
    For though he understands, he
    will not respond.

20 Do you *see* a man hasty in his
    words?
    There is more hope for a fool
    than for him.

21 He who pampers his servant
    from childhood
    Will have him as a son in the
    end.

22 An angry man stirs up strife,
    And a furious man abounds in
    transgression.

23 A man's pride will bring him low,
    But the humble in spirit will
    retain honor.

24 Whoever is a partner with a thief
    hates his own life;
    He swears to tell the truth, but
    reveals nothing.

25 The fear of man brings a snare,
    But whoever trusts in the LORD
    shall be safe.

26 Many seek the ruler's favor,
    But justice for man *comes* from
    the LORD.

27 An unjust man *is* an
    abomination to the righteous,
    And *he who is* upright in the way
    is an abomination to the
    wicked.

Amazing and wonderful things

30 The words of Agur the son of
Jakeh, *his* utterance. This man declared to Ithiel—to Ithiel and Ucal:

2 Surely I *am* more stupid than
    any man,
    And do not have the
    understanding of a man.
3 I neither learned wisdom
    Nor have knowledge of the Holy
    One.

4 Who has ascended into heaven,
    or descended?
    Who has gathered the wind in
    His fists?
    Who has bound the waters in a
    garment?
    Who has established all the ends
    of the earth?
    What *is* His name, and what *is*
    His Son's name,
    If you know?

5 Every word of God *is* pure;
    He *is* a shield to those who put
    their trust in Him.
6 Do not add to His words,
    Lest He rebuke you, and you
    be found a liar.

7 Two *things* I request of You
    (Deprive me not before I die):

What Agur Learned

Pronounce my name *AY-ger*, meaning "He Who Gathers." In John 3:13 Jesus told a great teacher that the Son of God is the only One who has come from and gone back to heaven. This is what I also learned in Proverbs 30:4. Even though I don't know the name of the Son of God yet, still I know who He is and I trust Him. This is man's greatest wisdom, and it comes from God.

Ever since the first people fell into sin (see Genesis 3), all of us have been foolish. The apostle Paul says, "There is none who understands" (Romans 3:11). So we should study God's Word and listen to Him in order to be wise. "Every word of God is pure; He is a shield to those who put their trust in Him" (Proverbs 30:5).

8 Remove falsehood and lies far
 from me;
 Give me neither poverty nor
 riches—
 Feed me with the food allotted
 to me;
9 Lest I be full and deny *You,*
 And say, "Who *is* the LORD?"
 Or lest I be poor and steal,
 And profane the name of my
 God.

10 Do not malign a servant to his
 master,
 Lest he curse you, and you be
 found guilty.

11 *There is* a generation *that* curses
 its father,
 And does not bless its mother.
12 *There is* a generation *that is* pure
 in its own eyes,
 Yet is not washed from its
 filthiness.
13 *There is* a generation— oh, how
 lofty are their *eyes!*
 And their eyelids are lifted up.
14 *There is* a generation whose
 teeth *are like* swords,
 And whose fangs *are like*
 knives,
 To devour the poor from off the
 earth,
 And the needy from *among*
 men.

15 The leech has two daughters—
 Give *and* Give!

There are three *things that* are
 never satisfied,
Four never say, "Enough!":
16 The grave,
 The barren womb,
 The earth *that* is not satisfied
 with water—
 And the fire never says,
 "Enough!"

17 The eye *that* mocks *his* father,
 And scorns obedience to *his*
 mother,
 The ravens of the valley will pick
 it out,
 And the young eagles will eat it.

18 There are three *things which* are
 too wonderful for me,
 Yes, four *which* I do not
 understand:
19 The way of an eagle in the air,
 The way of a serpent on a rock,
 The way of a ship in the midst
 of the sea,
 And the way of a man with a
 virgin.

20 This *is* the way of an adulterous
 woman:
 She eats and wipes her mouth,
 And says, "I have done no
 wickedness."

21 For three *things* the earth is
 perturbed,
 Yes, for four it cannot bear up:
22 For a servant when he reigns,

And does not turn away from
    any;
31 A greyhound,
A male goat also,
And a king *whose* troops *are*
    with him.

32 If you have been foolish in
    exalting yourself,
Or if you have devised evil, *put
    your* hand on *your* mouth.
33 For *as* the churning of milk
    produces butter,
And wringing the nose produces
    blood,
So the forcing of wrath produces
    strife.

A godly woman is praised by her family

31 The words of King Lemuel, the
utterance which his mother taught
him:

2 What, my son?
And what, son of my womb?
And what, son of my vows?
3 Do not give your strength to
    women,
Nor your ways to that which
    destroys kings.

4 *It is* not for kings, O Lemuel,
It is not for kings to drink wine,
Nor for princes intoxicating
    drink;
5 Lest they drink and forget the
    law,
And pervert the justice of all the
    afflicted.
6 Give strong drink to him who is
    perishing,
And wine to those who are bitter
    of heart.
7 Let him drink and forget his
    poverty,
And remember his misery no
    more.

8 Open your mouth for the
    speechless,
In the cause of all *who are*
    appointed to die.

God created the little rock badger to make his home in the crags.

A fool when he is filled with
    food,
23 A hateful *woman* when she is
    married,
And a maidservant who
    succeeds her mistress.

24 There are four *things which* are
    little on the earth,
But they *are* exceedingly wise:
25 The ants *are* a people not
    strong,
Yet they prepare their food in
    the summer;
26 The rock badgers are a feeble
    folk,
Yet they make their homes in
    the crags;
27 The locusts have no king,
Yet they all advance in ranks;
28 The spider skillfully grasps with
    its hands,
And it is in kings' palaces.

29 There are three *things which* are
    majestic in pace,
Yes, four *which* are stately in
    walk:
30 A lion, *which is* mighty among
    beasts

King Lemuel's Mother—Lemuel grew up in our home as a happy boy. His father and I taught him the Bible, but Lemuel also enjoyed all of the adventures that most boys enjoy. Pronounce his name *LEM-you-el* meaning "Devoted to God."

My words were the advice any good mother gives her boy as he begins a new life. I gave the words in chapter 31 to Lemuel on the day he was crowned king of Israel. Some people think "Lemuel" is another name for Solomon.

Now you and all young people can read the things I said to Lemuel just as though they were said to you. It is sad when boys or girls start out in a kind of life that only brings misery. Instead, learn the wisdom of bringing true happiness to yourself and those around you. Such happiness comes from knowing God as the Friend who never fails you.

This is my advice to my son Lemuel and to you.

9 Open your mouth, judge righteously,
And plead the cause of the poor and needy.

10 Who can find a virtuous wife?
For her worth *is* far above rubies.

11 The heart of her husband safely trusts her;
So he will have no lack of gain.

12 She does him good and not evil
All the days of her life.

13 She seeks wool and flax,
And willingly works with her hands.

14 She is like the merchant ships,
She brings her food from afar.

15 She also rises while it is yet night,
And provides food for her household,
And a portion for her maidservants.

16 She considers a field and buys it;
From her profits she plants a vineyard.

17 She girds herself with strength,
And strengthens her arms.

18 She perceives that her merchandise *is* good,
And her lamp does not go out by night.

19 She stretches out her hands to the distaff,
And her hand holds the spindle.

20 She extends her hand to the poor,
Yes, she reaches out her hands to the needy.

21 She is not afraid of snow for her household,
For all her household *is* clothed with scarlet.

22 She makes tapestry for herself;
Her clothing *is* fine linen and purple.

23 Her husband is known in the gates,
When he sits among the elders of the land.

24 She makes linen garments and sells *them*,
And supplies sashes for the merchants.

25 Strength and honor *are* her clothing;
She shall rejoice in time to come.

26 She opens her mouth with wisdom,
And on her tongue *is* the law of kindness.

27 She watches over the ways of her household,
And does not eat the bread of idleness.

28 Her children rise up and call her blessed;
Her husband *also,* and he praises her:

29 "Many daughters have done well,
But you excel them all."

A Great Woman of God—My husband honored me by writing the words in Proverbs 31:10–31. They have remained as God's idea of the kind of wife God honors.

I tried to live a life of virtue. Therefore, my husband valued me more than all of his friends and possessions. He trusted me in all of his business matters.

Sometimes I was up late or I rose early in the morning to be sure my children had enough clothing.

I was not afraid to try new things. I even learned how to buy and sell land. The poor were never turned away hungry from my door.

I may not be the most beautiful woman in the world, but with God's help, I have been a good mother. My children have grown up to praise me. They thank God for the wisdom I taught them while they were young.

30 Charm is deceitful and beauty
  is passing,
But a woman who fears the
  LORD, she shall be praised.

31 Give her of the fruit of her
  hands,
And let her own works praise her
  in the gates.

The Book of

ECCLESIASTES

> **The Preacher**—I'm glad I took the time to find out why I'm living in the world.
>
> At first I couldn't make much sense of life. The world was a very dull place to me. Nothing ever seemed to change. The sun rose and set. The rivers flowed into the ocean. The wind blew back and forth aimlessly.
>
> So I said to myself, "So what? There's no good reason for living in the world!" Even fun and games became dull after a while. Rich or poor, wise or foolish—all seemed the same to me. All was "vanity," which means emptiness.
>
> But one day God showed me I was wrong. At the end of my book, you will find that life can be happy and worthwhile. Each day you can wake up glad to be alive, because you can do something that day for God that will *last forever*.

Life is a soap bubble!

THE words of the Preacher, the son of David, king in Jerusalem.

2 "Vanity of vanities," says the
  Preacher;
  "Vanity of vanities, all *is* vanity."

3 What profit has a man from all
  his labor
  In which he toils under the
  sun?
4 *One* generation passes away,
  and *another* generation
  comes;
  But the earth abides forever.
5 The sun also rises, and the sun
  goes down,
  And hastens to the place where
  it arose.
6 The wind goes toward the south,
  And turns around to the north;
  The wind whirls about
  continually,
  And comes again on its circuit.
7 All the rivers run into the sea,
  Yet the sea *is* not full;
  To the place from which the
  rivers come,
  There they return again.
8 All things *are* full of labor;
  Man cannot express *it*.

The *eye* is not satisfied with
  seeing,
  Nor the ear filled with hearing.

9 That which has been *is* what will
  be,
  That which *is* done is what will
  be done,
  And *there is* nothing new under
  the sun.
10 Is there anything of which it may
  be said,
  "See, this *is* new"?
  It has already been in ancient
  times before us.
11 *There is* no remembrance of
  former *things,*
  Nor will there be any
  remembrance of *things* that
  are to come
  By *those* who will come after.

12 I, the Preacher, was king over Israel in Jerusalem. 13 And I set my heart to seek and search out by wisdom concerning all that is done under heaven; this burdensome task God has given to the sons of man, by which they may be exercised. 14 I have seen all the works that are done under the sun; and indeed, all *is* vanity and grasping for the wind.

15 *What is* crooked cannot be made
    straight,
    And what is lacking cannot be
    numbered.

16 I communed with my heart, saying, "Look, I have attained greatness,
and have gained more wisdom than
all who were before me in Jerusalem.
My heart has understood great wisdom
and knowledge." 17 And I set my heart
to know wisdom and to know madness
and folly. I perceived that this also is
grasping for the wind.

18 For in much wisdom *is* much
    grief,
    And he who increases
        knowledge increases sorrow.

Having fun isn't everything

2 I said in my heart, "Come now, I
will test you with mirth; therefore enjoy
pleasure"; but surely, this also *was*
vanity. 2 I said of laughter—"Madness!"; and of mirth, "What does it accomplish?" 3 I searched in my heart
how to gratify my flesh with wine, while
guiding my heart with wisdom, and

how to lay hold on folly, till I might
see what *was* good for the sons of men
to do under heaven all the days of their
lives.

4 I made my works great, I built myself houses, and planted myself vineyards. 5 I made myself gardens and or-
chards, and I planted all *kinds* of fruit
trees in them. 6 I made myself water
pools from which to water the growing
trees of the grove. 7 I acquired male
and female servants, and had servants
born in my house. Yes, I had greater
possessions of herds and flocks than
all who were in Jerusalem before me.
8 I also gathered for myself silver and
gold and the special treasures of kings
and of the provinces. I acquired male
and female singers, the delights of the
sons of men, *and* musical instruments
of all kinds.

9 So I became great and excelled
more than all who were before me in
Jerusalem. Also my wisdom remained
with me.

10 Whatever my *eyes* desired I did
    not keep from them.
    I did not withhold my heart from
        any pleasure,

⚒ DIGGING IN

1:13 Learn to Be Wise You can learn
a lot of facts, but you may never be wise.

A very important goal is to be wise. To
be wise means that you are able to use
the knowledge you have to make right decisions. A fool is a person who always
makes wrong decisions that hurt him and
others.

Sooner or later, trouble will catch up
to you if you try to live outside the law.
That's a fool's way of living. You will be
wise if you see early that laws (like drug
laws) are made to save your life.

You are not wise if you decide you can
get along without God, for then you will
have trouble all through life. But if you
make up your mind to study God's Word
and obey it, you will grow in wisdom. You
will win the battle of life because you see
everything God's way. That's wisdom.

2:10 Fun Is Not Happiness There's
nothing wrong with having fun as long as

you aren't hurting your health. You must
be careful to know when the fun you're
having may be harmful. Drinking alcohol
or driving a car too fast in traffic is fun to
some people. But this kind of fun doesn't
last. People who do these things often
end up ruining their lives. You can see
these folks at drug treatment centers,
hospitals, jails—and in morgues!

Even harmless fun is not the same as
happiness. *Happiness* is *joy* that lasts
when the *fun* is gone. Right now you can
play hard games and sports because your
body is strong and healthy. Someday you
won't be playing baseball, basketball,
football, soccer, or hockey because your
body won't be able to do those things anymore. But you can still be happy.

Happiness is joy that is *inside* you and
has nothing to do with *doing* things. Happiness is the constant joy that comes from
knowing you belong to God.

For my heart rejoiced in all my
   labor;
And this was my reward from
   all my labor.
11 Then I looked on all the works
   that my hands had done
And on the labor in which I had
   toiled;
And indeed all *was* vanity and
   grasping for the wind.
There was no profit under the
   sun.
12 Then I turned myself to consider
   wisdom and madness and
   folly;
For what *can* the man *do* who
   succeeds the king?—
Only what he has already done.
13 Then I saw that wisdom excels
   folly
As light excels darkness.
14 The wise man's eyes *are* in his
   head,
But the fool walks in darkness.
Yet I myself perceived
That the same event happens to
   them all.

15 So I said in my heart,
"As it happens to the fool,
It also happens to me,
And why was I then more wise?"
Then I said in my heart,
"This also *is* vanity."
16 For *there is* no more
   remembrance of the wise than
   of the fool forever,
Since all that now *is* will be
   forgotten in the days to come.
And how does a wise *man* die?
As the fool!

17 Therefore I hated life because the
work that was done under the sun *was*
distressing to me, for all *is* vanity and
grasping for the wind. 18 Then I hated all my labor in which
I had toiled under the sun, because I
must leave it to the man who will come
after me. 19 And who knows whether
he will be wise or a fool? Yet he will
rule over all my labor in which I toiled
and in which I have shown myself wise
under the sun. This also *is* vanity.

20 Therefore I turned my heart and despaired of all the labor in which I had
toiled under the sun. 21 For there is a
man whose labor *is* with wisdom,
knowledge, and skill; yet he must leave
his heritage to a man who has not labored for it. This also *is* vanity and a
great evil. 22 For what has man for all
his labor, and for the striving of his
heart with which he has toiled under
the sun? 23 For all his days *are* sorrowful, and his work burdensome; even
in the night his heart takes no rest. This
also is vanity.
24 Nothing *is* better for a man *than*
that he should eat and drink, and *that*
his soul should enjoy good in his labor.
This also, I saw, was from the hand
of God. 25 For who can eat, or who
can have enjoyment, more than I?
26 For *God* gives wisdom and knowledge and joy to a man who *is* good
in His sight; but to the sinner He gives
the work of gathering and collecting,
that he may give to *him who is* good
before God. This also *is* vanity and
grasping for the wind.

There is a proper time for everything

3 To everything *there is* a season,
   A time for every purpose under
   heaven:

2 A time to be born,
   And a time to die;
A time to plant,
   And a time to pluck *what is*
     planted;
3 A time to kill,
   And a time to heal;
A time to break down,
   And a time to build up;
4 A time to weep,
   And a time to laugh;
A time to mourn,
   And a time to dance;
5 A time to cast away stones,
   And a time to gather stones;
A time to embrace,
   And a time to refrain from
     embracing;

6   A time to gain,
    And a time to lose;
    A time to keep,
    And a time to throw away;
7   A time to tear,
    And a time to sew;
    A time to keep silence,
    And a time to speak;
8   A time to **love**,
    And a time to hate;
    A time of war,
    And a time of peace.

9 What profit has the worker from that in which he labors? 10 I have seen the God-given task with which the sons of men are to be occupied. 11 He has made everything beautiful in its time. Also He has put eternity in their hearts, except that no one can find out the work that God does from beginning to end.

12 I know that nothing *is* better for them than to rejoice, and to do good in their lives, 13 and also that every man should eat and drink and enjoy the good of all his labor—it *is* the gift of God.

14   I know that whatever God does,
     It shall be forever.
     Nothing can be added to it,
     And nothing taken from it.

God does *it*, that men should fear before Him.
15   That which is has already been,
     And what is to be has already been;
     And God requires an account of what is past.

16 Moreover I saw under the sun:

     In the place of judgment,
     Wickedness *was* there;
     And *in* the place of righteousness,
     Iniquity *was* there.

17 I said in my heart,

     "God shall judge the righteous and the wicked,
     For *there is* a time there for every purpose and for every work."

18 I said in my heart, "Concerning the condition of the sons of men, God tests them, that they may see that they themselves are *like* animals." 19 For what happens to the sons of men also happens to animals; one thing befalls them: as one dies, so dies the other. Surely, they all have one breath; man has no advantage over animals, for all

---

WORDFINDER

3:8 Love An attitude that leads to the behavior Paul describes in 1 Corinthians 13. Christian love is not selfish but always seeks the best for everybody. Such love is the greatest gift of God.

DIGGING IN

3:1–8 A Right Time for Everything Part of being wise is knowing *when* to do everything. It isn't wise to watch television when you need that time to study. It isn't wise to laugh when you're with someone who is suffering. The apostle Paul tells us to "weep with those who weep." But he also says to "rejoice with those who rejoice" (Romans 12:15).

When you want to talk with someone about something important, try to find a time when that person isn't busy. Other-

wise, you may just be wasting your breath, because he probably won't be able to think about what you're saying. There's a right time for doing everything. You need to pray for wisdom to learn those right times.

There's also "a time to be born and a time to die." Those are God's times for you. Jesus has planned a time when He will come and judge the world. Be ready for God's times.

is vanity. 20 All go to one place: all are from the dust, and all return to dust. 21 Who knows the spirit of the sons of men, which goes upward, and the spirit of the animal, which goes down to the earth? 22 So I perceived that nothing *is* better than that a man should rejoice in his own works, for that *is* his heritage. For who can bring him to see what will happen after him?

Becoming successful is like trying to catch the wind

4 Then I returned and considered all the oppression that is done under the sun:

> And look! The tears of the
>   oppressed,
> But they have no comforter—
> On the side of their oppressors
>   *there is* power,
> But they have no comforter.

2   Therefore I praised the dead
>   who *were* already dead,
>   More than the living who are still
>   alive.
3   Yet, better than both *is* he who
>   has never existed,
>   Who has not seen the evil work
>   that is done under the sun.

4 Again, I saw that for all toil and every skillful work a man is envied by his neighbor. This also *is* vanity and grasping for the wind.

5   The fool folds his hands
>   And consumes his own flesh.

6   Better a handful *with* quietness
>   Than both hands full, *together
>   with* toil and grasping for the
>   wind.

7 Then I returned, and I saw vanity under the sun:

8   There is one alone, without
>   companion:
>   He has neither son nor brother.
>   Yet *there is* no end to all his
>   labors,
>   Nor is his *eye* satisfied with
>   riches.
>   *But he never asks,*
>   "For whom do I toil and deprive
>   myself of good?"
>   This also *is* vanity and a grave
>   misfortune.

9   Two *are* better than one,
>   Because they have a good
>   reward for their labor.
10   For if they fall, one will lift up
>   his companion.
>   But woe to him *who is* alone
>   when he falls,
>   For *he has* no one to help him
>   up.
11   Again, if two lie down together,
>   they will keep warm;
>   But how can one be warm
>   *alone?*
12   Though one may be
>   overpowered by another, two
>   can withstand him.
>   And a threefold cord is not
>   quickly broken.

⚒ DIGGING IN

3:17 God Will Judge Our Works Your works will be judged when God comes to judge the world. Some of our works will be like precious stones that fire cannot hurt. Other works we have done will be like wood, hay, and straw. They won't stand the test of God's fire. (See 1 Corinthians 3:12, 13.)

How can you make sure your works will stand after God's judgment? The apostle Paul says that Jesus Christ is the true foundation to build on. So, if you build works that please Jesus, those works will remain forever. Jesus said that even a cup of cold water given for His sake is a work that God remembers.

Some people do some very great works, but they do those works just to make themselves look important. Such works don't count with God. All that lasts must be done because we love Jesus. Everything else will pass away.

13 Better a poor and wise youth
    Than an old and foolish king
        who will be admonished no
        more.
14 For he comes out of prison to
        be king,
    Although he was born poor in
        his kingdom.
15 I saw all the living who walk
        under the sun;
    They were with the second
        youth who stands in his place.
16 *There was* no end of all the
        people over whom he was
        made king;
    Yet those who come afterward
        will not rejoice in him.
    Surely this also *is* vanity and
        grasping for the wind.

Respect God and keep your promises

5 Walk prudently when you go to the
house of God; and draw near to hear
rather than to give the sacrifice of fools,
for they do not know that they do evil.

2   Do not be rash with your mouth,
    And let not your heart utter
        anything hastily before God.
    For God *is* in heaven, and you
        on earth;
    Therefore let your words be
        few.
3   For a dream comes through
        much activity,
    And a fool's voice *is known* by
        his many words.

DIGGING IN

4:8 Greedy People Are Never Satisfied No matter how much a greedy person gets, he is always unhappy. He just wants more and more. And the more he gets, the more miserable he is.

So don't imagine your happiness comes from having things. Many people say, "If only I had a bigger house," or "If only I had a bigger car" or "If only I had a bigger boat"—"then I would be happy."

A greedy person is never satisfied

But when greedy people get these things, they are soon tired of them and only want something more.

Maybe you think you need a new bicycle, or a new dress, or a bigger yard to play in. But you could be just like the unsatisfied greedy man. These things are new thrills that last for a day. Then you're back where you started—wanting something else. Please start early to be satisfied with the friendship of Jesus and doing what He asks. That's the secret of real happiness. Then He will supply all your other needs, too.

5:3 Don't Talk Too Much "A fool's voice is known by his many words."

A sure way to get in trouble is to talk every chance you get. Sooner or later, you're bound to say something foolish or even wicked. "Foot-in-mouth disease" is a problem too many people have.

A way to avoid talking too much is to become a good listener. First, be a good listener to what God says in His Word. When you listen to God and let His Spirit control you, you will always speak with wisdom. Second, listen to others. When everybody has had his say, then you will know how to speak. Besides, people listen more when you don't talk very much. They are more curious about what you have to say, and they trust you because you think more than you talk.

4   When you make a vow to God,
do not delay to pay it;
For *He has* no pleasure in fools.
Pay what you have vowed—
5   Better not to vow than to vow
and not pay.

6 Do not let your mouth cause your flesh to sin, nor say before the messenger *of God* that it *was* an error. Why should God be angry at your excuse and destroy the work of your hands? 7 For in the multitude of dreams and many words *there is* also vanity. But fear God.

8 If you see the oppression of the poor, and the violent perversion of justice and righteousness in a province, do not marvel at the matter; for high official watches over high official, and higher officials are over them. 9 Moreover the profit of the land is for all; *even* the king is served from the field.

10   He who loves silver will not be
satisfied with silver;
Nor he who loves abundance,
with increase.
This also *is* vanity.

11   When goods increase,
They increase who eat them;
So what profit have the owners
Except to see *them* with their
eyes?

12   The sleep of a laboring man *is*
sweet,
Whether he eats little or much;
But the abundance of the rich
will not permit him to sleep.

13   There is a severe evil *which* I
have seen under the sun:
Riches kept for their owner to
his hurt.

14   But those riches perish through
misfortune;
When he begets a son, *there is*
nothing in his hand.

15   As he came from his mother's
womb, naked shall he return,
To go as he came;

And he shall take nothing from
his labor
Which he may carry away in his
hand.

16   And this also *is* a severe evil—
Just exactly as he came, so shall
he go.
And what profit has he who has
labored for the wind?

17   All his days he also eats in
darkness,
And *he has* much sorrow and
sickness and anger.

18 Here is what I have seen: *It is* good and fitting *for one* to eat and drink, and to enjoy the good of all his labor in which he toils under the sun all the days of his life which God gives him; for it *is* his heritage. 19 As for every man to whom God has given riches and wealth, and given him power to eat of it, to receive his heritage and rejoice in his labor—this *is* the gift of God. 20 For he will not dwell unduly on the days of his life, because God keeps *him* busy with the joy of his heart.

Getting rich is not the goal

6 There is an evil which I have seen under the sun, and it *is* common among men: 2 A man to whom God has given riches and wealth and honor, so that he lacks nothing for himself of all he desires; yet God does not give him power to eat of it, but a foreigner consumes it. This *is* vanity, and it *is* an evil affliction.

3 If a man begets a hundred *children* and lives many years, so that the days of his years are many, but his soul is not satisfied with goodness, or indeed he has no burial, I say *that* a stillborn child *is* better than he— 4 for it comes in vanity and departs in darkness, and its name is covered with darkness. 5 Though it has not seen the sun or known *anything,* this has more rest than that man, 6 even if he lives a thousand years twice—but has not seen goodness. Do not all go to one place?

7 All the labor of man *is* for his
mouth,
And yet the soul is not satisfied.
8 For what more has the wise *man*
than the fool?
What does the poor man have,
Who knows *how* to walk before
the living?
9 Better *is* the sight of the eyes
than the wandering of
desire.
This also *is* vanity and grasping
for the wind.

10 Whatever one is, he has been
named already,
For it is known that he *is* man;
And he cannot contend with
Him who is mightier than he.
11 Since there are many things that
increase vanity,
How *is* man the better?

12 For who knows what *is* good for
man in life, all the days of his vain life
which he passes like a shadow? Who
can tell a man what will happen after
him under the sun?

Some very good advice

7 A good name *is* better than
precious ointment,
And the day of death than the
day of one's birth;
2 Better to go to the house of
mourning
Than to go to the house of
feasting,
For that *is* the end of all men;
And the living will take *it* to
heart.
3 Sorrow *is* better than laughter,
For by a sad countenance the
heart is made better.
4 The heart of the wise *is* in the
house of mourning,
But the heart of fools *is* in the
house of mirth.
5 *It is* better to hear the rebuke
of the wise
Than for a man to hear the song
of fools.

6 For like the crackling of thorns
under a pot,
So *is* the laughter of the fool.
This also is vanity.
7 Surely oppression destroys a
wise *man's* reason,
And a bribe debases the heart.
8 The end of a thing *is* better than
its beginning;
The patient in spirit *is* better than
the proud in spirit.
9 Do not hasten in your spirit to
be angry,
For anger rests in the bosom of
fools.
10 Do not say,
"Why were the former days better
than these?"
For you do not inquire wisely
concerning this.

11 Wisdom *is* good with an
inheritance,
And profitable to those who see
the sun.
12 For wisdom *is* a defense *as*
money *is* a defense,
But the excellence of knowledge
is that wisdom gives life to
those who have it.

13 Consider the work of God;
For who can make straight what
He has made crooked?
14 In the day of prosperity be
joyful,
But in the day of adversity
consider:
Surely God has appointed the
one as well as the other,
So that man can find out nothing
that will come after him.

15 I have seen everything in my days
of vanity:

There is a just *man* who perishes
in his righteousness,
And there is a wicked *man* who
prolongs *life* in his
wickedness.

16 Do not be overly righteous,
Nor be overly wise:

Why should you destroy
yourself?
17 Do not be overly wicked,
Nor be foolish:
Why should you die before your
time?
18 *It is* good that you grasp this,
And also not remove your hand
from the other;
For he who fears God will
escape them all.

19 Wisdom strengthens the wise
More than ten rulers of the city.

20 For *there is* not a just man on
earth who does good
And does not sin.

21 Also do not take to heart
everything people say,
Lest you hear your servant
cursing you.
22 For many times, also, your own
heart has known
That *even* you have cursed
others.

23 All this I have proved by
wisdom.
I said, "I will be wise";
But it *was* far from me.
24 As for that which is far off and
exceedingly deep,
Who can find it out?
25 I applied my heart to know,
To search and seek out wisdom
and the reason *of things,*
To know the wickedness of folly,

Even of foolishness *and*
madness.
26 And I find more bitter than death
The woman whose heart *is*
snares and nets,
Whose hands *are* fetters.
He who pleases God shall
escape from her,
But the sinner shall be trapped
by her.

27 "Here is what I have found," says
the Preacher,
"*Adding* one thing to the other
to find out the reason,
28 Which my soul still seeks but I
cannot find:
One man among a thousand I
have found,
But a woman among all these I
have not found.
29 Truly, this only I have found:
That God made man upright,
But they have sought out many
schemes."

Obey the rules
8 Who *is* like a wise *man?*
And who knows the
interpretation of a thing?
A man's wisdom makes his face
shine,
And the sternness of his face is
changed.

2 I *say,* "Keep the king's commandment for the sake of your oath to God.
3 Do not be hasty to go from his presence. Do not take your stand for an

⚒ DIGGING IN

8:2 Obey Your Country's Laws God has set up human governments to make laws for guiding our conduct. To disobey your country's laws is to disobey what God commanded. "Keep the king's commandment for the sake of your oath to God."

If you have promised your life to God, you must also obey the state. Then people will respect you as a law-abiding person. If you break your country's laws, then you will not be a useful witness for Jesus either.

Sometimes kings and nations have punished people for being Christians. The apostle Paul and nearly all of the other apostles were put to death for their faith. The emperor of Rome wanted to be worshiped as a god, and Christians who refused were killed. When anyone orders you to do something that is against God's law, then you must disobey that order. God is the Author of true law, and we must put His laws before any of man's laws.

evil thing, for he does whatever pleases him."

4   Where the word of a king *is*,
       there is power;
       And who may say to him, "What
       are you doing?"
5   He who keeps his command will
       experience nothing harmful;
       And a wise man's heart discerns
       both time and judgment.
6   Because for *every* matter there
       is a time and judgment,
       Though the misery of man
       increases greatly.
7   For he does not know what will
       happen;
       So who can tell him when it will
       occur?
8   No one has power over the spirit
       to retain the spirit,
       And no one has power in the
       day of death.
       There is no release from that
       war,
       And wickedness will not deliver
       those who are given to it.

9 All this I have seen, and applied my heart to *every* work that is done under the sun: *There is* a time in which one man rules over another to his own hurt. 10 Then I saw the wicked buried, who had come and gone from the place of holiness, and they were forgotten in the city where they had so done. This also *is* vanity. 11 Because the sentence against an evil work is not executed speedily, therefore the heart of the sons of men is fully set in them to do evil. 12 Though a sinner does evil a hundred *times,* and his *days* are prolonged, yet I surely know that it will be well with those who fear God, who fear before Him. 13 But it will not be well with the wicked; nor will he prolong *his* days, *which are* as a shadow, because he does not fear before God.

14 There is a vanity which occurs on earth, that there are just *men* to whom it happens according to the work of the wicked; again, there are wicked *men* to whom it happens according to

the work of the righteous. I said that this also *is* vanity.

15 So I commended enjoyment, because a man has nothing better under the sun than to eat, drink, and be merry; for this will remain with him in his labor *all* the days of his life which God gives him under the sun.

16 When I applied my heart to know wisdom and to *see* the business that is done on earth, even though one sees no sleep day or night, 17 then I saw all the work of God, that a man cannot find out the work that is done under the sun. For though a man labors to discover *it*, yet he will not find *it;* moreover, though a wise *man* attempts to know *it*, he will not be able to find *it*.

Everybody has to die

9 For I considered all this in my heart, so that I could declare it all: that the righteous and the wise and their works *are* in the hand of God. People know neither love nor hatred *by* anything *they see* before them. 2 All things *come* alike to all:

       One event *happens* to the
         righteous and the wicked;
       To the good, the clean, and the
         unclean;
       To him who sacrifices and him
         who does not sacrifice.
       As is the good, so *is* the sinner;
       He who takes an oath as *he* who
         fears an oath.

3 This *is* an evil in all that is done under the sun: that one thing *happens* to all. Truly the hearts of the sons of men are full of evil; madness *is* in their hearts while they live, and after that *they go* to the dead. 4 But for him who is joined to all the living there is hope, for a living dog is better than a dead lion.

5   For the living know that they will
       die;
       But the dead know nothing,
       And they have no more reward,
       For the memory of them is
         forgotten.

6 Also their love, their hatred, and
    their envy have now perished;
  Nevermore will they have a
    share
  In anything done under the sun.

7 Go, eat your bread with joy,
  And drink your wine with a
    merry heart;
  For God has already accepted
    your works.
8 Let your garments always be
    white,
  And let your head lack no oil.

9 Live joyfully with the wife whom you love all the days of your vain life which He has given you under the sun, all your days of vanity; for that is your portion in life, and in the labor which you perform under the sun. 10 Whatever your hand finds to do, do it with your might; for there is no work or device or knowledge or wisdom in the grave where you are going. 11 I returned and saw under the sun that—

  The race is not to the swift,
  Nor the battle to the strong,
  Nor bread to the wise,
  Nor riches to men of
    understanding,
  Nor favor to men of skill;
  But time and chance happen to
    them all.
12 For man also does not know his
    time:
  Like fish taken in a cruel net,
  Like birds caught in a snare,
  So the sons of men are snared
    in an evil time,
  When it falls suddenly upon
    them.

13 This wisdom I have also seen under the sun, and it seemed great to me: 14 There was a little city with few men in it; and a great king came against it, besieged it, and built great snares around it. 15 Now there was found in it a poor wise man, and he by his wisdom delivered the city. Yet no one remembered that same poor man.

16 Then I said:

  "Wisdom is better than strength.
  Nevertheless the poor man's
    wisdom is despised,
  And his words are not heard.
17 Words of the wise, spoken
    quietly, should be heard
  Rather than the shout of a ruler
    of fools.
18 Wisdom is better than weapons
    of war;
  But one sinner destroys much
    good."

Be wise, not foolish

10 Dead flies putrefy the perfumer's
    ointment,
  And cause it to give off a foul
    odor;
  So does a little folly to one
    respected for wisdom and
    honor.
2 A wise man's heart is at his right
    hand,
  But a fool's heart at his left.
3 Even when a fool walks along
    the way,
  He lacks wisdom,
  And he shows everyone that he
    is a fool.
4 If the spirit of the ruler rises
    against you,
  Do not leave your post;
  For conciliation pacifies great
    offenses.

5 There is an evil I have seen
    under the sun,
  As an error proceeding from the
    ruler:
6 Folly is set in great dignity,
  While the rich sit in a lowly
    place.
7 I have seen servants on horses,
  While princes walk on the
    ground like servants.

8 He who digs a pit will fall into
    it,
  And whoever breaks through a
    wall will be bitten by a
    serpent.

9 He who quarries stones may be
    hurt by them,
    And he who splits wood may be
    endangered by it.
10 If the ax is dull,
    And one does not sharpen the
    edge,
    Then he must use more
    strength;
    But wisdom brings success.
11 A serpent may bite when *it is*
    not charmed;
    The babbler is no different.
12 The words of a wise man's
    mouth *are* gracious,
    But the lips of a fool shall
    swallow him up;
13 The words of his mouth begin
    with foolishness,
    And the end of his talk *is* raving
    madness.
14 A fool also multiplies words.
    No man knows what is to be;
    Who can tell him what will be
    after him?
15 The labor of fools wearies
    them,
    For they do not even know how
    to go to the city!

16 Woe to you, O land, when your
    king *is* a child,
    And your princes feast in the
    morning!
17 Blessed *are* you, O land, when
    your king *is* the son of nobles,
    And your princes feast at the
    proper time—
    For strength and not for
    drunkenness!
18 Because of laziness the building
    decays,
    And through idleness of hands
    the house leaks.
19 A feast is made for laughter,
    And wine makes merry;
    But money answers everything.
20 Do not curse the king, even in
    your thought;
    Do not curse the rich, even in
    your bedroom;
    For a bird of the air may carry
    your voice,
    And a bird in flight may tell the
    matter.

Don't give up

11 Cast your bread upon the
    waters,

DIGGING IN

11:1 Share With Others Solomon had
ships that sailed to distant ports and
brought back wealth—"Cast your bread
[meaning, shiploads of grain] upon the
waters, for you will find it after many
days."

Solomon also saw a lesson for living
in his shipping business: By sharing your
good things with others, you will receive
good things in return. If you bless others
with your abilities, then others will bless
you, also. If you're musical and share your
music with others, then you will enjoy your
music even more.

Sharing is one of the greatest joys of
living. The bonus of sharing with others
is that others will then share their gifts
with you. Most of all, God will be pleased
with your life. The greatest gift you can
share with others is the gift of eternal life
as you tell them about your living Savior,
Jesus.

A person who shares receives many blessings.

For you will find it after many days.

2 Give a serving to seven, and also to eight,
For you do not know what evil will be on the earth.

3 If the clouds are full of rain,
They empty *themselves* upon the earth;
And if a tree falls to the south or the north,
In the place where the tree falls, there it shall lie.

4 He who observes the wind will not sow,
And he who regards the clouds will not reap.

5 As you do not know what *is* the way of the wind,
Or how the bones *grow* in the womb of her who is with child,
So you do not know the works of God who makes everything.

6 In the morning sow your seed,
And in the evening do not withhold your hand;
For you do not know which will prosper,
Either this or that,
Or whether both alike *will be* good.

7 Truly the light is sweet,
And *it is* pleasant for the eyes to behold the sun;

8 But if a man lives many years
And rejoices in them all,
Yet let him remember the days of darkness,
For they will be many.
All that is coming *is* vanity.

9 Rejoice, O young man, in your youth,
And let your heart cheer you in the days of your youth;
Walk in the ways of your heart,
And in the sight of your eyes;
But know that for all these
God will bring you into judgment.

10 Therefore remove sorrow from your heart,
And put away evil from your flesh,
For childhood and youth *are* vanity.

Seek God while you are young

12 Remember now your Creator in the days of your youth,
Before the difficult days come,
And the years draw near when you say,
"I have no pleasure in them":

2 While the sun and the light,
The moon and the stars,
Are not darkened,
And the clouds do not return after the rain;

3 In the day when the keepers of the house tremble,
And the strong men bow down;

🪓 DIGGING IN

12:1 Seek God When You Are Young
"Older" may not mean "wiser." The older you get, the harder it is to change your mind and learn new things. Sad to say, some people can't come to Christ because they have been without God for so long they don't know how to search for Him. They can't think anything new anymore.

But your mind is still young. Learning about God and God's ways is the most valuable thing you can do at this time of life. Seek Him now while you're still able.

Start by reading Genesis and learn in chapter 3 how we got lost from God. Then read in the Gospel of John how Jesus, the living Word of God, became a Man. See how He revealed His glory in the great works of healing and raising the dead. Then learn how He died to pay for your sins and how He rose again. Now He is alive forever, and He waits to live in you. Ask Him to come into your life today.

What the Preacher Learned

In the beginning I couldn't understand the meaning of my life. But I kept trying, and at last found out the reason for being in the world.

The whole truth is that God made me for *Himself,* so there is no use trying to enjoy my life without Him. The more I tried to satisfy myself, the more disappointed I was. Everything in this world dies and comes to an end.

But God never dies. He is the Author of life, the world, and everything we see. It makes good sense, then, to get to know God and learn to love Him more than anything He made.

When we love and enjoy our Creator just for being the wonderful Person He is, we can truly enjoy His creation, too.

When the grinders cease
  because they are few,
And those that look through the
  windows grow dim;
4 When the doors are shut in the
  streets,
And the sound of grinding is low;
When one rises up at the sound
  of a bird,
And all the daughters of music
  are brought low.
5 Also they are afraid of height,
And of terrors in the way;
When the almond tree
  blossoms,
The grasshopper is a burden,
And desire fails.
For man goes to his eternal
  home,
And the mourners go about the
  streets.

6 *Remember your Creator* before
  the silver cord is loosed,
Or the golden bowl is broken,
Or the pitcher shattered at the
  fountain,
Or the wheel broken at the
  well.
7 Then the dust will return to the
  earth as it was,
And the spirit will return to God
  who gave it.

8 "Vanity of vanities," says the
  Preacher,
"All *is* vanity."

9 And moreover, because the Preacher was wise, he still taught the people knowledge; yes, he pondered and sought out *and* set in order many proverbs. 10 The Preacher sought to find acceptable words; and *what was* written *was* upright—words of truth. 11 The words of the wise are like goads, and the words of scholars are like well-driven nails, given by one Shepherd. 12 And further, my son, be admonished by these. Of making many books *there* is no end, and much study *is* wearisome to the flesh.

13 Let us hear the conclusion of the whole matter:

Fear God and keep His
  commandments,
For this is man's all.
14 For God will bring every work
  into judgment,
Including every secret thing,
Whether good or evil.

The
SONG OF SOLOMON

The Girl from Shulem—Solomon was my husband, and he loved me very much. Because he loved me, I also loved him.

A boy should begin early to love and respect his mother. Then he will know how to love and honor that special girl God gives him when he marries. Look for kind things you can do for your mother—like helping with the chores around home. Someday she will die. Now you should make good memories of how you treated her.

Then, as you get older, you will begin to notice girls more. You will be building a happy life if you treat all girls with respect—just as you expect your father to treat your mother.

"Respect" means to appreciate the real value of a person. Love happens when you seek the best for that person.

Solomon sings a wedding song

THE song of songs, which *is* Solomon's.

THE SHULAMITE

2 Let him kiss me with the kisses
of his mouth—
For your love *is* better than
wine.
3 Because of the fragrance of your
good ointments,
Your name *is* ointment poured
forth;
Therefore the virgins love you.
4 Draw me away!

THE DAUGHTERS OF JERUSALEM

We will run after you.

THE SHULAMITE

The king has brought me into
his chambers.

THE DAUGHTERS OF JERUSALEM

We will be glad and rejoice in
you.

We will remember your love
more than wine.

THE SHULAMITE

Rightly do they love you.

5 I *am* dark, but lovely,
O daughters of Jerusalem,
Like the tents of Kedar,
Like the curtains of Solomon.
6 Do not look upon me, because
I *am* dark,
Because the sun has tanned me.
My mother's sons were angry
with me;
They made me the keeper of the
vineyards,
But my own vineyard I have not
kept.

(TO HER BELOVED)

7 Tell me, O you whom I love,
Where you feed *your flock*,
Where you make *it* rest at noon.
For why should I be as one who
veils herself
By the flocks of your
companions?

THE BELOVED

8 If you do not know, O fairest
among women,
Follow in the footsteps of the
flock,

And feed your little goats
Beside the shepherds' tents.
9   I have compared you, my
     love,
     To my filly among Pharaoh's
     chariots.
10   Your cheeks are lovely with
     ornaments,
     Your neck with chains *of gold.*

The Daughters of Jerusalem

11   We will make you ornaments of
     gold
     With studs of silver.

The Shulamite

12   While the king *is* at his table,
     My spikenard sends forth its
     fragrance.
13   A bundle of myrrh *is* my beloved
     to me,
     That lies all night between my
     breasts.
14   My beloved *is* to me a cluster
     of henna *blooms*
     In the vineyards of En Gedi.

The Beloved

15   Behold, you *are* fair, my love!
     Behold, you *are* fair!
     You *have* dove's eyes.

The Shulamite

16   Behold, you *are* handsome, my
     beloved!
     Yes, pleasant!
     Also our bed *is* green.
17   The beams of our houses *are*
     cedar,
     And our rafters of fir.

A country girl comes to the castle

2 I *am* the rose of Sharon,
     And the lily of the valleys.

The Beloved

2   Like a lily among thorns,
     So is my love among the
     daughters.

The Shulamite

3   Like an apple tree among the
     trees of the woods,
     So *is* my beloved among the
     sons.
     I sat down in his shade with great
     delight,
     And his fruit *was* sweet to my
     taste.

The Shulamite to the Daughters of Jerusalem

4   He brought me to the
     banqueting house,
     And his banner over me *was*
     love.
5   Sustain me with cakes of raisins,
     Refresh me with apples,
     For I *am* lovesick.
6   His left hand *is* under my head,
     And his right hand embraces
     me.
7   I charge you, O daughters of
     Jerusalem,
     By the gazelles or by the does
     of the field,
     Do not stir up nor awaken love
     Until it pleases.

The Shulamite

8   The voice of my beloved!
     Behold, he comes
     Leaping upon the mountains,
     Skipping upon the hills.
9   My beloved is like a gazelle or
     a young stag.
     Behold, he stands behind our
     wall;
     He is looking through the
     windows,
     Gazing through the lattice.
10   My beloved spoke, and said to
     me:
     "Rise up, my love, my fair one,
     And come away.
11   For lo, the winter is past,
     The rain is over *and* gone.
12   The flowers appear on the earth;
     The time of singing has come,
     And the voice of the turtledove
     Is heard in our land.
13   The fig tree puts forth her green
     figs,
     And the vines *with* the tender
     grapes

Give a good smell.
Rise up, my love, my fair one,
And come away!

14 "O my dove, in the clefts of the
rock,
In the secret *places* of the cliff,
Let me see your face,
Let me hear your voice;
For your voice *is* sweet,
And your face *is* lovely."

HER BROTHERS
15 Catch us the foxes,
The little foxes that spoil the
vines,
For our vines *have* tender
grapes.

THE SHULAMITE
16 My beloved *is* mine, and I *am*
his.
He feeds *his flock* among the
lilies.

(TO HER BELOVED)
17 Until the day breaks
And the shadows flee away,
Turn, my beloved,
And be like a gazelle
Or a young stag
Upon the mountains of Bether.

Looking for true love

THE SHULAMITE
3 By night on my bed I sought the
one I love;
I sought him, but I did not find
him.
2 "I will rise now," *I said,*
"And go about the city;
In the streets and in the squares
I will seek the one I love."
I sought him, but I did not find
him.
3 The watchmen who go about
the city found me;
I said,
"Have you seen the one I love?"

4 Scarcely had I passed by them,
When I found the one I love.
I held him and would not let him
go,

Until I had brought him to the
house of my mother,
And into the chamber of her
who conceived me.

5 I charge you, O daughters of
Jerusalem,
By the gazelles or by the does
of the field,
Do not stir up nor awaken love
Until it pleases.

THE SHULAMITE
6 Who *is* this coming out of the
wilderness
Like pillars of smoke,
Perfumed with myrrh and
frankincense,
With all the merchant's fragrant
powders?
7 Behold, it *is* Solomon's couch,
With sixty valiant men around it,
Of the valiant of Israel.
8 They all hold swords,
Being expert in war.
Every man *has* his sword on his
thigh
Because of fear in the night.

9 Of the wood of Lebanon
Solomon the King
Made himself a palanquin:
10 He made its pillars *of* silver,
Its support *of* gold,
Its seat *of* purple,
Its interior paved *with* love
By the daughters of Jerusalem.
11 Go forth, O daughters of Zion,
And see King Solomon with the
crown
With which his mother crowned
him
On the day of his wedding,
The day of the gladness of his
heart.

Solomon thinks the bride is beautiful

THE BELOVED
4 Behold, you *are* fair, my love!
Behold, you *are* fair!
You *have* dove's *eyes* behind
your veil.

Your hair *is* like a flock of goats,
Going down from Mount Gilead.

2 Your teeth *are* like a flock of
shorn *sheep*
Which have come up from the
washing,
Every one of which bears twins,
And none *is* barren among
them.

3 Your lips *are* like a strand of
scarlet,
And your mouth is lovely.
Your temples behind your veil
Are like a piece of pomegranate.

4 Your neck *is* like the tower of
David,
Built for an armory,
On which hang a thousand
bucklers,
All shields of mighty men.

5 Your two breasts *are* like two
fawns,
Twins of a gazelle,
Which feed among the lilies.

6 Until the day breaks
And the shadows flee away,
I will go my way to the mountain
of myrrh
And to the hill of frankincense.

7 You *are* all fair, my love,
And *there is* no spot in you.

8 Come with me from Lebanon,
my spouse,
With me from Lebanon.
Look from the top of Amana,
From the top of Senir and
Hermon,
From the lions' dens,
From the mountains of the
leopards.

9 You have ravished my heart,
My sister, *my* spouse;
You have ravished my heart
With one *look* of your eyes,
With one link of your necklace.

10 How fair is your love,
My sister, *my* spouse!
How much better than wine is
your love,
And the scent of your perfumes
Than all spices!

11 Your lips, O *my* spouse,
Drip as the honeycomb;
Honey and milk *are* under your
tongue;
And the fragrance of your
garments
Is like the fragrance of Lebanon.

12 A garden enclosed
Is my sister, *my* spouse,
A spring shut up,
A fountain sealed.

13 Your plants *are* an orchard of
pomegranates
With pleasant fruits,
Fragrant henna with spikenard,

14 Spikenard and saffron,
Calamus and cinnamon,
With all trees of frankincense,
Myrrh and aloes,
With all the chief spices—

15 A fountain of gardens,
A well of living waters,
And streams from Lebanon.

THE SHULAMITE

16 Awake, O north *wind,*
And come, O south!
Blow upon my garden,
That its spices may flow out.
Let my beloved come to his
garden
And eat its pleasant fruits.

How tanned and handsome is the bridegroom

THE BELOVED

5 I have come to my garden, my
sister, *my* spouse;
I have gathered my myrrh with
my spice;
I have eaten my honeycomb
with my honey;
I have drunk my wine with my
milk.

(TO HIS FRIENDS)

Eat, O friends!
Drink, yes, drink deeply,
O beloved ones!

THE SHULAMITE

2 I sleep, but my heart is awake;
It is the voice of my beloved!

He knocks, *saying,*
"Open for me, my sister, my
    love,
My dove, my perfect one;
For my head is covered with
    dew,
My locks with the drops of the
    night."

3   I have taken off my robe;
How can I put it on *again?*
I have washed my feet;
How can I defile them?
4   My beloved put his hand
By the latch *of the door,*
And my heart yearned for him.
5   I arose to open for my beloved,
And my hands dripped *with*
    myrrh,
My fingers with liquid myrrh,
On the handles of the lock.

6   I opened for my beloved,
But my beloved had turned
    away *and* was gone.
My heart leaped up when he
    spoke.
I sought him, but I could not find
    him;
I called him, but he gave me no
    answer.
7   The watchmen who went about
    the city found me.
They struck me, they wounded
    me;
The keepers of the walls
Took my veil away from me.
8   I charge you, O daughters of
    Jerusalem,
If you find my beloved,
That you tell him I *am* lovesick!

THE DAUGHTERS OF JERUSALEM

9   What *is* your beloved
More than *another* beloved,
O fairest among women?
What *is* your beloved
More than *another* beloved,
That you so charge us?

THE SHULAMITE

10   My beloved *is* white and ruddy,
Chief among ten thousand.
11   His head *is like* the finest gold;

His locks *are* wavy,
And black as a raven.
12   His eyes *are* like doves
By the rivers of waters,
Washed with milk,
And fitly set.
13   His cheeks *are* like a bed of
    spices,
Banks of scented herbs.
His lips *are* lilies,
Dripping liquid myrrh.

14   His hands *are* rods of gold
Set with beryl.
His body *is* carved ivory
Inlaid *with* sapphires.
15   His legs *are* pillars of marble
Set on bases of fine gold.
His countenance *is* like
    Lebanon,
Excellent as the cedars.
16   His mouth *is* most sweet,
Yes, he *is* altogether lovely.
This *is* my beloved,
And this *is* my friend,
O daughters of Jerusalem!

The bridesmaids serenade the wedding couple

THE DAUGHTERS OF JERUSALEM

6   Where has your beloved gone,
O fairest among women?
Where has your beloved turned
    aside,
That we may seek him with you?

THE SHULAMITE

2   My beloved has gone to his
    garden,
To the beds of spices,
To feed *his flock* in the gardens,
And to gather lilies.
3   I *am* my beloved's,
And my beloved *is* mine.
He feeds *his flock* among the
    lilies.

THE BELOVED

4   O my love, you *are as* beautiful
    as Tirzah,
Lovely as Jerusalem,

Awesome as *an army* with
   banners!
5 Turn your *eyes* away from me,
   For they have overcome me.
   Your hair *is* like a flock of goats
   Going down from Gilead.
6 Your teeth *are* like a flock of
   sheep
   Which have come up from the
   washing;
   Every one bears twins,
   And none *is* barren among
   them.
7 Like a piece of pomegranate
   Are your temples behind your
   veil.

8 There are sixty queens
   And eighty concubines,
   And virgins without number.
9 My dove, my perfect one,
   Is the only one,
   The only one of her mother,
   The favorite of the one who bore
   her.
   The daughters saw her
   And called her blessed,
   The queens and the concubines,
   And they praised her.

10 Who is she who looks forth as
   the morning,
   Fair as the moon,
   Clear as the sun,
   Awesome as *an army* with
   banners?

THE SHULAMITE
11 I went down to the garden of
   nuts
   To see the verdure of the valley,
   To see whether the vine had
   budded
   And the pomegranates had
   bloomed.
12 Before I was even aware,
   My soul had made me
   As the chariots of my noble
   people.

THE BELOVED AND HIS FRIENDS
13 Return, return, O Shulamite;
   Return, return, that we may look
   upon you!

THE SHULAMITE
   What would you see in the
   Shulamite—
   As it were, the dance of the two
   camps?

No other woman compares with the queen

THE BELOVED
7 How beautiful are your feet in
   sandals,
   O prince's daughter!
   The curves of your thighs *are*
   like jewels,
   The work of the hands of a
   skillful workman.
2 Your navel *is* a rounded goblet;
   It lacks no blended beverage.
   Your waist *is* a heap of wheat
   Set about with lilies.
3 Your two breasts *are* like two
   fawns,
   Twins of a gazelle.
4 Your neck *is* like an ivory tower,
   Your eyes *like* the pools in
   Heshbon
   By the gate of Bath Rabbim.
   Your nose *is* like the tower of
   Lebanon
   Which looks toward Damascus.
5 Your head *crowns* you like
   Mount Carmel,
   And the hair of your head *is* like
   purple;
   A king *is* held captive by *your*
   tresses.

6 How fair and how pleasant you
   are,
   O love, with your delights!
7 This stature of yours is like a
   palm tree,
   And your breasts *like* its clusters.
8 I said, "I will go up to the palm
   tree,
   I will take hold of its branches."
   Let now your breasts be like
   clusters of the vine,
   The fragrance of your breath like
   apples,
9 And the roof of your mouth like
   the best wine.

Solomon and the Shulamite woman walk in the vineyard.

THE SHULAMITE

> *The wine* goes *down* smoothly for my beloved,
> Moving gently the lips of sleepers.
> 10 I *am* my beloved's,
> And his desire *is* toward me.

> 11 Come, my beloved,
> Let us go forth to the field;
> Let us lodge in the villages.
> 12 Let us get up early to the vineyards;
> Let us see if the vine has budded,
> *Whether* the grape blossoms are open,
> *And* the pomegranates are in bloom.
> There I will give you my love.
> 13 The mandrakes give off a fragrance,
> And at our gates *are* pleasant *fruits,*
> All manner, new and old,
> Which I have laid up for you, my beloved.

Love is as strong as death

8 Oh, that you were like my brother,

Who nursed at my mother's breasts!
If I should find you outside,
I would kiss you;
I would not be despised.
2 I would lead you *and* bring you
Into the house of my mother,
She *who* used to instruct me.
I would cause you to drink of spiced wine,
Of the juice of my pomegranate.

(TO THE DAUGHTERS OF JERUSALEM)

> 3 His left hand *is* under my head,
> And his right hand embraces me.
> 4 I charge you, O daughters of Jerusalem,
> Do not stir up nor awaken love
> Until it pleases.

A RELATIVE

> 5 Who *is* this coming up from the wilderness,
> Leaning upon her beloved?

> I awakened you under the apple tree.
> There your mother brought you forth;
> There she *who* bore you brought *you* forth.

THE SHULAMITE TO HER BELOVED

> 6 Set me as a seal upon your heart,
> As a seal upon your arm;
> For love *is as* strong as death,
> Jealousy *as* cruel as the grave;
> Its flames *are* flames of fire,
> A most vehement flame.

> 7 Many waters cannot quench love,
> Nor can the floods drown it.
> If a man would give for love
> All the wealth of his house,
> It would be utterly despised.

THE SHULAMITE'S BROTHERS

> 8 We have a little sister,
> And she has no breasts.
> What shall *we* do for our sister

In the day when she is spoken
      for?
9   If she *is* a wall,
      We will build upon her
      A battlement of silver;
      And if she *is* a door,
      We will enclose her
      With boards of cedar.

The Shulamite

10   I *am* a wall,
      And my breasts like towers;
      Then I became in his eyes
      As one who found peace.
11   Solomon had a vineyard at Baal
      Hamon;
      He leased the vineyard to
      keepers;
      Everyone was to bring for its fruit
      A thousand silver coins.

(To Solomon)

12   My own vineyard *is* before me.
      You, O Solomon, *may have* a
      thousand,
      And those who tend its fruit two
      hundred.

The Beloved

13   You who dwell in the gardens,
      The companions listen for your
      voice—
      Let me hear it!

The Shulamite

14   Make haste, my beloved,
      And be like a gazelle
      Or a young stag
      On the mountains of spices.

⚒ DIGGING IN

8:14 Why Solomon Wrote His Song
The Song of Solomon, also called the
Song of Songs, is a long love poem. The
poem is written to show that God blesses
true love between a man and a woman.
Solomon writes about his love for a beautiful girl. But the young woman's heart remains faithful to her peasant lover who
is a young farmer. "Love is as strong as
death" (Song of Solomon 8:6).

But there is another great teaching in
the Song of Solomon. The Song speaks
of the love of Jesus for His people. Jesus
proved that love is as strong as death by
dying for those He loved. Then He rose
again so that His beloved people would
be His bride forever. Jesus will love you
forever also, if you surrender your life to
Him.

The Book of
ISAIAH

I am the first of the four major prophets. We are called the *major* prophets because our books are longer than those of the 12 minor prophets. My name is pronounced *eye-ZAY-uh* and means "The Lord Has Saved." I was a relative of the kings of Judah.

Sometimes people call me the gospel-preaching prophet because I speak more about the coming of Jesus and salvation than any of the other prophets do. I lived over seven hundred years before Jesus came and died for our sins.

My book of sixty-six chapters is divided into two parts. In the first section, chapters 1—39, I warn my people about the coming judgment of God. In chapters 40—66, God inspired me to comfort His people with His promises of salvation. The best-loved part of my book is chapter 53, where I tell how Jesus will be crucified for our sins.

Isaiah delivers God's message

THE vision of Isaiah the son of Amoz, which he saw concerning Judah and Jerusalem in the days of Uzziah, Jotham, Ahaz, *and* Hezekiah, kings of Judah.

2 Hear, O heavens, and give ear,
O earth!
For the LORD has spoken:
"I have nourished and brought up
children,
And they have rebelled against
Me;
3 The ox knows its owner
And the donkey its master's
crib;
But Israel does not know,
My people do not consider."

4 Alas, sinful nation,
A people laden with iniquity,
A brood of evildoers,
Children who are corrupters!
They have forsaken the
LORD,
They have provoked to anger
The Holy One of Israel,

They have turned away
backward.

5 Why should you be stricken
again?
You will revolt more and more.
The whole head is sick,
And the whole heart faints.
6 From the sole of the foot even
to the head,
There is no soundness in it,
But wounds and bruises and
putrefying sores;
They have not been closed or
bound up,
Or soothed with ointment.

7 Your country *is* desolate,
Your cities *are* burned with
fire;
Strangers devour your land in
your presence;
And *it is* desolate, as overthrown
by strangers.
8 So the daughter of Zion is left
as a booth in a vineyard,
As a hut in a garden of
cucumbers,
As a besieged city.

9   Unless the **LORD of hosts**
    Had left to us a very small
        remnant,
    We would have become like
        Sodom,
    We would have been made like
        Gomorrah.

10 Hear the word of the LORD,
    You rulers of Sodom;
    Give ear to the law of our
        God,
    You people of Gomorrah:
11 "To what purpose *is* the multitude
        of your sacrifices to Me?"
    Says the LORD.
    "I have had enough of burnt
        offerings of rams
    And the fat of fed cattle.
    I do not delight in the blood of
        bulls,
    Or of lambs or goats.

12 "When you come to appear
        before Me,
    Who has required this from your
        hand,
    To trample My courts?
13 Bring no more futile sacrifices;
    Incense is an abomination to
        Me.
    The New Moons, the Sabbaths,
        and the calling of
        assemblies—
    I cannot endure iniquity and the
        sacred meeting.
14 Your New Moons and your
        appointed feasts
    My soul hates;
    They are a trouble to Me,
    I am weary of bearing *them*.
15 When you spread out your
        hands,
    I will hide My eyes from you;
    Even though you make many
        prayers,
    I will not hear.
    Your hands are full of blood.

16 "Wash yourselves, make
        yourselves clean;
    Put away the evil of your doings
        from before My eyes.
    Cease to do evil,
17 Learn to do good;
    Seek justice,
    Rebuke the oppressor;
    Defend the fatherless,
    Plead for the widow.

18 "Come now, and let us reason
        together,"
    Says the LORD,
    "Though your sins are like scarlet,
    They shall be as white as snow;
    Though they are red like
        crimson,
    They shall be as wool.
19 If you are willing and obedient,
    You shall eat the good of the
        land;
20 But if you refuse and rebel,
    You shall be devoured by the
        sword";
    For the mouth of the LORD has
        spoken.

21 How the faithful city has become
        a harlot!
    It was full of justice;
    Righteousness lodged in it,
    But now murderers.
22 Your silver has become dross,
    Your wine mixed with water.
23 Your princes *are* rebellious,
    And companions of thieves;
    Everyone loves bribes,
    And follows after rewards.
    They do not defend the
        fatherless,
    Nor does the cause of the widow
        come before them.

24 Therefore the Lord says,
    The LORD of hosts, the Mighty
        One of Israel,
    "Ah, I will rid Myself of My
        adversaries,

WORDFINDER

1:9 Lord of Hosts A name for God as the leader of His heavenly armies. Lord Sabaoth (pronounced *SAB-ay-oth*), from the Hebrew, means the same.

And take vengeance on My
enemies.
25 I will turn My hand against you,
And thoroughly purge away
your dross,
And take away all your alloy.
26 I will restore your judges as at
the first,
And your counselors as at the
beginning.
Afterward you shall be called the
city of righteousness, the
faithful city."

27 Zion shall be redeemed with
justice,
And her penitents with
righteousness.
28 The destruction of transgressors
and of sinners *shall be*
together,
And those who forsake the LORD
shall be consumed.
29 For they shall be ashamed of the
terebinth trees
Which you have desired;
And you shall be embarrassed
because of the gardens
Which you have chosen.
30 For you shall be as a terebinth
whose leaf fades,
And as a garden that has no
water.
31 The strong shall be as tinder,
And the work of it as a spark;
Both will burn together,
And no one shall quench
them.

God punishes pride

2 The word that Isaiah the son of
Amoz saw concerning Judah and Jerusalem.

2 Now it shall come to pass in the
latter days
That the mountain of the LORD's
house
Shall be established on the top
of the mountains,
And shall be exalted above the
hills;
And all nations shall flow to it.

3 Many people shall come and
say,
"Come, and let us go up to the
mountain of the LORD,
To the house of the God of
Jacob;
He will teach us His ways,
And we shall walk in His paths."
For out of Zion shall go forth the
law,
And the word of the LORD from
Jerusalem.
4 He shall judge between the
nations,
And rebuke many people;
They shall beat their swords into
plowshares,
And their spears into pruning
hooks;
Nation shall not lift up sword
against nation,
Neither shall they learn war
anymore.

5 O house of Jacob, come and let
us walk
In the light of the LORD.

6 For You have forsaken Your
people, the house of Jacob,
Because they are filled with
eastern ways;
They *are* soothsayers like the
Philistines,
And they are pleased with the
children of foreigners.
7 Their land is also full of silver
and gold,
And there is no end to their
treasures;
Their land is also full of horses,
And there is no end to their
chariots.
8 Their land is also full of idols;
They worship the work of their
own hands,
That which their own fingers
have made.
9 People bow down,
And each man humbles himself;
Therefore do not forgive them.

10 Enter into the rock, and hide in
the dust,

From the terror of the L ORD
And the glory of His majesty.

11 The lofty looks of man shall be
humbled,
The haughtiness of men shall be
bowed down,
And the L ORD alone shall be
exalted in that day.

12 For the day of the L ORD of hosts
Shall come upon everything
proud and lofty,
Upon *everything* lifted up—
And it shall be brought low—

13 Upon all the cedars of Lebanon
that are high and lifted up,
And upon all the oaks of
Bashan;

14 Upon all the high mountains,
And upon all the hills *that are*
lifted up;

15 Upon every high tower,
And upon every fortified wall;

16 Upon all the ships of Tarshish,
And upon all the beautiful
sloops.

17 The loftiness of man shall be
bowed down,
And the haughtiness of men
shall be brought low;
The L ORD alone will be exalted
in that day,

18 But the idols He shall utterly
abolish.

19 They shall go into the holes of
the rocks,
And into the caves of the earth,
From the terror of the L ORD
And the glory of His majesty,
When He arises to shake the
earth mightily.

20 In that day a man will cast away
his idols of silver
And his idols of gold,
Which they made, *each* for
himself to worship,
To the moles and bats,

21 To go into the clefts of the rocks,
And into the crags of the rugged
rocks,
From the terror of the L ORD
And the glory of His majesty,

When He arises to shake the
earth mightily.

22 Sever yourselves from such a
man,
Whose breath *is* in his nostrils;
For of what account is he?

God's judgment on Judah

3 For behold, the Lord, the L ORD
of hosts,
Takes away from Jerusalem and
from Judah
The stock and the store,
The whole supply of bread and
the whole supply of water;

2 The mighty man and the man
of war,
The judge and the prophet,
And the diviner and the elder;

3 The captain of fifty and the
honorable man,
The counselor and the skillful
artisan,
And the expert enchanter.

4 "I will give children *to be* their
princes,
And babes shall rule over them.

5 The people will be oppressed,
Every one by another and every
one by his neighbor;
The child will be insolent toward
the elder,
And the base toward the
honorable."

6 When a man takes hold of his
brother
In the house of his father, *saying,*
"You have clothing;
You be our ruler,
And *let* these ruins *be* under
your power,"

7 In that day he will protest,
saying,
"I cannot cure *your* ills,
For in my house *is* neither food
nor clothing;
Do not make me a ruler of the
people."

8 For Jerusalem stumbled,
And Judah is fallen,

Because their tongue and their
doings
Are against the LORD,
To provoke the eyes of His
glory.

9 The look on their countenance
witnesses against them,
And they declare their sin as
Sodom;
They do not hide *it*.
Woe to their soul!
For they have brought evil upon
themselves.

10 "Say to the righteous that *it shall
be well with them,*
For they shall eat the fruit of their
doings.

11 Woe to the wicked! *It shall be
ill with him,*
For the reward of his hands shall
be given him.

12 *As for* My people, children *are*
their oppressors,
And women rule over them.
O My people! Those who lead
you cause *you* to err,
And destroy the way of your
paths."

13 The LORD stands up to plead,
And stands to judge the
people.

14 The LORD will enter into
judgment
With the elders of His people
And His princes:
"For you have eaten up the
vineyard;
The plunder of the poor *is* in
your houses.

15 What do you mean by crushing
My people
And grinding the faces of the
poor?"
Says the Lord GOD of hosts.

16 Moreover the LORD says:

"Because the daughters of Zion
are haughty,
And walk with outstretched
necks
And wanton eyes,

Walking and mincing *as* they go,
Making a jingling with their
feet,

17 Therefore the Lord will strike
with a scab
The crown of the head of the
daughters of Zion,
And the LORD will uncover their
secret parts."

18 In that day the Lord will take
away the finery:
The jingling anklets, the scarves,
and the crescents;

19 The pendants, the bracelets, and
the veils;

20 The headdresses, the leg
ornaments, and the
headbands;
The perfume boxes, the charms,

21 and the rings;
The nose jewels,

22 the festal apparel, and the
mantles;
The outer garments, the purses,

23 and the mirrors;
The fine linen, the turbans, and
the robes.

24 And so it shall be:

Instead of a sweet smell there
will be a stench;
Instead of a sash, a rope;
Instead of well-set hair,
baldness;
Instead of a rich robe, a girding
of sackcloth;
And branding instead of beauty.

25 Your men shall fall by the sword,
And your mighty in the war.

26 Her gates shall lament and
mourn,
And she *being* desolate shall sit
on the ground.

A glorious new city

4 And in that day seven women
shall take hold of one man,
saying,
"We will eat our own food and
wear our own apparel;

Only let us be called by your
name,
To take away our reproach."
2 In that day the **Branch of the
Lord** shall be beautiful and
glorious;
And the fruit of the earth *shall
be* excellent and appealing
For those of Israel who have
escaped.

³ And it shall come to pass that *he
who is* left in Zion and remains in Jerusalem will be called holy—everyone
who is recorded among the living in
Jerusalem. ⁴ When the Lord has
washed away the filth of the daughters
of Zion, and purged the blood of Jerusalem from her midst, by the spirit of
judgment and by the spirit of burning,
⁵ then the Lord will create above *every*
dwelling place of Mount Zion, and
above her assemblies, a cloud and
smoke by day and the shining of a
flaming fire by night. For over all the
glory there *will be* a covering. ⁶ And
there will be a tabernacle for shade in
the daytime from the heat, for a place
of refuge, and for a shelter from storm
and rain.

Wild grapes spoil the wine

5 Now let me sing to my
Well-beloved
A song of my Beloved regarding
His vineyard:

My Well-beloved has a vineyard
On a very fruitful hill.
2 He dug it up and cleared out its
stones,
And planted it with the choicest
vine.
He built a tower in its midst,
And also made a winepress in
it;

So He expected *it* to bring forth
good grapes,
But it brought forth wild grapes.

3 "And now, O inhabitants of
Jerusalem and men of Judah,
Judge, please, between Me and
My vineyard.
4 What more could have been
done to My vineyard
That I have not done in it?
Why then, when I expected *it*
to bring forth *good* grapes,
Did it bring forth wild grapes?
5 And now, please let Me tell you
what I will do to My vineyard:
I will take away its hedge, and
it shall be burned;
And break down its wall, and it
shall be trampled down.
6 I will lay it waste;
It shall not be pruned or dug,
But there shall come up briers
and thorns.
I will also command the clouds
That they rain no rain on it."

7 For the vineyard of the Lord of
hosts *is* the house of Israel,
And the men of Judah are His
pleasant plant.
He looked for justice, but
behold, oppression;
For righteousness, but behold, a
cry *for help.*

8 Woe to those who join house to
house;
They add field to field,
Till *there is* no place
Where they may dwell alone in
the midst of the land!
9 In my hearing the Lord of hosts
said,
"Truly, many houses shall be
desolate,
Great and beautiful ones,
without inhabitant.

WORDFINDER

4:2 Branch of the Lord   Used several times in the Old Testament as a title of
the coming Messiah, or Christ. Christ was a Branch coming from the family of King
David who lived a thousand years earlier.

10 For ten acres of vineyard shall
yield one bath,
And a homer of seed shall yield
one ephah."

11 Woe to those who rise early in
the morning,
That they may follow
intoxicating drink;
Who continue until night, *till*
wine inflames them!
12 The harp and the strings,
The tambourine and flute,
And wine are in their feasts;
But they do not regard the work
of the LORD,
Nor consider the operation of
His hands.

13 Therefore my people have gone
into captivity,
Because *they have* no
knowledge;
Their honorable men *are*
famished,
And their multitude dried up
with thirst.
14 Therefore Sheol has enlarged
itself
And opened its mouth beyond
measure;
Their glory and their multitude
and their pomp,
And he who is jubilant, shall
descend into it.
15 People shall be brought down,
Each man shall be humbled,
And the eyes of the lofty shall
be humbled.
16 But the LORD of hosts shall be
exalted in judgment,
And God who is holy shall be
hallowed in righteousness.
17 Then the lambs shall feed in
their pasture,
And in the waste places of the
fat ones strangers shall eat.

18 Woe to those who draw iniquity
with cords of vanity,
And sin as if with a cart rope;
19 That say, "Let Him make speed
and hasten His work,
That we may see *it;*

And let the counsel of the Holy
One of Israel draw near and
come,
That we may know *it.*"

20 Woe to those who call evil good,
and good evil;
Who put darkness for light, and
light for darkness;
Who put bitter for sweet, and
sweet for bitter!

21 Woe to *those who are* wise in
their own eyes,
And prudent in their own sight!

22 Woe to men mighty at drinking
wine,
Woe to men valiant for mixing
intoxicating drink,
23 Who justify the wicked for a
bribe,
And take away justice from the
righteous man!

24 Therefore, as the fire devours
the stubble,
And the flame consumes the
chaff,
So their root will be as
rottenness,
And their blossom will ascend
like dust;
Because they have rejected the
law of the LORD of hosts,
And despised the word of the
Holy One of Israel.
25 Therefore the anger of the
LORD is aroused against His
people;
He has stretched out His hand
against them
And stricken them,
And the hills trembled.
Their carcasses *were* as refuse
in the midst of the streets.

For all this His anger is not
turned away,
But His hand *is* stretched out
still.

26 He will lift up a banner to the
nations from afar,

Only let us be called by your
    name,
To take away our reproach."
2 In that day the **Branch of the
    Lord** shall be beautiful and
    glorious;
And the fruit of the earth *shall
    be* excellent and appealing
For those of Israel who have
    escaped.

3 And it shall come to pass that *he
who is* left in Zion and remains in Jerusalem will be called holy—everyone
who is recorded among the living in
Jerusalem. 4 When the Lord has
washed away the filth of the daughters
of Zion, and purged the blood of Jerusalem from her midst, by the spirit of
judgment and by the spirit of burning,
5 then the Lord will create above every
dwelling place of Mount Zion, and
above her assemblies, a cloud and
smoke by day and the shining of a
flaming fire by night. For over all the
glory there *will be* a covering. 6 And
there will be a tabernacle for shade in
the daytime from the heat, for a place
of refuge, and for a shelter from storm
and rain.

Wild grapes spoil the wine

5 Now let me sing to my
    Well-beloved
A song of my Beloved regarding
    His vineyard:

My Well-beloved has a vineyard
On a very fruitful hill.
2 He dug it up and cleared out its
    stones,
And planted it with the choicest
    vine.
He built a tower in its midst,
And also made a winepress in
    it;

So He expected *it* to bring forth
    good grapes,
But it brought forth wild grapes.

3 "And now, O inhabitants of
    Jerusalem and men of Judah,
Judge, please, between Me and
    My vineyard.
4 What more could have been
    done to My vineyard
That I have not done in it?
Why then, when I expected *it*
    to bring forth *good* grapes,
Did it bring forth wild grapes?
5 And now, please let Me tell you
    what I will do to My vineyard:
I will take away its hedge, and
    it shall be burned;
And break down its wall, and it
    shall be trampled down.
6 I will lay it waste;
It shall not be pruned or dug,
But there shall come up briers
    and thorns.
I will also command the clouds
That they rain no rain on it."

7 For the vineyard of the Lord of
    hosts *is* the house of Israel,
And the men of Judah are His
    pleasant plant.
He looked for justice, but
    behold, oppression;
For righteousness, but behold, a
    cry *for help*.

8 Woe to those who join house to
    house;
They add field to field,
Till *there is* no place
Where they may dwell alone in
    the midst of the land!
9 In my hearing the Lord of hosts
    said,
"Truly, many houses shall be
    desolate,
Great and beautiful ones,
    without inhabitant.

☉WORDFINDER

4:2 Branch of the Lord   Used several times in the Old Testament as a title of
the coming Messiah, or Christ. Christ was a Branch coming from the family of King
David who lived a thousand years earlier.

10 For ten acres of vineyard shall
    yield one bath,
And a homer of seed shall yield
    one ephah."

11 Woe to those who rise early in
    the morning,
That they may follow
    intoxicating drink;
Who continue until night, *till*
    wine inflames them!
12 The harp and the strings,
The tambourine and flute,
And wine are in their feasts;
But they do not regard the work
    of the LORD,
Nor consider the operation of
    His hands.

13 Therefore my people have gone
    into captivity,
Because *they have* no
    knowledge;
Their honorable men *are*
    famished,
And their multitude dried up
    with thirst.
14 Therefore Sheol has enlarged
    itself
And opened its mouth beyond
    measure;
Their glory and their multitude
    and their pomp,
And he who is jubilant, shall
    descend into it.
15 People shall be brought down,
Each man shall be humbled,
And the eyes of the lofty shall
    be humbled.
16 But the LORD of hosts shall be
    exalted in judgment,
And God who is holy shall be
    hallowed in righteousness.
17 Then the lambs shall feed in
    their pasture,
And in the waste places of the
    fat ones strangers shall eat.

18 Woe to those who draw iniquity
    with cords of vanity,
And sin as if with a cart rope;
19 That say, "Let Him make speed
    and hasten His work,
That we may *see it;*

And let the counsel of the Holy
    One of Israel draw near and
    come,
That we may know *it.*"

20 Woe to those who call evil good,
    and good evil;
Who put darkness for light, and
    light for darkness;
Who put bitter for sweet, and
    sweet for bitter!

21 Woe to *those who are* wise in
    their own eyes,
And prudent in their own sight!

22 Woe to men mighty at drinking
    wine,
Woe to men valiant for mixing
    intoxicating drink,
23 Who justify the wicked for a
    bribe,
And take away justice from the
    righteous man!

24 Therefore, as the fire devours
    the stubble,
And the flame consumes the
    chaff,
So their root will be as
    rottenness,
And their blossom will ascend
    like dust;
Because they have rejected the
    law of the LORD of hosts,
And despised the word of the
    Holy One of Israel.
25 Therefore the anger of the
    LORD is aroused against His
    people;
He has stretched out His hand
    against them
And stricken them,
And the hills trembled.
Their carcasses *were* as refuse
    in the midst of the streets.

For all this His anger is not
    turned away,
But His hand *is* stretched out
    still.

26 He will lift up a banner to the
    nations from afar,

What Isaiah Learned

Many people say I was one of the world's greatest poets. I could see and enjoy all the beautiful things God made. Because I was the king's cousin, I also had a lot of freedom to write and describe what I felt about my nation's failures and future.

Then one day something happened. I went into the temple—and there I saw the Lord Himself! He was on a high throne, surrounded by heavenly beings singing, "Holy! Holy! Holy!"

I had never seen such wonderful things. But I also saw what I was really like, and I felt like the worst sinner in the world.

The Lord forgave me and took away my sins. Now I'll spend the rest of my life praising His greatness!

And will whistle to them from the end of the earth;
Surely they shall come with speed, swiftly.

27 No one will be weary or stumble among them,
No one will slumber or sleep;
Nor will the belt on their loins be loosed,
Nor the strap of their sandals be broken;

28 Whose arrows *are* sharp,
And all their bows bent;
Their horses' hooves will seem like flint,
And their wheels like a whirlwind.

29 Their roaring *will be* like a lion,
They will roar like young lions;
Yes, they will roar
And lay hold of the prey;
They will carry *it* away safely,
And no one will deliver.

30 In that day they will roar against them
Like the roaring of the sea.
And if *one* looks to the land,
Behold, darkness *and* sorrow;
And the light is darkened by the clouds.

God calls Isaiah in a vision

6 In the year that King Uzziah died, I saw the Lord sitting on a throne, high and lifted up, and the train of His *robe* filled the **temple.** 2 Above it stood seraphim; each one had six wings: with two he covered his face, with two he covered his feet, and with two he flew. 3 And one cried to another and said:

"Holy, holy, holy *is* the LORD of hosts;
The whole earth *is* full of His glory!"

4 And the posts of the door were shaken by the voice of him who cried out, and the house was filled with smoke.

5 So I said:

"Woe *is* me, for I am undone!
Because I *am* a man of unclean lips,
And I dwell in the midst of a people of unclean lips;
For my eyes have seen the King, The LORD of hosts."

6 Then one of the seraphim flew to me, having in his hand a live coal

WORDFINDER

6:1 Temple Israel's place of worship after they settled in Canaan. It was a building of finished stone. Worship in the temple was the same as it had been in the tabernacle.

which he had taken with the tongs from the altar. ⁷And he touched my mouth *with it,* and said:

"Behold, this has touched your lips;
Your iniquity is taken away,
And your sin purged."

⁸Also I heard the voice of the Lord, saying:

"Whom shall I send,
And who will go for Us?"

Then I said, "Here *am* I! Send me." ⁹And He said, "Go, and tell this people:

'Keep on hearing, but do not understand;
Keep on seeing, but do not perceive.'

¹⁰ "Make the heart of this people dull,
And their ears heavy,
And shut their eyes;
Lest they see with their eyes,
And hear with their ears,
And understand with their heart,
And return and be healed."

¹¹ Then I said, "Lord, how long?" And He answered:

"Until the cities are laid waste and without inhabitant,
The houses are without a man,
The land is utterly desolate,
¹² The Lord has removed men far away,
And the forsaken places *are* many in the midst of the land.
¹³ But yet a tenth *will be* in it,
And will return and be for consuming,
As a terebinth tree or as an oak,
Whose stump *remains* when it is cut down.
So the holy seed *shall be* its stump."

God is with us

7 Now it came to pass in the days of Ahaz the son of Jotham, the son of Uzziah, king of Judah, *that* Rezin king of Syria and Pekah the son of Remaliah, king of Israel, went up to Jerusalem to *make* war against it, but could not prevail against it. ² And it was told to the house of David, saying, "Syria's forces are deployed in Ephraim." So his heart and the heart of his people were moved as the trees of the woods are moved with the wind.

³ Then the Lord said to Isaiah, "Go out now to meet Ahaz, you and Shear-Jashub your son, at the end of the aqueduct from the upper pool, on the highway to the Fuller's Field, ⁴ and say to him: 'Take heed, and be quiet; do not fear or be fainthearted for these two stubs of smoking firebrands, for the fierce anger of Rezin and Syria, and

---

What King Ahaz Learned

That prophet Isaiah really upsets me. He's always giving me news I don't want to hear.

The other day he came into my throne room babbling about a virgin's Son who was to be born. What really scared me was that he said the Baby's name would be "God-With-Us." The last thing I need is God coming down to live with us. I had enough trouble trying to keep that prophet off my back without having to listen to the Lord Himself!

Yes, this is bad news for me. I've given up on God. I'm worshiping false gods and even sacrificing my own children to them in fire. There is no hope for me. Pronounce my name *AY-haz,* meaning "He Has Grasped."

the son of Remaliah. 5 Because Syria, Ephraim, and the son of Remaliah have plotted evil against you, saying, 6 "Let us go up against Judah and trouble it, and let us make a gap in its wall for ourselves, and set a king over them, the son of Tabel"— 7 thus says the Lord GOD:

"It shall not stand,
Nor shall it come to pass.
8   For the head of Syria is
       Damascus,
     And the head of Damascus is
       Rezin.
     Within sixty-five years Ephraim
       will be broken,
     So that it will not be a people.
9   The head of Ephraim is Samaria,
     And the head of Samaria is
       Remaliah's son.
     If you will not believe,
     Surely you shall not be
       established.""'"

10 Moreover the LORD spoke again to Ahaz, saying, 11 "Ask a sign for yourself from the LORD your God; ask it either in the depth or in the height above."
12 But Ahaz said, "I will not ask, nor will I test the LORD!"
13 Then he said, "Hear now, O house of David! Is it a small thing for you to weary men, but will you weary my God also? 14 Therefore the Lord Himself will give you a sign: Behold, the virgin shall conceive and bear a Son, and shall call His name **Immanuel.** 15 Curds and honey He shall eat, that He may know to refuse the evil and choose the good. 16 For before the Child shall know to refuse the evil and choose the good, the land that you dread will be forsaken by both her kings. 17 The LORD will bring the king of Assyria upon you and your people and your father's house—days that

have not come since the day that Ephraim departed from Judah."

18 And it shall come to pass in that
      day
    That the LORD will whistle for the
      fly
    That is in the farthest part of the
      rivers of Egypt,
    And for the bee that is in the
      land of Assyria.
19 They will come, and all of them
      will rest
    In the desolate valleys and in the
      clefts of the rocks,
    And on all thorns and in all
      pastures.

20 In the same day the Lord will
      shave with a hired razor,
    With those from beyond the
      River, with the king of Assyria,
    The head and the hair of the
      legs,
    And will also remove the beard.

21 It shall be in that day
    That a man will keep alive a
      young cow and two sheep;
22 So it shall be, from the
      abundance of milk they give,
    That he will eat curds;
    For curds and honey everyone
      will eat who is left in the land.

23 It shall happen in that day,
    That wherever there could be a
      thousand vines
    Worth a thousand shekels of
      silver,
    It will be for briers and thorns.
24 With arrows and bows men will
      come there,
    Because all the land will become
      briers and thorns.

25 And to any hill which could be
      dug with the hoe,

WORDFINDER

7:14 Immanuel A Hebrew name meaning "God with us." The name refers to the coming Messiah, or Christ, in the New Testament. Jesus truly was and is "God with us."

You will not go there for fear of
   briers and thorns;
But it will become a range for
   oxen
And a place for sheep to roam.

Isaiah predicts the invasion of Assyria

8 Moreover the LORD said to me, "Take a large scroll, and write on it with a man's pen concerning Maher-Shalal-Hash-Baz. ² And I will take for Myself faithful witnesses to record, Uriah the priest and Zechariah the son of Jeberechiah."

³ Then I went to the prophetess, and she conceived and bore a son. Then the LORD said to me, "Call his name Maher-Shalal-Hash-Baz; ⁴ for before the child shall have knowledge to cry 'My father' and 'My mother,' the riches of Damascus and the spoil of Samaria will be taken away before the king of Assyria."

⁵ The LORD also spoke to me again, saying:

⁶   "Inasmuch as these people
     refused
    The waters of Shiloah that flow
     softly,
    And rejoice in Rezin and in
     Remaliah's son;
⁷   Now therefore, behold, the Lord
    brings up over them
    The waters of the River, strong
     and mighty—
    The king of Assyria and all his
     glory;
    He will go up over all his
     channels
    And go over all his banks.
⁸   He will pass through Judah,
    He will overflow and pass over,
    He will reach up to the neck;
    And the stretching out of his
     wings
    Will fill the breadth of Your land,
     O Immanuel.

⁹   "Be shattered, O you peoples,
    and be broken in pieces!

Give ear, all you from far
   countries.
Gird yourselves, but be broken
   in pieces;
Gird yourselves, but be broken
   in pieces.
¹⁰ Take counsel together, but it will
    come to nothing;
    Speak the word, but it will not
    stand,
    For God *is* with us."

¹¹ For the LORD spoke thus to me with a strong hand, and instructed me that I should not walk in the way of this people, saying:

¹² "Do not say, 'A conspiracy,'
    Concerning all that this people
     call a conspiracy,
    Nor be afraid of their threats, nor
     be troubled.
¹³ The LORD of hosts, Him you
    shall hallow;
    Let Him *be* your fear,
    And *let* Him *be* your dread.
¹⁴ He will be as a sanctuary,
    But a stone of stumbling and a
     rock of offense
    To both the houses of Israel,
    As a trap and a snare to the
     inhabitants of Jerusalem.
¹⁵ And many among them shall
    stumble;
    They shall fall and be broken,
    Be snared and taken."

¹⁶ Bind up the testimony,
    Seal the law among my
    disciples.
¹⁷ And I will wait on the LORD,
    Who hides His face from the
    house of Jacob;
    And I will hope in Him.
¹⁸ Here am I and the children
    whom the LORD has given me!
    We are for signs and wonders
     in Israel
    From the LORD of hosts,
    Who dwells in Mount Zion.

¹⁹ And when they say to you, "Seek those who are mediums and wizards, who whisper and mutter," should not

a people seek their God? *Should they seek* the dead on behalf of the living? ²⁰ To the law and to the testimony! If they do not speak according to this word, *it is* because *there is* no light in them.

²¹ They will pass through it hard-pressed and hungry; and it shall happen, when they are hungry, that they will be enraged and curse their king and their God, and look upward. ²² Then they will look to the earth, and see trouble and darkness, gloom of anguish; and *they will be* driven into darkness.

Isaiah predicts the Messiah's birth

9 Nevertheless the gloom *will* not
be upon her who *is* distressed,
As when at first He lightly
esteemed
The land of Zebulun and the
land of Naphtali,
And afterward more heavily
oppressed *her,*
By the way of the sea, beyond
the Jordan,
In Galilee of the Gentiles.
² The people who walked in
darkness
Have seen a great light;
Those who dwelt in the land of
the shadow of death,
Upon them a light has shined.

³ You have multiplied the nation
And increased its joy;
They rejoice before You
According to the joy of harvest,
As *men* rejoice when they divide
the spoil.
⁴ For You have broken the yoke
of his burden
And the staff of his shoulder,
The rod of his oppressor,
As in the day of Midian.
⁵ For *every* warrior's sandal from
the noisy battle,
And garments rolled in blood,
Will be used for burning *and* fuel
of fire.

⁶ For unto us a Child is born,
Unto us a Son is given;

Who Is Jesus?

Sometimes people think Jesus was just a very good man. You have to remember that the baby Jesus, who was born at Bethlehem, also lives forever in heaven as God. God caused Himself to be born into our world as Jesus of Nazareth. Jesus is God, the everlasting Son of the everlasting Father.

And the government will be
upon His shoulder.
And His name will be called
Wonderful, Counselor, Mighty
God,
Everlasting Father, Prince of
Peace.
⁷ Of the increase of *His*
government and peace
There will be no end,
Upon the throne of David and
over His kingdom,
To order it and establish it with
judgment and justice
From that time forward, *even*
forever.
The zeal of the LORD of hosts
will perform this.

⁸ The Lord sent a word against
Jacob,
And it has fallen on Israel.
⁹ All the people will know—
Ephraim and the inhabitant of
Samaria—
Who say in pride and arrogance
of heart:
¹⁰ "The bricks have fallen down,
But we will rebuild with hewn
stones;
The sycamores are cut down,
But we will replace *them* with
cedars."
¹¹ Therefore the LORD shall set up
The adversaries of Rezin against
him,
And spur his enemies on,
¹² The Syrians before and the
Philistines behind;
And they shall devour Israel with
an open mouth.

For all this His anger is not
 turned away,
But His hand *is* stretched out
 still.

13 For the people do not turn to
 Him who strikes them,
Nor do they seek the Lord of
 hosts.
14 Therefore the Lord will cut off
 head and tail from Israel,
Palm branch and bulrush in one
 day.
15 The elder and honorable, he *is*
 the head;
The prophet who teaches lies,
 he *is* the tail.
16 For the leaders of this people
 cause *them* to err,
And *those who are* led by them
 are destroyed.
17 Therefore the Lord will have no
 joy in their young men,
Nor have mercy on their
 fatherless and widows;
For everyone *is* a **hypocrite** and
 an evildoer,
And *every* mouth speaks folly.

For all this His anger is not
 turned away,
But His hand *is* stretched out
 still.

18 For wickedness burns as the fire;
It shall devour the briers and
 thorns,
And kindle in the thickets of the
 forest;
They shall mount up *like* rising
 smoke.
19 Through the wrath of the Lord
 of hosts
The land is burned up,
And the people shall be as fuel
 for the fire;
No man shall spare his brother.
20 And he shall snatch on the right
 hand

And be hungry;
He shall devour on the left hand
And not be satisfied;
Every man shall eat the flesh of
 his own arm.
21 Manasseh *shall devour* Ephraim,
 and Ephraim Manasseh;
Together they *shall be* against
 Judah.

For all this His anger is not
 turned away,
But His hand *is* stretched out
 still.

God will never forsake His people

10 "Woe to those who decree
 unrighteous decrees,
Who write misfortune,
Which they have prescribed
2 To rob the needy of justice,
And to take what is right from
 the poor of My people,
That widows may be their prey,
And *that* they may rob the
 fatherless.
3 What will you do in the day of
 punishment,
And in the desolation *which* will
 come from afar?
To whom will you flee for
 help?
And where will you leave your
 glory?
4 Without Me they shall bow
 down among the prisoners,
And they shall fall among the
 slain."

For all this His anger is not
 turned away,
But His hand *is* stretched out
 still.

5 "Woe to Assyria, the rod of My
 anger
And the staff in whose hand is
 My indignation.

WORDFINDER

9:17 Hypocrite Pronounced *HIP-puh-krit.* A person who pretends to be good or
godly, but who actually is not. Jesus later condemned hypocrites most of all.

6 I will send him against an
      ungodly nation,
   And against the people of My
      wrath
   I will give him charge,
   To seize the spoil, to take the
      prey,
   And to tread them down like the
      mire of the streets.
7 Yet he does not mean so,
   Nor does his heart think so;
   But *it is* in his heart to destroy,
   And cut off not a few nations.
8 For he says,
   'Are not my princes altogether
      kings?
9 *Is* not Calno like Carchemish?
   Is not Hamath like Arpad?
   Is not Samaria like Damascus?
10 As my hand has found the
      kingdoms of the idols,
   Whose carved images excelled
      those of Jerusalem and
      Samaria,
11 As I have done to Samaria and
      her idols,
   Shall I not do also to Jerusalem
      and her idols?' "

12 Therefore it shall come to pass,
when the Lord has performed all His
work on Mount Zion and on Jerusalem, *that He will say,* "I will punish
the fruit of the arrogant heart of the
king of Assyria, and the glory of his
haughty looks."
13 For he says:

   "By the strength of my hand I
      have done *it,*
   And by my wisdom, for I am
      prudent;
   Also I have removed the
      boundaries of the people,
   And have robbed their
      treasuries;
   So I have put down the
      inhabitants like a valiant
      man.
14 My hand has found like a nest
      the riches of the people,
   And as one gathers eggs *that are*
      left,
   I have gathered all the earth;

   And there was no one who
      moved *his* wing,
   Nor opened *his* mouth with even
      a peep."
15 Shall the ax boast itself against
      him who chops with it?
   Or shall the saw exalt itself
      against him who saws with it?
   As if a rod could wield *itself*
      against those who lift it up,
   Or as if a staff could lift up, *as
      if it were* not wood!
16 Therefore the Lord, the Lord of
      hosts,
   Will send leanness among his fat
      ones;
   And under his glory
   He will kindle a burning
   Like the burning of a fire.
17 So the Light of Israel will be for
      a fire,
   And his Holy One for a flame;
   It will burn and devour
   His thorns and his briers in one
      day.
18 And it will consume the glory of
      his forest and of his fruitful
      field,
   Both soul and body;
   And they will be as when a sick
      man wastes away.
19 Then the rest of the trees of his
      forest
   Will be so few in number
   That a child may write them.

20 And it shall come to pass in that
      day
   That the remnant of Israel,
   And such as have escaped of the
      house of Jacob,
   Will never again depend on him
      who defeated them,
   But will depend on the LORD,
      the Holy One of Israel, in
      truth.
21 The remnant will return, the
      remnant of Jacob,
   To the Mighty God.
22 For though your people, O
      Israel, be as the sand of the
      sea,
   A remnant of them will return;

The destruction decreed shall
overflow with righteousness.
23 For the Lord GOD of hosts
Will make a determined end
In the midst of all the land.

24 Therefore thus says the Lord GOD
of hosts: "O My people, who dwell in
Zion, do not be afraid of the Assyrian.
He shall strike you with a rod and lift
up his staff against you, in the manner
of Egypt. 25 For yet a very little while
and the indignation will cease, as will
My anger in their destruction." 26 And
the LORD of hosts will stir up a scourge
for him like the slaughter of Midian at
the rock of Oreb; as His rod was on
the sea, so will He lift it up in the manner of Egypt.

27 It shall come to pass in that day
That his burden will be taken
away from your shoulder,
And his yoke from your neck,
And the yoke will be destroyed
because of the anointing oil.
28 He has come to Aiath,
He has passed Migron;
At Michmash he has attended to
his equipment.
29 They have gone along the
ridge,
They have taken up lodging at
Geba.
Ramah is afraid,
Gibeah of Saul has fled.
30 Lift up your voice,
O daughter of Gallim!
Cause it to be heard as far as
Laish—
O poor Anathoth!
31 Madmenah has fled,
The inhabitants of Gebim seek
refuge.
32 As yet he will remain at Nob that
day;
He will shake his fist at the
mount of the daughter of
Zion,
The hill of Jerusalem.
33 Behold, the Lord,
The LORD of hosts,

Will lop off the bough with
terror;
Those of high stature *will be*
hewn down,
And the haughty will be
humbled.
34 He will cut down the thickets of
the forest with iron,
And Lebanon will fall by the
Mighty One.

When the Messiah comes

11 There shall come forth a Rod
from the stem of Jesse,
And a Branch shall grow out of
his roots.
2 The Spirit of the LORD shall rest
upon Him,
The Spirit of wisdom and
understanding,
The Spirit of counsel and might,
The Spirit of knowledge and of
the fear of the LORD.

3 His delight *is* in the fear of the
LORD,
And He shall not judge by the
sight of His eyes,
Nor decide by the hearing of His
ears;
4 But with righteousness He shall
judge the poor,
And decide with equity for the
meek of the earth;
He shall strike the earth with the
rod of His mouth,
And with the breath of His lips
He shall slay the wicked.
5 Righteousness shall be the belt
of His loins,
And faithfulness the belt of His
waist.

6 "The wolf also shall dwell with the
lamb,
The leopard shall lie down with
the young goat,
The calf and the young lion and
the fatling together;
And a little child shall lead them.
7 The cow and the bear shall
graze;

Their young ones shall lie down
   together;
And the lion shall eat straw like
   the ox.

8 The nursing child shall play by
   the cobra's hole,
And the weaned child shall put
   his hand in the viper's den.

9 They shall not hurt nor destroy
   in all My holy mountain,
For the earth shall be full of the
   knowledge of the LORD
As the waters cover the sea.

10 "And in that day there shall be a
   Root of Jesse,
Who shall stand as a banner to
   the people;
For the Gentiles shall seek Him,
And His resting place shall be
   glorious."

11 It shall come to pass in that
   day
That the Lord shall set His hand
   again the second time
To recover the remnant of His
   people who are left,
From Assyria and Egypt,
From Pathros and Cush,
From Elam and Shinar,
From Hamath and the islands of
   the sea.

12 He will set up a banner for the
   nations,
And will assemble the outcasts
   of Israel,
And gather together the
   dispersed of Judah
From the four corners of the
   earth.

13 Also the envy of Ephraim shall
   depart,
And the adversaries of Judah
   shall be cut off;
Ephraim shall not envy Judah,
And Judah shall not harass
   Ephraim.

14 But they shall fly down upon the
   shoulder of the Philistines
   toward the west;
Together they shall plunder the
   people of the East;

They shall lay their hand on
   Edom and Moab;
And the people of Ammon shall
   obey them.

15 The LORD will utterly destroy the
   tongue of the Sea of Egypt;
With His mighty wind He will
   shake His fist over the River,
And strike it in the seven
   streams,
And make *men* cross over
   dryshod.

16 There will be a highway for the
   remnant of His people
Who will be left from Assyria,
As it was for Israel
In the day that he came up from
   the land of Egypt.

A song of thanksgiving

12 And in that day you will say:

"O LORD, I will praise You;
Though You were angry with
   me,
Your anger is turned away, and
   You comfort me.

2 Behold, God *is* my salvation,
I will trust and not be afraid;
'For YAH, the LORD, *is* my
   strength and song;
He also has become my
   salvation.' "

3 Therefore with joy you will draw
   water
From the wells of salvation.

4 And in that day you will say:

"Praise the LORD, call upon His
   name;
Declare His deeds among the
   peoples,
Make mention that His name is
   exalted.

5 Sing to the LORD,
For He has done excellent
   things;
This *is* known in all the earth.

6 Cry out and shout, O inhabitant
   of Zion,

For great is the Holy One of
Israel in your midst!''

Babylon is doomed

13 The burden against Babylon
which Isaiah the son of Amoz saw.

2 "Lift up a banner on the high
    mountain,
Raise your voice to them;
Wave your hand, that they may
    enter the gates of the nobles.
3 I have commanded My
    sanctified ones;
I have also called My mighty
    ones for My anger—
Those who rejoice in My
    exaltation.''

4 The noise of a multitude in the
    mountains,
Like that of many people!
A tumultuous noise of the
    kingdoms of nations gathered
    together!
The LORD of hosts musters
The army for battle.
5 They come from a far country,
From the end of heaven—
The LORD and His weapons of
    indignation,
To destroy the whole land.

6 Wail, for the day of the LORD is
    at hand!
It will come as destruction from
    the Almighty.
7 Therefore all hands will be limp,
Every man's heart will melt,
8 And they will be afraid.
Pangs and sorrows will take hold
    of them;
They will be in pain as a woman
    in childbirth;
They will be amazed at one
    another;
Their faces will be like flames.

9 Behold, the day of the LORD
    comes,
Cruel, with both wrath and fierce
    anger,
To lay the land desolate;

And He will destroy its sinners
    from it.
10 For the stars of heaven and their
    constellations
Will not give their light;
The sun will be darkened in its
    going forth,
And the moon will not cause its
    light to shine.

11 "I will punish the world for its evil,
And the wicked for their iniquity;
I will halt the arrogance of the
    proud,
And will lay low the haughtiness
    of the terrible.
12 I will make a mortal more rare
    than fine gold,
A man more than the golden
    wedge of Ophir.
13 Therefore I will shake the
    heavens,
And the earth will move out of
    her place,
In the wrath of the LORD of hosts
And in the day of His fierce
    anger.
14 It shall be as the hunted gazelle,
And as a sheep that no man
    takes up;
Every man will turn to his own
    people,
And everyone will flee to his
    own land.
15 Everyone who is found will be
    thrust through,
And everyone who is captured
    will fall by the sword.
16 Their children also will be
    dashed to pieces before their
    eyes;
Their houses will be plundered
And their wives ravished.

17 "Behold, I will stir up the Medes
    against them,
Who will not regard silver;
And as for gold, they will not
    delight in it.
18 Also their bows will dash the
    young men to pieces,
And they will have no pity on
    the fruit of the womb;
Their eye will not spare children.

19 And Babylon, the glory of
kingdoms,
The beauty of the Chaldeans'
pride,
Will be as when God overthrew
Sodom and Gomorrah.
20 It will never be inhabited,
Nor will it be settled from
generation to generation;
Nor will the Arabian pitch tents
there,
Nor will the shepherds make
their sheepfolds there.
21 But wild beasts of the desert will
lie there,
And their houses will be full of
owls;
Ostriches will dwell there,
And wild goats will caper there.
22 The hyenas will howl in their
citadels,
And jackals in their pleasant
palaces.
Her time is near to come,
And her days will not be
prolonged."

How God will punish
the Babylonians

14 For the Lord will have mercy on
Jacob, and will still choose Israel, and
settle them in their own land. The
strangers will be joined with them, and
they will cling to the house of Jacob.
2 Then people will take them and bring
them to their place, and the house of
Israel will possess them for servants
and maids in the land of the Lord; they
will take them captive whose captives
they were, and rule over their oppressors.
3 It shall come to pass in the day the
Lord gives you rest from your sorrow,
and from your fear and the hard bondage in which you were made to serve,
4 that you will take up this proverb
against the king of Babylon, and say:

"How the oppressor has ceased,
The golden city ceased!
5 The Lord has broken the staff
of the wicked,
The scepter of the rulers;

6 He who struck the people in
wrath with a continual stroke,
He who ruled the nations in
anger,
Is persecuted and no one
hinders.
7 The whole earth is at rest and
quiet;
They break forth into singing.
8 Indeed the cypress trees rejoice
over you,
And the cedars of Lebanon,
Saying, 'Since you were cut
down,
No woodsman has come up
against us.'

9 "Hell from beneath is excited
about you,
To meet you at your coming;
It stirs up the dead for you,
All the chief ones of the earth;
It has raised up from their
thrones
All the kings of the nations.
10 They all shall speak and say to
you:
'Have you also become as weak
as we?
Have you become like us?
11 Your pomp is brought down to
Sheol,
And the sound of your stringed
instruments;
The maggot is spread under
you,
And worms cover you.'

12 "How you are fallen from
heaven,
O Lucifer, son of the morning!
How you are cut down to the
ground,

Who Is Lucifer?

Lucifer is another name for Satan, the
Devil. Satan was not always an evil
being. Once he was a favorite angel
of God, but he began to want to be
equal with God. That was foolish and
it was impossible. This is the way Satan became God's enemy.

You who weakened the nations!
13 For you have said in your heart:
'I will ascend into heaven,
I will exalt my throne above the
stars of God;
I will also sit on the mount of
the congregation
On the farthest sides of the
north;
14 I will ascend above the heights
of the clouds,
I will be like the Most High.'
15 Yet you shall be brought down
to Sheol,
To the lowest depths of the Pit.

16 "Those who see you will gaze at
you,
And consider you, *saying:*
'Is this the man who made the
earth tremble,
Who shook kingdoms,
17 Who made the world as a
wilderness
And destroyed its cities,
Who did not open the house of
his prisoners?'

18 "All the kings of the nations,
All of them, sleep in glory,
Everyone in his own house;
19 But you are cast out of your
grave
Like an abominable branch,
Like the garment of those who
are slain,
Thrust through with a sword,
Who go down to the stones of
the pit,
Like a corpse trodden
underfoot.
20 You will not be joined with them
in burial,
Because you have destroyed
your land
And slain your people.
The brood of evildoers shall
never be named.
21 Prepare slaughter for his
children
Because of the iniquity of their
fathers,
Lest they rise up and possess the
land,

And fill the face of the world with
cities."

22 "For I will rise up against them,"
says the LORD of hosts,
"And cut off from Babylon the
name and remnant,
And offspring and posterity,"
says the LORD.
23 "I will also make it a possession
for the porcupine,
And marshes of muddy water;
I will sweep it with the broom
of destruction," says the LORD
of hosts.

24 The LORD of hosts has sworn,
saying,
"Surely, as I have thought, so it
shall come to pass,
And as I have purposed, *so* it
shall stand:
25 That I will break the Assyrian in
My land,
And on My mountains tread him
underfoot.
Then his yoke shall be removed
from them,
And his burden removed from
their shoulders.
26 This *is* the purpose that is
purposed against the whole
earth,
And this *is* the hand that is
stretched out over all the
nations.
27 For the LORD of hosts has
purposed,
And who will annul *it?*
His hand *is* stretched out,
And who will turn it back?"

28 This is the burden which came in
the year that King Ahaz died.

29 "Do not rejoice, all you of
Philistia,
Because the rod that struck you
is broken;
For out of the serpent's roots will
come forth a viper,
And its offspring *will be* a fiery
flying serpent.

30 The firstborn of the poor will
 feed,
 And the needy will lie down in
  safety;
 I will kill your roots with famine,
 And it will slay your remnant.
31 Wail, O gate! Cry, O city!
 All you of Philistia *are* dissolved;
 For smoke will come from the
  north,
 And no one *will be* alone in his
  appointed times."

32 What will they answer the
  messengers of the nation?
 That the Lord has founded
  Zion,
 And the poor of His people shall
  take refuge in it.

Moab's days are numbered

15 The burden against Moab.

 Because in the night Ar of Moab
  is laid waste
 And destroyed,
 Because in the night Kir of Moab
  is laid waste
 And destroyed,
2 He has gone up to the temple
  and Dibon,
 To the high places to weep.
 Moab will wail over Nebo and
  over Medeba;
 On all their heads *will be*
  baldness,
 And every beard cut off.
3 In their streets they will clothe
  themselves with sackcloth;
 On the tops of their houses
 And in their streets
 Everyone will wail, weeping
  bitterly.
4 Heshbon and Elealeh will cry
  out,
 Their voice shall be heard as far
  as Jahaz;
 Therefore the armed soldiers of
  Moab will cry out;
 His life will be burdensome to
  him.
5 "My heart will cry out for Moab;
 His fugitives *shall flee* to Zoar,

Like a three-year-old heifer.
 For by the Ascent of Luhith
 They will go up with weeping;
 For in the way of Horonaim
 They will raise up a cry of
  destruction,
6 For the waters of Nimrim will be
  desolate,
 For the green grass has withered
  away;
 The grass fails, there is nothing
  green.
7 Therefore the abundance they
  have gained,
 And what they have laid up,
 They will carry away to the
  Brook of the Willows.
8 For the cry has gone all around
  the borders of Moab,
 Its wailing to Eglaim
 And its wailing to Beer Elim.
9 For the waters of Dimon will be
  full of blood;
 Because I will bring more upon
  Dimon,
 Lions upon him who escapes
  from Moab,
 And on the remnant of the
  land."

How God will punish the Moabites

16 Send the lamb to the ruler of
  the land,
 From Sela to the wilderness,
 To the mount of the daughter
  of Zion.
2 For it shall be as a wandering
  bird thrown out of the nest;
 So shall be the daughters of
  Moab at the fords of the
  Arnon.

3 "Take counsel, execute
  judgment;
 Make your shadow like the night
  in the middle of the day;
 Hide the outcasts,
 Do not betray him who escapes.
4 Let My outcasts dwell with you,
  O Moab;
 Be a shelter to them from the
  face of the spoiler.

For the extortioner is at an end,
Devastation ceases,
The oppressors are consumed
   out of the land.
5 In mercy the throne will be
   established;
And One will sit on it in truth,
   in the tabernacle of David,
Judging and seeking justice and
   hastening righteousness."

6 We have heard of the pride of
   Moab—
He is very proud—
Of his haughtiness and his pride
   and his wrath;
But his lies *shall* not *be* so.
7 Therefore Moab shall wail for
   Moab;
Everyone shall wail.
For the foundations of Kir
   Hareseth you shall mourn;
Surely *they are* stricken.

8 For the fields of Heshbon
   languish,
And the vine of Sibmah;
The lords of the nations have
   broken down its choice plants,
Which have reached to Jazer
And wandered through the
   wilderness.
Her branches are stretched out,
They are gone over the sea.
9 Therefore I will bewail the vine
   of Sibmah,
With the weeping of Jazer;
I will drench you with my tears,
O Heshbon and Elealeh;
For battle cries have fallen
Over your summer fruits and
   your harvest.

10 Gladness is taken away,
And joy from the plentiful field;
In the vineyards there will be no
   singing,
Nor will there be shouting;
No treaders will tread out wine
   in the presses;
I have made their shouting
   cease.
11 Therefore my heart shall
   resound like a harp for Moab,

And my inner being for Kir
   Heres.

12 And it shall come to pass,
When it is seen that Moab is
   weary on the high place,
That he will come to his
   sanctuary to pray;
But he will not prevail.

13 This *is* the word which the LORD has spoken concerning Moab since that time. 14 But now the LORD has spoken, saying, "Within three years, as the years of a hired man, the glory of Moab will be despised with all that great multitude, and the remnant *will be* very small *and* feeble."

How God will punish the Syrians

17 The burden against Damascus.

"Behold, Damascus will cease
   from *being* a city,
And it will be a ruinous heap.
2 The cities of Aroer *are* forsaken;
They will be for flocks
Which lie down, and no one will
   make *them* afraid.
3 The fortress also will cease from
   Ephraim,
The kingdom from Damascus,
And the remnant of Syria;
They will be as the glory of the
   children of Israel,"
Says the LORD of hosts.

4 "In that day it shall come to pass
That the glory of Jacob will
   wane,
And the fatness of his flesh grow
   lean.
5 It shall be as when the harvester
   gathers the grain,
And reaps the heads with his
   arm;
It shall be as he who gathers
   heads of grain
In the Valley of Rephaim.
6 Yet gleaning grapes will be left
   in it,
Like the shaking of an olive tree,

Two *or* three olives at the top
 of the uppermost bough,
Four *or* five in its most fruitful
 branches,"
Says the LORD God of Israel.

7 In that day a man will look to
 his Maker,
And his eyes will have respect
 for the Holy One of Israel.
8 He will not look to the altars,
The work of his hands;
He will not respect what his
 fingers have made,
Nor the wooden images nor the
 incense altars.

9 In that day his strong cities will
 be as a forsaken bough
And an uppermost branch,
Which they left because of the
 children of Israel;
And there will be desolation.

10 Because you have forgotten the
 God of your salvation,
And have not been mindful of
 the Rock of your stronghold,
Therefore you will plant pleasant
 plants
And set out foreign seedlings;
11 In the day you will make your
 plant to grow,
And in the morning you will
 make your seed to flourish;
But the harvest *will be* a heap
 of ruins
In the day of grief and desperate
 sorrow.

12 Woe to the multitude of many
 people
Who make a noise like the roar
 of the seas,
And to the rushing of nations
That make a rushing like the
 rushing of mighty waters!
13 The nations will rush like the
 rushing of many waters;
But *God* will rebuke them and
 they will flee far away,
And be chased like the chaff of
 the mountains before the
 wind,

Like a rolling thing before the
 whirlwind.
14 Then behold, at eventide,
 trouble!
And before the morning, he *is*
 no more.
This *is* the portion of those who
 plunder us,
And the lot of those who rob us.

How God will punish
the Ethiopians

18 Woe to the land shadowed with
 buzzing wings,
Which *is* beyond the rivers of
 Ethiopia,
2 Which sends ambassadors by
 sea,
Even in vessels of reed on the
 waters, *saying,*
"Go, swift messengers, to a
 nation tall and smooth *of skin,*
To a people terrible from their
 beginning onward,
A nation powerful and treading
 down,
Whose land the rivers divide."

3 All inhabitants of the world and
 dwellers on the earth:
When he lifts up a banner on
 the mountains, you see *it;*
And when he blows a trumpet,
 you hear *it.*
4 For so the LORD said to me,
"I will take My rest,
And I will look from My dwelling
 place
Like clear heat in sunshine,
Like a cloud of dew in the heat
 of harvest."
5 For before the harvest, when the
 bud is perfect
And the sour grape is ripening
 in the flower,
He will both cut off the sprigs
 with pruning hooks
And take away *and* cut down the
 branches.
6 They will be left together for the
 mountain birds of prey
And for the beasts of the earth;

The birds of prey will summer
  on them,
And all the beasts of the earth
  will winter on them.

7 In that time a present will be
   brought to the LORD of hosts
From a people tall and smooth
  of skin,
And from a people terrible from
  their beginning onward,
A nation powerful and treading
  down,
Whose land the rivers divide—
To the place of the name of the
  LORD of hosts,
To Mount Zion.

How God will punish the Egyptians

19 The burden against Egypt.

Behold, the LORD rides on a swift
  cloud,
And will come into Egypt;
The idols of Egypt will totter at
  His presence,
And the heart of Egypt will melt
  in its midst.

2 "I will set Egyptians against
   Egyptians;
Everyone will fight against his
  brother,
And everyone against his
  neighbor,
City against city, kingdom
  against kingdom.
3 The spirit of Egypt will fail in its
   midst;
I will destroy their counsel,
And they will consult the idols
  and the charmers,
The mediums and the sorcerers.
4 And the Egyptians I will give
   Into the hand of a cruel
   master,

And a fierce king will rule over
  them,"
Says the Lord, the LORD of
  hosts.

5 The waters will fail from the sea,
And the river will be wasted and
  dried up.
6 The rivers will turn foul;
The brooks of defense will be
  emptied and dried up;
The reeds and rushes will
  wither.
7 The **papyrus** reeds by the River,
  by the mouth of the River,
And everything sown by the
  River,
Will wither, be driven away, and
  be no more.
8 The fishermen also will mourn;
All those will lament who cast
  hooks into the River,
And they will languish who
  spread nets on the waters.
9 Moreover those who work in
  fine flax
And those who weave fine fabric
  will be ashamed;
10 And its foundations will be
   broken.
All who make wages *will be*
  troubled of soul.

11 Surely the princes of Zoan *are*
   fools;
Pharaoh's wise counselors give
  foolish counsel.
How do you say to Pharaoh, "I
  am the son of the wise,
The son of ancient kings?"
12 Where *are* they?
Where are your wise men?
Let them tell you now,
And let them know what the
  LORD of hosts has purposed
  against Egypt.
13 The princes of Zoan have
   become fools;

19:7 Papyrus Pronounced *puh-PIE-rus.* A reed that grows in northern Africa and southern Europe. In ancient times, these reeds were cut and pressed chiefly to make a kind of writing paper.

The princes of Noph are
deceived;
They have also deluded Egypt,
Those who are the mainstay of
its tribes.
14 The Lᴏʀᴅ has mingled a
perverse spirit in her midst;
And they have caused Egypt to
err in all her work,
As a drunken man staggers in
his vomit.
15 Neither will there be *any* work
for Egypt,
Which the head or tail,
Palm branch or bulrush, may
do.

16 In that day Egypt will be like women, and will be afraid and fear because of the waving of the hand of the Lᴏʀᴅ of hosts, which He waves over it. 17 And the land of Judah will be a terror to Egypt; everyone who makes mention of it will be afraid in himself, because of the counsel of the Lᴏʀᴅ of hosts which He has determined against it.

18 In that day five cities in the land of Egypt will speak the language of Canaan and swear by the Lᴏʀᴅ of hosts; one will be called the City of Destruction.

19 In that day there will be an altar to the Lᴏʀᴅ in the midst of the land of Egypt, and a pillar to the Lᴏʀᴅ at its border. 20 And it will be for a sign and for a witness to the Lᴏʀᴅ of hosts in the land of Egypt; for they will cry to the Lᴏʀᴅ because of the oppressors, and He will send them a Savior and a Mighty One, and He will deliver them. 21 Then the Lᴏʀᴅ will be known to Egypt, and the Egyptians will know the Lᴏʀᴅ in that day, and will make sacrifice and offering; yes, they will make a vow to the Lᴏʀᴅ and perform *it*. 22 And the Lᴏʀᴅ will strike Egypt, He will strike and heal *it;* they will return to the Lᴏʀᴅ, and He will be entreated by them and heal them.

23 In that day there will be a highway from Egypt to Assyria, and the Assyrian will come into Egypt and the Egyptian into Assyria, and the Egyptians will serve with the Assyrians.

24 In that day Israel will be one of three with Egypt and Assyria—a blessing in the midst of the land, 25 whom the Lᴏʀᴅ of hosts shall bless, saying, "Blessed *is* Egypt My people, and Assyria the work of My hands, and Israel My inheritance."

Isaiah goes barefoot

20 In the year that Tartan came to Ashdod, when Sargon the king of Assyria sent him, and he fought against Ashdod and took it, 2 at the same time the Lᴏʀᴅ spoke by Isaiah the son of Amoz, saying, "Go, and remove the sackcloth from your body, and take your sandals off your feet." And he did so, walking naked and barefoot.

3 Then the Lᴏʀᴅ said, "Just as My servant Isaiah has walked naked and barefoot three years *for* a sign and a wonder against Egypt and Ethiopia, 4 so shall the king of Assyria lead away the Egyptians as prisoners and the Ethiopians as captives, young and old, naked and barefoot, with their buttocks uncovered, to the shame of Egypt. 5 Then they shall be afraid and ashamed of Ethiopia their expectation

King Sargon II of Assyria.

and Egypt their glory. 6 And the inhabitant of this territory will say in that day, 'Surely such *is* our expectation, wherever we flee for help to be delivered from the king of Assyria; and how shall we escape?' "

Isaiah predicts the fall of Babylon

21 The burden against the Wilderness of the Sea.

As whirlwinds in the South pass
    through,
So it comes from the desert,
    from a terrible land.
2 A distressing vision is declared
    to me;
The treacherous dealer deals
    treacherously,
And the plunderer plunders.
Go up, O Elam!
Besiege, O Media!
All its sighing I have made to
    cease.

3 Therefore my loins are filled with
    pain;
Pangs have taken hold of me,
    like the pangs of a woman in
    labor.
I was distressed when *I* heard *it*;
I was dismayed when *I* saw *it*.
4 My heart wavered, fearfulness
    frightened me;
The night for which I longed He
    turned into fear for me.
5 Prepare the table,
Set a watchman in the tower,
Eat and drink.
Arise, you princes,
Anoint the shield!

6 For thus has the Lord said to
    me:
"Go, set a watchman,
Let him declare what he *sees*."
7 And he saw a chariot *with* a pair
    of horsemen,
A chariot of donkeys, *and* a
    chariot of camels,
And he listened earnestly with
    great care.
8 Then he cried, "A lion, my Lord!

I stand continually on the
    watchtower in the daytime;
I have sat at my post every night.
9 And look, here comes a chariot
    of men *with* a pair of
    horsemen!"
Then he answered and said,
"Babylon is fallen, is fallen!
And all the carved images of her
    gods
He has broken to the ground."

10 Oh, my threshing and the grain
    of my floor!
That which I have heard from
    the LORD of hosts,
The God of Israel,
I have declared to you.

11 The burden against Dumah.

He calls to me out of Seir,
"Watchman, what of the night?
Watchman, what of the night?"
12 The watchman said,
"The morning comes, and also
    the night.
If you will inquire, inquire;
Return! Come back!"

13 The burden against Arabia.

In the forest in Arabia you will
    lodge,
O you traveling companies of
    Dedanites.
14 O inhabitants of the land of
    Tema,
Bring water to him who is thirsty;
With their bread they met him
    who fled.
15 For they fled from the swords,
    from the drawn sword,
From the bent bow, and from
    the distress of war.

16 For thus the LORD has said to me: "Within a year, according to the year of a hired man, all the glory of Kedar will fail; 17 and the remainder of the number of archers, the mighty men of the people of Kedar, will be diminished; for the LORD God of Israel has spoken *it*."

Isaiah predicts Jerusalem's downfall

22 The burden against the Valley of Vision.

What ails you now, that you
  have all gone up to the
  housetops,
2 You who are full of noise,
A tumultuous city, a joyous
  city?
Your slain *men are* not slain with
  the sword,
Nor dead in battle.
3 All your rulers have fled
  together;
They are captured by the
  archers.
All who are found in you are
  bound together;
They have fled from afar.
4 Therefore I said, "Look away
  from me,
I will weep bitterly;
Do not labor to comfort me
Because of the plundering of the
  daughter of my people."

5 For *it is* a day of trouble and
  treading down and perplexity
By the Lord GOD of hosts
In the Valley of Vision—
Breaking down the walls
And of crying to the mountain.
6 Elam bore the quiver
With chariots of men *and*
  horsemen,
And Kir uncovered the shield.
7 It shall come to pass *that* your
  choicest valleys
Shall be full of chariots,
And the horsemen shall set
  themselves in array at the
  gate.
8 He removed the protection of
  Judah.
You looked in that day to the
  armor of the House of the
  Forest;
9 You also saw the damage to the
  city of David,
That it was great;

And you gathered together the
  waters of the lower pool.
10 You numbered the houses of
  Jerusalem,
And the houses you broke down
To fortify the wall.
11 You also made a reservoir
  between the two walls
For the water of the old pool.
But you did not look to its
  Maker,
Nor did you have respect for
  Him who fashioned it long
  ago.

12 And in that day the Lord GOD
  of hosts
Called for weeping and for
  mourning,
For baldness and for girding with
  sackcloth.
13 But instead, joy and gladness,
Slaying oxen and killing sheep,
Eating meat and drinking wine:
"Let us eat and drink, for
  tomorrow we die!"

14 Then it was revealed in my
  hearing by the LORD of hosts,
"Surely for this iniquity there will
  be no atonement for you,
Even to your death," says the
  Lord GOD of hosts.

15 Thus says the Lord GOD of hosts:

"Go, proceed to this steward,
To Shebna, who *is* over the
  house, *and say:*
16 'What have you here, and whom
  have you here,
That you have hewn a sepulcher
  here,
As he who hews himself a
  sepulcher on high,
Who carves a tomb for himself
  in a rock?
17 Indeed, the LORD will throw you
  away violently,
O mighty man,
And will surely seize you.
18 He will surely turn violently and
  toss you like a ball
Into a large country;

There you shall die, and there
     your glorious chariots
Shall be the shame of your
     master's house.
19 So I will drive you out of your
     office,
And from your position he will
     pull you down.

20 'Then it shall be in that day,
That I will call My servant
     Eliakim the son of Hilkiah;
21 I will clothe him with your robe
And strengthen him with your
     belt;
I will commit your responsibility
     into his hand.
He shall be a father to the
     inhabitants of Jerusalem
And to the house of Judah.
22 The key of the house of David
I will lay on his shoulder;
So he shall open, and no one
     shall shut;
And he shall shut, and no one
     shall open.
23 I will fasten him *as* a peg in a
     secure place,
And he will become a glorious
     throne to his father's house.

24 'They will hang on him all the
glory of his father's house, the offspring
and the posterity, all vessels of small
quantity, from the cups to all the pitchers. 25 In that day,' says the LORD of
hosts, 'the peg that is fastened in the
secure place will be removed and be
cut down and fall, and the burden that
was on it will be cut off; for the LORD
has spoken.' ''

God's plans for the wicked city of Tyre

23 The burden against Tyre.

Wail, you ships of Tarshish!
For it is laid waste,
So that there is no house, no
     harbor;
From the land of Cyprus it is
     revealed to them.

2 Be still, you inhabitants of the
     coastland,
You merchants of Sidon,
Whom those who cross the sea
     have filled.
3 And on great waters the grain
     of Shihor,
The harvest of the River, *is* her
     revenue;
And she is a marketplace for the
     nations.

4 Be ashamed, O Sidon;
For the sea has spoken,
The strength of the sea, saying,
"I do not labor, nor bring forth
     children;
Neither do I rear young men,
Nor bring up virgins."
5 When the report *reaches* Egypt,
They also will be in agony at the
     report of Tyre.

6 Cross over to Tarshish;
Wail, you inhabitants of the
     coastland!
7 *Is* this your joyous *city,*
Whose antiquity *is* from ancient
     days,
Whose feet carried her far off to
     dwell?
8 Who has taken this counsel
     against Tyre, the crowning
     city,
Whose merchants *are* princes,
Whose traders *are* the honorable
     of the earth?
9 The LORD of hosts has purposed
     it,
To bring to dishonor the pride
     of all glory,
To bring into contempt all the
     honorable of the earth.

10 Overflow through your land like
     the River,
O daughter of Tarshish;
There is no more strength.
11 He stretched out His hand over
     the sea,
He shook the kingdoms;
The LORD has given a
     commandment against
     Canaan
To destroy its strongholds.

12 And He said, "You will rejoice
    no more,
   O you oppressed virgin daughter
    of Sidon.
   Arise, cross over to Cyprus;
   There also you will have no
    rest."

13 Behold, the land of the
    Chaldeans,
   This people *which* was not;
   Assyria founded it for wild beasts
    of the desert.
   They set up its towers,
   They raised up its palaces,
   And brought it to ruin.

14 Wail, you ships of Tarshish!
   For your strength is laid waste.

15 Now it shall come to pass in that
day that Tyre will be forgotten seventy
years, according to the days of one
king. At the end of seventy years it will
happen to Tyre as *in* the song of the
harlot:

16 "Take a harp, go about the city,
    You forgotten harlot;
    Make sweet melody, sing many
     songs,
    That you may be remembered."

17 And it shall be, at the end of seventy years, that the Lord will deal with
Tyre. She will return to her hire, and
commit fornication with all the kingdoms of the world on the face of the
earth. 18 Her gain and her pay will be
set apart for the Lord; it will not be
treasured nor laid up, for her gain will
be for those who dwell before the
Lord, to eat sufficiently, and for fine
clothing.

The whole earth will be judged

24 Behold, the Lord makes the
    earth empty and makes it
     waste,
   Distorts its surface
   And scatters abroad its
    inhabitants.
2 And it shall be:

   As with the people, so with the
    priest;
   As with the servant, so with his
    master;
   As with the maid, so with her
    mistress;
   As with the buyer, so with the
    seller;
   As with the lender, so with the
    borrower;
   As with the creditor, so with the
    debtor.
3 The land shall be entirely
    emptied and utterly
     plundered,
   For the Lord has spoken this
    word.

4 The earth mourns *and* fades
    away,
   The world languishes *and* fades
    away;
   The haughty people of the earth
    languish.
5 The earth is also defiled under
    its inhabitants,
   Because they have transgressed
    the laws,
   Changed the ordinance,
   Broken the everlasting
    covenant.
6 Therefore the curse has
    devoured the earth,
   And those who dwell in it are
    desolate.
   Therefore the inhabitants of the
    earth are burned,
   And few men *are* left.

7 The new wine fails, the vine
    languishes,
   All the merry-hearted sigh.
8 The mirth of the tambourine
    ceases,
   The noise of the jubilant ends,
   The joy of the harp ceases.
9 They shall not drink wine with
    a song;
   Strong drink is bitter to those
    who drink it.
10 The city of confusion is broken
    down;
   Every house is shut up, so that
    none may go in.

11 *There is* a cry for wine in the
     streets,
   All joy is darkened,
   The mirth of the land is gone.
12 In the city desolation is left,
   And the gate is stricken with
     destruction.
13 When it shall be thus in the
     midst of the land among the
     people,
   It shall be like the shaking of an
     olive tree,
   Like the gleaning of grapes
     when the vintage is done.

14 They shall lift up their voice, they
     shall sing;
   For the majesty of the LORD
   They shall cry aloud from the
     sea.
15 Therefore glorify the LORD in the
     dawning light,
   The name of the LORD God of
     Israel in the coastlands of the
     sea.
16 From the ends of the earth we
     have heard songs:
   "Glory to the righteous!"
   But I said, "I am ruined, ruined!
   Woe to me!
   The treacherous dealers have
     dealt treacherously,
   Indeed, the treacherous dealers
     have dealt very
     treacherously."

17 Fear and the pit and the snare
   Are upon you, O inhabitant of
     the earth.
18 And it shall be
   That he who flees from the noise
     of the fear
   Shall fall into the pit,
   And he who comes up from the
     midst of the pit
   Shall be caught in the snare;
   For the windows from on high
     are open,
   And the foundations of the earth
     are shaken.

19 The earth is violently broken,
   The earth is split open,
   The earth is shaken exceedingly.

20 The earth shall reel to and fro
     like a drunkard,
   And shall totter like a hut;
   Its transgression shall be heavy
     upon it,
   And it will fall, and not rise again.

21 It shall come to pass in that day
   That the LORD will punish on
     high the host of exalted ones,
   And on the earth the kings of
     the earth.
22 They will be gathered together,
   As prisoners are gathered in the
     pit,
   And will be shut up in the prison;
   After many days they will be
     punished.
23 Then the moon will be disgraced
   And the sun ashamed;
   For the LORD of hosts will reign
   On Mount Zion and in
     Jerusalem
   And before His elders,
     gloriously.

The Lord will wipe away all tears

25 O LORD, You *are* my God.
   I will exalt You,
   I will praise Your name,
   For You have done wonderful
     things;
   Your counsels of old *are*
     faithfulness *and* truth.
2 For You have made a city a ruin,
   A fortified city a ruin,
   A palace of foreigners to be a
     city no more;
   It will never be rebuilt.
3 Therefore the strong people will
     glorify You;
   The city of the terrible nations
     will fear You.
4 For You have been a strength
     to the poor,
   A strength to the needy in his
     distress,
   A refuge from the storm,
   A shade from the heat;
   For the blast of the terrible ones
     is as a storm *against* the wall.
5 You will reduce the noise of
     aliens,

As heat in a dry place;
As heat in the shadow of a
cloud,
The song of the terrible ones will
be diminished.

6 And in this mountain
The LORD of hosts will make for
all people
A feast of choice pieces,
A feast of wines on the lees,
Of fat things full of marrow,
Of well-refined wines on the
lees.
7 And He will destroy on this
mountain
The surface of the covering cast
over all people,
And the veil that is spread over
all nations.
8 He will swallow up death
forever,
And the Lord GOD will wipe
away tears from all faces;
The rebuke of His people
He will take away from all the
earth;
For the LORD has spoken.

9 And it will be said in that day:
"Behold, this is our God;
We have waited for Him, and
He will save us.
This is the LORD;
We have waited for Him;
We will be glad and rejoice in
His salvation."

10 For on this mountain the hand
of the LORD will rest,
And Moab shall be trampled
down under Him,
As straw is trampled down for
the refuse heap.
11 And He will spread out His
hands in their midst
As a swimmer reaches out to
swim,
And He will bring down their
pride
Together with the trickery of
their hands.
12 The fortress of the high fort of
your walls

He will bring down, lay low,
And bring to the ground, down
to the dust.

Song of praise

26 In that day this song will be sung
in the land of Judah:

"We have a strong city;
God will appoint salvation for
walls and bulwarks.
2 Open the gates,
That the righteous nation which
keeps the truth may enter in.
3 You will keep him in perfect
peace,
Whose mind is stayed on You,
Because he trusts in You.
4 Trust in the LORD forever,
For in YAH, the LORD, is
everlasting strength.
5 For He brings down those who
dwell on high,
The lofty city;
He lays it low,
He lays it low to the ground,
He brings it down to the dust.
6 The foot shall tread it down—
The feet of the poor
And the steps of the needy."

7 The way of the just is
uprightness;
O Most Upright,
You weigh the path of the just.
8 Yes, in the way of Your
judgments,
O LORD, we have waited for
You;
The desire of our soul is for Your
name
And for the remembrance of
You.
9 With my soul I have desired You
in the night,
Yes, by my spirit within me I will
seek You early;
For when Your judgments are
in the earth,
The inhabitants of the world will
learn righteousness.
10 Let grace be shown to the
wicked,

Yet he will not learn righteousness;
In the land of uprightness he will deal unjustly,
And will not behold the majesty of the LORD.

11 LORD, *when* Your hand is lifted up, they will not *see.*
But they will see and be ashamed
For *their* envy of people;
Yes, the fire of Your enemies shall devour them.

12 LORD, You will establish peace for us,
For You have also done all our works in us.

13 O LORD our God, masters besides You
Have had dominion over us;
But by You only we make mention of Your name.

14 *They are* dead, they will not live;
They are deceased, they will not rise.
Therefore You have punished and destroyed them,
And made all their memory to perish.

15 You have increased the nation, O LORD,
You have increased the nation;
You are glorified;
You have expanded all the borders of the land.

16 LORD, in trouble they have visited You,
They poured out a prayer *when* Your chastening *was* upon them.

17 As a woman with child
Is in pain and cries out in her pangs,
When she draws near the time of her delivery,
So have we been in Your sight, O LORD.

18 We have been with child, we have been in pain;
We have, as it were, brought forth wind;

We have not accomplished any deliverance in the earth,
Nor have the inhabitants of the world fallen.

19 Your dead shall live;
Together with my dead body they shall arise.
Awake and sing, you who dwell in dust;
For your dew *is like* the dew of herbs,
And the earth shall cast out the dead.

20 Come, my people, enter your chambers,
And shut your doors behind you;
Hide yourself, as it were, for a little moment,
Until the indignation is past.

21 For behold, the LORD comes out of His place
To punish the inhabitants of the earth for their iniquity;
The earth will also disclose her blood,
And will no more cover her slain.

God is not angry anymore

27 In that day the LORD with His severe sword, great and strong,
Will punish Leviathan the fleeing serpent,
Leviathan that twisted serpent;
And He will slay the reptile that *is* in the sea.

2 In that day sing to her,
"A vineyard of red wine!

3 I, the LORD, keep it,
I water it *every* moment;
Lest any hurt it,
I keep it night and day.

4 Fury *is* not in Me.
Who would set briers *and* thorns Against Me in battle?
I would go through them,
I would burn them together.

5 Or let him take hold of My strength,

That he may make peace with
   Me;
And he shall make peace with
   Me."

6   Those who come He shall cause
   to take root in Jacob;
Israel shall blossom and bud,
And fill the face of the world with
   fruit.

7   Has He struck Israel as He struck
   those who struck him?
Or has He been slain according
   to the slaughter of those who
   were slain by Him?
8   In measure, by sending it away,
You contended with it.
He removes *it* by His rough wind
In the day of the east wind.
9   Therefore by this the iniquity of
   Jacob will be covered;
And this *is* all the fruit of taking
   away his sin:
When he makes all the stones
   of the altar
Like chalkstones that are beaten
   to dust,
Wooden images and incense
   altars shall not stand.

10   Yet the fortified city *will be*
   desolate,
The habitation forsaken and left
   like a wilderness;
There the calf will feed, and
   there it will lie down
And consume its branches.
11   When its boughs are withered,
   they will be broken off;
The women come *and* set them
   on fire.
For it *is* a people of no
   understanding;
Therefore He who made them
   will not have mercy on them,
And He who formed them will
   show them no favor.

12   And it shall come to pass in that
   day
That the Lᴏʀᴅ will thresh,
From the channel of the River
   to the Brook of Egypt;

And you will be gathered one
   by one,
O you children of Israel.

13   So it shall be in that day:
The great trumpet will be
   blown;
They will come, who are about
   to perish in the land of
   Assyria,
And they who are outcasts in the
   land of Egypt,
And shall worship the Lᴏʀᴅ in
   the holy mount at Jerusalem.

The Lord is our Cornerstone

28   Woe to the crown of pride, to
   the drunkards of Ephraim,
Whose glorious beauty *is* a
   fading flower
Which *is* at the head of the
   verdant valleys,
To those who are overcome with
   wine!
2   Behold, the Lord has a mighty
   and strong one,
Like a tempest of hail and a
   destroying storm,
Like a flood of mighty waters
   overflowing,
Who will bring *them* down to the
   earth with *His* hand.
3   The crown of pride, the
   drunkards of Ephraim,
Will be trampled underfoot;
4   And the glorious beauty is a
   fading flower
Which *is* at the head of the
   verdant valley,
Like the first fruit before the
   summer,
Which an observer sees;
He eats it up while it is still in
   his hand.

5   In that day the Lᴏʀᴅ of hosts will
   be
For a crown of glory and a
   diadem of beauty
To the remnant of His people,
6   For a spirit of justice to him who
   sits in judgment,
And for strength to those who

turn back the battle at the
gate.

7 But they also have erred through
wine,
And through intoxicating drink
are out of the way;
The priest and the prophet have
erred through intoxicating
drink,
They are swallowed up by wine,
They are out of the way through
intoxicating drink;
They err in vision, they stumble
in judgment.

8 For all tables are full of vomit
and filth;
No place *is clean.*

9 "Whom will he teach knowledge?
And whom will he make to
understand the message?
Those *just* weaned from milk?
Those *just* drawn from the
breasts?

10 For precept *must be* upon
precept, precept upon
precept,
Line upon line, line upon line,
Here a little, there a little."

11 For with stammering lips and
another tongue
He will speak to this people,

12 To whom He said, "This *is* the
rest *with which*
You may cause the weary to
rest,"
And, "This *is* the refreshing";
Yet they would not hear.

13 But the word of the LORD was
to them,
"Precept upon precept, precept
upon precept,
Line upon line, line upon line,
Here a little, there a little,"
That they might go and fall
backward, and be broken
And snared and caught.

14 Therefore hear the word of the
LORD, you scornful men,
Who rule this people who *are*
in Jerusalem,

15 Because you have said, "We
have made a covenant with
death,
And with Sheol we are in
agreement.
When the overflowing scourge
passes through,
It will not come to us,
For we have made lies our
refuge,
And under falsehood we have
hidden ourselves."

16 Therefore thus says the Lord GOD:

"Behold, I lay in Zion a stone for
a foundation,
A tried stone, a precious
cornerstone, a sure
foundation;
Whoever believes will not act
hastily.

17 Also I will make justice the
measuring line,
And righteousness the plummet;
The hail will sweep away the
refuge of lies,
And the waters will overflow the
hiding place.

18 Your covenant with death will be
annulled,
And your agreement with Sheol
will not stand;
When the overflowing scourge
passes through,
Then you will be trampled down
by it.

19 As often as it goes out it will take
you;
For morning by morning it will
pass over,
And by day and by night;
It will be a terror just to
understand the report."

20 For the bed is too short to stretch
out *on,*
And the covering so narrow
that one cannot wrap himself
in it.

21 For the LORD will rise up as *at*
Mount Perazim,
He will be angry as in the Valley
of Gibeon—

That He may do His work, His
    awesome work,
And bring to pass His act, His
    unusual act.
22 Now therefore, do not be
    mockers,
Lest your bonds be made
    strong;
For I have heard from the Lord
    GOD of hosts,
A destruction determined even
    upon the whole earth.

23 Give ear and hear my voice,
    Listen and hear my speech.
24 Does the plowman keep plowing
    all day to sow?
Does he keep turning his soil
    and breaking the clods?
25 When he has leveled its
    surface,
Does he not sow the black
    cummin
And scatter the cummin,
Plant the wheat in rows,
The barley in the appointed
    place,
And the spelt in its place?
26 For He instructs him in right
    judgment,
His God teaches him.

27 For the black cummin is not
    threshed with a threshing
    sledge,
Nor is a cartwheel rolled over the
    cummin;
But the black cummin is beaten
    out with a stick,
And the cummin with a rod.
28 Bread *flour* must be ground;
Therefore he does not thresh it
    forever,
Break *it with* his cartwheel,
Or crush *it with* his horsemen.
29 This also comes from the LORD
    of hosts,
Who is wonderful in counsel *and*
    excellent in guidance.

Israel is like a blind man

29 "Woe to Ariel, to Ariel, the city
    where David dwelt!

Add year to year;
Let feasts come around.
2 Yet I will distress Ariel;
There shall be heaviness and
    sorrow,
And it shall be to Me as Ariel.
3 I will encamp against you all
    around,
I will lay siege against you with
    a mound,
And I will raise siegeworks
    against you.
4 You shall be brought down,
You shall speak out of the
    ground;
Your speech shall be low, out
    of the dust;
Your voice shall be like a
    medium's, out of the ground;
And your speech shall whisper
    out of the dust.

5 "Moreover the multitude of your
    foes
Shall be like fine dust,
And the multitude of the terrible
    ones
Like chaff that passes away;
Yes, it shall be in an instant,
    suddenly.
6 You will be punished by the
    LORD of hosts
With thunder and earthquake
    and great noise,
With storm and tempest
And the flame of devouring fire.
7 The multitude of all the nations
    who fight against Ariel,
Even all who fight against her
    and her fortress,
And distress her,
Shall be as a dream of a night
    vision.
8 It shall even be as when a
    hungry man dreams,
And look—he eats;
But he awakes, and his soul is
    still empty;
Or as when a thirsty man
    dreams,
And look—he drinks;
But he awakes, and indeed *he*
    is faint,
And his soul still craves:

So the multitude of all the
   nations shall be,
Who fight against Mount Zion."

9 Pause and wonder!
   Blind yourselves and be blind!
   They are drunk, but not with
      wine;
   They stagger, but not with
      intoxicating drink.
10 For the LORD has poured out on
      you
   The spirit of deep sleep,
   And has closed your eyes,
      namely, the prophets;
   And He has covered your heads,
      namely, the seers.

11 The whole vision has become to
you like the words of a book that
is sealed, which *men* deliver to one
who is literate, saying, "Read this,
please."
   And he says, "I cannot, for it *is*
sealed."
12 Then the book is delivered to one
who is illiterate, saying, "Read this,
please."
   And he says, "I am not literate."
13 Therefore the Lord said:

   "Inasmuch as these people draw
      near with their mouths
   And honor Me with their lips,
   But have removed their hearts
      far from Me,
   And their fear toward Me is
      taught by the commandment
      of men,
14 Therefore, behold, I will again
      do a marvelous work
   Among this people,
   A marvelous work and a
      wonder;
   For the wisdom of their wise
      men shall perish,
   And the understanding of their
      prudent *men* shall be
      hidden."

15 Woe to those who seek deep to
      hide their counsel far from the
      LORD,
   And their works are in the dark;

   They say, "Who sees us?" and,
      "Who knows us?"
16 Surely you have things turned
      around!
   Shall the potter be esteemed as
      the clay;
   For shall the thing made say of
      him who made it,
   "He did not make me"?
   Or shall the thing formed say of
      him who formed it,
   "He has no understanding"?

17 *Is* it not yet a very little while
   Till Lebanon shall be turned into
      a fruitful field,
   And the fruitful field be
      esteemed as a forest?
18 In that day the deaf shall hear
      the words of the book,
   And the eyes of the blind shall
      see out of obscurity and out
      of darkness.
19 The humble also shall increase
      their joy in the LORD,
   And the poor among men shall
      rejoice
   In the Holy One of Israel.
20 For the terrible one is brought
      to nothing,
   The scornful one is consumed,
   And all who watch for iniquity
      are cut off—
21 Who make a man an offender
      by a word,
   And lay a snare for him who
      reproves in the gate,
   And turn aside the just by empty
      words.

22 Therefore thus says the LORD,
who redeemed Abraham, concerning
the house of Jacob:

   "Jacob shall not now be
      ashamed,
   Nor shall his face now grow pale;
23 But when he sees his children,
   The work of My hands, in his
      midst,
   They will hallow My name,
   And hallow the Holy One of
      Jacob,
   And fear the God of Israel.

24 These also who erred in spirit
will come to understanding,
And those who complained will
learn doctrine."

God promises wonderful blessings

30 "Woe to the rebellious children,"
says the LORD,
"Who take counsel, but not of
Me,
And who devise plans, but not
of My Spirit,
That they may add sin to sin;
2 Who walk to go down to Egypt,
And have not asked My advice,
To strengthen themselves in the
strength of Pharaoh,
And to trust in the shadow of
Egypt!
3 Therefore the strength of
Pharaoh
Shall be your shame,
And trust in the shadow of Egypt
Shall be your humiliation.
4 For his princes were at Zoan,
And his ambassadors came to
Hanes.
5 They were all ashamed of a
people who could not benefit
them,
Or be help or benefit,
But a shame and also a
reproach."

6 The burden against the beasts of
the South.

Through a land of trouble and
anguish,
From which came the lioness
and lion,
The viper and fiery flying
serpent,
They will carry their riches on
the backs of young donkeys,
And their treasures on the
humps of camels,
To a people who shall not profit;
7 For the Egyptians shall help in
vain and to no purpose.
Therefore I have called her
Rahab-Hem-Shebeth.

8 Now go, write it before them on
a tablet,
And note it on a scroll,
That it may be for time to come,
Forever and ever:
9 That this is a rebellious people,
Lying children,
Children who will not hear the
law of the LORD;
10 Who say to the seers, "Do not
see,"
And to the prophets, "Do not
prophesy to us right things;
Speak to us smooth things,
prophesy deceits.
11 Get out of the way,
Turn aside from the path,
Cause the Holy One of Israel
To cease from before us."

12 Therefore thus says the Holy One
of Israel:

"Because you despise this word,
And trust in oppression and
perversity,
And rely on them,
13 Therefore this iniquity shall be
to you
Like a breach ready to fall,
A bulge in a high wall,
Whose breaking comes
suddenly, in an instant.
14 And He shall break it like the
breaking of the potter's vessel,
Which is broken in pieces;
He shall not spare.
So there shall not be found
among its fragments
A shard to take fire from the
hearth,
Or to take water from the
cistern."

15 For thus says the Lord GOD, the
Holy One of Israel:

"In returning and rest you shall
be saved;
In quietness and confidence
shall be your strength."
But you would not,
16 And you said, "No, for we will
flee on horses"—

Therefore you shall flee!
And, "We will ride on swift
   horses"—
Therefore those who pursue you
   shall be swift!
17 One thousand *shall flee* at the
   threat of one,
At the threat of five you shall
   flee,
Till you are left as a pole on top
   of a mountain
And as a banner on a hill.

18 Therefore the LORD will wait,
   that He may be gracious to
   you;
And therefore He will be
   exalted, that He may have
   mercy on you.
For the LORD *is* a God of justice;
Blessed *are* all those who wait
   for Him.

19 For the people shall dwell in
   Zion at Jerusalem;
You shall weep no more.
He will be very gracious to you
   at the sound of your cry;
When He hears it, He will
   answer you.
20 And *though* the Lord gives you
The bread of adversity and the
   water of affliction,
Yet your teachers will not be
   moved into a corner anymore,
But your eyes shall see your
   teachers.
21 Your ears shall hear a word
   behind you, saying,
"This *is* the way, walk in it,"
Whenever you turn to the right
   hand
Or whenever you turn to the left.
22 You will also defile the covering
   of your images of silver,
And the ornament of your
   molded images of gold.
You will throw them away as an
   unclean thing;
You will say to them, "Get
   away!"

23 Then He will give the rain for
   your seed

With which you sow the ground,
And bread of the increase of the
   earth;
It will be fat and plentiful.
In that day your cattle will feed
In large pastures.
24 Likewise the oxen and the
   young donkeys that work the
   ground
Will eat cured fodder,
Which has been winnowed with
   the shovel and fan.
25 There will be on every high
   mountain
And on every high hill
Rivers *and* streams of waters,
In the day of the great slaughter,
When the towers fall.
26 Moreover the light of the moon
   will be as the light of the sun,
And the light of the sun will be
   sevenfold,
As the light of seven days,
In the day that the LORD binds
   up the bruise of His people
And heals the stroke of their
   wound.

27 Behold, the name of the LORD
   comes from afar,
Burning *with* His anger,
And *His* burden *is* heavy;
His lips are full of indignation,
And His tongue like a devouring
   fire.
28 His breath is like an overflowing
   stream,
Which reaches up to the neck,
To sift the nations with the sieve
   of futility;
And *there shall be* a bridle in the
   jaws of the people,
Causing *them* to err.

29 You shall have a song
As in the night *when* a holy
   festival is kept,
And gladness of heart as when
   one goes with a flute,
To come into the mountain of
   the LORD,
To the Mighty One of Israel.
30 The LORD will cause His glorious
   voice to be heard,

And show the descent of His
  arm,
With the indignation of *His*
  anger
And the flame of a devouring
  fire,
With scattering, tempest, and
  hailstones.
31 For through the voice of the
  LORD
Assyria will be beaten down,
As He strikes with the rod.
32 And *in* every place where the
  staff of punishment passes,
Which the LORD lays on him,
It will be with tambourines and
  harps;
And in battles of brandishing He
  will fight with it.
33 For Tophet *was* established of
  old,
Yes, for the king it is prepared.
He has made *it* deep and large;
Its pyre *is* fire with much wood;
The breath of the LORD, like a
  stream of brimstone,
Kindles it.

Don't trust in weapons, trust in God

31 Woe to those who go down to
  Egypt for help,
And rely on horses,
Who trust in chariots because
  they are many,
And in horsemen because they
  are very strong,
But who do not look to the Holy
  One of Israel,
Nor *seek* the LORD!
2 Yet He also *is* wise and will bring
  disaster,
And will not call back His words,
But will arise against the house
  of evildoers,
And against the help of those
  who work iniquity.
3 Now the Egyptians *are* men, and
  not God;
And their horses are flesh, and
  not spirit.
When the LORD stretches out His
  hand,

Both he who helps will fall,
And he who is helped will fall
  down;
They all will perish together.

4 For thus the LORD has spoken to
me:

"As a lion roars,
And a young lion over his prey
(When a multitude of shepherds
  is summoned against him,
He will not be afraid of their
  voice
Nor be disturbed by their noise),
So the LORD of hosts will come
  down
To fight for Mount Zion and for
  its hill.
5 Like birds flying about,
So will the LORD of hosts defend
  Jerusalem.
Defending, He will also deliver
  it;
Passing over, He will preserve
  it."

6 Return *to Him* against whom the
children of Israel have deeply revolted.
7 For in that day every man shall throw
away his idols of silver and his idols
of gold—sin, which your own hands
have made for yourselves.

8 "Then Assyria shall fall by a
  sword not of man,
And a sword not of mankind
  shall devour him.
But he shall flee from the sword,
And his young men shall
  become forced labor.
9 He shall cross over to his
  stronghold for fear,
And his princes shall be afraid
  of the banner,"
Says the LORD,
Whose fire *is* in Zion
And whose furnace *is* in
  Jerusalem.

Women of Jerusalem, beware!

32 Behold, a king will reign in
  righteousness,
And princes will rule with justice.

2 A man will be as a hiding place
 from the wind,
 And a cover from the tempest,
 As rivers of water in a dry
 place,
 As the shadow of a great rock
 in a weary land.
3 The eyes of those who see will
 not be dim,
 And the ears of those who hear
 will listen.
4 Also the heart of the rash will
 understand knowledge,
 And the tongue of the
 stammerers will be ready to
 speak plainly.

5 The foolish person will no longer
 be called generous,
 Nor the miser said to be
 bountiful;
6 For the foolish person will speak
 foolishness,
 And his heart will work
 iniquity:
 To practice ungodliness,
 To utter error against the
 LORD,
 To keep the hungry
 unsatisfied,
 And he will cause the drink of
 the thirsty to fail.
7 Also the schemes of the schemer
 are evil;
 He devises wicked plans
 To destroy the poor with lying
 words,
 Even when the needy speaks
 justice.
8 But a generous man devises
 generous things,
 And by generosity he shall
 stand.

9 Rise up, you women who are
 at ease,
 Hear my voice;
 You complacent daughters,
 Give ear to my speech.
10 In a year and some days
 You will be troubled, you
 complacent women;
 For the vintage will fail,
 The gathering will not come.

11 Tremble, you women who are
 at ease;
 Be troubled, you complacent
 ones;
 Strip yourselves, make
 yourselves bare,
 And gird sackcloth on your
 waists.
12 People shall mourn upon their
 breasts
 For the pleasant fields, for the
 fruitful vine.
13 On the land of my people will
 come up thorns and briers,
 Yes, on all the happy homes in
 the joyous city;
14 Because the palaces will be
 forsaken,
 The bustling city will be
 deserted.
 The forts and towers will
 become lairs forever,
 A joy of wild donkeys, a pasture
 of flocks—
15 Until the Spirit is poured upon
 us from on high,
 And the wilderness becomes a
 fruitful field,
 And the fruitful field is counted
 as a forest.

16 Then justice will dwell in the
 wilderness,
 And righteousness remain in the
 fruitful field.
17 The work of righteousness will
 be peace,
 And the effect of righteousness,
 quietness and assurance
 forever.
18 My people will dwell in a
 peaceful habitation,
 In secure dwellings, and in quiet
 resting places,
19 Though hail comes down on the
 forest,
 And the city is brought low in
 humiliation.

20 Blessed are you who sow beside
 all waters,
 Who send out freely the feet of
 the ox and the donkey.

s is for all who

God's forgiv
trust Him who plunder,

33 ou *have* not *been*

ho deal
ously, though they
t dealt treacherously
u!
u cease plundering,
be plundered;
ou make an end of
g treacherously,
ll deal treacherously with

Lᴏʀᴅ, be gracious to us;
We have waited for You.
Be their arm every morning,
Our salvation also in the time of
trouble.

3 At the noise of the tumult the
people shall flee;
When You lift Yourself up, the
nations shall be scattered;

4 And Your plunder shall be
gathered
Like the gathering of the
caterpillar;
As the running to and fro of
locusts,
He shall run upon them.

5 The Lᴏʀᴅ is exalted, for He
dwells on high;
He has filled Zion with justice
and righteousness.

6 Wisdom and knowledge will
be the stability of your
times,
And the strength of salvation;
The fear of the Lᴏʀᴅ *is* His
treasure.

7 Surely their valiant ones shall cry
outside,
The ambassadors of peace shall
weep bitterly.

8 The highways lie waste,
The traveling man ceases.
He has broken the covenant,
He has despised the cities,
He regards no man.

9 The earth mourns *and*
languishes,
Lebanon is shamed *and*
shriveled;
Sharon is like a wilderness,
And Bashan and Carmel shake
off *their fruits.*

10 "Now I will rise," says the Lᴏʀᴅ;
"Now I will be exalted,
Now I will lift Myself up.

11 You shall conceive chaff,
You shall bring forth stubble;
Your breath, *as* fire, shall devour
you.

12 And the people shall be *like* the
burnings of lime;
Like thorns cut up they shall be
burned in the fire.

13 Hear, you *who are* afar off, what
I have done;
And you *who are* near,
acknowledge My might."

14 The sinners in Zion are afraid;
Fearfulness has seized the
hypocrites:
"Who among us shall dwell with
the devouring fire?
Who among us shall dwell with
everlasting burnings?"

15 He who walks righteously and
speaks uprightly,
He who despises the gain of
oppressions,
Who gestures with his hands,
refusing bribes,
Who stops his ears from hearing
of bloodshed,
And shuts his eyes from seeing
evil:

16 He will dwell on high;
His place of defense *will be* the
fortress of rocks;
Bread will be given him,
His water *will be* sure.

17 Your eyes will see the King in
His beauty;
They will see the land that is very
far off.

18 Your heart will meditate on
terror:
"Where *is* the scribe?

Where *is* he who weighs?
Where *is* he who counts the
   towers?"
19 You will not see a fierce people,
A people of obscure speech,
   beyond perception,
Of a stammering tongue *that*
   you cannot understand.

20 Look upon Zion, the city of our
   appointed feasts;
Your *eyes* will see Jerusalem, a
   quiet home,
A tabernacle *that* will not be
   taken down;
Not one of its stakes will *ever*
   be removed,
Nor will any of its cords be
   broken.
21 But there the majestic LORD *will*
   be for us
A place of broad rivers *and*
   streams,
In which no galley with oars will
   sail,
Nor majestic ships pass by
22 (For the LORD *is* our Judge,
The LORD *is* our Lawgiver,
The LORD *is* our King;
He will save us);
23 Your tackle is loosed,
They could not strengthen their
   mast,
They could not spread the sail.

Then the prey of great plunder
   is divided;
The lame take the prey.
24 And the inhabitant will not say,
   "I am sick";
The people who dwell in it *will*
   be forgiven *their* iniquity.

Edom will be called "The Land of Nothing"

34 Come near, you nations, to
   hear;
And heed, you people!
Let the earth hear, and all that
   is in it,
The world and all things that
   come forth from it.

2 For the indigna
   is against all n
And *His* fury agaiⁿe LORD
   armies;
He has utterly destr
He has given them o
   slaughter.
3 Also their slain shall be
   out;
Their stench shall rise fro
   corpses,
And the mountains shall b
   melted with their blood.
4 All the host of heaven shall b
   dissolved,
And the heavens shall be rolle
   up like a scroll;
All their host shall fall down
As the leaf falls from the vine,
And as *fruit* falling from a fig
   tree.

5 "For My sword shall be bathed
   in heaven;
Indeed it shall come down on
   Edom,
And on the people of My curse,
   for judgment.
6 The sword of the LORD is filled
   with blood,
It is made overflowing with
   fatness,
With the blood of lambs and
   goats,
With the fat of the kidneys of
   rams.
For the LORD has a sacrifice in
   Bozrah,
And a great slaughter in the land
   of Edom.
7 The wild oxen shall come down
   with them,
And the young bulls with the
   mighty bulls;
Their land shall be soaked with
   blood,
And their dust saturated with
   fatness."

8 For *it is* the day of the LORD's
   vengeance,
The year of recompense for the
   cause of Zion.

9 Its streams shall be turned into
    pitch,
  And its dust into brimstone;
  Its land shall become burning
    pitch.
10 It shall not be quenched night
    or day;
  Its smoke shall ascend forever.
  From generation to generation
    it shall lie waste;
  No one shall pass through it
    forever and ever.
11 But the pelican and the
    porcupine shall possess it,
  Also the owl and the raven shall
    dwell in it.
  And He shall stretch out over it
  The line of confusion and the
    stones of emptiness.
12 They shall call its nobles to the
    kingdom,
  But none *shall be* there, and all
    its princes shall be nothing.

13 And thorns shall come up in its
    palaces,
  Nettles and brambles in its
    fortresses;
  It shall be a habitation of jackals,
  A courtyard for ostriches.
14 The wild beasts of the desert
    shall also meet with the
    jackals,
  And the wild goat shall bleat to
    its companion;
  Also the night creature shall rest
    there,
  And find for herself a place of
    rest.
15 There the arrow snake shall
    make her nest and lay *eggs*
  And hatch, and gather *them*
    under her shadow;
  There also shall the hawks be
    gathered,
  Every one with her mate.

16 "Search from the book of the
    LORD, and read:
  Not one of these shall fail;
  Not one shall lack her mate.
  For My mouth has commanded
    it, and His Spirit has gathered
    them.

17 He has cast the lot for them,
  And His hand has divided it
    among them with a measuring
    line.
  They shall possess it forever;
  From generation to generation
    they shall dwell in it."

The desert will bloom with flowers

35 The wilderness and the
    wasteland shall be glad for
    them;
  And the desert shall rejoice and
    blossom as the rose;
2 It shall blossom abundantly and
    rejoice,
  Even with joy and singing.
  The glory of Lebanon shall be
    given to it,
  The excellence of Carmel and
    Sharon.
  They shall see the glory of the
    LORD,
  The excellency of our God.

3 Strengthen the weak hands,
  And make firm the feeble
    knees.
4 Say to those *who are* fearful-
    hearted,
  "Be strong, do not fear!
  Behold, your God will come
    with vengeance,
  With the recompense of God;
  He will come and save you."

5 Then the eyes of the blind shall
    be opened,
  And the ears of the deaf shall
    be unstopped.
6 Then the lame shall leap like a
    deer,
  And the tongue of the dumb
    sing.
  For waters shall burst forth in the
    wilderness,
  And streams in the desert.
7 The parched ground shall
    become a pool,
  And the thirsty land springs of
    water;
  In the habitation of jackals,
    where each lay,

There shall be grass with reeds
and rushes.

8 A highway shall be there, and a
road,
And it shall be called the
Highway of Holiness.
The unclean shall not pass over
it,
But it *shall be* for others.
Whoever walks the road,
although a fool,
Shall not go astray.

9 No lion shall be there,
Nor shall *any* ravenous beast go
up on it;
It shall not be found there.
But the redeemed shall walk
there,

10 And the ransomed of the LORD
shall return,
And come to Zion with singing,
With everlasting joy on their
heads.
They shall obtain joy and
gladness,
And sorrow and sighing shall flee
away.

*King Sennacherib's victory over Jerusalem
was recorded on this stone prism.*

Little Judah faces big Assyria

36 Now it came to pass in the fourteenth year of King Hezekiah *that* Sennacherib king of Assyria came up
against all the fortified cities of Judah
and took them. 2 Then the king of Assyria sent *the* Rabshakeh with a great
army from Lachish to King Hezekiah
at Jerusalem. And he stood by the aqueduct from the upper pool, on the
highway to the Fuller's Field. 3 And
Eliakim the son of Hilkiah, who was
over the household, Shebna the scribe,
and Joah the son of Asaph, the recorder, came out to him.

4 Then *the* Rabshakeh said to them,
"Say now to Hezekiah, 'Thus says the
great king, the king of Assyria: "What
confidence is this in which you trust?
5 I say you speak of having plans and
power for war; but *they are* mere
words. Now in whom do you trust, that
you rebel against me? 6 Look! You are
trusting in the staff of this broken reed,
Egypt, on which if a man leans, it will
go into his hand and pierce it. So *is*
Pharaoh king of Egypt to all who trust
in him.

7 "But if you say to me, 'We trust
in the LORD our God,' *is it* not He
whose high places and whose altars
Hezekiah has taken away, and said to
Judah and Jerusalem, 'You shall worship before this altar'?" ' 8 Now therefore, I urge you, give a pledge to my
master the king of Assyria, and I will
give you two thousand horses—if you
are able on your part to put riders on
them! 9 How then will you repel one
captain of the least of my master's servants, and put your trust in Egypt for
chariots and horsemen? 10 Have I now
come up without the LORD against this
land to destroy it? The LORD said to
me, 'Go up against this land, and destroy it.' "

11 Then Eliakim, Shebna, and Joah
said to *the* Rabshakeh, "Please speak
to your servants in Aramaic, for we understand *it;* and do not speak to us in
Hebrew in the hearing of the people
who *are* on the wall."

¹² But *the* Rabshakeh said, "Has my master sent me to your master and to you to speak these words, and not to the men who sit on the wall, who will eat and drink their own waste with you?"

¹³ Then *the* Rabshakeh stood and called out with a loud voice in Hebrew, and said, "Hear the words of the great king, the king of Assyria! ¹⁴ Thus says the king: 'Do not let Hezekiah deceive you, for he will not be able to deliver you; ¹⁵ nor let Hezekiah make you trust in the LORD, saying, "The LORD will surely deliver us; this city will not be given into the hand of the king of Assyria." ' ¹⁶ Do not listen to Hezekiah; for thus says the king of Assyria: 'Make peace with me *by a* present and come out to me; and every one of you eat from his own vine and every one from his own fig tree, and every one of you drink the waters of his own cistern; ¹⁷ until I come and take you away to a land like your own land, a land of grain and new wine, a land of bread and vineyards. ¹⁸ *Beware* lest Hezekiah persuade you, saying, "The LORD will deliver us." Has any one of the gods of the nations delivered its land from the hand of the king of Assyria? ¹⁹ Where *are* the gods of Hamath and Arpad? Where *are* the gods of Sepharvaim? Indeed, have they delivered Samaria from my hand? ²⁰ Who among all the gods of these lands have delivered their countries from my hand, that the LORD should deliver Jerusalem from my hand?' "

²¹ But they held their peace and answered him not a word; for the king's commandment was, "Do not answer him." ²² Then Eliakim the son of Hilkiah, who *was* over the household, Shebna the scribe, and Joah the son of Asaph, the recorder, came to Hezekiah with *their* clothes torn, and told him the words of *the* Rabshakeh.

An Angel rescues Judah

37 And so it was, when King Hezekiah heard *it,* that he tore his clothes, covered himself with sackcloth, and went into the house of the LORD. ² Then he sent Eliakim, who *was* over the household, Shebna the scribe, and the elders of the priests, covered with sackcloth, to Isaiah the prophet, the son of Amoz. ³ And they said to him, "Thus says Hezekiah: 'This day *is* a day of trouble and rebuke and blasphemy; for the children have come to birth, but *there is* no strength to bring them forth. ⁴ It may be that the LORD your God will hear the words of *the* Rabshakeh, whom his master the king of Assyria has sent to reproach the living God, and will rebuke the words which the LORD your God has heard. Therefore lift up *your* prayer for the remnant that is left.' "

⁵ So the servants of King Hezekiah came to Isaiah. ⁶ And Isaiah said to them, "Thus you shall say to your master, 'Thus says the LORD: "Do not be afraid of the words which you have heard, with which the servants of the king of Assyria have blasphemed Me. ⁷ Surely I will send a spirit upon him, and he shall hear a rumor and return to his own land; and I will cause him to fall by the sword in his own land." ' "

⁸ Then *the* Rabshakeh returned, and found the king of Assyria warring against Libnah, for he heard that he had departed from Lachish. ⁹ And the king heard concerning Tirhakah king of Ethiopia, "He has come out to make war with you." So when he heard *it,* he sent messengers to Hezekiah, saying, ¹⁰ "Thus you shall speak to Hezekiah king of Judah, saying: 'Do not let your God in whom you trust deceive you, saying, "Jerusalem shall not be given into the hand of the king of Assyria." ¹¹ Look! You have heard what the kings of Assyria have done to all lands by utterly destroying them; and shall you be delivered? ¹² Have the gods of the nations delivered those whom my fathers have destroyed, Gozan and Haran and Rezeph, and the people of Eden who *were* in Telassar? ¹³ Where *is* the king of Hamath, the king of Arpad, and the king of the city of Sepharvaim, Hena, and Ivah?' "

14 And Hezekiah received the letter from the hand of the messengers, and read it; and Hezekiah went up to the house of the LORD, and spread it before the LORD. 15 Then Hezekiah prayed to the LORD, saying: 16 "O LORD of hosts, God of Israel, *the One* who dwells *between* the cherubim, You *are* God, You alone, of all the kingdoms of the earth. You have made heaven and earth. 17 Incline Your ear, O LORD, and hear; open Your eyes, O LORD, and *see*; and hear all the words of Sennacherib, which he has sent to reproach the living God. 18 Truly, LORD, the kings of Assyria have laid waste all the nations and their lands, 19 and have cast their gods into the fire; for they *were* not gods, but the work of men's hands—wood and stone. Therefore they destroyed them. 20 Now therefore, O LORD our God, save us from his hand, that all the kingdoms of the earth may know that You *are* the LORD, You alone."

21 Then Isaiah the son of Amoz sent to Hezekiah, saying, "Thus says the LORD God of Israel, 'Because you have prayed to Me against Sennacherib king of Assyria, 22 this *is* the word which the LORD has spoken concerning him:

"The virgin, the daughter of Zion,
Has despised you, laughed you to scorn;
The daughter of Jerusalem
Has shaken *her* head behind your back!

23 "Whom have you reproached and blasphemed?
Against whom have you raised *your* voice,
And lifted up your eyes on high?
Against the Holy One of Israel.
24 By your servants you have reproached the Lord,
And said, 'By the multitude of my chariots
I have come up to the height of the mountains,
To the limits of Lebanon;
I will cut down its tall cedars
And its choice cypress trees;

I will enter its farthest height,
To its fruitful forest.
25 I have dug and drunk water,
And with the soles of my feet I have dried up
All the brooks of defense.'

26 "Did you not hear long ago
How I made it,
From ancient times that I formed it?
Now I have brought it to pass,
That you should be
For crushing fortified cities *into* heaps of ruins.
27 Therefore their inhabitants *had* little power;
They were dismayed and confounded;
They were *as* the grass of the field
And the green herb,
As the grass on the housetops
And grain blighted before it is grown.

28 "But I know your dwelling place,
Your going out and your coming in,
And your rage against Me.
29 Because your rage against Me and your tumult
Have come up to My ears,
Therefore I will put My hook in your nose
And My bridle in your lips,
And I will turn you back
By the way which you came." '

30 "This *shall be* a sign to you:

You shall eat this year such as grows of itself,
And the second year what springs from the same;
Also in the third year sow and reap,
Plant vineyards and eat the fruit of them.
31 And the remnant who have escaped of the house of Judah
Shall again take root downward,
And bear fruit upward.

Assyrian Army Wiped Out in Jerusalem

The Assyrian National News Network—A special report to be released immediately:

The army of King Sennacherib (pronounced *suh-NAK-er-rib*) has been destroyed. After conquering all of Judah, the troops were at the gates of Jerusalem, the capital. In one night, all the soldiers died from some mysterious cause. King Sennacherib has returned home with only a few of his bodyguards.

This is a great tragedy for our capital, Nineveh (pronounced *NIN-uh-vuh*), and for the whole nation. Many families have lost sons in the calamity at Jerusalem.

Government officials have now questioned the wisdom of the king in leading the troops against the Jews. But the king cannot be reached for comment. He is in mourning and spends most of his time in the temple. It is believed that we will try no further acts of war in the near future.

BULLETIN: King Sennacherib was found murdered this morning in the temple. His sons are being held for questioning.

32 For out of Jerusalem shall go a
    remnant,
    And those who escape from
      Mount Zion.
    The zeal of the LORD of hosts
      will do this.

33 "Therefore thus says the LORD concerning the king of Assyria:

    'He shall not come into this city,
    Nor shoot an arrow there,
    Nor come before it with shield,
    Nor build a siege mound against
      it.
34   By the way that he came,
    By the same shall he return;
    And he shall not come into this
      city,'
    Says the LORD.
35   'For I will defend this city, to save
      it
    For My own sake and for My
      servant David's sake.' "

36 Then the angel of the LORD went out, and killed in the camp of the Assyrians one hundred and eighty-five thousand; and when *people* arose early in the morning, there were the corpses—all dead. 37 So Sennacherib king of Assyria departed and went away, returned *home,* and remained at Nineveh. 38 Now it came to pass, as he was worshiping in the house of Nisroch his god, that his sons Adrammelech and Sharezer struck him down with the sword; and they escaped into the land of Ararat. Then Esarhaddon his son reigned in his place.

King Hezekiah asks for a miracle

38 In those days Hezekiah was sick and near death. And Isaiah the prophet, the son of Amoz, went to him and said to him, "Thus says the LORD: 'Set your house in order, for you shall die and not live.' "

2 Then Hezekiah turned his face toward the wall, and prayed to the LORD, 3 and said, "Remember now, O LORD, I pray, how I have walked before You in truth and with a loyal heart, and have done *what is* good in Your sight." And Hezekiah wept bitterly.

4 And the word of the LORD came to Isaiah, saying, 5 "Go and tell Hezekiah, 'Thus says the LORD, the God of David your father: "I have heard your prayer, I have seen your tears; surely I will add to your days fifteen years. 6 I will deliver you and this city from the hand of the king of Assyria, and I will defend this city." ' 7 And this *is* the sign to you from the LORD, that the LORD will do this thing which He has spoken: 8 Behold, I will bring the shadow on the sundial, which has gone down with the sun on the sundial of

King's Life Saved by Miracle

The Jerusalem Times

JERUSALEM—King Hezekiah (pronounced *hez-uh-KIGH-uh*) has recovered from a serious illness. The prophet Isaiah had stated earlier that the king's sickness could not be cured and that death seemed certain.

We now understand that King Hezekiah later prayed to the Lord. At that time God answered the king and promised he would get well. The Lord also told Hezekiah that He would show the king proof of the promise by special sign: The shadow made by our sun clock would go backward ten steps! Scientists have confirmed this event.

Experts on the movement of the sun have been unable to answer our reporters' questions. One scientist simply shook his head and replied, "It's an act of God. What more can I say?"

This edition of *The Jerusalem Times* includes a beautiful poem written by the king when he was healed. (See Isaiah 38:10–20.)

Ahaz, ten degrees backward." So the sun returned ten degrees on the dial by which it had gone down.

9 This is the writing of Hezekiah king of Judah, when he had been sick and had recovered from his sickness:

10 I said,
    "In the prime of my life
    I shall go to the gates of Sheol;
    I am deprived of the remainder
       of my years."
11 I said,
    "I shall not see YAH,
    The LORD in the land of the
       living;
    I shall observe man no more
       among the inhabitants of the
       world.
12 My life span is gone,
    Taken from me like a shepherd's
       tent;
    I have cut off my life like a
       weaver.
    He cuts me off from the loom;
    From day until night You make
       an end of me.
13 I have considered until
       morning—
    Like a lion,
    So He breaks all my bones;
    From day until night You make
       an end of me.

14 Like a crane *or* a swallow, so I
       chattered;
    I mourned like a dove;
    My eyes fail *from looking*
       upward.
    O LORD, I am oppressed;
    Undertake for me!
15 "What shall I say?
    He has both spoken to me,
    And He Himself has done *it*.
    I shall walk carefully all my
       years
    In the bitterness of my soul.
16 O Lord, by these *things men*
       live;
    And in all these *things is* the life
       of my spirit;
    So You will restore me and
       make me live.
17 Indeed *it was* for *my own* peace
    That I had great bitterness;
    But You have lovingly *delivered*
       my soul from the pit of
       corruption,
    For You have cast all my sins
       behind Your back.
18 For Sheol cannot thank You,
    Death cannot praise You;
    Those who go down to the pit
       cannot hope for Your truth.
19 The living, the living man, he
       shall praise You,
    As I *do* this day;

919 ISAIAH 40:3

The father shall make known
Your truth to the children.

20 "The LORD *was ready* to save me;
Therefore we will sing my songs
with stringed instruments
All the days of our life, in the
house of the LORD."

21 Now Isaiah had said, "Let them take a lump of figs, and apply *it* as a poultice on the boil, and he shall recover."

22 And Hezekiah had said, "What *is* the sign that I shall go up to the house of the LORD?"

Judah will be captured

39 At that time Merodach-Baladan the son of Baladan, king of Babylon, sent letters and a present to Hezekiah, for he heard that he had been sick and had recovered. 2 And Hezekiah was pleased with them, and showed them the house of his treasures—the silver and gold, the spices and precious ointment, and all his armory—all that was found among his treasures. There was nothing in his house or in all his dominion that Hezekiah did not show them.

3 Then Isaiah the prophet went to King Hezekiah, and said to him, "What did these men say, and from where did they come to you?"

So Hezekiah said, "They came to me from a far country, from Babylon."

4 And he said, "What have they seen in your house?"

So Hezekiah answered, "They have seen all that *is* in my house; there is nothing among my treasures that I have not shown them."

5 Then Isaiah said to Hezekiah, "Hear the word of the LORD of hosts: 6 'Behold, the days are coming when all that *is* in your house, and what your fathers have accumulated until this day, shall be carried to Babylon; nothing shall be left,' says the LORD. 7 'And they shall take away *some* of your sons who will descend from you, whom you will beget; and they shall be eunuchs in the palace of the king of Babylon.'"

8 So Hezekiah said to Isaiah, "The word of the LORD which you have spoken *is* good!" For he said, "At least there will be peace and truth in my days."

Our great and awesome God

40 "Comfort, yes, comfort My people!"
Says your God.
2 "Speak comfort to Jerusalem,
and cry out to her,
That her warfare is ended,
That her iniquity is pardoned;
For she has received from the
LORD's hand
Double for all her sins."

3 The voice of one crying in the
wilderness:
"Prepare the way of the LORD;

What Hezekiah Learned

Pronounce my name *hez-uh-KIGH-un,* meaning "The Lord Is Strength." What I did was a result of self-importance and good nature. I wanted to show that foreign king's messengers how rich and powerful I am. At the same time, I wanted to be a nice friendly host. My big mistake was I forgot to be *wise.* In fact, what I did was very foolish!

Then Isaiah the prophet came and gave me the bad news: My stupid action means that the King of Babylon (pronounced *BAB-ih-lon*) will come and take away everything I showed those messengers.

False pride leads to destruction, and my pride is the proof of it. I only wish I could have learned this lesson before I sold out my country.

Make straight in the desert
A highway for our God.

4   Every valley shall be exalted
    And *every* mountain and hill
        brought low;
    The crooked places shall be
        made straight
    And the rough places smooth;
5   The glory of the LORD shall be
        revealed,
    And all flesh shall *see it* together;
    For the mouth of the LORD has
        spoken."

6   The voice said, "Cry out!"
    And he said, "What shall I cry?"

    "All flesh *is* grass,
    And all its loveliness *is* like the
        flower of the field.
7   The grass withers, the flower
        fades,
    Because the breath of the LORD
        blows upon it;
    Surely the people *are* grass.
8   The grass withers, the flower
        fades,
    But the word of our God stands
        forever."

9   O Zion,
    You who bring good tidings,
    Get up into the high mountain;
    O Jerusalem,
    You who bring good tidings,
    Lift up your voice with strength,
    Lift *it* up, be not afraid;
    Say to the cities of Judah,
        "Behold your God!"

10 Behold, the Lord GOD shall
        come with a strong *hand,*
    And His arm shall rule for Him;
    Behold, His reward *is* with Him,
    And His work before Him.
11 He will feed His flock like a
        shepherd;
    He will gather the lambs with His
        arm,
    And carry *them* in His bosom,
    And gently lead those who are
        with young.

12 Who has measured the waters
        in the hollow of His hand,
    Measured heaven with a span
    And calculated the dust of the
        earth in a measure?
    Weighed the mountains in scales
    And the hills in a balance?
13 Who has directed the Spirit of
        the LORD,
    Or *as* His counselor has taught
        Him?
14 With whom did He take counsel,
        and *who* instructed Him,
    And taught Him in the path of
        justice?
    Who taught Him knowledge,
    And showed Him the way of
        understanding?

15 Behold, the nations *are* as a
        drop in a bucket,
    And are counted as the small
        dust on the scales;
    Look, He lifts up the isles as a
        very little thing.
16 And Lebanon *is* not sufficient to
        burn,
    Nor its beasts sufficient for a
        burnt offering.
17 All nations before Him *are* as
        nothing,
    And they are counted by Him
        less than nothing and
        worthless.

18 To whom then will you liken
        God?
    Or what likeness will you
        compare to Him?
19 The workman molds an image,
    The goldsmith overspreads it
        with gold,
    And the silversmith casts silver
        chains.
20 Whoever *is* too impoverished for
        such a contribution
    Chooses a tree *that* will not rot;
    He seeks for himself a skillful
        workman
    To prepare a carved image *that*
        will not totter.

21 Have you not known?
    Have you not heard?
    Has it not been told you from
        the beginning?

Have you not understood from
the foundations of the earth?
22 *It is* He who sits above the circle
of the earth,
And its inhabitants *are* like
grasshoppers,
Who stretches out the heavens
like a curtain,
And spreads them out like a tent
to dwell in.
23 He brings the princes to nothing;
He makes the judges of the earth
useless.

24 Scarcely shall they be planted,
Scarcely shall they be sown,
Scarcely shall their stock take
root in the earth,
When He will also blow on
them,
And they will wither,
And the whirlwind will take them
away like stubble.

25 "To whom then will you liken
Me,
Or *to whom* shall I be equal?"
says the Holy One.
26 Lift up your eyes on high,
And see who has created these
things,
Who brings out their host by
number;
He calls them all by name,
By the greatness of His might
And the strength of *His* power;
Not one is missing.

27 Why do you say, O Jacob,
And speak, O Israel:

"My way is hidden from the
Lord,
And my just claim is passed over
by my God"?
28 Have you not known?
Have you not heard?
The everlasting God, the Lord,
The Creator of the ends of the
earth,
Neither faints nor is weary.
His understanding is
unsearchable.
29 He gives power to the weak,
And to *those who have* no might
He increases strength.
30 Even the youths shall faint and
be weary,
And the young men shall utterly
fall,
31 But those who wait on the Lord
Shall renew *their* strength;
They shall mount up with wings
like eagles,
They shall run and not be
weary,
They shall walk and not faint.

God will help His people

41 "Keep silence before Me, O
coastlands,
And let the people renew *their*
strength!
Let them come near, then let
them speak;
Let us come near together for
judgment.

2 "Who raised up one from the
east?

⚒ DIGGING IN

40:31 You Can Be Strong Not everybody can be built like a lineman on a football team, but everyone can be strong in spirit.

There is only one way to be strong spiritually: "Wait on the Lord." Does that sound strange? How do you *wait* on the Lord? Isn't God everywhere?

Yes, God is everywhere at the same time because He is infinite. But He

doesn't *act* the same everywhere at the same time. What the Lord is saying in this text is, "I want to change your life. So wait for Me in prayer and trust. Ask Me to come into your life." Then you will become strong like an eagle. You will run and never be tired of working for God. Serving Him will be the greatest happiness of your life!

Who in righteousness called him
to His feet?
Who gave the nations before
him,
And made *him* rule over kings?
Who gave *them* as the dust *to*
his sword,
As driven stubble to his bow?

3 Who pursued them, *and* passed
safely
By the way *that* he had not gone
with his feet?

4 Who has performed and done
it,
Calling the generations from the
beginning?
'I, the LORD, am the first;
And with the last I *am* He.' "

5 The coastlands saw *it* and
feared,
The ends of the earth were
afraid;
They drew near and came.

6 Everyone helped his neighbor,
And said to his brother,
"Be of good courage!"

7 So the craftsman encouraged
the goldsmith;
He who smooths *with* the
hammer *inspired* him who
strikes the anvil,
Saying, "It *is* ready for the
soldering";
Then he fastened it with pegs,
That it might not totter.

8 "But you, Israel, *are* My servant,
Jacob whom I have chosen,
The descendants of Abraham
My friend.

9 *You* whom I have taken from
the ends of the earth,
And called from its farthest
regions,
And said to you,
'You *are* My servant,
I have chosen you and have not
cast you away:

10 Fear not, for I *am* with you;
Be not dismayed, for I *am* your
God.
I will strengthen you,
Yes, I will help you,
I will uphold you with My
righteous right hand.'

11 "Behold, all those who were
incensed against you
Shall be ashamed and
disgraced;
They shall be as nothing,
And those who strive with you
shall perish.

12 You shall seek them and not find
them—
Those who contended with you.
Those who war against you
Shall be as nothing,
As a nonexistent thing.

13 For I, the LORD your God, will
hold your right hand,
Saying to you, 'Fear not, I will
help you.'

14 "Fear not, you worm Jacob,
You men of Israel!
I will help you," says the LORD
And your Redeemer, the Holy
One of Israel.

15 "Behold, I will make you into a
new threshing sledge with
sharp teeth;
You shall thresh the mountains
and beat *them* small,
And make the hills like chaff.

16 You shall winnow them, the
wind shall carry them away,
And the whirlwind shall scatter
them;
You shall rejoice in the LORD,
And glory in the Holy One of
Israel.

17 "The poor and needy seek water,
but *there is* none,
Their tongues fail for thirst.
I, the LORD, will hear them;
I, the God of Israel, will not
forsake them.

18 I will open rivers in desolate
heights,
And fountains in the midst of the
valleys;
I will make the wilderness a pool
of water,
And the dry land springs of
water.

19 I will plant in the wilderness the
cedar and the acacia tree,
The myrtle and the oil tree;
I will set in the desert the cypress
tree *and* the pine
And the box tree together,
20 That they may see and know,
And consider and understand
together,
That the hand of the LORD has
done this,
And the Holy One of Israel has
created it.

21 "Present your case," says the
LORD.
"Bring forth your strong
reasons," says the King of
Jacob.
22 "Let them bring forth and show
us what will happen;
Let them show the former
things, what they *were*,
That *we* may consider them,
And know the latter end of
them;
Or declare to us things to come.
23 Show the things that are to come
hereafter,
That we may know that you *are*
gods;
Yes, do good or do evil,
That *we* may be dismayed and
see *it* together.
24 Indeed you *are* nothing,
And your work *is* nothing;
He who chooses you *is* an
abomination.

25 "I have raised up one from the
north,
And he shall come;
From the rising of the sun he
shall call on My name;
And he shall come against
princes as *though* mortar,
As the potter treads clay.
26 Who has declared from the
beginning, that we may
know?
And former times, that we may
say, 'He *is* righteous'?
Surely *there is* no one who
shows,

Surely *there is* no one who
declares,
Surely *there is* no one who hears
your words.
27 The first time *I said* to Zion,
'Look, there they are!'
And I will give to Jerusalem one
who brings good tidings.
28 For I looked, and *there was* no
man;
I looked among them, but *there
was* no counselor,
Who, when I asked of them,
could answer a word.
29 Indeed they *are* all worthless;
Their works *are* nothing;
Their molded images *are* wind
and confusion.

The Chosen One is a mighty warrior

42 "Behold! My Servant whom I
uphold,
My Elect One *in whom* My soul
delights!
I have put My Spirit upon Him;
He will bring forth justice to the
Gentiles.
2 He will not cry out, nor raise *His
voice*,
Nor cause His voice to be heard
in the street.
3 A bruised reed He will not break,
And smoking flax He will not
quench;
He will bring forth justice for
truth.
4 He will not fail nor be
discouraged,
Till He has established justice in
the earth;
And the coastlands shall wait for
His law."

5 Thus says God the LORD,
Who created the heavens and
stretched them out,
Who spread forth the earth and
that which comes from it,
Who gives breath to the people
on it,
And spirit to those who walk on
it:

6 "I, the LORD, have called You in
      righteousness,
   And will hold Your hand;
   I will keep You and give You
      as a covenant to the people,
   As a light to the Gentiles,
7 To open blind eyes,
   To bring out prisoners from the
      prison,
   Those who sit in darkness from
      the prison house.
8 I *am* the LORD, that *is* My name;
   And My glory I will not give to
      another,
   Nor My praise to carved images.
9 Behold, the former things have
      come to pass,
   And new things I declare;
   Before they spring forth I tell you
      of them."

10 Sing to the LORD a new song,
   And His praise from the ends of
      the earth,
   You who go down to the sea,
      and all that is in it,
   You coastlands and you
      inhabitants of them!
11 Let the wilderness and its cities
      lift up *their voice,*
   The villages *that* Kedar inhabits.
   Let the inhabitants of Sela sing,
   Let them shout from the top of
      the mountains.
12 Let them give glory to the LORD,
   And declare His praise in the
      coastlands.
13 The LORD shall go forth like a
      mighty man;
   He shall stir up *His* zeal like a
      man of war.
   He shall cry out, yes, shout
      aloud;
   He shall prevail against His
      enemies.

14 "I have held My peace a long
      time,
   I have been still and restrained
      Myself.
   Now I will cry like a woman in
      labor,
   I will pant and gasp at once.
15 I will lay waste the mountains
      and hills,

   And dry up all their vegetation;
   I will make the rivers coastlands,
   And I will dry up the pools.
16 I will bring the blind by a way
      they did not know;
   I will lead them in paths they
      have not known.
   I will make darkness light before
      them,
   And crooked places straight.
   These things I will do for them,
   And not forsake them.
17 They shall be turned back,
   They shall be greatly ashamed,
   Who trust in carved images,
   Who say to the molded images,
   'You *are* our gods.'

18 "Hear, you deaf;
   And look, you blind, that you
      may *see.*
19 Who *is* blind but My servant,
   Or deaf as My messenger *whom*
      I send?
   Who *is* blind as *he who is*
      perfect,
   And blind as the LORD's servant?
20 Seeing many things, but you do
      not observe;
   Opening the ears, but he does
      not hear."

21 The LORD is well pleased for His
      righteousness' sake;
   He will exalt the law and make
      it honorable.
22 But this *is* a people robbed and
      plundered;
   All of them are snared in holes,
   And they are hidden in prison
      houses;
   They are for prey, and no one
      delivers;
   For plunder, and no one says,
      "Restore!"

23 Who among you will give ear to
      this?
   Who will listen and hear for the
      time to come?
24 Who gave Jacob for plunder,
      and Israel to the robbers?
   Was it not the LORD,
   He against whom we have
      sinned?

For they would not walk in His
ways,
Nor were they obedient to His
law.
25 Therefore He has poured on
him the fury of His anger
And the strength of battle;
It has set him on fire all around,
Yet he did not know;
And it burned him,
Yet he did not take *it* to heart.

God forgets His people's sins

43 But now, thus says the LORD,
who created you, O Jacob,
And He who formed you, O
Israel:
"Fear not, for I have redeemed
you;
I have called *you* by your name;
You *are* Mine.
2 When you pass through the
waters, I *will be* with you;
And through the rivers, they
shall not overflow you.
When you walk through the fire,
you shall not be burned,
Nor shall the flame scorch you.
3 For I *am* the LORD your God,
The Holy One of Israel, your
Savior;
I gave Egypt for your ransom,
Ethiopia and Seba in your place.
4 Since you were precious in My
sight,
You have been honored,
And I have loved you;
Therefore I will give men for
you,
And people for your life.

5 Fear not, for I *am* with you;
I will bring your descendants
from the east,
And gather you from the
west;
6 I will say to the north, 'Give
them up!'
And to the south, 'Do not keep
them back!'
Bring My sons from afar,
And My daughters from the ends
of the earth—
7 Everyone who is called by My
name,
Whom I have created for My
glory;
I have formed him, yes, I have
made him."

8 Bring out the blind people who
have eyes,
And the deaf who have ears.
9 Let all the nations be gathered
together,
And let the people be
assembled.
Who among them can declare
this,
And show us former things?
Let them bring out their
witnesses, that they may be
justified;
Or let them hear and say, "*It is
truth.*"
10 "You *are* My witnesses," says the
LORD,
"And My servant whom I have
chosen,
That you may know and believe
Me,
And understand that I *am* He.

43:7 Why God Created You Sometimes you may be disappointed because you aren't all you'd like to be. Maybe you aren't great at sports, or maybe you don't get the highest grades. But you can still be great because your life glorifies God. A person who can't walk or see can bring honor to God in ways that other people can't. Some have wonderful stories of how Jesus saved them and put a beautiful song in their hearts. The world is blessed by people like that.

Christians should be different because they have eternal life, not because they're VIPs. Such a Christian glorifies God because his or her life proves that Christ makes a difference. Such people make others want to be Christians, too. That's why God created you—to bring that kind of honor to Him.

Who Is Your Redeemer?

A "redeemer" is someone who buys back something that was sold to someone else. We were once sold to Satan because of our sins. But God has *redeemed* us. The Lord bought us back from slavery to Satan. The price of redeeming us was the blood of God's only Son, Jesus.

Before Me there was no God formed,
Nor shall there be after Me.
11 I, *even* I, am the LORD,
And besides Me *there is* no savior.
12 I have declared and saved,
I have proclaimed,
And *there was* no foreign *god* among you;
Therefore you *are* My witnesses,"
Says the LORD, "that I *am* God.
13 Indeed before the day *was*, I *am* He;
And *there is* no one who can deliver out of My hand;
I work, and who will reverse it?"

14 Thus says the LORD, your Redeemer,
The Holy One of Israel:
"For your sake I will send to Babylon,
And bring them all down as fugitives—
The Chaldeans, who rejoice in their ships.
15 I *am* the LORD, your Holy One,
The Creator of Israel, your King."

16 Thus says the LORD, who makes a way in the sea
And a path through the mighty waters,
17 Who brings forth the chariot and horse,
The army and the power
(They shall lie down together, they shall not rise;
They are extinguished, they are quenched like a wick):

18 "Do not remember the former things,
Nor consider the things of old.
19 Behold, I will do a new thing,
Now it shall spring forth;
Shall you not know it?
I will even make a road in the wilderness
And rivers in the desert.
20 The beast of the field will honor Me,
The jackals and the ostriches,
Because I give waters in the wilderness
And rivers in the desert,
To give drink to My people, My chosen.
21 This people I have formed for Myself;
They shall declare My praise.

22 "But you have not called upon Me, O Jacob;
And you have been weary of Me, O Israel.
23 You have not brought Me the sheep for your burnt offerings,
Nor have you honored Me with your sacrifices.
I have not caused you to serve with grain offerings,
Nor wearied you with incense.
24 You have bought Me no sweet cane with money,
Nor have you satisfied Me with the fat of your sacrifices;
But you have burdened Me with your sins,
You have wearied Me with your iniquities.

25 "I, *even* I, am He who blots out your transgressions for My own sake;
And I will not remember your sins.
26 Put Me in remembrance;
Let us contend together;
State your *case*, that you may be acquitted.
27 Your first father sinned,
And your mediators have transgressed against Me.

28 Therefore I will profane the
   princes of the sanctuary;
I will give Jacob to the curse,
And Israel to reproaches.

How stupid it is to worship a block of wood!

44 "Yet hear me now, O Jacob **My servant,**
   And Israel whom I have
   chosen.
2 Thus says the LORD who made
   you
   And formed you from the
   womb, *who* will help you:
'Fear not, O Jacob My servant;
And you, Jeshurun, whom I
   have chosen.
3 For I will pour water on him who
   is thirsty,
   And floods on the dry ground;
I will pour My Spirit on your
   descendants,
   And My blessing on your
   offspring;
4 They will spring up among the
   grass
   Like willows by the
   watercourses.'
5 One will say, 'I *am* the LORD's';
   Another will call *himself* by the
   name of Jacob;
Another will write *with* his hand,
   'The LORD's,'

And name *himself* by the name
   of Israel.
6 "Thus says the LORD, the King of
   Israel,
   And his Redeemer, the LORD of
   hosts:
'I *am* the First and I *am* the Last;
Besides Me *there is* no God.
7 And who can proclaim as I do?
   Then let him declare it and set
   it in order for Me,
   Since I appointed the ancient
   people.
   And the things that are coming
   and shall come,
   Let them show these to them.
8 Do not fear, nor be afraid;
   Have I not told you from that
   time, and declared *it*?
You *are* My witnesses.
Is there a God besides Me?
Indeed *there is* no other Rock;
I know not *one.*' "

9 Those who make an image, all
   of them *are* useless,
   And their precious things shall
   not profit;
They *are* their own witnesses;
They neither see nor know, that
   they may be ashamed.
10 Who would form a god or mold
   an image
   That profits him nothing?

WORDFINDER

44:1 My Servant Refers here to Israel, but in Isaiah 49:6, the term refers to the coming Messiah, or Christ, in the New Testament.

DIGGING IN

44:6 Who Is God? God says "I am the First and I am the Last." So God is the One we have to begin with when we start thinking about anything. If God didn't create all the things in the world, then all you see around you may be only your imagination.

You heard long ago that 2 + 2 = 4. Who decided that? Not just your school-teacher! God made 2 + 2 = 4 because He created a world where numbers make

sense. Right and wrong exist because God gives His Law to live by.

If you take God away, you can never be sure that 2 + 2 = 4 or that good is better than evil. Who would decide for us? What would be the use of learning? The apostle Paul says that people without God can never know the truth (see 2 Timothy 3:7). *But God created all the things in the universe and He is Truth.*

11 Surely all his companions would
be ashamed;
And the workmen, they *are*
mere men.
Let them all be gathered
together,
Let them stand up;
Yet they shall fear,
They shall be ashamed together.

12 The blacksmith with the tongs
works one in the coals,
Fashions it with hammers,
And works it with the strength
of his arms.
Even so, he is hungry, and his
strength fails;
He drinks no water and is faint.

13 The craftsman stretches out *his*
rule,
He marks one out with chalk;
He fashions it with a plane,
He marks it out with the
compass,
And makes it like the figure of
a man,
According to the beauty of a
man, that it may remain in the
house.

14 He cuts down cedars for himself,
And takes the cypress and the
oak;
He secures *it* for himself among
the trees of the forest.
He plants a pine, and the rain
nourishes *it*.

15 Then it shall be for a man to
burn,
For he will take some of it and
warm himself;
Yes, he kindles *it* and bakes
bread;
Indeed he makes a god and
worships *it*;
He makes it a carved image, and
falls down to it.

16 He burns half of it in the fire;
With this half he eats meat;
He roasts a roast, and is satisfied.
He even warms *himself* and
says,
"Ah! I am warm,
I have seen the fire."

17 And the rest of it he makes into
a god,
His carved image.
He falls down before it and
worships *it,*
Prays to it and says,
"Deliver me, for you *are* my
god!"

18 They do not know nor
understand;
For He has shut their eyes, so
that they cannot see,
And their hearts, so that they
cannot understand.

19 And no one considers in his
heart,
Nor *is there* knowledge nor
understanding to say,
"I have burned half of it in the
fire,
Yes, I have also baked bread on
its coals;
I have roasted meat and eaten
it;
And shall I make the rest of it
an abomination?
Shall I fall down before a block
of wood?"

20 He feeds on ashes;
A deceived heart has turned him
aside;
And he cannot deliver his soul,
Nor say, "*Is there* not a lie in
my right hand?"

21 "Remember these, O Jacob,
And Israel, for you *are* My
servant;
I have formed you, you *are* My
servant;
O Israel, you will not be
forgotten by Me!

22 I have blotted out, like a thick
cloud, your transgressions,
And like a cloud, your sins.
Return to Me, for I have
redeemed you."

23 Sing, O heavens, for the LORD
has done *it!*
Shout, you lower parts of the
earth;
Break forth into singing, you
mountains,

O forest, and *every* tree in it!
For the LORD has redeemed
  Jacob,
And glorified Himself in Israel.

24 Thus says the LORD, your
  Redeemer,
And He who formed you from
  the womb:
"I *am* the LORD, who makes all
  things,
Who stretches out the heavens
  all alone,
Who spreads abroad the earth
  by Myself;
25 Who frustrates the signs of the
  babblers,
And drives diviners mad;
Who turns wise men backward,
And makes their knowledge
  foolishness;
26 Who confirms the word of His
  servant,
And performs the counsel of His
  messengers;
Who says to Jerusalem, 'You
  shall be inhabited,'
To the cities of Judah, 'You shall
  be built,'
And I will raise up her waste
  places;
27 Who says to the deep, 'Be dry!
And I will dry up your rivers';
28 Who says of Cyrus, '*He is* My
  shepherd,
And he shall perform all My
  pleasure,
Saying to Jerusalem, "You shall
  be built,"
And to the temple, "Your
  foundation shall be laid." '

Only the true God can save us

45 "Thus says the LORD to His
  anointed,
To Cyrus, whose right hand I
  have held—
To subdue nations before him
And loose the armor of kings,
To open before him the double
  doors,
So that the gates will not be shut:
2 'I will go before you

And make the crooked places
  straight;
I will break in pieces the gates
  of bronze
And cut the bars of iron.
3 I will give you the treasures of
  darkness
And hidden riches of secret
  places,
That you may know that I, the
  LORD,
Who call *you* by your name,
Am the God of Israel.
4 For Jacob My servant's sake,
And Israel My elect,
I have even called you by your
  name;
I have named you, though you
  have not known Me.
5 I *am* the LORD, and *there is* no
  other;
There is no God besides Me.
I will gird you, though you have
  not known Me,
6 That they may know from the
  rising of the sun to its setting
That *there is* none besides Me.
I *am* the LORD, and *there is* no
  other;
7 I form the light and create
  darkness,
I make peace and create
  calamity;
I, the LORD, do all these *things.*'

8 "Rain down, you heavens, from
  above,
And let the skies pour down
  righteousness;
Let the earth open, let them
  bring forth salvation,
And let righteousness spring up
  together.
I, the LORD, have created it.

9 "Woe to him who strives with his
  Maker!
Let the potsherd *strive* with the
  potsherds of the earth!
Shall the clay say to him who
  forms it, 'What are you
  making?'
Or shall your handiwork *say,*
  'He has no hands'?

10 Woe to him who says to *his*
   father, 'What are you
   begetting?'
   Or to the woman, 'What have
   you brought forth?' "

11 Thus says the LORD,
   The Holy One of Israel, and his
   Maker:
   "Ask Me of things to come
   concerning My sons;
   And concerning the work of My
   hands, you command Me.

12 I have made the earth,
   And created man on it.
   I—My hands—stretched out the
   heavens,
   And all their host I have
   commanded.

13 I have raised him up in
   righteousness,
   And I will direct all his ways;
   He shall build My city
   And let My exiles go free,
   Not for price nor reward,"
   Says the LORD of hosts.

14 Thus says the LORD:

   "The labor of Egypt and
   merchandise of Cush
   And of the Sabeans, men of
   stature,
   Shall come over to you, and
   they shall be yours;
   They shall walk behind you,
   They shall come over in chains;
   And they shall bow down to
   you.
   They will make supplication to
   you, *saying,* 'Surely God *is* in
   you,
   And *there is* no other;
   There is no other God.' "

15 Truly You *are* God, who hide
   Yourself,
   O God of Israel, the **Savior!**

16 They shall be ashamed

And also disgraced, all of them;
They shall go in confusion
   together,
Who are makers of idols.

17 *But* Israel shall be saved by the
   LORD
   With an everlasting salvation;
   You shall not be ashamed or
   disgraced
   Forever and ever.

18 For thus says the LORD,
   Who created the heavens,
   Who is God,
   Who formed the earth and made
   it,
   Who has established it,
   Who did not create it in vain,
   Who formed it to be inhabited:
   "I *am* the LORD, and *there is* no
   other.

19 I have not spoken in secret,
   In a dark place of the earth;
   I did not say to the seed of
   Jacob,
   'Seek Me in vain';
   I, the LORD, speak righteousness,
   I declare things that are right.

20 "Assemble yourselves and come;
   Draw near together,
   You *who have* escaped from the
   nations.
   They have no knowledge,
   Who carry the wood of their
   carved image,
   And pray to a god *that* cannot
   save.

21 Tell and bring forth *your case;*
   Yes, let them take counsel
   together.
   Who has declared this from
   ancient time?
   Who has told it from that time?
   Have not I, the LORD?
   And *there is* no other God
   besides Me,
   A just God and a Savior;
   There is none besides Me.

22 "Look to Me, and be saved,
All you ends of the earth!
For I *am* God, and *there is* no
    other.
23 I have sworn by Myself;
The word has gone out of My
    mouth *in* righteousness,
And shall not return,
That to Me every knee shall
    bow,
Every tongue shall take an oath.
24 He shall say,
'Surely in the LORD I have
    righteousness and strength.
To Him *men* shall come,
And all shall be ashamed
Who are incensed against Him.
25 In the LORD all the descendants
    of Israel
Shall be justified, and shall
    glory.' "

Helpless idols can't compare to our powerful God

46 Bel bows down, Nebo stoops;
Their idols were on the beasts
    and on the cattle.
Your carriages *were* heavily
    loaded,

A burden to the weary *beast.*
2 They stoop, they bow down
    together;
They could not deliver the
    burden,
But have themselves gone into
    captivity.

3 "Listen to Me, O house of Jacob,
And all the remnant of the house
    of Israel,
Who have been upheld *by Me*
    from birth,
Who have been carried from the
    womb:
4 Even to *your* old age, I *am* He,
And *even* to gray hairs I will
    carry *you!*
I have made, and I will bear;
Even I will carry, and will deliver
    you.

5 "To whom will you liken Me, and
    make *Me* equal
And compare Me, that we
    should be alike?
6 They lavish gold out of the bag,
And weigh silver on the scales;
They hire a goldsmith, and he
    makes it a god;

The ruins of the Temple of Bel, an important god of Babylon.

They prostrate themselves, yes,
  they worship.
7 They bear it on the shoulder,
    they carry it
And set it in its place, and it
    stands;
From its place it shall not move.
Though *one* cries out to it, yet
    it cannot answer
Nor save him out of his trouble.

8 "Remember this, and show
    yourselves men;
Recall to mind, O you
    transgressors.
9 Remember the former things of
    old,
For I *am* God, and *there is* no
    other;
I am God, and *there is* none like
    Me,
10 Declaring the end from the
    beginning,
And from ancient times *things*
    that are not *yet* done,
Saying, 'My counsel shall stand,
And I will do all My pleasure,'
11 Calling a bird of prey from the
    east,
The man who executes My
    counsel, from a far country.
Indeed I have spoken *it;*
I will also bring it to pass.
I have purposed *it;*
I will also do it.

12 "Listen to Me, you
    stubborn-hearted,
Who *are* far from righteousness:
13 I bring My righteousness near,
    it shall not be far off;
My salvation shall not linger.
And I will place salvation in Zion,
For Israel My glory.

God will take revenge

47 "Come down and sit in the dust,
    O virgin daughter of Babylon;
Sit on the ground without a
    throne,
O daughter of the Chaldeans!
For you shall no more be called
Tender and delicate.

2 Take the millstones and grind
    meal.
Remove your veil,
Take off the skirt,
Uncover the thigh,
Pass through the rivers.
3 Your nakedness shall be
    uncovered,
Yes, your shame will be seen;
I will take vengeance,
And I will not arbitrate with a
    man."

4 *As for* our Redeemer, the LORD
    of hosts *is* His name,
The Holy One of Israel.

5 "Sit in silence, and go into
    darkness,
O daughter of the Chaldeans;
For you shall no longer be called
The Lady of Kingdoms.
6 I was angry with My people;
I have profaned My inheritance,
And given them into your hand.
You showed them no mercy;
On the elderly you laid your
    yoke very heavily.
7 And you said, 'I shall be a lady
    forever,'
So that you did not take these
    things to heart,
Nor remember the latter end of
    them.

8 "Therefore hear this now, *you
    who are* given to pleasures,
Who dwell securely,
Who say in your heart, 'I *am,*
    and *there is* no one else
    besides me;
I shall not sit *as* a widow,
Nor shall I know the loss of
    children';
9 But these two *things* shall come
    to you
In a moment, in one day:
The loss of children, and
    widowhood.
They shall come upon you in
    their fullness
Because of the multitude of your
    sorceries,
For the great abundance of your
    enchantments.

10 "For you have trusted in your
wickedness;
You have said, 'No one *sees*
me';
Your wisdom and your
knowledge have warped
you;
And you have said in your heart,
'I *am,* and *there is* no one else
besides me.'
11 Therefore evil shall come upon
you;
You shall not know from where
it arises.
And trouble shall fall upon
you;
You will not be able to put it
off.
And desolation shall come upon
you suddenly,
Which you shall not know.

12 "Stand now with your
enchantments
And the multitude of your
sorceries,
In which you have labored from
your youth—
Perhaps you will be able to
profit,
Perhaps you will prevail.
13 You are wearied in the multitude
of your counsels;
Let now the astrologers, the
stargazers,
And the monthly prognosticators
Stand up and save you
From what shall come upon
you.
14 Behold, they shall be as stubble,
The fire shall burn them;
They shall not deliver
themselves
From the power of the flame;
It shall not *be* a coal to be
warmed by,
Nor a fire to sit before!
15 Thus shall they be to you
With whom you have labored,
Your merchants from your
youth;
They shall wander each one to
his quarter.
No one shall save you.

Israel is stubborn and hard-headed

48 "Hear this, O house of Jacob,
Who are called by the name of
Israel,
And have come forth from the
wellsprings of Judah;
Who swear by the name of the
LORD,
And make mention of the God
of Israel,
But not in truth or in
righteousness;
2 For they call themselves after the
holy city,
And lean on the God of Israel;
The LORD of hosts *is* His name:

3 "I have declared the former things
from the beginning;
They went forth from My mouth,
and I caused them to hear it.
Suddenly I did *them,* and they
came to pass.
4 Because I knew that you *were*
obstinate,
And your neck *was* an iron
sinew,
And your brow bronze,
5 Even from the beginning I have
declared *it* to you;
Before it came to pass I
proclaimed *it* to you,
Lest you should say, 'My idol
has done them,
And my carved image and my
molded image
Have commanded them.'

6 "You have heard;
See all this.
And will you not declare *it?*
I have made you hear new
things from this time,
Even hidden things, and you did
not know them.
7 They are created now and not
from the beginning;
And before this day you have
not heard them,
Lest you should say, 'Of course
I knew them.'
8 Surely you did not hear,

Surely you did not know;
Surely from long ago your ear
was not opened.
For I knew that you would deal
very treacherously,
And were called a transgressor
from the womb.

9 "For My name's sake I will defer
My anger,
And *for* My praise I will restrain
it from you,
So that I do not cut you off.
10 Behold, I have refined you, but
not as silver;
I have tested you in the furnace
of affliction.
11 For My own sake, for My own
sake, I will do *it;*
For how should *My name* be
profaned?
And I will not give My glory to
another.

12 "Listen to Me, O Jacob,
And Israel, My called:
I *am* He, I *am* the First,
I *am* also the Last.
13 Indeed My hand has laid the
foundation of the earth,
And My right hand has stretched
out the heavens;
When I call to them,
They stand up together.

14 "All of you, assemble yourselves,
and hear!
Who among them has declared
these *things?*
The LORD loves him;
He shall do His pleasure on
Babylon,
And His arm *shall be against* the
Chaldeans.
15 I, *even* I, have spoken;
Yes, I have called him,
I have brought him, and his way
will prosper.

16 "Come near to Me, hear this:
I have not spoken in secret from
the beginning;
From the time that it was, I *was*
there."

And now the Lord GOD and His
Spirit
Have sent Me."

17 Thus says the LORD, your
Redeemer,
The Holy One of Israel:
"I *am* the LORD your God,
Who teaches you to profit,
Who leads you by the way you
should go.
18 Oh, that you had heeded My
commandments!
Then your peace would have
been like a river,
And your righteousness like the
waves of the sea.
19 Your descendants also would
have been like the sand,
And the offspring of your body
like the grains of sand;
His name would not have been
cut off
Nor destroyed from before Me."

20 Go forth from Babylon!
Flee from the Chaldeans!
With a voice of singing,
Declare, proclaim this,
Utter it to the end of the earth;
Say, "The LORD has redeemed
His servant Jacob!"
21 And they did not thirst
When He led them through the
deserts;
He caused the waters to flow
from the rock for them;
He also split the rock, and the
waters gushed out.

22 "*There is* no peace," says the
LORD, "for the wicked."

The Messiah is a Light for the world

49 "Listen, O coastlands, to Me,
And take heed, you peoples
from afar!
The LORD has called Me from
the womb;
From the matrix of My mother
He has made mention of My
name.

2 And He has made My mouth
   like a sharp sword;
In the shadow of His hand He
   has hidden Me,
And made Me a polished shaft;
In His quiver He has hidden
   Me."

3 "And He said to me,
  'You *are* My servant, O Israel,
  In whom I will be glorified.'
4 Then I said, 'I have labored in
   vain,
I have spent my strength for
   nothing and in vain;
Yet surely my just reward *is* with
   the Lord,
And my work with my God.' "

5 "And now the Lord says,
Who formed Me from the womb
   to be His Servant,
To bring Jacob back to Him,
So that Israel is gathered to Him
(For I shall be glorious in the
   eyes of the Lord,
And My God shall be My
   strength),
6 Indeed He says,
'It is too small a thing that You
   should be **My Servant**
To raise up the tribes of Jacob,
And to restore the preserved
   ones of Israel;
I will also give You as a light to
   the Gentiles,
That You should be My
   salvation to the ends of the
   earth.' "

7 Thus says the Lord,
The Redeemer of Israel, their
   Holy One,
To Him whom man despises,
To Him whom the nation
   abhors,
To the Servant of rulers:
"Kings shall *see* and arise,
Princes also shall worship,

Because of the Lord who is
   faithful,
The Holy One of Israel;
And He has chosen You."

8 Thus says the Lord:

"In an acceptable time I have
   heard You,
And in the day of salvation I
   have helped You;
I will preserve You and give You
As a covenant to the people,
To restore the earth,
To cause them to inherit the
   desolate heritages;
9 That You may say to the
   prisoners, 'Go forth,'
To those who *are* in darkness,
   'Show yourselves.'

"They shall feed along the
   roads,
And their pastures *shall be* on
   all desolate heights.
10 They shall neither hunger nor
   thirst,
Neither heat nor sun shall strike
   them;
For He who has mercy on them
   will lead them,
Even by the springs of water He
   will guide them.
11 I will make each of My
   mountains a road,
And My highways shall be
   elevated.
12 Surely these shall come from
   afar;
Look! Those from the north and
   the west,
And these from the land of
   Sinim."

13 Sing, O heavens!
Be joyful, O earth!
And break out in singing, O
   mountains!
For the Lord has comforted His
   people,

WORDFINDER

49:6 My Servant   Sometimes refers to Israel (44:1), but here refers to the coming Messiah, or Christ, in the New Testament.

And will have mercy on His
    afflicted.

14   But Zion said, "The LORD has
       forsaken me,
       And my Lord has forgotten me."

15   "Can a woman forget her nursing
       child,
       And not have compassion on
         the son of her womb?
       Surely they may forget,
       Yet I will not forget you.
16   See, I have inscribed you on the
       palms *of My hands;*
       Your walls *are* continually before
         Me.
17   Your sons shall make haste;
       Your destroyers and those who
         laid you waste
       Shall go away from you.
18   Lift up your eyes, look around
       and *see;*
       All these gather together *and*
         come to you.
       As I live," says the LORD,
       "You shall surely clothe
         yourselves with them all as an
         ornament,
       And bind them *on you* as a bride
         does.

19   "For your waste and desolate
       places,
       And the land of your
         destruction,
       Will even now be too small for
         the inhabitants;
       And those who swallowed you
         up will be far away.
20   The children you will have,
       After you have lost the others,
       Will say again in your ears,
       'The place *is* too small for me;
       Give me a place where I may
         dwell.'
21   Then you will say in your heart,
       'Who has begotten these for me,
       Since I have lost my children
         and am desolate,
       A captive, and wandering to and
         fro?
       And who has brought these up?
       There I was, left alone;
       But these, where *were* they?' "

22   Thus says the Lord GOD:

     "Behold, I will lift My hand in an
       oath to the nations,
       And set up My standard for the
         peoples;
       They shall bring your sons in
         their arms,
       And your daughters shall be
         carried on *their* shoulders;
23   Kings shall be your foster
       fathers,
       And their queens your nursing
         mothers;
       They shall bow down to you
         with *their* faces to the earth,
       And lick up the dust of your feet.
       Then you will know that I *am*
         the LORD,
       For they shall not be ashamed
         who wait for Me."

24   Shall the prey be taken from the
       mighty,
       Or the captives of the righteous
         be delivered?

25   But thus says the LORD:

     "Even the captives of the mighty
       shall be taken away,
       And the prey of the terrible be
         delivered;
       For I will contend with him who
         contends with you,
       And I will save your children.
26   I will feed those who oppress
       you with their own flesh,
       And they shall be drunk with
         their own blood as with sweet
         wine.
       All flesh shall know
       That I, the LORD, *am* your
         Savior,
       And your Redeemer, the Mighty
         One of Jacob."

The Messiah is our Hope

50 Thus says the LORD:

     "Where *is* the certificate of your
       mother's divorce,
       Whom I have put away?

Or which of My creditors *is it* to
whom I have sold you?
For your iniquities you have sold
yourselves,
And for your transgressions your
mother has been put away.
2 Why, when I came, *was there*
no man?
Why, when I called, *was there*
none to answer?
Is My hand shortened at all that
it cannot redeem?
Or have I no power to deliver?
Indeed with My rebuke I dry up
the sea,
I make the rivers a wilderness;
Their fish stink because *there is*
no water,
And die of thirst.
3 I clothe the heavens with
blackness,
And I make sackcloth their
covering."

4 "The Lord God has given Me
The tongue of the learned,
That I should know how to
speak
A word in season to *him who is*
weary.
He awakens Me morning by
morning,
He awakens My ear
To hear as the learned.
5 The Lord God has opened My
ear;
And I was not rebellious,
Nor did I turn away.
6 I gave My back to those who
struck *Me,*
And My cheeks to those who
plucked out the beard;
I did not hide My face from
shame and spitting.

7 "For the Lord God will help Me;
Therefore I will not be disgraced;
Therefore I have set My face like
a flint,
And I know that I will not be
ashamed.
8 *He is* near who justifies Me;
Who will contend with Me?
Let us stand together.

Who *is* My adversary?
Let him come near Me.
9 Surely the Lord God will help
Me;
Who *is* he *who* will condemn
Me?
Indeed they will all grow old like
a garment;
The moth will eat them up.

10 "Who among you fears the Lord?
Who obeys the voice of His
Servant?
Who walks in darkness
And has no light?
Let him trust in the name of the
Lord
And rely upon his God.
11 Look, all you who kindle a fire,
Who encircle *yourselves* with
sparks:
Walk in the light of your fire and
in the sparks you have
kindled—
This you shall have from My
hand:
You shall lie down in torment.

Israel will be a great nation

51 "Listen to Me, you who follow
after righteousness,
You who seek the Lord:
Look to the rock *from which* you
were hewn,
And to the hole of the pit *from
which* you were dug.
2 Look to Abraham your father,
And to Sarah *who* bore you;
For I called him alone,
And blessed him and increased
him."

3 For the Lord will comfort Zion,
He will comfort all her waste
places;
He will make her wilderness like
Eden,
And her desert like the garden
of the Lord;
Joy and gladness will be found
in it,
Thanksgiving and the voice of
melody.

4 "Listen to Me, My people;
  And give ear to Me, O My
      nation:
  For law will proceed from Me,
  And I will make My justice rest
  As a light of the peoples.
5 My righteousness *is* near,
  My salvation has gone forth,
  And My arms will judge the
      peoples;
  The coastlands will wait upon
      Me,
  And on My arm they will trust.
6 Lift up your eyes to the heavens,
  And look on the earth beneath.
  For the heavens will vanish away
      like smoke,
  The earth will grow old like a
      garment,
  And those who dwell in it will
      die in like manner;
  But My salvation will be forever,
  And My righteousness will not
      be abolished.

7 "Listen to Me, you who know
      righteousness,
  You people in whose heart *is* My
      law:
  Do not fear the reproach of men,
  Nor be afraid of their insults.
8 For the moth will eat them up
      like a garment,
  And the worm will eat them like
      wool;
  But My righteousness will be
      forever,
  And My salvation from
      generation to generation."

9 Awake, awake, put on strength,
  O arm of the LORD!
  Awake as in the ancient days,
  In the generations of old.
  Are You not *the arm* that cut
      Rahab apart,
  And wounded the serpent?

10 *Are* You not *the One* who dried
      up the sea,
  The waters of the great deep;
  That made the depths of the sea
      a road
  For the redeemed to cross over?

11 So the ransomed of the LORD
      shall return,
  And come to Zion with singing,
  With everlasting joy on their
      heads.
  They shall obtain joy and
      gladness;
  Sorrow and sighing shall flee
      away.

12 "I, *even* I, *am* He who comforts
      you.
  Who *are* you that you should be
      afraid
  Of a man *who* will die,
  And of the son of a man *who*
      will be made like grass?
13 And you forget the LORD your
      Maker,
  Who stretched out the heavens
  And laid the foundations of the
      earth;
  You have feared continually
      every day
  Because of the fury of the
      oppressor,
  When *he has* prepared to
      destroy.
  And where *is* the fury of the
      oppressor?
14 The captive exile hastens, that
      he may be loosed,
  That he should not die in the
      pit,
  And that his bread should not
      fail.
15 But I *am* the LORD your God,
  Who divided the sea whose
      waves roared—
  The LORD of hosts *is* His name.
16 And I have put My words in your
      mouth;
  I have covered you with the
      shadow of My hand,
  That I may plant the heavens,
  Lay the foundations of the earth,
  And say to Zion, 'You *are* My
      people.' "

17 Awake, awake!
  Stand up, O Jerusalem,
  You who have drunk at the
      hand of the LORD
  The cup of His fury;

You have drunk the dregs of the
cup of trembling,
And drained *it* out.

18 *There is* no one to guide her
Among all the sons she has
brought forth;
Nor *is there any* who takes her
by the hand
Among all the sons she has
brought up.

19 These two *things* have come to
you;
Who will be sorry for you?—
Desolation and destruction,
famine and sword—
By whom will I comfort you?

20 Your sons have fainted,
They lie at the head of all the
streets,
Like an antelope in a net;
They are full of the fury of the
LORD,
The rebuke of your God.

21 Therefore please hear this, you
afflicted,
And drunk but not with wine.

22 Thus says your Lord,
The LORD and your God,
Who pleads the cause of His
people:
"See, I have taken out of your
hand
The cup of trembling,
The dregs of the cup of My
fury;
You shall no longer drink it.

23 But I will put it into the hand of
those who afflict you,
Who have said to you,
'Lie down, that we may walk
over you.'
And you have laid your body
like the ground,
And as the street, for those who
walk over."

God's holy city will be
at peace again

52 Awake, awake!
Put on your strength, O Zion;
Put on your beautiful garments,
O Jerusalem, the holy city!

For the uncircumcised and the
unclean
Shall no longer come to you.

2 Shake yourself from the dust,
arise;
Sit down, O Jerusalem!
Loose yourself from the bonds
of your neck,
O captive daughter of Zion!

3 For thus says the LORD:

"You have sold yourselves for
nothing,
And you shall be redeemed
without money."

4 For thus says the Lord GOD:

"My people went down at first
Into Egypt to dwell there;
Then the Assyrian oppressed
them without cause.

5 Now therefore, what have I
here," says the LORD,
"That My people are taken away
for nothing?
Those who rule over them
Make them wail," says the LORD,
"And My name *is* blasphemed
continually every day.

6 Therefore My people shall know
My name;
Therefore *they shall know* in that
day
That I *am* He who speaks:
'Behold, *it is* I.' "

7 How beautiful upon the
mountains
Are the feet of him who brings
good news,
Who proclaims peace,
Who brings glad tidings of good
things,
Who proclaims salvation,
Who says to Zion,
"Your God reigns!"

8 Your watchmen shall lift up *their*
voices,
With their voices they shall sing
together;
For they shall see eye to eye

When the LORD brings back
Zion.
9 Break forth into joy, sing
together,
You waste places of Jerusalem!
For the LORD has comforted His
people,
He has redeemed Jerusalem.
10 The LORD has made bare His
holy arm
In the eyes of all the nations;
And all the ends of the earth
shall see
The salvation of our God.

11 Depart! Depart! Go out from
there,
Touch no unclean *thing;*
Go out from the midst of her,
Be clean,
You who bear the vessels of the
LORD.
12 For you shall not go out with
haste,
Nor go by flight;
For the LORD will go before
you,
And the God of Israel *will be*
your rear guard.

13 Behold, My Servant shall deal
prudently;
He shall be exalted and extolled
and be very high.
14 Just as many were astonished at
you,
So His visage was marred more
than any man,
And His form more than the
sons of men;
15 So shall He sprinkle many
nations.
Kings shall shut their mouths at
Him;
For what had not been told them
they shall see,
And what they had not heard
they shall consider.

The Messiah carries all our sins

53 Who has believed our report?
And to whom has the arm of the
LORD been revealed?

2 For He shall grow up before Him
as a tender plant,
And as a root out of dry ground.
He has no form or comeliness;
And when we *see* Him,
There is no beauty that we
should desire Him.
3 He is despised and rejected by
men,
A Man of sorrows and
acquainted with grief.
And we hid, as it were, *our* faces
from Him;
He was despised, and we did not
esteem Him.

4 Surely He has borne our griefs
And carried our sorrows;
Yet we esteemed Him stricken,
Smitten by God, and afflicted.
5 But He *was* wounded for our
transgressions,
He was bruised for our
iniquities;
The chastisement for our peace
was upon Him,
And by His stripes we are
healed.
6 All we like sheep have gone
astray;
We have turned, every one, to
his own way;
And the LORD has laid on Him
the iniquity of us all.

7 He was oppressed and He was
afflicted,
Yet He opened not His mouth;
He was led as a lamb to the
slaughter,
And as a sheep before its
shearers is silent,
So He opened not His mouth.
8 He was taken from prison and
from judgment,
And who will declare His
generation?
For He was cut off from the land
of the living;
For the transgressions of My
people He was stricken.
9 And they made His grave with
the wicked—
But with the rich at His death,

Because He had done no
violence,
Nor *was any* deceit in His
mouth.

10 Yet it pleased the Lord to bruise
Him;
He has put *Him* to grief.
When You make His soul an
offering for sin,
He shall see *His* seed, He shall
prolong *His* days,

And the pleasure of the Lord
shall prosper in His hand.
11 He shall see the labor of His
soul, *and* be satisfied.
By His knowledge **My
righteous Servant** shall justify
many,
For He shall bear their iniquities.
12 Therefore I will divide Him a
portion with the great,
And He shall divide the spoil
with the strong,

WORDFINDER

53:11 My Righteous Servant   Sometimes refers to Israel (see Isaiah 44:1). Here,
the term refers to Christ, your sin-bearing Servant.

DIGGING IN

53:6 Jesus Carried Our Sins You
have heard many times that Jesus paid
for your sins by dying on the Cross at
Calvary. What is so amazing is that Jesus
died because of a great plan that God
had in mind for a long time. Jesus didn't
die just because He made some Jews angry in Palestine two thousand years ago.
It was all planned in long ages past.
That's why Isaiah (pronounced *eye-ZAY-
uh*) could tell you all about the suffering
and death of Jesus over seven hundred

years before Jesus was born.
But the prophet told not only about
Jesus' death, he also told about the *reason* for it—"All we like sheep have gone
astray; we have turned, every one, to his
own way; and the Lord has laid on Him
the iniquity of us all." God would lay your
sins on His beloved Son. Then the Lord
would pronounce you "innocent" of all sin
because His Son died in your place.
Wasn't that a most amazing plan?

"By His stripes we are healed."

Because He poured out His soul
 unto death,
And He was numbered with the
 transgressors,
And He bore the sin of many,
And made intercession for the
 transgressors.

God's kindness never ends

54 "Sing, O barren,
 You *who* have not borne!
Break forth into singing, and cry
 aloud,
You *who* have not labored with
 child!
For more *are* the children of the
 desolate
Than the children of the married
 woman," says the LORD.
2 "Enlarge the place of your tent,
And let them stretch out the
 curtains of your dwellings;
Do not spare;
Lengthen your cords,
And strengthen your stakes.
3 For you shall expand to the right
 and to the left,
And your descendants will
 inherit the nations,
And make the desolate cities
 inhabited.

4 "Do not fear, for you will not be
 ashamed;
Neither be disgraced, for you will
 not be put to shame;
For you will forget the shame of
 your youth,
And will not remember the
 reproach of your widowhood
 anymore.
5 For your Maker *is* your husband,
The LORD of hosts *is* His name;
And your Redeemer *is* the Holy
 One of Israel;
He is called the God of the
 whole earth.
6 For the LORD has called you
Like a woman forsaken and
 grieved in spirit,
Like a youthful wife when you
 were refused,"
Says your God.

7 "For a mere moment I have
 forsaken you,
But with great mercies I will
 gather you.
8 With a little wrath I hid My face
 from you for a moment;
But with everlasting kindness I
 will have mercy on you,"
Says the LORD, your Redeemer.

9 "For this *is* like the waters of Noah
 to Me;
For as I have sworn
That the waters of Noah would
 no longer cover the earth,
So have I sworn
That I would not be angry with
 you, nor rebuke you.
10 For the mountains shall depart
And the hills be removed,
But My kindness shall not depart
 from you,
Nor shall My covenant of peace
 be removed,"
Says the LORD, who has mercy
 on you.

11 "O you afflicted one,
Tossed with tempest, *and* not
 comforted,
Behold, I will lay your stones
 with colorful gems,
And lay your foundations with
 sapphires.
12 I will make your pinnacles of
 rubies,
Your gates of crystal,
And all your walls of precious
 stones.
13 All your children *shall be* taught
 by the LORD,
And great *shall be* the peace of
 your children.
14 In righteousness you shall be
 established;
You shall be far from
 oppression, for you shall not
 fear;
And from terror, for it shall not
 come near you.
15 Indeed they shall surely
 assemble, *but* not because of
 Me.

Whoever assembles against you
shall fall for your sake.

16 "Behold, I have created the
blacksmith
Who blows the coals in the fire,
Who brings forth an instrument
for his work;
And I have created the spoiler
to destroy.
17 No weapon formed against you
shall prosper,
And every tongue *which* rises
against you in judgment
You shall condemn.
This *is* the heritage of the
servants of the LORD,
And their righteousness *is* from
Me,"
Says the LORD.

The trees will clap their hands for joy!

55 "Ho! Everyone who thirsts,
Come to the waters;
And you who have no money,
Come, buy and eat.
Yes, come, buy wine and milk
Without money and without
price.
2 Why do you spend money for
what is not bread,
And your wages for *what* does
not satisfy?
Listen carefully to Me, and eat
what is good,
And let your soul delight itself
in abundance.

3 Incline your ear, and come to
Me.
Hear, and your soul shall live;
And I will make an everlasting
covenant with you—
The sure mercies of David.
4 Indeed I have given him *as* a
witness to the people,
A leader and commander for the
people.
5 Surely you shall call a nation you
do not know,
And nations *who* do not know
you shall run to you,
Because of the LORD your God,
And the Holy One of Israel;
For He has glorified you."

6 Seek the LORD while He may be
found,
Call upon Him while He is
near.
7 Let the wicked forsake his way,
And the unrighteous man his
thoughts;
Let him return to the LORD,
And He will have mercy on him;
And to our God,
For He will abundantly pardon.

8 "For My thoughts *are* not your
thoughts,
Nor *are* your ways My ways,"
says the LORD.
9 "For *as* the heavens are higher
than the earth,
So are My ways higher than
your ways,
And My thoughts than your
thoughts.

⛏ DIGGING IN

55:1 Are You Thirsty? Of course you're thirsty sometimes. At those times, a cold soda or a glass of ice water is the greatest thing in the world. There's another kind of thirst that a cool can of soda can't quench. That's the thirst of the soul. Everybody's soul is thirsty sometimes, too.

Those are the times when nothing will satisfy you but God. Jesus said, "He who believes in Me shall never thirst" (John 6:35). Truly you can't drink from Jesus the way you drink water. But the way He satisfies you is *like* a river of living water (see John 7:38).

Imagine Jesus to be *like* a deep well of cool, pure spring water. As you drink from Him, you become filled with His life. Then you find that the life He fills you with overflows and satisfies those around you, too. Ask to be filled with that living water that only Jesus can give.

10 "For as the rain comes down, and
the snow from heaven,
And do not return there,
But water the earth,
And make it bring forth and bud,
That it may give seed to the
sower
And bread to the eater,

11 So shall My word be that goes
forth from My mouth;
It shall not return to Me void,
But it shall accomplish what I
please,
And it shall prosper *in the thing*
for which I sent it.

12 "For you shall go out with joy,
And be led out with peace;
The mountains and the hills
Shall break forth into singing
before you,
And all the trees of the field shall
clap *their* hands.
13 Instead of the thorn shall come
up the cypress tree,
And instead of the brier shall
come up the myrtle tree;
And it shall be to the LORD for
a name,
For an everlasting sign *that* shall
not be cut off."

God comes to the rescue

56 Thus says the LORD:

"Keep justice, and do
righteousness,
For My salvation *is* about to
come,
And My righteousness to be
revealed.
2 Blessed *is* the man *who* does
this,
And the son of man *who* lays
hold on it;
Who keeps from defiling the
Sabbath,
And keeps his hand from doing
any evil."

3 Do not let the son of the
foreigner

Who has joined himself to the
LORD
Speak, saying,
"The LORD has utterly separated
me from His people";
Nor let the eunuch say,
"Here I am, a dry tree."
4 For thus says the LORD:
"To the eunuchs who keep My
Sabbaths,
And choose what pleases Me,
And hold fast My covenant,
5 Even to them I will give in My
house
And within My walls a place and
a name
Better than that of sons and
daughters;
I will give them an everlasting
name
That shall not be cut off.

6 "Also the sons of the foreigner
Who join themselves to the
LORD, to serve Him,
And to love the name of the
LORD, to be His servants—
Everyone who keeps from
defiling the Sabbath,
And holds fast My covenant—
7 Even them I will bring to My holy
mountain,
And make them joyful in My
house of prayer.
Their burnt offerings and their
sacrifices
Will be accepted on My altar;
For My house shall be called a
house of prayer for all
nations."
8 The Lord GOD, who gathers the
outcasts of Israel, says,
"Yet I will gather to him
Others besides those who are
gathered to him."

9 All you beasts of the field, come
to devour,
All you beasts in the forest.
10 His watchmen *are* blind,
They are all ignorant;
They *are* all dumb dogs,
They cannot bark;

Sleeping, lying down, loving to
   slumber.
11 Yes, *they are* greedy dogs
   Which never have enough.
   And they *are* shepherds
   Who cannot understand;
   They all look to their own way,
   Every one for his own gain,
   From his *own* territory.
12 "Come," *one says,* "I will bring
   wine,
   And we will fill ourselves with
   intoxicating drink;
   Tomorrow will be as today,
   And much more abundant."

There is no peace for the wicked

57 The righteous perishes,
   And no man takes *it* to heart;
   Merciful men *are* taken away,
   While no one considers
   That the righteous is taken away
   from evil.
2 He shall enter into peace;
   They shall rest in their beds,
   Each one walking *in* his
   uprightness.

3 "But come here,
   You sons of the sorceress,
   You offspring of the adulterer
   and the harlot!
4 Whom do you ridicule?
   Against whom do you make a
   wide mouth
   And stick out the tongue?
   Are you not children of
   transgression,
   Offspring of falsehood,
5 Inflaming yourselves with gods
   under *every* green tree,
   Slaying the children in the
   valleys,
   Under the clefts of the rocks?
6 Among the smooth *stones* of the
   stream
   Is your portion;
   They, they, *are* your lot!
   Even to them you have poured
   a drink offering,
   You have offered a grain
   offering.
   Should I receive comfort in
   these?

7 "On a lofty and high mountain
   You have set your bed;
   Even there you went up
   To offer sacrifice.
8 Also behind the doors and their
   posts
   You have set up your
   remembrance;
   For you have uncovered
   yourself *to those other* than
   Me,
   And have gone up to them;
   You have enlarged your bed
   And made *a covenant* with
   them;
   You have loved their bed,
   Where you saw *their* nudity.
9 You went to the king with
   ointment,
   And increased your perfumes;
   You sent your messengers far
   off,
   And *even* descended to Sheol.
10 You are wearied in the length
   of your way;
   Yet you did not say, 'There is
   no hope.'
   You have found the life of your
   hand;
   Therefore you were not
   grieved.

11 "And of whom have you been
   afraid, or feared,
   That you have lied
   And not remembered Me,
   Nor taken *it* to your heart?
   Is it not because I have held My
   peace from of old
   That you do not fear Me?
12 I will declare your
   righteousness
   And your works,
   For they will not profit you.
13 When you cry out,
   Let your collection *of idols*
   deliver you.
   But the wind will carry them all
   away,
   A breath will take *them.*
   But he who puts his trust in Me
   shall possess the land,
   And shall inherit My holy
   mountain."

14 And one shall say,
    "Heap it up! Heap it up!
    Prepare the way,
    Take the stumbling block out of
        the way of My people."

15 For thus says the High and Lofty
        One
    Who inhabits eternity, whose
        name is Holy:
    "I dwell in the high and holy
        place,
    With him who has a contrite and
        humble spirit,
    To revive the spirit of the
        humble,
    And to revive the heart of the
        contrite ones.

16 For I will not contend forever,
    Nor will I always be angry;
    For the spirit would fail before
        Me,
    And the souls which I have
        made.

17 For the iniquity of his
        covetousness
    I was angry and struck him;
    I hid and was angry,
    And he went on backsliding in
        the way of his heart.

18 I have seen his ways, and will
        heal him;
    I will also lead him,
    And restore comforts to him
    And to his mourners.

19 "I create the fruit of the lips:
    Peace, peace to him who is far
        off and to him who is near,"
    Says the LORD,
    "And I will heal him."

20 But the wicked are like the
        troubled sea,
    When it cannot rest,
    Whose waters cast up mire and
        dirt.

21 "There is no peace,"
    Says my God, "for the wicked."

How to really please God

58 "Cry aloud, spare not;
    Lift up your voice like a trumpet;

Tell My people their
    transgression,
And the house of Jacob their
    sins.

2   Yet they seek Me daily,
    And delight to know My ways,
    As a nation that did
        righteousness,
    And did not forsake the
        ordinance of their God.
    They ask of Me the ordinances
        of justice;
    They take delight in approaching
        God.

3   'Why have we fasted,' they say,
        'and You have not seen?
    Why have we afflicted our souls,
        and You take no notice?'

    "In fact, in the day of your fast
        you find pleasure,
    And exploit all your laborers.

4   Indeed you fast for strife and
        debate,
    And to strike with the fist of
        wickedness.
    You will not fast as you do this
        day,
    To make your voice heard on
        high.

5   Is it a fast that I have chosen,
    A day for a man to afflict his
        soul?
    Is it to bow down his head like
        a bulrush,
    And to spread out sackcloth and
        ashes?
    Would you call this a fast,
    And an acceptable day to the
        LORD?

6   "Is this not the fast that I have
        chosen:
    To loose the bonds of
        wickedness,
    To undo the heavy burdens,
    To let the oppressed go free,
    And that you break every
        yoke?

7   Is it not to share your bread with
        the hungry,
    And that you bring to your
        house the poor who are cast
        out;

When you see the naked, that
   you cover him,
And not hide yourself from your
   own flesh?
8 Then your light shall break forth
   like the morning,
Your healing shall spring forth
   speedily,
And your righteousness shall go
   before you;
The glory of the LORD shall be
   your rear guard.
9 Then you shall call, and the
   LORD will answer;
You shall cry, and He will say,
   'Here I *am*.'

"If you take away the yoke from
   your midst,
The pointing of the finger, and
   speaking wickedness,
10 *If* you extend your soul to the
   hungry
And satisfy the afflicted soul,
Then your light shall dawn in the
   darkness,
And your darkness shall *be* as
   the noonday.
11 The LORD will guide you
   continually,
And satisfy your soul in drought,
And strengthen your bones;
You shall be like a watered
   garden,
And like a spring of water,
   whose waters do not fail.
12 Those from among you
Shall build the old waste
   places;
You shall raise up the
   foundations of many
   generations;
And you shall be called the
   Repairer of the Breach,
The Restorer of Streets to Dwell
   In.

13 "If you turn away your foot from
   the Sabbath,
From doing your pleasure on My
   holy day,
And call the Sabbath a delight,
The holy *day* of the LORD
   honorable,

And shall honor Him, not doing
   your own ways,
Nor finding your own pleasure,
Nor speaking *your own* words,
14 Then you shall delight yourself
   in the LORD;
And I will cause you to ride on
   the high hills of the earth,
And feed you with the heritage
   of Jacob your father.
The mouth of the LORD has
   spoken."

Sin hides God's face from us

59 Behold, the LORD's hand is not
   shortened,
   That it cannot save;
   Nor His ear heavy,
   That it cannot hear.
2 But your iniquities have
   separated you from your
   God;
And your sins have hidden *His*
   face from you,
So that He will not hear.
3 For your hands are defiled with
   blood,
And your fingers with iniquity;
Your lips have spoken lies,
Your tongue has muttered
   perversity.

4 No one calls for justice,
Nor does *any* plead for truth.
They trust in empty words and
   speak lies;
They conceive evil and bring
   forth iniquity.
5 They hatch vipers' eggs and
   weave the spider's web;
He who eats of their eggs dies,
And *from* that which is crushed
   a viper breaks out.

6 Their webs will not become
   garments,
Nor will they cover themselves
   with their works;
Their works *are* works of
   iniquity,
And the act of violence *is* in their
   hands.
7 Their feet run to evil,

And they make haste to shed
  innocent blood;
Their thoughts *are* thoughts of
  iniquity;
Wasting and destruction *are* in
  their paths.
8 The way of peace they have not
  known,
And *there is* no justice in their
  ways;
They have made themselves
  crooked paths;
Whoever takes that way shall
  not know peace.

9 Therefore justice is far from us,
Nor does righteousness overtake
  us;
We look for light, but there is
  darkness!
For brightness, *but* we walk in
  blackness!
10 We grope for the wall like the
  blind,
And we grope as if *we had* no
  eyes;
We stumble at noonday as at
  twilight;
We are as dead *men* in desolate
  places.
11 We all growl like bears,
And moan sadly like doves;
We look for justice, but *there is*
  none;
For salvation, *but* it is far from
  us.
12 For our transgressions are
  multiplied before You,
And our sins testify against us;
For our transgressions *are* with
  us,
And *as for* our iniquities, we
  know them:
13 In transgressing and lying against
  the LORD,
And departing from our God,
Speaking oppression and revolt,
Conceiving and uttering from
  the heart words of falsehood.
14 Justice is turned back,
And righteousness stands afar
  off;
For truth is fallen in the street,
And equity cannot enter.

15 So truth fails,
And he *who* departs from evil
  makes himself a prey.

Then the LORD saw *it,* and it
  displeased Him
That *there was* no justice.
16 He saw that *there was* no man,
And wondered that *there was* no
  intercessor;
Therefore His own arm brought
  salvation for Him;
And His own righteousness, it
  sustained Him.
17 For He put on righteousness as
  a breastplate,
And a helmet of salvation on His
  head;
He put on the garments of
  vengeance for clothing,
And was clad with zeal as a
  cloak.
18 According to *their* deeds,
  accordingly He will repay,
Fury to His adversaries,
Recompense to His enemies;
The coastlands He will fully
  repay.
19 So shall they fear
The name of the LORD from the
  west,
And His glory from the rising of
  the sun;
When the enemy comes in like
  a flood,
The Spirit of the LORD will lift
  up a standard against him.

20 "The Redeemer will come to
  Zion,
And to those who turn from
  transgression in Jacob,"
Says the LORD.

21 "As for Me," says the LORD, "this
is My covenant with them: My Spirit
who *is* upon you, and My words which
I have put in your mouth, shall not
depart from your mouth, nor from the
mouth of your descendants, nor from
the mouth of your descendants' descendants," says the LORD, "from this
time and forevermore."

The glory of God

60 Arise, shine;
For your light has come!
And the glory of the Lord is
risen upon you.
2 For behold, the darkness shall
cover the earth,
And deep darkness the people;
But the Lord will arise over
you,
And His glory will be seen upon
you.
3 The Gentiles shall come to your
light,
And kings to the brightness of
your rising.

4 "Lift up your eyes all around, and
see:
They all gather together, they
come to you;
Your sons shall come from afar,
And your daughters shall be
nursed at *your* side.
5 Then you shall *see* and become
radiant,
And your heart shall swell with
joy;
Because the abundance of the
sea shall be turned to you,
The wealth of the Gentiles shall
come to you.
6 The multitude of camels shall
cover your *land,*
The dromedaries of Midian and
Ephah;
All those from Sheba shall come;
They shall bring gold and
incense,
And they shall proclaim the
praises of the Lord.
7 All the flocks of Kedar shall be
gathered together to you,
The rams of Nebaioth shall
minister to you;
They shall ascend with
acceptance on My altar,
And I will glorify the house of
My glory.

8 "Who *are* these *who* fly like a
cloud,
And like doves to their roosts?

9 Surely the coastlands shall wait
for Me;
And the ships of Tarshish *will*
come first,
To bring your sons from afar,
Their silver and their gold with
them,
To the name of the Lord your
God,
And to the Holy One of Israel,
Because He has glorified you.

10 "The sons of foreigners shall build
up your walls,
And their kings shall minister to
you;
For in My wrath I struck you,
But in My favor I have had
mercy on you.
11 Therefore your gates shall be
open continually;
They shall not be shut day or
night,
That *men* may bring to you the
wealth of the Gentiles,
And their kings in procession.
12 For the nation and kingdom
which will not serve you shall
perish,
And *those* nations shall be
utterly ruined.

13 "The glory of Lebanon shall
come to you,
The cypress, the pine, and the
box tree together,
To beautify the place of My
sanctuary;
And I will make the place of My
feet glorious.
14 Also the sons of those who
afflicted you
Shall come bowing to you,
And all those who despised you
shall fall prostrate at the soles
of your feet;
And they shall call you The City
of the Lord,
Zion of the Holy One of Israel.

15 "Whereas you have been
forsaken and hated,
So that no one went through
you,

I will make you an eternal
excellence,
A joy of many generations.
16 You shall drink the milk of the
Gentiles,
And milk the breast of kings;
You shall know that I, the LORD,
am your Savior
And your Redeemer, the Mighty
One of Jacob.

17 "Instead of bronze I will bring
gold,
Instead of iron I will bring
silver,
Instead of wood, bronze,
And instead of stones, iron.
I will also make your officers
peace,
And your magistrates
righteousness.
18 Violence shall no longer be
heard in your land,
Neither wasting nor destruction
within your borders;
But you shall call your walls
Salvation,
And your gates Praise.

19 "The sun shall no longer be your
light by day,
Nor for brightness shall the
moon give light to you;
But the LORD will be to you an
everlasting light,
And your God your glory.
20 Your sun shall no longer go
down,
Nor shall your moon withdraw
itself;
For the LORD will be your
everlasting light,
And the days of your mourning
shall be ended.
21 Also your people *shall* all *be*
righteous;
They shall inherit the land
forever,
The branch of My planting,

The work of My hands,
That I may be glorified.
22 A little one shall become a
thousand,
And a small one a strong nation.
I, the LORD, will hasten it in its
time."

God has Good News for you

61 "The Spirit of the Lord GOD *is*
upon Me,
Because the LORD has anointed
Me
To preach good tidings to the
poor;
He has sent Me to heal the
brokenhearted,
To proclaim liberty to the
captives,
And the opening of the prison
to *those who are* bound;
2 To proclaim the acceptable year
of the LORD,
And the day of vengeance of our
God;
To comfort all who mourn,
3 To console those who mourn in
Zion,
To give them beauty for ashes,
The oil of joy for mourning,
The garment of praise for the
spirit of heaviness;
That they may be called trees
of righteousness,
The planting of the LORD, that
He may be **glorified.**"

4 And they shall rebuild the old
ruins,
They shall raise up the former
desolations,
And they shall repair the ruined
cities,
The desolations of many
generations.
5 Strangers shall stand and feed
your flocks,
And the sons of the foreigner

WORDFINDER

61:3 Glorified Pronounced *GLORY-fyed.* When Jesus comes back to earth, He
will give those who loved Him new bodies. They can never sin again.

Shall be your plowmen and your
vinedressers.
6 But you shall be named the
priests of the LORD,
They shall call you the servants
of our God.
You shall eat the riches of the
Gentiles,
And in their glory you shall
boast.
7 Instead of your shame *you shall
have* double *honor,*
And *instead of* confusion they
shall rejoice in their portion.
Therefore in their land they shall
possess double;
Everlasting joy shall be theirs.

8 "For I, the LORD, love justice;
I hate robbery for burnt
offering;
I will direct their work in truth,
And will make with them an
everlasting covenant.
9 Their descendants shall be
known among the Gentiles,
And their offspring among the
people.
All who see them shall
acknowledge them,
That they *are* the posterity
whom the LORD has blessed."

10 I will greatly rejoice in the
LORD,
My soul shall be joyful in my
God;
For He has clothed me with the
garments of salvation,
He has covered me with the
robe of righteousness,
As a bridegroom decks *himself*
with ornaments,
And as a bride adorns *herself*
with her jewels.
11 For as the earth brings forth its
bud,
As the garden causes the things
that are sown in it to spring
forth,
So the Lord GOD will cause
righteousness and praise to
spring forth before all the
nations.

The Land of God's Delight

62 For Zion's sake I will not hold
My peace,
And for Jerusalem's sake I will
not rest,
Until her righteousness goes
forth as brightness,
And her salvation as a lamp *that*
burns.
2 The Gentiles shall see your
righteousness,
And all kings your glory.
You shall be called by a new
name,
Which the mouth of the LORD
will name.
3 You shall also be a crown of
glory
In the hand of the LORD,
And a royal diadem
In the hand of your God.
4 You shall no longer be termed
Forsaken,
Nor shall your land any more be
termed Desolate;
But you shall be called
Hephzibah, and your land
Beulah;
For the LORD delights in you,
And your land shall be married.
5 For *as* a young man marries a
virgin,
So shall your sons marry you;
And *as* the bridegroom rejoices
over the bride,
So shall your God rejoice over
you.

6 I have set watchmen on your
walls, O Jerusalem;
They shall never hold their
peace day or night.
You who make mention of the
LORD, do not keep silent,
7 And give Him no rest till He
establishes
And till He makes Jerusalem a
praise in the earth.

8 The LORD has sworn by His right
hand
And by the arm of His strength:

"Surely I will no longer give your
    grain
As food for your enemies;
And the sons of the foreigner
    shall not drink your new wine,
For which you have labored.
9   But those who have gathered it
    shall eat it,
And praise the LORD;
Those who have brought it
    together shall drink it in My
    holy courts."

10 Go through,
Go through the gates!
Prepare the way for the people;
Build up,
Build up the highway!
Take out the stones,
Lift up a banner for the peoples!

11 Indeed the LORD has proclaimed
To the end of the world:
"Say to the daughter of Zion,
'Surely your salvation is coming;
Behold, His reward *is* with Him,
And His work before Him.' "
12 And they shall call them The
    Holy People,
The Redeemed of the LORD;
And you shall be called Sought
    Out,
A City Not Forsaken.

God gently carries His people

63 Who *is* this who comes from
    Edom,
With dyed garments from
    Bozrah,
This *One who is* glorious in His
    apparel,
Traveling in the greatness of His
    strength?—

"I who speak in righteousness,
    mighty to save."

2   Why *is* Your apparel red,
And Your garments like one
    who treads in the winepress?

3   "I have trodden the winepress
    alone,

And from the peoples no one
    was with Me.
For I have trodden them in My
    anger,
And trampled them in My fury;
Their blood is sprinkled upon
    My garments,
And I have stained all My robes.
4   For the day of vengeance *is* in
    My heart,
And the year of My redeemed
    has come.
5   I looked, but *there was* no one
    to help,
And I wondered
That *there was* no one to
    uphold;
Therefore My own arm brought
    salvation for Me;
And My own fury, it sustained
    Me.
6   I have trodden down the
    peoples in My anger,
Made them drunk in My fury,
And brought down their strength
    to the earth."

7   I will mention the
    lovingkindnesses of the LORD
And the praises of the LORD,
According to all that the LORD
    has bestowed on us,
And the great goodness toward
    the house of Israel,
Which He has bestowed on
    them according to His
    mercies,
According to the multitude of
    His lovingkindnesses.
8   For He said, "Surely they *are*
    My people,
Children *who* will not lie."
So He became their Savior.
9   In all their affliction He was
    afflicted,
And the Angel of His Presence
    saved them;
In His love and in His pity He
    redeemed them;
And He bore them and carried
    them
All the days of old.
10 But they rebelled and grieved
    His Holy Spirit;

So He turned Himself against
  them as an enemy,
And He fought against them.

11 Then he remembered the days
  of old,
Moses *and* his people, *saying:*
"Where *is* He who brought them
  up out of the sea
With the shepherd of His flock?
Where *is* He who put His Holy
  Spirit within them,
12 Who led *them* by the right hand
  of Moses,
With His glorious arm,
Dividing the water before them
To make for Himself an
  everlasting name,
13 Who led them through the deep,
As a horse in the wilderness,
That they might not stumble?"

14 As a beast goes down into the
  valley,
And the Spirit of the LORD
  causes him to rest,
So You lead Your people,
To make Yourself a glorious
  name.

15 Look down from heaven,
And *see* from Your habitation,
  holy and glorious.
Where *are* Your zeal and Your
  strength,
The yearning of Your heart and
  Your mercies toward me?
Are they restrained?
16 Doubtless You *are* our Father,
Though Abraham was ignorant
  of us,
And Israel does not
  acknowledge us.
You, O LORD, *are* our Father;
Our Redeemer from Everlasting
  is Your name.
17 O LORD, why have You made
  us stray from Your ways,
And hardened our heart from
  Your fear?
Return for Your servants' sake,
The tribes of Your inheritance.
18 Your holy people have
  possessed *it* but a little while;

Our adversaries have trodden
  down Your sanctuary.
19 We have become *like* those of
  old, over whom You never
  ruled,
Those who were never called by
  Your name.

In His presence
the mountains shake

64 Oh, that You would rend the
  heavens!
That You would come down!
That the mountains might shake
  at Your presence—
2 As fire burns brushwood,
As fire causes water to boil—
To make Your name known to
  Your adversaries,
That the nations may tremble at
  Your presence!
3 When You did awesome things
  for which we did not look,
You came down,
The mountains shook at Your
  presence.
4 For since the beginning of the
  world
Men have not heard nor
  perceived by the ear,
Nor has the eye seen any God
  besides You,
Who acts for the one who waits
  for Him.
5 You meet him who rejoices and
  does righteousness,
Who remembers You in Your
  ways.
You are indeed angry, for we
  have sinned—
In these ways we continue;
And we need to be saved.

6 But we are all like an unclean
  thing,
And all our righteousnesses *are*
  like filthy rags;
We all fade as a leaf,
And our iniquities, like the
  wind,
Have taken us away.
7 And *there is* no one who calls
  on Your name,

Who stirs himself up to take hold
    of You;
For You have hidden Your face
    from us,
And have consumed us because
    of our iniquities.

8 But now, O LORD,
    You *are* our Father;
    We *are* the clay, and You our
        potter;
    And all *we are* the work of Your
        hand.
9 Do not be furious, O LORD,
    Nor remember iniquity forever;
    Indeed, please look—we all *are*
        Your people!
10 Your holy cities are a wilderness,
    Zion is a wilderness,
    Jerusalem a desolation.
11 Our holy and beautiful temple,
    Where our fathers praised You,
    Is burned up with fire;
    And all our pleasant things are
        laid waste.
12 Will You restrain Yourself
        because of these *things*, O
        LORD?
    Will You hold Your peace, and
        afflict us very severely?

The lamb and the lion
will lie down together

65 "I was sought by *those who* did
        not ask *for Me;*
    I was found by *those who* did
        not seek Me.
    I said, 'Here I am, here I am,'
    To a nation *that* was not called
        by My name.
2 I have stretched out My hands
        all day long to a rebellious
        people,
    Who walk in a way *that is* not
        good,
    According to their own thoughts;
3 A people who provoke Me to
        anger continually to My
        face;
    Who sacrifice in gardens,
    And burn incense on altars of
        brick;
4 Who sit among the graves,

And spend the night in the
    tombs;
Who eat swine's flesh,
And the broth of abominable
    things is *in* their vessels;
5 Who say, 'Keep to yourself,
    Do not come near me,
    For I am holier than you!'
    These *are* smoke in My nostrils,
    A fire that burns all the day.

6 "Behold, *it is* written before Me:
    I will not keep silence, but will
        repay—
    Even repay into their bosom—
7 Your iniquities and the iniquities
        of your fathers together,"
    Says the LORD,
    "Who have burned incense on
        the mountains
    And blasphemed Me on the hills;
    Therefore I will measure their
        former work into their
        bosom."

8 Thus says the LORD:

    "As the new wine is found in the
        cluster,
    And *one* says, 'Do not destroy
        it,
    For a blessing *is* in it,'
    So will I do for My servants'
        sake,
    That I may not destroy them
        all.
9 I will bring forth descendants
        from Jacob,
    And from Judah an heir of My
        mountains;
    My elect shall inherit it,
    And My servants shall dwell
        there.
10 Sharon shall be a fold of
        flocks,
    And the Valley of Achor a place
        for herds to lie down,
    For My people who have sought
        Me.

11 "But you *are* those who forsake
        the LORD,
    Who forget My holy mountain,
    Who prepare a table for Gad,

And who furnish a drink offering
   for Meni.
12 Therefore I will number you for
   the sword,
And you shall all bow down to
   the slaughter;
Because, when I called, you did
   not answer;
When I spoke, you did not
   hear,
But did evil before My eyes,
And chose *that* in which I do not
   delight."

13 Therefore thus says the Lord GOD:

"Behold, My servants shall eat,
   But you shall be hungry;
Behold, My servants shall drink,
   But you shall be thirsty;
Behold, My servants shall
   rejoice,
But you shall be ashamed;
14 Behold, My servants shall sing
   for joy of heart,
But you shall cry for sorrow of
   heart,
And wail for grief of spirit.
15 You shall leave your name as a
   curse to My chosen;
For the Lord GOD will slay
   you,
And call His servants by another
   name;
16 So that he who blesses himself
   in the earth
Shall bless himself in the God
   of truth;
And he who swears in the
   earth
Shall swear by the God of
   truth;
Because the former troubles are
   forgotten,
And because they are hidden
   from My eyes.

17 "For behold, I create new
   heavens and a new earth;
And the former shall not be
   remembered or come to
   mind.
18 But be glad and rejoice forever
   in what I create;

For behold, I create Jerusalem
   as a rejoicing,
And her people a joy.
19 I will rejoice in Jerusalem,
And joy in My people;
The voice of weeping shall no
   longer be heard in her,
Nor the voice of crying.

20 "No more shall an infant from
   there *live but a few* days,
Nor an old man who has not
   fulfilled his days;
For the child shall die one
   hundred years old,
But the sinner *being* one
   hundred years old shall be
   accursed.
21 They shall build houses and
   inhabit *them;*
They shall plant vineyards and
   eat their fruit.
22 They shall not build and another
   inhabit;
They shall not plant and another
   eat;
For as the days of a tree, *so
   shall be* the days of My
   people,
And My elect shall long enjoy
   the work of their hands.
23 They shall not labor in vain,
Nor bring forth children for
   trouble;
For they *shall be* the
   descendants of the blessed of
   the LORD,
And their offspring with them.

24 "It shall come to pass
That before they call, I will
   answer;
And while they are still speaking,
   I will hear.
25 The wolf and the lamb shall feed
   together,
The lion shall eat straw like the
   ox,
And dust *shall be* the serpent's
   food.
They shall not hurt nor destroy
   in all My holy mountain,"
Says the LORD.

All the world will worship God

66 Thus says the LORD:

Heaven *is* My throne,
And earth *is* My footstool.
Where *is* the house that you will
build Me?
And where *is* the place of My
rest?
2 For all those *things* My hand has
made,
And all those *things* exist,"
Says the LORD.
"But on this *one* will I look:
On *him who is* poor and of a
contrite spirit,
And who trembles at My word.

3 "He who kills a bull *is as if* he
slays a man;
He who sacrifices a lamb, *as if*
he breaks a dog's neck;
He who offers a grain offering,
as if he offers swine's blood;
He who burns incense, *as if he*
blesses an idol.
Just as they have chosen their
own ways,
And their soul delights in their
abominations,
4 So will I choose their delusions,
And bring their fears on them;
Because, when I called, no one
answered,
When I spoke they did not hear;
But they did evil before My eyes,
And chose *that* in which I do not
delight."

5 Hear the word of the LORD,
You who tremble at His word:
"Your brethren who hated you,
Who cast you out for My name's
sake, said,
'Let the LORD be glorified,
That *we* may see your joy.'
But they shall be ashamed."

6 The sound of noise from the city!
A voice from the temple!
The voice of the LORD,
Who fully repays His enemies!

7 "Before she was in labor, she
gave birth;
Before her pain came,
She delivered a male child.
8 Who has heard such a thing?
Who has seen such things?
Shall the earth be made to give
birth in one day?
Or shall a nation be born at
once?
For as soon as Zion was in labor,
She gave birth to her children.
9 Shall I bring to the time of birth,
and not cause delivery?" says
the LORD.
"Shall I who cause delivery shut
up *the womb?*" says your
God.
10 "Rejoice with Jerusalem,
And be glad with her, all you
who love her;
Rejoice for joy with her, all you
who mourn for her;
11 That you may feed and be
satisfied
With the consolation of her
bosom,
That you may drink deeply and
be delighted
With the abundance of her
glory."

12 For thus says the LORD:

"Behold, I will extend peace to
her like a river,
And the glory of the Gentiles like
a flowing stream.
Then you shall feed;
On *her* sides shall you be
carried,
And be dandled on *her* knees.
13 As one whom his mother
comforts,

🔲 **WORDFINDER**

66:1 Heaven The dwelling place of God, angels, and souls of the dead who belong
to God. That heaven is not part of our universe, but sometimes the word just refers
to the sky (see Genesis 1:8).

So I will comfort you;
And you shall be comforted in
     Jerusalem."

14 When you see *this,* your heart
     shall rejoice,
   And your bones shall flourish
     like grass;
   The hand of the LORD shall be
     known to His servants,
   And *His* indignation to His
     enemies.
15 For behold, the LORD will come
     with fire
   And with His chariots, like a
     whirlwind,
   To render His anger with fury,
   And His rebuke with flames of
     fire.
16 For by fire and by His sword
   The LORD will judge all flesh;
   And the slain of the LORD shall
     be many.

17 "Those who sanctify themselves
     and purify themselves,
   To go to the gardens
   After an *idol* in the midst,
   Eating swine's flesh and the
     abomination and the mouse,
   Shall be consumed together,"
     says the LORD.

18 "For I *know* their works and their
thoughts. It shall be that I will gather
all nations and tongues; and they shall
come and see My glory. 19 I will set a
sign among them; and those among
them who escape I will send to the nations: *to* Tarshish and Pul and Lud,
who draw the bow, and Tubal and Javan, *to* the coastlands afar off who
have not heard My fame nor seen My
glory. And they shall declare My glory
among the Gentiles. 20 Then they shall
bring all your brethren for an offering
to the LORD out of all nations, on
horses and in chariots and in litters,
on mules and on camels, to My holy
mountain Jerusalem," says the LORD,
"as the children of Israel bring an offering in a clean vessel into the house of
the LORD. 21 And I will also take some
of them for priests *and* Levites," says
the LORD.

22 "For as the new heavens and the
     new earth
   Which I will make shall remain
     before Me," says the LORD,
   "So shall your descendants and
     your name remain.
23 And it shall come to pass
   That from one New Moon to
     another,
   And from one Sabbath to
     another,
   All flesh shall come to worship
     before Me," says the LORD.

24 "And they shall go forth and look
   Upon the corpses of the men
   Who have transgressed against
     Me.
   For their worm does not die,
   And their fire is not quenched.
   They shall be an abhorrence to
     all flesh."

⚒ DIGGING IN

66:22 A New World Coming If you
think about it for a while, you have to admit that the world we live in is a pretty
sad place. There is constant war, crime,
sickness, starvation, and death. Our world
population doubles and triples, while energy supplies get scarcer and scarcer. Everywhere the earth is polluted. This isn't
what God had in mind for those who love
Him.

God has in mind new heavens and a
new earth, where all the pain and suffering will be no more. He promises it in Isaiah's words, "The new heavens and the
new earth which I make shall remain"
(verse 22). That means that the old heavens and our present dying world will be
gone.

So let's look forward to the new and
better things God has in mind—a happy
world where death and disease and violence are not present. Ask God to bring
in His new world soon, and to make you
a citizen of that eternal country.

The Book of
JEREMIAH

My name is pronounced *jer-uh-MY-uh* and means "The Lord Lifts Up." Sometimes people call me "the weeping prophet" because of the sadness I felt for my people Israel.

My people didn't believe me when I warned them about the suffering that was coming. The armies of Babylon (pronounced *BAB-ih-lon*) would come from the East and burn the city of Jerusalem. Our people would be taken as prisoners to Babylon, and our last king, Zedekiah, would be killed. The king's name is pronounced *zed-uh-KIGH-uh* and means "The Lord My Righteousness," but Zedekiah was not very righteous.

My people said I was a traitor because I said our enemies would destroy us. But I was only God's spokesman to warn them to turn away from their sins.

In the end, our beloved city was burned and our nation ceased to exist for that time. I was kidnapped and taken to Egypt, where I died in my sorrow for Israel.

Do My work, Jeremiah!

THE words of Jeremiah the son of Hilkiah, of the priests who *were* in Anathoth in the land of Benjamin, 2 to whom the word of the LORD came in the days of Josiah the son of Amon, king of Judah, in the thirteenth year of his reign. 3 It came also in the days of Jehoiakim the son of Josiah, king of Judah, until the end of the eleventh year of Zedekiah the son of Josiah, king of Judah, until the carrying away of Jerusalem captive in the fifth month.

4 Then the word of the LORD came to me, saying:

5 "Before I formed you in the
    womb I knew you;
Before you were born I
    sanctified you;
I ordained you a prophet to the
    nations."

6 Then said I:

"Ah, Lord GOD!
Behold, I cannot speak, for I *am*
    a youth."

7 But the LORD said to me:

"Do not say, 'I *am* a youth,'
For you shall go to all to whom
    I send you,
And whatever I command you,
    you shall speak.
8   Do not be afraid of their faces,
For I *am* with you to deliver
    you," says the LORD.

9 Then the LORD put forth His hand and touched my mouth, and the LORD said to me:

"Behold, I have put My words in
    your mouth.
10 See, I have this day set you over
    the nations and over the
    kingdoms,
To root out and to pull down,
To destroy and to throw down,
To build and to plant."

11 Moreover the word of the LORD came to me, saying, "Jeremiah, what do you see?"

And I said, "I see a branch of an almond tree."

12 Then the LORD said to me, "You have seen well, for I am ready to perform My word."

13 And the word of the LORD came to me the second time, saying, "What do you see?"

And I said, "I see a boiling pot, and it is facing away from the north."

14 Then the LORD said to me:

"Out of the north calamity shall
    break forth
On all the inhabitants of the
    land.
15 For behold, I am calling
All the families of the kingdoms
    of the north," says the LORD;
"They shall come and each one
    set his throne
At the entrance of the gates of
    Jerusalem,
Against all its walls all around,
And against all the cities of
    Judah.
16 I will utter My judgments
Against them concerning all their
    wickedness,
Because they have forsaken
    Me,
Burned incense to other gods,
And worshiped the works of
    their own hands.

17 "Therefore prepare yourself and
    arise,
And speak to them all that I
    command you.
Do not be dismayed before their
    faces,
Lest I dismay you before them.
18 For behold, I have made you
    this day
A fortified city and an iron
    pillar,
And bronze walls against the
    whole land—
Against the kings of Judah,
Against its princes,
Against its priests,
And against the people of the
    land.
19 They will fight against you,

But they shall not prevail against
    you.
For I am with you," says the
    LORD, "to deliver you."

God's people turn their backs on Him

2 Moreover the word of the LORD came to me, saying, 2 "Go and cry in the hearing of Jerusalem, saying, 'Thus says the LORD:

"I remember you,
The kindness of your youth,
The love of your betrothal,
When you went after Me in the
    wilderness,
In a land not sown.
3 Israel was holiness to the LORD,
The firstfruits of His increase.
All that devour him will offend;
Disaster will come upon them,"
    says the LORD.' "

4 Hear the word of the LORD, O house of Jacob and all the families of the house of Israel. 5 Thus says the LORD:

"What injustice have your fathers
    found in Me,
That they have gone far from
    Me,
Have followed idols,
And have become idolaters?
6 Neither did they say, 'Where is
    the LORD,
Who brought us up out of the
    land of Egypt,
Who led us through the
    wilderness,
Through a land of deserts and
    pits,
Through a land of drought and
    the shadow of death,
Through a land that no one
    crossed
And where no one dwelt?'
7 I brought you into a bountiful
    country,
To eat its fruit and its goodness.
But when you entered, you
    defiled My land

And made My heritage an
abomination.

8 The priests did not say, 'Where
is the LORD?'
And those who handle the law
did not know Me;
The rulers also transgressed
against Me;
The prophets prophesied by
Baal,
And walked after *things that* do
not profit.

9 "Therefore I will yet bring charges
against you," says the LORD,
"And against your children's
children I will bring charges.
10 For pass beyond the coasts of
Cyprus and see,
Send to Kedar and consider
diligently,
And see if there has been such
a thing.
11 Has a nation changed *its*
gods,
Which *are* not gods?
But My people have changed
their Glory
For *what* does not profit.
12 Be astonished, O heavens, at
this,
And be horribly afraid;
Be very desolate," says the
LORD.
13 "For My people have committed
two evils:
They have forsaken Me, the
fountain of living waters,
And hewn themselves cisterns—
broken cisterns that can hold
no water.

14 "*Is* Israel a servant?
Is he a homeborn *slave?*
Why is he plundered?
15 The young lions roared at him,
and growled;
They made his land waste;
His cities are burned, without
inhabitant.
16 Also the people of Noph and
Tahpanhes
Have broken the crown of your
head.

17 Have you not brought this on
yourself,
In that you have forsaken the
LORD your God
When He led you in the way?
18 And now why take the road to
Egypt,
To drink the waters of Sihor?
Or why take the road to Assyria,
To drink the waters of the
River?
19 Your own wickedness will
correct you,
And your backslidings will
rebuke you.
Know therefore and see that *it
is* an evil and bitter *thing*
That you have forsaken the
LORD your God,
And the fear of Me *is* not in
you,"
Says the Lord GOD of hosts.

20 "For of old I have broken your
yoke *and* burst your bonds;
And you said, 'I will not
transgress,'
When on every high hill and
under every green tree
You lay down, playing the
harlot.
21 Yet I had planted you a noble
vine, a seed of highest quality.
How then have you turned
before Me
Into the degenerate plant of an
alien vine?
22 For though you wash yourself
with lye, and use much soap,
Yet your iniquity is marked
before Me," says the Lord
GOD.

23 "How can you say, 'I am not
polluted,
I have not gone after the Baals'?
See your way in the valley;
Know what you have done:
You are a swift dromedary
breaking loose in her ways,
24 A wild donkey used to the
wilderness,
That sniffs at the wind in her
desire;

In her time of mating, who can
    turn her away?
All those who seek her will not
    weary themselves;
In her month they will find
    her.
25 Withhold your foot from being
    unshod, and your throat from
    thirst.
But you said, 'There is no hope.
No! For I have loved aliens, and
    after them I will go.'

26 "As the thief is ashamed when he
    is found out,
So is the house of Israel
    ashamed;
They and their kings and their
    princes, and their priests and
    their prophets,
27 Saying to a tree, 'You *are* my
    father,'
And to a stone, 'You gave birth
    to me.'
For they have turned *their* back
    to Me, and not *their* face.
But in the time of their trouble
They will say, 'Arise and save
    us.'
28 But where *are* your gods that
    you have made for
    yourselves?
Let them arise,
If they can save you in the time
    of your trouble;
For *according to* the number of
    your cities
Are your gods, O Judah.

29 "Why will you plead with Me?
You all have transgressed
    against Me," says the LORD.
30 "In vain I have chastened your
    children;
They received no correction.
Your sword has devoured your
    prophets
Like a destroying lion.

31 "O generation, see the word of
    the LORD!
Have I been a wilderness to
    Israel,
Or a land of darkness?

Why do My people say, 'We are
    lords;
We will come no more to You'?
32 Can a virgin forget her
    ornaments,
Or a bride her attire?
Yet My people have forgotten
    Me days without number.

33 "Why do you beautify your way
    to seek love?
Therefore you have also taught
The wicked women your ways.
34 Also on your skirts is found
The blood of the lives of the
    poor innocents.
I have not found it by secret
    search,
But plainly on all these things.
35 Yet you say, 'Because I am
    innocent,
Surely His anger shall turn from
    me.'
Behold, I will plead My case
    against you,
Because you say, 'I have not
    sinned.'
36 Why do you gad about so much
    to change your way?
Also you shall be ashamed of
    Egypt as you were ashamed
    of Assyria.
37 Indeed you will go forth from
    him
With your hands on your head;
For the LORD has rejected your
    trusted allies,
And you will not prosper by
    them.

God's mercy is greater than their sin

3   "They say, 'If a man divorces his
            wife,
And she goes from him
And becomes another man's,
May he return to her again?'
Would not that land be greatly
    polluted?
But you have played the harlot
    with many lovers;
Yet return to Me," says the
    LORD.

2 "Lift up your eyes to the desolate
heights and see:
Where have you not lain *with
men?*
By the road you have sat for
them
Like an Arabian in the
wilderness;
And you have polluted the
land
With your harlotries and your
wickedness.
3 Therefore the showers have
been withheld,
And there has been no latter
rain.
You have had a harlot's
forehead;
You refuse to be ashamed.
4 Will you not from this time cry
to Me,
'My Father, You *are* the guide
of my youth?
5 Will He remain angry forever?
Will He keep *it* to the end?'
Behold, you have spoken and
done evil things,
As you were able."

6 The LORD said also to me in the
days of Josiah the king: "Have you
seen what backsliding Israel has done?
She has gone up on every high mountain and under every green tree, and
there played the harlot. 7 And I said,
after she had done all these *things,* 'Return to Me.' But she did not return.
And her treacherous sister Judah saw
it. 8 Then I saw that for all the causes
for which backsliding Israel had committed adultery, I had put her away
and given her a certificate of divorce;
yet her treacherous sister Judah did not
fear, but went and played the harlot
also. 9 So it came to pass, through her
casual harlotry, that she defiled the
land and committed adultery with
stones and trees. 10 And yet for all this
her treacherous sister Judah has not
turned to Me with her whole heart, but
in pretense," says the LORD.
11 Then the LORD said to me, "Backsliding Israel has shown herself more
righteous than treacherous Judah.

12 Go and proclaim these words toward the north, and say:

'Return, backsliding Israel,' says
the LORD;
'I will not cause My anger to fall
on you.
For I *am* merciful,' says the
LORD;
'I will not remain angry forever.
13 Only acknowledge your iniquity,
That you have transgressed
against the LORD your God,
And have scattered your
charms
To alien deities under every
green tree,
And you have not obeyed My
voice,' says the LORD.

14 "Return, O backsliding children,"
says the LORD; "for I am married to
you. I will take you, one from a city
and two from a family, and I will bring
you to Zion. 15 And I will give you
shepherds according to My heart, who
will feed you with knowledge and understanding.
16 "Then it shall come to pass, when
you are multiplied and increased in the
land in those days," says the LORD,
"that they will say no more, 'The ark
of the covenant of the LORD.' It shall
not come to mind, nor shall they remember it, nor shall they visit *it,* nor
shall it be made anymore.
17 "At that time Jerusalem shall be
called The Throne of the LORD, and
all the nations shall be gathered to it,
to the name of the LORD, to Jerusalem.
No more shall they follow the dictates
of their evil hearts.
18 "In those days the house of Judah
shall walk with the house of Israel, and
they shall come together out of the
land of the north to the land that I have
given as an inheritance to your fathers.
19 "But I said:

'How can I put you among the
children
And give you a pleasant land,
A beautiful heritage of the hosts
of nations?'

"And I said:

'You shall call Me, "My Father,"
And not turn away from Me.'
20 Surely, *as* a wife treacherously
    departs from her husband,
So have you dealt treacherously
    with Me,
O house of Israel," says the
    LORD.

21 A voice was heard on the
    desolate heights,
Weeping *and* supplications of
    the children of Israel.
For they have perverted their
    way;
They have forgotten the LORD
    their God.

22 "Return, you backsliding
    children,
And I will heal your
    backslidings."

"Indeed we do come to You,
For You are the LORD our
    God.
23 Truly, in vain *is salvation hoped
    for* from the hills,
And from the multitude of
    mountains;
Truly, in the LORD our God
Is the salvation of Israel.
24 For shame has devoured
The labor of our fathers from our
    youth—
Their flocks and their herds,
Their sons and their daughters.
25 We lie down in our shame,
And our reproach covers us.
For we have sinned against the
    LORD our God,
We and our fathers,
From our youth even to this
    day,
And have not obeyed the voice
    of the LORD our God."

Jeremiah cries over Judah

4 "If you will return, O Israel," says
    the LORD,
"Return to Me;

And if you will put away your
    abominations out of My sight,
Then you shall not be moved.
2 And you shall swear, 'The LORD
    lives,'
In truth, in judgment, and in
    righteousness;
The nations shall bless
    themselves in Him,
And in Him they shall glory."

3 For thus says the LORD to the men
of Judah and Jerusalem:

"Break up your fallow ground,
And do not sow among thorns.
4 Circumcise yourselves to the
    LORD,
And take away the foreskins of
    your hearts,
You men of Judah and
    inhabitants of Jerusalem,
Lest My fury come forth like fire,
And burn so that no one can
    quench *it*,
Because of the evil of your
    doings."

5 Declare in Judah and proclaim in
Jerusalem, and say:

"Blow the trumpet in the land;
Cry, 'Gather together,'
And say, 'Assemble yourselves,
And let us go into the fortified
    cities.'
6 Set up the standard toward Zion.
Take refuge! Do not delay!
For I will bring disaster from the
    north,
And great destruction."

7 The lion has come up from his
    thicket,
And the destroyer of nations is
    on his way.
He has gone forth from his
    place
To make your land desolate.
Your cities will be laid waste,
Without inhabitant.
8 For this, clothe yourself with
    sackcloth,
Lament and wail.

For the fierce anger of the LORD
Has not turned back from us.

9 "And it shall come to pass in that
     day," says the LORD,
"*That* the heart of the king shall
     perish,
And the heart of the princes;
The priests shall be astonished,
And the prophets shall wonder."

10 Then I said, "Ah, Lord GOD!
Surely You have greatly
     deceived this people and
     Jerusalem,
Saying, 'You shall have peace,'
Whereas the sword reaches to
     the heart."

11 At that time it will be said
To this people and to Jerusalem,
"A dry wind of the desolate
     heights *blows* in the
     wilderness
Toward the daughter of My
     people—
Not to fan or to cleanse—
12 A wind too strong for these will
     come for Me;
Now I will also speak judgment
     against them."

13 "Behold, he shall come up like
     clouds,
And his chariots like a whirlwind.
His horses are swifter than
     eagles.
Woe to us, for we are
     plundered!"

14 O Jerusalem, wash your heart
     from wickedness,
That you may be saved.
How long shall your evil
     thoughts lodge within you?
15 For a voice declares from Dan
And proclaims affliction from
     Mount Ephraim:
16 "Make mention to the nations,
Yes, proclaim against Jerusalem,
That watchers come from a far
     country
And raise their voice against the
     cities of Judah.

17 Like keepers of a field they are
     against her all around,
Because she has been rebellious
     against Me," says the LORD.
18 "Your ways and your doings
Have procured these *things* for
     you.
This *is* your wickedness,
Because it is bitter,
Because it reaches to your
     heart."

19 O my soul, my soul!
I am pained in my very heart!
My heart makes a noise in me;
I cannot hold my peace,
Because you have heard, O my
     soul,
The sound of the trumpet,
The alarm of war.
20 Destruction upon destruction is
     cried,
For the whole land is plundered.
Suddenly my tents are
     plundered,
And my curtains in a moment.
21 How long will I see the standard,
And hear the sound of the
     trumpet?

22 "For My people *are* foolish,
They have not known Me.
They *are* silly children,
And they have no
     understanding.
They *are* wise to do evil,
But to do good they have no
     knowledge."

23 I beheld the earth, and indeed
     it was without form, and
     void;
And the heavens, they *had* no
     light.
24 I beheld the mountains, and
     indeed they trembled,
And all the hills moved back and
     forth.
25 I beheld, and indeed *there was*
     no man,
And all the birds of the heavens
     had fled.
26 I beheld, and indeed the fruitful
     land *was* a wilderness,

And all its cities were broken
    down
At the presence of the LORD,
    By His fierce anger.

27 For thus says the LORD:

    "The whole land shall be
        desolate;
    Yet I will not make a full end.
28 For this shall the earth mourn,
    And the heavens above be
        black,
    Because I have spoken.
    I have purposed and will not
        relent,
    Nor will I turn back from it.
29 The whole city shall flee from the
        noise of the horsemen and
        bowmen.
    They shall go into thickets and
        climb up on the rocks.
    Every city *shall be* forsaken,
    And not a man shall dwell in it.

30 "And *when* you *are* plundered,
    What will you do?
    Though you clothe yourself with
        crimson,
    Though you adorn *yourself* with
        ornaments of gold,
    Though you enlarge your *eyes*
        with paint,
    In vain you will make yourself
        fair;
    Your lovers will despise you;
    They will seek your life.

31 "For I have heard a voice as of
        a woman in labor,
    The anguish as of her who
        brings forth her first child,
    The voice of the daughter of
        Zion bewailing herself;
    She spreads her hands, *saying,*
    'Woe *is* me now, for my soul is
        weary
    Because of murderers!'

Judah's terrible sins

5   "Run to and fro through the
        streets of Jerusalem;
    See now and know;

    And seek in her open places
    If you can find a man,
    If there is *anyone* who executes
        judgment,
    Who seeks the truth,
    And I will pardon her.
2 Though they say, 'As the LORD
        lives,'
    Surely they swear falsely."

3 O LORD, *are* not Your eyes on
        the truth?
    You have stricken them,
    But they have not grieved;
    You have consumed them,
    But they have refused to receive
        correction.
    They have made their faces
        harder than rock;
    They have refused to return.

4 Therefore I said, "Surely these
        are poor.
    They are foolish;
    For they do not know the way
        of the LORD,
    The judgment of their God.
5 I will go to the great men and
        speak to them,
    For they have known the way
        of the LORD,
    The judgment of their God."

    But these have altogether
        broken the yoke
    And burst the bonds.
6 Therefore a lion from the forest
        shall slay them,
    A wolf of the deserts shall
        destroy them;
    A leopard will watch over their
        cities.
    Everyone who goes out from
        there shall be torn in pieces,
    Because their transgressions are
        many;
    Their backslidings have
        increased.

7 "How shall I pardon you for this?
    Your children have forsaken Me
    And sworn by *those that are* not
        gods.
    When I had fed them to the full,

Then they committed adultery
And assembled themselves by
   troops in the harlots' houses.
8   They were *like* well-fed lusty
      stallions;
   Every one neighed after his
      neighbor's wife.
9   Shall I not punish *them* for these
      things?" says the LORD.
   "And shall I not avenge Myself
      on such a nation as this?

10 "Go up on her walls and destroy,
   But do not make a complete
      end.
   Take away her branches,
   For they *are* not the LORD's.
11 For the house of Israel and the
      house of Judah
   Have dealt very treacherously
      with Me," says the LORD.

12 They have lied about the LORD,
   And said, "*It is* not He.
   Neither will evil come upon us,
   Nor shall we see sword or
      famine.
13 And the prophets become wind,
   For the word *is* not in them.
   Thus shall it be done to them."

14 Therefore thus says the LORD God
of hosts:

   "Because you speak this word,
   Behold, I will make My words
      in your mouth fire,
   And this people wood,
   And it shall devour them.
15 Behold, I will bring a nation
      against you from afar,
   O house of Israel," says the
      LORD.
   "It *is* a mighty nation,
   It *is* an ancient nation,
   A nation whose language you do
      not know,
   Nor can you understand what
      they say.
16 Their quiver *is* like an open
      tomb;
   They *are* all mighty men.
17 And they shall eat up your
      harvest and your bread,

Which your sons and daughters
   should eat.
They shall eat up your flocks and
   your herds;
They shall eat up your vines and
   your fig trees;
They shall destroy your fortified
   cities,
In which you trust, with the
   sword.

18 "Nevertheless in those days,"
says the LORD, "I will not make a complete end of you. 19 And it will be when
you say, 'Why does the LORD our God
do all these *things* to us?' then you
shall answer them, 'Just as you have
forsaken Me and served foreign gods
in your land, so you shall serve aliens
in a land *that is* not yours.'

20 "Declare this in the house of
      Jacob
   And proclaim it in Judah,
      saying,
21 'Hear this now, O foolish people,
   Without understanding,
   Who have eyes and see not,
   And who have ears and hear
      not:
22 Do you not fear Me?' says the
      LORD.
   'Will you not tremble at My
      presence,
   Who have placed the sand as
      the bound of the sea,
   By a perpetual decree, that it
      cannot pass beyond it?
   And though its waves toss to and
      fro,
   Yet they cannot prevail;
   Though they roar, yet they
      cannot pass over it.
23 But this people has a defiant and
      rebellious heart;
   They have revolted and
      departed.
24 They do not say in their heart,
   "Let us now fear the LORD our
      God,
   Who gives rain, both the former
      and the latter, in its season.
   He reserves for us the appointed
      weeks of the harvest."

25 Your iniquities have turned
   these *things* away,
   And your sins have withheld
   good from you.

26 'For among My people are found
   wicked *men*;
   They lie in wait as one who sets
   snares;
   They set a trap;
   They catch men.
27 As a cage is full of birds,
   So their houses *are* full of deceit.
   Therefore they have become
   great and grown rich.
28 They have grown fat, they are
   sleek;
   Yes, they surpass the deeds of
   the wicked;
   They do not plead the cause,
   The cause of the fatherless;
   Yet they prosper,
   And the right of the needy they
   do not defend.
29 Shall I not punish *them* for these
   things?' says the LORD.
   'Shall I not avenge Myself on
   such a nation as this?'

30 "An astonishing and horrible
   thing
   Has been committed in the land:
31 The prophets prophesy falsely,
   And the priests rule by their *own*
   power;
   And My people love *to have it*
   so.
   But what will you do in the end?

Jeremiah gives Judah one last warning

6 "O you children of Benjamin,
   Gather yourselves to flee from
   the midst of Jerusalem!
   Blow the trumpet in Tekoa,
   And set up a signal-fire in Beth
   Haccerem;
   For disaster appears out of the
   north,
   And great destruction.
2 I have likened the daughter of
   Zion
   To a lovely and delicate woman.

3 The shepherds with their flocks
   shall come to her.
   They shall pitch *their* tents
   against her all around.
   Each one shall pasture in his
   own place."

4 "Prepare war against her;
   Arise, and let us go up at noon.
   Woe to us, for the day goes
   away,
   For the shadows of the evening
   are lengthening.
5 Arise, and let us go by night,
   And let us destroy her palaces."

6 For thus has the LORD of hosts said:

   "Cut down trees,
   And build a mound against
   Jerusalem.
   This *is* the city to be punished.
   She *is* full of oppression in her
   midst.
7 As a fountain wells up with
   water,
   So she wells up with her
   wickedness.
   Violence and plundering are
   heard in her.
   Before Me continually *are* grief
   and wounds.
8 Be instructed, O Jerusalem,
   Lest My soul depart from you;
   Lest I make you desolate,
   A land not inhabited."

9 Thus says the LORD of hosts:

   "They shall thoroughly glean as
   a vine the remnant of Israel;
   As a grape-gatherer, put your
   hand back into the branches."

10 To whom shall I speak and give
   warning,
   That they may hear?
   Indeed their ear *is*
   uncircumcised,
   And they cannot give heed.
   Behold, the word of the LORD
   is a reproach to them;
   They have no delight in it.

11 Therefore I am full of the fury
　　of the LORD.
　I am weary of holding *it* in.
　"I will pour it out on the children
　　outside,
　And on the assembly of young
　　men together;
　For even the husband shall be
　　taken with the wife,
　The aged with *him who is* full
　　of days.
12 And their houses shall be turned
　　over to others,
　Fields and wives together;
　For I will stretch out My hand
　Against the inhabitants of the
　　land," says the LORD.
13 "Because from the least of
　　them *even* to the greatest
　　of them,
　Everyone *is* given to
　　covetousness;
　And from the prophet even to
　　the priest,
　Everyone deals falsely.
14 They have also healed the hurt
　　of My people slightly,
　Saying, 'Peace, peace!'
　When *there is* no peace.
15 Were they ashamed when they
　　had committed abomination?
　No! They were not at all
　　ashamed;
　Nor did they know how to blush.
　Therefore they shall fall among
　　those who fall;
　At the time I punish them,
　They shall be cast down," says
　　the LORD.

16 Thus says the LORD:

　"Stand in the ways and see,
　And ask for the old paths, where
　　the good way *is*,
　And walk in it;
　Then you will find rest for your
　　souls.
　But they said, 'We will not walk
　　in it.'
17 Also, I set watchmen over you,
　　saying,
　'Listen to the sound of the
　　trumpet!'

But they said, 'We will not
　listen.'
18 Therefore hear, you nations,
　And know, O congregation,
　　what *is* among them.
19 Hear, O earth!
　Behold, I will certainly bring
　　calamity on this people—
　The fruit of their thoughts,
　Because they have not heeded
　　My words
　Nor My law, but rejected it.
20 For what purpose to Me
　Comes frankincense from
　　Sheba,
　And sweet cane from a far
　　country?
　Your burnt offerings *are* not
　　acceptable,
　Nor your sacrifices sweet to
　　Me."

21 Therefore thus says the LORD:

　"Behold, I will lay stumbling
　　blocks before this people,
　And the fathers and the sons
　　together shall fall on them.
　The neighbor and his friend shall
　　perish."

22 Thus says the LORD:

　"Behold, a people comes from
　　the north country,
　And a great nation will be raised
　　from the farthest parts of the
　　earth.
23 They will lay hold on bow and
　　spear;
　They *are* cruel and have no
　　mercy;
　Their voice roars like the sea;
　And they ride on horses,
　As men of war set in array
　　against you, O daughter of
　　Zion."

24 We have heard the report of it;
　Our hands grow feeble.
　Anguish has taken hold of us,
　Pain as of a woman in labor.
25 Do not go out into the field,
　Nor walk by the way.

Because of the sword of the
enemy,
Fear *is* on every side.
26 O daughter of my people,
Dress in sackcloth
And roll about in ashes!
Make mourning *as for* an only
son, most bitter lamentation;
For the plunderer will suddenly
come upon us.

27 "I have set you as an assayer *and*
a fortress among My people,
That you may know and test
their way.
28 They *are* all stubborn rebels,
walking as slanderers.
They are bronze and iron,
They *are* all corrupters;
29 The bellows blow fiercely,
The lead is consumed by the
fire;
The smelter refines in vain,
For the wicked are not drawn
off.
30 *People* will call them rejected
silver,
Because the LORD has rejected
them."

Obey God before it is too late

7 The word that came to Jeremiah
from the LORD, saying, 2 "Stand in the
gate of the LORD's house, and proclaim
there this word, and say, 'Hear the
word of the LORD, all *you of* Judah
who enter in at these gates to worship
the LORD!' " 3 Thus says the LORD of
hosts, the God of Israel: "Amend your
ways and your doings, and I will cause
you to dwell in this place. 4 Do not trust
in these lying words, saying, 'The temple of the LORD, the temple of the
LORD, the temple of the LORD *are*
these.'
5 "For if you thoroughly amend your
ways and your doings, if you thoroughly execute judgment between a
man and his neighbor, 6 *if* you do not
oppress the stranger, the fatherless,
and the widow, and do not shed innocent blood in this place, or walk after
other gods to your hurt, 7 then I will

cause you to dwell in this place, in the
land that I gave to your fathers forever
and ever.
8 "Behold, you trust in lying words
that cannot profit. 9 Will you steal, murder, commit adultery, swear falsely,
burn incense to Baal, and walk after
other gods whom you do not know,
10 and *then* come and stand before Me
in this house which is called by My
name, and say, 'We are delivered to
do all these abominations'? 11 Has this
house, which is called by My name,
become a den of thieves in your eyes?
Behold, I, even I, have seen *it*," says
the LORD.
12 "But go now to My place which
was in Shiloh, where I set My name
at the first, and see what I did to it
because of the wickedness of My people Israel. 13 And now, because you
have done all these works," says the
LORD, "and I spoke to you, rising up
early and speaking, but you did not
hear, and I called you, but you did not
answer, 14 therefore I will do to the
house which is called by My name, in
which you trust, and to this place which
I gave to you and your fathers, as I
have done to Shiloh. 15 And I will cast
you out of My sight, as I have cast out
all your brethren—the whole posterity
of Ephraim.
16 "Therefore do not pray for this
people, nor lift up a cry or prayer for
them, nor make intercession to Me; for
I will not hear you. 17 Do you not see
what they do in the cities of Judah and
in the streets of Jerusalem? 18 The children gather wood, the fathers kindle
the fire, and the women knead dough,
to make cakes for the queen of
heaven; and *they* pour out drink offerings to other gods, that they may provoke Me to anger. 19 Do they provoke
Me to anger?" says the LORD. "*Do they*
not *provoke* themselves, to the shame
of their own faces?"
20 Therefore thus says the Lord GOD:
"Behold, My anger and My fury will
be poured out on this place—on man
and on beast, on the trees of the field
and on the fruit of the ground. And it
will burn and not be quenched."

21 Thus says the LORD of hosts, the God of Israel: "Add your burnt offerings to your sacrifices and eat meat. 22 For I did not speak to your fathers, or command them in the day that I brought them out of the land of Egypt, concerning burnt offerings or sacrifices. 23 But this is what I commanded them, saying, 'Obey My voice, and I will be your God, and you shall be My people. And walk in all the ways that I have commanded you, that it may be well with you.' 24 Yet they did not obey or incline their ear, but followed the counsels and the dictates of their evil hearts, and went backward and not forward. 25 Since the day that your fathers came out of the land of Egypt until this day, I have even sent to you all My servants the prophets, daily rising up early and sending them. 26 Yet they did not obey Me or incline their ear, but stiffened their neck. They did worse than their fathers.

27 "Therefore you shall speak all these words to them, but they will not obey you. You shall also call to them, but they will not answer you.

28 "So you shall say to them, 'This is a nation that does not obey the voice of the LORD their God nor receive correction. Truth has perished and has been cut off from their mouth. 29 Cut off your hair and cast it away, and take up a lamentation on the desolate heights; for the LORD has rejected and forsaken the generation of His wrath.'

30 For the children of Judah have done evil in My sight," says the LORD. "They have set their abominations in the house which is called by My name, to pollute it. 31 And they have built the high places of Tophet, which is in the Valley of the Son of Hinnom, to burn their sons and their daughters in the fire, which I did not command, nor did it come into My heart.

32 "Therefore behold, the days are coming," says the LORD, "when it will no more be called Tophet, or the Valley of the Son of Hinnom, but the Valley of Slaughter; for they will bury in Tophet until there is no room. 33 The corpses of this people will be food for the birds of the heaven and for the beasts of the earth. And no one will frighten them away. 34 Then I will cause to cease from the cities of Judah and from the streets of Jerusalem the voice of mirth and the voice of gladness, the voice of the bridegroom and the voice of the bride. For the land shall be desolate.

God's people won't listen

8 "At that time," says the LORD, "they shall bring out the bones of the kings of Judah, and the bones of its princes, and the bones of the priests, and the bones of the prophets, and the bones of the inhabitants of Jerusalem, out of their graves. 2 They shall spread them before the sun and the moon and all the host of heaven, which they have loved and which they have served and after which they have walked, which they have sought and which they have worshiped. They shall not be gathered nor buried; they shall be like refuse on the face of the earth. 3 Then death shall be chosen rather than life by all the residue of those who remain of this evil family, who remain in all the places where I have driven them," says the LORD of hosts.

4 "Moreover you shall say to them, 'Thus says the LORD:

"Will they fall and not rise?
  Will one turn away and not return?
5 Why has this people slidden back,
  Jerusalem, in a perpetual backsliding?
  They hold fast to deceit,
  They refuse to return.
6 I listened and heard,
  But they do not speak aright.
  No man repented of his wickedness,
  Saying, 'What have I done?'
  Everyone turned to his own course,
  As the horse rushes into the battle.

7 "Even the stork in the heavens
    Knows her appointed times;
    And the turtledove, the swift,
        and the swallow
    Observe the time of their
        coming.
    But My people do not know the
        judgment of the LORD.

8 "How can you say, 'We *are* wise,
    And the law of the LORD *is* with
        us'?
    Look, the false pen of the scribe
        certainly works falsehood.

9   The wise men are ashamed,
    They are dismayed and taken.
    Behold, they have rejected the
        word of the LORD;
    So what wisdom do they have?

10 Therefore I will give their wives
        to others,
    And their fields to those who will
        inherit *them;*
    Because from the least *even* to
        the greatest
    Everyone is given to
        covetousness;
    From the prophet *even* to the
        priest
    Everyone deals falsely.

11 For they have healed the hurt
        of the daughter of My people
        slightly,
    Saying, 'Peace, peace!'
    When *there is* no peace.

12 Were they ashamed when
        they had committed
        abomination?
    No! They were not at all
        ashamed,
    Nor did they know how to
        blush.
    Therefore they shall fall among
        those who fall;
    In the time of their punishment
    They shall be cast down," says
        the LORD.

13 "I will surely consume them,"
        says the LORD.
    "No grapes *shall be* on the vine,
    Nor figs on the fig tree,
    And the leaf shall fade;
    And *the things* I have given them

shall pass away from
    them.'""

14 "Why do we sit still?
    Assemble yourselves,
    And let us enter the fortified
        cities,
    And let us be silent there.
    For the LORD our God has put
        us to silence
    And given us water of gall to
        drink,
    Because we have sinned against
        the LORD.

15 "We looked for peace, but no
        good *came;*
    And for a time of health, and
        there was trouble!

16 The snorting of His horses was
        heard from Dan.
    The whole land trembled at the
        sound of the neighing of His
        strong ones;
    For they have come and
        devoured the land and all that
        is in it,
    The city and those who dwell in
        it."

17 "For behold, I will send serpents
        among you,
    Vipers which cannot be
        charmed,
    And they shall bite you," says
        the LORD.

18 I would comfort myself in
        sorrow;
    My heart *is* faint in me.

19 Listen! The voice,
    The cry of the daughter of my
        people
    From a far country:
    "*Is* not the LORD in Zion?
    Is not her King in her?"

    "Why have they provoked Me to
        anger
    With their carved images—
    With foreign idols?"

20 "The harvest is past,
    The summer is ended,
    And we are not saved!"

21 For the hurt of the daughter of
    my people I am hurt.
I am mourning;
Astonishment has taken hold of
    me.
22 *Is there* no balm in Gilead,
    Is there no physician there?
Why then is there no recovery
For the health of the daughter
    of my people?

Jeremiah cries for the people

9 Oh, that my head were waters,
And my eyes a fountain of tears,
That I might weep day and night
For the slain of the daughter of
    my people!
2 Oh, that I had in the wilderness
A lodging place for travelers;
That I might leave my people,
And go from them!
For they *are* all adulterers,
An assembly of treacherous
    men.
3 "And *like* their bow they have
    bent their tongues *for* lies.
They are not valiant for the truth
    on the earth.
For they proceed from evil to
    evil,
And they do not know Me," says
    the LORD.
4 "Everyone take heed to his
    neighbor,
And do not trust any brother;
For every brother will utterly
    supplant,
And every neighbor will walk
    with slanderers.
5 Everyone will deceive his
    neighbor,
And will not speak the truth;
They have taught their tongue
    to speak lies;
They weary themselves to
    commit iniquity.
6 Your dwelling place *is* in the
    midst of deceit;
Through deceit they refuse to
    know Me," says the LORD.

7 Therefore thus says the LORD of
hosts:

"Behold, I will refine them and
    try them;
For how shall I deal with the
    daughter of My people?
8 Their tongue *is* an arrow shot
    out;
It speaks deceit;
One speaks peaceably to his
    neighbor with his mouth,
But in his heart he lies in wait.
9 Shall I not punish them for these
    things?" says the LORD.
"Shall I not avenge Myself on
    such a nation as this?"

10 I will take up a weeping and
    wailing for the mountains,
And for the dwelling places of
    the wilderness a lamentation,
Because they are burned up,
So that no one can pass
    through;
Nor can *men* hear the voice of
    the cattle.
Both the birds of the heavens
    and the beasts have fled;
They are gone.

11 "I will make Jerusalem a heap of
    ruins, a den of jackals.
I will make the cities of Judah
    desolate, without an
    inhabitant."

12 Who *is* the wise man who may understand this? And *who is he* to whom the mouth of the LORD has spoken, that he may declare it? Why does the land perish *and* burn up like a wilderness, so that no one can pass through? 13 And the LORD said, "Because they have forsaken My law which I set before them, and have not obeyed My voice, nor walked according to it, 14 but they have walked according to the dictates of their own hearts and after the Baals, which their fathers taught them," 15 therefore thus says the LORD of hosts, the God of Israel: "Behold, I will feed them, this people, with wormwood, and give them water of gall to drink. 16 I will scatter them also among the Gentiles, whom neither they nor

their fathers have known. And I will send a sword after them until I have consumed them."

17 Thus says the LORD of hosts:

"Consider and call for the
    mourning women,
That they may come;
And send for skillful wailing
    women,
That they may come.
18 Let them make haste
And take up a wailing for us,
That our eyes may run with
    tears,
And our eyelids gush with water.
19 For a voice of wailing is heard
    from Zion:
'How we are plundered!
We are greatly ashamed,
Because we have forsaken the
    land,
Because we have been cast out
    of our dwellings.' "

20 Yet hear the word of the LORD,
    O women,
And let your ear receive the
    word of His mouth;
Teach your daughters wailing,
And everyone her neighbor a
    lamentation.
21 For death has come through our
    windows,
Has entered our palaces,
To kill off the children—*no
    longer to be* outside!
And the young men—*no longer*
    on the streets!

22 Speak, "Thus says the LORD:

'Even the carcasses of men shall
    fall as refuse on the open field,
Like cuttings after the harvester,
And no one shall gather *them.*' "

23 Thus says the LORD:

"Let not the wise *man* glory in
    his wisdom,
Let not the mighty *man* glory in
    his might,
Nor let the rich *man* glory in his
    riches;
24 But let him who glories glory in
    this,
That he understands and knows
    Me,
That I *am* the LORD, exercising
    lovingkindness, judgment,
    and righteousness in the
    earth.
For in these I delight," says the
    LORD.

25 "Behold, the days are coming," says the LORD, "that I will punish all *who are* circumcised with the uncircumcised— 26 Egypt, Judah, Edom, the people of Ammon, Moab, and all *who are* in the farthest corners, who dwell in the wilderness. For all *these* nations *are* uncircumcised, and all the house of Israel *are* uncircumcised in the heart."

No other god like our God

10 Hear the word which the LORD speaks to you, O house of Israel.
2 Thus says the LORD:

"Do not learn the way of the
    Gentiles;
Do not be dismayed at the signs
    of heaven,
For the Gentiles are dismayed
    at them.
3 For the customs of the peoples
    are futile;
For *one* cuts a tree from the
    forest,
The work of the hands of the
    workman, with the ax.
4 They decorate it with silver and
    gold;
They fasten it with nails and
    hammers
So that it will not topple.
5 They *are* upright, like a palm
    tree,
And they cannot speak;
They must be carried,
Because they cannot go *by
    themselves.*
Do not be afraid of them,
For they cannot do evil,
Nor can they do any good."

6 Inasmuch as *there is* none like
   You, O LORD
   (You *are* great, and Your name
   is great in might),
7 Who would not fear You, O
   King of the nations?
   For this is Your rightful due.
   For among all the wise *men* of
   the nations,
   And in all their kingdoms,
   There is none like You.
8 But they are altogether
   dull-hearted and foolish;
   A wooden idol *is* a worthless
   doctrine.
9 Silver is beaten into plates;
   It is brought from Tarshish,
   And gold from Uphaz,
   The work of the craftsman
   And of the hands of the
   metalsmith;
   Blue and purple *are* their
   clothing;
   They *are* all the work of skillful
   men.
10 But the LORD *is* the true God;
   He *is* the living God and the
   everlasting King.
   At His wrath the earth will
   tremble,
   And the nations will not be able
   to endure His indignation.

11 Thus you shall say to them: "The
gods that have not made the heavens
and the earth shall perish from the
earth and from under these heavens."

12 He has made the earth by His
   power,
   He has established the world by
   His wisdom,
   And has stretched out the
   heavens at His discretion.
13 When He utters His voice,
   There is a multitude of waters
   in the heavens:
   "And He causes the vapors to
   ascend from the ends of the
   earth.
   He makes lightning for the
   rain,
   He brings the wind out of His
   treasuries."

14 Everyone is dull-hearted,
   without knowledge;
   Every metalsmith is put to
   shame by an image;
   For his molded image *is*
   falsehood,
   And *there is* no breath in
   them.
15 They *are* futile, a work of errors;
   In the time of their punishment
   they shall perish.
16 The Portion of Jacob *is* not like
   them,
   For He *is* the Maker of all *things,*
   And Israel *is* the tribe of His
   inheritance;
   The LORD of hosts *is* His name.
17 Gather up your wares from the
   land,
   O inhabitant of the fortress!

18 For thus says the LORD:

   "Behold, I will throw out at this
   time
   The inhabitants of the land,
   And will distress them,
   That they may find *it* so."

19 Woe is me for my hurt!
   My wound is severe.
   But I say, "Truly this *is* an
   infirmity,
   And I must bear it."
20 My tent is plundered,
   And all my cords are broken;
   My children have gone from me,
   And they *are* no more.
   There is no one to pitch my tent
   anymore,
   Or set up my curtains.

21 For the shepherds have become
   dull-hearted,
   And have not sought the LORD;
   Therefore they shall not prosper,
   And all their flocks shall be
   scattered.
22 Behold, the noise of the report
   has come,
   And a great commotion out of
   the north country,
   To make the cities of Judah
   desolate, a den of jackals.

23 O Lord, I know the way of man
  is not in himself;
  It is not in man who walks to
  direct his own steps.
24 O Lord, correct me, but with
  justice;
  Not in Your anger, lest You
  bring me to nothing.
25 Pour out Your fury on the
  Gentiles, who do not know
  You,
  And on the families who do not
  call on Your name;
  For they have eaten up Jacob,
  Devoured him and consumed
  him,
  And made his dwelling place
  desolate.

Judah breaks a solemn promise

11 The word that came to Jeremiah from the Lord, saying, 2 "Hear the words of this covenant, and speak to the men of Judah and to the inhabitants of Jerusalem; 3 and say to them, 'Thus says the Lord God of Israel: "Cursed is the man who does not obey the words of this covenant 4 which I commanded your fathers in the day I brought them out of the land of Egypt, from the iron furnace, saying, 'Obey My voice, and do according to all that I command you; so shall you be My people, and I will be your God,' 5 that I may establish the oath which I have sworn to your fathers, to give them 'a land flowing with milk and honey,' as it is this day." ' " And I answered and said, "So be it, Lord."

6 Then the Lord said to me, "Proclaim all these words in the cities of Judah and in the streets of Jerusalem, saying: 'Hear the words of this covenant and do them. 7 For I earnestly exhorted your fathers in the day I brought them up out of the land of Egypt, until this day, rising early and exhorting, saying, "Obey My voice." 8 Yet they did not obey or incline their ear, but everyone followed the dictates of his evil heart; therefore I will bring upon them all the words of this cov-

enant, which I commanded them to do, but which they have not done.' "

9 And the Lord said to me, "A conspiracy has been found among the men of Judah and among the inhabitants of Jerusalem. 10 They have turned back to the iniquities of their forefathers who refused to hear My words, and they have gone after other gods to serve them; the house of Israel and the house of Judah have broken My covenant which I made with their fathers."

11 Therefore thus says the Lord: "Behold, I will surely bring calamity on them which they will not be able to escape; and though they cry out to Me, I will not listen to them. 12 Then the cities of Judah and the inhabitants of Jerusalem will go and cry out to the gods to whom they offer incense, but they will not save them at all in the time of their trouble. 13 For according to the number of your cities were your gods, O Judah; and according to the number of the streets of Jerusalem you have set up altars to that shameful thing, altars to burn incense to Baal.

14 "So do not pray for this people, or lift up a cry or prayer for them; for I will not hear them in the time that they cry out to Me because of their trouble.

15 "What has My beloved to do in
  My house,
  Having done lewd deeds with
  many?
  And the holy flesh has passed
  from you.
  When you do evil, then you
  rejoice.
16 The Lord called your name,
  Green Olive Tree, Lovely and
  of Good Fruit.
  With the noise of a great tumult
  He has kindled fire on it,
  And its branches are broken.

17 "For the Lord of hosts, who planted you, has pronounced doom against you for the evil of the house of Israel and of the house of Judah, which they have done against

themselves to provoke Me to anger in offering incense to Baal."

18 Now the LORD gave me knowledge *of it,* and I know *it;* for You showed me their doings. 19 But I *was* like a docile lamb brought to the slaughter; and I did not know that they had devised schemes against me, *saying,* "Let us destroy the tree with its fruit, and let us cut him off from the land of the living, that his name may be remembered no more."

20   But, O LORD of hosts,
       You who judge righteously,
       Testing the mind and the heart,
       Let me see Your vengeance on
          them,
       For to You I have revealed my
          cause.

21 "Therefore thus says the LORD concerning the men of Anathoth who seek your life, saying, 'Do not prophesy in the name of the LORD, lest you die by our hand'— 22 therefore thus says the LORD of hosts: 'Behold, I will punish them. The young men shall die by the sword, their sons and their daughters shall die by famine; 23 and there shall be no remnant of them, for I will bring catastrophe on the men of Anathoth, *even* the year of their punishment.' "

Jeremiah complains to God

12   Righteous *are* You, O LORD,
          when I plead with You;
       Yet let me talk with You about
          Your judgments.
       Why does the way of the wicked
          prosper?
       Why are those happy who deal
          so treacherously?
2   You have planted them, yes,
          they have taken root;
       They grow, yes, they bear fruit.
       You *are* near in their mouth
       But far from their mind.

3   But You, O LORD, know me;
       You have seen me,
       And You have tested my heart
          toward You.

       Pull them out like sheep for the
          slaughter,
       And prepare them for the day
          of slaughter.
4   How long will the land mourn,
       And the herbs of every field
          wither?
       The beasts and birds are
          consumed,
       For the wickedness of those who
          dwell there,
       Because they said, "He will not
          see our final end."

5   "If you have run with the
          footmen, and they have
          wearied you,
       Then how can you contend with
          horses?
       And *if* in the land of peace,
       In which you trusted, *they
          wearied you,*
       Then how will you do in the
          floodplain of the Jordan?
6   For even your brothers, the
          house of your father,
       Even they have dealt
          treacherously with you;
       Yes, they have called a
          multitude after you.
       Do not believe them,
       Even though they speak smooth
          words to you.

7   "I have forsaken My house, I
          have left My heritage;
       I have given the dearly beloved
          of My soul into the hand of
          her enemies.
8   My heritage is to Me like a lion
          in the forest;
       It cries out against Me;
       Therefore I have hated it.
9   My heritage *is* to Me *like* a
          speckled vulture;
       The vultures all around *are*
          against her.
       Come, assemble all the beasts
          of the field,
       Bring them to devour!

10   "Many rulers have destroyed My
          vineyard,
       They have trodden My portion
          underfoot;

They have made My pleasant
portion a desolate wilderness.
11 They have made it desolate;
Desolate, it mourns to Me;
The whole land is made
desolate,
Because no one takes *it* to heart.
12 The plunderers have come
On all the desolate heights in the
wilderness,
For the sword of the LORD shall
devour
From *one* end of the land to the
other end of the land;
No flesh shall have peace.
13 They have sown wheat but
reaped thorns;
They have put themselves to
pain *but* do not profit.
But be ashamed of your harvest
Because of the fierce anger of
the LORD."

14 Thus says the LORD: "Against all
My evil neighbors who touch the inheritance which I have caused My people
Israel to inherit—behold, I will pluck
them out of their land and pluck out
the house of Judah from among them.
15 Then it shall be, after I have plucked
them out, that I will return and have
compassion on them and bring them
back, everyone to his heritage and everyone to his land. 16 And it shall be,
if they will learn carefully the ways of
My people, to swear by My name, 'As
the LORD lives,' as they taught My people to swear by Baal, then they shall
be established in the midst of My people. 17 But if they do not obey, I will
utterly pluck up and destroy that nation," says the LORD.

Wicked Judah is like a rotten cord

13 Thus the LORD said to me: "Go
and get yourself a linen sash, and put
it around your waist, but do not put it
in water." 2 So I got a sash according
to the word of the LORD, and put *it*
around my waist.

3 And the word of the LORD came
to me the second time, saying, 4 "Take
the sash that you acquired, which *is*
around your waist, and arise, go to the
Euphrates, and hide it there in a hole
in the rock." 5 So I went and hid it by
the Euphrates, as the LORD commanded me.

6 Now it came to pass after many
days that the LORD said to me, "Arise,
go to the Euphrates, and take from
there the sash which I commanded you
to hide there." 7 Then I went to the
Euphrates and dug, and I took the sash
from the place where I had hidden it;
and there was the sash, ruined. It was
profitable for nothing.

8 Then the word of the LORD came
to me, saying, 9 "Thus says the LORD:
'In this manner I will ruin the pride of
Judah and the great pride of Jerusalem. 10 This evil people, who refuse to
hear My words, who follow the dictates
of their hearts, and walk after other
gods to serve them and worship them,
shall be just like this sash which is profitable for nothing. 11 For as the sash
clings to the waist of a man, so I have
caused the whole house of Israel and
the whole house of Judah to cling to
Me,' says the LORD, 'that they may become My people, for renown, for
praise, and for glory; but they would
not hear.'

12 "Therefore you shall speak to
them this word: 'Thus says the LORD
God of Israel: "Every bottle shall be
filled with wine." '

"And they will say to you, 'Do we
not certainly know that every bottle will
be filled with wine?'

13 "Then you shall say to them,
'Thus says the LORD: "Behold, I will
fill all the inhabitants of this land—even
the kings who sit on David's throne,
the priests, the prophets, and all the
inhabitants of Jerusalem—with drunkenness! 14 And I will dash them one
against another, even the fathers and
the sons together," says the LORD. "I
will not pity nor spare nor have mercy,
but will destroy them." '

15   Hear and give ear:
Do not be proud,
For the LORD has spoken.
16   Give glory to the LORD your God

Before He causes darkness,
And before your feet stumble
On the dark mountains,
And while you are looking for
light,
He turns it into the shadow of
death
And makes *it* dense darkness.
17 But if you will not hear it,
My soul will weep in secret for
your pride;
My eyes will weep bitterly
And run down with tears,
Because the LORD's flock has
been taken captive.

18 Say to the king and to the queen
mother,
"Humble yourselves;
Sit down,
For your rule shall collapse, the
crown of your glory."
19 The cities of the South shall be
shut up,
And no one shall open *them;*
Judah shall be carried away
captive, all of it;
It shall be wholly carried away
captive.

20 Lift up your eyes and see
Those who come from the
north.
Where *is* the flock *that* was given
to you,
Your beautiful sheep?
21 What will you say when He
punishes you?
For you have taught them
To be chieftains, to be head over
you.
Will not pangs seize you,
Like a woman in labor?
22 And if you say in your heart,
"Why have these things come
upon me?"
For the greatness of your iniquity
Your skirts have been
uncovered,
Your heels made bare.
23 Can the Ethiopian change
his skin or the leopard its
spots?
Then may you also do good

who are accustomed to do
evil.
24 "Therefore I will scatter them like
stubble
That passes away by the wind
of the wilderness.
25 This is your lot,
The portion of your measures
from Me," says the LORD,
"Because you have forgotten Me
And trusted in falsehood.
26 Therefore I will uncover your
skirts over your face,
That your shame may appear.
27 I have seen your adulteries
And your *lustful* neighings,
The lewdness of your harlotry,
Your abominations on the hills
in the fields.
Woe to you, O Jerusalem!
Will you still not be made
clean?"

God speaks in the drought

14 The word of the LORD that came
to Jeremiah concerning the droughts.

2 "Judah mourns,
And her gates languish;
They mourn for the land,
And the cry of Jerusalem has
gone up.
3 Their nobles have sent their lads
for water;
They went to the cisterns *and*
found no water.
They returned with their vessels
empty;
They were ashamed and
confounded
And covered their heads.
4 Because the ground is parched,
For there was no rain in the land,
The plowmen were ashamed;
They covered their heads.
5 Yes, the deer also gave birth in
the field,
But left because there was no
grass.
6 And the wild donkeys stood in
the desolate heights;

They sniffed at the wind like
    jackals;
Their eyes failed because *there
    was* no grass."

7 O LORD, though our iniquities
    testify against us,
Do it for Your name's sake;
For our backslidings are many,
We have sinned against You.
8 O the Hope of Israel, his Savior
    in time of trouble,
Why should You be like a
    stranger in the land,
And like a traveler *who* turns
    aside to tarry for a night?
9 Why should You be like a man
    astonished,
Like a mighty one *who* cannot
    save?
Yet You, O LORD, *are* in our
    midst,
And we are called by Your
    name;
Do not leave us!

10 Thus says the LORD to this people:

"Thus they have loved to wander;
They have not restrained their
    feet.
Therefore the LORD does not
    accept them;
He will remember their iniquity
    now,
And punish their sins."

11 Then the LORD said to me, "Do
not pray for this people, for *their* good.
12 When they fast, I will not hear their
cry; and when they offer burnt offering
and grain offering, I will not accept
them. But I will consume them by the
sword, by the famine, and by the pestilence."
13 Then I said, "Ah, Lord GOD! Behold, the prophets say to them, 'You
shall not see the sword, nor shall you
have famine, but I will give you assured
peace in this place.' "
14 And the LORD said to me, "The
prophets prophesy lies in My name.
I have not sent them, commanded
them, nor spoken to them; they

prophesy to you a false vision, divination, a worthless thing, and the deceit
of their heart. 15 Therefore thus says
the LORD concerning the prophets who
prophesy in My name, whom I did not
send, and who say, 'Sword and famine
shall not be in this land'—'By sword
and famine those prophets shall be
consumed! 16 And the people to whom
they prophesy shall be cast out in the
streets of Jerusalem because of the
famine and the sword; they will have
no one to bury them—them nor their
wives, their sons nor their daughters—
for I will pour their wickedness on
them.'
17 "Therefore you shall say this word
to them:

'Let my eyes flow with tears night
    and day,
And let them not cease;
For the virgin daughter of my
    people
Has been broken with a mighty
    stroke, with a very severe
    blow.
18 If I go out to the field,
Then behold, those slain with
    the sword!
And if I enter the city,
Then behold, those sick from
    famine!
Yes, both prophet and priest go
    about in a land they do not
    know.' "

19 Have You utterly rejected
    Judah?
Has Your soul loathed Zion?
Why have You stricken us so
    that *there is* no healing for us?
We looked for peace, but *there
    was* no good;
And for the time of healing, and
    there was trouble.
20 We acknowledge, O LORD, our
    wickedness
And the iniquity of our fathers,
For we have sinned against You.
21 Do not abhor *us,* for Your
    name's sake;
Do not disgrace the throne of
    Your glory.

Remember, do not break Your
covenant with us.
22 Are there any among the idols
of the nations that can cause
rain?
Or can the heavens give
showers?
Are You not He, O LORD our
God?
Therefore we will wait for You,
Since You have made all these.

The Lord is angry with His people

15 Then the LORD said to me,
"*Even* if Moses and Samuel stood before Me, My mind *would* not *be* favorable toward this people. Cast *them* out
of My sight, and let them go forth.
2 And it shall be, if they say to you,
'Where should we go?' then you shall
tell them, 'Thus says the LORD:

"Such as *are* for death, to death;
And such as *are* for the sword,
to the sword;
And such as *are* for the famine,
to the famine;
And such as *are* for the captivity,
to the captivity." '

3 "And I will appoint over them four
forms *of destruction*," says the LORD:
"the sword to slay, the dogs to drag,
the birds of the heavens and the beasts
of the earth to devour and destroy.
4 I will hand them over to trouble, to
all kingdoms of the earth, because of
Manasseh the son of Hezekiah, king
of Judah, for what he did in Jerusalem.

5 "For who will have pity on you,
O Jerusalem?
Or who will bemoan you?
Or who will turn aside to ask
how you are doing?
6 You have forsaken Me," says
the LORD,
"You have gone backward.
Therefore I will stretch out My
hand against you and destroy
you;
I am weary of relenting!
7 And I will winnow them with a

winnowing fan in the gates of
the land;
I will bereave *them* of children;
I will destroy My people,
Since they do not return from
their ways.
8 Their widows will be increased
to Me more than the sand of
the seas;
I will bring against them,
Against the mother of the young
men,
A plunderer at noonday;
I will cause anguish and terror
to fall on them suddenly.

9 "She languishes who has borne
seven;
She has breathed her last;
Her sun has gone down
While *it was* yet day;
She has been ashamed and
confounded.
And the remnant of them I will
deliver to the sword
Before their enemies," says the
LORD.

10 Woe is me, my mother,
That you have borne me,
A man of strife and a man of
contention to the whole
earth!
I have neither lent for interest,
Nor have men lent to me for
interest.
Every one of them curses me.

11 The LORD said:

"Surely it will be well with your
remnant;
Surely I will cause the enemy to
intercede with you
In the time of adversity and in
the time of affliction.
12 Can anyone break iron,
The northern iron and the
bronze?
13 Your wealth and your treasures
I will give as plunder without
price,
Because of all your sins,
Throughout your territories.

14 And I will make *you* cross over
     with your enemies
  Into a land *which* you do not
     know;
  For a fire is kindled in My anger,
  Which shall burn upon you."

15 O LORD, You know;
  Remember me and visit me,
  And take vengeance for me on
     my persecutors.
  In Your enduring patience, do
     not take me away.
  Know that for Your sake I have
     suffered rebuke.

16 Your words were found, and I
     ate them,
  And Your word was to me the
     joy and rejoicing of my heart;
  For I am called by Your name,
  O LORD God of hosts.

17 I did not sit in the assembly of
     the mockers,
  Nor did I rejoice;
  I sat alone because of Your
     hand,
  For You have filled me with
     indignation.

18 Why is my pain perpetual
  And my wound incurable,
  Which refuses to be healed?
  Will You surely be to me like an
     unreliable stream,
  As waters *that* fail?

19 Therefore thus says the LORD:

  "If you return,
  Then I will bring you back;
  You shall stand before Me;
  If you take out the precious from
     the vile,
  You shall be as My mouth.
  Let them return to you,
  But you must not return to them.

20 And I will make you to this
     people a fortified bronze wall;
  And they will fight against you,
  But they shall not prevail against
     you;
  For I *am* with you to save you
  And deliver you," says the
     LORD.

21 "I will deliver you from the hand
     of the wicked,

  And I will redeem you from the
     grip of the terrible."

God will hunt His lost sheep

16 The word of the LORD also came to me, saying, 2 "You shall not take a wife, nor shall you have sons or daughters in this place." 3 For thus says the LORD concerning the sons and daughters who are born in this place, and concerning their mothers who bore them and their fathers who begot them in this land: 4 "They shall die gruesome deaths; they shall not be lamented nor shall they be buried, *but* they shall be like refuse on the face of the earth. They shall be consumed by the sword and by famine, and their corpses shall be meat for the birds of heaven and for the beasts of the earth."

5 For thus says the LORD: "Do not enter the house of mourning, nor go to lament or bemoan them; for I have taken away My peace from this people," says the LORD, "lovingkindness and mercies. 6 Both the great and the small shall die in this land. They shall not be buried; neither shall men lament for them, cut themselves, nor make themselves bald for them. 7 Nor shall *men* break *bread* in mourning for them, to comfort them for the dead; nor shall *men* give them the cup of consolation to drink for their father or their mother. 8 Also you shall not go into the house of feasting to sit with them, to eat and drink."

9 For thus says the LORD of hosts, the God of Israel: "Behold, I will cause to cease from this place, before your eyes and in your days, the voice of mirth and the voice of gladness, the voice of the bridegroom and the voice of the bride.

10 "And it shall be, when you show this people all these words, and they say to you, 'Why has the LORD pronounced all this great disaster against us? Or what *is* our iniquity? Or what *is* our sin that we have committed against the LORD our God?' 11 then you shall say to them, 'Because your fathers have forsaken Me,' says the

LORD; 'they have walked after other gods and have served them and worshiped them, and have forsaken Me and not kept My law. 12 And you have done worse than your fathers, for behold, each one follows the dictates of his own evil heart, so that no one listens to Me. 13 Therefore I will cast you out of this land into a land that you do not know, neither you nor your fathers; and there you shall serve other gods day and night, where I will not show you favor.'

14 "Therefore behold, the days are coming," says the LORD, "that it shall no more be said, 'The LORD lives who brought up the children of Israel from the land of Egypt,' 15 but, 'The LORD lives who brought up the children of Israel from the land of the north and from all the lands where He had driven them.' For I will bring them back into their land which I gave to their fathers.

16 "Behold, I will send for many fishermen," says the LORD, "and they shall fish them; and afterward I will send for many hunters, and they shall hunt them from every mountain and every hill, and out of the holes of the rocks. 17 For My eyes are on all their ways; they are not hidden from My face, nor is their iniquity hidden from My eyes. 18 And first I will repay double for their iniquity and their sin, because they have defiled My land; they have filled My inheritance with the carcasses of their detestable and abominable idols."

19 O LORD, my strength and my
    fortress,
    My refuge in the day of affliction,
    The Gentiles shall come to
      You
    From the ends of the earth and
      say,
    "Surely our fathers have inherited
      lies,
    Worthlessness and unprofitable
      things."
20 Will a man make gods for
    himself,
    Which are not gods?

21 "Therefore behold, I will this once
    cause them to know,
    I will cause them to know
    My hand and My might;
    And they shall know that My
      name is the LORD.

Double trouble for Judah

17 "The sin of Judah is written with
    a pen of iron;
    With the point of a diamond it
      is engraved
    On the tablet of their heart,
    And on the horns of your altars,
2   While their children remember
    Their altars and their wooden
      images
    By the green trees on the high
      hills.
3   O My mountain in the field,
    I will give as plunder your
      wealth, all your treasures,
    And your high places of sin
      within all your borders.
4   And you, even yourself,
    Shall let go of your heritage
      which I gave you;
    And I will cause you to serve
      your enemies
    In the land which you do not
      know;
    For you have kindled a fire in
      My anger which shall burn
      forever."

5 Thus says the LORD:

"Cursed is the man who trusts in
    man
    And makes flesh his strength,
    Whose heart departs from the
      LORD.
6   For he shall be like a shrub in
      the desert,
    And shall not see when good
      comes,
    But shall inhabit the parched
      places in the wilderness,
    In a salt land which is not
      inhabited.

7   "Blessed is the man who trusts
      in the LORD,
    And whose hope is the LORD.

8 For he shall be like a tree planted
   by the waters,
   Which spreads out its roots by
   the river,
   And will not fear when heat
   comes;
   But its leaf will be green,
   And will not be anxious in the
   year of drought,
   Nor will cease from yielding fruit.

9 "The heart *is* deceitful above all
   things,
   And desperately wicked;
   Who can know it?
10 I, the LORD, search the heart,
   I test the mind,
   Even to give every man
   according to his ways,
   According to the fruit of his
   doings.

11 "*As* a partridge that broods but
   does not hatch,
   So is he who gets riches, but not
   by right;
   It will leave him in the midst of
   his days,
   And at his end he will be a fool."

12 A glorious high throne from the
   beginning
   Is the place of our sanctuary.
13 O LORD, the hope of Israel,
   All who forsake You shall be
   ashamed.

   "Those who depart from Me
   Shall be written in the earth,
   Because they have forsaken the
   LORD,
   The fountain of living waters."

14 Heal me, O LORD, and I shall
   be healed;
   Save me, and I shall be saved,
   For You *are* my praise.
15 Indeed they say to me,
   "Where *is* the word of the
   LORD?
   Let it come now!"
16 As for me, I have not hurried
   away from *being* a shepherd
   who follows You,

   Nor have I desired the woeful
   day;
   You know what came out of my
   lips;
   It was right there before You.
17 Do not be a terror to me;
   You *are* my hope in the day of
   doom.
18 Let them be ashamed who
   persecute me,
   But do not let me be put to
   shame;
   Let them be dismayed,
   But do not let me be dismayed.
   Bring on them the day of doom,
   And destroy them with double
   destruction!

19 Thus the LORD said to me: "Go and stand in the gate of the children of the people, by which the kings of Judah come in and by which they go out, and in all the gates of Jerusalem; 20 and say to them, 'Hear the word of the LORD, you kings of Judah, and all Judah, and all the inhabitants of Jerusalem, who enter by these gates. 21 Thus says the LORD: "Take heed to yourselves, and bear no burden on the Sabbath day, nor bring *it* in by the gates of Jerusalem; 22 nor carry a burden out of your houses on the Sabbath day, nor do any work, but hallow the Sabbath day, as I commanded your fathers. 23 But they did not obey nor incline their ear, but made their neck stiff, that they might not hear nor receive instruction.

24 "And it shall be, if you heed Me carefully," says the LORD, "to bring no burden through the gates of this city on the Sabbath day, but hallow the Sabbath day, to do no work in it, 25 then shall enter the gates of this city kings and princes sitting on the throne of David, riding in chariots and on horses, they and their princes, accompanied by the men of Judah and the inhabitants of Jerusalem; and this city shall remain forever. 26 And they shall come from the cities of Judah and from the places around Jerusalem, from the land of Benjamin and from the lowland, from the mountains and from the

South, bringing burnt offerings and sacrifices, grain offerings and incense, bringing sacrifices of praise to the house of the LORD.

27 "But if you will not heed Me to hallow the Sabbath day, such as not carrying a burden when entering the gates of Jerusalem on the Sabbath day, then I will kindle a fire in its gates, and it shall devour the palaces of Jerusalem, and it shall not be quenched." ' "

Israel is like clay in the Potter's hands

18 The word which came to Jeremiah from the LORD, saying: 2 "Arise and go down to the potter's house, and there I will cause you to hear My words." 3 Then I went down to the potter's house, and there he was, making something at the wheel. 4 And the vessel that he made of clay was marred in the hand of the potter; so he made it again into another vessel, as it seemed good to the potter to make.

5 Then the word of the LORD came

A potter forms a jar from a lump of clay.

to me, saying: 6 "O house of Israel, can I not do with you as this potter?" says the LORD. "Look, as the clay is in the potter's hand, so are you in My hand, O house of Israel! 7 The instant I speak concerning a nation and concerning a kingdom, to pluck up, to pull down, and to destroy it, 8 if that nation against whom I have spoken turns from its evil, I will relent of the disaster that I thought to bring upon it. 9 And the instant I speak concerning a nation and concerning a kingdom, to build and to plant it, 10 if it does evil in My sight so that it does not obey My voice, then I will relent concerning the good with which I said I would benefit it.

11 "Now therefore, speak to the men of Judah and to the inhabitants of Jerusalem, saying, 'Thus says the LORD: "Behold, I am fashioning a disaster and devising a plan against you. Return now every one from his evil way, and make your ways and your doings good." ' "

12 And they said, "That is hopeless! So we will walk according to our own plans, and we will every one obey the dictates of his evil heart."

13 Therefore thus says the LORD:

"Ask now among the Gentiles,
Who has heard such things?
The virgin of Israel has done a
very horrible thing.
14 Will a man leave the snow water
of Lebanon,
Which comes from the rock of
the field?
Will the cold flowing waters be
forsaken for strange waters?
15 "Because My people have
forgotten Me,
They have burned incense to
worthless idols.
And they have caused
themselves to stumble in their
ways,
From the ancient paths,
To walk in pathways and not on
a highway,
16 To make their land desolate and
a perpetual hissing;

Everyone who passes by it will
be astonished
And shake his head.
17 I will scatter them as with an east
wind before the enemy;
I will show them the back and
not the face
In the day of their calamity."

18 Then they said, "Come and let
us devise plans against Jeremiah; for
the law shall not perish from the priest,
nor counsel from the wise, nor the
word from the prophet. Come and let
us attack him with the tongue, and
let us not give heed to any of his
words."

19   Give heed to me, O LORD,
And listen to the voice of those
who contend with me!
20   Shall evil be repaid for good?
For they have dug a pit for my
life.
Remember that I stood before
You
To speak good for them,
To turn away Your wrath from
them.
21   Therefore deliver up their
children to the famine,
And pour out their *blood*
By the force of the sword;
Let their wives *become* widows
And bereaved of their children.
Let their men be put to death,
Their young men *be* slain
By the sword in battle.
22   Let a cry be heard from their
houses,
When You bring a troop
suddenly upon them;
For they have dug a pit to take
me,
And hidden snares for my feet.
23   Yet, LORD, You know all their
counsel
Which is against me, to slay *me*.
Provide no atonement for their
iniquity,
Nor blot out their sin from Your
sight;
But let them be overthrown
before You.

Deal *thus* with them
In the time of Your anger.

A lesson from a broken bottle

19 Thus says the LORD: "Go and get
a potter's earthen flask, and *take* some
of the elders of the people and some
of the elders of the priests. 2 And go
out to the Valley of the Son of Hinnom, which *is* by the entry of the
Potsherd Gate; and proclaim there the
words that I will tell you, 3 and say,
'Hear the word of the LORD, O kings
of Judah and inhabitants of Jerusalem.
Thus says the LORD of hosts, the God
of Israel: "Behold, I will bring such a
catastrophe on this place, that whoever
hears of it, his ears will tingle.

4 "Because they have forsaken Me
and made this an alien place, because
they have burned incense in it to other
gods whom neither they, their fathers,
nor the kings of Judah have known,
and have filled this place with the
blood of the innocents 5 (they have
also built the high places of Baal, to
burn their sons with fire *for* burnt offerings to Baal, which I did not command
or speak, nor did it come into My
mind), 6 therefore behold, the days are
coming," says the LORD, "that this
place shall no more be called Tophet
or the Valley of the Son of Hinnom,
but the Valley of Slaughter. 7 And I will
make void the counsel of Judah and
Jerusalem in this place, and I will cause
them to fall by the sword before their
enemies and by the hands of those
who seek their lives; their corpses I will
give as meat for the birds of the heaven
and for the beasts of the earth. 8 I will
make this city desolate and a hissing;
everyone who passes by it will be astonished and hiss because of all its
plagues. 9 And I will cause them to eat
the flesh of their sons and the flesh of
their daughters, and everyone shall eat
the flesh of his friend in the siege and
in the desperation with which their enemies and those who seek their lives
shall drive them to despair." '
10 "Then you shall break the flask
in the sight of the men who go with

you, ¹¹ and say to them, 'Thus says the LORD of hosts: "Even so I will break this people and this city, as *one* breaks a potter's vessel, which cannot be made whole again; and they shall bury *them* in Tophet till *there is* no place to bury. ¹² Thus I will do to this place," says the LORD, "and to its inhabitants, and make this city like Tophet. ¹³ And the houses of Jerusalem and the houses of the kings of Judah shall be defiled like the place of Tophet, because of all the houses on whose roofs they have burned incense to all the host of heaven, and poured out drink offerings to other gods." ' "

¹⁴ Then Jeremiah came from Tophet, where the LORD had sent him to prophesy; and he stood in the court of the Lord's house and said to all the people, ¹⁵ "Thus says the LORD of hosts, the God of Israel: 'Behold, I will bring on this city and on all her towns all the doom that I have pronounced against it, because they have stiffened their necks that they might not hear My words.' "

Jeremiah is put in prison

20 Now Pashhur the son of Immer, the priest who *was* also chief governor in the house of the LORD, heard that Jeremiah prophesied these things. ² Then Pashhur struck Jeremiah the prophet, and put him in the stocks that *were* in the high gate of Benjamin, which *was* by the house of the LORD.

³ And it happened on the next day that Pashhur brought Jeremiah out of the stocks. Then Jeremiah said to him, "The LORD has not called your name Pashhur, but Magor-Missabib. ⁴ For thus says the LORD: 'Behold, I will make you a terror to yourself and to all your friends; and they shall fall by the sword of their enemies, and your eyes shall see *it*. I will give all Judah into the hand of the king of Babylon, and he shall carry them captive to Babylon and slay them with the sword. ⁵ Moreover I will deliver all the wealth of this city, all its produce, and all its precious things; all the treasures of the

kings of Judah I will give into the hand of their enemies, who will plunder them, seize them, and carry them to Babylon. ⁶ And you, Pashhur, and all who dwell in your house, shall go into captivity. You shall go to Babylon, and there you shall die, and be buried there, you and all your friends, to whom you have prophesied lies.' "

⁷   O LORD, You induced me, and
      I was persuaded;
    You are stronger than I, and
      have prevailed.
    I am in derision daily;
      Everyone mocks me.
⁸   For when I spoke, I cried out;
    I shouted, "Violence and
      plunder!"
    Because the word of the LORD
      was made to me
    A reproach and a derision daily.
⁹   Then I said, "I will not make
      mention of Him,
    Nor speak anymore in His
      name."
    But *His word* was in my heart
      like a burning fire
    Shut up in my bones;
    I was weary of holding *it* back,
    And I could not.
¹⁰ For I heard many mocking:
    "Fear on every side!"
    "Report," *they say*, "and we will
      report it!"
    All my acquaintances watched
      for my stumbling, *saying*,
    "Perhaps he can be induced;
    Then we will prevail against
      him,
    And we will take our revenge on
      him."

¹¹ But the LORD *is* with me as a
      mighty, awesome One.
    Therefore my persecutors will
      stumble, and will not prevail.
    They will be greatly ashamed,
      for they will not prosper.
    Their everlasting confusion will
      never be forgotten.
¹² But, O LORD of hosts,
    You who test the righteous,
    And see the mind and heart,

Let me see Your vengeance on
   them;
For I have pleaded my cause
   before You.

13 Sing to the LORD! Praise the
   LORD!
For He has delivered the life of
   the poor
From the hand of evildoers.

14 Cursed be the day in which I was
   born!
Let the day not be blessed in
   which my mother bore me!
15 Let the man be cursed
Who brought news to my father,
   saying,
"A male child has been born to
   you!"
Making him very glad.
16 And let that man be like the
   cities
Which the LORD overthrew, and
   did not relent;
Let him hear the cry in the
   morning
And the shouting at noon,
17 Because he did not kill me from
   the womb,
That my mother might have
   been my grave,
And her womb always enlarged
   with me.
18 Why did I come forth from the
   womb to see labor and
   sorrow,
That my days should be
   consumed with shame?

The Lord gives Judah one more chance

21 The word which came to Jeremiah from the LORD when King Zedekiah sent to him Pashhur the son of Melchiah, and Zephaniah the son of Maaseiah, the priest, saying, 2 "Please inquire of the LORD for us, for Nebuchadnezzar king of Babylon makes war against us. Perhaps the LORD will deal with us according to all His wonderful works, that the king may go away from us."

3 Then Jeremiah said to them, "Thus you shall say to Zedekiah, 4 'Thus says the LORD God of Israel: "Behold, I will turn back the weapons of war that are in your hands, with which you fight against the king of Babylon and the Chaldeans who besiege you outside the walls; and I will assemble them in the midst of this city. 5 I Myself will fight against you with an outstretched hand and with a strong arm, even in anger and fury and great wrath. 6 I will strike the inhabitants of this city, both man and beast; they shall die of a great pestilence. 7 And afterward," says the LORD, "I will deliver Zedekiah king of Judah, his servants and the people, and such as are left in this city from the pestilence and the sword and the famine, into the hand of Nebuchadnezzar king of Babylon, into the hand of their enemies, and into the hand of those who seek their life; and he shall strike them with the edge of the sword. He shall not spare them, or have pity or mercy." '

8 "Now you shall say to this people, 'Thus says the LORD: "Behold, I set before you the way of life and the way of death. 9 He who remains in this city shall die by the sword, by famine, and by pestilence; but he who goes out and defects to the Chaldeans who besiege you, he shall live, and his life shall be as a prize to him. 10 For I have set My face against this city for adversity and not for good," says the LORD. "It shall be given into the hand of the king of Babylon, and he shall burn it with fire." '

11 "And concerning the house of the king of Judah, say, 'Hear the word of the LORD, 12 O house of David! Thus says the LORD:

"Execute judgment in the
   morning;
And deliver him who is
   plundered
Out of the hand of the
   oppressor,
Lest My fury go forth like fire
And burn so that no one can
   quench it,

Because of the evil of your
doings.

13 "Behold, I *am* against you, O
inhabitant of the valley,
And rock of the plain," says the
LORD,
"Who say, 'Who shall come
down against us?
Or who shall enter our
dwellings?'
14 But I will punish you according
to the fruit of your doings,"
says the LORD;
"I will kindle a fire in its forest,
And it shall devour all things
around it."'"

Wicked kings will be punished

22 Thus says the LORD: "Go down
to the house of the king of Judah, and
there speak this word, 2 and say, 'Hear
the word of the LORD, O king of Judah,
you who sit on the throne of David,
you and your servants and your people
who enter these gates! 3 Thus says the
LORD: "Execute judgment and righteousness, and deliver the plundered
out of the hand of the oppressor. Do
no wrong and do no violence to the
stranger, the fatherless, or the widow,
nor shed innocent blood in this place.
4 For if you indeed do this thing, then
shall enter the gates of this house,
riding on horses and in chariots, accompanied by servants and people,
kings who sit on the throne of David.
5 But if you will not hear these words,
I swear by Myself," says the LORD,
"that this house shall become a desolation."'"

6 For thus says the LORD to the
house of the king of Judah:

"You *are* Gilead to Me,
The head of Lebanon;
Yet I surely will make you a
wilderness,
Cities *which* are not inhabited.
7 I will prepare destroyers against
you,
Everyone with his weapons;

They shall cut down your choice
cedars
And cast *them* into the fire.

8 And many nations will pass by this
city; and everyone will say to his neighbor, 'Why has the LORD done so to
this great city?' 9 Then they will answer,
'Because they have forsaken the covenant of the LORD their God, and worshiped other gods and served them.'"

10 Weep not for the dead, nor
bemoan him;
Weep bitterly for him who goes
away,
For he shall return no more,
Nor see his native country.

11 For thus says the LORD concerning
Shallum the son of Josiah, king of Judah, who reigned instead of Josiah his
father, who went from this place: "He
shall not return here anymore, 12 but
he shall die in the place where they
have led him captive, and shall see this
land no more.

13 "Woe to him who builds his
house by unrighteousness
And his chambers by injustice,
Who uses his neighbor's service
without wages
And gives him nothing for his
work,
14 Who says, 'I will build myself a
wide house with spacious
chambers,
And cut out windows for it,
Paneling *it* with cedar
And painting *it* with vermilion.'

15 "Shall you reign because you
enclose *yourself* in cedar?
Did not your father eat and
drink,
And do justice and
righteousness?
Then *it was* well with him.
16 He judged the cause of the poor
and needy;
Then *it was* well.
Was not this knowing Me?" says
the LORD.

17 "Yet your eyes and your heart *are*
    for nothing but your
    covetousness,
    For shedding innocent blood,
    And practicing oppression and
    violence."

18 Therefore thus says the LORD concerning Jehoiakim the son of Josiah,
king of Judah:

    "They shall not lament for him,
    Saying, 'Alas, my brother!' or
      'Alas, my sister!'
    They shall not lament for him,
    Saying, 'Alas, master!' or 'Alas,
      his glory!'
19 He shall be buried with the
    burial of a donkey,
    Dragged and cast out beyond
    the gates of Jerusalem.

20 "Go up to Lebanon, and cry out,
    And lift up your voice in Bashan;
    Cry from Abarim,
    For all your lovers are destroyed.
21 I spoke to you in your
    prosperity,
    But you said, 'I will not hear.'
    This *has been* your manner from
    your youth,
    That you did not obey My voice.
22 The wind shall eat up all your
    rulers,
    And your lovers shall go into
    captivity;
    Surely then you will be ashamed
    and humiliated
    For all your wickedness.
23 O inhabitant of Lebanon,
    Making your nest in the cedars,
    How gracious will you be when
      pangs come upon you,
    Like the pain of a woman in
    labor?

24 "*As* I live," says the LORD,
"though Coniah the son of Jehoiakim,
king of Judah, were the signet on My
right hand, yet I would pluck you off;
25 and I will give you into the hand of
those who seek your life, and into the
hand *of those* whose face you fear—
the hand of Nebuchadnezzar king of
Babylon and the hand of the **Chaldeans.** 26 So I will cast you out, and your
mother who bore you, into another
country where you *were* not born; and
there you shall die. 27 But to the land
to which they desire to return, there
they shall not return.

28 "Is this man Coniah a despised,
    broken idol—
    A vessel in which *is* no pleasure?
    Why are they cast out, he and
      his descendants,
    And cast into a land which they
    do not know?
29 O earth, earth, earth,
    Hear the word of the LORD!
30 Thus says the LORD:
    'Write this man down as
    childless,
    A man *who* shall not prosper in
    his days;
    For none of his descendants
    shall prosper,
    Sitting on the throne of David,
    And ruling anymore in Judah.' "

The true King is coming

23 "Woe to the shepherds who destroy and scatter the sheep of My pasture!" says the LORD. 2 Therefore thus
says the LORD God of Israel against the
shepherds who feed My people: "You
have scattered My flock, driven them
away, and not attended to them. Behold, I will attend to you for the evil
of your doings," says the LORD.
3 "But I will gather the remnant of My
flock out of all countries where I have
driven them, and bring them back to
their folds; and they shall be fruitful

and increase. ⁴ I will set up shepherds over them who will feed them; and they shall fear no more, nor be dismayed, nor shall they be lacking," says the LORD.

⁵ "Behold, *the* days are coming," says the LORD,
"That I will raise to David a Branch of righteousness;
A King shall reign and prosper,
And execute judgment and righteousness in the earth.
⁶ In His days Judah will be saved,
And Israel will dwell safely;
Now this *is* His name by which He will be called:

THE LORD OUR RIGHTEOUSNESS.

⁷ "Therefore, behold, *the* days are coming," says the LORD, "that they shall no longer say, 'As the LORD lives who brought up the children of Israel from the land of Egypt,' ⁸ but, 'As the LORD lives who brought up and led the descendants of the house of Israel from the north country and from all the countries where I had driven them.' And they shall dwell in their own land."

⁹ My heart within me is broken Because of the prophets;
All my bones shake.
I am like a drunken man,
And like a man whom wine has overcome,

Because of the LORD,
And because of His holy words.
¹⁰ For the land is full of adulterers;
For because of a curse the land mourns.
The pleasant places of the wilderness are dried up.
Their course of life is evil,
And their might *is* not right.

¹¹ "For both prophet and priest are profane;
Yes, in My house I have found their wickedness," says the LORD.
¹² "Therefore their way shall be to them
Like slippery *ways;*
In the darkness they shall be driven on
And fall in them;
For I will bring disaster on them,
The year of their punishment," says the LORD.
¹³ "And I have seen folly in the prophets of Samaria:
They prophesied by Baal
And caused My people Israel to err.
¹⁴ Also I have seen a horrible thing in the prophets of Jerusalem:
They commit adultery and walk in lies;
They also strengthen the hands of evildoers,
So that no one turns back from his wickedness.
All of them are like Sodom to Me,

DIGGING IN

23:6 The Lord Our Righteousness "Righteousness" (pronounced *RIGH-chuss-ness*) usually means something we possess because we do everything "right." But you and I know that we *never* do anything right as God measures it. The Bible says that all our righteousness is like "filthy rags" (see Isaiah 64:6). So there goes any idea that we can be righteous all by ourselves.

God doesn't cause us to be actually perfect, and He knows we are sinners.

But He said, *"I* will be your righteousness. If you will just accept Jesus as payment for your sins, I will treat you just as if you are as righteous as My own Son." That's amazing! God doesn't see you anymore *just as you are;* God sees you *just as if you were His very own Son!*

Wouldn't you say that's the greatest love you've ever heard of? Doesn't it make you want to leave your sins behind and be His son or daughter forever?

And her inhabitants like Gomorrah.

15 "Therefore thus says the LORD of hosts concerning the prophets:

'Behold, I will feed them with wormwood,
And make them drink the water of gall;
For from the prophets of Jerusalem
Profaneness has gone out into all the land.' "

16 Thus says the LORD of hosts:

"Do not listen to the words of the prophets who prophesy to you.
They make you worthless;
They speak a vision of their own heart,
Not from the mouth of the LORD.
17 They continually say to those who despise Me,
'The LORD has said, "You shall have peace" ';
And to everyone who walks according to the dictates of his own heart, they say,
'No evil shall come upon you.' "

18 For who has stood in the counsel of the LORD,
And has perceived and heard His word?
Who has marked His word and heard it?
19 Behold, a whirlwind of the LORD has gone forth in fury—
A violent whirlwind!
It will fall violently on the head of the wicked.
20 The anger of the LORD will not turn back
Until He has executed and performed the thoughts of His heart.
In the latter days you will understand it perfectly.

21 "I have not sent these prophets, yet they ran.

I have not spoken to them, yet they prophesied.
22 But if they had stood in My counsel,
And had caused My people to hear My words,
Then they would have turned them from their evil way
And from the evil of their doings.

23 "Am I a God near at hand," says the LORD,
"And not a God afar off?
24 Can anyone hide himself in secret places,
So I shall not see him?" says the LORD;
"Do I not fill heaven and earth?" says the LORD.

25 "I have heard what the prophets have said who prophesy lies in My name, saying, 'I have dreamed, I have dreamed!' 26 How long will this be in the heart of the prophets who prophesy lies? Indeed they are prophets of the deceit of their own heart, 27 who try to make My people forget My name by their dreams which everyone tells his neighbor, as their fathers forgot My name for Baal.

28 "The prophet who has a dream, let him tell a dream;
And he who has My word, let him speak My word faithfully.
What is the chaff to the wheat?" says the LORD.
29 "Is not My word like a fire?" says the LORD,
"And like a hammer that breaks the rock in pieces?

30 "Therefore behold, I am against the prophets," says the LORD, "who steal My words every one from his neighbor. 31 Behold, I am against the prophets," says the LORD, "who use their tongues and say, 'He says.' 32 Behold, I am against those who prophesy false dreams," says the LORD, "and tell them, and cause My people to err by their lies and by their recklessness. Yet I did not send them or

command them; therefore they shall not profit this people at all," says the LORD.

33 "So when these people or the prophet or the priest ask you, saying, 'What is the oracle of the LORD?' you shall then say to them, 'What oracle?' I will even forsake you," says the LORD. 34 "And as for the prophet and the priest and the people who say, 'The oracle of the LORD!' I will even punish that man and his house. 35 Thus every one of you shall say to his neighbor, and every one to his brother, 'What has the LORD answered?' and, 'What has the LORD spoken?' 36 And the oracle of the LORD you shall mention no more. For every man's word will be his oracle, for you have perverted the words of the living God, the LORD of hosts, our God. 37 Thus you shall say to the prophet, 'What has the LORD answered you?' and, 'What has the LORD spoken?' 38 But since you say, 'The oracle of the LORD!' therefore thus says the LORD: 'Because you say this word, "The oracle of the LORD!" and I have sent to you, saying, "Do not say, 'The oracle of the LORD!' " 39 therefore behold, I, even I, will utterly forget you and forsake you, and the city that I gave you and your fathers, and will cast you out of My presence. 40 And I will bring an everlasting reproach upon you, and a perpetual shame, which shall not be forgotten.' "

The lesson of the good and bad figs

24 The LORD showed me, and there were two baskets of figs set before the temple of the LORD, after Nebuchadnezzar king of Babylon had carried away captive Jeconiah the son of Jehoiakim, king of Judah, and the princes of Judah with the craftsmen and smiths, from Jerusalem, and had brought them to Babylon. 2 One basket had very good figs, like the figs that are first ripe; and the other basket had very bad figs which could not be eaten, they were so bad. 3 Then the LORD said to me, "What do you see, Jeremiah?"

And I said, "Figs, the good figs, very good; and the bad, very bad, which cannot be eaten, they are so bad."

4 Again the word of the LORD came to me, saying, 5 "Thus says the LORD, the God of Israel: 'Like these good figs, so will I acknowledge those who are carried away captive from Judah, whom I have sent out of this place for their own good, into the land of the Chaldeans. 6 For I will set My eyes on them for good, and I will bring them back to this land; I will build them and not pull them down, and I will plant them and not pluck them up. 7 Then I will give them a heart to know Me, that I am the LORD; and they shall be My people, and I will be their God, for they shall return to Me with their whole heart.

8 'And as the bad figs which cannot be eaten, they are so bad'—surely thus says the LORD—'so will I give up Zedekiah the king of Judah, his princes, the residue of Jerusalem who remain in this land, and those who dwell in the land of Egypt. 9 I will deliver them to trouble into all the kingdoms of the earth, for their harm, to be a reproach and a byword, a taunt and a curse, in all places where I shall drive them. 10 And I will send the sword, the famine, and the pestilence among them, till they are consumed from the land that I gave to them and their fathers.' "

Homesick for seventy years

25 The word that came to Jeremiah concerning all the people of Judah, in the fourth year of Jehoiakim the son of Josiah, king of Judah (which was the first year of Nebuchadnezzar king of Babylon), 2 which Jeremiah the prophet spoke to all the people of Judah and to all the inhabitants of Jerusalem, saying: 3 "From the thirteenth year of Josiah the son of Amon, king of Judah, even to this day, this is the twenty-third year in which the word of the LORD has come to me; and I have spoken to you, rising early and speaking, but you have not listened. 4 And the LORD has sent to you all His ser-

vants the prophets, rising early and sending *them,* but you have not listened nor inclined your ear to hear. 5 They said, 'Repent now everyone of his evil way and his evil doings, and dwell in the land that the LORD has given to you and your fathers forever and ever. 6 Do not go after other gods to serve them and worship them, and do not provoke Me to anger with the works of your hands; and I will not harm you.' 7 Yet you have not listened to Me," says the LORD, "that you might provoke Me to anger with the works of your hands to your own hurt.

8 "Therefore thus says the LORD of hosts: 'Because you have not heard My words, 9 behold, I will send and take all the families of the north,' says the LORD, 'and Nebuchadnezzar the king of Babylon, My servant, and will bring them against this land, against its inhabitants, and against these nations all around, and will utterly destroy them, and make them an astonishment, a hissing, and perpetual desolations. 10 Moreover I will take from them the voice of mirth and the voice of gladness, the voice of the bridegroom and the voice of the bride, the sound of the millstones and the light of the lamp. 11 And this whole land shall be a desolation *and* an astonishment, and these nations shall serve the king of Babylon seventy years.

12 'Then it will come to pass, when seventy years are completed, *that* I will punish the king of Babylon and that nation, the land of the Chaldeans, for their iniquity,' says the LORD; 'and I will make it a perpetual desolation. 13 So I will bring on that land all My words which I have pronounced against it, all that is written in this book, which Jeremiah has prophesied concerning all the nations. 14 (For many nations and great kings shall be served by them also; and I will repay them according to their deeds and according to the works of their own hands.)' "

15 For thus says the LORD God of Israel to me: "Take this wine cup of fury from My hand, and cause all the nations, to whom I send you, to drink

it. 16 And they will drink and stagger and go mad because of the sword that I will send among them."

17 Then I took the cup from the LORD's hand, and made all the nations drink, to whom the LORD had sent me: 18 Jerusalem and the cities of Judah, its kings and its princes, to make them a desolation, an astonishment, a hissing, and a curse, as *it is* this day; 19 Pharaoh king of Egypt, his servants, his princes, and all his people; 20 all the mixed multitude, all the kings of the land of Uz, all the kings of the land of the Philistines (namely, Ashkelon, Gaza, Ekron, and the remnant of Ashdod); 21 Edom, Moab, and the people of Ammon; 22 all the kings of Tyre, all the kings of Sidon, and the kings of the coastlands which *are* across the sea; 23 Dedan, Tema, Buz, and all *who are* in the farthest corners; 24 all the kings of Arabia and all the kings of the mixed multitude who dwell in the desert; 25 all the kings of Zimri, all the kings of Elam, and all the kings of the Medes; 26 all the kings of the north, far and near, one with another; and all the kingdoms of the world which *are* on the face of the earth. Also the king of Sheshach shall drink after them.

27 "Therefore you shall say to them, 'Thus says the LORD of hosts, the God of Israel: "Drink, be drunk, and vomit! Fall and rise no more, because of the sword which I will send among you." ' 28 And it shall be, if they refuse to take the cup from your hand to drink, then you shall say to them, 'Thus says the LORD of hosts: "You shall certainly drink! 29 For behold, I begin to bring calamity on the city which is called by My name, and should you be utterly unpunished? You shall not be unpunished, for I will call for a sword on all the inhabitants of the earth," says the LORD of hosts.'

30 "Therefore prophesy against them all these words, and say to them:

'The LORD will roar from on high,
And utter His voice from His
    holy habitation;

He will roar mightily against His
    fold.
He will give a shout, as those
    who tread *the grapes,*
Against all the inhabitants of the
    earth.
31 A noise will come to the ends
    of the earth—
For the LORD has a controversy
    with the nations;
He will plead His case with all
    flesh.
He will give those *who are*
    wicked to the sword,' says the
    LORD."

32 Thus says the LORD of hosts:

"Behold, disaster shall go forth
    From nation to nation,
And a great whirlwind shall be
    raised up
From the farthest parts of the
    earth.

33 "And at that day the slain of the
LORD shall be from *one* end of the
earth *even* to the *other* end of
the earth. They shall not be lamented,
or gathered, or buried; they shall become refuse on the ground.

34 "Wail, shepherds, and cry!
    Roll about *in the ashes,*
    You leaders of the flock!
For the days of your slaughter
    and your **dispersions** are
    fulfilled;
You shall fall like a precious
    vessel.
35 And the shepherds will have no
    way to flee,
Nor the leaders of the flock to
    escape.
36 A voice of the cry of the
    shepherds,
And a wailing of the leaders to
    the flock *will be heard.*

For the LORD has plundered
    their pasture,
37 And the peaceful dwellings are
    cut down
Because of the fierce anger of
    the LORD.
38 He has left His lair like the lion;
For their land is desolate
Because of the fierceness of the
    Oppressor,
And because of His fierce
    anger."

Jeremiah escapes death

26 In the beginning of the reign of
Jehoiakim the son of Josiah, king of
Judah, this word came from the LORD,
saying, 2 "Thus says the LORD: 'Stand
in the court of the LORD's house, and
speak to all the cities of Judah, which
come to worship *in* the LORD's house,
all the words that I command you to
speak to them. Do not diminish a
word. 3 Perhaps everyone will listen
and turn from his evil way, that I may
relent concerning the calamity which I
purpose to bring on them because of
the evil of their doings.' 4 And you shall
say to them, 'Thus says the LORD: "If
you will not listen to Me, to walk in
My law which I have set before you,
5 to heed the words of My servants the
prophets whom I sent to you, both rising up early and sending *them* (but you
have not heeded), 6 then I will make
this house like Shiloh, and will make
this city a curse to all the nations of
the earth." ' "

7 So the priests and the prophets and
all the people heard Jeremiah speaking
these words in the house of the LORD.
8 Now it happened, when Jeremiah
had made an end of speaking all that
the LORD had commanded *him* to
speak to all the people, that the priests
and the prophets and all the people
seized him, saying, "You will surely

WORDFINDER

25:34 Dispersion Pronounced *dis-PUR-zhun.* The Jews who were scattered
throughout the world of Peter's time (see 1 Peter 1:1). They were scattered mainly
because of the invasion of foreign nations throughout Jewish history.

die! 9 Why have you prophesied in the name of the Lord, saying, 'This house shall be like Shiloh, and this city shall be desolate, without an inhabitant'?" And all the people were gathered against Jeremiah in the house of the Lord.

10 When the princes of Judah heard these things, they came up from the king's house to the house of the Lord and sat down in the entry of the New Gate of the Lord's *house.* 11 And the priests and the prophets spoke to the princes and all the people, saying, "This man deserves to die! For he has prophesied against this city, as you have heard with your ears."

12 Then Jeremiah spoke to all the princes and all the people, saying: "The Lord sent me to prophesy against this house and against this city with all the words that you have heard. 13 Now therefore, amend your ways and your doings, and obey the voice of the Lord your God; then the Lord will relent concerning the doom that He has pronounced against you. 14 As for me, here I am, in your hand; do with me as seems good and proper to you. 15 But know for certain that if you put me to death, you will surely bring innocent blood on yourselves, on this city, and on its inhabitants; for truly the Lord has sent me to you to speak all these words in your hearing."

16 So the princes and all the people said to the priests and the prophets, "This man does not deserve to die. For he has spoken to us in the name of the Lord our God."

17 Then certain of the elders of the land rose up and spoke to all the assembly of the people, saying: 18 "Micah of Moresheth prophesied in the days of Hezekiah king of Judah, and spoke to all the people of Judah, saying, 'Thus says the Lord of hosts:

"Zion shall be plowed *like* a field,
    Jerusalem shall become heaps
        of ruins,
    And the mountain of the temple
    Like the bare hills of the
        forest." '

19 Did Hezekiah king of Judah and all Judah ever put him to death? Did he not fear the Lord and seek the Lord's favor? And the Lord relented concerning the doom which He had pronounced against them. But we are doing great evil against ourselves."

20 Now there was also a man who prophesied in the name of the Lord, Urijah the son of Shemaiah of Kirjath Jearim, who prophesied against this city and against this land according to all the words of Jeremiah. 21 And when Jehoiakim the king, with all his mighty men and all the princes, heard his words, the king sought to put him to death; but when Urijah heard *it,* he was afraid and fled, and went to Egypt. 22 Then Jehoiakim the king sent men to Egypt: Elnathan the son of Achbor, and *other* men *who went* with him to Egypt. 23 And they brought Urijah from Egypt and brought him to Jehoiakim the king, who killed him with the sword and cast his dead body into the graves of the common people.

24 Nevertheless the hand of Ahikam the son of Shaphan was with Jeremiah, so that they should not give him into the hand of the people to put him to death.

The people will be slaves

27 In the beginning of the reign of Jehoiakim the son of Josiah, king of Judah, this word came to Jeremiah from the Lord, saying, 2 "Thus says the Lord to me: 'Make for yourselves bonds and yokes, and put them on your neck, 3 and send them to the king of Edom, the king of Moab, the king of the Ammonites, the king of Tyre, and the king of Sidon, by the hand of the messengers who come to Jerusalem to Zedekiah king of Judah. 4 And command them to say to their masters, "Thus says the Lord of hosts, the God of Israel—thus you shall say to your masters: 5 'I have made the earth, the man and the beast that *are* on the ground, by My great power and by My outstretched arm, and have given it to whom it seemed proper to Me. 6 And now I have given all these lands into the hand of Nebuchadnezzar the king of Babylon, My servant; and the beasts of the field I have also given him to serve him. 7 So all nations shall serve him and his son and his son's son, until the time of his land comes; and then many nations and great kings shall make him serve them. 8 And it shall be, *that* the nation and kingdom which will not serve Nebuchadnezzar the king of Babylon, and which will not put its neck under the yoke of the king of Babylon, that nation I will punish,' says the LORD, 'with the sword, the famine, and the pestilence, until I have consumed them by his hand. 9 Therefore do not listen to your prophets, your diviners, your dreamers, your soothsayers, or your sorcerers, who speak to you, saying, "You shall not serve the king of Babylon." 10 For they prophesy a lie to you, to remove you far from your land; and I will drive you out, and you will perish. 11 But the nations that bring their necks under the yoke of the king of Babylon and serve him, I will let them remain in their own land,' says the LORD, 'and they shall till it and dwell in it.' " ' "

12 I also spoke to Zedekiah king of Judah according to all these words, saying, "Bring your necks under the yoke of the king of Babylon, and serve him and his people, and live! 13 Why will you die, you and your people, by the sword, by the famine, and by the pestilence, as the LORD has spoken against the nation that will not serve the king of Babylon? 14 Therefore do not listen to the words of the prophets who speak to you, saying, 'You shall not serve the king of Babylon,' for they prophesy a lie to you; 15 for I have not sent them," says the LORD, "yet they prophesy a lie in My name, that I may drive you out, and that you may perish, you and the prophets who prophesy to you."

16 Also I spoke to the priests and to all this people, saying, "Thus says the LORD: 'Do not listen to the words of your prophets who prophesy to you, saying, "Behold, the vessels of the

LORD's house will now shortly be brought back from Babylon"; for they prophesy a lie to you. 17 Do not listen to them; serve the king of Babylon, and live! Why should this city be laid waste? 18 But if they *are* prophets, and if the word of the LORD is with them, let them now make intercession to the LORD of hosts, that the vessels which are left in the house of the LORD, *in* the house of the king of Judah, and at Jerusalem, do not go to Babylon.'

19 "For thus says the LORD of hosts concerning the pillars, concerning the Sea, concerning the carts, and concerning the remainder of the vessels that remain in this city, 20 which Nebuchadnezzar king of Babylon did not take, when he carried away captive Jeconiah the son of Jehoiakim, king of Judah, from Jerusalem to Babylon, and all the nobles of Judah and Jerusalem— 21 yes, thus says the LORD of hosts, the God of Israel, concerning the vessels that remain in the house of the LORD, and in the house of the king of Judah and of Jerusalem: 22 'They shall be carried to Babylon, and there they shall be until the day that I visit them,' says the LORD. 'Then I will bring them up and restore them to this place.' "

Hananiah tells a lie

28 And it happened in the same year, at the beginning of the reign of Zedekiah king of Judah, in the fourth year *and* in the fifth month, *that* Hananiah the son of Azur the prophet, who *was* from Gibeon, spoke to me in the house of the LORD in the presence of the priests and of all the people, saying, 2 "Thus speaks the LORD of hosts, the God of Israel, saying: 'I have broken the yoke of the king of Babylon. 3 Within two full years I will bring back to this place all the vessels of the LORD's house, that Nebuchadnezzar king of Babylon took away from this place and carried to Babylon. 4 And I will bring back to this place Jeconiah the son of Jehoiakim, king of Judah, with all the captives of Judah who went to Babylon,' says the LORD, 'for I will

break the yoke of the king of Babylon.' "

5 Then the prophet Jeremiah spoke to the prophet Hananiah in the presence of the priests and in the presence of all the people who stood in the house of the LORD, 6 and the prophet Jeremiah said, "Amen! The LORD do so; the LORD perform your words which you have prophesied, to bring back the vessels of the LORD's house and all who were carried away captive, from Babylon to this place. 7 Nevertheless hear now this word that I speak in your hearing and in the hearing of all the people: 8 The prophets who have been before me and before you of old prophesied against many countries and great kingdoms—of war and disaster and pestilence. 9 As for the prophet who prophesies of peace, when the word of the prophet comes to pass, the prophet will be known as one whom the LORD has truly sent."

10 Then Hananiah the prophet took the yoke off the prophet Jeremiah's neck and broke it. 11 And Hananiah spoke in the presence of all the people, saying, "Thus says the LORD: 'Even so I will break the yoke of Nebuchadnezzar king of Babylon from the neck of all nations within the space of two full years.' " And the prophet Jeremiah went his way.

12 Now the word of the LORD came to Jeremiah, after Hananiah the prophet had broken the yoke from the neck of the prophet Jeremiah, saying, 13 "Go and tell Hananiah, saying, 'Thus says the LORD: "You have broken the yokes of wood, but you have made in their place yokes of iron." 14 For thus says the LORD of hosts, the God of Israel: "I have put a yoke of iron on the neck of all these nations, that they may serve Nebuchadnezzar king of Babylon; and they shall serve him. I have given him the beasts of the field also." ' "

15 Then the prophet Jeremiah said to Hananiah the prophet, "Hear now, Hananiah, the LORD has not sent you, but you make this people trust in a lie. 16 Therefore thus says the LORD: 'Behold, I will cast you from the face of the earth. This year you shall die, because you have taught rebellion against the LORD.' "

17 So Hananiah the prophet died the same year in the seventh month.

Jeremiah writes a letter

29 Now these are the words of the letter that Jeremiah the prophet sent from Jerusalem to the remainder of the elders who were carried away captive—to the priests, the prophets, and all the people whom Nebuchadnezzar had carried away captive from Jerusalem to Babylon. 2 (This happened after Jeconiah the king, the queen mother, the eunuchs, the princes of Judah and Jerusalem, the craftsmen, and the smiths had departed from Jerusalem.) 3 The letter was sent by the hand of Elasah the son of Shaphan, and Gemariah the son of Hilkiah, whom Zedekiah king of Judah sent to Babylon, to Nebuchadnezzar king of Babylon, saying,

4 Thus says the LORD of hosts, the God of Israel, to all who were carried away captive, whom I have caused to be carried away from Jerusalem to Babylon:

5 Build houses and dwell in them; plant gardens and eat their fruit. 6 Take wives and beget sons and daughters; and take wives for your sons and give your daughters to husbands, so that they may bear sons and daughters—that you may be increased there, and not diminished. 7 And seek the peace of the city where I have caused you to be carried away captive, and pray to the LORD for it; for in its peace you will have peace. 8 For thus says the LORD of hosts, the God of Israel: Do not let your prophets and your diviners who are in your midst deceive you, nor listen to

your dreams which you cause to be dreamed. ⁹ For they prophesy falsely to you in My name; I have not sent them, says the LORD.

10 For thus says the LORD: After seventy years are completed at Babylon, I will visit you and perform My good word toward you, and cause you to return to this place. ¹¹ For I know the thoughts that I think toward you, says the LORD, thoughts of peace and not of evil, to give you a future and a hope. ¹² Then you will call upon Me and go and pray to Me, and I will listen to you. ¹³ And you will seek Me and find *Me*, when you search for Me with all your heart. ¹⁴ I will be found by you, says the LORD, and I will bring you back from your captivity; I will gather you from all the nations and from all the places where I have driven you, says the LORD, and I will bring you to the place from which I cause you to be carried away captive.

15 Because you have said, "The LORD has raised up prophets for us in Babylon"— ¹⁶ therefore thus says the LORD concerning the king who sits on the throne of David, concerning all the people who dwell in this city, and concerning your brethren who have not gone out with you into captivity— ¹⁷ thus says the LORD of hosts: Behold, I will send on them the sword, the famine, and the pestilence, and will make them like rotten figs that cannot be eaten, they are so bad. ¹⁸ And I will pursue them with the sword, with famine, and with pestilence; and I will deliver them to trouble among all the kingdoms of the earth—to be a curse, an astonishment, a hissing, and a reproach among all the nations where I have

driven them, ¹⁹ because they have not heeded My words, says the LORD, which I sent to them by My servants the prophets, rising up early and sending *them;* neither would you heed, says the LORD. ²⁰ Therefore hear the word of the LORD, all you of the captivity, whom I have sent from Jerusalem to Babylon.

21 Thus says the LORD of hosts, the God of Israel, concerning Ahab the son of Kolaiah, and Zedekiah the son of Maaseiah, who prophesy a lie to you in My name: Behold, I will deliver them into the hand of Nebuchadnezzar king of Babylon, and he shall slay them before your eyes. ²² And because of them a curse shall be taken up by all the captivity of Judah who *are* in Babylon, saying, "The LORD make you like Zedekiah and Ahab, whom the king of Babylon roasted in the fire"; ²³ because they have done disgraceful things in Israel, have committed adultery with their neighbors' wives, and have spoken lying words in My name, which I have not commanded them. Indeed I know, and *am* a witness, says the LORD.

24 You shall also speak to Shemaiah the Nehelamite, saying, ²⁵ Thus speaks the LORD of hosts, the God of Israel, saying: You have sent letters in your name to all the people who *are* at Jerusalem, to Zephaniah the son of Maaseiah the priest, and to all the priests, saying, ²⁶ "The LORD has made you priest instead of Jehoiada the priest, so that there should be officers *in* the house of the LORD over every man *who* is demented and considers himself a prophet, that you should put him in prison and in the stocks. ²⁷ Now therefore, why have you

not rebuked Jeremiah of Anathoth who makes himself a prophet to you? 28 For he has sent to us *in* Babylon, saying, 'This *captivity is* long; build houses and dwell *in them,* and plant gardens and eat their fruit.'"

29 Now Zephaniah the priest read this letter in the hearing of Jeremiah the prophet. 30 Then the word of the LORD came to Jeremiah, saying: 31 Send to all those in captivity, saying, Thus says the LORD concerning Shemaiah the Nehelamite: Because Shemaiah has prophesied to you, and I have not sent him, and he has caused you to trust in a lie— 32 therefore thus says the LORD: Behold, I will punish Shemaiah the Nehelamite and his family: he shall not have anyone to dwell among this people, nor shall he see the good that I will do for My people, says the LORD, because he has taught rebellion against the LORD.

The Lord will bring the people home

30 The word that came to Jeremiah from the LORD, saying, 2 "Thus speaks the LORD God of Israel, saying: 'Write in a book for yourself all the words that I have spoken to you. 3 For behold, the days are coming,' says the LORD, 'that I will bring back from captivity My people Israel and Judah,' says the LORD. 'And I will cause them to return to the land that I gave to their fathers, and they shall possess it.'"

4 Now these *are* the words that the LORD spoke concerning Israel and Judah.

5 "For thus says the LORD:

'We have heard a voice of
    trembling,
Of fear, and not of peace.

6 Ask now, and see,
Whether a man is ever in labor
    with child?
So why do I see every man *with*
    his hands on his loins
Like a woman in labor,
And all faces turned pale?

7 Alas! For that day *is* great,
So that none *is* like it;
And it *is* the time of Jacob's
    trouble,
But he shall be saved out of it.

8 'For it shall come to pass in that
    day,'
Says the LORD of hosts,
'That I will break his yoke from
    your neck,
And will burst your bonds;
Foreigners shall no more enslave
    them.

9 But they shall serve the LORD
    their God,
And David their king,
Whom I will raise up for them.

10 'Therefore do not fear, O My
    servant Jacob,' says the LORD,
'Nor be dismayed, O Israel;
For behold, I will save you from
    afar,
And your seed from the land of
    their captivity.
Jacob shall return, have rest and
    be quiet,
And no one shall make *him*
    afraid.

11 For I *am* with you,' says the
    LORD, 'to save you;
Though I make a full end of all
    nations where I have scattered
    you,
Yet I will not make a complete
    end of you.
But I will correct you in justice,
And will not let you go
    altogether unpunished.'

12 "For thus says the LORD:

'Your affliction *is* incurable,
Your wound *is* severe.

13 *There is* no one to plead your
    cause,

That you may be bound up;
You have no healing medicines.
14 All your lovers have forgotten
    you;
They do not seek you;
For I have wounded you with
    the wound of an enemy,
With the chastisement of a cruel
    one,
For the multitude of your
    iniquities,
Because your sins have
    increased.
15 Why do you cry about your
    affliction?
Your sorrow *is* incurable.
Because of the multitude of your
    iniquities,
Because your sins have
    increased,
I have done these things to you.

16 'Therefore all those who devour
    you shall be devoured;
And all your adversaries, every
    one of them, shall go into
    captivity;
Those who plunder you shall
    become plunder,
And all who prey upon you I will
    make a prey.
17 For I will restore health to you
And heal you of your wounds,'
    says the LORD,
'Because they called you an
    outcast *saying:*
"This *is* Zion;
No one seeks her." '

18 "Thus says the LORD:

'Behold, I will bring back the
    captivity of Jacob's tents,
And have mercy on his dwelling
    places;
The city shall be built upon its
    own mound,
And the palace shall remain
    according to its own plan.
19 Then out of them shall proceed
    thanksgiving
And the voice of those who
    make merry;

I will multiply them, and they
    shall not diminish;
I will also glorify them, and they
    shall not be small.
20 Their children also shall be as
    before,
And their congregation shall be
    established before Me;
And I will punish all who oppress
    them.
21 Their nobles shall be from
    among them,
And their governor shall come
    from their midst;
Then I will cause him to draw
    near,
And he shall approach Me;
For who *is* this who pledged his
    heart to approach Me?' says
    the LORD.
22 'You shall be My people,
And I will be your God.' "

23 Behold, the whirlwind of the
    LORD
Goes forth with fury,
A continuing whirlwind;
It will fall violently on the head
    of the wicked.
24 The fierce anger of the LORD will
    not return until He has done
    it,
And until He has performed the
    intents of His heart.

In the latter days you will
    consider it.

I will always love you

31 "At the same time," says the
LORD, "I will be the God of all the families of Israel, and they shall be My people."
2 Thus says the LORD:

"The people who survived the
    sword
Found grace in the wilderness—
Israel, when I went to give him
    rest."

3 The LORD has appeared of old
    to me, *saying:*

"Yes, I have loved you with an
everlasting love;
Therefore with lovingkindness I
have drawn you.
4   Again I will build you, and you
shall be rebuilt,
O virgin of Israel!
You shall again be adorned with
your tambourines,
And shall go forth in the dances
of those who rejoice.
5   You shall yet plant vines on the
mountains of Samaria;
The planters shall plant and eat
them as ordinary food.
6   For there shall be a day
When the watchmen will cry on
Mount Ephraim,
'Arise, and let us go up *to*
Zion,
To the LORD our God.' "

7 For thus says the LORD:

"Sing with gladness for Jacob,
And shout among the chief of
the nations;
Proclaim, give praise, and say,
'O LORD, save Your people,
The remnant of Israel!'
8   Behold, I will bring them from
the north country,
And gather them from the ends
of the earth,
Among them the blind and the
lame,
The woman with child
And the one who labors with
child, together;
A great throng shall return there.
9   They shall come with weeping,
And with supplications I will lead
them.
I will cause them to walk by the
rivers of waters,
In a straight way in which they
shall not stumble;
For I am a Father to Israel,
And Ephraim *is* My firstborn.

10 "Hear the word of the LORD, O
nations,
And declare *it* in the isles afar
off, and say,

'He who scattered Israel will
gather him,
And keep him as a shepherd
does his flock.'
11 For the LORD has redeemed
Jacob,
And ransomed him from the
hand of one stronger than he.
12 Therefore they shall come and
sing in the height of Zion,
Streaming to the goodness of
the LORD—
For wheat and new wine and oil,
For the young of the flock and
the herd;
Their souls shall be like a
well-watered garden,
And they shall sorrow no more
at all.
13 "Then shall the virgin rejoice in
the dance,
And the young men and the old,
together;
For I will turn their mourning to
joy,
Will comfort them,
And make them rejoice rather
than sorrow.
14 I will satiate the soul of the
priests with abundance,
And My people shall be satisfied
with My goodness, says the
LORD."

15 Thus says the LORD:

"A voice was heard in Ramah,
Lamentation *and* bitter weeping,
Rachel weeping for her children,
Refusing to be comforted for her
children,
Because they *are* no more."

16 Thus says the LORD:

"Refrain your voice from
weeping,
And your eyes from tears;
For your work shall be
rewarded, says the LORD,
And they shall come back from
the land of the enemy.

17 There is hope in your future,
  says the LORD,
  That *your* children shall come
  back to their own border.

18 "I have surely heard Ephraim
  bemoaning himself:
  'You have chastised me, and I
  was chastised,
  Like an untrained bull;
  Restore me, and I will return,
  For You *are* the LORD my
  God.

19 Surely, after my turning, I
  repented;
  And after I was instructed, I
  struck myself on the thigh;
  I was ashamed, yes, even
  humiliated,
  Because I bore the reproach of
  my youth.'

20 *Is* Ephraim My dear son?
  Is he a pleasant child?
  For though I spoke against him,
  I earnestly remember him still;
  Therefore My heart yearns for
  him;
  I will surely have mercy on him,
  says the LORD.

21 "Set up signposts,
  Make landmarks;
  Set your heart toward the
  highway,
  The way in *which* you went.
  Turn back, O virgin of Israel,
  Turn back to these your cities.

22 How long will you gad about,
  O you backsliding daughter?
  For the LORD has created a new
  thing in the earth—
  A woman shall encompass a
  man."

23 Thus says the LORD of hosts, the
God of Israel: "They shall again use
this speech in the land of Judah and
in its cities, when I bring back their captivity: 'The LORD bless you, O home
of justice, *and* mountain of holiness!'
24 And there shall dwell in Judah itself,
and in all its cities together, farmers and
those going out with flocks. 25 For I
have satiated the weary soul, and I

have replenished every sorrowful
soul."

26 After this I awoke and looked
around, and my sleep was sweet to
me.

27 "Behold, the days are coming,
says the LORD, that I will sow the house
of Israel and the house of Judah with
the seed of man and the seed of beast.
28 And it shall come to pass, *that* as I
have watched over them to pluck up,
to break down, to throw down, to destroy, and to afflict, so I will watch over
them to build and to plant, says the
LORD. 29 In those days they shall say
no more:

'The fathers have eaten sour
  grapes,
  And the children's teeth are set
  on edge.'

30 But *every* one shall die for his own
iniquity; every man who eats the sour
grapes, his teeth shall be set on edge.

31 "Behold, the days are coming,
says the LORD, when I will make a new
covenant with the house of Israel and
with the house of Judah— 32 not according to the covenant that I made
with their fathers in the day *that* I took
them by the hand to lead them out of
the land of Egypt, My covenant which
they broke, though I was a husband
to them, says the LORD. 33 But this *is*
the covenant that I will make with the
house of Israel after those days, says
the LORD: I will put My law in their
minds, and write it on their hearts; and
I will be their God, and they shall be
My people. 34 No more shall every
man teach his neighbor, and every
man his brother, saying, 'Know the
LORD,' for they all shall know Me, from
the least of them to the greatest of
them, says the LORD. For I will forgive
their iniquity, and their sin I will remember no more."

35 Thus says the LORD,
  Who gives the sun for a light by
  day,
  The ordinances of the moon and
  the stars for a light by night,

Who disturbs the sea,
And its waves roar
(The LORD of hosts *is* His name):

36 "If those ordinances depart
From before Me, says the LORD,
Then the seed of Israel shall also
cease
From being a nation before Me
forever."

37 Thus says the LORD:

"If heaven above can be
measured,
And the foundations of the earth
searched out beneath,
I will also cast off all the seed
of Israel
For all that they have done, says
the LORD.

38 "Behold, the days are coming, says the LORD, that the city shall be built for the LORD from the Tower of Hananel to the Corner Gate. 39 The surveyor's line shall again extend straight forward over the hill Gareb; then it shall turn toward Goath. 40 And the whole valley of the dead bodies and of the ashes, and all the fields as far as the Brook Kidron, to the corner of the Horse Gate toward the east, *shall be* holy to the LORD. It shall not be plucked up or thrown down anymore forever."

Jeremiah buys some land

32 The word that came to Jeremiah from the LORD in the tenth year of Zedekiah king of Judah, which was the eighteenth year of Nebuchadnezzar. 2 For then the king of Babylon's army besieged Jerusalem, and Jeremiah the prophet was shut up in the court of the prison, which *was in* the king of Judah's house. 3 For Zedekiah king of Judah had shut him up, saying, "Why do you prophesy and say, 'Thus says the LORD: "Behold, I will give this city into the hand of the king of Babylon, and he shall take it; 4 and Zedekiah king of Judah shall not escape from

the hand of the Chaldeans, but shall surely be delivered into the hand of the king of Babylon, and shall speak with him face to face, and see him eye to eye; 5 then he shall lead Zedekiah to Babylon, and there he shall be until I visit him," says the LORD; "though you fight with the Chaldeans, you shall not succeed" ' ?"

6 And Jeremiah said, "The word of the LORD came to me, saying, 7 'Behold, Hanamel the son of Shallum your uncle will come to you, saying, "Buy my field which *is* in Anathoth, for the right of redemption *is* yours to buy *it*." ' 8 Then Hanamel my uncle's son came to me in the court of the prison according to the word of the LORD, and said to me, 'Please buy my field that *is* in Anathoth, which *is* in the country of Benjamin; for the right of inheritance *is* yours, and the redemption yours; buy *it* for yourself.' Then I knew that this was the word of the LORD. 9 So I bought the field from Hanamel, the son of my uncle who *was* in Anathoth, and weighed *out* to him the money—seventeen shekels of silver. 10 And I signed the deed and sealed *it,* took witnesses, and weighed the money on the scales. 11 So I took the purchase deed, *both* that which was sealed *according* to the law and custom, and that which was open; 12 and I gave the purchase deed to Baruch the son of Neriah, son of Mahseiah, in the presence of Hanamel my uncle's *son,* and in the presence of the witnesses who signed the purchase deed, before all the Jews who sat in the court of the prison.

13 "Then I charged Baruch before them, saying, 14 'Thus says the LORD of hosts, the God of Israel: "Take these deeds, both this purchase deed which is sealed and this deed which is open, and put them in an earthen vessel, that they may last many days." 15 For thus says the LORD of hosts, the God of Israel: "Houses and fields and vineyards shall be possessed again in this land." '

16 "Now when I had delivered the purchase deed to Baruch the son of Neriah, I prayed to the LORD, saying:

17 'Ah, Lord GOD! Behold, You have made the heavens and the earth by Your great power and outstretched arm. There is nothing too hard for You. 18 *You* show lovingkindness to thousands, and repay the iniquity of the fathers into the bosom of their children after them—the Great, the Mighty God, whose name *is* the LORD of hosts. 19 *You are* great in counsel and mighty in work, for your *eyes are* open to all the ways of the sons of men, to give everyone according to his ways and according to the fruit of his doings. 20 You have set signs and wonders in the land of Egypt, to this day, and in Israel and among *other* men; and You have made Yourself a name, as it is this day. 21 You have brought Your people Israel out of the land of Egypt with signs and wonders, with a strong hand and an outstretched arm, and with great terror; 22 You have given them this land, of which You swore to their fathers to give them—"a land flowing with milk and honey." 23 And they came in and took possession of it, but they have not obeyed Your voice or walked in Your law. They have done nothing of all that You commanded them to do; therefore You have caused all this calamity to come upon them.

24 'Look, the siege mounds! They have come to the city to take it; and the city has been given into the hand of the Chaldeans who fight against it, because of the sword and famine and pestilence. What You have spoken has happened; there You see *it!* 25 And You have said to me, O Lord GOD, "Buy the field for money, and take witnesses"!—yet the city has been given into the hand of the Chaldeans.' "

26 Then the word of the LORD came to Jeremiah, saying, 27 "Behold, I *am* the LORD, the God of all flesh. Is there anything too hard for Me? 28 Therefore thus says the LORD: 'Behold, I will give this city into the hand of the Chaldeans, into the hand of Nebuchadnezzar king of Babylon, and he shall take it. 29 And the Chaldeans who fight against this city shall come and set fire to this city and burn it, with the houses on whose roofs they have offered incense to Baal and poured out drink offerings to other gods, to provoke Me to anger; 30 because the children of Israel and the children of Judah have done only evil before Me from their youth. For the children of Israel have provoked Me only to anger with the work of their hands,' says the LORD. 31 'For this city has been to Me *a provocation of* My anger and My fury from the day that they built it, even to this day; so I will remove it from before My face 32 because of all the evil of the children of Israel and the children of Judah, which they have done to provoke Me to anger—they, their kings, their princes, their priests, their prophets, the men of Judah, and the inhabitants of Jerusalem. 33 And they have turned to Me the back, and not the face; though I taught them, rising up early and teaching *them,* yet they have not listened to receive instruction. 34 But they set their abominations in the house which is called by My name, to defile it. 35 And they built the high places of Baal which *are* in the Valley of the Son of Hinnom, to cause their sons and their daughters to pass through *the fire* to Molech, which I did not command them, nor did it come into My mind that they should do this abomination, to cause Judah to sin.'

36 "Now therefore, thus says the LORD, the God of Israel, concerning this city of which you say, 'It shall be delivered into the hand of the king of Babylon by the sword, by the famine, and by the pestilence: 37 Behold, I will gather them out of all countries where I have driven them in My anger, in My fury, and in great wrath; I will bring them back to this place, and I will cause them to dwell safely. 38 They shall be My people, and I will be their God; 39 then I will give them one heart and one way, that they may fear Me forever, for the good of them and their children after them. 40 And I will make an everlasting covenant with them, that I will not turn away from doing them good; but I will put My fear in their

hearts so that they will not depart from Me. 41 Yes, I will rejoice over them to do them good, and I will assuredly plant them in this land, with all My heart and with all My soul.'

42 "For thus says the LORD: 'Just as I have brought all this great calamity on this people, so I will bring on them all the good that I have promised them. 43 And fields will be bought in this land of which you say, "It is desolate, without man or beast; it has been given into the hand of the Chaldeans." 44 Men will buy fields for money, sign deeds and seal them, and take witnesses, in the land of Benjamin, in the places around Jerusalem, in the cities of Judah, in the cities of the mountains, in the cities of the lowland, and in the cities of the South; for I will cause their captives to return,' says the LORD."

God tells some great secrets

33 Moreover the word of the LORD came to Jeremiah a second time, while he was still shut up in the court of the prison, saying, 2 "Thus says the LORD who made it, the LORD who formed it to establish it (the LORD is His name): 3 'Call to Me, and I will answer you, and show you great and mighty things, which you do not know.'

4 "For thus says the LORD, the God of Israel, concerning the houses of this city and the houses of the kings of Judah, which have been pulled down to fortify against the siege mounds and the sword: 5 'They come to fight with the Chaldeans, but only to fill their places with the dead bodies of men whom I will slay in My anger and My fury, all for whose wickedness I have hidden My face from this city. 6 Behold, I will bring it health and healing; I will heal them and reveal to them the abundance of peace and truth. 7 And I will cause the captives of Judah and the captives of Israel to return, and will rebuild those places as at the first. 8 I will cleanse them from all their iniquity by which they have sinned against Me, and I will pardon all their iniquities by which they have sinned

and by which they have transgressed against Me. 9 Then it shall be to Me a name of joy, a praise, and an honor before all nations of the earth, who shall hear all the good that I do to them; they shall fear and tremble for all the goodness and all the prosperity that I provide for it.'

10 "Thus says the LORD: 'Again there shall be heard in this place—of which you say, "It is desolate, without man and without beast"—in the cities of Judah, in the streets of Jerusalem that are desolate, without man and without inhabitant and without beast, 11 the voice of joy and the voice of gladness, the voice of the bridegroom and the voice of the bride, the voice of those who will say:

"Praise the LORD of hosts,
For the LORD is good,
For His mercy endures
forever"—

and of those who will bring the sacrifice of praise into the house of the LORD. For I will cause the captives of the land to return as at the first,' says the LORD.

12 "Thus says the LORD of hosts: 'In this place which is desolate, without man and without beast, and in all its cities, there shall again be a dwelling place of shepherds causing their flocks to lie down. 13 In the cities of the mountains, in the cities of the lowland, in the cities of the South, in the land of Benjamin, in the places around Jerusalem, and in the cities of Judah, the flocks shall again pass under the hands of him who counts them,' says the LORD.

14 'Behold, the days are coming,' says the LORD, 'that I will perform that good thing which I have promised to the house of Israel and to the house of Judah:

15 'In those days and at that time
I will cause to grow up to David
A Branch of righteousness;
He shall execute judgment and
righteousness in the earth.

16 In those days Judah will be
saved,
And Jerusalem will dwell safely.
And this *is the name* by which
she will be called:

THE LORD OUR
RIGHTEOUSNESS.'

17 "For thus says the LORD: 'David shall never lack a man to sit on the throne of the house of Israel; 18 nor shall the priests, the Levites, lack a man to offer burnt offerings before Me, to kindle grain offerings, and to sacrifice continually.' "

19 And the word of the LORD came to Jeremiah, saying, 20 "Thus says the LORD: 'If you can break My covenant with the day and My covenant with the night, so that there will not be day and night in their season, 21 then My covenant may also be broken with David My servant, so that he shall not have a son to reign on his throne, and with the Levites, the priests, My ministers. 22 As the host of heaven cannot be numbered, nor the sand of the sea measured, so will I multiply the descendants of David My servant and the Levites who minister to Me.' "

23 Moreover the word of the LORD came to Jeremiah, saying, 24 "Have you not considered what these people have spoken, saying, 'The two families which the LORD has chosen, He has also cast them off'? Thus they have despised My people, as if they should no more be a nation before them.

25 "Thus says the LORD: 'If My covenant *is* not with day and night, *and if* I have not appointed the ordinances of heaven and earth, 26 then I will cast away the descendants of Jacob and David My servant, *so* that I will not take *any* of his descendants *to be* rulers over the descendants of Abraham, Isaac, and Jacob. For I will cause their captives to return, and will have mercy on them.' "

God gives the king fair warning

34 The word which came to Jeremiah from the LORD, when Nebuchadnezzar king of Babylon and all his army, all the kingdoms of the earth under his dominion, and all the people, fought against Jerusalem and all its cities, saying, 2 "Thus says the LORD, the God of Israel: 'Go and speak to Zedekiah king of Judah and tell him, "Thus says the LORD: 'Behold, I will give this city into the hand of the king of Babylon, and he shall burn it with fire. 3 And you shall not escape from his hand, but shall surely be taken and delivered into his hand; your eyes shall see the eyes of the king of Babylon, he shall speak with you face to face, and you shall go to Babylon.' " ' 4 Yet hear the word of the LORD, O Zedekiah king of Judah! Thus says the LORD concerning you: 'You shall not

---

King Zedekiah—What in the world did that gloomy Jeremiah expect me to do anyway? Our nation was wealthy, and I had stayed on friendly terms with Babylon. Now that fool wanted me to believe we were going to be destroyed. He even wanted us to surrender to our enemies!

No! I told him we must fight, so I put Jeremiah in prison (see Jeremiah 37:21). I told him that Egypt's army would come to help us. But then Jeremiah had the nerve to tell me we would be destroyed anyway, and Egypt would not be able to help us.

I admit I was getting frightened as time passed by. So I promised Jeremiah I would spare his life if he would only give me some good news, but he just kept saying we should surrender to Babylon.

Then the army of Babylon did come and destroy our city. They put out my eyes (see Jeremiah 39:7) and later killed me.

Lachish, a Hebrew city, was destroyed by Babylon.

die by the sword. ⁵ You shall die in peace; as in the ceremonies of your fathers, the former kings who were before you, so they shall burn incense for you and lament for you, *saying,* "Alas, lord!" For I have pronounced the word, says the LORD.' "

⁶ Then Jeremiah the prophet spoke all these words to Zedekiah king of Judah in Jerusalem, ⁷ when the king of Babylon's army fought against Jerusalem and all the cities of Judah that were left, against Lachish and Azekah; for *only* these fortified cities remained of the cities of Judah.

⁸ *This is* the word that came to Jeremiah from the LORD, after King Zedekiah had made a covenant with all the people who *were* at Jerusalem to proclaim liberty to them: ⁹ that every man should set free his male and female slave—a Hebrew man or woman—that no one should keep a Jewish brother in bondage. ¹⁰ Now when all the princes and all the people, who had entered into the covenant, heard that everyone should set free his male and female slaves, that no one should keep them in bondage anymore, they obeyed and let *them* go. ¹¹ But afterward they changed their minds and made the male and female slaves return, whom they had set free, and brought them into subjection as male and female slaves.

¹² Therefore the word of the LORD came to Jeremiah from the LORD, saying, ¹³ "Thus says the LORD, the God of Israel: 'I made a covenant with your fathers in the day that I brought them out of the land of Egypt, out of the house of bondage, saying, ¹⁴ "At the end of seven years let every man set free his Hebrew brother, who has been sold to him; and when he has served you six years, you shall let him go free from you." But your fathers did not obey Me nor incline their ear. ¹⁵ Then you recently turned and did what was right in My sight—every man proclaiming liberty to his neighbor; and you made a covenant before Me in the house which is called by My name. ¹⁶ Then you turned around and profaned My name, and every one of you brought back his male and female slaves, whom he had set at liberty, at their pleasure, and brought them back into subjection, to be your male and female slaves.'

¹⁷ "Therefore thus says the LORD: 'You have not obeyed Me in proclaiming liberty, every one to his brother and every one to his neighbor. Behold, I proclaim liberty to you,' says the LORD—'to the sword, to pestilence, and to famine! And I will deliver you to trouble among all the kingdoms of the earth. ¹⁸ And I will give the men who have transgressed My covenant,

who have not performed the words of the covenant which they made before Me, when they cut the calf in two and passed between the parts of it— ¹⁹ the princes of Judah, the princes of Jerusalem, the eunuchs, the priests, and all the people of the land who passed between the parts of the calf— ²⁰ I will give them into the hand of their enemies and into the hand of those who seek their life. Their dead bodies shall be for meat for the birds of the heaven and the beasts of the earth. ²¹ And I will give Zedekiah king of Judah and his princes into the hand of their enemies, into the hand of those who seek their life, and into the hand of the king of Babylon's army which has gone back from you. ²² Behold, I will command,' says the LORD, 'and cause them to return to this city. They will fight against it and take it and burn it with fire; and I will make the cities of Judah a desolation without inhabitant.' ''

The rewards for obeying God

35 The word which came to Jeremiah from the LORD in the days of Jehoiakim the son of Josiah, king of Judah, saying, ² "Go to the house of the Rechabites, speak to them, and bring them into the house of the LORD, into one of the chambers, and give them wine to drink."

³ Then I took Jaazaniah the son of Jeremiah, the son of Habazziniah, his brothers and all his sons, and the whole house of the Rechabites, ⁴ and I brought them into the house of the LORD, into the chamber of the sons of Hanan the son of Igdaliah, a man of God, which *was* by the chamber of the princes, above the chamber of Maaseiah the son of Shallum, the keeper of the door. ⁵ Then I set before the sons of the house of the Rechabites bowls full of wine, and cups; and I said to them, "Drink wine."

⁶ But they said, "We will drink no wine, for Jonadab the son of Rechab, our father, commanded us, saying, 'You shall drink no wine, you nor your

sons, forever. ⁷ You shall not build a house, sow seed, plant a vineyard, nor have *any of these;* but all your days you shall dwell in tents, that you may live many days in the land where you are sojourners.' ⁸ Thus we have obeyed the voice of Jonadab the son of Rechab, our father, in all that he charged us, to drink no wine all our days, we, our wives, our sons, or our daughters, ⁹ nor to build ourselves houses to dwell in; nor do we have vineyard, field, or seed. ¹⁰ But we have dwelt in tents, and have obeyed and done according to all that Jonadab our father commanded us. ¹¹ But it came to pass, when Nebuchadnezzar king of Babylon came up into the land, that we said, 'Come, let us go to Jerusalem for fear of the army of the Chaldeans and for fear of the army of the Syrians.' So we dwell at Jerusalem.''

¹² Then came the word of the LORD to Jeremiah, saying, ¹³ "Thus says the LORD of hosts, the God of Israel: 'Go and tell the men of Judah and the inhabitants of Jerusalem, ''Will you not receive instruction to obey My words?'' says the LORD. ¹⁴ "The words of Jonadab the son of Rechab, which he commanded his sons, not to drink wine, are performed; for to this day they drink none, and obey their father's commandment. But although I have spoken to you, rising early and speaking, you did not obey Me. ¹⁵ I have also sent to you all My servants the prophets, rising up early and sending *them,* saying, 'Turn now everyone from his evil way, amend your doings, and do not go after other gods to serve them; then you will dwell in the land which I have given you and your fathers.' But you have not inclined your ear, nor obeyed Me. ¹⁶ Surely the sons of Jonadab the son of Rechab have performed the commandment of their father, which he commanded them, but this people has not obeyed Me.'' '

¹⁷ "Therefore thus says the LORD God of hosts, the God of Israel: 'Behold, I will bring on Judah and on all the inhabitants of Jerusalem all the doom that I have pronounced against

Bible Heroes

New Testament

As you get to know these New Testament friends, try to discover what makes each of them special in God's sight. Can you see that many of them often made mistakes, just like you? But God forgave them, and He will forgive you if you ask Him. Read these riddles, then guess who is speaking:

My friends and I came from the East
To Bethlehem, as strangers,
With birthday presents for a King,
But we found Him in a *manger!*

WHO AM I?

—— —— —— —— —— ——

(Find out more about us in Matthew 2:1–12.)

I killed many Christians;
They often ran from me,
Until a light from heaven
Made me *blind* so I could *see!*

WHO AM I?

—— —— ——

(Read about my Damascus Road experience in Acts 9:1–9.)

I've always been a little man,
But I'm not sad at all.
Once Jesus stopped and spoke to me,
And I felt ten feet tall!

WHO AM I?

—— —— —— —— ——

(Learn what my Lord did for me in Luke 19:1–10.)

Bible Heroes

I was a leader of the Jews,
Yet Jesus was my Friend.
Though I'm a *man*, He taught me that
I must be born again!
WHO AM I?

— — — — — — — — —

(This midnight meeting is described in John 3:1–21.)

I used to be a fisherman,
My big mouth was my sin.
But Jesus told me I could change,
And now I fish for men!
WHO AM I?

— — — — —

*(Find out what happened when
Jesus called me to be
His disciple in Matthew 4:18–20.)*

I have to see before I'm sure
That things are really true.
When Jesus came back from the dead,
I said, "O Lord, it's You!"
WHO AM I?

— — — — —

*(Read how Jesus made a special
appearance just for me
in John 20:24–28.)*

them; because I have spoken to them but they have not heard, and I have called to them but they have not answered.' "

18 And Jeremiah said to the house of the Rechabites, "Thus says the LORD of hosts, the God of Israel: 'Because you have obeyed the commandment of Jonadab your father, and kept all his precepts and done according to all that he commanded you, 19 therefore thus says the LORD of hosts, the God of Israel: "Jonadab the son of Rechab shall not lack a man to stand before Me forever." ' "

A king burns the Bible

36 Now it came to pass in the fourth year of Jehoiakim the son of Josiah, king of Judah, *that* this word came to Jeremiah from the LORD, saying: 2 "Take a scroll of a book and write on it all the words that I have spoken to you against Israel, against Judah, and against all the nations, from the day I spoke to you, from the days of Josiah even to this day. 3 It may be that the house of Judah will hear all the adversities which I purpose to bring upon them, that everyone may turn from his evil way, that I may forgive their iniquity and their sin."

4 Then Jeremiah called Baruch the son of Neriah; and Baruch wrote on a scroll of a book, at the instruction of Jeremiah, all the words of the LORD which He had spoken to him. 5 And Jeremiah commanded Baruch, saying, "I *am* confined, I cannot go into the house of the LORD. 6 You go, therefore, and read from the scroll which you have written at my instruction, the words of the LORD, in the hearing of the people in the LORD's house on the day of fasting. And you shall also read them in the hearing of all Judah who come from their cities. 7 It may be that they will present their supplication before the LORD, and everyone will turn from his evil way. For great *is* the anger and the fury that the LORD has pronounced against this people." 8 And Baruch the son of Neriah did according to all that Jeremiah the prophet commanded him, reading from the book the words of the LORD in the LORD's house.

9 Now it came to pass in the fifth year of Jehoiakim the son of Josiah, king of Judah, in the ninth month, *that* they proclaimed a fast before the LORD to all the people in Jerusalem, and to all the people who came from the cities of Judah to Jerusalem. 10 Then Baruch read from the book the words of Jeremiah in the house of the LORD, in the chamber of Gemariah the son of Shaphan the scribe, in the upper court at the entry of the New Gate of the LORD's house, in the hearing of all the people.

11 When Michaiah the son of Gemariah, the son of Shaphan, heard all the words of the LORD from the book, 12 he then went down to the king's house, into the scribe's chamber; and there all the princes were sitting— Elishama the scribe, Delaiah the son of Shemaiah, Elnathan the son of

---

Jeremiah's Scribe—My name is Baruch (pronounced *bar-OOK*), and I was honored that the prophet chose me to be his writer. I wrote down all the words the Lord gave him in those days before Babylon destroyed us. I read the message to the people of Israel. When King Jehoiakim (pronounced *jeh-HOY-ah-kim*) was given my scroll, he burned it up!

Of course, I was only Jeremiah's servant. It was Jeremiah himself who was hated by the king and the nation. It was Jeremiah who went to prison for telling the people what God said. So you can see that being "Number One" for God is an honor, but it often means suffering. Jesus was the greatest of all, but they mistreated Him more than any of us.

Achbor, Gemariah the son of Shaphan, Zedekiah the son of Hananiah, and all the princes. 13 Then Michaiah declared to them all the words that he had heard when Baruch read the book in the hearing of the people. 14 Therefore all the princes sent Jehudi the son of Nethaniah, the son of Shelemiah, the son of Cushi, to Baruch, saying, "Take in your hand the scroll from which you have read in the hearing of the people, and come." So Baruch the son of Neriah took the scroll in his hand and came to them. 15 And they said to him, "Sit down now, and read it in our hearing." So Baruch read it in their hearing.

16 Now it happened, when they had heard all the words, that they looked in fear from one to another, and said to Baruch, "We will surely tell the king of all these words." 17 And they asked Baruch, saying, "Tell us now, how did you write all these words—at his instruction?"

18 So Baruch answered them, "He proclaimed with his mouth all these words to me, and I wrote them with ink in the book."

19 Then the princes said to Baruch, "Go and hide, you and Jeremiah; and let no one know where you are."

20 And they went to the king, into the court; but they stored the scroll in the chamber of Elishama the scribe, and told all the words in the hearing of the king. 21 So the king sent Jehudi to bring the scroll, and he took it from Elishama the scribe's chamber. And Jehudi read it in the hearing of the king and in the hearing of all the princes who stood beside the king. 22 Now the king was sitting in the winter house in the ninth month, with a fire burning on the hearth before him. 23 And it happened, when Jehudi had read three or four columns, that the king cut it with the scribe's knife and cast it into the fire that was on the hearth, until all the scroll was consumed in the fire that was on the hearth. 24 Yet they were not afraid, nor did they tear their garments, the king nor any of his servants who heard all these words. 25 Nevertheless Elnathan, Delaiah, and

Jeremiah dictated the words that Baruch the scribe wrote on a scroll.

Gemariah implored the king not to burn the scroll; but he would not listen to them. 26 And the king commanded Jerahmeel the king's son, Seraiah the son of Azriel, and Shelemiah the son of Abdeel, to seize Baruch the scribe and Jeremiah the prophet, but the LORD hid them.

27 Now after the king had burned the scroll with the words which Baruch had written at the instruction of Jeremiah, the word of the LORD came to Jeremiah, saying: 28 "Take yet another scroll, and write on it all the former words that were in the first scroll which Jehoiakim the king of Judah has burned. 29 And you shall say to Jehoiakim king of Judah, 'Thus says LORD: "You have burned this scroll, saying, 'Why have you written in it that the king of Babylon will certainly come and destroy this land, and cause man and beast to cease from here?' " 30 Therefore thus says the LORD concerning Jehoiakim king of Judah: "He shall have no one to sit on the throne of David; and his dead body shall be cast out to the heat of the day and the frost of the night. 31 I will punish him, his family, and his servants for their iniquity; and I will bring on them,

on the inhabitants of Jerusalem, and on the men of Judah all the doom that I have pronounced against them; but they did not heed." ' "

³² Then Jeremiah took another scroll and gave it to Baruch the scribe, the son of Neriah, who wrote on it at the instruction of Jeremiah all the words of the book which Jehoiakim king of Judah had burned in the fire. And besides, there were added to them many similar words.

"I'm innocent!" pleads Jeremiah

37 Now King Zedekiah the son of Josiah reigned instead of Coniah the son of Jehoiakim, whom Nebuchadnezzar king of Babylon made king in the land of Judah. ² But neither he nor his servants nor the people of the land gave heed to the words of the LORD which He spoke by the prophet Jeremiah.

³ And Zedekiah the king sent Jehucal the son of Shelemiah, and Zephaniah the son of Maaseiah, the priest, to the prophet Jeremiah, saying, "Pray now to the LORD our God for us." ⁴ Now Jeremiah was coming and going among the people, for they had not *yet* put him in prison. ⁵ Then Pharaoh's army came up from Egypt; and when the Chaldeans who were besieging Jerusalem heard news of them, they departed from Jerusalem.

⁶ Then the word of the LORD came to the prophet Jeremiah, saying, ⁷ "Thus says the LORD, the God of Israel, 'Thus you shall say to the king of Judah, who sent you to Me to inquire of Me: "Behold, Pharaoh's army which has come up to help you will return to Egypt, to their own land. ⁸ And the Chaldeans shall come back and fight against this city, and take it and burn it with fire." ' ⁹ Thus says the LORD: 'Do not deceive yourselves, saying, "The Chaldeans will surely depart from us," for they will not depart. ¹⁰ For though you had defeated the whole army of the Chaldeans who fight against you, and there remained *only* wounded men among them, they

would rise up, every man in his tent, and burn the city with fire.' "

¹¹ And it happened, when the army of the Chaldeans left *the siege* of Jerusalem for fear of Pharaoh's army, ¹² that Jeremiah went out of Jerusalem to go into the land of Benjamin to claim his property there among the people. ¹³ And when he was in the Gate of Benjamin, a captain of the guard *was* there whose name *was* Irijah the son of Shelemiah, the son of Hananiah; and he seized Jeremiah the prophet, saying, "You are defecting to the Chaldeans!" ¹⁴ Then Jeremiah said, "False! I am not defecting to the Chaldeans." But he did not listen to him.

So Irijah seized Jeremiah and brought him to the princes. ¹⁵ Therefore the princes were angry with Jeremiah, and they struck him and put him in prison in the house of Jonathan the scribe. For they had made that the prison.

¹⁶ When Jeremiah entered the dungeon and the cells, and Jeremiah had remained there many days, ¹⁷ then Zedekiah the king sent and took him *out.* The king asked him secretly in his house, and said, "Is there *any* word from the LORD?"

And Jeremiah said, "There is." Then he said, "You shall be delivered into the hand of the king of Babylon!"

¹⁸ Moreover Jeremiah said to King Zedekiah, "What offense have I committed against you, against your servants, or against this people, that you have put me in prison? ¹⁹ Where now *are* your prophets who prophesied to you, saying, 'The king of Babylon will not come against you or against this land?' ²⁰ Therefore please hear now, O my lord the king. Please, let my petition be accepted before you, and do not make me return to the house of Jonathan the scribe, lest I die there."

²¹ Then Zedekiah the king commanded that they should commit Jeremiah to the court of the prison, and that they should give him daily a piece of bread from the bakers' street, until all the bread in the city was gone. Thus

Jeremiah remained in the court of the prison.

Jeremiah is thrown into a well

38 Now Shephatiah the son of Mattan, Gedaliah the son of Pashhur, Jucal the son of Shelemiah, and Pashhur the son of Malchiah heard the words that Jeremiah had spoken to all the people, saying, 2 "Thus says the LORD: 'He who remains in this city shall die by the sword, by famine, and by pestilence; but he who goes over to the Chaldeans shall live; his life shall be as a prize to him, and he shall live.' 3 Thus says the LORD: 'This city shall surely be given into the hand of the king of Babylon's army, which shall take it.' "

4 Therefore the princes said to the king, "Please, let this man be put to death, for thus he weakens the hands of the men of war who remain in this city, and the hands of all the people, by speaking such words to them. For this man does not seek the welfare of this people, but their harm."

5 Then Zedekiah the king said, "Look, he is in your hand. For the king can do nothing against you." 6 So they took Jeremiah and cast him into the dungeon of Malchiah the king's son, which was in the court of the prison, and they let Jeremiah down with ropes. And in the dungeon there was no water, but mire. So Jeremiah sank in the mire.

7 Now Ebed-Melech the Ethiopian, one of the eunuchs, who was in the king's house, heard that they had put Jeremiah in the dungeon. When the king was sitting at the Gate of Benjamin, 8 Ebed-Melech went out of the king's house and spoke to the king, saying: 9 "My lord the king, these men have done evil in all that they have done to Jeremiah the prophet, whom they have cast into the dungeon, and he is likely to die from hunger in the place where he is. For there is no more bread in the city." 10 Then the king commanded Ebed-Melech the Ethiopian, saying, "Take from here thirty men with you, and lift Jeremiah the prophet out of the dungeon before he dies." 11 So Ebed-Melech took the men with him and went into the house of the king under the treasury, and took from there old clothes and old rags, and let them down by ropes into the dungeon to Jeremiah. 12 Then Ebed-Melech the Ethiopian said to Jeremiah, "Please put these old clothes and rags under your armpits, under the ropes." And Jeremiah did so. 13 So they pulled Jeremiah up with ropes and lifted him out of the dungeon. And Jeremiah remained in the court of the prison.

14 Then Zedekiah the king sent and had Jeremiah the prophet brought to him at the third entrance of the house of the LORD. And the king said to Jeremiah, "I will ask you something. Hide nothing from me."

15 Jeremiah said to Zedekiah, "If I declare it to you, will you not surely

🪓 DIGGING IN

38:6 Good People Often Suffer Jeremiah is actually the longest book of the prophets, although Isaiah has more chapters. The prophet Jeremiah had done nothing wrong. He had been a patient spokesman for God to the people of his time, almost six hundred years before Jesus was born. But the people didn't want Jeremiah to tell them God would punish them for their disobedience. So King Zedekiah put the great prophet of God in a filthy dungeon.

You have to realize that God's greatest servants have often been hated by their own people. This is hard to understand until you see that most people don't really seem to love God, even when they pretend they do. It's a lonely job to be God's messenger to such people.

God's true people always understand that they may have to lose everything in this world to be on God's side. Jeremiah did, the apostle Paul did—and Jesus did.

put me to death? And if I give you advice, you will not listen to me."

16 So Zedekiah the king swore secretly to Jeremiah, saying, "As the LORD lives, who made our very souls, I will not put you to death, nor will I give you into the hand of these men who seek your life."

17 Then Jeremiah said to Zedekiah, "Thus says the LORD, the God of hosts, the God of Israel: 'If you surely surrender to the king of Babylon's princes, then your soul shall live; this city shall not be burned with fire, and you and your house shall live. 18 But if you do not surrender to the king of Babylon's princes, then this city shall be given into the hand of the Chaldeans; they shall burn it with fire, and you shall not escape from their hand.' "

19 And Zedekiah the king said to Jeremiah, "I am afraid of the Jews who have defected to the Chaldeans, lest they deliver me into their hand, and they abuse me."

20 But Jeremiah said, "They shall not deliver you. Please, obey the voice of the LORD which I speak to you. So it shall be well with you, and your soul shall live. 21 But if you refuse to surrender, this is the word that the LORD has shown me: 22 'Now behold, all the women who are left in the king of Judah's house shall be surrendered to the king of Babylon's princes, and those women shall say:

"Your close friends have set upon you

And prevailed against you;
Your feet have sunk in the mire,
And they have turned away again.' "

23 'So they shall surrender all your wives and children to the Chaldeans. You shall not escape from their hand, but shall be taken by the hand of the king of Babylon. And you shall cause this city to be burned with fire.' "

24 Then Zedekiah said to Jeremiah, "Let no one know of these words, and you shall not die. 25 But if the princes hear that I have talked with you, and they come to you and say to you, 'Declare to us now what you have said to the king, and also what the king said to you; do not hide it from us, and we will not put you to death,' 26 then you shall say to them, 'I presented my request before the king, that he would not make me return to Jonathan's house to die there.' "

27 Then all the princes came to Jeremiah and asked him. And he told them according to all these words that the king had commanded. So they stopped speaking with him, for the conversation had not been heard. 28 Now Jeremiah remained in the court of the prison until the day that Jerusalem was taken. And he was there when Jerusalem was taken.

Jerusalem is captured

39 In the ninth year of Zedekiah king of Judah, in the tenth month,

DIGGING IN

38:17–23 It Makes Sense to Obey God King Zedekiah (pronounced zed-uh-KIGH-uh) was a wicked man. God had left him alone, so He didn't know what to do when the armies of Babylon were about to destroy Israel. Then Zedekiah brought Jeremiah the prophet out of prison to ask him what to do. Jeremiah told the king to surrender to Babylon. But the king wouldn't obey, even though the Lord promised to save him from the enemy. God also warned Zedekiah that all

would be destroyed if he didn't give up.

Sometimes you have to decide that God is right and you are wrong. Your idea may seem to be the safe way. For example, it may seem like the smart thing to lie to cover up some wrong you've done. But God's way is to tell the truth. God will honor you for obeying Him.

God would have honored King Zedekiah, too, if only he had done what the prophet told him. But the king didn't listen, and he lost everything.

Nebuchadnezzar king of Babylon and all his army came against Jerusalem, and besieged it. 2 In the eleventh year of Zedekiah, in the fourth month, on the ninth *day* of the month, the city was penetrated.

3 Then all the princes of the king of Babylon came in and sat in the Middle Gate: Nergal-Sharezer, Samgar-Nebo, Sarsechim, Rabsaris, Nergal-Sarezer, Rabmag, with the rest of the princes of the king of Babylon.

4 So it was, when Zedekiah the king of Judah and all the men of war saw them, that they fled and went out of the city by night, by way of the king's garden, by the gate between the two walls. And he went out by way of the plain. 5 But the Chaldean army pursued them and overtook Zedekiah in the plains of Jericho. And when they had captured him, they brought him up to Nebuchadnezzar king of Babylon, to Riblah in the land of Hamath, where he pronounced judgment on him. 6 Then the king of Babylon killed the sons of Zedekiah before his eyes in Riblah; the king of Babylon also killed all the nobles of Judah. 7 Moreover he put out Zedekiah's eyes, and bound him with bronze fetters to carry him off to Babylon. 8 And the Chaldeans burned the king's house and the houses of the people with fire, and broke down the walls of Jerusalem. 9 Then Nebuzaradan the captain of the guard carried away captive to Babylon the remnant of the people who remained in the city and those who defected to him, with the rest of the people who remained. 10 But Nebuzaradan the captain of the guard left in the land of Judah the poor people, who had nothing, and gave them vineyards and fields at the same time.

11 Now Nebuchadnezzar king of Babylon gave charge concerning Jeremiah to Nebuzaradan the captain of the guard, saying, 12 "Take him and look after him, and do him no harm; but do to him just as he says to you." 13 So Nebuzaradan the captain of the guard sent Nebushasban, Rabsaris, Nergal-Sharezer, Rabmag, and all the king of Babylon's chief officers; 14 then they sent *someone* to take Jeremiah from the court of the prison, and committed him to Gedaliah the son of Ahikam, the son of Shaphan, that he should take him home. So he dwelt among the people.

15 Meanwhile the word of the LORD had come to Jeremiah while he was shut up in the court of the prison, saying, 16 "Go and speak to Ebed-Melech the Ethiopian, saying, 'Thus says the LORD of hosts, the God of Israel: "Behold, I will bring My words upon this city for adversity and not for good, and they shall be *performed* in that day before you. 17 But I will deliver you in that day," says the LORD, "and you shall not be given into the hand of the men of whom you *are* afraid. 18 For I will surely deliver you, and you shall not fall by the sword; but your life shall

---

The Captain of the Guard—My name is Nebuzaradan (pronounced *neb-you-zar-AY-dan*). I was the army officer in charge of destroying Jerusalem and the temple, as the king of Babylon had commanded.

When I came to Jerusalem, Jeremiah the prophet was in prison where the Hebrew King Zedekiah had left him. But the king of Babylon ordered me to release Jeremiah and to look after his needs. Later I learned that Jeremiah was told by his God that he would be set free.

I treated Jeremiah with respect and courtesy, and I even offered to take him as my guest to Babylon, but Jeremiah didn't want to act like a traitor to his people. That is why he decided to stay in Israel and accept what his God provided him there. Only the poorest people were left in the land, and Jeremiah stayed with them.

The Plot Against Governor Gedaliah

The Babylon News-Press

MIZPAH—A Jewish man, Gedaliah (pronounced *ged-uh-LIE-uh*), was recently named governor of Judah. Governor Gedaliah will rule the Jews left in that country after the fall of Jerusalem.

King Nebuchadnezzar of Babylon (pronounced *neb-you-kad-NEZ-zer*) has promised peace to the Jews. But reports received from Judah are causing concern among our leaders. The king of Ammon, east of the Jordan River, is said to be plotting against Gedaliah. That king is reported to have hired one of Gedaliah's own men to murder him.

So far, Gedaliah does not believe the report. But the *News-Press* plans to follow up on the story.

---

be as a prize to you, because you have put your trust in Me," says the LORD.' "

Jeremiah, free at last

40 The word that came to Jeremiah from the LORD after Nebuzaradan the captain of the guard had let him go from Ramah, when he had taken him bound in chains among all who were carried away captive from Jerusalem and Judah, who were carried away captive to Babylon.

2 And the captain of the guard took Jeremiah and said to him: "The LORD your God has pronounced this doom on this place. 3 Now the LORD has brought *it*, and has done just as He said. Because you *people* have sinned against the LORD, and not obeyed His voice, therefore this thing has come upon you. 4 And now look, I free you this day from the chains that *were* on your hand. If it seems good to you to come with me to Babylon, come, and I will look after you. But if it seems wrong for you to come with me to Babylon, remain here. See, all the land *is* before you; wherever it seems good and convenient for you to go, go there."

5 Now while Jeremiah had not yet gone back, *Nebuzaradan said*, "Go back to Gedaliah the son of Ahikam, the son of Shaphan, whom the king of Babylon has made governor over the cities of Judah, and dwell with him

among the people. Or go wherever it seems convenient for you to go." So the captain of the guard gave him rations and a gift and let him go. 6 Then Jeremiah went to Gedaliah the son of Ahikam, to Mizpah, and dwelt with him among the people who were left in the land.

7 And when all the captains of the armies who *were* in the fields, they and their men, heard that the king of Babylon had made Gedaliah the son of Ahikam governor in the land, and had committed to him men, women, children, and the poorest of the land who had not been carried away captive to Babylon, 8 then they came to Gedaliah at Mizpah—Ishmael the son of Nethaniah, Johanan and Jonathan the sons of Kareah, Seraiah the son of Tanhumeth, the sons of Ephai the Netophathite, and Jezaniah the son of a Maachathite, they and their men. 9 And Gedaliah the son of Ahikam, the son of Shaphan, took an oath before them and their men, saying, "Do not be afraid to serve the Chaldeans. Dwell in the land and serve the king of Babylon, and it shall be well with you. 10 As for me, I will indeed dwell at Mizpah and serve the Chaldeans who come to us. But you, gather wine and summer fruit and oil, put *them* in your vessels, and dwell in your cities that you have taken." 11 Likewise, when all the Jews who *were* in Moab, among the Ammonites, in Edom, and who

were in all the countries, heard that the king of Babylon had left a remnant of Judah, and that he had set over them Gedaliah the son of Ahikam, the son of Shaphan, 12 then all the Jews returned out of all places where they had been driven, and came to the land of Judah, to Gedaliah at Mizpah, and gathered wine and summer fruit in abundance.

13 Moreover Johanan the son of Kareah and all the captains of the forces that *were* in the fields came to Gedaliah at Mizpah, 14 and said to him, "Do you certainly know that Baalis the king of the Ammonites has sent Ishmael the son of Nethaniah to murder you?" But Gedaliah the son of Ahikam did not believe them.

15 Then Johanan the son of Kareah spoke secretly to Gedaliah in Mizpah, saying, "Let me go, please, and I will kill Ishmael the son of Nethaniah, and no one will know *it*. Why should he murder you, so that all the Jews who are gathered to you would be scattered, and the remnant in Judah perish?"

16 But Gedaliah the son of Ahikam said to Johanan the son of Kareah, "You shall not do this thing, for you speak falsely concerning Ishmael."

The governor is killed

41 Now it came to pass in the seventh month *that* Ishmael the son of Nethaniah, the son of Elishama, of the royal family and of the officers of the king, came with ten men to Gedaliah the son of Ahikam, at Mizpah. And there they ate bread together in Mizpah. 2 Then Ishmael the son of Nethaniah, and the ten men who were with him, arose and struck Gedaliah the son of Ahikam, the son of Shaphan, with the sword, and killed him whom the king of Babylon had made governor over the land. 3 Ishmael also struck down all the Jews who were with him, *that is,* with Gedaliah at Mizpah, and the Chaldeans who were found there, the men of war.

4 And it happened, on the second day after he had killed Gedaliah, when as yet no one knew *it,* 5 that certain men came from Shechem, from Shiloh, and from Samaria, eighty men with their beards shaved and their clothes torn, having cut themselves, with offerings and incense in their hand, to bring *them* to the house of the LORD. 6 Now Ishmael the son of Nethaniah went out from Mizpah to meet them, weeping as he went along; and it happened as he met them that he said to them, "Come to Gedaliah the son of Ahikam!" 7 So it was, when they came into the midst of the city, that Ishmael the son of Nethaniah killed them *and cast them* into the midst of a pit, he and the men who were with him. 8 But ten men were found among them who said to Ishmael, "Do not kill us, for we have treasures of wheat, barley, oil, and honey in the field." So he desisted and did not kill them among their brethren. 9 Now the pit into which Ishmael had cast all the dead bodies of the men whom he had slain, because of Gedaliah, *was* the same one Asa the king had made for fear of Baasha king of Israel. Ishmael the son of Nethaniah filled it with *the* slain. 10 Then Ishmael carried away captive all the rest of the people who *were* in Mizpah, the king's daughters and all the people who remained in Mizpah, whom Nebuzaradan the captain of the guard had committed to Gedaliah the son of Ahikam. And Ishmael the son of Nethaniah carried them away captive and departed to go over to the Ammonites.

11 But when Johanan the son of Kareah and all the captains of the forces that *were* with him heard of all the evil that Ishmael the son of Nethaniah had done, 12 they took all the men and went to fight with Ishmael the son of Nethaniah; and they found him by the great pool that *is* in Gibeon. 13 So it was, when all the people who *were* with Ishmael saw Johanan the son of Kareah, and all the captains of the forces who *were* with him, that they were glad. 14 Then all the people whom Ishmael had carried away cap-

The Plot Against Governor Gedaliah

The Babylon News-Press

tive from Mizpah turned around and came back, and went to Johanan the son of Kareah. 15 But Ishmael the son of Nethaniah escaped from Johanan with eight men and went to the Ammonites.

16 Then Johanan the son of Kareah, and all the captains of the forces that were with him, took from Mizpah all the rest of the people whom he had recovered from Ishmael the son of Nethaniah after he had murdered Gedaliah the son of Ahikam—the mighty men of war and the women and the children and the eunuchs, whom he had brought back from Gibeon. 17 And they departed and dwelt in the habitation of Chimham, which is near Bethlehem, as they went on their way to Egypt, 18 because of the Chaldeans; for they were afraid of them, because Ishmael the son of Nethaniah had murdered Gedaliah the son of Ahikam, whom the king of Babylon had made governor in the land.

No escape to Egypt

42 Now all the captains of the forces, Johanan the son of Kareah, Jezaniah the son of Hoshaiah, and all the people, from the least to the greatest, came near 2 and said to Jeremiah the prophet, "Please, let our petition be acceptable to you, and pray for us to the LORD your God, for all this remnant (since we are left but a few of many, as you can see), 3 that the LORD your God may show us the way in which we should walk and the thing we should do."

4 Then Jeremiah the prophet said to them, "I have heard. Indeed, I will pray to the LORD your God according to your words, and it shall be, that whatever the LORD answers you, I will declare it to you. I will keep nothing back from you."

5 So they said to Jeremiah, "Let the LORD be a true and faithful witness between us, if we do not do according to everything which the LORD your God sends us by you. 6 Whether it is pleasing or displeasing, we will obey the voice of the LORD our God to whom we send you, that it may be well with us when we obey the voice of the LORD our God."

7 And it happened after ten days that the word of the LORD came to Jeremiah. 8 Then he called Johanan the son of Kareah, all the captains of the forces which were with him, and all the people from the least even to the greatest, 9 and said to them, "Thus says the LORD, the God of Israel, to whom you sent me to present your petition before Him: 10 'If you will still remain in this land, then I will build you and not pull you down, and I will plant you and not pluck you up. For I relent concerning the disaster that I have brought upon you. 11 Do not be afraid of the king of Babylon, of whom you are afraid; do not be afraid of him,' says the LORD, 'for I am with you, to save you and deliver you from his hand. 12 And I will show you mercy, that he may have mercy on you and cause you to return to your own land.'

13 "But if you say, 'We will not dwell in this land,' disobeying the voice of the LORD your God, 14 saying, 'No, but we will go to the land of Egypt where we shall see no war, nor hear the sound of the trumpet, nor be hungry for bread, and there we will dwell'— 15 Then hear now the word of the LORD, O remnant of Judah! Thus says the LORD of hosts, the God of Israel: 'If you wholly set your faces to enter Egypt, and go to dwell there, 16 then it shall be that the sword which you feared shall overtake you there in the land of Egypt; the famine of which you were afraid shall follow close after you there in Egypt; and there you shall die. 17 So shall it be with all the men who set their faces to go to Egypt to dwell there. They shall die by the sword, by famine, and by pestilence. And none of them shall remain or escape from the disaster that I will bring upon them.'

18 "For thus says the LORD of hosts, the God of Israel: 'As My anger and My fury have been poured out on the inhabitants of Jerusalem, so will My

Gedaliah Murdered, Jeremiah Kidnapped

The Babylon News-Press

MIZPAH—Further grim reports from Judah, the land lately conquered by our armies, indicate that Governor Gedaliah has been murdered. Also, Jeremiah the prophet has been kidnapped in a plan to take many Jews to Egypt.

This journey to Egypt is expected to end unhappily. Egypt is the land where the people of Israel were slaves for many years. At that time God called Moses to lead the people back to the land of Canaan, now called Israel. Now the Jews have chosen to return to the very land where they were once slaves!

Reports indicate that the Lord has told Jeremiah the prophet that the people will die in Egypt.

---

fury be poured out on you when you enter Egypt. And you shall be an oath, an astonishment, a curse, and a reproach; and you shall see this place no more.'

19 "The LORD has said concerning you, O remnant of Judah, 'Do not go to Egypt!' Know certainly that I have admonished you this day. 20 For you were hypocrites in your hearts when you sent me to the LORD your God, saying, 'Pray for us to the LORD our God, and according to all that the LORD your God says, so declare to us and we will do it.' 21 And I have this day declared it to you, but you have not obeyed the voice of the LORD your God, or anything which He has sent you by me. 22 Now therefore, know certainly that you shall die by the sword, by famine, and by pestilence in the place where you desire to go to dwell."

Jeremiah prophesies in Egypt

43 Now it happened, when Jeremiah had stopped speaking to all the people all the words of the LORD their God, for which the LORD their God had sent him to them, all these words, 2 that Azariah the son of Hoshaiah, Johanan the son of Kareah, and all the proud men spoke, saying to Jeremiah, "You speak falsely! The LORD our God has not sent you to say, 'Do not go to Egypt to dwell there.' 3 But Baruch the son of Neriah has set you against us, to deliver us into the hand of the Chaldeans, that they may put us to death or carry us away captive to Babylon." 4 So Johanan the son of Kareah, all the captains of the forces, and all the people would not obey the voice of the LORD, to remain in the land of Judah. 5 But Johanan the son of Kareah and all the captains of the forces took all the remnant of Judah who had returned to dwell in the land of Judah, from all nations where they had been driven— 6 men, women, children, the king's daughters, and every person whom Nebuzaradan the captain of the guard had left with Gedaliah the son of Ahikam, the son of Shaphan, and Jeremiah the prophet and Baruch the son of Neriah. 7 So they went to the land of Egypt, for they did not obey the voice of the LORD. And they went as far as Tahpanhes.

8 Then the word of the LORD came to Jeremiah in Tahpanhes, saying, 9 "Take large stones in your hand, and hide them in the sight of the men of Judah, in the clay in the brick courtyard which is at the entrance to Pharaoh's house in Tahpanhes; 10 and say to them, 'Thus says the LORD of hosts, the God of Israel: "Behold, I will send and bring Nebuchadnezzar the king of Babylon, My servant, and will set his throne above these stones that I have hidden. And he will spread his royal pavilion over them. 11 When he comes, he shall strike the land of Egypt and deliver to death those appointed for

death, and to captivity *those appointed* for captivity, and to the sword *those appointed* for the sword. ¹² I will kindle a fire in the houses of the gods of Egypt, and he shall burn them and carry them away captive. And he shall array himself with the land of Egypt, as a shepherd puts on his garment, and he shall go out from there in peace. ¹³ He shall also break the sacred pillars of Beth Shemesh that *are* in the land of Egypt; and the houses of the gods of the Egyptians he shall burn with fire." '"

The people make God angry

44 The word that came to Jeremiah concerning all the Jews who dwell in the land of Egypt, who dwell at Migdol, at Tahpanhes, at Noph, and in the country of Pathros, saying, ² "Thus says the LORD of hosts, the God of Israel: 'You have seen all the calamity that I have brought on Jerusalem and on all the cities of Judah; and behold, this day they *are* a desolation, and no one dwells in them, ³ because of their wickedness which they have committed to provoke Me to anger, in that they went to burn incense *and* to serve other gods whom they did not know, they nor you nor your fathers. ⁴ However I have sent to you all My servants the prophets, rising early and sending *them,* saying, "Oh, do not do this abominable thing that I hate!" ⁵ But they did not listen or incline their ear to turn from their wickedness, to burn no incense to other gods. ⁶ So My fury and My anger were poured out and kindled in the cities of Judah and in the streets of Jerusalem; and they are wasted *and* desolate, as it is this day.'

⁷ "Now therefore, thus says the LORD, the God of hosts, the God of Israel: 'Why do you commit *this* great evil against yourselves, to cut off from you man and woman, child and infant, out of Judah, leaving none to remain, ⁸ in that you provoke Me to wrath with the works of your hands, burning incense to other gods in the land of Egypt where you have gone to dwell, that you may cut yourselves off and be a curse and a reproach among all the nations of the earth? ⁹ Have you forgotten the wickedness of your fathers, the wickedness of the kings of Judah, the wickedness of their wives, your own wickedness, and the wickedness of your wives, which they committed in the land of Judah and in the streets of Jerusalem? ¹⁰ They have not been humbled, to this day, nor have they feared; they have not walked in My law or in My statutes that I set before you and your fathers.'

¹¹ "Therefore thus says the LORD of hosts, the God of Israel: 'Behold, I will set My face against you for catastrophe and for cutting off all Judah. ¹² And I will take the remnant of Judah who have set their faces to go into the land of Egypt to dwell there, and they shall all be consumed *and* fall in the land of Egypt. They shall be consumed by the sword *and* by famine. They shall die, from the least to the greatest, by the sword and by famine; and they shall be an oath, an astonishment, a curse and a reproach! ¹³ For I will punish those who dwell in the land of Egypt, as I have punished Jerusalem, by the sword, by famine, and by pestilence, ¹⁴ so that none of the remnant of Judah who have gone into the land of Egypt to dwell there shall escape or survive, lest they return to the land of Judah, to which they desire to return and dwell. For none shall return except those who escape.' "

¹⁵ Then all the men who knew that their wives had burned incense to other gods, with all the women who stood by, a great multitude, and all the people who dwelt in the land of Egypt, in Pathros, answered Jeremiah, saying: ¹⁶ "*As for* the word that you have spoken to us in the name of the LORD, we will not listen to you! ¹⁷ But we will certainly do whatever has gone out of our own mouth, to burn incense to the queen of heaven and pour out drink offerings to her, as we have done, we and our fathers, our kings and our princes, in the cities of Judah and in

the streets of Jerusalem. For *then* we had plenty of food, were well-off, and saw no trouble. 18 But since we stopped burning incense to the queen of heaven and pouring out drink offerings to her, we have lacked everything and have been consumed by the sword and by famine."

19 *The women also said,* "And when we burned incense to the queen of heaven and poured out drink offerings to her, did we make cakes for her, to worship her, and pour out drink offerings to her without our husbands' *permission?*"

20 Then Jeremiah spoke to all the people—the men, the women, and all the people who had given him *that* answer—saying: 21 "The incense that you burned in the cities of Judah and in the streets of Jerusalem, you and your fathers, your kings and your princes, and the people of the land, did not the LORD remember them, and did it *not* come into His mind? 22 So the LORD could no longer bear *it,* because of the evil of your doings *and* because of the abominations which you committed. Therefore your land is a desolation, an astonishment, a curse, and without an inhabitant, as *it is* this day. 23 Because you have burned incense and because you have sinned against the LORD, and have not obeyed the voice of the LORD or walked in His law, in His statutes or in His testimonies, therefore this calamity has happened to you, as *at* this day."

24 Moreover Jeremiah said to all the people and to all the women, "Hear the word of the LORD, all Judah who *are* in the land of Egypt! 25 Thus says the LORD of hosts, the God of Israel, saying: 'You and your wives have spoken with your mouths and fulfilled with your hands, saying, "We will surely keep our vows that we have made, to burn incense to the queen of heaven and pour out drink offerings to her." You will surely keep your vows and perform your vows!' 26 Therefore hear the word of the LORD, all Judah who dwell in the land of Egypt: 'Behold, I

have sworn by My great name,' says the LORD, 'that My name shall no more be named in the mouth of any man of Judah in all the land of Egypt, saying, "The Lord GOD lives." 27 Behold, I will watch over them for adversity and not for good. And all the men of Judah who *are* in the land of Egypt shall be consumed by the sword and by famine, until there is an end to them. 28 Yet a small number who escape the sword shall return from the land of Egypt to the land of Judah; and all the remnant of Judah, who have gone to the land of Egypt to dwell there, shall know whose words will stand, Mine or theirs. 29 And this *shall be* a sign to you,' says the LORD, 'that I will punish you in this place, that you may know that My words will surely stand against you for adversity.'

30 "Thus says the LORD: 'Behold, I will give Pharaoh Hophra king of Egypt into the hand of his enemies and into the hand of those who seek his life, as I gave Zedekiah king of Judah into the hand of Nebuchadnezzar king of Babylon, his enemy who sought his life.'"

God's message to Baruch

45 The word that Jeremiah the prophet spoke to Baruch the son of Neriah, when he had written these words in a book at the instruction of Jeremiah, in the fourth year of Jehoiakim the son of Josiah, king of Judah, saying, 2 "Thus says the LORD, the God of Israel, to you, O Baruch: 3 'You said, "Woe is me now! For the LORD has added grief to my sorrow. I fainted in my sighing, and I find no rest."'

4 "Thus you shall say to him, 'Thus says the LORD: "Behold, what I have built I will break down, and what I have planted I will pluck up, that is, this whole land. 5 And do you seek great things for yourself? Do not seek *them;* for behold, I will bring adversity on all flesh," says the LORD. "But I will give your life to you as a prize in all places, wherever you go."'"

God's message to the Egyptians

46 The word of the LORD which came to Jeremiah the prophet against the nations. ²Against Egypt.

Concerning the army of Pharaoh Necho, king of Egypt, which was by the River Euphrates in Carchemish, and which Nebuchadnezzar king of Babylon defeated in the fourth year of Jehoiakim the son of Josiah, king of Judah:

3 "Order the buckler and shield,
   And draw near to battle!
4 Harness the horses,
   And mount up, you horsemen!
   Stand forth with *your* helmets,
   Polish the spears,
   Put on the armor!
5 Why have I seen them dismayed
   and turned back?
   Their mighty ones are beaten
       down;
   They have speedily fled,
   And did not look back,
   For fear was all around," says
       the LORD.
6 "Do not let the swift flee away,
   Nor the mighty man escape;
   They will stumble and fall
   Toward the north, by the River
       Euphrates.

7 "Who *is* this coming up like a
       flood,
   Whose waters move like the
       rivers?
8 Egypt rises up like a flood,
   And *its* waters move like the
       rivers;
   And he says, 'I will go up *and*
       cover the earth,
   I will destroy the city and its
       inhabitants.'
9 Come up, O horses, and rage,
       O chariots!
   And let the mighty men come
       forth:
   The Ethiopians and the Libyans
       who handle the shield,
   And the Lydians who handle
       and bend the bow.

10 For this *is* the day of the Lord
       GOD of hosts,
   A day of vengeance,
   That He may avenge Himself on
       His adversaries.
   The sword shall devour;
   It shall be satiated and made
       drunk with their blood;
   For the Lord GOD of hosts has
       a sacrifice
   In the north country by the River
       Euphrates.

11 "Go up to Gilead and take balm,
       O virgin, the daughter of Egypt;
   In vain you will use many
       medicines;
   You shall not be cured.
12 The nations have heard of your
       shame,
   And your cry has filled the
       land;
   For the mighty man has
       stumbled against the mighty;
   They both have fallen together."

13 The word that the LORD spoke to Jeremiah the prophet, how Nebuchadnezzar king of Babylon would come *and* strike the land of Egypt.

14 "Declare in Egypt, and proclaim
       in Migdol;
   Proclaim in Noph and in
       Tahpanhes;
   Say, 'Stand fast and prepare
       yourselves,
   For the sword devours all
       around you.'
15 Why are your valiant *men* swept
       away?
   They did not stand
   Because the LORD drove them
       away.
16 He made many fall;
   Yes, one fell upon another.
   And they said, 'Arise!
   Let us go back to our own
       people
   And to the land of our nativity
   From the oppressing sword.'
17 They cried there,
   'Pharaoh, king of Egypt, *is but* a
       noise.

He has passed by the appointed time!'

18 "As I live," says the King,
Whose name *is* the LORD of hosts,
"Surely as Tabor *is* among the mountains
And as Carmel by the sea, *so* he shall come.

19 O you daughter dwelling in Egypt,
Prepare yourself to go into captivity!
For Noph shall be waste and desolate, without inhabitant.

20 "Egypt *is* a very pretty heifer,
But destruction comes, it comes from the north.

21 Also her mercenaries are in her midst like fat bulls,
For they also are turned back,
They have fled away together.
They did not stand,

For the day of their calamity had come upon them,
The time of their punishment.

22 Her noise shall go like a serpent,
For they shall march with an army
And come against her with axes,
Like those who chop wood.

23 "They shall cut down her forest," says the LORD,
"Though it cannot be searched,
Because they *are* innumerable,
And more numerous than grasshoppers.

24 The daughter of Egypt shall be ashamed;
She shall be delivered into the hand
Of the people of the north."

25 The LORD of hosts, the God of Israel, says: "Behold, I will bring punishment on Amon of No, and Pharaoh and Egypt, with their gods and their kings—Pharaoh and those who trust

Seti I offers sacrifices to Ra, a false god.

in him. 26 And I will deliver them into the hand of those who seek their lives, into the hand of Nebuchadnezzar king of Babylon and the hand of his servants. Afterward it shall be inhabited as in the days of old," says the LORD.

27 "But do not fear, O My servant
  Jacob,
  And do not be dismayed, O
    Israel!
  For behold, I will save you from
    afar,
  And your offspring from the land
    of their captivity;
  Jacob shall return, have rest and
    be at ease;
  No one shall make *him* afraid.
28 Do not fear, O Jacob My
    servant," says the LORD,
  "For I *am* with you;
  For I will make a complete end
    of all the nations
  To which I have driven you,
  But I will not make a complete
    end of you.
  I will rightly correct you,
  For I will not leave you wholly
    unpunished."

God's message to the Philistines

47 The word of the LORD that came to Jeremiah the prophet against the Philistines, before Pharaoh attacked Gaza.
2 Thus says the LORD:

  "Behold, waters rise out of the
    north,
  And shall be an overflowing
    flood;
  They shall overflow the land and
    all that is in it,
  The city and those who dwell
    within;
  Then the men shall cry,
  And all the inhabitants of the
    land shall wail.
3 At the noise of the stamping
    hooves of his strong horses,
  At the rushing of his chariots,
  At the rumbling of his wheels,

  The fathers will not look back
    for *their* children,
  Lacking courage,
4 Because of the day that comes
    to plunder all the Philistines,
  To cut off from Tyre and Sidon
    every helper who remains;
  For the LORD shall plunder the
    Philistines,
  The remnant of the country of
    Caphtor.
5 Baldness has come upon Gaza,
  Ashkelon is cut off
  With the remnant of their valley.
  How long will you cut yourself?

6 "O you sword of the LORD,
  How long until you are quiet?
  Put yourself up into your
    scabbard,
  Rest and be still!
7 How can it be quiet,
  Seeing the LORD has given it a
    charge
  Against Ashkelon and against
    the seashore?
  There He has appointed it."

God's message to the Moabites

48 Against Moab.
Thus says the LORD of hosts, the God of Israel:

  "Woe to Nebo!
  For it is plundered,
  Kirjathaim is shamed *and* taken;
  The high stronghold is shamed
    and dismayed—
2 No more praise of Moab.
  In Heshbon they have devised
    evil against her:
  'Come, and let us cut her off as
    a nation.'
  You also shall be cut down, O
    Madmen!
  The sword shall pursue you;
3 A voice of crying *shall be* from
    Horonaim:
  'Plundering and great
    destruction!'

4 "Moab is destroyed;
  Her little ones have caused a cry
    to be heard;

5 For in the Ascent of Luhith they
    ascend with continual
    weeping;
For in the descent of Horonaim
    the enemies have heard a cry
    of destruction.

6 "Flee, save your lives!
    And be like the juniper in the
    wilderness.
7 For because you have trusted in
    your works and your
    treasures,
You also shall be taken.
And Chemosh shall go forth into
    captivity,
His priests and his princes
    together.
8 And the plunderer shall come
    against every city;
No one shall escape.
The valley also shall perish,
And the plain shall be destroyed,
As the LORD has spoken.

9 "Give wings to Moab,
    That she may flee and get away;
For her cities shall be desolate,
    Without any to dwell in them.
10 Cursed is he who does the work
    of the LORD deceitfully,
And cursed is he who keeps
    back his sword from blood.

11 "Moab has been at ease from his
    youth;
He has settled on his dregs,
And has not been emptied from
    vessel to vessel,
Nor has he gone into captivity.
Therefore his taste remained in
    him,
And his scent has not changed.

12 "Therefore behold, the days are
    coming," says the LORD,
"That I shall send him
    wine-workers
Who will tip him over
And empty his vessels
And break the bottles.
13 Moab shall be ashamed of
    Chemosh,
As the house of Israel was

ashamed of Bethel, their
    confidence.

14 "How can you say, 'We are
    mighty
And strong men for the war'?
15 Moab is plundered and gone up
    from her cities;
Her chosen young men have
    gone down to the slaughter,"
says the King,
Whose name is the LORD of
    hosts.

16 "The calamity of Moab is near at
    hand,
And his affliction comes quickly.
17 Bemoan him, all you who are
    around him;
And all you who know his name,
Say, 'How the strong staff is
    broken,
The beautiful rod!'

18 "O daughter inhabiting Dibon,
Come down from your glory,
And sit in thirst;
For the plunderer of Moab has
    come against you,
He has destroyed your
    strongholds.
19 O inhabitant of Aroer,
Stand by the way and watch;
Ask him who flees
And her who escapes;
Say, 'What has happened?'
20 Moab is shamed, for he is
    broken down.
Wail and cry!
Tell it in Arnon, that Moab is
    plundered.

21 "And judgment has come on the
    plain country:
On Holon and Jahzah and
    Mephaath,
22 On Dibon and Nebo and Beth
    Diblathaim,
23 On Kirjathaim and Beth Gamul
    and Beth Meon,
24 On Kerioth and Bozrah,
On all the cities of the land of
    Moab,
Far or near.

25 The horn of Moab is cut off,
And his arm is broken," says the
LORD.

26 "Make him drunk,
Because he exalted *himself*
against the LORD.
Moab shall wallow in his vomit,
And he shall also be in derision.
27 For was not Israel a derision to
you?
Was he found among thieves?
For whenever you speak of him,
You shake *your head in scorn.*
28 You who dwell in Moab,
Leave the cities and dwell in the
rock,
And be like the dove *which*
makes her nest
In the sides of the cave's mouth.

29 "We have heard the pride of
Moab
(He *is* exceedingly proud),
Of his loftiness and arrogance
and pride,
And of the haughtiness of his
heart."

30 "I know his wrath," says the
LORD,
"But it *is* not right;
His lies have made nothing right.
31 Therefore I will wail for Moab,
And I will cry out for all Moab;
I will mourn for the men of Kir
Heres.
32 O vine of Sibmah! I will weep
for you with the weeping of
Jazer.
Your plants have gone over the
sea,
They reach to the sea of Jazer.
The plunderer has fallen on your
summer fruit and your
vintage.
33 Joy and gladness are taken
From the plentiful field
And from the land of Moab;
I have caused wine to fail from
the winepresses;
No one will tread with joyous
shouting—
Not joyous shouting!

34 "From the cry of Heshbon to
Elealeh and to Jahaz
They have uttered their voice,
From Zoar to Horonaim,
Like a three-year-old heifer;
For the waters of Nimrim also
shall be desolate.

35 "Moreover," says the LORD,
"I will cause to cease in Moab
The one who offers *sacrifices* in
the high places
And burns incense to his gods.
36 Therefore My heart shall wail
like flutes for Moab,
And like flutes My heart shall
wail
For the men of Kir Heres.
Therefore the riches they have
acquired have perished.

37 "For every head *shall be* bald,
and every beard clipped;
On all the hands *shall be* cuts,
and on the loins sackcloth—
38 A general lamentation
On all the housetops of Moab,
And in its streets;
For I have broken Moab like a
vessel in which *is* no
pleasure," says the LORD.
39 "They shall wail:
'How she is broken down!
How Moab has turned her back
with shame!'
So Moab shall be a derision
And a dismay to all those about
her."

40 For thus says the LORD:

"Behold, one shall fly like an
eagle,
And spread his wings over
Moab.
41 Kerioth is taken,
And the strongholds are
surprised;
The mighty men's hearts in
Moab on that day shall be
Like the heart of a woman in
birth pangs.
42 And Moab shall be destroyed as
a people,

Because he exalted *himself*
against the LORD.

43 Fear and the pit and the snare
shall be upon you,
O inhabitant of Moab," says the
LORD.

44 "He who flees from the fear shall
fall into the pit,
And he who gets out of the pit
shall be caught in the snare.
For upon Moab, upon it I will
bring
The year of their punishment,"
says the LORD.

45 "Those who fled stood under the
shadow of Heshbon
Because of exhaustion.
But a fire shall come out of
Heshbon,
A flame from the midst of Sihon,
And shall devour the brow of
Moab,
The crown of the head of the
sons of tumult.

46 Woe to you, O Moab!
The people of Chemosh perish;
For your sons have been taken
captive,
And your daughters captive.

47 "Yet I will bring back the captives
of Moab
In the latter days," says the
LORD.

Thus far *is* the judgment of Moab.

God's message to the Ammonites

49 Against the Ammonites.
Thus says the LORD:

"Has Israel no sons?
Has he no heir?
Why *then* does Milcom inherit
Gad,
And his people dwell in its
cities?

2 Therefore behold, the days are
coming," says the LORD,
"That I will cause to be heard an
alarm of war
In Rabbah of the Ammonites;

What Is a Tell?

We usually think of the word *tell* as a verb meaning to speak, but *tell* can also be a noun. The noun *tell* means a hill or mound formed by ruined cities over hundreds of years. Many cities grew up and were destroyed on the same spot to form a tell.

It shall be a desolate mound,
And her villages shall be burned
with fire.
Then Israel shall take possession
of his inheritance," says the
LORD.

3 "Wail, O Heshbon, for Ai is
plundered!
Cry, you daughters of Rabbah,
Gird yourselves with sackcloth!
Lament and run to and fro by
the walls;
For Milcom shall go into captivity
With his priests and his princes
together.

4 Why do you boast in the valleys,
Your flowing valley, O
backsliding daughter?
Who trusted in her treasures,
saying,
'Who will come against me?'

5 Behold, I will bring fear upon
you,"
Says the Lord GOD of hosts,
"From all those who are around
you;
You shall be driven out,
everyone headlong,
And no one will gather those
who wander off.

6 But afterward I will bring back
The captives of the people of
Ammon," says the LORD.

7 Against Edom.
Thus says the LORD of hosts:

"*Is* wisdom no more in Teman?
Has counsel perished from the
prudent?
Has their wisdom vanished?

8 Flee, turn back, dwell in the

depths, O inhabitants of
   Dedan!
For I will bring the calamity of
   Esau upon him,
The time *that* I will punish him.
9 If grape gatherers came to
      you,
   Would they not leave *some*
      gleaning grapes?
   If thieves by night,
   Would they not destroy until
      they have enough?
10 But I have made Esau bare;
   I have uncovered his *secret*
      places,
   And he shall not be able to hide
      himself.
   His descendants are plundered,
   His brethren and his neighbors,
   And he *is* no more.
11 Leave your fatherless children,
   I will preserve *them* alive;
   And let your widows trust in
      Me."

12 For thus says the LORD: "Behold,
those whose judgment *was* not to drink
of the cup have assuredly drunk. And
are you the one who will altogether
go unpunished? You shall not go unpunished, but you shall surely drink *of
it.* 13 For I have sworn by Myself," says
the LORD, "that Bozrah shall become
a desolation, a reproach, a waste, and
a curse. And all its cities shall be perpetual wastes."

14 I have heard a message from the
      LORD,
   And an ambassador has been
      sent to the nations:
   "Gather together, come against
      her,
   And rise up to battle!

15 "For indeed, I will make you small
      among nations,
   Despised among men.
16 Your fierceness has deceived
      you,
   The pride of your heart,
   O you who dwell in the clefts
      of the rock,
   Who hold the height of the hill!

Though you make your nest as
   high as the eagle,
I will bring you down from
   there," says the LORD.

17 "Edom also shall be an
      astonishment;
   Everyone who goes by it will be
      astonished
   And will hiss at all its plagues.
18 As in the overthrow of Sodom
      and Gomorrah
   And their neighbors," says the
      LORD,
   "No one shall remain there,
   Nor shall a son of man dwell in
      it.

19 "Behold, he shall come up like a
      lion from the floodplain of the
      Jordan
   Against the dwelling place of the
      strong;
   But I will suddenly make him run
      away from her.
   And who *is* a chosen *man that*
      I may appoint over her?
   For who *is* like Me?
   Who will arraign Me?
   And who *is* that shepherd
   Who will withstand Me?"

20 Therefore hear the counsel of
      the LORD that He has taken
      against Edom,
   And His purposes that He has
      proposed against the
      inhabitants of Teman:
   Surely the least of the flock shall
      draw them out;
   Surely He shall make their
      dwelling places desolate with
      them.
21 The earth shakes at the noise of
      their fall;
   At the cry its noise is heard at
      the Red Sea.
22 Behold, He shall come up and
      fly like the eagle,
   And spread His wings over
      Bozrah;
   The heart of the mighty men of
      Edom in that day shall be

Like the heart of a woman in
    birth pangs.

23 Against Damascus.

"Hamath and Arpad are shamed,
For they have heard bad news.
They are fainthearted;
There is trouble on the sea;
It cannot be quiet.
24 Damascus has grown feeble;
    She turns to flee,
And fear has seized *her*.
Anguish and sorrows have
    taken her like a woman in
    labor.
25 Why is the city of praise not
    deserted, the city of My joy?
26 Therefore her young men shall
    fall in her streets,
And all the men of war shall be
    cut off in that day," says the
    LORD of hosts.
27 "I will kindle a fire in the wall of
    Damascus,
And it shall consume the palaces
    of Ben-Hadad."

28 Against Kedar and against the
kingdoms of Hazor, which Nebuchadnezzar king of Babylon shall strike.
Thus says the LORD:

"Arise, go up to Kedar,
And devastate the men of the
    East!
29 Their tents and their flocks they
    shall take away.
They shall take for themselves
    their curtains,
All their vessels and their camels;
And they shall cry out to them,
'Fear *is* on every side!'

30 "Flee, get far away! Dwell in the
    depths,
O inhabitants of Hazor!" says
    the LORD.
"For Nebuchadnezzar king of
    Babylon has taken counsel
    against you,
And has conceived a plan
    against you.

31 "Arise, go up to the wealthy
    nation that dwells securely,"
    says the LORD,
"Which has neither gates nor
    bars,
Dwelling alone.
32 Their camels shall be for booty,
And the multitude of their cattle
    for plunder.
I will scatter to all winds those
    in the farthest corners,
And I will bring their calamity
    from all its sides," says the
    LORD.
33 "Hazor shall be a dwelling for
    jackals, a desolation forever;
No one shall reside there,
Nor son of man dwell in it."

34 The word of the LORD that came
to Jeremiah the prophet against Elam,
in the beginning of the reign of Zedekiah king of Judah, saying, 35 "Thus
says the LORD of hosts:

'Behold, I will break the bow of
    Elam,
The foremost of their might.
36 Against Elam I will bring the four
    winds
From the four quarters of
    heaven,
And scatter them toward all
    those winds;
There shall be no nations where
    the outcasts of Elam will not
    go.
37 For I will cause Elam to be
    dismayed before their
    enemies
And before those who seek their
    life.
I will bring disaster upon them,
My fierce anger,' says the LORD;
'And I will send the sword after
    them
Until I have consumed them.
38 I will set My throne in Elam,
And will destroy from there the
    king and the princes,' says the
    LORD.

39 'But it shall come to pass in the
    latter days:

I will bring back the captives of Elam,' says the LORD."

God's message to the Babylonians

50 The word that the LORD spoke against Babylon *and* against the land of the Chaldeans by Jeremiah the prophet.

2 "Declare among the nations,
  Proclaim, and set up a standard;
  Proclaim—do not conceal *it*—
  Say, 'Babylon is taken, Bel is shamed.
  Merodach is broken in pieces;
  Her idols are humiliated,
  Her images are broken in pieces.'
3 For out of the north a nation comes up against her,
  Which shall make her land desolate,
  And no one shall dwell therein.
  They shall move, they shall depart,
  Both man and beast.

4 "In those days and in that time," says the LORD,
  "The children of Israel shall come,
  They and the children of Judah together;
  With continual weeping they shall come,
  And seek the LORD their God.
5 They shall ask the way to Zion,
  With their faces toward it,
    saying,
  'Come and let us join ourselves to the LORD
  In a perpetual covenant
  That will not be forgotten.'

6 "My people have been lost sheep.
  Their shepherds have led them astray;
  They have turned them away *on* the mountains.
  They have gone from mountain to hill;
  They have forgotten their resting place.

7 All who found them have devoured them;
  And their adversaries said, 'We have not offended,
  Because they have sinned against the LORD, the habitation of justice,
  The LORD, the hope of their fathers.'

8 "Move from the midst of Babylon,
  Go out of the land of the Chaldeans;
  And be like the rams before the flocks.
9 For behold, I will raise and cause to come up against Babylon
  An assembly of great nations from the north country,
  And they shall array themselves against her;
  From there she shall be captured.
  Their arrows *shall be* like *those* of an expert warrior;
  None shall return in vain.
10 And Chaldea shall become plunder;
  All who plunder her shall be satisfied," says the LORD.

11 "Because you were glad, because you rejoiced,
  You destroyers of My heritage,
  Because you have grown fat like a heifer threshing grain,
  And you bellow like bulls,
12 Your mother shall be deeply ashamed;
  She who bore you shall be ashamed.
  Behold, the least of the nations *shall be* a wilderness,
  A dry land and a desert.
13 Because of the wrath of the LORD
  She shall not be inhabited,
  But she shall be wholly desolate.
  Everyone who goes by Babylon shall be horrified
  And hiss at all her plagues.

14 "Put yourselves in array against
    Babylon all around,
All you who bend the bow;
Shoot at her, spare no arrows,
For she has sinned against the
    LORD.
15 Shout against her all around;
She has given her hand,
Her foundations have fallen,
Her walls are thrown down;
For it is the vengeance of the
    LORD.
Take vengeance on her.
As she has done, so do to her.
16 Cut off the sower from Babylon,
And him who handles the sickle
    at harvest time.
For fear of the oppressing
    sword
Everyone shall turn to his own
    people,
And everyone shall flee to his
    own land.

17 "Israel is like scattered sheep;
The lions have driven him away.
First the king of Assyria
    devoured him;
Now at last this Nebuchadnezzar
    king of Babylon has broken
    his bones."

18 Therefore thus says the LORD of
hosts, the God of Israel:

"Behold, I will punish the king of
    Babylon and his land,
As I have punished the king of
    Assyria.
19 But I will bring back Israel to his
    home,
And he shall feed on Carmel and
    Bashan;
His soul shall be satisfied on
    Mount Ephraim and Gilead.
20 In those days and in that time,"
    says the LORD,
"The iniquity of Israel shall be
    sought, but there shall be
    none;
And the sins of Judah, but they
    shall not be found;
For I will pardon those whom I
    preserve.

21 "Go up against the land of
    Merathaim, against it,
And against the inhabitants of
    Pekod.
Waste and utterly destroy
    them," says the LORD,
"And do according to all that I
    have commanded you.
22 A sound of battle is in the land,
And of great destruction.
23 How the hammer of the whole
    earth has been cut apart and
    broken!
How Babylon has become a
    desolation among the nations!
I have laid a snare for you;
24 You have indeed been trapped,
    O Babylon,
And you were not aware;
You have been found and also
    caught,
Because you have contended
    against the LORD.
25 The LORD has opened His
    armory,
And has brought out the
    weapons of His indignation;
For this is the work of the Lord
    GOD of hosts
In the land of the Chaldeans.
26 Come against her from the
    farthest border;
Open her storehouses;
Cast her up as heaps of ruins,
And destroy her utterly;
Let nothing of her be left.
27 Slay all her bulls,
Let them go down to the
    slaughter.
Woe to them!
For their day has come, the time
    of their punishment.
28 The voice of those who flee and
    escape from the land of
    Babylon
Declares in Zion the vengeance
    of the LORD our God,
The vengeance of His temple.

29 "Call together the archers against
    Babylon.
All you who bend the bow,
    encamp against it all around;
Let none of them escape.

Repay her according to her
work;
According to all she has done,
do to her;
For she has been proud against
the LORD,
Against the Holy One of Israel.
30 Therefore her young men shall
fall in the streets,
And all her men of war shall be
cut off in that day," says the
LORD.
31 "Behold, I am against you,
O most haughty one!" says the
Lord GOD of hosts;
"For your day has come,
The time that I will punish you.
32 The most proud shall stumble
and fall,
And no one will raise him up;
I will kindle a fire in his cities,
And it will devour all around
him."

33 Thus says the LORD of hosts:

"The children of Israel were
oppressed,
Along with the children of
Judah;
All who took them captive have
held them fast;
They have refused to let them
go.
34 Their Redeemer is strong;
The LORD of hosts is His
name.
He will thoroughly plead their
case,
That He may give rest to the
land,
And disquiet the inhabitants of
Babylon.

35 "A sword is against the
Chaldeans," says the LORD,
"Against the inhabitants of
Babylon,
And against her princes and her
wise men.
36 A sword is against the
soothsayers, and they will be
fools.
A sword is against her mighty

men, and they will be
dismayed.
37 A sword is against their horses,
Against their chariots,
And against all the mixed
peoples who are in her midst;
And they will become like
women.
A sword is against her treasures,
and they will be robbed.
38 A drought is against her waters,
and they will be dried up.
For it is the land of carved
images,
And they are insane with their
idols.

39 "Therefore the wild desert beasts
shall dwell there with the
jackals,
And the ostriches shall dwell in
it.
It shall be inhabited no more
forever,
Nor shall it be dwelt in from
generation to generation.
40 As God overthrew Sodom and
Gomorrah
And their neighbors," says the
LORD,
"So no one shall reside there,
Nor son of man dwell in it.

41 "Behold, a people shall come
from the north,
And a great nation and many
kings
Shall be raised up from the ends
of the earth.
42 They shall hold the bow and the
lance;
They are cruel and shall not
show mercy.
Their voice shall roar like the
sea;
They shall ride on horses,
Set in array, like a man for the
battle,
Against you, O daughter of
Babylon.

43 "The king of Babylon has heard
the report about them,
And his hands grow feeble;

Anguish has taken hold of him,
Pangs as of a woman in
childbirth.

44 "Behold, he shall come up like a
lion from the floodplain of the
Jordan
Against the dwelling place of the
strong;
But I will make them suddenly
run away from her.
And who is a chosen man that
I may appoint over her?
For who is like Me?
Who will arraign Me?
And who is that shepherd
Who will withstand Me?"

45 Therefore hear the counsel of
the LORD that He has taken
against Babylon,
And His purposes that He has
proposed against the land of
the Chaldeans:
Surely the least of the flock shall
draw them out;
Surely He will make their
dwelling place desolate with
them.
46 At the noise of the taking of
Babylon
The earth trembles,
And the cry is heard among the
nations.

Babylon, God's battle-ax, will be broken

51 Thus says the LORD:

"Behold, I will raise up against
Babylon,
Against those who dwell in Leb
Kamai,
A destroying wind.
2 And I will send winnowers to
Babylon,
Who shall winnow her and
empty her land.
For in the day of doom
They shall be against her all
around.
3 Against her let the archer bend
his bow,

And lift himself up against her
in his armor.
Do not spare her young men;
Utterly destroy all her army.
4 Thus the slain shall fall in the
land of the Chaldeans,
And those thrust through in her
streets.
5 For Israel is not forsaken, nor
Judah,
By his God, the LORD of hosts,
Though their land was filled with
sin against the Holy One of
Israel."

6 Flee from the midst of Babylon,
And every one save his life!
Do not be cut off in her iniquity,
For this is the time of the LORD's
vengeance;
He shall recompense her.
7 Babylon was a golden cup in the
LORD's hand,
That made all the earth drunk.
The nations drank her wine;
Therefore the nations are
deranged.
8 Babylon has suddenly fallen and
been destroyed.
Wail for her!
Take balm for her pain;
Perhaps she may be healed.
9 We would have healed Babylon,
But she is not healed.
Forsake her, and let us go
everyone to his own country;
For her judgment reaches to
heaven and is lifted up to the
skies.
10 The LORD has revealed our
righteousness.
Come and let us declare in Zion
the work of the LORD our
God.

11 Make the arrows bright!
Gather the shields!
The LORD has raised up the spirit
of the kings of the Medes.
For His plan is against Babylon
to destroy it,
Because it is the vengeance of
the LORD,

The vengeance for His temple.
12 Set up the standard on the walls
of Babylon;
Make the guard strong,
Set up the watchmen,
Prepare the ambushes.
For the LORD has both devised
and done
What He spoke against the
inhabitants of Babylon.
13 O you who dwell by many
waters,
Abundant in treasures,
Your end has come,
The measure of your
covetousness.
14 The LORD of hosts has sworn by
Himself:
"Surely I will fill you with men,
as with locusts,
And they shall lift up a shout
against you."

15 He has made the earth by His
power;
He has established the world by
His wisdom,
And stretched out the heaven by
His understanding.
16 When He utters *His* voice—
There is a multitude of waters
in the heavens:
"He causes the vapors to ascend
from the ends of the earth;
He makes lightnings for the rain;
He brings the wind out of His
treasuries."

17 Everyone is dull-hearted,
without knowledge;
Every metalsmith is put to
shame by the carved image;
For his molded image *is*
falsehood,
And *there is* no breath in them.
18 They *are* futile, a work of errors;
In the time of their punishment
they shall perish.
19 The Portion of Jacob *is* not like
them,
For He *is* the Maker of all things;
And *Israel is* the tribe of His
inheritance.
The LORD of hosts *is* His name.

20 "You *are* My battle-ax *and*
weapons of war:
For with you I will break the
nation in pieces;
With you I will destroy
kingdoms;
21 With you I will break in pieces
the horse and its rider;
With you I will break in pieces
the chariot and its rider;
22 With you also I will break in
pieces man and woman;
With you I will break in pieces
old and young;
With you I will break in pieces
the young man and the
maiden;
23 With you also I will break in
pieces the shepherd and his
flock;
With you I will break in pieces
the farmer and his yoke of
oxen;
And with you I will break in
pieces governors and rulers.

24 "And I will repay Babylon
And all the inhabitants of
Chaldea
For all the evil they have done
In Zion in your sight," says the
LORD.

25 "Behold, I *am* against you, O
destroying mountain,
Who destroys all the earth," says
the LORD.
"And I will stretch out My hand
against you,
Roll you down from the rocks,
And make you a burnt
mountain.
26 They shall not take from you a
stone for a corner
Nor a stone for a foundation,
But you shall be desolate
forever," says the LORD.

27 Set up a banner in the land,
Blow the trumpet among the
nations!
Prepare the nations against her,
Call the kingdoms together
against her:

Ararat, Minni, and Ashkenaz.
Appoint a general against her;
Cause the horses to come up
   like the bristling locusts.
28 Prepare against her the nations,
With the kings of the Medes,
Its governors and all its rulers,
All the land of his dominion.
29 And the land will tremble and
   sorrow;
For every purpose of the LORD
   shall be performed against
   Babylon,
To make the land of Babylon a
   desolation without inhabitant.
30 The mighty men of Babylon
   have ceased fighting,
They have remained in their
   strongholds;
Their might has failed,
They became *like* women;
They have burned her dwelling
   places,
The bars of her *gate* are broken.
31 One runner will run to meet
   another,
And one messenger to meet
   another,
To show the king of Babylon
   that his city is taken on *all*
   sides;
32 The passages are blocked,
The reeds they have burned
   with fire,
And the men of war are terrified.

33 For thus says the LORD of hosts,
the God of Israel:

   "The daughter of Babylon *is* like
      a threshing floor
   When it is time to thresh her;
   Yet a little while
   And the time of her harvest will
      come."

34 "Nebuchadnezzar the king of
      Babylon
   Has devoured me, he has
      crushed me;
   He has made me an empty
      vessel,
   He has swallowed me up like a
      monster;

He has filled his stomach with
   my delicacies,
He has spit me out.
35 Let the violence *done* to me
   and my flesh *be* upon
   Babylon,"
The inhabitant of Zion will say;
"And my blood be upon the
   inhabitants of Chaldea!"
Jerusalem will say.

36 Therefore thus says the LORD:

   "Behold, I will plead your case
      and take vengeance for you.
   I will dry up her sea and make
      her springs dry.
37 Babylon shall become a heap,
   A dwelling place for jackals,
   An astonishment and a hissing,
   Without an inhabitant.
38 They shall roar together like
      lions,
   They shall growl like lions'
      whelps.
39 In their excitement I will prepare
      their feasts;
   I will make them drunk,
   That they may rejoice,
   And sleep a perpetual sleep
   And not awake," says the LORD.
40 "I will bring them down
   Like lambs to the slaughter,
   Like rams with male goats.

41 "Oh, how Sheshach is taken!
   Oh, how the praise of the whole
      earth is seized!
   How Babylon has become
      desolate among the nations!
42 The sea has come up over
      Babylon;
   She is covered with the
      multitude of its waves.
43 Her cities are a desolation,
   A dry land and a wilderness,
   A land where no one dwells,
   Through which no son of man
      passes.
44 I will punish Bel in Babylon,
   And I will bring out of his mouth
      what he has swallowed;
   And the nations shall not stream
      to him anymore.

Will Babylon Be Destroyed?

The Babylon News-Press

MIZPAH—Jeremiah the prophet has recently published a poem describing a future conquest of Babylon.

Jeremiah's poem tells of the suffering of his people caused by Babylon's invasion of Judah: "Nebuchadnezzar the king of Babylon has devoured me, he has crushed me; he has made me an empty vessel, he has swallowed me up like a monster" (verse 34).

The poem is a great work of word pictures that point out the sufferings of the Jews and God's coming punishment of our own nation of Babylonia (pronounced *bab-ih-LOW-nih-uh*). The Lord God of Israel is described as Babylonia's great Conqueror.

At that time, writes Jeremiah, the people of Israel will be freed to return to their own land.

(Your history books will tell you what happened to Babylonia and how God kept His promise to the Jews.)

Yes, the wall of Babylon shall
    fall.

45 "My people, go out of the midst
        of her!
    And let everyone deliver himself
        from the fierce anger of the
        LORD.
46 And lest your heart faint,
    And you fear for the rumor that
        will be heard in the land
    (A rumor will come *one* year,
    And after that, in *another* year

    A rumor *will come,*
    And violence in the land,
    Ruler against ruler),
47 Therefore behold, the days are
        coming
    That I will bring judgment on the
        carved images of Babylon;
    Her whole land shall be
        ashamed,
    And all her slain shall fall in her
        midst.
48 Then the heavens and the earth
        and all that *is* in them

Babylon was once one of the leading cities of the world.

Shall sing joyously over
    Babylon;
For the plunderers shall come to
    her from the north," says the
    LORD.

49 As Babylon *has caused* the slain
    of Israel to fall,
    So at Babylon the slain of all the
    earth shall fall.
50 You who have escaped the
    sword,
    Get away! Do not stand still!
    Remember the LORD afar off,
    And let Jerusalem come to your
    mind.

51 We are ashamed because *we*
    have heard reproach.
    Shame has covered our faces,
    For strangers have come into the
    sanctuaries of the LORD's
    house.

52 "Therefore behold, the days are
    coming," says the LORD,
    "That I will bring judgment on her
    carved images,
    And throughout all her land the
    wounded shall groan.
53 Though Babylon *were* to mount
    up to heaven,
    And though she *were* to fortify
    the height of her strength,
    Yet from Me plunderers would
    come to her," says the
    LORD.

54 The sound of a cry *comes* from
    Babylon,
    And great destruction from the
    land of the Chaldeans,
55 Because the LORD is plundering
    Babylon
    And silencing her loud voice,
    Though her waves roar like great
    waters,
    And the noise of their voice is
    uttered,
56 Because the plunderer comes
    against her, against Babylon,
    And her mighty men are taken.
    Every one of their bows is
    broken;

For the LORD *is* the God of
    recompense,
    He will surely repay.

57 "And I will make drunk
    Her princes and wise men,
    Her governors, her deputies,
    and her mighty men.
    And they shall sleep a perpetual
    sleep
    And not awake," says the King,
    Whose name *is* the LORD of
    hosts.

58 Thus says the LORD of hosts:

    "The broad walls of Babylon shall
    be utterly broken,
    And her high gates shall be
    burned with fire;
    The people will labor in vain,
    And the nations, because of the
    fire;
    And they shall be weary."

59 The word which Jeremiah the prophet commanded Seraiah the son of Neriah, the son of Mahseiah, when he went with Zedekiah the king of Judah to Babylon in the fourth year of his reign. And Seraiah *was* the quartermaster. 60 So Jeremiah wrote in a book all the evil that would come upon Babylon, all these words that are written against Babylon. 61 And Jeremiah said to Seraiah, "When you arrive in Babylon and see it, and read all these words, 62 then you shall say, 'O LORD, You have spoken against this place to cut it off, so that none shall remain in it, neither man nor beast, but it shall be desolate forever.' 63 Now it shall be, when you have finished reading this book, *that* you shall tie a stone to it and throw it out into the Euphrates. 64 Then you shall say, 'Thus Babylon shall sink and not rise from the catastrophe that I will bring upon her. And they shall be weary.'"

Thus far *are* the words of Jeremiah.

Looking back

52 Zedekiah *was* twenty-one years old when he became king, and he

reigned eleven years in Jerusalem. His mother's name *was* Hamutal the daughter of Jeremiah of Libnah. ² He also did evil in the sight of the LORD, according to all that Jehoiakim had done. ³ For because of the anger of the LORD *this* happened in Jerusalem and Judah, till He finally cast them out from His presence. Then Zedekiah rebelled against the king of Babylon.

⁴ Now it came to pass in the ninth year of his reign, in the tenth month, on the tenth *day* of the month, *that* Nebuchadnezzar king of Babylon and all his army came against Jerusalem and encamped against it; and *they* built a siege wall against it all around. ⁵ So the city was besieged until the eleventh year of King Zedekiah. ⁶ By the fourth month, on the ninth day of the month, the famine had become so severe in the city that there was no food for the people of the land. ⁷ Then the city wall was broken through, and all the men of war fled and went out of the city at night by way of the gate between the two walls, which *was* by the king's garden, even though the Chaldeans *were* near the city all around. And they went by way of the plain.

⁸ But the army of the Chaldeans pursued the king, and they overtook Zedekiah in the plains of Jericho. All his army was scattered from him. ⁹ So they took the king and brought him up to the king of Babylon at Riblah in the land of Hamath, and he pronounced judgment on him. ¹⁰ Then the king of Babylon killed the sons of Zedekiah before his eyes. And he killed all the princes of Judah in Riblah. ¹¹ He also put out the eyes of Zedekiah; and the king of Babylon bound him in bronze fetters, took him to Babylon, and put him in prison till the day of his death.

¹² Now in the fifth month, on the tenth *day* of the month (which *was* the nineteenth year of King Nebuchadnezzar king of Babylon), Nebuzaradan, the captain of the guard, *who* served the king of Babylon, came to Jerusalem. ¹³ He burned the house of the LORD and the king's house; all the houses of Jerusalem, that is, all the houses of the great, he burned with fire. ¹⁴ And all the army of the Chaldeans who *were* with the captain of the guard broke down all the walls of Jerusalem all around. ¹⁵ Then Nebuzaradan the captain of the guard carried away captive *some* of the poor people, the rest of the people who remained in the city, the defectors who had deserted to the king of Babylon, and the rest of the craftsmen. ¹⁶ But Nebuzaradan the captain of the guard left *some* of the poor of the land as vinedressers and farmers.

¹⁷ The bronze pillars that *were* in the house of the LORD, and the carts and the bronze Sea that *were* in the house of the LORD, the Chaldeans broke in pieces, and carried all their bronze to Babylon. ¹⁸ They also took away the pots, the shovels, the trimmers, the bowls, the spoons, and all the bronze utensils with which the priests ministered. ¹⁹ The basins, the firepans, the bowls, the pots, the lampstands, the spoons, and the cups, whatever *was* solid gold and whatever *was* solid silver, the captain of the guard took away. ²⁰ The two pillars, one Sea, the twelve bronze bulls which *were* under *it, and* the carts, which King Solomon had made for the house of the LORD— the bronze of all these articles was beyond measure. ²¹ Now *concerning* the pillars: the height of one pillar *was* eighteen cubits, a measuring line of twelve cubits could measure its circumference, and its thickness *was* four fingers; *it was* hollow. ²² A capital of bronze *was* on it; and the height of one capital *was* five cubits, with a network and pomegranates all around the capital, all of bronze. The second pillar, with pomegranates was the same. ²³ There were ninety-six pomegranates on the sides; all the pomegranates, all around on the network, *were* one hundred.

²⁴ The captain of the guard took Seraiah the chief priest, Zephaniah the second priest, and the three doorkeepers. ²⁵ He also took out of the city an officer who had charge of the men

of war, seven men of the king's close associates who were found in the city, the principal scribe of the army who mustered the people of the land, and sixty men of the people of the land who were found in the midst of the city. 26 And Nebuzaradan the captain of the guard took these and brought them to the king of Babylon at Riblah. 27 Then the king of Babylon struck them and put them to death at Riblah in the land of Hamath. Thus Judah was carried away captive from its own land.

28 These are the people whom Nebuchadnezzar carried away captive: in the seventh year, three thousand and twenty-three Jews; 29 in the eighteenth year of Nebuchadnezzar he carried away captive from Jerusalem eight hundred and thirty-two persons; 30 in the twenty-third year of Nebuchadnezzar, Nebuzaradan the captain of the guard carried away captive of the Jews seven hundred and forty-five persons. All the persons were four thousand six hundred.

31 Now it came to pass in the thirty-seventh year of the captivity of Jehoiachin king of Judah, in the twelfth month, on the twenty-fifth day of the month, that Evil-Merodach king of Babylon, in the first year of his reign, lifted up the head of Jehoiachin king of Judah and brought him out of prison. 32 And he spoke kindly to him and gave him a more prominent seat than those of the kings who were with him in Babylon. 33 So Jehoiachin changed from his prison garments, and he ate bread regularly before the king all the days of his life. 34 And as for his provisions, there was a regular ration given him by the king of Babylon, a portion for each day until the day of his death, all the days of his life.

The Book of
LAMENTATIONS

The Weeping Prophet—I sat down and cried when I looked around at the smoking ashes of Jerusalem and saw the temple furnishings being carried away by our enemies.

Along the road leading out of Jerusalem were long lines of my people being led away to Babylon, where they would be prisoners for many years. The smoke of the city was heavy and choking.

As I sat and wept, I prayed to God. I knew that Israel, my people, had been disobedient for hundreds of years. God had given us every chance to change our ways, but we only grew worse. I still loved my people, even though they hated me because I had spoken the Word of God to them.

I cried for them, even though I knew that one day the Lord would bring them back to their land.

Jeremiah is very sad

HOW lonely sits the city
   That was full of people!
   How like a widow is she,
Who *was* great among the
      nations!
The princess among the
      provinces
Has become a slave!

2   She weeps bitterly in the night,
Her tears *are* on her cheeks;
Among all her lovers
She has none to comfort *her*.
All her friends have dealt
      treacherously with her;
They have become her
      enemies.

3   Judah has gone into captivity,
Under affliction and hard
      servitude;
She dwells among the nations,
She finds no rest;
All her persecutors overtake her
      in dire straits.

4   The roads to Zion mourn
Because no one comes to the
      set feasts.
All her gates are desolate;
Her priests sigh,

Her virgins are afflicted,
And she *is* in bitterness.

5   Her adversaries have become
      the master,
Her enemies prosper;
For the LORD has afflicted her
Because of the multitude of her
      transgressions.
Her children have gone into
      captivity before the enemy.

6   And from the daughter of Zion
All her splendor has departed.
Her princes have become like
      deer
That find no pasture,
That flee without strength
Before the pursuer.

7   In the days of her affliction and
      roaming,
Jerusalem remembers all her
      pleasant things
That she had in the days of old.
When her people fell into the
      hand of the enemy,
With no one to help her,
The adversaries saw her
And mocked at her downfall.

8   Jerusalem has sinned gravely,
Therefore she has become vile.

All who honored her despise her
Because they have seen her
nakedness;
Yes, she sighs and turns away.

9   Her uncleanness *is* in her skirts;
She did not consider her destiny;
Therefore her collapse was
awesome;
She had no comforter.
"O LORD, behold my affliction,
For *the* enemy is exalted!"

10   The adversary has spread his
hand
Over all her pleasant things;
For she has seen the nations
enter her sanctuary,
Those whom You commanded
Not to enter Your assembly.

11   All her people sigh,
They seek bread;
They have given their valuables
for food to restore life.
"See, O LORD, and consider,
For I am scorned."

12   "*Is it* nothing to you, all you who
pass by?
Behold and see
If there is any sorrow like my
sorrow,
Which has been brought on me,
Which the LORD has inflicted
In the day of His fierce anger.

13   "From above He has sent fire into
my bones,
And it overpowered them;
He has spread a net for my feet
And turned me back;
He has made me desolate
And faint all the day.

14   "The yoke of my transgressions
was bound;
They were woven together by
His hands,
And thrust upon my neck.
He made my strength fail;
The Lord delivered me into the
hands of *those whom* I am not
able to withstand.

15   "The Lord has trampled
underfoot all my mighty *men*
in my midst;
He has called an assembly
against me
To crush my young men;
The Lord trampled *as* in a
winepress
The virgin daughter of Judah.

16   "For these *things* I weep;
My eye, my eye overflows with
water;
Because the comforter, who
should restore my life,
Is far from me.
My children are desolate
Because the enemy prevailed."

17   Zion spreads out her hands,
But no one comforts her;
The LORD has commanded
concerning Jacob
That those around him *become*
his adversaries;
Jerusalem has become an
unclean thing among them.

18   "The LORD is righteous,
For I rebelled against His
commandment.
Hear now, all peoples,
And behold my sorrow;
My virgins and my young men
Have gone into captivity.

19   "I called for my lovers,
But they deceived me;
My priests and my elders
Breathed their last in the city,
While they sought food
To restore their life.

20   "See, O LORD, that I *am* in
distress;
My soul is troubled;
My heart is overturned within
me,
For I have been very rebellious.
Outside the sword bereaves,
At home *it is* like death.

21   "They have heard that I sigh,
But no one comforts me.

All my enemies have heard of
my trouble;
They are glad that You have
done *it*.
Bring on the day You have
announced,
That they may become like me.

22 "Let all their wickedness come
before You,
And do to them as You have
done to me
For all my transgressions;
For my sighs *are* many,
And my heart *is* faint."

God is angry with Jerusalem

2 How the Lord has covered the
daughter of Zion
With a cloud in His anger!
He cast down from heaven to
the earth
The beauty of Israel,
And did not remember His
footstool
In the day of His anger.

2 The Lord has swallowed up and
has not pitied
All the dwelling places of
Jacob.
He has thrown down in His
wrath
The strongholds of the daughter
of Judah;
He has brought *them* down to
the ground;
He has profaned the kingdom
and its princes.

3 He has cut off in fierce anger
Every horn of Israel;
He has drawn back His right
hand
From before the enemy.
He has blazed against Jacob like
a flaming fire
Devouring all around.

4 Standing like an enemy, He has
bent His bow;
With His right hand, like an
adversary,

He has slain all *who were*
pleasing to His eye;
On the tent of the daughter of
Zion,
He has poured out His fury like
fire.

5 The Lord was like an enemy.
He has swallowed up Israel,
He has swallowed up all her
palaces;
He has destroyed her
strongholds,
And has increased mourning
and lamentation
In the daughter of Judah.

6 He has done violence to His
tabernacle,
As if it were a garden;
He has destroyed His place of
assembly;
The LORD has caused
The appointed feasts and
Sabbaths to be forgotten in
Zion.
In His burning indignation He
has spurned the king and the
priest.

7 The Lord has spurned His altar,
He has abandoned His
sanctuary;
He has given up the walls of her
palaces
Into the hand of the enemy.
They have made a noise in the
house of the LORD
As on the day of a set feast.

8 The LORD has purposed to
destroy
The wall of the daughter of Zion.
He has stretched out a line;
He has not withdrawn His hand
from destroying;
Therefore He has caused the
rampart and wall to lament;
They languished together.

9 Her gates have sunk into the
ground;
He has destroyed and broken
her bars.

Her king and her princes *are*
among the nations;
The Law *is* no *more,*
And her prophets find no vision
from the LORD.

10 The elders of the daughter of
Zion
Sit on the ground *and* keep
silence;
They throw dust on their heads
And gird themselves with
sackcloth.
The virgins of Jerusalem
Bow their heads to the ground.

11 My eyes fail with tears,
My heart is troubled;
My bile is poured on the ground
Because of the destruction of the
daughter of my people,
Because the children and the
infants
Faint in the streets of the city.

12 They say to their mothers,
"Where *is* grain and wine?"
As they swoon like the wounded
In the streets of the city,
As their life is poured out
In their mothers' bosom.

13 How shall I console you?
To what shall I liken you,
O daughter of Jerusalem?
What shall I compare with you,
that I may comfort you,
O virgin daughter of Zion?
For your ruin *is* spread wide as
the sea;
Who can heal you?

14 Your prophets have seen for you
False and deceptive visions;
They have not uncovered your
iniquity,
To bring back your captives,
But have envisioned for you
false prophecies and
delusions.

15 All who pass by clap *their* hands
at you;
They hiss and shake their heads

At the daughter of Jerusalem:
"*Is* this the city that is called
'The perfection of beauty,
The joy of the whole earth'?"

16 All your enemies have opened
their mouth against you;
They hiss and gnash *their* teeth.
They say, "We have swallowed
her up!
Surely this *is* the day we have
waited for;
We have found *it,* we have seen
it!"

17 The LORD has done what He
purposed;
He has fulfilled His word
Which He commanded in days
of old.
He has thrown down and has
not pitied,
And He has caused an enemy
to rejoice over you;
He has exalted the horn of your
adversaries.

18 Their heart cried out to the Lord,
"O wall of the daughter of Zion,
Let tears run down like a river
day and night;
Give yourself no relief;
Give your eyes no rest.

19 "Arise, cry out in the night,
At the beginning of the watches;
Pour out your heart like water
before the face of the Lord.
Lift your hands toward Him
For the life of your young
children,
Who faint from hunger at the
head of every street."

20 "See, O LORD, and consider!
To whom have You done this?
Should the women eat their
offspring,
The children they have cuddled?
Should the priest and prophet
be slain
In the sanctuary of the Lord?

21 "Young and old lie
On the ground in the streets;

My virgins and my young men
Have fallen by the sword;
You have slain *them* in the day
    of Your anger,
You have slaughtered *and* not
    pitied.

22 "You have invited as to a feast
    day
The terrors that surround me.
In the day of the LORD's anger
There was no refugee or
    survivor.
Those whom I have borne and
    brought up
My enemies have destroyed."

The Lord never stops loving

3   I *am* the man *who* has seen
    affliction by the rod of His
    wrath.
2   He has led me and made *me*
    walk
    In darkness and not *in* light.
3   Surely He has turned His hand
    against me
    Time and time again throughout
    the day.

4   He has aged my flesh and my
    skin,
    And broken my bones.
5   He has besieged me
    And surrounded *me* with
    bitterness and woe.
6   He has set me in dark places
    Like the dead of long ago.

7   He has hedged me in so that I
    cannot get out;
    He has made my chain heavy.
8   Even when I cry and shout,
    He shuts out my prayer.
9   He has blocked my ways with
    hewn stone;
    He has made my paths crooked.

10   He *has been* to me a bear lying
    in wait,
    Like a lion in ambush.
11   He has turned aside my ways
    and torn me in pieces;
    He has made me desolate.
12   He has bent His bow

And set me up as a target for
    the arrow.
13   He has caused the arrows of His
    quiver
    To pierce my loins.
14   I have become the ridicule of all
    my people—
    Their taunting song all the day.
15   He has filled me with bitterness,
    He has made me drink
    wormwood.

16   He has also broken my teeth
    with gravel,
    And covered me with ashes.
17   You have moved my soul far
    from peace;
    I have forgotten prosperity.
18   And I said, "My strength and my
    hope
    Have perished from the LORD."

19   Remember my affliction and
    roaming,
    The wormwood and the gall.
20   My soul still remembers
    And sinks within me.
21   This I recall to my mind,
    Therefore I have hope.

22   *Through* the LORD's mercies we
    are not consumed,
    Because His compassions fail
    not.
23   *They are* new every morning;
    Great *is* Your faithfulness.
24   "The LORD *is* my portion," says
    my soul,
    "Therefore I hope in Him!"

25   The LORD *is* good to those who
    wait for Him,
    To the soul *who* seeks Him.
26   *It is* good that *one* should hope
    and wait quietly
    For the salvation of the LORD.
27   *It is* good for a man to bear
    The yoke in his youth.

28   Let him sit alone and keep silent,
    Because *God* has laid *it* on him;
29   Let him put his mouth in the
    dust—

What the Prophet Learned

I was very sad when I walked the ruined streets of my beloved city. Our enemies had left Jerusalem in ashes.

At first, I lost all hope. The smoke that filled the air shut out the sunshine. Everything seemed gloomy, and all the beauty of our nation was gone.

Then God opened my eyes. We still had His promise. Our people and our king were taken prisoners, but the Lord would not forget His promise. Because of this, I could sing, "Great is Your faithfulness." Sometimes you sing a hymn in church with a similar title.

You must remember the message of that hymn always. No matter how bad things seem to get, God is still behind the clouds. He knows all your needs, and He will help you. Jesus never fails.

There may yet be hope.

30 Let him give *his* cheek to the one
who strikes him,
And be full of reproach.

31 For the Lord will not cast off
forever.
32 Though He causes grief,
Yet He will show compassion
According to the multitude of
His mercies.
33 For He does not afflict willingly,
Nor grieve the children of men.

34 To crush under one's feet
All the prisoners of the earth,
35 To turn aside the justice *due* a
man
Before the face of the Most
High,
36 Or subvert a man in his cause—
The Lord does not approve.

37 Who *is* he *who* speaks and it
comes to pass,
When the Lord has not
commanded *it?*
38 *Is it* not from the mouth of the
Most High
That woe and well-being
proceed?
39 Why should a living man
complain,
A man for the punishment of his
sins?

40 Let us search out and examine
our ways,
And turn back to the LORD;
41 Let us lift our hearts and hands
To God in heaven.
42 We have transgressed and
rebelled;
You have not pardoned.

43 You have covered *Yourself* with
anger
And pursued us;
You have slain *and* not pitied.
44 You have covered Yourself with
a cloud,
That prayer should not pass
through.
45 You have made us an
offscouring and refuse
In the midst of the peoples.

46 All our enemies
Have opened their mouths
against us.
47 Fear and a snare have come
upon us,
Desolation and destruction.
48 My eyes overflow with rivers of
water
For the destruction of the
daughter of my people.

49 My eyes flow and do not cease,
Without interruption,
50 Till the LORD from heaven
Looks down and sees.
51 My eyes bring suffering to my
soul
Because of all the daughters of
my city.

52 My enemies without cause
Hunted me down like a bird.
53 They silenced my life in the pit
And threw stones at me.
54 The waters flowed over my
head;
I said, "I am cut off!"

55 I called on Your name, O LORD,
From the lowest pit.
56 You have heard my voice:
"Do not hide Your ear
From my sighing, from my cry
for help."
57 You drew near on the day I
called on You,
And said, "Do not fear!"

58 O Lord, You have pleaded the
case for my soul;
You have redeemed my life.
59 O LORD, You have seen *how* I
am wronged;
Judge my case.
60 You have seen all their
vengeance,
All their schemes against me.

61 You have heard their reproach,
O LORD,
All their schemes against me,
62 The lips of my enemies
And their whispering against me
all the day.
63 Look at their sitting down and
their rising up;
I *am* their taunting song.

64 Repay them, O LORD,
According to the work of their
hands.
65 Give them a veiled heart;
Your curse *be* upon them!
66 In Your anger,
Pursue and destroy them
From under the heavens of the
LORD.

The golden city has lost its shine

4 How the gold has become dim!
How changed the fine gold!
The stones of the sanctuary are
scattered
At the head of every street.

2 The precious sons of Zion,
Valuable as fine gold,
How they are regarded as clay
pots,
The work of the hands of the
potter!

3 Even the jackals present their
breasts
To nurse their young;
But the daughter of my people
is cruel,
Like ostriches in the wilderness.

4 The tongue of the infant clings
To the roof of its mouth for
thirst;
The young children ask for
bread,
But no one breaks *it* for them.

5 Those who ate delicacies
Are desolate in the streets;
Those who were brought up in
scarlet
Embrace ash heaps.

6 The punishment of the iniquity
of the daughter of my people
Is greater than the punishment
of the sin of Sodom,
Which was overthrown in a
moment,
With no hand to help her!

7 Her Nazirites were brighter than
snow
And whiter than milk;
They were more ruddy in body
than rubies,
Like sapphire in their
appearance.

8 *Now* their appearance is blacker
than soot;
They go unrecognized in the
streets;
Their skin clings to their bones,
It has become as dry as wood.

9 *Those* slain by the sword are
better off
Than *those* who die of hunger;
For these pine away,

Stricken *for lack* of the fruits of
the field.

10 The hands of the compassionate
women
Have cooked their own children;
They became food for them
In the destruction of the
daughter of my people.

11 The LORD has fulfilled His fury,
He has poured out His fierce
anger.
He kindled a fire in Zion,
And it has devoured its
foundations.

12 The kings of the earth,
And all inhabitants of the world,
Would not have believed
That the adversary and the
enemy
Could enter the gates of
Jerusalem—

13 Because of the sins of her
prophets
And the iniquities of her priests,
Who shed in her midst
The blood of the just.

14 They wandered blind in the
streets;
They have defiled themselves
with blood,
So that no one would touch their
garments.

15 They cried out to them,
"Go away, unclean!
Go away, go away,
Do not touch us!"
When they fled and wandered,
Those among the nations said,
"They shall no longer dwell
here."

16 The face of the LORD scattered
them;
He no longer regards them.
The people do not respect the
priests
Nor show favor to the elders.

17 Still our eyes failed us,
Watching vainly for our help;

In our watching we watched
For a nation *that* could not save
us.

18 They tracked our steps
So that we could not walk in our
streets.
Our end was near;
Our days were over,
For our end had come.

19 Our pursuers were swifter
Than the eagles of the heavens.
They pursued us on the
mountains
And lay in wait for us in the
wilderness.

20 The breath of our nostrils, the
anointed of the LORD,
Was caught in their pits,
Of whom we said, "Under his
shadow
We shall live among the
nations."

21 Rejoice and be glad, O daughter
of Edom,
You who dwell in the land of
Uz!
The cup shall also pass over to
you
And you shall become drunk
and make yourself naked.

22 *The punishment of* your iniquity
is accomplished,
O daughter of Zion;
He will no longer send you into
captivity.
He will punish your iniquity,
O daughter of Edom;
He will uncover your sins!

Turn us around, Lord, and bring us back to You

5 Remember, O LORD, what has
come upon us;
Look, and behold our reproach!
2 Our inheritance has been turned
over to aliens,
And our houses to foreigners.
3 We have become orphans and
waifs,
Our mothers *are* like widows.

4 We pay for the water we drink,
And our wood comes at a
price.
5 *They* pursue at our heels;
We labor *and* have no rest.
6 We have given our hand *to* the
Egyptians
And the Assyrians, to be satisfied
with bread.

7 Our fathers sinned *and are* no
more,
But we bear their iniquities.
8 Servants rule over us;
There is none to deliver *us* from
their hand.
9 We get our bread *at the risk* of
our lives,
Because of the sword in the
wilderness.

10 Our skin is hot as an oven,
Because of the fever of famine.
11 They ravished the women in
Zion,
The maidens in the cities of
Judah.
12 Princes were hung up by their
hands,
And elders were not respected.
13 Young men ground at the
millstones;

Boys staggered under *loads of*
wood.
14 The elders have ceased
gathering at the gate,
And the young men from their
music.
15 The joy of our heart has ceased;
Our dance has turned into
mourning.
16 The crown has fallen *from* our
head.
Woe to us, for we have sinned!
17 Because of this our heart is faint;
Because of these *things* our eyes
grow dim;
18 Because of Mount Zion which is
desolate,
With foxes walking about on it.

19 You, O Lord, remain forever;
Your throne from generation to
generation.
20 Why do You forget us forever,
And forsake us for so long a
time?
21 Turn us back to You, O Lord,
and we will be restored;
Renew our days as of old,
22 Unless You have utterly rejected
us,
And are very angry with us!

Fallen Jerusalem lies in ruins.

The Book of
EZEKIEL

My name is pronounced *ee-ZEEK-yell* and means "God Will Strengthen." I was one of the Hebrew captives in Babylon 11 years before they destroyed Jerusalem and 597 years before Jesus came to earth.

Five years after I arrived in Babylon, God called me to be a prophet. I was about 25 years old and was already a priest. Since then I have been very thankful for the amazing visions God gave me of His glory. You can read about these wonderful visions in chapters 1 and 10 of my book. These visions show God's greatness, His power, and how He knows all things.

Through me, God revealed His great sorrow for disobedient Israel. But in the end, He showed me the eternal city where the Lord's people will dwell safely forever.

Ezekiel sees a vision of God's glory

NOW it came to pass in the thirtieth year, in the fourth *month,* on the fifth *day* of the month, as I *was* among the captives by the River Chebar, *that* the heavens were opened and I saw visions of God. 2 On the fifth *day* of the month, which *was* in the fifth year of King Jehoiachin's captivity, 3 the word of the LORD came expressly to Ezekiel the priest, the son of Buzi, in the land of the Chaldeans by the River Chebar; and the hand of the LORD was upon him there.

4 Then I looked, and behold, a whirl- wind was coming out of the north, a great cloud with raging fire engulfing itself; and brightness *was* all around it and radiating out of its midst like the color of amber, out of the midst of the fire. 5 Also from within it *came* the likeness of four living creatures. And this *was* their appearance: they had the likeness of a man. 6 Each one had four faces, and each one had four wings. 7 Their legs *were* straight, and the soles of their feet *were* like the soles of calves' feet. They sparkled like the color of burnished bronze. 8 The hands of a man *were* under their wings on their four sides; and each of the four had faces and wings. 9 Their wings

⛏ DIGGING IN

1:4–28 An Amazing Vision of God Sometimes a picture is better than a thousand words. We can't see or describe God completely because He is invisible. But God shows Himself by *living pictures,* or "visions," to people in the Bible.

To Abraham, God came as a burning torch (Genesis 15). In this way God was telling Abraham, "I am a consuming fire. I don't break My promises, and be sure you don't break yours, either!" To Jacob, the Lord came as a wrestler (Genesis 32).

God was saying to Jacob, "Don't fight against My will!" To Moses, God came as a burning bush that didn't burn up (Exodus 3). God was telling Moses, "My judgment burns like a fire, but My promise to My people will never be broken!"

Ezekiel, (pronounced *ee-ZEEK-yell*), now sees God in living pictures he can hardly describe. Ezekiel is being shown that God is high above human understanding. But in special ways, God visits people who truly look for Him.

touched one another. *The creatures did not turn when they went, but each one went straight forward.

¹⁰ As for the likeness of their faces, *each* had the face of a man; each of the four had the face of a lion on the right side, each of the four had the face of an ox on the left side, and each of the four had the face of an eagle. ¹¹ Thus *were* their faces. Their wings stretched upward; two *wings* of each one touched one another, and two covered their bodies. ¹² And each one went straight forward; they went wherever the spirit wanted to go, and they did not turn when they went.

¹³ As for the likeness of the living creatures, their appearance *was* like burning coals of fire, like the appearance of torches going back and forth among the living creatures. The fire was bright, and out of the fire went lightning. ¹⁴ And the living creatures ran back and forth, in appearance like a flash of lightning.

¹⁵ Now as I looked at the living creatures, behold, a wheel *was* on the earth beside each living creature with its four faces. ¹⁶ The appearance of the wheels and their workings *was* like the color of beryl, and all four had the same likeness. The appearance of their workings *was*, as it were, a wheel in the middle of a wheel. ¹⁷ When they moved, they went toward any one of four directions; they did not turn aside when they went. ¹⁸ As for their rims, they were so high they were awesome; and their rims *were* full of eyes, all around the four of them. ¹⁹ When the living creatures went, the wheels went beside them; and when the living creatures were lifted up from the earth, the wheels were lifted up. ²⁰ Wherever the spirit wanted to go, they went, *because* there the spirit went; and the wheels were lifted together with them, for the spirit of the living creatures *was* in the wheels. ²¹ When those went, *these*

went; when those stood, *these* stood; and when those were lifted up from the earth, the wheels were lifted up together with them, for the spirit of the living creatures *was* in the wheels.

²² The likeness of the firmament above the heads of the living creatures *was* like the color of an awesome crystal, stretched out over their heads. ²³ And under the firmament their wings *spread out* straight, one toward another. Each one had two which covered one side, and each one had two which covered the other side of the body. ²⁴ When they went, I heard the noise of their wings, like the noise of many waters, like the voice of the Almighty, a tumult like the noise of an army; and when they stood still, they let down their wings. ²⁵ A voice came from above the firmament that *was* over their heads; whenever they stood, they let down their wings.

²⁶ And above the firmament over their heads *was* the likeness of a throne, in appearance like a sapphire stone; on the likeness of the throne *was* a likeness with the appearance of a man high above it. ²⁷ Also from the appearance of His waist and upward I saw, as it were, the color of amber with the appearance of fire all around within it; and from the appearance of His waist and downward I saw, as it were, the appearance of fire with brightness all around. ²⁸ Like the appearance of a rainbow in a cloud on a rainy day, so *was* the appearance of the brightness all around it. This *was* the appearance of the likeness of the glory of the LORD.

So when I saw *it*, I fell on my face, and I heard a voice of One speaking.

God calls Ezekiel to be a prophet

2 And He said to me, "**Son of man**, stand on your feet, and I will speak to you." ² Then the Spirit entered me

WORDFINDER

2:1 Son of Man A title first used by the prophet Ezekiel. Jesus used the title in a special way to refer to His divine authority as the supreme Man (see Luke 6:22).

when He spoke to me, and set me on my feet; and I heard Him who spoke to me. ³ And He said to me: "Son of man, I am sending you to the children of Israel, to a rebellious nation that has rebelled against Me; they and their fathers have transgressed against Me to this very day. ⁴ For *they are* impudent and stubborn children. I am sending you to them, and you shall say to them, 'Thus says the Lord GOD.' ⁵ As for them, whether they hear or whether they refuse—for they *are* a rebellious house—yet they will know that a prophet has been among them.

⁶ "And you, son of man, do not be afraid of them nor be afraid of their words, though briers and thorns *are* with you and you dwell among scorpions; do not be afraid of their words or dismayed by their looks, though they *are* a rebellious house. ⁷ You shall speak My words to them, whether they hear or whether they refuse, for they *are* rebellious. ⁸ But you, son of man, hear what I say to you. Do not be rebellious like that rebellious house; open your mouth and eat what I give you."

⁹ Now when I looked, there was a hand stretched out to me; and behold, a scroll of a book *was* in it. ¹⁰ Then He spread it before me; and *there was* writing on the inside and on the outside, and written on it *were* lamentations and mourning and woe.

God warns Ezekiel that the people won't listen

3 Moreover He said to me, "Son of man, eat what you find; eat this scroll, and go, speak to the house of Israel." ² So I opened my mouth, and He caused me to eat that scroll.

³ And He said to me, "Son of man, feed your belly, and fill your stomach with this scroll that I give you." So I ate, and it was in my mouth like honey in sweetness.

⁴ Then He said to me: "Son of man, go to the house of Israel and speak with My words to them. ⁵ For you *are* not sent to a people of unfamiliar speech and of hard language, *but* to the house of Israel, ⁶ not to many people of unfamiliar speech and of hard language, whose words you cannot understand. Surely, had I sent you to them, they would have listened to you. ⁷ But the house of Israel will not listen to you, because they will not listen to Me; for all the house of Israel *are* impudent and hard-hearted. ⁸ Behold, I have made your face strong against their faces, and your forehead strong against their foreheads. ⁹ Like adamant stone, harder than flint, I have made your forehead; do not be afraid of them, nor be dismayed at their looks, though they *are* a rebellious house."

¹⁰ Moreover He said to me: "Son of man, receive into your heart all My words that I speak to you, and hear with your ears. ¹¹ And go, get to the captives, to the children of your people, and speak to them and tell them, 'Thus says the Lord GOD,' whether they hear, or whether they refuse."

¹² Then the Spirit lifted me up, and I heard behind me a great thunderous voice: "Blessed *is* the glory of the LORD from His place!" ¹³ *I* also *heard* the noise of the wings of the living creatures that touched one another, and the noise of the wheels beside them, and a great thunderous noise. ¹⁴ So the Spirit lifted me up and took me away, and I went in bitterness, in the heat of my spirit; but the hand of the LORD was strong upon me. ¹⁵ Then I came to the captives at Tel Abib, who dwelt by the River Chebar; and I sat where they sat, and remained there astonished among them seven days.

¹⁶ Now it came to pass at the end of seven days that the word of the LORD came to me, saying, ¹⁷ "Son of man, I have made you a watchman for the house of Israel; therefore hear a word from My mouth, and give them warning from Me: ¹⁸ When I say to the wicked, 'You shall surely die,' and you give him no warning, nor speak to warn the wicked from his wicked way, to save his life, that same wicked *man* shall die in his iniquity; but his blood I will require at your hand. ¹⁹ Yet, if

you warn the wicked, and he does not turn from his wickedness, nor from his wicked way, he shall die in his iniquity; but you have delivered your soul.

20 "Again, when a righteous *man* turns from his righteousness and commits iniquity, and I lay a stumbling block before him, he shall die; because you did not give him warning, he shall die in his sin, and his righteousness which he has done shall not be remembered; but his blood I will require at your hand. 21 Nevertheless if you warn the righteous *man* that the righteous should not sin, and he does not sin, he shall surely live because he took warning; also you will have delivered your soul."

22 Then the hand of the LORD was upon me there, and He said to me, "Arise, go out into the plain, and there I shall talk with you."

23 So I arose and went out into the plain, and behold, the glory of the LORD stood there, like the glory which I saw by the River Chebar; and I fell on my face. 24 Then the Spirit entered me and set me on my feet, and spoke with me and said to me: "Go, shut yourself inside your house. 25 And you, O son of man, surely they will put ropes on you and bind you with them, so that you cannot go out among them. 26 I will make your tongue cling to the roof of your mouth, so that you shall be mute and not be one to rebuke them, for they *are* a rebellious house. 27 But when I speak with you, I will open your mouth, and you shall say to them, 'Thus says the Lord GOD.' He who hears, let him hear; and he who refuses, let him refuse; for they *are* a rebellious house.

Ezekiel draws a map

4 "You also, son of man, take a clay tablet and lay it before you, and portray on it a city, Jerusalem. 2 Lay siege against it, build a siege wall against it, and heap up a mound against it; set camps against it also, and place battering rams against it all around. 3 Moreover take for yourself an iron plate, and set it *as* an iron wall between you and the city. Set your face against it, and it shall be besieged, and you shall lay siege against it. This *will be* a sign to the house of Israel.

4 "Lie also on your left side, and lay the iniquity of the house of Israel upon it. *According* to the number of the days that you lie on it, you shall bear their iniquity. 5 For I have laid on you the years of their iniquity, according to the number of the days, three hundred and ninety days; so you shall bear the iniquity of the house of Israel. 6 And when you have completed them, lie again on your right side; then you shall bear the iniquity of the house of Judah forty days. I have laid on you a day for each year.

7 "Therefore you shall set your face toward the siege of Jerusalem; your arm *shall be* uncovered, and you shall prophesy against it. 8 And surely I will restrain you so that you cannot turn from one side to another till you have ended the days of your siege.

9 "Also take for yourself wheat, barley, beans, lentils, millet, and spelt; put them into one vessel, and make bread of them for yourself. *During* the number of days that you lie on your side, three hundred and ninety days, you shall eat it. 10 And your food which you eat *shall be* by weight, twenty shekels a day; from time to time you shall eat it. 11 You shall also drink water by measure, one-sixth of a hin; from time to time you shall drink. 12 And you shall eat it *as* barley cakes; and bake it using fuel of human waste in their sight."

13 Then the LORD said, "So shall the children of Israel eat their defiled bread among the Gentiles, where I will drive them."

14 So I said, "Ah, Lord GOD! Indeed I have never defiled myself from my youth till now; I have never eaten what died of itself or was torn by beasts, nor has abominable flesh ever come into my mouth."

15 Then He said to me, "See, I am giving you cow dung instead of human waste, and you shall prepare your bread over it."

Street Drama Pictures Coming Fall of Jerusalem

The Babylon News-Press

MIZPAH—Shoppers are being amused these days by a one-man show staged by the prophet Ezekiel on our main street. Ezekiel has built a clay model of Jerusalem. Outside the walls of the clay city are models of camps of enemy troops. Following is an interview with Ezekiel by a reporter from *The Babylon News-Press:*

Reporter: "And just what are you trying to do here, Ezekiel?"

Ezekiel: "I'm showing our people that their holy city is about to be destroyed."

Reporter: "But, Ezekiel, why do you want to show such an unhappy thing to your people?"

Ezekiel: "Because it's the sad truth. For too many years our nation has not lived up to its place as God's chosen people."

Reporter: "Is there any hope for your people?"

Ezekiel: "Oh, yes! After about 70 years in Babylon, my people will go back to the land God gave them."

Ezekiel was last seen lying on his side to show how many years it will be till Jerusalem is destroyed.

16 Moreover He said to me, "Son of man, surely I will cut off the supply of bread in Jerusalem; they shall eat bread by weight and with anxiety, and shall drink water by measure and with dread, 17 that they may lack bread and water, and be dismayed with one another, and waste away because of their iniquity.

What kind of haircut is *that?*

5 "And you, son of man, take a sharp sword, take it as a barber's razor, and pass *it* over your head and your beard; then take scales to weigh and divide the hair. 2 You shall burn with fire one-third in the midst of the city, when the days of the siege are finished; then you shall take one-third and strike around *it* with the sword, and one-third you shall scatter in the wind: I will draw out a sword after them. 3 You shall also take a small number of them and bind them in the edge of your *garment.* 4 Then take some of them again and throw them into the midst of the fire, and burn them in the fire. From there a fire will go out into all the house of Israel.

5 "Thus says the Lord GOD: 'This is Jerusalem; I have set her in the midst of the nations and the countries all around her. 6 She has rebelled against My judgments by doing wickedness more than the nations, and against My statutes more than the countries that *are* all around her; for they have refused My judgments, and they have not walked in My statutes.' 7 Therefore thus says the Lord GOD: 'Because you

God told Ezekiel to shave his hair and beard as a sign of what would happen to Israel.

have multiplied *disobedience* more than the nations that *are* all around you, have not walked in My statutes nor kept My judgments, nor even done according to the judgments of the nations that *are* all around you'— 8 therefore thus says the Lord GOD: 'Indeed I, *even* I, *am* against you and will execute judgments in your midst in the sight of the nations. 9 And I will do among you what I have never done, and the like of which I will never do again, because of all your abominations. 10 Therefore fathers shall eat *their* sons in your midst, and sons shall eat their fathers; and I will execute judgments among you, and all of you who remain I will scatter to all the winds.

11 'Therefore, *as* I live,' says the Lord GOD, 'surely, because you have defiled My sanctuary with all your detestable things and with all your abominations, therefore I will also diminish *you; My* eye will not spare, nor will I have any pity. 12 One-third of you shall die of the pestilence, and be consumed with famine in your midst; and one-third shall fall by the sword all around you; and I will scatter another third to all the winds, and I will draw out a sword after them.

13 'Thus shall My anger be spent, and I will cause My fury to rest upon them, and I will be avenged; and they shall know that I, the LORD, have spoken *it* in My zeal, when I have spent My fury upon them. 14 Moreover I will make you a waste and a reproach among the nations that *are* all around you, in the sight of all who pass by.

15 'So it shall be a reproach, a taunt, a lesson, and an astonishment to the nations that *are* all around you, when I execute judgments among you in anger and in fury and in furious rebukes. I, the LORD, have spoken. 16 When I send against them the terrible arrows of famine which shall be for destruction, which I will send to destroy you, I will increase the famine upon you and cut off your supply of bread. 17 So I will send against you famine and wild beasts, and they will bereave you. Pes-

tilence and blood shall pass through you, and I will bring the sword against you. I, the LORD, have spoken.' "

Ezekiel speaks to the mountains

6 Now the word of the LORD came to me, saying: 2 "Son of man, set your face toward the mountains of Israel, and prophesy against them, 3 and say, 'O mountains of Israel, hear the word of the Lord GOD! Thus says the Lord GOD to the mountains, to the hills, to the ravines, and to the valleys: "Indeed I, *even* I, will bring a sword against you, and I will destroy your high places. 4 Then your altars shall be desolate, your incense altars shall be broken, and I will cast down your slain *men* before your idols. 5 And I will lay the corpses of the children of Israel before their idols, and I will scatter your bones all around your altars. 6 In all your dwelling places the cities shall be laid waste, and the high places shall be desolate, so that your altars may be laid waste and made desolate, your idols may be broken and made to cease, your incense altars may be cut down, and your works may be abolished. 7 The slain shall fall in your midst, and you shall know that I *am* the LORD.

8 "Yet I will leave a remnant, so that you may have *some* who escape the sword among the nations, when you are scattered through the countries. 9 Then those of you who escape will remember Me among the nations where they are carried captive, because I was crushed by their adulterous heart which has departed from Me, and by their eyes which play the harlot after their idols; they will loathe themselves for the evils which they committed in all their abominations. 10 And they shall know that I *am* the LORD; I have not said in vain that I would bring this calamity upon them."

11 'Thus says the Lord GOD: "Pound your fists and stamp your feet, and say, 'Alas, for all the evil abominations of the house of Israel! For they shall fall by the sword, by famine, and by pestilence. 12 He who is far off shall die by

the pestilence, he who is near shall fall by the sword, and he who remains and is besieged shall die by the famine. Thus will I spend My fury upon them. 13 Then you shall know that I *am* the LORD, when their slain are among their idols all around their altars, on every high hill, on all the mountaintops, under every green tree, and under every thick oak, wherever they offered sweet incense to all their idols. 14 So I will stretch out My hand against them and make the land desolate, yes, more desolate than the wilderness toward Diblah, in all their dwelling places. Then they shall know that I *am* the LORD.' " ' "

The end has come

7 Moreover the word of the LORD came to me, saying, 2 "And you, son of man, thus says the Lord GOD to the land of Israel:

'An end! The end has come upon the four corners of the land.
3   Now the end *has come* upon you,
     And I will send My anger against you;
     I will judge you according to your ways,
     And I will repay you for all your abominations.
4   My eye will not spare you,
     Nor will I have pity;
     But I will repay your ways,
     And your abominations will be in your midst;
     Then you shall know that I *am* the LORD!'

5 "Thus says the Lord GOD:

'A disaster, a singular disaster;
     Behold, it has come!
6   An end has come,
     The end has come;
     It has dawned for you;
     Behold, it has come!
7   Doom has come to you, you who dwell in the land;
     The time has come,

A day of trouble *is* near,
     And not of rejoicing in the mountains.
8   Now upon you I will soon pour out My fury,
     And spend My anger upon you;
     I will judge you according to your ways,
     And I will repay you for all your abominations.

9   'My eye will not spare,
     Nor will I have pity;
     I will repay you according to your ways,
     And your abominations will be in your midst.
     Then you shall know that I *am* the LORD who strikes.

10   'Behold, the day!
     Behold, it has come!
     Doom has gone out;
     The rod has blossomed,
     Pride has budded.
11   Violence has risen up into a rod of wickedness;
     None of them *shall remain,*
     None of their multitude,
     None of them;
     Nor *shall there be* wailing for them.
12   The time has come,
     The day draws near.

'Let not the buyer rejoice,
     Nor the seller mourn,
     For wrath *is* on their whole multitude.
13   For the seller shall not return to what has been sold,
     Though he may still be alive;
     For the vision concerns the whole multitude,
     And it shall not turn back;
     No one will strengthen himself Who lives in iniquity.

14   'They have blown the trumpet and made everyone ready,
     But no one goes to battle;
     For My wrath *is* on all their multitude.
15   The sword *is* outside,

And the pestilence and famine
   within.
Whoever *is* in the field
Will die by the sword;
And whoever *is* in the city,
Famine and pestilence will
   devour him.

16 'Those who survive will escape
   and be on the mountains
Like doves of the valleys,
All of them mourning,
Each for his iniquity.

17 Every hand will be feeble,
And *every* knee will be *as* weak
   as water.

18 They will also be girded with
   sackcloth;
Horror will cover them;
Shame *will be* on every face,
Baldness on all their heads.

19 'They will throw their silver into
   the streets,
And their gold will be like
   refuse;
Their silver and their gold will
   not be able to deliver them
In the day of the wrath of the
   LORD;
They will not satisfy their souls,
Nor fill their stomachs,
Because it became their
   stumbling block of iniquity.

20 'As for the beauty of his
   ornaments,
He set it in majesty;
But they made from it
The images of their
   abominations—
Their detestable things;
Therefore I have made it
Like refuse to them.

21 I will give it as plunder
Into the hands of strangers,
And to the wicked of the earth
   as spoil;
And they shall defile it.

22 I will turn My face from them,
And they will defile My secret
   place;
For robbers shall enter it and
   defile it.

23 'Make a chain,
For the land is filled with crimes
   of blood,
And the city is full of violence.

24 Therefore I will bring the worst
   of the Gentiles,
And they will possess their
   houses;
I will cause the pomp of the
   strong to cease,
And their holy places shall be
   defiled.

25 Destruction comes;
They will seek peace, but *there
   shall be* none.

26 Disaster will come upon disaster,
And rumor will be upon rumor.
Then they will seek a vision from
   a prophet;
But the law will perish from the
   priest,
And counsel from the elders.

27 'The king will mourn,
The prince will be clothed with
   desolation,
And the hands of the common
   people will tremble.
I will do to them according to
   their way,
And according to what they
   deserve I will judge them;
Then they shall know that I *am*
   the LORD!' "

Ezekiel finds a secret room

8 And it came to pass in the sixth
year, in the sixth *month,* on the fifth
day of the month, as I sat in my house
with the elders of Judah sitting before
me, that the hand of the Lord GOD
fell upon me there. 2 Then I looked,
and there was a likeness, like the appearance of fire—from the appearance
of His waist and downward, fire; and
from His waist and upward, like the
appearance of brightness, like the color
of amber. 3 He stretched out the form
of a hand, and took me by a lock of
my hair; and the Spirit lifted me up
between earth and heaven, and
brought me in visions of God to Jerusalem, to the door of the north gate

of the inner *court,* where the seat of the image of jealousy *was,* which provokes to jealousy. 4 And behold, the glory of the God of Israel *was* there, like the vision that I saw in the plain.

5 Then He said to me, "Son of man, lift your eyes now toward the north." So I lifted my eyes toward the north, and there, north of the altar gate, was this image of jealousy in the entrance.

6 Furthermore He said to me, "Son of man, do you see what they are doing, the great abominations that the house of Israel commits here, to make Me go far away from My sanctuary? Now turn again, you will see greater abominations." 7 So He brought me to the door of the court; and when I looked, there was a hole in the wall. 8 Then He said to me, "Son of man, dig into the wall"; and when I dug into the wall, there was a door.

9 And He said to me, "Go in, and see the wicked abominations which they are doing there." 10 So I went in and saw, and there—every sort of creeping thing, abominable beasts, and all the idols of the house of Israel, portrayed all around on the walls. 11 And there stood before them seventy men of the elders of the house of Israel, and in their midst stood Jaazaniah the son of Shaphan. Each man had a censer in his hand, and a thick cloud of incense went up. 12 Then He said to me, "Son of man, have you seen what the elders of the house of Israel do in the dark, every man in the room of his idols? For they say, 'The LORD does not see us, the LORD has forsaken the land.' "

13 And He said to me, "Turn again, *and* you will see greater abominations that they are doing." 14 So He brought me to the door of the north gate of the LORD's house; and to my dismay, women were sitting there weeping for Tammuz.

15 Then He said to me, "Have you seen *this,* O son of man? Turn again, you will see greater abominations than these." 16 So He brought me into the inner court of the LORD's house; and there, at the door of the temple of the LORD, between the porch and the altar, *were* about twenty-five men with their backs toward the temple of the LORD and their faces toward the east, and they were worshiping the sun toward the east.

17 And He said to me, "Have you seen *this,* O son of man? Is it a trivial thing to the house of Judah to commit the abominations which they commit here? For they have filled the land with violence; then they have returned to provoke Me to anger. Indeed they put the branch to their nose. 18 Therefore I also will act in fury. My eye will not spare nor will I have pity; and though they cry in My ears with a loud voice, I will not hear them."

The innocent are spared

9 Then He called out in my hearing with a loud voice, saying, "Let those who have charge over the city draw near, each *with* a deadly weapon in his hand." 2 And suddenly six men came from the direction of the upper gate, which faces north, each with his battle-ax in his hand. One man among them *was* clothed with linen and had a writer's inkhorn at his side. They went in and stood beside the bronze altar.

3 Now the glory of the God of Israel had gone up from the cherub, where it had been, to the threshold of the temple. And He called to the man clothed with linen, who *had* the writer's inkhorn at his side; 4 and the LORD said to him, "Go through the midst of the city, through the midst of Jerusalem, and put a mark on the foreheads of the men who sigh and cry over all the abominations that are done within it."

5 To the others He said in my hearing, "Go after him through the city and kill; do not let your eye spare, nor have any pity. 6 Utterly slay old *and* young men, maidens and little children and women; but do not come near anyone on whom *is* the mark; and begin at My sanctuary." So they began with the elders who *were* before the temple. 7 Then He said to them, "Defile the

temple, and fill the courts with the slain. Go out!" And they went out and killed in the city.

8 So it was, that while they were killing them, I was left *alone;* and I fell on my face and cried out, and said, "Ah, Lord GOD! Will You destroy all the remnant of Israel in pouring out Your fury on Jerusalem?"

9 Then He said to me, "The iniquity of the house of Israel and Judah *is* exceedingly great, and the land is full of bloodshed, and the city full of perversity; for they say, 'The LORD has forsaken the land, and the LORD does not see!' 10 And as for Me also, My *eye* will neither spare, nor will I have pity, *but* I will recompense their deeds on their own head."

11 Just then, the man clothed with linen, who *had* the inkhorn at his side, reported back and said, "I have done as You commanded me."

Angels, wheels, and coals of fire

10 And I looked, and there in the firmament that was above the head of the cherubim, there appeared something like a sapphire stone, having the appearance of the likeness of a throne. 2 Then He spoke to the man clothed with linen, and said, "Go in among the wheels, under the cherub, fill your hands with coals of fire from among the cherubim, and scatter *them* over the city." And he went in as I watched.

3 Now the cherubim were standing on the south side of the temple when the man went in, and the cloud filled the inner court. 4 Then the glory of the LORD went up from the cherub, *and* paused over the threshold of the temple; and the house was filled with the cloud, and the court was full of the brightness of the LORD's glory. 5 And the sound of the wings of the **cherubim** was heard *even* in the outer court,

like the voice of Almighty God when He speaks.

6 Then it happened, when He commanded the man clothed in linen, saying, "Take fire from among the wheels, from among the cherubim," that he went in and stood beside the wheels. 7 And the cherub stretched out his hand from among the cherubim to the fire that *was* among the cherubim, and took *some of it* and put *it* into the hands of the *man* clothed with linen, who took *it* and went out. 8 The cherubim appeared to have the form of a man's hand under their wings.

9 And when I looked, there were four wheels by the cherubim, one wheel by one cherub and another wheel by each other cherub; the wheels appeared *to have* the color of a beryl stone. 10 *As for* their appearance, all four looked alike—as it were, a wheel in the middle of a wheel. 11 When they went, they went toward *any of* their four directions; they did not turn aside when they went, but followed in the direction the head was facing. They did not turn aside when they went. 12 And their whole body, with their back, their hands, their wings, and the wheels that the four had, *were* full of eyes all around. 13 As for the wheels, they were called in my hearing, "Wheel."

14 Each one had four faces: the first face *was* the face of a cherub, the second face the face of a man, the third the face of a lion, and the fourth the face of an eagle. 15 And the cherubim were lifted up. This *was* the living creature I saw by the River Chebar. 16 When the cherubim went, the wheels went beside them; and when the cherubim lifted their wings to mount up from the earth, the same wheels also did not turn from beside them. 17 When *the cherubim* stood still, *the wheels* stood still, and when *one* was lifted up, *the other* lifted itself up,

WORDFINDER

10:5 Cherubim Pronounced *CHER-uh-bim.* Plural of cherub. These are special angels who are always in the presence of God and continually praise Him.

for the spirit of the living creature *was* in them.

18 Then the glory of the LORD departed from the threshold of the temple and stood over the cherubim. 19 And the cherubim lifted their wings and mounted up from the earth in my sight. When they went out, the wheels *were* beside them; and they stood at the door of the east gate of the LORD's house, and the glory of the God of Israel *was* above them.

20 This *is* the living creature I saw under the God of Israel by the River Chebar, and I knew they *were* cherubim. 21 Each one had four faces and each one four wings, and the likeness of the hands of a man *was* under their wings. 22 And the likeness of their faces *was* the same *as* the faces which I had seen by the River Chebar, their appearance and their persons. They each went straight forward.

Copying others brings punishment

11 Then the Spirit lifted me up and brought me to the East Gate of the LORD's house, which faces eastward; and there at the door of the gate were twenty-five men, among whom I saw Jaazaniah the son of Azzur, and Pelatiah the son of Benaiah, princes of the people. 2 And He said to me: "Son of man, these *are* the men who devise iniquity and give wicked counsel in this city, 3 who say, 'The time *is* not near to build houses; this *city is* the caldron, and we *are* the meat.' 4 Therefore prophesy against them, prophesy, O son of man!"

5 Then the Spirit of the LORD fell upon me, and said to me, "Speak! 'Thus says the LORD: "Thus you have said, O house of Israel; for I know the things that come into your mind. 6 You have multiplied your slain in this city, and you have filled its streets with the slain." 7 Therefore thus says the Lord GOD: "Your slain whom you have laid in its midst, they *are* the meat, and this *city is* the caldron; but I shall bring you out of the midst of it.

8 You have feared the sword; and I will bring a sword upon you," says the Lord GOD. 9 "And I will bring you out of its midst, and deliver you into the hands of strangers, and execute judgments on you. 10 You shall fall by the sword. I will judge you at the border of Israel. Then you shall know that I *am* the LORD. 11 This *city* shall not be your caldron, nor shall you be the meat in its midst. I will judge you at the border of Israel. 12 And you shall know that I *am* the LORD; for you have not walked in My statutes nor executed My judgments, but have done according to the customs of the Gentiles which *are* all around you." ' "

13 Now it happened, while I was prophesying, that Pelatiah the son of Benaiah died. Then I fell on my face and cried with a loud voice, and said, "Ah, Lord GOD! Will You make a complete end of the remnant of Israel?"

14 Again the word of the LORD came to me, saying, 15 "Son of man, your brethren, your relatives, your countrymen, and all the house of Israel in its entirety, *are* those about whom the inhabitants of Jerusalem have said, 'Get far away from the LORD; this land has been given to us as a possession.' 16 Therefore say, 'Thus says the Lord GOD: "Although I have cast them far off among the Gentiles, and although I have scattered them among the countries, yet I shall be a little sanctuary for them in the countries where they have gone." ' 17 Therefore say, 'Thus says the Lord GOD: "I will gather you from the peoples, assemble you from the countries where you have been scattered, and I will give you the land of Israel." ' 18 And they will go there, and they will take away all its detestable things and all its abominations from there. 19 Then I will give them one heart, and I will put a new spirit within them, and take the stony heart out of their flesh, and give them a heart of flesh, 20 that they may walk in My statutes and keep My judgments and do them; and they shall be My people, and I will be their God. 21 But *as for* those whose hearts follow the desire

Prophet Shows How Jerusalem Will Be Captured

The Babylon News-Press

MIZPAH—The famous prophet Eze-kiel, who has lived among us since 597 B.C., has been behaving strangely. First, we reported to you that he built the model of Jerusalem (see Ezekiel 4, 5).

Now Ezekiel has dug a hole through the wall of his house. Each day he comes out through the wall, carrying his belongings around the city. Then he returns at night and carries his be-longings through the wall and back into his house.

A reporter from *The Babylon News-Press* says the prophet explains his ac-tions as follows: "When I go out in the morning carrying my belongings, I am showing my people what is going to happen to Jerusalem. The city will be broken down. Then they will carry their belongings to another place where they will be prisoners for many years."

---

for their detestable things and their abominations, I will recompense their deeds on their own heads," says the Lord GOD.

22 So the cherubim lifted up their wings, with the wheels beside them, and the glory of the God of Israel *was* high above them. 23 And the glory of the LORD went up from the midst of the city and stood on the mountain, which *is* on the east side of the city.

24 Then the Spirit took me up and brought me in a vision by the Spirit of God into Chaldea, to those in cap-tivity. And the vision that I had seen went up from me. 25 So I spoke to those in captivity of all the things the LORD had shown me.

Ezekiel digs a tunnel

12 Now the word of the LORD came to me, saying: 2 "Son of man, you dwell in the midst of a rebellious house, which has eyes to see but does not see, and ears to hear but does not hear; for they *are* a rebellious house.

3 "Therefore, son of man, prepare your belongings for captivity, and go into captivity by day in their sight. You shall go from your place into captivity to another place in their sight. It may be that they will consider, though they *are* a rebellious house. 4 By day you shall bring out your belongings in their sight, as though going into captivity;

and at evening you shall go in their sight, like those who go into captivity. 5 Dig through the wall in their sight, and carry your belongings out through it. 6 In their sight you shall bear *them* on *your* shoulders *and* carry *them* out at twilight; you shall cover your face, so that you cannot see the ground, for I have made you a sign to the house of Israel."

7 So I did as I was commanded. I brought out my belongings by day, as though going into captivity, and at eve-ning I dug through the wall with my hand. I brought *them* out at twilight, *and* I bore *them* on *my* shoulder in their sight.

8 And in the morning the word of the LORD came to me, saying, 9 "Son of man, has not the house of Israel, the rebellious house, said to you, 'What are you doing?' 10 Say to them, 'Thus says the Lord GOD: "This bur-den *concerns* the prince in Jerusalem and all the house of Israel who are among them." ' 11 Say, 'I *am* a sign to you. As I have done, so shall it be done to them; they shall be carried away into captivity.' 12 And the prince who *is* among them shall bear *his* be-longings on *his* shoulder at twilight and go out. They shall dig through the wall to carry *them* out through it. He shall cover his face, so that he cannot see the ground with *his* eyes. 13 I will also spread My net over him, and he shall

be caught in My snare. I will bring him to Babylon, *to* the land of the Chaldeans; yet he shall not see it, though he shall die there. 14 I will scatter to *every* wind all who *are* around him to help him, and all his troops; and I will draw out the sword after them.

15 "Then they shall know that I *am* the LORD, when I scatter them among the nations and disperse them throughout the countries. 16 But I will spare a few of their men from the sword, from famine, and from pestilence, that they may declare all their abominations among the Gentiles wherever they go. Then they shall know that I *am* the LORD."

17 Moreover the word of the LORD came to me, saying, 18 "Son of man, eat your bread with quaking, and drink your water with trembling and anxiety. 19 And say to the people of the land, 'Thus says the Lord GOD to the inhabitants of Jerusalem *and* to the land of Israel: "They shall eat their bread with anxiety, and drink their water with dread, so that her land may be emptied of all who are in it, because of the violence of all those who dwell in it. 20 Then the cities that are inhabited shall be laid waste, and the land shall become desolate; and you shall know that I *am* the LORD." ' "

21 And the word of the LORD came to me, saying, 22 "Son of man, what *is* this proverb *that* you *people* have about the land of Israel, which says, 'The days are prolonged, and every vision fails'? 23 Tell them therefore, 'Thus says the Lord GOD: "I will lay this proverb to rest, and they shall no more use it as a proverb in Israel." But say to them, "The days are at hand, and the fulfillment of every vision. 24 For no more shall there be any false vision or flattering divination within the house of Israel. 25 For I *am* the LORD. I speak, and the word which I speak will come to pass; it will no more be postponed; for in your days, O rebellious house, I will say the word and perform it," says the Lord GOD.' "

26 Again the word of the LORD came to me, saying, 27 "Son of man, look,

the house of Israel is saying, 'The vision that he *sees is* for many days *from now,* and he prophesies of times far off.' 28 Therefore say to them, 'Thus says the Lord GOD: "None of My words will be postponed any more, but the word which I speak will be done," says the Lord GOD.' "

False prophets lie to the people

13 And the word of the LORD came to me, saying, 2 "Son of man, prophesy against the prophets of Israel who prophesy, and say to those who prophesy out of their own heart, 'Hear the word of the LORD!' "

3 Thus says the Lord GOD: "Woe to the foolish prophets, who follow their own spirit and have seen nothing! 4 O Israel, your prophets are like foxes in the deserts. 5 You have not gone up into the gaps to build a wall for the house of Israel to stand in battle on the day of the LORD. 6 They have envisioned futility and false divination, saying, 'Thus says the LORD!' But the LORD has not sent them; yet they hope that the word may be confirmed. 7 Have you not seen a futile vision, and have you not spoken false divination? You say, 'The LORD says,' but I have not spoken."

8 Therefore thus says the Lord GOD: "Because you have spoken nonsense and envisioned lies, therefore I *am* indeed against you," says the Lord GOD. 9 "My hand will be against the prophets who envision futility and who divine lies; they shall not be in the assembly of My people, nor be written in the record of the house of Israel, nor shall they enter into the land of Israel. Then you shall know that I *am* the Lord GOD.

10 "Because, indeed, because they have seduced My people, saying, 'Peace!' when *there is* no peace—and one builds a wall, and they plaster it with untempered *mortar*— 11 say to those who plaster *it* with untempered *mortar,* that it will fall. There will be flooding rain, and you, O great hailstones, shall fall; and a stormy wind shall tear *it* down. 12 Surely, when the

wall has fallen, will it not be said to you, 'Where is the mortar with which you plastered it?' "

13 Therefore thus says the Lord GOD: "I will cause a stormy wind to break forth in My fury; and there shall be a flooding rain in My anger, and great hailstones in fury to consume it. 14 So I will break down the wall you have plastered with untempered mortar, and bring it down to the ground, so that its foundation will be uncovered; it will fall, and you shall be consumed in the midst of it. Then you shall know that I am the LORD.

15 "Thus will I accomplish My wrath on the wall and on those who have plastered it with untempered mortar; and I will say to you, 'The wall is no more, nor those who plastered it, 16 that is, the prophets of Israel who prophesy concerning Jerusalem, and who see visions of peace for her when there is no peace,' " says the Lord GOD.

17 "Likewise, son of man, set your face against the daughters of your people, who prophesy out of their own heart; prophesy against them, 18 and say, 'Thus says the Lord GOD: "Woe to the women who sew magic charms on their sleeves and make veils for the heads of people of every height to hunt souls! Will you hunt the souls of My people, and keep yourselves alive? 19 And will you profane Me among My people for handfuls of barley and for pieces of bread, killing people who should not die, and keeping people alive who should not live, by your lying to My people who listen to lies?"

20 'Therefore thus says the Lord GOD: "Behold, I am against your magic charms by which you hunt souls there like birds. I will tear them from your arms, and let the souls go, the souls you hunt like birds. 21 I will also tear off your veils and deliver My people out of your hand, and they shall no longer be as prey in your hand. Then you shall know that I am the LORD.

22 "Because with lies you have made the heart of the righteous sad, whom I have not made sad; and you have

strengthened the hands of the wicked, so that he does not turn from his wicked way to save his life. 23 Therefore you shall no longer envision futility nor practice divination; for I will deliver My people out of your hand, and you shall know that I am the LORD.' "

War, hunger, wild animals, and disease

14 Now some of the elders of Israel came to me and sat before me. 2 And the word of the LORD came to me, saying, 3 "Son of man, these men have set up their idols in their hearts, and put before them that which causes them to stumble into iniquity. Should I let Myself be inquired of at all by them?

4 "Therefore speak to them, and say to them, 'Thus says the Lord GOD: "Everyone of the house of Israel who sets up his idols in his heart, and puts before him what causes him to stumble into iniquity, and then comes to the prophet, I the LORD will answer him who comes, according to the multitude of his idols, 5 that I may seize the house of Israel by their heart, because they are all estranged from Me by their idols." '

6 "Therefore say to the house of Israel, 'Thus says the Lord GOD: "Repent, turn away from your idols, and turn your faces away from all your abominations. 7 For anyone of the house of Israel, or of the strangers who dwell in Israel, who separates himself from Me and sets up his idols in his heart and puts before him what causes him to stumble into iniquity, then comes to a prophet to inquire of him concerning Me, I the LORD will answer him by Myself. 8 I will set My face against that man and make him a sign and a proverb, and I will cut him off from the midst of My people. Then you shall know that I am the LORD.

9 "And if the prophet is induced to speak anything, I the LORD have induced that prophet, and I will stretch out My hand against him and destroy

him from among My people Israel. 10 And they shall bear their iniquity; the punishment of the prophet shall be the same as the punishment of the one who inquired, 11 that the house of Israel may no longer stray from Me, nor be profaned anymore with all their transgressions, but that they may be My people and I may be their God,'' says the Lord GOD.' ''

12 The word of the LORD came again to me, saying: 13 ''Son of man, when a land sins against Me by persistent unfaithfulness, I will stretch out My hand against it; I will cut off its supply of bread, send famine on it, and cut off man and beast from it. 14 Even *if* these three men, Noah, Daniel, and Job, were in it, they would deliver *only* themselves by their righteousness,'' says the Lord GOD.

15 ''If I cause wild beasts to pass through the land, and they empty it, and make it so desolate that no man may pass through because of the beasts, 16 *even though* these three men *were* in it, *as* I live,'' says the Lord GOD, ''they would deliver neither sons nor daughters; only they would be delivered, and the land would be desolate.

17 ''Or *if* I bring a sword on that land, and say, 'Sword, go through the land,' and I cut off man and beast from it, 18 even *though* these three men *were* in it, *as* I live,'' says the Lord GOD, ''they would deliver neither sons nor daughters, but only they themselves would be delivered.

19 ''Or *if* I send a pestilence into that land and pour out My fury on it in blood, and cut off from it man and beast, 20 even *though* Noah, Daniel, and Job *were* in it, *as* I live,'' says the Lord GOD, ''they would deliver neither son nor daughter; they would deliver *only* themselves by their righteousness.''

21 For thus says the Lord GOD: ''How much more it shall be when I send My four severe judgments on Jerusalem—the sword and famine and wild beasts and pestilence—to cut off man and beast from it? 22 Yet behold, there shall be left in it a remnant who will be brought out, *both* sons and daughters; surely they will come out to you, and you will see their ways and their doings. Then you will be comforted concerning the disaster that I have brought upon Jerusalem, all that I have brought upon it. 23 And they will comfort you, when you see their ways and their doings; and you shall know that I have done nothing without cause that I have done in it,'' says the Lord GOD.

Jerusalem is like a useless vine

15 Then the word of the LORD came to me, saying: 2 ''Son of man, how is the wood of the vine *better* than any other wood, the vine branch which is among the trees of the forest? 3 Is wood taken from it to make any object? Or can *men* make a peg from it to hang any vessel on? 4 Instead, it is thrown into the fire for fuel; the fire devours both ends of it, and its middle is burned. Is it useful for *any* work? 5 Indeed, when it was whole, no object could be made from it. How much less will it be useful for *any* work when the fire has devoured it, and it is burned?

6 ''Therefore thus says the Lord GOD: 'Like the wood of the vine among the trees of the forest, which I have given to the fire for fuel, so I will give up the inhabitants of Jerusalem; 7 and I will set My face against them. They will go out from *one* fire, but *another* fire shall devour them. Then you shall know that I *am* the LORD, when I set My face against them. 8 Thus I will make the land desolate, because they have persisted in unfaithfulness,' says the Lord GOD.''

Jerusalem is like an unfaithful wife

16 Again the word of the LORD came to me, saying, 2 ''Son of man, cause Jerusalem to know her abominations, 3 and say, 'Thus says the Lord GOD to Jerusalem: ''Your birth and your nativity *are* from the land of Canaan; your father *was* an Amorite and

Some Bible-time people wore clothing made of fine linen, silk, and embroidered cloth.

your mother a Hittite. ⁴ *As for* your nativity, on the day you were born your navel cord was not cut, nor were you washed in water to cleanse *you;* you were not rubbed with salt nor wrapped in **swaddling cloths**. ⁵ No eye pitied you, to do any of these things for you, to have compassion on you; but you were thrown out into the open field, when you yourself were loathed on the day you were born.

⁶ "And when I passed by you and saw you struggling in your own blood, I said to you in your blood, 'Live!' Yes, I said to you in your blood, 'Live!' ⁷ I made you thrive like a plant in the field; and you grew, matured, and became very beautiful. *Your* breasts were formed, your hair grew, but you *were* naked and bare.

⁸ "When I passed by you again and looked upon you, indeed your time *was* the time of love; so I spread My wing over you and covered your nakedness. Yes, I swore an oath to you and entered into a covenant with you,

and you became Mine," says the Lord GOD.

⁹ "Then I washed you in water; yes, I thoroughly washed off your blood, and I anointed you with oil. ¹⁰ I clothed you in embroidered cloth and gave you sandals of badger skin; I clothed you with fine linen and covered you with silk. ¹¹ I adorned you with ornaments, put bracelets on your wrists, and a chain on your neck. ¹² And I put a jewel in your nose, earrings in your ears, and a beautiful crown on your head. ¹³ Thus you were adorned with gold and silver, and your clothing *was of* fine linen, silk, and embroidered cloth. You ate *pastry of* fine flour, honey, and oil. You were exceedingly beautiful, and succeeded to royalty. ¹⁴ Your fame went out among the nations because of your beauty, for it *was* perfect through My splendor which I had bestowed on you," says the Lord GOD.

¹⁵ "But you trusted in your own beauty, played the harlot because of

WORDFINDER

16:4 Swaddling Cloths   Cloths, like bandages, to wrap newborn babies. In Jesus' time, swaddling cloths were used to keep a baby's limbs straight.

your fame, and poured out your harlotry on everyone passing by who *would have* it. 16 You took some of your garments and adorned multicolored high places for yourself, and played the harlot on them. *Such* things should not happen, nor be. 17 You have also taken your beautiful jewelry from My gold and My silver, which I had given you, and made for yourself male images and played the harlot with them. 18 You took your embroidered garments and covered them, and you set My oil and My incense before them. 19 Also My food which I gave you— the pastry of fine flour, oil, and honey *which* I fed you—you set it before them as sweet incense; and *so* it was," says the Lord GOD.

20 "Moreover you took your sons and your daughters, whom you bore to Me, and these you sacrificed to them to be devoured. *Were* your *acts* of harlotry a small matter, 21 that you have slain My children and offered them up to them by causing them to pass through *the fire?* 22 And in all your abominations and acts of harlotry you did not remember the days of your youth, when you were naked and bare, struggling in your blood.

23 "Then it was so, after all your wickedness—'Woe, woe to you!' says the Lord GOD— 24 *that* you also built for yourself a shrine, and made a high place for yourself in *every* street. 25 You built your high places at the head of *every* road, and made your beauty to be abhorred. You offered yourself to everyone who passed by, and multiplied your acts of harlotry. 26 You also committed harlotry with the Egyptians, your very fleshly neighbors, and increased your acts of harlotry to provoke Me to anger.

27 "Behold, therefore, I stretched out My hand against you, diminished your allotment, and gave you up to the will of those who hate you, the daughters of the Philistines, who were ashamed of your lewd behavior. 28 You also played the harlot with the Assyrians, because you were insatiable; indeed you played the harlot with them and

still were not satisfied. 29 Moreover you multiplied your acts of harlotry as far as the land of the trader, Chaldea; and even then you were not satisfied.

30 "How degenerate is your heart!" says the Lord GOD, "seeing you do all these *things,* the deeds of a brazen harlot.

31 "You erected your shrine at the head of *every* road, and built your high place in *every* street. Yet you were not like a harlot, because you scorned payment. 32 *You are* an adulterous wife, *who* takes strangers instead of her husband. 33 Men make payment to all harlots, but you made your payments to all your lovers, and hired them to come to you from all around for your harlotry. 34 You are the opposite of *other* women in your harlotry, because no one solicited you to be a harlot. In that you gave payment but no payment was given you, therefore you are the opposite."

35 'Now then, O harlot, hear the word of the LORD! 36 Thus says the Lord GOD: "Because your filthiness was poured out and your nakedness uncovered in your harlotry with your lovers, and with all your abominable idols, and because of the blood of your children which you gave to them, 37 surely, therefore, I will gather all your lovers with whom you took pleasure, all those you loved, *and* all those you hated; I will gather them from all around against you and will uncover your nakedness to them, that they may see all your nakedness. 38 And I will judge you as women who break wedlock or shed blood are judged; I will bring blood upon you in fury and jealousy. 39 I will also give you into their hand, and they shall throw down your shrines and break down your high places. They shall also strip you of your clothes, take your beautiful jewelry, and leave you naked and bare.

40 "They shall also bring up an assembly against you, and they shall stone you with stones and thrust you through with their swords. 41 They shall burn your houses with fire, and exe-

cute judgments on you in the sight of many women; and I will make you cease playing the harlot, and you shall no longer hire lovers. 42 So I will lay to rest My fury toward you, and My jealousy shall depart from you. I will be quiet, and be angry no more. 43 Because you did not remember the days of your youth, but agitated Me with all these *things,* surely I will also recompense your deeds on *your own* head," says the Lord God. "And you shall not commit lewdness in addition to all your abominations.

44 "Indeed everyone who quotes proverbs will use *this* proverb against you: 'Like mother, like daughter!' 45 You *are* your mother's daughter, loathing husband and children; and you *are* the sister of your sisters, who loathed their husbands and children; your mother *was* a Hittite and your father an Amorite.

46 "Your elder sister *is* Samaria, who dwells with her daughters to the north of you; and your younger sister, who dwells to the south of you, *is* Sodom and her daughters. 47 You did not walk in their ways nor act according to their abominations; but, as *if that were* too little, you became more corrupt than they in all your ways.

48 "As I live," says the Lord God, "neither your sister Sodom nor her daughters have done as you and your daughters have done. 49 Look, this was the iniquity of your sister Sodom: She and her daughter had pride, fullness of food, and abundance of idleness; neither did she strengthen the hand of the poor and needy. 50 And they were haughty and committed abomination before Me; therefore I took them away as I saw *fit.*

51 "Samaria did not commit half of your sins; but you have multiplied your abominations more than they, and have justified your sisters by all the abominations which you have done. 52 You who judged your sisters, bear your own shame also, because the sins which you committed were more abominable than theirs; they are more righteous than you. Yes, be disgraced

also, and bear your own shame, because you justified your sisters.

53 "When I bring back their captives, the captives of Sodom and her daughters, and the captives of Samaria and her daughters, then *I will also bring back* the captives of your captivity among them, 54 that you may bear your own shame and be disgraced by all that you did when you comforted them. 55 When your sisters, Sodom and her daughters, return to their former state, and Samaria and her daughters return to their former state, then you and your daughters will return to your former state. 56 For your sister Sodom was not a byword in your mouth in the days of your pride, 57 before your wickedness was uncovered. It was like the time of the reproach of the daughters of Syria and all *those* around her, and of the daughters of the Philistines, who despise you everywhere. 58 You have paid for your lewdness and your abominations," says the Lord. 59 For thus says the Lord God: "I will deal with you as you have done, who despised the oath by breaking the covenant.

60 "Nevertheless I will remember My covenant with you in the days of your youth, and I will establish an everlasting covenant with you. 61 Then you will remember your ways and be ashamed, when you receive your older and your younger sisters; for I will give them to you for daughters, but not because of My covenant with you. 62 And I will establish My covenant with you. Then you shall know that I *am* the Lord, 63 that you may remember and be ashamed, and never open your mouth anymore because of your shame, when I provide you an atonement for all you have done," says the Lord God.' "

Ezekiel asks a riddle of eagles

17 And the word of the Lord came to me, saying, 2 "Son of man, pose a riddle, and speak a parable to the house of Israel, 3 and say, 'Thus says the Lord God:

"A great eagle with large wings
    and long pinions,
Full of feathers of various colors,
Came to Lebanon
And took from the cedar the
    highest branch.
4   He cropped off its topmost
    young twig
And carried it to a land of trade;
He set it in a city of merchants.
5   Then he took some of the seed
    of the land
And planted it in a fertile field;
He placed *it* by abundant waters
And set it like a willow tree.
6   And it grew and became a
    spreading vine of low stature;
Its branches turned toward him,
But its roots were under it.
So it became a vine,
Brought forth branches,
And put forth shoots.

7   "But there was another great
    eagle with large wings and
    many feathers;
And behold, this vine bent its
    roots toward him,
And stretched its branches
    toward him,
From the garden terrace where
    it had been planted,
That he might water it.
8   It was planted in good soil by
    many waters,
To bring forth branches, bear
    fruit,
And become a majestic vine.'"'

9 "Say, 'Thus says the Lord GOD:

"Will it thrive?
Will he not pull up its roots,
Cut off its fruit,
And leave it to wither?
All of its spring leaves will wither,
And no great power or many
    people
Will be needed to pluck it up by
    its roots.
10   Behold, *it is* planted,
Will it thrive?
Will it not utterly wither when
    the east wind touches it?

It will wither in the garden
    terrace where it grew." ' "

11 Moreover the word of the LORD came to me, saying, 12 "Say now to the rebellious house: 'Do you not know what these *things mean?*' Tell *them,* 'Indeed the king of Babylon went to Jerusalem and took its king and princes, and led them with him to Babylon. 13 And he took the king's offspring, made a covenant with him, and put him under oath. He also took away the mighty of the land, 14 that the kingdom might be brought low and not lift itself up, *but* that by keeping his covenant it might stand. 15 But he rebelled against him by sending his ambassadors to Egypt, that they might give him horses and many people. Will he prosper? Will he who does such *things* escape? Can he break a covenant and still be delivered?

16 'As I live,' says the Lord GOD, 'surely in the place *where* the king *dwells* who made him king, whose oath he despised and whose covenant he broke—with him in the midst of Babylon he shall die. 17 Nor will Pharaoh with *his* mighty army and great company do anything in the war, when they heap up a siege mound and build a wall to cut off many persons. 18 Since he despised the oath by breaking the covenant, and in fact gave his hand and still did all these *things,* he shall not escape.'"

19 Therefore thus says the Lord GOD: "As I live, surely My oath which he despised, and My covenant which he broke, I will recompense on his own head. 20 I will spread My net over him, and he shall be taken in My snare. I will bring him to Babylon and try him there for the treason which he committed against Me. 21 All his fugitives with all his troops shall fall by the sword, and those who remain shall be scattered to every wind; and you shall know that I, the LORD, have spoken."

22 Thus says the Lord GOD: "I will take also *one* of the highest branches of the high cedar and set *it* out. I will crop off from the topmost of its young

twigs a tender one, and will plant *it* on a high and prominent mountain. 23 On the mountain height of Israel I will plant it; and it will bring forth boughs, and bear fruit, and be a majestic cedar. Under it will dwell birds of every sort; in the shadow of its branches they will dwell. 24 And all the trees of the field shall know that I, the LORD, have brought down the high tree and exalted the low tree, dried up the green tree and made the dry tree flourish; I, the LORD, have spoken and have done *it*."

God is not unfair

18 The word of the LORD came to me again, saying, 2 "What do you mean when you use this proverb concerning the land of Israel, saying:

'The fathers have eaten sour grapes,
And the children's teeth are set on edge'?

3 "As I live," says the Lord GOD, "you shall no longer use this proverb in Israel.

4 "Behold, all souls are Mine;
The soul of the father
As well as the soul of the son is Mine;
The soul who sins shall die.
5 But if a man is just
And does what is lawful and right;
6 If he has not eaten on the mountains,

Nor lifted up his eyes to the idols of the house of Israel,
Nor defiled his neighbor's wife,
Nor approached a woman during her impurity;
7 If he has not oppressed anyone,
But has restored to the debtor his pledge;
Has robbed no one by violence,
But has given his bread to the hungry
And covered the naked with clothing;
8 If he has not exacted usury
Nor taken any increase,
But has withdrawn his hand from iniquity
And executed true judgment between man and man;
9 *If* he has walked in My statutes
And kept My judgments faithfully—
He *is* just;
He shall surely live!"
Says the Lord GOD.

10 "If he begets a son *who is* a robber
Or a shedder of blood,
Who does any of these *things*
11 And does none of those *duties,*
But has eaten on the mountains
Or defiled his neighbor's wife;
12 If he has oppressed the poor and needy,
Robbed by violence,
Not restored the pledge,
Lifted his eyes to the idols,
Or committed abomination;
13 If he has exacted usury
Or taken increase—

⚒ DIGGING IN

18:1–21 It's Up to You Some people try to blame all their problems on someone else. And we sometimes do go wrong because of someone else's actions. But, in the end, what you do with your life is up to you.

In this passage, Israel was reading God's commandment that says the parents' sins affect their children (Exodus 20:4, 5). So they thought all their suffering could be blamed on the sins of their parents. Read how Ezekiel showed the people they were wrong about that.

If you aren't careful, you may make the same mistake Israel made. In fact, some people today say young people from unhappy homes can't help the sins they commit later in life. That's false! Are you going God's way—or your own way? It's up to you.

Shall he then live?
He shall not live!
If he has done any of these
  abominations,
He shall surely die;
His blood shall be upon him.

14 "If, however, he begets a son
  Who sees all the sins which his
    father has done,
  And considers but does not do
    likewise;
15 Who has not eaten on the
    mountains,
  Nor lifted his eyes to the idols
    of the house of Israel,
  Nor defiled his neighbor's wife;
16 Has not oppressed anyone,
  Nor withheld a pledge,
  Nor robbed by violence,
  But has given his bread to the
    hungry
  And covered the naked with
    clothing;
17 Who has withdrawn his hand
    from the poor
  And not received usury or
    increase,
  But has executed My judgments
  And walked in My statutes—
  He shall not die for the iniquity
    of his father;
  He shall surely live!

18 "As for his father,
  Because he cruelly oppressed,
  Robbed his brother by violence,
  And did what is not good among
    his people,
  Behold, he shall die for his
    iniquity.

19 "Yet you say, 'Why should the son not bear the guilt of the father?' Because the son has done what is lawful and right, and has kept all My statutes and observed them, he shall surely live. 20 The soul who sins shall die. The son shall not bear the guilt of the father, nor the father bear the guilt of the son. The righteousness of the righteous shall be upon himself, and the wickedness of the wicked shall be upon himself.

21 "But if a wicked man turns from all his sins which he has committed, keeps all My statutes, and does what is lawful and right, he shall surely live; he shall not die. 22 None of the transgressions which he has committed shall be remembered against him; because of the righteousness which he has done, he shall live. 23 Do I have any pleasure at all that the wicked should die?" says the Lord GOD, "and not that he should turn from his ways and live?

24 "But when a righteous man turns away from his righteousness and commits iniquity, and does according to all the abominations that the wicked man does, shall he live? All the righteousness which he has done shall not be remembered; because of the unfaithfulness of which he is guilty and the sin which he has committed, because of them he shall die.

25 "Yet you say, 'The way of the Lord is not fair.' Hear now, O house of Israel, is it not My way which is fair, and your ways which are not fair? 26 When a righteous man turns away from his righteousness, commits iniquity, and dies in it, it is because of the iniquity which he has done that he dies. 27 Again, when a wicked man turns away from the wickedness which he committed, and does what is lawful and right, he preserves himself alive. 28 Because he considers and turns away from all the transgressions which he committed, he shall surely live; he shall not die. 29 Yet the house of Israel says, 'The way of the Lord is not fair.' O house of Israel, is it not My ways which are fair, and your ways which are not fair?

30 "Therefore I will judge you, O house of Israel, every one according to his ways," says the Lord GOD. "Repent, and turn from all your transgressions, so that iniquity will not be your ruin. 31 Cast away from you all the transgressions which you have committed, and get yourselves a new heart and a new spirit. For why should you die, O house of Israel? 32 For I have no pleasure in the death of one who

dies," says the Lord God. "Therefore turn and live!"

Ezekiel sings a mourning song

19 "Moreover take up a lamentation for the princes of Israel, ² and say:

> 'What *is* your mother? A lioness:
> She lay down among the lions;
> Among the young lions she
>   nourished her cubs.
> ³ She brought up one of her cubs,
> And he became a young lion;
> He learned to catch prey,
> And he devoured men.
> ⁴ The nations also heard of him;
> He was trapped in their pit,
> And they brought him with
>   chains to the land of Egypt.

> ⁵ 'When she saw that she waited,
>   *that* her hope was lost,
> She took another of her cubs
>   *and* made him a young lion.
> ⁶ He roved among the lions,
> And became a young lion;
> He learned to catch prey;
> He devoured men.
> ⁷ He knew their desolate places,
> And laid waste their cities;
> The land with its fullness was
>   desolated
> By the noise of his roaring.
> ⁸ Then the nations set against him
>   from the provinces on *every*
>   side,
> And spread their net over him;
> He was trapped in their pit.
> ⁹ They put him in a cage with
>   chains,
> And brought him to the king of
>   Babylon;
> They brought him in nets,
> That his voice should no longer
>   be heard on the mountains of
>   Israel.

> ¹⁰ 'Your mother *was* like a vine in
>   your bloodline,
> Planted by the waters,
> Fruitful and full of branches
> Because of many waters.

> ¹¹ She had strong branches for
>   scepters of rulers.
> She towered in stature above
>   the thick branches,
> And was seen in her height amid
>   the dense foliage.
> ¹² But she was plucked up in fury,
> She was cast down to the
>   ground,
> And the east wind dried her fruit.
> Her strong branches were
>   broken and withered;
> The fire consumed them.
> ¹³ And now she *is* planted in the
>   wilderness,
> In a dry and thirsty land.
> ¹⁴ Fire has come out from a rod
>   of her branches
> *And* devoured her fruit,
> So that she has no strong
>   branch— a scepter for
>   ruling.' "

This *is* a lamentation, and has become a lamentation.

Won't Israel ever learn?

20 It came to pass in the seventh year, in the fifth *month,* on the tenth *day* of the month, *that* certain of the elders of Israel came to inquire of the Lord, and sat before me. ² Then the word of the Lord came to me, saying, ³ "Son of man, speak to the elders of Israel, and say to them, 'Thus says the Lord God: "Have you come to inquire of Me? *As* I live," says the Lord God, "I will not be inquired of by you." ' ⁴ Will you judge them, son of man, will you judge *them?* Then make known to them the abominations of their fathers.

⁵ "Say to them, 'Thus says the Lord God: "On the day when I chose Israel and raised My hand in an oath to the descendants of the house of Jacob, and made Myself known to them in the land of Egypt, I raised My hand in an oath to them, saying, 'I *am* the Lord your God.' ⁶ On that day I raised My hand in an oath to them, to bring them out of the land of Egypt into a land that I had searched out for them,

'flowing with milk and honey,' the glory of all lands. 7 Then I said to them, 'Each of you, throw away the abominations which are before his eyes, and do not defile yourselves with the idols of Egypt. I *am* the LORD your God.' 8 But they rebelled against Me and would not obey Me. They did not all cast away the abominations which were before their eyes, nor did they forsake the idols of Egypt. Then I said, 'I will pour out My fury on them and fulfill My anger against them in the midst of the land of Egypt.' 9 But I acted for My name's sake, that it should not be profaned before the Gentiles among whom they *were,* in whose sight I had made Myself known to them, to bring them out of the land of Egypt.

10 "Therefore I made them go out of the land of Egypt and brought them into the wilderness. 11 And I gave them My statutes and showed them My judgments, 'which, *if* a man does, he shall live by them.' 12 Moreover I also gave them My Sabbaths, to be a sign between them and Me, that they might know that I *am* the LORD who sanctifies them. 13 Yet the house of Israel rebelled against Me in the wilderness; they did not walk in My statutes; they despised My judgments, 'which, *if* a man does, he shall live by them'; and they greatly defiled My Sabbaths. Then I said I would pour out My fury on them in the wilderness, to consume them. 14 But I acted for My name's sake, that it should not be profaned before the Gentiles, in whose sight I had brought them out. 15 So I also raised My hand in an oath to them in the wilderness, that I would not bring them into the land which I had given *them,* 'flowing with milk and honey,' the glory of all lands, 16 because they despised My judgments and did not walk in My statutes, but profaned My Sabbaths; for their heart went after their idols. 17 Nevertheless My eye spared them from destruction. I did not make an end of them in the wilderness.

18 "But I said to their children in the wilderness, 'Do not walk in the statutes of your fathers, nor observe their judgments, nor defile yourselves with their idols. 19 I *am* the LORD your God: Walk in My statutes, keep My judgments, and do them; 20 hallow My Sabbaths, and they will be a sign between Me and you, that you may know that I *am* the LORD your God.'

21 "Notwithstanding, the children rebelled against Me; they did not walk in My statutes, and were not careful to observe My judgments, 'which, *if* a man does, he shall live by them'; but they profaned My Sabbaths. Then I said I would pour out My fury on them and fulfill My anger against them in the wilderness. 22 Nevertheless I withdrew My hand and acted for My name's sake, that it should not be profaned in the sight of the Gentiles, in whose sight I had brought them out. 23 Also I raised My hand in an oath to those in the wilderness, that I would scatter them among the Gentiles and disperse them throughout the countries, 24 because they had not executed My judgments, but had despised My statutes, profaned My Sabbaths, and their eyes were fixed on their fathers' idols.

25 "Therefore I also gave them up to statutes *that were* not good, and judgments by which they could not live; 26 and I pronounced them unclean because of their ritual gifts, in that they caused all their firstborn to pass through *the fire,* that I might make them desolate and that they might know that I am the LORD."'

27 "Therefore, son of man, speak to the house of Israel, and say to them, 'Thus says the Lord GOD: "In this too your fathers have blasphemed Me, by being unfaithful to Me. 28 When I brought them into the land *concerning* which I had raised My hand in an oath to give them, and they saw all the high hills and all the thick trees, there they offered their sacrifices and provoked Me with their offerings. There they also sent up their sweet aroma and poured out their drink offerings. 29 Then I said to them, 'What *is* this high place to which you go?' So its name is called Bamah to this day."' 30 Therefore say

to the house of Israel, 'Thus says the Lord GOD: "Are you defiling yourselves in the manner of your fathers, and committing harlotry according to their abominations? 31 For when you offer your gifts and make your sons pass through the fire, you defile yourselves with all your idols, even to this day. So shall I be inquired of by you, O house of Israel? As I live," says the Lord GOD, "I will not be inquired of by you. 32 What you have in your mind shall never be, when you say, 'We will be like the Gentiles, like the families in other countries, serving wood and stone.'

33 "As I live," says the Lord GOD, "surely with a mighty hand, with an outstretched arm, and with fury poured out, I will rule over you. 34 I will bring you out from the peoples and gather you out of the countries where you are scattered, with a mighty hand, with an outstretched arm, and with fury poured out. 35 And I will bring you into the wilderness of the peoples, and there I will plead My case with you face to face. 36 Just as I pleaded My case with your fathers in the wilderness of the land of Egypt, so I will plead My case with you," says the Lord GOD.

37 "I will make you pass under the rod, and I will bring you into the bond of the covenant; 38 I will purge the rebels from among you, and those who transgress against Me; I will bring them out of the country where they dwell, but they shall not enter the land of Israel. Then you will know that I am the LORD.

39 "As for you, O house of Israel," thus says the Lord GOD: "Go, serve every one of you his idols—and hereafter—if you will not obey Me; but profane My holy name no more with your gifts and your idols. 40 For on My holy mountain, on the mountain height of Israel," says the Lord GOD, "there all the house of Israel, all of them in the land, shall serve Me; there I will accept them, and there I will require your offerings and the firstfruits of your sacrifices, together with all your holy things. 41 I will accept you as a sweet aroma when I bring you out from the peoples and gather you out of the countries where you have been scattered; and I will be hallowed in you before the Gentiles. 42 Then you shall know that I am the LORD, when I bring you into the land of Israel, into the country for which I raised My hand in an oath to give to your fathers. 43 And there you shall remember your ways and all your doings with which you were defiled; and you shall loathe yourselves in your own sight because of all the evils that you have committed. 44 Then you shall know that I am the LORD, when I have dealt with you for My name's sake, not according to your wicked ways nor according to your corrupt doings, O house of Israel," says the Lord GOD.' "

45 Furthermore the word of the LORD came to me, saying, 46 "Son of man, set your face toward the south; preach against the south and prophesy against the forest land, the South, 47 and say to the forest of the South, 'Hear the word of the LORD! Thus says the Lord GOD: "Behold, I will kindle a fire in you, and it shall devour every green tree and every dry tree in you; the blazing flame shall not be quenched, and all faces from the south to the north shall be scorched by it. 48 All flesh shall see that I, the LORD, have kindled it; it shall not be quenched." ' "

49 Then I said, "Ah, Lord GOD! They say of me, 'Does he not speak **parables?**' "

A sword that flashes like lightning

21 And the word of the LORD came to me, saying, 2 "Son of man, set your face toward Jerusalem, preach against

---

WORDFINDER

20:49 Parable Pronounced PAIR-uh-bull. A story that teaches a lesson. The story may or may not be based on a true fact. Jesus used parables to teach spiritual truths.

the holy places, and prophesy against the land of Israel; 3 and say to the land of Israel, 'Thus says the LORD: "Behold, I am against you, and I will draw My sword out of its sheath and cut off both righteous and wicked from you. 4 Because I will cut off both righteous and wicked from you, therefore My sword shall go out of its sheath against all flesh from south to north, 5 that all flesh may know that I, the LORD, have drawn My sword out of its sheath; it shall not return anymore." ' 6 Sigh therefore, son of man, with a breaking heart, and sigh with bitterness before their eyes. 7 And it shall be when they say to you, 'Why are you sighing?' that you shall answer, 'Because of the news; when it comes, every heart will melt, all hands will be feeble, every spirit will faint, and all knees will be weak as water. Behold, it is coming and shall be brought to pass,' says the Lord GOD."

8 Again the word of the LORD came to me, saying, 9 "Son of man, prophesy and say, 'Thus says the LORD!' Say:

'A sword, a sword is sharpened
And also polished!
10   Sharpened to make a dreadful slaughter,
Polished to flash like lightning!
Should we then make mirth?
It despises the scepter of My son,
As it does all wood.
11   And He has given it to be polished,
That it may be handled;
This sword is sharpened, and it is polished
To be given into the hand of the slayer.'

12 "Cry and wail, son of man;
For it will be against My people,
Against all the princes of Israel.
Terrors including the sword will be against My people;
Therefore strike your thigh.

13 "Because it is a testing,
And what if the sword despises even the scepter?
The scepter shall be no more,"

says the Lord GOD.

14 "You therefore, son of man, prophesy,
And strike your hands together.
The third time let the sword do double damage.
It is the sword that slays,
The sword that slays the great men,
That enters their private chambers.
15   I have set the point of the sword against all their gates,
That the heart may melt and many may stumble.
Ah! It is made bright;
It is grasped for slaughter:

16 "Swords at the ready!
Thrust right!
Set your blade!
Thrust left—
Wherever your edge is ordered!

17 "I also will beat My fists together,
And I will cause My fury to rest;
I, the LORD, have spoken."

18 The word of the LORD came to me again, saying: 19 "And son of man, appoint for yourself two ways for the sword of the king of Babylon to go; both of them shall go from the same land. Make a sign; put it at the head of the road to the city. 20 Appoint a road for the sword to go to Rabbah of the Ammonites, and to Judah, into fortified Jerusalem. 21 For the king of Babylon stands at the parting of the road, at the fork of the two roads, to use divination: he shakes the arrows, he consults the images, he looks at the liver. 22 In his right hand is the divination for Jerusalem: to set up battering rams, to call for a slaughter, to lift the voice with shouting, to set battering rams against the gates, to heap up a siege mound, and to build a wall.

23 And it will be to them like a false divination in the eyes of those who have sworn oaths with them; but he will bring their iniquity to remembrance, that they may be taken.

24 "Therefore thus says the Lord GOD: 'Because you have made your iniquity to be remembered, in that your transgressions are uncovered, so that in all your doings your sins appear— because you have come to remembrance, you shall be taken in hand.

25 'Now to you, O profane, wicked prince of Israel, whose day has come, whose iniquity *shall* end, 26 thus says the Lord GOD:

"Remove the turban, and take off
the crown;
Nothing *shall remain* the same.
Exalt the humble, and humble
the exalted.
27 Overthrown, overthrown,
I will make it overthrown!
It shall be no *longer,*
Until He comes whose right it
is,
And I will give it *to Him."* '

28 "And you, son of man, prophesy and say, 'Thus says the Lord GOD concerning the Ammonites and concerning their reproach,' and say:

'A sword, a sword *is* drawn,
Polished for slaughter,
For consuming, for flashing—
29 While they *see* false visions for
you,
While they divine a lie to you,
To bring you on the necks of
the wicked, the slain
Whose day has come,
Whose iniquity *shall* end.

30 'Return *it* to its sheath.
I will judge you
In the place where you were
created,
In the land of your nativity.
31 I will pour out My indignation
on you;
I will blow against you with the
fire of My wrath,

And deliver you into the hands
of brutal men *who are* skillful
to destroy.
32 You shall be fuel for the fire;
Your blood shall be in the midst
of the land.
You shall not be remembered,
For I the LORD have spoken.' "

God spells out the people's sins

22 Moreover the word of the LORD came to me, saying, 2 "Now, son of man, will you judge, will you judge the bloody city? Yes, show her all her abominations! 3 Then say, 'Thus says the Lord GOD: "The city sheds blood in her own midst, that her time may come; and she makes idols within herself to defile herself. 4 You have become guilty by the blood which you have shed, and have defiled yourself with the idols which you have made. You have caused your days to draw near, and have come to *the end of* your years; therefore I have made you a reproach to the nations, and a mockery to all countries. 5 *Those* near and *those* far from you will mock you as infamous *and* full of tumult.

6 "Look, the princes of Israel: each one has used his power to shed blood in you. 7 In you they have made light of father and mother; in your midst they have oppressed the stranger; in you they have mistreated the fatherless and the widow. 8 You have despised My holy things and profaned My Sabbaths. 9 In you are men who slander to cause bloodshed; in you are those who eat on the mountains; in your midst they commit lewdness. 10 In you men uncover their fathers' nakedness; in you they violate women who are set apart during their impurity. 11 One commits abomination with his neighbor's wife; another lewdly defiles his daughter-in-law; and another in you violates his sister, his father's daughter. 12 In you they take bribes to shed blood; you take usury and increase; you have made profit from your neighbors by extortion, and have forgotten Me," says the Lord GOD.

13 "Behold, therefore, I beat My fists at the dishonest profit which you have made, and at the bloodshed which has been in your midst. 14 Can your heart endure, or can your hands remain strong, in the days when I shall deal with you? I, the LORD, have spoken, and will do it. 15 I will scatter you among the nations, disperse you throughout the countries, and remove your filthiness completely from you. 16 You shall defile yourself in the sight of the nations; then you shall know that I am the LORD." '"

17 The word of the LORD came to me, saying, 18 "Son of man, the house of Israel has become dross to Me; they are all bronze, tin, iron, and lead, in the midst of a furnace; they have become dross from silver. 19 Therefore thus says the Lord GOD: 'Because you have all become dross, therefore behold, I will gather you into the midst of Jerusalem. 20 As men gather silver, bronze, iron, lead, and tin into the midst of a furnace, to blow fire on it, to melt it; so I will gather you in My anger and in My fury, and I will leave you there and melt you. 21 Yes, I will gather you and blow on you with the fire of My wrath, and you shall be melted in its midst. 22 As silver is melted in the midst of a furnace, so shall you be melted in its midst; then you shall know that I, the LORD, have poured out My fury on you.' "

23 And the word of the LORD came to me, saying, 24 "Son of man, say to her: 'You are a land that is not cleansed or rained on in the day of indignation.' 25 The conspiracy of her prophets in her midst is like a roaring lion tearing the prey; they have devoured people; they have taken treasure and precious things; they have made many widows in her midst. 26 Her priests have violated My law and profaned My holy things; they have not distinguished between the holy and unholy, nor have they made known the difference between the unclean and the clean; and they have hidden their eyes from My Sabbaths, so that I am profaned among them. 27 Her princes in her midst are like wolves tearing the prey, to shed blood, to destroy people, and to get dishonest gain. 28 Her prophets plastered them with untempered mortar, seeing false visions, and divining lies for them, saying, 'Thus says the Lord GOD,' when the LORD had not spoken. 29 The people of the land have used oppressions, committed robbery, and mistreated the poor and needy; and they wrongfully oppress the stranger. 30 So I sought for a man among them who would make a wall, and stand in the gap before Me on behalf of the land, that I should not destroy it; but I found no one. 31 Therefore I have poured out My indignation on them; I have consumed them with the fire of My wrath; and I have recompensed their deeds on their own heads," says the Lord GOD.

A tale of two sisters

23 The word of the LORD came again to me, saying:

2   "Son of man, there were two
        women,
        The daughters of one mother.
3   They committed harlotry in
            Egypt,
        They committed harlotry in their
            youth;
        Their breasts were there
            embraced,
        Their virgin bosom was there
            pressed.
4   Their names: Oholah the elder
            and Oholibah her sister;
        They were Mine,
        And they bore sons and
            daughters.
        As for their names,
        Samaria is Oholah, and
            Jerusalem is Oholibah.

5   "Oholah played the harlot even
            though she was Mine;
        And she lusted for her lovers, the
            neighboring Assyrians,
6   Who were clothed in purple,
        Captains and rulers,

All of them desirable young
       men,
Horsemen riding on horses.
7 Thus she committed her harlotry
       with them,
   All of them choice men of
       Assyria;
   And with all for whom she
       lusted,
   With all their idols, she defiled
       herself.
8 She has never given up her
       harlotry *brought* from Egypt,
   For in her youth they had lain
       with her,
   Pressed her virgin bosom,
   And poured out their immorality
       upon her.

9 "Therefore I have delivered her
       Into the hand of her lovers,
       Into the hand of the Assyrians,
       For whom she lusted.
10 They uncovered her nakedness,
   Took away her sons and
       daughters,
   And slew her with the sword;
   She became a byword among
       women,
   For they had executed judgment
       on her.

11 "Now although her sister Oholibah saw *this,* she became more corrupt
in her lust than she, and in her harlotry
more corrupt than her sister's harlotry.

12 "She lusted for the neighboring
       Assyrians,
   Captains and rulers,
   Clothed most gorgeously,
   Horsemen riding on horses,
   All of them desirable young
       men.
13 Then I saw that she was defiled;
   Both *took* the same way.
14 But she increased her harlotry;
   She looked at men portrayed on
       the wall,
   Images of Chaldeans portrayed
       in vermilion,
15 Girded with belts around their
       waists,
   Flowing turbans on their heads,

   All of them looking like captains,
   In the manner of the
       Babylonians of Chaldea,
   The land of their nativity.
16 As soon as her eyes saw them,
   She lusted for them
   And sent messengers to them in
       Chaldea.

17 "Then the Babylonians came to
       her, into the bed of love,
   And they defiled her with their
       immorality;
   So she was defiled by them, and
       alienated herself from them.
18 She revealed her harlotry and
       uncovered her nakedness.
   Then I alienated Myself from
       her,
   As I had alienated Myself from
       her sister.

19 "Yet she multiplied her harlotry
   In calling to remembrance the
       days of her youth,
   When she had played the harlot
       in the land of Egypt.
20 For she lusted for her
       paramours,
   Whose flesh *is like* the flesh of
       donkeys,
   And whose issue *is like* the issue
       of horses.
21 Thus you called to
       remembrance the lewdness of
       your youth,
   When the Egyptians pressed
       your bosom
   Because of your youthful
       breasts.

22 "Therefore, Oholibah, thus says
the Lord GOD:

   'Behold, I will stir up your lovers
       against you,
   From whom you have alienated
       yourself,
   And I will bring them against you
       from every side:
23 The Babylonians,
   All the Chaldeans,
   Pekod, Shoa, Koa,
   All the Assyrians with them,

All of them desirable young
    men,
Governors and rulers,
Captains and men of renown,
All of them riding on horses.
24 And they shall come against you
    With chariots, wagons, and war-
      horses,
    With a horde of people.
    They shall array against you
    Buckler, shield, and helmet all
      around.

    'I will delegate judgment to them,
    And they shall judge you
      according to their judgments.
25 I will set My jealousy against
      you,
    And they shall deal furiously
      with you;
    They shall remove your nose
      and your ears,
    And your remnant shall fall by
      the sword;
    They shall take your sons and
      your daughters,
    And your remnant shall be
      devoured by fire.
26 They shall also strip you of your
    clothes
    And take away your beautiful
      jewelry.

27 'Thus I will make you cease your
    lewdness and your harlotry
    Brought from the land of Egypt,
    So that you will not lift your eyes
      to them,
    Nor remember Egypt anymore.'

28 "For thus says the Lord God:
'Surely I will deliver you into the hand
of those you hate, into the hand *of
those* from whom you alienated yourself. 29 They will deal hatefully with
you, take away all you have worked
for, and leave you naked and bare.
The nakedness of your harlotry shall
be uncovered, both your lewdness and
your harlotry. 30 I will do these *things*
to you because you have gone as a
harlot after the Gentiles, because you
have become defiled by their idols.
31 You have walked in the way of your

sister; therefore I will put her cup in
your hand.'
32 "Thus says the Lord God:

    'You shall drink of your sister's
      cup,
    The deep and wide one;
    You shall be laughed to scorn
    And held in derision;
    It contains much.
33 You will be filled with
      drunkenness and sorrow,
    The cup of horror and
      desolation,
    The cup of your sister Samaria.
34 You shall drink and drain it,
    You shall break its shards,
    And tear at your own breasts;
    For I have spoken,'
    Says the Lord God.

35 "Therefore thus says the Lord
God:

    'Because you have forgotten Me
      and cast Me behind your
      back,
    Therefore you shall bear the
      penalty
    Of your lewdness and your
      harlotry.' "

36 The Lord also said to me: "Son
of man, will you judge Oholah and
Oholibah? Then declare to them their
abominations. 37 For they have committed adultery, and blood *is* on their
hands. They have committed adultery
with their idols, and even sacrificed
their sons whom they bore to Me, passing them through *the fire,* to devour
them. 38 Moreover they have done this
to Me: They have defiled My sanctuary
on the same day and profaned My
Sabbaths. 39 For after they had slain
their children for their idols, on the
same day they came into My sanctuary
to profane it; and indeed thus they
have done in the midst of My house.
40 "Furthermore you sent for men
to come from afar, to whom a messenger *was* sent; and there they came.
And you washed yourself for them,
painted your eyes, and adorned your-

self with ornaments. ⁴¹ You sat on a stately couch, with a table prepared before it, on which you had set My incense and My oil. ⁴² The sound of a carefree multitude *was* with her, and Sabeans *were* brought from the wilderness with men of the common sort, who put bracelets on their wrists and beautiful crowns on their heads. ⁴³ Then I said concerning *her who had grown* old in adulteries, 'Will they commit harlotry with her now, and she *with them?*' ⁴⁴ Yet they went in to her, as men go in to a woman who plays the harlot; thus they went in to Oholah and Oholibah, the lewd women. ⁴⁵ But righteous men will judge them after the manner of adulteresses, and after the manner of women who shed blood, because they *are* adulteresses, and blood *is* on their hands.

⁴⁶ "For thus says the Lord GOD: 'Bring up an assembly against them, give them up to trouble and plunder. ⁴⁷ The assembly shall stone them with stones and execute them with their swords; they shall slay their sons and their daughters, and burn their houses with fire. ⁴⁸ Thus I will cause lewdness to cease from the land, that all women may be taught not to practice your lewdness. ⁴⁹ They shall repay you for your lewdness, and you shall pay for your idolatrous sins. Then you shall know that I *am* the Lord GOD.' "

The parable of the rusty cooking pot

24 Again, in the ninth year, in the tenth month, on the tenth *day* of the month, the word of the LORD came to me, saying, ² "Son of man, write down the name of the day, this very day— the king of Babylon started his siege against Jerusalem this very day. ³ And utter a parable to the rebellious house, and say to them, 'Thus says the Lord GOD:

"Put on a pot, set *it* on,
And also pour water into it.
4   Gather pieces *of meat* in it,
Every good piece,

The thigh and the shoulder.
Fill *it* with choice cuts;
5   Take the choice of the flock.
Also pile *fuel* bones under it,
Make it boil well,
And let the cuts simmer in it."

⁶ 'Therefore thus says the Lord GOD:

"Woe to the bloody city,
To the pot whose scum *is* in it,
And whose scum is not gone from it!
Bring it out piece by piece,
On which no lot has fallen.
7   For her blood is in her midst;
She set it on top of a rock;
She did not pour it on the ground,
To cover it with dust.
8   That it may raise up fury and take vengeance,
I have set her blood on top of a rock,
That it may not be covered."

⁹ 'Therefore thus says the Lord GOD:

"Woe to the bloody city!
I too will make the pyre great.
10   Heap on the wood,
Kindle the fire;
Cook the meat well,
Mix in the spices,
And let the cuts be burned up.

11   "Then set the pot empty on the coals,
That it may become hot and its bronze may burn,
That its filthiness may be melted in it,
That its scum may be consumed.
12   She has grown weary with lies,
And her great scum has not gone from her.
Let her scum *be* in the fire!
13   In your filthiness *is* lewdness.
Because I have cleansed you, and you were not cleansed,
You will not be cleansed of your filthiness anymore,
Till I have caused My fury to rest upon you.

Prophet Doesn't Mourn Wife's Death

The Babylon News-Press

MIZPAH—Reporters in Babylon have grown used to the strange behavior of Ezekiel the prophet.

First, he performed that strange street drama with the clay model of Jerusalem (Ezekiel 4, 5). Then he broke a hole through the wall of his house (Ezekiel 12). Now the prophet's wife has died, but he has not mourned for her. He carries on his daily life as though nothing has happened. He doesn't even shed a tear!

When a *News-Press* reporter asked him about this strange response, he gave the following explanation: "I behave this way to let the people of Jerusalem know that the time is coming when their temple will be destroyed. Just as I loved my wife, so they also love their temple. But they will not be allowed to mourn for the temple, just as I was not allowed to mourn for my wife."

14 I, the LORD, have spoken *it;*
    It shall come to pass, and I will
        do *it;*
    I will not hold back,
    Nor will I spare,
    Nor will I relent;
    According to your ways
    And according to your deeds
    They will judge you,"
    Says the Lord GOD.' "

15 Also the word of the LORD came to me, saying, 16 "Son of man, behold, I take away from you the desire of your eyes with one stroke; yet you shall neither mourn nor weep, nor shall your tears run down. 17 Sigh in silence, make no mourning for the dead; bind your turban on your head, and put your sandals on your feet; do not cover *your* lips, and do not eat man's bread *of sorrow.*"

18 So I spoke to the people in the morning, and at evening my wife died; and the next morning I did as I was commanded.

19 And the people said to me, "Will you not tell us what these *things signify* to us, that you behave so?"

20 Then I answered them, "The word of the LORD came to me, saying, 21 'Speak to the house of Israel, "Thus says the Lord GOD: 'Behold, I will profane My sanctuary, your arrogant boast, the desire of your eyes, the de-light of your soul; and your sons and daughters whom you left behind shall fall by the sword. 22 And you shall do as I have done; you shall not cover *your* lips nor eat man's bread *of sorrow.* 23 Your turbans shall be on your heads and your sandals on your feet; you shall neither mourn nor weep, but you shall pine away in your iniquities and mourn with one another. 24 Thus Ezekiel is a sign to you; according to all that he has done you shall do; and when this comes, you shall know that I *am* the Lord GOD.' "

25 'And you, son of man—*will it* not *be* in the day when I take from them their stronghold, their joy and their glory, the desire of their eyes, and that on which they set their minds, their sons and their daughters: 26 on that day one who escapes will come to you to let *you* hear *it* with *your* ears; 27 on that day your mouth will be opened to him who has escaped; you shall speak and no longer be mute. Thus you will be a sign to them, and they shall know that I *am* the LORD.' "

God sends punishment on the evil nations

25 The word of the LORD came to me, saying, 2 "Son of man, set your face against the Ammonites, and prophesy against them. 3 Say to the

Ammonites, 'Hear the word of the Lord GOD! Thus says the Lord GOD: "Because you said, 'Aha!' against My sanctuary when it was profaned, and against the land of Israel when it was desolate, and against the house of Judah when they went into captivity, 4 indeed, therefore, I will deliver you as a possession to the men of the East, and they shall set their encampments among you and make their dwellings among you; they shall eat your fruit, and they shall drink your milk. 5 And I will make Rabbah a stable for camels and Ammon a resting place for flocks. Then you shall know that I *am* the LORD."

6 'For thus says the Lord GOD: "Because you clapped *your* hands, stamped your feet, and rejoiced in heart with all your disdain for the land of Israel, 7 indeed, therefore, I will stretch out My hand against you, and give you as plunder to the nations; I will cut you off from the peoples, and I will cause you to perish from the countries; I will destroy you, and you shall know that I *am* the LORD."

8 'Thus says the Lord GOD: "Because Moab and Seir say, 'Look! The house of Judah *is* like all the nations,' 9 therefore, behold, I will clear the territory of Moab of cities, of the cities on its frontier, the glory of the country, Beth Jeshimoth, Baal Meon, and Kirjathaim. 10 To the men of the East I will give it as a possession, together with the Ammonites, that the Ammonites may not be remembered among the nations. 11 And I will execute judgments upon Moab, and they shall know that I *am* the LORD."

12 'Thus says the Lord GOD: "Because of what Edom did against the house of Judah by taking vengeance, and has greatly offended by avenging itself on them," 13 therefore thus says the Lord GOD: "I will also stretch out My hand against Edom, cut off man and beast from it, and make it desolate from Teman; Dedan shall fall by the sword. 14 I will lay My vengeance on Edom by the hand of My people Israel, that they may do in Edom according

to My anger and according to My fury; and they shall know My vengeance," says the Lord GOD.

15 'Thus says the Lord GOD: "Because the Philistines dealt vengefully and took vengeance with a spiteful heart, to destroy because of the old hatred," 16 therefore thus says the Lord GOD: "I will stretch out My hand against the Philistines, and I will cut off the Cherethites and destroy the remnant of the seacoast. 17 I will execute great vengeance on them with furious rebukes; and they shall know that I *am* the LORD, when I lay My vengeance upon them." ' "

Tyre's towers will be torn down

26 And it came to pass in the eleventh year, on the first *day* of the month, *that* the word of the LORD came to me, saying, 2 "Son of man, because Tyre has said against Jerusalem, 'Aha! She is broken who *was* the gateway of the peoples; now she is turned over to me; I shall be filled; she is laid waste.'

3 "Therefore thus says the Lord GOD: 'Behold, I *am* against you, O Tyre, and will cause many nations to come up against you, as the sea causes its waves to come up. 4 And they shall destroy the walls of Tyre and break down her towers; I will also scrape her dust from her, and make her like the top of a rock. 5 It shall be *a place for* spreading nets in the midst of the sea, for I have spoken,' says the Lord GOD; 'it shall become plunder for the nations. 6 Also her daughter *villages* which *are* in the fields shall be slain by the sword. Then they shall know that I am the LORD.'

7 "For thus says the Lord GOD: 'Behold, I will bring against Tyre from the north Nebuchadnezzar king of Babylon, king of kings, with horses, with chariots, and with horsemen, and an army with many people. 8 He will slay with the sword your daughter *villages* in the fields; he will heap up a siege mound against you, build a wall against you, and raise a defense

against you. ⁹ He will direct his battering rams against your walls, and with his axes he will break down your towers. ¹⁰ Because of the abundance of his horses, their dust will cover you; your walls will shake at the noise of the horsemen, the wagons, and the chariots, when he enters your gates, as men enter a city that has been breached. ¹¹ With the hooves of his horses he will trample all your streets; he will slay your people by the sword, and your strong pillars will fall to the ground. ¹² They will plunder your riches and pillage your merchandise; they will break down your walls and destroy your pleasant houses; they will lay your stones, your timber, and your soil in the midst of the water. ¹³ I will put an end to the sound of your songs, and the sound of your harps shall be heard no more. ¹⁴ I will make you like the top of a rock; you shall be *a place for* spreading nets, and you shall never be rebuilt, for I the Lᴏʀᴅ have spoken,' says the Lord Gᴏᴅ.

¹⁵ "Thus says the Lord Gᴏᴅ to Tyre: 'Will the coastlands not shake at the sound of your fall, when the wounded cry, when slaughter is made in the midst of you? ¹⁶ Then all the princes of the sea will come down from their thrones, lay aside their robes, and take off their embroidered garments; they will clothe themselves with trembling; they will sit on the ground, tremble *every* moment, and be astonished at you. ¹⁷ And they will take up a lamentation for you, and say to you:

"How you have perished,
O one inhabited by seafaring
   men,
O renowned city,
Who was strong at sea,
She and her inhabitants,
Who caused their terror *to be*
   on all her inhabitants!
¹⁸ Now the coastlands tremble on
   the day of your fall;
Yes, the coastlands by the sea
   are troubled at your
   departure.'"'

¹⁹ "For thus says the Lord Gᴏᴅ: 'When I make you a desolate city, like cities that are not inhabited, when I bring the deep upon you, and great waters cover you, ²⁰ then I will bring you down with those who descend into the Pit, to the people of old, and I will make you dwell in the lowest part of the earth, in places desolate from antiquity, with those who go down to the Pit, so that you may never be inhabited; and I shall establish glory in the land of the living. ²¹ I will make you a terror, and you *shall be* no *more;* though you are sought for, you will never be found again,' says the Lord Gᴏᴅ."

Ezekiel sings a sad song

27 The word of the Lᴏʀᴅ came again to me, saying, ² "Now, son of man, take up a lamentation for Tyre, ³ and say to Tyre, 'You who are situated at the entrance of the sea, merchant of the peoples on many coastlands, thus says the Lord Gᴏᴅ:

"O Tyre, you have said,
'I *am* perfect in beauty.'
4   Your borders *are* in the midst of
   the seas.
Your builders have perfected
   your beauty.
5   They made all *your* planks of fir
   trees from Senir;
They took a cedar from
   Lebanon to make you a mast.
6   *Of* oaks from Bashan they made
   your oars;
The company of Ashurites have
   inlaid your planks
With ivory from the coasts of
   Cyprus.
7   Fine embroidered linen from
   Egypt was what you spread
   for your sail;
Blue and purple from the coasts
   of Elishah was what covered
   you.

8   "Inhabitants of Sidon and Arvad
   were your oarsmen;

Your wise men, O Tyre, were
   in you;
They became your pilots.
9   Elders of Gebal and its wise men
   Were in you to caulk your
      seams;
   All the ships of the sea
   And their oarsmen were in you
   To market your merchandise.

10   "Those from Persia, Lydia, and
      Libya
   Were in your army as men of
      war;
   They hung shield and helmet in
      you;
   They gave splendor to you.
11   Men of Arvad with your army
      were on your walls *all* around,
   And the men of Gammad were
      in your towers;
   They hung their shields on your
      walls *all* around;
   They made your beauty perfect.

12 "Tarshish *was* your merchant because of your many luxury goods.
They gave you silver, iron, tin, and
lead for your goods. 13 Javan, Tubal,
and Meshech *were* your traders. They
bartered human lives and vessels of
bronze for your merchandise. 14 Those
from the house of Togarmah traded
for your wares with horses, steeds, and
mules. 15 The men of Dedan *were* your
traders; many isles *were* the market of
your hand. They brought you ivory
tusks and ebony as payment. 16 Syria
was your merchant because of the
abundance of goods you made. They
gave you for your wares emeralds,
purple, embroidery, fine linen, corals,
and rubies. 17 Judah and the land of Israel *were* your traders. They traded
for your merchandise wheat of Minnith, millet, honey, oil, and balm.
18 Damascus *was* your merchant because of the abundance of goods you
made, because of your many luxury
items, with the wine of Helbon and
with white wool. 19 Dan and Javan
paid for your wares, traversing back
and forth. Wrought iron, cassia, and
cane were among your merchandise.

20 Dedan *was* your merchant in saddle-
cloths for riding. 21 Arabia and all the
princes of Kedar *were* your regular
merchants. They traded with you in
lambs, rams, and goats. 22 The merchants of Sheba and Raamah *were*
your merchants. They traded for your
wares the choicest spices, all kinds of
precious stones, and gold. 23 Haran,
Canneh, Eden, the merchants of
Sheba, Assyria, *and* Chilmad *were*
your merchants. 24 These *were* your
merchants in choice items—in purple
clothes, in embroidered garments, in
chests of multicolored apparel, in
sturdy woven cords, which were in
your marketplace.

25   "The ships of Tarshish *were*
      carriers of your merchandise.
   You were filled and very glorious
      in the midst of the seas.
26   Your oarsmen brought you into
      many waters,
   But the east wind broke you in
      the midst of the seas.

27 "Your riches, wares, and
      merchandise,
   Your mariners and pilots,
   Your caulkers and
      merchandisers,
   All your men of war who *are* in
      you,
   And the entire company which
      is in your midst,
   Will fall into the midst of the seas
      on the day of your ruin.
28   The common-land will shake at
      the sound of the cry of your
      pilots.

29 "All who handle the oar,
   The mariners,
   All the pilots of the sea
   Will come down from their ships
      and stand on the shore.
30   They will make their voice heard
      because of you;
   They will cry bitterly and cast
      dust on their heads;
   They will roll about in ashes;
31   They will shave themselves

completely bald because of
   you,
Gird themselves with sackcloth,
And weep for you
With bitterness of heart *and*
   bitter wailing.
32 In their wailing for you
They will take up a lamentation,
And lament for you:
'What *city is* like Tyre,
Destroyed in the midst of the
   sea?

33 'When your wares went out by
   sea,
You satisfied many people;
You enriched the kings of the
   earth
With your many luxury goods
   and your merchandise.
34 But you are broken by the seas
   in the depths of the waters;
Your merchandise and the entire
   company Will fall in your
   midst.
35 All the inhabitants of the isles will
   be astonished at you;
Their kings will be greatly afraid,
And *their* countenance will be
   troubled.
36 The merchants among the
   peoples will hiss at you;
You will become a horror, and
   be no more forever.' " ' "

The proud prince of Tyre

28 The word of the LORD came to
me again, saying, 2 "Son of man, say
to the prince of Tyre, 'Thus says the
Lord GOD:

"Because your heart *is* lifted up,
And you say, 'I *am* a god,
I sit *in* the seat of gods,
In the midst of the seas,'
Yet you *are* a man, and not a
   god,
Though you *set* your heart as
   the heart of a god
3 (Behold, you *are* wiser than
   Daniel!
There is no secret that can be
   hidden from you!

4 With your wisdom and your
   understanding
You have gained riches for
   yourself,
And gathered gold and silver
   into your treasuries;
5 By your great wisdom in trade
   you have increased your
   riches,
And your heart is lifted up
   because of your riches),"

6 'Therefore thus says the Lord
GOD:

"Because you have set your heart
   as the heart of a god,
7 Behold, therefore, I will bring
   strangers against you,
The most terrible of the
   nations;
And they shall draw their swords
   against the beauty of your
   wisdom,
And defile your splendor.
8 They shall throw you down into
   the Pit,
And you shall die the death of
   the slain
In the midst of the seas.

9 "Will you still say before him who
   slays you,
'I *am* a god'?
But you *shall be* a man, and not
   a god,
In the hand of him who slays
   you.
10 You shall die the death of the
   uncircumcised
By the hand of aliens;
For I have spoken," says the
   Lord GOD.' "

11 Moreover the word of the LORD
came to me, saying, 12 "Son of man,
take up a lamentation for the king of
Tyre, and say to him, 'Thus says the
Lord GOD:

"You *were* the seal of perfection,
Full of wisdom and perfect in
   beauty.

13 You were in Eden, the garden
   of God;
   Every precious stone *was* your
      covering:
   The sardius, topaz, and
      diamond,
   Beryl, onyx, and jasper,
   Sapphire, turquoise, and
      emerald with gold.
   The workmanship of your
      timbrels and pipes
   Was prepared for you on the
      day you were created.

14 "You *were* the anointed cherub
      who covers;
   I established you;
   You were on the holy mountain
      of God;
   You walked back and forth in
      the midst of fiery stones.
15 You *were* perfect in your ways
      from the day you were
      created,
   Till iniquity was found in you.

16 "By the abundance of your
      trading
   You became filled with violence
      within,
   And you sinned;
   Therefore I cast you as a profane
      thing
   Out of the mountain of God;
   And I destroyed you, O covering
      cherub,
   From the midst of the fiery
      stones.

17 "Your heart was lifted up because
      of your beauty;
   You corrupted your wisdom for
      the sake of your splendor;
   I cast you to the ground,
   I laid you before kings,
   That they might gaze at you.

18 "You defiled your sanctuaries
   By the multitude of your
      iniquities,
   By the iniquity of your trading;
   Therefore I brought fire from
      your midst;
   It devoured you,
   And I turned you to ashes upon
      the earth
   In the sight of all who saw you.
19 All who knew you among the
      peoples are astonished at
      you;
   You have become a horror,
   And *shall be* no more
      forever." ' "

20 Then the word of the LORD came
to me, saying, 21 "Son of man, set your
face toward Sidon, and prophesy
against her, 22 and say, 'Thus says the
Lord GOD:

   "Behold, I *am* against you, O
      Sidon;
   I will be glorified in your midst;
   And they shall know that I *am*
      the LORD,
   When I execute judgments in
      her and am hallowed in her.
23 For I will send pestilence upon
      her,
   And blood in her streets;
   The wounded shall be judged in
      her midst
   By the sword against her on
      every side;
   Then they shall know that I *am*
      the LORD.

24 "And there shall no longer be a
pricking brier or a painful thorn for the
house of Israel from among all *who
are* around them, who despise them.
Then they shall know that I *am* the
Lord GOD."
25 'Thus says the Lord GOD: "When

DIGGING IN

**28:25, 26 God Is Bringing Israel
Home Again** God loves the nation of Is-
rael because of His promise to Abra-
ham—"I will make you a great nation"
(Genesis 12:2). It is the only nation in his-
tory that was destroyed in ancient times
but has risen again in modern times.
   Israel was destroyed by Assyria and
Babylonia hundreds of years before
Christ. Israel was destroyed again by the

I have gathered the house of Israel from the peoples among whom they are scattered, and am hallowed in them in the sight of the Gentiles, then they will dwell in their own land which I gave to My servant Jacob. 26 And they will dwell safely there, build houses, and plant vineyards; yes, they will dwell securely, when I execute judgments on all those around them who despise them. Then they shall know that I *am* the LORD their God." ' "

The river monster

29 In the tenth year, in the tenth *month*, on the twelfth *day* of the month, the word of the LORD came to me, saying, 2 "Son of man, set your face against Pharaoh king of Egypt, and prophesy against him, and against all Egypt. 3 Speak, and say, 'Thus says the Lord GOD:

"Behold, I *am* against you,
  O Pharaoh king of Egypt,
O great monster who lies in the
  midst of his rivers,
Who has said, 'My River *is* my
  own;
I have made *it* for myself.'
4 But I will put hooks in your jaws,
And cause the fish of your rivers
  to stick to your scales;
I will bring you up out of the
  midst of your rivers,
And all the fish in your rivers will
  stick to your scales.
5 I will leave you in the wilderness,
You and all the fish of your
  rivers;
You shall fall on the open field;
You shall not be picked up or
  gathered.
I have given you as food

To the beasts of the field
And to the birds of the heavens.
6 "Then all the inhabitants of Egypt
Shall know that I *am* the LORD,
Because they have been a staff
  of reed to the house of Israel.
7 When they took hold of you with
  the hand,
You broke and tore all their
  shoulders;
When they leaned on you,
You broke and made all their
  backs quiver."

8 'Therefore thus says the Lord GOD: "Surely I will bring a sword upon you and cut off from you man and beast. 9 And the land of Egypt shall become desolate and waste; then they will know that I *am* the LORD, because he said, 'The River *is* mine, and I have made *it*.' 10 Indeed, therefore, I *am* against you and against your rivers, and I will make the land of Egypt utterly waste and desolate, from Migdol *to* Syene, as far as the border of Ethiopia. 11 Neither foot of man shall pass through it nor foot of beast pass through it, and it shall be uninhabited forty years. 12 I will make the land of Egypt desolate in the midst of the countries *that are* desolate; and among the cities *that are* laid waste, her cities shall be desolate forty years; and I will scatter the Egyptians among the nations and disperse them throughout the countries."

13 'Yet, thus says the Lord GOD: "At the end of forty years I will gather the Egyptians from the peoples among whom they were scattered. 14 I will bring back the captives of Egypt and cause them to return to the land of Pathros, to the land of their origin, and there they shall be a lowly kingdom.

⚒ DIGGING IN

Syrians almost two hundred years before Christ came. Finally, the Romans completely wiped out the nation between seventy and one hundred years after Christ.

Most people thought the Jewish nation was destroyed forever, but Israel remained as a people scattered over the earth. Then, in 1948, the United Nations Organization gave Israel back its land. Although surrounded by enemies, Israel stands to this day. God is keeping His promise to Israel.

Israel has been a suffering people, but God has not forgotten His promise.

15 It shall be the lowliest of kingdoms; it shall never again exalt itself above the nations, for I will diminish them so that they will not rule over the nations anymore. 16 No longer shall it be the confidence of the house of Israel, but will remind them of *their* iniquity when they turned to follow them. Then they shall know that I *am* the Lord God." ' "

17 And it came to pass in the twenty-seventh year, in the first *month,* on the first *day* of the month, *that* the word of the Lord came to me, saying, 18 "Son of man, Nebuchadnezzar king of Babylon caused his army to labor strenuously against Tyre; *every* head *was* made bald, and *every* shoulder rubbed raw; yet neither he nor his army received wages from Tyre, for the labor which they expended on it. 19 Therefore thus says the Lord God: 'Surely I will give the land of Egypt to Nebuchadnezzar king of Babylon; he shall take away her wealth, carry off her spoil, and remove her pillage; and that will be the wages for his army. 20 I have given him the land of Egypt *for* his labor, because they worked for Me,' says the Lord God. 21 'In that day I will cause the horn of the house of Israel to spring forth, and I will open your mouth to speak in their midst. Then they shall know that I *am* the Lord.' "

A day of dark clouds and despair

30 The word of the Lord came to me again, saying, 2 "Son of man, prophesy and say, 'Thus says the Lord God:

"Wail, 'Woe to the day!'
3   For the day *is* near,
    Even the day of the Lord *is* near;
    It will be a day of clouds, the time of the Gentiles.
4   The sword shall come upon Egypt,
    And great anguish shall be in Ethiopia,
    When the slain fall in Egypt,

    And they take away her wealth,
    And her foundations are broken down.

5 "Ethiopia, Libya, Lydia, all the mingled people, Chub, and the men of the lands who are allied, shall fall with them by the sword."

6 'Thus says the Lord:

"Those who uphold Egypt shall fall,
    And the pride of her power shall come down.
    From Migdol *to* Syene
    Those within her shall fall by the sword,"
    Says the Lord God.

7   "They shall be desolate in the midst of the desolate countries,
    And her cities shall be in the midst of the cities *that are* laid waste.
8   Then they will know that I *am* the Lord,
    When I have set a fire in Egypt
    And all her helpers are destroyed.
9   On that day messengers shall go forth from Me in ships
    To make the careless Ethiopians afraid,
    And great anguish shall come upon them,
    As on the day of Egypt;
    For indeed it is coming!"

10 'Thus says the Lord God:

"I will also make a multitude of Egypt to cease
    By the hand of Nebuchadnezzar king of Babylon.
11   He and his people with him, the most terrible of the nations,
    Shall be brought to destroy the land;
    They shall draw their swords against Egypt,
    And fill the land with the slain.
12   I will make the rivers dry,

The Egyptian city of Luxor is called No in the Bible.

And sell the land into the hand
    of the wicked;
I will make the land waste, and
    all that is in it,
By the hand of aliens.
I, the LORD, have spoken."

13 'Thus says the Lord GOD:

"I will also destroy the idols,
    And cause the images to cease
        from Noph;
There shall no longer be princes
    from the land of Egypt;
I will put fear in the land of
    Egypt.
14 I will make Pathros desolate,
    Set fire to Zoan,
    And execute judgments in No.
15 I will pour My fury on Sin, the
        strength of Egypt;
    I will cut off the multitude of No,
16 And set a fire in Egypt;
    Sin shall have great pain,
    No shall be split open,
    And Noph *shall be in* distress
        daily.
17 The young men of Aven and Pi
        Beseth shall fall by the sword,

And these *cities* shall go into
    captivity.
18 At Tehaphnehes the day shall
        also be darkened,
    When I break the yokes of Egypt
        there.
    And her arrogant strength shall
        cease in her;
    As for her, a cloud shall cover
        her,
    And her daughters shall go into
        captivity.
19 Thus I will execute judgments on
        Egypt,
    Then they shall know that I *am*
        the LORD." ' "

20 And it came to pass in the eleventh year, in the first *month,* on the seventh *day* of the month, *that* the word of the LORD came to me, saying, 21 "Son of man, I have broken the arm of Pharaoh king of Egypt; and see, it has not been bandaged for healing, nor a splint put on to bind it, to make it strong enough to hold a sword. 22 Therefore thus says the Lord GOD: 'Surely I *am* against Pharaoh king of Egypt, and will break his arms, both

the strong one and the one that was broken; and I will make the sword fall out of his hand. ²³ I will scatter the Egyptians among the nations, and disperse them throughout the countries. ²⁴ I will strengthen the arms of the king of Babylon and put My sword in his hand; but I will break Pharaoh's arms, and he will groan before him with the groanings of a mortally wounded *man.* ²⁵ Thus I will strengthen the arms of the king of Babylon, but the arms of Pharaoh shall fall down; they shall know that I *am* the LORD, when I put My sword into the hand of the king of Babylon and he stretches it out against the land of Egypt. ²⁶ I will scatter the Egyptians among the nations and disperse them throughout the countries. Then they shall know that I *am* the LORD.' "

A giant tree in God's garden

31 Now it came to pass in the eleventh year, in the third *month,* on the first *day* of the month, *that* the word of the LORD came to me, saying, ² "Son of man, say to Pharaoh king of Egypt and to his multitude:

'Whom are you like in your
greatness?
³   Indeed Assyria *was* a cedar in
Lebanon,
With fine branches that shaded
the forest,
And of high stature;
And its top was among the thick
boughs.
⁴   The waters made it grow;
Underground waters gave it
height,
With their rivers running around
the place where it was
planted,
And sent out rivulets to all the
trees of the field.
⁵   'Therefore its height was exalted
above all the trees of the
field;
Its boughs were multiplied,
And its branches became long

because of the abundance of
water,
As it sent them out.
⁶   All the birds of the heavens
made their nests in its boughs;
Under its branches all the beasts
of the field brought forth their
young;
And in its shadow all great
nations made their home.

⁷   'Thus it was beautiful in greatness
and in the length of its
branches,
Because its roots reached to
abundant waters.
⁸   The cedars in the garden of God
could not hide it;
The fir trees were not like its
boughs,
And the chestnut trees were not
like its branches;
No tree in the garden of God
was like it in beauty.
⁹   I made it beautiful with a
multitude of branches,
So that all the trees of Eden
envied it,
That *were* in the garden of God.'

¹⁰ "Therefore thus says the Lord GOD: 'Because you have increased in height, and it set its top among the thick boughs, and its heart was lifted up in its height, ¹¹ therefore I will deliver it into the hand of the mighty one of the nations, and he shall surely deal with it; I have driven it out for its wickedness. ¹² And aliens, the most terrible of the nations, have cut it down and left it; its branches have fallen on the mountains and in all the valleys; its boughs lie broken by all the rivers of the land; and all the peoples of the earth have gone from under its shadow and left it.

¹³   'On its ruin will remain all the
birds of the heavens,
And all the beasts of the field
will come to its branches—

¹⁴ 'So that no trees by the waters may ever again exalt themselves for their

height, nor set their tops among the thick boughs, that no tree which drinks water may *ever* be high enough to reach up to them.

'For they have all been delivered to death,
To the depths of the earth,
Among the children of men who go down to the Pit.'

15 "Thus says the Lord God: 'In the day when it went down to hell, I caused mourning. I covered the deep because of it. I restrained its rivers, and the great waters were held back. I caused Lebanon to mourn for it, and all the trees of the field wilted because of it. 16 I made the nations shake at the sound of its fall, when I cast it down to hell together with those who descend into the Pit; and all the trees of Eden, the choice and best of Lebanon, all that drink water, were comforted in the depths of the earth. 17 They also went down to hell with it, with those *slain* by the sword; and *those who were* its *strong* arm dwelt in its shadows among the nations.

18 'To which of the trees in Eden will you then be likened in glory and greatness? Yet you shall be brought down with the trees of Eden to the depths of the earth; you shall lie in the midst of the uncircumcised, with *those* slain by the sword. This *is* Pharaoh and all his multitude,' says the Lord God."

The crocodile who muddied the waters

32 And it came to pass in the twelfth year, in the twelfth *month*, on the first *day* of the month, *that* the word of the Lord came to me, saying, 2 "Son of man, take up a lamentation for Pharaoh king of Egypt, and say to him:

'You are like a young lion among the nations,
And you *are* like a monster in the seas,
Bursting forth in your rivers,

Troubling the waters with your feet,
And fouling their rivers.'

3 "Thus says the Lord God:

'I will therefore spread My net over you with a company of many people,
And they will draw you up in My net.
4 Then I will leave you on the land;
I will cast you out on the open fields,
And cause to settle on you all the birds of the heavens.
And with you I will fill the beasts of the whole earth.
5 I will lay your flesh on the mountains,
And fill the valleys with your carcass.
6 'I will also water the land with the flow of your blood,
Even to the mountains;
And the riverbeds will be full of you.
7 When *I* put out your light,
I will cover the heavens, and make its stars dark;
I will cover the sun with a cloud,
And the moon shall not give her light.
8 All the bright lights of the heavens I will make dark over you,
And bring darkness upon your land,'
Says the Lord God.

9 'I will also trouble the hearts of many peoples, when I bring your destruction among the nations, into the countries which you have not known. 10 Yes, I will make many peoples astonished at you, and their kings shall be horribly afraid of you when I brandish My sword before them; and they shall tremble *every* moment, every man for his own life, in the day of your fall.'

11 "For thus says the Lord God: 'The

sword of the king of Babylon shall come upon you. ¹²By the swords of the mighty warriors, all of them the most terrible of the nations, I will cause your multitude to fall.

'They shall plunder the pomp of
    Egypt,
And all its multitude shall be
    destroyed.
¹³ Also I will destroy all its animals
From beside its great waters;
The foot of man shall muddy
    them no more,
Nor shall the hooves of animals
    muddy them.
¹⁴ Then I will make their waters
    clear,
And make their rivers run like
    oil,'
Says the Lord GOD.

¹⁵ 'When I make the land of Egypt
    desolate,
And the country is destitute of
    all that once filled it,
When I strike all who dwell in
    it,
Then they shall know that I am
    the LORD.

¹⁶ 'This is the lamentation
With which they shall lament
    her;
The daughters of the nations
    shall lament her;
They shall lament for her, for
    Egypt,
And for all her multitude,'
Says the Lord GOD."

¹⁷ It came to pass also in the twelfth year, on the fifteenth day of the month, that the word of the LORD came to me, saying:

¹⁸ "Son of man, wail over the
    multitude of Egypt,
And cast them down to the
    depths of the earth,
Her and the daughters of the
    famous nations,
With those who go down to the
    Pit:

¹⁹ 'Whom do you surpass in
    beauty?
Go down, be placed with the
    uncircumcised.'

²⁰ "They shall fall in the midst of
    those slain by the sword;
She is delivered to the sword,
Drawing her and all her
    multitudes.
²¹ The strong among the mighty
Shall speak to him out of the
    midst of hell
With those who help him:
'They have gone down,
They lie with the uncircumcised,
    slain by the sword.'

²² "Assyria is there, and all her
    company,
With their graves all around her,
All of them slain, fallen by the
    sword.
²³ Her graves are set in the recesses
    of the Pit,
And her company is all around
    her grave,
All of them slain, fallen by the
    sword,
Who caused terror in the land
    of the living.

²⁴ "There is Elam and all her
    multitude,
All around her grave,
All of them slain, fallen by the
    sword,
Who have gone down
    uncircumcised to the lower
    parts of the earth,
Who caused their terror in the
    land of the living;
Now they bear their shame with
    those who go down to the
    Pit.
²⁵ They have set her bed in the
    midst of the slain,
With all her multitude,
With her graves all around it,
All of them uncircumcised, slain
    by the sword;
Though their terror was caused
In the land of the living,
Yet they bear their shame

With those who go down to the
Pit;
It was put in the midst of the
slain.

26 "There *are* Meshech and Tubal
and all their multitudes,
With all their graves around it,
All of them uncircumcised, slain
by the sword,
Though they caused their terror
in the land of the living.
27 They do not lie with the mighty
Who are fallen of the
uncircumcised,
Who have gone down to hell
with their weapons of war;
They have laid their swords
under their heads,
But their iniquities will be on
their bones,
Because of the terror of the
mighty in the land of the
living.
28 Yes, you shall be broken in the
midst of the uncircumcised,
And lie with *those* slain by the
sword.

29 "There *is* Edom,
Her kings and all her princes,
Who despite their might
Are laid beside *those* slain by the
sword;
They shall lie with the
uncircumcised,
And with those who go down
to the Pit.
30 There *are* the princes of the
north,
All of them, and all the
Sidonians,
Who have gone down with the
slain
In shame at the terror which they
caused by their might;
They lie uncircumcised with
those slain by the sword,
And bear their shame with those
who go down to the Pit.

31 "Pharaoh will see them
And be comforted over all his
multitude,

Pharaoh and all his army,
Slain by the sword,"
Says the Lord God.

32 "For I have caused My terror in
the land of the living;
And he shall be placed in the
midst of the uncircumcised
With *those* slain by the sword,
Pharaoh and all his multitude,"
Says the Lord God.

God always warns the wicked

33 Again the word of the Lord
came to me, saying, 2 "Son of man,
speak to the children of your people,
and say to them: 'When I bring the
sword upon a land, and the people of
the land take a man from their territory
and make him their watchman, 3 when
he sees the sword coming upon the
land, if he blows the trumpet and
warns the people, 4 then whoever
hears the sound of the trumpet and
does not take warning, if the sword
comes and takes him away, his blood
shall be on his *own* head. 5 He heard
the sound of the trumpet, but did not
take warning; his blood shall be upon
himself. But he who takes warning will
save his life. 6 But if the watchman sees
the sword coming and does not blow
the trumpet, and the people are not
warned, and the sword comes and
takes *any* person from among them,
he is taken away in his iniquity; but
his blood I will require at the watchman's hand.'

7 "So you, son of man: I have made
you a watchman for the house of Israel; therefore you shall hear a word
from My mouth and warn them for Me.
8 When I say to the wicked, 'O wicked
man, you shall surely die!' and you do
not speak to warn the wicked from his
way, that wicked *man* shall die in his
iniquity; but his blood I will require at
your hand. 9 Nevertheless if you warn
the wicked to turn from his way, and
he does not turn from his way, he shall
die in his iniquity; but you have delivered your soul.

10 "Therefore you, O son of man,

say to the house of Israel: 'Thus you say, "If our transgressions and our sins *lie* upon us, and we pine away in them, how can we then live?"' ¹¹ Say to them: '*As* I live,' says the Lord GOD, 'I have no pleasure in the death of the wicked, but that the wicked turn from his way and live. Turn, turn from your evil ways! For why should you die, O house of Israel?'

¹² "Therefore you, O son of man, say to the children of your people: 'The righteousness of the righteous man shall not deliver him in the day of his transgression; as for the wickedness of the wicked, he shall not fall because of it in the day that he turns from his wickedness; nor shall the righteous be able to live because of *his righteousness* in the day that he sins.' ¹³ When I say to the righteous *that* he shall surely live, but he trusts in his own righteousness and commits iniquity, none of his righteous works shall be remembered; but because of the iniquity that he has committed, he shall die. ¹⁴ Again, when I say to the wicked, 'You shall surely die,' if he turns from his sin and does what is lawful and right, ¹⁵ *if* the wicked restores the pledge, gives back what he has stolen, and walks in the statutes of life without committing iniquity, he shall surely live; he shall not die. ¹⁶ None of his sins which he has committed shall be remembered against him; he has done what is lawful and right; he shall surely live.

¹⁷ "Yet the children of your people say, 'The way of the LORD is not fair.' But it is their way which is not fair! ¹⁸ When the righteous turns from his righteousness and commits iniquity, he shall die because of it. ¹⁹ But when the wicked turns from his wickedness and does what is lawful and right, he shall live because of it. ²⁰ Yet you say, 'The way of the LORD is not fair.' O house of Israel, I will judge every one of you according to his own ways."

²¹ And it came to pass in the twelfth year of our captivity, in the tenth *month*, on the fifth *day* of the month, *that* one who had escaped from Jeru-

salem came to me and said, "The city has been captured!"

²² Now the hand of the LORD had been upon me the evening before the man came who had escaped. And He had opened my mouth; so when he came to me in the morning, my mouth was opened, and I was no longer mute.

²³ Then the word of the LORD came to me, saying: ²⁴ "Son of man, they who inhabit those ruins in the land of Israel are saying, 'Abraham was only one, and he inherited the land. But we *are* many; the land has been given to us as a possession.'

²⁵ "Therefore say to them, 'Thus says the Lord GOD: "You eat *meat* with blood, you lift up your eyes toward your idols, and shed blood. Should you then possess the land? ²⁶ You rely on your sword, you commit abominations, and you defile one another's wives. Should you then possess the land?"'

²⁷ "Say thus to them, 'Thus says the Lord GOD: "As I live, surely those who *are* in the ruins shall fall by the sword, and the one who *is* in the open field I will give to the beasts to be devoured, and those who *are* in the strongholds and caves shall die of the pestilence. ²⁸ For I will make the land most desolate, her arrogant strength shall cease, and the mountains of Israel shall be so desolate that no one will pass through. ²⁹ Then they shall know that I *am* the LORD, when I have made the land most desolate because of all their abominations which they have committed."'

³⁰ "As for you, son of man, the children of your people are talking about you beside the walls and in the doors of the houses; and they speak to one another, everyone saying to his brother, 'Please come and hear what the word is that comes from the LORD.' ³¹ So they come to you as people do, they sit before you *as* My people, and they hear your words, but they do not do them; for with their mouth they show much love, *but* their hearts pursue their *own* gain. ³² Indeed you *are* to them as a very lovely song of one

who has a pleasant voice and can play well on an instrument; for they hear your words, but they do not do them. 33 And when this comes to pass— surely it will come—then they will know that a prophet has been among them."

The Shepherd and the sheep

34 And the word of the LORD came to me, saying, 2 "Son of man, prophesy against the shepherds of Israel, prophesy and say to them, 'Thus says the Lord GOD to the shepherds: "Woe to the shepherds of Israel who feed themselves! Should not the shepherds feed the flocks? 3 You eat the fat and clothe yourselves with the wool; you slaughter the fatlings, *but* you do not feed the flock. 4 The weak you have not strengthened, nor have you healed those who were sick, nor bound up the broken, nor brought back what was driven away, nor sought what was lost; but with force and cruelty you have ruled them. 5 So they were scattered because *there was* no shepherd; and they became food for all the beasts of the field when they were scattered. 6 My sheep wandered through all the mountains, and on every high hill; yes, My flock was scattered over the whole face of the earth, and no one was seeking or searching *for them*."

7 'Therefore, you shepherds, hear the word of the LORD: 8 "As I live," says the Lord GOD, "surely because My flock became a prey, and My flock became food for every beast of the field, because *there was* no shepherd, nor did My shepherds search for My flock, but the shepherds fed themselves and did not feed My flock"— 9 therefore, O shepherds, hear the word of the LORD! 10 Thus says the Lord GOD: "Behold, I *am* against the shepherds, and I will require My flock at their hand; I will cause them to cease feeding the sheep, and the shepherds shall feed themselves no more; for I will deliver My flock from their mouths, that they may no longer be food for them."

11 'For thus says the Lord GOD: "Indeed I Myself will search for My sheep and seek them out. 12 As a shepherd seeks out his flock on the day he is among his scattered sheep, so will I seek out My sheep and deliver them from all the places where they were scattered on a cloudy and dark day. 13 And I will bring them out from the peoples and gather them from the countries, and will bring them to their own land; I will feed them on the mountains of Israel, in the valleys and in all the inhabited places of the country. 14 I will feed them in good pasture, and their fold shall be on the high mountains of Israel. There they shall lie down in a good fold and feed in rich pasture on the mountains of Israel. 15 I will feed My flock, and I will make them lie down," says the Lord GOD. 16 "I will seek what was lost and bring back what was driven away, bind up the broken and strengthen what was sick; but I will destroy the fat and the strong, and feed them in judgment."

17 'And *as for* you, O My flock, thus says the Lord GOD: "Behold, I shall judge between sheep and sheep, between rams and goats. 18 *Is it* too little for you to have eaten up the good pasture, that you must tread down with your feet the residue of your pasture— and to have drunk of the clear waters, that you must foul the residue with your feet? 19 And *as for* My flock, they eat what you have trampled with your feet, and they drink what you have fouled with your feet."

20 'Therefore thus says the Lord GOD to them: "Behold, I Myself will judge between the fat and the lean sheep. 21 Because you have pushed with side and shoulder, butted all the weak ones with your horns, and scattered them abroad, 22 therefore I will save My flock, and they shall no longer be a prey; and I will judge between sheep and sheep. 23 I will establish one shepherd over them, and he shall feed them—My servant David. He shall feed them and be their shepherd. 24 And I, the LORD, will be their God,

and My servant David a prince among them; I, the LORD, have spoken.

25 "I will make a covenant of peace with them, and cause wild beasts to cease from the land; and they will dwell safely in the wilderness and sleep in the woods. 26 I will make them and the places all around My hill a blessing; and I will cause showers to come down in their season; there shall be showers of blessing. 27 Then the trees of the field shall yield their fruit, and the earth shall yield her increase. They shall be safe in their land; and they shall know that I am the LORD, when I have broken the bands of their yoke and delivered them from the hand of those who enslaved them. 28 And they shall no longer be a prey for the nations, nor shall beasts of the land devour them; but they shall dwell safely, and no one shall make them afraid. 29 I will raise up for them a garden of renown, and they shall no longer be consumed with hunger in the land, nor bear the shame of the Gentiles anymore. 30 Thus they shall know that I, the LORD their God, am with them, and they, the house of Israel, are My people," says the Lord GOD.' "

31 "You are My flock, the flock of My pasture; you are men, and I am your God," says the Lord GOD.

Edom will be smashed with God's fist

35 Moreover the word of the LORD came to me, saying, 2 "Son of man, set your face against Mount Seir and prophesy against it, 3 and say to it, 'Thus says the Lord GOD:

"Behold, O Mount Seir, I am against you;
I will stretch out My hand against you,
And make you most desolate;
4   I shall lay your cities waste,
And you shall be desolate.
Then you shall know that I am the LORD.

5 "Because you have had an ancient hatred, and have shed the blood of the children of Israel by the power of the sword at the time of their calamity, when their iniquity came to an end, 6 therefore, as I live," says the Lord GOD, "I will prepare you for blood, and blood shall pursue you; since you have not hated blood, therefore blood shall pursue you. 7 Thus I will make Mount Seir most desolate, and cut off from it the one who leaves and the one who returns. 8 And I will fill its mountains with the slain; on your hills and in your valleys and in all your ravines those who are slain by the sword shall fall. 9 I will make you perpetually desolate, and your cities shall be uninhabited; then you shall know that I am the LORD.

10 "Because you have said, 'These two nations and these two countries shall be mine, and we will possess them,' although the LORD was there, 11 therefore, as I live," says the Lord GOD, "I will do according to your anger and according to the envy which you showed in your hatred against them; and I will make Myself known among them when I judge you. 12 Then you shall know that I am the LORD. I have heard all your blasphemies which you have spoken against the mountains of Israel, saying, 'They are desolate; they are given to us to consume.' 13 Thus with your mouth you have boasted against Me and multiplied your words against Me; I have heard them."

14 'Thus says the Lord GOD: "The whole earth will rejoice when I make you desolate. 15 As you rejoiced because the inheritance of the house of Israel was desolate, so I will do to you; you shall be desolate, O Mount Seir, as well as all of Edom—all of it! Then they shall know that I am the LORD." '

Hearts of love for hearts of stone

36 "And you, son of man, prophesy to the mountains of Israel, and say, 'O mountains of Israel, hear the word of the LORD! 2 Thus says the Lord GOD: "Because the enemy has said of you, 'Aha! The ancient heights have become our possession,' " ' 3 therefore

prophesy, and say, 'Thus says the Lord God: "Because they made *you* desolate and swallowed you up on every side, so that you became the possession of the rest of the nations, and you are taken up by the lips of talkers and slandered by the people"— ⁴ therefore, O mountains of Israel, hear the word of the Lord God! Thus says the Lord God to the mountains, the hills, the rivers, the valleys, the desolate wastes, and the cities that have been forsaken, which became plunder and mockery to the rest of the nations all around— ⁵ therefore thus says the Lord God: "Surely I have spoken in My burning jealousy against the rest of the nations and against all Edom, who gave My land to themselves as a possession, with wholehearted joy *and* spiteful minds, in order to plunder its open country." '

⁶ "Therefore prophesy concerning the land of Israel, and say to the mountains, the hills, the rivers, and the valleys, 'Thus says the Lord God: "Behold, I have spoken in My jealousy and My fury, because you have borne the shame of the nations." ⁷ Therefore thus says the Lord God: "I have raised My hand in an oath that surely the nations that *are* around you shall bear their own shame. ⁸ But you, O mountains of Israel, you shall shoot forth your branches and yield your fruit to My people Israel, for they are about to come. ⁹ For indeed I *am* for you, and I will turn to you, and you shall be tilled and sown. ¹⁰ I will multiply men upon you, all the house of Israel, all of it; and the cities shall be inhabited and the ruins rebuilt. ¹¹ I will multiply upon you man and beast; and they shall increase and bear young; I will make you inhabited as in former times, and do better *for you* than at your beginnings. Then you shall know that I *am* the Lord. ¹² Yes, I will cause men to walk on you, My people Israel; they shall take possession of you, and you shall be their inheritance; no more shall you bereave them *of children.*"

¹³ 'Thus says the Lord God: "Because they say to you, 'You devour men and bereave your nation *of children,*' ¹⁴ therefore you shall devour men no more, nor bereave your nation anymore," says the Lord God. ¹⁵ Nor will I let you hear the taunts of the nations anymore, nor bear the reproach of the peoples anymore, nor shall you cause your nation to stumble anymore," says the Lord God.' "

¹⁶ Moreover the word of the Lord came to me, saying: ¹⁷ "Son of man, when the house of Israel dwelt in their own land, they defiled it by their own ways and deeds; to Me their way was like the uncleanness of a woman in her customary impurity. ¹⁸ Therefore I poured out My fury on them for the blood they had shed on the land, and for their idols *with which* they had defiled it. ¹⁹ So I scattered them among the nations, and they were dispersed throughout the countries; I judged them according to their ways and their deeds. ²⁰ When they came to the nations, wherever they went, they profaned My holy name—when they said of them, 'These *are* the people of the Lord, *and* yet they have gone out of His land.' ²¹ But I had concern for My holy name, which the house of Israel had profaned among the nations wherever they went.

²² "Therefore say to the house of Israel, 'Thus says the Lord God: "I do not do *this* for your sake, O house of Israel, but for My holy name's sake, which you have profaned among the nations wherever you went. ²³ And I will sanctify My great name, which has been profaned among the nations, which you have profaned in their midst; and the nations shall know that I *am* the Lord," says the Lord God, "when I am hallowed in you before their eyes. ²⁴ For I will take you from among the nations, gather you out of all countries, and bring you into your own land. ²⁵ Then I will sprinkle clean water on you, and you shall be clean; I will cleanse you from all your filthiness and from all your idols. ²⁶ I will give you a new heart and put a new spirit within you; I will take the heart of stone out of your flesh and give you

a heart of flesh. 27 I will put My Spirit within you and cause you to walk in My statutes, and you will keep My judgments and do *them*. 28 Then you shall dwell in the land that I gave to your fathers; you shall be My people, and I will be your God. 29 I will deliver you from all your uncleannesses. I will call for the grain and multiply it, and bring no famine upon you. 30 And I will multiply the fruit of your trees and the increase of your fields, so that you need never again bear the reproach of famine among the nations. 31 Then you will remember your evil ways and your deeds that *were* not good; and you will loathe yourselves in your own sight, for your iniquities and your abominations. 32 Not for your sake do I do *this*," says the Lord God, "let it be known to you. Be ashamed and confounded for your own ways, O house of Israel!"

33 'Thus says the Lord God: "On the day that I cleanse you from all your iniquities, I will also enable *you* to dwell in the cities, and the ruins shall be rebuilt. 34 The desolate land shall be tilled instead of lying desolate in the sight of all who pass by. 35 So they will say, 'This land that was desolate has become like the garden of Eden; and the wasted, desolate, and ruined cities *are now* fortified *and* inhabited.' 36 Then the nations which are left all around you shall know that I, the Lord, have rebuilt the ruined places *and* planted what was desolate. I, the Lord, have spoken *it*, and I will do *it*."

37 'Thus says the Lord God: "I will also let the house of Israel inquire of Me to do this for them: I will increase their men like a flock. 38 Like a flock *offered as* holy *sacrifices*, like the flock at Jerusalem on its feast days, so shall the ruined cities be filled with flocks of men. Then they shall know that I *am* the Lord." ' "

The valley of dry bones

37 The hand of the Lord came upon me and brought me out in the Spirit of the Lord, and set me down in the midst of the valley; and it *was* full of bones. 2 Then He caused me to pass by them all around, and behold, *there were* very many in the open valley; and indeed *they were* very dry. 3 And He said to me, "Son of man, can these bones live?"

So I answered, "O Lord God, You know."

4 Again He said to me, "Prophesy to these bones, and say to them, 'O dry bones, hear the word of the Lord! 5 Thus says the Lord God to these bones: "Surely I will cause breath to enter into you, and you shall live. 6 I will put sinews on you and bring flesh upon you, cover you with skin and put breath in you; and you shall live. Then you shall know that I *am* the Lord." ' "

DIGGING IN

37:1–14 Can Dry Bones Really Live Again? If you have heard about the history of Israel in this century, you know how much they have suffered. Some say as many as six million Jews were murdered by the Nazis from 1933 through 1945. This was not the first time the Jews had suffered.

You can read in Exodus 1 about the slavery of Israel in Egypt until fifteen hundred years before Christ. Then see 2 Kings 25 and Jeremiah 52 about the destruction of Israel by Babylon. The Greeks and the Romans also persecuted the Jews before and after the time of Christ. Israel was then scattered all over the world.

So it is a miracle of history that the Jews have continued to be a nation all this time. We showed in the note on Ezekiel 28 how the United Nations Organization gave Israel back its land in 1948.

The dry bones in Ezekiel 37 are the restored nation of Israel. God is telling us that bringing them back to their land is like bringing their bones up from the grave.

7 So I prophesied as I was commanded; and as I prophesied, there was a noise, and suddenly a rattling; and the bones came together, bone to bone. 8 Indeed, as I looked, the sinews and the flesh came upon them, and the skin covered them over; but *there was* no breath in them.

9 Also He said to me, "Prophesy to the breath, prophesy, son of man, and say to the breath, 'Thus says the Lord GOD: "Come from the four winds, O breath, and breathe on these slain, that they may live." ' " 10 So I prophesied as He commanded me, and breath came into them, and they lived, and stood upon their feet, an exceedingly great army.

11 Then He said to me, "Son of man, these bones are the whole house of Israel. They indeed say, 'Our bones are dry, our hope is lost, and we ourselves are cut off!' 12 Therefore prophesy and say to them, 'Thus says the Lord GOD: "Behold, O My people, I will open your graves and cause you to come up from your graves, and bring you into the land of Israel. 13 Then you shall know that I *am* the LORD, when I have opened your graves, O My people, and brought you up from your graves. 14 I will put My Spirit in you, and you shall live, and I will place you in your own land. Then you shall know that I, the LORD, have spoken *it* and performed *it,*" says the LORD.' "

15 Again the word of the LORD came to me, saying, 16 "As for you, son of man, take a stick for yourself and write on it: 'For Judah and for the children of Israel, his companions.' Then take another stick and write on it, 'For Joseph, the stick of Ephraim, and *for* all the house of Israel, his companions.' 17 Then join them one to another for yourself into one stick, and they will become one in your hand.

18 "And when the children of your people speak to you, saying, 'Will you not show us what you *mean* by these?'— 19 say to them, 'Thus says the Lord GOD: "Surely I will take the stick of Joseph, which *is* in the hand of Ephraim, and the tribes of Israel, his companions; and I will join them with it, with the stick of Judah, and make them one stick, and they will be one in My hand." ' 20 And the sticks on which you write will be in your hand before their eyes.

21 "Then say to them, 'Thus says the Lord GOD: "Surely I will take the children of Israel from among the nations, wherever they have gone, and will gather them from every side and bring them into their own land; 22 and I will make them one nation in the land, on the mountains of Israel; and one king shall be king over them all; they shall no longer be two nations, nor shall they ever be divided into two kingdoms again. 23 They shall not defile themselves anymore with their idols, nor with their detestable things, nor with any of their transgressions; but I will deliver them from all their dwelling places in which they have sinned, and will cleanse them. Then they shall be My people, and I will be their God.

24 "David My servant *shall be* king over them, and they shall all have one shepherd; they shall also walk in My judgments and observe My statutes, and do them. 25 Then they shall dwell in the land that I have given to Jacob My servant, where your fathers dwelt; and they shall dwell there, they, their children, and their children's children, forever; and My servant David *shall be* their prince forever. 26 Moreover I will make a covenant of peace with them, and it shall be an everlasting covenant with them; I will establish them and multiply them, and I will set My sanctuary in their midst forevermore. 27 My tabernacle also shall be with them; indeed I will be their God, and they shall be My people. 28 The nations also will know that I, the LORD, sanctify Israel, when My sanctuary is in their midst forevermore." ' "

Flood, hail, fire, and brimstone

38 Now the word of the LORD came to me, saying, 2 "Son of man, set your

face against **Gog**, of the land of **Ma-gog**, the prince of Rosh, Meshech, and Tubal, and prophesy against him, 3 and say, 'Thus says the Lord GOD: "Behold, I *am* against you, O Gog, the prince of Rosh, Meshech, and Tubal. 4 I will turn you around, put hooks into your jaws, and lead you out, with all your army, horses, and horsemen, all splendidly clothed, a great company *with* bucklers and shields, all of them handling swords. 5 Persia, Ethiopia, and Libya are with them, all of them *with* shield and helmet; 6 Gomer and all its troops; the house of Togarmah *from* the far north and all its troops— many people *are* with you.

7 "Prepare yourself and be ready, you and all your companies that are gathered about you; and be a guard for them. 8 After many days you will be visited. In the latter years you will come into the land of those brought back from the sword *and* gathered from many people on the mountains of Israel, which had long been desolate; they *were* brought out of the nations, and now all of them dwell safely. 9 You will ascend, coming like a storm, covering the land like a cloud, you and all your troops and many peoples with you."

10 'Thus says the Lord GOD: "On that day it shall come to pass *that* thoughts will arise in your mind, and you will make an evil plan: 11 You will say, 'I will go up against a land of un-walled villages; I will go to a peaceful people, who dwell safely, all of them dwelling without walls, and having neither bars nor gates'— 12 to take plunder and to take booty, to stretch out your hand against the waste places *that are again* inhabited, and against a people gathered from the nations, who have acquired livestock and goods, who dwell in the midst of the land. 13 Sheba, Dedan, the merchants of Tarshish, and all their young lions will

say to you, 'Have you come to take plunder? Have you gathered your army to take booty, to carry away silver and gold, to take away livestock and goods, to take great plunder?' " '

14 "Therefore, son of man, prophesy and say to Gog, 'Thus says the Lord GOD: "On that day when My people Israel dwell safely, will you not know *it?* 15 Then you will come from your place out of the far north, you and many peoples with you, all of them riding on horses, a great company and a mighty army. 16 You will come up against My people Israel like a cloud, to cover the land. It will be in the latter days that I will bring you against My land, so that the nations may know Me, when I am hallowed in you, O Gog, before their eyes." 17 Thus says the Lord GOD: "Are *you* he of whom I have spoken in former days by My servants the prophets of Israel, who prophesied for years in those days that I would bring you against them?

18 "And it will come to pass at the same time, when Gog comes against the land of Israel," says the Lord GOD, "*that* My fury will show in My face. 19 For in My jealousy *and* in the fire of My wrath I have spoken: 'Surely in that day there shall be a great earthquake in the land of Israel, 20 so that the fish of the sea, the birds of the heavens, the beasts of the field, all creeping things that creep on the earth, and all men who *are* on the face of the earth shall shake at My presence. The mountains shall be thrown down, the steep places shall fall, and every wall shall fall to the ground.' 21 I will call for a sword against Gog throughout all My mountains," says the Lord GOD. "Every man's sword will be against his brother. 22 And I will bring him to judgment with pestilence and bloodshed; I will rain down on him, on his troops, and on the many peoples who *are* with him, flooding rain,

---

🌐 **WORDFINDER** _____

38:2, 3 Gog and Magog See Revelation 20:8. Gog is the future leader of an army against Israel. Magog is his country to the far north of Israel.

great hailstones, fire, and brimstone. 23 Thus I will magnify Myself and sanctify Myself, and I will be known in the eyes of many nations. Then they shall know that I *am* the LORD." '

Gog's weapons will be burned for firewood

39 "And you, son of man, prophesy against Gog, and say, 'Thus says the Lord GOD: "Behold, I *am* against you, O Gog, the prince of Rosh, Meshech, and Tubal; 2 and I will turn you around and lead you on, bringing you up from the far north, and bring you against the mountains of Israel. 3 Then I will knock the bow out of your left hand, and cause the arrows to fall out of your right hand. 4 You shall fall upon the mountains of Israel, you and all your troops and the peoples who *are* with you; I will give you to birds of prey of every sort and *to* the beasts of the field to be devoured. 5 You shall fall on the open field; for I have spoken," says the Lord GOD. 6 "And I will send fire on Magog and on those who live in security in the coastlands. Then they shall know that I *am* the LORD. 7 So I will make My holy name known in the midst of My people Israel, and I will not *let them* profane My holy name anymore. Then the nations shall know that *I am* the LORD, the Holy One in Israel. 8 Surely it is coming, and it shall be done," says the Lord GOD. "This *is* the day of which I have spoken.

9 "Then those who dwell in the cities of Israel will go out and set on fire and burn the weapons, both the shields and bucklers, the bows and arrows, the javelins and spears; and they will make fires with them for seven years. 10 They will not take wood from the field nor cut down *any* from the forests, because they will make fires with the weapons; and they will plunder those who plundered them, and pillage those who pillaged them," says the Lord GOD.

11 "It will come to pass in that day *that* I will give Gog a burial place there in Israel, the valley of those who pass by east of the sea; and it will obstruct travelers, because there they will bury Gog and all his multitude. Therefore they will call *it* the Valley of Hamon Gog. 12 For seven months the house of Israel will be burying them, in order to cleanse the land. 13 Indeed all the people of the land will be burying, and they will gain renown for it on the day that I am glorified," says the Lord GOD. 14 "They will set apart men regularly employed, with the help of a search party, to pass through the land and bury those bodies remaining on the ground, in order to cleanse it. At the end of seven months they will make a search. 15 The search party will pass through the land; and *when anyone* sees a man's bone, he shall set up a marker by it, till the buriers have buried it in the Valley of Hamon Gog. 16 *The* name of *the* city *will* also *be* Hamonah. Thus they shall cleanse the land."

17 "And as for you, son of man, thus says the Lord GOD, 'Speak to every sort of bird and to every beast of the field:

"Assemble yourselves and come;
  Gather together from all sides to
    My sacrificial meal
  Which I am sacrificing for you,
  A great sacrificial meal on the
    mountains of Israel,
  That you may eat flesh and drink
    blood.
18 You shall eat the flesh of the
    mighty,
  Drink the blood of the princes
    of the earth,
  Of rams and lambs,
  Of goats and bulls,
  All of them fatlings of Bashan.
19 You shall eat fat till you are
    full,
  And drink blood till you are
    drunk,
  At My sacrificial meal
  Which I am sacrificing for you.
20 You shall be filled at My table
  With horses and riders,
  With mighty men
  And with all the men of war,"
    says the Lord GOD.

21 "I will set My glory among the nations; all the nations shall see My judgment which I have executed, and My hand which I have laid on them. 22 So the house of Israel shall know that I *am* the LORD their God from that day forward. 23 The Gentiles shall know that the house of Israel went into captivity for their iniquity; because they were unfaithful to Me, therefore I hid My face from them. I gave them into the hand of their enemies, and they all fell by the sword. 24 According to their uncleanness and according to their transgressions I have dealt with them, and hidden My face from them." '

25 "Therefore thus says the Lord GOD: 'Now I will bring back the captives of Jacob, and have mercy on the whole house of Israel; and I will be jealous for My holy name— 26 after they have borne their shame, and all their unfaithfulness in which they were unfaithful to Me, when they dwelt safely in their *own* land and no one made *them* afraid. 27 When I have brought them back from the peoples and gathered them out of their enemies' lands, and I am hallowed in them in the sight of many nations, 28 then they shall know that I *am* the LORD their God, who sent them into captivity among the nations, but also brought them back to their land, and left none of them captive any longer. 29 And I will not hide My face from them anymore; for I shall have poured out My Spirit on the house of Israel,' says the Lord GOD."

The man who measured the temple

40 In the twenty-fifth year of our captivity, at the beginning of the year, on the tenth *day* of the month, in the fourteenth year after the city was captured, on the very same day the hand of the LORD was upon me; and He took me there. 2 In the visions of God He took me into the land of Israel and set me on a very high mountain; on it toward the south *was* something like the

structure of a city. 3 He took me there, and behold, *there was* a man whose appearance *was* like the appearance of bronze. He had a line of flax and a measuring rod in his hand, and he stood in the gateway.

4 And the man said to me, "Son of man, look with your eyes and hear with your ears, and fix your mind on everything I show you; for you *were* brought here so that I might show *them* to you. Declare to the house of Israel everything you see." 5 Now there was a wall all around the outside of the temple. In the man's hand was a measuring rod six cubits *long, each being a* cubit and a handbreadth; and he measured the width of the wall structure, one rod; and the height, one rod.

6 Then he went to the gateway which faced east; and he went up its stairs and measured the threshold of the gateway, *which was* one rod wide, and the other threshold *was* one rod wide. 7 Each gate chamber *was* one rod long and one rod wide; between the gate chambers *was a space of* five cubits; and the threshold of the gateway by the vestibule of the inside gate *was* one rod. 8 He also measured the vestibule of the inside gate, one rod. 9 Then he measured the vestibule of the gateway, eight cubits; and the gateposts, two cubits. The vestibule of the gate *was* on the inside. 10 In the eastern gateway *were* three gate chambers on one side and three on the other; the three *were* all the same size; also the gateposts were of the same size on this side and that side.

11 He measured the width of the entrance to the gateway, ten cubits; *and* the length of the gate, thirteen cubits. 12 *There was* a space in front of the gate chambers, one cubit *on this side* and one cubit on that side; the gate chambers *were* six cubits on this side and six cubits on that side. 13 Then he measured the gateway from the roof of *one* gate chamber to the roof of the other; the width *was* twenty-five cubits, as door faces door. 14 He measured the gateposts, sixty cubits high, and the

court all around the gateway *extended* to the gatepost. 15 *From* the front of the entrance gate to the front of the vestibule of the inner gate *was* fifty cubits. 16 *There were* beveled window *frames* in the gate chambers and in their intervening archways on the inside of the gateway all around, and likewise in the vestibules. *There were* windows all around on the inside. And on each gatepost *were* palm trees.

17 Then he brought me into the outer court; and *there were* chambers and a pavement made all around the court; thirty chambers faced the pavement. 18 The pavement was by the side of the gateways, corresponding to the length of the gateways; *this was* the lower pavement. 19 Then he measured the width from the front of the lower gateway to the front of the inner court exterior, one hundred cubits toward the east and the north.

20 On the outer court was also a gateway facing north, and he measured its length and its width. 21 Its gate chambers, three on this side and three on that side, its gateposts and its archways, had the same measurements as the first gate; its length *was* fifty cubits and its width twenty-five cubits. 22 Its windows and those of its archways, and also its palm trees, *had* the same measurements as the gateway facing east; it was ascended by seven steps, and its archway *was* in front of it. 23 A gate of the inner court was opposite the northern gateway, just as the eastern *gateway;* and he measured from gateway to gateway, one hundred cubits.

24 After that he brought me toward the south, and there a gateway was facing south; and he measured its gateposts and archways according to these same measurements. 25 *There were* windows in it and in its archways all around like those windows; its length *was* fifty cubits and its width twenty-five cubits. 26 Seven steps led up to it, and its archway *was* in front of them; and it had palm trees on its gateposts, one on this side and one on that side. 27 *There was* also a gateway on the inner court, facing south; and he measured from gateway to gateway toward the south, one hundred cubits.

28 Then he brought me to the inner court through the southern gateway; he measured the southern gateway according to these same measurements. 29 Also its gate chambers, its gateposts, and its archways *were* according to these same measurements; *there were* windows in it and in its archways all around; *it was* fifty cubits long and twenty-five cubits wide. 30 *There were* archways all around, twenty-five cubits long and five cubits wide. 31 Its archways faced the outer court, palm trees *were* on its gateposts, and going up to it *were* eight steps.

32 And he brought me into the inner court facing east; he measured the gateway according to these same measurements. 33 Also its gate chambers, its gateposts, and its archways *were* according to these same measurements; and *there were* windows in it and in its archways all around; *it was* fifty cubits long and twenty-five cubits wide. 34 Its archways faced the outer court, and palm trees *were* on its gateposts on this side and on that side; and going up to it *were* eight steps.

35 Then he brought me to the north gateway and measured *it* according to these same measurements— 36 also its gate chambers, its gateposts, and its archways. It had windows all around; its length *was* fifty cubits and its width twenty-five cubits. 37 Its gateposts faced the outer court, palm trees *were* on its gateposts on this side and on that side, and going up to it *were* eight steps.

38 *There was* a chamber and its entrance by the gateposts of the gateway, where they washed the burnt offering. 39 In the vestibule of the gateway *were* two tables on this side and two tables on that side, on which to slay the burnt offering, the sin offering, and the trespass offering. 40 At the outer side of the vestibule, as one goes up to the entrance of the northern gateway, *were* two tables; and on the other side of the vestibule of the gateway *were*

two tables. ⁴¹ Four tables *were* on this side and four tables on that side, by the side of the gateway, eight tables on which they slaughtered *the sacrifices.* ⁴² *There were* also four tables of hewn stone for the burnt offering, one cubit and a half long, one cubit and a half wide, and one cubit high; on these they laid the instruments with which they slaughtered the burnt offering and the sacrifice. ⁴³ Inside *were* hooks, a handbreadth wide, fastened all around; and the flesh of the sacrifices *was* on the tables.

⁴⁴ Outside the inner gate *were* the chambers for the singers in the inner court, one facing south at the side of the northern gateway, and the other facing north at the side of the southern gateway. ⁴⁵ Then he said to me, "This chamber which faces south *is* for the priests who have charge of the temple. ⁴⁶ The chamber which faces north *is* for the priests who have charge of the altar; these *are* the sons of Zadok, from the sons of Levi, who come near the LORD to minister to Him."

⁴⁷ And he measured the court, one hundred cubits long and one hundred cubits wide, foursquare. The altar *was* in front of the temple. ⁴⁸ Then he brought me to the vestibule of the temple and measured the doorposts of the vestibule, five cubits on this side and five cubits on that side; and the width of the gateway was three cubits on this side and three cubits on that side. ⁴⁹ The length of the vestibule *was* twenty cubits, and the width eleven cubits; and by the steps which led up to it *there were* pillars by the doorposts, one on this side and another on that side.

Ezekiel enters the Holy of Holies

41 Then he brought me into the sanctuary and measured the doorposts, six cubits wide on one side and six cubits wide on the other side—the width of the tabernacle. ² The width of the entryway *was* ten cubits, and the side walls of the entrance *were* five cubits on this side and five cubits on the other side; and he measured its length, forty cubits, and its width, twenty cubits.

³ Also he went inside and measured the doorposts, two cubits; and the entrance, six cubits *high;* and the width of the entrance, seven cubits. ⁴ He measured the length, twenty cubits; and the width, twenty cubits, beyond the sanctuary; and he said to me, "This is the Most Holy *Place.*"

⁵ Next, he measured the wall of the temple, six cubits. The width of each side chamber all around the temple *was* four cubits on every side. ⁶ The side chambers *were* in three stories, one above the other, thirty chambers in each story; they rested on ledges which *were* for the side chambers all around, that they might be supported, but not fastened to the wall of the temple. ⁷ As one went up from story to story, the side chambers became wider all around, because their supporting ledges in the wall of the temple ascended like steps; therefore the width of the structure increased as one went up *from* the lowest *story* to the highest by way of the middle one. ⁸ I also saw an elevation all around the temple; it was the foundation of the side chambers, a full rod, *that is,* six cubits *high.* ⁹ The thickness of the outer wall of the side chambers *was* five cubits, and so also the remaining terrace by the place of the side chambers of the temple. ¹⁰ And between *it and* the *wall* chambers was a width of twenty cubits all around the temple on every side. ¹¹ The doors of the side chambers opened on the terrace, one door toward the north and another toward the south; and the width of the terrace *was* five cubits all around.

¹² The building that faced the separating courtyard at its western end *was* seventy cubits wide; the wall of the building *was* five cubits thick all around, and its length ninety cubits.

¹³ So he measured the temple, one hundred cubits long; and the separating courtyard with the building and its walls *was* one hundred cubits long;

14 also the width of the eastern face of the temple, including the separating courtyard, *was* one hundred cubits. 15 He measured the length of the building behind it, facing the separating courtyard, with its galleries on the one side and on the other side, one hundred cubits, as well as the inner temple and the porches of the court, 16 their doorposts and the beveled window frames. And the galleries all around their three stories opposite the threshold were paneled with wood from the ground to the windows—the windows were covered— 17 from the space above the door, even to the inner room, as well as outside, and on *every* wall all around, inside and outside, by measure.

18 And *it was* made with cherubim and palm trees, a palm tree between cherub and cherub. *Each* cherub had two faces, 19 so that the face of a man *was* toward a palm tree on one side, and the face of a young lion toward a palm tree on the other side; thus *it was* made throughout the temple all around. 20 From the floor to the space above the door, and on the wall of the sanctuary, cherubim and palm trees *were* carved.

21 The doorposts of the temple *were* square, *as was* the front of the sanctuary; their appearance was similar. 22 The altar *was* of wood, three cubits high, and its length two cubits. Its corners, its length, and its sides *were* of wood; and he said to me, "This *is* the table that *is* before the LORD."

23 The temple and the sanctuary had two doors. 24 The doors had two panels *apiece,* two folding panels: two *panels* for one door and two panels for the other *door.* 25 Cherubim and palm trees *were* carved on the doors of the temple just as they *were* carved on the walls. A wooden canopy *was* on the front of the vestibule outside. 26 *There were* beveled window *frames* and palm trees on one side and on the other, on the sides of the vestibule—also on the side chambers of the temple and on the canopies.

Ezekiel visits the priests' rooms

42 Then he brought me out into the outer court, by the way toward the north; and he brought me into the chamber which *was* opposite the separating courtyard, and which *was* opposite the building toward the north. 2 Facing the length, *which was* one hundred cubits (the width was fifty cubits), was the north door. 3 Opposite the inner court of twenty *cubits,* and opposite the pavement of the outer court, *was* gallery against gallery in three *stories.* 4 In front of the chambers, toward the inside, *was* a walk ten cubits wide, at a distance of one cubit; and their doors faced north. 5 Now the upper chambers *were* shorter, because the galleries took away *space* from them more than from the lower and middle stories of the building. 6 For they *were* in three *stories* and did not have pillars like the pillars of the courts; therefore *the upper level* was shortened more than the lower and middle levels from the ground up. 7 And a wall which *was* outside ran parallel to the chambers, at the front of the chambers, toward the outer court; its length *was* fifty cubits. 8 The length of the chambers toward the outer court *was* fifty cubits, whereas that facing the temple *was* one hundred cubits. 9 At the lower chambers *was* the entrance on the east side, as one goes into them from the outer court.

10 Also *there were* chambers in the thickness of the wall of the court toward the east, opposite the separating courtyard and opposite the building. 11 *There was* a walk in front of them also, and their appearance *was* like the chambers which *were* toward the north; they *were* as long and as wide as the others, and all their exits and entrances *were* according to plan. 12 And corresponding to the doors of the chambers that *were* facing south, as one enters them, *there was* a door in front of the walk, the way directly in front of the wall toward the east.

13 Then he said to me, "The north

chambers *and* the south chambers, which *are* opposite the separating courtyard, *are* the holy chambers where the priests who approach the LORD shall eat the most holy offerings. There they shall lay the most holy offerings—the grain offering, the sin offering, and the trespass offering—for the place *is* holy. 14 When the priests enter them, they shall not go out of the holy *chamber* into the outer court; but there they shall leave their garments in which they minister, for they *are* holy. They shall put on other garments; then they may approach *that* which *is* for the people."

15 Now when he had finished measuring the inner temple, he brought me out through the gateway that faces toward the east, and measured it all around. 16 He measured the east side with the measuring rod, five hundred rods by the measuring rod all around. 17 He measured the north side, five hundred rods by the measuring rod all around. 18 He measured the south side, five hundred rods by the measuring rod. 19 He came around to the west side *and* measured five hundred rods by the measuring rod. 20 He measured it on the four sides; it had a wall all around, five hundred *cubits* long and five hundred wide, to separate the holy areas from the common.

Ezekiel describes the temple and its rules

43 Afterward he brought me to the gate, the gate that faces toward the east. 2 And behold, the glory of the God of Israel came from the way of the east. His voice *was* like the sound of many waters; and the earth shone with His glory. 3 *It was* like the appearance of the vision which I saw—like the vision which I saw when I came to destroy the city. The visions *were* like the vision which I saw by the River Chebar; and I fell on my face. 4 And the glory of the LORD came into the temple by way of the gate which faces toward the east. 5 The Spirit lifted me

up and brought me into the inner court; and behold, the glory of the LORD filled the temple.

6 Then I heard *Him* speaking to me from the temple, while a man stood beside me. 7 And He said to me, "Son of man, *this is* the place of My throne and the place of the soles of My feet, where I will dwell in the midst of the children of Israel forever. No more shall the house of Israel defile My holy name, they nor their kings, by their harlotry or with the carcasses of their kings on their high places. 8 When they set their threshold by My threshold, and their doorpost by My doorpost, with a wall between them and Me, they defiled My holy name by the abominations which they committed; therefore I have consumed them in My anger. 9 Now let them put their harlotry and the carcasses of their kings far away from Me, and I will dwell in their midst forever.

10 "Son of man, describe the temple to the house of Israel, that they may be ashamed of their iniquities; and let them measure the pattern. 11 And if they are ashamed of all that they have done, make known to them the design of the temple and its arrangement, its exits and its entrances, its entire design and all its ordinances, all its forms and all its laws. Write *it* down in their sight, so that they may keep its whole design and all its ordinances, and perform them. 12 This *is* the law of the temple: The whole area surrounding the mountaintop *is* most holy. Behold, this *is* the law of the temple.

13 "These are the measurements of the altar in cubits (the *cubit is* one cubit and a handbreadth): the base one cubit high and one cubit wide, with a rim all around its edge of one span. This *is* the height of the altar: 14 from the base on the ground to the lower ledge, two cubits; the width of the ledge, one cubit; from the smaller ledge to the larger ledge, four cubits; and the width of the ledge, *one* cubit. 15 The altar hearth *is* four cubits high, with four horns extending upward from the hearth. 16 The altar hearth *is* twelve

cubits long, twelve wide, square at its four corners; 17 the ledge, fourteen *cubits* long and fourteen wide on its four sides, with a rim of half a cubit around it; its base, one cubit all around; and its steps face toward the east."

18 And He said to me, "Son of man, thus says the Lord GOD: 'These *are* the ordinances for the altar on the day when it is made, for sacrificing burnt offerings on it, and for sprinkling blood on it. 19 You shall give a young bull for a sin offering to the priests, the Levites, who are of the seed of Zadok, who approach Me to minister to Me,' says the Lord GOD. 20 You shall take some of its blood and put *it* on the four horns of the altar, on the four corners of the ledge, and on the rim around it; thus you shall cleanse it and make atonement for it. 21 Then you shall also take the bull of the sin offering, and burn it in the appointed place of the temple, outside the sanctuary. 22 On the second day you shall offer a kid of the goats without blemish for a sin offering; and they shall cleanse the altar, as they cleansed *it* with the bull. 23 When you have finished cleansing *it,* you shall offer a young bull without blemish, and a ram from the flock without blemish. 24 When you offer them before the LORD, the priests shall throw salt on them, and they will offer them up *as* a burnt offering to the LORD. 25 Every day for seven days you shall prepare a goat *for* a sin offering; they shall also prepare a young bull and a ram from the flock, both without blemish. 26 Seven days they shall make atonement for the altar and purify it, and so **consecrate** it. 27 When these days are over it shall be, on the eighth day and thereafter, that the priests shall offer your burnt offerings and your peace offerings on the altar; and I will accept you,' says the Lord GOD."

God tells Ezekiel what the priests should do

44 Then He brought me back to the outer gate of the sanctuary which faces toward the east, but it *was* shut. 2 And the LORD said to me, "This gate shall be shut; it shall not be opened, and no man shall enter by it, because the LORD God of Israel has entered by it; therefore it shall be shut. 3 As *for* the prince, *because* he is the prince, he may sit in it to eat bread before the LORD; he shall enter by way of the vestibule of the gateway, and go out the same way."

4 Also He brought me by way of the north gate to the front of the temple; so I looked, and behold, the glory of the LORD filled the house of the LORD; and I fell on my face. 5 And the LORD said to me, "Son of man, mark well, see with your eyes and hear with your ears, all that I say to you concerning all the ordinances of the house of the LORD and all its laws. Mark well who may enter the house and all who go out from the sanctuary.

6 "Now say to the rebellious, to the house of Israel, 'Thus says the Lord GOD: "O house of Israel, let Us have no more of all your abominations. 7 When you brought in foreigners, uncircumcised in heart and uncircumcised in flesh, to be in My sanctuary to defile it—My house—and when you offered My food, the fat and the blood, then they broke My covenant because of all your abominations. 8 And you have not kept charge of My holy things, but you have set *others* to keep charge of My sanctuary for you." 9 Thus says the Lord GOD: "No foreigner, uncircumcised in heart or uncircumcised in flesh, shall enter My sanctuary, including any foreigner who is among the children of Israel.

10 "And the Levites who went far

WORDFINDER

43:26 Consecrate Pronounced *KON-see-krate.* A verb meaning "set apart" for God's use. Holy places and holy objects are consecrated, but people also must be consecrated.

from Me, when Israel went astray, who strayed away from Me after their idols, they shall bear their iniquity. 11 Yet they shall be ministers in My sanctuary, as gatekeepers of the house and ministers of the house; they shall slay the burnt offering and the sacrifice for the people, and they shall stand before them to minister to them. 12 Because they ministered to them before their idols and caused the house of Israel to fall into iniquity, therefore I have raised My hand in an oath against them," says the Lord GOD, "that they shall bear their iniquity. 13 And they shall not come near Me to minister to Me as priest, nor come near any of My holy things, nor into the Most Holy Place; but they shall bear their shame and their abominations which they have committed. 14 Nevertheless I will make them keep charge of the temple, for all its work, and for all that has to be done in it.

15 "But the priests, the Levites, the sons of Zadok, who kept charge of My sanctuary when the children of Israel went astray from Me, they shall come near Me to minister to Me; and they shall stand before Me to offer to Me the fat and the blood," says the Lord GOD. 16 "They shall enter My sanctuary, and they shall come near My table to minister to Me, and they shall keep My charge. 17 And it shall be, whenever they enter the gates of the inner court, that they shall put on linen garments; no wool shall come upon them while they minister within the gates of the inner court or within the house. 18 They shall have linen turbans on their heads and linen trousers on their bodies; they shall not clothe themselves with anything that causes sweat. 19 When they go out to the outer court, to the outer court to the people, they shall take off their garments in which they have ministered, leave them in the holy chambers, and put on other garments; and in their holy garments they shall not sanctify the people. 20 "They shall neither shave their heads, nor let their hair grow long, but they shall keep their hair well trimmed.

21 No priest shall drink wine when he enters the inner court. 22 They shall not take as wife a widow or a divorced woman, but take virgins of the descendants of the house of Israel, or widows of priests.

23 "And they shall teach My people the difference between the holy and the unholy, and cause them to discern between the unclean and the clean. 24 In controversy they shall stand as judges, and judge it according to My judgments. They shall keep My laws and My statutes in all My appointed meetings, and they shall hallow My Sabbaths.

25 "They shall not defile themselves by coming near a dead person. Only for father or mother, for son or daughter, for brother or unmarried sister may they defile themselves. 26 After he is cleansed, they shall count seven days for him. 27 And on the day that he goes to the sanctuary to minister in the sanctuary, he must offer his sin offering in the inner court," says the Lord GOD.

28 "It shall be, in regard to their inheritance, that I am their inheritance. You shall give them no possession in Israel, for I am their possession. 29 They shall eat the grain offering, the sin offering, and the trespass offering; every dedicated thing in Israel shall be theirs. 30 The best of all firstfruits of any kind, and every sacrifice of any kind from all your sacrifices, shall be the priest's; also you shall give to the priest the first of your ground meal, to cause a blessing to rest on your house. 31 The priests shall not eat anything, bird or beast, that died naturally or was torn by wild beasts.

Some land is for the Lord

45 "Moreover, when you divide the land by lot into inheritance, you shall set apart a district for the LORD, a holy section of the land; its length shall be twenty-five thousand cubits, and the width ten thousand. It shall be holy throughout its territory all around. 2 Of this there shall be a square plot for the sanctuary, five hundred by five hundred *rods,* with fifty cubits around it for an open space. ³ So this is the district you shall measure: twenty-five thousand *cubits* long and ten thousand wide; in it shall be the sanctuary, the Most Holy *Place.* ⁴ It shall be a holy *section* of the land, belonging to the priests, the ministers of the sanctuary, who come near to minister to the LORD; it shall be a place for their houses and a holy place for the sanctuary. ⁵ An *area* twenty-five thousand *cubits* long and ten thousand wide shall belong to the Levites, the ministers of the temple; they shall have twenty chambers as a possession.

⁶ "You shall appoint as the property of the city an *area* five thousand *cubits* wide and twenty-five thousand long, adjacent to the district of the holy *section;* it shall belong to the whole house of Israel.

⁷ "The prince shall have *a section* on one side and the other of the holy district and the city's property; and bordering on the holy district and the city's property, extending westward on the west side and eastward on the east side, the length *shall be* side by side with one of the *tribal* portions, from the west border to the east border. ⁸ The land shall be his possession in Israel; and My princes shall no more oppress My people, but they shall give *the rest of* the land to the house of Israel, according to their tribes."

⁹ 'Thus says the Lord GOD: "Enough, O princes of Israel! Remove violence and plundering, *execute* justice and righteousness, and stop dispossessing My people," says the Lord GOD. ¹⁰ "You shall have honest scales, an honest ephah, and an honest bath. ¹¹ The ephah and the bath shall be of the same measure, so that the bath contains one-tenth of a homer, and the ephah one-tenth of a homer; their measure shall be according to the homer. ¹² The shekel *shall be* twenty gerahs; twenty shekels, twenty-five shekels, *and* fifteen shekels shall be your mina.

¹³ "This *is* the offering which you shall offer: you shall give one-sixth of an ephah from a homer of wheat, and one-sixth of an ephah from a homer of barley. ¹⁴ The ordinance concerning oil, the bath of oil, *is* one-tenth of a bath from a kor. A kor *is* a homer or ten baths, for ten baths *are* a homer. ¹⁵ And one lamb shall be given from a flock of two hundred, from the rich pastures of Israel. These shall be for grain offerings, burnt offerings, and peace offerings, to make atonement for them," says the Lord GOD. ¹⁶ "All the people of the land shall give this offering for the prince in Israel. ¹⁷ Then it shall be the prince's part *to give* burnt offerings, grain offerings, and drink offerings, at the feasts, the New Moons, the Sabbaths, and at all the appointed seasons of the house of Israel. He shall prepare the sin offering, the grain offering, the burnt offering, and the peace offerings to make atonement for the house of Israel."

¹⁸ 'Thus says the Lord GOD: "In the first *month,* on the first *day* of the month, you shall take a young bull without blemish and cleanse the sanctuary. ¹⁹ The priest shall take some of the blood of the sin offering and put *it* on the doorposts of the temple, on the four corners of the ledge of the altar, and on the gateposts of the gate of the inner court. ²⁰ And so you shall do on the seventh *day* of the month for everyone who has sinned unintentionally or in ignorance. Thus you shall make atonement for the temple.

²¹ "In the first *month,* on the fourteenth day of the month, you shall observe the Passover, a feast of seven days; unleavened bread shall be eaten. ²² And on that day the prince shall prepare for himself and for all the people of the land a bull *for* a sin offering. ²³ On the seven days of the feast he shall prepare a burnt offering to the LORD, seven bulls and seven rams without blemish, daily for seven days, and a kid of the goats daily *for* a sin offering. ²⁴ And he shall prepare a grain offering of one ephah for each bull and one ephah for each ram, together with a hin of oil for each ephah.

²⁵ "In the seventh *month,* on the fif-

teenth day of the month, at the feast, he shall do likewise for seven days, according to the sin offering, the burnt offering, the grain offering, and the oil."

Feast days and special offerings

46 Thus says the Lord GOD: "The gateway of the inner court that faces toward the east shall be shut the six working days; but on the Sabbath it shall be opened, and on the day of the New Moon it shall be opened. ² The prince shall enter by way of the vestibule of the gateway from the outside, and stand by the gatepost. The priests shall prepare his burnt offering and his peace offerings. He shall worship at the threshold of the gate. Then he shall go out, but the gate shall not be shut until evening. ³ Likewise the people of the land shall worship at the entrance to this gateway before the LORD on the Sabbaths and the New Moons. ⁴ The burnt offering that the prince offers to the LORD on the Sabbath day *shall be* six lambs without blemish, and a ram without blemish; ⁵ and the grain offering *shall be one* ephah for a ram, and the grain offering for the lambs, as much as he wants to give, as well as a hin of oil with *every* ephah. ⁶ On the day of the New Moon *it shall be* a young bull without blemish, six lambs, and a ram; they shall be without blemish. ⁷ He shall prepare a grain offering of an ephah for a bull, an ephah for a ram, as much as he wants to give for the lambs, and a hin of oil with *every* ephah. ⁸ When the prince enters, he shall go in by way of the vestibule of the gateway, and go out the same way.

⁹ "But when the people of the land come before the LORD on the appointed feast days, whoever enters by way of the north gate to worship shall go out by way of the south gate; and whoever enters by way of the south gate shall go out by way of the north gate. He shall not return by way of the gate through which he came, but shall go out through the opposite gate.

¹⁰ The prince shall then be in their midst. When they go in, he shall go in; and when they go out, he shall go out. ¹¹ At the festivals and the appointed feast days the grain offering shall be an ephah for a bull, an ephah for a ram, as much as he wants to give for the lambs, and a hin of oil with every ephah.

¹² "Now when the prince makes a voluntary burnt offering or voluntary peace offering to the LORD, the gate that faces toward the east shall then be opened for him; and he shall prepare his burnt offering and his peace offerings as he did on the Sabbath day. Then he shall go out, and after he goes out the gate shall be shut.

¹³ "You shall daily make a burnt offering to the LORD *of* a lamb of the first year without blemish; you shall prepare it *every* morning. ¹⁴ And you shall prepare a grain offering with it every morning, a sixth of an ephah, and a third of a hin of oil to moisten the fine flour. This grain offering is a perpetual ordinance, to be made regularly to the LORD. ¹⁵ Thus they shall prepare the lamb, the grain offering, and the oil, *as* a regular burnt offering every morning."

¹⁶ Thus says the Lord GOD: "If the prince gives a gift *of some* of his inheritance to any of his sons, it shall belong to his sons; it is their possession by inheritance. ¹⁷ But if he gives a gift of some of his inheritance to one of his servants, it shall be his until the year of liberty, after which it shall return to the prince. But his inheritance shall belong to his sons; it shall become theirs. ¹⁸ Moreover the prince shall not take any of the people's inheritance by evicting them from their property; he shall provide an inheritance for his sons from his own property, so that none of My people may be scattered from his property.' "

¹⁹ Now he brought me through the entrance, which *was* at the side of the gate, into the holy chambers of the priests which face toward the north; and there a place *was* situated at their extreme western end. ²⁰ And he said

to me, "This *is* the place where the priests shall boil the trespass offering and the sin offering, *and* where they shall bake the grain offering, so that they do not bring *them* out into the outer court to sanctify the people."

21 Then he brought me out into the outer court and caused me to pass by the four corners of the court; and in fact, in every corner of the court *there was another* court. 22 In the four corners of the court *were* enclosed courts, forty *cubits* long and thirty wide; all four corners *were* the same size. 23 *There was* a row *of building stones* all around in them, all around the four of them; and cooking hearths were made under the rows of stones all around. 24 And he said to me, "These *are* the kitchens where the ministers of the temple shall boil the sacrifices of the people."

The River of Healing flows from the temple

47 Then he brought me back to the door of the temple; and there was water, flowing from under the threshold of the temple toward the east, for the front of the temple faced east; the water was flowing from under the right side of the temple, south of the altar. 2 He brought me out by way of the north gate, and led me around on the outside to the outer gateway that faces east; and there was water, running out on the right side.

3 And when the man went out to the east with the line in his hand, he measured one thousand cubits, and he brought me through the waters; the water *came up to my* ankles. 4 Again he measured one thousand and brought me through the waters; the water *came up to my* knees. Again he measured one thousand and brought me through; the water *came up to my* waist. 5 Again he measured one thousand, *and it was* a river that I could not cross; for the water was too deep, water in which one must swim, a river that could not be crossed. 6 He said to me, "Son of man, have you seen

this?" Then he brought me and returned me to the bank of the river.

7 When I returned, there, along the bank of the river, *were* very many trees on one side and the other. 8 Then he said to me: "This water flows toward the eastern region, goes down into the valley, and enters the sea. *When it* reaches the sea, *its* waters are healed. 9 And it shall be *that* every living thing that moves, wherever the rivers go, will live. There will be a very great multitude of fish, because these waters go there; for they will be healed, and everything will live wherever the river goes. 10 It shall be *that* fishermen will stand by it from En Gedi to En Eglaim; they will be *places* for spreading their nets. Their fish will be of the same kinds as the fish of the Great Sea, exceedingly many. 11 But its swamps and marshes will not be healed; they will be given over to salt. 12 Along the bank of the river, on this side and that, will grow all *kinds of* trees used for food; their leaves will not wither, and their fruit will not fail. They will bear fruit every month, because their water flows from the sanctuary. Their fruit will be for food, and their leaves for medicine."

13 Thus says the Lord GOD: "These *are* the borders by which you shall divide the land as an inheritance among the twelve tribes of Israel. Joseph *shall have two* portions. 14 You shall inherit it equally with one another; for I raised My hand in an oath to give it to your fathers, and this land shall fall to you as your inheritance.

15 "This *shall be* the border of the land on the north: from the Great Sea, *by* the road to Hethlon, as one goes to Zedad, 16 Hamath, Berothah, Sibraim (which *is* between the border of Damascus and the border of Hamath), to Hazar Hatticon (which *is* on the border of Hauran). 17 Thus the boundary shall be from the Sea to Hazar Enan, the border of Damascus; and as for the north, northward, it is the border of Hamath. *This is* the north side.

18 "On the east side you shall mark out the border from between Hauran

and Damascus, and between Gilead and the land of Israel, along the Jordan, and along the eastern side of the sea. *This is* the east side.

19 "The south side, toward the South, *shall be* from Tamar to the waters of Meribah by Kadesh, along the brook to the Great Sea. *This is* the south side, toward the South.

20 "The west side *shall be* the Great Sea, from the *southern* boundary until one comes to a point opposite Hamath. This *is* the west side.

21 "Thus you shall divide this land among yourselves according to the tribes of Israel. 22 It shall be that you will divide it by lot as an inheritance for yourselves, and for the strangers who dwell among you and who bear children among you. They shall be to you as native-born among the children of Israel; they shall have an inheritance with you among the tribes of Israel. 23 And it shall be *that* in whatever tribe the stranger dwells, there you shall give *him* his inheritance," says the Lord GOD.

The City of God

48 "Now these *are* the names of the tribes: From the northern border along the road to Hethlon at the entrance of Hamath, to Hazar Enan, the border of Damascus northward, in the direction of Hamath, *there shall be* one section *for* Dan from its east to its west side; 2 by the border of Dan, from the east side to the west, one section *for* Asher; 3 by the border of Asher, from the east side to the west, one section *for* Naphtali; 4 by the border of Naphtali, from the east side to the west, one section *for* Manasseh; 5 by the border of Manasseh, from the east side to the west, one section *for* Ephraim; 6 by the border of Ephraim, from the east side to the west, one section *for* Reuben; 7 by the border of Reuben, from the east side to the west, one section *for* Judah; 8 by the border of Judah, from the east side to the west, shall be the district which you shall set apart, twenty-five thousand *cubits* in width,

and *in* length the same as one of the *other* portions, from the east side to the west, with the sanctuary in the center.

9 "The district that you shall set apart for the LORD *shall be* twenty-five thousand *cubits* in length and ten thousand in width. 10 To these—to the priests—the holy district shall belong: on the north twenty-five thousand *cubits in length,* on the west ten thousand in width, on the east ten thousand in width, and on the south twenty-five thousand in length. The sanctuary of the LORD shall be in the center. 11 *It shall be* for the priests of the sons of Zadok, who are sanctified, who have kept My charge, who did not go astray when the children of Israel went astray, as the Levites went astray. 12 And *this* district of land that is set apart shall be to them a thing most holy by the border of the Levites.

13 "Opposite the border of the priests, the Levites *shall have an area* twenty-five thousand *cubits* in length and ten thousand in width; its entire length *shall be* twenty-five thousand and its width ten thousand. 14 And they shall not sell or exchange any of it; they may not alienate this best *part* of the land, for *it is* holy to the LORD.

15 "The five thousand *cubits* in width that remain, along the edge of the twenty-five thousand, shall be for general use by the city, for dwellings and common-land; and the city shall be in the center. 16 These *shall be* its measurements: the north side four thousand five hundred *cubits,* the south side four thousand five hundred, the east side four thousand five hundred, and the west side four thousand five hundred. 17 The common-land of the city shall be: to the north two hundred and fifty *cubits,* to the south two hundred and fifty, to the east two hundred and fifty, and to the west two hundred and fifty. 18 The rest of the length, alongside the district of the holy *section, shall be* ten thousand *cubits* to the east and ten thousand to the west. It shall be adjacent to the district of the holy *section,* and its produce shall

be food for the workers of the city.
19 The workers of the city, from all the
tribes of Israel, shall cultivate it. 20 The
entire district *shall be* twenty-five thousand *cubits* by twenty-five thousand
cubits, foursquare. You shall set apart
the holy district with the property of
the city.

21 "The rest *shall belong* to the
prince, on one side and on the other
of the holy district and of the city's
property, next to the twenty-five thousand *cubits* of the *holy* district as far
as the eastern border, and westward
next to the twenty-five thousand as far
as the western border, adjacent to the
tribal portions; *it shall belong* to the
prince. It shall be the holy district, and
the sanctuary of the temple *shall be*
in the center. 22 Moreover, apart from
the possession of the Levites and the
possession of the city *which are* in the
midst of what *belongs* to the prince,
the area between the border of Judah
and the border of Benjamin shall belong to the prince.

23 "As for the rest of the tribes, from
the east side to the west, Benjamin
shall have one *section;* 24 by the border
of Benjamin, from the east side to the
west, Simeon *shall have* one *section;*
25 by the border of Simeon, from the
east side to the west, Issachar *shall
have* one *section;* 26 by the border of
Issachar, from the east side to the west,

Zebulun *shall have* one *section;*
27 by the border of Zebulun, from the
east side to the west, Gad *shall have*
one *section;* 28 by the border of
Gad, on the south side, toward the
South, the border shall be from
Tamar *to* the waters of Meribah *by*
Kadesh, along the brook to the Great
Sea. 29 This *is* the land which you
shall divide by lot as an inheritance
among the tribes of Israel, and these
are their portions," says the Lord
God.

30 "These *are* the exits of the city.
On the north side, measuring four
thousand five hundred *cubits* 31 (the
gates of the city *shall be* named after
the tribes of Israel), the three gates
northward: one gate for Reuben, one
gate for Judah, and one gate for Levi;
32 on the east side, four thousand five
hundred *cubits,* three gates: one gate
for Joseph, one gate for Benjamin, and
one gate for Dan; 33 on the south side,
measuring four thousand five hundred
cubits, three gates: one gate for Simeon, one gate for Issachar, and one
gate for Zebulun; 34 on the west side,
four thousand five hundred *cubits* with
their three gates: one gate for Gad, one
gate for Asher, and one gate for Naphtali. 35 All the way around *shall be* eighteen thousand *cubits;* and the name
of the city from *that* day *shall be:* THE
LORD *IS* THERE."

⚒ DIGGING IN

48:35 The Name of the New City
What makes heaven really heaven? Is it
because the streets are all gold? They
are. But that isn't why heaven is heaven.
Is it because you'll meet loved ones there
who left you long ago? Yes, you will see
all those dear ones. You may have
watched them die, and you know they
went to the great house that Jesus describes in John 14:2. And won't it be wonderful to talk to the apostle Paul and the

prophet Isaiah? All of these joys wait for
you in heaven. But being able to see all
those you love isn't what makes heaven,
either.

Heaven is really heaven because the
Lord is there. We will actually be able
to see the Lord Jesus and talk with Him.
Jesus will be our eternal Brother, and
His Father will be our eternal Father *for-
ever.*

The Book of
DANIEL

My name is pronounced *DAN-yell* and means "God Is My Judge." I was a teenager when I was taken to Babylon 605 years before Jesus was born.

For more than 60 years, I served the Lord in Babylon as a prophet. I also became governor of the province of Babylon, and I was chief of the king's wise men there.

My first great experience in Babylon came when my three friends and I refused to eat food that was not right for Jews to eat. That's how the king learned that we were wiser than all his experts in Babylon.

But my big chance came when I explained the king's dream to him. That was when the king promoted my three friends and me to become leaders in the nation.

Daniel won't eat the king's rich food

IN the third year of the reign of Jehoiakim king of Judah, Nebuchadnezzar king of Babylon came to Jerusalem and besieged it. 2 And the Lord gave Jehoiakim king of Judah into his hand, with some of the articles of the house of God, which he carried into the land of Shinar to the house of his god; and he brought the articles into the treasure house of his god.

3 Then the king instructed Ashpenaz, the master of his eunuchs, to bring some of the children of Israel and some of the king's descendants and some of the nobles, 4 young men in whom *there was* no blemish, but good-looking, gifted in all wisdom, possessing knowledge and quick to understand, who *had* ability to serve in the king's palace, and whom they might teach the language and literature of the Chaldeans. 5 And the king appointed for them a daily provision of the king's delicacies and of the wine which he drank, and three years of training for them, so that at the end of *that time* they might serve before the king. 6 Now from among those of the sons of Judah were Daniel, Hananiah, Mishael, and Azariah.

7 To them the chief of the eunuchs gave names: he gave Daniel *the name* Belteshazzar; to Hananiah, Shadrach; to Mishael, Meshach; and to Azariah, Abed-Nego.

8 But Daniel purposed in his heart that he would not defile himself with the portion of the king's delicacies, nor with the wine which he drank; therefore he requested of the chief of the eunuchs that he might not defile himself. 9 Now God had brought Daniel into the favor and goodwill of the chief of the eunuchs. 10 And the chief of the eunuchs said to Daniel, "I fear my lord the king, who has appointed your food and drink. For why should he see your faces looking worse than the young men who *are* your age? Then you would endanger my head before the king."

11 So Daniel said to the steward whom the chief of the eunuchs had set over Daniel, Hananiah, Mishael, and Azariah, 12 "Please test your servants for ten days, and let them give us vegetables to eat and water to drink. 13 Then let our appearance be examined before you, and the appearance of the young men who eat the portion of the king's delicacies; and as you see fit, *so* deal with your servants." 14 So

he consented with them in this matter, and tested them ten days.

15 And at the end of ten days their features appeared better and fatter in flesh than all the young men who ate the portion of the king's delicacies. 16 Thus the steward took away their portion of delicacies and the wine that they were to drink, and gave them vegetables.

17 As for these four young men, God gave them knowledge and skill in all literature and wisdom; and Daniel had understanding in all visions and dreams.

18 Now at the end of the days, when the king had said that they should be brought in, the chief of the eunuchs brought them in before Nebuchadnezzar. 19 Then the king interviewed them, and among them all none was found like Daniel, Hananiah, Mishael, and Azariah; therefore they served before the king. 20 And in all matters of wisdom *and* understanding about which the king examined them, he found them ten times better than all the magicians *and* astrologers who *were* in all his realm. 21 Thus Daniel continued until the first year of King Cyrus.

Daniel explains a strange dream

2 Now in the second year of Nebuchadnezzar's reign, Nebuchadnezzar had dreams; and his spirit was so troubled that his sleep left him. 2 Then the king gave the command to call the magicians, the astrologers, the sorcerers, and the Chaldeans to tell the king his dreams. So they came and stood before the king. 3 And the king said to them, "I have had a dream, and my spirit is anxious to know the dream."

4 Then the Chaldeans spoke to the king in Aramaic, "O king, live forever! Tell your servants the dream, and we will give the interpretation."

5 The king answered and said to the Chaldeans, "My decision is firm: if you do not make known the dream to me, and its interpretation, you shall be cut in pieces, and your houses shall be made an ash heap. 6 However, if you tell the dream and its interpretation, you shall receive from me gifts, rewards, and great honor. Therefore tell me the dream and its interpretation."

7 They answered again and said, "Let the king tell his servants the dream, and we will give its interpretation."

8 The king answered and said, "I know for certain that you would gain time, because you see that my decision is firm: 9 if you do not make known the dream to me, *there is only* one decree for you! For you have agreed to speak lying and corrupt words before me till the time has changed. Therefore tell me the dream, and I shall know

---

King Nebuchadnezzar—My name is pronounced *neb-you-kad-NEZ-er.* I am the great king of Babylon who conquered the Hebrews and destroyed Jerusalem 586 years before Christ came.

My magicians and sorcerers couldn't explain a dream I had. The problem was that I couldn't even remember what I had dreamed!

Then somebody told me about a Jewish man named Daniel who could explain my dream. So I called him in, and he told me that His God, the Lord of heaven and earth, could explain dreams.

Then Daniel told me about the big statue I had seen in my dream. The statue was a sign of the four great empires of the ancient world. Mine was the first and greatest empire. We would be followed by the Persians, then by the Greeks, and finally by the Romans.

When you read your history books, you will learn that everything happened just as I saw in my dream.

that you can give me its interpretation."

10 The Chaldeans answered the king, and said, "There is not a man on earth who can tell the king's matter; therefore no king, lord, or ruler has *ever* asked such things of any magician, astrologer, or Chaldean. 11 *It is* a difficult thing that the king requests, and there is no other who can tell it to the king except the gods, whose dwelling is not with flesh."

12 For this reason the king was angry and very furious, and gave the command to destroy all the wise *men* of Babylon. 13 So the decree went out, and they began killing the wise *men;* and they sought Daniel and his companions, to kill *them.*

14 Then with counsel and wisdom Daniel answered Arioch, the captain of the king's guard, who had gone out to kill the wise *men* of Babylon; 15 he answered and said to Arioch the king's captain, "Why is the decree from the king so urgent?" Then Arioch made the decision known to Daniel.

16 So Daniel went in and asked the king to give him time, that he might tell the king the interpretation. 17 Then Daniel went to his house, and made the decision known to Hananiah, Mishael, and Azariah, his companions, 18 that they might seek mercies from the God of heaven concerning this secret, so that Daniel and his companions might not perish with the rest of the wise *men* of Babylon. 19 Then the secret was revealed to Daniel in a night vision. So Daniel blessed the God of heaven.

20 Daniel answered and said:

"Blessed be the name of God
    forever and ever,
For wisdom and might are
    His.
21 And He changes the times and
    the seasons;
He removes kings and raises up
    kings;
He gives wisdom to the wise
And knowledge to those who
    have understanding.

22 He reveals deep and secret
    things;
He knows what *is* in the
    darkness,
And light dwells with Him.

23 "I thank You and praise You,
    O God of my fathers;
You have given me wisdom and
    might,
And have now made known to
    me what we asked of You,
For You have made known to
    us the king's demand."

24 Therefore Daniel went to Arioch, whom the king had appointed to destroy the wise *men* of Babylon. He went and said thus to him: "Do not destroy the wise *men* of Babylon; take me before the king, and I will tell the king the interpretation."

25 Then Arioch quickly brought Daniel before the king, and said thus to him, "I have found a man of the captives of Judah, who will make known to the king the interpretation."

26 The king answered and said to Daniel, whose name *was* Belteshazzar, "Are you able to make known to me the dream which I have seen, and its interpretation?"

27 Daniel answered in the presence of the king, and said, "The secret which the king has demanded, the wise *men,* the astrologers, the magicians, and the soothsayers cannot declare to the king. 28 But there is a God in heaven who reveals secrets, and He has made known to King Nebuchadnezzar what will be in the latter days. Your dream, and the visions of your head upon your bed, were these: 29 As for you, O king, thoughts came *to* your *mind while* on your bed, *about* what would come to pass after this; and He who reveals secrets has made known to you what will be. 30 But as for me, this secret has not been revealed to me because I have more wisdom than anyone living, but for *our* sakes who make known the interpretation to the king, and that you may know the thoughts of your heart.

31 "You, O king, were watching; and behold, a great image! This great image, whose splendor *was* excellent, stood before you; and its form *was* awesome. 32 This image's head *was* of fine gold, its chest and arms of silver, its belly and thighs of bronze, 33 its legs of iron, its feet partly of iron and partly of clay. 34 You watched while a stone was cut out without hands, which struck the image on its feet of iron and clay, and broke them in pieces. 35 Then the iron, the clay, the bronze, the silver, and the gold were crushed together, and became like chaff from the summer threshing floors; the wind carried them away so that no trace of them was found. And the stone that struck the image became a great mountain and filled the whole earth.

36 "This *is* the dream. Now we will tell the interpretation of it before the king. 37 You, O king, *are* a king of kings. For the God of heaven has given you a kingdom, power, strength, and glory; 38 and wherever the children of men dwell, or the beasts of the field and the birds of the heaven, He has given *them* into your hand, and has made you ruler over them all—you *are* this head of gold. 39 But after you shall arise another kingdom inferior to yours; then another, a third kingdom of bronze, which shall rule over all the earth. 40 And the fourth kingdom shall be as strong as iron, inasmuch as iron breaks in pieces and shatters everything; and like iron that crushes, *that kingdom* will break in pieces and crush all the others. 41 Whereas you saw the feet and toes, partly of potter's clay and partly of iron, the kingdom shall be divided; yet the strength of the iron shall be in it, just as you saw the iron mixed with ceramic clay. 42 And *as* the toes of the feet *were* partly of iron and partly of clay, *so* the kingdom shall be partly strong and partly fragile. 43 As you saw iron mixed with ceramic clay, they will mingle with the seed of men; but they will not adhere to one another, just as iron does not mix with clay. 44 And in the days of these kings the God of heaven will set up a kingdom which shall never be destroyed; and the kingdom shall not be left to other people; it shall break in pieces and consume all these kingdoms, and it shall stand forever. 45 Inasmuch as you saw that the stone was cut out of the mountain without hands, and that it broke in pieces the iron, the bronze, the clay, the silver, and the gold—the great God has made known to the king what will come to pass after this. The dream is certain, and its interpretation is sure."

46 Then King Nebuchadnezzar fell on his face, prostrate before Daniel, and commanded that they should present an offering and incense to him. 47 The king answered Daniel, and said, "Truly your God *is* the God of gods, the Lord of kings, and a revealer of secrets, since you could reveal this secret." 48 Then the king promoted Daniel and gave him many great gifts; and he made him ruler over the whole province of Babylon, and chief administrator over all the wise *men* of Bab-

---

What King Nebuchadnezzar Learned

I was really amazed at what Daniel told me about my dream. Then I realized that Daniel's God was the One who had shown me about the coming empires of the world.

I had never known this God. In fact, I think I always believed I was the greatest power in the universe. But even though I was a great king, I was nothing at all compared to Daniel's God.

Now I know my real place in the world. God is the true King, and I am His servant. My great ambition now is to do His will in all things. That is the true road to happiness—for you, too!

ylon. 49 Also Daniel petitioned the king, and he set Shadrach, Meshach, and Abed-Nego over the affairs of the province of Babylon; but Daniel *sat* in the gate of the king.

They walked in the fire, but were not burned

3 Nebuchadnezzar the king made an image of gold, whose height *was* sixty cubits *and* its width six cubits. He set it up in the plain of Dura, in the province of Babylon. 2 And King Nebuchadnezzar sent *word* to gather together the satraps, the administrators, the governors, the counselors, the treasurers, the judges, the magistrates, and all the officials of the provinces, to come to the dedication of the image which King Nebuchadnezzar had set up. 3 So the satraps, the administrators, the governors, the counselors, the treasurers, the judges, the magistrates, and all the officials of the provinces gathered together for the dedication of the image that King Nebuchadnezzar had set up; and they stood before the image that Nebuchadnezzar had set up. 4 Then a herald cried aloud: "To you it is commanded, O peoples, nations, and languages, 5 *that* at the time you hear the sound of the horn, flute, harp, lyre, *and* psaltery, in symphony with all kinds of music, you shall fall down and worship the gold image that King Nebuchadnezzar has set up; 6 and whoever does not fall down and wor-

ship shall be cast immediately into the midst of a burning fiery furnace."

7 So at that time, when all the people heard the sound of the horn, flute, harp, *and* lyre, in symphony with all kinds of music, all the people, nations, and languages fell down *and* worshiped the gold image which King Nebuchadnezzar had set up.

8 Therefore at that time certain Chaldeans came forward and accused the Jews. 9 They spoke and said to King Nebuchadnezzar, "O king, live forever! 10 You, O king, have made a decree that everyone who hears the sound of the horn, flute, harp, lyre, *and* psaltery, in symphony with all kinds of music, shall fall down and worship the gold image; 11 and whoever does not fall down and worship shall be cast into the midst of a burning fiery furnace. 12 There are certain Jews whom you have set over the affairs of the province of Babylon: Shadrach, Meshach, and Abed-Nego; these men, O king, have not paid due regard to you. They do not serve your gods or worship the gold image which you have set up."

13 Then Nebuchadnezzar, in rage and fury, gave the command to bring Shadrach, Meshach, and Abed-Nego. So they brought these men before the king. 14 Nebuchadnezzar spoke, saying to them, "*Is it* true, Shadrach, Meshach, and Abed-Nego, *that* you do not serve my gods or worship the gold image which I have set up? 15 Now if you are ready at the time you hear the

DIGGING IN

3:12–30 Three Brave Boys King Nebuchadnezzar (pronounced *neb-you-kad-NEZ-er*) did not understand that there is only one God. So he set up a gold image about 90 feet high and ordered everybody to worship the image. Daniel's three friends—Shadrach, Meshach, and Abed-Nego—refused to worship the image. (Pronounce their names *SHAD-rack, ME-shack,* and *ah-BED-nee-go.*)

Of course, the king was angry, and he told the boys they would be burned alive in a fiery furnace. But the three boys

replied that God could save them—and *even if God didn't save them,* they would *never* worship the gold image.

So the king put the boys in the furnace. But when he looked into the furnace, the boys were not hurt. Someone "like the Son of God" was walking with them in the fire. Then King Nebuchadnezzar praised God and gave the three boys important jobs in his government.

You may go through hard places in life. But if you trust Him, the Son of God will walk through them with you.

sound of the horn, flute, harp, lyre, *and* psaltery, in symphony with all kinds of music, and you fall down and worship the image which I have made, *good!* But if you do not worship, you shall be cast immediately into the midst of a burning fiery furnace. And who *is* the god who will deliver you from my hands?''

16 Shadrach, Meshach, and Abed-Nego answered and said to the king, "O Nebuchadnezzar, we have no need to answer you in this matter. 17 If that *is the case,* our God whom we serve is able to deliver us from the burning fiery furnace, and He will deliver *us* from your hand, O king. 18 But if not, let it be known to you, O king, that we do not serve your gods, nor will we worship the gold image which you have set up.''

19 Then Nebuchadnezzar was full of fury, and the expression on his face changed toward Shadrach, Meshach, and Abed-Nego. He spoke and commanded that they heat the furnace seven times more than it was usually heated. 20 And he commanded certain mighty men of valor who *were* in his army to bind Shadrach, Meshach, and Abed-Nego, *and* cast *them* into the burning fiery furnace. 21 Then these men were bound in their coats, their trousers, their turbans, and their *other* garments, and were cast into the midst of the burning fiery furnace. 22 Therefore, because the king's command was urgent, and the furnace exceedingly hot, the flame of the fire killed those men who took up Shadrach, Meshach, and Abed-Nego. 23 And these three men, Shadrach, Meshach, and Abed-Nego, fell down bound into the midst of the burning fiery furnace.

24 Then King Nebuchadnezzar was astonished; and he rose in haste *and* spoke, saying to his counselors, "Did we not cast three men bound into the midst of the fire?''

They answered and said to the king, "True, O king.''

25 "Look!'' he answered, "I see four men loose, walking in the midst of the fire; and they are not hurt, and the form of the fourth is like the Son of God.''

26 Then Nebuchadnezzar went near the mouth of the burning fiery furnace *and* spoke, saying, "Shadrach, Meshach, and Abed-Nego, servants of the Most High God, come out, and come here.'' Then Shadrach, Meshach, and Abed-Nego came from the midst of the fire. 27 And the satraps, administrators, governors, and the king's counselors gathered together, and they saw these men on whose bodies the fire had no power; the hair of their head was not singed nor were their garments affected, and the smell of fire was not on them.

28 Nebuchadnezzar spoke, saying, "Blessed be the God of Shadrach, Meshach, and Abed-Nego, who sent His Angel and delivered His servants who trusted in Him, and they have frustrated the king's word, and yielded their bodies, that they should not serve nor worship any god except their own God! 29 Therefore I make a decree that any people, nation, or language which speaks anything amiss against the God of Shadrach, Meshach, and Abed-Nego shall be cut in pieces, and their houses shall be made an ash heap; because there is no other God who can deliver like this.''

30 Then the king promoted Shadrach, Meshach, and Abed-Nego in the province of Babylon.

The tree that reached to heaven

4 Nebuchadnezzar the king,

> To all peoples, nations, and languages that dwell in all the earth:
>
> Peace be multiplied to you.

2 I thought it good to declare the signs and wonders that the Most High God has worked for me.

3 How great *are* His signs,
And how mighty His wonders!

His kingdom *is* an everlasting
  kingdom,
And His dominion *is* from
  generation to generation.

4 I, Nebuchadnezzar, was at rest
in my house, and flourishing in
my palace. ⁵ I saw a dream
which made me afraid, and the
thoughts on my bed and the
visions of my head troubled me.
⁶ Therefore I issued a decree to
bring in all the wise *men* of
Babylon before me, that they
might make known to me the
interpretation of the dream.
⁷ Then the magicians, the
astrologers, the Chaldeans, and
the soothsayers came in, and I
told them the dream; but they
did not make known to me its
interpretation. ⁸ But at last
Daniel came before me (his
name *is* Belteshazzar, according
to the name of my god; in him
is the Spirit of the Holy God),
and I told the dream before him,
saying: 9 "Belteshazzar, chief of
the magicians, because I know
that the Spirit of the Holy God
is in you, and no secret troubles
you, explain to me the visions
of my dream that I have seen,
and its interpretation.

10 "These *were* the visions of my
head *while* on my bed:

"I was looking, and behold,
A tree in the midst of the earth,
And its height was great.
11 The tree grew and became
  strong;
Its height reached to the
  heavens,
And it could be seen to the ends
  of all the earth.
12 Its leaves *were* lovely,
Its fruit abundant,
And in it *was* food for all.
The beasts of the field found
  shade under it,
The birds of the heavens dwelt
  in its branches,
And all flesh was fed from it.

13 "I saw in the visions of my head
while on my bed, and there was
a watcher, a holy one, coming
down from heaven. 14 He cried
aloud and said thus:

'Chop down the tree and cut off
  its branches,
Strip off its leaves and scatter its
  fruit.
Let the beasts get out from
  under it,
And the birds from its branches.
15 Nevertheless leave the stump
  and roots in the earth,
Bound with a band of iron and
  bronze,
In the tender grass of the field.
Let it be wet with the dew of
  heaven,
And *let* him graze with the beasts
On the grass of the earth.
16 Let his heart be changed from
  that of a man,
Let him be given the heart of a
  beast,
And let seven times pass over
  him.

17 'This decision *is* by the decree of
  the watchers,
And the sentence by the word
  of the holy ones,
In order that the living may
  know
That the Most High rules in the
  kingdom of men,
Gives it to whomever He will,
And sets over it the lowest of
  men.'

18 "This dream I, King
Nebuchadnezzar, have seen.
Now you, Belteshazzar, declare
its interpretation, since all the
wise *men* of my kingdom are not
able to make known to me the
interpretation; but *you are* able,
for the Spirit of the Holy God
is in you."

19 Then Daniel, whose name was
Belteshazzar, was astonished for
a time, and his thoughts troubled

him. *So* the king spoke, and said, "Belteshazzar, do not let the dream or its interpretation trouble you."

Belteshazzar answered and said, "My lord, *may* the dream concern those who hate you, and its interpretation concern your enemies!

20 "The tree that you saw, which grew and became strong, whose height reached to the heavens and which *could be seen* by all the earth, 21 whose leaves *were* lovely and its fruit abundant, in which *was* food for all, under which the beasts of the field dwelt, and in whose branches the birds of the heaven had their home— 22 it *is* you, O king, who have grown and become strong; for your greatness has grown and reaches to the heavens, and your dominion to the end of the earth.

23 "And inasmuch as the king saw a watcher, a holy one, coming down from heaven and saying, 'Chop down the tree and destroy it, but leave its stump and roots in the earth, *bound* with a band of iron and bronze in the tender grass of the field; let it be wet with the dew of heaven, and let him graze with the beasts of the field, till seven times pass over him'; 24 this is the interpretation, O king, and this is the decree of the Most High, which has come upon my lord the king: 25 They shall drive you from men, your dwelling shall be with the beasts of the field, and they shall make you eat grass like oxen. They shall wet you with the dew of heaven, and seven times shall pass over you, till you know that the Most High rules in the kingdom of men, and gives it to whomever He chooses.

26 "And inasmuch as they gave the command to leave the stump *and* roots of the tree, your kingdom shall be assured to you, after you come to know that Heaven rules. 27 Therefore, O king, let my advice be acceptable to you; break off your sins by *being* righteous, and your iniquities by showing mercy to *the* poor. Perhaps there may be a lengthening of your prosperity."

28 All *this* came upon King Nebuchadnezzar. 29 At the end of the twelve months he was walking about the royal palace of Babylon. 30 The king spoke, saying, "Is not this great Babylon, that I have built for a royal dwelling by my mighty power and for the honor of my majesty?"

31 While the word *was still* in the king's mouth, a voice fell from heaven: "King Nebuchadnezzar, to you it is spoken: the kingdom has departed from you! 32 And they shall drive you from men, and your dwelling *shall be* with the beasts of the field. They shall make you eat grass like oxen; and seven times shall pass over you, until you know that the Most High rules in the kingdom of men, and gives it to whomever He chooses."

33 That very hour the word was fulfilled concerning Nebuchadnezzar; he was driven from men and ate grass like oxen; his body was wet with the dew of heaven till his hair had grown like eagles' *feathers* and his nails like birds' *claws.*

34 And at the end of the time I, Nebuchadnezzar, lifted my eyes to heaven, and my

Strange Happenings at Feast, King Slain

BTV (Babylonian Television)—With Channel 4 news teams on the scene to cover a royal party held at the palace last night, we are able to bring you this eyewitness report of some unusual events.

King Belshazzar (pronounced *bell-SHAZ-er*), who invited a thousand of the leading people of Babylon to a feast, shocked guests when he ordered the servants to bring in the sacred gold and silver cups and plates from the Jewish temple. These priceless items were taken by his father, King Nebuchadnezzar (pronounced *neb-you-kad-NEZ-er*),

when the Jews were brought to Babylon as prisoners many years ago. No one thought the king would dare to use the dishes at a party. But last night, he did!

King Belshazzar also praised his false gods at the banquet. Right away, some strange handwriting appeared on the wall. Reporters at the scene say the king was so scared his knees knocked together! He called in his wise men, but only the prophet Daniel could explain the writing. "It is the handwriting of God," he said. "It means that the kingdom of Belshazzar is over!" (See Ezekiel 5:25–27.)

understanding returned to me;
and I blessed the Most High and
praised and honored Him who
lives forever:

For His dominion *is* an
   everlasting dominion,
And His kingdom *is* from
   generation to generation.
35 All the inhabitants of the earth
   are reputed as nothing;
He does according to His will in
   the army of heaven
And *among* the inhabitants of
   the earth.
No one can restrain His hand
Or say to Him, "What have You
   done?"

36 At the same time my reason
returned to me, and for the glory
of my kingdom, my honor and
splendor returned to me. My
counselors and nobles resorted
to me, I was restored to my
kingdom, and excellent majesty
was added to me. 37 Now I,
Nebuchadnezzar, praise and
extol and honor the King of
heaven, all of whose works *are*
truth, and His ways justice. And
those who walk in pride He is
able to put down.

A giant hand writes on a wall

5 Belshazzar the king made a great feast for a thousand of his lords, and drank wine in the presence of the thousand. 2 While he tasted the wine, Belshazzar gave the command to bring the gold and silver vessels which his father Nebuchadnezzar had taken from the temple which *had been* in Jerusalem, that the king and his lords, his wives, and his concubines might drink from them. 3 Then they brought the gold vessels that had been taken from the temple of the house of God which *had been* in Jerusalem; and the king and his lords, his wives, and his concubines drank from them. 4 They drank wine, and praised the gods of gold and silver, bronze and iron, wood and stone.

5 In the same hour the fingers of a man's hand appeared and wrote opposite the lampstand on the plaster of the wall of the king's palace; and the king saw the part of the hand that wrote. 6 Then the king's countenance changed, and his thoughts troubled him, so that the joints of his hips were loosened and his knees knocked against each other. 7 The king cried aloud to bring in the astrologers, the Chaldeans, and the soothsayers. The king spoke, saying to the wise *men* of Babylon, "Whoever reads this writing,

and tells me its interpretation, shall be clothed with purple and *have* a chain of gold around his neck; and he shall be the third ruler in the kingdom."
8 Now all the king's wise *men* came, but they could not read the writing, or make known to the king its interpretation. 9 Then King Belshazzar was greatly troubled, his countenance was changed, and his lords were astonished.

10 The queen, because of the words of the king and his lords, came to the banquet hall. The queen spoke, saying, "O king, live forever! Do not let your thoughts trouble you, nor let your countenance change. 11 There is a man in your kingdom in whom *is* the Spirit of the Holy God. And in the days of your father, light and understanding and wisdom, like the wisdom of the gods, were found in him; and King Nebuchadnezzar your father—your father the king—made him chief of the magicians, astrologers, Chaldeans, *and* soothsayers. 12 Inasmuch as an excellent spirit, knowledge, understanding, interpreting dreams, solving riddles, and explaining enigmas were found in this Daniel, whom the king named Belteshazzar, now let Daniel be called, and he will give the interpretation."

13 Then Daniel was brought in before the king. The king spoke, and said to Daniel, "*Are* you that Daniel who is one of the captives from Judah, whom my father the king brought from Judah? 14 I have heard of you, that the Spirit of God *is* in you, and *that* light and understanding and excellent wisdom are found in you. 15 Now the wise *men*, the astrologers, have been brought in before me, that they should read this writing and make known to me its interpretation, but they could not give the interpretation of the thing. 16 And I have heard of you, that you can give interpretations and explain enigmas. Now if you can read the writing and make known to me its interpretation, you shall be clothed with purple and *have* a chain of gold around your neck, and shall be the third ruler in the kingdom."

17 Then Daniel answered, and said before the king, "Let your gifts be for yourself, and give your rewards to another; yet I will read the writing to the king, and make known to him the interpretation. 18 O king, the Most High God gave Nebuchadnezzar your father a kingdom and majesty, glory and honor. 19 And because of the majesty that He gave him, all peoples, nations, and languages trembled and feared before him. Whomever he wished, he executed; whomever he wished, he kept alive; whomever he wished, he set up; and whomever he wished, he put down. 20 But when his heart was lifted up, and his spirit was hardened in pride, he was deposed from his kingly throne, and they took his glory from him. 21 Then he was driven from the sons of men, his heart was made like the beasts, and his dwelling *was* with the wild donkeys. They fed him with grass like oxen, and his body was wet with the dew of heaven, till he knew that the Most High God rules in the kingdom of men, and appoints over it whomever He chooses.

22 "But you his son, Belshazzar, have not humbled your heart, although you knew all this. 23 And you have lifted yourself up against the Lord of heaven. They have brought the vessels of His house before you, and you and your lords, your wives and your concubines, have drunk wine from them. And you have praised the gods of silver and gold, bronze and iron, wood and stone, which do not see or hear or know; and the God who *holds* your breath in His hand and owns all your ways, you have not glorified. 24 Then the fingers of the hand were sent from Him, and this writing was written.

25 "And this is the inscription that was written:

MENE, MENE, TEKEL, UPHARSIN.

26 This *is* the interpretation of *each* word. MENE: God has numbered your kingdom, and finished it; 27 TEKEL: You have been weighed in the balances, and found wanting; 28 PERES: Your

kingdom has been divided, and given to the Medes and Persians." 29 Then Belshazzar gave the command, and they clothed Daniel with purple and *put* a chain of gold around his neck, and made a proclamation concerning him that he should be the third ruler in the kingdom.

30 That very night Belshazzar, king of the Chaldeans, was slain. 31 And Darius the Mede received the kingdom, *being* about sixty-two years old.

Guess who's coming to dinner!

6 It pleased Darius to set over the kingdom one hundred and twenty satraps, to be over the whole kingdom; 2 and over these, three governors, of whom Daniel *was* one, that the satraps might give account to them, so that the king would suffer no loss. 3 Then this Daniel distinguished himself above the governors and satraps, because an excellent spirit *was* in him; and the king gave thought to setting him over the whole realm. 4 So the governors and satraps sought to find *some* charge against Daniel concerning the kingdom; but they could find no charge or fault, because he *was* faithful; nor was there any error or fault found in him. 5 Then these men said, "We shall not find any charge against this Daniel unless we find *it* against him concerning the law of his God."

6 So these governors and satraps thronged before the king, and said thus to him: "King Darius, live forever! 7 All the governors of the kingdom, the administrators and satraps, the counselors and advisors, have consulted together to establish a royal statute and to make a firm decree, that whoever petitions any god or man for thirty days, except you, O king, shall be cast into the den of lions. 8 Now, O king, establish the decree and sign the writing, so that it cannot be changed, according to the law of the Medes and Persians, which does not alter." 9 Therefore King Darius signed the written decree.

10 Now when Daniel knew that the writing was signed, he went home. And in his upper room, with his windows open toward Jerusalem, he knelt down on his knees three times that day, and prayed and gave thanks before his God, as was his custom since early days.

11 Then these men assembled and found Daniel praying and making supplication before his God. 12 And they went before the king, and spoke concerning the king's decree: "Have you not signed a decree that every man who petitions any god or man within thirty days, except you, O king, shall be cast into the den of lions?"

The king answered and said, "The thing *is* true, according to the law of the Medes and Persians, which does not alter."

King Darius—Darius was not really my name but a title given to several Persian kings. The word is pronounced *duh-RIGH-us*. I inherited the kingdom of Babylonia from King Belshazzar, who also reigned in Babylon during the time of Daniel. That king's name is pronounced *bell-SHAZ-er*.

I was very fond of Daniel. He had served Nebuchadnezzar and Belshazzar well, so I made Daniel one of the three governors over the other leaders of Persia. These leaders were called satraps. There were 120 satraps who ruled 120 districts of Persia, and you can read about them in your history books.

A day came when I thought Daniel should be ruler over all the other governors. When I decided to do this, the governors and satraps were angry and jealous and plotted to kill Daniel. As you will see, God saved my friend Daniel from their evil scheme.

Prisoner Unhurt After Stay in Lions' Den

BTN (Babylonian Television Network)—Nearly everybody in Babylon is celebrating Daniel's narrow escape from a den of lions last night.

At a news conference with King Darius (pronounced *duh-RIGH-us*), we learned that some jealous members of the government had tried to destroy Daniel. They tricked the king into signing a law ordering everyone in the kingdom to pray only to the king for 30 days. Anyone breaking that law would be thrown to the lions!

King Darius agreed to the idea, just to please his officials. But Daniel, a faithful believer in God, would pray only to Him. That was the trap! Daniel's enemies quickly reported his illegal prayers, and the king was forced to put Daniel in the lions' den.

The king was all smiles today as he told our news team that the lions had not hurt Daniel. Daniel's God saved him from the cruel plot of the jealous officials.

13 So they answered and said before the king, "That Daniel, who is one of the captives from Judah, does not show due regard for you, O king, or for the decree that you have signed, but makes his petition three times a day."

14 And the king, when he heard *these* words, was greatly displeased with himself, and set *his* heart on Daniel to deliver him; and he labored till the going down of the sun to deliver him. 15 Then these men approached the king, and said to the king, "Know, O king, that *it is* the law of the Medes and Persians that no decree or statute which the king establishes may be changed."

16 So the king gave the command, and they brought Daniel and cast *him* into the den of lions. *But* the king spoke, saying to Daniel, "Your God, whom you serve continually, He will deliver you." 17 Then a stone was brought and laid on the mouth of the den, and the king sealed it with his own signet ring and with the signets of his lords, that the purpose concerning Daniel might not be changed.

18 Now the king went to his palace

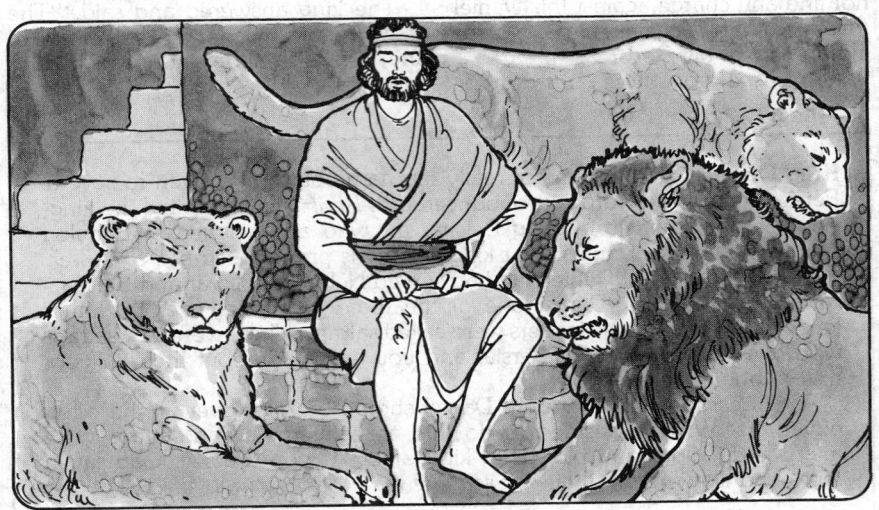

Daniel spends the night in a den of lions, but an angel closes their mouths.

and spent the night fasting; and no musicians were brought before him. Also his sleep went from him. ¹⁹ Then the king arose very early in the morning and went in haste to the den of lions. ²⁰ And when he came to the den, he cried out with a lamenting voice to Daniel. The king spoke, saying to Daniel, "Daniel, servant of the living God, has your God, whom you serve continually, been able to deliver you from the lions?"

²¹ Then Daniel said to the king, "O king, live forever! ²² My God sent His angel and shut the lions' mouths, so that they have not hurt me, because I was found innocent before Him; and also, O king, I have done no wrong before you."

²³ Now the king was exceedingly glad for him, and commanded that they should take Daniel up out of the den. So Daniel was taken up out of the den, and no injury whatever was found on him, because he believed in his God.

²⁴ And the king gave the command, and they brought those men who had accused Daniel, and they cast them into the den of lions—them, their children, and their wives; and the lions overpowered them, and broke all their bones in pieces before they ever came to the bottom of the den.

²⁵ Then King Darius wrote:

To all peoples, nations, and languages that dwell in all the earth:

Peace be multiplied to you.

²⁶ I make a decree that in every dominion of my kingdom men must tremble and fear before the God of Daniel.

For He is the living God,
And steadfast forever;
His kingdom is the one which
    shall not be destroyed,
And His dominion shall endure
    to the end.
²⁷ He delivers and rescues,

And He works signs and
    wonders
In heaven and on earth,
Who has delivered Daniel from
    the power of the lions.

²⁸ So this Daniel prospered in the reign of Darius and in the reign of Cyrus the Persian.

The beast with ten horns

7 In the first year of Belshazzar king of Babylon, Daniel had a dream and visions of his head while on his bed. Then he wrote down the dream, telling the main facts.

² Daniel spoke, saying, "I saw in my vision by night, and behold, the four winds of heaven were stirring up the Great Sea. ³ And four great beasts came up from the sea, each different from the other. ⁴ The first was like a lion, and had eagle's wings. I watched till its wings were plucked off; and it was lifted up from the earth and made to stand on two feet like a man, and a man's heart was given to it.

⁵ "And suddenly another beast, a second, like a bear. It was raised up on one side, and had three ribs in its mouth between its teeth. And they said thus to it: 'Arise, devour much flesh!'

⁶ "After this I looked, and there was another, like a leopard, which had on its back four wings of a bird. The beast also had four heads, and dominion was given to it.

⁷ "After this I saw in the night visions, and behold, a fourth beast, dreadful and terrible, exceedingly strong. It had huge iron teeth; it was devouring, breaking in pieces, and trampling the residue with its feet. It was different from all the beasts that were before it, and it had ten horns. ⁸ I was considering the horns, and there was another horn, a little one, coming up among them, before whom three of the first horns were plucked out by the roots. And there, in this horn, were eyes like the eyes of a man, and a mouth speaking pompous words.

9 "I watched till thrones were put
   in place,
   And the Ancient of Days was
      seated;
   His garment *was* white as snow,
   And the hair of His head *was*
      like pure wool.
   His throne *was* a fiery flame,
   Its wheels a burning fire;
10 A fiery stream issued
   And came forth from before
      Him.
   A thousand thousands
      ministered to Him;
   Ten thousand times ten
      thousand stood before Him.
   The court was seated,
   And the books *were* opened.

11 "I watched then because of the
sound of the pompous words which
the horn was speaking; I watched till
the beast was slain, and its body destroyed and given to the burning flame.
12 As for the rest of the beasts, they
had their dominion taken away, yet
their lives were prolonged for a season
and a time.

13 "I was watching in the night
      visions,
   And behold, *One* like the Son
      of Man,
   Coming with the clouds of
      heaven!
   He came to the Ancient of Days,
   And they brought Him near
      before Him.
14 Then to Him was given
      dominion and glory and a
      kingdom,
   That all peoples, nations, and
      languages should serve Him.
   His dominion *is* an everlasting
      dominion,
   Which shall not pass away,
   And His kingdom *the one*
   Which shall not be destroyed.

15 "I, Daniel, was grieved in my spirit
within *my* body, and the visions of my
head troubled me. 16 I came near to
one of those who stood by, and asked
him the truth of all this. So he told

me and made known to me the interpretation of these things: 17 'Those
great beasts, which are four, *are* four
kings *which* arise out of the earth.
18 But the saints of the Most High shall
receive the kingdom, and possess the
kingdom forever, even forever and
ever.'

19 "Then I wished to know the truth
about the fourth beast, which was different from all the others, exceedingly
dreadful, *with* its teeth of iron and its
nails of bronze, *which* devoured, broke
in pieces, and trampled the residue
with its feet; 20 and the ten horns that
were on its head, and the other *horn*
which came up, before which three fell,
namely, that horn which had eyes and
a mouth which spoke pompous words,
whose appearance *was* greater than his
fellows.

21 "I was watching; and the same
horn was making war against the
saints, and prevailing against them,
22 until the Ancient of Days came, and
a judgment was made *in favor* of the
saints of the Most High, and the time
came for the saints to possess the kingdom.

23 "Thus he said:

   'The fourth beast shall be
   A fourth kingdom on earth,
   Which shall be different from all
      other kingdoms,
   And shall devour the whole
      earth,
   Trample it and break it in pieces.
24 The ten horns *are* ten kings
   Who shall arise from this
      kingdom.
   And another shall rise after
      them;
   He shall be different from the
      first *ones,*
   And shall subdue three kings.
25 He shall speak *pompous* words
      against the Most High,
   Shall persecute the saints of the
      Most High,
   And shall intend to change times
      and law.
   Then *the saints* shall be given
      into his hand

For a time and times and half a
time.

26 'But the court shall be seated,
And they shall take away his
dominion,
To consume and destroy it
forever.
27 Then the kingdom and
dominion,
And the greatness of the
kingdoms under the whole
heaven,
Shall be given to the people, the
saints of the Most High.
His kingdom is an everlasting
kingdom,
And all dominions shall serve
and obey Him.'

28 "This is the end of the account.
As for me, Daniel, my thoughts greatly
troubled me, and my countenance
changed; but I kept the matter in my
heart."

The angry ram and the shaggy-haired goat

8 In the third year of the reign of King
Belshazzar a vision appeared to me—
to me, Daniel—after the one that appeared to me the first time. 2 I saw in
the vision, and it so happened while I
was looking, that I was in Shushan,
the citadel, which is in the province of
Elam; and I saw in the vision that I
was by the River Ulai. 3 Then I lifted
my eyes and saw, and there, standing
beside the river, was a ram which had
two horns, and the two horns were
high; but one was higher than the
other, and the higher one came up last.
4 I saw the ram pushing westward,
northward, and southward, so that no
animal could withstand him; nor was
there any that could deliver from his
hand, but he did according to his will
and became great.

5 And as I was considering, suddenly
a male goat came from the west, across
the surface of the whole earth, without
touching the ground; and the goat had

a notable horn between his eyes.
6 Then he came to the ram that had
two horns, which I had seen standing
beside the river, and ran at him with
furious power. 7 And I saw him con-
fronting the ram; he was moved with
rage against him, attacked the ram,
and broke his two horns. There was
no power in the ram to withstand him,
but he cast him down to the ground
and trampled him; and there was no
one that could deliver the ram from
his hand.

8 Therefore the male goat grew very
great; but when he became strong, the
large horn was broken, and in place
of it four notable ones came up toward
the four winds of heaven. 9 And out
of one of them came a little horn which
grew exceedingly great toward the
south, toward the east, and toward the
Glorious Land. 10 And it grew up to
the host of heaven; and it cast down
some of the host and some of the stars
to the ground, and trampled them.
11 He even exalted himself as high as
the Prince of the host; and by him the
daily sacrifices were taken away, and
the place of His sanctuary was cast
down. 12 Because of transgression, an
army was given over to the horn to
oppose the daily sacrifices; and he cast
truth down to the ground. He did all
this and prospered.

13 Then I heard a holy one speaking;
and another holy one said to that certain one who was speaking, "How long
will the vision be, concerning the daily
sacrifices and the transgression of desolation, the giving of both the sanctuary and the host to be trampled underfoot?"

14 And he said to me, "For two thousand three hundred days; then the
sanctuary shall be cleansed."

15 Then it happened, when I, Daniel,
had seen the vision and was seeking
the meaning, that suddenly there stood
before me one having the appearance
of a man. 16 And I heard a man's voice
between the banks of the Ulai, who
called, and said, "Gabriel, make this
man understand the vision." 17 So he
came near where I stood, and when

he came I was afraid and fell on my face; but he said to me, "Understand, son of man, that the vision *refers* to the time of the end."

18 Now, as he was speaking with me, I was in a deep sleep with my face to the ground; but he touched me, and stood me upright. 19 And he said, "Look, I am making known to you what shall happen in the latter time of the indignation; for at the appointed time the end *shall be.* 20 The ram which you saw, having the two horns—*they are* the kings of Media and Persia. 21 And the male goat *is* the kingdom of Greece. The large horn that *is* between its *eyes is* the first king. 22 As for the broken *horn* and the four that stood up in its place, four kingdoms shall arise out of that nation, but not with its power.

23 "And in the latter time of their
   kingdom,
   When the transgressors have
      reached their fullness,
   A king shall arise,
   Having fierce features,
   Who understands sinister
      schemes.
24 His power shall be mighty, but
      not by his own power;
   He shall destroy fearfully,
   And shall prosper and thrive;
   He shall destroy the mighty, and
      also the holy people.

25 "Through his cunning
   He shall cause deceit to prosper
      under his rule;
   And he shall exalt *himself* in his
      heart.
   He shall destroy many in *their*
      prosperity.
   He shall even rise against the
      Prince of princes;
   But he shall be broken without
      human means.

26 "And the vision of the evenings
      and mornings
   Which was told is true;
   Therefore seal up the vision,

For *it refers* to many days *in the
      future.*"

27 And I, Daniel, fainted and was sick for days; afterward I arose and went about the king's business. I was astonished by the vision, but no one understood it.

Daniel prays for his people

9 In the first year of Darius the son of Ahasuerus, of the lineage of the Medes, who was made king over the realm of the Chaldeans— 2 in the first year of his reign I, Daniel, understood by the books the number of the years *specified* by the word of the LORD through Jeremiah the prophet, that He would accomplish seventy years in the desolations of Jerusalem.

3 Then I set my face toward the Lord God to make request by prayer and supplications, with fasting, sackcloth, and ashes. 4 And I prayed to the LORD my God, and made confession, and said, "O Lord, great and awesome God, who keeps His covenant and mercy with those who love Him, and with those who keep His command-

Daniel prays for the people in sackcloth and ashes.

ments, 5 we have sinned and committed iniquity, we have done wickedly and rebelled, even by departing from Your precepts and Your judgments. 6 Neither have we heeded Your servants the prophets, who spoke in Your name to our kings and our princes, to our fathers and all the people of the land. 7 O Lord, righteousness *belongs* to You, but to us shame of face, as *it is* this day—to the men of Judah, to the inhabitants of Jerusalem and all Israel, those near and those far off in all the countries to which You have driven them, because of the unfaithfulness which they have committed against You.

8 "O Lord, to us *belongs* shame of face, to our kings, our princes, and our fathers, because we have sinned against You. 9 To the Lord our God *belong* mercy and forgiveness, though we have rebelled against Him. 10 We have not obeyed the voice of the Lord our God, to walk in His laws, which He set before us by His servants the prophets. 11 Yes, all Israel has transgressed Your law, and has departed so as not to obey Your voice; therefore the curse and the oath written in the Law of Moses the servant of God have been poured out on us, because we have sinned against Him. 12 And He has confirmed His words, which He spoke against us and against our judges who judged us, by bringing upon us a great disaster; for under the whole heaven such has never been done as what has been done to Jerusalem.

13 "As *it is* written in the Law of Moses, all this disaster has come upon us; yet we have not made our prayer before the Lord our God, that we might turn from our iniquities and understand Your truth. 14 Therefore the Lord has kept the disaster in mind, and brought it upon us; for the Lord our God *is* righteous in all the works which He does, though we have not obeyed His voice. 15 And now, O Lord our God, who brought Your people out of the land of Egypt with a mighty hand, and made Yourself a name, as *it is* this day—we have sinned, we have done wickedly!

16 "O Lord, according to all Your righteousness, I pray, let Your anger and Your fury be turned away from Your city Jerusalem, Your holy mountain; because for our sins, and for the iniquities of our fathers, Jerusalem and Your people *are* a reproach to all *those* around us. 17 Now therefore, our God, hear the prayer of Your servant, and his supplications, and for the Lord's sake cause Your face to shine on Your sanctuary, which is desolate. 18 O my God, incline Your ear and hear; open Your eyes and see our desolations, and the city which is called by Your name; for we do not present our supplications before You because of our righteous deeds, but because of Your great mercies. 19 O Lord, hear! O Lord, forgive! O Lord, listen and act! Do not delay for Your own sake, my God, for Your city and Your people are called by Your name."

20 Now while I *was* speaking, praying, and confessing my sin and the sin of my people Israel, and presenting my supplication before the Lord my God for the holy mountain of my God, 21 yes, while I *was* speaking in prayer, the man Gabriel, whom I had seen in the vision at the beginning, being caused to fly swiftly, reached me about the time of the evening offering. 22 And he informed *me,* and talked with me, and said, "O Daniel, I have now come forth to give you skill to understand. 23 At the beginning of your supplications the command went out, and I have come to tell *you,* for you *are* greatly beloved; therefore consider the matter, and understand the vision:

24 "Seventy weeks are determined
    For your people and for your
        holy city,
    To finish the transgression,
    To make an end of sins,
    To make reconciliation for
        iniquity,
    To bring in everlasting
        righteousness,

Who Is Messiah the Prince?

The angel Gabriel told Daniel that God's Messiah was coming. The word *Messiah* means Anointed One. All Old Testament people looked forward to His coming. Of course, the Messiah is Jesus. The Hebrew word *Messiah* is translated "Christ" in the New Testament, and both words mean the same Person. "Anointed One" means that Jesus was filled with the Spirit of God.

abominations shall be one
who makes desolate,
Even until the consummation,
which is determined,
Is poured out on the desolate.' "

The man with the message from heaven

10 In the third year of Cyrus king of Persia a message was revealed to Daniel, whose name was called Belteshazzar. The message *was* true, but the appointed time *was* long; and he understood the message, and had understanding of the vision. ² In those days I, Daniel, was mourning three full weeks. ³ I ate no pleasant food, no meat or wine came into my mouth, nor did I anoint myself at all, till three whole weeks were fulfilled.

⁴ Now on the twenty-fourth day of the first month, as I was by the side of the great river, that *is,* the Tigris, ⁵ I lifted my eyes and looked, and behold, a certain man clothed in linen, whose waist *was* girded with gold of Uphaz! ⁶ His body *was* like beryl, his face like the appearance of lightning, his eyes like torches of fire, his arms and feet like burnished bronze in color, and the sound of his words like the voice of a multitude.

⁷ And I, Daniel, alone saw the vision, for the men who were with me did not see the vision; but a great terror fell upon them, so that they fled to hide themselves. ⁸ Therefore I was left alone when I saw this great vision, and no strength remained in me; for my vigor was turned to frailty in me, and I retained no strength. ⁹ Yet I heard the sound of his words; and while I heard the sound of his words I was in a deep sleep on my face, with my face to the ground.

¹⁰ Suddenly, a hand touched me, which made me tremble on my knees

> To seal up vision and prophecy,
> And to anoint the Most Holy.

25 "Know therefore and understand,
That from the going forth of the
command
To restore and build Jerusalem
Until **Messiah** the Prince,
There shall be seven weeks and
sixty-two weeks;
The street shall be built again,
and the wall,
Even in troublesome times.

26 "And after the sixty-two weeks
Messiah shall be cut off, but not
for Himself;
And the people of the prince
who is to come
Shall destroy the city and the
sanctuary.
The end of it *shall be* with a
flood,
And till the end of the war
desolations are determined.
27 Then he shall confirm a
covenant with many for one
week;
But in the middle of the week
He shall bring an end to sacrifice
and offering.
And on the wing of

WORDFINDER

9:25, 26 Messiah Pronounced *muh-SIGH-uh.* A Hebrew word meaning "Anointed One." *Christos* (pronounced *KRISS-tos*) is a Greek word from which we get the word "Christ" and means the same as "Messiah."

and *on* the palms of my hands. ¹¹ And he said to me, "O Daniel, man greatly beloved, understand the words that I speak to you, and stand upright, for I have now been sent to you." While he was speaking this word to me, I stood trembling.

¹² Then he said to me, "Do not fear, Daniel, for from the first day that you set your heart to understand, and to humble yourself before your God, your words were heard; and I have come because of your words. ¹³ But the prince of the kingdom of Persia withstood me twenty-one days; and behold, Michael, one of the chief princes, came to help me, for I had been left alone there with the kings of Persia. ¹⁴ Now I have come to make you understand what will happen to your people in the latter days, for the vision *refers* to *many* days yet *to come*."

¹⁵ When he had spoken such words to me, I turned my face toward the ground and became speechless. ¹⁶ And suddenly, *one* having the likeness of the sons of men touched my lips; then I opened my mouth and spoke, saying to him who stood before me, "My lord, because of the vision my sorrows have overwhelmed me, and I have retained no strength. ¹⁷ For how can this servant of my lord talk with you, my lord? As for me, no strength remains in me now, nor is any breath left in me."

¹⁸ Then again, *the one* having the likeness of a man touched me and strengthened me. ¹⁹ And he said, "O man greatly beloved, fear not! Peace *be* to you; be strong, yes, be strong!"

So when he spoke to me I was strengthened, and said, "Let my lord speak, for you have strengthened me."

²⁰ Then he said, "Do you know why I have come to you? And now I must return to fight with the prince of Persia; and when I have gone forth, indeed the prince of Greece will come. ²¹ But I will tell you what is noted in the Scripture of Truth. (No one upholds me against these, except Michael your prince.

The messenger tells what is going to happen

11 "Also in the first year of Darius the Mede, I, *even* I, stood up to confirm and strengthen him.) ² And now I will tell you the truth: Behold, three more kings will arise in Persia, and the fourth shall be far richer than *them* all; by his strength, through his riches, he shall stir up all against the realm of Greece. ³ Then a mighty king shall arise, who shall rule with great dominion, and do according to his will. ⁴ And when he has arisen, his kingdom shall be broken up and divided toward the four winds of heaven, but not among his posterity nor according to his dominion with which he ruled; for his kingdom shall be uprooted, even for others besides these.

⁵ "Also the king of the South shall become strong, as well as *one* of his princes; and he shall gain power over him and have dominion. His dominion *shall be* a great dominion. ⁶ And at the end of *some* years they shall join forces, for the daughter of the king of the South shall go to the king of the North to make an agreement; but she shall not retain the power of her authority, and neither he nor his authority shall stand; but she shall be given up, with those who brought her, and with him who begot her, and with him who strengthened her in *those* times. ⁷ But from a branch of her roots *one* shall arise in his place, who shall come with an army, enter the fortress of the king of the North, and deal with them and prevail. ⁸ And he shall also carry their gods captive to Egypt, with their princes *and* their precious articles of silver and gold; and he shall continue *more* years than the king of the North.

⁹ "Also *the king of the North* shall come to the kingdom of the king of the South, but shall return to his own land. ¹⁰ However his sons shall stir up strife, and assemble a multitude of great forces; and *one* shall certainly come and overwhelm and pass through; then he shall return to his fortress and stir up strife.

11 "And the king of the South shall be moved with rage, and go out and fight with him, with the king of the North, who shall muster a great multitude; but the multitude shall be given into the hand of his *enemy*. 12 When he has taken away the multitude, his heart will be lifted up; and he will cast down tens of thousands, but he will not prevail. 13 For the king of the North will return and muster a multitude greater than the former, and shall certainly come at the end of some years with a great army and much equipment.

14 "Now in those times many shall rise up against the king of the South. Also, violent men of your people shall exalt themselves in fulfillment of the vision, but they shall fall. 15 So the king of the North shall come and build a siege mound, and take a fortified city; and the forces of the South shall not withstand *him*. Even his choice troops *shall have* no strength to resist. 16 But he who comes against him shall do according to his own will, and no one shall stand against him. He shall stand in the Glorious Land with destruction in his power.

17 "He shall also set his face to enter with the strength of his whole kingdom, and upright ones with him; thus shall he do. And he shall give him the daughter of women to destroy it; but she shall not stand *with him*, or be for him. 18 After this he shall turn his face to the coastlands, and shall take many. But a ruler shall bring the reproach against them to an end; and with the reproach removed, he shall turn back on him. 19 Then he shall turn his face toward the fortress of his own land; but he shall stumble and fall, and not be found.

20 "There shall arise in his place one who imposes taxes *on* the glorious kingdom; but within a few days he shall be destroyed, but not in anger or in battle. 21 And in his place shall arise a vile person, to whom they will not give the honor of royalty; but he shall come in peaceably, and seize the kingdom by intrigue. 22 With the force of a flood they shall be swept away from before him and be broken, and also the prince of the covenant. 23 And after the league *is made* with him he shall act deceitfully, for he shall come up and become strong with a small *number of* people. 24 He shall enter peaceably, even into the richest places of the province; and he shall do *what* his fathers have not done, nor his forefathers: he shall disperse among them the plunder, spoil, and riches; and he shall devise his plans against the strongholds, but *only* for a time.

25 "He shall stir up his power and his courage against the king of the South with a great army. And the king of the South shall be stirred up to battle with a very great and mighty army; but he shall not stand, for they shall devise plans against him. 26 Yes, those who eat of the portion of his delicacies shall destroy him; his army shall be swept away, and many shall fall down slain. 27 Both these kings' hearts *shall be* bent on evil, and they shall speak lies at the same table; but it shall not prosper, for the end *will* still *be* at the appointed time. 28 While returning to his land with great riches, his heart shall be *moved* against the holy covenant; so he shall do *damage* and return to his own land.

29 "At the appointed time he shall return and go toward the south; but it shall not be like the former or the latter. 30 For ships from Cyprus shall come against him; therefore he shall be grieved, and return in rage against the holy covenant, and do *damage*.

"So he shall return and show regard for those who forsake the holy covenant. 31 And forces shall be mustered by him, and they shall defile the sanctuary fortress; then they shall take away the daily *sacrifices,* and place *there* the abomination of desolation. 32 Those who do wickedly against the covenant he shall corrupt with flattery; but the people who know their God shall be strong, and carry out *great exploits.* 33 And those of the people who understand shall instruct many; yet *for many* days they shall fall by sword and

flame, by captivity and plundering.
34 Now when they fall, they shall be
aided with a little help; but many shall
join with them by intrigue. 35 And *some*
of those of understanding shall fall, to
refine them, purify *them,* and make
them white, *until* the time of the end;
because *it is* still for the appointed
time.

36 "Then the king shall do according
to his own will: he shall exalt and magnify himself above every god, shall
speak blasphemies against the God of
gods, and shall prosper till the wrath
has been accomplished; for what has
been determined shall be done.
37 He shall regard neither the God of
his fathers nor the desire of women,
nor regard any god; for he shall exalt
himself above *them* all. 38 But in their
place he shall honor a god of fortresses; and a god which his fathers
did not know he shall honor with
gold and silver, with precious stones
and pleasant things. 39 Thus he shall
act against the strongest fortresses
with a foreign god, which he shall acknowledge, *and* advance *its* glory;
and he shall cause them to rule
over many, and divide the land for
gain.

40 "At the time of the end the king
of the South shall attack him; and the
king of the North shall come against
him like a whirlwind, with chariots,
horsemen, and with many ships; and
he shall enter the countries, overwhelm
them, and pass through. 41 He shall
also enter the Glorious Land, and
many *countries* shall be overthrown;
but these shall escape from his hand:
Edom, Moab, and the prominent people of Ammon. 42 He shall stretch out
his hand against the countries, and the
land of Egypt shall not escape. 43 He
shall have power over the treasures of
gold and silver, and over all the precious things of Egypt; also the Libyans
and Ethiopians *shall follow* at his heels.
44 But news from the east and the
north shall trouble him; therefore he
shall go out with great fury to destroy
and annihilate many. 45 And he shall
plant the tents of his palace between

the seas and the glorious holy mountain; yet he shall come to his end, and
no one will help him.

The end of time

12 "At that time Michael shall stand
up,
The great prince who stands
watch over the sons of your
people;
And there shall be a time of
trouble,
Such as never was since there
was a nation,
Even to that time.
And at that time your people
shall be delivered,
Every one who is found written
in the book.
2 And many of those who sleep
in the dust of the earth shall
awake,
Some to everlasting life,
Some to shame *and* everlasting
contempt.
3 Those who are wise shall
shine
Like the brightness of the
firmament,
And those who turn many to
righteousness
Like the stars forever and *ever.*

4 "But you, Daniel, shut up the
words, and seal the book until the time
of the end; many shall run to and fro,
and knowledge shall increase."

5 Then I, Daniel, looked; and there
stood two others, one on this riverbank
and the other on that riverbank.
6 And *one* said to the man clothed in
linen, who *was* above the waters of
the river, "How long shall the fulfillment of these wonders *be?*"

7 Then I heard the man clothed in
linen, who *was* above the waters of
the river, when he held up his right
hand and his left hand to heaven, and
swore by Him who lives forever, that
it shall be for a time, times, and half *a
time;* and when the power of the holy
people has been completely shattered,
all these *things* shall be finished.

8 Although I heard, I did not understand. Then I said, "My lord, what *shall
be the end of these things?"*

9 And he said, "Go *your way,* Daniel, for the words *are* closed up and
sealed till the time of the end. 10 Many
shall be purified, made white, and refined, but the wicked shall do wickedly;
and none of the wicked shall understand, but the wise shall understand.

11 "And from the time *that* the daily
sacrifice is taken away, and the abomination of desolation is set up, *there
shall be* one thousand two hundred
and ninety days. 12 Blessed *is* he who
waits, and comes to the one thousand
three hundred and thirty-five days.

13 "But you, go *your way* till the end;
for you shall rest, and will arise to your
inheritance at the end of the days."

The Book of
HOSEA

My name is pronounced *ho-ZAY-uh* and means "Deliverance." My work as a prophet took place during the time that Isaiah lived. You will notice that the same kings were reigning in Judah when Isaiah and I were prophets (see Isaiah 1:1). Isaiah was a great preacher in the Southern Kingdom of Judah, but I preached in the Northern Kingdom of Israel just before the army of Assyria conquered us 722 years before the coming of Jesus.

People have often been puzzled about me because I married a young woman who had been a great sinner. But God forgave her and I loved her. God loves you and me that way, too. He forgives our sins because Jesus died.

I knew the hardships that Israel would soon experience when the army of Assyria came. But I also was thankful for God's promise that He would bring back our nation one day.

Hosea marries an unfaithful woman

THE word of the LORD that came to Hosea the son of Beeri, in the days of Uzziah, Jotham, Ahaz, *and* Hezekiah, kings of Judah, and in the days of Jeroboam the son of Joash, king of Israel. 2 When the LORD began to speak by Hosea, the LORD said to Hosea:

"Go, take yourself a wife of
harlotry
And children of harlotry,

For the land has committed
great harlotry
By departing from the LORD."

3 So he went and took Gomer the daughter of Diblaim, and she conceived and bore him a son. 4 Then the LORD said to him:

"Call his name Jezreel,
For in a little *while*
I will avenge the bloodshed of
Jezreel on the house of Jehu,
And bring an end to the
kingdom of the house of
Israel.

Gomer—My name is pronounced *GO-mer* and means "Complete." I am one of the greatest examples in the Bible of how much God loves people. As Hosea told you, I was an immoral woman, but God commanded him to love me. Then Hosea won my love, and I became his wife. So God really did make my life "complete."

Later, I became unfaithful to my husband. I ran away from him and went back to my ways of sin. Although I nearly broke Hosea's heart, he still loved me enough to come and bring me home again. Since then, I have stayed with Hosea and our children, and I love them.

Please learn a great lesson from my story. Be careful not to judge people harshly. God hates sin, but He also is like my husband Hosea. God cares for His lost people the way a shepherd cares for and seeks His lost sheep.

5   It shall come to pass in that
       day
    That I will break the bow of
       Israel in the Valley of Jezreel.''

6 And she conceived again and
bore a daughter. Then God said to
him:

    "Call her name Lo-Ruhamah,
    For I will no longer have mercy
       on the house of Israel,
    But I will utterly take them away.
7   Yet I will have mercy on the
       house of Judah,
    Will save them by the LORD their
       God,
    And will not save them by bow,
    Nor by sword or battle,
    By horses or horsemen.''

8 Now when she had weaned Lo-
Ruhamah, she conceived and bore a
son. 9 Then God said:

    "Call his name Lo-Ammi,
    For you are not My people,
    And I will not be your God.

10 "Yet the number of the children
       of Israel
    Shall be as the sand of the sea,
    Which cannot be measured or
       numbered.
    And it shall come to pass
    In the place where it was said
       to them,
    'You are not My people,'
    There it shall be said to them,
    'You are sons of the living God.'
11 Then the children of Judah and
       the children of Israel
    Shall be gathered together,
    And appoint for themselves one
       head;
    And they shall come up out of
       the land,
    For great will be the day of
       Jezreel!

Gomer runs away from home

2   Say to your brethren, 'My
       people,'

    And to your sisters, 'Mercy is
       shown.'
2   "Bring charges against your
       mother, bring charges;
    For she is not My wife, nor am
       I her Husband!
    Let her put away her harlotries
       from her sight,
    And her adulteries from between
       her breasts;
3   Lest I strip her naked
    And expose her, as in the day
       she was born,
    And make her like a
       wilderness,
    And set her like a dry land,
    And slay her with thirst.

4   "I will not have mercy on her
       children,
    For they are the children of
       harlotry.
5   For their mother has played the
       harlot;
    She who conceived them has
       behaved shamefully.
    For she said, 'I will go after my
       lovers,
    Who give me my bread and my
       water,
    My wool and my linen,
    My oil and my drink.'

6   "Therefore, behold,
    I will hedge up your way with
       thorns,
    And wall her in,
    So that she cannot find her
       paths.
7   She will chase her lovers,
    But not overtake them;
    Yes, she will seek them, but not
       find them.
    Then she will say,
    'I will go and return to my first
       husband,
    For then it was better for me
       than now.'
8   For she did not know
    That I gave her grain, new wine,
       and oil,
    And multiplied her silver and
       gold—

Which they prepared for
Baal.

9 "Therefore I will return and take
   away
My grain in its time
And My new wine in its season,
And will take back My wool and
   My linen,
Given to cover her nakedness.
10 Now I will uncover her lewdness
   in the sight of her lovers,
And no one shall deliver her
   from My hand.
11 I will also cause all her mirth to
   cease,
Her feast days,
Her New Moons,
Her Sabbaths—
All her appointed feasts.

12 "And I will destroy her vines and
   her fig trees,
Of which she has said,
'These *are* my wages that my
   lovers have given me.'
So I will make them a forest,
And the beasts of the field shall
   eat them.
13 I will punish her
For the days of the Baals to
   which she burned incense.
She decked herself with her
   earrings and jewelry,
And went after her lovers;
But Me she forgot," says the
   Lord.

14 "Therefore, behold, I will allure
   her,
Will bring her into the
   wilderness,
And speak comfort to her.
15 I will give her her vineyards from
   there,

And the Valley of Achor as a
   door of hope;
She shall sing there,
As in the days of her youth,
As in the day when she came
   up from the land of Egypt.

16 "And it shall be, in that day,"
Says the Lord,
"*That* you will call Me 'My
   Husband,'
And no longer call Me 'My
   Master,'
17 For I will take from her mouth
   the names of the Baals,
And they shall be remembered
   by their name no more.
18 In that day I will make a
   covenant for them
With the beasts of the field,
With the birds of the air,
And *with* the creeping things of
   the ground.
Bow and sword of battle I will
   shatter from the earth,
To make them lie down safely.

19 "I will **betroth** you to Me forever;
Yes, I will betroth you to Me
In righteousness and justice,
In lovingkindness and mercy;
20 I will betroth you to Me in
   faithfulness,
And you shall know the Lord.

21 "It shall come to pass in that day
That I will answer," says the
   Lord;
"I will answer the heavens,
And they shall answer the earth.
22 The earth shall answer
With grain,
With new wine,
And with oil;
They shall answer Jezreel.

WORDFINDER

2:8 Baal   The chief false god of the Canaanites (pronounced *KAY-nuh-nights*) and
Phoenicians (pronounced *fe-NISH-she-uns*). He was a nature god and was worshiped
in immoral ceremonies forbidden to Israel.
   2:19 Betroth   (Pronounced *be-TROTH*). Like being engaged to be married, but to
be betrothed in Bible times was more serious and legally binding than being engaged
today.

What Some Unhappy People Learned

We thought God had forgotten us when He allowed our enemies to destroy our nation and take us as prisoners to Babylon.

Then Hosea told us that even though the Lord did punish us for a time, He would not forget us. Even though He said, "You are not My people," He would still love us and one day again call us His people.

We learned that God never forgets His promises. Even when we act like disobedient children, He is still our Father.

No matter how alone you may feel in the world, we want you to know that God has not forgotten you either. God really cares, and He will prove this to you if you only ask Him.

---

23 Then I will sow her for Myself
    in the earth,
And I will have mercy on *her*
    who had not obtained mercy;
Then I will say to *those who*
    were not My people,
'You *are* My people!'
And they shall say, '*You are* my
    God!' "

Hosea brings his wife back and loves her

3 Then the Lord said to me, "Go again, love a woman *who is* loved by a lover and is committing adultery, just like the love of the Lord for the children of Israel, who look to other gods and love *the* raisin cakes *of the* **pagans**."

2 So I bought her for myself for fifteen *shekels* of silver, and one and one-half homers of barley. 3 And I said to her, "You shall stay with me many days; you shall not play the harlot, nor shall you have a man—so, too, *will I* be toward you."

4 For the children of Israel shall abide many days without king or prince, without sacrifice or sacred pillar, without ephod or teraphim. 5 Afterward the children of Israel shall return and seek the Lord their God and David their

king. They shall fear the Lord and His goodness in the latter days.

God is disappointed in Israel, too

4 Hear the word of the Lord,
    You children of Israel,
For the Lord *brings* a charge
    against the inhabitants of the
    land:

"There is no truth or mercy
    Or knowledge of God in the
    land.
2 *By* swearing and lying,
Killing and stealing and
    committing adultery,
They break all restraint,
With bloodshed upon
    bloodshed.
3 Therefore the land will mourn;
And everyone who dwells there
    will waste away
With the beasts of the field
And the birds of the air;
Even the fish of the sea will be
    taken away.

4 "Now let no man contend, or
    rebuke another;
For your people *are* like those
    who contend with the priest.
5 Therefore you shall stumble in
    the day;

WORDFINDER

3:1 Pagans People who worship false gods or whose minds are mainly on material things, physical pleasure, and this present world.

The prophet also shall stumble
  with you in the night;
And I will destroy your mother.
6 My people are destroyed for lack
    of knowledge.
  Because you have rejected
    knowledge,
  I also will reject you from being
    priest for Me;
  Because you have forgotten the
    law of your God,
  I also will forget your children.

7 "The more they increased,
  The more they sinned against
    Me;
  I will change their glory into
    shame.
8 They eat up the sin of My
    people;
  They set their heart on their
    iniquity.
9 And it shall be: like people, like
    priest.
  So I will punish them for their
    ways,
  And reward them for their
    deeds.
10 For they shall eat, but not have
    enough;
  They shall commit harlotry, but
    not increase;
  Because they have ceased
    obeying the LORD.

11 "Harlotry, wine, and new wine
    enslave the heart.
12 My people ask counsel from
    their wooden *idols*,
  And their staff informs them.
  For the spirit of harlotry has
    caused *them* to stray,
  And they have played the harlot
    against their God.
13 They offer sacrifices on the
    mountaintops,
  And burn incense on the hills,
  Under oaks, poplars, and
    terebinths,
  Because their shade *is* good.
  Therefore your daughters
    commit harlotry,
  And your brides commit
    adultery.

14 "I will not punish your daughters
    when they commit harlotry,
  Nor your brides when they
    commit adultery;
  For *the men* themselves go apart
    with harlots,
  And offer sacrifices with a ritual
    harlot.
  Therefore people *who* do not
    understand will be trampled.

15 "Though you, Israel, play the
    harlot,
  Let not Judah offend.
  Do not come up to Gilgal,
  Nor go up to Beth Aven,
  Nor swear an oath, *saying,* 'As
    the LORD lives'—

16 "For Israel is stubborn
  Like a stubborn calf;
  Now the LORD will let them
    forage
  Like a lamb in open country.

17 "Ephraim *is* joined to idols,
  Let him alone.
18 Their drink is rebellion,
  They commit harlotry
    continually.
  Her rulers dearly love dishonor.
19 The wind has wrapped her up
    in its wings,
  And they shall be ashamed
    because of their sacrifices.

Their faithfulness disappears like dew on the grass

5 "Hear this, O priests!
  Take heed, O house of Israel!
  Give ear, O house of the king!
  For yours *is* the judgment,
  Because you have been a snare
    to Mizpah
  And a net spread on Tabor.
2 The revolters are deeply
    involved in slaughter,
  Though I rebuke them all.
3 I know Ephraim,
  And Israel is not hidden from
    Me;
  For now, O Ephraim, you
    commit harlotry;
  Israel is defiled.

4 "They do not direct their deeds
    Toward turning to their God,
    For the spirit of harlotry is in their
      midst,
    And they do not know the LORD.
5   The pride of Israel testifies to his
      face;
    Therefore Israel and Ephraim
      stumble in their iniquity;
    Judah also stumbles with them.

6 "With their flocks and herds
    They shall go to seek the LORD,
    But they will not find *Him;*
    He has withdrawn Himself from
      them.
7   They have dealt treacherously
      with the LORD,
    For they have begotten pagan
      children.
    Now a New Moon shall devour
      them and their heritage.

8 "Blow the ram's horn in Gibeah,
    The trumpet in Ramah!
    Cry aloud *at* Beth Aven,
    '*Look* behind you, O Benjamin!'
9   Ephraim shall be desolate in the
      day of rebuke;
    Among the tribes of Israel I make
      known what is sure.

10 "The princes of Judah are like
      those who remove a
      landmark;
    I will pour out my wrath on them
      like water.
11   Ephraim is oppressed *and*
      broken in judgment,
    Because he willingly walked by
      human precept.
12   Therefore I *will be* to Ephraim
      like a moth,
    And to the house of Judah like
      rottenness.

13 "When Ephraim saw his sickness,
    And Judah *saw* his wound,
    Then Ephraim went to Assyria
    And sent to King Jareb;
    Yet he cannot cure you,
    Nor heal you of your wound.
14   For I *will be* like a lion to
      Ephraim,

And like a young lion to the
    house of Judah.
I, *even* I, will tear *them* and go
    away;
I will take *them* away, and no
    one shall rescue.
15   I will return again to My place
    Till they acknowledge their
      offense.
    Then they will seek My face;
    In their affliction they will
      earnestly seek Me."

God wants Israel's love, not their sacrifices

6   Come, and let us return to the
      LORD;
    For He has torn, but He will heal
      us;
    He has stricken, but He will bind
      us up.
2   After two days He will revive us;
    On the third day He will raise
      us up,
    That we may live in His sight.
3   Let us know,
    Let us pursue the knowledge of
      the LORD.
    His going forth is established as
      the morning;
    He will come to us like the
      rain,
    Like the latter *and* former rain
      to the earth.
4   "O Ephraim, what shall I do to
      you?
    O Judah, what shall I do to
      you?
    For your faithfulness is like a
      morning cloud,
    And like the early dew it goes
      away.
5   Therefore I have hewn *them* by
      the prophets,
    I have slain them by the words
      of My mouth;
    And your judgments *are like*
      light *that* goes forth.
6   For I desire mercy and not
      sacrifice,
    And the knowledge of God
      more than burnt offerings.

7 "But like men they transgressed
    the covenant;
There they dealt treacherously
    with Me.
8 Gilead *is* a city of evildoers
    And defiled with blood.
9 As bands of robbers lie in wait
    for a man,
So the company of priests
    murder on the way to
    Shechem;
Surely they commit lewdness.
10 I have seen a horrible thing in
    the house of Israel:
There *is* the harlotry of Ephraim;
Israel is defiled.
11 Also, O Judah, a harvest is
    appointed for you,
When I return the captives of My
    people.

Israel is like a crooked bow that does not shoot straight

7 "When I would have healed
    Israel,
Then the iniquity of Ephraim
    was uncovered,
And the wickedness of Samaria.
For they have committed
    fraud;
A thief comes in;
A band of robbers takes spoil
    outside.
2 They do not consider in their
    hearts
That I remember all their
    wickedness;
Now their own deeds have
    surrounded them;
They are before My face.
3 They make a king glad with their
    wickedness,
And princes with their lies.

4 "They *are* all adulterers.
Like an oven heated by a
    baker—
He ceases stirring *the fire* after
    kneading the dough,
Until it is leavened.
5 In the day of our king
Princes have made *him* sick,
    inflamed with wine;

He stretched out his hand with
    scoffers.
6 They prepare their heart like an
    oven,
While they lie in wait;
Their baker sleeps all night;
In the morning it burns like a
    flaming fire.
7 They are all hot, like an oven,
And have devoured their
    judges;
All their kings have fallen.
None among them calls upon
    Me.

8 "Ephraim has mixed himself
    among the peoples;
Ephraim is a cake unturned.
9 Aliens have devoured his
    strength,
But he does not know *it;*
Yes, gray hairs are here and
    there on him,
Yet he does not know *it.*
10 And the pride of Israel testifies
    to his face,
But they do not return to the
    LORD their God,
Nor seek Him for all this.

11 "Ephraim also is like a silly dove,
    without sense—
They call to Egypt,
They go to Assyria.
12 Wherever they go, I will spread
    My net on them;
I will bring them down like birds
    of the air;
I will chastise them
According to what their
    congregation has heard.

13 "Woe to them, for they have fled
    from Me!
Destruction to them,
Because they have transgressed
    against Me!
Though I redeemed them,
Yet they have spoken lies
    against Me.
14 They did not cry out to Me with
    their heart
When they wailed upon their
    beds.

"They assemble together for grain
 and new wine,
They rebel against Me;
15 Though I disciplined *and*
 strengthened their arms,
Yet they devise evil against
 Me;
16 They return, *but* not to the Most
 High;
They are like a treacherous bow.
Their princes shall fall by the
 sword
For the cursings of their tongue.
This *shall be* their derision in the
 land of Egypt.

Israel will reap what she has sown

8 "*Set* the trumpet to your
 mouth!
He shall come like an eagle
 against the house of the LORD,
Because they have transgressed
 My covenant
And rebelled against My **law.**
2 Israel will cry to Me,
'My God, we know You!'
3 Israel has rejected the good;
The enemy will pursue him.

4 "They set up kings, but not by
 Me;
They made princes, but I did not
 acknowledge *them.*
From their silver and gold
They made idols for
 themselves—
That they might be cut off.
5 Your calf is rejected, O Samaria!
My anger is aroused against
 them—
How long until they attain to
 innocence?
6 For from Israel *is* even this:
A workman made it, and it *is* not
 God;
But the calf of Samaria shall be
 broken to pieces.

7 "They sow the wind,
And reap the whirlwind.
The stalk has no bud;
It shall never produce meal.
If it should produce,
Aliens would swallow it up.
8 Israel is swallowed up;
Now they are among the
 Gentiles
Like a vessel in which *is* no
 pleasure.
9 For they have gone up to
 Assyria,
Like a wild donkey alone by
 itself;
Ephraim has hired lovers.
10 Yes, though they have hired
 among the nations,
Now I will gather them;
And they shall sorrow a little,
Because of the burden of the
 king of princes.

11 "Because Ephraim has made
 many altars for sin,
They have become for him altars
 for sinning.
12 I have written for him the great
 things of My law,
But they were considered a
 strange thing.
13 *For* the sacrifices of My offerings
 they sacrifice flesh and eat
 it,
But the LORD does not accept
 them.
Now He will remember their
 iniquity and punish their sins.
They shall return to Egypt.

14 "For Israel has forgotten his
 Maker,
And has built temples;
Judah also has multiplied
 fortified cities;
But I will send fire upon his
 cities,
And it shall devour his palaces."

WORDFINDER

8:1 Law The words of God that we must live by. Sometimes the Law refers to the Ten Commandments. At other times it includes all things that God says in the Scriptures.

The day of judgment is coming

9 Do not rejoice, O Israel, with joy
  like *other* peoples,
  For you have played the harlot
    against your God.
  You have made love *for* hire on
    every threshing floor.
2 The threshing floor and the
    winepress
  Shall not feed them,
  And the new wine shall fail in
    her.

3 They shall not dwell in the
    Lord's land,
  But Ephraim shall return to
    Egypt,
  And shall eat unclean *things* in
    Assyria.
4 They shall not offer wine
    offerings to the Lord,
  Nor shall their sacrifices be
    pleasing to Him.
  It shall be like bread of mourners
    to them;
  All who eat it shall be defiled.
  For their bread *shall be* for their
    own life;
  It shall not come into the house
    of the Lord.

5 What will you do in the
    appointed day,
  And in the day of the feast of
    the Lord?
6 For indeed they are gone
    because of destruction.
  Egypt shall gather them up;
  Memphis shall bury them.
  Nettles shall possess their
    valuables of silver;
  Thorns *shall be* in their tents.

7 The days of punishment have
    come;
  The days of recompense have
    come.
  Israel knows!
  The prophet *is* a fool,
  The spiritual man *is* insane,
  Because of the greatness of your
    iniquity and great enmity.

8 The watchman of Ephraim *is*
    with my God;
  But the prophet *is* a fowler's
    snare in all his ways—
  Enmity in the house of his God.
9 They are deeply corrupted,
  As in the days of Gibeah.
  He will remember their iniquity;
  He will punish their sins.

10 "I found Israel
  Like grapes in the wilderness;
  I saw your fathers
  As the firstfruits on the fig tree
    in its first season.
  But they went to Baal Peor,
  And separated themselves *to*
    that shame;
  They became an abomination
    like the thing they loved.
11 *As for* Ephraim, their glory shall
    fly away like a bird—
  No birth, no pregnancy, and no
    conception!
12 Though they bring up their
    children,
  Yet I will bereave them to the
    last man.
  Yes, woe to them when I depart
    from them!
13 Just as I saw Ephraim like Tyre,
    planted in a pleasant place,
  So Ephraim will bring out his
    children to the murderer."

14 Give them, O Lord—
  What will You give?
  Give them a miscarrying womb
  And dry breasts!

15 "All their wickedness *is* in Gilgal,
  For there I hated them.
  Because of the evil of their
    deeds
  I will drive them from My
    house;
  I will love them no more.
  All their princes *are* rebellious.
16 Ephraim is stricken,
  Their root is dried up;
  They shall bear no fruit.
  Yes, were they to bear children,
  I would kill the darlings of their
    womb."

17 My God will cast them away,
   Because they did not obey Him;
   And they shall be wanderers
      among the nations.

Israel gives all she has to idols

10 Israel empties *his* vine;
   He brings forth fruit for himself.
   According to the multitude of his
      fruit
   He has increased the altars;
   According to the bounty of his
      land
   They have embellished *his*
      sacred pillars.
2 Their heart is divided;
   Now they are held guilty.
   He will break down their altars;
   He will ruin their sacred pillars.

3 For now they say,
   "We have no king,
   Because we did not fear the
      LORD.
   And as for a king, what would
      he do for us?"
4 They have spoken words,
   Swearing falsely in making a
      covenant.
   Thus judgment springs up like
      hemlock in the furrows of the
      field.

5 The inhabitants of Samaria fear
   Because of the calf of Beth
      Aven.
   For its people mourn for it,
   And its priests shriek for it—
   Because its glory has departed
      from it.
6 *The idol* also shall be carried to
      Assyria
   As a present for King Jareb.
   Ephraim shall receive shame,
   And Israel shall be ashamed of
      his own counsel.

7 *As for* Samaria, her king is cut
      off
   Like a twig on the water.
8 Also the high places of Aven, the
      sin of Israel,
   Shall be destroyed.

The thorn and thistle shall grow
   on their altars;
They shall say to the mountains,
   "Cover us!"
And to the hills, "Fall on us!"

9 "O Israel, you have sinned from
      the days of Gibeah;
   There they stood.
   The battle in Gibeah against the
      children of iniquity
   Did not overtake them.
10 When *it is* My desire, I will
      chasten them.
   Peoples shall be gathered
      against them
   When I bind them for their two
      transgressions.
11 Ephraim *is* a trained heifer
   That loves to thresh *grain;*
   But I harnessed her fair neck,
   I will make Ephraim pull *a plow.*
   Judah shall plow;
   Jacob shall break his clods."

12 Sow for yourselves
      righteousness;
   Reap in mercy;
   Break up your fallow ground,
   For *it is* time to seek the LORD,
   Till He comes and rains
      righteousness on you.

13 You have plowed wickedness;
   You have reaped iniquity.
   You have eaten the fruit of lies,
   Because you trusted in your own
      way,
   In the multitude of your mighty
      men.
14 Therefore tumult shall arise
      among your people,
   And all your fortresses shall be
      plundered
   As Shalman plundered Beth
      Arbel in the day of battle—
   A mother dashed in pieces upon
      her children.
15 Thus it shall be done to you, O
      Bethel,
   Because of your great
      wickedness.
   At dawn the king of Israel
   Shall be cut off utterly.

The Lord loves Israel like a child

11 "When Israel *was* a child, I loved
him,
And out of Egypt I called My
son.

2 As they called them,
So they went from them;
They sacrificed to the Baals,
And burned incense to carved
images.

3 "I taught Ephraim to walk,
Taking them by their arms;
But they did not know that I
healed them.

4 I drew them with gentle cords,
With bands of love,
And I was to them as those who
take the yoke from their neck.
I stooped *and* fed them.

5 "He shall not return to the land
of Egypt;
But the Assyrian shall be his
king,
Because they refused to repent.

6 And the sword shall slash in his
cities,
Devour his districts,
And consume *them,*
Because of their own counsels.

7 My people are bent on
backsliding from Me.
Though they call to the Most
High,
None at all exalt *Him.*

8 "How can I give you up,
Ephraim?

How can I hand you over,
Israel?
How can I make you like
Admah?
How can I set you like Zeboiim?
My heart churns within Me;
My sympathy is stirred.

9 I will not *execute* the fierceness
of My anger;
I will not again destroy Ephraim.
For I *am* God, and not man,
The Holy One in your midst;
And I will not come with terror.

10 "They shall walk after the LORD.
He will roar like a lion.
When He roars,
Then *His* sons shall come
trembling from the west;

11 They shall come trembling like
a bird from Egypt,
Like a dove from the land of
Assyria.
And I will let them dwell in their
houses,"
Says the LORD.

12 "Ephraim has encircled Me with
lies,
And the house of Israel with
deceit;
But Judah still walks with God,
Even with the Holy One *who is*
faithful.

Come back to the One who loves you, Israel

12 "Ephraim feeds on the wind,
And pursues the east wind;

DIGGING IN

11:1–4 God's Love for Israel The
prophet Hosea's unhappy life with his
wife, Gomer, also shows God's unhappy
experience with His people Israel. Gomer
was unfaithful to Hosea, and Israel was
unfaithful to the Lord. Hosea still loved
Gomer, and God still loved Israel.

In this book God reminds Israel how
He loved them when they were slaves in
Egypt. The Lord led them out of their slavery. But for hundreds of years, Israel kept
turning away from God. So Israel was always a rebel against God.

Now the Lord continues to love His disobedient people. He has been trying to
win them back to Himself all these long
centuries. Someday they will return to
serve Him.

The Book of Hosea also describes how
much God loves *you.* He will plead with
you till you turn to Him.

He daily increases lies and
   desolation.
Also they make a covenant with
   the Assyrians,
And oil is carried to Egypt.

2 "The LORD also *brings* a charge
   against Judah,
And will punish Jacob according
   to his ways;
According to his deeds He will
   recompense him.
3 He took his brother by the heel
   in the womb,
And in his strength he struggled
   with God.
4 Yes, he struggled with the Angel
   and prevailed;
He wept, and sought favor from
   Him.
He found Him *in* Bethel,
And there He spoke to us—
5 That is, the LORD God of
   hosts.
The LORD *is* His memorable
   name.
6 So you, by *the help of* your
   God, return;
Observe mercy and justice,
And wait on your God
   continually.

7 "A cunning Canaanite!
Deceitful scales *are* in his
   hand;
He loves to oppress.
8 And Ephraim said,
'Surely I have become rich,
I have found wealth for myself;
In all my labors
They shall find in me no iniquity
   that *is* sin.'

9 "But I *am* the LORD your God,
Ever since the land of Egypt;
I will again make you dwell in
   tents,
As in the days of the appointed
   feast.
10 I have also spoken by the
   prophets,
And have multiplied visions;
I have given symbols through
   the witness of the prophets."

11 Though Gilead *has* idols—
Surely they are vanity—
Though they sacrifice bulls in
   Gilgal,
Indeed their altars *shall be* heaps
   in the furrows of the field.

12 Jacob fled to the country of
   Syria;
Israel served for a spouse,
And for a wife he tended
   sheep.
13 By a prophet the LORD brought
   Israel out of Egypt,
And by a prophet he was
   preserved.
14 Ephraim provoked *Him* to anger
   most bitterly;
Therefore his Lord will leave the
   guilt of his bloodshed upon
   him,
And return his reproach upon
   him.

The people anger God

13 When Ephraim spoke,
   trembling,
He exalted *himself* in Israel;
But when he offended through
   Baal *worship*, he died.
2 Now they sin more and more,
And have made for themselves
   molded images,
Idols of their silver, according to
   their skill;
All of it *is* the work of
   craftsmen.
They say of them,
"Let the men who sacrifice kiss
   the calves!"
3 Therefore they shall be like the
   morning cloud
And like the early dew that
   passes away,
Like chaff blown off from a
   threshing floor
And like smoke from a
   chimney.

4 "Yet I *am* the LORD your God
Ever since the land of Egypt,
And you shall know no God but
   Me;

For *there is* no **savior** besides Me.

5 I knew you in the wilderness,
In the land of great drought.
6 When they had pasture, they were filled;
They were filled and their heart was exalted;
Therefore they forgot Me.

7 "So I will be to them like a lion;
Like a leopard by the road I will lurk;
8 I will meet them like a bear deprived *of her cubs;*
I will tear open their rib cage,
And there I will devour them like a lion.
The wild beast shall tear them.

9 "O Israel, you are destroyed,
But your help *is* from Me.
10 I will be your King;
Where *is any other,*
That he may save you in all your cities?
And your judges to whom you said,
'Give me a king and princes'?
11 I gave you a king in My anger,
And took *him* away in My wrath.

12 "The iniquity of Ephraim *is* bound up;
His sin *is* stored up.
13 The sorrows of a woman in childbirth shall come upon him.
He *is* an unwise son,
For he should not stay long where children are born.

14 "I will ransom them from the power of the grave;
I will redeem them from death.
O Death, I will be your plagues!
O Grave, I will be your destruction!
Pity is hidden from My eyes."

15 Though he is fruitful among *his* brethren,
An east wind shall come;
The wind of the LORD shall come up from the wilderness.
Then his spring shall become dry,
And his fountain shall be dried up.
He shall plunder the treasury of every desirable prize.
16 Samaria is held guilty,
For she has rebelled against her God.
They shall fall by the sword,
Their infants shall be dashed in pieces,
And their women with child ripped open.

God will forgive and take His people back

14 O Israel, return to the LORD your God,
For you have stumbled because of your iniquity;
2 Take words with you,
And return to the LORD.
Say to Him,
"Take away all iniquity;
Receive *us* graciously,
For we will offer the sacrifices of our lips.
3 Assyria shall not save us,
We will not ride on horses,
Nor will we say anymore to the work of our hands, 'You are our gods.'
For in You the fatherless finds mercy."

4 "I will heal their backsliding,
I will love them freely,

What Is Backsliding?

Backsliding is a word that comes from the Bible. If you climb a hill and slide back, that's backsliding, too. The Bible word means to "slide back" into sin after we've climbed out of it. It's comforting to know that God can put an end to our backsliding.

For My anger has turned away
    from him.
5 I will be like the dew to Israel;
    He shall grow like the lily,
    And lengthen his roots like
        Lebanon.
6 His branches shall spread;
    His beauty shall be like an olive
        tree,
    And his fragrance like
        Lebanon.

7 Those who dwell under his
    shadow shall return;
    They shall be revived *like* grain,
    And grow like a vine.
    Their scent *shall be* like the wine
        of Lebanon.

8 "Ephraim *shall say,* 'What have I
        to do anymore with idols?'
    I have heard and observed him.
    I *am* like a green cypress tree;
    Your fruit is found in Me."

9 Who *is* wise?
    Let him understand these things.
    Who is prudent?
    Let him know them.
    For the ways of the LORD *are*
       right;
    The righteous walk in them,
    But transgressors stumble in
       them.

What Hosea Learned

Have you ever wondered if God is really in charge of the world? Will He really do right and make evil come to an end?

I used to ask these questions, too. But after a long time I learned that God always does the right thing. Because I didn't always understand Him, I doubted Him. But in the end I could see that His way is always the right way.

If we refuse to learn this lesson, then we trip over our own stubborn attitude. If we trip often enough, though, maybe we will learn to trust God's wisdom. Then we see that God's way is always the *best* way.

The Book of
JOEL

My name is pronounced *JO-el* and means "The Lord Is God." People remember me because I told about the coming of the Holy Spirit hundreds of years later. You can read about this great happening in Acts 2 in the New Testament.

My book also describes God's future judgment, which I call "the day of the Lord." We should always be expecting that great "Day" when God will bring all nations before Him for judgment. He is going to judge you and me, too, according to what we have done. See Revelation 20:12 in the New Testament.

You can escape God's judgment if you learn to be sorry for sin and turn to Jesus. Even though we don't talk about Jesus by name in the Old Testament, He was our Savior, too.

An army of locusts with teeth like lions

T HE word of the LORD that came to Joel the son of Pethuel.

2 Hear this, you elders,
And give ear, all you inhabitants of the land!
Has *anything like* this happened in your days,
Or even in the days of your fathers?
3 Tell your children about it,
Let your children *tell* their children,
And their children another generation.

4 What the chewing locust left, the swarming locust has eaten;
What the swarming locust left, the crawling locust has eaten;
And what the crawling locust left, the consuming locust has eaten.

5 Awake, you drunkards, and weep;
And wail, all you drinkers of wine,
Because of the new wine,
For it has been cut off from your mouth.
6 For a nation has come up against My land,
Strong, and without number;
His teeth *are* the teeth of a lion,
And he has the fangs of a fierce lion.
7 He has laid waste My vine,
And ruined My fig tree;
He has stripped it bare and thrown *it* away;
Its branches are made white.

8 Lament like a virgin girded with sackcloth
For the husband of her youth.
9 The grain offering and the drink offering
Have been cut off from the house of the LORD;
The priests mourn, who minister to the LORD.
10 The field is wasted,
The land mourns;
For the grain is ruined,
The new wine is dried up,
The oil fails.

11 Be ashamed, you farmers,
Wail, you vinedressers,
For the wheat and the barley;

Because the harvest of the field
    has perished.
12 The vine has dried up,
    And the fig tree has withered;
    The pomegranate tree,
    The palm tree also,
    And the apple tree—
    All the trees of the field are
        withered;
    Surely joy has withered away
        from the sons of men.

13 Gird yourselves and lament, you
        priests;
    Wail, you who minister before
        the altar;
    Come, lie all night in sackcloth,
    You who minister to my God;
    For the grain offering and the
        drink offering
    Are withheld from the house of
        your God.
14 Consecrate a fast,
    Call a sacred assembly;
    Gather the elders
    And all the inhabitants of the
        land
    Into the house of the LORD your
        God,
    And cry out to the LORD.

15 Alas for the day!
    For the day of the LORD *is* at
        hand;
    It shall come as destruction from
        the Almighty.
16 Is not the food cut off before our
        eyes,
    Joy and gladness from the house
        of our God?
17 The seed shrivels under the
        clods,
    Storehouses are in shambles;
    Barns are broken down,
    For the grain has withered.
18 How the animals groan!
    The herds of cattle are restless,
    Because they have no pasture;
    Even the flocks of sheep suffer
        punishment.

19 O LORD, to You I cry out;
    For fire has devoured the open
        pastures,

What Is the Day of the Lord?

God uses the word *day* in different
ways. Sometimes the word means 24
hours, sometimes it means daytime,
and sometimes it means at least a
thousand years (see 2 Peter 3:8).
Here Joel is writing about the great
Day of Judgment. Then God will call
all nations before Him and judge them.

    And a flame has burned all the
        trees of the field.
20 The beasts of the field also cry
        out to You,
    For the water brooks are dried
        up,
    And fire has devoured the open
        pastures.

Judgment strips the land bare

2 Blow the trumpet in Zion,
    And sound an alarm in My holy
        mountain!
    Let all the inhabitants of the land
        tremble;
    For the day of the LORD is
        coming,
    For it is at hand:
2 A day of darkness and
        gloominess,
    A day of clouds and thick
        darkness,
    Like the morning *clouds* spread
        over the mountains.
    A people *come,* great and
        strong,
    The like of whom has never
        been;
    Nor will there *ever* be any *such*
        after them,
    Even for many successive
        generations.

3 A fire devours before them,
    And behind them a flame burns;
    The land *is* like the Garden of
        Eden before them,
    And behind them a desolate
        wilderness;
    Surely nothing shall escape
        them.

4 Their appearance is like the
appearance of horses;
And like swift steeds, so they
run.
5 With a noise like chariots
Over mountaintops they leap,
Like the noise of a flaming fire
that devours the stubble,
Like a strong people set in battle
array.

6 Before them the people writhe
in pain;
All faces are drained of color.
7 They run like mighty men,
They climb the wall like men of
war;
Every one marches in formation,
And they do not break ranks.
8 They do not push one another;
Every one marches in his own
column.
Though they lunge between the
weapons,
They are not cut down.
9 They run to and fro in the city,
They run on the wall;
They climb into the houses,
They enter at the windows like
a thief.

10 The earth quakes before them,
The heavens tremble;
The sun and moon grow dark,
And the stars diminish their
brightness.
11 The Lord gives voice before His
army,
For His camp is very great;
For strong is the One who
executes His word.
For the day of the Lord is great
and very terrible;
Who can endure it?

12 "Now, therefore," says the
Lord,
"Turn to Me with all your heart,
With fasting, with weeping, and
with mourning."
13 So rend your heart, and not
your garments;
Return to the Lord your God,
For He is gracious and merciful,

Slow to anger, and of great
kindness;
And He relents from doing
harm.
14 Who knows if He will turn and
relent,
And leave a blessing behind
Him—
A grain offering and a drink
offering
For the Lord your God?

15 Blow the trumpet in Zion,
Consecrate a fast,
Call a sacred assembly;
16 Gather the people,
Sanctify the congregation,
Assemble the elders,
Gather the children and nursing
babes;
Let the bridegroom go out from
his chamber,
And the bride from her dressing
room.
17 Let the priests, who minister to
the Lord,
Weep between the porch and
the altar;
Let them say, "Spare Your
people, O Lord,
And do not give Your heritage
to reproach,
That the nations should rule
over them.
Why should they say among the
peoples,
'Where is their God?' "

18 Then the Lord will be zealous
for His land,
And pity His people.
19 The Lord will answer and say
to His people,
"Behold, I will send you grain and
new wine and oil,
And you will be satisfied by
them;
I will no longer make you a
reproach among the nations.

20 "But I will remove far from you
the northern army,
And will drive him away into a
barren and desolate land,

With his face toward the eastern
    sea
And his back toward the western
    sea;
His stench will come up,
And his foul odor will rise,
Because he has done monstrous
    things."

21 Fear not, O land;
    Be glad and rejoice,
    For the LORD has done
        marvelous things!
22 Do not be afraid, you beasts of
    the field;
    For the open pastures are
        springing up,
    And the tree bears its fruit;
    The fig tree and the vine yield
        their strength.
23 Be glad then, you children of
    Zion,
    And rejoice in the LORD your
        God;
    For He has given you the former
        rain faithfully,
    And He will cause the rain to
        come down for you—
    The former rain,
    And the latter rain in the first
        month.
24 The threshing floors shall be full
    of wheat,
    And the vats shall overflow with
    new wine and oil.

25 "So I will restore to you the years
    that the swarming locust has
    eaten,

The crawling locust,
The consuming locust,
And the chewing locust,
My great army which I sent
    among you.
26 You shall eat in plenty and be
    satisfied,
    And praise the name of the LORD
        your God,
    Who has dealt wondrously with
        you;
    And My people shall never be
        put to shame.
27 Then you shall know that I *am*
    in the midst of Israel:
    I *am* the LORD your God
    And there is no other.
    My people shall never be put to
        shame.

28 "And it shall come to pass
    afterward
    That I will pour out My Spirit on
        all flesh;
    Your sons and your daughters
        shall prophesy,
    Your old men shall dream
        dreams,
    Your young men shall see
        visions.
29 And also on *My* menservants
    and on *My* maidservants
    I will pour out My Spirit in those
    days.

30 "And I will show wonders in the
    heavens and in the earth:
    Blood and fire and pillars of
    smoke.

⛏ DIGGING IN

2:28, 29 God Has Sent His Spirit
There are *three Persons* in the *one God.*
They are the Father, the Son, and the
Holy Spirit. The Holy Spirit helped at Creation (see Genesis 1:2), and He spoke
through the prophets of the Old Testament.

But in the New Testament, the Holy
Spirit came in greater power to believers
than He did in the Old Testament. The
Holy Spirit came in that greater power after Jesus rose from the dead and went

back to heaven.

In Acts 2:16–21, you can read how
Joel's promise of the Holy Spirit was fulfilled in the New Testament. The Holy
Spirit not only spoke through the apostles
in the New Testament, but He also came
to live in all believers. Jesus called the
Holy Spirit the "Helper" (see John 14:16).
If you are a Christian, you have the Holy
Spirit living in you. The Holy Spirit helps
you know you are God's child, and He
helps you understand God's Word.

31 The sun shall be turned into
     darkness,
   And the moon into blood,
   Before the coming of the great
     and awesome day of the
     LORD.
32 And it shall come to pass
   That whoever calls on the name
     of the LORD
   Shall be saved.
   For in Mount Zion and in
     Jerusalem there shall be
     deliverance,
   As the LORD has said,
   Among the remnant whom the
     LORD calls.

The fields will be green again

3   "For behold, in those days and
       at that time,
     When I bring back the captives
       of Judah and Jerusalem,
2   I will also gather all nations,
     And bring them down to the
       Valley of Jehoshaphat;
     And I will enter into judgment
       with them there
     On account of My people, My
       heritage Israel,
     Whom they have scattered
       among the nations;
     They have also divided up My
       land.
3   They have cast lots for My
       people,
     Have given a boy *as payment*
       for a harlot,
     And sold a girl for wine, that they
       may drink.

4   "Indeed, what have you to do
       with Me,
     O Tyre and Sidon, and all the
       coasts of Philistia?
     Will you retaliate against Me?
     But if you retaliate against Me,
     Swiftly and speedily I will
       return your retaliation upon
       your own head;
5   Because you have taken My
       silver and My gold,
     And have carried into your

   temples My prized
     possessions.
6 Also the people of Judah and
     the people of Jerusalem
   You have sold to the Greeks,
   That you may remove them far
     from their borders.

7 "Behold, I will raise them
     Out of the place to which you
       have sold them,
     And will return your retaliation
       upon your own head.
8 I will sell your sons and your
     daughters
   Into the hand of the people of
     Judah,
   And they will sell them to the
     Sabeans,
   To a people far off;
   For the LORD has spoken."

9 Proclaim this among the
     nations:
   "Prepare for war!
   Wake up the mighty men,
   Let all the men of war draw
     near,
   Let them come up.
10 Beat your plowshares into
     swords
   And your pruning hooks into
     spears;
   Let the weak say, 'I *am*
     strong.'"
11 Assemble and come, all you
     nations,
   And gather together all
     around.
   Cause Your mighty ones to go
     down there, O LORD.

12 "Let the nations be wakened, and
     come up to the Valley of
     Jehoshaphat;
   For there I will sit to judge all
     the surrounding nations.
13 Put in the sickle, for the harvest
     is ripe.
   Come, go down;
   For the winepress is full,
   The vats overflow—
   For their wickedness *is* great."

14 Multitudes, multitudes in the
   valley of decision!
   For the day of the LORD *is* near
   in the valley of decision.
15 The sun and moon will grow
   dark,
   And the stars will diminish their
   brightness.
16 The LORD also will roar from
   Zion,
   And utter His voice from
   Jerusalem;
   The heavens and earth will
   shake;
   But the LORD will be a shelter
   for His people,
   And the strength of the children
   of Israel.

17 "So you shall know that I *am* the
   LORD your God,
   Dwelling in Zion My holy
   mountain.
   Then Jerusalem shall be holy,
   And no aliens shall *ever* pass
   through her again."

18 And it will come to pass in that
   day
   That the mountains shall drip
   with new wine,
   The hills shall flow with milk,
   And all the brooks of Judah shall
   be flooded with water;
   A fountain shall flow from the
   house of the LORD
   And water the Valley of
   Acacias.

19 "Egypt shall be a desolation,
   And Edom a desolate
   wilderness,
   Because of violence *against* the
   people of Judah,
   For they have shed innocent
   blood in their land.
20 But Judah shall abide forever,
   And Jerusalem from generation
   to generation.
21 For I will acquit them of the guilt
   of bloodshed, whom I had not
   acquitted;
   For the LORD dwells in Zion."

The Book of
AMOS

Strange to say, I was not always a prophet, and none of my family were prophets. I was a farmer. Just the same, God called me from my home in the Southern Kingdom of Judah to be a prophet to the Northern Kingdom of Israel.

They didn't like me much in Israel. I warned the rich people that they were making God angry by cheating the poor with heavy taxes. Some of the religious leaders complained about my tough words, but I had to be a good "Burden Bearer," which is the meaning of my name, pronounced AY-mos. I had to carry the burden of God's message.

When the people didn't listen, the army of Assyria came and conquered the Northern Kingdom.

Israel's neighbors will be punished

THE words of Amos, who was among the sheepbreeders of Tekoa, which he saw concerning Israel in the days of Uzziah king of Judah, and in the days of Jeroboam the son of Joash, king of Israel, two years before the earthquake.
2 And he said:

"The LORD roars from Zion,
And utters His voice from
    Jerusalem;
The pastures of the shepherds
    mourn,
And the top of Carmel withers."

3 Thus says the LORD:

"For three transgressions of
    Damascus, and for four,
I will not turn away its
    punishment,
Because they have threshed
    Gilead with implements of
    iron.
4   But I will send a fire into the
    house of Hazael,
Which shall devour the palaces
    of Ben-Hadad.
5   I will also break the *gate* bar of
    Damascus,

And cut off the inhabitant from
    the Valley of Aven,
And the one who holds the
    scepter from Beth Eden.
The people of Syria shall go
    captive to Kir,"
Says the LORD.

6 Thus says the LORD:

"For three transgressions of Gaza,
    and for four,
I will not turn away its
    punishment,
Because they took captive the
    whole captivity
To deliver *them* up to Edom.
7   But I will send a fire upon the
    wall of Gaza,
Which shall devour its palaces.
8   I will cut off the inhabitant from
    Ashdod,
And the one who holds the
    scepter from Ashkelon;
I will turn My hand against
    Ekron,
And the remnant of the
    Philistines shall perish,"
Says the Lord GOD.

9 Thus says the LORD:

"For three transgressions of Tyre,
    and for four,

I will not turn away its
    punishment,
Because they delivered up the
    whole captivity to Edom,
And did not remember the
    covenant of brotherhood.
10 But I will send a fire upon the
    wall of Tyre,
    Which shall devour its palaces."

11 Thus says the LORD:

    "For three transgressions of
        Edom, and for four,
    I will not turn away its
        punishment,
    Because he pursued his brother
        with the sword,
    And cast off all pity;
    His anger tore perpetually,
    And he kept his wrath forever.
12 But I will send a fire upon
    Teman,
    Which shall devour the palaces
        of Bozrah."

13 Thus says the LORD:

    "For three transgressions of the
        people of Ammon, and for
        four,
    I will not turn away its
        punishment,
    Because they ripped open the
        women with child in Gilead,
    That they might enlarge their
        territory.
14 But I will kindle a fire in the wall
    of Rabbah,
    And it shall devour its palaces,
    Amid shouting in the day of
        battle,
    And a tempest in the day of the
        whirlwind.
15 Their king shall go into captivity,
    He and his princes together,"
    Says the LORD.

God will punish Israel, too

2 Thus says the LORD:

    "For three transgressions of
        Moab, and for four,

I will not turn away its
    punishment,
Because he burned the bones of
    the king of Edom to lime.
2   But I will send a fire upon
    Moab,
    And it shall devour the palaces
        of Kerioth;
    Moab shall die with tumult,
    With shouting and trumpet
        sound.
3   And I will cut off the judge from
        its midst,
    And slay all its princes with
        him,"
    Says the LORD.

4 Thus says the LORD:

    "For three transgressions of
        Judah, and for four,
    I will not turn away its
        punishment,
    Because they have despised the
        law of the LORD,
    And have not kept His
        commandments.
    Their lies lead them astray,
    Lies which their fathers followed.
5   But I will send a fire upon
    Judah,
    And it shall devour the palaces
        of Jerusalem."

6 Thus says the LORD:

    "For three transgressions of Israel,
        and for four,
    I will not turn away its
        punishment,
    Because they sell the righteous
        for silver,
    And the poor for a pair of
        sandals.
7   They pant after the dust of the
        earth which is on the head of
        the poor,
    And pervert the way of the
        humble.
    A man and his father go in to
        the same girl,
    To defile My holy name.
8   They lie down by every altar on
        clothes taken in pledge,

Wicked Israel "sells the righteous for silver, and the poor for a pair of sandals" (2:6).

And drink the wine of the
    condemned *in* the house of
    their god.

9 "Yet *it was* I *who* destroyed the
    Amorite before them,
Whose height *was* like the height
    of the cedars,
And he *was as* strong as the
    oaks;
Yet I destroyed his fruit above
And his roots beneath.
10 Also *it was* I *who* brought you
    up from the land of Egypt,
And led you forty years through
    the wilderness,
To possess the land of the
    Amorite.
11 I raised up some of your sons
    as prophets,
And some of your young men
    as Nazirites.

Is it not so, O you children of
    Israel?"
Says the LORD.
12 "But you gave the Nazirites wine
    to drink,
And commanded the prophets
    saying,
'Do not prophesy!'

13 "Behold, I am weighed down by
    you,
As a cart full of sheaves is
    weighed down.
14 Therefore flight shall perish from
    the swift,
The strong shall not strengthen
    his power,
Nor shall the mighty deliver
    himself;
15 He shall not stand who handles
    the bow,
The swift of foot shall not
    escape,
Nor shall he who rides a horse
    deliver himself.
16 The most courageous men of
    might
Shall flee naked in that day,"
Says the LORD.

The Lion has roared

3 Hear this word that the LORD has
spoken against you, O children of Israel, against the whole family which I
brought up from the land of Egypt,
saying:

2 "You only have I known of all
    the families of the earth;
Therefore I will punish you for
    all your iniquities."
3 Can two walk together, unless
    they are agreed?
4 Will a lion roar in the forest,
    when he has no prey?
Will a young lion cry out of his
    den, if he has caught nothing?
5 Will a bird fall into a snare on
    the earth, where there is no
    trap for it?
Will a snare spring up from the
    earth, if it has caught nothing
    at all?

6 If a trumpet is blown in a city,
      will not the people be afraid?
   If there is calamity in a city, will
      not the LORD have done *it?*

7 Surely the Lord GOD does
      nothing,
   Unless He reveals His secret to
      His servants the prophets.
8 A lion has roared!
   Who will not fear?
   The Lord GOD has spoken!
   Who can but prophesy?

9 "Proclaim in the palaces at
      Ashdod,
   And in the palaces in the land
      of Egypt, and say:
   'Assemble on the mountains of
      Samaria;
   See great tumults in her midst,
   And the oppressed within her.
10 For they do not know to do
      right,'
   Says the LORD,
   'Who store up violence and
      robbery in their palaces.' "

11 Therefore thus says the Lord GOD:

   "An adversary *shall be* all around
      the land;
   He shall sap your strength from
      you,
   And your palaces shall be
      plundered."

12 Thus says the LORD:

   "As a shepherd takes from the
      mouth of a lion
   Two legs or a piece of an ear,
   So shall the children of Israel be
      taken out
   Who dwell in Samaria—
   In the corner of a bed and on
      the edge of a couch!
13 Hear and testify against the
      house of Jacob,"

Says the Lord GOD, the God of
   hosts,
14 "That in the day I punish Israel
      for their transgressions,
   I will also visit *destruction* on the
      altars of Bethel;
   And the horns of the altar shall
      be cut off
   And fall to the ground.
15 I will destroy the winter house
      along with the summer house;
   The houses of ivory shall perish,
   And the great houses shall have
      an end,"
Says the LORD.

The people keep on doing wrong

4 Hear this word, you cows of
      Bashan, who *are* on the
      mountain of Samaria,
   Who oppress the poor,
   Who crush the needy,
   Who say to your husbands,
      "Bring *wine,* let us drink!"
2 The Lord GOD has sworn by His
      holiness:
   "Behold, the days shall come
      upon you
   When He will take you away
      with fishhooks,
   And your posterity with
      fishhooks.
3 You will go out *through* broken
      walls,
   Each one straight ahead of
      her,
   And you will be cast into
      Harmon,"
Says the LORD.

4 "Come to Bethel and transgress,
   At Gilgal multiply transgression;
   Bring your sacrifices every
      morning,
   Your tithes *every* three days.
5 Offer a **sacrifice** of thanksgiving
      with leaven,

WORDFINDER

4:5 Sacrifice Pronounced *SACK-rih-fyce.* An offering to God. In the Old Testament, the people sacrificed the blood of animals for sin. In the New Testament, Christ is our only sacrifice for sin.

Proclaim *and* announce the
    freewill offerings;
For this you love,
You children of Israel!"
Says the Lord GOD.
6 "Also I gave you cleanness of
    teeth in all your cities.
And lack of bread in all your
    places;
Yet you have not returned to
    Me,"
Says the LORD.

7 "I also withheld rain from you,
When *there were* still three
    months to the harvest.
I made it rain on one city,
I withheld rain from another
    city.
One part was rained upon,
And where it did not rain the
    part withered.
8 So two *or* three cities wandered
    to another city to drink water,
But they were not satisfied;
Yet you have not returned to
    Me,"
Says the LORD.

9 "I blasted you with blight and
    mildew.
When your gardens increased,
Your vineyards,
Your fig trees,
And your olive trees,
The locust devoured *them;*
Yet you have not returned to
    Me,"
Says the LORD.

10 "I sent among you a plague after
    the manner of Egypt;
Your young men I killed with a
    sword,
Along with your captive horses;
I made the stench of your camps
    come up into your nostrils;
Yet you have not returned to
    Me,"
Says the LORD.

11 "I overthrew *some* of you,
As God overthrew Sodom and
    Gomorrah,

And you were like a firebrand
    plucked from the burning;
Yet you have not returned to
    Me,"
Says the LORD.

12 "Therefore thus will I do to you,
    O Israel;
Because I will do this to you,
Prepare to meet your God, O
    Israel!"

13   For behold,
He who forms mountains,
And creates the wind,
Who declares to man what his
    thought *is,*
And makes the morning
    darkness,
Who treads the high places of
    the earth—
The LORD God of hosts *is* His
    name.

Amos sings a sad song

5 Hear this word which I take up
against you, a lamentation, O house
of Israel:

2   The virgin of Israel has fallen;
    She will rise no more.
    She lies forsaken on her land;
    There is no one to raise her up.

3 For thus says the Lord GOD:

    "The city that goes out by a
        thousand
    Shall have a hundred left,
    And that which goes out by a
        hundred
    Shall have ten left to the house
        of Israel."

4 For thus says the LORD to the
house of Israel:

    "Seek Me and live;
5   But do not seek Bethel,
    Nor enter Gilgal,
    Nor pass over to Beersheba;
    For Gilgal shall surely go into
        captivity,

And Bethel shall come to
nothing.
6 Seek the LORD and live,
Lest He break out like fire *in the
house of Joseph,
And devour *it,
With no one to quench *it* in
Bethel—
7 You who turn justice to
wormwood,
And lay righteousness to rest in
the earth!"

8 He made the Pleiades and
Orion;
He turns the shadow of death
into morning
And makes the day dark as
night;
He calls for the waters of the sea
And pours them out on the face
of the earth;
The LORD *is* His name.
9 He rains ruin upon the strong,
So that fury comes upon the
fortress.

10 They hate the one who rebukes
in the gate,
And they abhor the one who
speaks uprightly.
11 Therefore, because you tread
down the poor
And take grain taxes from him,
Though you have built houses
of hewn stone,
Yet you shall not dwell in them;
You have planted pleasant
vineyards,
But you shall not drink wine
from them.
12 For I know your manifold
transgressions
And your mighty sins:
Afflicting the just *and* taking
bribes;
Diverting the poor *from justice*
at the gate.
13 Therefore the prudent keep
silent at that time,
For it *is* an evil time.

14 Seek good and not evil,
That you may live;

So the LORD God of hosts will
be with you,
As you have spoken.
15 Hate evil, love good;
Establish justice in the gate.
It may be that the LORD God of
hosts
Will be gracious to the remnant
of Joseph.

16 Therefore the LORD God of hosts,
the Lord, says this:

"*There shall be* wailing in all
streets,
And they shall say in all the
highways,
'Alas! Alas!'
They shall call the farmer to
mourning,
And skillful lamenters to wailing.
17 In all vineyards *there shall be*
wailing,
For I will pass through you,"
Says the LORD.

18 Woe to you who desire the day
of the LORD!
For what good *is* the day of the
LORD to you?
It *will be* darkness, and not light.
19 It *will be* as though a man fled
from a lion,
And a bear met him!
Or *as though* he went into the
house,
Leaned his hand on the wall,
And a serpent bit him!
20 *Is* not the day of the LORD
darkness, and not light?
Is it not very dark, with no
brightness in it?

21 "I hate, I despise your feast days,
And I do not savor your sacred
assemblies.
22 Though you offer Me burnt
offerings and your grain
offerings,
I will not accept *them,*
Nor will I regard your fattened
peace offerings.
23 Take away from Me the noise
of your songs,

For I will not hear the melody
   of your stringed instruments.
24 But let justice run down like
   water,
   And righteousness like a mighty
   stream.

25 "Did you offer Me sacrifices and
   offerings
   In the wilderness forty years, O
   house of Israel?
26 You also carried Sikkuth your
   king
   And Chiun, your idols,
   The star of your gods,
   Which you made for yourselves.
27 Therefore I will send you into
   captivity beyond Damascus,"
   Says the LORD, whose name *is*
   the God of hosts.

The party is over!

6
Woe to you *who are* at ease in
   Zion,
   And trust in Mount Samaria,
   Notable persons in the chief
   nation,
   To whom the house of Israel
   comes!
2 Go over to Calneh and see;
   And from there go to Hamath
   the great;
   Then go down to Gath of the
   Philistines.
   Are you better than these
   kingdoms?
   Or is their territory greater than
   your territory?

3 *Woe to* you who put far off the
   day of doom,
   Who cause the seat of violence
   to come near;
4 Who lie on beds of ivory,
   Stretch out on your couches,
   Eat lambs from the flock
   And calves from the midst of the
   stall;
5 Who sing idly to the sound of
   stringed instruments,
   And invent for yourselves
   musical instruments like
   David;

6 Who drink wine from bowls,
   And anoint yourselves with the
   best ointments,
   But are not grieved for the
   affliction of Joseph.
7 Therefore they shall now go
   captive as the first of the
   captives,
   And those who recline at
   banquets shall be removed.

8 The Lord GOD has sworn by
   Himself,
   The LORD God of hosts says:
   "I abhor the pride of Jacob,
   And hate his palaces;
   Therefore I will deliver up *the*
   city
   And all that is in it."

9 Then it shall come to pass, that if ten men remain in one house, they shall die. 10 And when a relative *of the dead,* with one who will burn *the bodies,* picks up the bodies to take them out of the house, he will say to one inside the house, *"Are there* any more with you?"
Then someone will say, "None."
And he will say, "Hold your tongue! For we dare not mention the name of the LORD."

11 For behold, the LORD gives a
   command:
   He will break the great house
   into bits,
   And the little house into pieces.

12 Do horses run on rocks?
   Does *one* plow *there* with oxen?
   Yet you have turned justice into
   gall,
   And the fruit of righteousness
   into wormwood,
13 You who rejoice over Lo Debar,
   Who say, "Have we not taken
   Karnaim for ourselves
   By our own strength?"

14 "But, behold, I will raise up a
   nation against you,
   O house of Israel,"
   Says the LORD God of hosts;

"And they will afflict you from the
    entrance of Hamath
To the Valley of the Arabah."

Locusts, fire, and a plumb line

7 Thus the Lord GOD showed me:
Behold, He formed locust swarms at
the beginning of the late crop; indeed
it was the late crop after the king's
mowings. ²And so it was, when they
had finished eating the grass of the
land, that I said:

"O Lord GOD, forgive, I pray!
Oh, that Jacob may stand,
For he *is* small!"
3   *So* the LORD relented concerning
        this.
"It shall not be," said the LORD.

⁴Thus the Lord GOD showed me:
Behold, the Lord GOD called for conflict by fire, and it consumed the great
deep and devoured the territory.
⁵Then I said:

"O Lord GOD, cease, I pray!
Oh, that Jacob may stand,
For he *is* small!"
6   *So* the LORD relented concerning
        this.
"This also shall not be," said the
    Lord GOD.

⁷Thus He showed me: Behold, the
Lord stood on a wall *made* with a
plumb line, with a plumb line in His
hand. ⁸And the LORD said to me,
"Amos, what do you see?"
And I said, "A plumb line."
Then the Lord said:

"Behold, I am setting a plumb line
In the midst of My people Israel;
I will not pass by them anymore.
9   The high places of Isaac shall be
        desolate,
    And the sanctuaries of Israel
        shall be laid waste.
    I will rise with the sword against
        the house of Jeroboam."

¹⁰Then Amaziah the priest of Bethel
sent to Jeroboam king of Israel, saying,

*A builder tests a wall with a plumb line to see
if it is straight from top to bottom.*

"Amos has conspired against you in
the midst of the house of Israel. The
land is not able to bear all his words.
¹¹For thus Amos has said:

'Jeroboam shall die by the
    sword,
And Israel shall surely be led
    away captive
From their own land.'"

¹²Then Amaziah said to Amos:

"Go, you seer!
Flee to the land of Judah.
There eat bread,
And there prophesy.
13   But never again prophesy at
        Bethel,
    For it *is* the king's sanctuary,
    And it *is* the royal residence."

14 Then Amos answered, and said to Amaziah:

"I *was* no prophet,
Nor *was* I a son of a prophet,
But I *was* a sheepbreeder
And a tender of sycamore fruit.
15 Then the LORD took me as I
   followed the flock,
And the LORD said to me,
'Go, prophesy to My people
   Israel.'
16 Now therefore, hear the word of
   the LORD:
You say, 'Do not prophesy
   against Israel,
And do not spout against the
   house of Isaac.'

17 "Therefore thus says the LORD:

'Your wife shall be a harlot in the
   city;
Your sons and daughters shall
   fall by the sword;
Your land shall be divided by
   survey line;
You shall die in a defiled land;
And Israel shall surely be led
   away captive
From his own land.' "

A basket of summer fruit

8 Thus the Lord GOD showed me:
Behold, a basket of summer fruit.
2 And He said, "Amos, what do you
see?"
So I said, "A basket of summer
fruit."
Then the LORD said to me:

"The end has come upon My
   people Israel;
I will not pass by them anymore.
3 And the songs of the temple
Shall be wailing in that day,"
Says the Lord GOD—
"Many dead bodies everywhere,
They shall be thrown out in
   silence."

4 Hear this, you who swallow up
   the needy,

And make the poor of the land
   fail,

5 Saying:

"When will the New Moon be
   past,
That we may sell grain?
And the Sabbath,
That we may trade wheat?
Making the ephah small and the
   shekel large,
Falsifying the scales by deceit,
6 That we may buy the poor for
   silver,
And the needy for a pair of
   sandals—
Even sell the bad wheat?"

7 The LORD has sworn by the
   pride of Jacob:
"Surely I will never forget any of
   their works.
8 Shall the land not tremble for
   this,
And everyone mourn who
   dwells in it?
All of it shall swell like the River,
Heave and subside
Like the River of Egypt.

9 "And it shall come to pass in that
   day," says the Lord GOD,
"That I will make the sun go
   down at noon,
And I will darken the earth in
   broad daylight;
10 I will turn your feasts into
   mourning,
And all your songs into
   lamentation;
I will bring sackcloth on every
   waist,
And baldness on every head;
I will make it like mourning for
   an only *son*,
And its end like a bitter day.

11 "Behold, the days are coming,"
   says the Lord GOD,
"That I will send a famine on the
   land,
Not a famine of bread,
Nor a thirst for water,

But of hearing the words of the
Lord.
12 They shall wander from sea to
sea,
And from north to east;
They shall run to and fro,
seeking the word of the Lord,
But shall not find *it*.

13 "In that day the fair virgins
And strong young men
Shall faint from thirst.
14 Those who swear by the sin of
Samaria,
Who say,
'As your god lives, O Dan!'
And, 'As the way of Beersheba
lives!'
They shall fall and never rise
again."

The people cannot escape, but God will rebuild

9 I saw the Lord standing by the altar, and He said:

"Strike the doorposts, that the
thresholds may shake,
And break them on the heads
of them all.
I will slay the last of them with
the sword.
He who flees from them shall
not get away,
And he who escapes from them
shall not be delivered.

2 "Though they dig into hell,
From there My hand shall take
them;

Though they climb up to
heaven,
From there I will bring them
down;
3 And though they hide
themselves on top of Carmel,
From there I will search and take
them;
Though they hide from My sight
at the bottom of the sea,
From there I will command the
serpent, and it shall bite them;
4 Though they go into captivity
before their enemies,
From there I will command the
sword,
And it shall slay them.
I will set My eyes on them for
harm and not for good."

5 The Lord God of hosts,
He who touches the earth and
it melts,
And all who dwell there mourn;
All of it shall swell like the River,
And subside like the River of
Egypt.
6 He who builds His layers in the
sky,
And has founded His strata in
the earth;
Who calls for the waters of the
sea,
And pours them out on the face
of the earth—
The Lord *is* His name.

7 "*Are* you not like the people of
Ethiopia to Me,
O children of Israel?" says the
Lord.

DIGGING IN

8:11–13 Treasure God's Word The prophet Amos warns you that a time is coming when young people will search for the Word of God and not be able to find it anymore.

Perhaps you don't open your Bible very often. You have to go to school every day and do all the things your teacher tells you. Then you have sports and parties to go to. You may find less and less time for reading God's Word.

These are days when your memory is sharp and strong. Now is the time to store the Scriptures in your mind. "Your word I have hidden in my heart, that I might not sin against You" (Psalm 119:11). If you are going to know God as He really is, and love Him as He wants you to, the Bible must be your best-loved Book. Make a habit of reading God's Word at the same time every day.

What Amos Learned

I used to think prophets were smart. Now I know we aren't. We only know what God tells us. I thought God's work was finished when He allowed Assyria to destroy the Northern Kingdom of Israel over seven hundred years before Jesus came.

Then the Lord showed me what He really had in mind. He was going to bring back His people someday. Not only that, but He had an even bigger plan. He was going to save people of other nations (called Gentiles). In Acts 15:16, 17, you will read where James uses my words to show that God would save everyone.

I sure have a lot to learn about God's wonderful ways.

"Did I not bring up Israel from
   the land of Egypt,
The Philistines from Caphtor,
And the Syrians from Kir?

8 "Behold, the eyes of the Lord
   GOD *are* on the sinful
   kingdom,
And I will destroy it from the face
   of the earth;
Yet I will not utterly destroy the
   house of Jacob,"
Says the LORD.

9 "For surely I will command,
And will sift the house of Israel
   among all nations,
As *grain* is sifted in a sieve;
Yet not the smallest grain shall
   fall to the ground.
10 All the sinners of My people shall
   die by the sword,
Who say, 'The calamity shall not
   overtake nor confront us.'

11 "On that day I will raise up
The tabernacle of David, which
   has fallen down,
And repair its damages;
I will raise up its ruins,
And rebuild it as in the days of
   old;

12 That they may possess the
   remnant of Edom,
And all the **Gentiles** who are
   called by My name,"
Says the LORD who does this
   thing.

13 "Behold, the days are coming,"
   says the LORD,
"When the plowman shall
   overtake the reaper,
And the treader of grapes him
   who sows seed;
The mountains shall drip with
   sweet wine,
And all the hills shall flow *with*
   it.
14 I will bring back the captives of
   My people Israel;
They shall build the waste cities
   and inhabit *them;*
They shall plant vineyards and
   drink wine from them;
They shall also make gardens
   and eat fruit from them.
15 I will plant them in their
   land,
And no longer shall they be
   pulled up
From the land I have given
   them,"
Says the LORD your God.

WORDFINDER

9:12 Gentiles All peoples and nations who are not of the Hebrew race. God promised that the Jews would be a blessing to the Gentiles. Jesus fulfilled that promise.

The Book of
OBADIAH

Mine is the shortest book in the Bible. My name is pronounced *oh-buh-DIE-uh* and means "Servant of the Lord."

In Genesis 27, you can read how Jacob and Esau became enemies. When God chose Jacob to be the father of Israel, Esau went to live in a land south of Israel that became known as Edom (pronounced *EE-dom*), another name for Esau.

My prophecy is against the people of Edom because they persecuted Israel. In my prophecy, I told the people of Edom that God would destroy them, even though they felt safe in their mountain fortress. History books tell us that the people of Edom were forced to leave their high place in the mountains because the traders didn't bring food to their city anymore.

Edom will be destroyed, but God will rebuild

THE vision of Obadiah.

Thus says the Lord GOD
concerning Edom
(We have heard a report from
the LORD,
And a messenger has been
sent among the nations,
saying,
"Arise, and let us rise up against
her for battle"):

2 "Behold, I will make you small
among the nations;
You shall be greatly despised.
3 The pride of your heart has
deceived you,
You who dwell in the clefts of
the rock,
Whose habitation is high;
You who say in your heart,
'Who will bring me down to
the ground?'
4 Though you ascend *as* high as
the eagle,
And though you set your nest
among the stars,
From there I will bring you
down," says the LORD.

5 "If thieves had come to you,
If robbers by night—
Oh, how you will be cut off!—
Would they not have stolen till
they had enough?
If grape-gatherers had come to
you,
Would they not have left *some*
gleanings?

6 "Oh, how Esau shall be searched
out!
How his hidden treasures shall
be sought after!
7 All the men in your
confederacy
Shall force you to the border;
The men at peace with you
Shall deceive you *and* prevail
against you.
Those who eat your bread shall
lay a trap for you.
No one is aware of it.

8 "Will I not in that day," says the
LORD,
"Even destroy the wise *men* from
Edom,
And understanding from the
mountains of Esau?
9 Then your mighty men, O
Teman, shall be dismayed,

To the end that everyone from
the mountains of Esau
May be cut off by slaughter.

10 "For violence against your
brother Jacob,
Shame shall cover you,
And you shall be cut off forever.
11 In the day that you stood on the
other side—
In the day that strangers carried
captive his forces,
When foreigners entered his
gates

And cast lots for Jerusalem—
Even you *were* as one of them.

12 "But you should not have gazed
on the day of your brother
In the day of his captivity;
Nor should you have rejoiced
over the children of Judah
In the day of their destruction;
Nor should you have spoken
proudly
In the day of distress.
13 You should not have entered the
gate of My people

DIGGING IN

2—4 The City of Petra Petra means "rocky" and is called Sela in the Bible. It was the capital of Edom, the last home of Esau, the brother of Jacob. (See Genesis 33:16, 17.) Petra was a city, south of Israel, that was actually carved out of the rock of Mount Seir (pronounced *SEE-ir*).

Esau's descendants were enemies of Israel until his nation of Edom came to an end. That was about two thousand years ago, soon after the time of Christ.

Obadiah tells about the coming fall of Edom and Petra because they tormented God's people.

There was only a narrow pass that went into Petra, so Edom's soldiers could easily defend the city against foreign troops. Then the trade routes changed; and because the city of Petra had no source of food, the people had to leave.

The empty, rocky city of Petra is a standing reminder that God's judgment is always carried out in the end.

The city of Petra in ancient Edom was carved out of sandstone cliffs about three hundred years before Christ.

In the day of their calamity.
Indeed, you should not have
   gazed on their affliction
In the day of their calamity,
Nor laid *hands* on their
   substance
In the day of their calamity.
14 You should not have stood at
   the crossroads
To cut off those among them
   who *escaped*;
Nor should you have delivered
   up those among them who
   remained
In the day of distress.

15 "For the day of the LORD upon
   all the nations *is* near;
As you have done, it shall be
   done to you;
Your reprisal shall return upon
   your own head.
16 For as you drank on my holy
   mountain,
So shall all the nations drink
   continually;
Yes, they shall drink, and
   swallow,
And they shall be as though they
   had never been.

17 "But on Mount Zion there shall
   be deliverance,
And there shall be holiness;
The house of Jacob shall possess
   their possessions.

18 The house of Jacob shall be a
   fire,
And the house of Joseph a
   flame;
But the house of Esau *shall be*
   stubble;
They shall kindle them and
   devour them,
And no survivor shall *remain* of
   the house of Esau,"
For the LORD has spoken.

19 The South shall possess the
   mountains of Esau,
And the Lowland shall possess
   Philistia.
They shall possess the fields of
   Ephraim
And the fields of Samaria.
Benjamin *shall possess* Gilead.
20 And the captives of this host of
   the children of Israel
Shall possess the land of the
   Canaanites
As far as Zarephath.
The captives of Jerusalem who
   are in Sepharad
Shall possess the cities of the
   South.
21 Then saviors shall come to
   Mount Zion
To judge the mountains of
   Esau,
And the kingdom shall be the
   LORD's.

The Book of
JONAH

I'm that amazing prophet who was swallowed alive by a very big fish—and lived to tell the story!

But God had a far more important reason for putting my book in the Bible. One day He commanded me to go and warn the wicked citizens of Nineveh (pronounced *NIN-uh-vuh*) that their city was going to be destroyed.

But the Lord sent a powerful storm on the sea, and our ship nearly sank. You can read in *The Tarshish Times* of all the terrifying things that changed my mind about obeying God. So I finally decided to go preach to the people in Nineveh.

To my surprise the people gave up their sins and accepted the Lord as their God. Therefore, the Lord didn't destroy Nineveh after all.

A big fish swallows Jonah

NOW the word of the LORD came to Jonah the son of Amittai, saying, 2 "Arise, go to Nineveh, that great city, and cry out against it; for their wickedness has come up before Me." 3 But Jonah arose to flee to Tarshish from the presence of the LORD. He went down to Joppa, and found a ship going to Tarshish; so he paid the fare, and went down into it, to go with them to Tarshish from the presence of the LORD.

4 But the LORD sent out a great wind on the sea, and there was a mighty tempest on the sea, so that the ship was about to be broken up.

5 Then the mariners were afraid; and every man cried out to his god, and threw the cargo that *was* in the ship into the sea, to lighten the load. But

God sent a great storm at sea, and Jonah's ship almost sank.

Sailors Toss Passenger Overboard!

Old Testament News Service

TARSHISH—Crewmen from the freighter *Joppa Queen* recounted the following bizarre tale to *Times* reporters yesterday.

It seems the ship had sailed over a month ago from Joppa, Palestine, with ivory, spices, and Persian fabrics for Tarshish.

While the vessel was passing south of Crete, a violent storm arose. It appeared certain the *Joppa Queen* would break up and all on board would drown. Attempts to save the ship by praying to various gods and throwing cargo overboard proved useless.

An Israeli passenger, a prophet named Jonah, then confessed that he himself was the reason for the storm. The man told a fantastic tale of how he had run away from God. He was sure the ship's crew could be saved only if they threw him into the sea. When they finally did so, the storm ceased immediately.

This newspaper is amazed by eyewitness reports that Jonah is alive and well in Nineveh. The prophet has shocked audiences in that city by declaring that he was even swallowed alive by a mysterious sea creature!

Jonah had gone down into the lowest parts of the ship, had lain down, and was fast asleep.

⁶ So the captain came to him, and said to him, "What do you mean, sleeper? Arise, call on your God; perhaps your God will consider us, so that we may not perish."

⁷ And they said to one another, "Come, let us **cast lots,** that we may know for whose cause this trouble *has come* upon us." So they cast lots, and the lot fell on Jonah. ⁸ Then they said to him, "Please tell us! For whose cause *is* this trouble upon us? What is your occupation? And where do you come from? What is your country? And of what people are you?"

⁹ So he said to them, "I *am* a Hebrew; and I fear the LORD, the God of heaven, who made the sea and the dry *land.*"

¹⁰ Then the men were exceedingly afraid, and said to him, "Why have you done this?" For the men knew that he fled from the presence of the LORD, because he had told them. ¹¹ Then they said to him, "What shall we do to you that the sea may be calm for us?"—for the sea was growing more tempestuous.

¹² And he said to them, "Pick me up and throw me into the sea; then the sea will become calm for you. For I know that this great tempest *is* because of me."

¹³ Nevertheless the men rowed hard to return to land, but they could not, for the sea continued to grow more tempestuous against them. ¹⁴ Therefore they cried out to the LORD and said, "We pray, O LORD, please do not let us perish for this man's life, and do not charge us with innocent blood; for You, O LORD, have done as it pleased You." ¹⁵ So they picked up Jonah and threw him into the sea, and the sea ceased from its raging. ¹⁶ Then the men feared the LORD exceedingly, and offered a sacrifice to the LORD and took vows.

¹⁷ Now the LORD had prepared a

⊕**WORDFINDER**

1:7 Casting Lots The way people in ancient times often made difficult choices— by closing their eyes and picking marked "lots" (like dice) out of a jar. See also Acts 1:26.

great fish to swallow Jonah. And Jonah was in the belly of the fish three days and three nights.

God hears Jonah's prayer and rescues him

2 Then Jonah prayed to the LORD his God from the fish's belly. ²And he said:

"I cried out to the LORD because
    of my affliction,
And He answered me.

"Out of the belly of **Sheol** I cried,
    And You heard my voice.
³ For You cast me into the deep,
    Into the heart of the seas,
    And the floods surrounded me;
    All Your billows and Your waves
        passed over me.
⁴ Then I said, 'I have been cast
        out of Your sight;
    Yet I will look again toward Your
        holy temple.'
⁵ The waters surrounded me,
        even to my soul;
    The deep closed around me;
    Weeds were wrapped around
        my head.
⁶ I went down to the moorings of
        the mountains;
    The earth with its bars *closed*
        behind me forever;
    Yet You have brought up my life
        from the pit,
    O LORD, my God.

⁷ "When my soul fainted within
        me,
    I remembered the LORD;
    And my prayer went *up* to
        You,
    Into Your holy temple.

A big fish spit me out on dry land.

⁸ "Those who regard worthless
        idols
    Forsake their own Mercy.
⁹ But I will sacrifice to You
    With the voice of thanksgiving;
    I will pay what I have vowed.
    Salvation *is* of the LORD.''

¹⁰ So the LORD spoke to the fish, and it vomited Jonah onto dry *land.*

A wicked city repents

3 Now the word of the LORD came to Jonah the second time, saying, ²"Arise, go to Nineveh, that great city, and preach to it the message that I tell you.'' ³So Jonah arose and went to Nineveh, according to the word of the LORD. Now Nineveh was an exceedingly great city, a three-day journey *in extent.* ⁴And Jonah began to enter the city on the first day's walk. Then he cried out and said, "Yet forty days, and Nineveh shall be overthrown!''

⁵So the people of Nineveh believed God, proclaimed a fast, and put on sackcloth, from the greatest to the least of them. ⁶Then word came to the king of Nineveh; and he arose from his

---

🔍 **WORDFINDER**

2:2 Sheol Sometimes means "grave." Also a place where souls live after death if they reject God's offer of salvation during their earthly lives.

2:9 Salvation Pronounced *sal-VAY-shun.* A work of saving someone from danger or death. In the Bible, salvation is Christ's work of dying to save us from sin and hell.

How Did Jesus Use Jonah's Story?

Jonah, whose name means "Dove," was born in Gath-Hepher, five miles from Nazareth, where Jesus grew up. Jonah lived more than 760 years before Jesus was born. Jesus compared His time in the tomb, after He was crucified, to the three days and nights Jonah spent in the fish's belly (see Matthew 12:39–41).

throne and laid aside his robe, covered *himself* with sackcloth and sat in ashes. 7 And he caused *it* to be proclaimed and published throughout Nineveh by the decree of the king and his nobles, saying,

Let neither man nor beast, herd nor flock, taste anything; do not let them eat, or drink water. 8 But let man and beast be covered with sackcloth, and cry mightily to God; yes, let every one turn from his evil way and from the violence that is in his hands. 9 Who can tell *if* God will turn and relent, and turn away from His fierce anger, so that we may not perish?

10 Then God saw their works, that they turned from their evil way; and God relented from the disaster that He

had said He would bring upon them, and He did not do it.

God teaches Jonah a lesson

4 But it displeased Jonah exceedingly, and he became angry. 2 So he prayed to the LORD, and said, "Ah, LORD, was not this what I said when I was still in my country? Therefore I fled previously to Tarshish; for I know that You *are* a gracious and merciful God, slow to anger and abundant in lovingkindness, One who relents from doing harm. 3 Therefore now, O LORD, please take my life from me, for *it is* better for me to die than to live!"

4 Then the LORD said, "*Is it* right for you to be angry?"

5 So Jonah went out of the city and sat on the east side of the city. There he made himself a shelter and sat under it in the shade, till he might see what would become of the city. 6 And the LORD God prepared a plant and made it come up over Jonah, that it might be shade for his head to deliver him from his misery. So Jonah was very grateful for the plant. 7 But as morning dawned the next day God prepared a worm, and it *so* damaged the plant that it withered. 8 And it happened, when the sun arose, that God prepared a vehement east wind; and the sun beat on Jonah's head, so that he grew faint. Then he wished death for himself, and said, "*It is* better for me to die than to live."

9 Then God said to Jonah, "*Is it* right

DIGGING IN

3:2 Nineveh Nineveh, the capital of ancient Assyria, was one of the largest and oldest cities of the world in Jonah's day. It had been founded by Nimrod, a great-grandson of Noah (see Genesis 10:8–11).

Surrounding nations destroyed Nineveh in 612 B.C. For hundreds of years no one knew exactly where the city was located. But about 150 years ago Sir Austen Layard discovered and dug up its ruins. So now we know a great deal about Nineveh.

You can read about King Sennacherib (pronounced Sen-AK-er-ib) in Isaiah 36 and 37. He built a wall fifty feet high surrounding inner Nineveh. Scholars have also discovered there the beautiful palaces of King Sennacherib and King Ashurbanipal, as well as a huge library.

In 763 B.C. Jonah warned the people of Nineveh that the city would be destroyed because of their wickedness. But the Ninevites repented of their sins, and the city was spared for nearly two hundred years more.

What Jonah Learned

When I tried to run away to Tarshish, I learned two important lessons—

First, God is always near me. When He sent the storm, and the sailors threw me into the sea, that was bad enough. But then that huge fish swallowed me, and I was sure I had come to the end of my life! *But God saved me.* So I learned that God will never leave me (see Hebrews 13:5).

The second thing I learned was that God always makes sure His orders are carried out. So I discovered that it is better to obey God the first time He tells me to do something. That makes more sense than obeying God only after I've been *swallowed by a huge problem,* doesn't it?

for you to be angry about the plant?''

And he said, "*It is right for me to be angry, even to death!*"

10 But the LORD said, "You have had pity on the plant for which you have not labored, nor made it grow, which came up in a night and perished in a night. 11 And should I not pity Nineveh, that great city, in which are more than one hundred and twenty thousand persons who cannot discern between their right hand and their left—and much livestock?"

The Book of
MICAH

My name is pronounced *MY-ka* and means "Who Is Like the Lord?" Most people remember me because, like Isaiah, I told about the birth of Jesus, who was born over seven hundred years later. See Micah 5:2; then look at Isaiah 9:6.

And like Amos, who was a prophet to the Northern Kingdom, I warned the rich about their actions in the Southern Kingdom. God wanted everyone in Israel to live on the land without paying rent, but rich landowners were cruel to people whose land had been stolen from them. Also, some of the merchants were cheating the people and bribing the leaders.

But I was glad I could promise my people that God would someday take away all our sins.

Hard times ahead for Israel and Judah

THE word of the LORD that came to Micah of Moresheth in the days of Jotham, Ahaz, *and* Hezekiah, kings of Judah, which he saw concerning Samaria and Jerusalem.

2 Hear, all you peoples!
Listen, O earth, and all that is in it!
Let the Lord GOD be a witness against you,
The Lord from His holy temple.

3 For behold, the LORD is coming out of His place;
He will come down
And tread on the high places of the earth.

4 The mountains will melt under Him,
And the valleys will split
Like wax before the fire,
Like waters poured down a steep place.

5 All this is for the transgression of Jacob
And for the sins of the house of Israel.
What *is* the transgression of Jacob?

Is it not Samaria?
And what *are* the high places of Judah?
Are they not Jerusalem?

6 "Therefore I will make Samaria a heap of ruins in the field,
Places for planting a vineyard;
I will pour down her stones into the valley,
And I will uncover her foundations.

7 All her carved images shall be beaten to pieces,
And all her pay as a harlot shall be burned with the fire;
All her idols I will lay desolate,
For she gathered *it* from the pay of a harlot,
And they shall return to the pay of a harlot."

8 Therefore I will wail and howl,
I will go stripped and naked;
I will make a wailing like the jackals
And a mourning like the ostriches,

9 For her wounds *are* incurable.
For it has come to Judah;
It has come to the gate of My people—
To Jerusalem.

10 Tell *it* not in Gath,
    Weep not at all;
    In Beth Aphrah
    Roll yourself in the dust.
11 Pass by in naked shame, you
        inhabitant of Shaphir;
    The inhabitant of Zaanan does
        not go out.
    Beth Ezel mourns;
    Its place to stand is taken away
        from you.

12 For the inhabitant of Maroth
        pined for good,
    But disaster came down from
        the LORD
    To the gate of Jerusalem.
13 O inhabitant of Lachish,
    Harness the chariot to the swift
        steeds
    (She *was* the beginning of sin
        to the daughter of Zion),
    For the transgressions of Israel
        were found in you.

14 Therefore you shall give
        presents to Moresheth Gath;
    The houses of Achzib *shall be* a
        lie to the kings of Israel.
15 I will yet bring an heir to you,
        O inhabitant of Mareshah;
    The glory of Israel shall come to
        Adullam.
16 Make yourself bald and cut off
        your hair,
    Because of your precious
        children;
    Enlarge your baldness like an
        eagle,
    For they shall go from you into
        captivity.

God despises unfairness

2 Woe to those who devise
        iniquity,
    And work out evil on their
        beds!
    At morning light they practice it,
    Because it is in the power of their
        hand.
2 They covet fields and take *them*
        by violence,
    Also houses, and seize *them*.

So they oppress a man and his
    house,
A man and his inheritance.

3 Therefore thus says the LORD:

"Behold, against this family I am
    devising disaster,
From which you cannot remove
    your necks;
Nor shall you walk haughtily,
For this *is* an evil time.
4 In that day *one* shall take up a
    proverb against you,
And lament with a bitter
    lamentation, saying:
'We are utterly destroyed!
He has changed the heritage of
    my people;
How He has removed *it* from
    me!
To a turncoat He has divided
    our fields.' "

5 Therefore you will have no one
    to determine boundaries by
    lot
In the assembly of the LORD.

6 "Do not prattle," *you say to those*
    who prophesy.
So they shall not prophesy to
    you;
They shall not return insult for
    insult.
7 *You who are* named the house
    of Jacob:
"Is the Spirit of the LORD
    restricted?
Are these His doings?
Do not My words do good
To him who walks uprightly?

8 "Lately My people have risen up
    as an enemy—
You pull off the robe with the
    garment
From those who trust *you*, as
    they pass by,
Like men returned from war.
9 The women of My people you
    cast out
From their pleasant houses;
From their children

You have taken away My glory
    forever.

10 "Arise and depart,
    For this *is* not *your* rest;
    Because it is defiled, it shall
      destroy,
    Yes, with utter destruction.
11 If a man should walk in a false
      spirit
    And speak a lie, *saying,*
    'I will prophesy to you of wine
      and drink,'
    Even he would be the prattler
      of this people.

12 "I will surely assemble all of you,
      O Jacob,
    I will surely gather the remnant
      of Israel;
    I will put them together like
      sheep of the fold,
    Like a flock in the midst of their
      pasture;
    They shall make a loud noise
      because of *so many* people.
13 The one who breaks open will
      come up before them;
    They will break out,
    Pass through the gate,
    And go out by it;
    Their king will pass before them,
    With the LORD at their head."

Wicked leaders are punished

3 And I said:

    "Hear now, O heads of Jacob,
    And you rulers of the house of
      Israel:
    Is it not for you to know justice?
2 You who hate good and love
      evil;
    Who strip the skin from My
      people,
    And the flesh from their bones;
3 Who also eat the flesh of My
      people,
    Flay their skin from them,
    Break their bones,
    And chop *them* in pieces
    Like *meat* for the pot,
    Like flesh in the caldron."

4 Then they will cry to the LORD,
    But He will not hear them;
    He will even hide His face from
      them at that time,
    Because they have been evil in
      their deeds.
5 Thus says the LORD concerning
      the prophets
    Who make my people stray;
    Who chant "Peace"
    While they chew with their teeth,
    But who prepare war against
      him
    Who puts nothing into their
      mouths:
6 "Therefore you shall have night
      without vision,
    And you shall have darkness
      without divination;
    The sun shall go down on the
      prophets,
    And the day shall be dark for
      them.
7 So the seers shall be ashamed,
    And the diviners abashed;
    Indeed they shall all cover their
      lips;
    For *there is* no answer from
      God."

8 But truly I am full of power by
      the Spirit of the LORD,
    And of justice and might,
    To declare to Jacob his
      transgression
    And to Israel his sin.
9 Now hear this,
    You heads of the house of Jacob
    And rulers of the house of Israel,
    Who abhor justice
    And pervert all equity,
10 Who build up Zion with
      bloodshed
    And Jerusalem with iniquity:
11 Her heads judge for a bribe,
    Her priests teach for pay,
    And her prophets divine for
      money.
    Yet they lean on the LORD, and
      say,
    "Is not the LORD among us?
    No harm can come upon us."
12 Therefore because of you

Zion shall be plowed *like* a field,
Jerusalem shall become heaps
  of ruins,
And the mountain of the temple
Like the bare hills of the forest.

Someday there will be no more war

4 Now it shall come to pass in the
    latter days
  That the mountain of the LORD's
    house
  Shall be established on the top
    of the mountains,
  And shall be exalted above the
    hills;
  And peoples shall flow to it.
2 Many nations shall come and
    say,
  "Come, and let us go up to the
    mountain of the LORD,
  To the house of the God of
    Jacob;
  He will teach us His ways,
  And we shall walk in His paths."
  For out of Zion the law shall go
    forth,
  And the word of the LORD from
    Jerusalem.
3 He shall judge between many
    peoples,
  And rebuke strong nations afar
    off;
  They shall beat their swords into
    plowshares,
  And their spears into pruning
    hooks;
  Nation shall not lift up sword
    against nation,
  Neither shall they learn war
    anymore.

4 But everyone shall sit under his
    vine and under his fig tree,
  And no one shall make *them*
    afraid;
  For the mouth of the LORD of
    hosts has spoken.
5 For all people walk each in the
    name of his god,
  But we will walk in the name of
    the LORD our God
  Forever and ever.

6 "In that day," says the LORD,
  "I will assemble the lame,
  I will gather the outcast
  And those whom I have afflicted;
7 I will make the lame a remnant,
  And the outcast a strong nation;
  So the LORD will reign over them
    in Mount Zion
  From now on, even forever.
8 And you, O tower of the flock,
  The stronghold of the daughter
    of Zion,
  To you shall it come,
  Even the former dominion shall
    come,
  The kingdom of the daughter of
    Jerusalem."

9 Now why do you cry aloud?
  Is there no king in your midst?
  Has your counselor perished?
  For pangs have seized you like
    a woman in labor.
10 Be in pain, and labor to bring
     forth,
   O daughter of Zion,
   Like a woman in birth pangs.
   For now you shall go forth from
     the city,
   You shall dwell in the field,
   And to Babylon you shall go.
   There you shall be delivered;
   There the LORD will redeem you
   From the hand of your enemies.

11 Now also many nations have
     gathered against you,
   Who say, "Let her be defiled,
   And let our eye look upon
     Zion."
12 But they do not know the
     thoughts of the LORD,
   Nor do they understand His
     counsel;
   For He will gather them like
     sheaves to the threshing floor.

13 "Arise and thresh, O daughter of
     Zion;
   For I will make your horn iron,
   And I will make your hooves
     bronze;
   You shall beat in pieces many
     peoples;

I will consecrate their gain to the
  LORD,
And their substance to the Lord
  of the whole earth."

The Messiah will come from Bethlehem

5 Now gather yourself in troops,
  O daughter of troops;
He has laid siege against us;
They will strike the judge of
  Israel with a rod on the
  cheek.
2 "But you, Bethlehem Ephrathah,
  Though you are little among the
  thousands of Judah,

Yet out of you shall come forth
  to Me
The One to be Ruler in Israel,
Whose goings forth *are* from of
  old,
From everlasting."

3   Therefore He shall give them up,
  Until the time *that* she who is
    in labor has given birth;
  Then the remnant of His
    brethren
  Shall return to the children of
    Israel.
4   And He shall stand and feed *His
    flock*
  In the strength of the LORD,

DIGGING IN

5:2 Jesus Will Be Born in Bethlehem
Did you know that the Christmas story is also told in the Old Testament? Isaiah 7:14 and Micah 5:2 tell about the birth of Jesus, the coming Messiah—over seven hundred years before He was born!

Micah even tells where Jesus would be born—in Bethlehem. This city of Israel has a long history. Bethlehem became famous first in the Book of Ruth. Ruth was the great-grandmother of David, who called Bethlehem "the city of David." A

thousand years later, Mary and Joseph came from the family of David. At that time, the Roman government made a law that everyone had to go back to his hometown to sign his name in a government book. Therefore, Mary and Joseph had to go to Bethlehem (see Luke 2:3, 4).

Bethlehem means "House of Bread." The city truly was a house of bread, because Jesus, "the Bread of Life," came from Bethlehem (see John 6:35).

This church was built over the place where Jesus is thought to have been born in Bethlehem.

In the majesty of the name of
   the Lord His God;
And they shall abide,
For now He shall be great
To the ends of the earth;
5 And this *One* shall be peace.

When the Assyrian comes into
   our land,
And when he treads in our
   palaces,
Then we will raise against him
Seven shepherds and eight
   princely men.
6 They shall waste with the sword
   the land of Assyria,
And the land of Nimrod at its
   entrances;
Thus He shall deliver *us* from the
   Assyrian,
When he comes into our land
And when he treads within our
   borders.

7 Then the remnant of Jacob
Shall be in the midst of many
   peoples,
Like dew from the Lord,
Like showers on the grass,
That tarry for no man
Nor wait for the sons of men.
8 And the remnant of Jacob
Shall be among the **Gentiles**,
In the midst of many peoples,
Like a lion among the beasts of
   the forest,
Like a young lion among flocks
   of sheep,
Who, if he passes through,
Both treads down and tears in
   pieces,
And none can deliver.
9 Your hand shall be lifted against
   your adversaries,
And all your enemies shall be
   cut off.

10 "And it shall be in that day," says
   the Lord,

"That I will cut off your horses
   from your midst
And destroy your chariots.
11 I will cut off the cities of your
   land
And throw down all your
   strongholds.
12 I will cut off sorceries from your
   hand,
And you shall have no
   soothsayers.
13 Your carved images I will also
   cut off,
And your sacred pillars from
   your midst;
You shall no more worship the
   work of your hands;
14 I will pluck your wooden images
   from your midst;
Thus I will destroy your cities.
15 And I will execute vengeance in
   anger and fury
On the nations that have not
   heard."

God asks His people to state their case

6 Hear now what the Lord says:

"Arise, plead your case before the
   mountains,
And let the hills hear your voice.
2 Hear, O you mountains, the
   Lord's complaint,
And you strong foundations of
   the earth;
For the Lord has a complaint
   against His people,
And He will contend with Israel.

3 "O My people, what have I done
   to you?
And how have I wearied you?
Testify against Me.
4 For I brought you up from the
   land of Egypt,
I redeemed you from the house
   of bondage;

WORDFINDER

5:8 Gentiles All peoples and nations who are not of the Hebrew race. God promised that the Jews would be a blessing to the Gentiles. Jesus fulfilled that promise.

What We All Must Learn

In Old Testament times, we used to think God mainly wanted us to offer sacrifices. And He did command us to worship by making sacrifices until Jesus came. Jesus would give Himself as the great sacrifice for our sins.

But God was not impressed by our sacrifices. More than anything else, He wanted us to live in a way that proved we really were His special people. When we didn't, God was angry with our sacrifices.

Saying "Jesus died for my sins" means nothing to God if we go on living as though He never died. If we ask Him, and we mean it, Jesus will take away our sins, and we will please Him in the way we live. "Do justly, love mercy, and walk humbly with your God."

And I sent before you Moses,
Aaron, and Miriam.

5 O My people, remember now
What Balak king of Moab
counseled,
And what Balaam the son of
Beor answered him,
From Acacia Grove to Gilgal,
That you may know the
righteousness of the LORD."

6 With what shall I come before
the LORD,
And bow myself before the High
God?
Shall I come before Him with
burnt offerings,
With calves a year old?

7 Will the LORD be pleased with
thousands of rams,
Ten thousand rivers of oil?
Shall I give my firstborn *for* my
transgression,
The fruit of my body *for* the sin
of my soul?

8 He has shown you, O man, what
is good;
And what does the LORD require
of you
But to do justly,
To love mercy,
And to walk humbly with your
God?

9 The LORD's voice cries to the
city—
Wisdom shall see Your name:

"Hear the rod!
Who has appointed it?

10 Are there yet the treasures of
wickedness
In the house of the wicked,
And the short measure *that is* an
abomination?

11 Shall I count pure *those* with the
wicked scales,
And with the bag of deceitful
weights?

12 For her rich men are full of
violence,
Her inhabitants have spoken
lies,
And their tongue is deceitful in
their mouth.

13 "Therefore I will also make *you*
sick by striking you,
By making *you* desolate because
of your sins.

14 You shall eat, but not be
satisfied;
Hunger *shall be* in your midst.
You may carry *some* away, but
shall not save *them;*
And what you do rescue I will
give over to the sword.

15 "You shall sow, but not reap;
You shall tread the olives, but
not anoint yourselves with oil;
And *make* sweet wine, but not
drink wine.

16 For the statutes of Omri are
kept;
All the works of Ahab's house
are done;

And you walk in their counsels,
That I may make you a
    desolation,
And your inhabitants a hissing.
Therefore you shall bear the
    reproach of My people."

God will be kind to Israel

7 Woe is me!
For I am like those who gather
    summer fruits,
Like those who glean vintage
    grapes;
There is no cluster to eat
Of the first-ripe fruit *which* my
    soul desires.

2 The faithful *man* has perished
    from the *earth,*
And *there is* no one upright
    among men.
They all lie in wait for blood;
Every man hunts his brother
    with a net.

3 That they may successfully do
    evil with both hands—
The prince asks *for gifts,*
The judge *seeks* a bribe,
And the great *man* utters his evil
    desire;
So they scheme together.

4 The best of them *is* like a
    brier;
The most upright *is sharper* than
    a thorn hedge;
The day of your watchman and
    your punishment comes;
Now shall be their perplexity.

5 Do not trust in a friend;
Do not put your confidence in
    a companion;
Guard the doors of your mouth
From her who lies in your
    bosom.

6 For son dishonors father,
Daughter rises against her
    mother,
Daughter-in-law against her
    mother-in-law;
A man's enemies *are* the men
    of his own household.

7 Therefore I will look to the LORD;
I will wait for the God of my
    salvation;
My God will hear me.

8 Do not rejoice over me, my
    enemy;
When I fall, I will arise;
When I sit in darkness,
The LORD *will be* a light to me.

9 I will bear the indignation of the
    LORD,
Because I have sinned against
    Him,
Until He pleads my case
And executes justice for me.
He will bring me forth to the
    light;
I will see His righteousness.

10 Then *she who is* my enemy will
    see,
And shame will cover her who
    said to me,
"Where is the LORD your God?"
My eyes will see her;
Now she will be trampled down
Like mud in the streets.

What Micah Learned

I always wanted a friend I could trust. A true friend is a wonderful gift.
But I learned that no human friend can be trusted completely.

It isn't fair to expect my friends to be more faithful than I am. I know I
often fail. And even my dearest friends fail me sometimes. But if we love
our friends, we shouldn't expect them to be perfect.

We can be more patient with those we love when we know we can
count on the Lord never to fail us. Someday, when we come to the end
of our lives, we will find out that Jesus is the Friend who sticks closer
than a brother (see Proverbs 18:24).

What Israel Learned

Our sins have been very great, but there is hope for us now. We have suffered a lot for our sins in a foreign land, and we realize we need God's forgiveness.

We also know we can't make ourselves good. Only God can make us what He wants us to be. So we are going to trust in Him to lead us.

God has told us He is going to bury our sins in the depths of the sea. That means He is going to forgive and forget all our disobedience. Also, He is going to teach us His truth.

What is God's truth? Years after I lived and wrote and prophesied, Jesus said, "I am the Truth." So please accept Jesus as the Truth who makes you free from sin.

11 In the day when your walls are
        to be built,
    In that day the decree shall go
        far and wide.
12 In that day they shall come to
        you
    From Assyria and the fortified
        cities,
    From the fortress to the River,
    From sea to sea,
    And mountain to mountain.
13 Yet the land shall be desolate
    Because of those who dwell in
        it,
    And for the fruit of their deeds.

14 Shepherd Your people with
        Your staff,
    The flock of Your heritage,
    Who dwell solitarily in a
        woodland,
    In the midst of Carmel;
    Let them feed in Bashan and
        Gilead,
    As in days of old.

15 "As in the days when you came
        out of the land of Egypt,
    I will show them wonders."

16 The nations shall see and be
        ashamed of all their might;

    They shall put their hand over
        their mouth;
    Their ears shall be deaf.
17 They shall lick the dust like a
        serpent;
    They shall crawl from their holes
        like snakes of the earth.
    They shall be afraid of the LORD
        our God,
    And shall fear because of You.
18 Who is a God like You,
    Pardoning iniquity
    And passing over the
        transgression of the remnant
        of His heritage?

    He does not retain His anger
        forever,
    Because He delights in mercy.
19 He will again have compassion
        on us,
    And will subdue our iniquities.

    You will cast all our sins
    Into the depths of the sea.
20 You will give truth to Jacob
    And mercy to Abraham,
    Which You have sworn to our
        fathers
    From days of old.

The Book of
NAHUM

My name is pronounced *NAY-hum* and means "Compassionate." My little book should be read along with Jonah's prophecy, because both books are about the city of Nineveh.

Jonah was sent to preach the gospel to Nineveh 623 years before Christ, and to Jonah's surprise the people believed him and repented. Because the people turned to God, Nineveh was not destroyed that time.

Years later, I again warned that Nineveh was going to be destroyed, but the people didn't listen to me. So my book describes how Nineveh was destroyed in a terrible street battle. You can almost hear the clatter of the horses' hooves, see the flash of the spears, and smell the smoke of the burning city!

Over one hundred years before, the army of Assyria had conquered the Northern Kingdom of Israel. But now Nineveh, the capital of Assyria itself, was destroyed.

The Lord will judge Nineveh with mercy

THE burden against Nineveh. The book of the vision of Nahum the Elkoshite.

2   God *is* jealous, and the LORD avenges;
    The LORD avenges and *is* furious.
    The LORD will take vengeance on His adversaries,
    And He reserves *wrath* for His enemies;
3   The LORD *is* slow to anger and great in power,
    And will not at all acquit *the wicked.*

    The LORD has His way
    In the whirlwind and in the storm,
    And the clouds *are* the dust of His feet.
4   He rebukes the sea and makes it dry,
    And dries up all the rivers.
    Bashan and Carmel wither,

And the flower of Lebanon wilts.
5   The mountains quake before Him,
    The hills melt,
    And the earth heaves at His presence,
    Yes, the world and all who dwell in it.

6   Who can stand before His indignation?
    And who can endure the fierceness of His anger?
    His fury is poured out like fire,
    And the rocks are thrown down by Him.

7   The LORD *is* good,
    A stronghold in the day of trouble;
    And He knows those who trust in Him.
8   But with an overflowing flood
    He will make an utter end of its place,
    And darkness will pursue His enemies.

9 What do you conspire against
the Lord?
He will make an utter end *of it.*
Affliction will not rise up a
second time.
10 For while tangled *like* thorns,
And while drunken *like*
drunkards,
They shall be devoured like
stubble fully dried.
11 From you comes forth *one*
Who plots evil against the Lord,
A wicked counselor.

12 Thus says the Lord:

"Though *they are* safe, and
likewise many,
Yet in this manner they will be
cut down
When he passes through.
Though I have afflicted you,
I will afflict you no more;
13 For now I will break off his yoke
from you,
And burst your bonds apart."

14 The Lord has given a command
concerning you:
"Your name shall be perpetuated
no longer.
Out of the house of your gods
I will cut off the carved image
and the molded image.
I will dig your grave,
For you are vile."

15 Behold, on the mountains
The feet of him who brings good
tidings,
Who proclaims peace!
O Judah, keep your appointed
feasts,
Perform your vows.
For the wicked one shall no
more pass through you;
He is utterly cut off.

A great city will fall

2 He who scatters has come up
before your face.
Man the fort!
Watch the road!

Strengthen *your* flanks!
Fortify *your* power mightily.

2 For the Lord will restore the
excellence of Jacob
Like the excellence of Israel,
For the emptiers have emptied
them out
And ruined their vine branches.

3 The shields of his mighty men
are made red,
The valiant men *are* in scarlet.
The chariots *come* with flaming
torches
In the day of his preparation,
And the spears are brandished.
4 The chariots rage in the streets,
They jostle one another in the
broad roads;
They seem like torches,
They run like lightning.

5 He remembers his nobles;
They stumble in their walk;
They make haste to her walls,
And the defense is prepared.
6 The gates of the rivers are
opened,
And the palace is dissolved.
7 It is decreed:
She shall be led away captive,
She shall be brought up;
And her maidservants shall lead
her as with the voice of doves,
Beating their breasts.

8 Though Nineveh of old *was* like
a pool of water,
Now they flee away.
"Halt! Halt!" *they cry;*
But no one turns back.
9 Take spoil of silver!
Take spoil of gold!
There is no end of treasure,
Or wealth of *every* desirable
prize.
10 She is empty, desolate, and
waste!
The heart melts, and the knees
shake;
Much pain *is* in every side,
And all their faces are drained
of color.

Nineveh in Ashes

World Press International

NINEVEH—News teams from around the world are watching as Nineveh (pronounced *NIN-uh-uuh*) goes up in smoke. This capital of Assyria (pronounced *ah-SEER-ih-ah*), dating back for centuries before our time, is in ruins.

The army of Babylon has run over the troops of Nineveh, and the enemy chariots are racing through the streets. Everywhere there is death and destruction.

Everyone present at this scene remembers Jonah's prophecy in 660 B.C.

When Jonah preached to the city, the people repented and the Lord spared Nineveh. But later generations did not repent. Now God's judgment is being carried out on the nation that destroyed the Northern Kingdom of Israel in 722 B.C.

How the mighty are fallen in Nineveh! Today all nations are seeing that the Lord is kind and patient while He waits for His people. But they must call on Him while he is still waiting!

11 Where *is* the dwelling of the
        lions,
    And the feeding place of the
        young lions,
    Where the lion walked, the
        lioness *and* lion's cub,
    And no one made *them* afraid?
12 The lion tore in pieces enough
        for his cubs,
    Killed for his lionesses,
    Filled his caves with prey,
    And his dens with flesh.

13 "Behold, I *am* against you," says
the LORD of hosts, "I will burn your
chariots in smoke, and the sword shall
devour your young lions; I will cut off
your prey from the earth, and the voice
of your messengers shall be heard no
more."

Nineveh's wounds will not heal

3 Woe to the bloody city!
    It *is* all full of lies *and* robbery.
    Its victim never departs.
2   The noise of a whip
    And the noise of rattling wheels,
    Of galloping horses,
    Of clattering chariots!
3   Horsemen charge with bright
        sword and glittering spear.
    There is a multitude of slain,
    A great number of bodies,

    Countless corpses—
    They stumble over the
        corpses—
4   Because of the multitude of
        harlotries of the seductive
        harlot,
    The mistress of sorceries,
    Who sells nations through her
        harlotries,
    And families through her
        sorceries.

5   "Behold, I *am* against you," says
        the LORD of hosts;
    "I will lift your skirts over your
        face,
    I will show the nations your
        nakedness,
    And the kingdoms your shame.
6   I will cast abominable filth upon
        you,
    Make you vile,
    And make you a spectacle.
7   It shall come to pass *that* all who
        look upon you
    Will flee from you, and say,
    'Nineveh is laid waste!
    Who will bemoan her?'
    Where shall I seek comforters for
        you?"

8   Are you better than No Amon
    That was situated by the River,
    That had the waters around her,

The ruins of ancient Thebes in Egypt. Nahum called this city No Amon.

Whose rampart *was* the sea,
Whose wall *was* the sea?
9 Ethiopia and Egypt *were* her
strength,
And *it was* boundless;
Put and Lubim *were* your
helpers.
10 Yet she *was* carried away,
She went into captivity;
Her young children also were
dashed to pieces
At the head of every street;
They cast lots for her honorable
men,
And all her great men *were*
bound in chains.
11 You also will be drunk;
You will be hidden;
You also will seek refuge from
the enemy.

12 All your strongholds *are* fig trees
with ripened figs:
If they are shaken,
They fall into the mouth of the
eater.
13 Surely, your people in your
midst *are* women!
The gates of your land are wide
open for your enemies;

Fire shall devour the bars of your
gates.
14 Draw your water for the siege!
Fortify your strongholds!
Go into the clay and tread the
mortar!
Make strong the brick kiln!
15 There the fire will devour you,
The sword will cut you off;
It will eat you up like a locust.

Make yourself many—like the
locust!
Make yourself many— like the
swarming locusts!
16 You have multiplied your
merchants more than the stars
of heaven.
The locust plunders and flies
away.
17 Your commanders *are* like
swarming locusts,
And your generals like great
grasshoppers,
Which camp in the hedges on
a cold day;
When the sun rises they flee
away,

And the place where they *are* is
   not known.

18 Your shepherds slumber, O king
   of Assyria;
Your nobles rest *in the dust.*
Your people are scattered on the
   mountains,

And no one gathers them.
19 Your injury *has* no healing,
Your wound is severe.
All who hear news of you
Will clap *their* hands over you,
For upon whom has not your
   wickedness passed
   continually?

The Book of
HABAKKUK

I wrote my book to tell you how I waited until God answered my hard questions. My name is pronounced *huh-BACK-kuk* and means "Embraced by God."

I wanted the Lord to tell me why He was allowing so much crime in our land. You may sometimes hear your folks ask the same question about your own country.

But God told me He was only giving our people time to change their ways. If they didn't, He would send our enemies against us. I was sad because I couldn't believe the Lord would destroy our cities. So I waited for the Lord's answer, like a man watching on a tower.

God proved that I could trust Him always to do what is right. He did punish us as we deserved, but later He helped us build our cities again. So I have learned to sing for joy to God my Savior.

Why do bad things happen to good people?

THE burden which the prophet Habakkuk saw.

2 O LORD, how long shall I cry,
And You will not hear?
Even cry out to You,
"Violence!"
And You will not save.
3 Why do You show me iniquity,
And cause *me* to see trouble?
For plundering and violence *are*
before me;
There is strife, and contention
arises.
4 Therefore the law is powerless,
And justice never goes forth.
For the wicked surround the
righteous;
Therefore perverse judgment
proceeds.

5 "Look among the nations and
watch—
Be utterly astounded!
For *I will* work a work in your
days
Which you would not believe,
though it were told *you*.
6 For indeed I am raising up the
Chaldeans,

A bitter and hasty nation
Which marches through the
breadth of the earth,
To possess dwelling places *that
are* not theirs.
7 They are terrible and dreadful;
Their judgment and their
dignity proceed from
themselves.
8 Their horses also are swifter than
leopards,
And more fierce than evening
wolves.
Their chargers charge ahead;
Their cavalry comes from afar;
They fly as the eagle *that* hastens
to eat.

9 "They all come for violence;
Their faces are set *like* the east
wind.
They gather captives like sand.
10 They scoff at kings,
And princes are scorned by
them.
They deride every stronghold,
For they heap up earthen
mounds and seize it.
11 Then *his* mind changes, and he
transgresses;
He commits offense,
Ascribing this power to his
god."

12 Are You not from everlasting,
   O LORD my God, my Holy
   One?
   We shall not die.
   O LORD, You have appointed
   them for judgment;
   O Rock, You have marked them
   for correction.
13 *You are* of purer eyes than to
   behold evil,
   And cannot look on wickedness.
   Why do You look on those who
   deal treacherously,
   And hold Your tongue when the
   wicked devours
   A *person* more righteous than
   he?
14 *Why* do You make men like fish
   of the sea,
   Like creeping things *that have*
   no ruler over them?

15 They take up all of them with a
   hook,
   They catch them in their net,
   And gather them in their
   dragnet.
   Therefore they rejoice and are
   glad.
16 Therefore they sacrifice to their
   net,
   And burn incense to their
   dragnet;
   Because by them their share *is*
   sumptuous
   And their food plentiful.
17 Shall they therefore empty their
   net,
   And continue to slay nations
   without pity?

God gives Habakkuk some answers

2 I will stand my watch
   And set myself on the rampart,
   And watch to see what He will
   say to me,
   And what I will answer when I
   am corrected.

2 Then the LORD answered me and
said:

What Is a Watchtower?

The prophet Habakkuk was like a man
waiting on a watchtower for God's answers to his questions. You have seen
pictures of watchtowers used to watch
for forest fires. An Old Testament
watchtower was used to watch for riders coming toward the city. But Habakkuk was watching for God.

"Write the vision
   And make *it* plain on tablets,
   That he may run who reads it.
3 For the vision *is* yet for an
   appointed time;
   But at the end it will speak, and
   it will not lie.
   Though it tarries, wait for it;
   Because it will surely come,
   It will not tarry.

*Tall watchtowers made it possible for
landowners to spot wild animals and other
enemies.*

4 "Behold the proud,
  His soul is not upright in him;
  But the just shall live by his faith.

5 "Indeed, because he transgresses
    by wine,
  He is a proud man,
  And he does not stay at home.
  Because he enlarges his desire
    as hell,
  And he *is* like death, and cannot
    be satisfied,
  He gathers to himself all nations
  And heaps up for himself all
    peoples.

6 "Will not all these take up a
    proverb against him,
  And a taunting riddle against
    him, and say,
  'Woe to him who increases
  What is not his—how long?
  And to him who loads himself
    with many pledges'?

7 Will not your creditors rise up
    suddenly?
  Will they not awaken who
    oppress you?
  And you will become their
    booty.

8 Because you have plundered
    many nations,
  All the remnant of the people
    shall plunder you,
  Because of men's blood
  And the violence of the land *and*
    the city,
  And of all who dwell in it.

9 "Woe to him who covets evil gain
    for his house,
  That he may set his nest on high,
  That he may be delivered from
    the power of disaster!

10 You give shameful counsel to
    your house,
  Cutting off many peoples,
  And sin *against* your soul.

11 For the stone will cry out from
    the wall,
  And the beam from the timbers
    will answer it.

12 "Woe to him who builds a town
    with bloodshed,

Who establishes a city by
  iniquity!

13 Behold, *is it* not of the LORD of
    hosts
  That the peoples labor to feed
    the fire,
  And nations weary themselves in
    vain?

14 For the earth will be filled
  With the knowledge of the glory
    of the LORD,
  As the waters cover the sea.

15 "Woe to him who gives drink to
    his neighbor,
  Pressing *him to* your bottle,
  Even to make *him* drunk,
  That you may look on his
    nakedness!

16 You are filled with shame
    instead of glory.
  You also—drink!
  And be exposed as
    uncircumcised!
  The cup of the LORD's right hand
    will be turned against you,
  And utter shame will be on your
    glory.

17 For the violence *done to*
    Lebanon will cover you,
  And the plunder of beasts *which*
    made them afraid,
  Because of men's blood
  And the violence of the land *and*
    the city,
  And of all who dwell in it.

18 "What profit is the image, that its
    maker should carve it,
  The molded image, a teacher of
    lies,
  That the maker of its mold
    should trust in it,
  To make mute idols?

19 Woe to him who says to wood,
    'Awake!'
  To silent stone, 'Arise! It shall
    teach!'
  Behold, it is overlaid with gold
    and silver,
  Yet in it there is no breath at
    all.

20 "But the LORD is in His holy
    temple.

Let all the earth keep silence
   before Him."

Habakkuk sings a song of triumph

3 A prayer of Habakkuk the prophet,
on Shigionoth.

2   O LORD, I have heard Your
      speech *and* was afraid;
   O LORD, revive Your work in the
      midst of the years!
   In the midst of the years make
      it known;
   In wrath remember mercy.

3   God came from Teman,
   The Holy One from Mount
      Paran.   Selah

   His glory covered the heavens,
   And the earth was full of His
      praise.
4   *His* brightness was like the light;
   He had rays *flashing* from His
      hand,
   And there His power *was*
      hidden.
5   Before Him went pestilence,
   And fever followed at His feet.

6   He stood and measured the
      earth;
   He looked and startled the
      nations.
   And the everlasting mountains
      were scattered,
   The perpetual hills bowed.
   His ways *are* everlasting.

7   I saw the tents of Cushan in
      affliction;
   The curtains of the land of
      Midian trembled.

8   O LORD, were *You* displeased
      with the rivers,
   Was Your anger against the
      rivers,
   Was Your wrath against the sea,
   That You rode on Your horses,
   Your chariots of salvation?
9   Your bow was made quite
      ready;
   Oaths were sworn over *Your*
      arrows.   Selah

   You divided the earth with
      rivers.
10 The mountains saw You *and*
      trembled.
   The overflowing of the water
      passed by.
   The deep uttered its voice,
   And lifted its hands on high.
11 The sun and moon stood still in
      their habitation;
   At the light of Your arrows they
      went,
   At the shining of Your glittering
      spear.

12 You marched through the land
      in indignation;
   You trampled the nations in
      anger.
13 You went forth for the salvation
      of Your people,

What Habakkuk Learned

I feel much better since the Lord answered my questions (Habakkuk 1
and 2). Now I realize that God is going to keep all of His promises. No
matter how hard my life becomes, I know I can still trust Him. This is
why I wrote my prayer (chapter 3).

I told the Lord in my prayer that I was glad about everything He was
doing. I know we will be prisoners in Babylon for a long time, but in the
end everything is going to be beautiful. Looking ahead to that time, "I
will rejoice in the Lord, I will joy in the God of my salvation" (3:18).
Now I am obeying what the Lord commanded me to do (2:4). I am
living by faith in Him.

For salvation with Your
Anointed.
You struck the head from the
house of the wicked,
By laying bare from foundation
to neck.   Selah

14 You thrust through with his own
arrows
The head of his villages.
They came out like a whirlwind
to scatter me;
Their rejoicing was like feasting
on the poor in secret.
15 You walked through the sea with
Your horses,
Through the heap of great
waters.

16 When I heard, my body
trembled;
My lips quivered at *the* voice;
Rottenness entered my bones;
And I trembled in myself,
That I might rest in the day of
trouble.

When he comes up to the
people,
He will invade them with his
troops.

17 Though the fig tree may not
blossom,
Nor fruit be on the vines;
Though the labor of the olive
may fail,
And the fields yield no food;
Though the flock may be cut off
from the fold,
And there be no herd in the
stalls—
18 Yet I will rejoice in the LORD,
I will joy in the God of my
salvation.

19 The LORD God is my strength;
He will make my feet like deer's
feet,
And He will make me walk on
my high hills.

To the Chief Musician. With my
stringed instruments.

The Book of
ZEPHANIAH

 My name is pronounced *zef-uh-NIGH-uh* and means "The Lord Has Hidden." God does hide some things from us until we are ready to understand them. I spoke my message to my people during the reign of good King Josiah about 640 years before Jesus was born. The great Jeremiah was also a prophet during my time.

I spoke very sternly to my people, using strong words to describe God's coming judgment on us and our neighbors. The "great day of the Lord" would be dark and gloomy. I described the Lord as searching Jerusalem with lamps to discover our sins.

But in the end I told my people to sing and shout for joy because God would forgive our sins, and after we had been captives for a while in a foreign country, the Lord would bring us back to our own land.

An awesome day of judgment

THE word of the LORD which came to Zephaniah the son of Cushi, the son of Gedaliah, the son of Amariah, the son of Hezekiah, in the days of Josiah the son of Amon, king of Judah.

2 "I will utterly consume everything
From the face of the land,"
Says the LORD;
3 "I will consume man and beast;
I will consume the birds of the heavens,
The fish of the sea,
And the stumbling blocks along with the wicked.
I will cut off man from the face of the land,"
Says the LORD.

4 "I will stretch out My hand against Judah,
And against all the inhabitants of Jerusalem.

I will cut off *every* trace of Baal from this place,
The names of the idolatrous priests with the **pagan** priests—
5 Those who worship the host of heaven on the housetops;
Those who worship and swear *oaths* by the LORD,
But who *also* swear by Milcom;
6 Those who have turned back from *following* the LORD,
And have not sought the LORD, nor inquired of Him."

7 Be silent in the presence of the Lord GOD;
For the day of the LORD *is* at hand,
For the LORD has prepared a sacrifice;
He has invited His guests.

8 "And it shall be,
In the day of the LORD's sacrifice,
That I will punish the princes and the king's children,

WORDFINDER

1:4 Pagan People who worship false gods or whose minds are mainly on material things, physical pleasure, and this present world.

And all such as are clothed with
   foreign apparel.
9 In the same day I will punish
All those who leap over the
   threshold,
Who fill their masters' houses
   with violence and deceit.

10 "And there shall be on that day,"
   says the LORD,
"The sound of a mournful cry
   from the Fish Gate,
A wailing from the Second
   Quarter,
And a loud crashing from the
   hills.
11 Wail, you inhabitants of
   Maktesh!
For all the merchant people are
   cut down;
All those who handle money are
   cut off.

12 "And it shall come to pass at that
   time
That I will search Jerusalem with
   lamps,
And punish the men
Who are settled in complacency,
Who say in their heart,
'The LORD will not do good,
Nor will He do evil.'
13 Therefore their goods shall
   become booty,
And their houses a desolation;
They shall build houses, but not
   inhabit *them;*
They shall plant vineyards, but
   not drink their wine."

14 The great day of the LORD *is*
   near;
It is near and hastens quickly.
The noise of the day of the LORD
   is bitter;
There the mighty men shall cry
   out.
15 That day *is* a day of wrath,
A day of trouble and distress,
A day of devastation and
   desolation,
A day of darkness and
   gloominess,

A day of clouds and thick
   darkness,
16 A day of trumpet and alarm
Against the fortified cities
And against the high towers.

17 "I will bring distress upon men,
And they shall walk like blind
   men,
Because they have sinned
   against the LORD;
Their blood shall be poured out
   like dust,
And their flesh like refuse."

18 Neither their silver nor their gold
Shall be able to deliver them
In the day of the LORD's wrath;
But the whole land shall be
   devoured
By the fire of His jealousy,
For He will make speedy
   riddance
Of all those who dwell in the
   land.

Repent, Israel, and God may save you

2 Gather yourselves together, yes,
   gather together,
O undesirable nation,
2 Before the decree is issued,
Or the day passes like chaff,
Before the LORD's fierce anger
   comes upon you,
Before the day of the LORD's
   anger comes upon you!
3 Seek the LORD, all you meek of
   the earth,
Who have upheld His justice.
Seek righteousness, seek
   humility.
It may be that you will be hidden
In the day of the LORD's anger.

4 For Gaza shall be forsaken,
And Ashkelon desolate;
They shall drive out Ashdod at
   noonday,
And Ekron shall be uprooted.
5 Woe to the inhabitants of the
   seacoast,
The nation of the Cherethites!

What Is the Remnant?

A remnant is what remains after everything else is used up. Part of a loaf of bread is a remnant of the whole loaf. God promised Israel that He would preserve a remnant of their nation and bring them back to Himself at last.

The word of the LORD *is* against you,
O Canaan, land of the Philistines:
"I will destroy you;
So there shall be no inhabitant."

6 The seacoast shall be pastures,
With shelters for shepherds and folds for flocks.
7 The coast shall be for the remnant of the house of Judah;
They shall feed *their* flocks there;
In the houses of Ashkelon they shall lie down at evening.
For the LORD their God will intervene for them,
And return their captives.

8 "I have heard the reproach of Moab,
And the insults of the people of Ammon,
With which they have reproached My people,
And made arrogant threats against their borders.
9 Therefore, as I live,"
Says the LORD of hosts, the God of Israel,
"Surely Moab shall be like Sodom,
And the people of Ammon like Gomorrah—
Overrun with weeds and saltpits,
And a perpetual desolation.
The residue of My people shall plunder them,
And the remnant of My people shall possess them."

10 This they shall have for their pride,
Because they have reproached and made arrogant threats
Against the people of the LORD of hosts.
11 The LORD *will be* awesome to them,
For He will reduce to nothing all the gods of the earth;
People shall worship Him,
Each one from his place,

"The herds shall lie down in her midst" (2:14).

Indeed all the shores of the
nations.

12 "You Ethiopians also,
You shall be slain by My sword."

13 And He will stretch out His hand
against the north,
Destroy Assyria,
And make Nineveh a desolation,
As dry as the wilderness.
14 The herds shall lie down in her
midst,
Every beast of the nation.
Both the pelican and the bittern
Shall lodge on the capitals *of* her
pillars;
Their voice shall sing in the
windows;
Desolation *shall be* at the
threshold;
For He will lay bare the cedar
work.
15 This is the rejoicing city
That dwelt securely,
That said in her heart,
"I *am it,* and *there is* none besides
me."
How has she become a
desolation,
A place for beasts to lie down!
Everyone who passes by her
Shall hiss and shake his fist.

The Lord Himself sings a happy song

3 Woe to her who is rebellious and
polluted,
To the oppressing city!
2 She has not obeyed *His* voice,
She has not received correction;
She has not trusted in the LORD,
She has not drawn near to her
God.

3 Her princes in her midst *are*
roaring lions;
Her judges *are* evening wolves
That leave not a bone till
morning.
4 Her prophets are insolent,
treacherous people;

Her priests have polluted the
sanctuary,
They have done violence to the
law.
5 The LORD *is* righteous in her
midst,
He will do no unrighteousness.
Every morning He brings His
justice to light;
He never fails,
But the unjust knows no shame.

6 "I have cut off nations,
Their fortresses are devastated;
I have made their streets
desolate,
With none passing by.
Their cities are destroyed;
There is no one, no inhabitant.
7 I said, 'Surely you will fear Me,
You will receive instruction'—
So that her dwelling would not
be cut off,
Despite everything for which I
punished her.
But they rose early and
corrupted all their deeds.

8 "Therefore wait for Me," says the
LORD,
"Until the day I rise up for
plunder;
My determination *is* to gather
the nations
To My assembly of kingdoms,
To pour on them My
indignation,
All My fierce anger;
All the earth shall be devoured
With the fire of My jealousy.

9 "For then I will restore to the
peoples a pure language,
That they all may call on the
name of the LORD,
To serve Him with one accord.
10 From beyond the rivers of
Ethiopia
My worshipers,
The daughter of My dispersed
ones,
Shall bring My offering.
11 In that day you shall not be
shamed for any of your deeds

In which you transgress against
  Me;
For then I will take away from
  your midst
Those who rejoice in your pride,
And you shall no longer be
  haughty
In My holy mountain.
12 I will leave in your midst
A meek and humble people,
And they shall trust in the name
  of the LORD.
13 The remnant of Israel shall do
  no unrighteousness
And speak no lies,
Nor shall a deceitful tongue be
  found in their mouth;
For they shall feed *their* flocks
  and lie down,
And no one shall make *them*
  afraid."

14 Sing, O daughter of Zion!
Shout, O Israel!
Be glad and rejoice with all *your*
  heart,
O daughter of Jerusalem!
15 The LORD has taken away your
  judgments,
He has cast out your enemy.
The King of Israel, the LORD, *is*
  in your midst;
You shall *see* disaster no more.

16 In that day it shall be said to
  Jerusalem:

"Do not fear;
Zion, let not your hands be
  weak.
17 The LORD your God in your
  midst,
The Mighty One, will save;
He will rejoice over you with
  gladness,
He will quiet *you* with His love,
He will rejoice over you with
  singing."

18 "I will gather those who sorrow
  over the appointed assembly,
Who are among you,
To whom its reproach *is* a
  burden.
19 Behold, at that time
I will deal with all who afflict you;
I will save the lame,
And gather those who were
  driven out;
I will appoint them for praise and
  fame
In *every* land where they were
  put to shame.
20 At that time I will bring you
  back,
Even at the time I gather you;
For I will give you fame and
  praise
Among all the peoples of the
  earth,
When I return your captives
  before your eyes,"
Says the LORD.

⚒ DIGGING IN

3:14, 15 Be Glad with God God is glad because Satan, the Enemy of your soul, has been thrown out. Satan's power over you was destroyed when Jesus died on the Cross for you. So God commands you, "Sing, O daughter of Zion! Shout, O Israel!" You and all who believe in Jesus are the sons and daughters of God. You belong to Him forever because Jesus paid for you with His own life at Calvary.

Some days aren't as bright as others. And sometimes your plans don't work out the way you would like. Even Jesus said you would be disappointed sometimes, but He also said He conquered evil for you.

Be glad. No need to be gloomy or sad anymore. God is preparing an eternal home for you that can never be destroyed. The present starry heavens and earth will pass away, but the home He has made ready for you will never pass away. Be glad with God.

The Book of
HAGGAI

My name is pronounced *HAG-ay-eye* and means "Festive." It surely was a festive time when King Cyrus of Persia let Israel, my people, come back to their own country. We danced for joy! We had been prisoners in faraway Babylon for about 70 years.

My task was to encourage my people to finish rebuilding the temple at Jerusalem, and we finally did finish the work 515 years before Jesus came.

You must remember that the Old Testament building called "the temple" was only temporary. When Jesus came, He said that His own body was the real temple. When Jesus was crucified, the great curtain in the temple was torn in two. So God showed that He would not always live in a temple made by hands.

Now God wants you to be a temple where He can live.

Rebuild My temple, Israel

IN the second year of King Darius, in the sixth month, on the first day of the month, the word of the LORD came by Haggai the prophet to Zerubbabel the son of Shealtiel, governor of Judah, and to Joshua the son of Jehozadak, the high priest, saying, 2 "Thus speaks the LORD of hosts, saying: 'This people says, "The time has not come, the time that the LORD's house should be built." ' "

3 Then the word of the LORD came by Haggai the prophet, saying, 4 *"Is it* time for you yourselves to dwell in your paneled houses, and this temple *to lie* in ruins?" 5 Now therefore, thus says the LORD of hosts: "Consider your ways!

6 "You have sown much, and bring in little;
You eat, but do not have enough;
You drink, but you are not filled with drink;
You clothe yourselves, but no one is warm;
And he who earns wages,
Earns wages *to put* into a bag with holes."

7 Thus says the LORD of hosts: "Consider your ways! 8 Go up to the mountains and bring wood and build the temple, that I may take pleasure in it and be glorified," says the LORD. 9 *"You* looked for much, but indeed *it came to* little; and when you brought it home, I blew it away. Why?" says the LORD of hosts. "Because of My house that *is in* ruins, while *every* one of you runs to his own house. 10 Therefore the heavens above you withhold the dew, and the earth withholds its fruit. 11 For I called for a drought on the land and the mountains, on the grain and the new wine and the oil, on whatever the ground brings forth, on men and livestock, and on all the labor of *your* hands."

12 Then Zerubbabel the son of Shealtiel, and Joshua the son of Jehozadak, the high priest, with all the remnant of the people, obeyed the voice of the LORD their God, and the words of Haggai the prophet, as the LORD their God had sent him; and the people feared the presence of the LORD. 13 Then Haggai, the LORD's messenger, spoke the LORD's message to the people, saying, "I *am* with you, says the LORD." 14 So the LORD stirred up the spirit of Zerubbabel the son of

What Zerubbabel Learned

Pronounce my name *zeh-RUB-uh-bell,* meaning "Child of Babylon." That is a good name for me, because I am a Jew who was born in Babylon.

We have had no kings since the Babylonians conquered us. I was the first governor of the people who returned to Israel from Babylon 536 years before Jesus came.

After I led the people back to our land, we rebuilt the temple in Jerusalem. Actually, the new temple was not as beautiful as the one Solomon built. But the Lord said it would be even more beautiful.

That puzzled me. But many years later, the Lord Jesus Christ came to the temple. The Lord Himself was the beauty of His own house (See John 2:13–22).

Shealtiel, governor of Judah, and the spirit of Joshua the son of Jehozadak, the high priest, and the spirit of all the remnant of the people; and they came and worked on the house of the Lord of hosts, their God, 15 on the twenty-fourth day of the sixth month, in the second year of King Darius.

Work and don't be afraid

2 In the seventh *month,* on the twenty-first of the month, the word of the Lord came by Haggai the prophet, saying: 2 "Speak now to Zerubbabel the son of Shealtiel, governor of Judah, and to Joshua the son of Jehozadak, the high priest, and to the remnant of the people, saying: 3 'Who is left among you who saw this temple in its former glory? And how do you see it now? In comparison with it, *is this* not in your eyes as nothing? 4 Yet now be strong, Zerubbabel,' says the Lord; 'and be strong, Joshua, son of Jehozadak, the high priest; and be strong, all you people of the land,' says the Lord, 'and work; for I *am* with you,' says the Lord of hosts. 5 'According to the word that I covenanted with you when you came out of Egypt, so My Spirit remains among you; do not fear!'

6 "For thus says the Lord of hosts: 'Once more (it *is* a little while) I will shake heaven and earth, the sea and dry land; 7 and I will shake all nations, and they shall come to the **Desire of All Nations**, and I will fill this temple with glory,' says the Lord of hosts. 8 'The silver *is* Mine, and the gold *is* Mine,' says the Lord of hosts. 9 'The

WORDFINDER

2:7 The Desire of All Nations A reference to the coming Messiah, or Christ, in the New Testament. There are several names for Christ in the Old Testament.

DIGGING IN

2:9 The Beauty of God's House Just like Israel in the days of Zerubbabel (pronounced *zeh-RUB-uh-bell*), we often think the beauty of God's house must be something you can see with your eyes. We look at the sunset, and we say, "How beautiful!" And this is true. Many church buildings also are truly beautiful works of art. Solomon's temple was very beautiful. It was so beautiful that, when the Jews later built a new temple, they were disappointed in it. But when Jesus came into the temple, His presence there made the temple beautiful. (See John 2:13–22.)

Can we, too, find the beauty of Jesus? We find His beauty whenever we come into His presence to pray. His beauty is the beauty of the holy God you can't see with your eyes; you see Him with your heart.

glory of this latter temple shall be greater than the former,' says the LORD of hosts. 'And in this place I will give peace,' says the LORD of hosts."

¹⁰ On the twenty-fourth *day* of the ninth *month,* in the second year of Darius, the word of the LORD came by Haggai the prophet, saying, ¹¹ "Thus says the LORD of hosts: 'Now, ask the priests *concerning the* law, saying, ¹² "If one carries holy meat in the fold of his garment, and with the edge he touches bread or stew, wine or oil, or any food, will it become holy?" ' "

Then the priests answered and said, "No."

¹³ And Haggai said, "If *one who is* unclean *because* of a dead body touches any of these, will it be unclean?"

So the priests answered and said, "It shall be unclean."

¹⁴ Then Haggai answered and said, " 'So is this people, and so is this nation before Me,' says the LORD, 'and so is *every* work of their hands; and what they offer there is unclean.

¹⁵ 'And now, carefully consider from this day forward: from before stone was laid upon stone in the temple of the LORD— ¹⁶ since those *days,* when *one* came to a heap of twenty ephahs, there were *but* ten; when *one* came to the wine vat to draw out fifty baths from the press, there were *but* twenty. ¹⁷ I struck you with blight and mildew

and hail in all the labors of your hands; yet you did not *turn* to Me,' says the LORD. ¹⁸ 'Consider now from this day forward, from the twenty-fourth day of the ninth month, from the day that the foundation of the LORD's temple was laid—consider it: ¹⁹ Is the seed still in the barn? As yet the vine, the fig tree, the pomegranate, and the olive tree have not yielded *fruit. But* from this day I will bless *you.*' "

²⁰ And again the word of the LORD came to Haggai on the twenty-fourth day of the month, saying, ²¹ "Speak to Zerubbabel, governor of Judah, saying:

'I will shake heaven and earth.
²² I will overthrow the throne of
    kingdoms;
I will destroy the strength of the
    Gentile kingdoms.
I will overthrow the chariots
And those who ride in them;
The horses and their riders shall
    come down,
Every one by the sword of his
    brother.

²³ 'In that day,' says the LORD of hosts, 'I will take you, Zerubbabel My servant, the son of Shealtiel,' says the LORD, 'and will make you like a signet *ring;* for I have chosen you,' says the LORD of hosts."

The Book of
ZECHARIAH

I served as a prophet in Judah along with Haggai when my people came back from being prisoners in Babylon. My name is pronounced *zek-uh-RIGH-uh* and means "The Lord Remembers." The Lord really did remember His promises to us when He brought us home to our own land over five hundred years before Jesus came.

I speak of Jesus eight times in my book. In Zechariah 9:9, you can read how Jesus is going to enter Jerusalem like a humble Man, riding on a donkey. You can read how this really happened in Matthew 21:5 of the New Testament.

In Zechariah 12:10, you can also read how my people will someday be sorry because they crucified their Messiah, the Lord Jesus Christ.

The vision of a rider on a red horse

IN the eighth month of the second year of Darius, the word of the LORD came to Zechariah the son of Berechiah, the son of Iddo the prophet, saying, 2 "The LORD has been very angry with your fathers. 3 Therefore say to them, 'Thus says the LORD of hosts: "Return to Me," says the LORD of hosts, "and I will return to you," says the LORD of hosts. 4 "Do not be like your fathers, to whom the former prophets preached, saying, 'Thus says the LORD of hosts: "Turn now from your evil ways and your evil deeds." ' But they did not hear nor heed Me," says the LORD.

5 "Your fathers, where *are* they?
    And the prophets, do they live forever?
6 Yet surely My words and My statutes,
    Which I commanded My servants the prophets,
    Did they not overtake your fathers?

"So they returned and said:

'Just as the LORD of hosts determined to do to us,
According to our ways and
    according to our deeds,
So He has dealt with us.' ' "

7 On the twenty-fourth day of the eleventh month, which is the month Shebat, in the second year of Darius, the word of the LORD came to Zechariah the son of Berechiah, the son of Iddo the prophet: 8 I saw by night, and behold, a man riding on a red horse, and it stood among the myrtle trees in the hollow; and behind him *were* horses: red, sorrel, and white. 9 Then I said, "My lord, what *are* these?" So the angel who talked with me said to me, "I will show you what they *are*."

10 And the man who stood among the myrtle trees answered and said, "These *are the ones* whom the LORD has sent to walk to and fro throughout the earth."

11 So they answered the Angel of the LORD, who stood among the myrtle trees, and said, "We have walked to and fro throughout the earth, and behold, all the earth is resting quietly."

12 Then the Angel of the LORD answered and said, "O LORD of hosts, how long will You not have mercy on Jerusalem and on the cities of Judah,

against which You were angry these seventy years?"

13 And the LORD answered the angel who talked to me, *with* good *and* comforting words. 14 So the angel who spoke with me said to me, "Proclaim, saying, 'Thus says the LORD of hosts:

"I am zealous for Jerusalem
And for Zion with great zeal.
15 I am exceedingly angry with the
    nations at ease;
For I was a little angry,
And they helped—*but* with evil
    intent."

16 'Therefore thus says the LORD:

"I am returning to Jerusalem with
    mercy;
My house shall be built in it,"
    says the LORD of hosts,
"And a *surveyor's* line shall be
    stretched out over
    Jerusalem."'

17 "Again proclaim, saying, 'Thus says the LORD of hosts:

"My cities shall again spread out
    through prosperity;
The LORD will again comfort
    Zion,
And will again choose
    Jerusalem."'"

18 Then I raised my eyes and looked, and there *were* four horns. 19 And I said to the angel who talked with me, "What *are* these?"

So he answered me, "These *are* the horns that have scattered Judah, Israel, and Jerusalem."

20 Then the LORD showed me four craftsmen. 21 And I said, "What are these coming to do?"

So he said, "These *are* the horns that scattered Judah, so that no one could lift up his head; but *the craftsmen* are coming to terrify them, to cast out the horns of the nations that lifted up *their* horn against the land of Judah to scatter it."

The vision of a man with a yardstick

2 Then I raised my eyes and looked, and behold, a man with a measuring line in his hand. 2 So I said, "Where are you going?"

And he said to me, "To measure Jerusalem, to see what *is* its width and what *is* its length."

3 And there *was* the angel who talked with me, going out; and another angel was coming out to meet him, 4 who said to him, "Run, speak to this young man, saying: 'Jerusalem shall be inhabited *as* towns without walls, because of the multitude of men and livestock in it. 5 For I,' says the LORD, 'will be a wall of fire all around her, and I will be the glory in her midst.'"

6 "Up, up! Flee from the land of the north," says the LORD; "for I have spread you abroad like the four winds of heaven," says the LORD. 7 Up, Zion! Escape, you who dwell with the daughter of Babylon."

8 For thus says the LORD of hosts: "He sent Me after glory, to the nations which plunder you; for he who touches you touches the apple of His eye. 9 For surely I will shake My hand against them, and they shall become spoil for their servants. Then you will know that the LORD of hosts has sent Me.

10 "Sing and rejoice, O daughter of Zion! For behold, I am coming and I will dwell in your midst," says the LORD. 11 "Many nations shall be joined to the LORD in that day, and they shall become My people. And I will dwell in your midst. Then you will know that the LORD of hosts has sent Me to you. 12 And the LORD will take possession of Judah as His inheritance in the Holy Land, and will again choose Jerusalem. 13 Be silent, all flesh, before the LORD, for He is aroused from His holy habitation!"

The vision of the Angel and Satan

3 Then he showed me Joshua the high priest standing before the Angel

of the LORD, and Satan standing at his right hand to oppose him. 2 And the LORD said to Satan, "The LORD rebuke you, Satan! The LORD who has chosen Jerusalem rebuke you! *Is* this not a brand plucked from the fire?"

3 Now Joshua was clothed with filthy garments, and was standing before the Angel.

4 Then He answered and spoke to those who stood before Him, saying, "Take away the filthy garments from him." And to him He said, "See, I have removed your iniquity from you, and I will clothe you with rich robes."

5 And I said, "Let them put a clean turban on his head."

So they put a clean turban on his head, and they put the clothes on him. And the Angel of the LORD stood by.

6 Then the Angel of the LORD admonished Joshua, saying, 7 "Thus says the LORD of hosts:

'If you will walk in My ways,
And if you will keep My
     command,
Then you shall also judge My
     house,
And likewise have charge of My
     courts;
I will give you places to walk
Among these who stand here.

8 'Hear, O Joshua, the high priest,
You and your companions who
     sit before you,

For they are a wondrous sign;
For behold, I am bringing forth
     My Servant the BRANCH.
9 For behold, the stone
That I have laid before Joshua:
Upon the stone *are* seven eyes.
Behold, I will engrave its
     inscription,'
Says the LORD of hosts,
'And I will remove the iniquity
     of that land in one day.
10 In that day,' says the LORD of
     hosts,
'Everyone will invite his
     neighbor
Under his vine and under his fig
     tree.' "

The vision of the golden lampstand

4 Now the angel who talked with me came back and wakened me, as a man who is wakened out of his sleep. 2 And he said to me, "What do you see?"

So I said, "I am looking, and there *is* a lampstand of solid gold with a bowl on top of it, and on the *stand* seven lamps with seven pipes to the seven lamps. 3 Two olive trees *are* by it, one at the right of the bowl and the other at its left." 4 So I answered and spoke to the angel who talked with me, saying, "What *are* these, my lord?"

5 Then the angel who talked with me

What Zechariah Learned

I didn't know what to think when I saw my vision of the gold lampstand with its seven branches. God had commanded Moses to make one like it for our place of worship. See Exodus 25 for a picture of the gold lampstand.

The priests had to supply the oil to keep its seven lamps lit. But the oil for the lampstand in my vision was supplied by two living olive trees. Then an angel of God told me what my vision meant.

The light of God's truth and God's kingdom is not kept burning by human power. God's work on earth must be done in the strength of the Holy Spirit. The Holy Spirit is God's own visible presence. The Holy Spirit is the One who makes your works for God succeed.

answered and said to me, "Do you not know what these are?"

And I said, "No, my lord."

6 So he answered and said to me:

"This is the word of the LORD to Zerubbabel:
  'Not by might nor by power, but by My Spirit,'
  Says the LORD of hosts.
7 'Who are you, O great mountain?
  Before Zerubbabel you shall become a plain!
  And he shall bring forth the capstone
  With shouts of "Grace, grace to it!" ' "

8 Moreover the word of the LORD came to me, saying:

9 "The hands of Zerubbabel
  Have laid the foundation of this temple;
  His hands shall also finish it.
  Then you will know
  That the LORD of hosts has sent Me to you.
10 For who has despised the day of small things?
  For these seven rejoice to see
  The plumb line in the hand of Zerubbabel.
  They are the eyes of the LORD,
  Which scan to and fro throughout the whole earth."

11 Then I answered and said to him, "What are these two olive trees—at the right of the lampstand and at its left?" 12 And I further answered and said to him, "What are these two olive branches that drip into the receptacles of the two gold pipes from which the golden oil drains?"

13 Then he answered me and said, "Do you not know what these are?"

And I said, "No, my lord."

14 So he said, "These are the two anointed ones, who stand beside the Lord of the whole earth."

The vision of a flying scroll

5 Then I turned and raised my eyes, and saw there a flying scroll.

2 And he said to me, "What do you see?"

So I answered, "I see a flying scroll. Its length is twenty cubits and its width ten cubits."

3 Then he said to me, "This is the curse that goes out over the face of the whole earth: 'Every thief shall be expelled,' according to this side of the scroll; and, 'Every perjurer shall be expelled,' according to that side of it."

4 "I will send out the curse," says the LORD of hosts;
  "It shall enter the house of the thief
  And the house of the one who swears falsely by My name.
  It shall remain in the midst of his house
  And consume it, with its timber and stones."

5 Then the angel who talked with me came out and said to me, "Lift your eyes now, and see what this is that goes forth."

6 So I asked, "What is it?" And he said, "It is a basket that is going forth."

He also said, "This is their resemblance throughout the earth: 7 Here is a lead disc lifted up, and this is a woman sitting inside the basket"; 8 then he said, "This is Wickedness!" And he thrust her down into the basket, and threw the lead cover over its mouth. 9 Then I raised my eyes and looked, and there were two women, coming with the wind in their wings; for they had wings like the wings of a stork, and they lifted up the basket between earth and heaven.

10 So I said to the angel who talked with me, "Where are they carrying the basket?"

11 And he said to me, "To build a house for it in the land of Shinar; when it is ready, the basket will be set there on its base."

The vision of the four chariots

6 Then I turned and raised my *eyes* and looked, and behold, four chariots *were* coming from between two mountains, and the mountains *were* mountains of bronze. ² With the first chariot *were* red horses, with the second chariot black horses, ³ with the third chariot white horses, and with the fourth chariot dappled horses—strong *steeds*. ⁴ Then I answered and said to the angel who talked with me, "What *are* these, my lord?"

⁵ And the angel answered and said to me, "These *are* four spirits of heaven, who go out from *their* station before the Lord of all the earth. ⁶ The one with the black horses is going to the north country, the white are going after them, and the dappled are going toward the south country."

⁷ Then the strong *steeds* went out, eager to go, that they might walk to and fro throughout the earth. And He said, "Go, walk to and fro throughout the earth." So they walked to and fro throughout the earth. ⁸ And He called to me, and spoke to me, saying, "See, those who go toward the north country have given rest to My Spirit in the north country."

⁹ Then the word of the Lord came to me, saying: ¹⁰ "Receive *the gift* from the captives—from Heldai, Tobijah, and Jedaiah, who have come from Babylon—and go the same day and enter the house of Josiah the son of Zephaniah. ¹¹ Take the silver and gold, make an elaborate crown, and set *it* on the head of Joshua the son of Jehozadak, the high priest. ¹² Then speak to him, saying, 'Thus says the Lord of hosts, saying:

Zechariah saw a vision of four chariots, with red, black, white, and dappled horses.

"Behold, the Man whose name
  is the BRANCH!
From His place He shall branch
  out,
And He shall build the temple
  of the LORD;
13 Yes, He shall build the temple
  of the LORD.
He shall bear the glory,
And shall sit and rule on His
  throne;
So He shall be a priest on His
  throne,
And the counsel of peace shall
  be between them both.'"'

14 "Now the elaborate crown shall be for a memorial in the temple of the LORD for Helem, Tobijah, Jedaiah, and Hen the son of Zephaniah. 15 Even those from afar shall come and build the temple of the LORD. Then you shall know that the LORD of hosts has sent Me to you. And *this* shall come to pass if you diligently obey the voice of the LORD your God."

God tells Israel to be kind and fair

7 Now in the fourth year of King Darius it came to pass *that* the word of the LORD came to Zechariah, on the fourth day of the ninth month, Chislev, 2 when *the people* sent Sherezer, with Regem-Melech and his men, *to* the house of God, to pray before the LORD, 3 *and* to ask the priests who *were* in the house of the LORD of hosts, and the prophets, saying, "Should I weep in the fifth month and fast as I have done for so many years?"

4 Then the word of the LORD of hosts came to me, saying, 5 "Say to all the people of the land, and to the priests: 'When you fasted and mourned in the fifth and seventh *months* during those seventy years, did you really fast for Me—for Me? 6 When you eat and when you drink, do you not eat and drink *for yourselves?* 7 *Should you* not *have obeyed* the words which the LORD proclaimed through the former prophets when Jerusalem and the cities around it were inhabited and pros-

perous, and the South and the Lowland were inhabited?' "

8 Then the word of the LORD came to Zechariah, saying, 9 "Thus says the LORD of hosts:

'Execute true justice,
  Show mercy and compassion
  Everyone to his brother.
10 Do not oppress the widow or the
  fatherless,
The alien or the poor.
Let none of you plan evil in his
  heart
Against his brother.'

11 But they refused to heed, shrugged their shoulders, and stopped their ears so that they could not hear. 12 Yes, they made their hearts like flint, refusing to hear the law and the words which the LORD of hosts had sent by His Spirit through the former prophets. Thus great wrath came from the LORD of hosts. 13 Therefore it happened, *that* just as He proclaimed and they would not hear, so they called out and I would not listen," says the LORD of hosts. 14 "But I scattered them with a whirlwind among all the nations which they had not known. Thus the land became desolate after them, so that no one passed through or returned; for they made the pleasant land desolate."

The Lord has a burning love for Jerusalem

8 Again the word of the LORD of hosts came, saying, 2 "Thus says the LORD of hosts:

'I am zealous for Zion with great
  zeal;
With great fervor I am zealous
  for her.'

3 "Thus says the LORD:

'I will return to Zion,
And dwell in the midst of
  Jerusalem.
Jerusalem shall be called the
  City of Truth,

The Mountain of the LORD of
hosts,
The Holy Mountain.'

4 "Thus says the LORD of hosts:

'Old men and old women shall
again sit
In the streets of Jerusalem,
Each one with his staff in his
hand
Because of great age.
5   The streets of the city
Shall be full of boys and girls
Playing in its streets.'

6 "Thus says the LORD of hosts:

'If it is marvelous in the eyes of
the remnant of this people in
these days,

Will it also be marvelous in My
eyes?"
Says the LORD of hosts.

7 "Thus says the LORD of hosts:

'Behold, I will save My people
from the land of the east
And from the land of the west;
8   I will bring them *back*,
And they shall dwell in the midst
of Jerusalem.
They shall be My people
And I will be their God,
In truth and righteousness.'

9 "Thus says the LORD of hosts:

'Let your hands be strong,
You who have been hearing in
these days

⛏ DIGGING IN

8:5 Games Boys and Girls Played Although young people in Bible times didn't
have as much free time as you have, they
did have time for play. Simple toys like
carts and wagons have been found in the
ancient tombs of Egypt. Boys and girls
learned dances and songs early in life.
Jesus described children sitting in the
marketplace playing musical instruments
(see Matthew 11:16, 17). Wrestling and
tug-of-war were games played by Egyptian children and probably by Jewish
children, also. They played hopscotch
and ran footraces much as you do today.

We know that David could use a sling
very well, and other young people would
have practiced that art also. Israel's soldiers used spears; and the boys imitated
them by playing war games, using toy
spears and other weapons.

See the drawing which shows you
some kinds of games played in Bible
times. Some of them look a little like
Parcheesi.

*"The streets of the city shall be full of boys
and girls playing in its streets"* (8:5).

These words by the mouth of
the prophets,
Who *spoke* in the day the
foundation was laid
For the house of the LORD of
hosts,
That the temple might be built.
10 For before these days
There were no wages for man
nor any hire for beast;
There was no peace from the
enemy for whoever went out
or came in;
For I set all men, everyone,
against his neighbor.

11 But now I *will* not *treat* the remnant
of this people as in the former days,'
says the LORD of hosts.

12 'For the seed *shall be*
prosperous,
The vine shall give its fruit,
The ground shall give her
increase,
And the heavens shall give their
dew—
I will cause the remnant of this
people
To possess all these.
13 And it shall come to pass
That just as you were a curse
among the nations,
O house of Judah and house of
Israel,
So I will save you, and you shall
be a blessing.
Do not fear,
Let your hands be strong.'

14 "For thus says the LORD of hosts:

'Just as I determined to punish
you
When your fathers provoked Me
to wrath,'
Says the LORD of hosts,
'And I would not relent,
15 So again in these days
I am determined to do good
To Jerusalem and to the house
of Judah.
Do not fear.
16 These *are* the things you shall
do:

Speak each man the truth to his
neighbor;
Give judgment in your gates for
truth, justice, and peace;
17 Let none of you think evil in
your heart against your
neighbor;
And do not love a false oath.
For all these *are things* that I
hate,'
Says the LORD.''

18 Then the word of the LORD of
hosts came to me, saying, 19 "Thus
says the LORD of hosts:

'The fast of the fourth *month*,
The fast of the fifth,
The fast of the seventh,
And the fast of the tenth,
Shall be joy and gladness and
cheerful feasts
For the house of Judah.
Therefore love truth and peace.'

20 "Thus says the LORD of hosts:

'Peoples shall yet come,
Inhabitants of many cities;
21 The inhabitants of one *city* shall
go to another, saying,
"Let us continue to go and pray
before the LORD,
And seek the LORD of hosts.
I myself will go also."
22 Yes, many peoples and strong
nations
Shall come to seek the LORD of
hosts in Jerusalem,
And to pray before the LORD.'

23 "Thus says the LORD of hosts: 'In
those days ten men from every language of the nations shall grasp the
sleeve of a Jewish man, saying, "Let
us go with you, for we have heard *that*
God *is* with you." ' "

Zion's King will come, riding on a donkey

9   The burden of the word of the
LORD
Against the land of Hadrach,

And Damascus its resting place
(For the eyes of men
And all the tribes of Israel
Are on the Lord);
2 Also *against* Hamath, *which*
borders on it,
And *against* Tyre and Sidon,
though they are very wise.

3 For Tyre built herself a tower,
Heaped up silver like the dust,
And gold like the mire of the
streets.
4 Behold, the Lord will cast her
out;
He will destroy her power in the
sea,
And she will be devoured by fire.

5 Ashkelon shall *see it* and fear;
Gaza also shall be very
sorrowful;
And Ekron, for He dried up her
expectation.
The king shall perish from
Gaza,
And Ashkelon shall not be
inhabited.

6 "A mixed race shall settle in
Ashdod,
And I will cut off the pride of
the Philistines.
7 I will take away the blood from
his mouth,
And the abominations from
between his teeth.
But he who remains, *even he
shall be* for our God,
And shall be like a leader in
Judah,
And Ekron like a Jebusite.
8 I will camp around My house
Because of the army,
Because of him who passes by
and him who returns.
No more shall an oppressor pass
through them,
For now I have seen with My
eyes.

9 "Rejoice greatly, O daughter of
Zion!
Shout, O daughter of Jerusalem!

Behold, your King is coming to
you;
He *is* just and having salvation,
Lowly and riding on a donkey,
A colt, the foal of a donkey.
10 I will cut off the chariot from
Ephraim
And the horse from Jerusalem;
The battle bow shall be cut off.
He shall speak peace to the
nations;
His dominion *shall be* 'from sea
to sea,
And from the River to the ends
of the earth.'

11 "As for you also,
Because of the blood of your
covenant,
I will set your prisoners free from
the waterless pit.
12 Return to the stronghold,
You prisoners of hope.
Even today I declare
That I will restore double to
you.
13 For I have bent Judah, My *bow,*
Fitted the bow with Ephraim,
And raised up your sons, O
Zion,
Against your sons, O Greece,
And made you like the sword
of a mighty man."

14 Then the Lord will be seen over
them,
And His arrow will go forth like
lightning.
The Lord God will blow the
trumpet,
And go with whirlwinds from the
south.
15 The Lord of hosts will defend
them;
They shall devour and subdue
with slingstones.
They shall drink *and* roar as if
with wine;
They shall be filled *with blood*
like basins,
Like the corners of the altar.
16 The Lord their God will save
them in that day,
As the flock of His people.

For they *shall be like* the jewels
   of a crown,
Lifted like a banner over His
   land—
17 For how great is its goodness
   And how great its beauty!
   Grain shall make the young men
     thrive,
   And new wine the young
     women.

God will comfort Judah and Israel

10 Ask the LORD for rain
   In the time of the latter rain.
   The LORD will make flashing
     clouds;
   He will give them showers of
     rain,
   Grass in the field for *everyone.*

2 For the idols speak delusion;
   The diviners envision lies,
   And tell false dreams;
   They comfort in vain.
   Therefore *the people* wend their
     way like sheep;
   They are in trouble because
     there is no shepherd.

3 "My anger is kindled against the
     shepherds,
   And I will punish the goatherds.
   For the LORD of hosts will visit
     His flock,
   The house of Judah,
   And will make them as His royal
     horse in the battle.
4 From him comes the
     cornerstone,
   From him the tent peg,
   From him the battle bow,
   From him *every* ruler together.
5 They shall be like mighty
     men,
   Who tread down *their*
     enemies
   In the mire of the streets in the
     battle.
   They shall fight because the
     LORD is with them,
   And the riders on horses shall
     be put to shame.

6 "I will strengthen the house of
     Judah,
   And I will save the house of
     Joseph.
   I will bring them back,
   Because I have mercy on them.
   They shall be as though I had
     not cast them aside;
   For I *am* the LORD their God,
   And I will hear them.
7 *Those of* Ephraim shall be like
     a mighty man,
   And their heart shall rejoice as
     if with wine.
   Yes, their children shall see *it*
     and be glad;
   Their heart shall rejoice in the
     LORD.
8 I will whistle for them and gather
     them,
   For I will redeem them;
   And they shall increase as they
     once increased.

9 "I will sow them among the
     peoples,
   And they shall remember Me in
     far countries;
   They shall live, together with
     their children,
   And they shall return.
10 I will also bring them back from
     the land of Egypt,
   And gather them from Assyria.
   I will bring them into the land
     of Gilead and Lebanon,
   Until no *more room* is found for
     them.
11 He shall pass through the sea
     with affliction,
   And strike the waves of the sea:
   All the depths of the River shall
     dry up.
   Then the pride of Assyria shall
     be brought down,
   And the scepter of Egypt shall
     depart.

12 "So I will strengthen them in the
     LORD,
   And they shall walk up and
     down in His name,"
   Says the LORD.

The wailing shepherds and the worthless shepherd

11 Open your doors, O Lebanon,
That fire may devour your
cedars.
2 Wail, O cypress, for the cedar
has fallen,
Because the mighty *trees* are
ruined.
Wail, O oaks of Bashan,
For the thick forest has come
down.
3 *There is* the sound of wailing
shepherds!
For their glory is in ruins.
There is the sound of roaring
lions!
For the pride of the Jordan is
in ruins.

4 Thus says the LORD my God,
"Feed the flock for slaughter, 5 whose
owners slaughter them and feel no
guilt; those who sell them say, 'Blessed
be the LORD, for I am rich'; and their
shepherds do not pity them. 6 For I
will no longer pity the inhabitants
of the land," says the LORD. "But
indeed I will give everyone into his
neighbor's hand and into the hand of
his king. They shall attack the land,
and I will not deliver *them* from their
hand."

7 So I fed the flock for slaughter, in
particular the poor of the flock. I took
for myself two staffs: the one I called
Beauty, and the other I called Bonds;
and I fed the flock. 8 I dismissed the
three shepherds in one month. My soul
loathed them, and their soul also
abhorred me. 9 Then I said, "I will not
feed you. Let what is dying die, and
what is perishing perish. Let those that
are left eat each other's flesh." 10 And
I took my staff, Beauty, and cut it in
two, that I might break the covenant
which I had made with all the peoples.
11 So it was broken on that day. Thus
the poor of the flock, who were watching me, knew that it *was* the word of
the LORD. 12 Then I said to them, "If
it is agreeable to you, give *me* my
wages; and if not, refrain." So they
weighed out for my wages thirty *pieces*
of silver.

13 And the LORD said to me, "Throw
it to the potter"—that princely price
they set on me. So I took the thirty
pieces of silver and threw them into
the house of the LORD for the potter.
14 Then I cut in two my other staff,
Bonds, that I might break the brotherhood between Judah and Israel.

15 And the LORD said to me, "Next,
take for yourself the implements of a
foolish shepherd. 16 For indeed I will
raise up a shepherd in the land *who*
will not care for those who are cut off,
nor seek the young, nor heal those that
are broken, nor feed those that still
stand. But he will eat the flesh of the
fat and tear their hooves in pieces.

17 "Woe to the worthless shepherd,
Who leaves the flock!
A sword *shall be* against his arm
And against his right *eye*;
His arm shall completely wither,
And his right *eye* shall be totally
blinded."

Israel will weep for the One they have pierced

12 The burden of the word of the
LORD against Israel. Thus says the
LORD, who stretches out the heavens,
lays the foundation of the earth, and
forms the spirit of man within him:
2 "Behold, I will make Jerusalem a cup
of drunkenness to all the surrounding
peoples, when they lay siege against
Judah and Jerusalem. 3 And it shall
happen in that day that I will make
Jerusalem a very heavy stone for all
peoples; all who would heave it away
will surely be cut in pieces, though all
nations of the earth are gathered
against it. 4 In that day," says the LORD,
"I will strike every horse with confusion, and its rider with madness; I will
open My eyes on the house of Judah,
and will strike every horse of the peoples with blindness. 5 And the governors of Judah shall say in their heart,
'The inhabitants of Jerusalem *are* my
strength in the LORD of hosts, their

God.' 6 In that day I will make the governors of Judah like a firepan in the woodpile, and like a fiery torch in the sheaves; they shall devour all the surrounding peoples on the right hand and on the left, but Jerusalem shall be inhabited again in her own place—Jerusalem.

7 "The LORD will save the tents of Judah first, so that the glory of the house of David and the glory of the inhabitants of Jerusalem shall not become greater than that of Judah. 8 In that day the LORD will defend the inhabitants of Jerusalem; the one who is feeble among them in that day shall be like David, and the house of David shall be like God, like the Angel of the LORD before them. 9 It shall be in that day that I will seek to destroy all the nations that come against Jerusalem.

10 "And I will pour on the house of David and on the inhabitants of Jerusalem the Spirit of grace and supplication; then they will look on Me whom they pierced. Yes, they will mourn for Him as one mourns for his only son, and grieve for Him as one grieves for a firstborn. 11 In that day there shall be a great mourning in Jerusalem, like the mourning at Hadad Rimmon in the plain of Megiddo. 12 And the land shall mourn, every family by itself: the family of the house of David by itself, and their wives by themselves; the family of the house of Nathan by itself, and their wives by themselves; 13 the family of the house of Levi by itself, and their wives by themselves; the family of Shimei by itself, and their wives by themselves; 14 all the families that remain, every family by itself, and their wives by themselves.

The Shepherd is my Savior

13 "In that day a fountain shall be opened for the house of David and for the inhabitants of Jerusalem, for sin and for uncleanness.

2 "It shall be in that day," says the LORD of hosts, "that I will cut off the names of the idols from the land, and they shall no longer be remembered. I will also cause the prophets and the unclean spirit to depart from the land. 3 It shall come to pass that if anyone still prophesies, then his father and mother who begot him will say to him, 'You shall not live, because you have spoken lies in the name of the LORD.' And his father and mother who begot him shall thrust him through when he prophesies.

4 "And it shall be in that day that every prophet will be ashamed of his vision when he prophesies; they will not wear a robe of coarse hair to deceive. 5 But he will say, 'I am no prophet, I am a farmer; for a man taught me to keep cattle from my youth.' 6 And one will say to him, 'What are these wounds between your arms?' Then he will answer, 'Those with which I was wounded in the house of my friends.'

7   "Awake, O sword, against My
        Shepherd,
     Against the Man who is My
        Companion,"
     Says the LORD of hosts.
     "Strike the Shepherd,
     And the sheep will be scattered;
     Then I will turn My hand against
        the little ones.
8   And it shall come to pass in all
        the land,"
     Says the LORD,
     "That two-thirds in it shall be cut
        off and die,
     But one-third shall be left in it:
9   I will bring the one-third through
        the fire,
     Will refine them as silver is
        refined,
     And test them as gold is tested.
     They will call on My name,
     And I will answer them.
     I will say, 'This is My people';
     And each one will say, 'The
        LORD is my God.' "

The King of all the earth

14 Behold, the day of the LORD is
        coming,

And your spoil will be divided in your midst.

2 For I will gather all the nations to battle against Jerusalem;
The city shall be taken,
The houses rifled,
And the women ravished.
Half of the city shall go into captivity,
But the remnant of the people shall not be cut off from the city.

3 Then the LORD will go forth
And fight against those nations,
As He fights in the day of battle.

4 And in that day His feet will stand on the Mount of Olives,
Which faces Jerusalem on the east.
And the Mount of Olives shall be split in two,
From east to west,
Making a very large valley;
Half of the mountain shall move toward the north
And half of it toward the south.

5 Then you shall flee *through* My mountain valley,
For the mountain valley shall reach to Azal.
Yes, you shall flee
As you fled from the earthquake
In the days of Uzziah king of Judah.

Thus the LORD my God will come,
And all the saints with You.

6 It shall come to pass in that day
That there will be no light;
The lights will diminish.

7 It shall be one day
Which is known to the LORD—
Neither day nor night.
But at evening time it shall happen
That it will be light.

8 And in that day it shall be
That living waters shall flow from Jerusalem,

Half of them toward the eastern sea
And half of them toward the western sea;
In both summer and winter it shall occur.

9 And the LORD shall be King over all the earth.
In that day it shall be—
"The LORD *is* one,"
And His name one.

10 All the land shall be turned into a plain from Geba to Rimmon south of Jerusalem. *Jerusalem* shall be raised up and inhabited in her place from Benjamin's Gate to the place of the First Gate and the Corner Gate, and *from* the Tower of Hananel to the king's winepresses.

11 *The people* shall dwell in it;
And no longer shall there be utter destruction,
But Jerusalem shall be safely inhabited.

12 And this shall be the plague with which the LORD will strike all the people who fought against Jerusalem:

Their flesh shall dissolve while they stand on their feet,
Their eyes shall dissolve in their sockets,
And their tongues shall dissolve in their mouths.

13 It shall come to pass in that day
That a great panic from the LORD will be among them.
Everyone will seize the hand of his neighbor,
And raise his hand against his neighbor's hand;

14 Judah also will fight at Jerusalem.
And the wealth of all the surrounding nations
Shall be gathered together:
Gold, silver, and apparel in great abundance.

15 Such also shall be the plague
   On the horse *and* the mule,
   On the camel and the
      donkey,
   And on all the cattle that will be
      in those camps.
   So *shall* this plague *be.*

16 And it shall come to pass *that* everyone who is left of all the nations which came against Jerusalem shall go up from year to year to worship the King, the LORD of hosts, and to keep the Feast of Tabernacles. 17 And it shall be *that* whichever of the families of the earth do not come up to Jerusalem to worship the King, the LORD of hosts, on them there will be no rain. 18 If the family of Egypt will not come up and enter in, they *shall have* no *rain;* they shall receive the plague with which the LORD strikes the nations who do not come up to keep the Feast of Tabernacles. 19 This shall be the punishment of Egypt and the punishment of all the nations that do not come up to keep the Feast of Tabernacles.

20 In that day "HOLINESS TO THE LORD" shall be *engraved* on the bells of the horses. The pots in the LORD's house shall be like the bowls before the altar. 21 Yes, every pot in Jerusalem and Judah shall be holiness to the LORD of hosts. Everyone who sacrifices shall come and take them and cook in them. In that day there shall no longer be a Canaanite in the house of the LORD of hosts.

The Book of
MALACHI

I have the honor of being the prophet who brings the Old Testament to a close. My name is pronounced *MAL-uh-kigh* and means "My Messenger."

After my prophecy, God did not speak to us again until John the Baptist baptized Jesus in the River Jordan (see Matthew 3) four hundred years later.

I warned my people about robbing God. This means they were not supporting God's house with their tithes. A "tithe" is a tenth of the money you earn. This tenth belongs to the Lord to help in His great work of the gospel.

Most of all, I had the great joy of promising my people the coming Jesus. I called Him the "Sun of Righteousness," who would rise and heal all our sins.

Israel's offerings to God are polluted

THE burden of the word of the Lord to Israel by Malachi.

2 "I have loved you," says the Lord.
"Yet you say, 'In what way have You loved us?'
Was not Esau Jacob's brother?"
Says the Lord.
"Yet Jacob I have loved;
3 But Esau I have hated,
And laid waste his mountains and his heritage
For the jackals of the wilderness."

4 Even though Edom has said,
"We have been impoverished,
But we will return and build the desolate places,"

Thus says the Lord of hosts:

"They may build, but I will throw down;
They shall be called the Territory of Wickedness,
And the people against whom the Lord will have indignation forever.

5 Your eyes shall see,
And you shall say,
'The Lord is magnified beyond the border of Israel.'

6 "A son honors *his* father,
And a servant *his* master.
If then I am the Father,
Where *is* My honor?
And if I *am* a Master,
Where *is* My reverence?
Says the Lord of hosts
To you priests who despise My name.
Yet you say, 'In what way have we despised Your name?'

7 "You offer defiled food on My altar,
But say,
'In what way have we defiled You?'
By saying,
'The table of the Lord is contemptible.'
8 And when you offer the blind as a sacrifice,
Is it not evil?
And when you offer the lame and sick,
Is it not evil?
Offer it then to your governor!
Would he be pleased with you?

Would he accept you
favorably?''
Says the LORD of hosts.

9 "But now entreat God's favor,
That He may be gracious to
us.
While this is being *done* by your
hands,
Will He accept you favorably?''
Says the LORD of hosts.
10 "Who *is there* even among you
who would shut the doors,
So that you would not kindle fire
on My altar in vain?
I have no pleasure in you,''
Says the LORD of hosts,
"Nor will I accept an offering from
your hands.
11 For from the rising of the sun,
even to its going down,
My name *shall be* great among
the Gentiles;
In every place incense *shall be*
offered to My name,
And a pure offering;
For My name shall be great
among the nations,''
Says the LORD of hosts.

12 "But you profane it,
In that you say,
'The table of the LORD is defiled;
And its fruit, its food, *is*
contemptible.'
13 You also say,
'Oh, what a weariness!'
And you sneer at it,''
Says the LORD of hosts.
"And you bring the stolen, the
lame, and the sick;
Thus you bring an offering!
Should I accept this from your
hand?''
Says the LORD.
14 "But cursed *be* the deceiver
Who has in his flock a male,
And takes a vow,
But sacrifices to the Lord what
is blemished—
For I *am* a great King,''
Says the LORD of hosts,
"And My name *is to be* feared
among the nations.

The priests are corrupt

2 "And now, O priests, this
commandment is for you.
2 If you will not hear,
And if you will not take *it* to
heart,
To give glory to My name,''
Says the LORD of hosts,
"I will send a curse upon you,
And I will curse your blessings.
Yes, I have cursed them already,
Because you do not take *it* to
heart.

3 "Behold, I will rebuke your
descendants
And spread refuse on your faces,
The refuse of your solemn
feasts;
And *one* will take you away with
it.
4 Then you shall know that I have
sent this commandment to
you,
That My covenant with Levi may
continue,''
Says the LORD of hosts.
5 "My covenant was with him, *one*
of life and peace,
And I gave them to him *that he
might* fear *Me;*
So he feared Me
And was reverent before My
name.
6 The law of truth was in his
mouth,
And injustice was not found on
his lips.
He walked with Me in peace and
equity,
And turned many away from
iniquity.

7 "For the lips of a priest should
keep knowledge,
And *people* should seek the law
from his mouth;
For he is the messenger of the
LORD of hosts.
8 But you have departed from the
way;
You have caused many to
stumble at the law.

You have corrupted the
covenant of Levi,"
Says the LORD of hosts.
9 "Therefore I also have made you
contemptible and base
Before all the people,
Because you have not kept My
ways
But have shown partiality in the
law."

10 Have we not all one Father?
Has not one God created us?
Why do we deal treacherously
with one another
By profaning the covenant of the
fathers?
11 Judah has dealt treacherously,
And an abomination has been
committed in Israel and in
Jerusalem,
For Judah has profaned
The LORD's holy *institution*
which He loves:
He has married the daughter of
a foreign god.
12 May the LORD cut off from the
tents of Jacob
The man who does this, being
awake and aware,
Yet who brings an offering to the
LORD of hosts!

13 And this is the second thing you
do:
You cover the altar of the LORD
with tears,
With weeping and crying;
So He does not regard the
offering anymore,
Nor receive *it* with goodwill from
your hands.
14 Yet you say, "For what reason?"
Because the LORD has been
witness
Between you and the wife of
your youth,
With whom you have dealt
treacherously;
Yet she is your companion
And your wife by covenant.
15 But did He not make *them* one,
Having a remnant of the Spirit?
And why one?

He seeks godly offspring.
Therefore take heed to your
spirit,
And let none deal treacherously
with the wife of his youth.

16 "For the LORD God of Israel says
That He hates divorce,
For it covers one's garment with
violence,"
Says the LORD of hosts.
"Therefore take heed to your
spirit,
That you do not deal
treacherously."

17 You have wearied the LORD with
your words;
Yet you say,
"In what way have we wearied
Him?"
In that you say,
"Everyone who does evil
Is good in the sight of the
LORD,
And He delights in them,"
Or, "Where *is* the God of
justice?"

The people have robbed God

3 "Behold, I send My messenger,
And he will prepare the way
before Me.
And the Lord, whom you seek,
Will suddenly come to His
temple,
Even the Messenger of the
covenant,
In whom you delight.
Behold, He is coming,"
Says the LORD of hosts.

2 "But who can endure the day of
His coming?
And who can stand when He
appears?
For He *is* like a refiner's fire
And like launderers' soap.
3 He will sit as a refiner and a
purifier of silver;
He will purify the sons of Levi,
And purge them as gold and
silver,

That they may offer to the LORD
  An offering in righteousness.

4 "Then the offering of Judah and
    Jerusalem
  Will be pleasant to the LORD,
  As in the days of old,
  As in former years.
5 And I will come near you for
    judgment;
  I will be a swift witness
  Against sorcerers,
  Against adulterers,
  Against perjurers,
  Against those who exploit wage
    earners and widows and
    orphans,
  And against those who turn
    away an alien—
  Because they do not fear Me,"
  Says the LORD of hosts.

6 "For I *am* the LORD, I do not
    change;
  Therefore you are not
    consumed, O sons of Jacob.
7 Yet from the days of your
    fathers
  You have gone away from My
    ordinances
  And have not kept *them*.
  Return to Me, and I will return
    to you,"
  Says the LORD of hosts.
  "But you said,
  'In what way shall we return?'

8 "Will a man rob God?
  Yet you have robbed Me!
  But you say,

'In what way have we robbed
    You?'
  In tithes and offerings.
9 You are cursed with a curse,
  For you have robbed Me,
  Even this whole nation.
10 Bring all the tithes into the
    storehouse,
  That there may be food in My
    house,
  And try Me now in this,"
  Says the LORD of hosts,
  "If I will not open for you the
    windows of heaven
  And pour out for you *such*
    blessing
  That *there will* not *be room*
    enough *to receive it*.

11 "And I will rebuke the devourer
    for your sakes,
  So that he will not destroy the
    fruit of your ground,
  Nor shall the vine fail to
    bear fruit for you in the
    field,"
  Says the LORD of hosts;
12 And all nations will call you
    blessed,
  For you will be a delightful
    land,"
  Says the LORD of hosts.
13 "Your words have been harsh
    against Me,"
  Says the LORD,
  "Yet you say,
  'What have we spoken against
    You?'
14 You have said,
  'It is useless to serve God;

⚒ DIGGING IN

3:1 Jesus Comes to the Temple You should review how Jesus came and drove the merchants out of the temple (see John 2:13–22). Over four hundred years before Jesus was born, the prophet Malachi described Jesus coming "suddenly" to the temple.

Usually we think of Jesus as being a quiet, mild Man, but Matthew, Mark, Luke, and John all describe Jesus' violent actions when He drove out the people who were doing business in the temple. Jesus said His Father's House should be a place of prayer. You need to help others remember this, too. God's House and God's work are not places where we make ourselves rich. It is where we serve God and preach His Word.

Jesus also comes *wherever* we worship and serve Him. Let us be sure that *all we do* brings honor to Him wherever we are—at church or in the streets.

What profit *is it* that we have
   kept His ordinance,
And that we have walked as
   mourners
Before the Lord of hosts?
15 So now we call the proud
   blessed,
For those who do wickedness
   are raised up;
They even tempt God and go
   free.' "

16 Then those who feared the Lord
   spoke to one another,
And the Lord listened and heard
   them;
So a book of remembrance was
   written before Him
For those who fear the Lord
And who meditate on His
   name.

The deeds of the wicked will burn up as in an oven.

17 "They shall be Mine," says the
   Lord of hosts,
  "On the day that I make them
   My jewels.
And I will spare them
As a man spares his own son
   who serves him."
18 Then you shall again discern
Between the righteous and the
   wicked,
Between one who serves
   God
And one who does not serve
   Him.

The day of judgment will burn like an oven

4   "For behold, the day is coming,
   Burning like an oven,
   And all the proud, yes, all who
     do wickedly will be stubble.
   And the day which is coming
     shall burn them up,"
   Says the Lord of hosts,
  "That will leave them neither root
     nor branch.
2   But to you who fear My name

What Malachi Learned

God showed me something very wonderful as I was
bringing the Old Testament to an end.
    My people had lived through very hard times of suf-
fering. Often there seemed to be no hope. Was there
anything in our future that could comfort them?
    Then the Lord showed me that someday He would
come and live among us. That would be the beginning
of God's great plan to build a kingdom that would
last forever. I didn't understand all that He meant. But now I know that
Jesus did come and show the world that He is God, "the Sun of Righteousness," who heals sin, disease, and death.

The Sun of Righteousness shall
arise
With healing in His wings;
And you shall go out
And grow fat like stall-fed
calves.
3 You shall trample the wicked,
For they shall be ashes under the
soles of your feet
On the day that I do *this*,"
Says the LORD of hosts.

4 "Remember the Law of Moses,
My servant,

Which I commanded him in
Horeb for all Israel,
With the statutes and judgments.
5 Behold, I will send you Elijah the
prophet
Before the coming of the great
and dreadful day of the LORD.
6 And he will turn
The hearts of the fathers to the
children,
And the hearts of the children
to their fathers,
Lest I come and strike the earth
with a curse."

WORDFINDER

4:3 Lord of Hosts A name for God as the leader of His heavenly armies. Lord
Sabaoth (pronounced *SAB-ay-oth*), from the Hebrew, means the same.

WHAT HAPPENED BETWEEN THE OLD AND NEW TESTAMENTS

By now you may know that the people of Israel were captives in Babylonia (pronounced *bab-ih-LOW-nee-uh*) between the years 606 B.C. and 536 B.C. Most of them were taken there in 586 B.C. The people were in Babylonia for a total of 70 years. You can read about these times in places like 2 Kings 25 and the books of Ezra, Nehemiah, and Esther. The prophets Jeremiah, Ezekiel, and Daniel also tell about this time. The prophet Malachi and the Book of Nehemiah bring the history of ancient Israel up to about 400 B.C., when Persia ruled the world. By this time King Cyrus of Persia had allowed the Jews to return to Palestine in 536 B.C. (see Ezra 1).

Alexander the Great

In 333 B.C., Alexander the Great of Greece conquered the Persian world. Ten years later, Alexander died at the early age of 33. Then his generals in Syria and Egypt ruled Palestine.

At about 167 B.C., the Syrian King, Antiochus IV, tried to destroy the Jewish religion. He even sacrificed a pig on the temple altar! This was an insult because pork was forbidden to the Jews. (Pronounce the king's name *an-TIE-oh-kus*.)

The Maccabees

At that time the Hasmon family led a Jewish revolt against their Syrian ene-

Alexander the Great conquered Palestine 300 years before Christ.

mies and drove them out. That Jewish family was also called the Maccabees—meaning "Hammers"—because they "hammered" the Syrians out of Palestine. This began a period of Jewish independence that lasted about a hundred years.

It is interesting that the Pharisees you meet in the New Testament arose during the revolt of the Maccabees. So the Pharisees saw themselves as the defenders of the Jewish religion—even against Jesus.

Julius Caesar

Julius Caesar was a brilliant general who became the father of the Roman Empire. Through a series of well-planned battles, Caesar was able to expand the empire throughout the known world.

As he assumed more and more power, he ordered that a month of the calendar—July—would bear his name and that coins

Pompey, a Roman general

with his image stamped on them would be issued.

In spite of his earthly power, however, Caesar could not protect himself from those who were secretly plotting to overthrow his government. And on March 15, at a Senate meeting, he was stabbed to death by some former "friends."

Pompey

The power of the Roman Empire was first felt in Judea during an invasion by General Pompey. In 63 B.C., he captured Jerusalem, breaking down part of the wall surrounding the city.

Pompey actually broke into the Holy of Holies at the temple, where only the high priest was allowed to enter. But he did not disturb anything there and even permitted temple worship to continue.

By the time Jesus was born, the Romans were in full control of the country. Herod, an evil man, had been named Procurator of Judea, with the promise that one day he would be king of the Jews. He certainly did not welcome the news that a rival King, the true King of the Jews, was about to be born!

The Famous Dead Sea Scrolls

In 1947 a shepherd boy lost one of his goats along the west bank of the Dead Sea. While trying to find the goat, he threw a stone into one of the many caves

Julius Caesar, a Roman emperor, conquered Palestine 63 years before Christ.

in that place. But instead of hearing a goat's cry, the boy heard the sound of a breaking pot.

In that cave and others were found many pots or jars containing ancient writings. Some of these writings were Hebrew copies of the Old Testament. The complete scroll of the prophecy of Isaiah is the most famous of all.

These scrolls, or rolls, were carefully written on leather and copper by people living in the community of Qumran (pronounced *KUM-ran*). It is believed that these people had left the cities of Israel to live a simple life of worship by the Dead Sea. The scrolls were copied during the time between a hundred years before Jesus lived and a hundred years afterward. The Dead Sea Scrolls show that God's Word in the Old Testament was very carefully preserved for our own time.

The most famous scroll contains the entire Book of Isaiah, beautifully handwritten on the hairy side of animal skins.

The
New Testament

What is the New Testament About?
At the beginning of the Old Testament, we said that the whole Bible is God's great story of salvation. When we are born into the world, we don't like to please God. We even imagine we can only be happy if we live to please ourselves. That's what sin is—going against God's plan for our lives in the world He created.

The second part of the story of salvation is contained in the 27 books of the New Testament. These books tell how God sent His promised Messiah, Jesus Christ, to finish the work of salvation begun in the Old Testament. God would create us *all over again* with a mind and a will that enjoys pleasing Him. That is what we mean by "salvation." Than you would be fit to live with God forever in a new world that He is planning for those who love Him.

The first four books of the New Testament tell you the story of the life of Jesus the Savior. They are called *Gospels,* meaning "Good News"—that is, the Good News of salvation. The fifth book, the Acts of the Apostles, tells how the first Christians told the story of salvation everywhere and began the first churches in Palestine, Asia, and Europe. The next 21 books are letters from the apostles to Christians in different parts of the ancient world. These letters contain the main body of teaching that God wants us to know so that we can live the Christian life. The last book is Revelation, which shows God's great plan for His new world of the future.

The Book of
MATTHEW

My name is pronounced *MATH-you* and means "The Gift of the Lord." Some people were surprised when Jesus called me to be one of His twelve disciples.

I was a tax collector. Everybody hated tax collectors because we took our people's money and gave it to our Roman enemies. Even the Romans themselves treated us with hatred because we didn't care about our own people.

Jesus was different, though. He didn't hate me, and He was the first Person who ever made me feel wanted. One day He came to the shop where I collected taxes. He just looked into my eyes and said two words: "Follow Me!"

I never knew such love as Jesus showed me that day, and I have been His disciple ever since. A disciple is a learner, and you can be a disciple, too.

Jesus' family tree

THE book of the **genealogy** of Jesus Christ, the Son of David, the Son of Abraham:

2 Abraham begot Isaac, Isaac begot Jacob, and Jacob begot Judah and his brothers. 3 Judah begot Perez and Zerah by Tamar, Perez begot Hezron, and Hezron begot Ram. 4 Ram begot Amminadab, Amminadab begot Nahshon, and Nahshon begot Salmon. 5 Salmon begot Boaz by Rahab, Boaz begot Obed by Ruth, Obed begot Jesse, 6 and Jesse begot David the king.

David the king begot Solomon by her *who had been the wife* of Uriah. 7 Solomon begot Rehoboam, Rehoboam begot Abijah, and Abijah begot

WORDFINDER

1:1 Genealogy The history of a family showing the family members of each generation from the beginning. This genealogy of Jesus begins with Abraham and ends with Joseph, husband of Mary.

DIGGING IN

1:1–17 The Family of Jesus God is a TRINITY (pronounced *TRIN-uh-tee*). This means that the one God is three Persons. God is our Father in heaven, Christ is the everlasting Son of the Father, and the Holy Spirit is the Third Person of God. Each Person is part of the one God in a special way, and each Person works along with the other two Persons.

For example, three separate glasses of water can be poured into one pitcher and become one container of water. In a similar way, the one God is also three Persons.

Jesus was always in heaven as God the Son, along with His Father and the Holy Spirit. But the Father sent His Son into the world to be born just like you were born. So the Son of God became Mary's Baby and grew up to be your Savior. As you read Matthew 1, you can see the list of the members of Jesus' earthly family going all the way back to Abraham two thousand years earlier.

Asa. ⁸ Asa begot Jehoshaphat, Jehoshaphat begot Joram, and Joram begot Uzziah. ⁹ Uzziah begot Jotham, Jotham begot Ahaz, and Ahaz begot Hezekiah. ¹⁰ Hezekiah begot Manasseh, Manasseh begot Amon, and Amon begot Josiah. ¹¹ Josiah begot Jeconiah and his brothers about the time they were carried away to Babylon.

¹² And after they were brought to Babylon, Jeconiah begot Shealtiel, and Shealtiel begot Zerubbabel. ¹³ Zerubbabel begot Abiud, Abiud begot Eliakim, and Eliakim begot Azor. ¹⁴ Azor begot Zadok, Zadok begot Achim, and Achim begot Eliud. ¹⁵ Eliud begot Eleazar, Eleazar begot Matthan, and Matthan begot Jacob. ¹⁶ And Jacob begot Joseph the husband of Mary, of whom was born Jesus who is called **Christ**.

¹⁷ So all the generations from Abraham to David *are* fourteen generations, from David until the captivity in Babylon *are* fourteen generations, and from the captivity in Babylon until the Christ *are* fourteen generations.

¹⁸ Now the birth of Jesus Christ was as follows: After His mother Mary was betrothed to Joseph, before they came together, she was found with child of the Holy Spirit. ¹⁹ Then Joseph her husband, being a just *man*, and not wanting to make her a public example, was minded to put her away secretly. ²⁰ But while he thought about these things, behold, an **angel** of the Lord appeared to him in a dream, saying, "Joseph, son of David, do not be afraid to take to you Mary your wife, for that which is conceived in her is of the Holy Spirit. ²¹ And she will bring forth a Son, and you shall call His name JESUS, for He will save His people from their sins."

²² So all this was done that it might be fulfilled which was spoken by the Lord through the prophet, saying: ²³ "Behold, the virgin shall be with child, and bear a Son, and they shall call His name **Immanuel**," which is translated, "God with us."

²⁴ Then Joseph, being aroused from sleep, did as the angel of the Lord commanded him and took to him his wife, ²⁵ and did not know her till she had brought forth her firstborn Son. And he called His name JESUS.

Why Was His Name "Jesus"?

The name *Jesus* comes from the Old Testament name *Yeshua* (pronounced *yesh-YOU-uh*) or Joshua. In the New Testament, the name was written in the Greek language, Jesus, pronounced *YAY-soos*. Both of these spellings have the same meaning. They mean "The Lord Is Salvation."

Who Was the King of the Jews?

The ancient true kings of the Jews came from the family of David. God promised David that his throne and kingdom would last forever (see 2 Samuel 7:13). The Romans later placed Herod on the Jewish throne—but he was not even a Jew! Jesus was the true King from the family of David.

WORDFINDER

1:16 Christ The divine title of the Man Jesus. The word means "the Anointed" (by the Holy Spirit). *Christos* is a Greek word translated from the Hebrew *Messiah*.

1:20 Angel Means "messenger." The messenger is usually from heaven, but sometimes the messenger is human. For example, Malachi, the name of the Old Testament prophet, means "my angel" or "my messenger."

1:23 Immanuel A Hebrew name meaning "God with us." The name refers to the coming Messiah, or Christ, in the New Testament. Jesus truly was and is "God with us."

Scholars Announce Birth of New King

New Testament News Service

BETHLEHEM—The wire services of the world are buzzing with the startling events in Bethlehem of Judea. A group of scholars from Persia has announced the birth of a new and unusual King in that city. The scholars are so excited about the event that they have traveled all the way from Persia to Judea to see the Child.

Persian National Television (PNTV) sent a news team to the location, but all they found was a poor family with a new Baby!

In an interview with one of the scholars, reporters asked: "Sir, are you sure this is the King that you announced to the world?" The scholar replied: "No doubt about it! Our calculations have never been mistaken. The signs are very clear by the star we have seen in the heavens. Even King Herod believes us."

Three wise men and a wicked king

2 Now after Jesus was born in Bethlehem of Judea in the days of Herod the king, behold, wise men from the East came to Jerusalem, ² saying, "Where is He who has been born King of the Jews? For we have seen His star in the East and have come to worship Him."

³ When Herod the king heard *this,* he was troubled, and all Jerusalem with him. ⁴ And when he had gathered all the chief priests and scribes of the people together, he inquired of them where the Christ was to be born.

⁵ So they said to him, "In Bethlehem of Judea, for thus it is written by the prophet:

⁶ 'But you, Bethlehem, *in* the land of Judah,
Are not the least among the rulers of Judah;
For out of you shall come a Ruler
Who will shepherd My people Israel.' "

⁷ Then Herod, when he had secretly called the wise men, determined from them what time the star appeared. ⁸ And he sent them to Bethlehem and said, "Go and search carefully for the young Child, and when you have found *Him,* bring back word to me, that I may come and worship Him also."

⁹ When they heard the king, they departed; and behold, the star which they had seen in the East went before them,

⚒ DIGGING IN

2:1 Wise Men from the East In Luke 2, you can read about the visit of the shepherds on the first Christmas Eve, when Jesus was born. Later, some wise men from the Middle East also came to worship the Baby Jesus. You read about these men in Matthew 2.

We know that these wise men came from Persia, which is called Iran today. They were magi (pronounced *MAY-ji*). The magi were scholars in a Persian religion called Zoroastrianism (pronounced *zorro-AS-tree-uh-nism*). Some of these Persians had learned to admire the Hebrew God when the Jews were captives in Babylon over five hundred years before Jesus was born.

When these scholars saw the sign of Jesus' birth in the heavens, they knew that the promised King of the Jews was going to be born. So they traveled to Israel across hundreds of miles of desert to worship Him.

Ruins of the castle of Herod the Great, who reigned during the time of Jesus.

till it came and stood over where the young Child was. ¹⁰ When they saw the star, they rejoiced with exceedingly great joy. ¹¹ And when they had come into the house, they saw the young Child with Mary His mother, and fell down and worshiped Him. And when they had opened their treasures, they presented gifts to Him: gold, frankincense, and myrrh.

¹² Then, being divinely warned in a dream that they should not return to Herod, they departed for their own country another way.

¹³ Now when they had departed, behold, an angel of the Lord appeared to Joseph in a dream, saying, "Arise, take the young Child and His mother, flee to Egypt, and stay there until I bring you word; for Herod will seek the young Child to destroy Him."

¹⁴ When he arose, he took the young Child and His mother by night and departed for Egypt, ¹⁵ and was

there until the death of Herod, that it might be fulfilled which was spoken by the Lord through the prophet, saying, "Out of Egypt I called My Son."

¹⁶ Then Herod, when he saw that he was deceived by the wise men, was exceedingly angry; and he sent forth and put to death all the male children who were in Bethlehem and in all its districts, from two years old and under, according to the time which he had determined from the wise men. ¹⁷ Then was fulfilled what was spoken by Jeremiah the prophet, saying:

¹⁸ "A voice was heard in Ramah,
    Lamentation, weeping, and
        great mourning,
    Rachel weeping *for* her children,
    Refusing to be comforted,
    Because they are no more."

¹⁹ Now when Herod was dead, behold, an angel of the Lord appeared

DIGGING IN

2:19 The Four Herods The "King Herod" described in Matthew 2 ruled Palestine when Jesus was born. He was not a Jew. He was actually a descendant of Esau, who lived almost two thousand years earlier. The descendants of Esau (called Edomites) were enemies of the Jewish people for a long time. (See Gene-

Boy Babies Killed at Bethlehem

PNTV (Persian National Television)—We interrupt this broadcast to bring you the following report: All babies two years old and younger in Bethlehem of Judea have been killed by King Herod's soldiers!

A group of scholars, who have recently returned from a visit to that country, have revealed important information that may explain the reason for this action. When the scholars were in Judea, they saw an infant King who may prove a threat to Herod. Apparently, King Herod got news of the birth and

was afraid that the Child would take his place on the throne. He then sent his soldiers to Bethlehem to kill all baby boys around the age of this Child.

The Persian scholars also reveal that Herod is not the true king of the Jews. In fact, he is not even a Jew! The true King of the Jews must come from the family of King David who lived a thousand years ago.

In a late-breaking news flash, PNTV reports that the family visited by the Persian scholars has fled to Egypt to protect the life of their Child.

in a dream to Joseph in Egypt, 20 saying, "Arise, take the young Child and His mother, and go to the land of Israel, for those who sought the young Child's life are dead." 21 Then he arose, took the young Child and His mother, and came into the land of Israel. 22 But when he heard that Archelaus was reigning over Judea instead of his father Herod, he was afraid to go there. And being warned by God in a dream, he turned aside into the region of Galilee. 23 And he came and dwelt in a city called Nazareth, that it might be fulfilled which was spoken by the prophets, "He shall be called a Nazarene."

John baptizes Jesus in the Jordan River

3 In those days John the Baptist came preaching in the wilderness of Judea, 2 and saying, "Repent, for the kingdom of heaven is at hand!" 3 For this is he who was spoken of by the prophet Isaiah, saying:

> "The voice of one crying in the wilderness:
> 'Prepare the way of the LORD;
> Make His paths straight.' "

4 Now John himself was clothed in camel's hair, with a leather belt around his waist; and his food was locusts and wild honey. 5 Then Jerusalem, all

DIGGING IN

sis 27:30–42.) So it was cruel for the emperor of Rome to make Esau's descendant, Herod, 'King of the Jews' just before Jesus was born. Jesus was the lawful King of the Jews because He came from the family of David, the ancient Jewish king that God loved.

We meet three other Herods in the New Testament: (1) Herod Antipas (pronounced AN-tih-pass), (2) Herod Agrippa I, and (3) Herod Agrippa II (pronounce their names uh-GRIP-uh).

Herod Antipas, son of Herod the Great, was the Herod who executed John the Baptist (see Matthew 14). He was first called "Herod the tetrarch." The word "te-

trarch" means ruler of a fourth part. This meant that Herod Antipas ruled the province of Galilee and Perea before he became king of all Palestine. Herod Antipas and his men made fun of Jesus during His trial. Then Antipas sent Jesus back to Pilate for sentencing (see Luke 23:6–12).

The last two Herods appear in the book of Acts. Herod Agrippa I executed James, brother of the apostle John (Acts 21). Herod Agrippa's son was Herod Agrippa II, and he took part in the trial of the apostle Paul (Acts 25). Agrippa II was the last of the Herod kings.

Crowds Hear Preacher at Jordan River

AJTN (The All-Judea Television Network)—Channel 3 has been providing coverage of recent happenings at the Jordan River. "John the Baptizer," as he is called, is holding daily meetings at the river. Thousands are coming to hear him preach. Many have confessed their sins, and John has been baptizing these people in the river.

Some of the religious leaders who have attended John's meetings have left angry because John tells them their lives have not really changed.

A Man named Jesus recently came for baptism. It is reported that John seemed surprised and said, "You should baptize *me!*" But Jesus insisted that John baptize Him. Reporters are saying that, when Jesus came up from the water, a heavenly voice spoke.

We are all wondering who this Man Jesus is.

Judea, and all the region around the Jordan went out to him 6 and were baptized by him in the Jordan, confessing their sins.

Who Were the Sadducees?

The Sadducees (pronounced *SAD-you-sees*) were a religious and political group who didn't believe in miracles or in a resurrection of the body after death. They disagreed with the Pharisees (pronounced *FAIR-uh-sees*). We will look at the Pharisees in Matthew 9. The Sadducees, like the Pharisees, were against Jesus.

7 But when he saw many of the Pharisees and Sadducees coming to his baptism, he said to them, "Brood of vipers! Who warned you to flee from the wrath to come? 8 Therefore bear fruits worthy of repentance, 9 and do not think to say to yourselves, 'We have Abraham as *our* father.' For I say to you that God is able to raise up children to Abraham from these stones. 10 And even now the ax is laid to the root of the trees. Therefore every tree which does not bear good fruit is cut down and thrown into the fire. 11 I indeed baptize you with water unto repentance, but He who is coming after me is mightier than I, whose sandals I am not worthy to carry. He will baptize you with the Holy Spirit and fire. 12 His winnowing fan *is* in His hand, and He will thoroughly clean out His threshing floor, and gather His wheat into the barn; but He will burn up the chaff with unquenchable fire."

13 Then Jesus came from Galilee to John at the Jordan to be baptized by him. 14 And John *tried to* prevent Him, saying, "I need to be baptized by You, and are You coming to me?"

15 But Jesus answered and said to him, "Permit *it to be so* now, for thus it is fitting for us to fulfill all righteousness." Then he allowed Him.

16 When He had been baptized, Jesus came up immediately from the water; and behold, the heavens were opened to Him, and He saw the Spirit of God descending like a dove and alighting upon Him. 17 And suddenly a voice *came* from heaven, saying, "This is My beloved Son, in whom I am well pleased."

Who Is the Son of God?

Jesus was the great Son of David a thousand years after David lived, but Jesus was also the Son of God. The prophets had long foretold the coming of the Son of God (see Isaiah 7:14). Jesus didn't become the Son of God by being born in the world. He was always the Son of God in heaven.

What the Religious Leaders Learned

For a long time we Pharisees and Sadducees thought we were God's favorite people. (Pronounce our names *FAIR-uh-sees* and *SAD-you-sees*.) When we heard that John the Baptist was preaching and baptizing people in the River Jordan, we decided to go, too. We were sure he would take us first in line to be baptized.

We were very disappointed when John told us God didn't care that we had descended from Abraham, the father of the Jews. He even said we were a bunch of snakes! Can you imagine that? He said that to *us*— the religious leaders of the people!

Some of us were beginning to wonder if we were as good as we thought we were. We always watched for other people's sins, but we closed our eyes to our own! God says *everybody* has to leave his sin behind. Do you think that includes you?

Satan tempts Jesus to do wrong

4 Then Jesus was led up by the Spirit into the wilderness to be tempted by the **devil**. ² And when He had fasted forty days and forty nights, afterward He was hungry. ³ Now when the tempter came to Him, he said, "If You are the Son of God, command that these stones become bread."

⁴ But He answered and said, "It is written, 'Man shall not live by bread alone, but by every word that proceeds from the mouth of God.'"

⁵ Then the devil took Him up into the holy city, set Him on the pinnacle of the temple, ⁶ and said to Him, "If You are the Son of God, throw Yourself down. For it is written:

'He shall give His angels charge over you,'

and,

'In *their* hands they shall bear you up,

Lest you dash your foot against a stone.'"

⁷ Jesus said to him, "It is written again, 'You shall not tempt the LORD your God.'"

⁸ Again, the devil took Him up on an exceedingly high mountain, and showed Him all the kingdoms of the world and their glory. ⁹ And he said to Him, "All these things I will give You if You will fall down and worship me."

¹⁰ Then Jesus said to him, "Away with you, Satan! For it is written, 'You shall worship the LORD your God, and Him only you shall serve.'"

¹¹ Then the devil left Him, and behold, angels came and ministered to Him.

¹² Now when Jesus heard that John had been put in prison, He departed to Galilee. ¹³ And leaving Nazareth, He came and dwelt in Capernaum, which is by the sea, in the regions of Zebulun and Naphtali, ¹⁴ that it might be fulfilled which was spoken by Isaiah the prophet, saying:

WORDFINDER

4:1 The Devil The title of the angel who rebelled against God's authority. The word means "liar," "slanderer," or "accuser." Satan, meaning "Enemy," is his personal name.

What the Devil Learned

I must have been out of my mind to think I could get Jesus to disobey His Father. But I sure tried!

First, I tried to get Him to do a couple of miracles just to prove He was the Son of God, but Jesus didn't fall for that. He didn't even seem to care if I believed in Him or not.

Then I offered Him all the nations of the world. All He had to do was worship me. I guess that was pretty stupid. I was offering the world to the One who created everything!

Nothing worked. Jesus just brushed me off. Since I couldn't get anywhere, I left Him. But it really made me mad to see those angels come and comfort Him!

A house at Capernaum, where Jesus set up His ministry.

15 "The land of Zebulun and the
        land of Naphtali,
    By the way of the sea, beyond
        the Jordan,
    Galilee of the Gentiles:
16   The people who sat in darkness
        have seen a great light,
    And upon those who sat in the
        region and shadow of death
    Light has dawned."

17 From that time Jesus began to preach and to say, "Repent, for the kingdom of heaven is at hand."

18 And Jesus, walking by the Sea of Galilee, saw two brothers, Simon called Peter, and Andrew his brother, casting a net into the sea; for they were fishermen. 19 Then He said to them, "Follow Me, and I will make you fishers of men." 20 They immediately left *their* nets and followed Him.

21 Going on from there, He saw two other brothers, James *the son* of Zebedee, and John his brother, in the boat with Zebedee their father, mending their nets. He called them, 22 and immediately they left the boat and their father, and followed Him.

23 And Jesus went about all Galilee, teaching in their synagogues, preach-

"Follow Me, and I will make you fishers of men."

This chapel, overlooking the Sea of Galilee, marks the place where Jesus preached the Sermon on the Mount.

ing the **gospel** of the kingdom, and healing all kinds of sickness and all kinds of disease among the people. 24 Then His fame went throughout all Syria; and they brought to Him all sick people who were afflicted with various diseases and torments, and those who were **demon-possessed,** epileptics, and paralytics; and He healed them. 25 Great multitudes followed Him— from Galilee, and *from* Decapolis, Je-

rusalem, Judea, and beyond the Jordan.

Jesus teaches His followers how to be happy

5 And seeing the multitudes, He went up on a mountain, and when He was seated His disciples came to Him. 2 Then He opened His mouth and taught them, saying:

WORDFINDER

4:23 Gospel Means "good news." The word is taken from the early English word *godspel*. In the New Testament, it is the Good News about Jesus Christ.

4:24 Demon-Possessed A person controlled by one or more demons living in him. A demon is an invisible spirit-being who serves Satan.

DIGGING IN

5:2–12 The Beatitudes Christians have always loved the Beatitudes of Jesus. The word *beatitude* is pronounced *bee-AT-uh-tyood* and might be called a "blessed attitude."

If you truly love Jesus, you will not be proud, but "poor in spirit." God will comfort you if you "mourn" (are sorry) for your sins. God will supply all your needs if you are "meek," or gentle. If you desire to be a good person ("righteous"), God will make you *truly* good. If you show mercy

to suffering people, God will show *you* mercy. If you are determined to please God (have a "pure heart"), then someday you will see Jesus in heaven. If you bring peace to the lives of others, you will be a true child of God. If you are "persecuted" (suffer) for Jesus, you will be a member of God's kingdom.

All these Beatitudes of Jesus describe how a Christian lives for God. You should memorize the Beatitudes.

3 "**Blessed** *are* the poor in spirit,
    For theirs is the kingdom of
    heaven.
4 Blessed *are* those who mourn,
    For they shall be comforted.
5 Blessed *are* the meek,
    For they shall inherit the earth.
6 Blessed *are* those who hunger
    and thirst for righteousness,
    For they shall be filled.
7 Blessed *are* the merciful,
    For they shall obtain mercy.
8 Blessed *are* the pure in heart,
    For they shall see God.
9 Blessed *are* the peacemakers,
    For they shall be called sons
    of God.
10 Blessed are those who are
    persecuted for
    righteousness' sake,
    For theirs is the kingdom of
    heaven.

11 "Blessed are you when they revile and persecute you, and say all kinds of evil against you falsely for My sake. 12 Rejoice and be exceedingly glad, for great is your reward in heaven, for so they persecuted the prophets who were before you.

13 "You are the salt of the earth; but if the salt loses its flavor, how shall it be seasoned? It is then good for nothing but to be thrown out and trampled underfoot by men.

14 "You are the light of the world. A city that is set on a hill cannot be hidden. 15 Nor do they light a lamp and put it under a basket, but on a **lampstand,** and it gives light to all *who are* in the house. 16 Let your light so shine before men, that they may see your good works and glorify your Father in heaven.

17 "Do not think that I came to destroy the Law or the Prophets. I did

Why Are Christians Called "Light"?

Jesus says He is "the Light of the world" (John 8:12). But He also says His followers are lights in the world. They bring the light of God's truth into a world dark with ignorance and sin. Jesus says Christians must not hide their light. Do you?

not come to destroy but to fulfill. 18 For assuredly, I say to you, till heaven and earth pass away, one jot or one tittle will by no means pass from the law till all is fulfilled. 19 Whoever therefore breaks one of the least of these commandments, and teaches men so, shall be called least in the kingdom of heaven; but whoever does and teaches *them,* he shall be called great in the kingdom of heaven. 20 For I say to you, that unless your righteousness exceeds *the righteousness* of the scribes and Pharisees, you will by no means enter the kingdom of heaven.

21 "You have heard that it was said to those of old, 'You shall not murder, and whoever murders will be in danger of the judgment.' 22 But I say to you

What Is Hatred?

God commanded us not to murder (see Exodus 20:13). But Jesus says that saying and doing unkind things to people is like murder. You can help people who are downhearted by a word or deed of kindness. Your kindness is the only way some people can see Jesus.

WORDFINDER

5:3 Blessed An adjective that means a person is favored by God and His kindness. Sometimes the word means "the happiness that God gives."

5:15 Lampstand An ornate, gold lamp of seven branches. It was a symbol of God's presence in what was called the Holy Place of Israel's place of worship.

that whoever is angry with his brother without a cause shall be in danger of the judgment. And whoever says to his brother, 'Raca!' shall be in danger of the council. But whoever says, 'You fool!' shall be in danger of **hell** fire. 23 Therefore if you bring your gift to the altar, and there remember that your brother has something against you, 24 leave your gift there before the altar, and go your way. First be **reconciled** to your brother, and then come and offer your gift. 25 Agree with your adversary quickly, while you are on the way with him, lest your adversary deliver you to the judge, the judge hand you over to the officer, and you be thrown into prison. 26 Assuredly, I say to you, you will by no means get out of there till you have paid the last penny.

27 "You have heard that it was said to those of old, 'You shall not commit adultery.' 28 But I say to you that whoever looks at a woman to lust for her has already committed adultery with her in his heart. 29 If your right eye causes you to sin, pluck it out and cast it from you; for it is more profitable for you that one of your members perish, than for your whole body to be cast into hell. 30 And if your right hand causes you to sin, cut it off and cast it from you; for it is more profitable for you that one of your members perish, than for your whole body to be cast into hell.

31 "Furthermore it has been said, 'Whoever divorces his wife, let him give her a certificate of divorce.' 32 But I say to you that whoever divorces his wife for any reason except sexual immorality causes her to commit adultery; and whoever marries a woman who is divorced commits adultery.

33 "Again you have heard that it was said to those of old, 'You shall not swear falsely, but shall perform your oaths to the Lord.' 34 But I say to you, do not swear at all: neither by heaven, for it is God's throne; 35 nor by the earth, for it is His footstool; nor by Jerusalem, for it is the city of the great King. 36 Nor shall you swear by your head, because you cannot make one hair white or black. 37 But let your 'Yes' be 'Yes,' and your 'No,' 'No.' For whatever is more than these is from the evil one.

38 "You have heard that it was said, 'An eye for an eye and a tooth for a tooth.' 39 But I tell you not to resist an evil person. But whoever slaps you on your right cheek, turn the other to him also. 40 If anyone wants to sue you and take away your tunic, let him have your cloak also. 41 And whoever compels you to go one mile, go with him two. 42 Give to him who asks you, and from him who wants to borrow from you do not turn away.

43 "You have heard that it was said, 'You shall love your neighbor and hate your enemy.' 44 But I say to you, love your enemies, bless those who curse you, do good to those who hate you, and pray for those who spitefully use you and persecute you, 45 that you may be sons of your Father in heaven; for He makes His sun rise on the evil and on the good, and sends rain on the just and on the unjust. 46 For if you love those who love you, what reward have you? Do not even the tax collectors do the same? 47 And if you greet your brethren only, what do you do more *than others?* Do not even the

WORDFINDER

5:22 Hell A place of endless misery where ungodly people go when they die. It is translated from a word for the burning dumping ground outside Jerusalem in Jesus' time.

5:24 Reconciled Pronounced *RECK-un-syld*. To be at peace with someone. God is at peace with us because Christ died for our sins. So now we should be at peace with God.

tax collectors do so? 48 Therefore you shall be perfect, just as your Father in heaven is perfect.

Jesus teaches His disciples how to pray

6 "Take heed that you do not do your charitable deeds before men, to be seen by them. Otherwise you have no reward from your Father in heaven. 2 Therefore, when you do a charitable deed, do not sound a trumpet before you as the hypocrites do in the synagogues and in the streets, that they may have glory from men. Assuredly, I say to you, they have their reward. 3 But when you do a charitable deed, do not let your left hand know what your right hand is doing, 4 that your charitable deed may be in secret; and your Father who sees in secret will Himself reward you openly.

How Do You Show Kindness?

Some people do kind deeds because they want everybody to think they are good people. But it's what God sees that counts. You can't help it if people find out you're a kind person, but God wants you to live for His praise, not for the praise of others.

---

5 "And when you pray, you shall not be like the hypocrites. For they love to pray standing in the synagogues and on the corners of the streets, that they may be seen by men. Assuredly, I say to you, they have their reward. 6 But you, when you pray, go into your room, and when you have shut your door, pray to your Father who is in the secret *place;* and your Father who sees in secret will reward you openly. 7 And when you pray, do not use vain repetitions as the heathen *do.* For they think that they will be heard for their many words.

8 "Therefore do not be like them. For your Father knows the things you have need of before you ask Him. 9 In this manner, therefore, pray:

> Our Father in heaven,
> Hallowed be Your name.
> 10 Your kingdom come.
> Your will be done
> On earth as *it is* in heaven.
> 11 Give us this day our daily bread.
> 12 And forgive us our debts,
> As we forgive our debtors.
> 13 And do not lead us into temptation,
> But deliver us from the evil one.
> For Yours is the kingdom and the power and the glory forever. Amen.

14 "For if you forgive men their trespasses, your heavenly Father will also forgive you. 15 But if you do not forgive men their trespasses, neither will your Father forgive your trespasses.

16 "Moreover, when you fast, do not be like the hypocrites, with a sad countenance. For they disfigure their faces that they may appear to men to be

---

⚒ DIGGING IN

6:9–13 How to Pray Prayer is not just telling God everything that comes into your mind. Jesus taught us how to pray. We don't always use His words, but we should always pray for the kinds of things He lists in His prayer.

You should remember that God is your Father in heaven, and His "name" is to be used carefully. God isn't your buddy. He is *the Lord.* A Christian wants to see God's kingdom coming everywhere, and not just at the end of the world. God's kingdom also comes when He rules your life. That means that His will is being done in you as well as in heaven. Remember that you depend on Him for all your earthly needs. Ask Him to help you not give in to evil desires ("temptation") and to keep you from the power of Satan ("the Evil One"). Be sure that God's "glory" (honor) is what you care most about in all your prayers.

fasting. Assuredly, I say to you, they have their reward. 17 But you, when you fast, anoint your head and wash your face, 18 so that you do not appear to men to be fasting, but to your Father who *is* in the secret *place;* and your Father who sees in secret will reward you openly.

19 "Do not lay up for yourselves treasures on earth, where moth and rust destroy and where thieves break in and steal; 20 but lay up for yourselves treasures in heaven, where neither moth nor rust destroys and where thieves do not break in and steal.

Where Is the Real Treasure?

Maybe you've read stories about finding buried treasure. But you don't have to dig up the earth to find real treasure. The best treasure is in heaven where God is. God wants you to find that heavenly treasure. You can find it by giving your life to Him for whatever He asks you to do.

---

21 For where your treasure is, there your heart will be also.

22 "The lamp of the body is the *eye.* If therefore your *eye* is good, your whole body will be full of light. 23 But if your *eye* is bad, your whole body will be full of darkness. If therefore the light that is in you is darkness, how great *is* that darkness!

24 "No one can serve two masters; for either he will hate the one and love the other, or else he will be loyal to the one and despise the other. You cannot serve God and **mammon.**

25 "Therefore I say to you, do not worry about your life, what you will eat or what you will drink; nor about your body, what you will put on. Is not life more than food and the body more than clothing? 26 Look at the birds of the air, for they neither sow nor reap nor gather into barns; yet your heavenly Father feeds them. Are you not of more value than they? 27 Which of you by worrying can add one cubit to his stature?

28 "So why do you worry about clothing? Consider the lilies of the field, how they grow: they neither toil nor spin; 29 and yet I say to you that even Solomon in all his glory was not arrayed like one of these. 30 Now if God so clothes the grass of the field, which today is, and tomorrow is thrown into the oven, *will He* not much more *clothe* you, O you of little faith?

31 "Therefore do not worry, saying, 'What shall we eat?' or 'What shall we drink?' or 'What shall we wear?' 32 For after all these things the Gentiles seek. For your heavenly Father knows that you need all these things. 33 But seek first the kingdom of God and His righteousness, and all these things shall be added to you. 34 Therefore do not worry about tomorrow, for tomorrow will worry about its own things. Sufficient for the day *is* its own trouble.

The most important things

7 "Judge not, that you be not judged. 2 For with what judgment you judge, you will be judged; and with the measure you use, it will be measured back to you. 3 And why do you look at the speck in your brother's eye, but do not consider the plank in your own eye? 4 Or how can you say to your brother, 'Let me remove the speck from your eye'; and look, a plank *is* in your own eye? 5 **Hypocrite!** First remove the plank from your own eye, and then you will see clearly to remove the speck from your brother's eye.

🌐 **WORDFINDER**

6:24 Mammon   Money, wealth, or material goods that are treated as more important than God. To serve mammon is to worship money instead of God.

7:5 Hypocrite   Pronounced *HIP-puh-krit.* A person who pretends to be good or godly, but who actually is not. Jesus condemned hypocrites most of all.

6 "Do not give what is holy to the dogs; nor cast your pearls before swine, lest they trample them under their feet, and turn and tear you in pieces.

7 "Ask, and it will be given to you; seek, and you will find; knock, and it will be opened to you. 8 For everyone who asks receives, and he who seeks finds, and to him who knocks it will be opened. 9 Or what man is there among you who, if his son asks for bread, will give him a stone? 10 Or if he asks for a fish, will he give him a serpent? 11 If you then, being evil, know how to give good gifts to your children, how much more will your Father who is in heaven give good things to those who ask Him! 12 Therefore, whatever you want men to do to you, do also to them, for this is the Law and the Prophets.

13 "Enter by the narrow gate; for wide is the gate and broad is the way that leads to destruction, and there are many who go in by it. 14 Because narrow is the gate and difficult is the way which leads to life, and there are few who find it.

15 "Beware of false prophets, who come to you in sheep's clothing, but inwardly they are ravenous wolves. 16 You will know them by their fruits. Do men gather grapes from thornbushes or figs from thistles? 17 Even so, every good tree bears good fruit, but a bad tree bears bad fruit. 18 A good tree cannot bear bad fruit, nor can a bad tree bear good fruit. 19 Every tree that does not bear good fruit is cut down and thrown into the fire. 20 Therefore by their fruits you will know them.

21 "Not everyone who says to Me, 'Lord, Lord,' shall enter the kingdom of heaven, but he who does the will of My Father in heaven. 22 Many will say to Me in that day, 'Lord, Lord, have we not prophesied in Your name, cast out demons in Your name, and done many wonders in Your name?' 23 And then I will declare to them, 'I never knew you; depart from Me, you who practice lawlessness!'

24 "Therefore whoever hears these sayings of Mine, and does them, I will liken him to a wise man who built his house on the rock: 25 and the rain descended, the floods came, and the winds blew and beat on that house;

⚒ DIGGING IN

7:12 The Golden Rule What do you do when someone does something mean to you? The first thing you may want to do is to hit back and make that person suffer. But that's mostly what's wrong with our world. Too many of us are hitting back.

Doing to others what you would like others to do to you only makes sense. You feel pain when someone hurts you. So do the people you hurt. Loving your neighbor as you want to be loved is what Jesus is talking about. If the whole world would love instead of hate, then we would have heaven on earth.

People in the world need God every bit as much as the people we put in prison. Everybody's heart needs to be changed. Only then do we start caring about others. Do you care?

7:13, 14 The Two Gates Jesus says that every believer must choose between a "wide gate" and a "narrow gate."

For most people, the wide gate may appear easier to enter. For example, it may seem easier to steal someone else's bicycle than to earn the money to buy your own. But have you thought what would happen if you were caught with the stolen bike? And stealing is not the only "wide gate," of course. There are many others—like swearing, lying, disobeying your parents, and taking drugs and alcohol.

No, the narrow gate is really the best gate in the long run. Even though you will have to obey God in order to walk through this gate, you will find that it pays off in the end because it leads to a full and joyful life. In fact, Jesus Himself is the "narrow gate" that leads to life. He said, "I am the way."

Which gate will you choose as you start out on the journey of your life?

and it did not fall, for it was founded on the rock.

26 "But everyone who hears these sayings of Mine, and does not do them, will be like a foolish man who built his house on the sand: 27 and the rain descended, the floods came, and the winds blew and beat on that house; and it fell. And great was its fall."

28 And so it was, when Jesus had ended these sayings, that the people were astonished at His teaching, 29 for He taught them as one having authority, and not as the scribes.

Jesus heals many sick people

8 When He had come down from the mountain, great multitudes followed Him. 2 And behold, a leper came and worshiped Him, saying, "Lord, if You are willing, You can make me clean."

3 Then Jesus put out *His* hand and touched him, saying, "I am willing; be cleansed." Immediately his leprosy was cleansed.

4 And Jesus said to him, "See that you tell no one; but go your way, show yourself to the priest, and offer the gift that Moses commanded, as a testimony to them."

5 Now when Jesus had entered Capernaum, a centurion came to Him, pleading with Him, 6 saying, "Lord, my servant is lying at home paralyzed, dreadfully tormented."

7 And Jesus said to him, "I will come and heal him."

8 The centurion answered and said, "Lord, I am not worthy that You should come under my roof. But only speak a word, and my servant will be healed. 9 For I also am a man under authority, having soldiers under me. And I say to this *one*, 'Go,' and he goes; and to another, 'Come,' and he comes; and to my servant, 'Do this,' and he does *it.*"

10 When Jesus heard *it*, He marveled, and said to those who followed, "Assuredly, I say to you, I have not found such great faith, not even in Israel! 11 And I say to you that many will come from east and west, and sit down with Abraham, Isaac, and Jacob in the kingdom of heaven. 12 But the sons of the kingdom will be cast out into outer darkness. There will be weeping and gnashing of teeth." 13 Then Jesus said to the centurion, "Go your way; and as you have believed, *so* let it be done for you." And his servant was healed that same hour.

14 Now when Jesus had come into Peter's house, He saw his wife's mother lying sick with a fever. 15 So He touched her hand, and the fever left her. And she arose and served them.

16 When evening had come, they brought to Him many who were demon-possessed. And He cast out the spirits with a word, and healed all who were sick, 17 that it might be fulfilled which was spoken by Isaiah the prophet, saying:

> "He Himself took our infirmities
> And bore *our* sicknesses."

18 And when Jesus saw great multitudes about Him, He gave a command to depart to the other side. 19 Then a certain scribe came and said to Him, "Teacher, I will follow You wherever You go."

20 And Jesus said to him, "Foxes have holes and birds of the air *have* nests, but the Son of Man has nowhere to lay *His* head."

21 Then another of His disciples said to Him, "Lord, let me first go and bury my father."

22 But Jesus said to him, "Follow Me, and let the dead bury their own dead."

23 Now when He got into a boat, His disciples followed Him. 24 And suddenly a great tempest arose on the sea, so that the boat was covered with the waves. But He was asleep. 25 Then His disciples came to *Him* and awoke Him, saying, "Lord, save us! We are perishing!"

Army Officer's Servant Healed by Miracle

The Jerusalem Times

JERUSALEM—A Roman army officer recently related a strange tale to reporters at our *Times* office here in Jerusalem. The officer told of a paralyzed man who worked for him. The soldier then went to the Man named Jesus and pleaded with Him to heal his servant. Jesus promised to come at once.

But the officer told our reporters that he begged Jesus *not* to come to his house! He felt unworthy to have the great Man there. The officer went on to say that he understood how orders work—a man who commands other men can tell others what to do and they

do it. Jesus could simply speak, he felt, and the paralyzed servant would be healed.

The officer was surprised, however, when Jesus complimented him before the crowd, saying that this Roman had more faith than anyone in all of Israel! When the soldier arrived home, his servant was well!

Members of our news staff following up on this story say that this same Roman has become a follower of Jesus. Wherever Jesus is preaching or teaching, the uniformed soldier is seen in the crowd.

26 But He said to them, "Why are you fearful, O you of little faith?" Then He arose and rebuked the winds and the sea, and there was a great calm. 27 So the men marveled, saying, "Who can this be, that even the winds and the sea obey Him?"

28 When He had come to the other side, to the country of the Gergesenes, there met Him two demon-possessed *men,* coming out of the tombs, exceedingly fierce, so that no one could pass that way. 29 And suddenly they cried out, saying, "What have we to do with

You, Jesus, You Son of God? Have You come here to torment us before the time?"

30 Now a good way off from them there was a herd of many swine feeding. 31 So the demons begged Him, saying, "If You cast us out, permit us to go away into the herd of swine."

32 And He said to them, "Go." So when they had come out, they went into the herd of swine. And suddenly the whole herd of swine ran violently down the steep place into the sea, and perished in the water.

A Centurion—I was a Roman officer in charge of one hundred soldiers. I was called a "centurion" (pronounced *sen-TU-rih-un*).

I had heard about Jesus, the great Jewish Messiah. When my personal servant became very ill, I decided I would take a chance and ask Jesus to help him. It did seem very strange for me, a Roman, to be asking a favor from a Jew. But when I met Jesus, I felt very humble and small before the Master. I fell on my knees and begged Him to heal my servant.

Jesus said He would come at once, but I stopped Him because I was not fit to have this great Man come to my home. Then Jesus told me my servant would be healed anyway, and when I got home, my servant was well again.

Now I am honored to be Jesus' disciple forever.

33 Then those who kept *them* fled; and they went away into the city and told everything, including what *had happened* to the **demon-possessed men.** 34 And behold, the whole city came out to meet Jesus. And when they saw Him, they begged *Him* to depart from their region.

Jesus invites Matthew to follow Him

9 So He got into a boat, crossed over, and came to His own city. 2 Then behold, they brought to Him a paralytic lying on a bed. When Jesus saw their faith, He said to the paralytic, "Son, be of good cheer; your sins are forgiven you."

3 And at once some of the scribes said within themselves, "This Man blasphemes!"

4 But Jesus, knowing their thoughts, said, "Why do you think evil in your hearts? 5 For which is easier, to say, 'Your sins are forgiven you,' or to say, 'Arise and walk'? 6 But that you may know that the Son of Man has power on earth to forgive sins"—then He said to the paralytic, "Arise, take up your bed, and go to your house." 7 And he arose and departed to his house.

8 Now when the multitudes saw *it,* they marveled and glorified God, who had given such power to men.

9 As Jesus passed on from there, He saw a man named Matthew sitting at the tax office. And He said to him, "Follow Me." So he arose and followed Him.

10 Now it happened, as Jesus sat at the table in the house, *that* behold, many tax collectors and sinners came and sat down with Him and His disciples. 11 And when the Pharisees saw *it,* they said to His disciples, "Why does your Teacher eat with tax collectors and sinners?"

12 When Jesus heard *that,* He said to them, "Those who are well have no need of a physician, but those who are sick. 13 But go and learn what *this* means: 'I desire mercy and not sacrifice.' For I did not come to call the righteous, but sinners, to repentance."

14 Then the disciples of John came to Him, saying, "Why do we and the Pharisees fast often, but Your disciples do not fast?"

15 And Jesus said to them, "Can the friends of the bridegroom mourn as long as the bridegroom is with them? But the days will come when the bridegroom will be taken away from them, and then they will fast. 16 No one puts a piece of unshrunk cloth on an old garment; for the patch pulls away from the garment, and the tear is made worse. 17 Nor do they put new wine into old wineskins, or else the wineskins break, the wine is spilled, and the wineskins are ruined. But they put new wine into new wineskins, and both are preserved."

18 While He spoke these things to them, behold, a ruler came and worshiped Him, saying, "My daughter has just died, but come and lay Your hand on her and she will live." 19 So Jesus arose and followed him, and so *did* His disciples.

20 And suddenly, a woman who had a flow of blood for twelve years came from behind and touched the hem of His garment. 21 For she said to herself, "If only I may touch His garment, I shall be made well." 22 But Jesus turned around, and when He saw her He said, "Be of good cheer, daughter; your faith has made you well." And the woman was made well from that hour.

23 When Jesus came into the ruler's house, and saw the flute players and the noisy crowd wailing, 24 He said to them, "Make room, for the girl is not dead, but sleeping." And they ridiculed Him. 25 But when the crowd was put

---

WORDFINDER

8:33 Demon-Possessed A person controlled by one or more demons living in him. A demon is an invisible spirit-being who serves Satan.

outside, He went in and took her by the hand, and the girl arose. 26 And the report of this went out into all that land.

27 When Jesus departed from there, two blind men followed Him, crying out and saying, "Son of David, have mercy on us!"

28 And when He had come into the house, the blind men came to Him. And Jesus said to them, "Do you believe that I am able to do this?"

They said to Him, "Yes, Lord."

29 Then He touched their eyes, saying, "According to your faith let it be to you." 30 And their eyes were opened. And Jesus sternly warned them, saying, "See that no one knows it." 31 But when they had departed, they spread the news about Him in all that country.

32 As they went out, behold, they brought to Him a man, mute and demon-possessed. 33 And when the **demon** was cast out, the mute spoke. And the multitudes marveled, saying, "It was never seen like this in Israel!"

34 But the Pharisees said, "He casts out demons by the ruler of the demons."

35 Then Jesus went about all the cities and villages, teaching in their syn-

Who Were the Pharisees?

Pharisee (pronounced *FAIR-uh-see*) means "Separated One." These men were strict in keeping many details of Jewish law. Jesus condemned them, however, because they didn't really love God or other people. They even refused to associate with ordinary Jews.

agogues, preaching the gospel of the kingdom, and healing every sickness and every disease among the people. 36 But when He saw the multitudes, He was moved with compassion for them, because they were weary and scattered, like sheep having no shepherd. 37 Then He said to His disciples, "The harvest truly is plentiful, but the laborers are few. 38 Therefore pray the Lord of the harvest to send out laborers into His harvest."

Jesus tells His disciples to be brave

10 And when He had called His twelve disciples to *Him*, He gave them power *over* unclean spirits, to cast them out, and to heal all kinds of sick-

WORDFINDER

9:33 Demon An invisible spirit-being who is a servant of Satan. Demons can live in people and hurt them. Demons also cause people to curse God and His people.

DIGGING IN

9:36–38 Jesus Needs Workers Have you ever seen a big grain field all grown and ready to be cut? What would happen if the farmer didn't have enough help to cut his grain and get it safely stored? That grain would wither and become useless.

Have you ever seen a flock of sheep or a herd of cattle? What would happen to them if there were no helpers to round them all up? They would get lost and hurt, and they would die at last.

That's the way Jesus sees the people of God's world. They are like a grain field without workers or like a flock without shepherds to care for them. Jesus is look-

ing for a boy or a girl who will be His helper to bring other lives to Him. He needs you to show and tell others about your great Savior. Will you offer Him your life to take His Good News of salvation to an unhappy world?

10:1–4 The Twelve Apostles Aren't God's ways amazing? You might think God would call up a big army of apostles and cover the earth with them. But God could get His work done with just a few if only those few would truly give their lives to Him. Jesus didn't put a big ad in the paper for workers. He didn't need a lot of people right away. Have you seen

---

What the Sick People Learned

The Pharisees (pronounced *FAIR-uh-sees*) said Jesus did His works of healing by the power of demons, but we know better. When did a demon ever heal anybody or do anyone any good?

It should have been enough that Jesus came and taught us at our place of worship. But He did more than that. He wanted everyone to know He was not just a Man of words, but a Man of deeds. The sin of mankind was the cause of all our diseases. Someday Jesus will give us new bodies that can never be sick again. And sin will be gone forever.

He proved this to us by healing many of us when He lived among us. Now we will love Him forever.

---

ness and all kinds of disease. 2 Now the names of the twelve **apostles** are these: first, Simon, who is called Peter, and Andrew his brother; James the *son* of Zebedee, and John his brother; 3 Philip and Bartholomew; Thomas and Matthew the tax collector; James the *son* of Alphaeus, and Lebbaeus, whose surname was Thaddaeus; 4 Simon the Cananite, and Judas Iscariot, who also betrayed Him.

5 These twelve Jesus sent out and commanded them, saying: "Do not go into the way of the Gentiles, and do not enter a city of the Samaritans. 6 But go rather to the lost sheep of the house of Israel. 7 And as you go, preach, saying, 'The kingdom of heaven is at hand.' 8 Heal the sick, cleanse the lepers, raise the dead, cast out demons. Freely you have received, freely give. 9 Provide neither gold nor silver nor copper in your money belts, 10 nor bag for *your* journey, nor two tunics, nor sandals, nor staffs; for a worker is worthy of his food.

11 "Now whatever city or town you enter, inquire who in it is worthy, and stay there till you go out. 12 And when you go into a household, greet it. 13 If the household is worthy, let your peace come upon it. But if it is not worthy, let your peace return to you. 14 And whoever will not receive you nor hear your words, when you depart from that house or city, shake off the dust from your feet. 15 Assuredly, I say to you, it will be more tolerable for the land of Sodom and Gomorrah in the day of judgment than for that city!

16 "Behold, I send you out as sheep in the midst of wolves. Therefore be wise as serpents and harmless as doves. 17 But beware of men, for they will deliver you up to councils and scourge you in their synagogues. 18 You will be brought before governors and kings for My sake, as a

---

WORDFINDER

10:2 Apostle Pronounced *uh-POSS-ul*. One of the men Jesus sent to preach the Good News of salvation. The word comes from a Greek word meaning "sent."

DIGGING IN

those signs along the road: "THE MARINES ARE LOOKING FOR A FEW GOOD MEN"? Jesus needed just a few good men He could train and send out into the world for Him.

Wouldn't you like to be one of Jesus' chosen few to go out and serve Him?

What an honor! If you don't believe it, ask anyone who is a missionary.

Notice that Judas was also among the disciples Jesus called. But he didn't remain faithful. If you've promised to serve the Lord, be sure to follow Him till the end of your life.

testimony to them and to the Gentiles. [19] But when they deliver you up, do not worry about how or what you should speak. For it will be given to you in that hour what you should speak; [20] for it is not you who speak, but the Spirit of your Father who speaks in you.

[21] "Now brother will deliver up brother to death, and a father *his* child; and children will rise up against parents and cause them to be put to death. [22] And you will be hated by all for My name's sake. But he who endures to the end will be saved. [23] When they persecute you in this city, flee to another. For assuredly, I say to you, you will not have gone through the cities of Israel before the Son of Man comes.

[24] "A **disciple** is not above *his* teacher, nor a servant above his master. [25] It is enough for a disciple that he be like his teacher, and a servant like his master. If they have called the master of the house Beelzebub, how much more *will they call* those of his household! [26] Therefore do not fear them. For there is nothing covered that will not be revealed, and hidden that will not be known.

[27] "Whatever I tell you in the dark, speak in the light; and what you hear in the ear, preach on the housetops. [28] And do not fear those who kill the body but cannot kill the soul. But rather fear Him who is able to destroy both soul and body in hell. [29] Are not two sparrows sold for a copper coin? And not one of them falls to the ground apart from your Father's will. [30] But the very hairs of your head are all numbered. [31] Do not fear therefore; you are of more value than many sparrows.

[32] "Therefore whoever confesses Me before men, him I will also confess before My Father who is in heaven. [33] But whoever denies Me before men, him I will also deny before My Father who is in heaven.

[34] "Do not think that I came to bring peace on earth. I did not come to bring peace but a sword. [35] For I have come to 'set a man against his father, a daughter against her mother, and a daughter-in-law against her mother-in-law'; [36] and 'a man's enemies will be those of his *own* household.' [37] He who loves father or mother more than Me is not worthy of Me. And he who loves son or daughter more than Me is not worthy of Me. [38] And he who does not take his cross and follow after Me is not worthy of Me. [39] He who finds his life will lose it, and he who loses his life for My sake will find it.

[40] "He who receives you receives Me, and he who receives Me receives Him who sent Me. [41] He who receives a prophet in the name of a prophet shall receive a prophet's reward. And he who receives a righteous man in the name of a righteous man shall receive a righteous man's reward. [42] And whoever gives one of these little ones only a cup of cold *water* in the name of a disciple, assuredly, I say to you, he shall by no means lose his reward."

Who Is Beelzebub?

Beelzebub, pronounced *bee-EL-zee-bub*, was the name of an ancient Philistine god. (See "Who Were the Philistines?" at 1 Chronicles 14:16.) *Beelzebub* was a word that also referred to Satan. But leaders of the Jews were calling *Jesus*, Beelzebub—that is, Satan.

Jesus explains why He has come

11 Now it came to pass, when Jesus finished commanding His twelve disci-

---

WORDFINDER

10:24 Disciple Pronounced *dih-SIGH-pul*. A learner or pupil. A Christian is a pupil of Jesus. The Holy Spirit teaches us to become like Jesus, as we are shown in the Bible.

ples, that He departed from there to teach and to preach in their cities.

2 And when John had heard in prison about the works of Christ, he sent two of his disciples 3 and said to Him, "Are You the Coming One, or do we look for another?"

4 Jesus answered and said to them, "Go and tell John the things which you hear and see: 5 The blind see and the lame walk; the lepers are cleansed and the deaf hear; the dead are raised up and the poor have the gospel preached to them. 6 And blessed is he who is not offended because of Me."

7 As they departed, Jesus began to say to the multitudes concerning John: "What did you go out into the wilderness to see? A reed shaken by the wind? 8 But what did you go out to see? A man clothed in soft clothing? Indeed, those who wear soft clothing are in kings' houses. 9 But what did you go out to see? A prophet? Yes, I say to you, and more than a prophet. 10 For this is he of whom it is written:

'Behold, I send My messenger
   before Your face,
Who will prepare Your way
   before You.'

11 "Assuredly, I say to you, among those born of women there has not risen one greater than John the Baptist; but he who is least in the kingdom of heaven is greater than he. 12 And from the days of John the Baptist until now the kingdom of heaven suffers violence, and the violent take it by force. 13 For all the prophets and the law prophesied until John. 14 And if you are willing to receive it, he is Elijah who is to come. 15 He who has ears to hear, let him hear!

16 "But to what shall I liken this generation? It is like children sitting in the marketplaces and calling to their companions, 17 and saying:

'We played the flute for you,
   And you did not dance;
We mourned to you,
   And you did not lament.'

18 For John came neither eating nor drinking, and they say, 'He has a demon.' 19 The Son of Man came eating and drinking, and they say, 'Look, a glutton and a winebibber, a friend of tax collectors and sinners!' But wisdom is justified by her children."

20 Then He began to rebuke the cities in which most of His mighty works had been done, because they did not repent: 21 "Woe to you, Chorazin! Woe to you, Bethsaida! For if the mighty works which were done in you had been done in Tyre and Sidon, they would have repented long ago in sackcloth and ashes. 22 But I say to you, it will be more tolerable for Tyre and Sidon in the day of judgment than for you. 23 And you, Capernaum, who are exalted to heaven, will be brought down to Hades; for if the mighty works which were done in you had been done in Sodom, it would have remained until this day. 24 But I say to you that it shall be more tolerable for the land of Sodom in the day of judgment than for you."

25 At that time Jesus answered and said, "I thank You, Father, Lord of heaven and earth, that You have hidden these things from the wise and prudent and have revealed them to babes. 26 Even so, Father, for so it seemed good in Your sight. 27 All things have been delivered to Me by My Father, and no one knows the Son except the Father. Nor does anyone know the Father except the Son, and the one to whom the Son wills to reveal Him. 28 Come to Me, all you who labor and are heavy laden, and I will give you rest. 29 Take My yoke upon you and learn from Me, for I am gentle and lowly in heart, and you will find rest for your souls. 30 For My yoke is easy and My burden is light."

Jesus is Lord of the Sabbath

12 At that time Jesus went through the grainfields on the Sabbath. And His disciples were hungry, and began to pluck heads of grain and to eat. 2 And when the Pharisees saw it, they

said to Him, "Look, Your disciples are doing what is not lawful to do on the Sabbath!"

3 But He said to them, "Have you not read what David did when he was hungry, he and those who were with him: 4 how he entered the house of God and ate the showbread which was not lawful for him to eat, nor for those who were with him, but only for the priests? 5 Or have you not read in the law that on the Sabbath the priests in the temple profane the Sabbath, and are blameless? 6 Yet I say to you that in this place there is *One* greater than the temple. 7 But if you had known what *this* means, 'I desire mercy and not sacrifice,' you would not have condemned the guiltless. 8 For the Son of Man is Lord even of the Sabbath."

9 Now when He had departed from there, He went into their **synagogue.** 10 And behold, there was a man who had a withered hand. And they asked Him, saying, "Is it lawful to heal on the Sabbath?"—that they might accuse Him.

11 Then He said to them, "What man is there among you who has one sheep, and if it falls into a pit on the Sabbath, will not lay hold of it and lift *it* out? 12 Of how much more value then is a man than a sheep? Therefore it is lawful to do good on the Sabbath." 13 Then He said to the man, "Stretch out your hand." And he stretched *it* out, and it was restored as whole as the other. 14 Then the Pharisees went out and plotted against Him, how they might destroy Him.

15 But when Jesus knew *it,* He withdrew from there. And great multitudes followed Him, and He healed them all. 16 Yet He warned them not to make Him known, 17 that it might be fulfilled which was spoken by Isaiah the prophet, saying:

Who Is the Servant of the Lord?

In the Old Testament the "Servant of the Lord" is sometimes the Jewish nation (see Isaiah 44:1). But the name also refers to the coming Messiah, or Christ (see Isaiah 42:1). In Isaiah 53:11, we see Jesus as the suffering Servant who takes upon Himself the punishment for our sins.

18 "Behold! My Servant whom I
    have chosen,
My Beloved in whom My soul
    is well pleased!
I will put My Spirit upon Him,
And He will declare justice to the
    Gentiles.
19 He will not quarrel nor cry out,
    Nor will anyone hear His voice
    in the streets.
20 A bruised reed He will not
    break,
    And smoking flax He will not
    quench,
    Till He sends forth justice to
    victory;
21 And in His name Gentiles will
    trust."

22 Then one was brought to Him who was demon-possessed, blind and mute; and He healed him, so that the blind and mute man both spoke and saw. 23 And all the multitudes were amazed and said, "Could this be the Son of David?"

24 Now when the Pharisees heard *it* they said, "This *fellow* does not cast out demons except by Beelzebub, the ruler of the demons."

25 But Jesus knew their thoughts, and said to them: "Every kingdom divided against itself is brought to desolation, and *every* city or house divided

WORDFINDER

12:9 Synagogue Pronounced *SIN-uh-gog.* From a Greek word meaning "gather together." The Jews have worshiped at buildings called synagogues ever since they lived in countries where they could no longer come to the temple.

against itself will not stand. 26 If Satan casts out Satan, he is divided against himself. How then will his kingdom stand? 27 And if I cast out demons by Beelzebub, by whom do your sons cast *them* out? Therefore they shall be your judges. 28 But if I cast out demons by the Spirit of God, surely the kingdom of God has come upon you. 29 Or how can one enter a strong man's house and plunder his goods, unless he first binds the strong man? And then he will plunder his house. 30 He who is not with Me is against Me, and he who does not gather with Me scatters abroad.

31 "Therefore I say to you, every sin and blasphemy will be forgiven men, but the blasphemy *against* the Spirit will not be forgiven men. 32 Anyone who speaks a word against the Son of Man, it will be forgiven him; but whoever speaks against the Holy Spirit, it will not be forgiven him, either in this age or in the *age* to come.

33 "Either make the tree good and its fruit good, or else make the tree bad and its fruit bad; for a tree is known by *its* fruit. 34 Brood of vipers! How can you, being evil, speak good things? For out of the abundance of the heart the mouth speaks. 35 A good man out of the good treasure of his heart brings forth good things, and an evil man out of the evil treasure brings forth evil things. 36 But I say to you that for *every* idle word men may speak, they will give account of it in the day of judgment. 37 For by your words you will be justified, and by your words you will be condemned."

38 Then some of the scribes and Pharisees answered, saying, "Teacher, we want to see a sign from You."

39 But He answered and said to them, "An evil and adulterous generation seeks after a sign, and no sign will be given to it except the sign of the prophet Jonah. 40 For as Jonah was three days and three nights in the belly of the great fish, so will the Son of Man be three days and three nights in the heart of the earth. 41 The men of Nineveh will rise up in the judgment with this generation and condemn it, because they repented at the preaching of Jonah; and indeed a greater than Jonah *is* here. 42 The queen of the South will rise up in the judgment with this generation and condemn it, for she came from the ends of the earth to hear the wisdom of Solomon; and indeed a greater than Solomon *is* here.

43 "When an unclean spirit goes out of a man, he goes through dry places, seeking rest, and finds none. 44 Then he says, 'I will return to my house from which I came.' And when he comes, he finds *it* empty, swept, and put in order. 45 Then he goes and takes with him seven other spirits more wicked than himself, and they enter and dwell there; and the last *state* of that man is worse than the first. So shall it also be with this wicked generation."

46 While He was still talking to the multitudes, behold, His mother and brothers stood outside, seeking to speak with Him. 47 Then one said to Him, "Look, Your mother and Your brothers are standing outside, seeking to speak with You."

🪓 DIGGING IN

12:33 What Is a Good Fruit Tree? Sometimes people think being a Christian is like being a Christmas tree. You trim your tree every Christmas with pretty ornaments and lights. Then you say, "What a beautiful tree!" Of course you know the tree won't last. The ornaments and lights will be taken down after New Year, and the tree will be thrown in the trash.

But a real, growing tree isn't like that. It's full of life-giving sap coming up from its roots. If it's a fruit tree, pretty soon you'll see delicious apples, pears, peaches, or cherries growing on its branches.

The Christian, too, is like a living tree, not a dead one. A Christian doesn't try to show off so he or she can *look* good for just a little while. A Christian bears the *real fruit* of deeds that please God and help people in need.

48 But He answered and said to the one who told Him, "Who is My mother and who are My brothers?" 49 And He stretched out His hand toward His disciples and said, "Here are My mother and My brothers! 50 For whoever does the will of My Father in heaven is My brother and sister and mother."

Jesus teaches through stories

13 On the same day Jesus went out of the house and sat by the sea. 2 And great multitudes were gathered together to Him, so that He got into a boat and sat; and the whole multitude stood on the shore. 3 Then He spoke many things to them in parables, saying: "Behold, a sower went out to sow. 4 And as he sowed, some seed fell by the wayside; and the birds came and devoured them. 5 Some fell on stony places, where they did not have much earth; and they immediately sprang up because they had no depth of earth. 6 But when the sun was up they were scorched, and because they had no root they withered away. 7 And some fell among thorns, and the thorns sprang up and choked them. 8 But others fell on good ground and yielded a crop: some a hundredfold, some sixty, some thirty. 9 He who has ears to hear, let him hear!"

10 And the disciples came and said to Him, "Why do You speak to them in parables?"

11 He answered and said to them, "Because it has been given to you to know the mysteries of the kingdom of heaven, but to them it has not been given. 12 For whoever has, to him more will be given, and he will have abundance; but whoever does not have, even what he has will be taken away from him. 13 Therefore I speak to them in parables, because seeing they do not see, and hearing they do not hear, nor do they understand. 14 And in them the **prophecy** of Isaiah is fulfilled, which says:

'Hearing you will hear and shall not understand,
And seeing you will see and not perceive;
15 For the hearts of this people have grown dull.
Their ears are hard of hearing,
And their eyes they have closed,
Lest they should see with their eyes and hear with their ears,
Lest they should understand with their hearts and turn,
So that I should heal them.'

16 But blessed are your eyes for they see, and your ears for they hear; 17 for assuredly, I say to you that many prophets and righteous men desired to see what you see, and did not see it,

WORDFINDER

13:14 Prophecy Pronounced *PROFF-uh-see*. A message or messages from God. Such messages in the Bible often tell about God's plans for the future.

DIGGING IN

13:3–9 Four Kinds of Soil Telling others about Jesus is like planting wheat. In order to have a good crop, you have to scatter seed everywhere in the field. Some of the seed falls on bad ground and never grows, but the farmer expects that much of his seed will come up and multiply.

Jesus says that spreading the gospel is like that. Some people are like the hard ground. They're too hard-hearted to listen to the Good News of Jesus. Others aren't very serious about being Christians. They're like shallow, stony ground. Still others are more concerned about making money than pleasing God. They're like the seed choked by thorny weeds.

Are you like the good kind of soil? If so, you will grow up and multiply yourself many times by leading many others to know the Savior.

and to hear what you hear, and did not hear *it.*

18 "Therefore hear the **parable** of the sower: 19 When anyone hears the word of the kingdom, and does not understand *it,* then the wicked *one* comes and snatches away what was sown in his heart. This is he who received seed by the wayside. 20 But he who received the seed on stony places, this is he who hears the word and immediately receives it with joy; 21 yet he has no root in himself, but endures only for a while. For when tribulation or persecution arises because of the word, immediately he stumbles. 22 Now he who received seed among the thorns is he who hears the word, and the cares of this world and the deceitfulness of riches choke the word, and he becomes unfruitful. 23 But he who received seed on the good ground is he who hears the word and understands *it,* who indeed bears fruit and produces: some a hundredfold, some sixty, some thirty."

24 Another parable He put forth to them, saying: "The kingdom of heaven is like a man who sowed good seed in his field; 25 but while men slept, his enemy came and sowed tares among the wheat and went his way. 26 But when the grain had sprouted and produced a crop, then the tares also appeared. 27 So the servants of the owner came and said to him, 'Sir, did you not sow good seed in your field? How then does it have tares?' 28 He said to them, 'An enemy has done this.' The servants said to him, 'Do you want us then to go and gather them up?' 29 But he said, 'No, lest while you gather up the tares you also uproot the wheat with them. 30 Let both grow together until the harvest, and at the time of harvest I will say to the reapers,

The mustard seed, the smallest of all seeds, grows up to be a tree!

"First gather together the tares and bind them in bundles to burn them, but gather the wheat into my barn." ' "

31 Another parable He put forth to them, saying: "The kingdom of heaven is like a mustard seed, which a man took and sowed in his field, 32 which indeed is the least of all the seeds; but when it is grown it is greater than the herbs and becomes a tree, so that the birds of the air come and nest in its branches."

33 Another parable He spoke to them: "The kingdom of heaven is like **leaven,** which a woman took and hid in three measures of meal till it was all leavened."

34 All these things Jesus spoke to the multitude in parables; and without a

---

⚜ WORDFINDER

13:18 Parable　Pronounced *PAIR-uh-bull.* A story that teaches a lesson. The story may or may not be true. Jesus used parables to teach spiritual truths.

13:33 Leaven　Pronounced *LEV-in.* A substance used in ancient times to make bread dough rise. Today bakers use yeast to do this. Jesus compared the growth of God's kingdom to the slow work of leaven.

parable He did not speak to them, 35 that it might be fulfilled which was spoken by the prophet, saying:

> "I will open My mouth in
> parables;
> I will utter things kept secret from
> the foundation of the world."

36 Then Jesus sent the multitude away and went into the house. And His disciples came to Him, saying, "Explain to us the parable of the tares of the field."

37 He answered and said to them: "He who sows the good seed is the Son of Man. 38 The field is the world, the good seeds are the sons of the kingdom, but the tares are the sons of the wicked one. 39 The enemy who sowed them is the devil, the harvest is the end of the age, and the reapers are the angels. 40 Therefore as the tares are gathered and burned in the fire, so it will be at the end of this age. 41 The Son of Man will send out His angels, and they will gather out of His kingdom all things that offend, and those who practice lawlessness, 42 and will cast them into the furnace of fire. There will be wailing and gnashing of teeth. 43 Then the righteous will shine forth as the sun in the kingdom of their Father. He who has ears to hear, let him hear!

44 "Again, the kingdom of heaven is like treasure hidden in a field, which a man found and hid; and for joy over it he goes and sells all that he has and buys that field.

45 "Again, the kingdom of heaven is like a merchant seeking beautiful pearls, 46 who, when he had found one pearl of great price, went and sold all that he had and bought it.

47 "Again, the kingdom of heaven is like a dragnet that was cast into the sea and gathered some of every kind, 48 which, when it was full, they drew to shore; and they sat down and gathered the good into vessels, but threw the bad away. 49 So it will be at the end of the age. The angels will come forth, separate the wicked from among the just, 50 and cast them into the furnace of fire. There will be wailing and gnashing of teeth."

51 Jesus said to them, "Have you understood all these things?"

They said to Him, "Yes, Lord."

52 Then He said to them, "Therefore every scribe instructed concerning the kingdom of heaven is like a householder who brings out of his treasure things new and old."

53 Now it came to pass, when Jesus had finished these parables, that He departed from there. 54 When He had come to His own country, He taught them in their synagogue, so that they were astonished and said, "Where did this Man get this wisdom and these mighty works? 55 Is this not the carpenter's son? Is not His mother called Mary? And His brothers James, Joses, Simon, and Judas? 56 And His sisters, are they not all with us? Where then did this Man get all these things?" 57 So they were offended at Him.

But Jesus said to them, "A prophet is not without honor except in his own country and in his own house."

⚒ DIGGING IN

13:45, 46 The Expensive Pearl Do you want to be a Christian, a real disciple of Jesus? If you do, it will cost you everything, including your life itself. You may not have to die for your faith, but your life must be given over to pleasing your Master, the Lord Jesus Christ.

Just imagine the pearl collector who found the greatest pearl he had ever seen! What else could he do but sell all his other pearls to buy that greatest pearl of all? That's the way it is when you come to see Jesus as He really is. He is like that greatest pearl. Of course, Jesus is worth far, far more than anything else you might find in life. So you say, "Yes, I want Jesus more than anything in the world. I now give Him my poor life. Take me, Lord Jesus, and use me just as You wish."

Jesus Feeds Large Crowd with Small Supper

New Testament News Service

GALILEE—A large crowd that had gathered to hear Jesus speak last week got much more than they expected.

The audience of more than five thousand men, plus women and children, were out in the country all day with nothing to eat. It is reported that the disciples wanted to send the hungry crowd away.

Late in the afternoon, Jesus commanded His disciples to feed the crowd.

But they were not sure what to do since they had only five loaves of bread and two fish available.

Jesus told the people to sit down on the green grass and, after He asked the blessing, everybody ate supper. All of those thousands of people had plenty to eat!

People are still talking about the miracle meal!

---

58 Now He did not do many mighty works there because of their unbelief.

A small lunch feeds five thousand people

14 At that time Herod the tetrarch heard the report about Jesus 2 and said to his servants, "This is John the Baptist; he is risen from the dead, and therefore these powers are at work in him." 3 For Herod had laid hold of John and bound him, and put him in prison for the sake of Herodias, his brother Philip's wife. 4 Because John had said to him, "It is not lawful for you to have her." 5 And although he wanted to put him to death, he feared the multitude, because they counted him as a prophet.

6 But when Herod's birthday was celebrated, the daughter of Herodias danced before them and pleased Herod. 7 Therefore he promised with an oath to give her whatever she might ask.

8 So she, having been prompted by her mother, said, "Give me John the Baptist's head here on a platter."

9 And the king was sorry; nevertheless, because of the oaths and because of those who sat with him, he commanded it to be given to her. 10 So he sent and had John beheaded in prison. 11 And his head was brought

on a platter and given to the girl, and she brought it to her mother. 12 Then his disciples came and took away the body and buried it, and went and told Jesus.

13 When Jesus heard it, He departed from there by boat to a deserted place by Himself. But when the multitudes heard it, they followed Him on foot from the cities. 14 And when Jesus went out He saw a great multitude; and He was moved with compassion for them, and healed their sick. 15 When it was evening, His disciples came to Him, saying, "This is a deserted place, and the hour is already late. Send the multitudes away, that they may go into the villages and buy themselves food."

16 But Jesus said to them, "They do not need to go away. You give them something to eat."

17 And they said to Him, "We have here only five loaves and two fish."

18 He said, "Bring them here to Me." 19 Then He commanded the multitudes to sit down on the grass. And He took the five loaves and the two fish, and looking up to heaven, He blessed and broke and gave the loaves to the disciples; and the disciples gave to the multitudes. 20 So they all ate and were filled, and they took up twelve baskets full of the fragments that remained. 21 Now those who had eaten

were about five thousand men, besides women and children.

22 Immediately Jesus made His disciples get into the boat and go before Him to the other side, while He sent the multitudes away. 23 And when He had sent the multitudes away, He went up on the mountain by Himself to pray. Now when evening came, He was alone there. 24 But the boat was now in the middle of the sea, tossed by the waves, for the wind was contrary.

25 Now in the fourth watch of the night Jesus went to them, walking on the sea. 26 And when the disciples saw Him walking on the sea, they were troubled, saying, "It is a ghost!" And they cried out for fear.

27 But immediately Jesus spoke to them, saying, "Be of good cheer! It is I; do not be afraid."

28 And Peter answered Him and said, "Lord, if it is You, command me to come to You on the water."

29 So He said, "Come." And when Peter had come down out of the boat, he walked on the water to go to Jesus. 30 But when he saw that the wind was boisterous, he was afraid; and beginning to sink he cried out, saying, "Lord, save me!"

31 And immediately Jesus stretched out His hand and caught him, and said to him, "O you of little faith, why did you doubt?" 32 And when they got into the boat, the wind ceased.

33 Then those who were in the boat came and worshiped Him, saying, "Truly You are the Son of God."

34 When they had crossed over, they came to the land of Gennesaret. 35 And when the men of that place recognized Him, they sent out into all that surrounding region, brought to Him all who were sick, 36 and begged Him that they might only touch the hem of His garment. And as many as touched it were made perfectly well.

God's rules or man's traditions?

15 Then the scribes and Pharisees who were from Jerusalem came to Jesus, saying, 2 "Why do Your disciples transgress the tradition of the elders? For they do not wash their hands when they eat bread."

3 He answered and said to them, "Why do you also transgress the commandment of God because of your tradition? 4 For God commanded, saying, 'Honor your father and your mother'; and, 'He who curses father or mother, let him be put to death.' 5 But you say, 'Whoever says to his father or mother, "Whatever profit you might have received from me is a gift to God"— 6 then he need not honor his father or mother.' Thus you have made the commandment of God of no effect by your tradition. 7 Hypocrites! Well did Isaiah prophesy about you, saying:

8   'These people draw near to Me
     with their mouth,
    And honor Me with their lips,
    But their heart is far from Me.
9   And in vain they worship Me,
    Teaching as doctrines the
     commandments of men.' "

⚒ DIGGING IN

14:25–33 Jesus Controls Nature Sometimes you see the lightning flashing and hear the thunder crashing, and you are afraid. If you have ever seen a hurricane, you know how powerful nature can be. The wind just smashes everything in its path. If you're in a ship at sea during a hurricane, you see waves coming at you 60, 75, 90 feet high. You can't believe how frightening the sea can be in such a storm.

But Jesus is Lord of nature. Notice that the disciples were out in the boat in a storm, but Jesus was praying on a mountain. Then out of the darkness, Jesus came walking on the water toward the little boat. Soon He was in the boat, and He commanded the sea to be calm.

Nothing in the world can scare you when you know Jesus is in control. Winds can blow, lightning can flash, nations can rise or fall. But Jesus is Master of all.

The ruins of the city of Tyre. Jesus once walked the fifty miles from Jerusalem to Tyre.

10 When He had called the multitude to *Himself*, He said to them, "Hear and understand: 11 Not what goes into the mouth defiles a man; but what comes out of the mouth, this defiles a man."

12 Then His disciples came and said to Him, "Do You know that the Pharisees were offended when they heard this saying?"

13 But He answered and said, "Every plant which My heavenly Father has not planted will be uprooted. 14 Let them alone. They are blind leaders of the blind. And if the blind leads the blind, both will fall into a ditch."

15 Then Peter answered and said to Him, "Explain this parable to us."

16 So Jesus said, "Are you also still without understanding? 17 Do you not yet understand that whatever enters the mouth goes into the stomach and is eliminated? 18 But those things which proceed out of the mouth come from the heart, and they defile a man. 19 For out of the heart proceed evil thoughts, murders, adulteries, fornications, thefts, false witness, blasphemies. 20 These are *the things* which defile a man, but to eat with unwashed hands does not defile a man."

21 Then Jesus went out from there and departed to the region of Tyre and Sidon. 22 And behold, a woman of Canaan came from that region and cried out to Him, saying, "Have mercy on me, O Lord, Son of David! My daughter is severely demon-possessed."

23 But He answered her not a word. And His disciples came and urged Him, saying, "Send her away, for she cries out after us."

24 But He answered and said, "I was not sent except to the lost sheep of the house of Israel."

25 Then she came and worshiped Him, saying, "Lord, help me!"

26 But He answered and said, "It is not good to take the children's bread and throw *it* to the little dogs."

27 And she said, "Yes, Lord, yet even the little dogs eat the crumbs which fall from their masters' table."

28 Then Jesus answered and said to her, "O woman, great *is* your faith! Let it be to you as you desire." And her daughter was healed from that very hour.

29 Jesus departed from there, skirted the Sea of Galilee, and went up on the mountain and sat down there. 30 Then great multitudes came to Him, having with them *the* lame, blind, mute, maimed, and many others; and they laid them down at Jesus' feet, and He healed them. 31 So the multitude marveled when they saw *the* mute speaking, *the* maimed made whole, *the* lame walking, and *the* blind seeing; and they glorified the God of Israel.

32 Now Jesus called His disciples to *Himself* and said, "I have compassion on the multitude, because they have now continued with Me three days and have nothing to eat. And I do not want to send them away hungry, lest they faint on the way."

33 Then His disciples said to Him, "Where could we get enough bread in the wilderness to fill such a great multitude?"

34 Jesus said to them, "How many loaves do you have?"

And they said, "Seven, and a few little fish."

35 So He commanded the multitude to sit down on the ground. 36 And He took the seven loaves and the fish and gave thanks, broke *them* and gave *them* to His disciples; and the disciples *gave* to the multitude. 37 So they all ate and were filled, and they took up seven large baskets full of the fragments that were left. 38 Now those who ate were four thousand men, besides women and children. 39 And He sent away the multitude, got into the boat, and came to the region of Magdala.

Peter says Jesus is the Messiah

16 Then the Pharisees and Sadducees came, and testing Him asked that He would show them a sign from heaven. 2 He answered and said to them, "When it is evening you say, '*It will be* fair weather, for the sky is red'; 3 and in the morning, '*It will be* foul weather today, for the sky is red and threatening.' Hypocrites! You know how to discern the face of the sky, but you cannot *discern* the signs of the times. 4 A wicked and adulterous generation seeks after a sign, and no sign shall be given to it except the sign of the prophet Jonah." And He left them and departed.

5 Now when His disciples had come to the other side, they had forgotten to take bread. 6 Then Jesus said to them, "Take heed and beware of the leaven of the Pharisees and the Sadducees."

7 And they reasoned among themselves, saying, "*It is* because we have taken no bread."

8 But Jesus, being aware of *it,* said to them, "O you of little faith, why do you reason among yourselves because you have brought no bread? 9 Do you not yet understand, or remember the five loaves of the five thousand and how many baskets you took up? 10 Nor the seven loaves of the four thousand and how many large baskets

🪓 DIGGING IN

15:32–38 Jesus Feeds More Than Four Thousand People Jesus actually fed four thousand men, *besides women and children.* So the number of people Jesus fed was several times more than four thousand.

The disciples only had seven loaves of bread and a few fish. Yet Jesus fed everybody! You and I are the disciples of Jesus, and we don't have very much to offer Him. But He will take the little we have and multiply it many times over.

Like the disciples long ago, you must be willing to give Jesus what you have. As you give to Him your little gift, He surprises you by making it big. Then many people are blessed.

When the offering plate is passed at church on Sunday, don't say, "My little bit won't do any good. I'm only one person." Say instead, "I don't have much, Jesus. But you can have it. Please use it to bless many." Then you will see how very much He can do with your little bit.

you took up? [11] How is it you do not understand that I did not speak to you concerning bread?—*but* to beware of the leaven of the Pharisees and Sadducees." [12] Then they understood that He did not tell *them* to beware of the leaven of bread, but of the doctrine of the Pharisees and Sadducees.

[13] When Jesus came into the region of Caesarea Philippi, He asked His disciples, saying, "Who do men say that I, the Son of Man, am?"

[14] So they said, "Some *say* John the Baptist, some Elijah, and others Jeremiah or one of the prophets."

[15] He said to them, "But who do you say that I am?"

[16] Simon Peter answered and said, "You are the Christ, the Son of the living God."

[17] Jesus answered and said to him, "Blessed are you, Simon Bar-Jonah, for flesh and blood has not revealed *this* to you, but My Father who is in heaven. [18] And I also say to you that you are Peter, and on this rock I will build My church, and the gates of Hades shall not prevail against it. [19] And I will give you the keys of the kingdom of heaven, and whatever you bind on earth will be bound in heaven, and whatever you loose on earth will be loosed in heaven."

[20] Then He commanded His disciples that they should tell no one that He was Jesus the Christ.

[21] From that time Jesus began to show to His disciples that He must go to Jerusalem, and suffer many things from the elders and chief priests and scribes, and be killed, and be raised the third day.

[22] Then Peter took Him aside and began to rebuke Him, saying, "Far be it from You, Lord; this shall not happen to You!"

[23] But He turned and said to Peter, "Get behind Me, Satan! You are an offense to Me, for you are not mindful of the things of God, but the things of men."

[24] Then Jesus said to His disciples, "If anyone desires to come after Me, let him deny himself, and take up his cross, and follow Me. [25] For whoever desires to save his life will lose it, but whoever loses his life for My sake will find it. [26] For what profit is it to a man if he gains the whole world, and loses his own soul? Or what will a man give in exchange for his soul? [27] For the Son of Man will come in the glory of His Father with His angels, and then He will reward each according to his works. [28] Assuredly, I say to you, there are some standing here who shall not taste death till they *see* the Son of Man coming in His kingdom."

Jesus shines like the sun

17 Now after six days Jesus took Peter, James, and John his brother, led them up on a high mountain by themselves; [2] and He was transfigured before them. His face shone like the sun, and His clothes became as white as the light. [3] And behold, Moses and Elijah appeared to them, talking with Him. [4] Then Peter answered and said

---

⚒ DIGGING IN

16:25 You Can't Save Your Life You hear a lot about saving lives. But if you stop to think about it, none of us can really *save* anybody's life. All we can do is hope to make their lives last a little longer. Very few people live to be a hundred years old. Even before that time, most people get pretty tired of living in the world. So Jesus was telling the truth everybody can understand: "Whoever desires to save his life will lose it."

But then Jesus said something amazing: "Whoever loses his life for My sake will find it." How can you "find" your life by losing it? God is the Author of your life. Every moment of your life is in His hand. So if you lose your life by giving it back to Him, you don't really lose it. Jesus *gives His eternal life to you* when you *give your short life to Him.* That's a pretty good trade!

to Jesus, "Lord, it is good for us to be here; if You wish, let us make here three tabernacles: one for You, one for Moses, and one for Elijah."

5 While he was still speaking, behold, a bright cloud overshadowed them; and suddenly a voice came out of the cloud, saying, "This is My beloved Son, in whom I am well pleased. Hear Him!" 6 And when the disciples heard *it,* they fell on their faces and were greatly afraid. 7 But Jesus came and touched them and said, "Arise, and do not be afraid." 8 When they had lifted up their eyes, they saw no one but Jesus only.

9 Now as they came down from the mountain, Jesus commanded them, saying, "Tell the vision to no one until the Son of Man is risen from the dead."

10 And His disciples asked Him, saying, "Why then do the scribes say that Elijah must come first?"

11 Jesus answered and said to them, "Indeed, Elijah is coming first and will restore all things. 12 But I say to you that Elijah has come already, and they did not know him but did to him whatever they wished. Likewise the Son of Man is also about to suffer at their hands." 13 Then the disciples understood that He spoke to them of John the Baptist.

14 And when they had come to the multitude, a man came to Him, kneeling down to Him and saying, 15 "Lord, have mercy on my son, for he is an epileptic and suffers severely; for he often falls into the fire and often into the water. 16 So I brought him to Your dis-

ciples, but they could not cure him."

17 Then Jesus answered and said, "O faithless and perverse generation, how long shall I be with you? How long shall I bear with you? Bring him here to Me." 18 And Jesus rebuked the demon, and it came out of him; and the child was cured from that very hour.

19 Then the disciples came to Jesus privately and said, "Why could we not cast it out?"

20 So Jesus said to them, "Because of your unbelief; for assuredly, I say to you, if you have faith as a mustard seed, you will say to this mountain, 'Move from here to there,' and it will move; and nothing will be impossible for you. 21 However, this kind does not go out except by prayer and fasting."

22 Now while they were staying in Galilee, Jesus said to them, "The Son of Man is about to be betrayed into the hands of men, 23 and they will kill Him, and the third day He will be raised up." And they were exceedingly sorrowful.

24 When they had come to Capernaum, those who received the *temple* tax came to Peter and said, "Does your Teacher not pay the *temple* tax?"

25 He said, "Yes."

And when he had come into the house, Jesus anticipated him, saying, "What do you think, Simon? From whom do the kings of the earth take customs or taxes, from their sons or from strangers?"

26 Peter said to Him, "From strangers."

Jesus said to him, "Then the sons

⛏ DIGGING IN

17:22, 23 Jesus Came to Die for Our Sins Some people think you can cure sin by just teaching people what is good and right. But Jesus knew His teaching would do no good unless He died on the Cross to destroy our sins. Sin is not just the bad things we do. Sin is deep inside us, in our wills. Only God can change our deep rebellion against Him and His ways.

You can see your temperature rise with a thermometer, but you can't see the disease that causes you to feel hot and uncomfortable. In the same way, you can feel the unhappiness that sin causes, but you can't see the sin deep inside.

Jesus is the great Doctor who cures sin. The medicine is His blood poured out on the Cross. Tell Jesus you want Him to heal the deep sin of your heart and be your Friend forever.

are free. 27 Nevertheless, lest we offend them, go to the sea, cast in a hook, and take the fish that comes up first. And when you have opened its mouth, you will find a piece of money; take that and give it to them for Me and you.''

Who is the greatest?

18 At that time the disciples came to Jesus, saying, "Who then is greatest in the kingdom of heaven?"
2 Then Jesus called a little child to Him, set him in the midst of them, 3 and said, "Assuredly, I say to you, unless you are converted and become as little children, you will by no means enter the kingdom of heaven. 4 Therefore whoever humbles himself as this little child is the greatest in the kingdom of heaven. 5 Whoever receives one little child like this in My name receives Me.
6 "Whoever causes one of these little ones who believe in Me to sin, it would be better for him if a millstone were hung around his neck, and he were drowned in the depth of the sea.

7 Woe to the world because of offenses! For offenses must come, but woe to that man by whom the offense comes!
8 "If your hand or foot causes you to sin, cut it off and cast it from you. It is better for you to enter into life lame or maimed, rather than having two hands or two feet, to be cast into the everlasting fire. 9 And if your eye causes you to sin, pluck it out and cast it from you. It is better for you to enter into life with one eye, rather than having two eyes, to be cast into hell fire.
10 "Take heed that you do not despise one of these little ones, for I say to you that in heaven their angels always see the face of My Father who is in heaven. 11 For the Son of Man has come to save that which was lost.
12 "What do you think? If a man has a hundred sheep, and one of them goes astray, does he not leave the ninety-nine and go to the mountains to seek the one that is straying? 13 And if he should find it, assuredly, I say to you, he rejoices more over that sheep than over the ninety-nine that did not go astray. 14 Even so it is not

⛏ DIGGING IN

18:3 We Must Always Be Like Children Everybody wants to "grow up," and that's good. But in growing up, we often just become more clever at deceiving, cheating, and hurting one another. When you're young, you may want to punch someone in the nose. But later in life, instead of punching someone, you may just start a mean story about him that hurts his good name.

Jesus wouldn't agree with punching someone in the nose, but He would agree even less with the evil tricks grown-ups sometimes play on one another. So He said we must always be like children in our treatment of people. Young people get angry, but they forgive quickly.

Also, you learn new things quickly when you are young. You don't argue when we ask you to believe in Jesus. You're ready to listen. We all need to stay young in our willingness to listen to God speaking to us.

18:11 Why Jesus Lived with Us By the time Jesus was born, people had some very strange ideas about God. Many Jews thought God cared only about them, so they hated people who were not Jews. Others in Jesus' day imagined God had forgotten all about them because He allowed their Roman enemies to rule over them. So they had given up hope and were becoming hard-hearted and unloving because of these false ideas.

Jesus came to be a mirror-image of what God is really like. First of all, Jesus went about doing good among all people, teaching them that God really loved them. He also showed them that God is willing to live in humble people like Himself. God doesn't favor the proud and those who think they are better than others. Jesus showed that patience and love for your enemies is God's desire, even if you have to die as He did.

A good shepherd is happy when he finds his lost sheep.

the will of your Father who is in heaven that one of these little ones should perish.

15 "Moreover if your brother sins against you, go and tell him his fault between you and him alone. If he hears you, you have gained your brother. 16 But if he will not hear, take with you one or two more, that 'by the mouth of two or three witnesses every word may be established.' 17 And if he refuses to hear them, tell *it* to the church. But if he refuses even to hear the church, let him be to you like a heathen and a tax collector.

18 "Assuredly, I say to you, whatever you bind on earth will be bound in heaven, and whatever you loose on earth will be loosed in heaven.

19 "Again I say to you that if two of you agree on earth concerning anything that they ask, it will be done for them by My Father in heaven. 20 For where two or three are gathered together in My name, I am there in the midst of them."

21 Then Peter came to Him and said, "Lord, how often shall my brother sin against me, and I forgive him? Up to seven times?"

22 Jesus said to him, "I do not say to you, up to seven times, but up to seventy times seven. 23 Therefore the kingdom of heaven is like a certain king who wanted to settle accounts with his servants. 24 And when he had begun to settle accounts, one was brought to him who owed him ten thousand talents. 25 But as he was not able to pay, his master commanded that he be sold, with his wife and children and all that he had, and that payment be made. 26 The servant therefore fell down before him, saying, 'Master, have patience with me, and I will pay you all.' 27 Then the master of that servant was moved with compassion, released him, and forgave him the debt.

28 "But that servant went out and found one of his fellow servants who owed him a hundred denarii; and he laid hands on him and took *him* by the throat, saying, 'Pay me what you owe!' 29 So his fellow servant fell down at his feet and begged him, saying, 'Have patience with me, and I will pay you all.' 30 And he would not, but went and threw him into prison till he should pay the debt. 31 So when his fellow servants saw what had been done, they were very grieved, and came and told their master all that had been done. 32 Then his master, after he had called him, said to him, 'You wicked servant! I forgave you all that debt because you begged me. 33 Should you not also have had compassion on your fellow servant, just as I had pity on you?' 34 And his master was angry, and delivered him to the torturers until he should pay all that was due to him.

35 "So My heavenly Father also will do to you if each of you, from his heart, does not forgive his brother his trespasses."

Jesus talks about divorce

19 Now it came to pass, when Jesus had finished these sayings, *that* He departed from Galilee and came to the region of Judea beyond the Jordan. 2 And great multitudes followed Him, and He healed them there.

3 The Pharisees also came to Him, testing Him, and saying to Him, "Is it

lawful for a man to divorce his wife for *just* any reason?"

4 And He answered and said to them, "Have you not read that He who made *them* at the beginning 'made them male and female,' 5 and said, 'For this reason a man shall leave his father and mother and be joined to his wife, and the two shall become one flesh'? 6 So then, they are no longer two but one flesh. Therefore what God has joined together, let not man separate."

7 They said to Him, "Why then did Moses command to give a certificate of divorce, and to put her away?"

8 He said to them, "Moses, because of the hardness of your hearts, permitted you to divorce your wives, but from the beginning it was not so. 9 And I say to you, whoever divorces his wife, except for sexual immorality, and marries another, commits adultery; and whoever marries her who is divorced commits adultery."

10 His disciples said to Him, "If such is the case of the man with *his* wife, it is better not to marry."

11 But He said to them, "All cannot accept this saying, but only *those* to whom it has been given: 12 For there are eunuchs who were born thus from *their* mother's womb, and there are eunuchs who were made eunuchs by men, and there are eunuchs who have made themselves eunuchs for the kingdom of heaven's sake. He who is able to accept *it,* let him accept *it.*"

13 Then little children were brought to Him that He might put *His* hands on them and pray, but the disciples rebuked them. 14 But Jesus said, "Let the little children come to Me, and do not forbid them; for of such is the kingdom of heaven." 15 And He laid *His* hands on them and departed from there.

16 Now behold, one came and said to Him, "Good Teacher, what good thing shall I do that I may have eternal life?"

17 So He said to him, "Why do you call Me good? No one *is* good but One, *that is,* God. But if you want to enter into life, keep the commandments."

18 He said to Him, "Which ones?"

Jesus said, "'You shall not murder,' 'You shall not commit adultery,' 'You shall not steal,' 'You shall not bear false witness,' 19 'Honor your father and *your* mother,' and, 'You shall love your neighbor as yourself.' "

20 The young man said to Him, "All these things I have kept from my youth. What do I still lack?"

21 Jesus said to him, "If you want to be perfect, go, sell what you have and give to the poor, and you will have treasure in heaven; and come, follow Me."

22 But when the young man heard that saying, he went away sorrowful, for he had great possessions.

23 Then Jesus said to His disciples, "Assuredly, I say to you that it is hard for a rich man to enter the kingdom of heaven. 24 And again I say to you, it is easier for a camel to go through the eye of a needle than for a rich man to enter the kingdom of God."

DIGGING IN

19:14 You, Too, Can Come to Jesus

Jesus didn't say you had to be a certain age before you could come to Him. He even invited little children. You're no longer a little child, but you're still a young person, and Jesus is calling you to be His disciple. Becoming a believer in Jesus is the most important decision you will ever make.

It may seem hard to decide to follow Jesus because He asks you to choose one of two opposite ways. You may choose to turn your back on God and chase after things that don't last. But that way leads to a lonely end without God.

Happily, you can begin the other way of life by choosing Jesus instead. Having the friendship of Jesus is worth far more than having all the other great things you could imagine. And Jesus will be your Friend forever.

Preacher from Galilee Says God Can Do Anything

The Jordan Journal—Editorial

TRANSJORDAN—Reporters from this newspaper were on hand the other day when Jesus was teaching on many subjects. At that time, He welcomed children into the kingdom of God. Our people can't help admiring the new Teacher for His love and kindness to all kinds of people, young and old.

One thing that caught our reporter's attention was the way Jesus spoke to a certain rich young man. The young man wanted to know how he could have eternal life. Jesus told him to keep the Ten Commandments. The young fellow answered, "I've *always* done those things!"

Jesus then directed him to give his wealth to the poor. Of course, the young man was disappointed. Jesus was asking him to love God more than his money, but the young man did not seem able to do that. His heart evidently needed to be changed.

Before the young man walked away, Jesus said God could change his heart. Can we believe that?

25 When His disciples heard *it,* they were greatly astonished, saying, "Who then can be saved?"

26 But Jesus looked at *them* and said to them, "With men this is impossible, but with God all things are possible."

27 Then Peter answered and said to Him, "See, we have left all and followed You. Therefore what shall we have?"

28 So Jesus said to them, "Assuredly I say to you, that in the **regeneration,** when the Son of Man sits on the throne of His glory, you who have followed Me will also sit on twelve thrones, judging the twelve tribes of Israel. 29 And everyone who has left houses or brothers or sisters or father or mother or wife or children or lands, for My name's sake, shall receive a hundredfold, and inherit eternal life. 30 But many *who are* first will be last, and the last first.

What will happen to Jesus?

20 "For the kingdom of heaven is like a landowner who went out early in the morning to hire laborers for his vineyard. 2 Now when he had agreed with the laborers for a denarius a day, he sent them into his vineyard. 3 And he went out about the third hour and saw others standing idle in the marketplace, 4 and said to them, 'You also go into the vineyard, and whatever is right I will give you.' So they went. 5 Again he went out about the sixth and the ninth hour, and did likewise. 6 And about the eleventh hour he went out and found others standing idle, and said to them, 'Why have you been standing here idle all day?' 7 They said to him, 'Because no one hired us.' He said to them, 'You also go into the vineyard, and whatever is right you will receive.'

8 "So when evening had come, the owner of the vineyard said to his steward, 'Call the laborers and give them *their* wages, beginning with the last to the first.' 9 And when those came who *were hired* about the eleventh hour, they each received a denarius. 10 But when the first came, they supposed that they would receive more; and they

WORDFINDER

19:28 Regeneration   Pronounced *re-jen-uh-RAY-shun.* A word meaning to "create all over again." Regeneration is what God does for us when we are "born again" (see definition at John 3:3).

likewise received each a denarius.
11 And when they had received *it,* they
complained against the landowner,
12 saying, 'These last *men* have worked
only one hour, and you made them
equal to us who have borne the burden and the heat of the day.' 13 But
he answered one of them and said,
'Friend, I am doing you no wrong. Did
you not agree with me for a denarius?
14 Take *what is* yours and go your way.
I wish to give to this last man *the same*
as to you. 15 Is it not lawful for me to
do what I wish with my own things?
Or is your *eye* evil because I am good?'
16 So the last will be first, and the first
last. For many are called, but few chosen."

17 Now Jesus, going up to Jerusalem, took the twelve disciples aside on
the road and said to them, 18 "Behold,
we are going up to Jerusalem, and
the Son of Man will be betrayed to
the chief priests and to the scribes;
and they will condemn Him to
death, 19 and deliver Him to the Gentiles to mock and to scourge and to
crucify. And the third day He will rise
again."

20 Then the mother of Zebedee's
sons came to Him with her sons, kneeling down and asking something from
Him.

21 And He said to her, "What do you
wish?"

She said to Him, "Grant that these
two sons of mine may sit, one on Your
right hand and the other on the left,
in Your kingdom."

22 But Jesus answered and said,
"You do not know what you ask.
Are you able to drink the cup that I
am about to drink, and be baptized
with the baptism that I am baptized
with?"

They said to Him, "We are able."

23 So He said to them, "You will indeed drink My cup, and be baptized
with the baptism that I am baptized
with; but to sit on My right hand and
on My left is not Mine to give, but *it
is for those* for whom it is prepared
by My Father."

24 And when the ten heard *it,* they
were greatly displeased with the two
brothers. 25 But Jesus called them to
Himself and said, "You know that the
rulers of the Gentiles lord it over them,
and those who are great exercise authority over them. 26 Yet it shall not
be so among you; but whoever desires
to become great among you, let him
be your servant. 27 And whoever desires to be first among you, let him be
your slave— 28 just as the Son of Man
did not come to be served, but to
serve, and to give His life a ransom
for many."

29 Now as they went out of Jericho,
a great multitude followed Him.
30 And behold, two blind men sitting
by the road, when they heard that
Jesus was passing by, cried out, saying,
"Have mercy on us, O Lord, Son of
David!"

31 Then the multitude warned them
that they should be quiet; but they
cried out all the more, saying, "Have

⛏ DIGGING IN

20:20–28 Who Will Be Number One?
Have you been watching the football
games? Sometimes you'll see a fast full-
back outrun his tacklers and speed across
the goal line. Then he spikes the ball on
the ground and runs around waving his
finger in the air. He's saying to the crowd,
"I'm Number One!"

Being "Number One" in sports is great.
And you should be the very best you can
be in all the contests of life. But remember, God has a reason for your being

"Number One." That's so you can be of
more use to others in a needy world.

Some of Jesus' followers wanted to be
"Number One" just so they could look important. People like that are selfish. Jesus
made it clear to His disciples that He
came into the world *to serve,* not *to be
served* by others. Have you heard about
Mother Teresa, the famous missionary to
India? She gave her life for others. She's
a really good example of how to be a
"Number One"!

mercy on us, O Lord, Son of David!"
32 So Jesus stood still and called them, and said, "What do you want Me to do for you?"
33 They said to Him, "Lord, that our eyes may be opened." 34 So Jesus had compassion and touched their eyes. And immediately their eyes received sight, and they followed Him.

Jesus rides into Jerusalem on a donkey

21 Now when they drew near Jerusalem, and came to Bethphage, at the Mount of Olives, then Jesus sent two disciples, 2 saying to them, "Go into the village opposite you, and immediately you will find a donkey tied, and a colt with her. Loose *them* and bring *them* to Me. 3 And if anyone says anything to you, you shall say, 'The Lord has need of them,' and immediately he will send them.' "

4 All this was done that it might be fulfilled which was spoken by the prophet, saying:

5 "Tell the daughter of Zion,
  'Behold, your King is coming to
    you,
   Lowly, and sitting on a donkey,
   A colt, the foal of a donkey.' "

6 So the disciples went and did as Jesus commanded them. 7 They brought the donkey and the colt, laid their clothes on them, and set *Him* on them. 8 And a very great multitude spread their clothes on the road; others cut down branches from the trees and spread *them* on the road. 9 Then the multitudes who went before and those who followed cried out, saying:

"Hosanna to the Son of David!
 'Blessed *is* He who comes in the
    name of the LORD!'
 Hosanna in the highest!"

Money changers charged large fees to exchange coins for the temple tax.

10 And when He had come into Jerusalem, all the city was moved, saying, "Who is this?"
11 So the multitudes said, "This is Jesus, the prophet from Nazareth of Galilee."
12 Then Jesus went into the temple of God and drove out all those who bought and sold in the temple, and overturned the tables of the **money changers** and the seats of those who sold doves. 13 And He said to them, "It is written, 'My house shall be called a house of prayer,' but you have made it a 'den of thieves.' "
14 Then *the* blind and *the* lame came to Him in the temple, and He healed them. 15 But when the chief priests and scribes saw the wonderful things that He did, and the children crying out in the temple and saying, "Hosanna to the Son of David!" they were indignant 16 and said to Him, "Do You hear what these are saying?"
And Jesus said to them, "Yes. Have you never read,

WORDFINDER

21:12 Money Changers Bankers who exchanged temple money for the money of another nation. Some money changers in the temple charged a large fee.

New Preacher Gets Tough at Temple

The Jerusalem Times—Editorial

JERUSALEM—Something happened in the temple recently that is causing our local clergy to wonder about the Preacher from Galilee.

It has been our custom for many years to buy and sell and change money in the temple. No one has ever objected. Now this Jesus has come storming into our holy temple, telling us what we can and can't do! At one point, He even became violent, drove out our merchants, and upset the tables of money.

Some people are wondering if the authorities should put a stop to this Man's actions. In fact, there has been talk about arresting Jesus.

We are asking our readers to write and tell us their thoughts about the Preacher from Galilee. What do you think about Jesus?

'Out of the mouth of babes and nursing infants
You have perfected praise'?''

17 Then He left them and went out of the city to Bethany, and He lodged there.

18 Now in the morning, as He returned to the city, He was hungry. 19 And seeing a fig tree by the road, He came to it and found nothing on it but leaves, and said to it, "Let no fruit grow on you ever again." Immediately the fig tree withered away.

20 And when the disciples saw it, they marveled, saying, "How did the fig tree wither away so soon?"

21 So Jesus answered and said to them, "Assuredly, I say to you, if you have faith and do not doubt, you will not only do what was done to the fig tree, but also if you say to this mountain, 'Be removed and be cast into the sea,' it will be done. 22 And whatever things you ask in prayer, believing, you will receive."

23 Now when He came into the temple, the chief priests and the elders of the people confronted Him as He was teaching, and said, "By what authority are You doing these things? And who gave You this authority?"

24 But Jesus answered and said to them, "I also will ask you one thing, which if you tell Me, I likewise will tell you by what authority I do these things: 25 The baptism of John—where was it from? From heaven or from men?"

And they reasoned among themselves, saying, "If we say, 'From heaven,' He will say to us, 'Why then did you not believe him?' 26 But if we say, 'From men,' we fear the multitude, for all count John as a prophet." 27 So they answered Jesus and said, "We do not know."

And He said to them, "Neither will I tell you by what authority I do these things.

28 "But what do you think? A man had two sons, and he came to the first and said, 'Son, go, work today in my vineyard.' 29 He answered and said, 'I will not,' but afterward he regretted it and went. 30 Then he came to the second and said likewise. And he answered and said, 'I go, sir,' but he did not go. 31 Which of the two did the will of his father?"

They said to Him, "The first."

Jesus said to them, "Assuredly, I say to you that tax collectors and harlots enter the kingdom of God before you. 32 For John came to you in the way of righteousness, and you did not believe him; but tax collectors and harlots believed him; and when you saw it, you did not afterward relent and believe him.

33 "Hear another parable: There was a certain landowner who planted a vineyard and set a hedge around it, dug a winepress in it and built a tower.

And he leased it to vinedressers and went into a far country. 34 Now when vintage-time drew near, he sent his servants to the vinedressers, that they might receive its fruit. 35 And the vinedressers took his servants, beat one, killed one, and stoned another. 36 Again he sent other servants, more than the first, and they did likewise to them. 37 Then last of all he sent his son to them, saying, 'They will respect my son.' 38 But when the vinedressers saw the son, they said among themselves, 'This is the heir. Come, let us kill him and seize his inheritance.' 39 So they took him and cast *him* out of the vineyard and killed *him.*

40 "Therefore, when the owner of the vineyard comes, what will he do to those vinedressers?"

41 They said to Him, "He will destroy those wicked men miserably, and lease *his* vineyard to other vinedressers who will render to him the fruits in their seasons."

42 Jesus said to them, "Have you never read in the Scriptures:

'The stone which the builders
      rejected
   Has become the chief
      cornerstone.
   This was the LORD's doing,
      And it is marvelous in our eyes' ?

43 "Therefore I say to you, the kingdom of God will be taken from you and given to a nation bearing the fruits of it. 44 And whoever falls on this stone will be broken; but on whomever it falls, it will grind him to powder."

45 Now when the chief priests and Pharisees heard His parables, they perceived that He was speaking of them. 46 But when they sought to lay hands on Him, they feared the multitudes, because they took Him for a prophet.

A royal wedding

22 And Jesus answered and spoke to them again by parables and said: 2 "The kingdom of heaven is like a certain king who arranged a marriage for his son, 3 and sent out his servants to call those who were invited to the wedding; and they were not willing to come. 4 Again, he sent out other servants, saying, 'Tell those who are invited, "See, I have prepared my dinner; my oxen and fatted cattle *are* killed, and all things *are* ready. Come to the wedding." ' 5 But they made light of it and went their ways, one to his own farm, another to his business. 6 And the rest seized his servants, treated *them* spitefully, and killed *them.* 7 But when the king heard *about it,* he was furious. And he sent out his armies, destroyed those murderers, and burned up their city. 8 Then he said to his servants, 'The wedding is ready, but those who were invited were not worthy. 9 Therefore go into the highways, and as many as you find, invite to the wedding.' 10 So those servants went out into the highways and gathered together all whom they found, both bad and good. And the wedding *hall* was filled with guests.

11 "But when the king came in to see the guests, he saw a man there who did not have on a wedding garment. 12 So he said to him, 'Friend, how did you come in here without a wedding garment?' And he was speechless. 13 Then the king said to the servants, 'Bind him hand and foot, take him away, and cast *him* into outer darkness; there will be weeping and gnashing of teeth.'

14 "For many are called, but few *are* chosen."

15 Then the Pharisees went and plotted how they might entangle Him in His talk. 16 And they sent to Him their disciples with the **Herodians,** saying,

WORDFINDER

22:16 Herodians Pronounced *huh-ROH-dih-uns.* A group of Jews in Jesus' time who supported the Herod kings and the rule of Rome. They also wanted to bring Greek pagan customs into Jewish life.

Superhero

The Life of Jesus Christ

The Old Testament is full of clues about the coming of Jesus. In fact, as early as Genesis, we learned that God would send a Savior. In the chart of Jesus' life below, find the Old Testament clue to that event!

His Birth And Boyhood

	WHAT HAPPENED?	WHERE?	READ ABOUT IT:
JESUS	is born	in Bethlehem	Luke 2:1–7 *(Isaiah 7:14)*
JESUS	is worshiped by the shepherds	in Bethlehem	Luke 2:15–20
JESUS	is hidden from the soldiers	in Egypt	Matthew 2:13–18 *(Jeremiah 31:15)*
JESUS	visits the temple	in Jerusalem	Luke 2:41–50
JESUS	grows strong and wise	in Nazareth	Luke 2:51, 52

His Ministry Begins

When Jesus was a young man of thirty, He began the mission for which He came into the world. Everywhere He went, He preached the Good News of God's love, taught the people how to live together happily, and healed their diseases.

	WHAT HAPPENED?	WHERE?	READ ABOUT IT:
JESUS	is baptized	in the Jordan River	Matthew 3:13–17 *(Psalm 2:7)*
JESUS	is tempted by Satan	in the Desert	Matthew 4:1–11 *(Psalm 91:11)*
JESUS	chooses His disciples	in Galilee	John 1:35–51
JESUS	performs His first miracle	in Cana	John 2:1–11

Superhero

His Ministry

	WHAT HAPPENED?	WHERE?	READ ABOUT IT:
JESUS	heals Peter's mother-in-law	in Capernaum	Matthew 8:14–18 *(Isaiah 53:4)*
JESUS	heals a lame man	in Jerusalem	John 5:1–47 *(Exodus 20:10)*
JESUS	preaches the Sermon on the Mount	near Capernaum	Luke 6:20–49
JESUS	raises the widow's son	in Nain	Luke 7:11–17 *(Job 19:25)*
JESUS	walks on the water	Sea of Galilee	Matthew 14:22–33
JESUS	heals a man born blind	in Jerusalem	John 9:1–41
JESUS	teaches a lesson on prayer	in Judea?	Luke 11:1–13
JESUS	heals a crippled woman on the Sabbath	in Perea?	Luke 13:10–17 *(Deuteronomy 5:12)*
JESUS	tells stories about a lost sheep, a lost coin and a lost boy	in Perea	Luke 15:1–32
JESUS	raises Lazarus from the dead	in Bethany	John 11:1–44
JESUS	heals ten lepers	in Samaria	Luke 17:12–19 *(Leviticus 13:45)*
JESUS	blesses the children	in Perea	Matthew 19:13–15 *(Psalm 131:2)*
JESUS	speaks to the rich young ruler	in Perea	Mark 10:17–31 *(Exodus 20:1–17)*
JESUS	meets Zacchaeus	in Jericho	Luke 19:1–10

"Teacher, we know that You are true, and teach the way of God in truth; nor do You care about anyone, for You do not regard the person of men. 17 Tell us, therefore, what do You think? Is it lawful to pay taxes to Caesar, or not?"

18 But Jesus perceived their wickedness, and said, "Why do you test Me, you hypocrites? 19 Show Me the tax money."

So they brought Him a denarius.

20 And He said to them, "Whose image and inscription is this?"

21 They said to Him, "Caesar's."

And He said to them, "Render therefore to Caesar the things that are Caesar's, and to God the things that are God's." 22 When they had heard these words, they marveled, and left Him and went their way.

23 The same day the Sadducees, who say there is no resurrection, came to Him and asked Him, 24 saying: "Teacher, Moses said that if a man dies, having no children, his brother shall marry his wife and raise up offspring for his brother. 25 Now there were with us seven brothers. The first died after he had married, and having no offspring, left his wife to his brother. 26 Likewise the second also, and the third, even to the seventh. 27 Last of all the woman died also. 28 Therefore, in the resurrection, whose wife of the seven will she be? For they all had her."

29 Jesus answered and said to them, "You are mistaken, not knowing the Scriptures nor the power of God. 30 For in the resurrection they neither marry nor are given in marriage, but are like angels of God in heaven. 31 But concerning the resurrection of the dead, have you not read what was spoken to you by God, saying, 32 'I am the God of Abraham, the God of Isaac, and the God of Jacob' ? God is not the God of the dead, but of the living." 33 And when the multitudes heard this, they were astonished at His teaching.

34 But when the Pharisees heard that He had silenced the Sadducees, they gathered together. 35 Then one of them, a lawyer, asked Him a question, testing Him, and saying, 36 "Teacher, which is the great commandment in the law?"

37 Jesus said to him, " 'You shall love the LORD your God with all your heart, with all your soul, and with all your mind.' 38 This is the first and great commandment. 39 And the second is like it: 'You shall love your neighbor as yourself.' 40 On these two commandments hang all the Law and the Prophets."

41 While the Pharisees were gathered together, Jesus asked them,

---

⊕WORDFINDER

22:37 Love   An attitude that leads to the behavior Paul describes in 1 Corinthians 13. Christian love is not selfish but always seeks the best for everybody. Such love is the greatest gift of God.

⚒DIGGING IN

22:37 The Great Commandment Some people say we should love others, but they don't think loving God is important. They say you can't see God, but you can see people, so you should just love people.

What if your parents took a trip and left you in charge of your little brother and sister? Which would you love most—your parents, or your brother and sister? The fact is, you would still care most about your father and mother even though you could not see them. You would care for your brother and sister just because they were your parents' children.

That's why we care about other people, too—they are our heavenly Father's children. And we love Him too much to neglect those in the world He commanded us to love. The whole world belongs to our Father, and we love Him first because He is Lord of the world He created.

42 saying, "What do you think about the Christ? Whose Son is He?"

They said to Him, "*The Son* of David."

43 He said to them, "How then does David in the Spirit call Him 'Lord,' saying:

44   'The LORD said to my Lord,
   "Sit at My right hand,
   Till I make Your enemies Your
      footstool" ' ?

45 If David then calls Him 'Lord,' how is He his Son?" 46 And no one was able to answer Him a word, nor from that day on did anyone dare question Him anymore.

Jesus rebukes the religious leaders

23 Then Jesus spoke to the multitudes and to His disciples, 2 saying: "The scribes and the Pharisees sit in Moses' seat. 3 Therefore whatever they tell you to observe, *that* observe and do, but do not do according to their works; for they say, and do not do. 4 For they bind heavy burdens, hard to bear, and lay *them* on men's shoulders; but they *themselves* will not move them with one of their fingers. 5 But all their works they do to be seen by men. They make their phylacteries broad and enlarge the borders of their garments. 6 They love the best places at feasts, the best seats in the synagogues, 7 greetings in the marketplaces, and to be called by men,

A Pharisee was a religious leader who often didn't practice what he preached!

'Rabbi, Rabbi.' 8 But you, do not be called 'Rabbi'; for One is your Teacher, the Christ, and you are all brethren. 9 Do not call anyone on earth your father; for One is your Father, He who is in heaven. 10 And do not be called teachers; for One is your Teacher, the Christ. 11 But he who is greatest among you shall be your servant. 12 And whoever exalts himself will be humbled, and he who humbles himself will be exalted.

13 "But woe to you, scribes and Pharisees, hypocrites! For you shut up the kingdom of heaven against men; for you neither go in *yourselves,* nor do you allow those who are entering to go in. 14 Woe to you, scribes and Pharisees, hypocrites! For you devour widows' houses, and for a pretense make long prayers. Therefore you will receive greater condemnation.

What Was a Rabbi?

The word *Rabbi* (pronounced *RAB-eye*) means teacher or master. One who taught Jewish law was called a rabbi. So Jesus was sometimes called "Rabbi." Jesus said that people who loved to be called "Rabbi" were not true lovers of God or His truth. They really cared more about being very important persons, or "VIPs."

What the Scribes and Pharisees Learned

We always thought we were the faithful servants of God. We were often at the temple, and we said a lot of prayers in public places. We also did many good works—mostly when other people were watching us. Even our clothing was different from everybody else's. That way the people knew we were Scribes and Pharisees. So the people were always very careful to greet us, "Good Pharisee!" or "Good Scribe!"

We truly felt that we were much better than other people.

Then Jesus insulted us in public. He even called us names like "fools" and "blind guides"! We knew we would have to get rid of this Jesus so we could keep our honored place among the people.

---

15 "Woe to you, scribes and Pharisees, hypocrites! For you travel land and sea to win one proselyte, and when he is won, you make him twice as much a son of hell as yourselves.

16 "Woe to you, blind guides, who say, 'Whoever swears by the temple, it is nothing; but whoever swears by the gold of the temple, he is obliged *to perform it.*' 17 Fools and blind! For which is greater, the gold or the temple that sanctifies the gold? 18 And, 'Whoever swears by the altar, it is nothing; but whoever swears by the gift that is on it, he is obliged *to perform it.*' 19 Fools and blind! For which is greater, the gift or the altar that sanctifies the gift? 20 Therefore he who swears by the altar, swears by it and by all things on it. 21 He who swears by the temple, swears by it and by Him who dwells in it. 22 And he who swears by heaven, swears by the throne of God and by Him who sits on it.

23 "Woe to you, scribes and Pharisees, hypocrites! For you pay tithe of mint and anise and cummin, and have neglected the weightier *matters* of the law: justice and mercy and faith. These you ought to have done, without leaving the others undone. 24 Blind guides, who strain out a gnat and swallow a camel!

25 "Woe to you, scribes and Pharisees, hypocrites! For you cleanse the outside of the cup and dish, but inside they are full of extortion and self-indulgence. 26 Blind Pharisee, first cleanse the inside of the cup and dish, that the outside of them may be clean also.

27 "Woe to you, scribes and Pharisees, hypocrites! For you are like whitewashed tombs which indeed appear beautiful outwardly, but inside are full of dead *men's* bones and all uncleanness. 28 Even so you also outwardly appear righteous to men, but inside you are full of hypocrisy and lawlessness.

29 "Woe to you, scribes and Pharisees, hypocrites! Because you build the tombs of the prophets and adorn the monuments of the righteous, 30 and say, 'If we had lived in the days of our fathers, we would not have been partakers with them in the blood of the prophets.'

31 "Therefore you are witnesses against yourselves that you are sons of those who murdered the prophets. 32 Fill up, then, the measure of your fathers' *guilt.* 33 Serpents, brood of vipers! How can you escape the condemnation of hell? 34 Therefore, indeed, I send you prophets, wise men, and scribes: *some* of them you will kill and crucify, and *some* of them you will scourge in your synagogues and persecute from city to city, 35 that on you may come all the righteous blood shed on the earth, from the blood of righteous Abel to the blood of Zechariah, son of Berechiah, whom you murdered between the temple and the altar. 36 Assuredly, I say to you, all these things will come upon this generation. 37 "O Jerusalem, Jerusalem, the one

who kills the prophets and stones those who are sent to her! How often I wanted to gather your children together, as a hen gathers her chicks under *her* wings, but you were not willing! 38 See! Your house is left to you desolate; 39 for I say to you, you shall see Me no more till you say, 'Blessed *is* He who comes in the name of the LORD!' "

Jesus knows all about the future

24 Then Jesus went out and departed from the temple, and His disciples came up to show Him the buildings of the temple. 2 And Jesus said to them, "Do you not see all these things? Assuredly, I say to you, not *one* stone shall be left here upon another, that shall not be thrown down."

3 Now as He sat on the Mount of Olives, the disciples came to Him privately, saying, "Tell us, when will these things be? And what *will be* the sign of Your coming, and of the end of the age?"

4 And Jesus answered and said to them: "Take heed that no one deceives you. 5 For many will come in My name, saying, 'I am the Christ,' and will deceive many. 6 And you will hear of wars and rumors of wars. See that you are not troubled; for all *these things* must come to pass, but the end is not yet. 7 For nation will rise against nation, and kingdom against kingdom. And there will be famines, pestilences, and earthquakes in various places. 8 All these *are* the beginning of sorrows.

9 "Then they will deliver you up to tribulation and kill you, and you will be hated by all nations for My name's sake. 10 And then many will be offended, will betray one another, and will hate one another. 11 Then many false prophets will rise up and deceive many. 12 And because lawlessness will abound, the love of many will grow cold. 13 But he who endures to the end shall be saved. 14 And this gospel of the kingdom will be preached in all the world as a witness to all the nations, and then the end will come.

15 "Therefore when you see the 'abomination of desolation,' spoken of by Daniel the prophet, standing in the holy place" (whoever reads, let him understand), 16 "then let those who are in Judea flee to the mountains. 17 Let him who is on the housetop not go down to take anything out of his house. 18 And let him who is in the field not go back to get his clothes. 19 But woe to those who are pregnant and to those who are nursing babies in those days! 20 And pray that your flight may not be in winter or on the Sabbath. 21 For then there will be great tribulation, such as has not been since the beginning of the world until this time, no, nor ever shall be. 22 And unless those days were shortened, no flesh would be saved; but for the elect's sake those days will be shortened.

23 "Then if anyone says to you, 'Look, here is the Christ!' or 'There!' do not believe *it*. 24 For false christs and false prophets will rise and show great signs and wonders to deceive, if possible, even the elect. 25 See, I have told you beforehand.

26 "Therefore if they say to you, 'Look, He is in the desert!' do not go out; *or* 'Look, *He is* in the inner rooms!' do not believe *it*. 27 For as the lightning comes from the east and flashes to the west, so also will the coming of the Son of Man be. 28 For wherever the carcass is, there the eagles will be gathered together.

29 "Immediately after the tribulation of those days the sun will be darkened, and the moon will not give its light; the stars will fall from heaven, and the powers of the heavens will be shaken. 30 Then the sign of the Son of Man will appear in heaven, and then all the tribes of the earth will mourn, and they will see the Son of Man coming on the clouds of heaven with power and great glory. 31 And He will send His angels with a great sound of a trumpet, and they will gather together His elect from the four winds, from one end of heaven to the other.

32 "Now learn this parable from the fig tree: When its branch has already

become tender and puts forth leaves, you know that summer *is* near. ³³ So you also, when you see all these things, know that it is near—at the doors! ³⁴ Assuredly, I say to you, this generation will by no means pass away till all these things take place. ³⁵ Heaven and earth will pass away, but My words will by no means pass away.

³⁶ "But of that day and hour no one knows, not even the angels of heaven, but My Father only. ³⁷ But as the days of Noah *were,* so also will the coming of the Son of Man be. ³⁸ For as in the days before the flood, they were eating and drinking, marrying and giving in marriage, until the day that Noah entered the ark, ³⁹ and did not know until the flood came and took them all away, so also will the coming of the Son of Man be. ⁴⁰ Then two *men* will be in the field: one will be taken and the other left. ⁴¹ Two *women will be* grinding at the mill: one will be taken and the other left. ⁴² Watch therefore, for you do not know what hour your Lord is coming. ⁴³ But know this, that if the master of the house had known what hour the thief would come, he would have watched and not allowed his house to be broken into. ⁴⁴ Therefore you also be ready, for the Son of Man is coming at an hour you do not expect.

⁴⁵ "Who then is a faithful and wise servant, whom his master made ruler over his household, to give them food in due season? ⁴⁶ Blessed *is* that servant whom his master, when he comes, will find so doing. ⁴⁷ Assuredly, I say to you that he will make him ruler over all his goods. ⁴⁸ But if that evil servant says in his heart, 'My master is delaying his coming,' ⁴⁹ and begins to beat *his* fellow servants, and to eat and drink with the drunkards, ⁵⁰ the master of that servant will come on a day when he is not looking for *him* and at an hour that he is not aware of, ⁵¹ and will cut him in two and appoint *him* his portion with the hypocrites. There shall be weeping and gnashing of teeth.

⛏ DIGGING IN

24:44 Jesus Is Coming Back Again
When you study your history lessons, you may wonder where the world is heading. The books can't tell you, because they can only describe what has happened in the past.

It's a wonderful thing to learn that God is in charge of all of history. The more you read and study your Bible, the more you will realize that what happens in our world is not pointless. Everything that happens has a purpose in God's plan.

God keeps history going to give people the chance to obey Him. We notice in the Old Testament that God gave Israel many chances—for many hundreds of years—to follow His commandments. Only then came God's severe punishment.

God is now giving our world a chance to return to Him and His laws. One day, though, the Lord will come and judge His world "at an hour when you do not expect." Are you ready to meet God when He comes? Have you surrendered your life to Him?

"Watch, therefore, for you do not know what hour your Lord is coming" (verse 42).

The kingdom of heaven is like ten bridesmaids; five were prepared to meet the groom, and five were not.

Five wise and five foolish bridesmaids

25 "Then the kingdom of heaven shall be likened to ten virgins who took their lamps and went out to meet the bridegroom. ² Now five of them were wise, and five *were* foolish. ³ Those who *were* foolish took their lamps and took no oil with them, ⁴ but the wise took oil in their vessels with their lamps. ⁵ But while the bridegroom was delayed, they all slumbered and slept. ⁶ "And at midnight a cry was *heard:* 'Behold, the bridegroom is coming; go out to meet him!' ⁷ Then all those virgins arose and trimmed their lamps. ⁸ And the foolish said to the wise, 'Give us *some* of your oil, for our lamps are going out.' ⁹ But the wise answered, saying, '*No,* lest there should not be enough for us and you; but go rather

---

What We Learned About Good and Evil

Before Jesus came and taught us, we used to think the only *good* people were the Pharisees, the Sadducees (pronounced *FAIR-uh-sees* and *SAD-you-sees*), and other religious leaders.

Then Jesus told us it doesn't make any difference how important or famous you are. God cares about how we treat other people.

If people are hungry, we must feed them. If they need clothing, we should clothe them. If they are sick or in prison, we must visit them. Jesus even said that the good or bad we do to people is the same as if we did it to *Him!* This made us think a lot about what pleases God. Does it make you think?

---

to those who sell, and buy for yourselves.' ¹⁰And while they went to buy, the bridegroom came, and those who were ready went in with him to the wedding; and the door was shut.

¹¹ "Afterward the other virgins came also, saying, 'Lord, Lord, open to us!' ¹²But he answered and said, 'Assuredly, I say to you, I do not know you.'

¹³ "Watch therefore, for you know neither the day nor the hour in which the Son of Man is coming.

¹⁴ "For *the kingdom of heaven is* like a man traveling to a far country, *who* called his own servants and delivered his goods to them. ¹⁵And to one he gave five talents, to another two, and to another one, to each according to his own ability; and immediately he went on a journey. ¹⁶Then he who had received the five talents went and traded with them, and made another five talents. ¹⁷And likewise he who *had received* two gained two more also. ¹⁸But he who had received one went and dug in the ground, and hid his lord's money. ¹⁹After a long time the lord of those servants came and settled accounts with them.

²⁰ "So he who had received five talents came and brought five other talents, saying, 'Lord, you delivered to me five talents; look, I have gained five more talents besides them.' ²¹ His lord said to him, 'Well *done,* good and faithful servant; you were faithful over a few things, I will make you ruler over many things. Enter into the joy of your lord.' ²² He also who had received two talents came and said, 'Lord, you delivered to me two talents; look, I have gained two more talents besides them.' ²³His lord said to him, 'Well *done,* good and faithful servant; you have been faithful over a few things, I will make you ruler over many things. Enter into the joy of your lord.'

²⁴ "Then he who had received the one talent came and said, 'Lord, I knew you to be a hard man, reaping where you have not sown, and gathering where you have not scattered seed. ²⁵And I was afraid, and went and hid your talent in the ground. Look, *there* you have *what is* yours.'

²⁶ "But his lord answered and said to him, 'You wicked and lazy servant, you knew that I reap where I have not sown, and gather where I have not scattered seed. ²⁷So you ought to have deposited my money with the bankers, and at my coming I would have received back my own with interest. ²⁸So take the talent from him, and give *it* to him who has ten talents.

²⁹ 'For to everyone who has, more will be given, and he will have abundance; but from him who does not have, even what he has will be taken away. ³⁰And cast the unprofitable servant into the outer darkness. There will be weeping and gnashing of teeth.'

³¹ "When the Son of Man comes in His glory, and all the holy angels with Him, then He will sit on the throne of

His glory. 32 All the nations will be gathered before Him, and He will separate them one from another, as a shepherd divides *his* sheep from the goats. 33 And He will set the sheep on His right hand, but the goats on the left. 34 Then the King will say to those on His right hand, 'Come, you blessed of My Father, inherit the kingdom prepared for you from the foundation of the world: 35 for I was hungry and you gave Me food; I was thirsty and you gave Me drink; I was a stranger and you took Me in; 36 I *was* naked and you clothed Me; I was sick and you visited Me; I was in prison and you came to Me.'

37 "Then the righteous will answer Him, saying, 'Lord, when did *we* see You hungry and feed *You,* or thirsty and give *You* drink? 38 When did *we* see You a stranger and take *You* in, or naked and clothe *You?* 39 Or when did *we* see You sick, or in prison, and come to You?' 40 And the King will answer and say to them, 'Assuredly, I say to you, inasmuch as you did *it* to one of the least of these My brethren, you did *it* to Me.'

41 "Then He will also say to those on the left hand, 'Depart from Me, you cursed, into the everlasting fire prepared for the devil and his angels: 42 for I was hungry and you gave Me no food; I was thirsty and you gave Me no drink; 43 I was a stranger and you did not take Me in, naked and you did not clothe Me, sick and in prison and you did not visit Me.'

44 "Then they also will answer Him, saying, 'Lord, when did *we* see You hungry or thirsty or a stranger or naked or sick or in prison, and did not minister to You?' 45 Then He will answer them, saying, 'Assuredly, I say to you, inasmuch as you did not do *it* to one of the least of these, you did not do *it*

to Me.' 46 And these will go away into everlasting punishment, but the righteous into **eternal life."**

Jesus and His disciples eat the Lord's supper

26 Now it came to pass, when Jesus had finished all these sayings, *that* He said to His disciples, 2 "You know that after two days is the Passover, and the **Son of Man** will be delivered up to be crucified."

3 Then the chief priests, the scribes, and the elders of the people assembled at the palace of the high priest, who was called Caiaphas, 4 and plotted to take Jesus by trickery and kill *Him.* 5 But they said, "Not during the feast, lest there be an uproar among the people."

6 And when Jesus was in Bethany at the house of Simon the leper, 7 a woman came to Him having an alabaster flask of very costly fragrant oil, and she poured *it* on His head as He sat *at the table.* 8 But when His disciples saw *it,* they were indignant, saying, "Why this waste? 9 For this fragrant oil might have been sold for much and given to *the* poor."

10 But when Jesus was aware of *it,* He said to them, "Why do you trouble the woman? For she has done a good work for Me. 11 For you have the poor with you always, but Me you do not have always. 12 For in pouring this fragrant oil on My body, she did *it* for My burial. 13 Assuredly, I say to you, wherever this gospel is preached in the whole world, what this woman has done will also be told as a memorial to her."

14 Then one of the twelve, called Judas Iscariot, went to the chief priests 15 and said, "What are you willing to give me if I deliver Him to you?" And

they counted out to him thirty pieces of silver. 16 So from that time he sought opportunity to betray Him.

17 Now on the first *day of the Feast of* Unleavened Bread the disciples came to Jesus, saying to Him, "Where do You want us to prepare for You to eat the Passover?"

18 And He said, "Go into the city to a certain man, and say to him, 'The Teacher says, "My time is at hand; I will keep the Passover at your house with My disciples." ' "

19 So the disciples did as Jesus had directed them; and they prepared the Passover.

20 When evening had come, He sat down with the twelve. 21 Now as they were eating, He said, "Assuredly, I say to you, one of you will betray Me."

22 And they were exceedingly sorrowful, and each of them began to say to Him, "Lord, is it I?"

23 He answered and said, "He who dipped *his* hand with Me in the dish will betray Me. 24 The Son of Man indeed goes just as it is written of Him, but woe to that man by whom the Son of Man is betrayed! It would have been good for that man if he had not been born."

25 Then Judas, who was betraying Him, answered and said, "Rabbi, is it I?"

He said to him, "You have said it."

26 And as they were eating, Jesus took bread, blessed and broke *it,* and gave *it* to the disciples and said, "Take, eat; this is My body."

27 Then He took the cup, and gave thanks, and gave *it* to them, saying, "Drink from it, all of you. 28 For this is My blood of the new covenant, which is shed for many for the remission of sins. 29 But I say to you, I will not drink of this fruit of the vine from now on until that day when I drink it new with you in My Father's kingdom."

30 And when they had sung a hymn, they went out to the Mount of Olives.

31 Then Jesus said to them, "All of you will be made to stumble because of Me this night, for it is written:

'I will strike the Shepherd,
    And the sheep of the flock will
        be scattered.'

32 But after I have been raised, I will go before you to Galilee."

33 Peter answered and said to Him, "Even if all are made to stumble because of You, I will never be made to stumble."

34 Jesus said to him, "Assuredly, I say to you that this night, before the rooster crows, you will deny Me three times."

35 Peter said to Him, "Even if I have to die with You, I will not deny You!" And so said all the disciples.

36 Then Jesus came with them to a place called Gethsemane, and said to the disciples, "Sit here while I go and pray over there." 37 And He took with Him Peter and the two sons of Zebedee, and He began to be sorrowful and deeply distressed. 38 Then He said to them, "My soul is exceedingly sorrowful, even to death. Stay here and watch with Me."

39 He went a little farther and fell on His face, and prayed, saying, "O My Father, if it is possible, let this cup pass from Me; nevertheless, not as I will, but as You *will.*"

40 Then He came to the disciples and found them sleeping, and said to Peter, "What! Could you not watch with Me one hour? 41 Watch and pray, lest you enter into temptation. The spirit indeed is willing, but the flesh is weak."

42 Again, a second time, He went away and prayed, saying, "O My Father, if this cup cannot pass away from Me unless I drink it, Your will be done." 43 And He came and found them asleep again, for their eyes were heavy.

44 So He left them, went away again, and prayed the third time, saying the same words. 45 Then He came to His disciples and said to them, "Are *you* still sleeping and resting? Behold, the hour is at hand, and the Son of Man is being betrayed into the hands of sinners. 46 Rise, let us be going. See, My betrayer is at hand."

⁴⁷ And while He was still speaking, behold, Judas, one of the twelve, with a great multitude with swords and clubs, came from the chief priests and elders of the people.

⁴⁸ Now His betrayer had given them a sign, saying, "Whomever I kiss, He is the One; seize Him." ⁴⁹ Immediately he went up to Jesus and said, "Greetings, Rabbi!" and kissed Him.

⁵⁰ But Jesus said to him, "Friend, why have you come?"

Then they came and laid hands on Jesus and took Him. ⁵¹ And suddenly, one of those *who were* with Jesus stretched out *his* hand and drew his sword, struck the servant of the high priest, and cut off his ear.

⁵² But Jesus said to him, "Put your sword in its place, for all who take the sword will perish by the sword. ⁵³ Or do you think that I cannot now pray to My Father, and He will provide Me with more than twelve legions of angels? ⁵⁴ How then could the Scriptures be fulfilled, that it must happen thus?"

⁵⁵ In that hour Jesus said to the multitudes, "Have you come out, as against a robber, with swords and clubs to take Me? I sat daily with you, teaching in the temple, and you did not seize Me. ⁵⁶ But all this was done that the Scriptures of the prophets might be fulfilled."

Then all the disciples forsook Him and fled.

⁵⁷ And those who had laid hold of Jesus led *Him* away to Caiaphas the high priest, where the scribes and the elders were assembled. ⁵⁸ But Peter followed Him at a distance to the high priest's courtyard. And he went in and sat with the servants to see the end.

⁵⁹ Now the chief priests, the elders, and all the council sought false testimony against Jesus to put Him to death, ⁶⁰ but found none. Even though many false witnesses came forward, they found none. But at last two false witnesses came forward ⁶¹ and said, "This *fellow* said, 'I am able to destroy the temple of God and to build it in three days.' "

⁶² And the high priest arose and said to Him, "Do You answer nothing? What *is it* these men testify against

DIGGING IN

26:36–46 Jesus Prays in the Garden Jesus planned to die, but He didn't want to die! You may wonder how death could hurt Jesus, the Son of God! Remember, Jesus was also a Man, and dying was a horrible thought for this special Man who was still so young.

It's hard to think about. But try to imagine yourself having nails driven through your hands and feet. Then imagine hanging on a cross for hours before death comes. It's horrible, isn't it?

But that isn't all there was to it. No, Jesus, the very Son of God, would carry all of the sins of the whole world on the Cross. And that was the suffering He feared most. Even His own Father would have to leave Him alone during those long hours. Jesus was judged for your sins so you wouldn't have to be judged.

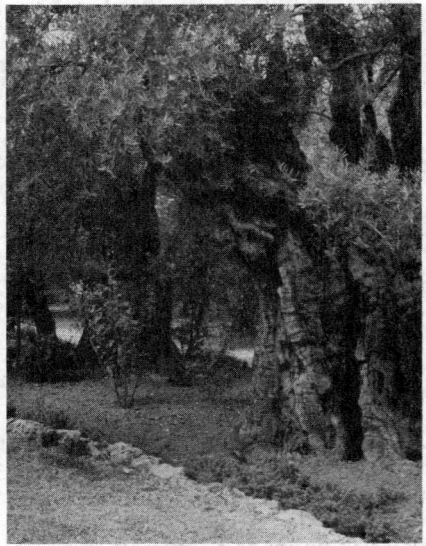

The Garden of Gethsemane, where Jesus prayed before He was arrested.

You?" **63** But Jesus kept silent. And the high priest answered and said to Him, "I put You under oath by the living God: Tell us if You are the Christ, the Son of God!"

64 Jesus said to him, "*It is as* you said. Nevertheless, I say to you, hereafter you will see the Son of Man sitting at the right hand of the Power, and coming on the clouds of heaven."

65 Then the high priest tore his clothes, saying, "He has spoken **blasphemy!** What further need do we have of witnesses? Look, now you have heard His blasphemy! **66** What do you think?"

They answered and said, "He is deserving of death."

67 Then they spat in His face and beat Him; and others struck *Him* with the palms of their hands, **68** saying, "Prophesy to us, Christ! Who is the one who struck You?"

69 Now Peter sat outside in the courtyard. And a servant girl came to him, saying, "You also were with Jesus of Galilee."

70 But he denied it before *them* all, saying, "I do not know what you are saying."

71 And when he had gone out to the gateway, another *girl* saw him and said to those *who were* there, "This *fellow* also was with Jesus of Nazareth."

72 But again he denied with an oath, "I do not know the Man!"

73 And a little later those who stood by came up and said to Peter, "Surely you also are *one* of them, for your speech betrays you."

74 Then he began to curse and swear, *saying,* "I do not know the Man!"

Immediately a rooster crowed. **75** And Peter remembered the word of Jesus who had said to him, "Before the rooster crows, you will deny Me three times." So he went out and wept bitterly.

Jesus dies on the Cross

27 When morning came, all the chief priests and elders of the people plotted against Jesus to put Him to death. **2** And when they had bound Him, they led Him away and delivered Him to Pontius Pilate the governor.

3 Then Judas, His betrayer, seeing

WORDFINDER

26:65 Blasphemy Pronounced *BLASS-fuh-mee*. Profanity, cursing, or insulting God.

DIGGING IN

26:72 Confessing Jesus Like Peter, you, too, may get into tight places where it will be hard for you to confess you are a Christian. But these are places in life where you should pray to be ready to speak for Jesus in a way that will change the lives of others. For example, someday you may find yourself with someone who is doing drugs. Then he or she says to you, "What about you? Would you like a sniff of cocaine?" or "Would you like a joint of marijuana?" What do you do? Do you just sneak away in shame?

No, you can say, "I'm a Christian. I wish you would come to know my Savior, too, so you wouldn't need drugs anymore."

That person may be angry at you, but that can't hurt you. It will hurt a lot, though, if later you realize you missed the chance to tell that needy boy or girl about Jesus.

27:3–5 A Traitor Dies Poor Judas! He had walked and talked with the Lord for over three years. What a privilege! But then he threw it all away. He even led the soldiers to Jesus so they could arrest Him. The religious leaders had paid Judas 30 pieces of silver to sell out his Lord!

You mustn't think the silver was the only thing Judas wanted. He even tried to return the money later. But Judas had allowed the Devil to do his thinking for him. He thought Jesus should have that He had been condemned, was remorseful and brought back the thirty pieces of silver to the chief priests and elders, 4 saying, "I have sinned by betraying innocent blood."

And they said, "What *is that* to us? You *see to it!*"

5 Then he threw down the pieces of silver in the temple and departed, and went and hanged himself.

6 But the chief priests took the silver pieces and said, "It is not lawful to put them into the treasury, because they are the price of blood." 7 And they consulted together and bought with them the potter's field, to bury strangers in. 8 Therefore that field has been called the Field of Blood to this day.

9 Then was fulfilled what was spoken by Jeremiah the prophet, saying, "And they took the thirty pieces of silver, the value of Him who was priced, whom they of the children of Israel priced, 10 and gave them for the potter's field, as the LORD directed me."

11 Now Jesus stood before the governor. And the governor asked Him, saying, "Are You the King of the Jews?"

Jesus said to him, "*It is as you say.*"

12 And while He was being accused by the chief priests and elders, He answered nothing.

13 Then Pilate said to Him, "Do You not hear how many things they testify against You?" 14 But He answered him not one word, so that the governor marveled greatly.

15 Now at the feast the governor was accustomed to releasing to the multitude one prisoner whom they wished. 16 And at that time they had a notorious prisoner called Barabbas. 17 Therefore, when they had gathered together, Pilate said to them, "Whom do you want me to release to you? Barabbas,

or Jesus who is called Christ?" 18 For he knew that they had handed Him over because of envy.

19 While he was sitting on the judgment seat, his wife sent to him, saying, "Have nothing to do with that just Man, for I have suffered many things today in a dream because of Him."

20 But the chief priests and elders persuaded the multitudes that they should ask for Barabbas and destroy Jesus. 21 The governor answered and said to them, "Which of the two do you want me to release to you?"

They said, "Barabbas!"

22 Pilate said to them, "What then shall I do with Jesus who is called Christ?"

They all said to him, "Let Him be crucified!"

23 Then the governor said, "Why, what evil has He done?"

But they cried out all the more, saying, "Let Him be crucified!"

24 When Pilate saw that he could not prevail at all, but rather *that* a tumult was rising, he took water and washed *his* hands before the multitude, saying, "I am innocent of the blood of this just Person. You *see to it.*"

25 And all the people answered and said, "His blood *be* on us and on our children."

26 Then he released Barabbas to them; and when he had scourged Jesus, he delivered *Him* to be crucified.

27 Then the soldiers of the governor took Jesus into the Praetorium and gathered the whole garrison around Him. 28 And they stripped Him and put a scarlet robe on Him. 29 When they had twisted a crown of thorns, they put *it* on His head, and a reed in His right hand. And they bowed the knee before Him and mocked Him, saying, "Hail, King of the Jews!" 30 Then they

---

DIGGING IN

brought in the kingdom of God right away. Judas wanted *everything now,* but that didn't happen.

Don't get tricked into thinking Jesus should make everything perfect *right now.*

In this world you serve as a soldier of Christ your King. His friendship is enough until one day you see Him face to face in heaven.

spat on Him, and took the reed and struck Him on the head. 31 And when they had mocked Him, they took the robe off Him, put His *own* clothes on Him, and led Him away to be crucified.

32 Now as they came out, they found a man of Cyrene, Simon by name. Him they compelled to bear His cross. 33 And when they had come to a place called Golgotha, that is to say, Place of a Skull, 34 they gave Him sour wine mingled with gall to drink. But when He had tasted *it,* He would not drink.

35 Then they crucified Him, and divided His garments, casting lots, that it might be fulfilled which was spoken by the prophet:

"They divided My garments
    among them,
And for My clothing they cast
    lots."

36 Sitting down, they kept watch over Him there. 37 And they put up over His head the accusation written against Him:

THIS IS JESUS THE KING
OF THE JEWS.

38 Then two robbers were crucified with Him, one on the right and another on the left.

39 And those who passed by blasphemed Him, wagging their heads 40 and saying, "You who destroy the temple and build *it* in three days, save Yourself! If You are the Son of God, come down from the cross."

41 Likewise the chief priests also, mocking with the scribes and elders, said, 42 "He saved others; Himself He cannot save. If He is the King of Israel, let Him now come down from the cross, and we will believe Him. 43 He trusted in God; let Him deliver Him now if He will have Him; for He said, 'I am the Son of God.' "

44 Even the robbers who were crucified with Him reviled Him with the same thing.

45 Now from the sixth hour until the ninth hour there was darkness over all the land. 46 And about the ninth hour Jesus cried out with a loud voice, saying, "Eli, Eli, lama sabachthani?" that is, "My God, My God, why have You forsaken Me?"

47 Some of those who stood there, when they heard *that,* said, "This Man is calling for Elijah!" 48 Immediately one of them ran and took a sponge, filled *it* with sour wine and put *it* on a reed, and offered it to Him to drink. 49 The rest said, "Let Him alone; let us *see* if Elijah will come to save Him."

50 And Jesus cried out again with a loud voice, and yielded up His spirit.

51 Then, behold, the veil of the temple was torn in two from top to bottom; and the earth quaked, and the rocks were split, 52 and the graves were opened; and many bodies of the saints who had fallen asleep were raised; 53 and coming out of the graves after His resurrection, they went into the holy city and appeared to many.

54 So when the centurion and those with him, who were guarding Jesus, saw the earthquake and the things that had happened, they feared greatly, saying, "Truly this was the Son of God!"

55 And many women who followed Jesus from Galilee, ministering to Him, were there looking on from afar, 56 among whom were Mary Magdalene, Mary the mother of James and Joses, and the mother of Zebedee's sons.

57 Now when evening had come, there came a rich man from Arimathea, named Joseph, who himself had also become a disciple of Jesus. 58 This man went to Pilate and asked for the body of Jesus. Then Pilate commanded the body to be given to him. 59 When Joseph had taken the body, he wrapped it in a clean linen cloth, 60 and laid it in his new tomb which he had hewn out of the rock; and he rolled a large stone against the door of the tomb, and departed. 61 And Mary Magdalene was there, and the other Mary, sitting opposite the tomb.

62 On the next day, which followed the Day of Preparation, the chief priests and Pharisees gathered together

Jesus Dies on Cross

The Jerusalem Times—Editorial

JERUSALEM—This newspaper has not always agreed with everything Jesus of Galilee said and did, but now that He has been crucified, we have a lot of new thoughts about Him.

The Times believes that Jesus didn't get a fair trial. A lot of lies were told about Him, in our opinion. Besides, what real harm has He done? We have heard only that Jesus healed the sick, opened the eyes of the blind, and made the lame walk. We can't find fault with that!

We wonder how many of Jesus' enemies showed up when He suffered that awful Roman death on the Cross. Did this Man really deserve that kind of treatment? Whatever Jesus said and did, He was no murderer or robber, like the others who died with Him.

Our hearts are heavy because we believe Jerusalem has committed a great sin in killing Jesus. *The Times* calls for a public inquiry into this great crime!

to Pilate, 63 saying, "Sir, we remember, while He was still alive, how that deceiver said, 'After three days I will rise.' 64 Therefore command that the tomb be made secure until the third day, lest His disciples come by night and steal Him *away,* and say to the people, 'He has risen from the dead.' So the last deception will be worse than the first."

65 Pilate said to them, "You have a guard; go your way, make *it* as secure as you know how." 66 So they went

Jesus was laid in a tomb like this one, owned by a rich Hebrew.

and made the tomb secure, sealing the stone and setting the guard.

Jesus comes back to life!

28 Now after the Sabbath, as the first *day* of the week began to dawn, Mary Magdalene and the other Mary came to see the tomb. 2 And behold, there was a great earthquake; for an angel of the Lord descended from heaven, and came and rolled back the stone from the door, and sat on it. 3 His countenance was like lightning, and his clothing as white as snow. 4 And the guards shook for fear of him, and became like dead *men.*

5 But the angel answered and said to the women, "Do not be afraid, for I know that you seek Jesus who was crucified. 6 He is not here; for He is risen, as He said. Come, see the place where the Lord lay. 7 And go quickly and tell His disciples that He is risen from the dead, and indeed He is going before you into Galilee; there you will see Him. Behold, I have told you."

8 So they went out quickly from the tomb with fear and great joy, and ran to bring His disciples word.

9 And as they went to tell His disciples, behold, Jesus met them, saying, "Rejoice!" So they came and held Him by the feet and worshiped Him. 10 Then Jesus said to them, "Do not

Soldiers Report Strange Happenings at Tomb

The Jerusalem Times

JERUSALEM—Jesus of Nazareth was crucified in this city last week, but now rumors are flying that He isn't dead.

Some of the soldiers on guard duty at the tomb say Jesus' enemies paid them to say His disciples stole the body while the guards were sleeping. But how could the guards know what happened if they were asleep? Others have told of an angel from heaven who reportedly rolled back the stone from the door of the tomb.

In fact, reports have come in that there was no body in the tomb. Jesus is gone! But where? The soldiers either don't know or are afraid to tell. An angel has said He is risen from the dead!

Other stories from the tomb in the garden are just as amazing. Jesus' disciples say that they have seen Him alive. Meanwhile, eyewitnesses report seeing Jesus in the north country of Galilee.

The Times will continue to check out the story that Jesus is risen.

---

be afraid. Go *and* tell My brethren to go to Galilee, and there they will see Me."

11 Now while they were going, behold, some of the guard came into the city and reported to the chief priests all the things that had happened. 12 When they had assembled with the elders and consulted together, they gave a large sum of money to the soldiers, 13 saying, "Tell them, 'His disciples came at night and stole Him *away* while we slept.' 14 And if this comes to the governor's ears, we will appease him and make you secure." 15 So they took the money and did as they were instructed; and this saying is commonly reported among the Jews until this day.

16 Then the eleven disciples went away into Galilee, to the mountain which Jesus had appointed for them. 17 When they saw Him, they worshiped Him; but some doubted.

18 And Jesus came and spoke to

 DIGGING IN

28:11–15 Jesus Is Alive! The guards at Jesus' tomb were bribed to say Jesus didn't come back from death. Besides, the guards even admitted they were asleep when it happened.

Some people today say the disciples of Jesus made up the story that He arose alive from the tomb. But if that is true, what happened to Jesus' body? Jesus' enemies wanted to prove He was still dead. They could have forced someone to tell them where His dead body was. But they never found Jesus' body—*Jesus was alive!*

Also, why did all of the disciples spend *their whole lives* gladly telling us Jesus was risen if it was all a lie? The disciples even let themselves be killed for saying He was alive. Would you let yourself be killed for something that wasn't true? No,

and neither would the disciples. They changed the world by telling about their risen Savior.

28:18–29 Jesus Commands You to Tell About Him We call these last verses of Matthew's Gospel the "Great Commission." A commission (pronounced *kuh-MISH-shun*) is a command by an authority to carry out his orders. Jesus had "all authority" (verse 18) to command His disciples to go and tell the nations about His victory over sin and death. He also gave them the power to speak for Him.

This commission was not only given to the disciples of Jesus' own time, but it was also given to the disciples of Jesus today. Are you a disciple, a pupil of Jesus? Then the Great Commission is for you, too.

Now is the time to think about how your

them, saying, "All authority has been given to Me in heaven and on earth. 19 Go therefore and make disciples of all the nations, baptizing them in the name of the Father and of the Son and of the Holy Spirit, 20 teaching them to observe all things that I have commanded you; and lo, I am with you always, *even* to the end of the age." Amen.

DIGGING IN

life is going to be spent. You will make a bad mistake if you only ask, How much money can I make? Yes, you need money to live in the world, but only what you do for Jesus will last forever. What will you do to carry out *your* Great Commission?

The Book of
MARK

 I think I was the youngest of Jesus' disciples. In fact, I was too young to understand a lot of the things Jesus said when I used to come and listen to Him, but I couldn't stay away from Him. He seemed like a great older Brother to me. When He was crucified, I was afraid. Like most of the others, I ran away from Calvary where they killed the best Brother I ever knew.

When I grew up, I became a useful helper to the apostles, Paul and Peter. An apostle was someone "sent" by God with the gospel. While we were living in Rome, Peter helped me write this earliest Gospel about the life and work of Jesus on earth.

Mine is the shortest of the four Gospels. I wrote it so that the Roman people would be able to know and love my great Brother who is now in heaven.

John the Baptist gets the world ready for Jesus

The beginning of the **gospel** of Jesus Christ, the Son of God. ² As it is written in the Prophets:

"Behold, I send My messenger
   before Your face,
Who will prepare Your way
   before You."
³ "The voice of one crying in the
   wilderness:
'Prepare the way of the LORD;
Make His paths straight.' "

⁴ John came baptizing in the wilderness and preaching a baptism of repentance for the remission of sins. ⁵ Then all the land of Judea, and those from Jerusalem, went out to him and were all baptized by him in the Jordan River, confessing their sins.

⁶ Now John was clothed with camel's hair and with a leather belt around his waist, and he ate locusts and wild honey. ⁷ And he preached, saying, "There comes One after me who is mightier than I, whose sandal strap I am not worthy to stoop down and loose. ⁸ I indeed baptized you with water, but He will baptize you with the Holy Spirit."

What Is Baptism?

Jesus commands us to baptize people who believe the Good News of salvation. Baptism by water is a sign that a person's sins are forgiven. Jesus also baptizes with the Holy Spirit (see verse 8). This means that the Spirit of Christ Himself comes to live in us and gives us a new nature.

WORDFINDER

1:1 Gospel Means "good news." The word is taken from the early English word *godspel*. In the New Testament, it is the Good News about Jesus Christ.

If you visited Nazareth today, you would find modern buildings like these.

9 It came to pass in those days *that* Jesus came from Nazareth of Galilee, and was baptized by John in the Jordan. 10 And immediately, coming up from the water, He saw the heavens parting and the Spirit descending upon Him like a dove. 11 Then a voice came from heaven, "You are My beloved Son, in whom I am well pleased."

12 Immediately the Spirit drove Him into the wilderness. 13 And He was there in the wilderness forty days, tempted by Satan, and was with the wild beasts; and the angels ministered to Him.

14 Now after John was put in prison, Jesus came to Galilee, preaching the gospel of the kingdom of God, 15 and saying, "The time is fulfilled, and the kingdom of God is at hand. Repent, and believe in the gospel."

16 And as He walked by the Sea of Galilee, He saw Simon and Andrew his brother casting a net into the sea; for they were fishermen. 17 Then Jesus said to them, "Follow Me, and I will make you become fishers of men."

Why Did Jesus Choose Ordinary People to Be His Disciples?

Jesus calls ordinary people to show us that He doesn't need the most talented ones to do His work. Sometimes His followers are highly trained, like Luke and Paul. But Abraham Lincoln said, "The Lord must have loved the common people because He made so many of them."

DIGGING IN

1:15 Repent and Believe in the Gospel The New Testament was first written in Greek, and the word *repent* comes from a Greek word meaning "to turn around," or change your mind. So repenting doesn't mean simply being sorry for your sins. Being sorry alone doesn't change anything. Repenting means changing your mind about how you're going to live. You used to live for yourself. Now you'll live for Jesus.

To "believe in the gospel" simply means trusting Jesus. Trusting Jesus is something like learning to swim. As long as you keep fighting the water, you'll sink. But just as soon as you let yourself relax in the water, you'll float. In the same way, trusting Jesus is relaxing in what Jesus has promised. Then you will find out that everything He has promised will come true for you.

God sent His Son Jesus from heaven so that everybody could see what God is like, but nobody has ever seen Me, the Holy Spirit. I am like the wind that blows. You feel My presence, but you can't see Me. The word *spirit* comes from a Bible word meaning *wind*. I am the "Wind" of God, but I am also a Person just as much as Jesus and His Father are Persons. I have always been part of God, just as the Father and the Son are part of God.

My work is to make God's plans happen in the world. At the very beginning of time, I was the One who made the Creation happen when God spoke the command: "Let there be light." (See Genesis 1:2, 3.)

I am also the One who took the place of Jesus in the world, and I keep on doing His great works. I want to live in you so Jesus can do His works through you.

18 They immediately left their nets and followed Him.

19 When He had gone a little farther from there, He saw James the *son* of Zebedee, and John his brother, who also *were* in the boat mending their nets. 20 And immediately He called them, and they left their father Zebedee in the boat with the hired servants, and went after Him.

21 Then they went into Capernaum, and immediately on the Sabbath He entered the synagogue and taught.

22 And they were astonished at His teaching, for He taught them as one having authority, and not as the scribes.

23 Now there was a man in their synagogue with an unclean spirit. And he cried out, 24 saying, "Let *us* alone! What have we to do with You, Jesus of Nazareth? Did You come to destroy us? I know who You are—the Holy One of God!"

25 But Jesus rebuked him, saying, "Be quiet, and come out of him!"

Four fishermen left their nets to become Jesus' disciples.

26 And when the unclean spirit had convulsed him and cried out with a loud voice, he came out of him. 27 Then they were all amazed, so that they questioned among themselves, saying, "What is this? What new doctrine is this? For with authority He commands even the unclean spirits, and they obey Him." 28 And immediately His fame spread throughout all the region around Galilee.

29 Now as soon as they had come out of the synagogue, they entered the house of Simon and Andrew, with James and John. 30 But Simon's wife's mother lay sick with a fever, and they told Him about her at once. 31 So He came and took her by the hand and lifted her up, and immediately the fever left her. And she served them.

32 At evening, when the sun had set, they brought to Him all who were sick and those who were demon-possessed. 33 And the whole city was gathered together at the door. 34 Then He healed many who were sick with various diseases, and cast out many demons; and He did not allow the demons to speak, because they knew Him.

35 Now in the morning, having risen a long while before daylight, He went out and departed to a solitary place; and there He prayed. 36 And Simon and those who were with Him searched for Him. 37 When they found Him, they said to Him, "Everyone is looking for You."

38 But He said to them, "Let us go into the next towns, that I may preach there also, because for this purpose I have come forth."

39 And He was preaching in their synagogues throughout all Galilee, and casting out demons.

40 Now a leper came to Him, imploring Him, kneeling down to Him and saying to Him, "If You are willing, You can make me clean."

41 Then Jesus, moved with compassion, stretched out His hand and touched him, and said to him, "I am willing; be cleansed." 42 As soon as He had spoken, immediately the leprosy left him, and he was cleansed. 43 And He strictly warned him and sent him away at once, 44 and said to him, "See that you say nothing to anyone; but go your way, show yourself to the priest, and offer for your cleansing those things which Moses commanded, as a testimony to them."

45 However, he went out and began to proclaim it freely, and to spread the matter, so that Jesus could no longer openly enter the city, but was outside in deserted places; and they came to Him from every direction.

Jesus begins to heal the sick

2 And again He entered Capernaum after some days, and it was heard that He was in the house. 2 Immediately many gathered together, so that there was no longer room to receive them, not even near the door. And He preached the word to them. 3 Then they came to Him, bringing a paralytic who was carried by four men. 4 And

---

⚒ DIGGING IN

1:40–42 Jesus Heals a Leper This was a man who had the dreaded disease of leprosy. Leprosy is the name of several diseases today. But in Jesus' time it was a bad form of a skin disease we call "psoriasis" (pronounced *sore-EYE-uh-sis*).

Notice how the suffering man speaks to Jesus: "If you are willing, You can make me clean." The man's words show how much He really trusted Jesus. The man wasn't *demanding* anything. He didn't feel that he had a *right* to be healed. But he was just glad to put his life in Jesus' hands. Then he knew Jesus would do what was best.

Sometimes we come to Jesus and *tell* Him what we think is best for us. Then we expect Him to do what we want. That isn't a good way to get along with the Lord. Rather, we should always say, "If You are willing, please grant what I ask. But if not, I know You will do what is best."

when they could not come near Him because of the crowd, they uncovered the roof where He was. So when they had broken through, they let down the bed on which the paralytic was lying.

5 When Jesus saw their faith, He said to the paralytic, "Son, your sins are forgiven you."

6 And some of the scribes were sitting there and reasoning in their hearts, 7 "Why does this *Man* speak blasphemies like this? Who can forgive sins but God alone?"

8 But immediately, when Jesus perceived in His spirit that they reasoned thus within themselves, He said to them, "Why do you reason about these things in your hearts? 9 Which is easier, to say to the paralytic, 'Your sins are forgiven you,' or to say, 'Arise, take up your bed and walk'? 10 But that you may know that the Son of Man has power on earth to forgive sins"— He said to the paralytic, 11 "I say to you, arise, take up your bed, and go to your house." 12 Immediately he arose, took up the bed, and went out in the presence of them all, so that all were amazed and glorified God, saying, "We never saw *anything* like this!"

13 Then He went out again by the sea; and all the multitude came to Him, and He taught them. 14 As He passed by, He saw Levi the *son* of Alphaeus sitting at the tax office. And He said to him, "Follow Me." So he arose and followed Him.

15 Now it happened, as He was dining in *Levi's* house, that many tax collectors and sinners also sat together with Jesus and His disciples; for there were many, and they followed Him. 16 And when the scribes and Pharisees saw Him eating with the tax collectors and sinners, they said to His disciples, "How *is it* that He eats and drinks with tax collectors and sinners?"

17 When Jesus heard *it*, He said to them, "Those who are well have no need of a physician, but those who are sick. I did not come to call *the* righteous, but sinners, to **repentance.**"

18 The disciples of John and of the Pharisees were fasting. Then they came and said to Him, "Why do the disciples of John and of the Pharisees fast, but Your disciples do not fast?"

What Is Fasting?

Fasting means going without food for a time so that the whole time can be spent in prayer. Jesus teaches that fasting is necessary for some things (see Matthew 17:21). Sad to say, some people used to fast just to show off their religion (see Matthew 6:16).

WORDFINDER

2:17 Repentance Pronounced *re-PEN-tunce.* Turning away from sin to obey God. You repent when you leave your sins to receive Christ as your Savior and Master of your life.

DIGGING IN

2:5 Jesus Forgives Sinners If you were sick and Jesus came to your bedside and said, "Your sins are forgiven," what would you think?

The scribes were annoyed when Jesus said these words to a paralyzed man. Only God can forgive sins, they said. But Jesus and the paralyzed man understood each other. Being paralyzed gives you time to think a lot. And that paralyzed man knew Jesus was doing first things first. Sin, and not our other sicknesses, is our deepest disease. Jesus did a beautiful thing when He forgave the poor man's sins. *Then* He made him able to walk again.

Your first need is to have a new heart that loves God. That is the greatest gift God can give you. Jesus was the Son of God, so He had authority to forgive the paralyzed man and give him a new heart. Jesus wants to forgive you and give you a new heart, too.

19 And Jesus said to them, "Can the friends of the bridegroom fast while the bridegroom is with them? As long as they have the bridegroom with them they cannot fast. 20 But the days will come when the bridegroom will be taken away from them, and then they will fast in those days. 21 No one sews a piece of unshrunk cloth on an old garment; or else the new piece pulls away from the old, and the tear is made worse. 22 And no one puts new wine into old wineskins; or else the new wine bursts the wineskins, the wine is spilled, and the wineskins are ruined. But new wine must be put into new wineskins."

23 Now it happened that He went through the grainfields on the Sabbath; and as they went His disciples began to pluck the heads of grain. 24 And the Pharisees said to Him, "Look, why do they do what is not lawful on the Sabbath?"

25 But He said to them, "Have you never read what David did when he was in need and hungry, he and those with him: 26 how he went into the house of God *in the days* of Abiathar the high priest, and ate the **showbread,** which is not lawful to eat except for the priests, and also gave some to those who were with him?"

27 And He said to them, "The Sabbath was made for man, and not man for the Sabbath. 28 Therefore the Son of Man is also Lord of the Sabbath."

Jesus chooses His followers

3 And He entered the synagogue again, and a man was there who had a withered hand. 2 So they watched Him closely, whether He would heal him on the Sabbath, so that they might accuse Him. 3 And He said to the man who had the withered hand, "Step forward." 4 Then He said to them, "Is it lawful on the Sabbath to do good or to do evil, to save life or to kill?" But they kept silent. 5 And when He had looked around at them with anger, being grieved by the hardness of their hearts, He said to the man, "Stretch out your hand." And he stretched *it* out, and his hand was restored as whole as the other. 6 Then the Pharisees went out and immediately plotted with the **Herodians** against Him, how they might destroy Him.

7 But Jesus withdrew with His disciples to the sea. And a great multitude from Galilee followed Him, and from Judea 8 and Jerusalem and Idumea and beyond the Jordan; and those from Tyre and Sidon, a great multitude, when they heard how many things He was doing, came to Him. 9 So He told His disciples that a small boat should be kept ready for Him because of the multitude, lest they should crush Him. 10 For He healed many, so that as many as had afflictions pressed about Him to touch Him. 11 And the unclean spirits, whenever they saw Him, fell down before Him and cried out, saying, "You are the Son of God." 12 But He sternly warned them that they should not make Him known.

13 And He went up on the mountain and called to *Him* those He Himself wanted. And they came to Him. 14 Then He appointed twelve, that they might be with Him and that He might send them out to preach, 15 and to have power to heal sicknesses and to cast out demons: 16 Simon, to whom He gave the name Peter; 17 James the *son* of Zebedee and John the brother of James, to whom He gave the name Boanerges, that is, "Sons of Thunder"; 18 Andrew, Philip, Bartholomew, Mat-

WORDFINDER

2:26 Showbread A symbol of God's presence and supply. Every Sabbath 12 loaves of bread were arranged on a table about 36 inches long by 18 inches wide by 27 inches high.

3:6 Herodians Pronounced *huh-ROH-dih-uns.* A group of Jews in Jesus' time who supported the Herod kings and the rule of Rome. They also wanted to bring Greek pagan customs into Jewish life.

thew, Thomas, James the *son* of Alphaeus, Thaddaeus, Simon the Cananite; 19 and Judas Iscariot, who also betrayed Him. And they went into a house.

20 Then the multitude came together again, so that they could not so much as eat bread. 21 But when His own people heard *about this,* they went out to lay hold of Him, for they said, "He is out of His mind."

22 And the scribes who came down from Jerusalem said, "He has Beelzebub," and, "By the ruler of the demons He casts out demons."

23 So He called them to *Himself* and said to them in parables: "How can Satan cast out Satan? 24 If a kingdom is divided against itself, that kingdom cannot stand. 25 And if a house is divided against itself, that house cannot stand. 26 And if Satan has risen up against himself, and is divided, he cannot stand, but has an end. 27 No one can enter a strong man's house and plunder his goods, unless he first binds the strong man. And then he will plunder his house.

28 "Assuredly, I say to you, all sins will be forgiven the sons of men, and whatever blasphemies they may utter; 29 but he who blasphemes against the Holy Spirit never has forgiveness, but is subject to eternal condemnation"— 30 because they said, "He has an unclean spirit."

31 Then His brothers and His mother came, and standing outside they sent to Him, calling Him. 32 And a multitude was sitting around Him; and they said to Him, "Look, Your mother and Your brothers are outside seeking You."

33 But He answered them, saying, "Who is My mother, or My brothers?" 34 And He looked around in a circle at those who sat about Him, and said, "Here are My mother and My brothers! 35 For whoever does the will of God is My brother and My sister and mother."

Stories about seeds, soil, and a lamp

4 And again He began to teach by the sea. And a great multitude was gathered to Him, so that He got into a boat and sat *in it* on the sea; and the whole multitude was on the land facing the sea. 2 Then He taught them many things by parables, and said to them in His teaching:

3 "Listen! Behold, a sower went out to sow. 4 And it happened, as he sowed, *that* some *seed* fell by the wayside; and the birds of the air came and devoured it. 5 Some fell on stony ground, where it did not have much earth; and immediately it sprang up because it had no depth of earth. 6 But when the sun was up it was scorched, and because it had no root it withered away. 7 And some *seed* fell among thorns; and the thorns grew up and choked it, and it yielded no crop. 8 But other *seed* fell on good ground and yielded a crop that sprang up, increased and produced: some thirtyfold, some sixty, and some a hundred."

⚒ DIGGING IN

3:31–35 Are You a Member of Jesus' Family? This is a very puzzling part of Jesus' life. Jesus did belong to the family of Mary and Joseph. But Jesus was also the Son of God. So He had a higher duty than He owed Joseph and Mary. He had a duty to the whole great family of God. That's why He said, "Here are My mother and My brothers!" and pointed to His followers who were sitting there.

Jesus wasn't hard-hearted toward His earthly family. Later, we see that even when He was on the Cross, He really cared for Mary, His mother (see John 19:25–27). But Jesus had to follow the path His heavenly Father had set before Him. He had to be the older Brother who takes away the sin of God's great family.

Jesus wants you to be a member of that greater family of God. Then Jesus Himself will be your Brother forever.

9 And He said to them, "He who has ears to hear, let him hear!"

10 But when He was alone, those around Him with the twelve asked Him about the parable. 11 And He said to them, "To you it has been given to know the mystery of the kingdom of God; but to those who are outside, all things come in parables, 12 so that

'Seeing they may see and not perceive,
And hearing they may hear and not understand;
Lest they should turn,
And *their* sins be forgiven them.' "

13 And He said to them, "Do you not understand this parable? How then will you understand all the parables? 14 The sower sows the word. 15 And these are the ones by the wayside where the word is sown. When they hear, Satan comes immediately and takes away the word that was sown in their hearts. 16 These likewise are the ones sown on stony ground who, when they hear the word, immediately receive it with gladness; 17 and they have no root in themselves, and so endure only for a time. Afterward, when tribulation or persecution arises for the word's sake, immediately they stumble. 18 Now these are the ones sown among thorns; *they are* the ones who hear the word, 19 and the cares of this world, the deceitfulness of riches, and the desires for other things entering in choke the word, and it becomes unfruitful. 20 But these are the ones sown on good ground, those who hear the word, accept *it,* and bear fruit: some

thirtyfold, some sixty, and some a hundred."

21 Also He said to them, "Is a lamp brought to be put under a basket or under a bed? Is it not to be set on a lampstand? 22 For there is nothing hidden which will not be revealed, nor has anything been kept secret but that it should come to light. 23 If anyone has ears to hear, let him hear."

24 Then He said to them, "Take heed what you hear. With the same measure you use, it will be measured to you; and to you who hear, more will be given. 25 For whoever has, to him more will be given; but whoever does not have, even what he has will be taken away from him."

26 And He said, "The kingdom of God is as if a man should scatter seed on the ground, 27 and should sleep by night and rise by day, and the seed should sprout and grow, he himself does not know how. 28 For the earth yields crops by itself: first the blade, then the head, after that the full grain in the head. 29 But when the grain ripens, immediately he puts in the sickle, because the harvest has come."

30 Then He said, "To what shall we liken the kingdom of God? Or with what parable shall we picture it? 31 *It is* like a mustard seed which, when it is sown on the ground, is smaller than all the seeds on earth; 32 but when it is sown, it grows up and becomes greater than all herbs, and shoots out large branches, so that the birds of the air may nest under its shade."

33 And with many such parables He spoke the word to them as they were able to hear *it.* 34 But without a **parable** He did not speak to them. And when

---

WORDFINDER

4:34 Parable Pronounced *PAIR-uh-bull.* A story that teaches a lesson. The story may or may not be based on fact. Jesus used parables to teach spiritual truths.

DIGGING IN

4:33 Jesus Taught by Parables Jesus had a a lot of hard things to teach His followers, so He taught them mostly by parables (pronounced *PAIR-uh-bulls*).

A parable is a story. The story may or may not be true in every way, but each story teaches a true lesson. Jesus has just told the parable of the mustard seed.

What Jesus' Disciples Learned

Up until now, Jesus had healed people and taught us a lot of wonderful things. We thought He must be a very great prophet.

Then one day we were out on the sea in a boat, and a terrible storm came up. We were sure we were going to sink, but Jesus was fast asleep. We were frightened and asked Him how He could sleep when it looked as if we were all going to drown!

So Jesus just stood up and spoke to the storm, and the wind and waves became quiet. All was calm just as if the storm had never happened.

Then we began to realize that this Man must be more than a man. Only God commands the wind and the sea!

---

they were alone, He explained all things to His disciples.

35 On the same day, when evening had come, He said to them, "Let us cross over to the other side." 36 Now when they had left the multitude, they took Him along in the boat as He was. And other little boats were also with Him. 37 And a great windstorm arose, and the waves beat into the boat, so that it was already filling. 38 But He was in the stern, asleep on a pillow. And they awoke Him and said to Him, "Teacher, do You not care that we are perishing?"

39 Then He arose and rebuked the wind, and said to the sea, "Peace, be still!" And the wind ceased and there was a great calm. 40 But He said to them, "Why are you so fearful? How is it that you have no faith?" 41 And they feared exceedingly, and said to one another, "Who can this be, that even the wind and the sea obey Him!"

Jesus has power over demons, disease, and death

5 Then they came to the other side of the sea, to the country of the **Gadarenes.** 2 And when He had come out of the boat, immediately there met Him out of the tombs a man with an unclean spirit, 3 who had *his* dwelling among the tombs; and no one could bind him, not even with chains, 4 because he had often been bound with shackles and chains. And the chains had been pulled apart by him, and the shackles broken in pieces; neither could anyone tame him. 5 And always, night and day, he was in the mountains and in the tombs, crying out and cutting himself with stones.

6 When he saw Jesus from afar, he ran and worshiped Him. 7 And he cried out with a loud voice and said, "What have I to do with You, Jesus, Son of

---

WORDFINDER

5:1 Gadarenes (Pronounced *GAD-uh-reens*). People who lived in the city of Gadara, about six miles southeast of the Sea of Galilee. Gadara was one of the group called "Ten Cities."

DIGGING IN

The mustard seed was the smallest seed; but when it grew up, it was the largest kind of shrub. Jesus was saying the kingdom of God is like the mustard seed—at first God's kingdom is very small, but it is the greatest kingdom of all when it is grown.

Sometimes Jesus' enemies didn't understand His parables. That was because His enemies were so "know-it-all" that they couldn't be taught anything. People can only learn if they're listening. Are you listening?

the Most High God? I implore You by God that You do not torment me."

8 For He said to him, "Come out of the man, unclean spirit!" 9 Then He asked him, "What *is* your name?"

And he answered, saying, "My name is Legion; for we are many." 10 Also he begged Him earnestly that He would not send them out of the country.

11 Now a large herd of swine was feeding there near the mountains. 12 So all the demons begged Him, saying, "Send us to the swine, that we may enter them." 13 And at once Jesus gave them permission. Then the unclean spirits went out and entered the swine (there were about two thousand); and the herd ran violently down the steep place into the sea, and drowned in the sea.

14 So those who fed the swine fled, and they told *it* in the city and in the country. And they went out to see what it was that had happened. 15 Then they came to Jesus, and saw the one *who had been* demon-possessed and had the legion, sitting and clothed and in his right mind. And they were afraid. 16 And those who saw it told them how it happened to him *who had been* demon-possessed, and about the swine. 17 Then they began to plead with Him to depart from their region.

18 And when He got into the boat, he who had been demon-possessed begged Him that he might be with Him. 19 However, Jesus did not permit him, but said to him, "Go home to your friends, and tell them what great things the Lord has done for you, and how He has had compassion on you." 20 And he departed and began to proclaim in Decapolis all that Jesus had done for him; and all marveled.

21 Now when Jesus had crossed over again by boat to the other side, a great multitude gathered to Him; and He was by the sea. 22 And behold, one of the rulers of the synagogue came, Jairus by name. And when he saw Him, he fell at His feet 23 and begged Him earnestly, saying, "My little daughter lies at the point of death. Come and lay Your hands on her, that she may be healed, and she will live." 24 So *Jesus* went with him, and a great multitude followed Him and thronged Him.

25 Now a certain woman had a flow of blood for twelve years, 26 and had suffered many things from many physicians. She had spent all that she had and was no better, but rather grew worse. 27 When she heard about Jesus, she came behind *Him* in the crowd and touched His garment. 28 For she said, "If only I may touch His clothes, I shall be made well."

29 Immediately the fountain of her blood was dried up, and she felt in *her* body that she was healed of the affliction. 30 And Jesus, immediately knowing in Himself that power had gone out of Him, turned around in the crowd and said, "Who touched My clothes?"

31 But His disciples said to Him, "You see the multitude thronging You, and You say, 'Who touched Me?' "

32 And He looked around to see her who had done this thing. 33 But the woman, fearing and trembling, knowing what had happened to her, came and fell down before Him and told Him the whole truth. 34 And He said to her,

---

⚒ DIGGING IN

5:35–42 Jesus Brings a Dead Girl Back to Life Faith is the gift of God. And when Jesus was among people, He gave them great ability to have faith in Him, just as He gave great faith to the father of the little girl in this story. When her father "begged" Him, Jesus took the little girl by the hand and said, "Little girl, I say to you, arise." And the dead girl came back to life.

Jesus was the Lord from heaven, and He had all authority to command nature. He could even command the dead to live *because He was the Creator of life.*

We don't see many miracles today. Even in Jesus' time, He didn't go around

"Daughter, your faith has made you well. Go in peace, and be healed of your affliction."

35 While He was still speaking, *some* came from the ruler of the synagogue's *house* who said, "Your daughter is dead. Why trouble the Teacher any further?"

36 As soon as Jesus heard the word that was spoken, He said to the ruler of the synagogue, "Do not be afraid; only believe." 37 And He permitted no one to follow Him except Peter, James, and John the brother of James. 38 Then He came to the house of the ruler of the synagogue, and saw a tumult and those who wept and wailed loudly. 39 When He came in, He said to them, "Why make this commotion and weep? The child is not dead, but sleeping."

40 And they ridiculed Him. But when He had put them all outside, He took the father and the mother of the child, and those *who were* with Him, and entered where the child was lying. 41 Then He took the child by the hand, and said to her, "Talitha, cumi," which is translated, "Little girl, I say to you, arise." 42 Immediately the girl arose and walked, for she was twelve years *of age*. And they were overcome with great amazement. 43 But He commanded them strictly that no one should know it, and said that *something* should be given her to eat.

King Herod kills John the Baptist

6 Then He went out from there and came to His own country, and His disciples followed Him. 2 And when the Sabbath had come, He began to teach in the synagogue. And many hearing *Him* were astonished, saying, "Where did this Man *get* these things? And what wisdom *is* this which is given

Where Did Jesus Get His Wisdom?

People were amazed at what a great Teacher Jesus was. They couldn't understand how a carpenter's son could be such a scholar. They didn't yet know that Jesus was the Lord from heaven. The apostle Paul said that all wisdom and knowledge dwell in Jesus (Colossians 2:3).

to Him, that such mighty works are performed by His hands! 3 Is this not the carpenter, the Son of Mary, and

Jesus worked in Joseph's carpenter shop.

raising all the dead people. But He wanted us to know that He does have such authority. Sometimes Jesus still answers real faith by doing a great miracle.

These are signs of His saving power. Jesus is the same yesterday, today, and forever.

Herod Executes Prophet

AJTN (All-Judea Television Network)—A special bulletin:

We have confirmed a report that John the Baptist is dead. Eyewitnesses say the prophet was beheaded at the request of the king's stepdaughter.

At his birthday party held in the palace, Herod's stepdaughter danced for the guests. To reward her for her good performance, Herod told her he would give her whatever she wanted. It is reported that she asked her mother for a suggestion, and her mother told her to ask for John's head.

Herod the Great had arrested the prophet after he told the king he should not marry his brother's wife. Such a marriage is against the Law of God, of course. Apparently, Herod was determined to get even with John the Baptist.

We are shocked that the king would grant the young woman such an evil request.

---

brother of James, Joses, Judas, and Simon? And are not His sisters here with us?" So they were offended at Him.

4 But Jesus said to them, "A prophet is not without honor except in his own country, among his own relatives, and in his own house." 5 Now He could do no mighty work there, except that He laid His hands on a few sick people and healed *them.* 6 And He marveled because of their unbelief. Then He went about the villages in a circuit, teaching.

7 And He called the twelve to *Himself,* and began to send them out two by two, and gave them power over unclean spirits. 8 He commanded them to take nothing for the journey except a staff—no bag, no bread, no copper in *their* money belts— 9 but to wear sandals, and not to put on two tunics.

10 Also He said to them, "In whatever place you enter a house, stay there till you depart from that place. 11 And whoever will not receive you nor hear you, when you depart from there, shake off the dust under your feet as a testimony against them. Assuredly, I say to you, it will be more tolerable for Sodom and Gomorrah in the day of judgment than for that city!"

12 So they went out and preached that *people* should repent. 13 And they cast out many demons, and anointed with oil many who were sick, and healed *them.*

14 Now King Herod heard *of Him,* for His name had become well known. And he said, "John the Baptist is risen from the dead, and therefore these powers are at work in him."

15 Others said, "It is Elijah."

And others said, "It is the Prophet, or like one of the prophets."

16 But when Herod heard, he said, "This is John, whom I beheaded; he has been raised from the dead!" 17 For Herod himself had sent and laid hold of John, and bound him in prison for the sake of Herodias, his brother Philip's wife; for he had married her. 18 Because John had said to Herod, "It is not lawful for you to have your brother's wife."

19 Therefore Herodias held it against him and wanted to kill him, but she could not; 20 for Herod feared John, knowing that he *was* a just and holy man, and he protected him. And when he heard him, he did many things, and heard him gladly.

21 Then an opportune day came when Herod on his birthday gave a feast for his nobles, the high officers, and the chief *men* of Galilee. 22 And when Herodias' daughter herself came in and danced, and pleased Herod and those who sat with him, the king said to the girl, "Ask me whatever you want, and I will give *it* to you." 23 He also swore to her, "Whatever you ask me, I will give you, up to half my kingdom."

24 So she went out and said to her mother, "What shall I ask?"

And she said, "The head of John the Baptist!"

25 Immediately she came in with haste to the king and asked, saying, "I want you to give me at once the head of John the Baptist on a platter."

26 And the king was exceedingly sorry; yet, because of the oaths and because of those who sat with him, he did not want to refuse her. 27 Immediately the king sent an executioner and commanded his head to be brought. And he went and beheaded him in prison, 28 brought his head on a platter, and gave it to the girl; and the girl gave it to her mother. 29 When his disciples heard of it, they came and took away his corpse and laid it in a tomb.

30 Then the apostles gathered to Jesus and told Him all things, both what they had done and what they had taught. 31 And He said to them, "Come aside by yourselves to a deserted place and rest a while." For there were many coming and going, and they did not even have time to eat. 32 So they departed to a deserted place in the boat by themselves.

33 But the multitudes saw them departing, and many knew Him and ran there on foot from all the cities. They arrived before them and came together to Him. 34 And Jesus, when He came out, saw a great multitude and was moved with compassion for them, because they were like sheep not having a shepherd. So He began to teach them many things. 35 When the day was now far spent, His disciples came

to Him and said, "This is a deserted place, and already the hour is late. 36 Send them away, that they may go into the surrounding country and villages and buy themselves bread; for they have nothing to eat."

37 But He answered and said to them, "You give them something to eat."

And they said to Him, "Shall we go and buy two hundred denarii worth of bread and give them something to eat?"

38 But He said to them, "How many loaves do you have? Go and see."

And when they found out they said, "Five, and two fish."

39 Then He commanded them to make them all sit down in groups on the green grass. 40 So they sat down in ranks, in hundreds and in fifties. 41 And when He had taken the five loaves and the two fish, He looked up to heaven, blessed and broke the loaves, and gave them to His disciples to set before them; and the two fish He divided among them all. 42 So they all ate and were filled. 43 And they took up twelve baskets full of fragments and of the fish. 44 Now those who had eaten the loaves were about five thousand men.

45 Immediately He made His disciples get into the boat and go before Him to the other side, to Bethsaida, while He sent the multitude away. 46 And when He had sent them away, He departed to the mountain to pray. 47 Now when evening came, the boat was in the middle of the sea; and He was alone on the land. 48 Then He saw them straining at rowing, for the wind

DIGGING IN

6:46 Jesus Took Time to Pray Does your life seem to get busier every day? Not only do you have to go to school, but there are sports, parties, chores—and all that homework! There are just not enough hours for everything.

Let's learn a new verb that adults use these days—it's the verb *prioritize*. That's a tongue-twister that you pronounce *pry-OR-uh-tize*. To prioritize means to make

a list of of all the things you have to do. You put the most important things at the top of your list.

You should make a list like that. But be sure to put your prayer time with God *first*. When you do, then everything else on your list will work out better. Jesus proved that in His own life. And He said, "Without Me you can do nothing." You'd better believe that!

was against them. Now about the fourth watch of the night He came to them, walking on the sea, and would have passed them by. 49 And when they saw Him walking on the sea, they supposed it was a ghost, and cried out; 50 for they all saw Him and were troubled. But immediately He talked with them and said to them, "Be of good cheer! It is I; do not be afraid." 51 Then He went up into the boat to them, and the wind ceased. And they were greatly amazed in themselves beyond measure, and marveled. 52 For they had not understood about the loaves, because their heart was hardened.

53 When they had crossed over, they came to the land of Gennesaret and anchored there. 54 And when they came out of the boat, immediately the people recognized Him, 55 ran through that whole surrounding region, and began to carry about on beds those who were sick to wherever they heard He was. 56 Wherever He entered, into villages, cities, or the country, they laid the sick in the marketplaces, and begged Him that they might just touch the hem of His garment. And as many as touched Him were made well.

Jesus scolds the Pharisees

7 Then the Pharisees and some of the scribes came together to Him, having come from Jerusalem. 2 Now when they saw some of His disciples eat bread with defiled, that is, with unwashed hands, they found fault. 3 For the Pharisees and all the Jews do not eat unless they wash *their* hands in a special way, holding the tradition of the elders. 4 *When they come* from the marketplace, they do not eat unless they wash. And there are many other things which they have received and hold, *like* the washing of cups, pitchers, copper vessels, and couches.

5 Then the Pharisees and scribes asked Him, "Why do Your disciples not walk according to the tradition of the elders, but eat bread with unwashed hands?"

6 He answered and said to them, "Well did Isaiah prophesy of you hypocrites, as it is written:

'This people honors Me with *their* lips,
　　But their heart is far from Me.
7 　And in vain they worship Me,

⚒ DIGGING IN

6:56 You Can Touch Jesus There are different kinds of touching. Not all touching is done with the hands and fingers. Some kinds of touching are done with your heart and mind.

If you would like Jesus to be near you and if you would like to touch Him, you can touch Him *by prayer*. Just close your eyes and be very quiet. Then say the name "Jesus." Tell Him, "I need You more than anything in the world. I know I can't live without You. Please come into my life and let me know You're with me always. You said, 'I will never leave you.' Please give me faith to know You are near and will keep that promise to me."

If you will only pray this simple prayer, you can be certain that Jesus will answer you. He said, "You will seek Me and find Me, when you search for Me *with all your heart.*"

You can touch Jesus through prayer.

Teaching *as* doctrines the commandments of men.'

8 For laying aside the commandment of God, you hold the tradition of men—the washing of pitchers and cups, and many other such things you do."

9 He said to them, "*All too* well you reject the commandment of God, that you may keep your tradition. 10 For Moses said, 'Honor your father and your mother'; and, 'He who curses father or mother, let him be put to death.' 11 But you say, 'If a man says to his father or mother, "Whatever profit you might have received from me *is* Corban"—' (that is, a gift *to* God), 12 then you no longer let him do anything for his father or his mother, 13 making the word of God of no effect through your tradition which you have handed down. And many such things you do."

14 When He had called all the multitude to *Himself,* He said to them, "Hear Me, everyone, and understand: 15 There is nothing that enters a man from outside which can defile him; but the things which come out of him, those are the things that defile a man. 16 If anyone has ears to hear, let him hear!"

17 When He had entered a house away from the crowd, His disciples asked Him concerning the parable.

Why Were Tyre and Sidon Important?

These two cities were in the country of Phoenicia (pronounced *fe-NISH-she-uh*), north of Galilee. See the map of Palestine on page 1343. Phoenicia was a great trading nation, and Tyre and Sidon (pronounced *TIRE* and *SIGH-dun*) were seaports on the Mediterranean coast. These cities existed over twenty-five hundred years before Jesus was born.

18 So He said to them, "Are you thus without understanding also? Do you not perceive that whatever enters a man from outside cannot defile him, 19 because it does not enter his heart but his stomach, and is eliminated, *thus* purifying all foods?" 20 And He said, "What comes out of a man, that defiles a man. 21 For from within, out of the heart of men, proceed evil thoughts, adulteries, fornications, murders, 22 thefts, covetousness, wickedness, deceit, lewdness, an evil eye, **blasphemy,** pride, foolishness. 23 All these evil things come from within and defile a man."

24 From there He arose and went to the region of Tyre and Sidon. And He entered a house and wanted no one to know *it,* but He could not be hidden. 25 For a woman whose young daughter

WORDFINDER

7:22 Blasphemy Pronounced *BLASS-fuh-mee.* Profanity, cursing, or insulting God.

DIGGING IN

7:6–13 Obey God First Some leaders in Jesus' time were telling people to do extra things God had not commanded. So the people were asking themselves, Should I obey the Bible or should I do what these leaders tell me? These *extra* laws often made life hard for the people. But God meant His law to free the people from impossible burdens. (See 1 John 5:3.)

One of the extra laws even allowed a young man to neglect his parents if he gave his life to serve in the temple. But God's law said, "Honor your father and your mother." Loving your parents must come before your duty to other people. So these extra laws made Jesus angry because they kept people from obeying God.

First things must come first. Obey God's laws. Then you will know what to think about all the other rules for living.

What a Greek Woman Learned

I knew Jesus had come to our country to rest, but He was my only hope for my little girl.

My daughter had a demon, and I had heard how Jesus could drive out evil spirits from people. So I went to Jesus and fell at His feet, begging Him to heal my child.

At first it seemed as if He didn't care. Then He said He was not sent to work among the people in our nation. But I just kept on begging Him. At last He smiled, told me I was right to come to Him, and promised that my daughter would be well when I got home. It was true! When I saw my little girl, the demon was gone.

Now I know that Jesus is the Savior of all kinds of people.

had an unclean spirit heard about Him, and she came and fell at His feet. 26 The woman was a Greek, a Syro-Phoenician by birth, and she kept asking Him to cast the **demon** out of her daughter. 27 But Jesus said to her, "Let the children be filled first, for it is not good to take the children's bread and throw it to the little dogs."

28 And she answered and said to Him, "Yes, Lord, yet even the little dogs under the table eat from the children's crumbs."

29 Then He said to her, "For this saying go your way; the demon has gone out of your daughter."

30 And when she had come to her house, she found the demon gone out, and her daughter lying on the bed.

31 Again, departing from the region of Tyre and Sidon, He came through the midst of the region of Decapolis to the Sea of Galilee. 32 Then they brought to Him one who was deaf and had an impediment in his speech, and they begged Him to put His hand on him. 33 And He took him aside from the multitude, and put His fingers in his ears, and He spat and touched his tongue. 34 Then, looking up to heaven, He sighed, and said to him, "Ephphatha," that is, "Be opened."

35 Immediately his ears were opened, and the impediment of his tongue was loosed, and he spoke plainly. 36 Then He commanded them that they should tell no one; but the more He commanded them, the more widely they proclaimed it. 37 And they were astonished beyond measure, saying, "He has done all things well. He makes both the deaf to hear and the mute to speak."

Jesus works a miracle at a picnic

8 In those days, the multitude being very great and having nothing to eat, Jesus called His disciples to Him and said to them, 2 "I have compassion on the multitude, because they have now continued with Me three days and have nothing to eat. 3 And if I send them away hungry to their own houses, they will faint on the way; for some of them have come from afar."

4 Then His disciples answered Him, "How can one satisfy these people with bread here in the wilderness?"

5 He asked them, "How many loaves do you have?"

And they said, "Seven."

6 So He commanded the multitude to sit down on the ground. And He took the seven loaves and gave thanks, broke them and gave them to His disci-

⊕ WORDFINDER

7:26 Demon An invisible spirit-being who is a servant of Satan. Demons can live in people and hurt them. Demons also cause people to curse God and His people.

What Is a Sign?

The kind of sign that the Bible talks about is a special notice that God is doing a great work. The miracles of Jesus are sometimes called signs (see John 2:11). They are notices to us that God is going to save us from our sins.

ples to set before *them;* and they set *them* before the multitude. 7 They also had a few small fish; and having blessed them, He said to set them also before *them.* 8 So they ate and were filled, and they took up seven large baskets of leftover fragments. 9 Now those who had eaten were about four thousand. And He sent them away, 10 immediately got into the boat with His disciples, and came to the region of Dalmanutha.

11 Then the Pharisees came out and began to dispute with Him, seeking from Him a sign from heaven, testing Him. 12 But He sighed deeply in His spirit, and said, "Why does this generation seek a sign? Assuredly, I say to you, no sign shall be given to this generation."

13 And He left them, and getting into the boat again, departed to the other side. 14 Now the disciples had forgotten to take bread, and they did not have more than one loaf with them in the boat. 15 Then He charged them, saying, "Take heed, beware of the leaven of the Pharisees and the leaven of Herod."

16 And they reasoned among themselves, saying, *"It is* because we have no bread."

17 But Jesus, being aware of *it,* said to them, "Why do you reason because you have no bread? Do you not yet perceive nor understand? Is your heart still hardened? 18 Having eyes, do you not see? And having ears, do you not hear? And do you not remember? 19 When I broke the five loaves for the five thousand, how many baskets full of fragments did you take up?"

They said to Him, "Twelve."

20 "Also, when I broke the seven for

the four thousand, how many large baskets full of fragments did you take up?"

And they said, "Seven."

21 So He said to them, "How *is it* you do not understand?"

22 Then He came to Bethsaida; and they brought a blind man to Him, and begged Him to touch him. 23 So He took the blind man by the hand and led him out of the town. And when He had spit on his eyes and put His hands on him, He asked him if he saw anything.

24 And he looked up and said, "I see men like trees, walking."

25 Then He put *His* hands on his eyes again and made him look up. And he was restored and saw everyone clearly. 26 Then He sent him away to his house, saying, "Neither go into the town, nor tell anyone in the town."

27 Now Jesus and His disciples went out to the towns of Caesarea Philippi; and on the road He asked His disciples, saying to them, "Who do men say that I am?"

28 So they answered, "John the Baptist; but some *say,* Elijah; and others, one of the prophets."

29 He said to them, "But who do you say that I am?"

Peter answered and said to Him, "You are the Christ."

30 Then He strictly warned them that they should tell no one about Him.

31 And He began to teach them that the Son of Man must suffer many things, and be rejected by the elders and chief priests and scribes, and be killed, and after three days rise again. 32 He spoke this word openly. Then Peter took Him aside and began to rebuke Him. 33 But when He had turned around and looked at His disciples, He rebuked Peter, saying, "Get behind Me, Satan! For you are not mindful of the things of God, but the things of men."

34 When He had called the people to *Himself,* with His disciples also, He said to them, "Whoever desires to come after Me, let him deny himself, and take up his cross, and follow Me.

35 For whoever desires to save his life will lose it, but whoever loses his life for My sake and the gospel's will save it. 36 For what will it profit a man if he gains the whole world, and loses his own soul? 37 Or what will a man give in exchange for his soul? 38 For whoever is ashamed of Me and My words in this adulterous and sinful generation, of him the Son of Man also will be ashamed when He comes in the glory of His Father with the holy angels."

Jesus talks with Elijah and Moses

Mount Hermon, in the northeastern part of Palestine, is snow-capped all year round.

9 And He said to them, "Assuredly, I say to you that there are some standing here who will not taste death till they see the kingdom of God present with power."

2 Now after six days Jesus took Peter, James, and John, and led them up on a high mountain apart by themselves; and He was transfigured before them. 3 His clothes became shining, exceedingly white, like snow, such as no launderer on earth can whiten them. 4 And Elijah appeared to them with Moses, and they were talking with Jesus. 5 Then Peter answered and said to Jesus, "Rabbi, it is good for us to be here; and let us make three tabernacles: one for You, one for Moses, and one for Elijah"— 6 because he did not know what to say, for they were greatly afraid.

7 And a cloud came and overshadowed them; and a voice came out of the cloud, saying, "This is My beloved Son. Hear Him!" 8 Suddenly, when they had looked around, they saw no one anymore, but only Jesus with themselves.

9 Now as they came down from the mountain, He commanded them that they should tell no one the things they had seen, till the Son of Man had risen from the dead. 10 So they kept this word to themselves, questioning what the rising from the dead meant.

11 And they asked Him, saying, "Why do the scribes say that Elijah must come first?"

12 Then He answered and told them,

"Indeed, Elijah is coming first and restores all things. And how is it written concerning the Son of Man, that He must suffer many things and be treated with contempt? 13 But I say to you that Elijah has also come, and they did to him whatever they wished, as it is written of him."

14 And when He came to the disciples, He saw a great multitude around them, and scribes disputing with them. 15 Immediately, when they saw Him, all the people were greatly amazed, and running to *Him*, greeted Him. 16 And He asked the scribes, "What are you discussing with them?"

17 Then one of the crowd answered and said, "Teacher, I brought You my son, who has a mute spirit. 18 And wherever it seizes him, it throws him down; he foams at the mouth, gnashes his teeth, and becomes rigid. So I spoke to Your disciples, that they should cast it out, but they could not."

19 He answered him and said, "O faithless generation, how long shall I be with you? How long shall I bear with you? Bring him to Me." 20 Then they brought him to Him. And when he saw Him, immediately the spirit convulsed him, and he fell on the ground and wallowed, foaming at the mouth.

21 So He asked his father, "How long has this been happening to him?"

And he said, "From childhood. 22 And often he has thrown him both into the fire and into the water to destroy him. But if You can do anything, have compassion on us and help us."

23 Jesus said to him, "If you can believe, all things *are* possible to him who believes."

24 Immediately the father of the child cried out and said with tears, "Lord, I believe; help my unbelief!"

25 When Jesus saw that the people came running together, He rebuked the unclean spirit, saying to it, "Deaf and dumb spirit, I command you, come out of him and enter him no more!" 26 Then *the spirit* cried out, convulsed him greatly, and came out of him. And he became as one dead, so that many said, "He is dead." 27 But Jesus took him by the hand and lifted him up, and he arose.

28 And when He had come into the house, His disciples asked Him privately, "Why could we not cast it out?" 29 So He said to them, "This kind can come out by nothing but prayer and fasting."

30 Then they departed from there and passed through Galilee, and He did not want anyone to know *it.* 31 For He taught His disciples and said to them, "The Son of Man is being betrayed into the hands of men, and they will kill Him. And after He is killed, He will rise the third day." 32 But they did not understand this saying, and were afraid to ask Him.

33 Then He came to Capernaum. And when He was in the house He asked them, "What was it you disputed among yourselves on the road?" 34 But they kept silent, for on the road they had disputed among themselves who *would be the* greatest. 35 And He sat down, called the twelve, and said to them, "If anyone desires to be first, he shall be last of all and servant of all." 36 Then He took a little child and set him in the midst of them. And when He had taken him in His arms, He said to them, 37 "Whoever receives one of these little children in My name receives Me; and whoever receives Me, receives not Me but Him who sent Me."

38 Now John answered Him, saying, "Teacher, we saw someone who does not follow us casting out demons in Your name, and we forbade him because he does not follow us."

39 But Jesus said, "Do not forbid him, for no one who works a miracle in My name can soon afterward speak evil of Me. 40 For he who is not against us is on our side. 41 For whoever gives you a cup of water to drink in My name, because you belong to Christ, assuredly, I say to you, he will by no means lose his reward.

42 "But whoever causes one of these little ones who believe in Me to stumble, it would be better for him if a millstone were hung around his neck, and he were thrown into the sea. 43 If your hand causes you to sin, cut it off. It is better for you to enter into life maimed, rather than having two hands, to go to hell, into the fire that shall never be quenched— 44 where

'Their worm does not die
And the fire is not quenched.'

45 And if your foot causes you to sin, cut it off. It is better for you to enter life lame, rather than having two feet, to be cast into hell, into the fire that shall never be quenched— 46 where

'Their worm does not die
And the fire is not quenched.'

47 And if your eye causes you to sin, pluck it out. It is better for you to enter the kingdom of God with one eye, rather than having two eyes, to be cast into hell fire— 48 where

'Their worm does not die
And the fire is not quenched.'

49 "For everyone will be seasoned with fire, and every sacrifice will be seasoned with salt. 50 Salt *is* good, but if the salt loses its flavor, how will you season it? Have salt in yourselves, and have peace with one another."

How Can You Be Like Salt?

Salt makes food taste good. You are like salt when you live like a Christian. You have a Christian "flavor" when you show Jesus' mercy to people around you. If you're mean and unkind, then you'll taste bitter to others. If you hide your faith, then you'll taste flat!

Little children come to Jesus

10 Then He arose from there and came to the region of Judea by the other side of the Jordan. And multitudes gathered to Him again, and as He was accustomed, He taught them again.
2 The Pharisees came and asked Him, "Is it lawful for a man to divorce *his* wife?" testing Him.
3 And He answered and said to them, "What did Moses command you?"
4 They said, "Moses permitted *a man* to write a certificate of divorce, and to dismiss *her.*"
5 And Jesus answered and said to them, "Because of the hardness of your heart he wrote you this precept.
6 But from the beginning of the creation, God 'made them male and female.' 7 'For this reason a man shall leave his father and mother and be joined to his wife, 8 and the two shall become one flesh'; so then they are no longer two, but one flesh. 9 There-

fore what God has joined together, let not man separate."
10 In the house His disciples also asked Him again about the same *matter.* 11 So He said to them, "Whoever divorces his wife and marries another commits adultery against her. 12 And if a woman divorces her husband and marries another, she commits adultery."
13 Then they brought little children to Him, that He might touch them; but the disciples rebuked those who brought *them.* 14 But when Jesus saw *it,* He was greatly displeased and said to them, "Let the little children come to Me, and do not forbid them; for of such is the kingdom of God. 15 Assuredly, I say to you, whoever does not receive the kingdom of God as a little child will by no means enter it." 16 And He took them up in His arms, laid *His* hands on them, and blessed them.
17 Now as He was going out on the road, one came running, knelt before Him, and asked Him, "Good Teacher, what shall I do that I may inherit eternal life?"
18 So Jesus said to him, "Why do you call Me good? No one *is* good but One, *that is,* God. 19 You know the commandments: 'Do not commit adultery,' 'Do not murder,' 'Do not steal,' 'Do not bear false witness,' 'Do not defraud,' 'Honor your father and your mother.' "
20 And he answered and said to Him, "Teacher, all these things I have kept from my youth."

DIGGING IN

10:17–27 What Do You Put First in Your Life? Jesus had just been talking to a rich young man who found it hard to decide whether to put Jesus or his wealth first. Most of us are wealthy by the world's standards. We have more than we need to live.

Is there anything you care about more than everything else? What is it? For the young man in our story, it was his money. Maybe for you, it is being the top player

on your team, or the prettiest girl on your street, or the smartest student in school. Maybe you would give anything to be president of the United States someday.

But what if Jesus said to you, "I want you to go across the sea and spend your life with a strange people who have nothing?" Only God can give you the desire to put Him before everything else. "You shall have no other gods before Me" (Exodus 20:3).

21 Then Jesus, looking at him, loved him, and said to him, "One thing you lack: Go your way, sell whatever you have and give to the poor, and you will have treasure in heaven; and come, take up the cross, and follow Me."

22 But he was sad at this word, and went away sorrowful, for he had great possessions.

23 Then Jesus looked around and said to His disciples, "How hard it is for those who have riches to enter the kingdom of God!" 24 And the disciples were astonished at His words. But Jesus answered again and said to them, "Children, how hard it is for those who trust in riches to enter the kingdom of God! 25 It is easier for a camel to go through the eye of a needle than for a rich man to enter the kingdom of God."

26 And they were greatly astonished, saying among themselves, "Who then can be saved?"

27 But Jesus looked at them and said, "With men it is impossible, but not with God; for with God all things are possible."

28 Then Peter began to say to Him, "See, we have left all and followed You."

29 So Jesus answered and said, "Assuredly, I say to you, there is no one who has left house or brothers or sisters or father or mother or wife or children or lands, for My sake and the gospel's, 30 who shall not receive a hundredfold now in this time—houses and brothers and sisters and mothers and children and lands, with persecutions—and in the age to come, eternal life. 31 But many who are first will be last, and the last first."

32 Now they were on the road, going up to Jerusalem, and Jesus was going before them; and they were amazed. And as they followed they were afraid. Then He took the twelve aside again and began to tell them the things that would happen to Him: 33 "Behold, we are going up to Jerusalem, and the Son of Man will be betrayed to the chief priests and to the scribes; and they will

condemn Him to death and deliver Him to the Gentiles; 34 and they will mock Him, and scourge Him, and spit on Him, and kill Him. And the third day He will rise again."

35 Then James and John, the sons of Zebedee, came to Him, saying, "Teacher, we want You to do for us whatever we ask."

36 And He said to them, "What do you want Me to do for you?"

37 They said to Him, "Grant us that we may sit, one on Your right hand and the other on Your left, in Your glory."

38 But Jesus said to them, "You do not know what you ask. Are you able to drink the cup that I drink, and be baptized with the baptism that I am baptized with?"

39 They said to Him, "We are able."

So Jesus said to them, "You will indeed drink the cup that I drink, and with the baptism I am baptized with you will be baptized; 40 but to sit on My right hand and on My left is not Mine to give, but it is for those for whom it is prepared."

41 And when the ten heard it, they began to be greatly displeased with James and John. 42 But Jesus called them to Himself and said to them, "You know that those who are considered rulers over the Gentiles lord it over them, and their great ones exercise authority over them. 43 Yet it shall not be so among you; but whoever desires to become great among you shall be your servant. 44 And whoever of you desires to be first shall be slave of all. 45 For even the Son of Man did not come to be served, but to serve, and to give His life a ransom for many."

46 Now they came to Jericho. As He went out of Jericho with His disciples and a great multitude, blind Bartimaeus, the son of Timaeus, sat by the road begging. 47 And when he heard that it was Jesus of Nazareth, he began to cry out and say, "Jesus, Son of David, have mercy on me!"

48 Then many warned him to be quiet; but he cried out all the more,

"Son of David, have mercy on me!"

⁴⁹ So Jesus stood still and commanded him to be called.

Then they called the blind man, saying to him, "Be of good cheer. Rise, He is calling you."

⁵⁰ And throwing aside his garment, he rose and came to Jesus.

⁵¹ So Jesus answered and said to him, "What do you want Me to do for you?"

The blind man said to Him, "Rabboni, that I may receive my sight."

⁵² Then Jesus said to him, "Go your way; your faith has made you well." And immediately he received his sight and followed Jesus on the road.

Happy crowds welcome Jesus to Jerusalem

11 Now when they drew near Jerusalem, to Bethphage and Bethany, at the Mount of Olives, He sent two of His disciples; ² and He said to them, "Go into the village opposite you; and as soon as you have entered it you will find a colt tied, on which no one has sat. Loose it and bring *it.* ³ And if anyone says to you, 'Why are you doing this?' say, 'The Lord has need of it,' and immediately he will send it here."

⁴ So they went their way, and found the colt tied by the door outside on the street, and they loosed it. ⁵ But some of those who stood there said to them, "What are you doing, loosing the colt?"

⁶ And they spoke to them just as Jesus had commanded. So they let them go. ⁷ Then they brought the colt to Jesus and threw their clothes on it, and He sat on it. ⁸ And many spread their clothes on the road, and others cut down leafy branches from the trees and spread *them* on the road. ⁹ Then those who went before and those who followed cried out, saying:

"Hosanna!
'Blessed *is* He who comes in the name of the Lᴏʀᴅ!'
¹⁰ Blessed *is* the kingdom of our father David
That comes in the name of the Lord!
Hosanna in the highest!"

DIGGING IN

10:46–52 Jesus Can Make You See
Jesus cared about the blind man more than His disciples did, and Jesus gave him back his sight.

Jesus said the man's faith brought back his ability to see. What is faith? Is it just believing what is impossible? No! Faith is the ability to *see that God is always in charge of what is possible.* We don't trust our own faith to save us. Like the blind man, *we trust Jesus* to save us from whatever kind of blindness we have.

Sometimes you may become so mixed up about what to do about your life that you're all ready to give up. At a time like that, you need to remember that Jesus can make everything clear. You have to come to Jesus, who will give you what you need. Then, like the blind man, you will be glad to follow Jesus wherever He leads you.

11:7–10 Jesus Rode on a Donkey
What a strange thing! Jesus was the King of Glory. Yet He rode on a donkey as He entered God's beloved city of Jerusalem. Why didn't He find the most handsome white horse and enter the city in a great show of power? He easily could have, you know.

In a way, it seems funny to us that Jesus rode a donkey instead of a horse. He was saying to everybody, "I don't need to show off My power." Jesus didn't need to make a big hit with people. He was already "the Greatest"!

Jesus also showed you and me what is important. You don't have to act important if you're a son or daughter of the great King of heaven. You're already important to the God who created you and saved you at the cost of the royal blood of Jesus. It sure takes a lot of foolish strain out of life when you stop needing to be important.

11 And Jesus went into Jerusalem and into the temple. So when He had looked around at all things, as the hour was already late, He went out to Bethany with the twelve.

12 Now the next day, when they had come out from Bethany, He was hungry. 13 And seeing from afar a fig tree having leaves, He went to see if perhaps He would find something on it. When He came to it, He found nothing but leaves, for it was not the season for figs. 14 In response Jesus said to it, "Let no one eat fruit from you ever again."

And His disciples heard it.

15 So they came to Jerusalem. Then Jesus went into the temple and began to drive out those who bought and sold in the temple, and overturned the tables of the **money changers** and the seats of those who sold doves. 16 And He would not allow anyone to carry wares through the temple. 17 Then He taught, saying to them, "Is it not written, 'My house shall be called a house of prayer for all nations'? But you have made it a 'den of thieves.'"

18 And the scribes and chief priests heard it and sought how they might destroy Him; for they feared Him, because all the people were astonished at His teaching. 19 When evening had come, He went out of the city.

20 Now in the morning, as they passed by, they saw the fig tree dried up from the roots. 21 And Peter, re-membering, said to Him, "Rabbi, look! The fig tree which You cursed has withered away."

22 So Jesus answered and said to them, "Have faith in God. 23 For assuredly, I say to you, whoever says to this mountain, 'Be removed and be cast into the sea,' and does not doubt in his heart, but believes that those things he says will be done, he will have whatever he says. 24 Therefore I say to you, whatever things you ask when you pray, believe that you receive *them*, and you will have *them*. 25 "And whenever you stand praying, if you have anything against anyone, forgive him, that your Father in heaven may also forgive you your trespasses. 26 But if you do not forgive, neither will your Father in heaven forgive your trespasses."

27 Then they came again to Jerusalem. And as He was walking in the

Why Do Some People Worry?

Do you ever worry about things? Some people worry, but never try to solve their problems in a common-sense way. Worrying never makes sense, because God is always in charge even when things seem to go wrong. It makes sense to ask God about your problems.

WORDFINDER

11:15 Money Changers Bankers who exchanged temple money for the money of another nation. Some temple money changers often charged a large fee.

DIGGING IN

11:25, 26 Forgive and Be Forgiven
Holding a grudge is like poison in your mind. The more you hate, the more hateful you become. Bitterness toward others only makes you bitter inside yourself. Then you even hate yourself, and living becomes a very sour experience.

God can take away that grudge you have against somebody. The more you think of how much God has loved you, the less you will be able to think badly of others. Then you'll find yourself saying, "God has given me His friendship forever. So why not forgive my enemies? They can't really hurt me anyway." Then you'll be free from bitter feelings about people. Why be miserable? Do it God's way! A *forgiven* person is a *forgiving* person.

temple, the chief priests, the scribes, and the elders came to Him. 28 And they said to Him, "By what authority are You doing these things? And who gave You this authority to do these things?"

29 But Jesus answered and said to them, "I also will ask you one question; then answer Me, and I will tell you by what authority I do these things: 30 The baptism of John—was it from heaven or from men? Answer Me."

31 And they reasoned among themselves, saying, "If we say, 'From heaven,' He will say, 'Why then did you not believe him?' 32 But if we say, 'From men' "—they feared the people, for all counted John to have been a prophet indeed. 33 So they answered and said to Jesus, "We do not know."

And Jesus answered and said to them, "Neither will I tell you by what authority I do these things."

Some wicked men try to trap Jesus

12 Then He began to speak to them in parables: "A man planted a vineyard and set a hedge around it, dug a place for the wine vat and built a tower. And he leased it to vinedressers and went into a far country. 2 Now at vintage-time he sent a servant to the vinedressers, that he might receive some of the fruit of the vineyard from the vinedressers. 3 And they took him and beat him and sent him away empty-handed. 4 Again he sent them another servant, and at him they threw stones, wounded him in the head, and sent him away shamefully treated. 5 And again he sent another, and him they killed; and many others, beating some and killing some. 6 Therefore still having one son, his beloved, he also sent him to them last, saying, 'They will respect my son.' 7 But those vinedressers said among themselves, 'This is the heir. Come, let us kill him, and the inheritance will be ours.' 8 So they took him and killed him and cast him out of the vineyard.

9 "Therefore what will the owner of the vineyard do? He will come and destroy the vinedressers, and give the vineyard to others. 10 Have you not even read this Scripture:

'The stone which the builders rejected
Has become the chief cornerstone.
11 This was the LORD's doing,
And it is marvelous in our eyes'?"

12 And they sought to lay hands on Him, but feared the multitude, for they knew He had spoken the parable against them. So they left Him and went away.

13 Then they sent to Him some of the Pharisees and the Herodians, to catch Him in His words. 14 When they had come, they said to Him, "Teacher, we know that You are true, and care about no one; for You do not regard the person of men, but teach the way of God in truth. Is it lawful to pay taxes to Caesar, or not? 15 Shall we pay, or shall we not pay?"

But He, knowing their hypocrisy, said to them, "Why do you test Me? Bring Me a denarius that I may see it." 16 So they brought it.

And He said to them, "Whose image and inscription is this?" They said to Him, "Caesar's."

17 And Jesus answered and said to them, "Render to Caesar the things that are Caesar's, and to God the things that are God's."

And they marveled at Him.

18 Then some Sadducees, who say there is no resurrection, came to Him; and they asked Him, saying: 19 "Teacher, Moses wrote to us that if a man's brother dies, and leaves his wife behind, and leaves no children, his brother should take his wife and raise up offspring for his brother. 20 Now there were seven brothers. The first took a wife; and dying, he left no offspring. 21 And the second took her, and he died; nor did he leave any offspring. And the third likewise. 22 So the seven had her and left no offspring.

What the Scribe Learned

Listening to Jesus answer the Sadducees (pronounced *SAD-you-sees*) about rising from the dead (see Mark 12:18–27), I could see that this Man was very wise. I wanted to know Him better.

Finally, I dared to ask Him a question of my own: What is the most important commandment? When Jesus answered me, I knew He was no liar, as some of the Pharisees (pronounced *FAIR-uh-sees*) said He was. He believed in the same laws we all believed in. So why did the Pharisees hate Him so?

Then Jesus said something that gave me great hope. He told me I was not far from the kingdom of God. Yes, I was sure I had met my King, and I wanted to be in His kingdom! Do you?

Last of all the woman died also. 23 Therefore, in the resurrection, when they rise, whose wife will she be? For all seven had her as wife."

24 Jesus answered and said to them, "Are you not therefore mistaken, because you do not know the Scriptures nor the power of God? 25 For when they rise from the dead, they neither marry nor are given in marriage, but are like angels in heaven. 26 But concerning the dead, that they rise, have you not read in the book of Moses, in the *burning* bush *passage,* how God spoke to him, saying, 'I *am* the God of Abraham, the God of Isaac, and the God of Jacob'? 27 He is not the God of the dead, but the God of the living. You are therefore greatly mistaken."

28 Then one of the scribes came, and having heard them reasoning together, perceiving that He had answered them well, asked Him, "Which is the first commandment of all?"

29 Jesus answered him, "The first of all the commandments *is:* 'Hear, O Israel, the LORD our God, the LORD is one. 30 And you shall love the LORD your God with all your heart, with all your **soul,** with all your mind, and with

all your strength.' This *is* the first commandment. 31 And the second, like *it,* is this: 'You shall love your neighbor as yourself.' There is no other commandment greater than these."

32 So the scribe said to Him, "Well said, Teacher. You have spoken the truth, for there is one God, and there is no other but He. 33 And to love Him with all the heart, with all the understanding, with all the soul, and with all the strength, and to love one's neighbor as oneself, is more than all the whole burnt offerings and sacrifices."

34 Now when Jesus saw that he answered wisely, He said to him, "You are not far from the kingdom of God."

But after that no one dared question Him.

35 Then Jesus answered and said, while He taught in the temple, "How *is it* that the scribes say that the Christ is the Son of David? 36 For David himself said by the Holy Spirit:

'The LORD said to my Lord,
"Sit at My right hand,
Till I make Your enemies Your
footstool."'

WORDFINDER

12:30 Soul The inner life of a person that cannot die. The soul of a believing person who dies goes to be with God in heaven. But the unbelieving person's soul is cut off from God.

37 Therefore David himself calls Him 'Lord'; how is He *then* his Son?''

And the common people heard Him gladly.

38 Then He said to them in His teaching, ''Beware of the scribes, who desire to go around in long robes, *love* greetings in the marketplaces, 39 the best seats in the synagogues, and the best places at feasts, 40 who devour widows' houses, and for a pretense make long prayers. These will receive greater condemnation.''

41 Now Jesus sat opposite the treasury and saw how the people put money into the treasury. And many *who were* rich put in much. 42 Then one poor widow came and threw in two mites, which make a quadrans. 43 So He called His disciples to *Himself* and said to them, ''Assuredly, I say to you that this poor widow has put in more than all those who have given to the treasury; 44 for they all put in out of their abundance, but she out of her poverty put in all that she had, her whole livelihood.''

Jesus tells about His return

13 Then as He went out of the temple, one of His disciples said to Him, ''Teacher, see what manner of stones and what buildings *are here!*''

2 And Jesus answered and said to him, ''Do you see these great buildings? Not *one* stone shall be left upon another, that shall not be thrown down.''

3 Now as He sat on the Mount of Olives opposite the temple, Peter, James, John, and Andrew asked Him privately, 4 ''Tell us, when will these things be? And what *will be* the sign when all these things will be fulfilled?''

5 And Jesus, answering them, began to say: ''Take heed that no one deceives you. 6 For many will come in My name, saying, 'I am *He*,' and will deceive many. 7 But when you hear of wars and rumors of wars, do not be troubled; for *such things* must happen, but the end *is* not yet. 8 For nation will rise against nation, and kingdom against kingdom. And there will be earthquakes in various places, and

---

⚒ DIGGING IN

12:37 King David's King David was the greatest king in the Old Testament. No one was greater than David. Yet David looked forward to a greater King than himself. David lifted his eyes beyond his own little throne to the throne in heaven where God Himself sits.

There David could see the Lord of heaven giving all authority to the eternal Son of God. David called God's Son ''my Lord'' (see Psalm 110:1). This is why King David was such a humble man. He knew that he was only a king for a little while, but his King in heaven would rule forever.

Jesus reminded the Jewish officials that He was greater than David because David called Him ''Lord.'' So Jesus shocked everybody by saying that Christ is more than just ''the Son of David.'' Christ, the Messiah, had to be ''the Son of God.'' *David himself said so!*

12:41–44 When Do You Give Enough? God already owns everything,

so we can only give Him what is already His. But He still wants us to share in His work on earth.

The rich men in the story were giving a lot of money, but they had so much that they didn't miss what they gave. The poor widow had very little, but she gave all she had. That is why Jesus said she gave more than anybody.

How do you give to God? Not by saying, ''Only 10 percent of my life belongs to God, but 90 percent belongs to me.'' Remember, He really owns *every bit* of you.

So God would like you to open your heart and say, ''Take me, Lord, and all I have. Use my life and my things as You wish.'' Say that to God, and mean it from your heart. Then the next time you give your time or money to God, you won't be stingy. Remember, you owe Him everything, anyway.

The arch of the Emperor Titus, who destroyed Jerusalem in A.D. 70.

there will be famines and troubles. These *are* the beginnings of sorrows. 9 "But watch out for yourselves, for they will deliver you up to councils, and you will be beaten in the synagogues. You will be brought before rulers and kings for My sake, for a testimony to them. 10 And the gospel must first be preached to all the nations. 11 But when they arrest *you* and deliver you up, do not worry beforehand, or premeditate what you will speak. But whatever is given you in that hour, speak that; for it is not you who speak, but the Holy Spirit. 12 Now brother will betray brother to death, and a father *his* child; and children will rise up against parents and cause them to be put to death. 13 And you will be hated by all for My name's sake. But he who endures to the end shall be saved.

14 "So when you see the 'abomination of desolation,' spoken of by Daniel the prophet, standing where it ought not" (let the reader understand), "then let those who are in Judea flee to the mountains. 15 Let him who is on the housetop not go down into the house, nor enter to take anything out of his house. 16 And let him who is in the field not go back to get his clothes. 17 But woe to those who are pregnant and to those who are nursing babies in those days! 18 And pray that your flight may not be in winter. 19 For *in* those days there will be tribulation, such as has not been since the beginning of the creation which God created until this time, nor ever shall be. 20 And unless the Lord had shortened those days, no flesh would be saved; but for the elect's sake, whom He chose, He shortened the days.

21 "Then if anyone says to you, 'Look, here *is* the Christ!' or, 'Look, *He is* there!' do not believe it. 22 For

false christs and false prophets will rise and show signs and wonders to deceive, if possible, even the elect. 23 But take heed; see, I have told you all things beforehand.

24 "But in those days, after that tribulation, the sun will be darkened, and the moon will not give its light; 25 the stars of heaven will fall, and the powers in the heavens will be shaken. 26 Then they will see the Son of Man coming in the clouds with great power and glory. 27 And then He will send His angels, and gather together His elect from the four winds, from the farthest part of earth to the farthest part of heaven.

28 "Now learn this parable from the fig tree: When its branch has already become tender, and puts forth leaves, you know that summer is near. 29 So you also, when you see these things happening, know that it is near—at the doors! 30 Assuredly, I say to you, this generation will by no means pass away till all these things take place. 31 Heaven and earth will pass away, but My words will by no means pass away.

32 "But of that day and hour no one knows, not even the angels in heaven, nor the Son, but only the Father. 33 Take heed, watch and pray; for you do not know when the time is. 34 It is like a man going to a far country, who left his house and gave authority to his servants, and to each his work, and commanded the doorkeeper to watch. 35 Watch therefore, for you do not know when the master of the house is coming—in the evening, at midnight, at the crowing of the rooster, or in the morning— 36 lest, coming suddenly, he find you sleeping. 37 And what I say to you, I say to all: Watch!"

The Jewish leaders plot to kill Jesus

14 After two days it was the Passover and the Feast of Unleavened Bread. And the chief priests and the scribes sought how they might take Him by trickery and put Him to death. 2 But they said, "Not during the feast, lest there be an uproar of the people."

3 And being in Bethany at the house of Simon the leper, as He sat at the table, a woman came having an ala-

DIGGING IN

13:24–37 Watch for the Coming of Jesus This present world will come to an end. Even modern science tells us so. Then Jesus will come and set up His government over a new world that will never pass away.

God has a better plan for the ages than the disease, destruction, and death we see around us every day. Now you can see around the world in an instant by turning the television knob, but what do you see? There is misery everywhere.

So it makes a lot of sense that Jesus, who came and died and rose again, will come back to bring His beautiful life into a grand new world. Jesus commands one thing—"Watch!" This means making sure you are getting ready to meet Him. He wants you to have a part in His new world.

We know that summer is near when the fig tree puts out leaves.

baster flask of very costly oil of spikenard. Then she broke the flask and poured it on His head. 4 But there were some who were indignant among themselves, and said, "Why was this fragrant oil wasted? 5 For it might have been sold for more than three hundred denarii and given to the poor." And they criticized her sharply.

6 But Jesus said, "Let her alone. Why do you trouble her? She has done a good work for Me. 7 For you have the poor with you always, and whenever you wish you may do them good; but Me you do not have always. 8 She has done what she could. She has come beforehand to anoint My body for burial. 9 Assuredly, I say to you, wherever this gospel is preached in the whole world, what this woman has done will also be told as a memorial to her."

10 Then Judas Iscariot, one of the twelve, went to the chief priests to betray Him to them. 11 And when they heard it, they were glad, and promised to give him money. So he sought how he might conveniently betray Him.

12 Now on the first day of Unleavened Bread, when they killed the Passover lamb, His disciples said to Him, "Where do You want us to go and prepare, that You may eat the Passover?"

13 And He sent out two of His disciples and said to them, "Go into the city, and a man will meet you carrying a pitcher of water; follow him. 14 Wherever he goes in, say to the master of the house, 'The Teacher says, "Where is the guest room in which I may eat the Passover with My disciples?"' 15 Then he will show you a large upper room, furnished and prepared; there make ready for us."

16 So His disciples went out, and came into the city, and found it just as He had said to them; and they prepared the Passover.

17 In the evening He came with the twelve. 18 Now as they sat and ate, Jesus said, "Assuredly, I say to you, one of you who eats with Me will betray Me."

19 And they began to be sorrowful, and to say to Him one by one, "Is it I?" And another said, "Is it I?"

20 He answered and said to them, "It is one of the twelve, who dips with Me in the dish. 21 The Son of Man indeed goes just as it is written of Him, but woe to that man by whom the Son of Man is betrayed! It would have been good for that man if he had never been born."

22 And as they were eating, Jesus took bread, blessed and broke it, and gave it to them and said, "Take, eat; this is My body."

23 Then He took the cup, and when He had given thanks He gave it to them, and they all drank from it. 24 And He said to them, "This is My blood of the new covenant, which is shed for many. 25 Assuredly, I say to you, I will no longer drink of the fruit of the vine until that day when I drink it new in the kingdom of God."

26 And when they had sung a hymn, they went out to the Mount of Olives.

27 Then Jesus said to them, "All of you will be made to stumble because of Me this night, for it is written:

'I will strike the Shepherd,
   And the sheep will be scattered.'

28 "But after I have been raised, I will go before you to Galilee."

29 Peter said to Him, "Even if all are made to stumble, yet I will not be."

30 Jesus said to him, "Assuredly, I say to you that today, even this night, before the rooster crows twice, you will deny Me three times."

31 But he spoke more vehemently, "If I have to die with You, I will not deny You!"

And they all said likewise.

32 Then they came to a place which was named Gethsemane; and He said to His disciples, "Sit here while I pray." 33 And He took Peter, James, and John with Him, and He began to be troubled and deeply distressed. 34 Then He said to them, "My soul is exceedingly sorrowful, even to death. Stay here and watch."

35 He went a little farther, and fell on the ground, and prayed that if it were possible, the hour might pass from Him. 36 And He said, **"Abba,** Father, all things *are* possible for You. Take this cup away from Me; nevertheless, not what I will, but what You *will."*

37 Then He came and found them sleeping, and said to Peter, "Simon, are you sleeping? Could you not watch one hour? 38 Watch and pray, lest you enter into temptation. The spirit indeed *is* willing, but the flesh *is* weak."

39 Again He went away and prayed, and spoke the same words. 40 And when He returned, He found them asleep again, for their eyes were heavy; and they did not know what to answer Him.

41 Then He came the third time and said to them, "Are you still sleeping and resting? It is enough! The hour has come; behold, the Son of Man is being betrayed into the hands of sinners. 42 Rise, let us be going. See, My betrayer is at hand."

43 And immediately, while He was still speaking, Judas, one of the twelve, with a great multitude with swords and clubs, came from the chief priests and the scribes and the elders. 44 Now His betrayer had given them a signal, saying, "Whomever I kiss, He is the One; seize Him and lead *Him* away safely."

45 As soon as He had come, immediately he went up to Him and said to Him, "Rabbi, Rabbi!" and kissed Him.

46 Then they laid their hands on Him and took Him. 47 And one of those who stood by drew his sword and struck the servant of the high priest, and cut off his ear.

48 Then Jesus answered and said to them, "Have you come out, as against a robber, with swords and clubs to take Me? 49 I was daily with you in the temple teaching, and you did not seize Me. But the Scriptures must be fulfilled."

50 Then they all forsook Him and fled.

51 Now a certain young man followed Him, having a linen cloth thrown around *his* naked *body.* And the young men laid hold of him, 52 and he left the linen cloth and fled from them naked.

53 And they led Jesus away to the high priest; and with him were assembled all the chief priests, the elders, and the scribes. 54 But Peter followed Him at a distance, right into the courtyard of the high priest. And he sat with the servants and warmed himself at the fire.

55 Now the chief priests and all the council sought testimony against Jesus to put Him to death, but found none. 56 For many bore false witness against Him, but their testimonies did not agree.

WORDFINDER

14:36 Abba A word for father from the ancient Aramaic language (pronounced *air-uh-MAY-ik*). The word is like our words *daddy* and *papa.*

DIGGING IN

14:53–59 Lying About Jesus The Scriptures of the Old Testament said a person could be put to death for a crime only if witnesses agreed about what that person had done (see Deuteronomy 17:6). So some people just got up and told lies about Jesus (Mark 14:57, 58).

Some people today still say Jesus was just a man and not the Son of God. Other people say Jesus was a troublemaker, and some even say He never lived.

But we know Jesus was the Son of God because even today He changes sinful people and gives them His new life. We also know that Jesus was not a troublemaker because He taught people to love one another. And we know Jesus lived, because even the history writers of His time tell about Him. One ancient writer says Jesus seemed to be more than a man and that He came back from the dead. The writer's name was Josephus (pronounced *jo-SEE-fus*).

What Peter Learned

The Lord had told me I was going to deny Him, but I thought that was impossible, and I told Him so (see Mark 14:30, 31).

Now it has actually happened. When the real test came, I was a miserable failure. I wonder now if Jesus will ever be able to forgive me.

Yet my failure has taught me a great lesson. I'll never boast again about how much I'm going to do for Jesus. Without His help, I can never do anything at all to please Him. Next time I'll be quiet and simply trust Him to help me do whatever He commands me. Don't you think that's wise?

---

57 Then some rose up and bore false witness against Him, saying, 58 "We heard Him say, 'I will destroy this temple made with hands, and within three days I will build another made without hands.' " 59 But not even then did their testimony agree.

60 And the high priest stood up in the midst and asked Jesus, saying, "Do You answer nothing? What *is* it these men testify against You?" 61 But He kept silent and answered nothing.

Again the high priest asked Him, saying to Him, "Are You the Christ, the Son of the Blessed?"

62 Jesus said, "I am. And you will see the Son of Man sitting at the right hand of the Power, and coming with the clouds of heaven."

63 Then the high priest tore his clothes and said, "What further need do we have of witnesses? 64 You have heard the blasphemy! What do you think?"

And they all condemned Him to be deserving of death.

65 Then some began to spit on Him, and to blindfold Him, and to beat Him, and to say to Him, "Prophesy!" And the officers struck Him with the palms of their hands.

66 Now as Peter was below in the courtyard, one of the servant girls of the high priest came. 67 And when she saw Peter warming himself, she looked at him and said, "You also were with Jesus of Nazareth."

68 But he denied it, saying, "I neither know nor understand what you are saying." And he went out on the porch, and a rooster crowed.

69 And the servant girl saw him again, and began to say to those who stood by, "This is one of them." 70 But he denied it again.

And a little later those who stood by said to Peter again, "Surely you are *one* of them; for you are a Galilean, and your speech shows *it.*"

71 Then he began to curse and swear, "I do not know this Man of whom you speak!"

72 A second time *the* rooster crowed. Then Peter called to mind the word that Jesus had said to him, "Before the rooster crows twice, you will deny Me three times." And when he thought about it, he wept.

Jesus is arrested and crucified

15 Immediately, in the morning, the chief priests held a consultation with the elders and scribes and the whole council; and they bound Jesus, led *Him* away, and delivered *Him* to Pilate. 2 Then Pilate asked Him, "Are You the King of the Jews?"

He answered and said to him, "*It is as* you say."

3 And the chief priests accused Him of many things, but He answered nothing. 4 Then Pilate asked Him again, saying, "Do You answer nothing? See how many things they testify against You!" 5 But Jesus still answered nothing, so that Pilate marveled.

6 Now at the feast he was accustomed to releasing one prisoner to

them, whomever they requested.
7 And there was one named Barabbas,
who was chained with his fellow rebels;
they had committed murder in the rebellion. 8 Then the multitude, crying
aloud, began to ask *him to do* just as
he had always done for them. 9 But
Pilate answered them, saying, "Do you
want me to release to you the King of
the Jews?" 10 For he knew that the
chief priests had handed Him over because of envy.
  11 But the chief priests stirred up the
crowd, so that he should rather release Barabbas to them. 12 Pilate answered and said to them again,
"What then do you want me to do
with Him whom you call the King
of the Jews?"
  13 So they cried out again, "Crucify
Him!"
  14 Then Pilate said to them, "Why,
what evil has He done?"
  But they cried out all the more,
"Crucify Him!"
  15 So Pilate, wanting to gratify the
crowd, released Barabbas to them; and
he delivered Jesus, after he had
scourged *Him,* to be crucified.
  16 Then the soldiers led Him away
into the hall called **Praetorium,** and
they called together the whole garrison. 17 And they clothed Him with purple; and they twisted a crown of thorns,
put it on His *head,* 18 and began to
salute Him, "Hail, King of the Jews!"
19 Then they struck Him on the head
with a reed and spat on Him; and bowing the knee, they worshiped Him.
20 And when they had mocked Him,
they took the purple off Him, put His
own clothes on Him, and led Him out
to crucify Him.
  21 Then they compelled a certain
man, Simon a Cyrenian, the father of
Alexander and Rufus, as he was coming out of the country and passing by,
to bear His cross. 22 And they brought
Him to the place Golgotha, which is

translated, Place of a Skull. 23 Then
they gave Him wine mingled with
myrrh to drink, but He did not take
it. 24 And when they crucified Him,
they divided His garments, casting lots
for them to determine what every man
should take.
  25 Now it was the third hour, and
they crucified Him. 26 And the inscription of His accusation was written
above:

THE KING OF THE JEWS.

27 With Him they also crucified two
robbers, one on His right and the other
on His left. 28 So the Scripture was fulfilled which says, "And He was numbered with the transgressors."
  29 And those who passed by blasphemed Him, wagging their heads and
saying, "Aha! *You* who destroy the
temple and build *it* in three days,
30 save Yourself, and come down from
the cross!"
  31 Likewise the chief priests also,
mocking among themselves with the
scribes, said, "He saved others; Himself He cannot save. 32 Let the Christ,
the King of Israel, descend now from
the cross, that we may see and believe."
  Even those who were crucified with
Him reviled Him.
  33 Now when the sixth hour had
come, there was darkness over the
whole land until the ninth hour.
34 And at the ninth hour Jesus cried
out with a loud voice, saying, "Eloi,
Eloi, lama sabachthani?" which is
translated, "My God, My God, why
have You forsaken Me?"
  35 Some of those who stood by,
when they heard *that,* said, "Look, He
is calling for Elijah!" 36 Then someone
ran and filled a sponge full of sour
wine, put *it* on a reed, and offered *it*
to Him to drink, saying, "Let Him
alone; let us see if Elijah will come to
take Him down."

15:16 Praetorium Pronounced *prih-TOE-rih-um.* The headquarters of the Roman
governor of Judea. This was located at Antonia Castle, where Pilate questioned Jesus.

"This Man Was the Son of God!"

AJTN (All Judea Television Network)—Special news bulletin: For the past few hours, startling reports have been coming in from the scene of the crucifixion of Jesus of Nazareth.

Early this morning, Jesus, the Preacher from Galilee, was made to carry the heavy wooden Cross. When He appeared to be getting weak, the soldiers forced a man named Simon to carry the Cross for Jesus.

At the hill of Calvary outside Jerusalem, Jesus was nailed to the Cross. There He suffered for several hours.

About three o'clock in the afternoon, the Man from Galilee cried out with a loud voice to God and died. There was a frightening earthquake, and the sky became very dark.

Then one of the soldiers standing by Jesus declared, "Truly this Man was the Son of God!" Other eyewitnesses confirm that what the soldier said was true: Jesus was the Son of God! A dreadful crime has been committed. We have crucified the King of Kings—the Son of God Himself!

37 And Jesus cried out with a loud voice, and breathed His last. 38 Then the veil of the temple was torn in two from top to bottom. 39 So when the centurion, who stood opposite Him, saw that He cried out like this and breathed His last, he said, "Truly this Man was the Son of God!"

40 There were also women looking on from afar, among whom were Mary Magdalene, Mary the mother of James the Less and of Joses, and Salome, 41 who also followed Him and ministered to Him when He was in Galilee, and many other women who came up with Him to Jerusalem.

42 Now when evening had come, because it was the Preparation Day, that is, the day before the Sabbath, 43 Joseph of Arimathea, a prominent council member, who was himself waiting for the kingdom of God, coming and taking courage, went in to Pilate and asked for the body of Jesus. 44 Pilate marveled that He was already dead; and summoning the centurion, he asked him if He had been dead for some time. 45 So when he found out from the centurion, he granted the body to Joseph. 46 Then he bought fine linen, took Him down, and wrapped Him in the linen. And he laid Him in a tomb which had been hewn out of the rock, and rolled a stone against the door of the tomb. 47 And Mary Magdalene and Mary the mother of Joses observed where He was laid.

A Roman centurion, like the one who confessed Christ, commanded a hundred men.

Jesus rises and returns to heaven

16 Now when the Sabbath was past, Mary Magdalene, Mary *the mother* of James, and Salome bought spices, that they might come and anoint Him. 2 Very early in the morning, on the first *day* of the week, they came to the tomb when the sun had risen. 3 And they said among themselves, "Who will roll away the stone from the door of the tomb for us?" 4 But when they looked up, they saw that the stone had been rolled away— for it was very large. 5 And entering the tomb, they saw a young man clothed in a long white robe sitting on the right side; and they were alarmed.

6 But he said to them, "Do not be alarmed. You seek Jesus of Nazareth, who was crucified. He is risen! He is not here. See the place where they laid Him. 7 But go, tell His disciples—and Peter—that He is going before you into Galilee; there you will see Him, as He said to you."

8 So they went out quickly and fled from the tomb, for they trembled and were amazed. And they said nothing to anyone, for they were afraid.

9 Now when *He* rose early on the first *day* of the week, He appeared first to Mary Magdalene, out of whom He had cast seven demons. 10 She went and told those who had been with Him, as they mourned and wept. 11 And when they heard that He was

The lion of John Mark, an ancient symbol of the author of this Gospel.

alive and had been seen by her, they did not believe.

12 After that, He appeared in another form to two of them as they walked and went into the country. 13 And they went and told *it* to the rest, *but* they did not believe them either.

14 Later He appeared to the eleven as they sat at the table; and He rebuked their unbelief and hardness of heart, because they did not believe those who had seen Him after He had risen. 15 And He said to them, "Go into all the world and preach the gospel to every creature. 16 He who believes and

---

What Believers Learned

Many of us were with Jesus for more than three years. We heard His teaching, and we saw His wonderful miracles. Then we saw Him die on the Cross.

All this would have meant nothing if we had never seen Jesus again. He would have been just another great teacher who died.

But we saw Jesus alive for 40 days. He showed us the nail marks made in His body when He died on the Cross. We touched Him, and He ate with us. Then we saw Him go back to heaven.

After that, God gave us power to go and tell everyone everywhere about our risen, living Savior. If you ask Him, Jesus will give you power to tell others about Him, too.

Where Is Jesus Now?

Jesus came from His Father in heaven. Now He has gone back to be with His Father in heaven. Someday you can be there with Him, too. Even now Jesus can make your life like heaven by sending the Holy Spirit to live in you. The Holy Spirit tells you that God will love you forever.

is baptized will be saved; but he who does not believe will be condemned. ¹⁷ And these signs will follow

those who believe: In My name they will cast out demons; they will speak with new tongues; ¹⁸ they will take up serpents; and if they drink anything deadly, it will by no means hurt them; they will lay hands on the sick, and they will recover."

¹⁹ So then, after the Lord had spoken to them, He was received up into heaven, and sat down at the right hand of God. ²⁰ And they went out and preached everywhere, the Lord working with *them* and confirming the word through the accompanying signs. Amen.

The Book of
LUKE

I felt unworthy to write about Jesus because I hadn't known Him well, but God guided me to do just that.

I was Greek by birth. As a medical doctor, the birth of Jesus was important to me. First, I talked to Mary the mother of Jesus and to Joseph, her husband. Then I got more facts from the parents of John the Baptizer.

I even went out to meet the shepherds in the hills of Bethlehem. They had been visited by the angels who sent them to a stable where they found the Baby Jesus.

I came to believe that Jesus truly was the Son of God, and I have trusted in Him ever since.

Later, I also wrote the Book of Acts. In that book, I tell about the work of Jesus' apostles after He went back to heaven. You should read the Book of Acts after you read my Gospel about Jesus.

John the Baptist is born

INASMUCH as many have taken in hand to set in order a narrative of those things which have been fulfilled among us, 2 just as those who from the beginning were eyewitnesses and ministers of the word delivered them to us, 3 it seemed good to me also, having had perfect understanding of all things from the very first, to write to you an orderly account, most excellent Theophilus, 4 that you may know the certainty of those things in which you were instructed.

5 There was in the days of Herod, the king of Judea, a certain priest named Zacharias, of the division of Abijah. His wife *was* of the daughters of Aaron, and her name *was* Elizabeth. 6 And they were both righteous before God, walking in all the commandments and ordinances of the Lord blameless. 7 But they had no child, because Elizabeth was barren, and they were both well advanced in years.

8 So it was, that while he was serving as priest before God in the order of his division, 9 according to the custom of the priesthood, his lot fell to burn incense when he went into the temple of the Lord. 10 And the whole multitude of the people was praying outside at the hour of incense. 11 Then an angel of the Lord appeared to him, standing on the right side of the altar of incense. 12 And when Zacharias saw *him,* he was troubled, and fear fell upon him.

13 But the angel said to him, "Do not be afraid, Zacharias, for your prayer is heard; and your wife Elizabeth will bear you a son, and you shall call his name John. 14 And you will have joy and gladness, and many will rejoice at his birth. 15 For he will be great in the sight of the Lord, and shall drink neither wine nor strong drink. He will also be filled with the Holy Spirit, even from his mother's womb. 16 And he will turn many of the children of Israel to the Lord their God. 17 He will also go before Him in the spirit and power of Elijah, 'to turn the hearts of the fathers to the children,' and the disobedient to the wisdom of the just, to make ready a people prepared for the Lord."

I, Mary, was an ordinary young woman living in Nazareth, a town in the Roman province of Galilee. One day I was surprised by a visit from Gabriel, a man from heaven. He was an angel whose name is pronounced GAY-brih-ell and means "My God Is Great."

Gabriel told me I was going to be the mother of the Son of God! I didn't know what to say, so I just said, "Let it be to me according to your word." Then I sang the beautiful song you can read in this chapter.

At first, Joseph, the man I was going to marry, was very upset, but he understood later. Our Savior from heaven was going to be born, just as the ancient prophets had said (see Isaiah 7:14).

As my Son grew up, I realized He could never really belong to me. He was the Son of God. Sorrow would come to me because one day they would crucify Him.

18 And Zacharias said to the angel, "How shall I know this? For I am an old man, and my wife is well advanced in years."

19 And the angel answered and said to him, "I am Gabriel, who stands in the presence of God, and was sent to speak to you and bring you these glad tidings. 20 But behold, you will be mute and not able to speak until the day these things take place, because you did not believe my words which will be fulfilled in their own time."

21 And the people waited for Zacharias, and marveled that he lingered so long in the temple. 22 But when he came out, he could not speak to them; and they perceived that he had seen a vision in the temple, for he beckoned to them and remained speechless.

23 So it was, as soon as the days of his service were completed, that he departed to his own house. 24 Now after those days his wife Elizabeth conceived; and she hid herself five months, saying, 25 "Thus the Lord has dealt with me, in the days when He looked on me, to take away my reproach among people."

26 Now in the sixth month the angel Gabriel was sent by God to a city of Galilee named Nazareth, 27 to a virgin **betrothed** to a man whose name was Joseph, of the house of David. The virgin's name was Mary. 28 And having come in, the angel said to her, "Rejoice, highly favored one, the Lord is with you; blessed are you among women!"

29 But when she saw him, she was troubled at his saying, and considered what manner of greeting this was. 30 Then the angel said to her, "Do not be afraid, Mary, for you have found favor with God. 31 And behold, you will conceive in your womb and bring forth a Son, and shall call His name JESUS. 32 He will be great, and will be called the Son of the Highest; and the Lord God will give Him the throne of His father David. 33 And He will reign over the house of Jacob forever, and of His kingdom there will be no end."

34 Then Mary said to the angel, "How can this be, since I do not know a man?"

35 And the angel answered and said to her, "The Holy Spirit will come

WORDFINDER

1:27 Betrothed (Pronounced be-TROTHD). Like being engaged to be married, but in Bible times, to be betrothed was more serious and legally permanent than being engaged today.

upon you, and the power of the Highest will overshadow you; therefore,
also, that Holy One who is to be born
will be called the Son of God. 36 Now
indeed, Elizabeth your relative has also
conceived a son in her old age; and
this is now the sixth month for her who
was called barren. 37 For with God
nothing will be impossible."

38 Then Mary said, "Behold the
maidservant of the Lord! Let it be to
me according to your word." And the
angel departed from her.

39 Now Mary arose in those days and
went into the hill country with haste,
to a city of Judah, 40 and entered the
house of Zacharias and greeted Elizabeth. 41 And it happened, when Elizabeth heard the greeting of Mary, that
the babe leaped in her womb; and Elizabeth was filled with the Holy Spirit.
42 Then she spoke out with a loud
voice and said, "Blessed are you
among women, and blessed is the fruit
of your womb! 43 But why is this
granted to me, that the mother of my
Lord should come to me? 44 For indeed, as soon as the voice of your
greeting sounded in my ears, the babe
leaped in my womb for joy. 45 Blessed
is she who believed, for there will be
a fulfillment of those things which were
told her from the Lord."

46 And Mary said:

"My soul magnifies the Lord,
47   And my spirit has rejoiced in
       God my Savior.
48   For He has regarded the lowly
       state of His maidservant;
     For behold, henceforth all
       generations will call me
       blessed.
49   For He who is mighty has done
       great things for me,
     And holy is His name.
50   And His mercy is on those who
       fear Him
     From generation to generation.
51   He has shown strength with His
       arm;
     He has scattered the proud in
       the imagination of their
       hearts.

52   He has put down the mighty
       from their thrones,
     And exalted the lowly.
53   He has filled the hungry with
       good things,
     And the rich He has sent away
       empty.
54   He has helped His servant Israel,
     In remembrance of His mercy,
55   As He spoke to our fathers,
     To Abraham and to his seed
       forever."

56 And Mary remained with her
about three months, and returned to
her house.

57 Now Elizabeth's full time came for
her to be delivered, and she brought
forth a son. 58 When her neighbors and
relatives heard how the Lord had
shown great mercy to her, they rejoiced with her.

59 So it was, on the eighth day, that
they came to circumcise the child; and
they would have called him by the
name of his father, Zacharias. 60 His
mother answered and said, "No; he
shall be called John."

61 But they said to her, "There is no
one among your relatives who is called
by this name." 62 So they made signs
to his father—what he would have him
called.

63 And he asked for a writing tablet,
and wrote, saying, "His name is
John." So they all marveled. 64 Immediately his mouth was opened
and his tongue loosed, and he spoke,
praising God. 65 Then fear came on all
who dwelt around them; and all these
sayings were discussed throughout all
the hill country of Judea. 66 And all
those who heard them kept them in
their hearts, saying, "What kind of
child will this be?" And the hand of
the Lord was with him.

67 Now his father Zacharias was filled
with the Holy Spirit, and prophesied,
saying:

68 "Blessed is the Lord God of
     Israel,
   For He has visited and
     redeemed His people,

My name is pronounced *zak-uh-RIGH-us* and means "God Has Remembered."

Gabriel, the same man from heaven who visited Mary, visited me, too. He announced that my wife and I would be the parents of John the Baptist. But we had no children, and now it seemed too late for us. Because I didn't believe him, the angel made me unable to speak until the boy was born.

Gabriel reminded me of God's promise that Elijah would come again to get us ready for the coming of our Savior from heaven. Our son was to be like that amazing prophet, Elijah, from Old Testament times. His name is pronounced *ih-LIE-jah* and means "The Lord Is My God."

Everyone wondered why Gabriel had said the boy was to be named John since we usually gave our children the names of our relatives. John means "The Lord Has Been Gracious." The word *gracious* means "kind." The Lord was very kind to send us the Savior, of course!

69 And has raised up a horn of
   salvation for us
   In the house of His servant
   David,
70 As He spoke by the mouth of
   His holy prophets,
   Who *have been* since the world
   began,
71 That we should be saved from
   our enemies
   And from the hand of all who
   hate us,
72 To perform the mercy *promised*
   to our fathers
   And to remember His holy
   covenant,
73 The oath which He swore to our
   father Abraham:
74 To grant us that we,
   Being delivered from the hand
   of our enemies,
   Might serve Him without fear,
75 In holiness and righteousness
   before Him all the days of our
   life.
76 "And you, child, will be called the
   prophet of the Highest;
   For you will go before the face
   of the Lord to prepare His
   ways,
77 To give knowledge of salvation
   to His people
   By the remission of their sins,

78 Through the tender mercy of our
   God,
   With which the Dayspring from
   on high has visited us;
79 To give light to those who sit in
   darkness and the shadow of
   death,
   To guide our feet into the way
   of peace."

80 So the child grew and became strong in spirit, and was in the deserts till the day of his manifestation to Israel.

Angels announce Baby Jesus' birth to some shepherds

2 And it came to pass in those days *that* a decree went out from Caesar Augustus that all the world should be registered. 2 This census first took place while Quirinius was governing Syria. 3 So all went to be registered, everyone to his own city.

4 Joseph also went up from Galilee, out of the city of Nazareth, into Judea, to the city of David, which is called Bethlehem, because he was of the house and lineage of David, 5 to be registered with Mary, his betrothed wife, who was with child. 6 So it was, that while they were there, the days were completed for her to be deliv-

ered. ⁷ And she brought forth her first-born Son, and wrapped Him in **swaddling cloths,** and laid Him in a manger, because there was no room for them in the inn.

⁸ Now there were in the same country shepherds living out in the fields, keeping watch over their flock by night. ⁹ And behold, an **angel of the Lord** stood before them, and the glory of the Lord shone around them, and they were greatly afraid. ¹⁰ Then the angel said to them, "Do not be afraid, for behold, I bring you good tidings of great joy which will be to all people. ¹¹ For there is born to you this day in the city of David a Savior, who is Christ the Lord. ¹² And this *will be* the sign to you: You will find a Babe wrapped in swaddling cloths, lying in a manger."

¹³ And suddenly there was with the angel a multitude of the heavenly host praising God and saying:

¹⁴ "Glory to God in the highest,
　　And on earth peace, goodwill
　　　toward men!"

¹⁵ So it was, when the angels had gone away from them into heaven, that the shepherds said to one another, "Let us now go to Bethlehem and see this thing that has come to pass, which the Lord has made known to us." ¹⁶ And they came with haste and found Mary and Joseph, and the Babe lying in a manger. ¹⁷ Now when they had seen *Him,* they made widely known the saying which was told them concerning this Child. ¹⁸ And all those who heard *it* marveled at those things which were told them by the shepherds.

WORDFINDER

2:7 Swaddling Cloths　Cloths, like bandages, to wrap newborn babies. In Jesus' time, swaddling cloths were used to keep a baby's limbs straight.

2:9 Angel of the Lord　*Angel* means "messenger." This messenger from God brings the Good News of the Savior's birth to the shepherds. In the Old Testament, the Angel of the Lord is God revealing Himself.

DIGGING IN

2:1 Caesar Augustus　Caesar Augustus (pronounced *SEE-zer aw-GUS-tus*) was the first emperor of Rome. His reign brought the Roman republic to an end and began the new Roman Empire. Jesus was born in Bethlehem of Judea when Augustus was emperor. Judea, where the Jews lived, was a Roman province.

Augustus' name was first "Octavian" (pronounced *ok-TAY-vee-un*). He was the nephew and adopted son of Julius Caesar, a great Roman general. Octavian became "Emperor Caesar Augustus" after Julius Caesar was murdered in 44 B.C. The word *Caesar* was a family name that later came to be used as a title for Roman emperors.

Augustus was the first Roman ruler who allowed himself to be worshiped as a god. Later, Christians were put to death for refusing to worship the emperor.

When Augustus Caesar ordered all the world to be registered, Mary and Joseph traveled to Bethlehem.

Bethlehem Shepherds Tell Amazing Story

The Jerusalem Times

JERUSALEM—Shepherds from the fields outside Bethlehem are telling a bizarre story to reporters of *The Times*.

While watching their flocks one night last week, the shepherds say they were visited by a shining heavenly messenger, an angel. At the same time, brilliant light shone all around them. Of course, the shepherds were terrified because they didn't understand what was happening.

The angel told them not to be afraid because he brought good and joyful news for the whole world. A Savior was being born in Bethlehem who is the Messiah we have been awaiting for many centuries. The angel went on to tell them where they would find the newborn Baby.

All at once the sky was filled with a great choir singing praises to God. When the angels were gone, the shepherds hurried to Bethlehem and found the Infant, just as the angel had reported to them.

Is it true that our Messiah has been born in a stable?

Swaddling cloths kept babies warm and straight.

19 But Mary kept all these things and pondered *them* in her heart. 20 Then the shepherds returned, glorifying and praising God for all the things that they had heard and seen, as it was told them.

21 And when eight days were completed for the circumcision of the Child, His name was called JESUS, the name given by the angel before He was conceived in the womb.

22 Now when the days of her purification according to the law of Moses were completed, they brought Him to Jerusalem to present *Him* to the Lord 23 (as it is written in the law of the Lord, "Every male who opens the womb shall be called holy to the LORD"), 24 and to offer a sacrifice according to what is said in the law of the Lord, "A pair of turtledoves or two young pigeons."

25 And behold, there was a man in Jerusalem whose name was Simeon, and this man was just and devout, waiting for the Consolation of Israel, and the Holy Spirit was upon him. 26 And it had been revealed to him by the Holy Spirit that he would not see death before he had seen the Lord's Christ. 27 So he came by the Spirit into the temple. And when the parents brought in the Child Jesus, to do for

On the night Jesus was born, shepherds were in the fields, guarding their sheep.

Him according to the custom of the law, 28 he took Him up in his arms and blessed God and said:

29 "Lord, now You are letting Your
    servant depart in peace,
    According to Your word;
30 For my eyes have seen Your
    salvation
31 Which You have prepared
    before the face of all peoples,
32 A light to *bring* revelation to the
    Gentiles,
    And the glory of Your people
    Israel."

33 And Joseph and His mother marveled at those things which were spoken of Him. 34 Then Simeon blessed them, and said to Mary His mother, "Behold, this *Child* is destined for the fall and rising of many in Israel, and for a sign which will be spoken against 35 (yes, a sword will pierce through your own soul also), that the thoughts of many hearts may be revealed."

36 Now there was one, Anna, a prophetess, the daughter of Phanuel, of the tribe of Asher. She was of a great age, and had lived with a husband seven years from her virginity; 37 and

---

What Simeon Learned

Pronounce my name *SIM-ee-un.* I had been waiting a long time for our "Messiah." This Hebrew word for *Christ* means "Anointed One" and is pronounced *muh-SIGH-uh.* He was the One who would save our people and bring many Gentiles to God.

When Mary and Joseph brought Jesus to the temple, the Lord showed me right away that this Baby was the One I was waiting for. So I gave thanks to God for letting me live to see Him.

Then I blessed the Baby Jesus, and I told Mary that the Child would bring wonderful changes to our people. I also foretold that He would suffer and that Mary, His mother, would be brokenhearted someday because of what people would do to her Son.

Besides Mary and Joseph, Simeon and I were the only people in Jerusalem who recognized the baby Jesus as our Savior from heaven. We were not important people in those days, but God often chooses to bless ordinary folks in very special ways.

My husband died after seven years of a wonderful marriage. The Lord didn't want me to marry anyone else, so I was a widow for 84 years.

God gave me a special gift of prophecy. I spent nearly all my time at the temple in Jerusalem, speaking God's words of comfort to all who came there.

Seeing my Savior in His mother's arms was the greatest moment in my long life. At once I gave thanks to God that I had lived to see that day!

Why Did Jesus Live in Nazareth?

Jesus was born in Bethlehem as the prophet Micah foretold (see Micah 5:2). The prophets also said that Jesus would be called a "Nazarene" (pronounced NAZ-uh-reen), meaning a man from Nazareth. Jesus lived in Nazareth at first because it was the home of Mary and Joseph. Find Nazareth on the map of Palestine (page 1343).

this woman *was* a widow of about eighty-four years, who did not depart from the temple, but served *God* with fastings and prayers night and day. 38 And coming in that instant she gave thanks to the Lord, and spoke of Him

to all those who looked for redemption in Jerusalem.

39 So when they had performed all things according to the law of the Lord, they returned to Galilee, to their *own* city, Nazareth. 40 And the Child grew and became strong in spirit, filled with wisdom; and the grace of God was upon Him.

41 His parents went to Jerusalem every year at the Feast of the Passover. 42 And when He was twelve years old, they went up to Jerusalem according to the custom of the feast. 43 When they had finished the days, as they returned, the Boy Jesus lingered behind in Jerusalem. And Joseph and His mother did not know *it;* 44 but supposing Him to have been in the company, they went a day's journey, and sought Him among *their* relatives and ac-

DIGGING IN

2:42–50 Caring for My Father's Business Jesus was 12 years old, and He had been missing for three days in Jerusalem. Can you imagine how worried your family would be if they didn't know where you were for three days?

When Mary and Joseph found Jesus, He told them they shouldn't have worried. He had to care for *His Father's business*. They had forgotten that Jesus was different from ordinary sons because He was also *the Son of God*. This meant that He

had to obey His heavenly Father before all His other duties.

Where had Jesus been those three days? He had been sitting in the temple discussing the Scriptures with the great teachers of His time. Even at age 12, Jesus had the wisdom of God, and His hearers were amazed. The Bible says you, too, can have "the mind of Christ" (1 Corinthians 2:16). As you study the Scriptures, the Holy Spirit helps you share in the wisdom of Jesus.

Boy Wonder Stumps Scholars

The Jerusalem Times

JERUSALEM—A twelve-year-old Boy has created a lot of excitement among the scholars who meet to discuss the Bible and other spiritual matters.

The Boy, whose name is Jesus, talked with the scholars for several hours last week. His wisdom and knowledge of the Scriptures have surprised all who were present. He was able to recite the whole Creation story of Genesis, the Ten Commandments, and many psalms.

Most interesting of all is His great knowledge of the coming Messiah. Everyone knows that our Messiah will come from the family of King David. But, quoting from Psalm 110, young Jesus asked the teachers how our Messiah could be David's great Son if David also called Him "Lord"?

When the scholars couldn't give Him an answer, Jesus told them that the Messiah, or Christ, was "the Mighty God" from heaven (see Isaiah 9:6).

quaintances. 45 So when they did not find Him, they returned to Jerusalem, seeking Him. 46 Now so it was *that* after three days they found Him in the temple, sitting in the midst of the teachers, both listening to them and asking them questions. 47 And all who heard Him were astonished at His understanding and answers. 48 So when they saw Him, they were amazed; and His mother said to Him, "Son, why have You done this to us? Look, Your father and I have sought You anxiously."

49 And He said to them, "Why did you seek Me? Did you not know that I must be about My Father's business?" 50 But they did not understand the statement which He spoke to them.

51 Then He went down with them and came to Nazareth, and was subject to them, but His mother kept all these things in her heart. 52 And Jesus increased in **wisdom** and stature, and in favor with God and men.

John prepares the way for Jesus

3 Now in the fifteenth year of the reign of Tiberius Caesar, Pontius Pilate being governor of Judea, Herod being tetrarch of Galilee, his brother Philip tetrarch of Iturea and the region of Tra-

---

WORDFINDER

2:52 Wisdom The ability to use facts to bring about good results. The so-called wisdom of this world could not do this. Jesus Christ is the source of true wisdom.

DIGGING IN

2:52 Growing Up God's Way What will you be when you are an adult? That depends on what you are doing now.

With so many careers to choose from, you should be careful to choose a future that will be exciting and useful at the same time. What kinds of things do you enjoy most now? Do you like making things with your hands? Then maybe someday you can be a successful clothing or engineering designer. Do you enjoy science? Per-

haps you may think about becoming a medical doctor or research scientist.

The important thing is to ask God what *He* wants you to be. Then ask Him how He wants you to train for that career. God wants you to honor Him in whatever path of life you follow. If you really mean to honor Him, He will show you how to grow up His way. God's way is the way that will really satisfy you and bless other people.

chonitis, and Lysanias tetrarch of Abilene, 2 while Annas and Caiaphas were high priests, the word of God came to John the son of Zacharias in the wilderness. 3 And he went into all the region around the Jordan, preaching a baptism of repentance for the remission of sins, 4 as it is written in the book of the words of Isaiah the prophet, saying:

"The voice of one crying in the wilderness:
'Prepare the way of the LORD;
Make His paths straight.
5 Every valley shall be filled
And every mountain and hill brought low;
The crooked places shall be made straight
And the rough ways smooth;
6 And all flesh shall see the salvation of God.' "

7 Then he said to the multitudes that came out to be baptized by him, "Brood of vipers! Who warned you to flee from the wrath to come? 8 Therefore bear fruits worthy of repentance, and do not begin to say to yourselves, 'We have Abraham as our father.' For I say to you that God is able to raise up children to Abraham from these stones. 9 And even now the ax is laid to the root of the trees. Therefore every tree which does not bear good fruit is cut down and thrown into the fire."

10 So the people asked him, saying, "What shall we do then?"

11 He answered and said to them, "He who has two tunics, let him give to him who has none; and he who has food, let him do likewise."

12 Then tax collectors also came to be baptized, and said to him, "Teacher, what shall we do?"

13 And he said to them, "Collect no more than what is appointed for you."

14 Likewise the soldiers asked him, saying, "And what shall we do?"

So he said to them, "Do not intimidate anyone or accuse falsely, and be content with your wages."

15 Now as the people were in expectation, and all reasoned in their hearts about John, whether he was the Christ or not, 16 John answered, saying to all, "I indeed baptize you with water; but One mightier than I is coming, whose sandal strap I am not worthy to loose.

DIGGING IN

3:1 Caesar Tiberius Caesar Tiberius (pronounced *tie-BEER-ih-us*) became Roman emperor after the death of Caesar Augustus (pronounced *SEE-zer aw-GUS-tus*) in A.D. 14. Tiberius was born in 42 B.C. and reigned until his death in A.D. 37. This was the emperor who ruled the Roman Empire, including Palestine, during the time of Jesus' manhood. The city of Tiberias, on the Sea of Galilee, was built in honor of Emperor Tiberius by Herod Antipas (pronounced *AN-tih-pass*), the son of Herod the Great (see Matthew 2:3–20). The Sea of Galilee was also renamed the "Sea of Tiberias."

Tiberius tried to carry on the plans of Caesar Augustus in ruling the empire. Tiberius was a brilliant soldier and leader, but he didn't trust his government leaders. So he executed many of them for treason. Tiberius himself had no part in crucifying Jesus, however.

He will baptize you with the Holy Spirit and fire. 17 His winnowing fan *is* in His hand, and He will thoroughly clean out His threshing floor, and gather the wheat into His barn; but the chaff He will burn with unquenchable fire."

18 And with many other exhortations he preached to the people. 19 But Herod the tetrarch, being rebuked by him concerning Herodias, his brother Philip's wife, and for all the evils which Herod had done, 20 also added this, above all, that he shut John up in prison.

21 When all the people were baptized, it came to pass that Jesus also was baptized; and while He prayed, the heaven was opened. 22 And the Holy Spirit descended in bodily form like a dove upon Him, and a voice came from heaven which said, "You are My beloved Son; in You I am well pleased."

23 Now Jesus Himself began *His ministry at* about thirty years of age, being (as was supposed) *the* son of Joseph, *the son* of Heli, 24 *the son* of

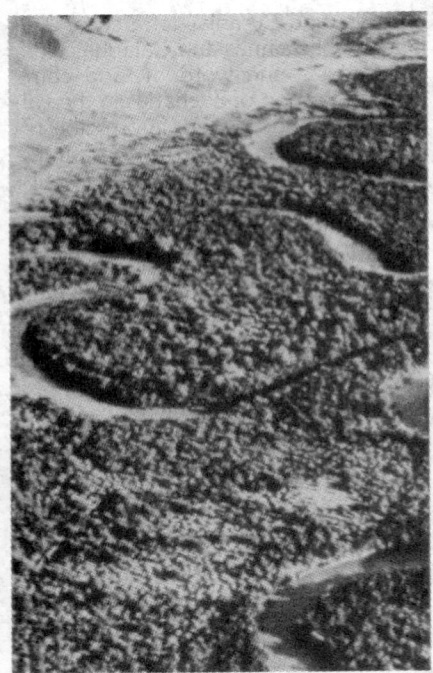

Jesus was baptized in the Jordan River.

WORDFINDER

3:23 Son of . . . (Genealogy) The history of a family showing the family members of each generation from the beginning. This genealogy of Jesus begins with Abraham and ends with Joseph, husband of Mary.

DIGGING IN

3:7–20 John the Baptist John the Baptist was the first prophet sent by God since Malachi, the last Old Testament prophet, who lived four hundred years before John. Malachi had promised that God would send a prophet who would prepare the way for the coming Messiah.

So John prepared the people for the coming of Jesus. He preached all around the Jordan River (see the map on page 1343). John preached that the people needed to "repent" of their sins. He meant that they must leave *their sins behind* and promise God they would live according to His law.

The people came to John and asked to be baptized in the Jordan River. So John baptized the people as a sign that they had repented.

Farmers separated wheat from chaff by tossing it into the air (John 3:17).

Matthat, *the son* of Levi, *the son* of Melchi, *the son* of Janna, *the son* of Joseph, 25 *the son* of Mattathiah, *the son* of Amos, *the son* of Nahum, *the son* of Esli, *the son* of Naggai, 26 *the son* of Maath, *the son* of Mattathiah, *the son* of Semei, *the son* of Joseph, *the son* of Judah, 27 *the son* of Joannas, *the son* of Rhesa, *the son* of Zerubbabel, *the son* of Shealtiel, *the son* of Neri, 28 *the son* of Melchi, *the son* of Addi, *the son* of Cosam, *the son* of Elmodam, *the son* of Er, 29 *the son* of Jose, *the son* of Eliezer, *the son* of Jorim, *the son* of Matthat, *the son* of Levi, 30 *the son* of Simeon, *the son* of Judah, *the son* of Joseph, *the son* of Jonan, *the son* of Eliakim, 31 *the son* of Melea, *the son* of Menan, *the son* of Mattathah, *the son* of Nathan, *the son* of David, 32 *the son* of Jesse, *the son* of Obed, *the son* of Boaz, *the son* of Salmon, *the son* of Nahshon, 33 *the son* of Amminadab, *the son* of Ram, *the son* of Hezron, *the son* of Perez, *the son* of Judah, 34 *the son* of Jacob, *the son* of Isaac, *the son* of Abraham, *the son* of Terah, *the son* of Nahor, 35 *the son* of Serug, *the son* of Reu, *the son* of Peleg, *the son* of Eber, *the son* of Shelah, 36 *the son* of Cainan, *the son* of Arphaxad, *the son* of Shem, *the son* of Noah, *the son* of Lamech, 37 *the son* of Methuselah, *the son* of Enoch, *the son* of Jared, *the son* of Mahalalel, *the son* of Cainan, 38 *the son* of Enosh, *the son* of Seth, *the son* of Adam, *the son* of God.

Satan tempts Jesus in the wilderness

4 Then Jesus, being filled with the Holy Spirit, returned from the Jordan and was led by the Spirit into the wilderness, 2 being tempted for forty days by the devil. And in those days He ate

In the distance, as seen from Jericho, is the mountain where Satan tempted Jesus.

nothing, and afterward, when they had ended, He was hungry.

3 And the devil said to Him, "If You are the Son of God, command this stone to become bread."

4 But Jesus answered him, saying, "It is written, 'Man shall not live by bread alone, but by every word of God.'"

5 Then the devil, taking Him up on a high mountain, showed Him all the kingdoms of the world in a moment of time. 6 And the devil said to Him, "All this authority I will give You, and their glory; for *this* has been delivered to me, and I give it to whomever I wish. 7 Therefore, if You will worship before me, all will be Yours."

8 And Jesus answered and said to him, "Get behind Me, **Satan!** For it is written, 'You shall worship the Lᴏʀᴅ

WORDFINDER

4:8 Satan Pronounced *SAY-tun*. The personal name of the Devil. The name means "Adversary" or "Enemy." Satan is the chief spiritual enemy of God. He is an angel who rebelled against the Lord.

New Religious Leader?

Nazareth News Leader

NAZARETH—Announcement of a new Teacher in the area of Galilee appeared yesterday in this newspaper. Jesus, of the family of Joseph and Mary of Nazareth, has been a carpenter in Joseph's shop for many years.

However, Jesus has been away from the shop for some time now. Neighbors say He was seen at one of the meetings held by John the Baptizer at the Jordan River, after which He disappeared for many days.

Having returned from a long stay in the desert, He has been teaching around the Sea of Galilee. Those who have heard Him speak report that He teaches with great power. Some have even said His words are so wonderful that it is as if "the people who walked in darkness have seen a great light" (see Isaiah 9:2).

Recently Jesus spoke in His own synagogue (pronounced SIN-uh-gog). But the people of Nazareth were angry at some of the things He was saying, and threw Him out. Fortunately, He was able to slip away from the angry mob before they could kill Him.

your God, and Him only you shall serve.' "

9 Then he brought Him to Jerusalem, set Him on the pinnacle of the temple, and said to Him, "If You are the Son of God, throw Yourself down from here. 10 For it is written:

'He shall give His angels charge over you,
To keep you,'

11 and,

'In their hands they shall bear you up,
Lest you dash your foot against a stone.' "

12 And Jesus answered and said to him, "It has been said, 'You shall not tempt the LORD your God.' "

13 Now when the devil had ended every temptation, he departed from Him until an opportune time.

14 Then Jesus returned in the power of the Spirit to Galilee, and news of Him went out through all the surrounding region. 15 And He taught in their synagogues, being glorified by all.

16 So He came to Nazareth, where He had been brought up. And as His custom was, He went into the synagogue on the Sabbath day, and stood up to read. 17 And He was handed the book of the prophet Isaiah. And when He had opened the book, He found the place where it was written:

18 "The Spirit of the LORD is upon Me,
Because He has anointed Me
To preach the gospel to the poor;
He has sent Me to heal the brokenhearted,
To proclaim liberty to the captives
And recovery of sight to the blind,
To set at liberty those who are oppressed;

WORDFINDER

4:16 Synagogue Pronounced SIN-uh-gog. From a Greek word meaning "gather together." The Jews have worshiped at buildings called synagogues ever since they lived in countries where they could no longer come to the temple.

19 To proclaim the acceptable year of the LORD.''

20 Then He closed the book, and gave *it* back to the attendant and sat down. And the eyes of all who were in the synagogue were fixed on Him. 21 And He began to say to them, ''Today this Scripture is fulfilled in your hearing.'' 22 So all bore witness to Him, and marveled at the gracious words which proceeded out of His mouth. And they said, ''Is this not Joseph's son?''

23 He said to them, ''You will surely say this proverb to Me, 'Physician, heal yourself! Whatever we have heard done in Capernaum, do also here in Your country.' '' 24 Then He said, ''Assuredly, I say to you, no prophet is accepted in his own country. 25 But I tell you truly, many widows were in Israel in the days of Elijah, when the heaven was shut up three years and six months, and there was a great famine throughout all the land; 26 but to none of them was Elijah sent except to Zarephath, *in the region* of Sidon, to a woman *who was* a widow. 27 And many lepers were in Israel in the time of Elisha the prophet, and none of them was cleansed except Naaman the Syrian.''

28 So all those in the synagogue, when they heard these things, were filled with wrath, 29 and rose up and thrust Him out of the city; and they led Him to the brow of the hill on which their city was built, that they might throw Him down over the cliff.

30 Then passing through the midst of them, He went His way.

31 Then He went down to Capernaum, a city of Galilee, and was teaching them on the Sabbaths. 32 And they were astonished at His teaching, for His word was with authority. 33 Now in the synagogue there was a man who had a spirit of an unclean demon. And he cried out with a loud voice, 34 saying, ''Let *us* alone! What have we to do with You, Jesus of Nazareth? Did You come to destroy us? I know who You are—the Holy One of God!''

35 But Jesus rebuked him, saying, ''Be quiet, and come out of him!'' And when the demon had thrown him in *their* midst, it came out of him and did not hurt him. 36 Then they were all amazed and spoke among themselves, saying, ''What a word this *is!* For with authority and power He commands the unclean spirits, and they come out.'' 37 And the report about Him went out into every place in the surrounding region.

38 Now He arose from the synagogue and entered Simon's house. But Simon's wife's mother was sick with a high fever, and they made request of Him concerning her. 39 So He stood over her and rebuked the fever, and it left her. And immediately she arose and served them.

40 When the sun was setting, all those who had any that were sick with various diseases brought them to Him; and He laid His hands on every one of them and healed them. 41 And demons also came out of many, crying

---

✗ DIGGING IN

4:24–30 Jesus Hated in His Hometown Jesus' first earthly home was in Nazareth, near the Sea of Galilee (see the map on page 1343). He grew up helping in Joseph's carpenter's shop until He was thirty years old. (Remember that Jesus was the Son of God, but Joseph raised Jesus like his own son.)

Then Jesus announced that He was the promised Messiah. This confused the citizens of Nazareth, who remembered Him only as a humble carpenter. They certainly weren't looking for a carpenter to be their Messiah, and they were offended at the idea.

The Jews thought their Messiah should be a very important person, like a king. But Jesus didn't act like royalty. He didn't wear expensive clothes, ride on the finest horse, or have soldiers to protect Him. This wonderful, humble Man was their King from heaven.

out and saying, "You are the **Christ, the Son of God!**"

And He, rebuking *them,* did not allow them to speak, for they knew that He was the Christ.

42 Now when it was day, He departed and went into a deserted place. And the crowd sought Him and came to Him, and tried to keep Him from leaving them; 43 but He said to them, "I must preach the kingdom of God to the other cities also, because for this purpose I have been sent." 44 And He was preaching in the synagogues of Galilee.

Jesus is a friend to the sick and sinful

5 So it was, as the multitude pressed about Him to hear the word of God, that He stood by the Lake of Gennesaret, 2 and saw two boats standing by the lake; but the fishermen had gone from them and were washing *their* nets. 3 Then He got into one of the boats, which was Simon's, and asked him to put out a little from the land. And He sat down and taught the multitudes from the boat.

4 When He had stopped speaking, He said to Simon, "Launch out into the deep and let down your nets for a catch."

5 But Simon answered and said to Him, "Master, we have toiled all night and caught nothing; nevertheless at Your word I will let down the net." 6 And when they had done this, they caught a great number of fish, and their net was breaking. 7 So they signaled to *their* partners in the other boat to come and help them. And they came and filled both the boats, so that they began to sink. 8 When Simon Peter saw *it,* he fell down at Jesus' knees, saying, "Depart from me, for I am a sinful man, O Lord!"

9 For he and all who were with him were astonished at the catch of fish which they had taken; 10 and so also *were* James and John, the sons of Zeb-

DIGGING IN

4:40 Diseases in Bible Times Most of the diseases you read about in the Bible also exist today.

Pestilence (pronounced *PEST-ih-lunce*) and *plague* (pronounced *PLAYG*) are common words to describe severe contagious diseases. The dreaded bubonic plague was one of these. This was a terrible disease that also broke out in Europe three hundred years ago and killed many people. It was carried by the fleas on rats. Job suffered from boils (see Book of Job). Deafness and the inability to speak (deaf-mute) was a physical problem that Jesus often healed.

Other diseases were eczema, tumors, epilepsy, leprosy, paralysis, and tuberculosis (called "wasting disease" in the Bible).

Jesus is the Great Physician.

New Preacher Becoming Famous

Nazareth News Leader

NAZARETH—The Carpenter-Preacher named Jesus is fast becoming one of the most popular speakers in the country of Galilee. People are reporting amazing things about Him.

Jesus is teaching that evil spirits, or demons, can actually live in people. He often commands these demons to leave. In Capernaum (pronounced *kuh-PURR-nih-um*), where Jesus is now living, He recently drove a demon out of a man. A reliable eyewitness states that some of the spirits even confessed that Jesus is the Christ, the Son of God!

Not only this, but many people are bringing sick members of their families to Jesus, and He heals all of them!

Can this Man Jesus really be the Christ as some are saying? Evidence in favor of this opinion seems to be growing. Reporters of the *News Leader* will follow this story with interest.

edee, who were partners with Simon. And Jesus said to Simon, "Do not be afraid. From now on you will catch men." ¹¹ So when they had brought their boats to land, they forsook all and followed Him.

¹² And it happened when He was in a certain city, that behold, a man who was full of leprosy saw Jesus; and he fell on *his* face and implored Him, saying, "Lord, if You are willing, You can make me clean."

What Is Leprosy?

There are several diseases called leprosy (pronounced *LEP-rah-see*), but leprosy in the Bible was a bad form of a modern skin disease called psoriasis (pronounced *so-RIGH-uh-sis*). Moses' sister Miriam and King Uzziah (pronounced *uh-ZIGH-uh*) were struck with leprosy when they sinned (see Numbers 12 and 2 Chronicles 26). Jesus healed many lepers.

¹³ Then He put out *His* hand and touched him, saying, "I am willing; be cleansed." Immediately the leprosy left him. ¹⁴ And He charged him to tell no one, "But go and show yourself to the priest, and make an offering for your cleansing, as a testimony to them, just as Moses commanded."

¹⁵ However, the report went around concerning Him all the more; and great multitudes came together to hear, and to be healed by Him of their infirmities. ¹⁶ So He Himself *often* withdrew into the wilderness and prayed.

¹⁷ Now it happened on a certain day, as He was teaching, that there were Pharisees and teachers of the law sitting by, who had come out of every town of Galilee, Judea, and Jerusalem. And the power of the Lord was *present* to heal them. ¹⁸ Then behold, men brought on a bed a man who was

Leprosy, a serious skin disease, afflicted many people in Jesus' day.

paralyzed, whom they sought to bring in and lay before Him. ¹⁹ And when they could not find how they might bring him in, because of the crowd, they went up on the housetop and let him down with *his* bed through the tiling into the midst before Jesus.

²⁰ When He saw their faith, He said to him, "Man, your sins are forgiven you."

²¹ And the scribes and the Pharisees began to reason, saying, "Who is this who speaks blasphemies? Who can forgive sins but God alone?"

²² But when Jesus perceived their thoughts, He answered and said to them, "Why are you reasoning in your hearts? ²³ Which is easier, to say, 'Your sins are forgiven you,' or to say, 'Rise up and walk'? ²⁴ But that you may know that the Son of Man has power on earth to forgive sins"—He said to

How Could Jesus Heal a Man Who Couldn't Walk?

Not everybody can command lame people to walk, but Jesus could. In fact, He healed a lot of people with many diseases. By doing this, Jesus was teaching us that He has all power over nature because He is the Son of God. We need to know that Jesus is still all-powerful.

the man who was paralyzed, "I say to you, arise, take up your bed, and go to your house."

²⁵ Immediately he rose up before them, took up what he had been lying on, and departed to his own house, glorifying God. ²⁶ And they were all amazed, and they glorified God and

DIGGING IN

5:28 Who Were the Tax Collectors?
The Roman government, which ruled the Jews in Jesus' day, required several kinds of taxes, including a land tax and a personal tax.

The Jewish tax collectors were despised because they worked for the hated Romans. Besides, some tax collectors kept tax money for themselves. So these men were treated as "sinners" by the rest of the people. John the Baptist warned the tax collectors to be honest in their work (see Luke 3:12, 13).

It may seem strange that Jesus befriended tax collectors. He even asked Matthew, a tax collector, to be one of His disciples! Matthew is the disciple who wrote the first Gospel of the New Testament.

Jesus loved men and women that most people hated! Doesn't that make you stop and think?

Levi (Matthew), a tax collector, was chosen by Jesus to be one of His disciples.

were filled with fear, saying, "We have seen strange things today!"

27 After these things He went out and saw a tax collector named Levi, sitting at the tax office. And He said to him, "Follow Me." 28 So he left all, rose up, and followed Him.

29 Then Levi gave Him a great feast in his own house. And there were a great number of tax collectors and others who sat down with them. 30 And their scribes and the Pharisees complained against His disciples, saying, "Why do You eat and drink with tax collectors and sinners?"

31 Jesus answered and said to them, "Those who are well have no need of a physician, but those who are sick. 32 I have not come to call *the* righteous, but sinners, to repentance."

33 Then they said to Him, "Why do the disciples of John fast often and make prayers, and likewise those of the Pharisees, but Yours eat and drink?" 34 And He said to them, "Can you make the friends of the bridegroom fast while the bridegroom is with them? 35 But the days will come when the bridegroom will be taken away from them; then they will fast in those days."

36 Then He spoke a parable to them: "No one puts a piece from a new garment on an old one; otherwise the new makes a tear, and also the piece that was *taken* out of the new does not match the old. 37 And no one puts new wine into old wineskins; or else the new wine will burst the wineskins and be spilled, and the wineskins will be ruined. 38 But new wine must be put into new wineskins, and both are preserved. 39 And no one, having drunk old *wine,* immediately desires new; for he says, 'The old is better.' "

Jesus begins to teach His disciples

6 Now it happened on the second Sabbath after the first that He went through the grainfields. And His disciples plucked the heads of grain and ate *them,* rubbing *them* in *their* hands. 2 And some of the Pharisees said to them, "Why are you doing what is not lawful to do on the Sabbath?"

3 But Jesus answering them said, "Have you not even read this, what David did when he was hungry, he and those who were with him: 4 how he went into the house of God, took and ate the showbread, and also gave some to those with him, which is not lawful for any but the priests to eat?" 5 And He said to them, "The Son of Man is also Lord of the Sabbath."

6 Now it happened on another Sabbath, also, that He entered the synagogue and taught. And a man was there whose right hand was withered. 7 So the scribes and Pharisees watched Him closely, whether He would heal on the Sabbath, that they might find an accusation against Him. 8 But He knew their thoughts, and said to the man who had the withered hand, "Arise and stand here." And he arose and stood. 9 Then Jesus said to them, "I will ask you one thing: Is it lawful on the Sabbath to do good or to do evil, to save life or to destroy?" 10 And when He had looked around at them all, He said to the man, "Stretch out your hand." And he did so, and his hand was restored as whole as the other. 11 But they were filled with rage, and discussed with one another what they might do to Jesus.

12 Now it came to pass in those days that He went out to the mountain to pray, and continued all night in prayer to God. 13 And when it was day, He called His disciples to *Himself;* and from them He chose twelve whom He also named apostles: 14 Simon, whom He also named Peter, and Andrew his brother; James and John; Philip and Bartholomew; 15 Matthew and Thomas; James the *son* of Alphaeus, and Simon called the **Zealot;** 16 Judas

---

WORDFINDER

6:15 Zealot Pronounced ZELL-ut. A member of the Zealot political party in Jesus' time. This group of Jews was trying to raise a military revolt against the Romans.

Jesus of Nazareth Stirs Up Trouble

Nazareth News Leader

NAZARETH—The new Preacher in Galilee is being praised by the people as an even greater Teacher than John the Baptizer. John didn't heal sick people or drive out demons, but Jesus does, as many have reported.

Some of our religious authorities, however, are angry. They say the Man Jesus is really a false teacher and should be punished. Following are some of the reasons for their opinion:

Our people have always honored God's law about the Sabbath (see Exodus 20:8–11). But the Pharisees say Jesus breaks the Sabbath. His disciples were seen picking grain in the fields and eating it on God's day. This amounts to reaping on the Sabbath!

Jesus has also been seen healing people on the Sabbath. Our leaders are greatly disturbed by these actions. They are now trying to decide what to do about the new Preacher.

What do our readers think?

the son of James, and Judas Iscariot who also became a traitor.

17 And He came down with them and stood on a level place with a crowd of His disciples and a great multitude of people from all Judea and Jerusalem, and from the seacoast of Tyre and Sidon, who came to hear Him and be healed of their diseases, 18 as well as those who were tormented with unclean spirits. And they were healed. 19 And the whole multitude sought to touch Him, for power went out from Him and healed them all.

20 Then He lifted up His eyes toward His disciples, and said:

"Blessed are you poor,
    For yours is the kingdom of God.
21 Blessed are you who hunger now,
    For you shall be filled.
Blessed are you who weep now,
    For you shall laugh.
22 Blessed are you when men hate you,

And when they exclude you,
And revile you, and cast out your name as evil,
    For the **Son of Man's** sake.
23 Rejoice in that day and leap for joy!
    For indeed your reward is great in **heaven**,
    For in like manner their fathers did to the prophets.

24 "But woe to you who are rich,
    For you have received your consolation.
25 Woe to you who are full,
    For you shall hunger.
Woe to you who laugh now,
    For you shall mourn and weep.
26 Woe to you when all men speak well of you,
    For so did their fathers to the false prophets.

27 "But I say to you who hear: Love your enemies, do good to those who hate you, 28 bless those who curse you, and pray for those who spitefully use

WORDFINDER

6:22 Son of Man A title first used by the prophet Ezekiel (see Ezekiel 2:1). Jesus used the title in a special way to refer to His divine authority as the supreme Man.

6:23 Heaven The dwelling place of God, angels, and souls of the dead who belong to God. That heaven is not part of our universe, but sometimes the word refers to the sky (see Genesis 1:8).

you. ²⁹ To him who strikes you on the *one* cheek, offer the other also. And from him who takes away your cloak, do not withhold *your* tunic either. ³⁰ Give to everyone who asks of you. And from him who takes away your goods do not ask *them* back. ³¹ And just as you want men to do to you, you also do to them likewise.

³² "But if you love those who love you, what credit is that to you? For even sinners love those who love them. ³³ And if you do good to those who do good to you, what credit is that to you? For even sinners do the same. ³⁴ And if you lend *to those* from whom you hope to receive back, what credit is that to you? For even sinners lend to sinners to receive as much back. ³⁵ But love your enemies, do good, and lend, hoping for nothing in return; and your reward will be great, and you will be sons of the Most High. For He is kind to the unthankful and evil. ³⁶ Therefore be merciful, just as your Father also is merciful.

³⁷ "Judge not, and you shall not be judged. Condemn not, and you shall not be condemned. Forgive, and you will be forgiven. ³⁸ Give, and it will be given to you: good measure, pressed down, shaken together, and running over will be put into your bosom. For with the same measure that you use, it will be measured back to you."

³⁹ And He spoke a parable to them: "Can the blind lead the blind? Will they not both fall into the ditch? ⁴⁰ A disciple is not above his teacher, but everyone who is perfectly trained will be like his teacher. ⁴¹ And why do you look at the speck in your brother's eye, but do not perceive the plank in your own eye? ⁴² Or how can you say to your brother, 'Brother, let me remove the speck that *is* in your eye,' when you yourself do not see the plank that *is* in your own eye? Hypocrite! First remove the plank from your own eye, and then you will see clearly to remove the speck that is in your brother's eye.

⁴³ "For a good tree does not bear bad fruit, nor does a bad tree bear good fruit. ⁴⁴ For every tree is known by its own fruit. For *men* do not gather figs from thorns, nor do they gather grapes from a bramble bush. ⁴⁵ A good man out of the good treasure of his heart brings forth good; and an evil man out of the evil treasure of his heart brings forth evil. For out of the abundance of the heart his mouth speaks.

⁴⁶ "But why do you call Me 'Lord, Lord,' and not do the things which I say? ⁴⁷ Whoever comes to Me, and hears My sayings and does them, I will show you whom he is like: ⁴⁸ He is like a man building a house, who dug deep and laid the foundation on the rock. And when the flood arose, the stream beat vehemently against that house, and could not shake it, for it was founded on the rock. ⁴⁹ But he who heard and did nothing is like a man who built a house on the earth without a foundation, against which the stream beat vehemently; and immediately it fell. And the ruin of that house was great."

⚒ DIGGING IN

6:46–49 Build Your Life on Jesus

You build your life on another person by following his example and doing what he says.

Jesus rightly complains that many people only pretend to be His disciples. They say, "Lord, Lord!" But their worship is only words and no deeds. They don't do what Jesus says.

Jesus spent His early years as a carpenter, and He knew about building a strong foundation. If you don't have a good foundation, the whole building will come tumbling down when the wind and the rain beat on the house.

You are like that house. Jesus is the foundation you can build your life on. Take the things Jesus says—like building blocks—into your mind and heart. Then you will be like a strong house that the powerful winds of life can't blow down. Yes, your house will stand forever!

Jesus heals the sick and raises the dead

7 Now when He concluded all His sayings in the hearing of the people, He entered Capernaum. ² And a certain centurion's servant, who was dear to him, was sick and ready to die. ³ So when he heard about Jesus, he sent elders of the Jews to Him, pleading with Him to come and heal his servant. ⁴ And when they came to Jesus, they begged Him earnestly, saying that the one for whom He should do this was deserving, ⁵ "for he loves our nation, and has built us a synagogue."

⁶ Then Jesus went with them. And when He was already not far from the house, the centurion sent friends to Him, saying to Him, "Lord, do not trouble Yourself, for I am not worthy that You should enter under my roof. ⁷ Therefore I did not even think myself worthy to come to You. But say the word, and my servant will be healed. ⁸ For I also am a man placed under authority, having soldiers under me. And I say to one, 'Go,' and he goes; and to another, 'Come,' and he comes; and to my servant, 'Do this,' and he does it."

⁹ When Jesus heard these things, He marveled at him, and turned around and said to the crowd that followed Him, "I say to you, I have not found such great faith, not even in Israel!"

¹⁰ And those who were sent, returning to the house, found the servant well who had been sick.

¹¹ Now it happened, the day after, that He went into a city called Nain; and many of His disciples went with Him, and a large crowd. ¹² And when He came near the gate of the city, behold, a dead man was being carried out, the only son of his mother; and she was a widow. And a large crowd from the city was with her. ¹³ When the Lord saw her, He had compassion on her and said to her, "Do not weep." ¹⁴ Then He came and touched the open coffin, and those who carried him stood still. And He said, "Young man, I say to you, arise." ¹⁵ So he who was dead sat up and began to speak. And He presented him to his mother.

¹⁶ Then fear came upon all, and they glorified God, saying, "A great prophet has risen up among us"; and, "God has visited His people." ¹⁷ And this report about Him went throughout all Judea and all the surrounding region.

¹⁸ Then the disciples of John reported to him concerning all these things. ¹⁹ And John, calling two of his disciples to him, sent them to Jesus, saying, "Are You the Coming One, or do we look for another?"

²⁰ When the men had come to Him, they said, "John the Baptist has sent us to You, saying, 'Are You the Coming One, or do we look for another?'"

What John the Baptist Learned

For some time I had been preaching that the Messiah was coming and that we should get ready to meet Him.

I was expecting the Messiah to drive out our Roman enemies. Then He would set up His kingdom in Jerusalem and rule over the whole world. But it didn't happen that way. Because of my preaching, I was arrested and put in jail.

So I sent word to ask Jesus why He had not set up His kingdom. But He only answered that people were being saved from their diseases and other miseries.

That was very hard for me to understand right then. Later, I realized Jesus knew just what He was doing. He was the King who came to give us the life of God. You can have that life, too.

21 And that very hour He cured many of infirmities, afflictions, and evil spirits; and to many blind He gave sight.

22 Jesus answered and said to them, "Go and tell John the things you have seen and heard: that *the* blind see, *the* lame walk, *the* lepers are cleansed, *the* deaf hear, *the* dead are raised, *the* poor have the gospel preached to them. 23 And blessed is *he* who is not offended because of Me."

24 When the messengers of John had departed, He began to speak to the multitudes concerning John: "What did you go out into the wilderness to see? A reed shaken by the wind? 25 But what did you go out to see? A man clothed in soft garments? Indeed those who are gorgeously apparelled and live in luxury are in kings' courts. 26 But what did you go out to see? A prophet? Yes, I say to you, and more than a prophet. 27 This is *he* of whom it is written:

'Behold, I send My messenger
    before Your face,
Who will prepare Your way
    before You.'

28 For I say to you, among those born of women there is not a greater prophet than John the Baptist; but he who is least in the kingdom of God is greater than he."

29 And when all the people heard *Him,* even the tax collectors justified God, having been baptized with the baptism of John. 30 But the Pharisees and lawyers rejected the will of God for themselves, not having been baptized by him.

31 And the Lord said, "To what then shall I liken the men of this generation, and what are they like? 32 They are like children sitting in the marketplace and calling to one another, saying:

'We played the flute for you,
    And you did not dance;
We mourned to you,
    And you did not weep.'

33 For John the Baptist came neither eating bread nor drinking wine, and you say, 'He has a demon.' 34 The Son of Man has come eating and drinking, and you say, 'Look, a glutton and a winebibber, a friend of tax collectors and sinners!' 35 But wisdom is justified by all her children."

36 Then one of the Pharisees asked Him to eat with him. And He went to the Pharisee's house, and sat down to eat. 37 And behold, a woman in the city who was a sinner, when she knew that *Jesus* sat at the table in the Pharisee's house, brought an alabaster flask of fragrant oil, 38 and stood at His feet behind *Him* weeping; and she began to wash His feet with her tears, and wiped *them* with the hair of her head; and she kissed His feet and anointed *them* with the fragrant oil. 39 Now when the Pharisee who had invited Him saw *this,* he spoke to himself, saying, "This Man, if He were a prophet, would know who and what manner of woman *this is* who is touching Him, for she is a sinner."

40 And Jesus answered and said to him, "Simon, I have something to say to you."

So he said, "Teacher, say it."

41 "There was a certain creditor who had two debtors. One owed five hundred denarii, and the other fifty. 42 And when they had nothing with which to repay, he freely forgave them both. Tell Me, therefore, which of them will love him more?"

43 Simon answered and said, "I suppose the *one* whom he forgave more."

And He said to him, "You have rightly judged." 44 Then He turned to the woman and said to Simon, "Do you see this woman? I entered your house; you gave Me no water for My feet, but she has washed My feet with her tears and wiped *them* with the hair of her head. 45 You gave Me no kiss, but this woman has not ceased to kiss My feet since the time I came in. 46 You did not anoint My head with oil, but this woman has anointed My feet with fragrant oil. 47 Therefore I say to you, her sins, *which are* many, are forgiven, for she loved much. But to whom little is forgiven, *the same* loves little."

⁴⁸ Then He said to her, "Your sins are forgiven."

⁴⁹ And those who sat at the table with Him began to say to themselves, "Who is this who even forgives sins?"

⁵⁰ Then He said to the woman, "Your faith has saved you. Go in peace."

Jesus tells stories about His kingdom

8 Now it came to pass, afterward, that He went through every city and village, preaching and bringing the glad tidings of the kingdom of God. And the twelve *were* with Him, ² and certain women who had been healed of evil spirits and infirmities—Mary called Magdalene, out of whom had come seven demons, ³ and Joanna the wife of Chuza, Herod's steward, and Susanna, and many others who provided for Him from their substance.

⁴ And when a great multitude had gathered, and they had come to Him from every city, He spoke by a parable: ⁵ "A sower went out to sow his seed. And as he sowed, some fell by the wayside; and it was trampled down, and the birds of the air devoured it. ⁶ Some fell on rock; and as soon as it sprang up, it withered away because it lacked moisture. ⁷ And some fell among thorns, and the thorns sprang

up with it and choked it. ⁸ But others fell on good ground, sprang up, and yielded a crop a hundredfold." When He had said these things He cried, "He who has ears to hear, let him hear!"

⁹ Then His disciples asked Him, saying, "What does this parable mean?"

¹⁰ And He said, "To you it has been given to know the **mysteries** of the kingdom of God, but to the rest *it is given* in parables, that

'Seeing they may not see,
And hearing they may not
   understand.'

¹¹ "Now the parable is this: The seed is the word of God. ¹² Those by the wayside are the ones who hear; then the devil comes and takes away the word out of their hearts, lest they should believe and be saved. ¹³ But the ones on the rock *are those* who, when they hear, receive the word with joy; and these have no root, who believe for a while and in time of temptation fall away. ¹⁴ Now the ones *that* fell among thorns are those who, when they have heard, go out and are choked with cares, riches, and pleasures of life, and bring no fruit to maturity. ¹⁵ But the ones *that* fell on the good ground are those who, having heard the word with a noble and good heart, keep *it* and bear fruit with patience.

¹⁶ "No one, when he has lit a lamp,

WORDFINDER

8:10 Mysteries Things that are not known. Paul spoke about "the mysteries of God." These were things that weren't known until Jesus came and revealed the gospel.

DIGGING IN

8:16–18 Let Your Light Shine What good is a light if it doesn't help you see in the dark? What would you think if your parents went around covering all the lamps in your home? Wouldn't that be foolish!

Jesus commands you to *let your light shine*. What light? Let the light of Jesus shine in your life. Your actions must show that Jesus lives in you. People look for a light when it is dark. They need the light

of Jesus to show them the way through a dark and frightening world.

Some Christians hide their light. They seem afraid to let others know how much Jesus means to them. If people can see how much Jesus has done for you, then they, too, will come to Jesus. Jesus is this dark world's true light (see John 9:5). He is the only One who can light our way to heaven.

What Jesus' Family Learned

Jesus grew up in the same home with us, so it seemed very strange that He was too busy to talk to us when we came to see Him.

Then Jesus said something we always remembered. He told us that His real mother and brothers are those who hear God's Word and do it! Jesus did love our mother. Even when He was dying on the Cross, He told John to take care of her. You can read this in John 19:26, 27.

Jesus could be with us for only a little while. He had come from His Father's throne to do His Father's work. Now the Holy Spirit will help us be the disciples of Jesus. He can help you follow Jesus, too.

---

covers it with a vessel or puts *it* under a bed, but sets *it* on a lampstand, that those who enter may see the light. 17 For nothing is secret that will not be revealed, nor *anything* hidden that will not be known and come to light. 18 Therefore take heed how you hear. For whoever has, to him *more* will be given; and whoever does not have, even what he seems to have will be taken from him."

19 Then His mother and brothers came to Him, and could not approach Him because of the crowd. 20 And it was told Him *by some,* who said, "Your mother and Your brothers are standing outside, desiring to see You."

21 But He answered and said to them, "My mother and My brothers are these who hear the word of God and do it."

22 Now it happened, on a certain day, that He got into a boat with His disciples. And He said to them, "Let us cross over to the other side of the lake." And they launched out. 23 But as they sailed He fell asleep. And a windstorm came down on the lake, and they were filling *with water,* and were in jeopardy. 24 And they came to Him and awoke Him, saying, "Master, Master, we are perishing!"

Then He arose and rebuked the wind and the raging of the water. And they ceased, and there was a calm. 25 But He said to them, "Where is your faith?"

And they were afraid, and marveled, saying to one another, "Who can this be? For He commands even the winds and water, and they obey Him!"

26 Then they sailed to the country of the **Gadarenes,** which is opposite Galilee. 27 And when He stepped out on the land, there met Him a certain man from the city who had demons for a long time. And he wore no clothes, nor did he live in a house but in the tombs. 28 When he saw Jesus, he cried out, fell down before Him, and with a loud voice said, "What have I to do with You, Jesus, Son of the Most High God? I beg You, do not torment me!" 29 For He had commanded the unclean spirit to come out of the man. For it had often seized him, and he was kept under guard, bound with chains and shackles; and he broke the bonds and was driven by the demon into the wilderness.

30 Jesus asked him, saying, "What is your name?"

And he said, "Legion," because many demons had entered him. 31 And they begged Him that He would not command them to go out into the abyss.

32 Now a herd of many swine was

WORDFINDER

8:26 Gadarenes (Pronounced *GAD-uh-reens*). People who lived in the city of Gadara, about six miles southeast of the Sea of Galilee. Gadara was one of the group called "Ten Cities."

The village of Gadara, where Jesus drove demons out of a man.

feeding there on the mountain. So they begged Him that He would permit them to enter them. And He permitted them. 33 Then the demons went out of the man and entered the swine, and the herd ran violently down the steep place into the lake and drowned.

34 When those who fed *them* saw what had happened, they fled and told *it* in the city and in the country. 35 Then they went out to see what had happened, and came to Jesus, and found the man from whom the demons had departed, sitting at the feet of Jesus, clothed and in his right mind. And they were afraid. 36 They also who had seen *it* told them by what means he who had been demon-possessed was healed. 37 Then the whole multitude of the surrounding region of the Gadarenes asked Him to depart from them, for they were seized with great fear. And He got into the boat and returned.

38 Now the man from whom the demons had departed begged Him that he might be with Him. But Jesus sent him away, saying, 39 "Return to your own house, and tell what great things God has done for you." And he went his way and proclaimed throughout the whole city what great things Jesus had done for him.

40 So it was, when Jesus returned, that the multitude welcomed Him, for they were all waiting for Him. 41 And behold, there came a man named Jairus, and he was a ruler of the synagogue. And he fell down at Jesus' feet and begged Him to come to his house, 42 for he had an only daughter about twelve years of age, and she was dying.

But as He went, the multitudes thronged Him. 43 Now a woman, having a flow of blood for twelve years, who had spent all her livelihood on physicians and could not be healed by any, 44 came from behind and touched the border of His garment. And immediately her flow of blood stopped.

45 And Jesus said, "Who touched Me?"

When all denied it, Peter and those with him said, "Master, the multitudes throng and press You, and You say, 'Who touched Me?'"

46 But Jesus said, "Somebody touched Me, for I perceived power going out from Me." 47 Now when the woman saw that she was not hidden, she came trembling; and falling down before Him, she declared to Him in

the presence of all the people the reason she had touched Him and how she was healed immediately.

48 And He said to her, "Daughter, be of good cheer; your faith has made you well. Go in peace."

49 While He was still speaking, someone came from the ruler of the synagogue's *house,* saying to him, "Your daughter is dead. Do not trouble the Teacher."

50 But when Jesus heard *it,* He answered him, saying, "Do not be afraid; only believe, and she will be made well." 51 When He came into the house, He permitted no one to go in except Peter, James, and John, and the father and mother of the girl. 52 Now all wept and mourned for her; but He said, "Do not weep; she is not dead, but sleeping." 53 And they ridiculed Him, knowing that she was dead.

54 But He put them all outside, took her by the hand and called, saying, "Little girl, arise." 55 Then her spirit returned, and she arose immediately. And He commanded that she be given *something* to eat. 56 And her parents were astonished, but He charged them to tell no one what had happened.

What does it cost to follow Jesus?

9 Then He called His twelve disciples together and gave them power and authority over all demons, and to cure diseases. 2 He sent them to preach the kingdom of God and to heal the sick. 3 And He said to them, "Take nothing for the journey, neither staffs nor bag nor bread nor money; and do not have two tunics apiece.

4 "Whatever house you enter, stay there, and from there depart. 5 And whoever will not receive you, when you go out of that city, shake off the very dust from your feet as a testimony against them."

6 So they departed and went through the towns, preaching the gospel and healing everywhere.

7 Now Herod the tetrarch heard of all that was done by Him; and he was perplexed, because it was said by some that John had risen from the dead, 8 and by some that Elijah had appeared, and by others that one of the old prophets had risen again. 9 Herod said, "John I have beheaded, but who is this of whom I hear such things?" So he sought to see Him.

10 And the apostles, when they had returned, told Him all that they had done. Then He took them and went aside privately into a deserted place belonging to the city called Bethsaida. 11 But when the multitudes knew *it,* they followed Him; and He received them and spoke to them about the kingdom of God, and healed those who had need of healing. 12 When the day began to wear away, the twelve came and said to Him, "Send the multitude away, that they may go into the surrounding towns and country, and lodge and get provisions; for we are in a deserted place here."

13 But He said to them, "You give them something to eat."

And they said, "We have no more than five loaves and two fish, unless we go and buy food for all these people." 14 For there were about five thousand men.

Then He said to His disciples, "Make them sit down in groups of fifty." 15 And they did so, and made them all sit down.

16 Then He took the five loaves and the two fish, and looking up to heaven, He blessed and broke *them,* and gave *them* to the disciples to set before the multitude. 17 So they all ate and were filled, and twelve baskets of the leftover fragments were taken up by them.

18 And it happened, as He was alone

 DIGGING IN

9:18–20 Confessing Christ Jesus left His throne in heaven to live among us like a servant. The apostle Paul says He "made Himself of no reputation" (Philippians 2:7). In other words, Jesus tried very hard to *look unimportant.* If He was really praying, *that* His disciples joined Him, and He asked them, saying, "Who do the crowds say that I am?"

19 So they answered and said, "John the Baptist, but some *say* Elijah; and others *say* that one of the old prophets has risen again."

20 He said to them, "But who do you say that I am?"

Peter answered and said, "The Christ of God."

21 And He strictly warned and commanded them to tell this to no one, 22 saying, "The Son of Man must suffer many things, and be rejected by the elders and chief priests and scribes, and be killed, and be raised the third day."

23 Then He said to *them* all, "If anyone desires to come after Me, let him deny himself, and take up his cross daily, and follow Me. 24 For whoever desires to save his life will lose it, but whoever loses his life for My sake will save it. 25 For what profit is it to a man if he gains the whole world, and is himself destroyed or lost? 26 For whoever is ashamed of Me and My words, of him the Son of Man will be ashamed when He comes in His *own* glory, and *in His* Father's, and of the holy angels.

27 But I tell you truly, there are some standing here who shall not taste death till they see the kingdom of God."

28 Now it came to pass, about eight days after these sayings, that He took Peter, John, and James and went up on the mountain to pray. 29 As He prayed, the appearance of His face was altered, and His robe *became* white *and* glistening. 30 And behold, two men talked with Him, who were Moses and Elijah, 31 who appeared in glory and spoke of His decease which He was about to accomplish at Jerusalem. 32 But Peter and those with him were heavy with sleep; and when they were fully awake, they saw His glory and the two men who stood with Him. 33 Then it happened, as they were parting from Him, *that* Peter said to Jesus, "Master, it is good for us to be here; and let us make three tabernacles: one for You, one for Moses, and one for Elijah"—not knowing what he said.

34 While he was saying this, a cloud came and overshadowed them; and they were fearful as they entered the cloud. 35 And a voice came out of the cloud, saying, "This is My beloved Son. Hear Him!" 36 When the voice had ceased, Jesus was found alone. But they kept quiet, and told no one in those days any of the things they had seen.

37 Now it happened on the next day, when they had come down from the mountain, that a great multitude met Him. 38 Suddenly a man from the multitude cried out, saying, "Teacher, I implore You, look on my son, for he is my only child. 39 And behold, a spirit seizes him, and he suddenly cries out; it convulses him so that he foams *at the mouth;* and it departs from him with great difficulty, bruising him. 40 So I implored Your disciples to cast it out, but they could not."

41 Then Jesus answered and said, "O faithless and perverse generation, how long shall I be with you and bear with you? Bring your son here." 42 And as he was still coming, the demon threw him down and convulsed *him.* Then Jesus rebuked the unclean

DIGGING IN

the Messiah, why didn't He show off His great power? But Jesus refused to do that.

For a long time, even the 12 disciples weren't really sure who He was. Then one day He asked them, "Who do you say I am?" Peter gave the right answer—"The Christ of God." Now the disciples knew who Jesus was. Even so, they all ran away when He was crucified.

Do you know who Jesus is? If you do, then pray every day that you will never deny Him as the disciples did. Peter promised he would never deny Jesus, but he did! As Jesus said, "Without Me you can do nothing" (John 15:5).

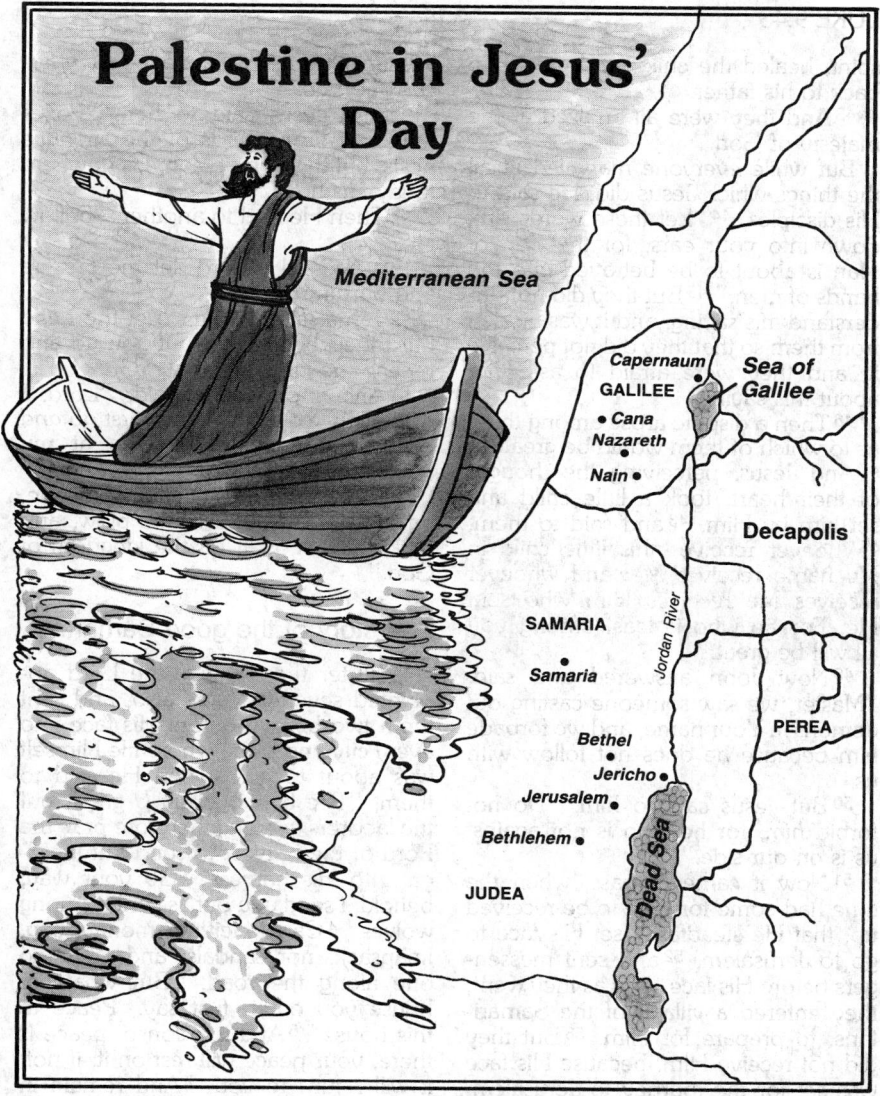

Palestine in Jesus' Day

Mediterranean Sea

Capernaum
GALILEE
Sea of Galilee
Cana
Nazareth
Nain
Decapolis
SAMARIA
Samaria
Jordan River
PEREA
Bethel
Jericho
Jerusalem
Bethlehem
Dead Sea
JUDEA

Jesus never traveled very far from his hometown of Nazareth in Galilee. But everywhere He went, He brought joy, peace, and healing.

In Cana, He attended a wedding where He helped the hostess when she ran out of refreshments (John 2:1–11).

In Capernaum, He invited Matthew to be His disciple (Mark 2:14), healed a soldier's paralyzed servant (Matthew 8:5–13), and healed Peter's mother-in-law of a fever (vv. 14, 15).

In a boat on the Sea of Galilee, He quieted a storm and saved His disciples from capsizing in the high waves (Mark 4:35–41).

In Samaria, He healed ten lepers (Luke 17:11–19).

In Jericho, He restored the sight of a blind man (Luke 18:35–43) and went home with Zaccheus, the tax collector (Luke 19:1–10).

"Jesus went about doing good."

spirit, healed the child, and gave him back to his father.

43 And they were all amazed at the majesty of God.

But while everyone marveled at all the things which Jesus did, He said to His disciples, 44 "Let these words sink down into your ears, for the Son of Man is about to be betrayed into the hands of men." 45 But they did not understand this saying, and it was hidden from them so that they did not perceive it; and they were afraid to ask Him about this saying.

46 Then a dispute arose among them as to which of them would be greatest. 47 And Jesus, perceiving the thought of their heart, took a little child and set him by Him, 48 and said to them, "Whoever receives this little child in My name receives Me; and whoever receives Me receives Him who sent Me. For he who is least among you all will be great."

49 Now John answered and said, "Master, we saw someone casting out demons in Your name, and we forbade him because he does not follow with us."

50 But Jesus said to him, "Do not forbid him, for he who is not against us is on our side."

51 Now it came to pass, when the time had come for Him to be received up, that He steadfastly set His face to go to Jerusalem, 52 and sent messengers before His face. And as they went, they entered a village of the Samaritans, to prepare for Him. 53 But they did not receive Him, because His face was set for the journey to Jerusalem. 54 And when His disciples James and John saw this, they said, "Lord, do You want us to command fire to come down from heaven and consume them, just as Elijah did?"

55 But He turned and rebuked them, and said, "You do not know what manner of spirit you are of. 56 For the Son of Man did not come to destroy men's lives but to save them." And they went to another village.

57 Now it happened as they journeyed on the road, that someone said to Him, "Lord, I will follow You wherever You go."

58 And Jesus said to him, "Foxes have holes and birds of the air have nests, but the Son of Man has nowhere to lay His head."

59 Then He said to another, "Follow Me."

But he said, "Lord, let me first go and bury my father."

60 Jesus said to him, "Let the dead bury their own dead, but you go and preach the kingdom of God."

61 And another also said, "Lord, I will follow You, but let me first go and bid them farewell who are at my house."

62 But Jesus said to him, "No one, having put his hand to the plow, and looking back, is fit for the kingdom of God."

The story of the good Samaritan

10 After these things the Lord appointed seventy others also, and sent them two by two before His face into every city and place where He Himself was about to go. 2 Then He said to them, "The harvest truly is great, but the laborers are few; therefore pray the Lord of the harvest to send out laborers into His harvest. 3 Go your way; behold, I send you out as lambs among wolves. 4 Carry neither money bag, knapsack, nor sandals; and greet no one along the road. 5 But whatever house you enter, first say, 'Peace to this house.' 6 And if a son of peace is there, your peace will rest on it; if not, it will return to you. 7 And remain in the same house, eating and drinking such things as they give, for the laborer is worthy of his wages. Do not go from house to house. 8 Whatever city you enter, and they receive you, eat such things as are set before you. 9 And heal the sick there, and say to them, 'The kingdom of God has come near to you.' 10 But whatever city you enter, and they do not receive you, go out into its streets and say, 11 'The very dust of your city which clings to us we wipe off against you. Nevertheless

What the Lawyer Learned

I've been an expert in the law for many years, and one day I tried to trick Jesus with a question about the law. But He only answered me from God's Word. He told me I must love God and my neighbor. Now how could I find fault with that?

Then I asked Him just whom He expected me to love. So He told me a story about a good Samaritan (pronounced *suh-MARE-ih-tun*), one of the hated people from Samaria (pronounced *suh-MARE-ee-ah*). Now who ever heard of a *good* Samaritan?

But Jesus actually had the nerve to tell me—a good Jew—that I had to be as good as the Samaritan in His story! I felt like a fool in front of my friends.

I'm still thinking about what Jesus told me.

know this, that the kingdom of God has come near you.' 12 But I say to you that it will be more tolerable in that Day for Sodom than for that city.

13 "Woe to you, Chorazin! Woe to you, Bethsaida! For if the mighty works which were done in you had been done in Tyre and Sidon, they would have repented long ago, sitting in sackcloth and ashes. 14 But it will be more tolerable for Tyre and Sidon at the judgment than for you. 15 And you, Capernaum, who are exalted to heaven, will be brought down to Hades. 16 He who hears you hears Me, he who rejects you rejects Me, and he who rejects Me rejects Him who sent Me."

17 Then the seventy returned with joy, saying, "Lord, even the demons are subject to us in Your name."

18 And He said to them, "I saw Satan fall like lightning from heaven. 19 Behold, I give you the authority to trample on serpents and scorpions, and over all the power of the enemy, and nothing shall by any means hurt you. 20 Nevertheless do not rejoice in this, that the spirits are subject to you, but rather rejoice because your names are written in heaven."

21 In that hour Jesus rejoiced in the Spirit and said, "I thank You, Father, Lord of heaven and earth, that You have hidden these things from *the* wise and prudent and revealed them to babes. Even so, Father, for so it seemed good in Your sight. 22 All things have been delivered to Me by My Father, and no one knows who the Son is except the Father, and who the Father is except the Son, and *the one* to whom the Son wills to reveal *Him*."

23 Then He turned to *His* disciples and said privately, "Blessed *are* the eyes which see the things you see; 24 for I tell you that many prophets and kings have desired to see what you see, and have not seen *it,* and to hear what you hear, and have not heard *it.*"

25 And behold, a certain lawyer stood up and tested Him, saying, "Teacher, what shall I do to inherit eternal life?"

26 He said to him, "What is written in the law? What is your reading *of it?*"

27 So he answered and said, "'You shall love the LORD your God with all your heart, with all your soul, with all your strength, and with all your mind,' and 'your neighbor as yourself.'"

28 And He said to him, "You have answered rightly; do this and you will live."

29 But he, wanting to justify himself, said to Jesus, "And who is my neighbor?"

30 Then Jesus answered and said: "A certain *man* went down from Jerusalem to Jericho, and fell among thieves, who stripped him of his clothing, wounded *him,* and departed, leaving *him* half dead. 31 Now by chance

a certain priest came down that road. And when he saw him, he passed by on the other side. 32 Likewise a Levite, when he arrived at the place, came and looked, and passed by on the other side. 33 But a certain **Samaritan,** as he journeyed, came where he was. And when he saw him, he had compassion. 34 So he went to *him* and bandaged his wounds, pouring on oil and wine; and he set him on his own animal, brought him to an inn, and took care of him. 35 On the next day, when he departed, he took out two denarii, gave *them* to the innkeeper, and said to him, 'Take care of him; and whatever more you spend, when I come again, I will repay you.' 36 So which of these three do you think was neighbor to him who fell among the thieves?"

37 And he said, "He who showed mercy on him."

Then Jesus said to him, "Go and do likewise."

38 Now it happened as they went that He entered a certain village; and a certain woman named Martha welcomed Him into her house. 39 And she had a sister called Mary, who also sat at Jesus' feet and heard His word. 40 But Martha was distracted with much serving, and she approached Him and said, "Lord, do You not care

that my sister has left me to serve alone? Therefore tell her to help me."

41 And Jesus answered and said to her, "Martha, Martha, you are worried and troubled about many things. 42 But one thing is needed, and Mary has chosen that good part, which will not be taken away from her."

Jesus teaches the disciples how to pray

11 Now it came to pass, as He was praying in a certain place, when He ceased, *that* one of His disciples said to Him, "Lord, teach us to pray, as John also taught his disciples."

2 So He said to them, "When you pray, say:

Our Father in heaven,
Hallowed be Your name.
Your kingdom come.
Your will be done
On earth as *it is* in heaven.
3 Give us day by day our daily
    bread.
4 And forgive us our sins,
   For we also forgive everyone
    who is indebted to us.
   And do not lead us into
    temptation,
   But deliver us from the evil
    one."

🔍 **WORDFINDER**

10:33 Samaritan (Pronounced *suh-MARE-ih-tun*). A person who lived in Samaria (pronounced *suh-MARE-ee-ah*), a district north of Judea (see map on page 1343). Jews hated Samaritans, partly because they were a mixed race.

⛏ **DIGGING IN**

10:33 Who Were the Samaritans? The Samaritans (pronounced *suh-MARE-ih-tuns*) were a mixed race of Jewish and non-Jewish people. They lived in the land north of Judea after the Northern Kingdom of Israel was conquered by Assyria (pronounced *ah-SEER-ih-uh*) in 722 B.C. The Samaritans later built their own temple and gave up the Jewish religion. Then the Jews started to hate the Samaritans.

This is why Jesus told the story of the

"good Samaritan." He knew the Jews would be shocked because the hero in his parable was "one of those awful Samaritan people!"

Jesus' way of treating people was often different from our way. Jesus was a Friend to people that others hated. Yes, the Samaritans were sinners, but they were sinners Jesus came to save. Will you remember that the next time you meet someone you don't like?

What the Disciples Learned

We had seen the Scribes and the Pharisees (pronounced *FAIR-uh-sees*) stand in the streets making long prayers. Everybody admired those men because they always looked so holy. That's why we couldn't understand why Jesus was always putting them down. Later, we found out that those fellows who prayed in the streets were just fakes, and Jesus knew it all along.

Jesus taught us *not* to pray to show off before people. Prayer is *talking to God,* and we must be very honest and very plain when we speak to Him. God sees our hearts.

Then Jesus gave us a model prayer that contains everything we could ever ask God. You should also read Matthew 6:5–15 to learn all that Jesus taught us about prayer.

⁵And He said to them, "Which of you shall have a friend, and go to him at midnight and say to him, 'Friend, lend me three loaves; ⁶for a friend of mine has come to me on his journey, and I have nothing to set before him'; ⁷and he will answer from within and say, 'Do not trouble me; the door is now shut, and my children are with me in bed; I cannot rise and give to you'? ⁸I say to you, though he will not rise and give to him because he is his friend, yet because of his persistence he will rise and give him as many as he needs.

⁹"So I say to you, ask, and it will be given to you; seek, and you will find; knock, and it will be opened to you. ¹⁰For everyone who asks receives, and he who seeks finds, and to him who knocks it will be opened. ¹¹If a son asks for bread from any father among you, will he give him a stone? Or if *he asks* for a fish, will he give him a serpent instead of a fish? ¹²Or if he asks for an egg, will he offer him a scorpion? ¹³If you then, being evil, know how to give good gifts to your children, how much more will *your* heavenly Father give the Holy Spirit to those who ask Him!"

¹⁴And He was casting out a demon, and it was mute. So it was, when the demon had gone out, that the mute spoke; and the multitudes marveled. ¹⁵But some of them said, "He casts out demons by Beelzebub, the ruler of the demons."

¹⁶Others, testing *Him,* sought from Him a sign from heaven. ¹⁷But He, knowing their thoughts, said to them: "Every kingdom divided against itself is brought to desolation, and a house *divided* against a house falls. ¹⁸If Satan

DIGGING IN

11:9 Ask, Seek, Knock Maybe you pray to God sometimes, but did you know that He really hears and understands your feelings?

People who think God is far away are called "deists" (pronounced *DEE-ists*). God is then seen as the One who created the universe but has nothing to do with how people get along. Deists think the world is like a machine that just runs on its own.

Another false idea is that everyone and everything is *part of God,* so there is no difference between God and us. That way of thinking is called "pantheism" (pronounced *PAN-thee-ism*).

Jesus tells us that God is *our Father* who is closer to us than breath. When you pray to Him, He hears you. Jesus means that you should keep on knocking at the door of your heavenly Father. He will open the door and answer your needs.

...so is divided against himself, how will his kingdom stand? Because you say I cast out demons by Beelzebub. 19 And if I cast out demons by Beelzebub, by whom do your sons cast *them* out? Therefore they will be your judges. 20 But if I cast out demons with the finger of God, surely the kingdom of God has come upon you. 21 When a strong man, fully armed, guards his own palace, his goods are in peace. 22 But when a stronger than he comes upon him and overcomes him, he takes from him all his armor in which he trusted, and divides his spoils. 23 He who is not with Me is against Me, and he who does not gather with Me scatters.

24 "When an unclean spirit goes out of a man, he goes through dry places, seeking rest; and finding none, he says, 'I will return to my house from which I came.' 25 And when he comes, he finds *it* swept and put in order. 26 Then he goes and takes with *him* seven other spirits more wicked than himself, and they enter and dwell there; and the last *state* of that man is worse than the first."

27 And it happened, as He spoke these things, that a certain woman from the crowd raised her voice and said to Him, "Blessed *is* the womb that bore You, and *the* breasts which nursed You!"

28 But He said, "More than that, blessed *are* those who hear the word of God and keep it!"

29 And while the crowds were thickly gathered together, He began to say, "This is an evil generation. It seeks a sign, and no sign will be given to it except the sign of Jonah the prophet. 30 For as Jonah became a sign to the Ninevites, so also the Son of Man will be to this generation. 31 The queen of the South will rise up in the judgment with the men of this generation and condemn them, for she came from the ends of the earth to hear the wisdom of Solomon; and indeed a greater than Solomon *is* here. 32 The men of Nineveh will rise up in the judgment with this generation and condemn it, for

they repented at the preaching of Jonah; and indeed a greater than Jonah *is* here.

33 "No one, when he has lit a lamp, puts *it* in a secret place or under a basket, but on a lampstand, that those who come in may see the light. 34 The lamp of the body is the eye. Therefore, when your eye is good, your whole body also is full of light. But when *your* eye is bad, your body also *is* full of darkness. 35 Therefore take heed that the light which is in you is not darkness. 36 If then your whole body *is* full of light, having no part dark, *the* whole *body* will be full of light, as when the bright shining of a lamp gives you light."

37 And as He spoke, a certain Pharisee asked Him to dine with him. So He went in and sat down to eat. 38 When the Pharisee saw *it,* he marveled that He had not first washed before dinner.

39 Then the Lord said to him, "Now you Pharisees make the outside of the cup and dish clean, but your inward part is full of greed and wickedness. 40 Foolish ones! Did not He who made the outside make the inside also? 41 But rather give alms of such things as you have; then indeed all things are clean to you.

42 "But woe to you Pharisees! For you tithe mint and rue and all manner of herbs, and pass by justice and the love of God. These you ought to have done, without leaving the others undone. 43 Woe to you Pharisees! For you love the best seats in the synagogues and greetings in the marketplaces. 44 Woe to you, scribes and Pharisees, hypocrites! For you are like graves which are not seen, and the men who walk over *them* are not aware *of them.*"

45 Then one of the lawyers answered and said to Him, "Teacher, by saying these things You reproach us also."

46 And He said, "Woe to you also, lawyers! For you load men with burdens hard to bear, and you yourselves do not touch the burdens with one of your fingers. 47 Woe to you! For you

build the tombs of the prophets, and your fathers killed them. 48 In fact, you bear witness that you approve the deeds of your fathers; for they indeed killed them, and you build their tombs. 49 Therefore the wisdom of God also said, 'I will send them prophets and apostles, and *some* of them they will kill and persecute,' 50 that the blood of all the prophets which was shed from the foundation of the world may be required of this generation, 51 from the blood of Abel to the blood of Zechariah who perished between the altar and the temple. Yes, I say to you, it shall be required of this generation.

52 "Woe to you lawyers! For you have taken away the key of knowledge. You did not enter in yourselves, and those who were entering in you hindered."

53 And as He said these things to them, the scribes and the Pharisees began to assail *Him* vehemently, and to cross-examine Him about many things, 54 lying in wait for Him, and seeking to catch Him in something He might say, that they might accuse Him.

Who is the richest man in the world?

12 In the meantime, when an innumerable multitude of people had gathered together, so that they trampled one another, He began to say to His disciples first *of all,* "Beware of the leaven of the Pharisees, which is hypocrisy. 2 For there is nothing covered that will not be revealed, nor hidden that will not be known. 3 Therefore whatever you have spoken in the dark will be heard in the light, and what you have spoken in the ear in inner rooms will be proclaimed on the housetops.

4 "And I say to you, My friends, do not be afraid of those who kill the body, and after that have no more that they can do. 5 But I will show you whom you should fear: Fear Him who, after He has killed, has power to cast into **hell**; yes, I say to you, fear Him! 6 "Are not five sparrows sold for two copper coins? And not one of them is forgotten before God. 7 But the very hairs of your head are all numbered. Do not fear therefore; you are of more value than many sparrows.

8 "Also I say to you, whoever confesses Me before men, him the Son of Man also will confess before the angels of God. 9 But he who denies Me before men will be denied before the angels of God.

10 "And anyone who speaks a word against the Son of Man, it will be forgiven him; but to him who blasphemes against the Holy Spirit, it will not be forgiven.

11 "Now when they bring you to the

WORDFINDER

12:5 Hell A place of endless misery where ungodly people go when they die. It is translated from a word for the burning dumping ground outside Jerusalem in Jesus' time.

DIGGING IN

12:1 Make-Believe Christians Jesus said the Pharisees were "hypocrites" (pronounced *HIP-puh-krits*). A hypocrite is someone who pretends to be something he is not.

The Pharisees were a special sect of Jewish people who pretended they were better than the ordinary people. The Pharisees knew the Scriptures very well and looked at themselves as the defenders of the Jewish religion. The sad truth was that their forefathers were men of great faith, but the Pharisees themselves were like hollow men. God did not live in them.

A building may be infested with termites for years. Then one day the whole beautiful building falls. The termites have eaten out the inside of that building. Jesus said the Pharisees were like buildings with termites—hollow inside.

What the Rich Fool Learned

What a fool I've been! I've made myself richer and richer, but I never stopped to think I would soon die, and I couldn't take my money with me.

It would have been a lot better if I had only sent my wealth ahead to God. I could have helped so many needy people, and I could have given my money to spread the gospel. God would have put my gifts in my heavenly bank account.

Now I'm going to die, and I have all this money! What am I going to do with it all? Quick, call my bank! I want to give my money where it will do the most good because I now realize that's why God trusted me with so much.

synagogues and magistrates and authorities, do not worry about how or what you should answer, or what you should say. 12 For the Holy Spirit will teach you in that very hour what you ought to say."

13 Then one from the crowd said to Him, "Teacher, tell my brother to divide the inheritance with me."

14 But He said to him, "Man, who made Me a judge or an arbitrator over you?" 15 And He said to them, "Take heed and beware of **covetousness,** for one's life does not consist in the abundance of the things he possesses."

16 Then He spoke a parable to them, saying: "The ground of a certain rich man yielded plentifully. 17 And he thought within himself, saying, 'What shall I do, since I have no room to store my crops?' 18 So he said, 'I will do this: I will pull down my barns and build greater, and there I will store all my crops and my goods. 19 And I will say to my soul, "Soul, you have many goods laid up for many years; take your ease; eat, drink, and be merry." '

20 But God said to him, 'Fool! This night your soul will be required of you; then whose will those things be which you have provided?'

21 "So is he who lays up treasure for himself, and is not rich toward God."

22 Then He said to His disciples, "Therefore I say to you, do not worry about your life, what you will eat; nor about the body, what you will put on. 23 Life is more than food, and the body is more than clothing. 24 Consider the ravens, for they neither sow nor reap, which have neither storehouse nor barn; and God feeds them. Of how much more value are you than the birds? 25 And which of you by worrying can add one cubit to his stature? 26 If you then are not able to do the least, why are you anxious for the rest? 27 Consider the lilies, how they grow: they neither toil nor spin; and yet I say to you, even Solomon in all his glory was not arrayed like one of these. 28 If then God so clothes the grass, which today is in the field and tomor-

WORDFINDER

12:15 Covetousness Pronounced *KUV-ih-tuss-ness.* Envy or the extreme and wrong desire to own what belongs to someone else.

DIGGING IN

12:28 God Will Take Care of You Let's be honest. Sometimes we all wonder what's going to happen tomorrow. We do have to think about tomorrow, but we don't need to *worry.* God takes care of us if we are trying to *please Him first.*

row is thrown into the oven, how much more *will He clothe* you, O *you* of little faith?

29 "And do not seek what you should eat or what you should drink, nor have an anxious mind. 30 For all these things the nations of the world seek after, and your Father knows that you need these things. 31 But seek the kingdom of God, and all these things shall be added to you.

32 "Do not fear, little flock, for it is your Father's good pleasure to give you the kingdom. 33 Sell what you have and give alms; provide yourselves money bags which do not grow old, a treasure in the heavens that does not fail, where no thief approaches nor moth destroys. 34 For where your treasure is, there your heart will be also.

35 "Let your waist be girded and *your* lamps burning; 36 and you yourselves be like men who wait for their master, when he will return from the wedding, that when he comes and knocks they may open to him immediately. 37 Blessed *are* those servants whom the master, when he comes, will find watching. Assuredly, I say to you that he will gird himself and have them sit down *to eat,* and will come and serve them. 38 And if he should come in the second watch, or come in the third watch, and find *them* so, blessed are those servants. 39 But know this, that if the master of the house had known what hour the thief would come, he would have watched and not allowed his house to be broken into. 40 Therefore you also be ready, for the Son of Man is coming at an hour you do not expect."

41 Then Peter said to Him, "Lord, do You speak this parable *only* to us, or to all *people?*"

42 And the Lord said, "Who then is that faithful and wise steward, whom *his* master will make ruler over his household, to give *them their* portion of food in due season? 43 Blessed *is* that servant whom his master will find so doing when he comes. 44 Truly, I say to you that he will make him ruler over all that he has. 45 But if that servant says in his heart, 'My master is delaying his coming,' and begins to beat the male and female servants, and to eat and drink and be drunk, 46 the master of that servant will come on a day when he is not looking for *him,* and at an hour when he is not aware, and will cut him in two and appoint *him* his portion with the unbelievers. 47 And that servant who knew his master's will, and did not prepare *himself* or do according to his will, shall be beaten with many *stripes.* 48 But he who did not know, yet committed things deserving of stripes, shall be beaten with few. For everyone to whom much is given, from him much will be required; and to whom much has been committed, of him they will ask the more.

49 "I came to send fire on the earth, and how I wish it were already kindled! 50 But I have a baptism to be baptized with, and how distressed I am till it is accomplished! 51 Do *you* suppose that I came to give peace on earth? I tell you, not at all, but rather division. 52 For from now on five in one house will be divided: three against two, and two against three. 53 Father will be divided against son and son against father, mother against daughter and

DIGGING IN

Jesus tells us to look at the flowers—more beautiful than Solomon in all his robes. God clothes the flowers. The birds aren't farmers. They can't plant crops, but God feeds them just the same.

We want lots of things—the most popular sport shoes or high-fashion jeans. Sometimes you see your friends with those things. So maybe you think you should have them, too. But God will not give you what you *want* just so you can have what your friends have. The Bible calls wanting what someone else has, *coveting,* or envy (see Exodus 20:17). God may not always give you exactly what you want, but He does always supply your needs when you try to please Him above everything else.

daughter against mother, mother-in-law against her daughter-in-law and daughter-in-law against her mother-in-law."

54 Then He also said to the multitudes, "Whenever *you see* a cloud rising out of the west, immediately you say, 'A shower is coming'; and so it is. 55 And when you see the south wind blow, you say, 'There will be hot weather'; and there is. 56 Hypocrites! You can discern the face of the sky and of the earth, but how *is it* you do not discern this time?

57 "Yes, and why, even of yourselves, do you not judge what is right? 58 When you go with your adversary to the magistrate, make every effort along the way to settle with him, lest he drag you to the judge, the judge deliver you to the officer, and the officer throw you into prison. 59 I tell you, you shall not depart from there till you have paid the very last mite."

Jesus heals a woman on the Sabbath

13 There were present at that season some who told Him about the Gal-

ileans whose blood Pilate had mingled with their sacrifices. 2 And Jesus answered and said to them, "Do you suppose that these Galileans were worse sinners than all *other* Galileans, because they suffered such things? 3 I tell you, no; but unless you repent you will all likewise perish. 4 Or those eighteen on whom the tower in Siloam fell and killed them, do you think that they were worse sinners than all *other* men who dwelt in Jerusalem? 5 I tell you, no; but unless you repent you will all likewise perish."

6 He also spoke this parable: "A certain *man* had a fig tree planted in his vineyard, and he came seeking fruit on it and found none. 7 Then he said to the keeper of his vineyard, 'Look, for three years I have come seeking fruit on this fig tree and find none. Cut it down; why does it use up the ground?' 8 But he answered and said to him, 'Sir, let it alone this year also, until I dig around it and fertilize *it.* 9 And if it bears fruit, *well.* But if not, after that you can cut it down.'"

10 Now He was teaching in one of the synagogues on the Sabbath. 11 And behold, there was a woman

---

⚒ DIGGING IN

13:5 You Need to Repent Daily Repenting is something you do when you first trust in Jesus for salvation (see Mark 1:15).

Then, as you go through life, you begin to notice that you aren't perfect. Sometimes you speak roughly to your brother or sister. Maybe you complain if your mother asks you to do your chores. Perhaps you're holding a grudge against a classmate at school. Or some bad habit may be getting a hold on your life.

Remember, repenting isn't just being sorry about sin. Repenting is *turning around* and walking away from sin. Every Christian has to begin every day by asking, "Search me, O God . . . and see if there is any wicked way in me" (Psalm 139:23, 24). So start each day like a new page in your life. Try to walk with God in ways that please Him.

A Christian, like a fig tree, should produce fruit.

who had a spirit of infirmity eighteen years, and was bent over and could in no way raise *herself* up. 12 But when Jesus saw her, He called *her* to *Him* and said to her, "Woman, you are loosed from your infirmity." 13 And He laid *His* hands on her, and immediately she was made straight, and glorified God.

14 But the ruler of the synagogue answered with indignation, because Jesus had healed on the Sabbath; and he said to the crowd, "There are six days on which men ought to work; therefore come and be healed on them, and not on the Sabbath day."

15 The Lord then answered him and said, "Hypocrite! Does not each one of you on the Sabbath loose his ox or donkey from the stall, and lead *it* away to water it? 16 So ought not this woman, being a daughter of Abraham, whom Satan has bound—think of it— for eighteen years, be loosed from this bond on the Sabbath?" 17 And when He said these things, all His adversaries were put to shame; and all the multitude rejoiced for all the glorious things that were done by Him.

18 Then He said, "What is the kingdom of God like? And to what shall I compare it? 19 It is like a mustard seed, which a man took and put in his garden; and it grew and became a large tree, and the birds of the air nested in its branches."

20 And again He said, "To what shall I liken the kingdom of God? 21 It is like leaven, which a woman took and hid in three measures of meal till it was all leavened."

22 And He went through the cities and villages, teaching, and journeying toward Jerusalem. 23 Then one said to Him, "Lord, are there few who are saved?"

And He said to them, 24 "Strive to enter through the narrow gate, for many, I say to you, will seek to enter and will not be able. 25 When once the Master of the house has risen up and shut the door, and you begin to stand outside and knock at the door, saying, 'Lord, Lord, open for us,' and He will

answer and say to you, 'I do not know you, where you are from,' 26 then you will begin to say, 'We ate and drank in Your presence, and You taught in our streets.' 27 But He will say, 'I tell you I do not know you, where you are from. Depart from Me, all you workers of iniquity.' 28 There will be weeping and gnashing of teeth, when you see Abraham and Isaac and Jacob and all the prophets in the kingdom of God, and yourselves thrust out. 29 They will come from the east and the west, from the north and the south, and sit down in the kingdom of God. 30 And indeed there are last who will be first, and there are first who will be last."

31 On that very day some Pharisees came, saying to Him, "Get out and depart from here, for Herod wants to kill You."

32 And He said to them, "Go, tell that fox, 'Behold, I cast out demons and perform cures today and tomorrow, and the third *day* I shall be perfected.' 33 Nevertheless I must journey today, tomorrow, and the *day* following; for it cannot be that a prophet should perish outside of Jerusalem.

34 "O Jerusalem, Jerusalem, the one who kills the prophets and stones those who are sent to her! How often I wanted to gather your children together, as a hen *gathers* her brood under *her* wings, but you were not willing! 35 See! Your house is left to you desolate; and assuredly, I say to you, you shall not see Me until *the time* comes when you say, 'Blessed is He who comes in the name of the LORD!' "

The story of a wedding supper

14 Now it happened, as He went into the house of one of the rulers of the Pharisees to eat bread on the Sabbath, that they watched Him closely. 2 And behold, there was a certain man before Him who had dropsy. 3 And Jesus, answering, spoke to the lawyers and Pharisees, saying, "Is it lawful to heal on the Sabbath?"

4 But they kept silent. And He took

him and healed him, and let him go. 5 Then He answered them, saying, "Which of you, having a donkey or an ox that has fallen into a pit, will not immediately pull him out on the Sabbath day?" 6 And they could not answer Him regarding these things.

7 So He told a parable to those who were invited, when He noted how they chose the best places, saying to them: 8 "When you are invited by anyone to a wedding feast, do not sit down in the best place, lest one more honorable than you be invited by him; 9 and he who invited you and him come and say to you, 'Give place to this man,' and then you begin with shame to take the lowest place. 10 But when you are invited, go and sit down in the lowest place, so that when he who invited you comes he may say to you, 'Friend, go up higher.' Then you will have glory in the presence of those who sit at the table with you. 11 For whoever exalts himself will be humbled, and he who humbles himself will be exalted."

12 Then He also said to him who invited Him, "When you give a dinner or a supper, do not ask your friends, your brothers, your relatives, nor rich neighbors, lest they also invite you back, and you be repaid. 13 But when you give a feast, invite *the* poor, *the* maimed, *the* lame, *the* blind. 14 And you will be blessed, because they cannot repay you; for you shall be repaid at the resurrection of the just."

15 Now when one of those who sat at the table with Him heard these things, he said to Him, "Blessed *is* he who shall eat bread in the kingdom of God!"

16 Then He said to him, "A certain man gave a great supper and invited many, 17 and sent his servant at supper time to say to those who were invited, 'Come, for all things are now ready.' 18 But they all with one *accord* began to make excuses. The first said to him, 'I have bought a piece of ground, and I must go and see it. I ask you to have me excused.' 19 And another said, 'I have bought five yoke of oxen, and I am going to test them. I ask you to have me excused.' 20 Still another said, 'I have married a wife, and therefore I cannot come.' 21 So that servant came and reported these things to his master. Then the master of the house, being angry, said to his servant, 'Go out quickly into the streets and lanes of the city, and bring in here *the* poor and *the* maimed and *the* lame and *the* blind.' 22 And the servant said, 'Master, it is done as you commanded, and still there is room.' 23 Then the master said to the servant, 'Go out into the highways and hedges, and compel *them* to come in, that my house may be filled. 24 For I say to you that none of those men who were invited shall taste my supper.' "

25 Now great multitudes went with Him. And He turned and said to them, 26 "If anyone comes to Me and does not hate his father and mother, wife and children, brothers and sisters, yes, and his own life also, he cannot be My disciple. 27 And whoever does not bear his cross and come after Me cannot be My disciple. 28 For which of you, intending to build a tower, does not sit down first and count the cost, whether he has *enough* to finish *it*— 29 lest, after he has laid the foundation, and is not able to finish, all who see *it* begin to mock him, 30 saying, 'This man began to build and was not able to finish.' 31 Or what king, going to make war against another king, does not sit down first and consider whether he is able with ten thousand to meet him who comes against him with twenty thousand? 32 Or else, while the other is still a great way off, he sends a delegation and asks conditions of peace. 33 So likewise, whoever of you

---

⚒ **DIGGING IN**

14:33 Leaving All for Jesus You might think someone who dies has lost everything. But if that one lived for Jesus, he has only left everything here to gain does not forsake all that he has cannot be My disciple.

34 "Salt *is* good; but if the salt has lost its flavor, how shall it be seasoned? 35 It is neither fit for the land nor for the dunghill, *but* men throw it out. He who has ears to hear, let him hear!''

The lost sheep, the lost coin, and the lost son

15 Then all the tax collectors and the sinners drew near to Him to hear Him. 2 And the Pharisees and scribes complained, saying, "This Man receives sinners and eats with them." 3 So He spoke this parable to them, saying:

4 "What man of you, having a hundred sheep, if he loses one of them, does not leave the ninety-nine in the wilderness, and go after the one which is lost until he finds it? 5 And when he has found *it,* he lays *it* on his shoulders, rejoicing. 6 And when he comes home, he calls together *his* friends and neighbors, saying to them, 'Rejoice with me, for I have found my sheep which was lost!' 7 I say to you that likewise there will be more joy in heaven over one sinner who repents than over ninety-nine just persons who need no repentance.

8 "Or what woman, having ten silver coins, if she loses one coin, does not light a lamp, sweep the house, and search carefully until she finds *it?* 9 And when she has found *it,* she calls *her* friends and neighbors together, saying, 'Rejoice with me, for I have found the piece which I lost!' 10 Likewise, I say to you, there is joy in the presence of the angels of God over one sinner who repents."

11 Then He said: "A certain man had two sons. 12 And the younger of them said to *his* father, 'Father, give me the portion of goods that falls *to me.*' So he divided to them *his* livelihood. 13 And not many days after, the younger son gathered all together, journeyed to a far country, and there wasted his possessions with prodigal living. 14 But when he had spent all, there arose a severe famine in that land, and he began to be in want. 15 Then he went and joined himself to a citizen of that country, and he sent him into his fields to feed swine. 16 And he would gladly have filled his stomach with the pods that the swine ate, and no one gave him *anything.*

17 "But when he came to himself, he said, 'How many of my father's hired servants have bread enough and to spare, and I perish with hunger! 18 I will arise and go to my father, and

DIGGING IN

all the wealth of heaven. *Jesus Himself* is the real wealth of heaven. Heaven is the place where we see Jesus and know Him as our Friend—forever and ever!

So Jesus is asking you to be like that Christian who has died. Once you know Jesus, the good things of this life don't matter so much anymore.

To know Jesus is to have Jesus Himself living in you. That's heaven! Like that Christian who dies, you no longer care about being wealthy or poor. All of your life and your things belong to Jesus. Jesus Himself is worth more than all this world can offer.

15:1–32 Jesus Is Looking for You
Have you ever lost something you cared about very much? That's the way Jesus cares about people. He sees you and me as "lost" until we come to know His love.

No matter where you go or what you do, Jesus is looking for you. You may spend a long time trying to get away from Him, but He keeps looking for you everywhere.

Like the lost sheep, the lost coin, and the lost son, you are very special to Him. He looks for you on the street where you walk, in the classroom where you sit, and in your bed at night. He calls out to you where your heart can hear Him—in your conscience. He reminds you that you belong to Him. He made you for Himself, but you may be wandering far away from Him. You can answer Him by saying, "Yes, my life belongs to You. Now I want to give myself back to You."

will say to him, "Father, I have sinned against heaven and before you, 19 and I am no longer worthy to be called your son. Make me like one of your hired servants.' "

20 "And he arose and came to his father. But when he was still a great way off, his father saw him and had compassion, and ran and fell on his neck and kissed him. 21 And the son said to him, 'Father, I have sinned against heaven and in your sight, and am no longer worthy to be called your son.'

22 "But the father said to his servants, 'Bring out the best robe and put *it* on him, and put a ring on his hand and sandals on *his* feet. 23 And bring the fatted calf here and kill *it,* and let us eat and be merry; 24 for this my son was dead and is alive again; he was lost and is found.' And they began to be merry.

25 "Now his older son was in the field. And as he came and drew near to the house, he heard music and dancing. 26 So he called one of the servants and asked what these things meant. 27 And he said to him, 'Your brother has come, and because he has received him safe and sound, your father has killed the fatted calf.'

28 "But he was angry and would not go in. Therefore his father came out and pleaded with him. 29 So he answered and said to *his* father, 'Lo, these many years I have been serving you; I never transgressed your commandment at any time; and yet you never gave me a young goat, that I might make merry with my friends. 30 But as soon as this son of yours came, who has devoured your livelihood with harlots, you killed the fatted calf for him.'

31 "And he said to him, 'Son, you are always with me, and all that I have is yours. 32 It was right that we should make merry and be glad, for your

brother was dead and is alive again, and was lost and is found.' "

The story of a dishonest employee

16 He also said to His disciples: "There was a certain rich man who had a steward, and an accusation was brought to him that this man was wasting his goods. 2 So he called him and said to him, 'What is this I hear about you? Give an account of your stewardship, for you can no longer be steward.'

3 "Then the steward said within himself, 'What shall I do? For my master is taking the stewardship away from me. I cannot dig; I am ashamed to beg. 4 I have resolved what to do, that when I am put out of the stewardship, they may receive me into their houses.'

5 "So he called every one of his master's debtors to *him,* and said to the first, 'How much do you owe my master?' 6 And he said, 'A hundred measures of oil.' So he said to him, 'Take your bill, and sit down quickly and write fifty.' 7 Then he said to another, 'And how much do you owe?' So he said, 'A hundred measures of wheat.' And he said to him, 'Take your bill, and write eighty.' 8 So the master commended the unjust steward because he had dealt shrewdly. For the sons of this world are more shrewd in their generation than the sons of light.

9 "And I say to you, make friends for yourselves by unrighteous mammon, that when you fail, they may receive you into an everlasting home. 10 He who *is* faithful in *what is* least is faithful also in much; and he who is unjust in *what is* least is unjust also in much. 11 Therefore if you have not been faithful in the unrighteous **mammon,** who will commit to your trust the true *riches?* 12 And if you have not been faithful in what is another man's,

16:11 Mammon Money, wealth, or material goods that are treated as more important than God. To serve mammon is to worship money instead of God.

who will give you what is your own? 13 "No servant can serve two masters; for either he will hate the one and love the other, or else he will be loyal to the one and despise the other. You cannot serve God and mammon."

14 Now the Pharisees, who were lovers of money, also heard all these things, and they derided Him. 15 And He said to them, "You are those who justify yourselves before men, but God knows your hearts. For what is highly esteemed among men is an abomination in the sight of God.

16 "The law and the prophets *were* until John. Since that time the kingdom of God has been preached, and everyone is pressing into it. 17 And it is easier for heaven and earth to pass away than for one tittle of the law to fail.

18 "Whoever divorces his wife and marries another commits adultery; and whoever marries her who is divorced from *her* husband commits adultery.

19 "There was a certain rich man who was clothed in purple and fine linen and fared sumptuously every day. 20 But there was a certain beggar named Lazarus, full of sores, who was laid at his gate, 21 desiring to be fed with the crumbs which fell from the rich man's table. Moreover the dogs came and licked his sores. 22 So it was that the beggar died, and was carried by the angels to Abraham's bosom. The rich man also died and was buried. 23 And being in torments in Hades, he lifted up his eyes and saw Abraham afar off, and Lazarus in his bosom.

24 "Then he cried and said, 'Father Abraham, have mercy on me, and send Lazarus that he may dip the tip of his finger in water and cool my tongue; for I am tormented in this flame.' 25 But Abraham said, 'Son, remember that in your lifetime you received your good things, and likewise Lazarus evil things; but now he is comforted and you are tormented. 26 And besides all this, between us and you there is a great gulf fixed, so that those who want to pass from here to you cannot, nor can those from there pass to us.'

27 "Then he said, 'I beg you therefore, father, that you would send him

⚒ DIGGING IN

16:23 What Is Hell Like? Will everybody live in heaven with God forever? No, because God's love can't be where people go on loving their sins. Jesus said the kingdom of heaven is like a great plant that grows from a small seed. The kingdom of hell also grows up from a small seed until it crowds out everything lovely.

Have you ever been angry at somebody? The more you thought about that person, the more angry you became. Finally, you got so mad you couldn't stand yourself anymore. You were miserable until God made you sorry for your anger. Hell is like that kind of misery. Hell is a place where people can no longer think lovely thoughts. Everyone who rejects the great love Jesus showed in dying for them must go there. Let Jesus drive out all bitter thoughts. Then heaven will begin to grow in you and last forever. Which do you prefer—heaven or hell?

"Father Abraham . . . send Lazarus that he may . . . cool my tongue; for I am tormented in this flame."

to my father's house, 28 for I have five brothers, that he may testify to them, lest they also come to this place of torment.' 29 Abraham said to him, 'They have Moses and the prophets; let them hear them.' 30 And he said, 'No, father Abraham; but if one goes to them from the dead, they will repent.' 31 But he said to him, 'If they do not hear Moses and the prophets, neither will they be persuaded though one rise from the dead.' "

What will the world be like when Jesus returns?

17 Then He said to the disciples, "It is impossible that no offenses should come, but woe to him through whom they do come! 2 It would be better for him if a millstone were hung around his neck, and he were thrown into the sea, than that he should offend one of these little ones. 3 Take heed to yourselves. If your brother sins against you, rebuke him; and if he repents, forgive him. 4 And if he sins against you seven times in a day, and seven times in a day returns to you, saying, 'I repent,' you shall forgive him."

5 And the apostles said to the Lord, "Increase our faith."

6 So the Lord said, "If you have faith as a mustard seed, you can say to this mulberry tree, 'Be pulled up by the roots and be planted in the sea,' and it would obey you. 7 And which of you, having a servant plowing or tending sheep, will say to him when he has come in from the field, 'Come at once and sit down to eat'? 8 But will he not rather say to him, 'Prepare something for my supper, and gird yourself and serve me till I have eaten and drunk, and afterward you will eat and drink'? 9 Does he thank that servant because he did the things that were commanded him? I think not. 10 So likewise you, when you have done all those things which you are commanded, say, 'We are unprofitable servants. We have done what was our duty to do.' "

11 Now it happened as He went to Jerusalem that He passed through the midst of Samaria and Galilee. 12 Then as He entered a certain village, there met Him ten men who were lepers, who stood afar off. 13 And they lifted up their voices and said, "Jesus, Master, have mercy on us!"

14 So when He saw them, He said to them, "Go, show yourselves to the priests." And so it was that as they went, they were cleansed.

15 And one of them, when he saw that he was healed, returned, and with a loud voice glorified God, 16 and fell down on his face at His feet, giving Him thanks. And he was a Samaritan.

17 So Jesus answered and said, "Were there not ten cleansed? But where are the nine? 18 Were there not any found who returned to give glory to God except this foreigner?" 19 And He said to him, "Arise, go your way. Your faith has made you well."

20 Now when He was asked by the Pharisees when the kingdom of God

---

What the Pharisees Learned

We Pharisees (pronounced FAIR-uh-sees) always enjoyed arguing about when the kingdom of God would come. We had many opinions.

One day we asked that new Teacher, Jesus, what He thought about the kingdom of God. We wanted to find out how good a scholar He really was!

But Jesus gave us a strange answer. He told us we must first look into our own hearts. If the kingdom of God isn't in our hearts, we won't see it at all! Of course, that's just what we wicked Pharisees needed to hear.

Later, Jesus told His disciples just what was going to happen when the Son of God comes back from heaven (see Luke 17:22–37).

would come, He answered them and said, "The kingdom of God does not come with observation; 21 nor will they say, 'See here!' or 'See there!' For indeed, the kingdom of God is within you."

22 Then He said to the disciples, "The days will come when you will desire to see one of the days of the Son of Man, and you will not see it. 23 And they will say to you, 'Look here!' or 'Look there!' Do not go after them or follow them. 24 For as the lightning that flashes out of one part under heaven shines to the other part under heaven, so also the Son of Man will be in His day. 25 But first He must suffer many things and be rejected by this generation. 26 And as it was in the days of Noah, so it will be also in the days of the Son of Man: 27 They ate, they drank, they married wives, they were given in marriage, until the day that Noah entered the ark, and the flood came and destroyed them all. 28 Likewise as it was also in the days of Lot: They ate, they drank, they bought, they sold, they planted, they built; 29 but on the day that Lot went out of Sodom it rained fire and brimstone from heaven and destroyed them all. 30 Even so will it be in the day when the Son of Man is revealed.

31 "In that day, he who is on the housetop, and his goods are in the house, let him not come down to take them away. And likewise the one who is in the field, let him not turn back. 32 Remember Lot's wife. 33 Whoever seeks to save his life will lose it, and whoever loses his life will preserve it. 34 I tell you, in that night there will be two men in one bed: the one will be taken and the other will be left. 35 Two women will be grinding together: the

one will be taken and the other left. 36 Two men will be in the field: the one will be taken and the other left."

37 And they answered and said to Him, "Where, Lord?"

So He said to them, "Wherever the body is, there the eagles will be gathered together."

Jesus tells more stories

18 Then He spoke a parable to them, that men always ought to pray and not lose heart, 2 saying: "There was in a certain city a judge who did not fear God nor regard man. 3 Now there was a widow in that city; and she came to him, saying, 'Get justice for me from my adversary.' 4 And he would not for a while; but afterward he said within himself, 'Though I do not fear God nor regard man, 5 yet because this widow troubles me I will avenge her, lest by her continual coming she weary me.' "

6 Then the Lord said, "Hear what the unjust judge said. 7 And shall God not avenge His own elect who cry out day and night to Him, though He bears long with them? 8 I tell you that He will avenge them speedily. Nevertheless, when the Son of Man comes, will He really find faith on the earth?"

9 Also He spoke this parable to some who trusted in themselves that they were righteous, and despised others: 10 "Two men went up to the temple to pray, one a Pharisee and the other a tax collector. 11 The Pharisee stood and prayed thus with himself, 'God, I thank You that I am not like other men—extortioners, unjust, adulterers, or even as this tax collector. 12 I fast twice a week; I give tithes of all that I possess.' 13 And the tax collector,

---

⚒ DIGGING IN

18:13 Be Honest with God Do you have a clear conscience? Or do you just have a bad memory?

One man in Jesus' story seemed to have a bad memory. He didn't remember any sin he had done. He was very

pleased with himself. The other man was a hated tax collector, but he knew he was a sinner, and he knew he needed God's forgiveness.

Let's all pray that we never become like the proud Pharisee. All he could rememstanding afar off, would not so much as raise *his* eyes to heaven, but beat his breast, saying, 'God, be merciful to me a sinner!' ¹⁴ I tell you, this man went down to his house justified *rather* than the other; for everyone who exalts himself will be humbled, and he who humbles himself will be exalted."

¹⁵ Then they also brought infants to Him that He might touch them; but when the disciples saw *it,* they rebuked them. ¹⁶ But Jesus called them to *Him* and said, "Let the little children come to Me, and do not forbid them; for of such is the kingdom of God. ¹⁷ Assuredly, I say to you, whoever does not receive the kingdom of God as a little child will by no means enter it."

¹⁸ Now a certain ruler asked Him, saying, "Good Teacher, what shall I do to inherit eternal life?"

¹⁹ So Jesus said to him, "Why do you call Me good? No one *is* good but One, *that is,* God. ²⁰ You know the commandments: 'Do not commit adultery,' 'Do not murder,' 'Do not steal,' 'Do not bear false witness,' 'Honor your father and your mother.' "

²¹ And he said, "All these things I have kept from my youth."

²² So when Jesus heard these things, He said to him, "You still lack one thing. Sell all that you have and distribute to the poor, and you will have treasure in heaven; and come, follow Me."

²³ But when he heard this, he became very sorrowful, for he was very rich.

²⁴ And when Jesus saw that he became very sorrowful, He said, "How hard it is for those who have riches to enter the kingdom of God! ²⁵ For it is easier for a camel to go through the eye of a needle than for a rich man to enter the kingdom of God."

²⁶ And those who heard it said, "Who then can be saved?"

²⁷ But He said, "The things which are impossible with men are possible with God."

²⁸ Then Peter said, "See, we have left all and followed You."

²⁹ So He said to them, "Assuredly, I say to you, there is no one who has left house or parents or brothers or wife or children, for the sake of the kingdom of God, ³⁰ who shall not receive many times more in this present time, and in the age to come eternal life."

³¹ Then He took the twelve aside and said to them, "Behold, we are going up to Jerusalem, and all things that are written by the prophets concerning the Son of Man will be accomplished. ³² For He will be delivered to the Gentiles and will be mocked and insulted and spit upon. ³³ They will scourge *Him* and kill Him. And the third day He will rise again."

³⁴ But they understood none of these things; this saying was hidden from them, and they did not know the things which were spoken.

³⁵ Then it happened, as He was coming near Jericho, that a certain blind man sat by the road begging. ³⁶ And hearing a multitude passing by, he asked what it meant. ³⁷ So they told him that Jesus of Nazareth was passing by. ³⁸ And he cried out, saying, "Jesus, Son of David, have mercy on me!"

³⁹ Then those who went before warned him that he should be quiet; but he cried out all the more, "Son of David, have mercy on me!"

⁴⁰ So Jesus stood still and commanded him to be brought to Him. And when he had come near, He asked him, ⁴¹ saying, "What do you want Me to do for you?"

⚒ DIGGING IN

ber were all the good works he thought he had done. But the Pharisee's good works were useless because they weren't works of love. His deeds were done just to show off before a watching world.

Pray, too, that your conscience will always be like the tax collector's. You are closest to God when you feel that you are a sinner.

Jesus Befriends Our Enemies

The Jericho Journal

JERICHO—Today, as Jesus of Nazareth was passing through Jericho (pronounced *JERRY-ko*), he made a surprise visit to the home of one of the rich tax collectors of our city.

Zacchaeus (pronounced *zack-KEY-us*) had hoped to see Jesus as he passed in the streets. But, being very short, Zacchaeus had to climb a tree in order to see the great Teacher.

When Jesus saw Zacchaeus, He called to the little man and said that He wanted to go home with him. Jesus also said that Zacchaeus was one of the "lost sheep" He had come to save.

With that strange riddle in mind, many people are wondering about this Man Jesus who seems to enjoy being with sinners. Everyone knows we have nothing to do with the tax collectors. Our people hate tax collectors because they are Jews themselves, yet they take our money and give it to our Roman enemies.

Jesus seems to care about sinners like Zacchaeus. Such a thing seems very strange to us. What do our readers think?

He said, "Lord, that I may receive my sight."

42 Then Jesus said to him, "Receive your sight; your faith has made you well." 43 And immediately he received his sight, and followed Him, glorifying God. And all the people, when they saw *it,* gave praise to God.

A little man climbs a tree to see Jesus

19 Then *Jesus* entered and passed through Jericho. 2 Now behold, *there was* a man named Zacchaeus who was a chief tax collector, and he was rich. 3 And he sought to see who Jesus was, but could not because of the crowd, for he was of short stature. 4 So he ran ahead and climbed up into a sycamore tree to see Him, for He was going to pass that *way.* 5 And when Jesus came to the place, He looked up and saw him, and said to him, "Zacchaeus, make haste and come down, for today I must stay at your house." 6 So he made haste and came down, and received Him joyfully. 7 But when they saw *it,* they all complained, saying, "He has gone to be a guest with a man who is a sinner."

8 Then Zacchaeus stood and said to the Lord, "Look, Lord, I give half of my goods to the poor; and if I have taken anything from anyone by false accusation, I restore fourfold."

9 And Jesus said to him, "Today salvation has come to this house, because he also is a son of Abraham; 10 for the Son of Man has come to seek and to save that which was lost."

11 Now as they heard these things, He spoke another parable, because He was near Jerusalem and because they thought the kingdom of God would appear immediately. 12 Therefore He said: "A certain nobleman went into a far country to receive for himself a kingdom and to return. 13 So he called ten of his servants, delivered to them ten minas, and said to them, 'Do business till I come.' 14 But his citizens hated him, and sent a delegation after him, saying, 'We will not have this *man* to reign over us.'

15 "And so it was that when he returned, having received the kingdom, he then commanded these servants, to whom he had given the money, to be called to him, that he might know how much every man had gained by trading. 16 Then came the first, saying, 'Master, your mina has earned ten minas.' 17 And he said to him, 'Well *done,* good servant; because you were faithful in a very little, have authority over

ten cities.' 18 And the second came, saying, 'Master, your mina has earned five minas.' 19 Likewise he said to him, 'You also be over five cities.'

20 "Then another came, saying, 'Master, here is your mina, which I have kept put away in a handkerchief. 21 For I feared you, because you are an austere man. You collect what you did not deposit, and reap what you did not sow.' 22 And he said to him, 'Out of your own mouth I will judge you, you wicked servant. You knew that I was an austere man, collecting what I did not deposit and reaping what I did not sow. 23 Why then did you not put my money in the bank, that at my coming I might have collected it with interest?'

24 "And he said to those who stood by, 'Take the mina from him, and give it to him who has ten minas.' 25 (But they said to him, 'Master, he has ten minas.') 26 'For I say to you, that to everyone who has will be given; and from him who does not have, even what he has will be taken away from him. 27 But bring here those enemies of mine, who did not want me to reign over them, and slay them before me.' "

28 When He had said this, He went on ahead, going up to Jerusalem. 29 And it came to pass, when He drew near to Bethphage and Bethany, at the mountain called Olivet, that He sent two of His disciples, 30 saying, "Go into the village opposite you, where as you enter you will find a colt tied, on which no one has ever sat. Loose it and bring it here. 31 And if anyone asks you, 'Why are you loosing it?' thus you shall say to him, 'Because the Lord has need of it.' "

32 So those who were sent went their way and found it just as He had said to them. 33 But as they were loosing the colt, the owners of it said to them, "Why are you loosing the colt?"

34 And they said, "The Lord has need of him." 35 Then they brought him to Jesus. And they threw their own clothes on the colt, and they set Jesus on him. 36 And as He went, many spread their clothes on the road.

37 Then, as He was now drawing near the descent of the Mount of Olives, the whole multitude of the disciples began to rejoice and praise God with a loud voice for all the mighty works they had seen, 38 saying:

" 'Blessed is the King who comes
    in the name of the LORD!'
Peace in heaven and glory in the
    highest!"

39 And some of the Pharisees called to Him from the crowd, "Teacher, rebuke Your disciples."

40 But He answered and said to them, "I tell you that if these should keep silent, the stones would immediately cry out."

41 Now as He drew near, He saw the city and wept over it, 42 saying, "If you had known, even you, especially in this your day, the things that make for your peace! But now they are hidden from your eyes. 43 For days will come upon you when your enemies will build an embankment around you, surround you and close you in on every side, 44 and level you, and your children within you, to the ground; and they will not leave in you one stone upon another, because you did not know the time of your visitation."

45 Then He went into the temple and began to drive out those who bought

---

DIGGING IN

19:45—20:2 How Could Jesus Do These Things? What was Jesus doing that made the elders angry? Jesus drove out the people who were turning the temple into a shopping mall.

What would you do if some stranger came into your house and began to buy and sell things in it? You would be very upset.

That's exactly how Jesus felt about the buying and selling in His Father's house. Those merchants had no right to be there.

and sold in it, ⁴⁶ saying to them, "It is written, 'My house is a house of prayer,' but you have made it a 'den of thieves.' "

⁴⁷ And He was teaching daily in the temple. But the chief priests, the scribes, and the leaders of the people sought to destroy Him, ⁴⁸ and were unable to do anything; for all the people were very attentive to hear Him.

The religious leaders argue with Jesus

20 Now it happened on one of those days, as He taught the people in the temple and preached the gospel, *that* the chief priests and the scribes, together with the elders, confronted *Him* ² and spoke to Him, saying, "Tell us, by what authority are You doing these things? Or who is he who gave You this authority?"

³ But He answered and said to them, "I also will ask you one thing, and answer Me: ⁴ The baptism of John—was it from heaven or from men?"

⁵ And they reasoned among themselves, saying, "If we say, 'From heaven,' He will say, 'Why then did you not believe him?' ⁶ But if we say, 'From men,' all the people will stone us, for they are persuaded that John was a prophet." ⁷ So they answered that they did not know where *it was* from.

⁸ And Jesus said to them, "Neither will I tell you by what authority I do these things."

⁹ Then He began to tell the people this parable: "A certain man planted a vineyard, leased it to vinedressers, and went into a far country for a long time. ¹⁰ Now at vintage-time he sent a servant to the vinedressers, that they might give him some of the fruit of the

vineyard. But the vinedressers beat him and sent *him* away empty-handed. ¹¹ Again he sent another servant; and they beat him also, treated *him* shamefully, and sent *him* away empty-handed. ¹² And again he sent a third; and they wounded him also and cast *him* out.

¹³ "Then the owner of the vineyard said, 'What shall I do? I will send my beloved son. Probably they will respect *him* when they see him.' ¹⁴ But when the vinedressers saw him, they reasoned among themselves, saying, 'This is the heir. Come, let us kill him, that the inheritance may be ours.' ¹⁵ So they cast him out of the vineyard and killed *him*. Therefore what will the owner of the vineyard do to them? ¹⁶ He will come and destroy those vinedressers and give the vineyard to others."

And when they heard *it* they said, "Certainly not!"

¹⁷ Then He looked at them and said, "What then is this that is written:

'The stone which the builders rejected
Has become the chief cornerstone' ?

¹⁸ Whoever falls on that stone will be broken; but on whomever it falls, it will grind him to powder."

¹⁹ And the chief priests and the scribes that very hour sought to lay hands on Him, but they feared the people—for they knew He had spoken this parable against them.

²⁰ So they watched *Him,* and sent spies who pretended to be righteous, that they might seize on His words, in order to deliver Him to the power and the authority of the governor.

²¹ Then they asked Him, saying,

⛏ DIGGING IN

So Jesus, the Son of God, had all the authority He needed to drive out those salespeople.

We ought to be careful about making the gospel a means of making ourselves rich. God understands the need to support His servants with money. But if we're not careful, we can make God look bad by turning the gospel into a big business for the purpose of getting wealthy.

"Teacher, we know that You say and teach rightly, and You do not show personal favoritism, but teach the way of God in truth: 22 Is it lawful for us to pay taxes to Caesar or not?"

23 But He perceived their craftiness, and said to them, "Why do you test Me? 24 Show Me a denarius. Whose image and inscription does it have?"

They answered and said, "Caesar's."

25 And He said to them, "Render therefore to Caesar the things that are Caesar's, and to God the things that are God's."

26 But they could not catch Him in His words in the presence of the people. And they marveled at His answer and kept silent.

27 Then some of the Sadducees, who deny that there is a resurrection, came to Him and asked Him, 28 saying: "Teacher, Moses wrote to us that if a man's brother dies, having a wife, and he dies without children, his brother should take his wife and raise up offspring for his brother. 29 Now there were seven brothers. And the first took a wife, and died without children. 30 And the second took her as wife, and he died childless. 31 Then the third took her, and in like manner the seven also; and they left no children, and died. 32 Last of all the woman died also. 33 Therefore, in the resurrection, whose wife does she become? For all seven had her as wife."

34 Jesus answered and said to them, "The sons of this age marry and are given in marriage. 35 But those who are counted worthy to attain that age, and the resurrection from the dead, neither marry nor are given in marriage; 36 nor can they die anymore, for they are equal to the angels and are sons of God, being sons of the resurrection. 37 But even Moses showed in the burning bush passage that the dead are raised, when he called the Lord 'the God of Abraham, the God of Isaac, and the God of Jacob.' 38 For He is not the God of the dead but of the living, for all live to Him."

39 Then some of the scribes an-

Who Were the Scribes?

Sometimes the scribes are called lawyers in the New Testament. This is because the scribes were experts in Jewish law. They explained the law for the people when they wanted to know if something was right or wrong. The scribes' sin was that they claimed to have more authority than the Scriptures.

swered and said, "Teacher, You have spoken well." 40 But after that they dared not question Him anymore.

41 And He said to them, "How can they say that the Christ is the Son of David? 42 Now David himself said in the Book of Psalms:

'The LORD said to my Lord,
  "Sit at My right hand,
43   Till I make Your enemies Your
     footstool." '

44 Therefore David calls Him 'Lord'; how is He then his Son?"

45 Then, in the hearing of all the people, He said to His disciples, 46 "Beware of the scribes, who desire to go around in long robes, love greetings in the marketplaces, the best seats in the synagogues, and the best places at feasts, 47 who devour widows' houses, and for a pretense make long prayers. These will receive greater condemnation."

Jesus describes the future

21 And He looked up and saw the rich putting their gifts into the treasury, 2 and He saw also a certain poor widow putting in two mites. 3 So He said, "Truly I say to you that this poor widow has put in more than all; 4 for all these out of their abundance have put in offerings for God, but she out of her poverty put in all the livelihood that she had."

5 Then, as some spoke of the temple, how it was adorned with beautiful stones and donations, He said,

6 "These things which you see—the days will come in which not *one* stone shall be left upon another that shall not be thrown down."

7 So they asked Him, saying, "Teacher, but when will these things be? And what sign *will there be* when these things are about to take place?"

8 And He said: "Take heed that you not be deceived. For many will come in My name, saying, 'I am *He*,' and, 'The time has drawn near.' Therefore do not go after them. 9 But when you hear of wars and commotions, do not be terrified; for these things must come to pass first, but the end *will not come* immediately."

10 Then He said to them, "Nation will rise against nation, and kingdom against kingdom. 11 And there will be great earthquakes in various places, and famines and pestilences; and there will be fearful sights and great signs from heaven. 12 But before all these things, they will lay their hands on you and persecute *you*, delivering *you* up to the synagogues and prisons. You will be brought before kings and rulers for My name's sake. 13 But it will turn out for you as an occasion for testimony. 14 Therefore settle *it* in your hearts not to meditate beforehand on what you will answer; 15 for I will give you a mouth and wisdom which all your adversaries will not be able to contradict or resist. 16 You will be betrayed even by parents and brothers, relatives and friends; and they will put *some* of you to death. 17 And you will be hated by all for My name's sake.

⚒ DIGGING IN

21:20 Jerusalem Will Be Destroyed
Jerusalem has been destroyed several times. First, it was destroyed by the Babylonian Empire in 586 B.C. Then it was destroyed by the Syrians in about 167 B.C. Finally, Jesus said Jerusalem would be destroyed again after His time. This would be God's judgment on the city for rejecting its Messiah.

The Romans did destroy Jerusalem in A.D. 70, about 40 years after Jesus was crucified. The Jews had long hated their Roman tyrants. So the Jews started a revolt against them.

Then the Roman army surrounded Jerusalem. Finally, the Romans under General Titus (pronounced *TIGHT-us*) entered the city. The people were starving, and a history writer named Josephus says that mothers were even eating their infant children! After this, the Jews were scattered over the earth until the modern Jewish nation was restored by the United Nations in 1948.

The Roman emperor, Titus, who destroyed Jerusalem.

18 But not a hair of your head shall be lost. 19 By your patience possess your souls.

20 "But when you see Jerusalem surrounded by armies, then know that its desolation is near. 21 Then let those who are in Judea flee to the mountains, let those who are in the midst of her depart, and let not those who are in the country enter her. 22 For these are the days of vengeance, that all things which are written may be fulfilled. 23 But woe to those who are pregnant and to those who are nursing babies in those days! For there will be great distress in the land and wrath upon this people. 24 And they will fall by the edge of the sword, and be led away captive into all nations. And Jerusalem will be trampled by Gentiles until the times of the Gentiles are fulfilled.

25 "And there will be signs in the sun, in the moon, and in the stars; and on the earth distress of nations, with perplexity, the sea and the waves roaring; 26 men's hearts failing them from fear and the expectation of those things which are coming on the earth, for the powers of the heavens will be shaken. 27 Then they will see the Son of Man coming in a cloud with power and great glory. 28 Now when these things begin to happen, look up and lift up your heads, because your redemption draws near."

29 Then He spoke to them a **parable:** "Look at the fig tree, and all the trees. 30 When they are already budding, you see and know for yourselves that summer is now near. 31 So you also, when you see these things happening, know that the kingdom of God is near. 32 Assuredly, I say to you, this generation will by no means pass away till all things take place. 33 Heaven and earth will pass away, but My words will by no means pass away.

34 "But take heed to yourselves, lest your hearts be weighed down with ca-

rousing, drunkenness, and cares of this life, and that Day come on you unexpectedly. 35 For it will come as a snare on all those who dwell on the face of the whole earth. 36 Watch therefore, and pray always that you may be counted worthy to escape all these things that will come to pass, and to stand before the Son of Man."

37 And in the daytime He was teaching in the temple, but at night He went out and stayed on the mountain called Olivet. 38 Then early in the morning all the people came to Him in the temple to hear Him.

Jesus' last supper

22 Now the Feast of Unleavened Bread drew near, which is called Passover. 2 And the chief priests and the scribes sought how they might kill Him, for they feared the people.

Who Was Satan?

Remember that Satan was Eve's enemy in the Garden of Eden (Genesis 3) and Job's enemy (Job 1 and 2). Satan is the personal name of the Devil. The word *Satan* means "Enemy," and *Devil* means "Accuser" or "Liar." Satan was put out of heaven when he tried to be equal with God. (See Isaiah 14:12–15.)

---

3 Then Satan entered Judas, surnamed Iscariot, who was numbered among the twelve. 4 So he went his way and conferred with the chief priests and captains, how he might betray Him to them. 5 And they were glad, and agreed to give him money. 6 So he promised and sought opportunity to betray Him to them in the absence of the multitude.

7 Then came the Day of Unleavened Bread, when the Passover must be killed. 8 And He sent Peter and John,

---

🔍 **WORDFINDER**

21:29 Parable Pronounced *PAIR-uh-bull.* A story that teaches a lesson. The story may or may not be true. Jesus used parables to teach spiritual truths.

saying, "Go and prepare the Passover for us, that we may eat."

9 So they said to Him, "Where do You want us to prepare?"

10 And He said to them, "Behold, when you have entered the city, a man will meet you carrying a pitcher of water; follow him into the house which he enters. 11 Then you shall say to the master of the house, 'The Teacher says to you, "Where is the guest room where I may eat the Passover with My disciples?" ' 12 Then he will show you a large, furnished upper room; there make ready."

13 So they went and found it just as He had said to them, and they prepared the Passover.

14 When the hour had come, He sat down, and the twelve apostles with Him. 15 Then He said to them, "With *fervent* desire I have desired to eat this Passover with you before I suffer; 16 for I say to you, I will no longer eat of it until it is fulfilled in the kingdom of God."

17 Then He took the cup, and gave thanks, and said, "Take this and divide *it* among yourselves; 18 for I say to you, I will not drink of the fruit of the vine until the kingdom of God comes."

19 And He took bread, gave thanks and broke *it,* and gave *it* to them, saying, "This is My body which is given for you; do this in remembrance of Me."

20 Likewise He also *took* the cup after supper, saying, "This cup *is* the **new covenant** in My blood, which is shed for you. 21 But behold, the hand of My betrayer *is* with Me on the table. 22 And truly the Son of Man goes as it has been determined, but woe to that man by whom He is betrayed!"

23 Then they began to question among themselves, which of them it was who would do this thing.

24 Now there was also a dispute among them, as to which of them should be considered the greatest. 25 And He said to them, "The kings of the Gentiles exercise lordship over them, and those who exercise authority over them are called 'benefactors.' 26 But not so *among* you; on the contrary, he who is greatest among you, let him be as the younger, and he who governs as he who serves. 27 For who *is* greater, he who sits at the table, or he who serves? *Is* it not he who sits at the table? Yet I am among you as the One who serves.

28 "But you are those who have continued with Me in My trials. 29 And I bestow upon you a kingdom, just as My Father bestowed *one* upon Me, 30 that you may eat and drink at My table in My kingdom, and sit on thrones judging the twelve tribes of Israel."

31 And the Lord said, "Simon, Simon! Indeed, Satan has asked for you, that he may sift *you* as wheat. 32 But I have prayed for you, that your faith should not fail; and when you have returned to *Me,* strengthen your brethren."

33 But he said to Him, "Lord, I am ready to go with You, both to prison and to death."

34 Then He said, "I tell you, Peter, the rooster shall not crow this day before you will deny three times that you know Me."

35 And He said to them, "When I sent you without money bag, knapsack, and sandals, did you lack anything?"

So they said, "Nothing."

36 Then He said to them, "But now, he who has a money bag, let him take *it,* and likewise a knapsack; and he who has no sword, let him sell his garment and buy one. 37 For I say to you that this which is written must still be accomplished in Me: 'And He was

WORDFINDER

22:20 New Covenant A covenant (pronounced *KUV-uh-nunt*) is a legal agreement. Under the Old Covenant (or Old Testament), God agreed to save His people through the blood of animals, which was a symbol for Christ's blood. Under the New Covenant (or New Testament), God agrees to save His people by the blood of Christ Himself.

I am only a servant girl, but I felt sorry for Jesus, the Man they arrested. Everybody was sitting around a fire, and Jesus' hands and feet were tied with chains. He spoke softly and didn't seem upset at all.

There was also another man who followed the crowd into the yard—a disciple of Jesus whose name was Peter. When I told him I had seen him with Jesus, he just got angry and told me I was making a mistake, so I kept quiet after that.

A second and a third time someone spoke to Peter, but Peter denied that he even knew Jesus.

Something happened then that I'll never forget. A rooster crowed. Then Peter looked at Jesus, and for the longest time Jesus stared at him with more pity than I have ever seen.

Peter then got up and rushed out into the night, sobbing.

numbered with the transgressors.' For the things concerning Me have an end.''

38 So they said, "Lord, look, here *are* two swords."

And He said to them, "It is enough."

39 Coming out, He went to the Mount of Olives, as He was accustomed, and His disciples also followed Him. 40 When He came to the place, He said to them, "Pray that you may not enter into temptation."

41 And He was withdrawn from them about a stone's throw, and He knelt down and prayed, 42 saying, "Father, if it is Your will, take this cup away from Me; nevertheless not My will, but Yours, be done." 43 Then an angel appeared to Him from heaven, strengthening Him. 44 And being in agony, He prayed more earnestly. Then His sweat became like great drops of blood falling down to the ground.

45 When He rose up from prayer, and had come to His disciples, He found them sleeping from sorrow. 46 Then He said to them, "Why do you sleep? Rise and pray, lest you enter into temptation."

47 And while He was still speaking, behold, a multitude; and he who was called Judas, one of the twelve, went before them and drew near to Jesus to kiss Him. 48 But Jesus said to him,

"Judas, are you betraying the Son of Man with a kiss?"

49 When those around Him saw what was going to happen, they said to Him, "Lord, shall we strike with the sword?" 50 And one of them struck the servant of the high priest and cut off his right ear.

51 But Jesus answered and said, "Permit even this." And He touched his ear and healed him.

52 Then Jesus said to the chief priests, captains of the temple, and the elders who had come to Him, "Have you come out, as against a robber, with swords and clubs? 53 When I was with you daily in the temple, you did not try to seize Me. But this is your hour, and the power of darkness."

54 Having arrested Him, they led *Him* and brought Him into the high priest's house. But Peter followed at a distance. 55 Now when they had kindled a fire in the midst of the courtyard and sat down together, Peter sat among them. 56 And a certain servant girl, seeing him as he sat by the fire, looked intently at him and said, "This man was also with Him."

57 But he denied Him, saying, "Woman, I do not know Him."

58 And after a little while another saw him and said, "You also are of them."

But Peter said, "Man, I am not!"

Jesus Claims to Be Son of God

The Jerusalem Times

JERUSALEM—Religious leaders questioned Jesus of Nazareth today about a claim He has made publicly, that He, a mere Carpenter, is the Son of God!

Jesus was accused of blasphemy (pronounced *BLASS-fuh-mee*). This meant that leaders believe He *falsely* claims to be the Messiah (or Christ). Our leaders insist they are certain that His actions prove He certainly is not our expected Messiah. After all, this Man has

often been seen in the company of sinners, and His followers are very ordinary men, mostly common fishermen.

The court has continued all day to try to get Jesus to admit that He is the Christ. Finally, He did admit to them that He is the Son of God. This was the proof they needed to convict the Preacher from Galilee.

But this newspaper is not convinced that the leaders are correct. Just who is this Man from Galilee?

---

⁵⁹ Then after about an hour had passed, another confidently affirmed, saying, "Surely this *fellow* also was with Him, for he is a Galilean."

⁶⁰ But Peter said, "Man, I do not know what you are saying!"

Immediately, while he was still speaking, the rooster crowed. ⁶¹ And the Lord turned and looked at Peter. Then Peter remembered the word of the Lord, how He had said to him, "Before the rooster crows, you will deny Me three times." ⁶² So Peter went out and wept bitterly.

⁶³ Now the men who held Jesus mocked Him and beat Him. ⁶⁴ And having blindfolded Him, they struck Him on the face and asked Him, saying, "Prophesy! Who is the one who struck You?" ⁶⁵ And many other things they blasphemously spoke against Him.

⁶⁶ As soon as it was day, the elders

of the people, both chief priests and scribes, came together and led Him into their council, saying, ⁶⁷ "If You are the Christ, tell us."

But He said to them, "If I tell you, you will by no means believe. ⁶⁸ And if I also ask *you,* you will by no means answer Me or let *Me* go. ⁶⁹ Hereafter the Son of Man will sit on the right hand of the power of God."

⁷⁰ Then they all said, "Are You then the Son of God?"

So He said to them, "You *rightly* say that I am."

⁷¹ And they said, "What further testimony do we need? For we have heard it ourselves from His own mouth."

Jesus is betrayed, arrested, and crucified

23 Then the whole multitude of them arose and led Him to Pilate.

DIGGING IN

23:1–25 Pontius Pilate Pontius Pilate (pronounced *PON-chus PIE-lat*) was the fifth Roman governor of Judea. He actually ruled over Judea and Samaria and as far south as the Dead Sea (see the map on page 1343). He ruled from A.D. 26 until A.D. 36. Pilate's official title was "procurator" (pronounced *PROK-you-ray-ter*). Pilate had to decide what to do with

Jesus because the Jewish authorities wanted to crucify Him. But they were not allowed to crucify people without Roman permission. Pilate was puzzled because he "found no reason for death in Him" (verse 22). Since Pilate thought he must please the Jews, he let them crucify Jesus.

Pilate was willing to sacrifice what was

Pilate Lets Barabbas Go!

The Jerusalem Times

JERUSALEM—Two men were brought before Governor Pilate for judgment today. Our religious officials wanted the death sentence for Jesus of Nazareth, but the law doesn't permit our Jewish nation to execute anyone by crucifixion. Only the Roman governor has that power.

The second man on trial before Pilate is a murderer. At the hearing, Jewish leaders stirred up the crowd to persuade Pilate to let Barabbas (pronounced *bar-RAB-bus*) go free. The Roman custom at the Jewish feast of Passover is to release one Jewish criminal. (See Exodus 12 for more information about Passover.)

This newspaper knows of no real crimes that Jesus of Galilee has committed. Yet the crowd kept shouting, "Crucify Him!" Pilate listened to the crowd and, after several delays, freed Barabbas. Jesus was led away to be crucified.

Apparently, the people are willing for a murderer to go free while a harmless religious Teacher has to die!

2 And they began to accuse Him, saying, "We found this *fellow* perverting the nation, and forbidding to pay taxes to Caesar, saying that He Himself is Christ, a King."

3 Then Pilate asked Him, saying, "Are You the King of the Jews?"

He answered him and said, *"It is as you say."*

4 So Pilate said to the chief priests and the crowd, "I find no fault in this Man."

5 But they were the more fierce, saying, "He stirs up the people, teaching throughout all Judea, beginning from Galilee to this place."

6 When Pilate heard of Galilee, he asked if the Man were a Galilean. 7 And as soon as he knew that He belonged to Herod's jurisdiction, he sent Him to Herod, who was also in Jerusalem at that time. 8 Now when Herod saw Jesus, he was exceedingly glad; for he had desired for a long *time* to see Him, because he had heard many things about Him, and he hoped to see some miracle done by Him. 9 Then he questioned Him with many words, but He answered him nothing. 10 And the chief priests and scribes stood and vehemently accused Him. 11 Then Herod, with his men of war, treated Him with contempt and mocked *Him,* arrayed Him in a gorgeous robe, and sent Him back to Pilate. 12 That very day Pilate and Herod became friends with each other, for previously they had been at enmity with each other.

13 Then Pilate, when he had called together the chief priests, the rulers, and the people, 14 said to them, "You have brought this Man to me, as one who misleads the people. And indeed, having examined *Him* in your presence, I have found no fault in this Man concerning those things of which you accuse Him; 15 no, neither did Herod, for I sent you back to him; and indeed nothing deserving of death has been done by Him. 16 I will therefore chastise Him and release *Him*" 17 (for it was necessary for him to release one to them at the feast).

18 And they all cried out at once, saying, "Away with this *Man,* and release

DIGGING IN

right in order to keep his place in the world. He knew Jesus was innocent, but he condemned Him anyway just to satisfy the mob. Some history writers say that Pilate later killed himself.

to us Barabbas"— 19 who had been thrown into prison for a certain rebellion made in the city, and for murder.

20 Pilate, therefore, wishing to release Jesus, again called out to them. 21 But they shouted, saying, "Crucify *Him,* crucify Him!"

22 Then he said to them the third time, "Why, what evil has He done? I have found no reason for death in Him. I will therefore chastise Him and let *Him* go."

23 But they were insistent, demanding with loud voices that He be crucified. And the voices of these men and of the chief priests prevailed. 24 So Pilate gave sentence that it should be as they requested. 25 And he released to them the one they requested, who for rebellion and murder had been thrown into prison; but he delivered Jesus to their will.

26 Now as they led Him away, they laid hold of a certain man, Simon a Cyrenian, who was coming from the country, and on him they laid the cross that he might bear *it* after Jesus.

27 And a great multitude of the people followed Him, and women who also mourned and lamented Him. 28 But Jesus, turning to them, said, "Daughters of Jerusalem, do not weep for Me, but weep for yourselves and for your children. 29 For indeed the days are coming in which they will say, 'Blessed *are* the barren, wombs that never bore, and breasts which never nursed!' 30 Then they will begin 'to say to the mountains, "Fall on us!" and to the hills, "Cover us!" ' 31 For if they do these things in the green wood, what will be done in the dry?"

32 There were also two others, criminals, led with Him to be put to death. 33 And when they had come to the place called **Calvary,** there they crucified Him, and the criminals, one on the right hand and the other on the

left. 34 Then Jesus said, "Father, forgive them, for they do not know what they do."

And they divided His garments and cast lots. 35 And the people stood looking on. But even the rulers with them sneered, saying, "He saved others; let Him save Himself if He is the Christ, the chosen of God."

36 The soldiers also mocked Him, coming and offering Him sour wine, 37 and saying, "If You are the King of the Jews, save Yourself."

38 And an inscription also was written over Him in letters of Greek, Latin, and Hebrew:

THIS IS THE KING OF THE JEWS.

39 Then one of the criminals who were hanged blasphemed Him, saying, "If You are the Christ, save Yourself and us."

40 But the other, answering, rebuked him, saying, "Do you not even fear God, seeing you are under the same condemnation? 41 And we indeed justly, for we receive the due reward of our deeds; but this Man has done nothing wrong." 42 Then he said to Jesus, "Lord, remember me when You come into Your kingdom."

43 And Jesus said to him, "Assuredly, I say to you, today you will be with Me in Paradise."

44 Now it was about the sixth hour, and there was darkness over all the earth until the ninth hour. 45 Then the sun was darkened, and the veil of the temple was torn in two. 46 And when Jesus had cried out with a loud voice, He said, "Father, 'into Your hands I commit My spirit.' " Having said this, He breathed His last.

47 So when the centurion saw what had happened, he glorified God, saying, "Certainly this was a righteous Man!"

48 And the whole crowd who came

⊛WORDFINDER

23:33 Calvary Pronounced *KAL-vuh-ree.* From a Latin word meaning "the skull." It seems to be the place outside Jerusalem where criminals were put to death and where Jesus, also, was crucified.

together to that sight, seeing what had been done, beat their breasts and returned. 49 But all His acquaintances, and the women who followed Him from Galilee, stood at a distance, watching these things.

50 Now behold, *there was* a man named Joseph, a council member, a good and just man. 51 He had not consented to their decision and deed. *He was* from Arimathea, a city of the Jews, who himself was also waiting for the kingdom of God. 52 This man went to Pilate and asked for the body of Jesus. 53 Then he took it down, wrapped it in linen, and laid it in a tomb *that was* hewn out of the rock, where no one had ever lain before. 54 That day was the Preparation, and the Sabbath drew near.

55 And the women who had come with Him from Galilee followed after, and they observed the tomb and how His body was laid. 56 Then they returned and prepared spices and fragrant oils. And they rested on the Sabbath according to the commandment.

Jesus is alive!

24 Now on the first *day* of the week, very early in the morning, they, and certain *other women* with them, came to the tomb bringing the spices which they had prepared. 2 But they found the stone rolled away from the tomb. 3 Then they went in and did not find the body of the Lord Jesus. 4 And it happened, as they were greatly perplexed about this, that behold, two men stood by them in shining garments. 5 Then, as they were afraid and bowed *their* faces to the earth, they said to them, "Why do you seek the living among the dead? 6 He is not here, but is risen! Remember how He spoke to you when He was still in Galilee, 7 saying, 'The Son of Man must be delivered into the hands of sinful men, and be crucified, and the third day rise again.' "

8 And they remembered His words. 9 Then they returned from the tomb and told all these things to the eleven and to all the rest. 10 It was Mary Magdalene, Joanna, Mary *the mother* of James, and the other *women* with them, who told these things to the apostles. 11 And their words seemed to them like idle tales, and they did not believe them. 12 But Peter arose and ran to the tomb; and stooping down, he saw the linen cloths lying by themselves; and he departed, marveling to himself at what had happened.

13 Now behold, two of them were traveling that same day to a village called Emmaus, which was seven miles from Jerusalem. 14 And they talked together of all these things which had happened. 15 So it was, while they conversed and reasoned, that Jesus Himself drew near and went with them. 16 But their eyes were restrained, so that they did not know Him.

17 And He said to them, "What kind of conversation *is* this that you have with one another as you walk and are sad?"

18 Then the one whose name was Cleopas answered and said to Him, "Are You the only stranger in Jerusalem, and have You not known the things which happened there in these days?"

19 And He said to them, "What things?"

So they said to Him, "The things concerning Jesus of Nazareth, who was a Prophet mighty in deed and word before God and all the people, 20 and how the chief priests and our rulers delivered Him to be condemned to death, and crucified Him. 21 But we were hoping that it was He who was going to redeem Israel. Indeed, besides all this, today is the third day since these things happened. 22 Yes, and certain women of our company, who arrived at the tomb early, astonished us. 23 When they did not find His body, they came saying that they had also seen a vision of angels who said He was alive. 24 And certain of those *who were* with us went to the tomb and found *it* just as the women had said; but Him they did not see."

25 Then He said to them, "O foolish

ones, and slow of heart to believe in all that the prophets have spoken! 26 Ought not the Christ to have suffered these things and to enter into His glory?" 27 And beginning at Moses and all the Prophets, He expounded to them in all the Scriptures the things concerning Himself.

28 Then they drew near to the village where they were going, and He indicated that He would have gone farther. 29 But they constrained Him, saying, "Abide with us, for it is toward eve-

ning, and the day is far spent." And He went in to stay with them.

30 Now it came to pass, as He sat at the table with them, that He took bread, blessed and broke it, and gave it to them. 31 Then their eyes were opened and they knew Him; and He vanished from their sight.

32 And they said to one another, "Did not our heart burn within us while He talked with us on the road, and while He opened the Scriptures to us?" 33 So they rose up that very hour and

---

⛏DIGGING IN

24:13–35 Jesus Walks with His Friends Two of Jesus' disciples were walking from Jerusalem to the village of Emmaus (pronounced *eh-MAY-us*) about seven miles away. The disciples, sad because Jesus had been crucified, felt that all their hopes had come to an end.

Then, as these two disciples walked along the road, Jesus came and walked beside them. For some reason, they didn't recognize Him.

It was not until they had arrived in Emmaus that they discovered who He was. While they were sitting at the table, Jesus broke off some bread. Since He had often broken bread with His disciples in this very same way, they knew at last who had been walking and talking with them.

Jesus will also walk beside you in life. Even though you can't see Him, you can know Him, and He will sit with you at your table.

24:26 Jesus Had to Die Do you think Jesus was crucified just because a mob in Jerusalem wanted Him to die? No! God had always planned that Jesus would be crucified for our sins. If Jesus had not died, we all would have been condemned for our sins, just as we deserved.

The Old Testament sacrifice was an example of the sacrifice of Jesus on the Cross. The priests of the Old Testament brought a lamb for sacrifice and killed it. This was a terrible act. But the sacrifice of the lamb on the Old Testament altar is a dreadful picture of the even more awesome cost of sin—the death of God's own Son!

Everything has a price, and sin has its own price. God loved you so much that He was willing to pay with the life of His own Son so you would not have to pay for your sins.

Emmaus, the village where Jesus showed two disciples that He was alive!

What We All Can Learn

God gave us His Word in the Bible, but we need Jesus to help us understand what the Bible says. That's why Jesus taught His disciples.

The Bible is really about Jesus. He is the Living Word of God. Jesus
always existed, but He revealed Himself in a human body to His disciples.

Jesus came to show us the true way to God. He even said, "I am the
way." So the Bible is really one long story leading up to Jesus. He made
what the Old Testament prophets said come true.

Since Adam and Eve first disobeyed God, people have needed a Savior
to take away their sins. That's what the Bible is about, and that's why
Jesus came.

returned to Jerusalem, and found the eleven and those *who were* with them gathered together, 34 saying, "The Lord is risen indeed, and has appeared to Simon!" 35 And they told about the things *that had happened* on the road, and how He was known to them in the breaking of bread.

36 Now as they said these things, Jesus Himself stood in the midst of them, and said to them, "Peace to you." 37 But they were terrified and frightened, and supposed they had seen a spirit. 38 And He said to them, "Why are you troubled? And why do doubts arise in your hearts? 39 Behold My hands and My feet, that it is I My-self. Handle Me and see, for a spirit does not have flesh and bones as you see I have."

40 When He had said this, He showed them His hands and His feet. 41 But while they still did not believe for joy, and marveled, He said to them,

"Have you any food here?" 42 So they gave Him a piece of a broiled fish and some honeycomb. 43 And He took *it* and ate in their presence.

44 Then He said to them, "These *are* the words which I spoke to you while I was still with you, that all things must be fulfilled which *were* written in the Law of Moses and *the* Prophets and *the* Psalms concerning Me." 45 And He opened their understanding, that they might comprehend the Scriptures.

46 Then He said to them, "Thus it is written, and thus it was necessary for the Christ to suffer and to rise from the dead the third day, 47 and that re-pentance and remission of sins should be preached in His name to all nations, beginning at Jerusalem. 48 And you are witnesses of these things. 49 Behold, I send the Promise of My Father upon you; but tarry in the city of Jerusalem until you are endued with power from on high."

DIGGING IN

24:46, 47 What Is the Gospel? Jesus explained to His disciples that He died and rose again to carry out what the Old Testament Scriptures promised. The promise was that Jesus would die in order to send the gospel to "all nations." The gospel means "the Good News."

The Good News is that because Jesus died for us and rose again, we can be forgiven if we turn away from our sins. That is great news! Strange to say, many people just throw this Good News away

like trash. They don't care that Jesus died for them, and they don't want their sins forgiven.

God has been very patient for many hundreds of years. If we throw away the sacrifice of God's Son, and if we do not repent, then we have no other hope for God's forgiveness. Have you accepted the Good News of Jesus' sacrifice for your sins? He is living now to give you His peace.

50 And He led them out as far as Bethany, and He lifted up His hands and blessed them. 51 Now it came to pass, while He blessed them, that He was parted from them and carried up into heaven. 52 And they worshiped Him, and returned to Jerusalem with great joy, 53 and were continually in the temple praising and blessing God. Amen.

The Book of
JOHN

The four Gospels are all about My coming to earth, My life here, and how I went back to heaven. John will tell you about My reason for coming to the world.

In order to know who I am, you must begin by realizing that My life didn't begin in Bethlehem. Christmas is only the story of how I began My life *on earth.*

Always and forever, I have lived in heaven with My Father and with the Holy Spirit. We three are One. My Father is God, I am God, the Holy Spirit is God.

Sometimes in the Old Testament, I showed myself in strange ways like when I wrestled with Jacob all night (see Genesis 32). But in the New Testament, I was the ''Word Who Became Flesh.'' Then everybody could see what God is like by watching how I lived and the works I did. You know who I am. My name is Jesus.

God left heaven to become one of us

IN the beginning was the Word, and the Word was with God, and the Word was God. 2 He was in the beginning with God. 3 All things were made through Him, and without Him nothing was made that was made. 4 In Him was life, and the life was the light of men. 5 And the light shines in the darkness, and the darkness did not comprehend it.

6 There was a man sent from God, whose name *was* John. 7 This man came for a witness, to bear witness of the Light, that all through him might believe. 8 He was not that Light, but *was sent* to bear witness of that Light. 9 That was the true Light which gives light to every man coming into the world.

10 He was in the world, and the world was made through Him, and the world did not know Him. 11 He came to His own, and His own did not receive Him. 12 But as many as received Him, to them He gave the right to become children of God, to those who believe in His name: 13 who were born, not of blood, nor of the will of the flesh, nor of the will of man, but of God.

14 And the Word became flesh and dwelt among us, and we beheld His

⛏ DIGGING IN

1:1 Jesus Christ Is God Have you ever wondered what it would be like to live in the form of an animal—say, a beautiful German Shepherd dog? You would still have all your abilities as a human being. You could think human thoughts and do mathematics. You would be able to read books and enjoy beautiful scenery just like a human being. But to others, you would *seem* like that German Shepherd in every other way.

This may help you understand just a little of what it was like for the unlimited God to become a Man. He always was God, but about two thousand years ago, He was born and lived as a sinless Man called Jesus. He lived as God's special Man to show you what God's love is like. God lived as this Man so He could die for your sins.

What the Priests and Levites Learned

We were important people in Israel when John the Baptist lived, and we thought we had a right to know just who John thought he was. That's why we went to him and asked, "Who are you?"

Of course, he knew we were trying to trap him, and so he didn't tell us what we wanted to hear. If he had said he was Christ or the great prophet who would come before Christ, then we would have arrested him.

John did say something that made us think. He used the words of Isaiah the prophet: "I am 'the voice of one crying in the wilderness: "make straight the way of the LORD." ' " Then he announced that Christ would come after him. We came away, shaking our heads.

glory, the glory as of the only begotten of the Father, full of grace and truth.

15 John bore witness of Him and cried out, saying, "This was He of whom I said, 'He who comes after me is preferred before me, for He was before me.' "

16 And of His fullness we have all received, and grace for grace. 17 For the law was given through Moses, *but* grace and truth came through Jesus Christ. 18 No one has seen God at any time. The only begotten Son, who is in the bosom of the Father, He has declared *Him*.

19 Now this is the testimony of John, when the Jews sent priests and Levites from Jerusalem to ask him, "Who are you?"

20 He confessed, and did not deny, but confessed, "I am not the Christ."

21 And they asked him, "What then? Are you Elijah?"

He said, "I am not."

"Are you the Prophet?"

And he answered, "No."

22 Then they said to him, "Who are you, that we may give an answer to those who sent us? What do you say about yourself?"

23 He said: "I *am*

'The voice of one crying in the
    wilderness:
"Make straight the way of the
    LORD," '

as the prophet Isaiah said."

24 Now those who were sent were from the Pharisees. 25 And they asked him, saying, "Why then do you baptize if you are not the Christ, nor Elijah, nor the Prophet?"

26 John answered them, saying, "I baptize with water, but there stands One among you whom you do not know. 27 It is He who, coming after me, is preferred before me, whose sandal strap I am not worthy to loose."

28 These things were done in Bethabara beyond the Jordan, where John was baptizing.

29 The next day John saw Jesus coming toward him, and said, "Behold! The Lamb of God who takes away the sin of the world! 30 This is He of whom I said, 'After me comes a Man who is preferred before me, for He was before me.' 31 I did not know Him; but that He should be revealed to Israel, therefore I came baptizing with water."

32 And John bore witness, saying, "I saw the Spirit descending from heaven like a dove, and He remained upon Him. 33 I did not know Him, but He who sent me to baptize with water said to me, 'Upon whom you see the Spirit descending, and remaining on Him, this is He who baptizes with the Holy Spirit.' 34 And I have seen and testified that this is the Son of God."

35 Again, the next day, John stood with two of his disciples. 36 And looking at Jesus as He walked, he said, "Behold the Lamb of God!"

37 The two disciples heard him speak, and they followed Jesus. 38 Then Jesus turned, and seeing them following, said to them, "What do you seek?"

They said to Him, "Rabbi" (which is to say, when translated, Teacher), "where are You staying?"

39 He said to them, "Come and see." They came and saw where He was staying, and remained with Him that day (now it was about the tenth hour).

40 One of the two who heard John speak, and followed Him, was Andrew, Simon Peter's brother. 41 He first found his own brother Simon, and said to him, "We have found the **Messiah**" (which is translated, the Christ). 42 And he brought him to Jesus.

Now when Jesus looked at him, He said, "You are Simon the son of Jonah. You shall be called Cephas" (which is translated, A Stone).

43 The following day Jesus wanted to go to Galilee, and He found Philip and said to him, "Follow Me." 44 Now Philip was from Bethsaida, the city of Andrew and Peter. 45 Philip found Nathanael and said to him, "We have found Him of whom Moses in the law, and also the prophets, wrote—Jesus of Nazareth, the son of Joseph."

46 And Nathanael said to him, "Can anything good come out of Nazareth?" Philip said to him, "Come and see."

47 Jesus saw Nathanael coming toward Him, and said of him, "Behold, an Israelite indeed, in whom is no deceit!"

48 Nathanael said to Him, "How do You know me?"

Jesus answered and said to him, "Before Philip called you, when you were under the fig tree, I saw you."

49 Nathanael answered and said to Him, "Rabbi, You are the Son of God! You are the King of Israel!"

50 Jesus answered and said to him, "Because I said to you, 'I saw you under the fig tree,' do you believe? You will see greater things than these." 51 And He said to him, "Most assuredly, I say to you, hereafter you shall see heaven open, and the angels of God ascending and descending upon the Son of Man."

Jesus changes water into wine

2 On the third day there was a wedding in Cana of Galilee, and the mother of Jesus was there. 2 Now both Jesus and His disciples were invited to the wedding. 3 And when they ran out of wine, the mother of Jesus said to Him, "They have no wine."

4 Jesus said to her, "Woman, what does your concern have to do with Me? My hour has not yet come."

5 His mother said to the servants, "Whatever He says to you, do it."

6 Now there were set there six waterpots of stone, according to the manner of purification of the Jews, containing twenty or thirty gallons apiece. 7 Jesus said to them, "Fill the waterpots with water." And they filled them up to the brim. 8 And He said to them, "Draw some out now, and take it to the master of the feast." And they took it. 9 When the master of the feast had tasted the water that was made wine, and did not know where it came from (but the servants who had drawn the water knew), the master of the feast called the bridegroom. 10 And he said to him, "Every man at the beginning sets out the good wine, and when the guests have well drunk, then the inferior. You have kept the good wine until now!"

11 This beginning of signs Jesus did in Cana of Galilee, and manifested His glory; and His disciples believed in Him.

🔍 WORDFINDER

1:41 Messiah Pronounced *muh-SIGH-uh*. A Hebrew word meaning "Anointed One." *Christos* (pronounced *KRISS-tos*) is a Greek word from which we get the word "Christ" and means the same as "Messiah."

Can Water Become Wine?

The Cana News

CANA—At a wedding dinner in Cana of Galilee, a Man has turned water into the very best wine!

Jesus, a local Preacher, recently attended the wedding with His mother and His disciples. But the servants at the dinner were upset when they found there was no wine to serve the guests. Jesus' mother told him about the prob-lem, then instructed the servants to do whatever Jesus said.

Jesus told the servants to fill six large water jugs with water. After they did that, they served the best wine of all from those same water jugs!

Though it appears this Jesus pulled off a miracle, we understand the bridegroom got all the thanks for the wine!

¹² After this He went down to Capernaum, He, His mother, His brothers, and His disciples; and they did not stay there many days.

¹³ Now the **Passover** of the Jews was at hand, and Jesus went up to Jerusalem. ¹⁴ And He found in the temple those who sold oxen and sheep and doves, and the **money changers** doing business. ¹⁵ When He had made

Cana, where Jesus turned water to wine at a wedding.

WORDFINDER

2:13 Passover   The greatest Hebrew celebration. The people remember that the Lord "passed over" their homes in Egypt because a lamb's blood was applied to their doorways (see Exodus 12). After the death of the firstborn in Egypt, Pharaoh freed God's people.

2:14 Money changers   Bankers who changed common money for the temple money needed for the purchase of ceremonial animals. Some temple money changers often charged a large fee.

What Nicodemus Learned

We Pharisees (pronounced *FAIR-uh-sees*) were among the leaders of our Jewish people for centuries before Jesus came. Now the crowds were following Him.

Well, I was determined to find out just who this Man was. The people said He could even heal the sick. There couldn't be any harm in talking to Him, I thought. But I decided to go at night so none of my friends would see me.

The new Teacher really upset me at first. He told me I "must be born again." When I asked Him what this meant, He said I had to be born all over again from God. Because I trusted Him, I'm a new person now.

Would you like to be born again?

a whip of cords, He drove them all out of the **temple,** with the sheep and the oxen, and poured out the changers' money and overturned the tables. 16 And He said to those who sold doves, "Take these things away! Do not make My Father's house a house of merchandise!" 17 Then His disciples remembered that it was written, "Zeal for Your house has eaten Me up."

18 So the Jews answered and said to Him, "What sign do You show to us, since You do these things?"

19 Jesus answered and said to them, "Destroy this temple, and in three days I will raise it up."

20 Then the Jews said, "It has taken forty-six years to build this temple, and will You raise it up in three days?"

21 But He was speaking of the temple of His body. 22 Therefore, when He had risen from the dead, His disciples remembered that He had said this to them; and they believed the Scripture and the word which Jesus had said.

23 Now when He was in Jerusalem at the Passover, during the feast, many believed in His name when they saw the signs which He did. 24 But Jesus did not commit Himself to them, be-cause He knew all *men,* 25 and had no need that anyone should testify of man, for He knew what was in man.

Jesus tells Nicodemus how to be born again

3 There was a man of the Pharisees named Nicodemus, a ruler of the Jews. 2 This man came to Jesus by night and said to Him, "Rabbi, we know that You are a teacher come from God; for no one can do these signs that You do unless God is with him."

3 Jesus answered and said to him, "Most assuredly, I say to you, unless one is **born again,** he cannot see the kingdom of God."

4 Nicodemus said to Him, "How can a man be born when he is old? Can he enter a second time into his mother's womb and be born?"

5 Jesus answered, "Most assuredly, I say to you, unless one is born of water and the Spirit, he cannot enter the kingdom of God. 6 That which is born of the flesh is flesh, and that which is born of the Spirit is spirit. 7 Do not marvel that I said to you, 'You must be born again.' 8 The wind blows where

WORDFINDER

2:15 Temple Israel's place of worship after they settled in Canaan. It was a building of finished stone. Worship in the temple was the same as it had been in the tabernacle.

3:3 Born Again When God changes a person to become a Christian. The change is so great that Jesus said it is like being born all over again.

it wishes, and you hear the sound of it, but cannot tell where it comes from and where it goes. So is everyone who is born of the Spirit."

9 Nicodemus answered and said to Him, "How can these things be?"

10 Jesus answered and said to him, "Are you the teacher of Israel, and do not know these things? 11 Most assuredly, I say to you, We speak what We know and testify what We have seen, and you do not receive Our witness. 12 If I have told you earthly things and you do not believe, how will you believe if I tell you heavenly things? 13 No one has ascended to heaven but He who came down from heaven, *that is,* the Son of Man who is in heaven. 14 And as Moses lifted up the serpent in the wilderness, even so must the Son of Man be lifted up, 15 that whoever believes in Him should not perish but have eternal life. 16 For God so loved the world that He gave His only begotten Son, that whoever **believes** in Him should not perish but have everlasting life. 17 For God did not send His Son into the world to condemn the world, but that the world through Him might be saved.

18 "He who believes in Him is not condemned; but he who does not believe is condemned already, because he has not believed in the name of the only begotten Son of God. 19 And this is the condemnation, that the light has come into the world, and men loved darkness rather than light, because their deeds were evil. 20 For everyone practicing evil hates the light and does not come to the light, lest his deeds should be exposed. 21 But he who does the truth comes to the light, that his deeds may be clearly seen, that they have been done in God."

22 After these things Jesus and His disciples came into the land of Judea, and there He remained with them and baptized. 23 Now John also was baptizing in Aenon near Salim, because there was much water there. And they came and were baptized. 24 For John had not yet been thrown into prison.

25 Then there arose a dispute between *some* of John's disciples and the Jews about purification. 26 And they came to John and said to him, "Rabbi, He who was with you beyond the Jordan, to whom you have testified—behold, He is baptizing, and all are coming to Him!"

27 John answered and said, "A man can receive nothing unless it has been given to him from heaven. 28 You yourselves bear me witness, that I said, 'I am not the Christ,' but, 'I have been sent before Him.' 29 He who has the bride is the bridegroom; but the friend of the bridegroom, who stands and

WORDFINDER

3:16 Believes To accept what God has said in the Bible and to trust Jesus to save you from your sins. To believe as a Christian is to receive Jesus Christ into your life.

DIGGING IN

3:16 How Much Did God Love You?
You are a son or daughter of Adam and Eve. Long ago Adam and Eve disobeyed God in a way that said, "We don't want You to be our God. We want to do our own thing." You and I have received that rebel nature from Adam and Eve. We, too, want to do our own thing. We don't want God in our thoughts and our lives.

Suppose you had a speedboat that broke down. If you couldn't fix it for a good price, you would just get rid of it. But God didn't get rid of Adam and Eve, and He doesn't want to get rid of you, either.

God has been patient with us for thousands of years, and He has paid for us with the blood of His only beloved Son. God is still patiently waiting for you to love Him as He has loved you.

hears him, rejoices greatly because of the bridegroom's voice. Therefore this joy of mine is fulfilled. 30 He must increase, but I *must* decrease. 31 He who comes from above is above all; he who is of the earth is earthly and speaks of the earth. He who comes from heaven is above all. 32 And what He has seen and heard, that He testifies; and no one receives His testimony. 33 He who has received His testimony has certified that God is true. 34 For He whom God has sent speaks the words of God, for God does not give the Spirit by measure. 35 The Father loves the Son, and has given all things into His hand. 36 He who believes in the Son has everlasting life; and he who does not believe the Son shall not see life, but the wrath of God abides on him."

Jesus talks with a Samaritan woman

4 Therefore, when the Lord knew that the Pharisees had heard that Jesus made and baptized more disciples than John 2 (though Jesus Himself did not baptize, but His disciples), 3 He left Judea and departed again to Galilee. 4 But He needed to go through Samaria.

5 So He came to a city of Samaria which is called Sychar, near the plot of ground that Jacob gave to his son Joseph. 6 Now Jacob's well was there. Jesus therefore, being wearied from *His* journey, sat thus by the well. It was about the sixth hour.

7 A woman of Samaria came to draw water. Jesus said to her, "Give Me a drink." 8 For His disciples had gone away into the city to buy food.

9 Then the woman of Samaria said to Him, "How is it that You, being a Jew, ask a drink from me, a Samaritan woman?" For Jews have no dealings with Samaritans.

10 Jesus answered and said to her, "If you knew the gift of God, and who it is who says to you, 'Give Me a drink,' you would have asked Him, and He would have given you living water."

11 The woman said to Him, "Sir, You have nothing to draw with, and the well is deep. Where then do You get that living water? 12 Are You greater than our father Jacob, who gave us the well, and drank from it himself, as well as his sons and his livestock?"

13 Jesus answered and said to her, "Whoever drinks of this water will thirst again, 14 but whoever drinks of the water that I shall give him will never thirst. But the water that I shall give him will become in him a fountain of water springing up into everlasting life."

15 The woman said to Him, "Sir, give me this water, that I may not thirst, nor come here to draw."

16 Jesus said to her, "Go, call your husband, and come here."

17 The woman answered and said, "I have no husband."

Jesus said to her, "You have well said, 'I have no husband,' 18 for you have had five husbands, and the one whom you now have is not your husband; in that you spoke truly."

19 The woman said to Him, "Sir, I perceive that You are a prophet.

⚒ DIGGING IN

4:14 Have You Ever Drunk Living Water? When you're thirsty nothing tastes so good as a huge drink of cool water. Of course, that water can only satisfy you for a while. Then you need another drink.

But Jesus said He could give you a drink of water that would last forever! Of course He wasn't talking about the water that comes out of your kitchen faucet. Jesus was talking about a special kind of water—*the water of everlasting life*. This can be a waterspring deep inside you. It just keeps bubbling up and refreshing you, and it never runs dry.

Who wouldn't like to have this kind of water? Nobody ever satisfied thirst by just *looking* at water, though. You have to *drink* it. That means you have to come to Jesus. He said, "He who believes in Me shall never thirst" (John 6:35). He will give you "living water."

Jacob's well, where Jesus talked to a Samaritan woman.

20 Our fathers worshiped on this mountain, and you *Jews* say that in Jerusalem is the place where one ought to worship."

21 Jesus said to her, "Woman, believe Me, the hour is coming when you will neither on this mountain, nor in Jerusalem, worship the Father. 22 You worship what you do not know; we know what we worship, for salvation is of the Jews. 23 But the hour is coming, and now is, when the true worshipers will worship the Father in spirit and truth; for the Father is seeking such

---

🪓 DIGGING IN

4:20 Who Were the Jews of the New Testament? The Jews had been God's chosen people for a long time. Two thousand years before Jesus was born, God called Abraham from his hometown in what is modern Iraq to come and live in Palestine. There Abraham became the great father of the Jewish nation. (See Genesis 11:12.)

After Abraham's time, the Jews often rebelled against the Lord. You have seen in the Old Testament how God had to punish the Jews. He allowed foreign nations, like the Assyrians and Babylonians, to conquer His people. Finally, the Romans became the rulers of the Jews. The Jewish people had long been a conquered people when Jesus came and offered them God's friendship and salvation.

The Jews of Jesus' time were proud of their temple and their religious customs. In their pride, they made a mistake that some Christians also make—they avoided unbelievers. God wants us to share the Good News of His love with everyone we meet.

to worship Him. ²⁴ God *is* Spirit, and those who worship Him must worship in spirit and truth."

²⁵ The woman said to Him, "I know that Messiah is coming" (who is called Christ). "When He comes, He will tell us all things."

²⁶ Jesus said to her, "I who speak to you am *He*."

²⁷ And at this *point* His disciples came, and they marveled that He talked with a woman; yet no one said, "What do You seek?" or, "Why are You talking with her?"

²⁸ The woman then left her waterpot, went her way into the city, and said to the men, ²⁹ "Come, see a Man who told me all things that I ever did. Could this be the Christ?" ³⁰ Then they went out of the city and came to Him.

Who Is Christ?

The woman at the well knew that Jesus was "the Christ." The word *Christ* means the "Anointed One" from God. Jesus was the One that people had expected since Old Testament times. The Old Testament word for Christ was *Messiah.*

³¹ In the meantime His disciples urged Him, saying, "Rabbi, eat."

³² But He said to them, "I have food to eat of which you do not know."

³³ Therefore the disciples said to one another, "Has anyone brought Him *anything* to eat?"

³⁴ Jesus said to them, "My food is to do the will of Him who sent Me, and to finish His work. ³⁵ Do you not say, 'There are still four months and *then* comes the harvest'? Behold, I say to you, lift up your eyes and look at the fields, for they are already white for harvest! ³⁶ And he who reaps receives wages, and gathers fruit for eternal life, that both he who sows and he who reaps may rejoice together. ³⁷ For in this the saying is true: 'One sows and another reaps.' ³⁸ I sent you to reap that for which you have not

labored; others have labored, and you have entered into their labors."

³⁹ And many of the Samaritans of that city believed in Him because of the word of the woman who testified, "He told me all that *ever* did." ⁴⁰ So when the Samaritans had come to Him, they urged Him to stay with them; and He stayed there two days. ⁴¹ And many more believed because of His own word.

⁴² Then they said to the woman, "Now we believe, not because of what you said, for we ourselves have heard *Him* and we know that this is indeed the Christ, the Savior of the world."

⁴³ Now after the two days He departed from there and went to Galilee. ⁴⁴ For Jesus Himself testified that a prophet has no honor in his own country. ⁴⁵ So when He came to Galilee, the Galileans received Him, having seen all the things He did in Jerusalem at the feast; for they also had gone to the feast.

⁴⁶ So Jesus came again to Cana of Galilee where He had made the water wine. And there was a certain nobleman whose son was sick at Capernaum. ⁴⁷ When he heard that Jesus had come out of Judea into Galilee, he went to Him and implored Him to come down and heal his son, for he was at the point of death. ⁴⁸ Then Jesus said to him, "Unless you *people* see signs and wonders, you will by no means believe."

⁴⁹ The nobleman said to Him, "Sir, come down before my child dies!"

⁵⁰ Jesus said to him, "Go your way; your son lives." So the man believed the word that Jesus spoke to him, and he went his way. ⁵¹ And as he was now going down, his servants met him and told *him,* saying, "Your son lives!"

⁵² Then he inquired of them the hour when he got better. And they said to him, "Yesterday at the seventh hour the fever left him." ⁵³ So the father knew that *it was* at the same hour in which Jesus said to him, "Your son lives." And he himself believed, and his whole household.

⁵⁴ This again *is* the second sign Jesus

What the Samaritans Learned

We were really surprised that the Jewish Prophet would come to our country. Usually, Jews had nothing to do with us. They hated us because of something that happened long ago.

Now this Jesus had come and talked with one of our worst citizens. She was that awful woman who had several husbands! But something has happened to her since she talked to Jesus. Now she seems completely changed and has started a new life.

Some of us went to see this Man Jesus. After He stayed with us for two days, many of us believed in Him as our Savior. This is an amazing thing. God sent His very own Son to save sinners—even Samaritans like us! How about you?

did when He had come out of Judea into Galilee.

A sick man is healed

5 After this there was a feast of the Jews, and Jesus went up to Jerusalem. ² Now there is in Jerusalem by the Sheep *Gate* a pool, which is called in Hebrew, Bethesda, having five porches. ³ In these lay a great multitude of sick people, blind, lame, paralyzed, waiting for the moving of the water. ⁴ For an angel went down at a certain time into the pool and stirred up the water; then whoever stepped in first, after the stirring of the water, was made well of whatever disease he had. ⁵ Now a certain man was there who had an infirmity thirty-eight years. ⁶ When Jesus saw him lying there, and knew that he already had been *in that condition* a long time, He said to him, "Do you want to be made well?"

⁷ The sick man answered Him, "Sir, I have no man to put me into the pool

Jacob's well is a half mile from Sychar, a town located at the foot of Mount Gerizim.

Paralyzed Man Walks!

The Jerusalem Times

JERUSALEM—At the Bethesda Pool today, where reporters from *The Times* have been covering the many healings that take place there, a man who had been paralyzed for thirty-eight years walked away!

Jesus, the Teacher from Galilee, saw the man lying there, unable to get into the pool because he had no one to help him. Jesus asked the crippled man if he wanted to be well. When the man answered Him, Jesus gave a simple command: "Rise, take up your bed and walk."

Eyewitnesses report an amazing happening. At once, the man stood up and carried away his bedroll. He walked as if nothing had ever been wrong with his legs.

Some of the religious leaders told the man he was breaking the Sabbath by carrying his bed. There is a growing belief among other people, however, that God created the Sabbath for doing His works, like healing the crippled man!

when the water is stirred up; but while I am coming, another steps down before me."

8 Jesus said to him, "Rise, take up your bed and walk." 9 And immediately the man was made well, took up his bed, and walked.

And that day was the Sabbath. 10 The Jews therefore said to him who was cured, "It is the Sabbath; it is not lawful for you to carry your bed."

The Pool of Bethesda where Jesus healed the man who had been lame for thirty-eight years.

11 He answered them, "He who made me well said to me, 'Take up your bed and walk.' "

12 Then they asked him, "Who is the Man who said to you, 'Take up your bed and walk'?" 13 But the one who was healed did not know who it was, for Jesus had withdrawn, a multitude being in *that* place. 14 Afterward Jesus found him in the temple, and said to him, "See, you have been made well. Sin no more, lest a worse thing come upon you."

15 The man departed and told the Jews that it was Jesus who had made him well.

16 For this reason the Jews persecuted Jesus, and sought to kill Him, because He had done these things on the Sabbath. 17 But Jesus answered them, "My Father has been working until now, and I have been working."

18 Therefore the Jews sought all the more to kill Him, because He not only broke the Sabbath, but also said that God was His Father, making Himself equal with God. 19 Then Jesus answered and said to them, "Most assuredly, I say to you, the Son can do nothing of Himself, but what He sees the Father do; for whatever He does, the Son also does in like manner. 20 For the Father loves the Son, and

shows Him all things that He Himself does; and He will show Him greater works than these, that you may marvel. 21 For as the Father raises the dead and gives life to *them*, even so the Son gives life to whom He will. 22 For the Father judges no one, but has committed all judgment to the Son, 23 that all should honor the Son just as they honor the Father. He who does not honor the Son does not honor the Father who sent Him.

24 "Most assuredly, I say to you, he who hears My word and believes in Him who sent Me has everlasting life, and shall not come into judgment, but has passed from death into life. 25 Most assuredly, I say to you, the hour is coming, and now is, when the dead will hear the voice of the Son of God; and those who hear will live. 26 For as the Father has life in Himself, so He has granted the Son to have life in Himself, 27 and has given Him authority to execute judgment also, because He is the Son of Man. 28 Do not marvel at this; for the hour is coming in which all who are in the graves will hear His voice 29 and come forth—those who have done good, to the resurrection of life, and those who have done evil, to the resurrection of condemnation. 30 I can of Myself do nothing. As I hear, I judge; and My judgment is righteous, because I do not seek My own will but the will of the Father who sent Me.

31 "If I bear witness of Myself, My witness is not true. 32 There is another who bears witness of Me, and I know that the witness which He witnesses of Me is true. 33 You have sent to John, and he has borne witness to the truth. 34 Yet I do not receive testimony from man, but I say these things that you may be saved. 35 He was the burning and shining lamp, and you were willing for a time to rejoice in his light. 36 But I have a greater witness than John's; for the works which the Father has given Me to finish—the very works that I do—bear witness of Me, that the Father has sent Me. 37 And the Father Himself, who sent Me, has testified of

Me. You have neither heard His voice at any time, nor seen His form. 38 But you do not have His word abiding in you, because whom He sent, Him you do not believe. 39 You search the Scriptures, for in them you think you have eternal life; and these are they which testify of Me. 40 But you are not willing to come to Me that you may have life.

41 "I do not receive honor from men. 42 But I know you, that you do not have the love of God in you. 43 I have come in My Father's name, and you do not receive Me; if another comes in his own name, him you will receive. 44 How can you believe, who receive honor from one another, and do not seek the honor that *comes* from the only God? 45 Do not think that I shall accuse you to the Father; there is *one* who accuses you—Moses, in whom you trust. 46 For if you believed Moses, you would believe Me; for he wrote about Me. 47 But if you do not believe his writings, how will you believe My words?"

Jesus multiplies food for the crowd

6 After these things Jesus went over the Sea of Galilee, which is *the Sea* of Tiberias. 2 Then a great multitude followed Him, because they saw His signs which He performed on those who were diseased. 3 And Jesus went up on the mountain, and there He sat with His disciples.

4 Now the Passover, a feast of the Jews, was near. 5 Then Jesus lifted up *His* eyes, and seeing a great multitude coming toward Him, He said to Philip, "Where shall we buy bread, that these may eat?" 6 But this He said to test him, for He Himself knew what He would do.

7 Philip answered Him, "Two hundred denarii worth of bread is not sufficient for them, that *every* one of them may have a little."

8 One of His disciples, Andrew, Simon Peter's brother, said to Him, 9 "There is a lad here who has five

What a Certain Boy Learned

I was only one boy in a big crowd of people who had come to hear a Man named Jesus. He was preaching around the country in those days. I couldn't see much, but I enjoyed hearing Him talk. One day I brought a good supply of food along for myself so I could stay for a while.

Then one of His followers came and said the Teacher wanted my lunch. I looked at my bag of lunch, and I looked at the man. Then I said, "OK, Jesus can have it."

Next thing I knew, the disciples were passing out my lunch to everybody there—five thousand of them! When I think about it, I still scratch my head and wonder how Jesus did that. He must be the true Messiah. I'm glad He could use what I had.

barley loaves and two small fish, but what are they among so many?"

10 Then Jesus said, "Make the people sit down." Now there was much grass in the place. So the men sat down, in number about five thousand. 11 And Jesus took the loaves, and when He had given thanks He distributed *them* to the disciples, and the disciples to those sitting down; and likewise of the fish, as much as they wanted. 12 So when they were filled, He said to His disciples, "Gather up the fragments that remain, so that nothing is lost." 13 Therefore they gathered *them* up, and filled twelve baskets with the fragments of the five barley loaves which were left over by those who had eaten. 14 Then those men, when they had seen the sign that Jesus did, said, "This is truly the Prophet who is to come into the world."

15 Therefore when Jesus perceived that they were about to come and take Him by force to make Him king, He departed again to the mountain by Himself alone.

16 Now when evening came, His disciples went down to the sea, 17 got into the boat, and went over the sea toward Capernaum. And it was already dark, and Jesus had not come to them. 18 Then the sea arose because a great wind was blowing. 19 So when they had rowed about three or four miles, they saw Jesus walking on the sea and drawing near the boat; and they were

afraid. 20 But He said to them, "It is I; do not be afraid." 21 Then they willingly received Him into the boat, and immediately the boat was at the land where they were going.

22 On the following day, when the people who were standing on the other side of the sea saw that there was no other boat there, except that one which His disciples had entered, and that Jesus had not entered the boat with His disciples, but His disciples had gone away alone— 23 however, other boats came from Tiberias, near the place where they ate bread after the Lord had given thanks— 24 when the people therefore saw that Jesus was not there, nor His disciples, they also got into boats and came to Capernaum, seeking Jesus. 25 And when they found Him on the other side of the sea, they said to Him, "Rabbi, when did You come here?"

26 Jesus answered them and said, "Most assuredly, I say to you, you seek Me, not because you saw the signs, but because you ate of the loaves and were filled. 27 Do not labor for the food which perishes, but for the food which endures to everlasting life, which the Son of Man will give you, because God the Father has set His seal on Him."

28 Then they said to Him, "What shall we do, that we may work the works of God?"

29 Jesus answered and said to them,

"This is the work of God, that you believe in Him whom He sent."

30 Therefore they said to Him, "What sign will You perform then, that we may see it and believe You? What work will You do? 31 Our fathers ate the **manna** in the desert; as it is written, 'He gave them bread from heaven to eat.'"

32 Then Jesus said to them, "Most assuredly, I say to you, Moses did not give you the bread from heaven, but My Father gives you the true bread from heaven. 33 For the bread of God is He who comes down from heaven and gives life to the world."

34 Then they said to Him, "Lord, give us this bread always."

35 And Jesus said to them, "I am the bread of life. He who comes to Me shall never hunger, and he who believes in Me shall never thirst. 36 But I said to you that you have seen Me and yet do not believe. 37 All that the Father gives Me will come to Me, and the one who comes to Me I will by no means cast out. 38 For I have come down from heaven, not to do My own will, but the will of Him who sent Me. 39 This is the will of the Father who sent Me, that of all He has given Me I should lose nothing, but should raise it up at the last day. 40 And this is the will of Him who sent Me, that everyone who sees the Son and believes in Him may

have everlasting life; and I will raise him up at the last day."

41 The Jews then complained about Him, because He said, "I am the bread which came down from heaven." 42 And they said, "Is not this Jesus, the son of Joseph, whose father and mother we know? How is it then that He says, 'I have come down from heaven'?"

43 Jesus therefore answered and said to them, "Do not murmur among yourselves. 44 No one can come to Me unless the Father who sent Me draws him; and I will raise him up at the last day. 45 It is written in the prophets, 'And they shall all be taught by God.' Therefore everyone who has heard and learned from the Father comes to Me. 46 Not that anyone has seen the Father, except He who is from God; He has seen the Father. 47 Most assuredly, I say to you, he who believes in Me has everlasting life. 48 I am the bread of life. 49 Your fathers ate the manna in the wilderness, and are dead. 50 This is the bread which comes down from heaven, that one may eat of it and not die. 51 I am the living bread which came down from heaven. If anyone eats of this bread, he will live forever; and the bread that I shall give is My flesh, which I shall give for the life of the world."

52 The Jews therefore quarreled

WORDFINDER

6:31 Manna The miraculous food God gave Israel in the desert. It looked like frost, and when cooked, tasted like pastry. The Hebrew word means "What Is It?".

DIGGING IN

6:35 Have You Eaten the Bread of Heaven? Bread is a basic food around the world. It is made from nourishing grain and satisfies hunger. We take bread for granted because we live in a land of plenty. We have lots of meat, fish, poultry, and vegetables. We also enjoy sweet things—candy and cookies and ice cream!

Jesus compared Himself to bread because bread is so basic to life. He said,

"I am the bread of life." If we feed on Jesus, He promises us we will never hunger again. Of course, we will still need our daily meals. But the bread that Jesus gives us is the bread of heaven. Sometimes we sing the words of the Welsh hymnwriter, William Williams, "Bread of heaven . . . feed me till I want no more!" So Jesus simply says that He is our source of the greatest kind of life—life that is perfect and never ends.

among themselves, saying, "How can this Man give us *His* flesh to eat?"

53 Then Jesus said to them, "Most assuredly, I say to you, unless you eat the flesh of the Son of Man and drink His blood, you have no life in you. 54 Whoever eats My flesh and drinks My blood has eternal life, and I will raise him up at the last day. 55 For My flesh is food indeed, and My blood is drink indeed. 56 He who eats My flesh and drinks My blood abides in Me, and I in him. 57 As the living Father sent Me, and I live because of the Father, so he who feeds on Me will live because of Me. 58 This is the bread which came down from heaven—not as your fathers ate the manna, and are dead. He who eats this bread will live forever."

59 These things He said in the synagogue as He taught in Capernaum.

60 Therefore many of His disciples, when they heard *this,* said, "This is a hard saying; who can understand it?"

61 When Jesus knew in Himself that His disciples complained about this, He said to them, "Does this offend you? 62 *What* then if you should *see* the Son of Man ascend where He was before? 63 It is the Spirit who gives life; the flesh profits nothing. The words that I speak to you are spirit, and *they* are life. 64 But there are some of you who do not believe." For Jesus knew from the beginning who they were who did not believe, and who would betray Him. 65 And He said, "Therefore I have said

to you that no one can come to Me unless it has been granted to him by My Father."

66 From that *time* many of His disciples went back and walked with Him no more. 67 Then Jesus said to the twelve, "Do you also want to go away?"

68 But Simon Peter answered Him, "Lord, to whom shall we go? You have the words of eternal life. 69 Also we have come to believe and know that You are the Christ, the Son of the living God."

70 Jesus answered them, "Did I not choose you, the twelve, and one of you is a devil?" 71 He spoke of Judas Iscariot, *the son* of Simon, for it was he who would betray Him, being one of the twelve.

Jesus teaches at the temple

7 After these things Jesus walked in Galilee; for He did not want to walk in Judea, because the Jews sought to kill Him. 2 Now the Jews' Feast of Tabernacles was at hand. 3 His brothers therefore said to Him, "Depart from here and go into Judea, that Your disciples also may see the works that You are doing. 4 For no one does anything in secret while he himself seeks to be known openly. If You do these things, show Yourself to the world." 5 For even His brothers did not believe in Him.

6 Then Jesus said to them, "My time

What Peter Learned

It was a sad day for Jesus. Many people who had followed Him were now leaving Him. Jesus told them they would have to share in His suffering, but they didn't want to do that. I think they imagined He was going to set up His kingdom right away, and they would all sit on thrones beside Him.

Instead, Jesus was going to be crucified. Who ever heard of a king who could reign on a cross? Yet that was exactly how Jesus planned to rule over our sins. It was our sins that separated us from God's love. So, many of Jesus' disciples left Him.

That's when I found out how much I loved and trusted Jesus. He had the words that gave me eternal life. That was all that mattered to me.

What the Jerusalem Crowd Learned

One day when Jesus was teaching in the temple, some of our leaders tried to prove He was wrong. But they couldn't. His wisdom was so great they had to be quiet. They wanted to arrest Him, but they were too afraid of Him to try just then.

Some of us began to realize that Jesus really was the Son of God. No one could speak as He did unless he came from heaven. Then many of us believed in Him, even though our leaders were furious.

After that, Jesus told us that the truth would make us free. Later, we realized that Jesus Himself is the Truth. Now He has made us free forever!

---

has not yet come, but your time is always ready. 7 The world cannot hate you, but it hates Me because I testify of it that its works are evil. 8 You go up to this feast. I am not yet going up to this feast, for My time has not yet fully come." 9 When He had said these things to them, He remained in Galilee.

10 But when His brothers had gone up, then He also went up to the feast, not openly, but as it were in secret. 11 Then the Jews sought Him at the feast, and said, "Where is He?" 12 And there was much complaining among the people concerning Him. Some said, "He is good"; others said, "No, on the contrary, He deceives the people." 13 However, no one spoke openly of Him for fear of the Jews.

14 Now about the middle of the feast Jesus went up into the temple and taught. 15 And the Jews marveled, saying, "How does this Man know letters, having never studied?"

16 Jesus answered them and said, "My **doctrine** is not Mine, but His who sent Me. 17 If anyone wills to do His will, he shall know concerning the doctrine, whether it is from God or whether I speak on My own authority. 18 He who speaks from himself seeks his own glory; but He who seeks the glory of the One who sent Him is true,

and no unrighteousness is in Him. 19 Did not Moses give you the law, yet none of you keeps the law? Why do you seek to kill Me?"

20 The people answered and said, "You have a demon. Who is seeking to kill You?"

21 Jesus answered and said to them, "I did one work, and you all marvel. 22 Moses therefore gave you circumcision (not that it is from Moses, but from the fathers), and you circumcise a man on the Sabbath. 23 If a man receives circumcision on the Sabbath, so that the law of Moses should not be broken, are you angry with Me because I made a man completely well on the Sabbath? 24 Do not judge according to appearance, but judge with righteous judgment."

25 Now some of them from Jerusalem said, "Is this not He whom they seek to kill? 26 But look! He speaks boldly, and they say nothing to Him. Do the rulers know indeed that this is truly the Christ? 27 However, we know where this Man is from; but when the Christ comes, no one knows where He is from."

28 Then Jesus cried out, as He taught in the temple, saying, "You both know Me, and you know where I am from; and I have not come of Myself, but He who sent Me is true, whom you

WORDFINDER

7:16 Doctrine Pronounced *DOK-trin.* The truth taught in the Bible. Christians believe all of God's doctrine or teaching as their foundation for salvation and living in the world.

do not know. 29 But I know Him, for I am from Him, and He sent Me.''

30 Therefore they sought to take Him; but no one laid a hand on Him, because His hour had not yet come. 31 And many of the people believed in Him, and said, ''When the Christ comes, will He do more signs than these which this *Man* has done?''

32 The Pharisees heard the crowd murmuring these things concerning Him, and the Pharisees and the chief priests sent officers to take Him. 33 Then Jesus said to them, ''I shall be with you a little while longer, and *then* I go to Him who sent Me. 34 You will seek Me and not find *Me,* and where I am you cannot come.''

35 Then the Jews said among themselves, ''Where does He intend to go that we shall not find Him? Does He intend to go to the Dispersion among the Greeks and teach the Greeks? 36 What is this thing that He said, 'You will seek Me and not find Me, and where I am you cannot come'?''

37 On the last day, that great *day* of the feast, Jesus stood and cried out, saying, ''If anyone thirsts, let him come to Me and drink. 38 He who believes in Me, as the Scripture has said, out of his heart will flow rivers of living water.'' 39 But this He spoke concerning the Spirit, whom those believing in Him would receive; for the Holy Spirit was not yet *given,* because Jesus was not yet **glorified.**

40 Therefore many from the crowd, when they heard this saying, said, ''Truly this is the Prophet.'' 41 Others said, ''This is the Christ.''

But some said, ''Will the Christ come out of Galilee? 42 Has not the Scripture said that the Christ comes from the seed of David and from the town of Bethlehem, where David was?'' 43 So there was a division among the people because of Him. 44 Now some of them wanted to take Him, but no one laid hands on Him.

45 Then the officers came to the chief priests and Pharisees, who said to them, ''Why have you not brought Him?''

46 The officers answered, ''No man ever spoke like this Man!''

47 Then the Pharisees answered them, ''Are you also deceived? 48 Have any of the rulers or the Pharisees believed in Him? 49 But this crowd that does not know the law is accursed.''

50 Nicodemus (he who came to Jesus by night, being one of them) said to them, 51 ''Does our law judge a man before it hears him and knows what he is doing?''

52 They answered and said to him, ''Are you also from Galilee? Search and look, for no prophet has arisen out of Galilee.''

53 And *everyone* went to his *own* house.

God sent Jesus into the world

8 But Jesus went to the Mount of Olives.

2 Now early in the morning He came again into the temple, and all the people came to Him; and He sat down and taught them. 3 Then the scribes and Pharisees brought to Him a woman caught in adultery. And when they had set her in the midst, 4 they said to Him, ''Teacher, this woman was caught in adultery, in the very act. 5 Now Moses, in the law, commanded us that such should be stoned. But what do You say?'' 6 This they said, testing Him, that they might have *something* of which to accuse Him. But Jesus stooped down and wrote on the ground with *His* finger, as though He did not hear.

7 So when they continued asking Him, He raised Himself up and said to them, ''He who is without sin among you, let him throw a stone at her first.'' 8 And again He stooped down and wrote on the ground. 9 Then those

---

WORDFINDER

7:39 Glorified Pronounced *GLORY-fyed.* When Jesus comes back to earth, He will give those who loved Him new bodies. They will never sin again.

Superhero

His Last Days

In the last week of of Jesus' life on earth,
He spent most of His time in Jerusalem, speaking with
His disciples, praying, and getting ready for the great sacrifice
He would make for all of us.

	WHAT HAPPENED?	WHERE?	READ ABOUT IT:
JESUS	rides on a donkey	into Jerusalem	Luke 19:28–44 *(Zechariah 9:9)*
JESUS	drives out the money changers	in the temple	Mark 11:15–18 *(Jeremiah 7:11)*
JESUS	eats the Last Supper	in the Upper Room	Matthew 26:17–29 *(Psalm 41:9)*
JESUS	prays	in the Garden of Gethsemane	Matthew 26:36–46 *(Psalm 42:6)*
JESUS	is arrested	in Jerusalem	Luke 22:47–53
JESUS	is crucified	on Golgotha	Matthew 27:27–56 *(Psalm 22:1,18)*
JESUS	is buried	in the tomb of Joseph of Arimathea	Matthew 27:57–66 *(Exodus 12:46)*
JESUS	comes back to life	in Jerusalem	Mark 16:1–8

Superhero

HE'S ALIVE! HE'S ALIVE!

*Before He went back to heaven,
Jesus appeared to many people. Some of them were frightened
when they saw Him. Some could scarcely believe their eyes!
Others praised God that their Friend Jesus was alive again!*

How did each of the following feel
when they saw Jesus for the first time after
He arose from the dead?

Mary Magdalene
(Mark 16:9; John 20:11–18)
The other women
(Matthew 28:8–10)
Peter
(Luke 24:34)
The ten disciples
(Luke 24:36–43; John 20:19–25)
Thomas
(John 20:26–29)
The disciples, on the road to Emmaus
(Mark 16:12)
The crowd of five hundred people
(1 Corinthians 15:6)
James and the apostles
(1 Corinthians 15:7)
Paul, on the road to Damascus
(Acts 9:1–6; 18:9,10; 22:1–8; 23:11; 26:12–18)
**The people who watched Jesus
ascend to heaven**
(Mark 16:19, 20; Luke 24:50–53; Acts 1:4–12)

Jesus is alive today! He lives in heaven and in the hearts
of those who love Him and want to give their lives
to Him. Does He live in your heart?

who heard *it,* being convicted by *their* conscience, went out one by one, beginning with the oldest *even* to the last. And Jesus was left alone, and the woman standing in the midst. ¹⁰ When Jesus had raised Himself up and saw no one but the woman, He said to her, "Woman, where are those accusers of yours? Has no one condemned you?"

¹¹ She said, "No one, Lord."

And Jesus said to her, "Neither do I condemn you; go and sin no more."

¹² Then Jesus spoke to them again, saying, "I am the light of the world. He who follows Me shall not walk in darkness, but have the light of life."

¹³ The Pharisees therefore said to Him, "You bear witness of Yourself; Your witness is not true."

¹⁴ Jesus answered and said to them, "Even if I bear witness of Myself, My witness is true, for I know where I came from and where I am going; but you do not know where I come from and where I am going. ¹⁵ You judge according to the flesh; I judge no one. ¹⁶ And yet if I do judge, My judgment is true; for I am not alone, but I *am* with the Father who sent Me. ¹⁷ It is also written in your law that the testimony of two men is true. ¹⁸ I am One who bears witness of Myself, and the Father who sent Me bears witness of Me."

¹⁹ Then they said to Him, "Where is Your Father?"

Jesus answered, "You know neither Me nor My Father. If you had known Me, you would have known My Father also."

²⁰ These words Jesus spoke in the treasury, as He taught in the temple; and no one laid hands on Him, for His hour had not yet come.

²¹ Then Jesus said to them again, "I am going away, and you will seek Me, and will die in your sin. Where I go you cannot come."

²² So the Jews said, "Will He kill Himself, because He says, 'Where I go you cannot come'?"

²³ And He said to them, "You are from beneath; I am from above. You are of this world; I am not of this world. ²⁴ Therefore I said to you that you will die in your sins; for if you do not believe that I am *He,* you will die in your sins."

²⁵ Then they said to Him, "Who are You?"

And Jesus said to them, "Just what I have been saying to you from the beginning. ²⁶ I have many things to say and to judge concerning you, but He who sent Me is true; and I speak to the world those things which I heard from Him."

²⁷ They did not understand that He spoke to them of the Father.

²⁸ Then Jesus said to them, "When you lift up the Son of Man, then you will know that I am *He,* and *that* I do nothing of Myself; but as My Father taught Me, I speak these things. ²⁹ And He who sent Me is with Me. The Father has not left Me alone, for I always do those things that please Him." ³⁰ As He spoke these words, many believed in Him.

³¹ Then Jesus said to those Jews

DIGGING IN

8:12 Have You Seen the Light of the World? Just like food, light is necessary for life. No one can live very long in darkness. Even plants need light to grow. And without light, we can't see.

God says we are like people who live in darkness if we don't know Him. When Jesus came, the Old Testament prophecy also came true: "The people who walked in darkness have seen a great light" (Isaiah 9:2). That is why Jesus

could say, "I am the light of the world."

As you look around you, you will see many people who are walking in darkness. Many are prisoners of dark habits and life-styles that lead to disappointment, disease, and even death.

Jesus came to be the Light to the dark world around you. Will you carry His light wherever you go? His light can shine in you and lead others to know Him, but you must first ask Jesus to live in you.

who believed Him, "If you abide in My word, you are My disciples indeed. 32 And you shall know the truth, and the truth shall make you free."

33 They answered Him, "We are Abraham's descendants, and have never been in bondage to anyone. How *can* you say, 'You will be made free'?"

34 Jesus answered them, "Most assuredly, I say to you, whoever commits sin is a slave of sin. 35 And a slave does not abide in the house forever, *but* a son abides forever. 36 Therefore if the Son makes you free, you shall be free indeed.

37 "I know that you are Abraham's descendants, but you seek to kill Me, because My word has no place in you. 38 I speak what I have seen with My Father, and you do what you have seen with your father."

39 They answered and said to Him, "Abraham is our father."

Jesus said to them, "If you were Abraham's children, you would do the works of Abraham. 40 But now you seek to kill Me, a Man who has told you the truth which I heard from God. Abraham did not do this. 41 You do the deeds of your father."

Then they said to Him, "We were not born of fornication; we have one Father—God."

42 Jesus said to them, "If God were your Father, you would love Me, for I proceeded forth and came from God; nor have I come of Myself, but He sent Me. 43 Why do you not understand My speech? Because you are not able to listen to My word. 44 You are of *your* father the devil, and the desires of your father you want to do. He was a murderer from the beginning, and *does not* stand in the truth, because there is no truth in him. When he speaks a lie, he speaks from his own *resources,* for he is a liar and the father of it. 45 But because I tell the truth, you do not believe Me. 46 Which of you convicts Me of sin? And if I tell the truth, why do you not believe Me? 47 He who is of God hears God's words; therefore you do not hear, because you are not of God."

48 Then the Jews answered and said to Him, "Do we not say rightly that You are a **Samaritan** and have a demon?"

49 Jesus answered, "I do not have a demon; but I honor My Father, and you dishonor Me. 50 And I do not seek My *own* glory; there is One who seeks and judges. 51 Most assuredly, I say to you, if anyone keeps My word he shall never see death."

52 Then the Jews said to Him, "Now we know that You have a demon!

WORDFINDER

8:48 Samaritan (Pronounced *suh-MARE-ih-tun*). A person who lived in Samaria (pronounced *suh-MARE-ee-ah*), a district north of Judea (see map on page 1343). Jews hated Samaritans, partly because they were a mixed race.

DIGGING IN

8:32 The Truth Makes You Free Ignorance is caused by sin. When people don't understand the world around them, they become afraid. Fear comes from not knowing the truth. Such fear often leads to anger and violence as people try to defend themselves against what they fear.

Ignorance exists only where God is not known. But knowing God causes you to understand the meaning of life. When God is first in your life, then the world is no longer a strange and frightening place.

A little boy needed a light on at night when his father was away. But when his dad came home, the boy said, "You can turn the light off now. Daddy's home!"

Jesus is the living Truth who sets you free from fear of living in the dark unknown. It is enough that the One who knows all is at home in your heart. Now you, too, can sleep in peace.

What the Blind Man Learned

Can you imagine what it must be like never to see? I had been blind all my life when Jesus found me. I never knew what people meant when they talked about the sky, the mountains, the trees, and so many other beautiful things God made. But Jesus changed all that for me.

He told me to do the strangest thing! He put mud on my eyes and told me to wash them in a water pool. Jesus seemed to know what He was doing, so I did what he said. Then I could see for the very first time in my life.

Jesus told His disciples I wasn't blind because of any sin. God just wanted to do a beautiful thing for me. So He did.

Abraham is dead, and the prophets; and You say, 'If anyone keeps My word he shall never taste death.' 53 Are You greater than our father Abraham, who is dead? And the prophets are dead. Who do You make Yourself out to be?"

54 Jesus answered, "If I honor Myself, My honor is nothing. It is My Father who honors Me, of whom you say that He is your God. 55 Yet you have not known Him, but I know Him. And if I say, 'I do not know Him,' I shall be a liar like you; but I do know Him and keep His word. 56 Your father Abraham rejoiced to see My day, and he saw it and was glad."

57 Then the Jews said to Him, "You are not yet fifty years old, and have You seen Abraham?"

58 Jesus said to them, "Most assuredly, I say to you, before Abraham was, I AM."

59 Then they took up stones to throw at Him; but Jesus hid Himself and went out of the temple, going through the midst of them, and so passed by.

Jesus heals a man born blind

9 Now as *Jesus* passed by, He saw a man who was blind from birth. 2 And His disciples asked Him, saying, "Rabbi, who sinned, this man or his parents, that he was born blind?"

3 Jesus answered, "Neither this man nor his parents sinned, but that the works of God should be revealed in him. 4 I must work the works of Him who sent Me while it is day; the night is coming when no one can work. 5 As long as I am in the world, I am the light of the world."

6 When He had said these things, He spat on the ground and made clay with the saliva; and He anointed the eyes of the blind man with the clay. 7 And He said to him, "Go, wash in the pool of Siloam" (which is translated, Sent).

DIGGING IN

8:58 Jesus Has Always Lived Jesus could have said, "I was before Abraham." That would be saying quite a lot, because Abraham lived two thousand years before the time of Jesus! But Jesus wanted to say more than that. Jesus had lived even before there was time at all! Jesus is eternal. He had no beginning and He has no ending.

Of course, you should know that Jesus was both God and Man. As a *Man,* Jesus had lived only since His birth at Bethlehem. As *God,* He has always lived and will live forever and ever. Jesus' earthly body could die, and you know that He did die—on the Cross. Then something wonderful happened. That part of Jesus that was *God* took over His dead body and brought it back to life. When Jesus rose up in His body, it was a body that could never die again. Now Jesus can share that same *undying life* with you!

Former Blind Man Angers Local Leaders

The Jerusalem Times

JERUSALEM—A man who was born blind has been healed by Jesus, the Teacher from Galilee. The man has been telling all of Jerusalem how Jesus made him see.

Now some of the religious leaders are angry with the former blind man. They have asked him many questions and have tried to convince him that Jesus is a false teacher. But the man sticks to his story: "He put clay on my eyes, and I washed, and I see."

The former blind man also proved how wrong Jesus' accusers were when he told them that no one has ever before healed someone who was born blind. He said Jesus must have come from God. This made Jesus' enemies very angry, and they ordered the man never to come to the synagogue (pronounced SIN-uh-gog) again.

So he went and washed, and came back seeing.

8 Therefore the neighbors and those who previously had seen that he was blind said, "Is not this he who sat and begged?"

9 Some said, "This is he." Others said, "He is like him."

He said, "I am he."

10 Therefore they said to him, "How were your eyes opened?"

11 He answered and said, "A Man called Jesus made clay and anointed my eyes and said to me, 'Go to the pool of Siloam and wash.' So I went and washed, and I received sight."

12 Then they said to him, "Where is He?"

He said, "I do not know."

13 They brought him who formerly was blind to the Pharisees. 14 Now it was a Sabbath when Jesus made the clay and opened his eyes. 15 Then the Pharisees also asked him again how he had received his sight. He said to them, "He put clay on my eyes, and I washed, and I see."

16 Therefore some of the Pharisees said, "This Man is not from God, because He does not keep the Sabbath."

Others said, "How can a man who is a sinner do such signs?" And there was a division among them.

17 They said to the blind man again, "What do you say about Him because He opened your eyes?"

He said, "He is a prophet."

18 But the Jews did not believe concerning him, that he had been blind and received his sight, until they called the parents of him who had received his sight. 19 And they asked them, saying, "Is this your son, who you say was born blind? How then does he now see?"

20 His parents answered them and said, "We know that this is our son, and that he was born blind; 21 but by

The Pool of Siloam, where the blind man washed and received his sight.

what means he now sees we do not know, or who opened his eyes we do not know. He is of age; ask him. He will speak for himself." 22 His parents said these *things* because they feared the Jews, for the Jews had agreed already that if anyone confessed *that He was* Christ, he would be put out of the synagogue. 23 Therefore his parents said, "He is of age; ask him."

24 So they again called the man who was blind, and said to him, "Give God the glory! We know that this Man is a sinner."

25 He answered and said, "Whether He is a sinner *or not* I do not know. One thing I know: that though I was blind, now I see."

26 Then they said to him again, "What did He do to you? How did He open your eyes?"

27 He answered them, "I told you already, and you did not listen. Why do you want to hear *it* again? Do you also want to become His disciples?"

28 Then they reviled him and said, "You are His **disciple,** but we are Moses' disciples. 29 We know that God spoke to Moses; *as for* this *fellow,* we do not know where He is from."

30 The man answered and said to them, "Why, this is a marvelous thing, that you do not know where He is from; yet He has opened my eyes! 31 Now we know that God does not hear sinners; but if anyone is a worshiper of God and does His will, He hears him. 32 Since the world began it has been unheard of that anyone opened the eyes of one who was born blind. 33 If this Man were not from God, He could do nothing."

34 They answered and said to him, "You were completely born in sins, and are you teaching us?" And they cast him out.

35 Jesus heard that they had cast him out; and when He had found him, He said to him, "Do you believe in the Son of God?"

36 He answered and said, "Who is He, Lord, that I may believe in Him?"

37 And Jesus said to him, "You have both seen Him and it is He who is talking with you."

38 Then he said, "Lord, I believe!" And he worshiped Him.

39 And Jesus said, "For judgment I have come into this world, that those who do not see may see, and that those who see may be made blind."

40 Then *some* of the Pharisees who were with Him heard these words, and said to Him, "Are we blind also?"

41 Jesus said to them, "If you were blind, you would have no sin; but now you say, 'We see.' Therefore your sin remains.

Jesus is the Good Shepherd

10 "Most assuredly, I say to you, he who does not enter the sheepfold by the door, but climbs up some other way, the same is a thief and a robber. 2 But he who enters by the door is the shepherd of the sheep. 3 To him the doorkeeper opens, and the sheep hear his voice; and he calls his own sheep by name and leads them out. 4 And when he brings out his own sheep, he goes before them; and the sheep follow him, for they know his voice. 5 Yet they will by no means follow a stranger, but will flee from him, for they do not know the voice of strangers." 6 Jesus used this illustration, but they did not understand the things which He spoke to them.

7 Then Jesus said to them again, "Most assuredly, I say to you, I am the door of the sheep. 8 All who *ever* came before Me are thieves and robbers, but the sheep did not hear them. 9 I am the door. If anyone enters by Me, he will be saved, and will go in and out and find pasture. 10 The thief

9:28 Disciple Pronounced *dih-SIGH-pul.* A learner or pupil. A Christian is a pupil of Jesus. The Holy Spirit teaches us to become like Jesus, as we are shown in the Bible.

does not come except to steal, and to kill, and to destroy. I have come that they may have life, and that they may have *it* more abundantly.

11 "I am the good shepherd. The good shepherd gives His life for the sheep. 12 But a hireling, *he who* is not the shepherd, one who does not own the sheep, sees the wolf coming and leaves the sheep and flees; and the wolf catches the sheep and scatters them. 13 The hireling flees because he is a hireling and does not care about the sheep. 14 I am the good shepherd; and I know My *sheep,* and am known by My own. 15 As the Father knows Me, even so I know the Father; and I lay down My life for the sheep. 16 And other sheep I have which are not of this fold; them also I must bring, and they will hear My voice; and there will be one flock *and* one shepherd.

17 "Therefore My Father loves Me, because I lay down My life that I may take it again. 18 No one takes it from Me, but I lay it down of Myself. I have power to lay it down, and I have power to take it again. This command I have received from My Father."

19 Therefore there was a division again among the Jews because of these sayings. 20 And many of them said, "He has a demon and is mad. Why do you listen to Him?"

21 Others said, "These are not the words of one who has a **demon.** Can a

⊕WORDFINDER

10:21 Demon An invisible spirit-being who is a servant of Satan. Demons can live in people and hurt them. Demons also cause people to curse God and His people.

⛏DIGGING IN

10:11 I Am the Good Shepherd In chapter 8 Jesus said, "Before Abraham was, I AM." Those two words are the name that God gave Himself when He met with Moses in Exodus 3. So Jesus is making it clear that He is the same God who appeared to Moses in the burning bush.

Jesus goes on to use the words "I AM" to show the various ways in which He comes to you. In verse 11 He tells you, *"I am* the good shepherd." All through the Old Testament, God describes Himself as the Shepherd of His people. They understood this because many of the people were shepherds, and they knew how much care their sheep needed. Jesus also knows how much care you need, and He wants to be your Shepherd. He wants to lead you in the right and happy ways that David talks about in Psalm 23.

Will you let Jesus be the Shepherd of your life?

"I am the Good Shepherd."

demon open the eyes of the blind?"

22 Now it was the Feast of Dedication in Jerusalem, and it was winter. 23 And Jesus walked in the temple, in Solomon's porch. 24 Then the Jews surrounded Him and said to Him, "How long do You keep us in doubt? If You are the Christ, tell us plainly."

25 Jesus answered them, "I told you, and you do not believe. The works that I do in My Father's name, they bear witness of Me. 26 But you do not believe, because you are not of My sheep, as I said to you. 27 My sheep hear My voice, and I know them, and they follow Me. 28 And I give them eternal life, and they shall never perish; neither shall anyone snatch them out of My hand. 29 My Father, who has given *them* to Me, is greater than all; and no one is able to snatch *them* out of My Father's hand. 30 I and *My* Father are one."

31 Then the Jews took up stones again to stone Him. 32 Jesus answered them, "Many good works I have shown you from My Father. For which of those works do you stone Me?"

33 The Jews answered Him, saying, "For a good work we do not stone You, but for blasphemy, and because You, being a Man, make Yourself God."

34 Jesus answered them, "Is it not written in your law, 'I said, "You are gods" '? 35 If He called them gods, to whom the **word of God** came (and the Scripture cannot be broken), 36 do you say of Him whom the Father sanctified and sent into the world, 'You are blaspheming,' because I said, 'I am the Son of God'? 37 If I do not do the works of My Father, do not believe Me; 38 but if I do, though you do not believe Me, believe the works, that you may know and believe that the Father *is* in Me, and I in Him." 39 Therefore they sought again to seize Him, but He escaped out of their hand.

40 And He went away again beyond the Jordan to the place where John was baptizing at first, and there He stayed. 41 Then many came to Him and said, "John performed no sign, but all the things that John spoke about this Man were true." 42 And many believed in Him there.

Jesus brings Lazarus back to life

11 Now a certain *man* was sick, Lazarus of Bethany, the town of Mary and her sister Martha. 2 It was *that* Mary who anointed the Lord with fragrant oil and wiped His feet with her hair, whose brother Lazarus was sick. 3 Therefore the sisters sent to Him, saying, "Lord, behold, he whom You love is sick."

4 When Jesus heard *that,* He said, "This sickness is not unto death, but for the glory of God, that the Son of God may be glorified through it."

5 Now Jesus loved Martha and her sister and Lazarus. 6 So, when He heard that he was sick, He stayed two more days in the place where He was. 7 Then after this He said to *the* disciples, "Let us go to Judea again."

8 *The* disciples said to Him, "Rabbi, lately the Jews sought to stone You, and are You going there again?"

9 Jesus answered, "Are there not twelve hours in the day? If anyone walks in the day, he does not stumble, because he sees the light of this world. 10 But if one walks in the night, he stumbles, because the light is not in him." 11 These things He said, and after that He said to them, "Our friend Lazarus sleeps, but I go that I may wake him up."

12 Then His disciples said, "Lord, if he sleeps he will get well." 13 However, Jesus spoke of his death, but they thought that He was speaking about taking rest in sleep.

WORDFINDER

10:35 Word of God God speaking in the Scriptures of the Old and New Testaments. Jesus also is called "the Word" (John 1:1) because He is God's *personal* Word.

What Martha Learned

I was almost angry at Jesus because He didn't come sooner and save Lazarus when my brother got sick and died. Yet I still hoped Jesus could do something. (Pronounce my brother's name *LAZ-uh-rus.*)

I was surprised when Jesus said, "Your brother will rise again." Of course, I believed Lazarus would rise with everybody else on the day of Judgment.

Then Jesus said something I'll never forget. He said, "I am the resurrection and the life. . . . Whoever lives and believes in Me shall never die" (John 11:25, 26).

For the first time I think I saw Jesus as He really is. He has eternal life in Himself, and He gives that life to all who truly ask Him. Yes, Jesus is my Savior.

14 Then Jesus said to them plainly, "Lazarus is dead. 15 And I am glad for your sakes that I was not there, that you may believe. Nevertheless let us go to him."

16 Then Thomas, who is called the Twin, said to his fellow disciples, "Let us also go, that we may die with Him."

17 So when Jesus came, He found that he had already been in the tomb four days. 18 Now Bethany was near Jerusalem, about two miles away. 19 And many of the Jews had joined the women around Martha and Mary, to comfort them concerning their brother.

20 Now Martha, as soon as she heard that Jesus was coming, went and met Him, but Mary was sitting in the house. 21 Now Martha said to Jesus, "Lord, if You had been here, my brother would not have died. 22 But even now I know that whatever You ask of God, God will give You."

23 Jesus said to her, "Your brother will rise again."

24 Martha said to Him, "I know that he will rise again in the resurrection at the last day."

25 Jesus said to her, "I am the resurrection and the life. He who believes in Me, though he may die, he shall live. 26 And whoever lives and believes in Me shall never die. Do you believe this?"

27 She said to Him, "Yes, Lord, I believe that You are the Christ, the Son of God, who is to come into the world."

28 And when she had said these things, she went her way and secretly called Mary her sister, saying, "The Teacher has come and is calling for you." 29 As soon as she heard *that,* she arose quickly and came to Him. 30 Now Jesus had not yet come into the town, but was in the place where Martha met Him. 31 Then the Jews who were with her in the house, and comforting her, when they saw that Mary rose up quickly and went out, followed her, saying, "She is going to the tomb to weep there."

32 Then, when Mary came where Jesus was, and saw Him, she fell down at His feet, saying to Him, "Lord, if You had been here, my brother would not have died."

33 Therefore, when Jesus saw her weeping, and the Jews who came with her weeping, He groaned in the spirit and was troubled. 34 And He said, "Where have you laid him?"

WORDFINDER

11:25 Resurrection Pronounced *rez-er-RECK-shun.* The rising of Jesus from death. Jesus has promised that those who trust Him will also be raised up as He was.

Can This Man Raise the Dead?

The Jerusalem Times

JERUSALEM—Reporters from this newspaper were present yesterday when Jesus arrived at the home of Mary and Martha of Bethany, a small town about two miles outside Jerusalem. It is thought that Jesus had meant to attend the funeral of their brother Lazarus, who died four days ago.

In spite of the loss of His friend, Jesus appeared calm, though some people were angry that He had not come sooner to heal Lazarus. It is noted, however, that Jesus had tears in His eyes when He came near the tomb and ordered the stone to be taken away from the door.

Then Jesus shouted, "Lazarus, come forth!" People standing by were shocked when the dead man, still wrapped in his graveclothes, came out of the tomb!

Since this incident, local leaders have decided this Jesus has become very dangerous. It is thought they will try to stop Him once and for all.

They said to Him, "Lord, come and see."

35 Jesus wept. 36 Then the Jews said, "See how He loved him!"

37 And some of them said, "Could not this Man, who opened the eyes of the blind, also have kept this man from dying?"

38 Then Jesus, again groaning in Himself, came to the tomb. It was a cave, and a stone lay against it. 39 Jesus said, "Take away the stone."

Jesus raises His friend Lazarus from the dead.

Martha, the sister of him who was dead, said to Him, "Lord, by this time there is a stench, for he has been *dead* four days."

40 Jesus said to her, "Did I not say to you that if you would believe you would see the glory of God?" 41 Then they took away the stone *from the place* where the dead man was lying. And Jesus lifted up *His* eyes and said, "Father, I thank You that You have heard Me. 42 And I know that You always hear Me, but because of the people who are standing by I said *this*, that they may believe that You sent Me." 43 Now when He had said these things, He cried with a loud voice, "Lazarus, come forth!" 44 And he who had died came out bound hand and foot with graveclothes, and his face was wrapped with a cloth. Jesus said to them, "Loose him, and let him go."

45 Then many of the Jews who had come to Mary, and had seen the things Jesus did, believed in Him. 46 But some of them went away to the Pharisees and told them the things Jesus did. 47 Then the chief priests and the Pharisees gathered a council and said, "What shall we do? For this Man works many signs. 48 If we let Him alone like this, everyone will believe in Him, and the Romans will come and take away both our place and nation."

A floor plan of the temple.

Most Holy Place

49 And one of them, Caiaphas, being high priest that year, said to them, "You know nothing at all, 50 nor do you consider that it is expedient for us that one man should die for the people, and not that the whole nation should perish." 51 Now this he did not say on his own *authority;* but being high priest that year he prophesied that Jesus would die for the nation, 52 and not for that nation only, but also that He would gather together in one the children of God who were scattered abroad.

53 Then, from that day on, they plotted to put Him to death. 54 Therefore Jesus no longer walked openly among the Jews, but went from there into the country near the wilderness, to a city called Ephraim, and there remained with His disciples.

55 And the Passover of the Jews was near, and many went from the country up to Jerusalem before the Passover, to purify themselves. 56 Then they sought Jesus, and spoke among themselves as they stood in the temple, "What do you think—that He will not come to the feast?" 57 Now both the chief priests and the Pharisees had given a command, that if anyone knew where He was, he should report *it,* that they might seize Him.

Jesus leads the parade into Jerusalem

12 Then, six days before the Passover, Jesus came to Bethany, where Lazarus was who had been dead, whom He had raised from the dead. 2 There they made Him a supper; and Martha served, but Lazarus was one of those who sat at the table with Him. 3 Then Mary took a pound of very costly oil of spikenard, anointed the feet of Jesus, and wiped His feet with her hair. And the house was filled with the fragrance of the oil.

4 But one of His disciples, Judas Iscariot, Simon's *son,* who would betray Him, said, 5 "Why was this fragrant oil not sold for three hundred denarii and given to the poor?" 6 This he said, not that he cared for the poor, but because he was a thief, and had the money box; and he used to take what was put in it.

7 But Jesus said, "Let her alone; she has kept this for the day of My burial. 8 For the poor you have with you always, but Me you do not have always."

9 Now a great many of the Jews knew that He was there; and they came, not for Jesus' sake only, but that they might also see Lazarus, whom He had raised from the dead. 10 But the chief priests plotted to put Lazarus to death also, 11 because on account of him many of the Jews went away and believed in Jesus.

12 The next day a great multitude that had come to the feast, when they heard that Jesus was coming to Jerusalem, 13 took branches of palm trees and went out to meet Him, and cried out:

> "Hosanna!
> 'Blessed is He who comes in the
> name of the LORD!'
> The King of Israel!"

I am Mary, the sister of Martha and Lazarus. Jesus often came to stay with us when He visited Jerusalem because we lived at Bethany, just a short distance from the city.

The last time Jesus was with us was a sad day. Jesus had told us He was going to Jerusalem to be crucified. Martha and I made supper while Lazarus sat at the table with Jesus and His disciples.

After the meal, I poured a pound of special oil made from the nard plant over Jesus' feet. As I did this the whole house was filled with a beautiful fragrance.

Judas, the disciple, was angry and said the oil could have been sold to feed the poor. But he didn't really care about the poor because he was a thief.

Jesus accepted my gift as an offering of love before His death. I will always be glad I gave Jesus the best I had. Shouldn't you?

14 Then Jesus, when He had found a young donkey, sat on it; as it is written:

15 "Fear not, daughter of Zion;
    Behold, your King is coming,
    Sitting on a donkey's colt."

16 His disciples did not understand these things at first; but when Jesus was glorified, then they remembered that these things were written about Him and *that* they had done these things to Him. 17 Therefore the people, who were with Him when He called Lazarus out of his tomb and raised him from the dead, bore witness. 18 For this reason

Mary anoints Jesus' feet with oil.

the people also met Him, because they heard that He had done this sign. 19 The Pharisees therefore said among themselves, "You see that you are accomplishing nothing. Look, the world has gone after Him!"

20 Now there were certain Greeks among those who came up to worship at the feast. 21 Then they came to Philip, who was from Bethsaida of Galilee, and asked him, saying, "Sir, we wish to see Jesus."

22 Philip came and told Andrew, and in turn Andrew and Philip told Jesus.

23 But Jesus answered them, saying, "The hour has come that the Son of Man should be glorified. 24 Most assuredly, I say to you, unless a grain of wheat falls into the ground and dies, it remains alone; but if it dies, it produces much grain. 25 He who loves his life will lose it, and he who hates his life in this world will keep it for eternal life. 26 If anyone serves Me, let him follow Me; and where I am, there My servant will be also. If anyone serves Me, him *My* Father will honor.

27 "Now My soul is troubled, and what shall I say? 'Father, save Me from this hour'? But for this purpose I came to this hour. 28 Father, glorify Your name."

Then a voice came from heaven, *saying,* "I have both glorified *it* and will glorify *it* again."

29 Therefore the people who stood

by and heard *it* said that it had thundered. Others said, "An angel has spoken to Him."

30 Jesus answered and said, "This voice did not come because of Me, but for your sake. 31 Now is the judgment of this world; now the ruler of this world will be cast out. 32 And I, if I am lifted up from the earth, will draw all peoples to Myself." 33 This He said, signifying by what death He would die.

34 The people answered Him, "We have heard from the law that the Christ remains forever; and how *can* You say, 'The Son of Man must be lifted up'? Who is this Son of Man?"

35 Then Jesus said to them, "A little while longer the light is with you. Walk while you have the light, lest darkness overtake you; he who walks in darkness does not know where he is going. 36 While you have the light, believe in the light, that you may become sons of light." These things Jesus spoke, and departed, and was hidden from them.

37 But although He had done so many signs before them, they did not believe in Him, 38 that the word of Isaiah the prophet might be fulfilled, which he spoke:

"Lord, who has believed our
    report?
And to whom has the arm of the
    LORD been revealed?"

39 Therefore they could not believe, because Isaiah said again:

40 "He has blinded their eyes and
    hardened their hearts,
Lest they should see with *their*
    eyes,
Lest they should understand
    with *their* hearts and turn,
So that I should heal them."

41 These things Isaiah said when he saw His glory and spoke of Him.

42 Nevertheless even among the rulers many believed in Him, but because of the Pharisees they did not confess Him, lest they should be put out of the synagogue; 43 for they loved the praise of men more than the praise of God.

44 Then Jesus cried out and said, "He who believes in Me, believes not in Me but in Him who sent Me. 45 And he who sees Me sees Him who sent Me. 46 I have come *as* a light into the world, that whoever believes in Me should not abide in darkness. 47 And if anyone hears My words and does not believe, I do not judge him; for I did not come to judge the world but to save the world. 48 He who rejects Me, and does not receive My words, has that which judges him—the word that I have spoken will judge him in the last day. 49 For I have not spoken on My own *authority;* but the Father who sent Me gave Me a command, what I should say and what I should speak. 50 And I know that His command is everlasting life. Therefore, whatever I speak, just as the Father has told Me, so I speak."

Jesus washes the disciples' feet

13 Now before the Feast of the Passover, when Jesus knew that His hour had come that He should depart from this world to the Father, having loved His own who were in the world, He loved them to the end.

2 And supper being ended, the devil having already put it into the heart of Judas Iscariot, Simon's *son,* to betray Him, 3 Jesus, knowing that the Father had given all things into His hands, and that He had come from God and was going to God, 4 rose from supper and laid aside His garments, took a towel and girded Himself. 5 After that, He poured water into a basin and began to wash the disciples' feet, and to wipe *them* with the towel with which He was girded. 6 Then He came to Simon Peter. And *Peter* said to Him, "Lord, are You washing my feet?"

7 Jesus answered and said to him, "What I am doing you do not understand now, but you will know after this."

8 Peter said to Him, "You shall never wash my feet!"

Jesus answered him, "If I do not wash you, you have no part with Me."

9 Simon Peter said to Him, "Lord, not my feet only, but also *my* hands and *my* head!"

10 Jesus said to him, "He who is bathed needs only to wash *his* feet, but is completely clean; and you are clean, but not all of you." 11 For He knew who would betray Him; therefore He said, "You are not all clean."

12 So when He had washed their feet, taken His garments, and sat down again, He said to them, "Do you know what I have done to you? 13 You call Me Teacher and Lord, and you say well, for *so* I am. 14 If I then, *your* Lord and Teacher, have washed your feet, you also ought to wash one another's feet. 15 For I have given you an example, that you should do as I have done to you. 16 Most assuredly, I say to you, a servant is not greater than his master; nor is he who is sent greater than he who sent him. 17 If you know these things, blessed are you if you do them.

18 "I do not speak concerning all of you. I know whom I have chosen; but that the Scripture may be fulfilled, 'He who eats bread with Me has lifted up his heel against Me.' 19 Now I tell you before it comes, that when it does come to pass, you may believe that I am *He.* 20 Most assuredly, I say to you, he who receives whomever I send receives Me; and he who receives Me receives Him who sent Me."

21 When Jesus had said these things,

He was troubled in spirit, and testified and said, "Most assuredly, I say to you, one of you will betray Me." 22 Then the disciples looked at one another, perplexed about whom He spoke.

23 Now there was leaning on Jesus' bosom one of His disciples, whom Jesus loved. 24 Simon Peter therefore motioned to him to ask who it was of whom He spoke.

25 Then, leaning back on Jesus' breast, he said to Him, "Lord, who is it?"

26 Jesus answered, "It is he to whom I shall give a piece of bread when I have dipped *it.*" And having dipped the bread, He gave *it* to Judas Iscariot, *the son* of Simon. 27 Now after the piece of bread, Satan entered him. Then Jesus said to him, "What you do, do quickly." 28 But no one at the table knew for what reason He said this to him. 29 For some thought, because Judas had the money box, that Jesus had said to him, "Buy *those things* we need for the feast," or that he should give something to the poor.

30 Having received the piece of bread, he then went out immediately. And it was night.

31 So, when he had gone out, Jesus said, "Now the Son of Man is glorified, and God is glorified in Him. 32 If God is glorified in Him, God will also glorify Him in Himself, and glorify Him immediately. 33 Little children, I shall be with you a little while longer. You will seek Me; and as I said to the Jews, 'Where I am going, you cannot come,' so now I say to you. 34 A **new commandment**

 WORDFINDER

13:34 New Commandment (Covenant) A covenant (pronounced *KUV-uh-nunt*) is a legal agreement. Under the Old Covenant (or Old Testament), God agreed to save His people through the blood of animals, which was a symbol for Christ's blood. Under the New Covenant (or New Testament), God agrees to save His people by the blood of Christ Himself.

DIGGING IN

13:34 Love One Another You hear the word *love* quite a lot. But the love Jesus talks about is much different and more wonderful than the love you hear about. You love your special friends, but Jesus asks you to love *everybody* in the same way that God loves them. God created us and He cares about us, even

I give to you, that you love one another; as I have loved you, that you also love one another. 35 By this all will know that you are My disciples, if you have love for one another."

36 Simon Peter said to Him, "Lord, where are You going?"

Jesus answered him, "Where I am going you cannot follow Me now, but you shall follow Me afterward."

37 Peter said to Him, "Lord, why can I not follow You now? I will lay down my life for Your sake."

38 Jesus answered him, "Will you lay down your life for My sake? Most assuredly, I say to you, the rooster shall not crow till you have denied Me three times.

Jesus is the Way, the Truth, and the Life

14 "Let not your heart be troubled; you believe in God, believe also in Me.

2 In My Father's house are many mansions; if *it were* not *so,* I would have told you. I go to prepare a place for you. 3 And if I go and prepare a place for you, I will come again and receive you to Myself; that where I am, *there* you may be also. 4 And where I go you know, and the way you know."

5 Thomas said to Him, "Lord, we do not know where You are going, and how can we know the way?"

6 Jesus said to him, "I am the way, the truth, and the life. No one comes to the Father except through Me.

7 "If you had known Me, you would have known My Father also; and from now on you know Him and have seen Him."

8 Philip said to Him, "Lord, show us the Father, and it is sufficient for us."

9 Jesus said to him, "Have I been with you so long, and yet you have not known Me, Philip? He who has seen Me has seen the Father; so how

---

⚒ DIGGING IN

when we don't love Him. He follows us with goodness and mercy all of our lives.

When you meet someone who is different from you, how do you treat that person? Do you say, "He's strange! I don't like him." Then God says to you, "I made that boy or girl for Myself. So I want you to care about that person. I want you to care about people who are hungry or lonely or caught in sin. I want you to be always ready to help them. That's what I mean when I say, 'Love one another.'"

14:2 Jesus Is Building You a House It's nice to have a house to live in. But a lot of people don't have houses. Many, many people in the world don't have any home at all. They live and sleep in the streets. That's a very sad thing in a world where there is so much. Jesus cares about people like that.

Someday all our homes will fall into ruin or be destroyed. But Jesus is building a place for you in heaven. One day He would like to invite you there to your new home that will last forever. God made you so that you can live forever with Him.

You may rise to great fame in this world, or you may fall into deep disgrace. But God made you for Himself, and it would be your highest honor to be asked to live in that special house that Jesus is building for you.

14:6 I Am the Way Here is another I AM that Jesus spoke. Many people have written and talked about a way of life that will bring them to heaven.

Some people think you can go to heaven by living a certain way. They say you have to sit cross-legged every day and say long prayers. Strange as it seems, they say you must even punish your body and starve a lot to go to heaven. Other people say you must earn your place in heaven by doing good works. This last way comes closest, but it still isn't true. If you love God, you will do good works, but your good works won't get you into heaven.

The ONLY way to heaven is Jesus. Jesus has made the path to heaven FOR you. He died and rose again to GIVE you a new life that will last forever. When you surrender your life to Him, He gives His life to you. Jesus is the Way to heaven.

can you say, 'Show us the Father'? 10 Do you not believe that I am in the Father, and the Father in Me? The words that I speak to you I do not speak on My own *authority;* but the Father who dwells in Me does the works. 11 Believe Me that I *am* in the Father and the Father in Me, or else believe Me for the sake of the works themselves.

12 "Most assuredly, I say to you, he who believes in Me, the works that I do he will do also; and greater *works* than these he will do, because I go to My Father. 13 And whatever you ask in My name, that I will do, that the Father may be glorified in the Son. 14 If you ask anything in My name, I will do *it.*

15 "If you love Me, keep My commandments. 16 And I will pray the Father, and He will give you another **Helper,** that He may abide with you forever— 17 the Spirit of truth, whom the world cannot receive, because it neither sees Him nor knows Him; but you know Him, for He dwells with you and will be in you. 18 I will not leave you orphans; I will come to you.

19 "A little while longer and the world will see Me no more, but you will see Me. Because I live, you will live also. 20 At that day you will know that I *am* in My Father, and you in Me, and I in you. 21 He who has My commandments and keeps them, it is he who loves Me. And he who loves Me will be loved by My Father, and I will love him and manifest Myself to him."

22 Judas (not Iscariot) said to Him, "Lord, how is it that You will manifest Yourself to us, and not to the world?"

23 Jesus answered and said to him, "If anyone loves Me, he will keep My word; and My Father will love him, and We will come to him and make Our home with him. 24 He who does not love Me does not keep My words; and the word which you hear is not Mine but the Father's who sent Me.

25 "These things I have spoken to you while being present with you. 26 But the Helper, the Holy Spirit, whom the Father will send in My name, He will teach you all things, and bring to your remembrance all things that I said to you. 27 Peace I leave with you, My peace I give to you; not as the world gives do I give to you. Let not your heart be troubled, neither let it be afraid. 28 You have heard Me say to you, 'I am going away and coming *back* to you.' If you loved Me, you would rejoice because I said, 'I am going to the Father,' for My Father is greater than I.

29 "And now I have told you before it comes, that when it does come to pass, you may believe. 30 I will no longer talk much with you, for the ruler of this world is coming, and he has nothing in Me. 31 But that the world may know that I love the Father, and as the Father gave Me commandment, so I do. Arise, let us go from here.

Jesus is the vine, we are the branches

15 "I am the true vine, and My Father is the vinedresser. 2 Every branch

---

ⓦ WORDFINDER

14:16 Helper The Holy Spirit, who is sometimes called "the Comforter." The Holy Spirit lives in you when you receive Jesus. He is your "Helper" in understanding God's Word.

⚒ DIGGING IN

15:1 I Am the True Vine This is the last I AM of Jesus. Why does Jesus describe Himself as a vine?

If you ever see a grapevine, you will notice that it is a mass of many branches.

Some of the branches have luscious grapes on them. Other branches just use up the life of the vine by making big leaves, but they never make any grapes! So they have to be cut away to let the in Me that does not bear fruit He takes away; and every *branch* that bears fruit He prunes, that it may bear more fruit. ³ You are already clean because of the word which I have spoken to you. ⁴ Abide in Me, and I in you. As the branch cannot bear fruit of itself, unless it abides in the vine, neither can you, unless you abide in Me.

⁵ "I am the vine, you *are* the branches. He who abides in Me, and I in him, bears much fruit; for without Me you can do nothing. ⁶ If anyone does not abide in Me, he is cast out as a branch and is withered; and they gather them and throw *them* into the fire, and they are burned. ⁷ If you abide in Me, and My words abide in you, you will ask what you desire, and it shall be done for you. ⁸ By this My Father is glorified, that you bear much fruit; so you will be My disciples.

⁹ "As the Father loved Me, I also have loved you; abide in My love. ¹⁰ If you keep My commandments, you will abide in My love, just as I have kept My Father's commandments and abide in His love.

¹¹ "These things I have spoken to you, that My joy may remain in you, and *that* your joy may be full. ¹² This is My commandment, that you love one another as I have loved you. ¹³ Greater love has no one than this, than to lay down one's life for his friends. ¹⁴ You are My friends if you do whatever I command you. ¹⁵ No longer do I call you servants, for a servant does not know what his master is doing; but I have called you friends, for all things that I heard from My Father I have made known to you. ¹⁶ You did not choose Me, but I chose you and appointed you that you

should go and bear fruit, and *that* your fruit should remain, that whatever you ask the Father in My name He may give you. ¹⁷ These things I command you, that you love one another.

Who Is a Servant of Jesus?

A servant of Jesus is someone who lives to please Him (see John 14:15). Jesus' servants are sometimes treated badly. But it is enough that the Lord loves you and you love Him. A servant of Jesus is also called a "disciple" (pronounced *dih-SIGH-pul*) or learner.

¹⁸ "If the world hates you, you know that it hated Me before *it hated* you. ¹⁹ If you were of the world, the world would love its own. Yet because you are not of the world, but I chose you out of the world, therefore the world hates you. ²⁰ Remember the word that I said to you, 'A servant is not greater than his master.' If they persecuted Me, they will also persecute you. If they kept My word, they will keep yours also. ²¹ But all these things they will do to you for My name's sake, because they do not know Him who sent Me. ²² If I had not come and spoken to them, they would have no sin, but now they have no excuse for their sin. ²³ He who hates Me hates My Father also. ²⁴ If I had not done among them the works which no one else did, they would have no sin; but now they have seen and also hated both Me and My Father. ²⁵ But *this happened* that the word might be fulfilled which is written in their law, 'They hated Me without a cause.'

DIGGING IN

good branches produce more grapes.

The many branches in Jesus are the people who say they are Christians. Many people are like the vine branches with big leaves, but they don't live for Jesus and they don't do anything for Him that lasts.

They LOOK great—but they have no fruit!

Make up your mind that you're going to find out how Jesus wants to work through you. If His life is in you, you will do things for God that will last forever.

26 "But when the **Helper** comes, whom I shall send to you from the Father, the Spirit of truth who proceeds from the Father, He will testify of Me. 27 And you also will bear witness, because you have been with Me from the beginning.

The disciples believe Jesus

16 "These things I have spoken to you, that you should not be made to stumble. 2 They will put you out of the synagogues; yes, the time is coming that whoever kills you will think that he offers God service. 3 And these things they will do to you because they have not known the Father nor Me. 4 But these things I have told you, that when the time comes, you may remember that I told you of them.

"And these things I did not say to you at the beginning, because I was with you.

5 "But now I go away to Him who sent Me, and none of you asks Me, 'Where are You going?' 6 But because I have said these things to you, sorrow has filled your heart. 7 Nevertheless I tell you the truth. It is to your advantage that I go away; for if I do not go away, the Helper will not come to you; but if I depart, I will send Him to you. 8 And when He has come, He will convict the world of sin, and of righteousness, and of judgment: 9 of sin, because they do not believe in Me; 10 of righteousness, because I go to My Father and you see Me no more; 11 of judgment, because the ruler of this world is judged.

12 "I still have many things to say to you, but you cannot bear *them* now. 13 However, when He, the Spirit of truth, has come, He will guide you into all truth; for He will not speak on His own *authority,* but whatever He hears He will speak; and He will tell you

things to come. 14 He will glorify Me, for He will take of what is Mine and declare *it* to you. 15 All things that the Father has are Mine. Therefore I said that He will take of Mine and declare *it* to you.

16 "A little while, and you will not see Me; and again a little while, and you will see Me, because I go to the Father."

17 Then *some* of His disciples said among themselves, "What is this that He says to us, 'A little while, and you will not see Me; and again a little while, and you will see Me'; and, 'because I go to the Father'?" 18 They said therefore, "What is this that He says, 'A little while'? We do not know what He is saying."

19 Now Jesus knew that they desired to ask Him, and He said to them, "Are you inquiring among yourselves about what I said, 'A little while, and you will not see Me; and again a little while, and you will see Me'? 20 Most assuredly, I say to you that you will weep and lament, but the world will rejoice; and you will be sorrowful, but your sorrow will be turned into joy. 21 A woman, when she is in labor, has sorrow because her hour has come; but as soon as she has given birth to the child, she no longer remembers the anguish, for joy that a human being has been born into the world. 22 Therefore you now have sorrow; but I will see you again and your heart will rejoice, and your joy no one will take from you.

23 "And in that day you will ask Me nothing. Most assuredly, I say to you, whatever you ask the Father in My name He will give you. 24 Until now you have asked nothing in My name. Ask, and you will receive, that your joy may be full.

25 "These things I have spoken to you in figurative language; but the time is coming when I will no longer speak

WORDFINDER

15:26 Helper The Holy Spirit, who is sometimes called "the Comforter." The Holy Spirit lives in you when you receive Jesus. He is your "Helper" in understanding God's Word.

What the Disciples Learned

In the beginning we were puzzled by what Jesus said: "A little while, and you will not see Me; and again a little while, and you will see Me."

Then He told us what He meant: He had come into the world from His Father, and now He was going back to His Father.

We understood clearly that Jesus was not just a teacher who would die. He truly was the Son of God, and He would live forever. Because He lived, we also would live with Him.

This is the most important truth for us to learn. Those who believe in Jesus will be with Him forever.

---

to you in figurative language, but I will tell you plainly about the Father. 26 In that day you will ask in My name, and I do not say to you that I shall pray the Father for you; 27 for the Father Himself loves you, because you have loved Me, and have believed that I came forth from God. 28 I came forth from the Father and have come into the world. Again, I leave the world and go to the Father."

29 His disciples said to Him, "See, now You are speaking plainly, and using no figure of speech! 30 Now we are sure that You know all things, and have no need that anyone should question You. By this we believe that You came forth from God."

31 Jesus answered them, "Do you now believe? 32 Indeed the hour is coming, yes, has now come, that you will be scattered, each to his own, and will leave Me alone. And yet I am not alone, because the Father is with Me. 33 These things I have spoken to you, that in Me you may have peace. In the world you will have tribulation; but be of good cheer, I have overcome the world."

Jesus prays for His disciples

17 Jesus spoke these words, lifted up His eyes to heaven, and said: "Father, the hour has come. Glorify Your Son, that Your Son also may glorify You, 2 as You have given Him authority over all flesh, that He should give eternal life to as many as You have given Him. 3 And this is eternal life, that they may know You, the only true God, and Jesus Christ whom You have sent. 4 I have glorified You on the earth. I have finished the work which You have given Me to do. 5 And now, O Father, glorify Me together with Yourself, with the glory which I had with You before the world was.

6 "I have manifested Your name to the men whom You have given Me out of the world. They were Yours, You gave them to Me, and they have

---

⛏ DIGGING IN

16:33 Don't Be Afraid Some people are afraid of the dark. Others are afraid of heights. Many people are just afraid of being in a world of so many sights and sounds.

We're sometimes afraid of the things we don't understand. That's one reason Jesus came—so that you could know the truth. Then you would never need to be afraid again.

You aren't God, and you can't know all

that God knows. So you have to live in a world you often don't understand. What can you do about that? Of course, you can read a lot and learn more about your world and yourself, but you soon find out that the more you learn, *the more there is still to learn.*

God knows all, and He will take care of you. You can trust Him with your life and with everything you don't understand. Then you won't be afraid anymore.

kept Your word. 7 Now they have known that all things which You have given Me are from You. 8 For I have given to them the words which You have given Me; and they have received *them,* and have known surely that I came forth from You; and they have believed that You sent Me.

9 "I pray for them. I do not pray for the world but for those whom You have given Me, for they are Yours. 10 And all Mine are Yours, and Yours are Mine, and I am glorified in them. 11 Now I am no longer in the world, but these are in the world, and I come to You. Holy Father, keep through Your name those whom You have given Me, that they may be one as We *are.* 12 While I was with them in the world, I kept them in Your name. Those whom You gave Me I have kept; and none of them is lost except the son of perdition, that the Scripture might be fulfilled. 13 But now I come to You, and these things I speak in the world, that they may have My joy fulfilled in themselves. 14 I have given them Your word; and the world has hated them because they are not of the world, just as I am not of the world. 15 I do not pray that You should take them out of the world, but that You should keep them from the evil one. 16 They are not of the world, just as I am not of the world. 17 **Sanctify** them by Your truth. Your word is truth. 18 As You sent Me into the world, I also have sent them into the world. 19 And for their sakes I sanctify Myself, that they also may be sanctified by the truth.

20 "I do not pray for these alone, but also for those who will believe in Me through their word; 21 that they all may be one, as You, Father, *are* in Me, and I in You; that they also may be one in Us, that the world may believe that You sent Me. 22 And the glory which You gave Me I have given them, that

they may be one just as We are one: 23 I in them, and You in Me; that they may be made perfect in one, and that the world may know that You have sent Me, and have loved them as You have loved Me.

24 "Father, I desire that they also whom You gave Me may be with Me where I am, that they may behold My glory which You have given Me; for You loved Me before the foundation of the world. 25 O righteous Father! The world has not known You, but I have known You; and these have known that You sent Me. 26 And I have declared to them Your name, and will declare *it,* that the love with which You loved Me may be in them, and I in them."

The soldiers arrest Jesus in the Garden

18 When Jesus had spoken these words, He went out with His disciples over the Brook Kidron, where there was a garden, which He and His disciples entered. 2 And Judas, who betrayed Him, also knew the place; for Jesus often met there with His disciples. 3 Then Judas, having received a detachment *of troops,* and officers from the chief priests and Pharisees, came there with lanterns, torches, and weapons. 4 Jesus therefore, knowing all things that would come upon Him, went forward and said to them, "Whom are you seeking?"

5 They answered Him, "Jesus of Nazareth."

Jesus said to them, "I am He." And Judas, who betrayed Him, also stood with them. 6 Now when He said to them, "I am He," they drew back and fell to the ground.

7 Then He asked them again, "Whom are you seeking?"

And they said, "Jesus of Nazareth."

8 Jesus answered, "I have told you

⊕ WORDFINDER

17:17 Sanctify Pronounced *SANK-tih-fy.* Means "set apart" for God's use. The Scriptures teach you to be useful to God when you have trusted Him.

Passion Week

Read about Jesus' last week
in Matthew 26:1 — 27:54.

† Gordon's Calvary

(10) Antonia Fortress
(Praetorium)

(3) Temple

(2)

(11) Church of the Holy
Sepulchre

Mount of
Olives

(6)

(9) Hasmoneon Palace

Kidron Valley

(8) Herod's Palace

(1) Bethany

Mount Zion

Tyropoeon Valley

Hill
Ophel

(7) House of
(4) Caiaphas

(5) Upper Room
(Last Supper)

Pool of Siloam

Hinnom Valley
(Gehenna)

1. Jesus stays with His friends—Mary, Martha and Lazarus—in **BETHANY**.
2. Entering **JERUSALEM** on a donkey, Jesus is greeted by happy people.
3. Going into the **TEMPLE**, Jesus drives out the money changers.
4. **HOUSE OF CAIAPHAS** the high priest, the religious leaders plot to kill Jesus.
5. Jesus and His disciples celebrate the Passover in an UPPER ROOM.
6. Jesus prays in the **GARDEN OF GETHSEMANE**.
7. Jesus is arrested and taken to the **HOUSE OF CAIAPHAS** for trial.
8. Jesus is moved to **'HEROD'S PALACE** to appear before Pilate.
9. Governor Pilate sends Jesus to Herod who was probably living in the
   'HASMONEON PALACE.
10. After questioning, Herod returns Jesus to Pilate at the **PRAETORIUM** in the
    'FORTRESS OF ANTONIO.
11. Jesus is sentenced to die on a cross at **GOLGOTHA**. (The **CHURCH OF THE
    HOLY SEPULCHRE** is built over the traditional spot where He died.)

*Some teachers think Herod and Pilate were living in these quarters during Jesus' last week on earth.

that I am *He*. Therefore, if you seek Me, let these go their way," ⁹ that the saying might be fulfilled which He spoke, "Of those whom You gave Me I have lost none."

¹⁰ Then Simon Peter, having a sword, drew it and struck the high priest's servant, and cut off his right ear. The servant's name was Malchus.

¹¹ So Jesus said to Peter, "Put your sword into the sheath. Shall I not drink the cup which My Father has given Me?"

¹² Then the detachment *of troops* and the captain and the officers of the Jews arrested Jesus and bound Him. ¹³ And they led Him away to Annas first, for he was the father-in-law of Caiaphas who was high priest that year. ¹⁴ Now it was Caiaphas who advised the Jews that it was expedient that one man should die for the people.

¹⁵ And Simon Peter followed Jesus, and so *did* another disciple. Now that disciple was known to the high priest, and went with Jesus into the courtyard of the high priest. ¹⁶ But Peter stood at the door outside. Then the other disciple, who was known to the high priest, went out and spoke to her who kept the door, and brought Peter in. ¹⁷ Then the servant girl who kept the door said to Peter, "You are not also *one* of this Man's disciples, are you?"

He said, "I am not."

¹⁸ Now the servants and officers who had made a fire of coals stood there, for it was cold, and they warmed themselves. And Peter stood with them and warmed himself.

¹⁹ The high priest then asked Jesus about His disciples and His doctrine.

²⁰ Jesus answered him, "I spoke openly to the world. I always taught in synagogues and in the temple, where the Jews always meet, and in secret I have said nothing. ²¹ Why do you ask Me? Ask those who have heard Me what I said to them. Indeed they know what I said."

²² And when He had said these things, one of the officers who stood by struck Jesus with the palm of his hand, saying, "Do You answer the high priest like that?"

²³ Jesus answered him, "If I have spoken evil, bear witness of the evil; but if well, why do you strike Me?"

²⁴ Then Annas sent Him bound to Caiaphas the **high priest.**

²⁵ Now Simon Peter stood and warmed himself. Therefore they said to him, "You are not also *one* of His disciples, are you?"

He denied *it* and said, "I am not!"

²⁶ One of the servants of the high priest, a relative *of him* whose ear Peter cut off, said, "Did I not see you in the garden with Him?" ²⁷ Peter then denied again; and immediately a rooster crowed.

²⁸ Then they led Jesus from Caiaphas to the **Praetorium,** and it was early morning. But they themselves did not go into the Praetorium, lest they should be defiled, but that they might eat the Passover. ²⁹ Pilate then went out to them and said, "What accusation do you bring against this Man?"

³⁰ They answered and said to him, "If He were not an evildoer, we would not have delivered Him up to you."

³¹ Then Pilate said to them, "You take Him and judge Him according to your law."

Therefore the Jews said to him, "It is not lawful for us to put anyone to death," ³² that the saying of Jesus might be fulfilled which He spoke, signifying by what death He would die.

³³ Then Pilate entered the Praetorium again, called Jesus, and said to Him, "Are You the King of the Jews?"

WORDFINDER

18:24 High Priest The priest who was over the other priests in Old Testament worship. Aaron, Moses' brother, was the first. Christ is now our High Priest.

18:28 Praetorium Pronounced *prih-TOE-rih-um*. The headquarters of the Roman governor of Judea. This was located at Antonia Castle, where Pilate questioned Jesus.

Barabbas—My life will always belong to Jesus. I lived because He died.

You see, I was sentenced to die for murder (Luke 23:18, 19). When Pilate, the governor, had to free one prisoner at the Jewish Passover feast, he let the screaming mob decide who it should be—Jesus or me. And the crowd just shouted "Barabbas! Barabbas!" Even Pilate was shocked.

I couldn't believe I was free. As I looked back, there stood Jesus, the Son of God, who had done no wrong. Pilate was sending Him away to be crucified instead of me.

How can I ever forget what Jesus did for me? By dying, that good Man gave me back my life. And so I want to give myself to Him.

Did you know that Jesus died in your place, too? What does Jesus mean to you?

34 Jesus answered him, "Are you speaking for yourself about this, or did others tell you this concerning Me?"

35 Pilate answered, "Am I a Jew? Your own nation and the chief priests have delivered You to me. What have You done?"

36 Jesus answered, "My kingdom is not of this world. If My kingdom were of this world, My servants would fight, so that I should not be delivered to the Jews; but now My kingdom is not from here."

37 Pilate therefore said to Him, "Are You a king then?"

Jesus answered, "You say *rightly* that I am a king. For this cause I was born, and for this cause I have come into the world, that I should bear witness to the truth. Everyone who is of the truth hears My voice."

38 Pilate said to Him, "What is truth?" And when he had said this, he went out again to the Jews, and said to them, "I find no fault in Him at all.

39 "But you have a custom that I should release someone to you at the Passover. Do you therefore want me to release to you the King of the Jews?"

40 Then they all cried again, saying, "Not this Man, but Barabbas!" Now Barabbas was a robber.

Jesus gives His life and is buried

19 So then Pilate took Jesus and scourged *Him*. 2 And the soldiers twisted a crown of thorns and put *it* on His head, and they put on Him a purple robe. 3 Then they said, "Hail, King of the Jews!" And they struck Him with their hands.

4 Pilate then went out again, and said to them, "Behold, I am bringing Him out to you, that you may know that I find no fault in Him."

5 Then Jesus came out, wearing the crown of thorns and the purple robe. And *Pilate* said to them, "Behold the Man!"

6 Therefore, when the chief priests and officers saw Him, they cried out, saying, "Crucify *Him*, crucify *Him*!"

"Jesus died in my place."

What Pilate Learned

I never did trust those religious leaders who brought Jesus to me for trial. They hated Jesus because He made them look foolish. Now the good Man stood before me. What should I do?

The more I talked with Jesus, the more I hated my job. Jesus was at least an honest person. Maybe He really was the Son of God after all! How could I crucify the Son of God?

I tried to get those stupid Jewish leaders to drop their silly charges against Jesus, but they wouldn't. I even told them they were going to crucify their King!

I knew who Jesus was. But I let them crucify Him anyway because I was afraid of the mob.

Pilate said to them, "You take Him and crucify *Him,* for I find no fault in Him."

⁷ The Jews answered him, "We have a law, and according to our law He ought to die, because He made Himself the Son of God."

⁸ Therefore, when Pilate heard that saying, he was the more afraid, ⁹ and went again into the Praetorium, and said to Jesus, "Where are You from?" But Jesus gave him no answer.

¹⁰ Then Pilate said to Him, "Are You not speaking to me? Do You not know that I have power to crucify You, and power to release You?"

¹¹ Jesus answered, "You could have no power at all against Me unless it had been given you from above. Therefore the one who delivered Me to you has the greater sin."

¹² From then on Pilate sought to release Him, but the Jews cried out, saying, "If you let this Man go, you are not Caesar's friend. Whoever makes himself a king speaks against Caesar."

¹³ When Pilate therefore heard that saying, he brought Jesus out and sat

The place called "The Pavement," where Jesus was judged by Pilate.

down in the judgment seat in a place that is called *The* Pavement, but in Hebrew, Gabbatha. 14 Now it was the Preparation Day of the Passover, and about the sixth hour. And he said to the Jews, "Behold your King!"

15 But they cried out, "Away with *Him,* away with *Him!* Crucify Him!"

Pilate said to them, "Shall I crucify your King?"

The chief priests answered, "We have no king but Caesar!"

16 Then he delivered Him to them to be crucified. Then they took Jesus and led *Him* away.

17 And He, bearing His cross, went out to a place called *the Place* of a Skull, which is called in Hebrew, Golgotha, 18 where they crucified Him, and two others with Him, one on either side, and Jesus in the center. 19 Now Pilate wrote a title and put *it* on the cross. And the writing was:

JESUS OF NAZARETH, THE KING OF THE JEWS.

20 Then many of the Jews read this title, for the place where Jesus was crucified was near the city; and it was written in Hebrew, Greek, *and* Latin.

21 Therefore the chief priests of the Jews said to Pilate, "Do not write, 'The King of the Jews,' but, 'He said, "I am the King of the Jews." ' "

22 Pilate answered, "What I have written, I have written."

23 Then the soldiers, when they had crucified Jesus, took His garments and made four parts, to each soldier a part, and also the tunic. Now the tunic was without seam, woven from the top in one piece. 24 They said therefore among themselves, "Let us not tear it, but cast lots for it, whose it shall be," that the Scripture might be fulfilled which says:

> "They divided My garments
>   among them,
> And for My clothing they cast
>   lots."

Therefore the soldiers did these things.

25 Now there stood by the cross of Jesus His mother, and His mother's sister, Mary the *wife* of Clopas, and Mary Magdalene. 26 When Jesus therefore saw His mother, and the disciple whom He loved standing by, He said to His mother, "Woman, behold your son!" 27 Then He said to the disciple, "Behold your mother!" And from that hour that disciple took her to his own *home.*

28 After this, Jesus, knowing that all things were now accomplished, that the Scripture might be fulfilled, said, "I thirst!" 29 Now a vessel full of sour wine was sitting there; and they filled a sponge with sour wine, put *it* on hyssop, and put *it* to His mouth. 30 So when Jesus had received the sour wine, He said, "It is finished!" And bowing His head, He gave up His spirit.

31 Therefore, because it was the Preparation *Day,* that the bodies should not remain on the cross on the Sabbath (for that Sabbath was a high day), the Jews asked Pilate that their

DIGGING IN

19:30 Jesus Finished His Work
There's a special happiness in finishing your work and knowing it is done well. Jesus was given a very hard assignment by His Father—to go into a world that hated Him and then to die to save that world.

For more than three years, Jesus carried out the task His Father had given Him. He went everywhere showing His Father's love. Where there was sickness, He brought health. Where there was blindness, He brought sight. Where there was hunger, He brought food. Where there was death, He brought life. We see Jesus working day and night to carry out His Father's command. Then He died.

At that moment, He finished the dreadful task of carrying your sins, even though you weren't born yet! The weight of that load of sin broke His heart. He died in pain and darkness and alone, but He finished the work. Now you can go free simply by trusting Him to take away your sins.

Joseph of Arimathea—My home was in Arimathea (pronounced *air-ih-muh-THEE-ah*) in Palestine. After I grew up, I was honored to be a member of the council called the Sanhedrin (pronounced *san-HEE-drin*). That council had 71 members, and most of them voted to crucify Jesus, but I didn't. Actually, I was a secret disciple of Jesus.

After they crucified Him, I went to Pilate, the Roman governor, and asked for Jesus' body. When Pilate gave his permission, I placed Jesus in my own personal tomb in a beautiful garden.

Jesus forgave me for being a secret disciple, but I had a hard time forgiving myself. Always be ready to share Jesus your Savior with those you meet.

---

legs might be broken, and *that* they might be taken away. 32 Then the soldiers came and broke the legs of the first and of the other who was crucified with Him. 33 But when they came to Jesus and saw that He was already dead, they did not break His legs. 34 But one of the soldiers pierced His side with a spear, and immediately blood and water came out. 35 And he who has seen has testified, and his testimony is true; and he knows that he is telling the truth, so that you may believe. 36 For these things were done that the Scripture should be fulfilled, "Not one of His bones shall be broken." 37 And again another Scripture says, "They shall look on Him whom they pierced."

38 After this, Joseph of Arimathea, being a disciple of Jesus, but secretly, for fear of the Jews, asked Pilate that he might take away the body of Jesus; and Pilate gave *him* permission. So he came and took the body of Jesus. 39 And Nicodemus, who at first came to Jesus by night, also came, bringing a mixture of myrrh and aloes, about a hundred pounds. 40 Then they took the body of Jesus, and bound it in strips of linen with the spices, as the custom of the Jews is to bury. 41 Now in the place where He was crucified there was a garden, and in the garden a new tomb in which no one had yet been laid. 42 So there they laid Jesus, because of the Jews' Preparation *Day*, for the tomb was nearby.

Jesus lives again and appears to the disciples

20 Now the first *day* of the week Mary Magdalene went to the tomb early, while it was still dark, and saw *that* the stone had been taken away from the tomb. 2 Then she ran and came to Simon Peter, and to the other disciple, whom Jesus loved, and said to them, "They have taken away the Lord out of the tomb, and we do not know where they have laid Him."

3 Peter therefore went out, and the other disciple, and were going to the tomb. 4 So they both ran together, and the other disciple outran Peter and came to the tomb first. 5 And he, stooping down and looking in, saw the linen cloths lying *there;* yet he did not go in. 6 Then Simon Peter came, following him, and went into the tomb; and he saw the linen cloths lying *there,* 7 and the handkerchief that had been around His head, not lying with the linen cloths, but folded together in a place by itself. 8 Then the other disciple, who came to the tomb first, went in also; and he saw and believed. 9 For as yet they did not know the Scripture, that He must rise again from the dead. 10 Then the disciples went away again to their own homes.

11 But Mary stood outside by the tomb weeping, and as she wept she stooped down *and looked* into the tomb. 12 And she saw two angels in white sitting, one at the head and the

What Mary Magdalene Learned

I am called Mary Magdalene (pronounced *MAG-dah-leen*) because I am from Magdala (pronounced *MAG-dah-lah*) on the shore of the Sea of Galilee.

Jesus had promised us He would rise from the dead on the third day after He was killed. I wanted to believe it, but I wasn't sure. So I went to His tomb on Sunday morning before dawn, and I found it empty! John and Peter also came, and they saw the empty tomb. I thought someone had stolen Jesus' body.

As I waited there in the dark, a man called my name. At first I thought it was the gardener. But just as the sun was rising, He called my name and I saw His face. It was my Lord! Then He told me He was going back to His Father in heaven.

Later, He appeared to all the other disciples. Yes, my Savior is alive!

other at the feet, where the body of Jesus had lain. 13 Then they said to her, "Woman, why are you weeping?"

She said to them, "Because they have taken away my Lord, and I do not know where they have laid Him."

14 Now when she had said this, she turned around and saw Jesus standing *there,* and did not know that it was Jesus. 15 Jesus said to her, "Woman, why are you weeping? Whom are you seeking?"

She, supposing Him to be the gardener, said to Him, "Sir, if You have carried Him away, tell me where You have laid Him, and I will take Him away."

16 Jesus said to her, "Mary!"

She turned and said to Him, "Rabboni!" (which is to say, Teacher).

17 Jesus said to her, "Do not cling to Me, for I have not yet ascended to My Father; but go to My brethren and say to them, 'I am ascending to My Father and your Father, and *to* My God and your God.' "

18 Mary Magdalene came and told the disciples that she had seen the Lord, and *that* He had spoken these things to her.

19 Then, the same day at evening, being the first *day* of the week, when the doors were shut where the disciples were assembled, for fear of the Jews,

Jesus came and stood in the midst, and said to them, "Peace *be* with you." 20 When He had said this, He showed them *His* hands and His side. Then the disciples were glad when they saw the Lord.

21 So Jesus said to them again, "Peace to you! As the Father has sent Me, I also send you." 22 And when He had said this, He breathed on *them,* and said to them, "Receive the Holy Spirit. 23 If you forgive the sins of any, they are forgiven them; if you retain the *sins* of any, they are retained."

24 Now Thomas, called the Twin, one of the twelve, was not with them when Jesus came. 25 The other disciples therefore said to him, "We have seen the Lord."

Thomas recognizes Jesus after His resurrection: "My Lord and my God!"

Like the other disciples, I, Thomas, was brokenhearted when they crucified our Lord. All we had hoped and dreamed seemed to come to an end, so many of us went back to our earlier life as fishermen.

When we heard the reports of the women that Jesus was alive, we didn't believe them.

One evening the disciples were all together hiding from the authorities. Even though the doors were shut, somehow Jesus came and stood before them. He showed them the nail wounds in His hands and feet.

But I wasn't there when Jesus came, so I said I wouldn't believe He was risen from the dead unless I touched Him myself.

Some days later, Jesus came to us again, even though the doors were shut. Then He invited me to touch the wounds in His hands and side.

I needed no further proof. I saw and believed my Lord and my God. Jesus really did rise from the dead!

So he said to them, "Unless I see in His hands the print of the nails, and put my finger into the print of the nails, and put my hand into His side, I will not believe."

²⁶ And after eight days His disciples were again inside, and Thomas with them. Jesus came, the doors being shut, and stood in the midst, and said, "Peace to you!" ²⁷ Then He said to Thomas, "Reach your finger here, and look at My hands; and reach your hand *here,* and put *it* into My side. Do not be unbelieving, but believing."

²⁸ And Thomas answered and said to Him, "My Lord and my God!"

²⁹ Jesus said to him, "Thomas, because you have seen Me, you have believed. Blessed *are* those who have not seen and *yet* have believed."

³⁰ And truly Jesus did many other signs in the presence of His disciples, which are not written in this book; ³¹ but these are written that you may believe that Jesus is the Christ, the Son of God, and that believing you may have life in His name.

Jesus cooks breakfast on the seashore

21 After these things Jesus showed Himself again to the disciples at the Sea of Tiberias, and in this way He showed *Himself:* ² Simon Peter, Thomas called the Twin, Nathanael of Cana in Galilee, the *sons* of Zebedee, and two others of His disciples were together. ³ Simon Peter said to them, "I am going fishing."

They said to him, "We are going with you also." They went out and immediately got into the boat, and that night they caught nothing. ⁴ But when the morning had now come, Jesus stood on the shore; yet the disciples did not know that it was Jesus. ⁵ Then Jesus said to them, "Children, have you any food?"

They answered Him, "No."

⁶ And He said to them, "Cast the net on the right side of the boat, and you will find *some.*" So they cast, and now they were not able to draw it in because of the multitude of fish.

⁷ Therefore that disciple whom Jesus loved said to Peter, "It is the Lord!" Now when Simon Peter heard that it was the Lord, he put on *his* outer garment (for he had removed it), and plunged into the sea. ⁸ But the other disciples came in the little boat (for they were not far from land, but about two hundred cubits), dragging the net with fish. ⁹ Then, as soon as they had come to land, they saw a fire of coals there, and fish laid on it, and bread. ¹⁰ Jesus

Nearly everybody loves my Gospel because I, John, tell them clearly who Jesus really is. He was not just a wonderful man who became our Savior. He is the Lord from heaven.

I like to tell the stories of how Jesus told lonely and needy people that He came to give them a whole new life. Nicodemus and the woman at the well were two such people.

Jesus told us He was the true Bread of Life. He also said that He would be like a spring of Everlasting Water living in people.

One day His friend Lazarus became sick and died, but Jesus said that those who trust Him never really die. Then Jesus raised Lazarus from death.

The Lord Jesus Himself later arose from the tomb. He now wants you to know Him as the One who can keep you safe for Himself. Whoever believes in Jesus lives with Him forever.

said to them, "Bring some of the fish which you have just caught."

11 Simon Peter went up and dragged the net to land, full of large fish, one hundred and fifty-three; and although there were so many, the net was not broken. 12 Jesus said to them, "Come and eat breakfast." Yet none of the disciples dared ask Him, "Who are You?"—knowing that it was the Lord. 13 Jesus then came and took the bread and gave it to them, and likewise the fish.

14 This is now the third time Jesus showed Himself to His disciples after He was raised from the dead.

15 So when they had eaten breakfast, Jesus said to Simon Peter, "Simon, son of Jonah, do you love Me more than these?"

He said to Him, "Yes, Lord; You know that I love You."

He said to him, "Feed My lambs."

16 He said to him again a second time, "Simon, son of Jonah, do you love Me?"

He said to Him, "Yes, Lord; You know that I love You."

He said to him, "Tend My sheep."

17 He said to him the third time, "Simon, son of Jonah, do you love Me?" Peter was grieved because He said to him the third time, "Do you love Me?"

And he said to Him, "Lord, You know all things; You know that I love You."

Jesus said to him, "Feed My sheep. 18 Most assuredly, I say to you, when you were younger, you girded yourself and walked where you wished; but when you are old, you will stretch out your hands, and another will gird you and carry you where you do not wish." 19 This He spoke, signifying by what death he would glorify God. And when He had spoken this, He said to him, "Follow Me."

20 Then Peter, turning around, saw the disciple whom Jesus loved following, who also had leaned on His breast at the supper, and said, "Lord, who is the one who betrays You?" 21 Peter, seeing him, said to Jesus, "But Lord, what about this man?"

22 Jesus said to him, "If I will that he remain till I come, what is that to you? You follow Me."

23 Then this saying went out among the brethren that this disciple would not die. Yet Jesus did not say to him that he would not die, but, "If I will that he remain till I come, what is that to you?"

24 This is the disciple who testifies of these things, and wrote these things; and we know that his testimony is true.

25 And there are also many other things that Jesus did, which if they were written one by one, I suppose that even the world itself could not contain the books that would be written. Amen.

DIGGING IN

21:25 How Much Does God Know? John tells you that the whole story of Jesus' life could not be told, because it would take too many books. So God hasn't told us everything there is to know. But in the Bible God tells us what we need to know to be saved from our sins. Getting to know all that is contained between the covers of the Bible will take a lifetime.

Just think of the vastness of God's knowledge! His knowledge is infinite—unlimited! Our mightiest computers can store immense amounts of information, and we can bring up that information in an instant of time. Yet, computers only know what we put into them. We also are like computers, and we know what God shows to us in His created universe.

Although you will never know as much as God knows, your life can be spent learning all you can about what He has created. Then you can use that knowledge as He does—to bless others in whatever work God calls you to do.

The Book of
ACTS

Theophilus—I was a leading citizen of Greek society. My name is pronounced *thee-OFF-ah-luss.*

Luke and I both grew up in Antioch. We had been friends a long time, so I was honored when he sent his Gospel and this book to me.

I always admired my Christian brother, Luke, because he was such a careful scholar. Luke loved the truth. When he heard the story of Jesus the Savior, he studied very hard to find out all the facts about Him. Luke also studied medicine at the great universities of our time.

Some of us trusted Luke more because he was a Gentile like ourselves. In those days we Greeks didn't understand the Jews very well.

But I'm glad Luke became a Christian, and now he has led me to become a disciple of Jesus, too.

Jesus returns to heaven

THE former account I made, O Theophilus, of all that Jesus began both to do and teach, 2 until the day in which He was taken up, after He through the Holy Spirit had given commandments to the apostles whom He had chosen, 3 to whom He also presented Himself alive after His suffering by many infallible proofs, being seen by them during forty days and speaking of the things pertaining to the kingdom of God.

4 And being assembled together with *them,* He commanded them not to depart from Jerusalem, but to wait for the Promise of the Father, "which," *He said,* "you have heard from Me; 5 for John truly baptized with water, but you shall be baptized with the Holy Spirit not many days from now."

6 Therefore, when they had come together, they asked Him, saying, "Lord, will You at this time restore the kingdom to Israel?" 7 And He said to them, "It is not for you to know times or seasons which the Father has put in His own authority. 8 But you shall receive power when the Holy Spirit has come upon you; and you shall be witnesses to Me in Jerusalem, and in all Judea and Samaria, and to the end of the earth."

9 Now when He had spoken these things, while they watched, He was

⚒ DIGGING IN

1:3 The Second Book of Luke The biblical book we call "Acts of the Apostles" could also be called the "Second Book of Luke." In the first book, the Gospel of Luke, the author tells all that Jesus *began* to do and teach. In the second book written by Luke, the author tells of all that Jesus *continued* to do.

When Jesus rose from the dead, He went to be with His Father. From there, Jesus sent the Holy Spirit to help the apostles *continue* the work that Jesus be-

gan in the Gospel of Luke. In a way, the Book of Acts is still being written today. The servants of Jesus Christ continue to carry out His work of spreading the gospel in the world.

As you read the Book of Acts, you will meet Luke as a friend of the apostle Paul. Luke traveled with Paul and reported happenings along the way.

Luke was a Greek medical doctor, and he was the only non-Jewish author of Bible writings.

taken up, and a cloud received Him out of their sight. 10 And while they looked steadfastly toward heaven as He went up, behold, two men stood by them in white apparel, 11 who also said, "Men of Galilee, why do you stand gazing up into heaven? This *same* Jesus, who was taken up from you into heaven, will so come in like manner as you saw Him go into heaven."

12 Then they returned to Jerusalem from the mount called Olivet, which is near Jerusalem, a Sabbath day's journey. 13 And when they had entered, they went up into the upper room where they were staying: Peter, James, John, and Andrew; Philip and Thomas; Bartholomew and Matthew; James *the son* of Alphaeus and Simon the **Zealot**; and Judas *the son* of James. 14 These all continued with one accord in prayer and supplication, with the women and Mary the mother of Jesus, and with His brothers.

15 And in those days Peter stood up in the midst of the disciples (altogether the number of names was about a hundred and twenty), and said, 16 "Men *and* brethren, this Scripture had to be fulfilled, which the Holy Spirit spoke before by the mouth of David concerning Judas, who became a guide to those who arrested Jesus; 17 for he was numbered with us and obtained a part in this ministry."

18 (Now this man purchased a field with the wages of iniquity; and falling headlong, he burst open in the middle and all his entrails gushed out. 19 And it became known to all those dwelling in Jerusalem; so that field is called in their own language, Akel Dama, that is, Field of Blood.)

20 "For it is written in the Book of Psalms:

🔍 WORDFINDER

1:13 Zealot Pronounced *ZELL-ut*. A member of the Zealot political party in Jesus' time. This group of Jews was trying to cause a military revolt against the Romans.

⛏ DIGGING IN

1:8 Are You a Witness for Jesus? What is a witness? A witness is someone who can tell you what really happened because he or she was there. We believe witnesses in court only when they have seen and heard what really happened. They didn't hear the news from someone else. *They were there!*

You and I weren't there to see Jesus healing the sick. You didn't see Him die on the Cross or rise from the dead. But you can know that He did those things just as if you were there yourself. How? The Spirit of God travels across time and takes you there. He shows your *inner* eyes those things the Bible tells you about. More than that, the Holy Spirit breathes the risen life of Jesus into your being. Then you *know* Jesus is risen and alive and living in you! So you can be a real witness of what He has done to make you a new person.

1:11 How Jesus Will Come Back Jesus said, "I will come again." Do you wonder how He will come back? Jesus came the first time as a little Baby who grew up to be a servant of mankind. Then He died on the Cross. He rose up from death, and He is alive forever.

You can't see Jesus now because He has gone up to heaven. But someday you will see Him again. Then He will come, not as a little child, but as the mighty God. He will judge all people by the way they have believed and lived.

Some people will be judged because they did not receive the free gift of salvation. Others will be judged because they said they were Christians, but they lied. They never really loved Jesus. But if you have truly given your life to Him, you have no need to fear His coming. You can pray, "Come quickly, Lord Jesus."

'Let his dwelling place be desolate,
    And let no one live in it';

and,

'Let another take his office.'

21 "Therefore, of these men who have accompanied us all the time that the Lord Jesus went in and out among us, 22 beginning from the baptism of John to that day when He was taken up from us, one of these must become a witness with us of His resurrection."

23 And they proposed two: Joseph called Barsabas, who was surnamed Justus, and Matthias. 24 And they prayed and said, "You, O Lord, who know the hearts of all, show which of these two You have chosen 25 to take part in this ministry and apostleship from which Judas by transgression fell, that he might go to his own place." 26 And they cast their lots, and the lot fell on Matthias. And he was numbered with the eleven apostles.

The Holy Spirit fills the disciples

2 When the **Day of Pentecost** had fully come, they were all with one accord in one place. 2 And suddenly there came a sound from heaven, as of a rushing mighty wind, and it filled the whole house where they were sitting. 3 Then there appeared to them divided tongues, as of fire, and *one* sat upon each of them. 4 And they were all filled with the Holy Spirit and began to speak with other tongues, as the Spirit gave them utterance.

5 And there were dwelling in Jerusalem Jews, devout men, from every nation under heaven. 6 And when this sound occurred, the multitude came together, and were confused, because everyone heard them speak in his own language. 7 Then they were all amazed and marveled, saying to one another, "Look, are not all these who speak Galileans? 8 And how *is it that* we hear, each in our own language in which we were born? 9 Parthians and Medes and Elamites, those dwelling in Mesopotamia, Judea and Cappadocia, Pontus and Asia, 10 Phrygia and Pamphylia, Egypt and the parts of Libya adjoining Cyrene, visitors from Rome, both Jews and proselytes, 11 Cretans and Arabs— we hear them speaking in our own tongues the wonderful works of God." 12 So they were all amazed and perplexed, saying to one another, "Whatever could this mean?"

13 Others mocking said, "They are full of new wine."

14 But Peter, standing up with the

🌐 WORDFINDER

2:1 Day of Pentecost The day coming fifty days after the Jewish Passover (see definition of *Passover* at John 2:13). Pentecost (pronounced *PEN-tih-cost*) is also called the Feast of Harvest.

⛏ DIGGING IN

2:4 The Holy Spirit Has Come Before He went back to heaven, Jesus promised He would send the Holy Spirit to be with us while He was gone (see John 16:7). So it was on the Jewish holiday of Pentecost (pronounced *PEN-tih-cost*) that the Holy Spirit came. Pentecost was held fifty days after the Jewish Passover, a time that celebrated the night of the Jews' escape from Egypt (see Exodus 12).

The Holy Spirit is the real presence of *God Himself,* and He now lives in every-one who believes in Jesus. The Holy Spirit teaches you about Jesus, and He reminds you that you will be a son or daughter of God forever. He also helps you to live like Jesus. When the Holy Spirit lives in you, it means that Jesus Himself lives in you, too.

The Holy Spirit made the disciples able to preach the Good News about Jesus in everybody's language. He also made the disciples able to do miracles.

eleven, raised his voice and said to them, "Men of Judea and all who dwell in Jerusalem, let this be known to you, and heed my words. 15 For these are not drunk, as you suppose, since it is *only* the third hour of the day. 16 But this is what was spoken by the prophet Joel:

17 'And it shall come to pass in the last days, says God,
That I will pour out of My Spirit on all flesh;
Your sons and your daughters shall prophesy,
Your young men shall see visions,
Your old men shall dream dreams.
18 And on My menservants and on My maidservants
I will pour out My Spirit in those days;

Simon, the fisherman, became Peter, the fisher of men.

And they shall prophesy.
19 I will show wonders in heaven above
And signs in the earth beneath:
Blood and fire and vapor of smoke.
20 The sun shall be turned into darkness,
And the moon into blood,
Before the coming of the great and awesome day of the LORD.
21 And it shall come to pass
That whoever calls on the name of the LORD
Shall be saved.'

22 "Men of Israel, hear these words: Jesus of Nazareth, a Man attested by God to you by miracles, wonders, and signs which God did through Him in your midst, as you yourselves also know— 23 Him, being delivered by the determined purpose and foreknowledge of God, you have taken by lawless hands, have crucified, and put to death; 24 whom God raised up, having loosed the pains of death, because it was not possible that He should be held by it. 25 For David says concerning Him:

'I foresaw the LORD always before my face,
For He is at my right hand, that I may not be shaken.
26 Therefore my heart rejoiced, and my tongue was glad;
Moreover my flesh also will rest in hope.
27 For You will not leave my soul in Hades,
Nor will You allow Your Holy One to see corruption.
28 You have made known to me the ways of life;
You will make me full of joy in Your presence.'

29 "Men *and* brethren, let *me* speak freely to you of the patriarch David, that he is both dead and buried, and his tomb is with us to this day. 30 Therefore, being a prophet, and

Was This Man the Christ?

AJTN (All-Judea Television Network)—The city of Jerusalem is in an uproar! Our camera crews have been on the scene all day, covering the events of this Day of Pentecost.

Jews from all over the world are in the city for the special holiday. While here, many of them have accepted the new faith of Jesus Christ. At a recent meeting of some Christian disciples, the sound of a great rushing wind was heard. Then these disciples began preaching in the native language of all the foreigners present!

They say that this is the birthday of Christianity in the world. After this, the gospel of the crucified Christ will be told to every nation.

AJTN believes that something very unusual and wonderful has happened since Jesus was seen alive several days ago. After what we have seen today, we find it hard to deny that Jesus Christ is working powerfully by His Spirit living in these Christians.

knowing that God had sworn with an oath to him that of the fruit of his body, according to the flesh, He would raise up the Christ to sit on his throne, ³¹ he, foreseeing this, spoke concerning the resurrection of the Christ, that His soul was not left in Hades, nor did His flesh see corruption. ³² This Jesus God has raised up, of which we are all witnesses. ³³ Therefore being exalted to the right hand of God, and having received from the Father the promise of the Holy Spirit, He poured out this which you now see and hear.

³⁴ "For David did not ascend into the heavens, but he says himself:

'The LORD said to my Lord,
"Sit at My right hand,
35   Till I make Your enemies Your
       footstool." '

³⁶ "Therefore let all the house of Israel know assuredly that God has made this Jesus, whom you crucified, both Lord and Christ."

³⁷ Now when they heard *this,* they were cut to the heart, and said to Peter and the rest of the apostles, "Men *and* brethren, what shall we do?"

³⁸ Then Peter said to them, "Repent, and let every one of you be baptized in the name of Jesus Christ for the remission of sins; and you shall receive the gift of the Holy Spirit. ³⁹ For the promise is to you and to your children, and to all who are afar off, as many as the Lord our God will call."

⁴⁰ And with many other words he testified and exhorted them, saying, "Be saved from this perverse generation." ⁴¹ Then those who gladly received his word were baptized; and that day about three thousand souls were added *to them.* ⁴² And they continued steadfastly in the apostles' doctrine and fellowship, in the breaking of bread, and in prayers. ⁴³ Then fear came upon every soul, and many wonders and signs were done through the apostles. ⁴⁴ Now all who believed were together, and had all things in common, ⁴⁵ and sold their possessions and goods, and divided them among all, as anyone had need.

⁴⁶ So continuing daily with one ac-

What Is the Promise?

Four thousand years ago, God promised that all nations would be blessed because of Abraham (pronounced *AY-bruh-ham*). (See Genesis 12:3.) Now God is keeping His promise. Jews and all nations are being invited into the kingdom of God. This is the great news of salvation through Jesus. (See Acts 2:39.)

What the First Christians Learned

After Jesus left us, we wondered what was going to happen. Then the Holy Spirit came, and Peter preached His first great message to the people gathered in Jerusalem. We were surprised when about three thousand men, women, boys, and girls believed the gospel and were saved. So we learned that Jesus had not really left us.

The Holy Spirit is the Spirit of God Himself. The Spirit gives us power to do what God wants us to do and to tell others about Him.

Now we can obey Jesus' command to spread the news about Him all over the world. If you trust Jesus yourself, you will be able to lead others to know Him as their Savior, too.

---

cord in the temple, and breaking bread from house to house, they ate their food with gladness and simplicity of heart, [47] praising God and having favor with all the people. And the Lord added to the church daily those who were being saved.

Peter and John heal a crippled man

3 Now Peter and John went up together to the temple at the hour of prayer, the ninth *hour*. [2] And a certain man lame from his mother's womb was carried, whom they laid daily at the gate of the temple which is called Beautiful, to ask alms from those who entered the temple; [3] who, seeing Peter and John about to go into the temple, asked for alms. [4] And fixing his eyes on him, with John, Peter said, "Look at us." [5] So he gave them his attention, expecting to receive something from them. [6] Then Peter said, "Silver and gold I do not have, but what I do have I give you: In the name of Jesus Christ of Nazareth, rise up and walk." [7] And he took him by the right hand and lifted *him* up, and immediately his feet and ankle bones received

strength. [8] So he, leaping up, stood and walked and entered the temple with them—walking, leaping, and praising God. [9] And all the people saw him walking and praising God. [10] Then they knew that it was he who sat begging alms at the Beautiful Gate of the temple; and they were filled with wonder and amazement at what had happened to him.

[11] Now as the lame man who was healed held on to Peter and John, all the people ran together to them in the porch which is called Solomon's, greatly amazed. [12] So when Peter saw *it*, he responded to the people: "Men of Israel, why do you marvel at this? Or why look so intently at us, as though by our own power or godliness we had made this man walk? [13] The God of Abraham, Isaac, and Jacob, the God of our fathers, glorified His Servant Jesus, whom you delivered up and denied in the presence of Pilate, when he was determined to let *Him* go. [14] But you denied the Holy One and the Just, and asked for a murderer to be granted to you, [15] and killed the Prince of life, whom God raised from the dead, of which we are witnesses. [16] And His name, through faith in His

---

⚒ DIGGING IN

3:16 Trusting Jesus Changes Us Peter had just healed a lame man (Acts 3:6, 7). Now Peter tells everybody how it happened—by the lame man's faith in Jesus.

Everyone who trusts Jesus is changed in some way. The lame man walked again. More than that—*the lame man became a new person inside!* Do you think name, has made this man strong, whom you see and know. Yes, the faith which *comes* through Him has given him this perfect soundness in the presence of you all.

17 "Yet now, brethren, I know that you did *it* in ignorance, as *did* also your rulers. 18 But those things which God foretold by the mouth of all His prophets, that the Christ would suffer, He has thus fulfilled. 19 Repent therefore and be converted, that your sins may be blotted out, so that times of refreshing may come from the presence of the Lord, 20 and that He may send Jesus Christ, who was preached to you before, 21 whom heaven must receive until the times of restoration of all things, which God has spoken by the mouth of all His holy prophets since the world began. 22 For Moses truly said to the fathers, 'The LORD your God will raise up for you a Prophet like me from your brethren. Him you shall hear in all things, whatever He says to you. 23 And it shall be *that* every soul who will not hear that Prophet shall be utterly destroyed from among the people.' 24 Yes, and all the prophets, from Samuel and those who follow, as many as have spoken, have also foretold these days. 25 You are sons of the prophets, and of the covenant which God made with our fathers, saying to Abraham, 'And in your seed all the families of the earth shall be **blessed.**' 26 To you first, God, having raised up His Servant Jesus, sent Him to bless you, in turning away every one *of* you from your iniquities."

Brave Peter and John are put in prison

4 Now as they spoke to the people, the priests, the captain of the temple, and the Sadducees came upon them, 2 being greatly disturbed that they taught the people and preached in Jesus the resurrection from the dead. 3 And they laid hands on them, and put *them* in custody until the next day, for it was already evening. 4 However, many of those who heard the word believed; and the number of the men came to be about five thousand.

5 And it came to pass, on the next day, that their rulers, elders, and scribes, 6 as well as Annas the high priest, Caiaphas, John, and Alexander, and as many as were of the family of the high priest, were gathered together at Jerusalem. 7 And when they had set them in the midst, they asked, "By what power or by what name have you done this?"

8 Then Peter, filled with the Holy Spirit, said to them, "Rulers of the people and elders of Israel: 9 If we this day are judged for a good deed *done* to a helpless man, by what means he has been made well, 10 let it be known to you all, and to all the people of Israel, that by the name of Jesus Christ of Nazareth, whom you crucified, whom God raised from the dead, by Him this man stands here before you whole. 11 This is the 'stone which was rejected by you builders, which has become the

---

WORDFINDER

3:25 Blessed An adjective that means a person is favored by God and His kindness. Sometimes the word means "the happiness that God gives."

DIGGING IN

the lame man could ever forget what Jesus did for his legs? Never! Wherever he went, he told people about the great miracle.

Jesus wants to do wonders for you, too. The most wonderful thing Jesus does for people is to give them a whole new life.

Yes, Jesus changes people so they are never the same again. He can give you lasting joy and peace by believing in Him. Have you trusted Jesus? Do you believe He died for your sins? Then give your life to Him. That is what it means to trust Jesus.

chief cornerstone.' 12 Nor is there **salvation** in any other, for there is no other name under heaven given among men by which we must be saved."

13 Now when they saw the boldness of Peter and John, and perceived that they were uneducated and untrained men, they marveled. And they realized that they had been with Jesus. 14 And seeing the man who had been healed standing with them, they could say nothing against it. 15 But when they had commanded them to go aside out of the council, they conferred among themselves, 16 saying, "What shall we do to these men? For, indeed, that a notable miracle has been done through them is evident to all who dwell in Jerusalem, and we cannot deny it. 17 But so that it spreads no further among the people, let us severely threaten them, that from now on they speak to no man in this name."

18 So they called them and commanded them not to speak at all nor teach in the name of Jesus. 19 But Peter and John answered and said to them, "Whether it is right in the sight of God to listen to you more than to God, you judge. 20 For we cannot but speak the things which we have seen and heard." 21 So when they had further threatened them, they let them go, finding no way of punishing them, because of the people, since they all glorified God for what had been done. 22 For the man was over forty years old on whom this miracle of healing had been performed.

23 And being let go, they went to their own *companions* and reported all that the chief priests and elders had said to them. 24 So when they heard that, they raised their voice to God with one accord and said: "Lord, You *are* God, who made heaven and earth and the sea, and all that is in them, 25 who by the mouth of Your servant David have said:

'Why did the nations rage,
　And the people plot vain things?
26　The kings of the earth took their
　　stand,
　And the rulers were gathered
　　together
　Against the LORD and against His
　　Christ.'

27 "For truly against Your holy Servant Jesus, whom You anointed, both Herod and Pontius Pilate, with the Gentiles and the people of Israel, were gathered together 28 to do whatever Your hand and Your purpose

---

WORDFINDER

4:12 Salvation Pronounced *sal-VAY-shun*. A work of saving someone from danger or death. In the Bible, salvation is Christ's work of dying to save us from sin and hell.

DIGGING IN

4:12 Jesus Your Only Savior As you grow up, you will hear the names of people who taught many wonderful things about how to live.

Buddha (pronounced *BOO-duh*) taught that by living right, you can live forever. The only trouble was, he couldn't tell you what was good and how to make yourself good.

Mohammed (pronounced *mo-HAM-id*) taught that if you believed in one god (Allah), you would go to heaven. Your place in heaven would be guaranteed if you died in battle for Allah.

Zoroaster (pronounced *zorro-AS-ter*) taught about a god of light, but this god was no stronger than the evil spirit in the world.

Hindus (pronounced *HEN-doos*) teach that by spending long periods of time in thought, you can become part of the whole universe.

You can't take away your sins by trying. Only Jesus can take away the sin that prevents you from knowing and loving God.

determined before to be done. 29 Now, Lord, look on their threats, and grant to Your servants that with all boldness they may speak Your word, 30 by stretching out Your hand to heal, and that signs and wonders may be done through the name of Your holy Servant Jesus."

31 And when they had prayed, the place where they were assembled together was shaken; and they were all filled with the Holy Spirit, and they spoke the word of God with boldness.

32 Now the multitude of those who believed were of one heart and one soul; neither did anyone say that any of the things he possessed was his own, but they had all things in common. 33 And with great power the apostles gave witness to the **resurrection** of the Lord Jesus. And great grace was upon them all. 34 Nor was there anyone among them who lacked; for all who were possessors of lands or houses sold them, and brought the proceeds of the things that were sold, 35 and laid *them* at the apostles' feet; and they distributed to each as anyone had need.

36 And Joses, who was also named Barnabas by the apostles (which is translated Son of Encouragement), a Levite of the country of Cyprus, 37 having land, sold *it,* and brought the money and laid *it* at the apostles' feet.

A man and his wife lie to God

5 But a certain man named Ananias, with Sapphira his wife, sold a possession. 2 And he kept back *part* of the proceeds, his wife also being aware *of it,* and brought a certain part and laid *it* at the apostles' feet. 3 But Peter said, "Ananias, why has Satan filled your heart to lie to the Holy Spirit and keep back *part* of the price of the land for yourself? 4 While it remained, was it not your own? And after it was sold, was it not in your own control? Why have you conceived this thing in your heart? You have not lied to men but to God."

5 Then Ananias, hearing these words, fell down and breathed his last. So great fear came upon all those who heard these things. 6 And the young men arose and wrapped him up, carried *him* out, and buried *him.*

7 Now it was about three hours later when his wife came in, not knowing what had happened. 8 And Peter answered her, "Tell me whether you sold the land for so much?"

She said, "Yes, for so much."

9 Then Peter said to her, "How is it that you have agreed together to test the Spirit of the Lord? Look, the feet of those who have buried your husband *are* at the door, and they will

🌐 WORDFINDER

4:33 Resurrection   Pronounced *rez-er-RECK-shun.* The rising of Jesus from death. Jesus has promised that those who trust Him will also be raised up as He was.

⛏ DIGGING IN

4:31 Prayer Makes You Brave John and Peter were put in jail for telling people about Jesus. Do you think that's strange? Why should people be arrested just for talking? Yet even today, people can get in trouble with the law for talking about Jesus. If you tell about Jesus in the streets or in public school, you can be in great trouble. This is something new in our country, where people used to be free to preach the gospel anywhere.

When Peter and John were released from jail, they told the other Christians what happened. But the Christians didn't complain to anyone about how they were treated. *They prayed!* Then God made them strong and brave enough to tell about Jesus even more than they had before.

Christians can't expect much help from the world. The place to go when you need help is to God. He gives strength for all things.

They Dared to Lie to God

The Jerusalem Times

JERUSALEM—A man and his wife lost their lives recently after telling a lie about some money they were donating to their church.

The man, Ananias (pronounced *ann-uh-NIGH-us*) and his wife, Sapphira (pronounced *suh-FIRE-uh*) had kept for themselves part of the money from the sale of something they owned. They wanted the church to think they were making a big gift. That was a lie.

Many of the disciples had already given away their goods and money to be used for supporting people who had lost their jobs because they were Christians. Everyone was sharing everything. Ananias and Sapphira were not willing to share everything they had and even lied about what they had done.

According to eyewitness reports, both of them fell dead when their lie became known. Someone has said, "You can't mock God." God demands truth, and lying to Him is very dangerous.

carry you out." 10 Then immediately she fell down at his feet and breathed her last. And the young men came in and found her dead, and carrying *her* out, buried *her* by her husband. 11 So great fear came upon all the church and upon all who heard these things.

12 And through the hands of the apostles many signs and wonders were done among the people. And they were all with one accord in Solomon's Porch. 13 Yet none of the rest dared join them, but the people esteemed them highly. 14 And believers were increasingly added to the Lord, multitudes of both men and women, 15 so that they brought the sick out into the streets and laid *them* on beds and couches, that at least the shadow of Peter passing by might fall on some of them. 16 Also a multitude gathered from the surrounding cities to Jerusalem, bringing sick people and those who were tormented by unclean spirits, and they were all healed.

17 Then the high priest rose up, and all those who *were* with him (which is the sect of the Sadducees), and they were filled with indignation, 18 and laid their hands on the apostles and put them in the common prison. 19 But at night an angel of the Lord opened the prison doors and brought them out, and said, 20 "Go, stand in the temple and speak to the people all the words of this life."

21 And when they heard *that,* they entered the temple early in the morning and taught. But the high priest and those with him came and called the council together, with all the elders of the children of Israel, and sent to the prison to have them brought.

22 But when the officers came and did not find them in the prison, they returned and reported, 23 saying, "Indeed we found the prison shut securely, and the guards standing outside before the doors; but when we opened them, we found no one inside!" 24 Now when the high priest, the captain of the temple, and the chief priests heard these things, they wondered what the outcome would be. 25 So one came and told them, saying, "Look, the men whom you put in prison are standing in the temple and teaching the people!"

26 Then the captain went with the officers and brought them without violence, for they feared the people, lest they should be stoned. 27 And when they had brought them, they set *them* before the council. And the high priest asked them, 28 saying, "Did we not strictly command you not to teach in this name? And look, you have filled Jerusalem with your doctrine, and intend to bring this Man's blood on us!"

29 But Peter and the *other* apostles answered and said: "We ought to obey God rather than men. 30 The God of our fathers raised up Jesus whom you murdered by hanging on a tree. 31 Him God has exalted to His right hand *to be* Prince and Savior, to give repentance to Israel and forgiveness of sins. 32 And we are His witnesses to these things, and *so* also *is* the Holy Spirit whom God has given to those who obey Him."

33 When they heard *this,* they were furious and plotted to kill them. 34 Then one in the council stood up, a Pharisee named Gamaliel, a teacher of the law held in respect by all the people, and commanded them to put the apostles outside for a little while. 35 And he said to them: "Men of Israel, take heed to yourselves what you intend to do regarding these men. 36 For some time ago Theudas rose up, claiming to be somebody. A number of men, about four hundred, joined him. He was slain, and all who obeyed him were scattered and came to nothing. 37 After this man, Judas of Galilee rose up in the days of the census, and drew away many people after him. He also perished, and all who obeyed him were dispersed. 38 And now I say to you, keep away from these men and let them alone; for if this plan or this work is of men, it will come to nothing; 39 but if it is of God, you cannot overthrow it—lest you even be found to fight against God."

40 And they agreed with him, and when they had called for the apostles and beaten *them,* they commanded that they should not speak in the name of Jesus, and let them go. 41 So they departed from the presence of the council, rejoicing that they were counted worthy to suffer shame for His name. 42 And daily in the temple, and in every house, they did not cease teaching and preaching Jesus *as* the Christ.

Seven men are chosen for special work

6 Now in those days, when *the number of* the disciples was multiplying, there arose a complaint against the Hebrews by the **Hellenists,** because their widows were neglected in the daily distribution. 2 Then the twelve summoned the multitude of the disciples and said, "It is not desirable that we should leave the word of God and serve tables. 3 Therefore, brethren, seek out from among you seven men of *good* reputation, full of the Holy Spirit and wisdom, whom we may appoint over this business; 4 but we will give ourselves continually to prayer and to the ministry of the word."

5 And the saying pleased the whole multitude. And they chose Stephen, a man full of faith and the Holy Spirit, and Philip, Prochorus, Nicanor, Timon, Parmenas, and Nicolas, a proselyte from Antioch, 6 whom they set before the apostles; and when they had prayed, they laid hands on them.

7 Then the word of God spread, and the number of the disciples multiplied greatly in Jerusalem, and a great many of the priests were obedient to the faith.

8 And Stephen, full of faith and power, did great wonders and signs among the people. 9 Then there arose some from what is called the Synagogue of the Freedmen (Cyrenians, Alexandrians, and those from Cilicia and Asia), disputing with Stephen. 10 And they were not able to resist the wisdom and the Spirit by which he spoke. 11 Then they secretly induced men to say, "We have heard him speak blasphemous words against Moses and God." 12 And they stirred up

WORDFINDER

6:1 Hellenists Pronounced *HELL-ih-nists.* Jews in Jesus' time who spoke Greek and tried to follow the ancient Greek style of living and thinking. That style was called Hellenism.

My name, Stephen (pronounced STEVE-un), means "A Crown." I was one of the seven men chosen to serve the needs of our Greek-speaking widows in Jerusalem. I never planned to be a preacher, but God gave me the gift of speaking and debate. That was when my trouble started.

Some of the Jews hated Jesus. I preached that the temple and the old ways of worship were passing away. Jesus had already told them that His own body was the true temple of God.

So they brought me before the council of men that had also condemned Jesus. When they asked me if what they heard about me was true, I told them they had always disobeyed the Lord, and now they had killed Jesus, His only Son. Then they threw stones at me till I died.

But I could see Jesus standing at God's right hand. He was calling me home to heaven.

the people, the elders, and the scribes; and they came upon *him,* seized him, and brought *him* to the council. 13 They also set up false witnesses who said, "This man does not cease to speak blasphemous words against this holy place and the law; 14 for we have heard him say that this Jesus of Nazareth will destroy this place and change the customs which Moses delivered to us." 15 And all who sat in the council, looking steadfastly at him, saw his face as the face of an angel.

Angry men throw rocks at Stephen

7 Then the high priest said, "Are these things so?"

2 And he said, "Brethren and fathers, listen: The God of glory appeared to our father Abraham when he was in Mesopotamia, before he dwelt in Haran, 3 and said to him, 'Get out of your country and from your relatives, and come to a land that I will show you.' 4 Then he came out of the land of the **Chaldeans** and dwelt in Haran. And from there, when his father was dead, He moved him to this land in which you now dwell. 5 And

God gave him no inheritance in it, not even *enough* to set his foot on. But even when *Abraham* had no child, He promised to give it to him for a possession, and to his descendants after him. 6 But God spoke in this way: that his descendants would dwell in a foreign land, and that they would bring them into bondage and oppress *them* four hundred years. 7 'And the nation to whom they will be in bondage I will judge,' said God, 'and after that they shall come out and serve Me in this place.' 8 Then He gave him the covenant of circumcision; and so *Abraham* begot Isaac and circumcised him on the eighth day; and Isaac *begot* Jacob, and Jacob *begot* the twelve patriarchs.

9 "And the patriarchs, becoming envious, sold Joseph into Egypt. But God was with him 10 and delivered him out of all his troubles, and gave him favor and wisdom in the presence of Pharaoh, king of Egypt; and he made him governor over Egypt and all his house. 11 Now a famine and great trouble came over all the land of Egypt and Canaan, and our fathers found no sustenance. 12 But when Jacob heard that there was grain in Egypt, he sent out our fathers first. 13 And the second

WORDFINDER

7:4 Chaldeans The people who lived in Chaldea (pronounced *kal-DEE-uh*), a land found in the region of modern Iran and Iraq. Chaldea later included nearly all of Babylonia (pronounced *bab-ih-LOW-nih-uh*).

time Joseph was made known to his brothers, and Joseph's family became known to the Pharaoh. ¹⁴ Then Joseph sent and called his father Jacob and all his relatives to *him,* seventy-five people. ¹⁵ So Jacob went down to Egypt; and he died, he and our fathers. ¹⁶ And they were carried back to Shechem and laid in the tomb that Abraham bought for a sum of money from the sons of Hamor, *the father* of Shechem.

¹⁷ "But when the time of the promise drew near which God had sworn to Abraham, the people grew and multiplied in Egypt ¹⁸ till another king arose who did not know Joseph. ¹⁹ This man dealt treacherously with our people, and oppressed our forefathers, making them expose their babies, so that they might not live. ²⁰ At this time Moses was born, and was well pleasing to God; and he was brought up in his father's house for three months. ²¹ But when he was set out, Pharaoh's daughter took him away and brought him up as her own son. ²² And Moses was learned in all the wisdom of the Egyptians, and was mighty in words and deeds.

²³ "Now when he was forty years old, it came into his heart to visit his brethren, the children of Israel. ²⁴ And seeing one of *them* suffer wrong, he defended and avenged him who was oppressed, and struck down the Egyptian. ²⁵ For he supposed that his brethren would have understood that God would deliver them by his hand, but they did not understand. ²⁶ And the next day he appeared to two of them

as they were fighting, and *tried to* reconcile them, saying, 'Men, you are brethren; why do you wrong one another?' ²⁷ But he who did his neighbor wrong pushed him away, saying, 'Who made you a ruler and a judge over us? ²⁸ Do you want to kill me as you did the Egyptian yesterday?' ²⁹ Then, at this saying, Moses fled and became a dweller in the land of Midian, where he had two sons.

³⁰ "And when forty years had passed, an Angel of the Lord appeared to him in a flame of fire in a bush, in the wilderness of Mount Sinai. ³¹ When Moses saw *it,* he marveled at the sight; and as he drew near to observe, the voice of the Lord came to him, ³² *saying,* 'I *am* the God of your fathers—the God of Abraham, the God of Isaac, and the God of Jacob.' And Moses trembled and dared not look. ³³ 'Then the LORD said to him, "Take your sandals off your feet, for the place where you stand is holy ground. ³⁴ I have surely seen the oppression of My people who are in Egypt; I have heard their groaning and have come down to deliver them. And now come, I will send you to Egypt." '

³⁵ "This Moses whom they rejected, saying, 'Who made you a ruler and a judge?' is the one God sent *to be* a ruler and a deliverer by the hand of the Angel who appeared to him in the bush. ³⁶ He brought them out, after he had shown wonders and signs in the land of Egypt, and in the Red Sea, and in the wilderness forty years.

³⁷ "This is that Moses who said to the children of Israel, 'The LORD your

---

⛏ DIGGING IN

7:37 What Is a Prophet? The word *prophet* comes from a Hebrew word meaning "mouthpiece." Sometimes you may hear an attorney referred to in slang as a "mouthpiece." An attorney *speaks for* his client in a court of law. In the same way, a prophet speaks for the Lord. The prophet doesn't speak about his own beliefs or thoughts. He tells what God tells him to say.

You have read about a lot of prophets in the Old Testament. Moses, the first great prophet, told the people only what God told him to say. Moses said that someday a greater Prophet would come. He was referring to Jesus, who would come about fifteen hundred years after Moses. Jesus would be the perfect Prophet because He was the Son of God from heaven. Every Christian should also be a prophet who can tell people what God says in His Word.

Why Was This Man Killed?

The Jerusalem Times

JERUSALEM—Reporters from this newspaper have been following the growth of the followers of the Teacher called Jesus who was crucified outside this city some time ago.

One of the disciples of Jesus, a man named Stephen (pronounced *STEVE-un*) was accused of blasphemy (pronounced *BLASS-fuh-mee*), meaning an insult to God. When he was brought before our council, he made a long speech and told how our people, the Jews, always seem to resist God. Then he accused us of murdering Jesus.

Eyewitnesses report that Stephen was dragged outside the city, where he died after the people threw heavy stones at him.

This newspaper is trying to decide if those who follow Jesus are right. We have noticed that they seem to be a loving and peaceful people. There is much angry feeling against the group, but *The Times* hopes that the opposition will remain calm and think carefully about how the Jesus followers should be treated.

God will raise up for you a Prophet like me from your brethren. Him you shall hear.'

38 "This is he who was in the congregation in the wilderness with the Angel who spoke to him on Mount Sinai, and *with* our fathers, the one who received the living oracles to give to us, 39 whom our fathers would not obey, but rejected. And in their hearts they turned back to Egypt, 40 saying to Aaron, 'Make us gods to go before us; *as for* this Moses who brought us out of the land of Egypt, we do not know what has become of him.' 41 And they made a calf in those days, offered sacrifices to the idol, and rejoiced in the works of their own hands. 42 Then God turned and gave them up to worship the host of heaven, as it is written in the book of the Prophets:

'Did you offer Me slaughtered
    animals and sacrifices *during*
    forty years in the wilderness,
    O house of Israel?
43 You also took up the tabernacle
    of Moloch,
And the star of your god
    Remphan,
Images which you made to
    worship;

And I will carry you away
    beyond Babylon.'

44 "Our fathers had the tabernacle of witness in the wilderness, as He appointed, instructing Moses to make it according to the pattern that he had seen, 45 which our fathers, having received it in turn, also brought with Joshua into the land possessed by the Gentiles, whom God drove out before the face of our fathers until the days of David, 46 who found favor before God and asked to find a dwelling for the God of Jacob. 47 But Solomon built Him a house.

48 "However, the Most High does not dwell in temples made with hands, as the prophet says:

49 'Heaven *is* My throne,
    And earth *is* My footstool.
    What house will you build for
        Me? says the LORD,
    Or what *is* the place of My rest?
50   Has My hand not made all these
        things?'

51 "*You* stiff-necked and uncircumcised in heart and ears! You always resist the Holy Spirit; as your fathers *did,* so *do* you. 52 Which of the prophets did your fathers not persecute? And

they killed those who foretold the coming of the Just One, of whom you now have become the betrayers and murderers, 53 who have received the law by the direction of angels and have not kept *it*."

54 When they heard these things they were cut to the heart, and they gnashed at him with *their* teeth. 55 But he, being full of the Holy Spirit, gazed into heaven and saw the glory of God, and Jesus standing at the right hand of God, 56 and said, "Look! I see the heavens opened and the Son of Man standing at the right hand of God!"

57 Then they cried out with a loud voice, stopped their ears, and ran at him with one accord; 58 and they cast *him* out of the city and stoned *him*. And the witnesses laid down their clothes at the feet of a young man named Saul. 59 And they stoned Stephen as he was calling on *God* and saying, "Lord Jesus, receive my spirit." 60 Then he knelt down and cried out with a loud voice, "Lord, do not charge them with this sin." And when he had said this, he fell asleep.

Saul tries to destroy the Christians

8 Now Saul was consenting to his death.

At that time a great persecution arose against the church which was at Jerusalem; and they were all scattered throughout the regions of Judea and

---

⚒ DIGGING IN

7:56 Jesus Our Friend in Death What an exciting moment! Stephen had just made a great speech about Jesus and Israel's long history of disobedience to God. Suddenly, Stephen looked up to heaven and saw Jesus standing there at the right hand of God. Who wouldn't give everything for that sight of Jesus?

No one wants to die, because death is our great enemy, but in a few minutes, Stephen was going to die. By himself, he would have lost courage. The Lord knew this, and so Jesus kindly opened Stephen's eyes to see His Lord in heaven. Now Stephen could face anything!

Someday everyone will die. You, too, will die, unless Jesus comes first. But trust Jesus the way Stephen did. In that hour of death, Jesus will come and put His arms around you. You will not be afraid anymore, and in a moment you will be with Him forever.

7:59 Stephen Killed by Stoning There were several methods of putting people to death during Bible times. Stoning—throwing stones—was the usual method. People were killed by stoning for the following crimes—idolatry, or worshiping other gods; leading others to worship other gods; breaking the Sabbath; adultery.

It seems that Stephen was executed by stoning because he was leading people to worship Jesus. Stephen also made the people angry by telling them they had always been unfaithful to the Lord. So they dragged Stephen outside the city and threw stones at him until he died.

When people were put to death by stoning, the witnesses of the crime laid their hands on the condemned person. Then the witnesses threw the first stones. Finally, a heap of stones was piled over the victim. Do you think Stephen deserved to die that way? How do you think the crowd should have acted when Stephen preached to them?

Stephen is stoned to death after confessing his belief in Jesus.

Samaria, except the apostles. 2 And devout men carried Stephen *to his burial,* and made great lamentation over him.

3 As for Saul, he made havoc of the church, entering every house, and dragging off men and women, committing *them* to prison.

4 Therefore those who were scattered went everywhere preaching the word. 5 Then Philip went down to the city of Samaria and preached Christ to them. 6 And the multitudes with one accord heeded the things spoken by Philip, hearing and seeing the miracles which he did. 7 For unclean spirits, crying with a loud voice, came out of many who were possessed; and many who were paralyzed and lame were healed. 8 And there was great joy in that city.

9 But there was a certain man called Simon, who previously practiced **sorcery** in the city and astonished the people of Samaria, claiming that he was someone great, 10 to whom they all gave heed, from the least to the greatest, saying, "This man is the great power of God." 11 And they heeded him because he had astonished them with his sorceries for a long time. 12 But when they believed Philip as he preached the things concerning the kingdom of God and the name of Jesus Christ, both men and women were baptized. 13 Then Simon himself also believed; and when he was baptized he continued with Philip, and was amazed, seeing the miracles and signs which were done.

14 Now when the apostles who were at Jerusalem heard that Samaria had received the word of God, they sent Peter and John to them, 15 who, when they had come down, prayed for them that they might receive the Holy Spirit. 16 For as yet He had fallen upon none of them. They had only been baptized in the name of the Lord Jesus. 17 Then they laid hands on them, and they received the Holy Spirit.

18 And when Simon saw that through the laying on of the apostles' hands the Holy Spirit was given, he offered them money, 19 saying, "Give me this power also, that anyone on whom I lay hands may receive the Holy Spirit."

20 But Peter said to him, "Your money perish with you, because you thought that the gift of God could be purchased with money! 21 You have neither part nor portion in this matter, for your heart is not right in the sight of God. 22 Repent therefore of this your wickedness, and pray God if perhaps the thought of your heart may be forgiven you. 23 For I see that you are poisoned by bitterness and bound by iniquity."

24 Then Simon answered and said, "Pray to the Lord for me, that none of the things which you have spoken may come upon me."

25 So when they had testified and preached the word of the Lord, they returned to Jerusalem, preaching the gospel in many villages of the Samaritans.

26 Now an angel of the Lord spoke to Philip, saying, "Arise and go toward the south along the road which goes down from Jerusalem to Gaza." This is desert. 27 So he arose and went. And behold, a man of Ethiopia, a eunuch of great authority under Candace the queen of the Ethiopians, who had charge of all her treasury, and had come to Jerusalem to worship, 28 was returning. And sitting in his chariot, he was reading Isaiah the prophet. 29 Then the Spirit said to Philip, "Go near and overtake this chariot."

30 So Philip ran to him, and heard him reading the prophet Isaiah, and said, "Do you understand what you are reading?"

31 And he said, "How can I, unless

WORDFINDER

8:9–13 Sorcery Pronounced *SORE-sah-ree.* The practice of magic using secret potions and spells to control nature and persons. The Bible forbids sorcery.

someone guides me?'' And he asked Philip to come up and sit with him. 32 The place in the Scripture which he read was this:

"He was led as a sheep to the slaughter;
And as a lamb before its shearer is silent,
So He opened not His mouth.
33 In His humiliation His justice was taken away,
And who will declare His generation?
For His life is taken from the earth.''

34 So the eunuch answered Philip and said, "I ask you, of whom does the prophet say this, of himself or of some other man?'' 35 Then Philip opened his mouth, and beginning at this Scripture, preached Jesus to him. 36 Now as they went down the road, they came to some water. And the eunuch said, "See, *here is* water. What hinders me from being baptized?''

37 Then Philip said, "If you believe with all your heart, you may.''

And he answered and said, "I **believe** that Jesus Christ is the Son of God.''

38 So he commanded the chariot to stand still. And both Philip and the eunuch went down into the water, and he baptized him. 39 Now when they came up out of the water, the Spirit of the Lord caught Philip away, so that the eunuch saw him no more; and he went on his way rejoicing. 40 But Philip was found at Azotus. And passing through, he preached in all the cities till he came to Caesarea.

Saul meets Jesus on the road to Damascus

9 Then Saul, still breathing threats and murder against the disciples of the Lord, went to the high priest 2 and asked letters from him to the synagogues of Damascus, so that if he found any who were of the Way, whether men or women, he might bring them bound to Jerusalem.

3 As he journeyed he came near Damascus, and suddenly a light shone around him from heaven. 4 Then he fell to the ground, and heard a voice saying to him, "Saul, Saul, why are you persecuting Me?''

5 And he said, "Who are You, Lord?''

Then the Lord said, "I am Jesus, whom you are persecuting. It *is* hard for you to kick against the goads.''

6 So he, trembling and astonished,

WORDFINDER

8:37 Believe To accept what God has said in the Bible and to trust Jesus to save you from your sins. To believe as a Christian is to receive Jesus Christ into your life.

DIGGING IN

8:37 An African Man Finds Christ Jesus came to offer eternal life to people of every race. Not only Jewish, but Greek, Roman, Asian, and African people are part of the family of Christ. You should not be surprised, then, that a man from Ethiopia became an early Christian.

Christians have to remember that all people have the stamp of God on their natures. The gospel of Jesus is open to all people, no matter what their color or local customs. Christians should not need to be taught to accept people of other races. Love is always your first rule for living, and that means loving and caring about people of all nations and languages.

Do you ever hear people say unkind things about people of other races? When you hear these things, remember that in God's sight, you were once an outsider, too. But God loved you just the same and sent Jesus to die for you. Now it's your turn to love the outsider.

Saul the Pharisee Now Claims To Be a Christian

The Jerusalem Times

JERUSALEM—Saul the Pharisee (pronounced *FAIR-uh-see*), one of our brightest young scholars and a member of our great council, has been converted to faith in Jesus!

Ordered to arrest as many followers of Jesus as he could find, Saul was on his way to Damascus (pronounced *duh-MASK-us*) when something very strange happened. Since that experience, Saul has considered himself a "Christian," as this group is sometimes called.

The Times has always tried to be fair in the argument about the crucified Carpenter, but it is a bad sign for our leaders when even Saul decides to follow Him.

We must think carefully about the so-called "risen Christ." He has been seen alive by as many as five hundred people at one time. If what our brother Saul tells us is true, then we are a very guilty people who need God's forgiveness!

said, "Lord, what do You want me to do?"

Then the Lord *said* to him, "Arise and go into the city, and you will be told what you must do."

[7] And the men who journeyed with him stood speechless, hearing a voice but seeing no one. [8] Then Saul arose from the ground, and when his eyes were opened he saw no one. But they led him by the hand and brought *him* into Damascus. [9] And he was three days without sight, and neither ate nor drank.

[10] Now there was a certain disciple at Damascus named Ananias; and to him the Lord said in a vision, "Ananias."

And he said, "Here I am, Lord."

[11] So the Lord *said* to him, "Arise and go to the street called Straight, and inquire at the house of Judas for *one* called Saul of Tarsus, for behold, he is praying. [12] And in a vision he has seen a man named Ananias coming in and putting *his* hand on him, so that he might receive his sight."

[13] Then Ananias answered, "Lord, I have heard from many about this man, how much harm he has done to Your saints in Jerusalem. [14] And here he has authority from the chief priests to bind all who call on Your name."

[15] But the Lord said to him, "Go, for he is a chosen vessel of Mine to bear My name before Gentiles, kings, and the children of Israel. [16] For I will show him how many things he must suffer for My name's sake."

DIGGING IN

9:5 Saul Meets Jesus Saul was a VIP (very important person) in Israel. He was a young man and well educated. He had been to all the best schools.

Saul was also an ambitious member of the Jewish council, called the Sanhedrin (pronounced *san-HEE-drin*). He was a Pharisee (pronounced *FAIR-uh-see*), which meant he was a leading teacher of the Jews. Remember that the Pharisees had bitterly argued with Jesus during His ministry.

Saul was also determined to stamp out early Christianity. He was arresting and killing as many Christians as he could. In fact, Saul was on his way to arrest Christians at Damascus in Syria when a frightening thing happened. He actually met the risen Christ Himself! As you can read, Saul was blinded by the sight. Later He believed in Jesus, and his sight was restored.

You, too, must have a meeting with Jesus. When you meet Him, He will change your life completely, just as He changed Saul's life.

17 And Ananias went his way and entered the house; and laying his hands on him he said, "Brother Saul, the Lord Jesus, who appeared to you on the road as you came, has sent me that you may receive your sight and be filled with the Holy Spirit." 18 Immediately there fell from his eyes *something* like scales, and he received his sight at once; and he arose and was baptized.

19 So when he had received food, he was strengthened. Then Saul spent some days with the disciples at Damascus.

20 Immediately he preached the Christ in the synagogues, that He is the Son of God.

21 Then all who heard were amazed, and said, "Is this not he who destroyed those who called on this name in Jerusalem, and has come here for that purpose, so that he might bring them bound to the chief priests?"

22 But Saul increased all the more in strength, and confounded the Jews who dwelt in Damascus, proving that this *Jesus* is the Christ.

23 Now after many days were past, the Jews plotted to kill him. 24 But their plot became known to Saul. And they watched the gates day and night, to kill him. 25 Then the disciples took him by night and let *him* down through the wall in a large basket.

26 And when Saul had come to Jerusalem, he tried to join the disciples; but they were all afraid of him, and did not believe that he was a disciple. 27 But Barnabas took him and brought *him* to the apostles. And he declared to them how he had seen the Lord on the road, and that He had spoken to him, and how he had preached boldly at Damascus in the name of Jesus. 28 So he was with them at Jerusalem, coming in and going out. 29 And he spoke boldly in the name

Saul is let down in a basket and escapes from an angry crowd.

of the Lord Jesus and disputed against the **Hellenists,** but they attempted to kill him. 30 When the brethren found out, they brought him down to Caesarea and sent him out to Tarsus.

31 Then the churches throughout all Judea, Galilee, and Samaria had peace and were edified. And walking in the fear of the Lord and in the comfort of the Holy Spirit, they were multiplied.

32 Now it came to pass, as Peter went through all *parts of the country,* that he also came down to the saints who dwelt in Lydda. 33 There he found a certain man named Aeneas, who had been bedridden eight years and was

🕮 **WORDFINDER**

9:29 Hellenists Pronounced *HELL-ih-nists.* Jews in Jesus' time who spoke Greek and tried to follow the ancient Greek style of living and thinking. That style was called Hellenism.

Joppa Woman Raised from the Dead

The Joppa News

JOPPA—Dorcas (pronounced *DOOR-kus*), a woman of the seaport town of Joppa, died recently. Well known in the town as a doer of good works, she was greatly loved. No one seemed to mind that she was a Christian because she was so kind, especially to the poor.

People in Joppa have even said that they, too, might become Christians if only all Christians were like Dorcas.

Even though Dorcas became sick and died, she is alive again! Peter, one of the Christian leaders, simply commanded her to rise from the dead. Now the whole town is talking about Dorcas, and many citizens are believing in Jesus.

paralyzed. ³⁴ And Peter said to him, "Aeneas, Jesus the Christ heals you. Arise and make your bed." Then he arose immediately. ³⁵ So all who dwelt at Lydda and Sharon saw him and turned to the Lord.

³⁶ At Joppa there was a certain disciple named Tabitha, which is translated Dorcas. This woman was full of good works and charitable deeds which she did. ³⁷ But it happened in those days that she became sick and died. When they had washed her, they laid *her* in an upper room. ³⁸ And since Lydda was near Joppa, and the disciples had heard that Peter was there, they sent two men to him, imploring *him* not to delay in coming to them. ³⁹ Then Peter arose and went with them. When he had come, they brought *him* to the upper room. And all the widows stood by him weeping, showing the tunics and garments which Dorcas had made while she was with them. ⁴⁰ But Peter put them all out, and knelt down and prayed. And turning to the body he

Peter brings Dorcas back to life.

Tanners, like Simon of Joppa, made leather from the skins of animals.

Gentile Believes in Christ

The Seaside Sentinel

CAESAREA—Until recently, everyone in this country believed that only Jews could become Christians. Now we have learned that a leading Gentile has also become a follower of Jesus.

Cornelius (pronounced *kor-NEEL-yus*), a Roman army officer living in this seaport town of Caesarea (sess-uh-REE-uh), says he saw a vision one day. In the vision, an angel told him to send for Peter, the Christian apostle living at Joppa. We are told that Peter also saw a vision the next day in which God commanded him to accept people who are not Jews. Just then the men sent from Cornelius arrived at Peter's house, and the Lord told Peter to go with them to Caesarea where Cornelius lives.

When Peter arrived, it is reported that Cornelius wanted to worship him, but Peter wouldn't allow it. Peter then preached the Good News about Jesus to Cornelius and his family. They all became Christians and were baptized.

---

said, "Tabitha, arise." And she opened her eyes, and when she saw Peter she sat up. 41 Then he gave her *his* hand and lifted her up; and when he had called the saints and widows, he presented her alive. 42 And it became known throughout all Joppa, and many believed on the Lord. 43 So it was that he stayed many days in Joppa with Simon, a tanner.

Peter preaches to a Roman captain

10 There was a certain man in Caesarea called Cornelius, a centurion of what was called the Italian Regiment, 2 a devout *man* and one who feared God with all his household, who gave alms generously to the people, and prayed to God always. 3 About the ninth hour of the day he saw clearly in a vision an angel of God coming in and saying to him, "Cornelius!"

4 And when he observed him, he was afraid, and said, "What is it, lord?"

So he said to him, "Your prayers and your alms have come up for a memorial before God. 5 Now send men to Joppa, and send for Simon whose surname is Peter. 6 He is lodging with Simon, a tanner, whose house is by the sea. He will tell you what you must do." 7 And when the angel who spoke to him had departed, Cornelius called two of his household servants and a devout soldier from among those who waited on him continually. 8 So when he had explained all *these* things to them, he sent them to Joppa.

9 The next day, as they went on their journey and drew near the city, Peter went up on the housetop to pray, about the sixth hour. 10 Then he became very hungry and wanted to eat; but while they made ready, he fell into a trance 11 and saw heaven opened and an object like a great sheet bound at the four corners, descending to him and let down to the earth. 12 In it were all kinds of four-footed animals of the earth, wild beasts, creeping things, and birds of the air. 13 And a voice came to him, "Rise, Peter; kill and eat."

14 But Peter said, "Not so, Lord! For I have never eaten anything common or unclean."

15 And a voice *spoke* to him again the second time, "What God has cleansed you must not call common." 16 This was done three times. And the object was taken up into heaven again.

17 Now while Peter wondered within himself what this vision which he had seen meant, behold, the men who had been sent from Cornelius had made inquiry for Simon's house, and stood before the gate. 18 And they called and

asked whether Simon, whose surname was Peter, was lodging there.

19 While Peter thought about the vision, the Spirit said to him, "Behold, three men are seeking you. 20 Arise therefore, go down and go with them, doubting nothing; for I have sent them."

21 Then Peter went down to the men who had been sent to him from Cornelius, and said, "Yes, I am he whom you seek. For what reason have you come?"

22 And they said, "Cornelius the centurion, a just man, one who fears God and has a good reputation among all the nation of the Jews, was divinely instructed by a holy angel to summon you to his house, and to hear words from you." 23 Then he invited them in and lodged them.

On the next day Peter went away with them, and some brethren from Joppa accompanied him.

24 And the following day they entered Caesarea. Now Cornelius was waiting for them, and had called together his relatives and close friends. 25 As Peter was coming in, Cornelius met him and fell down at his feet and worshiped him. 26 But Peter lifted him up, saying, "Stand up; I myself am also a man." 27 And as he talked with him, he went in and found many who had come together. 28 Then he said to them, "You know how unlawful it is for a Jewish man to keep company with or go to one of another nation. But God has shown me that I should not call any man common or unclean. 29 Therefore I came without objection as soon as I was sent for. I ask, then, for what reason have you sent for me?"

30 So Cornelius said, "Four days ago I was fasting until this hour; and at the ninth hour I prayed in my house, and behold, a man stood before me in bright clothing, 31 and said, 'Cornelius, your prayer has been heard, and your alms are remembered in the sight of God. 32 Send therefore to Joppa and call Simon here, whose surname is Peter. He is lodging in the house of Si-

mon, a tanner, by the sea. When he comes, he will speak to you.' 33 So I sent to you immediately, and you have done well to come. Now therefore, we are all present before God, to hear all the things commanded you by God."

34 Then Peter opened his mouth and said: "In truth I perceive that God shows no partiality. 35 But in every nation whoever fears Him and works righteousness is accepted by Him. 36 The word which God sent to the children of Israel, preaching peace through Jesus Christ—He is Lord of all— 37 that word you know, which was proclaimed throughout all Judea, and began from Galilee after the baptism which John preached: 38 how God anointed Jesus of Nazareth with the Holy Spirit and with power, who went about doing good and healing all who were oppressed by the devil, for God was with Him. 39 And we are witnesses of all things which He did both in the land of the Jews and in Jerusalem, whom they killed by hanging on a tree. 40 Him God raised up on the third day, and showed Him openly, 41 not to all the people, but to witnesses chosen before by God, even to us who ate and drank with Him after He arose from the dead. 42 And He commanded us to preach to the people, and to testify that it is He who was ordained by God to be Judge of the living and the dead. 43 To Him all the prophets witness that, through His name, whoever believes in Him will receive remission of sins."

44 While Peter was still speaking these words, the Holy Spirit fell upon all those who heard the word. 45 And those of the circumcision who believed were astonished, as many as came with Peter, because the gift of the Holy Spirit had been poured out on the Gentiles also. 46 For they heard them speak with tongues and magnify God.

Then Peter answered, 47 "Can anyone forbid water, that these should not be baptized who have received the Holy Spirit just as we have?" 48 And he commanded them to be baptized in the name of the Lord. Then they asked him to stay a few days.

Christians start a church in Antioch

11 Now the apostles and brethren who were in Judea heard that the Gentiles had also received the word of God. ² And when Peter came up to Jerusalem, those of the circumcision contended with him, ³ saying, "You went in to uncircumcised men and ate with them!"

⁴ But Peter explained *it* to them in order from the beginning, saying: ⁵ "I was in the city of Joppa praying; and in a trance I saw a vision, an object descending like a great sheet, let down from heaven by four corners; and it came to me. ⁶ When I observed it intently and considered, I saw four-footed animals of the earth, wild beasts, creeping things, and birds of the air. ⁷ And I heard a voice saying to me, 'Rise, Peter; kill and eat.' ⁸ But I said, 'Not so, Lord! For nothing common or unclean has at any time entered my mouth.' ⁹ But the voice answered me again from heaven, 'What God has cleansed you must not call common.' ¹⁰ Now this was done three times, and all were drawn up again into heaven. ¹¹ At that very moment, three men stood before the house where I was, having been sent to me from Caesarea. ¹² Then the Spirit told me to go with them, doubting nothing. Moreover these six brethren accompanied me, and we entered the man's house. ¹³ And he told us how he had seen an angel standing in his house, who said to him, 'Send men to Joppa, and call for Simon whose surname is Peter, ¹⁴ who will tell you words by which you and all your household will be saved.' ¹⁵ And as I began to speak, the Holy Spirit fell upon them, as upon us at the beginning. ¹⁶ Then I remembered the word of the Lord, how He said, 'John indeed baptized with water, but you shall be baptized with the Holy Spirit.' ¹⁷ If therefore God gave them the same gift as *He gave* us when we believed on the Lord Jesus Christ, who was I that I could withstand God?"

¹⁸ When they heard these things they became silent; and they glorified God, saying, "Then God has also granted to the Gentiles repentance to life."

¹⁹ Now those who were scattered after the persecution that arose over Stephen traveled as far as Phoenicia, Cyprus, and Antioch, preaching the word to no one but the Jews only. ²⁰ But some of them were men from Cyprus

Christian Good News Spreads

New Testament News Service

JERUSALEM—Following the death of Stephen (see Acts 7), the Jesus followers have scattered across the map, to the dismay of leaders at Jerusalem who thought this would be the end of the new religious group.

Now a new report from Antioch (pronounced *ANN-tee-ock*), confirms that there are now many believers in Jesus in that city. We understand that the disciples of Jesus there are now called "Christians." Since Antioch is in Syria, these followers of the crucified Carpenter are reaching beyond the borders of Palestine.

Reports of Christians living in Cyprus and Phoenicia (pronounced *SIGH-pruss* and *fe-NISH-she-uh*) have also been received. Saul, the Pharisee who became a Christian, is living and preaching at his hometown of Tarsus in the country of Cilicia (pronounced *suh-LISH-she-uh*).

The Christians may soon become a worldwide group. Rather than ending the gospel, the death of Stephen has caused the spread of the Good News he preached.

Believers were first called Christians in Antioch of Syria.

and Cyrene, who, when they had come to Antioch, spoke to the Hellenists, preaching the Lord Jesus. 21 And the hand of the Lord was with them, and a great number believed and turned to the Lord.

22 Then news of these things came to the ears of the church in Jerusalem, and they sent out Barnabas to go as far as Antioch. 23 When he came and had seen the grace of God, he was glad, and encouraged them all that with purpose of heart they should continue with the Lord. 24 For he was a good man, full of the Holy Spirit and of faith. And a great many people were added to the Lord.

25 Then Barnabas departed for Tarsus to seek Saul. 26 And when he had found him, he brought him to Antioch. So it was that for a whole year they assembled with the church and taught a great many people. And the disciples were first called **Christians** in Antioch.

27 And in these days prophets came from Jerusalem to Antioch. 28 Then one of them, named Agabus, stood up and showed by the Spirit that there was going to be a great famine throughout all the world, which also happened in the days of Claudius Caesar. 29 Then the disciples, each according to his ability, determined to send relief to the brethren dwelling in Judea.

WORDFINDER

11:26 Christians A person who believes in and follows Jesus Christ. People were first called Christians after Jesus rose from death.

Apostle James Murdered

The Jerusalem Times

JERUSALEM—Our nation is shocked by official news that King Herod Agrippa has put the apostle James to death. The king's news office gave no reason for the execution.

This newspaper believes that James Zebedee was killed to please some of our people who hated the Christians. This is the second violent death among the innocent Christians of our society. Stephen was the first (see Acts 7). Now James, the apostle of Christ, has been murdered for no reason except that Herod wanted to please some anti-Christian members of our society.

Where will the killing stop? Do the rights of any king include killing people without a fair trial?

James Zebedee was the brother of the apostle John. James was a gentle and harmless man who earlier worked at the fishing trade with his father and brother. Later, the two brothers became followers of Jesus.

30 This they also did, and sent it to the elders by the hands of Barnabas and Saul.

An angel rescues Peter from prison

12 Now about that time Herod the king stretched out *his* hand to harass some from the church. 2 Then he killed James the brother of John with the sword. 3 And because he saw that it pleased the Jews, he proceeded further to seize Peter also. Now it was *during* the Days of Unleavened Bread. 4 So when he had arrested him, he put *him* in prison, and delivered *him* to four squads of soldiers to keep him, intend ing to bring him before the people after Passover.

5 Peter was therefore kept in prison, but constant prayer was offered to God for him by the church. 6 And when Herod was about to bring him out, that night Peter was sleeping, bound with two chains between two soldiers; and the guards before the door were keeping the prison. 7 Now behold, an angel of the Lord stood by *him,* and a light shone in the prison; and he struck Peter on the side and raised him up, saying, "Arise quickly!" And his chains fell off *his* hands. 8 Then the angel said to him, "Gird yourself and tie on your sandals"; and so he did. And he said to him, "Put on your garment and fol-

What Peter Learned

King Herod had killed James, the brother of the apostle John who wrote the Gospel of John. The Herod I'm telling you about was King Herod Agrippa I, grandson of Herod the Great who lived when Jesus was born.

Now the same Herod who killed James also put me in prison, and I thought my own life would soon end, too. But then an angel came and unlocked my chains. As soon as I could tie on my sandals, the angel led me out through the prison gates. At first, I thought I was dreaming. Can you imagine how surprised I was to be really free?

This experience showed me that no one can change God's plans. When the Lord wants you to serve Him, nothing can stop you.

Rhoda—My name is pronounced *ROW-duh* and means "A Rose."

The Christians were having a prayer meeting at the home of Mary, the mother of John Mark. You may remember him as the apostle who wrote the Gospel of Mark.

Often Jesus' disciples would meet at Mary's house in Jerusalem. I was about your age then, and I used to come to the meetings with my parents.

On that special night, we were all praying for our friend Peter, who was in prison. We didn't know Peter was being set free by an angel just as we were praying!

When Peter came to our door and knocked, I was so surprised I didn't even let him in! When I ran back to tell the others, they just laughed at me. But the joke was on them when they saw Peter.

God sometimes answers our prayers faster than we believe He will.

low me." 9 So he went out and followed him, and did not know that what was done by the angel was real, but thought he was seeing a vision. 10 When they were past the first and the second guard posts, they came to the iron gate that leads to the city, which opened to them of its own accord; and they went out and went down one street, and immediately the angel departed from him.

11 And when Peter had come to himself, he said, "Now I know for certain that the Lord has sent His angel, and has delivered me from the hand of Herod and *from* all the expectation of the Jewish people."

12 So, when he had considered *this,* he came to the house of Mary, the mother of John whose surname was Mark, where many were gathered together praying. 13 And as Peter knocked at the door of the gate, a girl named Rhoda came to answer. 14 When she recognized Peter's voice, because of *her* gladness she did not open the gate, but ran in and announced that Peter stood before the gate. 15 But they said to her, "You are beside yourself!" Yet she kept insisting that it was so. So they said, "It is his angel."

16 Now Peter continued knocking; and when they opened *the door* and saw him, they were astonished. 17 But motioning to them with his hand to keep silent, he declared to them how the Lord had brought him out of the prison. And he said, "Go, tell these things to James and to the brethren." And he departed and went to another place.

18 Then, as soon as it was day, there was no small stir among the soldiers about what had become of Peter. 19 But when Herod had searched for him and not found him, he examined the guards and commanded that *they* should be put to death.

And he went down from Judea to Caesarea, and stayed *there.*

20 Now Herod had been very angry with the people of Tyre and Sidon; but they came to him with one accord, and having made Blastus the king's personal aide their friend, they asked for peace, because their country was supplied with food by the king's *country.*

21 So on a set day Herod, arrayed in royal apparel, sat on his throne and gave an oration to them. 22 And the people kept shouting, "The voice of a god and not of a man!" 23 Then immediately an angel of the Lord struck him, because he did not give glory to God. And he was eaten by worms and died.

24 But the word of God grew and multiplied.

25 And Barnabas and Saul returned from Jerusalem when they had fulfilled *their* ministry, and they also took with them John whose surname was Mark.

The Island of Cyprus, where Paul preached in the synagogue at Salamis.

Paul and Barnabas preach to the Gentiles

13 Now in the church that was at Antioch there were certain prophets and teachers: Barnabas, Simeon who was called Niger, Lucius of Cyrene, Manaen who had been brought up with Herod the tetrarch, and Saul. ²As they ministered to the Lord and fasted, the Holy Spirit said, "Now separate to Me Barnabas and Saul for the work to which I have called them." ³Then, having fasted and prayed, and laid hands on them, they sent *them* away.

⁴So, being sent out by the Holy Spirit, they went down to Seleucia, and from there they sailed to Cyprus. ⁵And when they arrived in Salamis, they preached the word of God in the synagogues of the Jews. They also had John as *their* assistant.

⁶Now when they had gone through the island to Paphos, they found a certain sorcerer, a false prophet, a Jew whose name *was* Bar-Jesus, ⁷who was with the proconsul, Sergius Paulus, an intelligent man. This man called for Barnabas and Saul and sought to hear the word of God. ⁸But Elymas the sorcerer (for so his name is translated) withstood them, seeking to turn the proconsul away from the faith. ⁹Then

DIGGING IN

13:8 Paul Meets a Sorcerer After Saul became a Christian, his name became "Paul." Peter was preaching the gospel mainly to the Jews, but the Lord sent Paul to lead the Gentiles (non-Jews) to Christ.

Paul's first challenge as an apostle was a meeting with a sorcerer on the island of Cyprus. (See the map on pages 1452–53.) A sorcerer is a magician. This magician was deceiving the island's governor, whose name was Paulus. Some people think Paul took his own name from that governor.

What did Paul do with the sorcerer? He didn't argue. He commanded the sorcerer to become blind, and it became clear at once that the sorcerer was a false teacher. Then Governor Paulus believed the gospel.

The main thing to remember is that you can't always waste time arguing with evil. Just show Satan up to be the liar he is. Light drives away darkness, and the truth of God's Word drives away falsehood.

Christian Gospel Comes to Asia Minor

The Jerusalem Times

JERUSALEM—Late reports say that the church in Antioch has sent Saul and another Christian apostle named Barnabas (pronounced *BAR-nuh-bus*) as missionaries to Asia Minor. They are winning new believers there.

Saul and Barnabas have already preached on the island of Cyprus (pronounced *SIGH-pruss*) and have arrived on the mainland of Asia Minor. A younger man, John Mark, is also reported to be traveling with the two men.

Saul has preached a powerful message at the Jewish synagogue in Antioch of Pisidia (pronounced *pih-SID-ee-uh*). This is not the same Antioch as the city in Syria. Both cities are named after ancient Syrian kings.

Saul, the former Pharisee (pronounced *FAIR-uh-see*), has boldly declared Jesus Christ to be the risen Savior. Many Gentiles have believed in Jesus because of Saul's preaching, but the Jews are angry and have driven the apostles out of the city.

Saul, who also *is called* Paul, filled with the Holy Spirit, looked intently at him ¹⁰ and said, "O full of all deceit and all fraud, *you* son of the devil, *you* enemy of all righteousness, will you not cease perverting the straight ways of the Lord? ¹¹ And now, indeed, the hand of the Lord *is* upon you, and you shall be blind, not seeing the sun for a time."

And immediately a dark mist fell on him, and he went around seeking someone to lead him by the hand. ¹² Then the proconsul believed, when he saw what had been done, being astonished at the teaching of the Lord.

¹³ Now when Paul and his party set sail from Paphos, they came to Perga in Pamphylia; and John, departing from them, returned to Jerusalem. ¹⁴ But when they departed from Perga, they came to Antioch in Pisidia, and went into the synagogue on the Sabbath day and sat down. ¹⁵ And after the reading of the Law and the Prophets, the rulers of the synagogue sent to them, saying, "Men *and* brethren, if you have any word of **exhortation** for the people, say on."

Who Was John Mark?

John Mark was the nephew of Barnabas (pronounced *BARN-nuh-bus*). John Mark went with Paul and Barnabas on their first missionary journey. Then that young man became discouraged and went home. Later, he was helpful in Paul's work (see 2 Timothy 4:11). John Mark wrote the Gospel of Mark.

¹⁶ Then Paul stood up, and motioning with *his* hand said, "Men of Israel, and you who fear God, listen: ¹⁷ The God of this people Israel chose our fathers, and exalted the people when they dwelt as strangers in the land of Egypt, and with an uplifted arm He brought them out of it. ¹⁸ Now for a time of about forty years He put up with their ways in the wilderness. ¹⁹ And when He had destroyed seven nations in the land of Canaan, He distributed their land to them by allotment.

²⁰ "After that He gave *them* judges for about four hundred and fifty years,

WORDFINDER

13:15 Exhortation Pronounced *egg-zor-TAY-shun*. A speech or writing that is meant to warn or encourage people.

until Samuel the prophet. 21 And afterward they asked for a king; so God gave them Saul the son of Kish, a man of the tribe of Benjamin, for forty years. 22 And when He had removed him, He raised up for them David as king, to whom also He gave testimony and said, 'I have found David the *son* of Jesse, a man after My *own* heart, who will do all My will.' 23 From this man's seed, according to *the* promise, God raised up for Israel a Savior—Jesus— 24 after John had first preached, before His coming, the baptism of repentance to all the people of Israel. 25 And as John was finishing his course, he said, 'Who do you think I am? I am not *He.* But behold, there comes One after me, the sandals of whose feet I am not worthy to loose.'

26 "Men *and* brethren, sons of the family of Abraham, and those among you who fear God, to you the word of this salvation has been sent. 27 For those who dwell in Jerusalem, and their rulers, because they did not know Him, nor even the voices of the Prophets which are read every Sabbath, have fulfilled *them* in condemning *Him.* 28 And though they found no cause for death *in Him,* they asked Pilate that He should be put to death. 29 Now when they had fulfilled all that was written concerning Him, they took *Him* down from the tree and laid *Him* in a tomb. 30 But God raised Him from the dead. 31 He was seen for many days by those who came up with Him from Galilee to Jerusalem, who are His witnesses to the people. 32 And we declare to you glad tidings—that promise which was made to the fathers. 33 God has fulfilled this for us their children, in that He has raised up Jesus. As it is also written in the second Psalm:

'You are My Son,
Today I have begotten You.'

34 And that He raised Him from the dead, no more to return to corruption, He has spoken thus:

'I will give you the sure mercies of David.'

35 Therefore He also says in another *Psalm:*

'You will not allow Your Holy
One to see corruption.'

36 "For David, after he had served his own generation by the will of God, fell asleep, was buried with his fathers, and saw corruption; 37 but He whom God raised up saw no corruption. 38 Therefore let it be known to you, brethren, that through this Man is preached to you the forgiveness of sins; 39 and by Him everyone who believes is justified from all things from which you could not be justified by the law of Moses. 40 Beware therefore, lest what has been spoken in the prophets come upon you:

41 'Behold, you despisers,
Marvel and perish!
For I work a work in your days,
A work which you will by no
means believe,
Though one were to declare it
to you.' "

42 So when the Jews went out of the synagogue, the Gentiles begged that these words might be preached to them the next Sabbath. 43 Now when the congregation had broken up, many of the Jews and devout proselytes followed Paul and Barnabas, who, speaking to them, persuaded them to continue in the grace of God.

44 On the next Sabbath almost the whole city came together to hear the word of God. 45 But when the Jews saw the multitudes, they were filled with envy; and contradicting and blaspheming, they opposed the things spoken by Paul. 46 Then Paul and Barnabas grew bold and said, "It was necessary that the word of God should be spoken to you first; but since you reject it, and judge yourselves unworthy of everlasting life, behold, we turn

to the Gentiles. 47 For so the Lord has commanded us:

'I have set you as a light to the Gentiles,
That you should be for salvation to the ends of the earth.' "

48 Now when the Gentiles heard this, they were glad and glorified the word of the Lord. And as many as had been appointed to eternal life believed.
49 And the word of the Lord was being spread throughout all the region. 50 But the Jews stirred up the devout and prominent women and the chief men of the city, raised up persecution against Paul and Barnabas, and expelled them from their region. 51 But they shook off the dust from their feet against them, and came to Iconium. 52 And the disciples were filled with joy and with the Holy Spirit.

Some unbelievers stone Paul

14 Now it happened in Iconium that they went together to the synagogue of the Jews, and so spoke that a great multitude both of the Jews and of the Greeks believed. 2 But the unbelieving Jews stirred up the Gentiles and poisoned their minds against the brethren. 3 Therefore they stayed there a long time, speaking boldly in the Lord, who was bearing witness to the word of His grace, granting signs and wonders to be done by their hands.
4 But the multitude of the city was divided: part sided with the Jews, and part with the apostles. 5 And when a violent attempt was made by both the Gentiles and Jews, with their rulers, to abuse and stone them, 6 they became aware of it and fled to Lystra and Derbe, cities of Lycaonia, and to the surrounding region. 7 And they were preaching the gospel there.
8 And in Lystra a certain man without strength in his feet was sitting, a cripple from his mother's womb, who had never walked. 9 This man heard Paul speaking. Paul, observing him intently and seeing that he had faith to

be healed, 10 said with a loud voice, "Stand up straight on your feet!" And he leaped and walked. 11 Now when the people saw what Paul had done, they raised their voices, saying in the Lycaonian language, "The gods have come down to us in the likeness of men!" 12 And Barnabas they called Zeus, and Paul, Hermes, because he was the chief speaker. 13 Then the priest of Zeus, whose temple was in front of their city, brought oxen and garlands to the gates, intending to sacrifice with the multitudes.
14 But when the apostles Barnabas and Paul heard this, they tore their clothes and ran in among the multitude, crying out 15 and saying, "Men, why are you doing these things? We also are men with the same nature as you, and preach to you that you should turn from these useless things to the living God, who made the heaven, the earth, the sea, and all things that are in them, 16 who in bygone generations allowed all nations to walk in their own ways. 17 Nevertheless He did not leave Himself without witness, in that He did good, gave us rain from heaven and fruitful seasons, filling our hearts with food and gladness." 18 And with these sayings they could scarcely restrain the multitudes from sacrificing to them.
19 Then Jews from Antioch and Iconium came there; and having persuaded the multitudes, they stoned Paul and dragged him out of the city, supposing him to be dead. 20 However, when the disciples gathered around him, he rose up and went into the city. And the next day he departed with Barnabas to Derbe.
21 And when they had preached the gospel to that city and made many disciples, they returned to Lystra, Iconium, and Antioch, 22 strengthening the souls of the disciples, exhorting them to continue in the faith, and saying, "We must through many tribulations enter the kingdom of God." 23 So when they had appointed elders in every church, and prayed with fasting, they commended them to the

Paul's Missionary Journeys

Come with Paul and Barnabus as they sail for the Island of Cyprus! After telling many people about Jesus, they travel to Pamphylia, and from there to the cities of Galatia –Derbe, Lystra, and Iconium, and to Antioch in Pisidia. Can you find these cities on the map? What happens to Paul in Derbe? (14:19) What does he do in all these places? (14:21–23)

On their second journey, Paul and Silas return to visit the baby Christians in the churches they have started. But one of their most exciting adventures takes place in Macedonia (present-day Greece), where they go after they leave Galatia.

MACEDONIA
Thessalonica
Philippi
Berea
Troas
Aegean Sea
GALATIA
Athens
Antioch of Pisidia
Corinth
Ephesus
Iconium
Lystra
Derbe
Attalia
Tarsus
Antioch
Rhodes
SYRIA
Cyprus
Crete
Salamis
Paphos
Mediterranean Sea
Caesarea
Jerusalem

Black Sea

FIRST MISSIONARY JOURNEY- - - - →
SECOND MISSIONARY JOURNEY ●━━●

After being arrested in Philippi for casting a demon out of a slave girl, Paul and Silas are beaten and put in a dungeon.(16:23–24) While they are singing hymns in the prison at midnight, there is a miracle! What is it? (16:25–26) The poor jailer is sure all the prisoners have escaped and is about to kill himself when Paul speaks up. What happens next? (16:29–33)

The jailer will never forget the night of the earthquake when he found Jesus in his jail! You don't have to travel to Bible lands or look for Jesus only in sacred places. You can find Him anywhere, at any time. He is as close as your next breath. Ask Him to be your Savior.

Lord in whom they had believed. 24 And after they had passed through Pisidia, they came to Pamphylia. 25 Now when they had preached the word in Perga, they went down to Attalia. 26 From there they sailed to Antioch, where they had been commended to the grace of God for the work which they had completed.

27 Now when they had come and gathered the church together, they reported all that God had done with them, and that He had opened the door of faith to the Gentiles. 28 So they stayed there a long time with the disciples.

Christians have a special meeting in Jerusalem

15 And certain *men* came down from Judea and taught the brethren, "Unless you are circumcised according to the custom of Moses, you cannot be saved." 2 Therefore, when Paul and Barnabas had no small dissension and dispute with them, they determined that Paul and Barnabas and certain others of them should go up to Jerusalem, to the apostles and elders, about this question.

3 So, being sent on their way by the church, they passed through Phoenicia and Samaria, describing the **conversion** of the Gentiles; and they caused great joy to all the brethren. 4 And when they had come to Jerusalem, they were received by the church and the apostles and the elders; and they reported all things that God had done with them. 5 But some of the sect of the Pharisees who believed rose up, saying, "It is necessary to circumcise them, and to command *them* to keep the law of Moses."

6 Now the apostles and elders came

WORDFINDER

15:3 Conversion Pronounced *kon-VERR-zhun*. Means changing over from one kind of life to another kind. A person is "converted" by being "born again" (see definition at John 3:3).

DIGGING IN

14:28 Paul in Asia Minor Find Asia Minor on the map on pages 1452–53. Paul traveled all over that country, telling people about Jesus and forming new Christian churches.

As you read about Paul's travels in these chapters, remember that there were no planes or cars in those days. Some of the traveling was by donkey or by ship, but much of it was on foot. So Paul did a lot of walking for the gospel. He was the greatest of the apostles and wrote thirteen of the twenty-seven books in the New Testament.

We have told you before that Paul was sent by Jesus to be the special apostle to the Gentiles, or non-Jews. Isn't that exciting? Paul, who had been the most determined hater of Christians now became the most determined preacher of the Christian gospel! But you should know that some of Paul's education was in the college town of Tarsus, in Asia Minor,

where he grew up. There the great Gentile teacher, Athenadorus (pronounced *ah-then-uh-DOOR-us*) taught about the great Greek thinkers. So Paul knew all about Gentile beliefs. You can better help people to know Jesus if you understand what they believe.

15:6 The Jerusalem Meeting Paul was a determined missionary to the Gentile world. The Jewish Christians were still following strict Old Testament laws of worship, but Paul didn't expect his Gentile converts to follow the Jewish rituals. This upset some of the Christian Jews. They held a meeting at Jerusalem to decide what to about the Gentiles. This was the first great council of churches, and it became an example of how decisions are made in churches today.

So the apostles and elders of the churches listened to both sides. Even Peter, the apostle to the Jews, agreed with Paul. Then everyone decided that Gen-

Who Were the Gentiles?

Remember that God promised that Abraham would be a blessing to all nations (see Genesis 12:3). The Jews called the other nations "Gentiles." Peter and Paul had to teach the Jewish Christians that Gentiles also could be Christians.

together to consider this matter. 7 And when there had been much dispute, Peter rose up and said to them: "Men and brethren, you know that a good while ago God chose among us, that by my mouth the Gentiles should hear the word of the **gospel** and believe. 8 So God, who knows the heart, acknowledged them by giving them the Holy Spirit, just as *He did* to us, 9 and made no distinction between us and them, purifying their hearts by faith. 10 Now therefore, why do you test God by putting a yoke on the neck of the disciples which neither our fathers nor we were able to bear? 11 But we believe that through the grace of the Lord Jesus Christ we shall be saved in the same manner as they."

12 Then all the multitude kept silent and listened to Barnabas and Paul declaring how many miracles and wonders God had worked through them among the Gentiles. 13 And after they had become silent, James answered,

saying, "Men *and* brethren, listen to me: 14 Simon has declared how God at the first visited the Gentiles to take out of them a people for His name. 15 And with this the words of the prophets agree, just as it is written:

16 'After this I will return
    And will rebuild the tabernacle
        of David, which has fallen
        down;
    I will rebuild its ruins,
    And I will set it up;
17 So that the rest of mankind may
        seek the LORD,
    Even all the Gentiles who are
        called by My name,
    Says the LORD who does all
        these things.'

18 "Known to God from eternity are all His works. 19 Therefore I judge that we should not trouble those from among the Gentiles who are turning to God, 20 but that we write to them to abstain from things polluted by idols, *from* sexual immorality, *from* things strangled, and *from* blood. 21 For Moses has had throughout many generations those who preach him in every city, being read in the **synagogues** every Sabbath."

22 Then it pleased the apostles and elders, with the whole church, to send chosen men of their own company to Antioch with Paul and Barnabas, *namely,* Judas who was also named

WORDFINDER

15:7 Gospel Means "good news." The word is taken from the early English word *godspel.* In the New Testament, it is the good news about Jesus Christ.

15:21 Synagogue Pronounced *SIN-uh-gog.* From a Greek word meaning "gather together." The Jews have worshiped at buildings called synagogues ever since they lived in countries where they could no longer come to the temple.

DIGGING IN

tiles didn't have to obey the Jewish laws or customs after all.

As time went by, Christians realized they were not tied to the Old Testament customs. Jesus had died for their sins.

So they no longer needed the ceremonies that only pointed to the first coming of Jesus. Now they had Jesus Himself, and so do we.

Leaders Say Anyone May Be Christian

The Jerusalem Times

JERUSALEM—A surprising report has come from a special meeting of Christian leaders held recently in Jerusalem.

Jewish Christians have always believed that their religion is for Jews and others who are willing to accept the Jewish laws and customs. Now a larger number of non-Jews (also called Gentiles) have been accepting Christ as their Savior. These Gentiles do not keep the Jewish laws and customs. Jewish Christians have disagreed with Saul (who is now called Paul) because he allows Gentiles to become Christians without accepting the Jewish laws.

In a meeting of a special council, called at Jerusalem to discuss this problem about the Gentiles, the apostle Peter made a speech in which he said Gentiles should not have to keep Jewish law. James, the pastor of the church at Jerusalem, agrees with Peter.

The council at Jerusalem has now written a statement telling Gentile Christians they need not follow the Jewish customs. This means that the Christian church is no longer a branch of the Jewish religion.

Barsabas, and Silas, leading men among the brethren.

23 They wrote this *letter* by them:

The apostles, the elders, and the brethren,

To the brethren who are of the Gentiles in Antioch, Syria, and Cilicia:

Greetings.

24 Since we have heard that some who went out from us have troubled you with words, unsettling your souls, saying, "*You must* be circumcised and keep the law"—to whom we gave no *such* commandment— 25 it seemed good to us, being assembled with one accord, to send chosen men to you with our beloved Barnabas and Paul, 26 men who have risked their lives for the name of our Lord Jesus Christ. 27 We have therefore sent Judas and Silas, who will also report the same things by word of mouth. 28 For it seemed good to the Holy Spirit, and to us, to lay upon you no greater burden than these necessary things: 29 that you abstain from things offered to idols, from blood, from things strangled, and from sexual immorality. If you keep yourselves from these, you will do well.

Farewell.

30 So when they were sent off, they came to Antioch; and when they had gathered the multitude together, they delivered the letter. 31 When they had read it, they rejoiced over its encouragement. 32 Now Judas and Silas, themselves being prophets also, exhorted and strengthened the brethren with many words. 33 And after they had stayed *there* for a time, they were sent back with greetings from the brethren to the apostles. 34 However, it seemed good to Silas to remain there. 35 Paul and Barnabas also remained in Antioch, teaching and preaching the word of the Lord, with many others also.

36 Then after some days Paul said to Barnabas, "Let us now go back and

visit our brethren in every city where we have preached the word of the Lord, *and see* how they are doing." 37 Now Barnabas was determined to take with them John called Mark. 38 But Paul insisted that they should not take with them the one who had departed from them in Pamphylia, and had not gone with them to the work. 39 Then the contention became so sharp that they parted from one another. And so Barnabas took Mark and sailed to Cyprus; 40 but Paul chose Silas and departed, being commended by the brethren to the grace of God. 41 And he went through Syria and Cilicia, strengthening the churches.

Timothy is Paul's new helper

16 Then he came to Derbe and Lystra. And behold, a certain disciple was there, named Timothy, *the* son of a certain Jewish woman who believed, but his father *was* Greek. 2 He was well spoken of by the brethren who were at Lystra and Iconium. 3 Paul wanted to have him go on with him. And he took *him* and circumcised him because of the Jews who were in that region, for they all knew that his father was Greek. 4 And as they went through the cities, they delivered to them the decrees to keep, which were determined by the apostles and elders at Jerusalem. 5 So the churches were strengthened in the faith, and increased in number daily.

6 Now when they had gone through Phrygia and the region of Galatia, they were forbidden by the Holy Spirit to preach the word in Asia. 7 After they had come to Mysia, they tried to go into Bithynia, but the Spirit did not permit them. 8 So passing by Mysia, they came down to Troas. 9 And a vision appeared to Paul in the night. A man of Macedonia stood and pleaded with him, saying, "Come over to Macedonia and help us." 10 Now after he had seen the vision, immediately we sought to go to Macedonia, concluding that the Lord had called us to preach the gospel to them.

11 Therefore, sailing from Troas, we ran a straight course to Samothrace, and the next *day* came to Neapolis, 12 and from there to Philippi, which is the foremost city of that part of Macedonia, a colony. And we were staying in that city for some days. 13 And on the Sabbath day we went out of the city to the riverside, where prayer was customarily made; and we sat down and spoke to the women who met there. 14 Now a certain woman named Lydia heard *us*. She was a seller of purple from the city of Thyatira, who worshiped God. The Lord opened her heart to heed the things spoken by Paul. 15 And when she and her household were baptized, she begged *us,* saying, "If you have judged me to be faithful to the Lord, come to my house and stay." So she persuaded us.

16 Now it happened, as we went to prayer, that a certain slave girl possessed with a spirit of divination met us, who brought her masters much profit by fortune-telling. 17 This girl followed Paul and us, and cried out, saying, "These men are the servants of the Most High God, who proclaim to us the way of salvation." 18 And this she did for many days.

But Paul, greatly annoyed, turned and said to the spirit, "I command you in the name of Jesus Christ to come out of her." And he came out that very hour. 19 But when her masters saw that their hope of profit was gone, they seized Paul and Silas and dragged *them* into the marketplace to the authorities.

20 And they brought them to the magistrates, and said, "These men, being Jews, exceedingly trouble our city; 21 and they teach customs which are not lawful for us, being Romans, to receive or observe." 22 Then the multitude rose up together against them; and the magistrates tore off their clothes and commanded *them* to be beaten with rods. 23 And when they had laid many stripes on them, they threw *them* into prison, commanding the jailer to keep them securely. 24 Having received such a charge, he

> **Lydia**—You should pronounce my name *LID-ee-ah*. I was a wealthy businesswoman in the city of Philippi (pronounced *FILL-ih-pie*). The city was named for King Philip, the father of Alexander the Great.
>
> My original home was in Thyatira (pronounced *thigh-uh-TIE-ruh*). Thyatira was in Asia Minor, across the Aegean Sea from Greece. I sold purple cloth that was used to make clothing for royalty and wealthy people.
>
> On the Sabbath day, I always went with Jewish believers to pray by a river outside Philippi. One day the apostle Paul came with his friends—Luke, Silas, and Timothy—and told us about Jesus the Savior.
>
> My whole family and I believed in Jesus as our Lord and Savior that day, and we were all baptized.

put them into the inner prison and fastened their feet in the stocks.

25 But at midnight Paul and Silas were praying and singing hymns to God, and the prisoners were listening to them. 26 Suddenly there was a great earthquake, so that the foundations of the prison were shaken; and immediately all the doors were opened and everyone's chains were loosed. 27 And the keeper of the prison, awaking from sleep and seeing the prison doors open, supposing the prisoners had fled, drew his sword and was about to kill himself. 28 But Paul called with a loud voice, saying, "Do yourself no harm, for we are all here."

29 Then he called for a light, ran in, and fell down trembling before Paul and Silas. 30 And he brought them out and said, "Sirs, what must I do to be saved?"

31 So they said, "Believe on the Lord Jesus Christ, and you will be

The Chapel of Lydia, who became a Christian after hearing Paul tell about Jesus.

What the Jailer Learned

I'm the jail keeper at Philippi (pronounced *FILL-ih-pie*). Our city was named after Philip II, father of Alexander the Great. You can read about Alexander in your history books.

Paul and Silas came to our town with their friends, Luke and Timothy. You remember that Luke wrote a Gospel, and Paul later wrote two letters to Timothy.

There was a slave girl at Philippi who told fortunes by means of an evil spirit. When Paul drove the spirit out of the girl, the citizens who had been making money from her fortune-telling put Paul and Silas in my prison.

That night there was an earthquake, and the prison gates and locks were all opened. I was terrified and asked Paul how to be saved. Then he told me to believe in Jesus, and that same night my whole family became Christians.

---

saved, you and your household." 32 Then they spoke the word of the Lord to him and to all who were in his house. 33 And he took them the same hour of the night and washed *their* stripes. And immediately he and all his family were baptized. 34 Now when he had brought them into his house, he set food before them; and he rejoiced, having believed in God with all his household.

35 And when it was day, the magistrates sent the officers, saying, "Let those men go."

36 So the keeper of the prison reported these words to Paul, saying, "The magistrates have sent to let you go. Now therefore depart, and go in peace."

37 But Paul said to them, "They have beaten us openly, uncondemned Romans, *and* have thrown *us* into prison. And now do they put us out secretly? No indeed! Let them come themselves and get us out."

38 And the officers told these words to the magistrates, and they were afraid when they heard that they were Romans. 39 Then they came and pleaded with them and brought *them* out, and asked *them* to depart from the city. 40 So they went out of the prison and entered *the house of* Lydia; and when they had seen the brethren, they encouraged them and departed.

Paul preaches in Athens

17 Now when they had passed through Amphipolis and Apollonia, they came to Thessalonica, where there was a synagogue of the Jews. 2 Then Paul, as his custom was, went in to them, and for three Sabbaths reasoned with them from the Scriptures, 3 explaining and demonstrating that the Christ had to suffer and rise again from the dead, and *saying,* "This Jesus whom I preach to you is the Christ." 4 And some of them were persuaded; and a great multitude of the devout Greeks, and not a few of the leading women, joined Paul and Silas.

5 But the Jews who were not persuaded, becoming envious, took some of the evil men from the marketplace, and gathering a mob, set all the city in an uproar and attacked the house of Jason, and sought to bring them out to the people. 6 But when they did not find them, they dragged Jason and some brethren to the rulers of the city, crying out, "These who have turned the world upside down have come here too. 7 Jason has harbored them, and these are all acting contrary to the decrees of Caesar, saying there is another king—Jesus." 8 And they troubled the crowd and the rulers of the city when they heard these things. 9 So when they had taken security

Paul's Missionary Journeys

Paul sets out once more from Antioch (pronounced ANN-tee-ock) to revisit the churches he has started in Galatia (pronounced guh-LAY-she-ah) and Greece. (Acts 18:23) This time he goes on to Ephesus (pronounced EFF-uh-sus), where he stays for two years, teaching about Jesus and working miracles in His name. Some of the Ephesians have been practicing magic. What happens to their magic books? (Acts 19:19–20) On this journey, Paul writes three letters that later become books of the Bible (1 and 2 Corinthians and Romans).

Back home in Jerusalem, Paul's missionary work is interrupted when he is arrested in the temple on false charges. (Acts 21:30–33) He is moved to Caesarea (pronounced SESS-uh-ree-uh), where he is held by Roman soldiers for many months before sailing to Rome to appeal to Caesar as a Roman citizen. Trace Paul's journey from Sidon to Crete.

En route from Fair Havens on the coast of Crete, Paul's ship is caught in a sudden winter storm and is blown off course. Paul tells his Roman guard that God has promised to spare all their lives if they will only follow His instructions. (Acts 27:30–38) They escape safely to land——the island of Malta——where they have many more exciting adventures before Paul is able to complete his trip. Follow the path, by sea and by land, that finally leads Paul to Rome.

Adriatic Sea

Rome
Three Inns
Appii Forum
ITALY

Rhegium

Sicily

Malta

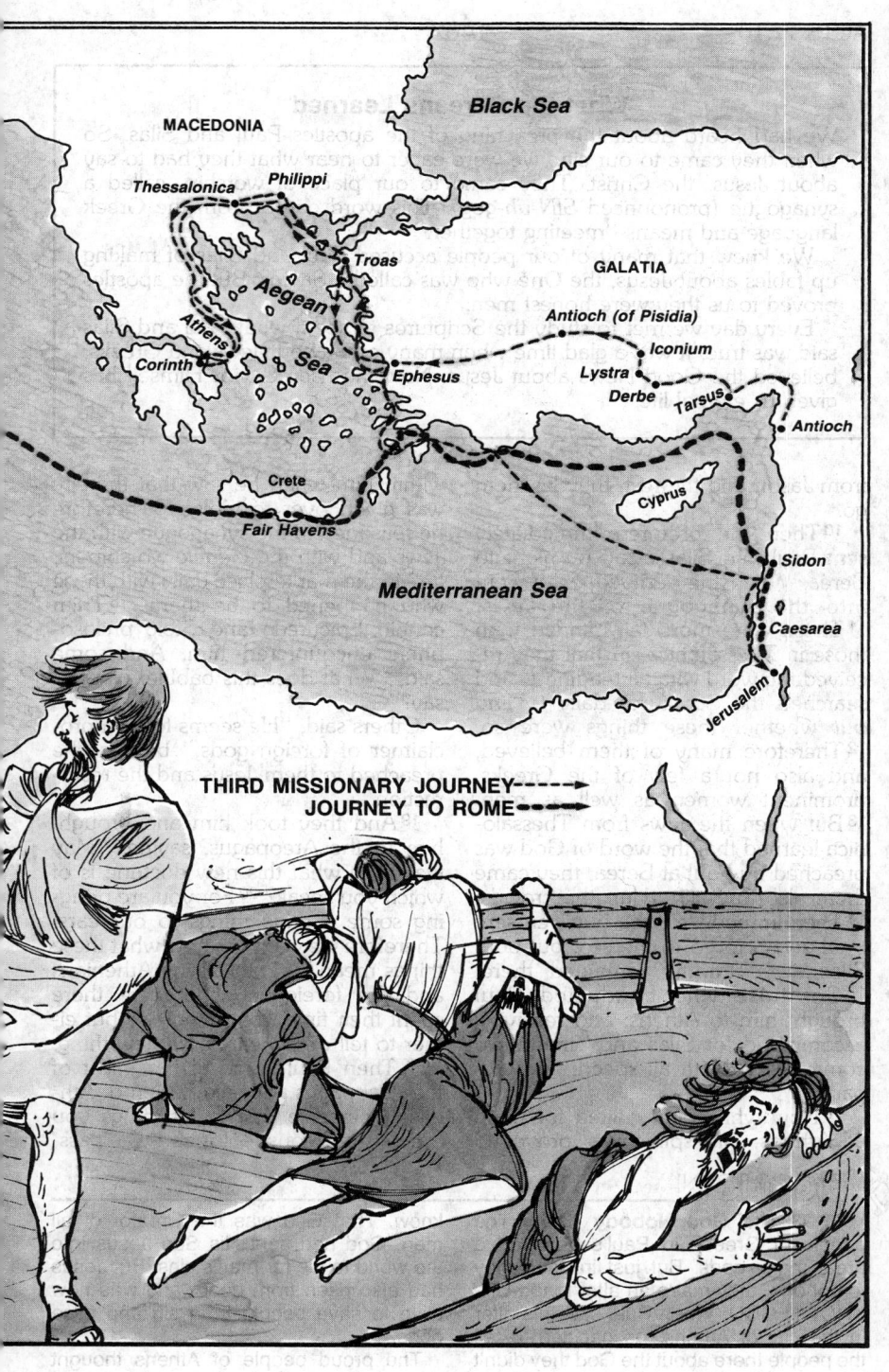

Black Sea

MACEDONIA

Thessalonica   Philippi

Troas

GALATIA

Aegean

Sea

Athens   Antioch (of Pisidia)

Corinth   Iconium

Ephesus   Lystra

Derbe   Tarsus

Antioch

Crete

Cyprus

Fair Havens

Mediterranean Sea   Sidon

Caesarea

Jerusalem

THIRD MISSIONARY JOURNEY --->
JOURNEY TO ROME ---->

What the Bereans Learned

We had heard about the preaching of the apostles Paul and Silas. So when they came to our city, we were eager to hear what they had to say about Jesus, the Christ. They came to our place of worship, called a synagogue (pronounced *SIN-uh-gog*). This word comes from the Greek language and means "meeting together."

We knew that many of our people accused Paul and Silas of making up fables about Jesus, the One who was called a Savior. But the apostles proved to us they were honest men.

Every day we met to study the Scriptures to see if what Paul and Silas said was true. It was a glad time when many of us, both Jews and Greeks, believed the Good News about Jesus. Now the risen Savior Himself has given us eternal life.

from Jason and the rest, they let them go.

10 Then the brethren immediately sent Paul and Silas away by night to Berea. When they arrived, they went into the synagogue of the Jews. 11 These were more fair-minded than those in Thessalonica, in that they received the word with all readiness, and searched the Scriptures daily *to find out* whether these things *were* so. 12 Therefore many of them believed, and also not a few of the Greeks, prominent women as well as men. 13 But when the Jews from Thessalonica learned that the word of God was preached by Paul at Berea, they came there also and stirred up the crowds. 14 Then immediately the brethren sent Paul away, to go to the sea; but both Silas and Timothy remained there. 15 So those who conducted Paul brought him to Athens; and receiving a command for Silas and Timothy to come to him with all speed, they departed.

16 Now while Paul waited for them at Athens, his spirit was provoked within him when he saw that the city was given over to idols. 17 Therefore he reasoned in the synagogue with the Jews and with the *Gentile* worshipers, and in the marketplace daily with those who happened to be there. 18 Then certain Epicurean and Stoic philosophers encountered him. And some said, "What does this babbler want to say?"

Others said, "He seems to be a proclaimer of foreign gods," because he preached to them Jesus and the resurrection.

19 And they took him and brought him to the Areopagus, saying, "May we know what this new doctrine *is* of which you speak? 20 For you are bringing some strange things to our ears. Therefore we want to know what these things mean." 21 For all the Athenians and the foreigners who were there spent their time in nothing else but either to tell or to hear some new thing.

22 Then Paul stood in the midst of the Areopagus and said, "Men of Athens, I perceive that in all things you are very religious; 23 for as I was pass-

DIGGING IN

17:23 The God Nobody Knew The people of Greece in Paul's day had a great many gods. But just in case they forgot one, they made an altar to the UNKNOWN GOD. When Paul saw this altar in the city of Athens, he decided to tell the people there about the God they didn't know. That God was the Creator of all men. God had sent His Son Jesus into the world to die for men's sins. But Jesus had also risen from death and was now alive to save people from sin and false gods.

The proud people of Athens thought

ing through and considering the objects of your worship, I even found an altar with this inscription:

TO THE UNKNOWN GOD.

Therefore, the One whom you worship without knowing, Him I proclaim to you: 24 God, who made the world and everything in it, since He is Lord of heaven and earth, does not dwell in temples made with hands. 25 Nor is He worshiped with men's hands, as though He needed anything, since He gives to all life, breath, and all things. 26 And He has made from one blood every nation of men to dwell on all the face of the earth, and has determined their preappointed times and the boundaries of their dwellings, 27 so that they should seek the Lord, in the hope that they might grope for Him and find Him, though He is not far from each one of us; 28 for in Him we live and move and have our being, as also some of your own poets have said, 'For we are also His offspring.' 29 Therefore, since we are the offspring of God, we ought not to think that the Divine Nature is like gold or silver or stone, something shaped by art and man's devising. 30 Truly, these times of ignorance God overlooked, but now commands all men everywhere to repent, 31 because He has appointed a day on which He will judge the world in righteousness by the Man whom He has ordained. He has given assurance of this to all by raising Him from the dead.''

32 And when they heard of the resurrection of the dead, some mocked, while others said, "We will hear you again on this *matter*." 33 So Paul departed from among them. 34 However, some men joined him and believed, among them Dionysius the Areopagite,

a woman named Damaris, and others with them.

Paul makes tents with Aquila and Priscilla

18 After these things Paul departed from Athens and went to Corinth. 2 And he found a certain Jew named Aquila, born in Pontus, who had recently come from Italy with his wife Priscilla (because Claudius had commanded all the Jews to depart from Rome); and he came to them. 3 So,

The Roman Emperor Claudius, who commanded all the Jews to leave Rome.

⚒ DIGGING IN

Paul was foolish for talking about a risen Savior. They believed the human body was just a worthless prison for the soul. But Paul preached that Christ arose to redeem our bodies so that we would rise

from death, too.

Only a few people at Athens believed Paul's gospel. They were proud because their great thinkers—Socrates, Plato, and Aristotle—had lived among them.

Paul works with Priscilla and Aquila, making tents.

because he was of the same trade, he stayed with them and worked; for by occupation they were tentmakers. 4 And he reasoned in the synagogue every Sabbath, and persuaded both Jews and Greeks.

5 When Silas and Timothy had come from Macedonia, Paul was compelled by the Spirit, and testified to the Jews *that* Jesus *is* the Christ. 6 But when they opposed him and blasphemed, he shook *his* garments and said to them, "Your blood *be* upon your *own* heads; I *am* clean. From now on I will go to the Gentiles." 7 And he departed from there and entered the house of a certain *man* named Justus, *one* who worshiped God, whose house was next door to the synagogue. 8 Then Crispus, the ruler of the synagogue, believed on the Lord with all his household. And many of the Corinthians, hearing, believed and were baptized.

9 Now the Lord spoke to Paul in the night by a vision, "Do not be afraid, but speak, and do not keep silent; 10 for I am with you, and no one will attack you to hurt you; for I have many people in this city." 11 And he continued *there* a year and six months, teaching the word of God among them.

12 When Gallio was proconsul of Achaia, the Jews with one accord rose up against Paul and brought him to the judgment seat, 13 saying, "This *fellow* persuades men to worship God contrary to the law."

14 And when Paul was about to open *his* mouth, Gallio said to the Jews, "If it were a matter of wrongdoing or wicked crimes, O Jews, there would be reason why I should bear with you. 15 But if it is a question of words and names and your own law, look *to it* yourselves; for I do not want to be a

judge of such *matters.*" ¹⁶ And he drove them from the judgment seat. ¹⁷ Then all the Greeks took Sosthenes, the ruler of the synagogue, and beat *him* before the judgment seat. But Gallio took no notice of these things.

¹⁸ So Paul still remained a good while. Then he took leave of the brethren and sailed for Syria, and Priscilla and Aquila *were* with him. He had *his* hair cut off at Cenchrea, for he had taken a vow. ¹⁹ And he came to Ephesus, and left them there; but he himself entered the synagogue and reasoned with the Jews. ²⁰ When they asked *him* to stay a longer time with them, he did not consent, ²¹ but took leave of them, saying, "I must by all means keep this coming feast in Jerusalem; but I will return again to you, God willing." And he sailed from Ephesus.

²² And when he had landed at Caesarea, and gone up and greeted the church, he went down to Antioch. ²³ After he had spent some time *there,* he departed and went over the region of Galatia and Phrygia in order, strengthening all the disciples.

²⁴ Now a certain Jew named Apollos, born at Alexandria, an eloquent man *and* mighty in the Scriptures, came to Ephesus. ²⁵ This man had been instructed in the way of the Lord; and being fervent in spirit, he spoke and taught accurately the things of the

Lord, though he knew only the baptism of John. ²⁶ So he began to speak boldly in the synagogue. When Aquila and Priscilla heard him, they took him aside and explained to him the way of God more accurately. ²⁷ And when he desired to cross to Achaia, the brethren wrote, exhorting the disciples to receive him; and when he arrived, he greatly helped those who had believed through grace; ²⁸ for he vigorously refuted the Jews publicly, showing from the Scriptures that Jesus is the Christ.

Paul's preaching causes a riot in Ephesus

19 And it happened, while Apollos was at Corinth, that Paul, having passed through the upper regions, came to Ephesus. And finding some disciples ² he said to them, "Did you receive the Holy Spirit when you believed?"

So they said to him, "We have not so much as heard whether there is a Holy Spirit."

³ And he said to them, "Into what then were you baptized?"

So they said, "Into John's baptism."

⁴ Then Paul said, "John indeed baptized with a baptism of repentance, saying to the people that they should believe on Him who would come after him, that is, on Christ Jesus."

Apollos—People remember me because I was a good public speaker. When I preached about Jesus, great crowds would come to hear me. Although I am Jewish, my name is Greek and means "Destroyer." My name is pronounced *uh-POLL-us*.

Although I could speak well, I wasn't a great apostle like Paul. Some people said harsh things about Paul because he wasn't a great preacher. They wanted to hear me instead. I was really ashamed for them because they were wrong. (See 1 Corinthians 3:4.)

I was very glad when I met Aquila and his wife Priscilla (pronounced *ak-WILL-uh* and *prih-SILL-uh*). They were older disciples and knew more about Jesus than I did. So they carefully taught me more about the Scriptures, and I became a better preacher.

Then I was able to show more of my people that Jesus really was the Savior from heaven.

5 When they heard *this,* they were baptized in the name of the Lord Jesus. 6 And when Paul had laid hands on them, the Holy Spirit came upon them, and they spoke with tongues and prophesied. 7 Now the men were about twelve in all.

8 And he went into the synagogue and spoke boldly for three months, reasoning and persuading concerning the things of the kingdom of God. 9 But when some were hardened and did not believe, but spoke evil of the Way before the multitude, he departed from them and withdrew the disciples, reasoning daily in the school of Tyrannus. 10 And this continued for two years, so that all who dwelt in Asia heard the word of the Lord Jesus, both Jews and Greeks.

11 Now God worked unusual miracles by the hands of Paul, 12 so that even handkerchiefs or aprons were brought from his body to the sick, and the diseases left them and the evil spirits went out of them. 13 Then some of the itinerant Jewish exorcists took it upon themselves to call the name of the Lord Jesus over those who had evil spirits, saying, "We exorcise you by the Jesus whom Paul preaches." 14 Also there were seven sons of Sceva, a Jewish chief priest, who did so.

15 And the evil spirit answered and said, "Jesus I know, and Paul I know; but who are you?"

16 Then the man in whom the evil spirit was leaped on them, overpowered them, and prevailed against them, so that they fled out of that house naked and wounded. 17 This became known both to all Jews and Greeks dwelling in Ephesus; and fear fell on them all, and the name of the Lord Jesus was magnified. 18 And many who had believed came confessing and telling their deeds. 19 Also, many of those who had practiced magic brought their books together and burned *them* in the sight of all. And they counted up the value of them, and *it* totaled fifty thousand *pieces* of silver. 20 So the word of the Lord grew mightily and prevailed.

21 When these things were accomplished, Paul purposed in the Spirit, when he had passed through Macedonia and Achaia, to go to Jerusalem, saying, "After I have been there, I must also see Rome." 22 So he sent into Macedonia two of those who ministered to him, Timothy and Erastus, but he himself stayed in Asia for a time.

23 And about that time there arose a great commotion about the Way. 24 For a certain man named Demetrius, a silversmith, who made silver shrines of Diana, brought no small profit to the craftsmen. 25 He called them together with the workers of similar occupation, and said: "Men, you know that we have our prosperity by this trade. 26 Moreover you see and hear that not only at Ephesus, but throughout almost all Asia, this Paul has persuaded and turned away many people, saying that they are not gods which are made with hands. 27 So not only is this trade of ours in danger of falling into disrepute, but also the temple of the great

---

⛏ DIGGING IN

19:9 How Do You Spend Your Time? Paul traveled far and wide to tell people about His Savior, Jesus. He could have spent his time just enjoying the scenery and beautiful buildings of the Greek world. But Paul had made up his mind to use his time for the gospel. He didn't even spend a lot of time arguing with people. He spent his time teaching the people who believed his message. When even 12 people believed, he took them to a school and taught them the Word of God.

How do you spend your time? God needs boys and girls who not only do the fun things that everybody enjoys. God needs young folks who will spend time studying and preparing to serve Him in time to come. Jesus needs teachers and preachers—yes. But He also needs doctors, plumbers, lawyers, and carpenters—all kinds of people to be His witnesses in every walk of life.

goddess Diana may be despised and her magnificence destroyed, whom all Asia and the world worship."

28 Now when they heard *this,* they were full of wrath and cried out, saying, "Great *is* Diana of the Ephesians!" 29 So the whole city was filled with confusion, and rushed into the theater with one accord, having seized Gaius and Aristarchus, Macedonians, Paul's travel companions. 30 And when Paul wanted to go in to the people, the disciples would not allow him. 31 Then some of the officials of Asia, who were his friends, sent to him pleading that he would not venture into the theater. 32 Some therefore cried one thing and some another, for the assembly was confused, and most of them did not know why they had come together. 33 And they drew Alexander out of the multitude, the Jews putting him forward. And Alexander motioned with his hand, and wanted to make his defense to the people. 34 But when they found out that he was a Jew, all with one voice cried out for about two hours, "Great *is* Diana of the Ephesians!"

35 And when the city clerk had quieted the crowd, he said: "Men of Ephesus, what man is there who does not know that the city of the Ephesians is temple guardian of the great goddess Diana, and of the *image* which fell down from Zeus? 36 Therefore, since these things cannot be denied, you ought to be quiet and do nothing rashly. 37 For you have brought these men here who are neither robbers of temples nor blasphemers of your goddess. 38 Therefore, if Demetrius and his fellow craftsmen have a case against anyone, the courts are open and there are proconsuls. Let them bring charges against one another. 39 But if you have any other inquiry to make, it shall be determined in the lawful assembly. 40 For we are in danger of being called in question for today's uproar, there being no reason which we may give to account for this disorderly gathering." 41 And when he had said these things, he dismissed the assembly.

A young man falls out of a window

20 After the uproar had ceased, Paul called the disciples to *himself,* embraced *them,* and departed to go to Macedonia. 2 Now when he had gone over that region and encouraged them with many words, he came to Greece 3 and stayed three months. And when the Jews plotted against him as he was about to sail to Syria, he decided to return through Macedonia. 4 And Sopater of Berea accompanied him to Asia—also Aristarchus and Secundus of the Thessalonians, and Gaius of Derbe, and Timothy, and Tychicus and Trophimus of Asia. 5 These men, going ahead, waited for us at Troas. 6 But we sailed away from Philippi after the Days of Unleavened Bread, and in five days joined them at Troas, where we stayed seven days.

7 Now on the first *day* of the week, when the disciples came together to break bread, Paul, ready to depart the

---

⛏ DIGGING IN

19:28 The Riot Over Diana "Diana" was the Roman name for the Greek goddess Artemis (pronounced *ARE-teh-miss*). She was the goddess of the moon, hunting, wild animals, and purity. Diana was the main god at Ephesus (pronounced *EFF-uh-sus*). A great statue of Diana stood at the head of the harbor of Ephesus, and silver workers made a lot of money by selling small silver idols of Diana.

That was how Paul got in trouble. He told the people of Ephesus that anything made by human hands could not be a god. So the silver workers of Ephesus began to lose their business, and they started a riot.

Sometimes you have to expect trouble when you tell people the truth. The truth may even hurt some people—just as it hurt those silversmiths. But we can never be free by living in error and making money by doing so.

Boy Revived After Fatal Fall

New Testament News Service

TROAS—In a recent meeting in Troas (pronounced *TROH-az*), Saul the former Pharisee, now called Paul, a boy fell from the upstairs window where Paul was preaching. The boy's name was Eutychus (pronounced *YOU-tih-kus*).

Witnesses say the young man was killed by the fall, but Paul immediately spread his body over Eutychus. The next morning at daybreak, the young fellow was found to be alive and well! The boy's family and friends are delighted to have him back.

Is it possible that the Christ that Christians worship is still living? Can this living Christ also raise the dead?

---

next day, spoke to them and continued his message until midnight. 8 There were many lamps in the upper room where they were gathered together. 9 And in a window sat a certain young man named Eutychus, who was sinking into a deep sleep. He was overcome by sleep; and as Paul continued speaking, he fell down from the third story and was taken up dead. 10 But Paul went down, fell on him, and embracing *him* said, "Do not trouble yourselves, for his life is in him." 11 Now when he had come up, had broken bread and eaten, and talked a long while, even till daybreak, he departed. 12 And they brought the young man in alive, and they were not a little comforted.

13 Then we went ahead to the ship and sailed to Assos, there intending to take Paul on board; for so he had given orders, intending himself to go on foot. 14 And when he met us at Assos, we took him on board and came to Mitylene. 15 We sailed from there, and the next *day* came opposite Chios. The following *day* we arrived at Samos and stayed at Trogyllium. The next *day* we came to Miletus. 16 For Paul had decided to sail past Ephesus, so that he would not have to spend time in Asia; for he was hurrying to be at Jerusalem, if possible, on the Day of Pentecost.

17 From Miletus he sent to Ephesus and called for the elders of the church. 18 And when they had come to him, he said to them: "You know, from the first day that I came to Asia, in what manner I always lived among you, 19 serving the Lord with all humility, with many tears and trials which happened to me by the plotting of the Jews; 20 how I kept back nothing that was helpful, but proclaimed it to you, and taught you publicly and from house to house, 21 testifying to Jews, and also to Greeks, repentance toward God and faith toward our Lord Jesus Christ. 22 And see, now I go bound in the spirit to Jerusalem, not knowing the things that will happen to me there, 23 except that the Holy Spirit testifies in every city, saying that chains and tribulations await me. 24 But none of these things move me; nor do I count my life dear to myself, so that I may finish my race with joy, and the ministry which I received from the Lord Jesus, to testify to the gospel of the grace of God.

25 "And indeed, now I know that you all, among whom I have gone preaching the kingdom of God, will see my face no more. 26 Therefore I testify to you this day that I *am* innocent of the blood of all *men*. 27 For I have not shunned to declare to you the whole counsel of God. 28 Therefore take heed to yourselves and to all the flock, among which the Holy Spirit has made you overseers, to shepherd the church of God which He purchased with His own blood. 29 For I know this, that after

my departure savage wolves will come in among you, not sparing the flock. 30 Also from among yourselves men will rise up, speaking perverse things, to draw away the disciples after themselves. 31 Therefore watch, and remember that for three years I did not cease to warn everyone night and day with tears.

32 "So now, brethren, I commend you to God and to the word of His grace, which is able to build you up and give you an inheritance among all those who are sanctified. 33 I have coveted no one's silver or gold or apparel. 34 Yes, you yourselves know that these hands have provided for my necessities, and for those who were with me. 35 I have shown you in every way, by laboring like this, that you must support the weak. And remember the words of the Lord Jesus, that He said, 'It is more blessed to give than to receive.' "

36 And when he had said these things, he knelt down and prayed with them all. 37 Then they all wept freely, and fell on Paul's neck and kissed him, 38 sorrowing most of all for the words which he spoke, that they would see his face no more. And they accompanied him to the ship.

Paul journeys to Jersualem and is arrested

21 Now it came to pass, that when we had departed from them and set sail, running a straight course we came to Cos, the following day to Rhodes, and from there to Patara. 2 And finding a ship sailing over to Phoenicia, we went aboard and set sail. 3 When we had sighted Cyprus, we passed it on the left, sailed to Syria, and landed at Tyre; for there the ship was to unload her cargo. 4 And finding disciples, we stayed there seven days. They told Paul through the Spirit not to go up to Jerusalem. 5 When we had come to the end of those days, we departed and went on our way; and they all accompanied us, with wives and children, till we were out of the city. And we knelt down on the shore and prayed. 6 When we had taken our leave of one another, we boarded the ship, and they returned home.

7 And when we had finished our voyage from Tyre, we came to Ptolemais, greeted the brethren, and stayed with them one day. 8 On the next day we who were Paul's companions departed and came to Caesarea, and

Paul sailed on a Phoenician ship like this one.

entered the house of Philip the **evange-list,** who was *one* of the seven, and stayed with him. 9 Now this man had four virgin daughters who prophesied. 10 And as *we* stayed many days, a certain prophet named Agabus came down from Judea. 11 When he had come to us, he took Paul's belt, bound his *own* hands and feet, and said, "Thus says the Holy Spirit, 'So shall the Jews at Jerusalem bind the man who owns this belt, and deliver *him* into the hands of the Gentiles.' "

12 Now when we heard these things, both *we* and those from that place pleaded with him not to go up to Jerusalem. 13 Then Paul answered, "What do you mean by weeping and breaking my heart? For I am ready not only to be bound, but also to die at Jerusalem for the name of the Lord Jesus."

14 So when he would not be persuaded, we ceased, saying, "The will of the Lord be done."

15 And after those days we packed and went up to Jerusalem. 16 Also some of the disciples from Caesarea went with us and brought with them a certain Mnason of Cyprus, an early disciple, with whom we were to lodge.

17 And when we had come to Jerusalem, the brethren received us gladly. 18 On the following *day* Paul went in with us to James, and all the elders were present. 19 When he had greeted them, he told in detail those things which God had done among the Gentiles through his ministry. 20 And when they heard *it,* they glorified the Lord. And they said to him, "You see, brother, how many myriads of Jews there are who have believed, and they are all zealous for the law; 21 but they have been informed about you that you teach all the Jews who are among the Gentiles to forsake Moses, saying that they ought not to circumcise *their* children nor to walk according to the customs. 22 What then? The assembly must certainly meet, for they will hear that you have come. 23 Therefore do what we tell you: We have four men who have taken a vow. 24 Take them and be purified with them, and pay their expenses so that they may shave *their* heads, and that all may know that those things of which they were informed concerning you are nothing, but *that* you yourself also walk orderly and keep the law. 25 But concerning the Gentiles who believe, we have written *and* decided that they should observe no such thing, except that they should keep themselves from *things* offered to idols, from blood, from things strangled, and from sexual immorality."

26 Then Paul took the men, and the next day, having been purified with them, entered the temple to announce the expiration of the days of purification, at which time an offering should be made for each one of them.

27 Now when the seven days were almost ended, the Jews from Asia, seeing him in the temple, stirred up the whole crowd and laid hands on him, 28 crying out, "Men of Israel, help! This is the man who teaches all *men* everywhere against the people, the law, and this place; and furthermore he also brought Greeks into the temple and has defiled this holy place." 29 (For they had previously seen Trophimus the Ephesian with him in the city, whom they supposed that Paul had brought into the temple.)

30 And all the city was disturbed; and the people ran together, seized Paul, and dragged him out of the temple; and immediately the doors were shut. 31 Now as they were seeking to kill him, news came to the commander of the garrison that all Jerusalem was in an uproar. 32 He immediately took soldiers and centurions, and ran down to

---

🌐 WORDFINDER ━━━━━━━━━━━━━━━━━━━━━━━━━━━━━━━━━

21:8 Evangelist Pronounced *ih-VAN-juh-list.* A person who preaches the Good News of salvation through Jesus Christ. The word comes from a Greek word meaning "preach the gospel."

St. Paul's Gate at the City of Tarsus, where the apostle was born.

them. And when they saw the commander and the soldiers, they stopped beating Paul. 33 Then the commander came near and took him, and commanded *him* to be bound with two chains; and he asked who he was and what he had done. 34 And some among the multitude cried one thing and some another.

So when he could not ascertain the truth because of the tumult, he commanded him to be taken into the barracks. 35 When he reached the stairs, he had to be carried by the soldiers because of the violence of the mob.

36 For the multitude of the people followed after, crying out, "Away with him!"

37 Then as Paul was about to be led into the barracks, he said to the commander, "May I speak to you?"

He replied, "Can you speak Greek? 38 Are you not the Egyptian who some time ago stirred up a rebellion and led the four thousand assassins out into the wilderness?"

39 But Paul said, "I am a Jew from Tarsus, in Cilicia, a citizen of no mean city; and I implore you, permit me to speak to the people."

🔨 DIGGING IN

21:33 Paul Arrested for Preaching the Gospel People often don't want what's best for them. Sometimes you'd rather not eat the things your mother tells you are "good for you." The people at Jerusalem were like that. All through their long history, God had been telling the people of Jerusalem that He loved them. He wanted them to love Him and leave their sins behind. After all, their sins were only destroying their lives.

So Paul came to Jerusalem to bring God's Good News once more. Now the Jews were very proud of their temple at Jerusalem, but Paul told them their temple and their law could not save them. He said their sins could be forgiven only because Jesus died. Then the people accused Paul of bringing a Greek man into the temple, which was against the law. That wasn't true, but they wanted that excuse to kill Paul.

40 So when he had given him permission, Paul stood on the stairs and motioned with his hand to the people. And when there was a great silence, he spoke to *them* in the Hebrew language, saying,

Paul gives his testimony

22 "Brethren and fathers, hear my defense before you now." 2 And when they heard that he spoke to them in the Hebrew language, they kept all the more silent.

Then he said: 3 "I am indeed a Jew, born in Tarsus of Cilicia, but brought up in this city at the feet of Gamaliel, taught according to the strictness of our fathers' law, and was zealous toward God as you all are today. 4 I persecuted this Way to the death, binding and delivering into prisons both men and women, 5 as also the high priest bears me witness, and all the council of the elders, from whom I also received letters to the brethren, and went to Damascus to bring in chains even those who were there to Jerusalem to be punished.

6 "Now it happened, as I journeyed and came near Damascus at about noon, suddenly a great light from heaven shone around me. 7 And I fell to the ground and heard a voice saying to me, 'Saul, Saul, why are you persecuting Me?' 8 So I answered, 'Who are You, Lord?' And He said to me, 'I am Jesus of Nazareth, whom you are persecuting.'

9 "And those who were with me indeed saw the light and were afraid, but they did not hear the voice of Him who spoke to me. 10 So I said, 'What shall I do, Lord?' And the Lord said to me, 'Arise and go into Damascus, and there you will be told all things which are appointed for you to do.' 11 And since I could not see for the glory of that light, being led by the hand of those

who were with me, I came into Damascus.

12 "Then a certain Ananias, a devout man according to the law, having a good testimony with all the Jews who dwelt *there*, 13 came to me; and he stood and said to me, 'Brother Saul, receive your sight.' And at that same hour I looked up at him. 14 Then he said, 'The God of our fathers has chosen you that you should know His will, and see the Just One, and hear the voice of His mouth. 15 For you will be His witness to all men of what you have seen and heard. 16 And now why are you waiting? Arise and be baptized, and wash away your sins, calling on the name of the Lord.'

17 "Now it happened, when I returned to Jerusalem and was praying in the temple, that I was in a trance 18 and saw Him saying to me, 'Make haste and get out of Jerusalem quickly, for they will not receive your testimony concerning Me.' 19 So I said, 'Lord, they know that in every synagogue I imprisoned and beat those who believe on You. 20 And when the blood of Your **martyr** Stephen was shed, I also was standing by consenting to his death, and guarding the clothes of those who were killing him.' 21 Then He said to me, 'Depart, for I will send you far from here to the Gentiles.' "

22 And they listened to him until this word, and *then* they raised their voices and said, "Away with such a *fellow* from the earth, for he is not fit to live!" 23 Then, as they cried out and tore off *their* clothes and threw dust into the air, 24 the commander ordered him to be brought into the barracks, and said that he should be examined under scourging, so that he might know why they shouted so against him. 25 And as they bound him with thongs, Paul said to the centurion who stood by, "Is it lawful for you to scourge a man who is a Roman, and uncondemned?"

WORDFINDER

22:20 Martyr Pronounced *MAR-ter*. A person who is put to death for being a Christian. The word comes from a Greek word meaning "witness."

26 When the centurion heard *that,* he went and told the commander, saying, "Take care what you do, for this man is a Roman."

27 Then the commander came and said to him, "Tell me, are you a Roman?"

He said, "Yes."

28 The commander answered, "With a large sum I obtained this citizenship."

And Paul said, "But I was born *a citizen.*"

29 Then immediately those who were about to examine him withdrew from him; and the commander was also afraid after he found out that he was a Roman, and because he had bound him.

30 The next day, because he wanted to know for certain why he was accused by the Jews, he released him from *his* bonds, and commanded the chief priests and all their council to appear, and brought Paul down and set him before them.

Paul takes his stand for the Lord and is comforted

23 Then Paul, looking earnestly at the council, said, "Men *and* brethren, I have lived in all good conscience before God until this day." 2 And the high priest Ananias commanded those who stood by him to strike him on the mouth. 3 Then Paul said to him, "God will strike you, *you* whitewashed wall! For you sit to judge me according to the law, and do you command me to be struck contrary to the law?"

4 And those who stood by said, "Do you revile God's high priest?"

5 Then Paul said, "I did not know, brethren, that he was the high priest; for it is written, 'You shall not speak evil of a ruler of your people.' "

6 But when Paul perceived that one part were Sadducees and the other Pharisees, he cried out in the council, "Men *and* brethren, I am a Pharisee, the son of a Pharisee; concerning the hope and resurrection of the dead I am being judged!"

7 And when he had said this, a dissension arose between the Pharisees and the Sadducees; and the assembly was divided. 8 For Sadducees say that there is no resurrection—and no angel or spirit; but the Pharisees confess both. 9 Then there arose a loud outcry. And the scribes of the Pharisees' party arose and protested, saying, "We find no evil in this man; but if a spirit or an angel has spoken to him, let us not fight against God."

10 Now when there arose a great dissension, the commander, fearing lest Paul might be pulled to pieces by them, commanded the soldiers to go down and take him by force from among them, and bring *him* into the barracks.

11 But the following night the Lord stood by him and said, "Be of good cheer, Paul; for as you have testified for Me in Jerusalem, so you must also bear witness at Rome."

12 And when it was day, some of the Jews banded together and bound themselves under an oath, saying that

DIGGING IN

22:26 Paul the Roman Citizen Of all things! This Jewish preacher was a Roman citizen! How could that be?

To be a Roman citizen, you had to be born in Italy—usually. But sometimes people from lands conquered by the Romans were also made Roman citizens. This meant that their families were also Romans.

Paul had grown up in the important city of Tarsus in the Roman province of Cilicia (pronounced *suh-LISH-she-uh*) in Asia

Minor. (See the map on pages 1460–61). It is likely that Paul's father had done a valuable service for the Roman government. Therefore, even though he was a Jew, the government rewarded Paul's father by making him a Roman citizen. This meant that Paul also was a Roman. As a citizen, Paul had the right to have his case tried at Rome. So Paul traveled at government expense to Rome where he also preached the gospel.

they would neither eat nor drink till they had killed Paul. 13 Now there were more than forty who had formed this conspiracy. 14 They came to the chief priests and elders, and said, "We have bound ourselves under a great oath that we will eat nothing until we have killed Paul. 15 Now you, therefore, together with the council, suggest to the commander that he be brought down to you tomorrow, as though you were going to make further inquiries concerning him; but we are ready to kill him before he comes near."

16 So when Paul's sister's son heard of their ambush, he went and entered the barracks and told Paul. 17 Then Paul called one of the centurions to him and said, "Take this young man to the commander, for he has something to tell him." 18 So he took him and brought him to the commander and said, "Paul the prisoner called me to him and asked me to bring this young man to you. He has something to say to you."

19 Then the commander took him by the hand, went aside, and asked privately, "What is it that you have to tell me?"

20 And he said, "The Jews have

⛏ DIGGING IN

23:6 Paul on Trial You must remember that the Jewish people of Paul's time were a very proud people. God had brought their ancestors out of slavery in Egypt. Then the Lord gave them their great Law. These facts made the Jews very proud.

Paul understood the Jews because he, too, had been a very important Jew—a Pharisee. Now Paul was a Christian. He realized that God only wanted to use the Jewish people to bring salvation to the world. Since Paul had met Jesus, this was all that Paul could think about—telling the world about Jesus the Savior.

But Paul made the Jews angry. They had crucified Jesus, and Paul was now Jesus' friend and apostle. For these reasons, they wanted to kill Paul also.

Paul used his head. He got the Jews into an argument among themselves about whether people could rise from the dead. Then the Roman police had to come and break up the fight. Always be ready to use your head for Jesus.

Paul tells the Sanhedrin, a council of Jewish leaders, about meeting Jesus on the road to Damascus.

agreed to ask that you bring Paul down to the council tomorrow, as though they were going to inquire more fully about him. 21 But do not yield to them, for more than forty of them lie in wait for him, men who have bound themselves by an oath that they will neither eat nor drink till they have killed him; and now they are ready, waiting for the promise from you.''

22 So the commander let the young man depart, and commanded *him*, ''Tell no one that you have revealed these things to me.''

23 And he called for two centurions, saying, ''Prepare two hundred soldiers, seventy horsemen, and two hundred spearmen to go to Caesarea at the third hour of the night; 24 and provide mounts to set Paul on, and bring *him* safely to Felix the governor.'' 25 He wrote a letter in the following manner:

26   Claudius Lysias,

To the most excellent governor Felix:

Greetings.

27   This man was seized by the Jews and was about to be killed by them. Coming with the troops I rescued him, having learned that he was a Roman. 28 And when I wanted to know the reason they accused him, I brought him before their council. 29 I found out that he was accused concerning questions of their law, but had nothing charged against him deserving of death or chains. 30 And when it was told me that the Jews lay in wait for the man, I sent him immediately to you, and also commanded his accusers to state before you the charges against him.

Farewell.

31 Then the soldiers, as they were commanded, took Paul and brought him by night to Antipatris. 32 The next day they left the horsemen to go on with him, and returned to the barracks. 33 When they came to Caesarea and had delivered the letter to the governor, they also presented Paul to him. 34 And when the governor had read *it*, he asked what province he was from. And when he understood that *he was* from Cilicia, 35 he said, ''I will hear you when your accusers also have come.'' And he commanded him to be kept in Herod's Praetorium.

Paul is brought before Governor Felix

24 Now after five days Ananias the high priest came down with the elders and a certain orator *named* Tertullus. These gave evidence to the governor against Paul.

2 And when he was called upon, Tertullus began his accusation, saying: ''Seeing that through you we enjoy great peace, and prosperity is being brought to this nation by your foresight, 3 we accept *it* always and in all places, most noble Felix, with all thankfulness. 4 Nevertheless, not to be tedious to you any further, I beg you to hear, by your courtesy, a few words from us. 5 For we have found this man a plague, a creator of dissension among all the Jews throughout the world, and a ringleader of the sect of the Nazarenes. 6 He even tried to profane the temple, and we seized him, and wanted to judge him according to our law. 7 But the commander Lysias came by and with great violence took *him* out of our hands, 8 commanding his accusers to come to you. By examining him yourself you may ascertain all these things of which we accuse him.'' 9 And the Jews also assented, maintaining that these things were so.

10 Then Paul, after the governor had nodded to him to speak, answered: ''Inasmuch as I know that you have been for many years a judge of this nation, I do the more cheerfully answer for myself, 11 because you may ascertain that it is no more than twelve days

Apostle Arrested, Will Be Judged at Rome

The Jerusalem Times

JERUSALEM—After the religious leaders of this city accused Paul of bringing a Gentile into the temple, which is a crime among our people, the apostle was arrested.

The mob would have killed Paul if the Roman police had not arrived in time to save him. When the Romans learned that some of our Jewish people planned to kill Paul, they put him on a horse one night and took him to the seaport town of Caesarea (pronounced *sess-uh-REE-uh*). There Governor Felix put Paul on trial for crimes against Rome. Paul has been held in Caesarea for two years.

Now *The Times* has learned that Paul has demanded to be tried at Rome. It seems that Paul is actually a Jewish citizen of that city. Since he has full Roman rights, the apostle will be taken to Rome for trial.

---

since I went up to Jerusalem to worship. 12 And they neither found me in the temple disputing with anyone nor inciting the crowd, either in the synagogues or in the city. 13 Nor can they prove the things of which they now accuse me. 14 But this I confess to you, that according to the Way which they call a sect, so I worship the God of my fathers, believing all things which are written in the Law and in the Prophets. 15 I have hope in God, which they themselves also accept, that there will be a resurrection of *the* dead, both of *the* just and *the* unjust. 16 This *being* so, I myself always strive to have a conscience without offense toward God and men.

17 "Now after many years I came to bring alms and offerings to my nation, 18 in the midst of which some Jews from Asia found me purified in the temple, neither with a mob nor with tumult. 19 They ought to have been here before you to object if they had anything against me. 20 Or else let those who are *here* themselves say if they found any wrongdoing in me while I stood before the council, 21 unless *it is* for this one statement which I cried out, standing among them, 'Concerning the resurrection of the dead I am being judged by you this day.'"

22 But when Felix heard these things, having more accurate knowledge of *the* Way, he adjourned the proceedings and said, "When Lysias the commander comes down, I will make a decision on your case." 23 So he commanded the centurion to keep Paul and to let *him* have liberty, and told him not to forbid any of his friends to provide for or visit him.

24 And after some days, when Felix came with his wife Drusilla, who was Jewish, he sent for Paul and heard him concerning the faith in Christ. 25 Now as he reasoned about righteousness, self-control, and the judgment to come, Felix was afraid and answered, "Go away for now; when I have a convenient time I will call for you." 26 Meanwhile he also hoped that money would be given him by Paul, that he might release him. Therefore he sent for him more often and conversed with him.

27 But after two years Porcius Festus succeeded Felix; and Felix, wanting to do the Jews a favor, left Paul bound.

Paul appears to Caesar

25 Now when Festus had come to the province, after three days he went up from Caesarea to Jerusalem. 2 Then the high priest and the chief men of the Jews informed him against

Paul; and they petitioned him, ³ asking a favor against him, that he would summon him to Jerusalem—while *they* lay in ambush along the road to kill him. ⁴ But Festus answered that Paul should be kept at Caesarea, and that he himself was going *there* shortly. ⁵ "Therefore," he said, "let those who have authority among you go down with *me* and accuse this man, to see if there is any fault in him."

⁶ And when he had remained among them more than ten days, he went down to Caesarea. And the next day, sitting on the judgment seat, he commanded Paul to be brought. ⁷ When he had come, the Jews who had come down from Jerusalem stood about and laid many serious complaints against Paul, which they could not prove, ⁸ while he answered for himself, "Neither against the law of the Jews, nor against the temple, nor against Caesar have I offended in anything at all."

⁹ But Festus, wanting to do the Jews a favor, answered Paul and said, "Are you willing to go up to Jerusalem and there be judged before me concerning these things?"

¹⁰ So Paul said, "I stand at Caesar's judgment seat, where I ought to be judged. To the Jews I have done no wrong, as you very well know. ¹¹ For if I am an offender, or have committed anything deserving of death, I do not object to dying; but if there is nothing in these things of which these men accuse me, no one can deliver me to them. I appeal to Caesar."

¹² Then Festus, when he had conferred with the council, answered, "You have appealed to Caesar? To Caesar you shall go!"

¹³ And after some days King Agrippa and Bernice came to Caesarea to greet Festus. ¹⁴ When they had been there many days, Festus laid Paul's case before the king, saying: "There is a certain man left a prisoner by Felix, ¹⁵ about whom the chief priests and the elders of the Jews informed *me*, when I was in Jerusalem, asking for a judgment against him. ¹⁶ To them I answered, 'It is not the custom of the Romans to deliver any man to destruction before the accused meets the accusers face to face, and has opportunity to answer for himself concerning the charge against him.' ¹⁷ Therefore when they had come together, without any delay, the next day I sat on the judgment seat and commanded the man to be brought in. ¹⁸ When the accusers stood up, they brought no accusation against him of such things as I supposed, ¹⁹ but had some questions against him about their own religion and about a certain Jesus, who had died, whom Paul affirmed to be alive. ²⁰ And because I was uncertain of such questions, I asked whether he was willing to go to Jerusalem and there be judged concerning these matters. ²¹ But when Paul appealed to be reserved for the decision of Augustus, I commanded him to be kept till I could send him to Caesar."

²² Then Agrippa said to Festus, "I also would like to hear the man myself."

"Tomorrow," he said, "you shall hear him."

²³ So the next day, when Agrippa and Bernice had come with great pomp, and had entered the auditorium with the commanders and the prominent men of the city, at Festus' command Paul was brought in. ²⁴ And Festus said: "King Agrippa and all the men who are here present with us, you see this man about whom the whole assembly of the Jews petitioned me, both at Jerusalem and here, crying out that he was not fit to live any longer. ²⁵ But when I found that he had committed nothing deserving of death, and that he himself had appealed to Augustus, I decided to send him. ²⁶ I have nothing certain to write to my lord concerning him. Therefore I have brought him out before you, and especially before you, King Agrippa, so that after the examination has taken place I may have something to write. ²⁷ For it seems to me unreasonable to send a prisoner and not to specify the charges against him."

King Agrippa *almost* becomes a Christian

26 Then Agrippa said to Paul, "You are permitted to speak for yourself."

So Paul stretched out his hand and answered for himself: 2 "I think myself happy, King Agrippa, because today I shall answer for myself before you concerning all the things of which I am accused by the Jews, 3 especially because you are expert in all customs and questions which have to do with the Jews. Therefore I beg you to hear me patiently.

4 "My manner of life from my youth, which was spent from the beginning among my own nation at Jerusalem, all the Jews know. 5 They knew me from the first, if they were willing to testify, that according to the strictest sect of our religion I lived a Pharisee. 6 And now I stand and am judged for the hope of the promise made by God to our fathers. 7 To this *promise* our twelve tribes, earnestly serving *God* night and day, hope to attain. For this hope's sake, King Agrippa, I am accused by the Jews. 8 Why should it be thought incredible by you that God raises the dead?

9 "Indeed, I myself thought I must do many things contrary to the name of Jesus of Nazareth. 10 This I also did in Jerusalem, and many of the saints I shut up in prison, having received authority from the chief priests; and when they were put to death, I cast my vote against *them*. 11 And I punished them often in every synagogue and compelled *them* to blaspheme; and being exceedingly enraged against them, I persecuted *them* even to foreign cities.

12 "While thus occupied, as I journeyed to Damascus with authority and commission from the chief priests, 13 at midday, O king, along the road I saw a light from heaven, brighter than the sun, shining around me and those who journeyed with me. 14 And when we all had fallen to the ground, I heard a voice speaking to me and saying in the Hebrew language, 'Saul, Saul, why are you persecuting Me? *It is* hard for you to kick against the goads.' 15 So I said, 'Who are You, Lord?' And He said, 'I am Jesus, whom you are persecuting. 16 But rise and stand on your feet; for I have appeared to you for this purpose, to make you a minister and a witness both of the things which you have seen and of the things which I will yet reveal to you. 17 I will deliver you from the *Jewish* people, as well as *from* the Gentiles, to whom I now send you, 18 to open their eyes, *in order* to turn *them* from darkness to light, and *from* the power of Satan to God, that they may receive forgiveness of sins and an inheritance among those who are sanctified by faith in Me.'

19 "Therefore, King Agrippa, I was not disobedient to the heavenly vision, 20 but declared first to those in Damascus and in Jerusalem, and throughout all the region of Judea, and *then* to the Gentiles, that they should repent, turn to God, and do works befitting repentance. 21 For these reasons the Jews seized me in the temple and tried to kill *me*. 22 Therefore, having obtained help from God, to this day I stand, witnessing both to small and great, saying no other things than those which the prophets and Moses said would come— 23 that the Christ would suffer, that He would be the first to rise from the dead, and would proclaim light to the *Jewish* people and to the Gentiles."

24 Now as he thus made his defense, Festus said with a loud voice, "Paul, you are beside yourself! Much learning is driving you mad!"

25 But he said, "I am not mad, most noble Festus, but speak the words of truth and reason. 26 For the king, before whom I also speak freely, knows these things; for I am convinced that none of these things escapes his attention, since this thing was not done in a corner. 27 King Agrippa, do you believe the prophets? I know that you do believe."

28 Then Agrippa said to Paul, "You

almost persuade me to become a **Christian**."

²⁹ And Paul said, "I would to God that not only you, but also all who hear me today, might become both almost and altogether such as I am, except for these chains."

³⁰ When he had said these things, the king stood up, as well as the governor and Bernice and those who sat with them; ³¹ and when they had gone aside, they talked among themselves, saying, "This man is doing nothing deserving of death or chains."

³² Then Agrippa said to Festus, "This man might have been set free if he had not appealed to Caesar."

Paul's ship is caught in a storm

27 And when it was decided that we should sail to Italy, they delivered Paul and some other prisoners to *one* named Julius, a centurion of the Augustan Regiment. ² So, entering a ship of Adramyttium, we put to sea, meaning to sail along the coasts of Asia. Aristarchus, a Macedonian of Thessalonica, was with us. ³ And the next *day* we landed at Sidon. And Julius treated Paul kindly and gave *him* liberty to go to his friends and receive care. ⁴ When we had put to sea from there, we sailed under *the shelter of* Cyprus, because

the winds were contrary. ⁵ And when we had sailed over the sea which is off Cilicia and Pamphylia, we came to Myra, *a city* of Lycia. ⁶ There the centurion found an Alexandrian ship sailing to Italy, and he put us on board.

⁷ When we had sailed slowly many days, and arrived with difficulty off Cnidus, the wind not permitting us to proceed, we sailed under *the shelter of* Crete off Salmone. ⁸ Passing it with difficulty, we came to a place called Fair Havens, near the city *of* Lasea.

⁹ Now when much time had been spent, and sailing was now dangerous because the Fast was already over, Paul advised them, ¹⁰ saying, "Men, I perceive that this voyage will end with disaster and much loss, not only of the cargo and ship, but also our lives." ¹¹ Nevertheless the centurion was more persuaded by the helmsman and the owner of the ship than by the things spoken by Paul. ¹² And because the harbor was not suitable to winter in, the majority advised to set sail from there also, if by any means they could reach Phoenix, a harbor of Crete opening toward the southwest and northwest, *and* winter *there*.

¹³ When the south wind blew softly, supposing that they had obtained *their* desire, putting out to sea, they sailed close by Crete. ¹⁴ But not long after,

---

WORDFINDER

26:28 Christian A person who believes in and follows Jesus Christ. People were first called Christians after Jesus rose from death (see 11:26).

DIGGING IN

26:29 How to Answer Your Enemies
Being a Christian isn't always smooth sailing. In fact, sometimes it can be rough. The Roman police who rescued Paul from the Jewish mob (see Acts 23) had taken Paul by horseback down to the seaport of Caesarea (see map on pages 1460–61). Paul was kept there for two years because Felix, the Roman governor, expected a bribe from Paul.

Finally, Paul was brought before King Herod Agrippa II. Then Paul told the great

story of how he had been a Pharisee, and how Jesus had appeared to him, causing Paul to believe in Him and become a Christian. King Herod Agrippa was so impressed by Paul's speech that he even admitted he would almost like to be a Christian himself.

Paul didn't attack or argue with his enemies. He simply told them how God had changed his life. That's a model for you to follow when you have a chance to speak for Jesus.

Paul's ship is wrecked off the island of Malta.

a tempestuous head wind arose, called **Euroclydon.** 15 So when the ship was caught, and could not head into the wind, we let *her* drive. 16 And running under *the shelter of* an island called Clauda, we secured the skiff with difficulty. 17 When they had taken it on board, they used cables to undergird the ship; and fearing lest they should run aground on the Syrtis *Sands,* they struck sail and so were driven. 18 And because we were exceedingly tempesttossed, the next *day* they lightened the ship. 19 On the third *day* we threw the ship's tackle overboard with our own hands. 20 Now when neither sun nor stars appeared for many days, and no small tempest beat on *us,* all hope that we would be saved was finally given up.

21 But after long abstinence from food, then Paul stood in the midst of them and said, "Men, you should have listened to me, and not have sailed from Crete and incurred this disaster and loss. 22 And now I urge you to take heart, for there will be no loss of life among you, but only of the ship. 23 For there stood by me this night an angel of the God to whom I belong and whom I serve, 24 saying, 'Do not be afraid, Paul; you must be brought before Caesar; and indeed God has granted you all those who sail with

WORDFINDER

27:14 Euroclydon Pronounced *you-ROCK-lah-din.* A powerful wind that often blows in the eastern Mediterranean Sea in the springtime. The word means "east wind" because it comes from the northeast.

you.' 25 Therefore take heart, men, for I believe God that it will be just as it was told me. 26 However, we must run aground on a certain island."

27 Now when the fourteenth night had come, as we were driven up and down in the Adriatic *Sea,* about midnight the sailors sensed that they were drawing near some land. 28 And they took soundings and found *it* to be twenty fathoms; and when they had gone a little farther, they took soundings again and found *it* to be fifteen fathoms. 29 Then, fearing lest we should run aground on the rocks, they dropped four anchors from the stern, and prayed for day to come. 30 And as the sailors were seeking to escape from the ship, when they had let down the skiff into the sea, under pretense of putting out anchors from the prow, 31 Paul said to the centurion and the soldiers, "Unless these men stay in the ship, you cannot be saved." 32 Then the soldiers cut away the ropes of the skiff and let it fall off.

33 And as day was about to dawn, Paul implored *them* all to take food, saying, "Today is the fourteenth day you have waited and continued without food, and eaten nothing. 34 Therefore I urge you to take nourishment, for this is for your survival, since not a hair will fall from the head of any of you." 35 And when he had said these things, he took bread and gave thanks to God in the presence of them all; and when he had broken *it* he began to eat. 36 Then they were all encouraged, and also took food themselves. 37 And in all we were two hundred and seventy-six persons on the ship. 38 So when they had eaten enough, they lightened the ship and threw out the wheat into the sea.

39 When it was day, they did not recognize the land; but they observed a bay with a beach, onto which they planned to run the ship if possible. 40 And they let go the anchors and left *them* in the sea, meanwhile loosing the rudder ropes; and they hoisted the mainsail to the wind and made for shore. 41 But striking a place where two

seas met, they ran the ship aground; and the prow stuck fast and remained immovable, but the stern was being broken up by the violence of the waves.

42 And the soldiers' plan was to kill the prisoners, lest any of them should swim away and escape. 43 But the centurion, wanting to save Paul, kept them from *their* purpose, and commanded that those who could swim should jump *overboard* first and get to land, 44 and the rest, some on boards and some on *parts* of the ship. And so it was that they all escaped safely to land.

Paul is shipwrecked on an island

28 Now when they had escaped, they then found out that the island was called Malta. 2 And the natives showed us unusual kindness; for they kindled a fire and made us all welcome, because of the rain that was falling and because of the cold. 3 But when Paul had gathered a bundle of sticks and laid *them* on the fire, a viper came out because of the heat, and fastened on his hand. 4 So when the natives saw the creature hanging from his hand, they said to one another, "No doubt this man is a murderer, whom, though he has escaped the sea, yet justice does not allow to live." 5 But he shook off the creature into the fire and suffered no harm. 6 However, they were expecting that he would swell up or suddenly fall down dead. But after they had looked for a long time and saw no harm come to him, they changed their minds and said that he was a god.

7 In that region there was an estate of the leading citizen of the island, whose name was Publius, who received us and entertained us courteously for three days. 8 And it happened that the father of Publius lay sick of a fever and dysentery. Paul went in to him and prayed, and he laid his hands on him and healed him. 9 So when this was done, the rest of those on the island who had diseases also came and were healed. 10 They also honored us in many ways; and when we departed,

they provided such things as were necessary.

11 After three months we sailed in an Alexandrian ship whose figurehead was the Twin Brothers, which had wintered at the island. 12 And landing at Syracuse, we stayed three days. 13 From there we circled round and reached Rhegium. And after one day the south wind blew; and the next day we came to Puteoli, 14 where we found brethren, and were invited to stay with them seven days. And so we went toward Rome. 15 And from there, when the brethren heard about us, they came to meet us as far as Appii Forum and Three Inns. When Paul saw them, he thanked God and took courage.

16 Now when we came to Rome, the centurion delivered the prisoners to the captain of the guard; but Paul was permitted to dwell by himself with the soldier who guarded him.

17 And it came to pass after three days that Paul called the leaders of the Jews together. So when they had come together, he said to them: "Men *and* brethren, though I have done nothing against our people or the customs of our fathers, yet I was delivered as a prisoner from Jerusalem into the hands of the Romans, 18 who, when they had examined me, wanted to let *me* go, because there was no cause for putting me to death. 19 But when the Jews spoke against *it,* I was compelled to appeal to Caesar, not that I had anything of which to accuse my nation. 20 For this reason therefore I have called for you, to see *you* and speak with *you,* because for the hope of Israel I am bound with this chain."

21 Then they said to him, "We neither received letters from Judea concerning you, nor have any of the

DIGGING IN

28:16 Paul at Rome God had worked everything out in a wonderful way for Paul. Paul had used his right to be tried at Rome. There Paul was allowed to rent his own house where a Roman soldier guarded him. Of course, the Roman government found no fault with Paul. They didn't care what the Jews said about him, because Paul hadn't broken any Roman laws. Later, we read in Paul's letters how he was able to win many to Christ at Rome—even people who lived at the emperor's palace!

After two years, Paul was set free. After that, we think he was able to go as far as Spain and preach the gospel. Later, Paul was arrested again and accused of treason. Like many other Christians, he refused to worship Emperor Nero. So the great apostle was beheaded at the Mamartine prison. (See Paul's second letter to Timothy.)

Paul is arrested in Rome.

brethren who came reported or spoken any evil of you. 22 But we desire to hear from you what you think; for concerning this sect, we know that it is spoken against everywhere."

23 So when they had appointed him a day, many came to him at *his* lodging, to whom he explained and solemnly testified of the kingdom of God, persuading them concerning Jesus from both the Law of Moses and the Prophets, from morning till evening. 24 And some were persuaded by the things which were spoken, and some disbelieved. 25 So when they did not agree among themselves, they departed after Paul had said one word: "The Holy Spirit spoke rightly through Isaiah the prophet to our fathers, 26 saying,

'Go to this people and say:
"Hearing you will hear, and shall
    not understand;

And seeing you will see, and not
    perceive;
27 For the hearts of this people
    have grown dull.
Their ears are hard of hearing,
And their eyes they have closed,
Lest they should see with *their*
    eyes and hear with *their* ears,
Lest they should understand
    with *their* hearts and turn,
So that I should heal them." '

28 "Therefore let it be known to you that the salvation of God has been sent to the Gentiles, and they will hear it!" 29 And when he had said these words, the Jews departed and had a great dispute among themselves.

30 Then Paul dwelt two whole years in his own rented house, and received all who came to him, 31 preaching the kingdom of God and teaching the things which concern the Lord Jesus Christ with all confidence, no one forbidding him.

The Book of
ROMANS

I, Paul, don't deserve to be an apostle for Jesus. I tried to destroy His people who make up the church. I even gave permission to the mob that stoned poor Stephen to death (see Acts 7), but I am comforted to know that young man is in heaven today.

I realize now that by doing those evil things, I was really doing them to Jesus Himself. One day the risen Savior met me on a lonely road to Damascus (pronounced *duh-MASK-us*), where I was going to punish the Christians. Jesus was as bright as the sun shining in my eyes, and I was blinded. Soon after that I, too, became a Christian, and I have served Him ever since. I wrote most of the letters to people in the New Testament.

Now I know Jesus is the only One who can save you and me. He died on the Cross to pay for our sins.

Paul writes a letter to the Christians at Rome

PAUL, a bondservant of Jesus Christ, called *to be* an **apostle,** separated to the gospel of God 2 which He promised before through His prophets in the Holy Scriptures, 3 concerning His Son Jesus Christ our Lord, who was born of the seed of David according to the flesh, 4 *and* declared *to be* the Son of God with power according to the Spirit of holiness, by the resurrection from the dead. 5 Through Him we have received grace and apostleship for obedience to the faith among all nations for His name, 6 among whom you also are the called of Jesus Christ;

7 To all who are in Rome, beloved of God, called *to be* **saints:**

Grace to you and peace from God our Father and the Lord Jesus Christ.

8 First, I thank my God through Jesus Christ for you all, that your faith is spoken of throughout the whole world. 9 For God is my witness, whom I serve with my spirit in the gospel of His Son, that without ceasing I make mention of you always in my prayers, 10 making request if, by some means,

What Is the Gospel?

The word *gospel* means "good news." The Good News is that Jesus has come and died to pay for our sins just as God promised the people in Old Testament times. The *great* news is that Jesus rose from the dead and will save from sin all who ask Him.

✒ WORDFINDER

1:1 Apostle Pronounced *uh-POSS-ul.* One of the men Jesus sent to preach the Good News of salvation. The word comes from a Greek word meaning "sent."

1:7 Saints People who are set apart by God. They believe in Jesus for salvation. The word comes from a Greek word meaning "holy" or "set apart."

The Roman Forum, a big plaza in the center of Rome.

now at last I may find a way in the will of God to come to you. ¹¹ For I long to see you, that I may impart to you some spiritual gift, so that you may be established— ¹² that is, that I may be encouraged together with you by the mutual faith both of you and me.

¹³ Now I do not want you to be unaware, brethren, that I often planned to come to you (but was hindered until now), that I might have some fruit among you also, just as among the other Gentiles. ¹⁴ I am a debtor both to Greeks and to barbarians, both to wise and to unwise. ¹⁵ So, as much as is in me, *I am* ready to preach the gospel to you who are in Rome also.

¹⁶ For I am not ashamed of the **gospel** of Christ, for it is the power of God to salvation for everyone who believes, for the Jew first and also for the Greek.

🌐 WORDFINDER

1:16 Gospel Means "good news." The word is taken from the early English word *godspel.* In the New Testament, it is the good news about Jesus Christ.

⛏ DIGGING IN

1:16 Paul and the Gospel By now you know that the word *gospel* means "good news." The Good News from God is that His Son Jesus has died in your place so you can also be a son or daughter of God.

Paul had been a very religious man. He had been a Pharisee—a Jewish scholar who tried to please God by keeping the Jewish law. But one day Jesus appeared to Paul. Then he realized that his sins were too great to fight all by himself. He needed Jesus to change him so he would love to please God in all things.

Jesus changed Paul and gave him a new nature. Then Paul loved God and others in a way he never could before. Now he wanted to share that Good News with everybody.

Has Jesus come into your life? He wants to make you a new person who loves God and others as Paul did.

17 For in it the righteousness of God is revealed from faith to faith; as it is written, "The just shall live by faith."

18 For the wrath of God is revealed from heaven against all ungodliness and unrighteousness of men, who suppress the truth in unrighteousness, 19 because what may be known of God is manifest in them, for God has shown *it* to them. 20 For since the creation of the world His invisible *attributes* are clearly seen, being understood by the things that are made, *even* His eternal power and Godhead, so that they are without excuse, 21 because, although they knew God, they did not glorify *Him* as God, nor were thankful, but became futile in their thoughts, and their foolish hearts were darkened. 22 Professing to be wise, they became fools, 23 and changed the glory of the incorruptible God into an image made like corruptible man—and birds and four-footed animals and creeping things.

24 Therefore God also gave them up to uncleanness, in the lusts of their hearts, to dishonor their bodies among themselves, 25 who exchanged the truth of God for the lie, and worshiped and served the creature rather than the Creator, who is blessed forever. Amen.

26 For this reason God gave them up to vile passions. For even their women exchanged the natural use for what is against nature. 27 Likewise also the men, leaving the natural use of the woman, burned in their lust for one another, men with men committing what is shameful, and receiving in themselves the penalty of their error which was due.

28 And even as they did not like to retain God in *their* knowledge, God gave them over to a debased mind, to do those things which are not fitting; 29 being filled with all unrighteousness, sexual immorality, wickedness, covetousness, maliciousness; full of envy, murder, strife, deceit, evil-mindedness; *they are* whisperers, 30 backbiters, haters of God, violent, proud, boasters, inventors of evil things, disobedient to parents, 31 undiscerning, untrustworthy, unloving, unforgiving, unmerciful; 32 who, knowing the righteous judgment of God, that those who practice such things are deserving of death, not

⚒ DIGGING IN

1:17 Living by Faith How can you live by faith? Right now, when you're young and strong, you might think you're living just fine without faith. Sooner or later, though, you will need more help than anybody can give you, and you won't be able to help yourself either. What will you do when you're sick or hurt or in bad trouble?

The Bible says you have a Friend who sticks closer than a brother (Proverbs 18:24). That Friend is Jesus. But a friend, even Jesus, can only help you if you trust Him.

The wise thing is to start trusting Jesus right now. Then you can live every day and know that nothing can really harm you. Even if you do get sick or hurt, Jesus will be right there to make you strong. You will be able to be happy because you live by faith in a Friend who sticks closer than a brother.

1:20 You Can See God's Work Everywhere Some people *look* but they don't *see*. They don't see the grand plan of God in the world around them. In fact, they never even think about it! They enjoy all the good things of the world—food, shelter, clothing, and even luxuries. But they're never thankful because they have never seen the hand of God providing all these things.

Life becomes exciting when you begin to realize that the world and everything in it didn't just *happen*. Nature has no mind of its own. The weather can't think. The seasons of the year don't plan their own changes. Life didn't happen all by itself. In everything you see around you, God is saying to you, "As you enjoy all these good things, remember that your greatest joy comes from knowing Me." Then nature and the world will come to life in a new way for you. Your life will be more exciting than you could ever dream.

only do the same but also approve of those who practice them.

True believers trust God

2 Therefore you are inexcusable, O man, whoever you are who judge, for in whatever you judge another you condemn yourself; for you who judge practice the same things. 2 But we know that the judgment of God is according to truth against those who practice such things. 3 And do you think this, O man, you who judge those practicing such things, and doing the same, that you will escape the judgment of God? 4 Or do you despise the riches of His goodness, forbearance, and longsuffering, not knowing that the goodness of God leads you to **repentance**? 5 But in accordance with your hardness and your impenitent heart you are treasuring up for yourself wrath in the day of wrath and revelation of the righteous judgment of God, 6 who "will render to each one according to his deeds": 7 eternal life to those who by patient continuance in doing good seek for glory, honor, and **immortality;** 8 but to those who are self-seeking and do not obey the truth, but obey unrighteousness—indignation and wrath, 9 tribulation and anguish, on every soul of man who does evil, of the Jew first and also of the Greek; 10 but glory, honor, and peace to everyone who works what is good, to the Jew first and also to the Greek. 11 For there is no partiality with God.

12 For as many as have sinned without law will also perish without law, and as many as have sinned in the law will be judged by the law 13 (for not the hearers of the law are just in the sight of God, but the doers of the law will be justified; 14 for when Gentiles, who do not have the law, by nature do the things in the law, these, although not having the law, are a law to themselves, 15 who show the work of the law written in their hearts, their conscience also bearing witness, and between themselves their thoughts accusing or else excusing them) 16 in the day when God will judge the secrets of men by Jesus Christ, according to my gospel.

17 Indeed you are called a Jew, and rest on the law, and make your boast in God, 18 and know His will, and approve the things that are excellent, being instructed out of the law, 19 and are confident that you yourself are a guide to the blind, a light to those who are in darkness, 20 an instructor of the foolish, a teacher of babes, having the form of knowledge and truth in the law. 21 You, therefore, who teach another, do you not teach yourself? You who preach that a man should not steal, do you steal? 22 You who say, "Do not commit adultery," do you commit adultery? You who abhor idols, do you rob temples? 23 You who make your boast in the law, do you dishonor God through breaking the law? 24 For "the name of God is blasphemed among the Gentiles because of you," as it is written.

25 For circumcision is indeed profitable if you keep the law; but if you are a breaker of the law, your circumcision has become uncircumcision. 26 Therefore, if an uncircumcised man keeps the righteous requirements of the law, will not his uncircumcision be counted as circumcision? 27 And will not the physically uncircumcised, if he fulfills the law, judge you who, even with your written code and circumcision, are a transgressor of the law? 28 For he is not a Jew who is one

---

🔶 **WORDFINDER** _____

2:4 Repentance Pronounced re-PEN-tunce. Turning away from sin to obey God. You repent when you leave your sins to receive Christ as your Savior and Master of your life.

2:7 Immortality Pronounce im-or-TAL-ih-tee. Life that never ends. Paul uses it to describe our everlasting life with God.

outwardly, nor *is* circumcision that which *is* outward in the flesh; 29 but *he is* a Jew who *is one* inwardly; and circumcision *is that* of the heart, in the Spirit, not in the letter; whose praise *is* not from men but from God.

Everyone has sinned and deserves punishment

3 What advantage then has the Jew, or what *is* the profit of circumcision? 2 Much in every way! Chiefly because to them *were* committed the oracles of God. 3 For what if some did not believe? Will their unbelief make the faithfulness of God without effect? 4 Certainly not! Indeed, let God be true but every man a liar. As it is written:

> "That You may be justified in Your words,
> And may overcome when You are judged."

5 But if our unrighteousness demonstrates the righteousness of God, what shall we say? *Is* God unjust who inflicts wrath? (I speak as a man.) 6 Certainly not! For then how will God judge the world? 7 For if the truth of God has increased through my lie to His glory, why am I also still judged as a sinner? 8 And *why* not *say,* "Let us do evil that good may come"?—as we are slanderously reported and as some affirm that we say. Their condemnation is just.

9 What then? Are *we* better *than*

they? Not at all. For we have previously charged both Jews and Greeks that they are all under sin.

10 As it is written:

> "There is none righteous, no, not one;
>
> 11 There is none who understands;
> There is none who seeks after God.
> 12 They have all turned aside;
> They have together become unprofitable;
> There is none who does good, no, not one."
> 13 "Their throat *is* an open tomb;
> With their tongues they have practiced deceit";
> "The poison of asps *is* under their lips";
> 14 "Whose mouth *is* full of cursing and bitterness."
> 15 "Their feet *are* swift to shed blood;
> 16 Destruction and misery *are* in their ways;
> 17 And the way of peace they have not known."
> 18 "There is no fear of God before their eyes."

19 Now we know that whatever the law says, it says to those who are under the law, that every mouth may be stopped, and all the world may become guilty before God. 20 Therefore by the deeds of the law no flesh will be justified in His sight, for by the law *is* the knowledge of sin.

DIGGING IN

3:2 God Gave His Words to the Jews
The nation God first showed Himself to was a nation of slaves—the Jews. They were prisoners in Egypt when God sent Moses to lead them out of slavery. How did God do this? With military power? No, God didn't need an army to set the Jews free. He did it by His powerful words. He sent Moses to the king of Egypt and said, "Let my people go!" The king tried to resist God's Word, but in the end, God conquered him. Then the people simply

walked out of Egypt.

After that, God used the Jews to bring salvation to the rest of us. Yes, the ancient Jews later became a disobedient people. But in spite of that, God sent His heavenly Son to be born of a Jewish mother. Jesus was a Jew, the Son of a slave nation, yet He spoke the words and did the work that makes us free from sin. Because of Jesus, we have God's words today.

21 But now the righteousness of God apart from the law is revealed, being witnessed by the Law and the Prophets, 22 even the righteousness of God, through faith in Jesus Christ, to all and on all who believe. For there is no difference; 23 for all have sinned and fall short of the glory of God, 24 being justified freely by His grace through the redemption that is in Christ Jesus, 25 whom God set forth *as* a **propitiation** by His blood, through faith, to demonstrate His righteousness, because in His forbearance God had passed over the sins that *were* previously committed, 26 to demonstrate at the present time His righteousness, that He might be just and the justifier of the one who has faith in Jesus.

27 Where *is* boasting then? It is excluded. By what law? Of works? No,

but by the law of faith. 28 Therefore we conclude that a man is **justified** by faith apart from the deeds of the law. 29 Or *is He* the God of the Jews only? *Is He* not also the God of the Gentiles? Yes, of the Gentiles also, 30 since *there* is one God who will justify the circumcised by faith and the uncircumcised through faith. 31 Do we then make void the law through faith? Certainly not! On the contrary, we establish the law.

God says Abraham was "not guilty"

4 What then shall we say that Abraham our father has found according to the flesh? 2 For if Abraham was justified by works, he has *something* to boast about, but not before God. 3 For what does the Scripture say?

🌐 WORDFINDER

3:25 Propitiation Pronounced *pro-pish-ee-AY-shun*. The work of Jesus on the Cross. By dying for us, Jesus paid the penalty we owed God for breaking His laws.

3:28 Justified (pronounced *JUSS-tih-fyed*). To be considered righteous by God because you trust in Jesus Christ as your Savior.

⛏ DIGGING IN

3:23 Everyone Has Sinned Let's stop making excuses. Sin isn't just the nasty things we do to people. Sin is what lives deep inside us. That is the sin that constantly is saying "No!" to God. Lying, stealing, bad language, hate, and anger all come from that deep-inside sin. And the more we say "No" to God, the deeper we get into doing things that hurt ourselves and others.

Wouldn't you like to start saying "Yes" to God? What a big difference it would make! Then you would also enjoy saying "Yes" to your parents, and you would enjoy being kind to others. Life is really beautiful when God says, "I am taking away your sinful heart and giving you a new heart that loves Me." That's life worth living!

3:28 Good Deeds Can't Save You In verse 23 you saw that sin is saying "No" to God deep inside yourself. Some people think they can cover up that big NO by doing a good deed now and then. But,

deep inside, those people are still saying "No" to God. The good deeds they do are not to please God, but to make themselves look good to other people. Then they can brag to the world, "See what a good guy I am—I dropped a quarter in the beggar's cup!"

Nothing you can do will ever please God until you gratefully accept HIS GOOD DEED FOR YOU—giving His Son to die on the Cross because of your sin of saying "No" to God. When you say, "Yes, I thank You for Jesus," and mean it, then Jesus comes to live within you. Now your good deeds can please God because you do everything to thank God for the gift of His Son.

4:3 How Abraham Became a Son of God Abraham lived in the Middle East country we call Iran today. In Abraham's day, it was called "Chaldea" (pronounced *kal-DEE-uh*).

Abraham didn't know God as we do. But one day God spoke to him and said,

The Appian Way, the road on which Paul traveled to Rome.

"Abraham believed God, and it was accounted to him for righteousness."
4 Now to him who works, the wages are not counted as grace but as debt.

5 But to him who does not work but believes on Him who justifies the ungodly, his faith is accounted for righteousness, 6 just as David also describes the blessedness of the man to whom God imputes righteousness apart from works:

7 "Blessed *are those* whose lawless
    deeds are forgiven,
And whose sins are covered;
8 Blessed *is the* man to whom the
    LORD shall not **impute** sin."

9 *Does* this blessedness then *come* upon the circumcised *only*, or upon the uncircumcised also? For we say that faith was accounted to Abraham for righteousness. 10 How then was it ac-

WORDFINDER

4:8 Impute Pronounced *im-PYOOT*. To consider a person guilty or not guilty. God *imputes* the goodness of Christ to people who believe the gospel. He no longer *imputes* sin to them (no longer considers them guilty).

DIGGING IN

"Get out of this country. I'm going to show you another land where your descendants will live forever." God also told Abraham that the whole world would be blessed because of him.

Just think of it! Abraham might have just ignored what God told him, but he didn't. Abraham left Chaldea and lived in Palestine. The Jews came from Abraham,

and Jesus came from the Jews two thousand years later. Now almost the whole world has heard about Jesus the Savior. So God kept His promise to Abraham.

That's how Abraham became a great son of God. How? When Abraham believed God, he also did what God told him. That's how you, too, can become a son or daughter of God.

counted? While he was circumcised, or uncircumcised? Not while circumcised, but while uncircumcised. 11 And he received the sign of circumcision, a seal of the righteousness of the faith which *he had while still* uncircumcised, that he might be the father of all those who believe, though they are uncircumcised, that righteousness might be imputed to them also, 12 and the father of circumcision to those who not only *are* of the circumcision, but who also walk in the steps of the faith which our father Abraham *had while still* uncircumcised.

13 For the promise that he would be the heir of the world *was* not to Abraham or to his seed through the law, but through the righteousness of faith. 14 For if those who are of the law *are* heirs, faith is made void and the promise made of no effect, 15 because the law brings about wrath; for where there is no law *there is* no transgression.

16 Therefore *it is* of faith that *it might be* according to grace, so that the promise might be sure to all the seed, not only to those who are of the law, but also to those who are of the faith of Abraham, who is the father of us all 17 (as it is written, "I have made you a father of many nations") in the presence of Him whom he believed—God, who gives life to the dead and calls those things which do not exist as though they did; 18 who, contrary to hope, in hope believed, so that he became the father of many nations, according to what was spoken, "So shall your descendants be." 19 And not being weak in faith, he did not consider his own body, already dead (since he was about a hundred years old), and the deadness of Sarah's womb. 20 He did not waver at the promise of God through unbelief, but was strengthened in faith, giving glory to God, 21 and being fully convinced that what He had promised He was also able to perform. 22 And therefore "it was accounted to him for righteousness."

23 Now it was not written for his sake alone that it was imputed to him, 24 but also for us. It shall be imputed to us who believe in Him who raised up Jesus our Lord from the dead, 25 who was delivered up because of our offenses, and was raised because of our justification.

Christ brought forgiveness for sin

5 Therefore, having been **justified** by faith, we have peace with God through our Lord Jesus Christ, 2 through whom also we have access by faith into this

---

⊕ WORDFINDER

5:1 Justified Pronounced *JUSS-tih-fyed.* To be considered righteous by God because you trust in Jesus Christ as your Savior from sin.

⚒ DIGGING IN

5:1 Trusting Jesus Brings Peace As you get a little older you may hear more about being "justified by faith." This means that God accepts you as His son or daughter. He does this when you confess your sins and trust that Jesus has taken them away by dying on the Cross. When you're trusting Jesus to save you from your sins, you also receive PEACE from God.

Right now you may be having a lot of trouble. Maybe you've lost a friend. Perhaps someone special to you has died.

Possibly you've done something really wrong. We do sometimes, no matter how hard we try to be good. What are you going to do to fix it?

Whatever happens, God can give you peace in the world. First of all, get alone with Jesus in prayer. Tell Him all that troubles you. Jesus will show you how to make everything right, and you will have God's peace. Whether you are sick or hurt or even have to go to prison, God will be right there with you always.

grace in which we stand, and rejoice in hope of the glory of God. 3 And not only *that,* but we also glory in tribulations, knowing that tribulation produces perseverance; 4 and perseverance, character; and character, hope. 5 Now hope does not disappoint, because the love of God has been poured out in our hearts by the Holy Spirit who was given to us.

6 For when we were still without strength, in due time **Christ** died for the ungodly. 7 For scarcely for a righteous man will one die; yet perhaps for a good man someone would even dare to die. 8 But God demonstrates His own love toward us, in that while we were still sinners, Christ died for us. 9 Much more then, having now been justified by His blood, we shall be saved from wrath through Him. 10 For if when we were enemies we were reconciled to God through the death of His Son, much more, having been reconciled, we shall be saved by His life. 11 And not only *that,* but we also rejoice in God through our Lord Jesus Christ, through whom we have now received the **reconciliation.**

12 Therefore, just as through one man sin entered the world, and death through sin, and thus death spread to all men, because all sinned— 13 (For until the law sin was in the world, but sin is not imputed when there is no law. 14 Nevertheless death reigned from Adam to Moses, even over those who had not sinned according to the likeness of the transgression of Adam, who is a type of Him who was to come. 15 But the free gift *is* not like the offense. For if by the one man's offense many died, much more the grace of God and the gift by the grace of the one Man, Jesus Christ, abounded to many. 16 And the gift *is* not like *that which came* through the one who sinned. For the judgment *which came* from one *offense resulted* in condemnation, but the free gift *which came* from many offenses *resulted* in justification. 17 For if by the one man's offense death reigned through the one, much more those who receive abundance of grace and of the gift of righteousness will reign in life through the One, Jesus Christ.)

18 Therefore, as through one man's offense *judgment* came to all men, resulting in condemnation, even so through one Man's righteous act *the free gift came* to all men, resulting in justification of life. 19 For as by one man's disobedience many were made

WORDFINDER

5:6 Christ   The divine title of the Man Jesus. The word means "the Anointed" (by the Holy Spirit). *Christos* is a Greek word translated from the Hebrew *Messiah.*

5:11 Reconciliation   The state of being at peace with someone. God is at peace with us because Christ died for our sins. So now we should be at peace with God.

DIGGING IN

5:8 Jesus Died for Sinful People   When people break the law, we put them in prison where we hope they'll learn better. And a lot of times, we hear people say, "I just wish they would never let that man out of prison." So people often hate criminals. To us, that could seem to make sense.

It doesn't make sense to God, though. Are you ready to hear this? GOD LOVES SINNERS! But how could a perfect, holy, and loving God love hateful sinners. The answer is—just BECAUSE He is perfect, holy, and loving! It's our nature to hate, but it's God's nature to love. Because God IS love, He doesn't love just the good and lovely. He also loves the hateful and the unlovely. That includes you and me. We were the sinners Jesus came to save. And we'll spend forever and ever trying to understand how God could love us so much that Jesus bled and died for us on the Cross.

sinners, so also by one Man's obedience many will be made righteous.

20 Moreover the law entered that the offense might abound. But where sin abounded, grace abounded much more, 21 so that as sin reigned in death, even so grace might reign through righteousness to eternal life through Jesus Christ our Lord.

Sin makes us die, but Christ gives us life

6 What shall we say then? Shall we continue in sin that grace may abound? 2 Certainly not! How shall we who died to sin live any longer in it? 3 Or do you not know that as many of us as were baptized into Christ Jesus were baptized into His death? 4 Therefore we were buried with Him through baptism into death, that just as Christ was raised from the dead by the glory of the Father, even so we also should walk in newness of life.

5 For if we have been united together in the likeness of His death, certainly we also shall be in the likeness of His resurrection, 6 knowing this, that our old man was crucified with Him, that the body of sin might be done away with, that we should no longer be slaves of sin. 7 For he who has died has been freed from sin. 8 Now if we died with Christ, we believe that we shall also live with Him, 9 knowing that Christ, having been raised from the dead, dies no more. Death no longer has dominion over Him. 10 For the death that He died, He died to sin once for all; but the life that He lives, He

lives to God. 11 Likewise you also, reckon yourselves to be dead indeed to sin, but alive to God in Christ Jesus our Lord.

12 Therefore do not let sin reign in your **mortal** body, that you should obey it in its lusts. 13 And do not present your members as instruments of unrighteousness to sin, but present yourselves to God as being alive from the dead, and your members as instruments of righteousness to God. 14 For sin shall not have dominion over you, for you are not under law but under grace.

15 What then? Shall we sin because we are not under law but under grace? Certainly not! 16 Do you not know that to whom you present yourselves slaves to obey, you are that one's slaves whom you obey, whether of sin leading to death, or of obedience leading to righteousness? 17 But God be thanked that though you were slaves of sin, yet you obeyed from the heart that form of doctrine to which you were delivered. 18 And having been set free from sin, you became slaves of righteousness. 19 I speak in human terms because of the weakness of your flesh. For just as you presented your members as slaves of uncleanness, and of lawlessness leading to more lawlessness, so now present your members as slaves of righteousness for holiness.

20 For when you were slaves of sin, you were free in regard to righteousness. 21 What fruit did you have then in the things of which you are now ashamed? For the end of those things is death. 22 But now having been

set free from sin, and having become slaves of God, you have your fruit to holiness, and the end, everlasting life. 23 For the wages of sin is death, but the gift of God is **eternal life** in Christ Jesus our Lord.

God's law is like a mirror that shows us our sin

7 Or do you not know, brethren (for I speak to those who know the law), that the law has dominion over a man as long as he lives? 2 For the woman who has a husband is bound by the law to her husband as long as he lives. But if the husband dies, she is released from the law of her husband. 3 So then if, while her husband lives, she marries another man, she will be called an adulteress; but if her husband dies, she is free from that law, so that she is no adulteress, though she has married another man. 4 Therefore, my brethren, you also have become dead to the law through the body of Christ, that you may be married to another—to Him who was raised from the dead, that

we should bear fruit to God. 5 For when we were in the flesh, the sinful passions which were aroused by the law were at work in our members to bear fruit to death. 6 But now we have been delivered from the law, having died to what we were held by, so that we should serve in the newness of the Spirit and not in the oldness of the letter.

7 What shall we say then? Is the law sin? Certainly not! On the contrary, I would not have known sin except through the law. For I would not have known covetousness unless the law had said, "You shall not covet." 8 But sin, taking opportunity by the commandment, produced in me all manner of evil desire. For apart from the law sin was dead. 9 I was alive once without the law, but when the commandment came, sin revived and I died. 10 And the commandment, which was to bring life, I found to bring death. 11 For sin, taking occasion by the commandment, deceived me, and by it killed me. 12 Therefore the law is holy, and the commandment holy and just and good.

WORDFINDER

6:23 Eternal Life The endless life of God. God gives His eternal life to people who trust in Jesus as their Savior. God Himself comes to live in them.

DIGGING IN

we are free to destroy ourselves and others. That's why we have laws even in a free country—to protect us from destructive behavior.

But real freedom comes from being a willing slave of God. That means you will want to love only the things that God loves. That's perfect freedom because you no longer love things that hurt you. Now you love the things that help you and bless other people. A Christian is a free slave of God.

6:23 The Greatest Gift Everyone can think of something they want more than anything. What would you like? A million dollars? A new bike? A trip to Disneyworld?

God wants to give you a gift so great that you can't even imagine it. If you knew what that gift was, you would never trade it for anything. It's called ETERNAL LIFE!

We know that everybody's soul is going to live forever somewhere. For many people, that will mean everlasting misery because God won't be there. But listen! That isn't the same as "eternal life." Eternal life is a special kind of life that God has, and He can give that life to you. Eternal life means enjoying God's special kind of life forever and ever. That life can start right now for you. Just tell God you're sorry for your sins, and ask Him to give you His gift of eternal life.

13 Has then what is good become death to me? Certainly not! But sin, that it might appear sin, was producing death in me through what is good, so that sin through the commandment might become exceedingly sinful. 14 For we know that the law is spiritual, but I am carnal, sold under sin. 15 For what I am doing, I do not understand. For what I will to do, that I do not practice; but what I hate, that I do. 16 If, then, I do what I will not to do, I agree with the law that *it is* good. 17 But now, *it is* no longer I who do it, but sin that dwells in me. 18 For I know that in me (that is, in my flesh) nothing good dwells; for to will is present with me, but *how* to perform what is good I do not find. 19 For the good that I will *to do,* I do not do; but the evil I will not *to do,* that I practice. 20 Now if I do what I will not *to do,* it is no longer I who do it, but sin that dwells in me.

21 I find then a law, that evil is present with me, the one who wills to do

good. 22 For I delight in the law of God according to the inward man. 23 But I see another law in my members, warring against the law of my mind, and bringing me into captivity to the law of sin which is in my members. 24 O wretched man that I am! Who will deliver me from this body of death? 25 I thank God—through Jesus Christ our Lord!

So then, with the mind I myself serve the law of God, but with the flesh the law of sin.

Nothing can separate us from God's love

8 *There is* therefore now no condemnation to those who are in Christ Jesus, who do not walk according to the flesh, but according to the Spirit. 2 For the law of the Spirit of life in Christ Jesus has made me free from the law of sin and death. 3 For what the law could not do in that it was weak through the flesh, God *did* by sending His own Son

DIGGING IN

7:13 Why God's Law Makes Us Miserable You may have been at school or some public place when a fire alarm went off. And maybe you said, "Oh, there goes that alarm again! Why don't they leave us alone?" But having your peace disturbed is better than burning up in a fire. Without the alarm, you might not even know when there's danger.

God also gave us an alarm called His law—the Ten Commandments. Without that alarm, we would not even know we do things that finally destroy us. God didn't create us to do such things. Just like driving a car a hundred miles an hour on a crowded highway, we're heading for disaster when we break God's law. So it's good that God's law is upsetting. See the story of Adam and Eve in Genesis 3:7–13, and how their sin made them unhappy.

God gives us the law so we will feel bad about the sins that destroy us. Then we come and ask God to make us want the good things He loves.

8:2 God's Spirit Makes You Glad God's Spirit is most often called "the Holy Spirit," but He is also called "the Spirit of God," "the Spirit of Christ," and "the Spirit of Truth." All these are names for *God the Holy Spirit.* Remember, God is *one Being,* but He is also *three Persons.*

These three Persons are God the Father, God the Son, and God the Holy Spirit. The Father is the Person most active in Creation and in providing for us. Jesus the Son is the Person most active in saving us from our sins. The Holy Spirit is the Person most active in making the Father and the Son real in our lives. All three Persons of God work together.

In Romans 8, Paul says that the Spirit of God makes you glad by setting you free from sin and death. This gladness is also called "a fruit" of the Spirit. Other fruits, or results of the Spirit in your life, are love, joy, peace, gentleness, patience, kindness, goodness, faithfulness, and self-control (see Galatians 5:22–23).

in the likeness of sinful flesh, on account of sin: He condemned sin in the flesh, 4 that the righteous requirement of the law might be fulfilled in us who do not walk according to the flesh but according to the Spirit. 5 For those who live according to the flesh set their minds on the things of the flesh, but those *who live* according to the Spirit, the things of the Spirit. 6 For to be carnally minded *is* death, but to be spiritually minded *is* life and peace. 7 Because the carnal mind *is* enmity against God; for it is not subject to the law of God, nor indeed can be. 8 So then, those who are in the flesh cannot please God.

9 But you are not in the flesh but in the Spirit, if indeed the Spirit of God dwells in you. Now if anyone does not have the Spirit of Christ, he is not His. 10 And if Christ *is* in you, the body *is* dead because of sin, but the Spirit *is* life because of righteousness. 11 But if the Spirit of Him who raised Jesus from the dead dwells in you, He who raised Christ from the dead will also give life to your mortal bodies through His Spirit who dwells in you.

12 Therefore, brethren, we are debtors—not to the flesh, to live according to the flesh. 13 For if you live according to the flesh you will die; but if by the Spirit you put to death the deeds of the body, you will live. 14 For as many as are led by the Spirit of God, these are sons of God. 15 For you did not receive the spirit of bondage again to fear, but you received the Spirit of **adoption** by whom we cry out, **"Abba,** Father." 16 The Spirit Himself bears witness with our spirit that we are children of God, 17 and if children, then heirs—heirs of God and joint heirs with Christ, if indeed we suffer with *Him,* that we may also be glorified together.

18 For I consider that the sufferings of this present time are not worthy *to be compared* with the glory which shall be revealed in us. 19 For the earnest expectation of the creation eagerly waits for the revealing of the sons of God. 20 For the creation was subjected to futility, not willingly, but because of Him who subjected *it* in hope; 21 because the creation itself also will be delivered from the bondage of corruption into the glorious liberty of the children of God. 22 For we know that the whole creation groans and labors with birth pangs together until now. 23 Not only *that,* but we also who have the firstfruits of the Spirit, even we ourselves groan within ourselves, eagerly waiting for the adoption, the redemption of our body. 24 For we were saved in this hope, but hope that is seen is

---

🔍 WORDFINDER

8:15 Adoption Pronounced *uh-DOP-shun*. God's work of making us His sons and daughters. When we believe in Jesus for salvation, God sends His Spirit to live in us. The Spirit of God teaches us that we are God's children.

8:15 Abba A word for father from the ancient Aramaic language (pronounced *air-uh-MAY-ik*). The word is like our words *daddy* and *papa.*

⛏ DIGGING IN

8:16 Sons and Daughters of God When you believe in Jesus as your Savior, then the Holy Spirit of God Himself comes to live in you. As the Holy Spirit lives in you, He makes you know that you're God's very own child. This means that God has ADOPTED you. So the Bible also calls the Holy Spirit the "Spirit of Adoption," because He reminds us that God has taken us to be His own sons and daughters.

Remember, having the Holy Spirit is the same as having the Spirit of Jesus Himself living in you.

When you know you're an adopted son or daughter of God, then you know Jesus died for your sins. You also have a deep desire to be like Jesus in every way. Sons and daughters are like their parents. So sons and daughters of God are like God.

not hope; for why does one still hope for what he sees? 25 But if we hope for what we do not see, we eagerly wait for it with perseverance.

26 Likewise the Spirit also helps in our weaknesses. For we do not know what we should pray for as we ought, but the Spirit Himself makes intercession for us with groanings which cannot be uttered. 27 Now He who searches the hearts knows what the mind of the Spirit is, because He makes intercession for the saints according to the will of God.

28 And we know that all things work together for good to those who love God, to those who are the called according to His purpose. 29 For whom He foreknew, He also predestined to be conformed to the image of His Son, that He might be the firstborn among many brethren. 30 Moreover whom He predestined, these He also called; whom He called, these He also justified; and whom He justified, these He also glorified.

31 What then shall we say to these things? If God is for us, who can be against us? 32 He who did not spare His own Son, but delivered Him up for us all, how shall He not with Him also freely give us all things? 33 Who shall bring a charge against God's elect? It is God who justifies. 34 Who is he who condemns? It is Christ who died, and furthermore is also risen, who is even at the right hand of God, who also makes intercession for us. 35 Who shall separate us from the love of Christ? Shall tribulation, or distress, or persecution, or famine, or nakedness, or peril, or sword? 36 As it is written:

"For Your sake we are killed all
    day long;
We are accounted as sheep for
    the slaughter."

37 Yet in all these things we are more than conquerors through Him who loved us. 38 For I am persuaded that

WORDFINDER

8:29 Foreknew To know beforehand. Because God is all-knowing, He foreknows the people who will become believers. This also means that He loved them before they knew Him.

8:30 Predestined Pronounced pre-DESS-tend. All that God decided before time existed. Everything that ever happens has always been part of God's never-changing, forever plan.

8:30 Called The way God draws people to Himself. He calls them when they hear the gospel. By calling people, God gives them the desire to come to Him.

8:30 Justified Pronounced JUSS-tih-fyed. To be considered righteous by God because you trust in Jesus Christ as your Savior from sin.

8:30 Glorified Pronounced GLORY-fyed. When Jesus comes back to earth, He will give those who loved Him new bodies. They can never sin again.

DIGGING IN

8:37 You Win with Christ All around you are people who seem to be losing the battle of living in the world. Some are in prison, some are in terrible debt, some are unhappy where they live or where they work.

This didn't have to happen to them, and it doesn't have to happen to you. With Jesus, everybody wins! That doesn't mean life will always be smooth and easy. Sometimes life with Jesus can be hard,

but life with Jesus is always exciting—and you win in the end!

Sometimes you will make mistakes, and sometimes you will even sin. Jesus understands all that. The main question is, Do you love Him? Is Jesus your personal Friend? Then you can only win. Jesus said you may even lose your life because of Him, but then you win eternal life with Him. That's real winning!

neither death nor life, nor angels nor principalities nor powers, nor things present nor things to come, 39 nor height nor depth, nor any other created thing, shall be able to separate us from the love of God which is in Christ Jesus our Lord.

God has the right to do what He pleases

9 I tell the truth in Christ, I am not lying, my conscience also bearing me witness in the Holy Spirit, 2 that I have great sorrow and continual grief in my heart. 3 For I could wish that I myself were accursed from Christ for my brethren, my countrymen according to the flesh, 4 who are Israelites, to whom *pertain* the adoption, the glory, the covenants, the giving of the law, the service *of God,* and the promises; 5 of whom *are* the fathers and from whom, according to the flesh, Christ *came,* who is over all, *the* eternally blessed God. Amen.

6 But it is not that the word of God has taken no effect. For they *are* not all Israel who *are* of Israel, 7 nor *are* they all children because they are the seed of Abraham; but, "In Isaac your seed shall be called." 8 That is, those who *are* the children of the flesh, these *are* not the children of God; but the children of the promise are counted as the seed. 9 For this *is* the word of promise: "At this time I will come and Sarah shall have a son."

10 And not only *this,* but when Rebecca also had conceived by one man, *even* by our father Isaac 11 (for *the children* not yet being born, nor having done any good or evil, that the purpose of God according to election might stand, not of works but of Him who calls), 12 it was said to her, "The older shall serve the younger." 13 As it is written, "Jacob I have loved, but Esau I have hated."

14 What shall we say then? *Is there* unrighteousness with God? Certainly not! 15 For He says to Moses, "I will have mercy on whomever I will have

God is like a potter who shapes the clay into useful and beautiful vessels.

mercy, and I will have compassion on whomever I will have compassion." 16 So then *it is* not of him who wills, nor of him who runs, but of God who shows mercy. 17 For the Scripture says to the Pharaoh, "For this very purpose I have raised you up, that I may show My power in you, and that My name may be declared in all the earth." 18 Therefore He has mercy on whom He wills, and whom He wills He hardens.

19 You will say to me then, "Why does He still find fault? For who has resisted His will?" 20 But indeed, O man, who are you to reply against God? Will the thing formed say to him who formed *it,* "Why have you made me like this?" 21 Does not the potter have power over the clay, from the same lump to make one vessel for honor and another for dishonor?

22 *What* if God, wanting to show *His* wrath and to make His power known, endured with much longsuffering the vessels of wrath prepared for destruction, 23 and that He might make known the riches of His glory on the vessels of mercy, which He had prepared beforehand for glory, 24 *even* us whom

He called, not of the Jews only, but also of the Gentiles?

25 As He says also in Hosea:

"I will call them My people, who
    were not My people,
And her beloved, who was not
    beloved."

26 "And it shall come to pass in the
    place where it was said to
    them,
'You are not My people,'
There they shall be called sons
    of the living God."

27 Isaiah also cries out concerning Israel:

"Though the number of the
    children of Israel be as the
    sand of the sea,
The remnant will be saved.

28   For He will finish the work and
    cut it short in righteousness,
Because the LORD will make a
    short work upon the earth."

29 And as Isaiah said before:

"Unless the LORD of Sabaoth had
    left us a seed,
We would have become like
    Sodom,
And we would have been made
    like Gomorrah."

30 What shall we say then? That Gentiles, who did not pursue righteousness, have attained to righteousness, even the righteousness of faith; 31 but Israel, pursuing the law of righteousness, has not attained to the law of righteousness. 32 Why? Because they did not seek it by faith, but as it were, by the works of the law. For they stumbled at that stumbling stone. 33 As it is written:

"Behold, I lay in Zion a stumbling
    stone and rock of offense,
And whoever believes on Him
    will not be put to shame."

Everyone can ask to be saved

10 Brethren, my heart's desire and prayer to God for Israel is that they may be saved. 2 For I bear them witness that they have a zeal for God, but not according to knowledge. 3 For they being ignorant of God's righteousness, and seeking to establish their own righteousness, have not submitted to the righteousness of God. 4 For Christ is the end of the law for righteousness to everyone who believes.

5 For Moses writes about the righteousness which is of the law, "The man who does those things shall live by them." 6 But the righteousness of faith speaks in this way, "Do not say in your heart, 'Who will ascend into heaven?'" (that is, to bring Christ down from above) 7 or, "'Who will descend into the abyss?'" (that is, to bring Christ up from the dead). 8 But what does it say? "The word is near you, in your mouth and in your heart" (that is, the word of faith which we preach): 9 that if you confess with your

---

⛏ DIGGING IN

10:1 We Want Our Friends to Be Saved Paul the apostle was not just a great preacher. He was a man who cared about people. Because he cared so much, his greatest wish was for the salvation of his friends and others.

How much do you care about your friends? Do you share your time and your possessions with them? The greatest possession you can have is the gift of salvation from God. If it is, your greatest desire should be to share your salvation with others. God wants you to give away everything you know about Jesus.

What do you talk about when you meet your friends at school or on the street or in their homes? Ask God to help you find ways and times to tell them what Jesus means to you and what He can mean to them.

mouth the Lord Jesus and **believe** in your heart that God has raised Him from the dead, you will be saved. 10 For with the heart one believes unto righteousness, and with the mouth confession is made unto salvation. 11 For the Scripture says, "Whoever believes on Him will not be put to shame." 12 For there is no distinction between Jew and Greek, for the same Lord over all is rich to all who call upon Him. 13 For "whoever calls on the name of the LORD shall be saved."

14 How then shall they call on Him in whom they have not believed? And how shall they believe in Him of whom they have not heard? And how shall they hear without a preacher? 15 And how shall they preach unless they are sent? As it is written:

"How beautiful are the feet of
  those who preach the gospel
  of peace,
Who bring glad tidings of good
  things!"

16 But they have not all obeyed the gospel. For Isaiah says, "Lord, who has believed our report?" 17 So then faith *comes* by hearing, and hearing by the word of God.

18 But I say, have they not heard? Yes indeed:

"Their sound has gone out to all
  the earth,
And their words to the ends of
  the world."

19 But I say, did Israel not know? First Moses says:

"I will provoke you to jealousy by
  those who are not a nation,
I will move you to anger by a
  foolish nation."

20 But Isaiah is very bold and says:

"I was found by those who did
  not seek Me;
I was made manifest to those
  who did not ask for Me."

21 But to Israel he says:

"All day long I have stretched out
  My hands
To a disobedient and contrary
  people."

God's forgiveness is for all people

11 I say then, has God cast away His people? Certainly not! For I also

WORDFINDER

10:9 Believe To accept what God has said in the Bible and to trust Jesus to save you from your sins. To believe as a Christian is to receive Jesus Christ into your life.

DIGGING IN

11:1 God Remembers All His Promises Someone has joked, "How odd of God to choose the Jews!" Israel was a small nation unlike many others—such as Assyria, Persia, Greece, and Rome.

The Jews were not only an important people, they were also a rebellious people. They seemed to disobey nearly every time God told them to do something. Usually they made a good start, but they would soon forget God, and do their own thing.

Even so, God made some special promises to the Jews. God wanted to do

a great work of worldwide salvation. He chose the Jews to be the people who would bring that salvation to us. Jesus, the Jewish Messiah, would keep that promise.

God also promised Abraham, the father of the Jews, that Israel would become a great nation. Though they have suffered more than any other people, God is keeping that promise to Abraham. Today, after nearly two thousand years, the Jews are living again in the land God promised them. And that is a sure proof that God will keep all His promises to you, too.

am an Israelite, of the seed of Abraham, *of* the tribe of Benjamin. ²God has not cast away His people whom He foreknew. Or do you not know what the Scripture says of Elijah, how he pleads with God against Israel, saying, ³"LORD, they have killed Your prophets and torn down Your altars, and I alone am left, and they seek my life"? ⁴But what does the divine response say to him? "I have reserved for Myself seven thousand men who have not bowed the knee to Baal." ⁵Even so then, at this present time there is a remnant according to the election of grace. ⁶And if by grace, then *it is* no longer of works; otherwise grace is no longer grace. But if *it is* of works, it is no longer grace; otherwise work is no longer work.

⁷What then? Israel has not obtained what it seeks; but the elect have obtained it, and the rest were blinded. ⁸Just as it is written:

"God has given them a spirit of
      stupor,
Eyes that they should not *see*
And ears that they should not
      hear,
To this very day."

⁹And David says:

"Let their table become a snare
      and a trap,
A stumbling block and a
      recompense to them.

¹⁰Let their eyes be darkened, so
      that they do not *see*,
And bow down their back
      always."

¹¹I say then, have they stumbled that they should fall? Certainly not! But through their fall, to provoke them to jealousy, salvation *has come* to the Gentiles. ¹²Now if their fall *is* riches for the world, and their failure riches for the Gentiles, how much more their fullness!

¹³For I speak to you Gentiles; inasmuch as I am an **apostle** to the Gentiles, I magnify my ministry, ¹⁴if by any means I may provoke to jealousy *those who are* my flesh and save some of them. ¹⁵For if their being cast away *is* the reconciling of the world, what *will* their acceptance *be* but life from the dead?

¹⁶For if the firstfruit *is* holy, the lump *is* also *holy;* and if the root *is* holy, so *are* the branches. ¹⁷And if some of the branches were broken off, and you, being a wild olive tree, were grafted in among them, and with them became a partaker of the root and fatness of the olive tree, ¹⁸do not boast against the branches. But if you do boast, *remember that* you do not support the root, but the root supports you.

¹⁹You will say then, "Branches were broken off that I might be grafted in." ²⁰Well *said.* Because of unbelief they were broken off, and you stand by faith. Do not be haughty, but fear.

WORDFINDER

11:13 Apostle Pronounced *uh-POSS-ul.* One of the men Jesus sent to preach the Good News of salvation. The word comes from a Greek word meaning "sent."

DIGGING IN

11:20 Pride Is the Greatest Danger Pride was the first sin: Adam and Eve dreamed of being as great as God! You might say pride is being cocky: "I can do anything I want to do without help from God or anyone." Pride also makes you feel superior to other people.

But the first thing a Christian feels is,

"I am the worst of all sinners." The next thing a Christian feels is, "I can't do anything right without God helping me every minute of my life."

Some people feel they are better than other races of people. About the middle of the twentieth century, Adolph Hitler taught his nation that they were superior to

21 For if God did not spare the natural branches, He may not spare you either. 22 Therefore consider the goodness and severity of God: on those who fell, severity; but toward you, goodness, if you continue in *His* goodness. Otherwise you also will be cut off. 23 And they also, if they do not continue in unbelief, will be grafted in, for God is able to graft them in again. 24 For if you were cut out of the olive tree which is wild by nature, and were grafted contrary to nature into a cultivated olive tree, how much more will these, who *are* natural *branches*, be grafted into their own olive tree?

25 For I do not desire, brethren, that you should be ignorant of this mystery, lest you should be wise in your own opinion, that blindness in part has happened to Israel until the fullness of the Gentiles has come in. 26 And so all Israel will be saved, as it is written:

"The Deliverer will come out of
    Zion,
And He will turn away
    ungodliness from Jacob;
27 For this *is* My covenant with
    them,
When I take away their sins."

28 Concerning the gospel *they are* enemies for your sake, but concerning the election *they are* beloved for the sake of the fathers. 29 For the gifts and the calling of God *are* irrevocable. 30 For as you were once disobedient to God, yet have now obtained mercy through their disobedience, 31 even so these also have now been disobedient, that through the mercy shown you they also may obtain mercy. 32 For God has committed them all to disobedience, that He might have mercy on all.

33 Oh, the depth of the riches both of the wisdom and knowledge of God! How unsearchable *are* His judgments and His ways past finding out!

34 "For who has known the mind
        of the LORD?
    Or who has become His
        counselor?"
35 "Or who has first given to Him
    And it shall be repaid to him?"

36 For of Him and through Him and to Him *are* all things, to whom *be* glory forever. Amen.

Let God change your life

12 I beseech you therefore, brethren, by the mercies of God, that you present your bodies a living **sacrifice, holy,** acceptable to God, *which is* your

---

✒ WORDFINDER

12:1 Sacrifice Pronounced *SACK-rih-fyce.* An offering to God. In the Old Testament, the people sacrificed the blood of animals for sin. In the New Testament, Christ is our only sacrifice for sin.

12:1 Holy An adjective meaning "separate," but includes the idea of moral purity and being like God.

⚒ DIGGING IN

the Jews, so millions of Jews were killed.

Jesus was a Servant of mankind. To the outside world, this is how a Christian should look—like someone who wants to serve others. People will see Jesus if they can see Him in your actions.

12:1 Give Yourself to God If you wanted to give God a present, what do you think He would like? Some of your money? Some of your talents? Some of your time? God can use all these things, but He only wants them on one condition—these gifts must come with the gift of your whole self.

God is looking for your undivided loyalty. That kind of giving yourself is the simplest way after all. Then you don't have to worry about how much of you is reasonable service. 2 And do not be conformed to this world, but be transformed by the renewing of your mind, that you may prove what *is* that good and acceptable and perfect will of God.

3 For I say, through the grace given to me, to everyone who is among you, not to think *of himself* more highly than he ought to think, but to think soberly, as God has dealt to each one a measure of faith. 4 For as we have many members in one body, but all the members do not have the same function, 5 so we, *being* many, are one body in Christ, and individually members of one another. 6 Having then gifts differing according to the grace that is given to us, *let us use them:* if prophecy, *let us prophesy* in proportion to our faith; 7 or ministry, *let us use it* in *our* ministering; he who teaches, in teaching; 8 he who exhorts, in exhortation; he who gives, with liberality; he who leads, with diligence; he who shows mercy, with cheerfulness.

9 *Let* love *be* without hypocrisy. Abhor what is evil. Cling to what is good. 10 *Be* kindly affectionate to one another with brotherly love, in honor giving preference to one another; 11 not lagging in diligence, fervent in spirit, serving the Lord; 12 rejoicing in hope, patient in tribulation, continuing steadfastly in prayer; 13 distributing to the needs of the saints, given to hospitality.

14 Bless those who persecute you; bless and do not curse. 15 Rejoice with those who rejoice, and weep with those who weep. 16 Be of the same mind toward one another. Do not set your mind on high things, but associate with the humble. Do not be wise in your own opinion.

17 Repay no one evil for evil. Have regard for good things in the sight of all men. 18 If it is possible, as much as depends on you, live peaceably with all men. 19 Beloved, do not avenge yourselves, but *rather* give place to wrath; for it is written, "Vengeance *is* Mine, I will repay," says the Lord. 20 Therefore

> "If your enemy is hungry, feed him;
> If he is thirsty, give him a drink;
> For in so doing you will heap coals of fire on his head."

21 Do not be overcome by evil, but overcome evil with good.

Obey your rulers

13 Let every soul be subject to the governing authorities. For there is no

---

⚒ DIGGING IN

being given to God, and how much you're keeping. Just give it all! Then, wherever you are, all your hours and days will be spent doing the things God enjoys seeing you do. Jesus DIED for you. Will you LIVE for Him?

12:18 Get Along with People If you're a Christian, you will often find yourself disagreeing with a lot of opinions you hear. And sometimes you *should* disagree! But that doesn't mean you should quarrel with people—even people you know are wrong.

God knows all about the evil and false opinions in the world. When you have the chance, you may try to help people who are mistaken. But very often you will drive people farther away from Jesus by arguing with them. Instead of being their friend, you become their enemy.

So, as much as possible, get along with people. After all, your best argument is a cheerful attitude and a kind deed. Then people will be less afraid to talk to you about Jesus. But remember, you can't please everybody. The Devil will see to that.

13:1 Obey Your Government That could be hard advice. Christians have always tried to obey the laws of their country—and they should! But sometimes their country passes laws Christians can't obey. An example is when the Romans made laws demanding that everybody authority except from God, and the authorities that exist are appointed by God. 2 Therefore whoever resists the authority resists the ordinance of God, and those who resist will bring judgment on themselves. 3 For rulers are not a terror to good works, but to evil. Do you want to be unafraid of the authority? Do what is good, and you will have praise from the same. 4 For he is God's minister to you for good. But if you do evil, be afraid; for he does not bear the sword in vain; for he is God's minister, an avenger to execute wrath on him who practices evil. 5 Therefore you must be subject, not only because of wrath but also for conscience' sake. 6 For because of this you also pay taxes, for they are God's ministers attending continually to this very thing. 7 Render therefore to all their due: taxes to whom taxes are due, customs to whom customs, fear to whom fear, honor to whom honor.

8 Owe no one anything except to love one another, for he who loves another has fulfilled the law. 9 For the commandments, "You shall not commit adultery," "You shall not murder," "You shall not steal," "You shall not bear false witness," "You shall not covet," and if there is any other commandment, are all summed up in this saying, namely, "You shall love your neighbor as yourself." 10 Love does no harm to a neighbor; therefore love is the fulfillment of the law.

11 And do this, knowing the time, that now it is high time to awake out of sleep; for now our salvation is nearer than when we first believed. 12 The night is far spent, the day is at hand. Therefore let us cast off the works of darkness, and let us put on the armor of light. 13 Let us walk properly, as in the day, not in revelry and drunkenness, not in lewdness and lust, not in strife and envy. 14 But put on the Lord Jesus Christ, and make no provision for the flesh, to fulfill its lusts.

Treat other Christians with respect

14 Receive one who is weak in the faith, but not to disputes over doubtful things. 2 For one believes he may eat all things, but he who is weak eats only vegetables. 3 Let not him who eats despise him who does not eat, and let not him who does not eat judge him who eats; for God has received him. 4 Who are you to judge another's servant? To his own master he stands or falls. Indeed, he will be made to stand, for God is able to make him stand.

5 One person esteems one day above another; another esteems every

---

⚒ DIGGING IN

must worship the emperor. Many Christians died horrible deaths because they refused to worship that man. A Christian should never obey a law that forces him or her to disobey God.

But, most often, you should seek to be a model citizen by obeying your country's laws. Our own nation grew up because people who cared about God made laws that honored God and were good for people. In time to come, Christians can show by their happy lives that a nation is happiest when it is a nation under God.

13:8 What Really Pleases God? Some people think that if you go around with a long face or pray a lot or go to church, you're pleasing God.

Christians love to go to church and to pray, but if they are miserable doing those things, they aren't pleasing God. "The Lord loves a cheerful giver"—that includes the time you give to praying and going to church.

What really counts with God is LOVE. That means CARING ABOUT OTHERS. If we aren't loving people, we're probably only wasting God's time by going to church. At church we hear God's Word. But God's Word should change our lives so that we bring some sunshine into the lives of others. "He who loves another has fulfilled the law." That's what pleases God.

day *alike.* Let each be fully convinced in his own mind. 6 He who observes the day, observes *it* to the Lord; and he who does not observe the day, to the Lord he does not observe *it.* He who eats, eats to the Lord, for he gives God thanks; and he who does not eat, to the Lord he does not eat, and gives God thanks. 7 For none of us lives to himself, and no one dies to himself. 8 For if we live, we live to the Lord; and if we die, we die to the Lord. Therefore, whether we live or die, we are the Lord's. 9 For to this end Christ died and rose and lived again, that He might be Lord of both the dead and the living. 10 But why do you judge your brother? Or why do you show contempt for your brother? For we shall all stand before the judgment seat of Christ. 11 For it is written:

"As I live, says the LORD,
   Every knee shall bow to Me,
   And every tongue shall confess
      to God."

12 So then each of us shall give account of himself to God. 13 Therefore let us not judge one another anymore, but rather resolve this, not to put a stumbling block or a cause to fall in *our* brother's way.

14 I know and am convinced by the Lord Jesus that *there is* nothing unclean of itself; but to him who considers anything to be unclean, to him *it is* unclean. 15 Yet if your brother is grieved because of *your* food, you are no longer walking in love. Do not destroy with your food the one for whom Christ died. 16 Therefore do not let your good be spoken of as evil; 17 for the kingdom of God is not eating and drinking, but righteousness and peace and joy in the Holy Spirit. 18 For he who serves Christ in these things *is* acceptable to God and approved by men.

19 Therefore let us pursue the things *which make* for peace and the things by which one may edify another. 20 Do not destroy the work of God for the sake of food. All things indeed *are* pure, but *it is* evil for the man who eats with offense. 21 *It is* good neither to eat meat nor drink wine nor *do anything* by which your brother stumbles or is offended or is made weak. 22 Do you have faith? Have *it* to yourself before God. Happy *is* he who does not condemn himself in what he approves. 23 But he who doubts is condemned if he eats, because *he does* not *eat* from faith; for whatever *is* not from faith is sin.

Paul makes travel plans

15 We then who are strong ought to bear with the scruples of the weak, and not to please ourselves. 2 Let each

---

⚒ DIGGING IN

14:15 Don't Lead Others Astray You've heard the word *life-style. Life-style* just means the way you live in the world. Some people's life-styles are wrong because they go against God's plan for living in the world. Therefore, those life-styles often cause sickness and death, and many people go to prison. A wrong life-style even leads to hell.

For the sake of others, you have to be careful about how you live in the world. A couple asked a boy to keep house for them while they were away. They didn't know the boy was a drug user. In their home the adults had some drugs that a doctor had given them when they were sick, and the boy took those drugs and hurt himself.

Something that may be good for you may be bad for someone else. You have to think about that in today's world. You can lead others into sin by an innocent but thoughtless act. A motto might be: "Consider others before you act."

15:1 Do Your Best to Please Other People Everybody likes to be pleased. Mostly we like to please ourselves. So why in the world does Paul tell us to please others? Did Paul know something we don't know? Yes, he did.

Believe it or not, a sure way to become unhappy is always to be pleasing of us please *his* neighbor for *his* good, leading to edification. ³ For even Christ did not please Himself; but as it is written, "The reproaches of those who reproached You fell on Me." ⁴ For whatever things were written before were written for our learning, that we through the patience and comfort of the Scriptures might have hope. ⁵ Now may the God of patience and comfort grant you to be like-minded toward one another, according to Christ Jesus, ⁶ that you may with one mind *and* one mouth glorify the God and Father of our Lord Jesus Christ.

⁷ Therefore receive one another, just as Christ also received us, to the glory of God. ⁸ Now I say that Jesus Christ has become a servant to the circumcision for the truth of God, to confirm the promises *made* to the fathers, ⁹ and that the Gentiles might glorify God for *His* mercy, as it is written:

"For this reason I will confess to
    You among the Gentiles,
And sing to Your name."

¹⁰ And again he says:

"Rejoice, O Gentiles, with His
    people!"

¹¹ And again:

"Praise the Lord, all you
    Gentiles!
Laud Him, all you peoples!"

¹² And again, Isaiah says:

"There shall be a root of Jesse;
And He who shall rise to reign
    over the Gentiles,
In Him the Gentiles shall hope."

¹³ Now may the God of hope fill you with all joy and peace in believing, that you may abound in hope by the power of the Holy Spirit.

¹⁴ Now I myself am confident concerning you, my brethren, that you also are full of goodness, filled with all knowledge, able also to admonish one another. ¹⁵ Nevertheless, brethren, I have written more boldly to you on *some* points, as reminding you, because of the grace given to me by God, ¹⁶ that I might be a minister of Jesus Christ to the Gentiles, ministering the gospel of God, that the offering of the Gentiles might be acceptable, sanctified by the Holy Spirit. ¹⁷ Therefore I have reason to glory in Christ Jesus in the things *which pertain* to God. ¹⁸ For I will not dare to speak of any of those things which Christ has not accomplished through me, in word and deed, to make the Gentiles obedient— ¹⁹ in mighty signs and wonders, by the

---

⚒ DIGGING IN

yourself. When you live only to please yourself, you get very lonely because you've been *thinking only about yourself.* Suddenly you find you really are all alone, and you have no friends.

You see, God wants us to be a *family.* In a real family, everybody cares for the happiness of the others. That means doing things that bring happiness to others. Have you tried to be a friend to a lonely boy or girl at school? Have you visited a sick friend lately? Try to think of ways to make life bright for people around you.

15:16 Take a Present to God Paul gave a present to God. This is what he means by his words "the offering of the Gentiles." The Gentiles were the non-

Jews, the Greeks and the Romans of Paul's time. And Paul had brought many of these people to God as "an offering"— a gift to God. That's a nice way to say it, isn't it? Whenever you lead another person to know Jesus, you are bringing that person as "an offering" or gift to God.

Have you brought any offerings like that to God? Maybe you go to church on Sunday, and you put an offering in the collection plate. God appreciates offerings like that, but the best offering you can make is someone you bring to Jesus. Has Jesus come into your heart? Then why not share Him with someone else, too? That is the greatest present you can give to God.

power of the Spirit of God, so that from Jerusalem and round about to Illyricum I have fully preached the gospel of Christ. 20 And so I have made it my aim to preach the gospel, not where Christ was named, lest I should build on another man's foundation, 21 but as it is written:

"To whom He was not
    announced, they shall see;
And those who have not heard
    shall understand."

22 For this reason I also have been much hindered from coming to you. 23 But now no longer having a place in these parts, and having a great desire these many years to come to you, 24 whenever I journey to Spain, I shall come to you. For I hope to see you on my journey, and to be helped on my way there by you, if first I may

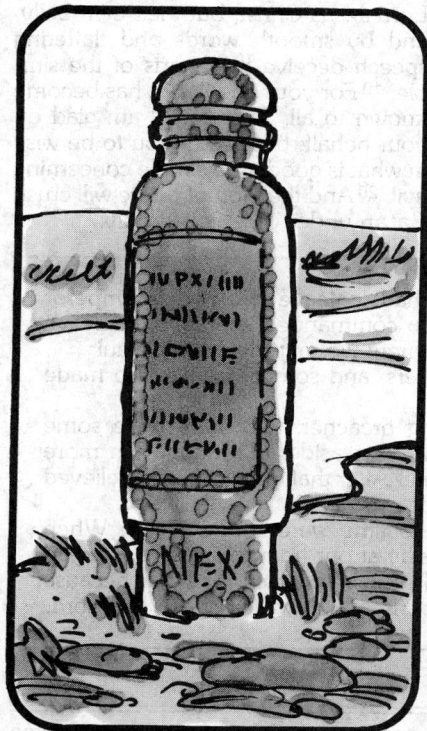

A milestone on a Roman road, showing the distance between cities.

enjoy your *company* for a while. 25 But now I am going to Jerusalem to minister to the saints. 26 For it pleased those from Macedonia and Achaia to make a certain contribution for the poor among the saints who are in Jerusalem. 27 It pleased them indeed, and they are their debtors. For if the Gentiles have been partakers of their spiritual things, their duty is also to minister to them in material things. 28 Therefore, when I have performed this and have sealed to them this fruit, I shall go by way of you to Spain. 29 But I know that when I come to you, I shall come in the fullness of the blessing of the gospel of Christ.

30 Now I beg you, brethren, through the Lord Jesus Christ, and through the love of the Spirit, that you strive together with me in prayers to God for me, 31 that I may be delivered from those in Judea who do not believe, and that my service for Jerusalem may be acceptable to the saints, 32 that I may come to you with joy by the will of God, and may be refreshed together with you. 33 Now the God of peace *be* with you all. Amen.

Paul tells his friends good-bye

16 I commend to you Phoebe our sister, who is a servant of the church in Cenchrea, 2 that you may receive her in the Lord in a manner worthy of the saints, and assist her in whatever business she has need of you; for indeed she has been a helper of many and of myself also.

3 Greet Priscilla and Aquila, my fellow workers in Christ Jesus, 4 who risked their own necks for my life, to whom not only I give thanks, but also all the churches of the Gentiles. 5 Likewise *greet* the church that is in their house.

Greet my beloved Epaenetus, who is the firstfruits of Achaia to Christ. 6 Greet Mary, who labored much for us. 7 Greet Andronicus and Junia, my countrymen and my fellow prisoners, who are of note among the apostles, who also were in Christ before me.

Phoebe—My name is pronounced *FEE-bee* and means "Radiant" or "Shining." My home was a port town called Cenchrea (pronounced *SEN-kree-ah*).

Like Lydia, the lady you met in the Book of Acts, I, too, was a wealthy businesswoman, but it was more important to me that I was a Christian. I was able to be of some help to the apostle Paul in His ministry. Some people say I even carried this letter to the Christians at Rome.

I am very honored that Paul would speak so kindly about me in his letter. I was not a very important person, but I did what God asked me to do.

You should learn from me that it is not great deeds God expects. God just wants us to do well *whatever* He gives us to do.

8 Greet Amplias, my beloved in the Lord. 9 Greet Urbanus, our fellow worker in Christ, and Stachys, my beloved. 10 Greet Apelles, approved in Christ. Greet those who are of the *household* of Aristobulus. 11 Greet Herodion, my countryman. Greet those who are of the *household* of Narcissus who are in the Lord.

12 Greet Tryphena and Tryphosa, who have labored in the Lord. Greet the beloved Persis, who labored much in the Lord. 13 Greet Rufus, chosen in the Lord, and his mother and mine. 14 Greet Asyncritus, Phlegon, Hermas, Patrobas, Hermes, and the brethren who are with them. 15 Greet Philologus and Julia, Nereus and his sister, and Olympas, and all the saints who are with them.

16 Greet one another with a holy kiss. The churches of Christ greet you.

17 Now I urge you, brethren, note those who cause divisions and offenses, contrary to the doctrine which you learned, and avoid them. 18 For those who are such do not serve our Lord Jesus Christ, but their own belly, and by smooth words and flattering speech deceive the hearts of the simple. 19 For your obedience has become known to all. Therefore I am glad on your behalf; but I want you to be wise in what is good, and simple concerning evil. 20 And the God of peace will crush **Satan** under your feet shortly.

Priscilla—My husband Aquila and I had to leave Italy when Emperor Claudius (pronounced *CLAW-dee-us*) commanded all Jews to leave Rome. So we went to live at Corinth where we met the apostle Paul.

Paul, Aquila, and I were all tentmakers, and sometimes we also made sails for boats.

Later we met Apollos, a fine young preacher. But there were some things Apollos had to learn, so we took him aside and taught him more about the Good News of Jesus the Savior. After that, many people believed in Jesus when they heard Apollos preach.

Our meetings with Paul from time to time were special treats. When he passed through Corinth, he would stay at our home. Once Paul stayed with us for 18 months. We were glad to have a place for Paul, because he had no home or wife. His whole Christian life was spent for his Lord.

WORDFINDER

16:20 Satan Pronounced *SAY-tun.* The personal name of the Devil. The name means "Adversary" or "Enemy." Satan is the chief spiritual enemy of God. He is an angel who rebelled against the Lord.

What the Romans Learned

The Good News about Jesus first came to us when some of the people came back from the Day of Pentecost at Jerusalem (see Acts 2).

But a lot of things were still not clear to us. We Romans had worshiped the same gods as the Greeks. According to legends, some of those so-called gods lived very unclean lives. Also, the government expected us to worship the emperor of Rome as a god.

When Paul wrote to us, though, we realized we had to forget all those things we used to do. We would worship only the true God (see Romans 1:25).

Now we are saved by faith in the living Son of God, and we are learning to live by the power of God's Spirit who dwells in us (see Romans 8:1, 2).

The grace of our Lord Jesus Christ *be* with you. Amen.

21 Timothy, my fellow worker, and Lucius, Jason, and Sosipater, my countrymen, greet you.

22 I, Tertius, who wrote *this* epistle, greet you in the Lord.

23 Gaius, my host and *the host* of the whole church, greets you. Erastus, the treasurer of the city, greets you,

A Roman marketplace was a center of activity.

and Quartus, a brother. 24 The grace of our Lord Jesus Christ *be* with you all. Amen.

25 Now to Him who is able to establish you according to my gospel and the preaching of Jesus Christ, according to the **revelation** of the mystery kept secret since the world began 26 but now made manifest, and by the prophetic Scriptures made known to all nations, according to the commandment of the everlasting God, for obedience to the faith— 27 to God, alone wise, *be* glory through Jesus Christ forever. Amen.

WORDFINDER

16:25 Revelation Pronounced *rev-uh-LAY-shun*. *What God has revealed or shown about His plan for all time. This revelation is the gospel or Good News the whole Bible tells about.*

The Book of

1 CORINTHIANS

Our city will go down in history as one of the worst cities of the ancient world. Any person of bad character was often called a "Corinthian" (pronounced *ko-RIN-thee-un*).

Strange to say, though, our city was a place where the gospel of Jesus grew very strong. Many of our people became Christians, and a large church was planted here.

How wonderful that the gospel did so well in our town! But in Athens, where the great thinkers were, few showed any interest when Paul told them about Jesus.

Perhaps this is what Paul meant when He said that God didn't call many wise men to Himself. And Jesus said He came to invite sinners to His Father's kingdom.

But remember, we're all sinners! We Corinthians knew this was true, but the people of Athens were proud of their "wisdom" and "goodness." That was their foolish mistake.

Paul writes a letter to the church at Corinth

PAUL, called *to be* an apostle of Jesus Christ through the will of God, and Sosthenes *our* brother,

2 To the church of God which is at Corinth, to those who are sanctified in Christ Jesus, called *to be* saints, with all who in every place call on the name of Jesus Christ our Lord, both theirs and ours:

3 Grace to you and peace from God our Father and the Lord Jesus Christ.

4 I thank my God always concerning you for the grace of God which was given to you by Christ Jesus, 5 that you

Some columns from the Temple of Apollo, a god worshiped by the Corinthians.

What Is the Church?

The word *church* comes from a Greek word meaning "assembly" (pronounced *ah-SEM-blee*). The church is the assembly or gathering of all who believe in Jesus as their Savior. The church is not just a building of wood or ordinary stones. It is a living building of *living stones*. (See 1 Peter 2:4, 5.)

were enriched in everything by Him in all utterance and all knowledge, 6 even as the testimony of Christ was confirmed in you, 7 so that you come short in no gift, eagerly waiting for the revelation of our Lord Jesus Christ, 8 who will also confirm you to the end, *that you may be* blameless in the day of our Lord Jesus Christ. 9 God *is* faithful, by whom you were called into the fellowship of His Son, Jesus Christ our Lord.

10 Now I plead with you, brethren, by the name of our Lord Jesus Christ, that you all speak the same thing, and *that* there be no divisions among you, but *that* you be perfectly joined together in the same mind and in the same judgment. 11 For it has been declared to me concerning you, my brethren, by those of Chloe's *household,* that there are contentions among you. 12 Now I say this, that each of you says, "I am of Paul," or "I am of Apollos," or "I am of Cephas," or "I am of Christ." 13 Is Christ divided? Was

Paul crucified for you? Or were you baptized in the name of Paul?

14 I thank God that I baptized none of you except Crispus and Gaius, 15 lest anyone should say that I had baptized in my own name. 16 Yes, I also baptized the household of Stephanas. Besides, I do not know whether I baptized any other. 17 For Christ did not send me to baptize, but to preach the gospel, not with wisdom of words, lest the cross of Christ should be made of no effect.

18 For the message of the cross is foolishness to those who are perishing, but to us who are being saved it is the power of God. 19 For it is written:

"I will destroy the wisdom of the
    wise,
And bring to nothing the
    understanding of the
    prudent."

20 Where *is* the wise? Where *is* the scribe? Where *is* the disputer of this age? Has not God made foolish the **wisdom** of this world? 21 For since, in

What Is God's Wisdom?

Many people thought Jesus was foolish to die on the Cross. They still think so. Some people even think it's wise to stay alive by killing other people. But God showed His wisdom by giving His Son to bring everlasting life to others.

WORDFINDER

1:20 Wisdom The ability to use facts to bring about good results. The so-called wisdom of this world could not do this. Jesus Christ is the source of true wisdom.

DIGGING IN

1:12 Jesus Is Your True Leader A lot of people in Corinth (pronounced *KOR-inth*) were trusting in human leaders like Paul and Peter, instead of trusting in Jesus.

God gives you human helpers along the way. And you should honor them—including your parents, your pastor, and your teachers.

But these folks are all human, and

sometimes they fail. That's why many people are mad at the world. Some human being failed to do his job, and people are disappointed. The trouble is we expect too much of people.

But Jesus never fails. Prove it to yourself by trusting Him with your problems. You'll see how He always takes care of the things that trouble you. Jesus is the great and true Leader of your life.

A scribe reads the Law.

the wisdom of God, the world through wisdom did not know God, it pleased God through the foolishness of the message preached to save those who believe. 22 For Jews request a sign, and Greeks seek after wisdom; 23 but we preach Christ crucified, to the Jews a stumbling block and to the Greeks foolishness, 24 but to those who are called, both Jews and Greeks, Christ the power of God and the wisdom of God. 25 Because the foolishness of God is wiser than men, and the weakness of God is stronger than men.

26 For you see your calling, brethren, that not many wise according to the flesh, not many mighty, not many noble, *are called.* 27 But God has chosen the foolish things of the world to put

to shame the wise, and God has chosen the weak things of the world to put to shame the things which are mighty; 28 and the base things of the world and the things which are despised God has chosen, and the things which are not, to bring to nothing the things that are, 29 that no flesh should glory in His presence. 30 But of Him you are in Christ Jesus, who became for us wisdom from God—and righteousness and sanctification and redemption— 31 that, as it is written, "He who glories, let him glory in the LORD."

Paul uses the Holy Spirit's words and wisdom

2 And I, brethren, when I came to you, did not come with excellence of speech or of wisdom declaring to you the testimony of God. 2 For I determined not to know anything among you except Jesus Christ and Him crucified. 3 I was with you in weakness, in fear, and in much trembling. 4 And my speech and my preaching *were* not with persuasive words of human wisdom, but in demonstration of the Spirit and of power, 5 that your faith should not be in the wisdom of men but in the power of God.

6 However, we speak wisdom among those who are mature, yet not the wisdom of this age, nor of the rulers of this age, who are coming to nothing. 7 But we speak the wisdom of God in a mystery, the hidden *wisdom* which God ordained before the ages for our

⚒ DIGGING IN

2:7 Gain the Wisdom of God How wise are you? Maybe you would like to be wise enough to be rich and famous someday. That's what wisdom means to a lot of people. The trouble comes when people get rich and famous, but aren't wise in how they use their riches and fame. History is full of stories of people who became rich and famous, but many of them were ruined in the end because they weren't wise after all.

So ask God to give you wisdom to take care of whatever He asks you to do in life. The higher your place in the world, the more wisdom you will need. Having power and wealth is really a means for better serving others.

Paul says Jesus Himself is your true wisdom. So make sure to ask God to send Jesus into your life. Then you will be wise because you have the wisdom of Jesus.

glory, 8 which none of the rulers of this age knew; for had they known, they would not have crucified the Lord of glory.

9 But as it is written:

"Eye has not seen, nor ear heard,
Nor have entered into the heart
    of man
The things which God has
    prepared for those who love
    Him."

10 But God has revealed *them* to us through His Spirit. For the Spirit searches all things, yes, the deep things of God. 11 For what man knows the things of a man except the spirit of the man which is in him? Even so no one knows the things of God except the Spirit of God. 12 Now we have received, not the spirit of the world, but the Spirit who is from God, that we might know the things that have been freely given to us by God.

13 These things we also speak, not in words which man's wisdom teaches but which the Holy Spirit teaches, comparing spiritual things with spiritual. 14 But the natural man does not receive the things of the Spirit of God, for they are foolishness to him; nor can he know *them,* because they are spiritually discerned. 15 But he who is spiritual judges all things, yet he himself is *rightly* judged by no one. 16 For "who has known the mind of the LORD that he may instruct Him?" But we have the mind of Christ.

Paul talks to baby Christians

3 And I, brethren, could not speak to you as to spiritual *people* but as to carnal, as to babes in Christ. 2 I fed you with milk and not with solid food; for until now you were not able *to receive it,* and even now you are still not able; 3 for you are still carnal. For where *there are* envy, strife, and divisions among you, are you not carnal and behaving like *mere* men? 4 For when one says, "I am of Paul," and another, "I *am* of Apollos," are you not carnal?

5 Who then is Paul, and who *is* Apollos, but ministers through whom you believed, as the Lord gave to each one? 6 I planted, Apollos watered, but God gave the increase. 7 So then neither he who plants is anything, nor he who waters, but God who gives the increase. 8 Now he who plants and he who waters are one, and each one will receive his own reward according to his own labor.

9 For we are God's fellow workers; you are God's field, *you are* God's building. 10 According to the grace of God which was given to me, as a wise master builder I have laid the foundation, and another builds on it. But let each one take heed how he builds on it. 11 For no other foundation can anyone lay than that which is laid, which is Jesus Christ. 12 Now if anyone builds on this foundation *with* gold, silver, precious stones, wood, hay, straw, 13 each one's work will become clear; for the Day will declare it, because it will be revealed by fire; and the fire will test each one's work, of what sort it is. 14 If anyone's work which he has built on *it* endures, he will receive a reward. 15 If anyone's work is burned, he will suffer loss; but he himself will be saved, yet so as through fire.

16 Do you not know that you are the temple of God and *that* the Spirit of God dwells in you? 17 If anyone defiles

DIGGING IN

3:16 Your Body Is God's Temple In Romans 8 you can read how the Spirit of God makes you an adopted son or daughter of God. The Spirit of God, also called "the Holy Spirit," does this by coming to live in your body. The Holy Spirit lives in you when you surrender your life to Jesus as your Savior and Lord.

This truth is almost frightening: *God Himself* really comes to live in our bodies! Of course God is "infinite" (pronounced *IN-fih-nit*), which means God has no lim-the temple of God, God will destroy him. For the temple of God is holy, which *temple* you are.

18 Let no one deceive himself. If anyone among you seems to be wise in this age, let him become a fool that he may become wise. 19 For the wisdom of this world is foolishness with God. For it is written, "He catches the wise in their *own* craftiness"; 20 and again, "The LORD knows the thoughts of the wise, that they are futile." 21 Therefore let no one boast in men. For all things are yours: 22 whether Paul or Apollos or Cephas, or the world or life or death, or things present or things to come—all are yours. 23 And you *are* Christ's, and Christ *is* God's.

Christians should not judge other Christians

4 Let a man so consider us, as servants of Christ and **stewards** of the **mysteries** of God. 2 Moreover it is required in stewards that one be found faithful. 3 But with me it is a very small thing that I should be judged by you or by a human court. In fact, I do not even judge myself. 4 For I know of nothing against myself, yet I am not justified by this; but He who judges me is the Lord. 5 Therefore judge nothing before the time, until the Lord comes, who will both bring to light the hidden

things of darkness and reveal the counsels of the hearts. Then each one's praise will come from God.

6 Now these things, brethren, I have figuratively transferred to myself and Apollos for your sakes, that you may learn in us not to think beyond what is written, that none of you may be puffed up on behalf of one against the other. 7 For who makes you differ *from another*? And what do you have that you did not receive? Now if you did indeed receive *it*, why do you boast as if you had not received *it*?

8 You are already full! You are already rich! You have reigned as kings without us—and indeed I could wish you did reign, that we also might reign with you! 9 For I think that God has displayed us, the apostles, last, as men condemned to death; for *we* have been made a spectacle to the world, both to angels and to men. 10 We *are* fools for Christ's sake, but *you are* wise in Christ! We *are* weak, but *you are* strong! *You are* distinguished, but we *are* dishonored! 11 To the present hour we both hunger and thirst, and we are poorly clothed, and beaten, and homeless. 12 And we labor, working with our own hands. Being reviled, we bless; being persecuted, we endure; 13 being defamed, we entreat. We have been made as the filth of the world, the offscouring of all things until now.

14 I do not write these things to shame you, but as my beloved children

🐟 WORDFINDER

4:1 Stewards Those in charge of property or an area of work. The apostles were "stewards of the mysteries of God." They were in charge of the work of preaching the gospel.

4:1 Mysteries Things that are not known. Paul spoke about "the mysteries of God." These were things that weren't known until Jesus came and revealed the gospel.

⛏ DIGGING IN

its. But the invisible Holy Spirit still comes to dwell in you and in everyone else who trusts in Jesus.

If the Holy Spirit lives in you, it should make a big difference how you use your body and how you spend your life. Your

body and your life are no longer your own to use as you please. They belong to God. So remember to study, work, and play in ways that please God, because He lives in you.

I warn *you.* 15 For though you might have ten thousand instructors in Christ, yet *you do* not *have* many fathers; for in Christ Jesus I have begotten you through the gospel. 16 Therefore I urge you, imitate me. 17 For this reason I have sent Timothy to you, who is my beloved and faithful son in the Lord, who will remind you of my ways in Christ, as I teach everywhere in every church.

18 Now some are puffed up, as though I were not coming to you. 19 But I will come to you shortly, if the Lord wills, and I will know, not the word of those who are puffed up, but the power. 20 For the kingdom of God is not in word but in power. 21 What do you want? Shall I come to you with a rod, or in love and a spirit of gentleness?

Be careful not to mix with evil people

5 It is actually reported *that there is* sexual immorality among you, and such sexual immorality as is not even named among the Gentiles—that a man has his father's wife! 2 And you are puffed up, and have not rather mourned, that he who has done this deed might be taken away from among you. 3 For I indeed, as absent in body but present in spirit, have already judged (as though I were present) him who has so done this deed. 4 In the name of our Lord Jesus Christ, when you are gathered together, along with my spirit, with the power of our Lord Jesus Christ, 5 deliver such a one to Satan for the destruction of the flesh, that his spirit may be saved in the day of the Lord Jesus.

6 Your glorying *is* not good. Do you not know that a little **leaven** leavens the whole lump? 7 Therefore purge out the old leaven, that you may be a new lump, since you truly are unleavened. For indeed **Christ,** our Passover, was sacrificed for us. 8 Therefore let us keep the feast, not with old leaven, nor with the leaven of malice and wickedness, but with the unleavened *bread* of sincerity and truth.

9 I wrote to you in my epistle not to keep company with sexually immoral people. 10 Yet *I* certainly *did* not *mean* with the sexually immoral people of this world, or with the covetous, or extortioners, or idolaters, since then you

WORDFINDER

5:6 Leaven Pronounced *LEV-in.* A substance used in ancient times to make bread dough rise. Today bakers use yeast to do this. Jesus compared the growth of God's kingdom to the slow work of leaven.

5:7 Christ The divine title of the Man Jesus. The word means "the Anointed" (by the Holy Spirit). *Christos* is a Greek word translated from the Hebrew *Messiah.*

DIGGING IN

4:10 Are You a Fool for Christ's Sake? Nobody wants to be a fool. But imagine what it would be like to live in another world where everybody was blind. You would be telling the people there how beautiful the sky, the earth, and the sea are. But the blind people of that other world would probably think you were crazy. After all, they would say, nobody has even heard of people *seeing* the things you talk about.

That's what it's like to be a Christian in this world. Most people don't know God or Jesus Christ, and they don't see the works of God. As a Christian, you'll want to tell others about Jesus and how wonderful it is to know Him. But sometimes people will say you're a *fool* to tell them about Jesus, because they don't even know He's alive. We have to be ready to be "fools for Christ's sake"—a small price compared to the price He paid to save us!

would need to go out of the world. ¹¹ But now I have written to you not to keep company with anyone named a brother, who is sexually immoral, or covetous, or an idolater, or a reviler, or a drunkard, or an extortioner—not even to eat with such a person.

¹² For what have I to do with judging those also who are outside? Do you not judge those who are inside? ¹³ But those who are outside God judges. Therefore "put away from yourselves the evil person."

Christians should not sue each other

6 Dare any of you, having a matter against another, go to law before the unrighteous, and not before the saints? ² Do you not know that the saints will judge the world? And if the world will be judged by you, are you unworthy to judge the smallest matters? ³ Do you not know that we shall judge angels? How much more, things that pertain to this life? ⁴ If then you have judgments concerning things pertaining to this life, do you appoint those who are least esteemed by the church to judge? ⁵ I say this to your shame. Is it so, that there is not a wise man among you, not even one, who will be able to judge between his brethren? ⁶ But brother goes to law against brother, and that before unbelievers!

⁷ Now therefore, it is already an utter failure for you that you go to law against one another. Why do you not rather accept wrong? Why do you not

rather let yourselves be cheated? ⁸ No, you yourselves do wrong and cheat, and you do these things to your brethren! ⁹ Do you not know that the unrighteous will not inherit the kingdom of God? Do not be deceived. Neither fornicators, nor idolaters, nor adulterers, nor homosexuals, nor sodomites, ¹⁰ nor thieves, nor covetous, nor drunkards, nor revilers, nor extortioners will inherit the kingdom of God. ¹¹ And such were some of you. But you were washed, but you were sanctified, but you were justified in the name of the Lord Jesus and by the Spirit of our God.

¹² All things are lawful for me, but all things are not helpful. All things are lawful for me, but I will not be brought under the power of any. ¹³ Foods for the stomach and the stomach for foods, but God will destroy both it and them. Now the body is not for sexual immorality but for the Lord, and the Lord for the body. ¹⁴ And God both raised up the Lord and will also raise us up by His power.

¹⁵ Do you not know that your bodies are members of Christ? Shall I then take the members of Christ and make them members of a harlot? Certainly not! ¹⁶ Or do you not know that he who is joined to a harlot is one body with her? For "the two," He says, "shall become one flesh." ¹⁷ But he who is joined to the Lord is one spirit with Him.

¹⁸ Flee sexual immorality. Every sin that a man does is outside the body, but he who commits sexual immorality sins against his own body. ¹⁹ Or do you

⚒ DIGGING IN

6:12 Can You Do as You Please? Some people say, "I can do anything I please." And so they can. But what happens when they do?

What happens if you ride your bicycle over a cliff? You know the answer to that. What happens if you go swimming in the middle of the ocean with nobody around to pick you up? That story has a bad ending, too. How about jumping out of an airplane at thirty thousand feet—without a

parachute? That would be your last day on earth.

So you can do anything you please, but a lot of things are not very good for you. In fact, they really hurt you. You can spend your life just playing games, or even doing nothing at all. But then you've lost a lifetime that you can never replace. "Only one life—'twill soon be past—only what's done for Christ will last."

not know that your body is the temple of the Holy Spirit *who is* in you, whom you have from God, and you are not your own? ²⁰ For you were bought at a price; therefore glorify God in your body and in your spirit, which are God's.

Families should not split up

7 Now concerning the things of which you wrote to me:

It is good for a man not to touch a woman. ² Nevertheless, because of sexual immorality, let each man have his own wife, and let each woman have her own husband. ³ Let the husband render to his wife the affection due her, and likewise also the wife to her husband. ⁴ The wife does not have authority over her own body, but the husband *does.* And likewise the husband does not have authority over his own body, but the wife *does.* ⁵ Do not deprive one another except with consent for a time, that you may give yourselves to fasting and prayer; and come together again so that Satan does not tempt you because of your lack of self-control. ⁶ But I say this as a concession, not as a commandment. ⁷ For I wish that all men were even as I myself. But each one has his own gift from God, one in this manner and another in that.

⁸ But I say to the unmarried and to the widows: It is good for them if they remain even as I am; ⁹ but if they cannot exercise self-control, let them marry. For it is better to marry than to burn *with passion.*

¹⁰ Now to the married I command, *yet* not I but the Lord: A wife is not to depart from *her* husband. ¹¹ But even if she does depart, let her remain unmarried or be reconciled to *her* husband. And a husband is not to divorce *his* wife.

¹² But to the rest I, not the Lord, say: If any brother has a wife who does not believe, and she is willing to live with him, let him not divorce her. ¹³ And a woman who has a husband who does not believe, if he is willing to live with her, let her not divorce him.

¹⁴ For the unbelieving husband is sanctified by the wife, and the unbelieving wife is sanctified by the husband; otherwise your children would be unclean, but now they are holy. ¹⁵ But if the unbeliever departs, let him depart; a brother or a sister is not under bondage in such *cases.* But God has called us to peace. ¹⁶ For how do you know, O wife, whether you will save *your* husband? Or how do you know, O husband, whether you will save *your* wife?

¹⁷ But as God has distributed to each one, as the Lord has called each one, so let him walk. And so I ordain in all the churches. ¹⁸ Was anyone called while circumcised? Let him not become uncircumcised. Was anyone called while uncircumcised? Let him not be circumcised. ¹⁹ Circumcision is nothing and uncircumcision is nothing, but keeping the commandments of God *is what matters.* ²⁰ Let each one remain in the same calling in which he was called. ²¹ Were you called *while* a slave? Do not be concerned about it; but if you can be made free, rather use *it.* ²² For he who is called in the Lord *while* a slave is the Lord's freedman. Likewise he who is called *while* free is Christ's slave. ²³ You were bought at a price; do not become slaves of men. ²⁴ Brethren, let each one remain with God in that *state* in which he was called.

²⁵ Now concerning virgins: I have no commandment from the Lord; yet I give judgment as one whom the Lord in His mercy *has made* trustworthy. ²⁶ I suppose therefore that this is good because of the present distress—that *it is* good for a man to remain as he is: ²⁷ Are you bound to a wife? Do not seek to be loosed. Are you loosed from a wife? Do not seek a wife. ²⁸ But even if you do marry, you have not sinned; and if a virgin marries, she has not sinned. Nevertheless such will have trouble in the flesh, but I would spare you.

²⁹ But this I say, brethren, the time *is* short, so that from now on even those who have wives should be as though they had none, ³⁰ those who weep as though they did not weep,

those who rejoice as though they did not rejoice, those who buy as though they did not possess, 31 and those who use this world as not misusing *it.* For the form of this world is passing away.

32 But I want you to be without care. He who is unmarried cares for the things of the Lord—how he may please the Lord. 33 But he who is married cares about the things of the world—how he may please *his* wife. 34 There is a difference between a wife and a virgin. The unmarried woman cares about the things of the Lord, that she may be holy both in body and in spirit. But she who is married cares about the things of the world—how she may please *her* husband. 35 And this I say for your own profit, not that I may put a leash on you, but for what is proper, and that you may serve the Lord without distraction.

36 But if any man thinks he is behaving improperly toward his virgin, if she is past the flower of youth, and thus it must be, let him do what he wishes. He does not sin; let them marry. 37 Nevertheless he who stands steadfast in his heart, having no necessity, but has power over his own will, and has so determined in his heart that he will keep his virgin, does well. 38 So then he who gives *her* in marriage does well, but he who does not give *her* in marriage does better.

39 A wife is bound by law as long as her husband lives; but if her husband dies, she is at liberty to be married to whom she wishes, only in the Lord. 40 But she is happier if she remains as she is, according to my judgment—and I think I also have the Spirit of God.

Should Christians eat food offered to idols?

8 Now concerning things offered to idols: We know that we all have knowledge. Knowledge puffs up, but love edifies. 2 And if anyone thinks that he knows anything, he knows nothing yet as he ought to know. 3 But if anyone loves God, this one is known by Him.

4 Therefore concerning the eating of things offered to idols, we know that an idol *is* nothing in the world, and that *there is* no other God but one. 5 For even if there are so-called gods, whether in heaven or on earth (as there are many gods and many lords), 6 yet for us *there is* one God, the Father, of whom *are* all things, and we for Him; and one Lord Jesus Christ, through whom *are* all things, and through whom we *live.*

7 However, *there is* not in everyone that knowledge; for some, with consciousness of the idol, until now eat *it* as a thing offered to an idol; and their conscience, being weak, is defiled. 8 But food does not commend us to God; for neither if we eat are we the better, nor if we do not eat are we the worse.

9 But beware lest somehow this liberty of yours become a stumbling block to those who are weak. 10 For if anyone sees you who have knowledge eating in an idol's temple, will not the conscience of him who is weak be emboldened to eat those things offered

⚒DIGGING IN

8:2 We Have a Lot to Learn No wonder someone has said God will laugh at us (see Psalm 2:4). We think we know so much. Right now you may be very excited about science. We have learned a lot from science. But as you get older, you may begin to notice that many of the things scientists believe today will be debunked later.

We must keep on trying to learn all we can. But when we have learned as much as we can, we're not much closer to knowing everything than we were before. The universe keeps getting older and older, and even scientists tell us it will die one day. But God will live forever. Knowing Him is what matters when everything else is passing away.

to idols? 11 And because of your knowledge shall the weak brother perish, for whom Christ died? 12 But when you thus sin against the brethren, and wound their weak conscience, you sin against Christ. 13 Therefore, if food makes my brother stumble, I will never again eat meat, lest I make my brother stumble.

Paul's pay is the joy of preaching the Good News

9 Am I not an apostle? Am I not free? Have I not seen Jesus Christ our Lord? Are you not my work in the Lord? 2 If I am not an apostle to others, yet doubtless I am to you. For you are the seal of my apostleship in the Lord.

3 My defense to those who examine me is this: 4 Do we have no right to eat and drink? 5 Do we have no right to take along a believing wife, as *do* also the other apostles, the brothers of the Lord, and Cephas? 6 Or *is it* only Barnabas and I *who* have no right to refrain from working? 7 Who ever goes to war at his own expense? Who plants a vineyard and does not eat of its fruit? Or who tends a flock and does not drink of the milk of the flock?

8 Do I say these things as a *mere* man? Or does not the law say the same also? 9 For it is written in the law of Moses, "You shall not muzzle an ox while it treads out the grain." Is it oxen God is concerned about? 10 Or does He say *it* altogether for our sakes? For our sakes, no doubt, *this* is written, that he who plows should plow in hope,

and he who threshes in hope should be partaker of his hope. 11 If we have sown spiritual things for you, *is it* a great thing if we reap your material things? 12 If others are partakers of *this* right over you, *are* we not even more?

Nevertheless we have not used this right, but endure all things lest we hinder the gospel of Christ. 13 Do you not know that those who minister the holy things eat *of the things* of the temple, and those who serve at the altar partake of *the offerings of* the altar? 14 Even so the Lord has commanded that those who preach the gospel should live from the gospel.

15 But I have used none of these things, nor have I written these things that it should be done so to me; for it *would be* better for me to die than that anyone should make my boasting void. 16 For if I preach the gospel, I have nothing to boast of, for necessity is laid upon me; yes, woe is me if I do not preach the gospel! 17 For if I do this willingly, I have a reward; but if against my will, I have been entrusted with a stewardship. 18 What is my reward then? That when I preach the gospel, I may present the gospel of Christ without charge, that I may not abuse my authority in the gospel.

19 For though I am free from all *men,* I have made myself a servant to all, that I might win the more; 20 and to the Jews I became as a Jew, that I might win Jews; to those *who are* under the law, as under the law, that I might win those *who are* under the law; 21 to those *who are* without law,

DIGGING IN

9:19 Learn to Be a Servant Everybody wants to be the boss. Nobody wants to be a servant. But can you believe that God's way UP is DOWN? Jesus was the Son of the Highest, but He made Himself a servant. That was a long way down for Jesus. Why did He do that?

There were two reasons. First, Jesus had to be a servant to die for our sins. Jesus was greater than Pilate and greater than the emperor of Rome, but He made

Himself the servant of all. He let Himself be nailed to a cross by the Jews and the Romans. He was the Highest, but He let Himself be treated like the lowest of men.

The second reason was that Jesus wanted to show you what true greatness is like. Real greatness is being a successful servant of people. You may be the president or you may be the janitor. But God calls you to be His SERVANT in both places.

Happy Thoughts For Children

(The Beatitudes—Matthew 5:3–12, adapted)

Jesus once preached a special Sermon to His close friends and other followers who had gathered on the side of a mountain to hear Him. In that Sermon, He gave us all some happy thoughts:

HAPPY ARE THE CHILDREN
who know they need Me; I will give them My kingdom.
HAPPY ARE THE CHILDREN
who are sad; I will comfort them.
HAPPY ARE THE CHILDREN
who are gentle to others; I will bless them here on
earth and in heaven, too.
HAPPY ARE THE CHILDREN
who "hunger" to be good; I will fill them up with goodness.
HAPPY ARE THE CHILDREN
who are kind and forgiving; I will forgive *them*, too.
HAPPY ARE THE CHILDREN
with pure, unpolluted hearts; someday they will see Me face to face.
HAPPY ARE THE CHILDREN
who try to stop fights; they are just like Me!
HAPPY ARE THE CHILDREN
who are mistreated because of Me;
they will be with Me always in My Forever Life.

When others make fun of you, hurt
you, and say mean things about
you because you believe in Me,
you can sing and be happy! I have a
big reward for you in heaven, and
for all My other faithful children
who lived long ago.

Love Lines

(1 Corinthians 13, adapted)

If I can speak many languages, even the language of angels, but do not say the words with Jesus' kind of love, I sound like rusty hinges on a banging door.

If I know everything before it happens, and if I am the smartest kid in the world, and if I am positive that God can do anything, but do not tell about it with Jesus' kind of love, I can't help anybody.

If I give away all my toys to kids who don't have any, and if I am even willing to die for what I believe, but do not love as Jesus did, it means nothing at all.

LOVE takes turns.
LOVE is gentle and kind.
LOVE does not wish for what belongs to someone else.
LOVE does not brag or try to get ahead of others.
LOVE is not rude; it does not demand its own way.
LOVE puts others first.
LOVE does not get mad in a hurry.
LOVE does not keep score when someone wrongs me.
LOVE is not happy when the bad guys are winning, but gets excited when truth comes out on top.
LOVE puts up with a lot, always trusts in God, never lets me down, never ends.
LOVE keeps on going when everything else fails. Someday all talking will be hushed. All I have learned will not matter anymore. Besides, I know only part of the truth, but when the whole truth comes, even the part I know will disappear.

Now I am a little child. I talk like a child, understand like a child, think like a child. But when I grow up, I won't act like a child anymore. Right now I can only see God's reflection as in a piece of polished metal, like the mirrors of the people of Corinth. But someday I will be able to see His face, and I will know Him as well as He already knows me.

Of these three—faith, hope, and love—
the greatest of all is LOVE!

as without law (not being without law toward God, but under law toward Christ), that I might win those *who are* without law; 22 to the weak I became as weak, that I might win the weak. I have become all things to all *men,* that I might by all means save some. 23 Now this I do for the gospel's sake, that I may be partaker of it with *you.*

24 Do you not know that those who run in a race all run, but one receives the prize? Run in such a way that you may obtain *it.* 25 And everyone who competes *for the prize* is temperate in all things. Now they *do it* to obtain a perishable crown, but we *for* an imperishable *crown.* 26 Therefore I run thus: not with uncertainty. Thus I fight: not as *one who* beats the air. 27 But I **discipline** my body and bring *it* into subjection, lest, when I have preached to others, I myself should become disqualified.

Don't do anything that might cause a brother to stumble

10 Moreover, brethren, I do not want you to be unaware that all our fathers were under the cloud, all passed through the sea, 2 all were baptized into Moses in the cloud and in the sea, 3 all ate the same spiritual food, 4 and all drank the same spiritual drink. For they drank of that spiritual Rock that followed them, and that Rock was Christ. 5 But with most of them God was not well pleased, for *their bodies* were scattered in the wilderness.

6 Now these things became our examples, to the intent that we should not lust after evil things as they also lusted. 7 And do not become idolaters as *were* some of them. As it is written, "The people sat down to eat and drink, and rose up to play." 8 Nor let us commit sexual immorality, as some of them did, and in one day twenty-three thousand fell; 9 nor let us tempt Christ, as some of them also tempted, and were destroyed by serpents; 10 nor complain, as some of them also complained, and were destroyed by the destroyer. 11 Now all these things happened to them as examples, and they were written for our admonition, upon whom the ends of the ages have come.

12 Therefore let him who thinks he stands take heed lest he fall. 13 No temptation has overtaken you except such as is common to man; but God is faithful, who will not allow you to be tempted beyond what you are able, but with the temptation will also make the way of escape, that you may be able to bear *it.*

14 Therefore, my beloved, flee from

🔍 WORDFINDER

9:27 Discipline Pronounced *DIS-ih-plin.* Comes from the same word as "disciple." To discipline means to "train" or "teach."

⛏ DIGGING IN

9:24 Run for the Prize Have you ever been in a race? Why did you run? You ran as hard as you could because you wanted to win. That's the only way to run a race.

That's the only way to run the race of life, too. In the race Paul is talking about, the important thing is to stay in the race. Don't quit! The only way to lose is to drop out. You may not finish first in the contest, but you have to cross the finish line to get the prize.

In the games long ago, the emperor held the crown while the race was on, and then he placed the crown on the winner's head. Jesus waits to place on your head a crown that will last forever. The rule of the Christian race is, "Keep on living for Jesus." To see His face is your goal and your prize.

idolatry. 15 I speak as to wise men; judge for yourselves what I say. 16 The cup of blessing which we bless, is it not the communion of the blood of Christ? The bread which we break, is it not the communion of the body of Christ? 17 For we, *though* many, are one bread *and* one body; for we all partake of that one bread.

18 Observe Israel after the flesh: Are not those who eat of the sacrifices partakers of the altar? 19 What am I saying then? That an idol is anything, or what is offered to idols is anything? 20 Rather, that the things which the Gentiles sacrifice they sacrifice to demons and not to God, and I do not want you to have fellowship with demons. 21 You cannot drink the cup of the Lord and the cup of demons; you cannot partake of the Lord's table and of the table of demons. 22 Or do we provoke the Lord to jealousy? Are we stronger than He?

23 All things are lawful for me, but not all things are helpful; all things are lawful for me, but not all things edify. 24 Let no one seek his own, but each one the other's *well-being.*

25 Eat whatever is sold in the meat market, asking no questions for conscience' sake; 26 for "the earth *is* the LORD's, and all its fullness."

27 If any of those who do not believe invites you to *dinner,* and you desire to go, eat whatever is set before you, asking no question for conscience' sake. 28 But if anyone says to you, "This was offered to idols," do not eat it for the sake of the one who told you, and for conscience' sake; for "the earth is the LORD's, and all its fullness." 29 "Conscience," I say, not your own, but that of the other. For why is my liberty judged by another *man's* conscience? 30 But if I partake with thanks, why am I evil spoken of for *the food* over which I give thanks?

31 Therefore, whether you eat or drink, or whatever you do, do all to the glory of God. 32 Give no offense, either to the Jews or to the Greeks or to the church of God, 33 just as I also please all *men* in all *things,* not seeking my own profit, but the *profit* of many, that they may be saved.

Take the Lord's Supper with reverence and remembrance

11 Imitate me, just as I also *imitate* Christ.

2 Now I praise you, brethren, that you remember me in all things and keep the traditions just as I delivered *them* to you. 3 But I want you to know that the head of every man is Christ, the head of woman *is* man, and the head of Christ *is* God. 4 Every man praying or prophesying, having *his* head covered, dishonors his head. 5 But *every* woman who prays or prophesies with *her* head uncovered dishonors her head, for that is one and the same as if her head were shaved. 6 For if a woman is not covered, let her also be shorn. But if it is shameful for a woman to be shorn or shaved, let her be covered. 7 For a man indeed ought not to cover *his* head, since he is the image and glory of God; but woman is the glory of man. 8 For man is not from woman, but woman from man. 9 Nor was man created for the woman, but woman for the man. 10 For this reason the woman ought to have *a symbol of* authority on *her* head, because of the angels. 11 Nevertheless, neither *is* man independent of woman, nor woman independent of man, in the Lord. 12 For as woman *came* from man, even so man also *comes* through woman; but all things are from God.

13 Judge among yourselves. Is it

WORDFINDER

10:14 Idolatry Pronounced *eye-DOLL-uh-tree.* The worship of idols and false gods. Unless you work or serve God, you will serve something or someone less than God.

proper for a woman to pray to God with her head uncovered? 14 Does not even nature itself teach you that if a man has long hair, it is a dishonor to him? 15 But if a woman has long hair, it is a glory to her; for *her* hair is given to her for a covering. 16 But if anyone seems to be contentious, we have no such custom, nor *do* the churches of God.

17 Now in giving these instructions I do not praise *you,* since you come together not for the better but for the worse. 18 For first of all, when you come together as a church, I hear that there are divisions among you, and in part I believe it. 19 For there must also be factions among you, that those who are approved may be recognized among you. 20 Therefore when you come together in one place, it is not to eat the Lord's Supper. 21 For in eating, each one takes his own supper ahead of *others;* and one is hungry and another is drunk. 22 What! Do you not have houses to eat and drink in? Or do you despise the church of God and shame those who have nothing? What shall I say to you? Shall I praise you in this? I do not praise *you.*

What Does the Lord's Supper Mean?

Sometimes when you go to church, you will see Christians eating and drinking a small meal called the Lord's Supper. We do this to obey Jesus' command to remember His death. The bread stands for His body, and the drink stands for His blood. That is how we show we believe Jesus died for us.

23 For I received from the Lord that which I also delivered to you: that the Lord Jesus on the *same* night in which He was betrayed took bread; 24 and when He had given thanks, He broke

it and said, "Take, eat; this is My body which is broken for you; do this in remembrance of Me." 25 In the same manner *He* also *took* the cup after supper, saying, "This cup is the new covenant in My blood. This do, as often as you drink *it,* in remembrance of Me."

26 For as often as you eat this bread and drink this cup, you proclaim the Lord's death till He comes.

27 Therefore whoever eats this bread or drinks *this* cup of the Lord in an unworthy manner will be guilty of the body and blood of the Lord. 28 But let a man examine himself, and so let him eat of the bread and drink of the cup. 29 For he who eats and drinks in an unworthy manner eats and drinks judgment to himself, not discerning the Lord's body. 30 For this reason many *are* weak and sick among you, and many sleep. 31 For if we would judge ourselves, we would not be judged. 32 But when we are judged, we are chastened by the Lord, that we may not be condemned with the world.

33 Therefore, my brethren, when you come together to eat, wait for one another. 34 But if anyone is hungry, let him eat at home, lest you come together for judgment. And the rest I will set in order when I come.

Gifts of the Holy Spirit are to help the church

12 Now concerning **spiritual** *gifts,* brethren, I do not want you to be ignorant: 2 You know that you were Gentiles, carried away to these dumb idols, however you were led. 3 Therefore I make known to you that no one speaking by the Spirit of God calls Jesus accursed, and no one can say that Jesus is Lord except by the Holy Spirit.

WORDFINDER

12:1 Spiritual Gifts The abilities God gives to all believers for serving Him in different ways. Every Christian has one or more spiritual gifts as described by Paul.

4 There are diversities of gifts, but the same Spirit. 5 There are differences of ministries, but the same Lord. 6 And there are diversities of activities, but it is the same God who works all in all. 7 But the manifestation of the Spirit is given to each one for the profit *of all:* 8 for to one is given the word of wisdom through the Spirit, to another the word of knowledge through the same Spirit, 9 to another faith by the same Spirit, to another gifts of healings by the same Spirit, 10 to another the working of miracles, to another prophecy, to another discerning of spirits, to another *different* kinds of tongues, to another the interpretation of tongues. 11 But one and the same Spirit works all these things, distributing to each one individually as He wills.

12 For as the body is one and has many members, but all the members of that one body, being many, are one body, so also *is* Christ. 13 For by one Spirit we *were* all baptized into one body—whether Jews or Greeks, whether slaves or free—and have all been made to drink into one Spirit. 14 For in fact the body is not one member but many.

15 If the foot should say, "Because I am not a hand, I am not of the body," is it therefore not of the body? 16 And if the ear should say, "Because I am not an *eye,* I am not of the body," is it therefore not of the body? 17 If the whole body *were* an eye, where *would be* the hearing? If the whole *were* hearing, where *would be* the smelling?

18 But now God has set the members, each one of them, in the body just as He pleased. 19 And if they *were* all one member, where *would* the body be?

20 But now indeed *there are* many members, yet one body. 21 And the eye cannot say to the hand, "I have no need of you"; nor again the head to the feet, "I have no need of you." 22 No, much rather, those members of the body which seem to be weaker are necessary. 23 And those *members* of the body which we think to be less honorable, on these we bestow greater honor; and our unpresentable *parts* have greater modesty, 24 but our presentable *parts* have no need. But God composed the body, having given greater honor to that *part* which lacks it, 25 that there should be no schism in the body, but *that* the members should have the same care for one another. 26 And if one member suffers, all the members suffer with *it;* or if one member is honored, all the members rejoice with *it.*

27 Now you are the body of Christ, and members individually. 28 And God has appointed these in the church: first apostles, second prophets, third teachers, after that miracles, then gifts of healings, helps, administrations, varieties of tongues. 29 *Are* all apostles? *Are* all prophets? *Are* all teachers? *Are* all workers of miracles? 30 Do all have gifts of healings? Do all speak with tongues? Do all interpret? 31 But earnestly desire the best gifts. And yet I show you a more excellent way.

DIGGING IN

12:27 Are You the Hands and Feet of Jesus? The apostle Paul says we are all parts of the body of Jesus. Of course, he means that each Christian possesses the real life of Christ. Your body becomes His for doing His work today. Jesus is in heaven, but you can continue to do His works on earth.

You don't need to rely on your own strength to do the works of Jesus. In fact, you can't do His works by your strength.

Your hands, your feet, your brain, and your mouth become only the CHANNELS Jesus uses to help and to speak to people now.

At one time Jesus walked the dusty roads of Palestine. Today He walks the streets and halls where you live. You are the one in whom Jesus now lives, speaks, and acts to bless other lives all around you.

Love is the greatest gift of all

13 Though I speak with the tongues of men and of angels, but have not **love,** I have become sounding brass or a clanging cymbal. ² And though I have *the gift of* prophecy, and understand all **mysteries** and all knowledge, and though I have all faith, so that I could remove mountains, but have not love, I am nothing. ³ And though I bestow all my goods to *feed the poor,* and though I give my body to be burned, but have not love, it profits me nothing.

⁴ Love suffers long *and* is kind; love does not envy; love does not parade itself, is not puffed up; ⁵ does not behave rudely, does not seek its own, is not provoked, thinks no evil; ⁶ does not rejoice in iniquity, but rejoices in the truth; ⁷ bears all things, believes all things, hopes all things, endures all things.

⁸ Love never fails. But whether *there are* prophecies, they will fail; whether *there are* tongues, they will cease; whether *there is* knowledge, it will vanish away. ⁹ For we know in part and we prophesy in part. ¹⁰ But when that which is perfect has come, then that which is in part will be done away.

¹¹ When I was a child, I spoke as a child, I understood as a child, I thought as a child; but when I became a man, I put away childish things. ¹² For now we see in a mirror, dimly, but then face to face. Now I know in part, but then I shall know just as I also am known.

¹³ And now abide faith, hope, love, these three; but the greatest of these *is* love.

"Now we can only see God's reflection, as in a piece of polished metal like the mirrors the Corinthians used."

The gift of prophecy helps unsaved people find God

14 Pursue love, and desire **spiritual gifts,** but especially that you may prophesy. ² For he who speaks in a tongue does not speak to men but to God, for no one understands *him;* however, in the spirit he speaks mysteries. ³ But he who prophesies speaks

---

ᴺᴷᴱ WORDFINDER

13:1 Love An attitude that leads to the behavior Paul describes in this chapter. Christian love is not selfish but always seeks the best for everybody. Such love is the greatest gift of God.

13:2 Mysteries Things that are not known. Paul spoke about "the mysteries of God." These were things that weren't known until Jesus came and revealed the gospel.

14:1 Spiritual Gifts The abilities God gives to all believers for serving Him in different ways. Every Christian has one or more spiritual gifts as described by Paul.

edification and exhortation and comfort to men. ⁴He who speaks in a tongue edifies himself, but he who prophesies edifies the church. ⁵I wish you all spoke with tongues, but even more that you prophesied; for he who prophesies is greater than he who speaks with tongues, unless indeed he interprets, that the church may receive edification.

⁶But now, brethren, if I come to you speaking with tongues, what shall I profit you unless I speak to you either by revelation, by knowledge, by prophesying, or by teaching? ⁷Even things without life, whether flute or harp, when they make a sound, unless they make a distinction in the sounds, how will it be known what is piped or played? ⁸For if the trumpet makes an uncertain sound, who will prepare for battle? ⁹So likewise you, unless you utter by the tongue words easy to understand, how will it be known what is spoken? For you will be speaking into the air. ¹⁰There are, it may be, so many kinds of languages in the world, and none of them is without significance. ¹¹Therefore, if I do not know the meaning of the language, I shall be a foreigner to him who speaks, and he who speaks will be a foreigner to me. ¹²Even so you, since you are zeal-

ous for spiritual gifts, let it be for the edification of the church that you seek to excel.

¹³Therefore let him who speaks in a tongue pray that he may interpret. ¹⁴For if I pray in a tongue, my spirit prays, but my understanding is unfruitful. ¹⁵What is the conclusion then? I will pray with the spirit, and I will also pray with the understanding. I will sing with the spirit, and I will also sing with the understanding. ¹⁶Otherwise, if you bless with the spirit, how will he who occupies the place of the uninformed say "Amen" at your giving of thanks, since he does not understand what you say? ¹⁷For you indeed give thanks well, but the other is not edified.

¹⁸I thank my God I speak with tongues more than you all; ¹⁹yet in the church I would rather speak five words with my understanding, that I may teach others also, than ten thousand words in a tongue.

²⁰Brethren, do not be children in understanding; however, in malice be babes, but in understanding be mature.

²¹In the law it is written:

"With men of other tongues and other lips
I will speak to this people;

✦WORDFINDER

14:16 Amen   Pronounced *ah-MEN.* A Greek and Hebrew word meaning "let it be so." Jesus is also called "the Amen" because He is faithful and true (Revelation 3:14).

⚒DIGGING IN

13:13 Your Greatest Gift from God Some people would like to have great FAITH. Then they could do great miracles and surprise everybody with their power. Such people could put on a show and make millions of dollars. Other people would like to have great HOPE. Then nothing could ever make them afraid. But remember, there probably has never been a Christian who was not sad and afraid sometimes.

But Paul says the greatest gift from God

is LOVE. What is love? Paul tells us what love is like in 1 Corinthians 13. Love is different from just *liking* somebody. We *like* people who please us by their appearance or actions, but we truly *love* people when we care about them even when they aren't nice. That's like the love of Jesus for us. He loved us when we were ugly with sin. Love is what really proves us as Christians. But that kind of love is God's greatest gift to you.

And yet, for all that, they will not hear Me,'' says the Lord.

22 Therefore tongues are for a sign, not to those who believe but to unbelievers; but prophesying is not for unbelievers but for those who believe. 23 Therefore if the whole church comes together in one place, and all speak with tongues, and there come in *those who are* uninformed or unbelievers, will they not say that you are out of your mind? 24 But if all prophesy, and an unbeliever or an uninformed person comes in, he is convinced by all, he is convicted by all. 25 And thus the secrets of his heart are revealed; and so, falling down on *his* face, he will worship God and report that God is truly among you.

26 How is it then, brethren? Whenever you come together, each of you has a psalm, has a teaching, has a tongue, has a revelation, has an interpretation. Let all things be done for edification. 27 If anyone speaks in a tongue, *let there be* two or at the most three, *each* in turn, and let one interpret. 28 But if there is no interpreter, let him keep silent in church, and let him speak to himself and to God. 29 Let two or three prophets speak, and let the others judge. 30 But if *anything* is revealed to another who sits by, let the first keep silent. 31 For you can all prophesy one by one, that all may learn and all may be encouraged. 32 And the spirits of the prophets are subject to the prophets. 33 For God is not *the author* of confusion but of peace, as in all the churches of the saints.

34 Let your women keep silent in the churches, for they are not permitted to speak; but *they are* to be submissive, as the law also says. 35 And if they want to learn something, let them ask their own husbands at home; for it is shameful for women to speak in church.

36 Or did the word of God come *originally* from you? Or *was it* you only that it reached? 37 If anyone thinks himself to be a prophet or spiritual, let

him acknowledge that the things which I write to you are the commandments of the Lord. 38 But if anyone is ignorant, let him be ignorant.

39 Therefore, brethren, desire earnestly to prophesy, and do not forbid to speak with tongues. 40 Let all things be done decently and in order.

Jesus Christ rose from the dead, and so will we

15 Moreover, brethren, I declare to you the gospel which I preached to you, which also you received and in which you stand, 2 by which also you are saved, if you hold fast that word which I preached to you—unless you believed in vain.

3 For I delivered to you first of all that which I also received: that Christ died for our sins according to the Scriptures, 4 and that He was buried, and that He rose again the third day according to the Scriptures, 5 and that He was seen by Cephas, then by the twelve. 6 After that He was seen by over five hundred brethren at once, of whom the greater part remain to the present, but some have fallen asleep. 7 After that He was seen by James, then by all the apostles. 8 Then last of all He was seen by me also, as by one born out of due time.

9 For I am the least of the apostles, who am not worthy to be called an apostle, because I persecuted the church of God. 10 But by the grace of God I am what I am, and His grace toward me was not in vain; but I labored more abundantly than they all, yet not I, but the grace of God *which was* with me. 11 Therefore, whether *it was* I or they, so we preach and so you believed.

12 Now if Christ is preached that He has been raised from the dead, how do some among you say that there is no resurrection of the dead? 13 But if there is no resurrection of the dead, then Christ is not risen. 14 And if Christ is not risen, then our preaching *is* empty and your faith *is* also empty.

15 Yes, and we are found false witnesses of God, because we have testified of God that He raised up Christ, whom He did not raise up—if in fact the dead do not rise. 16 For if *the* dead do not rise, then Christ is not risen. 17 And if Christ is not risen, your faith *is* futile; you are still in your sins! 18 Then also those who have fallen asleep in Christ have perished. 19 If in this life only we have hope in Christ, we are of all men the most pitiable.

20 But now Christ is risen from the dead, *and* has become the **firstfruits** of those who have fallen asleep. 21 For since by man *came* death, by Man also *came* the resurrection of the dead. 22 For as in Adam all die, *even* so in Christ all shall be made alive. 23 But each one in his own order: Christ the firstfruits, afterward those *who are* Christ's at His coming. 24 Then *comes* the end, when He delivers the kingdom to God the Father, when He puts an end to all rule and all authority and power. 25 For He must reign till He has put all enemies under His *feet.* 26 The last enemy *that* will be destroyed *is* death. 27 For "He has put all things under His feet." But when He says "all things are put under *Him,*" *it is* evident that He who put all things under Him

is excepted. 28 Now when all things are made subject to Him, then the Son Himself will also be subject to Him who put all things under Him, that God may be all in all.

29 Otherwise, what will they do who are baptized for the dead, if the dead do not rise at all? Why then are they baptized for the dead? 30 And why do we stand in jeopardy every hour? 31 I affirm, by the boasting in you which I have in Christ Jesus our Lord, I die daily. 32 If, in the manner of men, I have fought with beasts at Ephesus, what advantage *is it* to me? If *the* dead do not rise, "Let us eat and drink, for tomorrow we die!"

33 Do not be deceived: "Evil company corrupts good habits." 34 Awake to righteousness, and do not sin; for some do not have the knowledge of God. I speak *this* to your shame.

35 But someone will say, "How are the dead raised up? And with what body do they come?" 36 Foolish one, what you sow is not made alive unless it dies. 37 And what you sow, you do not sow that body that shall be, but mere grain—perhaps wheat or some other *grain.* 38 But God gives it a body as He pleases, and to each *seed* its own body.

39 All flesh *is* not the same flesh, but

WORDFINDER

15:20 Firstfruits Israel's offering to God at the Feast of Harvest. They gave God the first and best of their work. Our first and best also belong to God.

DIGGING IN

15:20 The Greatest Truth of All What is the most amazing thing you ever heard? For many people living today, the greatest discovery was splitting the atom, resulting in nuclear energy. And can you imagine what people said when they saw the first television picture? "Amazing!"

Then think of what the people of Jesus' day said when they saw His miracles. Yet changing water to wine, multiplying the loaves and fish, and healing a withered hand were easy for Jesus.

The hardest thing for Jesus was letting

Himself be led to a cross and having nails driven through His hands and feet. He was the sinless Son of God, and He didn't deserve to be crucified.

But the greatest truth of all is that Jesus conquered sin and death when He rose up on that first Easter. Without the resurrection of Jesus, no other truth in the world could ever matter. We would all be slaves of death. But now you can have eternal life because Jesus is alive forevermore.

there is one kind of flesh of men, another flesh of animals, another of fish, and another of birds.

40 There are also celestial bodies and terrestrial bodies; but the glory of the celestial is one, and the glory of the terrestrial is another. 41 There is one glory of the sun, another glory of the moon, and another glory of the stars; for one star differs from another star in glory.

42 So also is the resurrection of the dead. The body is sown in corruption, it is raised in incorruption. 43 It is sown in dishonor, it is raised in glory. It is sown in weakness, it is raised in power. 44 It is sown a natural body, it is raised a spiritual body. There is a natural body, and there is a spiritual body. 45 And so it is written, "The first man Adam became a living being." The last Adam became a life-giving spirit.

46 However, the spiritual is not first, but the natural, and afterward the spiritual. 47 The first man was of the earth, made of dust; the second Man is the Lord from heaven. 48 As was the man of dust, so also are those who are made of dust; and as is the heavenly Man, so also are those who are heavenly. 49 And as we have borne the image of the man of dust, we shall also bear the image of the heavenly Man.

50 Now this I say, brethren, that flesh and blood cannot inherit the kingdom of God; nor does corruption inherit incorruption. 51 Behold, I tell you a mystery: We shall not all sleep, but we shall all be changed— 52 in a moment, in the twinkling of an eye, at the last trumpet. For the trumpet will sound, and the dead will be raised incorruptible, and we shall be changed. 53 For this corruptible must put on incorruption, and this mortal must put on immortality. 54 So when this corruptible

has put on incorruption, and this mortal has put on immortality, then shall be brought to pass the saying that is written: "Death is swallowed up in victory."

55 "O Death, where is your sting?
O Hades, where is your
victory?"

56 The sting of death is sin, and the strength of sin is the law. 57 But thanks be to God, who gives us the victory through our Lord Jesus Christ. 58 Therefore, my beloved brethren, be steadfast, immovable, always abounding in the work of the Lord, knowing that your labor is not in vain in the Lord.

Taking a collection for the churches in Galatia

16 Now concerning the collection for the saints, as I have given orders to the churches of Galatia, so you must do also: 2 On the first day of the week let each one of you lay something aside, storing up as he may prosper, that there be no collections when I come. 3 And when I come, whomever you approve by your letters I will send to bear your gift to Jerusalem. 4 But if it is fitting that I go also, they will go with me.

5 Now I will come to you when I pass through Macedonia (for I am passing through Macedonia). 6 And it may be that I will remain, or even spend the winter with you, that you may send me on my journey, wherever I go. 7 For I do not wish to see you now on the way; but I hope to stay a while with you, if the Lord permits.

8 But I will tarry in Ephesus until

🌐 WORDFINDER _____

15:53–54 Mortal The opposite of immortal (see definition at Romans 2:7). Your present body will die, but your soul is immortal (cannot die). Someday believers will receive immortal bodies like Christ's body.

15:53–54 Immortality Pronounce im-or-TAL-ih-tee. Life that never ends. Paul uses it to describe our everlasting life with God.

Pentecost. 9 For a great and *effective* door has opened to me, and *there are* many adversaries.

10 And if Timothy comes, see that he may be with you without fear; for he does the work of the Lord, as I also *do.* 11 Therefore let no one despise him. But send him on his journey in peace, that he may come to me; for I am waiting for him with the brethren.

12 Now concerning *our* brother Apollos, I strongly urged him to come to you with the brethren, but he was quite unwilling to come at this time; however, he will come when he has a convenient time.

13 Watch, stand fast in the faith, be brave, be strong. 14 Let all *that* you *do* be done with love.

15 I urge you, brethren—you know the household of Stephanas, that it is the firstfruits of Achaia, and *that* they have devoted themselves to the minis-

try of the saints— 16 that you also submit to such, and to everyone who works and labors with *us.*

17 I am glad about the coming of Stephanas, Fortunatus, and Achaicus, for what was lacking on your part they supplied. 18 For they refreshed my spirit and yours. Therefore acknowledge such men.

19 The churches of Asia greet you. Aquila and Priscilla greet you heartily in the Lord, with the church that is in their house. 20 All the brethren greet you.

Greet one another with a holy kiss. 21 The salutation with my own hand—Paul's.

22 If anyone does not love the Lord Jesus Christ, let him be accursed. O Lord, come!

23 The grace of our Lord Jesus Christ *be* with you. 24 My love *be* with you all in Christ Jesus. Amen.

WORDFINDER

16:8 The Day of Pentecost   The day coming fifty days after the Jewish Passover (see definition of *Passover* at John 2:13). Pentecost (pronounced *PEN-tih-cost*) is also called the Feast of Harvest.

The Book of
2 CORINTHIANS

We owe our lives to the apostle Paul. He was like a father to us, but we made his life very hard.

When Paul first came to Corinth, we were all living in terrible sin. We were the awful "Corinthians" you read about in our first letter from Paul.

Then Paul came and shared with us his wonderful Good News about Jesus, the Savior who died for our sins. So our lives were changed. We believed the gospel and became like people who were dead but now are alive again.

Somehow we forgot our good beginnings, though, and began to fight among ourselves about who our leader should be. Should it be Paul? Or Peter? Or Apollos?

Then Paul had to explain that Jesus was our only true Leader. He had to tell us some things about ourselves that made us ashamed of ourselves. Now we pray we may never act like Christian babies again.

Paul comforts the Christians in Corinth

PAUL, an **apostle** of Jesus Christ by the will of God, and Timothy our brother,

To the church of God which is at Corinth, with all the saints who are in all Achaia:

2 Grace to you and peace from God our Father and the Lord Jesus Christ.

3 Blessed be the God and Father of our Lord Jesus Christ, the Father of mercies and God of all comfort, 4 who comforts us in all our tribulation, that we may be able to comfort those who are in any trouble, with the comfort with which we ourselves are comforted by God. 5 For as the sufferings of Christ abound in us, so our consolation also abounds through Christ. 6 Now if we are afflicted, it is for your consolation and salvation, which is

WORDFINDER

1:1 Apostle Pronounced *uh-POSS-ul*. One of the men Jesus sent to preach the Good News of salvation. The word comes from a Greek word meaning "sent."

DIGGING IN

1:6 How Much Should We Love People? The question isn't so hard, but the answer may be. Paul loved the people at Corinth more than anyone could expect, even though a lot of people at Corinth didn't like Paul very much. They said he was a boring speaker, and he wasn't good-looking!

But Paul had led many of those people to know Jesus, and Paul started the church at Corinth. Paul had spent himself beyond human limits to do what was best for the people of Corinth.

Real love has no limits. Love sometimes suffers long and may never be appreciated by those who are loved. There are lots of monuments built to honor people who loved much but were not loved in their own time. The world may be unkind and even cruel to you, but it is your privilege to go on loving that world because Jesus loves you—and because He died for that world.

A view of the mountain beyond Corinth, with the marketplace or public square in the foreground.

effective for enduring the same sufferings which we also suffer. Or if we are comforted, *it is* for your consolation and salvation. ⁷ And our hope for you *is* steadfast, because we know that as you are partakers of the sufferings, so also *you will partake* of the consolation.

⁸ For we do not want you to be ignorant, brethren, of our trouble which came to us in Asia: that we were burdened beyond measure, above strength, so that we despaired even of life. ⁹ Yes, we had the sentence of death in ourselves, that we should not trust in ourselves but in God who raises the dead, ¹⁰ who delivered us from so great a death, and does deliver us; in whom we trust that He will still deliver us, ¹¹ you also helping together in prayer for us, that thanks may be given by many persons on our behalf for the gift *granted* to us through many.

¹² For our boasting is this: the testimony of our conscience that we conducted ourselves in the world in simplicity and godly sincerity, not with fleshly wisdom but by the grace of God, and more abundantly toward you. ¹³ For we are not writing any other things to you than what you read or understand. Now I trust you will understand, even to the end ¹⁴ (as also you have understood us in part), that we are your boast as you also *are* ours, in the day of the Lord Jesus.

¹⁵ And in this confidence I intended to come to you before, that you might have a second benefit— ¹⁶ to pass by way of you to Macedonia, to come again from Macedonia to you, and be helped by you on my way to Judea. ¹⁷ Therefore, when I was planning this, did I do it lightly? Or the things I plan, do I plan according to the flesh, that

with me there should be Yes, Yes, and No, No? 18 But *as* God *is* faithful, our word to you was not Yes and No. 19 For the Son of God, Jesus Christ, who was preached among you by us—by me, Silvanus, and Timothy—was not Yes and No, but in Him was Yes. 20 For all the promises of God in Him *are* Yes, and in Him Amen, to the glory of God through us. 21 Now He who establishes us with you in Christ and has anointed us *is* God, 22 who also has sealed us and given us the Spirit in our hearts as a guarantee.

23 Moreover I call God as witness against my soul, that to spare you I came no more to Corinth. 24 Not that we have dominion over your faith, but are fellow workers for your joy; for by faith you stand.

Spread the Good News like sweet perfume

2 But I determined this within myself, that I would not come again to you in sorrow. 2 For if I make you sorrowful, then who is he who makes me glad but the one who is made sorrowful by me? 3 And I wrote this very thing to you, lest, when I came, I should have sorrow over those from whom I ought to have joy, having confidence in you all that my joy is *the joy* of you all. 4 For out of much affliction and anguish of heart I wrote to you, with many

How Do You Treat Those Who Hurt You?

If someone does something unkind or mean to you, you often want to hurt that person. We have to ask God to give us the kind of heart that doesn't want to pay back the harm people do to us. Jesus said, "Father, forgive them, for they do not know what they do" (Luke 23:34).

tears, not that you should be grieved, but that you might know the love which I have so abundantly for you.

5 But if anyone has caused grief, he has not grieved me, but all of you to some extent—not to be too severe. 6 This punishment which *was inflicted* by the majority *is* sufficient for such a man, 7 so that, on the contrary, you *ought* rather to forgive and comfort *him,* lest perhaps such a one be swallowed up with too much sorrow. 8 Therefore I urge you to reaffirm *your* love to him. 9 For to this end I also wrote, that I might put you to the test, whether you are obedient in all things. 10 Now whom you forgive anything, I also *forgive.* For if indeed I have forgiven anything, I have forgiven that one for your sakes in the presence of Christ, 11 lest Satan should take advantage of us; for we are not ignorant of his devices.

12 Furthermore, when I came to

What the Forgiven Man Learned

You can read about me in the fifth chapter of Paul's first letter to the Corinthians. I had committed a great sin. At first everybody thought Paul was too harsh because he told the church at Corinth they must not allow me to worship with them.

But Paul was right. When I had time to think about it, I really missed my friends at the church. Worse than that, I knew Jesus was disappointed in me.

So I gave up my sin. Then Paul wrote right away to tell the people to welcome me back to church with them. He said Jesus had forgiven me and Paul had forgiven me, so the church must also forgive me.

Being forgiven is wonderful. I know my sins are forgotten. Best of all, God and I are friends again.

Troas to *preach* Christ's gospel, and a door was opened to me by the Lord, ¹³ I had no rest in my spirit, because I did not find Titus my brother; but taking my leave of them, I departed for Macedonia.

¹⁴ Now thanks *be* to God who always leads us in triumph in Christ, and through us diffuses the fragrance of His knowledge in every place. ¹⁵ For we are to God the fragrance of Christ among those who are being saved and among those who are perishing. ¹⁶ To the one *we are* the aroma of death *leading* to death, and to the other the aroma of life *leading* to life. And who *is* sufficient for these things? ¹⁷ For we are not, as so many, peddling the word of God; but as of sincerity, but as from God, we speak in the sight of God in Christ.

Christians are Christ's living love letters

3 Do we begin again to commend ourselves? Or do we need, as some *others,* epistles of commendation to you or *letters* of commendation from you? ² You are our epistle written in our hearts, known and read by all men; ³ clearly *you are* an epistle of Christ, ministered by us, written not with ink but by the Spirit of the living God, not on tablets of stone but on tablets of flesh, *that is,* of the heart.

⁴ And we have such trust through Christ toward God. ⁵ Not that we are sufficient of ourselves to think of anything as *being* from ourselves, but our

sufficiency *is* from God, ⁶ who also made us sufficient as ministers of the new covenant, not of the letter but of the Spirit; for the letter kills, but the Spirit gives life.

⁷ But if the ministry of death, written *and* engraved on stones, was glorious, so that the children of Israel could not look steadily at the face of Moses because of the glory of his countenance, which *glory* was passing away, ⁸ how will the ministry of the Spirit not be more glorious? ⁹ For if the ministry of condemnation *had* glory, the ministry of righteousness exceeds much more in glory. ¹⁰ For even what was made glorious had no glory in this respect, because of the glory that excels. ¹¹ For if what is passing away *was* glorious, what remains *is* much more glorious.

¹² Therefore, since we have such hope, we use great boldness of speech— ¹³ unlike Moses, *who* put a veil over his face so that the children of Israel could not look steadily at the end of what was passing away. ¹⁴ But their minds were blinded. For until this day the same veil remains unlifted in the reading of the Old Testament, because the *veil* is taken away in Christ. ¹⁵ But even to this day, when Moses is read, a veil lies on their heart. ¹⁶ Nevertheless when one turns to the Lord, the veil is taken away. ¹⁷ Now the Lord is the Spirit; and where the Spirit of the Lord *is,* there *is* liberty. ¹⁸ But we all, with unveiled face, beholding as in a mirror the glory of the Lord, are being transformed into the

---

⚒ DIGGING IN

3:2 Be a Walking Bible It's hard to get everybody to read the Bible. But in a real way, you can be a walking Bible that everyone can read.

God doesn't want the thoughts in the Bible to stay between the covers of that great Book. He wants those words to leap out of the pages and into your life. As the words of God pass through your eyes and ears, they are something like vitamins. The words of God give you the

strength of Jesus inside. After a while you begin to be a walking Bible. Even more than that, you begin to live and speak and think the way Jesus would. Jesus said, "The words I speak . . . are life."

That's a thrilling idea, isn't it? You can actually become like Jesus in the world. And the more you become like Jesus, the more your life will change people around you—just the way Jesus' life did.

same image from glory to glory, just as by the Spirit of the Lord.

Paul is excited about preaching the gospel

4 Therefore, since we have this ministry, as we have received mercy, we do not lose heart. 2 But we have renounced the hidden things of shame, not walking in craftiness nor handling the word of God deceitfully, but by manifestation of the truth commending ourselves to every man's conscience in the sight of God. 3 But even if our gospel is veiled, it is veiled to those who are perishing, 4 whose minds the god of this age has blinded, who do not believe, lest the light of the gospel of the glory of Christ, who is the image of God, should shine on them. 5 For we do not preach ourselves, but Christ Jesus the Lord, and ourselves your bondservants for Jesus' sake. 6 For it is the God who commanded light to shine out of darkness, who has shone in our hearts to *give* the light of the knowledge of the glory of God in the face of Jesus Christ.

7 But we have this treasure in earthen vessels, that the excellence of the power may be of God and not of us. 8 *We are* hard-pressed on every side, yet not crushed; *we are* perplexed, but not in despair; 9 persecuted, but not forsaken; struck down, but not destroyed— 10 always carrying about in the body the dying of the Lord Jesus, that the life of Jesus also may be manifested in our body. 11 For we who live are always delivered to death for Jesus' sake, that the life of Jesus also may be manifested in our mortal flesh. 12 So then death is working in us, but life in you.

13 And since we have the same spirit of faith, according to what is written, "I believed and therefore I spoke," we also believe and therefore speak, 14 knowing that He who raised up the Lord Jesus will also raise us up with Jesus, and will present *us* with you. 15 For all things *are* for your sakes, that grace, having spread through the many, may cause thanksgiving to abound to the glory of God.

16 Therefore we do not lose heart. Even though our outward man is

DIGGING IN

4:7 God Wants to Live in You God is not just "the man in the sky." God is the INFINITE CREATOR. Even though God is unlimited, He came to live in the form of a special Man named Jesus. Jesus was GOD WITH US—that was one of His names (see Matthew 1:23). Jesus was the way God showed us what He is like—and also what we should be like.

But you can't be like God just by making up your mind to be like Him. You can only be like God if God Himself comes to live inside you. In fact, the great plan of God is to make people become like LIVING BUILDINGS that God will live in forever. Doesn't that idea make chills go up and down your spine? Just think of it—the God of the universe living in you forever and ever!

That's the way God plans to make people become like He is. That's how you, too, can become like God.

4:16 Never Give In These are the words of the great English statesman, Sir Winston Churchill. He spoke these words to the British people when the bombs were falling on their cities during World War II.

On a hiking trip, you will sometimes feel like you can't take another step. You just want to drop your pack and sit down. But the leader urges you on and on. Soon you're back at camp, sitting down to a big meal and a long rest.

Being a Christian is like that. You may get tired of the long journey through this world. You may even feel like quitting sometimes, but then a verse comes to you, such as, "I can do all things through Christ who strengthens me" (Philippians 4:13). Now you can go on and do greater things for Jesus than you ever did before. One day you will arrive at the heavenly camp where Jesus is your Leader. Then you'll say, "I'm glad I never gave in."

perishing, yet the inward *man* is being renewed day by day. ¹⁷ For our light affliction, which is but for a moment, is working for us a far more exceeding *and* eternal weight of glory, ¹⁸ while we do not look at the things which are seen, but at the things which are not seen. For the things which are seen *are* temporary, but the things which are not seen *are* eternal.

In heaven we will have wonderful new bodies

5 For we know that if our earthly house, *this* tent, is destroyed, we have a building from God, a house not made with hands, eternal in the heavens. ² For in this we groan, earnestly desiring to be clothed with our habitation which is from heaven, ³ if indeed, having been clothed, we shall not be found naked. ⁴ For we who are in *this* tent groan, being burdened, not because we want to be unclothed, but further clothed, that mortality may be swallowed up by life. ⁵ Now He who has prepared us for this very thing *is* God, who also has given us the Spirit as a guarantee.

⁶ So *we are* always confident, knowing that while we are at home in the body we are absent from the Lord. ⁷ For we walk by faith, not by sight. ⁸ We are confident, yes, well pleased rather to be absent from the body and to be present with the Lord.

⁹ Therefore we make it our aim, whether present or absent, to be well pleasing to Him. ¹⁰ For we must all appear before the judgment seat of Christ, that each one may receive the things *done* in the body, according to what he has done, whether good or bad. ¹¹ Knowing, therefore, the terror of the Lord, we persuade men; but we are well known to God, and I also trust are well known in your consciences.

¹² For we do not commend ourselves again to you, but give you opportunity to boast on our behalf, that you may have an *answer* for those who boast in appearance and not in heart. ¹³ For if we are beside ourselves, *it is* for God; or if we are of sound mind, *it is* for you. ¹⁴ For the love of Christ compels us, because we judge thus: that if One died for all, then all died; ¹⁵ and He died for all, that those who live should live no longer for themselves, but for Him who died for them and rose again.

¹⁶ Therefore, from now on, we regard no one according to the flesh. Even though we have known Christ according to the flesh, yet now we know *Him thus* no longer. ¹⁷ Therefore, if anyone *is* in Christ, *he is* a new creation; old things have passed away; behold, all things have become new. ¹⁸ Now all things *are* of God, who has reconciled us to Himself through Jesus Christ, and has given us the ministry of reconciliation, ¹⁹ that is, that God was in Christ reconciling the world to Himself, not imputing their trespasses to them, and has committed to us the word of reconciliation.

²⁰ Now then, we are ambassadors for Christ, as though God were pleading through us: we implore *you* on Christ's behalf, be **reconciled** to God.

WORDFINDER

5:20 Reconciled Pronounced *REK-un-syld*. To be at peace with someone. God is at peace with us because Christ died for our sins. So now we should be at peace with God.

DIGGING IN

5:21 Jesus Carried All Your Sins
Why did Jesus die on the Cross? We say, "He died for our sins." But what does that mean?

Something happened when Jesus was

crucified that never happened to anyone else, and it can never happen again. Jesus was totally innocent, but when He died He was blamed for ALL your sin, and He took ALL your punishment. It was as

21 For He made Him who knew no sin *to be* sin for us, that we might become the righteousness of God in Him.

Paul is God's partner

6 We then, *as* workers together *with Him* also plead with *you* not to receive the grace of God in vain. 2 For He says:

"In an acceptable time I have heard you,
And in the day of salvation I have helped you."

Behold, now *is* the accepted time; behold, now *is* the day of salvation.

3 We give no offense in anything, that our ministry may not be blamed. 4 But in all *things* we commend ourselves as ministers of God: in much patience, in tribulations, in needs, in distresses, 5 in stripes, in imprisonments, in tumults, in labors, in sleeplessness, in fastings; 6 by purity, by knowledge, by longsuffering, by kindness, by the Holy Spirit, by sincere love, 7 by the word of truth, by the power of God, by the armor of righteousness on the right hand and on the left, 8 by honor and dishonor, by evil report and good report; as deceivers, and *yet* true; 9 as unknown, and *yet* well known; as dying, and behold we live; as chastened, and *yet* not

killed; 10 as sorrowful, yet always rejoicing; as poor, yet making many rich; as having nothing, and *yet* possessing all things.

11 O Corinthians! We have spoken openly to you, our heart is wide open. 12 You are not restricted by us, but you are restricted by your *own* affections. 13 Now in return for the same (I speak as to children), you also be open.

14 Do not be unequally yoked together with unbelievers. For what fellowship has righteousness with lawlessness? And what communion has light with darkness? 15 And what accord has Christ with Belial? Or what part has a believer with an unbeliever? 16 And what agreement has the temple of God with idols? For you are the temple of the living God. As God has said:

"I will dwell in them
And walk among *them*.
I will be their God,
And they shall be My people."

17 Therefore

"Come out from among them
And be separate, says the Lord.
Do not touch what is unclean,
And I will receive you."
18 "I will be a Father to you,
And you shall be My sons and daughters,
Says the LORD Almighty."

⛏ DIGGING IN

if Jesus actually went to hell for you. No one can ever thank Him enough for suffering what you and I can never understand.

At the same time, something just as amazing happened. When Jesus died, ALL of the goodness of Jesus was given to you. It's just as if you are arrested for a terrible crime, but when the judge gives the sentence, he doesn't blame *you.* A friend of yours has offered Himself in your place and said, "Punish me instead, Judge, and let my friend go free." Jesus is that Friend who died in your place.

6:14 Make God's Friends Your Friends You become like your friends, and your friends become like you. If your friends are interested in sports, you will

likely be someone who likes sports, too. If your friends are into drugs, you also are in danger of becoming a drug user. So it matters a lot who your friends are since we like to be with people who enjoy what we enjoy.

Christians mostly enjoy God. In fact, Christians know their greatest reason for living is to honor God in their lives and to *enjoy* Him forever. Making friends with people who enjoy God's friends is a pretty good idea. After all, these are the people you're going to be in heaven with forever. If you don't enjoy the friendship of other Christians, it may be a sign that you don't enjoy God's friendship either. People who enjoy God enjoy one another also.

Paul is proud of the Corinthian Christians

7 Therefore, having these promises, beloved, let us cleanse ourselves from all filthiness of the flesh and spirit, perfecting holiness in the fear of God.

2 Open *your hearts* to us. We have wronged no one, we have corrupted no one, we have cheated no one. 3 I do not say *this* to condemn; for I have said before that you are in our hearts, to die together and to live together. 4 Great *is* my boldness of speech toward you, great *is* my boasting on your behalf. I am filled with comfort. I am exceedingly joyful in all our tribulation.

5 For indeed, when we came to Macedonia, our bodies had no rest, but we were troubled on every side. Outside *were* conflicts, inside *were* fears. 6 Nevertheless God, who comforts the downcast, comforted us by the coming of Titus, 7 and not only by his coming, but also by the consolation with which he was comforted in you, when he told us of your earnest desire, your mourning, your zeal for me, so that I rejoiced even more.

8 For even if I made you sorry with my letter, I do not regret it; though I did regret it. For I perceive that the same epistle made you sorry, though only for a while. 9 Now I rejoice, not that you were made sorry, but that your sorrow led to repentance. For you were made sorry in a godly manner, that you might suffer loss from us in nothing. 10 For godly sorrow produces repentance *leading* to salvation, not to be regretted; but the sorrow of the world produces death. 11 For observe this very thing, that you sorrowed in a godly manner: What diligence it produced in you, *what* clearing *of yourselves, what* indignation, *what* fear, *what* vehement desire, *what* zeal, *what* vindication! In all *things* you proved yourselves to be clear in this matter. 12 Therefore, although I wrote to you, I *did* not *do it* for the sake of him who had done the wrong, nor for the sake of him who suffered wrong, but that our care for you in the sight of God might appear to you.

13 Therefore we have been comforted in your comfort. And we rejoiced exceedingly more for the joy of Titus, because his spirit has been refreshed by you all. 14 For if in anything I have boasted to him about you, I am not ashamed. But as we spoke all things to you in truth, even so our boasting to Titus was found true. 15 And his affections are greater for you as he remembers the obedience of you all, how with fear and trembling you received him. 16 Therefore I rejoice that I have confidence in you in everything.

WORDFINDER

7:10 Repentance Pronounced *re-PEN-tunce*. Turning away from sin to obey God. You repent when you leave your sins to receive Christ as your Savior and Master of your life.

DIGGING IN

7:1 Lead a Clean Life John Wesley, a great preacher, once said, "Cleanliness is next to godliness." But there are different kinds of dirt. There's the dirt you get from doing a dirty job or from playing sports. That kind of dirt can be washed off. Every day you have to wash off the dirt of living in a dirty world.

Then there's that other kind of dirt. People may not see it, but God can. It's the dirt INSIDE you—in your inner life, where God should live. Jesus died to make you clean inside, but every day you find yourself getting dirty all over again. Sin creeps in daily. So every day you need to ask Jesus to make you clean *inside*. Then you will be able to live clean before God and before a watching world.

Share with those who are in need

8 Moreover, brethren, we make known to you the grace of God bestowed on the churches of Macedonia: 2 that in a great trial of affliction the abundance of their joy and their deep poverty abounded in the riches of their liberality. 3 For I bear witness that according to their ability, yes, and beyond their ability, they were freely willing, 4 imploring us with much urgency that we would receive the gift and the fellowship of the ministering to the saints. 5 And not only as we had hoped, but they first gave themselves to the Lord, and then to us by the will of God. 6 So we urged Titus, that as he had begun, so he would also complete this grace in you as well. 7 But as you abound in everything—in faith, in speech, in knowledge, in all diligence, and in your love for us—see that you abound in this grace also.

8 I speak not by commandment, but I am testing the sincerity of your love by the diligence of others. 9 For you know the grace of our Lord Jesus Christ, that though He was rich, yet for your sakes He became poor, that you through His poverty might become rich.

10 And in this I give advice: It is to your advantage not only to be doing what you began and were desiring to do a year ago; 11 but now you also must complete the doing of it; that as there was a readiness to desire it, so there also may be a completion out of what you have. 12 For if there is first a willing mind, it is accepted according to what one has, and not according to what he does not have.

13 For I do not mean that others should be eased and you burdened; 14 but by an equality, that now at this time your abundance may supply their lack, that their abundance also may supply your lack—that there may be equality. 15 As it is written, "He who gathered much had nothing left over, and he who gathered little had no lack."

16 But thanks be to God who puts the same earnest care for you into the heart of Titus. 17 For he not only accepted the exhortation, but being more diligent, he went to you of his own accord. 18 And we have sent with him the brother whose praise is in the gospel throughout all the churches, 19 and not only that, but who was also chosen by the churches to travel with us with this gift, which is administered by us to the glory of the Lord Himself and to show your ready mind, 20 avoiding this: that anyone should blame us in this lavish gift which is administered by us— 21 providing honorable things, not only in the sight of the Lord, but also in the sight of men.

22 And we have sent with them our brother whom we have often proved diligent in many things, but now much more diligent, because of the great confidence which we have in you. 23 If anyone inquires about Titus, he is my partner and fellow worker concerning you. Or if our brethren are inquired about, they are messengers of the churches, the glory of Christ. 24 Therefore show to them, and before the churches the proof of your love and of our boasting on your behalf.

Cheerful givers please God

9 Now concerning the ministering to the saints, it is superfluous for me to write to you; 2 for I know your willingness, about which I boast of you to the Macedonians, that Achaia was ready a year ago; and your zeal has stirred up the majority. 3 Yet I have sent the brethren, lest our boasting of

Are You a Happy Giver?

Jesus was glad to come and die for you. He received joy by giving Himself. God doesn't look at how much you can give to Him. He looks at your heart. We are giving to a great work when we give to spread the Good News of Jesus. Let us be glad to be part of God's work.

you should be in vain in this respect, that, as I said, you may be ready; 4 lest if *some* Macedonians come with me and find you unprepared, we (not to mention you!) should be ashamed of this confident boasting. 5 Therefore I thought it necessary to exhort the brethren to go to you ahead of time, and prepare your generous gift beforehand, which *you had* previously promised, that it may be ready as *a matter of* generosity and not as a grudging obligation.

6 But this *I say:* He who sows sparingly will also reap sparingly, and he who sows bountifully will also reap bountifully. 7 *So let* each one *give* as he purposes in his heart, not grudgingly or of necessity; for God loves a cheerful giver. 8 And God *is* able to make all grace abound toward you, that you, always having all sufficiency in all *things,* may have an abundance for every good work. 9 As it is written:

"He has dispersed abroad,
He has given to the poor;
His righteousness endures
forever."

10 Now may He who supplies seed to the sower, and bread for food, supply and multiply the seed you have *sown* and increase the fruits of your righteousness, 11 while *you are* enriched in everything for all liberality, which causes thanksgiving through us to God. 12 For the administration of this service not only supplies the needs of the saints, but also is abounding through many thanksgivings to God, 13 while, through the proof of this ministry, they glorify God for the obedience of your confession to the gospel of Christ, and for *your* liberal sharing with them and all *men,* 14 and by their prayer for you, who long for you because of the exceeding grace of God in you. 15 Thanks *be* to God for His indescribable gift!

Paul's authority comes from God

10 Now I, Paul, myself am pleading with you by the meekness and gentleness of Christ—who in presence *am* lowly among you, but being absent am bold toward you. 2 But I beg *you* that when I am present I may not be bold with that confidence by which I intend to be bold against some, who think of us as if we walked according to the flesh. 3 For though we walk in the flesh, we do not war according to the flesh. 4 For the weapons of our warfare *are* not carnal but mighty in God for pulling down strongholds, 5 casting down arguments and every high thing that exalts itself against the knowledge of God, bringing every thought into captivity to the obedience of Christ, 6 and being ready to punish all disobedience when your obedience is fulfilled.

7 Do you look at things according to the outward appearance? If anyone is convinced in himself that he is Christ's,

⚒ DIGGING IN

9:7 Be a Cheerful Giver What do you think to yourself when you give a gift to someone? Do you say, "I wish that gift hadn't cost so much," or, "I wish I had the money back that I spent on that gift"? Nobody wants a gift like that. Most of all, God doesn't want gifts that come from a grudging heart. God loves a cheerful giver.

But how can you be cheerful when giving to others takes away your money? That question has a mistake in it. It isn't "your" money! "Your" money comes from God. Everything you have comes from Him. There's a little hymn that goes like this: "We give You what You gave. . . . all that we have is Yours alone, a gift, O Lord, from You."

You can't beat God in your giving. The more you give to God, the more He gives back to you. Just try giving with a thankful heart. You'll see how generous God can be.

Apostle Paul Gives News Conference at Corinth

The Corinthian Chronicle

CORINTH—Following is a statement to the press by the now-famous apostle Paul:

"No doubt my Jewish fellow-citizens and others believe I am a fool. I left a good position among my people in Jerusalem where I was a respected Pharisee (pronounced *FAIR-uh-see*) and member of the Jewish council.

"My career as an apostle began while I was on the road to Damascus (pronounced *duh-MASK-us*) in Syria. I had orders to arrest the Christians there, but then something happened to change my mind. Jesus Himself appeared to me, and He has changed my life completely.

"Since then, all that matters to me is telling the world about my risen Savior, though I have suffered a lot for doing so. But I have been glad to lose my important place in the world so that I may win Christ. When my time comes to die, I will be glad because then I will be with Jesus forever."

---

let him again consider this in himself, that just as he *is* Christ's, even so we *are* Christ's. 8 For even if I should boast somewhat more about our authority, which the Lord gave us for edification and not for your destruction, I shall not be ashamed— 9 lest I seem to terrify you by letters. 10 "For *his* letters," they say, "*are* weighty and powerful, but *his* bodily presence *is* weak, and *his* speech contemptible." 11 Let such a person consider this, that what we are in word by letters when we are absent, such *we will* also *be* in deed when we are present.

12 For we dare not class ourselves or compare ourselves with those who commend themselves. But they, measuring themselves by themselves, and comparing themselves among themselves, are not wise. 13 We, however, will not boast beyond measure, but within the limits of the sphere which God appointed us—a sphere which especially includes you. 14 For we are not overextending ourselves (as though *our authority* did not extend to you), for it was to you that we came with the gospel of Christ; 15 not boasting of things beyond measure, *that is,* in other men's labors, but having hope, *that* as your faith is increased, we shall be greatly enlarged by you in our sphere, 16 to preach the gospel in the *regions* beyond you, *and* not to boast in another man's sphere of accomplishment.

17 But "he who glories, let him glory in the Lord." 18 For not he who commends himself is approved, but whom the Lord commends.

Beware of phony teachers

11 Oh, that you would bear with me in a little folly—and indeed you do bear with me. 2 For I am jealous for you with godly jealousy. For I have betrothed you to one husband, that I may present *you as* a chaste virgin to Christ. 3 But I fear, lest somehow, as the serpent deceived Eve by his craftiness, so your minds may be corrupted from the simplicity that is in Christ. 4 For if he who comes preaches another Jesus whom we have not preached, or *if* you receive a different spirit which you have not received, or a different gospel which you have not accepted—you may well put up with it!

5 For I consider that I am not at all inferior to the most eminent apostles. 6 Even though *I am* untrained in speech, yet *I am* not in knowledge. But we have been thoroughly manifested among you in all things.

7 Did I commit sin in humbling myself that you might be exalted, because I preached the gospel of God to you free of charge? 8 I robbed other

churches, taking wages *from them* to minister to you. 9 And when I was present with you, and in need, I was a burden to no one, for what I lacked the brethren who came from Macedonia supplied. And in *everything* I kept myself from being burdensome to you, and so I will keep *myself*. 10 As the truth of Christ is in me, no one shall stop me from this boasting in the regions of Achaia. 11 Why? Because I do not love you? God knows!

12 But what I do, I will also continue to do, that I may cut off the opportunity from those who desire an opportunity to be regarded just as we are in the things of which they boast. 13 For such *are* false apostles, deceitful workers, transforming themselves into apostles of Christ. 14 And no wonder! For Satan himself transforms himself into an angel of light. 15 Therefore *it is* no great thing if his ministers also transform themselves into ministers of righteousness, whose end will be according to their works.

16 I say again, let no one think me a fool. If otherwise, at least receive me as a fool, that I also may boast a little. 17 What I speak, I speak not according to the Lord, but as it were, foolishly, in this confidence of boasting. 18 Seeing that many boast according to the flesh, I also will boast. 19 For you put up with fools gladly, since you *yourselves* are wise! 20 For you put up with it if one brings you into bondage, if one devours *you,* if one takes *from you,* if one exalts himself, if one strikes you on the face. 21 To *our*

shame I say that we were too weak for that! But in whatever anyone is bold—I speak foolishly—I am bold also.

22 Are they Hebrews? So *am* I. Are they Israelites? So *am* I. Are they the seed of Abraham? So *am* I. 23 Are they ministers of Christ?—I speak as a fool—I *am* more: in labors more abundant, in stripes above measure, in prisons more frequently, in deaths often. 24 From the Jews five times I received forty *stripes* minus one. 25 Three times I was beaten with rods; once I was stoned; three times I was shipwrecked; a night and a day I have been in the deep; 26 *in* journeys often, *in* perils of waters, *in* perils of robbers, *in* perils of *my own* countrymen, *in* perils of the Gentiles, *in* perils in the city, *in* perils in the wilderness, *in* perils in the sea, *in* perils among false brethren; 27 *in* weariness and toil, in sleeplessness often, in hunger and thirst, in fastings often, in cold and nakedness— 28 besides the other things, what comes upon me daily: my deep concern for all the churches. 29 Who is weak, and I am not weak? Who is made to stumble, and I do not burn *with indignation?*

30 If I must boast, I will boast in the things which concern my infirmity. 31 The God and Father of our Lord Jesus Christ, who is blessed forever, knows that I am not lying. 32 In Damascus the governor, under Aretas the king, was guarding the city of the Damascenes with a garrison, desiring to arrest me; 33 but I was let down in a bas-

---

⛏ DIGGING IN

11:14 Don't Be Fooled by Satan Satan likes to dress up like an angel. But he's no angel! *Satan* means "Enemy." Satan has been the enemy of God ever since he tried to be equal with God. He is also a liar and a deceiver. In the Garden of Eden, he deceived Eve by making her believe she could be equal with God.

Satan usually tries to look charming and beautiful. So when you're tempted to

sin, does the sin look ugly? No, of course it doesn't! Satan has made sure it looks nice and attractive.

A lot of things in the world can make you feel good—for a little while! But those very things can also kill you. People used to think cigarettes made them look stylish. Now everybody knows that cigarettes cause cancer. Alcohol is also a poison that makes you feel good—but it can also kill. Yes, Satan is a liar.

ket through a window in the wall, and escaped from his hands.

Paul brags about his weakness

12 It is doubtless not profitable for me to boast. I will come to visions and revelations of the Lord: 2 I know a man in Christ who fourteen years ago— whether in the body I do not know, or whether out of the body I do not know, God knows—such a one was caught up to the third heaven. 3 And I know such a man—whether in the body or out of the body I do not know, God knows— 4 how he was caught up into Paradise and heard inexpressible words, which it is not lawful for a man to utter. 5 Of such a one I will boast; yet of myself I will not boast, except in my infirmities. 6 For though I might desire to boast, I will not be a fool; for I will speak the truth. But I refrain, lest anyone should think of me above what he sees me *to be* or hears from me.

7 And lest I should be exalted above measure by the abundance of the revelations, a thorn in the flesh was given to me, a messenger of Satan to buffet me, lest I be exalted above measure. 8 Concerning this thing I pleaded with the Lord three times that it might depart from me. 9 And He said to me, "My **grace** is sufficient for you, for My strength is made perfect in weakness." Therefore most gladly I will rather boast in my infirmities, that the power of Christ may rest upon me. 10 Therefore I take pleasure in infirmities, in reproaches, in needs, in persecutions, in distresses, for Christ's sake. For when I am weak, then I am strong.

11 I have become a fool in boasting; you have compelled me. For I ought to have been commended by you; for in nothing was I behind the most eminent apostles, though I am nothing. 12 Truly the signs of an apostle were

accomplished among you with all perseverance, in signs and wonders and mighty deeds. 13 For what is it in which you were inferior to other churches, except that I myself was not burdensome to you? Forgive me this wrong!

14 Now *for* the third time I am ready to come to you. And I will not be burdensome to you; for I do not seek yours, but you. For the children ought not to lay up for the parents, but the parents for the children. 15 And I will very gladly spend and be spent for your souls; though the more abundantly I love you, the less I am loved.

16 But be that *as it may,* I did not burden you. Nevertheless, being crafty, I caught you by cunning! 17 Did I take advantage of you by any of those whom I sent to you? 18 I urged Titus, and sent our brother with *him.* Did Titus take advantage of you? Did we not walk in the same spirit? Did *we* not *walk* in the same steps?

19 Again, do you think that we excuse ourselves to you? We speak before God in Christ. But *we do* all things, beloved, for your edification. 20 For I fear lest, when I come, I shall not find you such as I wish, and *that* I shall be found by you such as you do not wish; lest *there be* contentions, jealousies, outbursts of wrath, selfish ambitions, backbitings, whisperings, conceits, tumults; 21 lest, when I come again, my God will humble me among you, and I shall mourn for many who have sinned before and have not repented of the uncleanness, fornication, and lewdness which they have practiced.

Paul warns the Christians to test themselves

13 This *will be* the third *time* I am coming to you. "By the mouth of two or three witnesses every word shall be

12:9 Grace The undeserved kindness of God. We are saved from sin by this grace of God. All the good we enjoy is due to His grace.

established." ²I have told you before, and foretell as if I were present the second time, and now being absent I write to those who have sinned before, and to all the rest, that if I come again I will not spare— ³since you seek a proof of Christ speaking in me, who is not weak toward you, but mighty in you. ⁴For though He was crucified in weakness, yet He lives by the power of God. For we also are weak in Him, but we shall live with Him by the power of God toward you.

⁵Examine yourselves *as to* whether you are in the faith. Test yourselves. Do you not know yourselves, that Jesus Christ is in you?—unless indeed you are disqualified. ⁶But I trust that you will know that we are not disqualified.

⁷Now I pray to God that you do no evil, not that we should appear approved, but that you should do what is honorable, though we may seem disqualified. ⁸For we can do nothing against the truth, but for the truth. ⁹For we are glad when we are weak and you are strong. And this also we pray, that you may be made complete. ¹⁰Therefore I write these things being absent, lest being present I should use sharpness, according to the authority which the Lord has given me for edification and not for destruction.

¹¹Finally, brethren, farewell. Become complete. Be of good comfort, be of one mind, live in peace; and the God of love and peace will be with you.

¹²Greet one another with a holy kiss.

¹³All the saints greet you.

¹⁴The grace of the Lord Jesus Christ, and the love of God, and the communion of the Holy Spirit *be* with you all. Amen.

The Book of
GALATIANS

We are the church Paul describes in his letter as the "foolish Galatians." We lived in the Roman province of Asia called Galatia (pronounced *guh-LAY-she-ah*). Today you call that area "Asia Minor."

We were like the plant Jesus describes in Matthew 13:20, 21. We grew up fast, but we had no roots and so we soon wilted. We loved the Good News Paul preached. If we had just believed what Paul told us, we needn't have worried about anything else.

But other preachers came after Paul left. They said Paul was not a real apostle. They also told us that we non-Jews would have to obey the Jewish religious customs. They said the death of Jesus on the Cross was not enough to save us, and we foolishly believed those men.

We are very thankful that Paul wrote this letter and showed us our mistake.

Paul writes to the Galatian Christians

PAUL, an apostle (not from men nor through man, but through Jesus Christ and God the Father who raised Him from the dead), 2 and all the brethren who are with me,

To the churches of Galatia:

3 Grace to you and peace from God the Father and our Lord Jesus Christ, 4 who gave Himself for our sins, that He might deliver us from this present evil age, according to the will of our God and Father, 5 to whom *be* glory forever and ever. Amen.

6 I marvel that you are turning away so soon from Him who called you in the grace of Christ, to a different gospel, 7 which is not another; but there are some who trouble you and want to pervert the gospel of Christ. 8 But even if we, or an angel from heaven, preach any other gospel to you than what we have preached to you, let him be accursed. 9 As we have said before, so now I say again, if anyone preaches any other gospel to you than what you have received, let him be accursed.

10 For do I now persuade men, or God? Or do I seek to please men? For if I still pleased men, I would not be a bondservant of Christ.

11 But I make known to you,

⚒ DIGGING IN

1:6 There Is Only One Gospel The word *gospel* means "good news." Everyone likes to hear good news of all kinds. But God has just one message of Good News—Jesus Christ died to take away our sins so we can be with Him in heaven forever.

The poor Galatians had truly believed this gospel. Then some false teachers came along and filled their minds with lies. So the Galatians began to believe another so-called gospel that was not "good news" at all. In fact it was very *bad news*. The false teachers made the Galatians believe they had to obey a lot of man-made rules to go to heaven. Actually, nobody could ever perfectly keep all those rules. So that "bad news" nearly ruined the Galatians. The happy ending is that Paul was able to help the Galatians see their mistake.

Jesus is your only way to heaven. He paid your way completely.

brethren, that the gospel which was preached by me is not according to man. 12 For I neither received it from man, nor was I taught it, but it came through the **revelation** of Jesus Christ.

13 For you have heard of my former conduct in Judaism, how I persecuted the church of God beyond measure and tried to destroy it. 14 And I advanced in Judaism beyond many of my contemporaries in my own nation, being more exceedingly zealous for the traditions of my fathers.

15 But when it pleased God, who separated me from my mother's womb and called me through His grace, 16 to reveal His Son in me, that I might preach Him among the Gentiles, I did not immediately confer with flesh and blood, 17 nor did I go up to Jerusalem to those who were apostles before me; but I went to Arabia, and returned again to Damascus.

18 Then after three years I went up to Jerusalem to see Peter, and remained with him fifteen days. 19 But I saw none of the other apostles except James, the Lord's brother. 20 (Now concerning the things which I write to you, indeed, before God, I do not lie.)

21 Afterward I went into the regions of Syria and Cilicia. 22 And I was unknown by face to the churches of Judea which were in Christ. 23 But they were hearing only, "He who formerly persecuted us now preaches the faith which he once tried to destroy." 24 And they glorified God in me.

Peter and Paul disagree about faith and law

2 Then after fourteen years I went up again to Jerusalem with Barnabas, and also took Titus with me. 2 And I went up by revelation, and communicated to them that gospel which I preach among the **Gentiles,** but privately to those who were of reputation, lest by any means I might run, or had run, in vain. 3 Yet not even Titus who was with me, being a Greek, was compelled to be circumcised. 4 And this occurred because of false brethren secretly brought in (who came in by stealth to spy out our liberty which we have in Christ Jesus, that they might bring us into bondage), 5 to whom we did not yield submission even for an hour, that the truth of the gospel might continue with you.

6 But from those who seemed to be something—whatever they were, it makes no difference to me; God shows personal favoritism to no man—for those who seemed to be something added nothing to me. 7 But on the contrary, when they saw that the gospel for the uncircumcised had been committed to me, as the gospel for the circumcised was to Peter 8 (for He who worked effectively in Peter for the apostleship to the circumcised also worked effectively in me toward the Gentiles), 9 and when James, Cephas, and John, who seemed to be pillars, perceived the grace that had been given to me, they gave me and Barnabas the right hand of fellowship, that we should go to the Gentiles and they to the circumcised. 10 They desired only that we should remember the poor, the very thing which I also was eager to do.

11 Now when Peter had come to Antioch, I withstood him to his face, because he was to be blamed; 12 for before certain men came from James, he would eat with the Gentiles; but when they came, he withdrew and separated himself, fearing those who were of the circumcision. 13 And the rest of the

WORDFINDER

1:12 Revelation Pronounced rev-uh-LAY-shun. What God has revealed or shown about His plan for all time. This revelation is the gospel or Good News the whole Bible tells about.

2:2 Gentiles All peoples and nations who are not of the Hebrew race. God promised that the Jews would be a blessing to the Gentiles. Jesus fulfilled that promise.

Jews also played the hypocrite with him, so that even Barnabas was carried away with their hypocrisy.

14 But when I saw that they were not straightforward about the truth of the gospel, I said to Peter before *them* all, "If you, being a Jew, live in the manner of Gentiles and not as the Jews, why do you compel Gentiles to live as Jews? 15 We *who are* Jews by nature, and not sinners of the Gentiles, 16 knowing that a man is not justified by the works of the law but by faith in Jesus Christ, even we have believed in Christ Jesus, that we might be justified by faith in Christ and not by the works of the law; for by the works of the law no flesh shall be justified.

17 "But if, while we seek to be justified by Christ, we ourselves also are found sinners, *is* Christ therefore a minister of sin? Certainly not! 18 For if I build again those things which I destroyed, I make myself a transgressor. 19 For I through the law died to the law that I might live to God. 20 I have been crucified with Christ; it is no longer I who live, but Christ lives in me; and the *life* which I now live in the flesh I live by faith in the Son of God, who loved me and gave Himself for me. 21 I do not set aside the grace of God; for if righteousness *comes* through the law, then Christ died in vain."

Jewish laws do not give life

3 O foolish Galatians! Who has bewitched you that you should not obey

Why Were the Galatians Foolish?

The Galatians (pronounced *guh-LAY-shuns*) were *foolish* because they thought their own deeds could get them to heaven. We ought to pray, and we ought to go to church, and we ought to do kind deeds; but none of these things can bring us eternal life. Only Jesus can put heaven in our hearts.

the truth, before whose eyes Jesus Christ was clearly portrayed among you as crucified? 2 This only I want to learn from you: Did you receive the Spirit by the works of the law, or by the hearing of faith? 3 Are you so foolish? Having begun in the Spirit, are you now being made perfect by the flesh? 4 Have you suffered so many things in vain—if indeed *it was* in vain?

5 Therefore He who supplies the Spirit to you and works miracles among you, *does He do it* by the works of the law, or by the hearing of faith?— 6 just as Abraham "believed God, and it was accounted to him for righteousness." 7 Therefore know that *only* those who are of faith are sons of Abraham. 8 And the Scripture, foreseeing that God would justify the Gentiles by faith, preached the gospel to Abraham beforehand, *saying,* "In you all the nations shall be blessed." 9 So then those who *are* of faith are blessed with believing Abraham.

10 For as many as are of the works

DIGGING IN

2:20 Jesus Lives in You We should say, "Jesus lives in you if you have trusted Him with your life." Have you put your life in the hands of Jesus? If so, then Jesus lives in you, and He now gives you the power to live for Him.

Paul said, "I am crucified with Christ." That's a big statement. It means that the OLD Paul (the one who lived before he trusted in Jesus) is *dead.* Now a NEW Paul is living. The new Paul is the Paul

that lives by the power of Jesus who lives in him.

Jesus wants to live in you, too. He wants you to leave behind the old person you used to be. Then that old person is dead. Now the new person is living because *Jesus lives in you.*

Jesus won a new life for you when He rose from the dead after they killed Him. He gives you that new life by coming to live in your body.

of the law are under the curse; for it is written, "Cursed is everyone who does not continue in all things which are written in the book of the law, to do them." 11 But that no one is justified by the law in the sight of God is evident, for "the just shall live by faith." 12 Yet the law is not of faith, but "the man who does them shall live by them."

13 Christ has redeemed us from the curse of the law, having become a curse for us (for it is written, "Cursed is everyone who hangs on a tree"), 14 that the blessing of Abraham might come upon the Gentiles in Christ Jesus, that we might receive the promise of the Spirit through faith.

15 Brethren, I speak in the manner of men: Though it is only a man's covenant, yet if it is confirmed, no one annuls or adds to it. 16 Now to Abraham and his Seed were the promises made. He does not say, "And to seeds," as of many, but as of one, "And to your Seed," who is Christ. 17 And this I say, that the law, which was four hundred and thirty years later, cannot annul the covenant that was confirmed before by God in Christ, that it should make the promise of no effect. 18 For if the inheritance is of the law, it is no longer of promise; but God gave it to Abraham by promise.

19 What purpose then does the law serve? It was added because of transgressions, till the Seed should come to whom the promise was made; and it was appointed through angels by the hand of a mediator. 20 Now a mediator does not mediate for one only, but God is one.

21 Is the law then against the promises of God? Certainly not! For if there had been a law given which could have given life, truly righteousness would have been by the law. 22 But the Scripture has confined all under sin, that the promise by faith in Jesus Christ might be given to those who believe. 23 But before faith came, we were kept under guard by the law, kept for the faith which would afterward be revealed. 24 Therefore the **law** was our tutor to bring us to Christ, that we might be justified by faith. 25 But after faith has come, we are no longer under a tutor.

26 For you are all sons of God through faith in Christ Jesus. 27 For as many of you as were baptized into Christ have put on Christ. 28 There is neither Jew nor Greek, there is neither slave nor free, there is neither male nor female; for you are all one in Christ Jesus. 29 And if you are Christ's, then you are Abraham's seed, and heirs according to the promise.

Paul hopes the Galatians won't back out

4 Now I say that the heir, as long as he is a child, does not differ at all from a slave, though he is master of all, 2 but is under guardians and stewards until the time appointed by the father. 3 Even so we, when we were children, were in bondage under the elements of the world. 4 But when the fullness of the time had come, God sent forth His Son, born of a woman, born under the law, 5 to **redeem** those who were under the law, that we might receive the adoption as sons.

6 And because you are sons, God has sent forth the Spirit of His Son into your hearts, crying out, "**Abba,** Fa-

---

⟨WF⟩ WORDFINDER

3:24, 25 Law The words of God that we must live by. Sometimes the law refers to the Ten Commandments. At other times it includes all things that God says in the Scriptures.

4:5 Redeem To buy something back from someone. Jesus bought back believers from the slavery of sin.

4:6 Abba A word for father from the ancient Aramaic language (pronounced air-uh-MAY-ik). The word is like our words daddy and papa.

ther!'' 7 Therefore you are no longer a slave but a son, and if a son, then an heir of God through Christ.

8 But then, indeed, when you did not know God, you served those which by nature are not gods. 9 But now after you have known God, or rather are known by God, how *is it that* you turn again to the weak and beggarly elements, to which you desire again to be in bondage? 10 You observe days and months and seasons and years. 11 I am afraid for you, lest I have labored for you in vain.

12 Brethren, I urge you to become like me, for I *became* like you. You have not injured me at all. 13 You know that because of physical infirmity I preached the gospel to you at the first. 14 And my trial which was in my flesh you did not despise or reject, but you received me as an angel of God, *even* as Christ Jesus. 15 What then was the blessing you *enjoyed?* For I bear you witness that, if possible, you would have plucked out your own eyes and given them to me. 16 Have I therefore become your enemy because I tell you the truth?

17 They zealously court you, *but* for no good; yes, they want to exclude you, that you may be zealous for them. 18 But it is good to be zealous in a good thing always, and not only when I am present with you. 19 My little children, for whom I labor in birth again until Christ is formed in you, 20 I would like to be present with you now and to change my tone; for I have doubts about you.

21 Tell me, you who desire to be under the law, do you not hear the law? 22 For it is written that Abraham had two sons: the one by a bondwoman, the other by a freewoman. 23 But he *who was* of the bondwoman was born according to the flesh, and he of the freewoman through promise, 24 which things are symbolic. For these are the two covenants: the one from Mount Sinai which gives birth to bondage, which is Hagar— 25 for this Hagar is Mount Sinai in Arabia, and corresponds to Jerusalem which now is, and

is in bondage with her children— 26 but the Jerusalem above is free, which is the mother of us all. 27 For it is written:

"Rejoice, O barren,
You who do not bear!
Break forth and shout,
You who are not in labor!
For the desolate has many more children
Than she who has a husband."

28 Now we, brethren, as Isaac *was,* are children of promise. 29 But, as he who was born according to the flesh then persecuted him *who was born* according to the Spirit, even so *it is* now. 30 Nevertheless what does the Scripture say? "Cast out the bondwoman and her son, for the son of the bondwoman shall not be heir with the son of the freewoman." 31 So then, brethren, we are not children of the bondwoman but of the free.

Christ makes us free from laws

5 Stand fast therefore in the liberty by which Christ has made us free, and do not be entangled again with a yoke of bondage. 2 Indeed I, Paul, say to you that if you become circumcised, Christ will profit you nothing. 3 And I testify again to every man who becomes circumcised that he is a debtor to keep the whole law. 4 You have become estranged from Christ, you who *attempt to* be justified by law; you have fallen from grace. 5 For we through the Spirit eagerly wait for the hope of righteousness by faith. 6 For in Christ Jesus neither circumcision nor uncircumcision avails anything, but faith working through love.

7 You ran well. Who hindered you from obeying the truth? 8 This persuasion does not *come* from Him who calls you. 9 A little leaven leavens the whole lump. 10 I have confidence in you, in the Lord, that you will have no other mind; but he who troubles you shall bear his judgment, whoever he is.

11 And I, brethren, if I still preach

circumcision, why do I still suffer persecution? Then the offense of the cross has ceased. 12 I could wish that those who trouble you would even cut themselves off!

13 For you, brethren, have been called to liberty; only do not *use* liberty as an opportunity for the flesh, but through love serve one another. 14 For all the law is fulfilled in one word, *even* in this: "You shall love your neighbor as yourself." 15 But if you bite and devour one another, beware lest you be consumed by one another!

16 I say then: Walk in the Spirit, and you shall not fulfill the lust of the flesh. 17 For the flesh lusts against the Spirit, and the Spirit against the flesh; and these are contrary to one another, so that you do not do the things that you wish. 18 But if you are led by the Spirit, you are not under the law.

19 Now the works of the flesh are evident, which are: adultery, fornication, uncleanness, lewdness, 20 **idolatry, sorcery,** hatred, contentions, jealousies, outbursts of wrath, selfish ambitions, dissensions, **heresies,** 21 envy, murders, drunkenness, revelries, and the like; of which I tell you beforehand, just as I also told *you* in time past, that those who practice such things will not inherit the kingdom of God.

22 But the fruit of the Spirit is love, joy, peace, longsuffering, kindness, goodness, faithfulness, 23 gentleness, self-control. Against such there is no law. 24 And those *who are* Christ's have crucified the flesh with its passions and desires. 25 If we live in the Spirit, let us also walk in the Spirit. 26 Let us not become conceited, provoking one another, envying one another.

WORDFINDER

5:20 Idolatry Pronounced *eye-DOLL-uh-tree*. The worship of idols and false gods. Unless you work or serve God, you will serve something or someone less than God.

5:20 Sorcery Pronounced *SORE-sah-ree*. The practice of magic using secret potions and spells to control nature and persons. The Bible forbids sorcery. See Acts 8:9–13.

5:20 Heresies Pronounced *HERR-uh-sees*. False teaching. Any teaching or society that contradicts the Word of God is a heresy.

DIGGING IN

5:1 Jesus Christ Makes You Free Democracy stands for freedom. But even though we have democracy, we aren't free as long as we are slaves to sin.

Jesus is the One who can make you free from the sins that make you a slave. A slave is the property of someone else. And people without God are slaves to sin. When a slave is made free, he can go and do what he wishes. When Jesus makes you free, then your whole wish is to please Him who made you free.

Serving someone we love is not slavery. So serving Jesus is the greatest joy of our lives because He has made us free citizens of the kingdom of heaven. A citizen isn't a slave anymore. You aren't a slave either if you give your life to Jesus.

Jesus' yoke is "easy and His burden is light."

Do your best and you will be blessed

6 Brethren, if a man is overtaken in any trespass, you who *are* spiritual restore such a one in a spirit of gentleness, considering yourself lest you also be tempted. ² Bear one another's burdens, and so fulfill the law of Christ. ³ For if anyone thinks himself to be something, when he is nothing, he deceives himself. ⁴ But let each one examine his own work, and then he will have rejoicing in himself alone, and not in another. ⁵ For each one shall bear his own load.

⁶ Let him who is taught the word share in all good things with him who teaches.

⁷ Do not be deceived, God is not mocked; for whatever a man sows, that he will also reap. ⁸ For he who sows to his flesh will of the flesh reap corruption, but he who sows to the Spirit will of the Spirit reap everlasting life. ⁹ And let us not grow weary while doing good, for in due season we shall

What Do You Boast About?

Some people boast about how strong they are, and some boast about how rich they are. Jesus had done so much for Paul by dying for him that Paul wanted to boast everywhere about it. When you count up what Jesus did for you, then you will boast about Jesus, too.

reap if we do not lose heart. ¹⁰ Therefore, as we have opportunity, let us do good to all, especially to those who are of the household of faith.

¹¹ See with what large letters I have written to you with my own hand! ¹² As many as desire to make a good showing in the flesh, these *would* compel you to be circumcised, only that they may not suffer persecution for the cross of Christ. ¹³ For not even those who are circumcised keep the law, but they desire to have you circumcised that they may boast in your flesh.

What the Galatians Learned

You've already read in Galatians 3 how foolish we were. Paul has shown us that God's way is the wise way.

Everybody knew how fickle Galatian people were. We could believe something one day, and next month we would believe something else. We were people of weak character, like quicksilver. When you touch quicksilver, it runs in all directions. That's what we were like.

But we've made a new start since Paul wrote to us. We want to be steady for Jesus all our lives. No more foolish thoughts! Jesus is not only "Number One." He is the *only* One!

DIGGING IN

6:2 Keeping the Law of Christ When Jesus died on the Cross, He took away all our guilt. This means you never have to stand trial before God for your sins. You're free from what Paul calls "the law of sin and death." What is that law?

All laws aren't written on paper or in books. The law of gravity is one of those laws. The law of SIN AND DEATH is another. That's the law that drives us to sin

even when we know better. We may not realize that sin leads to death, but it does.

There is also a law of LIFE that Jesus causes to work inside us—to "love one another as I have loved you." Paul commanded the same thing when he told us to "bear one another's burdens and so fulfill the law of Christ." That's the law that drives us to care about others. Ask Jesus to keep that law working in your life.

14 But God forbid that I should boast except in the cross of our Lord Jesus Christ, by whom the world has been crucified to me, and I to the world. 15 For in Christ Jesus neither circumcision nor uncircumcision avails anything, but a new creation.

16 And as many as walk according to this rule, peace and mercy be upon them, and upon the Israel of God.

17 From now on let no one trouble me, for I bear in my body the marks of the Lord Jesus.

18 Brethren, the grace of our Lord Jesus Christ be with your spirit. Amen.

The Book of
EPHESIANS

Ours was one of the most important cities in the world of Paul's time almost two thousand years ago in Asia Minor. Its name is pronounced *EFF-uh-sus.*

We had beautiful buildings and a street 35 feet wide that led to our harbor on the Aegean (pronounced *ee-JEE-un*) Sea. One of our buildings was a temple to the goddess Diana. The Greeks called her Artemis (pronounced *ARE-teh-miss*). Sometimes we called her the moon goddess, or the goddess of the hunt, or the goddess of young girls. We also believed that a statue of Diana fell from heaven.

When Paul came and preached about Jesus, we all heard him gladly at first. But then Paul said you couldn't make a god with your hands. One of the men who made silver statues of Diana started a riot against Paul.

Paul spent over two years in our city. Then he left his friend Timothy to be our pastor.

Paul writes to the church at Ephesus

PAUL, an apostle of Jesus Christ by the will of God,

To the saints who are in Ephesus, and faithful in Christ Jesus:

2 Grace to you and peace from God our Father and the Lord Jesus Christ. 3 Blessed *be* the God and Father of our Lord Jesus Christ, who has blessed us with *every* spiritual blessing in the heavenly *places* in Christ, 4 just as He chose us in Him before the foundation of the world, that we should be holy

A map of the city of Ephesus.

⚒ DIGGING IN

1:3 Living in Heavenly Places You don't have to die to be in heaven. Heaven is where Jesus is. If you know Jesus as your Friend, you have some of heaven right now.

Often this world is not a very happy place. There is a lot of anger and hatred and violence. But you can live in this unhappy world and carry some of heaven around with you just the same.

What happens when you turn on a light in a dark room? The room is filled with light, and *the darkness can't stop the light.* That's what happens when you carry Jesus around in your life. You bring the light of heaven to people living in misery. Do you have some unhappy friends from unhappy homes? You can bring some of heaven into their lives by showing Jesus to them in all the things you do and say. Then they will want to know Him, too.

and without blame before Him in love, ⁵ having predestined us to **adoption** as sons by Jesus Christ to Himself, according to the good pleasure of His will, ⁶ to the praise of the glory of His grace, by which He made us accepted in the Beloved.

7 In Him we have redemption through His blood, the forgiveness of sins, according to the riches of His grace ⁸ which He made to abound toward us in all wisdom and prudence, ⁹ having made known to us the mystery of His will, according to His good pleasure which He purposed in Himself, ¹⁰ that in the dispensation of the fullness of the times He might gather together in one all things in Christ, both which are in heaven and which are on earth—in Him. ¹¹ In Him also we have obtained an inheritance, being **predestined** according to the purpose of Him who works all things according to the counsel of His will, ¹² that we who first trusted in Christ should be to the praise of His glory.

¹³ In Him you also *trusted,* after you heard the word of truth, the gospel of your salvation; in whom also, having believed, you were sealed with the Holy Spirit of promise, ¹⁴ who is the guarantee of our inheritance until the redemption of the purchased possession, to the praise of His glory.

¹⁵ Therefore I also, after I heard of your faith in the Lord Jesus and your love for all the saints, ¹⁶ do not cease to give thanks for you, making mention of you in my prayers: ¹⁷ that the God of our Lord Jesus Christ, the Father of glory, may give to you the spirit of wisdom and revelation in the knowledge of Him, ¹⁸ the eyes of your understanding being enlightened; that you may know what is the hope of His calling, what are the riches of the glory of His inheritance in the saints, ¹⁹ and what *is* the exceeding greatness of His power toward us who believe, according to the working of His mighty power ²⁰ which He worked in Christ when He raised Him from the dead and seated *Him* at His right hand in the heavenly *places,* ²¹ far above all principality and power and might and dominion, and every name that is named, not only in this age but also in that which is to come.

²² And He put all *things* under His feet, and gave Him *to be* head over all *things* to the church, ²³ which is His body, the fullness of Him who fills all in all.

Christ is the way to peace

2 And you He *made alive,* who were dead in trespasses and sins, ² in which you once walked according to the course of this world, according to the prince of the power of the air, the spirit who now works in the sons of disobedience; ³ among whom also we all once conducted ourselves in the lusts of our flesh, fulfilling the desires of the flesh and of the mind, and were by nature children of wrath, just as the others.

⁴ But God, who is rich in mercy, because of His great love with which He loved us, ⁵ even when we were dead in trespasses, made us alive together with Christ (by **grace** you have been saved), ⁶ and raised *us* up together, and made *us* sit together in the heavenly *places* in Christ Jesus, ⁷ that in the

WORDFINDER

1:5 Adoption Pronounced *uh-DOP-shun.* God's work of making us His sons and daughters. When we believe in Jesus for salvation, God sends His Spirit to live in us. The Spirit of God teaches us that we are God's children.

1:11 Predestined Pronounced *pre-DESS-tend.* All that God decided before time existed. Everything that ever happens has always been part of God's never-changing, forever plan.

2:5 Grace The undeserved kindness of God. We are saved from sin by this grace of God. All the good we enjoy is due to His grace.

What the Ephesians Learned

We were very thankful to God for what Paul taught us. We also were truly humbled.

At one time we imagined that we had to create our own faith in God. All we had to do was make up our minds to believe Him, but we couldn't really. God was too hard for us to understand. That makes sense because no one can see God, so we didn't know what He is like.

Then Paul showed us that we are saved by grace. *God Himself shows us* what He is like. The invisible Holy Spirit of God works in our minds to make us able to understand God. When we see God with our inner eye of understanding, then it is easy to believe in Him. If you ask Him, God will make you able to understand and believe in Him.

ages to come He might show the exceeding riches of His grace in *His* kindness toward us in Christ Jesus. 8 For by grace you have been saved through faith, and that not of yourselves; *it is* the gift of God, 9 not of works, lest anyone should boast. 10 For we are His workmanship, created in Christ Jesus for good works, which God prepared beforehand that we should walk in them.

11 Therefore remember that you, once Gentiles in the flesh—who are called Uncircumcision by what is called the Circumcision made in the flesh by hands— 12 that at that time you were without Christ, being aliens from the commonwealth of Israel and strangers from the covenants of promise, having no hope and without God in the world. 13 But now in Christ Jesus you who once were far off have been brought near by the blood of Christ.

14 For He Himself is our peace, who has made both one, and has broken down the middle wall of separation,

⚒ DIGGING IN

2:1 Jesus Makes You Alive "But I'm not dead!" you say. There are different ways of being dead. One kind of death is when your body functions stop. Then your body can't hear, see, or feel anything. But another way of being dead is when you can't enjoy God and His love. That's a worse kind of death because your spirit will live forever. If you can't know and enjoy God now, then you never will enjoy Him.

What can you do about being dead to God? Jesus can make you alive. That's why He rose up from death in a body that can never die. Now He can share His life with you, and you can be alive to enjoy God forever . . . and ever . . . and ever—starting this very minute!

Just close your eyes and say, "Jesus, I need You more than anything in the world. Without You, I'm dead. Please come in and make me alive to God."

2:14 Jesus Is Your Peace Every day,

the newspapers and television talk about peace, but peace never seems to come. One war just follows another all around the world.

When you really think hard about it, there isn't much chance that peace can soon come to the world. Few people want to serve others. Many people want to be "Number One." So there isn't much hope of peace when people will fight just so they can be ahead of others.

Can peace still exist in such a world? Yes, it can. But peace has to live inside people before they can be people of peace. The desire to be "Number One" must disappear, and the desire to serve others must take its place. You don't have to fight to be first in line anymore when you know you have a home with God forever. You can know you have that home with God when Jesus comes to live in you. Jesus IS your peace.

A street paved with marble in Ephesus.

15 having abolished in His flesh the enmity, *that is,* the law of commandments *contained* in ordinances, so as to create in Himself one new man *from* the two, *thus* making peace, 16 and that He might reconcile them both to God in one body through the cross, thereby putting to death the enmity. 17 And He came and preached peace to you who were afar off and to those who were near. 18 For through Him we both have access by one Spirit to the Father.

19 Now, therefore, you are no longer strangers and foreigners, but fellow citizens with the saints and members of the household of God, 20 having been built on the foundation of the apostles and prophets, Jesus Christ Himself being the chief cornerstone, 21 in whom the whole building, being fitted together, grows into a holy temple in the Lord, 22 in whom you also are being built together for a dwelling place of God in the Spirit.

God's secret plan for the Gentiles

3 For this reason I, Paul, the prisoner of Christ Jesus for you Gentiles— 2 if indeed you have heard of the dispensation of the grace of God which was given to me for you, 3 how that by revelation He made known to me the mystery (as I have briefly written already, 4 by which, when you read, you may understand my knowledge in the mystery of Christ), 5 which in other ages was not made known to the sons of men, as it has now been revealed by the Spirit to His holy apostles and prophets: 6 that the Gentiles should be fellow heirs, of the same body, and partakers of His promise in Christ through the gospel, 7 of which I became a minister according to the gift of the grace of God given to me by the effective working of His power.

8 To me, who am less than the least of all the saints, this grace was given, that I should preach among the Gentiles the unsearchable riches of Christ, 9 and to make all see what *is* the fellowship of the mystery, which from the beginning of the ages has been hidden in God who created all things through Jesus Christ; 10 to the intent that now the manifold wisdom of God might be made known by the church to the principalities and powers in the heavenly *places,* 11 according to the eternal pur-

pose which He accomplished in Christ Jesus our Lord, 12 in whom we have boldness and access with confidence through faith in Him. 13 Therefore I ask that you do not lose heart at my tribulations for you, which is your glory.

14 For this reason I bow my knees to the Father of our Lord Jesus Christ, 15 from whom the whole family in heaven and earth is named, 16 that He would grant you, according to the riches of His glory, to be strengthened with might through His Spirit in the inner man, 17 that Christ may dwell in your hearts through faith; that you, being rooted and grounded in love, 18 may be able to comprehend with all the saints what is the width and length and depth and height— 19 to know the love of Christ which passes knowledge; that you may be filled with all the fullness of God.

20 Now to Him who is able to do exceedingly abundantly above all that we ask or think, according to the power that works in us, 21 to Him be glory in the church by Christ Jesus to all generations, forever and ever. Amen.

We need to grow up

4 I, therefore, the prisoner of the Lord, beseech you to walk worthy of the calling with which you were called, 2 with all lowliness and gentleness, with longsuffering, bearing with one another in love, 3 endeavoring to keep the unity of the Spirit in the bond of peace. 4 There is one body and one Spirit, just as you were called in one hope of your calling; 5 one Lord, one faith, one baptism; 6 one God and Father of all, who is above all, and through all, and in you all.

7 But to each one of us grace was given according to the measure of Christ's gift. 8 Therefore He says:

"When He ascended on high,
He led captivity captive,
And gave gifts to men."

9 (Now this, "He ascended"—what does it mean but that He also first descended into the lower parts of the earth? 10 He who descended is also the One who ascended far above all the heavens, that He might fill all things.)

11 And He Himself gave some to be apostles, some prophets, some evangelists, and some pastors and teachers, 12 for the equipping of the **saints** for the work of ministry, for the edifying of the body of Christ, 13 till we all come to the unity of the faith and of the knowledge of the Son of God, to a perfect man, to the measure of the stature of the fullness of Christ; 14 that we should no longer be children, tossed to and fro and carried about with every wind of doctrine, by the trickery of men, in the cunning craftiness of deceitful plotting, 15 but, speaking the truth in love, may grow up in all things into Him who is the head—Christ— 16 from whom the whole body, joined and knit together by what every joint supplies, according to the effective working by which every part does its share, causes growth of the body for the edifying of itself in love.

17 This I say, therefore, and testify in the Lord, that you should no longer walk as the rest of the Gentiles walk, in the futility of their mind, 18 having their understanding darkened, being alienated from the life of God, because of the ignorance that is in them, because of the blindness of their heart; 19 who, being past feeling, have given themselves over to lewdness, to work all uncleanness with greediness.

20 But you have not so learned Christ, 21 if indeed you have heard Him and have been taught by Him, as the truth is in Jesus: 22 that you put off, concerning your former conduct,

---

WORDFINDER

4:12 Saints People who are set apart by God. They believe in Jesus for salvation. The word comes from a Greek word meaning "holy" or "set apart."

the old man which grows corrupt according to the deceitful lusts, 23 and be renewed in the spirit of your mind, 24 and that you put on the new man which was created according to God, in true righteousness and holiness.

25 Therefore, putting away lying, "Let each one of you speak truth with his neighbor," for we are members of one another. 26 "Be angry, and do not sin": do not let the sun go down on your wrath, 27 nor give place to the devil. 28 Let him who stole steal no longer, but rather let him labor, working with his hands what is good, that he may have something to give him who has need. 29 Let no corrupt word proceed out of your mouth, but what is good for necessary edification, that it may impart grace to the hearers. 30 And do not grieve the Holy Spirit of God, by whom you were sealed for the day of redemption. 31 Let all bitterness, wrath, anger, clamor, and evil speaking be put away from you, with all malice. 32 And be kind to one another, tenderhearted, forgiving one another, even as God in Christ forgave you.

Learn to please God in everything

5 Therefore be imitators of God as dear children. 2 And walk in love, as Christ also has loved us and given Himself for us, an offering and a sacrifice to God for a sweet-smelling aroma.

3 But fornication and all uncleanness or covetousness, let it not even be named among you, as is fitting for saints; 4 neither filthiness, nor foolish talking, nor coarse jesting, which are not fitting, but rather giving of thanks. 5 For this you know, that no fornicator, unclean person, nor covetous man, who is an idolater, has any inheritance in the kingdom of Christ and God. 6 Let no one deceive you with empty words, for because of these things the wrath of God comes upon the sons of disobedience. 7 Therefore do not be partakers with them.

8 For you were once darkness, but now you are light in the Lord. Walk as children of light 9 (for the fruit of the Spirit is in all goodness, righteousness, and truth), 10 finding out what is acceptable to the Lord. 11 And have no fellowship with the unfruitful works of darkness, but rather expose

🔨 DIGGING IN

4:24 Be Your New Self Paul says, "Put on the new man." Are you a Christian? Have you trusted Jesus with your life? Then TAKE OFF THE OLD CLOTHES of your old life without Christ, and PUT ON THE NEW CLOTHES of your new life with Christ.

Jesus lives in you now. So your "inside" life has been made new. Now all you have to do is throw away all those old habits and actions that aren't part of your new life. Then your "inside" life will be happy with your "outside" life.

Do you have a habit of lying? Throw away that habit. Do you use bad words or profanity? You can put an end to that now. Are you bad-tempered? Just "take off" your bad temper and trash it. Who needs those things anymore? Let your "outside" life show to everyone what you're like inside—where Jesus now lives.

5:1 Be God's Person The way you act tells the world what you're like. But even more than that, the way you act tells everybody what your parents or guardians are like. We hope you love them. Because, if you do, you'll want to show the world what really great folks they are. Nobody should want to make someone who cares for them look bad in public.

But it's even more important in the world to be God's person. God made you so you would show everybody what He is like. The greatest tragedy in the world is that so many people give God a bad name by the way they act. That's very sad. God deserves better treatment.

So be God's person in the world. Be cheerful in doing all the great things God has asked you to do in His world. Then you'll prove to everybody that GOD IS TRULY GREAT.

them. 12 For it is shameful even to speak of those things which are done by them in secret. 13 But all things that are exposed are made manifest by the light, for whatever makes manifest is light. 14 Therefore He says:

"Awake, you who sleep,
Arise from the dead,
And Christ will give you light."

15 See then that you walk circumspectly, not as fools but as wise, 16 redeeming the time, because the days are evil.

17 Therefore do not be unwise, but understand what the will of the Lord *is.* 18 And do not be drunk with wine, in which is dissipation; but be filled with the Spirit, 19 speaking to one another in psalms and hymns and spiritual songs, singing and making melody in your heart to the Lord, 20 giving thanks always for all things to God the Father in the name of our Lord Jesus Christ, 21 submitting to one another in the fear of God.

22 Wives, submit to your own husbands, as to the Lord. 23 For the husband is head of the wife, as also Christ is head of the church; and He is the Savior of the body. 24 Therefore, just as the church is subject to Christ, so *let* the wives *be* to their own husbands in everything.

25 Husbands, love your wives, just

A happy family in Ephesus.

as Christ also loved the church and gave Himself for her, 26 that He might **sanctify** and cleanse her with the washing of water by the word, 27 that He might present her to Himself a glorious church, not having spot or wrinkle or any such thing, but that she should be holy and without blemish. 28 So husbands ought to love their own wives as their own bodies; he who loves his wife loves himself. 29 For no one ever hated his own flesh, but nourishes and cherishes it, just as the Lord

WORDFINDER

5:26 Sanctify Pronounced *SANK-tih-fy.* Means "set apart" for God's use. The Scriptures teach you to be useful to God when you have trusted Him.

DIGGING IN

5:19 Teach Your Heart to Sing "The hills are alive with the sound of music." This line from the great musical show, *The Sound of Music,* expresses the truth very well. God filled His universe with music. Some people even say there is a kind of music in outer space. Everywhere the sounds of nature are a chorus of praise to the Creator of all things. One of our hymns by M. D. Babock even reflects this: "All nature sings, and round me rings the music of the spheres."

If nature sings to its Creator, it only makes sense that man should also sing to God. We hope you'll learn to love the songs in your hymnbook. Then, everywhere you go, you can always have a song in your heart, like the song by William Featherstone that says, "My Jesus I love Thee, I know Thou art mine. For Thee all the pleasures of sin I resign. My gracious Redeemer, my Savior art Thou. If ever I loved Thee, my Jesus 'tis now."

does the church. 30 For we are members of His body, of His flesh and of His bones. 31 "For this reason a man shall leave his father and mother and be joined to his wife, and the two shall become one flesh." 32 This is a great mystery, but I speak concerning Christ and the church. 33 Nevertheless let each one of you in particular so love his own wife as himself, and let the wife *see* that she respects *her* husband.

Put on God's armor

6 Children, obey your parents in the Lord, for this is right. 2 "Honor your father and mother," which is the first commandment with promise: 3 "that it may be well with you and you may live long on the earth."

4 And you, fathers, do not provoke your children to wrath, but bring them up in the training and admonition of the Lord.

5 Bondservants, be obedient to those who are your masters according to the flesh, with fear and trembling, in sincerity of heart, as to Christ; 6 not with **eyeservice,** as men-pleasers, but as bondservants of Christ, doing the will of God from the heart, 7 with goodwill doing service, as to the Lord,

WORDFINDER

6:6 Eyeservice Living in a way that looks good to people but doesn't please God. We may deceive others, but we can't deceive God.

DIGGING IN

6:11 A Good Soldier of Jesus Christ
A good soldier of Jesus is like the Roman soldier in the days of the apostle Paul. The Christian soldier must have:

(1) The heavy belt of truth. This is the belt on which the soldier hung his sword and other weapons. The truth is our best defense.

(2) The breastplate of righteousness. Righteousness protects you from being wounded by your own weakness.

(3) Footwear that makes the soldier able to walk in rough terrain. You need a good understanding of the gospel because Jesus calls you to places of hard service.

(4) The shield of faith. Satan's lies can't affect you when your faith is strong.

(5) The helmet of salvation. When you know Jesus is your Savior, nothing can hurt you.

(6) The sword of the Spirit. This is the Word of God, the weapon that destroys the falsehoods of Satan.

(7) A good knowledge of battle tactics. The Christian soldier gets his battle orders through prayer.

"The whole armor of God" gives protection from evil and temptation.

Where Is Heaven?

We know just a little about heaven. We know that heaven is where God is, and we know that God plans to gather all of His loved ones with Him forever in heaven. There you can have perfect love, joy, and peace. Right now you can have heaven in your life if you truly ask Jesus to live in you.

and not to men, 8 knowing that whatever good anyone does, he will receive the same from the Lord, whether *he is* a slave or free.

9 And you, masters, do the same things to them, giving up threatening, knowing that your own Master also is in heaven, and there is no partiality with Him.

10 Finally, my brethren, be strong in the Lord and in the power of His might. 11 Put on the whole armor of God, that you may be able to stand against the wiles of **the devil.** 12 For we do not wrestle against flesh and blood, but against principalities, against powers, against the rulers of the darkness of this age, against spiritual *hosts* of wickedness in the heavenly *places.* 13 Therefore take up the whole armor of God, that you may be able to withstand in the evil day, and having done all, to stand.

14 Stand therefore, having girded your waist with truth, having put on the breastplate of righteousness, 15 and having shod your feet with the preparation of the gospel of peace; 16 above all, taking the shield of faith with which you will be able to quench all the fiery darts of the wicked one. 17 And take the helmet of salvation, and the sword of the Spirit, which is the word of God; 18 praying always with all prayer and supplication in the Spirit, being watchful to this end with all perseverance and supplication for all the saints— 19 and for me, that utterance may be given to me, that I may open my mouth boldly to make known the mystery of the gospel, 20 for which I am an ambassador in chains; that in it I may speak boldly, as I ought to speak.

21 But that you also may know my affairs *and* how I am doing, Tychicus, a beloved brother and faithful minister in the Lord, will make all things known to you; 22 whom I have sent to you for this very purpose, that you may know our affairs, and *that* he may comfort your hearts.

23 Peace to the brethren, and love with faith, from God the Father and the Lord Jesus Christ. 24 Grace *be* with all those who love our Lord Jesus Christ in sincerity. Amen.

WORDFINDER

6:11 The Devil The title of the angel who rebelled against God's authority. The word means "liar," "slanderer," or "accuser." Satan, meaning "Enemy," is his personal name.

The Book of
PHILIPPIANS

Pronounce the name of our city *FILL-ih-pie.* We named our city for Philip the Second, father of Alexander the Great. Philippi was a leading city of Macedonia (pronounced *mass-uh-DOH-nee-uh*) in northern Greece.

The apostle Paul visited us about 20 years after the time of Jesus. Paul had spoken to some of our women who worshiped the God of the Hebrews. He told them about Jesus who died for the sins of the world. Some of the women became Christians.

Later, Paul wrote this letter to us when he was in prison at Rome. He encouraged us to make Christ, who rose from death, the most important Person in our lives and to let Him live His life in us. Now, like Paul, we know we can do all things through Christ who lives in us.

Paul is a slave of Jesus Christ

PAUL and Timothy, bondservants of Jesus Christ,

To all the saints in Christ Jesus who are in Philippi, with the bishops and **deacons:**

2 Grace to you and peace from God our Father and the Lord Jesus Christ.

3 I thank my God upon *every* remembrance of you, 4 always in every prayer of mine making request for you all with joy, 5 for your fellowship in the gospel from the first day until now, 6 being confident of this very thing, that He who has begun a good work in you will complete *it* until the day of Jesus Christ; 7 just as it is right for me to think this of you all, because I have you in my heart, inasmuch as both in my chains and in the defense and confirmation of the gospel, you all are partakers with me of grace. 8 For God is my witness, how greatly I long for you all with the affection of Jesus Christ.

9 And this I pray, that your love may abound still more and more in knowledge and all discernment, 10 that you may approve the things that are excellent, that you may be sincere and without offense till the day of Christ, 11 being filled with the fruits of righteousness which *are* by Jesus Christ, to the glory and praise of God.

12 But I want you to know, brethren, that the things *which happened* to me have actually turned out for the furtherance of the gospel, 13 so that it has become evident to the whole palace guard, and to all the rest, that my chains are in Christ; 14 and most of the brethren in the Lord, having become confident by my chains, are much

Are You Thankful?

We feel good that Paul thanked God every time he remembered his friends. Jesus also remembers us when He prays before His Father's throne. He died for us, and He prays for us right now. You can be filled with thankfulness as you remember all that Jesus did for you.

WORDFINDER

1:1 Deacons Pronounced *DEE-kuns*. From a Greek word meaning "servant." Sometimes deacons are ministers, and sometimes they are not. *Minister* also means "servant."

What the Philippians Learned

Paul told us he was sure we would continue in our Christian faith to the end of our lives. Even more, he said our faith would grow more and more until Jesus comes.

How could Paul be sure of this? Then we thought about what he really said. Paul didn't say we were going to keep *ourselves* strong in faith. He said *Jesus* would keep us and make us grow stronger in our Christian lives.

Then we understood. Jesus is the only One who can *save* us, but He is also the only One who can *keep* us. Now we don't have to worry anymore. We may fail sometimes, but Jesus can never fail. When you trust Him, He will keep you forever.

more bold to speak the word without fear.

15 Some indeed preach Christ even from envy and strife, and some also from goodwill: 16 The former preach Christ from selfish ambition, not sincerely, supposing to add affliction to my chains; 17 but the latter out of love, knowing that I am appointed for the defense of the gospel. 18 What then? Only *that* in every way, whether in pretense or in truth, Christ is preached; and in this I rejoice, yes, and will rejoice.

19 For I know that this will turn out for my deliverance through your prayer and the supply of the Spirit of Jesus Christ, 20 according to my earnest expectation and hope that in nothing I shall be ashamed, but with all boldness, as always, so now also Christ will be magnified in my body, whether by life or by death. 21 For to me, to live *is* Christ, and to die *is* gain. 22 But

if *I* live on in the flesh, this *will mean* fruit from *my* labor; yet what I shall choose I cannot tell. 23 For I am hard-pressed between the two, having a desire to depart and be with Christ, *which is* far better. 24 Nevertheless to remain in the flesh *is* more needful for you. 25 And being confident of this, I know that I shall remain and continue with you all for your progress and joy of faith, 26 that your rejoicing for me may be more abundant in Jesus Christ by my coming to you again.

27 Only let your conduct be worthy of the gospel of Christ, so that whether I come and see you or am absent, I may hear of your affairs, that you stand fast in one spirit, with one mind striving together for the faith of the gospel, 28 and not in any way terrified by your adversaries, which is to them a proof of perdition, but to you of salvation, and that from God. 29 For to you it has been granted on behalf of Christ,

⚒ DIGGING IN

1:21 Let Christ Live in You Becoming a Christian is a little like learning a new language. At first the language is hard for you, but as time goes by, you can speak the new language without even thinking about how to say the words. The language becomes part of you.

You may spend a lot of time reading the Bible and learning how God wants you to live. At first it seems very puzzling. But then one day you realize what it really

means to be a Christian—Christ Himself must take over your life until He is EVERYTHING and you are NOTHING. Then you live as a Christian because Jesus lives in you and *through* you. You no longer live by a set of rules. Living, loving, and speaking as Jesus did become *part of you.*

Yes, you do go on living, but in a real way your new life is Jesus living in you.

Ruins of the marketplace in Philippi.

not only to believe in Him, but also to suffer for His sake, 30 having the same conflict which you saw in me and now hear *is* in me.

Work together with God's help

2 Therefore if *there is* any consolation in Christ, if any comfort of love, if any fellowship of the Spirit, if any affection and mercy, 2 fulfill my joy by being like-minded, having the same love, *being* of one accord, of one mind. 3 *Let* nothing *be done* through selfish ambition or conceit, but in lowliness of mind let each esteem others better than himself. 4 Let each of you look out not only for his own interests, but also for the interests of others.

5 Let this mind be in you which was also in Christ Jesus, 6 who, being in the form of God, did not consider it robbery to be equal with God, 7 but made Himself of no reputation, taking the form of a bondservant, *and* coming in the likeness of men. 8 And being found in appearance as a man, He humbled Himself and became obedient to *the point of* death, *even the* death of the cross. 9 Therefore God

DIGGING IN

2:8 Christ Became a Man So He Could Die These are some things God can't do—God can't sin, and He can't die. That means that Christ, the Son of God, couldn't die either.

Yet someone had to die in your place to pay for your sins. That person would have to be perfect and without sin. So God did something very special—He sent His own Son to take the form of a Man. Then He could die and pay the penalty for your sins! That was a work of divine genius.

Have you ever thought how much it must have meant for God's Son to become a Man? He gave up His privileges and honor as the King of Glory. He had to come in contact with sin, and that was something Jesus never had to do in heaven. He had to let Himself be treated like a criminal and be abused and beaten by men. Then He had to let Himself be crucified—the most horrible death of that time. That's why Jesus became a Man.

also has highly exalted Him and given Him the name which is above every name, 10 that at the name of Jesus every knee should bow, of those in heaven, and of those on earth, and of those under the earth, 11 and *that* every tongue should confess that Jesus Christ *is* Lord, to the glory of God the Father.

12 Therefore, my beloved, as you have always obeyed, not as in my presence only, but now much more in my absence, work out your own salvation with fear and trembling; 13 for it is God who works in you both to will and to do for *His* good pleasure.

14 Do all things without complaining and disputing, 15 that you may become blameless and harmless, children of God without fault in the midst of a crooked and perverse generation, among whom you shine as lights in the world, 16 holding fast the word of life, so that I may rejoice in the day of Christ that I have not run in vain or labored in vain.

17 Yes, and if I am being poured out *as a drink offering* on the sacrifice and service of your faith, I am glad and rejoice with you all. 18 For the same reason you also be glad and rejoice with me.

19 But I trust in the Lord Jesus to send Timothy to you shortly, that I also may be encouraged when I know your state. 20 For I have no one like-minded, who will sincerely care for your state. 21 For all seek their own, not the things which are of Christ Jesus. 22 But you know his proven character, that as a son with *his* father he served with me in the gospel. 23 Therefore I hope to send him at once, as soon as I see how it goes with me. 24 But I trust in the Lord that I myself shall also come shortly.

25 Yet I considered it necessary to send to you Epaphroditus, my brother, fellow worker, and fellow soldier, but your messenger and the one who ministered to my need; 26 since he was longing for you all, and was distressed because you had heard that he was sick. 27 For indeed he was sick almost

unto death; but God had mercy on him, and not only on him but on me also, lest I should have sorrow upon sorrow. 28 Therefore I sent him the more eagerly, that when you see him again you may rejoice, and I may be less sorrowful. 29 Receive him therefore in the Lord with all gladness, and hold such men in esteem; 30 because for the work of Christ he came close to death, not regarding his life, to supply what was lacking in your service toward me.

Forget the past and look ahead

3 Finally, my brethren, rejoice in the Lord. For me to write the same things to you is not tedious, but for you *it is* safe.

2 Beware of dogs, beware of evil workers, beware of the mutilation! 3 For we are the circumcision, who worship God in the Spirit, rejoice in Christ Jesus, and have no confidence in the flesh, 4 though I also might have confidence in the flesh. If anyone else thinks he may have confidence in the flesh, I more so: 5 circumcised the eighth day, of the stock of Israel, *of* the tribe of Benjamin, a Hebrew of the Hebrews; concerning the law, a Pharisee; 6 concerning zeal, persecuting the church; concerning the righteousness which is in the law, blameless.

7 But what things were gain to me, these I have counted loss for Christ. 8 Yet indeed I also count all things loss for the excellence of the knowledge of Christ Jesus my Lord, for whom I have suffered the loss of all things, and count them as rubbish, that I may gain Christ 9 and be found in Him, not having my own righteousness, which *is* from the law, but that which *is* through faith in Christ, the righteousness which is from God by faith; 10 that I may know Him and the power of His resurrection, and the fellowship of His sufferings, being conformed to His death, 11 if, by any means, I may attain to the resurrection from the dead.

12 Not that I have already attained,

What Is a Citizen of Heaven?

As a citizen of your country, you must obey its laws. Christians are also citizens of heaven, and they also must obey the laws of heaven. The first law of heaven is to love God with all your being. The next law is that you love your neighbor as yourself. Each person you meet is your neighbor.

or am already perfected; but I press on, that I may lay hold of that for which Christ Jesus has also laid hold of me. 13 Brethren, I do not count myself to have apprehended; but one thing I do, forgetting those things which are behind and reaching forward to those things which are ahead, 14 I press toward the goal for the prize of the upward call of God in Christ Jesus.

15 Therefore let us, as many as are mature, have this mind; and if in anything you think otherwise, God will reveal even this to you. 16 Nevertheless, to the degree that we have already attained, let us walk by the same rule, let us be of the same mind.

17 Brethren, join in following my example, and note those who so walk, as you have us for a pattern. 18 For many walk, of whom I have told you

often, and now tell you even weeping, that they are the enemies of the cross of Christ: 19 whose end is destruction, whose god is their belly, and whose glory is in their shame—who set their mind on earthly things. 20 For our citizenship is in heaven, from which we also eagerly wait for the Savior, the Lord Jesus Christ, 21 who will transform our lowly body that it may be conformed to His glorious body, according to the working by which He is able even to subdue all things to Himself.

God will take care of all our needs

4 Therefore, my beloved and longed-for brethren, my joy and crown, so stand fast in the Lord, beloved.

2 I implore Euodia and I implore Syntyche to be of the same mind in the Lord. 3 And I urge you also, true companion, help these women who labored with me in the gospel, with Clement also, and the rest of my fellow workers, whose names are in the Book of Life.

4 Rejoice in the Lord always. Again I will say, rejoice!

5 Let your gentleness be known to all men. The Lord is at hand.

6 Be anxious for nothing, but in

WORDFINDER

3:20 Savior Someone who saves our lives. Jesus is our Savior from heaven who died on the Cross to save our souls from sin and hell.

4:3 Book of Life The book containing the names of all of God's people saved by faith in Christ.

DIGGING IN

3:8 Trade Everything for Jesus You may ask yourself, "What do I want more than anything in the world?" What is the answer? A trip around the world? To be president of your country? To be the richest person you know?

The trouble with all these things—and a lot more—is that THEY DON'T LAST. Anything you might want more than everything else is something that comes to an end all too soon. Where are all the

millionaires of the year 1900? What do you do after a trip around the world? What do you know about the man who was president in 1893?

All these things and many more are soon gone, but the friendship of Jesus Christ is the same yesterday, today, and forever. So you would be wise to trade all your dreams for the friendship of Jesus.

What Paul Learned

Jesus said we shouldn't worry about what we're going to eat or wear tomorrow. God will take care of tomorrow just as He takes care of today.

That was hard for me to learn at first. I have traveled to many countries and have suffered many things for Jesus. But I have learned that He looks out for all my real needs.

Sometimes I haven't had all the comforts I would like to have, but happiness doesn't mean having nice things. Happiness comes from inside you, where Jesus lives. When you have Jesus in your heart, you don't feel hungry, even if you have to miss a meal or two.

---

everything by prayer and supplication, with thanksgiving, let your requests be made known to God; 7 and the peace of God, which surpasses all understanding, will guard your hearts and minds through Christ Jesus.

8 Finally, brethren, whatever things are true, whatever things *are* noble, whatever things *are* just, whatever things *are* pure, whatever things *are* lovely, whatever things *are* of good report, if *there is* any virtue and if *there is* anything praiseworthy—meditate on these things. 9 The things which you learned and received and heard and saw in me, these do, and the God of peace will be with you.

10 But I rejoiced in the Lord greatly that now at last your care for me has flourished again; though you surely did care, but you lacked opportunity. 11 Not that I speak in regard to need, for I have learned in whatever state I am, to be content: 12 I know how to be abased, and I know how to abound. Everywhere and in all things I have learned both to be full and to be hungry, both to abound and to suffer need. 13 I can do all things through **Christ** who strengthens me.

14 Nevertheless you have done well that you shared in my distress. 15 Now you Philippians know also that in the beginning of the gospel, when I departed from Macedonia, no church shared with me concerning giving and receiving but you only. 16 For even in

---

WORDFINDER

4:13 Christ The divine title of the Man Jesus. The word means "the Anointed" (by the Holy Spirit). *Christos* is a Greek word translated from the Hebrew *Messiah*.

DIGGING IN

4:8 Think Great Thoughts What do you like to think about? Maybe you spend a lot of time thinking about when the school day will end so you can play baseball, soccer, or do other things with your friends. That's OK. But try to understand that *you're going to become what you think*. Solomon said, "As anyone thinks . . . that's what he is."

That's scary, isn't it? You don't really want to become some of the things you think about, do you? What should you think about then?

Think first about the things that are TRUE. That guarantees a sound mind. Then think about things that are NOBLE—thoughts that rise above ordinary, everyday happenings, like the great deeds of the world. Then think about things that are PURE. Don't allow unclean ideas into your mind. Instead, think about LOVELY things. There are so many beautiful things in God's world. The secret is to see the world as God sees it, and to think about life the way He does.

Paul and Silas were beaten and imprisoned as troublemakers for their preaching in Philippi.

Thessalonica you sent *aid* once and again for my necessities. ¹⁷ Not that I seek the gift, but I seek the fruit that abounds to your account. ¹⁸ Indeed I have all and abound. I am full, having received from Epaphroditus the things *sent* from you, a sweet-smelling aroma, an acceptable sacrifice, well pleasing to God. ¹⁹ And my God shall supply all your need according to His riches in glory by Christ Jesus. ²⁰ Now to our God and Father *be* glory forever and ever. Amen.

²¹ Greet *every* saint in Christ Jesus. The brethren who are with me greet you. ²² All the saints greet you, but especially those who are of Caesar's household.

²³ The grace of our Lord Jesus Christ be with you all. Amen.

The Book of
COLOSSIANS

Colosse (pronounced *ko-LAH-see*) was about a hundred miles east of the coast of Asia Minor. Like the books of Ephesians and Philippians this letter to the Colossians was written while Paul was in prison at Rome.

When the apostle Paul came and taught us about Jesus the Savior, we believed him. We trusted in Jesus as the risen Son of God.

But we also held on to some of our earlier beliefs. We kept some of the Hebrew feast days, and we practiced astrology (pronounced *ah-STRAH-lo-gee*). This is a false belief that you can tell the future by studying the stars. We also worshiped angels.

You may wonder how we could have mixed these things up with the Good News about Jesus. But early Christians like ourselves were not as well taught as you are. That is why Paul had to write us this letter.

Paul prays for the Colossians

PAUL, an apostle of Jesus Christ by the will of God, and Timothy our brother,

2 To the saints and faithful brethren in Christ *who are* in Colosse:

Grace to you and peace from God our Father and the Lord Jesus Christ.

3 We give thanks to the God and Father of our Lord Jesus Christ, praying always for you, 4 since we heard of your faith in Christ Jesus and of your love for all the saints; 5 because of the hope which is laid up for you in heaven, of which you heard before in the word of the truth of the gospel, 6 which has come to you, as *it has* also in all the world, and is bringing forth fruit, as *it is* also among you since the day you heard and knew the grace of God in truth; 7 as you also learned from Epaphras, our dear fellow servant, who is a faithful minister of Christ on your behalf, 8 who also declared to us your love in the Spirit.

9 For this reason we also, since the day we heard it, do not cease to pray for you, and to ask that you may be filled with the knowledge of His will in all wisdom and spiritual understanding; 10 that you may walk worthy of the Lord, fully pleasing *Him,* being fruitful in every good work and increasing in the knowledge of God; 11 strengthened with all might, according to His glorious power, for all patience and longsuffering with joy; 12 giving thanks to the Father who has qualified us to be partakers of the inheritance of the saints in the light. 13 He has delivered us from the power of darkness and conveyed *us* into the kingdom of the Son of His love, 14 in whom we have redemption through His blood, the forgiveness of sins.

15 He is the image of the invisible God, the firstborn over all creation. 16 For by Him all things were created that are in heaven and that are on

What Was the First Work Jesus Did?

Long ago in heaven, Jesus agreed with His Father and the Holy Spirit to create the world. That was the first work Jesus did that we can see. Only Jesus had the wisdom and power to imagine and make the world around you. We can work with Him to keep the world as beautiful as He made it.

earth, visible and invisible, whether thrones or dominions or principalities or powers. All things were created through Him and for Him. ¹⁷ And He is before all things, and in Him all things consist. ¹⁸ And He is the head of the body, the church, who is the beginning, the firstborn from the dead, that in all things He may have the preeminence.

¹⁹ For it pleased *the Father that* in Him all the fullness should dwell,

²⁰ and by Him to reconcile all things to Himself, by Him, whether things on earth or things in heaven, having made peace through the blood of His cross.

²¹ And you, who once were alienated and enemies in your mind by wicked works, yet now He has reconciled ²² in the body of His flesh through death, to present you **holy,** and blameless, and above reproach in His sight— ²³ if indeed you continue in the faith,

WORDFINDER

1:22 Holy   An adjective meaning "separate," but includes the idea of moral purity and being like God.

DIGGING IN

1:17 Jesus Holds All Things Together When you think about the world and the universe, do you ever wonder how it all stays together? Marvelous, isn't it?

Every galaxy, every star, every planet in the immense universe stays right in its place for ages and ages! And yet the whole system is constantly moving! The sun never fails to give light right on time every day. The seas don't overrun our continents. Even that amazing world you

can see only through a microscope lives and moves and grows exactly in the way it must.

We often take all this wonderful order for granted. But that's a sad mistake. No matter how much you learn about the universe, you always have to ask the question, "What holds it all in place?" The Bible rightly tells you that Jesus who was BEFORE all things also CONTROLS all things.

Only God has the power to create the world around you.

grounded and steadfast, and are not moved away from the hope of the gospel which you heard, which was preached to every creature under heaven, of which I, Paul, became a minister.

24 I now rejoice in my sufferings for you, and fill up in my flesh what is lacking in the afflictions of Christ, for the sake of His body, which is the church, 25 of which I became a minister according to the stewardship from God which was given to me for you, to fulfill the word of God, 26 the mystery which has been hidden from ages and from generations, but now has been revealed to His saints. 27 To them God willed to make known what are the riches of the glory of this mystery among the Gentiles: which is Christ in you, the hope of glory. 28 Him we preach, warning every man and teaching every man in all wisdom, that we may present every man perfect in Christ Jesus. 29 To this end I also labor, striving according to His working which works in me mightily.

Rules that were made to be broken

2 For I want you to know what a great conflict I have for you and those in Laodicea, and for as many as have not seen my face in the flesh, 2 that their hearts may be encouraged, being knit together in love, and attaining to all riches of the full assurance of understanding, to the knowledge of the mystery of God, both of the Father and of Christ, 3 in whom are hidden all the treasures of wisdom and knowledge.

4 Now this I say lest anyone should deceive you with persuasive words. 5 For though I am absent in the flesh, yet I am with you in spirit, rejoicing to see your good order and the steadfastness of your faith in Christ.

6 As you therefore have received Christ Jesus the Lord, so walk in Him, 7 rooted and built up in Him and established in the faith, as you have been taught, abounding in it with thanksgiving.

8 Beware lest anyone cheat you

DIGGING IN

1:27 How Can You Know You're Going to Heaven? Just saying something doesn't make it true. So, if somebody says, "I'm going to heaven," how can he know? Not even by saying it over and over!

The answer is simple. You can know you're going to heaven because you have heaven inside you now. That's another way of saying you have Jesus inside you. When you have Jesus living in you, then you know you have heaven, because Jesus lives forever. So you and He will live forever together.

Maybe you're saying, "I don't know that Jesus is living in me." Well, that's easy. All you have to do is go someplace quiet and say something like this: "Jesus, I don't have You in my life, but I want to. I want to give my life to You right now. So please come and live in me forever." Say it and mean it. Then you'll know that Jesus and you will always be together. That's heaven.

2:3 Jesus Makes You Able To Think God's Thoughts Just how smart are you? If you're honest, you will have to say, "Not as smart as I'd like to be." Nobody knows as much as he could know. As time goes by, you'll realize how little you do understand about living in the world.

This is God's world. You have to live in it just the way He planned for you to live, or else you'll always be in some kind of trouble. How can you know what God wants you to know?

Jesus Himself is your wisdom, and Jesus has to take over your brain. That's what Paul means when he says, "We have the mind of Christ" (see 1 Corinthians 2:16). So, learning how to live in God's world means letting Jesus control your thoughts. The Spirit of God will help you do this as you read God's thoughts in the Bible. Then let God's thoughts become your thoughts.

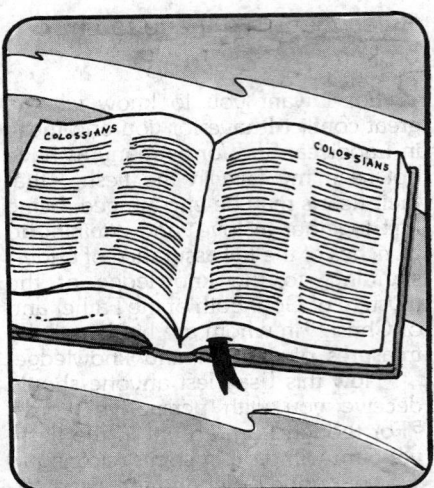

God's Word guards us against "philosophy and empty deceit."

through **philosophy** and empty deceit, according to the tradition of men, according to the basic principles of the world, and not according to Christ. 9 For in Him dwells all the fullness of the Godhead bodily; 10 and you are complete in Him, who is the head of all principality and power.

11 In Him you were also circumcised with the circumcision made without hands, by putting off the body of the sins of the flesh, by the circumcision of Christ, 12 buried with Him in baptism, in which you also were raised with *Him* through faith in the working of God, who raised Him from the dead. 13 And you, being dead in your trespasses and the uncircumcision of your flesh, He has made alive together with Him, having forgiven you all trespasses, 14 having wiped out the handwriting of requirements that was against us, which was contrary to us. And He has taken it out of the way, having nailed it to the cross. 15 Having

disarmed principalities and powers, He made a public spectacle of them, triumphing over them in it.

16 So let no one judge you in food or in drink, or regarding a festival or a new moon or sabbaths, 17 which are a shadow of things to come, but the substance is of Christ. 18 Let no one cheat you of your reward, taking delight in *false* humility and worship of angels, intruding into those things which he has not seen, vainly puffed up by his fleshly mind, 19 and not holding fast to the Head, from whom all the body, nourished and knit together by joints and ligaments, grows with the increase *that is* from God.

20 Therefore, if you died with Christ from the basic principles of the world, why, as *though* living in the world, do you subject yourselves to regulations— 21 "Do not touch, do not taste, do not handle," 22 which all concern things which perish with the using—according to the commandments and doctrines of men? 23 These things indeed have an appearance of wisdom in self-imposed religion, *false* humility, and neglect of the body, *but are* of no value against the indulgence of the flesh.

Rules for families and friends

3 If then you were raised with Christ, seek those things which are above, where Christ is, sitting at the right hand of God. 2 Set your mind on things above, not on things on the earth. 3 For you died, and your life is hidden with Christ in God. 4 When Christ *who is* our life appears, then you also will appear with Him in glory.

5 Therefore put to death your members which are on the earth: fornication, uncleanness, passion, evil desire,

🌎 **WORDFINDER**

2:8 Philosophy Pronounced *fih-LOS-uh-fee.* A word meaning "love of wisdom." Many ancient Greeks worshiped human wisdom. They believed they could solve all problems by thinking. True wisdom comes from God's Word in the Bible.

What the Colossians Learned

You may have already read how we mixed up our faith in Jesus with all kinds of strange ideas. Finally, we saw the plain truth about Jesus, and we aren't confused anymore.

We know now that when Jesus rose from death, He shared His new risen life with us. Jesus' very own Spirit now lives in us. So our main interests are in heavenly things. We have no need to waste time with all those weird ideas we used to think about. We've given up all that nonsense. Now we know we have a living Savior.

Jesus will come back someday. Then we will be with Him. Until then, the Holy Spirit gives us inner sight to see Him continually.

and **covetousness,** which is idolatry. 6 Because of these things the wrath of God is coming upon the sons of disobedience, 7 in which you yourselves once walked when you lived in them.

8 But now you yourselves are to put off all these: anger, wrath, malice, blasphemy, filthy language out of your mouth. 9 Do not lie to one another, since you have put off the old man with his deeds, 10 and have put on the new *man* who is renewed in knowledge according to the image of Him who created him, 11 where there is neither Greek nor Jew, circumcised nor uncircumcised, barbarian, Scythian, slave *nor* free, but Christ *is* all and in all.

12 Therefore, as *the* elect of God, holy and beloved, put on tender mercies, kindness, humility, meekness, longsuffering; 13 bearing with one another, and forgiving one another, if anyone has a complaint against another; even as Christ forgave you, so you also *must do.* 14 But above all these things put on love, which is the bond of perfection. 15 And let the peace of God rule in your hearts, to which also you *were* called in one body; and be thankful. 16 Let the word of Christ dwell in you richly in all wisdom, teaching and admonishing one another in psalms and hymns and spiri-

We are all equal in God's sight.

tual songs, singing with grace in your hearts to the Lord. 17 And *whatever* you do in word or deed, *do* all in the

WORDFINDER

3:5 Covetousness Pronounced *KUV-ih-tuss-ness.* Envy or the extreme and wrong desire to own what belongs to someone else.

name of the Lord Jesus, giving thanks to God the Father through Him.

18 Wives, submit to your own husbands, as is fitting in the Lord.

19 Husbands, love your wives and do not be bitter toward them.

20 Children, obey your parents in all things, for this is well pleasing to the Lord.

21 Fathers, do not provoke your children, lest they become discouraged.

22 Bondservants, obey in all things your masters according to the flesh, not with **eyeservice,** as men-pleasers, but in sincerity of heart, fearing God. 23 And whatever you do, do it heartily, as to the Lord and not to men, 24 knowing that from the Lord you will receive the reward of the inheritance; for you serve the Lord Christ. 25 But he who does wrong will be repaid for what he has done, and there is no partiality.

Paul asks his friends to pray for him

4 Masters, give your bondservants what is just and fair, knowing that you also have a Master in heaven.

2 Continue earnestly in prayer, being vigilant in it with thanksgiving; 3 meanwhile praying also for us, that God would open to us a door for the word, to speak the mystery of Christ, for which I am also in chains, 4 that I may make it manifest, as I ought to speak.

5 Walk in wisdom toward those *who are* outside, redeeming the time. 6 *Let* your speech always *be* with grace, seasoned with salt, that you may know how you ought to answer each one.

7 Tychicus, a beloved brother, faithful minister, and fellow servant in the Lord, will tell you all the news about me. 8 I am sending him to you for this

WORDFINDER

3:22 Eyeservice Living in a way that looks good to people but doesn't please God. We may deceive others, but we can't deceive God.

DIGGING IN

3:25 What You Do Will Come Back to You Can you remember a mean thing you once said or did to somebody? Maybe you think it's all past and forgotten. But don't count on it!

Better go to that person and make right what you did. If you don't, someday that mean thing will come back to you. When you remember the mean thing you did, you'll feel so bad you could almost wish to die. By that time it may be too late to say you're sorry. The person you hurt may even be dead. Then all you can do is ask God to forgive you because Jesus died for you. You can also ask Him to help you never do anything like that again.

But the best policy is to learn to do kind things to people every chance you get. Then you'll always have good memories.

4:6 Be Careful What You Say There are too many words in the world. That's another way of saying people often talk

too much. If you talk too much, sooner or later you're likely to say something you shouldn't.

How can we solve this problem of too much talking? The answer is simple, but doing it may not be easy: THINK MORE than you talk, and always THINK BEFORE you speak.

Just imagine that you carry a "talk meter" around with you. The talk meter flashes GREAT when you say something good. But every time you speak before you think, your talk meter flashes, YOU GOOFED!

When you think more than you talk, then you'll usually have something worth saying. Also, people will listen to you more. But if you just babble on and on, nobody will listen to you.

All of us need to ask God to help us control our talking at all times.

very purpose, that he may know your circumstances and comfort your hearts, 9 with Onesimus, a faithful and beloved brother, who is *one* of you. They will make known to you all things which *are happening* here.

10 Aristarchus my fellow prisoner greets you, with Mark the cousin of Barnabas (about whom you received instructions: if he comes to you, welcome him), 11 and Jesus who is called Justus. These *are my* only fellow workers for the kingdom of God who are of the circumcision; they have proved to be a comfort to me.

12 Epaphras, who is *one* of you, a bondservant of Christ, greets you, always laboring fervently for you in prayers, that you may stand perfect and complete in all the will of God. 13 For I bear him witness that he has a great zeal for you, and those who are in Laodicea, and those in Hierapolis. 14 Luke the beloved physician and Demas greet you. 15 Greet the brethren who are in Laodicea, and Nymphas and the church that *is* in his house.

16 Now when this epistle is read among you, see that it is read also in the church of the Laodiceans, and that you likewise read the epistle from Laodicea. 17 And say to Archippus, "Take heed to the ministry which you have received in the Lord, that you may fulfill it."

18 This salutation by my own hand— Paul. Remember my chains. Grace *be* with you. Amen.

The Book of
1 THESSALONIANS

Like Philippi, our city of Thessalonica (pronounced *thess-uh-low-NIGH-kuh*) was located in the Roman province of Macedonia. The apostle Paul visited us about 20 years after Jesus was crucified.

Our city was founded about 315 years before Christ by Cassander, the Syrian general. He named it for his wife, Thessalonica, a sister of Alexander the Great. Alexander later conquered the whole world of that time. A citizen of Thessalonica is called a "Thessalonian" (pronounced *thess-uh-LOW-nee-un*).

Before Paul's time, the Romans made Thessalonica the capital city of Macedonia. The leading Roman road to the Eastern world, called the Egnatian (pronounced *egg-NAY-shun*) Way, ran through our city. A wall surrounded Thessalonica, and parts of that wall are still standing today.

A great Christian church grew up in our city after Paul's visit.

The Thessalonians are good examples

PAUL, Silvanus, and Timothy,

To the church of the Thessalonians in God the Father and the Lord Jesus Christ:

Grace to you and peace from God our Father and the Lord Jesus Christ.

2 We give thanks to God always for you all, making mention of you in our prayers, 3 remembering without ceasing your work of faith, labor of love, and patience of hope in our Lord Jesus Christ in the sight of our God and Father, 4 knowing, beloved brethren, your election by God. 5 For our gospel did not come to you in word only, but also in power, and in the Holy Spirit

Thessalonica's natural harbor made it an important trading center. People came from many places to do business here.

Are You an Example?

An "example" is something or someone to imitate. Christians like to imitate Jesus. We also need to be living and walking examples. For someone else, you may be the only example of what a Christian is like. It's very important, then, to show what it means to be a Christian by how you act.

and in much assurance, as you know what kind of men we were among you for your sake.

6 And you became followers of us and of the Lord, having received the word in much affliction, with joy of the Holy Spirit, 7 so that you became examples to all in Macedonia and Achaia who believe. 8 For from you the word of the Lord has sounded forth, not only in Macedonia and Achaia, but also in every place. Your faith toward God has gone out, so that we do not need to say anything. 9 For they themselves declare concerning us what manner of entry we had to you, and how you turned to God from idols to serve the living and true God, 10 and to wait for His Son from heaven, whom He raised from the dead, even Jesus who delivers us from the wrath to come.

Paul remembers his friends with affection

2 For you yourselves know, brethren, that our coming to you was not in vain.

2 But even after we had suffered before and were spitefully treated at Philippi, as you know, we were bold in our God to speak to you the gospel of God in much conflict. 3 For our exhortation did not come from error or uncleanness, nor was it in deceit.

4 But as we have been approved by God to be entrusted with the gospel, even so we speak, not as pleasing men, but God who tests our hearts. 5 For neither at any time did we use flattering words, as you know, nor a cloak for covetousness—God is witness. 6 Nor did we seek glory from men, either from you or from others, when we might have made demands as apostles of Christ. 7 But we were gentle among you, just as a nursing mother cherishes her own children. 8 So, affectionately longing for you, we were well pleased to impart to you not only the gospel of God, but also our own lives, because you had become dear to us. 9 For you remember, brethren, our labor and toil; for laboring night and day, that we might not be a burden to any of you, we preached to you the gospel of God.

10 You are witnesses, and God also, how devoutly and justly and blamelessly we behaved ourselves among you who believe; 11 as you know how we exhorted, and comforted, and charged every one of you, as a father does his own children, 12 that you would walk worthy of God who calls you into His own kingdom and glory. 13 For this reason we also thank God

⚒ DIGGING IN

2:13 Believing What God Says God speaks in the Bible, which is His Word. When the Spirit of God (also called the Spirit of Christ) lives in you, then He tells you that the Bible is the Word of God, and you believe and obey what God says.

There are a lot of voices in the world. Some voices make good sense and others don't, but God's Word is the gauge by which you measure the truth of what people say.

God's Word also must be the gauge by which you measure the truth of what YOU say. If you're always guessing at the truth, or if you're just lying, then you have broken God's Word. The Bible says, "You shall not bear false witness [tell lies]" (Matthew 19:18).

But BELIEVING what God says is the key to OBEYING what God says. When you believe that God has spoken in the Bible, then you know you must obey because God Himself has spoken to you.

without ceasing, because when you received the word of God which you heard from us, you welcomed *it* not *as* the word of men, but as it is in truth, the word of God, which also *effectively* works in you who believe. 14 For you, brethren, became imitators of the churches of God which are in Judea in Christ Jesus. For you also suffered the same things from your own countrymen, just as they *did* from the Judeans, 15 who killed both the Lord Jesus and their own prophets, and have persecuted us; and they do not please God and are contrary to all men, 16 forbidding us to speak to the Gentiles that they may be saved, so as always to fill up *the measure of* their sins; but wrath has come upon them to the uttermost.

17 But *we*, brethren, having been taken away from you for a short time in presence, not in heart, endeavored more eagerly to see your face with great desire. 18 Therefore we wanted to come to you—even I, Paul, time and again—but Satan hindered us. 19 For what *is* our hope, or joy, or crown of rejoicing? *Is it* not even you in the presence of our Lord Jesus Christ at His coming? 20 For you are our glory and joy.

Paul receives good news about the church

3 Therefore, when we could no longer endure it, we thought it good to be left in Athens alone, 2 and sent Timothy, our brother and minister of God, and our fellow laborer in the gospel of Christ, to establish you and encourage you concerning your faith, 3 that no one should be shaken by these afflictions; for you yourselves know that we are appointed to this. 4 For, in fact, we told you before when we were with you that we would suffer tribulation, just as it happened, and you know. 5 For this reason, when I could no longer endure it, I sent to know your faith, lest by some means the tempter had tempted you, and our labor might be in vain.

6 But now that Timothy has come to us from you, and brought us good news of your faith and love, and that you always have good remembrance of us, greatly desiring to see us, as we also *to see* you— 7 therefore, brethren, in all our affliction and distress we were comforted concerning you by your faith. 8 For now we live, if you stand fast in the Lord.

9 For what thanks can we render to God for you, for all the joy with which we rejoice for your sake before our God, 10 night and day praying exceedingly that we may see your face and perfect what is lacking in your faith? 11 Now may our God and Father Himself, and our Lord Jesus Christ, direct our way to you. 12 And may the Lord make you increase and abound in love to one another and to all, just as we *do* to you, 13 so that He may establish your hearts blameless in holiness before our God and Father at the coming of our Lord Jesus Christ with all His saints.

How to get ready for Christ's return

4 Finally then, brethren, we urge and exhort in the Lord Jesus that you should abound more and more, just as you received from us how you ought to walk and to please God; 2 for you know what commandments we gave you through the Lord Jesus. 3 For this is the will of God, your sanctification: that you should abstain from sexual immorality; 4 that each of you should know how to possess his own vessel in sanctification and honor, 5 not in passion of lust, like the Gentiles who do not know God; 6 that no one should take advantage of and defraud his brother in this matter, because the Lord *is* the avenger of all such, as we also forewarned you and testified. 7 For God did not call us to uncleanness, but in holiness. 8 Therefore he who rejects *this* does not reject man, but God, who has also given us His Holy Spirit.

9 But concerning brotherly love you

have no need that I should write to you, for you yourselves are taught by God to love one another; 10 and indeed you do so toward all the brethren who are in all Macedonia. But we urge you, brethren, that you increase more and more; 11 that you also aspire to lead a quiet life, to mind your own business, and to work with your own hands, as we commanded you, 12 that you may walk properly toward those who are outside, and *that* you may lack nothing.

13 But I do not want you to be ignorant, brethren, concerning those who have fallen asleep, lest you sorrow as others who have no hope. 14 For if we believe that Jesus died and rose again, even so God will bring with Him those who sleep in Jesus.

15 For this we say to you by the word of the Lord, that we who are alive *and* remain until the coming of the Lord will by no means precede those who are asleep. 16 For the Lord Himself will descend from heaven with a shout, with the voice of an archangel, and with the trumpet of God. And the dead in Christ will rise first. 17 Then we who are alive *and* remain shall be caught up together with them in the clouds to meet the Lord in the air. And thus we shall always be with the Lord. 18 Therefore comfort one another with these words.

When will the Lord come again?

5 But concerning the times and the seasons, brethren, you have no need that I should write to you. 2 For you yourselves know perfectly that the day of the Lord so comes as a thief in the night. 3 For when they say, "Peace and safety!" then sudden destruction comes upon them, as labor pains upon a pregnant woman. And they shall not escape. 4 But you, brethren, are not in darkness, so that this Day should overtake you as a thief. 5 You are all sons of light and sons of the day. We are not of the night nor of darkness. 6 Therefore let us not sleep, as others *do,* but let us watch and be sober. 7 For those who sleep, sleep at night, and those who get drunk are drunk at night. 8 But let us who are of the day be sober, putting on the breastplate of faith and love, and *as* a helmet the hope of salvation. 9 For God did not appoint us to wrath, but to obtain salvation through our Lord Jesus Christ, 10 who died for us, that whether we wake or sleep, we should live together with Him.

11 Therefore comfort each other and edify one another, just as you also are doing.

12 And we urge you, brethren, to recognize those who labor among you, and are over you in the Lord and admonish you, 13 and to esteem them very highly in love for their work's sake. Be at peace among yourselves.

14 Now we exhort you, brethren, warn those who are unruly, comfort the fainthearted, uphold the weak, be patient with all. 15 See that no one renders evil for evil to anyone, but always pursue what is good both for yourselves and for all.

16 Rejoice always, 17 pray without

 DIGGING IN

4:14 We Will Live Forever With Jesus Jesus didn't die and rise again from death just to prove He could do it. Jesus was no "show-off." He had a great purpose in what He did. He died to take away your sins. But He rose again so that death would never have real power over you. He rose again so that you could have the kind of life that He brought back from the dead. That is life that lasts forever. That

is the life of God Himself.

So if you have trusted your life to Jesus, then you have the very life of Jesus in your life. Some people will EXIST forever, but they won't have the life of God. To exist without God is worse than death. We call that kind of existence HELL. So being saved from sin and hell means having the life of Christ Himself. We call that kind of life ETERNAL LIFE.

ceasing, 18 in everything give thanks; for this is the will of God in Christ Jesus for you.

19 Do not quench the Spirit. 20 Do not despise prophecies. 21 Test all things; hold fast what is good. 22 Abstain from every form of evil.

23 Now may the God of peace Himself sanctify you completely; and may your whole spirit, soul, and body be preserved blameless at the coming of our Lord Jesus Christ. 24 He who calls you is faithful, who also will do it.

25 Brethren, pray for us.

26 Greet all the brethren with a holy kiss.

27 I charge you by the Lord that this epistle be read to all the holy brethren.

28 The grace of our Lord Jesus Christ be with you. Amen.

The Book of
2 THESSALONIANS

We are the church of the Thessalonians. Some of us believed in Jesus when Paul preached at Thessalonica, but Paul had to leave soon after that because other citizens accused him of being disloyal to the emperor of Rome. He left his friend Timothy in charge.

Some of our people were worried about what would happen to Christians who died. They wondered how they could be ready when Jesus returns. But Paul told us in his first letter that the dead would be raised when Jesus comes, just as the body of Jesus was raised up. Believers will always be with the Lord.

Paul also warned us that there would be a lot of trouble in the world before Jesus returns. But Jesus will judge the wicked troublemakers.

Paul writes another letter to the Thessalonians

PAUL, Silvanus, and Timothy,

To the church of the Thessalonians in God our Father and the Lord Jesus Christ:

2 Grace to you and peace from God our Father and the Lord Jesus Christ. 3 We are bound to thank God always for you, brethren, as it is fitting, because your faith grows exceedingly, and the love of every one of you all abounds toward each other, 4 so that we ourselves boast of you among the churches of God for your patience and faith in all your persecutions and tribulations that you endure, 5 *which is* manifest evidence of the righteous judgment of God, that you may be counted worthy of the kingdom of God, for which you also suffer; 6 since *it is* a righteous thing with God to repay with tribulation those who trouble you, 7 and to *give* you who are troubled rest with us when the Lord Jesus is revealed from heaven with His mighty angels, 8 in flaming fire taking vengeance on those who do not know God, and on those who do not obey the gospel of our Lord Jesus Christ. 9 These shall be punished with everlasting destruction from the presence of the Lord and from the glory of His

DIGGING IN

1:3 Let Your Faith Grow Anything that lives also grows. If you have LIVING faith, you also have GROWING faith. Your faith is growing if you are living more and more in friendship with Jesus.

Your body lives and grows by breathing, drinking, eating, resting, and exercise. Your faith is BREATHING if you receive the Holy Spirit every moment. Do you know the hymn, "Breathe on Me, Breath of God"? Your faith also grows by EATING and DRINKING the life of Jesus Himself: "He who comes to Me shall never hunger, and he who believes in Me shall never thirst"(John 6:35). Find this LIFE of Jesus in His words in the Bible. Jesus also says, "Come to Me, . . . and I will give you rest" (Matthew 11:28). That means TRUSTING Jesus so you don't have to be afraid of anything in the world.

Finally, your growing faith needs EXERCISE in doing all the things Jesus commands you. By works of love and mercy, show and tell others what Jesus is like. Then you will have a living and growing faith.

The city walls of Thessalonica.

power, 10 when He comes, in that Day, to be glorified in His saints and to be admired among all those who believe, because our testimony among you was believed.

11 Therefore we also pray always for you that our God would count you worthy of *this* calling, and fulfill all the good pleasure of *His* goodness and the work of faith with power, 12 that the name of our Lord Jesus Christ may be glorified in you, and you in Him, according to the grace of our God and the Lord Jesus Christ.

The Antichrist will trick everyone

2 Now, brethren, concerning the coming of our Lord Jesus Christ and our gathering together to Him, we ask you, 2 not to be soon shaken in mind or troubled, either by spirit or by word or by letter, as if from us, as though the day of Christ had come. 3 Let no one deceive you by any means; for *that Day will not come* unless the falling away comes first, and the man of sin is revealed, the son of perdition, 4 who opposes and exalts himself above all that is called God or that is worshiped, so that he sits as God in the temple of God, showing himself that he is God.

5 Do you not remember that when I was still with you I told you these things? 6 And now you know what is restraining, that he may be revealed in his own time. 7 For the mystery of lawlessness is already at work; only He who now restrains *will do so* until He is taken out of the way. 8 And then the lawless one will be revealed, whom the Lord will consume with the breath of His mouth and destroy with the brightness of His coming. 9 The coming of the *lawless one* is according to the working of Satan, with all power, signs, and lying wonders, 10 and with all unrighteous deception among those who perish, because they did not receive the love of the truth, that they might be saved. 11 And for this reason God will send them strong delusion, that they should believe the lie, 12 that

🪓 DIGGING IN

2:3–10 Who Is "the Man of Sin"? In his letters John the apostle calls the Man of Sin "the Antichrist." John also says that the spirit of Antichrist is already in the world. As time goes by, you will realize that many people hate Christ and His followers in the world. This is the spirit of Antichrist that John talks about in his first and second letters.

But Paul says that the Antichrist will be an actual man someday. This man will be very powerful and will be controlled by Satan. He will even do miracles and will deceive a lot of people.

Jesus also warns you about false christs. As you learn more, you will be amazed at how many religious fakes are in the world. Such people often take advantage of simple people and make a lot of wild promises to them. The only safety against these false teachers and the Antichrist is to know what the Bible says. The Bible teaches you the difference between true and false teachings.

they all may be condemned who did not believe the truth but had pleasure in unrighteousness.

13 But we are bound to give thanks to God always for you, brethren beloved by the Lord, because God from the beginning chose you for salvation through sanctification by the Spirit and belief in the truth, 14 to which He called you by our gospel, for the obtaining of the glory of our Lord Jesus Christ. 15 Therefore, brethren, stand fast and hold the traditions which you were taught, whether by word or our epistle.

16 Now may our Lord Jesus Christ Himself, and our God and Father, who has loved us and given us everlasting consolation and good hope by grace, 17 comfort your hearts and establish you in every good word and work.

God will guard us from Satan

3 Finally, brethren, pray for us, that the word of the Lord may run *swiftly* and be glorified, just as *it is* with you, 2 and that we may be delivered from unreasonable and wicked men; for not all have faith. 3 But the Lord is faithful, who will establish you and guard *you* from the evil one. 4 And we have confidence in the Lord concerning you, both that you do and will do the things we command you.

5 Now may the Lord direct your hearts into the love of God and into the patience of Christ.

6 But we command you, brethren, in the name of our Lord Jesus Christ, that you withdraw from every brother who walks disorderly and not according to the tradition which he received from us. 7 For you yourselves know how you ought to follow us, for we were not disorderly among you; 8 nor did we eat anyone's bread free of charge, but worked with labor and toil night and day, that we might not be a burden to any of you, 9 not because we do not have authority, but to make ourselves an example of how you should follow us.

10 For even when we were with you, we commanded you this: If anyone will not work, neither shall he eat. 11 For we hear that there are some who walk among you in a disorderly manner, not working at all, but are **busybodies.** 12 Now those who are such we command and exhort through our Lord Jesus Christ that they work in quietness and eat their own bread.

13 But *as for* you, brethren, do not grow weary *in* doing good. 14 And if anyone does not obey our word in this epistle, note that person and do not

⊕WORDFINDER

3:11 Busybodies People who mind other people's business. Paul said that some Christians were not doing their own work but were meddling in other people's affairs.

⛏DIGGING IN

3:6 Choose Your Friends When you read about the life of Jesus in Matthew, Mark, Luke, and John, you notice that Jesus mixed with many kinds of people. But He always kept His place as the Son of God, and He witnessed to everybody.

Jesus chose His friends carefully. He said, "You are My friends if you do what I command you." Your friends must also be Jesus' friends. You cannot become close friends with young people who swear, lie, steal, use drugs, or don't believe in Jesus. If you do, chances are you will become like them. They will not become like you.

Remember, this doesn't mean you should hate young people who are not friends of Jesus, but you must make up your mind not to do the things they do. If you do, you can get into real trouble with God—and with people, too.

What the Thessalonians Learned

We Christians at Thessalonica learned how to live both in God's present time and for God's future time.

Our *present* time is not our own. We should spend the time God now gives us in useful ways. We must not be lazy, but find joy in all our work, because God uses our work for His great purposes.

Some of us had been spending too much time dreaming about God's *future* time and the Lord's return. So we became useless as workers for God in this present time. The Lord will return. But until He comes, Jesus said we must be busy doing whatever He calls us to do.

---

keep company with him, that he may be ashamed. ¹⁵ Yet do not count *him* as an enemy, but admonish *him* as a brother.

¹⁶ Now may the Lord of peace Himself give you peace always in every way. The Lord *be* with you all.

¹⁷ The salutation of Paul with my own hand, which is a sign in *every* epistle; so I write.

¹⁸ The grace of our Lord Jesus Christ *be* with you all. Amen.

The Book of
1 TIMOTHY

I grew up in Lystra (pronounced *LISS-trah*) where my Hebrew mother and grandmother taught me the Old Testament Scriptures. My father was Greek. My name, Timothy, means "Honored By God." I also had the honor of being the apostle Paul's friend. Paul even referred to me as his "beloved and faithful son in the Lord."

After meeting Paul during his second preaching trip, I traveled with him. Paul had to leave Thessalonica when they accused him of treason against the emperor of Rome. So I stayed in that city and helped to strengthen the Christians. I also helped Paul in his hard ministry at Corinth.

During Paul's first time as a prisoner at Rome, I was able to stand by and help him. But the second time, he was sent to jail for treason against the cruel Emperor Nero, and they put Paul to death. Before he was killed, he wrote another beautiful letter to me.

Paul writes to his son in the Lord

PAUL, an apostle of Jesus Christ, by the commandment of God our Savior and the Lord Jesus Christ, our hope,

2 To Timothy, a true son in the faith:

Grace, mercy, *and* peace from God our Father and Jesus Christ our Lord.

3 As I urged you when I went into Macedonia—remain in Ephesus that you may charge some that they teach no other doctrine, 4 nor give heed to fables and endless genealogies, which cause disputes rather than godly edification which is in faith. 5 Now the purpose of the commandment is love from a pure heart, *from* a good conscience, and *from* sincere faith, 6 from which some, having strayed, have turned aside to idle talk, 7 desiring to be teachers of the law, understanding neither what they say nor the things which they affirm.

8 But we know that the law *is* good if one uses it lawfully, 9 knowing this: that the law is not made for a righteous person, but for *the* lawless and insub-ordinate, for *the* ungodly and for sinners, for *the* unholy and profane, for murderers of fathers and murderers of mothers, for manslayers, 10 for fornicators, for sodomites, for kidnappers, for liars, for perjurers, and if there is any other thing that is contrary to sound doctrine, 11 according to the glorious gospel of the blessed God which was committed to my trust.

12 And I thank Christ Jesus our Lord who has enabled me, because He counted me faithful, putting *me* into the ministry, 13 although I was formerly a blasphemer, a persecutor, and an insolent man; but I obtained mercy because I did *it* ignorantly in unbelief. 14 And the grace of our Lord was exceedingly abundant, with faith and love which are in Christ Jesus. 15 This is a faithful saying and worthy of all acceptance, that Christ Jesus came into the world to save sinners, of whom I am chief. 16 However, for this reason I obtained mercy, that in me first Jesus Christ might show all longsuffering, as a pattern to those who are going to believe on Him for everlasting life. 17 Now to the King eternal, immortal, invisible, to God who alone is wise,

How Does Jesus Save Sinners?

All of us are sinners. By nature we don't like to please God. But Jesus can change your nature so that you love God and the things that please Him. Jesus died and rose again so that He could give you His new life that will please God forever.

be honor and glory forever and ever. Amen.

18 This charge I commit to you, son Timothy, according to the prophecies previously made concerning you, that by them you may wage the good warfare, 19 having faith and a good conscience, which some having rejected, concerning the faith have suffered shipwreck, 20 of whom are Hymenaeus

and Alexander, whom I delivered to Satan that they may learn not to blaspheme.

How to pray for ourselves and others

2 Therefore I exhort first of all that supplications, prayers, intercessions, and giving of thanks be made for all men, 2 for kings and all who are in authority, that we may lead a quiet and peaceable life in all godliness and reverence. 3 For this is good and acceptable in the sight of God our Savior, 4 who desires all men to be saved and to come to the knowledge of the truth. 5 For there is one God and one **Mediator** between God and men, the Man Christ Jesus, 6 who gave Himself a ransom for all, to be testified in due time, 7 for which I was appointed a preacher

WORDFINDER

2:5 Mediator Pronounced MEE-dee-ay-tor. Someone who brings two groups or individuals to agreement. Jesus is the Mediator who brings God and people to agreement by His death on the Cross.

DIGGING IN

2:1 Pray for All Kinds of People What do you do when you pray? Do you just ask God to give you the things you need or want today? Of course you should pray for your family, too. Then remember to pray for your pastor and your friends at church. Perhaps you have met some missionaries from around the world. They need your prayers as well.

Pray also for your teachers at school and for your classmates. Some of them probably aren't Christians. Pray that you may show them what Jesus is like, and that they will want to become Christians, too. Always remember to pray for members of your government. They carry heavy burdens, and they need God's help.

Remember that you aren't all alone when you pray. The Spirit of God—also called "the Holy Spirit"—helps you to pray! Ask the Holy Spirit to show you what you need in your own life and what others need in theirs.

2:6 Jesus Became Your Ransom Ransom is a word you may have seen from time to time. A ransom is the price that people have to pay to get back their loved ones who have been kidnapped. A ransom is usually a lot of money.

But the Bible uses the word ransom to explain what Jesus did when He died for your sins. You were, in a real way, kidnapped by Satan, who planned to keep you as his prisoner. Then came Jesus and said, "I will pay the ransom price to set My loved ones free." And you know what that ransom price was—it was the very blood of Jesus Himself. He gave His life and even suffered the punishment of hell to buy back your soul from Satan's power.

Now you belong to Jesus—unless you want to be Satan's prisoner! Jesus has broken down the door of Satan's prison, and you can come out a free person. Jesus paid for your freedom.

and an apostle—I am speaking the truth in Christ *and* not lying—a teacher of the Gentiles in faith and truth.

8 I desire therefore that the men pray everywhere, lifting up holy hands, without wrath and doubting; 9 in like manner also, that the women adorn themselves in modest apparel, with propriety and moderation, not with braided hair or gold or pearls or costly clothing, 10 but, which is proper for women professing godliness, with good works. 11 Let a woman learn in silence with all submission. 12 And I do not permit a woman to teach or to have authority over a man, but to be in silence. 13 For Adam was formed first, then Eve. 14 And Adam was not deceived, but the woman being deceived, fell into transgression. 15 Nevertheless she will be saved in childbearing if they continue in faith, love, and holiness, with self-control.

Some guidelines for church leaders

3 This *is* a faithful saying: If a man desires the position of a bishop, he desires a good work. 2 A bishop then must be blameless, the husband of one wife, temperate, sober-minded, of good behavior, hospitable, able to teach; 3 not given to wine, not violent, not greedy for money, but gentle, not quarrelsome, not covetous; 4 one who rules his own house well, having *his* children in submission with all reverence 5 (for if a man does not know how to rule his own house, how will he take care of the church of God?); 6 not a novice, lest being puffed up with pride he fall into the *same* condemnation as the devil. 7 Moreover he must have a good testimony among those who are outside, lest he fall into reproach and the snare of the devil.

8 Likewise **deacons** *must be* rever-

ent, not double-tongued, not given to much wine, not greedy for money, 9 holding the mystery of the faith with a pure conscience. 10 But let these also first be tested; then let them serve as deacons, being *found* blameless. 11 Likewise, *their* wives *must be* reverent, not slanderers, temperate, faithful in all things. 12 Let deacons be the husbands of one wife, ruling *their* children and their own houses well. 13 For those who have served well as deacons obtain for themselves a good standing and great boldness in the faith which is in Christ Jesus.

14 These things I write to you, though I hope to come to you shortly; 15 but if I am delayed, *I write* so that you may know how you ought to conduct yourself in the house of God, which is the church of the living God, the pillar and ground of the truth. 16 And without controversy great is the mystery of godliness:

God was manifested in the flesh,
Justified in the Spirit,
Seen by angels,
Preached among the Gentiles,
Believed on in the world,
Received up in glory.

Don't waste time arguing over silly ideas

4 Now the Spirit expressly says that in latter times some will depart from the faith, giving heed to deceiving spirits and doctrines of demons, 2 speaking lies in hypocrisy, having their own conscience seared with a hot iron, 3 forbidding to marry, *and commanding* to abstain from foods which God created to be received with thanksgiving by those who believe and know the truth. 4 For *every* creature of God *is* good, and nothing is to be refused if it is received with thanksgiving;

WORDFINDER

3:8 Deacons Pronounced *DEE-kuns.* From a Greek word meaning "servant." Sometimes deacons are ministers, and sometimes they are not. Minister also means "servant."

⁵ for it is sanctified by the word of God and prayer.

⁶ If you instruct the brethren in these things, you will be a good minister of Jesus Christ, nourished in the words of faith and of the good doctrine which you have carefully followed. ⁷ But reject profane and old wives' fables, and exercise yourself toward godliness. ⁸ For bodily exercise profits a little, but godliness is profitable for all things, having promise of the life that now is and of that which is to come. ⁹ This is a faithful saying and worthy of all acceptance. ¹⁰ For to this *end* we both labor and suffer reproach, because we trust in the living God, who is *the* Savior of all men, especially of those who believe. ¹¹ These things command and teach.

¹² Let no one despise your youth, but be an example to the believers in word, in conduct, in love, in spirit, in faith, in purity. ¹³ Till I come, give attention to reading, to **exhortation,** to doctrine. ¹⁴ Do not neglect the gift that is in you, which was given to you by prophecy with the laying on of the hands of the **eldership.** ¹⁵ Meditate on these things; give yourself entirely to them, that your progress may be evident to all. ¹⁶ Take heed to yourself and to the doctrine. Continue in them, for in doing this you will save both yourself and those who hear you.

How to care for God's family

5 Do not rebuke an older man, but exhort *him* as a father, younger men

WORDFINDER

4:13 Exhortation Pronounced *egg-zor-TAY-shun.* A speech or writing that is meant to warn or encourage people. Paul says Timothy must exhort his people.

4:14 Eldership The council of men who governed God's people in Old Testament and New Testament times. Sometimes these "elders" were teachers and preachers.

DIGGING IN

4:13 Keep On Learning There never will be a time to stop learning. School days are only the beginning of learning. As time goes by, you will see that life itself is one big school, and learning about life gets more and more exciting all the time.

You have to learn by experience, but experience is not your best teacher, no matter what some people say. Some kinds of experience are too unpleasant. Going to prison is learning by experience, but who wants to go to prison?

So where do we begin to learn? From God! In the Scriptures God has shown you every secret of living a successful life in His world. When you listen to God's teaching, you can avoid a lot of painful experience. Better to learn now that God's way is always the best way. Talk to someone who has spent years living without God. They'll tell you that was a hard way to learn a lesson!

5:1, 2 Honor Your Elders It's sad that many young people snub older folks. When young people do this, they miss

out on all that the older people could have taught them. Older people can save you a lot of grief by sharing what they have learned about living in the world.

There's another side to honoring older folks, too. God's plan for a happy and prosperous society says that we should respect our elders. If we refuse to follow God's plan, He will let us get into lots of trouble. An ancient king of Judah refused to listen to his senior advisers, so he lost most of his kingdom (see 1 Kings 12:8–24).

"Honor your father and your mother" also means that you should have respect for everyone who has authority. You may not always agree with your elders, but you should always consider that God expects you to treat them with respect.

A special way of showing respect for elders is the way you care for them when they are too old to care for themselves. "Blessed are the merciful, for they shall receive mercy."

as brothers, 2 older women as mothers, younger women as sisters, with all purity.

3 Honor widows who are really widows. 4 But if any widow has children or grandchildren, let them first learn to show piety at home and to repay their parents; for this is good and acceptable before God. 5 Now she who is really a widow, and left alone, trusts in God and continues in supplications and prayers night and day. 6 But she who lives in pleasure is dead while she lives. 7 And these things command, that they may be blameless. 8 But if anyone does not provide for his own, and especially for those of his household, he has denied the faith and is worse than an unbeliever.

9 Do not let a widow under sixty years old be taken into the number, *and not unless* she has been the wife of one man, 10 well reported for good works: if she has brought up children, if she has lodged strangers, if she has washed the saints' feet, if she has relieved the afflicted, if she has diligently followed *every* good work.

11 But refuse *the* younger widows; for when they have begun to grow wanton against Christ, they desire to marry, 12 having condemnation because they have cast off their first faith. 13 And besides they learn *to be* idle, wandering about from house to house, and not only idle but also gossips and **busybodies,** saying things which they ought not. 14 Therefore I desire that *the* younger *widows* marry, bear children, manage the house, give no opportunity to the adversary to speak reproachfully. 15 For some have already turned aside after Satan. 16 If any believing man or woman has widows, let them relieve them, and do not let the church be burdened, that it may relieve those who are really widows.

17 Let the elders who rule well be counted worthy of double honor, especially those who labor in the word and doctrine. 18 For the Scripture says, "You shall not muzzle an ox while it treads out the grain," and, "The laborer *is* worthy of his wages." 19 Do not receive an accusation against an elder except from two or three witnesses. 20 Those who are sinning rebuke in the presence of all, that the rest also may fear.

21 I charge *you* before God and the Lord Jesus Christ and the elect angels that you observe these things without prejudice, doing nothing with partiality. 22 Do not lay hands on anyone hastily, nor share in other people's sins; keep yourself pure.

23 No longer drink only water, but use a little wine for your stomach's sake and your frequent infirmities.

24 Some men's sins are clearly evident, preceding *them* to judgment, but those of some *men* follow later. 25 Likewise, the good works *of some* are clearly evident, and those that are otherwise cannot be hidden.

How to live for God in a godless world

6 Let as many bondservants as are under the yoke count their own masters worthy of all honor, so that the name of God and *His* doctrine may not be blasphemed. 2 And those who have believing masters, let them not despise *them* because they are brethren, but rather serve *them* because those who are benefited are believers and beloved. Teach and exhort these things.

3 If anyone teaches otherwise and does not consent to wholesome words, *even* the words of our Lord Jesus Christ, and to the doctrine which accords with godliness, 4 he is proud, knowing nothing, but is obsessed with disputes and arguments over words, from which come envy, strife, reviling,

WORDFINDER

5:13 Busybodies People who mind other people's business. Paul said that some Christians were not doing their own work but were meddling in other people's affairs.

evil suspicions, 5 useless wranglings of men of corrupt minds and destitute of the truth, who suppose that godliness is a *means of* gain. From such withdraw yourself.

6 Now godliness with contentment is great gain. 7 For we brought nothing into *this* world, *and it is* certain we can carry nothing out. 8 And having food and clothing, with these we shall be content. 9 But those who desire to be rich fall into temptation and a snare, and *into* many foolish and harmful lusts which drown men in destruction and perdition. 10 For the love of money is a root of all *kinds of* evil, for which some have strayed from the faith in their greediness, and pierced themselves through with many sorrows.

11 But you, O man of God, flee these things and pursue righteousness, godliness, faith, love, patience, gentleness. 12 Fight the good fight of faith, lay hold on eternal life, to which you were also called and have confessed the good confession in the presence of many witnesses. 13 I urge you in the sight of God who gives life to all things, and *before* Christ Jesus who witnessed the good confession before Pontius Pilate, 14 that you keep *this* commandment without spot, blameless until our Lord Jesus Christ's appearing, 15 which He will manifest in His own time, *He who is* the blessed and only Potentate, the King of kings and Lord of lords, 16 who alone has immortality, dwelling in unapproachable light, whom no man has seen or can see, to whom *be* honor and everlasting power. Amen.

17 Command those who are rich in this present age not to be haughty, nor to trust in uncertain riches but in the living God, who gives us richly all things to enjoy. 18 *Let them* do good, that they be rich in good works, ready to give, willing to share, 19 storing up for themselves a good foundation for the time to come, that they may lay hold on eternal life.

20 O Timothy! Guard what was committed to your trust, avoiding the profane *and* idle babblings and contradictions of what is falsely called knowledge— 21 by professing it some have strayed concerning the faith.

Grace *be* with you. Amen.

The Book of
2 TIMOTHY

Eunice—I am Timothy's mother and my name is pronounced *YOU-niss.* Our family met the apostle Paul on one of his travels through our town of Lystra (pronounced *LISS-trah*) in Asia Minor.

At that time my Greek husband and I were very proud of our young son Timothy. His grandmother and I had been careful to teach him the Scriptures ever since he was a young boy.

When Paul came and preached in our town, we accepted Jesus as our Lord and Savior. Timothy wanted to travel with Paul to other countries to help preach the gospel, so we all agreed that he should go with Paul and Luke, the doctor.

We will always prize the two letters our beloved Paul wrote to our son. Timothy's grandmother is with the Lord now and Timothy is a pastor at Ephesus (pronounced *EFF-uh-sus*).

Keep up the good work!

PAUL, an apostle of Jesus Christ by the will of God, according to the promise of life which is in Christ Jesus,

2 To Timothy, a beloved son:

Grace, mercy, *and* peace from God the Father and Christ Jesus our Lord.

3 I thank God, whom I serve with a pure conscience, as *my* forefathers *did,* as without ceasing I remember you in my prayers night and day, 4 greatly desiring to see you, being mindful of your tears, that I may be filled with joy, 5 when I call to remembrance the genuine faith that is in you, which dwelt first in your grandmother Lois and your mother Eunice, and I am persuaded is in you also. 6 Therefore I remind you to stir up the gift of God which is in you through the laying on of my hands. 7 For God has not given us a spirit of fear, but of power and of love and of a sound mind.

8 Therefore do not be ashamed of the testimony of our Lord, nor of me His prisoner, but share with me in the sufferings for the gospel according to the power of God, 9 who has saved us and called *us* with a holy calling, not according to our works, but according to His own purpose and grace which was given to us in Christ Jesus before time began, 10 but has now been revealed by the appearing of our Savior Jesus Christ, *who* has abolished death and brought life and immortality to light through the gospel, 11 to which I was appointed a preacher, an apostle, and a teacher of the Gentiles. 12 For this reason I also suffer these things; nevertheless I am not ashamed, for I know whom I have believed and am persuaded that He is able to keep what I have committed to Him until that Day.

13 Hold fast the pattern of sound words which you have heard from me, in faith and love which are in Christ Jesus. 14 That good thing which was committed to you, keep by the Holy Spirit who dwells in us.

15 This you know, that all those in Asia have turned away from me, among whom are Phygellus and Hermogenes. 16 The Lord grant mercy to the household of Onesiphorus, for he often refreshed me, and was not ashamed of my chain; 17 but when he

Timothy learned about God from his mother when he was a small boy.

arrived in Rome, he sought me out very zealously and found *me*. [18] The Lord grant to him that he may find mercy from the Lord in that Day— and you know very well how many ways he ministered *to me* at Ephesus.

Be a good soldier of Jesus Christ

2 You therefore, my son, be strong in the grace that is in Christ Jesus. [2] And the things that you have heard from me among many witnesses, commit these to faithful men who will be able to teach others also. [3] You therefore must endure hardship as a good soldier of Jesus Christ. [4] No one engaged in warfare entangles himself with the affairs of *this* life, that he may please him who enlisted him as a soldier. [5] And also if anyone competes in athletics, he is not crowned unless he competes according to the rules. [6] The hardworking farmer must be first to partake of the crops. [7] Consider what I say, and may the Lord give you understanding in all things.

[8] Remember that Jesus Christ, of the seed of David, was raised from the dead according to my gospel, [9] for which I suffer trouble as an evildoer, *even* to the point of chains; but the

---

Is It Easy to Be a Christian?

Christians are the happiest people in the world. But their lives aren't always easy. Sometimes being a Christian is very hard. Even nowadays many people lose their lives simply because they are Christians. You have to be like a strong soldier to be a Christian.

word of God is not chained. [10] Therefore I endure all things for the sake of the elect, that they also may obtain the **salvation** which is in Christ Jesus with eternal glory.

[11] *This is* a faithful saying:

For if we died with *Him,*
We shall also live with *Him.*
[12] If we endure,
We shall also reign with *Him.*
If we deny *Him,*
He also will deny us.
[13] If we are faithless,
He remains faithful;
He cannot deny Himself.

[14] Remind *them* of these things, charging *them* before the Lord not to strive about words to no profit, to the ruin of the hearers. [15] Be diligent to present yourself approved to God, a worker who does not need to be ashamed, rightly dividing the word of truth. [16] But shun profane *and* idle babblings, for they will increase to more ungodliness. [17] And their message will spread like cancer. Hymenaeus and Philetus are of this sort, [18] who have strayed concerning the truth, saying that the resurrection is already past; and they overthrow the faith of some. [19] Nevertheless the solid foundation of God stands, having this seal: "The Lord knows those who are His," and, "Let everyone who names the name of Christ depart from iniquity."

[20] But in a great house there are not only vessels of gold and silver, but also of wood and clay, some for honor and some for dishonor. [21] Therefore if anyone cleanses himself from the latter, he will be a vessel for honor, sanctified and useful for the Master, prepared for every good work. [22] Flee also youthful lusts; but pursue righteousness, faith, love, peace with those who call on the Lord out of a pure heart. [23] But avoid foolish and ignorant disputes, knowing that they generate strife. [24] And a servant of the Lord must not quarrel but be gentle to all, able to teach, patient, [25] in humility correcting those who are in opposition, if God perhaps will grant them repentance, so that they may know the truth, [26] and *that* they may come to their senses *and escape* the snare of the devil, having been taken captive by him to *do* his will.

It isn't easy being a Christian

3 But know this, that in the last days perilous times will come: [2] For men will

---

WORDFINDER

2:9 Word of God   God speaking in the Scriptures of the Old and New Testaments. Jesus also is called "the Word" (John 1:1) because He is God's *personal* Word.

2:10 Salvation   Pronounced *sal-VAY-shun.* A work of saving someone from danger or death. In the Bible, salvation is Christ's work of dying to save us from sin and hell.

DIGGING IN

2:16 Foolish Arguments Often someone who doesn't believe in Jesus will say something against the gospel. Right away you may want to argue with that person. Then a quarrel starts, and there will be angry feelings. No good can come from an argument like that. The unbeliever will be more against the gospel than before. But you, too, may have sinned by getting angry.

What's the answer? Some arguments are OK if people will agree to listen to each other with courtesy, but usually arguments should be avoided. Satan loves to get a quarrel going so that he can create more confusion and lies.

The best course is not to answer somebody's unkind insults. By your calm and gentle attitude, show that person what it is really like to be a Christian. That's your strongest argument because action is more convincing than words.

Is Life on Earth Getting Better?

Some people live in a fool's paradise. This means that they pretend everything is OK while life around them gets worse. Paul tells Timothy that it will get harder to live in the world. In these times, you need to live nearer to Jesus everyday.

be lovers of themselves, lovers of money, boasters, proud, blasphemers, disobedient to parents, unthankful, unholy, 3 unloving, unforgiving, slanderers, without self-control, brutal, despisers of good, 4 traitors, headstrong, haughty, lovers of pleasure rather than lovers of God, 5 having a form of godliness but denying its power. And from such people turn away! 6 For of this sort are those who creep into households and make captives of gullible women loaded down with sins, led away by various lusts, 7 always learning and never able to come to the knowledge of the truth. 8 Now as Jannes and Jambres resisted Moses, so do these also resist the truth: men of corrupt minds, disapproved concerning the faith; 9 but they will progress no further, for their folly will be manifest to all, as theirs also was.

10 But you have carefully followed my doctrine, manner of life, purpose, faith, longsuffering, love, perseverance, 11 persecutions, afflictions, which happened to me at Antioch, at Iconium, at Lystra—what persecutions I endured. And out of *them* all the Lord delivered me. 12 Yes, and all who desire to live godly in Christ Jesus will suffer persecution. 13 But evil men and impostors will grow worse and worse, deceiving and being deceived. 14 But you must continue in the things which you have learned and been assured of, knowing from whom you have learned *them,* 15 and that from childhood you have known the Holy Scriptures, which are able to make you wise for salvation through faith which is in Christ Jesus.

16 All Scripture *is* given by inspiration of God, and *is* profitable for doctrine, for reproof, for correction, for instruction in righteousness, 17 that the man of God may be complete, thoroughly equipped for *every* good work.

Tell others about the Lord

4 I charge *you* therefore before God and the Lord Jesus Christ, who will

What Timothy Learned

When I was growing up, my Jewish mother and grandmother taught me the scriptures of the Old Testament. We didn't have the New Testament yet.

As I studied the Old Testament writings, I learned to look for our coming Messiah, the Christ. He would take away our sins.

So when Paul came to our town of Lystra (pronounced *LISS-trah*), I was eager to hear the message he preached. Our Messiah had come! Paul had been a wicked Pharisee (pronounced *FAIR-uh-see*), but now he believed in Jesus the Messiah. I was excited about the story of how the risen Christ met Paul on the road and changed his life.

Now Jesus has changed my life, too. I'm so glad I learned to love God's Word when I was young. That Word gave me wisdom to accept Jesus as my Lord and Savior.

Paul Sentenced to Death at Rome

Rome Daily Press

The apostle Paul has been sentenced to death by Emperor Nero.

After Paul's arrest in Jerusalem (see Acts 21—26) and his transport to Rome by ship, Paul was allowed some freedom as a prisoner in his own rented house (see Acts 28:30). Two years later, Paul was released because he really had done nothing against the law.

For some time Paul has continued preaching throughout the Roman world. Some people say Paul even traveled as far as Spain.

Lately, the apostle was arrested again. This time he was accused of treason against Rome. Like all Christians, Paul believes he must serve Christ above all other kings. Emperor Nero now views Paul as an enemy of Rome.

BULLETIN: In this year 68, it is now reported that Paul has been beheaded in Rome. Many other Christians have also been put to death during this time.

judge the living and the dead at His appearing and His kingdom: 2 Preach the word! Be ready in season *and* out of season. Convince, rebuke, exhort, with all longsuffering and teaching. 3 For the time will come when they will not endure sound doctrine, but according to their own desires, *because* they have itching ears, they will heap up for themselves teachers; 4 and they will turn *their* ears away from the truth, and be turned aside to fables. 5 But you be watchful in all things, endure afflictions, do the work of an **evangelist,** fulfill your ministry.

6 For I am already being poured out as a drink offering, and the time of my departure is at hand. 7 I have fought the good fight, I have finished the race, I have kept the faith. 8 Finally, there is laid up for me the crown of righteousness, which the Lord, the righteous Judge, will give to me on that Day, and not to me only but also to all who have loved His appearing.

9 Be diligent to come to me quickly; 10 for Demas has forsaken me, having loved this present world, and has departed for Thessalonica—Crescens for Galatia, Titus for Dalmatia. 11 Only Luke is with me. Get Mark and bring him with you, for he is useful to me for ministry. 12 And Tychicus I have sent to Ephesus. 13 Bring the cloak that I left with Carpus at Troas when you come—and the books, especially the parchments.

14 Alexander the coppersmith did me much harm. May the Lord repay him according to his works. 15 You also must beware of him, for he has greatly resisted our words.

16 At my first defense no one stood with me, but all forsook me. May it not be charged against them.

17 But the Lord stood with me and strengthened me, so that the message might be preached fully through me, and *that* all the Gentiles might hear. Also I was delivered out of the mouth of the lion. 18 And the Lord will deliver me from every evil work and preserve *me* for His heavenly kingdom. To Him *be* glory forever and ever. Amen!

WORDFINDER

(4:5) Evangelist Pronounced *ih-VAN-juh-list.* A person who preaches the Good News of salvation through Jesus Christ. The word comes from a Greek word meaning "preach the gospel."

19 Greet Prisca and Aquila, and the household of Onesiphorus. 20 Erastus stayed in Corinth, but Trophimus I have left in Miletus sick.

21 Do your utmost to come before winter.

Eubulus greets you, as well as Pudens, Linus, Claudia, and all the brethren.

22 The Lord Jesus Christ be with your spirit. Grace be with you. Amen.

The Book of
TITUS

Titus—My name is pronounced *TIGHT-us* and means "Pleasant." You don't read about me in the Book of Acts, but the apostle Paul thought very highly of me and my ministry.

You first read about me in Galatians 2:1–3. I traveled with Paul and Barnabas to Jerusalem. There Paul showed the Jewish Christians that non-Jews don't have to obey the religious customs of the Jews.

When some members of the church at Corinth were in trouble, Paul sent me to help them. I solved the problems of quarreling and sinful living there, and Paul was very pleased.

My next big task came when Paul sent me to be pastor of some churches on the island of Crete. Later I went on a mission journey to Dalmatia (pronounced *dal-MAY-she-ah*), a country you now call Yugoslavia.

Paul gives Titus some guidelines for church leaders

PAUL, a bondservant of God and an apostle of Jesus Christ, according to the faith of God's elect and the acknowledgment of the truth which accords with godliness, 2 in hope of eternal life which God, who cannot lie, promised before time began, 3 but has in due time manifested His word through preaching, which was committed to me according to the commandment of God our Savior;

4 To Titus, a true son in *our* common faith:

Grace, mercy, *and* peace from God the Father and the Lord Jesus Christ our Savior.

5 For this reason I left you in Crete, that you should set in order the things that are lacking, and appoint elders in every city as I commanded you— 6 if a man is blameless, the husband of one wife, having faithful children not accused of dissipation or insubordination. 7 For a bishop must be blameless, as a **steward** of God, not self-willed, not quick-tempered, not given to wine, not violent, not greedy for money, 8 but hospitable, a lover of what is good, sober-minded, just, holy, self-controlled, 9 holding fast the faithful word as he has been taught, that he may be able, by sound doctrine, both to exhort and convict those who contradict.

10 For there are many insubordinate, both idle talkers and deceivers, especially those of the circumcision, 11 whose mouths must be stopped, who subvert whole households, teaching things which they ought not, for the sake of dishonest gain. 12 One of them, a prophet of their own, said, "Cretans *are* always liars, evil beasts, lazy gluttons." 13 This testimony is true. Therefore rebuke them sharply, that they may be sound in the faith, 14 not giving heed to Jewish fables and commandments of men who turn from the

---

🌐 **WORDFINDER**

1:7 Steward Those in charge of property or an area of work. The apostles were "stewards of the mysteries of God." They were in charge of the work of preaching the gospel.

The island of Crete, where Titus was the pastor of a church.

truth. ¹⁵ To the pure all things are pure, but to those who are defiled and unbelieving nothing is pure; but even their mind and conscience are defiled. ¹⁶ They profess to know God, but in works they deny Him, being abominable, disobedient, and disqualified for every good work.

What Is a Pure Mind?

Jesus said the pure in heart would see God. Paul tells Titus that impure thoughts separate us from God. There are many beautiful things in God's world and God's heaven to think about. If we would teach ourselves to think about these things, there would be no room for impure thoughts and deeds.

Marks of a strong church

2 But as for you, speak the things which are proper for sound doctrine: ² that the older men be sober, reverent, temperate, sound in faith, in love, in patience; ³ the older women likewise, that they be reverent in behavior, not slanderers, not given to much wine, teachers of good things— ⁴ that they

DIGGING IN

1:10, 11 Listen to Good Teachers As you live in the world, you will find out that some teachers have strange ideas. Jesus described these teachers as "wolves in sheep's clothing" (see Matthew 7:15). It's hard to explain why some people get these strange notions. For example, some teachers even deny that Jesus was really the Savior from heaven. They say He was just a good man who was also a good teacher. That sounds great to some

people, but it's a lie! Satan, the great liar, puts such lies into people's minds.

The important thing is to know the Scriptures so well that you won't be tricked by the false teachers of the world. Jesus said His people would not follow strangers (see John 10:5). Be sure to attend a gospel-preaching, Bible-teaching church. There you will find teachers who will help you understand the Bible more and more every day.

admonish the young women to love their husbands, to love their children, [5] to be discreet, chaste, homemakers, good, obedient to their own husbands, that the word of God may not be blasphemed.

[6] Likewise, exhort the young men to be sober-minded, [7] in all things showing yourself *to be* a pattern of good works; in doctrine *showing* integrity, **reverence,** incorruptibility, [8] sound speech that cannot be condemned, that one who is an opponent may be ashamed, having nothing evil to say of you.

[9] *Exhort* bondservants to be obedient to their own masters, to be well pleasing in all *things,* not answering back, [10] not pilfering, but showing all good fidelity, that they may adorn the doctrine of God our Savior in all things.

[11] For the grace of God that brings salvation has appeared to all men, [12] teaching us that, denying ungodliness and worldly lusts, we should live soberly, righteously, and godly in the present age, [13] looking for the blessed hope and glorious appearing of our great God and Savior Jesus Christ, [14] who gave Himself for us, that He might redeem us from every lawless deed and purify for Himself *His* own special people, zealous for good works. [15] Speak these things, exhort, and rebuke with all authority. Let no one despise you.

How Christians should act

3 Remind them to be subject to rulers and authorities, to obey, to be ready for *every* good work, [2] to speak evil of no one, to be peaceable, gentle,

showing all humility to all men. [3] For we ourselves were also once foolish, disobedient, deceived, serving various lusts and pleasures, living in malice and envy, hateful and hating one another. [4] But when the kindness and the love of God our Savior toward man appeared, [5] not by works of righteousness which we have done, but according to His mercy He saved us, through the washing of **regeneration** and renewing of the Holy Spirit, [6] whom He poured out on us abundantly through Jesus Christ our Savior, [7] that having been justified by His grace we should become heirs according to the hope of eternal life.

[8] This is a faithful saying, and these things I want you to affirm constantly, that those who have believed in God should be careful to maintain good works. These things are good and profitable to men.

[9] But avoid foolish disputes, genealogies, contentions, and strivings about the law; for they are unprofitable and useless. [10] Reject a divisive man after the first and second admonition, [11] knowing that such a person is warped and sinning, being self-condemned.

[12] When I send Artemas to you, or Tychicus, be diligent to come to me at Nicopolis, for I have decided to spend the winter there. [13] Send Zenas the lawyer and Apollos on their journey with haste, that they may lack nothing. [14] And let our *people* also learn to maintain good works, to *meet* urgent needs, that they may not be unfruitful.

[15] All who *are* with me greet you. Greet those who love us in the faith.

Grace *be* with you all. Amen.

WORDFINDER

2:7 Reverence Pronounced *REV-er-ents.* An attitude of respect and awe. Reverence is an attitude we should have for God in worship and in serving Him.

3:5 Regeneration Pronounced *re-jen-uh-RAY-shun.* A word meaning to "create all over again." Regeneration is what God does for us when we are "born again" (see definition at John 3:3).

The Book of
PHILEMON

My name, Onesimus, is pronounced *oh-NESS-ih-muss* and means "Useful." I think I am the happiest slave in the whole world!

Paul the apostle used to visit my master Philemon (pronounced *fy-LEE-mun*). I loved to hear Paul preach, and I came to think of him as my own father. So I later ran away from my master and went to live in Rome where Paul was then a prisoner.

Paul was glad to see me, and we had good times together. He was allowed to live at his own house at that time. There Paul led me to become a Christian.

But Paul began to realize we were not treating my master Philemon right by letting me stay in Rome. We both agreed, then, that I should go back to Philemon in Colosse (pronounced *ko-LAH-see*), so Paul sent me back to Philemon with this letter about myself. Since then, Philemon and I have been true brothers in Christ, and I am not like a slave anymore.

Paul sends a runaway slave home to his master

PAUL, a prisoner of Christ Jesus, and Timothy *our* brother,

To Philemon our beloved *friend* and fellow laborer, 2 to the beloved Apphia, Archippus our fellow soldier, and to the church in your house:

3 Grace to you and peace from God our Father and the Lord Jesus Christ.

4 I thank my God, making mention of you always in my prayers, 5 hearing of your love and faith which you have toward the Lord Jesus and toward all the saints, 6 that the sharing of your faith may become effective by the acknowledgment of every good thing which is in you in Christ Jesus. 7 For we have great joy and consolation in your love, because the hearts of the saints have been refreshed by you, brother.

8 Therefore, though I might be very bold in Christ to command you what is fitting, 9 *yet* for love's sake I rather appeal *to you*—being such a one as Paul, the aged, and now also a prisoner of Jesus Christ— 10 I appeal to

🔨 DIGGING IN

10 Be a Soul Winner What is a soul winner? A soul winner is someone who wins people to trust in Jesus. Soul winning calls for three main personal traits: (1) love, (2) gentleness, and (3) wisdom.

Paul had all these personal traits. When the slave Onesimus (pronounced *oh-NESS-ih-muss*) came to him, Paul wasn't angry because the young man had run away. Paul loved Onesimus. Also, Paul was gentle to Onesimus, and led him to know Jesus as Savior and Lord. Then both Paul and Onesimus agreed that Onesimus should go back home and face

his master, Philemon (pronounced *fih-LEE-mun*).

After that, Paul and Philemon were probably better friends than ever. Some scholars say Onesimus later became pastor of the church at Ephesus (pronounced *EFF-uh-sus*) in Asia Minor (see map on pages 1460–61). So you can see that winning just one soul was a great benefit to many people.

Philemon is one of the most beautiful books in the New Testament. Paul wrote it from prison, and it shows how much he loved a slave.

you for my son Onesimus, whom I have begotten *while* in my chains, 11 who once was unprofitable to you, but now is profitable to you and to me.

12 I am sending him back. You therefore receive him, that is, my own heart, 13 whom I wished to keep with me, that on your behalf he might minister to me in my chains for the gospel. 14 But without your consent I wanted to do nothing, that your good deed might not be by compulsion, as it were, but voluntary.

15 For perhaps he departed for a while for this *purpose,* that you might receive him forever, 16 no longer as a slave but more than a slave—a beloved brother, especially to me but how much more to you, both in the flesh and in the Lord.

17 If then you count me as a partner, receive him as *you would* me. 18 But if he has wronged you or owes anything, put that on my account. 19 I, Paul, am writing with my own hand. I will repay—not to mention to you that you owe me even your own self besides. 20 Yes, brother, let me have joy from you in the Lord; refresh my heart in the Lord.

21 Having confidence in your obedience, I write to you, knowing that you will do even more than I say. 22 But, meanwhile, also prepare a guest room for me, for I trust that through your prayers I shall be granted to you.

23 Epaphras, my fellow prisoner in Christ Jesus, greets you, 24 *as do* Mark, Aristarchus, Demas, Luke, my fellow laborers.

25 The grace of our Lord Jesus Christ *be* with your spirit. Amen.

The Book of
HEBREWS

As high priest, I was both the religious and civic leader of the Old Testament people after Moses died. I presented the people's sacrifices to God. Once every year, on the Day of Atonement (pronounced *ah-TONE-ment*), I came before the Lord in the Most Holy Place of the tent of meeting. There I sprinkled the blood of the sacrifice on the mercy seat. The Lord Himself would appear there as a fiery light called the Shekinah (pronounced *shih-KIGH-nuh*). (In Leviticus 8, you will see that Aaron, the brother of Moses, was the earliest high priest.)

Often I failed to live up to what God called me to be. This was one reason God allowed our enemies to destroy our nation several times.

But in the Book of Hebrews, you will learn that Jesus is your real High Priest forever.

God has spoken to us by His Son

GOD, who at various times and in various ways spoke in time past to the fathers by the prophets, 2 has in these last days spoken to us by *His* Son, whom He has appointed heir of all things, through whom also He made the worlds; 3 who being the brightness of *His* glory and the express image of His person, and upholding all things by the word of His power, when He had by Himself purged our sins, sat down at the right hand of the Majesty on high, 4 having become so much better than the angels, as He has by inheritance obtained a more excellent name than they.

5 For to which of the angels did He ever say:

"You are My Son,
    Today I have begotten You"?

And again:

"I will be to Him a Father,
    And He shall be to Me a Son"?

6 But when He again brings the first-born into the world, He says:

"Let all the angels of God worship Him."

7 And of the angels He says:

"Who makes His angels spirits
    And His ministers a flame of fire."

8 But to the Son *He says:*

"Your throne, O God, *is* forever and *ever;*
    A scepter of righteousness *is* the scepter of Your kingdom.
9   You have loved righteousness and hated lawlessness;
    Therefore God, Your God, has anointed You

Who Is Greater Than Angels?

God created angels, so God is greater than angels. This means that Jesus, the Son of God, is also greater than angels. But Jesus is greater for another reason. He came to earth and obeyed His Father by dying for our sins. No angel could do that.

With the oil of gladness more
than Your companions.''

10 And:

"You, LORD, in the beginning laid
the foundation of the earth,
And the heavens are the work
of Your hands.
11 They will perish, but You
remain;
And they will all grow old like a
garment;
12 Like a cloak You will fold them
up,
And they will be changed.
But You are the same,
And Your years will not fail.''

13 But to which of the angels has He
ever said:

"Sit at My right hand,
Till I make Your enemies Your
footstool'' ?

14 Are they not all ministering spirits
sent forth to minister for those who will
inherit salvation?

Christ became a human being like you and me

2 Therefore we must give the more
earnest heed to the things we have
heard, lest we drift away. 2 For if the
word spoken through angels proved
steadfast, and every transgression and
disobedience received a just reward,

3 how shall we escape if we neglect so
great a salvation, which at the first began to be spoken by the Lord, and
was confirmed to us by those who
heard Him, 4 God also bearing witness
both with signs and wonders, with various miracles, and gifts of the Holy
Spirit, according to His own will?

5 For He has not put the world to
come, of which we speak, in subjection
to angels. 6 But one testified in a certain
place, saying:

"What is man that You are
mindful of him,
Or the son of man that You take
care of him?
7 You have made him a little lower
than the angels;
You have crowned him with
glory and honor,
And set him over the works of
Your hands.
8 You have put all things in
subjection under his feet.''

For in that He put all in subjection under him, He left nothing that is not put
under him. But now we do not yet see
all things put under him. 9 But we see
Jesus, who was made a little lower than
the angels, for the suffering of death
crowned with glory and honor, that
He, by the grace of God, might taste
death for everyone.

10 For it was fitting for Him, for
whom are all things and by whom are
all things, in bringing many sons to
glory, to make the captain of their

⛏ DIGGING IN

2:10 The Author of Your Salvation
You know that "salvation" means that
your sins are forgiven, and you belong
to God because Jesus died in your place.
So salvation is a work that somebody did
FOR YOU because you couldn't do it for
yourself.

Imagine that you fall out of a boat into
a lake, but you can't swim. You're splash-
ing and floundering in the water, and
you're going down for the last time. Just
then a lifeguard puts his arm under you

and pulls you to shore. You've been
saved! That's a real kind of salvation.

So the lifeguard is not only your savior
from drowning. He is also the AUTHOR
of your salvation. He trained a long time
for the day when he would have to jump
into the water to save you.

Jesus also is the Author of your salvation. You couldn't save yourself. But
Jesus carried out His ancient plan to rescue you from your sins.

salvation perfect through sufferings. [11] For both He who sanctifies and those who are being sanctified *are* all of one, for which reason He is not ashamed to call them brethren, [12] saying:

> "I will declare Your name to My brethren;
> In the midst of the assembly I will sing praise to You."

[13] And again:

> "I will put My trust in Him."

And again:

> "Here am I and the children whom God has given Me."

[14] Inasmuch then as the children have partaken of flesh and blood, He Himself likewise shared in the same, that through death He might destroy him who had the power of death, that is, the devil, [15] and release those who through fear of death were all their lifetime subject to bondage. [16] For indeed He does not give aid to angels, but He does give aid to the seed of Abraham. [17] Therefore, in all things He had to be made like *His* brethren, that He might be a merciful and faithful High Priest in things *pertaining* to God, to make **propitiation** for the sins of the people. [18] For in that He Himself has suffered, being tempted, He is able to aid those who are tempted.

Christis our model

3 Therefore, holy brethren, partakers of the heavenly calling, consider the Apostle and High Priest of our confession, Christ Jesus, [2] who was faithful to Him who appointed Him, as Moses also *was faithful* in all His house. [3] For this One has been counted worthy of more glory than Moses, inasmuch as He who built the house has more honor than the house. [4] For every house is built by someone, but He who built all things *is* God. [5] And Moses indeed *was* faithful in all His house as a servant, for a testimony of those things which would be spoken *afterward*, [6] but Christ as a Son over His own house, whose house we are if we hold fast the confidence and the rejoicing of the hope firm to the end.

[7] Therefore, as the Holy Spirit says:

> "Today, if you will hear His voice,
> [8]   Do not harden your hearts as in the rebellion,
>   In the day of trial in the wilderness,
> [9]   Where your fathers tested Me, tried Me,
>   And saw My works forty years.
> [10]   Therefore I was angry with that generation,
>   And said, 'They always go astray in *their* heart,
>   And they have not known My ways.'
> [11]   So I swore in My wrath,
>   'They shall not enter My rest.' "

[12] Beware, brethren, lest there be in any of you an evil heart of unbelief in departing from the living God; [13] but exhort one another daily, while it is called "Today," lest any of you be hardened through the deceitfulness of sin. [14] For we have become partakers of Christ if we hold the beginning of our confidence steadfast to the end, [15] while it is said:

> "Today, if you will hear His voice,
> Do not harden your hearts as in the rebellion."

[16] For who, having heard, rebelled? Indeed, *was it* not all who came out of Egypt, *led* by Moses? [17] Now with

---

2:17 Propitiation Pronounced *pro-pish-ee-AY-shun*. The work of Jesus on the Cross. By dying for us, Jesus paid the penalty we owed God for breaking His laws.

whom was He angry forty years? *Was it* not with those who sinned, whose corpses fell in the wilderness? [18] And to whom did He swear that they would not enter His rest, but to those who did not obey? [19] So we see that they could not enter in because of unbelief.

God's Word is sharper than a sword

4 Therefore, since a promise remains of entering His rest, let us fear lest any of you seem to have come short of it. [2] For indeed the gospel was preached to us as well as to them; but the word which they heard did not profit them, not being mixed with faith in those who heard *it*. [3] For we who have believed do enter that rest, as He has said:

"So I swore in My wrath,
'They shall not enter My rest,' "

although the works were finished from the foundation of the world. [4] For He has spoken in a certain place of the seventh *day* in this way: "And God rested on the seventh day from all His works"; [5] and again in this *place:* "They shall not enter My rest."

[6] Since therefore it remains that some *must* enter it, and those to whom it was first preached did not enter because of disobedience, [7] again He designates a certain day, saying in David, "Today," after such a long time, as it has been said:

"Today, if you will hear His voice,
Do not harden your hearts."

[8] For if Joshua had given them rest, then He would not afterward have spoken of another day. [9] There remains therefore a rest for the people of God. [10] For he who has entered His rest has himself also ceased from his works as God *did* from His.

[11] Let us therefore be diligent to enter that rest, lest anyone fall according to the same example of disobedience. [12] For the **word of God** *is* living and powerful, and sharper than any two-edged sword, piercing even to the division of soul and spirit, and of joints and marrow, and is a discerner of the thoughts and intents of the heart. [13] And there is no creature hidden from His sight, but all things *are* naked and open to the eyes of Him to whom we *must give* account.

[14] Seeing then that we have a great High Priest who has passed through the heavens, Jesus the Son of God, let us hold fast *our* confession. [15] For we do not have a High Priest who cannot sympathize with our weaknesses, but was in all *points* tempted as *we are, yet* without **sin.** [16] Let us therefore come boldly to the throne of **grace,** that we may obtain mercy and find grace to help in time of need.

God chose Christ to be our High Priest

5 For every high priest taken from among men is appointed for men in things *pertaining* to God, that he may offer both gifts and sacrifices for sins. [2] He can have compassion on those who are ignorant and going astray, since he himself is also subject to weakness. [3] Because of this he is required as for the people, so also for himself, to offer *sacrifices* for sins. [4] And no man takes this honor to himself, but he who is called by God, just as Aaron *was.*

WORDFINDER

4:12 Word of God   God speaking in the Scriptures of the Old and New Testaments. Jesus also is called "the Word" (John 1:1) because He is God's *personal* Word.

4:15 Sin   Disobedience of God's law or rebellion against His will. All people sin, but Christ died to take sin away.

4:16 Grace   The undeserved kindness of God. We are saved from sin by this grace of God. All the good we enjoy is due to His grace.

5 So also Christ did not glorify Himself to become High Priest, *but it* was He who said to Him:

"You are My Son,
Today I have begotten You."

6 As *He* also *says* in another *place:*

"You *are* a priest forever
According to the order of
Melchizedek";

7 who, in the days of His flesh, when He had offered up prayers and supplications, with vehement cries and tears to Him who was able to save Him from death, and was heard because of His godly fear, 8 though He was a Son, *yet* He learned obedience by the things which He suffered. 9 And having been perfected, He became the author of eternal salvation to all who obey Him, 10 called by God as High Priest "according to the order of Melchizedek," 11 of whom we have much to say, and hard to explain, since you have become dull of hearing.

12 For though by this time you ought to be teachers, you need *someone* to teach you again the first principles of the oracles of God; and you have come to need milk and not solid food. 13 For *everyone* who partakes *only* of milk *is* unskilled in the word of righteousness, for he is a babe. 14 But solid food belongs to those who are of full age, *that is,* those who by reason of use have their senses exercised to discern both good and evil.

Baby Christians need to grow up

6 Therefore, leaving the discussion of the elementary *principles* of Christ, let us go on to perfection, not laying again the foundation of repentance from dead works and of faith toward God, 2 of the doctrine of baptisms, of laying on of hands, of resurrection of the dead, and of eternal judgment. 3 And this we will do if God permits.

4 For *it is* impossible for those who were once enlightened, and have tasted the heavenly gift, and have become partakers of the Holy Spirit, 5 and have tasted the good word of God and the powers of the age to come, 6 if they fall away, to renew them again to repentance, since they crucify again for themselves the Son of God, and put *Him* to an open shame.

7 For the earth which drinks in the rain that often comes upon it, and bears herbs useful for those by whom it is cultivated, receives blessing from God; 8 but if it bears thorns and briers, *it is* rejected and near to being cursed, whose end *is* to be burned.

9 But, beloved, we are confident of better things concerning you, yes, things that accompany salvation, though we speak in this manner. 10 For God *is* not unjust to forget your work and labor of love which you have shown toward His name, *in that* you have ministered to the saints, and do minister. 11 And we desire that each one of you show the same diligence to the full assurance of hope until the end, 12 that you do not become sluggish, but imitate those who through faith and patience inherit the promises.

13 For when God made a promise to Abraham, because He could swear by no one greater, He swore by Himself, 14 saying, "Surely blessing I will bless you, and multiplying I will multiply you." 15 And so, after he had patiently endured, he obtained the promise. 16 For men indeed swear by the greater, and an oath for confirmation is for them an end of all dispute. 17 Thus God, determining to show more abundantly to the heirs of promise the immutability of His counsel, confirmed *it* by an oath, 18 that by two **immutable** things, in which it *is* impos-

WORDFINDER

6:18 Immutable Pronounced *im-MYOOT-uh-bull*. Unchanging. God does not change in His character, His truth, or His promises.

sible for God to lie, we might have strong consolation, who have fled for refuge to lay hold of the hope set before us.

19 This *hope* we have as an anchor of the **soul**, both sure and steadfast, and which enters the Presence *behind* the veil, 20 where the forerunner has entered for us, *even* Jesus, having become High Priest forever according to the order of Melchizedek.

Christ is a priest forever like Melchizedek

7 For this Melchizedek, king of Salem, priest of the Most High God, who met Abraham returning from the slaughter of the kings and blessed him, 2 to whom also Abraham gave a tenth part of all, first being translated "king of righteousness," and then also king of Salem, meaning "king of peace," 3 without father, without mother, without genealogy, having neither beginning of days nor end of life, but made like the Son of God, remains a priest continually.

4 Now consider how great this man *was,* to whom even the patriarch Abraham gave a tenth of the spoils. 5 And indeed those who are of the sons of Levi, who receive the priesthood, have

Who Was Melchizedek?

Melchizedek (pronounced *mel-KIZ-uh-dek*) means "King of Righteousness." This king and priest met Abraham in the Old Testament two thousand years before Jesus was born (see Genesis 14:18–20). The real King of Righteousness is Jesus Christ, the Son of God. So Jesus was the one who long ago visited Abraham in the form of Melchizedek, the priest of God.

a commandment to receive tithes from the people according to the law, that is, from their brethren, though they have come from the loins of Abraham; 6 but he whose genealogy is not derived from them received tithes from Abraham and blessed him who had the promises. 7 Now beyond all contradiction the lesser is blessed by the better. 8 Here mortal men receive tithes, but there he *receives them,* of whom it is witnessed that he lives. 9 Even Levi, who receives tithes, paid tithes through Abraham, so to speak, 10 for he was still in the loins of his father when Melchizedek met him.

11 Therefore, if perfection were through the Levitical priesthood (for under it the people received the law), what further need *was there* that another priest should rise according to the order of Melchizedek, and not be called according to the order of Aaron? 12 For the priesthood being changed, of necessity there is also a change of the law. 13 For He of whom these things are spoken belongs to another tribe, from which no man has officiated at the altar.

14 For *it is* evident that our Lord arose from Judah, of which tribe Moses spoke nothing concerning priesthood. 15 And it is yet far more evident if, in the likeness of Melchizedek, there arises another priest 16 who has come, not according to the law of a fleshly commandment, but according to the power of an endless life. 17 For He testifies:

"You *are* a priest forever
According to the order of
Melchizedek."

18 For on the one hand there is an annulling of the former commandment because of its weakness and unprofitableness, 19 for the law made nothing

WORDFINDER

6:19 Soul The inner life of a person that cannot die. The soul of a believing person who dies goes to be with God in heaven. But the unbelieving person's soul is cut off from God.

perfect; on the other hand, *there is the* bringing in of a better hope, through which we draw near to God.

20 And inasmuch as *He was* not *made priest* without an oath 21 (for they have become priests without an oath, but He with an oath by Him who said to Him:

> "The LORD has sworn
> And will not relent,
> 'You *are* a priest forever
> According to the order of
>   Melchizedek' "),

22 by so much more Jesus has become a surety of a better covenant.

23 Also there were many priests, because they were prevented by death from continuing. 24 But He, because He continues forever, has an unchangeable priesthood. 25 Therefore He is also able to save to the uttermost those who come to God through Him, since He always lives to make intercession for them.

26 For such a High Priest was fitting for us, *who is* holy, harmless, undefiled, separate from sinners, and has become higher than the heavens; 27 who does not need daily, as those high priests, to offer up sacrifices, first for His own sins and then for the people's, for this He did once for all when He offered up Himself. 28 For the law appoints as high priests men who have weakness, but the word of the oath, which came after the law, *appoints* the Son who has been perfected forever.

God makes a new agreement with Israel

8 Now *this is* the main point of the things we are saying: We have such a High Priest, who is seated at the right hand of the throne of the Majesty in the heavens, 2 a Minister of the sanctu-ary and of the true tabernacle which the Lord erected, and not man.

3 For every high priest is appointed to offer both gifts and sacrifices. Therefore *it is* necessary that this One also have something to offer. 4 For if He were on earth, He would not be a priest, since there are priests who offer the gifts according to the law; 5 who serve the copy and shadow of the heavenly things, as Moses was divinely instructed when he was about to make the tabernacle. For He said, "See *that* you make all things according to the pattern shown you on the mountain." 6 But now He has obtained a more excellent ministry, inasmuch as He is also Mediator of a better covenant, which was established on better promises.

7 For if that first *covenant* had been faultless, then no place would have been sought for a second. 8 Because finding fault with them, He says: "Behold, the days are coming, says the LORD, when I will make a new covenant with the house of Israel and with the house of Judah— 9 not according to the **covenant** that I made with their fathers in the day when I took them by the hand to lead them out of the land of Egypt; because they did not continue in My covenant, and I disregarded them, says the LORD. 10 For this *is* the covenant that I will make with the house of Israel after those days, says the LORD: I will put My laws in their mind and write them on their hearts; and I will be their God, and they shall be My people. 11 None of them shall teach his neighbor, and none his brother, saying, 'Know the LORD,' for all shall know Me, from the least of them to the greatest of them. 12 For I will be merciful to their unrighteousness, and their sins and their lawless deeds I will remember no more."

🌐 WORDFINDER

8:8 Covenant Pronounced *KUV-uh-nunt*. A legal agreement. God made a covenant with Abraham to give the land of Canaan to his descendants and to make Abraham a blessing to the whole world.

13 In that He says, "A **new cov-enant**," He has made the first obsolete. Now what is becoming obsolete and growing old is ready to vanish away.

Christ is the perfect Sacrifice

9 Then indeed, even the first *covenant* had ordinances of divine service and the earthly sanctuary. 2 For a tabernacle was prepared: the first *part,* in which *was* the lampstand, the table, and the showbread, which is called the sanctuary; 3 and behind the second veil, the part of the tabernacle which is called the Holiest of All, 4 which had the golden censer and the **ark of the covenant** overlaid on all sides with gold, in which *were* the golden pot that had the manna, Aaron's rod that budded, and the tablets of the covenant; 5 and above it were the **cherubim** of glory overshadowing the **mercy seat.**

Of these things we cannot now speak in detail.

6 Now when these things had been thus prepared, the priests always went into the first part of the tabernacle, performing *the services.* 7 But into the second part the high priest *went* alone once a year, not without blood, which he offered for himself and *for* the people's sins *committed* in ignorance; 8 the Holy Spirit indicating this, that the way into the Holiest of All was not yet made manifest while the first tabernacle was still standing. 9 It *was* symbolic for the present time in which both gifts and sacrifices are offered which cannot make him who performed the service perfect in regard to the conscience— 10 *concerned* only with foods and drinks, various washings, and fleshly ordinances imposed until the time of reformation.

11 But Christ came *as* **High Priest** of the good things to come, with the

---

WORDFINDER

8:13 New Covenant A covenant (pronounced *KUV-uh-nunt*) is a legal agreement. Under the Old Covenant (or Old Testament), God agreed to save His people through the blood of animals, which was a symbol for Christ's blood. Under the New Covenant (or New Testament), God agrees to save His people by the blood of Christ Himself.

9:4 Ark of the Covenant A gold-covered wooden chest about 45 inches long by 27 inches wide by 27 inches high. The chest first contained the Ten Commandments, but later also contained some manna and Aaron's wooden staff (see Numbers 11:6).

9:5 Cherubim Pronounced *CHER-uh-bim*. Plural of cherub. These are special angels who are always in the presence of God and continually praise Him.

9:5 Mercy Seat A flat gold seat that covered the top of the ark of the covenant. In the Old Testament, God revealed Himself in a cloud and fire over the mercy seat.

9:11 High Priest The priest who was over the other priests in Old Testament worship. Aaron, Moses' brother, was the first. Christ is now our High Priest.

DIGGING IN

8:13 God's New Covenant God has always had one wonderful plan for saving you from your sins. He always planned to send His Son Jesus Christ to die in your place (read Isaiah 53).

But for hundreds of years, in Old Testament times, God had to teach people how serious sin is. During that time God taught the people to bring lambs, goats, and calves to be sacrificed every day. This was a way of teaching people that sin

costs a life. *Sin causes death.* That method of coming to God was called the "Old Covenant"—the method of worship during Old Testament times.

Then God finally did send His only Son to die in our place. He did this once for all, and He brought to an end the sacrifices of the Old Covenant. Jesus was the *real sacrifice* that God had planned from the beginning. Jesus' sacrifice for us is called the "New Covenant."

greater and more perfect tabernacle not made with hands, that is, not of this creation. 12 Not with the blood of goats and calves, but with His own blood He entered the Most Holy Place once for all, having obtained eternal redemption. 13 For if the blood of bulls and goats and the ashes of a heifer, sprinkling the unclean, sanctifies for the purifying of the flesh, 14 how much more shall the blood of Christ, who through the eternal Spirit offered Himself without spot to God, cleanse your conscience from dead works to serve the living God? 15 And for this reason He is the Mediator of the new covenant, by means of death, for the redemption of the transgressions under the first covenant, that those who are called may receive the promise of the eternal inheritance.

16 For where there is a testament, there must also of necessity be the death of the testator. 17 For a testament is in force after men are dead, since it has no power at all while the testator lives. 18 Therefore not even the first covenant was dedicated without blood. 19 For when Moses had spoken every precept to all the people according to the law, he took the blood of calves and goats, with water, scarlet wool, and hyssop, and sprinkled both the book itself and all the people, 20 saying, "This is the blood of the covenant which God has commanded you." 21 Then likewise he sprinkled with blood both the tabernacle and all the vessels of the ministry. 22 And according to the law almost all things are purified with blood, and without shedding of blood there is no remission.

23 Therefore it was necessary that the copies of the things in the heavens should be purified with these, but the heavenly things themselves with better

Christians are freed from making the sacrifices taught in the Old Testament.

sacrifices than these. 24 For Christ has not entered the holy places made with hands, *which are* copies of the true, but into heaven itself, now to appear in the presence of God for us; 25 not that He should offer Himself often, as the high priest enters the Most Holy Place every year with blood of another— 26 He then would have had to suffer often since the foundation of the world; but now, once at the end of the ages, He has appeared to put away sin by the **sacrifice** of Himself. 27 And as it is appointed for men to die once, but after this the judgment, 28 so Christ was offered once to bear the sins of many. To those who eagerly wait for Him He will appear a second time, apart from sin, for salvation.

Christ died for our sins as one offering for all time

10 For the law, having a shadow of the good things to come, *and* not the very image of the things, can never with these same sacrifices, which they offer continually year by year, make those who approach perfect. 2 For then would they not have ceased to be offered? For the worshipers, once purified, would have had no more consciousness of sins. 3 But in those *sacrifices there is* a reminder of sins every year. 4 For *it is* not possible that the blood of bulls and goats could take away sins.

5 Therefore, when He came into the world, He said:

"Sacrifice and offering You did not desire,
But a body You have prepared for Me.
6 In burnt offerings and *sacrifices* for sin
You had no pleasure.

7 Then I said, 'Behold, I have come—
In the volume of the book it is written of Me—
To do Your will, O God.' "

8 Previously saying, "Sacrifice and offering, burnt offerings, and *offerings* for sin You did not desire, nor had pleasure *in them*" (which are offered according to the law), 9 then He said, "Behold, I have come to do Your will, O God." He takes away the first that He may establish the second. 10 By that will we have been sanctified through the offering of the body of Jesus Christ once *for all.*

11 And every priest stands ministering daily and offering repeatedly the same sacrifices, which can never take away sins. 12 But this Man, after He had offered one sacrifice for sins forever, sat down at the right hand of God, 13 from that time waiting till His enemies are made His footstool. 14 For by one offering He has perfected forever those who are being sanctified. 15 But the Holy Spirit also witnesses to us; for after He had said before,

16 "This *is* the covenant that I will make with them after those days, says the LORD: I will put My laws into their hearts, and in their minds I will write them," 17 *then He adds,* "Their sins and their lawless deeds I will remember no more." 18 Now where there is remission of these, *there is* no longer an offering for sin.

19 Therefore, brethren, having boldness to enter the Holiest by the blood of Jesus, 20 by a new and living way which He consecrated for us, through the veil, that is, His flesh, 21 and *having* a High Priest over the house of God, 22 let us draw near with a true heart in full assurance of faith, having our hearts sprinkled from an evil conscience and our bodies washed with

---

WORDFINDER

9:26 Sacrifice Pronounced *SACK-rih-fyce.* An offering to God. In the Old Testament, the people sacrificed the blood of animals for sin. In the New Testament, Christ is our only sacrifice for sin.

Jesus made one sacrifice for sins forever.

pure water. 23 Let us hold fast the confession of *our* hope without wavering, for He who promised *is* faithful. 24 And let us consider one another in order to stir up love and good works, 25 not forsaking the assembling of ourselves together, as *is* the manner of some, but exhorting *one another,* and so much the more as you see the Day approaching.

26 For if we sin willfully after we have received the knowledge of the truth, there no longer remains a sacrifice for sins, 27 but a certain fearful expectation of judgment, and fiery indignation which will devour the adversaries. 28 Anyone who has rejected Moses' law dies without mercy on the testimony of two or three witnesses. 29 Of how much worse punishment, do you suppose, will he be thought worthy who has trampled the Son of God underfoot, counted the blood of the

covenant by which he was sanctified a common thing, and insulted the Spirit of grace? 30 For we know Him who said, "Vengeance is Mine, I will repay," says the Lord. And again, "The LORD will judge His people." 31 It is a fearful thing to fall into the hands of the living God.

32 But recall the former days in which, after you were illuminated, you endured a great struggle with sufferings: 33 partly while you were made a spectacle both by reproaches and tribulations, and partly while you became companions of those who were so treated; 34 for you had compassion on me in my chains, and joyfully accepted the plundering of your goods, knowing that you have a better and an enduring possession for yourselves in heaven. 35 Therefore do not cast away your confidence, which has great reward. 36 For you have need of endurance, so that after you have done the will of God, you may receive the promise:

37 "For yet a little while,
       And He who is coming will come
           and will not tarry.
38   Now the just shall live by faith;
       But if *anyone* draws back,
       My soul has no pleasure in him."

39 But we are not of those who draw back to perdition, but of those who believe to the saving of the soul.

Heroes of the faith

11 Now faith is the substance of things hoped for, the evidence of things not seen. 2 For by it the elders obtained a *good* testimony.

3 By faith we understand that the worlds were framed by the word of God, so that the things which are seen were not made of things which are visible.

4 By faith Abel offered to God a more excellent sacrifice than Cain, through which he obtained witness that he was righteous, God testifying of his

gifts; and through it he being dead still speaks.

⁵ By faith Enoch was taken away so that he did not see death, "and was not found, because God had taken him"; for before he was taken he had this testimony, that he pleased God. ⁶ But without faith *it is* impossible to please *Him,* for he who comes to God must believe that He is, and *that* He is a rewarder of those who diligently seek Him.

⁷ By faith Noah, being divinely warned of things not yet seen, moved with godly fear, prepared an ark for the saving of his household, by which he condemned the world and became heir of the righteousness which is according to faith.

⁸ By faith Abraham obeyed when he was called to go out to the place which he would receive as an inheritance. And he went out, not knowing where he was going. ⁹ By faith he dwelt in the land of promise as *in* a foreign country, dwelling in tents with Isaac and Jacob, the heirs with him of the same promise; ¹⁰ for he waited for the city which has foundations, whose builder and maker *is* God.

¹¹ By faith Sarah herself also received strength to conceive seed, and she bore a child when she was past the age, because she judged Him faithful who had promised. ¹² Therefore from one man, and him as good as dead, were born *as many* as the stars of the sky in multitude—innumerable as the sand which is by the seashore.

¹³ These all died in faith, not having received the promises, but having seen them afar off were assured of them, embraced *them* and confessed that they were strangers and pilgrims on the earth. ¹⁴ For those who say such things declare plainly that they seek a homeland. ¹⁵ And truly if they had called to mind that *country* from which they had come out, they would have had opportunity to return. ¹⁶ But now they desire a better, that is, a heavenly *country.* Therefore God is not ashamed to be called their God, for He has prepared a city for them.

¹⁷ By faith Abraham, when he was tested, offered up Isaac, and he who had received the promises offered up his only begotten *son,* ¹⁸ of whom it was said, "In Isaac your seed shall be called," ¹⁹ concluding that God *was* able to raise *him* up, even from the dead, from which he also received him in a figurative sense.

²⁰ By faith Isaac blessed Jacob and Esau concerning things to come.

²¹ By faith Jacob, when he was dying, blessed each of the sons of Joseph, and worshiped, *leaning* on the top of his staff.

²² By faith Joseph, when he was dying, made mention of the departure of the children of Israel, and gave instructions concerning his bones.

²³ By faith Moses, when he was born, was hidden three months by his parents, because they saw *he was* a beautiful child; and they were not afraid of the king's command.

²⁴ By faith Moses, when he became of age, refused to be called the son of

🪓 DIGGING IN

11:1–40 God's Hall of Fame Many of us know about the football Hall of Fame. That's where we remember the great football heroes of all time.

God also has a hall of fame. That is a memorial of all the great heroes of faith. Hebrews 11 lists only the Old Testament heroes. We also know a lot of brave New Testament leaders whose names we will always remember—John, James, Peter, Paul, and many others.

Isn't it thrilling to read about Moses, a prince of Egypt, who left the palace to join the Hebrew slaves? After the end of the New Testament time, the story is told of a Roman army officer who left his own troops and stood with a group of Christians who were condemned to die. One day we shall see Abraham and Sarah, Joshua and Rahab, Boaz and Ruth. Would you like to join that hall of fame with them? You can!

Pharaoh's daughter, 25 choosing rather to suffer affliction with the people of God than to enjoy the passing pleasures of sin, 26 esteeming the reproach of Christ greater riches than the treasures in Egypt; for he looked to the reward.

27 By faith he forsook Egypt, not fearing the wrath of the king; for he endured as seeing Him who is invisible. 28 By faith he kept the **Passover** and the sprinkling of blood, lest he who destroyed the firstborn should touch them.

29 By faith they passed through the Red Sea as by dry *land, whereas* the Egyptians, attempting *to do* so, were drowned.

30 By faith the walls of Jericho fell down after they were encircled for seven days. 31 By faith the harlot Rahab did not perish with those who did not believe, when she had received the spies with peace.

32 And what more shall I say? For the time would fail me to tell of Gideon and Barak and Samson and Jephthah, also *of* David and Samuel and the prophets: 33 who through faith subdued kingdoms, worked righteousness, obtained promises, stopped the mouths of lions, 34 quenched the vio-

lence of fire, escaped the edge of the sword, out of weakness were made strong, became valiant in battle, turned to flight the armies of the aliens. 35 Women received their dead raised to life again.

Others were tortured, not accepting deliverance, that they might obtain a better resurrection. 36 Still others had trial of mockings and scourgings, yes, and of chains and imprisonment. 37 They were stoned, they were sawn in two, were tempted, were slain with the sword. They wandered about in sheepskins and goatskins, being destitute, afflicted, tormented— 38 of whom the world was not worthy. They wandered in deserts and mountains, *in* dens and caves of the earth.

39 And all these, having obtained a good testimony through faith, did not receive the promise, 40 God having provided something better for us, that they should not be made perfect apart from us.

Running the race that God has set before us

12 Therefore we also, since we are surrounded by so great a cloud of wit-

11:28 Passover The greatest Hebrew celebration. The people remember that the Lord "passed over" their homes in Egypt because a lamb's blood was applied to their doorways. See Exodus 12. After the death of the firstborn in Egypt, God's people were freed to leave.

DIGGING IN

12:1, 2 Run the Race of Faith Sometimes we describe faith in Jesus as resting in Jesus. This means that the world around you can't frighten you because you trust Jesus for everything. In a way that's resting.

But faith in Jesus is also like running a race. This means trusting Jesus in a way that makes sure you reach the goal of life that Jesus sets for you. The goal of life is to reach heaven and to be given the prize of doing the work Jesus gives

you to do on earth.

The first thing you must do in training to run is to be sure tobacco, alcohol, or drugs don't make you short of breath. Those things also make you unable to run your race for Jesus in the world.

The next thing you think about is getting rid of any extra weight. There are many good things a Christian can enjoy in the world. But even the weight of too many good things leaves no time for serving Jesus.

nesses, let us lay aside every weight, and the sin which so easily ensnares us, and let us run with endurance the race that is set before us, ² looking unto Jesus, the author and finisher of our faith, who for the joy that was set before Him endured the cross, despising the shame, and has sat down at the right hand of the throne of God.

³ For consider Him who endured such hostility from sinners against Himself, lest you become weary and discouraged in your souls. ⁴ You have not yet resisted to bloodshed, striving against sin. ⁵ And you have forgotten the exhortation which speaks to you as to sons:

"My son, do not despise the
   chastening of the LORD,
Nor be discouraged when you
   are rebuked by Him;
6   For whom the LORD loves He
   chastens,
And scourges every son whom
   He receives."

⁷ If you endure chastening, God deals with you as with sons; for what son is there whom a father does not chasten? ⁸ But if you are without chastening, of which all have become partakers, then you are illegitimate and not sons. ⁹ Furthermore, we have had human fathers who corrected us, and we paid them respect. Shall we not much more readily be in subjection to the Father of spirits and live? ¹⁰ For they indeed for a few days chastened us as seemed best to them, but He for our profit, that we may be partakers of His holiness. ¹¹ Now no chastening seems to be joyful for the present, but painful; nevertheless, afterward it yields the peaceable fruit of righteousness to those who have been trained by it.

¹² Therefore strengthen the hands which hang down, and the feeble knees, ¹³ and make straight paths for your feet, so that what is lame may not be dislocated, but rather be healed.

¹⁴ Pursue peace with all people, and holiness, without which no one will see the Lord: ¹⁵ looking carefully lest anyone fall short of the grace of God; lest any root of bitterness springing up cause trouble, and by this many become defiled; ¹⁶ lest there be any fornicator or profane person like Esau, who for one morsel of food sold his birthright. ¹⁷ For you know that afterward, when he wanted to inherit the blessing, he was rejected, for he found no place for repentance, though he sought it diligently with tears.

¹⁸ For you have not come to the mountain that may be touched and that burned with fire, and to blackness and darkness and tempest, ¹⁹ and the sound of a trumpet and the voice of words, so that those who heard it begged that the word should not be spoken to them anymore. ²⁰ (For they could not endure what was commanded: "And if so much as a beast touches the mountain, it shall be stoned or shot with an arrow." ²¹ And so terrifying was the sight that Moses said, "I am exceedingly afraid and trembling.")

²² But you have come to Mount Zion and to the city of the living God, the heavenly Jerusalem, to an innumerable company of angels, ²³ to the general assembly and church of the firstborn who are registered in heaven, to God the Judge of all, to the spirits of just men made perfect, ²⁴ to Jesus the **Mediator** of the new covenant, and to the blood of sprinkling that speaks better things than that of Abel.

²⁵ See that you do not refuse Him who speaks. For if they did not escape who refused Him who spoke on earth, much more shall we not escape if we

---

WORDFINDER

12:24 Mediator Pronounced *MEE-dee-ay-tor.* Someone who brings two groups or individuals to agreement. Jesus is the Mediator who brings God and people to agreement by His death on the Cross.

turn away from Him who *speaks* from heaven, [26] whose voice then shook the earth; but now He has promised, saying, "Yet once more I shake not only the earth, but also heaven." [27] Now this, "Yet once more," indicates the removal of those things that are being shaken, as of things that are made, that the things which cannot be shaken may remain.

[28] Therefore, since we are receiving a kingdom which cannot be shaken, let us have grace, by which we may serve God acceptably with **reverence** and godly fear. [29] For our God *is* a consuming fire.

How to live a good life

13 Let brotherly love continue. [2] Do not forget to entertain strangers, for by so *doing* some have unwittingly entertained angels. [3] Remember the prisoners as if chained with them—

those who are mistreated—since you yourselves are in the body also.

[4] Marriage *is* honorable among all, and the bed undefiled; but fornicators and adulterers God will judge.

[5] *Let your* conduct *be* without covetousness; *be* content with such things as you have. For He Himself has said, "I will never leave you nor forsake you." [6] So we may boldly say:

"The LORD *is* my helper;
I will not fear.
What can man do to me?"

[7] Remember those who rule over you, who have spoken the word of God to you, whose faith follow, considering the outcome of *their* conduct. [8] Jesus Christ *is* the same yesterday, today, and forever. [9] Do not be carried about with various and strange doctrines. For *it is* good that the heart be

---

WORDFINDER

12:28 Reverence   Pronounced *REV-er-ents*. An attitude of respect and awe. Reverence is an attitude we should have for God in worship and in serving Him.

DIGGING IN

12:28 Fear Can Be Healthy Nobody likes to be afraid. But being afraid is a lot better than getting into a bad accident. So you look both ways when you cross the street. That's healthy fear.

It would be wonderful if we loved God so much that we would just obey him all the time. But we fail sometimes, and we often get hurt because we didn't do it God's way.

Getting burned once gives you a healthy fear of fire. Getting in trouble with the police can make you afraid of getting in trouble again. You should also be afraid of God's holy anger. "For our God is a consuming fire" (verse 29). God means business about the way He wants you to live. He is serious about obedience to His commands. Although He forgives you over and over, there is an end to God's patience. God will always love you, but He may have to teach you

some hard lessons.

13:5 Jesus Never Leaves You Have you ever been alone? Do you remember what it was like not to know when your parents would come home? It was frightening not to have someone near.

It's nice and comforting to have friends and those who love you, but what if they were all taken away? Would you be alone then?

Jesus has given you perhaps the greatest promise in the Bible—"I will never leave you." If Jesus is always with you, then you really need no one else.

Do you know Jesus as your Friend forever from heaven? You can. All you have to do is ask Him. Right now, say, "Lord Jesus, come into my life and be my Friend forever." He'll do it. As you talk to Him every day, you'll find He is a Friend who never leaves you.

What the Hebrews Learned

We are the Hebrews, also called Jews, and now we have become Christians. This was hard for us because we had to forget a lot of our early religious customs.

God commanded Moses to teach our people all the sacrifices that were made in Old Testament times. Now that we have received Jesus as our Messiah, we have had to stop making those sacrifices. Jesus made the only sacrifice His Father would now accept. Jesus sacrificed His own body on the Cross.

So we learned that our old religious customs couldn't take away our sins. Those sacrifices only showed how Jesus would be the true Lamb of sacrifice for us. We're glad now that Jesus, our Sacrifice, is in heaven. Someday we shall be with Him. Will you?

Does Jesus Change?

The whole world changes every day. You grow a little taller and your parents get older. Someday you, too, will become old; but Jesus never grows old. Jesus grew up in the world and He died. Then He rose again in a body that can never change. Because He lives, someday He can give you an unchanging body also.

established by grace, not with foods which have not profited those who have been occupied with them.

10 We have an altar from which those who serve the tabernacle have no right to eat. 11 For the bodies of those animals, whose blood is brought into the sanctuary by the high priest for sin, are burned outside the camp. 12 Therefore Jesus also, that He might sanctify the people with His own blood, suffered outside the gate. 13 Therefore let us go forth to Him, outside the camp, bearing His reproach. 14 For here we have no continuing city, but we seek the one to come. 15 Therefore by Him let us continually offer the sacrifice of praise to God, that is, the fruit of our lips, giving thanks to His name. 16 But do not forget to do good and to share, for with such sacrifices God is well pleased.

17 Obey those who rule over you, and be submissive, for they watch out for your souls, as those who must give account. Let them do so with joy and not with grief, for that would be unprofitable for you.

18 Pray for us; for we are confident that we have a good conscience, in all things desiring to live honorably. 19 But I especially urge you to do this, that I may be restored to you the sooner.

20 Now may the God of peace who brought up our Lord Jesus from the dead, that great Shepherd of the sheep, through the blood of the everlasting covenant, 21 make you complete in every good work to do His will, working in you what is well pleasing in His sight, through Jesus Christ, to whom be glory forever and ever. Amen.

22 And I appeal to you, brethren, bear with the word of exhortation, for I have written to you in few words. 23 Know that our brother Timothy has been set free, with whom I shall see you if he comes shortly.

24 Greet all those who rule over you, and all the saints. Those from Italy greet you.

25 Grace be with you all. Amen.

The Book of

JAMES

You meet me first in Matthew 13:55, also in Mark 6:3. I was, James, the oldest of Jesus' younger brothers. My mother Mary was also the mother of Jesus, but His Father was God.

At first my brothers and I didn't believe in Jesus as the Son of God. Later, after Jesus rose from death, I believed in Him as my Savior and Lord. Since that time, the apostles of Jesus have given me the task of being leader of the Christians in Jerusalem.

You meet me again in Acts 15. Paul and his friends came to Jerusalem to show us why non-Jewish Christians did not need to keep the Jewish religious customs. So we understood that those special customs couldn't help to take away sin.

My older Brother's death on the Cross paid the whole cost of your salvation.

Trouble builds patience

JAMES, a bondservant of God and of the Lord Jesus Christ,

To the twelve tribes which are scattered abroad:

Greetings.

2 My brethren, count it all joy when you fall into various trials, 3 knowing that the testing of your faith produces patience. 4 But let patience have *its* perfect work, that you may be perfect and complete, lacking nothing. 5 If any of you lacks wisdom, let him ask of God, who gives to all liberally and without reproach, and it will be given to him. 6 But let him ask in faith, with no doubting, for he who doubts is like a wave of the sea driven and tossed by the wind. 7 For let not that man suppose that he will receive anything from the Lord; 8 *he is* a double-minded man, unstable in all his ways.

9 Let the lowly brother glory in his exaltation, 10 but the rich in his humilia-tion, because as a flower of the field he will pass away. 11 For no sooner has the sun risen with a burning heat than it withers the grass; its flower falls, and its beautiful appearance perishes. So the rich man also will fade away in his pursuits.

12 Blessed *is* the man who endures temptation; for when he has been approved, he will receive the crown of life which the Lord has promised to those who **love** Him. 13 Let no one say when he is tempted, "I am tempted by God"; for God cannot be tempted by evil, nor does He Himself tempt anyone. 14 But each one is tempted when he is drawn away by his own desires and enticed. 15 Then, when desire has conceived, it gives birth to sin; and sin, when it is full-grown, brings forth death.

16 Do not be deceived, my beloved brethren. 17 Every good gift and every perfect gift is from above, and comes down from the Father of lights, with whom there is no variation or shadow

of turning. 18 Of His own will He brought us forth by the word of truth, that we might be a kind of firstfruits of His creatures.

19 So then, my beloved brethren, let every man be swift to hear, slow to speak, slow to wrath; 20 for the wrath of man does not produce the righteousness of God.

21 Therefore lay aside all filthiness and overflow of wickedness, and receive with meekness the implanted word, which is able to save your souls. 22 But be doers of the word, and not hearers only, deceiving yourselves. 23 For if anyone is a hearer of the word and not a doer, he is like a man observing his natural face in a mirror; 24 for he observes himself, goes away, and immediately forgets what kind of man he was. 25 But he who looks into the perfect law of liberty and continues in it, and is not a forgetful hearer but a doer of the work, this one will be blessed in what he does.

26 If anyone among you thinks he is religious, and does not bridle his tongue but deceives his own heart, this one's religion is useless. 27 Pure and undefiled religion before God and the Father is this: to visit orphans and widows in their trouble, and to keep oneself unspotted from the world.

Prove your faith by your actions

2 My brethren, do not hold the faith of our Lord Jesus Christ, the Lord of glory, with partiality. 2 For if there should come into your assembly a man with gold rings, in fine apparel, and there should also come in a poor man in filthy clothes, 3 and you pay attention to the one wearing the fine clothes and say to him, "You sit here in a good place," and say to the poor man, "You stand there," or, "Sit here at my footstool," 4 have you not shown partiality among yourselves, and become judges with evil thoughts?

5 Listen, my beloved brethren: Has God not chosen the poor of this world to be rich in faith and heirs of the kingdom which He promised to those who love Him? 6 But you have dishonored the poor man. Do not the rich oppress you and drag you into the courts? 7 Do they not blaspheme that noble name by which you are called?

8 If you really fulfill the royal law according to the Scripture, "You shall love your neighbor as yourself," you do well; 9 but if you show partiality, you commit sin, and are convicted by the law as transgressors. 10 For whoever shall keep the whole law, and yet stumble in one point, he is guilty of all. 11 For He who said, "Do not commit adultery," also said, "Do not murder." Now if you do not commit adultery, but you do murder, you have become a transgressor of the law. 12 So speak and so do as those who will be judged by the law of liberty. 13 For judgment is without mercy to the one who has shown no mercy. Mercy triumphs over judgment.

14 What does it profit, my brethren,

🏹 DIGGING IN

1:22 Hearing Is Not Enough Too many times we may hear someone talking, but we aren't listening to what that person is saying. Do you sometimes hear your teacher say, "Now pay attention, class!" That's because the teacher can see you're not really listening. The same thing happens when you go to church. You hear the teacher or the pastor talking on and on—but you aren't paying attention.

There's another way of hearing but not listening. That's when you listen to everything someone says, and then go away and forget about it. That's like the story Jesus told in Matthew 13. Some of the farmer's seeds fell on hard ground. They didn't take root, and the birds ate up the seeds. In the same way, sometimes you hear or read God's words, but you don't think about what God says. You don't let His words take root and become part of your life. Then you become a HEARER, but you're not a DOER. That kind of hearing is useless. God is looking for people who will do what He commands.

Faith without kind deeds is useless.

Can Others See Your Faith?

John Bunyan wrote *Pilgrim's Progress,* and someday you should read it. In this book Bunyan describes a man named "Talkative." The man talked a lot about his faith, but he really didn't have any. So he came to a bad end. You can show your faith by living and loving as Jesus did.

received the messengers and sent *them* out another way? 26 For as the body without the spirit is dead, so faith without works is dead also.

The tongue is like the rudder of a ship

3 My brethren, let not many of you become teachers, knowing that we shall receive a stricter judgment. 2 For we all stumble in many things. If anyone does not stumble in word, he *is* a perfect man, able also to bridle the whole body. 3 Indeed, we put bits in horses' mouths that they may obey us, and we turn their whole body. 4 Look also at ships: although they are so large and are driven by fierce winds, they are turned by a very small rudder wherever the pilot desires. 5 Even so the tongue is a little member and boasts great things.

See how great a forest a little fire kindles! 6 And the tongue *is* a fire, a world of iniquity. The tongue is so set among our members that it defiles the whole body, and sets on fire the course of nature; and it is set on fire by hell. 7 For every kind of beast and bird, of reptile and creature of the sea, is tamed and has been tamed by mankind. 8 But no man can tame the tongue. *It is* an unruly evil, full of deadly poison. 9 With it we bless our God and Father, and with it we curse men, who have been made in the similitude of God. 10 Out of the same mouth proceed blessing and cursing. My brethren, these things ought not to be so. 11 Does a spring send forth fresh *water*

if someone says he has faith but does not have works? Can faith save him? 15 If a brother or sister is naked and destitute of daily food, 16 and one of you says to them, "Depart in peace, be warmed and filled," but you do not give them the things which are needed for the body, what *does it* profit? 17 Thus also faith by itself, if it does not have works, is dead.

18 But someone will say, "You have faith, and I have works." Show me your faith without your works, and I will show you my faith by my works. 19 You believe that there is one God. You do well. Even the demons believe—and tremble! 20 But do you want to know, O foolish man, that faith without works is dead? 21 Was not Abraham our father justified by works when he offered Isaac his son on the altar? 22 Do you see that faith was working together with his works, and by works faith was made perfect? 23 And the Scripture was fulfilled which says, "Abraham believed God, and it was accounted to him for righteousness." And he was called the friend of God. 24 You see then that a man is justified by works, and not by faith only.

25 Likewise, was not Rahab the harlot also justified by works when she

and bitter from the same opening?
¹² Can a fig tree, my brethren, bear
olives, or a grapevine bear figs? Thus
no spring yields both salt water and
fresh.

¹³ Who *is* wise and understanding
among you? Let him show by good
conduct *that* his works *are done* in the
meekness of wisdom. ¹⁴ But if you

have bitter envy and self-seeking in
your hearts, do not boast and lie
against the truth. ¹⁵ This wisdom does
not descend from above, but *is* earthly,
sensual, demonic. ¹⁶ For where envy
and self-seeking *exist,* confusion and
every evil thing *are* there. ¹⁷ But the
wisdom that is from above is first pure,
then peaceable, gentle, willing to yield,

⛏ DIGGING IN

3:5 Your Tongue Can Start a Fire
You've probably never thought about that.
Fires are started with matches, not
tongues! Just the same, God says the
tongue starts its own kind of fire.

When you say mean things about
someone, you're starting a fire. Just like
a fire, your ugly story can travel all
around. Pretty soon no one is speaking
to the one you hurt with the fiery words
of your tongue.

People have lost their jobs, and others
have taken their own lives, all because
of mean stories someone told about
them.

A story doesn't have to be a lie to hurt
someone. You may hear something true
that can do a lot of harm. Make up your
mind not to tell anyone else. And ask the
person who told you to stop talking about
it. Stop the fire from spreading.

3:17 Learn the Wisdom of God True
wisdom comes from God:

(1) The wisdom of God is pure. It isn't
mixed with selfishness. It seeks the good
of others.

(2) The wisdom of God is peaceable.
It doesn't quarrel. It is willing to be insulted
but doesn't insult others.

(3) The wisdom of God is gentle. It isn't
noisy or forceful. It listens to others and
speaks at the right time.

(4) The wisdom of God is merciful. It
doesn't pass by people in need. It reaches
out to help wherever it can.

(5) The wisdom of God treats everyone
fairly. It doesn't play favorites. It cares
about all kinds of people, rich or poor, of
all races.

(6) The wisdom of God is sincere. It
doesn't pretend to be something it is not.
It loves the truth.

Talking too much is dangerous.

full of mercy and good fruits, without partiality and without hypocrisy. ¹⁸ Now the fruit of righteousness is sown in peace by those who make peace.

God has plans for you

4 Where do wars and fights *come* from among you? Do *they* not *come* from your *desires for* pleasure that war in your members? ² You lust and do not have. You murder and covet and cannot obtain. You fight and war. Yet you do not have because you do not ask. ³ You ask and do not receive, because you ask amiss, that you may spend *it* on your pleasures. ⁴ Adulterers and adulteresses! Do you not know that friendship with the world is enmity with God? Whoever therefore wants to be a friend of the world makes himself an enemy of God. ⁵ Or do you think that the Scripture says in vain, "The Spirit who dwells in us yearns jealously"?

⁶ But He gives more grace. Therefore He says:

"God resists the proud,
But gives grace to the humble."

⁷ Therefore submit to God. Resist the devil and he will flee from you. ⁸ Draw near to God and He will draw near to you. Cleanse your hands, you sinners; and purify your hearts, you double-minded. ⁹ Lament and mourn and weep! Let your laughter be turned

What Is Pride?

Some people are proud of being clever. Others are proud of their good looks. God gives a gift to everybody. If we have a gift that someone else doesn't have, we aren't better than they are. Instead, we should be thankful for all gifts.

to mourning and *your* joy to gloom. ¹⁰ Humble yourselves in the sight of the Lord, and He will lift you up.

¹¹ Do not speak evil of one another, brethren. He who speaks evil of a brother and judges his brother, speaks evil of the law and judges the law. But if you judge the law, you are not a doer of the law but a judge. ¹² There is one Lawgiver, who is able to save and to destroy. Who are you to judge another?

¹³ Come now, you who say, "Today or tomorrow we will go to such and such a city, spend a year there, buy and sell, and make a profit"; ¹⁴ whereas you do not know what *will happen* tomorrow. For what *is* your life? It is even a vapor that appears for a little time and then vanishes away. ¹⁵ Instead you *ought* to say, "If the Lord wills, we shall live and do this or that." ¹⁶ But now you boast in your arrogance. All such boasting is evil.

¹⁷ Therefore, to him who knows to do good and does not do *it*, to him it is sin.

DIGGING IN

4:7 Submit to God, Resist the Devil
It's a mistake to think you can ever really be your own boss. Right now you have to obey your parents or your teachers. Someday you might like to be free so you can do what you want to do in the world. But that day will never really come. Even grown-ups have to obey someone else where they work.

You can choose who your great Master is going to be. And you will be very wise

if you decide right now that God is going to run your life. When you decide to do that, then you won't be all upset because you have to obey other people, too.

Making God your Master will also mean that the Devil can't run your life anymore. The Devil can have his way with you as long as God isn't in your life. But when you put Jesus first, the Devil can't lead you into trouble.

Be patient and pray

5 Come now, *you* rich, weep and howl for your miseries that are coming upon *you!* ² Your riches are corrupted, and your garments are moth-eaten. ³ Your gold and silver are corroded, and their corrosion will be a witness against you and will eat your flesh like fire. You have heaped up treasure in the last days. ⁴ Indeed the wages of the laborers who mowed your fields, which you kept back by fraud, cry out; and the cries of the reapers have reached the ears of the Lord of Sabaoth. ⁵ You have lived on the earth in pleasure and luxury; you have fattened your hearts as in a day of slaughter. ⁶ You have condemned, you have murdered the just; he does not resist you.

⁷ Therefore be patient, brethren, until the coming of the Lord. See *how* the farmer waits for the precious fruit of the earth, waiting patiently for it until it receives the early and latter rain. ⁸ You also be patient. Establish your hearts, for the coming of the Lord is at hand.

⁹ Do not grumble against one another, brethren, lest you be condemned. Behold, the Judge is standing at the door! ¹⁰ My brethren, take the prophets, who spoke in the name of the Lord, as an example of suffering and patience. ¹¹ Indeed we count them blessed who endure. You have heard of the perseverance of Job and seen the end *intended by* the Lord—that the Lord is very compassionate and merciful.

¹² But above all, my brethren, do not swear, either by heaven or by earth or with any other oath. But let your "Yes" be "Yes," and *your* "No," "No," lest you fall into judgment.

¹³ Is anyone among you suffering? Let him pray. Is anyone cheerful? Let him sing psalms. ¹⁴ Is anyone among you sick? Let him call for the elders of the church, and let them pray over him, anointing him with oil in the name of the Lord. ¹⁵ And the prayer of faith will save the sick, and the Lord will raise him up. And if he has committed sins, he will be forgiven. ¹⁶ Confess *your* trespasses to one another, and pray for one another, that you may be healed. The effective, fervent prayer of a righteous man avails much. ¹⁷ Elijah was a man with a nature like ours, and he prayed earnestly that it would not rain; and it did not rain on the land for three years and six months. ¹⁸ And he prayed again, and the heaven gave rain, and the earth produced its fruit.

¹⁹ Brethren, if anyone among you wanders from the truth, and someone turns him back, ²⁰ let him know that he who turns a sinner from the error of his way will save a soul from death and cover a multitude of sins.

DIGGING IN

5:15 God Heals the Sick In the Books of Matthew, Mark, Luke, and John, you can read how Jesus had power over sickness and death. He proved He was Lord of both the body and the soul.

But none of the people Jesus healed lived forever. They all finally died from some kind of disease, violence, or old age. Yet Jesus had to show them that He really was Lord over their bodies. When they died, they knew He would give them a new life and a new body like His that could never be sick or destroyed again.

There are also people today who can tell you that Jesus has healed their bodies of some disease. But even now, though Jesus doesn't heal everyone, He does heal some people as a sign that He is Lord over the body.

Someday you may be there when a Christian dies. Then you will know that death is not your greatest enemy. Christians *don't really die.* They just go to be with Jesus. "Whoever lives and believes in Me shall never die" (John 11:26).

The Book of
1 PETER

Peter—I used to think I loved Jesus so much that I would do anything for Him. I even told Him I would die for Him.

Imagine my shock when the Lord Jesus told me I would be the very one to deny I ever knew Him! That seemed impossible for me.

Then they came and arrested our Master. I was crushed. How could He let them do that to Him? It seemed to me that He had failed as our Messiah, the One God would send to save us, so I was very disappointed. Then I denied that I knew Him. At that very moment, Jesus turned and looked in my eyes, and I remembered His warning (Luke 22:59–61). I cried because I had failed Him.

Then they crucified my Jesus, and all seemed lost.

But one morning Jesus met us again by the seashore and made breakfast for us. Then He forgave my sins. Jesus was alive again!

The prophets told about Christ's coming

PETER, an apostle of Jesus Christ,

To the pilgrims of the **Dispersion** in Pontus, Galatia, Cappadocia, Asia, and Bithynia, 2 elect according to the foreknowledge of God the Father, in sanctification of the Spirit, for obedience and sprinkling of the blood of Jesus Christ:

Grace to you and peace be multiplied.

3 Blessed be the God and Father of our Lord Jesus Christ, who according to His abundant mercy has begotten us again to a living hope through the resurrection of Jesus Christ from the dead, 4 to an inheritance incorruptible and undefiled and that does not fade away, reserved in heaven for you, 5 who are kept by the power of God through faith for salvation ready to be revealed in the last time.

6 In this you greatly rejoice, though now for a little while, if need be, you have been grieved by various trials, 7 that the genuineness of your faith, being much more precious than gold that perishes, though it is tested by fire, may be found to praise, honor, and glory at the revelation of Jesus Christ, 8 whom having not seen you love. Though now you do not see *Him*, yet believing, you rejoice with joy inexpressible and full of glory, 9 receiving the end of your faith—the salvation of *your* souls.

10 Of this salvation the prophets have inquired and searched carefully, who prophesied of the grace *that would come* to you, 11 searching what, or what manner of time, the Spirit of Christ who was in them was indicating when He testified beforehand the sufferings of Christ and the glories that would follow. 12 To them it was revealed that, not to themselves, but to us they were ministering the things

---

WORDFINDER

1:1 Dispersion Pronounced dis-PUR-zhun. The Jews who were scattered throughout the world of Peter's time. They were scattered mainly because of the invasion of foreign nations throughout Jewish history.

which now have been reported to you through those who have preached the **gospel** to you by the Holy Spirit sent from heaven—things which angels desire to look into.

13 Therefore gird up the loins of your mind, be sober, and rest *your* hope fully upon the grace that is to be brought to you at the revelation of Jesus Christ; 14 as obedient children, not conforming yourselves to the former lusts, *as* in your ignorance; 15 but as He who **called** you *is* holy, you also be holy in all *your* conduct, 16 because it is written, "Be holy, for I am holy."

17 And if you call on the Father, who without partiality judges according to each one's work, conduct yourselves throughout the time of your stay *here* in fear; 18 knowing that you were not redeemed with corruptible things, *like* silver or gold, from your aimless conduct *received* by tradition from your fathers, 19 but with the precious blood of Christ, as of a lamb without blemish and without spot. 20 He indeed was foreordained before the foundation of the world, but was manifest in these last times for you 21 who through Him believe in God, who raised Him from the dead and gave Him glory, so that your faith and hope are in God.

22 Since you have purified your souls in obeying the truth through the Spirit in sincere love of the brethren, love one another fervently with a pure heart, 23 having been **born again,** not of corruptible seed but incorruptible, through the word of God which lives and abides forever, 24 because

WORDFINDER

1:12 Gospel Means "good news." The word is taken from the early English word *godspel.* In the New Testament, it is the Good News about Jesus Christ.

1:15 Called The way God draws people to Himself. He *calls* them when they hear the gospel. By calling people, God gives them the desire to come to Him.

1:23 Born Again When God changes a person to become a Christian. The change is so great that Jesus said it is like being born all over again.

DIGGING IN

1:7 The Emperor Nero, Enemy of Christ In this letter Peter speaks of the persecution of Christians during the reign of Emperor Nero. Nero ruled Rome during the years A.D. 54–68. In the early years of his reign, Nero brought reform and prosperity to the Roman Empire. Later, he became corrupt and cruel. He murdered his own mother and his first wife.

In the year A.D. 64, a great fire broke out in Rome. Some writers of history say that Nero himself started the fire. He blamed the Christians instead and killed many of them. He even used some of the Christians as human torches to entertain his guests at an outdoor party. Both Paul and Peter were put to death during the time of Nero. It was also during Nero's reign that the Jews revolted against Rome.

Nero committed suicide after the Roman senate sentenced him to death.

The Roman Emperor Nero was a cruel enemy of early Christians.

Can You Live Forever?

When someone you love dies, it makes you sad. The death of that loved one reminds you that all life in this world comes to an end. This should cause you to think about God. God is the Author of life, and He wants you to live forever with Him. He gives eternal life to those who ask Him.

"All flesh is as grass,
And all the glory of man as the
flower of the grass.
The grass withers,
And its flower falls away,
25 But the word of the LORD
endures forever."

Now this is the word which by the gospel was preached to you.

Our real home is in heaven

2 Therefore, laying aside all malice, all deceit, hypocrisy, envy, and all evil speaking, ² as newborn babes, desire the pure milk of the word, that you may grow thereby, ³ if indeed you have tasted that the Lord is gracious.

⁴ Coming to Him as to a living stone, rejected indeed by men, but chosen by God and precious, ⁵ you also, as living stones, are being built up a spiritual house, a holy priesthood, to offer up spiritual sacrifices acceptable to God through Jesus Christ. ⁶ Therefore it is also contained in the Scripture,

"Behold, I lay in Zion
A chief cornerstone, elect,
precious,
And he who believes on Him will
by no means be put to
shame."

⁷ Therefore, to you who believe, He is precious; but to those who are disobedient,

"The stone which the builders
rejected
Has become the chief
cornerstone,"

⚒ DIGGING IN

1:25 God's Word Lasts Forever Everywhere you look, you can see a world that has lasted a very long time, but it won't last forever. Jesus said that the heavens and the earth would pass away, but His words would never pass away (see Matthew 24:35).

What does God mean when He says His Word will last forever? He means that everything He ever promised will happen just as He said. He promised Abraham that his descendants would possess their land forever. So, in the new world that God has promised, the people of Israel will have their own land.

One day God is going to judge the world. People who believe His Word and accept Jesus as Savior and Lord will live with God forever. But people who refuse to accept God's free offer of salvation will be separated from God. Then there will be everlasting crying and sorrow. That's what Jesus called hell (see Matthew 10:28.)

2:5 God Needs You to Be a Living Rock Buildings are often made of rocks or stones, and those buildings last a long time. But God is also building a big house in heaven that can never be destroyed. It's made of living stones. Those living stones are people like you. God calls that building His "church." So churches aren't really made of wood or stone. Yes, the building is made of such materials, but the real church is the people. God will dwell in the living building of His people forever.

Every living stone in God's building fits in a special place with all the other stones. That means you have a special place in God's building, the church. He has a special work in the church that only you can do, and that work will last FOREVER!

There are lots of stones in the world, but they are of no use until they become part of a building. You're useful to God when you become part of His building, the church of Jesus Christ.

8 and

"A stone of stumbling
And a rock of offense."

They stumble, being disobedient to the word, to which they also were appointed.

9 But you *are* a chosen generation, a royal priesthood, a holy nation, His own special people, that you may proclaim the praises of Him who called you out of darkness into His marvelous light; 10 who once *were* not a people but *are* now the people of God, who had not obtained mercy but now have obtained mercy.

11 Beloved, I beg *you* as sojourners and pilgrims, abstain from fleshly lusts which war against the soul, 12 having your conduct honorable among the Gentiles, that when they speak against you as evildoers, they may, by *your* good works which they observe, glorify God in the day of visitation.

13 Therefore submit yourselves to every ordinance of man for the Lord's sake, whether to the king as supreme, 14 or to governors, as to those who are sent by him for the punishment of evildoers and *for the* praise of those who do good. 15 For this is the will of God, that by doing good you may put to silence the ignorance of foolish men— 16 as *free*, yet not using liberty as a cloak for vice, but as bondservants of God. 17 Honor all *people*. Love the brotherhood. Fear God. Honor the king.

18 Servants, *be* submissive to *your* masters with all fear, not only to the good and gentle, but also to the harsh. 19 For this *is* commendable, if because of conscience toward God one endures grief, suffering wrongfully. 20 For what credit *is it* if, when you are beaten for your faults, you take it patiently? But when you do good and suffer, if you take it patiently, this *is* commendable before God. 21 For to this you were called, because Christ also suffered for us, leaving us an example, that you should follow His steps:

22 "Who committed no sin,
Nor was deceit found in His mouth";

23 who, when He was reviled, did not revile in return; when He suffered, He did not threaten, but committed *Himself* to Him who judges righteously; 24 who Himself bore our sins in His own body on the tree, that we, having died to sins, might live for righteousness—by whose stripes you were healed. 25 For you were like sheep going astray, but have now returned to the Shepherd and Overseer of your souls.

Wise words for husbands and wives

3 Wives, likewise, *be* submissive to your own husbands, that even if some do not obey the word, they, without a word, may be won by the conduct of their wives, 2 when they observe your chaste conduct *accompanied* by fear. 3 Do not let your adornment be *merely* outward—arranging the hair, wearing gold, or putting on *fine* apparel— 4 rather *let it be* the hidden person of the heart, with the incorruptible *beauty* of a gentle and quiet spirit, which is very precious in the sight of God. 5 For in this manner, in former times, the holy women who trusted in God also adorned themselves, being submissive to their own husbands, 6 as Sarah obeyed Abraham, calling him lord, whose daughters you are if you do good and are not afraid with any terror.

7 Husbands, likewise, dwell with *them* with understanding, giving honor to the wife, as to the weaker vessel, and as *being* heirs together of the grace of life, that your prayers may not be hindered.

8 Finally, all *of you be* of one mind, having compassion for one another; love as brothers, *be* tenderhearted, *be* courteous; 9 not returning evil for evil or reviling for reviling, but on the contrary blessing, knowing that you were

called to this, that you may inherit a blessing. ¹⁰ For

> "He who would love life
> And see good days,
> Let him refrain his tongue from evil,
> And his lips from speaking deceit.
> ¹¹ Let him turn away from evil and do good;
> Let him seek peace and pursue it.
> ¹² For the eyes of the LORD *are* on the righteous,
> And His ears *are open* to their prayers;
> But the face of the LORD *is* against those who do evil."

¹³ And who *is* he who will harm you if you become followers of what is good? ¹⁴ But even if you should suffer for righteousness' sake, *you are* blessed. "And do not be afraid of their threats, nor be troubled." ¹⁵ But sanctify the Lord God in your hearts, and always *be* ready to *give* a defense to everyone who asks you a reason for the hope that is in you, with meekness and fear; ¹⁶ having a good conscience, that when they defame you as evildoers, those who revile your good conduct in Christ may be ashamed. ¹⁷ For *it is* better, if it is the will of God, to suffer for doing good than for doing evil.

¹⁸ For **Christ** also suffered once for sins, the just for the unjust, that He might bring us to God, being put to death in the flesh but made alive by the Spirit, ¹⁹ by whom also He went and preached to the spirits in prison, ²⁰ who formerly were disobedient, when once the Divine longsuffering waited in the days of Noah, while the ark was being prepared, in which a few, that is, eight souls, were saved through water. ²¹ There is also an antitype which now saves us—baptism (not the removal of the filth of the flesh, but the answer of a good conscience toward God), through the **resurrection** of Jesus Christ, ²² who has gone into heaven and is at the right hand of God, angels and authorities and powers having been made subject to Him.

Christ is our Partner

4 Therefore, since Christ suffered for us in the flesh, arm yourselves also with the same mind, for he who has suffered in the flesh has ceased from sin, ² that he no longer should live the rest of *his* time in the flesh for the lusts of men, but for the will of God. ³ For we *have spent* enough of our past lifetime in doing the will of the Gentiles—when we walked in lewdness, lusts, drunkenness, revelries, drinking parties, and abominable idolatries. ⁴ In regard to these, they think it strange that you do not run with *them* in the same flood of dissipation, speaking evil of *you*. ⁵ They will give an account to Him who is ready to judge the living and the dead. ⁶ For this reason the gospel was preached also to those who are dead, that they might be judged according to men in the flesh, but live according to God in the spirit.

⁷ But the end of all things is at hand; therefore be serious and watchful in your prayers. ⁸ And above all things have fervent love for one another, for "love will cover a multitude of sins." ⁹ *Be* hospitable to one another without grumbling. ¹⁰ As each one has received a gift, minister it to one another, as good stewards of the manifold grace of God. ¹¹ If anyone speaks, *let him*

WORDFINDER

3:18 Christ The divine title of the Man Jesus. The word means "the Anointed" (by the Holy Spirit). *Christos* is a Greek word translated from the Hebrew *Messiah*.

3:21 Resurrection Pronounced *rez-er-RECK-shun*. The rising of Jesus from death. Jesus has promised that those who trust Him will also be raised up as He was.

What Peter's Readers Learned

When we believed the Good News about Jesus, we thought life would be a lot easier. In one way we were happier because we had the Spirit of Jesus with us always.

But we were upset because so many of our earlier friends wouldn't speak to us anymore. Also, the government made life hard for us. Some of us lost our jobs, our homes, and even our lives—just because we were Christians and we wouldn't worship the emperor. They said we didn't love our country.

We still do love our country and obey its laws, but we can't worship a man. So Peter explained to us that Christians should expect to suffer sometimes. Why should we be treated any better than Jesus was?

---

speak as the oracles of God. If anyone ministers, *let him do it* as with the ability which God supplies, that in all things God may be glorified through Jesus Christ, to whom belong the glory and the dominion forever and ever. Amen.

12 Beloved, do not think it strange concerning the fiery trial which is to try you, as though some strange thing happened to you; 13 but rejoice to the extent that you partake of Christ's sufferings, that when His glory is revealed, you may also be glad with exceeding joy. 14 If you are reproached for the name of Christ, blessed *are you,* for the Spirit of glory and of God rests upon you. On their part He is blasphemed, but on your part He is glorified. 15 But let none of you suffer as a murderer, a thief, an evildoer, or as a **busybody** in other people's matters. 16 Yet if *anyone suffers* as a **Christian,** let him not be ashamed, but let him glorify God in this matter.

17 For the time *has come* for judgment to begin at the house of God; and if *it begins* with us first, what will *be* the end of those who do not obey the gospel of God? 18 Now

"If the righteous one is scarcely saved,
Where will the ungodly and the sinner appear?"

19 Therefore let those who suffer according to the will of God commit their souls *to Him* in doing good, as to a faithful Creator.

Don't worry about anything

5 The elders who are among you I exhort, I who am a fellow elder and a witness of the sufferings of Christ, and also a partaker of the glory that will be revealed: 2 Shepherd the flock of God which is among you, serving as overseers, not by compulsion but willingly, not for dishonest gain but eagerly; 3 nor as being lords over those entrusted to you, but being examples to the flock; 4 and when the Chief Shepherd appears, you will receive the crown of glory that does not fade away.

5 Likewise you younger people, submit yourselves to *your* elders. Yes, all of *you* be submissive to one another, and be clothed with humility, for

WORDFINDER

4:15 Busybody People who mind other people's business. Paul said that some Christians were not doing their own work but were meddling in other people's affairs.

4:16 Christian A person who believes in and follows Jesus Christ. People were first called Christians after Jesus rose from death (see 11:26).

"God resists the proud,
But gives grace to the humble."

6 Therefore humble yourselves under the mighty hand of God, that He may exalt you in due time, 7 casting all your care upon Him, for He cares for you.

8 Be sober, be vigilant; because your adversary the devil walks about like a roaring lion, seeking whom he may devour. 9 Resist him, steadfast in the faith, knowing that the same sufferings are experienced by your brotherhood in the world. 10 But may the God of all grace, who called us to His eternal glory by Christ Jesus, after you have suffered a while, perfect, establish, strengthen, and settle you. 11 To Him be the glory and the dominion forever and ever. Amen.

12 By Silvanus, our faithful brother as I consider him, I have written to you briefly, exhorting and testifying that this is the true grace of God in which you stand.

13 She who is in Babylon, elect together with you, greets you; and so does Mark my son. 14 Greet one another with a kiss of love.

Peace to you all who are in Christ Jesus. Amen.

⚒ DIGGING IN

5:5 Why Should You Obey Your Elders? Not all boys and girls have two living parents. If you do, you're very lucky. Many young people have only one parent, and some have none at all. But God has placed someone in charge of your life. You will be wise to obey your parents or the elders you live with.

First of all, your elders have to answer to God for how you grow up in the world. Don't make your folks ashamed of you.

Remember, too, your elders know a lot more about getting along in the world than you do. They've been in the world longer. So doesn't it make sense to listen to what they say?

Sometimes you'll think you know better than your parents or teachers. You won't always feel like obeying them. But someday you'll be glad you did. A lot of young people get into serious trouble because they just won't listen.

The Book of
2 PETER

Growing in Christian character

SIMON Peter, a bondservant and apostle of Jesus Christ,

To those who have obtained like precious faith with us by the righteousness of our God and Savior Jesus Christ:

2 Grace and peace be multiplied to you in the knowledge of God and of Jesus our Lord, 3 as His divine power has given to us all things that *pertain* to life and godliness, through the knowledge of Him who called us by glory and virtue, 4 by which have been given to us exceedingly great and precious promises, that through these you may be partakers of the divine nature, having escaped the corruption *that is* in the world through lust.

5 But also for this very reason, giving all diligence, add to your faith virtue, to virtue knowledge, 6 to knowledge self-control, to self-control perseverance, to perseverance godliness, 7 to godliness brotherly kindness, and to brotherly kindness love. 8 For if these things are yours and abound, *you will be* neither barren nor unfruitful in the knowledge of our Lord Jesus Christ. 9 For he who lacks these things is shortsighted, even to blindness, and has forgotten that he was cleansed from his old sins.

10 Therefore, brethren, be even more diligent to make your call and election sure, for if you do these things you will never stumble; 11 for so an entrance will be supplied to you abundantly into the everlasting kingdom of our Lord and Savior Jesus Christ.

12 For this reason I will not be negligent to remind you always of these things, though you know and are established in the present truth. 13 Yes, I think it is right, as long as I am in this tent, to stir you up by reminding *you,* 14 knowing that shortly I *must* put off my tent, just as our Lord Jesus Christ showed me. 15 Moreover I will be careful to ensure that you always have a reminder of these things after my decease.

16 For we did not follow cunningly

What Peter Learned

When Jesus was still living and teaching among us, I denied that I knew Him. You can read about this in Matthew 26 and Mark 14.

I had to learn a very bitter lesson. For a while I really thought I had failed so badly that Jesus would never forgive me. The marvel is that He did forgive me after all. See John 21.

I learned that I must be careful never to act that way again. Next time I might keep right on denying my Savior. Then I would forget that I owed Him my life.

I will always remember what I did, and I want you to learn from my bitter experience. Be thankful Jesus called you to be His own, and pray that you will never deny Him.

1:1 Apostle Pronounced *uh-POSS-ul.* One of the men Jesus sent to preach the Good News of salvation. The word comes from a Greek word meaning "sent."

devised fables when we made known to you the power and coming of our Lord Jesus Christ, but were eye-witnesses of His majesty. ¹⁷For He received from God the Father honor and glory when such a voice came to Him from the Excellent Glory: "This is My beloved Son, in whom I am well pleased." ¹⁸And we heard this voice which came from heaven when we were with Him on the holy mountain.

¹⁹And so we have the prophetic word confirmed, which you do well to heed as a light that shines in a dark place, until the day dawns and the morning star rises in your hearts; ²⁰knowing this first, that no prophecy of Scripture is of any private interpretation, ²¹for prophecy never came by the will of man, but holy men of God spoke *as they were* moved by the Holy Spirit.

False teachers are wells without water

2 But there were also false prophets among the people, even as there will be false teachers among you, who will secretly bring in destructive heresies, even denying the Lord who bought them, *and* bring on themselves swift destruction. ²And many will follow their destructive ways, because of whom the way of truth will be blasphemed. ³By covetousness they will exploit you with deceptive words; for a long time their judgment has not been idle, and their destruction does not slumber.

⁴For if God did not spare the angels who sinned, but cast *them* down to hell and delivered *them* into chains of darkness, to be reserved for judgment; ⁵and did not spare the ancient world, but saved Noah, *one of* eight *people,* a preacher of righteousness, bringing in the flood on the world of the ungodly; ⁶and turning the cities of Sodom and Gomorrah into ashes, condemned *them* to destruction, making *them* an example to those who afterward would live ungodly; ⁷and delivered righteous Lot, *who was* oppressed by the filthy conduct of the wicked ⁸(for that righteous man, dwelling among them, tormented *his* righteous soul from day to day by seeing and hearing *their* lawless deeds)— ⁹*then* the Lord knows how to deliver the godly out of temptations and to reserve the unjust under punishment for the day of judgment, ¹⁰and especially those who walk according to the flesh in the lust of uncleanness and despise authority. *They are* presumptuous, self-willed. They are not afraid to speak evil of dignitaries, ¹¹whereas angels, who are greater in power and might, do not bring a reviling accusation against them before the Lord.

¹²But these, like natural brute beasts made to be caught and destroyed, speak evil of the things they do not understand, and will utterly perish in their own corruption, ¹³*and* will receive the wages of unrighteousness, *as* those who count it pleasure to carouse in the daytime. *They are* spots and blemishes, carousing in their own de-

---

 DIGGING IN

1:19 A Light Shines in the Darkness It's dangerous to be in a strange and dark place without a light to show you the way. That's why a car needs headlights. And the greatest friend of a ship at sea may be a lighthouse along the shore. The lighthouse tells the sailors there are rocks nearby that could destroy the ship's hull.

Peter is also talking about a lighthouse that shines in a dark world. That light-

house is the Bible. Light brings knowledge. The Bible is a lighthouse that lights your way in a dark, dangerous, and often evil world.

Remember that Jesus said, "I am the light of the world" (John 8:12). He also said, "I am the truth" (John 14:6). There can be no ignorance where the light of truth is shining.

ceptions while they feast with you,
¹⁴ having eyes full of adultery and that
cannot cease from sin, enticing unsta-
ble souls. *They have* a heart trained
in covetous practices, *and are* accursed
children. ¹⁵ They have forsaken the
right way and gone astray, following
the way of Balaam the *son* of Beor,
who loved the wages of unrighteousness; ¹⁶ but he was rebuked for
his iniquity: a dumb donkey speaking
with a man's voice restrained the madness of the prophet.

¹⁷ These are wells without water,
clouds carried by a tempest, for whom
is reserved the blackness of darkness
forever.

¹⁸ For when they speak great swell-
ing *words* of emptiness, they allure
through the lusts of the flesh, through
lewdness, the ones who have actually
escaped from those who live in error.
¹⁹ While they promise them liberty,
they themselves are slaves of corruption; for by whom a person is overcome, by him also he is brought into
bondage. ²⁰ For if, after they have escaped the pollutions of the world
through the knowledge of the Lord
and Savior Jesus Christ, they are again
entangled in them and overcome, the
latter end is worse for them than the
beginning. ²¹ For it would have been
better for them not to have known the
way of righteousness, than having
known *it,* to turn from the holy commandment delivered to them. ²² But
it has happened to them according to
the true proverb: "A dog returns to

his own vomit," and, "a sow, having
washed, to her wallowing in the
mire."

There is hope for growing Christians

3 Beloved, I now write to you this
second epistle (in *both of* which I stir
up your pure minds by way of re-
minder), ² that you may be mindful of
the words which were spoken before
by the holy prophets, and of the commandment of us, the apostles of the
Lord and Savior, ³ knowing this first:
that scoffers will come in the last days,
walking according to their own lusts,
⁴ and saying, "Where is the promise
of His coming? For since the fathers
fell asleep, all things continue as *they
were* from the beginning of creation."
⁵ For this they willfully forget: that by
the word of God the heavens were of
old, and the earth standing out of water
and in the water, ⁶ by which the world
that then existed perished, being
flooded with water. ⁷ But the heavens
and the earth *which* are now preserved
by the same word, are reserved for fire
until the day of judgment and perdition
of ungodly men.

⁸ But, beloved, do not forget this one
thing, that with the Lord one day *is*
as a thousand years, and a thousand
years as one day. ⁹ The Lord is not
slack concerning *His* promise, as some
count slackness, but is longsuffering toward us, not willing that any should

Peter—I hear a lot of people asking, "Is the Lord really coming back?"
The Lord Jesus promised He would return, and some people think He
should have come back by now.

So I want to remind you that God has lots of time. You and I only
have a few years to do our work, but God has *forever!*

If you were the Lord, you wouldn't hurry about coming back, either.
There are many who haven't heard the Good News about Jesus yet.
Maybe He wants you to tell people on the other side of the world about
Him as well as the ones in your own neighborhood.

Jesus did say He will come quickly. Many things in this world don't
last. Will you spend your life doing something for Jesus that will last forever?

perish but that all should come to **repentance.**

10 But the day of the Lord will come as a thief in the night, in which the heavens will pass away with a great noise, and the elements will melt with fervent heat; both the earth and the works that are in it will be burned up. 11 Therefore, since all these things will be dissolved, what manner *of persons* ought you to be in holy conduct and godliness, 12 looking for and hastening the coming of the day of God, because of which the heavens will be dissolved, being on fire, and the elements will melt with fervent heat? 13 Nevertheless we, according to His promise, look for new heavens and a new earth in which righteousness dwells.

14 Therefore, beloved, looking forward to these things, be diligent to be found by Him in peace, without spot and blameless; 15 and consider *that* the longsuffering of our Lord *is* salvation— as also our beloved brother Paul, according to the wisdom given to him, has written to you, 16 as also in all his epistles, speaking in them of these things, in which are some things hard to understand, which untaught and unstable *people* twist to their own destruction, as *they do* also the rest of the Scriptures.

17 You therefore, beloved, since you know *this* beforehand, beware lest you also fall from your own steadfastness, being led away with the error of the wicked; 18 but grow in the grace and knowledge of our Lord and Savior Jesus Christ.

To Him *be* the glory both now and forever. Amen.

 WORDFINDER

3:9 Repentance Pronounced *re-PEN-tunce.* Turning away from sin to obey God. You repent when you leave your sins to receive Christ as your Savior and Master of your life.

The Book of
1 JOHN

John—I saw and heard with my own eyes and ears what Jesus did and said.

When the Lord Jesus came from heaven to earth two thousand years ago, He came to show us what God is like. So He went about doing good—healing the sick, giving sight to the blind, and even bringing some dead people back to life. He also taught us that His Father wants us to love one another, just the way Jesus loved us.

I was also there when they nailed Jesus my Savior to a cross. But that wasn't the end of the story! Three days later He came back to life in a body that could never die again. How do I know this? I was there, and I even touched Him with my own hands! Then I saw Him go back to heaven.

I didn't just hear about what Jesus did. *I was there!*

God's light erases darkness

THAT which was from the beginning, which we have heard, which we have seen with our eyes, which we have looked upon, and our hands have handled, concerning the Word of life— 2 the life was manifested, and we have seen, and bear witness, and declare to you that eternal life which was with the Father and was manifested to us— 3 that which we have seen and heard we declare to you, that you also may have fellowship with us; and truly our fellowship is with the Father and with His Son Jesus Christ. 4 And these things we write to you that your joy may be full.

5 This is the message which we have heard from Him and declare to you, that God is light and in Him is no darkness at all. 6 If we say that we have fellowship with Him, and walk in darkness, we lie and do not practice the truth. 7 But if we walk in the light as He is in the light, we have fellowship with one another, and the blood of Jesus Christ His Son cleanses us from all sin.

8 If we say that we have no sin, we deceive ourselves, and the truth is not in us. 9 If we confess our sins, He is

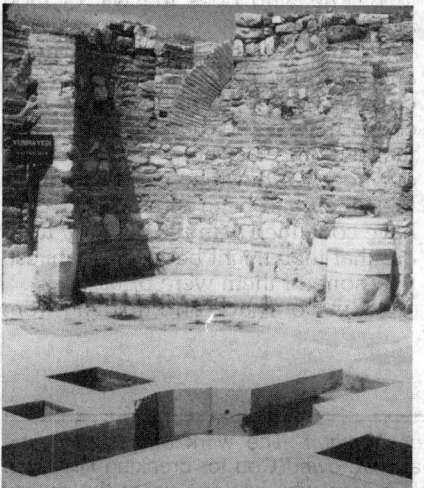

The place where John the apostle is buried.

Should Christians Confess Their Sins?

Sometimes Christians don't remember to confess their sins to God. When such forgetting becomes a habit, we may even forget that we are still sinners saved by God's kindness. When you remember that Jesus died for you, then you will hate the smallest sin that caused His death.

faithful and just to forgive us *our* sins and to cleanse us from all unrighteousness. ¹⁰ If we say that we have not sinned, we make Him a liar, and His word is not in us.

How well do you know Christ?

2 My little children, these things I write to you, so that you may not sin. And if anyone sins, we have an Advocate with the Father, Jesus Christ the righteous. ² And He Himself is the **propitiation** for our sins, and not for ours only but also for the whole world.

³ Now by this we know that we know Him, if we keep His commandments. ⁴ He who says, "I know Him," and does not keep His commandments, is a liar, and the truth is not in him. ⁵ But whoever keeps His word, truly the love of God is perfected in him. By this we know that we are in Him. ⁶ He who says he abides in Him ought himself also to walk just as He walked.

⁷ Brethren, I write no new commandment to you, but an old commandment which you have had from the beginning. The old commandment is the word which you heard from the beginning. ⁸ Again, a new commandment I write to you, which thing is true in Him and in you, because the darkness is passing away, and the true light is already shining.

⁹ He who says he is in the light, and hates his brother, is in darkness until now. ¹⁰ He who loves his brother abides in the light, and there is no cause for stumbling in him. ¹¹ But who hates his brother is in darkness and walks in darkness, and does not know where he is going, because the darkness has blinded his eyes.

¹² I write to you, little children,
Because your sins are forgiven
you for His name's sake.
¹³ I write to you, fathers,
Because you have known
Him *who is* from the
beginning.
I write to you, young men,
Because you have overcome
the wicked one.
I write to you, little children,
Because you have known the
Father.
¹⁴ I have written to you, fathers,
Because you have known
Him *who is* from the
beginning.
I have written to you, young
men,
Because you are strong, and
the word of God abides in
you,
And you have overcome the
wicked one.

¹⁵ Do not love the world or the things in the world. If anyone loves the world, the love of the Father is not in him. ¹⁶ For all that *is* in the world— the lust of the flesh, the lust of the eyes, and the pride of life—is not of the Father but is of the world. ¹⁷ And the world is passing away, and the lust of it; but he who does the will of God abides forever.

¹⁸ Little children, it is the last hour; and as you have heard that the **Antichrist** is coming, even now many antichrists have come, by which we know that it is the last hour. ¹⁹ They went out from us, but they were not of us; for if they had been of us, they would have continued with us; but *they went out* that they might be made manifest, that none of them were of us. ²⁰ But you have an anointing from

---

2:2 Propitiation Pronounced *pro-pish-ee-AY-shun*. The work of Jesus on the Cross. By dying for us, Jesus paid the penalty we owed God for breaking His laws.

2:18 Antichrist Pronounced *AN-tih-krist*. A man who will rise up at the end of this age to lead the forces of evil against Christ and His church in the world.

the Holy One, and you know all things. 21 I have not written to you because you do not know the truth, but because you know it, and that no lie is of the truth.

22 Who is a liar but he who denies that Jesus is the Christ? He is antichrist who denies the Father and the Son. 23 Whoever denies the Son does not have the Father either; he who acknowledges the Son has the Father also.

24 Therefore let that abide in you which you heard from the beginning. If what you heard from the beginning abides in you, you also will abide in the Son and in the Father. 25 And this is the promise that He has promised us—eternal life.

26 These things I have written to you concerning those who *try to* deceive you. 27 But the anointing which you have received from Him abides in you, and you do not need that anyone teach you; but as the same anointing teaches you concerning all things, and is true, and is not a lie, and just as it has taught you, you will abide in Him.

28 And now, little children, abide in Him, that when He appears, we may have confidence and not be ashamed before Him at His coming. 29 If you know that He is righteous, you know

that everyone who practices righteousness is born of Him.

We are His little children

3 Behold what manner of love the Father has bestowed on us, that we should be called children of God! Therefore the world does not know us, because it did not know Him. 2 Beloved, now we are children of God; and it has not yet been revealed what we shall be, but we know that when He is revealed, we shall be like Him, for we shall see Him as He is. 3 And everyone who has this hope in Him purifies himself, just as He is pure.

4 Whoever commits **sin** also commits lawlessness, and sin is lawlessness. 5 And you know that He was manifested to take away our sins, and in Him there is no sin. 6 Whoever abides in Him does not sin. Whoever sins has neither seen Him nor known Him.

7 Little children, let no one deceive you. He who practices righteousness is righteous, just as He is righteous. 8 He who sins is of the devil, for the devil has sinned from the beginning. For this purpose the Son of God was manifested, that He might destroy the works of the devil. 9 Whoever has been born of God does not sin, for His seed

WORDFINDER

3:4 Sin Disobedience of God's law or rebellion against His will. All people sin, but Christ died to take sin away.

DIGGING IN

2:17 You Can Live Forever One thing is certain, and John says it: "The world is passing away." As you look around you, it almost seems that the world could go on and on forever. Cars and planes zoom back and forth. Streets, stores, and offices are filled with busy people. The world's business speeds on. Everything keeps going faster and faster without ever stopping.

But one day it *will* all stop! People don't like to think about it, but they know the

world has to stop sometime. For one thing the world's energy supply is running out. Scientists say the planet will just die out someday.

Whatever happens, though, you can live forever. Ask Christ the Creator to fill you with His eternal life. Then you will be with Him always. He rose from death so you could live forever. Jesus said, "Because I live, you will live also" (John 14:19).

What Is the Message from the Beginning?

John tells us that the earliest message from Jesus is that we should love one another. Loving people also keep the Ten Commandments. Jesus knew that, and that is why He commanded us to love. To love means to help when people around us are in trouble. Love doesn't destroy. Love builds up.

remains in him; and he cannot sin, because he has been born of God.

10 In this the children of God and the children of the devil are manifest: Whoever does not practice righteousness is not of God, nor is he who does not love his brother. 11 For this is the message that you heard from the beginning, that we should love one another, 12 not as Cain who was of the wicked one and murdered his brother. And why did he murder him? Because his works were evil and his brother's righteous.

13 Do not marvel, my brethren, if the world hates you. 14 We know that we have passed from death to life, because we love the brethren. He who does not love his brother abides in death. 15 Whoever hates his brother is a murderer, and you know that no murderer has eternal life abiding in him.

16 By this we know love, because He laid down His life for us. And we also ought to lay down our lives for the brethren. 17 But whoever has this world's goods, and sees his brother in need, and shuts up his heart from him, how does the love of God abide in him?

18 My little children, let us not love in word or in tongue, but in deed and in truth. 19 And by this we know that we are of the truth, and shall assure our hearts before Him. 20 For if our heart condemns us, God is greater than our heart, and knows all things. 21 Beloved, if our heart does not condemn us, we have confidence toward God. 22 And whatever we ask we receive from Him, because we keep His commandments and do those things that are pleasing in His sight. 23 And this is His commandment: that we should **believe** on the name of His Son Jesus Christ and love one another, as He gave us commandment.

24 Now he who keeps His commandments abides in Him, and He in him. And by this we know that He abides in us, by the Spirit whom He has given us.

Loving God means we will love others, too

4 Beloved, do not believe every spirit, but test the spirits, whether they are of God; because many false prophets have gone out into the world. 2 By this you know the Spirit of God: Every spirit that confesses that Jesus Christ has come in the flesh is of God, 3 and every spirit that does not confess that Jesus Christ has come in the flesh is not of God. And this is the spirit of the Antichrist, which you have heard was coming, and is now already in the world.

4 You are of God, little children, and have overcome them, because He who is in you is greater than he who is in the world. 5 They are of the world. Therefore they speak as of the world, and the world hears them. 6 We are of God. He who knows God hears us; he who is not of God does not hear us. By this we know the spirit of truth and the spirit of error.

7 Beloved, let us love one another,

WORDFINDER

3:23 Believe To accept what God has said in the Bible and to trust Jesus to save you from your sins. To believe as a Christian is to receive Jesus Christ into your life.

for love is of God; and everyone who loves is born of God and knows God. **8** He who does not love does not know God, for God is love. **9** In this the love of God was manifested toward us, that God has sent His only begotten Son into the world, that we might live through Him. **10** In this is love, not that we loved God, but that He loved us and sent His Son *to be* the propitiation for our sins. **11** Beloved, if God so loved us, we also ought to love one another.

12 No one has seen God at any time. If we love one another, God abides in us, and His love has been perfected in us. **13** By this we know that we abide in Him, and He in us, because He has given us of His Spirit. **14** And we have seen and testify that the Father has sent the Son *as* **Savior** of the world. **15** Whoever confesses that Jesus is the Son of God, God abides in him, and he in God. **16** And we have known and believed the love that God has for us. God is love, and he who abides in love abides in God, and God in him.

17 Love has been perfected among us in this: that we may have boldness in the day of judgment; because as He is, so are we in this world. **18** There is no fear in love; but perfect love casts out fear, because fear involves torment. But he who fears has not been made perfect in love. **19** We love Him because He first loved us.

20 If someone says, "I love God," and hates his brother, he is a liar; for he who does not love his brother whom he has seen, how can he love God whom he has not seen? **21** And this commandment we have from Him: that he who loves God *must* love his brother also.

If we love God, we will obey Him

5 Whoever believes that Jesus is the Christ is born of God, and everyone who loves Him who begot also loves him who is begotten of Him. **2** By this we know that we love the children of God, when we love God and keep His commandments. **3** For this is the love of God, that we keep His commandments. And His commandments are not burdensome. **4** For whatever is born of God overcomes the world. And this is the victory that has overcome the world—our faith. **5** Who is he who overcomes the world, but he who believes that Jesus is the Son of God?

6 This is He who came by water and blood—Jesus Christ; not only by water, but by water and blood. And it is the Spirit who bears witness, because the Spirit is truth. **7** For there are three

WORDFINDER

4:14 Savior Someone who saves our lives. Jesus is our Savior from heaven who died on the Cross to save our souls from sin and hell.

DIGGING IN

4:2 Confessing Christ Is Important Just saying you believe in Jesus doesn't make you a Christian. You belong to Jesus when you *believe in your heart* that God raised Him from the dead (see Romans 10:9).

To believe "in your heart" means you believe *truly*. That's a lot different than just saying some nice words about Jesus. But when you truly believe in Jesus, it's important to tell others about Him, too. That's what we mean when we talk about "confessing Christ."

Are you ashamed to tell people whose son or daughter you are? Of course not! Right away you tell people, "I'm Mrs. Jones's daughter," or "I'm Mr. Smith's son." Be proud, also, to say, "I belong to Jesus. He died for my sins. I'd like Him to be your Savior, too." You tell others about Jesus because you want them to know the joy that Jesus gives to you.

that bear witness in heaven: the Father, the Word, and the Holy Spirit; and these three are one. 8 And there are three that bear witness on earth: the Spirit, the water, and the blood; and these three agree as one.

9 If we receive the witness of men, the witness of God is greater; for this is the witness of God which He has testified of His Son. 10 He who believes in the Son of God has the witness in himself; he who does not believe God has made Him a liar, because he has not believed the testimony that God has given of His Son. 11 And this is the testimony: that God has given us eternal life, and this life is in His Son. 12 He who has the Son has life; he who does not have the Son of God does not have life. 13 These things I have written to you who believe in the name of the Son of God, that you may know that you have eternal life, and that you may continue to believe in the name of the Son of God.

14 Now this is the confidence that we have in Him, that if we ask anything according to His will, He hears us.

15 And if we know that He hears us, whatever we ask, we know that we have the petitions that we have asked of Him.

16 If anyone sees his brother sinning a sin which does not lead to death, he will ask, and He will give him life for those who commit sin not leading to death. There is sin leading to death. I do not say that he should pray about that. 17 All unrighteousness is sin, and there is sin not leading to death.

18 We know that whoever is born of God does not sin; but he who has been born of God keeps himself, and the wicked one does not touch him.

19 We know that we are of God, and the whole world lies under the sway of the wicked one.

20 And we know that the Son of God has come and has given us an understanding, that we may know Him who is true; and we are in Him who is true, in His Son Jesus Christ. This is the true God and eternal life.

21 Little children, keep yourselves from idols. Amen.

WORDFINDER

5:13 Eternal Life   The endless life of God. God gives His eternal life to people who trust in Jesus as their Savior. God Himself comes to live in them.

DIGGING IN

5:12 Having Jesus Is Eternal Life
There's probably a big bank near where you live. Just imagine you have ten million dollars in that bank. If you live wisely, you'll probably never spend it all. You'll always have enough for all you need every day. You'll never have to work to earn your living because it's all in the bank.

That's what it's like to have Jesus. You never run out of eternal life with Jesus.

You can get back to Him every day, and He keeps giving you more and more life. When something bad happens to you, like getting sick, you go to Jesus. Then He gives you more eternal life, and you don't mind being sick anymore. When your bank is out of money, you can go to Jesus, and He gives you eternal life. Then you don't mind being poor. You have Jesus, and He is all you need now and forever. "He who has the Son has life."

The Book of
2 JOHN

The Chosen Lady—John wrote to me, a widow with children! Wasn't that just like the good man he was? No wonder people call him the "Beloved Apostle."

I'll never forget the day John came to our town. We were all a little afraid of him at first. After all, he was a Jew and we were Greeks. But he came to my door and simply said, "Lady, I'm bringing Good News for you and your little ones."

It wasn't so much what he said, but the compassion and love I saw in his eyes. Besides, I could see he was tired and hungry, and so I asked the poor man in to share what little food we had.

After supper, he told us the most wonderful story about Jesus the Savior. Now we have Jesus as our Friend forever.

Watch out for teachers who counterfeit Christianity

THE Elder,

To the elect lady and her children, whom I love in truth, and not only I, but also all those who have known the truth, 2 because of the truth which abides in us and will be with us forever:

3 Grace, mercy, *and* peace will be with you from God the Father and from the Lord Jesus Christ, the Son of the Father, in truth and love.

4 I rejoiced greatly that I have found *some* of your children walking in truth, as we received commandment from the Father. 5 And now I plead with you, lady, not as though I wrote a new commandment to you, but that which we have had from the beginning: that we love one another. 6 This is love, that we walk according to His commandments. This is the commandment, that as you have heard from the beginning, you should walk in it.

7 For many deceivers have gone out into the world who do not confess

---

Do You Walk in the Truth?

The truth isn't a street where you live, but you can still walk in the truth as you go through life. Jesus said that God's Word is the truth. When you let God's Word become part of you, then you will walk in that truth. Jesus also said, "I am the Truth."

⚒ DIGGING IN

6 The Old Commandment John isn't teaching anything new. He is only reminding us of what Jesus had said a long time before: "Love one another as I have loved you" (John 13:34).

Love is not that excitement you feel when you see a pretty girl or when you meet a nice boy. Real love like that happens when you meet someone you admire and want to care for all your life.

The love John is talking about also means caring for everyone in the same way Jesus did.

Love doesn't *just happen*. You have to *decide* you're going to love some people even when you don't feel like loving them. That means you're going to make the best things happen for as many people as you can. After a while that kind of love becomes a good habit of life.

Jesus Christ *as* coming in the flesh. This is a deceiver and an **antichrist.** [8] Look to yourselves, that we do not lose those things we worked for, but *that* we may receive a full reward.

[9] Whoever transgresses and does not abide in the doctrine of Christ does not have God. He who abides in the doctrine of Christ has both the Father and the Son. [10] If anyone comes to you and does not bring this doctrine, do not receive him into your house nor greet him; [11] for he who greets him shares in his evil deeds.

[12] Having many things to write to you, I did not wish *to do so* with paper and ink; but I hope to come to you and speak face to face, that our joy may be full.

[13] The children of your elect sister greet you. Amen.

WORDFINDER

7 Antichrist Pronounced *AN-tih-krist*. A man who will rise up at the end of this age to lead the forces of evil against Christ and His church in the world.

The Book of
3 JOHN

Gaius—My name is pronounced *GAY-us*. Some of my friends at the church told the apostle John some kind things about Demetrius (pronounced *dih-MEE-tree-us*) and me, so John wrote me this letter.

I was honored to receive such a letter from the Beloved Apostle. He did try to write to our church once before, but one of our leaders wouldn't let us read John's letter. You will hear more about that bad leader later.

I never performed any miracles, and everybody knows I'm not much of a preacher. But I do sincerely love the Lord Jesus, and I try to live as He taught.

God doesn't want me to be big in my own eyes. He does want me to obey Him in the everyday things He gives me to do. When I can be trusted in the little things, then someday He will give me greater things to do for Him.

Entertaining God's workers pleases Him

THE Elder,

To the beloved Gaius, whom I love in truth:

2 Beloved, I pray that you may prosper in all things and be in health, just as your soul prospers. 3 For I rejoiced greatly when brethren came and testified of the truth *that is* in you, just as you walk in the truth. 4 I have no greater joy than to hear that my children walk in truth.

5 Beloved, you do faithfully whatever you do for the brethren and for strangers, 6 who have borne witness of your love before the church. *If* you send them forward on their journey in a manner worthy of God, you will do well, 7 because they went forth for His name's sake, taking nothing from the Gentiles. 8 We therefore ought to receive such, that we may become fellow workers for the truth.

9 I wrote to the church, but Diotrephes, who loves to have the preeminence among them, does not receive us. 10 Therefore, if I come, I will call to mind his deeds which he does, prating against us with malicious words. And not content with that, he himself does not receive the brethren, and forbids those who wish to, putting *them* out of the church.

11 Beloved, do not imitate what is

⚒ DIGGING IN

9 The First Shall Be Last In many places in today's world, you will be first if you can scare somebody else into being second. Being "the greatest" is very important to many people. That leaves no room for everyone else.

If you want to get God's attention, you can't be trying to grab first place. God says, "Come and let Me put you in the place I have chosen for you. That's where you'll be happy." But if you're just trying

to be important all the time, you're going to be miserable. You won't win most of the time, but you will wear yourself out by trying.

The man in John's story, Diotrephes (pronounced *die-OT-rah-fees*), wanted to be first, so he ended up being last. But Demetrius (pronounced *dih-MEE-tree-us*) was a good friend to everyone, so he ended up first.

evil, but what is good. He who does good is of God, but he who does evil has not seen God.

12 Demetrius has a *good* testimony from all, and from the truth itself. And we also bear witness, and you know that our testimony is true.

13 I had many things to write, but I do not wish to write to you with pen and ink; 14 but I hope to see you shortly, and we shall speak face to face.

Peace to you. Our friends greet you. Greet the friends by name.

The Book of
JUDE

My brother James and I don't like to call ourselves the brothers of the Lord. Yes, we were both younger sons of Mary and Joseph, but only Jesus was the Son of God.

My main reason for writing this letter is that some men are teaching lies to the people in our churches. Followers of Jesus need to know what these men are saying.

These false teachers deny that Jesus is the Lord from heaven, and they are not examples of how Christians should live. Such men are complainers and noisy talkers. You should learn to recognize such men as Satan's workers. You may remember that Satan told the first lie to Eve in the Garden of Eden.

Be sure to store up God's Word in your thoughts. Then you may even help false teachers to see their falsehoods.

God can keep us from falling

JUDE, a bondservant of Jesus Christ, and brother of James,

To those who are called, sanctified by God the Father, and preserved in Jesus Christ:

2 Mercy, peace, and love be multiplied to you.

3 Beloved, while I was very diligent to write to you concerning our common salvation, I found it necessary to write to you exhorting you to contend earnestly for the faith which was once for all delivered to the saints. 4 For certain men have crept in unnoticed, who long ago were marked out for this condemnation, ungodly men, who turn the grace of our God into lewdness and deny the only Lord God and our Lord Jesus Christ.

5 But I want to remind you, though you once knew this, that the Lord, having saved the people out of the land of Egypt, afterward destroyed those who did not believe. 6 And the angels who did not keep their proper domain, but left their own abode, He has reserved in everlasting chains under darkness for the judgment of the great day; 7 as Sodom and Gomorrah, and the cities around them in a similar manner to these, having given themselves over to sexual immorality and gone after strange flesh, are set forth as an example, suffering the vengeance of eternal fire.

8 Likewise also these dreamers defile the flesh, reject authority, and speak evil of dignitaries. 9 Yet Michael the archangel, in contending with the devil, when he disputed about the body of Moses, dared not bring against him a reviling accusation, but said, "The Lord rebuke you!" 10 But these speak evil of whatever they do not know; and whatever they know naturally, like brute beasts, in these things they corrupt themselves. 11 Woe to them! For they have gone in the way of Cain, have run greedily in the error of Balaam for profit, and perished in the rebellion of Korah.

12 These are spots in your love feasts, while they feast with you without fear, serving only themselves. They are clouds without water, carried about by the winds; late autumn trees without fruit, twice dead, pulled up by the roots; 13 raging waves of the sea,

foaming up their own shame; wandering stars for whom is reserved the blackness of darkness forever.

14 Now Enoch, the seventh from Adam, prophesied about these men also, saying, "Behold, the Lord comes with ten thousands of His saints, 15 to execute judgment on all, to convict all who are ungodly among them of all their ungodly deeds which they have committed in an ungodly way, and of all the harsh things which ungodly sinners have spoken against Him."

16 These are grumblers, complainers, walking according to their own lusts; and they mouth great swelling *words,* flattering people to gain advantage. 17 But you, beloved, remember the words which were spoken before by the apostles of our Lord Jesus Christ: 18 how they told you that there would be mockers in the last time who would walk according to their own ungodly lusts. 19 These are sensual persons, who cause divisions, not having the Spirit.

20 But you, beloved, building yourselves up on your most holy faith, praying in the Holy Spirit, 21 keep yourselves in the love of God, looking for the mercy of our Lord Jesus Christ unto eternal life.

22 And on some have compassion, making a distinction; 23 but others save with fear, pulling *them* out of the fire, hating even the garment defiled by the flesh.

24   Now to Him who is able to keep
     you from stumbling,
   And to present *you* faultless
   Before the presence of His glory
     with exceeding joy,
25   To God our Savior,
   Who alone is wise,
   Be glory and majesty,
   Dominion and power,
   Both now and forever.
   Amen.

DIGGING IN

24 God Can Keep You From Stumbling It's not fatal to stumble if you don't fall and break your neck!

God knows you may stumble over some sin sometimes. You say words that you're ashamed of. You do something in secret that should never be done. You allow hateful thoughts to come into your mind. You stumble in those ways. The important thing is to *know when you stumble, then tell it to God.* He will always understand and forgive you if you honestly love Him. He will also prevent you from destroying your life when you stumble.

Some people just fall all the way down to hell. That's stumbling in a way that destroys them. That's when they say to themselves, "We don't care about God anymore. We're going our own way." Ask God to keep you from falling into the dangerous sin of just ignoring Him.

The Book of
REVELATION

The world has not been as cruel to me, John, as to my 11 brother apostles. Each of them died for Jesus' sake, and some died very painful deaths.

But I lived to be about a hundred years old. After I became too old to travel and lead the life of a missionary, I became pastor of the church at Ephesus (pronounced *EFF-uh-sus*).

Christians were treated badly during the reign of the Roman Emperor Domitian (pronounced *do-MISH-shun*). The emperor said we were atheists because we wouldn't worship him as a god.

Domitian made me a prisoner on Patmos Island, about 60 miles from Ephesus. Then I couldn't preach at our church anymore. But it was on Patmos Island that the Lord showed me the amazing visions in this book.

Later, I was allowed to go home again to Ephesus, where I ended my days with my beloved people.

John sees Jesus coming in the clouds

THE **Revelation** of Jesus Christ, which God gave Him to show His servants—things which must shortly take place. And He sent and signified it by His angel to His servant John, 2 who bore witness to the word of God, and to the testimony of Jesus Christ, to all things that he saw. 3 Blessed is he who reads and those who hear the words of this prophecy, and keep those things which are written in it; for the time is near.

4 John, to the seven churches which are in Asia:

WORDFINDER

1:1 Revelation Pronounced *rev-uh-LAY-shun.* What God has revealed or shown about His plan for all time. This revelation is the gospel or Good News the whole Bible tells about.

DIGGING IN

1:1 Jesus Is Revealed What do we mean when we say something is "revealed"? We mean that something hidden has now become known.

All through the Bible, God revealed Himself in many ways—as the Angel of the Lord, then as the strange priest, Melchizedek (pronounced *mel-KIZ-uh-dek*) (Genesis 14), as a burning torch (Genesis 15), as a wrestler (Genesis 32), as a burning bush (Exodus 3), and in voices and visions given to people throughout the Old Testament. Still, God was mostly hidden from people—like the sun just peeping through the clouds.

Then Jesus came, and John says, "We beheld [saw] His glory" (John 1:14). Finally, in the book of Revelation, we see God in all His majesty (see Revelation 1:13–15; also see Revelation 4:3–5). The Bible is really a book that gradually unfolds or "reveals" the mighty God and His Son, Jesus Christ.

Grace to you and peace from Him who is and who was and who is to come, and from the seven Spirits who are before His throne, 5 and from Jesus Christ, the faithful witness, the firstborn from the dead, and the ruler over the kings of the earth.

To Him who loved us and washed us from our sins in His own blood, 6 and has made us kings and priests to His God and Father, to Him *be* glory and dominion forever and ever. Amen.

7 Behold, He is coming with clouds, and *every eye* will see Him, even they who pierced Him. And all the tribes of the earth will mourn because of Him. Even so, Amen.

8 "I am the **Alpha and the Omega,** *the* Beginning and *the* End," says the Lord, "who is and who was and who is to come, the Almighty."

9 I, John, both your brother and companion in the tribulation and kingdom and patience of Jesus Christ, was on the island that is called Patmos for the word of God and for the testimony of Jesus Christ. 10 I was in the Spirit on the Lord's Day, and I heard behind me a loud voice, as of a trumpet, 11 saying, "I am the Alpha and the Omega, the First and the Last," and,

"I am the Alpha and the Omega, the Beginning and the End."

Who Sent John to Patmos Island?

The apostle John was pastor of the church at Ephesus (pronounced *EFF-uh-sus*) when he was very old. The Roman emperor Domitian (pronounced *doh-MISH-shun*) was persecuting Christians all over the Roman Empire about 90 years after Jesus died. So Domitian sent John to be a prisoner on Patmos Island in the Mediterranean Sea.

"What you see, write in a book and send *it* to the seven churches which are in Asia: to Ephesus, to Smyrna, to Pergamos, to Thyatira, to Sardis, to Philadelphia, and to Laodicea."

12 Then I turned to see the voice that spoke with me. And having turned I saw seven golden lampstands, 13 and in the midst of the seven lampstands *One* like the Son of Man, clothed with a garment down to the feet and girded about the chest with a golden band. 14 His head and hair *were* white like wool, as white as snow, and His eyes like a flame of fire; 15 His feet *were* like fine brass, as if refined in a furnace, and His voice as the sound of many waters; 16 He had in His right hand seven stars, out of His mouth went a sharp two-edged sword, and His countenance *was* like the sun shining in its strength. 17 And when I saw Him, I fell at His feet as dead. But He laid His right hand on me, saying to me, "Do not be afraid; I am the First and the Last. 18 I *am* He who lives, and was dead, and behold, I am alive forevermore. Amen. And I have the keys of Hades and of Death. 19 Write the things which you have seen, and the things which are, and the things which will take place after this. 20 The mystery of the seven stars which you saw in

---

WORDFINDER

1:8 The Alpha and the Omega Pronounced *Al-fuh* and *oh-MEG-uh*. The first and last letters of the Greek alphabet. This is one of the names for Christ who is the First and the Last of all things.

My right hand, and the seven golden lampstands: The seven stars are the angels of the seven churches, and the seven lampstands which you saw are the seven churches.

John writes to four churches

2 "To the angel of the church of Ephesus write,

'These things says He who holds the seven stars in His right hand, who walks in the midst of the seven golden lampstands: 2 "I know your works, your labor, your patience, and that you cannot bear those who are evil. And you have tested those who say they are apostles and are not, and have found them liars; 3 and you have persevered and have patience, and have labored for My name's sake and have not become weary. 4 Nevertheless I have *this* against you, that you have left your first love. 5 Remember therefore from where you have fallen; repent and do the first works, or else I will come to you quickly and remove your lampstand from its place—unless you repent. 6 But this you have, that you hate the deeds of the **Nicolaitans,** which I also hate.

7 "He who has an ear, let him hear what the Spirit says to the churches. To him who overcomes I will give to eat from the tree of life, which is in the midst of the Paradise of God." '

8 "And to the angel of the church in Smyrna write,

'These things says the First and the Last, who was dead, and came to life: 9 "I know your works, tribulation, and poverty (but you are rich); and *I know* the blasphemy of those who say they are Jews and are not, but *are* a synagogue of Satan. 10 Do not fear any of those things which you are about to suffer. Indeed, the devil is about to throw *some* of you into prison, that you may be tested, and you will have tribulation ten days. Be faithful until death, and I will give you the crown of life.

11 "He who has an ear, let him hear what the Spirit says to the churches. He who overcomes shall not be hurt by the second death." '

12 "And to the angel of the church in Pergamos write,

'These things says He who has the sharp two-edged sword: 13 "I know your works, and where you dwell, where Satan's throne *is*. And you hold fast to My name, and did not deny My faith even in the days in which Antipas

---

WORDFINDER

2:6 Nicolaitans Pronounced *nick-oh-LAY-ih-tons.* A group led by a false teacher named Nicolas. This was a group who believed they could be immoral and still be Christians.

DIGGING IN

2:7 The Seven Churches In Revelation 2 and 3 you read about "the seven churches of Asia" (called Asia Minor today). These were actual churches. The majestic Christ that John saw sends a letter to each of these churches. To most of the seven churches, Jesus pays a compliment. But He finds some faults in all except two of them—Smyrna and Philadelphia.

As you look at each of these churches, you are reminded of what some Christians are like today. One church has left its "first love." That means the people don't love Christ as much as they did in the beginning. Two churches are allowing filthy and indecent behavior by their members. One church is "dead"—they still pretend to be Christians, but they don't really love Jesus anymore. Another church is "lukewarm"— they are only halfhearted for Jesus. But Jesus says He wishes they were either hot or cold—all or nothing!

Are you like any of these churches?

The ancient city of Smyrna, where Paul started a church, is now Izmir, Turkey.

was My faithful **martyr,** who was killed among you, where Satan dwells. ¹⁴ But I have a few things against you, because you have there those who hold the doctrine of Balaam, who taught Balak to put a stumbling block before the children of Israel, to eat things sacrificed to idols, and to commit sexual immorality. ¹⁵ Thus you also have those who hold the doctrine of the Nicolaitans, which thing I hate. ¹⁶ Repent, or else I will come to you quickly and will fight against them with the sword of My mouth.

What Is the Second Death?

You already know that the first death is what happens to everybody. The second or final death is what happens to people who don't ask Jesus to forgive their sins (see Revelation 20:14, 15). The second death means to be cut off from God and all goodness forever.

---

¹⁷ "He who has an ear, let him hear what the Spirit says to the churches. To him who overcomes I will give some of the hidden manna to eat. And I will give him a white stone, and on the stone a new name written which no one knows except him who receives *it.*" '

¹⁸ "And to the angel of the church in Thyatira write,

'These things says the Son of God, who has eyes like a flame of fire, and His feet like fine brass: ¹⁹ I know your works, love, service, faith, and your patience; and *as* for your works, the last *are* more than the first. ²⁰ Nevertheless I have a few things against you, because you allow that woman Jezebel, who calls herself a prophetess, to teach and seduce My servants to commit sexual immorality and eat things sacrificed to idols. ²¹ And I gave her time to repent of her sexual immorality, and she did not repent. ²² Indeed I will cast her into a sickbed, and those who commit adultery with her into great tribulation,

---

WORDFINDER

2:13 Martyr Pronounced *MAR-ter.* A person who is put to death for being a Christian. The word comes from a Greek word meaning "witness."

unless they repent of their deeds. 23 I will kill her children with death, and all the churches shall know that I am He who searches the minds and hearts. And I will give to each one of you according to your works.

24 "Now to you I say, and to the rest in Thyatira, as many as do not have this doctrine, who have not known the depths of Satan, as they say, I will put on you no other burden. 25 But hold fast what you have till I come. 26 And he who overcomes, and keeps My works until the end, to him I will give power over the nations—

27 'He shall rule them with a rod
of iron;
They shall be dashed to pieces
like the potter's vessels'—

as I also have received from My Father; 28 and I will give him the morning star. 29 "He who has an ear, let him hear what the Spirit says to the churches." '

Hear what Christ says to the churches

3 "And to the angel of the church in Sardis write,

'These things says He who has the seven Spirits of God and the seven stars: "I know your works, that you have a name that you are alive, but you are dead. 2 Be watchful, and strengthen the things which remain, that are ready to die, for I have not found your works perfect before God. 3 Remember therefore how you have received and heard; hold fast and repent. Therefore if you will not watch, I will come upon you as a thief, and you will not know what hour I will come upon you. 4 You have a few names even in Sardis who have not defiled their garments; and they shall walk with Me in white, for they are worthy. 5 He who overcomes shall be clothed in white garments, and I will not blot out his name from the Book of Life; but I will confess his name before My Father and before His angels. 6 "He who has an ear, let him hear what the Spirit says to the churches." '

7 "And to the angel of the church in Philadelphia write,

'These things says He who is holy, He who is true, "He who has the key of David, He who opens and no one shuts, and shuts and no one opens":

Alasehir, Turkey is the site of the biblical city of Philadelphia.

Ruins of a church at Laodicea, mentioned by Jesus in the Book of Revelation.

⁸ I know your works. See, I have set before you an open door, and no one can shut it; for you have a little strength, have kept My word, and have not denied My name. ⁹ Indeed I will make *those* of the synagogue of Satan, who say they are Jews and are not, but lie—indeed I will make them come and worship before your feet, and to know that I have loved you. ¹⁰ Because you have kept My command to persevere, I also will keep you from the hour of trial which shall come upon the whole world, to test those who dwell on the earth. ¹¹ Behold, I am coming quickly! Hold fast what you have, that no one may take your crown. ¹² He who overcomes, I will make him a pillar in the temple of My God, and he shall go out no more. I will write on him the name of My God and the name of the city of My God, the New Jerusalem, which comes down out of heaven from My God. And *I will write on him* My new name.

¹³ "He who has an ear, let him hear what the Spirit says to the churches." '

¹⁴ "And to the angel of the church of the Laodiceans write,

'These things says the **Amen,** the Faithful and True Witness, the Beginning of the creation of God: ¹⁵ "I know your works, that you are neither cold nor hot. I could wish you were cold or hot. ¹⁶ So then, because you are lukewarm, and neither cold nor hot, I will vomit you out of My mouth. ¹⁷ Because you say, 'I am rich, have become wealthy, and have need of nothing'—and do not know that you are wretched, miserable, poor, blind, and naked— ¹⁸ I counsel you to buy from Me gold refined in the fire, that you may be rich; and white garments, that you may be clothed, *that* the

🌐 WORDFINDER

3:14 Amen Pronounced *ah-MEN.* A Greek and Hebrew word meaning "let it be so." Jesus is also called "the Amen" because He is faithful and true.

shame of your nakedness may not be revealed; and anoint your eyes with eye salve, that you may see. ¹⁹ As many as I love, I rebuke and chasten. Therefore be zealous and repent. ²⁰ Behold, I stand at the door and knock. If anyone hears My voice and opens the door, I will come in to him and dine with him, and he with Me. ²¹ To him who overcomes I will grant to sit with Me on My throne, as I also overcame and sat down with My Father on His throne.

²² "He who has an ear, let him hear what the Spirit says to the churches." ' "

John sees God's throne in heaven

4 After these things I looked, and behold, a door *standing* open in heaven. And the first voice which I heard *was* like a trumpet speaking with me, saying, "Come up here, and I will show you things which must take place after this."

² Immediately I was in the Spirit; and behold, a throne set in heaven, and *One* sat on the throne. ³ And He who sat there was like a jasper and a sardius stone in appearance; and *there was* a rainbow around the throne, in appearance like an emerald. ⁴ Around the throne *were* twenty-four thrones, and on the thrones I saw twenty-four elders sitting, clothed in white robes; and they had crowns of gold on their heads.

⁵ And from the throne proceeded lightnings, thunderings, and voices. Seven lamps of fire *were* burning before the throne, which are the seven Spirits of God.

⁶ Before the throne *there was* a sea of glass, like crystal. And in the midst of the throne, and around the throne, *were* four living creatures full of eyes in front and in back. ⁷ The first living creature *was* like a lion, the second living creature like a calf, the third living creature had a face like a man, and the fourth living creature *was* like a flying eagle. ⁸ *The* four living creatures, each having six wings, were full of eyes around and within. And they do not rest day or night, saying:

> "Holy, holy, holy,
> Lord God Almighty,
> Who was and is and is to come!"

⁹ Whenever the living creatures give glory and honor and thanks to Him who sits on the throne, who lives forever and ever, ¹⁰ the twenty-four elders fall down before Him who sits on the throne and worship Him who lives forever and ever, and cast their crowns before the throne, saying:

> ¹¹ "You are worthy, O Lord,
> To receive glory and honor and power;
> For You created all things,
> And by Your will they exist and were created."

⚒ DIGGING IN

4:2–5 What God Is Like in Heaven John, the author of this book, could not see everything clearly in heaven. There was a rainbow, like a mist, that surrounded God on His throne. It was hard for John to describe all that he saw. He could see a mixture of the beauty of two precious stones—the jasper and the sardius. The jasper stone stands for purity, while the sardius (or sard) is reddish in color. This scene reminds you that God is glorious to behold.

Part of that glory of God is the red blood of Jesus, the Lamb of God who died for your sins. It is good to be reminded that Jesus in heaven is still God's sacrifice for sins. Jesus is the Lamb of God whose red blood is always before God's throne. You can see Jesus the Lamb in Revelation 5:6. You, too, will be allowed to see God like this only because Jesus died for you.

A scroll sealed with seven seals

5 And I saw in the right *hand* of Him who sat on the throne a scroll written inside and on the back, sealed with seven seals. ² Then I saw a strong angel proclaiming with a loud voice, "Who is worthy to open the scroll and to loose its seals?" ³ And no one in heaven or on the earth or under the earth was able to open the scroll, or to look at it.

⁴ So I wept much, because no one was found worthy to open and read the scroll, or to look at it. ⁵ But one of the elders said to me, "Do not weep. Behold, the Lion of the tribe of Judah, the Root of David, has prevailed to open the scroll and to loose its seven seals."

⁶ And I looked, and behold, in the midst of the throne and of the four living creatures, and in the midst of the elders, stood a Lamb as though it had been slain, having seven horns and seven eyes, which are the seven Spirits of God sent out into all the earth. ⁷ Then He came and took the scroll out of the right hand of Him who sat on the throne.

⁸ Now when He had taken the scroll, the four living creatures and the twenty-four elders fell down before the Lamb, each having a harp, and golden bowls full of incense, which are the prayers of the saints. ⁹ And they sang a new song, saying:

"You are worthy to take the scroll,

And to open its seals;
For You were slain,
And have redeemed us to God by Your blood
Out of every tribe and tongue and people and nation,
10 And have made us kings and priests to our God;
And we shall reign on the earth."

¹¹ Then I looked, and I heard the voice of many angels around the throne, the living creatures, and the elders; and the number of them was ten thousand times ten thousand, and thousands of thousands, ¹² saying with a loud voice:

"Worthy is the Lamb who was slain
To receive power and riches and wisdom,
And strength and honor and glory and blessing!"

¹³ And every creature which is in heaven and on the earth and under the earth and such as are in the sea, and all that are in them, I heard saying:

"Blessing and honor and glory and power
Be to Him who sits on the throne,
And to the Lamb, forever and ever!"

¹⁴ Then the four living creatures said, "Amen!" And the twenty-four elders

⛏ DIGGING IN

5:1 The Book of the Future Lots of people have written books about the past. That's why you can study history in school. But God has written the book about the future. The book (or scroll) John sees in heaven contains God's complete plan for all time. The remaining chapters of the Book of Revelation show the main outlines of God's great scheme for the coming time.

One thing you will notice is that no man or angel was able to open God's book.

Jesus, the Lamb of God (verse 5), is the only One who can unlock the book of the future for us. When Jesus opens the book, you can go on to read about the coming judgments of God on the earth. When Jesus returns to earth, Satan and his people and nations are thrown into hell. But in the end, the Lord brings in His beautiful new heavens and new earth. Then He reigns over all in peace forever and ever.

fell down and worshiped Him who lives forever and ever.

The Lamb opens six seals

6 Now I saw when the Lamb opened one of the seals; and I heard one of the four living creatures saying with a voice like thunder, "Come and see." 2 And I looked, and behold, a white horse. He who sat on it had a bow; and a crown was given to him, and he went out conquering and to conquer.

3 When He opened the second seal, I heard the second living creature saying, "Come and see." 4 Another horse, fiery red, went out. And it was granted to the one who sat on it to take peace from the earth, and that *people* should kill one another; and there was given to him a great sword.

5 When He opened the third seal, I heard the third living creature say, "Come and see." So I looked, and behold, a black horse, and he who sat on it had a pair of scales in his hand. 6 And I heard a voice in the midst of the four living creatures saying, "A quart of wheat for a denarius, and three quarts of barley for a denarius; and do not harm the oil and the wine."

7 When He opened the fourth seal, I heard the voice of the fourth living creature saying, "Come and see." 8 So I looked, and behold, a pale horse. And the name of him who sat on it was Death, and Hades followed with him. And power was given to them over a fourth of the earth, to kill with sword, with hunger, with death, and by the beasts of the earth.

9 When He opened the fifth seal, I saw under the altar the souls of those who had been slain for the word of God and for the testimony which they held. 10 And they cried with a loud voice, saying, "How long, O Lord, holy and true, until You judge and avenge our blood on those who dwell on the earth?" 11 Then a white robe was given to each of them; and it was said to them that they should rest a little while longer, until both *the number of* their fellow servants and their brethren, who would be killed as they *were,* was completed.

12 I looked when He opened the sixth seal, and behold, there was a great earthquake; and the sun became black as sackcloth of hair, and the moon became like blood. 13 And the stars of heaven fell to the earth, as a fig tree drops its late figs when it is shaken by a mighty wind. 14 Then the sky receded as a scroll when it is rolled up, and every mountain and island was moved out of its place. 15 And the kings of the earth, the great men, the rich men, the commanders, the mighty men, every slave and every free man, hid themselves in the caves and in the rocks of the mountains, 16 and said to the mountains and rocks, "Fall on us and hide us from the face of Him who sits on the throne and from the wrath of the Lamb! 17 For the great day of His wrath has come, and who is able to stand?"

144,000 are chosen by God

7 After these things I saw four angels standing at the four corners of the earth, holding the four winds of the earth, that the wind should not blow on the earth, on the sea, or on any tree. 2 Then I saw another angel ascending from the east, having the seal of the living God. And he cried with a loud voice to the four angels to whom it was granted to harm the earth and the sea, 3 saying, "Do not harm the earth, the sea, or the trees till we have sealed the servants of our God on their foreheads." 4 And I heard the number of those who were sealed. One hundred *and* forty-four thousand of all the tribes of the children of Israel *were* sealed:

5   of the tribe of Judah twelve
       thousand *were* sealed;
       of the tribe of Reuben twelve
       thousand *were* sealed;
       of the tribe of Gad twelve
       thousand *were* sealed;

6   of the tribe of Asher twelve
       thousand *were* sealed;
     of the tribe of Naphtali twelve
       thousand *were* sealed;
     of the tribe of Manasseh twelve
       thousand *were* sealed;
7   of the tribe of Simeon twelve
       thousand *were* sealed;
     of the tribe of Levi twelve
       thousand *were* sealed;
     of the tribe of Issachar twelve
       thousand *were* sealed;
8   of the tribe of Zebulun twelve
       thousand *were* sealed;
     of the tribe of Joseph twelve
       thousand *were* sealed;
     of the tribe of Benjamin twelve
       thousand *were* sealed.

9 After these things I looked, and behold, a great multitude which no one
could number, of all nations, tribes,
peoples, and tongues, standing before
the throne and before the Lamb,
clothed with white robes, with palm
branches in their hands, 10 and crying
out with a loud voice, saying, "Salvation *belongs* to our God who sits on
the throne, and to the Lamb!" 11 All
the angels stood around the throne
and the elders and the four living creatures, and fell on their faces before the
throne and worshiped God, 12 saying:

    "Amen! Blessing and glory and
       wisdom,
    Thanksgiving and honor and
       power and might,
    Be to our God forever and ever.
    Amen."

13 Then one of the elders answered,
saying to me, "Who are these arrayed
in white robes, and where did they
come from?"
14 And I said to him, "Sir, you
know."
    So he said to me, "These are the
ones who come out of the great tribulation, and washed their robes and made
them white in the blood of the Lamb.
15 Therefore they are before the throne
of God, and serve Him day and night
in His temple. And He who sits on the
throne will dwell among them. 16 They
shall neither hunger anymore nor thirst
anymore; the sun shall not strike them,
nor any heat; 17 for the Lamb who is
in the midst of the throne will shepherd
them and lead them to living fountains
of waters. And God will wipe away
every tear from their eyes."

The seventh seal is broken

8 When He opened the seventh seal,
there was silence in heaven for about
half an hour. 2 And I saw the seven
angels who stand before God, and to
them *were* given seven trumpets.
3 Then another angel, having a golden
censer, came and stood at the altar.
He was given much incense, that he
should offer *it* with the prayers of all
the saints upon the golden altar which
was before the throne. 4 And the
smoke of the incense, with the prayers
of the saints, ascended before God
from the angel's hand. 5 Then the angel took the censer, filled it with fire
from the altar, and threw *it* to the earth.
And there *were* noises, thunderings,
lightnings, and an earthquake.

6 So the seven angels who had the
seven trumpets prepared themselves to
sound.

7 The first angel sounded: And hail
and fire followed, mingled with blood,
and they were thrown to the earth.
And a third of the trees were burned
up, and all green grass was burned up.

8 Then the second angel sounded:
And *something* like a great mountain
burning with fire was thrown into the
sea, and a third of the sea became
blood. 9 And a third of the living creatures in the sea died, and a third of
the ships were destroyed.

10 Then the third angel sounded:
And a great star fell from heaven, burning like a torch, and it fell on a third
of the rivers and on the springs of water. 11 The name of the star is Wormwood. A third of the waters became
wormwood, and many men died from
the water, because it was made bitter.

12 Then the fourth angel sounded:
And a third of the sun was struck, a

third of the moon, and a third of the stars, so that a third of them were darkened. A third of the day did not shine, and likewise the night.

13 And I looked, and I heard an angel flying through the midst of heaven, saying with a loud voice, "Woe, woe, woe to the inhabitants of the earth, because of the remaining blasts of the trumpet of the three angels who are about to sound!"

Angels sound the trumpets and plagues begin

9 Then the fifth angel sounded: And I saw a star fallen from heaven to the earth. To him was given the key to the bottomless pit. 2 And he opened the bottomless pit, and smoke arose out of the pit like the smoke of a great furnace. So the sun and the air were darkened because of the smoke of the pit. 3 Then out of the smoke locusts came upon the earth. And to them was given power, as the scorpions of the earth have power. 4 They were commanded not to harm the grass of the earth, or any green thing, or any tree, but only those men who do not have the seal of God on their foreheads. 5 And they were not given *authority* to kill them, but to torment them *for* five months. Their torment *was* like the torment of a scorpion when it strikes a man. 6 In those days men will seek death and will not find it; they will desire to die, and death will flee from them.

7 The shape of the locusts was like horses prepared for battle. On their heads were crowns of something like gold, and their faces *were* like the faces of men. 8 They had hair like women's hair, and their teeth *were* like lions' *teeth.* 9 And they had breastplates like breastplates of iron, and the sound of their wings *was* like the sound of chariots with many horses running into battle. 10 They had tails like scorpions, and there were stings in their tails. Their power *was* to hurt men five months. 11 And they had as king over them the

The painful sting of a scorpion reminds us of God's judgment.

angel of the bottomless pit, whose name in Hebrew is Abaddon, but in Greek he has the name Apollyon.

12 One woe is past. Behold, still two more woes are coming after these things.

13 Then the sixth angel sounded: And I heard a voice from the four horns of the golden altar which is before God, 14 saying to the sixth angel who had the trumpet, "Release the four angels who are bound at the great river Euphrates." 15 So the four angels, who had been prepared for the hour and day and month and year, were released to kill a third of mankind. 16 Now the number of the army of the horsemen *was* two hundred million; I heard the number of them. 17 And thus I saw the horses in the vision: those who sat on them had breastplates of fiery red, hyacinth blue, and sulfur yellow; and the heads of the horses *were* like the heads of lions; and out of their mouths came fire, smoke, and brimstone. 18 By these three *plagues* a third of mankind was killed—by the fire and the smoke and the brimstone which came out of their mouths. 19 For their power is in their mouth and in their tails; for their tails *are* like serpents,

having heads; and with them they do harm.

20 But the rest of mankind, who were not killed by these plagues, did not repent of the works of their hands, that they should not worship demons, and idols of gold, silver, brass, stone, and wood, which can neither see nor hear nor walk. 21 And they did not repent of their murders or their sorceries or their sexual immorality or their thefts.

A mighty angel eats a little scroll

10 I saw still another mighty angel coming down from heaven, clothed with a cloud. And a rainbow *was* on his head, his face *was* like the sun, and his feet like pillars of fire. 2 He had a little book open in his hand. And he set his right foot on the sea and *his* left *foot* on the land, 3 and cried with a loud voice, as *when* a lion roars. When he cried out, seven thunders uttered their voices. 4 Now when the seven thunders uttered their voices, I was about to write; but I heard a voice from heaven saying to me, "Seal up the things which the seven thunders uttered, and do not write them."

5 The angel whom I saw standing on the sea and on the land raised up his hand to heaven 6 and swore by Him who lives forever and ever, who created heaven and the things that are in it, the earth and the things that are in it, and the sea and the things that are in it, that there should be delay no longer, 7 but in the days of the sounding of the seventh angel, when he is about to sound, the mystery of God would be finished, as He declared to His servants the prophets.

8 Then the voice which I heard from heaven spoke to me again and said, "Go, take the little book which is open in the hand of the angel who stands on the sea and on the earth."

9 So I went to the angel and said to him, "Give me the little book."

And he said to me, "Take and eat it; and it will make your stomach bitter, but it will be as sweet as honey in your mouth."

10 Then I took the little book out of the angel's hand and ate it, and it was as sweet as honey in my mouth. But when I had eaten it, my stomach became bitter. 11 And he said to me, "You must prophesy again about many peoples, nations, tongues, and kings."

Two witnesses prophesy

11 Then I was given a reed like a measuring rod. And the angel stood, saying, "Rise and measure the temple of God, the altar, and those who worship there. 2 But leave out the court which is outside the temple, and do not measure it, for it has been given to the **Gentiles.** And they will tread the holy city underfoot *for* forty-two months. 3 And I will give *power* to my two witnesses, and they will prophesy one thousand two hundred and sixty days, clothed in sackcloth."

4 These are the two olive trees and the two lampstands standing before the God of the earth. 5 And if anyone wants to harm them, fire proceeds from their mouth and devours their enemies. And if anyone wants to harm them, he must be killed in this manner. 6 These have power to shut heaven, so that no rain falls in the days of their prophecy; and they have power over waters to turn them to blood, and to strike the earth with all plagues, as often as they desire.

7 When they finish their testimony, the beast that ascends out of the bottomless pit will make war against them, overcome them, and kill them. 8 And their dead bodies *will lie* in the street

11:2 Gentiles All peoples and nations who are not of the Hebrew race. God promised that the Jews would be a blessing to the Gentiles. Jesus fulfilled that promise.

of the great city which spiritually is called Sodom and Egypt, where also our Lord was crucified. 9 Then *those* from the peoples, tribes, tongues, and nations will see their dead bodies three-and-a-half days, and not allow their dead bodies to be put into graves. 10 And those who dwell on the earth will rejoice over them, make merry, and send gifts to one another, because these two prophets tormented those who dwell on the earth.

11 Now after the three-and-a-half days the breath of life from God entered them, and they stood on their feet, and great fear fell on those who saw them. 12 And they heard a loud voice from heaven saying to them, "Come up here." And they ascended to heaven in a cloud, and their enemies saw them. 13 In the same hour there was a great earthquake, and a tenth of the city fell. In the earthquake seven thousand people were killed, and the rest were afraid and gave glory to the God of heaven.

14 The second woe is past. Behold, the third woe is coming quickly.

15 Then the seventh angel sounded: And there were loud voices in heaven, saying, "The kingdoms of this world have become *the kingdoms* of our Lord and of His Christ, and He shall reign forever and ever!" 16 And the twenty-four elders who sat before God on their thrones fell on their faces and worshiped God, 17 saying:

"We give You thanks, O Lord
      God Almighty,
The One who is and who was
      and who is to come,
Because You have taken
      Your great power and
      reigned.
18   The nations were angry, and
      Your wrath has come,
And the time of the dead, that
      they should be judged,
And that You should reward
      Your servants the prophets
      and the saints,
And those who fear Your name,
      small and great,

And should destroy those who
      destroy the earth."

19 Then the temple of God was opened in heaven, and the ark of His covenant was seen in His temple. And there were lightnings, noises, thunderings, an earthquake, and great hail.

The woman, the Child, and the dragon

12 Now a great sign appeared in heaven: a woman clothed with the sun, with the moon under her feet, and on her head a garland of twelve stars. 2 Then being with child, she cried out in labor and in pain to give birth.

3 And another sign appeared in heaven: behold, a great, fiery red dragon having seven heads and ten horns, and seven diadems on his heads. 4 His tail drew a third of the stars of heaven and threw them to the earth. And the dragon stood before the woman who was ready to give birth, to devour her Child as soon as it was born. 5 She bore a male Child who was to rule all nations with a rod of iron. And her Child was caught up to God and His throne. 6 Then the woman fled into the wilderness, where she has a place prepared by God, that they should feed her there one thousand two hundred and sixty days.

7 And war broke out in heaven: Michael and his angels fought with the dragon; and the dragon and his angels fought, 8 but they did not prevail, nor was a place found for them in heaven any longer. 9 So the great dragon was cast out, that serpent of old, called the Devil and Satan, who deceives the whole world; he was cast to the earth, and his angels were cast out with him.

10 Then I heard a loud voice saying in heaven, "Now salvation, and strength, and the kingdom of our God, and the power of His Christ have come, for the accuser of our brethren, who accused them before our God day and night, has been cast down. 11 And they overcame him by the blood of

the Lamb and by the word of their testimony, and they did not love their lives to the death. 12 Therefore rejoice, O heavens, and you who dwell in them! Woe to the inhabitants of the earth and the sea! For the devil has come down to you, having great wrath, because he knows that he has a short time."

13 Now when the dragon saw that he had been cast to the earth, he persecuted the woman who gave birth to the male *Child.* 14 But the woman was given two wings of a great eagle, that she might fly into the wilderness to her place, where she is nourished for a time and times and half a time, from the presence of the serpent. 15 So the serpent spewed water out of his mouth like a flood after the woman, that he might cause her to be carried away by the flood. 16 But the earth helped the woman, and the earth opened its mouth and swallowed up the flood which the dragon had spewed out of his mouth. 17 And the dragon was enraged with the woman, and he went to make war with the rest of her offspring, who keep the commandments of God and have the testimony of Jesus Christ.

The beast with seven horns

13 Then I stood on the sand of the sea. And I saw a beast rising up out of the sea, having seven heads and ten horns, and on his horns ten crowns, and on his heads a blasphemous name. 2 Now the beast which I saw was like a leopard, his feet were like *the feet of* a bear, and his mouth like the mouth of a lion. The dragon gave him his power, his throne, and great authority. 3 And *I saw* one of his heads as if it had been mortally wounded, and his deadly wound was healed. And all the world marveled and followed the beast. 4 So they worshiped the dragon who gave authority to the beast; and they worshiped the beast, saying, "Who *is* like the beast? Who is able to make war with him?"

5 And he was given a mouth speaking great things and blasphemies, and he was given authority to continue for forty-two months. 6 Then he opened his mouth in blasphemy against God, to blaspheme His name, His tabernacle, and those who dwell in heaven. 7 It was granted to him to make war with the saints and to overcome them. And authority was given him over every tribe, tongue, and nation. 8 All who dwell on the earth will worship him, whose names have not been written in the Book of Life of the Lamb slain from the foundation of the world.

9 If anyone has an ear, let him hear. 10 He who leads into captivity shall go into captivity; he who kills with the sword must be killed with the sword. Here is the patience and the faith of the saints.

11 Then I saw another beast coming up out of the earth, and he had two horns like a lamb and spoke like a dragon. 12 And he exercises all the authority of the first beast in his presence, and causes the earth and those who dwell in it to worship the first beast, whose deadly wound was healed. 13 He performs great signs, so that he even makes fire come down from heaven on the earth in the sight of men. 14 And he deceives those who dwell on the earth by those signs which he was granted to do in the sight of the beast, telling those who dwell on the earth to make an image to the beast who was wounded by the sword and lived. 15 He was granted *power* to give breath to the image of the beast, that the image of the beast should both speak and cause as many as would not worship the image of the beast to be killed. 16 He causes all, both small and great, rich and poor, free and slave, to receive a mark on their right hand or on their foreheads, 17 and that no one may buy or sell except one who has the mark or the name of the beast, or the number of his name.

18 Here is wisdom. Let him who has understanding calculate the number of the beast, for it is the number of a man: His number *is* 666.

The Son of Man will reap a great harvest

14 Then I looked, and behold, a Lamb standing on Mount Zion, and with Him one hundred *and* forty-four thousand, having His Father's name written on their foreheads. ²And I heard a voice from heaven, like the voice of many waters, and like the voice of loud thunder. And I heard the sound of harpists playing their harps. ³They sang as it were a new song before the throne, before the four living creatures, and the elders; and no one could learn that song except the hundred *and* forty-four thousand who were redeemed from the earth. ⁴These are the ones who were not defiled with women, for they are virgins. These are the ones who follow the Lamb wherever He goes. These were redeemed from *among* men, *being* firstfruits to God and to the Lamb. ⁵And in their mouth was found no deceit, for they are without fault before the throne of God.

⁶Then I saw another angel flying in the midst of heaven, having the everlasting gospel to preach to those who dwell on the earth—to every nation, tribe, tongue, and people— ⁷saying with a loud voice, "Fear God and give glory to Him, for the hour of His judgment has come; and worship Him who made heaven and earth, the sea and springs of water."

⁸And another angel followed, saying, "Babylon is fallen, is fallen, that great city, because she has made all nations drink of the wine of the wrath of her fornication."

⁹Then a third angel followed them, saying with a loud voice, "If anyone worships the beast and his image, and receives *his* mark on his forehead or on his hand, ¹⁰he himself shall also drink of the wine of the wrath of God, which is poured out full strength into the cup of His indignation. He shall be tormented with fire and brimstone in the presence of the holy angels and in the presence of the Lamb. ¹¹And the smoke of their torment ascends for-

ever and ever; and they have no rest day or night, who worship the beast and his image, and whoever receives the mark of his name."

¹²Here is the patience of the saints; here *are* those who keep the commandments of God and the faith of Jesus.

¹³Then I heard a voice from heaven saying to me, "Write: 'Blessed *are* the dead who die in the Lord from now on.'"

"Yes," says the Spirit, "that they may rest from their labors, and their works follow them."

¹⁴Then I looked, and behold, a white cloud, and on the cloud sat *One* like the Son of Man, having on His head a golden crown, and in His hand a sharp sickle. ¹⁵And another angel came out of the temple, crying with a loud voice to Him who sat on the cloud, "Thrust in Your sickle and reap, for the time has come for You to reap, for the harvest of the earth is ripe." ¹⁶So He who sat on the cloud thrust in His sickle on the earth, and the earth was reaped.

¹⁷Then another angel came out of the temple which is in heaven, he also having a sharp sickle.

¹⁸And another angel came out from the altar, who had power over fire, and he cried with a loud cry to him who had the sharp sickle, saying, "Thrust in your sharp sickle and gather the clusters of the vine of the earth, for her grapes are fully ripe." ¹⁹So the angel thrust his sickle into the earth and gathered the vine of the earth, and threw *it* into the great winepress of the wrath of God. ²⁰And the winepress was trampled outside the city, and blood came out of the winepress, up to the horses' bridles, for one thousand six hundred furlongs.

Seven angels with seven plagues

15 Then I saw another sign in heaven, great and marvelous: seven angels having the seven last plagues, for in them the wrath of God is complete.

2 And I saw *something* like a sea of glass mingled with fire, and those who have the victory over the beast, over his image and over his mark *and* over the number of his name, standing on the sea of glass, having harps of God. 3 They sing the song of Moses, the servant of God, and the song of the Lamb, saying:

"Great and marvelous *are* Your works,
Lord God Almighty!
Just and true *are* Your ways,
O King of the saints!
4 Who shall not fear You, O Lord, and glorify Your name?
For *You* alone *are* holy.
For all nations shall come and worship before You,
For Your judgments have been manifested."

5 After these things I looked, and behold, the temple of the tabernacle of the testimony in heaven was opened. 6 And out of the temple came the seven angels having the seven plagues, clothed in pure bright linen, and having their chests girded with golden bands. 7 Then one of the four living creatures gave to the seven angels seven golden bowls full of the wrath of God who lives forever and ever. 8 The temple was filled with smoke from the glory of God and from His power, and no one was able to enter the temple till the seven plagues of the seven angels were completed.

Seven bowls of God's wrath

16 Then I heard a loud voice from the temple saying to the seven angels, "Go and pour out the bowls of the wrath of God on the earth."
2 So the first went and poured out his bowl upon the earth, and a foul and loathsome sore came upon the men who had the mark of the beast and those who worshiped his image.
3 Then the second angel poured out his bowl on the sea, and it became blood as of a dead *man;* and every living creature in the sea died.
4 Then the third angel poured out his bowl on the rivers and springs of water, and they became blood. 5 And I heard the angel of the waters saying:

"You are righteous, O Lord,
The One who is and who was and who is to be,
Because You have judged these things.
6 For they have shed the blood of saints and prophets,
And You have given them blood to drink.
For it is their just due."

7 And I heard another from the altar saying, "Even so, Lord God Almighty, true and righteous *are* Your judgments."
8 Then the fourth angel poured out his bowl on the sun, and power was given to him to scorch men with fire. 9 And men were scorched with great heat, and they blasphemed the name of God who has power over these plagues; and they did not repent and give Him glory.
10 Then the fifth angel poured out his bowl on the throne of the beast, and his kingdom became full of darkness; and they gnawed their tongues because of the pain. 11 They blasphemed the God of heaven because of their pains and their sores, and did not repent of their deeds.
12 Then the sixth angel poured out his bowl on the great river Euphrates, and its water was dried up, so that the way of the kings from the east might be prepared. 13 And I saw three unclean spirits like frogs *coming* out of the mouth of the dragon, out of the mouth of the beast, and out of the mouth of the false prophet. 14 For they are spirits of demons, performing signs, *which* go out to the kings of the earth and of the whole world, to gather them to the battle of that great day of God Almighty.
15 "Behold, I am coming as a thief. Blessed *is* he who watches, and keeps

A model of the fortress city of Megiddo, called Armageddon in the Book of Revelation.

his garments, lest he walk naked and they see his shame."

16 And they gathered them together to the place called in Hebrew, **Armageddon.**

17 Then the seventh angel poured out his bowl into the air, and a loud voice came out of the temple of heaven, from the throne, saying, "It is done!" 18 And there were noises and thunderings and lightnings; and there was a great earthquake, such a mighty and great earthquake as had not occurred since men were on the earth. 19 Now the great city was divided into three parts, and the cities of the nations fell. And great Babylon was remembered before God, to give her the cup of the wine of the fierceness of His wrath. 20 Then every island fled away, and the mountains were not found. 21 And great hail from heaven fell upon men, *each hailstone* about the weight of a talent. Men blasphemed God be-

cause of the plague of the hail, since that plague was exceedingly great.

The drunken woman and the beast with ten horns

17 Then one of the seven angels who had the seven bowls came and talked with me, saying to me, "Come, I will show you the judgment of the great harlot who sits on many waters, 2 with whom the kings of the earth committed fornication, and the inhabitants of the earth were made drunk with the wine of her fornication."

3 So he carried me away in the Spirit into the wilderness. And I saw a woman sitting on a scarlet beast *which was* full of names of blasphemy, having seven heads and ten horns. 4 The woman was arrayed in purple and scarlet, and adorned with gold and precious stones and pearls, having in her

WORDFINDER

16:16 Armageddon Pronounced *are-muh-GED-un.* From two Hebrew words meaning "the hill of Megiddo." It was the place of many ancient battles in northern Palestine.

hand a golden cup full of abominations and the filthiness of her fornication. 5 And on her forehead a name *was* written:

MYSTERY,
BABYLON THE GREAT,
THE MOTHER OF HARLOTS AND
OF THE ABOMINATIONS OF THE
EARTH.

6 I saw the woman, drunk with the blood of the saints and with the blood of the martyrs of Jesus. And when I saw her, I marveled with great amazement.

7 But the angel said to me, "Why did you marvel? I will tell you the mystery of the woman and of the beast that carries her, which has the seven heads and the ten horns. 8 The beast that you saw was, and is not, and will ascend out of the bottomless pit and go to perdition. And those who dwell on the earth will marvel, whose names are not written in the Book of Life from the foundation of the world, when they see the beast that was, and is not, and yet is.

9 "Here *is* the mind which has wisdom: The seven heads are seven mountains on which the woman sits. 10 There are also seven kings. Five have fallen, one is, *and* the other has not yet come. And when he comes, he must continue a short time. 11 The beast that was, and is not, is himself also the eighth, and is of the seven, and is going to perdition.

12 "The ten horns which you saw are ten kings who have received no kingdom as yet, but they receive authority for one hour as kings with the beast. 13 These are of one mind, and they will give their power and authority to the beast. 14 These will make war with the Lamb, and the Lamb will overcome them, for He is Lord of lords and King of kings; and those *who are* with Him *are* called, chosen, and faithful."

15 Then he said to me, "The waters which you saw, where the harlot sits, are peoples, multitudes, nations, and tongues. 16 And the ten horns which you saw on the beast, these will hate the harlot, make her desolate and naked, eat her flesh and burn her with fire. 17 For God has put it into their hearts to fulfill His purpose, to be of one mind, and to give their kingdom to the beast, until the words of God are fulfilled. 18 And the woman whom you saw is that great city which reigns over the kings of the earth."

Wicked Babylon will fall

18 After these things I saw another angel coming down from heaven, having great authority, and the earth was illuminated with his glory. 2 And he cried mightily with a loud voice, saying, "Babylon the great is fallen, is fallen, and has become a dwelling place of demons, a prison for every foul spirit, and a cage for every unclean and hated bird! 3 For all the nations have drunk of the wine of the wrath of her fornication, the kings of the earth have committed fornication with her, and the merchants of the earth have become rich through the abundance of her luxury."

4 And I heard another voice from heaven saying, "Come out of her, my people, lest you share in her sins, and lest you receive of her plagues. 5 For her sins have reached to heaven, and God has remembered her iniquities. 6 Render to her just as she rendered to you, and repay her double according to her works; in the cup which she has mixed, mix double for her. 7 In the measure that she glorified herself and lived luxuriously, in the same measure give her torment and sorrow; for she says in her heart, 'I sit *as* queen, and am no widow, and will not see sorrow.' 8 Therefore her plagues will come in one day—death and mourning and famine. And she will be utterly burned with fire, for strong *is* the Lord God who judges her.

9 "The kings of the earth who committed fornication and lived luxuriously with her will weep and lament for her, when they see the smoke of her burning, 10 standing at a distance for fear of her torment, saying, 'Alas, alas, that

great city Babylon, that mighty city! For in one hour your judgment has come.'

11 "And the merchants of the earth will weep and mourn over her, for no one buys their merchandise anymore: 12 merchandise of gold and silver, precious stones and pearls, fine linen and purple, silk and scarlet, every kind of citron wood, every kind of object of ivory, every kind of object of most precious wood, bronze, iron, and marble; 13 and cinnamon and incense, fragrant oil and frankincense, wine and oil, fine flour and wheat, cattle and sheep, horses and chariots, and bodies and souls of men. 14 The fruit that your soul longed for has gone from you, and all the things which are rich and splendid have gone from you, and you shall find them no more at all. 15 The merchants of these things, who became rich by her, will stand at a distance for fear of her torment, weeping and wailing, 16 and saying, 'Alas, alas, that great city that was clothed in fine linen, purple, and scarlet, and adorned with gold and precious stones and pearls! 17 For in one hour such great riches came to nothing.' Every shipmaster, all who travel by ship, sailors, and as many as trade on the sea, stood at a distance 18 and cried out when they saw the smoke of her burning, saying, 'What is like this great city?'

19 "They threw dust on their heads and cried out, weeping and wailing, and saying, 'Alas, alas, that great city, in which all who had ships on the sea became rich by her wealth! For in one hour she is made desolate.'

20 "Rejoice over her, O heaven, and you holy apostles and prophets, for God has avenged you on her!"

21 Then a mighty angel took up a stone like a great millstone and threw it into the sea, saying, "Thus with violence the great city Babylon shall be thrown down, and shall not be found anymore. 22 The sound of harpists, musicians, flutists, and trumpeters shall not be heard in you anymore. No craftsman of any craft shall be found in you anymore, and the sound of a millstone shall not be heard in you anymore. 23 The light of a lamp shall not shine in you anymore, and the voice of bridegroom and bride shall not be heard in you anymore. For your merchants were the great men of the earth, for by your sorcery all the nations were deceived. 24 And in her was found the blood of prophets and saints, and of all who were slain on the earth."

The wedding feast of the Lamb

19 After these things I heard a loud voice of a great multitude in heaven, saying, "Alleluia! Salvation and glory and honor and power *belong* to the Lord our God! 2 For true and righteous *are* His judgments, because He has judged the great harlot who corrupted the earth with her fornication; and He has avenged on her the blood of His servants *shed* by her." 3 Again they said, "Alleluia! Her smoke rises up forever and ever!" 4 And the twenty-four elders and the four living creatures fell down and worshiped God who sat on the throne, saying, "Amen! Alleluia!" 5 Then a voice came from the throne, saying, "Praise our God, all you His servants and those who fear Him, both small and great!"

6 And I heard, as it were, the voice of a great multitude, as the sound of many waters and as the sound of mighty thunderings, saying, "**Alleluia!** For the Lord God **Omnipotent** reigns! 7 Let us be glad and rejoice and give Him glory, for the marriage of the Lamb has come, and His wife has made herself ready." 8 And to her it

---

WORDFINDER

19:6 Alleluia Pronounced *al-uh-LOO-yah*. From the Hebrew word *Hallelujah* (pronounced *hal-uh-LOO-yah*), meaning "Praise the Lord."

19:6 Omnipotent Pronounced *ahm-NIP-uh-tent*. Almighty or All-powerful.

was granted to be arrayed in fine linen, clean and bright, for the fine linen is the righteous acts of the saints.

9 Then he said to me, "Write: 'Blessed *are* those who are called to the marriage supper of the Lamb!' " And he said to me, "These are the true sayings of God." 10 And I fell at his feet to worship him. But he said to me, "See *that you do* not *do that!* I am your fellow servant, and of your brethren who have the testimony of Jesus. Worship God! For the testimony of Jesus is the spirit of prophecy."

11 Now I saw heaven opened, and behold, a white horse. And He who sat on him *was* called Faithful and True, and in righteousness He judges and makes war. 12 His eyes *were* like a flame of fire, and on His head *were* many crowns. He had a name written that no one knew except Himself. 13 He *was* clothed with a robe dipped in blood, and His name is called The Word of God. 14 And the armies in heaven, clothed in fine linen, white and clean, followed Him on white horses. 15 Now out of His mouth goes a sharp sword, that with it He should strike the nations. And He Himself will rule them

DIGGING IN

19:16 Jesus the King of Kings When you read Matthew, Mark, Luke, and John, you see Jesus as the *Servant* of God. He came to do His heavenly Father's will. God told His Son Jesus to come and be the Servant of mankind, then die on a cross for their sins. That is the Jesus we know most about.

In heaven, Jesus had always been God, the Son of the Father, forever and ever. The earthly Jesus you know had to change His appearance. He became a Man who went about doing good. Jesus, the heavenly Son of God, went all the way to the Cross to convince you that God loves you. What more can God do for you? But in Revelation 19 we no longer see Jesus as a Servant, but *as He really is*—the King of Kings who comes to rule over the world at last. Will you be glad to see Him, or will you be afraid because you didn't listen to Him?

Many battles have been fought here in the Valley of Jezreel.

with a rod of iron. He Himself treads the winepress of the fierceness and wrath of Almighty God. 16 And He has on *His* robe and on His thigh a name written:

KING OF KINGS
AND LORD OF LORDS.

17 Then I saw an angel standing in the sun; and he cried with a loud voice, saying to all the birds that fly in the midst of heaven, "Come and gather together for the supper of the great God, 18 that you may eat the flesh of kings, the flesh of captains, the flesh of mighty men, the flesh of horses and of those who sit on them, and the flesh of all *people,* free and slave, both small and great."

19 And I saw the beast, the kings of the earth, and their armies, gathered together to make war against Him who sat on the horse and against His army. 20 Then the beast was captured, and with him the false prophet who worked signs in his presence, by which he deceived those who received the mark of the beast and those who worshiped his image. These two were cast alive into the lake of fire burning with brimstone. 21 And the rest were killed with the sword which proceeded from the mouth of Him who sat on the horse. And all the birds were filled with their flesh.

Christ will reign for 1,000 years

20 Then I saw an angel coming down from heaven, having the key to the bottomless pit and a great chain in his hand. 2 He laid hold of the dragon, that serpent of old, who is *the* Devil and Satan, and bound him for a thousand years; 3 and he cast him into the bottomless pit, and shut him up, and set a seal on him, so that he should deceive the nations no more till the thousand years were finished. But after these things he must be released for a little while.

4 And I saw thrones, and they sat on them, and judgment was committed to them. Then *I saw* the souls of those who had been beheaded for their witness to Jesus and for the word of God, who had not worshiped the beast or his image, and had not received *his* mark on their foreheads or on their hands. And they lived and reigned with Christ for a thousand years. 5 But the

---

WORDFINDER

20:2 The Devil The title of the angel who rebelled against God's authority. The word means "liar," "slanderer," or "accuser." Satan, meaning "Enemy," is his personal name.

DIGGING IN

20:4 You Can Be a King A long time ago there were great kings, and small kings ruled under the great kings. The kings of the Herod family of Judea ruled during the time of Jesus and Paul on earth. But the Herods were small kings who ruled under the authority of the great Roman emperors.

You are a king if you are in charge of what God gives you to do. Right now God wants you to take charge of your own life. By surrendering your body to Him, you become a king ruling under God. As you prove you can rule over your own life, then God will give you greater work to do. He will be your great King, but you will be a king under Him.

People get in trouble because they believe they can be kings and queens without God. So, sad to say, such people usually end up in ruin. God has to be King of your life because He is your Creator. Your life belongs to Him. (See Revelation 3:21.)

rest of the dead did not live again until the thousand years were finished. This *is* the first resurrection. 6 Blessed and holy *is* he who has part in the first resurrection. Over such the second death has no power, but they shall be priests of God and of Christ, and shall reign with Him a thousand years.

7 Now when the thousand years have expired, Satan will be released from his prison 8 and will go out to deceive the nations which are in the four corners of the earth, **Gog and Magog**, to gather them together to battle, whose number *is* as the sand of the sea. 9 They went up on the breadth of the earth and surrounded the camp of the saints and the beloved city. And fire came down from God out of heaven and devoured them. 10 The devil, who deceived them, was cast into the lake of fire and brimstone where the beast and the false prophet *are*. And they will be tormented day and night forever and ever.

11 Then I saw a great white throne and Him who sat on it, from whose face the earth and the heaven fled away. And there was found no place

for them. 12 And I saw the dead, small and great, standing before God, and books were opened. And another book was opened, which is *the Book* of Life. And the dead were judged according to their works, by the things which were written in the books. 13 The sea gave up the dead who were in it, and Death and Hades delivered up the dead who were in them. And they were judged, each one according to his works. 14 Then Death and Hades were cast into the lake of fire. This is the second death. 15 And anyone not found written in the **Book of Life** was cast into the lake of fire.

John sees a new heaven and a new earth

21 Now I saw a new heaven and a new earth, for the first heaven and the first earth had passed away. Also there was no more sea. 2 Then I, John, saw the holy city, New Jerusalem, coming down out of heaven from God, prepared as a bride adorned for her husband. 3 And I heard a loud voice from heaven saying, "Behold, the taberna-

WORDFINDER

20:8 Gog and Magog   Gog is the future leader of an army against Israel. Magog is his country to the far north of Israel. See Ezekiel 38:2, 3.

20:15 Book of Life   The book containing the names of all of God's people saved by faith in Christ.

DIGGING IN

20:12–15 The Last Judgment Quite often you have to take exams at school. The grades you get will help decide what you're going to be later in life. There are many good careers, but your exams will help guide you to the best career for you.

Someday God also is going to give everybody a big exam. Some people will pass—but others will fail the test. You don't have to be clever to pass God's exam. All you have to do is listen to your conscience. Your conscience tells you

that you don't measure up to the way God planned you should be. The Bible says "all have sinned and fall short of God's glory" (Romans 3:23).

So what can you do? You can't go back and fix all your failures. The good news is that *God* can fix them! Jesus took your place and died instead of you. If you give yourself to Jesus, you don't need to fear the Last Judgment of God. Jesus took that final test for you.

cle of God *is* with men, and He will dwell with them, and they shall be His people. God Himself will be with them *and be* their God. 4 And God will wipe away every tear from their eyes; there shall be no more death, nor sorrow, nor crying. There shall be no more pain, for the former things have passed away."

5 Then He who sat on the throne said, "Behold, I make all things new." And He said to me, "Write, for these words are true and faithful."

6 And He said to me, "It is done! I am the Alpha and the Omega, the Beginning and the End. I will give of the fountain of the water of life freely to him who thirsts. 7 He who overcomes shall inherit all things, and I will be his God and he shall be My son. 8 But the cowardly, unbelieving, abominable, murderers, sexually immoral, sorcerers, idolaters, and all liars shall have their part in the lake which burns with fire and brimstone, which is the second death."

9 Then one of the seven angels who had the seven bowls filled with the seven last plagues came to me and talked with me, saying, "Come, I will show you the bride, the Lamb's wife." 10 And he carried me away in the Spirit to a great and high mountain, and showed me the great city, the holy Jerusalem, descending out of heaven from God, 11 having the glory of God. Her light *was* like a most precious stone, like a jasper stone, clear as crystal. 12 Also she had a great and high

wall with twelve gates, and twelve angels at the gates, and names written on them, which are *the names* of the twelve tribes of the children of Israel: 13 three gates on the east, three gates on the north, three gates on the south, and three gates on the west.

14 Now the wall of the city had twelve foundations, and on them were the names of the twelve apostles of the Lamb. 15 And he who talked with me had a gold reed to measure the city, its gates, and its wall. 16 The city is laid out as a square; its length is as great as its breadth. And he measured the city with the reed: twelve thousand furlongs. Its length, breadth, and height are equal. 17 Then he measured its wall: one hundred *and* forty-four cubits, *according* to the measure of a man, that is, of an angel. 18 The construction of its wall was *of* jasper; and the city *was* pure gold, like clear glass. 19 The foundations of the wall of the city *were* adorned with all kinds of precious stones: the first foundation *was* jasper, the second sapphire, the third chalcedony, the fourth emerald, 20 the fifth sardonyx, the sixth sardius, the seventh chrysolite, the eighth beryl, the ninth topaz, the tenth chrysoprase, the eleventh jacinth, and the twelfth amethyst. 21 The twelve gates *were* twelve pearls: each individual gate was of one pearl. And the street of the city *was* pure gold, like transparent glass.

22 But I saw no temple in it, for the

DIGGING IN

21:5 God Makes All Things New God enjoys creating things. He enjoyed creating the world, even though we later spoiled His world by our sins. Someday He is going to create the world all over again. Sin and the miseries of sin will be gone forever.

In fact, God has already begun His new creation. He is making people new again everywhere in the world. You can be part of God's new creation if you ask Him to give you His new life. Jesus said, "Unless

one is born again, he cannot see the kingdom of God" (John 3:3). You become a new creation of God when you are "born again."

Of course, you can't be born again the way you were born the first time, but God can change you inside. What a thrilling idea! A new start! A brand-new life! And God will do it for you in a single moment if you will sincerely ask Him.

Lord God Almighty and the Lamb are its temple. 23 The city had no need of the sun or of the moon to shine in it, for the glory of God illuminated it. The Lamb *is* its light. 24 And the nations of those who are saved shall walk in its light, and the kings of the earth bring their glory and honor into it. 25 Its gates shall not be shut at all by day (there shall be no night there). 26 And they shall bring the glory and the honor of the nations into it. 27 But there shall by no means enter it anything that defiles, or causes an abomination or a lie, but only those who are written in the Lamb's Book of Life.

Jesus is coming again . . . quickly!

22 And he showed me a pure river of water of life, clear as crystal, proceeding from the throne of God and of the Lamb. 2 In the middle of its street, and on either side of the river, *was* the tree of life, which bore twelve fruits, each *tree* yielding its fruit every month. The leaves of the tree *were* for the healing of the nations. 3 And there shall be no more curse, but the throne of God and of the Lamb shall be in it, and His servants shall serve Him. 4 They shall see His face, and His name *shall be* on their foreheads. 5 There shall be no night there: They need no lamp nor light of the sun, for the Lord God gives them light. And they shall reign forever and ever.

6 Then he said to me, "These words *are* faithful and true." And the Lord God of the holy prophets sent His angel to show His servants the things which must shortly take place.

7 "Behold, I am coming quickly! Blessed *is* he who keeps the words of the prophecy of this book."

8 Now I, John, saw and heard these things. And when I heard and saw, I fell down to worship before the feet of the angel who showed me these things.

9 Then he said to me, "See *that you do* not *do that.* For I am your fellow servant, and of your brethren the prophets, and of those who keep the words of this book. Worship God."

10 And he said to me, "Do not seal the words of the **prophecy** of this book, for the time is at hand. 11 He who is unjust, let him be unjust still; he who is filthy, let him be filthy still; he who is righteous, let him be righteous still; he who is holy, let him be holy still."

12 "And behold, I am coming quickly, and My reward *is* with Me, to give to every one according to his work. 13 I am **the Alpha and the Omega,** *the* Beginning and *the* End, the First and the Last."

14 Blessed *are* those who do His commandments, that they may have the right to the tree of life, and may enter through the gates into the city. 15 But outside *are* dogs and sorcerers and sexually immoral and murderers and idolaters, and whoever loves and practices a lie.

16 "I, Jesus, have sent My **angel** to testify to you these things in the churches. I am the Root and the Offspring of David, the Bright and Morning Star."

WORDFINDER

22:10 Prophecy Pronounced *PROFF-uh-see.* A message or messages from God. Such messages in the Bible often tell about God's plans for the future.

22:13 Alpha and the Omega Pronounced *Al-fuh* and *oh-MEG-uh.* The first and last letters of the Greek alphabet. This is one of the names for Christ who is the First and the Last of all things.

22:16 Angel Means "messenger." The messenger is usually from heaven, but sometimes the messenger is human. For example, Malachi, the name of the Old Testament prophet, means "my angel" or "my messenger."

¹⁷ And the Spirit and the bride say, "Come!" And let him who hears say, "Come!" And let him who thirsts come. Whoever desires, let him take the water of life freely.

¹⁸ For I testify to everyone who hears the words of the prophecy of this book: If anyone adds to these things, God will add to him the plagues that are written in this book; ¹⁹ and if anyone takes away from the words of the book of this prophecy, God shall take away his part from the Book of Life, from the holy city, and *from* the things which are written in this book.

DIGGING IN

22:20 Jesus Is Coming Quickly Remember the last promise in the Bible— "Surely I am coming quickly"? Jesus came first to a world that was sick and dying because we had refused to live God's way.

So far God has given us two thousand more years to change our minds. He has invited the whole world to come and receive His friendship and healing for sin. But a day is coming when God must judge the world. When people live in sin, they ruin their lives until there is only unhappiness and disease everywhere.

God will not allow us to completely destroy the world He created. Jesus will come quickly and save His loved ones from destruction and hell. You will be ready to meet Jesus if you give your life to Him now and live for Him every day. Are you praying with the apostle John, "Even so, come, Lord Jesus"?

Jesus invites all people everywhere to come to Him.

I am the One you first met in Genesis 1. I created the universe and all things in it. I love to create beautiful things, and I love all the beautiful things I have created.

You can never completely understand My sorrow when man, My special creation, decided to live in the world without Me (see Genesis 3). I knew his decision would be the beginning of suffering and death. But you can begin to understand My love when I tell you that right away I planned a way to save My beautiful creation. Yes, I would even find a way to *die* so that those who decided to love Me could live with Me forever. That is what the Bible has been saying all along. My very own Son would become a Man and die in your place.

Now I am making all things new. You are invited to become a member of My NEW CREATION. My Son Jesus will reign as King forever and ever.

20 He who testifies to these things says, "Surely I am coming quickly."
Amen. Even so, come, Lord Jesus!

21 The **grace** of our Lord Jesus Christ *be* with you all. Amen.

 WORDFINDER

22:21 Grace The undeserved kindness of God. We are saved from sin by this grace of God. All the good we enjoy is due to His grace.

DICTIONARY-CONCORDANCE

This dictionary-concordance will help you to find the meanings of words used in the Bible and also to locate key passages in which those words occur.

The more difficult words show pronunciation. The meaning follows the word itself (or the pronunciation) and this is followed by the concordance listing. In the concordance listing only the first letter of the word is used—"l." for "love." The references give you the name of the Bible book, then the chapter, and then the verse or verses. Thus, Lk 24:30-51 would be Luke, chapter 24, verses 30 through 51. See the abbreviations for Bible books listed below.

Abbreviations for the Books of the Bible

Acts	Acts	Judges	Judg
Amos	Amos	1 Kings	1 Kgs
1 Chronicles	1 Chr	2 Kings	2 Kgs
2 Chronicles	2 Chr	Lamentations	Lam
Colossians	Col	Leviticus	Lev
1 Corinthians	1 Cor	Luke	Lk
2 Corinthians	2 Cor	Malachi	Mal
Daniel	Dan	Mark	Mk
Deuteronomy	Deut	Matthew	Mt
Ecclesiastes	Eccles	Micah	Mic
Ephesians	Eph	Nahum	Nah
Esther	Esther	Nehemiah	Neh
Exodus	Ex	Numbers	Num
Ezekiel	Ezek	Obadiah	Obad
Ezra	Ezra	1 Peter	1 Pet
Galatians	Gal	2 Peter	2 Pet
Genesis	Gen	Philemon	Philem
Habakkuk	Hab	Philippians	Phil
Haggai	Hag	Proverbs	Prov
Hebrews	Heb	Psalms	Ps
Hosea	Hos	Revelation	Rev
Isaiah	Isa	Romans	Rom
James	Jas	Ruth	Ruth
Jeremiah	Jer	1 Samuel	1 Sam
Job	Job	2 Samuel	2 Sam
Joel	Joel	Song of Solomon	Song
John (Gospel)	Jn	1 Thessalonians	1 Thess
1 John	1 Jn	2 Thessalonians	2 Thess
2 John	2 Jn	1 Timothy	1 Tim
3 John	3 Jn	2 Timothy	2 Tim
Jonah	Jon	Titus	Tit
Joshua	Josh	Zechariah	Zech
Jude	Jude	Zephaniah	Zeph

BOOKS OF THE BIBLE

Old Testament

Genesis (JEN-ih-sis)
Exodus (EX-oh-dus)
Leviticus (leh-VIT-ih-kus)
Numbers
Deuteronomy (dew-ter-ONN-oh-mee)
Joshua (JOSH-you-uh)
Judges
Ruth
Samuel (SAM-you-ell)
1 and 2 Kings
1 and 2 Chronicles (KRON-ih-kuls)
Ezra (EZ-ruh)
Nehemiah (nee-huh-MY-uh)
Esther (ESS-ter)
Job (JOBE)
Psalms (SALMS)
Proverbs (PRAH-verbs)
Ecclesiastes (ih-klee-zih-ASS-tees)

Song of Solomon
Isaiah (eye-ZAY-uh)
Jeremiah (jer-uh-MY-uh)
Lamentations (lam-men-TAY-shuns)
Ezekiel (ee-ZEEK-yell)
Daniel (DAN-yell)
Hosea (ho-ZAY-uh)
Joel (JO-ell)
Amos (AY-mus)
Obadiah (oh-buh-DIE-uh)
Jonah (JO-nuh)
Micah (MY-kuh)
Nahum (NAY-hum)
Habakkuk (huh-BACK-kuk)
Zephaniah (zef-uh-NIGH-uh)
Haggai (HAG-ay-eye)
Zechariah (zek-uh-RIGH-uh)
Malachi (MAL-uh-kigh)

New Testament

Matthew (MATH-you)
Mark
Luke
John
Acts
Romans (ROW-muns)
1 and 2 Corinthians (ko-RIN-thee-uns)
Galatians (guh-LAY-shuns)
Ephesians (ee-FEE-zhuns)
Colossians (ko-LOSH-shuns)

1 and 2 Thessalonians (thess-uh-
    LOW-nih-uns)
1 and 2 Timothy
Titus (TIGHT-us)
Philemon (fih-LEE-mun)
Hebrews (HE-brews)
James
1 and 2 Peter
1, 2, and 3 John
Jude (JEWD)
Revelation (rev-uh-LAY-shun)

A

Aaron (AIR-un) The older brother of Moses
(Ex 6:20; 7:7); the spokesman for Moses
(Ex 7:1); brings on plagues with his rod (Ex
7:10—8:17); from him are descended the
class of priests in Israel (Ex 29:9); he makes
atonement and stops a plague (Num
16:41-50); his rod buds (Num 17:1-11);
his death (Num 20:22-29).

Abba (AB-buh) Aramaic for "Father" (Mk
14:36; Rom 8:15; Gal 4:6).

Abed-Nego (ah-BED-nee-go) Babylonian
name of one of Daniel's companions (Dan
1:7; 3:16).

Abel (AY-bull) Son of Adam; murdered by
his brother Cain (Gen 4:2ff). He is described as righteous (Mt 23:35; 1 Jn 3:12).
In Hebrews 11:4 he stands at the head of
the heroes of faith.

abhor To despise, hate.
I hate and a. lying Ps 119:163
Nations will a. him Prov 24:24
A. what is evil Rom 12:9

abomination (ah-bom-ih-NAY-shun)
Something loathsome.
Wickedness is an a. Prov 8:7
is an a. in the sight of God Lk 16:15

Abraham; Abram (AY-bruh-ham; AY-
brum) Israel's first great patriarch or leader.
Through faith in God's promise to make of
him a great nation, he is led from Ur to Canaan (Gen 11:31—15:7). God makes a
covenant with him (Gen 15:7-21); an angel of God promises that Sarah shall give
birth to a son (Gen 18:10); God tests Abraham's faith (Gen 22:1-19). He stands as
the father of all the faithful (Gal 3:7).

Absalom (AB-suh-lum) Son of David and
Maacah; turned the people against his father; was defeated and then slain by Joab,
to the great sorrow of David (2 Sam 3:3;
13:20—19:10).

Adam (ADD-um) The first man, from whom
is descended all mankind. Created on the
same day as the animals, he is particularly
blessed by God (Gen 1:27, 28). He and
Eve were driven from the Garden of Eden
because of their disobedience (Gen
3:1-24).

adultery (ah-DULL-ter-ih) Unchastity; unfaithfulness to one's husband or wife.
You shall not commit a. Ex 20:14
You shall not commit a. Deut 5:18
has already committed a. with her Mt 5:28

advise To tell, inform.
I will a. you what Num 24:14

advocate One who speaks in defense of another. Christ is so called (1 Jn 2:1).

affliction

affliction Distress; pain; adversity.
God has seen my a. Gen 31:42

agape (ah-GAH-pe) A Greek word meaning "love." It is also used to denote the "love
feasts" of the early Christians (Jude 12).

Agrippa (ah-GRIP-uh) King of Judea before
whom Paul appeared to plead his defense
(Acts 25:13—26:32).

Ahab (AY-hab) An evil king of the northern
kingdom of Israel in the time of Elijah; married Jezebel, a Sidonian princess, which
caused religious turmoil; robbed Naboth of
his vineyard and then caused his death
(1 Kgs 16:29—22:40).

Ahasuerus (ah-haz-you-EAR-us) The
name of two kings in the Old Testament.
1. A king of Persia and the husband
of the Jewess, Esther (Esther 1:2, 19;
2:16-17). Through her guardian, Mordecai, Esther was able to save her people, Israel, from an evil plan. 2. A king of the
Medes and the father of Darius (Dan 9:1).

Ahaz (AY-haz) A name which means "he has
grasped." 1. A wicked king of Judah who
worshiped idols on the "high places" and
even offered one of his own sons on an altar (2 Kgs 16:3-4); refused to listen to the
prophet Isaiah when he encouraged the

king to call on God instead of seeking foreign aid against the army of Syria (Isa 7:1-16); heard the wonderful announcement of the promised Messiah. Hosea and Micah also prophesied during the reign of Ahaz (Hos 1:1; Mic 1:1). 2. A descendant of King Saul, the son of Micah and the father of Jehoaddah (1 Chr 8:35-36; 9:42).

alien A foreigner.
give it to the a. Deut 14:21

Alleluia (al-uh-LOO-yah) Hallelujah; "Praise the Lord" (Rev 19:1, 3, 4, 6).

Almighty, the God, as being all powerful.
I am A. God Gen 17:1
as God A. Ex 6:3
Holy, holy, holy, Lord God A. Rev 4:8

Alpha and Omega (Al-fuh; oh-MEE-guh) The first and last letters of the Greek alphabet; hence, "the First and the Last." Applied to God (Rev 1:8, 11; 21:6) and to Christ (Rev 22:13).

altar

altar Table of sacrifice.
Noah built an a. Gen 8:20
Moses built an a. Ex 17:15

Am Exist; be. The reply to Moses' question for the name of the Deity, "I AM WHO I AM" (Ex 3:14), indicates that the Lord makes Himself present as He wills.

Amen Verily; so be it (Mt 6:13; Rev 3:14).

Amos (AY-mus) A prophet of Israel; the first to proclaim that God is the ruler of the whole universe; foretold the downfall of the northern kingdom. The OT Book of Amos is the third of the 12 Minor Prophets.

Ananias (ann-uh-NIGH-us) 1. A Christian of Jerusalem who lost his life for lying and attempting to hold back part of the price of property he had sold (Acts 5:1-10). 2. A Christian of Damascus who received Paul into Christian fellowship (Acts 9:10-17; 22:12-16). 3. A Jewish high priest before whom Paul was tried in Jerusalem (Acts 23:2; 24:1).

Ancient of Days The judge in Daniel's vision; probably intended to be God Himself (Dan 7:9, 13, 22).

Andrew One of the first of the 12 apostles of Jesus; brother of Simon Peter (Mt 4:18; 10:2-4; Mk 1:16-20, 29; 3:16-19; 13:3; 6:14-16; Jn 1:35-42, 44; 6:8; 12:20-22; 21:15-17; Acts 1:13). He was a former disciple of John the Baptist (Jn 1:35-40). *See* Simon.

angel A heavenly messenger.
an a. spoke to me 1 Kgs 13:18
a little lower than the a. Ps 8:5
a. came and ministered Mt 4:11
the a. Gabriel was sent Lk 1:26
a. of the bottomless pit Rev 9:11

Angel of the Lord The heavenly messenger whose presence is evidence of God Himself (Gen 16:7; Ex 3:2; Num 22:23; 1 Kgs 19:7; Mt 28:2; Lk 1:11; 2:9).

anoint To consecrate; to pour oil upon in a ceremony.
a. my head with oil Ps 23:5
to a. My body Mk 14:8
You did not a. Lk 7:46

answer A reply.
soft a. turns away wrath Prov 15:1

ant An insect.
Go to the a., you sluggard Prov 6:6

antichrist (AN-tih-krist) Opponent or enemy of Christ.
He is a. who denies 1 Jn 2:22
deceiver and an a. 2 Jn 7

Antioch (ANN-tee-ock) 1. In Syria; the name "Christian" was first used here (Acts 11:26). 2. In Pisidia; visited by Paul and Barnabas (Acts 13:14-52).

anxious Worried; careful.
Be a. for nothing Phil 4:6

Apollos (uh-POLL-us) A well-educated Jew and a follower of John the Baptist; knew the Old Testament well and taught others (Acts 18:24-28); learned of the Holy Spirit from Aquila and Priscilla in Ephesus; preached in Corinth (1 Cor 1:12; 3:4-6, 22; 4:6). Some teachers think Apollos wrote the Letter to the Hebrews.

apostle (uh-POSS-ul) One of the 12 disciples chosen by Jesus (Mt 10:2-4) or cer-

tain other early Christian leaders (Acts 14:14; Rom 16:7; Gal 1:1).
apple A fruit.
a. of His eye Deut 32:10; Ps 17:8
appoint 1. To consecrate, or set apart as for the ministry.
a. elders in every church Acts 14:23
a. elders in every city Tit 1:5
2. To establish.
I will a. a place 1 Chr 17:9
Aquila (ak-WILL-uh) A Jew who lived in Rome with his wife Priscilla until the emperor ordered all Jewish people to leave; moved to Corinth where he worked as a tentmaker with Paul (Acts 18:1-3); traveled with Paul to Syria (Acts 18:18, 19).
Arabia; Arabians The NW part of the large peninsula in SW Asia; scene of many biblical events. The peoples of the area were nomads.
Arameans (air-uh-ME-uns) A Semitic people, traditionally descendants of Shem, the oldest son of Noah (Gen 10:1, 22, 23). They were nomads, wandering along the W side of the Syrian desert.
Ararat (AIR-uh-rat) The mountain on which the ark came to rest after the Flood (Gen 8:4); the land of Ararat is Armenia.
archangel (ark-AYN-jel) An angel of the highest order.
the voice of an a. 1 Thess 4:16
Michael the a. Jude 9
ark A floating vessel; ship.
Noah's a. Gen 6:14—8:19
Noah entered the a. Mt 24:38
ark of the Testimony The chest which held the two stone tablets on which were inscribed the Ten Commandments (Ex 25:10-22). Also called the ark of the covenant (1 Kgs 8:6; 2 Chr 5:2).
Armageddon (are-muh-GED-un) The name means "mountain of Megiddo." The large valley of Jezreel or Plain of Esdraelon near the ancient fortified city of Megiddo in northern Israel. According to prophecy, this is the place where the last battle of this age will be fought between the forces of good and evil.
Artaxerxes (are-tack-SURK-sees) The name of two Persian kings: the first, mentioned in Ezra 7 and Nehemiah 2; 13; his grandson, the second, may have been the builder of the palace described in Esther 1:5, 6.
Ascension (ah-SEN-shun) The return of the risen Christ to heaven (Lk 24:51; Acts

1:9) on the fortieth day after the Resurrection.
Ascents, Song of A title given to each of Psalms 120—134; probably so called because of their use in a procession ascending to the temple or for pilgrims going up to Jerusalem.

ark of the Testimony

Asher (ASH-er) The eighth son of Jacob, the second by Zilpah (Gen 30:12ff); one of the 12 tribes of Israel.
Asherah (ah-SHE-rah) The wife of the Canaanite god, Baal. Asherah often refers to a wooden pole that stood near Canaanite high places of worship ("grove"). Gideon was ordered by the Lord to destroy the wooden image beside the altar (Judg 6:25).
Asia (AY-zhuh) A Roman province in the western part of what we call Asia Minor (Acts 16:6; 20:18; 1 Pet 1:1; Rev 1:4).
ask To request.
A., and it will be given Mt 7:7
a. in prayer, believing Mt 21:22
do not know what you a. Mk 10:38
Assyria (ah-SEER-ih-uh) A kingdom between the Tigris and Euphrates Rivers in Mesopotamia; ruled over the ancient world from the 9th to the 7th centuries B.C. (before Christ). After defeating the northern kingdom of Israel in 722 B.C., the Assyrians captured and carried away thousands of Israelites to their country. In 701 B.C.,

Assyria attacked the southern kingdom of Judah, but did not succeed because a plague from the "Angel of the Lord" struck down the soldiers (2 Kgs 19:35). Thousands died, and Jerusalem, the capital, was saved. (Find out more about Assyria in the Book of Jonah and in Isa 10:5, Ezek 16:28, and Hos 8:9).

Athens (ATH-ins) The capital city of the ancient Greeks as well as the modern capital, located on the southern coast of Attica; center of Greek art, architecture, literature, and politics during the golden age of Grecian history. The world's most famous building—the Parthenon—stands here in ruins. During his second missionary journey, the apostle Paul preached his famous sermon on Areopagus, Mars' Hill (Acts 17:15—18:1).

Atonement, Day of An annual fast day of the Jews. Ordained in the Law as a day of humbling oneself and making amends for sins (Lev 23:27).

B

Baal (BAYL) One of the fertility gods of Canaan. There were many local Baals. Elijah met the prophets of Baal in a contest (1 Kgs 18:1-40).

Babel (BAY-bull) Hebrew form of the name "Babylon," capital of Babylonia; site of the Tower of Babel (Gen 11:1-9).

babes Infants; small children.
Out of the mouth of b. Ps 8:2; Mt 21:16

Babylon (BAB-ih-lun) An ancient walled city, once the capital of the Babylonian Empire, located between the Tigris and Euphrates Rivers. In 586 B.C., the leading citizens of Judah were taken captive by King Nebuchadnezzar and brought to Babylon where they stayed for 70 years during the period called the Exile. (You can read about this period of history in the books of Isaiah, Jeremiah, Ezekiel, and Daniel.) Here were the famous hanging gardens and, nearby, the Tower of Babel (Gen 11:1-9).

baptism A ceremony in which one enters the church family. It is a way of showing that you have been washed free of sin by the death and rising from the dead of Jesus Christ.
John's b. of Jesus Mt 3:13-17
b. by the disciples Jn 4:1, 2

Barabbas (bar-RAB-bus) A robber held in prison by the Roman authorities at the time of Jesus' trial; Pilate freed him and condemned Jesus to death (Mt 27:20-26; Mk 15:7-15; Lk 23:18-25; Jn 18:39, 40).

Barnabas (BARN-nuh-bus) The surname given by the apostles to Joses or Joseph, a Levite of Cyprus, who was sent by them to Antioch to confirm the church there. Accompanied Paul on his first missionary journey (Acts 4:36, 37; 9:27; 11:22, 25, 30; 12:25; 13:1-13, 43-52; 14:12, 14, 20; 15:2ff; 1 Cor 9:6; Gal 2:1, 9, 13; Col 4:10).

Bartholomew (bar-THAHL-uh-mew) One of the 12 apostles of Jesus (Mt 10:3; Mk 3:18; Lk 6:14; Acts 1:13).

Baruch (bar-OOK) Jeremiah's scribe, or secretary (Jer 36:4ff).

basket The container for holding a dry measure.
under a b. Mt 5:15; Mk 4:21; Lk 11:33

bath A liquid measure equal to the dry measure ephah (Ezek 45:11); about six gallons.
just ephah, and a just b. Ezek 45:10

Bathsheba (bath-SHE-bah) The wife of Uriah, the Hittite, and King David (2 Sam 11; 12:24); the woman with whom David sinned. David had her husband, Uriah, killed in battle. Then David married her and she became the mother of Solomon, who ruled after David's death.

beard The growth of hair on the lower part of a man's face. The Hebrews were forbidden to cut the edges of their beards (Lev 19:27). The shaving off of beards was an indignity (2 Sam 10:4, 5).

beast Animal (used for all living things other than man, as a general term); in the Book of Revelation the word is used of both "heavenly" beasts and "beasts from the bottomless pit."

Beatitudes (bee-AT-ih-tyoods) The blessings listed by Jesus in the Sermon on the Mount (Mt 5:3-12; Lk 6:20-23).

Beelzebub (bee-EL-zee-bub) The prince of demons whom Jesus refers to as Satan (Mt 10:25; 12:26; Mk 3:23; Lk 11:15, 18). The Jews considered this heathen god as the supreme evil spirit.

beginning Outset; start.
In the b. God created Gen 1:1
In the b. was the Word Jn 1:1

begotten Having been brought into being.
The only b. Son Jn 1:18

benediction (ben-ih-DICK-shun) An asking for God's blessing, as by a minister or priest at the conclusion of a church service; a blessing.

Benjamin The youngest son of Jacob. His mother, Rachel, died at his birth (Gen 35:18). Especially beloved by his father and by Joseph, his only full brother (Gen 42:4, 36; 43:14-16, 29, 34; 44:12; 45:12, 14, 22). Ancestor of the tribe of Benjamin, the smallest of the 12 tribes of Israel.

Bethany (BETH-uh-nee) A small village on the E slope of the Mount of Olives, about one and one-half mi. E of Jerusalem. From here Jesus made His triumphal entry into Jerusalem (Mk 11:1-11); the home of Simon the leper (Mt 26:6; Mk 14:3); home of Lazarus, Mary, and Martha (Jn 11:1-44); site of Jesus' final parting from His disciples (Lk 24:50, 51).

Bethel (BETH-ul) City 14 mi. N of Jerusalem. Near here Abraham built an altar (Gen 12:8; 13:3, 4); here Jacob's name was changed to Israel (Gen 35:10-15); the ark of the Testimony rested here (Judg 20:18-28); Jeroboam made it a place of idolatry (1 Kgs 12:29—13:32), which Josiah destroyed (2 Kgs 23:4-15).

Bethlehem A very old town about six mi. SSW of Jerusalem; the birthplace of Jesus (Mt 2:1-16; Lk 2:4-15; Jn 7:42); also associated with David (1 Sam 16:1-13; 17:12, 15; 20:6, 28), Ruth (Ruth 1:1, 2, 19, 22; 2:4; 4:11), and other persons of the OT.

bird A winged creature.
let b. fly above Gen 1:20
b. of the air Gen 6:7; Mt 6:26

birthright Privilege of the firstborn of a family.
Esau despised his b. Gen 25:34

bishop A high-ranking minister, head of a district or diocese.
A b. then must be blameless 1 Tim 3:2

blood The life-giving fluid of the body. In the OT it is regarded as the seat of life; but since shed blood signifies death, the word is used of both life and death.
you shall not eat any b. Lev 7:26; Deut 12:16
this is My b. Mt 26:28; Mk 14:24
new covenant in My b. Lk 22:20
eats My flesh and drinks My b. Jn 6:54
redemption through His b. Eph 1:7; Col 1:14
precious b. of Christ 1 Pet 1:19

Boaz (BOH-az) A wealthy Bethlehemite who married Ruth (Ruth 2:1—4:22).

body The physical human being or animal. The church is called "the body of Christ" as the living spiritual community of which Christ is the head and all believers are members. At the Lord's Supper, Jesus broke bread to represent His body given in sacrifice for sinners.
touches the dead b. Num 19:11
lamp of the b. is the eye Mt 6:22
this is My b. Mt 26:26; Mk 14:22; Lk 22:19; 1 Cor 11:24
many members in one b. Rom 12:4
you are the b. of Christ 1 Cor 12:27

Booths, Feast of See Feast of Tabernacles.

bread A food made of a dough of flour or meal and water and baked; sustenance in general. Often used in offerings by OT peoples. In the NT, also used in reference to the coming of the kingdom of God or to Jesus Himself.
not live by b. alone Deut 8:3
shall eat unleavened b. Deut 16:8
Cast your b. upon the Eccles 11:1
not live by b. alone Mt 4:4
Give us this day our daily b. Mt 6:11; Lk 11:3
eat b. in the kingdom Lk 14:15
the true b. from heaven Jn 6:32
I am the b. of life Jn 6:35

bread, breaking of Since the earliest form of the Lord's Supper involved the "breaking of bread," the term has been used for worship in general (Acts 2:42).

bread from heaven The food miraculously provided by God for the Israelites in their wanderings through the wilderness (Ex 16:15).

brother A male relative of the same parents; a close associate.
Am I my b.'s keeper Gen 4:9
b. is born for adversity Prov 17:17
sticks closer than a b. Prov 18:24
is My b. and sister and Mt 12:50

C

Cain Son of Adam; murdered his brother Abel (Gen 4:2ff); prototype of wicked men (1 Jn 3:12; Jude 11).

Calvary (KAL-vuh-ree) From the Latin word meaning "skull." A place outside the second wall of Jerusalem where Jesus was crucified (Lk 23:33). Since Jerusalem has been destroyed and rebuilt so many times, no one knows for sure where this event took place, but there are at least two opinions: (1) A spot under the Church of the Holy Sepulcher; (2) "Gordon's Calvary," named for General Charles Gordon, a British soldier and explorer. The Hebrew name for the place where Jesus was crucified is *Golgotha* (Mt 27:33; Mk 15:22; Jn 19:17).

camel A large animal of desert areas.
a c. to go through Mt 19:24
and swallow a c. Mt 23:24

Canaan; Canaanites (KAY-nun; KAY-nuh-nights) 1. The fourth son of Ham and grandson of Noah (Gen 9:18-27; 10:6, 15). 2. The region along the Mediterranean Sea known as the Promised Land—the land given by God to Abraham and the Children of Israel; known as Israel today; the land bridge between three continents—Africa, Europe, and Asia. Because of its position, this narrow strip of land has always been very important to invading armies as well as to traders.

Capernaum (kuh-PURR-nah-um) A city on the NW shore of the Sea of Galilee. Jesus lived there (Mk 2:1); home of Peter and Andrew (Mt 8:5, 14); here Jesus healed the man with an unclean spirit (Mk 1:21-28) and the paralytic (Mk 2:1-12) and held discussions about true greatness (Mk 9:33-37) and paying the half-shekel tax (Mt 17:24-27).

Carmel, Mount (KAR-mel) A mountain range in northern Palestine, Israel; stretches SE from the Mediterranean Sea about thirteen miles. Here Elijah held his famous contest with the Baal priests (1 Kgs 18:19-20); saw the cloud which marked the end of a long drought (1 Kgs 18:44).

cheek The side of the face.
slaps you on your right c. Mt 5:39; Lk 6:29

cherubim (CHER-uh-bim) Winged creatures, statues of which were fixed to the mercy seat of the ark of the Testimony. Two cherubim carved from olive wood were placed within the inner room of the temple.
two c. of gold Ex 25:18
made two c. of olive 1 Kgs 6:23

child A young person of either sex.
a c. is known by his Prov 20:11
unto us a C. is born Isa 9:6
little c. shall lead Isa 11:6

children Young persons of either sex.
become as little c. Mt 18:3
Let the little c. come Mt 19:14

Christians Followers of Christ.
first called C. in Antioch Acts 11:26

Christmas The holiday on December 25 which celebrates the birth of Jesus Christ.

church The people of God; those destined to inherit the kingdom of God. Also, any local group of believers.
I will build My c. Mt 16:18
Christ is head of the c. Eph 5:23
head of the body, the c. Col 1:18
the seven c. Rev 1:4, 11, 20

child

clean Free from defilement or dirt. Under the Hebrew law certain animals are declared clean and others unclean (Lev 11:1-47; Deut 14:3-21).
c. hands and a pure heart Ps 24:4
can make me c. Mt 8:2; Mk 1:40; Lk 5:12
c. the outside of the cup Mt 23:25; Lk 11:39
all things are c. Lk 11:41

cloud A visible mass of water particles in the air above the earth.
pillar of c. Ex 13:21; Num 12:5
c. covered the mountain Ex 24:15

Colosse; Colossians (ko-LAH-see; ko-LOSH-uns) A city in Asia Minor. Paul wrote an epistle to the Christians of this city.

commandment Any of the Ten Commandments or laws given to Moses by God at Mount Sinai (Ex 20:1-17; Deut 5:6-21); other OT laws.
keep the c. Mt 19:17

which is the great c. Mt 22:36
you love Me, keep My c. Jn 14:15
confess To admit to a fault or sin, particularly as a sign of repentance; to acknowledge God's redeeming acts and openly acknowledge that Jesus is the Messiah, Lord, and Son of God (as Peter's great confession in Mt 16:16; Mk 8:29; Lk 9:20); to offer praise and thanksgiving to God.
c. that he has sinned Lev 5:5
c. Me before men Mt 10:32; Lk 12:8
c. their sins Mk 1:5
c. that Jesus Christ is Phil 2:11
C. your trespasses to one Jas 5:16
congregation An assembly; gathering.
c. of the righteous Ps 1:5
God stands in the c. Ps 82:1
in the c. of saints Ps 149:1
converted Changed, as one's religion or belief.
unless you are c. Mt 18:3
Repent . . . and be c. Acts 3:19
Corinth (KOR-inth) Most important trade city of ancient Greece (Acts 18:1; 19:1; 1 Cor 1:2; 2 Cor 1:1; 2 Tim 4:20); situated on the Isthmus of Corinth, a narrow strip of land between the Aegean and Ionian Seas. Today a deep canal saves scores of miles of sea travel. Corinth was a very wealthy and wicked city in Paul's day. He did establish a strong church here to which he wrote letters—1 and 2 Corinthians.
Cornelius (kor-NEEL-yus) A Roman soldier stationed in Caesarea who was the first recorded Gentile convert to Christianity (Acts 10:1-33). Even before his conversion, he was a God-fearing man who believed in the Jewish teaching of one God (monotheism) and opposed the worship of idols. The apostle Peter took part in Cornelius' conversion.
counselor An adviser or teacher. Counselors seem to have been court officials of the Israelite kings (1 Chr 27:33; Job 3:14; Prov 11:14). The coming Messiah is so called (Isa 9:6).
courier Messenger.
letters were sent by c. Esther 3:13
c. who rode on royal horses Esther 8:14
covenant (KUV-uh-nunt) A binding agreement. The great covenant between God and Israel was made at Sinai (Ex 24:3-8); the tablets on which the Ten Commandments were engraved were called "the tablets of the covenant" (Deut 9:11). The chest in which these tablets were placed

was called the "ark of the Testimony" (Ex 25:22). The new covenant came into being through the blood of Christ.
My blood of the new c. Mk 14:24
cup is the new c. 1 Cor 11:25
creation The act of God in making heaven and earth and bringing forth all life; the whole universe.
the story of c. Gen 1:1—2:25
c. which God created Mk 13:19
the whole c. groans Rom 8:22
creator; Creator The maker; originator; hence, **Creator:** God; the Lord.
Remember now your C. Eccles 12:1
C. of the ends of the Isa 40:28
creature rather than the C. Rom 1:25

creature

creature Any living thing that God has made.
great sea c. Gen 1:21
called each living c. Gen 2:19
every c. of God is good 1 Tim 4:4
creeping thing Reptile.
every c. that creeps Gen 1:26
C. and flying fowl Ps 148:10
wild beasts, c. Acts 10:12
cross An upright post with cross-beam on which victims of execution were nailed; used by the Romans. A symbol of Christianity.
who does not take his c. Mt 10:38
take up his c. Mt 16:24; Mk 8:34

come down from the c. Mt 27:40
Simon . . . . to bear His c. Mk 15:21
stood by the c. of Jesus Jn 19:25
crown A headdress of gold, precious stones,
etc.; a wreath encircling the head.
A c. of glory Prov 4:9; 16:31
excellent wife is the c. Prov 12:4
c. of thorns Mt 27:29; Mk 15:17; Jn 19:2, 5
perishable c. 1 Cor 9:25

The Crucifixion

Crucifixion, the (crew-sih-FIX-shun) Jesus' execution on the Cross by the Romans at the instigation of the Jewish leaders (Mt 27; Mk 15; Lk 23; Jn 19).
crucify (CREW-sih-fy) To put to death by fastening to a cross.
scourge and to c. Mt 20:19
Let Him be c. Mt 27:22
C. Him Mk 15:13; Lk 23:21; Jn 19:6
cubit A measure of length of about 18 inches.
add one c. to Mt 6:27; Lk 12:25
cup A vessel from which to drink.
My c. runs over Ps 23:5
c. of cold water Mt 10:42; Mk 9:41
drink the c. Mt 20:22; Mk 10:39
outside of the c. Mt 23:25
took the c. Mt 26:27; Mk 14:23; Lk 22:17; 1 Cor 11:25
c. pass from Me Mt 26:39; Mk 14:36; Lk 22:42
c. which My Father Jn 18:11
curse To call on God to punish.

c. him who curses you Gen 12:3
Whoever c. his God Lev 24:15
C. God and die Job 2:9
bless those who c. you Mt 5:44; Lk 6:28
began to c. Mt 26:74; Mk 14:71
fig tree which You c. Mk 11:21

cubit

Cyrus (SIGH-rus) The powerful king of Persia (559–530 B.C.), sometimes called "Cyrus the Great." In 536 B.C., he wrote an edict or law which allowed the Jewish captives in Babylon to return to their homeland in Jerusalem; praised in the OT as God's "shepherd" and "anointed" (Isa 44:28; 45:1); encouraged the rebuilding of the temple. God often uses nonbelievers in working out His plans for His people. (Find out more about Cyrus in Ezra 3:7; 4:3, 5; 5:13, 14, 17; 6:3, 14; Dan 1:21; 6:28; 10:1.)

D

Dagon (DAY-gun) The chief god of the Philistines (1 Sam 5:2-7). When the Philistines defeated Israel, they captured the ark of the covenant and took it to the temple of Dagon in Ashdod. Samson, blinded by his captors, had been brought into the temple and tied between the two pillars which supported the roof. When he called on the Lord to return his strength, he brought down the building with his bare hands and

died along with hundreds of Philistines
(Judg 16:23-30).

Dagon

Damascus (duh-MASK-us) A very ancient
city, capital of Syria; in OT times the capital
of the Aramean kingdom. Site of Saul's
conversion (Acts 9:1-22).

Dan The fifth son of Jacob, born of Bilhah
(Gen 30:1-6); one of the 12 tribes of Israel.

dance To move in rhythm, usually to the
sound of music.

mourn, And a time to d. Eccles 3:4
you did not d. Mt 11:17; Lk 7:32

Daniel The Jewish prophet at the Babylonian court about whom the OT Book of
Daniel is written. Interpreted dreams (Dan
2:1-45) and the handwriting on the wall
(5:17-30); saved by God from the lions
(6:16-24).

David The second and greatest king over Israel; youngest son of Jesse (1 Sam 17:12,
14); slew Goliath (1 Sam 17:41-50);
friend of Jonathan (1 Sam 19:1—20:42);
a fugitive from Saul's wrath (1 Sam
21—27; 30); king of Judah (2 Sam
1:1—5:5); king of Israel (2 Sam 3:6—
1 Kgs 2:11); brought the ark of the Testimony to Jerusalem (2 Sam 6:1-17); his
great sin in coveting Bathsheba (2 Sam
11:1-27); rebellion of his son Absalom
(2 Sam 14—18); his psalm of thanksgiving
(2 Sam 22); names Solomon, his son, to
succeed him (1 Kgs 1:11—2:12).

day The time between sunrise and sunset; a
period of 24 hours.
God called the light D. Gen 1:5
neither the d. nor Mt 25:13

D. come on you unexpectedly Lk 21:34
day of the Lord In the OT, the day when
God punishes evil (Amos 5:18-20); a day
of universal disaster (Isa 2; 13; 24; Zeph
1:7-18; 2:2, 3; 3:8). In the NT, the day of
the Last Judgment and the end of the world
(1 Cor 4:5; 5:5; 1 Thess 5:2; Rev 16:14).

deacon A servant or minister; an officer of a
local church who assists the minister or
priest.
with the bishops and d. Phil 1:1
d. must be reverent, not 1 Tim 3:8

Dead Sea The salt lake at the mouth of the
Jordan River. Biblical names: "Salt Sea"
(Gen 14:3; Num 34:3, 12; Deut 3:17;
Josh 3:16; 12:3; 15:2, 5; 18:19); "eastern
sea" (Joel 2:20).

death The condition of being without life; the
act of dying. Symbol of the final state of the
unsaved (Jn 8:51; Rom 6:23; Rev 20:6),
and of the power that rules over man in the
age of sin (Rom 5:14; Rev 6:8).
valley of the shadow of d. Ps 23:4
swallow up d. forever Isa 25:8
not taste d. Mt 16:28; Mk 9:1; Lk 9:27
D., where is your sting 1 Cor 15:55

Deborah 1. Rebekah's nurse and companion (Gen 35:8). 2. An early "judge" of
Israel; aroused the scattered tribes to opposition to Canaanite oppression; Song
of Deborah (Judg 5:2-31) celebrates her
achievement.

debts Obligations; anything owed to another.
forgive us our d. Mt 6:12

Dedication, Feast of An eight-day festival
observing the victories of Judas Mac-
cabaeus and the purification and rededica-
tion of the temple (Jn 10:22). Also called
Feast of Lights; Hanukkah; Chanukah.

Delilah (dih-LIE-luh) A woman from the
Valley of Sorek; betrayed Samson to the
Philistines (Judg 16:4-22).

deliverer, the In five OT passages (2 Sam
22:2; Ps 18:2; 40:17; 70:5; 144:2) God is
referred to as "the deliverer"; but even
though Christ is the instrument of God's deliverance of mankind from sin, the NT does
not use the word except when Paul repeats
Isaiah 59:20, using "Deliverer" instead of
"Redeemer" (Rom 11:26).

demon An evil spirit.
sacrifices to d. Lev 17:7; Deut 32:17
who were d.-possessed Mt 4:24; 9:32;
12:22
He has a d. Mt 11:18; Lk 7:33

den Lair; cave of a wild animal.
into the d. of lions Dan 6:7
a 'd. of thieves Mt 21:13; Mk 11:17
detestable Abominable; loathsome.
not eat any d. thing Deut 14:3
Deuteronomy (dew-ter-ONN-oh-mee) The fifth book of the Law in the OT; teaches that God's laws are given for our own good—to help us stay close to Him in attitude and action. The name means "second law" or the second time the Law was given. (Look up Ex 20:1-17 for the first giving of the Law.)
Devil The chief demon, Satan.
Jesus . . . tempted by the d. Mt 4:1-11
serpent of old, called the D. Rev 12:9; 20:2
die Perish; lose life.
you shall surely d. Gen 2:17
born, And a time to d. Eccles 3:2
for tomorrow we d. Isa 22:13
in Me shall never d. Jn 11:26
disciple (dih-SIGH-pul) A learner; a follower, particularly one who follows Jesus Christ.
called His twelve d. Mt 10:1; Lk 6:13
sent two of his d. Mt 11:2
d. rebuked them Mt 19:13
d. were first called Christians Acts 11:26

door

Dispersion (dis-PURR-zhun) The widespread settlement of Jews outside of Palestine from the time of the Exile through the following centuries.

doctrine Teaching or instruction, particularly that of Jesus or the apostles concerning God's will.
My d. is pure Job 11:4
My d. is not Mine Jn 7:16
the d. of baptisms Heb 6:2
door Entrance way.
will pass over the d. Ex 12:23
and the d. was shut Mt 25:10
I am the d. Jn 10:9
d. standing open in heaven Rev 4:1
doxology A hymn, usually in a set formula, for expressing praise to God. Luke 2:14 ("Glory to God in the highest") has influenced Christian doxologies.
dreadful Awesome; feared; terrible.
d. day of the LORD Mal 4:5
dust Fine, dry, powdery earth.
God formed man of the d. Gen 2:7
d. you are, And to d. Gen 3:19

E

earth The planet on which we live; the soil.
God created the . . . e. Gen 1:1
The e. is the LORD's Ps 24:1
meek shall inherit the e. Ps 37:11
And e. is My footstool Isa 66:1
meek, . . . shall inherit the e. Mt 5:5
Your will be done On e. Mt 6:10
on e. peace, good will Lk 2:14
new heaven and a new e. Rev 21:1
Easter A Christian festival celebrating the Resurrection of Jesus; on a Sunday between March 22 and April 25.
eat To consume food.
shall not e. of every Gen 3:1
e. and drink, for tomorrow Isa 22:13
Take, e.; this is My body Mt 26:26
Ebal, Mount (EE-bull) A mountain in N Israel opposite Mt. Gerizim (Deut 11:29). It became known as the Mount of Cursing when Joshua read the curses of the Law. People on the mountain cried out with an "Amen!" When he read the blessings, people on nearby Mt. Gerizim responded in the same way. These two mountains marked the center of the land of the Samaritans in the OT. See Gerizim, Mount.
Eden, Garden of A garden of trees planted by the Lord (Gen 2:8) in which Adam and Eve first lived; actual site unknown; symbolically identified with Paradise.
Edom; Edomites (EE-dum; EE-duh-mights) A country to the E and S of Israel;

its people had a close relationship to the Israelites, being descendants of Esau.

Egypt A land of NE Africa. Temporary home of Abraham (Gen 12:10-20); Joseph sold "into Egypt" (Gen 37:28, 36); Joseph as governor (Gen 41:37—47:26); Israel in bondage (Ex 1:1—12:36); the Exodus (Ex 12:37—14:31); Jesus taken there (Mt 2:13).

Elah, Valley of (EE-luh) A narrow valley surrounded by low hills, SW of Jerusalem, where David killed Goliath (1 Sam 17:2; 21:9).

Elohim (EL-oh-heem) One of the names of God; the other is Yahweh (YAH-way). Elohim appears first in Gen 1:1 and is plural, meaning to Christians—"Trinity"—not three gods! The abbreviated form, El, is found in many biblical names—Beth*el*, Ezeki*el*, Dani*el*, *El*izabeth.

elders Seniors; among the Jews, the old and mature men who were civil and religious leaders; in the Christian church, leaders of the local church.
seventy of the e. of Israel Ex 24:9
tradition of the e. Mt 15:2; Mk 7:3
appointed e. in every Acts 14:23
the e. who rule well 1 Tim 5:17
twenty-four e. Rev 4:4

Eli (EE-lie) The priest of Shiloh to whom the boy Samuel was brought (1 Sam 1—4).

Elijah (ih-LIE-jah) A prophet from Tishbe to Gilead in the northern kingdom; fed by ravens (1 Kgs 17:6); performs miracles (1 Kgs 17:14-24; 20:30; 2 Kgs 1:10-12; 2:8); taken up by a whirlwind into heaven (2 Kgs 2:11). Malachi prophesies his return before the day of the Lord (Mal 4:5). In NT times, some thought Jesus to be Elijah (Mt 16:14; Lk 9:8); others thought John the Baptist to be Elijah (Jn 1:21). In the early church, John was regarded as the heir to the spirit and power of Elijah (Lk 1:17) or as Elijah reborn (Mt 11:14; 17:10-13). At the Transfiguration, Elijah appears with Moses (Mt 17:3, 4; Mk 9:4, 5).

Elisha (ih-LIE-shuh) A prophet; disciple and successor to Elijah; performed many miracles (2 Kgs 2:14-24; 3:16-20; 4:2-7, 32-44; 5:10-14, 27; 6:5-7, 18-20); contact with his bones revives a dead man (2 Kgs 13:20, 21).

Elizabeth Wife of the priest, Zacharias, and mother of John the Baptist (Lk 1:5-66).

ephah (EE-fah) A dry measure equal to the liquid measure bath; estimated as three-eighths to two-thirds of a bushel.
balances, a just e. Ezek 45:10

Emmanuel (em-MAN-you-el) *See* Immanuel.

Emmaus (em-MAY-us) A village in Judea, probably NW of Jerusalem, where Jesus revealed Himself to two disciples on the road after His resurrection from the grave (Lk 24:13-29).

enemies Foes; opponents.
presence of my e. Ps 23:5
love your e. Mt 5:44; Lk 6:27, 35

enter To go or come into.
E. into His gates with Ps 100:4
E. by the narrow gate Mt 7:13; Lk 13:24

Ephesus; Ephesians (EFF-uh-sus; ee-FEE-zhuns) A seaport in the Roman province of Asia; visited by Paul on his second and third journeys. Paul's NT Epistle to the Ephesians seems to be a general letter to the churches of Asia Minor.

Ephraim (EE-frah-im) The younger son of Joseph; adopted by Jacob (Gen 48:1ff); ancestor of one of the most powerful of the 12 tribes of Israel.

epistle (ee-PIS-ul) Letter; specifically those letters written by the apostles that are included in the NT. **Pastoral Epistles:** The NT books of 1 and 2 Timothy and Titus, which are written in the name of Paul as the chief pastor of the churches. **General (Catholic) Epistles:** The NT books of James, 1 and 2 Peter, 1, 2 and 3 John, and Jude.

Esau (EE-saw) Son of Isaac and Rebekah who traded his birthright to his younger twin brother Jacob for a bowl of pottage (Gen 25:22-34; 27; 33:1-16).

Essenes A Jewish community in Palestine at the time of Jesus; strict adherents of Jewish law.

Esther A Jewess of Shushan who became Ahasuerus's queen and thwarted a plot to kill all the Jews, later commemorated by the Jewish festival of Purim. The Book of Esther tells the story.

Euphrates (you-FRAY-tees) Means "that which waters." The longest river in W Asia and one of the two major rivers in Mesopotamia; begins in the mountains of Turkey and runs down to the Persian Gulf, almost two thousand miles away. The ruins of many ancient cities, including Babylon, Nippur, and Ur of the Chaldees, are located along this river in Iraq.

Eve The first woman; wife of Adam (Gen 2:21-25); tempted by the serpent (Gen 3:1-5).

everlasting Eternal; never ending.
the E. God Gen 21:33; Isa 40:28
underneath are the e. arms Deut 33:27
into the e. fire Mt 18:8; 25:41
inherit e. life Mt 19:29
have e. life Jn 3:16, 36; 5:24

evil Wickedness; slanderous or injurious actions.
tree . . . of good and e. Gen 2:9
I will fear no e. Ps 23:4
Depart from e. Ps 37:27
deliver us from the e. Mt 6:13
what e. has He done Mt 27:23; Mk 15:14; Lk 23:22
love of money is a root of all kinds of e. 1 Tim 6:10

Exile, the A period during which most of the people of Judah and Jerusalem were forced to live in Babylonia.

Exodus The going out of Israel from Egypt as recorded in the second book of the OT. It includes the deliverance from slavery, the wandering through the wilderness, the covenant with the Lord at Mount Sinai, and the provision of the tabernacle and ark of the covenant.

eye The organ of sight.
e. of both of them were opened Gen 3:7
e. for e. Ex 21:24; Lev 24:20; Deut 19:21; Mt 5:38
lift up my e. to the hills Ps 121:1
wise in your own e. Prov 3:7
if your right e. causes you Mt 5:29; 18:9; Mk 9:47

Ezekiel (ee-ZEEK-yell) A major Jewish prophet; author of the OT Book of Ezekiel; one of the captives of the Babylonian exile. Vision of God (Ezek 1:4-28); parable of the two eagles and the vine (17:1-24); the fall of Jerusalem (24:1-27); various prophecies about other nations (25—32).

Ezra (EZ-ruh) A priest and scribe; supposed author of the OT Book of Ezra, which details the first return of the Israelites from Babylon and the rebuilding of the temple.

F

face The front of the head; the surface or top side; frequently used to indicate the presence of God. Among the Hebrews, "seeking the face of God" referred to attendance at public worship (Ps 27:8).

on the f. of the deep Gen 1:2
In the sweat of your f. you shall Gen 3:19
LORD spoke to Moses f. to f. Ex 33:11
make His f. shine upon you Num 6:25
Seek My f. Ps 27:8
f. of the LORD is against Ps 34:16
the f. of My Father Mt 18:10
My messenger before Your f. Mk 1:2
but then f. to f. 1 Cor 13:12

faith Belief or trust in someone or something. Among Christians, belief in the Holy Trinity.
your f. has made you Mt 9:22; Mk 5:34; 10:52; Lk 8:48; 17:19
f. as a mustard seed Mt 17:20; Lk 17:6
just shall live by f. Rom 1:17
man is justified by f. Rom 3:28; 5:1; Gal 2:16; 3:24
f. is accounted for righteousness Rom 4:5
saved through f. Eph 2:8
one Lord, one f., one Eph 4:5
f. is the substance of Heb 11:1
f. without works is dead Jas 2:20

Fall, the A sinking into sin; the disobedience of Adam and Eve whereby sin entered the world (Gen 3).

falsehood Lying.
love worthlessness And seek f. Ps 4:2
destroy those who speak f. Ps 5:6

fast To go without food.
when you f., do not be Mt 6:16
Pharisees f. often Mt 9:14; Mk 2:18

father The male parent or ancestor. In the OT, used of God as the One who made a covenant with the people of Israel.
be a f. of many nations Gen 17:4
Honor your f. and Ex 20:12; Lev 19:3; Deut 5:16
who curses his f. Ex 21:17; Lev 20:9
David rested with his f. 1 Kgs 2:10
f. of the fatherless, . . . Is God Ps 68:5
LORD, You are our F. Isa 64:8

Father The First Person of the Holy Trinity.
your F. in heaven Mt 5:16, 45
Our F. in Mt 6:9; Lk 11:2
Abba, F. Mk 14:36; Rom 8:15; Gal 4:6
baptizing them in the name of the F. Mt 28:19
about My F.'s business Lk 2:49
who the F. is but the Son Lk 10:22
the Promise of My F. Lk 24:49
the only begotten of the F. Jn 1:14
one F.—God Jn 8:41
I and My F. are one Jn 10:30
comes to the F. except through Me Jn 14:6
ask the F. in My name Jn 15:16

fear To dread; to be afraid of; to be anxious.

I will f. no evil Ps 23:4
Whom shall I f. Ps 27:1
F. not, for I am Isa 41:10; 43:5
fear of the LORD The term used in the OT
for "religion" (Deut 6:2; 10:20; 28:58; Ps
111:10; Prov 1:7; 8:13; Eccles 12:13). In
the NT, "those who fear the Lord" are the
faithful (Lk 1:50; 18:4) or converts to Judaism (Acts 10:2; 13:26).
feast A festival; in ancient Israel associated
with occasions of religious joy. Those mentioned in the Bible: 1. **Passover and
Feast of Unleavened Bread** (Ex
12:1-30; Lev 23:4-14; Deut 16:1-8).
2. **Feast of Weeks or Pentecost** (Lev
23:15-21; Deut 16:9-12). 3. **Feast of
Tabernacles** (Lev 23:34-36; Deut
16:13-15). 4. **Purim** (Esther 9:20-28).
5. **Feast of Dedication or Feast of
Lights** (Jn 10:22).
fellowship Companionship; a group of persons with a common interest. Among
Christians, the common bond is their faith
in Christ, particularly in partaking of the
Lord's Supper.
into the f. of His Son 1 Cor 1:9
the right hand of f. Gal 2:9
any f. of the Spirit Phil 2:1
our f. is with the Father 1 Jn 1:3
fight Struggle against; do battle.
F. the good f. of faith 1 Tim 6:12
firmament Sky; heavens.
Let there be a f. in Gen 1:6
f. shows His handiwork Ps 19:1
first Before all others.
f. will be last Mt 19:30; Mk 10:31
First and the Last, the A title used by Isaiah (Isa 41:4; 44:6; 48:12) to convey the
idea of God's everlasting sovereignty and
eternal majesty and power. The same title
is used in Revelation (1:11, 17; 2:8;
22:13) implying God's sovereign lordship
manifest in Jesus Christ.
firstborn, firstfruits The eldest; the earliest fruits harvested. The consecration of
the first of the male children, of animals,
and of fruits was an important part of the religion of Israel.
LORD struck all the f. Ex 12:29
flesh The soft part of the human body; all
mankind.
All f. is grass Isa 40:6; 1 Pet 1:24
but the f. is weak Mt 26:41; Mk 14:38
the Word became f. Jn 1:14
Flood, the The covering of the earth with
water because of man's wickedness. Noah's

family and the animals of the earth are
saved in an ark (Gen 6:1-8:19).
fool A silly or senseless person.
f. despise wisdom Prov 1:7
f. is right in his own eyes Prov 12:15
folly of f. is deceit Prov 14:8
f. for Christ's sake 1 Cor 4:10
foolish Silly; unwise. Parables of Jesus deal
with: foolish and wise virgins (Mt 25:1-13)
and a foolish rich man (Lk 12:16-21).
forgive To pardon; show mercy to.
f. us . . . , As we f. Mt 6:12; Lk 11:4
F., and you will be Lk 6:37
Father, f. them Lk 23:34
fountain The source, as the spring from
which water flows. The Lord is called "the
fountain of living waters" (Jer 2:13; cf. Jn
4:14) and the "fountain of life" (Ps 36:9).
frankincense A fragrant incense.
spices . . . and pure f. Ex 30:34
gold, f., and myrrh Mt 2:11
friend An associate whom one likes.
the rich has many f. Prov 14:20
A f. loves at all times Prov 17:17
a f. who sticks closer Prov 18:24

G

Gabriel (GAY-brih-el) An angel of high rank
(Dan 8:16; 9:21; Lk 1:19, 26).
Gad The seventh son of Jacob; born of
Leah's maid Zilpah (Gen 30:10, 11); an-
cestor of the tribe of Gad.
Galatia; Galatians (guh-LAY-she-uh;
guh-LAY-shuns) A region and Roman
province in Asia Minor. Paul, in the NT
Epistle to the Galatians, tells of his own
conversion.
Galilee (GAL-ih-lee) A region of N Palestine, including the Sea of Galilee on the E
side. OT references include: Solomon gives
20 cities of Galilee to Hiram (1 Kgs 9:11);
the prophecy of Isaiah (Isa 9:1) concerning
"Galilee of the Gentiles" (cf. Mt 4:13).
Called "land of Gennesaret" (Mt 14:34;
Mk 6:53). Jesus' active ministry was almost
entirely within its borders.
Galilee, Sea of The larger of the two fresh-
water lakes on the Jordan River system.
Site of miracles: the great catch of fish (Lk
5:1-11); Jesus stills the sea (Mt 8:23-26;
Mk 4:35-39; Lk 8:22-24); Jesus walks on
the sea (Mt 14:25-27; Mk 6:48-51; Jn
6:19, 20). Also called "Chinnereth" (Num
34:11; Deut 3:17; Josh 13:27); "Chin-

neroth" (Josh 12:3); "Gennesaret" (Lk 5:1); and "Tiberias" (Jn 6:1; 21:1).

Gamaliel (guh-MAY-lih-el) A famous member of the Jewish Sanhedrin and a teacher of the Law; taught Paul in Tarsus (Acts 22:3); advised the Sanhedrin in Jerusalem to treat well the apostles of the young Christian church. His approach was simple: If Jesus was a false prophet, Christianity would soon fail. If the movement was of God, "You cannot overthrow it!" (Acts 5:39).

gate Doorway.
Enter into His g. with Ps 100:4
Enter by the narrow g. Mt 7:13

Gaza (GAY-zuh; GAH-zuh) One of the five principal cities of the Philistines, located along the southern Mediterranean coast of Israel, on the great caravan route between Mesopotamia and Egypt. Philip preached to the Ethiopian eunuch on the road to Gaza and baptized him (Acts 8:26-40).

Gehenna (geh-HEN-uh) Or "Valley of Hinnom" in the NT. A deep, narrow, curving valley at the south end of Jerusalem, used as a garbage dump where waste and dead animals were burned; children sacrificed to the god Molech (2 Kgs 23:10); high places of heathen worship destroyed by good King Josiah; "hell" (NKJV).

Gerizim, Mount (geh-RIGH-zim) A mountain in N Israel, close to Mt. Ebal in the district of Samaria. The main north-south road through central Palestine ran between these mountains. Jacob's Well, where Jesus talked with the Samaritan woman, is situated at the foot of Mt. Gerizim (Jn 4:14). See Ebal, Mount.

Gethsemane (geth-SEM-uh-neh) A garden on the Mount of Olives where Jesus prayed and where He was betrayed by Judas (Mt 26:36; Mk 14:32).

Gideon (GID-ee-un) A prophet of Israel especially favored by the Lord with revelations and unusual powers (Judg 6:11-8:35).

Gilead (GILL-ih-ud) A rugged, mountainous region E of the Jordan. Possibly also a city (Judg 10:17; Hos 6:8) and a tribe (Judg 5:17).

Gilgal (GILL-gal) The name of several places in the OT, one of them a city of the tribe of Benjamin, near Jericho; site of the first encampment of the Israelites after crossing the Jordan (Josh 3-4); there Saul was made king (1 Sam 11:14, 15).

give To bestow; hand over to another.
G. us this day our daily Mt 6:11
it will be g. to you Mt 7:7; Lk 6:38; 11:9
more blessed to g. than Acts 20:35

giver One who bestows.
God loves a cheerful g. 2 Cor 9:7

glad tidings Good news; the gospel (used in Lk 1:19; 8:1; Acts 13:32; and Rom 10:15).

Gloria in Excelsis The proclamation of the heavenly host at the birth of Christ, "Glory to God in the highest" (Lk 2:14).

glory of the Lord The word *glory* is sometimes synonymous with "God" to avoid referring to God in human form (Ex 33:22). In the OT, used of the fiery presence at Sinai (Ex 24:16, 17) and of the radiance that filled the tabernacle (Ex 40:34). In the NT, used of the divine Presence (Mk 8:38; Lk 2:9), of the quality of Jesus' appearance in His transfiguration (Lk 9:29, 31), and of Jesus' Second Coming (Mt 25:31).

gnat A tiny insect.
strain out a g. and swallow Mt 23:24

God, kingdom of *See* kingdom of God; heaven, kingdom of.

gods Idols.
have no other g. before Ex 20:3

Golden Gate The eastern gate of Jerusalem, sometimes called the Gate Beautiful on the Temple Mount, directly across the Kidron Valley from the Garden of Gethsemane where Judas betrayed Jesus. According to prophecy, this gate will be opened when the Messiah, Jesus, returns the second time.

Golden Rule A commandment given by Jesus in the Sermon on the Mount (Mt 7:12; Lk 6:31).

Golgotha (GOLL-goth-uh) Place where Jesus was crucified (Mt 27:33, 35; Mk 15:22; Jn 19:17).

Goliath (go-LIE-uth) A Philistine giant about 9½ to 11 feet tall; from a family of giants called the Anakim, who lived in Gath (Num 13:33). David, while still a young man, killed Goliath with a stone from his sling (1 Sam 17:4-51).

Gomer (GO-mer) A prostitute whom God told the prophet Hosea to marry as a lesson to Israel about their relationship to Him. Hosea's forgiveness of his wife symbolized God's forgiving love toward Israel (Hos 1:2; 14:1-4).

Gomorrah (go-MAR-uh) One of the two

cities destroyed by the Lord because of their wickedness (Gen 19:24-28).

good Virtuous; honorable.

g. name . . . rather than great Prov 22:1

No one is g. but One Mt 19:17; Lk 18:19

Good Friday The Friday before Easter; the anniversary of the Crucifixion of Jesus.

Goshen (GO-shun) A fertile part of the Nile delta in N Egypt, given to the family of Joseph by Pharaoh because of the famine in Israel (Gen 45:10-13).

gospel Good news; glad tidings. Hence, the teachings of Jesus and of the apostles. The NT books of Matthew, Mark, Luke, and John are called the Gospels.

g. of the kingdom Mt 4:23

the g. of Jesus Christ Mk 1:1

and believe in the g. Mk 1:15

preach the g. Lk 4:18

hear the word of the g. Acts 15:7

the g. of Christ Rom 1:16

grace OT usage: "favor" in the expression "found g. in the eyes of" (Gen 6:8). In NT usage: "the unmerited and abundant gift of God's love and favor to man," particularly made effective in Jesus Christ for the Christian. Used by Paul as an opening and fare-well greeting (Rom 16:24; 1 Cor 1:3).

g. and truth came through Jesus Jn 1:17

g. of God and the gift by the g. Rom 5:15

G. to you and 1 Cor 1:3; Eph 1:2

by the g. of God I am 1 Cor 15:10

g. of God in vain 2 Cor 6:1

g. of our Lord Jesus 2 Cor 8:9; 13:14

by g. you have been saved Eph 2:5

guarantee A pledge.

given us the Spirit as a g. 2 Cor 5:5

who is the g. of our inheritance Eph 1:14

H

Habakkuk (huh-BACK-kuk) A prophet of Judah; the OT book which bears his name is the eighth of the 12 Minor Prophets.

Hagar (HAY-gar) The Egyptian servant of Sarah, Abraham's wife; mother of Abra-ham's son, Ishmael (Gen 16:1-16). When Sarah was very old, God gave her a son, Isaac, who became the father of the Jewish nation. Hagar's son Ishmael, his half-brother, became the father of the Arab na-tion. The two nations cannot get along to this day!

Haggai (HAG-ay-eye) A Jewish prophet contemporary with Zechariah; the tenth of the 12 Minor Prophets of the OT.

Hallelujah (hal-luh-LOO-yah) "Praise the Lord" (not used in the NKJV). See Alle-luia.

hallowed Made sacred; consecrated.

H. be Your name Mt 6:9

hand The end of the arm.

Into Your h. I commit Ps 31:5

not let your left h. know Mt 6:3

if your h. or foot Mt 18:8; Mk 9:43

hands, laying on of A symbolic ritual: 1. Of divine blessing (Mt 19:13-15), sometimes accompanied by the gift of the Holy Spirit (Acts 19:6). 2. Of divine healing (Mk 7:32). 3. Of consecration of a man for a specific office (Acts 13:2, 3; 1 Tim 4:14). 4. Of dedication of an animal as for sacrifice (Lev 16:21).

Hannah (HAN-uh) The wife of Elkanah the priest and mother of Samuel. For many years, Hannah prayed for a child, promis-ing God that she would dedicate him to the Lord's service. Samuel, who became a great judge, priest, and prophet, was God's answer to her prayers (1 Sam 1:11-17, 22).

Hanukkah (HAH-nuh-kah) Hebrew word for "dedication." See Feast of Dedication.

Haran (HAY-ran) A city of N Mesopotamia, on one of the main trade routes between Babylon and the Mediterranean Sea; home of Abraham and his father Terah (Gen 11:31-32; 12:4-5); home of Jacob and his wives, Leah and Rachel (Gen 28:10; 29:4-6).

harp A stringed musical instrument.

play the h. and flute Gen 4:21

David would take a h. and 1 Sam 16:23

haughty Overbearing; proud.

h. spirit before a fall Prov 16:18

Hazael (HAY-zay-el) A Syrian official whom the prophet Elijah anointed king of Syria at God's command (1 Kgs 19:15); sent by Ben-Hadad, king of Syria, to the prophet Elisha to ask whether the king would re-cover from an illness; assassinated Ben-Hadad and took the throne (2 Kgs 8:7-15); fought against God's people when the Lord's anger "became aroused against Israel" (2 Kgs 13:3).

heart The physical organ thought of as being the seat of the affections.

A broken and a contrite h. Ps 51:17

Blessed are the pure in h. Mt 5:8

not your h. be troubled Jn 14:1

heaven A term sometimes used for "God."

I have sinned against h. Lk 15:18

it has been given to him from h. Jn 3:27

heaven; heavens 1. The sky; the space in which the sun, the moon, and the stars move; the firmament.

God called the firmament H. Gen 1:8
He adorned the h. Job 26:13
h. declare the glory of God Ps 19:1
stretch out the h. Ps 104:2; Isa 40:22
saw h. opened and Acts 10:11

2. The place where God, the risen Christ, the angels, and the saints reside; the future home of the redeemed.

new h. and Isa 65:17; Rev 21:1
till h. and earth pass Mt 5:18
Father in h. Mt 6:9; Lk 11:2
looked . . . toward h. as Acts 1:10
eternal in the h. 2 Cor 5:1

harp

heaven, kingdom of Used throughout the Gospel of Matthew for "kingdom of God." *See* kingdom of God.

the kingdom of h. is at hand Mt 3:2; 10:7
theirs is the kingdom of h. Mt 5:3, 10
least in the kingdom of h. Mt 5:19; 11:11
kingdom of h. is like Mt 13:24
such is the kingdom of h. Mt 19:14

heavenly host *See* host, heavenly.

Hebrews (HE-brews) The descendants of Eber (Gen 10:21); sometimes used interchangeably with "Israelites."

Hebron (HE-brun) An ancient city in the mountains of Judah, 19 mi. S of Jerusalem. Here Abraham purchased a cave for a family burial place (Gen 23:1-20). David's capital city for the first seven and one-half years of his reign (2 Sam 2:1—5:5).

Helper The Holy Spirit; the intercessor promised by Christ to help and guide believers (Jn 14:26; 15:26; 16:7).

heresy (HERR-uh-see) False doctrine or teaching which denies the truth about God or Jesus Christ. In the Book of 2 Corinthians, Paul spoke against "false apostles" and "deceitful workers" who claimed to be "apostles of Christ" (2 Cor 11:13); in 1 John, the writer also condemned a group known as the gnostics, who denied that Jesus was the Son of God (1 Jn 2:22).

Hermon, Mount (HUR-man) "Sacred mountain." The highest mountain in the area (9,232 feet), which marks the N boundary of Canaan; the major source of the Jordan River because of its melting snows and glaciers. Some scholars think Jesus' Transfiguration took place near Caesarea Philippi, at the southern base of Mt. Hermon.

Herod (HERR-ud) 1. Ruler of Jewish Palestine under Rome (37-4 B.C.); sent the wise men to search out the infant Jesus (Mt 2:1-9). 2. **Herod Antipas:** Tetrarch of Galilee (4 B.C.—A.D. 39); put John the Baptist to death (Mt 14:1-12; Mk 6:14-29; Lk 3:19, 20; 9:7-9).

Hezekiah (hez-uh-KIGH-uh) The name of four persons in the OT, one of whom was king of Judah (715-687 B.C.; 2 Kgs 18—20; 2 Chr 29—32; Isa 36—39).

Hinnom, Valley of (HEN-um) See "Gehenna," the Greek term for the same location.

Hiram (HIGH-rum) A king of Tyre and friend of both David and Solomon (2 Sam 5:11; 1 Kgs 10:11, 22; 2 Chr 8:2, 18); furnished cedar wood from the famous Cedars of Lebanon and workmen to help David build his palace; sent supplies and skilled laborers to help Solomon build the temple in Jerusalem.

Hittites (HIT-tights) A people of the ancient world who lived in Asia Minor between 1900 and 1200 B.C.; spread into N Syria and later into the land promised Abraham; had to be driven out when Israel conquered Canaan under Joshua (Ex 3:8, 17; Deut 7:1; Judg 3:5). The most famous Hittite was Uriah, the husband of Bathsheba. David had Uriah killed in battle so he could marry Bathsheba.

holy of holies The innermost room of the temple or tabernacle in which the ark of the Testimony was kept.

Holy Spirit *See* Spirit, Holy.

Holy Trinity *See* Trinity.

Holy Week The week before Easter.

honor To esteem; to give respect.

H. your father and your mother Ex 20:12; Mt 15:4

before h. is humility Prov 15:33

prophet is not without h. Mt 13:57

h. to whom h. Rom 13:7

Horeb, Mount (HOE-reb) A sacred mountain (Ex 3:1; Deut 1:2, 6, 19; 4:10; 5:2) which may be the same mountain as Mount Sinai.

Hosea (ho-ZAY-uh) A prophet of Israel; the first of the 12 Minor Prophets of the OT.

host, heavenly 1. The celestial bodies—the sun, moon, and stars.

all the h. of heaven Deut 4:19; Jer 8:2

worshiped all the h. of 2 Kgs 17:16

2. The mighty army in God's service, including the angels.

all the h. of them Gen 2:1

heavens, with all their h. Neh 9:6

the h. of them by Ps 33:6

brings out their h. Isa 40:26

worship the h. of heaven Acts 7:42

Hosts, LORD of God, first as leader of the armies of Israel (1 Sam 17:45), then as leader of the "heavenly host."

LORD of h., He is the King Ps 24:10

LORD of h. is His name Isa 47:4; 51:15; Jer 10:16; 31:35

name is the God of h. Amos 5:27

house 1. A dwelling place.

not covet your neighbor's h. Ex 20:17

Set your h. in order 2 Kgs 20:1

dwell in the h. of the LORD Ps 23:6

Father's h. are many mansions Jn 14:2

2. A family group; a nation.

h. divided against itself Mt 12:25; Lk 11:17

hypocrite (HIP-puh-krit) A person who pretends to be what he or she is not. In the Greek theater of NT times, a hypocrite was an actor who wore a mask and played a part on the stage. **hypocrisy** (hip-POCK-rih-see) Jesus spoke against the hypocrisy of many persons who opposed Him, especially the scribes and Pharisees, who tried to give the appearance of being godly, but were actually blind to the truth of God (Lk 20:19-20).

for everyone is a h. Isa 9:17

You are full of h. Mt 23:28

Let love be without h. Rom 12:9

I

idol A false god; an image or figure regarded as an object of worship.

Do not turn to i. Lev 19:4

who regard vain i. Ps 31:6

gods of the peoples are i. Ps 96:5

And with foreign i. Jer 8:19

the i. of the nations Jer 14:22

keep yourselves from i. 1 Jn 5:21

image A likeness; an idol.

make man in Our i. Gen 1:26

not make . . . any carved i. Ex 20:4

Immanuel (em-MAN-you-el) A Hebrew name meaning "God With Us," used by Isaiah in foretelling the birth of the Messiah.

call His name I. Isa 7:14

of Your land, O I. Isa 8:8

shall call His name I. Mt 1:23

immediately Right now.

i. he stumbles Mt 13:21

end will not come i. Lk 21:9

Incarnation (in-car-NAY-shun) The taking by God of human characteristics in the person of Jesus; God's presence on earth.

iniquity (ih-NICK-kwih-tih) Sin; wickedness. *See* sin.

the i. of the fathers Ex 20:5; Deut 5:9

Pardon my i. Ps 25:11

we bear their i. Lam 5:7

intercession A plea on behalf of another; for example, Christ's prayer for His followers (Jn 17:6-26).

i. for the transgressors Isa 53:12

the Spirit Himself makes i. Rom 8:26

He ever lives to make i. Heb 7:25

Isaac (EYE-zik) The son of Abraham and Sarah, and half brother of Ishmael; by his wife Rebekah he was the father of Jacob and Esau (Gen 21:1-12; 22:1-19; 24:62-67; 25:9-11, 19, 20; 26:1—28:5; 35:27-29).

Isaiah (eye-ZAY-uh) A prophet of Israel; the first book of the OT Major Prophets.

Ishmael (ISH-may-el) The name of six persons in the OT, one of them Abraham's son by Hagar (Gen 16; 17:18-26; 21:8-21; 25:12-18).

Israel (IZ-ray-el) The name that Jacob received after his mysterious struggle at Jabbok (Gen 32:22-30); also the name of the whole people descended from him. After the separation into two kingdoms under Jeroboam, the name was confined to the northern kingdom of the ten tribes.

Israelites (IZ-ray-el-lights) A name applied to Israel (the people); also called "Hebrews," mostly by foreigners, as was the name "Jews"; the latter arose at the time when Judah, after the fall of the northern kingdom, represented the entire people.

Issachar (IZ-uh-kar) The ninth son of Jacob, the fifth by Leah (Gen 30:17, 18); ancestor of the tribe of Issachar.

J

Jacob (JAY-kob) Son of Isaac and Rebekah; younger twin brother of Esau; father of the people of Israel. Gained by craft the blessing meant for Esau; married Leah and Rachel, the daughters of his uncle Laban; received the name Israel; finally found refuge in Egypt with his favorite son, Joseph (Gen 25:21-34; 27—35; 37:1-3; 47:28—49:33).

Jacob's Well An ancient well near Shechem and Mt. Ebal and Gerizim in central Palestine; dug by hand and crude tools; site of a conversation between Jesus and a Samaritan woman, in which He told her how to find "living water" (Jn 4:5-10).

James The name of several persons in the NT. 1. "The Elder," son of Zebedee and brother of John; one of the 12 apostles; martyred under Herod Agrippa (Mt 4:21; 10:2; 17:1; 20:20; 26:37; Mk 1:19, 20, 29; 3:17; 5:37; 9:2; 10:35, 41; 13:3; 14:33; Lk 5:10; 6:14; 8:51; 9:28, 54; Acts 1:13; 12:1, 2). 2. The son of Alphaeus, also one of the 12 apostles (Mt 10:3; Mk 3:18; Lk 6:15; Acts 1:13). 3. One of the sons of Mary; known as "the Less" (Mt 27:56; Mk 15:40; 16:1; Lk 24:10). Tradition regards James (3) to be the same person as James (2). 4. The father of Judas (Lk 6:16; Acts 1:13). 5. "The brother of the Lord"; a pillar of the church at Jerusalem; called "James the Just"; traditionally the author of the Epistle of James (Mt 13:55; Mk 6:3; Acts 12:17; 15:13; 21:18; 1 Cor 15:7; Gal 1:19; 2:9, 12; Jas 1:1; Jude 1).

jealous Envious; suspicious; full of zeal. When used of God, jealousy describes either His anger against His unfaithful people or His zeal to protect His persecuted people.

a j. God Ex 20:5; Deut 4:24

Jehovah (jeh-HOE-vuh) The LORD; God. Used by some Bible translators for the name of the covenant God of Israel (Ex 6:3; Ps 83:18; Isa 12:2; 26:4). See tetragrammaton.

Jephthah (JEFF-thah) A warrior of Gilead; sacrificed his daughter in fulfillment of a vow (Judg 11:1—12:7).

Jeremiah (jer-uh-MY-uh) The name of ten persons in the OT, one of them the prophet Jeremiah (c. 626-580 B.C.). His prophecies, visions, and life story are narrated in the second book of the OT Major Prophets, which bears his name. The almond rod and the boiling pot (1:11-19); the potter's wheel (18:2-10); the good and bad figs (24); Baruch records Jeremiah's prophecies (36:4-32).

Jericho (JERRY-ko) An ancient city at the S end of the Jordan Valley; the fall of the city is told in Joshua 6:1-25.

Jeroboam (jer-uh-BOW-um) 1. The first king of Israel (c. 922-901 B.C.); son of Nebat (1 Kgs 11:26—14:20; 2 Kgs 17:21, 22; 2 Chr 10:2-15; 13:1-20). 2. King of Israel (c. 786-747 B.C.); son and successor of Joash (2 Kgs 14:23-29).

Jerusalem (jeh-ROO-suh-lem) The chief city of Palestine; most sacred city of both Jews and Christians; mentioned under one name or another (Shalem; Salem; City of David; Moriah; Jebus; Zion; Ariel) in about 40 of the 66 books of the Bible. David captured the city (2 Sam 5:6-9; 1 Chr 11:4-8) and made it his capital; brought the ark of the Testimony to the city (2 Sam 6:1-17). Solomon built the temple and other buildings there (1 Kgs 5—7). Captured by Nebuchadnezzar (Jer 39); rebuilt by Ezra and Nehemiah. Several events in the life of Jesus occurred there: His presentation in the temple (Lk 2:22-38); the cleansing of the temple (Jn 2:13-25); the conversation with Nicodemus (Jn 2:23; 3:1-21); and the events of the last week of His life (Mt 21—28; Mk 11—16; Lk 19:28—24; Jn 12:12—21).

Jesse (JESS-ih) Son of Obed; grandson of Boaz and Ruth; father of David (1 Sam 16:1-13; 17:12ff).

Jesus Christ The personal name of the One whose title gave its name to the Christian religion. Since "Jesus" was a fairly common name in the first century, distinguishing phrases were used when referring to Him (Jesus of Nazareth; Jesus, Son of David; Christ Jesus; the Messiah Jesus; and Jesus Christ). The four Gospels detail His life and ministry: birth (Mt 1:18-25; Lk 2:1-20); baptism (Mt 3:13-17; Mk 1:9-11; Lk 3:21, 22); makes water into wine (Jn 2:1-12); the Sermon on the Mount (Mt 5:1—7:29; Lk 6:20-49); stilling of the storm (Mk 4:35-41; Lk 8:22-25); sending the unclean spirits into the swine (Mk 5:1-20); feeding of the 5,000 (Mt 14:13-21; Mk 6:30-44; Lk 9:10-17; Jn 6:1-14); walking on the water (Mt 14:22-33; Mk 6:45-52; Jn 6:15-21); feeding of the 4,000 (Mt 15:32-39; Mk 8:1-10); the Transfiguration (Mt 17:1-8; Mk 9:2-8; Lk 9:28-36); entry into Jerusalem (Mt 21:1-10; Mk 11:1-11; Lk 19:28-44; Jn 12:12-19); raises Lazarus from the dead (Jn 11:1-44); the Lord's Supper (Mt 26:26-29; Mk 14:22-25; Lk 22:15-20); is arrested (Mt 26:47-56; Mk 14:43-52; Lk 22:47-50; Jn 18:2-12); trial before Pilate (Mt 27:11-14; Mk 15:1-5; Lk 23:1-5; Jn 18:33-38); the Crucifixion and burial (Mt 27:32-61; Mk 15:21-47; Lk 23:26-56; Jn 19:17-42); the Resurrection and Ascension (Mt 28:1-20; Mk 16:1-20; Lk 24:1-53; Jn 20; 21).

Job (JOBE) Chief character in the OT Book of Job; unknown otherwise.

Joel (JO-ell) The name of several persons in the OT, including the prophet, son of Pethuel, author of the second book of the 12 Minor Prophets.

John The name of five persons in the NT, among them: 1. **John the apostle:** A son of Zebedee, brother of James (Mt 4:21, 22; Mk 1:19, 20; Lk 5:10); sometimes called "the beloved disciple" and "Saint John"; traditional author of the Fourth Gospel, the three epistles of John, and the Book of Revelation. 2. **John the Baptist:** The son of Elizabeth and Zacharias (Lk 1:5-25, 57-66); a prophet, called the forerunner of Jesus (Jn 1:15-28); baptized Jesus (Mt 3:13-17; Mk 1:9-11; Lk 3:21, 22; Jn 1:29-34); imprisoned by Herod and beheaded (Mt 14:3-12; Mk 6:17-29). 3. **John Mark:** See Mark.

Jonah (JO-nuh) The name of two persons of the OT, one of whom was the prophet about whom the fifth book of the 12 Minor Prophets is written. Swallowed by a great fish (Jon 1:17—2:10).

Jonathan (JOHN-uh-thun) The name of 15 persons in the OT, one of whom was the oldest son of Saul; David's friend (1 Sam 13:2; 14:1-45; 19:1-7; 20).

Jordan (JOR-dun) The chief river of Palestine, flowing from the slopes of Mount Hermon through Lake Huleh and the Sea of Galilee to the Dead Sea. The waters were miraculously stopped for the Israelites to

Jordan River

pass (Josh 3:14—4:24). Jesus was baptized there (Mt 3:13; Mk 1:9).

Joseph; Joses (JOE-sef; JOE-sus) The name of 14 persons in the Bible, among them: 1. The son of Jacob and Rachel (Gen 30:22-24); his coat of many colors (Gen 37:3); sold into Egypt by his brothers (Gen 37:18-36); imprisoned on false accusations (Gen 39:7-23); interpreted Pharaoh's dreams, thus gaining favor (Gen 41:1-36); as administrator of Egypt (Gen 41:37—50:26); his brothers come to him for food (Gen 42—45). 2. The husband of Mary mother of Jesus; resident of Nazareth; descended from David (Mt 1:16-25; Lk 2:4-7; Jn 1:45). 3. **Joseph of Arimathea:** A member of the Sanhedrin; buried the body of Jesus on his own property (Mt 27:57-60; Mk 15:43-46; Lk 23:50-53; Jn 19:38-42).

Joshua; Jeshua (JOSH-you-ah; JESH-you-ah) The name of several persons in the OT, the most important being Joshua, son of Nun, the central figure of the Book of Joshua. This book tells the story of Moses' successor as leader of the Israelites, the conquest of Canaan, and the division of the country among the 12 tribes. His miraculous crossing of the Jordan (Josh 3:14—4:24); conquest of Jericho (Josh 6:1-21).

Josiah (jo-SIGH-uh) One of the few good kings of Judah; son of Amon and grandson of Manasseh (2 Kgs 21:23—23:30); became king at the age of 8; found the Book of the Law while the house of the Lord was being repaired (2 Chr 34:14); read the Book to the inhabitants of Judah (2 Chr 34:29-32), resulting in repentance and reform.

Judah (JEW-duh) The fourth son of Jacob, by Leah (Gen 29:31, 35); ancestor of the tribe of Judah.

Judas (JEW-dus) The name of six persons in the NT, including: 1. A brother of Jesus (Mt 13:55; Mk 6:3). See Jude, The General Epistle of. 2. **Judas Iscariot** (iz-CARE-ih-ut): One of the 12 apostles; the betrayer of Jesus (Mt 26:20-25, 47-50; Mk 14:18-20, 43-46; Lk 22:47, 48; Jn 13:21-26). 3. The brother of James; one of the 12 apostles (Lk 6:16; Jn 14:22; Acts 1:13). See Thaddaeus. 4. **Judas Barsabas** (BAR-sab-bus): A Jewish Christian (Acts 15:22, 27, 32).

Jude, The General Epistle of This NT letter designates its author as a "servant of Jesus Christ, and brother of James." See Judas (1).

Judea (jew-DEE-uh) An area of SW Palestine; formerly called Judah.

judge To decide; form an opinion.
J. not, that you be not Mt 7:1

judge One who forms an opinion. In the OT Book of Judges, one chosen by God to save the people from foreign oppressors; a military leader with both legislative and executive authority.
made you . . . a j. over us Ex 2:14

Judge God; Christ.
J. of all the earth Gen 18:25
J. of the living and the dead Acts 10:42
to God the J. of all Heb 12:23

justified (JUS-tih-fyed) The way sinful human beings are made acceptable to a holy God. Christianity is different from all other religions because of its teaching of being justified by grace (Rom 3:24)—an act of love from God to undeserving sinners. We can have grace and be justified when we believe and have faith that Jesus died on the Cross to save us from our sins (Rom 3:25-30; 4:3, 5, 9; Jn 6:28-29; Phil 1:29).

K

keeper One who guards or takes care of someone or something.
Am I my brother's k. Gen 4:9

Kidron Valley (KID-run) A very important valley E of the walls of Jerusalem and extending all the way to the Dead Sea; site of Nehemiah's inspection of the broken-down walls of Jerusalem (Neh 2:13-15); site of a common burial ground (2 Kgs 23:6); dumping ground for ashes of idols (1 Kgs 15:13; 2 Kgs 23:4; 2 Chron 29:16; 30:14). Jesus crossed the valley to go to the Garden of Gethsemane to pray just before He was arrested and crucified (John 18:1).

king A chief ruler; among ancient peoples, a religious leader often held to be divine. God and Jesus Christ are called "King."
trees . . . anoint a k. Judg 9:8
My K. and my God Ps 5:2; 84:3
the K. of glory shall Ps 24:7
seen the K., The Lord Isa 6:5
no k. but Caesar Jn 19:15
K. of kings and Lord 1 Tim 6:15

kingdom of God The eternal sovereignty

or kingly rule of God, manifested in its acceptance by men on earth and the hope for the future; the central theme of Jesus' teaching. The phrase does not occur in the OT, but the idea is present in "Your kingdom," "My kingdom," etc., which are also sometimes used in the NT. "Kingdom of heaven" is used in Matthew's gospel; "kingdom of the Son of His love" (Col 1:13); "kingdom of our Lord and Savior Jesus Christ" (2 Pet 1:11).

Yours is the k., O Lord 1 Chr 29:11
the scepter of Your k. Ps 45:6
Your k. come Mt 6:10; Lk 11:2
seek first the k. of God Mt 6:33; Lk 12:31
with you in My Father's k. Mt 26:29
k. of God is at hand Mk 1:15
cannot see the k. of God Jn 3:3
inherit the k. of God 1 Cor 6:10; Gal 5:21

L

Laban (LAY-bun) Brother of Rebekah and father-in-law of Jacob; lived near Haran where Abraham once lived; instrumental in two important marriages—Isaac to Rebekah (Gen 24) and Jacob to Leah and Rachel (Gen 29).

ladder A framework of uprights and crosspieces on which one may ascend or descend. Jacob dreams of a ladder (Gen 28:12).

lamb The young of a sheep, commonly used as the sacrificial animal of the Passover.

God will provide . . . l. Gen 22:8
a l. to the slaughter Isa 53:7
wolf and the l. shall feed Isa 65:25
Feed My l. Jn 21:15

Lamb (of God) Christ, whose sacrificial death removed the sins of the world. By extension of "lamb" as the most common victim of OT sacrifices, particularly the "Passover." Christ, our Passover (1 Cor 5:7).

Behold! The L. of God Jn 1:29, 36
a l. without blemish 1 Pet 1:19
stood a L. as though it had Rev 5:6
L. slain from the foundation Rev 13:8
L. will overcome them Rev 17:14

lamp A device producing light.

spirit of a man is the l. Prov 20:27
light a l. and put it Mt 5:15
ten virgins who took their l. Mt 25:1
light of a l. shall not shine Rev 18:23

lampstand

lampstand Particularly the seven-branched lampstand of the tabernacle and the temple, and the symbolic one of Revelation.

make a l. of pure gold Ex 25:31
I saw seven golden l. Rev 1:12

last The final one.

first will be l. Mt 19:30; Mk 10:31
I am the First and the L. Rev 1:17

Last Supper The last meal eaten by Jesus with His apostles, on the night before His crucifixion. *See* Holy Communion.

laver (LAY-ver) A basin in which priests washed their hands for purification purposes while serving at the altar of the tabernacle or temple; made by Moses so Aaron and the priests could wash their hands and feet before offering sacrifices (Ex 30:18-21). Ten bronze lavers, decorated with lions, oxen, and cherubim, were made by Hiram for Solomon's temple (1 Kgs 7:27-39).

law Rules of conduct; particularly rules given by God to Moses by which the Israelites were to live and which were defined in the Pentateuch (the Law of Moses).

l. of the Lord is perfect Ps 19:7
not . . . to destroy the L. Mt 5:17
l. was given through Moses Jn 1:17

Lazarus (LAZ-uh-rus) 1. The beggar in a parable told by Jesus (Lk 16:19-31). 2. A friend of Jesus; brother of Martha and Mary (Jn 11:1-44; 12:1-11).

Leah (LEE-uh) Elder daughter of Laban; Jacob's first wife to whom were born six of his sons (Gen 29:16—30:21).

leaven (LEV-in) Yeast or other fermenting agent. It was forbidden to the Israelites in all offerings made with fire (Lev 2:11; 6:17) and at the Passover (Ex 12:17-19).
beware of the l. Mt 16:6
a little l. leavens 1 Cor 5:6

laver

Lebanon (LEB-uh-nun) A nation just N of Israel (ancient Phoenicia in Bible times); named for the snow-capped range of mountains running the entire length of the country; has been conquered by the Egyptians, Assyrians, Persians, Greeks, Romans, Arabs, and Turks; famous for the Cedars of Lebanon, the wood of which was used in Solomon's temple and palace. Well-known cities include Byblos, from which we get the word "Bible," Sidon, and Tyre (Gen 10:19; Mt 15:21-28; Mk 7:24-31).

Lent The 40 weekdays preceding Easter; a period of fasting and repentance in Christian churches.

leopard (LEPP-urd) A wild animal of the cat family.
l. shall lie down with the Isa 11:6

let Allow.
l. me first go Mt 8:21
L. the little children Mt 19:14; Mk 10:14; Lk 18:16

Levi; Levites (LEE-vigh; LEE-vights) Third

son of Jacob and Leah (Gen 29:31, 34); ancestor of the tribe of Levites, who were charged with the care of the tabernacle and the temple.

Leviticus (leh-VIT-ih-kus) The third book of the OT; it deals mainly with the priests and their duties.

life The union of body and soul. Christ is called the "Prince of life" (Acts 3:15).
The tree of l. was also Gen 2:9
the resurrection and the l. Jn 11:25

light Brightness; radiance.
Let there be l. Gen 1:3
my l. and my salvation Ps 27:1
the l. of the world Mt 5:14
I am the l. of the world Jn 8:12

Lights, Feast of *See* Dedication, Feast of.

lilies Flowering plants that grow from bulbs.
He feeds his flock among the l. Song 6:3
Consider the l. of the Mt 6:28

lord One who has authority over persons or things; hence, **Lord:** God, as the supreme authority; Jesus, as leader during His ministry and as the Son of God. When large and small capitals are used for Lord, the original Hebrew reads YHWH (*See* tetragrammaton).
L. Himself is God Deut 4:35; 1 Kgs 18:39
the L. is one Deut 6:4
L. of the whole earth Ps 97:5
says to Me, L., L. Mt 7:21
L. of heaven and earth Mt 11:25
Son of Man is also L. Mk 2:28
My L. and my God Jn 20:28
both L. and Christ Acts 2:36
crucified the L. of glory 1 Cor 2:8
is L. of l. and King Rev 17:14

Lord of Hosts *See* Hosts, Lord of.

Lord's Day Sunday (Rev 1:10).

Lord's Prayer The prayer, taught by Jesus to His disciples, that begins "Our Father" (Mt 6:9-13; Lk 11:2-4).

Lord's Supper 1. Holy Communion (1 Cor 11:20). 2. Last Supper.

lost Mislaid; not to be found.
the lost sheep Mt 18:12-14; Lk 15:4-7
the lost coin Lk 15:8-10
the lost (prodigal) son Lk 15:11-32

Lot The nephew of Abraham who came with him to Canaan (Gen 11:27—13:12). Saved from Sodom's destruction (Gen 19:1-38). His wife was turned into a pillar of salt (Gen 19:26).

love 1. A deep affection; devotion.
l. covers all sins Prov 10:12
Greater l. has no one Jn 15:13

l. of money is a root 1 Tim 6:10
God is l. 1 Jn 4:8
  2. To have deep affection for someone or something.
l. your neighbor Lev 19:18; Mt 22:39; Jas 2:8
l. the LORD your God Deut 6:5; Mt 22:37
l. your enemies Mt 5:44; Lk 6:27
God so l. the world Jn 3:16

Luke Probable author of the Book of Luke and the Acts of the Apostles; Gentile, the only non-Jewish writer of a NT book; a "fellow laborer" of the apostle Paul, who accompanied him on parts of the second and third missionary journeys and the journey to Rome (2 Tim 4:11; Philem 24); a physician by profession (Col 4:14).

Lydia (LID-ee-uh) A prosperous businesswoman from the city of Thyatira in W Asia Minor (Turkey), a seller of purple cloth; lived in Philippi in N Greece, where she heard Paul preach about Jesus and became the first convert to Christianity in Europe (Acts 16:14-15, 40).

Lystra (LISS-trah) A city of Lycaonia in central Asia Minor (Turkey); home of Timothy (Acts 16:1-2). Paul preached and healed here on his first and second missionary journeys, was stoned and left for dead (Acts 14:6-21; 2 Tim 3:11).

M

Macedonia (mass-uh-DOH-nee-uh) A mountainous country N of Greece which Paul visited on his missionary journeys after receiving his "Macedonian call" (Acts 16:9); at Philippi, the first European convert to Christianity was Lydia, a businesswoman (Acts 16:14-15, 40). Philip II of Macedon, father of Alexander the Great, established his capital at Philippi and made Macedon internationally important.

Machpelah (mack-PEA-luh) The name of a field, a cave, and the surrounding land which Abraham bought as a burial place for his wife, Sarah, from Ephron the Hittite. Abraham, Sarah, Isaac, Rebekah, Jacob, and Leah are all buried in this cave (Gen 49:31; 50:13). The modern city of Hebron was built around this site, now covered by a large Muslim mosque.

Magi (MAY-ji) The wise men who came to worship the infant Jesus (Mt 2:1-12); because they offered three gifts, it is often assumed that there were three Magi.

maker One who brings into being; creator; hence, **Maker:** God.
more pure than his M. Job 4:17
man will look to his M. Isa 17:7
builder and m. is God Heb 11:10

Malachi (MAL-uh-kigh) An OT prophet, author of the last book of the OT, one of the 12 Minor Prophets.

man A male human being; the whole human race.
God is not a m. Num 23:19
m. is born to trouble Job 5:7
M. shall not live by Mt 4:4
not m. for the Sabbath Mk 2:27

Manasseh (mah-NASS-uh) 1. Joseph's eldest son, born in Egypt (Gen 41:50-51). Like his younger brother, Ephraim, Manasseh was half Hebrew and half Egyptian. Both of Joseph's sons were "adopted" by Jacob and became two of the heads of the tribes of Israel. 2. King of Judah (2 Kgs 21:1-18); reigned longer than any of the Israelite kings, but was the most wicked; rebuilt the altars to idols that had been destroyed by King Hezekiah and even sacrificed his own son to the heathen god Molech; deported to Babylon where he repented (2 Chr 33:11-13); tried to introduce reforms when he returned, but was opposed by his wicked son Amon, who succeeded him.

mark A sign.
set a m. on Cain Gen 4:15
his m. on his forehead Rev 14:9

Mark; John Mark Son of Mary of Jerusalem; companion of Paul and other early Christian missionaries; the traditional author of the Second Gospel (Acts 12:12, 25; 15:37).

marriage The union of one man and one woman. Explained by Jesus (Mk 10:6-9).
are given in m. Mt 22:30
M. is honorable among all Heb 13:4

martyr (MAR-ter) A witness. Because the early Christians often suffered for their faith, the word soon came to mean one who suffered or died because of his witness to Christ. The apostle Paul called Stephen a martyr (Acts 22:20); the Book of Revelation mentions "the martyrs of Jesus" (Rev 17:6).

Mary The name of seven persons in the NT, among them: 1. The mother of Jesus (Mt 1:16, 18-25; Lk 2:5-20). 2. **Mary Magdalene:** A Galilean follower of Jesus (Mt 27:55, 56, 61; 28:1; Mk 15:40, 47; 16:1;

Lk 8:2; 24:10; Jn 19:25; 20:1, 18). 3.
The sister of Martha and Lazarus (Lk
10:38-42; Jn 11:1-45; 12:1-8). 4. The
mother of James "the Less" (Mt 27:55, 56,
61; 28:1-10; Mk 15:40, 41, 47; 16:1-8;
Lk 24:1-11). 5. The mother of John Mark
(Acts 12:12).

martyr

master A male person in authority; one who
controls someone or something; owner.
is free from his m. Job 3:19
can serve two m. Mt 6:24; Lk 16:13
nor a servant above his m. Mt 10:24
Matthew (MATH-you) One of the 12 apostles; called "Levi the son of Alphaeus" in
Mark 2:14; traditional author of the First
Gospel.
measure A certain amount; capacity.
have a . . . just m. Deut 25:15
same m. you use Mt 7:2; Mk 4:24; Lk 6:38
good m., pressed down Lk 6:38
mediator (MEE-dee-ay-tor) One who acts
as a go-between in making an agreement
between two parties. Moses is so designated (Gal 3:19) in making the covenant at
Sinai. Christ is called the "one Mediator between God and men" (1 Tim 2:5).
meditate To study; contemplate.
he m. day and night Ps 1:2
meek Humble; gentle.
m. shall inherit the earth Ps 37:11
Blessed are the m. Mt 5:5
Megiddo (muh-GID-oh) A fortified, walled
city at the foot of the Carmel mountain
range in N Israel, overlooking the Valley of
Jezreel where the last battle between good
and evil will be fought (Rev 16:16); a chariot city for Kings Solomon and Ahab; site of

many important OT battles. Megiddo is an-
other name for Armageddon.
Melchizedek (mel-KIZ-uh-dek) A king of
Salem (Jerusalem) and priest of the Most
High God (Gen 14:18-20; Ps 110:4; Heb
5:6-11; 6:20—7:21); appeared and disappeared somewhat mysteriously in the
Book of Genesis; bestowed a blessing on
Abraham and praised God for giving him
a victory in battle (Gen 14:18-20). Melchizedek is seen as a type of Christ in both
Psalm 110 and the Book of Hebrews.
"Mene, Mene, Tekel, Upharsin" (ME-
neh, ME-neh, TEK-ul, you-FAR-sin)
Means "numbered, numbered, weighed,
and divided." An inscription that appeared
on the wall of the palace of King Belshazzar
in Babylon, written by a mysterious hand
during a feast (Dan 5:1-29). The king ordered that the gold vessels taken from the
temple of Jerusalem be brought in for the
guests to use in eating and drinking. When
the words appeared on the wall, Daniel
was called in to interpret. Daniel told the
king that God had weighed him on the
scales of righteousness, and he did not
measure up. The kingdom would be divided between his enemies, the Medes and
the Persians. That very night, Belshazzar
was killed and his kingdom fell.
Mephibosheth (meh-FIB-oh-sheth) A son
of Jonathan and grandson of King Saul;
only five years old when his father and
grandfather were killed on Mount Gilboa in
the Battle of Jezreel (2 Sam 4:4); dropped
by his nurse and crippled for the rest of his
life (2 Sam 4:4); treated kindly by King David because of an agreement made between the king and his father, Jonathan
(2 Sam 9:7-13).
merciful Forgiving; unwilling to punish.
LORD God, m. and gracious Ex 34:6
God be m. to us Ps 67:1
Blessed are the m. Mt 5:7
m. to me a sinner Lk 18:13
mercy Forgiveness or kindness, particularly
to a wrongdoer.
His m. endures forever Ezra 3:11
they shall obtain m. Mt 5:7
mercy seat Literally, "covering." The lid of
the ark of the testimony, from above which
God spoke to His people (Ex 25:22).
merry Joyous; happy.
m. heart makes a cheerful Prov 15:13
m. heart does good Prov 17:22
eat, drink, and be m. Eccles 8:15; Lk 12:19

Meshach (ME-shack) The Babylonian name of one of Daniel's friends (Dan 1:7; 3:12).

Mesopotamia (mess-uh-puh-TAY-mee-uh) "Land between the rivers." A region between the Tigris and Euphrates Rivers in the modern countries of Iraq and Iran; the "cradle of civilization"; traditional site of the Garden of Eden; Ur of the Chaldees is located in the S part of the region (Acts 7:2).

Messiah (muh-SIGH-uh) Literally, "anointed one"; one sent by God to save others. In Hebrew belief, the coming savior of the Jewish people; in Christianity, Jesus.

Methuselah (meh-THOO-zuh-luh) Noah's grandfather; lived for 969 years, the oldest person mentioned in the Bible (Gen 5:27).

Micah (MY-kuh) A Judean prophet, contemporary of Isaiah, whose prophecies appear in the OT Book of Micah, the sixth of the 12 Minor Prophets.

mighty Powerful; very strong.
He was a m. hunter Gen 10:9
a great and m. nation Gen 18:18
How the m. have fallen 2 Sam 1:19
m. in deed and word Lk 24:19

ministry God's service.
to the m. of the word Acts 6:4
m. of reconciliation 2 Cor 5:18

miracle An event that exceeds the known laws of nature and science. Usually an act of God done through human agents. The OT miracles include:
ten plagues of Egypt Ex 7:14—12:30
parting of the Red Sea Ex 14:21-31
feeding with bread from heaven Ex 16:14-35
walls of Jericho fall Josh 6:1-21
strength of Samson Judg 14:1—16:30
Elijah taken by a whirlwind 2 Kgs 2:11
Elisha revives dead child 2 Kgs 4:18-37
three men saved from furnace Dan 3:19-27
Daniel saved from lions Dan 6:16-23
Jonah saved Jon 1:10—2:10
  The NT miracles of Jesus include:
the leper cured Mt 8:2, 3; Mk 1:40-42; Lk 5:12, 13
centurion's servant healed Mt 8:5-13; Lk 7:1-10
the storm stilled Mt 8:23-26; Mk 4:35-39; Lk 8:22-24
demons entered into swine Mt 8:28-32; Mk 5:1-13; Lk 8:26-33
dumb demoniac healed Mt 9:32, 33
feeding the 5,000 Mt 14:15-21; Mk 6:35-44; Lk 9:10-17; Jn 6:1-14

Jesus walks on the sea Mt 14:25-27; Mk 6:48-51; Jn 6:19-21
feeding the 4,000 Mt 15:32-38; Mk 8:1-9
ten lepers cleansed Lk 17:11-19
water changed to wine Jn 2:1-11
Lazarus raised from dead Jn 11:38-44
  Other NT miracles include:
the gift of tongues Acts 2:4-11
Peter restores Tabitha Acts 9:36-41
Peter's release from prison Acts 12:5-10

mite A copper coin of small value.
widow . . . threw in two m. Mk 12:42

money Riches; coins.
the tax m. Mt 22:19
no copper in their m. belts Mk 6:8
love of m. is a root of all . . . evil 1 Tim 6:10

money changer

money changers Bankers who exchanged one nation's currency for another, often charging too much for this service. Twice, Jesus found them in the temple, made a whip of cords, and drove them out, along with those who sold oxen, sheep, and doves (Jn 2:13-16; Mt 21:12-13). Jesus said, "Do not make My Father's house a house of merchandise" (Jn 2:16).

Mordecai (MOR-duh-kigh) The Jewish hero of the OT Book of Esther.

Moses (MO-zez) The great deliverer and lawgiver of Israel; born during the oppression of the Israelites in Egypt (Ex 1:22—2:2); brought up in Pharaoh's house (Ex 2:5-10); fled to Midian where he lived

40 years (Ex 2:15-25); called by God from the burning bush (Ex 3:2-5) to deliver the Israelites; after performing ten miracles of plagues (Ex 7:14—12:30) he got Pharaoh's consent to take the Israelites from Egypt; led them 40 years through the wilderness; received the Ten Commandments from God (Ex 20). The OT books of Exodus, Leviticus, Numbers, and Deuteronomy detail his life and deeds.

Most High, the A name used of God.
When the Most H. divided Deut 32:8
the Most H. rules in Dan 4:25
the Most H. does not dwell Acts 7:48

mother Female parent.
Honor . . . your m. Ex 20:12; Mt 19:19
Like m., like daughter Ezek 16:44
disciple, "Behold your m. Jn 19:27

Mount of Olives A ridge of hills E of Jerusalem, where Jesus was betrayed by Judas on the night before His crucifixion; site of Jesus' triumphal entry into Jerusalem, when He wept over the city because the people would not believe (Lk 19:37-41); traditional location of the tomb of Mary, Jesus' mother; site of Jesus' ascension (Mt 28:16).

mourn To grieve for.
Blessed are those who m. Mt 5:4

murder To kill; cause the death of.
You shall not m. Ex 20:13; Deut 5:17; Mt 5:21

myrrh An aromatic, resinous substance used in incense and perfumes.
of liquid m. Ex 30:23
frankincense, and m. Mt 2:11
wine mingled with m. Mk 15:23

N

Naaman (NAY-uh-mun) Commander of the Syrian army, who was "a great and honorable man in the eyes of his master (Ben-Hadad, king of Syria) . . . but he was a leper" (2 Kgs 5:1-27); served by a young Israelite girl who had been captured on one of Syria's frequent raids of Israel; encouraged to see the prophet Elisha, who could heal his leprosy; finally following Elisha's instructions, dipped himself seven times in the Jordan River and was healed; became a worshiper of God.

Nahum (NAY-hum) A prophet, the prophecies of whom are given in the OT Book of Nahum, the seventh of the 12 Minor Prophets.

name The word by which a person, place, or thing is called.
n. of the LORD your God in vain Ex 20:7
How excellent is Your n. Ps 8:1
Hallowed be Your n. Mt 6:9; Lk 11:2
in My n. Mt 24:5; Mk 13:6; Lk 21:8
My n. is Legion Mk 5:9
ask the Father in My n. Jn 15:16

Naomi (nay-OH-mee) The mother-in-law of Ruth, the Moabitess. After her husband and two sons died, Naomi returned to Bethlehem with her daughter-in-law Ruth, who insisted on going with her (Ruth 1:16-17). Ruth became an ancestor of Jesus Christ when she married her kinsman, Boaz (Ruth 4:21-22; Mt 1:5).

Naphtali (NAF-tah-ligh) The sixth son of Jacob, the second born of Bilhah (Gen 30:7, 8); ancestor of one of the 12 tribes of Israel.

narrow Not wide; small in width.
n. is the gate . . . which Mt 7:14

Nathan (NAY-thun) A prophet during the reign of David and Solomon; told David that he would not be the one to build the temple at Jerusalem (1 Chr 17:1-15); confronted David after he had Uriah killed in battle so he could marry his wife, Bathsheba (2 Sam 12:9-15).

nation A group of people under one government or sharing the same history.
make you a great n. Gen 12:2
n. will rise against n. Mt 24:7; Mk 13:8

Nazareth (NAZ-uh-reth) The town in Lower Galilee where Jesus was brought up (Lk 2:39, 51).

Nazirite (NAZ-uh-right) A person who took a vow to be separated from the world and completely dedicated to God (Num 6:1-8). They promised not to touch strong drink, not to shave or cut their hair (Samson), not to touch or go near a dead body, not even to bury a relative (Num 6:5-12; Prov 20:1; Eph 5:17-18), etc.

Nebuchadnezzar (neb-you-kad-NEZ-zer) King of Babylonia (605-562 B.C.).

Nehemiah (nee-huh-MY-uh) The name of three persons in the OT, one of whom was the rebuilder of Jerusalem after the Babylonian Exile. The Book of Nehemiah tells his story.

neighbor A person who lives near another.
false witness against your n. Ex 20:16
love your n. as yourself Lev 19:18; Mt 19:19

Nicodemus (nick-uh-DEE-mus) A wealthy, well-educated and well-respected Pharisee and member of the Sanhedrin, who probably became a disciple of Jesus; visited Jesus at night to learn more about His teachings (Jn 3:1-8; 7:50). On this visit Jesus told Him he must be "born again" (Jn 3:7); later gave him the Gospel in one verse: John 3:16! Nicodemus defended Jesus before the Sanhedrin; purchased a hundred pounds of spices to be placed between the folds of the cloth in which Jesus was buried (Jn 19:39).

night The period of darkness between sunset and sunrise.
darkness He called N. Gen 1:5
Watchman, what of the n. Isa 21:11
the n. is coming when no Jn 9:4

Nineveh (NIN-uh-vuh) One of the oldest and greatest cities of Mesopotamia; capital of Assyria; destroyed 612 B.C. (Gen 10:11, 12; 2 Kgs 19:36; Isa 37:37; Jon 1:2; 4:11; Nah 1:1; 2:8; 3:7).

Nisan (NIGH-san) The name given, after the captivity lasting 70 years, to the former month of Abib—the first month of the Jewish sacred year (Esther 3:7).

Noah (NO-uh) The ninth descendant of Adam; the survivor, with his family, of the Flood (Gen 6—9).

O

Obadiah (oh-buh-DIE-uh) The name of 11 persons in the OT, none of whom can be assumed to be the author of the Book of Obadiah, the shortest OT book and fourth of the 12 Minor Prophets.

offering Something given in worship. In the OT we find offerings of: 1. **grain:** Consisting of unleavened bread, cakes, wafers, or grain mixed with salt and, except when a sin offering, with olive oil (Lev 2:1-16; 5:11; 6:14-23; Num 15:4, 6, 9). Sometimes accepted from the poor as a sin offering in place of the burnt offering (Lev 5:11-13). 2. **drink:** Consisting of wine and used with the grain and burnt offerings, except in the sin and trespass offerings (Num 6:17; 15:5, 10). 3. **animals,** or **sacrifice:** Cattle, sheep, and goats that were free from blemish (Lev 1:3). These were used with: a. The **burnt offering** in which a male lamb, ram, goat, bull, dove, or pigeon was entirely consumed on the altar (Lev 1; 6:9-13). b. The **sin offering** in which a bull, a male or female goat, a female lamb, a dove, or a pigeon was given

(Lev 4; 5:7; 6:25-30). c. The **trespass offering** in which a ram or lamb was used (Lev 5:6, 15; 6:6; 7:1-8; 14:12, 21). d. The **peace offering,** including the giving of thanks (Lev 7:12-15), the payment of a vow (Lev 7:16-20; Num 6:13-21), and the voluntary or freewill offering (Lev 7:16-20); for these any animal without blemish of either sex could be used, except birds (Lev 3; 7:11-27). In sacrifices, the term "wave offering" is used of those portions consecrated to the Lord by the rite of "waving" (Lev 7:30-34; Num 6:17-20); and the term "heave offering" is used of those portions taken away and set apart for the Lord (Lev 7:14, 32-34; Num 18:8-32).

oil Any of several greasy liquids that can be burned.
anoint my head with o. Ps 23:5

Olives, Mount of; Olivet, mount called A mountain E of Jerusalem (2 Sam 15:30; Zech 14:4). Closely associated with the last days in the life of Jesus (in the four Gospels and Acts 1:12).

P

Palestine (PAL-es-tine) The Greek and Roman names for Canaan; modern usage applies the name to the territory alloted to the 12 tribes of Israel.

Palm Sunday The Sunday before Easter; commemorates the triumphal entry of Jesus into Jerusalem (Jn 12:12, 13).

parable (PAIR-uh-bull) A short story teaching a moral lesson. Among those of the OT are:
Samson's riddle Judg 14:14
field of the slothful Prov 24:30-34
two harlots Ezek 23
healing waters Ezek 47:1-12
  In the NT, parables are only by Jesus, and include:
lamp under a basket Mt 5:14-16; Mk 4:21-23; Lk 8:16-18
unshrunk cloth on an old garment Mt 9:16, 17; Mk 2:21, 22; Lk 5:36-39
weeds among wheat Mt 13:24-30
the mustard seed Mt 13:31, 32; Mk 4:30-32; Lk 13:18, 19
lost sheep Mt 18:12-14; Lk 15:4-7
laborers in vineyard Mt 20:1-16
wise and foolish virgins Mt 25:1-13
the talents Mt 25:14-30
two debtors Lk 7:41-50

Good Samaritan Lk 10:30-37
Prodigal Son Lk 15:11-32
Pharisee and tax collector Lk 18:9-14
shepherd and the sheep Jn 10:1-30

Passover 1. A seven-day Jewish festival held in March or April, commemorating the slaying of the firstborn just before the Israelites were freed from slavery in Egypt (Ex 12); combined with the Feast of Unleavened Bread which commemorates the actual Exodus flight (Ex 13:3-16). 2. The sacrificial lamb of the Passover (Ex 12:11, 21, 27). Paul refers to Christ as the Paschal Lamb.
Christ, our P., was sacrificed 1 Cor 5:7

Pastoral Epistles The epistles to Timothy and Titus are so called because they deal chiefly with directions about the work of the pastor of a church.

pasture Grassy land where cattle and sheep graze.
me to lie down in green p. Ps 23:2

Patmos, Island of (PAT-mus) A small, rocky, irregularly shaped island off the western coast of Asia Minor or modern Turkey; used by the Romans to hold exiled criminals, one of whom was the apostle John, who received messages from the Lord, which became the Book of Revelation (Rev 1:9-11).

Paul As Saul, the son of Hebrew parents, he persecuted the followers of Jesus (Acts 8:3; Gal 1:13). Miraculously converted (Acts 9:1ff) and name changed to Paul (Acts 13:9), he became the leading missionary of early Christianity. His life is detailed in the NT Book of Acts. He founded many churches in Asia Minor and Greece and carried on extensive correspondence with them.

peace Freedom from turmoil and war.
of war, And a time of p. Eccles 3:8
is no p. . . . for the wicked Isa 57:21
not come to bring p. but a sword Mt 10:34
on earth p., good will Lk 2:14
P. to you Lk 24:36; Jn 20:19

peeled Stripped off the bark.
rods which he had p. Gen 30:38

Pentecost (PEN-tih-cost) A Jewish festival on the fiftieth day after Passover; also called Feast of Weeks (Lev 23:15, 16). Observed by the Christian church as the day on which the gift of the Holy Spirit was given to the church (Acts 2:1).

perish To die; to be destroyed.
way of the ungodly shall p. Ps 1:6

believes in Him should not p. Jn 3:15

Peter; Simon Peter A fisherman on the Sea of Galilee who was called with his brother Andrew by Jesus (Mt 4:18-20; Mk 1:16-18; Lk 5:1-11; Jn 1:35-41). He became the "first" of the 12 apostles (Mt 10:2), and sometimes spoke for all the disciples. Jesus changed his name from Simon to Peter (Mt 16:18; Mk 3:16; Lk 6:14; Jn 1:42). His mother-in-law healed by Jesus (Mt 8:14, 15; Mk 1:30, 31; Lk 4:38, 39); his confession that Jesus is the Christ (Mt 16:16; Mk 8:29; Lk 9:20); his denial of Jesus (Mt 26:69-75; Mk 14:66-72; Lk 22:54-62). The traditional author of two NT epistles.

Pharaoh

Pharaoh (FAY-row) A title used as a name, or prefixed to a name, of the king of Egypt. Joseph interprets Pharaoh's dream (Gen 41:1-36); the Pharaoh of the Exodus (Ex 7-14).

Pharisee (FAIR-uh-see) A member of a strict Jewish sect, holding the Mosaic Law and their own traditions as binding. The parable of the Pharisee and the publican (Lk 18:9-14).

Philemon (fih-LEE-mun) A Christian of Colosse to whom the NT Epistle to Philemon was written by Paul. In the letter Paul asks Philemon to pardon Onesimus, a runaway slave whom Paul has converted.

Philip The name of four persons in the NT, among them: 1. The apostle (Mt 10:3; Mk 3:18; Lk 6:14; Jn 1:43-48; 6:5, 7; 12:21,

22; 14:8, 9; Acts 1:13). 2. The evangelist (Acts 6:5; 8:5-40; 21:8).

Philippi; Philippians (FILL-ih-pie; fih-LIP-ih-uns) A city of Macedonia where Paul founded his first Christian congregation in Europe. The NT Epistle to the Philippians was written by Paul to the church there.

Philistines (fih-LIS-teens) The people who lived along the S coast of Palestine; often at war with the Israelites. Goliath was a champion of the Philistines (1 Sam 17:23-51).

Phoenicia (fe-NISH-she-uh) A country W of the Lebanon range and Galilee on the coast of the Mediterranean Sea (Acts 11:19; 15:3; 21:2); its chief cities were Tyre and Sidon.

physician A medical doctor.
Is there no p. there Jer 8:22
who are well have no need of a p. Mt 9:12
P., heal yourself Lk 4:23
Luke the beloved p. Col 4:14

Pilate; Pontius Pilate (PIE-lut; PON-chus) The Roman governor of Judea (A.D. 26-36); the judge in the trial and execution of Jesus (Mt 27:1-26; Mk 15:1-15; Lk 23:1-25; Jn 18:28—19:16).

pillar An upright column.
became a p. of salt Gen 19:26
by day in a p. of cloud Ex 13:21
by night in a p. of fire Ex 13:21

plank A log; a piece of timber.
remove the p. Mt 7:5

plowing
will be neither p. nor harvesting Gen 45:6
in p. time and in harvest Ex 34:21

plowshare

plowshare The cutting blade of a plow.
their swords into p. Isa 2:4
Beat your p. into swords Joel 3:10

poor Needy; having little or no goods or money.
the p. shall not give less Ex 30:15
Blessed are the p. in spirit Mt 5:3
have the p. with you always Mt 26:11; Mk 14:7

prayer Words addressed to God.
house of p. Isa 56:7; Mt 21:13; Mk 11:17; Lk 19:46
by p. and fasting Mt 17:21; Mk 9:29
you ask in p. Mt 21:22

pride Conceit; vanity.
P. goes before destruction Prov 16:18

priest A minister. Aaron and his sons, of the tribe of Levi, were appointed to the priesthood at Sinai; the office became hereditary and restricted to that family (Ex 28:1; 40:12-15).
p. of God Most High Gen 14:18

prince One who has authority or influence; a ruler; hence, **Prince:** the Messiah; Christ.
made you a p. . . . over us Ex 2:14
Do not put your trust in p. Ps 146:3
P. of Peace Isa 9:6
the P. of princes Dan 8:25
killed the P. of life Acts 3:15

prodigal (PROD-ih-gul) Wasteful. The parable of the Prodigal Son is given in Luke 15:11-32.

prophet (PROFF-et) A man called by God to be His spokesman.
I will raise up for them a P. Deut 18:18
p. is not without honor Mt 13:57; Mk 6:4; Jn 4:44
no p. is accepted in his Lk 4:24

propitiation (pro-pish-ee-AY-shun) Expiation; removal of guilt by atonement (Rom 3:25; 1 Jn 2:2; 4:10).

proverb (PRAH-verb); **Proverbs, the Book of** A short, meaningful saying about the nature of man and life. Proverbs in the Bible, most of which were written down by Solomon (1 Kgs 4:32), help to explain God's truths for wise and godly living.

psalm; Psalms, the Book of The hymn book of the Bible—a collection of prayers, poems, and hymns that focus the worshiper's thoughts on God in praise; the longest (150 psalms) book in the Bible. The title comes from a Greek word which means "a song sung to the accompaniment of a musical instrument." Subjects include God and His creation, war, worship, wisdom, sin and evil, judgment, justice, and the coming of the Messiah. Psalms are grouped by subject—thanksgiving, repentance, praise, confession, messianic, as well as psalms to be sung by pilgrims as they traveled to Jerusalem.

Purim (PEW-reem) A Jewish festival celebrating the deliverance from massacre (Esther 9:20–28).

R

Rabbi (RAB-eye) Master; teacher.
They said to Him, "R. Jn 1:38

rabbi

Rachel (RAY-chul) The younger daughter of Laban; Jacob's second wife; mother of Joseph and Benjamin (Gen 29:1—31:35; 35:16-19).

Rebekah (ree-BECK-uh) Wife of Isaac; mother of Esau and Jacob (Gen 24:10-67; 25:20-26, 28; 26:6-11; 27:5-17).

redeemer One who buys back, rescues (as from sin), or ransoms. Jesus is called "the Redeemer," through His sacrificial death, although the word does not appear in the NT.

I know that my R. lives Job 19:25
LORD, my strength and my r. Ps 19:14
R. will come to Zion Isa 59:20

Red Sea; Sea of Reeds The body of water between Arabia and Africa; the miraculous parting of the sea (Ex 14:21-31) enabled the Israelites to escape the Egyptians.

remember To bring to mind again.
R. the Sabbath day Ex 20:8
R. Lot's wife Lk 17:32

repent To feel regret; to change one's mind about.
r. in dust and ashes Job 42:6

R., for the kingdom Mt 3:2
unless you r. you will Lk 13:3
R., and . . . be baptized Acts 2:38
R. therefore and be Acts 3:19

resurrection (rez-er-RECK-shun) A rising from the dead; a return to life; hence, **Resurrection:** The rising of Christ from the dead (Mt 28; Mk 16; Lk 24; Jn 20; 1 Cor 15).

there is no r. Mt 22:23; Mk 12:18
I am the r. and the life Jn 11:25
This is the first r. Rev 20:5

Reuben; Reubenites (ROO-bin; ROO-bin-nights) The firstborn son of Jacob, by Leah (Gen 29:32); the ancestor of the tribe of Reuben.

revelation (rev-uh-LAY-shun) The making known of something previously concealed.
through the r. of Jesus Christ Gal 1:12
The R. of Jesus Christ Rev 1:1

reward To give payment for something done; used particularly of God's blessing upon the obedient and His punishment of the wicked.
r. in heaven Mt 5:12; Lk 6:23
receive his own r. 1 Cor 3:8

rich Wealthy; having money or property.
Do not overwork to be r. Prov 23:4
for he was very r. Lk 18:23

riches Wealth; property; material goods.
r. are not forever Prov 27:24
deceitfulness of r. Mt 13:22; Mk 4:19

resurrection

righteous One who does what is right; a virtuous person.

LORD knows the way of the r. Ps 1:6

not come to call the r. Mt 9:13

righteousness Virtue; right action; particularly, conformity to God's will.

in the paths of r. Ps 23:3

hunger and thirst for r. Mt 5:6

grace might reign through r. Rom 5:21

rock A mass of stone; anything hard like a rock.

are my r. and my fortress Ps 31:3

on this r. I will build Mt 16:18

Rock The Lord.

Of the R. who begot you Deut 32:18

The LORD is my r. Ps 18:2

Rome; Romans The capital of the Roman Empire; Christianity probably came to Rome early in the apostolic age. Paul wrote the NT Epistle to the Romans to the Christian community there.

rooster

before the r. crows Mt 26:34, 75

Ruth A Moabite woman who became an ancestress of David through her second marriage, to Boaz. Her story of devotion is told in the OT Book of Ruth.

S

sabbath The day of rest ordained by God. Among Jews, the seventh day (Saturday); among Christians, the first day of the week (Sunday), the day of divine worship (1 Cor 16:2).

Remember the S. day Ex 20:8

a s. of solemn rest for you Lev 16:31

S. was made for man Mk 2:27

sacrifice (SACK-rih-fyce) An offering, usually of the life of a person or an animal, made to God.

s. to the LORD Ex 5:17

love . . . is more than . . . s. Mk 12:33

put away sin by the s. of Heb 9:26

Sadducees (SAD-you-sees) The aristocratic party of the Jews at the time of Christ. They collaborated with the Romans to maintain their favorable status.

salt A seasoning; a preservative.

became a pillar of s. Gen 19:26

You are the s. of the earth Mt 5:13

salvation (sal-VAY-shun) Deliverance from evil, danger, or trouble; God's gift, through Christ, to save men's souls.

the God of my s. Ps 25:5

to the Rock of our s. Ps 95:1

shall see the s. of God Lk 3:6

this will turn out for my s. Phil 1:19

grace of God that brings s. Tit 2:11

the author of their s. Heb 2:10

Samaria; Samaritans (suh-MARE-ee-ah; suh-MARE-ih-tuns) The capital city of the northern kingdom, Israel. Also the name of the territory near the city. The term "Samaritan" is usually applied to a member of a religious sect living in that area. The parable of the Good Samaritan told by Jesus (Lk 10:30-37).

Samson A hero of the tribe of Dan, noted for his great strength (Judg 13—16).

Samuel (SAM-you-ell) The last "judge" of Israel; a prophet of the eleventh century B.C. The two OT books of Samuel record his life and deeds and the history of Israel through the reigns of Solomon and David. The Lord calls Samuel (1 Sam 3); Samuel anoints David (1 Sam 16:11-13).

sanctify (SANK-tih-fy) To set apart as holy; to consecrate to religious use; to make holy.

seventh day and s. it Gen 2:3

s. by the Holy Spirit Rom 15:16

sanctuary (SANK-shoe-air-ih) A building or place set apart for religious worship; in the OT, the tabernacle (Ex 25:8) or the temple (1 Chr 22:19).

sandal strap Thong to fasten a sandal.

whose s.s. I am not worthy Jn 1:27

Sanhedrin (SAN-hee-drun) A council or assembly, the highest ruling body and court of justice among the Jewish people in the time of Jesus; headed by the high priest of Israel; composed of 71 members, among whom were Joseph of Arimathea (Mk 15:43), Gamaliel, Paul's teacher (Acts 5:34), Nicodemus (Jn 3:1; 7:50), the high priests, Annas and Caiaphas (Lk 3:2) and Ananias (Acts 23:2); given limited authority over certain religious, civil, and criminal matters involving foreign nations that dominated Israel at various times in its history.

Sarah; Sarai The wife of Abraham; mother of Isaac in accord with divine promise (Gen 17:15-21; 18:1-15).

Satan (SAY-tun) The Devil; the adversary of God and Christ.

S. casts out S. Mt 12:26; Mk 3:23

forty days, tempted by S. Mk 1:13

lest S. should take advantage 2 Cor 2:11

S. will be released from Rev 20:7

Saul Son of Kish, of the tribe of Benjamin; first king over Israel. The prophet Samuel anoints him to be king (1 Sam 10:1); he disobeys the Lord (1 Sam 15); David enters his service (1 Sam 16:14-23); he tries to kill David (1 Sam 19:9, 10); David spares his life (1 Sam 26:6-24).

sandal strap

Saul of Tarsus *See* Paul.

Savior Literally, "one who saves or delivers"; Christ, as the One who delivers us from the sins of this life and through whom salvation is obtained; God, as the deliverer of the Israelites from oppression and as the redeemer of all peoples.

my refuge; My S. 2 Sam 22:3

A just God and a S. Isa 45:21

rejoiced in God my S. Lk 1:47

Christ, the S. of the world Jn 4:42

Christ . . . the S. of the body Eph 5:23

S., the Lord Jesus Christ Phil 3:20

God our S., Who alone is wise Jude 25

scripture; Scriptures, the Any writing, particularly that of a sacred nature; hence, the Bible. Also "Scriptures"; "Holy Scripture"; "Holy Scriptures."

Have you not read this S. Mk 12:10

search the S. Jn 5:39

S. is given by inspiration 2 Tim 3:16

seek To search for; to try to find.

s., and you will find Mt 7:7; Lk 11:9

none who s. after God Rom 3:11

Sermon on the Mount Name given to a talk by Jesus while teaching His disciples in the hill country of Galilee early in His ministry (Mt 5:3—7:27). It includes a series of blessings, the Beatitudes (5:3-12); the Lord's Prayer (6:9-13); and the Golden Rule (7:12). A similar discourse in Luke 6:17-49 is called the "Sermon on the Plain."

serpent

serpent A snake; in biblical usage, many times synonymous with "Satan."

s. was more cunning than Gen 3:1

will take up s. Mk 16:18

s. deceived Eve 2 Cor 11:3

s. of old, who is the Devil Rev 20:2

Shadrach (SHAD-rack) The Babylonian name of one of Daniel's companions (Dan 1:7; 3:12).

Sheba, queen of (SHE-bah) A queen, probably Arabian, who came to test Solomon's wisdom (1 Kgs 10:1-13; 2 Chr 9:1-12).

Shem The eldest son of Noah who stands as the ancestor of the Semites generally and of the Hebrews specifically (Gen 5:32; 9:18-27; 10:21-31; Lk 3:36).

shepherd One who herds and takes care of sheep; by extension, the ruler or king of a people. The Lord is the shepherd of Israel; Christ is the Good Shepherd (Jn 10:7-18).

The LORD is my s. Ps 23:1

s. . . . keeping watch over Lk 2:8

one flock and one s. Jn 10:16

Lord Jesus . . . that great S. Heb 13:20

Silas; Silvanus (SIGH-lus; sil-VAY-nus) One of the earliest of the apostolic missionaries, associated with both Paul (Acts 16:19ff; 1 Thess 1:1; 2:1, 2) and Peter (1 Pet 5:12).

Siloam, Pool of (sigh-LOW-um) A storage pool and tunnel that provided a water supply for the residents of Jerusalem, fed by the Gihon Spring; dug through solid rock in the time of King Hezekiah of Judah (2 Chr 32:30). Water still flows through the tunnel to this day!

Simeon (SIM-ee-un) The name of six persons in the Bible, including: 1. The second son of Jacob, by Leah (Gen 29:33); ancestor of the tribe of Simeon. 2. A devout man who blessed the infant Jesus when His parents presented Him in the temple (Lk 2:25-35).

Simon (SIGH-mun) The name of nine persons in the NT, including: 1. **Simon Peter:** See Peter (Mt 16:17, 18; Jn 1:42). 2. **Simon the Zealot:** Also one of the 12 apostles (Lk 6:15). 3. **Simon the Pharisee,** in whose home Jesus was anointed by the sinful woman (Lk 7:36-50). 4. **Simon the leper,** in whose home Jesus was anointed by Mary (Mk 14:3-9; Jn 12:1-8). 5. **Simon of Cyrene,** who was forced to carry Jesus' cross (Mt 27:32; Mk 15:21; Lk 23:26). 6. **Simon the sorcerer,** who offered money to Peter and John for the power of the Holy Spirit (Acts 8:9-24).

sin 1. An offense or revolt against God (as Adam and Eve in the Garden of Eden); deliberate defiance; wickedness; iniquity; ungodliness.

put to death for his own s. Deut 24:16

our s. testify against us Isa 59:12

power on earth to forgive s. Mt 9:6

Who can forgive s. Mk 2:7; Lk 5:21

takes away the s. of Jn 1:29

He who is without s. Jn 8:7

gave Himself for our s. Gal 1:4

2. To commit an offense against God; to be wicked.

is no one who does not s. 1 Kgs 8:46

soul who s. shall die Ezek 18:4

S. no more, lest a Jn 5:14

cannot s., because he has been born of God 1 Jn 3:9

Sinai, Mount (SIGH-nigh) The name of a peninsula, a wilderness, and a mountain. 1. The barren, triangular-shaped peninsula stands between Egypt and Israel. 2. In the wilderness, there are no flowing streams or rivers, only wadis (dry stream beds which carry off the occasional rains). 3. The traditional mountain where Moses received the Ten Commandments (Ex 19:3-20) is in the Sinai range and is called Jebel Musa, the mountain of Moses. When the Israelites camped there, it was called Sinai (Ex 19:11), or sometimes called Horeb (Ex 3:1).

sinful Wicked; full of iniquity.

s. nation, A people laden Isa 1:4

in the likeness of s. flesh Rom 8:3

sinner One who commits an offense against God.

stands in the path of s. Ps 1:1

Why does your Teacher eat with . . . s. Mt 9:11; Mk 2:16; Lk 5:30

come to call . . . s., to repentance Mt 9:13; Mk 2:17; Lk 5:32

over one s. who repents Lk 15:7

be merciful to me a s. Lk 18:13

Sodom (SOD-um) One of the two cities destroyed by the Lord because of their wickedness (Gen 19:24-28).

Solomon Son of David and Bathsheba; third king of Israel; under his reign the kingdom reached its zenith; noted for his wisdom (1 Kgs 3:16-28) and his gift of expressing himself. The OT books of Proverbs, Ecclesiastes, and Song of Solomon, and Psalms 72 and 127 are attributed to him. He built the temple (1 Kgs 6—7; 2 Chr 3); was visited by the queen of Sheba (1 Kgs 10:1-13; 2 Chr 9:1-12).

son A male child or man as related to his parents; a male descendant.

wise s. makes a glad father Prov 10:1

Unto us a S. is given Isa 9:6

Is this not the carpenter's s. Mt 13:55

Son; Son of God The Second Person of the Trinity; Christ.

is My beloved S. Mt 3:17; 17:5; Mk 1:11; Lk 9:35

S. of the living God Mt 16:16; Jn 6:69

this is the S. of God Jn 1:34

gave His only begotten S. Jn 3:16

son of man Any human being (Ps 8:4); the prophet Ezekiel (used throughout the OT Book of Ezekiel); in the Gospels, Jesus uses "Son of Man" as a self-designation, particularly in the passages relating to His Second Coming.

sons of God Angels (Job 1:6; Dan 3:25); any human beings, as created in God's image (Hos 1:10); Christians (Rom 8:14).

soul The life principle of a human being; the immortal element of man; the spirit; the living individual.

obey . . . with all your s. Deut 30:2

Hear, and your s. shall live Isa 55:3

all s. are Mine Ezek 18:4

destroy both s. and body Mt 10:28

loses his own s. Mt 16:26; Mk 8:36

s. be subject to the governing Rom 13:1

sow To plant.

s. in tears Shall reap in joy Ps 126:5

man s., that he will also reap Gal 6:7

spirit That part of a person's being thought of as the center of life, the will, thinking, feeling; that part of man that survives death.

Into Your hand I commit my s. Ps 31:5

a haughty s. before Prov 16:18

yielded up His s. Mt 27:50; Jn 19:30

the s. indeed is willing Mt 26:41; Mk 14:38

to the s. of just men Heb 12:23

Spirit, Holy The Third Person of the Trinity; that divine Spirit, referred to in the OT as "Spirit of the LORD" or "Spirit of God," through which men receive power, particularly effective through Jesus Christ in bringing men into fellowship with God. Some Bible translators use "Holy Ghost" rather than "Holy Spirit."

in the name of the . . . Holy S. Mt 28:19

baptize you with the Holy S. Mt 3:11; Mk 1:8; Lk 3:16; Jn 1:33

be filled with the Holy S. Lk 1:15

Holy S. was not yet given Jn 7:39

Helper, the Holy S. Jn 14:26

promise of the Holy S. Acts 2:33

witness in the Holy S. Rom 9:1

except by the Holy S. 1 Cor 12:3

communion of the Holy S. 2 Cor 13:14

Spirit of the Lord; Spirit of God; Holy Spirit The divine source of all life; a special manifestation of God's divine Presence.

S. of God was hovering Gen 1:2

S. is poured upon us Isa 32:15

S. of the Lord GOD is Isa 61:1; Lk 4:18

S. descending . . . like a dove Mk 1:10; Jn 1:32

God is S. Jn 4:24

not grieve the Holy S. of Eph 4:30

Stephen The first Christian martyr; one of the seven men chosen by the apostles for the special "service of tables"; his death was the signal for a general persecution of the Christians (Acts 6:1—8:3).

stew A thick soup.

Esau sells birthright for s. Gen 25:29-34

steward A manager of a household or of property; used of Christians, particularly ministers, as guardians of the affairs of God.

faithful and wise s. Lk 12:42

s. of the mysteries of God 1 Cor 4:1

s. of the manifold grace of God 1 Pet 4:10

stone A rock; a hard mineral.

dash your foot against a s. Ps 91:12; Mt 4:6; Lk 4:11

not one s. . . . upon another Mt 24:2; Mk 13:2; Lk 19:44; 21:6

s. to become bread Lk 4:3

sufficient Enough; ample.

S. for the day is its own Mt 6:34

Supper, Last *See* Last Supper.

Supper, Lord's *See* Holy Communion.

swear To declare under oath.

not s. by My name falsely Lev 19:12

not s. at all Mt 5:34

sword A sharp-bladed weapon with a hilt or handle.

beat their s. into plowshares Isa 2:4; Mic 4:3

Beat your plowshares into s. Joel 3:10

sharper than any two-edged s. Heb 4:12

synagogue (SIN-uh-gog) A building where Jewish religious services and schools and other meetings are held.

preached the word of God in the s. Acts 13:5

T

tabernacle (TAB-er-nak-kel) Literally, "tent of meeting"; the portable shelter used by the Israelites as a place of worship.

pattern of the t. Ex 25:9

Tabernacles, Feast of One of the three great joyous festivals of the Jewish year; held in autumn at the end of the harvest; celebrates a renewal of the covenant and recalls the wilderness pilgrimage (Ex 23:16; Lev 23:34-36; Deut 16:13-15). Also called "Feast of Booths" (Lev 23:42); "the Feast of Ingathering" (Ex 23:16; 34:22).

tablets Flat stones bearing inscriptions.
two t. of the Testimony Ex 31:18

talent A unit of money or of weight. Parable of the talents (Mt 25:14-30).

Tarsus (TAR-sus) The birthplace of Saul, who, after his conversion, was called Paul (Acts 9:11; 22:3); chief city of Cilicia, a province in SW Asia Minor or modern Turkey; located on the banks of the Cydnus River, about ten miles from the Mediterranean Sea; a learning center of the world. "I am a Jew from Tarsus, in Cilicia, a citizen of no mean city," declared Paul (Acts 21:39).

tax collector One who collects taxes.
Matthew the t. Mt 10:3
a friend of t. and sinners Mt 11:19
saw a t. named Levi Lk 5:27

Teacher Title, used of Jesus during His ministry.
your T., the Christ Mt 23:8, 10
trouble the T. Mk 5:35
call Me T. and Lord Jn 13:13

temple A building for the worship of a deity; hence, the temple at Jerusalem. *See* 1 Kings 5—8 for description of Solomon's temple.
LORD is in His holy t. Ps 11:4
destroy the t. of God Mt 26:61; 27:40; Mk 15:29; Jn 2:19

temptation An attempt to get someone to do something wrong; a test of character.
not lead us into t. Mt 6:13; Lk 11:4

temptations of Jesus *See* Matthew 4:1-11; Luke 4:1-13.

Ten Commandments The ten laws given by God to Moses on Mount Sinai (Ex 20:1-17; Deut 5:6-21).

tent of meeting *See* tabernacle.

testimony In OT: the divine law, especially the Ten Commandments; in NT: witness.
law and to the t. Isa 8:20
know that his t. is true Jn 21:24
to the t. of Jesus Christ Rev 1:2

Thaddaeus (THAD-ee-us) One of the twelve apostles of Jesus (Mk 3:18), also called Lebbaeus (Mt 10:3) and probably Judas. *See* Judas (3).

Thessalonica; Thessalonians (thess-uh-low-NIGH-kuh; thess-uh-LOW-nih-uns) An important city of Macedonia where Paul and his associates founded an early Christian church. The two NT epistles to the Thessalonians were among the earliest written by Paul.

Thomas One of the 12 apostles; his incredulity of Jesus' resurrection gained him the name "doubting Thomas" (Mt 10:3; Mk 3:18; Lk 6:15; Jn 11:16; 14:5; 20:24-29; Acts 1:13).

Timothy A trusted companion and assistant of Paul, from the early part of the latter's second missionary journey. According to tradition the two epistles to Timothy were written near the close of Paul's life.

tithe The tenth part of one's income paid to support God's work (Lev 27:30-32).

Titus (TIGHT-us) A gentile Christian associate of Paul (2 Cor 7:5-7); according to Titus 1:4, 5, Paul wrote the letter bearing his name in order to encourage him in his work in the churches of Crete.

tomb

tomb A place of burial.
like whitewashed t. Mt 23:27

Torah (TOE-ruh) Guidance or direction from God to His people for living the covenant relationship—a total way of life; in earlier times, a term referring directly to the first five books of Moses (*see* Pentateuch), but came to mean both the hearing and doing of the Law (Deut 32:46). Later, the Hebrew OT included the books of wisdom and prophets, and this entire collection became known as the Torah.

Transfiguration Jesus' glorious and radiant change in appearance; witnessed by three disciples (Mt 17:1-9; Mk 9:2-10; Lk 9:28-36; 2 Pet 1:16-18).

transgression A sin; rebellion against God's will.
t. of Adam Rom 5:14

Trinity The doctrine held by most Christians that there are three divine Persons (Father, Son, and Holy Spirit) united in the one Supreme Divine Being. NT teachings (Mt 12:32; 28:19; Lk 12:10; Acts 2:33; 1 Cor 12:4-6; 2 Cor 13:14) support this doctrine.

trust To have or put confidence in someone or something.
T. in the LORD with all Prov 3:5
those who t. in riches Mk 10:24

truth A proven sincerity, verity, honesty; righteousness.
A God of t. and without Deut 32:4
t. shall make you free Jn 8:32
I am the way, the t. Jn 14:6
He, the Spirit of t., has Jn 16:13

tunic An outer garment.
made him a t. of many colors Gen 37:3
do not have two t. Lk 9:3

Tyropoeon Valley (tie-ROW-pih-un) A small valley in the city of Jerusalem, which divides hill Ophel, the original City of David, from the Western Hill, or Upper City.

U

unleavened bread Bread baked from unfermented dough, or dough without yeast or "leaven" (Gen 19:3; Josh 5:11; 1 Sam 28:24); the flat bread used in the Passover celebration and the priestly rituals, recalling the Exodus, when the Hebrews left Egypt so quickly that they had no time to wait for the bread to rise (Ex 12:8, 15-20, 34, 39; 13:6-7).

Ur An ancient city on the Euphrates, called "Ur of the Chaldees"; home of Abraham (Gen 11:28).

Uzziah (uh-ZIGH-uh) The name of three persons in the OT, one of them a king of Judah (c. 783-742 B.C.).

V

vanity Futility; emptiness.
V. of v., all is v. Eccles 1:2

viper A poisonous snake.
stings like a v. Prov 23:32

vision Something seen other than by ordinary sight, as in a dream. God's revelations to the prophets were usually by visions.
They err in v. Isa 28:7

revealed to Daniel in a night v. Dan 2:19
Tell the v. to no one Mt 17:9

voice A sound uttered through the mouth as in speaking.
a still small v. 1 Kgs 19:12
v. of the turtledove is heard Song 2:12
v. of one crying Isa 40:3; Mt 3:3; Mk 1:3; Lk 3:4; Jn 1:23

W

wadi (WAH-dih) A valley, ravine, or riverbed that usually remains dry except during the rainy season; similar to an arroyo in the western United States; also "brook" (Josh 15:47; 2 Kgs 23:12) and "torrent" (Judg 5:21) in the Bible.

wages The payment for services.
be content with your w. Lk 3:14
the w. of sin is death Rom 6:23

walk To move by stepping.
w. through the valley of Ps 23:4
saw Him w. on the sea Mt 14:26
shall not w. in darkness Jn 8:12

want To lack or need (not in the sense of "to desire").
I shall not w. Ps 23:1

war Fighting with weapons between large groups.
A time of w., And a time Eccles 3:8
w. and rumors of w. Mt 24:6; Mk 13:7; Lk 21:9

wash To clean with water or other liquid.
w. His feet with her tears Lk 7:38
w. the disciples' feet Jn 13:5

water The colorless fluid that falls as rain.
over the face of the w. Gen 1:2
the flood of w. was on Gen 7:6
Planted by the rivers of w. Ps 1:3
me beside the still w. Ps 23:2
Cast your bread upon the w. Eccles 11:1
baptized you with w. Mk 1:8; Lk 3:16; Jn 1:26

way The direction; path; man's mode of living.
the w. of the righteous Ps 1:6
Train up a child in the w. Prov 22:6
Prepare the w. of the LORD Isa 40:3; Mt 3:3; Mk 1:3; Lk 3:4; Jn 1:23
I am the w., the truth Jn 14:6

Weeks, Feast of Seven weeks after Passover (Lev 23:15-21; Deut 16:9-12). Also called Feast of Harvest (Ex 23:16). See Pentecost.

will Desire; something wished.
Your w. be done Mt 6:10; Lk 11:2

wine The fermented juice of fruits.
W. is a mocker Prov 20:1
new w. into new wineskins Mt 9:17; Mk 2:22; Lk 5:37
wise Having good judgment.
tree desirable to make one w. Gen 3:6
man w. in his own eyes Prov 26:12
w. men from the East Mt 2:1
witness Someone or something that bears testimony to the truthfulness of a statement or to the occurrence of a happening.
be a w. between you Gen 31:44
as a w. to all the nations Mt 24:14
My w. is true Jn 8:14
The people . . . bore w. Jn 12:17
God is my w., whom Rom 1:9
bore w. to the word Rev 1:2
word A spoken sound having meaning.
God spoke all these w. Ex 20:1
w. fitly spoken is like Prov 25:11
Word; Word of God; word of the Lord
God's revealed will; the Holy Scriptures.
the w. is very near Deut 30:14; Rom 10:8
By the w. of the LORD Ps 33:6
hear the w. of the LORD Jer 29:20
hear the w. of God Lk 8:21
for the w. of God Rev 1:9

Word of God

Word; Word of God A title of Christ.
the W. was God Jn 1:1
concerning the W. of life 1 Jn 1:1
's called The W. of God Rev 19:13

work 1. Labor; effort.
God ended His w. Gen 2:2
the w. of Your fingers Ps 8:3
2. To labor; to toil.
Father has been w. Jn 5:17
all things w. together Rom 8:28
faith w. through love Gal 5:6
works Deeds; efforts.
according to his w. Mt 16:27; 2 Tim 4:14
w. which the Father Jn 5:36
its w. are evil Jn 7:7
not of w., lest anyone Eph 2:9
world The earth; the universe.
the w. is Mine, and all Ps 50:12
You are the light of the w. Mt 5:14
gains the whole w. Mt 16:26
God so loved the w. Jn 3:16
I am the light of the w. Jn 8:12
brought nothing into this w. 1 Tim 6:7
worry Be or become anxious.
by w. can add one cubit Mt 6:27
do not w. about tomorrow Mt 6:34
do not w. beforehand Mk 13:11
do not w. about your life Lk 12:22
worship To honor; to show reverence for.
you shall w. no other god Ex 34:14
w. at His footstool Ps 99:5
w. the LORD your God Mt 4:10; Lk 4:8
where one ought to w. Jn 4:20
wrath Great anger, especially God's punishment of sin.
soft answer turns away w. Prov 15:1
w. to come Mt 3:7; Lk 3:7
w. in the day of w. Rom 2:5
delivers us from the w. 1 Thess 1:10

Y

Yahweh (YAH-way) The covenant God of Israel, YHWH in the original Hebrew. According to Jewish custom, because of reverence the divine name was not to be spoken, so the Hebrew words for Lord and God were substituted. Whenever the words LORD and GOD appear in large and small capital letters, the original Hebrew reads YHWH.

Z

Zacchaeus (zack-KEY-us) Chief tax collector of Jericho at the time of one of Jesus' visits (Lk 19:2-8).
Zealot (ZELL-ut) A term used to designate the more radical Jewish rebels against for-

...gn, particularly Roman, rule; one motivated by zeal for the Jewish law.

bedee (ZEB-uh-dee) The father of the apostles James and John (Mt 4:21; Mk 1:19, 20; Lk 5:10; Jn 21:2).

ebulun (ZEB-you-lun) The tenth son of Jacob, the sixth by Leah (Gen 30:19, 20); ancestor of the tribe of Zebulun.

Zechariah; Zecher; Zacharias (zek-uh-RIGH-uh; zek-ur; zack-uh-RIGH-us) The name of 33 persons in the Bible, including: 1. Son of the priest Jehoiada (2 Chr 24:20, 21). 2. One of the OT minor prophets; contemporary of Haggai; urged the rebuilding of the temple (Ezra 5:1; 6:14; Zech 1:1, 7; 7:1, 8). 3. The father of John the Baptist (Lk 1:5-67; 3:2).

Zedekiah (zed-uh-KIGH-uh) The name of three persons in the OT, including the last king of Judah (c. 597-587 B.C.). Also called Mattaniah.

Zephaniah (zef-uh-NIGH-uh) The name of four persons in the OT, including a prophet during the time of Josiah; his prophecies appear in the OT Book of Zephaniah, the ninth of the 12 Minor Prophets.

Zion; Sion (ZIGH-un; SIGH-un) Originally the name of the fortified hill of pre-Israelite Jerusalem; poetically extended to refer to the religious capital of Israel.